A New History *of* Gloucestershire

A New History *of* Gloucestershire

SAMUEL RUDDER

With a new Introduction by
Nicholas M. Herbert

Republished by Alan Sutton in collaboration with
Gloucestershire County Library.

Originally published in 1779

NONSUCH
2006

This work was first published in 1779. This reprint edition contains the additions of a postscript to the preface dated 3 April, 1783, and an extra leaf numbered [345] – [346] for Cirencester.

In this reprint edition the text had been photographically reduced by 35 per cent.

Nonsuch Publishing Limited
The Mill, Brimscombe Port, Stroud, Gloucestershire, GL5 2QG
www.nonsuch-publishing.com

British Library Cataloguing in Publication Data.
A catalogue record for this book is available from the British Library.

ISBN 1 84588 023 4
ISBN-13 (from January 2007) 978 1 84588 023 1

Printed in Great Britain by Oaklands Book Services Limited

INTRODUCTION

TO THE 1977 EDITION

The successive historians of Gloucestershire have tended to adopt an ambivalent attitude to their predecessors in the same field, treating them as both useful colleagues to be consulted and borrowed from and blundering rivals to be corrected and outshone. The attitude of Samuel Rudder, author, printer, and publisher of *A New History* of *Gloucestershire,* to Sir Robert Atkyns, whose *Ancient and Present State of Glostershire* had appeared in 1712, varied from a generous appreciation of 'the great labour and expense the compilation of that history must have cost him, which had been attempted by none before him,'[1] to some distinctly sarcastic allusions to the 'learned author' when correcting his mistakes.[2] Originally conceived as a revision of 'Atkyns', forced to make its way against the challenge of a second edition of 'Atkyns', and subject immediately to invidious comparison with 'Atkyns', the *New History* became associated with its predecessor in ways that were not always relished by its author, and for a while it seemed unable to escape that predecessor's shadow. Atkyns's book had become the accepted wisdom on the county's history and there were some who regarded as presumptuous Rudder's attempt to replace it. As further grounds for their prejudice, this latest venture into a field of study that cultivated gentlemen and learned clerics had annexed as their own was made by a tradesman of modest standing and humble origins.

Samuel Rudder was born at Uley near Dursley into a branch of the family which in his lifetime altered its name from Rutter. His grandfather was John Rutter, probably a weaver by trade, and his father was Roger Rutter or Rudder who married Lydia Hillier from Cam. In 1726 when Samuel was born Roger was apparently living at Stoutshill in Uley [4] but later and until his death in 1771 he had a cottage in the little hamlet of White Court just across the valley.5 At the time of his second marriage in 1754 Roger was described as a shopkeeper but later he worked as a pig-killer. Incongruously, as his tombstone in Uley churchyard announces, he was also a lifelong vegetarian. That Roger held his cottage on a lease and in 1770 was able to lend a neighbour £29[7] suggests a reasonable level of prosperity; more significant, perhaps, is the degree of education revealed by his son, who presumably went as a paying pupil to a local grammar school, or to a private academy.

How the Uley pig-killer's son came to set up as a printer in Cirencester has not been discovered. Family connexions may have played a part in his move to the town, for there were both Rutters and Hilliers in Cirencester at the period.[8] Samuel was in business as a bookseller in Cirencester by 1749 when he married Mary Hinton there.[9] She was the daughter of William Hinton, who was living at Cranham in 1724 when she was born[10] but in the 1740s was trading as a maltster in Cirencester[11] Mary's surname, may be significant, for she was possibly related

1 Glos. Collection (at Gloucester Library) JR 1.22.

2 e.g. A *New History of Glos.* pp. 701, 709 (where Atkyns was probably right), 836. The *New History* is referred to later in these footnotes by page numbers alone.

3 W. P. W. Phillimore, 'The Rudder Family': *Glos. Notes and Queries,* ii. 80-2.

4 p. 783.

5 Glos. Colln. RF 319.3.

6 *Glos. Parish Registers,* ed. W. P. W. Phillimore, ii. 103.

7 Glos. Record Office, D 2957/319, mortgage assignment 1779; Glos. Colln. RF 319.3.

8 Glos. R.O., D 2346; Bigland, *Collections Relative to the County of Gloucester,* i. 371-2.

9 Glos. R.O., D 1388/III/84; Cirencester parish registers.

10 Cranham parish registers.

11 Glos. R.O., D 2050/M 4, pp. 92-3.

to Thomas Hinton who was recorded as a printer at Cirencester between 1709 and 1724.[1] The first book printed by Samuel Rudder of which record survives was the Latin grammar which he advertised in 1752.[2] The following year he produced a collection of material concerning an acrimonious dispute over the choice of the parliamentary candidates for Cirencester; in that affair Rudder worked for the Bathurst family's interest while the opposing faction had the services of another of the town's printers, George Hill.[3] Hill died in 1767,[4] from which time until his own death in 1801 Rudder's was apparently the only press at work in Cirencester. In a town which was then second only to Gloucester in the county, an important centre of road communications, and, in spite of a decline in its market, still a seat of wool-stapling, edge-tool making, and other industries, his business was probably a brisk one. He was moreover able to supplement it by the sale of patent medicines, groceries, and other goods,[5] and by 1780 he was also widely employed as an auctioneer.[6] Though not among the leading inhabitants of Cirencester, he was a substantial and respected member of the community, chosen, for example, as a trustee of one of the town charities and as treasurer of a local prosecution society.[7]

Rudder's house and printing-office, which he held as a tenant of Lord Bathurst, occupied a central position in Dyer Street adjoining the market-place.[8] By his marriage he also came into possession of the White Hart inn in Dyer Street, a copyhold under Lord Bathurst. He sold his rights in the inn in 1792[9] and the land-tax assessments suggest that he gave up the tenancy of his house some time in the next two years,[10] though his history of Cirencester published in 1800 still gives his address as Dyer Street. By the time of his death in 1801 at the age of 84 he had presumably retired from business and, his wife having died the previous year,[11] he had probably left the town to live with a married daughter, Elizabeth Window; it was in her house at Chelsea that he died.[12] Most, if not all, of his family had left Cirencester. His son Samuel, the eldest of the five children who survived him,[13] was established in Birmingham as a steel button maker by 1792 and another son, William, also found employment in the metal-working industry of that town. Also living in Birmingham by 1792 were their sister Mary and her husband John Saunders, who as landlord of the Fleece inn had been the Rudders' next-door neighbour in Dyer Street.[14] To the younger Samuel the author bequeathed all his papers relating to the *New History,* while his main assets at the time of his death — shares in the Monmouthshire Canal Navigation and a Birmingham copper-mining company — were divided among the five children.[15]

The monument to Samuel Rudder in the north chapel of Cirencester church describes him as 'a man of the strictest honour and most inflexible integrity', a conventional enough characterization in such a context but in accord with the general impression to be gained from what we know of him and from some personal opinions which he interjects in the *New History*. His complaints of

1 Gloucester Diocesan Registry wills 1709/145; *Transactions of Bristol and Glos. Arch. Soc. xx. 48-9.* If Hinton was the man who died at Cirencester in 1741 it is possible that Rudder may have served him as an apprentice, but the Cirencester registers also record the burial of a Thos. Hinton in 1727.

2 *Gloucester Journal,* 4 Aug. 1752.

3 *Trans. B.G.A.S.* xcii. 159.

4 Cirencester parish registers.

5 R. Austin, 'Samuel Rudder': *The Library,* 3rd ser., vol. vi (1915), 237; *Glouc. Jnl.* 29 Nov. 1757.

6 Glos. R.O., D 214/B 4/4; cf. *Glouc. Jnl.* which carries many of his sale notices.

7 Glos. R.O., P 86/CH 10/2; Glos. Colln. 16962, p. 397.

8 Glos. R.O., Q/REl 1; cf. ibid. photocopy 236.

9 Ibid. D 2050/M 4, pp. 135-6; M 5, pp. 637-45.

10 Ibid. Q/REI 1.

11 Rudder monument in Cirencester church.

12 *Gentleman's Magazine,* lxxi (1801), 285.

13 Cirencester parish registers; Rudder monument.

14 Glos. R.O., D 2050/M 5, pp. 355-7, 411-16, 637-45, 645-7; Sam. Rudder's will: in Public Record Office, Prob. 11/1355.

15 Sam. Rudder's will.

Lidney.

This parish lies in the hundred of Blideslow, in the Forest division, ten miles south-east from Monmouth, eight north-east from Chepstow, and twenty south-west from Gloucester. The turnpike-road from that city through Newnham to Chepstow, and so on to Cardiff, Swansea, & Milford-haven, is carried through it.

It probably took its name from being situated upon a broad part of the river Severn, for **Llydan** in the British language signifies broad, and the termination **ey** denotes a watry situation; and consistently with this explanation of the name, the river is here between two and three miles over. [illegible]

[4] The parish is of large extent. It consists of rich meadow and pasture, with some arable, and a large proportion of woodland. It is well watered by several fine brooks which rise in the forest of Dean. Newerne-brook, after a long course, runs through the middle of the parish, and discharges itself into the Severn at Lidney-pill; Woodwards-brook rises at St. Briavells, and running along the side of this parish, parts it from Alvington, where it obtains the name of the Coln, and empties itself into the Severn at Coln-pill: — Linch-brook divides this parish from Aure, and falls into the Severn at — Purton-pill. The Asteria Columnaris, &c. as at this mark ✡ . to come in here.

[3] Here is a fine seat about a mile westward of the church, called **Lidney Park**, with large gardens, a park, and very extensive woods adjoining, the property and residence of Thomas Bathurst, esq. Of this seat he has obliged the public and the editor with the beautiful plate annexed. He has also a large right of fishery in the river Severn, wherein are taken great quantities of salmon and other sea-fish, and sometimes, tho' not often, the sturgeon is — taken there.

Upon the summit of a little hill, in that part of Mr. Bathurst's park which lies in the tithing of Ailberton, are the remains of a large encampment, with foundations of antient buildings; and the ruins of a Roman hypocaust now to be seen. [illegible] Square pieces of brick, like dice, have been found, which undoubtedly were the materials of a tessellated pavement. And notwithstanding

Part of the draft history of Lydney sent by Rudder to Thomas Bathurst

the spread of alehouses and their effects on the poor-rates[1] may be a common observation of the period but taken with his strictures on duelling, on pleasure-seeking absentee landlords, and on the rowdy revel held at St. George's, Bristol,[2] reveal a man of puritanical views. More important for the success of the *New History* he had a down-to-earth cast of mind that eschewed legend and romantic embroidery; a businessman's curiosity about the more practical matters in human affairs; and an element of stubbornness that made him persevere with his chosen project when it proved far more difficult and time-consuming than he had envisaged.

The first evidence of Rudder's interest in antiquities is a little pamphlet on the Fairford church windows which he printed, and presumably wrote, in 1763.[3] The *New History of Gloucestershire* had its origins in a growing demand for a revised edition of Atkyns's *Ancient and Present State of Glostershire* which had become scarce and expensive, copies selling for as much as £12 and £14 in the 1760's.[4] According to the dedication of the *New History* the idea of revising 'Atkyns' was first suggested to Rudder by his landlord and patron, Allen, 1st Earl Bathurst; if this was so, the friend of Pope and creator of Cirencester Park has a further claim on our gratitude. The idea of a new edition of 'Atkyns' also suggested itself to William Herbert, a London bookseller with an interest in antiquities,[5] who had acquired the plates of the engravings by Kip that were such an adornment to Atkyns's book. Hearing of Rudder's plans, Herbert suggested a meeting to discuss a possible collaboration on the project, but his approach was rejected by Rudder because, as he said, Herbert could promise no new material for the book and because the old Kip plates were no longer relevant, 'most of the houses being pulled down, and the gardens totally changed with the taste of the times.'[6] He had early determined it seems to attempt something that was much more than a corrected and updated 'Atkyns' and in a prospectus issued to attract subscribers in February 1767 he set out an ambitious scheme. Careful to stress his respect for Atkyns's work, he also emphasised the new matter on trade and industry he would provide and his 'heads of inquiry', listing topics on which he hoped local gentry in each parish would supply information, embraced such things as inclosures, manufactures, and (an item which perhaps not surprisingly he did not manage to include) the number of sheep, horses, and cattle in each parish. The new work was offered to subscribers at 2½ guineas and their deposits were guaranteed by a bond for £500 entered into with the Duke of Beaufort, Lord Bathurst, and others.[7] By the beginning of the next year he was far enough advanced with the project to publish the section on Hailes parish as a specimen of the book.[8]

Rudder was understandably put out when in September 1768 William Herbert published an unrevised second edition of Atkyns's history at the lower price of 2 guineas. This severe blow to his plans stung him into a provocative new advertisement which claimed that his new history

> will be found upon comparison to be a much more copious, accurate and elegant book than Sir Robert Atkyns's History, or the second edition of it with the old plates now advertised, which was hurried to the press to come out before this new history could be finished, though not begun 'till long after the proposals for it were published ...[9]

Herbert answered this by publishing a set of queries, of which the following will give the flavour:

1 Preface, p. vii.
2 pp. 250, 420, 461.
3 In its later editions it included the account of Fairford from the *New History: Cat. of Glos. Colln.* (1928), nos. 8619-26.
4 Glos. Colln. JR 1.22; *Glouc. Jnl.* 24 Oct. 1768.
5 For Herbert, see *Dictionary of National Biography.*
6 *Glouc. Jnl.* 24 Oct. 1768.
7 Glos. Colln. JR 1.22.
8 *Glouc. Jnl.* 25 Jan. 1768.
9 Ibid. 12 Sept. 1768.

Cirencester April 1, 1769.

S I R,

THE modern history of the parish of Alderley so far as the undermentioned particulars concern it, being brought down no lower than the year 1757, in the account I have received of it; I shall therefore esteem it a very particular favour if you will please to send me, as speedily as you can conveniently, answers to the undermentioned queries; that the matters may be inserted in the History of Gloucestershire now printing, and that the accounts of all the parishes may be brought down to the same year.

The article marked with a cross at the beginning need not be regarded. You will, I hope, Sir, excuse my taking so much liberty with you, which I should not have done in any business of a private nature.

QUERIES.

1. Who is the present lord of the manor, and what is his coat armour? — — — — — —

2. What were the disbursements to the poor in the years — — — —

	£. S. D.		£. S. D.
1761		1765	
1762		1766	
1763		1767	
1764			

3. What are the numbers of your births and burials for the last 10 years? — — — — —

4. How many inhabitants are there in the parish?

5. What number of cattle upon an average *com. ann.* viz. Horses for husbandry, — — — —

   Black cattle, — — — — —

   Sheep, — — — — — — — —

I am Sir,

Your very humble Servant

S. Rudder.

There is a mistake in Sr. R. A's acct. of your Arms. I have several Accts. particularly one in the heralds book for the county, where it is, Argent a fess sable, 3 cinque foils in chief Azure. I beg the favour to confirm me or correct me in this matter.

The topographical description in Sr. R. A's book is imperfect. The peculiarities in the situation should be mentioned; the bearings and distances should be in statute miles; I mean from Gloucester, and the nearest market towns. — As the parishes will stand in alphabetical order in the book, and not follow each other according to vicinity, it will be necessary to show by what other parishes each place is bounded. In these matters, Sr. as you must be perfectly acquainted with them, permit me to request the favor of your assistance.

Questionnaire sent by Rudder to Matthew Hale of Alderley, 1769.

Does the editor, in boasting that his work will be more copious than the second edition of Sir Robert Atkyns's History, mean only that it will be more *bulky;* and would he have us judge of its accuracy by the specimen already published?

When the editor roundly asserts, that "the second edition of Sir Robert Atkyns's *Old History* was hurried to the press to come out before this *New History* could be finished," does he assert this of his own real knowledge, or only on conjecture, and in a fit of petulance, because the proprietor of the re-published history did not deliver proposals in the year 1765, and defer the work itself 'till the year 1775!

The fruitless public dispute between the two men rumbled on in the newspapers in the same vein of heavy sarcasm until near the end of the year, when Rudder declared that 'though you should endeavour to eke out this dispute to a full page of the newspaper every week, it is probable I may never trouble you again,' and was apparently allowed to have the last word.[1] There is no doubt that the new edition of Atkyns's book had lost Rudder many potential subscribers, who preferred to buy the old well-tried history rather than wait for a new one of unknown quality. Those who did subscribe to the *New History* had in the event a long wait and as the years passed Herbert's sarcasm about the length of time Rudder would take with his work seemed justified. At the end of 1771 Rudder had to publish a notice to quell rumours that he had abandoned the task. He was, he said,

> surprized that any person can think him capable of relinquishing a work, which, if executed as he could wish, will yield him a solid satisfaction, independent of the advantages sought after by a tradesman. [2]

In 1776 several of the subscribers published a letter in the London papers demanding an explanation for the delay and Rudder replied, once more blaming the second edition of 'Atkyns' and promising the book the following summer.[3]

Rudder's determination to include as much new information as possible and the careful and conscientious way he set about gathering it was the main reason for the delay. Over the years he visited every parish,[4] questioning the inhabitants, consulting the parish registers, and making careful copies of monumental inscriptions. In the margins of his set of proof pages of the *New History* he later gratefully recorded the names of parish clergy and landowners who had given generous assistance in his travels around the county in search of information, some of them entertaining him at their houses for several days.[5] When he had to make do with the country inns he was not usually so comfortable: at St. Briavels he lodged at an inn kept in the old castle and had a room that was 'more suitable to the horrid works of murderers and assassins, than for the accommodation of travellers', and at a small inn at Hayden in Boddington parish he spent a sleepless night, tormented by fleas.[6] Much of the information was gathered, however, by postal enquiries to local gentry and clergy. In a letter of 1769 to a Mr. Beale, requesting information on Newent and an introduction to some people who could help with Dymock, Rudder confessed that 'for above these two years past I have been a very troublesome fellow, and to my friends more especially.'[7] He also circulated a standard printed letter repeating some of the 'heads of inquiry' of his original prospectus; one addressed to Matthew Hale of Alderley survives with additional queries added in manuscript.[8] Some at least of the parish histories were submitted in their final

1 Ibid. 24 Oct.; 14, 21, 28 Nov.; 19 Dec. 1768.
2 Ibid. 16 Dec. 1771.
3 Austin, op. cit, 246-7.
4 Preface, p. v.
5 *New History*, proof copy (in Glos. Colln. 35243), e.g. MS. notes on pp. 297, 308, 316, 802.
6 Ibid. notes on pp. 301, 307.
7 Austin, op. cit. 244-5.
8 Glos. Colln. JF 1.4.

manuscript draft to local gentry for their comments. The history of Lydney, neatly written out ready for printing, was sent to Thomas Bathurst, and the fact that the draft was never returned[1] and so must have had a duplicate emphasises the physical effort that went into the preparation of the volume.

Rudder's visits and postal enquiries produced the greater part of the new material that he was able to add to the information from 'Atkyns' in his parish histories. Much of it naturally concerned matters of contemporary or fairly recent date, but, using deeds, pedigrees, and other documents lent by his local contacts, he was also able to supplement and correct some of the details of more ancient matters given by Atkyns. Less often he or his helpers provided fresh information from the national archives which Sir Robert had made so much his own province.

Among Rudder's other sources the biggest single contribution was made by the work of Richard Furney (d. 1753), master of the Crypt School at Gloucester from 1719 to 1724 and later archdeacon of Surrey.[2] From his painstaking researches, particularly into documents in the cathedral library and bishop's registry, Furney had compiled a minutely detailed history of Gloucester, including sections on the city and its government, the earls of Gloucester, Gloucester Abbey, the cathedral, the bishopric, the chapter, and the individual city churches. A copy of Furney's manuscript was put at Rudder's disposal by the Revd. Richard Rogers, rector of St. Mary de Crypt,[3] and with some re-arrangement and editing but relatively little additional material it appeared as 'the history of the city and diocese of Gloucester' which forms such a significant part of the *New History.* Rudder's debt to Furney was greater than his rather perfunctory acknowledgement in his preface suggests; he used Furney's work in the history of the city and diocese in an even more undiluted form than he did that of Atkyns in the parish histories. His knowledge of his obligation to both men is no doubt one of the reasons why he preferred to style himself as editor rather then author of the *New History.*

Rudder also drew, but to a much lesser extent, on the collections of two of the other unpublished antiquaries of Gloucestershire, whose work like Furney's survives in manuscripts in the Bodleian Library. From the collections of Abel Wantner (d. 1714), a citizen of Gloucester who made an abortive attempt to publish a history of the county,[4] he drew selectively,[5] passing over most of the more fanciful stories that Wantner included in his account of the market towns: Rudder also took some additional details[6] from the manuscript of Chancellor Richard Parsons (d. 1711) which had been so extensively used by Atkyns.[7] Among published sources Rudder like all the old county historians turned to such standard works as Camden's *Britannia,* Dugdale's *Monasticon,* and Tanner's *Notitia Monastica,* and he also had the advantage, presumably denied to Atkyns, of seeing the *Itinerary* of John Leland, which was first published in the edition of Thomas Hearne in 1710.

In one part of his work on the *New History,* the preparation of the illustrations, Rudder met with a disappointment. Although he can never have hoped to rival Atkyns's book in this respect, if only because unlike Atkyns he was asking the owners of the houses to supply

1 Glos. R.O., D 421/E 27.

2 *Glos. N. & Q.* i. 384-7.

3 Preface, p. v. This copy was later acquired by the Hyett family of Painswick and is now in Glos. Record Office (D 327). Furney bequeathed another copy in two volumes to the Bodleian Library (now MSS. Top Glouc. c. 4-5), where it was deposited in 1755; Rudder probably also saw this, for he used Wantner's MSS. which formed part of the same bequest: see *Summary Cat. of Western MSS. in Bodl. Libr.* v. pp. 364-6.

4 p. 184; E. Moir, 'The Historians of Glos.': *Glos. Studies,* ed. H. P. R. Finberg (1957), 274-6. His collections are in Bodl. MSS. Top. Glouc. c. 2-3.

5 See pp. 222, 595, and Rudder's account of Minchinhampton which in parts follows closely MS. Top. Glouc. c. 3, f.166 and v.

6 e.g. pp. 583, 663.

7 See intro. by B. S. Smith to the facsimile reprint of Atkyns, *Glos.* (EP Publishing Ltd. 1974), pp. viii-xi. Parsons's MS. is Bodl. MS. Rawl. B 323.

the engravings at their own cost, he had nevertheless, intended to have many more than the 13 whole-sheet views of seats, which with 3 half-sheets, the inset of Fairford church, and the county map eventually provided the sum of the illustrations to the volume. In 1768 he claimed rashly that over 30 views of seats were assured,[1] and Thomas Bonnor, the Gloucester engraver who was responsible for 9 of the plates that finally appeared, advertised for further commissions for the *New History* in 1769.[2] Some who had planned to have their houses included must have been put off by the long delay in publication; two views were lost by the deaths of the clients;[3] and a view of Sherborne House was omitted because the owner disapproved of it.[4] Those owners who did finally come forward mostly left it too late or else found the engravers dilatory in executing their commissions, and Rudder had the chagrin of being able to issue only 5 of the whole-sheet views to the subscribers with the volume in 1779; the remaining 8 were issued in 1782.[5] For this reason few copies are found with the complete set inserted. The plates in the *New History* thus represent the rump of what might have been a valuable set of houses in 18th-century landscaped parks to put beside the formal gardens of an earlier age illustrated so well by the Kip plates of 'Atkyns'.

Printing of the volume went ahead while Rudder was still gathering information and extended over a period of years. He claimed in 1771 that about half the book was already printed, by which he evidently meant the introductory sections and the history of the city and diocese;[6] the printing of the parish histories, for which the material was not so easily forthcoming, followed more slowly and parishes low in the alphabetical order included information received as late as January 1778.[7] The type having to be broken up after each short section was completed, produced the features, strange to our eyes, of a list of addenda and corrigenda published with the volume and corrections to some of the earlier parish histories included in the later ones.[8] The modern luxury of revising and resetting from a completed set of proofs was unknown to the 18th-century printer.

It must have been an immense relief to Samuel Rudder when the *New History* was finally delivered to the subscribers in June 1779,[9] and another to see the good notices given it by the London reviews.[10] He would have been even more pleased if he could have seen a comment by Horace Walpole that '(Rudder's) additions to Sir Robert Atkyns make it the most sensible history of a county that we have had yet.[11] Nearer home he encountered some wounding criticisms and even had to suffer the suggestion that he had bribed the London reviewers. Rudder dismissed this hostility as merely the product of envy [12] but some unfavourable comparisons made between the *New History* and 'Atkyns' by an unnamed clergyman led him to publish an answer in a postscript to the preface, inserted into a second issue of the

1 *Glouc. Jnl. 24* Oct. 1768.

2 Ibid. 3 July 1769.

3 Preface, pp. vii-viii; the view of Rendcomb mentioned there was eventually included.

4 Postscript to preface, 1783.

5 In his advertisement announcing publication in June 1779 Rudder could only say for certain that 3 whole-sheet views (Sandywell, Bibury, New Mills) had been completed; but he also mentioned 4 others (Batsford, Williamstrip, Rendcomb, Highnam) that were in preparation, and 2 of those were presumably also completed in time to go out with the volume, for in 1782 he said that only 8 whole-sheet views had missed the publication. In 1782 he gave the final total of whole-sheets as 14, evidently including in that total the map, which with the 3 half-sheets presumably went out in 1779: *Glouc. Jnl.* 21 June 1779; 11 Mar. 1782.

6 *Glouc. Jnl.* 16 Dec. 1771.

7 pp. 783, 796.

8 e.g. pp. 334, 400, 617.

9 *Glouc. Jnl.* 21 June 1779.

10 *Critical Review,* xlviii. 301-8; *Monthly Review,* lxiii. 10-15.

11 Quoted by Austin, op, cit. 249.

12 *New History*, proof copy, MS. note at front.

book that he made in 1783.[1] The clergyman in question may have been Thomas Rudge, later himself the author of a more modest history of the county; Rudge, who was curate at Cirencester at the time of publication, is identified elsewhere by Rudder as one of his most eager critics.[2] Any justified criticisms and suggestions received after publication were carefully noted by Rudder on his set of proofs and he even made some attempt to keep his parish histories up to date, though it is unlikely that he can ever have contemplated the vast labour of a second edition. The sections on Cirencester and on the city and diocese of Gloucester were reprinted for sale as separate volumes in 1780 and 1781 respectively, and to the Cirencester section he later added a great deal more material to make the useful little history of the town published in 1800.[3]

The most obvious feature that the *New History* inherited from 'Atkyns' was its plan, introductory sections on the county as a whole, followed by the history of the city and diocese of Gloucester and then the parishes of the county in alphabetical order. Rudder probably never considered departing from the alphabetical arrangement of the parishes with its overriding advantage to the reader of ease of reference, but he recognised one of its disadvantages compared with some form of geographical grouping; it involved frequent repetition of details like agricultural produce and type of landscape which were common to groups of neighbouring parishes.[4] He managed to bring together some of his general observations on particular areas in his short chapters on the three geographical divisions of the county, and they remain among the most interesting of the introductory sections. The introductory matter on the county as a whole is followed by the first complete transcript of the Gloucestershire section of Domesday Book, and the decision to include this reflects both Rudder's good judgement as a historian and his willingness to spare himself no labour in doing a thorough job. In the event it only preceded by five years the complete edition of Domesday Book produced as a government commission by John Nichols. The history of the city and diocese of Gloucester which follows was, as mentioned above, largely the work of Archdeacon Furney, whose exhaustive compilation, extending to lists of all the occupants of the cathedral prebends and even the ushers of the city's schools, enabled Rudder to far outdo the equivalent part of 'Atkyns'. The detailed footnoting is also the work of Furney; Rudder attempted nothing similar in the rest of the volume. Although some of the sections have been largely superseded by more recent work this part of the *New History* remains a valuable quarry for information.

Any assessment of the parish histories which form the largest and most frequently consulted part of the *New History* must begin by stressing the great debt to the *Ancient and Present State of Glostershire.* There is little value in reviving the controversy over the relative merits of the two books. Remembering that it is always easier to come second to such a task, to have a solid basis of material to revise and build on, we can appreciate the wider scope and more enquiring mind of Rudder without demeaning the pioneering achievement of Sir Robert. Rudder himself was usually generous in his praise of his predecessor and open in acknowledging that he had 'availed himself of whatever was useful.' What he made use of in particular in his parish histories was Atkyns's manorial descents, often as he says, seeing no point in even altering the wording.[5] He added to the descents, however, a considerable fund

1 The postscript is one of the only two differences to be found between copies of the *New History.* The other is the new sheet, comprising pp. 345, 346, [345], [346], which Rudder issued in March 1782 to be inserted in place of the original pp. 345, 346: see his note on p. [346], and *Bibliographer's Manual of Glos. Literature*, ed. F. A. Hyett and W. Bazely, i (1895), 23-5.

2 *New History*, proof copy, MS. notes at front and on p. 516.

3 *Cat. of Glos. Colln.* nos. 7593-4, 3284. The 1800 Cirencester history is sometimes misleadingly described as though it was merely a new edition of that of 1780.

4 p. 396.

5 Preface, pp. v-vi.

of new information and pointed out many wrong attributions of records by Atkyns where two places had similar names. He also, of course, updated the descents by his enquiries to local landowners. In many cases, however, Rudder merely repeated Atkyns's mistakes and transmitted them with some new ones of his own to the next generation of antiquaries. The fact is that this most characteristic part of the old county histories is the one most soon made redundant. With the wider sources now available, many of them collected and catalogued in record offices or published by record societies, it is now possible to compile descents of a detail and accuracy that were beyond the reach of the old antiquaries.

The new information in Rudder's book that has proved of much more enduring value mainly concerns economic affairs, in which as a tradesman and a shareholder in business enterprises he took a natural interest. His brief sketches of Gloucestershire's towns, their industries, their rise or decline in prosperity, and the state of their markets and fairs, provide us with the kind of information that is difficult to recover from surviving documents. We learn, to give a few examples, of the expansion of Newnham's maritime trade, of Dursley's card-making industry, of the traffic through Sodbury to the coal-mines of south Gloucestershire, and of the decline of Cirencester's wool-market. A theme he returns to several times is the general decline of the market trade of the towns, attributing it to forestalling by dealers who travelled the countryside, buying up produce directly from the farmhouses.[1] At the lower level of the villages we learn, for example, of those places in the agricultural areas of the county where the women and children did spinning work for the Stroud Valley clothiers or for the Blockley silk-throwsters.

Rudder's own visits to the parishes result in a sense of place that is entirely lacking from 'Atkyns'. Although he was anxious to avoid the 'disgusting sameness in expression' he thought minute descriptions of the villages would produce,[2] he often — in a brief mention such as that of Salperton lying 'very high and bleak on the Coteswold', or in a more detailed picture such as that of the decayed state of Coaley village — gives us a direct glimpse at 18th-century Gloucestershire. That is not to claim for him any great descriptive powers; his descriptions of the countryside don't usually rise above the stilted phraseology that was current at the period, typified by the poem about Clifton that Rudder quotes under that parish. As with many of his contemporaries the landscapes which most engaged his sympathies were those that reflected the works of man — a fertile and skilfully-farmed stretch of countryside or a region where populous villages and well-built houses showed the influence of a prosperous industry. This is best illustrated in his description of the Stroud valleys as seen from Rodborough Hill:

There is a large tract of rich country in the foreground of the landscape, interspersed with good houses, gardens, and highly cultivated plantations and inclosures; and these are improved with the beautiful colouring of clothes on the tenters, accompanied with a variety of other objects, peculiar to a clothing country. Here the fancy glows, and agreeable ideas rise of the benefits and extensiveness of trade and manufactures, which flourish most in free countries; and of the affluence and riches which are at once incitements to, and the rewards of integrity and industry.[3] Bonnor's plate of New Mills at Stroud, with the elegant house and cloth-mill in the park-like setting, seems to give visual expression to this attitude.

It follows that Samuel Rudder was an advocate of improvement of all kinds and shared in the current preoccupation with agricultural innovation. He invariably records where inclosures had been carried through, often stressing the beneficial results, and he often includes tips on farming practice such as the use of marle and the 'drowning' of meadows.[4] The backward and

1 e.g. pp. 207, 344, 671-2.
2 Preface, p. v.
3 p. 629.
4 e g. pp. 327, 414, 418-19, 610.

badly-farmed parishes receive his censure, notably those owned by corporations such as the dean and chapter of Gloucester, whose usual system of granting their manors out on leases for lives with arbitrary fines for renewal apparently gave little incentive to improvements of the land.[1] The absence of many landowners from their estates was another hindrance to improvement. Again and again in his parish histories Rudder found himself recording manor-houses in disrepair, standing empty, or used as farm-houses, and in one passage reminiscent of Cobbett and some other writers on the English countryside he associates this with extravagant living, the lure of the London season, and a general decline in the old values.[2] One factor in the desertion of manor-houses in the 18th century was connected if not with extravagant living at least with a growing sophistication; this was a tendency among the more important landowning families, who in Atkyns's day often used more than one of the manor-houses on their various estates, to keep up only one residence, which they had perhaps rebuilt and landscaped in the modern style. By Rudder's time the Stephenses, for example, had abandoned their Eastington house to live exclusively at Chavenage in Horsley; the Guises at that period kept up Rendcomb rather than Elmore; and Lord Ducie used Woodchester in preference to Tortworth.

There was one aspect of the countryside where the need for improvement was brought home to Rudder in a direct way as he gathered material for his history: the state of the roads. He is particularly critical of the condition of the lanes of the Newent area where he was forced to dismount from his horse and struggle through the mud on foot.[3] On the more important roads the coming of the turnpike system had not proved a complete solution to the problem. In part of the Gloucester-Bristol road, one of the great thoroughfares of the county, he tells us of vehicles and horses almost sunk in the mire.[4] He was able to record some recent improvements, such as the new bridge on the Bath road at Tetbury, but many of the more significant improvements had to wait until the next century.

The state of the roads must have been a common topic of conversation in the 18th century. Another was personal health and the search for cures. Rudder like most contemporary topographers records numerous medicinal springs and the varied curative properties claimed for them. He also sets out to establish the relative healthiness of the parishes, inevitably contrasting the 'impure and unwholesome' air of Severnside, where 'agues and asthmatic disorders' afflicted the inhabitants,[5] with the breezy salubrity of the Cotswolds, which boasted many instances of remarkable longevity and where, according to Rudder, a Cirencester doctor once declared that nobody in his profession could make a living. In calculating the population figures for a few places by means of the parish registers he used a proportion of annual burials to total population of about 1 in 32 in the former area but about 1 in 40 or 1 in 50 in the latter.[6] Luckily for their value to us today his population figures are more often taken from estimates given him by the parish clergy or from locally-conducted censuses, and usually he employed his parish register statistics only as a comment on the healthiness of the places.

A topic eagerly discussed by 18th-century antiquaries, and the subject of much misguided speculation, was the derivation of place names. Literal interpretations were made with little appreciation that the modern forms of the names were usually the result of corruption over the centuries. Rudder, who recognised the need to recover the early forms of the names,[7] dismisses some of Atkyns's more naïve surmises, such as Winstone and Winrush (*sic*) as places where battles were fought and won or Dymock as a place darkened by oak trees, but in attempting his own interpretation he often further clouds the issue. This field of study,

1 pp. 237, 390, 634.
2 p. 420.
3 pp. 561, 589.
4 p.813.
5 p.644.
6 e.g. pp. 246, 249, 707.
7 Preface, p. v.

where even a name as apparently straightforward as Edgeworth given to a village on the edge of a hill may be deceptive, was not one for the amateur, and correct interpretations ad to await the specialized linguistic knowledge of the compilers of the English Place-Name Society volumes.

Archaeological remains were naturally another field of intense antiquarian speculation but here the discussions yield us much useful knowledge. Rudder's own interest was stimulated by his residence at Cirencester; in the addenda to the *New History* he included a note of a late discovery at a neighbour's house and the opportunity he had later to examine the remains of another of the town's Roman buildings caused him to put out a new sheet in 1782 to be inserted into the account of the town.[1] He carefully records many of the finds within the county that had been accidentally turned up by the ploughman and builder or brought to light by some local squire setting his farm labourers at a barrow in search of treasure. Modern archaeologists may smile at the contemporary misconceptions that saw all barrows as the tombs of those slain in battle and all Roman villas as military stations[2] and at the lengthy digressions on the identity of the *Abone* of the Antonine Itinerary — obviously a favourite source of dispute for antiquaries of the day;[3] but they welcome the accounts, however inadequate, of otherwise unrecorded discoveries.

Those then are among the themes that run through Rudder's parish histories, some of them throwing as much light on 18th-century attitudes as on the history of Gloucestershire. The *New History* was very much a book of its day in its wide range of reference, embracing not only history and antiquities, but also geology and natural history; hints on husbandry and thoughts on social problems; and 'curiosities' such as the giant eels of Arlingham and the monstrous child of Upper Slaughter. Some of the preoccupations of Rudder's time are of much less interest to us today and his general themes will in any case be lost on the average modern user of the volume, who turns to a specific parish in search of some particular detail. But even as a quarry for facts the *New History* is one that, thanks to Rudder's sound instinct for the significant and his careful use of evidence, will not easily be worked out.

Even as the *New History of Gloucestershire* joined the *Ancient and Present State of Glostershire* on the bookshelves of Gloucestershire's students of antiquity the work of writing the history of the county was continuing. 'A gentleman in the heralds office'[4] had begun researches that would eclipse at least one part of Rudder's work, the recording of inscriptions; though Ralph Bigland's *Collections* would take even longer than Samuel Rudder's *New History* to publish. Over the years the scope of enquiry has continued to be extended, so that modern county historians include topics that Rudder would have thought mundane and find interest and individuality in parishes that he dismissed as having 'nothing worth the traveller's attention'.[5] Nevertheless all students of the history of Gloucestershire still turn many times to the work of the conscientious Cirencester printer, who 230 years ago struggled through muddy lanes to remote villages, badgered the county gentry for information, and withstood the unkind comments about the late arrival of his volume.

N. M. Herbert, 1976

1 See note on p. [346].
2 e.g. pp. 226, 631, 841, 848.
3 pp. 211, 295, 525-6; now identified as Sea Mills, near Bristol.
4 Preface, p. vi.
5 pp. 221, 383, 636.

ILLUSTRATIONS

All of the original engravings in Samuel Rudder's *A New History of Gloucestershire* had dedications at the base. These have been removed in this edition, but the text is now provided below. All of the engravings were drawn and engraved by Thomas Bonnor unless stated below.

Between pages 262 and 263
Barrington Park the Seat of the Countess Talbot.
This Plate is Inscribed by his most Obliged humble Servant S: Rudder.

Between pages 264 and 265
Battesford the Seat of Thomas Edwards Freeman Esqr.
Drawn by E. Garvy, engraved by P. Benazech.

Between pages 268 and 269
Berkeley Castle
To the Right Honble the Earl of Berkeley, Viscount Dursley, Lord Lieutenant of the County of Gloucester, &c. &c. This Plate is Inscribed by his Lordships most Obliged humble Servant S: Rudder.

Between pages 284 and 285
To Estcourt Cresswell Esqr. Member of Parliament for Cirencester, in the County of Gloucester. This Plate is Inscribed by his most Obliged humble Servant S: Rudder.

Between pages 342 and 343
Highnam Court the Seat of John Guise Esqr.

Between pages 354 and 355
Plan of the Home Park at Cirencester belonging to Henry Earl Bathurst.

Between pages 356 and 357
Plan of the Oakley Great Park belonging to Henry Earl Bathurst.

Between pages 384 and 385
Williamstrip the Seat of Samuel Blackwell Esqr. To whom this Plate is inscribed by his most obliged and very obedient humble Servant Samuel Rudder.
Drawn by M. Hartley and engraved by Francis Chesham.

Between pages 414 and 415
Sandywell Park
To Thomas Tracy Esqr. Member of Parliament for the County of Gloucester.

Between pages 524 and 525
Lydney Park the Seat of Thomas Bathurst Esqr.
To whom this Plate is humbly inscribed by his most obliged and very obedient humble Servant Saml Rudder.
Drawn by Bathurst F. Lewis and engraved by Francis Chesham.

Between pages 574 and 575
Nibley
To Nicholas Smythe Esqr. of Nibley, in the County of Gloucetser. This Plate is inscribed by his most obliged humble Servant S. Rudder.

Between pages 620 and 621
Rendcomb
To Sir Willm. Guise Barv. Member of Parliament for the County of Gloucester. This Plate is Inscribed by his most Obliged humble Servant S: Rudder.

Between pages 638 and 639
To Samuel Hayward Esqr. of Wallsworth Hall in the County of Gloucester. This Plate is Inscribed by his most Obliged humble Servant S: Rudder.

Between pages 714 and 715
New Mills
To Thomas Baylis Esqr. of New Mills, in the County of Gloucester. This Plate is Inscribed by his most obliged humble Servant S: Rudder.

Between pages 716 and 717
Sudley Castle
Inscribed to the Right Honourable George Lord Rivers, By His Lordships most obliged and very dutiful Humble Servant Samuel Rudder.
Drawn by S. & N. Buck 1732, engraved by Bayly.

Between pages 796 and 797
Pen Park Hole
Drawn by W. White, engraved by Bayly.

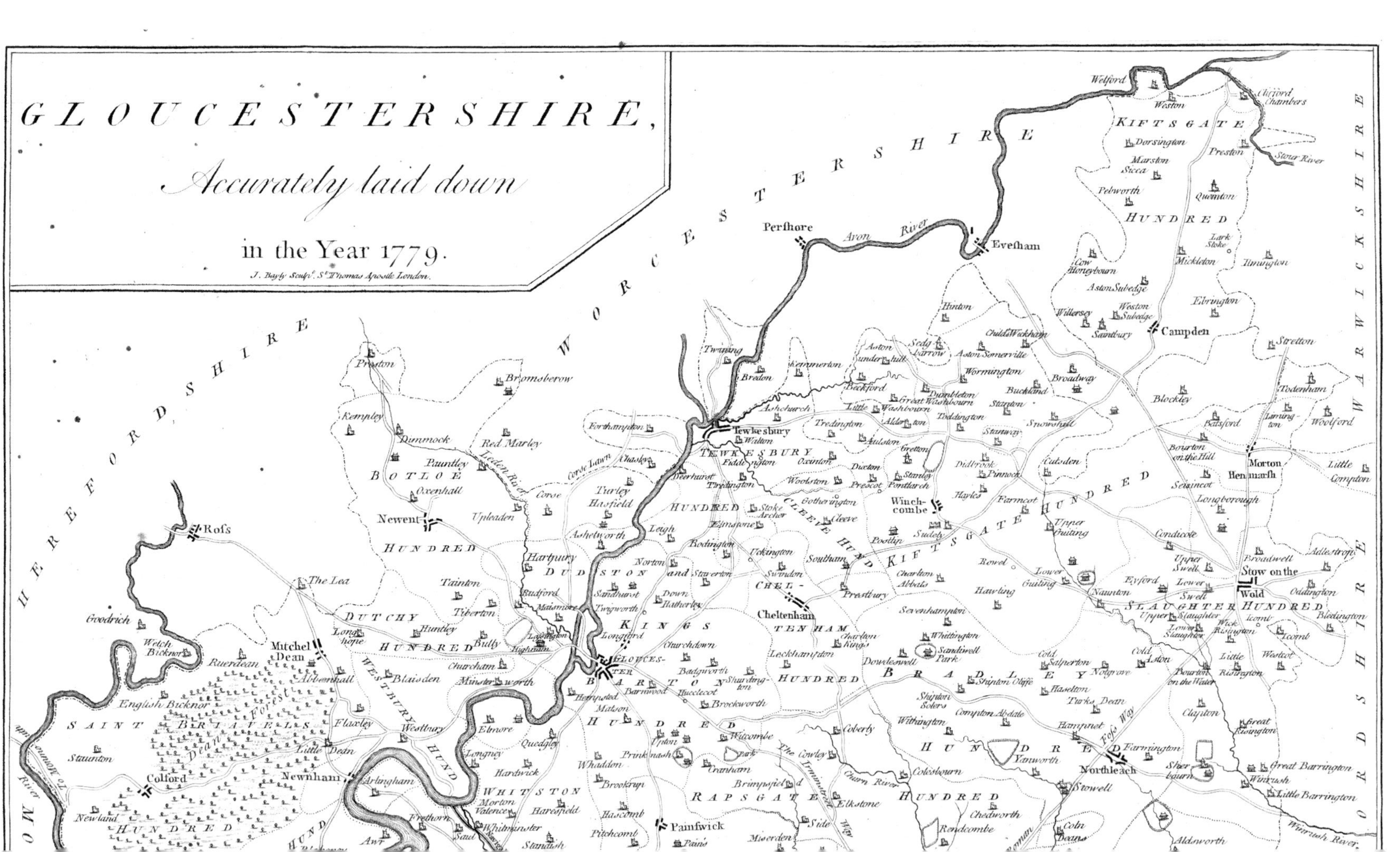
GLOUCESTERSHIRE,
Accurately laid down
in the Year 1779.
J. Bayly Sculpt. St. Thomas Apostle London.
WORCESTERSHIRE
HEREFORDSHIRE
WARWICKSHIRE
OXFORDSHIRE
Gloucester
Tewkesbury
Cheltenham
Winchcombe
Campden
Evesham
Pershore
Newent
Ross
Mitchel Dean
Newnham
Colford
Painswick
Northleach
Stow on the Wold
Morton Henmarsh
KIFTSGATE HUNDRED
SLAUGHTER HUNDRED
BRADLEY HUNDRED
RAPSGATE HUNDRED
BOTLOE HUNDRED
DUTCHY HUNDRED
WESTBURY HUND
SAINT BRIAVELS HUNDRED
Dean Forest

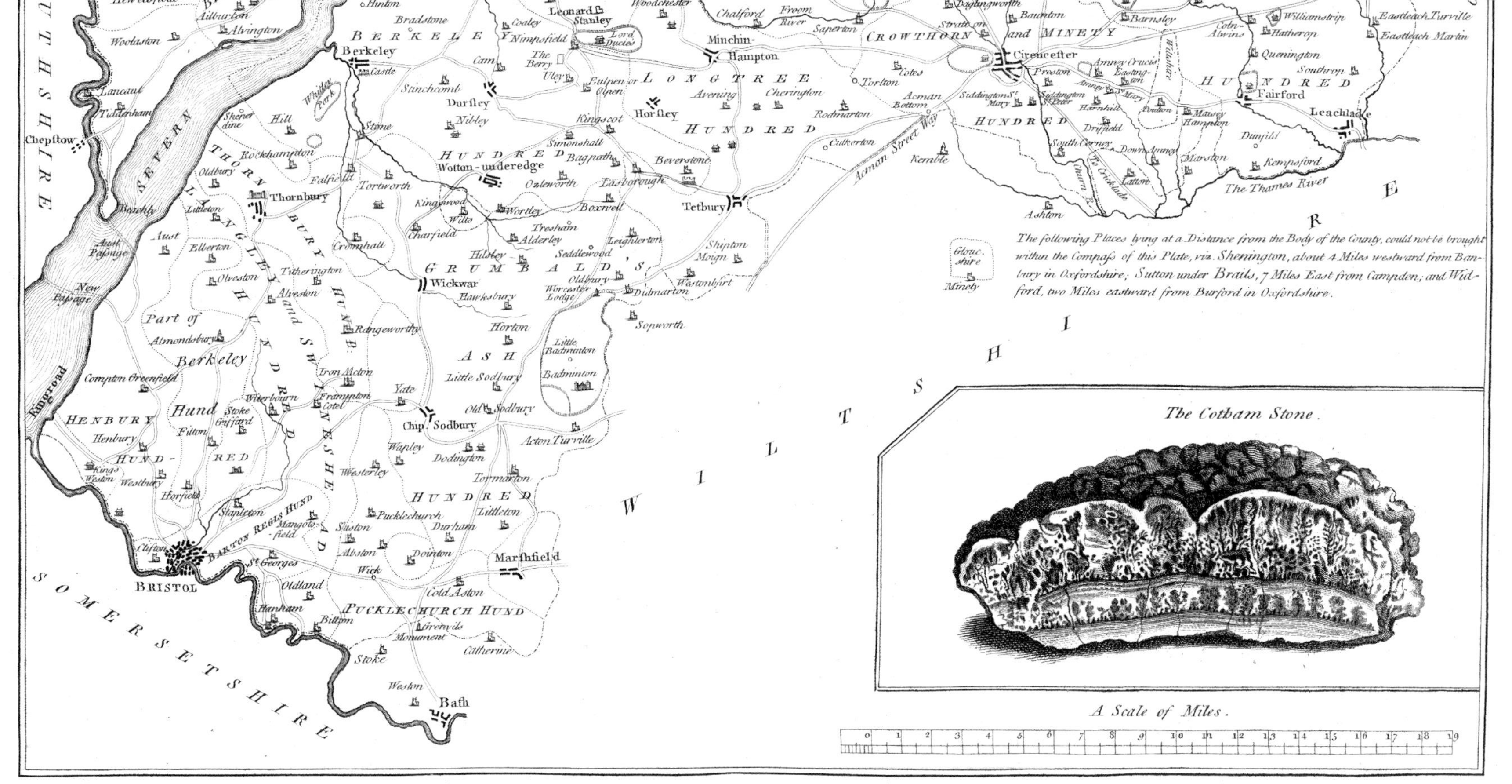

The following Places lying at a Distance from the Body of the County, could not be brought within the Compass of this Plate, viz. Shenington, about 4 Miles westward from Banbury in Oxfordshire; Sutton under Brails, 7 Miles East from Campden; and Widford, two Miles eastward from Burford in Oxfordshire.
The Cotham Stone.
A Scale of Miles.
0 1 2 3 4 5 6 7 8 9 10 11 12 13 14 15 16 17 18 19
W I L T S H I R E
S O M E R S E T S H I R E
SEVERN
Chepstow
Berkeley
Thornbury
Wotton-underedge
Wickwar
Chip. Sodbury
Marshfield
Bath
BRISTOL
Tetbury
Minchin-Hampton
Cirencester
Fairford
Leachlade
Leonard Stanley
Horsley
Durfley
B E R K E L E Y
T H O R N B U R Y H U N D.
L A N G L E Y and S W I N E S H E A D
G R U M B A L D'S A S H
L O N G T R E E H U N D R E D
C R O W T H O R N and M I N E T Y
P U C K L E C H U R C H H U N D
H E N B U R Y H U N D-R E D
Part of Berkeley Hund
BARTON REGIS HUND
Acman Street Way
The Thames River
Kingroad
New Passage
Aust Passage
Glouc. shire
Minety

A

NEW HISTORY

OF

Gloucesterſhire.

COMPRISING THE

TOPOGRAPHY,	PRODUCE,
ANTIQUITIES,	TRADE, and
CURIOSITIES,	MANUFACTURES

OF THAT COUNTY;

The Foundation-Charters *and* Endowments *of* Abbies, *and other* Religious Houſes;

The FOUNDATION of the BISHOPRICK, &c. with a ſhort Biographical Account of the BISHOPS and DEANS;

The Names of the PATRONS and INCUMBENTS, and the Antient and Preſent Value of all the ECCLESIASTICAL BENEFICES;

CHARTERS of INCORPORATION, and CIVIL GOVERNMENT Of the ſeveral BOROUGHS;

DESCRIPTIONS of the PRINCIPAL SEATS;

DESCENT of the MANORS; GENEALOGIES of FAMILIES, With their ARMS, MONUMENTAL INSCRIPTIONS, &c.

In the Courſe of this WORK is given

The Hiſtory of every Pariſh, Tithing, and Extraparochial Place in the County.

ALSO THE

ECCLESIASTICAL, CIVIL, AND MILITARY

HISTORY of the CITY of GLOUCESTER,

From its FIRST FOUNDATION to the PRESENT TIME.

With a Copy of DOMESDAY-BOOK for *GLOUCESTERSHIRE*, now firſt printed in the Language, and after the Manner of the Original.

Illuſtrated with a MAP of the COUNTY, VIEWS of GENTLEMEN's SEATS, &c. &c.

Par ſit Fortuna Labori.

CIRENCESTER: PRINTED BY SAMUEL RUDDER. 1779.

TO THE

RIGHT HONOURABLE

HENRY Earl *BATHURST.*

MY LORD,

IT was your Lordſhip's Noble Father ſuggeſting the Expediency of Reviſing Sir ROBERT ATKYNS's GLOUCESTERSHIRE, that gave Being to this Publication; and I beg Leave to preſent it to Your Lordſhip, his only ſurviving Son and Succeſſor.

I am not ſo vain, My Lord, as to think it worth your Acceptance, but if its Merit were to be eſtimated by the Greatneſs of the Subject, and the Time and Labour it has coſt me, it might have a better Claim to your Patronage.

Sir ROBERT ATKYNS's Book was well received by the County, and ſhould the preſent Publication be conſidered only as an Improvement upon it, my Ambition will be ſufficiently gratified. Your Opinion, My Lord, will fix its Character, and having your Approbation, there will be Nothing to fear from Men of Judgment and Candor.

I have the Honour to be,

With the utmoſt Deference and Reſpect,

My Lord,

Your Lordſhip's very dutiful

and obedient humble Servant,

SAMUEL RUDDER.

P R E F A C E.

SIR Robert Atkyns's *Ancient and Present State of Glosterſhire* was publiſhed in the year 1712. The extreme ſcarcity and great price of it encouraged the editor to offer the preſent work under the title of A New History of Gloucestershire: Soon after his propoſals were given out, another perſon republiſhed ſir Robert's book, without the leaſt addition or improvement. This is a fact very neceſſary to be ſtated, but it wants neither comment nor remark. The editor of the preſent work purſuing his plan, has at length completed it. How far the title he has aſſumed can be ſupported, muſt be left to the deciſion of the public: He does not, however, mean to inſinuate that he has made no uſe of ſir Robert Atkyns's book; on the contrary, he has adopted that gentleman's method of alphabetical arrangement, and has availed himſelf of whatever was uſeful. It is incumbent on him alſo to acknowledge many obligations to other writings and compilations.

The preliminary and introductory part is drawn from various ſources; the monaſtic hiſtory chiefly from Stevens's Supplement to ſir William Dugdale's *Monaſticon*, and doctor Burnet's *Hiſtory of the Reformation*. The other introductory matters are ſelected from Camden, Selden, lord Lyttelton, and various writers on the antient ſtate of affairs in Britain.

The Hiſtory of the county, in the three grand diviſions of Coteſwold, Vale, and Foreſt, with the account of its trade, is new; and that part of *Domeſday* which relates to Glouceſterſhire, and concludes the General Hiſtory, is now firſt printed in the language, and after the contracted manner of the original, ſo far as with common printing types could be effected. For the copy of that record the editor is indebted to Mr. Samuel Dixon, of Norfolk-ſtreet, London, who procured and ſent it to him; but it was afterwards very carefully collated with lord chief juſtice Hale's *Fac Simile* copy, depoſited in Lincoln's Inn library; and this, it is preſumed, will be thought a curious and valuable acquiſition.

The Hiſtory of the city and dioceſe of Glouceſter, making together 129 pages, is newly drawn up from materials collected by the late reverend Mr. Furney, archdeacon of Surrey, and communicated by Mr. Rogers of Glouceſter.

The parochial Hiſtory follows next in order; and the editor, to be correct, and to note every thing obſervable, has viſited the ſeveral pariſhes, and made diligent enquiries. He has given an account of their antiquities and natural curioſities, and has attempted to give the etymology of the names of places, agreeing with or diſſenting from ſir Robert Atkyns occaſionally.

In this part, it is preſumed, he has ſometimes ſucceeded; but to inveſtigate the meaning of names is no very eaſy province. Great length of time produces changes in circumſtances and things which otherwiſe might give light to the origin and ſignification of names; and vulgar pronunciation and incorrect writing have ſo diſtorted them, that many at preſent have very little reſemblance to their original. The peculiarities of ſituation, produce, and ſoil, were proper circumſtances from whence to derive the appellation of places; but where nature afforded no ſuch obvious aſſiſtance, the name-giver had one grand reſource, which was to add ſome common termination, as *don*, *ton*, *lege*, *ley*, *berg*, *&c.* to the proprietor's name; and as this was very eaſily done, ſo was it commonly practiced. There are certain names, however, which bid defiance to explanation; and if the editor has ſometimes failed in his conjectures, no wonder, eſpecially in a matter of ſo much uncertainty.

In the parochial Hiſtory, he has alſo given a deſcription of the market-towns, and moſt remarkable places, wherein ſir Robert Atkyns was defective; but to deſcend to a minute deſcription of every little village would have been ridiculous, as many of them have nothing more than their names, bearings, and diſtances to diſtinguiſh them; and without *differentia* in the ſubject, a diſguſting ſameneſs in expreſſion will inevitably recur. Let the brighteſt genius exert his abilities on a few inconſiderable places, and he will feel the truth of this aſſertion. A deſcription of two or three will indifferently ſuit almoſt all the reſt, and he that ſays much of them, reſembles one that talks a great deal about trifles.

The deſcent of the manors generally commences with an abſtract from *Domeſday*, faithfully, but as literally as poſſible, tranſlated from the original. Herein ſir Robert Atkyns was exceedingly imperfect. He has taken too great liberty with that record, and inſtead of tranſlating the whole paſſages, gives a paraphraſe of part only.

He uſually takes the quantity of land ſpecified in *Domeſday* to be preciſely what the manor was taxed at; but he was greatly miſtaken, as the record itſelf will prove concerning Alveſton, Newnham, Guiting, and ſeveral other places. Beſides theſe miſtakes, there are many inſtances of his applying the *Domeſday* accounts to places which they have no relation to, and not a few of their being totally omitted: But it is unneceſſary to enumerate them here, as they are commonly taken notice of in the accounts of thoſe places where the miſtakes have happened.

It was chiefly in the hiſtorical accounts of the ſucceſſive owners of manors and eſtates that ſir Robert Atkyns's book was of ſervice to the editor of this work; for as the ſhort and ſummary manner in which that part is written would not admit of great variety of expreſſion, he has very commonly uſed the words of that author, thinking it unneceſſary, without particular reaſon, to affect a different language. Sir Robert derived his accounts from the eſcheators books, original fines, and other records, to which he had free acceſs; and, excepting a few miſtakes which might happen in tranſcribing, he abſtracts them very faithfully. The editor has not only corrected thoſe miſtakes, ſo far as they have occurred to him, but alſo filled up ſome chaſms from the records, and quoted his authorities in both inſtances; but where no authority is given, the credibility in general reſts on ſir Robert Atkyns. The additions in deſcents ſince ſir Robert's time have been carefully made, and may ſafely be relied on; and genealogical accounts of families, with their arms, ſo far as they could be procured, are ſubjoined to the reſpective eſtates of which ſuch families are owners.

The next head principally concerns the clergy. Eccleſiaſtical benefices are greatly enhanced ſince ſir Robert's time. Here will be found the name of the patron, and the preſent value of every living, as nearly as could be aſcertained, together with all other particulars reſpecting the church, that are either curious or uſeful.

Sir Robert had taken notice of a few monuments in the churches for eminent perſons, but the editor conceiving it would be more ſatiſfactory to give the memorials at large, has accordingly placed under a diſtinct head many curious monumental inſcriptions, and the arms found with them, ſo exactly taken, that the particularities, and in ſome inſtances the errors, in the original, are deſignedly preſerved in the copy. Theſe exhibit very uſeful anecdotes of family hiſtory and connections, and making the living acquainted with the dead, not only ſhew us what they were, but often teach us what we ourſelves ought to be. Some hold monumental inſcriptions in light eſtimation, but it was the opinion of the author of the Plain Dealer, '*That every ſtone that we look upon in the repoſitory of paſt ages is both an entertainment and a monitor.*' Perhaps ſome inſcriptions have found admittance on account of the arms which accompany them, whilſt others have little more to recommend them than the particular caſt of the writer, or of the times when they were written. In this department there was no rule for ſelection, and the taſte even of men of judgment is ſo very different, that it is poſſible the editor may be equally cenſured for admitting ſo many, and for not inſerting more. The laws of this country take cognizance of moving or defacing a monumental ſtone in the church, as of an injury done to the family of the deceaſed, and the placing memorials in a book ſeems the moſt effectual ſecurity againſt ſuch injuries. But this part of the work, it is ſaid, is likely to be extended, with a view very different from the preſent publication, by a gentleman whoſe employment in the heralds office enables him to anſwer every expectation. 'Till that gentleman ſhall have finiſhed his undertaking, the editor flatters himſelf that the preſent collection may prove entertaining, and afterwards ſerve as an humble attendant upon it.

Next to the monumental inſcriptions, follows a liſt of benefactions to the poor, and other public charities, continued down to the preſent time, the utility of which is too obvious to need explanation.

Then follows the rate of the public taxes, and the comparative ſtate of population in each pariſh, between the time when ſir Robert Atkyns made his collections, and the preſent. Under this head the editor has given, in a variety of inſtances, the true proportion between the annual baptiſms and burials, and the whole number of inhabitants, which ſhews the degrees of healthineſs in different ſituations.

The alarm lately ſpread of the nation's depopulating, induced the editor to compare the average of births and burials about ſeventy years ago, with thoſe of the preſent time, taking the authority of the regiſters in both inſtances; but there are a few pariſhes of which accounts could not be obtained, ſome of the regiſters being loſt, or imperfectly kept. The reſult of the compariſon is, that the inhabitants of Glouceſterſhire are very conſiderably increaſed during that period, but not uniformly ſo. In ſome places their numbers are more than doubled, whilſt in others they continue nearly the ſame. This is owing to different cauſes: The growth of trade and improvements in agriculture encourage population, whilſt the decline of manufactures produces a contrary effect.

During the before-mentioned period, agriculture has been much improved, particularly in the hill country; and in the clothing and manufacturing parts, trade has equally increaſed: But in the Vale, moſt of thoſe incloſures that in the former part of this period were corn-fields, have ſince been laid down to paſture, which very ſenſibly affected population; and tho' even ſome

of

of thoſe places where that has happened, are more populous than they were before, yet the alteration has prevented them from increaſing ſo much as they would have done; for dairy and grazing-farms furniſh leſs employment than tillage, and many of the younger people have migrated to the hill-country, or to market-towns.

Another impediment to population has crept in during the latter part of this period, which is, the laying of two or three farms into one. The little pariſh of Aſton Subedge is chiefly in tillage, and ſir Robert Atkyns reports it to have conſiſted of 24 houſes, and 104 inhabitants. By an exact account taken in 1773, the houſholders were 20, and the inhabitants only 63; and upon inquiry into the cauſe of this ſtrange declenſion, it was given for a reaſon, that the pariſh had juſt then been incloſed, and ſeven farms, of which it conſiſted before, being laid into four, the occupiers of three little farms, with their families, had left the place. There are two or three other inſtances in the county, beſide this, of a like decreaſe of inhabitants.

Here ſome notice ſhould be taken of a practice prevailing in ſome places, leſt it become more general, and produce a train of evil conſequences to the community. It is ſaid, that in ſome pariſhes the lords of manors, and the principal landholders, conſidering it as a piece of refined policy, have pulled down their cottage-houſes, or ſuffered them to fall, on purpoſe to drive away the poor miſerable inhabitants, and to prevent the younger ſort from marrying and ſettling in their own pariſhes. Miſerable indeed! to be deſerted and abandoned by thoſe whoſe lands they have cultivated, and whoſe granaries they have filled. Miſerable! to be expelled from the place of their nativity, as unworthy to breathe the air in common with their lords and maſters; who, deaf to the calls of humanity, and inattentive to their own real intereſt, ſeem not to be ſenſible that without the labourer's hand their ample fields would be of no value, and that rents advance from labour and improved cultivation. If the poor are burthenſome, they ſhould be relieved, and not extirpated. The induſtrious part of them are the moſt profitable members of the community; the idle ſhould be reclaimed; but that will never be effected by penal laws, whilſt our towns and villages ſwarm with alehouſes. It is there they ſpend their time and money; there their morals are corrupted; there the ſot, the poacher, the petty thief and highwayman are gradually formed; and to thoſe ſeminaries of vice we chiefly owe the evils complained of among the lower claſs of people. Strike at the root of them; put down the alehouſe, not the cottage, in your village; ſo ſhall you ſoon find the poor more induſtrious, more honeſt, and leſs burthenſome.

This is a matter highly deſerving the attention of the magiſtrate, upon whoſe conduct, in the execution of his office, the morals of the people, and the well-being of the ſtate ſo much depend. It is a vulgar error that the drunkard injures nobody but himſelf: Hundreds are connected with him, and the community ſuffers more from one character of that ſort, than it is benefited by two ſober perſons. The editor has been led as it were inadvertently into theſe reflections, and tho' they may not be particularly applicable to Glouceſterſhire, yet as a general well-wiſher to his country, he hopes they are not altogether unſeaſonable.

But to return from this digreſſion: The Appendix ſtands after the parochial Hiſtory, and conſiſts of a variety of charters and papers of conſiderable length, taken from ſir Robert Atkyns's Gloſterſhire, and other ſources, and are proper to be referred to occaſionally. Some of them were originally written in Latin, but are here given in the Engliſh language, exactly as they were tranſlated by ſir Robert, except one or two of them, particularly the charter to the priory of Leonard Stanley, which in ſir Robert's book is blended and confuſed with part of the charter to the priory of Newent. The editor has rectified that miſtake, and added from the *Monaſticon* what was omitted.

Next follows a copious and uſeful Index, to which the reader muſt have recourſe to find the tithings and hamlets, which are not placed in alphabetical order in the body of the work, but inſerted in the pariſhes to which they reſpectively belong. By the Index alſo will be found the arms of the gentry, and the principal perſons and things treated of in the courſe of the work. With reſpect to the arms found upon monuments, they are in general blazoned as they appear there; but ſculptors and painters are not always the beſt heralds, and if they have made miſtakes, they ſhould not be imputed to the editor. Beſides, Guillim obſerves, that '*So great is the reſemblance* '*oftentimes of things borne in coat armour, which* '*yet in their exiſtence are much differing, that a* '*man well ſeen in heraldry may commit an error in* '*blazoning of them.*' Add to this, that colours fade in a long courſe of time, and as in a few inſtances the editor was to rely ſolely on the preſent appearance of them on monuments in the churches, he offers this apology, if he has at any time miſtaken one colour for another, as blue for green, or *vice verſa*.

Laſtly, there is interſperſed through the body of the work, a curious ſet of prints of the chief ſeats in the county, for which the editor returns ſincere thanks to thoſe gentlemen to whom they are addreſt, and at whoſe expence they were engraven. As they are well executed, they make a valuable part of the work, and together with the correct map of the county, will undoubtedly prove acceptable to the public. He laments, however, the loſs of the plates of Stoke Giffard, and King's Weſton, by the deaths of lord Botetourt, and lord Clifford; and Rendcombe Houſe was

was designed to have made its appearance in this History; but the person employ'd to take the drawing, could not be prevailed on to finish it in time.

The editor has now passed over in review the different heads of his work, and is far from being of opinion with Mela, an antient Roman geographer, who speaking of his own country, says, *De Italia, magis quia Ordo exigit, quam quia monstrari egeat, pauca dicuntur, nota sunt omnia.* — If many things generally known by the inhabitants of Gloucestershire be taken notice of in this work, they should not be considered as unnecessary or superfluous, because they are so known; for the book may fall into hands to whom the information may be acceptable. On the other hand, it would be altogether as unreasonable in strangers to take exception against such things as are serviceable chiefly to the inhabitants of this county; because it was for their use they were inserted. In short, what may seem trifling to one class of readers, another may value and esteem; and it was the editor's intention to accommodate himself to all.

Thus much he thought necessary by way of preface. How he has acquitted himself in the compilation, will be determined by the public voice. All he will venture to say further is, that he has endeavoured to investigate Truth, perhaps with various success. If he differ from others in matter of fact, he generally gives his authority; if in opinion, he thought himself at liberty to declare it with temper and moderation.

He affects not a cold indifference to the reception which his labours may meet with, for that would be unnatural, and an indignity to the highest tribunal in matters of Literature. Conscious of his imperfections, he is sensible he may have fallen into error; but he has traduced no character, nor wilfully misrepresented any transaction; and he doubts not but the generous public will extend that indulgence to him, which others in similar cases have experienced.

CIRENCESTER,
December 1, 1778.

SAM. RUDDER.

ADDENDA ET CORRIGENDA.

DURING the Printing of so large a Work, some Alterations in Property have happened by Death and Alienations, which cannot be imputed for Mistakes to the Editor. They principally relate to the following Places, *viz.*

ABBENHALL. By the death of John Howell, esq; in 1778, this manor passed to his grandson, Edmund Probyn, of Newland in this county, esq; who is the present lord of the manor, and whose arms are emblazoned under the account of monuments in the church of Newland.

ARLINGHAM. Mrs. Yate dying in the year 1776, this manor is vested in lady Mill, Powell Snell, of Guiting-Grange in this county, esq; and Mrs. Estcourt, of Burton Hill, in the county of Wilts, whose family name was Yate.

BARNSLEY. Mrs. Cassandra Perrot died in June, 1778, and by her will devised this manor and her other estates to James Musgrave, of the Middle Temple, esq; one of her nearest relations, who now resides at Barnsley-Park. He bears *Azure, six annulets,* 3, 2, 1, *Or.*

BATSFORD. The following monumental inscriptions were received too late to be inserted in the account of this parish:

To the Memory
Of The Right Hon[ble] RICHARD FREEMAN,
Lord High Chancellor of Ireland,
And ELIZABETH His Wife,
Daughter of S[r]. ANTHONY KECK:
MARY Wife of WALTER EDWARDS Esq[r].
Their only Child;
ANNA Daughter of RICH[d] MARSHALL Esq[r].
Second Wife of the said L[d]. Chancellor FREEMAN;
RICHARD FREEMAN Esq[r]. their only Son.
And ANNA their Daughter;
MARG[t]. ELIZ[th]. FREEMAN,
Wife of the said RICHARD FREEMAN;
And WALTER EDWARDS FREEMAN Esq[r].
Eldest Son of the abovenam'd WALTER EDWARDS,
by MARY his Wife.
This Monument is dedicated by
THOMAS EDWARDS FREEMAN Esq[r].
Surviving Son of the said WALTER EDWARDS
Ann. Dom. 1756.

The arms on this monument are the same with those given under the short account of this family, p. 266; and they are here accompanied with this well-chosen motto, very proper for a lord chancellor, NEC PRECE NEC PRETIO.

To

To the Memory of
the Rev[d]. THOMAS BURTON, D.D.
Rector of this Pariſh,
Prebendary of Durham,
and
Arch-Deacon of St. Davids,
Who dyed July 16, 1767,
In the fifty ſeventh Year of his Age,
And lies interr'd by his own Direction,
In the adjoining Church-Yard.
The Soundneſs of his Faith
Was evidenced by the beſt of Proofs
The exemplarineſs of his Practice.
The ſerious, friendly, & affectionate Attention
With which he conſcientiouſly diſcharged
Every Branch of his Miniſterial Function,
Engaged the Hearts, & influenced the Manners
Of all his People.
Thankful for the good things of this Life,
Which the Providence of GOD
Had amply beſtow'd upon Him,
He employ'd them to Purpoſes
Of real Uſefulneſs.
He was a Friend, a Father to the Poor,
A generous, indulgent Maſter
To a faithful & obſervant Houſhold,
A Lover of Hoſpitality,
And a chearful Promoter
Of every ſocial, every liberal Affection.
Juſtice, Humanity, Benevolence, & Charity
Mark'd the Character
of
This excellent Man.
Whoſe Life was ſo uniformly Good,
That Death, tho' ſudden, found him not unprepared.
Bleſſed ſhall that Servant be,
Whom his Lord when He cometh,
Shall find ſo Prepared.

BISLEY, PITCHCOMBE, STROUD, LYPIAT. On the death of John Stephens, eſq; in the year 1778, theſe manors were, by his will, veſted in his nephew, Thomas-Baghot Delabere, eſq; whoſe family arms are emblazoned under the account of Southam, in the pariſh of Cleeve.

BROCKWORTH. The following is the inſcription upon the monument mentioned to be in the chancel at Brockworth :

HIC SITUS EST ILLE HONORABILIS CHRISTOPHERUS GUISE IN HOC AGRO GLOCEST. MILES AC BARONET' NEC NON AB UTROQ. PRÆLUSTRIUM PROAVORUM SANGUINE LONGISSIMA SERIE PERINSIGNIS. VIR ERAT NON VULGARITER ERUDITUS, INDOLIS PERACUTÆ, MEMORIÆ TENACIS, INGENII VIVIDI, IUDICII PERQUAM SUBACTI. HINC PROPTER EXIMIAS DOTES FIDEM FORTITUDINEMQ' PROVINCIÆ SUÆ PRO-PRÆFECTUS ALTER A REGIO DIPLOMATE CONSTITUTUS EST UNDE POSTQUAM FIDELIS ILLE PATRIOTA REGI PATRIÆ SIBI SUISQ' SATIS FECISSET ET INTERIORES PROVINCIÆ SUÆ COMITATUS VRBEM GLOCESTRIÆ CIRCUMIACENTES, AB URBIS SERVITUDINE PERANTIQUA, INIQUISQ' CIVIUM PRIVILEGIIS EMANCIPASSET, IMMUNESQ' POSTERIS PERLIQUISSET, SAL. ÆRA M.DC.LXX. ÆT. 53. HEU NIMIS PROPERANT FATA. PRETIOSÆ CUIUS MEMORIÆ UNICUS FILIUS AC HAERES IOHANNES GUISE MILES AC BARONETUS HOC MONUMENTUM PARENTAVIT.

CIRENCESTER. To the account of the manor and hundred of Cirenceſter, with the Seven Hundreds, (pp. 354, 355) ſhould be ſubjoined as follows : Allen earl Bathurſt dying in 1775, was ſucceeded in title and eſtate by his lordſhip's only ſurviving ſon, Henry earl Bathurſt, who is lord of the manor and hundred of Cirenceſter, and likewiſe of the Seven Hundreds, by an accommodation between his lordſhip and the other claimants. There is a monument erected in this pariſh church for the late earl Bathurſt and his lady, with their buſts in white marble, and a weeping genius between them. Upon the tablet is the following inſcription :

Near this Place are depoſited the Remains of
ALLEN EARL BATHURST, and CATHERINE LADY BATHURST.

In the Legiſlative & Judicial departments
of the great Council of the Nation he ſerved his
Country 69 Years, wth honour, ability, & diligence.
Judgment & taſte directed his Learning,
Humanity tempered his Wit,
Benevolence guided all his Actions.
He died regretted by moſt, & praiſed by all,
The 16th day of September, 1775, aged 91.

Catherine his Conſort, by her milder Virtues,
added Luſtre to his great Qualities ;
Her domeſtic Oeconomy extended his Liberality,
Her judicious Charity his Munificence,
Her prudent government of her family, his hoſpitality.
She received the reward of her Exemplary life
The 8th day of June 1768, aged 79.

Married July the 6th. 1704.

Beneath the table are the following arms : Quarterly, 1ſt and 4th, Bathurſt ; 2d and 3d, *Argent, on a croſs of St. George gules five eſcallops Or*, for Villiers. A ſcutcheon of pretence, quarterly, 1ſt and 4th, *Barry of ſix argent and gules, a canton ermine*, for Apſley ; 2d and 3d, *Gules, a bend between two eſcallops Or*, for Petre.—The creſt, ſupporters, and motto, are ſet down in the ſhort genealogical account of his lordſhip's family, p. 355.

It is not improper to obſerve, that in May 1777, ſince the account of Cirenceſter was printed, ſome workmen, in digging a cellar in Dyer-ſtreet, now under the ſhop and warehouſes belonging to Meſſ. Robert and William Croome, diſcovered a curious teſſellated pavement about eighteen feet ſquare, of which they had deſtroy'd nearly half before it was taken notice of. The remainder was in good preſervation, and being waſhed, was expoſed for a few days to public view. It had a checkered border round it, about fourteen inches broad, compoſed of blue and white ſtones of an inch ſquare. Within the border, it conſiſted alſo of blue and white ſtones, and of red bricks, but in much ſmaller ſquares, worked into wreaths and other ornaments. It was divided into four compartments by the artful arrangement and diſpoſition of the different coloured ſtones and bricks into lines of hearts, linked together, and interlaced fretty-wiſe, which had a very pretty effect. The center of the pavement is ſtill preſerved. It conſiſts of an octagon border, incloſing a wreathed figure, with rays pointed to the angles of the octagon. There was alſo a ſmaller figure of the ſame kind in the middle of each compartment ; and the pavement together had very much the reſemblance of a rich Turkey carpet, the firſt idea of which I apprehend was ſuggeſted by a work of this kind. This pavement lay about ſix feet below the ſurface of the ground ; and there remained alſo part of the plaſtered walls of the houſe to which it belonged, which appeared to have been painted, but the figures were ſo decayed by time, that it was impoſſible to form any idea of the ſubject. It is very remarkable that one corner of the pavement lay next the ſtreet, and about eight or ten yards on the north ſide of it, the workmen found a road made of lime and gravel ; from which circumſtances it appears that antiently the ſtreets of the town lay in a different direction from what they do at preſent. This was undoubtedly a Roman work, and muſt be referred to the laſt-mentioned order of Roman pavements, in the ſhort account of them, p. 348.

DIMMOCK. The blank left for Mrs. Cam's arms in the cloſe of the account of this manor, ſhould be filled up thus : *Paly of ſix, argent and azure*. And in the account of population, the preſent number of inhabitants ſhould be 1282.

FLAXLEY. The antient manor houſe, taken notice of under this head, was burnt down in April, 1777.

FRAMPTON upon Severn. At the cloſe of the note, p. 453, concerning the late Mr. Richard Clutterbuck, read,----He died in 1775, and deviſed this eſtate

 to

to Mr. Phillips of Glouceſter, and to his wife, who was Mr. Clutterbuck's niece, for their lives; the remainder to Nathaniel Winchcombe, of Stroud, eſq; and his heirs.

LITTLETON upon Severn. By a late purchaſe, this manor is the property of ſir Henry Lippincot, who was created a baronet in the year 1778, ſince the printing of the account of Stoke Biſhop, where that gentleman reſides, and under which head his name occurs.

OLEPEN. To the genealogical account of the family of Daunt, in the note to p. 587, add as follows: By the death of Thomas Daunt, ſon of Thomas and Elizabeth, in the year 1777, his nephew, Thomas Daunt, eſq; ſucceeded to this eſtate, and is the preſent lord of the manor of Olepen.

OZLEWORTH. By the death of James Clutterbuck, eſq; this eſtate is veſted in Mrs. Clutterbuck, his widow.

WORMINGTON. Nathaniel Jefferys, late of London, eſq; purchaſed this manor, and the advowſon of the church, of the late Mr. Partridge, and preſented the reverend Mr. Thomas Stedman to the rectory. He alſo purchaſed Wormington Grange of lord Aylmer, ſo that he is proprietor of the greater part of the pariſh, and reſides at the Grange. He gives *Ermine, a lion rampant ſable, a canton of the ſecond within a double border argent.*

Page.	Column.	Line.
6	1	35 *for* rents houſes and, *read* rents and houſes.
6	2	45 *for* we, *read* were.
7	1	51 *for* for, *read* from.
11	2	16 *for* dioſceſes, *read* dioceſes.
13	2	In the explanation of berry, *read* a camp or fortification.
20	2	43 *for* Botloe, *read* Dudſton and King's Barton
24	1	45 *for* every Thurſday, *read* on Thurſday.
33	1	34 *for* a bible, *read* the bible.
59	2	3 *for* that purſue, *read* purſuing.
65	2	37 *for* writtin, *read* written.
66	1	17 *for* ſorth, *read* ſorts; and in the 2d line of the 2d column of the note, *for* conjecture, *read* conjuncture.
67	2	3&5 *for* preſtitit, *read* p'ſtitit; and in the 16th line of the ſame column, *for* poſiut, *read* poſuit; alſo, in the 22d line, *for* vill'e, *read* vill'ni.
82	1	11 *for* era, *read* æra.
84	2	6 from the bottom, *read* 9 E. 1.

P.	C.	L.
92	2	2 of the note, *for* alured, *read* allured.
98	1	laſt line, *read* 13 E. 1.
103	2	43 *for* wiſhfully, *read* wiſtfully.
137	2	31 *for* within, *read* with.
139	1	6 *for* legantine, *read* legatine.
143	2	6 *for* Linton, *read* Minſterworth.
161	2	12 *for* roundels, *read* roundlets.
165	1	52 *for* prebends, *read* prebendaries.
167	2	13 for that inſcription, ſee it more correct under Withington.
171	1	17 *for* Trinity college, *read* King's college.
175	2	38 *for* SVE, *read* SVÆ.
233	1	30 *for* Saliſbury, *read* Shrewſbury.
239	1	22 *for* ſable, *read* azure.
242	1	27 *for* Somerviles, *read* following.
264	2	12 *for* earl of Talbot, *read* earl Talbot.
271	2	7 after ſeven hides, *read* and one virgate. In Eldbertone five hides.
281	2	9 *for* a chevron, *read* a feſs.
285	2	7 *for* a bend wavy, *read* a bend wavy ſable.
351	1	39 *for* No. 1. *read* No. 31.
353	1	8 *for* 1775, *read* 1774.
354	2	18 *for* his, *read* her; and line 28, *for* earl of Bathurſt, *read* earl Bathurſt.
355	2	13 of the note, *for* earl of Bathurſt, *read* earl Bathurſt.
368	1	34 In the account of population, *for* 3878, *read* 3988. This miſtake was occaſioned by the family in the workhouſe having been intirely omitted.
374	2	19 *for* gules, *read* azure.
387	1	23 *for* York, *read* Canterbury.
421	2	4 from the bottom, *for* Elliot, *read* Elton.
425	2	13 *for* quicked, *read* quickened.
426	1	40 *for* againſt, *read* in favour of; and line 42, *for* 1 R. 3. *read* 1 H. 7.
429	2	32 *for* dures, *read* duros.
474	2	48 *for* Newland, *read* Newnham.
476	2	15 *for* daughters, *read* ſiſters.
495	2	49 *read* and his ſiſter, Mrs. Wilmot.
528	1	19 *for* 1776, *read* 1766.
546	1	44 *for* Thomas-Edwards Freeman of Batſford, *read* John Freeman, of Hidcote.
548	2	32 *for* leaſt, *read* left.
563	2	30 *dele* it.
634	2	44 *for* George, *read* Charles.
643	2	5&6 *read* Thomas Eſtcourt, eſq; is lord of the manor.
675	2	33 *for* George, *read* Gregory.
716	2	49 *for* Sheldon, *read* Selden.
775	2	24 *for* 32 E. 3. *read* 32 E. 1.
842	1	1 of the note, *for* paternally, as it is printed in part of the impreſſion, *read* maternally.

In the charter of the corporation of Tewkeſbury, *for* community, *read* commonalty, throughout.

PRELIMINARY

POSTSCRIPT to the PREFACE.

THE Editor, unwilling to appear arrogant and assuming, cautiously avoided a minute comparison, in the foregoing preface, between his Book and sir Robert Atkyns's *Ancient and Present State of Glocestershire.* Some additions and deviations are indeed cursorily mentioned; but experience evinces that he was too scrupulous, and Envy has taken advantage of it. He had both the Books in possession, and knew their contents better, perhaps, than any man. It was therefore the more easy for him to have shewn wherein they differ, and it was his interest to have it generally known.

Had he been more particular, Prejudice would have been less adventurous, and Malevolence have lost its aim. But it was a task disagreeable to him, and he passed it lightly over. He wished the Public to examine the NEW HISTORY with the OLD, and to decide upon their different merits; but he did not consider that to compare two large folio volumes requires much labour and attention. Few have leisure and opportunity to do it; fewer have inclination; but fewest of all are those who examine facts, to judge on which side Truth lies, where authorities differ. Hence Obloquy, ever forward and assuming, took occasion to exert itself, against which he thinks it not improper to enter his *caveat*, in the words of the poet:

> *Ne mea dona tibi studio dispôsta fideli,*
> *Intellecta prius quam sint, contempta relinquas.*
> Lucret. lib. 1.

The human mind appears to have been the same in all ages; subject to the same passions and affections. Inclination often warps the judgment, and reason is sway'd by the will. Were it not so, it is probable the Editor would not have been under obligations of a *very particular nature* to a gentleman whose duty it is to instruct, and not to injure him. That gentleman, however, speaking of the forementioned Histories, was pleased to decide in favour of the Old, though by confession it appeared he had never read the New. — Unhappy disposition! that could wish to deprive another of a little reputation that had been publicly allowed *him.! — Ill-fated Book! condemned without reading! — All the world must applaud such *distinguished candor* in a clergyman, whatever may be thought of his judgment!

It was that gentleman's decision that determined the Editor to subjoin the following particulars for the use of such who have, as well as those who have not, an opportunity to compare the two books together. They certainly differ very materially, but it will be found that this volume contains all the abstracts from the records, and whatever else is useful, in *Sir Robert Atkyns's Glocestershire*, besides great additions interspersed through the whole.

When the Editor first engaged in this undertaking, he thought it necessary to examine authorities; and his care and diligence will in some measure appear, from the numberless errors discovered in his predecessor's performance. Some of them are mentioned in the body of the work; but this uncandid attack makes it necessary for him, though reluctantly, to bring them, with some others, into one point of view.

Errors in Atkyns's *Glocestershire.*

It has been already observed, that sir Robert Atkyns has blended and confused the charter to the priory of Leonard Stanley with that to the priory of Newent. — In his account of the tithes of Abston and Wick, he mistakes that place for Wick in Berkeley. [See this volume, p. 212.]—Part of the records relating to Pirton in Lidney are misapplied to Pirton in Churchdown, 340. -- Those relating to the hamlet of Naunton in Winchcombe are placed erroneously to the parish of Naunton, 559.—The extracts from Domesday-Book which belong to Cold Aston, are misapplied to Acton, 213. — Those belonging to Aston Subedge stand under Aston Blank; — to Aston upon Carant, under Aston-under-Hill, 243; — to Bibury, under Barnsley; — to the tithing of Little Colesbourn, under the parish of Colesbourn; — to Dointon, under Dodington;—to Hampnet and Meysey-

* The writers of the CRITICAL REVIEW, announcing that the editor had published *A New History of Gloucestershire*, deliver themselves in the following terms: "This task he appears to "have executed with great attention and industry; not only "comprising in the work whatever was useful in the collection "of his predecessor, but enriching it with a variety of ad-"ditional information and materials. A correct map of Glou-"cestershire is prefixed to the volume; and through the work "are interspersed some excellent prints, representing the chief "seats in the county. Considered as an improved edition of Sir "Robert Atkyns's Glocestershire, this work is a valuable system "of provincial history; and its merit rises in proportion to the "numerous articles of information which have been added by "Mr. Rudder. The great expence of printing so large a work, "ought to entitle the author or editor to the public favour, "which will, therefore, we doubt not, be extended to this in-"dustrious collector." *Review for Aug.* 1779.

The authors of the MONTHLY REVIEW conclude their examination of this work in these words: "We shall finish our "account with observing, that the editor of this volume appears "to us to have been very industrious in preparing it for the "public eye, and we esteem it a work in its kind which justly "merits notice and approbation." *Review for July*, 1780.

And every other publication wherein this work is taken notice of, makes honourable mention of it. One of them has the following passage: "This is a work which we may venture to re-"commend to our readers. Many years since, Sir Robert "Atkyns gave the public the *Ancient and Present State of Glo-cestershire*; but the great scarcity of the remaining copies of "that work, and its high price, induced Mr. Rudder to engage "in the present production, which he has executed in a very "masterly manner, and illustrated and embellished it with a "correct map of Gloucestershire, and many excellent en-"gravings."

Hampton,

Hampton, under Minchin-Hampton; — to Horfield, under Haresfield; — to Hayles, under Hawling; — to Sodbury, under Henbury, 492; — to Norton in Wefton Subedge, under Morton-Henmarfh, 557; — to Wotton near Gloucefter, under Upton St. Leonard's; — to Wefton upon Avon, under Wefton Subedge; — and the extract proper to the tithing of Winfon in Bibury, ftands under the parifh of Winfton, in a different hundred.

Befides the foregoing obvious and grofs mifapplications, the following manors, &c. want the Domefday accounts properly belonging to them, *viz.* Gaunt's Urcot in Almondfbury, Afton Subedge, Bagendon, the extenfive and noble barony of Berkeley, Bourton on the Water, Cow Honeybourn, Cowley, Doynton, Ebberton, Frampton Cotterel, Hampnet, Hayles, Meyfey-Hampton, Hewelsfield, Olvefton, Painfwick, Pauntley, Adminton and Wincot in Queinton, 615; Rifington Wick, 625; Shenington, Shipton Oliffe, Little Sodbury, Old Sodbury, Southrop, Tainton, Upton St. Leonard's, Rodley in Weftbury, and Woollafton.

The following places have only a part of the record applied to them, *viz.* Awre, Bibury, Elkftone, Kemerton, Allifton in Lidney, 529; Prefbury, Quenington, Shipton Moign, Shipton Solers, Tewkefbury, Thornbury, Weftbury upon Trim, Hambrook in Winterbourn, and Woodchefter.

It has been obferved that fir Robert has rather paraphrafed than tranflated any part of Domefday-Book; and in many places he has perverted the fenfe, as under Alvefton, Broadwell, Cheltenham, Hidcot Bois in Ebberton, &c. &c. In others, the abftracts are interpolated with matters not mentioned in the original, as under Batsford, Brimpsfield, Horton, Kempsford, Long Hope, Little Rifington, Saperton, &c. And there is one very remarkable inconfiftency, where (under Amney St. Peter) fir Robert's quotation makes Domefday-Book give an account of a donation to the monaftery of St. Peter at Gloucefter, 26 H. 1. which was forty years after the compilation of the record.

In fir Robert's account of Newland, he takes notice of an antient tomb in the church-yard, with this infcription:

Here lyeth Jenkin Wyrral, chief Forefter in Fee;
A braver Fellow never was, nor never will thère be.

And in an advertifement for the publication of the *Antiquarian Repertory*, mention is made, that in the fecond volume of that work, there is a print of Jenkyn Wyrral's tomb; but unfortunately the tomb alluded to is not for *Jenkin Wyrral*, nor was there ever any fuch couplet upon it, as fir Robert mentions. The fides of it were very much over-grown with mofs, which the Editor carefully cleared away in 1776, and then copied the true reading, as it is printed in p. 570.

Were it neceffary, great numbers of other miftakes in the quotations from Domefday might be produced; for it is in that part efpecially that the learned author hath erred; but thefe will fatisfy a reafonable perfon that the Editor of the New History of Gloucestershire has confidered his fubject, and examined authorities. He has avoided fir Robert's errors, and fupplied his defects; but he refts not his caufe on thefe merits only.

It has been faid that the introductory part, the general hiftory, &c. are newly written, and greatly enlarged. The parochial hiftory has not been lefs improved; for the additions in topography, antiquities, biography, &c. are extended, in moft of the following parifhes, from one to four or five pages each; and are not inconfiderable in the reft. The chief improvements are under Abfton and Wick, Berkeley, Bifley, Bitton, Bourton on the Water, Cheltenham, Cirencefter, Cleeve, Clifton, Daglingworth, Derhurft, Dimmock, Driffield, [the method of improving meadow land, as defcribed under Driffield, is particularly recommended to the attention of the public;] Durfley, Elmore, Fairford, Flaxley, Frampton, St. George's, (a newly erected parifh;) Hampton, Hayles, Henbury, Kingfcot, Leachlade, Lidney, Longney, Marfhfield, Minety, Miferden, Newent, Newland, Newnham, Northleach, Painfwick, St. Philip's and Jacob's, Pucklechurch, Rodborough, Rodmarton, Slaughter and Eyford, Slimbridge, Sodbury, Stanley St. Leonard's, Stroud, Sudley, Tetbury, Tewkefbury, Thornbury, Uley, Weftbury, Welbury upon Trim, Winchcombe, Woodchefter, Wotton-under-edge, Acton, Almondfbury, Alvington, Arlingham, Afton Blank, Avening, Awre, Badgworth, Badminton, Bagendon, Barrington, Beverftone, Bibury, Boxwell, Brookrup, Buckland, Campden, Chedworth, Coates, Cranham, Dumbleton, Durham, Eaftington, Kemerton, Kempley, Lafborough, Mangotsfield, Naunton, Pauntley, Prefbury, Queinton, Randwick, Sandhurft, Saperton, Saul, Sherbourn, Sidington, Sifton, Stapleton, Stonehoufe, Stow, Tidenham, Titherington, Twining, Whitminfter, Wickwar, and Winterbourn.

The parochial hiftory is alfo neceffarily very much enlarged, by a continuation of the hiftory of property for feventy years lower than Sir Robert Atkyns had carried it; by the addition of numerous charities fince his time; the fupply of above fix hundred monumental infcriptions, fome of them very curious; and the blazoning of nearly as many family arms. So that all the additions and new materials, were they printed with as large a type as Sir Robert's, would alone make a volume nearly, if not altogether, as large as his.

Nor is it unworthy notice, that, including the map of the county, there are fourteen whole fheet prints, and three on half fheets, fuch as few county-hiftories can boaft of, to embellifh the work. The plate of Sherbourn-houfe, indeed, as mentioned p. 649, is not engraven, nor to be expected. The proprietor of that feat was pleafed to order a drawing of it, but difliking the draught, relinquifhed his original defign of giving a plate.

Why then, it may be afked, does not the reverend gentleman prefer the New Book to the Old?——Is it that the former oppofes fome of Sir Robert's chimeras, *That fenators fhould hold their places for life*, and other ftrange whims, that have as little to do with good fenfe as with a county-hiftory? Or is it——but there is no end to conjecture.——The Editor confines himfelf to facts. He wifhes not to irritate, but to reduce to candor and reafon.

April 3, 1783.

PRELIMINARY

PRELIMINARY MATTERS.

OF RELIGIOUS FOUNDATIONS, &c.

THERE were ſix mitred abbies in this county; thoſe of Glouceſter, Cirenceſter, Winchcombe, Tewkeſbury, Hayles, and Flaxley. The three firſt were peeral, the heads of which had ſeats in parliament till the diſſolution. This was more than a proportionable ſhare for the county, ſince there were only twenty-five abbats and two priors that held by barony in the whole kingdom. Beſides theſe, there were many other religious houſes of almoſt every denomination, which are mentioned in this book, under the names of the ſeveral places where they ſtood. But a ſhort account of the riſe, progreſs, and diſſolution of the monaſtic ſtate in general belongs more properly to this part of the work.

By religious houſes I mean cathedral churches, abbeys, priories, colleges, preceptories, &c. Few are ignorant of what is meant by cathedral churches, but the names and diſtinctions of the reſt are not ſo well underſtood.

An Abbey was a ſociety of religious people, over whom an abbat, [from the Syriac *abba*, father] or abbeſs, preſided as head. In every abbey was a prior immediately under the abbat, who, during the abbat's abſence, had the chief care of the houſe. Under him was the ſub-prior, and in great abbies the third and fourth prior, all removable at the will of the abbat. They had alſo four great *obedientiarii*, or officers, viz. 1. The *ſacriſta* or ſexton, who took care of the buildings, the veſſels, the books, and veſtments of the church. 2. The *theſaurarius*, or burſar, who received all the rents and revenues of the monaſtery, and diſburſed all expences. 3. The cellarer, who provided food for the houſe. 4. The *camerarius*, or chamberlain, who found the clothing. Beſides theſe, there were the almoner, infirmarer, and other inferior officers.

A Priory had for its head a prior or prioreſs, who was as abſolute as any abbat in his abbey. Theſe were called conventual priories, becauſe the head was choſen by the convent; but they could not proceed to election without a *Conge d'elire* from their patron; which is alſo the reaſon why the king grants a *Conge d'elire*, in order to the election of biſhops, for the crown is the patron of all biſhopricks. In ſome of theſe were alſo a ſub-prior, *ſacriſta*, &c. as in the abbey. But there was a ſubordinate kind of priory, being only a cell to ſome great abbey. In

B ſuch

ſuch, the prior was placed and removed at the will of the abbat-ſovereign. Alien-priories, or priories-alien, had their riſe in this manner: when eſtates were given to any foreign monaſtery, the monks, that they might have faithful ſtewards of their lands, built a convenient houſe upon them, for the reception of a ſmall convent, and then ſent over ſuch a number of their own houſe as they thought fit, conſtituting a prior over them.

Colleges, or Collegiate Churches, had a certain number of *Secular Canons*, living under the government of a dean, warden, provoſt, or maſter. There belonged to theſe foundations ſometimes chaplains, ſinging-men, clerks and choriſters.

Cells were of two kinds; ſome, where an abbat, or prior of a great monaſtery, had lands lying at a diſtance from it, on which account they found it convenient to ſend two or three monks to inſpect the revenues of the place, and to perform divine ſervice, allowing them a maintenance at diſcretion, and removing them at pleaſure. Other cells received their revenues, to their own uſe, of the head of ſome great monaſtery, who preſented to, and viſited them, as their patron.

Preceptories, or Commanderies, were houſes or cells to their principal manſions in London, erected by the Knights Templars, or Hoſpitallers, on their manors, in which ſome of their fraternity inhabited, who were under the government of the preceptors or commanders, and were to take care of the lands and rents, belonging to their order, in the neighbouring country.

Frieries differed from monaſteries, as they were not endowed with any certain revenues. They generally belonged to the *Franciſcans* and *Dominicans*, of the mendicant orders.

Chanteries were ſmall chapels, commonly built adjoining to the ſides or ends of churches, to which lands were given for prieſts to pray for the ſouls of the donors, their anceſtors and heirs; but theſe chanteries were not incorporate.

Hospitals were for the relief and maintenance of the ſick and impotent, who were lay-brethren, or ſiſters.

Guilds, from the Anglo-Saxon word *gild*, which ſignifies a ſociety, were maintained by the yearly contributions of well-diſpoſed perſons; but the maintenance of the prieſt was ſettled by the firſt founder.

The monaſtic orders belonging to theſe ſeveral houſes were either religious or military; of the firſt were all monks and canons. Of the monks the moſt antient are

The Benedictines, or thoſe that follow the rule of St. Benedict, or Bennet, who was born at Narſi, in Italy, about the year 480. He founded twelve monaſteries in his own country, the chief whereof was at Mont Caſſin, and gave them a rule, approved by pope Gregory the Great, A. D. 595. They were called the Black Monks, from the colour of their habit, which was a long, black, looſe, ſtuff coat, with a cowl or hood of the ſame, and a ſcapular. They wore a white flannel habit under it, and boots on their legs. Of this order were the three abbies of Glouceſter, Tewkeſbury, and Winchcombe; and the priories of Stanley St. Leonard, Deerhurſt, and Newent, in this county; as were indeed all the cathedral priories, except Carliol, or Carliſle, and moſt of the richeſt abbies in the kingdom. Odo biſhop of Cluny, in Burgundy, thinking ſome things too remiſs in St. Bennet's rule, about A. D. 912, took upon him to reform them, which was the riſe of

The Cluniac order. Moſt of our Engliſh houſes of this order were ſubordinate to the abbey of Cluny, or ſome other foreign monaſtery; and, as alien-priories, were ſeized during the wars with France, but were afterwards made *indigenæ*, and diſcharged from all ſubjection to any foreign abbey. Their habit was little different from that of the Benedictines.

The Carthusians were alſo a branch of the Benedictines, whoſe rule, with the addition of many ſeverities, they followed. Bruno, a native of Cologn in Germany, firſt inſtituted this order at Chartreuſe, in the dioceſe of Grenoble, about A. D. 1080; whence their monaſteries were corruptly called charter-houſes. They never eat fleſh, always wore a hair ſhirt next their ſkin, and none ever ſtirred out of the monaſtery, except the prior and procurator. Their habit was all white, except a plaited cloak, which was black.

The Cistertian order was ſo called, from Ciſtertium, or Citeaux, in the biſhoprick of Chalons, where it was firſt planted, A. D. 1098, by Robert Harding, an Engliſhman, abbat of Moliſme, in Burgundy. They were ſometimes called Bernardines, becauſe St. Bernard was a great propagator of this order; alſo, White Monks, becauſe their habit was a white caſſock, with a narrow ſcapulary; but they ſometimes wore a black gown, with long ſleeves, when they went abroad, but not to church. The abbies of Hayles, and Flaxley, in this county, were of this order.

Theſe were all the orders of monks that were to be met with in England. The canons were either ſecular or regular.

The Secular Canons were ſo called, becauſe, being clergymen, they ſerved the world, [*ſeculum*] in performing ſpiritual offices for the laity, and taking upon them the care of ſouls, which the regulars were incapable of. They were in no reſpect different from ordinary prieſts, except being under the government of ſome local ſtatutes; and were not ſo ſtrictly obliged to live under one roof as the monks and regular canons, but generally lived apart, and were ſeverally maintained by diſtinct prebends, in almoſt the ſame manner with the canons and prebendaries of our cathedral and collegiate churches at preſent. There was a college of theſe at Weſtbury, in Gouceſterſhire.

Regular Canons were ſo called, becauſe they were obliged to a ſtrict obſervance of the rule of St.

St. Auftin, or Auguftine, bifhop of Hippo, in Africa; who, they fay, was their founder, about the year 400; but they were not eminent till the tenth or eleventh century, and came not into England till after the conqueft; St. Gregory's, in Canterbury, being the firft, which was built by archbifhop Lanfranc, A.D. 1084. They were alfo called Black Canons, becaufe they wore a long black caffock, with a white rochet over it, and over all a black cloak and hood. They alfo wore beards, whereas the monks were all fhaved, and wore a cap upon their heads. The abbey of Cirencefter, the priory of St. Ofwald in the city of Gloucefter, and that of Lanthony, near Gloucefter, were of this order.

The PREMONSTRATENSIAN CANONS were inftituted at Premonftratum, in France, by one Norbert, about A.D. 1120. They were alfo called White Canons, from their wearing a white caffock, with a rochet over it, and a long white cloak.

The SEMPRINGHAM, or GILBERTINE CANONS were inftituted by St. Gilbert, at Sempringham, in Lincolnfhire, A. D. 1148. Their habit was a black caffock, over which they wore a furred cloak, and a hood lined with lamb-fkins. Their rule was compofed out of thofe of St. Auftin and St. Bennet, with fome fpecial ftatutes of their own. The monafteries of this order confifted both of men and women, living under the fame roof, but feparated by a wall.

The CANONS REGULAR OF THE HOLY SEPULCHRE were founded in imitation of thofe regulars inftituted in the church of that name at Jerufalem. Their habit was the fame as of other Black Canons, with a diftinction of a double red crofs upon the breaft of their cloak, or upper garment. The endeavours of thefe religious for the regaining of the Holy Land, after the lofs of Jerufalem, coming to nothing, their lands, revenues and privileges were transferred to the

MATURINES, or friers of the order of the Holy Trinity for the redemption of captives, who were inftituted by St. John de Matta, and Felix de Valois, about A. D. 1200; and confirmed by Innocent III, who gave them white robes, with a red and blue crofs on their breafts, and appointed that all the poffeffions which they enjoyed fhould be equally divided into three parts; one for the entertainment and reception of religious perfons, another to relieve the poor, and the third to redeem chriftians kept captive by the infidels. Thefe canons were alfo called Trinitarians, and here in England they were faid to be of the order of Ingham, becaufe the monaftery at Ingham, in Norfolk, was the chief of that rule.

The BONHOMMES, or GOODMEN, were firft brought into England A. D. 1283, by Edmund earl of Cornwall, and placed in a rectory or college founded by him at Afferug, or Afhridge, in Bucks. They followed St. Auftin's rule. At Edingdon, in Wiltfhire, was another houfe of this order, thefe two being all that were in England.

As for the nunneries of the Benedictine, Cluniac, Ciftertian, and Carthufian rules, and the Auftin, Premonftratenfian, and Gilbertine nuns, they were inftituted by the fame perfons as the monks of thofe orders, and followed the fame rules, and wore habits of the fame colour with the monks, their heads being always covered with a veil. Befides thefe, we had in England three other orders of religious females.

1. CLARISSES, or thofe of the order of St. Clare, who inftituted it about A.D. 1225.

2. BRIGETTAN nuns, founded by St. Bridget, queen of Sweden, about A. D. 1360.

3. Nuns of the order of FONTEVRAULT, wearing a black habit with a white veil; reformed from the Benedictines by Robert de Arbufculo, at Font Ebrald in Poictiers, A. D. 1117.

Of the military orders there is mention made but of two in this book, viz. of the Knights Hofpitallers of St. John of Jerufalem, and the Knights Templars.

The HOSPITALLERS, fince called Knights of Rhodes, or Malta, were firft taken notice of about A. D. 1090, and were greatly favoured by Godfrey of Bullen, or Bologne, and his fucceffor Baldwin, king of Jerufalem. They followed partly St. Auftin's rule, and wore a white crofs upon their black habit. There was alfo in England one houfe of nuns of the order of St. John of Jerufalem, viz. Buckland, in Somerfetfhire.

The KNIGHTS TEMPLARS, fo called from having their refidence in certain rooms adjoining to the temple at Jerufalem, were inftituted A. D. 1118. They followed the Ciftertian rule, and their duty was to guard pilgrims travelling to the Holy Land. Their habit was white, with a red crofs. They were at firft fo poor, that they had fcarce one horfe to two knights, therefore their coat of arms was two knights riding upon one horfe. The temple at London, now belonging to the focieties of the law, was confecrated to their ufe in the year 1185, in the prefence of king Henry the fecond, queen Elianor, and a great concourfe of nobles. They had a preceptory at Quenington, in this county.

The eftates belonging to religious houfes were valued by the king's commiffioners in the 26th year of Henry VIII. Of this valuation we have two very different copies, the one given us by Mr. Burton, or Mr. Speed, which was taken from the very original delivered to king Henry VIII. by the commiffioners; the other at the end of the firft Tome of the Monafticon, taken by Sir William Dugdale out of an antient copy in the Cottonian library. Thefe two valuations feldom agree, and for that reafon, becaufe there is fuch authority for both, it is thought fit that the revenues, according to both rates, fhould be inferted.

The original of monks in Britain may be dated from the firft planting of chriftianity here, though it is probable the monaftic rules were not introduced till the time of St. Patrick, who, after he had converted the Irish to the christian faith, A. D. 433, came over to England; and finding at Glastonbury twelve anchorites, gathered them together, and making himself abbat, taught them to live according to the monastic rules. In the next age, about A. D. 512, the British historians report, that St. Dubricius, archbishop of St. David's, founded twelve monasteries, and taught his monks to live after the manner of the Asiatics and Africans, by the labour of their own hands. And not long after, the abbey of Bangor was instituted, which, according to Bede, consisted of seven classes, each class containing three hundred monks, who all lived on their own labour. About A. D. 596, Austin, a monk of Rome, was sent over by pope Gregory the Great, to convert England to the christian faith; who being courteously entertained by Ethelbert, king of Kent, and made archbishop of Canterbury, founded a monastery there that bore his own name: Soon after which, upon the conversion of the West Saxons and Mercians, monasteries were erected in all parts where christianity had any footing, and liberally endowed by the Saxon kings.

At the end of the eighth century, the Danes made descents upon England, and finding most wealth, and least resistance, in the monasteries, generally plundered them; which forced the monks to quit their seats, and leave them to the secular clergy; so that in king Edgar's time, there was scarce one left in all England. Edgar was a lewd and cruel prince, and Dunstan, archbishop of Canterbury, with other monks, taking advantage from the horrors of conscience that seized him, persuaded him that the restoring of the monastic state would be matter of great merit; so he converted many of the chapters into monasteries, and it appears by the foundation of the priory of Worcester, that he had then founded forty-seven. By his authority also, all the lands which had been taken away from religious places were restored; and the king, by Dunstan's advice, made the second reformation of our antient English monks, in the council of Winchester, A. D. 965.

The monks being thus settled in their antient rights and privileges, quietly enjoyed their lands till the conquest; at which time monasteries had a deep share in the afflictions of the conquered nation.

It was in the conqueror's time that the third and last regulation of monks was made, by archbishop Lanfranc, in the council held at London, A. D. 1075.

The orders of regular canons of St. Austin, and of Cluniac monks, were brought into England, and six houses of each sort founded in this reign; as also sixteen Benedictine abbies and priories, besides fourteen alien priories. The king himself built and endowed two abbies, one priory, and five alien priories.

William Rufus succeeded. He was heir to the vices, not to the virtues of his father, and miserably oppressed the religious, seized upon the revenues of the vacant abbies, and bishopricks, and would never let them be filled without some simoniacal bargain. If we except about nine alien priories, there were only thirteen religious houses founded in the thirteen years of this reign; viz. seven of the Benedictine, four of the Cluniac, and two of the Austin order, and about nine alien priories; but not one collegiate church in this or the preceding reign. The king himself built only two small priories.

King Henry I. is recorded not only as an encourager of learning, but, according to the ideas of that age, as a very pious, good prince; and his founding of nine or ten monasteries confirms the truth of this character. In the beginning of his reign, the Knights Hospitallers settled in London. A. D. 1128, the Cistertians were first brought into England, and placed at Weverley, in Surrey; and about this time the canons of the Holy Sepulchre came to Warwick. The number of religious houses founded in the reign of king Henry I. were above one hundred; viz. about thirty of the Benedictine monasteries, forty of the Austin order, five of the Cluniac, ten Cistertian houses, four colleges, two preceptories, and thirteen alien priories.

King Stephen was virtuous, religious, and liberal; and after the wars between him and the empress Maud were ended, he became a great builder of religious houses. A. D. 1146, the Premonstratensian order was brought into England, their first monastery being Newhouse, in Lincolnshire. Two years after, the Gilbertine order had its rise, at Sempringham, in that county. In this reign were built fifteen monasteries of the Benedictine order, twenty-five priories of Black Canons, thirty-five Cistertian abbies, six houses of the Premonstratensian, six of the Gilbertine, and four of the Cluniac rule; one college, two preceptories, and three alien priories.

King Henry II. was very obliging to the clergy, especially after the murder of Thomas Becket, archbishop of Canterbury. He founded eight religious houses; and in his reign were built twenty-two Benedictine, thirty Austin, eight Premonstratensian, four Gilbertine, and six Cluniac monasteries; three collegiate churches, six preceptories, (for in the year 1185 the Templars came into England) eight alien priories, and, what is more remarkable, almost twenty Cistertian abbies, notwithstanding it was contrary to a canon made at the general chapter of the Cistertian order, in the year 1152; wherein the erecting of any more abbies of that rule was expressly forbid, because there were above five hundred of them already founded.

In the time of Richard I. the humour of going to recover the Holy Land from the Saracens mightily prevailed in England, as well as in all other parts of Christendom; and the money designed for pious uses being expended in those wars,

wars, and for the ranſom of the king, there were few monaſteries built in this reign, viz. only ſix of the Benedictine, four of the Auſtin, one of the Ciſtertian, four of the Premonſtratenſian, and two of the Gilbertine order, with one alien priory. The king is ſaid to have mortally hated the Black Monks, the Ciſtertians, and the Templars; and not only theſe three ſorts, but alſo all religious men, for we do not find that he built one monaſtery in all England.

King John, though he was always prejudiced againſt the eccleſiaſtics, founded a ſtately abbey for the Ciſtertians, at Beaulieu, *in Com.* Hants, and a nunnery for Benedictines, at Lambley in Northumberland. In this reign were built ſeven Benedictine abbies and priories, eleven for regular canons, ſeven for Ciſtertian monks, one preceptory, two Premonſtratenſian abbies, ſix of the Gilbertine order, and two alien priories.

In the reign of king Henry III. we find but four Benedictine abbies and priories built, fifteen of the Auſtin, nine of the Ciſtertian, and of the Gilbertine, Cluniac, and Premonſtratenſian orders each one, as alſo one alien priory. And the king himſelf founded only the ſmall Gilbertine cell of Fordham in Cambridgeſhire. For during this reign came the Dominican or preaching friars into this kingdom, A. D. 1217; and the Franciſcans, or Friars Minors, A. D. 1224; who, for the pretended ſeverity of their lives, and their frequent preaching, were at firſt greatly admired by the people, to the prejudice of the other regulars and pariſh prieſts.

King Edward I. ſucceeded next, who built the ſtately abbey of Vale-Royal, in Cheſhire.

Now the greatneſs and riches of the eccleſiaſtics began to be envied by the nobility and gentry, and the affections of the people were alienated by the ſermons, pamphlets, and ſecret inſinuations of the begging friars. In the ſeventh year of this king's reign, the ſtatute of *Mortmain* was enacted, by which all religious perſons were incapacitated from entering upon any fees, either to buy them, or to receive them of the gift of others, without licence of the chief lords, upon pain of forfeiture. There were ſeveral laws made to prevent this, for (as Frederick the abbot of Canterbury told William the Conqueror) the lands, which were for the maintenance of martial men, were converted to pious uſes, and beſtowed on holy votaries, by which means the military ſervices, neceſſary for the defence of the kingdom, were withdrawn; and beſides, the chief lords loſt their eſcheats, wardſhips, reliefs, &c. to prevent which, at the creating of a ſeignory, this clauſe was often inſerted in the deed of feoffment, viz. *Quod licitum ſit donatori, rem donatam dare vel vendere cui voluerit, exceptis viris religioſis, et Judæis.* Lord Coke, 2 Inſt. c. 36. has ſhewn how many ways the religious had to evade this law, of which they complained; and, to ſupply the loſs of new benefactions, procured penſions, privileges from paying tithes, and, what the church finds the inconvenience of to this day, impropriations.—— The king ſeized all the alien priories in the year 1295; the rents and profits, which iſſued out of them to foreign monaſteries, being conceived of advantage to his enemies. In this reign were founded three monaſteries of the Benedictine order, two Auſtin priories, three Ciſtertian abbies, one preceptory, nine colleges, and one Gilbertine priory.

In the reign of king Edward II. we find no great ſtir made about the monks, or their lands; indeed the Knights Templars were ſeized, and their goods and revenues confiſcated, though they were not appropriated to any ſecular uſe, but ſettled upon the Knights Hoſpitallers, by act of parliament, 17 Edw. 2. We do not meet with any monaſtery founded by this unhappy prince, nor indeed but two of the Benedictine, and two of the Auſtin order, by any other perſons, during this period.

King Edward III. is charactered by the monks to have been a pious as well as a valiant prince, for though his wars with France would not ſuffer him to give much to religious houſes, and forced him to be ſevere upon the alien priories; yet there were a great many monaſteries founded in his reign, viz. three Benedictine houſes, ſix of the Auſtin order, one Ciſtertian, and ſeventeen colleges. And notwithſtanding his own extraordinary charges, he founded, and liberally endowed, the Auſtin nunnery at Dartford, in Kent, with the two large colleges of St. George at Windſor, and St. Stephen at Weſtminſter.

In the reign of king Richard II. Wickliff's doctrines were eagerly embraced, and the mendicant friars began to loſe their reputation. There were only two or three Carthuſian monaſteries, and ten or eleven colleges founded during this period.

In the ſixth year of Henry IV. A. D. 1404, was held the *parliamentum indoctum*, ſo called, becauſe none that were learned in the laws of the land were ſuffered to be choſen members of it. A bill was brought into this parliament to deprive the clergy of all their temporal poſſeſſions, for the relief of the king's neceſſities; but by the mediation of Thomas Arundel, archbiſhop of Canterbury, it was ſet aſide. This king built the college of Battelfield *in com. Salop.* which, with two or three colleges more, and a Carthuſian priory, were all the foundations during this reign.

In the ſecond year of Henry V. there was another attempt made againſt the poſſeſſions of the church, but archbiſhop Chicheley, earneſtly preſſing the young king to recover his right to the crown of France; and for the vigorous carrying on of a war, promiſing in the name of the clergy ſuch a benevolence as ſcarce ever had been given by the ſubject, the king readily embraced the propoſal, and the church was once more preſerved from ſacrilege. But in a parliament held this year at Leicefter, all the alien priors were given to the king, with their lands, houfes, &c. except fuch as were conventual, *i. e.* fuch as had liberty to choofe their own prior. In this king's fhort reign were founded only fix colleges and an Auftin priory, befides the Carthufian abbey at Sheen *in com. Surr.* and the houfe of the Brigettan order at Syon, *in com. Middlef.* which were built, and liberally endowed by the king himfelf.

King Henry VI. a religious but unfortunate prince, fucceeded next, who founded Eaton college in Buckinghamfhire, and king's college in Cambridge, and endowed them chiefly out of the fuppreffed alien priories. Befides them there were fix other colleges founded in this reign.

During the civil wars between the York and Lancafter families, in the time of Edward IV. we muft not expect to meet with any confiderable additions to the church. In thofe troublefome times fhe was more fortunate than might have been expected, in keeping her own; but there were fome few colleges founded in this reign.

Note, the numbers of religious houfes built in every king's reign are not compleat and exact, for there are almoft two hundred and fifty abbies, priories and colleges, the dates of the foundations of which we are ignorant of.

Our hiftorians are filent concerning monaftic affairs in the reigns of Richard III. and Henry VII. fo that we conclude there was nothing remarkable in them till the reformation, which began to take place in the next reign. For all monafteries not having 200 *l. per ann.* (of which there were above 370) were diffolved, 27 H. 8. and all their lands, rents, and houfes, with their ftock of cattle, corn, &c. given to the king. In the 31ft year of his reign, all the great abbies, to the number of fix hundred and forty-five, met with the fame fate. The next year, the houfes, lands and goods of the knights of St. John of Jerufalem were feized by, or annexed to, the crown; as were ninety colleges, one hundred and ten hofpitals, and 2374 chanteries and free chapels, in the thirty-feventh year of that reign; which put a final period to the monaftic ftate in this kingdom.

The firft ftep that was made towards it, was that which cardinal Wolfey took, in the fixteenth and twentieth years of the king's reign. He projected and laid two noble foundations, the one at Oxford, and the other at Ipfwich, the place of his birth, both for the encouragement of the learned, and the inftruction of youth; and for that end obtained licenfe from the fee of Rome to diffolve above thirty fmall monafteries, which being executed, their lands by law fell to the king, and thereupon the cardinal took out grants of, and endowed his colleges with them. This made way for the ruin of the greater houfes.

Another thing was the difcovery of an impofture about this time, begun and carried on by one Elizabeth Barton, afterwards called the nun of Kent, and fome priefts that confederated with her. This woman had been for a while troubled with fits, or elfe counterfeited them, and fpoke fuch things as made thofe about her think fhe was infpired. The parfon of the parifh, hoping to draw advantages from this, engaged her for his purpofe, and taught her fo to counterfeit thofe fits, if they were ever real, that fhe became very ready at it. The matter was much noifed about, and the prieft intending to raife the credit of an image of the bleffed virgin's that was in this church, that fo pilgrimages and offerings might be made to it, alfo engaged one Bocking, a monk of Canterbury, in the fcheme. They taught her to declare in her fits, that the bleffed virgin appeared to her, and told her fhe could not be well till fhe vifited that image. She inveighed againft an ill courfe of life, herefy, and the king's fuit of divorce, then depending; and by many diftortions of her body, feemed to be inwardly poffeffed. A day was fet for her cure, and before an affembly of two thoufand people, fhe was carried to that image; where, having acted her fits all over, fhe feemed fuddenly to be recovered, which was afcribed to the interpofition of the virgin, and the virtue of the image. Upon this fhe entered into a religious life, and Bocking was her ghoftly father. There were violent fufpicions of incontinence between them, but the efteem fhe was in bore them down. Many thought her a prophetefs; and archbifhop Warham among the reft. A book was written of her revelations, and a letter fhewed in characters of gold, faid to be fent to her from heaven by Mary Magdalen. She pretended that when the king was laft at Calais, fhe was carried invifibly beyond fea, and brought back again; that an angel gave her the facrament; and that God revealed to her, that, if the king went on in his divorce, and married another wife, he fhould fall from his crown, and not live a month longer. Bifhop Fifher, and many monks, friers and nuns, gave credit to this, and grew very infolent upon it. Her confederates publifhed her revelations in all parts of the kingdom, whereupon fhe and nine of her accomplices we apprehended; who, without rack or torture, confeffed the whole confpiracy, and were appointed to go to St. Paul's; where, after a fermon preached on that occafion by the bifhop of Bangor, they repeated their confeffion in the hearing of the people, and were fent prifoners to the tower. But it was given out that all was extorted from them by violence, and meffages were fent to the nun, defiring her to deny all that fhe had confeffed; which made the king judge it neceffary to proceed to further extremities. So fhe and fix of her accomplices were attainted of treafon, and on the twentieth of April following, were executed at tyburn; where, freely acknowledging her impoftures, and the juftice of the fentence, fhe laid the blame on thofe that fuffered with her; and concluded her life, begging pardon both of God and the king.

If

If this impoſture had fallen out in a darker age, in which the world went mad after viſions, the king might have loſt his crown by it. This diſcovery diſpoſed all to look on older ſtories of the trances of monaſtical people, as contrivances to ſerve baſe purpoſes, and made way for the deſtruction of that order of men in England.

About the year 1535, the king, apprehenſive of a war from the emperor, intended to fortify his harbours, and to encourage trade and navigation, upon which the ballance of Europe began then to turn; and for that purpoſe, reſolving to make uſe of the wealth of the monaſteries, thought the beſt way to bring them into his own hands, would be to expoſe their vices.

Cranmer promoted this much, and a general viſitation of all the religious houſes in England, was begun in October 1535, and caſt into ſeveral precincts. Inſtructions were given to the viſitors, directing them what things to inquire after, concerning the revenues of the monaſteries, the lives and converſation of the monks, nuns, &c.

With theſe inſtructions they went over England, and found in many places monſtrous diſorders. The ſin of Sodom was found in ſeveral houſes; great factions and barbarous cruelties in others, and in ſome they found tools for coining. The report contained many abominable things, that are not fit to be mentioned. Some of theſe were printed, but the greateſt part is loſt; only a report of one hundred and forty-four houſes is yet extant. The abbat of Langden, in Kent, had been found in bed with a whore, who went in the habit of a lay brother; which perhaps diſpoſed him to comply with ſuch terms as were offered him, and he and ten of his monks were the firſt who ſigned a reſignation of their houſe to the king. Two other houſes in the ſame county, Folkeſtone and Dover, followed their example, as did four others in the following year.

In February a parliament met, and an act was paſſed for the ſuppreſſion of all monaſteries under 200 *l.* a year, and their revenues were given to the king. The report of the viſitors was read in the two houſes, and diſpoſed them to great eaſineſs in this matter. The monaſteries were much richer than they ſeemed to be from the rent-rolls of their eſtates, for it was the practice to let them at their firſt rates, tho' the value of lands was much enhanced, but inſtead of raiſing the rents, they exacted great fines from their tenants, upon the renewal of their leaſes; ſo that ſome houſes, rated only at 200 *l.* a year, were really worth many thouſands.

As ſoon as this act was paſſed, viſitors were ſent to examine into, and take inventories of their revenues, and to take their ſeals into their keeping: They were to try how many of the religious would take capacities, and return to a ſecular courſe of life; but thoſe who intended to continue in that ſtate, were to be ſent to ſome of the great monaſteries that lay neareſt. A penſion was alſo to be aſſigned to the abbat, or prior, during life; and they were particularly to examine what leaſes had been made all the laſt year; for the abbats, hearing what was coming upon them, had been raiſing all the money they could; and ſo it was intended to recover what was made away by ill bargains. There were great complaints made of the proceedings of the viſitors, of their violences and briberies, and perhaps not without reaſon. Ten thouſand of the religious were ſet to ſeek their fortunes, with forty ſhillings and a gown a man. Their goods and plate were eſtimated at 100,000 *l.* and the valued rents of their houſes was 32,000 *l.* but was really worth above ten times as much. The churches and cloiſters were in moſt places pulled down, and the materials ſold, leſt ſome accidental change might conduce to their reſtitution.

This gave a general diſcontent, and the monks were now as much pitied as they were formerly hated. It was thought ſtrange to ſee the king devour what his anceſtors had dedicated to the honour of God, and his ſaints. The nobility and gentry, who provided for their younger children and friends, by putting them in thoſe ſanctuaries, were ſenſible of their loſs. The people, who had been fed at the abbats tables, and as they travelled over the country, found the abbies to be places of reception for ſtrangers, ſaw what they were to loſe. But the more ſuperſtitious, who thought their friends muſt now ſtill continue in purgatory, whithout that relief which the maſſes procured them, were beyond meaſure offended at theſe proceedings.

To remove this general diſcontent, Cromwell adviſed the king to ſell the abbey lands, at very eaſy rates, to the nobility and gentry, and to oblige them to keep up the wonted hoſpitality. This would both be grateful to them, and would engage them to aſſiſt the crown in the maintenance of the changes that had been made; ſince their own intereſts would be interwoven with the rights of the crown; and the common people, whoſe grudges lay chiefly in their ſtomachs, would be eaſily pacified, if hoſpitality was ſtill kept up. Upon a clauſe in the act, impowering the king to found a-new ſuch houſes as he ſhould think fit, there were fifteen monaſteries, and ſixteen nunneries, new founded. It ſeems theſe had been more regular than the reſt, ſo that for a while, they were reprieved, till the general ſuppreſſion. They were bound to obey ſuch rules as the king ſhould ſend them, and to pay him tenths and firſt fruits.

All this did not pacify the people, for in the beginning of October, 20,000 roſe in Lincolnſhire, led by a prieſt, under the diſguiſe of a cobler; but upon the offer of a general pardon, they were ſoon diſperſed. At the ſame time there was a more formidable riſing in Yorkſhire, headed by one Aſk, who performed his part with great dexterity. They became 40,000 ſtrong in a few days, and met with no oppoſition. They forced the archbiſhop of York, and the lord Darcy, to

ſwear

ſwear to their covenant, and to go along with them. They beſieged Skipton, but the earl of Cumberland held it out againſt them; as Sir Ralph Evers did Scarborough caſtle; though for twenty days he and his men had no proviſions but bread and water. There was alſo an inſurrection in all the other northern counties, againſt whom the earl of Shrewſbury made head. But at length a proclamation of pardon, without any reſtrictions, being ſigned and ſent them, they were every where quieted. Aſk was invited to court, and well uſed by the king, with a view to learn from him all the ſecret correſpondences they had in other parts of the kingdom; but withdrawing without leave, he was taken, and hanged at York. This was followed by ſeveral little inſurrections but they were all quickly diſperſed by the vigilance of the duke of Norfolk.

As ſoon as the country was every where quieted, and this threatening ſtorm blown over, the king went on more reſolutely in his deſign of ſuppreſſing the monaſteries. A new viſitation was appointed, to inquire into the converſation of the monks, to examine how they ſtood affected to the pope, and how they promoted the king's ſupremacy. The viſitors were likewiſe ordered to examine what impoſtures might be carried on among them, with regard either to images or relics, by which the ſuperſtition of the credulous people was wrought upon. Some few houſes of greater value were prevailed with, the former year, to ſurrender to the king. Many of the houſes that had not been diſolved, though they were in the former act, were now ſuppreſt, and many of the greater abbats were perſuaded by ſeveral motives to ſurrender. Some had been faulty during the rebellion, and ſo, to prevent a ſtorm, offered a reſignation. Others liked the reformation, and did it on that account. Some were found guilty of great diſorders in their lives, and, to prevent a ſhameful diſcovery, offered their houſes to the king; and others had made ſuch waſte, and ſuffered dilapidations, that having taken care of themſelves, they were the leſs concerned for others. At St. Albans, the rents were fixed ſo low, that the abbat could not maintain the charge of the abbey. At Battel, the whole furniture of the houſe and chapel were not worth 100 *l.* and their plate not above 300 *l.* In ſome houſes there was ſcarce any plate or furniture left. Many abbats and monks were glad to accept of a penſion for life, which was proportioned to the value of their houſe, and to their innocence. The abbats of St. Albans and Tewkeſbury had each 400 marks a year: but the abbat of St. Edmondſbury was more innocent, and more reſolute. The viſitors wrote "that they found no ſcandals in that houſe," but at laſt he was prevailed with, for a penſion of 500 marks, to reſign. The inferior governors had ſome 30, 20, or 10 *l.* penſions, and the monks had generally 6 *l.* or 8 marks each. All that ſhould give good example to others, by a quick and chearful ſurrender, were made to hope for advancement; ſo 121 of theſe houſes were this year reſigned to the king. In moſt houſes, the viſitors made the monks ſign a confeſſion of their former vices and diſorders, of which there is only one original extant, that eſcaped a general raſure of all ſuch papers in queen Mary's time; wherein they acknowledged, in a long narrative, their former idleneſs, gluttony and ſenſuality.

The common preamble to moſt ſurrenders was, "that upon full deliberation, and of their own "proper motion, for juſt and reaſonable cauſes "moving their conſciences, they did freely give "up their houſes to the king." Though ſome ſurrendered without any preamble, to the viſitors, as feoffees in truſt for the king. In ſhort, they went on at ſuch a rate, that 159 reſignations were obtained before the parliament met, who afterwards declared them good in law.

Such of the abbats as refuſed to ſurrender were roughly handled. The abbat of Fountains, in Yorkſhire, was charged by the commiſſioners with theft and ſacrilege, for taking into his private hands ſome jewels belonging to that monaſtery; for which they pronounced him perjured, and having depoſed him, extorted a private reſignation. The monks of the Charter-houſe, in the ſuburbs of London, were committed to Newgate, where, with hard and barbarous uſage, five of them died, and five more lay at the point of death. The two priors of Wooburn and Burlington, with the abbats of Whaley, Jervaux, and Sawley, were ſuſpected of a correſpondence with the rebels, and of favouring the pope; ſo they were all taken, attainted of treaſon, and executed. The abbats of Glaſtonbury and Reading had alſo ſent a great deal of their plate to the rebels; the former, to diſguiſe it the better, had made a perſon break into the houſe where the plate was kept; ſo he was convicted both of burglary and treaſon, and being condemned to death, was drawn from Wells, upon a hurdle, then hanged upon the hill called the Tor, near Glaſtonbury; his head ſet upon the abbey-gate, and his quarters expoſed at Wells, Bath, Ilcheſter, and Bridgwater. At his execution, he confeſt his crime, and begged both God's and the king's pardon for it. The abbat of Colcheſter was alſo attainted and executed, the grounds of which proceeding are not known; for the records of their attainders are loſt.

Upon the attainders of theſe abbats, their abbies were ſeized, and they were confirmed to the king in the following parliament, in a ſpecial proviſo made for that purpoſe.

Great complaints were made of the viſitors, as if they had uſed undue practices to make the abbats and monks ſurrender. They, on the other hand, publiſhed many of the vile practices found in thoſe houſes; and no ſtory became ſo public, as that of the prior of the Croſſed Friars in London, who was found in bed with a whore at noon-day: He fell down on his knees, and begged thoſe

who

who ſurpriſed him, not to diſcover his ſhame: They made him give them 30 *l.* which he proteſted was all he had, and he promiſed them as much more; but as he did not keep his word, a ſuit followed upon it. Yet all theſe perſonal blemiſhes did not work much on the people. It ſeemed unreaſonable to extinguiſh noble foundations, for the fault of ſome individuals; therefore another way was taken, which had a better effect.

They diſcovered many impoſtures concerning reliques and wonderful images, to which pilgrimages had been uſually made. At Reading was an angel's wing, which brought over the point of the ſpear that pierced our ſaviour's ſide. As many pieces of the croſs were found, as joined together would have made a prodigious one. The rood of grace at Boxley, in Kent, had been much eſteemed, and had drawn many pilgrims to it. It was obſerved to bow and rowl its eyes, to look at times well pleaſed or angry, which the credulous multitude imputed to a divine power; but being brought to St. Paul's croſs; and all the ſprings openly expoſed, that governed its ſeveral motions, all was diſcovered to be a notorious cheat. At Hayles, in Glouceſterſhire, the blood of Chriſt was ſhewed in a phial, and it was taught, that none could ſee it that was in mortal ſin. But good preſents being made, the deluded pilgrims went away well ſatisfied with the ſight of it. This was the blood of a duck, renewed every week, put into a phial, very thick on one ſide, and thin on the other; and either ſide turned toward the pilgrim, as the prieſts were ſatisfied with their oblations. Several other ſuch like impoſtures were diſcovered, which contributed much to the undeceiving of the people.

The richeſt ſhrine in England was Thomas Becket's, at Canterbury, whoſe ſtory is well known. His altar drew far greater oblations than thoſe that were dedicated to Chriſt, or the Bleſſed Virgin, as appears by the account of them in two years. In one, 3 *l.* 2 *s.* 6 *d.* and in another, not a penny was offered at Chriſt's altar. The ſame years, 63 *l.* 5 *s.* 6 *d.* and 4 *l.* 1 *s.* 8 *d.* were offered at the Bleſſed Virgin's altar. But in theſe very years there were 832 *l.* 12 *s.* 3 *d.* and 964 *l.* 6 *l.* 3 *d.* offered at St. Thomas's. The ſhrine grew to be of ineſtimable value. Two days in the year were obſerved in honour of this ſaint; the twenty-ninth of December, called his martyrdom, and the ſeventh of July, the day of his tranſlation; and every fiftieth year was a jubilee, and an indulgence was granted to all that came and viſited his tomb, where 100,000 pilgrims are ſaid to have been at one time. Lewis VII. of France, came over in pilgrimage to viſit it, and offered a ſtone eſteemed the richeſt in Europe. It is hard to ſay which of the two, a hatred to Becket's ſeditious practices, or the love of his ſhrine, operated the ſtrongeſt on the king to unſaint him. However the ſhrine was broken, and the gold of it was ſo heavy, that it filled two cheſts, which took eight men each to carry them out of the church; and his ſcull, that had been ſo much worſhipped, was proved to be an impoſture; for the true ſcull was found with the reſt of his bones in his coffin.

The foundation of all this wealth was the belief of purgatory, and of the virtue that was in maſſes to redeem ſouls out of it; ſo it paſſed among all for a piece of piety to parents, and of care for the ſouls of themſelves and families, to endow religious houſes with lands, upon condition that they ſhould have maſſes ſaid for them, as it was agreed on, more or leſs frequently, according to the meaſure of the gift.

Some images were believed to have extraordinary virtue in them, and pilgrimages to theſe were much extolled. There was alſo great rivalry among the ſeveral orders, every one magnifying their own ſaints, images and reliques. The religious were generally very diſſolute, and groſſly ignorant. Their privileges were become a public grievance, and their lives were ill examples to the world; which, together with the proſpect of vaſt profit, through that deluge of wealth which was like to be diſperſed through the nation, upon the ſuppreſſion of monaſteries, diſpoſed the people the more eaſily to conſent to their diſſolution.

A parliament was ſummoned on the twenty-eight of April, 1539, in which twenty of the abbats ſat in perſon. During this ſeſſion, an act paſſed for confirming all reſignations of religious houſes already made, or to be made; and the king's right, founded either on ſurrenders, forfeitures, or attainders of treaſon, was thereby declared to be good in law; and though there were ſo many abbats ſitting in the houſe, none of them proteſted againſt it.

Fifty-ſeven ſurrenders were made this year, of which there were twelve parliamentary abbies, and twenty nunneries. Commiſſioners were appointed, by the court of augmentation, to ſeize on the revenues and goods belonging to thoſe houſes; to eſtabliſh the penſions that were to be given to every one that had been in them; and to pull down the churches, or other parts of the fabric, which they thought ſuperfluous, and to ſell the materials of them. The valued rents of the abbey lands, as they were then let, was 132,607 *l.* 6 *s.* 4 *d*; but this was not one tenth of the true value. The king had now in his hand the greateſt advantage that ever king of England had, both for enriching the crown, and making royal foundations. But ſuch was his extravagance, that all this melted away in a few years, and his deſigns, or pretended deſigns, were never accompliſhed. It is ſaid, he intended to have founded eighteen new biſhopricks, but theſe ſix only, Weſtminſter, Cheſter, Glouceſter, Peterborough, Oxford, and Briſtol, were eſtabliſhed.

In the year 1540, a bill was brought into parliament, for the ſuppreſſing of the Knights of St. John of Jeruſalem. Theſe were at firſt only eftablifhed in an hofpital, to entertain the pilgrims that went to vifit the holy grave, but afterwards became an order of knights; and they and the Knights Templars conducted and guarded the pilgrims. It was thought, for fome ages, one of the higheft expreffions of devotion to Chrift, to vifit the place where he was crucified, buried, and afcended to heaven; and it was efteemed to be highly meritorious, to fight for the recovery of the Holy Land out of the hands of infidels; fo that almoft every one that died, either vowed to go to the holy war, or left fomething to fuch as fhould go. If they recovered, they generally obtained a difpenfation from their vow, by giving lands for the entertainment of thofe knights. There were great complaints made againft the Templars, but whether it was their wealth that made them a defirable prey, or their guilt that drew ruin on them, is not certain; they were however fo univerfally hated, that a perfon whofe beard refembled the form of theirs, and which he had made a vow to continue, was neceffitated to carry about him a certificate, well attefted, that he was not of that order; otherwife he muft often have run the hazard of being knocked on the head. They were condemned in a council, and the whole order fuppreffed in 1312, and all of them that could be found were cruelly put to death. The Knights of St. John ftill continued, but when the Chriftians quitted Paleftine they fettled in Rhodes, out of which being expelled by the Turks, after a noble refiftance, they fixed themfelves in Malta, and ftill continue in poffeffion of that ifland. Since they could not be brought to furrender of their own accord here in England, they were fuppreffed by act of parliament.

When the order of the Templars were fuppreft, their lands, which were fimple gifts, went to the lords by efcheat; but there is a diftinction to be made betwixt fuch, and the lands given to abbies, in as much as thefe were given in confideration of the maffes to be faid for the donors and their families; and therefore it was inferred, that when the cheat of redeeming fouls out of purgatory was difcovered, and thefe houfes were fuppreft, the lands were to revert to the heirs of the donors; and upon that account it was thought neceffary to exclude them by a fpecial provifo.

When all this was done, the better to fatisfy the people, it was reprefented to them, that by the wealth of thefe houfes, the kingdom fhould be ftrengthened with an army of 40,000 men, and that for the future they fhould never be charged with fubfidies, loans, or common aids; and left they fhould take up arms upon this great and ftrange alteration, reports were fpread, that cardinal Pool laboured to excite our enemies to fend forces againft the kingdom, and that an invafion was threatened; which feemed the more credible, becaufe the truce concluded betwixt the emperor and the French was generally known, and neither of them wanted a pretence to break with us. Thefe apprehenfions were ftrengthened by the king's fudden journey to the fea coafts, whither alfo feveral of the nobility and great officers went, to vifit the ports and places of danger; who reprefented it to be every where fo great, as one would have thought each place had needed a fortification. The navy was immediately got ready, and mufters were ordered to be taken all over the kingdom. The expence of all thefe preparations, made againft a danger believed to be fo very imminent, was to be defraied out of the revenues of the monafteries, which faved the purfes of the people, who therefore became the better affected to the diffolution.

The monaftic ftate being now compleatly fubverted, let us turn our eyes for a moment on Cromwell, earl of Effex, lord vice-gerent, and high chancellor of England, vifitor-general, and knight of the garter; who having rifen by his great parts, to all thefe honors and high employments, from the low condition of a blackfmith's fon, excited the envy and hatred of the nobility; and having been the grand actor in this cataftrophe, drew upon him the further odium of the catholics. His numerous enemies did him every ill office with the king, who having no more ufe for him, and hoping to regain their affections, by cafting upon Cromwell all the blame of paft proceedings, gave way to their accufations, and made him a facrifice. He was arrefted by the duke of Norfolk at the council table, when he leaft dreamt of it, and commited to the tower; and by the fame parliament that ratified and confirmed what with fo much induftry he had brought to pafs, was himfelf condemned for herefy and treafon, unheard and little pitied; and on the twenty-eighth of July, had his head cut off on Tower-hill.

The temporal advantages refulting to the people from thefe furprizing changes, were not equal to their expectations, for by the hiftories of thofe times it appears, that fubfidies from the clergy, and fifteenths of laymen's goods, were foon after exacted; and that in the next reign, a new tax was levied on the fubject for three years, which grew fo exceeding heavy, that the commons applied to the king for a mitigation of it.

In this and the fucceeding reigns, Mary's excepted, the abbey lands were granted away, chiefly to the courtiers, and favorites of the crown, on very eafy terms, and hofpitality enjoined the purchafers, to compenfate for the lofs of that relief which the poor found in the monafteries; but the meafure of it being difcretionary, it fell fo far fhort of the intention, that in 39 Eliz. there were no lefs than eleven bills brought into the houfe of commons for their relief, which were the firft rudiments of the laws relating to the poor now in force.

In confequence of this great revolution, large eftates in Gloucefterfhire, as well as other counties, that belonged to the church, became the property of lay perfons; and fome of them ftill continue in the families to whom they were originally granted.

Here

Here it is proper to obſerve, that the demean lands that belonged to the Ciſtertians, Premonſtratenſes, Hoſpitallers, and Templars, whoſe houſes were founded before the council of Lateran, 1215, were diſcharged from the payment of tythes; as were all thoſe that belonged to the other houſes of the two firſt mentioned orders, though of a later foundation, which being above the value of 200 *l. per. ann.* were not diſſolved by the ſtatute of 27 H. 8. This accounts for many exemptions from tythes.

Of Advowſons, Patronage, Preſentation, &c.

The parochial clergy were formerly well provided for, till the patrons of churches found out a method of purchaſing maſſes and obits of the monaſteries at no expence, by giving, inſtead of lands, the advowſons of churches. The monaſteries ſent their vicar to officiate at the pariſh church, for the ſmall tythes and offerings, reſerving the great ones, or the greater part of them, to themſelves. At the diſſolution, ſome of theſe were diſpoſed of to the beſt bidders, or greateſt favorites, and ſo became lay property, and are what we now call *impropriations:* others of them were appointed to the erecting or augmenting of ſome biſhoprick, deanery, or religious foundation; and are called *appropriations*; theſe terms are often uſed indiſcriminately, but not by perſons of judgment.

Parſons have not the fee ſimple of their livings, but impropriations and appropriations are perpetuities; and becauſe thoſe who have them are owners of the fee, they are called *proprietarii.*

At the Norman conqueſt, when the nation was divided into 60,215 knights fees, 28,000 belonged to the clergy, beſides tythes, offerings, and other perquiſites; but there were then 45,000 churches, and 52,000 chapels in the kingdom; whereas the preſent number of both is about 10,000, whereof 3,845 are impropriations. There are 290 pariſh churches in Glouceſterſhire, of which 140 are impropriations; which is the reaſon that ſome of the parochial clergy have ſo ſcanty a pittance, under the miſapplied denomination of *livings.*

The learned hiſtorian, whoſe ſentiments and expreſſions I have ſo often adopted and uſed in the courſe of this work, thinks it reaſonable that the clergy ſhould have an income to enable them to live independently, and in proportion to the orders of the other learned profeſſions. It ſhould be certain, and keep pace with the price of proviſions. All theſe and many other good purpoſes, might be anſwered, by appointing a quantity of land in every pariſh to the miniſter, inſtead of tythes; concerning which there are ſo many diſputes betwixt them and their pariſhioners. And it is with pleaſure, that I find this method purſued, where new incloſures are made by act of parliament. It is uſual to allow the miniſter about one ſeventh, or one eighth of the land, for his portion.

When the chriſtian religion was firſt eſtabliſhed in England, kings began to build cathedral churches, and to make biſhops; and afterwards in imitation of them, ſeveral lords of manors founded particular churches, on ſome part of their own lands, and endowed them with glebe, reſerving to themſelves and their heirs a right to preſent a fit perſon to the biſhop, when the church ſhould become void. This right is called an *advowſon,* and he that hath it is called the patron. By the common law therefore, the right of patronage is a real right, and deſcends to the heirs and ſucceſſors, in ſome meaſure like lands and tenements. 1 *Nelſ. Abr.* 184. Originally, the right of nomination of fit perſons to officiate through the dioſceſes, was in the biſhops, but for the encouragement of pious undertakings, ſuch as building churches and endowing them, they permitted the benefactors to nominate, reſerving to themſelves an intire right to judge of the fitneſs of the perſons ſo nominated. And what was the practice, became, in proceſs of time, to be the law of the church. *Gibſ. Codex,* 2d. edit. 756.

If a preſentation be made to a chapel of eaſe as to a church, by the name of *eccleſia,* it will change the nature of it, and make it a church. *Nat. Brev.* 32. Alſo when the queſtion was, whether it were *eccleſia, aut capella, pertinens ad matricem eccleſiam?* the iſſue was, whether it had *baptyſterium et ſepulturam?* for if it had the adminiſtration of the ſacraments and ſepulture, it was in law judged a church. 2 *Inſt.* fol. 363.

A Rectory is an intire pariſh church, with all its rights, glebes, tythes, and other profits whatſoever. *Spelman.* But the word *rectoria* is often uſed for the rector's manſe, or parſonage houſe. *Paroch. Ant.* 179.

Parson, *perſona,* ſignifies the rector of a church; ſo called becauſe he is bound, by virtue of his office, *in propria perſona ſervire Deo.*

Vicar, *vicarius, quaſi vice fungens rectoris.* At firſt a vicar was a mere curate to the impropriator of the church, removable at pleaſure, as prieſts in antient times, when there were no particular pariſhes, were only curates to the biſhops; but by degrees the vicars got a ſettled maintenance of the glebe, and ſome kinds of tythes, and now claim their dues, either by endowment, or by preſcription. Where any church is a vicarage, it may be preſumed that it formerly belonged to ſome monaſtery. There were no vicarages earlier than king John.

A Donative is a ſpiritual preſentment, be it church, chapel or vicarage, which is in the free gift, or collation of the patron, without making any preſentation to, or having admiſſion, inſtitution, or induction, by or from the biſhop. And it is exempt from all eccleſiaſtical juriſdiction.

A Peculiar ſignifies a particular pariſh, or church, that hath juriſdiction within itſelf for probate of wills, &c. exempt from the ordinary, and the biſhop's courts. It is an antient privilege of of the fee of Canterbury, that all manors, or advowfons belonging to it are exempt from the ordinary, and are reputed peculiars, of which there are fifty-feven in the province.

Church-wardens are officers yearly chofen by the parifhioners, or by the minifter and parifhioners, according to the cuftom of the place, to look to the church and church-yard, and to fupprefs prophanenefs and immorality, &c. They are a corporation, and may fue for any thing belonging to their church, or the poor of their parifh. In the antient epifcopal fynods, the bifhops fummoned credible perfons out of every parifh, to give information of the diforders of clergy and people. Thefe were called *teftes fynodales*, and were in after times a kind of impannelled jury, who were upon oath to prefent all heretics, and other irregular perfons. *Kennet's Paroch. Antiq.* 649. And thefe in procefs of time became ftanding officers, efpecially in great cities, and from hence were called *fynodfmen*, and by corruption *fidefmen*. They are alfo fometimes called *queftmen*, from the nature of their office, in making inquiry concerning offences. But for the moft part this office is now devolved upon the church-wardens. *Dr. Burn's Ecclef. Law.*

Parifh regifters were inftituted by lord Cromwell, in September, *anno* 1538, while he was vicar-general to king H. 8.

Tythes, tenths, *difmes*, *decimæ*, all fignify the tenth part of the fruits of the earth, of beafts, &c. They are given to the clergy in recompence of their attending their office. Mr. Selden has fhewn that tythes were not introduced here in England till towards the end of the eighth century, about 786, when parifhes and ecclefiaftical benefices came to be fettled. In the early ages of the Chriftian church, the people difpofed of their offerings, in the room of which tythes are now legally fubftituted, in various manners; now to priefts, now to abbats, now to the poor; and when they were offered to baptifmal or epifcopal churches, they were received as indefinite offerings, the quantity whereof was wholly arbitrary, in refpect of any conftitution or general law in ufe; but fome kind of offering was neceffary to be made, on pain of excommunication. And it feems, the difpofition of the offerings was fo in the patron's power, by the practice of fome places, that he might affign a certain portion of them to the minifter of the church, and employ the reft at his pleafure. About the year 780 or 800, laws were made by Charles king of France, Italy, and Lombardy, and afterwards emperor, for the payment of tythes. Pope Innocent III. about the year 1200, decreed the tythes to be paid to the parifh prieft; and though fubjects of this nation were not bound by his decree, yet as it was judged reafonable, it became cuftomary here, and the cuftom in time grew into a law. Religious perfons antiently paid no tithes of lands in their own poffeffion, but this privilege was reftrained by pope Adrian.

Glebe is a portion of land, meadow or pafture, belonging to the parfonage or vicarage, over and above the tythes.

Composition, an agreement or contract between a parfon, patron and ordinary, &c. for money, or other things, in lieu of tythes, called real compofition. An agreement between the parfon and the parifhioners, to pay fo much inftead of tythes, is called a perfonal contract; and though confirmed by the ordinary, yet that doth not make it a real compofition, becaufe he ought to be a party to the deed. *March's Rep.* 87. And by 13 Eliz. c. 10. fhall not bind the fucceffor, unlefs made for twenty-one years, or three lives. Compofitions were made at firft for a valuable confideration, fo that though in procefs of time, upon the increafe of the value of lands, they do not amount to the value of the tythes, yet cuftom prevails, and from hence arifes a *modus decimandi*.

Procurations are fums of money which parifh priefts pay to the bifhop, or archdeacon, *ratione vifitationis*. They were antiently paid in neceffary victuals, for the vifitor and his attendants, but turned into money, on account of the many abufes of the vifitors. Complaint was made to pope Clement IV. that the archdeacon of Richmond, vifiting the diocefe, travelled with 103 horfes, twenty-one dogs, and three hawks, which vaft equipage was fo oppreffive to the religious houfes as to occafion the fpending in an hour as much as would have maintained the monks a long time. *Mon. Angl. 2 tom. p.* 165.

First-fruits, *annates*, *primitiæ*, are the profits of every fpiritual living for one year, given in antient time to the pope, through all Chriftendom; but tranflated to the king, here in England, by ftatute 26 H. 8. c. 3. But what pope firft impofed firft-fruits, hiftorians do not agree. 4 *Inft.* 120. Sir Robert Atkyns fays it was done in the year 1316.

Mortuary is a gift left by a man at his death to his parifh church, in recompence of his perfonal tythes and offerings, not duly paid in his life-time. It was antiently called *faulefceat*, which fignifies *fymbolum animæ*. Formerly, and until 21 H. 8. cap. 6. *ftatute-mortuaries* were paid in cattle, the beft to the lord for a heriot, the fecond for a mortuary. At the conqueft it was called a *corf-prefent*, becaufe the beaft was prefented with the body at the funeral. And fometimes a *principal*, of which fee a learned difcourfe in the *Antiquities of Warwickfhire*, fol. 679. And *Selden's Hift. of Tythes*, 287. There is no mortuary due by law, but by cuftom. 2 *Inft.* 491.

Synodal is a tribute in money paid to the bifhop, or archdeacon, by the inferior clergy, at Eafter vifitation; and it is called *Synodale*, becaufe it was paid yearly at the Eafter fynod. Thefe were the affemblies of the clergy, wherein they prefented their grievances for redrefs, which are now difcontinued.

Pentecostals, *denarii de caritate*, Whitfun-farthings, the cuftomary oblations made to the cathedral

thedral church about the time of Pentecoſt, when the pariſh prieſts, and many of the people, went in proceſſion to viſit the mother church. This contribution, though at firſt but a voluntary gift, to help to maintain and adorn the biſhop's ſee, or cathedral church, was afterwards charged as a ſettled due upon the pariſh prieſt.

SANCTUARIES were places privileged by the prince for the ſafe-guard of offenders. The Jews had cities of refuge; the Athenians and Romans had their ſanctuaries; but our antient kings of England had them in greater reverence than any others in their time; for ſuch as had committed even felonies and treaſons, were permitted to take ſhelter in them, provided they acknowleged their crimes within forty days, and ſubmitted themſelves to baniſhment; mean while, if any layman expelled them, he was excommunicated; if any clerk, he was made irregular; but afterwards, no man might relieve them. *Staunf. Pl. Cor.*——Sanctuaries were taken away by ſtat. 21 Jac. 1. *c.* 2. *ſ.* 7.

The coifs, which the judges wear on the crown of their heads, are ſaid to have come into uſe in the following manner. In early ages the clergy filled moſt of the places of great profit, truſt and power, in the gift of the crown, as indeed there were few in thoſe days who had learning enough to acquit themſelves properly beſide them. King Rich. I. having conſtituted Hubert Walter, (archbiſhop of Canterbury) the chief juſticiary of England, pope Innocent, by his brief, in the year 1198, required the king to remove the archbiſhop from that office, alledging that it did not become biſhops to be employed in ſecular affairs, and threatened the king with an interdict in caſe of refuſal. The king forthwith obeyed, and made Jeofry, the ſon of Peter, chief juſticiary in his place. However the clergy continued long after in civil employments belonging to juſtice; but, to ſave appearances, they changed their habit; and to cover their ſhaved heads, introduced the uſe of coifs, which the judges and ſerjeants at law have continued to wear ever ſince.

Many of the officers in chancery were antiently of the eccleſiaſtical order, and the lord chancellor himſelf was called *archicapellanus*. The ſix clerks, who are conſiderable officers in that court, ſtill bear their primitive names: and the original occaſion why ſo many preſentations to churches were annexed to the great office of lord chancellor, was, that he might thereby be enabled to reward the officers of his court.

Of the Names of Places, and Perſons; of Titles, Dignities, &c.

MOST of the names of places and perſons are ſignificant; the former being generally expreſſive of the ſituation, the latter of the various ſentiments or conditions of thoſe that gave them: yet it is often difficult to trace them to their origin.

The Britons were the antient inhabitants of this iſland, the Romans ſubdued it, to them ſucceeded the Saxons, after them the Danes got footing here, and laſt of all it ſubmitted to the Normans. It is probable that ſome perſons of each nation, gave names to places where they had authority. This being the caſe, how difficult, how uncertain muſt the etymology of names be, in many inſtances. Some appear to be of Britiſh, others of Saxon original; and there are ſtill others, probably ſo mutilated and corrupted in common uſe, or given for reaſons ſo remote and obſcure, that I have not ventured to ſay any thing about them.

The explanation of the following words, which enter into the compoſition of the names of places, will direct to the etymology:

Ab, in the beginning of the names of places is oftentimes a contraction of Abbot, and implies either that a monaſtery was there, or that the place belonged to ſome monaſtery.

Ac, from ac, *Saxon*, an oak.

Ar, (*Britiſh*) upon.

Bac, (*French*) a ferry.

Bach, *bec*, *beke*; a river, a ſtream. *Munſter*.

Bearne, a wood. *Bede*.

Beorh, beoɲh, (*Saxon*) *acervus*, a heap.

Bere, a court, the lord's court; or from beɲe, *A. S.* barley.

Berie, a flat ſituation.

Berry, a hill, from the *Dutch* word *berg*.

Berton, *barton*; from beɲe, *A. S.* barley; and tun, a vill, a town.

Beys, little rills or brooks.

Bod, (*Britiſh*) a manſion.

Bois, (*French*) wood.

Bolde, bolð; *A. S.* a village.

Borne, *bourn*, *burne*; buɲn, *A. S.* a river or brook.

Borow, *borough*, denote an antient town.

By at the end of the names of places ſignifies village, or dwelling-place. It is of Daniſh extraction, whence we have the term by-laws in England, *i. e.* ſuch laws as are peculiar to each town or village.

Câr,

Câr, *Câer*, *(Britiſh)* a fortified city. Alſo *Car* is ſometimes put for a low watry place, or pool where alders grow.

Carnes, a heap of ſtones.

Ced, the brow or deſcent of a place.

Cene, *A. S.* bold, valiant.

Charlton, the grange, the carle's or huſbandman's town.

Combe, (*Cwmm*, *Br.*) a valley between two hills.

Cope, the head, the top of a high hill.

Covert, *(French)* a ſhadowed place, or ſhade.

Cro, *croy*; marſhy lands.

Croft, *A. S.* a little cloſe. Our anceſtors uſed to ſay proverbially of a very poor man, "*He had ne toft, ne croft.*"

Dale, *dole*; (*Britiſh*) a plain near the ſea, or great river.

Delle, a dike.

Den, ꝺen, *(Saxon) vallis, locus ſylveſtris*; a valley, or a place near woods.

Der. Names of this beginning ſignify places where wild beaſts herd together, from the *Saxon* ꝺeoꞃ, *fera*, a wild beaſt; or a watry ſituation, from *dwr*, *C. Br.* water.

Dod, the ſedge on the bank of a river.

Don, *doun*, *dun*; a down, a high hill or mount. Alſo *don* is ſometimes put for *ton*, which ſee.

Droſſen, *dru*, *druſſ*, *druſſen*; a thicket, or wood in a valley.

Ea, or *ey*, *eia*; from *A. S.* Ea, water. Names of theſe terminations denote that the places are in a watry ſituation.

Ell, watry, or bottom.

Er. This ſyllable in the middle of words is contracted from the *Saxon* paꞃa, which ſignifies inhabitants; *e. g.* Canterbury, antiently written Cantwaraburgh.

Fell, *(Saxon)* craigs, barren and ſtony rocks.

Ferth and *Forth* (common terminations, ſays the editor of Camden) are the ſame as an army, in *Engliſh*, coming from the *Saxon* word ꝼyꞃð.

Flet, from ꝼloð, *A. S.* a river.

Ford, where there was a noted one.

Frith, a wood, a plain amidſt woods; alſo peace, the ſea, or a place which the tide overfloweth.

Ger, from ᵹeꞃ, *A. S.* mud.

Gers, from ᵹẏꞃaꞅ, ᵹeꞃeꞅ, *A. S.* fens.

Gill, a ſmall water. *Camden*.

Glade, from *klados*, *Gr.* a bough, a ſhady place.

Glyn, *(Britiſh)* a narrow vale thickly ſet with woods.

Gorſe, furz, a prickly ſhrub.

Grange, a farm, or houſe, generally at a conſiderable diſtance from the town.

Ham, often abridged into *am*; a houſe, a village, a town, a farm, a meadow.

Haugh, *hough*; a green plot, in a valley, as uſed in the North.

Hay, *(French)* a hedge. *Hay-boot*, wood to repair hedges.

Heal, from hæl, *A. S.* whole, health.

Hen, *(Britiſh)* old.

Here, *her*; from heꞃe, *A. S.* army.

Herne, *hurne*, or *horn*; a houſe, a corner. *Alfricus*.

Hirſt, *hurſt*, *herſt*; a little wood. *Domeſday*.

Holt, a wood. *Alfricus*.

Hore, from hoꞃh, *(Saxon)* filth.

Holm, an iſland, a place ſurrounded with water; and ſometimes meadow ground on the water ſide.

Hope, the ſide of an hill; but in the North a low ground amidſt the tops of hills. *Camden*.

How, *hou*, or *hoo*; a hill, riſing ground, high.

Ing, ınᵹ, *(Saxon)* a meadow or low ground, or watry place.

Kemp; from cempa, *A. S.* a ſoldier.

Knoll, the top of a hill.

Lade, *lod*, from laꝺian, *A. S.* to empty; a paſſage of waters, the mouth of a river.

Laith *(Britiſh)* moiſt.

Leag, *leg*, from leᵹ, *A. S.* a paſture.

Lle, *(Britiſh)* a place; *leag*, *leigh*, *lee*; *A. S.* a field; alſo the laſt in *Old Eng.* ſignifies a ſhelter.

Ley; from ley, *A. S.* upland paſture, untilled ground, ſtill called the leys.

Ling, fern.

Llys, *(Britiſh)* a palace, a court.

Lowe, an artificial mount or hill.

Llydan, *(Britiſh)* broad.

Lyd, from lıꝺa, *(Saxon)* the ſhore.

Maes, (*Br.*) a field; but in the name of a place, ſignifies ſometimes that a battle has been fought there.

Mâr, *mêr*, and *môr*, ſignified antiently water as well as ſea. Lluyd *in Baxter*.

Mer, *mere*; a fen, marſh, pool:—alſo *mere*, a fence or boundary.

March, meaꞃc, (*Sax.*) a limit or confine.

Marſh, from meꞃꞅc, *S.* a fenny place.

Mees, meadows.

Meſnil, or *menil*; in *Norman-French* a manſion-houſe.

Minſter, contracted from monaſtery, a church.

Mod, fr. moꝺ, *Sax.* valour; alſo proud or lofty.

Mouth, where a river falls into the ſea, or into another water.

Næſe, or *neſs*; næꞅe, *(Saxon)* a promontory, becauſe it runs into the ſea like a noſe.

Nore, north.

Oc, aac, *(Saxon)* oak.

Over. Words beginning or ending thus, are names of places ſituated near the bank of ſome river, from oꝼꞃe, *Saxon*, *ripa*, *ſuper*; a bank, over.

Pen, *ben*, *fen*; *(Britiſh)* the head; the top of a hill, mountain, or any other thing.

Plat, *(French)* plain ground.

Pré, *prey*; (*French*) a meadow.

Prindle, the ſame as *Croft*.

Rad, *rod*; from ꞃaꝺe, *A. S.* counſel.

Rein, (*Teut.*) pure.

Ric, (*Saxon*) a kingdom, rich; *Teut.* a government.

Rill, a ſmall brook.

Rithy, from *rhyd*, (*Britiſh*) a ford.

Rhôs,

Rhôs; (*British*) a mountain-meadow, a moiſt large plain; alſo a heath.

Row, from *rue*, (*French*) a ſtreet.

Ry, from *rive*, (*French*) a ſhore, coaſt or bank.

Sale (*Fr.*) a hall, an entrance; whence, *Saloon*, or *Salo*, which in *High Dutch* ſignifies a king's court.

Scarr, a craggy, ſtony hill.

Secce, *A. S.* a fight.

Sel, good, convenient.

Sett, habitation, or ſeat.

Shaw, many trees near together, or ſhadow of trees.

Sige, victory.

Slade, from ſleꝺ, (*Saxon*) a long, flat ſlip of ground, a valley.

Snoth, or *ſneath*; a lot or portion.

Socne, *A.S. libertas*, freedom.

Stan, a ſtone.

Sted, from *ſtadt*, *Dutch*; a ſtanding place, a ſtation.

Stoke, *Stow*, } a place. *Alfricus.*

Strand, a bank of a river.

Stroad, *Stroud*, } ſome think the ſame as ſtrand.

Sutton, ſouth town.

Tam, *Tim*, *Tav*, *Tiv*, } a great number of our larger rivers begin with theſe words; hence Thame, or Thames; Tav, Taüy.—This *tam* is probably the ſame with the Greek *tamos* in *Potamos*, *Po* in Greek being an old prepoſitive. *Lluyd in Baxter.*

Tein, an incloſure.

Tern, or *dern*; a ſtanding pool, a word uſual in the North.

Thet Thed, from Ðeoꝺ, *A. S.* the people.

Thorp, *threp*, *throp*; (*Saxon*) a ſtreet, village.

Thurn, a tower. *Ortelius.*

Tin, *Br.* narrow.

Toft, a piece of ground where there hath been a houſe.

Tor, a high place, or tower; alſo a hill in the Weſt.

Ton, *Tun*, } a town, village, fence, incloſure, farm, dwelling.

Trêf, *Tre*, (*Britiſh*) a town, houſe or home.

Treau, *treaw*; a tree.

Trey, from *tref*, (*Britiſh*) a town.

Wad, *A. S.* a ford.

Wald; *Weald*; *Wild*; } a wood.

Wara, (*Saxon*) *vid. Er.*

Wark, or *werk*; a work or building.

Warth; a cuſtomary payment for caſtle-guard.

Wath; a ford.

Wic, *wich*, *wick*; [ĭ ſhort] the curviture or reach of a river, or of the ſea; *Junius Rhenanus.*—But *Alfricus* and *Tillius* make it a caſtle or little port, others a dairy farm.—*Wica*, in old Engliſh, *vicus*; a ſtreet, or paſſage between rows of houſes.

Wich; [ī long] a ſalt ſpring.

Wia; (*Saxon*) *via*, a way.

Wig, a wood, foreſt, grove.

Win, (*Saxon*) *prælium*, a battle. At the beginning and end of the names of places, it denotes that ſome great battle was fought there.

Windaſs, *wandaſs*, and *wanlaſs*; a term in hunting, as *to drive the windaſs*. It ſignifies the chaſing a deer to a ſtand, where a perſon is ready with a bow or gun to ſhoot.

Wire, *A. S.* a foreſt.

Worth, from ƿorð, *Sax.* a village, ſtreet, croft. It was antiently written *werth*, *weorthid*. *Alfricus* makes it *prædium*, a poſſeſſion or farm. *Abbo* tranſlates it a court or place; *Killianus* a fort, and an iſle; a fortified place.

Well, watry, or bottom.

Would, a down.

Wye, *ey*; water: alſo *wy*, *gwy*, *Br.* wandering.

Some perſons have objected, that there is a great impropriety in ſuppoſing a word to be compounded of parts drawn from different languages; but Quintilian ſhews the contrary, and produceth for inſtances, *Epirhedium*, *Anti-cato*, *Biclinium*, *Epitogium*; being compounded of Greek, Latin and other languages. *Camden's Br. col.* cclx.

Names were given to men for diſtinction of perſons; but they were choſen upon occaſions too numerous to ſpecify. In early ages they were often given upon future good hope conceived by parents of their children. Among the Roman names we find Victor, a conqueror; Probus, honeſt, good; Caſtus, chaſte; Fauſtus, fortunate; &c. which Cicero calls *bona nomina*; for many wiſe men were of opinion that names were ominous. Claudius Rutillius hints at this notion in the following lines,

Nominibus certis credam decurrere mores?
Moribus, aut potius, nomina certa dari?

Antiently people had but one proper name, as David, Ulyſſes, Romulus, Caradoc, Hengiſt, Edmund, &c. The Romans were the firſt that took ſurnames, in confirmation of their league with the Sabines, whoſe names they uſed before their own; as the Sabines, in like manner, did the Roman.

Surnames obtained in France about the year 1000, and at the conqueſt, or a little before, were brought into England, from which time, by degrees, the better ſort took them; but they were not fully ſettled among the common people, till about the time of Ed. II. The cognomen was uſed by the Anglo-Saxons before this time, but that differed from the ſurname, becauſe it did not deſcend from the father to the ſon, but was a ſort of nickname. ſome perſons have been of opinion, that ſurnames were ſo called from the Latin *ſuper*, or the French *ſur*, over; becauſe in early ages it was uſual to write the titles of perſons over their names, as $\frac{\text{Earl}}{\text{William}}$; but the title was not the ſurname.

name. Others have thought them ſo called, as being the name of the ſire, or father; but the better reaſon ſeems to be, becauſe they are ſuperadded to Chriſtian names. Domeſday book is perhaps the earlieſt record in which they are to be found: moſt of them were names of places, where thoſe that aſſumed them had reſided, or of which they were lords; as *Roger de Laci*, *Roger de Belmont*, *Roger de Luri*, *Roger de Berchelai*, &c. Others are diſtinguiſhed with *filius*, as *Willielmus filius Norman*, *Drogo filius Ponz*, &c. others again with the name of their office, as *Robertus Diſpenſator*, *Walterius Baliſtarius*, *Humfridus Camerarius*, &c. but there are ſome ſingle names in that book, placed at the end of every ſhire, as men of leaſt account; for it ſoon became a diſgrace to have but one name, as baſtards had. Robert of Glouceſter ſays, when king H. 1. would have married the great heireſs of Fitz-Haimon, lord of Glouceſter, to his baſtard ſon Robert, ſhe firſt refuſing, anſwered,

So vair eritage as ich habbe, it were me grete ſhame
Vor to abbe an louerd, bote he had an to name.

This paſſage is expreſſed with ſome variation, and more like the preſent language, by another author,

—— It were to me a great ſhame
To have a lord withouten his twa name.

So the king gave him the name of Fitz-roy, who was afterwards earl of Glouceſter.

The moſt antient ſurnames, and of beſt account, are deduced from places in Normandy, where, Mr. Camden ſays, there is not a village but gives name to ſome family in England; they are known by having the French *de*, *du*, *des*, *de la*, prefixt; and beginning or ending with *font*, *fant*, *beau*, *belle*, *ſaint*, *mont*, *bois*, *aux*, *eux*, *val*, *vaux*, *cort*, *court*, *fort*, *champ*, *ville*, *&c.* which laſt termination ſome have corrupted into *field*, others into *well*, as Somerfield, for Somerville; Boſwell, for Baſſeville, &c. Many noble families take their names from places in Brittany, and other parts of France; and there is hardly a village in Great Britain but hath given a family name: which in old Engliſh writings had *of*, or *a*, commonly ſet before them; as Thomas of Breadſtone, John a Standiſh, &c.

Rivers gave names to families, as Derwentwater, Trent, Tamer; and trees, as Box, Aſh, Pine, Aſp, &c. which in former times had *at* prefixed to them, as well as to ſome other kinds of local names, *viz.* At More, At Bower, At Wood, At Down, At Ho, At Beech, At Well, &c. The prefix hath been retained in ſome, as Atwood, Atho, Atwell; but removed from others. The diſtinctions of local names [*de*, *of*, *a*, *at*, and *le*] were ſtrictly obſerved in records till about the time of Edw. IV.

Names have been taken from trades, as Brewer, Chapman, Fuller; from offices, as Chamberlain, Steward, Marſhal; from eccleſiaſtical functions, as Biſhop, Dean; from civil honours, as King, Prince, Duke; from the qualities of the mind, as Wiſe, Sharp, Prat, *i. e.* ſubtil; from habits of the body, as Strong, Long; from colours, flowers, beaſts, birds, fiſhes, from Chriſtian names, nick names, and a variety of other things and occaſions, to exemplify which would take up too much room, and therefore ſhall mention only one inſtance more, juſt as I find it, on account of its ſingularity, without vouching for the truth of the ſtory. It is of a Grecian family, that obtained the name of Gephyri, *i. e.* Bridges; of whom it is ſaid, that the mother being delivered of nine children at a birth, in a fooliſh fear ſent ſeven of them to be drowned; the father coming inſtantly by, ſaved them on the bridge of the river, and ſo gave them the above name.

It is a good proof of antient deſcent, when the name of the perſon is the ſame with the place where he reſides, as Codrington of Codrington, Aylworth of Aylworth, Slaughter of Slaughter, and ſuch others.

In times paſt, gentlemen changed their names upon many occaſions, but moſt commonly upon changing their habitation. The heir took the father's ſurname, and the younger ſons aſſumed the names of the lands allotted them, which is the cuſtom in France at this time. Thus Hugh de Sudington gave to his ſecond ſon his manor of Frydon; to his third, that of Pantley; the ſons called themſelves De Frydon, De Pantley; and their poſterity afterwards removed the particle *de*. Some took their mother's name, others that of their progenitors, benefactors, &c. in remembrance of them; others changed their names at the king's command, as in the inſtance of king Ed. IV. who often told the family of the Picards that he loved them, but not their names, upon which they changed it, one of them taking the name of Ruddle, where he was born.

A Welch gentleman, *temp.* H. 8. being called at the pannel of the jury by the name of Thomas Ap Williams, Ap Thomas, Ap Richard, Ap Hoel, Ap Evan Vaughan, &c. was adviſed by the judge to leave that old manner; whereupon he afterwards called himſelf Moſton, from his principal houſe, and left that ſurname to his family.

Many names are ſtrangely contracted, as At Aſh into Taſh, At Abbey into Tabbey, Saint Oyly into Toly, Saint Ebbe into Tabbe, Saint Oſyth into Tows; others again are ſo diſtorted by the ignorant vulgar, to make them, according to their apprehenſions, ſignificant, that there is but a faint likeneſs either in ſound or orthography left. We find Wormwood for Ormond, Drinkwater for Derwentwater, Cuckold for Coxwold, and many others of the ſame nature. There is a remarkable inſtance of this abuſe in my own family, who about thirty years ago always wrote their name Rutter; but were induced by an ignorant perſon to change it, becauſe it ſhould ſignify ſomething they had heard of; and I have fooliſhly followed them.

Tho

Tho' women with us, at their marriage, change their own ſurnames for thoſe of their huſbands, becauſe it is ſaid, *non ſunt duo, ſed caro una*; yet it is not ſo every where. In France, a woman of family retains her name, and uſeth it with her huſband's; as for inſtance, if Genevieve Villeville marry A. Belmont, ſhe then writes herſelf Genevieve Belmont Villeville;—and ſo of others.

The tranſlating of names into Greek or Latin is ſtill in uſe among the Germans, for he whoſe name is Ertſwept, or Blackland, will be Melancthon; if Newman, Neander; if Holiman, Oſiander; if Brook, Torrentius; if Fen, Paludanus, &c. And here in England there are a few that have two ſurnames, with *aliàs* betwixt them. Judge Catline having taken exception againſt a perſon in this reſpect, ſaid, no honeſt man had a double name, and came in with an *aliàs*; upon which the perſon aſked him, what exception his lordſhip could take to Jeſus Chriſt, *aliàs* Jeſus of Nazareth? which reply probably might ſoften his lordſhip's ſeverity.

It was uſual, among the antients, to give ſuch names to their kings and princes as ſhould contain the name of one of their deities. Thus the Tyrian, or Phænician princes were called Beleaſtartus, Abdaſtartus, Ithobaal, from their deities Baal and Aſtaroth. Nebo, a Babylonian idol, is a part of the names of Nebuchadonezar, Nabopollaſſar, and Nabonitus, kings of Babylon. Among the Egyptians were the kings Buſiris, Petoſiris, Oſiris, &c. having the Egyptian deity Siris in their names; as the Jewiſh kings Amaziah, Azariah, and divers others have in them one of the names of the true God. And the kings of our antient Britons had Belin, or Abellio, one of their deities in the names of Caſſibelin, Cynobelin, and of ſome others.

Adjuncts to names and titles are of very antient uſage. *Dominus* was attributed to the Roman emperors. Lucian ſays, ſpeaking of the beginning of the empire in Julius Cæſar,

Namq; omnes voces, per quas jam tempore tanto
Mentimur Dominis, hæc primum reperit ætas.

By which it ſhould ſeem, that thoſe titular attributes of greatneſs had their origin at Rome about that time. Auguſtus refuſed the title of *Dominus*, by public edict, perhaps becauſe it was then taken up by every private man. But Domitian was of another diſpoſition, for Suetonius informs us, that by his expreſs order, it was thus inſerted in the letters which carried his commands, *Dominus et Deus noſter ſic fieri jubet*. Diocleſian was the next of the emperors, after Domitian, that permitted himſelf to be ſo ſtiled. Conſtantine the Great was the firſt of the Chriſtian emperors that aſſumed it; and the learned Selden has ſhewn, that ſome title of the ſame ſignification hath been given to the princes of the Mahomedan ſtates, as well as to thoſe of every kingdom in Europe.

The Romans, under the late emperors, were very exact and particular in giving five ſorts of titles to their officers and great men. *Illuſtris* was the higheſt, appropriated to the *Præfecti Prætorio* of Italy and Gallia, the *Præfecti* of the city of Rome, the *Magiſter Equitum*, *Magiſter Peditum*, the *Quæſtor Palatii*, the *Comes Largitionis*, and to all that had voice in the ſenate.—*Spectabilis* was the ſecond title due to the lieutenants general, *Comites* of provinces, &c.—*Clariſſimus* was the third title peculiar to the *Conſulares*, *Correctores*, and *Præſtes* of provinces.—*Perfectiſſimus* was the fourth.—*Egregius* was the fifth; and none could have the two laſt but by patent, nor could *Clariſſimus* be otherwiſe obtained, except only by theſe great officers above ſpecified, in virtue of their offices.

The title of duke was antiently given to great men, in reſpect of their military employments. Under the Roman empire, he that had a province committed to him, not being a count, was called *Dux*. The firſt duke of the preſent acceptation, was the Black Prince, created duke of Cornwall by his father when in parliament, 11 Edw. 3. 1337. By this creation, not only the firſt born ſon of the kings of England, but the eldeſt living alſo, are always dukes of Cornwall.

As duke and earl were uſed with us for expreſſions of the ſame ſignification, many years before duke was made a diſtinct dignity; ſo earls and barons were ſometimes called marquiſſes. But *Marchia* or *Marchiſius*, of itſelf, did not antiently denote any title of honour, any more than *Commarchiones regni noſtri*, in the old Latin tranſlation of king Ina's laws, for ſuch as lived bınnan ðam gemæꞃum uꝼeꞃ ꞃiceꞅ, i. e. *in the frontiers of the kingdom*, which are called marches, from whence the word is derived. But afterwards it became a ſpecial dignity alſo, next beneath that of duke. The firſt of this ſort was Robert de Vere, earl of Oxford, created marquis of Dublin, 9 R. 2. which Walſingham ſays the lords took very ill, aſſigning their reaſons, *quia nec prudentia cæteris, nec armis valentior extitiſſet.*

Viſcount is a title of ſtill later date, and ſtands between earl and baron. The firſt was John Beaumont, created viſcount Beaumont, 18 E. 6.

Baron with us is the moſt antient title. Before the ſettling of the Norman monarchy, the kingdom was compoſed of earldoms and baronies. Moſt of the great barons fell in the battle of Eveſham, 1265, therefore others were called by writ; and becauſe they ſat in parliament with the former, they were called peers, [from *pares*,] being in every reſpect reputed equal to thoſe barons which were by tenure.

Coronets were firſt aſſigned to earls in the reign of king H. 3. to viſcounts by king J. 1. and to barons by king C. 2. after the reſtoration.

The title of baronet is hereditary. The firſt creation was by king James 1. on the twenty-ſecond day of May, in the ninth year of his reign. In the following year a decree was made that the baronets and their eldeſt ſons, being of full age, ſhould be knighted, and that they and their deſcendants ſhould bear the arms of Ulſter; *i. e.* on a field argent, a hand gules, either in a canton in their coat of arms, or in an eſcutcheon, at their own choiſe.

The name of knight, [in Latin, *eques*, *miles*; in French, *chevalier*] has been of various ſignifications. In Saxon it is written Cnıhꞇ or Cnẏhꞇ, and ſignifies a boy, a ſervant, an attendant; ſometimes a ſoldier. The chief gentlemen or freeholders of every county, becauſe they held by knights ſervice, were ſtiled *Chivallers* in the ſtatute of Weſtminſter the firſt, concerning the choiſe of coroners. Antiently great ſubjects, as well as their ſovereigns, gave this dignity; but the conferring of it has been long ſince confined to the ſovereign only. Various ceremonies have been uſed on this occaſion, ſuch as ſome antient knight girding the perſon with a ſword, and putting on his ſpurs, &c. &c. which the reader may ſee at large in *Seldon's Tit.* of *Honor*, c. 5. ſ. 34.

The eſquire [*armiger*, *ſcutifer*] is beneath the knight, and, in the opinion of the learned author juſt mentioned, is ſometimes ſupplied in our antient writings by *ſerviens*, or *ſerjeant*, which is the ſame word, and ſometimes diſtinguiſhed from it. In the ſtatute 23 H. 6. concerning the choiſe of knights of the ſhire, it is ſaid they muſt be either knights *ou autrement tielx notables eſquiers, gentileſhomes del nativitie des meſmes les counties come ſoient ables deſtre chevalier, & nul home deſtre tiel chivalier que eſtoite en le degrer de* Vadlet *et deſouth.* This word *vadlet* is the ſame as *varlet*, and has the ſignification of *knave* at preſent; though both of them were antiently names of civil degrees, or ſervice only. In the reign of R. 2. John de Kingſtone was created eſquire by patent; and Seldon thinks that then it might be acquired by ſervice or employment. At the time of creation, the eſquire received a collar of SS from the king, as an enſign of the dignity. It was the buſineſs of eſquires to attend their reſpective knights, each of whom had two, to the wars and elſewhere; but long before military ſervice was laid aſide, and ever ſince that time, thoſe whoſe birth or eminence have been thought worthy ſome note of diſtinction, above the rank of gentleman, have had that of eſquire given them.

I ſhall conclude this chapter with an obſervation of the learned Camden, who, ſpeaking of anceſtors, parentage, and names, recommends every man to ſay, " *Vix ea noſtra voco*; for, ſays he, " we are come to this preſent time by various " ſucceſſive deſcents, the low are deſcended from " the high, and contrariwiſe the high from the " low." He goes on. " If any vaunt of their " names, let them look to it, leſt they have *in-* " *ania nomina*; you know who ſaith, *veſtra nomina* " *nunquam ſum admiratus*; *viros qui ea vobis reli-* " *querunt, magnos arbitrabor*."

Gloucesterſhire.

CONSIDERED,

I. As INTIRE and UNDIVIDED.

II. As divided by Nature into the COTESWOLD, or *Hill-country*, the VALE, and the FOREST.

III. In its Political Diſtribution into *Hundreds*.

Of the Name, Situation, Extent, Antient State, Diviſions, Cuſtoms, Manufactures, Produce, &c. *of the County*.

GLOUCESTERSHIRE is ſo called from Glouceſter, a handſome city, its capital, and ſcyre, a Saxon word, ſignifying a diviſion, from ſcyran, to cut or ſeparate.

The inhabitants of this county and of Oxfordſhire were called by the Romans *Dobuni*, which Dion has miſtaken for *Bodunni*. The name is ſuppoſed to be derived from *Dwfn*, which in the Britiſh language ſignifies deep, * or low. By the *Dobuni*, therefore, were originally meant the inhabitants of the vale country; but gradually the word obtained a larger ſignification; for, as they increaſed, and removed to the higher lands, they were nevertheleſs conſidered as belonging to, and retained the ſame name with the people of the vale, whence they came; for in all countries the richer ſoils have been § firſt inhabited, but the people multiplying, extend their limits, till by degrees the leſs hoſpitable hills and woodlands yield to cultivation.

When the Romans were in Britain, there was no ſuch particular diſtrict as Glouceſterſhire. After they had ſubdued this part of the iſland almoſt as far as Scotland, they divided it into *Britannia Prima et Secunda*. The tract of country, which we now call Glouceſterſhire, lay in both provinces, becauſe the river Severn divided them for a conſiderable length. That part which lay on the S. E. of the river Severn was in *Britannia Prima*, under the government of the preſident reſiding at London. The other part, on the N. W. of the Severn, which was formerly much more woody than at preſent, and had been poſſeſſed by the Silures, was in *Britannia Secunda*, under the government of the preſident reſiding at Caerleon, in Monmouthſhire.

* Mr Camden has ſhewn, that many places have taken their names from ſuch a ſituation, of which *Catabathmos* in Africa, and *Deepdale* in Britain, are inſtances.

§ And men firſt building towns, themſelves did wiſely ſeat
Still in the bounteous vale; whoſe burthened paſture bears
The moſt abundant ſwarth. *Drayton's Poliolb. S.* 14.

After

After the Romans quitted Britain, in the 476th year from Julius Cæſar's coming over, the Saxons at length ſeized the reigns of government, and, the beſt part of the Iſland falling into their hands, was divided into ſeven kingdoms, of which Mercia was one. At this time we know nothing of any ſmaller diviſion of territory, for the name of the *Dobuni*, which diſtinguiſhed the inhabitants of Glouceſterſhire and Oxfordſhire, was utterly loſt.

When the Saxons, under the heptarchy, were firſt converted to chriſtianity, the kingdom and the dioceſe were of the ſame dimenſions, under one king and one biſhop. The firſt ſubdiviſion of kingdoms under them ſeems to be of eccleſiaſtical eſtabliſhment; for in the year 679, the kingdom of Mercia was divided into five biſhopricks, of which Florence of Worceſter ſaith, *Wiccia* † was the firſt.

This province of *Wiccia* was probably of the ſame extent with the antient biſhoprick of Worceſter, containing all that part of Glouceſterſhire ſituate on the S. E. of the Severn, with the city of Briſtol; the greateſt part of Worceſterſhire, and near the half of Warwickſhire, including the town of Warwick.

Why the Saxons gave this province and its inhabitants the reſpective names of *Wiccia* and *Wicces*, is not abſolutely certain. Mr. Camden, at the beginning of his account of Glouceſterſhire, with great diffidence conjectures, that the names might come from the Saxon word Wic, which ſome have thought to ſignify the creek of a river; and that becauſe the *Wicces* or *Wiccij* dwelt about the mouth of the Severn, they obtained that appellation. But if it be conſidered, that in Edgar's charter to Oſwald, the Coteſwold country about Blockley and Iccombe is called * *Mons Wicciſca*, Wiccian hill; and that Sceorſtan is expreſſly ſaid by Florentius to be in *Wiccia*, all at a great diſtance from any large river, one would willingly find a better reaſon for the name; which I think the ſame learned author has given in another place. In this province were many § briny wells, which the antient Engliſh in their language called *Wiches*, whence with little trouble they made ſalt; and 'tis not improbable but that *Wiccia* might thence obtain it's name, eſpecially as the Wiches were ſo conſiderable, that ſalt was antiently the chief article of commerce in that country. There is at preſent only one of them remaining, the others being cloſed up, becauſe it appears by antient writings that they were confined to one place for the making of ſalt, to prevent too great a conſumption of wood.

Glouceſterſhire was undoubtedly firſt ſo called when it was firſt made a county, which ſignifies the ſame as ſhire; the one coming from the French, the other from the Saxon language, both denoting one of thoſe portions into which the whole kingdom is divided, for the better government of it, and for the more eaſy adminiſtration of juſtice.

The dividing of the kingdom into counties has generally been attributed to king Alfred. Ingulphus affirms it; but Selden has clearly demonſtrated the contrary. The *Pagi* and *Provinciæ*, which Ingulphus mentions in the following paſſage, *Totius Angliæ pagos & provincias in comitatus primus omnium commutavit*, were the ſame with the *comitatus*, or ſhires. And, before Alfred's time, theſe *Pagi* had their ealdormen in them. Thoſe of Berkſhire, Devonſhire and Somerſetſhire, were Ethelwolfus, Ceorle, and Eanulf, under king Athelwolfe, father of Alfred; as they are expreſſly mentioned by Aſſerius Menevenſis, who lived in king Alfred's time. And we alſo learn by the ſame antient author, and by Ethelwerd, another writer of the Saxon times, that Ealhere, or Alchere was ealdorman of Kent, and Auda or Wuda, of Surry, at the ſame time that Oſric was ealdorman of Dorſet. Further, the charter of the foundation of Crowland abbey, granted by king Ethelbald, was ſubſcribed by the *comites* of Leiceſter and Lincoln: And laſtly, the original laws of Ina, king of Weſtſex, anno 720, ſay, That if an ealdorman were guilty of an eſcape, þolige hiſ ſcyre, *perdat comitatum ſuum*, *i. e.* he ſhould loſe his ſhire. Alfred therefore could not be the firſt that began to divide the kingdom into counties.

This county lies in the Oxford circuit, is bounded on the N. W. by Herefordſhire; on the E. by Oxfordſhire, and a ſmall part of Berkſhire; on the S. by Wiltſhire; and on the W. by part of Somerſetſhire, the Britiſh channel, and Monmouthſhire. It extends itſelf in length from the pariſh of Clifford-Chambers, near Stratford upon Avon, to Clifton, beyond the city of Briſtol, in a S. W. direction, about ſeventy ſtatute-miles; and in breadth, from Leachlade, north-weſtward to the pariſh of Preſton, in the hundred of Botloe, about forty ſuch miles. Draw a ſtraight line lengthwiſe through the county, to touch each of the two firſt mentioned places, and another line to croſs it, from one of thoſe points of extreme breadth to the other, and they will interſect about Shurdington, nearly at right angles.

The form of the county reſembles an ellipſis, the N. E. end of which is more acute than the other. If five miles of the length, and ſix of the breadth, be abated for irregular jettings out at thoſe extremities, the ſuperficial content of the whole county will be nearly 1,100,000 acres. Notwithſtanding

† Wiccia is ſaid to contain 300 hides of land. *Camd. col.* ccxxv.

* Spelman reads it corruptly *Monte Wittiſca*, and the *Monaſticon* more corruptly *Wibiſca*. *Add. to Camden*, *col.* 617.

§ The old Chartulary mentions a ſalt-pit in the boundaries of *Scepwæſcetune* [Shipſton upon Stour] a ſalt-well adjacent to Iccumb, on the weſt; a road called Salt-ſtreet near *Euinlode*; a ſalt-pit, or *Saltere wælan*, in the limits of Wulfrinton, to the eaſt of Worceſter. But the ſprings that were moſt famous and have ſurvived the memory of all their rivals, are thoſe near the river Salwarp, which gave both name and ſubſiſtence to a town, that grew up on their margin, now diſtinguiſhed by the name of Droit-wich; in Domeſday called Wich, in Saxon charters Wic, and ſometimes Salt Wic. *Green's Survey of Worceſter*, *P.* 15.

ſtanding this is conſiderably larger than a former eſtimate, [800,000] it will be found to come very near the truth.

A vaſt range of hills, covered with wood in many parts on the north-weſt ſide adjoining to the Vale, reaches from Campden, on the borders of Warwickſhire and Worceſterſhire, to Lanſdown, near Bath; and runs through the county length-wiſe, a little obliquely with the courſe of the Severn; dividing, not very unequally, the Vale and the Foreſt part of the county from the Coteſwold.

Various parts of this chain of hills are denominated from the pariſhes in or near which they lie, and many great roads are carried down them. The turnpike-road from London to Worceſter leads down Broadway-hill; that from Stow to Tewkeſbury, down Stanway-hill; from Cirenceſter to Cheltenham, down Windaſs-hill; from London through Oxford, to Glouceſter, down Crickley-hill; but through Cirenceſter to Glouceſter, you deſcend Birdlip-hill: From the eaſt part of the county, to either of the paſſages over the Severn at Framilode or Newnham, the road is down Rodborough-hill; from Bath to Glouceſter, down Froceſter-hill; from Cirenceſter to Wotton, Durſley, and Berkeley, down Wotton, Durſley, and Stinchcombe hills, reſpectively; from Oxford to Briſtol, down Sodbury-hill; but from Oxford to Bath, down Fryſon-hill; and the great road from London to Briſtol leads down Tog-hill; ſo that there is no poſſibility of paſſing directly from Oxfordſhire, Berkſhire, or Wiltſhire, to the vale of Glouceſterſhire, without deſcending one of the hills in this great chain, which ſtands as a boundary between the Coteſwold and the Vale, the latter being again ſeparated from the Foreſt by the interpoſition of the great river Severn.

Nature having thus divided the county into three parts, let us take her for our guide, and ſurvey each of them diſtinctly in its order.

Of the COTESWOLD.

UNDER the denomination of the Coteſwold, I now include all that high country on the ſouth-eaſt ſide of the beforementioned range of hills which runs through the county. It is a noble champaign country, the reſidence of many of the nobility and gentry, and abounds in verdant plains, downs, corn-fields, parks, woods, and little vallies, well ſupply'd with ſprings and rivulets, and enjoys a fine healthy air, which, however, in the higher and more expoſed parts, has been thought too thin and cold for perſons of very tender and delicate conſtitutions.

It was antiently much over-run with woods, whence I conjecture it obtained its double name, for *Coed*, in the Britiſh language, and *weold*, in the Saxon, both ſignify *a wood*, and together make a kind of tautology, of which there are many like inſtances in the names of other places. And with great deference to Mr. Camden, it ſeems probable that all thoſe that have *Cot*, or *Cotes* in their compoſition, are derived from the beforementioned Britiſh word; and the preſent woody ſtate of ſuch places ſerves to ſtrengthen this opinion.

Tho' this part of the county lies high with reſpect to the vale, yet in itſelf it is not very hilly; for when the traveller has gained the ſummit of the great ridge already mentioned, he finds himſelf on the verge of an extenſive country, finely diverſified with groves and plains, and gently riſing grounds; plentifully watered with pleaſant ſprings, purling rills, and winding brooks, ſome running north-weſtward into the Severn, whilſt others, taking a contrary courſe, empty themſelves into the Thames, which takes its riſe in Glouceſterſhire, and is navigable for veſſels of thirty or forty tons burthen, in the ſame county where it firſt becomes a river.

This country was always famous for feeding numerous flocks of ſheep. Drayton has done it no little honour, who, in his poetic way, invokes the muſe

————————— "to tell
How Ev'ſham's ferile vale at firſt in liking fell
With Cotſwold, that great king of ſhepherds; whoſe proud ſite
When that fair vale firſt ſaw, ſo nouriſh'd her delight
That him ſhe only lov'd; for wiſely ſhe beheld
The beauties clean throughout that on his ſurface dweld.
* * * * * * * * * * * * * *
T' whom Sarum's plain gives place, tho' famous for her flocks,
Yet hardly doth ſhe tythe our Cotſwold wealthy locks.
Though Lemſter him exceed for fineneſſe of her ore,
Yet quite he puts her downe for his abundant ſtore.
A match ſo fit as hee, contenting to her mind,
Few vales (as I ſuppoſe) like Ev'ſham hapt to find.
Nor any other wold like Cotſwold ever ſped,
So fair and rich a vale by fortuning to wed."

POLYOLBION. *14th Song*.

Within the laſt forty years, prodigious improvements have been made here, by a courſe of huſbandry, firſt introduced into theſe parts by the late Mr. Richard Biſhop, once the moſt conſiderable ſeedſman in the kingdom; who brought the graſs-ſeeds, turnips, and clover into uſe, and taught the coteſwold farmers how to become an opulent people. 'Till that time their ſheep and other cattle were ſent to winter in the vale for want of fodder; but the preſent method in huſbandry, enables them to keep more than double the live ſtock they were uſed to do, upon their own lands, throughout the year.

Planting of ſaintfoin, clover, and turnips, anſwers two grand purpoſes to the coteſwold farmer. His cattle, whilſt they feed and fatten upon them, dung and fertilize the ſoil, which infallibly inſures a good ſucceeding crop of corn; ſo that under favourable circumſtances, and judicious management,

ment, the produce of an acre in this country will fometimes equal that of a like quantity of land in the vale. However, if this be not always the cafe, it is generally allowed that the hill-country farmer has the advantage very confiderably, fince the vale lands are rented at double, or treble the price, and will not admit of proportionable improvement.

Saintfoin has long fince been the produce of the Cotefwolds. Gloucefterfhire has the honour of leading the county of Norfolk in the culture of this valuable grafs, which fir John Turner getting the knowledge of here, introduced into that county. The method of planting it is with barley or oats after turnips; but fome perfons think it better fown with wheat, to get ftrong and fecure againft a dry fummer, which is fo pernicious to it when planted in the fpring. This grafs is both fed and mow'd. It flourifhes on the moft ftony land, and will laft feven or eight years in pretty good vigour. When worn out, it is ufual to break it up, by paring and burning, preparatory for a crop of wheat or turnips.

The cotefwold hufbandry varies according to the ftrength of the foil, and the fkill of the farmer. The crops are planted in the following orders.——On good inclofed land, 1. Wheat. 2. Beans, or peafe. 3. Barley, or oats with clover. —Or, 1. Turnips. 2. Barley. 3. Peafe. 4. Oats and clover. 5. Wheat. 6. Turnips.——Or, 1. Barley. 2. Clover for two years. 3. Wheat. 4. Peafe.—Or, on very light land, they fometimes after a crop, lay down with ray-grafs and clover.

The common fields are cropped, every other year, with all forts of grain. And in fuch places where envy leaft prevails, and the farmers have difcernment enough to fee their own intereft, they take a hitching out of the common field, by general confent, and plant with turnips or peafe, in the year for fallowing.

There are many fpots of ftrong land on this fide the great ridge of hills, which are planted in the following order, 1. Turnips, to be fed with fheep 'till the fpring. 2. Barley with clover. 3. Wheat. 4. Peafe, or Beans. 5. Barley with clover. 6. Wheat. 7. Turnips.

The farmers pen their fheep upon the land univerfally, befides which they ufe no kind of manure except that of the yard and ftable. Perhaps a few, on the fide of Oxfordfhire, may have made the experiment of woollen rags, but they are not at prefent likely to come into general ufe.

The common methods of planting peafe here, are, fetting in rows, and fowing broad caft. In both ways, about four bufhels of feed go to the acre. But I would recommend an improved one, practifed in feveral parts of Wiltfhire. It is thus: With a plough, drawn by one horfe, they make three fhallow furrows in the dreffed land, about eighteen or twenty inches afunder; into which, women following, throw the peafe very regularly, at proper diftances. A man coming after, covers the feed with earth by means of his foot, or a hoe, according as the land requires.

About three weeks after the plants appear, they flat hoe them, and about the fame diftance of time afterwards, draw the earth that is on one fide of the rows, with a large hoe, over the roots and lower part of the plants, fo as to lay them flat on the ground. When the bloffoms are juft dropt, and the kids appear, a perfon going betwixt the rows, plucks up thofe plants that are backward in blow, which is called reaping them.

By this management the crop ripens together, and the corn is fo very even, and fo much fuperior to what is raifed in the common way, as to fell for at leaft 6*d.* a bufhel extraordinary. The two hoeings are done at about 5*s.* an acre, the expence of which, the faving in the feed will defray; for two bufhels and three pecks, or, at moft, three bufhels will plant an acre in this way.

The farms on the Cotefwold, are from one hundred to five or fix hundred pounds a year. The price of labour is 10*d.* a day in the winter; 1*s.* in the fpring, 1*s.* 6*d.* in grafs mowing, and 1*s.* 8*d.* or 2*s.* for about five weeks at corn harveft.

Many of the downs, common fields, and wafte lands, in this part of the county, have been lately inclofed, to the vaft advantage of the proprietors of eftates, and I apprehend of the kingdom in general; for, under favour, I will venture my opinion, that it is our intereft to encourage agriculture rather than grazing, to which we have been too much inclined.

In former times, there were two things that operated very powerfully to the hindrance of agriculture. The great barons preferred grazing, becaufe it required fewer hands than the plough employ'd, fo that their vaffals could be better fpared from it, to attend them in their wars with the crown, and with each other, in which they were almoft continually engaged.

Another thing was, before the woollen manufactures were brought into England, and from that time 'till the reign of queen Elizabeth, we were fuppofed to derive great advantages from the fale of unwrought wool to the Flemings; therefore breeding and feeding of fheep was the general practice, and it might perhaps be encouraged by government, for the king had a large revenue arifing from the fale of that article.

This neglect of agriculture occafioned frequent famines, and great peftilence enfued. In the reign of that unhappy prince, Edward the Second, in the years 1314, 1315, and 1317, wheat fold for 3*l.* 1*s.* 2*d.* a quarter; and the next year it advanced to 6*l.* 14*s.* 7*d.** which, confidering all circumftances at that time, was at leaft equal to 8*l.* a bufhel at prefent.

* See an inquiry into the Prices of wheat &c. But I think there muft be fome miftake in this account.

Peftilence

Peftilence and famine might fill the nation with horror; but nothing befides long experience could convince it of its error in the neglect of agriculture, which a few only of the moft fenfible men difcovered, and complained of, among whom was the great Sir Thomas More.—"Our flocks of fheep, fays he, which were formerly fo mild and gentle, are now become fo voracious, as not only to devour men, but even fields, houfes, and walled towns are laid wafte and depopulated by them;" meaning, no doubt, that the people, wanting that employment which agriculture afforded them, many were obliged to leave their habitations, and fo became thieves and ftrollers.

In the fourth year of king H. 7. the converting of arable land into pafture, was reftrained by a ftatute, which rather prevented things from growing worfe than made them better. But that which above all other things has moftly tended to promote agriculture, was the bounty on the exportation of corn, † firft granted by parliament in the year 1689, which has induced a general fpirit for inclofing the wafte lands and common fields throughout the kingdom; a method of improvement adopted very early in Gloucefterfhire.

Some objections have been raifed againft inclofing, but it would be extending this digreffion too far to take any notice of them here.

Mr. Camden, who was a diligent inquirer, and faithful hiftorian, takes notice of the wool of this country, for its whitenefs and finenefs, wherein he has been followed by a great number of writers who had either never feen, or feeing, had no judgment in that article. What kind of wool this may have been four or five hundred years ago, I can have no knowledge of, except from hiftory; but can fpeak with certainty as to the prefent condition of it. The fheep of this country incline to the large fize; for, fince by the improvements in agriculture, the quantity of food for cattle is greatly increafed, the farmers have both enlarged their flocks and improved the breed, by introducing the Leicefterfhire ram, which is fometimes brought hither in little carriages made for that purpofe. I have been informed, that 40*l*. has been paid for the ufe of one of thefe rams for a feafon only. They are efteemed the ftouteft fheep in the kingdom, and bear prodigious fleeces, the hair of which is coarfe and long; fo that the cotefwold wool, which was never fine within the memory of any man I have converfed with on that fubject, is now become ftill coarfer, by thus mixing the breed. The longeft fort of it is combed for worfted ftuffs, whilft the fhort is wrought up in cloth for the army, for the Eaft-India company trade, and other coarfe goods. Herefordfhire, one of the adjoining counties, may juftly boaft of the fineft fleeces in the kingdom. The difference in the quality may in fome meafure be judged of by their refpective prices in the fame year. In 1767, the beft cotefwold fleeces fold for 8*d*. 3 qrs. a pound, when the beft Herefordfhire brought two fhillings.

There is no coal-pit in this part of the county; but at Stratton, about a mile from Cirencefter, they have often found what the miners call plodding-coal; particularly as the labourers were digging a well, about four years fince, a good quantity was taken up there. I have now by me three fpecimens of different foffil fubftances found at that time, one of which is the common pit-coal; another is very black, with a grain perfectly refembling a piece of oak, and not fo heavy as the firft; the third is a piece of iron ore. There is a great probability that a good ftratum of coal might be found there, as every appearance feems to indicate it, and I am told that the plodding-coal is a circumftance of the ftrongeft prefumption of it.

About twenty years ago, the workmen difcovered a fmall vein of coal, of an inch thick, in one of the fine free-ftone quarries, in the parifh of Barnfley. It lay nine feet below the furface, upon a bed of blue clay. They traced it 'till 'twas imperceptible, and I don't find that circumftances encouraged them to examine further.

Coal has alfo been found in the parifh of Siddington St. Peter, by people that were digging a well there, the water of which was fo black and ftinking as not to be fit for culinary purpofes. Mr. Bathurft, who was lord of the manor, was informed of the difcovery, and it is aftonifhing that it was not followed by a ftrict and careful examination, in order to the opening of a pit, efpecially as there was a great probability of fuccefs. A good coal-mine in either of thefe places, round which for many miles firing is dear, would be a prodigious treafure to the proprietor, and a great advantage to the country, which is fupply'd by land carriage with that neceffary article, either from the pits beyond Sodbury, or from Gloucefter, both at great diftances.

On the Cotefwolds is a cuftomary annual meeting at Whitfuntide, vulgarly called an Ale, or Whitfun-ale. Perhaps the true word is Yule, for in the time of druidifm, the feafts of yule or the grove, were celebrated in the months of May or * December. Thefe fportsare reforted to by great numbers of young people of both fexes, and are conducted in the following manner. Two perfons are chofen, previous to the meeting, to be lord and lady of the yule, who drefs as fuitably as they can to the characters they affume. A large empty barn, or fome fuch building, is pro-

† The author of An Inquiry into the prices of wheat, malt, &c. as fold in England from the year 1000 to the year 1765, has fhewn, that 14,332,435 quarters and 3 bufhels of wheat; 2,543,096 quarters of barley; 13,653,186 quarters and 1 bufhel of malt; and 2,288,321 quarters and 7 bufhels of rye, have been exported with the bounty; which amounted in the whole to the fum of 6,658,702l. 10s. 11d. to the end of the year 1764.

* In the north of England Chriftmas is called, Chriftmas-yule, and Chriftmas gambols, yule games. Yule is the proper Scotch word for this feftival, *vide* 10 *Annæ c.* 13.

vided

vided for the lord's hall, and fitted up with feats to accommodate the company. Here they affemble to dance and to regale in the beft manner their circumftances and the place will afford, and each young fellow treats his girl with a ribband, or favour. The lord and lady honour the hall with their prefence, attended by the fteward, fwordbearer, purfe-bearer, and mace-bearer, with their feveral badges or enfigns of office. They have likewife a page, or train bearer, and a jefter, dreft in a party coloured jacket, whofe ribaldry and gefticulation contribute not a little to the entertainment of fome part of the company. The lord's mufic, confifting generally of a pipe and tabor, is employ'd to conduct the dance.

All thefe figures, handfomely reprefented in baffo-relievo, ftand in the north wall of the nave of Cirencefter church, which vouches fufficiently for the antiquity of the cuftom. Some people think it a commemoration of the antient drink-lean, a day of feftivity formerly obferved by the tenants and vaffals of the lord of the fee, within his manor, the memory of which, on account of the jollity of thofe meetings, the people have thus preferved ever fince. It may, notwithftanding, have its rife in druidifm, as on thefe occafions they always erect a may-pole, which is an eminent fign of it.

I fhall juft remark, that the mace is made of filk, finely plaited with ribbands on the top, and filled with fpices and perfume, for fuch of the company to fmell to as defire it. Does not this afford fome light towards difcovering the original ufe, and account for the name of the mace, now carried in oftentation before the fteward of the court, on court days, and before the chief magiftrate in corporations; as the prefenting of fpices by great men at their entertainments was a very antient practice?

Mr. Robert Dover, who lived in the reign of king J. I. inftituted certain diverfions on the Cotefwold, called after his name, which were annually exhibited about Willerfey and Campden. Even now there is fomething to be feen of them, every Thurfday in Whitfun-week, at a place about half a mile from Campden, called Dover's Hill.

The cotefwold games, and their patron, are celebrated in a fmall collection of poems, intituled *Annalia Dubrenfia*, written by Michael Drayton, Ben. Johnfon, and about thirty other eminent perfons of their time, moftly addreft to the patron of the games; by means of which, if you believe the poet,

Cotfwold, that barren was, and rough before,
Is Tempe now become, Cotfwold no more.
Pan may go pipe in barren Malvern chafe;
The fawns and Satyrs feek fome other place.
Cotfwold is now th' epitome of myrth;
And joy, prefaged erft, is come to birth.
Olympus' mount, that e'en to this day fills
The world with fame, fhall to thy Cotfwold hills
Give place and honour. Hercules was firft
Who thofe brave games begun: Thou, better nurft,
Doft in our anniverfe moft nobly ftrive
To do in one year what he did in five.

The meetings were very numerous, as may be collected from the following lines:

——————— On Cotfwold hills there meets
A greater troop of gallants than Rome's ftreets
E'er faw in Pompey's triumphs: Beauties too,
More than Diana's beavie of nymphes could fhow.
On their great hunting days, ————
——————— there in the morn,
When bright Aurora peeps, a bugle horn
The fummons gives, ftreight thoufands fill the plains
On ftately courfers.

I have felected out of this collection, part of an Eclogue, by Mr. Thomas Randall, of Cambridge, which is one of the beft of thofe pieces, defcribing the cotefwold diverfions. The fpeakers are Collen and Thenot.

* * * * * * * * *

Collen. Laft evening, lad, I met a noble fwayne,
That fpurr'd his fprightly palfry o'er the playne;
His head with ribbands crown'd, and deck'd as gay
As any laffe upon her bridal day.
I thought (what eafy faiths we fhepherds prove!)
This, not the bull, had been Europa's love.
I afk'd the caufe; they told me this was he
Whom this day's triumph crown'd with victory.
Many brave fteeds there were, fome you fhould find
So fleet as they had been fons of the winde.
Others with hoofs fo fwift beate o'er the race,
As if fome engine fhot 'um to the place.
So many, and fo well wing'd fteeds they were,
As all the broode of Pegafus had been there.
Rider and horfe could not diftinguifh'd be;
Both feem'd conjoin'd, a centaur's progeny.
A numerous troupe they were, yet all fo light,
Earth never groan'd, nor felt 'um in their flight.
Such royal paftimes Cotefwold mountains fill,
When gentle fwains vifit her glorious hill;
Where with fuch packs of hounds they hunting go,
As Cyrus never woon'd his bugle to;
Whofe noife is mufical, and with full cries
Beat o'er the fields, and eccho thro' the fkyes.
Orion hearing, wifh'd to leave his fphere,
And call his dogs from heaven, to fport it there.

* * * * * * * * * * * * * * * * * * *

There, fhepherd, there the folemn games be plaid,
Such as great Thefeus or Alcides made;
Such as Apollo wifhes he had feen,
And Jove defires had his invention been.
The Nemæan and the Ifthmian paftimes ftill,
Though dead in Greece, furvive on Cotfwold hill.

Thenott. Happy O hill! the gentle graces now
Shall trip o'er thine, and leave Citheron's brow;
Parnaffus' clift fhall finke below his fpring,
And ev'ry mufe fhall on thy frontlet fing:

The

The goddeffes again in ftrife fhall bee,
And from mount Ida, make appeal to thee;
Olympus pay thee homage, and in dread
The aged Alps fhall bow his fnowy head.
* * * * * * * * * * *

But gentle Collen, fay, what God or man
Fame we for this great worke, Daphnis or Pan?

COLL. Daphnis is dead, and Pan hath broke his reed;
Tell all your flocks 'tis jovial DOVER's deed.
Behold the fhepherds in their ribbands goe,
And fhortly all the nymphs fhall wear 'um too.
Amaz'd to fee fuch glorie meet together,
Blefs DOVER's pipe, whofe muficke call'd 'um hither.
Sport you, my rams, at found of DOVER's name;
Big-bellied ewes, make hafte to bring a lambe
For DOVER's fold. Go maids, and lillies get,
To make him up a glorious coronet.
Swains, keep his holiday, and each man fweare
To faint him in the fhepherd's kalendar.

Mr. William Durham, in another copy of verfes, hath thus prefaged the lafting fame of this public fpirited man:

Firft fhall the tender lambs with tygers dwell,
And fearful harts fhall lodge with lions fell;
Firft fhall the glorious ftar-beftudded fkie
Want light, and Neptune's regiment be drie;
Firft fhall the courtiers leave their fweet embraces;
Ladies to plafter o'er their furrow'd faces;
* * * * * * * * * * * *
Firft fhall Nyctimene, that bird of night,
To flie at noon take pleafure and delight,
Ere Cotfwold fhepherds, on their jointed reeds,
Shall ceafe to fing his fame-deferved deeds;
Who from their tombs, wherein they were in-thrall'd,
The antient dancing Druides hath call'd.

But thofe that allow Mr. Durham a competent fhare of merit as a poet, will probably refufe him their fuffrage as a prophet; for already we hear but little on the Cotefwolds of his worthy friend Mr. Dover, fince whofe time the diverfions have alfo much declined, for want of fo good a patron.

Damnofa quid non imminuit dies! HOR.

What doth not time's injurious hand impair!

Of the VALE.

THE Vale of Gloucefterfhire lies chiefly on the fouth-eaft of the river Severn, which gives life and fpirit to the foil. For extent and fertility, it is not exceeded, nor do I know that it can be equalled by any in the kingdom; therefore Drayton, perhaps with more hiftoric juftnefs than poetic licence, gives her the fovereignty, in the following lines:

——————— " I, which am the queene
Of all the Britifh vales, and fo have ever been
Since *Gomer's* giant brood inhabited this ifle,
And that of all the reft myfelf may fo enftile."

It is honoured with the refidence of feveral of the nobility and gentry, who have eftates in this county.

What it more antiently was, may be feen in a paffage taken by Mr. Camden out of a book intituled *De Pontificibus*, written by William of Malmefbury. "The Vale of Gloucefterfhire," fays he, "yields plenty of corn and fruit, in fome "places by the natural richnefs of the ground, in "others by the diligence of the country men; "enough to excite the idleft perfon to take pains, "when it repays his labour with the increafe of "an hundred fold. Here you may behold high-"ways and public roads full of fruit trees, not "planted, but growing naturally. The earth bears "fruit of its own accord, much exceeding others "both in tafte and beauty, many forts of which "continue frefh the year round, and ferve the "owner 'till he is fupplied by a new increafe. "No county in England has fo many or fo good "vineyards † as this, either for fertility, or fweet-"nefs of the grape. The wine has in it no un-"pleafant tartnefs, or eagernefs, and is little

† "Many places in this county, fays fir Robert Atkyns, bear "the name of vineyards, from thence it has been concluded that "wine has heretofore been made in thefe parts; but thefe vine-"yards were only apple-orchards, as may appear by many records "where manors were held of the king, and the tenants were "obliged to pay yearly veffels of wine, made of apple-fruit. One "record is 6 Joh. rot. 48. Walter de Hevene held the manor of "Runham, in the county of Norfolk, by yielding yearly two "veffels of wine, made of pearmains, to the king, at his "exchequer, on the feaft of St. Michael. Another record is full "to this point; William Mansfeld, 18 E. 2. was feized of a "vineyard, fix acres of arable, and there acres of wood, in Bifley. "Now it is wholly improbable than any other vineyard than "that of apples could grow in that cold barren place; one might "as foon gather grapes of thiftles." *Ancient and prefent State of Glocefterfhire*, p. 32.

Thus the learned author determines pofitively againft our vineyards; but let us examine the ftrength of his argument. In the firft record a certain liquor is termed, *wine made of pearmains*, by which it appears that fuch as wrote in Latin ufed a periphrafis to defcribe cider, and for this reafon, becaufe there is no Latin word for that liquor; but how does that prove that our *vineyards were only apple orchards?* The fecond record fir Robert declares to be *full to this point*; and indeed it is fully againft him, for it proves that William Mansfield was feized of a vineyard, &c. in Bifley. But befides this evidence, *Domefday* is fufficient to determine the difpute, where, in the account of Stonehoufe in this county, it is thus recorded: *Ibi duo arpenz vinee*; and I believe nobody will contend that *vinea*, in this place, fignifies an apple orchard, or any thing elfe but a plantation of vines. Laftly, fir Robert oppofes improbability to plain evidence, and thinks that no other vineyard than that of apples could grow in Bifley; but he might have known that about Chalford, in that parifh, are many warm and fheltered fpots of ground of a fouth afpect, extreamly fuitable to the purpofe in queftion. The monk of Malmefbury, who lived on the borders of this county, knew it well, and exprefsly mentions the Gloucefterfhire vineyards and grapes; and as his account is fupported by the evidence of *Domefday*, and other records, I give him full credit againft all vague opinions, that the vineyards he mentions were not apple-orchards, but plantations of the vine.

" inferior to the French in ſweetneſs. The " villages are very thick, the churches handſome, " and the towns populous and many."

Camden ſays, the reaſon why ſo many places in the county are called vineyards, was, on account of the plenty of wines made here; " and that " they yield none now, is rather to be imputed " to the ſloth of the inhabitants, than the in- " diſpoſition of the climate." But with Mr. Camden's leave, the lands are employ'd to better advantage, and it is for that reaſon that we have no vineyard in the county at preſent.

In this Vale is made that fine cheeſe, ſo deſervedly eſteemed not only in Great Britain, but in all countries wherever it has been carried. The hundreds of Berkeley, of Thornbury, and the lower diviſion of Grumbald's-aſh, produce the beſt. It is made of various thickneſſes, from about ten pounds to a quarter of a hundred weight each. The thick ſort is called double Glouceſterſhire, and double Berkeley, and uſually ſells upon the ſpot at ſix-pence a pound. It requires to be kept to an age proportionable to its ſize and richneſs, to make it ready for the table.

Cider is another production of this Vale, in which I believe no county in the kingdom can rival it. There is great variety of it, which I ſhall divide into three claſſes: 1. The ſtout-bodied, rough, maſculine cider, made of Longney-ruſſet, Hagley-crab, Winter-pippin, &c. 2. The full-bodied, rich, pleaſant cider, of the Harvey-ruſſet, woodcock, golden-pippin, winter-quinning, &c. and 3. A ſort made of the Bodnam apple, fox-whelp, and various ſpecies of kernel fruit; which, tho' I have placed laſt in order, might perhaps have ſtood with more propriety in the ſecond claſs, being of a middle nature between the other two, as partaking of the properties of both. There is alſo ſome ſtyre made in the vale, but not in that perfection as in the foreſt of Dean.

Perry being a liquor of a diſtinct ſpecies, muſt not be omitted. The beſt of the produce of this country is made of the Tainton ſquaſh pear, the Barland pear, and the mad pear. His late Royal Highneſs the prince of Wales, father of his preſent Majeſty, on his tour through this country in 1750, gave it the name of *La Champaigne d' Angleterre*. It is a delicious, ſprightly liquor, when in perfection; but a perſon when hot ſhould never drink of it freely.

Moſt places in Glouceſterſhire, within ten or twelve miles eaſt and north-eaſt of Briſtol, abound in coal mines, ſome of them of a prodigious depth, and are therefore greatly incommoded with water, which is taken off by the means of fire-engines. The coal is ſomething of the nature of that of Newcaſtle; about one half of it riſing in large lumps, the reſt about the ſize of gravel; but when thrown on a good fire, it melts, forms itſelf into one maſs, and is very durable. The upper part of the county is ſupply'd with coal out of Shropſhire, down the river Severn, which burns quick and lively, but is not ſo durable as our own.

It is aſſerted by ſir Robert Atkyns, p. 30. that if a line were laid from the mouth of the Severn to Newcaſtle, and ſo paſſed round the globe, coal is to be found within a degree of that line, and ſcarce any where elſe in the world. But the remark is unaccountably whimſical and ridiculous, as facts and experiments are wanting, and always muſt be wanting to ſupport it.

The veins of coal, found about Briſtol, are covered with a ſhell of black, hard, ſtrong ſubſtance, called *Wark*, which will ſplit like blue ſlate, but is much more brittle, and not nearly ſo hard. Upon dividing this Wark, there is often found upon one of the ſeparated ſurfaces, the perfect ſhape of a fern-leaf, as if it had been engraven by a ſkilful hand.

The lower part of the Vale from Arlingham downwards, on the ſouth-eaſt of the Severn, is very liable to inundations from that river. Several commiſſions have been iſſued for the preſervation of theſe lands, the firſt of which to be found on record was 5 E. 2. There were others as follow: 33, 36, 38, & 44 E. 3.—2, 4, 6, 8, 9, & 16 R. 2. 11 H. 4. 1 H. 5. *Dugdale on Fenns.*

The lands are divided into two levels, called the Upper and Lower. Commiſſions are occaſionally held, and orders and regulations made for ſupporting the banks of the river, on which the preſervation of the country depends. In each level, to receive and carry off the water, are ten or twelve pills, or inlets, which, as well as the ſea-wall, are repaired by thoſe whoſe eſtates lie next them. A ſmall ſum is annually raiſed to defray the expence of the court of ſewers, by rating the pariſhes at 2*d.* an acre, according to the following table, which ſhews the number of acres given in by the reſpective places, as particularly liable to inundation; but ſome of them have not charged themſelves with more than about one half, others two thirds of what is actually ſubject to floods.

Upper Level.	Acres.	Lower Level.	Acres.
Arlingham, —— —	738½	Auſt, —— —— —	272
Slimbridge, ——	412	Redwick and Northwick,	950
Hinton in Berkeley, —	161	Compton Greenfield, —	783
Ham, and Ham Fallow	1400	Stowick, —— —	1111
Hill, —— ——	600	Olveſton, ——	500
Elberton, ——	300	Tockington, — —	800
Rockhampton ——	300	Over, —— ——	150
Moreton in Thornbury,	426	Hempton and Patchway,	76
Oldbury upon Severn,	1247	Almondſbury, ——	200
Kington and Cowhill,	300	Lawrence Weſton, —	458
Littleton and Coat, —	100	King's Weſton, ——	530
Awre, a pariſh on the north-weſt of Severn.	200	Gaunt's Ircot, — —	116
	6184½		5946

In

In the reign of G. 2. another commiſſion was iſſued for the preſervation of lands, lying further up the river, above theſe levels; but nothing was ever done in conſequence of it.

Birdlip-hill and Crickley-hill, part of that ridge which has been already obſerved to divide the Coteſwolds from the Vale, ſtand about ſeven miles diſtant from the city of Glouceſter, and are nearly of the ſame height, the top of the firſt being about 450 yards above the water in the Severn, at that city, and on a level with a great part of the coteſwold country. It is therefore no wonder if the temperature of the air in the Vale ſhould be ſenſibly different from that on the coteſwolds; but Sir R. Atkyns has expreſſed the difference too ſtrongly in the following paſſage: "If it be objected againſt the cold air of the Coteſ- "wolds, that there are eight months winter, and "cold weather all the year beſides, it may be here "affirmed, that there are eight months ſummer, "and warm weather all the reſt of the year." The learned hiſtorian ſeems to have been led into this miſrepreſentation, by his affecting a perfectly contraſted mode of expreſſion: for tho' the difference be conſiderable, his account of it is very much exaggerated.

The Vale upon the whole is healthy, yet in ſome places, on the borders of the great river Severn, the inhabitants are very ſubject to agues.

Moſt of the other productions of the Vale, beſides thoſe particularly noted, being common to other countries, I paſs them over, and conclude this head with a ſhort obſervation, no leſs juſt than general, That they are no where to be found in greater plenty and perfection than here. For a further account of the productions of the Vale, ſee the latter part of the chapter on trade, &c.

Of the FOREST of DEAN.

THE Saxons called a foreſt Bucholt, *i. e. ſylva ferina, vel cervina*. Others define it to be *locus ſylveſtris et ſaltuoſus*; a territory of woody grounds and fruitful paſtures, privileged for wild beaſts and fowls of foreſt, chaſe and warren, to reſt and abide in, under the king's protection, † for his princely delight and pleaſure; incident to which are ſeveral courts and officers of record, which muſt appear on record.

The foreſts in England (the new foreſt in Hampſhire and that of Hampton Court excepted) are of ſuch antiquity, that hiſtory makes no mention when they were firſt erected; and as in England, ſo in other countries, the charge of them has always been committed to perſons of eminence.

Si canimus ſylvas, ſylvæ ſunt conſule dignæ. VIRG.

Or if ye chuſe to ſing the ſhady grove,
Make your theme worthy a great conſul's love.

For the Roman conſuls had the government of foreſts.

Before the obtaining of the Great Charter of the foreſts, the king claimed, *de jure*, to make a new foreſt wherever he pleaſed, and to incloſe, not only his own demeſnes, but the lands of other perſons, within its bounds and perambulation; but Lord Coke, whom with great confidence I follow, has ſhewn, that this was not agreeable to the laws then in force; for, ſays he, the act of *Carta de Foreſta* is but a declaratory law, reſtoring the ſubject to his former right; and that charter is directly againſt ſuch claim. Indeed originally, all the lands of the ſubject are derived from the crown, and our foreſts may have been made when the antient kings had the greateſt part in their own hands, and ſo having a lawful beginning, a foreſt may be, by preſcription, good in law over other men's grounds. But king H. 2. and his two ſons, Richard and John, enlarged the antient bounds of the foreſts, and under the notion of exerting the prerogative, exerciſed great ſeverities and oppreſſions on their ſubjects, who were afterwards reſtored to their former rights by the Great Charter. But for theſe, and other matters, concerning foreſts in general, having juſt ſhewn what they are, the reader is referred to the books written profeſſedly on that ſubject. I ſhall now confine myſelf particularly to examine into the bounds and extent, the government, peculiar cuſtoms, privileges and produce of the foreſt of Dean.

This Foreſt, which gives name to one of the four political diviſions of the county, is celebrated in Drayton's lofty ſtrains, as

——— "Queen of foreſts all that weſt of Severn lie;
Her broad and buſhy top DEAN holdeth up ſo high,
The leſſer are not ſeen, ſhe is ſo tall and large."

POLYOLB. *Song* 7.

It obtained the name of Dean, * or Dene, from the antient market-town of that name, lying within its bounds and perambulation; which town was ſo called, perhaps from its remarkable low ſituation, being almoſt encompaſſed round with high hills and woods. The word is of Saxon original,

† There was a miſtaken notion, that no ſubject could enjoy a foreſt; whereas the duke of Lancaſter had the foreſts of Pickering and Lancaſter; and the abbat of Whitby had the foreſt of Whitby, in Yorkſhire. *vid.* 4 *Inſt.* 314.

* Mr. Camden, whom Sir Robert Atkyns follows, was of opinion that the Gauls and Britons heretofore uſed the word *arden* for a wood, from whence, by rejecting the firſt ſyllable, the name of this foreſt might be derived; but I find no ſuch word of that general ſignification in their language. *Ardenne*, indeed, was the proper name of a wood or foreſt in Gaul.

original, and ſignifies a dale, a valley, or woody place; whence our Engliſh word *den*, a hole, or cave in the earth. *Giraldus*, and ſome others, gave this foreſt the name of *Danubia*, and *Danica Sylva*, or the Dane's woods, becauſe they ſheltered themſelves here.

In the Roman times it was part of the territory of the Silures, and after the Britons were driven by the Saxons beyond the Severn, it belonged to the dominions of Wales. All this part of Glouceſterſhire, together with Monmouthſhire, and part of Herefordſhire, was called by the general name of *Gwent*, 'till Wales was divided into counties. But king Athelſtan, drove the Welch beyond the Wye, which afterwards became the boundary between England and Wales, according to Alexander Neckham;

Inde vagos Vaga Cambrenſes, hinc reſpicit Anglos.

On this ſide, Wye the Engliſh views;
On that, the wandering Welch purſues.

Bounds *of the* FOREST.

King H. 2. as before obſerved, greatly extended the boundaries of the foreſt of Dean, and the ſucceeding kings, Richard and John, following his example, the whole country lying between the Wye and the Severn, and the road leading from Goodrich-caſtle, in Herefordſhire, thro' Weſton and Newent, to Glouceſter-bridge, was taken within the perambulation.

There was a perambulation made 9 H. 3. upon account of the monks of Flaxley. And a juſtice-ſeat was held at Glouceſter 10 E. 1. for ſettling the foreſt bounds. There were then ten bailiwicks, which included only the king's waſte ſoil, and ſuch aſſarted lands and purpreſtures as had been the waſte ſoil, and did not take in the antient manors, &c. tho' within the perambulation § of the foreſt. The extent of the bailiwicks, with the names of the woodwards, are ſet forth upon the oaths of twelve regarders; and the proceedings remain on record at the chapter-houſe, Weſtminſter.

Soon after the confirmation of the Great Charter, and of the Charter of the Foreſt, 25 E. 1. the king iſſued out his commiſſion to perambulate the new foreſt, taken into that of Dean, ſince the coronation of H 2. The commiſſioners returned † the names of all the vills, woods, and lands which were afforeſted after the coronation of king H. 2. and that they ought to be diſafforeſted; and 28° *regni*, another perambulation was made, leaving out all ſuch places as had been newly taken in. The woods ſo left out were called purlieus *, and ſome of them ſtill retain the name, as the biſhop's purlieu, and Pirton purlieu, in the manor of Lidney. The bounds of the foreſt of Dean were then ſettled; and always afterwards, reference was had to this perambulation, which was uſed by the officers of the foreſt from time to time 'till the 20th year of James the Firſt.

In the ſucceeding reign, ſome attempts were made to enlarge the bounds of it, and 10 C. 1. a juſtice-ſeat was holden at Glouceſter, before the earl of Holland, aſſiſted by juſtice Jones, baron Trevor, and ſerjeant Bridgman, when the jury was prevailed on to find the bounds as extenſive as in the time of H. 2. But an act paſſed in the 17th year of the ſame reign, for ſettling the boundaries of all foreſts, as they were reputed to be 20 Jac. 1.

In the next reign, the legiſlature taking the affairs of the foreſt into conſideration, the occaſion of which the reader will be acquainted with hereafter, an act paſſed 20 C. 2. by which many good regulations took place. Soon afterwards, the lord warden cauſed a perambulation ‡ to be made by the regarders, agreeably to that of 28 E. 1. and as it was reputed to be 20 Jac. which was returned upon their oaths.

Previous to the act 17 C. 1. a Survey was made of Dean foreſt, the particulars of which are exhibited in the following Table.

A Survey *of the Common of the* Forest *of* Dean, *taken Anno Domini*, 1641.

Woodwardſhips.	Acres.	Into Wood.	Clear.	Common alotted.	The poſſeſſors of the reſpective woodwardſhips, at that time.
Great Dean woodwardſhip containeth —	1794	508	1286	626	Maynard Colcheſter, at the Wilderneſs, Eſq;
Lea Bayley woodwardſhip containeth —	998	690	308	——	Maynard Colcheſter, Eſq;
Ruar-Dean woodwardſhip containeth —	1936	1339	597	597	John Clarke, of the Hill, Eſq;
Abinghall and Badcock's Bayley containeth	5049	3849	1200	459	John Howell, of Lincoln's Inn, Eſq;
Bicknor woodwardſhip containeth — —	1031	877	158	305	Thomas, Lord Viſcount Gage.
Staunton woodwardſhip containeth —	6096	3343	2753	873	Thomas, Lord Viſcount Gage.
Blakeney woodwardſhip containeth —	4297	1620	2677	600	The Rev. Mr. Thomas Savage, of Glouceſter.
Bloyſe Bayley woodwardſhip containeth	187	187	——	187	John Beal, of Newent, Eſq;
The Bearſe woodwardſhip containeth —	1190	890	300	——	Thomas Wyndham, of Clearwell, Eſq;
Abbot's Wood containeth —— ——	943	735	208	——	Thomas Crawley Bovey, of Flaxley, Eſq;
	23521	14034	9487	3647	

---

§ See Appendix, No. 1.
† Appendix, No. 2.

* From two French words *pur* and *lieu*, a pure place, exempt from ſervitude. *See* 4 *Inſt. p.* 103.
‡ See Appendix, No. 3.

It appears by the ſurvey, that the foreſt of Dean contains, within its perambulation, 23,521 acres of the king's waſte, lying within the hundred of St. Briavel's, beſides ſeveral antient manors, pariſhes, vills, and places, to the amount of above 20,000 acres more, ſome of which were taken from the Saxons by the Conqueror, and given to his Norman followers. But ſince that time, many thouſands of acres that were formerly foreſt, have been aſſarted, taken out by purpreſtures §, and granted away by the crown.

The whole foreſt, which is extraparochial, is divided into ſix walks, known by the names of their reſpective lodges or houſes, built for the reſidence of ſo many keepers, *viz.*

1. The king's lodge, but oftener called the ſpeech-houſe, ſtanding between Kenſlo-hill and Daniel's-moor.
2. York lodge, at the upper end of Lumbard's marſh.
3. Worceſter lodge, upon Wimbury-hill.
4. Danby lodge, upon the Old Baily-hill, near Lidney.
5. Herbert lodge, upon Ruerdean-hill.
6. Latimer lodge, upon Dane-Meen-hill †, not far from the beacon. The hill takes its name from ſome ſtones which ſtood there in memory of ſome great Dane ſlain in theſe parts.

Each keeper has a ſettled annual ſalary of 15*l.* paid out of the exchequer, and an incloſure of ground for his further encouragement.

Of ROYAL *and other* GRANTS, *&c.*

MILES or Milo, earl of Hereford, portreeve or conſtable of Glouceſter, was lord of the foreſt of Dean in the reign of H. 1. but Sir William Dugdale, in his Baronage, informs us, that Maud the empreſs, gave the whole foreſt of Dean, with the caſtle of St. Briavel's, to Miles, for his aſſiſtance againſt her brother, 4° Steph. However incompatible theſe accounts may ſeem at firſt, they may be reconciled, by ſuppoſing that the conſtable had been violently diſpoſſeſſed of his eſtate by Stephen, at the beginning of his reign. This great man had five ſons and three daughters. The ſons all died without iſſue; but Lucy, the youngeſt daughter, was married to Herbert Fitz-Herbert, chamberlain to the king, 5° Steph. who had for her portion the foreſt of Dean, and was therefore afterwards called lord of Dean. He was high-ſheriff of Glouceſterſhire during that reign. The following abſtracts from the records are ſet down in the order of the dates. The reigns are marked at the beginning of each paragraph.

HENRY II. granted to the abbey of Flaxley two oaks out of this foreſt every ſeven days, for the maintenance of a forge there.

JOHN.] Henry de Bohun releaſed all his right in this foreſt to the king 1° *regni*; who granted it 18° *regni* to John de Monemuta.

HENRY III.] It was found by inquiſition that the monks of Flaxley had a forge for making of iron there 4° *regni*. The ſame year the judges itinerant ordered that none ſhould have an iron forge in the foreſt, without ſpecial licence from the king.—Almarick of the Park had a grant of waſte lands in this foreſt the ſame year.—Walter de Aure, and Maud de Cantelupe, had each of them an iron forge 5° *regni*.—John de Standon had a grant of 12 acres of land, near Sitgrove, on the borders of the foreſt 8° *regni*.—Henry earl of Warwick had a forge in his woods at Lidney, and other iron forges in the foreſt 10° *regni*.—William de Alba Mara had a grant of the foreſt of Dean 40° *regni*.—The king finding the grant of the two oaks every week, which the abbat of Flaxley had obtained of his grandfather, ſo injurious and deſtructive to the foreſt, granted the monks a wood *, in recompenſe for the ſaid two oaks 42° *regni*.—William de Dean was ſeized of Great Dean, and of a bailiwick in the foreſt 43° *regni*.—William de Londres was ſeized of Eclawe 50° *regni*.

EDW. I.] Henry de Chauworth had a forge here 2° *regni*.—Alexander Blith held Blith bailiwick 6° *regni*.—Richard de Abbenhalle had the bailiwick of that name 7° *regni*, againſt whom a Quo Warranto was brought, to prove his right of common of paſture in 20 acres in Ridley.—The abbey of Glouceſter held Hope Malerſel 9° *regni*.—Bogo de Knovile had a licence to incloſe Kilcot wood, and convert it into a park the ſame year.—The ten bailiwicks were kept by the ten perſons following, as appears by the proceedings at a juſtice-ſeat, held 10° *regni*; *viz.* the bailiwick of Abbenhalle, by Ralph de Abbenhalle; of Blakeney, by Walter de Aſtune; of Bleythe, by Ralph Hatheway; of Berſe, by William Wodeard; of Bicknoure, by Cecilia de Michegros; Rywardyn, by the conſtable of St. Briavel's; The Lea, by Nicholas de Lacu; Great Dean, in the hands of the king, and kept by the conſtable of St. Briavel's; Little Dean, by Ralph de Abbenhalle; Stauntene, by Richard de la More.—William Boteler was ſeized of a bailiwick 13° *regni*.—Cecilia de Michegros was ſeized of a wood in the foreſt, and 28 acres of aſſart land, at Greenway, and 9 yard-

§ Aſſarts and Purpreſtures. The firſt ſo called from the French *aſſartir*, to make plain; or from *exertum*, to pull up by the roots; or *exaratum*, or *exartum*, to pull or cut up. The word ſignifies woodlands cleared and made fit for tillage.—Purpreſtures, from the French *pourpris*, *conſeptum*, an incloſure; but properly it ſignifies an incroachment.

† Mr. Borlace obſerves, that the common name of the circular monuments in Cornwall, is *Dawns Meen*, that is, ſays he, the ſtone-dance, ſo called of the common people on no other account, than that they are placed in a circular order, and ſo make an area for dancing. But with all deference to ſo reſpectable a perſon, I think the name is expreſſive of the nature of the thing; for in the Britiſh language, of which the Corniſh is a dialect, *Dane Maen*, ſignifies the Dane's ſtone, having no relation to dancing.

* Appendix No. 27.

lands and a half, at Brat-Forton 29° *regni*; and the ſame year, Ralph de Abbenhalle was alſo ſeized of a wood in the foreſt of Dean.—The tythes of all aſſart lands within the foreſt, were granted to the church of All Saints, in Newland, then belonging to John biſhop of Landaff, 34° *regni*.—And the ſame year, William Bleyth, and Joan his wife, had a grant of 104 acres of aſſart lands in this foreſt.—Alſo in the ſame year, Alexander de Bicknore was found ſeized of the bailiwick of Rywardyn. William Bleyth held the bailiwick of Bleyth 35° *regni*.

Edw. II.] John de Abbenhalle, 1° *regni*, held a certain bailiwick in this foreſt, of the king, *in capite, ad cuſtodiendum eam per corpus ſui cum arrou et ſagittis, et non valet ultra cuſtod*.—The ſame year, Bogo de Knovil was ſeized of Kilcot wood, in this foreſt.—Henry de Chaworth had a forge here 2° *regni*.—The prior and convent of Lanthony, near Glouceſter, was ſeized of 212 acres of aſſart lands 4° *regni*.—John Abbenhalle held a bailiwick 10° *regni*.—And the ſame year, John de Wiſham was ſeized of Noxton vineyard, in the foreſt, and 200 acres of waſte, to be aſſarted and incloſed.—John Barington held 40 acres of waſte, near Maleſcoyte-wood; and Ralph Hatheway was alſo ſeized of 40 acres in Holſtone, both in the year laſt mentioned.—William Joice was ſeized of 20 acres of waſte at Muchel-Clay, and 80 acres of waſte at Brakenherd, both in this foreſt 16° *regni*. —Robert de Aure held one meſſuage, and 12 acres of land here 19° *regni*.

Edw. III.] Tythes of the iron-mines were granted to the biſhop of Landaff 6° *regni*.—John Joice, and his heirs, had a grant of 116 acres in ſeveral parcels in the foreſt, at the yearly rent of 19*s*. 4*d*. 12° *regni*.

Richard II.] Thomas de Brug, and Elizabeth his wife, levied a fine of a bailiwick in Dean, and of lands in Lee-Walton, and in Lee, in Herefordſhire, to the uſe of Thomas in taile, remainder to Richard Curle 5° *regni*.—The king granted the caſtle of St. Briavel's and the foreſt of Dean to Thomas duke of Glouceſter, in ſpecial taile, 14° *regni*; whereby nothing paſſed but a frank chaſe, ſays lord Coke; but it was afterwards enacted in parliament, that the duke ſhould hold the ſaid foreſt, with power to conſtitute ſuch juſtices and officers as are incident and belonging to a foreſt.

Henry IV.] The foreſt was granted to John the king's ſon, in taile, 1° *regni*.

Edw. IV.] John Throgmorton was ſeized of a woodwardſhip 13° *regni*.

Henry VII.] The king by letters patents, 24 Sept. 1° *regni*, granted the mines of Newland to Thomas Motten for his life, without rent.—And by like letters patents, 1 Feb. 1° *regni*, he alſo granted the mines beneath the wood *vocat. Le Gawle*, to John Motten for his life, without rent.

Henry VIII.] After the diſſolution of monaſteries, 36° *regni*, Sir Anthony Kingſton obtained a grant, amongſt other things, of all the lands in this foreſt, formerly belonging to the abbey of Flaxley.

Eliz.] Richard Brain, eſq; died ſeized of a woodwardſhip and of a foreſter's place, in this foreſt, 15° *regni*.

James. I.] The king by letters patents, 7 Feb. 9° *regni*, granted to the earl of Pembroke a leaſe of the foreſt of Dean, together with the iron-ore, cinders, coal, and wood for making of charcoal, with many other extenſive liberties and privileges, for 21 years, at the rent of 2433*l*. 6*s*. 8*d*.—The king by his letters patents, 30 June 16° *regni*, granted to William Wintour, eſq; and William Bell, at the nomination of divers perſons therein mentioned purchaſers, in conſideration of 1074*l*. 8*s*. ſeveral meſſuages, lands and tenements, called aſſart lands, purpreſtures, and other lands and tenements belonging to the crown, lying in the foreſt of Dean, at the rent of 5*s*. ſaving to himſelf and his ſucceſſors, all mines, quarries of ſea-coal, &c. And Wintour and Bell covenanted that the lands ſhould remain under the foreſt laws.

Char. I.] The king by letters patents, 28 May 1° *regni*, granted to Sir Edward Villiers, knight, and to his heirs, a part of the waſte ſoil of the foreſt, called Malyſcott, together with all woods growing thereon, and all mines, &c.—The king, 16° *regni*, diſafforeſted the whole waſte ſoil, and by his letters patents dated March 31, the ſame year, in conſideration of 10,000*l*. then paid, and of 16,000*l*. more to be paid in ſix years, and of a fee-farm rent of 1950*l*. 6*s*. 8*d*. to be paid for ever, granted to Sir John Wintour, and to his heirs and aſſigns, the cheſnut-wood or coppice, in leaſe to Richard Brayne, and the Snead and Kidnals, in leaſe to Triſtram Flower, and others; and all thoſe his majeſty's coppices, woods, lands, and waſte ſoil in the foreſt, with their appurtenances, lying within the perambulation made 27° E. 1. containing in the whole 18,000 acres; and all the mines of iron, tin, lead and coals therein, and in the lands of his majeſty's ſubjects within that perambulation, reſerved by the crown; together with free warren and free chaſe, and power to make ſalteries in his own lands of Lidney, &c. all royal mines excepted.

The foreſters, as ſuch, had long enjoyed many conſiderable privileges and advantages, and tho' generally well affected to the king, could not with indifference ſee them granted away to a favourite with this prodigious eſtate, which Sir John began to incloſe. Therefore, in the great rebellion, the incloſures were broken down, and the foreſt was almoſt totally deſtroy'd.

Char. II.] After the reſtoration, Sir John would have repaired the mounds, but was oppoſed by the whole country round about; upon which a commiſſion iſſued out of the exchequer to Henry lord Herbert, to inquire into the condition of the foreſt, &c. and great numbers of the inhabitants ſubſcribed a paper, containing their claims to privileges,

privileges, and a kind of petition, deſiring that the 18,000 acres might be reafforeſted, and that the letters patents, for the ſale thereof, might be made void; which paper, the commiſſioners made a part of their return. *See App. No.* 4.

This repreſentation had its deſired effect. Sir John Wintour, in obedience to his majeſty, by indenture dated 28 July, 14° *regni*, in conſideration that he ſhould have the Snead and Kidnals, containing 280 acres, to himſelf and to his heirs forever; and alſo in conſideration of 30,000*l.* then due to him, on account of his patent, ſurrendered * and yielded up to his majeſty all the particulars granted to him by the late king, except the Snead and Kidnals, and except the authority of free warren, and of making ſalteries in his own lands. And an act paſſed 20° C. 2. c. 3. which made the diſafforeſting of thoſe lands, by the late king, null and void.

By this act, the waſte lands of the foreſt were reafforeſted, and are to be governed by foreſt laws, as in 10° C. 1. And all future grants of the waſtes, or incloſures, or of the mines, or quarries, are made void. The king is impowered to incloſe 11,000 acres, to remain in ſeveralty in the actual poſſeſſion of the crown for ever, as a nurſery for wood and timber only. There is a proviſo, that all leaſes made, or to be made, by the king, his heirs or ſucceſſors, to any perſon, for a term not exceeding thirty-one years, of the coal-mines and quarries of grindſtone, in the foreſt, ſhall be of like force as if this act had never been made, except of ſuch coal-mines, &c. as are, or ſhall be in any part of the 11,000 acres alotted for incloſing, whilſt they ſhall continue incloſed.

The foreſt of Dean is, at preſent, under the power of this law, ſince the making of which, there has been no alteration in matters relative to the government of this fine diſtrict of country.

Of the CASTLE *of* St. BRIAVEL's, *and* CONSTABLES *of the* CASTLE; *of the* WARDENSHIP *and* WARDENS *of the* FOREST, *and other Officers, &c.*

THE caſtle of St. Briavel's, antiently written Brulais, ſtands in the foreſt of Dean, and gives name to one of the hundreds in the foreſt diviſion. The king, *jure coronæ*, is ſeized of this caſtle, which is extraparochial. It is ſaid to have been built to curb the Welch, by Milo earl of Hereford, in the reign of Henry the Firſt. It was antiently the reſidence of men of eminence in the government, who exerciſed great power in the foreſt, demiſing the waſte lands, &c. and ſuch rents as were reſerved upon leaſes of foreſt lands, were made payable to the conſtable, *i. e.* the governor of this caſtle. The ruins ſhew it to have been ſtrong, and of large extent, and was formerly of great conſequence. It is remarkable for the death of Mahel, the youngeſt ſon of Miles earl of Hereford; for there, ſays Camden, the judgments of God overtook him for his rapacious ways, inhuman cruelties, and boundleſs avarice, always uſurping on other men's rights; for being courteouſly entertained there, by Sir Walter Clifford, and the caſtle taking fire, he loſt his life by the fall of a ſtone on his head, from the higheſt tower †. What now remains of the caſtle, ſerves as a priſon for criminals, offending againſt the vert and veniſon of the foreſt, and for ſuch as are convicted at the mine-law court, and at the court of pleas, of which hereafter.

CONSTABLES, &c.] John de Monemouth was conſtable of the caſtle, and warden of the foreſt 18° Joh.—As was John Giffard 47° H. 3. Taking part with the rebellious barons, he was excommunicated by the archbiſhop of Canterbury; but afterwards deſerting them, and fighting at the battle of Eveſham, the king pardoned him.—Thomas, brother to Gilbert the Red, earl of Glouceſter, was made governor of this caſtle by Simon Montfort, earl of Leiceſter, after the victory gained over king H. 3. at Lewes.—William de Beauchamp, earl of Warwick, was conſtable of the caſtle 10° E. 1.—John de Bottourt, deſcended from Ansfrid de Bottourt, who lived 2° H. 2. was made governor of it, and warden of the foreſt of Dean 19° E. 1. but was ſoon diſplaced;—for Thomas de Euerty held the caſtle 21° E. 1.—John de Handelo was governor thereof, and warden of the foreſt 27° E. 1.—Ralph de Abbenhalle held it 29° E. 1.—Almarick de St. Amand was governor of the caſtle, and warden of the foreſt in the latter part of this reign.—And John de Bottourt was reſtored 1° E. 2.—William de Staure held the caſtle 2° E. 2.—Hugh le Deſpencer, the elder, was governor of it, and warden of the foreſt 15° E. 2.—John de Nivers was made governor of this caſtle, and warden of the foreſt, to hold at pleaſure 18° E. 2.—John de Hardeſhull was alſo governor and warden 20° E. 2.—Roger Clifford was governor 14° E. 3. and had 55 marks yearly allowed him out of the exchequer; and all ſucceeding governors were from that time to have feeding, houſe-boot and hey-boot out of the foreſt.—This caſtle was granted to Thomas duke of Glouceſter 14° R. 2.—John duke of Bedford, third ſon of H. 4. had a grant, and died ſeized of it 14° H. 6.—John Tiptot, earl of Worceſter, had the cuſtody of it 39° H. 6.—Richard Nevil, earl of Warwick,

* The ſurrender is now in the poſſeſſion of Thomas Bathurſt, of Lidney, eſq;

† Mr. Camden ſpeaking of the caſtle of Aber-Gavenni, mentions this perſon by the name of William, ſon of earl Miles; and ſays, that he ſtained the caſtle of the laſt mentioned place, with the infamy of treachery, as William de Breos had done before, both having invited ſome of the Welch nobility thither upon public aſſurance, and under pretence of friendſhip, and then baſely murdered them. And then tells the above ſtory of his untimely death. *col.* 715.

and Ann his wife, levied a fine of it 6° E. 4.—The ſame counteſs levied a fine of it to the uſe of the king 3° H. 7.—The earl of Pembroke was conſtable of it, and warden of the foreſt 9° Jac. 1.—Henry lord Herbert of Ragland, afterwards duke of Beaufort, had a grant for life of the conſtablewick of this caſtle, with a fee of 40*l.* a year, 1660.

Beſides the conſtable, there are ſeveral ſubordinate officers *, all created by patent, *viz.* a clerk, a meſſor, or intinerant officer, two ſerjeants and a janitor; and a fee was annexed to each of their offices.

The VERDURERS of the foreſt, of which there are four, are elected by the freeholders of the county, by virtue of the king's writ, directed to the ſheriff for that purpoſe. They are, according to the order of time in which they were choſen, as follow, *viz.*

William Jones, of Naſs, eſq;
John Probyn, of the city of Glouceſter, eſq;
Maynard Colcheſter, of Weſtbury, eſq;
John Gyſe, of Highnam, eſq; elected 1769.

In the time of king Canute, their fee was yearly of the king's allowance, two horſes, one of which was ſaddled; one ſword, five javelins, one ſpear, one ſhield, and 10*l.* in money.

The GAVELLER is an officer appointed by the conſtable of the caſtle. The name is derived from Gapel, or Gapol, which in the Anglo-Saxon language ſignifies a tribute. This officer receives by way of perquiſite, or fee, a ſmall ſum of the miners, called the king's dues, and gives ſome directions concerning mining. At a juſtice-ſeat, held at Glouceſter 10° C. 1. the commiſſioners returned, that the office of Gaveller, or Gawler, was an antient office, and that he uſually attended at the mine-law courts; but I have not found upon record any ſuch officer in this foreſt before the year 1660, when the office was conferred upon Sir Baynham Throckmorton, and which ſome years afterwards William Wolſeley, eſq; held by patent. If there had been antiently ſuch an officer, he would probably have accounted to the king, and the name muſt then have been found in the exchequer; but as lately as 4° H. 7. William Lewellyn, the king's receiver, accounted for the mines of Newland and Le Gawle, and all the other king's mines in the foreſt, a copy of whoſe account I have by me.

Of the COURTS *of this* FOREST.

THERE are three courts incident to all foreſts. 1. The court of attachment. 2. The court of ſwanimote. 3. The juſtice-ſeat.

1. The court of attachment is held once in forty days before the verdurers, who receive the attachments, *de viridi & venatione*, taken by the reſt of the officers, and inroll them, that the offenders may be preſented and puniſhed at the next juſtice-ſeat; for this court can only inquire, but not convict.

2. The court of ſwanimote † is holden before the verdurers, as judges, by the ſteward of the ſwanimote, thrice in the year. The foreſters ought to preſent their attachments at the next ſwanimote court; and the freeholders within the foreſt are to appear at this court, to make inqueſt and juries. The court of ſwanimote may both inquire and convict, but cannot give judgment.

3. The juſtice-ſeat, which is the higheſt court, cannot be kept oftener than every third year. It is holden before the chief juſtice of the foreſt, or juſtice in Eire, of which there are two created by patent, one for the foreſts on this ſide of Trent, the other beyond. This court hath juriſdiction to inquire, hear, and determine all treſpaſſes within the foreſt, and all claims of franchiſes, privileges and liberties relative thereto. Before a juſtice-ſeat be holden, the regarders of the foreſt muſt go thro', and view the whole foreſt, in order to preſent all kinds of treſpaſſes.

About the middle of the foreſt ſtands a large building, called the Speech-houſe, where the courts of ſwanimote and attachment uſed to be holden; but they have now been neglected for ſome time.

Beſides theſe courts, which are common to all foreſts, the hundred of St. Briavel's, being in the crown, retains the privilege of a court-leet, which is held at the caſtle.

There are alſo two other courts held here, which being of peculiar natures, deſerve particular notice.

The firſt I ſhall mention is a court of record, held for the caſtle, the manor, and the hundred of St. Briavel's, before the conſtable of the caſtle, or his deputy, and the ſuitors of the manor; for trying of all perſonal actions, of what value ſoever, ariſing within the hundred. Fines of lands within the hundred are levied at this court, which is very antient, as appears by a record, *temp.* E. 1. where it is ſaid, *S'tus Briavellus h'et return' brevium.*

All proceſſes run in the name of the conſtable, or his deputy, only; yet the court, in its ſtile, is ſaid to be held before the conſtable of the caſtle of St. Briavel's, and the homagers, or ſuitors of the manor-court; upon which account, ſome perſons have been of opinion, that this cannot properly be a court of record, ſince the homagers, before whom, with the conſtable, the court is preſcribed to be holden, ſit as judges. But nothing can be concluded with certainty againſt its being of record, merely from the complexion of it, as it may formerly have derived its authority either

* Lately there have been only a clerk, a bailiff or meſſor, and caſtle-keeper, who have all been appointed by the conſtable of the caſtle for the time being.

† Lork Coke derives the word of *Swein*, that is, in Saxon, *miniſter*; and *mote*, or *gemote*, which is *curia*, i. e. *Curia miniſtrorum foreſtæ*; ſo called becauſe it is but a preparative for the juſtice-ſeat.

from

from act of parliament, letters patents, or preſcription, the three ſeveral ways by which courts of record are created.

To account for the homage ſitting in this court, it has been conjectured, that originally, when the caſtle was in its proſperity, three courts were held here, 1. a court of pleas or record, held before the conſtable, or his deputy only; 2. a court for the hundred, and 3. a court for the manor, held before the conſtable or his deputy, and the ſuitors or homagers. And it is thought, that, for the eaſe and convenience of the conſtable and country, theſe three courts might at ſome time be united by conſent, and ſo have continued down without any interruption, to the preſent time. But I give this as mere opinion, without the leaſt authority from the public records to ſupport it.

Another court, called the mine-law court, is held before the conſtable of St. Briavel's, as ſteward of the court, or his deputy, for the trial of all cauſes ariſing between the miners, &c. concerning the mines, &c. But from 4° Annæ to 5° G. 1. it was held before the deputies of Charles earl of Berkeley, who in the court papers is ſtiled, Lord high ſteward of her majeſty's court of pleas, courts leet, and of the mine-law court, within the foreſt; the earl having obtained a patent for theſe purpoſes, altho' he was not conſtable of the caſtle. At this court, none are to be preſent but the conſtable, or his deputy, the gaveller, caſtle-clerk, and free-miners, who muſt be natives of the hundred of St. Briavel's, and have worked in ſome of the mines at leaſt one year and a day. The parties and witneſſes are ſworn upon a bible, into which a piece of holly ſtick is put, and are obliged to wear the hooff, or working cap on their heads, during examination. The following particulars are drawn from the beſt authorities that could be procured.

I can find no mention made of the mine-law court in any record before 10° C. 1. when the earl of Pembroke, as conſtable of the caſtle of St. Briavel's, and warden of the foreſt of Dean, claimed to be judge of it.

In the act of parliament 20° C. 2. concerning this foreſt, is a clauſe, wherein the lawful rights and privileges in all lands and grounds lying within the perambulation and regard of the foreſt, are ſaved to the miners, and perſons uſing the trade of digging for iron ore, coal, and ochre.

Before the paſſing of this act, many diſputes had riſen between the miners and others, concerning rights and cuſtoms, which remained unſettled; but now the miners, conſidering the forementioned clauſe as a confirmation of their antient privileges, began to call themſelves the free-miners, and the king's miners; and their court a court of record.

Sir Baynham Throckmorton having been appointed gaveller, deputy conſtable of St. Briavel's, and duputy warden of the foreſt, preſided at this court; and, according to tradition, firſt introduced the examining of evidences upon oath.

At a court, holden the 16th of Jan. 28° C. 2. a jury of 48 miners, after ſetting forth, that ſeveral controverſies had lately riſen between the miners and others, concerning their rights and cuſtoms, ordered, That all the articles and clauſes contained in a certain writing, called an inquiſition, which they declare to contain their antient cuſtoms, rights and privileges, ſhall be inviolably obſerved by the miners.

At this court, an order was made to raiſe the price of coals, from 4 *d.* to 6 *d.* the horſeload, and another order was confirmed, for taxing every miner and carrier, with a quarterly ſum *, to defend themſelves in all ſuits that ſhould be brought againſt them. The inquiſition was then reviſed, and ingroſſed on parchment, and the jury ſet their hands and ſeals to it, that whenever it ſhould be produced, it might carry the force of an inſtrument executed with great deliberation, order, and ſolemnity. From this time the court proceeded with greater freedom; and I find of no oppoſition made to it 'till the year 1752, when its authority was put to the teſt.

In that year, Francis Jones commenced an action in the court of king's-bench, againſt Philips and others, for breaking his cloſe, and taking away and ſelling three mares. The defendants pleaded, that there had been immemorially in the foreſt of dean, a court of record, called the mine-law court; and that they had recovered 10 *l.* in an action brought againſt the plaintiff, in the ſaid court, and proſecuted and ſued out a precept, upon which the ſaid mares were levied.—Upon this plea, a verdict was found for the defendants.—Jones afterwards ſued out a writ of error, to which a return was made, and errors aſſigned; but they were never argued.

Cauſes tried at this court are not determined by the foreſt laws, or by any written laws of the realm, but by ſuch as are peculiar to the court itſelf. The miners exerciſe the legiſlative power, and make new laws for their convenience, as often as they ſee occaſion.

PRIVILEGES *of the* FORESTERS.

AT a juſtice-ſeat held at Glouceſter 10° E. 1. already mentioned, the ſeveral officers of the foreſt, and others, put in their claims to common of paſture, common of eſtovers, and to fees and other privileges and liberties, which I ſhall have occaſion to mention more particularly hereafter.

Alſo at a juſtice-ſeat holden at Glouceſter-caſtle, for the ſaid foreſt, 10° Car. all the officers of the foreſt, and above 120 of the inhabitants of the hundred of St. Briavel's, and other perſons

* They are ſaid to be able to raiſe about 40 *l.* at 6 *d.* per head.

bordering on the foreſt, put in their ſeveral claims to eſtovers*, commons, fees, franchiſes and other privileges within the foreſt; all which original claims are now on record in the tower of London.

The earl of Pembroke pleaded, that by letters patents he was conſtituted conſtable of the caſtle of St. Briavel's; that the office of warden of the foreſt is always appendant to it, and that, as warden, he claimed to be judge of the mine law court, held from time to time, whereof the memory of man is not to the contrary.

By 20° C. 2. c. 3. the occupiers and owners of land not being part of the waſte, or incloſures, within the bounds of the foreſt, are impowered to cut timber and wood in their ſeveral lands; to manure and improve them, by plowing, aſſarting, building, &c. and to keep dogs unexpedited, and to hunt, and kill beaſts of chace, or other game, without incurring any offence by the foreſt law. All perſons having right of common are to enjoy it, as they did 10° C. 1. and the metes and bounds of the foreſt to be taken as they were 20° Jac. 1. In this act is a ſaving to the inhabitants of St. Briavel's of their right of cutting wood in Hudnalls, which they had enjoyed from time immemorially.

The free miners claim a right by preſcription, of digging iron ore, and coal in the foreſt, and of carrying their coal works, begun there, into the incloſed lands adjoining. They alſo preſcribe to cut timber out of the foreſt, neceſſary for carrying on their works, as well in the lands of private perſons, as in the king's ſoil. Theſe are very extenſive privileges; and as it may be entertaining to ſome of my readers, I ſhall endeavour to trace out the gradual progreſs of their claim.

Very antiently, the crown erected works to manufacture the vaſt abundance of iron-ore, found in the foreſt; and generally, the works and mines of ore have been let to farm; and it appears by the inqueſt of the regarders, at a juſtice-ſeat, held 10° E. 1. that the miners had a penny a horſe-load paid them, for ſupplying the king's works with ore †. At the ſame *iter* ſome of the keepers of the bailiwicks claimed iron-ore and ſea-coal, *mortua et ſicca et vento proſtrata* [dead and dry wood and windfalls] and had their claims allowed, particularly the bailiff of Blakeney, and Sir Rauf de Abbenhalle §, as he and his anceſtors had enjoy'd the ſame ever ſince the conqueſt.

The ſame record ſhews that the keepers in the bailiwicks of Abbenhalle, Bikenore, Staunten, and Blakeneye had coal; and Nicholas de Lacu took the ſame in his wood of Lideneye; but it is ſaid, reſpecting all theſe, *et neſciunt quo warranto.* It is alſo expreſſly ſaid, that the king had the coal in the other bailiwicks, *viz.* Bers, Rywardyn, Magna Dene, and Parva Dene; but the record doth not ſhew upon what terms the coal-pits were worked, as in the caſe of the iron-mines. Indeed as the inhabitants were intituled to eſtovers, and the whole country was full of wood, it is probable that very little coal was uſed at that time.

That the chief property of the mines was antiently in the crown, ſeems evident from the above inquiſitions; and alſo from an antient grant which the abbat of Flaxley obtained 42° H. 3. of a large portion of the foreſt, wherein the mines are excepted and reſerved to the king. It is equally evident, that they were claimed by the crown, in James the Firſt's time, from the grant of the foreſt of Dean, made to the earl of Pembroke 9° *regni*, already noticed, wherein the ore, cinders, coal, &c. are expreſſly mentioned; and the king covenants, that the earl's ſervants and workmen employ'd in the foreſt, ſhould be protected as his majeſty's own ſervants had been. In ſeveral leaſes and grants made to others in the ſame reign, the mines are reſerved. *See Grants.*

Soon after this grant to the earl of Pembroke, the miners began to dig ore without the earl's conſent; and claiming a right of ſo doing, the attorney-general, at the earl's inſtance, filed an information in the exchequer againſt ſeveral of them. The court, upon the ſubmiſſion of the defendants, acknowledging the ſoil to be the king's, and that they had no intereſt therein; and repreſenting that they had been uſed to mining only, and had no other way to ſupport themſelves and families, made an ‡ order that the inhabitants of the ſaid foreſt, who had been uſed before that time to dig and carry mine, ore, and cinders, ſhould be permitted, of *favour and grace*, and not of *right*, to continue the ſame until the hearing of the cauſe, ſo that they carry them to his majeſty's works; and if there refuſed at the uſual prices, that then they be permitted to carry them elſewhere. This ſeems to be the foundation of the miners claim, as probably at that time all parties acquieſced.

Sir Richard Catchmaid farming ſome lands in the foreſt, 19° Jac. the miners dug, and claimed a right to dig, grindſtone on his farm, without

* Eſtovers, from the French, *eſtoffe*, i.e. *materia*. Weſt. Symb. part 2. ſect. 26. ſaith, That the word eſtovers includeth houſe-bote, hey-bote, and plow-bote; but it appears to have a larger ſignification, by a precept to John de Monmouth, 7 H. 3. which runs thus: Mandatum eſt Joh'i de Monemuta quod h'ere fac' hominibus manentibus in foreſta de Dene r'onabile eſtoverium ſuum in foreſta de Dene *tam de paſtura quam de boſco*, ſicut habere debent et ſolent tempore Joh' regis ante guerram motam inter ipſum et barones ſui Angliæ.

† Si d'nus rex h'et unam forgeam errantem p'dci operatores invenient ei mineam ad ſuſtentationem pred'ce forgee. Et d'us rex dabit eis p' qal' ſumma i. den'. It. D'us rex h'ebit de q'libt ſumma minee que ducet' extra foreſta un. ob. et omnia que D'us rex capit de min'ia pon't' ad firmam pro xlvi lib.

Lord Ch. Juſtice Hale's MSS. in Lincoln's Inn Library.

§ His claim runs thus:—Les demandes de Sire Rauf de Abbenhalle in ſa baillie. Sire Rauf de Abbenhalle tent la baillie de Abbenhalle e la terre en fee du roy rend X s. p' la terre e XX s. p' la baillie e garder de memes le terres. E ſi le roy vent guerrer il vendra a cheval od un haubergen od ces 2 valles od arkes e od ſetes e fere le commaundement le roy de deux le metes de la foreſt, &c.—Haubergen is an helmet, or head-piece, which covered the head and ſhoulders, ſo called from the German *hals*, *collum*, and *bergen*, *tegere*.

‡ See Appendix No. 4.

Sir

Sir Richard's leave; for which the attorney-general filed an information in the exchequer, againſt ſome of them. The court, without decreeing concerning the right, on account of their poverty, recommended it to Sir Richard, not to oppreſs them for ſo trifling an article, the ſtones not being worth more than the labour of raiſing them; and it ſeems they paid 3 *s.* 4 *d.* each, as an acknowledgement for digging.

About 27° C .2. they firſt carried their coal-works, which had been begun in the foreſt, into the incloſed lands adjoining, which occaſioned ſeveral conteſts at law, between the freeholders and miners. And in 1752, the governors and company of copper-miners, in England, commenced an action againſt one Philips and others, for breaking and entering their cloſe. The defendants juſtifying, pleaded the cuſtom of the free-miners entering the lands of all other perſons, as well as of the king, within the hundred of St. Briavel's, by the licence of the king's gaveller, entered, &c. and paying the king certain dues. Iſſue was joined, and the cuſtom found by the jury, before Mr. Juſtice Birch, at Glouceſter aſſizes.

As to their right to timber, it ſhould be obſerved, that ſoon after the paſſing of the act 20° C. 2. proper incloſures were made, and planted with young oaks and acorns, and new officers, with ſalaries, appointed for the preſervation of them. The foreſt courts were regularly holden, offenders puniſh'd, incroachments on the king's ſoil removed, and in ſhort, every meaſure was taken to raiſe a fine foreſt of timber. But there are always people ready to catch every opportunity to avail themſelves of public commotions; ſo at the revolution, the incloſures were again thrown open, and dreadful ſpoil made of the timber.

During king William's reign, and the latter part of queen Anne's, the miners were allowed to take wood, but not timber.

Orders having been iſſued in the latter part of her majeſty's reign, for cutting beech, and dead and dotard trees, not likely to become timber, great ſpoil was again committed; and upon information being filed by the attorney-general, againſt Richard Whetſtone and others, for cutting timber, the defendants ſet forth their cuſtom of taking it, upon application to, and obtaining an order from, the court of attachments, to the proper officers, for the delivery of it. But this cauſe never came to a hearing; for the queen dying, the warden, lord Weymouth, was removed, and proceedings were ſtayed. And ever ſince the miners have had timber alſo for carrying on their works, of which it is computed they uſe about 1000 tons yearly.

From the above records, act of parliament, grants, reſervations, and accounts extracted from antient papers, it may be ſeen what privileges the miners formerly had, and have claimed from time to time, and what they now enjoy.

SOIL, PRODUCE, MANUFACTURE, *&c. of the* FOREST.

THE face of this country is remarkably uneven, full of little hills, with ſprings and pleaſant rivulets purling down, and running between them. The ſoil is various, but much inclining to clay, proper for the growth of oak, which flouriſhes here exceedingly. Here is alſo plenty of beech, birch, holly, and other kinds of wood.

Our enemies * have always been ſenſible of the great advantage we derive from the oak timber of Dean foreſt, which is perhaps the beſt in the world for ſhip-building, being extremely tough and hard when dry, and not ſo apt to ſplinter as that of the growth of other countries.

The ſoil of the foreſt is alſo particularly agreeable to the cyder-apple. Styre cyder is almoſt peculiar to this diſtrict, and yields a moſt extraordinary price. But beſides this particular ſort, it is the opinion of very competent judges, that the foreſters make the beſt cyder in the kingdom. In the year 1763, was ſuch a plentiful crop of apples, that great quantities of them were ſuffered to rot, for want of caſks to put the cyder in; yet even in that year, the beſt old ſtyre ſold at fifteen guineas the hogſhead, and is ſince advanced to twenty. Indeed there is no fixing the price of it, being chiefly purchaſed by perſons of fortune. It is, however, aſſerted, that Glouceſterſhire cyder is worth more money in the maker's cellar, than the fineſt wines in the world, in the reſpective countries of their own growth. The reaſons generally alledged for this liquor bearing ſo great a price, are, that the ſtyre-apple is not a plentiful bearer, and the cyder in keeping is ſaid to be ſo particularly liable to injury, from accidents altogether unaccountable, that its proving good is very precarious.

There is not much corn planted here, but ſome people think the produce in that reſpect ſufficient for the uſe of the inhabitants.

The foreſt is full of iron-ore, coal, and ochre, and the waters of many of the ſprings and rivulets, as they run along, tinge the ſtones and other ſubſtances, lying in their courſes, with a reddiſh brown colour, received from the iron-mine, and ochre, thro' whoſe beds they paſs. I have ſeen great variety of iron-ore at Mr. Worrall's, at

* Mr. Evelyn obſerves, that the Spaniards, in queen Elizabeth's reign, ſent over an ambaſſador into England, on purpoſe to try if he could, either by private practices, great rewards, fair promiſes, or any other contrivances whatever, procure this wooden wall, the ſtrength of our kingdom, as they called it, to be deſtroyed, who, had he effected his majeſty's commiſſion, had right well deſerved his particular favour. But what the crafty Spaniard could not do by treachery, was in the time of the great rebellion nearly compleated thro' our own diviſions and diſſentions, by expoſing to ſale for fewel thoſe ſtout and ſturdy oaks, whoſe preſervation might have proved a ſure defence and bulwark on the water, if the frozen winter of that iron age had not deſtroy'd them by fire. *Evelyn's Sylva.*

Lidney,

Lidney, who is curious, and has collected many beautiful ſpecimens out of this country; the chief of which are,

1. *Minera ferri cryſtalliſata*; an ore of a cryſtaline form, not much attracted by the magnet.

2. *Minera ferri nigricans, magneti amica*; the dark-coloured ore, of which there are multitudes of varieties as to form, ſome being ſtriated or channelled; teſſulated, breaking into dice; radiated, &c. &c. The miners here call this ſpecies by the general name of bruſh ore. It is very rich, and the magnet attracts it ſtrongly.

The pipe ore is an aſſemblage of ſmall cylindrical columns, of various lengths, ſtanding cloſe together, and iſſuing at one end from a lump of the ſame kind of matter. The cylindrical ſhape is occaſioned by the metallic matter falling in a liquid ſtate from the maſs, to which the pipes are fixed, and like icicles gradually concreting into the various forms in which we find them.

Some of the ore is found in lumps, crowned with ſpar, reſembling a cawliflower, and other curious figures. I ſaw there a piece of kidney ore, ſo called from the figure of that gland always appearing at the end of it, when broken tranſverſely; one of the pieces ſhews it *in relievo*, the other impreſſed. It was almoſt pure metal, but I think this came from Lancaſhire.

The foreſt coal crackles much when firſt thrown on the fire, and burns very bright. It has a more ſhining and gloſſy appearance than the Kingſwood coal, but is not ſo bituminous and laſting; yet is more durable on the fire than the Shropſhire coal. The pits are not deep, for when the miners find themſelves much incommoded with water, they ſink a new one, rather than erect a fire-engine, which might anſwer the expence very well, yet there is not one of them in all this diviſion. They have indeed two or three pumps worked by cranks, that in ſome meaſure anſwer the intention.

Great quantities of iron cinders are found in all parts where blomaries were formerly erected. Some of them are very rich and valuable, and being mixed with the ore, not only help to flux it, but render the metal tougher, and of a better temper.

The furnaces for melting of the ore are built of a gritty ſtone, dug out of the foreſt, that will endure a fire intenſe enough to melt or break down almoſt any other material. The grains of this ſtone, ſays Dr. Grew, muſt therefore be inſuperable, yet not ſo united but that the ſtone is ſomewhat ſoft and crumbly, of a dirty colour, like fuller's earth.

Some furnaces are between twenty and thirty feet high. The cavity is in the ſhape of a crucible, and about ſeven or eight feet in diameter, at the mouth. They are generally built againſt a bank, or at leaſt one is thrown up againſt them, that the workmen may aſcend by a ſpiral kind of path, to throw in the materials at the mouth, which is done in the following manner; firſt ten baſkets of charcoal, then ten of cinders, and laſtly the ſame quantity of ore; which is repeated every half hour. The blaſt is made at a hole about three inches diameter, towards the bottom of the furnace, by two vaſt bellows near thirty feet long, which are driven by water, and work alternately. There is a hole ſtill lower, to which a plug is well adjuſted, where they let out the droſs, which by the violent action of the bellows, is ſeparated from the metal in fuſion, and being the lighteſt, lies at the top. Quite at the bottom of the furnace is another hole, with its plug, which is drawn out once in twenty-four hours, when the iron runs upon a bed of ſand, laid upon the earthen floor, from the furnace to the length of thirty feet. There is a large groove impreſſed in the ſand, from one end of the floor to the other, and ſhort ones all along the ſides of it, one end of each of which enters into the large one, that ſerves as a common conveyance to carry the metal into the ſhort ones, where the iron pigs are caſt. That which fills the large groove is called the ſow, and is broken into convenient lengths for working.

From the furnace the ſows and pigs of iron are carried to the forges, which are of two ſorts, one of which is called the finery, the other the chafery. On the hearth of the finery, is a large charcoal fire, excited by bellows like thoſe at the furnace, but not ſo large. They put the ends of two or three pigs or ſows into the finery together, where ſoftening gradually, they ſtir and work them 'till the metal runs together into one maſs or lump, which they call a half bloom. This they take out, and giving it a few ſtrokes with their ſledges, they carry it to a great weighty hammer, raiſed likewiſe by the motion of a water-wheel, where it is preſently beaten out into a thick, ſhort, ſquare figure. This is put into the finery again, and being made red hot, is worked under the ſame hammer, to the ſhape of a bar in the middle, with a ſquare knob at each end. Laſtly, they give it another heating in the chafery, and more workings under the hammer, 'till they have brought the iron into bars of the required ſhape and ſize.

About ſix years ago, an experiment was tried at Lidney, to make iron with pit-coal, charred to diſcharge it of the ſulphur, which renders the metal friable; but it was not found to anſwer, otherwiſe it would have been a prodigious ſaving to the iron-maſter, as wood gets dearer almoſt every ſeaſon, but the coal-mines are inexhauſtible.

The large iron furnaces now in uſe, were firſt erected by the crown, not long before 1617, as appears by the return to a commiſſion iſſued out of the exchequer in that year. The ſort in uſe 10° E. 1.* was called *forgeam errantem*. I con-

* In that reign there were ſeventy-two forges in Dean foreſt, as appears by a record of the affairs of this foreſt, preſerved in a collection of MSS. left by lord chief juſtice Hale, to Lincoln's Inn Library; where it is further ſaid, *Et quelibet forgia per annum dabit domino regi vij ſol. et forgia operans p' dimid. anni dabit iij ſol. vj den. et forgia operans per quartam partem unius anni dabit xxi. den.*

clude

clude this ſort was carried from place to place, and worked by hand. It was certainly owing to their uſing machines of little power, that our anceſtors left the cinders ſo rich and full of metal.

Some queſtions ariſing between the earl of Nottingham, juſtice in Eire in all the king's foreſts, and the earl of Dorſet, treaſurer of England, concerning the diſpoſing of the king's woods in his foreſts, all the judges of England were aſſembled, by the king's command, to reſolve them. After conference and deliberation, they delivered their anſwer; which, with the order of the exchequer in conſequence thereof, may be ſeen in 4 Inſt. p. 299.

Some paſſages in the courſe of this narration may, perhaps, excite the reader to lament with me the general neglect of the foreſt timber, which ought to be preſerved for public uſe. The produce of it to the crown is very trifling, as appears by the ſubſequent account, the authenticity of which may be depended on, as I had it from a gentleman of honour.

Trent, South. — An ACCOUNT of the Produce of TIMBER, together with the Bark, Lops, Tops, and Offal-wood thereof, felled and cut down in his Majeſty's Foreſt of Dean, in the County of Glouceſter, by a Medium of Seven Years laſt paſt, *viz.* from the 25th of March, 1745, to the 25th of March, 1752.

		£.	s.	d.	£.	s.	d.
Anno 1745,	It does not appear that any timber was felled in the ſaid foreſt, therefore charged ———				*Nil.*		
Anno 1746,	In the accompt of John Phillipſon, eſq; ſurveyor-general of his majeſty's woods on the ſouth ſide Trent, of wood ſales by him made in the ſaid foreſt, purſuant to a warrant from the Right Honourable the lords commiſſioners of his majeſty's treaſury, bearing date the 6th day of May, 1746, he is charged with the ſale of ſeveral quantities of timber, together with the bark thereof, valued and ſold to divers perſons, for the ſum of ——— ——— ———	570	13	9	1894	0	3 ¾
	In another accompt of the ſaid John Phillipſon, of wood ſales by him made in the ſaid foreſt, purſuant to a like warrant, dated the 3d day of July, 1746, he is charged with the ſale of wood, valued and ſold to divers perſons, for the ſum of ——— ——— ———	510	6	0			
	In another accompt of the ſaid John Phillipſon of wood ſales by him made in the ſaid foreſt, purſuant to a like warrant, dated the 17th day of February, 1746, he is charged with the ſale of ſeveral quantities of wood, felled and cut down in the ſaid foreſt, valued and ſold to divers perſons, for the ſum of ——— ——— ——— ———	813	0	6 ¾			
Anno 1747,	And in another accompt of the ſaid John Phillipſon of wood ſales, by him made in the ſaid foreſt, purſuant to a like warrant, dated the 31ſt day of March, 1747, he is charged with divers quantities of wood, felled and cut down in the ſaid foreſt, valued and ſold to divers perſons, for the ſum of ——— ——— ——— ———				499	4	2 ¼
Annis 1748, 1749, 1750, 1751,	It does not appear that any timber was felled in the ſaid foreſt; but there are two warrants directed to the ſaid John Phillipſon, to cut down timber there, one dated the 18th of January, 1749, to raiſe, clear of all charges, the ſum of 373*l.* 4*s.* for repairs in Windſor foreſt; and the other, dated the 29th of January, 1750, to raiſe the ſum of 6767*l.* 17*s.* 4*d.* ¼ to be paid to Mr. Whatley, for repairs at Hampton-court houſe, park, and Windſor great park, which the ſaid John Phillipſon has not accounted for, therefore is charged ——— ——— ——— ——— ———				*Nil.*		

If when the courts of ſwanimote and attachment were regularly holden, and offenders puniſhed, the very officers of the foreſt were daring enough to plunder it, as appears to have been the caſe *; it can be no wonder ſurely, now thoſe courts are diſcontinued, and the execution of the foreſt law, as to this place, has been laid aſide for nearly thirty years, that the foreſt ſhould become the object of avarice and rapine.

During the laſt war, great quantities of the timber were cut and ſent to Plymouth, for the uſe of the royal navy, which was a proper application of it, and proved a very ſeaſonable ſupply. And it were to be wiſhed, rather, I fear, than to be expected, in this age of prodigality and extravagance, of venality and corruption, that now, before it be too late, proper means may be uſed to preſerve the timber that remains; and that care may be ſpeedily taken to raiſe a future crop, to be ready for uſe before the preſent be intirely exhauſted. This is a matter of great and national concern, and ought not to be neglected.

This foreſt is winter-heined, or exempted from common, between the 11th of November and the 23d of April, by 20° C. 2. c. 3.

The gentry of the foreſt are courteous, hoſpitable and generous; and the poorer ſort of people, by their example, are now brought to an obliging kind of behaviour, which uſed not to diſtinguiſh their character: For this country was formerly ſo intirely covered with wood, ſo dark and terrible, and the roads ſo intricate, from their often croſſing each other, that it rendered the inhabitants barbarous, and emboldened them to commit many robberies and outrages, particularly on the banks of the

* A commiſſion iſſuing out of the exchequer 25 March, 1617, to William Cook, knight, and others, to inquire into the ſtate of the foreſt, they made this return, That George Caſtle and William Callow, the perſons appointed for the marking of trees and delivery of wood for the iron-works, within the foreſt, have felled 160 oaks of timber, at a place called the Hayts, of purpoſe to have the bark thereof; which bark they have ſold, as by the depoſition of John Dobbs. 14° *Jac.* 1.

Severn; inſomuch that an act of parliament was made 8° H. 6. on purpoſe to curb and reſtrain them. Mining is the chief employment of the poor, who, I am told, can earn more money than any common labourers in the kingdom beſides.

The foreſters boaſt of their independency, and ſay that the produce of their own country is ſufficient for them, without being obliged to any other part of the kingdom; which, that the reader may be the better diſpoſed to credit, I will give him, at the concluſion of the account of this country, an old proverb in its favour,

"*Happy is the eye betwixt the Severn and the Wye.*"

There was another foreſt in this county, called the foreſt of Kingſwood; but it was diſafforeſted in the reign of king H. 3. In the act of parliament for erecting the pariſh of St. George, near Briſtol, it is called the now or late foreſt of Kingſwood. It extended from Nibley-green northwards, to the river Avon, which runs to Briſtol, ſouthwards, being ſixteen or ſeventeen miles in length, and in ſome places near ſix miles broad. At preſent, what is called Kingſwood foreſt, lies in the pariſhes of Bitton, Mangotsfield, and St. George's, containing about 5000 acres of ground, ſeveral gentlemen being poſſeſſed of it, by patent from the crown, and it conſiſts chiefly of coal-mines.

Of the FOUR DIVISIONS of the COUNTY.

HAVING taken a ſhort view of the county, in the three grand diviſions made by nature, as at firſt propoſed, it now remains to be conſidered in the parts or diſtricts into which good policy hath divided it, for the ſake of order and government. Of theſe diviſions there are four, *viz.*

1. Kiftſgate diviſion, comprizing the north and north-eaſt parts, adjoining to Worceſterſhire, Warwickſhire, and Oxfordſhire.

2. The diviſion of the Seven Hundreds, lies S. and S.W. of the former, with Oxfordſhire and a part of Berkſhire on the E. and Wiltſhire on the S. and S.E. of it.

3. Berkeley diviſion extends from the Seven Hundreds to the extremity of the county towards Wiltſhire and Somerſetſhire, with the river Severn on the N.W. of it.

4. The foreſt diviſion takes in all that part of Glouceſterſhire which lies on the N.W. of the Severn, and that part of the hundred of Dudſton and King's-Barton, ſituated on the other ſide of that river.

When this diſtribution was made I have not diſcovered; but conjecture, that it took place for the convenience of the magiſtrates in their petty ſeſſions, ſome of whom reſiding near the extremity of the county, and not being able to attend buſineſs at large, might probably undertake ſuch diſtricts as lay moſt commodiouſly to their reſpective habitations.

The moſt antient diviſion of the counties is into hundreds and tythings, made by king Alfred, to preſerve peace and good order. He appointed, that all free-born men ſhould form themſelves into companies of ten perſons each, and that every of thoſe ten ſhould be ſurety and pledge for the appearance of his fellows; therefore thoſe companies were called tythings, as containing the number of ten free men, with their families. And as it was appointed that ten of theſe companies ſhould meet together at certain times, to conſult on matters of great moment, therefore that general aſſembly was called an hundred.

There are now twenty-eight hundreds in this county, reckoning the hundred of Cirenceſter and the reputed one of Crowthorne and Minety, to be one. *(See the diviſion of the Seven Hundreds.)* The city of Glouceſter, notwithſtanding its being taken into the foreſt diviſion, will be conſider'd ſeparately, as it is a diſtinct county. The names of the hundreds, with the pariſhes, and ſuch of the tythings and places as have their reſpective officers, are ſet down in the following tables.

KIFTSGATE DIVISION.

Containing the Hundreds of

1. KIFTSGATE.

Pariſhes in the Upper Part.

Aſton Subedge,
Batteſford,
Campden, (Chipping) *and its tythings, viz.*
  Berrington,
  Broad Campden,
  Weſtington *and* Comb.
Condicote, (part of)
Cowhonibourn,
Dorſington,
Ebrington, *with the tythings of*
  Charringworth,
  Hidcot Bois.

Lark Stoke,
Longborough,
Marſton Sicca,
Mickleton *and* Hidcot Batterham.
Pebworth,
Queinton, *with* Almington.
Saintbury,
Seiſincot,
Swell, (Upper)
Weſton Subedge,
Weſton ſuper Avon,
Willerſey,

Places

Places in the Lower Part.

Afton Somerville,	Sudley Manor,
Buckland,	Sudley Tenements,
Charlton Abbats,	Todington,
Child's Wickham,	Twining,
Didbrook,	Winchcombe, *with the tithings of*
Dumbleton,	Cotes,
Guiting Power, *with* Farmcot.	Cockbury,
Guiting Temple,	Corndean,
Hawling,	Greet,
Hayles,	Greton,
Pinnock,	Naunton,
Rowel, *extraparochial.*	Poftlip,
Snowfhill,	Stanley Pontlarch.
Stanton,	Wormington.

2. SLAUGHTER.

The Upper Part.

Adleftrop,	Stow, *with the tithings of*
Bledington,	Donington,
Broadwell,	Maugerfbury,
Condicote, (part of)	Swell, (Lower)
Icombe,	Weftcot.
Oddington,	

The Lower Part.

Barrington, (Great)	Rifington, (Wick)
Barrington, (Little)	Sherbourn,
Bourton on the Water,	Slaughter, (Upper) *with* Eyford,
Clapton,	Slaughter (Lower)
Naunton,	Widford,
Rifington, (Great)	Winrufh.
Rifington, (Little)	

3. TIBBLESTON.

Afhton-under-hill,	Grafton in Beckford.
Beckford, *and its tithings* Bangrove,	Hinton on the Green.

4. CLEEVE.

Cleeve, *with its tithings,*	Stoke Archer, (part of) in Cleeve,
Gotherington,	
Southam, &c.	Wodmancot in Cleeve.

5. CHELTENHAM.

Charlton King's,	Weftall, Naunton, and Sandford.
Cheltenham, *with its tithings, viz.*	Lechampton,
Alfton,	Swindon.
Arle,	

6. DERHURST.

The Upper Part.

Coln St. Dennis,	Prefton,
Compton, (Little)	Welford.

The Lower Part.

Derhurft,	Staverton,
Haw and Turley, (p^t. of)	Uckington, in Elmfton parifh,
Leigh,	
Prefbury,	Wolftone.

7. TEWKESBURY.

The Upper Part.

Alderton, *with* Dixton,	Lemington,
Afhton-under-hill, part of	Prefcot,
Bourton on the hill, part of	Shenington,
Clifford Chambers,	Stanway,
Didcot in Beckford,	Wafhbourn.

The Lower Part.

Afhchurch, *with its tithings, viz.*	Kemerton,
	Oxinton,
Afton fuper Carant,	Stoke Archer, (part of) in Cleeve parifh,
Fiddington and Natton,	Tewkefbury, *and the tithings of*
Northway and Newton,	Mythe, and Mythe-Hook,
Pamington,	Southwick,
Boddington, *with* Barrow,	Tredington,
Forthampton,	Walton Cardiff.

8. WESTMINSTER.

The Upper Part.

Bourton on the hill, (p^t.)	Sutton under Brayles,
Morton-henmarfh,	Todenham.

The Lower Part.

Apperley and Wightfield, in the parifh of Derhurft,	Hasfield,
	Heydon, in the parifh of Boddington,
Corfe,	Turley, (part of)
Evington, in the parifh of Leigh,	Walton, in the parifh of Derhurft.
Hardwick, in Derhurft,	

DIVISION *of the* SEVEN HUNDREDS.

Containing the Hundreds of

9. CIRENCESTER†.

Caftle Ward,	Gofditch Ward,
Cricklade Ward,	Inftrip Ward,
Dollar Ward,	St. Lawrence Ward,
Dyer Ward,	

The OUT TORN *and* MINETY†, *vulgarly* CROWTHORN *and* MINETY.

Amney St. Mary,	Amney Crucis,
Amney St. Peter,	Bagendon,

Barton

† Thefe two divifions make but the hundred of Cirencefter, as appears by the fheriff's return of all the hundreds, &c. in the county 9 E. I. inferted at the end of this chapter. But on account of the extent of it, the bufinefs was divided between feveral high

Barton tithing in Cirencester,
Baunton,
Chesterton tithing in Cirencester,
Cotes,
Daglingworth,
Down Amney,
Driffield,
Duntesbourn Abbats,
Duntesbourn Rous,
Harnhill,
Meysey Hampton,
Minety,
Oakley tithing in Cirencester.
Preston,
Siddington St. Mary.
Siddington St. Peter.
South Cerney,
Spitalgate, *vulgarly* Speringate tithing in Cirencester,
Stratton,
Wigold tithing in Cirencester.

10. BRITWEL'S BARROW.

Aldsworth,
Barnesley,
Bibury, *with the tithings of*
Ablington,
Arlington.
Coln St. Alwin's,
Eastleach Martin,
Eastleach Turville,
Fairford,
Hatherop,
Kempsford,
Leachlade,
Quenington,
Southrop,

11. BRADLEY.

Aston Blank, *or* Cold Aston,
Aylworth in Naunton,
Coln Rogers,
Compton Abdale,
Dowdeswell,
Farmington,
Hampnet,
Hasleton,
Northleach, *with* Eastington,
Notgrove,
Salperton,
Sevenhampton,
Shipton Oliffe,
Shipton Solers.
Stowell,
Turkdean,
Whittington,
Winson in Bibury,
Withington,
Yanworth in Hasleton.

12. RAPSGATE.

Brimpsfield,
Chedworth,
Colesbourn,
Cowley,
Cranham,
Cubberley,
Duntesbourn Lyre, in Duntesbourn Abbats,
Elkstone,
North Cerney,
Rendcombe,
Side.

13. BISLEY.

Bisley,
Edgworth,
Miserden,
Painswick,
Saperton,
Stroud,
Winston.

14. LONGTREE§.

Avening,
Cherington,
Hampton, (Minchin)
Horsley,
Rodborough,
Rodmarton,
Shipton Moign,
Tetbury, *and its tithings,*
Charlton,
Upton, &c.
Westonbirt,
Woodchester.

15. WHITSTON.

The Upper Part.

Frethren, or Frethorn,
Hardwick,
Haresfield, *and its tithing,*
Harescombe,
Longney,
Morton Valence,
Quedgley,
Randwick,
Saul,
Standish, *with its tithings*
Oxlinch,
Putloe.

The Lower Part.

Eastington, *with* Alkerton,
Frampton upon Severn,
Frocester,
Stanley, (King's)
Stanley, (St. Leonard's)
Stonehouse,
Wheatenhurst, *or* Whitminster.

BERKELEY DIVISION,

Containing the Hundreds of

16. BERKELEY.

The Upper Part.

Arlingham,
Ashelworth,
Berkeley, *and its tithings,*
Alkington,
Bradstone,
Ham,
Hamfallow,
Hinton,
Beverstone,
Cromhall Abbats, *with* Cromhall Ligon,
Cam,
Cowley, or Coaley,
Dursley,
Kingscot,
Newington, or Bagpath,
Nimpsfield,
North Nibley,
Olepen, *vulgarly* Oldpen,
Ozleworth,
Slimbridge,
Stinchcombe,
Stone,
Uley, or Ewley,
Wotton, *and its tithings,*
Huntingford,
Simondshall, and Combe,
Sinwell and Bradley,
Wortley.

The Lower Part.

Almondsbury,
Elberton,
Filton,
Hill, *alias* Hull,
Horfield,
King's Weston, in Henbury.

---

high constables; the borough was consigned to two, and the outparishes, with Minety, (which was a member of the manor of Cirencester) were appointed to another constable; whose division, to distinguish it from the *In-Torn*, (*i. e.* the court within the borough) was called *Th' Out-Torn and Minety*; and so by common use was at length corrupted to the unmeaning name by which it now passes. The name makes it appear to have been originally a distinct hundred, whereas it is only a part of the old hundred of Cirencester. Thus considered, the division of the Seven Hundreds contains its proper number: But if the Out Torn and Minety be taken as a distinct hundred, there will then be *Eight Hundreds* in this division of the *Seven Hundreds*. — A most glaring absurdity!

§ This was antiently written *Langetrev*, i.e. Long-town, &c. for *Trev*, or *Tref*, in the British language signifies a town, house, or home.

17. THORN-

17. Thornbury.

The Upper Part.

Marſhfield borough, *with its tythings.*

The Lower Part.

Gaunt's Urcot, in Almondeſbury,
Iron Acton,
Rangeworthy,
Titherington,
Thornbury, *with the tythings of*
Falfield,
Kington,
Morton,
Oldbury.

18. Pucklechurch.

Cold Aſhton,
Pucklechurch,
Syſton,
Weſterleigh,
Wick and Abſton.

19. Langley *and* Swineshead.

Alveſton,
Bitton, *with its tythings,*
Hanham,
Oldland.
Deynton,
Frampton Cotterel, *with* Wickwick.
Hempton, in Almondeſbury,
Littleton on Severn,
Olveſton, *with the tything* Tockington,
Over, in Almondeſbury,
Rockhampton,
Winterbourn, *with the tything of* Hambrook.

20. King's Barton.

Clifton,
Mangotsfield,
St. George's, [Eaſton.]
Stapleton.

21. Henbury.

Compton Greenfield,
Henbury, *and its tythings,*
Auſt,
Charlton,
Lawrence Weſton,
Redwick & Northwick,
Stowick.
Itchington, in Titherington,
Stoke Giffard,
Weſtbury on Trim, *with the tythings of*
Stoke Biſhop,
Shirehampton.
Yate.

22. Grumbald's Ash *.

The Upper Part.

Alderley,
Badminton, (Great)
Badminton, (Little)
Boxwell and Leighterton
Charfield,
Didmarton,
Hawkeſbury, *with its tythings,*
Hilſley,
Kilcot, Treſham, and Seddlewood,
Upton.
Horton,
Oldbury on the hill,
Tortworth,
Wickwar.

The Lower Part.

Acton Turville,
Acton Ilgar,
Doddington,
Dyrham and Hinton,
Sodbury (Chipping,)
Sodbury (Little,)
Sodbury (Old,)
Tormarton,
Wapley and Codrington,
Weſt Littleton.

FOREST DIVISION.

Containing the Hundreds of

23. St. Briavel's.

Abbenhall,
Bicknor,
Dean Magna, or Mitchel Dean,
Dean Parva,
Flaxley,
Hewelsfield,
The Lea,
Newland, *and its tythings,*
Bream,
Clowerwall,
Colford,
Lea Baily.
Rure Dean,
Saint Briavel's,
Staunton.

24. Blideslow.

Awr,
Alvington,
Lidney.

25. Westbury.

Blaiſden,
Churcham,
Newnham,
Tidenham,
Weſtbury,
Woolaſton.

26. Botloe.

Bromſborow,
Dimmock, *with its tythings, viz.*
Leddington,
Ryeland,
Woodend.
Kempley,
Newent, *with its tythings,*
Compton,
Cugley,
Maulſwick.
Oxenhall,
Pauntley,
Rudford,
Tainton,
Upleaden.

27. Dutchy *of* Lancaster.

Bully,
Huntley,
Long Hope,
Minſterworth,
Tiberton.

28. Dudston *and* King's-Barton.

Upper Part.

Brockworth,
Barnwood,
Badgworth,
Churchdown,
Down Hatherly,
Highleaden, in Rudford,
Hucklecot, in Churchdown,
King's Holm,
Laſſington,

* The antient name is *Grimboldeſtou*, or *Grimboldeſtowe*, *i. e.* Grimbolde's place.

Longford,	Twigworth,
North Hamlet,	Uphatherly,
Norton,	Witcombe Magna,
Sandhurſt,	Wotton,
Shurdington Magna,	

Middle Part.

Barton St. Mary, Glouceſter,	Matſon,
Barton St. Michael, Glouceſter,	Pitchcombe,
Brookrup, or Brookthrop,	Prinknaſh, (extraparochial)
Elmore,	South Hamlet,
Haſcombe,	Tuffly,
Hempſtead,	Upton, (St. Leonard's)
Littleworth,	Whaddon,
	Woolſtrop.

Lower Part.

Hartpury,	Maiſmore,
Highnam, Linton, and Over, in Churcham,	Preſton,

Thoſe hundreds that are divided, have a high conſtable for each diviſion.

A little after the Norman conqueſt, many of the above hundreds had different names, and ſome of thoſe which have ſtill preſerved their antient ones, have ſuffered alterations in their extent and dimenſions, as may be ſeen in the Domeſday account of Glouceſterſhire, from whence the antient names of the hundreds in the following table are extracted.

KIFTSGATE DIVISION.

Modern Names.	*Antient Names.*
Kiftſgate *nearly includes the hundreds of* —	Chelflede, Chelfleode, Chelfledeſtorn, Cheſteſiat. Witelai, Greteſtanes, Holefordes, Holiford.
Weſtminſter, — — Deerhurſt, — —	Derheſt.
Slaughter *comprizes the greateſt part of* —	Salemaneſberie, Berintone, Bernitone.
Cheltenham, ——	Chilteham.
Cleeve, — — — Tibbleſtone, — —	Tetboldeſtane.
Tewkeſbury, — —	Teodecheſberie.

DIVISION *of the* SEVEN HUNDREDS.

Modern Names.	*Antient Names.*
Cirenceſter *and* Crowthorn *and* Minety, *ſomewhat more extenſive than the hundreds of*	Cireceſtre, and Gerſdon, Gerſdunes.
Britwel's Barrow *equal to* — —	Brictwoldeſberg, Becheberie, Begeberie.
Bradley *nearly commenſurate with* ——	Bradelei, Bradelege, and Wacreſcumbe.
Rapſgate, *little different from* — — —	Reſpiet, Reſpigete.
Biſley *differs little from*	Biſeleie.
Longtree *differs little from*	Langetreu Langetrewes.
Whitſton *not fully comprized in* — —	Witeſtan and Blacelawes, Blacelew.

BERKELEY DIVISION.

Modern Names.	*Antient Names.*
Berkeley, — — —	Berkelai.
Thornbury *includes*	Edereſtan, and part of Bacheſtanes.
Langley *and* Swineſhead *nearly include* —	Langelei, Langenei, Suinheve, Sineſhovedes, Tuiferde.
King's Barton, *and* Henbury, — —	Bertune *apud* Briſtou, Part of Weſberie and Bernintreu.
Pucklechurch, —	Polcrecerce,
Grumbaldſaſh *includes*	Grimboldeſtowes, Bacheſtanes, and part of Polcrecerce, and Edredeſtane, Edereſtan.

FOREST DIVISION.

Modern Names.	*Antient Names.*
St. Briavel's *and* Weſtbury, *take part of the hundreds of* —	Weſtberie, Weſtberies, Ledenei, Letberge, and Tedeneham.
Blideſlow *includes* —	Bliteſlau, Blideſlawe and Ledenei.
Botloe *and* Dutchy *of* Lancaſter,	Botelau, and part of Weſtberie.
Dodſton *and* King's Barton *include* —	Dudeſtan, Duneſtane, Langebrige, Tolangebriges.

The king iſſued his writ to the ſheriff of Glouceſterſhire, 9° E. 2. commanding him to return into the exchequer the names of all the cities, boroughs, and vills in every hundred in the county, and who were the lords of them. In the ſheriff's return are two newly erected hundreds, *viz.* Thornbury and the Liberty of Weſtminſter; and ſome of the ſmaller hundreds are incorporated into others. They were then as follow:

Glouceſter,	Holford and Greſton,
Dudſton,	Derhurſt,
Botlowe,	Weſtbury,
Berkley,	Grymbaldeſaſhe,
Wiſton,	Swyneſhoved,
Kiftegate,	Langley,

Cirenceſter,

Cirencefter *,
Bradley,
Langetree,
Repfgate,
Brightwoldefberoe,
Tewxbury,
The liberty of Weft-minfter,
Blidellowe,
Chiltenham,
Salmonfbury,
Pokelchurche,
Berton *regis*, *juxt*. Gl.
Teobaldfton,
Saint Briavelle,
Thornburye,
Hendbury,
Bifley.

The fum of the vills of the whole county of Gloucefter, together with five boroughs, *viz.* Gloucefter, Briftol, Berkeley, Durfley and Newneham were then ccxxxiii. The vills are fet down in the hundreds to which they belong, which were then much altered in extent from thofe at the time of the general furvey, and were much more like what they now are. Gloucefter and Briftol have fince been made cities by the royal favour; but the other three antient boroughs are funk greatly to decay, yet they ftill keep their rank among the market towns, the whole number of which within the county, where markets are actually holden, is twenty-eight. They are as follow:

	Market-Days.		Market-Days.
Berkeley, - -	*Tuefday,*	Newent, - -	*Friday.*
Bifley, - - -	*Thurfday,*	Newnham, -	*Friday.*
Campden, - -	*Wednefd.*	Northleach, -	*Wednefd.*
Cheltenham,	*Thurfday.*	Painfwick, -	*Tuefday.*
Cirencefter, -	*Mo. & F.*	Stanley St. Le.	*Saturday.*
Coleford, -	*Friday.*	Sodbury, - -	*Thurfday.*
Dean, - - -	*Monday.*	Stow,- - - -	*Thurfday.*
Durfley, - -	*Thurfday.*	Stroud, - -	*Friday.*
Fairford, - -	*Thurfday.*	Tetbury, - -	*Wednefd.*
Gloucefter, -	*W. & S.*	Tewkefbury,	*W. & Sa.*
Hampton, -	*Tuefday.*	Thornbury, -	*Saturday.*
Horfley, - -	*Saturday.*	Wickwar, -	*Monday.*
Leachlade, -	*Tuefday.*	Winchcombe,	*Saturday.*
Marfhfield, -	*Tuefday.*	Wotton, - -	*Friday.*

By a ftatute made 17° E. 2. this county was indulged to continue its antient cuftom and privilege, that the lands of perfons who might forfeit their lives by felony, fhould defcend to their heirs; according to the words exprefs'd in the ftatute, *The father to the bough, and the fon to the plough.* The reafon of this was, becaufe Wales having newly fubmitted to England, and this county bordering upon Wales, it was thought convenient to humour the inhabitants with their old cuftoms. The Kentifhmen were allowed to enjoy the fame privilege upon a like account, becaufe that county bordered on France, and was therefore the more liable to fuffer from invafion. The cuftom may ftill fubfift in Kent, but in Gloucefterfhire, it has not been ufed within the reach of memory; and upon the ftricteft inquiry it does not appear to be claimed at prefent in any part of the county.

There is a common proverb refpecting this county, by different perfons a little varioufly expreffed. It is fometimes faid, *As fure as God's in Gloucefterfhire*; at others, *As fure as God's in Gloucefter.* I fhall not venture to fay which is the true reading, but Dr. Stukeley takes notice of the latter; and is of opinion, that it was occafioned by the great number of churches, and religious foundations, in that city; "for you can fcarcely "walk paft ten doors, fays he, but fomewhat of "that fort occurs." *Itin. Curiofa. p.* 64. Sir Robert Atkyns mentions the firft manner of expreffion, having perhaps, never heard the other; and fays, "the proverb was occafioned by "the words *God* and *Glofterfhire* beginning with "the fame letter, and not *from* the extraordinary "multitude of religious foundations, tho' that "was afterwards affigned for the reafon; for "Glofterfhire had not more religious houfes "in proportion than other counties." *p.* 4.

Upon this matter I fhall obferve, that whether the proverb originally related to the city, or to the county at large, I think it much more likely to take rife upon fome religious account, than on that trifling one of two words beginning with the fame letter. As relative to the former, the learned doctor has given his opinion. Let us now fee what ground there was for fuch a faying, upon account of religious foundations, fuppofing it ought to be apply'd to the latter.

Sir Robert fays, "there are eighteen † coun- "ties in England larger than this," which, for argument fake, fhall be granted him; yet four only of thofe paid fo much in penfions, to the members and fervants of diffolved religious houfes, in the year 1553, when the penfions in this county amounted to 1434*l.* 11*s.* 2*d.* And by an old account, copied by Stevens in his Supplement to the *Monafticon*, V 1. p. 23, it appears, that there were but four counties which exceeded Gloucefterfhire in the yearly value of their religious

* That the Out-Torn and Minety was part of the hundred of Cirencefter, will appear from the fheriff's lift of the vills in that hundred, *viz.*

In the hundred of Cirencefter are the underwritten vills, *viz.*

Cirencefter, and the abbat of Cirencefter is lord of the fame.

Upampney, and the abbat of Tewxbury, the abbat of Gloucefter, the abbat of Cirencefter, and Ifabella de Clare, are lords, &c.

Hampton Moyfey, and Nicholas de St. Maria is lord.

South Cerney, and the prior of Lanthony, near Glouc. John de St. Amando, and St. Auguftine Briftol are lords.

Down Ampney, and Margaret Valers is lady.

Sodington, and Hugo de Spencer, John de Langley, and Gualter de Langley are lords.

Dryfeild, and the abbat of Cirencefter, and Rob'tus de Harinhull are lords.

Prefton, and the abbat of Cyren' and Peter de ——— are lords.

Cotes, and Richard de Lymell, and the abbefs of Ramfey are lord and lady.

Duntefburne Abbats, and the abbat of Glouc. —— de Cadomo, and John de Rowfe are lords.

Daglingworth, and —— Blunt, and Richard de Hampton are lords.

Bawdinton, and Richard de Bageidden, Robert de Penynton, and Thomas Corbet are lords.

The fum of the vills in the hundred of Cyren. xii.

† I fuppofe he meant feventeen, becaufe he immediately refers to Mr. Houghton's table for the proportions of the counties to each other; by which it appears, that feventeen counties have a greater number of acres than Gloucefterfhire.

foundations,

foundations, at the time of the diſſolution; *viz.* York, Lincoln, Somerſet, and Middleſex, including the city of London. Therefore it may be preſumed this county had more, or at leaſt, better endowed houſes, than many others of greater extent, which might occaſion the proverb in queſtion.

By the above account, the clear yearly value of religious houſes, including the abbey of Kingſwood, in Wilts, becauſe it was intirely ſurrounded by Glouceſterſhire, and the priory of Lanthony, in the county of Monmouth, becauſe it was a cell to Lanthony, near Glouceſter, was 6672*l.* 19*s.* 2*d.* 3 farthings.

The cuſtom of waſſalling, or going from houſe to houſe at Chriſtmas, with a bowl to be filled with toaſt and ale, or cyder, is grown much out of uſe in this county. Lambard gives the following account of the riſe of the "auncient maner "of the Waſſallinge cuppe," which he takes from Galfride [Geoffry] of Monmouth: "Hengiſt hav-"ing finiſhed his caſtle, [now called Thong-caſtle, "in Lincolnſhire] for which he had obtained leave "of Vortigern, invited him to a banquet, and "after he had well pleaſed his taſte, he aſſayed, "by ſhewing of his daughter, to ſatisfy his ſight "alſo. The maid therefore (being of excellent "beautie) came forth with a cuppe of wine in her "hand, and kneeling downe in his ſight, ſaid, as "ſhe had been taught, laꝼoꞃꝺe cynẏnᵹ ƿaꞅꞅaıl, "*Lord king, be in health*; which, when the king "underſtood by his interpreter, he anſwered, "ꝺꞃıncheıl, *drink in health*; and ſo the maid drank "to him, and he pledged her ſo heartily, that be-"fore it was long he took her to wife."

Of PARISHES, &c.

HONORIUS, archbiſhop of Canterbury, about the year 640, divided that part of England which was then converted to chriſtianity into pariſhes.

The number of pariſhes has increaſed ever ſince the conqueſt. When they were firſt laid out, it is preſumed that due regard was had to the extent of them, and to the number of the inhabitants; for it was neceſſary to conſider both circumſtances together, in order to divide the duties of the pariſh prieſts equally amongſt them. But large members have been continually lopped off from the mother churches, and becoming independent, the pariſhes are now very diſproportionate. Under this head, Sir R. A. has obſerved, that "the pariſh of Newland, in the foreſt diviſion, is "30 miles in compaſs; the pariſh of Rudford, in "the ſame diviſion, is 3 miles in compaſs; ſo "that the one pariſh is an hundred times as large as "the other." But theſe premiſſes will not juſtify the learned author's concluſion; for though it ſhould be admitted, that Newland is an hundred times as large as Rudford, it is poſſible, notwithſtanding, that the latter might be the largeſt. No competent judgment can be formed of the ſize of a pariſh, from the circumference of it, without aſcertaining its ſhape and figure; for which reaſon I have ſeldom mentioned the circumference of places.

When the *Antient and Preſent State of Gloſterſhire* was firſt publiſhed, the following remarks were in ſome meaſure juſt and ſeaſonable. "It is," ſays the author, "a neglect that the "highways and footpaths are not better amended; "that lights in the dark nights are not ſet up in "market-towns, as they are in London; that "hoſpitals are not erected in the greater towns, "for the relief of the ſick and wounded, and for "the conveniency of women to lye in. Many "more ſuch public charities are neglected, be-"cauſe faith, like Pharaoh's lean kine, has de-"voured charity. It is hard to allow neither free "will nor good will."

The firſt objection is ſince in a great meaſure obviated, by the erecting of turnpikes on every conſiderable road in the kingdom; a mode of collecting money but little known to the author. That between Glouceſter and Birdlip was one of the firſt turnpike roads in the kingdom. I wiſh it might be ſaid to be one of the beſt.

As to the other objections, it is proper to obſerve, that the city of Glouceſter is enlightened with lamps, by virtue of an act of parliament; and that in the ſame city is a noble infirmary, erected and ſupported by ſubſcriptions and private donations; a more particular account of which will be found in a ſubſequent ſection of the general hiſtory.

Some perſons have conſidered the latter part of the quoted paragraph, as containing an unneceſſary, not to ſay injurious, inſinuation of the want of public charity; for my part, I underſtand the author as warmly expreſſing his zeal for the promotion of the practice of that great and noble virtue. That he never intended to reflect on the county, of which he had written the hiſtory, is evident from the following paſſage: "It appears, "ſays he, by examining the particular charities "in the ſeveral pariſhes, that this latter age "has been as fruitful in good works as any of "the former. There *has* not been ſo many "pompous buildings, and extravagant donations, "which are often the effects of proud and ſuper-"ſtitious minds; but the modern charities tend "to the relief of the ſick and poor, which proceed "from an humble and compaſſionate mind. "The others go away with the loud applauſe of "the world; but theſe are the *true* praiſe-wor-"thy, and ought to be encouraged." *p.* 16.

The

The *Monaſticon Anglicanum* of Sir William Dugdale, and the Supplement to it, by Mr. Stevens, have been ſometimes produced to ſhew the many and great acts of charity before the reformation, by way of depreciating the latter ones; but with how little reaſon, will appear to thoſe that will take the trouble to examine into the many public charities done ſince that time, and compare them with thoſe in any like number of years before it. By this method, ſuch a difference will be ſeen as to render the one unworthy of a compariſon with the other. Dr. Willet, in his *Synopſis Papiſmi*, has given us a ſhort ſpecimen with regard to the two univerſities, and the city of London; but vaſt numbers of benefactions have been made ſince that work was firſt publiſhed. Beſides, the author was not fully informed of all the charities, down to the time when he wrote.——All nations muſt acknowledge, that none enjoys freedom of ſentiment more fully than this, nor is charity any where more liberally diſpenced to the poor and needy. Whatever virtues have deſerted our country, charity ſtill continues to adorn it.

"There is no part of Gloſterſhire, ſays Sir "R. Atkyns, but what is within ſeven miles * of "ſome other county: This happens becauſe the "city of Gloſter is a diſtinct county, and the "pariſh of Kingſwood is in Wiltſhire;" to which he might have added, that Poulton, in the ſame county, and Broadway, in Worceſterſhire, are both completely ſurrounded by Glouceſterſhire. There are alſo ſeveral places in this county ſurrounded by Oxfordſhire, Wiltſhire, Worceſterſhire, and Warwickſhire, which will be particularly taken notice of under the reſpective pariſhes.—Theſe are a few of the vaſt number of inſtances that might be given of the great irregularity and confuſion in the antient diviſion of lands in the kingdom; which ſome perſons have ſuppoſed to have been occaſioned by the great influence of the barons after the conqueſt; who, jealous of the rights and honours of their manors, procured their lands on the borders, and within the limits of neighbouring counties, to be appropriated to thoſe in which their demeans, and chief places of reſidence lay.—But it is very certain that this diſtribution, as to Glouceſterſhire, took place before the conqueſt; becauſe, when the kingdom was ſurveyed, at the beginning of the conqueror's reign, neither of the places I have juſt mentioned, as belonging to other counties, were then reputed as part of this; and Widford, which is ſurrounded by Oxfordſhire, was then, as well as now, belonging to Glouceſterſhire. *See Domeſday-book.*

The ſame learned author, p. 23, has repreſented the pariſh of Keynſham to be in this county, whereas it is in Somerſetſhire. But this is one of thoſe trivial miſtakes which genius frequently overlooks; and which I mention not invidiouſly, being ſenſible that all men are ſubject to error.

Of the RIVERS.

THE principal rivers are the Severn; the Iſis, or Thames; the firſt Avon, at Tewkeſbury; the ſecond Avon, at Briſtol. Theſe receive all the others that either riſe in the county, or run through it.

The SEVERN. The Britiſh name of this river is *Hafren*, which was given it, if Giraldus Cambrenſis and Geoffry of Monmouth are to be credited, becauſe a virgin of the name of *Abren*, or *Hebren*, was drowned in it, by the command of queen Guendoloena, after the death of Locrine, her huſband, becauſe ſhe was the fruit of his unlawful love.

—— *In flumen præcipitatur* Abren;
Nomen Abren *fluvio de virgine*; *nomen eidem.*
Nomine corrupto, deinde Sabrina *datur.*

Headlong was *Abren* thrown into the ſtream,
And hence the river took the virgin's name.
Corrupted, thence at laſt *Sabrina* came.

But Leland deſervedly treats this ſtory as fabulous, and gives it as his opinion, that both this river and the Humber took their names of *Aber*, which in the Britiſh language ſignifies the mouth of any river.

It riſes out of Plinlimmon-hill, in Montgomeryſhire, and makes, ſays Camden, "ſuch a num-"ber of windings, that a perſon would think "many times he returns again to his fountain." It paſſes by Lanidlos and Welchpool, where it becomes navigable; and proceeding to Shrewſbury and Bridgenorth, enters Worceſterſhire above Bewdley; viſits Worceſter, and haſtens into Glouceſterſhire a little above Tewkeſbury, receiving the Avon from Warwickſhire, about half a mile below that town. Taking its courſe downwards "it "parts itſelf to make the iſle of Alney, which is "rich and beautiful, and then haſtens to Glou-"ceſter; a little below which place, uniting its "divided ſtreams, it waxeth broader and deeper

* When Sir Robert wrote the *Antient and Preſent State of Gloſterſhire*, the diſtances between places were not ſo commonly meaſured as they now are; therefore, when he ſpeaks of miles, candour will underſtand him to intend the common computation of the country.

" by the ebbing and flowing of the tide." Paſſing by the antient borough of Newnham, to a place below Chepſtow, after a courſe of more than forty miles thro' the county, it receives the Wye, which riſes out of the ſame hill, and loſes its name at the place of confluence, their united waters being called the Severn. Here the river becomes a boundary between Glouceſterſhire and Monmouthſhire, and continues ſo 'till it receives the Avon, which runs from Briſtol, at Kingroad. For many miles above this place, the ſevern is two or three miles over, but here it is three or four times as broad, and capable of receiving ſhips of great burthen.

On this river, from Glouceſter and Newnham, ſeveral brigs are employ'd in the trade to London and Ireland, and a great number of barges, or trows, run to and from Briſtol, Glouceſter, Tewkeſbury, Worceſter, and Bewdley, at which place, a communication is opened, by a canal, with the rivers Merſey and Trent, promiſing great advantages to this trading country.

The Severn is remarkable for its tide, which rolls in with a head of three or four feet high, foaming and roaring in its courſe, as if enraged by the oppoſition it meets with from a ſtrong current of freſh water, which ſeems to contend with it for the ſuperiority. They claſh in ſuch a manner as to daſh the waters to a conſiderable height. This conteſt between them is called the Hygre, or Eager, probably from the French *eau-guerre*, i. e. water-war. The tide getting the better, marches up the ſtream victoriouſly. Hear Drayton's deſcription of this turbulent river.

——————— " with whoſe tumultuous waves,
Shut up in narrow bounds, the Hygre wildry raves;
And 'frights the ſtraggling flocks, the neighbouring ſhores to fly
Afar, as from the main it comes with hideous cry.
And on the angry front the curling foam doth bring,
The billows 'gainſt the banks, when fiercely it doth fling:
Hurles up the ſlimy ooze, and makes the ſcaly brood
Leap madding to the land, affrighted, from the flood;
O'erturns the toiling barge, whoſe ſteerſman doth not launch,
And thruſts the furrowing beake into her ireful paunch.
As when we haply ſee a ſickly woman fall
Into a fit of that which we the mother call.
When from the grieved wombe ſhe feels the pain ariſe,
Breaks into grievous ſighs, with intermixed cries,
Bereaved of her ſenſe; and ſtruggling ſtill with thoſe
That 'gainſt her riſing paine their utmoſt ſtrength oppoſe,
Starts, toſſes, tumbles, ſtrikes, turns, touſes, ſpurns and ſprawls,
Caſting with furious limbs her holders to the walls.
But that the horrid pangs torment the grieved ſo,
One well might muſe from whence this ſudden ſtrength ſhould grow."

Sir Robert Atkyns attempts to account for the tide coming in as above deſcribed, and not ſwelling more gradually, as in ſome other rivers. It is occaſioned, he ſays, by the mouth of the Severn opening to the great Atlantic ocean, which pours in its tide with great violence, and the river growing narrow on a ſudden, it fills the channel at once.

The remark that the tides here are largeſt one year at full moon, and the next at the change; and that the night-tides are larger than the day-tides one year, and the contrary the next, is, I believe, rather a chimera, than the reſult of accurate obſervation.

The Severn has been ſaid to be a rapid river, yet there is not a lock upon it, from the top of the navigation downwards, which is a circumſtance not very conſiſtent with that notion, for rapid rivers are generally full of ſhallows. Like other great rivers, it overflows its banks after much rain, from which the vale of Glouceſterſhire ſuſtained great damage, particularly in the years 1606, 1687, and 1703.

This river does not boaſt of a great variety of fiſh, yet the ſalmon, of which there is great plenty, is truly excellent. To ſome perſons the flavour of the ſhad of this river is very grateful. This is a ſea-fiſh, of the herring kind, by ſome naturaliſts called *Clupea*. But the Severn is more eſpecially famed for the lamprey, in Latin, *lampetra*, a ſpecies of *Petromyzon*. It has ſeveral rows of teeth, without back-bone, or gills, but inſtead of the latter, on each ſide of the throat are ſeven holes to receive water. It is of a dark colour on the back, but of a fine, clear, light blue on the belly. It ſometimes grows to the weight of three pounds, and upwards of two feet and a half in length. They are very ſcarce, much eſteemed, and ſell at a high price.

The Severn alſo produces the elver, a ſpecies of fiſh which the editor of Camden, by miſtake, ſuppoſes not to be found in any county but Somerſetſhire. If the ſpring be mild and open, they generally appear about the middle of April, when they cover the ſurface of the water, more eſpecially about the mouths of the rivers that empty themſelves into the Severn. They are of a dark brown colour, about two or three inches long, and have the name from a ſuppoſition that they are young eels. The country people ſkim them up in great abundance, ſcour and boil them, and bring them to market as white as ſnow, where they uſually ſell at about two-pence a pound.

The bailiwick of the Severn is in the crown. John Arnold had a leaſe of it 1660, for thirty-one years at 10*l.* a year. Mr. Edward Baylis of Glouceſter is the preſent Water bailiff.—2° E. 6. Thomas Hennage and the lord Willoughby had a grant of a fiſhery, from Newnham-ladder to Boxgrove, which formerly belonged to the abbey of St. Auſtin's, Briſtol.

The places for paſſing of this river are as follow, viz.

At the Lower Load, a mile below Tewkeſbury, by ferry.

At the Haw, ſix miles above Glouceſter, by boat.

At Maiſmore bridge.

At the bridge at Glouceſter.

At Framilode, by boat, about ten miles below Glouceſter. The paſſage-houſe is on the S. E. ſide of the river. They land at Weſtbury.

At

At Newnham, two miles farther down, where the paſſage-houſe is on the contrary ſide. They land at Arlingham. Here is a ford, over which, at low water, waggons and people on horſeback, of more reſolution than prudence, ſometimes paſs; for many have loſt their lives in the attempt. The river is here about a mile over. At the above places they paſs almoſt at any time.

At Pirton, in the pariſh of Lidney. They land in Berkeley pariſh.

At Auſt, in the pariſh of Henbury, and Beachley, in that of Tidenham, are correſpondent paſſage-houſes. This paſſage communicates with the roads in Monmouthſhire on one ſide, and thoſe leading to Briſtol and Bath on the other. As it is of great importance to travellers to know the time of paſſing, the following obſervations will be uſeful. The paſſage here depends both on the wind and tide. The ſoutherly, weſterly, and northerly winds are proper for paſſing; but when the wind and tide go both the ſame way, there is no paſſing; therefore, when the wind is northerly it muſt be at flood, or coming in of the tide, and then you may paſs for five hours. On the contrary, when the wind is ſoutherly or weſterly, all paſſing muſt be at ebb, or going out of the tide, which affords ſeven hours good paſſing.

Knowing the age of the moon, by which all tides are governed, the following table ſhows at what hour to paſs every day in the year.

The Wind being above.	Time of paſſing.		The Wind being below.	Time of paſſing.	
Moon's age.	H. M.	H. M.	Moon's age.	H. M.	H. M.
1 and 16	2 : 00 to	7 : 00	1 and 16	7 : 00 to	2 : 00
2 and 17	2 : 48 to	7 : 48	2 and 17	7 : 48 to	2 : 48
3 and 18	3 : 36 to	8 : 36	3 and 18	8 : 36 to	3 : 36
4 and 19	4 : 24 to	9 : 24	4 and 19	9 : 24 to	4 : 24
5 and 20	5 : 12 to	10 : 12	5 and 20	10 : 12 to	5 : 12
6 and 21	6 : 00 to	11 : 00	6 and 21	11 : 00 to	6 : 00
7 and 22	6 : 48 to	11 : 48	7 and 22	11 : 48 to	6 : 48
8 and 23	7 : 36 to	12 : 36	8 and 23	12 : 36 to	7 : 36
9 and 24	8 : 24 to	1 : 24	9 and 24	1 : 24 to	8 : 24
10 and 25	9 : 12 to	2 : 12	10 and 25	2 : 12 to	9 : 12
11 and 26	10 : 00 to	3 : 00	11 and 26	3 : 00 to	10 : 00
12 and 27	10 : 48 to	3 : 48	12 and 27	3 : 48 to	10 : 48
13 and 28	11 : 36 to	4 : 36	13 and 28	4 : 36 to	11 : 36
14 and 29	12 : 24 to	5 : 24	14 and 29	5 : 24 to	12 : 24
15 and 30	1 : 12 to	6 : 12	15 and 30	6 : 12 to	1 : 12

Example. If the moon be 5 or 20 days old, and the wind above, there is paſſing from 12 minutes after 4, 'till 12 minutes after 10. If the wind be below, from 12 minutes after 10, to 12 minutes after 5.

When the tide is coming in, the wind being above, they paſs an hour earlier at the New Paſſage than here; but the tide going out, and wind below, they are an hour later at the New Paſſage; ſo that this table will ſerve for both paſſages.

This river was formerly the limit between England and Wales; and the acts 8° H. 6. c. 27, and 27° H. 8. were intended to prevent robberies upon it. The 20° C. 2. c. 9. is for the preſervation of fiſh therein.

The Avon. This river riſes near Naſeby, in Northamptonſhire, enters Warwickſhire at Colthrop, and paſſes by Rugby, Warwick, and Stratford, where it is navigable. Quitting that county, it haſtens by Eveſham to enter Glouceſterſhire, a little above Tewkeſbury; and about half a mile below the town, is diſcharged into the Severn. The name is Britiſh, and ſignifies a river.

The Iſbourne, a little river which riſes in Charlton Abbats, and runs by Winchcombe, empties itſelf into the Avon a little below Eveſham.

The Carrant, which riſes in Beckford, is a boundary, above Tewkeſbury, between the counties of Glouceſter and Worceſter, and empties itſelf into the Avon; as doth

The Swilyate, a little below that town.

The little river Chilt, riſes at Dowdeſwell, and running by Cheltenham is voided into the Severn at Wainload's-bridge.

The Badgworth river, after receiving a brook that runs thro' Brockworth, falls into the Severn at Sainthurſt, or Sandhurſt.

The Leaden or Leddon, riſes in Herefordſhire, and empties itſelf into the Severn almoſt oppoſite Glouceſter.

The Froome, or Stroud river, riſes at Brimpſfield, runs by Stroud, thro' Stonehouſe, Eaſington, and into the Severn at Framilode.

The Ewelm, riſes at Owlpen and Uly, runs by Durſley, and receives the Broad-well water. Paſſing on, it changes its firſt name for that of Cam, which it communicates to the next village; and collecting ſeveral little ſtreams in its courſe to Cowley and Slimbridge, falls into the Severn at the laſt mentioned pariſh.

The Berkeley Avon, riſes in two heads at Boxwell and Kilcot, and collecting other ſmall brooks in its courſe, paſſes by Berkeley, and a little below it, falls into the Severn.

The Isis. This river has generally been conſidered as the head of the Thames, which, according to the current opinion, had that name from the junction of the names of the two rivers, Thame and Iſis, as their waters alſo join near Dorcheſter, in Oxfordſhire. But however plauſible this etymology may ſeem, the learned author of the additions to Camden's *Britannia* has made it appear, that this river, which Camden and others have called *Iſis* and *Ouſe*, was antiently called *Thames* or *Tems*, before it came near the *Thame*, and produces the following authorities. " In an antient charter granted to abbat Aldhelm, there is particular mention made of certain lands upon the eaſt part of the river, *cujus vocabulum* Temis, *juxta vadum qui appellatur Summerford*; and this ford is in Wiltſhire. " The ſame thing appears from ſeveral other " charters granted to the abbey of Malmeſbury, " as well as that of Eveſham; and from the old " deeds relating to Cricklade. And perhaps it " may with ſafety be affirmed, that in any charter " or authentic hiſtory, it does not ever occur under the name of *Iſis*; which indeed is not ſo " much as heard of but among ſcholars; the

" common

" common people, all along from the head of it " to Oxford, calling it by no other name but that " of *Thames*. So alſo the Saxon Temeſe (from " whence our Tems immediately comes) is a plain " evidence that that people never dreamt of any " ſuch conjunction. But further: All our hiſ- " torians who mention the incurſions of Æthel- " wold into Wiltſhire, *A. D.* 905; or of Canute, " *A. D.* 1016, tell us, that they paſſed over the " Thames at Cricklade.——As for the original " of the word [Thames] it ſeems plainly to be " Britiſh, becauſe there are ſeveral rivers in ſeveral " parts of England of almoſt the ſame name " with it; as *Tame* in Staffordſhire, *Teme* in Here- " fordſhire, *Tamar* in Cornwall, &c. And a " learned perſon of that nation [Mr. Lhwyd] " affirms it to be the ſame with their *Tâf*, which " is the name of many rivers in Wales; the Ro- " mans changing the pronunciation of the *(f)* " into *(m)*, as the Latin word *Demetia*, is in " Welch *Dyfed*." *Camden's Brit. col.* 100,101.

Mr. Lhwyd has alſo ſhewn that where the Latins uſe an *(m)* the Britons have a *(v)*, as *Firmus*, *Firv*; *Terminus*, *Tervin*; *Amnis*, *Avon*; *Lima*, *Lhîv*, *&c.* and that the word *Tâv*, was, according to the old Britiſh orthography, written *Tam*; wherefore he thinks that *Tâv*, or *Taff*, is originally the ſame word with *Tame*, or *Thames*; and that *tamos* in *potamos* is probably no other.

The Thames has been reputed to riſe in the pariſh of Coats, out of a well that overflows in the winter, or in a very wet ſeaſon only; but in the ſummer, this river can be traced no higher than to ſome ſprings which riſe in the pariſh of Kemble, a little ſouth of the foſs road. The poetical deſcription of the ſource of this river may be found in the Marriage of Thame and Iſis, which Mr. Camden's Biographer ſuppoſes him to be the author of; it begins thus:

Lanigeros quà lata greges Cotſwaldia paſcit, &c.

The following tranſlation of it is taken from the *Britannia.*

Where Cotſwold's hillocks, fam'd for weighty ſheep,
Their eager courſe to the Dobunians keep;
Near the great foſſe a ſpacious plain there lies,
Where broken cliffs the ſecret top diſguiſe.
Hugh free-ſtones neatly carv'd adorn the gate
The porch with ivory ſhines, the roof with jeat,
And rows of pumice in the poſts are ſet.
But nature yields to art: the workman's ſkill
Does free-ſtone, ivory, pumice, jeat, excel.
* * * * * * * *
Here awful Isis fills his liquid throne;
Isis, whom Britiſh ſtreams their monarch own.
His never-wearied hands a ſpacious urn,
Down on his azure boſom gravely turn,
And flags and reeds his unpoll'd locks adorn.
Each waving horn the ſubject ſtream ſupplies,
And grateful light darts from his ſhining eyes.
His grizzly beard all wet hangs dropping down,
And guſhing veins in wat'ry channels run.
The little fiſh in joyful numbers crowd,
And ſilver ſwans fly o'er the cryſtal flood,
And clap their ſnowy wings, &c.——

The reader will be eaſily perſuaded that the poet has taken greater licence in deſcribing the ſource of this river, than will be allowed the topographer; and if he ſhould ſurvey the place called Thames-head, he will find, that the picture is not a very ſtriking likeneſs of nature.

This river is navigable as high as Cricklade, in Wiltſhire, from whence it runs to Leachlade, and viſits Oxford, Abingdon, Wallingford, Reading, Henly and Windſor, in its way to the great metropolis.

The Churn is another river, more antiently written, in compoſition, *Ceri*, *Cori*, *Corin*; as *Caer-Cori*, &c. The name is of Britiſh original; *Chwyrn*, in that language ſignifies rapid. This river riſes at Cubberly, ten miles north of Cirenceſter, and paſſing thro' that town, joins the Thames near Cricklade; and may with great propriety be called the head of that river, being the higheſt ſource from whence it derives its water.

The Coln riſing near Withington, runs by Compton, Foſs-bridge, Bibury, Coln St. Aldwin's, and Fairford, and pours its ſtream into the Thames, a little above Leachlade.

The Lech riſes in the pariſh of Hampnet, and paſſing by Northleach and Eaſtleach, empties itſelf into the Thames a little below Leachlade, which places all take their names from this river.

The Windruſh riſes near Guiting, and paſſing by Bourton-on-the-Water and Barrington, and ſo on to Burford and Witney, in Oxfordſhire, joins the Thames at Newbridge, in that county.

The Evenlode runs from a pariſh of the ſame name in Worceſterſhire, near Battesford, and after paſſing thro' the eaſt corner of Glouceſterſhire, enters Oxfordſhire, and mingles its waters with the Thames near Eanſham.

The Avon, or Briſtol Avon, takes its riſe at Tetbury, in this county, which it quits immediately; and paſſing by Malmeſbury, Chippenham, Bradford, and Bath, where it is navigable, runs to Briſtol, and from thence to Kingroad, where the Briſtol ſhips firſt ſpread their ſails when outward bound, and firſt caſt anchor upon their return home. This river waſhes the weſtern borders of Glouceſterſhire, and is the boundary between it and Somerſetſhire, for about twenty miles. By 11° and 12° W. 3. c. 23. the mayor, burgeſſes, and commonalty of the city of Briſtol, are conſervators of the Avon, from above the bridge there to Kingroad, and ſo down the Severn to the two iſlands called Holmes. And the preſervation of the rivers Avon and Froome, is the object of the 25th chapter of the ſame ſtatute; and of the 20th chapter of 22° G. 2. It was once propoſed to join the Avon with the Thames by a canal, and ſo to compleat an inland navigation betwixt London and Briſtol, which might be eaſily carried into execution.

The

The Boyd riſes at Codrington, and empties itſelf into the Avon at Bitton.

The Froome riſes in two heads at Doddington and Rangeworthy, and receiving ſeveral little brooks, paſſes on to the key at Briſtol, where it falls into the Avon.

The little river Trin, or Trim, runs from Weſtbury by a very ſhort courſe into the Avon.

The Wye has but little claim to a place in our liſt of rivers. It is a boundary between Glouceſterſhire and Monmouthſhire at Welch Bicknor, and at St. Briavel's. It then runs again into Herefordſhire to take its laſt farewell; and quitting it, as tho' with reluctance, divides the two firſt mentioned counties a little above Monmouth. Half the wooden-bridge over this river at Chepſtow is repaired by Glouceſterſhire, and the other half by Monmouthſhire, as directed by 18° Eliz. and 3° Jac. 1. This bridge is built near the confluence of the Wye with the Severn, at which place is one of the higheſt tides in the world, the flood ſometimes riſing ſixty feet. The Wye is well ſtored with excellent ſalmon, and other fiſh common to ſuch large rivers.

Of the LIEUTENANCY, &c. of the COUNTY.

IN the time of the Saxons, the governors of other counties were called earls, or dukes; but Glouceſterſhire had its vice-roys, or ſub-reguli. Oſrick, or Oſhire, was vice-roy of the Wiccij in the year 680. Huctred ſucceeded him, who was alſo followed by Eanbert and Aldred, his two brothers.

Mr. Camden is of opinion, that the *Cuſtodes Regni*, ſettled in every county by king Alfred, were of the ſame nature with our lieutenants. And that thoſe were afterwards known in the reign of H. 3. by the name of *Capitanei*, who, by the aſſiſtance of the ſheriffs were to curb the inſolence of the robbers.

The governors of counties are now called the king's lieutenants. The office of lieutenancy, under that particular name, is but of late eſtabliſhment, tho' of great honour and dignity. Lords lieutenants were at firſt appointed occaſionally by the crown, whoſe repreſentatives they are, with coercive power to keep order, within their reſpective counties, in time of great danger. They ſeem to have been firſt uſed on the ſuppreſſion of monaſteries, which cauſed a great ferment in the nation. They were afterwards eſtabliſhed by law 2° and 3° E. 6. c. 2. and 4° and 5° Ph. and M. c. 3. and confirmed by 13° and 14° Car. 2. c. 3.

The defence of the nation formerly depended on tenures, and on the forces raiſed by the ſheriffs in their counties. King H. 2 iſſued a proclamation, commanding all freeholders and burgeſſes of his dominions, on the continent, to provide themſelves with arms offenſive and defenſive, in proportion to their ſubſtance; an ordinance which afterwards took place in England, according to the regulation of the aſſize of arms, which was executed under the inſpection of the itinerant judges.

Every perſon poſſeſſed of a knight's fee, was obliged to have a coat of mail, a helmet, ſhield and lance, and ſuch a ſuit for every fee he poſſeſſed. Every free layman poſſeſſed of effects, or rents, to the value of ſixteen marks, was bound to have the ſame ſort of armour; and thoſe who had not above ten marks, were excuſed for a ſlighter coat of mail, an iron ſkull-cap and a lance. Burgeſſes were equipped with an iron cap, a lance, and a wambois, or quilted coat; and no perſon could pawn, or lend his armour, nor could a lord take it from his vaſſal by forfeiture, gift, ſecurity, or under any pretence whatſoever. When the poſſeſſor died, the armour deſcended to his heir; and during a minority, the guardian took it in charge, and provided a man for ſervice, until his ward was able to ſerve in perſon. *Benedict. p.* 365.

Queen Elizabeth, upon the great invaſion threatened by the Spaniard, 1588, by the advice of her council, began to iſſue out commiſſions of array, and to model a ſtanding militia. Lord Chandois was then appointed lieutenant of this county, and the trained bands conſiſted of 3000 foot under ten captains, and 250 horſe, divided into four troops.

The earl of Berkeley had a commiſſion of lieutenancy 7° Jac. when the militia was new modelled, but the county provided the ſame number of men as before. Berkeley diviſion was charged with 750 men, under three captains; the diviſion of the Seven Hundreds furniſhed 750 men, under three captains; Kiftſgate diviſion 750 men, under four captains; the Foreſt diviſion 400 men, under two captains; and the city of Glouceſter, with the hundred of Dudſton and King's-Barton, called the in-county, was charged with 350 men, under one captain.

This body was divided into 600 pike-men, 600 halbardeers, 600 muſketteers, and 1200 calivers. There were then only 200 horſe, under the command of four captains, of whom 20 were furniſhed with lances, and the reſt were called light horſe. The county was alſo charged with 400*l.* to provide ammunition.

The militia was then raiſed by the inhabitants in proportion to their eſtates. By the 13° and 14° C. 2. c. 3. every perſon having a revenue of 500*l. per ann.* or an eftate in goods or money of 6000*l.* value, was liable to find a horfe, horfe-man and arms; having a yearly revenue of 50*l.* or a perfonal eftate of 600*l.* in goods or money, other than ftock upon the ground, made him liable to find a foot-foldier and arms, and fo in proportion for a greater eftate in both inftances. But real and perfonal eftates were chargeable according to thefe proportions, tho' of a fmaller value, to the fupplying of arms, and pay.

But this law was repealed 30° G. 2. and a new one, very materially different from the former, took place of it, § which has been fince explained and amended by 2° G. 3. By the old laws, property was charged with the burthen of the fervice; which by the new, is determined by lot on perfons between the ages of eighteen and forty-five years, without any regard to property. By 30° G. 2. men were liable to be placed on the lifts from the age of eighteen to that of fifty; and according to lifts fo made out, one man out of twenty-nine was taken in Gloucefterfhire, to furnifh 960 men, which was the complement for this county, including the cities of Gloucefter and Briftol. But this proportion would have raifed a greater number, had the lifts been accurately made.

Among the Romans, the military age, according to Dionyfius and Polybius, was from feventeen to forty-five or forty-fix, and in dangerous times to fifty. Formerly our militia was compofed of perfons from the age of fixteen to fixty; fo that a great part of them muft have been old men and boys.

The earl of Berkeley is the prefent lieutenant of Gloucefterfhire. Many of his lordfhip's anceftors held this office of high truft, 'till the death of the late earl of Berkeley, when it was fucceffively filled by lord Ducie, the late lord Chedworth, and Norborne Berkeley, efq; now lord Botetourt; who, going to take upon himfelf the government of Virginia, was fucceeded as colonel of the militia by the earl of Berkeley. This nobleman is alfo Cuftos Rotulorum of the county.

Of the OFFICE of HIGH SHERIFF, With a Lift of Sheriffs of this County to the prefent Time.

EVERY county is governed by a yearly officer, whom we call the fheriff. The name is of Saxon original, compounded of Scype, already explained, and Gerefa, a governor, or conful; that is, a governor of a fhire or county. The fheriff was fometimes alfo called *Vifcount*, before the word was ufed to fignify a title of honour.

The principal functions of this office are thus defined by Mr. Madox, in his very accurate *Hiftory of the Exchequer*: "It was the fheriff's duty to "do the juftice of his county, to keep the public "peace, to ftock and improve the king's lands, "and to collect the king's revenue." It appears that in time of war, he alfo performed fome military functions; and the above-cited author has obferved, "that he ufually was the præfect, "or governor of the king's caftle in his county." In the fecond book of lord Littleton's *Life of king Henry the Second*, I find moft of the following further particulars relating to this office. It is faid, that among the Anglo-Saxons, the fheriff was elected in the county-court, by the people; and in the reign of king Henry the Firft, the citizens of London paid a fine to that prince, of a hundred marks of filver, that they might have the privilege of chufing their fheriffs themfelves. But no inftance occurs of fuch a liberty in the counties after the entrance of the Normans, 'till the ftatute made by Edward the Firft, in the 28th year of his reign, by which he granted to his people, *that they fhall have election of their fheriff in every fhire where the fhrivalty is not of fee, if they lift.* Nor did that act of parliament continue long unrepealed. In the times of which I write, fays his lordfhip, the fheriffs had the counties committed to them refpectively, by the king, at his pleafure, either in cuftody, or at ferm-certain.

It appears by the rolls, that, under Henry the Firft, Richard Baffet and Aubrey de Vere, were joint-fheriffs of *eleven counties*. This was extraordinary: but there are feveral inftances under different kings, of two or three being committed to the fame perfon. Urfo d' Abitot, in the reign of William the Conqueror, was made fheriff of Worcefterfhire, and the office was granted in fee to him and his heirs. Neverthelefs it appears that his fon was turned out of it by Henry the Firft, for having ordered one of the fervants of that king to be flain. But it went to his fifter, and in her right to her hufband, Walter de Beauchamp, from whom it defcended, by inheritance, to William their fon, who, in the reign of Henry the Second,

§ An order was publifh'd, 43 E. 3. requiring all ecclefiaftics in general, to be array'd and arm'd for the defence of the kingdom. Afterwards they were exempt from perfonal fervice, but were to find money to provide their quota of men and arms, which they were permitted to fettle themfelves. But by 30 G. 2. and 2 G. 3. all peers of the realm, the clergy, and members of both univerfities, with a few others, are intirely exempt from this fervice.

Second, was alſo ſheriff of three other counties, *viz.* thoſe of Hereford, Glouceſter, and Warwick. Archbiſhops and biſhops were ſometimes appointed ſheriffs. William biſhop of Ely, who was chancellor to king Richard the Firſt, offered to give the king for the ſhrivalty of the ſeveral counties of York, Lincoln, and Northampton, 1500 marks in hand, and 100 marks *increment*, (that is, above the uſual term) every year for each county. But the archbiſhop of York out-bid him for Yorkſhire, and was made ſheriff thereof, on the payment of 3000 marks for that county alone, and the yearly *increment* of 300. Three thouſand marks were then equivalent to 30,000*l.* in our days. This auction of a miniſterial and judicial office, of the higheſt truſt and importance, was a ſcandalous thing; and the permitting of an office of this kind to deſcend by inheritance, may be reckoned among the faults of our old conſtitution; from which the kingdom muſt have experienced great inconveniencies, therefore proviſion was at length made by ſtatute, that no perſon ſhould ſerve two years together, but ſhould be two years at leaſt diveſted of the office, and not 'till then be capable of ſerving again in the ſame county.

The following is a Liſt of the SHERIFFS of the County of Glouceſter, with the Years in which they ſerved, from 1 H. 2. to the preſent Time.

A. D. Henry II.

1154 Miles de Glouceſter.
5 Walter de Hereford.
6 William de Beauchamp.
7 the ſame.
8 the ſame.
9 the ſame.
1160 the ſame.
1 the ſame.
2 the ſame.
3 William Piperd.
4 the ſame.
5 the ſame.
6 the ſame.
7 Gilbert Piperd.
8 the ſame.
9 the ſame.
1170 the ſame.
1 Ralph Fitz Stephen, and William his brother.
2 the two ſame.
3 the two ſame.
4 the two ſame.
5 William Fitz Stephen.
6 the ſame.
7 the ſame.
8 the ſame.
9 the ſame.
1180 the ſame.
1 the ſame.
2 the ſame.
3 the ſame.
4 the ſame.
5 the ſame.
6 the ſame.

Richard I.

7 William Fitz Stephen, William Marſhal, and John Avenel.
8 the three ſame.
9 the three ſame.
1190 William Marſhal, and John Muſgros.
1 the two ſame.
2 the two ſame.

A. D.

1193 Herbert Fitz Herbert.
4 the ſame.
5 the ſame, and William de Romen.
6 Herbert Fitz Herbert.

John.

7 William earl Marſhal, and John Avenel.
8 the ſame.
9 William Marſhall, and Thomas Rochford.
1200 the ſame.
1 the ſame.
2 William Marſhal, and Richard Haſelrue.
3 the ſame.
4 Richard Muſgroſs, and Reginald Patenolt.
5 the ſame.
6 Gerard de Alcia, and Richard Burgeis.
7 Engelrad de Cumat, and Richard Burgeis.
8 the ſame.
9 the ſame.
1210 the ſame.
1 the ſame.
2 the ſame.

Henry III.

3 Ralph Muſard,
4 the ſame.
5 the ſame.
6 the ſame.
7 the ſame.
8 Ralph Muſard, and Peter Edgward.
9 Ralph Muſard.
1220 the ſame.
1 the ſame.
2 William Putot.
3 the ſame.
4 the ſame.
5 the ſame.
6 the ſame.

A. D.

1227 the ſame.
8 the ſame.
9 Henry Bade.
1230 the ſame.
1 William Talbot, Peter de Edgward, and Thomas de St. Martin.
2 the three ſame.
3 William Talbot.
4 Thurſtan de Spencer.
5 the ſame.
6 John Fitz Jeffry, and Jeffry de Derehurſt.
7 John Fitz Jeffry, and Marſdat Canomwite.
8 John Fitz Jeffry.
9 the ſame.
1240 the ſame.
1 the ſame.
2 the ſame.
3 Robert de Waleran, and Jeffery de Derehurſt.
4 Robert de Waleran, and Nicholas de Montacute.
5 Robert de Waleran, and Reginald Acle.
6 Robert Waleran.
7 John de Fleming.
8 the ſame.
9 Adam de Hitteſtre.
1250 the ſame.
1 the ſame.
2 the ſame.
3 William de Laſborowe.
4 the ſame.
5 Robert de Mayſey.
6 John de Brun.
7 the ſame.
8 the ſame.
9 Matthew Werill.
1260 the ſame.
1 the ſame.
2 Reginald de Acle, Roger de Chedney, and Peter de Coventry.

A. D.
1263 the fame.
4 the fame.
5 the fame.
6 the fame.
7 the fame.

EDWARD I.

8 Peter de Chanett, and fir Walter Boking.
9 Reginald de Acle.
1270 Adam de Botiler.
1 the fame.
2 the fame.
3 the fame.
4 the fame.
5 Richard de la Riviere.
6 Walter de Steuckly.
7 the fame.
8 the fame.
9 the fame.
1280 Roger de Lackington.
1 the fame.
2 the fame.
3 Jeffry de Maudiacre.
4 the fame.
5 Fulk de Lacy.
6 the fame.
7 Fulk de Lacy, and Thomas de Gardins.
8 the fame.
9 the fame.
1290 the fame.
1 the fame.
2 the fame.
3 the fame.
4 John de Langley.
5 Richard Talbot.
6 the fame.
7 John de Newborough.
8 Thomas de Gardens.
9 the fame.
1300 the fame.
1 the fame.
2 the fame.

EDWARD II.

3 John de Langley.
4 Nicholas de Kingfton, and John de Amefly.
5 the fame.
6 John de Amefly, and John de Acton
7 the fame.
8 William Manfell, and Robert Darcy.
9 the fame.
1310 Richard de la Rivere.
1 the fame.
2 the fame.
3 the fame.
4 John de Hampton.
5 the fame.
6 the fame.
7 the fame.

A. D.
1318 the fame.
9 John de Sulanfell, and William Tracy.
1320 the fame.
1 the fame.

EDWARD III.

2 Thomas de Rodborow.
3 the fame.
4 the fame.
5 William Gamage, and Thomas de Rodborow.
6 Thomas de Berkeley.
7 the fame.
8 Richard Foxcott.
9 the fame.
1330 the fame.
1 the fame.
2 the fame.
3 Thomas Berkeley of Cubberly, and Richard Foxcott.
4 Thomas de Berkeley.
5 the fame.
6 Walter de Daftin.
7 Simon Baffet.
8 the fame.
9 the fame.
1340 the fame.
1 the fame.
2 the fame.
3 the fame.
4 the fame.
5 the fame.
6 Walter Daftin, and Phillebert Moreftel.
7 John de Wrefton.
8 William de la Dene.
9 the fame.
1350 Thomas Berkeley of Cubberley, and William de la Dene.
1 Thomas Berkeley of Cubberly.
2 Robert de Hildeflee.
3 the fame.
4 the fame.
5 the fame.
6 Thomas Moigne.
7 the fame.
8 the fame.
9 Thomas Tracy.
1360 the fame.
1 the fame.
2 the fame.
3 John Pointz.
4 the fame.
5 the fame.
6 John Tracy.
7 John de Clifford.
8 Thomas de Ocle.
9 John de Joce.
1370 Nicholas de Berkeley.

A. D.
1371 Peter de Veale.
2 John de Joce.
3 Peter Chament.
4 the fame.
5 the fame.
6 the fame.
7 the fame.

RICHARD II.

8 Thomas Bradwell.
9 John Tracy.
1380 Ralph Walledge.
1 Thomas Bradwell.
2 Sir John Thorp.
3 Thomas Fitz Nicholas.
4 Ralph Wallery.
5 Thomas Berkeley.
6 Thomas Bruges.
7 Thomas Bradwell.
8 Thomas Berkeley of Cubberly.
9 Lawrence Leabrook.
1390 Thomas Bruges.
1 Maurice de Kenfell.
2 Henry de la River.
3 John de Berkeley.
4 Gilbert Dennis.
5 William Tracy.
6 Maurice Ruffel.
7 Robert Pointz.
8 John Berkeley.
9 John Browning.

HENRY IV.

1400 Henry de la Riviere.
1 Maurice Ruffel, and Robert Somerville.
2 Robert Whittington.
3 Sir William Beauchamp.
4 the fame.
5 John Grinder.
6 Maurice Ruffel.
7 Robert Whittington.
8 Richard Mawarden.
9 Alexander Clivedon.
1410 William Wallwynne.
1 Sir John Grinder.

HENRY V.

2 William Beauchamp of Powick.
3 Sir John Berkeley.
4 John Greville.
5 the fame.
6 William Tracy.
7 Bifhop Stone.
8 John Bruges.
9 John Willecots.
1420 the fame.

HENRY VI.

1 John Pauncefoot.
2 John Blacket.
3 Stephen Haytfield.

1424

A. D.
1424 John Greville.
5 John Pauncefoot.
6 Guy Whittington.
7 Robert Andrew.
8 Giles Bruges.
9 Sir Maurice Berkeley.
1430 Stephen Haytefield.
1 John Stourton.
2 Guy Whittington.
3 John Pauncefoot.
4 Sir Maurice Berkeley.
5 the ſame.
6 John Beauchamp.
7 William Stafford.
8 Sir John Sturton.
9 the ſame.
1440 John Boteler.
1 Robert Leverſey.
2 William Tracy.
3 the ſame.
4 William Gifford.
5 John Boteler.
6 Henry Clifford.
7 John Try.
8 John Giſe.
9 William Tracy.
1450 James Clifford.
1 John de Veale.
2 Giles Bruges.
3 John Giſe.
4 Sir Walter Devereux.
5 Sir John Barre.
6 Sir Edward Hungerford.
7 Nicholas Latimore.
8 Thomas Hungerford.

EDWARD IV.

9 John Greville, eſq;
1460 Maurice Dennis.
1 the ſame.
2 Maurice Berkeley, eſq;
3 Edward Hungerford, eſq;
4 John Hungerford, eſq;
5 —— Henton.
6 Sir John Grevill.
7 Robert Pointz, eſq;
8 John Caſſey, eſq;
9 Sir Richard Beauchamp.
1470 the ſame.
1 Humphrey Foſter.
2 John Boteler, eſq;
3 Thomas Whittington.
4
5 Thomas Norton, eſq;
6 Thomas Baynham, eſq;
7 Edward Langley.
8 Walter Dennis.
9 Sir John Sanctloe.
1480 Robert Poyntz, eſq;

RICHARD III.

1 Sir Alexander Baynham.
2 John Huddleſton, eſq;

A. D.
1483 Sir William Berkeley, and Robert Poyntz.

HENRY VII.

4 Sir Robert Poyntz.
5 John Sanctloe.
6 John Walſh, eſq;
7 Thomas Mourton.
8 Chriſtopher Throgmorton.
9 Sir Thomas Hungerford.
1490 Richard Pool, eſq;
1 Sir Robert Poyntz.
2 Sir Walter Dennys.
3 Sir Edward Berkeley.
4 Sir Robert Poyntz.
5 Robert Whittington, eſq;
6 Richard Pool, eſq;
7 Alexander Baynham.
8 Sir Giles Bruges.
9 John Huddleſton.
1500 Sir Robert Poyntz.
1 Alexander Baynham.
2 the ſame.
3 Giles Greville.
4 John Boteler, eſq;
5 Edmund Tame, eſq;
6 John Pauncefoot, eſq;
7 Anthony Poyntz, eſq;

HENRY VIII.

8 Sir Maurice Berkeley.
9 Thomas Poyntz, eſq;
1510 Chriſtopher Baynham, eſq;
1 Sir Robert Moreton.
2 Sir William Tracy.
3 Sir William Kingſton.
4 Sir Maurice Berkeley.
5 Sir Alexander Baynham.
6 Sir Chriſtopher Baynham.
7 John Whittington.
8 Sir William Dennis.
9 Sir Giles Tame.
1520 Thomas Poyntz.
1 Sir Thomas Berkeley.
2 Sir Anthony Pointz.
3 Sir Edmond Tame.
4 Sir Edward Wadham.
5 Sir John Walſh.
6 Sir William Dennis.
7 Sir Anthony Poyntz.
8 William Throgmorton eſq;
9 Sir John Walſh.
1530 Sir Edward Wadham.
1 Walter Dennis, eſq;
2 Anthony Kingſton.
3 Sir Richard Ligon.
4 Sir John Walſh.
5 Sir John Sainctloe.
6 Sir Edward Tame.
7 Sir Walter Dennis.
8 Sir Nicholas Poyntz.
9 Sir John Walſh.
1540 Sir Edward Wadham.

A. D.
1541 Sir Edward Tame.
2 Walter Dennis.
3 Sir George Baynham.
4 Sir Nicholas Poyntz.
5 Nicholas Wickers.

EDWARD VI.

9 Sir Miles Patrick.
7 Arthur Porter, eſq;
8 Sir Thomas Bridges.
9 Sir Anthony Kingſton.
1550 Sir Walter Dennis.
1 Hugh Dennis, eſq;

PHILIP and MARY.

2 Anthony Hungerford.
3 Nicholas Hicks, eſq;
4 Sir Walter Dennis.
5 Nicholas Pauncefoot.
6 Richard Brayne, eſq;
7 Thomas Throgmorton eſq;

ELIZABETH.

8 Nicholas Arnold.
9 the ſame.
1560 Richard Tracy, eſq;
1 Nicholas Walſh, eſq;
2 William Read, eſq;
3 George Huntly, eſq;
4 Richard Berkeley, eſq;
5 Sir Giles Pool.
6 William Palmer.
7 John Hungerford.
8 Robert Brayne, eſq;
9 Sir Nicholas Poyntz.
1570 Richard Baynham, eſq;
1 Thomas Smith, eſq;
2 John Higford, eſq;
3 Robert Strainge, eſq;
4 Sir Thomas Porter.
5 Thomas Wye, eſq;
6 Walter Compton, eſq;
7 Thomas Cheſter.
8 John Tracy, eſq;
9 William Read, eſq;
1580 Richard Peate, eſq;
1 Sir Thomas Porter.
2 Thomas Baynham, eſq;
3 Thomas Smith, eſq;
4 Anthony Hungerford, eſq;
5 John Higford, eſq;
6 Paul Tracy, eſq;
7 Sir Thomas Throgmorton.
8 Sir Henry Poole.
9 Thomas Lucy, eſq;
1590 William Dutton, eſq;
1 Sir John Poyntz.
2 William Cheſter, eſq;
3 Sir John Danvers.
4 Joſeph Baynham, eſq;
5 Sir Henry Winſtone.
6 John Chamberlain, eſq;
7 Sir John Hungerford.
8 Sir Edward Wintour.

A. D.
1599 George Huntly, efq;
1600 Sir Thomas Throgmorton.
1 William Dutton efq;
2 Thomas Baynham, efq;

JAMES I.

3 Sir Henry Poole.
4 Giles Reade, efq;
5 Sir Thomas Staymer.
6 William Norwood, efq;
7 Sir Thomas Eftcourt.
8 Sir Thomas Woodroff, who dying in May, William Guife was fheriff the reft of that year.
9 Sir John Tracy.
1610 Paul Tracy, efq;
1 Robert Bathurft, efq;
2 John Carter, efq;
3 William Kingfton, efq;
4 Richard Brent, efq;
5 Henry Finch, efq;
6 Ralph Cotton, efq;
7 Thomas Chefter, efq;
8 Sir Richard Hill.
9 Philip Langley, efq;
1620 Sir Thomas Baker.
1 Sir Thomas Thynne.
2 Thomas Hodges, efq;
3 Sir Richard Rogers.
4 John Dowle, efq;

CHARLES I.

5 Sir William Sandys.
6 Thomas Nicholas.
7 Sir William Mafters.
8 Sir Richard Tracy, bart.
9 Henry Dennis, efq;
1630 Sir Ralph Dutton.
1 Sir George Wintour.
2 Henry Poole, efq;
3 Sir George Fettiplace.
4 Edward Stephens, efq;
5 William Leigh, efq;
6 Sir Richard Ducy, bart.
7 Sir Robert Poyntz.
8 John Codrington, efq;
9 Sir Humphry Tracy, bart.
1640 Robert Pleydell, efq;
1 Francis Crefwick, efq;
2 Sir Baynham Throgmorton, bart.
3 William Moreton, efq; for the king.
Thomas Stephens, efq; for the parliament.
4 Thomas Stephens efq;
5 John Fettiplace, efq;
6 William Brown, efq;
7 William Guife, efq;
8 John Browning, efq;

CHARLES II.

9 John Dennis, efq;
1650 John Howe, efq;
1 John Keyte, efq;
2 John Goflet, efq;
3 Richard Talboys, efq;
4 Simon Bennet, efq;
5 George Raymond, efq;
6 the fame.
7 John Barnerd, efq;
8 the fame.
9 the fame.
1660 Sir William Ducy, bart.
1 Sir Humphry Hooke.
2 Sir Thomas Eftcourt.
3 William Cook, efq;
4 Sir John Hanmer.

A. D.
1665 Sir Richard Cocks, bart.
6 Richard Whitmore, efq;
7 William Dutton, efq;
8 Sir Richard Afhfield, bart.
9 John Browning, efq;
1670 Sir Robert Canne, bart.
1 Sir Thomas Stephens.
2 Henry Dennis, efq;
3 John Dowle, efq;
4 Abraham Clark, efq;
5 Sir John Fuft, bart.
6 Sir William Juxton, bart.
7 Richard Jones, efq;
8 Miles Sandys, efq;
9 Thomas Smith, efq;
1680 Sir Gabriel Lowe.
1 William Wall, efq;
2 Robert Pleydel, efq;
3 Charles Jones, efq;

JAMES II.

4 Charles Hancox, efq;
5 Sir Charles Wintour.
6 Sir Thomas Canne.
7 Henry Benedict Hall, efq;

WILLIAM III.

8 Sir Hele Hook, bart.
9 William Dennis, efq;
1690 John de la Bere, efq;
1 Samuel Barker, efq;
2 Sir Richard Cocks, bart.
3 Thomas Stephens, efq;
4 Nathaniel Ridler, efq;
5 Sir George Hanger.
6 Walter Yate, efq;
7 John Marriot, efq;
8 Nathaniel Stephens, efq;
9 Thomas Chefter, efq;
1700 Richard Haynes, efq;
1 Samuel Eckley, efq;

ANNE.

2 Sir Samuel Eckley.
3 Sir Edward Fuft, bart.
4 William Hayward, efq;
5 Edmond Chamberlain, efq;
6 Matthew Ducy Moreton, efq;
7 Francis Wyndham, efq;
8 Henry Wagftaff, efq;
9 Henry Sackvile, efq;
1710 William Batfon, efq;
1 George Smith, efq;
2 Thomas Winftone, efq;
3 Lawford Cole, efq;

GEORGE I.

4 William Whittington, efq;
5 William Kingfcott, efq;
6 Abraham Elton, efq;
7 Edmund Bray, efq;
8 Sir Edward Fuft, bart.
9 Chriftopher Bond, efq;
1720 Edward Saunders, efq;
1 John Baker Dowell, efq;
2 William Blathwait, efq;
3 Thomas Warner, efq;
4 Samuel Roch, efq;
5 Windfor Sandys, jun. efq;
6 John Sampfon, efq;

GEORGE II.

7 Sir Robert Cann, bart.
8 Robert Cocks, efq;
9 Jofeph Small, efq;
1730 Samuel Sheppard, efq;
1 Samuel Mee, efq;

A. D.
1732 Robert Martin, efq;
3 Reginald Winyatt, efq;
4 Richard Marriett, efq;
5 Thomas Lingen, efq;
6 John Gladwin, efq;
7 William Robins, efq;
8 Ambrofe Baldwyn, efq;
9 William Giles, efq;
1740 Edward Rogers, efq;
1 William Holbrow, efq;
2 Samuel Hawker, efq;
3 William Tayloe, efq;
4 Thomas Snell, efq;
5 Daniel Adye, jun. efq;
6 William Baghott Delabere, efq;
7 John Harding, efq;
8 Robert Ball, efq;
9 Thomas Winftone, efq;
1750 Henry-Toy Bridgman, efq;
1 Richard Hill, efq;
2 John Beale, efq;
3 Thomas Kemble, efq;
4 Thomas Ingram, efq;
5 John Coffins, efq;
6 Charles Wyndham, efq;
7 William Mills, efq;
8 Thomas Jones, efq;
9 Samuel Hayward, efq;

GEORGE III.

1760 Onefiphorus Paul, efq;
1 John Delafield Phelps, efq;
2 Peter Hancock, efq;
3 Samuel Paul, efq;
4 Giles Nafh, efq;
5 Robert Dobyns Yate, efq;
6 William Dallaway, efq;
7 Edmund Probyn, efq;
8 John Guife, efq;
9 William Singleton, efq;
1770 George Smyth. efq;
1 Thomas Mafter, efq;
2 Edmund Waller, efq;
3 Jofeph Pyrke, efq;
4 Henry Wyatt, efq;
5 Sir George Smith, bart.
6 Henry Lippincott, efq;
7 William-Hayward Winftone, efq;
8 Edward Sampfon, efq;

N. B. The dates from 1701, reprefent the years of their office at Michaelmas, after their appointment.

Of

Of KNIGHTS of the SHIRE, ſent from this County to Parliament, from 1° E. 6. to the preſent Time; with a few previous Obſervations on our antient Parliaments.

TO trace out exactly the original of our parliament, and to obſerve the ſeveral alterations it hath undergone, 'till it came to be modelled as we now ſee it, is a work of the greateſt difficulty, owing to the deſtruction of our records in the Saxon and other wars.

The Anglo-Saxons brought with them many of the laws and cuſtoms of the antient German nations, with whom all the freeholders enjoy'd an equal right with the nobles, to aſſiſt in deliberations on affairs of great moment. And it is highly probable, from a paſſage in Matthew of Weſtminſter, that the people's right of appearing in parliament, was exerciſed originally by the whole body of freeholders, aſſembling together in open plains. "The meadow near Steins," ſays he, "in which the *Great Charter* was granted by "king John, had the name of Runemeed; which "in the Saxon language, ſignifies *the meadow of* "*counſel*, becauſe, from antient times, it had been "uſual to conſult there, upon buſineſs which con- "cerned the peace of the kingdom."

The preſence of the people in the Saxon councils, either in perſon, or by repreſentation, and their having had a ſhare in the higheſt acts of legiſlature and government, may be proved, in the ſtrongeſt manner, by the preamble to laws, and other proceedings of thoſe councils.

About the year 800, Egbert, king of the Weſt-Saxons, overpower'd the other kingdoms, and united them under one monarchy. Soon after, the lords of the leet, and the repreſentatives of towns, who were choſen by the burgeſſes, were ſummoned by the king, and appeared at the Witena gemot, which in the Saxon language, ſignifies the aſſembly of wiſe men, who met once a year at leaſt, and generally twice, about Eaſter and Michaelmas. *Wilkins LL. Sax.*

We are not told where this meeting was holden; but 'tis probable, that at this time the cuſtom of aſſembling in the open fields had been diſuſed; nor do we find an inſtance of its being ever revived, 'till that extraordinary meeting in the reign of king John; all the parliaments, or great councils, whereof we have any accounts before, having been held in churches, abbies, or royal caſtles; it ſhould ſeem therefore, that the freeholders muſt have exerciſed their right, not perſonally, as they did in more antient times, but by repreſentatives; for no building could be ſufficient to contain all the freeholders in the kingdom, even in thoſe times.

On long uſage the people's right of going to parliament ſeems to have been eſtabliſhed, before the conqueſt; and it appears to have been continued under William the Conqueror, with other cuſtoms and rights, confirmed by him to the nation; and under his ſucceſſors, by like ſanctions of antient liberties, granted in repeated royal charters. But of what orders of men the Engliſh parliament was compoſed, for ſeveral reigns immediately ſucceeding the conqueſt, is a queſtion much diſputed, and which can never, perhaps, be ſo abſolutely decided as to put an end to any difference of opinion about it; but happily the inquiry is rather matter of curioſity, than of real importance; becauſe the right of the commons to a ſhare of the legiſlature and national councils, even according to the hypotheſis of thoſe who are not moſt favourable to them, has antiquity enough to give it all the eſtabliſhment which can be derived from long cuſtom, and all the reverence and authority, which time and experience can add to the ſpeculative reaſon and fitneſs of wiſe inſtitutions.

We learn from Hoveden, that William the Firſt, after having compelled all the Engliſh, as well as Normans, to take out patents of their lands, to be holden of him by knight-ſervice, ſummoned the moſt eminent of thoſe feodaries called * barons, with perſons learned in the law, to ſit with him in the great council, particularly in the 4th year of his reign, which was that in which he firſt brought the biſhops and abbats under the tenure of barony. To this council, twelve were returned out of every county, who ſhewed what the cuſtoms of the kingdom were, which Aldred archbiſhop of York, and Hugh biſhop of London took down in writing; and they were confirmed in that aſſembly, which was a parliament of that time.

At the coronation of H. 1. *Clerus Angliæ, et populus univerſus*, the clergy and all the people of England, ſaith Matthew Paris, were ſummoned to Weſtminſter, where ſeveral laws were made and publiſhed. And in the ſecond year of king H. 5. the houſe of commons aſſert, in their petition to the king, *that it ever hath been their liberty and freedom, that there ſhould no ſtatute or law be made without their aſſent*; *and that they are, and ever*

* There is no colourable teſtimony in any record or law, that ſo much as ſeems to juſtify the common notion of 13⅓ knights fees held *in capite*, making a great barony; and of 20 making an earldom. In truth the contrary is very plain. Jeffery lord Talbot held 20 knights fees in chief, of H. 1. the ſame which Walter de Meduana held afterwards of H. 2. yet neither of theſe were ever accounted to have had earldoms. The ſame may be ſaid of John de Port, who had 57 knights fees, &c. and many others, as may be ſeen in the records of the exchequer, where are ſome who have had fewer than 13, and yet are equally barons with the reſt. *Selden's Tit. of Honour.*

have been, a member of the parliament; which claim was not disallowed either by the lords or the king.

We are assured by a record which Dr. Brady has cited, that so late as in the 15th year of king John, not only the greater barons, but all the inferior tenants, in chief, of the crown, had a right to be summoned to parliament by particular writs; but these were far from being all the freeholders in the kingdom. We are therefore to inquire whether at this time the rest were excluded from parliament, or were present there by any kind of representation.

Sir Henry Spelman, and some other learned writers, have supposed, that every superior lord who held of the king immediately, and in chief, being the head of his tenants, in all the degrees of sub-infeudation, whatever he agreed to in making of laws, bound all his vassals, he being as it were, their tribune or procurator; in like manner as the freeholders are now bound by the acts of the knights of the shire. But it is to be observed, that the knights, citizens and burgesses, who are now the representatives of the commons of England, are *elected* by those for whom they serve; all their power is derived to them from their electors, and on the calling of a new parliament, those electors are at liberty to make a new choice; whereas the superior lords were neither *elected*, nor liable to be *changed*, at any period of time, by those whom, according to Sir H. Spelman's hypothesis, they represented; and indeed it seems improper, and a force on the words, to call them *representatives*, or *procurators*.

But further, if the barons, and superior lords of great fiefs, holden immediately of the crown, had, by virtue of the institutions of William the First, been supposed to represent their vassals in parliaments; and the notion was then, that every feudatory, holding by a mesne tenure, was bound by the parliamentary acts of his lord; how came that notion to be discarded in the reigns of H. 3. Edw. 1. Edw. 3. &c. since it is certain, that a baron who held of the crown, was to all intents and purposes *the head of his vassals* in those reigns, as much as in any of the preceding ones? How happened it then, that the consent of the vassals to the making of laws in those reigns, was not still included in the vote of their lord? And why was it given, against the course of former proceedings, not by *him*, as *their representative*, but by knights of the shires, or by citizens, or by burgesses, chosen by the vassals?

Some learned men have asserted, that this change was brought about by the power of the earl of Leicester, 49° H. 3. But we have a record that demonstrates that date to be false. A writ of summons directed to the sheriffs of Bedfordshire and Buckinghamshire, requiring two knights to be sent for those counties, is extant in the close roll of 38° H. 3. And there is a clause in the Great Charter, of the 9th of the same king, whereby it is declared, that together with the spiritual and temporal lords, other inferior freeholders, *et omnes de regno*, by which words I understand *the whole commonalty of the realm*, granted to the king the fifteenth part of all their moveable goods, in return for the liberties accorded to them in that charter. Nor can I discover, in the history of those times, any reason sufficient to render it probable, that so great an alteration should then have been made in the constitution of England. But if it had been made, it must naturally have produced some disputes, which would have been taken notice of by some of the many historians who lived in that age, and who have left very large and particular accounts of less important transactions; whereas they are quite silent as to any disputes between the nobility and the people, on this account, from the earliest times of the Saxon government, down to the reign of Ch. 1. wherefore I think we may presume, that the right of the commons must have been incontestably established by custom, and interwoven into the original frame of our government; and that the antient parliaments, from the conquest down to H. 3. contained in them *the first elements* of those we have now; but were only a *rough draught*, in which regularity and decorum were absolutely wanting.

The clergy had formerly their particular representatives in parliament. There are not, indeed, any writs of summons now remaining, which require proctors to be sent for them to the parliaments of this kingdom, before 23° E. 1. but from the annals of Burton it appears, that the whole body of the clergy was so represented, 39° H. 3. And the commons, in a petition to the king, 21° R. 2. shew'd, *That before those times, many judgments and ordinances, made in the times of the progenitors of our lord the king, in parliament, had been repealed and disannulled, because the state of the clergy were not present in parliament, at the making of the said judgments and ordinances.*

Upon the reformation of religion, in the reign of E. 6. an attempt was made in convocation, to have the lower house united to the house of commons, according to antient custom, *Sicut ab antiquo fieri consuevit*. It was also proposed to queen Elizabeth, but rejected. The clergy continued to tax themselves, in a separate body, 'till the restoration of Ch. 2. soon after which they were taxed in the same manner, and conjointly with the rest of the commons; and have ever since been represented in parliament by the same persons; which has more embodied them with the laity, and prevents the setting up of a church interest, distinct from that of the people. It is remarkable, that this very important alteration in the state of this kingdom, was made *without any law*, by agreement with the clergy.

A LIST of the KNIGHTS of the SHIRE for this COUNTY.

Anno Reg.		*A. D.*		*N A M E S.*	
Edw. 6.	1,	1547,	at Weſtminſter,	Nicholas Pointz, knight,	— — — — — —
	7,	1552-3,	ſame place,	Anthony Kingſton, knight,	Nicholas Arnold, knight.
Mary	1,	1553,	ſame place,	Edward Bridges, knight,	Anthony Hungerford, knight
	1,	1554,	at Oxford, but adjourned to Weſtminſter.	Giles Poole, knight,	Nicholas Wykes, eſq;
P. & M.	1 & 2,	1554,	at Weſtminſter,	Arthur Porter, eſq;	William Reede, eſq;
	2 & 3,	1555,	ſame place,	Ant. Kingſton, knight,	Nicholas Arnold, knight.
	4 & 5,	1557,	ſame place,	Walter Dennys, knight,	Henry Jerningham, knight.
Eliz.	1,	1558-9,	ſame place,	Arthur Porter, eſq;	— — — — — —
	5,	1563,	ſame place,	Nicholas Walſhe, eſq;	Richard Dennys, eſq;
	13,	1571,	ſame place,	Giles Poole, knight,	Nicholas Pointz, knight.
	14,	1572,	ſame place,	Giles Bridges, eſq; Thomas Cheſter, eſq; in the room of Bridges, created lord Chandois.	Nicholas Arnold, knight.
	27,	1585,	ſame place,	John Darcy, knight,	William Bruges, eſq;
	28,	1586,	ſame place,	William Bridges, eſq;	William Wintour, knight.
	31,	1588,	ſame place,	Thomas Throckmorton, kt.	Edward Winter, knight.
	35,	1592,	ſame place,	Henry Poole, knight,	John Pointz, knight.
	39,	1596,	ſame place,	John Tracy, eſq;	John Hungerford, knight.
	43,	1601,	ſame place,	Edward Wintour, knight,	John Throckmorton, knight.
Jac.	1,	1603,	ſame place,	Thomas Berkley, knight,	Richard Berkley, kt.—In the room of ſir Thomas Berkley, John Throckmorton, eſq;
	12,	1614,	ſame place,	Richard Berkely, knight,	— — — — — —
	18,	1620,	ſame place,	Robert Tracy, knight,	Maurice Berkeley, eſq;
	21,	1623,	ſame place,	Maurice Berkley, knight,	John Dutton, eſq;
Car. 1.	1,	1625	at Weſtminſter and at Oxford,	Robert Tracy, knight,	Robert Pointz, knight.
	1,	1625,	at Weſtminſter,	Maurice Berkley, knight,	John Dutton, eſq;
	3,	1628,	ſame place,	Robert Pointz, knight,	Nathaniel Stevens, eſq;
	15,	1640,	ſame place,	Robert Tracy, knight,	Robert Cooke, knight.
	16,	1640,	ſame place,	John Dutton, eſq; John Seymer, knight.	Nathaniel Stevens, eſq;
		1653,	ſame place,	John Crofts, William Neaſt, and Robert Holmes.—— ☞ Oliver Cromwell convened this, which was called the Little Parliament, to which no repreſentatives for the cities or boroughs were ſummoned, except for the city of London. It was compoſed of a few members returned from the counties in general; and, meeting July 5, ſat 'till December 12, 1653.	
Common Wealth Parliaments.		1654,	ſame place,	George Berkley, eſq;—Matthew Hale, one of the juſtices of the common bench.—John How, eſq;—Chriſtopher Guiſe, eſq;—Sylvanus Wood, eſq;—*N. B.* To this parliament Yorkſhire returned 13, Eſſex 12, Kent 11, Norfolk 10, and other counties more than their proportion, whilſt many cities and boroughs ſent but one each. Scotland ſent 21, Ireland 30.	
		1656,	ſame place,	George Berkley, eſq;—John Howe, eſq;—John Crofts, eſq; Baynham Throckmorton, eſq;—William Neaſt, eſq; *N. B.* Scotland ſent 28, Ireland 30.	
		1658,	ſame place,	John Grubham Howe, eſq;—John Crofts, eſq;—Baynham Throckmorton, eſq;	
		1658-9,	ſame place,	John Grubham Howe, eſq;—John Stephens, eſq;—*N. B.* At this parliament the counties and boroughs ſent the uſual numbers.—Scotland 21, Ireland 30.	

Reign	Year		Place		
The Convention Parliament.———				Baynham Throckmorton,	John Howe.
		1661,	at Weſtminſter,	The ſame,	The ſame.
		1678,	ſame place,	Sir John Guiſe,	Sir Ralph Dutton.
		1680,	ſame place,	The ſame,	The ſame.
		1680,	at Oxford,	The ſame,	The ſame.
Jac. 2.	1,	1685,	at Weſtminſter,	Charles Somerſet,	Sir Robert Atkyns.
	4,	1688,	ſame place,	Sir John Guiſe,	Sir Ralph Dutton.
W. & M.	1,	1689,	ſame place,	The ſame,	The ſame.
	7,	1695,	ſame place,	The ſame,	The ſame.
	10,	1698,	ſame place,	John Howe,	Richard Cocks.
	12,	1700,	ſame place,	The ſame,	The ſame.
	13,	1701,	ſame place,	Richard Cocks,	Maynard Colcheſter.
Anne,	1,	1702,	ſame place,	John Howe,	The ſame.
	3,	1705,	ſame place,	Sir John Guiſe,	The ſame.
	5,	1707,	ſame place,	The ſame,	The ſame.
	6,	1708,	ſame place,	The ſame,	Matthew Ducie Moreton.
	8,	1710,	ſame place,	John Berkeley,	The ſame.
	11,	1713,	ſame place,	The ſame,	Thomas Stephens.
Geo. 1.	1,	1714,	ſame place,	Matthew Ducie Moreton,	Thomas Stephens, who dying, in his place was choſen Henry Berkeley.
	9,	1722,	ſame place,	Henry Berkeley,	Kinnard De La Bere.
Geo. 2.	1,	1727,	ſame place,	The ſame,	Sir John Dutton.
	8,	1734,	ſame place,	Hon. Benjamin Bathurſt,	Thomas Cheſter.
	15,	1741,	ſame place,	Thomas Cheſter,	Norborne Berkeley.
	21,	1747,	ſame place,	The ſame,	The ſame.
	28,	1754,	ſame place,	The ſame,	The ſame.
Geo. 3.	1,	1761,	ſame place,	The ſame,	The ſame; but Norborne Berkeley being made a peer, there was elected in his ſtead———Thomas Tracy.
	8,	1768,	ſame place,	Edward Southwell,	Thomas Tracy, who dying in 1770, there was elected—Sir William Guiſe, baronet.
	14,	1774,	ſame place,	Sir William Guiſe,	Edward Southwell, on whoſe advancement to the barony of Clifford, in 1776, there was choſen in his ſtead—William-Bromley Cheſter.

The knights of the ſhire were formerly paid 4 *ſol.* and the citizens and burgeſſes 2 *ſol. per diem* each, for their attendance on the public buſineſs, which many of the boroughs thinking too great an expence for them to bear, got themſelves exempted.

In antient times, all mitred abbats ſat in the great council. In the 49° H. 3. 102 abbats and priors were ſummoned to parliament, and only 25 lay barons. 1° E. 2. 56 abbats and priors were ſummoned; but 4° E. 3. there were only 33, and in the reigns preceding the diſſolution of monaſteries, no more than 27 abbats and priors ſat in parliament; which ſhews the gradual decline of the power of the clergy.

When the commons formerly went to conſult by themſelves, upon any buſineſs of great moment, they returned their anſwer by a member of their own, whom they choſe upon that particular occaſion. Their firſt ſtanding ſpeaker was Sir Thomas Hungerford, 51° E. 3.

Sir Edward Coke, 4 Inſt. p. 2. ſays, "of antient "time both Houſes ſat together;" which is a miſtake he was led into by a miſtranſlation of the French word *grants*, in Sir Robert Cotton's Abridgment of the parliamentary rolls in the Tower, which he has rendered *commons*, whereas it ſignifies *great men*.

In Sir Robert Atkyns's *Ancient and Preſent State of Gloſterſhire*, p. 19, is the following obſervable paſſage, concerning the Britiſh parliament:

" The ambition of prieſts has aboliſhed the like
" conſtitution in Italy; the mutual wars betwixt
" contending princes have extinguiſh'd it in Ger-
" many; the pride of monarchs has deſtroy'd it
" in Spain; differences in religion have laid it
" aſide in France; the arrogancy of the lords has
" ſubverted it in Denmark; the madneſs of the
" commons has ruined it in Sweden; and the
" barbarity of the Muſcovites has not admitted
" it in Ruſſia*; but curſt be the man who ſhall
" attempt to undermine this happy conſtitution
" of Great Britain."

This ſentence diſcovers the goodneſs of the author's heart; I approve his patriotiſm, but can- not

* It has been the ſingular fortune and wiſdom of England, ſays lord Lyttleton, that whereas France, Spain, and other realms, in which much the ſame feudal policy had taken place, have, thro' an impatience of the oppreſſions which the people often ſuffered from the nobility, deſperately run into abſolute monarchy, or have been compelled to yield to it by force of arms; in the change which has gradually happened in ours, all that exceſs of power which the nobles have loſt, has been ſo divided between the crown and the commons, that the whole ſtate of the kingdom is much better poiſed, and all incroachments of any one part on the other are more effectually reſtrained. *Life of Henry II.*

not altogether ſubſcribe to his politicks; for in the ſame page he propoſes a plan, that in all probability, would ſoon ſubvert that very conſtitution he ſo ardently wiſhes to have preſerved. "Perhaps" ſays he, "it might be a good expedient, in Utopia, that ſenators ſhould hold their places for life, and their eſtates ſhould conſiſt of 500*l.* a year, which ought to undergo a ſtrict examination. If their members by theſe means ſhould be thought too many or two few, this might be regulated by fixing an age, either thirty or forty years old.—Theſe perſons would be above temptations, and all debauchery and animoſity in elections would be prevented; they would then be a venerable aſſembly of wealthy citizens."

I agree with the learned hiſtorian, that perſons of independent fortune are certainly the propereſt to repreſent the people. Such will probably be moſt careful of the public treaſure, who have contributed largely to the ſtock themſelves; but on the other hand, the hiſtory of the preſent age will furniſh inſtances of men whom no fortune will ſatisfy, and whoſe avaritious diſpoſitions will always expoſe them to temptations.

I am a declared enemy to riot and debauchery, but the expedient propoſed to prevent them, I fear, would be attended with greater inconveniencies. We have found, by dreadful experience, that in long parliaments, thoſe who at their firſt election were truly the repreſentatives of the people, become, in time, a cabal of men, that purſue their own intereſts more than the public ſervice.

Tho' ſome inconveniences attend elections, eſpecially in the preſent mode of conducting them, it is their frequency by which the good people of England hope to preſerve their liberties, and the conſtitution; for by how much the oftener elections recur, by ſo much the more dependant on the people will their repreſentatives be, as the conſtituents will not probably make thoſe the objects of their *ſecond* choice, whoſe former conduct they have diſapproved. I ſpeak now of counties, and of thoſe cities and boroughs only, which have too many voters to be purchaſed, if any ſuch there be: for corruption hath ſo univerſally ſpread her baleful influence through the petty ones, that I cannot ſuppoſe *ſuch* to be in the leaſt attentive to the conduct of *their* repreſentatives, who never made their characters, when candidates, the ſubject of inquiry among them; and to whom their perſons and very names have been totally unknown, 'till perhaps the day before polling.

If I have digreſſed from my ſubject, I have taken no greater liberty than the gentleman whoſe notions I have oppoſed, becauſe I think him miſtaken in a matter very eſſential to the good of my country.

Of the COUNTY INFIRMARY.

ABOUT the year 1756, a ſubſcription was opened for eſtabliſhing a county infirmary, which was filled with great ſucceſs, under the auſpices of Norborne Berkeley, eſq; now lord Botetourt, and the Honourable and Reverend Dr. Talbot, who contributed to this noble charity in a meaſure adequate to their great generoſity, and public ſpirit.

A large ſum of money being raiſed, and a piece of ground purchaſed in the ſouth-gate ſtreet, in the city of Glouceſter, a very handſome and commodious building was erected for the purpoſe, and patients were admitted as ſoon as it could be got ready for their reception, which was in the year 175 . But the charity was extended to proper objects long before this houſe was built; for the governors purchaſed the Crown-and-Sceptre, a large inn, in the Weſtgate-ſtreet, and fitted it up for the reception of patients, 'till the contributions were ſufficient for building the preſent infirmary, towards which his late majeſty granted 9,200 feet of timber, out of the foreſt of Dean. The building coſt 6,200*l.*

This extenſive charity is ſupported by annual ſubſcriptions, amounting to 997*l.* 10*s.* 6*d* in the year 1767; and by the intereſt of near 12,000*l*, placed out on government and land ſecurities. It is managed by a ſociety, called the governors of the infirmary, who have eſtabliſhed rules, by which the whole is orderly and prudently conducted.

All ſubſcribers of two guineas a year, or contributors of 20*l.* or more, at one time, are governors, and may attend and vote at the meetings.

Every ſubſcriber hath a right to recommend one in-patient, and one out-patient, every year, for each guinea *per ann.* ſubſcribed and paid, provided the in-patients do not exceed five. A benefactor of 50*l.* hath the privilege of a ſubſcriber of five guineas; of 20*l.* that of two guineas *per annum.* But no ſubſcriber can have more than one in-patient at a time; nor can a benefactor of leſs than 20*l.* at one time, recommend a patient. Only ſuch as are recommended by a ſubſcriber, or benefactor, and appear to the weekly board and receiving phyſician and ſurgeon to be curable, and real objects of charity, to be admitted, and that on Thurſdays only; except in ſuch caſes as will admit of no delay.

If at any time, more ſhould be recommended than there is room for, in caſes of equal exigence the preference

preference is given, firſt, to thoſe that come from the greateſt diſtance; ſecondly, to the recommendation of ſuch ſubſcribers as have not ſent any in-patient, within the year of their ſubſcription; thirdly, to the recommendation of the greateſt ſubſcribers to the charity.

Proper objects excluded at any time for want of room, are entered in the books as in-patients, and received by the matron, without order, on the firſt vacancy. And perſons recommended according to the rules, are received into this infirmary, from any country or nation.

Whilſt we admire the truly chriſtian charity of thoſe gentlemen who were moſt active in promoting this eſtabliſhment, we cannot too much applaud the beneficence of all that contribute to ſupport it.

Of the TRADE, MANUFACTURES, &c. of the COUNTY.

NOTWITHSTANDING the port of Glouceſter is furniſhed, by the favour of queen Elizabeth, with proper cuſtom-houſe officers, very few foreign entries are made there. Yet, if we import but little goods, this county ſupplies large quantities for exportation, part of which is the produce of the ſoil, and part the manufacture of the induſtrious inhabitants.

The manufactures are woollen cloths of various ſorts, harrateens, chenies, cotton and worſted ſtockings, carpets, blankets, rugs, men's hats, leather, pins, paper, bar-iron, edge-tools, nails, wire, tinned plates, braſs, &c. Of the growth of the county, the principal articles of commerce are, cheeſe and bacon, cyder and perry, fiſh, &c.

I ſhall firſt ſpeak of the cloathing manufacture, as it has a juſt claim to the preference on every account. It is probable that the colony of Flemings, who came into this kingdom in the reign of William the Conqeror, might bring with them the art of making woollen cloth, which their countrymen excelled in, and that in proceſs of time the Engliſh learnt it of them; for the records ſhew, that payments were made by various gilds of weavers in many parts of the kingdom, for the farm of their gilds, in the reign of Henry the Second, and Richard the Firſt; when, according to the learned Sir Matthew Hale, *this kingdom greatly flouriſhed in the art of manufacturing woollen cloth: but by the troubleſome wars in the time of king John and Henry the Third, and alſo of Edward the Firſt and Edward the Second, this manufacture was wholly loſt, and all our trade ran out in wool, woolfels, and leather, carried out in ſpecie.* It is alſo obſerved by Mr. Madox, in his Hiſtory of the Exchequer, that the cities of Worceſter, Glouceſter, Nottingham, Norwich, Bedford, and many other towns, paid fines to king John, *that they might buy and ſell dyed cloth, as they were accuſtomed to do in the time of king Henry the Second.* This ſhews, that both the cloathing and dying trades had then flouriſhed, and had been free from ſome oppreſſions with which they were afterwards loaded.

Many centuries ago, the city of Glouceſter was famous for its cloth manufacture, where Brookſtreet, ſituated upon Fullbrook, was the place of habitation for clothiers, dyers and ſhearmen; and even as lately as 1629, there was a company of clothiers in that city. It was conſiderable at Cirenceſter, in the reign of king H. 4. who granted a charter to a company of weavers there, which ſtill ſubſiſts. It has flouriſhed alſo at different times in various other parts of the county. But nature pointing out the moſt convenient ſituation for carrying on this manufacture, which requires plenty of water for driving the fulling mills, and ſcouring of wool; it has long ſince ſeated itſelf principally on the borders of the little rivers and brooks in the pariſhes of Biſley, Hampton, Stroud, Painſwick, Woodcheſter, Horſley, Stonehouſe, Stanley, Uley, Durſley, Wottonunderedge, and neighbouring places of leſs note. 'Tis there the maſter clothiers live, and the moſt curious operations of the manufacture are performed under their immediate inſpection; but the women and children all over the country are chiefly employ'd in carding of wool, and ſpinning of yarn; nor is the Glouceſterſhire cloathing bounded by the limits of the county, if it be allowable in point of language to ſay, that it furniſhes employment for great numbers of hands, from the borders of Wiltſhire to the edge of Saliſbury plain.

The manufacture has been gradually advancing in this county during the laſt century, but by very unequal ſteps, for it is ſenſibly affected by the ſituation of our public affairs. In time of war, there is an extraordinary demand for cloathing the army; and if it be with the French, who are our great rivals in this trade, it is an additional circumſtance in its favour, as they have uſually at ſuch time been much interrupted by our ſuperior fleets, in the conveyance of their goods to market: and then alſo the great internal enemies of our country, the ſmugglers and owlers of wool, find it it very hazardous to help our neighbours to that commodity, without which they could not ſucceed ſo well in the woollen † manufacture.

To enable the reader to judge of what importance this manufacture is to the nation, I have procured from ſome of the moſt intelligent clothiers, perſons of acknowledged judgment and integrity, the various particulars which, taken together, make the following account of the preſent ſtate of it. I ſhall conſider it under four heads, 1. The country trade, or inland trade. 2. The army trade, and that with the drapers in London. 3. The Turkey trade. 4. The Eaſt India company trade.

1. The inland trade, in the language of the manufacturer, muſt not be ſtrictly taken, as if confined to our own kingdom, for that is not the fact. It may be ſo called from its furniſhing the ſorts of cloth uſually worn in our own country, conſiſting of ſuperfines, ſeconds, foreſts, drabs, naps, duffils, and all that variety to be found in a well ſtored draper's ſhop.

This trade is governed by faſhion and fancy, and has been introduced into Glouceſterſhire within the laſt fifty or ſixty years. Great part of the goods are diſperſed by means of travelling thro' Great Britain and Ireland, by the manufacturers themſelves, or their ſervants. Many of them are likewiſe ſold to merchants, who ſend them to our colonies, and other foreign markets; and ſome go to the warehouſes in London, from whence they are diſperſed in like manner.

This branch has been ſupported with ſuch ſpirit and induſtry, as from ſmall beginnings to become very valuable.—Being leſs ſubject to fluctuation than the other branches, it employs more regularly and uniformly a number of hands, perhaps the moſt of any of them. Many perſons have ſucceeded in it, and ſome large fortunes have been made; but at preſent, thro' the dearneſs of proviſions, the diſagreement with our colonies, and other diſcouraging circumſtances, common to moſt trades at this time, 'tis in a languid condition, tho' the returns in it are eſtimated at 250,000 *l. per ann.*

2. The ſecond branch is the trade with the drapers in London, who take a variety of goods for their retail cuſtomers; and the cloth for the army, the marines and the militia paſſes thro' their hands. The demands in this part of the cloathing trade at different times is very diſproportionate. In time of war 'tis great; but not very conſiderable at preſent, the ſhare which this county has of it being eſtimated at 100,000 *l. per annum.*

3. The third branch is the trade to Turkey, which is much declined. The French, by reaſon of their political connections with the Porte, the ſituation of their country, the price of labour, and their method of conducting their trade, have gained a great ſuperiority over us at this market. But I am told that our ſuperfines ſtill ſupport their credit there, and that the ſhare of this country in the Turkey trade cannot be leſs than 50,000 *l. per annum.*

4. The cloth made for the Eaſt India company, is the laſt and moſt conſiderable branch of our foreign trade, yet from the preſent method of conducting it, 'tis far from being advantageous to the clothier. Very few perſons have ſucceeded in the coarſe trade, whilſt many, labouring all their time with great care and aſſiduity, have ruined their fortunes, without making a bad debt in it. In ſhort, there are not wanting perſons of obſervation, knowledge and integrity, who are confidently of opinion, that, averaging the profit and loſs on all the coarſe cloth, ſold to the company, for many years back, by the clothiers in this county, not a ſhilling has been gained by it.

This will ſeem ſtill more unaccountable to the reader, when he is informed, that the company never require of the clothier any abatement of price, nor doth it appear that they wiſh to withold from him, that reaſonable profit which ſhould be the reward of his ſkill and induſtry. This is a kind of paradox, which I ſhall endeavour to explain, as things have been often repreſented to me.

Firſt it ſhould be obſerved, that the buſineſs of the ſales to the company, is tranſacted by the Blackwell-hall factors, who are the clothiers agents; and the courſe cloth, which is by much the largeſt quantity, lies in the hands of a few, not more than four or five of them. The ſales are conducted in the following manner.

The company having given the factors previous notice of the time appointed for buying, they ſend in ſample cloths for the inſpection of the buying committee, with the prices, and number of cloths they have to ſell, correſponding with the reſpective ſamples. In buying, the company's ſervants impartially chooſe the beſt ſamples, according to the prices, 'till their quantity is ſupplied; and if ſuch as are deemed equal in quality and price ſhould amount to more than are wanted, they have lately taken a part of each lot, in order that every clothier might benefit by the ſale. Theſe meaſures are ſo prudent and equitable, that I have never heard any perſon object to them.

Let us now turn to the factor, and upon inquiry, inſtead of finding him a mere agent to the clothier, which he originally was, and ſtill ought to be, it will appear that he is now, by inſenſible degrees, become a very different kind of perſon; for the commiſſion on the ſales being great in proportion to the value of the goods, and the buſineſs attended with little trouble, he hath found out an expedient to eſtabliſh himſelf on a firmer foundation than the mere good opinion of the clothier; which was all, according to the original inſtitution, he had to depend on. By this expedient he hath virtually, in many inſtances, the power of the

† It is the common notion that all ſorts of wool are ſmuggled to France; but I have been informed that it is principally, if not ſolely, the long wool, for making of worſted ſtuffs. The French, beſides what is grown in their own country, are ſupply'd with the coarſe cloathing wool from Barbary.

principal, yet ftill preferves the appearance, the indemnity, and every other advantage of the agent. 'Tis thus: He feeks out perfons of little or no fortune; fome who have been fervants to clothiers, and may have worked at particular branches of the manufacture; others who underftand no branch of it. To fuch as thefe he lends money at common intereft, to make cloth for his warehoufe: And it can be no wonder, furely, if many embrace the offer, from a poffibility of gaining fomething by it.

By thefe means it may be conceived, that goods are too often ill made, to the difcredit of the manufacture; however, if they fell at any rate, the factor is not affected by abatements on them, his commiffion arifing from the *number* of cloths fold, without regard to the value of them. This being the cafe, 'tis the factor's bufinefs to bring large quantities of goods to market; and when there, the clothier is often induced, by fpecious arguments, to offer his goods at a lower rate than he can afford them, occafioned by the factor's endeavouring to appear at the fale to a greater advantage than his rivals in the fame bufinefs.

In order to this, as the fales approach, would it be matter of wonder, if the dependent clothiers in the country fhould be advifed of the general apprehenfion of a dull fale, on account of a great quantity of cloth in town; and with the report that the company will buy but little? The inference is eafy, *i. e.* that unlefs the goods are offered at a very low price, they can have no chance of being fold for that feafon. It fhould be obferved, that they are fit for no other market, and at *this* there is but one buyer.

Notwithftanding all this, fome manufacturers might be difpofed to wait an opportunity 'till they could fell their goods for a reafonable profit; but when a man, confiderably indebted, receives information that the money advanced in his favour will be fhortly wanted, he begins to be convinced that he is not abfolutely his own mafter, and finds himfelf under a neceffity of fubmitting to difagreeable terms.

Thus it happens, that cloths of eight or nine pounds value, are frequently offer'd at thirty or forty fhillings lefs than they coft the maker; and tho' not always fo, yet the many difadvantages and expences confider'd, fuch as fhort fales, a glutted market, occafioned by fetting up, and pufhing on fo many people in the trade; the lofs on returned goods fpoilt in the hurry of making; intereft of money, warehoufeage, * commiffion, &c. &c. it is not doubted, by fuch as beft underftand this branch of the manufacture, but that during the laft ten years, the Gloucefterfhire clothiers have been lofers upon an average.

Let us confider this matter a little further. In this inverted order of things, when the clothier becomes the factor's fervant, he fends his cloth as faft as 'tis made to the factor, to be a collateral fecurity for the money borrowed of him; with whom it remains 'till the fales begin. At firft the new adventurer is enabled to pay his creditors in the country, by draughts on the factor, in virtue of which he foon gets in debt, and enlarges his trade upon his credit with the woolftapler and yarnmaker; proceeding (as is too often the cafe) from time to time, 'till he has wormed himfelf fo deeply in their books, as to be unable to make good his payments. For having, to the factor's knowledge, been lofing confiderably in the courfe of trade, his draughts are no longer honoured, than the goods remitted to the factor are ample fecurity for them; who, knowing the fituation of this fort of people much better than any other perfon, generally takes care to abandon them when they appear to be no longer in a condition to ferve his purpofe.

Hitherto I have been fpeaking of the neceffitous clothier only; but what is the cafe of the man of capital in this branch?—After a moment's confideration will it not appear, that if others offer great quantities of goods at under rates, he will alfo be obliged to fell at the fame prices, if he fell at all. Befides, let it be confider'd, that if the factor hath it in his power to prefer one perfon before another, as no doubt in fome cafes it may be poffible, will not his intereft direct him to promote the manufacture where his money is employ'd at five *per cent.* and from which he may derive other confiderable advantages? Therefore many clothiers of property have declined the company trade, and ftruck into other employments. Some of them who continue ftill engaged in it, are convinced by experience, that unlefs fome regulations take place, it will never anfwer, tho' the returns in it are very confiderable, eftimated, for this county only, at 200,000 *l. per annum.*

Thus, if I am rightly informed, has the clothier in the courfe branch of the company trade, which is by much the greateft part of it, the trouble and hazard of a large bufinefs, without a reafonable advantage from it. The poor indeed have hitherto been employ'd by fits, but how long this branch may furnifh any work for them, when the manufacturer has no reafonable profpect of advantage to himfelf, I will not take upon me to determine.

Cloathing is the great manufacture of the nation, and that branch of it which *cet. par.* keeps the labouring hands moft conftantly employ'd, is certainly the moft valuable. But the meafures complained of render it unfteady, languid and convulfive. For a confiderable time back, we have had two or three bankrupt clothiers within the year, for many thoufands each, which without fuch connexions with the factors could never have happened, as few, if any of them, had ever been worth a fhilling. If one of them die, or break, which cafes differ but little in confequence,

* The commiffion on a cloth of 6*l.* or 7*l.* value is 5*s.* befides 6*d.* for drawing, and 6*d.* for cafh-money, which laft I don't well underftand.

the

the factor ſeizes the cloth in his hands unſold, and the debts outſtanding, to ſecure himſelf, leaving the woolſtapler, yarnmaker, ſhopkeeper, poor workmen, and other creditors in the country, to divide four, five, or perhaps two ſhillings in the pound, and ſometimes leſs.—A long train of dreadful conſequences always follow: Many of the creditors are greatly injured in their fortunes, ſome utterly ruined. The poor, who ſeldom ſave a penny in times of the greateſt plenty of work and proviſions, being out of employment, are reduced to the pariſh, to beggary, and ſome of them expoſed to famine itſelf.

Theſe evils which are growing, for bankruptcies are more and more frequent, ſeem to ariſe chiefly from the too great ſecurity of the factor, who, in caſes of failure, claims all the bankrupt's goods remaining in his cuſtody, and all debts upon contracts by him made, to indemnify himſelf, not for his commiſſion only, but for all monies advanced on intereſt to the clothier.

I have never been made ſenſible, by any good argument, why the factor ſhould be ſo highly privileged over other creditors. On the contrary, I apprehend it has a manifeſt tendency to diſcredit the manufacture, to advance the raw materials, to beggar middling tradeſmen; but to inrich, (beſides about half a dozen individuals) the moſt opulent trading company on earth; who ought, and 'tis probable would be willing, to give a fair price for the manufacture of their country.—If the factor was made equally liable to loſſes with other creditors, he would be more cautious to whom he lent his money, and it might prevent the ruin of numbers that are decoy'd, by ſpecious appearances, to credit thoſe that trade, or rather trifle with it. This is a matter that calls loudly for redreſs, which might probably be obtained; but many of the clothiers are ſo intirely in the power of the factors, as to make it unſafe for them to apply for it.

Thus, free from the leaſt intention of injuring any perſon, in eſtate or reputation; and without either an apprehenſion of offending, or the hope of pleaſing, any man, or ſett of men whatever, I have given the ſtate of the company trade, as fairly and impartially as poſſible, agreeably to the information received from ſeveral perſons of credit, who underſtand the ſubject, and will vouch for the facts. I am willing to believe, notwithſtanding, that there may be ſome inſtances of exception, among the body of people whoſe conduct is reprehended.—That regard to truth which I profeſs, and that juſtice which is equally due to all, will have it acknowleged, that there are at this time a few clothiers, who were ſet up by the factors, as already mentioned, that, either from their ſuperior ſkill, great application, or ſome other cauſe, too latent for me to diſcover, have flouriſhed in the trade, and continue to carry on buſineſs with credit and reputation.

The iron manufacture is of the next greateſt conſequence to this county. In the foreſt of Dean are ſeveral furnaces and forges, that afford employment for great numbers of miners, colliers, carriers, and other labourers. *See Foreſt, p.* 35.——At Froombridge, in the pariſh of Frampton upon Severn, has lately been erected one of the largeſt and completeſt works of the kind in the kingdom, conſiſting of a ſet of mills for making of iron and ſteel wire. And at Framilode is a tin-plate work, carried on by the ſame proprietors.

There are two very large braſs-works in this county; one at the Baptiſt-mills, near Briſtol, the other at Warmley, in the pariſh of Bitton. They are both carried on in company, by perſons of large fortune, and vaſt ſums are employ'd in the trade.

At Glouceſter is a valuable pin-manufacture, which employs great numbers of the women and children, and beſides a large country trade, returns near 20,000*l.* from London yearly.

The making of cards, for the uſe of the clothier, has ſeated itſelf at Durſley, Stroud, and Wottonunderedge.

Scarlet-dying is ſcarcely any where done in that perfection as about Stroud.

Worſted combing is carried on at Glouceſter, Cirenceſter, Tewkeſbury, and Tetbury. The markets for the goods are Kidderminſter, Andover, and Leiceſter, where they are manufactured into ſhalloons, ſtuffs, ſtockings, &c.

Stocking-frame knitting is found at Cirenceſter, Tewkeſbury, Newent, and a few villages in that neighbourhood.

Carpet-weaving has been lately brought into Cirenceſter, by two perſons, who make all the various ſizes and patterns, with good ſucceſs.

The heavy edge-tools, made at Cirenceſter, are in great reputation. Two families have enjoy'd one branch of that buſineſs for ſome time unrivalled throughout the world, at leaſt they know nothing to the contrary. It is that of making knives for curriers to ſhave the leather with, which the people of Birmingham have attempted in vain.

Harrateens, cheneys, and a few other woollen-ſtuffs are made at Cirenceſter, and ſent white to London.

Fine writing paper is made at Poſtlip, in the pariſh of Winchcombe, at Quenington, and at Abbenhall; and brown ſorts at a few other places in the county.

The manufacture of felt-hats, at Frampton Cotterel, deſerves a place in our account, becauſe it employs ſo many hands. Neither would it be juſt to paſs by, unnoticed, the rug and blanket manufactures, at Nailſworth, Durſley, Nibley, and other places of the clothing country, with which I ſhall cloſe this ſhort account of the Glouceſterſhire manufactures. Woolſtapling, or breaking of wool, is not mentioned in the number, becauſe it will hardly be admitted to be one, in the common acceptation of the word, tho' it is a very conſiderable trade; and the moſt eminent places

for

for it are Gloucester, Cirencester, and Tetbury. To be so particular as to enumerate every trade carried on in the county, would be impertinent, but I think I have omitted no manufacture that deserves notice.

The chief article of our produce is grain, of which large quantities are raised in the vale, and on the coteswolds. The city of Bristol is supply'd out of Gloucestershire with great part of its provisions, from whence it has been concluded, that this county grows a great quantity of corn more than it consumes. But if it be considered, what a vast consumption there is of every kind in the manufacturing and populous parts of the county; and that the meal-men and corn-dealers are continually supplying the markets in the south-eastern parts, with grain and flour, out of Oxfordshire and Berkshire, and that in common years a great quantity of corn is brought to Gloucester market from Herefordshire, in waggons, as well as by water from Upton upon Severn; there is good reason to believe that the corn of the growth of this county is not more than sufficient for its inhabitants; so that grain will not be an article in our account.

The quantity of cheese made in the county is calculated in the following manner: The vale is estimated at 500,000 acres, allowing for the Severn, &c. 350,000 of them are in pasture, of which admit 158,000 acres to be fed by milch cattle. Then at three acres to each cow, the stock will be 50,000. The most usual calculation is 3 C. weight of cheese to a cow, according to which the sum of the whole year's making, in the vale, will be 7,500 tons. But there are milch beasts kept in the other parts of the county. If you allow 20 to every 3000 acres, upon an average; then on 500,000 acres will be found 3333 milch cattle, from which, according to the above proportion, may be made about 500 tons of cheese: And together, the year's making will be 8,000 tons for the whole county.

For the three or four last years, cheese upon an average has sold at about 28 *l. per* ton; therefore the value of the whole will be 224,000 *l.* The greatest part of it is sent by the factors to London; a considerable quantity of it goes to Bristol, and to the fairs at Gloucester, Stow, Leachlade, &c. and so is dispersed thro' the country.

Gloucestershire bacon is in good repute; London and Bristol take large quantities of it annually.

Cyder is another article, of which we make more than we consume ourselves, to the amount, perhaps in a good year, of about 5,000 *l.*

Salmon is the only kind of fish that is sent from hence to London in any quantities, for which the metropholis pays us about 4,000 *l.* annually.

The value of fat cattle fed in the county, with their skins, hides and wool, must be very great, but I have not been able to collect particulars enough to make an estimate of the amount of them.

Of the antient SURVEY of the KINGDOM, but more especially as far as it relates to GLOUCESTERSHIRE.

OUR histories are almost wholly silent as to particular property in this county, 'till the 11th century, when there was a register made by the command of William the Conqueror, with great care and exactness, of all the lands in the kingdom, and the names of the owners of them, with the quantities and other particulars of their estates, except in the counties of Northumberland, Cumberland, Westmoreland, Durham, and part of Lancashire, with Wales, which were not then surveyed. The business was begun under the care of five justices in each county, appointed for that purpose, in the year 1081, and compleated in 1086. The materials of this survey were digested, and fairly entered in a book, which some have called *Liber Judiciarius, vel Censualis Angliæ*, others *Domesday-Book* §, from the Saxon word ꝺom, *census, vel estimatio.* It is a most antient record, and now remains in the exchequer, very fair and legible.

A soon as William had settled himself in his his new dominions, he made such alterations in

§ Ingulphus says, that king Alfred made such another roll, which he kept at Winchester, and called it *Domesday.* It referred to the time of king Æthelred, as that made by William the First refers to the time of Edward the Confessor. There is a third book in 4to, differing from the others which are in folio, more in form than matter, made by the command of the same king, which is more fairly written, hath fewer erasures, and seems to be more antient. A fourth *Domesday* is kept in the exchequer, being only an abridgement of the first; and there is a fifth, an exact copy of the last, kept in the remembrancer's office. There is also a book in the exchequer, something of the same nature, called *Nomina Villarum*, made at the command of king E. 2. containing the names of all the hundreds, cities, burghs, and vills in England, and the possessors of them, returned by the sheriffs of all the counties; I have a copy of the part concerning Gloucestershire. What is contained in the Domesday of W. 1. appears by these old verses.

Quid deberetur fisco, quæ, quanta tributa,
Nomine quid census, quæ vectigalia, quantum
Quisque teneretur feodali solvere jure,
Qui sunt exempti, vel quos angaria damnat,
Qui sunt vel glebæ servi, vel conditionis,
Quove manumissus patrono, jure ligatur.

the

the laws, partly from policy, and partly from prejudice, as to bring the whole conſtitution to as near a conformity as he could with that of Normandy, by ingrafting the feudal tenures, and other cuſtoms of that country, upon the old Saxon laws, which produced a different political ſyſtem, and changed both power and property in many reſpects; though the firſt principles of the feudal law, and general notions of it, had been in uſe among the Engliſh ſome ages before. But that the liberty of the ſubject was not deſtroy'd by theſe alterations, as ſome writers have ſuppoſed, plainly appears by the very ſtatutes that William enacted, in one of which we find an expreſs declaration, *That all the freemen in his kingdom ſhould hold and enjoy their lands and poſſeſſions free from all unjuſt exaction, and from all tallage; ſo that nothing ſhould be exacted or taken of them but their free ſervice, which they by right owed to the crown, and were bound to perform.* It is further ſaid, *That this was ordained and granted to them as an hereditary right for ever, by the common council of the kingdom.*

Some of our eminent lawyers have been of opinion, that 'till this time eſtates were not hereditary in England; but that William made them ſo, in imitation of the ſyſtem that had then lately obtained in the kingdom of France, where the nobility and gentry had had their honours and eſtates granted to them and to their heirs *in feodo* for ever; whereas before, the French held them only at will, or for life. But in objection to this opinion, it is moſt certain, that our Saxon anceſtors had their hereditary eſtates, which Spelman calls *thaneland*, and ſpeaks of it as ſynonymous to *Bocland*, which in antient writings has been interpreted by * *Allodium*, *Terra* † *hereditaria*, *Terra* || *libera*, *Terra* § *teſtamentalis*. But our Saxon anceſtors had other lands of a feudal nature, diſtinguiſhed from the former, by the name of *Folcland*, perhaps, becauſe they were ſuch as the common people poſſeſſed; yet the barons, or thanes, frequently held both ſorts together. Folkland was perſonal, and held only for life, and ſometimes indeed at the will of the lord, or for a certain number of years. But theſe eſtates were made hereditary fiefs under William the Conqueror, and moſt of the Bocland was converted into the ſame kind of tenure.

If we conſider this change with regard to *bocland* alone, in which before they had an abſolute property, and power to diſpoſe of it by will, it may ſeem at firſt a matter of aſtoniſhment, that freeholders thus poſſeſſed of alodial eſtates, ſhould ever have been diſpoſed to convert them into fiefs, ſubject to ſo many ſervices, entails and other burthens. Yet it is certain, that ſuch alterations were deſired. The reaſons given for it are theſe: The poſſeſſors of fiefs had ſeveral privileges, which other freemen had not; a higher value was ſet upon their perſons; the compoſitions for injuries done to them were greater, which was an important diſtinction, when moſt offences were puniſhed by pecuniary fines, according to rates aſcertained and fixed by law; and what ſeems to have weighed more than any other reaſons, the demeſne lands of thoſe who held by knight-ſervice, were exempted from tallage, and many other impoſitions, which fell heavy on the poſſeſſors of alodial eſtates.

Originally all *proper feuds*, I mean, all of a *military nature*, deſcended in equal proportions to all the ſons of a vaſſal, but not to daughters. This excluſion of females had been taken off in moſt countries, before the Normans came hither; but whether the equal diviſion of all military fiefs continued after that time, and when it abſolutely ceaſed, is not very clear. The impartibility of them is aſcribed, by many writers, to a conſtitution made by the emperor Barbaroſſa, in the year 1152. But earldoms and baronies, which that ordinance chiefly relates to, had before been indiviſible, both in England and in France, except in the caſe of a baron leaving ſeveral daughters, and no ſon, at his death. I ſhould therefore ſuppoſe that the cuſtom of preſerving knights-fees undivided, in the courſe of deſcent, which ſeemed neceſſary to enable the military tenant to perform his honourable ſervice with the requiſite dignity, began to prevail among the Engliſh ſome time before it was ſettled by law in the empire. And, together with that, was introduced the *right of primogeniture* in feudal ſucceſſions. For when, in order to preſerve the tenure intire, only one ſon could take it, the eldeſt was preferred as ſooneſt able to perform the duties of the fee, and moſt naturally coming into the place of his father. Certain it is, that when Glanvile's Treatiſe was writtin, it was the eſtabliſhed law of England, that in a military fief, the eldeſt ſon ſhould ſucceed to the whole inheritance. Yet it appears from records, that men frequently held by parts of a knight's-fee; but ſuch diviſions either aroſe from marriages with the daughters of a military tenant, who had no ſon, and ſeveral daughters; or were made by enfeoffments, and not in virtue of the rule and courſe of ſucceſſion. Lands held in *free ſocage* were equally divided among all the ſons, unleſs they were ſuch as had been impartible, by antient cuſtom; of which ſome went to the *eldeſt* ſon, and others to the *ſecond*.

William divided the kingdom into 60,215 knight's-fees, making 30,000 baronies, vills, or manors, the proprietors whereof were the only freeholders in the kingdom. The number of them in the whole county of Glouceſter was between ſixty and ſeventy, including the Cynınᵹeƿ Ðeᵹenƿ, or the king's *thanes*, by which I mean, thoſe that held of the king in chief by knight-ſervice; and all the lands, beſides what they held, were either in the crown or the church.

* *Textus Roffenſis.* † *Leges Aluredi.* || *Leges Ethelredi.* § *Leges Canuti.*

Theſe *thanes*, according to Mr. Selden, were honorary, and were of the ſame kind with them that were, after the Normans, parliamentary barons; and the *tainlands* only were the parliamentary baronies. But there was an inferior order of men called Meðmeꝛa Ðeȝen, or *middle thane*, who after the Normans, were often ſtiled *Vavoſors*, a name that never was honourary here, but only feudal, and occurs ſometimes in Domeſday book, as a ſynonymy with *liberi homines regis*.

Thoſe lands which were in the poſſeſſion of Edward the Confeſſor, and afterwards came to the Conqueror, and were ſet down in Domeſday-book under the title *Terra Regis*, are § antient demeſnes; and therefore, whether they are ſuch or not, can be tried only by that book.

Of theſe lands there were two ſorth of tenants, one that held them frankly by charter, the other by copy of court roll, or by the verge, at the will of the lord, according to the cuſtom of the manor. The privileges of this tenure conſiſted in three points; the tenants holding by charter could not be impleaded out of their manor; they were free from toll for all things concerning their livelihood, or huſbandry; and they were not liable to ſerve on juries. *F. N. B.* fol. 14, and 228. Theſe tenants held originally by plowing and cultivating of the king's lands, for the ſupplying of his houſhold with proviſions, wherefore ſuch liberties and privileges were allowed them, which ſtill belong to that kind of land, tho' the ſervice is now changed from labour to money.

The names of all the manors and their dependencies, together with the owners, and other particulars of them, at the time of the general ſurvey, are ſet down in Domeſday-book; a copy of which, in the contracted manner of that writing, as nearly as it could be imitated with the common printing types, is as follows. *Note, the* Apoſtrophe ['] *ſhews the place of contraction.*

COPY of *DOMESDAY* BOOK.

GLOWECEST'SCIRE.

TEMPORE REGIS EDWARDI reddebat Civitas de GLOWECESTRE xxxvj lib' numeratas & xii ſextaria mellis ad menſuram ejuſd' burgi & xxxvi dicras ferri & c virgas ferreas ductiles ad clavos navium Regis & quaſdam alias minutas conſuetudines in aula & in camera Regis. Modo reddit ipſa Civitas regi lx lib' de xx in ora & de moneta vero h't rex xx lib'

In d'inca t'ra Regis ten' Rogerius de Berchelai unam domum & unam piſcariam in ipſa villa & eſt extra manum Regis. hanc Balduinus tenuit T. R. E.

Oſb'nus ep's ten' terram & manſiones quas Edmarus tenuit redd x ſolid. cum alia conſuetudine.

Gaufridus de Mannevile ten' vi manſiones. he T. R. E. redd'b. vi ſolid. & viii denar' cum alia c'ſuetud.

Will's Baderon ii manſion' de xxx denar.

Will's Scriba i manſion' ten. de li denar.

Rogerius de Laci i manſion' de xxvi denar.

Oſb'nus ep's i manſion' de xli denar.

Bernerius i manſion' de xiv denar.

Will's Calvus i manſion' de xii denar.

Durandus Vicecom' ii manſion' de xiv denar.

Iſd' Durandus ten' i manſion' de xxvi den. & adhuc unam manſion' que nullam c'ſuetud' redd.

Hadeuuinus ten' i manſ' que dat gablum ſed aliam c'ſuetud. retinet.

Goſb'tus i manſionem Dunning i mans' Widardus i mans' Arnulfus p'br i mans' que redd. gablum et aliam c'ſuet. retin.

Om's iſte manſiones reddeb. regalem c'ſuetud. T. R. E. modo rex W. nichil inde h't nec Rotb'tus miniſter ejus. Iſte manſiones fuer' in firma regis E. die qua fuit vivus & mortuus modo vero ſunt ablate de firma & c'ſuetud. regis. T. R. E. erat d'nium regis in civitate totum hoſpitatum t' veſtitum. Quando comes W. ad firmam recep' ſimilit' veſtitum fuit.

Sedecim domus erant ubi ſedet caſtellum que modo deſunt & in burgo civitatis ſunt waſtate xiv domus.

CASTELLUM de ESTBRIGHOIEL fecit Will's Comes et ejus tempore reddeb. xl ſol. tantum de navibus in ſilvam euntibus. Tempore vero Com. Rogerij fiilij ejus reddid' ipſa villa xvi lib. et medietatem habeb. Rad. de Limeſi. Modo h't rex inde xii lib.

Int' redditionem de Carleion & i carucam que ibi eſt & vii piſcarias in Waie & Huſcham exeunt vii lib. & x ſolid.

In Wales ſunt iii harduices Lamecare et Poteſchiuet et Dinan. In his ſunt viii car. & xi vill'i dimidii & xv bord. cum vi car' Pro his iii harduices voleb. habere c ſolid. Rog' de Ivrei.

Sub Waſſunic p'poſito ſunt xiii ville. Sub Elmvi xiiii ville. Sub Bleio ſunt xiii ville. Sub Idhel ſunt xiv ville.

Hi reddunt xlvii ſextaria mellis & xl porc. & xli vaccas & xxviii ſolid. pro accipitrib' Tot. hoc val. ix lib. & x ſol. & iiii den.

De una waſta t'ra redd. Walter' Baliſtarius i ſext' mell. & i porc.

Berdic joculator regis h't iii villas & ibi v car. nil redd.

Morinus i villam Cheneſiis i filius Waſſunic i Seſſiſbert i.

Abraham pb'r ii villas. Hi h'nt vi car' & nichil reddunt. Hos miſit W. comes ad c'ſuetud. Grifin regis licentia regis W.

Sub eiſd. p'poſitis ſunt iiii ville waſtate p' regem Caraduech.

In Elemoſina regis eſt una villa que p' anima ejus redd. eccl'e ad feſt' S. Martini ii porc. & c panes cum cerviſia.

Ad ſc'm Michaelem eſt i carucata terre & ad ſc'm Deuum una carucata. He non redd't ſervitiam niſi ſc'is.

Unus Beluard de Caruen h't dimid. car. t're & nihil redd.

Sexaginta & ſex porci exeunt de paſuag' & app'tiant xliv ſol. H' omnia redd't xl lib. & xii ſol. & viii den.

Durandus vicecom. ded. h' ead. Will'o de OW p' lv lib. ad firmam.

Walt'ius Baliſtarius ten. de rege ii carucat. t're & ibi h't iii car. & iii ſervos & iii ancillas. Val. h' xx ſol.

Girardus h't ii caruc. t're & ibi ii car. val. xx ſol.

Ouus p'poſitus regis ii car. t're & ibi iiii car. val. xx ſol. Ibi eſt in d'nio regis i caruc' t're quam tenuit Dagob'tus.

Gozelinus Brito ten' v caruc' t're in Caroen & ibi ſunt ii car. cum ii Walenſibus val. xx ſol.

Ep's CONSTANTIENSIS ten. de rege v caruc' t're & de eo unus ho' ejus. Ibi ſunt ii car. in d'nio & iii villanorum val. xl ſol.

Rogerius de Berchelai ten. ii car. terre ad Strigoielg & ibi h't vi bord. cum i car. val. xx ſol.

Vicec' Durandus ten. de rege in Caroen i t'ra Nom. Coldecote Ibi h't in d'nio iii car. & xv dimid. vill'os & iiii ſervos & unum militem. Hi om's h'nt xii car. Ibi molin. de x ſolid Hoc totum val. vi lib.

Will's de Ow h't de Strigoielg ix lib. p' c'ſuetud. ut dicit. Sed Girardus & alii ho'es d'nt nil plus hab'e illum juſte de x lib. de c'ſuetud. Strigoielg etiam ſi app'rtiaret. c lib.

In Wales h't iſd. W. in feudo iii piſcarias in Waie redd't lxx ſolid. & in eodem feudo ded. Will's com' Rad. de Limeſi l carucatas t're ſic' fit in Normania. Hoc teſtant' Hugo & alii lib'atores q'd ita Rad. conceſſit.

Modo dic. W. de Ow non ſe hab'e de hac t'ra niſi xxxii car. Ibi ſunt in d'nio viii car. & ho'es h'nt xvi car. Ibi duo molini de x ſol. Tot. val. x lib. & x ſol.

§ The fee-farm rents remaining to the kings of England from their antient demeſnes, were many of them alienated from the crown, in the reign of king Charles the Second.——How doubtful people were of the title to alienations, of any nature, from the crown, may be gathered hence: Whilſt theſe rents were expoſed to ſale for ready money, there were very few purchaſers; but an expedient was found out, which ſerved as a ſpur; it was no leſs than ſtopping ſome of his majeſty's payments. People then began to purchaſe them, as the only method of getting their own in that conjecture; and by 22 C. 2. c. 6. ſ. 10. the letters patents by which theſe alienations are made, are confirmed, and declared to be good. ——— But alienations from the crown have been better ſecured to the ſubject, by the deciſion of the houſe of lords, in the caſe of the earl of Portland, in 1769, wherein the *Nullum Tempus*, ſo often pleaded by the crown in caſes of reſumption, was ſet aſide.

Rog' de Laci ten. in feudo de Strigoielg tant. t're hofpitat. cum uno molino q'd val. xxxvi folid.

Turftinus filius Rolf h't int' Hufcham & Waiam xvii carucas. De his funt in d'nio iiii & dimid. alie funt ho'um. Ibi xi bord. funt et molin. de vii folid. val. viiii lib. tot. De hac t'ra v caruc. & dimid. calumniant' p'pofiti regis dicentes q'd eas Turftinus fine dono affumpfit.

Ifd. Turftinus h't vi caruc. t're ult. Hufcham & ibi ho'es ejus h'nt iiii car. & molin redd. xv fol. & dimid. pifcaria de x fol. Tot. val. liiii fol. & vi den.

Aluredus Hifpanus h't in fendo ii carucat. t're. Ibi ii car. in d'nio Ifd. A. h't in Wales vii villas que fuer' Will'i Comitis & Rog' filii ejus in d'nio. He redd. vi mell. fextaria & vi porc. & x folid.

BURGUM de WINCELCUMBE reddeb. T. R. E. vi lib. de firma. De his habeb. Comes Heraldus terc'm denar' id eft xl fol. Poftea redd. xx lib. cum toto hund. ejufd. ville. Durandus vicecom. appofuit c fol. & Rogerius de Iurei lx folid.

Modo adjunctis iii hund. redd. xxviii lib. de xx in ora.

HIC ANNOTANT' TERRAM TENENTES IN GLOWEC'SCIRE.

I. REX WILLELMUS.
II. Archiep's Eboracenfis.
III. Ep's de Wireceftre.
IIII. Ep's de Hereforde.
V. Ep's de Execeftre.
VI. Ep's de S'co Laudo.
VII. Eccl'a de Bade.
VIII. Abbatia de Glaftingb'ie.
IX. Abbatia de Malmefb'ie.
X. Abbatia de Glouueceftre.
XI. Abbatia de Wincelcumbe.
XII. Abbatia de Evefham.
XIII. Abbatia de Abendone.
XIIII. Abbatia de Perfore.
XV. Abbatia de Coventreu.
XVI. Abbatia de Cormelies.
XVII. Abbatia de Lire.
XVIII. Abbatia de Eglefham.
XIX. Abbatia de Weftmonaft.
XX. Eccl'a S. Dionifij Parifij.
XXI. Eccl'a de Langheig.
XXII. Eccl'a S. Ebrulfi.
XXIII. Eccl'a S. TRINITAT. Cadom.
XXIIII. Eccl'a de Troarz.
XXV. Eccl'a de Cireceftre.
XXVI. Renbaldus P'br
XXVII. Comes Rogerius.
XXVIII. Comes Hugo.
XXIX. Comes Moritonienfis.
XXX. Ep's Liciac'fis Gifleb'tus Maminoth.
XXXI. Willelmus de OW.
XXXII. Will's filius Baderon.
XXXIII. Will's Camerarius.
XXXIIII. Will's Goizenboded.
XXXV. Will's filius Widon.
XXXVI. Will's Froiffeleuu.
XXXVII. Will's filius Norman.
XXXVIII. Will's Leuric.
XXXIX. Rogerius de Laci.
XL. Rogerius de Belmont.
XLI. Rogerius de Luri.
XLII. Rogerius de Berchelai.
XLIII. Radulfus frater ejus.
XLIIII. Radulfus Pagenel.
XLV. Radulfus de Todeni.
XLVI. Rob'tus de Todeni.
XLVII. Rob'tus Difpenfator.
XLVIII. Rob'tus de Oilgi.
XLIX. Ricardus Legatus.
L. Ofbernus Gifard.
LI. Goisfridus Orleteile.
LII. Gifleb'tus filius Turold.
LIII. Durandus Vicecomes.
LIIII. Drogo filius Ponz.
LV. Walterius filius Ponz.
LVI. Walterius filius Rog.
LVII. Walterius Diaconus.
LVIII. Walterius Baliftarius.
LIX. Henricus de Ferieres.
LX. Ernulfus de Hefding.
LXI. Heraldus filius Rad.
LXII. Hugo de Grentemaifn.
LXIII. Hugo Lafne.
LXIIII. Milo Crifpin.
LXV. Urfo de Abetot.
LXVI. Hafcoit Mufard.
LXVII. Turftinus filius Rolf.
LXVIII. Ansfridus de Cormel.
LXIX. Hunfridus Camerarius.
LXX. Hunfridus de Medehalle.
LXXI. Hunfridus Coquus.
LXXII. Sigar de Cioches.
LXXIII. Maci de Mauritanie.
LXXIIII Gozelingus Brito.
LXXV. Rogerius filius Radulfi.
LXXVI. Uxor Geri.
LXXVII. Balduinus.
LXXVIII. Elfi & alij taini regis.

GLOWEC'SCIRE.

I. TERRA REGIS.

Rex EDWARDUS tenuit CHINTENEHAM ibi erant viii hide & dim. Ad eccl'am p'tin. i hid. & dim.

Reinbaldus ten. eam. In d'ni'o erant iii car. & xx vill'i & x bord. & vii fervi cum xviii car. Pr'b'ri ii car. Ibi ii molini de xi fol. & viii denar.

Huic m. accrevit p'pofitus regis W. duos bord. & iv vill'os & iii molinos hor. ii funt regis t'cius prepofiti & i car. plus e. ibi T. R. E. redd'b. ix lib. & v fol. & ter mille panes canibus.

Modo redd. xx lib. & xx vaccas & xx porc. & xvi fol. pro panibus.

In BERTUNE habuit rex E. novem hid. De his erant vii in d'nio & ibi iii car. & xiv vill'i & x bord. cum ix car. Ibi vii fervi. De hoc m. ten. ii lib'i ho'es ii hid. h'nt ibi ix car. ipfi fe non poffunt nec t'ram feparare a manerio ibi molin. de iv folid. P'pofitus W. regis accrevit viii bord & ii molinos & i caruca. T. R. E. reddeb. ix lib. & v folid. & ter mille panes canibus.

Modo redd. xx lib. xx vaccas xx porc. & pro panibus xvi fol.

De hoc m. p'ftitit Ældred archiep's i membrum BREWERE ibi funt iii virg. t're & iii ho'es. Milo Crifpin tenet.

Alter membrum no'ie Optune preftitit Aluui vicecom. Ibi una hida t're & ibi funt iv ho'es. Hunfridus ten.

Tertium membrum no'ie MERWEN preftitit ifd. Aluui. Ibi funt iii virg. t're Nigellus medicus tenet.

In DUDESTAN Hund. habuit quidam tainus Edmar iii maner. Herferel & Athelai & Sanher. Ifte ho. poterat dare & vend'e t'ram fuam cui voluiffet pro ii hid. fe def'd'b. h. t'ra. In d'nio erant viii car. & iv vill'i & iv bord. & xxx fervi cum v car. Ibi p'tum fufficiens carucis.

In HERSECOME teneb. Wiflet iii virg. t're lib'as ficut & Edmer. Ibi babeb. ii car. & ii bord. & v fervos & prata carrucis.

In BROSTORP tenuit Aluric iii virg. t're hic habeb. ii car. et un. uillin iii bord. iv fervos. Has v t'ras abftulit Comes Herald. poft mortem regis E. Has eafd. Rog. de Lurei pofiut ad firmam pro xlvi lib. & xiii fol. & iv den.

In eod. HUND. juxta Civitatem habuit Uluuard dimid. hidam de rege E. quietam & ibi ii car. & iv fervi. Hanc ded. W. com. cuidam coquo fuo Vluuard enim utlag. fact. eft.

In CIRECESTRE Hund. habuit rex E. quinq; hid. t're Ibi in d'nio v car. & xxxi vill'ni cum x car. Ibi xiii fervi & x bord. & iii molini de xxx folid. prata & ii filvas de l. fol. & ibi ii lib'i ho'es ii car. h'ntes lanam o'nium regina habeb. T. R. E. reddeb. hoc m. iii modios frumenti & dimid. & braifi iii mod. & mell. fex fextar. & dimid. & ix lib. & v fol. & ter mille pan. canibus. Modo redd. xx lib. & v fol. & xx vaccas xx porc. & pro pan. xvi fol. & de nouo foro xx fol. quorum h't S Maria t'cium den.

In CIRECESTRE unus lib. ho. teneb. ii hid. t're & reddeb. xx fol. in firma & per totam Angliam vicecomiti fervitium faciebat.

Will's Com. hanc t'ram mifit ext. firmam & cuidam fuo ho'i. dedit eam.

In SUINHEVE Hund. erant T. R. E. ad firmam xxxvi hide. in BETUNE cum ii Membris Wapelei & Wintreborne.

In d'nio erant v car. & xli vill'i & xxix bord. cum xlv car. Ibi xviii fervi cum i molino.

Hoc m. T. R. E. reddeb. firmam unius noctis & mo. fimilit' facit.

In SALEMANESBERIE Hund. tenuit E. rex SCLOSTRE. Ibi erant vii hide. & in d'nio iii car. & ix vill'i & xi bord. cum viii car. Ibi vii fervi & ii molini de una Marka Arg'ti. prata de x fol. & de una ex his hid. x folid. & canib. v folid.

De hoc m. reddeb. q'd voleb. Vicecom. T. R. E. Ido' nefciunt app'ciari. Modo vicecom. accrev. ibi i car. & v bord. cum i car. Redd. nunc de m. iofo & de hund. xxvii lib. ad numerum.

In WESBERIE xxx hide. Ibi habeb. E. rex v car. in d'nio & xxxii vill'os & xv bord. cum xxviii car. Ibi i fervus. Hoc m. reddeb. unam noctem de firma T. R. E. Similiter T. R. W. per iv annos. Poftea ablate funt de ifto m. vi hide. In Chire & in Cliftone x hide. In Noent & Chingeftune viii hid. In Ladenent i hid.

Has t'ras ten. mo. abb. de Cormelijs & Ofb'nus & Will's f. Ricardi & tam. de remanenti inven. vicecom. totam firmam.

D'nt autem ho'es de comitatu q'd Sapina jacent in Weftberie ad firmam regis E.

In CHEFTESIAT Hund. tenuit E. rex LANGEBERGE cum uno membro no'e MENE. In utroq; erant viii hide. In d'nio iii car. & x vill'i & iv bord. cum vi car. & molin. de v fol. & vi fervi pratum de x fol. T. R. E. reddeb. vicecom. de hoc m. q'd exibat ad firmam. Modo redd. xv lib. cum ii hund. quos ibi vicece. appofuit.

In BLITESLAU Hund. tenuit E. rex AURE. Ibi v hide & in d'nio i car. & xii vill'i & viii bord. cum xiv car. Ibi unus fervus & molin. de xxx denar. & falina de xxx fummis falis & eccl'a cum i virg. t're.

Hoc m. reddeb. dim. firmam noctis T. R. E. & mo. fimiliter facit.

De eod. m. jacet waftata dimid. hida & ido. non redd. nifi xii lib. vicecom. tam. redd. totam firmam.

Extra m. funt iii membra que femper in eo fuer. & effe debent ut teftant' ho'es de comitatu id eft Peritone, Etellau, Bliteflau.

In his funt vii hide & in d'nio i car. & xx vill'i & iii bord. cum xiii car. & ii fervi & pifcaria.

Peritone eft in feudo Will'i Comitis, Etelau ten. Rog. de Berchelai, Bliteflau ten. Will's filius Baderon. Aluui vicecom. mifit h. extra firm.

In LANGELEI Hund. tenuit Comes Heraldus ALWESTAN. Ibi erant x hide. In d'nio i car. & xxiii vill'i & v bord. cum xxii & ii fervi. Ibi p'pofitus accrevit ii car. & v fervos. Redd. xii lib. ad penfum.

In

In BERCHELAI habuit E. rex v hid. & in d'nio v car. & xx vill'i & v bord. cum xi car. & ix fervi, & ii molini de xii folid. Ibi x radchenistres h'ntes vii hid. & vii car. Ibi unum forum in quo manent xvii ho'es & redd't cenfum in firma.

He BEREW. pertin. ad BERCHELAI.

In Hilla iv hide. In Almintune iv hide. In Hinetune iv hide. In Camma vi hide, & alie xi hide. In Gofintune iv hide. In Derfilege iii hide. In Couelege iv hide. In Euuelege ii hide. In Nimdesfelle iii hide. In Uutune xv hide & dimid. v'. In Simondefhale dimid. hida. In Chingefcote iv hide & dimid. In Beureftane x hid. In Ofleuuorde dimid. hida. In Almondefbere ii hid. In Horefelle viii hide. In Wefton vii hide & una v'. In Eldbertone v hide. In Cromale ii hide. In Erlingeham ix hide. In Efceleuuorde iii hide.

Hec fup'dicta membra om'a p'tinent ad Berchelai. Inter totum.——————

In his T. R. E. in d'nio xlix car. & dimid. & ccxlii vill'i & cxlii bord. cum cxxvi car. Ibi cxxvii fervi. Ibi xix lib'i ho'es Radchenift' h'ntes xlviii car. cum fuis ho'ibus. Ibi xxii colib'ti & xv ancille. Ibi viii molini de lvii fol. & vi denar.

In ifto M. tenuer. ii fr's T. R. E. in CROMHAL v hidas h'ntes in d'nio ii car. & vi vill. & v bord. h'ntes vi car.

Hi ii fr's cum t'ra fua fe poterant vertere quo volebant. T'c valeb. iv lib. m'o iii lib. hos W. Com. com'dauit p' pofito de Berchelai ut eorum hab'et fervitium fic. dicit Rogerius.

De hoc M. cum omnibus ad eum p'tinentibus redd. Rogerius ad firmam clxx lib. arfas & penfatas. Ipfe Rogerius h't de t'ra hujus m. in Hiflinbruge ii hid. Ad Claenhangare i hid. Ad Hirflege i hid.

Ad Neuetone vii hid. Ibi f't in d'nio x car. & xiii vill'i & xxi bord. cum xxii car. Ibi xvi fervi & molin. de v folid.

Tot' T. R. E. ual'b ix lib. modo xi lib. & x folid. Ifd. Rogerius ten. t'ra Bernardi p'bri v hid. Ibi h't iii car. & ii vill'os & vi bord. cum. v car. Val. & valuit lx fol.

In NESSE funt v hide p'tinent. ad Berchelai quas W. com. mifit extra ad faciendum un. caftellulum H. Rogerius calumniat.

In EDREDESTANE Hund. tenuit Eddit Regina MERESFELDE. Ibi xiiii hide. In d'nio v car. & xxxvi vill'i & xiii bord. cum xiii car. Ibi xviii fervi. P'br h't unam ex his hid. T. R. E. reddeb. xxxv lib. modo xlvii lib.

In BERTUNE apud BRISTOU erant vi hid. In d'nio iii car. & xxii vill'i & xv bord. cum xxv car. Ibi x fervi & xviii colib'ti h'ntes xiiii car. Ibi ii molini de xxvii folid. Q'do Rogerius recep. hoc m. de Rege inven. ibi ii hid. & ii car. in d'nio & xvii vill'i & xxiiii bord. cum xxi car. Ibi iv fervos & xiii colib'tos cum iii car.

In uno membro ejufd. m. Manegodesfelle vi boves in d'nio.

De ead. t'ra ten. Eccl'a de Briftou iii hid. & i car. habet ibi.

Unus Radchenift. ten. i hid. & h't i car. & iv bord. cum i car.

Hoc m. & BRISTOU redd't Regi cx mark.argenti burgenfes d'nt q'd ep's G. h't xxxiii mark. argenti & unam mark. auri p'ter firmam regis.

In BRADELEI Hund. habuit Balduinus f. Herluini m. unum in qo erant x hide. Hoc m. tenuit ep's Baioc'fis m'o eft in manu regis & geldat. Ibi funt in d'nio ii car. & vii vill'i & v bord. cum vi car. Ibi v fervi & ii molini de xx folid. Ibi p'br T. R. E. val'b. xii lib. modo vi lib.

In CIRECESTRE Hund. habuit Elmar HUNLAFESED. In quo erant iii hide & dim. ep's Baiocenfis tenuit m'o eft in manu regis. In d'nio eft i car. & iv vill'i & iv bord. cum iii car. Valuit iv lib. m'o l. fol.

In TEODECHESBERIE fuer. T. R. E. quat. xx. & xv hide. Ex his funt in d'nio xlv et erant quiete ab om'i fervitio Regali & geldo p'ter fervitium ipfius d'ni cujus erat m. In capitie m. erant in d'nio xii car. et l. int' fervos & ancillas & xvi bord. circa aulam manebant & ii molini de xx folid. & una pifcaria & una falina ap. Wicham p'tin. ad m.

Ap'd Sudwicham iii hid. In Trotintune vi hid. In Fitentone vi hide. In Pamintonie viii hide. In Natone iii hide & dim. In Waltone iii hide. In Eftone vi hide.

Ibi erant vill'i xxi & ix Radchenift. h'ntes xxvi car. & v colib'ti & unus bord. cum v car. Hi Radchenift. arabant & herciabant ad curiam d'ni.

In Glouueceftre erant viii burgenfes reddentes v folid. & iv den. & fervientes ad curiam.

In tota Teodechefberie funt cxx ac. p'ti & filva una leuga & dimid. l'g. & tant'd lat.

Ap' Teodekefberie funt modo xiii burgenfes reddentes xx fol. p' ann. mercat. q'd regina c'ftituit ibi redd. xi fol. & viii denar. Ibi eft una car. plus & xxii inter fervos & ancillas & una pifcaria & una falina ap. Wicham.

Ibi iii Radchenift. T. R. E. p'tineb. unus eorum tenebat in Eftone vi hid. modo ten. Girardus Alt. tenebat in Waltone iii hid. modo ten. Radulfus Tercius tenebat in Fitentone ii hid. modo ten. Bernardus.

In his xi hid. funt x car. in d'nio & iv vill'i & i bord. & ix fervi cum una car. Ibi xviii ac. p'ti tot. T. R. E. ual'b x lib. modo tant'd.

Ap. OXENDONE T. R. E. erat aula & v hide p'tin'tes ad Teodekefberie. Ibi funt v car. in d'nio & v vill'i & ii radchenift. h'ntes vii car. & inter fervos & ancill. xii. Ibi xxiv ac. p'ti. Ap' Wincecombe iii burgenfes redd. xl den. Tot. hoc val. & valuit viii lib.

Hec fubfcripta t'ra p'tin. eccl'e. de Teodekefberie.

In STANWEGE funt vii hide p'tin. eccl'ie. Ibi ii car. in d'nio & viii vill'i & ii bord. cum viii car. Ibi monafter. & inter fervos & ancillas v & ap. Wicham una falina & viii ac. p'ti filva iii qur. l'g & una lat. T. R. E. val'b viii lib. modo vii lib.

In TATINTONE iv hid. Ibi funt ii car. & xi vill'i & unus Radchen. cum ii car. & iii bord. & ix fervi valeb. vi lib. modo c fol.

In LIMENTONE iii hid. Ibi funt ii car. & viii vill'i cum iv car. & vi fervi & unus bord. Valuit lx fol. modo xl folid.

In WASEBORNE iii hid. Ibi funt ii car. & vi vill'i cum iii car. & i bord. & ix fervi cum ancill. Valuit & val. lx folid.

In FITENTONE ii hide. Ibi unus vill'us & ii colib'ti cum ii car. val. & valuit x fol. una ex his hid. qieta t'ra fuit.

In ATONE i hida q'ete t're et ibi i.car. val. x fol.

In STANLEGE iv hide & dimid. Ibi eft i car. & iv vill'i cum ii car. & iii bord. & v fervi. H. t'ra qieta fuit. Valuit iv lib. modo xl folid. Tota t'ra p'tin. Eccl'e. geldab. pro xx hid. T. R. E.

In eod. m. de Teodekefberie p'tineb. iv hid. fine d'nio que funt in Hanlege. Ibi T. R. E. erant in d'nio ii car. & int. vill'os & bord. xl & int. Servos & Ancillas viii & molin. de xvi den. filva in qua eft hai. H' t'ra fuit W. Comitis m'o eft ad firmam regis in Hereford. T. R. E. valuit xv lib. m'o x lib.

In Fortemeltone ix hide p'tineb. huic m. Ibi ii car. in d'nio & xx inter vill'os & bord. & vi int. fervos & ancillas. Ibi filva. Valuit x lib. T. R. E. m'o viii lib. Has ii t'ras tenuit W. Com. & geld'b p' p't Tedekefberie.

In Senendone x hide p'tin. eid. m. Ibi funt iv car. & viii vill'i & iv bord. & v radchenift. cum viii car. Ibi xii fervi & molin. de iii fol. H. t'ra geld. pro vii hid. T. R. E. val'b. xx lib. modo viii lib. In manu regis eft Rob'tus de Olgi ten. ad firmam.

In CLIFORT vii hide p'tin. eid. m. Ibi iii car. in d'nio & xiiii vill'i cum v car. & molin. de xii folid. & ii ac. p'ti. Ibi erant int. fervos & ancill. xiii & eccl'a & p'br cum i car. Val'b. viii lib. modo vi lib. hanc t'ram ded. regnia Rogero deBufli & geld'b. pro iv hid. in Tedechefb'rie. Quat. xx & xv hidas que p'tin. in Tedechefberie qinquaginta hide fup. memorate facieb. qietas & lib'as ab om'i geldo, & regali fervitio.

Manerium iftud Tedekefberie, cum erat tot. fimul T. R. E. val'b. c lib. Q'do Radulfus recep. xii lib. qia diftruct. & c'fufum erat. Modo app'ciatus xl lib. tam. Radulfus redd. l lib.

Hoc m. tenuit Brictric filius Algar T. R. E. & has fubfcriptas t'ras alior. Teinor. ipfo t'p're in fua poteftate habuit.

In ESETONE tenuit unus teinus iv hid. & m. erat modo ten. Girardus & ibi h't i car. & ii vill'os cum i car. val. & valuit xl folid.

In CHENEMERTONE tenuit Let viii hid. & m. erat. Modo ten. Girandus & ibi h't iii car. & xiv vill. cum iv car. Ibi viii fervi & iii molini de xv folid. Valuit viii lib. modo vi lib.

Ad hoc m. adjacent iii hide in Botintone. Ifd. Girard ten. & ibi h't ii car. & iv vill. cum iii car. & ibi iii fervi & molin. de viii folid. & viii ac. p'ti. Val. & valuit xl fol.

In WENECOTE tenuit unus teinus iii hid. regina ded. hanc t'ram Rainaldo capellano. Ibi funt iii vill'i cum dimid. car. Valuit xl folid.

In ALDRITONE tenuit Dunning vi hid. & dimid. & in Dridedone iv hid. & dimid. & in Hundeuuic i hid. tenuit i teinus.

Has ten. t'ras Hunfridus de Rege & ibi h't iv car. in d'nio & v vill'i & viii bord. cum iii car. & unus radchenift. cum i car. & in Wi'combe unus burg'fis & ibi h'ntur xii ac. p'ti. Tot. T. R. E. Val'b. xi lib. modo vi lib.

In TUNINGE teneb. iv vill'i ii hid. & unus teinus dimid hid. Ibi funt iv car. & iii ac. p'ti Regina ded. hanc t'ram Johi camerar. Val & valuit xxxv folid.

In STOCHES tenuer Hermer' & Aluuinus iii hid. una v'. minus. Modo ten. Bernardus de Rege & h't ibi i car. in d'nio & iv ac's p'ti. Valuit xvi folid. modo xl folid.

Qui T. R. E. has t'ras tenebant & fe & t'ras fuas fub Brictrici poteftate fummifer.

In LANGELEI Hund. BRICTRIC filius Algar tenuit TURNEBERIE. Ibi T. R. E. erant xi hide & iv car. in d'nio & xlii vill'i & xviii radechaniftres cum xxi car. & xxiv bord. & xv fervi & iv colib'ti. Ibi ii molini de vi folid. & iv den. filva de i leu. l'g & una lat. Ibi forum de xx folid. Modo accreuit p'pofitus molin. ibi de viii den.

Hoc m. fuit regine Mathildis Humphridus redd. de eo l lib. ad numer. In hoc m. eft un. p'tum de xl folid. & ad Wiche xl fext. falis vel xx den. & pifcaria de Glouueceftre de l. et viii denar.

In EDERESTAN Hund. Ipfe Brictric tenuit Sopeberie. Ibi T. R. E. erant x hide & iv car. in d'nio & xii vill'i cum v car. & iv bord. & xviii fervi & unus parcus & molin. de v fol. Modo crevit p'pofitus i molin. de xl denar. Ibi filva

de

de una leuua l'g & una lat. Hunfridus redd. de hoc m. xvi lib. & x solid.

Ad hoc m. p'tin. una v' in Wiche que reddeb. xxv sext. salis Ursus vicecom. ita vastavit ho'es q'd modo redd'e non possunt sal.

In LANGETREU Hund. Isd. Brictric tenuit AVENINGE. Ibi T. R. E. erant x hide & in d'nio viii car. & xxiiii vill'i & v bord. & xxx servi cum xvi car. Ibi iv molini de xix sol & ii den. modo crevit p'positus unum molin. de xl denar. Ibi silva ii leuuis l'g & dimid. leuua lat. Ibi est aira accipitris. Val. xxvii lib.

In BRISTOLDESBERG Hund. Isd. Brictric tenuit Fareforde. Ibi T. R. E. erant xxi hida, & lvi vill'os & viiii bord. cum xxx car. Ibi p'br qui teneb. unam v' t're de d'nio & iii molini de xxxii solid. & vi den. In d'nio non sunt nisi xiii hide & una v'.

Hoc M. tenuit Mathild Regina. Hunfridus redd. xxxviii lib. & x sol. ad numerum. De t'ra hujus M. ded. regina iv hid. Johi Camerario. Ibi sunt ii car. & ix vill'i & iv bord. cum iv car. Ibi xiiii servi redd. ix lib. de firma.

Ipsa regina ded. Balduino iii hid. & iii virg. de ead. t'ra & ibi h't ii car. & v servos & un. liberum hoe'm h'ntem i car. & ii bord. Val. iv lib.

Qui has ii t'ras tenuer. T. R. E. non poterant reced'e a capite. M.

In BOTELAU Hund. REX E. tenuit DIMOCH. Ibi erant xx hide & ii car. in d'nio & xlii vill'i & x bord. & xi colib'ti h'ntes xli car. Ibi p'br tenens xii ac's & iv radechenistre cum iv car. Ibi silva iii leuu. l'g & una lat.

De hoc M. reddeb. vicecom. q'd voleb. T. R. E.

Rex W. tenuit in d'nio suo iv annis postea habuit eum com. W. et Rogerius filius ejus. Ho'es de comitatu nesciunt quomodo. Modo redd. xxi lib.

In BLITESLAU Hund. Com. Heraldus tenuit NEST. Ibi erant v hide & in d'nio i car. & x vill'i & ii bord. cum ix car. T. R. E. non fuit ad firmam.

Comes v'o W. adjunx. illum duob. alijs M. scilicet Pontune et Peritune. In his erant ix hide et ii car. in d'nio et xv vill'i et ii bord. et ii servi cum ix car. ibi i piscaria. Modo crevit p'positus in Pontune i car. Peritune est in Calumnia ad firmam regis. Int. tot. redd. xi lib.

In LINDENEE fecit Com. W. un. M. de iv t'ris quas ab earum d'nis accepit. De d'nio ep'i de Hereford iii hid. De d'nico victu monachorum de Persore vi hid. ubi erant vi vill'i cum iv car. De duobus teinis accep. iii hid. et dim. Ibi sunt in d'nio iii car. et viii bord. et molin. de xl den. silva i leuu. l'g et dim. lat. Int. tot. redd. vii lib.

In TEDENEHAM Hund. habuit Abb. de Bade unum man. no'e TEDENEHAM. Ibi habebant xxx hide harum x erant in d'nio. Ibi erant xxxviii vill'i h'ntes xxxviii car. et x bord. In Saverna xi piscarie. in d'nio et xlii piscarie villanorum. In Waia i piscaria et villanorum ii piscarie et dimidia.

Rogerius Comes creuit in Waia ii piscarias. Ibi est silva ii leuu. l'g et dimid. leuua lat. et xii bord. plus sunt.

W. Com. ded. de hac t'ra fr'i suo O. ep'o unam v' t're cum i vill'o et Walterio de Laci ded. ii piscar. in Saverna et dimid. in Waia cum uno vill'o Rad. de Limesi ded. ii piscar. in Waia cum uno vill'o Abbatie de Lyra ded. dimid. hid. t're et eccl'am M. cum decima.

Hoc M. non reddeb. censum T. R. E. nisi victum monachis Stigandus archiep's teneb. illum q'do com. W. accep. eum. Modo redd. xxv lib. de xx in Ora et albas. Ibi est m'o molin. de xl denarijs.

In RESPIET Hund. WLWARDUS tenuit CEDEORDE. Ibi xv hide int. silvam et planum et pratum et vii car. in d'nio T. R. E. et xvi vill'i et iii bord. cum vi car. et iii molini de xiiii solid. et ii denar. et theloneum sal. q'd venieb. ad aulam. Ibi crevit vicecom. *viii* vill'os et iii bord. h'ntes iiii car.

In BEGEBERIE Hund. CHENVICHELLE teinus regis E. tenuit ALVREDINTVNE. Ibi erant *v* hide et iiii car. in d'nio et xii vill'i et unus bord. cum *vi* car. et *xvi* inter servos et ancillas et ii molini de *xx* solid. silva i leuua l'g et dim. lat. Horum ii maneriorum p'positi. q'd voleb. reddeb. T. R. E. Modo redd't *xl* lib. alborum nummorum de *xx* in ora. Rog' com. tenuit.

In TETBOLDESTANE Hund. ROTLESE Huscarle R. E. tenuit BECEFORD. Ibi erant *xi* hide et iii car. in d'nio et *xxxiv* vill'i et *xvii* bord. h'ntes *xxx* car. ibi *xii* servi et iiii ancille.

De hoc M. ded. W. com. iii hid. Ansfrido de Cormelijs. In quib; erant *xii* vill'i cum *v* car.

TURBERTUS teinus Com. Heraldi tenuit ESTONE. Ibi f't *viii* hide et iiii car. in d'nio et *x* vill'i et *iv* bord. cum *vi* car. Ibi *viii* servi et iii ancille.

De his ii vill'is fec. Com. W. unum M. et non erant ad firmam donec Rog' de Lurei misit ad *xxx* lib. firme. Decimam v'o et eccl'as cum ii vill'is et iii virg. t're ded. ipse Com. Abbatie de Cormelijs.

Ho'es de comitatu inquisiti dixer. se nunq. vidisse breuem regis q' hanc t'ra diceret datam e'e Comiti W.

In LANGENEI Hund. Wlgar teinus regis E. tenuit Tochintune. Ibi fuer. *viii* hide et *v* car. in d'nio et *xx* vill'i et *xii* bord. et *x* servi cum *xx* car.

Hoc M. non redd. firmam T. R. E. sed inde viveb. cujus erat. Com. W. tenuit in d'nio et ibi crevit p'positus i car. et molin. de *viii* denar.

Modo redd. *xxiv* lib. candidorum nummorum de *xx* in ora.

In DODESTAN Hund. EDRIC Lang teinus Com. Heraldi tenuit HECHANESTEDE. Ibi erant *v* hide et in d'nio iii car. et *vi* vill'i et *viii* bord. cum *vi* car. Ibi *vi* servi et dimid. piscaria. Hoc M. cep. W. com. in d'nio et non fuit ad firmam sed m'o vicecom. posuit eum ad *lx* sol. nu'o.

In LANGETREU Hund. Gueda mat. Com. Heraldi tenuit UDECESTRE. Goduinus emit ab Azor et ded. sue uxori ut inde viveret donec ad Berchelai maneret. Noleb. enim de ipso M. aliquid comedere pro distrucc'one Abbatie. Hanc t'ra ten. Eduuardus in firma de Wiltescire injuste ut dicit comitatus qia non p'tin. ad aliq' firmam. De quo M. nemo legatis regis reddid. rationem nec aliquis eorum venit ad hanc discriptionem. H. t'ra redd. *vii* lib.

In TUIFERDE Hund. Brictric tenuit iii hid. in MODIETE & geldab. In d'nio h't rex ibi ii piscarias Rog'us de Laci h't unam piscar. cum dimid. hida. Abb. de Malmesberiam h't unam piscar. cum dimid. hida et hoc dono regis sicut dicunt.

Will's de Ow h't ii hid. et ipsas *iv* piscarias calumniat. He piscarie sunt in Waia et reddeb. *iv* lib.

In GERSDON Hund. EDNOD tenuit OMENEL T. R. E. Ibi *xv* hid. geld. De his p'donavit rex E. Ednodo *v* hid. ut dicit scira et postea reddid. de *x* hid.

Hoc M. In d'nio *iv* car. et p'br et *xix* vill'i et iii bord. cum *x* car. Ibi *xii* servi.

Hoc M. fuit Ep'i Baioc'sis et val'b. *xx* lib. modo redd. *xxvi* lib. in firma regis.

In BERNITONE Hund. Tovi Widenesa Huscarle Comit. Heraldi tenuit BERNITONE. Ibi iiii hide. In d'nio sunt ii car. et *x* vill'i et *v* bord. cum *v* car. Ibi iiii servi et molin. de *v* solid. Val. et valuit *vii* lib. Elsi de Ferendone ten. in firma regis.

EILMER tenuit in BERNITONE iiii hid. pro M. T. R. E. In d'nio est i car. et *vii* vill'i et iii bord. cum iiii car. Ibi *vi* servi et molin. de *v* sol. Valuit c solid. modo *lx* solid. Goduinus de Stantone ten. in firma regis.

GLOWEC'SCIRE.

II. TERRA THOME ARCHIEP'I.

STIGANDUS Archiep's tenuit CIRCESDUNE. Ibi erant *xv* hide et dimid. et ii car. in d'nio et *xviii* vill'i et *v* bord. et *vii* radechenist. cum *xxx* car. Ibi silva dimid. leuua l'g et iii qr. lat. T'c valeb. *xiii* lib. m'o *xii* lib.

Isd. Stig. tenuit HOCHILICOTE. Ibi erant iiii hide et in d'nio ii car. et *xi* vill'i et *v* bord. cum *xi* car. Ibi est molin. de *xxxii* den. et silva i leuua l'g et dimid. lat. T'c et m'o val. iiii lib.

Isd. Stig. tenuit NORTUNE. Ibi erant *v* hide et dim. In d'nio ii car. et *xv* vill'i cum *xv* car. et iiii servi et molin. de *xxii* den. T'c et m'o val. iiii lib. Hos iii man. ten. m'o Thomas Archiep's. Nortune ten. Walchelinus de eo nepos Ep'i de Winton.

In SALMANSBERIE Hund. ELDREDUS Archiep's ten. OTINTUNE cum BEREW. Condicote. Ibi erant *x* hide et ii car. in d'nio et *xvi* vill'i et ii radechenist. et iiii bord cum *xiiii* car.

H. t'ra nunq. geldau. T. R. E. val'b. *vi* lib. m'o x lib.——

Thomas Archiep's ten. Sci. Petrus de Glouuecestre habuit in d'nio donec rex W. in Angliam venit.

In CILTEHAM Hund. Stigand. Archiep's tenuit SUINDONE. Ibi erant iii hide et ii car. in d'nio et *vii* vill'i et ii bord et h'nt *vii* car. Ibi f't iiii servi. T'c val'b. iii lib. m'o iiii lib. et x solid. Hoc M. ten. Thomas Arch. de t'ra S't Osuualdi et geldat.

In WACRESCUMBE Hund. Gundulf tenuit et ten. SCIPETUNE un. M. de una hida et geld. et ibi i car. in d'nio & val. viii solid. De Thoma Arch. ten.

PIN tenuit i M. de i hida in HAGEPINE & geld. Anſgerus ten. de Thoma Arch. & h't i car. in d'nio. Valuit xx ſol. modo x ſolid.

In BRADELEGE Hund. Sc's Petrus de Glouuec. tenuit LECCE & Eldred Archiep's tenuit cum Abbatia. Ibi erant xxiiii hide in d'nio ſunt iiii car. & xxxiii vill'i & xvi bord. cum xxx car. Ibi ſunt iiii ſervi & ii molini de vii ſolid. & iiii den.

Ad hoc M. adjacet Stanuuelle. Ibi ſunt ii car. in d'nio & v vill'i cum v car. & molin. de xl den. & iiii ſervi & ii ancille & in Culberlege eſt una hida p'tin. huic M.

De hac t'ra hujus M. ten. Walt. filius Pontii unum M. de xii hid. q't jacuit in eod M. T. R. E. Ibi ſunt ii car. in d'nio ap. Tormentone & xxv vill'i cum xii car. & iiii ſervi.

Tot. M. T. R. E. val'b. xviii lib. Thomas Arch. miſit ad firmam pro xxvii lib. Hida de Culberlege p'ciat xx ſol.

Q'd Walt'us ten. val. xiiii lib. Thomas Arch. calumniat. Stigandus Archiep's tenuit CUNTUNE. Ibi erant ix hide. Ibi ſunt ii car. & v ac. p'ti & xxii vill'i & v bord. cum xi car. Ibi v ſervi & molin. de v ſolid. T. R. E. val'b. viiii lib. modo vii lib. Thomas Arch. tenet. Unus h'o Rog. de Lurei ten. un. M. de iii hid. pertin. huic M. Hoc. ipſe Arch. calumniat.

In WITESTAN Hund. ELDRED Archiep's tenuit STANEDIS. De d'nio S. Petri de Glouuceſtre fuit. Ibi erant xv hide T. R. E. In d'nio ſunt iii car. & viiii vill'i & xiiii bord. cum xvi car. & vii radechenift. h'ntes xvii car. Ibi viii ſervi & dimid. piſcaria. Silva dim. leuua l'g & una qr. lat.

Tot. M. T. R. E. val'b. xvi lib. modo xii lib. Thomas Archiep's ten. & ſimilit. geldat.

De hac t'ra hujus M. ten. Abb. de Glouuec. ii hid. & jure deb. ten'e. Com. Hugo ten. unam hidam injuſte. Vicecom. Durandus ten. iii hid. q's W. Com. ded. fr'i ejus Rogerio. Has calumniat. Archiep's Thomas.

In BERNITON Hund. Sc's Oſwaldus de Glouuec. tenuit WIDIFORDE. Ibi T. R. E. erant ii hide & ii car. in d'nio & iiii vill'i & iii bord. cum ii car. Ibi iiii ſervi & viii ac. p'ti & molin. de x ſolid. T. R. E. Val'b. xl ſol. m'o lx ſol. Rannulfus ten. de eod. ſc'o. Qualis t'c fuit talis eſt modo.

In RESPIGETE Hund. Sc's Oſwaldus tenuit in CERNEI un. M. de iiii hid. T. R. E. Iſd. ſc's ten. adhuc & h't ii car. in d'nio & vi vill'i & ii bord. cum v car. Ibi i ſervus & molin. de vii ſol. & ii ac. p'ti. T'c valuit c ſol. modo iiii lib.

In LANGEBRIGE Hund. Ulchetel tenuit LESSEDUNE M. de ii hid. modo ten. Rog. de Thoma Arch. h. t'ra geld. In d'nio eſt una car. & v vill'i & ii bord. cum iii car. Ibi iii ſervi & xx ac. p'ti. Valuit xl ſol. modo xxx ſol.

III. TERRA ECCL'E DE WIRECESTRE.

In BERNINTREU Hund. SC'A MARIA de Wireceſtre tenuit & ten. HUESBERIE. Ibi fuer. & ſunt l. hide. In d'nio ſunt ii car. & viii vill'i & vi bord. cum viii car. Ibi iiii ſervi & una ancilla. Ad hoc M. p'tin. h. membra. Henberie. Redeuuiche. STOCHE. GIETE. In his ſunt viiii car in d'nio & xxvii vill'i & xxii bord. cum xxvi car. Ibi xx ſervi & ii ancille & xx colib'ti cum x car. & molin. de xx den.

Ad hoc M. p'tin. vi radechenift. h'ntes viii hid. & viii car. Non poterant a M. ſeperari & in Briftou ii dom. reddeb. xvi den.

De hac t'ra hujus M. ten. Turſtinus filius Rolf v hid. in Auſtreclive. & Giſleb'tus filius Turold iii hid. & dimid. in Contone. & Conſtantinus v hid. in Icetune. In his t'ris ſunt v car. in d'nio & xvi vill'i & xii bord. cum xii car. ibi xi ſervi.

De ead. t'ra hujus M. ten. Oſb'nus Gifard v hid. & nullum ſervitium facit.

Totum M. cum membris ſuis T. R. E. val'b. xxiiii lib. modo d'nium S. MARIE val. xxix lib. & xiiii ſol. & vi den. Q' ho'es ten. viii lib.

In RESPIGETE Hund. Ipſa Eccl'a tenuit COLESBORNE & Suein de ea non poterat recedere. Ibi viii hide geld. Walterius f. Rog. ten. de eccl'a. In d'nio eſt una car. & xviii vill'i & ii bord. cum v car. Ibi ii ſervi & iii ac. p'ti & ii molini de vii ſolid. & vi denar. T'c valuit viii lib. modo iiii lib.

Ipſa eccl'a ten. AICOTE & Ailricus de ea. In Begeberie jacet. Ibi una hida. In d'nio ſunt ii car. & ii vill'i & iiii bord. cum ii car. Ibi ii ſervi & viii ac. p'ti molin. de lxiiii den. Valuit xx ſol. modo xxx ſolid. Ordric ten. de Ep'o.

In BECHEBERIE Hund. Ipſa Eccl'a tenuit BECHEBERIE. Ibi xxi hida. In d'nio ſunt iiii car. & xix vill'i & ii bord. cum xi car. Ibi iii radchenift. h'ntes iiii hid. & iiii car. & p'br h'ns iii hid. & cum ſuis iiii car. Ibi xi int. ſervos & ancillas & ii molini de xvii ſolid. & x ac. p'ti. De ead. t'ra hujus M. ten. Durandus de Ep'o un. M. de iii hid. & unam v' in Berneſleis. & Eudo vii virgat. ibid. pro M.

In his ſunt v car. in d'nio & xii vill'i cum vi car. Ibi xii ſervi. Tot. M. T. R. E. valuit xviii lib. & m'o ſimilit. Ulſtanus Ep's ten. & geldat.

In WACRESCUMBE Hund. Ipſa Eccl'a ten. WIDINDVNE. Ibi xxx hide. Tres ex his nunq. geldauer. In d'nio ſunt ii car. & xvi vill'i & viii bord. cum vii car. Ibi vi ſervi & x ac. p'ti ſilva i leuua l'g & dim. lat. & in Contone eſt una car. & ii vill'i & ii bord. cum i car. & ii ſervi & molin. de v ſolid.

In eod. M. ſunt iiii radchenift. h'ntes ii hid. & iii virg. & h'nt ii car. & p'br h'ns dimid. & i car. In Glouuec. iiii Burgenſes redd. vii den. & obolum.

De hac t'ra hujus M. ten. de ep'o Morinus iii hid. in Fuſcote. Anſchitil ii hid. in Coleſburne & Willecot. Rob'tus iiii hid. & dimid. in Dodeſuuelle & Pecleſurde. Schelinus v hid. in Nategraue. Drogo x hid. in Eſtone.

In his t'ris ſunt xvi car. in d'nio & li vill's & vii bord. cum xxviii car. Ibi xli ſervus & iii molini de xiii ſolid. & iiii denar. In Wicelcumbe i Burg'ſis redd. iii ſolid. In qibuſdam locis p'tum & ſilva ſed non multa. Tot. M. T. R. E. val'b. xxxviii lib. modo xxxiii lib. in't om's. Ulſtanus Ep's ten. hoc M.

In TEDBOLDESTAN Hund. Ipſa Eccl'a tenuit CLIVE. Ibi xxx hide. In d'nio ſ't iii car. & xvi vill'i & xix bord. cum xvi car. Ibi viii ſervi & unus Afrus. Ibi p'br h't i hid. & ii car. & unus radchenift. h'ns unam hidam & ii car. Ibi ſilva paruula.

De hac t'ra ejuſd. M. ten. de eccl'a Vicec. Durandus vi hid. in Surham. Rad's iiii hid. in Sapletone. Turſtinus f. Rolf vi hid. in Godrinton. In his t'ris ſunt in d'nio viii car. & xxii vill'i & vii bord. cum xiii car. Ibi xx ſervi & iii afri & molin. de xii den. & aliq'tum p'ti. De ead. t'ra ten. Bernardus & Raynaldus vii hid. in STOCHES & ſervitium S. MARIE noluit facere.

Tot. M. T. R. E. valuit xxxvi lib. modo xxvi lib. in't om's. Hoc M. ten. Ulſtanus Ep's.

In WITELAI Hund. Ipſa Eccl'a ten. in CONDICOTE ii hid. & Oſb'nus de Ep'o. Val. & valuit xl ſolid.

IIII. TERRA ECCL'E DE HEREFORD.

In CILTEHAM Hund. EP'S DE HEREFORD tenuit PRESTEBERIE. Ibi xxx hide. In d'nio ſ't iii car. & xviii vill'i & v bord. cum viiii car. Ibi p'br & un. radchenift. cum ii car. & in Wicelcumbe i burg'ſis redd. xviii den. & int. ſervos & ancillas xi. Ibi xx ac. p'ti & ſilva de una leuua l'g & dimid. lat.

Ad hoc M. adjacet una villa SEVENHAMTONE ext. iſt. HUND. Ibi ſunt xx hide de ſup'dictis xxx hid. & ibi ſunt ii car. & xxi vill'i cum xi car. ibi iii lib'i ho'es h'ntes vii car. cum ſuis ho'ibus.

De his xx hid. ten. Durandus de Ep'o iii hid. Tot. M. T. R. E. valuit xii lib. modo xvi lib. Hoc M. ten. Rotb'tus Ep's eid. Urbis.

V. TERRA EP'I OSBERNI.

IN SINESHOVEDES Hund. EP'S de EXECESTRE ten. ALDELANDE Aluui tenuit ho. Com. Heraldi & poterat ire quo volebat. Ibi ii hide una geld. alia non. In d'nio ſunt ii car. & unus vill's & vi bord. cum i car. Ibi ii ſervi & x ac. p'ti. T'c valuit iiii lib. modo xx ſol.

In BACHESTANES Hund. Iſd. Ep's ten. Tidrentune. Aluui tenuit T. R. E. Ibi v hide & ii car. ſunt in d'nio & unus vill's & v bord. & ii ſervi & xx ac. p'ti ſilva dimid. leuu. in l'g & lat. Valuit c ſolid. m'o xl ſol.

VI. TERRA EP'I CONSTANTIEN'S.

In BACHESTANES Hund. EP'S de S. LAUDO ten. ACTUNE & Ilgerus de eo. Ibi ii hide & dimid. in d'nio eſt i car. & iiii vill'i & v bord. & i ſervus & ii ancille cum i car. & dimid. Ibi dimid. molin. de xvi den. & x ac. p'ti & una qr. ſilve. Val. & valuit xl ſolid. Ebbi tenuit hoc M. h'o Brictric f. Algar.

In SINESHOVEDES Hund. Iſd. Ep's ten HANBROC & Oſulfus de eo. Algar tenuit de Rege E. & poterat ire quo voleb. T'ra eſt v car. Ibi ii hide. In d'nio ſ't ii car. & ii vill'i cum ii car. & ii ſervi & vi ac. p'ti. Valuit c ſolid. modo lx ſolid.

Iſdem Ep's ten. unum MANER. de una hida & Goiſmerus de eo. In iſta hida q'do arat. non ſunt niſi lxiiii ac. t're. Ibi eſt in d'nio i car. Valuit xx ſol. modo xvi ſolid.

Iſd. Ep's ten. ESTOCH & Tetbaldus de eo. Eldred tenuit de Com. Heraldo & poterat ire quo voleb. Ibi ii hide una geld. al'ra non. In d'nio eſt una car. & ii vill'i & i bord. cum i car. Ibi vi ſervi & v ac. p'ti. Valuit xl ſolid. modo xx ſolid.

In POLCRECERCE Hund. Iſd. Ep's tenuit DIDINTONE & Rob'tus de eo. Aluuardus tenuit. teinus Regis E. Ibi v hide geld. In d'nio ſunt iii car. & xiiii vill'i & viii bord. cum

cum viii car. Ibi x ſervi & ii molin. de x ſol. & x den. & ii ho'es de v ſolid. & xii ac. p'ti ſilva dimid. leuua l'g & dim. lat. Val. & valuit viii lib.

Iſd. Ep's ten. WAPELIE & Aldredus de eo. Iſd. tenuit T. R. E. Ibi i hida in d'nio i car. & ii ſervi. Val. & valuit xx ſolid.

In LETBERGE Hund. Iſd. Ep's ten. LEGA & Rob'tus de eo. Algar tenuit T. R. E. Ibi i hida geld. & ii car. in d'nio & iii bord. & ii ſervi cum i car. Val. & valuit xx ſolid.

In LANGELIE Hund. Iſd. Ep's ten. HERDICOTE & Rob'tus de eo. Cuulf tenuit T. R. E. Ibi ii hide geld. & ii car. ſunt in d'nio & ii bord. & iiii ſervi & iiii vill'i & x ac. p'ti & ſilva. Val. & valuit xl ſol.

In EDREDESTAN Hund. Ipſe Ep's ten. DODINTONE & Rogerus de eo. Ulnod tenuit T. R. E. Ibi i hida & dim. & tertia pars dim. hide in d'nio eſt i car. & iiii vill'i & unus bord. cum i car. Ibi iii ſervi. Val. et valuit xxx ſolid.

VII. TERRA ECCL'E DE BADE.

In LANGELEI Hund. SC'S PETRUS DE BADA tenuit ALVESTONE. Ibi v hid. Tres geldant ex his ii non geld. c'ceſſu E. & W. regum. In d'nio ſunt ii car. & viii vill'i & vi bord. & p'br & unus radchen. cum x car. Ibi vii ſervi & p'ta & ſilva ad M. Suſtinend. valuit c ſol. modo iiii lib. Ipſa eccl'a ten. adhuc.

In PVLCRECERCE Hund. Ipſa eccl'a ten. ESCETONE ibi v hide harum ii ſunt a geldo quiete c'ceſſu E. & W. regum. Tres non geld. In d'nio eſt una car. & iii vill'i & iii bord. & unus radchen. Int. om's iii car. Ibi i colib'tus & molin. de l. denar. & vi ac. p'ti. Val. & valuit iiii lib.

VIII. TERRA ECCL'E GLASTINGBER.

In PVLCRECERCE Hund. S'CA MARIA DE GLASTINGEBERIE ten. PVLCRECERCE. Ibi xx hide in d'nio ſ't vi car. & xxiii vill'i & viii bord. cum xviii car. ibi x ſervi & vi ho'es redd't c maſſas ferri x minus & in Glouuecestre i burg'ſis redd. v den. & ii colib'ti redd. xxxiiii den. & iii francig. ſunt ibi & ii molini de c den. ibi lx ac. p'ti & ſilva dimid. leuua l'g & dimid. lat. Valuit xx lib. modo xxx lib.

IX. TERRA ECCL'E MALMESBER.

In LANGELEI Hund. SC'A MARIA de MALMESBERIE tent. LITELTONE. Ibi v hide harum ii & dimid. geld. aliæ ſunt quiete. In d'nio ſunt ii car. & xiii vill'i & ii bord. cum viii car. Ibi eccl'a & p'br & xxx ac. p'ti. Valuit lx ſolid. modo c ſolid.

X. TERRA S. PETRI DE GLOWEC.

In DVDESTANES Hund. SC'S PETRUS DE GLOWECESTRE tenuit T. R. E. M. BERTUNE cum membris adjacentibus Berneuude Tuffelege Mereuuent. Ibi xxii hide una v' minus. Ibi ſ't in d'nio viiii car. & xlii vill'i & xxi bord. cum xlv car. Ibi xii ſervi & molin. de v ſolid. & cxx ac. p'ti & ſilva v qr. l'g & iii lat. Valuit viii lib. modo xxiiii lib. Hoc M. qietum fuit ſemp. a geldo & ab omni regali ſervitio.

In BLACELAWES Hund. Ipſa ead. eccl'a tenuit FROWECESTRE. Ibi v hide. In d'nio ſunt iiii car. & viii vill'i & vii bord. cum vii car. ibi tres ſervi & x ac. p'ti & ſilva iii qr. l'g & ii qr. lat. Valuit iiii lib. m'o viii lib.

In GRIMBOLDESTOWES Hund. Ipſa eccl'a ten. BOXEWELLE. Ibi v hide. In d'nio ſunt ii car. & xii vill'i & i radchenift. h'entes xii car. ibi viii ſervi & molin. de v ſolid. Valuit lxx ſol. modo c ſol.

In BRICTWOLDESBERG Hund. Ipſa eccl'a ten. CULNE. ibi iiii hide. in d'nio ſunt iii car. & xi vill'i & vii bord. cum xii car. ibi iiii ſervi. Valuit vi lib. modo viii lib. Duo molini reddeb. xxv ſolid.

IN BEGEBRIGES Hund. Ipſa eccl'a ten. ALDESORDE. Ibi xi hide. In d'nio ſunt iii car. & xxi vill'i & v bord. & ii franchig. cum xv car. Ibi vi ſervi. Valuit c ſolid. modo viii lib.

In WIDELES Hund. Ipſa eccl'a ten. BOCHELANDE. Ibi x hide. In d'nio ſunt iii car. & xxii vill'i & vi bord. cum xii car. Ibi viii ſervi & x ac. p'ti. Valuit iii lib. modo viiii lib.

In TETBOLDESTANES Hund. Ipſa eccl'a ten. HINETUNE. Ibi xv hide. In d'nio ſ't ii car. & xxx vill'i & vii bord. cum xvi car. Ibi xi ſervi & un. francigena. Valuit iii lib. modo x lib. Hoc M. quietum eſt a geldo & ab o'i forenſi ſervitio p'ter eccl'e.

In TOLANGEBRIGES Hund. Ipſa eccl'a ten. HAMME. Ibi vii hide. In d'nio ſunt iii car. & xxii vill'i & iiii bord. cum vii car. Ibi viii ſervi & xxx ac. p'ti ſilva q'tm M. ſufficit. Valuit xl ſol. modo iiii lib.

Ipſa eccl'a ten. PRESTETUNE. Ibi ii hide. In d'nio ſunt ii car. & viii vill'i & iiii bord. cum viii car. ibi iiii ſervi. Valuit xxx ſol. modo iiii lib.

In BOTELEWES Hund. Ipſa eccl'a ten. LEDENE. Ibi iiii hide. In d'nio ſunt ii car. & viii vill'i & unus bord. cum viii car. Ibi iiii ſervi & molin. de iiii ſolid. & x ac. p'ti. Silva ii leuu. l'g & ii qr. lat. Vix val. xxx ſol.

In WESTBERIES Hund. Ipſa eccl'a ten. HAMME & MORTUNE. Int. ſilvam & plan. v hid. In d'nio ſunt ii car. & vii vill'i & ii bord. cum vi car. ſilva i leuu. l'g & una lat. Ibi habuit eccl'a venationem ſuam p' iii haias T. R. E. & t'pr W. Valuit xx ſol. modo xl ſol.

In GERSDVNES Hund. In Omenie ten. fr. Reinbaldi ii hid. Ibi ii car. & v vill'i cum iii car. & iiii ſervi & xxiiii ac. p'ti & molin. de v ſol. Valuit xl ſol. modo vix xx ſol.

In CIRECESTRE Hund. Uxor Walterij de Laci c'ceſſu Regis W. ded. ſc'o Petro pro anima viri ſui DUNTESBORNE Maner' de v hid. In d'nio iii car. & viii vill'i cum v car. Ibi xvi ſervi & molin. de ii ſolid. Val. iiii lib.

T. R. E. habeb. Sc's Petrus in Glouueceſtre de ſuis burgenſibus xix ſolid. & v den. & xvi ſalmons. Modo h't totid. ſalmons & l. ſol. Ibi eſt molin. de xii ſol. et iiii piſcarie ad uictum monachorum.

XI. TERRA ECCL'E DE WINCELCUMBE.

In SALEMONES Hund. ECCL'A S. MARIÆ de WINCELCUMBE ten. SCIREBURNE. Ibi xxx hid. ex his x ſunt libere ad curiam p'tin. Ibi ſunt in d'nio v car. & xl vill'i & vii bord. cum xxii car. ibi xii ſervi & iiii molini de xl ſol. & xxx ac. p'ti. T. R. E. val'b. xx lib. m'o xiiii lib.

Ipſa eccl'a ten. Bladintvn. Ibi vii hide. In d'nio ſunt ii car. & viii vill'i & iiii bord. cum v car. & viii ſervi & ii ancillæ. Ibi molin. de v ſol. & xxx ac. p'ti. Valuit iiii lib. modo iii lib.

In GRETESTANES Hund. Ipſa eccl'a ten. TUENINGE. Ibi iii hide geld. In d'nio ſunt ii car. & xxiiii vill'i & viii bord. cum xxvii car. Ibi viii ſervi & ii ancillæ & xl ac. p'ti ſilva ii qr. l'g & i lat. Valuit viii lib. modo vii lib.

Ipſa eccl'a ten. FREOLINTUNE. Ibi eſt una hida et in d'nio iiii car. & vi ſervi & ii ancillæ. h. t'ra lib'a fuit & qieta ab omni geldo & regali ſervitio. Valuit xl ſol. m'o l. ſolid.

Ipſa eccl'a ten. ALDRITONE & qidam Miles de Abbe. Ibi ii hide & dimid. In d'nio ſunt ii car. & unus vill's cum una car. & adhuc iii poſſunt e'e. Ibi iiii ſervi. Val. & valuit xxx ſol.

Ipſa eccl'a ten. NIWETONE et duo Milites de Abbe. Ibi iii hide & dim. In d'nio ſ't iii car. & iii ſervi & ii vill'i cum i car. & adhuc vi ibi poſſent e'e. Val. & valuit xl ſolid.

Ipſa eccl'e ten. STANTONE. Ibi iii hide. In d'nio ſunt ii car. & xiiii vill'i cum vii car. Ibi iii bord. & vi ſervi & vi ac. p'ti. Silva una leuua l'g & dimid. lat. Val. & valuit iii lib.

Ipſa eccl'a ten. CERLETONE. Ibi ii hide libere & quiete. In d'nio eſt i car. & iiii vill'i & ii bord. cum iiii car. ibi vi ſervi & molin. de xx den. & ii ac. p'ti. Val. & valuit xx ſolid.

In HOLEFORDES Hund. Ipſa eccl'a ten. SNAWESILLE. Ibi vii hide geldantes. In d'nio ſ't iii car. & xii vill'i & ii bord. cum vi car. Ibi vi ſervi. Val. & valuit c ſolid.

In CELFLEDE Hund. Ipſa eccl'a ten. HENIBERGE. Ibi x hide ſunt harum ii in d'nio & ad ſervitium viii. In d'nio ſunt v car. & xv vill'i cum v car. Ibi viiii ſervi & iii ancillæ. Valuit vi lib. m'o viii lib.

Ipſa eccl'a ten. EDELMINTONE. Ibi iii hide & dimidia. In d'nio ſunt ii car. & xiii vill'i cum vi car. ibi iiii ſervi & ii ancillæ. Valuit iiii lib. modo iii lib.

Ipſa eccl'a ten. HIDICOTE Ibi ii hide libere. In d'nio eſt i car. cum i ſervo. Val. & valuit xl ſolid.

T. R. E. deſd'b. ſe h' eccl'a in Gloweceſtreſcyre pro lx hid.

ELSI de Ferendone ten. de ipſa Abbatia iii hid. & dimid. in WENRIC. Bolle tenuit & Abbatie dedit q'i cum iſta t'ra poterat ire quo voleb. In d'nio ſunt v car. & ix vill'i & vii bord. cum i car. & x ſervi & molin. & dimid. de xii ſolid. & vi den. Val. int. totum viii lib. Uluric tenuit de hac t'ra ii hid. pro M. & Tovi v virg. pro M. & Leuuinus. i virg. pro M.

Hoc M. quem ten. Elſi de Abbe injuſte jacuit in Salemoneſberie hd. poſtq. Bolle mortuus fuit. Modo jacet in Bernitone hd. judicio ho'um. ejuſdem hund.

XII. TERRA S. MARIE DE EVESHAM.

In SALEMONES Hund. Eccl'a S. MARIE DE EVESHAM ten. MALGERESBERIE ad Eduuardeſtou. Ibi T. R. E. erant viii hide et nona hida jacet ad eccl'am S. Edwardi. Rex Adelredus qietam dedit ibi. In d'nio ſunt iii car. & xii vill'i et unus lib. hom. & p'br int. ſe h'ntes vii car. Ibi vi ſervi & molin. de viii ſolid. p'ti aliq'tum. T. R. E. val'b. c ſolid. modo vii lib.

Ipſa eccl'a ten. TEDESTROP. Ibi vii hide. In d'nio ſunt ii car. & x vill'i & ii bord. cum iii car. Ibi iiii ſervi & unus miles cum ii car. Ibi parum p'ti. Valuit iiii lib. modo c ſolid.

Ipſa eccl'a ten. BORTVNE. Ibi x hide. In d'nio ſunt vi car. & xvi vill'i & viii bord. & ii lib'i ho'es cum vii car. Ibi p'br cum dim. car. Valuit viii lib. modo xii lib.

Ipſa eccl'a ten. BRADEWELLE. Ibi x hide. ibi vi. car. ibi xiii ſervi in d'nio & xxv vill'i & viii bord. & unus lib. h'o & p'br. Int. om's h'nt xii car. In Glouuec. iiii burg'ſes & in Wicelcombe unus redd't xxvii den. Valuit tot. viii lib. modo xii lib.

In WIDELEI Hund. Ipſa eccl'a ten. SVELLE. Ibi iii hide & viiii vill'i & ii bord. et p'br. Int. om's iiii car. Ibi vi ſervi. Valuit iiii lib. modo v lib. In d'nio ſ't iii car. ibi iii molin. xx ſol.

Ipſa eccl'a ten. WILLERSEI. Ibi viii hide i ad Wiquennam. ibi iii car. in d'nio & xvi vill'os & iiii bord. & p'br cum vi car. Ibi ii ſervi & parum prati. Valuit iiii lib. modo c ſolid.

Ipſa eccl'a ten WESTUNE. Ibi iii hide & una libera. In d'nio ſ't ii car. & v vill'i & p'br cum ii car. Valuit xx ſol. m'o xl ſol.

Ipſa eccl'a ten. STOCH. Ibi ii hide. In d'nio eſt una car. & vii vill'i & ii bord. cum ii car. ibi i ſervus. Val. & valuit xl ſolid.

Ipſa eccl'a ten. HEDECOTE. Ibi iii hide. In d'nio eſt una car. & ii ſervi & uxores iiii vill'orum nuper defunctorum h'nt i car. Val. & valuit xx ſolid. Has ii villas h't abb. ii militibus ſuis comendatas.

In Ferdingo de WICELCOMBE habuit S. Maria de EVESHAM lvi hidas T. R. E.

XIII. TERRA S. MARIE DE ABENDONE.

In GRETESTAN Hund. ECCL'A S. MARIÆ de ABENDVNE ten. DUBENTONE. Ibi vii hide & dimid. In d'nio ſunt iiii car. & xiii vill'i & viii bord. cum viii car. Ibi vi ſervi & molin. de vi ſolid. T. R. E. Val'b. xii lib. modo viiii lib. Hoc. M. geldab. T. R. E.

XIIII. TERRA S'CE MARIE DE P'SORE.

In RESPIGETE Hund. Eccl'a S. MARIE de PERSORE ten. KVLEGE. Ibi v hide geld. In d'nio ſunt ii car. & xiiii vill'i & unus bord. cum vii car. Ibi v ſervi & molin. de l. den. & vi ac. p'ti & ſilva iii qr. l'g & una lat. Val. c ſolid.

In GRIMBOLDESTOV Hund. Ipſa eccl'a ten. HAVOCHESBERIE. Ibi xvii hide. In d'nio v car. & xviii vill'i & xxv bord. cum xv car. Ibi ii ſervi et vii colib'ti. Ibi iii molini de xix ſol. et ii den. et x ac. p'ti. Silva de ii leuu. l'g et una lat. Valuit xvi lib. modo x lib.

XV. TERRA S. MARIE DE COVENTREV.

In CELFLEODE Hund. ECCL'A S. MARIE de COVENTREV ten. MERESTONE. Ibi x hide. In d'nio ſ't iii car. et xv vill'i et iii bord. cum xii car. Ibi vi ſervi et p'tum de x ſol. Valuit viii lib. modo c ſolid.

XVI. TERRA S. MARIE DE CORMELIIS.

In BOTESLAU Hund. Eccl'a S. MARIE de CORMELIES ten. NOENT. Rex E. tenuit. Ibi vi hide. non geldauer. Rogerius Com. ded. huic eccl'ie pro Anima Patris ſui conceſſu Regis W. In d'nio ſunt iii car. et viiii vill'i et viiii bord. cum xii car. Ibi p'poſitus h'ns i vill'm et dim. et v bord. Int. om's h'nt v car. et molin. de xx den. Ibi ii ſervi et ii molin. de vi ſol. et viii den. De ſilva xxx den.

De hac t'ra ten. Durandus de Abbe i hid. et ibi h't i car. et v bord. et ii ſervos cum ii car. Ibi ii haie quas h't ſaiſitas rex.

Totum M. T. R. E. val'b. iiii lib. modo c ſol. hida Durandi xii ſol.

De t'ra hujus M. ten. Will's filius Baderon unam v' p. m'm.

XVII. TERRA S'CE MARIE DE LIRE.

In RESPIGET Hund. ECCL'A S. MARIE de LIRE ten. TANTESBORNE. Ibi i hida et una v'a. In d'nio eſt una car. et ii bord. Val. et valuit xx ſolid. Hanc t'ra ded. ip'i ecl'æ Rogerus de Laci. Edmer tenuit T. R. E.

XVIII. TERRA ECCL'E DE EGLESHAM.

In CELFLEDETORN Hund. ECCL'A DE EGLESHAM ten. MUCELTUDE. Ibi xiiii hide. In d'nio ſunt v car. et xx vill'i et viii bord. cum x car. Ibi viii ſervi et ii ancillæ et xxiiii menſuræ Salis de Wich. Val. et valuit x lib. Ead. eccl'a tenuit T. R. E.

XIX. TERRA S. PETRI WESTMON.

In DERHEST Hund. ECCL'A S. PETRI WESTMONAST. ten. DERHEST. Ibi ſ't lviiii hide. In capite M. erant T. R. E. v hide. Ibi ſunt iii car. et xx vill'i et viii bord. cum x car. Ibi vi ſervi et lx ac. p'ti ſilva ii leuu. l'g et dimid. leuu. lat. Val. et valuit x lib.

Ad hoc M. p'tin. he BEREW. Herdeuuic v hid. Bortune viii hid. Teodcha vii hid. Sudtune v hid. Int. tot. xxv hid. Ibi in d'nio ſunt xiii car. et xlv vill'i et xxvii bord. cum xxi car. Ibi xxxvii ſervi et iiii molini de xx ſolid. et xx ac. p'ti. Silva i leuu. l'g et dim. lat. et Broce iii qr. l'g et i lat.

De t'ra hujus M. teneb. radchen. id eſt lib'i ho'es T. R. E. qui tam. om's ad opus d'ini arabant et herciabant falcabant et metebant.

Ad Almundeſtan Brictric i hida. Reimbaldus ten. Ad Telinge Godric ii hid. Ad Wicfeld Eduui i hid. Ad Toteham Eduui i hid. H. ten. Walterius Pontherius. Ad Botingtune ii hid. Ad Bortune ii hid. Has tenuit Wluui. Ad Chinemertune dim. hid. Leuuinus tenuit. Girardus tenet iſtas t'ras. Ad Giningtune Eluui i hid. et unam v' Ad Tereige Leuuinus dimid. hid. Ad Trinleie Edricus ii virg. et dimid. H. ten. Will's filius Baderon. Ad Chinemertune Eluuinus dimid. hid. H. ten. Balduinus Abb. Ad Hasfelde Brictric i hid. et dimid. Turſtinus f. Rolf ten. Ad Lemingtune Anti iii hid. Giſleb'tus f. Turaldi ten. Ad Mortune Elfridus dimid. hid. Idem Ipſe tenet. In his t'ris ſunt in d'nio xi car. et dimid. et xiiii vill'i et xxvii bord. cum vii car. Ibi xiiii ſervi et xx ac. p'ti.

Preter hæc ten. Girardus Camerarius in Chenemertune viii hid. et in Botingtune iii hid. que ſemper geldaver. et Servitia alia fecer. in Derheſte hund. Sed poſtquam Girardus habuit nec geld. nec ſervitium reddidit.

Totum M. T. R. E. dabat de firma xli lib. et viii ſextaria mellis ad menſuram Regis. Modo val. xl lib. De his p'tin. ad d'nicum M. xxvi lib. et ad ho'es xiiii lib.

XX. TERRA S'CI DYONISII PARISII.

In DERHEST Hund. Eccl'a S. DYONISII tenet has villas. Hochinton v hid. Staruenton iii hid. Colne et Caldecote v hid. Contone xii hid. Preſton x hid. Welleford xv hid. In his t'ris ſunt in d'nio xv car. et lxxv vill'i et xii bord. cum *xxxiix* car. Ibi *xxxviii* ſervi et iiii molini de *xl* ſolid. et *xxxvi* ac. p'ti. Silva ii leuu. et dim. l'g et una leuu. et ii qr. lat.

De hac t'ra ſup'dicta ten. v lib'i ho'es iiii hid. et dimid. Ad eund. M. p'tin. ii hid. et dimid. ultra Saverne. In Olſendone v hid. In Lalege i hid. In Valton i hid. In Caneberton dim. hida. In his t'ris ſunt in d'nio v car. et v vill'i et *xviii* bord. cum viiii car. Ibi manet i lib. h'o. Ibi *xxxviii* ac. p'ti. Silva dim. leuua. l'g et ii qr. lat.

Ad hoc M. p'tin. *xxx* burgenſes in Glouuec. redd. *xv* ſol. et viii den. et in Wicelcombe ii burg'es redd. x denar.

T. R. E. Tot. M. valeb. *xxvi* lib. et x ſolid. modo *xxx* lib.

XXI. TERRA ECCL'E DE LANHEIE.

In CELFLEDETORN Hund. Eccl'a S. MARIÆ DE LANHEIE ten. ESTUNE Goda comitiſſa tenuit T. R. E. Ibi iiii hide. In d'nio ſ't iii car. et vi vill'i et unus miles cum iii car. et dimid. Ibi vi ſervi et iii ancillæ. Valuit c ſol. modo iiii lib.

XXII. TERRA S'CI EBRULFI.

In HOLEFORD Hund. Eccl'a S. EBRULFI ten. de Rege RAWELLE Wluuard tenuit T. R. E. Ibi x hide In d'nio ſunt iiii car. et *xvi* vill'i et ii bord. cum vi car. Ibi iii ſervi. Val. & valuit x lib. hoc M. nunq; geldavit.

XXIII. TERRA ECCL'E MONIALIUM DE CADOM.

In CIRECESTRE Hund. Eccl'a S. TRINIT. MONIALIUM de CADOMO ten. de Rege PENNEBERIE. Ibi iii hide. In d'nio ſunt iii car. et *viii* vill'i et unus faber cum iii car. Ibi ix ſervi et molin de *xl* den. Val. et valuit iiii lib.

In LANGETREU Hund. Ipſa eccl'a ten. HANTONE Goda Comitiſſa tenuit T. R. E. Ibi *viii* hide. In d'nio ſunt *v* car. et *xxxii* vill'i et x bord. cum *xxiiii* car. Ibi p'br et x ſervi et *viii* molini de xlv ſol. et *xx* ac. p'ti. Silva ii leuu. l'g et dimid. leuu. lat. Valet *xxviii* lib.

XXIIII. TERRA

XXIIII. TERRA ECCL'E DE TROARS.

In LANGETREW Hund. Eccl'a S. MARTINI de TROARS ten. HORSELEI dono Reg s W. Goda tenuit foror R. E. Ibi x hide. In d'nio funt iiii car. & vi vill'i & v bord. cum vi car. & un. Radchenift. & in Glouuecestre una domus de vi den. Ibi molin. de l. denar. Valuit xii lib. m'o xiiii lib.

XXV. TERRA ECCL'E DE CIRECESTRE.

In CIRECESTRE Hund. Eccl'a de CIRECESTRE ten. de rege ii hid. in Elemofina & de rege E. Tenuit quietas ab om'i confuetudine. Ibi funt vi ac. p'ti. Val. & valuit hoc xl fol.

XXVI. TERRA RENBALDI PR'BI.

In GERSDONES Hund. Reinbaldus ten. OMENIE de rege. Godricus tenuit T. R. E. Ibi iiii hide & una v'. In d'nio ii car. & viii vill'i & i bord. cum vi car. & p'bro. Ibi viii fervi & ii molini de x folid. & xx ac. p'ti. Val. & valuit c folid.

Ifd. Reinbaldus ten. DRIFELLE. Elaf tenuit de Comite Tofti. Ibi vii hide. In d'nio iiii car. & viii vill'i & ii bord. & p'br cum v car. Ibi xv fervi & molin. de v folid. & xx ac. p'ti. Val. & valuit viii lib.

In CIRECESTRE Hund. Ifd. Rainbaldus ten. in NORTCOTE i hid. Godricus tenuit T. R. E. In d'nio eft una car. & ii vill'i & ii bord. cum ii car. Ibi vi fervi. Val. xl folid. Hic tainus poterat ire quo volebat.

Ifd. Rainb. ten. PRESTETUNE. Elaf tenuit T. R. E. Ibi viii hide geld. p'ter d'nium. In d'nio funt iiii car. & vii vill'i & vi bord. cum vi car. Ibi viiii fervi & xii ac. p'ti. Val. & valuit viii lib. Ipfe Ealf poterat ire quo voleb.

XXVII. TERRA ROGERIJ COMITIS.

In GERSDONES Hund. COMES ROGERIUS ten. HANTONE & Turoldus de eo nepos Wiget. Leueric tenuit. Ibi v hide. In d'nio eft i car. & iiii vill'i & ii bord. & p'br & ii alij ho'es. Int. om's h'nt ii car. & dimid. Ibi vi fervi. Valuit viii lib. modo iii lib.

XXVIII. TERRA HUGONIS COMITIS.

In BISELEIE Hund. COMES HUGO ten. BISELEGE & Rob'tus de eo. Ibi viii hide. In d'nio funt iiii car. & xx vill'i & xxviii bord. cum xx car. Ibi vi fervi et iiii ancille. Ibi ii p'bri & viii radchenift. h'ntes x car. & alij xxiii ho'es redd'tes xliiii folid. & ii fextar. mell. Ibi v molini de xvi folid. & filva de xx folid. & in Glouuec. xi burg'fes redd'tes lxvi den. Valuit xxiiii lib. modo xx lib.

Ibid. ten. ipfe Comes i hid. ad Troham. Levenod tenuit de rege E. & poterat ire quo voleb. H. t'ra geld. Ibi funt iiii bord. cum i car. & iiii ac. p'ti. Val. xx folid.

Ibid. ten. ipfe com. dimid. hid. quam Rog. de Laci calumn'at. ad Egeifuurde tefte comitatu. Val. x fol. & geld.

In WITELAI Hund. Ipfe Comes ten. CAMPEDENE. Com. Haroldus tenuit. Ibi xv hide geldant. In d'nio vi car. & l. vill'i & viii bord. cum xxi car. Ibi xii fervi & ii molini de vi folid. & ii denar. Ibi iii ancille. Valuit xxx lib. modo xx lib.

In LANGETREU Hund. Ifdem Com. ten. WESTONE. Elnod tenuit. T. R. E. Ibi iii hide geld. In ip'o hund. tenuit Leuuinus i hid.

Ipfe Com. ten. ii M. de iiii hid. geldant & ii ho'es ejus de eo. Elnod & Leuuinus tenuer. T. R. E. non fuit qi refponderet de his t'ris fed p. ho'es comitatus app'ciant viii lib.

XXIX. TERRA COMITIS MORITON.

In WITELAI Hund. COMES MORITON. ten. LANGEBERGE. Toni tenuit T. R. E. Ibi ii hide. In d'nio f't ii car. & iii vill'i & unus bord. cum i car. & iiii fervi. Valuit iiii lib. m'o xl fol. & geld.

XXX. TERRA GISLEBERTI E'PI LISIAC'SIS.

In LANGETREW Hund. HUGO Maminot ten. REDMERTONE de Gifleb'to ep'o Lifiac'fi & ipfe de rege. Ibi ii hide. In d'nio funt ii car. & i vill' & ii bord. & p'br cum i car. Ibi ii fervi. Valuit iiii lib. modo iii lib. Leuuinus tenuit de rege E.

Ifdem Hugo ten. de ipfo ep'o LESSEBERGE. Leuuinus tenuit. Ibi v hide. In d'nio eft una car. & v vill'i & p'br cum ii car. Ibi vii fervi. Valuit x lib. modo l. folid.

In GRIMBOLDESTOU Hund. Ifd. Hugo ten. SOPEBERIE de eod. ep'o. Aluuardus tenuit T. R. E. Ibi v hide geld. In d'nio f't ii car. & iiii vill'i & ii bord. cum ii car. Ibi iiii fervi & xx ac. p'ti. Silvæ aliq'tulum. Valuit viii lib. modo iiii lib.

XXXI. TERRA WILLELMI DE OW.

In BLACHELEW Hund. WILL'S de OW ten. STANHUS. Toui tenuit T. R. E. Ibi erant vii hide. Ibi funt in d'nio ii car. & xxi vill'i & viiii bord. cum xx car. Ibi iiii fervi & ii molini de xvii folid. & vi denar. Ibi ii arpens. uinee. Val. & valuit viii lib. Hoc M. geldat.

In LEDENEI Hund. Ifd. Will's ten. ALVREDESTONE. Bondi tenuit T.R.E. Ibi iii hide. geldant nil. Ibi eft in d'nio fed v vill'i & iii bord. h'nt iii car. Ibi pifcaria de xii den. & x ac. p'ti. Silva dimid. leuua l'g & dimid. lat. Valuit xx folid. modo xxx folid. Henricus de Fererijs calumniat eo q'd Bondi tenuerit. Willi. v'o anteceffor tenuit Rad. de Limefi.

Ifd. W. ten. ibid ii hid. geld. & ibi funt ii vill'i cum ii car. Vlnod tenuit. Val. & valuit x folid

Ifd. W. tenuit WIGHEIETE & Rad. de Limefi ante eum. Aleftan tenuit. T. R. E. N'c eft juffu Regis in forefta fua. Ibi erant vi hide & geld'b. & valeb. lx folid. modo non eft nifi pifcaria de x folid.

In TWIFERDE Hund. Ifd. W. ten. ODELAVESTON. Brictric f. Algari tenuit. Ibi ii hide. Nil ibi eft in d'nio nifi v vill'i cum v car. Ibi una pifcaria in Saverna de v folid. & molin. de xl denar. Val. & valuit xx folid. h. t'ra geld.

Ifte W. ten. in TIDEHAM unam v' & dimid. geldant. Stigand Arch. tenuit. Ibi i vill'us cum i car. & ii pifcarie. Val. & valuit x fol.

In CIRECESTRE Hund. Ifdem W. ten. DUNTESBORNE. Aleftan tenuit T. R. E. Ibi v hide & dim. geld. In d'nio funt ii car. & vi vill'i & iiii bord. cum v car. & dimid. Ibi vii fervi & molin. de viii folid. Hoc M. ten. Radulius de Will'o & geld. fed ipfe geld. retin. de iii hid. Un. francig. ten. dimid. hid. de ipfa t'ra & ibi h't i car. cum fuis ho'ibus. Tot. T. R. E. val'b. x lib. modo viii lib.

Ifdem W. ten. in TORNENTONE i hid. & Herb'tus de eo. Leuricus tenuit. T. R. E. & potuit ire quo voluit. In d'nio eft una car. & iiii fervi. Valuit xl folid. modo xx fol.

In LANGETREV Hund. Ifd. W. ten. SCIPTONE fic' Rad. de Limefi teneb. Wlui tenuit T. R. E. Ibi ii hide. In d'nio funt ii car. & ii bord. & viii fervi. Val. & valuit xl fol. Ipfe Wluui poterat ire quo vellet. Hugo ten. de Will'o.

Ifd. W. ten. CULCORTORNE & Herb'tus de eo. Scireuold tenuit T. R. E. Ibi iii virg. & v acre. In d'nio eft una car. & iii fervi. Val. & valuit xxxv fol. Hanc t'ram tenuit Rad s de Limefi fed non fuit Aleftani.

In DUDESTANES Hund. Ifd. W. ten. BEIEWRDE. Aleftan tenuit. Ibi viii hid. In d'nio funt vi car. & xx vill'i & xiiii bord. cum xxiiii car. Ibi xvii fervi & molin. de xii denar. Silva ii leuu. l'g & una lat. Valuit xv lib. modo xiii lib.

In SALEMANESBERIE Hund. Ifd. W. ten. SUELLE. Ernefi tenuit T. R E. Ibi iii hide geld. Valuit xl fol. modo x fol.

XXXII. TERRA WILL'I FILIJ BADERON.

In CIRECESTRE Hund. Will's filius BADERON tenuit ii hid. in CIRECESTRE & Hugo ten. de eo. In d'nio eft una car. & unus vill's & dimid. & iiii bord. cum i car. Ibi ii fervi. Valuit c folid. modo lxx folid. Aluui tenuit hanc t'ram.

Ifd. Will's ten DUNTESBORNE. Chetel & Aluric tenuer. & poterant ire quo volebant. Ibi iii hide & dimid. In d'nio i car. & dimid. eft & unus vill's & ii bord. cum i car. Ibi i fervus. Valuit x lib. modo lxx fol.

Ifd. W. ten. in SUDITONE i hid. Ofuuid tenuit T. R. E. & potuit ire quo voluit. In d'nio eft i car. & iiii fervi. Val. & valuit xxiiii fol.

In LANGETREU Hund. Ifd. W. ten. Weftone. Bricfi tenuit T. R. E. Ibi iii hide. In d'nio f't ii car. & ii vill'i & iii bord. cum ii car. Ibi iiii fervi & vi ac. p'ti. Valuit vi lib. modo iii lib.

In BOTELAU Hund. Ifd. W. ten. TEBRISTON. Ibi v hide. Vlfelmus tenuit de rege E. & poterat ire quo vellet. In d'nio funt iii car. & x vill'i & viii bord. cum viii car. Ibi iiii fervi & filva iii leuu. l'g & una lat. Valuit vi lib. & x folid. modo c folid.

Ifd. W. ten. HVNTELEI. Aluuin tenuit de Ældred Archiep'o & poterat ire quo voleb. Ibi ii hide. In d'nio eft una car. & iiii vill'i & vi bord. cum iii car. Ibi i fervus. Silva ii leuu. l'g & i lat. Valuit xl fol. m'o xxx folid.

X In WEST-

In WESTBERIE Hund. Ifd. W. ten. HOPE. Forne & Ulfeg tenuer. de rege E. & ibi v hide geld. & poterant ipfi teini ire quo voleb. In d'nio funt ii car. & xii vill'i & unus bord. cum xii car. Ibi iii fervi & molin. de xvii denar. Valuit viii lib. modo c fol.

Ifd. W. ten. STAURE. Ulfeg tenuit T. R. E. Valuit x fol. modo v fol. Ibi eft una hida & non geldat.

Ifd. W. ten. ii virg. & dimid. & ibi h't i vill'm & i bord. Anteceffor ejus Wihanoc tenuit fed comitatus affirmat hanc t'ram effe de d'in'ca firma regis in Woftberie. Val. iii fol.

Ifd. W. ten. NEUNEHAM. Ibi i hida & iii vill'i & iii bord. redd'tes xx fol. H. t'ra non geldat. Silva ibi ii qr. l'g & una lat.

In LEDENEI Hund. Ifd. W ten. LEDENEI. Alfer tenuit T. R. E. Ibi vi hide geld. In d'nio funt ii car. & iii vill'i & v bord. cum ii car. Ibi iii fervi & molin. de v fol. & xx ac. p'ti & in Waie dimid. pifcar. Silva i leuu. l'g & dimid. lat. Valuit iiii lib. modo xl folid.

Ifd. W. ten. HIWOLDESTONE. Ulfeg tenuit T. R. E. Ibi iii hide. H. t'ra juffu regis eft in forefta. Valet xxx fol.

In WACRESCUMBE Hund. Ifd. W. ten. HAGENEPENE & Goisfridus de eo. Eduui tenuit. Ibi v hid. In d'nio funt ii car. & vi vill'i cum iii car. Ibi iiii fervi. H. t'ra geldat. Valuit c fol. modo lx fol.

XXXIII. TERRA WILLELMI CAMERARIJ.

In WITELAI Hund. Will's Camerarius ten. ——————————WENECOTE. Wenric tenuit T. R. E. Ibi iii hide. In d'nio funt iii car. & ii vill'i & ii bord. cum i car. Ibi iiii fervi. Val. & valuit iiii lib. Hoc. M. geldat.

XXXIIII. TERRA WILL'I GOIZENBODED.

In CEOLFLEDE Hund. Will's Goizenboded ten. PEBEWORDE de rege. Vluiet & Uluuardus tenuer. T. R. E. pro ii M. Ibi vi hide & una v'. In d'nio eft una car. & i bord. & unus feruus. Valuit vii lib. modo iiii lib. & x folid.

Ifd. W. ten. WENITONE. unus tainus tenuit T. R. E. Ibi v hide. In d'nio f't ii car. & ii vill'i & unus francig. ten. i hid. & dimid. cum i car.

Hoc M. mifit Algar Com. in Pebeuuorde. Valuit x fol. modo xl fol.

Ifd. W. ten. CLOPTUNE. Hufcarle tenuit T. R. E. Ibi x hide. In d'nio iii car. & xii vill'i & iiii bord. & unus radchenift. cum viiii car. In Wicelcombe unus burg'fis. Valuit viii lib. modo c folid.

In WITELAI Hund. Ifd. Will's ten BRISTENTUNE. Brifmar tenuit. Ibi x hide. In d'nio iiii car. & xviii vill'i & iiii bord. cum xiiii car. Ibi viii fervi & iii ancillæ & ii molini de xv folid. Valuit xii lib. modo vii lib.

In SALEMANESBERIE Hund. Ifd. Will's ten. Callicote & Rannulfus de eo. Aluuinus tenuit T. R. E. Ibi iii hide geld. In d'nio iii car. & viii inter fervos & ancillas. Valuit ix fol. modo xl fol.

Ifd W. ten. AILEWRDE. Aluuinus tenuit T. R. E. Ibi una hida geld. In d'nio i car. & ii fervi. Valuit vi fol. modo iii fol.

In HOLEFORD Hund. Ifd. Will's ten. FERNECOTE. Aluuinus tenuit. Ibi iii hide geld. In d'nio ii car. & iiii vill'i cum iiii car. & xiii inter fervos & ancillas. Goisfridus ten. de Will'o. Valuit x lib. modo iii lib.

Ifd. W. ten. GETINGE. Rex E. tenuit & accommodavit eum Aluuino, Vicecomiti fuo, ut in Vita fua habet. Non tam dono dedit ut comitatus teftat. Mortuo v'o Aluuino Rex W. dedit Richardo cuidam juveni uxorem ejus & t'ram. N'c Will's fucceffor Richardi ita ten. hanc t'ram. Ibi x hide harum viiii geldant. In d'nio funt iiii car. & iiii vill'i & iii francig. & ii radchenift. & p'br cum ii bord. Inter om's h'nt v car. Int. fervos & Ancillas xi & ii molini de xiiii folid. Ibi v falinæ redd't xx fummas falis. In Wicelcombe ii burgenfes redd't xi fol. & iiii denar. Valuit xvi lib. modo vi lib.

Ifd. W. ten. CATESLAT. Aluuinus tenuit. Ibi ii hide geld. In d'nio ii car. & iiii fervi & molin. de v folid. Valuit xl folid. modo x folid.

In BOTELAU Hund. Ifd. W. ten. TETINTON. Aluuinus tenuit. Ibi vi hide. In d'nio eft una car. & viiii vill'i & vii bord. cum viiii car. Valuit vi lib. modo iii lib.

In BERINTONE Hund. Ifd. W. ten. ii hide in BERINTONE & Radulfus de eo. Aluuinus tenuit T. R. E. In d'nio eft una car. & unus fervus & molin. de xl den. & vi ac. p'ti. Val. & valuit xl fol.

In WESTBERIE Hund. Ifd. W. ten. dimid. hid. t're & dimid. pifcaria. Aluuinus Vicecom. tenuit & uxori fue dedit. H. t'am fuer. de firma Regis in Weftberie.

In GRETESTAN Hund. Ifd. W. ten. in DVNBENTVNE i hid. Sauuinus tenuit T. R. E. & potuit ire quo voluit. Valuit xx folid. modo xii folid.

XXXV. TERRA WILL'I FILIJ WIDON.

In GRIMBOLDESTOU Hund. Will's filius Widonii ten. de rege DIRHAM. Aluric tenuit T. R. E. Ibi vii hide geld. In d'nio eft una car. & xiii vill'i & xiii bord. cum ii car. Ibi viii int. fervos & ancillas & iii molini de xv folid. & vi ac. p'ti. Valuit xii lib. modo viii lib.

Ifd. Will's tenuit iii hid. hujus M. Quibus Durandus vicecom. faifierat S. MARIAM de Perfore juffu regis quas W. Com. dederat Turftino filio Rolf cum hoc M.

XXXVI. TERRA WILL'I FROISSELEW.

In DUDESTAN Hund. Will's Froiffeleuu. ten. de rege ULETONE. Godric tenuit. Ibi ii hide. In d'nio funt ii car. & iiii bord. & iiii fervi. Valuit xxx fol. modo lx fol.

In WITELAI Hund. Ifd. W. ten. in CONNICOTE dimid. hid. geld. Ibi erat i car. & iiii fervi. Valuit xx fol. modo iii folid. Brittric tenuit T. R. E.

In GRETESTAN Hund. Ifd. W. ten. in LITENTUNE i hidam. Godric tenuit. In d'nio funt ii car. & ii bord. & iii fervi & molin. de iiii folid. Valuit xl fol. modo xxx fol. et geld.

XXXVII. TERRA WILL'I FILLIJ NORMAN.

In LANGEBRIGE Hund. Will's filius Norman ten. MORCOTE. Ulfegh tenuit T. R. E. Ibi i hida. In d'nio eft una car. cum ii bord. Valuit viii fol. modo x fol. H. t'ra non geld.

In WESTBERIE Hund. Ifd. Will's ten. BICANOFRE. Morganan tenuit. T. R. E. Ibi dimid. hida. In d'nio eft dim. car. cum vi bord. Valuit v fol. modo x fol.

Ifd. W. ten. in DENE ii hid. et ii virg. t'ræ et dimid. Has tenuer. iii teini, Godric, Elric, et Ernui, T. R E. In d'nio funt iii car. Ibi xxxviii bord. h'ntes vii car. et dimid. et tres ex eis redd't viii folid. Valuit xxxiii fol. modo xliiii folid. Has t'ras c'ceffit rex E. qietas a geldo pro forefta cuftod.

In BOTELAU Hund. Ifd. W. ten. TATINTON. Ulgar tenuit de rege E. H. t'ra lib'a eft. Ibi funt vi bord. cum i car. Val. et valuit xx folid. Ibi una virg. t'ræ jacet ad foreftam et redd. xii denar.

In BLIDESLAWE Hund. Ifd. W. ten. i hid. et dim. v' t're. Siuuardus et Winftan tenuer. In d'nio funt ii car. et xvii bord. cum v car. Valuit xv fol. modo xxx fol.

XXXVIII. TERRA WILL'I LEURIC.

In CILTEHAM Hund. Will's Leuric ten. de rege LECHANTONE. Ofgot tenuit T. R. E. Ibi iii hide geld. In d'nio funt ii car. et ii vill'i et viii bord. cum i car. Ibi iiii fervi. Silva una qr. l'g et una lat. Val. et valuit xl fol.

In GRETESTAN Hund. Ifd. W. ten. HEILE. Ofgot tenuit T. R. E. Ibi xi hide. In d'nio funt iii car. et viiii vill'i et xi bord. cum viii car. Ibi erant xii fervi quos Will'us liberos fecit. Ibi molin. de x folid. Silva una leuua l'g et dimid. lat. Valuit xii lib. modo viii lib. Hoc M. geldat.

In WACRESCUMBE Hund. Ifd. W. ten. WITETUNE. Ofgot tenuit. Ibi iii hide et geld. In d'nio funt ii car. et vi vill'i et unus radchen. et iiii bord. cum iiii car. Ibi molin. de x fol. Silva una leuua l'g et dimid. lat. Valuit c fol. modo lx fol.

Ifd. W. ten. in SCIPETVNE iii hid. una v' minus et geld. Goisfridus ten. de eo. Ofgot tenuit. In d'nio f't ii car. et p'br et i vill's et iiii fervi fine car. Valuit xl fol. modo xx fol.

In BRADELEG Hund. Ifd. W. ten. TVRGHEDENE et Goisfridus de eo. Ofgot tenuit. Ibi v hide et una v' et dimid. In d'nio nichil. Ibi funt ii vill'i et iii bord. cum i car. H. t'ra geld. Valuit iiii lib. modo x lib.

XXXIX. TERRA ROGERIJ DE LACI.

In BOTELAU Hund. ROGERIUS DE LACI ten. de rege CHENEPELEI. Edricus et Leuricus tenuer. T. R. E. pro ii M. et poterant ire quo volebant. Ibi iii hide. In d'nio funt iii car. et x vill'i et vii bord. cum xii car. Ibi vii fervi. Valuit iiii lib. modo c fol.

Ifd. Rogerius ten. HORSENEHAL. Turchil tenuit de Com. Heraldo et poterat ire quo voleb. Ibi iii hide. In d'nio funt ii car. et v vill'i vill'i et iii bord. cum v car. Ibi ii ſervi et in Glouueceſt. iii burgenſes de xv den. Val. et valuit xl ſol.

Iſd. Rog. ten. CRASOWEL & Odo de eo. Ulfel tenuit T. R. E. & poterat ire quo vellet. Ibi i hida & una v'. In d'nio eſt una car. & iii vill'i & un. bord. cum iii car. Val. & valuit xx ſol.

In SALEMANESBERIE Hund. Iſd. Rog. ten. Iccumbe & Radulfus de eo. Haldene tenuit. Ibi ii hide. In d'nio ſunt ii car. & ii vill'i & ii bord. cum una car. Ibi iiii ſervi & iii ancillæ. Val. & valuit xl ſol. H. t'ra geld.

Iſd. Rog. ten. RISEDUNE & Hugo de eo. Ibi viii hide geld'tes. Aluuard, & Aſchil, & Aluuard, & Uluui tenuer. pro iiii M. In d'nio ſunt vii car. & iiii vill'i cum ii car. Ibi xii ſervi & ii ancillæ. Ibi molin. de x ſolid. Val. & valuit vii lib. & x ſol.

In HOLEFORD Hund. Iſd. Rog. ten. GETINGE. Ibi x hide geld. p'ter d'nicum q'd non geld. Brictric tenuit teinus regis Ed. In d'nio ſunt v car. & xxv vill'i et p'br & vii radchen. cum xviii car. Ibi xviii int. ſervos & ancillas & iii molini de xxiiii ſolid. & ſalina de xx ſol. & xii ſummas ſalis & in Wincelcumbe iii burgenſes de xxxii den. & in Glouuec. ii burg'ſes de x den. De ſilva & paſtura xl gallinas. Val. & valuit x lib.

In RESPIGETE Hund. Iſd. Rog. ten. TANTESBORNE & Giſleb'tus de eo. Keneuuardus tenuit teinus regis E. & poterat ire quo voleb. Ibi ii hide. In d'nio eſt i car. & ii vill'i & ii bord. cum i car. & dimid. Ibi ii ſervi. Val. xl ſol. & valuit.

In BISELEGE Hund. Iſd. Rog. ten. Wiche. Ibi una hida geld. Erneſi tenuit. In d'nio eſt i car. & xxxv vill'i & xvi bord. & p'br & iii radchen. Inter om's h'nt lii car. Ibi xi ſervi & iiii molini de xxiiii ſol. Silva v leuu. l'g & ii lat. Valuit xx lib. modo xxiiii lib. Ipſe teinus poterat ire quo voleb.

In hac t'ra ten. S. MARIA de Cireceſtre i vill'm & partem ſilve. Hoc conceſſit ei W. Rex. Val. x ſol.

Iſdem Rog ten. EGESWORDE. Ibi i hida & dimid. geld. Eluuinus tenuit. In d'nio ſunt iiii car. & iiii vill'i et iii bord. cum ii car. Ibi ii lib'i ho'es cum ii car. Ibi xv ſervi & molin. de xxx den. & ii ac. p'ti. Silva i leuua l'g & dimid. lat. Val. & valuit vi lib.

Iſdem Rog. ten. dimid. hidam cum i piſcaria in Waie & ibi i vill's cum una car. H. t'ra vocatur MODIETE. Val. & valuit xx ſol. Brictric tenuit.

Iſd. Rog. ten. dimid. hida in TEDEHAM. Arch. Stigandus tenuit. Ibi i vill's cum i car. & iiii piſcarie & dimid. Val. et valuit xx ſol.

In BRICTWOLDESBERG Hund. Iſd. Rog. ten. QUENINTONE. Ibi viii hide. Tres lib'i ho'es tenuer. Dodo & alt. Dodo & Aluuoldus pro iii M. & poterant ire quo voleb. & geld. In d'nio ſunt iii car. & xx vill'i & vii bord. & p'br & p'poſitus. Inter om's h'nt xii car. & ii radchen. cum i car. Ibi xii ſervi & ii molin. de xx ſol. & x ac. pr'ti. In Glouuec. i burg'ſis redd. iiii ſoccos, & ſab. i redd. ii ſol. Valuit viii lib. modo x lib.

Iſd. Rog. ten. LECCE & Will's de eo. Ibi v hide. Alduinus tenuit T. R. E. In d'nio ſunt ii car. & xii vill'i & i bord. cum v car. Ibi v ſervi & viii ac. pr'ti. Val. & valuit vi lib.

Iſd. Rog. ten. HETROPE & Will's de eo. Ibi ii hide. Dunning tenuit T. R. E. In d'nio ſunt ii car. & iii vill'i & iii bord. cum i car. Ibi vi ſervi. Val. & valuit c ſol.

In BERNINTONE Hund. Iſd. Rog. ten. WENRIC & Radulfus de eo. Ibi ii hide. W. Luric tenuit T. R. E. In d'nio eſt i car. & iii vill'i & ii bord. cum i car. Ibi v ſervi & molin. de v ſol. & x ac. pr'ti. Valuit c ſol. modo iiii lib.

Iſd. Rog. ten. ibid. unam hid. & unam v' & Hugo de eo. Godric tenuit teinus regis E. In d'nio eſt i car. & ii bord. & unus ſervus & molin. de iii ſol. & viii ac. p'ti. Val. & valuit xxiiii ſolid.

In CIRECESTRE Hund. Iſd. Rog. ten. STRATONE. Ibi v hide geld. preter dominium. Edmundus tenuit T. R. E. In d'nio ſunt iii car. & xvi vill'i & vii bord. cum p'bro h'ntes ix car. Ibi v ſervi & ii molini de xx ſolid. Valuit viii lib. modo vi lib.

Iſd. Rog. ten. SUINTONE & mat. ejus ten. de ſua dote. Ibi vi hide. Godricus & Leuuinus tenuer. pro ii M. In d'nio ſunt iii car. & viiii vill'i & vi bord. & p'br cum vii car. Ibi ii ſervi & molinum de x ſol. Valuit viii lib. modo viiii lib.

Iſd. Rog. ten. ACHELIE. Ibi i hida & dimid. Leuuinus tenuit modo ten. Girardus de Rog. In d'nio ſunt ii car. & ii vill'i cum p'bro h'ntes ii car. & dimid. Ibi viiii ſervi. Valuit iiii lib. modo iii lib.

In SALESMANESBERIE Hund. Iſd. Roger & mat. ejus ten. SCLOSTRE. Ibi iii hide. Offa & Leuuinus tenuer. pro ii M. & poterant ire quo voleb. In d'nio ſunt iiii car. & iiii bord. & viii ſervi & molin. de xii ſolid. Val. & valuit vi lib. De his iii hid. geldab. i hid. ſingul. annis pro x ſolid. ad opus regis.

In GRETESTAN Hund. Iſd. Rog. ten. WORMETVN. Walt. f. Ercold. de eo. Ibi v hide geld. Eduui tenuit. In d'nio ſunt ii car. & vi vill'i cum ii car. Ibi ii ſervi & molin. de viii ſolid. & x ac. p'ti. Valuit c ſol. modo iiii lib.

XL. TERRA ROGERIJ DE BELMONT.

In CEOLFLEDE Hund. ROGERUS de Belmont ten. DORSINTUNE & Rob'tus de eo. Ibi x hide. Saxi tenuit. In d'nio iii car. & viii vill'i cum v car. & vi ſervi. Valuit viii lib. modo c ſolid.

XLI. TERRA ROGERIJ DE LUERI.

In BRADELEGE Hund. ROGERIUS DE LUREI ten. HANTONE. Ibi x hide. Arch. Eldred tenuit. Rex E. ded. ei ii hid. qietas ex his x ut dicunt. In d'nio ſunt iii car. & x vill'i cum pr'b'o & i bord. cum v car. Ibi xi ſervi & in Wincelcumbe x burg'ſes redd't lxv denar. Valuit viii lib. modo vi lib.

In LANGETREWES Hund. Iſdem Rog. ten. TETEBERIE Ibi xxiii hide geld. Siuuard tenuit T. R E. In d'nio ſ't viii car. & xxxii vill'i & ii bord. & ii radchen. cum p'bro inter om's h'ntes xiiii car. Ibi xviii ſervi & molin. de xv den. & paſtura de x ſolid. & x ac. p'ti.

Iſd. Roger ten. UPTONE. Ibi ii hide & una v' geld. Aluricus tenuit de rege E. In d'nio ſunt ii car. & v vill'i & iii bord. cum iii car. Ibi viii ſervi. Hec duo M. T. R. E. val'b. xxxiii lib. modo ſunt ad firmam pro l. lib.

Iſd. Rog. ten. Culcortone. Aluric tenuit & Anſchitil de eo. Ibi i hida & dim. In d'nio ii car. & iiii ſervi. Valuit xx ſol. modo xxx ſolid.

Iſd. Roger ten. HASEDENE. Ibi iii hide & iii virg. geld. Elnoc tenuit T. R. E. In d'nio ſunt iiii car. & vii dimidii vill'i & i bord. cum iii car. & xvii ſervi & dimid. molin. de xxx denar. & xv ac. p'ti. Hoc M. tenuit qidam ho. Rog. de ep'o baioc'ſi pro xvi lib. poſtea ded. ep's eidem Rogerio cum firma.

XLII. TERRA ROGERIJ DE BERCHELAI.

In RESPIGETE Hund. ROGERIUS de BERCHELAI ten. COBERLEIE. Ibi x hide. Dena tenuit teinus Regis E. In d'nio ſunt ii car. & xviiii vill'i & iiii bord. cum v car. Ibi iiii ſervi & v ac. p'ti. Silva iii qr. l'g & ii lat. Valuit vii lib. modo viii lib.

In HEDREDESTAN Hund. Iſd. Rog. ten. Dodintone. Ibi iii hide & ii p'tes dimid. hide. Aluuinus tenuit T. R. E. In d'nio eſt i car. & vii vill'i & iiii bord. cum iiii car. Ibi iiii ſervi & x ac. p'ti. Val. & valuit iii lib.

In PULCRECERCE Hund. Iſd. Rog. ten. SISTONE. Anne tenuit. Ibi v hide geld. In d'nio ſunt ii car. & viii vill'i & x bord. cum iiii car. Ibi iiii ſervi & viii ac. p'ti. Val. & valuit c ſolid.

XLIII. TERRA RADULFI DE BERCHELAI.

In PULCHECERCE Hund. RADULFUS frater ip'ius Rogerii ten. de rege WAPELIE. Ibi i hida. Godricus tenuit. In d'nio eſt una car. & iiii ſervi. Val. & valuit xx ſolid.

In BLACELEW Hund. Iſd. Rad. ten. STANLEGE. Ibi iiii hide & dim. Godricus & Wiſnodus tenuer. p. ii M. In d'nio ſunt ii car. & vi vill'i & xiiii bord. cum xii car. Ibi v ſervi & x ac. p'ti. Valuit & val. c ſolid.

XLIIII. TERRA RADULFI PAGENEL.

In CIRECESTRE Hund. RADVLFVS Pagenel ten. TORENTVNE et Radulfus de eo. Ibi iiii hide et dimid. geld. Merleſuen tenuit. In d'nio ſunt iii car. & x vill'i & i bord. cum iii car. Ibi x ſervi. Valuit x lib. modo c ſolid.

In LANGETREWES Hund. Teneb. Rog. de Iurei unam v' t'ræ & dimid. de Rad. Paganel quam utriq; derelinquerunt.

XLV. TERRA RADULFI DE TODENI.

In WITELAI Hund. RADULFUS de Todeni ten. CHEURINGAURDE & Rogerius de eo. Ibi x hide. Briſmar tenuit. In d'nio iii car. & xiii vill'i & unus radchen. cum vi car. & viiii inter ſervos & ancillas. Valuit viii lib. modo vi lib.

In SALEMANES-

In SALEMANESBERIE Hund. Ifd. Radulfus ten. Icumbe & Rog. de eo. Ibi x hide geldantes. In d'nio iii car. & xii vill'i & ii bord. cum vii car. Ibi viii fervi. Val. & valuit vii lib.

In BOTELAU Hund. Ifd. Rad. ten. BRUNMEBERGE. Ibi v hide. Com. Heraldus tenuit. In d'nio eft i car. & xi vill'i & viii bord. cum xiiii car. Ibi unus fervus. Silva ii leuu. l'g & una lat. Valuit viii lib. modo c folid.

In GERSDONES Hund. Ifd. Radulfus ten. HAREHILLE & Rogerius de eo. Ibi v hide. Elric Aluuinus & Uluricus tenuer. p. iii M.

Ifd. Radulfus ten. OMENIE & CERNEI & Rogerius de eo. Ibi iiii hide. Quatuor teini tenuer. p. iiii M. & poterant ire quo voleb. In d'nio x car. & i vill's & i bord. Ibi xxi ferv. & molin. de v fol. & xxx ac. pr'ti. Valeb. x lib. modo vi lib.

In SALEMANESBERIE Hund. Ifd. Rad. ten. SUELLE & Drogo de eo. Ernefi tenuit. Ibi vii hide geld. In d'nio funt iiii car. & x vill'i cum vi car. & molin. de vii fol. & vi den. Valuit viii lib. modo vii lib.

XLVI. TERRA ROBERTI DE TODENI.

In SALEMANESBERIE Hund. ROTBERTUS de Todeni ten. RISENDONE. Ulf tenuit. Ibi xiii hide geld. In d'nio funt iii car. & xxiii vill'i & vi bord. cum x car. Ibi viii inter fervos & ancillas & molinus de x fol. & unus burg'fis in Glouuecef t. de iii den. Valuit xii lib. modo x lib.

In GRIMBOLDESTOU Hund. Ifd. Rob'tus ten. HOREDONE. Ibi x hide geld. Ulf tenuit. In d'nio funt iii car. & xi vill'i & viii bord. cum viii car. Ibi vii fervi & molin. de vi folid. & xx ac. p'ti. Silva ii leuu. & una lat. Valuit xii lib. modo vii lib.

In BISELEGE Hund. Ifd. Rob'tus ten. SAPLETORNE & FRANTONE. In uno v hide & in alio v hide. Ulf tenuit. In d'nio funt vii car. & xvii vill'i & viiii bord. cum x car. Ibi xiii fervi & ii molini de vi folid. Silva dimid. leuua l'g & ii qr. lat. H. ii M. T. R. E. val'b. xiiii lib. fimul modo xvi lib.

XLVII. TERRA ROBERTI DISPENSAT.

In GRETESTANE Hund. ROTBERTUS Difpenfator ten. WICUENE. Ibi x hide geld. Balduinus tenuit. In d'nio funt iii car. & xxxii vill'i & x bord. cum xii car. Ibi i fervus & ii molini de x fol. & x ac. p'ti. In Wincelcumbe i burgenfis de xvi den. Valuit xii lib. modo xvi lib.

XLVIII. TERRA ROBERTI DE OILGI.

In SALEMANESBERIE Hund. ROTBERTUS de Olgi ten. RISENDVNE. Ibi x hide geld. Siuuard tenuit. In d'nio iiii car. & xii vill'i & ii bord. cum. v car. Ibi viii fervi & ii molini de xx folid. Valuit x lib. modo viii lib.

In BRADELEG Hund. Ifd. Rotb'tus ten. TURCHEDENE. Ibi v hide & ii virg. & dimid. geld. Siuuard tenuit. In d'nio funt iiii car et xii vill'i cum vi car. Ibi viii inter fervos et ancill. Valuit vi lib. modo c fol.

In SALEMANESBERIE Hund. ROGERUS de Olgi ten. NIWETONE de Ofb'no f. Ricardi. Ibi v hide geld. Turftan tenuit. In d'nio ii car. et viii vill'i cum iiii car. et dimid. Val. iii lib.

XLIX. TERRA RICARDI LEGATI.

In HEDREDESTAN. Hund. RICARDUS Legatus ten. de rege TORMENTONE. Ibi viii hide. Alricus tenuit de rege E. In d'nio f't vi car. et xx vill'i et iiii bord. et p'br et unus radechen. Int. om's xii car. h'nt. Ibi xii fervi. Valuit xii lib. modo xv lib.

L. TERRA OSBERNI GIFARD.

In LANGELEIE Hund. OSBERNUS Gifard ten. de rege ROCHEMTUNE. Ibi iii hide geld. Dunne tenuit T. R. E. In d'nio funt ii car. et vi vill'i et vii bord. cum iii car. Ibi v fervi et xx ac. p'ti et falina ad Wich de iiii fummis falis. Silva i leuua l'g et dim. lat. Val. vi lib.

In LETBERG Hund. Ifd. Ofb'nus ten. STOCHE. Ibi v hide geld. Dunne tenuit. In d'nio funt iiii car. et viii vill'i et iii bord. et p'br cum viii car. Ibi iiii fervi. Valuit vi lib. modo viii lib.

In RESPIGET Hund. Ifd. Ofb'nus ten. BRIMESFELDE. Ibi viiii hid. geld. Duns tenuit de Com. Heraldo. In d'nio funt iii car. et xvi vill'i et vi bord. et p'br cum xii car. Ibi viii fervi et iiii ancillæ et ii molini de lxiiii den. In Glouuec. v burg'fes de ii fol. Val. et valuit xii lib.

Ifd. Ofb'nus ten. ALDEBERIE fed non p'tinuit ad Duns h'o t'ra quam Ofb'nus ten. ut fcira dicit. Eilricus tenuit et potuit ire quo voluit. Ibi i hida et i car. Val. et valuit x fol.

LI. TERRA GOISFRIDI ORLETEILE.

GOISFRIDUS ORLETEILE ten. de rege in BAUDINTUNE ii hid. et unam v' geld. Bolli tenuit. Non eft in d'nio q'd. Ibi ii vill'i et viii bord. cum iii car. Val. et valuit lx fol. Ibi viii ac. p'ti.

LII. TERRA GISLEB'TI FILIJ TUROLD.

In CIRECESTRE Hund. GISLEBERTUS filius Turoldi ten. in ACHELIE i hid. de rege et Ofulfus de eo. Keneward tenuit T. R. E. In d'nio funt ii car. et iii bord. et vi fervi. Valuit xl folid. modo xxx folid.

Ifd. Gifleb'tus ten. in TURSBERIE dim. hida et Ofuuard de eo. Aluuardus tenuit. In d'nio eft i car. Valuit x fol. modo xv fol.

In RESPIGET Hund. Ifd. Gifleb'tus ten. CERNEI. Ibi vii hide. Elaf et fr. ejus duo teini tenuer. pro ii M. et poterant ire quo voleb. In d'nio f't iiii car. et vii vill'i et vi bord. cum v car. Ibi vi fervi et molin. de viii folid. et vi ac. pr'ti. Silva ii qr. l'g et una lat. Ibi iiii milites Gifleb'ti h'nt cum fuis ho'ibus vii car. et molin. de viii fol. Tot. T. R. E. val'b. xiiii lib. modo xii lib.

Ifd. Gifl. ten. RINDECOMBE. Ibi v hide geld. Aluricus tenuit. In d'nio eft i car. et iii vill'i et vii bord. cum iii car. Ibi vii fervi et unus francig. ten. t'ram duor. villor. et molin. de viii folid. et iiii ac. pr'ti. Valuit vii lib. modo c folid.

Ifd. Gifl. ten. RINDECUMBE et Walterius de eo. Ibi iii hide geld. In d'nio f't ii car. et iiii vill'i et iii bord. cum ii car. Ibi vi fervi et molin. de v folid. et iii ac. pr'ti. Val. et valuit vi lib.

In SALEMANESBERIE Hund. Ifd. Gifleb'tus ten. ELEWRDE et Walterus de eo. Aluuinus tenuit. Ibi iiii hide geld. In d'nio ii car. et iii vill'i cum ii car. et vi inter fervos et ancillas. Val et valuit xl fol.

Ifd. Gifl. ten. HURFORD. Alfer tenuit. Ibi i hida geld. In d'nio ii car. iiii vill'i et i bord. cum ii car. et ii fervi et molin. de v fol. Val. et valuit xl folid.

LIII. TERRA DURANDI DE GLOWEC.

In WESTBERIE Hund. DURANDUS Vicecomes ten. unum M. de iii hid. Aluuold tenuit et geldab. In d'nio eft i car. et iiii vill'i et iii bord. cum iiii car. Ibi ii fervi. Valuit lx fol. modo xl fol.

In GERSDONES Hund. Ifd. Durandus ten. in ESBROC i hid. et Miles ejus qidam de eo. In d'nio i car. et i bord. et i fervus. Val. et valuit x folid.

In CIRECESTRE Hund. Ifd. Durandus ten. ii hid. in DUNTESBORNE et Radulfus de eo. Wluuardus tenuit pro M. de rege E. In d'nio funt ii car. et iii vill'i et unus bord. cum i car. Ibi iiii fervi et ii ac. pr'ti. Val. et valuit xl fol.

In LANGETREU Hund. Ifd. Durandus ten. CULCORTONE et Rogerus Ivri de eo. Ibi ii hide et ii v' et dimid. Grim tenuit. In d'nio f't ii car. et vi vill'i cum iii car. Val. et valuit iiii lib.

In GRIMBOLDESTOU Hund. Ifd. Durandus ten. DEDMERTONE et Anfchitil de eo. Ibi iii hide geld. Leuuinus tenuit de Com. Heraldo. In d'nio funt iii car. et viii bord. cum i car. et iiii fervi et vi ac. pr'ti. Valuit xxx fol. modo xl fol.

In DVNESTANE Hund. Ifd. Durandus ten. WADUNE. Ibi v hide. Quinque fr's tenuer. pro v M. et poterant ire quo voleb. et pares erant. In d'nio f't v car. et unus vill's et vii bord. cum v car. T. R. E. valeb. viii lib. m'o c folid.

In CELFLEDETORNE Hund. Ifd. Durandus ten. CHIESNECOTE et Walterius de eo. Ibi ii hide et dim. Leuuinus et Leuui tenuer. pro ii M. In d'nio funt ii car. et iiii bord. Val. xl fol. modo lx folid.

In SALEMANESBERIE Hund. Ifd. Durandus ten. ICCUMBE et Walterius de eo. Ibi ii hide geld. Turftan tenuit. In d'nio ii car. et ii vill'i et ii bord. cum i car. et vi inter fervos et ancillas. Valuit xxx fol. modo xl fol.

In WACRES-

In WACRESCUMBE Hund. Ifd. Durandus ten. SCIPTUNE & Radulfus de eo. Eduui tenuit. Ibi iii hide & dimid. geld. In d'nio funt ii car. & iii vill'i cum ii car. & iiii fervi & x ac. pr'ti. Valuit iiii lib. modo xl fol.

In WITESTAN Hund. Ifd. Durandus ten. in HERSEFELD vii hide geld. Godrick & Edric ii fr's tenuer. pro ii M. & poterant ire quo voleb. In d'nio funt iii car. & viiii vill'i & xi bord. cum viiii car. Ibi iiii fervi & v figuli redd't xliiii den. Silva dimid. leuua l'g & iii qr. lat. Val. & valuit vi lib.

Ifd. Durandus ten. MORTUNE. Ibi iii hide geld. Anti tenuit. In d'nio eft i car. & iiii vill'i & vi bord. cum iii car. & dimid. Ibi iiii fervi & xx ac. p'ti. Valuit iiii lib. modo xl fol.

In GRETESTAN Hund. Ifd. Durandus ten. LITETUNE & Randulfus de eo. Ibi dimid. hida geld. Leuenot tenuit pro uno M. Ibi eft una car. Val. & valuit x folid.

In WITELAI Hund. In CONDICOTE ten. Ofb'nus de Durando i hid. & dimid. Val. & valuit xx fol.

LIIII. TERRA DROGONIS FILIJ PONZ.

In BLACHELEU Hund. DROGO Filius Ponz ten. de rege FRANTONE. Ibi x hide geld Ernefi tenuit. In d'nio funt iii car. & x vill'i & viii bord. cum vi car. Ibi ix fervi & molin. de x folid. & x ac. p'ti. Silva i leuua l'g & iii qr. lat. In Glouuec. i burg'fis de vi den. Val. & valuit c folid. De hoc M. ten. Rog. de Laci i hid. injufte.

In BRICSTUOLDES Hund. Ifdem Drogo ten. LECE. Ibi x hide geld. Cola tenuit. In d'nio funt iiii car. & xv vill'i & iiii bord. cum viiii car. Ibi viiii fervi & molin. de x folid. & x ac. p'ti. Valuit viii lib. modo x lib.

LV. TERRA WALTERIJ FILIJ PONZ.

In BRICSTUOLDES Hund. WALTERIUS Filius Ponz ten. de rege LECE. Ibi x hide geld. Tofti Com. tenuit. In d'nio funt iiii car. & xvi vill'i & vi bord. & p'br cum viii car. Ibi xii fervi & molin. de x folid. & xx ac. p'ti. Valuit xii lib. modo xv lib.

LVI. TERRA WALTERIJ FILIJ ROGER.

In BERNINTON Hund. Walterius Filius Rogerij ten. de rege BERNINTONE. Ibi viii hide. Turftan & Eduui tenuer. pro ii maner. In d'nio funt iiii car. & xiiii vill'i & p'br & ii bord. cum viiii car. Ibi xiiii fervi & molin. de x folid. & xx ac. p'ti. Val. & valuit viii lib.

In GERSDONES Hund. Ifd. Walterus ten. CERNEI. Ibi xiiii hide & una v'. Arch. Stigandus tenuit. In d'nio funt ii car. & xxv vill'i & p'br & viiii bord. cum x car. Ibi iiii fervi & c ac. p'ti & iii molini fuer. de xxx folid. Val'b. xvi lib. modo xii lib.

Hoc M. calumniatum eft ad eccl'am S. MARIE de Abendone fed om'is Commitatus teftificatus eft Arch. Stigandus x Annis tenuiffe vivente E. Rege. Hoc M. ded. W. Com. Rogerio vicecomiti patri Walterij.

LVII. TERRA WALTERIJ DIACONI.

In WITELAI Hund. Walterius Diaconus ten. de rege CHESNECOTE. Ibi iiii hide & dimid. Goduinus tenuit & potuit ire quo voluit. In d'nio ii car. & viii vill'i cum vi car. & x fervi Val. & valuit iii lib.

LVIII. TERRA WALTERIJ BALISTAR.

In WESTBERIE Hund. WALTERIUS Baliftarius ten. de rege BULELEGE. Ibi iiii hide geld. Tovi tenuit de rege E. In d'nio funt ii car. & iiii vill'i & vi bord. cum iiii car. Ibi iiii fervi & x ac. p'ti. In Glouuec. unus burg'fis redd. xviii den. Valuit lx fol. modo xl fol.

Ifd. Walter. ten. RODELE. Ibi i hida geld. Tovi tenuit. In d'nio eft i car. & ii vill'i & iiii bord. cum ii car. Valuit xl fol. modo x fol.

In BLIDESLAU Hund. Ifd. Walt. ten. dimid. hidam que non geldat. Palli tenuit. Ibi eft molin. Val. xviiii folid.

In LANGELEI Hund. Ifd. Walter. ten. FRANTONE. Ibi v hide geld. Aleftan tenuit de Bofcombe. In d'nio eft i car. & x vill'i & xi bord. cum v car. Ibi v fervi & ii molini de v folid. Ibi & eccl'a q. non fuit. Valuit viii lib. modo iii lib.

LIX. TERRA HENRICI DE FERIERES.

In BRICTUOLDEBERG Hund. HENRICUS de Ferreres ten. LECELADE. Bar. Siuuard tenuit. Ibi xv hide T. R. E. geldantes fed ipfe Rex c'ceffit vi hid. quietas a geldo. Hoc teftat. om'is comitatus & ipfe qi Sigillum Regis detulit. In d'nio funt iiii car. & xxviiii vill'i & x bord. & unus Francig. ten. t'ram unius vill'i. Int. om's h'nt xvi car. Ibi xiii fervi & iii molini de xxx folid. & pifcaria de cc anguill. xxv minus. De pratis vii lib. & vii fol. p'ter fenum boum. In Wicelcumbe ii burgenfes redd. xvi den. & unus in Glouuec. fine cenfu. Tot. M. T. R. E. val'b. xx lib. & modo fimiliter.

LX. TERRA ERNULFI DE HESDING.

In BRICTUOLDESBERG Hund. HERNULFUS de Hefding ten. CHENEMERESFORDE. Ibi xxi hida geld. Ofgot tenuit de Com. Heraldo. In d'nio funt vi car. & xxxviii vill'i & viiii bord. & i radchen. cum xviii car. Ibi xiiii fervi & iiii molini de xl fol. & xl den. Et de p'tis viiii lib. p't' pafturam boum & de ouili cxx penfas cafeorum. In Glouuec. vii burgenfes redd. ii folid. Tot. T. R. E. val'b. xxx lib. modo lxvi lib. & vi fol. & iii den.

Ifd. Hernulf. ten. Etherope. Ibi vii hide. Uluuardus tenuit. In d'nio funt vi car. & xxiii vill'i cum x car. Ibi xii fervi & molin. de xv folid. Valuit viii lib. modo xii lib.

In GERSDONES Hund. Ifd. Hernulf. ten. in OMENIE iiii hide & ii virg. & dim. Elricus & Godricus tenuer. pro ii M. In d'nio funt iii car. & vii vill'i & ii bord. cum ii car. Ibi iiii fervi. Tot. valuit & val. vi lib.

In GRIMBOLDESTOU Hund. Ifd. Hernulf. ten. ALDEBERIE. Ibi v hide geld. Edricus tenuit. In d'nio f't iii car. & iiii vill'i cum iiii car. & ibi viiii fervi & unus francig. h'ns i car. Ibi vi ac. p'ti. Val. & valuit x lib.

Ifd. Hernulfus ten. MADMINTUNE. Ibi iiii hide geld. Edricus tenuit. In d'nio f't ii car. & vi vill'i & viii bord. cum p'b'ro h'nt xiii car. Ibi viiii fervi & viii ac. p'ti. Val. & valuit x lib.

Ifd. Hernulfus ten. ACHETONE. Ibi v hide geld. Edricus tenuit. In d'nio f't iii car. & iiii vill'i & iii bord. cum iiii car. Ibi xv ac. p'ti. Val. & valuit c fol.

In SINESHOVEDES Hund. Ifd. Hernulfus ten. HANUN & Humbaldus de eo. Edric tenuit. Ibi dimid. hida. In d'nio f't ii car. cum viii bord. & iiii fervis. Val. & valuit xl folid.

LXI. TERRA HERALDI FILIJ COMITIS RAD.

HERALDUS filius Com. Radulfi ten. de rege SUDLEGE. Pat' ejus Radulfus tenuit. Ibi x hide geld. In d'nio funt iiii car. & xviii vill'i & viii bord. cum xiii car. Ibi xiiii int. fervos & ancillas & vi molini de lii folid. Silva iii leuu. l'g & ii lat.

Ifdem Heraldus ten. TODINTUN. Pat' ejus tenuit. Ibi x hide geld. In d'nio f't iii car. & xvii vill'i & vii bord. & ii lib. ho'es. Int. om's h'nt viii car. Ibi x int. fervos & ancill. & ii molin. de xx folid. De una falina l. mittas fal. H. duo M. Val. & valuer. xl lib.

LXII. TERRA HUGON. DE GRENTEM.

In CEOLFLEDE Hund. HUGO de Grentemaifnil ten. PEBEWORDE. Ibi ii hide & una v' Duo teini tenuer. pro ii M. Ibi iii car. & i vill's & unus bord. & vii fervi.

Ifd. Hugo ten. MERESTUNE. Ibi ii hid.

Ifd. Hugo ten. QUENINTUNE. Ibi ii hide. Unus teinus tenuit. In d'nio ii car. & v vill'i & i bord. cum iii car. Ibi iiii fervi & una ancilla. Valuer. vii lib. m'o iiii lib.

Ifd. Hugo ten. QUENINTUNE & Rogerus de eo. Ibi xii hide. Balduinus tenuit T. R. E. In d'nio iii car. & xvii vill'i & ii bord. cum viiii car. Ibi vi fervi. Valuit vii lib. modo vi lib.

Ifd. Hugo ten. WESTONE & Rogerus de eo. Ibi iiii hide. Balduinus tenuit. In d'nio ii car. & vi vill'i cum iii car. Ibi iiii fervi & v ancille & molin. de x fol. Val. vii lib. modo vi lib.

Ifd. Hugo ten. WILCOTE & Clericus ejus de eo. Ibi ii hide & dimid. In d'nio ii car. & ii vill'i & i bord. cum i car. Ibi iiii fervi & una ancilla. Valuit xl fol. modo xxx. Leuricus tenuit.

LXIII. TERRA HUGONIS LASNE.

In DUDESTAN Hund. HUGO Lafne ten. de rege BROCOWARDINGE. Ibi v hide. Turchil tenuit de rege E. In d'nio f't ii car. & viii vill'i & vi bord. & p'br & ii lib'i ho'es & p'pofitus. Int. om'es h'nt xv car. Ibi iiii fervi & molin. de ii folid. Silva una leuua l'g & dimid. lat. Valuit vi lib. modo c folid.

In WACRESCUMBE Hund. Ifd. Hugo ten. SCIPTVNE. Ibi v hide geld. Uuluard tenuit. In d'nio funt ii car. & iiii vill'i & i bord. cum ii car. Ibi v fervi & molin. de x folid. Valuit iiii lib. modo iii lib.

In BRADELEGE Hund. Ifd. Hugo ten. SALPRETUNE. Ibi x hide geld. Uuluuard tenuit. In d'nio f't iii car. & x vill'i & p'br cum vii car. ‖ et xi int. fervos et ancillas et v ac. p'ti. Valuit viiii lib. modo vii lib.

‖ In another copy after this mark [‖] it runs thus : *& vi fervi & molin. de x fol. & viii ac. p'ti.* Then follows *Valuit* as above, which is according to Sir Matthew Hale's copy.

In CIRECESTRE Hund. Ifd. Hugo ten. BENWEDENE & Gifleb'tus de eo. Ibi iii hide geld. Wluuard tenuit. In d'nio f't iii car. & v vill'i cum iii car. & vi fervi & molin. de x fol. & viii ac. p'ti. Val. & valuit iiii lib.

LXIIII. TERRA MILONIS CRISPIN.

In DUDESTAN Hund. MILO Crifpin ten. in BRUURNE iii virg. t're. Wigot tenuit. In d'nio i car. & vii bord. cum ii car. & dimid. pifcaria. Valuit xl fol. modo xxx fol.

In LANGETREU Hund. Ifd. Milo ten. CERINTONE & Goisfridus de eo. Haminc tenuit de rege E. Ibi ii hide geldant. In d'nio funt iii car. & iii vill'i & viii bord. cum iii car. & dimid. Ibi xii fervi & molin. de xxx den. & iiii ac. p'ti. Val. & valuit iiii lib.

In GRIMBOLDESTOU Hund. Ifd. Milo ten. ALRELIE. Wigot tenuit. Ibi una hida. In d'nio funt ii car. & vii vill'i & v bord. cum vii car. Ibi iiii fervi & molin. de x fol. & xii ac. p'ti. Val. & valuit c folid.

LXV. TERRA URSONIS DE ABETOT.

In WITELAI Hund. URSO de Wireceftre ten. in CHEISNECOTE unam hidam. Eluuinus tenuit pro M. & geld. In d'nio i car. & iiii fervi. Valuit xl fol. modo x folid.

LXVI. TERRA HASCOIT MUSARD.

In WITELAI Hund. Hafcoit Mufard ten. de rege SUINEBERIE. Chenuicelle tenuit. Ibi x hide. In d'nio iii car. & xviii vill'i & iii bord. cum viiii car. & x int. fervos & ancill. & molin. de vi den. Valuit xii lib. modo x lib.

Ifd. Hafcoit ten. i hidam in CHEISNECOTE & geld. Uluuinus tenuit pro M. Ibi i car. & i bord. Val. & valuit x fol.

In SALEMANESBERIE Hund. Ifd. Hafcoit ten. AIFORDE. Ibi v hide geld. Ernefi tenuit. In d'nio f't ii car. & xii vill'i & i bord. cum v car. Ibi viii int. fervos & ancill. Val. iiii lib.

In GRETESTAN Hund. Ifd. Hafc. ten. ESTUNE. Ibi vi hide geld. Ernefi tenuit. In d'nio f't iii car. & xii vill'i cum iiii car. & viiii int. fervos & ancill. Ibi molin. de viii folid. & xx ac. p'ti. Val. & valuit vi lib.

In CIRECESTRE Hund. Ifd. Hafcoit ten. SUDINTONE. Ibi x hide geld. p'ter d'nium. Ernefi tenuit. In d'nio f't iii car. & viii vill'i & x bord cum p'b'ro h'ntes v car. & dimid. Ibi vii fervi & xx ac. p'ti. Valuit x lib. modo viii lib.

In BISELEGE Hund. Ifd. Hafcoit ten. GRENHAMSTEDE. Ibi i hida geld. Ernefi tenuit. In d'nio f't iii car. & viii vill'i & v bord. & p'br & unus radchen. Int. om's h'nt viiii car. Ibi x fervi & viii ac. p'ti. Silva i leuua l'g & dimid. lat. Valuit c fol. m'o vii lib.

LXVII. TERRA TURSTINI FILIJ ROLF.

In GERSDONES Hund. TURSTINUS filius Rolf ten. de rege OMENIE. Ibi vii hide. Tovi tenuit de rege E. In d'nio f't iii car. & viii vill'i & p'br cum viii car. Ibi viii fervi. De hac t'ra ten. Tovi ii vill'orum t'ram & quidam Miles t'ram iiii vill'orum. Ad eccl'am p'tin. dim. hida & iiii ac. p'ti. Valuit viii lib. modo vi lib.

Ibid. ten. ipfe Turften i hid. Uluui tenuit pro M. et poterat ire quo voleb. In d'nio ii car. cum i bord. Valuit lx fol.

In CIRECETST. Hund. Ifd. Turften. ten. in Achelie unam hid. Brictric tenuit pro Manerio de rege E. In d'nio eft una car. & iii vill'i cum iii car. Ibi vi fervi & iiii ac. p'ti. Val. & valuit l. fol. Girvius ten. de Turftino.

In GRIMBOLDESTOU Hund. Ifd. Turftinus ten. HILDESLEI & Bernardus de eo. Ibi i hida. Aluricus tenuit. In d'nio f't ii car. & v dimidij vill'i & vii bord. cum ii car. Ibi viii fervi & iii molin. de xviii fol. & viii ac. p'ti. Valuit xl fol. m'o lx fol.

In BACHESTAN Hund. Ifd. Turft. ten. TORTEWORD. Ibi una hida. Aluuold tenuit. In d'nio funt ii car. & vi vill'i & vii bord. cum vii car. Ibi vi fervi et iii molini de xv folid. et x ac. p'ti. Silva i leuu. l'g et dimid. lat. redd. v folid. Valuit vii lib. modo c. folid.

In BLACHELAVE Hund. Ifd. Turft. ten. STANTONE. Ibi v hide. Tovi tenuit de rege E. In d'nio f't ii car. et viii vill'i et vi bord. cum x car. Ibi iiii fervi et ii molini de xxxv folid. et x ac. p'ti. Silva i leuua l'g et dimid. lat. Val. et valuit c fol. De hac t'ra ten. Tovi ii hid. Elemofina Regis W.

Ifd. Turftin. ten. FRIDORNE. Auti tenuit. Ibi iii hide geld. In d'nio eft una car. et iii vill'i et iii bord. cum ii car. et unus fervus. Val. lx folid. modo xxx fol.

LXVIII. TERRA ANSFRIDI DE CORMELIIS.

In BISELEGE Hund. ANSFRIDUS de Cormelies ten. WINESTANE. Ibi v hide. Uluuard tenuit. In d'nio f't iii car. et x vill'i et iiii bord. et unus francig. cum viii car. Ibi viii fervi et molin. de xx den. Val. et valuit vii lib.

In CELFLESTORN Hund. Ifd. Ansfr. ten. WESTONE. Duo teini tenuer. unus ho. Com. Heraldi. alter Leurici. Ibi x hide pro ii M. Et poterat ire quo voleb. In d'nio iiii car. et xviii vill'i et i bord. cum viiii car. et xii fervi. Valuit c fol. modo vii lib.

Ifd. Ansfr. ten. in NORTUNE v hid. Duo teini tenuer. pro ii M. et poterant ire quo voleb. In d'nio iiii car. et viiii vill'i et ii bord. cum iiii car. et x fervi. Valuer. iiii lib. modo vi lib.

In WITELAI Hund. Ifd. A. ten. BECESHORE. Brifmer tenuit. Ibi iii hide. In d'nio iii car. et x vill'i cum vi car. et xvi fervi et unus ho' redd. vi fochs. Valuit viii lib. modo vi lib.

In GRETESTAN Hund. Ifd. A. ten. POTESLEPE. Godric tenuit. Ibi iii hid. geld. In d'nio f't ii car. et iii vill'i et v bord. cum ii car. Ibi xi fervi et ii molini de xv fol. Silva i leuua l'g et una lat. Val. c fol. m'o iiii lib.

In WACRESCUMBE Hund. Ifd. A. ten. in SCIPTUNE iii virg. t're. Bil tenuit pro M. et geld. In d'nio eft i car. Val. et valuit x fol. Hic Bil potuit ire q'o voluit.

In BRADELEGE Hund. Ifd. A. ten. WINESTUNE. Edricus, et Leuric, et Elricus tenuer. pro iii M. et poterant ire quo voleb. Ibi v hide geld. In d'nio funt iiii car. et viiii vill'i & iiii bord. cum v car. Ibi x int. fervos et ancill. et molin. de vii fol. et vi den. et xv acre p'ti. Valb. viii lib. modo vii lib.

In CIRECESTRE Hund. Ifd. A. ten. i hid. in TANTESBORNE. Elmer tenuit pro M. et potuit ire q'o voluit. In d'nio eft una car. et unus vill's et ii bord. et v ancille. Valuit xl fol. m'o xx fol.

In RESPIGETE Hund. Ifd. A. ten. ELCHESTANE. Duo Leuuini tenuer. pro ii M. Ibi iiii hide et dimid. Et in COLESBORNE i hid. & dimid. Eluuinus tenuit pro M. et poterant ire q'o voleb. ifti iii teini. In d'nio f't ii car. et v vill'i et ii bord. cum iii car. et dimid. Ibi iiii fervi et x ac. p'ti. Silva dimid'. leuua l'g et ii qr. lat. Medietatem hujus M. ten. un. Miles de Ansfrido et ibi h't ii car. et v vill'i et ii bord. cum iii car. et alt. Miles ten. Colefburne de eo et h't ibi dimid. car. et ii vill'i et ii bord. cum i car. et molin. de l. denar. H. val'b. viii lib. m'o vii lib. et x folid.

Ifd. A. ten. SIDE et Turftinus de eo. Leuuinus tenuit de rege E. Ibi iii hide geld. In d'nio f't ii car. et i vill. cum p'br'o et iii bord. cum i car. et vi fervi et iiii ac. p'ti. Valuit iiii lib. m'o xl fol.

Ifd. A. ten. ii v' et dimid. in DANTESBORNE et Bernardus de eo. Elmer tenuit pro M et poterit ire quo voleb. Ibi eft i bord. Val. et valuit xl folid.

Ifd Ansfridus ten. i hid. & dimid. PANTELIE & i hid. CHILCOT & i hida. CHITIFORD & i hida. HEGE. Int. tot. iiii hid. et dimid. Ulfel et Eluuard et Wiga tenuer. pro iiii M. una hida et dim. lib'a a geldo. In d'nio f't ii car. et vii vill'i et iii bord. cum vii car. Ibi ii fervi et molin. de vii fol. et vi den. Val'b. iii lib. et x fol. modo iiii lib. Qui has t'ras teneb. poterant ire quo voleb.

Has t'ras et WINESTAN et TANTESBORNE fup'ius fcriptas habuit Ansfridus de Walterio de Laci cum ejus nep'te accepit. Alias v'o terras ten. de rege.

LXIX. TERRA HUNFRIDI CAMERARIJ.

In WITELAI Hund. HUNFRIDUS Camerarius ten. de rege LANGEBERGE. Ibi iiii hide geld. Elftan et Blacheman

Blacheman et Edric et Alric tenuer. pro iiii M. et poterant ire quo voleb. In d'nio erant iiii car. et iii vill'i et v bord. cum iii car. Ibi ix fervi. Valeb. xvi lib. modo c folid.

In GERSDONES Hund. Ifd. Hunfridus ten. in OMENIE i hidam. Æluui tenuit pro M. de rege E. In d'nio ii car. & iiii fervi & i bord. & molin. de v fol. Val. & valuit xxv fol.

In CIRECESTRE Hund. Ifd. H. ten. i hid. in PRESTITUNE. Æluuinus tenuit pro M. In d'nio eft una car. & ii fervi & iii bord. cum i car. Val. & valuit xxx fol. Hic q. teneb. poterat ire q'o voleb.

Ifd. H. ten. i hid. in NORCOTE. Eluuardus tenuit pro M. In d'nio funt ii car. & ii bord. cum dim. car. Val. & valuit xl fol. Has ii t'ras tenuit Will's de Hunfrido. Q. teneb. poterant ire q'o vol'b.

Ifd. H. ten. ii hid. in SUDINTONE & Anfchitil de eo. Aluuard tenuit pro M. In d'nio eft i car. & ii bord. cum dim. car. & molin. de v folid. Val. & valuit xl fol. Q. teneb. poterat ire q'o voleb.

In BACHESTANES Hund. Ifd. H. ten. ACTUNE. Heroldus tenuit. Ho. Eluui H'des q'i poterat ire quo voleb. Ibi ii hide & dimid. In d'nio eft i car. & iii vill'i & iii bord. cum dimid. car. Ibi ii fervi & molin. & dimid. de lxiiii den. & v ac. p'ti. Val. & valuit xl fol.

Ifd. H. ten. WICHEN. Ibi iiii hide. Tres ho'es F. Algar Briƈtrici tenuer. pro tribus Maner. T. R. E. & poterant ire q'o voleb. In d'nio erant iii car. & viiii vill'i & xiiii bord. cum viiii car. Ibi v fervi & xx ac. p'ti & vi qr. de filva. Val. & valuit xii lib. Has ii villas ded. Regina Hunfrido Actune & Wichen.

In GERSDONES Hund. Ifd. H. ten. i virg. t're in ESTBROCE & Will's de eo. Aluuine tenuit pro M. Ibi eft i vill's. Val. ii fol. & valuit.

LXX. TERRA HUNFRIDI DE MEDEHAL.

In DUNESTAN Hund. HUNFRIDUS de Medehalle ten. UTONE. Pagen tenuit. Ibi i hida. In d'nio i car. & iii fervi & iiii bord. cum ii car. Valuit xxx folid. modo xl fol.

In WITELAI Hund. Ifd. Hunfridus ten. i hid. in CHEISNECOT. Aluui tenuit pro M. & geld. In d'nio erant ii car. & vi fervi & i bord. & val'b. l. folid. modo xii den. tant. p'pt' prata.

LXXI. HUNFRIDI COCI.

In SALESMANESBERIE Hund. HUNFRIDUS Coqus ten. in LECHETONE i hid. & ibi h't i car. cum iiii bord. & val. xv fol. & geld. Ofb'nus de Kerefburg tenuit. Ordric tenuit pro M. T. R. E.

LXXII. TERRA SIGARI DE CIOCHES.

In HOLIFORDE Hund. SIGAR de Cioches ten. de rege HALLINGE. Comitiffa Goda tenuit. Ibi x hide geld. In d'nio funt iii car. & xx vill'i & v bord. cum viiii bord. Ibi vi fervi & iii ancille. Silva eft ibi. Valuit vii lib. modo viii lib.

In BRADELEGE Hund. Ifd. Sigar ten. HASEDENE. Goda tenuit. Ibi x hide. Will's Rex c'ceffit iii hid. ex his quietas a geldo ut teftat. comitatus. In d'nio f't iii car. & xiiii vill'i & p'br cum x car. Ibi vi fervi. Valuit viii lib. modo vii lib.

Ifd. Sigar ten. Jeneurde. Goda tenuit. Ibi v hide. Ex his iii f't qiete a geldo per W. Regem ut dicit h'o Sigardi. In d'nio f't iii car. & xiiii vill'i & ii bord. cum vii car. Ibi vii fervi & molin. de xl den. Silva iii qr. l'g & ii lat. Valuit vii lib. modo vi lib.

LXXIII. TERRA MATHIU DE MORETANIE.

In LANGETREWES Hund. MACI de Mauritania ten. de rege SCIPETONE. Danus Strang tenuit. Ibi x hide geld. In d'nio f't ii car. & iiii vill'i & ii bord. cum iiii car. Ibi iiii fervi & molin. de x folid. De paftura ii fol. Valuit xv lib. modo viii lib.

Ifd. Maci ten. SCIPETONE & Rumbaldus de eo. Ibi x hide geld. Joh's tenuit T. R. E. In d'nio f't iii car. & iiii vill'i & viii bord. cum iiii car. Ibi iiii fervi & molin. de xii fol. De paftura ii fol. Valuit xv lib. modo viii lib.

Ifd. Maci ten. ibi i hid. & Rumbaldus de eo. Aluuinus tenuit & potuit ire quo voluit & Rainb'tus Flandrenfis p'tea habuit. In d'nio eft i car. & i vill'i & i bord. cum dim. car. Valuit xx folid. modo xiiii folid.

LXXIIII. TERRA GOZELINI BRITONIS.

In BACHESTANES Hund. GOZELINUS Brito ten. de rege CIRVELDE. Elfelt tenuit de rege E. Ibi iii hide. In d'nio f't ii car. & iiii vill'i & vii bord. cum iiii car. Ibi iiii fervi & molin. de x folid. & viii ac. p'ti. Silva dimid. leuua l'g & lat. Valuit iiii lib. m'o xl fol.

LXXV. TERRA ROGERII FILIJ RAD. No'i'e CLISTONE.

In SINESHOVED Hund. Rogerius filius Rad. ten. unum Manerium q'd tenuit Seuuinus p'pofitus de Briftou de rege E. & poterat ire cum hac t'ra quo voleb. nec aliquam firmam inde dabat. Ibi iii hide. In d'nio f't iii car. & vi vill'i & vi bord. cum ii car. Ibi iii fervi & viii ac. p'ti. Val'b. c folid. modo lx folid.

In SINESHOVEDES Hund. Rogerius h't i manerium de i hida t're & ibi h't ii fervos. Hoc app'ciat' x folid. Non fuit qui de hac t'ra refpond'et. Walterius h't un. M. de i virg. t're. Valuit xx den. m'o ii folid.

LXXVI. TERRA UXORIS GERI.

In HOLIFORDE Hund. UXOR GERI de Loges ten. de rege iiii hid. in GETINGE. Tres taini tenuer. pro iii M. & geldab. Gulvert Tovi & Turbern. In d'nio eft i car. & i vill's cum dim. car. Val'b. xl fol. modo xx fol.

LXXVII. In GERSDONES Hund. Balduinus ten. de Rege iii v' t're in OMENIE. Aluuinus tenuit T. R. E. Ibi eft i car. cum ii bord. Val. & valuit x folid.

LXXVIII. TERRE TAINORUM REGIS.

In BERNINTONE Hund. ELSI de Ferendone ten. de rege in WENRIC iii hid. & dimid. Uuluric & Tovi & Leuuinus tenuer. pro iii maner. & poterant ire quo voleb. In d'nio f't v car. & i vill's & vii bord. cum i car. Ibi x fervi & molin. & dimid. de xii folid. & vi den. Val'b. iii lib. modo viii lib.

In GERSDONES Hund. Chetel ten. de rege i hid. & unam v' in WENRIC. Ipfe tenuit T. R. E. Ibi i car. & iiii fervi. Val. & valuit xx folid.

In RESPIGETE Hund. Ifd. Chetel ten. iii virg. & dimid. in DANTESBORNE. Ipfe tenuit T. R. E. Ibi i car. & ii bord. & ii fervi. Valuit x fol. modo xv.

In LANGETREU Hund. OSWARD ten. de rege REDMERTONE. Ibi iii virg. geld. Ipfe tenuit T. R. E. Ibi eft i car. Valuit xx fol. modo x fol.

In CIRECESTRE Hund. Edric f. Ketel ten. BAUDINTONE de rege. Pater ejus tenuit T. R. E. Ibi iii hid. & iii virg. geld. In d'nio funt ii car. & iii vill'i cum i car. & iiii fervi & xv ac. p'ti. Val. & valuit lx folid.

In DUNESTAN Hund. EDWARDUS ten. de rege dimid. hid. pro M. & ibi h't in d'nio i car. & vi bord. cum ii car. Val. xxx fol.

In CEOLFLEDE Hund. EDDIET ten. de rege BICHEMERSE. Ipfa tenuit T. R. E. Ibi i hida & in d'nio ii car. & i vill's & i bord. & iiii fervi. Valet & valuit xx folid.

In SALEMANESBERIE Hund. CVENILD Monial. ten. de rege viiii hid. in NIWETONE. Ex his iiii hide geld'b. Efmerus tenuit pro M. In d'nio funt iiii car. & vii vill'i cum v car. & m'o habet. i car. & molin. de v folid. & xiii inter fervos & ancillas. Valuit viii lib. m'o v lib.

In CILTENHAM Hund. BRICTRIC ten. de rege iiii hid. in LECHAMETONE & geld. Ipfe ii hid. T. R. E. & Ordric tenuit alias ii. Rex W. utranq; eid. Briƈtric c'ceffit p'gens in Norman. In d'nio h't i car. & viiii bord. cum iii car. & ii fervos & i ancill. Silva ii qr. l'g & ii lat. Val. xxx folid.

In HOLEFORD Hund. ALWOLD ten. de rege PIGNOCSIRE. Ipfe tenuit T. R. E. Ibi iiii hid. una ex his non geld'b. In d'nio funt iiii car. & xi vill'i & v bord. cum iiii car. Ibi viii fervi & molin. de xxx denar. In Wicelcumbe i burgenfis redd. viii den. Silva dimid. leuua l'g & una qr. lat. Val. & valuit iiii lib.

In BECHEBERIE Hund. ELWARD f. Reinbaldi ten. ALDESWRDE. Balchi tenuit. Ibi ii hide geld. In d'nio eft i car. & iiii vill'i & ii bord. cum ii car. & unus fervus. Valuit xl folid. modo xxx fol.

In WITESTAN Hund. ELSI ten. de rege LANGENEI. Ibi v hide geld. Ipfe tenuit T.R.E. In d'nio f't ii car.

ii car. & vi vill'i & xii bord. cum viiii car. Ibi iiii ſervi & x ac. p'ti & piſcaria. Valuit c ſolid. modo lx ſolid.

In SINESHOVEDES Hund. DONS ten. de rege BETONE. Ipſe tenuit T. R. E. Ibi ii hide una ex his geld'b. alia ad eccl'am p'tinebat. In d'nio ſunt ii car. & v vill'i & ii bord. cum v car. Ibi iiii ſervi & x ac. p'ti. Valuit vi lib. modo iii lib.

In BLACHELEU Hund. BRICTRIC ten. de rege WIDECESTRE. Ipſe tenuit T. R. E. Ibi i hida geld. Ibi ſunt xvi vill'i & xii bord. cum xvi car. In d'nio nichil. In Glouuec. i burgenſis redd. xx ferra. Ibi molin. de x ſolid. Val. & valuit c ſolid.

Hardinc ten. in Vadimonio de Brictric WITENHERST. Ipſe Brictric tenuit T. R. E. Ibi v hide geld. In d'nio eſt i car. & p'br & ii vill'i & vi bord. cum v car. Ibi iii ſervi & molin. de x ſol. & x ac. p'ti. Val. c ſol. modo xxx ſolid.

EDRIC f. Chetel ten. ALCRINTONE. Pater ejus tenuit T. R. E. Ibi iiii hide & dimid. geld. In d'nio eſt i car. & vi vill'i & iiii bord. cum viii car. Ibi iii ſervi & molin. de x ſolid. & viii ac. p'ti. Silva i leuua l'g & dimid. lat. Val. & valuit iii lib.

In BOTELAU Hund. MADOCH ten. de rege RUDEFORD. Ipſe tenuit T. R. E. Ibi ii hide. In d'nio ii car. & iii vill'i & iiii bord. cum iii car. & molendin. redd. annonam q'tum poteſt lucrari. Val. & valuit xl ſol.

END OF GLOUCESTERSHIRE IN DOMESDAY-BOOK.

The following EXPLANATIONS will elucidate ſome Paſſages in the ANTIENT SURVEY.

SOME authors derive the word *Villani* from the French, *vilain*, or from the Latin, *villa*, a country farm. Villenage was of two kinds, the one being a ſtate of ſervitude, which ſome were ſubject to from their birth, called *pure villenage*; from whom, ſays Bracton, *uncertain and undeterminate ſervice was due to the lord.* The other was villenage by *tenure*, by which the tenant was bound to perform *certain ſervices* agreed upon between him and his lord, ſuch as plowing of his ground, reaping of his corn, &c. Of this ſort the *Villani* ſo often mentioned in Domeſday are ſuppoſed to be.

The *Bordarii* were ſuch as held a cottage, or ſome ſmall parcel of land, on condition of ſupplying the lord with poultry, eggs, and other ſmall proviſions for his board and entertainment. Hence ſmall eſtates ſo held were uſually called *bord-lands*. *Gloſſ. to Kennett's Par. Antiq.* The *bordarii* held thoſe lands which we now call Demeſnes.

The *Servi* and *Ancillæ* were pure villeins, living under the arbitrary pleaſure of the lord, and received their wages according to his diſcretion.

Liberi homines were ſuch as might diſpoſe of their eſtates without leave of their lords.

Radchenistres are explained in Domeſday to be free men. See *Terra S. Petri Weſtmon. p. 72. col. 2.*

Sochs, for *Socmanni*. A certain number of free ſocmen appears to have been neceſſary to every lord of a manor, for holding the pleas of the manor court, which the Saxons called *Soke*, or *Soc*, a word ſignifying a franchiſe, or juriſdiction, to which a franchiſe was annexed. And it is from this that ſome derive the terms *ſocmen* and *ſocage*, with great appearance of truth. *Lord Lyttelton's Life of H. 2. vol. 2. p. 252.*

Francigena was a general name for all perſons who could not prove themſelves to be Engliſh. Canute, the Dane, having ſettled himſelf in the kingdom at peace, at the requeſt of his lords diſcharged his army, upon condition, that whoever ſhould kill an alien ſhould be liable to juſtice; and if the manſlayer eſcaped, the town where the man was killed ſhould forfeit 66 marks to the king; but if it was not able to pay the fine, it ſhould be levied on the hundred. And further, that every man murdered ſhould be accounted *francigena*, except he could be proved to be an Engliſhman before the coroner.

Coliberti, men who held in free ſocage, whom we ſometimes meet with under the names *Conditionales* and *Colones*, from which laſt the word *Clown* is ſuppoſed to be derived.

Ut ſcira dicit, (p. 76, col. 2. &c.) in the language of Domeſday, ſignifies the jury by which the ſurvey was made, the form of which remains now in the Cotton Library, beginning thus: *Hic ſcribuntur Inquiſitio terrarum quomodo barones Regis inquiſiverunt, videlicet, per ſacramentum Vicecomitis, Scire, & omnium Baronum, & earum Francigenarum, & totius Centuriatus, Preſbyteri, Prepoſiti, ſex Villani, uniuſcujuſque villæ.* Each article concludes in theſe words,—*& alii omnes Franci & Angli de hoc hundreto juraverunt.* Cott. Lib. Tib. A. vi.

Burgaris and *Burgenſes* are properly men of trade, or the inhabitants of a borough or walled town.

Hai, *Haia*, a hedge, and ſometimes it ſignifies a park, or incloſure. *Bracton.*

Harduices, is a word variouſly underſtood. Cowell derives it from *Heord-wic*, the herdſman's village, which ſeems to be a right interpretation.

Broce, a thicket, or covert of buſhes and bruſh wood.

The *Pound*, ſo often mentioned in Domeſday-Book for reſerved rent, was the weight of a pound of ſilver, conſiſting of twelve ounces.

The *Shilling*, conſiſted of twelve pence, and was equal in weight to ſomething more than three of our ſhillings; ſo that the Norman Pound, conſiſting of twenty of ſuch ſhillings, was worth three pounds two ſhillings of our preſent money. The Saxon *Shilling* was valued at five pence, and forty-eight of them went to the pound; but one of their pence was three times the weight of our preſent ſilver penny, conſequently the Saxon Pound was alſo worth three pounds ſterling of our preſent money. But it is obſervable that there was no ſuch piece of money as the ſhilling coined in this kingdom, 'till the year 1504. The penny was antiently the only current ſilver coin, 'till about the reign of king John, when the ſilver *half-penny* and *farthing* were introduced; but in the year 1353 king E. 3. began to coin larger pieces, which obtained the name of Groats from their ſize. Crowns and Half-Crowns were firſt coined in the year 1551.

The *Mark*, muſt be underſtood to be two thirds of a pound of ſilver, that is, twice the value of our preſent pound ſterling. And Mr. Madox has ſhewn, in his *Hiſtory of the Exchequer*, that, in the reign of king Steghen, nine marks of ſilver were accepted in payment for one mark of gold, as appears from the pipe-rolls. And that, in another inſtance, ſix pounds in ſilver were paid for one mark of gold.

Sir Robert Atkyns has endeavoured to ſhew what proportion the value of ſilver, at the time of the ſurvey, bore to the preſent value of it. "The rate of neceſſaries," ſays he, "which ſubſiſt "humane life, is the true eſtimate of money. Since therefore "wheat corn ſeems to be the moſt neceſſary of any one thing, "we may beſt value coin by the price of wheat in the ſeveral "ages. A buſhel of wheat, ſoon after the Norman conqueſt, "was ſold for a penny, which was equal in weight to our three "pence. At this day a buſhel of wheat, one year with another, "may be valued at four ſhillings, which is ſixteen times the value "of it ſix or ſeven hundred years ago. The concluſion will be, "that a man might live in that time as well on twenty ſhillings "a year of our money, as on ſixteen pounds a year at preſent. "And to carry it further, two pounds of their money would buy "as much wheat as ninety-ſix pounds of the preſent.

Oro, in *Domeſday*, ſignifies a Saxon piece of coin, value ſixteen pence, and ſometimes, according to the variation of the ſtandard, twenty pence. In the laws of king Canute fifteen *Oræ* make a pound.

The expreſſions *libras numeratas*, *penſatas*, *ad penſum*, *de numero*, *ad ſcala*, are to be underſtood in this manner. It has been already ſhewn that 240 ſilver pence, perfect as they came from the mint, weighed juſt a pound Troy. But much of the money being clipped, the words *penſatas*, *ad penſum*, were ſometimes inſerted to ſignify that the money ſhould not be received in payment by tale; but that if the coin had been any way diminiſhed, the payer ſhould make good the weight, by adding other money, altho' it amounted to more or leſs than ſix-pence in the pound, which was the *ſolutio ad ſcalam*. The *libra numerata*, or *ad numerum*, or *de numero*, was the pound by tale of 240 pence, without regard to the weight of them. The payment *ad numerum* was always intended in grants, unleſs the contrary was expreſſed.——*Arſas et penſatas. Arſas* ſignified lawful money, whoſe alloy was tried by fire.

Firma,—*Red. firmam unius noctis*,—*unam noctem de firma.*— The two latter of theſe expreſſions are to be underſtood of entertainment for ſo many nights. For our anceſtors computed time not by days, but by nights, which was not intirely out of uſe 'till about Henry the Firſt's time; and hence it is that we now ſay a fortnight, ſe'nnight. The A. S. word *Feormian* ſignifies to feed, or yield victuals; and thoſe who held the out-lands of the lord, as cuſtomary tenants, paid him a certain portion of victuals and things neceſſary for human life, which rent they called a *Feorm*; and tho' ever ſince the reign of H. 2. the rent has been changed from victuals into money, yet we ſtill retain the names *farm*, and *farmer*.

Geldat. *Geldum* with the A. S. ſignified *tributum*. So *geldare* here ſignifies to pay tax or tribute.

Menſura, was a buſhel.

Modius, uſually a buſhel, but various, according to the cuſtom of the country.

Dicra ferri, a quantity of iron, ſuppoſed to conſiſt of ten bars. *Gale's Hiſt. Brit.* 766.

Leuca, *Leuua*, a meaſure of land conſiſting of 1500 paces; but according to Ingulphus (p. 710.) of 2000 paces. In the *Monaſticom* (1 *tom. p.* 313.) 'tis 480 perches.

THE

T H E

HISTORY

Of the CITY and DIOCESE of

GLOUCESTER.

Of the Name, Foundation, Situation, Extent, &c. *of the* CITY.

GLOUCESTER is a handſome city, the capital of the ſurrounding county, to which it gives name. It is ſituated in lat. 51° 49′ ‖, longitude 101 miles W. from London; in the midſt of the fine and extenſive vale of * Glouceſter. It ſtands 36 miles N. E. from Briſtol, 25 S. W. from Worceſter, 32 S. from Hereford, and 26 E. from Monmouth.

The river Severn flows on the weſt ſide of it, where is a convenient key or wharf. It is the firſt port upon that river, with its proper officers, *viz.* a cuſtomer and collector, a controller, a ſearcher, a ſurveyor and two boatmen. Queen Elizabeth granted the city this privilege by her charter, dated the 20th of June in the 22d year of her reign.

The proſpect of the city, on the weſt ſide of it is delightful, being adorned with many beautiful towers and ſpires, but more eſpecially with the lofty and moſt elegant tower of the cathedral church, which, to uſe Leland's expreſſion, ſtands as a pharos to all parts around for a conſiderable diſtance.

From the middle of the city, where the four principal ſtreets meet, there is a deſcent every way, which makes it not only clean and healthy, but adds greatly to the beauty of the place.

The buildings are chiefly of brick, whereas formerly they were of wood. The ſtreets are well paved, and enlightened with lamps by authority of parliament. An act paſſed 12° E. 4. to oblige the inhabitants to pave the ſtreets, and the next year, the king by his charter impowered the corporation to do it. This had before been an object of royal care, for king E. 3. in the 9th year of his reign, gave the toll of Glouceſter for ſeven years for that purpoſe; and afterwards king H. 4.

‖ But according to Sir Robert Atkyns, 51° 53.

* This has ſometimes been called the *vale of Eveſham*, but I know not by what authority. Antiently this vale was denominated from the city of Glouceſter; for *Malmeſbury de Giſt. Pont. Aug.l.* 4. and Camden from him, ſays, this city ſtands in the *Vale of Glouceſter*. Ravelle in his *Giſt.* to the priory of Beckford, in *Mon. Ang.* ſays, Beckford is in the *Vale of Glouceſter*. In a confirmation of lands by king R. 1. to Almaric Deſpencer, Stanley is expreſsly ſaid to be in the *Vale of Glouceſter*. And Malmeſbury ſays, that Briſtol ſtands in the ſame vale.

in the 13th year of his reign, did the fame for five years, as appears by the city books and writings.

The Britons called this city *Caer Gloi*, *Caer Glou*, or *Caer Gloui*; which name, after the Romans had fubdued a great part of this ifland, was changed into *Glevum*, or *Clevum*, agreeable to the Latin idiom. This conqueft was made in their fecond expedition by Aulus Plautius, the prætor, under the emperor Claudius, about the 44th, 45th, or 46th year of the Chriftian æra. Many of the Britons fubmitted to the Roman government, and a colony was ftationed at Gloucefter, as a convenient fituation to curb the Silures, who gave the invaders more trouble than any other of the inhabitants of the ifland. It was called *Colonia Glevum*, as appears by an antient infcription to be feen on a ftone near the north gate at Bath. Dr. Gale has given his reading of it, which Mr. Hern, in his notes upon Leland's Itinerary, finds fault with, and fubftitutes the following:

DEC. COLONE GLEV.

VIXT AN. LXXXo VI.

The doctor thinks the decurio died at Bath, whither he is fuppofed to have gone to refrefh his forces.

When the Romans quitted this ifland, the Britons were mafters of the town for fome time; but it was taken from them by the Saxons in the year 570, or 577. They called it Gleauceꞅꞇeꞃ, Gleauceꞅꞇꞃe, Gleapanceaꞅꞇeꞃ, Glouceꞅꞇeꞃ, Gleuceꞅꞇeꞃ, Gleanceꞅꞇꞃe. By the modern Latinifts it is written *Glavorna*, *Glavornia*, *Glovernia*, *Gloveria*, *Glocejtria*, *Glauceftria*, *Gloeceftria*, and *Glouceftria*. By antient Englifh writers, Glocef-tar, Glouceftre, Glowcefter, Glouceftyre, Gloecefter; and now we write it Gloucefter, or, by contraction, Glocefter, but it is pronounced Glofter.

Varunnius and others have accounted differently for the name of this place. They would have us believe that the emperor Claudius, having here married his daughter Genuiffa to king Arviragus, commanded the town, and caftle, adds the mafter of St. Albans, to be § built, and ordered it to be called after his own name. Thus, according to them, have we the origin of *Claudia*, *Claudioceftria*, *Clauceftria*, *Claudiana civitas*, *Claudiaceftrienfis civitas*, *Claudioceftre*, *Clauceftre*, *&c.* A little after this, a fmall alteration is faid to have been made in the name, out of refpect to one Gloius, a general, whom Claudius begat here, and was fometime governor of Demetia, a part of South Wales. Robert of Gloucefter fays, (*Chron. p.* 66.) that before the emperor Claudius's time 'twas a little town, and that to render it more like to Gloius's name, it was called Glouceftre, inftead of Clauceftre, which was its former name.

But Dr. Plot, in his *Natural Hiftory of Oxfordfhire*, obferves, that notwithftanding the name *Claudii Caftrum* may feem to favour thefe ftories, yet in all likelihood there was never any fuch matter; for tho' Suetonius and Dion enumerate the emperor's daughters, and fhew to whom they were married, neither of them mentions any thing of this † Genuiffa; which might be expected, efpecially as the latter of thefe hiftorians lived in Claudius's time, and bore the office of conful. Befides, the beft hiftorians agree, that ‡ Arviragus was never heard of before the time of Domitian: So that this derivation of its name, founded on fo many fabulous ftories, muft be rejected.

Ninius advances an opinion of his own, that there were three brothers, the fons of Glouus, great grandfather to king Vortigern, who built this town, and called it after their father's name; but this ftory is as groundlefs as the former, for *Clevum*, or *Glevum*, with its diftance from *Durocornovium*, or *Corinium*, now Cirencefter, is mentioned long before that time by Antoninus, in his thirteenth journey.

Others have conjectured, that when the Romans divided Britain into five parts, the making of this town the head of *Flavia Cæfarienfis*, which was one of the five, gave rife to the name; for, fay ‖ they, Flavius in the Britifh language founds the fame as Glaui, which by a Britifh pronunciation might eafily pafs into Gloui.

But this etymology is alfo to be rejected for the better one of Minfhew, Skinner, and others, who are of opinion, that the Britons gave it the name of *Caer Glou*, or *Caer Gloyw*, which in their language fignifies the *bright* or * *fplendid town*, on account of its fituation, which is on a fine eminence in the midft of the flat and low part of the country of the *Dobuni*, and therefore it might juftly be efteemed fair, bright, and beautiful. Camden is of this opinion, and fays that upon the like account, the Greeks had their *Callipolis*, *Callidromos*, *Calliftratia*, and amongft the Englifh, *Brightftow*, and *Fairford*.

The Romans, as was ufual with them, altered the termination of the Britifh name, to make it

§ They pretend that this was the city mentioned by Seneca, *in Lib. de morte Claudij*, who fays, that the barbarians in Britain worfhiped him for a god, and built a city for his honour.

† Bale, (*Cent.* 1. *p.* 18.) fays, Genuiffa was the emperor Claudius's natural daughter. Her name is fometimes written Jeniffa, Gennifa, and Gewife.

‡ Bifhop Stillingfleet mentions Arviragus (*Ant. Brit.*) as a confiderable Britifh prince, and an enemy at firft to Cæfar; but he brings him down to the time of Domitian. He is otherwife called Armiragus, Armoger, Arivoger, or Arivog; by Hector Boetius, Protufagus; by the Britons, Gwerydh ap Arwenydog, brother to king Guiderius, and fon to king Cunobeline.

‖ Gale's Antoninus, *p.* 129.

* The word *Caer*, fignifies only a wall, fortrefs, or inclofure; which being prefixt to the names of Roman towns, becaufe fortified, has occafioned feveral to fuppofe the genuine fignification of it to be a town or city. We have divers camps on our mountains called *Caereu*, where we have not the leaft ground to fufpect that ever any cities were founded; and in fome places I have obferved the church-yard wall to be called *Caer y Vynwent*. Nor does it feem improbable that this *Kaer* was derived originally from *Kai*, which fignifies to fhut up or inclofe. *Camden col.* 822.

it more agreeable to their own language, and called it *Glevum*; whence, or from the Britiſh name, the Saxons called it Ᵹleauceaꞅꞇꞃe; for wherever they found the word *Caer*, in the Britiſh names of places, they always tranſlated it by ceaꞅꞇꞃe, which was of the ſame ſignification in their own language.

This is a place of conſiderable antiquity. Alfred of Beverly mentions *Kair Gloi*, i. e. *Glouceſtria*, as one of the twenty eight cities built by the Britons before the Roman invaſion. One of thoſe highways, called by the Romans *Vias Conſulares*, *Regias*, *Prætorias*, *Militares*, *&c.* paſſed thro' the town, from St. David's to Southampton, in Hampſhire. This was the Irminſtreet, and ſeems to have come from Newland or Dudſton, on the N. ſide of St. Mary de Cript church, along the ſchool-maſter's garden, and Mary-lane, and under the gate belonging to the ſchool, acroſs the ſouth-gate ſtreet, to the houſe directly oppoſite to the ſchool, and thence to the river Severn.

It is obſervable that this place is called a city, [*civitas*] when many others, at preſent much larger, are called only burghs. Alfred of Beverly ſays expreſſly, that it is a city; and Huntingdon affirms that there are more cities in England than biſhopricks, and then inſtances Glouceſter, &c. But notwithſtanding the title of *civitas*, or city, was frequently given to this place in ſeveral king's charters, pope's bulls, and other authentic records and regiſters, it cannot thence of neceſſity be inferred, that it was really ſuch. Antiently indeed there was little difference between cities and great boroughs; but afterwards a diſtinction aroſe, when cities, properly ſo called, were inveſted with particular privileges, and by particular charters made counties of themſelves. The word *Urbs*, which is often uſed when ſpeaking of this place, is of a more reſtrained ſignification than *Civitas*, and denotes a large and populous place.

This town being well ſituated to curb the Silures, was enlarged by the Roman emperors, as their occaſions and neceſſities of employing more forces required. It is ſaid to have been large and populous, when the conſul of it was ſummoned, together with other great perſons, to attend king Arthur's court, to ſolemnize his coronation.

In the year 577, according to the Saxon chronicle, when it was taken from the Britons by the Weſt Saxons, 'twas reputed one of their principal cities.

During the wars between the Britons and Saxons, and (after the Norman conqueſt) between the crown and the great barons, this place was thought very important, on account of its ſituation, which always gained it the favour of one party, and drew upon it the reſentment of the other; ſo that it hath experienced a great variety of fortune.

In the year 679, (as it is in *Mon. Anglic.*) Wolphere, ſon of king Penda, repaired it, having greatly ſuffered in the wars, and ſo enlarged and adorned it, as Bede informs us, that about the beginning of the eighth century, it was eſteemed one of the nobleſt cities in the kingdom. And in the year 918, it was very inſtrumental in routing and deſtroying the Daniſh army.

In § 1087, or according to ſome 1088, the greateſt part of the town was conſumed by fire, in the wars between the different parties of William Rufus and his brother Robert. And again in 1093, or according to others, 1095, William de Ewe, or Auco, with his Welch confederates, in an inſurrection to depoſe king William the Second, aſſaulted and greatly damaged the town and neighbourhood.

The town being antiently built of timber, made it extremely ſubject to fire. On the eighth ides of June, 1101, ſays Dunelm, (others will have it to be on the 11th of June, 1102) moſt of the town was burnt down; and on the 7th ides of March, 1121, *(Leland's Itin.)* or 1122, *(Antiq. Brit.)* it ſuffered the like calamity.

In the beginning of king Stephen's reign 'twas large and handſome, but ſiding with the empreſs Maud, and her adherents, greatly impoveriſhed it. And we learn by a MS. called the Glouceſter book, in the library of C. C. C. Oxon, that it was burnt on the 5th ides of May, 1150; and that again on the 17th of June, 1264, almoſt the whole town was deſtroyed by fire.

About 1487, there were 300 houſes in it fallen to decay; and an act of parliament was made 27 H. 8. to enforce the rebuilding of part of it, which had ſo good effect, that even in the ſame reign, there were ſeveral ſtreets and lanes which are now intirely demoliſhed and forgotten. But the terrible deſtruction made at the ‡ ſiege, Aug. 10th, 1643, in pulling down or burning 241 dwelling houſes and other buildings, reduced it ſo much, that it has ſcarcely yet recovered its former ſize and grandeur.

Mr. Camden ſays of Shrewſbury, when the Normans firſt ſettled here, it was a well built and well frequented city; for it appears by Domeſday-Book, that it was taxed at 7*l.* 16*s.* to the king yearly. Upon which it may be obſerved, that if the extent and riches of places, hold any proportion with the tax paid to the king at that time, Glouceſter muſt have been, and it certainly was, greatly ſuperior to Shrewſbury, as appears by the following account.

In Domeſday-Book, the groſs of the borough

§ Loyde, in his *Hiſtory of Wales*, ſays, that in 1087, the earls of Hereford and Shrewſbery, with the Welchmen, burnt all Worceſterſhire and Glouceſterſhire. The Saxon Chronicle mentions the commotions in that year.—Dugdale ſays, William de Auco, or Ewe, with his forces, did great miſchief in Glouceſterſhire 1 Willi Rufi; but by miſtake he calls this 1088. For the intent of this rebellion was to obtain the crown for Robert, upon his father's death, which was in 1087. But hiſtorians beginning the year at different times might occaſion this difference.

‡ Civ.

is

is furveyed at the beginning of the county, diftinctly from the Berton. The demefnes of the crown are placed firft, as follow, *viz.*

" In king Edward's time, the city of Gloucefter paid thirty-fix pounds in money; twelve fextaries [*gallons*] of honey, according to the meafure of the burgh; thirty-fix dicres of iron [*each of ten bars*]; a hundred iron rods drawn out for the nails of the king's fhips, and fome other fmall cuftoms in the king's hall and chamber. Now this city pays the king fixty pounds, twenty in *ora*, and of money the king hath twenty.

" In the demefne lands of the king, Rogerius de Berchelai holds one houfe, and one fifhery in the vill, and it is out of the king's hands. Balduinus held it in king Edward's time.

" Ofbernus Epifcopus [*Exon.*] holds the land and manfions which Edmarus held. They pay ten fhillings, with other cuftom.

" Gaufridus de Manneuile holds fix manfions. In king Edward's time, thefe paid fix fhillings and eight pence, with other cuftom.

" Willielmus Baderon, two manfions of thirty pence.

" Willielmus Scriba, holds one manfion of fifty one pence.

" Rogerius de Laci, one manfion of twenty fix pence.

" Ofbernus Epifcopus, one manfion of forty one pence.

" Bernerus, one manfion of fourteen pence.

" Willielmus Calvus, one manfion of twelve pence.

" Durandus the fheriff, two manfions of fourteen pence. The fame Durandus holds one manfion of twenty fix pence, and another manfion which pays no cuftom.

" Hadeuuinus holds one manfion which pays gabel, but witholds other cuftom.

" Gofbertus, one manfion; Dunning, one manfion; Widardus, one manfion; Arnulfus the prieft one manfion which pays gabel, and witholds other cuftom.

" All thefe manfions paid royal cuftom in the time of king Edward. Now king William hath nothing thence, nor Rotbertus his minifter.

" Thefe manfions were in the farm of king Edward when he was alive, and after his death; but now they are taken away from the farm and cuftom of the king. In king Edward's time, there was demefne of the king in the city, all his entertainment and clothing. When earl William was received to farm, he was likewife clothed.

" There were fixteen houfes where the caftle ftands, which are now wanting, [*demolifhed*] and in the burgh of the city, fourteen that are wafte.

The number of burgages and houfes with the names of the owners, fpecified in the above account, are twenty three, befides fixteen which were demolifhed for the building of the caftle; fourteen that were wafte; and fome that belonged to Ofbernus, that are not numbered; but they yielded the yearly rent of ten fhillings, which at five pence or fix pence a houfe, the ufual rate of houfes in Gloucefter at that time, will produce twenty in number. Befides thefe, there are mentioned in the fame furvey, under the titles of feveral owners of lands, as *Terra S'ti Dyonifij, &c.* about eighty two in all. Under the title *Terra S. Petri de Glouec'* it is faid, " In king Edward's time Saint Peter in Glouueceftre had from its burgages xix. *fol.* and v. *den.* and xvi. falmons. Now it hath the fame number of falmons and l. *fol.*" In this inftance alfo the number of burgages is not mentioned, but according to the above calculation, we may well fuppofe them to be a hundred. Admitting then this calculation, the total of burgages and houfes taken notice of in Domefday, are about two hundreds and fifty-five.

That Gloucefter was formerly a place of confiderable note, may alfo be collected from its fines, tallages, aids, and fee farm rents.

In Madox's *Hiftory of the Exchequer*, *pp.* 226, 227, 485, &c. are the following particulars. The ferm of the burgh, 16, 17, 19, 22 H. 2. was lv. *lib.* and the increment thereof v. *lib.* King Richard the Firft, by his charter dated the 5th and 6th of May, 5° *regni*, granted to the burgeffes to farm the whole borough, with the appurtenances, at the yearly rent of lv. *lib.* and x *lib.* increafe of farm. King John, by his charter in the firft year of his reign, granted it fo to them; and 8° *regni*, § they paid c. marks for having this to farm, according to the king's charter. 2° and 9° H. 3. the old increment of the borough was v. *lib.* and the new x. *lib.* more; and that king, by his charter 6 Apr. 11° *regni*, granted it to them exactly as king John did by his.

The king, by his letters patents, dated 10 Jan. 7° E. 3. for a fine § which they paid him, and for fome other caufes, granted to them the borough, with its rents, free from all charges, except lxv. *lib. per ann.* And it appearing that king H. 3. granted to Ely de Rochefter, and his heirs, v. *lib.* thereof, to be allowed, that allowance is yearly made, and the fee farm rent now paid is but lx. *lib. per ann.*

Gloucefter was antiently a diftinct hundred of itfelf, and 'tis probable that it continued fo 'till the reign of king E. 3. for before that time, feveral acts are expreflly faid to be done in the full hundred of Gloucefter. The high fheriff of Gloucefterfhire, in anfwer to the king's writ, dated 5° Mar. 9° E. 2. certified as follows: *Hundred de Gloucefter. Et D'na Margaret regina eft Domina ejufdem Hundred.* Hundred of Gloucefter. And the lady queen Margaret is lady of that hundred.

The perambulation or bounds of the town,

§ Civ.—Madox's Hift. of the Exchequer, p. 281. * A. 11.

which is generally walked every year, is about three miles. Thomas Styward and John de Elmore, bailiffs of the borough, *die Mercurij*, 44° E. 3. perambulated the liberties thereof; and the perambulation was then as follows, *viz.*

From the west-gate to the cross in the middle of the west bridge, the meadows of the abbot of S. Peter's on each side of the bridge excepted. Then from the river Severn, within the little gate towards the east, between the meadow of the archdeacon, and the garden of the Bartholomews, to Little Severn; and so from Little Severn to Tulliwell brooke, on which there is a bridge with iron bars. Thence from the highway to the gate of the monks garden, with the lane called Fetelane, to Newlands, by marks and bounds, as appears by the stones there fixed. Thence to the south-gate, to the limit there, the inn excepted, with the houses and lands on the other side. Thence from Rigley stile, to the tenements of the abbat of S. Peter's. Thence to the lane called Severn-street, to the key at the end of that street, the king's castle, and the meadows excepted, as it appears by the extent of the city, in the treasury of the kings of England. And, to prevent disputes, great stones with C. G. cut on them, are now set up at the limits thereof.

The West-Gate-Street

Is the modern name of the principal street, the lower part of which is called the *Island*, or *Between the Bridge*. It is 938 yards long, from the top of the street to the West-gate. Before 6° E. 2. it was termed *Ebrug-street*, as it has been also in several records and evidences since that time. Part of it was antiently, and is now, thus called:

On the North Side. (938 yards.)

The *Mercer's Row*, sometimes called *Zonaria*.
The *Cofery*.
The *Century*.
Craftis, or *Craftis Lane*, called also *Ironmonger's Row*, *Currier's Lane*, *Trinity-Lane*, or, because it joins the abbey or college, *Upper College Lane*; what was formerly within the walls, being now called the *College*.
Rotten Row, extending from near *Abbey Lane*, to near St. Nicholas church. Streets and lanes out of it are, *Grace Lane*, or *Maverdine's Lane*, so called from John Maverdine, who had possessions and lived there in the time of E. 1. *King Edward's Lane*, or *Lich-Lane*, or *Peter's Lane*, or *Lower College Lane*, because it leads into the abbey or college.
Abbey-Lane, or *Three-Cocks-Lane*.
Archdeacon-Lane, or Street; so called because the archdeacon of Gloucester had a house on the W. side thereof, and the first herbage of a meadow which contained 18 acres, and was, about 1473, exchanged by archdeacon Seydon with the abbey of Gloucester for Dursley rectory, which is now united to the archdeaconry. This is also called *Leathern Bottle-Lane*, because of an alehouse that was in it.---- And beyond these,
Mary de Lode Street.
St. Oswald's Priory, and because houses are built but on one side of the way, *Half Street*, which leads to
The Bridge-Gate.
Dockham, or *Dock-Lane*, because large barges or trows which were made use of in Severn, were built near it.
Pewke-Lane.

On the South Side.

Butcher Row. Lanes leading out of it, are
Mercer's Entry, formerly called *Love Alley*; and from this alley was another alley, which led from the Southgate street, tho' now quite destroyed.
The Bull Lane, or *Goose Lane*; perhaps because it joined to the Butcher's Row.
The Upper Key Lane, or *Castle Lane*, and beyond that,
The Bareland, and
The Castle.
Castle-Lane, or *Street*, on the E. side, and *Marybone-Park* on the W.
The Lower Key-Lane, or *Walker's Lane*, or *Fuller's Lane*.

N. B. The King's Board, *Trinity Tower*, and a statue of *King George*, stood in the middle of the street, but are taken down, of which hereafter.

In the Middle.

The West Gate.

The East-Gate-Street

Is 294 yards long, from the crossing of the four principal streets to the East Gate. 'Twas antiently, and is also now sometimes called, the *Hailes-Gate*, or **Ailes-gate-Street*. 'Twas formerly known by the name of *Jury-Street*, or *Judaismus*, on account of the Jews, many of whom were settled here. In the reign of H. 2. they had a synagogue, and § crucified a boy; and in that of H. 3. their school was here.

On the North Side, is	294 yards.	On the South Side.
Sir Thomas Rich's Hospital.		*St. Michael's Church.* *Stadenham*, or *Scathenam*.

In the Middle.

A Statue of King George I.
Removed in July 1767, from the middle of the Westgate-street, and placed here.

The Barley Market-House.

The Pillory and Stocks.

The East Gate.

* Perhaps it was called *Ailesgate-street* because here was antiently a place for the reception of persons who had ails and distempers. 32 H. 6. the abbey of Gloucester had a tenement next to the wall by the corner of the lane leading to the Fryers Preachers, wherein lay many sick and infirm people. Or it may be from *hail*, which formerly, as well as at present, was used to signify health, vigour and strength; and as 'tis likely this was antiently esteemed the strongest gate in the city, and particularly mentioned, which the other parts never are, as newly erected, about the reign of king H. 3. perhaps this gate hence received its denomination, and was called by way of eminence the *Hails*, or strong *Gate*.

§ Trevisa, fol. 355, has it, in the 7th of H. 2. Brompton says, in 1160. In MS. Coll. it is said, the Jews had a synagogue in or near the same place which is called St. Kimbro's chapel, near to the South-gate.

The Upper North-gate-Street

Is 180 yards long, from the crossing of the streets to the Upper Northgate.

On the West Side.	180 yards	On the East Side.
The upper part was antiently called *Cordwainer's Row.* *St. John's Church.* *St. John's Lane.*		*St. Martyn's Place.* *Graunt's Lane*, or *Ross Lane*; or because part of the New Inn, built by R. Twining, *New-Inn-Lane*; or, for the great resort of pilgrims and persons who undertook travelling on a religious account, and seem to have had proper accommodations prepared for them by the abbey, at this great inn, *Pilgrim-Lane.* *Oxbody-Lane*, so called from an alehouse, which is the sign of the ox's body. *St. Aldate's Lane*, which leads to St. Aldate's church, where are several houses. *Almesham.* *Postern*, or *Sally-Gate.*

In the Middle.

The Upper North-Gate.

For *Lower North-Gate*, see North Hamlets.

The South-Gate-Street

Is 391 yards long.

On the West Side.	391 yards.	On the East Side.
Mr. *Scriven's*, or Mr. *Longden's*, because they lived at the East end of it, and had possessions in it. *Long Smith-Street*, or *Old Smith Street*; or, because the priory of Lanthony had a school there, *The School-House-Lane*; or because the Bolt is now the chief alehouse in it, 'tis called *The Bolt-Lane.* *Austin's Place.* *Suter's Lane*, which leads to *The Black Fryers.* *St. Kyneburg's Lane.* There was another lane about the time of the conquest, called *Shepster's Lane*, which extended from the Southgate Street to the moat of the castle. But it seems to have been utterly destroyed not long after the foundation of Lanthony priory, at least in or near the reign of king Henry 3.		*Travail-Lane*, or *St. Peter's Lane*; or because the bellman or cryer lived therein, *The Bellman's Lane.* *Crypt-Alley*, which was formerly called *Mary-Lane.* *St. Mary-de-Crypt-School* and *Church.* *Fryer's Lane*, which leads to the Grey Fryers. There was formerly a lane called *Sheep-Lane*, in St. Owen's parish, which extended from the Southgate Street to the walls of the Grey Fryers.

In the Middle.

Queen Anne's Statue.

The Wheat Market.

Scriven's Conduit.

The South-Gate.

As to the streets, &c. without the walls of the city, see North and South Hamlets.

Probably *Pelleteria* and *Draperia*, which are mentioned as being in this town in the time of king H. 3. — *Suetaria*, 5° E. 1. — *Glovers Row*, 30° E. 3.—*Small Lane*, near *Brookstreet*, 34° E. 3. *Sueria*, 35° E. 3.—and *Fishmongers Row*, 8° H. 4. were in some part of the streets already named.

In the year 1562, the number of housholders in this city, according to bishop Cheiney, was 936, to which 16 more were added for St. Margaret's and St. Mary Magdalen's hospitals. About the year 1710, the number of houses is reckoned at 1003; of inhabitants, 4990. In Mr. Wantner's MS. Collections, about 1714, it is said that there were not less than 6000 souls within the precincts. In the year 1743, there were 1335 housholders, and about 5585 inhabitants in Gloucester; and in the hamlets which are within the liberties, 275 housholders and 936 inhabitants more.

Of its Strength, Walls, Gates, Bridges, &c.

EARL Eldol, in 489, and Edmund Ironside, in 1016, flying to this city for safety, protection and succour, against their adversaries, evidence that in those times 'twas of great strength. In king Stephen's reign, 'twas kept for the king, with a strong garrison. But the inhabitants of the town, who sided with the empress Maud, drove out the garrison, and frequently gave vigorous assaults to his adherents; particularly in November 1139, when they sent out a considerable army of horse and foot to spoil the city of Worcester, for refusing to espouse the empress's title. King John, in May 1216, fled hither for his defence, and continued here for some time. The parts about it that were open and undefended were frequently molested by war, and brought almost to ruin, by the great forces of Lewis, the French king's son. Upon king John's death, the pope's legate and the earl of Pembroke, took care to secure the young king, queen Isabel his mother, his brother Richard, with his sisters, and great numbers of the nobility, and chief of the realm, in this place, which then was esteemed the safest in the kingdom. One of that king's reasons for his being here often in his long reign was, as we are told in Fuller's *Church History*, because it was the strongest, and adhered to his interest. In 1326, king E. 2. retired hither, and the queen soon followed him, and had the gates opened to her. At this place she published a proclamation, inviting him to come and resume the government of the realm. Her army was very much increased by the addition of new forces, which, whilst she was here, came to her; particularly the lords of Percy and Wake, and others from the Northern parts, and from the Marches.

In 1473, queen Margaret, wife of king H. 6. having got together a great army at Bristol, would fain

fain have went thro' this town, but ſhe was refuſed by the governor; and there being no likelihood of taking it at the firſt aſſault, much leſs by laying ſiege to it in form, they reſolved to paſs the Severn at Tewkeſbury.

The walls occur in merlin's propheſy *, tho' 'tis ſaid § That they were founded, or rather perhaps regularly made round every part of the town by the ſame prince that founded thoſe at Chicheſter, who was Ciſſa, the ſecond king of the South Saxons. † King William the Conqueror, after he had ſettled the ſouthern parts of the kingdom, viſiting the weſtern ones, came to Glouceſter; and greatly liking the ſituation of this place, which he conſidered as a barrier between England and Wales, from which it was divided by the river Severn, he therefore cauſed the north-eaſt and ſouth ſides to be fortified with embattled ſtone walls, and gates, to repel the incurſions of the turbulent Welch, who had greatly diſquieted the peace of king Edward the Confeſſor.

Sir Thomas de Bradeſtan, or Bradſton, an active perſon in thoſe days, and eminent for his military employments, was very inſtrumental in repairing and ſuſtaining them, and it appears by the city books, that, 19° E. 3. he obtained a grant of the tolls, or rather the fee-farm rent of the town for this purpoſe. Before that time, as well as ſince, a great deal was expended for murage. And particular perſons, called Murage-gatherers, accounted for the money which they received for this uſe. In the time of H. 8. according to Leland, the town was ſtrongly defended by its walls, where it was not well ſecured by the river Severn, and ſo it continued 'till the ſiege in 1643 ‖; when, from the South-gate to the North-port, or Poſtern gate, was an antient wall, well lined with earth to a conſiderable height. Thence to the North-gate was a ſlender work, raiſed upon a low ground. From the North to the Weſt-gate was no antient defence, but a ſmall work newly raiſed, with the advantage of marſhy grounds without, and a line within, from the inner North-gate under the college wall, to the priory of S. Oſwald. From the Weſt towards the South-gate, along the river ſide, it had no more defence than the river itſelf, and the meadows being level with the town. From the caſtle to the South-port was a firm and lofty work, to command the high ground in the ſuburbs. The ditches or moats narrow, but watered round.

In 1662, the walls were demoliſhed by order of the commiſſioners appointed for the regulation of corporations.

Before the walls were taken down, four principal gates ſtood in them, denominated, as already obſerved, from their ſituation, Eaſt, Weſt, North and South, which are ſtill remaining.

The Weſt-Gate, belonging to the porter that attends the eldeſt ſheriff, was built in the reign of king H. 8. ** . It is a very handſome building, little impaired by time.

The Eaſt-Gate, belonging to the porter that attends the younger ſheriff, is now the houſe of correction. A charity ſchool alſo was kept here 57° H. 3. In antient deeds belonging to Bartholomew's hoſpital, 'tis called The New Eaſt-gate.

The North-Gate, which ſtands upon Fulbrook, is now the city priſon §§ for debtors and malefactors. Mr. Richard Pate, recorder of the city, bequeathed twenty marks for the repairing of the Eaſt and North-gates, provided it were done within two years after Feb. 2, 1588. The mayor and burgeſſes expended that ſum, and 40*l*. or, according to ſome MS. papers, 100 marks more, for building the houſe adjoining on the eaſt ſide of it, for the goaler's lodgings.

The South-Gate, belonging to the porter that attends the mayor's wife, was ſo battered ‡ at the ſiege, that very ſoon after it fell to the ground. In the ſame year it was rebuilt; and on it was cut in capital letters ‡‡ round the arch, on the one ſide, A CITY ASSAULTED BY MAN, BUT SAVED BY GOD. On the other ſide next the city, EVER REMEMBER THE FIFTH OF SEPTEMBER, 1643. GIVE GOD THE GLORY.

'Tis ſaid that the arms ‖‖ of the king, the prince, and the duke, were appointed to be erected here: but they were afterwards demoliſhed, and 1671, the two firſt were put up, and an inſcription was appointed to be cut thereon.

This gate remains almoſt intire. Part of the city wall, tho' reduced to the height of eight or nine feet, runs eaſtward of this gate, and is a boundary to the lands of the late friary of Franciſcans, or Gray Friars. On the weſt ſide alſo of the ſaid gate a ſmall part of the wall remains.

There are other gates of leſs note within the city, and they are,

King Edward's Gate, a noble one, and made of freeſtone. It was built by king E. 3. and

* The propheſy is, An Owl ſhall build her neſt upon the walls of Gloceſter, and in her neſt ſhall be brought forth an aſs. *Thompſon's Tranſlations*, *p.* 220. Alſo p. 221. Gloceſter ſhall ſend forth a lion, and ſhall diſturb him [the Bull of Totneſs] in his cruelty in ſeveral battles. He ſhall trample him under his feet, and ſhall terrify him with open jaws. At laſt the lion ſhall quarrel with the kingdom, and get upon the backs of the nobility. A bull ſhall come into the quarrel, and ſtrike the lion with his right foot. He ſhall drive him thro' all the inns in the kingdom, but ſhall break his horns againſt the walls of Oxford. But for the authority of this propheſy ſee *Camd. Brit. coll. x.* where Geoffry of Monmouth, who tranſlated them into Latin, is charged with adding a great deal of his own invention by William of Newborough, who was a contemporary writer.

§ Mr. Hearne's Notes to A. of Beverly, from an antient MS. in the Univ. Coll. Oxon.

† MS. C.

‖ Corbet's Military Government, p. 41. In the 1 R. 2. the burgeſſes of Glouceſter cleanſed and enlarged the ditch under the wall of the Friars-Preachers, to the quantity of twelve feet, ſo that ſeveral elms and aſhes in the bank, and in the churchyard of St. Kyneburg, were cut down. A. 11.

** Leland's Itinerary, V. 3.

§§ In the time of king James 1. the four principal gates of the city were then made priſons for the city, and the Boothall was the place to which the burgeſſes were committed for any miſdemeanor. MS. C.

‡ MS. C. ‡‡ Dorney's Speeches. MS. C. ‖‖ Civ.

repaired by abbat Parker, but almoft demolifhed in the civil wars.

Lady Bell's Gate, received its name from the Lady Bell, who, with Sir Thomas Bell, her hufband, lived at the Black Fryers, which from him was termed Bell's Place; and was called the Eaftgate of the Black Fryers. 'Twas neatly arched with freeftone, and lately fell down.

There were two other gates which led out of the city, and were in the walls thereof, but not of confiderable note, and they were,

The Poftern-Gate, which was in the middle between the Eaft and the North-gates, and had, as I fuppofe, on the eaft fide of it, a kennel for the hounds belonging to the city.

The Blind-Gate *, which is fometimes called St. Ofwald's gate, as being near, and leading to the church and priory of that name.

Thefe gates were within the liberties of the city, tho' without the walls.

Alvin-Gate, and the Lower North-Gate, are found in the Suburbs.

Within a little time after the reftoration, it is reported, generally, that the doors belonging to the gates, by the king's order, were pulled down, and moft of them given to the city of Worcefter, where they now are. A great many of the large iron hooks, which were part of the hinges thereof, ftill remain here.

Forreign Bridge §, which was antiently accounted to be over the chief arm of the Severn, was of feven great arches.

Cole-Bridge, which is a little below the Bartholomew's Hofpital, confifts of one arch, and ferves to drain the meads. It is likely it received its name from its fituation, as it is very convenient for conveying coals, fuel and other things, from Severn to St. Bartholomew's Hofpital.

The Weft-gate Bridge was built by † Nicholas Walred, clerk, in the reign of king H. 2. William Coxnel ‡, minifter of St. Nicholas, claimed, in right of his church, 5° H. 3. forty feet of pafture on each fide, for the repair and fuftaining thereof. William Fitz Catherine gave lands to it, about that king's reign. In the time of king E. 3. the brethren of St. Bartholomew's Hofpital claimed St. Nicholas's church, with all its cuftoms, efpecially for the fuftentation of it. The priors and brethren thereof frequently repaired it, as appears by a procefs in the King's Bench, 10° H. 7. And in divers records, that prior is called by the name of the keeper of the fame. Dame Joan Cook, 31° H. 8. gave to the mayor and burgeffes 5 *l. per ann.* towards the keeping of this bridge and the caufeys in repair. Alfo Sir Thomas Bell, 34° H. 8. gave 10 *l. per ann.* for the fame ufes. About the time of this reign, there were feveral ‖ benefactions to it. It is probable, that the acre of land in Winnals, in the parifh of Hasfield, called formerly *Bridge-Acre*, was given for it. This bridge confifts of five great arches over Severn. In 1691, the water works on the fouth fide were begun, and here perhaps the two water-mills, erected 30° H. 6. might ftand.

From the bridge there goes a great and lofty ** caufey of ftone, called, according to the name of the place at the other end of it, *Over's Caufeway*, thrown up, thro' the low meadows, acrofs the ifle of Alney. In it are feveral arched bridges, fome of one, fome of two, and fome of three arches, intended to draw the water off the meadows when they are overflowed. Part of it is within the liberties of the city, and is repaired by it to near the bridge. 'Twas made as it now is in the reign of king H. 8. and is about half a mile long, confifting of thirty-fix arches.

PUBLIC STRUCTURES.

IN the midft of the city ftood the lofty and beautiful HIGH CROSS, which received its name from its fituation, and to diftinguifh it from feveral other croffes in various parts of the city. There were feveral elegant ftatues at full length placed upon it, in diftinct niches, facing the feveral ftreets. Weftward ftood thofe of king John, and king Edw. 3. Eaftward, king H. 3. and queen Eleanor. Northward, queen Elizabeth, and king Charles the Firft. And Southward, the kings Richard the Second, and Richard the Third.

Leland takes notice of this building, and fays, *The beauty of the town lies in two croffing ftreets, and at the place of the middle meeting is an aqueduct incallated.* The Grey Fryers, in 1438, granted, that water might be brought hither from Mattesnoll, or Robin-Hood's hill, for the ufe of the city. *Civ.*

It was built in the reign of king Henry the Seventh, and has been repaired feveral times fince,

---

* Perhaps it was fo called becaufe it was but as a poftern, or little gate, out of the city, which had four others that were more confpicuous; whereas *that* was reputed as a dark and blind paffage thro' the walls, and no particular porter appointed to it. La Walchard, which was toward Brook-ftreet, and is mentioned 1255 Barth. 'tis probable was this, and fo called becaufe it is a fhoard or break made in the wall to pafs thro'.

§ It was called Forreign Bridge from its being outward, near the weft end of the town. Very antiently what was beyond it is faid to be *beyond the bridge*. And even in the reign of king H. 3. St. Bartholomew's hofpital is mentioned as fo ftanding. See the word *Forinfecus*, in the *Gloffary to Kennet's Paroch. Antiq.*

† Monaft. Anglic. v. 2. p. 456, and an antient copy now in the cuftody of the mayor and burgeffes.

‡ MS. of abbat Froucefter.

‖ Sir Thomas Hill gave certain houfes and lands to Dr. Greenwood and Mr. Woodwell, with an intent that the income thereof fhould be expended for the public benefit of this place; and a certificate of his having given fo much for the fupportation or maintenance of the city and bridge, was figned by the mayor and nine aldermen, and fealed with the feal of the mayoralty and their own feals on it, as in Madox's Forine Angl. p. 20.

** Lelands Itinerary, v. 4, and 8. Some MS. Coll. fay, that the Weft-Gate, and Over's Bridge of feven arches, were built in the reign of H. 8. That from Over's bridge, which leadeth over the rivulet Leddon, to the far end, or Foreign bridge, in the city, is half a mile at leaft, under which continued caufey there are thirty-fix arches for the draining of the water.

particularly in 1550, 1635, and 1712. But by act of parliament, 23 G. 2. it was taken down, becaufe, being fituated in the centre of the four principal ftreets, it greatly interrupted the paffage of carriages.

‡ Several felds ftood near the high crofs, and the burgeffes, 6 Joh. paid the king 20 *fol.* fine for amoving them §.

The TOLSEY, or TOLSEND, or TOLBOOTH, ‖ fo called, according to bifhop Kennet, becaufe it was the place where the lord of the manor received his dues, rents, and profits of the fair or market, called *Toll.* The Tolfey was antiently employ'd, as it is now, for the public affairs of the city.

By an act of parliament, 23 G. 2. the old Tolfey was taken down, and has been lately rebuilt from the ground, with a handfome front. Here the mayor, and juftices for the city and in-county, hold the quarter-feffions, and tranfact all public bufinefs. But the trial of criminals, and all civil caufes of importance, are carried before the judges of affize at the Boothall.

The BOOTHALL, fometimes called *Bohalle,* and *Guildhall.* Mr. Madox fays, that the burgeffes paid 2*s.* to the king, for a fine to buy and fell therein for the improvement of the borough, 5 R. 1. It was rebuilt in the year 1606, and by the charter of the city is made fubject to the jurifdiction both of the out-county and of the city; and here the affizes are held, and the quarter-feffions for the out-county only.

The KING'S BOARD*, (formerly affigned for the felling of butter and cheefe) was built or repaired by king Richard the Second, but it is now taken down†.

The KEY occurs by that name in the reign of king Edward the Fourth, as alfo *the lane leading to the key,* in that of king Henry the Seventh. In queen Elizabeth's time 'twas called the King's Key. In 1621, 1622, and 1713, 'twas greatly repaired and enlarged. In the prefent charter, exprefs mention is made of the Old and New Key; and there was lately a pillar of timber ftanding on the great key*, and the following infcription engraven on a brafs plate, at the top of it.

1650, QUI FELICITER OPTAT CIVITATI GLEVENSI, NON UT HERCULEAM COLUMNAM, SED PERPUSILLAM, HOC PIGNUS AMORIS ET GRATITUDINIS.

In the middle were thefe arms: *On a chevron three rofes; and on a canton a dexter hand gules,* to denote they belonged to a baronet.

The BARLEY-MARKET-HOUSE*, in the Eaftgate-ftreet, appointed for barley, beans, and oats, was built in 1655, or 1656. Margery Price gave 50*l.* towards it, and ftones were taken from the churches of St. Katherine, and St. Mary de Grace, and ufed in this market-houfe. Before that time, there was one which ftood nearer to the Eaftgate, many of the materials of which were alfo applied to the building of this.

The WHEAT-MARKET-HOUSE*, in the Southgate-ftreet, was built in 1606. Being very much battered and weakened at the fiege, another, with a poor ftatue of king Charles the Second, in a nich at the north end of it, was erected in 1660 and 1661.——Near it, in the midft of the ftreet, on a pedeftal inclofed with iron palifades, is a ftatue of queen Anne. And near to the fouth end of this market-houfe, in the middle of the ftreet alfo, is a Gothic building, of an octagonal form, inclofing a ciftern for the water of an antient aqueduct from Robinhood's hill, which at ftated hours is open for public ufe. On the fouth fide of it is an infcription. This was erected at the charge of alderman John Scriven, in 1636.

The STATUE of king George the Firft, upon an ornamented pedeftal, inclofed with iron palifades, ftands in the Eaft-gate-ftreet.

The CASTLE of Gloucefter. 'The caftle of 'Eftbrighoiel was built by earl William, and paid 'only 40 *fol.* in his time for fhips going to the 'foreft.' *Domefday,* p. 66. It is now the common jail for the out-county. Some part of the buildings is in private hands, held by leafe from the crown; but the greater part belongs to the county, and is fettled in the fheriff, by a ftatute 19 H. 7. It is extraparochial, and fo is the hill adjoining, called the Barbican, which, according to Camden, is an Arabic word, fignifying a watchtower, or military defence.

There were many other places of note in the city, which are now either converted into parifh dwellings, or totally deftroy'd, as

St. MARTIN'S PLACE*, near the fcite of the High Crofs, which king Edward the Third, in 1371, granted to the bailiffs, to erect a tower, and place a clock therein, for which the fheriffs of the city paid 12*d.* yearly.

‡ Madox's *Hiftory of the Exchequer,* p. 280.

§ R. Cole's Roll in Civ.

‖ It formerly confifted only of the council-chamber, and the room under it, (which were erected in 1602, upon the demolifhing of the former edifice, made in 1565) 'till 1648, when the north wall of All Saints church was taken away, and the whole church converted into a court for the fheriffs, and other public ufes. The chancel was turned into a ftair cafe, leading to a room over it, and to the council-chamber. Some lands between that church and the ftreet were afterwards purchafed to enlarge the place. And, in 1685, the chamber over the fheriff's court was made into a chapel, and king James the Second coming to Gloucefter, in his progrefs in 1686, was feated on a throne erected for him there, at the city charge; and from him it obtained the denomination of the King's Chapel. But foon after the revolution, in 1688, moft of the coftly furniture belonging to it was burnt and deftroy'd.

* Civ.

† It was a magnificent market-houfe, according to Dr. Stukeley, *of Gothic Architecture, uncommon and antient, but finely adorned.* Over the arches, and on the fides and ends of it, were carvings of many hiftorical parts of the Holy Scripture. At each corner was a large ftatue, and on the upper part a crofs upon a pyramid, between four effigies, and it had battlements round it. In 1572, the upper part was repaired, and about 1691, was taken down, that a large ciftern might be erected as a refervoir for water, conveyed thither from near the Weftgate.

The Meal-Market, joining to the eaft end of St. John's church. It was ordered to be repaired in 1619, and about 1657, was converted into a dwelling houfe. But upon rebuilding St. John's church, in 1733, or 1734, it was intirely demolifhed, as being very incommodious.

Formerly there were feveral conduits and public wells in the city, which are now deftroy'd, and there are no veftiges of them remaining.

The lands extending along where the workhoufe now is, to a moat which led to the caftle, and thence down to the key, were called Mary-Bone Park, and were inclofed in 1635, and afterwards built upon, in 1644.

By a voluntary fubfcription of the inhabitants of this city and county, an act of parliament was obtained 23 G. 2. whereby certain commiffioners were appointed, and impowered to purchafe and pull down feveral buildings, both public and private; among others, the antient High Crofs, as before obferved; the King's Board, or Butter-market-houfe, with the tower of the demolifhed church of the Holy Trinity, which ftood in the middle of the Weft-gate-ftreet, and were very incommodious to carriages. By this act, thefe buildings, with fome dwelling houfes, were taken down; and lately, feveral public nuifances and obftructions have been removed, and the ftreets new paved, greatly to the public conveniency, and beautifying of the city.

Of COINAGE, MINT, and MONEY.

THIS town, together with all other great places*, antiently enjoy'd the privilege of coining. King John's grant of a mint feems to be no more than a confirmation of a more antient grant, and 'tis very likely, that fome of the Britifh coins which have been found here in great plenty, were ftruck in this place. There is a filver coin of king Harold, the fon of king Canute, with this infcription,—HAROLD REX ANGLOrum. The king had crown and fceptre. The reverfe is, WVLFGEAT ON (de) GLEapecejτρe. With PAX in the middle.

In antient grants to this place, the *Monetarii* (moneyers, or coiners, who were minifters of the mint, and made, coined, and delivered out the king's money) are expreflly mentioned, and had particular privileges granted to them. It is probable that feveral of he coins, whereon are fleurs de lis, and this infcription, Ave Maria Gratia Pia et Plena, were ftruck in this place, fince they are fo frequently found here.

In 1657, a farthing was coined, with the city arms in the middle, and round them this infcription: FOR NECESSARY CHANGE. On the reverfe, in the middle, C. G. round which LUKE NOURSE MAIOR, 1657.

On another farthing, in the middle, the arms of the city; round them THOMAS PRICE MAIOR. On the reverfe, in the middle, C. G. round which, A GLOCESTER FARTHING.

On another farthing, in the middle, the city arms; round them, THE ARMS OF GLOVCESTER. On the reverfe, in the middle,

{ * * *
C * G
1669. }

Round it, A GLOVCESTER FARTHING.

Of COURTS.

THERE were courts held in this town very antiently, particularly before the reign of king John, who granted the burgeffes a charter, by which they were impowered to hold all pleas in the town for their lands, tenures, wages, juft debts, and whatfoever was due to them there. King Edward the Second, in the 6th year of his reign, granted them, that they might hold pleas of lands and tenures in the vill; and for the future, that they might hear complaints, and punifh offences, fo as not to be fubject to communicate with, or impart to foreigners, but only with their fellow burgeffes. King Richard the Second, by his charter, in the twenty-firft year of his reign, gave them like authority to hear and determine all caufes, and to punifh offenders in the town; at which time the court was held in the Guildhall.

And ever fince that king's reign, the burgeffes of the vill have had authority to hold pleas, real and perfonal, within their liberties. And 'tis expreflly granted, by former charters as well as the prefent §, That the mayor, &c. upon every Monday, may hold a court for this purpofe, as the fame ufed to be holden time out of mind. And that the fheriffs, for all debts, &c. may hold the Tolfey-court, from hour to hour, and from day to day, as there is occafion.

The fheriffs fhall, in every month, hold a county-court, and twice in the year a law-day.

The fuitors of this hundred, or law-day court, were as follow †, 18 H. 7.

The earl of Gloucefter.
The archbifhop of York.
The prior of Lanthony.

---

* As at the council, or fynod of Grateley, held by king Athelftan, in 928, and alfo by the king's own order, it was appointed, that there fhould be one mint for coining of money in all *Burghs*, as 'tis in the Saxon, which is rendered by Mr. Lambard in Latin, *oppida*, or towns; caftles, as 'tis in Cl. Wilkins's *Councils*, vol. 1, p. 206; great towns, as in Tindale's *Notes upon Rapin*, vol. 1, p. 114; it may thence be well concluded that there was a mint in Gloucefter long before the time of king John; and that *that* king only eftablifhed it by his charter.

Mr. Camden, in his *Remains*, p. 185, fays, There was in every good town one coiner, called *Monetarius*, in the time of our antient Saxon kings. The mint, or place particularly appointed for coinage, was near Trinity church, in the reign of king Henry the Second. A. 5. A. 6. A. 9.

§ See Appendix, No. 6. † Civ.

The

The prior of St. Bartholomew's, Gloucester.

The prior of the Hospital of St. John of Jerusalem.

The abbat of Wynchecombe.

The abbat of Eynesham.

The abbat of Tewxbury.

The abbat of S. Aug. in Bristol.

The abbat of Hayles.

The earl of Hereford.

The abbat of St. Peter's of Gloucester.

The prior of St. Oswald's of Gloucester.

The prior of Derehurst.

The abbess of Godestow.

The abbat of Keynesham.

The proctors of the service of St. Mary, in the Church of St. Michael, in Gloucester.

The abbat of Flaxley.

The abbat of Kingswood.

The heirs of Peter Flory.

§ All these are mentioned, 20° and 21° of H. 7. except the abbat of Hayles, and the heirs of Peter Flory, who are then omitted.

§ In 1657, the suitors of this court are mentioned thus:

The earl of Hereford and Gloucester.

Henry lord Stafford, for his honours of Hereford and Gloucester.

The several purchasers of the lands of the late dean and chapter of Gloucester.

Miles Clent, gentleman, for the lands of John Jennings, being St. Oswald's priory.

The heir of John Chamberlayne, esq; and the heir of Richard Pate, esq; being Edward Willoughby, esq; for the lands lately belonging to St. Mary, and St. Oswald, in Gloucester.

The heirs of Thomas Bell, for the lands lately belonging to the priory of Lanthony.

After the restoration, instead of the purchasers of the Dean and Chapter's lands, *the Dean and Chapter*, are suitors to this court.

In 1660 and 1688, Henry Sutton, D.D. occurs in the place of Miles Clent. October 8, 1688, John Webb, A. M. occurs, in the place of Dr. Sutton, as he does also in 1700. Saunders Saunders, gent. occurs in the place of Mr. Webb, as he does also in 1717. Since that time Saunders Saunders, gent. sold several possessions which he had in the city, to Mr. Bridges Pateshall, after which, his widow was reckoned suitor to this court.

‡ An act of parliament was passed in the first year of king William the Third, for the erecting of a court of requests, or court of conscience, for all debts under forty shillings, to be holden as often as the commissioners shall think fit, before three at least of them. This court being designed for the benefit and relief of the burgesses and inhabitants, the expences of proceedings are so moderate as not to frustrate the intention of it.

Besides this court of the town, there was also another court, which was commonly called the *Foreign court of the honour of Gloucester*, and was holden within the jurisdiction of the honour, but not within the liberties of the governors of the town. Maud, the wife of the last Gilbert de Clare, who was earl of this place, had for her dowry an assignment, among other things, of the *Foreign court of the honour of Gloucester*. Dug. Bar. v. 1. p. 217. And this foreign court is mentioned Claus. 8° E. 2. It was reserved by earl Mylo, the founder of Lanthony priory, and his descendants enjoyed the same for many ages after him. 'Tis said, that upon the death of Humphry de Bohun, Mary, his daughter, had assigned to her, amongst other things, for the purparty of her father's part, the court of the honour of Hereford, holden at Gloucester; which was worth ten shillings a year. And Henry of Lancaster, her husband, having sworn fealty to the king, his majesty commanded his escheater, by his charter, dated at Westminster, the 22d day of December, 8° R. 2. to give the said earl possession thereof.

Of the HONOUR *of* GLOUCESTER.

ALTHOUGH in a great many writers the *Honour* and *Title* are confused, and frequently put one for the other, I rather chuse to mention them distinctly and separately.

The honour of Gloucester was enjoy'd by several persons who never had any title of dignity taken from this place; whilst others took their titles hence, but were never possessors of the lands which belonged to this barony, which was very great.

What is affirmed of land baronies *, That they were divided and subdivided, 'till at length they were brought to little or nothing, may truely and properly be said of the honour of Gloucester, to which, being a noble seigneury or lordship, tho' several others did originally belong, yet was it afterwards greatly reduced, as will appear by the following short account of it.

Brictrick † (called also Brithrick) obtained it from Hailward Snow, before the conquest; but having incurred the hatred of Maud, William the Conqueror's queen, whom, when he was a public ambassador abroad, he had refused to marry, soon after the entrance of the Normans she revenged the insult, by procuring his imprisonment, and the confiscation of his estate.

The queen, after Brictric's death, enjoy'd it, and after her death king William the First, to whom succeeded king William the Second, who held it for some time, and then granted it to

Robert Fitz Haman, or Hayman, lord of Corboil and Thorigny, in Normandy; kinsman

§ Civ. ‡ Which was then printed. * Madox's Bar. Ang. p. 59. † Dugdale's Bar. vol. 1. p. 406.

and affiftant to the Conqueror, who had very large poffeffions in feveral places. This great perfon was the firft, I fuppofe, who held the honour and the title together. He was the chief actor in the conqueft || of Glamorganfhire, in 1091, and feated himfelf for the moft part at Cardiff, where, fays Camden, (col. 733) he fortified the town with walls and a caftle, and made it both a feat of war and a court of juftice. In 1102, he new built the abbey of Tewkefbury, with all its offices, and endow'd it with many lands, rents, and large poffeffions, and made Cranburne, in Dorfetfhire, a cell to it. In the retaking of Faleife, in Normandy, he was ftruck on the temples, which deprived him of his fenfes, but he lived a confiderable time after; and dying, he was buried in the chapter-houfe of Tewkefbury, in 1107; but was moved into the middle of the prefbytery in 1241. And in 1397, an admirable chapel was made by abbat Parker, on the north fide of the chancel, and certain offices were daily celebrated for him. Round the top of the chapel was written, but now not legible, "*In ifta capella jacet Dnus Robertus Filius Hammonis, hujus loci Fundator.*" His bones now lie wrapt in fine diaper in a plain tomb above ground, in the middle of the chapel.

But 'tis probable that king Stephen ‡ took this honour away from Earl Robert, and gave it to Miles of Gloucefter, who, I think, had it but a little time before his revolt to the emprefs. Afterwards 'twas again |||| in the king's hands; for Hugh Bardolf §§ 1° R. 1. was accountable for 42*l.* 13*s.* 6*d.* of the antient farm of the honour of Gloucefter; and likewife for 370*l.* 18*s.* 9*d.* for the farm of the manors belonging to it, for three quarters of a year, before the king gave it to his brother John; and for 32*l.* for the third part of the profits arifing from the pleas of the county for half a year. And by *Mag. Rot.* 9° R. 1. it appears, that William de Warrenna accounted for 340*l.* 8*s.* 7*d.* for the fcutage of the honour of Gloucefter, affifed for the king's redemption, after his return from Aleman; of the knights of the faid honour, which he can find, as he fays, in the treafury 196*l.* 0*s.* 10*d.* and of Euftace of Grainville of the fee of one knight, by the king's writ, which he holds *in capite* of the king, as the faid William fays. And he owes 143*l.* 7*s.* 9*d.* which ought to be required of the knights, whofe names are noted in the roll which the faid William delivered in the treafury, when he left off to have the cuftody of the faid honour. The fame accounts for the fame debt nothing. Alfo of Thomas de Sandford, 25 *fol.* who went to the fervice of the king by the faid writ, and he owes 145*l.* 12*s.* 9*d.* which ought to be required of the aforefaid knights, as he fays.

Robert Fitz-Haman left behind him † four daughters, *viz.* Mabel, by others called Sibil, or Maud, who afterwards married Robert Melhent; Cicily, afterwards abbefs of Shaftefbury, in Dorfetfhire; Hawife, abbefs of Winchefter, or, as Dugdale fays, of Wilton; and Amice, who married the earl of Britain. But among thefe four females king Henry the Firft would not have the honour divided, and therefore gave this whole honour to his natural fon Robert, concerning whom hereafter.

Earl Robert was fucceeded in this honour by his fon William, who dying, left three daughters.

John the fourth fon of king H. 2. received this honour of his brother king Richard, as a portion with Ifabel, one of the daughters of earl William; and tho' he was afterwards divorced from her, yet he retained ** the honour to himfelf; for it is faid, *Mag. Rot.* 1° Joh. that William de Faleife and Mafter Swain, rendered an account of the honour of Gloucefter, namely, 223*l.* 12*s.* 3*d.* for the ferms and iffues of the manor of this honour, which were in the king's hands for half a year; that is to fay, 18*l.* 10*s.* for the ferm of Bradeftede for half a year, it having been let to ferm at that rate by the faid William and Mafter Suein, 78 *fol.* arifing by the fale of wood, five marks for the ** affifed §§ aid in the faid vill, 46 *fol.* and three halfpence of the ** affifed §§ rent of Peteresfield, of the faid ferm; five marks in toll, and other perquifites; four marks for the tallage of the fame vill; 8*l.* 17*s.* 11*d.* for the rent affifed of Mapelderefham; 7*l.* 6*s.* 8*d.* for the tallage of the fame town, and in many other items.

* Guy de Chancels, 15° John, accounted for the fcutage of the honour of Gloucefter, as well of the old feoffment as of the new, *viz.* for 327 knights fees and a tenth, and a twelfth part of a fee. Several of the knights fees belonging to this honour, about twenty in number, could not at prefent be found, or afcertained.

|| This conqueft was made in the following manner: Jeftyn, lord of Glamorganfhire, having been defeated in a rebellion againft Rhees ap Tewdor, fent Eneon, a Welch gentleman, to Robert Fitz-Haimon, who was a great baron and a gentleman of the king's privy chamber, to follicit him to come to his affiftance, with promifes of great rewards and emoluments; and Eneon, if he fucceeded in his negotiation, was promifed Jeftyn's daughter in marriage. The propofal was agreeable to the fpirit of the times, and Fitz-Haimon, with twelve knights of confiderable note and diftinction, at the head of a large body of troops, joined thofe of Glamorganfhire, and invaded the territories of Rhees ap Tewdor, who met them near Brecknock, and giving them battle was vanquifhed by them, and flain in the action. Jeftyn kept his engagements with the Normans very faithfully, but broke his word with Eneon, who burning with refentment, followed the Normans who were already embarked for England, and complaining to them moft bitterly of his mafter's perfidioufnefs, incited them to turn their arms againft him; upon which, partly out of regard to the man, and partly being alured by the bait he propofed to them, of the conqueft of the country, they all returned with him, attack'd the lord of Glamorganfhire, defeated, and flew him. This is the account given by Caradoc of Lancarvon; but another account fays, that Jeftyn refufed to perform the covenants he had made with the Normans. However, Fitz-Haimon feized the country, and referving to himfelf fome principal parts, and the feignory of the whole, gave all the reft of that fertile province to be held as fiefs under him, by the twelve knights and fome others who had affifted him, particularly Eneon. *Lord Lyttelton's Life of H. 2. vol.* 2. p. 47, 48.

† Dug. Bar. V. 1. p. 407. ‡ Dug. Bar. V. 1. p. 537. Madox's Hift. Excheq. p. 134. |||| Madox's Bar. Anglic. p. 77. §§ Selden's Tit. Hon. ** Madox's Bar. Angl. p. 76.

* Madox's Hift. Excheq. p. 445. Mad. Bar. Angl. p. 92. 123.

John,

§ John, earl of Moreton, afterwards king of England, by his charter, granted the land or manor of Briftelton, belonging to the honour of Gloucefter, to John la Warre, to be holden by John la Warre and his heirs, of Earl John and his heirs, by the fervice of half a knight; and the fame grant was confirmed 8° John.

† In the fecond year of king Henry the Third, Gilbert earl of Gloucefter was vefted with this honour, and paid 100*l.* for the relief of it.

‡ Gilbert de Rue held it 27° H. 3.
Robert Mufgrofe was feized of it 38° H. 3.
Nicholas Berkeley held it 47° H. 3. as did Patronelle de La Mere in the fame year.

|| King Henry the Third, towards the latter end of his reign, granted feveral manors in the counties of Southampton and Kent, belonging to the honour of Gloucefter, to the then countefs of Gloucefter, and her fon Gilbert de Clare. I fuppofe this honour, at or before the time laft mentioned, was continually decreafing. In the fecond year of the reign of queen Mary, 'twas given by the queen, with other things, to the lady Urfula Stafford. And 13° Eliz. it appears that this honour was then worth but 19*s.* 11*d.* 'Tis certain, 32° H. 3. earl Gilbert de Clare, who then had this, gave to William, his brother, the inheritance of the manors of Maplederham and Petersfield in the county of Southampton, which formerly belonged to it, and that other eftates which were part thereof have been fince parted with.

Of the EARLS of GLOUCESTER.

THERE is no earldom in the kingdom fo antient as this of Gloucefter. Eldol, * or Edel, the Briton, by fome called earl, by others duke and conful, was earl of this place in the year 461; and attended king Vortigern at the treaty of peace at Ambrefbury, in Wiltfhire, to which they were invited by Hengift the Saxon, when it was agreed that neither party fhould go thither armed; but the Saxons concealing long knives under their cloathes, murdered great numbers of the Britons. At this time Eldol is faid to have taken up a ftake, which he found by chance, and to have laid about him with fuch courage and effect, that he flew no lefs than feventy of them; and having broke the heads, arms, and limbs of many more, got from them into Gloucefter, his own city. Alfo, that in the bloody battle fought between Ambrofius, king of the Britons, and Hengift, in 489, earl Eldol charging thro' the midft of the pagan army, took Hengift prifoner, and remembering his former treachery, cut off his head.

Swaine, ** or Suane, eldeft fon of Godwin, earl of Kent, was earl hereof in the time of king Edward the Confeffor, and going to Jerufalem barefooted, on penance, to expiate the murder of Beorne, his kinfman, took cold thereby, and died at Licia, in his return in the year 1053.

Some have obtruded §§ William Fitz Euftace, in 1094; but it does not †† appear that there ever was fuch a man.

Robert Melhent, or Fitz Roy, fometimes called Robert Rufus, conful of Gloucefter. He was natural fon of king Henry the Firft, born of Nefta, the beautiful daughter of Rhees ap Tudor, or Theodore, prince of South Wales, and was made firft earl after the conqueft. For as it was not efteemed honourable to be enriched with great poffeffions, without fome title or dignity, having married Sibil, the eldeft of the daughters of Robert Fitz Haman, he was created, in 1109, earl of this place, which was the moft eminent of her heritage. By the writers of that time, he is called the conful, and alfo earl of Gloucefter, and was a perfon above all others, of a great and undaunted fpirit, never dejected by misfortunes; and who being efteemed a prudent, learned, brave, and valiant prince ‡‡, fkilled in the arts of war and peace, performed many heroic and difficult exploits with great honour, in the caufe of his fifter Matilda, againft king Stephen. As his mother was daughter to Rhees ap Teudor, the laft king of South Wales, he derived from the affection of the Welch to her family a great intereft there,

---

§ Madox's Bar. Angl. p. 59. † *Ibid.* p. 33. ‡ Sir R. Atkyns p. 84. || In about the time of Henry the Third, amongft the king's tenants *in capitie*, in the county of Gloucefter, 'tis faid, the honour of Gloucefter holds of the king, in Gloucefterfhire, twenty-feven knights and a half, and one fourth part of one knight.——The honour of Gloucefter. Nicholas Pointz feven knights and three parts. Geffry fil. Roberti fix knights. Roger de Mayby eight knights. Roger Corbet one knight. William Camerarius one knight. Richard de Dickefdon two knights and a half. William de Kirdif one knight. John de Sor fourteen knights. (In the roll of the charters 'tis faid fifteen knights) Robert de Fifcham two knights. Robert Treham half a knight. Thomas de la Mare ten knights. Roger de Berkelegh two knights. Adam fil. Nigel the fifth part. Thomas Blundus half a knight. *Evidences extracted from the Red Book of the Exchequer*, *Roll* 156.

* Dugd. Bar. vol. 1. p. 1.—Robert of Gloucefter fays that earl Eldol was a ftrong knight, and has many particulars relating to him, agreeable to Matthew Weftminfter, p. 160.

** Dugdale's Bar. v. 1. p. 18. §§ Lloyd, in his *Hiftory of Wales*, p. 153, fays, he was flain between Cardiff and Brecknock by the Welchmen. He alfo affirms, That William de Albermarle was earl of this place in 1216, but he does not mention any authority for thefe affertions.

†† Camden's *Britannia*, v. 1. col. 287.

‡‡ All writers concur in their teftimony of the excellent character of this nobleman, "who had no inconfiderable tincture of learning, and was the patron of all who excelled in it; qualities rare at all times in a nobleman of his high rank, but particularly in an age when knowledge and valour were thought incompatible, and not to be able to read was a mark of nobility." *Lord Lyttelton's Life of H. 2. p.* 281. And in another place, "He was unqueftionably the wifeft man of thofe times; and his virtue was fuch, that even thofe times could not corrupt it. If when the nation was grown equally tired of Matilda and of Stephen, he had afpired to obtain the crown for himfelf, he might very poffibly have gained it from both; but he thought it lefs glorious to be a king, than to preferve his fidelity and honour inviolate. He feems to have acted only from the pureft and nobleft principles of juftice and duty, without pride, without paffion, without any private views, or felfifh ambition; and to this admirable temper of mind he joined all the addrefs and extenfive abilities, that are peculiarly neceffary for *the head of a party*; who muft connect and keep together great numbers of independent perfons, held by no regular bond of obedience; conciliate their different paffions and interefts, endure their abfurdities, footh their ill humour, manage their pride, and eftablifh an abfolute authority over them, without feeming to exercife any, but that of perfuafion." *p.* 344.

which was ftill increafed by a clofe union with two of the moft powerful lords in thofe parts, who were coufin-germans, and acted together in fupport of Matilda, namely, Brian Fitz-comte and Milo Fitz-walter. The former of thefe poffeffed the lordfhips of Abergavenny and Overwent, in what is now the county of Monmouth; the latter enjoyed the beft part of Brecknockfhire, in right of his wife, with ample poffeffions in Herefordfhire and Gloucefterfhire, having alfo the government of the royal caftle of Gloucefter, and being hereditary conftable of England. When king Stephen was taken, in 1140, he would furrender to none but this earl. And when the earl of Gloucefter was taken prifoner, in 1141, and by William de Ypre fent to Rochefter caftle; tho' an offer was foon made to releafe him for the king, he would not hearken to it without the emprefs's confent. And at length after fix months imprifonment, the emprefs agreed that the king and he fhould be fet at liberty; and this exchange, one for the other, was deemed equal.

This earl * had with his wife, befides this whole honour, a great inheritance in Normandy, and all the land of Hamo Dapifer, his wife's uncle. Mr. Tyrrel fays, that his father, king Henry the Firft, by his will, made him his executor, and is faid to have given him 60,000 *lib.* at his death. He died at Gloucefter of a fever, on October 31, 1147, and was buried under a great jafper ftone in the choir of St. James's priory, in Briftol, which he had founded upon his own demefne lands, and endowed with lands, ornaments, poffeffions and liberties, and made a cell to Tewkefbury abbey, whereof he had the abbat and twelve monks to dine with him conftantly every funday. He built the caftles of Briftol and Cardift, and of that at Briftol, which was made of ftone, brought from Caen in Normandy, he gave every tenth ftone towards the erecting of St. Mary's chapel §, in St. James's priory there. He alfo founded, in 1147 †, the priory of Morgan, in Glamorganfhire, valued at its diffolution at 181*l.* 7*s.* 4*d.* or 188*l.* 14*s.* And is faid ‡ to have founded a priory at Cardiff, and was a great benefactor to the priories of Nethe and Great Malvern ||, and to the abbies of Tewkefbury and Gloucefter. After his death the emprefs's caufe declined very much, and at length came to little, the chief fupport being gone. This great || and illuftrious earl had the town of Briftol, which Robert Fitz Haman, his father-in-law, held in fealty of king William the Conqueror. At his inftance the prince, afterwards king Henry the Second, came into England, and ftaying a confiderable time here, the earl, his uncle, conducted him into Normandy, on his return. He left iffue behind him, by the beforementioned Sibil, or Maud, his wife, four fons, *viz.* William, his fucceffor in that honour; Roger, bifhop of Worcefter; Haman, and Phillip; and one daughter, named Maud.

§§ William, his eldeft fon, fucceeded him in his earldom. In his father's time, he was made governor of the caftle of Warham; and 12° H. 2. upon levying the aid for marrying the king's daughter, certified his knight's fees in Kent to be twenty-two and an half and a third part, and elfewhere two hundred and fixty and a half *de veteri Feoffamento*, and thirteen and a half *de novo*. Having, with other gentlemen, oppofed the king in behalf of young Henry, 20° H. 2. he returned to his obedience. He had a great conteft with one Yvor, or Ivor, furnamed *Bâch*, a little man of ftature, but exceedingly refolute and couragious, who kept himfelf chiefly in the woods and mountains, of which this earl endeavoured to bereave him, or at leaft to ftraiten his limits. Yvor being irritated thereat, came in the night to Cardiff caftle, with his men, and tho' the walls were high, and there were no lefs than 120 foldiers, befides a large number of archers therein; he fcaled them, and took away this earl William, with his countefs, and their young fon, and carrying them to the woods, refufed to releafe them, until he had full reftitution of what had been wrongfully taken from him. This earl obtained the lordfhip of Caerleon from Meredith ap Howell, who was lord thereof. He died †† November 23, 1173, or as others 1183, and was buried in the abbey of Keynfham, which he founded, and amply endow'd and adorn'd, next his wife Hawife, the daughter of Robert Boffu, earl of Leicefter, and a fon called Robert, who is before mentioned. He alfo had three daughters, *viz.* Mabel, Amice, and Ifabel, or rather Avifa. This earl was a great benefactor to the monafteries of Bradenftoke, Co. Wilts; Nuneaton, Co. Warwick; Tewkefbury, Co. Gloucefter; Bermondfey, Co. Surrey; St. Auguftine's and St. James's, Briftol; Stanley, in Wilts; Neth, in Glamorganfhire; Lyra, in France; Dureford, in Suffex; and the cell of Goldcliff, in Monmouthfhire. Being unwilling that his inheritance fhould be divided amongft females, for reafons unknown, fays *Rapin's Hiftory*, being at Windelefhore, or Windfor, on the 4th or 6th

* Dug. Bar. V. I. p. 534.

§ Annal. Teux. in Mon. Angl.

† But Mr. Camden, *Britannia*, V. 2. col. 738, fays, that Morgan was founded by his fon William. And in the Note to Bifhop Tanner's *Notitia Monaft.* p. 713, the editor feems for a reafon there mentioned, to think, that this earl Robert only began this houfe a little before his death, and William, his fon and fucceffor, finifhed it fome time after; tho' it the firft edition of *Not. Monaft.* 'tis faid, That Morgan was built by earl Robert, not William, as in Speed.

‡ Tanner's *Notitia Monaft.* p. 715.

|| Dug. Bar. V. I. 535.

§§ Dug. Bar. V. I. p. 535, 536.

†† Annal Teux. in Mon. Ang. fay, That this earl William died in 1173, and his body was honourably buried, as it ought to be, in the abbey of the canons of Keynfham, near by his fon Robert, which abbey he had founded in memory of his fon, and endowed it with lands, ornaments, and liberties. Dug. Bar. V. I. p. 536, fays, That upon St. Clement's night, 1173, 20 H. 2. he departed this life. Sir R. Atkyns, p. 90, fays, that he died in 1183. And Wilkins's Counfels, V. I. p. 486, fay, This earl William was one of the witneffes at the council at Weftminfter, holden by king Henry the Second, in 1177, *regni* 23° in the firft week of lent.

of

of the kalends of October, in 1176, he conftituted for his heir,

John, commonly called *Sans-Terre*, or Lackland, fourth fon to king Henry the Second, and of all his children was the chiefeft favourite. But that king retained this honour in his own hands for many years. And, as 'tis in *Annal. Teux. in Mon. Anglic.* and fome other authors, in the laft year of his reign, gave one of earl William's three daughters in marriage to his fon John; who * had with his wife this whole earldom. He was alfo earl Moreton in Normandy, and, during the reign of his brother king Richard the Firft, built the long bridge at Tewkefbury, and gave the toll of the market there for the repair thereof. But becaufe earl John and his lady were in the third degree of confanguinity, (for king Henry the Firft was great grandfather to them both) Baldwin, archbifhop of Canterbury, put all the earl's lands under an interdict; but from that interdict he appealed to the fee of Rome. His appeal was confirmed, and he was releafed by the Pope's legate from it. This John was afterwards king of England, and having no child by his wife, after he had reigned one year, was divorced from her, whom, after he had retained in his hands part of her inheritance, 'tis faid §, he fold, with all her lands and fees, except the caftle of Briftol, and chaces thereto belonging, for 20,000 marks, to

Geofry de Mandeville †, earl of Effex, in the fifteenth year of his reign, and created him earl of Gloucefter, and gave him the county of Gloucefter. This earl Geofry, the fame year, delivered up the cuftody of the tower of London, which he before had, 17° Joh. He had feifin of all the liberties belonging to the honour of Gloucefter, of the inheritance of Ifabel his wife, as amply as William earl of Gloucefter, his father, had enjoyed them, having then the title of earl of Gloucefter. But foon after, ‡ adhering with the barons, who then were in arms againft the king, he was excommunicated by the Pope, and was one of the chief of thofe lords who would have affumed the whole fway of the realm in their own power. And about that time he was killed by a Frenchman at a tournament holden at London, and left no iffue. Ifabel, his wife, furvived him, and afterwards married to Hugh de Burgh, juftice of England, who was a great benefactor to Dureford priory, Co. Suffex. Ifabel died without iffue by either of her hufbands, whereby the honour of Gloucefter came to her nephew,

Almerick ‖, fon to the earl of Eureux, in Normandy, as being defcended from Maud, another daughter of earl William, before mentioned. But he enjoy'd this earldom only for a fhort time, and was buried at Keynfham, to which, and Dureford priory, he was a great benefactor. He died without children, whereby

Gilbert de Clare **, fon of Richard de Clare earl of Hertford, who married Amice, another daughter of earl William, was the firft earl of Gloucefter and Hertford jointly. The county §§ of Hertford had very antiently earls that were of the family of Clare, who therefore were more commonly called earls of Clare, from Clare, their principal feat in the county of Suffolk. But when this family, by right of inheritance as well as by their prince's favour, came to be alfo earls of Gloucefter, they bore the two titles jointly, and were fummoned to parliament by the names of earl of Gloucefter †† and Hertford. Leland fays, that he took thofe two earldoms into his poffeffion, in 1216, and was one of the chief of thofe barons who kept themfelves in arms againft king John, in the feventeenth year of his reign, feizing the city of London totally in their own power, and appointing that all things fhould be directed by twenty-five perfons, whereof he was one. He was excommunicated ‡‡ by Pope Innocent the Third, and adhering to Lewis the French king, was taken prifoner at the battle of Lincoln,

* But there is a great difpute concerning the perfon who gave this earldom to John. The pipe roll, 1° R. 1. implies that king Richard the Firft, had it in his hands for fome time before he gave it his brother. Robert of Gloucefter fays, that king Richard gave to his brother John this earldom, and many lands in England and beyong fea. Hoveden, p. 655, fays, that king Richard the Firft, came into England, and gave to his brother John the earldom of Moreton, and thofe of Cornwall, Dorfet, Somerfet, Nottingham, Derbyfhire, and Lancafter, and the caftles of Merleberg, and Lutegarefhale, with the foreft and all their appurtenances; and the honours of Wallingford, Tikehill, and Hain; and the county of Gloucefter, with the daughter of the earl, whom he made immediately to be married to him; and alfo *Le Peel*, and Bolefovers; but the duke (meaning the king) retained fome of the caftles of the faid earldom. Probably king Henry the Second verbally gave this earldom, &c. to his fon John; but the king died before earl John was legally poffeffed of it; for Brompton fays, that the duke (meaning king Richard the Firft) granted and gave to his brother John all the lands which his father gave him. He granted him alfo the daughter of the earl of Gloucefter, with that honour; and that this John married the faid daughter on the 4th of the kalends of September, at Marleberg. It is affrmed alfo by other hiftorians, that at king Richard's coronation, which was on the 3d of the nones of September, John was then called the earl of Gloucefter and Moreton, and carried one of the royal fwords before him.

§ Camden's Brit. v. 1. col. 288. Madox's Hift. Excheq. p. 322. Dug. Bar. v. 1. 706.

† Camden's Brit. v. 1. col. 288. But Annal. Teux. in Mon. Angl. as tranflated by Sir R. Atkyns, p. 728, miftake in faying that after the divorce made by earl John, *Walter* (not Geofry) was married to her. 'Tis faid in Madox's Hift. of the Excheq. p. 322. that he owed to the king 20,000 marks for marrying Ifabel, countefs of Gloucefter, with all the lands, tenements, and fees which belonged to her, as is contained in the roll, 16° king John.

‡ Dug. Bar. v. 1. p. 694, 705.

‖ Sir Robert Atkyns fays, that this *Almaric* affumed the title of earl of Gloucefter, upon the divorce of king John from Ifabel. But Dugdale in his Baronage, vol. 1. p. 536, fays, that upon the death of Elizabeth, Almaric had this earldom for a fhort fpace. Camden, in his Britannia, v. 1. col. 288, fays, that this Almaric had this honour, or earldom, *conferred* upon him.

** Dug. Bar. v. 1 p. 211.

§§ Camden's Britannia, vol. 1. col. 360, by miftake the Clares are called earls of Gloucefter and Hereford, inftead of Hertford.

†† If two or more baronies happened to be vefted in the fame man, they did not confolidate in his perfon, but he held them diftinct, and was chargeable with a feparate relief for each barony; fo it appears by the rolls, 20 H. 3. that this earl paid 100l. relief for the honour of Gloucefter; 100l. for the honour of Clare; 100l. for the honour of St. Hilary; and 50l. for the moiety of earl Giffard's honour. *Lord Lyttelton's H* 2. vol. 2. p. 214.

‡‡ Dug. Bar. v. 1. 211. Annal. Teux. in Mon. Ang. Walfingham's *Ypodigma Neuftra*, p. 57.

by

by William Marefchal, earl of Pembroke, and carried to fafe cuftody at Gloucefter. But after the peace was fettled, he married Ifabel, the third daughter, and at length coheir of that earl. He was in the expedition into Wales, 7° H. 3. and on that account had fcutage of all his tenants by military fervice. He was alfo one * of thofe Englifh noblemen who firft invaded Ireland, and fubdued it to the crown of England. He died at Penros, in Britanny, 14° H. 3. being then in his return from thofe parts, leaving iffue, by Ifabel his wife, three fons and three daughters, Richard, William, and Gilbert; Amice, Agnes, and Ifabel; and was buried in the middle of the choir at Tewkefbury, to which abbey he was a confiderable benefactor. At the S. W. end of that town, on an elevated fituation, at a place called *Holmes*, he and his fucceffors had an eminent caftle, which is now deftroyed. Leland fpeaking of it fays, *In the time of mind*, i. e. in memory, *fome ruins of bottoms of walls did then appear, and now it is called Holme Hill. The time of the building of it is uncertain. It is certain that the Clares, earls of Gloucefter, efpecially the Redde earl, lay much at Holmes.* His coat armour is, *Topaz*, 3 *Chevrons Ruby*, which may be feen in Tewkefbury church, and in the church windows; but on the covering of the tomb of this earl is the fame coat, with the addition in the firft quarter, of a *Label of three points Argent, each charged with a Canton Gules.*

Richard de Clare, his eldeft fon, fucceeded him; but in regard of his minority, the guardianfhip of him, with his lands and manors, was committed to Hubert de Burgh, then Jufticiary of England. In 1227, he took up arms with many other barons, and joined prince Richard, to compel king Henry the Third to reftore the charters to the duke of Cornwall, which he had lately annulled. In 1240, ‡ he went to the Holy Land, notwithftanding the pope's prohibition. Upon collecting the aid for marrying the king's daughter, 29° H. 3. he paid 261 *l.* 10 *s.* for 261 knights fees and a half, as alfo 43 *l.* for 43 knights fees, for the moiety of the honour of Giffard. And 38° H. 3. double as much, upon collecting the aid for making the king's eldeft fon knight; the fcutage then levied being according to that proportion. In that year, ‡ upon Whitfunday, the king celebrating that feftival at London, made him a knight, together with forty more brave young foldiers, for the greater honour of that folemnity. In 30° H. 3. ‡ he was one of thofe peers who fubfcribed a letter then fent to the pope, complaining of his oppreffions, and threatening to do themfelves juftice if they were not fpeedily redreffed. In 32° H. 3. ‡ this earl brought the Auguftine friars firft into England. In 34° H. 3. ‡ he travelled beyond fea to the pope at Lyons, whence he returned about rogation week. In 39° H. 3. ‡ he was fent by the king into Scotland, together with John Manfel, the king's fecretary, on the behalf of the king of Scotland, and the queen, fifter to king Henry, then kept in reftraint within the caftle of Edenborough, where he behaved with great fubtilty; for leaving his attendants at a diftance, he got into the caftle without any oppofition, and furprifing the guard, gave entrance to his followers, fo that the king and queen were foon relieved and refcued. In 40° H. 3. ‡ he was one of the chief perfons prefent in Weftminfter hall with the king, when Boniface, archbifhop of Canterbury, with divers other bifhops, pronounced that folemn curfe, with candles lighted, againft all thofe who fhould henceforth violate the Great Charter, and charter of the forefts; and the fame year paid a debt of 640 marks, due to the king for the dowry of Eleanor, the king's fifter, for the lands which belonged to the earl Marfhal, of Ireland. In 41° H. 3. ‡ upon an infurrection of the Welch, the king preparing a great power, he was made commander in chief of all the forces in the counties of Glamorgan and Pembroke, and other parts of South Wales. In 42° or 43° H. 3. § he and his brother William had poifon given to them, from which he hardly efcaped with his life, his hair, nails, and fkin coming off, and his brother died of it. In 1258, † he was chofen by the barons, one of the twelve appointed by them for the reformation of the kingdom. In that year, ‖ he and ten more fent to the pope concerning Sicily, and to recall Ethelmar, the bifhop elect of Winchefter. The inftrument for this purpofe was fealed with their own feals, inftead of that of the whole commonalty of the kingdom. In or about this year, ** he, by the advice of the parliament then fitting, was employ'd with fome others of the nobility, by the appointment of the king, in the great convention of the eftates of France met in the parliament of France, to carry king Henry the Third's refignation of Normandy, and to compofe all difficulties betwixt both crowns, and to treat of the moft important affairs; and at his return, he acquainted the king in open parliament, with what he had in charge from the French. In 1260, ‡‡ being jealous of the earl of Leicefter, who was alfo appointed one of the twelve to reform the kingdom, he endeavoured to form a party againft him, and accufed Edward, prince of Wales, of endeavouring to obtain the kingdom, during his father's life time. The prince was exceedingly incenfed at him, and the quarrel might have been attended

* Camd. Brit. v. 1. col. 1321, 1322, 1388.

‡ Dugdale's Baronage.

§ Dug. Bar. vol. 1. p. 212. 676. By Walter de Scatenay, or Scoteney, who, fays Wykes, p. 53, was one of his knights. But Dugdale calls him the principal perfon of council with the earl of Gloucefter, and likewife his fteward, as p. 676, his chief counfellor, as p. 212, and as 'tis p. 676, 'twas believed he committed this act of villainy for a great fum of money then given him by William de Valence; fhortly after which, having his trial by the country, and being found guilty thereof, he was drawn thro' the city of Winchefter, and there hanged. Vid. M. Paris. M. Weftm.

† Additions to M. Paris's Hift. p. 215. Annales Burton, p. 415.

‖ Ibid. ** Dugdale's Baronage vol. 1. p. 213, 715.

‡‡ Rapin's Hift. v. 1. p. 334, 335, 336.

with

with fatal consequences, had not the king of the Romans used his interest to end it, and appease the prince his nephew. In 1261, he and the earl of Leicester were reconciled, and swearing once more to the Oxford provisions, sent a threatening message to the king; but in the year 1262, the earl of Leicester retired into France, and the earl of Gloucester died. It is reported of him §, that being in Tewkesbury, 45° H. 3. and hearing that a Jew who had fallen into a jakes upon a Saturday, refused to be pulled out for the reverence he bore to that day, being his sabbath, he prohibited any help to be afforded him on the Sunday, being the Lord's day, deluding by this means his Jewish niceness, but forgetting in the mean time Christian charity and godliness; for the same day the poor wretch died for want of succour. Keeping his Christmas at Tewkesbury he made a feast there, at which sixty knights were present. He was a great benefactor to Thorney abbey †, and died July 14, or according to the *Monasticon*, on the 14th of the kalends of July, 1262. His bowels were buried ‡ at Canterbury, his heart in the church at Tunbridge, in Kent, where he had a castle, near the walls whereof he founded a priory of canons of the order of St. Augustine; and his body on the right hand of his father in Tewkesbury abbey, the bishops of Worcester ‖ and Landaff, twelve abbats, and a great number of barons, knights, and great men attending his funeral. His wife erected over him a very stately tomb, ornamented with gold and precious stones, the sword and spurs which he wore when alive, and other valuable materials. Upon the tomb was a large image of the earl in silver, and the following epitaph:

* *Hic pudor Hippolyti, Paridis gena, sensus Ulyssis,*
Æneæ pietas, Hectoris ira, jacet.

Which is thus translated by Weaver, in his *Funeral Monuments*.

Chaste Hippolite, and Paris faire; Ulysses wise and sly;
Æneas kinde, fierce Hector, here jointly entombed lye.

By an inquisition after his death it appears that he held the town and court of Gloucester. It is several times mentioned in Dugdale's *Baronage*, that this earl was poisoned at the table of Peter de Savoy, the queen's uncle, in July 1262, and with him Baldwin Redvin, earl of Devon, and several others who were of the king's houshold.

Gilbert de Clare, son of the last earl, born the 2d of September, at Christ-Church, in Hants, succeeded his father, at the age of about seventeen, and was commonly called the Red, from the colour of his hair. Upon the death of his father, he repaired to the king, at Guienne, in France, to be invested with his father's inheritance, but the king having no friendship for him, was solicited some time before he would do him that justice; and it was not 'till after receiving a considerable present that he sent him away satisfied in 1262. The next year he had livery of all his castles, manors, and lands in England and Ireland; but not long after, associating himself with Simon Montfort, earl of Leicester, and the rest of the mutinous barons, he was one of the framers of those unreasonable ordinances called *Provisiones Oxonij*, whereby they did, in effect, wholly divest the king of his royal power, which occasioned him soon after to arm. He was with the barons when the king and prince were taken prisoners at the battle of Lewes. The king of Almaine, or of the Romans, in 1264, surrendered to him, who then commanded one part of the army for the barons, and was sent prisoner by him to the priory of Lewes, in Sussex. The earl obtained §§ several lands and possessions for himself, and extorted a commission from the king, authorizing himself, with the bishop of Chichester, to nominate nine persons for the administration of public affairs for some time. But after this victory ††, not thinking himself sufficiently rewarded, and the profits and revenues, and half the money for the ransom of prisoners taken at this battle, which by agreement he was to have had, being absolutely refused him; and the earl of Leicester aspiring to the crown, and the sons of that earl growing insolent, he quitted their party, with whom, above all the rest of the barons, he was highly displeased; and, ‡‡ with several others, endeavoured to rescue the king's person. He was very active in procuring liberty for prince Edward, but first told him plainly, that he could not promise his assistance unless he would oblige himself, by oath, to use his utmost endeavours to restore the antient laws, and to banish all foreigners from about the king's person. Prince Edward promised and swore to do it in the presence of several barons, and then took the command of the troops raised by this earl, who afterwards assisted the king in the great battle of Evesham, 49° H. 3. wherein he commanded a second brigade of the royal army; and, for his service, obtained a full pardon for all his former offences, and soon after had the castle of Bergavenny for some time. In 1267, joining with some discontented lords ‖‖, probably of the Marches, who with their men had come to him

§ Dug. Bar. v. 1, p. 213. Trevisa's Chron.
† Mon. Anglic.
‡ Weaver's Funeral Monuments, p. 322.
‖ Annal. Teux. in Mon. Anglic.
* Dug. Bar. v. 1, p. 213.
§§ Dug. Bar. v. 1, p. 213.
†† Dug. Bar. v. 1, p. 213. Rapin's Hist. v. 1, p. 339, &c.
‡‡ Dug Bar. v. 1, p. 748.
‖‖ Rapin, v. 1, p. 344, calls them disinherited. Dugdale in his Baronage says, That he began to make head again in favour of those who were disherited. Walsingham Upod. Neust. p. 65, That an army being gathered by him in Wales, in favour of the Disinherited, came to London, and John de Civele, with great force of his accomplices meeting him, he seized the city, the citizens favouring him. The earl by messengers commanded the legate, who had the tower to dwell in, without delay to deliver up the same. And that he might hasten to do it, the earl forbad all persons to sell any victuals to him.

for his protection, he feized the city of London, and formally befieged the pope's legate, to whom it was committed, and took the tower at that time, with an army which he raifed in his own lands, and in Wales; but the king forgave him and his accomplices, and by the mediation of the king of the Romans was reconciled to them in a few days, the earl having engaged under the penalty of 10000 marks not to make any difturbance for the future. The next year, it is faid, the king, at the inftance of the prince, received him into his full favour and grace; whereupon he was figned with the fign of the crofs, at Northampton, for the expedition to the Holy Land. However, notwithftanding all this, perhaps there was no perfect reconciliation betwixt him and the king 'till 1270, when demanding from prince Edward the expences and cofts which he had fuftained at the battle of Evefham, wherein he had been inftrumental in the king's reftoration, with the livery of all his caftles and lands which his anceftors had enjoy'd, he obtained them about the feaft of Pentecoft next following; and from that time became fo firm to the royal intereft, that in 1272, the king, during his fon's abfence *, appointed him governor of the realm after his death, and he faithfully executed the great truft repofed in him. When the king died, the earl of Gloucefter was the principal of thofe noblemen who met at the New Temple, in London, and proclaimed prince Edward king, who was then in the Holy Land. At the king's funeral, the earls of Gloucefter and Warren, the clergy, and the people, went up to the altar, at Weftminfter, and there fwore fealty to the prince, as their king, by the name of Edward the Firft. Moreover, upon his arrival in England, the earl of Gloucefter entertained him, with his whole retinue, moft honourably for many days, in his caftle at Tunbridge, in Kent. About the 10th of Edward the Firft §, he had feveral encounters with the Welch, and near Lantilawir, or Lantilovawr, obtained a compleat victory over them; but five knights were killed on the earl's fide, one of which was William de Valenfis, the younger, kinfman to the king. In 1285 †, foon after the birth of prince Edward, (afterwards king Edward the Second) the king went to Snowdon, by Weft Wales, and came to Glamorgan, which belonged to this earl, and was received by him with the greateft honour, at his own expence. About 13° E. 3. he was divorced from Alice de March, his wife, daughter of Guy earl of Angoulefme, to whom, being very young, he was married in his father's life time, and to whom king Henry the Third, whofe niece ‖ fhe was, gave 500 marks for her portion. But tho' the divorce was at her fuit, he fettled feveral poffeffions ‡ upon her. He gave up all his inheritance, 17° E. 1. ** to the king and Joan of Acres, or Acon, (fo called from a place of that name in the Holy Land, where fhe was born) the king's fecond daughter, to whom he was prefently afterwards married. On the morrow preceding the kalends of May, the fame year, the king reftored to him all thofe lands again, and they were then entailed. The next year, there were great difputes between him and the earl of Hereford, concerning feveral of their poffeffions in Wales, and both earls were committed to prifon, each paying to the king a fine of 1000 marks, for an attonement. About 19° E. 1. there having been a ditch or trench caft up by the appointment of this earl and his lady, over the creft of Malvern hills, †† Godfrey Giffard, then bifhop of Worcefter, objected to it, as encroaching upon his territories. But by the mediation of Robert Burnel, bifhop of Bath and Wells, and others, this controverfy was ended, and the following agreement was made between them, That the earl and his countefs fhould pay yearly to the bifhop and his fucceffors, a brace of bucks and a brace of does, out of their chace at Malvern, at his palace at Kemfey; and in the vacancy of the fee, the fame to be paid to the prior and convent of Worcefter, demanding them by their attorney at the caftle of Henley. He was a confiderable benefactor §§ to Keynfham abbey, and Mr. Speed fays he built a nunnery at Markyate, now Market-ftreet, in Bedfordfhire, to the honour of St. Giles, 6° E. 1. Dying at his caftle at Monmouth, on the 7th of the ides of December, 1295, he was buried in the church of Tewkefbury next his father and grandfather, by Godefred bifhop of Worcefter, under a plain ftone, with an infcription on brafs round the edges, now defaced. He left iffue by Joan of Acres, his wife, Gilbert his fon and heir, and three daughters, Margaret, Ifabel, and Elizabeth.

Ralph de Monthermer, or Mortimer, a plain efquire ‡‡, foon after earl Gilbert's death, clandeftinely married Joan de Acres, and was fent by her to her father to receive the honour of knighthood.

* Dug. Bar. vol. 1, p. 214.

§ Walfingham's Hift. p. 10. Ypod. Neuft. p. 70. Dug. Bar. v. 1, p. 214, 500.

† Walfingham's Hift. p. 12.

‖ Dug. Bar. v. 1. p. 213.

‡ Dug. Bar. v. 1, p. 214. Prinne's Intolerable Ufurpations, v. 3, 344, where the poffeffions are mentioned, in the agreement then made between them

** Dugdale in his Baronage fays, That he did it, becoming ambitious to marry in the royal line. But Dr. Holland, in his Infertions in the text of Mr. Camden's Britannia, as mentioned by Dr. Gibfon, in his edition thereof, obferving of this earl, that he powerfully and prudently fway'd much in the baron's wars, as he inclined to the barons or the king, fays, That being obnoxious to king Edward the Firft, furrendered his lands unto him, and received them again by marrying of Joan of Acres, the king's daughter. And Sir Robert Atkyns, p. 92, fays, That he was fallen under the king's difpleafure for not accompanying him in his arms in Flanders, and all his lands were feized to the king's ufe. He afterwards took the king's daughter for his fecond wife, and upon this marriage all his lands were reftored to him.

†† Thomas's Survey of Worcefter Cathedral.

§§ Annal. of Teux. in Mon. Anglic. Notes to bifhop Tanner's Notitia Monaftica, p. 4.

‡‡ Dug. Bar. v. 1. p. 115. But in the notes to Rapin's Hift. v. 1. p. 386, 'tis faid, That he was fervant of her firft hufband, and that the marriage was done in 1296, with the knowledge of her father.

hood. The earl, her husband, being dead, she in frank marriage was infeoffed of great part of his lands. This Ralph held them for some time; but the king thinking Joan had much debased herself by this match, was very much incensed at it, and caused all her lands and castles to be seized, and her husband to be closely imprisoned. But by the mediation of Anthony Beke, bishop of Durham, he was restored, and afterwards beloved of the king, who, in the twenty-fifth year of his reign ‖, gave him livery of all the lands belonging to this great earldom, to hold by the service of fifty knights fees, in the war of Flanders, and was summoned to parliament from the 28th to the 35th of E. 1. inclusive, by the title of earl of Gloucester and Hertford; but after the death of his wife, which was 1° E. 2. he was never more summoned by these titles, but had subsequent summons, as a baron only, 'till the eighteenth year of that reign.

Gilbert de Clare, son of the last earl Gilbert and Joan of Acres, was the next who possessed this earldom, being, at his father's death, but about five years old. He, tho' in minority and in ward to the king, had his lands restored * him; and petitioning § to have all his socage rents and franchises in the town of Gloucester, and elsewhere, when he was about eighteen years of age they were delivered to him. Notwithstanding Ralph de Monthermer had been summoned to parliament, and acknowledged as earl of Gloucester, yet when this Gilbert came of age, he claimed and obtained that title, the summons 2° E. 2. being directed to *the knight, nephew Gilbert de Clare, earl of Gloucester and Hertford.* In 1307, Robert Bruce †, who was crowned king of Scotland, marched against the earl of Gloucester, who was at the head of another body for king Edward the First, and obliged him to retreat to the castle of Aire, which Robert besieged, tho' without success. In 1311, the great men of the nation ‡ being assembled at Bedford, they made the earl of Gloucester the keeper of England; and 4° E. 2. he was ‖‖ constituted guardian of the whole realm, during the king's abode in the wars with Scotland. In the dispute between the king and the peers concerning some of their antient liberties and privileges, the earl of Gloucester adhered to neither side, and therefore was appointed and acted as a mediator between them. He was also very instrumental in qualifying the great displeasure which the king bore to divers of the nobles on the death of Piers de Gaveston, and earnestly endeavouring to bring about a reconciliation between them, it was chiefly effected by his mediation, tho' several persons of great dignity had before attempted it in vain. The king going to France in 1313, appointed him regent in his absence. He was afterwards one of the ambassadors sent into France, and was a great supporter of the English state, and therefore much valued and esteemed by the nobility. Rushing precipitately upon the Scotch army, at the battle of Bannocksburne, where he was captain of the king's vanguard, he was killed June 24, 1314, in the twenty third year of his age, being much lamented, because, says Leland, he was a good man. The king of the Scots generously, and without any price or ransom, sent his body to king Edward, at Berwick **, which was buried on the left hand of his father, near his grandfather and great-grandfather, at Tewkesbury, the place of his nativity, in the virgin Mary's chapel, which was near an hundred feet long, then standing at the east end behind the altar, but now demolished, and the scite an orchard. It appears §§ that this earl was a promising young man, and beloved by the whole kingdom. After two years expectance of another son beside John, (who died in his father's life time, and was buried in the Lady's chapel, at Tewkesbury) to be born of Maud, his wife, daughter of John de Burgo, son to Richard earl of Ulster, several manors and possessions were assigned to her. Thus the most noble earldom of Gloucester, which was formerly called the second pillar of the kingdom of England, was divided into three baronies ††, and parted between this earl's three sisters, of whom Eleanor, the eldest, was married to lord Hugh Despencer; the second, named Margaret, to Hugh de Audley, and before that, to Peter, or Piers de Gaveston, sometime earl of Cornwall, king Edward the Second's great favourite, much to the earl's displeasure, and the king's desire; and the third, named Elizabeth, to lord Roger de Damori, or Tamori, and before that to John de Burgo, son and heir of the earl of Ulster, in Ireland. The lady Maud died 1315, and was buried on the left hand of her husband.

Hugh Despencer, or Spencer ‡‡, the younger son of the earl of Winchester, having married Eleanor before mentioned, doing his homage, had livery of her purparty of the lordships and lands which descended to her by the death of her brother; and obtained a confirmation of all those royalties within the territories and lordships of Glamorgan and Morganog, as Gilbert de Clare, earl of Glou-

‖ Dug. Bar. v. 1. p. 215, Walsingh. Hist. p. 36, calls him Ralph de Moynhermer, and reckons this as done in the year 1298, 25 E. 1.

* Walsingham's History, p. 98.

§ Dug. Bar. p. 217.

† Rapin's History, vol. 1. p. 385.

‡ Stow's Chron. p. 215, 216.

‖‖ Dug. Bar. vol. 1. p. 216.

** Annal. Teux. in Mon. Anglic.

§§ Leland's Itinerary. Walsingham's History, p. 71. And Ypodigma Neustriæ, p. 99.

†† Mon. Malmesbur. p. 191. Walsingham's Hist. p. 81. Dug. Bar. v. 1. p. 217.

‡‡ Mr. Tyrrel, in his History, vol. 3. questions whether Hugh de Spencer was really earl of Gloucester, or only called so by courtesy. Heylin, p. 329, and Sir R. Atkyns, p. 92, omit him among the earls hereof. But Sir Thomas de la Mare, and Dr. Brady affirm that he was earl hereof. And Mr. Camden, in his Britannia, not only reckons him among the earls of this place, but also says he is stiled by writers earl of Gloucester. Sir Robert Atkyns, p. 722, stiles him earl hereof, and says, p. 93, that he was sometimes called earl of Gloucester in right of his wife.

ceſter and Hertford, lately enjoy'd. But not content with the third part of this earldom ||, tho' then worth 5000 marks, he endeavoured to wreſt the other two from his wife's ſiſters, whoſe property they were. He was lord Chamberlain * and chief favourite to king Edward the Second, after Gaveſton. And, together with his father, being accuſed § of ſeducing the king, and oppreſſing the ſtate, was, by the queen's particular orders, drawn on a hurdle thro' all the ſtreets of Hereford, on St. Andrew's eve, in 1326, hanged on a gallows fifty feet high, beheaded and quartered, and his four quarters were ſent to ſeveral places in the kingdom, but his head was fixed upon London bridge. At his death he was poſſeſſed † of no leſs than fifty nine lordſhips, in ſundry counties, 28000 ſheep, 1000 oxen and ſteers, 1200 kine with their calves, 40 mares with their colts of two years, 160 draught horſes, 2000 hogs, 40 tuns of wine, 600 bacons, 8 carcaſes of Martinmas beef, 600 muttons in his larder, 10 tuns of cyder, armour, plate, jewels, and ready money better than 10000 pounds, 36 ſacks of wool, and a library of books. He left iſſue by his wife, three ſons, Hugh, Edward and Gilbert. The Deſpencers arms are, *Quarterly, argent and gules, a fret or, over all a bendlet ſable*, to be ſeen in the chancel windows at Tewkeſbury, and many places about the church.

Hugh de Audley, or Aldithley, the ſecond huſband of Margaret de Clare, as before obſerved, was ‡ by the favour of king Edward the Third, in the eleventh year of his reign, created earl in parliament, being in the wars againſt the Scots. Neglecting to ſerve king Edward the Second, and refuſing to come to |||| Glouceſter, on the third day of April, in the fourteenth year of that reign, in purſuance of the ſummons requiring him ſo to do, his caſtle at Thornbury, in this county, and his other lands, were ſeized by the king's order; but for ſome errors in the proſecution againſt him, they were reſtored in the firſt year of the next reign. In the 13th of E. 3. he was, amongſt others, aſſigned to array all the able men of Eſſex, for the defence of the ſea coaſts there, againſt an invaſion then apprehended. The ſame year being with the king in France, and conſtituted one of the marſhals of the Engliſh army, he was in that part of it which was drawn up for battle at Vironfoſſe, and led by king Edward himſelf. The next year, being ſent into Flanders upon the king's ſervice, he was in the memorable ſea-fight before Sluyce, between the Engliſh and French. Being ambaſſador beyond ſea, 15° E. 3. he had 230 marks allowed him for his expences in that journey. The next year he was one of thoſe gentlemen who then went into Brittany upon the king's ſervice, his troops conſiſting of 100 men at arms, himſelf accounted for one, one banneret, twenty knights, ſeventy-eight eſquires, and alſo 100 archers on horſeback. And in the next year he was ſent with the earl of Lancaſter and divers other great lords into Scotland, to raiſe the ſiege of Loughmaban-Caſtle. He died 21° E. 3. leaving iſſue only one daughter, called Margaret, the wife of Ralph lord Stafford, and thus the honour of Glouceſter came to the lord Stafford's heirs ‡‡. 'Tis remarkable, that the firſt mention made in a charter of creation of an earl, of ſome revenue given to him out of the profits of the county, for the better ſupport of his dignity, is that expreſſly mentioned in the creation charter of this earl; by which he had yearly *viginti libratas reditûs de exitibus Com. Gloceſtr*, it being in lieu of the *tertium denarium de placitis Comitatûs*. Dr. Holland, in his Inſertions in the text of Mr. Camden, as publiſh'd in the laſt edition of Camden's Britannia, ſays, That this earl built a houſe at Thornbury, which the duke of Buckingham took down when he built the caſtle there. This earl Hugh was buried at Tewkeſbury, on the north ſide of the high altar. He bore *Gules, a fret or, and a bordure argent*, to be ſeen about the church where he was buried.

Thomas of Woodſtock, ſo called by reaſon of his birth there, the ſixth, or according to ſome the ſeventh, and youngeſt ſon of king Edward the Third, was conſtituted lieutenant by his father in the twenty-ninth year of his reign, during his abſence in France, upon the occaſion of an intended expedition into that kingdom. Being earl of Buckingham, he was advanced in the parliament by his nephew king Richard the Second, 9° *regni*, to the dignity of ** duke of Glouceſter, and with his title had a grant of 1000*l.* a year, to be paid out of the cuſtoms of ſeveral ports. Having married Eleanor, the daughter and coheireſs of Humphry de Bohun, earl of Hereford, Eſſex and Northampton, he became poſſeſſed of thoſe earldoms. And 'tis generally ſaid, that his father-in-law being conſtable of England, he alſo ſucceeded him in that title. But Dugdale, in his Baronage, affirms, that in the reign of king Edward the Third, he was made conſtable of England, and others

|| Mon. Angl. v. 2. p. 223.

* Dugdale's Bar. v. 1. p. 392.

§ Ibid. vol. 1. p. 394. Annal. Teux. in Mon. Anglic.

† Dug. Bar. v. 1. p. 396.

‡ Camden's Britannia, v. 1. col. 288. Dug. Bar. v. 1. p. 751. But Leland's Collect. v. 1 p. 250, ſays, Audeley was made earl 10 E. 3. Mon. Malmeſb. p. 247, 1335, *Rex ordinavit Comitem ad Glouceſtriam.* Sir R. Atkyns ſays, That upon the death of earl Gilbert, this Hugh de Audley was created earl of Glouceſter in parliament, the ſecond year of king Edward the Third. But it may be what Sir R. Atkyns calls creating him earl, was only reſtoring to him in parliament thoſe poſſeſſions which had ſome time belonged to this earldom, and came to him by the death of his brother-in-law; but were taken away, or ſeized by king Edward the Second, as mentioned in Dugd. Bar. vol. 1. p. 751. And earl Gilbert's three ſiſters were, as 'tis ſaid Mon. Malmeſb. p. 191, called *Comites*, becauſe *Comitatus Glouceſtriæ* was divided between them.

|||| Dug. Bar. v. 1. p. 751.

‡‡ Dug. Bar. v. 1. p. 751.

** Dugdale's Baronage, vol. 2. p. 169. But the ceremony of his creation was performed at Hoſlelow Lodge, in Tividale, by girding with a ſword and putting a cap with a circle of gold upon his head. The parliament then ſitting at London, aſſenting thereto, at which time the king took his homage.

ſay,

ſay, that he was ſo to continue during the king's pleaſure. In all his employments, which were very great, he merited much. In king Richard the Second's reign, he was made knight of the Garter. Knighton ſays, that in 1394, he aſſembled a parliament at Weſtminſter, in the king's name. 18° R. 2. being by indenture retained to ſerve the king in his wars of France, with 100 men at arms, whereof three to be bannerets, and eight knights, he obtained a grant to himſelf and heirs male of his body, of the fee farm rent of the town of Glouceſter, and all fines, forfeitures, and amerciaments thereto belonging. Afterwards he was by the parliament, † and alſo by commiſſion from the king, appointed one of the fourteen perſons to inſpect the affairs of the realm, from the time of his father's death. Thomas Arundel, archbiſhop of Canterbury, being made lord chancellor, is ſaid to have granted to this duke the government of the realm, by virtue of which he took upon him regal power. ‡ He was alſo aſſigned with other commiſſioners to depoſe the king. And being of a fierce ||, head-ſtrong, ambitious and unquiet ſpirit, was * privately ſmothered between two feather beds, at Calais, by the privity and procurement of the king, who mortally hated him, upon Saturday next after the feaſt of St. Bartholomew, 1397. 'Tis ſaid that he made a confeſſion under his own hand, that he had arrogated too much. But perhaps this was only the ſchedule wrote by himſelf, in anſwer to his accuſation § ; which ſchedule †† was ſeen, and diſapproved of by the king, who was determined to deſtroy him, and commanded the earl of Nottingham to do it, on pain of death. In the articles againſt the king for his depoſition, 'twas objected to him, That notwithſtanding he had pardoned this earl in full parliament, and by ſolemn oath, made of his own accord, in the preſence of the dukes of Lancaſter and York, and many other lords, at the duke of York's chapel, at Langley, where duke Thomas was alſo preſent; yet when he had him afterwards in his power, he cauſed him to be arreſted and impriſoned, and horribly and cruelly to be murdered; damnably incurring the guilt of perjury. This duke at his manor of Plecy ‡‡, or Pleſhy, in Eſſex, 17° R. 2. founded a college, dedicated to the Holy Trinity, for a maſter and eight ſecular prieſts, two clerks, and two choiriſters, which was valued at its diſſolution at 139*l.* 3*s.* 10*d.* clear, and was buried at the church there, |||| or in the chapel at Weſtminſter abbey **. After his death, the king gave away a great part of his lands to the dukes and earls which he made. Stowe, p. 317, ſays, *That he was condemned to die after he was dead*; by which I ſuppoſe he means no more than what Dugdale and Camden have otherwiſe expreſſed, That he was attainted of high treaſon by act of parliament, after he was dead. Providence ſeems to have revenged this cruel murder, on the king and the duke of Aumerle; for it was not much more than two years after, that the king was depoſed from his government, and murdered in Pomfret caſtle. The duke of Aumerle, or earl of Rutland, did not die a natural death, but was afterwards ſlain in battle. Some of the perſons concerned in this fact were duly executed, and as for the reſt, ſays Dugdale, *I preſume they never returned into England, but if they did, they ſuffered accordingly* §§. Thomas Mowbray then earl of Nottingham, and earl marſhal of England, but afterwards duke of Norfolk, had a principal hand in the execrable murder of the duke, and was himſelf baniſhed for life, by the very king that had cauſed the duke to be murdered, on that day twelvemonth afterwards; which may ſerve as an example among others to deter all perſons from committing murder, however they may fancy themſelves covered and protected. The parliament prevailed with king Henry the Fourth to grant a general pardon in the firſt year of his reign, in which, however, the murderers of the duke of Glouceſter were excepted.

Thomas lord Deſpencer, commonly called Thomas Deſpencer of Glamorgan and Morganog, great grandſon to Hugh Deſpencer the younger, was created earl about the 4th of October, 21° R. 2. He was one of the perſecutors of duke Thomas of Woodſtock, and of the chief of thoſe peers who formally acted at the depoſition of king R. 2. Being attainted |||||| by act of parliament 1° H. 4. he was firſt ignominiouſly degraded from his title, and afterwards adjudged as a traytor, and beheaded at Briſtol. The lords in parliament, with the king's aſſent, adjudged and decreed, that he,

† Knighton's Chron. p. 2685, 2686. This earl was the patron of and a great benefactor to the priory of Lanthony St. Mary. For in Prior Chiriton's Regiſter, marked A. 7. is a grant made in the chapter-houſe of Lanthony, dated on the 25th of September, 1394, wherein 'tis ſaid, that conſidering the various excellent things done to them and to their priory in their difficult buſineſſes, the priory not being able to repay him in tranſitory things, leſt they ſhould afford a token of ingratitude, they purely, freely, voluntarily, and with their unanimous conſent, obliged themſelves and their ſucceſſors, to perform for all times the particulars following, *viz.* They aſſigned to him and Alinor his wife, one of their canons in prieſt orders, to celebrate the maſs of *Salus Populi*, in the chapel of the Holy Trinity, in their priory; and after their death, the maſs of *Requiem*, with the prayers which are uſed in their choir for the dead, as ought to be done in anniverſaries. And the priory ſhall have the ſouls of him and of Alienor, his wife, in ſpecial memory recommended.

‡ Knighton's Chron. Tyrrel's Hiſt.

|| Camden's Brit. v. 1. col. 288.

* Dug. Bar. vol. 1. p. 170, 171.

§ Peck's Antiquities of Stanford, B. 12. p. 36.

†† *Ibid. ibid.*

‡‡ Biſhop Tanner's Not. Mon. p. 136.

|||| Dug. Bar. vol. 2. p. 171, ſays, That his body being embalmed was buried in the church of Pleſhey, which he had founded in honour of the Holy Trinity.

** Stowe's Survey of London, B. 6. pp. 14, 24, 26. In the Notes to Rapin's Hiſt. v. 3. p. 469, 'tis ſaid, That his body was brought over to England ſoon after his death. But according to ſome, that it was firſt buried at his caſtle of Wadley, in Eſſex, and removed thence to the college, founded by him, at Pleſhy, and afterwards to Weſtminſter abbey, where his tomb is ſtill to be ſeen.

§§ Walſingham's Hiſt. p. 394. Dugd. Bar. v. 1. p. 129.

|||||| Camd. Brit. v. 1. col. 288. Dugd. Bar. v. 2. p. 397.

who was then preſent, ſhould loſe his dignity for himſelf and heirs, and all his caſtles, lordſhips, manors and lands granted ſince the arreſting of duke Thomas beforementioned. That he ſhould thenceforth give no liveries or cognizances, nor have any retainers, except his domeſtic ſervants.

His body was buried in the middle of the choir at Tewkeſbury, under a lamp that burned before the hoſt.

He married Conſtance, daughter of Edmund of Langley, duke of York, fifth ſon to E. 3. by whom he left one ſon, Richard, who having married Elizabeth, daughter of Ralph Nevil earl of Weſtmoreland, died October 7, 1414, without iſſue, and was alſo buried at Tewkeſbury. He had alſo two daughters, *viz.* Elizabeth and Iſabel. The firſt died an infant. Iſabel married Richard Beauchamp lord Bergavenny, and earl of Worceſter, and from her, the preſent lord Deſpencer is lineally deſcended. She afterwards married Richard Beauchamp earl of Warwick, by whom ſhe had iſſue alſo.

Humphry of Lancaſter, the fourth and youngeſt ſon of king Henry the Fourth, was created † duke of Glouceſter in the parliament held at Leiceſter by the king his brother, in the firſt year of his reign. And by that title, as alſo by the title of earl of Pembroke, had ſummons to the parliament held at Weſtminſter the following year. He behaved very valiantly in ſeveral encounters and battles, and was therefore, in recompence of his paſt ſervices, rewarded with large poſſeſſions. He uſed to ſtile ‡ himſelf ſon, brother, and uncle of kings, duke of Glouceſter, earl of Pembroke, and lord high chamberlain of England. He occurs as lieutenant of the kingdom, 5° and 10° H. 5, and was protector ‖ of his nephew king Henry the Sixth, in his minority, governing the kingdom with great prudence for twenty five years. But the king his nephew being very weak, and eaſy to be guided as thoſe about his perſon would have him, Margaret, queen to king Henry the Sixth, with his uncle the cardinal, who was alſo biſhop of Wincheſter, and ſeveral others, contrived and effected the duke's ruin. In February, 1447, he was ſummoned to parliament at St. Edmondſbury in Suffolk, and coming thither, was arreſted the firſt or ſecond day of the ſeſſions, by viſcount Beaumont, then high conſtable of England, accompanied by the duke of Buckingham and ſome others, and put into cloſe confinement, all his ſervants being taken from him, and thirty two of the chief of them ſent to divers priſons. In the night following he was found dead * in his bed, without any ſigns of violence on his body, which was ſoon after ſhewn to the lords and commons, as tho' he had died with ſome ſudden diſeaſe; but people were convinced that he ſuffered by violent hands.

For his eminent virtues, knowledge and literature, he was beloved by the commons, and greatly reſpected by all men, truely deſerving the name by which he was called, *the great duke of Glouceſter*. As he was a true friend and patron to his country, ſo he alſo was to learned men and learning §, whereof he himſelf had a great ſhare. Bale ſays of him, that he was *Nobilitatis omnis atque eruditionis, Phœnix ſane unicus*. And Camden in his Britannia, ſpeaking of St. Edmond's-bury, ſays, "If England ever ſuffered by the loſs of any man, it was in this place; for that true father of his country, Humphry duke of Glouceſter, (a ſtrict patron of juſtice, and one who had improved his own excellent natural endowments, by a courſe of ſevere ſtudies) after he had governed the kingdom under king Henry the Sixth, for twenty five years together, with ſo great applauſe and commendation, that neither the good could find reaſon for complaints, nor the bad for calumnies, was cut oft in this place by the malice of Margaret of Lorain ‡‡, who obſerving her huſband king Henry the Sixth to be of a low and narrow ſpirit, ſet about this villainous contrivance, to get the management of the government into her own hands. But in the iſſue, it was the greateſt misfortune that could have befallen either her or the kingdom, for Normandy and Aquitain were preſently loſt upon it, and a moſt lamentable civil war raiſed in England." In the parliament at Weſtminſter, 33° H. 6. it was openly declared, that this duke was a true ſubject to the king. This great duke had his herald ‖‖, who was called *Pembroke*, whom, in 1436 he ſent to defy the duke of Burgundy. Duke Humphry was honourably buried in the choir of the abbey of St. Alban's, to which he was a great benefactor ††, and a

† Dugd. Bar. v. 2. p. 198.

‡ Camd. Brit. v. 1. col. 288. Doctor Holland, (in his inſertions in Camden's Britannia) ſays, that he had ſeen an inſtrument of his with theſe titles, Humphry, by the grace of God, ſon, brother, and uncle to kings, duke of Glouceſter, earl of Hainault, Holland, Zeeland, and Pembroke, lord of Freſland, great chamberlain of the kingdom of England, protector and defender of the ſame kingdom and church of England.

‖ Stowe's Chron. p. 200.

* Some ſay he was ſmothered between two feather beds; others, that he underwent the ſame fate with king Edward the Second. *Rapin's Hiſtory*. Bale affirms that he was *pulvinis ſuffocatus*. And Stowe ſays, that ſeveral ſuſpected him to be ſtrangled.

§ This good duke had his education at Baliol college in Oxford, and became a great proficient in learning, eſpecially in aſtronomy. He alſo began the foundation of the famous library in Oxford, over the Divinity-School there, by him alſo built, and gave to that library 129 books, procured by him at a great expence from Italy and France, valued at above 1000*l.* In 1440, he gave 126 volumes more, and in 1443 a much greater number, beſides conſiderable additions at his death. Camden's Brit. v. 1. col. 311. Dugd. Bar. v. 2. p. 200.

‡‡ The outrage exerciſed on a prince of this character, ſo univerſally beloved and eſteemed by the people, drew upon the queen and the miniſters an almoſt univerſal hatred, which time could never efface. The queen eſpecially was publicly charged with the murder, and the reſpect due to her was not capable of bridling people's tongues. The queen's haughty carriage and partiality in diſpoſing of places, and above all, this duke's murder, had drawn upon her the hatred of the nation to ſuch a degree, that ſhe was every where talked of with very little reſpect. Rapin's Hiſtory, v. 1. pp. 570, 571, 573.

‖‖ Stowe's Survey of London, B. 1. p. 143.

†† Particularly, he gave them Monkton priory, in the ſuburbs of Pembroke, as a cell to their abbey, 21° H. 6. Tanner's Notitia Monaſtica, p. 719.

noble

noble monument was erected for him there, a draught of which may be feen in Sandford's *Genealogical Hiftory*. At one time, Sir John Beauchamp's tomb in St. Paul's cathedral was commonly miftaken for that of the duke of Gloucefter, out of refpect to whom, numbers of people went to view it, and fometimes ftaying longer than they expected, loft their dinner, which gave rife to the faying of *dining with duke Humphry*.

Richard Plantagenet, younger brother to king Edward the Fourth, was, fhortly after the coronation of the king, advanced to the title of duke * of Gloucefter, and for the better fupport of his dignity, he obtained a grant of the fee farm rent of that town, and alfo feveral other great and rich offices, lordfhips, honours, towns, caftles, and manors in the counties of Dorfet, York, Oxford, Cambridge, Cornwal, Suffolk, Effex, Middlefex, Bedford, Northampton, Rutland, Kent, Somerfet, Wilts, Gloucefter, and other parts of England and Wales. He was made conftable of England, and juftice of North Wales, 9° E. 4. and in the eleventh year of that reign was appointed lord chamberlain for life. But not being fatisfied with thefe and other poffeffions which he then had, endeavoured to obtain the crown immediately after his brother's death; for notwithftanding his oath and recognition of prince Edward, feveral perfons have judged, that before the death of his brother, he had a defign of mounting the throne to the prejudice of his nephews. King Edward the Fourth died April the 9th, 1483, and left his brother, the duke of Gloucefter, protector and guardian over the young king and kingdom: And on the 19th of June, in a proclamation then made at York, Richard was ftiled brother and uncle of kings, duke of Gloucefter, defender, protector, great chamberlain, and admiral of England. But on the 22d, the duke himfelf was proclaimed king of England, and crowned on the 6th of July following. After his coronation he went his progrefs; and before he proceeded to York, made fome ftay at the city of Gloucefter, becaufe he would not be too far from London, whilft his orders concerning his nephews were executed. His intimate friend the duke of Buckingham attended him thither, and during the king's ftay, fent an exprefs order to the governor of the tower to murder the two nephews. 'Tis probable that 'twas about this time that the community of Gloucefter offered the king money, which he refufed; and it feems to be about the month of Auguft, in 1483, that king Edward the Fifth and the duke of York were barbaroufly murdered by the inhuman uncle's command. This mercilefs fact was committed by fmothering them in bed about midnight. But in 1485, he was himfelf miferably flain by Henry earl of Richmond, afterwards king Henry the Seventh, in a pitch'd battle at Bofworth field, in Leicefterfhire; finding, by fad experience, fays Camden, *That ufurped power is never lafting*. The fame, however, cannot be faid of Richard as was of Galba, *That he had been thought fit for empire, had he not reigned*; for Galba, after he had fettled in the empire, deceived all men's expectations; but Richard had been moft worthy of a kingdom, had he not afpired to it by wicked ways; fo that in the opinion of the wife, he is to be reckoned in the number of *bad men*, but of *good princes*. *Britannia*, col. 290. When he was duke, he obtained two licences § from the king, in the 17th year of his reign, the one to found a college at Middleham in Yorkfhire, for one dean, fix chaplains, four clerks, fix choirifters, and a clergyman to officiate in the parifh church; but he never finifhed it. The other was, to found another college at Bernard's Caftle in the county of Durham, for a dean, twelve fecular priefts, ten clerks, and ten choirifters, in the chapel there; but there is nothing more faid of it. After the battle, Richard was carried in a very ignominious manner to Leicefter, and buried in St. Mary's chapel, belonging to the Grey Friars there.

Henry of Oatlands, the youngeft fon of king Charles the Firft, was born on the 8th of July, 1640, and declared ‡ duke of Gloucefter by his royal father, and fo always after entitled; but was not created 'till May 13, 1659, by his brother king Charles the Second, whom he accompanied into England at his reftoration, and who alfo made him earl of Cambridge. Lord Clarendon and others, in the hiftories of the great rebellion, have given us an account of the interview between his father and him, the day before the king was beheaded. The king then taking the duke of Gloucefter upon his knee, faid, *Sweetheart, now they will cut off thy father's head*; at which words, the child looked very wifhfully upon him; *Mark, child, what I fay*; *they will cut off my head, and perhaps make thee a king*; *but mark what I fay, you muft not be a king, fo long as your brothers Charles and James are alive*; *for they will cut off your brothers heads as foon as they can catch them, and cut thy head off too at laft*; *and therefore I charge you not to be made a king by them*. At which the child fighing, faid, *I will be torn in pieces firft*; which falling unexpectedly from a child fo young, made the king rejoice exceedingly. After the king was beheaded, the duke of Gloucefter was fent with two fervants to Dunkirk, with a promife, it is faid, of a fmall exhibition ‖ for his maintenance,

* Dug. Bar. v. 2. p. 165. ——— Out of refpect to the city of Gloucefter, from which he had his ducal title, after he was king, he erected a herald king at arms by the name of *Gloucefter*, and fubmitted all Wales to his jurifdiction.

§ Bifhop Tanner's Notitia Monaft. pp. 117, 697.

‡ In a fecond petition of the mayor and burgeffes of Gloucefter to king Charles the Second, concerning the uniting of the two hundreds of Dudfton and King's-barton to the out county, 'tis faid, The third fons of the royal family own the title, and are ftiled dukes of Gloucefter. And in the end of it, Your petitioners and your whole kingdom are in fo great hopes of feeing your majefty and themfelves alfo happy in your royal iffue, and your third fon to be duke of Gloucefter.

‖ Hiftory of England in 2 vol. 8vo, p. 325.

pro-

provided he would not come near his brother nor any of his relations. But as foon as he arrived on the other fide of the water, he was received according to his birth and quality, and was attended to the princefs of Orange at Breda, to the great joy of her and all the royal family. After he had been fome time at Breda, he was conducted to Paris by the earl of Lauderdale, to the king his brother, and to his mother the queen, and to his other relations, to whom he was as welcome as one rifen from the dead; and was very civilly treated by the king and queen-mother of France. In 1653, when the form of government was to be fettled, it is faid by Mr. Whitlock, that the foldiers were then for a republic, the lawyers for a mixt monarchy, and many for this duke to be made king. He died of the fmall pox, September 30, 1660, in the twentieth year of his age, being one of the king's privy council, and a knight of the garter, much lamented by his royal relations and all that knew him, as he is reprefented to have been wife and accomplifhed above his years, and a prince of great expectation. As to his religion, he was an invincible afferter of the proteftant faith againft all the errors of popery; to preferve him from the temptations of which, his fifter had for fome years parted with one half of her annual income that was left to her own difpofal. His body was buried in the royal chapel of king Henry the Seventh, at Weftminfter, under the tomb of Mary queen of Scotland, his great grandmother, and on his coffin, of black velve, was this infcription, on a filver plate.

Depofitum illuftriffimi Principis HENRICI Ducis Gloceftriæ,
Comitis Cantabrigiæ, Filij quarto geniti
Sereniffimi Regis Caroli (piæ femper memoriæ) defuncti;
Et fratris fereniffimi Regis Caroli ejus nominis Secundi.
Qui in Aulâ Regia apud Whitehall, die Jovis,
Decimo tertio die Septembris, Anno a Chrifto nato 1660,
In Domino abdormivit, Ætatis fuæ vicefimo.

William Henry, only fon of George prince of Denmark and the princefs Ann his wife, afterwards queen of England, was born at Hampton Court, July 24, 1689, and on the 27th following was chriftened by Henry bifhop of London; king William the Third, and the king of Denmark, by his proxy the earl of Dorfet, being godfathers; and the marchionefs of Halifax, godmother. As foon as he was chriftened, he was immediately declared * duke of Gloucefter by his uncle king William the Third, who was extremely fond of him. And, at a chapter of the garter, held at Kenfington January 6, 1695, was elected member thereof, having been firft knighted by the king with a fword of ftate, and was inftalled on the 24th of July following. He was a prince of a tender conftitution, but of incomparable parts, promifing whatever a nation could wifh or defire. He died in the twelfth year of his age, in the year 1700, being then the only remaining iffue of the prince and princefs above mentioned. His death in a great meafure was occafioned by over heating himfelf in the obfervation of his birth-day, (being Wednefday) July 24th, which caufed a fever, and foon after a dilirium, which lafted with his life.

Frederick Lewis, father to his prefent majefty king George the Third, was created duke of Gloucefter by his royal grandfather, January the 10th, 1718, N. S.

His royal highnefs William-Henry, third fon of his late royal highnefs Frederick prince of Wales, was born November 25, 1743, N. S. and on the 17th of November, 1764, his prefent majefty was pleafed to grant to him and to his heirs male, the dignities of a duke of the kingdom of Great Britain, and of an earl of the kingdom of Ireland, by the names, ftiles, and titles of duke of Gloucefter and Edinburgh in Great Britain, and Earl of Connaught, in Ireland.

Of COUNCILS, SYNODS, ROYAL and GRAND ASSEMBLIES, and PARLIAMENTS, at GLOUCESTER.

WHEN Aurelius Ambrofius, king of the Britons, in 489, had oppofed himfelf in a great battle againft Hengift, at Mafebell, beyond Humber in Yorkfhire; the king and his nobility affembled together at Gloucefter †, to confult what was to be done with their prifoner. Among others of the nobility, there were at that time of Gloucefter, three noble and renowned perfonages prefent; Edel, the earl; Eldad, the bifhop; and Eldo, the mayor or chief governor; and when the greateft part of the company feemed to favour the life of Hengift, Eldad the bifhop fpoke with fuch eloquence and power, that he moved all the company to be of his opinion; and by the common confent of all prefent, the prifoner was delivered to Eldo § the mayor, who leading him out of the city, put him to death.

In 804, Ethelrick, fon of king Ethelmund, at the requeft of a fynod held here, to which he was invited, was himfelf a great benefactor to the church of St. Peter.

In 896, here was a great meeting of the Mercnamen, when Werefrid, bifhop of Worcefter, recovered feveral laws.

It appears from the Saxon Chronicle, that Lanfrank, archbifhop of Canterbury, held two of his councils or fynods here, and by his confent, and at the king's command, at one of them, Thomas archbifhop of York confecrated William de S. Carilefo to the bifhoprick of Durham, in the prefence of the king; archbifhop Lanfrank, and

---

* Hift. of England v. 2. 8vo pp. 501, 550. In Heylyn's Help to Hiftory, p. 331, 'tis faid, That this duke William was nominated in 1689, but died before his creation, July 30, 1700.

† Dr. Hutton's Antiq. Oxford, in Mr. Hearne's Textus Roff. p. 352. M. Weftm.

§ In fome places 'tis faid Eldol the earl killed him, See p. 93.

Wol-

Wolftan, Ofbern, Gifo, and Rotbertus, at that time bifhops, affifted.

King Edgar, upon innocents-day 964, * in this royal city, as then expreffly called, gave to the monks of Worcefter certain lands and liberties. This grant was confirmed by the king with the confent of his princeffes and archbifhops; and figned by the king, the queen, the two archbifhops, fix bifhops, fix abbats, fix dukes, and twelve minifters.

In 1051, earl Euftace, king Edward the Confeffor's brother-in-law, fled for fhelter to Gloucefter, which is called the court, where the king had abode fome confiderable time. Leofwine, or Leofric, earl of Mercia, and earl Styward of Northumberland, came to him hither with great forces, where he continued a good while §. And a little after the feaft of St. Mary, in September, the king appointed a general affembly for all the nobility to meet here, which was very full. The fame king in 1063, kept his court here, and fent hence a body of horfe againft Griffin prince of South-Wales; and he is frequently mentioned as being at this place.

King William the Conqueror, every year when his affairs would permit him, kept his chriftmas here; and to render this affembly the more grand, magnificent and fumptuous, and that the ambaffadors of foreign nations might admire the appearance of the company; he, by his royal edicts, was attended by all the archbifhops, bifhops, abbats, earls, thanes, and knights. He wore his crown, and made a grand and delicate fare. The great men appeared in golden, or very fplendid robes, which were called *feftiva indumenta*, and the town found much of his entertainment and clothing, as it did for his fucceffors, when at this place. He was at no time more courteous, gentle and kind than at fuch affemblies, fo that thofe who came might fee that his bounty equalled his riches.

In 1076, Lanfrank held his council here, when Wulketul, abbat of Croyland was depofed.

In 1085, at chriftmas, the king with his nobles held his court here for five days; and afterwards, the archbifhop and clergy held a fynod for three days, and the king's three chaplains, Maurice of Lundene, [London] William of Northfolc, [Norwich] and Redbeard of Ceafterfcire, [now Litchfield and Coventry] were then made bifhops. *Sax. Chron.* Archbifhop Wake's *State of the Church*, &c. p. 160.

King William Rufus ufually kept his chriftmas here, which Brompton calls the cuftom of his father, and held it with great pomp. (p. 979.) Falling dangeroufly fick at Alveftan, in this county, which Dunelm calls the royal vill, in 1093, he removed in great hafte to this town, where he continued in a very weak condition during lent; and here he granted the archbifhoprick of Canterbury to Anfelm, and the bifhoprick of Lincoln to Robert Bloet, his chancellor, and lands to feveral monafteries, and reftored many rights and revenues which he had before detained. Notwithftanding articles of peace had been concluded between this king and Malcolm king of Scotland, fome things ftill remained to be fettled between them, wherefore Malcolm came to the Englifh court in this city, and was received in a very imperious manner by Rufus. At his court held here the next year, great complaints and menaces were fent to the king by his brother Robert's ambaffadors, concerning the king's mifbehaviour towards him. At another of his great councils held here at chriftmas, he granted fome poffeffions to the archbifhop of York, the two archbifhops, twelve bifhops, eight abbats, eight lords, and others being prefent.

King Henry the Firft held his court here at candlemas 1123, and fent his letters all over England, commanding all his bifhops, abbats and thanes to come to it for the choofing of an archbifhop of Canterbury: William Corbeil was then nominated, and the king confirmed the election.

In 1175, on the feaft of St. Peter and Paul, the king fummoned hither another great council of his earls and barons, and Refe, and other princes of Wales; when the king iffued orders to all his fubjects, that if any of the Welch made infurrections in their countries, they fhould unanimoufly fall upon them; and the earl of Gloucefter and the nobility were fworn to the obfervance thereof.

In 1190, William Longchamp, the pope's legate, protector of the kingdom in king Richard the Second's abfence, and bifhop of Ely, held a fynod here.

On the eve of St. Simon and Jude 1216, there came to Gloucefter, which was then thought the fafeft place in the realm, in the prefence of Walo the pope's legate, the bifhops of Winchefter, Bath, Litchfield, and Worcefter, the earls of Chefter, Pembroke, Ferrars, William the marfhal, John his brother, Philip of Albani, with abbats, priors, and a great company. On the morrow, the legate, with the bifhops, earls, and lords before mentioned, led prince Henry to the abbey-church with folemn proceffion, where he publickly fwore before the great altar, that he would pay due honour and reverence to God and his holy church all his life; adminifter juftice, obferve good laws and cuftoms, and abolifh all evil ones; and that he would pay one thoufand marks yearly to the pope for his kingdoms, according to his father's grant. Thefe things being done, the bifhops of Winchefter and Bath anointed and folemnly crowned him with the ufual ceremonies; after which, the bifhops, earls and lords led him, clad in royal veftments, to the table, where all things being fet in order, they dined in joyful ex-

* Mon. Angl. v. 1. p. 141. Homingi Cartil. v. 2. p. 521.

§ Dunelm p. 184. Flor. Wigorn. pp. 117, 627.

ultation. On the morrow, the king took the homage and fealty of all prefent; and continued in this town a confiderable time afterwards.

In 1233 or 1234, on Saturday the morrow after St. Catharine's day, being November 26, there was a provincial council holden here before the archbifhops and bifhops; and the king fent a writ dated at Hereford, Nov. 23, prohibiting them to treat of any thing prejudicial to his crown, ftate and dignity.

In 1233, 17° H. 3. the king kept the feaft of whitfuntide here, and girt with the fword of knighthood Thomas earl of Warwick, Roger Bigod, earl of Norfolk, and Hugh de Vere, earl of Oxford; and alfo iffued out his writs to all who held any lands of him by knight-fervice, commanding them to repair to him at this town, on the morrow after all-faints day, then next enfuing.

In 1234, on the Sunday after afcenfion-day, a colloquium was held at this place, when the difinherited barons were reftored to the king's favour. [*Hody.*] The fame year the king held his court here at chriftmas. *M. Weftm.*

In 1241 the court was here, when David ap Llewelyn prince of North-Wales came and did the king homage for the principality of Wales. Dr. Fuller has obferved that this place was more beloved by king Henry than London itfelf, becaufe it was ftrong and loyal, and where he was crowned, and did afterwards often refide.

In 1278 or 1279 king Edward the Firft, in the octaves of St. John Baptift, held a parliament in the long work-houfe of the abbey, on which fpot is built the houfe now extending from that belonging to the deanery, on the eaft, to the gate leading to the miller's green on the weft; and fummoned to it all perfons, to fhew by what authority and titles they held their lands or claimed their privileges, according to the ftatute of *Quo Warranto*; and to prevent the great mifchiefs, damages and difherifons which the people had before fuffered thro' the default of the laws, feveral laws were then enacted, which ever fince have gone by the name of the ftatutes of Gloucefter.

In 1301 there was another ftatute of *Quo Warranto* dated from this place.

Wednefday, October the 20th, 1378, Richard the Second held a parliament here, in which were great bickerings between the temporal lords and the bifhops, each complaining of the others incroachments. It continued twenty eight days, and much bufinefs was difpatched therein. On the day of the rifing of this parliament, November 16, Simon de Sudbury, archbifhop of Canterbury, held a provincial council in a chamber within the abbey, and made a decree concerning the ftipends of priefts.

On October 20, 1407, king Henry the Fourth held a parliament here, wherein feveral laws were made: it continued forty four or fifty four days, and Mr. Prynne affirms, that the members of it hufbanded well their time for the king and kingdom's advantage.

In 1420, February 15, king Henry the Fifth held a parliament here, which was adjourned to Weftminfter in about a fortnight's time.

R. Cole affirms in his roll, now in the cuftody of the city, " That kyng Harry iiij held a p'liament at Glouc. the ix yere of his regne, begynnyng the fayde p'leament at alhalontyd and fo contynued til midwynt' next fuyng.

Of BATTLES and SIEGES.

ONE of king Edgar's battles againft the Danes was fought here. After the king's death, Ethelwulph † his fon fucceeding in 836, the Danes returning to the kingdom with greater rage and cruelty than they had in the former reign, poffeffed themfelves of this place, and pitching their tents here, lorded it over this part of the country, and made themfelves mafters not only of the foreft of Dean, but likewife of great part of Herefordfhire.

In 978 Ethelred was crowned king, and not long after the beginning of his reign, the Danes again entered the kingdom, and began afrefh their intermixt cruelties, burning and deftroying moft of the eminent cities and places in the kingdom. Amongft the reft, this city was the third time ravaged by them, and almoft confumed by fire, for they had no refpect to places or perfons, facred or civil; but like a tempeftuous hurricane, drove the whole kingdom before them, and in the end brought the country into fervitude and flavery.

In 1172 ‡, Jorwerth lord of Caerleon upon Ufke gathered all his friends and forces together, and without mercy deftroyed all the country with fire and fword, even to the gates of Hereford and Gloucefter.

In 1263 ||, Sir Maci de Befile, (called alfo Matthias de Befille) a French knight, was made fheriff of Gloucefterfhire, and conftable of Gloucefter-caftle by the king. But the barons being greatly difpleafed at it, fet up Sir William Tracy, a knight of this country, in oppofition to him. Sir William, as he was holding a county court, was affaulted by a large body of the king's forces, with Maci at their head, who took him, and after ufing him with great barbarity, led him through the town to the caftle, and there caft him into prifon. When the barons heard of it, Sir Roger de Clifford and Sir John Giffard came to refcue Sir William, and befieged the caftle for four days. Sir Maci, who is characterifed to be a ftout and bold knight, refufed to yield it to them, and continued

† Manufcript Coll.
‡ Lloyd's Welch Hiftory, p. 233.
|| R. Glouc. Chron. pp. 535, 536, 537. Cont. M. Paris. Triveti Chron. M. Weftm. Walfingham's Upod. Neuft. Daniel's, and feveral other Hiftories of England.

to

to defend it and the town, 'till the firft gate leading to it was burnt, as was afterwards the wooden bridge belonging to the caftle. Some prifoners were releafed by the governor in expectation of their affiftance, but they treacheroufly made another entrance or poftern for the befiegers, and thereupon Sir Maci and his men flying to the high and ftrongeft tower, defended themfelves as well as they could, 'till the three iron gates and locks were broken down, and he himfelf was taken; and even then with invincible courage he refufed to furrender. Sir Roger de Clifford having taken the caftle, fent Sir Maci to the marches of Wales, where he was kept prifoner at Erdefley-Caftle.

Sir Roger de Clifford afterwards returned to his allegiance, and delivered the town and caftle of Gloucefter into the king's hands; but Sir John Giffard retired to Brimpsfield, and having affembled many of the moft valiant of his neighbours, there were frequent fkirmifhes between the garrifon of that caftle and this of Gloucefter. The next year the town was taken* by fome of the barons, and the following ftratagem was ufed to accomplifh it: Sir John Giffard, who is called a knight of wonderful probity and courage, and Sir John de Balun, being cloathed with Welch cloaks, and riding upon two woolpacks, after the manner of chapmen or woolmongers, were let into the town at the weft-gate. When it was unlock'd, they both leaped off their horfes, and cafting away their cloaks, appeared armed from head to foot. At this fight the porters were fo terrified as to deliver up the keys; and thereupon, the gates were thrown open to the forces which the two knights had procured, and were ready at hand. Prince Edward followed the barons clofe at their heels, and having fpeedily repaired the bridge over Severn, which they had burnt, came hither on Afhwednefday, and affaulted the town at the weft-gate. But the barons within defended themfelves fo well that he could not conquer them. Forces were fent from the caftle, which was ftill in the king's hands, to affift the prince; but Grimbald Pauncefoot attacking them, turned them back with the lofs of fome wounded. The prince feeing his condition, turned into the meadows, and was brought by a boat to the caftle, where he fet up his banner upon the high tower, which, when the barons faw, they were a little furprized. However on the town fide they prefently befieged the caftle, which was ftoutly defended by the garrifon. But Sir John Giffard coming from Brimpsfield, and burning the caftle-bridge which cut off the communication with the country; and the prince feeing Robert Ferrers earl of Derby, coming againft him with a great reinforcement, went unarmed and very privately to the barons, and upon oath granted them what they defired, upon which they left the town. But the prince revenged himfelf on the burgeffes, whom he put in prifon 'till they had paid 1000*l.* for their ranfom, and then, after very ill treatment, they were fet at liberty; but the town was miferably deftroyed. A little after this, the prince fortified the town, and about 1264, the earl of Leicefter got poffeffion of it; when the prince, the earl of Gloucefter, and others befieged it on the north fide, and entering at a breach which they had made in the wall leading to St. Ofwald's gate, took it from Leicefter.

In 1265, Robert de Ros, William de Vefti, and other knights and gentlemen, to the number of three hundred, entered the town to defend themfelves in it againft the prince, but they were obliged to furrender it, and were fuffered to depart, fwearing not to bear arms againft him for a month.

As foon as the civil war broke out in 1641, this city joined in the parliament intereft, and to put themfelves in a pofture of defence, added one company of voluntiers to the trained bands which affifted them; procured fome pieces of ordnance from London and Briftol; provided materials, and at a great expence raifed its fortifications. Thereupon, the king, by a letter from Oxford, dated February 12, 1642, fent to the fheriff and juftices of Gloucefterfhire, prohibiting his fubjects in that county from having any traffic or commerce with the city, 'till it fhould return to its obedience; which letter was publickly read in the churches and chapels in the city, that all perfons might know his majefty's pleafure, and do their duty accordingly. Prince Rupert on the 3d of the fame month, demanded the city for the king. Lieutenant colonel Maffie and the principal officers returned him for anfwer, That they were refolved with their lives and fortunes to defend the city for the ufe of the king and parliament, and would by no means furrender at the demand of a foreign prince: The mayor alfo fent another meffage, That according to his oath and allegiance, he was refolved to keep the city on his majefty's behalf, and would not deliver it up. Thereupon another fummons to the fame purpofe was fent by the prince, and it had a like effect.

About the middle of this month, lord Herbert, fon of the marquis of Worcefter, general of South-Wales, with a body of about 1500 foot and 500 horfe, well armed, which he had raifed with more expedition than was expected, came to reduce the garrifon. The horfe were put under the command of his brother lord John Somerfet, and the foot under Sir Jeremiah Bret, their major general. The laft of thefe foon after demanded the city for the king's fervice, but the fummons from a Welch brigade was received with fcorn; whereupon the Welch began to encamp at Highnam, within a mile and a half of the city. The garrifon deferting Sudely-Caftle

* R. Glouc. p. 537 et fequentes.

and

and other out garrisons, made good the guard of the bishop's palace on the Vineyard hill, and sometimes made slender sallies; for the governor had not 100 horse, and the Welch forces were double the number of the garrison, 'till 200 foot and dragoons from Bristol, commanded by captain John Fiennes, came to their supply. However the Welch lay still in their camp, and for five weeks together did not so much as attempt the out guards, or any considerable action, but expected that prince Maurice from Cirencester should take equal care to distress the city on the other side, which he did to a great degree; and 'twas thought that prince Rupert would speedily come to their assistance, which, on account of Bristol, he could not possibly do. Mean time, colonel Massie (by order of Sir William Waller) immediately after the taking of Malmesbury, drew out the garrison forces to Highnam, and kept them to very close play. But Sir William Waller, by the help of some flat bottom boats, crossing the river at Frampton passage, and advancing towards the Welch with a light body of about 2000; the Welch, tho' their works were too strong to be entered by horse and dragoons; their avenues narrow, with cannon planted in all of them; and though their number was near, if not equal to their enemy; without striking a stroke, sounded a parley, and surrendered on condition that they might receive quarter, and that the officers might have respect according to their quality, which was granted: So on the 24th or 25th of March, near 1300 foot and three troops of horse were led prisoners into the city, and several of them for some time, were kept under strict confinement in the churches of St. Mary de Load and the Holy Trinity. But many of the parliament garrisons being before filled with such persons, most of the common soldiers were, within ten days, sent back into their own country, having taken an oath never to serve against the parliament; others that offered themselves were entertained in the parliament's service: Several of the gentlemen and officers paid a ransom, and took the same oath with the soldiers; and the rest were sent to Bristol, but delivered at the taking of that city by prince Rupert.

This defeat, tho' it seem'd so inconsiderable, with the other preparations that were rendered useless by it, lord Herbert himself affirmed to cost 60,000*l.* tho' 'tis called a mushroom army that had not courage to defend itself. About this time a great deal of provision was laid in, and a considerable quantity of money provided by the city, and the king's forces frequently hovered over the hills, and now and then skirted upon the town; but no close siege was laid to it 'till the 10th of August following. This was then said to be the only garrison the parliament had between Bristol and Lancaster on the north of England, which, if the king could have taken, he would have been master of the Severn, and would have needed no forces in Wales.

The king did not himself approve the undertaking of the siege, but as it was a measure strongly recommended by his friends, he came in person against the city, and about two in the afternoon sent the following summons by two heralds, who would have read it openly in the street; but the mayor would not permit them to do it, so it was read in the Tolsey only, by Somerset herald.

Charles Rex.

Out of our tender compassion to our city of Gloucester, and that it may not receive prejudice by our army, which we cannot prevent if we be compelled to assault it; we are personally come before it to require the same, and are graciously pleased to let all the inhabitants of and all other persons within that city, as well soldiers as others, know, that if they shall immediately submit themselves, and deliver this city to us, we are contented freely and absolutely to pardon every one of them without exception; and do assure them in the word of a king, that they nor any of them shall receive the least damage or prejudice by our army in their persons or estates: But that we will appoint such a governor and a moderate garrison to abide there as shall be both for the ease and security of the city and the whole county. But if they shall neglect this offer of grace and favour, and compel us by the power of our army to reduce that place (which by the help of God we shall easily and shortly be able to doe) they must thank themselves for all the calamities and miseries that shall befall them. To this message we expect a clear and positive answer within two hours after the publishing hereof. And by these presents do give leave to any persons easily to repair to and return from us whom that city shall desire to employ unto us in that businesse, and we do require all the officers and souldiers of our army quietly to suffer them to pass accordingly.

The king immediately drew a part of his troops into Tredworth field, before the town, and being attended by prince Charles, the duke of York, prince Rupert, and general Ruthen, faced the city with about 6000 horse and foot, not above a quarter of a mile from it, and 2000 horse on the other side within cannon shot, the main of the army being not yet come up. The Governor, with the consent of several others, within less than the time prescribed, sent the following answer to the king by serjeant major Pudsey and Mr. Tobias Jordan; who, it is said, without any circumstance of duty or good manners, told his majesty, That they brought an answer from the godly city of Gloucester, the mayor being first satisfied in some scruples touching the oath of his mayoralty.

The ANSWER.

August 10, 1643.

We the inhabitants, magistrates, officers and soldiers within the garrison of Gloucester, unto his majesty's gracious message return this humble answer; that we do keep this city, according to our oaths and allegiance, to and for the use of his majesty and his royal

royal posterity; and do accordingly conceive ourselves wholly bound to obey the commands of his majesty, signed by both houses of parliament; and are resolved, by God's help, to keep this city accordingly.

De Wise, mayor §,	John Brewster,	G. Davidson,
Robert Maxwell,	Edw. Massie,	Con. Ferrer,
William Lugge,	My. Singleton,	Thomas Hill,
Thomas Pury,	John Scriven,	Nich. Webb,
Jo. Dorney,	Anth. Edwards,	John Halford,
Toby Jordan,	Hum. Mathews,	Isaac Dobson,
Edward Gray,	Charles Blount,	Peter Crispe,
Rob. Backhouse,	Ja. Harcus,	Tho. Pury, Jun.
Robert Stevenson,	Thomas Blayney.	

His majesty received this answer with great temper and mildness, only expressing a kind of wonder at their confidence, saying in the hearing of the messengers, *Waller is extinct, and Essex cannot come.* And indeed their resolution was wonderful, for at that time there were not in the city more than fourteen or fifteen hundred soldiers, and forty or fifty barrels of powder; they had a slender artillery, and their works were low and unfinished.

Upon the return of the messengers, the governor and council of war judged it absolutely necessary to pull down a few houses, and to set on fire all the rest of the suburbs, in which were many large, handsome houses, well inhabited. *By burning of the suburbs,* (says Mr. Dorney in his fourth speech, made October 8, 1646) *the city is a garment without skirts, which we were willing to part withall, lest our enemies should sit upon them.*

The earl of Brentford, the king's general, brought all the battering cannon that could be spared from Oxford; and all things were made ready for the siege. The Rev. Mr. Chillingworth had invented, after the manner of the Romans, *testudines cum pluteis,* which ran upon cart-wheels, with a blind of planks, musket proof, (each having four holes for musketteers to fire through) placed upon the axle tree, to defend the musketteers and those that thrust forward the engine, the fore-part of which was to serve for a bridge. In using these engines the wheels were to fall into the ditch, and the bridge to rest upon the town breast-works, and so each would become a compleat bridge by which to enter the city.

Sir William Vavasor drew all his forces to the west side, broke down all bridges, and after leaving a strong guard at the Vineyard, joined the Welch at Longford and Kingsholm, on the north-west side of the city, to the forces lately come from Worcester. General Ruthen had placed his men in some grounds behind Lanthony, about a quarter of a mile from the town. And Sir Jacob Ashley was quartered with a strong body in some part of the suburbs on the east side.

Many of the king's commanders were officers of the greatest skill and experience, and his army was increased by the arrival of two regiments out of Ireland, commanded by colonel Myn and Sir William St. Leger.

The king, almost all the time of the siege, quartered at Matson-house, on the east.

The south and south-east sides of the city, tho' really they were the strongest and best fortified, were represented to his majesty as most proper to be attacked, because there only the springs would not annoy the works of the besiegers, and if his majesty's troops could enter at a breach in these parts they would be instantly possessed of the highest ground in the city. These things the garrison were aware of, and to defend themselves raised a sconce, and strengthened all their inward works with earth.

During the siege there were frequent assaults on both sides. The king's troops endeavoured to fill up some part of the moat between the south and west gates; and sunk a mine under the east-gate, but it was countermined. In short, their efforts seem to have been very feeble and altogether unsuccessful. They made about 150 great shot against the wall, which shattered the stone-work considerably; but the garrison drew an inward work from the south side all along the friers orchard, southward, and stopt all the passages between that and the east port. They also threw up a strong work across the east-gate-street, which had a large trench before it filled with water. This work they intended to have raised to the height of the eaves of the houses, and to have planted cannon thereon if the siege had continued. And so indefatigable were the citizens, that the very women and children were daily employed in fetching of turf, and placing of cannon-baskets and earth, for repairing of the fortifications during the whole siege, which lasted twenty six days.

On Monday, the 4th of September, at night, the garrison discovered two fires on Wainload-hill, which was the signal for approaching relief, and answered them by lights from the college-tower. On the 5th, which was appointed for a public fast to be kept within the city, the siege was raised.

This great event was brought about by the earl of Essex, who determining to relieve Gloucester, had obtained from the committee for the militia in the city of London, two regiments of trained bands, three regiments of auxiliaries, and a regiment of horse, with eleven pieces of cannon and three drakes, by way of reinforcement to his army. On the 24th of August, the earl mustered his forces upon Hounslow-heath, when they were 10,000 compleat; after which he took up his quarters at Colebrook, and on the 26th marched to Beconsfield, and so forward to Beerton, where he cloathed his army. Upon intelligence of this advance, prince Rupert, with the greatest part of the king's horse, drew off from before Gloucester

§ Reliq. Carolinæ, p. 212; but in Rushworth's Collections Constance Ferrer is said to be mayor. Lord Clarendon says that the king sent the summons on August 10, 1643, which was Wednesday, but Dorney says the siege was laid on Thursday, August 10, 1643, and raised Tuesday, September 5.

to oppofe their march, whilft the king carried on the fiege. About Bicefter 400 of the king's troops fkirmifhed with a part of the parliament-army, but were forced by numbers to retire; and fcarce a day paffed in the whole march without fome fmall engagement, which obliged Effex's army to proceed with the greateft order and caution. The reinforcement from London, under colonel Manwaring, joined the earl of Effex on the firft of September at the general randezvous on Brackley-heath; after which the whole proceeded on their route for Gloucefter, but were attacked on the 4th, at Stow on the Would, by the prince, with about 4000 horfe, in which action the lofs on either fide was nearly equal. On the 5th, Effex advancing to Prefbury-hill, drew up his army in view of the city, and difcovered the huts in the royal camp on fire, and the fiege raifed as already related. The general himfelf marched to Cheltenham, but the king's troops often fkirmifhed with him and beat up his quarters. On the 8th the whole army entered Gloucefter, and were joyfully received; and having furnifhed the city with fome neceffaries during their ftay of two nights, moved to Tewkefbury, and lay there five days, that in the mean time Gloucefter might take in more provifions.

When the fiege was raifed, the city was reduced to two or three barrels of powder, and other provifions were fhort in proportion.

The king's army, which is faid to have been near 30,000, retreated in the night up Painfwick-hill. Their lofs before Gloucefter is computed to have been upwards of 1000 men, whilft that of the garrifon did not amount to 50, of which two only were officers.

The raifing of this fiege gave a greater turn to the king's affairs than his enemies expected, who were then in the loweft condition they had experienced during the war.

In an original letter wrote by bifhop Goodman, dated Chedfey, November 23, 1649, directed to the mayor and aldermen of Gloucefter, and now in the cuftody of the corporation, 'tis faid, *You have better deferved of the parliament than any city of England, not only for the enduring of a great fiege, but indeed the turning * of the wheel, for ever after the parliament-forces prevailed, which before they did not.* And 'tis faid in Mr. Dorney's fourth fpeech, *That the ftanding out of this place in the late fiege, made it the vertical point in this civil war; for from that time the enemies* [i. e. the king's forces] *more and more declined; infomuch as it pleafed that reverend judge ferjeant Wilde, in his late charge, fitting upon the commiffion of oyer and terminer here, to ftile us of this place the confervators of the parliament of England.*

A letter of thanks, accompanied with a prefent of 1000*l.* was fent to colonel Maffie as a reward for his fervices; proper largeffes were alfo fent to the inferior officers, and the private men of the garrifon had a month's pay over and above their arrears, by an order of both houfes of parliament made on the 15th of September, ten days after the raifing of the fiege. The 5th of September was ordered by the mayor and common council to be annually obferved as a day of thankfgiving for raifing the fiege. It was called *Gloucefter-holiday*, and kept accordingly 'till the reftoration.

Many attempts were afterwards made to recover the city, but none fucceeded. After Newbury fight, Sir William Vavafor was fent to Hereford with a ftrong party, to raife forces in thofe parts, and was ordered by the king to diftrefs Gloucefter on the Welch fide. Sir John Wintour, at his entering upon his government of Newnham, plundered the villages near the city; and about the latter end of 1643, upon intelligence of the governor's abfence, advanced with a confiderable body of men to furprize it; but the governor returning, he defeated and drove them back in great confufion.

After this, a project was formed to get the city by corrupting captain Backhoufe, one of the officers of the garrifon, in order to which lieutenant-colonel Stanford wrote him a letter §, which was carried by one of Backhoufe's particular friends, who told him, that if he would undertake the bufinefs he might have 5000 *l.* reward. Backhoufe fhewed a feeming readinefs to engage in the affair, but imparted it to the governor, and by his advice returned a complying anfwer, defiring that a correfpondence

* The unfortunate fiege of this city, fays Sir Robert Atkyns, gave a ftand to the king's victorious army; which being raifed as has been related, it turned the ftate of the war, and the king could never after obtain fuccefs; which confirms, that the greateft of kings, and the beft of men are not fecured from the violence of the wicked. This royal family will always be honoured in the memory of good men, and muft have been fo throughout the Chriftian world, had it been as profperous as it was deferving. King James the Firft was the moft learned king: King Charles the Firft was the moft religious king: King Charles the Second was the beft natured king; and king James the Second was the beft friend; which virtue was moft eminent in his tender love to his children, and in his fteady kindnefs to his fervants. This fucceffion of kings has been oppofed by their virtues; for peace, religion, good nature, and friendfhip ruined them. It is remarkable of this royal family, that the *witty* king was over reached by the Spanifh ambaffador: That the *religious* king was murdered by rebellious faints: The *voluptuary* was confpired againft by men of no religion; and the *beft friend* was betrayed and forfaken by them whom he moft intirely loved. It does not hence follow that this family will always be unfortunate. *Ancient and Prefent State of Glofterfhire.* pp. 88, 89. ——— The paffages in this note being *remarkable* will ferve as an apology for inferting them, to thofe who differ in fentiment from the learned hiftorian; to fuch as agree with him, I am fatisfied none will be thought neceffary.

§ The letter is as follows: Good Robin, It is not unknown to you that once I loved you, and therefore I fend this to advife you, whilft it is in your power, to make ufe of it, and take my word I am confident as yet you may not only have your pardon, but raife yourfelf a greater fortune than the condition of thofe you ferve *are* able to afford you. This you may gain by the delivery—you may guefs my meaning of what place, which is not hard for you to do. You know the old faying, *fallere fallentem non eft fraus.* This is the advice of him that, when you fhall defift the caufe, will ever be

Your loving friend

Edward Stanford.

refpondence might be fettled, which was done, and many letters paffed between them.

The defign being thus far advanced, it was thought neceffary that lord Digby fhould write to captain Backhoufe †, to give him a ftronger affurance of what had been promifed him, and to name feveral of the king's officers, that Backhoufe might approve of one who fhould affift in the execution of their project. Backhoufe chofe Sir William Vavafor: Afterwards meeting lieutenant colonel Stanford on Corfe-lawn, he received 200*l.* of him, when it was agreed between them, that on the 15th of January the king's troops fhould advance to the weft-gate, and Backhoufe fhould let them in, provided they came by nine o'clock or half an hour after; and early that evening he fent them the word, which was *Briftol.*

As foon as this meffage was difpatched, the governor called a council of war, acquainted them with the whole plot, and ordered both the foldiers and citizens under arms. Four men were placed under Over-bridge, which the king's troops were to pafs, with orders upon firing the firft gun to cut a large cable, which done, the bridge would have fallen in, and cut off the retreat of the royalifts, who, if they could not have conquered, muft all have been cut to pieces or made prifoners. But the troops intended for this expedition moved fo flowly, that when they came to Laffington-hill, within a mile of the town, it was almoft day break, whereupon they retreated to Newent, and Gloucefter expected them in vain.

Backhoufe endeavoured to draw them on again, but in a few days they had notice of his having difcovered the plot, and fo defifted from any further correfpondence with him.

This city was thought to be a place of fuch confequence to the king, that Sir William Vavafor was afterwards reinforced to reduce it, who advanced to Painfwick with a very ftrong brigade, which upon lord Hoptoun's defeat by Sir William Waller, was inftantly ordered to march to Oxford; otherwife, it is probable that Gloucefter might have been blocked up and befieged a fecond time.

The city fuffered greatly by the fiege, as appears by the following petition:

To the fupreme Authority, the Parliament of the Commonwealth of England.

The humble Petition of the Mayor, Burgeffes, and divers Hundreds of Inhabitants of the City of Glocefter, fheweth,

THAT the city of Glocefter *being a garrifon for the parliament's fervice, in* 1643, *and of vaft importance to the commonwealth, upon the approach of the late king's army, to befiege the faid city, it was refolved by the governour and council of war there, That the faid city and garrifon could not be preferved againft the enemy, unlefs the whole fuburbs of the faid city (which was a full third part thereof) were pulled down and demolifhed.*

That in purfuance of the faid refolve, two hundred forty and one houfes (befides barns, ftables, outhoufes, gardens, orchards and goods) of the fuburbs of the faid city, wherein fo many families lived, were burned, pulled down, and utterly deftroyed, the night before the leaguer was laid to the faid city, by the late king's forces; whereby moft of your petitioners were reduced to moft miferable poverty, and the eftates of moft of them much impaired, and the faid city, in general, very much impoverifhed.

That it was proved upon oath, to the grand inqueft, at an affizes held for the county of the faid city, that your petitioners loffes, by the burning and deftroying their faid houfes, amounted to the fum of twenty fix thoufand pounds and upwards; as by the certificate of the grand inqueft to the lord chief baron, a copy whereof is hereunto annexed, may appear.

That your petitioners willingly fuffered the lofs of their houfes and goods, for their affections to the parliament fervice; and it was a great means, under God, to preferve the faid city and garrifon, and by confequence the whole country, from the power of the enemy: And your petitioners have ever fince continued conftantly faithful to the commonwealth, and the prefent government thereof, in the times of greateft danger and tryal unto this day; and have always hoped, that according to the parliament's declarations, their loffes and ruins for the commonwealth's fervice, fhould be repaired out of the eftates of the commonwealth's enemies, who occafioned the fame.

Your petitioners therefore humbly pray, That their loffes and ruins may be repaired,

† His lordfhip's letter runs thus: Sir, You have fo far declared your defires to ferve his majefty, unto my very good friend Mr Stanford, that I think it fit you fhould now receive fome more authentic affurances of his majefty's gracious acceptance thereof, than perhaps you will think his bare engagement to be; therefore I do hereby folemnly engage my word unto you, both as a minifter of ftate and as a gentleman, that if you fhall perform faithfully what you promife there, you fhall punctually receive, immediately after, fuch a pardon as yourfelf fhall defire, and the fum of 2000*l.* As for the 300*l.* which you defire in prefent, fuch a confidence I will have in your word, that as foon as ever I fhall have received your anfwer to this, under your hand, it fhall be forthwith paid into what place foever you fhall appoint, and to what perfon. As for the particular way of effecting our defign, thofe you propofe are very rational, but the choife and difpofition of that muft be between you and thofe who are to execute it; with whom, if it were poffible, you fhould procure a meeting at fome unfufpected place. I do propofe to you your choife of feveral men, and whom of them you fhall like beft and think fitteft, by reafon of the place where his command is, to him alone and no other the bufinefs fhall be imparted; and whether Sir William Vavafour, commander in chief of the forces now in Gloucefterfhire; or colonel Mynne, commander of a brigade of Englifh come out of Ireland; or colonel Wafhington, who is at Evefham; or laftly, whether the governor of Berkeley caftle. As foon as you fhall fend me an anfwer, you fhall receive fatisfaction from him, who hopes you will fo behave yourfelf as to make me

Oxford, this 14th of December, 1643. Your friend

George Digby.

paired, and their diftreffed families relieved, out of the eftates of fuch delinquents as fhall be appointed to be fold; or in fuch other way as fhall feem beft to your wifdom, Juftice, and charity.

And they fhall be bound to pray, &c.

In 1644, feveral ordinances were made for recruiting and paying the garrifon, by which the county of Gloucefter was rated to pay 1000 *l.* and the city 100*l.* weekly; befides, the third part of the cuftoms payable upon currants was appropriated to that purpofe *. Another ordinance was made about June, that colonel Maffie fhould have an eftate of inheritance of 1000*l.* a year at leaft, fettled upon him by the committee of Gloucefter, out of fome eftates then efteemed to be forfeited §.

Colonel Maffie was appointed deputy-governor by the earl of Stanford, to whom the government of this garrifon was committed about 1641; but in 1643, Maffie was made governor himfelf, and continued fo 'till 1645, when the parliament appointed him lieutenant general of the weft, to the great regret of the inhabitants of the place; the whole garrifon, city and county unanimoufly petitioning for his continuance among them.

On the 3d of June, the mayor, alderman Singleton, and colonel Blount had the command given to them, 'till another governor fhould come down, or the parliament give further orders. Colonel Thomas Morgan occurs governor Auguft 13, 1645, and December 28, 1647. As does Sir William Conftable December 7, 1648, and December 27, 1650.

Major general Maffie had fignalized himfelf in feveral remarkable actions, and was therefore highly efteemed by the parliament, the army, and the city of London; but things having been carried to greater extremities than he expected, or could approve of, he withdrew himfelf from their party, and went out of the kingdom in the year 1647; but returning, was made prifoner at St. James's, (being one of the fecluded members) whence he efcaped January 18, 1648, and went to the prince in Holland. He afterwards formed a defign of furprizing Gloucefter, which was not then a garrifon, and conferred *incog.* with his friends in that city; but the defign took air, and was fruftrated. This was probably in 1659, when the keys of the city were ordered to be delivered out of the poffeffion of captain Hill, to the mayor, on account of fome matters imparted to the corporation.

The general lay concealed fome time in a little houfe near Simonfhall, belonging to Mr. Veal of that place, who was a friend to the royal caufe, and Maffie's relation; but at length he was difcovered, and taken there by fome troopers, who were made drunk before they left the place. However, they put him upon a horfe before one of the men, and carried him off; but going down Nimpsfield-hill, which is very fteep and woody, Maffie threw himfelf from the horfe, and being a ftout man, and his guards a little intoxicated, he made his efcape in a dark tempeftuous night.

Of the *GOVERNMENT* and *OFFICERS* of the *CITY*.

WHO were the governors in the time of the Britons I cannot tell, nor can I learn who they were when the Romans divided Britain into *Britannia Prima* and *Britannia Secunda*, and made the town fubject to a prefident refiding at London: But I conjecture that in this and all other changes which they made, the town was always under the dominion of a conful; for 'tis faid ‖, that in the time of the Romans, and fome time after, it was governed by perfons who had that title: And in the time of the Saxons, and fince, it was governed by a portgreve, præfect, or provoft ‡.

Morvid was conful in king Arthur's reign, and Wulpin le Rue 5° *regis Canuti*. Wihifide is called præfect in 1022, and Ofmund was provoft 16° and 22° H. 2: In the reign of king John, who made it a borough to be governed by two bailiffs, and in that of king H. 3. who made it a corporation, the head officers of the town who were afterwards termed bailiffs, were generally called *præpofiti* or *provofti*: And though the king appointed another perfon to be provoft of Gloucefter, yet it is probable this perfon did nothing more than receive the king's rents, and other payments due to him; and that 'till Henry the Third's time, there was not a regular fucceffion of provofts or bailiffs here. The firft in king Henry the Third's reign, were Thomas Felde, and John Blound or Blounte. Thofe which occur afterwards, in the writings which I have feen, will be found in a lift at the end of this chapter.

The following perfons are by charter or prefcription officers in the city.

The mayor, who is alfo the clerk of the market, and the marfhal and fteward of the king's houfhold when his majefty is in the city.

The high fteward.

The recorder.

The two members of parliament.

The twelve aldermen, out of whom the mayor is chofen. That alderman which was laft mayor is generally the coroner, and the prefident of the hofpitals.

* Civ.

§ Sir Robert Atkyns fays, that 1000*l.* a year was voted to him out of Sir John Wintour's eftate; and in the mean time, 200*l.* were paid him, and a penfion of 1000*l.* a year fettled on him for life.

‖ MS. Collections.—Mag. Brit. Ant. et Nov.—Sir R. Atkyns.

‡ G. Monmouth.——Mon. Angl.———Queen Mary's *Quo Warranto.*

The

The town clerk.
The fheriffs.
The common council.
The treafurer.
The chamberlain.
The fword-bearer.
The twelve conftables to the four wards ; *viz.* for the weft-ward four, north-ward four, eaft-ward two, fouth-ward two.
The four ferjeants at mace.
A cryer, or day-bellman.
A water bailiff.
Four porters.
A night-bellman.
A goaler.
A beadle and provoft-marfhal.

This city has the higheft marks of honour generally granted to magiftracy, *viz.* fcarlet gowns, a fword, and cap of maintenance, and four ferjeants at mace; but the ordinary robes are a black cloth gown, edged with velvet, and lined with velvet or fur.

The new mayor, when he is elected, wears upon his fcarlet gown, a fcarlet cloak or mantle, which was given by alderman Thomas Semys, in 1602 ; and ferved for this purpofe, 'till about 1738, when another was ufed in its ftead.

The mayor hath in his cuftody three fwords, *viz.* one with the figure of queen Elizabeth, and E. R. 1574, and the arms of the city, as they were then, on it; another, which is covered with black velvet, and has the prefent arms of the city on it; and laftly, that which is now ufually carried before him, and has the city-arms, and *Toby Jordan mayor*, thereon. He hath alfo the cap of maintenance, two large filver maces gilt, and feveral pieces of plate in his poffeffion.

The mayor hath for his hofpitality, and for his keeping the fword-bearer, two ferjeants, and two porters, 80 *l.* a year, befide wheat, capons, two falmons, and other perquifites.

Each of the fheriffs hath in his cuftody a large filver mace gilt ; and maintains a ferjeant at mace, and one of the porters.

A Lift of Provofts, Bailiffs, Mayors and Sheriffs down to the prefent Time.

1241, William le, or de, Somery or Sumery, Egeas Fifher, or Peffoner.
1245, William or Walter le Sumery. Roger Lenveife, or Danveife.
1248, William de Chiltenham, Herbert le Mercer.
1249, William Somery, or de Sumery. Richard Francis, or Franceys.
1252, John Simon, or Fitz Simon. Roger Lenveife.
1254, Luke Cornubienfis. Ege Pifcator.
1255, John Fitz Simon. William de Chiltenham.
1261, Robert Potel, or Putteley. Robert Sely, or Cely.
1262, The fame.
1263, William de Chiltenham. Philip Speciare.
1269, John Payn. Robert le Wife, or Lenweyfy, or Lenveife.
1270, William de Chiltenham. John Cornubienfis.

Several other perfons were fo called and enjoyed the office in or about the reign of king Henry the Third ; but as the writings wherein they are mentioned are without date, the precife time when any of them were in this office does not appear ; but they were

Helias Godman, William Burgens.
Richard Fitz William, Maurice Paumer, or Palmer.
Maurice Fitz Durand, or Durant, John Tixtor.
The fame, Gilbert Seifor, or le Taillor.
Walter Scriptor, Thomas Oye.
The fame, Richard Burgens.
* Richard Burgenfis, or Burgeys, Thomas Oye.
The fame, Maurice Fitz Durand.
The fame, Adam Croc, or Crok.
The fame, Thomas Ovenat.
The fame, David Dunning.
The fame, Walter Payn.
David Dunning, Thomas Oye.
The fame, Walter Hoch, or Hoich.
The fame, Walter Pain,
John Draper, William de Sandford, or Stanford
The fame, Thomas Oye.
The fame, Maurice Durant.
The fame, David Dunning.
Hugh Sciffor, or Tailer, Walter Kentwin.
Walter Hoy, or Hoich, Jeffery or Walter Cutteftich.
The fame, Walter Pain.
Walter Pain, Hugh de Aula Regis, or Kingfhall, or Kingfham.
The fame, Richard de Cellario.
Henry Dais, (or William Dais, jun. or Thomas Die,) Stephen Cornubienfis.
Henry Burgens, John de Gofeditch.
John de Gofeditch, or Gofdig§, Richard Fitz Walter Fitz Peter.
Richard de Cellario, Egeas Fifher.
Walter Cadomor, Robert Calvus, or Bald.
Adam Wahile or Walenfis John Rufus, or Red.
Elias Palmer, William Ruffel.
The fame, Ralph de Tudenham.
Hugh le Ceinter, or Seirvant, Alexander de la Broke.
Hernaldus, Henry Calvus, or Bald.
William de Somery, Stephen Cornubienfis.
The fame, Roger Lacrue.
The fame, John Innoud.
The fame, John Simund, or Fitz Roger or Fitz Simund.
The fame, Thomas de Evefham.
William de Chiltenham, Roger Lenveife.
The fame, Philip Apothecary.
William, or Robert, de Chiltenham, John Payn.
Roger Lenveife, or le Wife, William de Chiltenham.
Richard le Blund, Robert de Putteley.
Ralph de Andovere, Peter Flory.
John Payn, Robert de Honfum.
Philip Speciarius, or Lefpicer, Robert Honfum.
The fame, John Pain.
Walter de Saundon, William Chofe.
Richard Rufus, John Ruffus.

The head officers of the town were called Bailiffs during the reign of king Edward the Firft, and down to the firft of king Richard the

* This Robert Burgenfis is often called by the title of Mayor, and particularly when William Pain and Richard de Cellario were in the office of provoft. He has alfo this name when Walter Scriptor and Thomas Oye, Walter Pain and Hugh de Kingefhall, and David Dunning had that office. But perhaps fome of thefe were in the reign of king John; and that then it was when Hernaldus was Prætor or Mayor here, and Henry Calvus, his fellow. This Richard Burgeys was High Sheriff of the county of Gloucefter twice in the reign of king John. But perhaps by this mayor is meant no more than fenior; for Richard Burgeys of Gloucefter, the fon of Richard Burgeys, is mentioned in two charters in A. 5, fol. 108. And Richard Burgeys of Gloucefter is called Antiqui, or Old, A. 5, fol. 256.

§ This ditch extending from the South-gate to the Eaft-gate of the town, was antiently called Gofeditch.

Third, and they were, as they occur in antient records, as follow:

1273,	Alexander de Bikenore,	Robert Clerk.
1274,	Robert Clark,	William Chofe.
1277,	John le Draper,	Walter Sevare.
1283,	John de Wigornia,	Ralph Putteley.
1284,	John le Draper,	Richard de Pućteler.
1287,	Walter Sevare,	William Staward.
1288,	The fame,	James de Langeney.
1289,	Robert de Stanedifh,	
1290,	John de Gardino,	Robert de Stanedifh.
1291,	Alexander de Bikenore§,	Hugh le Clerk.
2,	John le Draper,	Walter Sevare.
3,	Hugh le Clerk,	Robert de Standifh.
4,	Henry de, or del Oka, or Oke,	Stephen Brown.
5,	John Lucas,	William Croc.
6,	Hugh le Clerk,	Henry le Draper.
7,	Walter Sevare,	William de Wytfield.
8,	Walter de Bikenore,	Roger le Heiberare.
9,	The fame,	The fame.
1300,	Roger le Heiberare,	Roger, or Robert Lefpicer.
1,	Robert de Stanedifh,	Robert Lefpicer.
2,	The fame,	The fame, or Apothecary.
3,	Alexander de Bikenor,	William de Riouns.
4,	William de Wythfield,	William de Hertford.
5,	John Lucas,	The fame.
6,	John de la Cumbe, or Combe,	John Northwyche.
7,	The fame,	The fame.

Bailiffs in the reign of king Edward the Firft, of whom the firft in the lift are without date.

	Henry Draper,	John Chofe.
	John Pamiar,	Alexander de Bikenore.
	John Chedworth,	William de Hertford.
	John Draper,	Alexander de Bikenore.
	John Payn,	John le Draper.
	The fame,	John de Wigornia.
	The fame,	Alexander de Bikenore.
	Alexander de Bikenore,	Germanus de Tunebrugg.
	The fame,	Robert Hauel.
	Alexander de Bikenore,	Ralph de Potel, or Putteley.
	The fame,	Walter Sefare.
	Ralph de Potel,	John le Draper.
	John le Draper,	William, or Gylemin Chofe.
	The fame,	Randal, or Ralf de Hamdene.
	The fame,	Alexander de Bikenore.
	Philip Apothecary,	John de Wigornia.
	John de Wigornia,	Robert de Sondhurft.
	John, or Walter de Wigornia,	Walter Sevar.
	Robert Apothecary,	Roger de Heyberer.
1308,	Walter le Spicer,	Thomas de Bernewode.
1309,	The fame,	Peter de la Hulle.
1310,	Peter de la Hulle,	Walter Lefpicer, or Apothecary.
1,	Walter Lefpicer,	Nicholas de Honfum.
2,	Robert de Goldhull,	Robert Pope.
3,	William de Marcle,	William de Aftone.
4,	Robert de Goldhull,	John de Northwich.
5,	Andrew de Pendock,	Owen de Wyndefore.
6,	Andrew, or Alexander, de Pendock,	Richard de Aftone.
7,	Stephen Brown,	John le Tanner.
8,	Andrew de Pendock,	John le Tanner.
9,	The fame,	The fame.
1320,	John le Tanner,	Randulph le Wheolare.
1,	Adam de la Hulle,	Walter Lefpicer.
2,	Alexander, or Andrew Pendock,	Walter le Southern.
3,	John de Boyfield,	Roger Hewed, or Hewet.
4,	John de Chedworth,	Thomas Foxcote.
5,	John de Chedworth,	William Lefpicer.

Bailiffs from the firft of Edward the Second, to the firft of Richard the Third.

Walter, or William Sevare, John Sage.

Alfo

1 E. 2. Robert Pope, and Robert de Goldhull, Friday after Epiphany.

9 E. 2. Andrew de Pendock, and Tweyn de la Bothalle, occur on St. Andrew's Day; and on the Tuefday next after, this Tweyn is called Audoen de la Bohalle.

6 E. 2. William de Afton, and Edmund de Baverton, or Barton, fometime in January.

1327,	(1 & 2 E. 3.) Edward de Leye,	Richard de Bromfhulf *.
8,	Thomas Sevare, or de Severne,	William Crifp.
9,	John de Boyfield,	Richard le Recevour.
1330,	Andrew de Pendock,	Randulph le Wheolare.
1,	Richard le Recevour,	John de Boyfield.
2,	Roger Heued,	Stephen Broun.
3,	Richard le Recevour,	Edward le Taverner.
4,	The fame,	John le Deyer.
5,	Richard Shot,	William Bruyn, or le Gruyin.
6,	Roger Heued,	John le Walfhe.
7,	Roger de Kingfleone,	John Cluet §.
8,	William Crifp,	Robert Hendy.
9,	William Ragoun,	Henry le Draper.
1340,	Henry le Draper,	Hugh de Chew.
1,	Adam de Hope,	Nicholas Attedoure.
2,	William de Bruyn, or Gruyn,	William de Kingefhaw.
3,	Henry le Draper,	Hugh de Chyw, or Chew.
4,	Roger de Kingfleon,	William de Kingefhagh.
5,	The fame,	The fame.
6,	William de Kingefhagh, or Kingefhaw,	Robert le Walour.
7,	Richard Schot,	Henry le Draper.
8,	Thomas Clech,	Edmund de Chedworth.
9,	Henry le Draper,	Walter de Elmore.
1350,	William de Ledene, or Loudene,	Thomas de Monynton.
2,	William de Ledene,	Edmund de Chedworth.
3,	The fame,	Thomas Monynton.
4,	Roger le Heiberare,	Robert Lefpicer.
1355,	Edmund de Chedworth,	Robert de Afton.
6,	William de Kingefhaw,	John Cluet.
7,	Robert le Walour,	Hugh le Parker.
8.	William de Kingefhawe,	The fame.
9,	Thomas de Ledebiry,	Thomas de Stoke.
1360,	Hugh le Parkere,	William de Tronefbury, or Trofebury.
1,	William Crocks,	William le Heyberare.
2,	William Heyberare,	Roger Crocks.
3,	William, or Walter le Heyberare,	William Crook.
7,	Thomas de Byfeley,	John de Aulep.
8,	Thomas de Byfeley,	William Crook.
9,	Thomas Styward,	John de Elmore
1370,	The fame,	John de Monemouth.
1,	William Heyberare,	Thomas de Byfeley.
2,	The fame,	John Pope.
4,	Thomas Byfeley,	William Foliot.
5,	Edward le Taverner,	Nicholas, or Richard Bridlep.
7,	William Heyberare,	Thomas Byfeley.
	John Cheverel,	Robert le Walour.
1378,	John Compton,	Robert Pope.
9,	William Crok,	John Ruffeby.
1310,	Roger Receyvour,	Richard Afhewell.
1,	Richard Barret,	Richard Afhwell.
2,	Richard Barret,	William Wightfield.
3,	John Rufby,	John Pope.
4,	William Heyberare,	William Crook.
5,	William Crok,	Roger Receyvour.
7,	John Hened,	The fame.
9,	Robert Pope,	William Crook.
1390,	The fame,	John Pope.
1,	John Bannebury,	Robert Pope.
2,	John Rofeby, or Riffeby,	Thomas Pope.

§ The following were chofen to fupply vacancies for part of a year.
10 E. 1. Alexander Bikenore, Peter Flory at Michaelmas.
18 E. 1. Hugh, called Clark, and Henry a Deane, Sunday next after Michaelmas.
1294, William Croc, John Bell occur fometimes in this year.
1297, Walter de Bikenore occurs with Sevare October 27.
31 E. 1. Robert Apothecary, Robert de Stanedifh occur.
1306, Robert de Goldhull, William de Hartford occur in July and Auguft.
31 E. 1. William de Withfield, Roger le Heyberare on Sunday next after St. Kenelm's.

* Alfo, 2 E. 3. John King, and William de Lyndefeye, Monday next after St. Barnabas.
6, 7 E. 3. Edward le Taverner fometimes occurs in Broun's place, and
8, 9 E. 3. Richard de Bromfhulf occurs with Deyer.

§ Alfo, 12 E. 3. 'Tis faid John Cluet, and Roger de Kingflone, were bailiffs on the Thurfday next after St. Scholaftica's day.

16 E. 3. Walter Lefpicer, and Adam Attehull, Monday next after St. Lawrence.

30, 31 E. 3. Thomas de Monynton, and John de Hafulton, occur at the latter end of the year.

1393, John Ruſby, or Biſley,	The ſame.
5, Richard Aſhwele,	William Crook.
6, John Need,	Robert Reſcevour.
7, Roger Balle,	Robert Swaynefey.
8, William Crook,	Roger Balle.
9, Robert But,	Simon Brok.
1400, Richard Barret,	John, or Roger Balle.
1, John Byeley	Roger Balle.
2, Robert But,	Thomas Compton.
3, Robert Butt,	William Brydlep.
4, Roger Balle,	Simon Brocke.
5, Simon Brocke,	Thomas Compton.
7, John Pope,	Simon Brocke.
8, Thomas Compton,	Thomas Saliſbury.
9, Robert But,	William Brydlep.
1411, Roger Balle,	Richard Chamberlayn.
12, Roger Balle,	William Bridlep.
13, John, or Robert Butte, or Balle,	Thomas More.
14, John Spencer,	Thomas Friville.
16, John Biſeley, ſen.	Roger Balle.
17, Robert Gilberd,	John Derhurſt.
18, John Streynſham,	Michael Saliſbury.
19, Richard Chamberleyn,	Thomas Hewes.
1422, Roger Balle,	Thomas Compton.
23, John Biſley,	Richard Dalby.
24, Robert Gilbert,	John Hamelyn.
25, John Byſſeley, ſen.	Richard Dalby.
26, Thomas Guldeford,	Henry Saliſbury.
27, William Butteler, or Botiler,	Thomas Hewis, or Hewes.
28, John Streynſham,	Richard Dalby.
29, Roger Balle,	Thomas Compton.
1430, Robert Gilbert,	Truſtan Power.
31, John Rede,	William Olyver.
32, Robert Gilbert,	John Steynſham.
33, John Hamelin,	John Luke.
34, John Streynſham,	Thomas Hughes.
36, William Olyver,	Philip Monger.
40, Thurſton Southern,	Walter Bauknot.
41, William Eldesfeld,	Walter Chauntrel or Chaunterell
42, William Oliver,	Walter Bauknot.
44, John Luke,	John Heydon.
45, Walter Chauntrell,	William Saunders.
46, William Oliver,	Henry Dood.
48, Thomas Hilley,	William Newman.
49, William Nottingham,	Henry Dood.
1453, William Eldersfield,	Thomas Bye.
55, The ſame,	Richard Skyamore.
56, Maurice Andrew,	John Kylray.
57, Thomas Bokeland,	John Hylley.
58, Maurice Andrew,	John Jeolyf.
1461, John Grove,	William Francomb.
62, Richard Barret,	Roger Balle.
63, William Brokewood,	William Gran, or Gean.
64, John Chauntrell,	John Pole.
65, Roger Balle,	Simon Brocke.
66, Nicholas Hill,	William Perkyns.
74, John Hartland,	John Farley.
75, John Barton,	John Caple.
76, John Farley,	William Poole.
1477, John Fry.	

Since the firſt of Richard the Third, the title of Bailiff hath ceaſed, and inſtead thereof were Mayors and Sheriffs, and they are as follow.

MAYORS.	SHERIFFS.
1483, John Trye.	William Francomb, John Poole.
4, John Caple, eſq;	Robert Cuffe, or Coofe, Thomas Hart.
5, William Framcomb.	Robert Rawlins, Philip Pridith.
6, John Poole.	William Cole, Thomas Franeford, or Fairford.
7, John Hilley.	James Ivie, John Elliott.
1488, William Cole, mercer	Walter Rowden, William Cooke.
9, Robert Poole.	Thomas Aſpline, Thomas Collins.
1490, Thomas Hart.	Ralph Graſton, John Natton.
1, Walter Rowden, gent	Robert Rawlins, William Graſewell.
2, William Cooke.	Philip Pridith, William Marmion.
3, John Caple.	John Cole, Garret, or Gerard Vanecke.
4, William Cole.	John Cooke, Philip Greenowe.
5, Robert Rawlins.	Thomas Studley, William Goldſmith. *
6, Walter Rowden.	James Ivie, William Hanſhaw.
7, Philip Pridith.	Garret, or Gerard Vanecke, Thomas Tayloe, or Teylowe.
8, William Cooke ‖.	John Cooke, David Vaughan.
9, Garret, or Gerard Vaneck.	Thomas Aſpline, Thomas Lane.
1500, John Caple.	Nicholas Elliotts, Richard Rowden
1, John Cooke, ‡ brewer	William Hanſhaw, John Hawkins.
2, Walter Rowden.	Thomas Teylowe, David Vaughan
3, William Hanſhaw, bell-founder.	John Allen, jun. Thomas Hertland
4, William Cole.	John Natton, Walter Beeche.
5, Garret, or Gerard Vanecke §.	Nicholas Elliots, Robert Plavys.
6, Thomas Telowe, or Taylowe.	John Norwood, or Morewood, William Byford.
7, John Cooke.	William Smyth, Ralph Sankey.
8, William Hanſhaw.	Richard Rowden, Robert Hawerdine.
9, William Hanſhaw.	Thomas Hertland William Jordan†
1510, John Natton.	John Hawkins, Ralph Halſey.
1, Thomas Porter **.	Ralph Sankey, William Greenow.
2, John Cook.	John Allen, jun. Thomas Oſborne
3, Thomas Teylowe.	Robert Plavys, William Haſſard.
4, Richard Rowden.	William Jordan, John Rowlins.
5, William Hanſhaw.	Ralph Halſey, John Fawkener.
6, Ralph Sankey.	William Marmion, William Matthews.
7, Thomas Hartland.	Walter Beeche, John Baſtel.
8, Robert Plavys ‖‖.	Robert Hawerdine, Adam Apowel
9, John Cook.	John Rawlins, Thomas Meſſenger
1520, William Hanſhaw.	John Fawkener, John Semys.
1, William Jordan.	William Haſſard, Henry Marmion.
2, Thomas Teylowe.	Thomas Oſborne, Jeffry Todde.
3, William Haſſard.	John Raſtel, Thomas Bell.
4, John Rawlyns.	William Matthews, Henry French.
5, John Fawkener, Capper.	John Chapman, John Semys.
6, Thomas Oſborne.	Adam Apowel, Robert Pool.
7, John Raſtell.	Thomas Maſſinger, Thomas Bell.
8, John Semys.	Henry Marmion, Philip Redvyn, or Redvern.
9, William Jordan.	Lewis Ap Rice, Thomas Payne.
1530, William Haſſard.	Robert Poole, Thomas Bell.
1, Thomas Maſſinger.	Maurice Vaughan, John Uggons.
2, William Matthews.	Philip Redyn, or Redvern, Ralph or Raphael Rawlyns.
3, Henry Marmion.	Lewis Ap Rice, Thomas Browne‡‡
4, John Fawkener.	Thomas Payne, Richard Edwards.
5, John Semys.	Thomas Bell, jun. Leonard Oſborne.
6, Thomas Bell, ſen.	Raphael Rawlyns, Thomas Clowterbuck.
7, William Haſſard.	Thomas Browne Thomas Loveday
8, William Matthews.	John Uggons, John Raſtel.
9, Robert Poole.	Maurice Vaughan, William Trahern.
1540, Thomas Payne.	Richard Edwards, William Michel
1, Henry Marmion §§.	John Todd, Thomas Pury.
2, John Fawkener.	Thomas Loveday, Philip Barker.
3, Thomas Bell, jun.	John Raſtel, William Haſſard.
4, Thomas Bell ††, ſen.	Thomas Clowterbuck, John Sandford.
5, Thomas Clowterbuck	Edmund Allen, William Jenkins.
6, Thomas Loveday.	William Trahern, Robert Moreton

* Thomas Cook occurs ſheriff with Goldſmith 20th of April, 1495.

‖ 1498, William Cole occurs mayor the 7th and 14th of Nov. *Old Book in Cuſtody of the City.*

‡ This John Cooke and William Cooke, John Trye, John Caple, John Poole, and other Gentlemen of Glouceſter, are ſaid to be made the firſt aldermen, juſtices of the peace, and chief burgeſſes of the town of Glouceſter, and county thereof, by king Richard the Third, in the firſt year of his reign. And beſide his founding Crypt ſchool, gave large poſſeſſions for other pious and charitable uſes.

§ Vanecke, mayor, *ob.* and was ſucceeded by Richard Rowden in 1505.

† Thomas Porter occurs ſheriff 21ſt December, 1509.

** Thomas Hartland occurs mayor the 21ſt of December, 1511.

‖‖ William Haſſard was elected mayor in 1518, Robert Plavys dying the 24th of Auguſt.

‡‡ 21ſt of December, 1533, Brown occurs as eldeſt ſheriff; the other was Edmund Allen, jun.

§§ Philip Redvyn, or Redvern, ſucceeded Marmion mayor, who died the 7th of March, 1541,

†† This Thomas Bell, in 1544, occurs as one of the gentlemen of the king's bed-chamber.

1547, Raphael

Mayors.	Sheriffs.
1547, Raphael Rawlyns ‡.	William Mitchel, William Bonde
8, John Raftel.	Thomas Pury, Thomas Maffinger.
9, William Michel, draper.	John Sandford, Lewis Lyfons.
1550, Thomas Pury, mercer	William Haffard, Henry Machen.
1, John Sandford †, draper.	Edmund Aphowel, John Aprichard
2, Thomas Payne.	Robert Morton, Robert Adams.
3, Thomas Bell, knight.	Thomas Hide, Thomas Heathe.
4, Thomas Bell, jun.	William Jenkins, William Bonde.
5, Thomas Loveday.	Henry Machen, Thomas Machen.
6, William Bonde.	Lawrence Singleton Richard Cooke
7, Robert Moreton.	John Aprichard, John Woodward ‖
8, Henry Machen.	Thomas Semys, Henry King.
9, Thomas Hide, tanner	John Kerbie, Humphrey Atkins.
1560, Thomas Pury.	Thomas Maffinger, Thomas Weekes, or Wyks.
1, William Bonde.	Lawrence Singleton, William Wyman.
2, Thomas Maffinger.	John Woodward, William Maffinger.
3, Lawrence Singleton, draper.	Thomas Semys, John Webly.
4, Thomas Hide.	Thomas Weekes, or Wykes, Hugh Hide.
5, Thomas Semys, clothier.	Luke Garnons, Richard Cugley.
6, John Woodward, mercer.	William Maffinger, John Kerby.
7, Henry King, mercer.	John Webly, William Weale.
8, John Kerby, clothier.	William Sandford, Peter Rumney.
9, William Maffinger, gent.	Luke Garnons Thomas Francombe
1570, Luke Garnons, draper	Thomas Lane, James Morfe.
1, Thomas Weekes, or Wykes *	Richard Cugley, Guy Symmons.
2, Peter Rumney, clothier.	Thomas Machen, John Moor §.
3, Richard Cugley baker	John Smith, Henry Horne.
4, Thomas Francomb, merchant.	James Morfe, John Raftal.
5, James Morfe, tanner.	John Cowdal, Richard Coxe.
6, John Kerby.	Thomas Machen, Thomas Lane.
7, Lawrence Singleton.	Guy Symmons, Lawrence Holliday
8, Thomas Semys.	John Browne, Robert Walkley.
9, Thomas Machen, mercer.	Thomas Beft, Maurice Apowel.
1580, Thomas Lane malfter	John Cowdale, Richard Webb.
1, John Smith, brewer.	Richard Cox, Walter Merry.
2, Lawrence Holliday, mercer.	John Browne, Robert Walkley.
3, John Webley, dyer.	Robert Hobbs, Richard Ward.
4, Thomas Beft, gent.	Richard Webb, John Taylor.
5, William Maffinger fen	John Ciely, Grumbald Hutchins.
6, Luke Garnons.	Walter Nurfe, Henry Haffard.
7, John Cowdale, tanner	John Jones, John White.
8, Thomas Machen.	Richard Hands, John Newman.
9, John Browne, mercer	John Dorney, John Walkley.
1590, Richard Webb, baker afterwards brewer.	John Taylor, *alias* Cook, Grumbald Hutchins,
1, Richard Cox, malfter.	Henry Haffard, Thomas Rich.
2. Robert Walkley, mercer.	Walter Nurfe, John Jones.
3, John Taylor.	Rowland Atkinfon, John Loathingham, or Luffingham.
4, Henry Haffard malfter	Chriftopher Caple, John Brewfter.
5, Richard Webb.	Thomas Rich, John Payne.
6, Grumbald Hutchins, draper.	John Baugh, Nicholas Langford.
7, John Jones, gent.	Henry Darbye, Lawrence Wilfhire
8, Chriftopher Caple, mercer.	John Brewfter, John Little.
9, Thomas Semys.	Thomas Barnes, John Maddock.
1600, Luke Garnons.	John Thorne, William Hill.
1, Thomas Machen.	Henry Darbye, Lawrence Wilfhire
2, Richard Cox.	Nicholas Langford Thomas Adams

Mayors.	Sheriffs.
1603, Thomas Rich, mercer	John Browne, Thomas Kerbye.
4, Henry Haffard.	Edmund Clements, Robert Pettifer
5, Henry Darby, baker.	Matthew Price, Nathaniel Bifhop.
6, Lawrence Wilfhire, clothier.	Richard Smith, Jeffry Beale.
7, John Baugh, mercer.	Thomas Adams, William Lock.
8, John Brewfter, furrier	Edmund Clements, Robert Pettifer
9, John Thorne, brewer	Toby Bullock, Humphry Holman.
1610, John Browne, brewer	Richard Smith, Henry Browne.
1, William Hill, mercer	Thomas Field, William Price.
2, Thomas Adams, clothier.	John Webb, John Brewfter.
3, John Taylor.	John Walton, Richard Beard.
4, Edmund Clements, mercer.	Thomas Ruffel, Richard Hoar.
5, Richard Smith, tanner	Thomas Field, John Reynolds.
6, Matthew Price tanner	Toby Bullock, Anthony Robinfon
7, Jeffry Beale, mercer.	John Brewfter, William Lugg.
8, John Jones.	Robert Bifhop, William Singleton
9, Chriftopher Caple.	William Bubb, William Caple.
1620, John Baugh ††.	John Deighton, John Gwilliam.
1, John Browne.	John Hayward, James Powel.
2, William Hill.	Thomas Morfe, John Scriven.
3, Edmund Clements.	Henry Redvyn, or Redverne, Peter Lugg.
4, Richard Smith.	John Deighton, Edward Michel.
5, John Jones.	John Gwilliam, John Read.
6, Matthew Price.	Thomas Hill, Thomas Pury.
7, Richard Beard mercer	Richard Keylock, Dennis Wife.
8, Henry Browne.	Abel Angel, John Price.
9, Anthony Robinfon efq	Richard Green, Nicholas Webb.
1630, William Price.	Luke Nurfe, Leonard Tarn.
1, Toby Bullock.	Richard Window, Jafper Clutterbuck.
2, John Brewfter.	John Woodward, Henry Price.
3, John Webb.	Nathaniel Hodges, Richard Hayward, or Harwood.
4, John Browne.	Charles Hoar, Lawrence Singleton.
5, William Hill ‡‡.	Nicholas Webb, John Nelme.
6, William Lugg.	Edward Wagftaffe, James Wood.
7, William Singleton.	Anthony Edwards, Richard Grimes ‖‖.
8, William Caple.	John Maddock, Henry Cugley.
9, James Powel.	Richard Cugley, James Stephens.
1640, Thomas Hill.	Anthony Hathway Edmund Palmer
1, John Scriven, ironmonger.	Edmund Collet, John Wood.
2, Dennis Wife.	Edward Wagftaffe, James Wood.
3, Nicholas Webb.	James Stephens, Robert Tyther.
4, Luke Nurfe.	Toby Jordan, John Edwards.
5, Lawrence Singleton.	Anthony Edwards, Walter Lane.
6, Jafper Clutterbuck.	Thomas Prichard, Henry Ellis **.
7, John Maddock.	Thomas Pearfe, Thomas Lugg.
8, Henry Cugley.	William Clark, Richard Tayler.
9, James Stephens.	Robert Tyther, William Fowler.
1650, Anthony Edwards.	Henry Robins, Daniel Lyfons.
1, William Singleton.	John Purlewent, Thomas Witcomb.
2, William Caple.	William Ruffel, John Singleton.
3, Thomas Pury.	Robert Hill, William Bubb.
4, Edmund Collett.	Thomas Cooke, James Comeline.
5, Dennis Wife.	John Purlewent, Nicholas Webb.
6, Luke Nurfe.	Jeffry Beale, John Toms.
7, Lawrence Singleton.	Thomas Witcomb, William Ruffel
8, Robert Tyther.	John Singleton, Richard Maffinger
9, Toby Jordan, bookfeller.	William Scudamore, Nicholas Snell
1660, Robert Payne.	John Powel, Samuel Brewfter.
1, Thomas Peirce.	Thomas Yate, Thomas Price.
2, William Ruffel furrier	Edward Tyther, Toby Longford.
3, John Powel.	Walter Harris, Clement Dowle.
4, Robert Fielding M.D.	Robert Longden, William Hodges
5, Thomas Yate.	Ifaac Williams, John Gythens.
6, Thomas Price.	Thomas Aram, Richard Stephens
7, John Woodward §§.	John Rogers, John Marfton.

‡ Raphael Rawlyns mayor, *ob.* 27 July, and was fucceeded by Philip Redvin, or Redvern, and this Redvyn, *alias* Clerk, mercer, made his Laft Will the 7th of June, 1547, and thereby ordained that a yearly *obit* fhould be kept for him, and that he fhould be buried without the choir in St. John's Church, (Regift.) but died the 15th of September, 3 Edw. 6. *Civit.*

† A licence under the king's feal, dated February 4, 1551, was granted to John Sandford of the city of Gloucefter, draper, that he, with two of his guefts at his table, might eat flefh and white meats during all the Lent, and all other fafting days in the year; and this licence was during his life. *Strype's Memor.* Vol. 2, p. 32. And I fuppofe, being an active man in the former reign, was, the 16th of January, 1 Mary, amoved from being alderman; the reafon of his amoval is faid to be for certain caufes (then) moving.

‖ John Aprichard, and Chriftopher Moore were fheriffs, 17th of March, 4 and 5 Philip and Mary. (Regift.)

* 1571, Weekes, mayor, *ob.* Aug. 15, and was fucceeded by Thomas Hide.

§ 1572, Moore, fheriff, *ob.* July 29, and was fucceeded by William Waite, who alfo dying September the 19th, following, Walter Knight fucceeded him.

†† 1620, Baugh, mayor, *ob.* Chriftopher Caple elected January the 9th.

‡‡ 1635, Hill, mayor, *ob.* Auguft the 29th, John Browne elected Aug. 30.

‖‖ 1637, Grimes, fheriff, *ob.* July the 7th, John Woodward fucceeded him July the 10th.

** 1646, Ellis, fheriff, *ob.* and Robert Payne elected July the 6th.

§§ 1667, Woodward, mayor, *ob.* October the 30th. Anthony Arnold elected November the 4th.

1668, Henry

Mayors.	Sheriffs.
1668, Henry Ockold †, attorney at law.	John Ewins, George Taylor.
9, John Wagftaff.	Richard Broad, William Maffinger
1670, Henry Fowler.	Edward Tyther, Nicholas Phelps.
1, Henry Fowler.	William Lambe, Samuel Rofe.
2, Henry Norwood, efq;	William Jordan, John Price.
3, William Cook, efq;	Richard Stephens, Nicholas Phelps
4, Sir Duncomb Colchefter, knight.	John Campion, Walter Veifey.
5, William Selwyn, efq;	William Carfley, Nicholas Lane.
6, William Ruffel.	John Bifhop, Richard Bofley ‡.
7, Thomas Price.	John Marfton, Samuel Rofe.
8, John Wagftaff,	Benjamin Hyett, Thomas Mills.
9, Henry Fowler.	John Smallwood, John Rodway.
1680, John Gythens, draper	Ifaac Williams, William Phelps.
1, John Rogers, brewer and inn-holder.	John Hill, John Wilcox.
2, John Webb.	George Broad, Richard Chandler.
3, John Price.	Gyles Rodway, Jofias Randle.
4, William Lamb.	Thomas Wilcox, James Price.
5, William Jordan, apothecary.	John Chapman, Ntahaniel Cooke, *alias* Caftle.
6, John Hill ‖.	Jofeph Phelph, Robert Punter.
7, John Hill.	William Reeves, Ifaac Lambard.
8, Anfelm Fowler *.	William Reeves, Thomas Longden
9, William Hodges.	Samuel Palmer, Benjamin Rofe.
1690, Sir John Guife baronet	Peter Haines, Thomas Webb.
1, Thomas Browne.	Samuel Lye, John Bell.
2, Robert Payne, mercer	Caple Payne, William Nicholls.
3, John Ewins.	Samuel Hayward Samuel Burroughs
4, William Taylor, ironmonger.	Thomas Edwards, William Edwards.
5, Thomas Longden, ironmonger.	Thomas Veifey, Richard Corfnett.
6, John Hyett, mercer.	John Guillim, Edmund Gregory.
7, Gyles Rodway mercer	William Randle, Thomas Farley.
8, Thomas Wilcox.	James Furney, Thomas Field.
9, Thomas Snell.	Henry Plat, Samuel Beale.
1700, Nicholas Webb.	Richard Maffinger, John Cowdale.
1, Thomas Webb, mercer.	Thomas Nicholls, Thomas Lewis.
2, Sir Samuel Eckley, kt.	Richard Partridge, Samuel Browne
3, Robert Payne.	Edmund Gregory, Nicholas Lane.
4, John Hyett.	Richard Cofsley, Thomas Ludlow
5, Samuel Lye, grocer.	Gabriel Harris, John White.
6, John Bell, mercer.	William Branch, John Gammond.
7, Caple Payne, mercer.	Edward Nicholls, Daniel Collerick
8, Gyles Rodway.	John King, Daniel Wafhborne.
9, Edmund Gregory, furrier.	John Rodway, Jofhua Worrel.
1710, Caple Payne.	William Haynes, Thomas Carill.
1, Samuel Hayward, grocer.	Thomas Hill, Thomas Cole §.
2, James Furney, ironmonger.	John Watfon, Ifaac Wood,
3, Richard Green, malfter.	John Green, John Bonner.
4, Samuel Brown, malfter.	Daniel Wafhborne, John Rodway.
5, Thomas Ludlow, draper.	James Gregory, John Hayward.
6, Thomas Nicholls, plumber.	Richard Lewis, William Nicholls.
7, John Bell.	Jofhua Worrel, William Ireland †.
8, James Furney.	William Haynes, Edward Machen
9, Richard Cofsley, goldfmith.	Thomas Carill, John Motlow.
1720, John King, dyer.	Edward Stephens, Richard Cofffley, jun.
1, Gabriel Harris, bookfeller.	Ifaac Wood, John Green.
2, Daniel Wafhborne, malfter.	John Hayward, Richard Lewis.
3, John Rodway, mercer	Samuel Worrel, Thomas Rogers.
4, Richard Green.	Thomas Smyth, Richard Finch.
5, Samuel Browne.	Thomas Hill, John Bonner.
6, Thomas Ludlow,	Thomas Payne, Lawrence Crump.

Mayors.	Sheriffs.
1727, John Selwyn, efq;	John Small, William Bell.
8, John King.	Richard Finch, John Blackwell.
9, Thomas Carill, hofier	William Nicholls, Thomas Bower
1730, John Small, efq;	Richard Coffley, Samuel Worrel.
1, William Bell.	Edward Machen, Benjamin Saunders.
2, Gabriel Harris, fen.	Thomas Steel, Gabriel Harris, jun.
3, John Selwyn.	Edward Stephens, Michael Bailey.
4, John Hayward mercer	Thomas Smyth, Samuel Farmer.
5, Richard Lewis, goldfmith.	Lawrence Crump, John Blackwell
6, Charles Selwyn, efq;	Benjamin Saunders, James Herbert.
7, Thomas Hill, apothecary.	Thomas Steel, John Knight.
8, William Nicholls, tanner.	James Elly, William Robins.
9, Edward Machen ‡.	Thomas Ratcliff, Miles Bell.
1740, Samuel Worrel.	Michael Bailey, William Bell, jun.
1, Thomas Hayward, efq	Gabriel Harris, jun. Richard Webb.
2, Richard Finch.	Samuel Farmer, Thomas Branch,
3, Lawrence Crump, upholder.	John Heath, Jofeph Chefton.
4, John Blackwell.	John Carrell, George Worrell.
5, Benjamin Saunders.	Jafper Herbert, John Baylis.
6, Gabriel Harris.	John Knight, Edward Baylis.
7, Michael Baily.	William Robbins, William Afhmeade.
8, William Bell.	William Bell, jun. Martin Lloyd.
9, Samuel Farmer.	Richard Webb, John Jefferis.
1750, Lawrence Crump.	Thomas Branch, Thomas Price.
1, Richard Roberts.	William Dimmock William Crump
2, James Herbert.	Jofeph Chefton, Cornelius Gardiner
3, Thomas Hill.	Edward Baylis, James Wintle.
4, John Blackwell.	George Worrall, John Baylis
5, Thomas Hayward.	Martin Lloyd, Thomas Vernon.
6, Benjamin Saunders.	John Jefferis, John Webb.
7, Gabriel Harris.	Thomas Price, Daniel Quarrington
8, George Auguftus Selwyn.	William Crump, Benjamin Baylis.
9, Jofeph Chefton.	James Wintle, Abraham Saunders
1760, Richard Webb.	John Box, James Sadler.
1, John Baylis.	John Webb, William Lane.
2, Edward Baylis.	Daniel Quarrington, Benjamin Baylis.
3, Samuel Farmer.	Abraham Saunders, Mofes Randall
4, Thomas Branch.	Richard Crump, William Cowcher
5, George Auguftus Selwyn.	Ralph Fletcher, Richard Webb.
6, Jofeph Chefton.	John Box, Henry Wintle.
7, Richard Webb.	James Sadler, John Bufh.
1768, Edward Baylis.	William Lane, Thomas Weaver.

HIGH STEWARDS.

The Marquis of Winchefter occurs 5° *Mariæ* 1.

William Compton, earl of Northampton, occurs in the reign of king James the Firft.

Sir Edward Cooke, knight, lord chief juftice of England, and one of the king's privy council, was elected the 26th of Auguft, 1615.

Oliver Cromwell, then lord protector, was elected on the 30th of September, 1651.

Henry Lord Cromwell, elected February 16, 1653; and according to fome accounts,

Richard Cromwell was elected, and occurs in 1656.

Henry Duke of Gloucefter elected June 13, 1660.

Henry Lord Herbert, upon the duke of Glou-

† 1668, Ockold, mayor, *ob.* Robert Fielding M. D. elected Aug. the 26th.

‡ 1676, Bofley, fheriff, *ob.* May 30. Daniel Lyfons elected June 7th.

‖ In 1686, 1687, feveral memorandums and difpenfations were fent by king James the Second to the corporation, That Hill fhould be obliged to take no oath, but that of mayoralty, at his admiffion into that office; That Anfelm Fowler fhould be made a burgefs, and elected an alderman. The mayor and aldermen fhould not proceed to the election of officers in the city for the year enfuing 'till his farther pleafure fhould be known. John Hill fhould be mayor for 1687; William Reeves and Ifaac Lambard then fheriffs, and no oaths fhould be tendered to them, except thofe of mayoralty and fhrievalty, refpectively. The recorder, three of the aldermen, and ten of the common council fhould be turned out, and others admitted in their ftead without having any oaths adminiftered to them, except that appointed for the recorder, aldermen and common council.

* 1688, Fowler, mayor, refigned November the 29th, William Cook fucceeded him in the fame year. Reeves, fheriff, refigned, Robert Longden fucceeded him then as eldeft fheriff, and William Scudamore was then made youngeft.

§ 1711, Cole, fheriff, *ob.* John King elected April the 8th.

† 1717, Ireland, fheriff, *ob.* Daniel Collerick elected July 4th.

‡ 1739, Machen, mayor, *ob.* 20 September, John Hayward elected.

cefter's death, elected January 14, 1660-1. He was afterwards duke of Beaufort, and being amoved, was fucceeded by

Charles earl of Macclesfield, who was elected Auguft 6, 1690, and upon his death

Charles Lord Durfley, afterwards earl of Berkeley, was elected February 11, 1694-5.

James Earl of Berkeley, upon his father's death, was elected September 28, 1710, and was alfo vifcount Durfley and baron Berkeley of Berkeley caftle; and fome years before, and 'till his death, ranger of Dean foreft, lord lieutenant, and cuftos rotulorum of the county of Gloucefter.

Auguftus earl of Berkeley, upon his father's death, was elected September 16, 1737, fucceeding him in moft of his titles, and upon his deceafe in 1755,

Matthew lord Ducie was elected high fteward in his ftead, but his lordfhip refigned this office in favour of

Frederick-Auguftus earl of Berkeley, who was elected in the year 1766, and is now the high fteward.

The High-Steward, at prefent, receiveth no falary; but in old papers concerning the city, it is faid, he receiveth for the acknowledgment of his office, five guineas yearly.

RECORDERS.

Thomas Lane, gent. was recorder in the reign of king H. 8. He was fteward of the priory of Stanley, and manor of Standifh, belonging to the abbey of Gloucefter; and after the diffolution thereof, was made fteward to the dean and chapter. He died in the reign of king H. 8. and was buried in the north-crofs-ifle of the cathedral.

Richard Morgan, ferjeant at law, occurs 1° E. 6. and 1552, and afterwards being a judge, uttered feveral opprobious words againft bifhop Hooper.

John Pollard, efq; occurs 1553, and 1555.

Richard Pate, efq; occurs in 1556, and was confirmed by queen Elizabeth's charter, 1561. He was a commiffioner to king H. 8. and E. 6. for taking a furvey of all religious foundations in Gloucefter, Briftol, &c. then fuppreffed, and the lands belonging to them given to the crown; and he, with Thomas Chamberlayn, efq; purchafed of king E. 6. many of thofe lands in Gloucefter and elfewhere. He is frequently termed of Minfterworth, where 'tis probable he fometimes refided; and was a good benefactor to St. Bartholomew's hofpital, and this city. He was buried in 1588, near the fouth wall of the fouth-croffifle of the cathedral, where there is a monument erected for him, which has been of late years repaired by Corpus Chrifti college in Oxford; to which he gave the nomination of a fchool-mafter and ufher at Cheltenham, in this county; the hofpital there, and fome other benefactions. Upon the monument is the effigies of an old man in a lawyer's gown, and a boy kneeling behind him; and of a woman, with three girls behind her. Over them is this infcription:

Richardus Pates, Arm. huic nuper Civitati a memoria, qui vixit Annos 73, et ob. 29 Oct. 1588, fibi et conjugi, et natis fuis, pofuit.

Quid ftulti vitæ mortales ftamina duci
Longa volunt miferæ, non minus atq; malæ.
Dic quotus eft, cujus non ficcat cura medullas,
Cui mens non fceleris confcia, dic quotus eft.
In cœlis expers curarum et criminis infons
Vita eft, hæc vera eft, cætera vita necat.

Over the monument is a board or wainfcot to keep off the duft, and upon it are thefe arms; *Argent, a cheveron fable, between three pellets: In chief, three croffes patee fitchy of the firft.* Creft, *a lion vaire crowned, fable and argent*; and thefe words at top: *Mihi vita Chriftus, Chriftus mea fpes unica.*

William Oldifworth, efq; was elected 29° Eliz.

Nicholas Overbury, efq; afterwards knight, was elected April 15, 1° Jac. 1. upon Oldifworth's death, and confirmed in the charters of king James 1. and king Charles 1.

Sir John Bridgman, knight, chief juftice of Chefter, was elected March 21, 1626, upon Overbury's refignation.

William Lenthal, efq; mafter of the benchers of Lincoln's-inn, and reader there, was elected January 23, 13° C. 1. He was afterwards fpeaker and one of the principal agents of the long parliament, and mafter of the rolls; and being amoved November 23, 1660, from this office,

Evan Selis, ferjeant at law, was elected on the fame day.

Sir William Morton, knight, ferjeant at law, upon Selis's refignation, was elected April 1, 1662; and died one of the juftices of the common pleas, in 1672, and was buried in the Temple church in London.

William Gregory, efq; elected October 3, 1672, was afterwards knighted, and made one of the barons of the exchequer; but by a mandate from the king he was amoved, and by another royal mandate dated November 21, 1687,

Charles Trinder, efq; was appointed to fucceed him; and by virtue of this nomination was elected December 8, 1687; but he refigned, and thereupon

Sir John Somers, knight, was elected, Aug. 29, 1690, and was afterwards lord high chancellor of England, and baron of Evefham.

Nicholas Lechmere, efq; upon lord Somers's death, was elected, May 18, 1716. He was afterwards chancellor of the dutchy of Lancafter, and baron of Evefham; and upon his death

Thomas Windham, efq; was elected, July 1, 1727.

Philip lord Hardwick, upon Mr. Windham's refignation, was elected December 9, 1734. On February 21, 1736-7, his lordfhip was appointed lord high chancellor of Great Britain; and on April 2, 1754, his majefty was pleafed to advance him

him to the titles of viscount Royston, and earl of Hardwick, in the county of Gloucester *.

On his lordship's death, his second son, the honourable Charles York, esq; was elected to this office in the year 1764, and since his decease, lord North has been chosen, who is the present recorder.

The recorder's salary is 6*l.* 13*s.* 4*d.* yearly.

Altho' the title of recorder is not in any charter of the city before that of queen Elizabeth, yet it is certain that several persons were so called, long before that charter, particularly Thomas Lane, in the time of king Henry the Eighth; Richard Morgan, 1 E. 6. and 6 E. 6. John Pollard, esq; 1553; John Pollard, knight, 1555; Richard Pate, esq; 4 & 5 Phil. & Mar. and 1 Eliz.

TOWN or *COMMON CLERKS.*

Christopher White occurs 28 H. 8. and 1557.

Humphry Ulton, 1558, 1562.

Thomas Atkins, esq; the queen's attorney in the marches of Wales, 1563.

Richard Bird, esq; upon Atkins's resignation, was elected July 13, 21 Eliz.

Richard Baker, esq; upon Bird's resignation, elected June 20, 37 Eliz. and dying at Abergavenny, October 7, 1598, was there buried.

Thomas Atkins, esq; upon Baker's death, elected October 17, 40 Eliz. He was probably the same with the before-mentioned Thomas Atkins.

Henry Robins, esq; upon the resignation of Atkins, who is said to be then very old and weak, was elected January 18, 45 Eliz. This Robins was buried near alderman Machen's monument in the cathedral, and upon the grave stone was this inscription:

Here lyeth the body
of Henry Ro-
bins, esq; who departed this life the 11 day
of Nov. 1613.

And on a brass plate on the same stone,

Causidicus fueram, dum me mea fata finebant;
Nunc mea stellifero causa peracta foro est.
Tristis et indignor tu, (cui licet) argue causas:
O quanto mitior sors mea, sorte tua est.

William Locksmith, esq; upon Robins's death, was elected January 13, 1613.

William Guys, or Guise, esq; upon Locksmith's death, was elected August 26, 1615; and the same year gave to the corporation a great silver cup, or bowl, and cover, double gilt, to remain with the mayor for the time being, for ever; but they were sold to contribute to the fortifications of the city, 18 C. 1.

John Dorney, esq; upon Guise's death, elected January 11, 1640; but being amoved by the commissioners appointed for the regulation of corporations, he was succeeded by

Thomas Williams, esq; elected August 15, 1662. He has the following memorial on a monument erected for him against the wall of the middle chancel of St. Mary de Crypt:

Memoriæ
Thomæ Williams, Armigeri,
Legum Anglicarum peritissimi, Medii Templi apud Londinates
Bancarii, Comitatui Glevensi Irenarchæ regii,
Hujus Civitatis Communis Clerici, simul
ac Ornamenti;
Viri
Clara stirpe, (Williamsorum, sc. de Guerne Knevot, in agro
Brecon) probis moribus, candido ingenio, pietate summâ,
Quem omnes amarunt,
adhuc deflent,
In posterum desiderabunt.
Crochthruppiæ, in agro Oxon nati, Glocestriæ denati, juxta sepulti,
ad tubæ sonitum resurrecturi.
Monumentum hoc, mœrens extruxit Elizabetha Williams,
delectissima conjux.
Obiit Nov. 27, Anno { Ætatis 50.
Salutis 1667.

In a shield are these arms: *Argent, a chevron between three fighting cocks gules, on a chief sable, three spears heads of the first*; impaling, *Argent, a chevron between three squirrels seiant gules.* The crest, *A cock gules, armed Or.*—There are memorials for several of this family in Winchcombe church.

John Dorney, esq; upon Williams's death, was re-elected December 23, 1667.

John Powell, esq; upon Dorney's death, elected March 8, 1674; but being amoved, was succeeded by

Robert Price, esq; who was elected September 22, 1685; but soon resigned. He was afterwards baron of the exchequer, and thence removed to be justice of the common pleas.

John Powell, esq; was, upon Price's resignation, re-elected July 5, 1687. Against the north wall in the lady's chapel, is a magnificent monument of white marble, with his effigies at length, in a judge's habit, and this inscription for him underneath it:

H. S. E.

IOHANNES POWELL Eq; Aurat. Generosâ & Antiquâ Gente oriundus, cum Sedem apud Herefordienses per plurimos Anōs fixisset, inde ad Glocestrienses jam olim Comigravit. Nobilitatem quam à Majoribus accepit, ipse vitâ Summâ cum Laude transactâ, egregie honestavit.

Legum Patriarum consultissimus Patronus diu, postea per XXII Anōs continuos Collegij Iudicum in Foro Londinensi triplicis Sodalis, Integritatis illibatæ, Industriæ indefessæ, Probitatis Fortitudinisq; et in protegendis Inōcentibus, et in puniendis Reis Semper Conspicuæ, nec promissis nec minis unquam dimovendæ Famam meruit.

IV. Vir Stlitibus Fisci judicandis nominatus Sub Gul: III° Cal. Nov. MDCXCI.

IV. Vir Stlit. Banc. Comūn. judicand. Sub Gul. III° VII Cal. Nov. MDCXCV.

IV. Vir Stlit. Banc. Reg. judicand. Sub. Reg. ANNA IX Cal. Iulij MDCCII.

VIX. ANN. LXVIII. DIES XIX OBIIT XVII Cal. Jul. MDCCXIII.

Iohannes Snell Arm.
Testamento ex Asse Hæres, Gratitudinis Amoris et Officij sui Monumentum hoc, Avunculo Optimo, opitimeq; de se merito
P. C.
Nisi utile est quod facimus, Stulta est Gloria.

Over his head are these arms, *Party per pale azure and gules, three lioncels rampant argent.*—On a black marble grave-stone underneath, is

* For a further account of his lordship, see the parish of Hardwick.

H. S. I.
Johannes Powell, miles, qui obiit 14 Junii, An. Dom. 1713,
Annoque Ætatis 69.
In cujus Memoriam, Monumentum prope ædificatum eft.

Thomas Powell, efq; on the refignation of his brother John Powell, was elected September 1, 1692. He was buried in the lady's chapel, but has no memorial.

John Cocks, efq; upon Powell's death, was elected April 22, 1700.

Thomas Stephens, efq; upon Cocks's refignation, was elected January 19, 1719. When he died, he was principal regifter to the bifhop of Gloucefter, and clerk of the peace for the county of Gloucefter; and dying at Briftol, was buried there, under the communion table of Little St. Auguftine's.

Caple Payne, efq; fucceeded Mr. Stephens, and died in 1764, to whom

William Selwyn, efq; fucceeded, and is the prefent town-clerk.

The yearly falary is 12*l.* 13*s.* 4*d.* and feveral other particulars of confiderable value.

A LIST of the REPRESENTATIVES of the City in Parliament.

N. B. The Parliaments mark'd thus (*) were held at London.
(§) —— at York.
(†) —— at Carlifle.
(‡) —— at Lincoln.
(‖) —— at Nottingham.
(**) —— at Northampton
(§§) —— at Winchefter.
(††) —— at Cambridge.
(‡‡) —— at New Sarum.
(‖‖) —— at Gloucefter.
(§§§) —— at Oxford.
(‡‡‡) —— at Leicefter.
(‖‖‖) —— at Reading.
And thofe which have no mark after the date were holden —— at Weftminfter.

Anno Regni			
Edw. I.	23	Henry de Chounger,	Roger de Heyberare.
	26 §	Richard de Bryt-hampton,	Robert le Efpicer.
	30 *	Robert le Efpicer,	John le Bale.
	33	William de Hartford,	John de Comb.
	34	Richard le Clerk,	Richard le Blehfton.
	35 †	Andrew de Pevedock,	Thomas de Hannely.
Edw. II.	2	William Hertford,	John de Norwich.
	4	Walter le Spicer,	John Lucas.
	5 *	Walter le Spicer,	John King.
	6	William Tidderington,	William de Hertford.
	6	Walter de Hertford,	John le King.
	7	Walter Lefpicer,	John King.
	8	John Bury,	Thomas Copperich.
	12 §	John de Hertford,	Andrew de Pentoker.
	12 §	Walter Lefpicer,	Stephen de Maifmor.
	15	Walter Lefpicer,	John King.
	15	Andrew Pendock,	Walter le Spicer.
	16 §	John Hertford,	Richard Kift.
	19	Andrew de Pendock,	John de Coveley.
	20	Andrew Pendock,	John de Coveley.
Edw. III.	1	Elias Ailbirton,	John Coggefhall.
	1 ‡	John Brayton,	John Nichfield.
	2	Thomas Copperych,	Walter le Spicer.
	4	Walter le Spicer,	Richard Fifher.
	4	The fame,	Edmund Beverton.
	6 §	The fame,	Richard Coumbe.
	6	The fame,	William Hertford.
	7 §	Robert de Goldhull,	Walter Norfolke.
	8 §	Robert de Goldhull,	Walter de Wawepoll.
	9	William Tidderington,	John Walfhe.
	9 §	Thomas Gloucefter,	Walter le Spicer.
Edw. III.	10 ‖	Walter le Spicer,	William Cowbrigge.
	12	The fame,	Stephen Merciber.
	12	John de Coveleye,	Hugh de Albrighton.
	12 **	Andrew Pendock,	John de Gloucefter.
	14	William Kingfhagh,	Roger Kingflove.
	14	Andrew Pendock,	John de Brugge.
	15	William Ringfhagh,	Robert le Valour.
	17	Andrew Pendock,	Richard Gradenftok.
	20	Adam le Hope,	Hugh de Aylbrighton.
	21	John Duyerfay,	John Wynfton.
	22	William Bruyn,	John Wynfton.
	24	John Coles,	The fame.
	27	Robert Broun,	Richard North.
	29	Thomas Okynton,	Nicholas Cricklade.
	31	Robert Waley,	Robert Broun.
	33	William Hertford,	John Comb.
	34	Thomas Stoke,	Thomas Stiwarde.
	34	John Halefton,	William Hibberere.
	36	William Hibberere,	Hugh Parkere.
	38	William Hibberere,	John de Monmouth.
	39	John Butte,	John Elianore.
	42	Thomas Stiward,	William de Veftare.
	43	The fame,	William Crooke.
	45 §§	John Heyberere,	
	46	William Heyberere,	Thomas Styward.
	47	The fame,	John Stiward.
	50	John Auleper,	Richard Barret.
Ric. II.	1	William de Heyberere,	John Dowlop.
	2 ‖‖	John Dulep,	Richard Barret.
	3	William Heyberere,	William Nightfield.
	6	John Hafelton,	John Bifeley.
	7	William Baret,	The fame.
	7 ‡‡	John Hed,	Robert Pope.
	8	John Compton,	John Pope.
	10	William Crook,	The fame.
	12 ††	Stephen Pope,	The fame.
	13	William Heyberere,	John Bannbery.
	15	Richard Afhewell,	John Bifeley.
	16 §§	Thomas Pope,	Simon Brock.
	18	Roger Ball,	William Scevok.
	20	Thomas Pope,	Richard Barret.
	21	John Pope,	The fame.
Hen. IV.	1	Richard Barret,	Simon Brook.
	3	William Bridley,	The fame.
	4 ‖‖	John Bifley,	Roger Balle.
	8 ‖‖	The fame,	The fame.
	12	The fame,	William Bridelep.
Hen. V.	1	John Streynfham,	John Clipfton.
	2	John Bifley,	Thomas Moore.
	3	No Return.	
	5	William Bridlep,	John Boifley.
	6	The fame	John Bifley.
	7	Robert Gilbert,	The fame.
	8	Thomas Moor,	Thomas Stevens.
	9	Robert Gilbert,	Richard Dalby.
Hen. VI.	1	The fame,	Thomas Stevens.
	2	John Streynfham,	The fame.
	3	Robert Gilbert,	Richard Dalby.
	4 ‡‡‡	Thomas Hewes,	John Beifley, jun.
	8	Thomas Bifeley,	John Edwards.
	9	John Hamelyn,	Thomas Stevens.
	11	The fame,	Thomas Derehurft.
	13	Thomas Hewes,	Richard Dalby.
	15	Thomas Derehurft,	John Andrew.
	20	Thomas Stephens,	William Oliver.
	25 ††	Thomas Derehurft,	Walter Chaunterell.
	27	The fame,	John Andreaux.
	28	William Nottingham,	Henry Dod.
	29	John Andreaux,	Thomas Bokeland.
	31 ‖‖‖	Robert Bentham,	William Eldelsfeld.
	33	John Andreaux,	John Dodding.
	38	Nicholas Hert,	William Brokwood.
Edw. IV.	7	John Hilley,	John Try.
	12	Alexander Colly,	The fame.
	17	Alexander Cely,	John Farley.

N. B. All the Returns are left out of the Tower from 17 Edw. 4. to 1 Edw. 6.

Edw. VI.	1	Thomas Bell, knight,	Rich. Morgan, recorder.
	6	The fame,	The fame.
Mariæ I.	1	Thomas Payne,	Thomas Loveday.
	1 §§§	The fame,	The fame.
P.&M.	1.&2	Thomas Bell, knight,	William Maffinger.
	2&3	Arthur Porter, efq;	The fame.
	4&5	Richard Pate, efq;	Thomas Paine, gent.
Eliz.	1	The fame,	Nicholas Arnold, kt.
	5	The fame,	The fame.
	13	William Maffinger gent.	Thomas Atkins, gent.

14 Thomas

Anno Regni.			
	14	Tho. Semys, alderman,	Thomas Atkins, the queen's attorney in her council, in the marches of Wales.
	27	Luke Garnons, eſq;	Thomas Atkins, gent.
	28	Richard Pate, recorder,	Thomas Atkins, eſq;
	31	Luke Garnons, alderm.	Thomas Atkins, eſq;
	35	Richard Birde, eſq;	The ſame.
	39	William Oldiſworth eſq;	Luke Garnons, eſq;
	43	The ſame,	The ſame.
Jac. I.	1	Nich. Overbury recorder	John Jones, eſq; alderm.
	12	The ſame,	Chriſtopher Caple, ald.
	18	John Browne, eſq; ald.	Anthony Robinſon, gent
	21	John Browne, eſq; ald.	The ſame.
Car. I.	1	Chriſt. Caple, eſq; ald.	John Browne, eſq;
	1	The ſame,	The ſame.
	3	John Browne, eſq;	John Hanbury, eſq;
Car. I.	15	William Singleton,	Henry Brett, eſq;
	16	Thomas Pury, alderman	Henry Brett, eſq; is mentioned as member of the city, who went to Oxford; and John Lenthall, in 1640, is ſaid to be in his ſtead probably on the parliament ſide.
Commonwealth Parliaments.	1654	William Lenthall, eſq; maſter of the rolls,	Thomas Pury, ſen. alderman.
	1656	General John Deſborough,	Thomas Pury, jun.
	1659	James Stephens,	Lawrence Singleton, ald.
	1660	Edward Maſſey,	James Stephens.
Car. II.	12	Edward Maſſey, eſq;	James Stephens, eſq:
	13	Edward Maſſey, kt.	Evan Seys, ſerjeant at law
	31	William Cook, eſq;	The ſame.
	31	Charles Barkley, kt.	The ſame.
	32§§	Charles lord Durſley,	Charles Somerſet, lord Herbert.
Jac. II.	1	John Wagſtaffe, eſq;	John Powell, eſq;
Will. III. M. II.			
	1	Duncomb Colcheſter kt.	William Cook, eſq;
	2	William Trye, eſq;	The ſame.
Will. III.	7	The ſame,	Robert Payne, gent.
	10	William Rich, baronet,	William Selwyn, eſq;
	12	John Bridgman, eſq;	The ſame.
	13	James lord Durſley,	John Hanbury, eſq;
Anæn	1	Right Honourable John Howe, eſq; *	William Trye, eſq;
	4	John Hanbury, eſq;	William Cook, eſq;
Annæ	7	Thomas Webb, eſq;	William Cook, eſq; §
	9	Thomas Webb, eſq;	John Blanch, eſq;
	12	John Snell, eſq;	Charles Cox, eſq;
Geo. I.	1	The ſame,	The ſame.
Geo. I.	9	Charles Hyett, eſq;	John Snell, eſq; and upon his death, John Howe, eſq; was elected. He was afterwards created baron of Chedworth, in this county, by king G. 2.
Geo. II.	1	Benjamin Bathurſt, eſq;	John Selwyn, eſq;
	8	John Selwyn, eſq;	Benjamin Bathurſt, eſq;
	15	The ſame,	The ſame.
	21	The ſame,	The ſame.
	28	Charles Barrow,	Geo. Auguſtus Selwyn.
Geo. III.	1	The ſame,	The ſame.
	8	The ſame,	The ſame.

It was uſually to aſſeſs the burgeſſes of the city for the wages of the burgeſſes in parliament, who were allowed two *ſol. per diem* each for every day that he ſat. Six days were appointed for their going to and returning from parliament every ſeſſions; and ſix ſhillings were then paid to the ſerjeant for his fee.

The election of members of parliament for this city is now very popular and tumultuous; but formerly it ſeems to have been otherwiſe, for in the indenture ‡ for this borough, fixed to the writ of 28° H. 6. and ſealed with the ſeals of the bailiffs, and of the high ſheriff of this county, 'tis ſaid as follows:

Burgeſſes elected, { William Nottingham, Henry Dodd.

The electors of the ſaid burgeſſes.

Thomas Hulley,	Walter Bauknot,	Thomas Barbour,
William Newman,	William Benſon,	William Shepiſtouk,
Thomas Biſley,	Thomas Heſt,	Richard Bunbury,
William Eldresfeld,	Thomas Bye,	John Coteler.

The number of burgeſſes, or freemen, that might vote in 1741, living

Within the city, about 950,
Out of the city, about 950,
In all — 1900,

In 1623 the inhabitants of the county of the city endeavoured in parliament to have a knight for their in-ſhire, which the city oppoſed, and occaſioned a proper clauſe to be inſerted in the city charter.

Of the LIBERTIES, PRIVILEGES, *and* CUSTOMS *of the* CITY; *of the* TWELVE COMPANIES *in the* CORPORATION, *the* CITY ARMS, *its* TRADES, MANUFACTURES, *&c.*

IN the time of king Edward the Confeſſor, this place was an antient borough, whoſe inhabitants were ſtiled the burgeſſes of the town of Glouceſter, and ſo they continued to be, 'till king John, by his letters patents, incorporated them; and indeed they were ſo called in the charters of king Henry the Second and Richard the Firſt.

King Henry the Second granted to his burgeſſes of Glouceſter the ſame cuſtoms and liberties, through his whole land, of toll and all other things, as the better citizens of London, and they of Weſtminſter enjoyed, in the reign of king Henry the Firſt.

King Richard the Firſt, on the 5th of May, in the 5th year of his reign, granted them the borough with its appurtenances, already mentioned page 84.

And king John granted them, *inter alia*, That they ſhould be quit of toll, laſtage, pontage and ſtallage, in and out of fair, and thro' all the ſeaports belonging to the king on this ſide and beyond the ſeas, the liberties of the city of London reſerved.—That the burgeſſes may elect two diſcreet burgeſſes to be bailiffs, who may not be amoved from their bailiwick, called alſo *præpoſitura*, as long as they behave well, but by the common council of the borough; and four coroners, to keep the pleas of the crown there.

* In the Honourable John Howe's place, John Hanbury, eſq; was elected.

§ In the place of William Cook, eſq; deceaſed, Francis Wyndham, eſq; was elected.

‡ Prine's Brev. Parl. page 662.

King Henry the Third confirms his father's grants, [p. 84] and granted to them further, that they fhould have for ever all their prefcribed liberties, and that if there were any particulars formerly granted to them which they did not then fully exercife, they might fully ufe the fame.

The kings Edward the * Second and Third confirmed the former grants, and the latter added, That they fhould be quit of murage, keyage, paviage, gildage, &c. thro' the kingdom.

King Richard the Second alfo confirmed them, and further granted them the chattels of outlaws, felons and fugitives, and deodands; all iffues, fines, redemptions and amerciaments of all the burgeffes; and all pleas real and perfonal within the vill, to be held in Gild-hall, with power and authority, as juftices, to hear and determine all offences committed in the vill, except felony, which they were not to determine without fpecial licence from the king,: That they might take recognizances according to the ftatute of Acton Burnel, and attach the body and goods of all perfons within the vill, except thofe of the abbat of St. Peter, his fucceffors, tenants and fervants.

King Henry the Fourth, Dec. 4, *regni* 1°; king Henry the Fifth, Feb. 5, *regni* 2°; king Henry the Sixth, Oct. 26. *regni* 2°; and king Edward the Fourth, May 5, *regni* 2°, confirmed all former grants to them; as did alfo

King Richard the Third, Sept. 2, *regni* 1°; and added, That 45 *l.* of the fee-farm rent fhould be abated; that on Monday next after Michaelmas then enfuing, a mayor fhould be elected, and that they be henceforth incorporated by the name of the mayor and burgeffes of the town of Gloucefter, and by that name to plead or be impleaded; that they of the corporation might choofe twelve aldermen to act as the aldermen of London do; that the hundreds of Dudfton and King's-Barton fhould be diftinct and feparate from the county of Gloucefter, and from the Monday aforefaid to be called the county of the town of Gloucefter; and that from and after that time the bailiffs of the town fhould alfo execute the office of fheriffs, and be fworn as fuch before the mayor, who fhould, under the feal of his office, certify their names in chancery when fworn; that the fheriffs fhould hold a county-court, and all precepts within the town and hundreds aforefaid fhould be executed by them; and that the mayor fhould be elected by the twelve aldermen, and twelve of the moft difcreet burgeffes. That there fhould be four ferjeants at mace, two whereof to wait upon the mayor, and two upon the fheriffs. The mayor to be clerk of the market, and fteward and marfhal of the king's houfhold, and the king's efcheator. But that the town of Tewkefbury fhould be exempted from tolls in Gloucefter.

King Henry the Seventh confirmed all former grants and privileges, except the abatement of 45 *l.* out of the fee-farm rent; and the mayor and burgeffes petitioning for the faid abatement, on account of 300 houfes being decayed and other great charges, he granted them an abatement of 5 *l.* for ever.

King Henry the Eighth alfo confirmed them, and September 3, *regni* 33° erecting a bifhoprick here, by a particular claufe in his charter, ordered that the whole town be thenceforth and for ever a city, to be called the § city of Gloucefter.

King Edward the Sixth, March 1, *regni* 5° confirmed the former grants as his father had done.

Queen Elizabeth, February 21, *regni* 3°, alfo confirmed them, and added, that Richard Pates, efq; fhould be recorder of the city during the pleafure of the mayor and burgeffes, to execute his office by himfelf, or by his deputy, to be called the town-clerk. That the mayor, recorder, and aldermen be juftices of the peace within the city, and no other juftice of the peace to intermeddle therein. That the mayor and burgeffes, or the majority of them, might choofe a recorder, and tax the inhabitants for the fafety, neceffity, or profit of the city; with feveral other particulars.

King James the Firft granted, that they fhould have a common feal; that the mayor and burgeffes might elect fheriffs, efcheators, coroners, bailiffs, chamberlains, conftables, ferjeants at mace, and other inferior officers, as have been accuftomed, with many other particulars.

King Charles the Firft granted, among other things, that they might elect and increafe the number of the common council as they thought proper; that on the Monday next after Michaelmas the twenty-four electors fhall choofe an alderman to be mayor, another to be coroner, two of the common council to be fheriffs, and four of the common council to be ftewards, all which fhould take their perfonal oaths. The mayor and burgeffes to elect a town-clerk, and other officers as formerly.

By an ordinance of parliament, which was made April 3, 1648, all former letters patents, and charters of liberties, tolls, &c. granted to the city, were confirmed under the great feal of England.

On Monday after Michaelmas 1671, in the morning, eight of the aldermen, the oldeft fheriffs, and others of the common council to make up the number twenty-four, affembled at Gild-hall, and there elected officers for the year enfuing. In the afternoon of the fame day, the mayor, who was not at the election, came to the Gild-hall to elect, and being told that the election was made in the morning, he, one of the aldermen, and fixteen of the council, protefted againft it, as being contrary to the charter of the city, upon which the charter was thought to be forfeited, and was furrendered.

It has been remarked, that of all the charters of corporations which the king took into his

* The original charter of king Edward the Second, is not now in the cuftody of the city, but is confirmed by *Infpeximus*.

§ See the faid Charter in Appendix, No. 7.

hands,

hands, that of this city, upon the pretence before-mentioned, was the firft.

Upon proper application, however, king Charles the Second, April 18, 24° *regni*, granted them another, dated at Weftminfter, which is the prefent * one, wherein their former privileges are confirmed; but it coft the corporation 679*l.* 4*s.* 9*d.* to procure it.

By this charter the corporation muft confift of thirty members at leaft, but cannot exceed forty; of which the mayor and aldermen are twelve, and the reft are the common council.

There are twelve companies in the corporation, who attend on the mayor, with their ftreamers, upon folemn occafions, *viz.*

1. Mercers, under which are alfo included apothecaries, grocers, and chandlers.

2. Weavers, who, 24° H. 7. were ftiled the warden and ftewards of the fraternity of St. Anne, and continued proctors of St. Anne's fervice in St. Michael's church 'till its diffolution; and were afterwards fo very confiderable, that when Thomas Machen was mayor, 44° Eliz. a writing or agreement, in behalf of their journeymen was then made, and approved by two juftices of affize, at their being in this city.

3. Tanners.

4. Butchers.

5. Bakers.

6. Smiths and hammer-men, among which are alfo ironmongers, cutlers, fadlers and glaziers.

7. Joiners and coopers.

8. Shoemakers.

9. Metalmen; to which belong goldfmiths, braziers, pewterers, and pin-makers.

10. Taylors.

11. Barbers.

12. Glovers.

Befides thefe there were formerly the companies of cappers and furriers, fhearmen and dyers, which became united 21° Eliz. and were quite decayed in 1634; of cooks and innholders, which became united 24° Eliz. and with their companies attended the mayor upon folemn occafions in 1629; of clothiers, of haberdafhers, and of brewers.

Borough Englifh, whereby lands and eftates defcend to the youngeft fon, and are forfeited to the king for felony but for a year and a day, was an antient cuftom and privilege, enjoyed by the town and fome part of the county of Gloucefter, and confirmed by a ftatute made 17° E. 2. And tho' 'tis now loft through difufe, and not claimed, in any part of the county; the ufage, was preferved in the city, as appears by an inquifition taken before the mayor as efcheator, and affirmed upon oath 28° Eliz.

Every fon of a burgefs is free-born, and as fuch is intituled to his freedom.

Each burgefs has free common all the year in the Town-ham, and in Portham after the hay is moved and carried away, which were purchafed of the abbey of St Peter's 21° H. 3. Alfo in Oxleafe, Meanham, and Little-meadow, after the firft vefture is taken off. And about June or July yearly, fome of the corporation are chofen to be officers of the commons.

On the 14th of February. 43° E. 3. the abbey of St. Peter's § granted, that the bailiffs and better fort of the burgeffes of Gloucefter, might fifh in their fmall fifhery in the Severn at and near to Gloucefter, at all times at their pleafure; but the common fifhers, who catch fifh to fell, fhould pay one penny a year to the kitchener of the abbey. The mayor has now this fifhery, and a fmall acknowledgement is paid for it.

A writ of *Quo Warranto* was brought againft the city 1ft and 2d Ph. and M. to prove their right to their feveral liberties; and upon their anfwer, all the former grants were confirmed. Another *Quo Warranto* was alfo brought againft it 15° Jac. 1. and thereupon a *Non Pros.* was obtained.

The town had a kind of market as long fince as the reign of king John, who commanded that all perfons coming hither with their wares might peaceably, and without moleftation, come, ftay, or depart hence. But the markets, as they now are, were granted by king Henry the Third, weekly on Wednefday and Saturday, of which the mayor is clerk.

King Edward the Third, in 1356, granted a fair, yearly to be holden on the eve and feaft of St. John Baptift, with five days immediately fucceeding. King James the Firft granted one upon the 25th of March, with two days fucceeding; and another on the 17th of November, and two days after. Barton fair, which is on September 17, was obtained in or about 5° Edw. 4. by St. Peter's abbey, to whom the manor and farm of that name did formerly belong; but after the diffolution, king Henry the Eighth, September 11, 34° *regni*, in confideration of 493*l.* 14*s.* 2*d.* granted to the corporation fome part of the lands of the manor, which they now enjoy, and feveral other particulars which were foon granted away.

The matters relating to tolls may be learnt from the various charters and other records ftill remaining in the city treafury, particularly that in the 32d year of Edward the Firft, the bailiffs of the town paid to the king 100*l.* for the tolls of the borough. And that, 35° Edw. 1. an agreement was made between Worcefter and Gloucefter, that the burgeffes fhould each be toll-free to the other. And in the reigns of king Rich. 2. H. 4. H. 5. H. 6. Edw. 4. H. 8. and Edw. 6. certain fines were paid to the bailiffs in the earlier times, and afterwards to the fheriffs of the town, by fuch as

* See Appendix No. 6.

§ The original grant in the cuftody of the city.

were

were not free of it. In 1629, fines were paid for the fame; and by a decree made in the ftar-chamber, in the reign of Charles the Second, they were ratified and confirmed. In 1589, Mr. Pain and others had feveral difputes with the corporation of the city, concerning the market-overt here, and the right of felling and taking toll at any time was determined in the queen's court of the marches, in behalf of the corporation of the city.

The chief employment of the town in and before the reign of king William the Conqueror, was making and forging of iron; and in the times of king Richard the Second and Henry the Fourth, 'twas eminent for its iron manufacture. The ore was brought from Robin-Hood's hill, at the diftance of about two miles from the city, where it is faid to have been found in great abundance.

Here was a ftreet antiently called Smith-ftreet *, moftly inhabited by perfons employ'd in the ironworks, on which account I prefume it had its name; but there were many furnaces and forges in other parts of the city. Thefe engines were then worked by hand, which, fince the bufinefs has been carried on in a larger way, are moved by water; and the town then loft that manufacture which could no longer be carried on there but under great difadvantages.

Some have been of opinion that this city had formerly a greater fhare of the foreign trade of the nation than it now enjoys, and urge, that feveral benefactions have been expreflly given to the merchant inhabitants; but probably, at that time, every confiderable fhopkeeper was called merchant, as is the cafe at prefent in Scotland, and fome other parts of the kingdom. However, without determining this matter, it is certain, that foon after the conqueft many of the Jews, who fubfifted intirely on trade and ufury, and were a fort of wandering merchants, refided here; but what was the nature of their trade in this place I have not been able to difcover any further with certainty. At prefent the foreign imports of the city are confined to the fole article of wines, which are in good repute.

The cloathing bufinefs, was formerly very eminent here, and Brook-ftreet, fituate upon Fullbrook, was the place of habitation for fuch as were concerned in that manufacture. As lately as the year 1629, here was a company of clothiers, who with the other companies attended the mayor on folemn occafions.

Cap-making was alfo a very confiderable trade here, and employ'd a great many hands, but that, as well as the clothing, has long fince deferted the city.

In the year 1626, at the decline of the clothing trade, that the poor inhabitants might not be deftitute of employment, John Tilfley, to his great honour, brought hither the art of pinmaking §, which was fo properly encouraged and promoted, that it foon grew to be confiderable, and has been gradually increafing ever fince. In 1712, this trade is faid to have returned 80*l.* a week; but in 1744 the wages in this branch amounted to about the fame fum, exclufive of materials, and together made a return of about 300*l.* a week. At prefent the manufacture returns about 20,000 *l. per ann.* from London, befides a very extenfive trade with the country.

This place had very antiently its proper fignature. On an old feal in the time of king Edward the Third, which is ftill ufed for recognizances, on each fide of that king's head is a horfe-fhoe, one horfe-nail near it, and three below it, two and one; with the like number above it, placed in the fame order. And it is affirmed, that king Richard the Third, when he made this a mayor town, gave it his fword and cap of maintenance; accordingly we find the following arms on the fouth fide of the gate leading into Crypt-fchool, which was built by alderman Cooke, who died 1529, viz. *A fword erect, with a cap of maintenance on the point, on each fide an horfe-fhoe and three horfe-nails at length in the bafe.*

On another old feal, ufed in the reign of king Henry the Third, and in the 38th year of Edward the Third, is *a caftle*, which appears to have had battlements from the turrets at each corner. And on another antient one in the middle is *a caftle, with a turret on each fide*, and round it this infcription, SIGILLUM BURGENSIUM DE GILDA MERCATORUM GLOUC.

In the reign of queen Elizabeth, the city ufed a feal which had, in the middle, *a fword in bend, the pomel in bafe, between fix horfefhoes, and ten horfe-nails*; and round it, SIGILLUM MAJORALITATIS GLOUC.

Chriftopher Barker, efq; garter principal king at arms, October 18, 1538, granted ‡ to the city of Gloucefter the following arms, viz. *Vert, a pale or, a fword azure befanted, the hilt and pomel gules; upon the point a cap of maintenance purple, lined ermine; upon the field two horfe-fhoes argent, pierced fable, between fix horfe-nails in triangle. On a chief, party per pale, or and purple, a boar's head coupee argent; in his mouth a quince apple gules between two rofes.* Thefe arms were ufed on the city feal from the time they were granted 'till 1652; but part of the time, with this addition, *viz.* Over the arms, 1564, and on each fide, *two maces, the one furmounted of the other*; which arms are upon feveral grave-ftones, &c. in the churches within the

* In king Henry the Third's time there was a place in fmith-ftreet called Colftall, M. S. *Frouc.* Perhaps the fmiths put their coles here. It was generally afterwards called the Bareland; becaufe it was bare or wafte ground, not built upon, next to the bridge, and the way into the caftle.

§ Pins were firft made in England in the year 1543, before which the ladies ufed fkewers, or rather, I fuppofe, the prickles of thorns, curioufly fcraped, trimmed and dried; which the poor women in Wales call *pin draen*, and have ferved with them for the purpofe of pins 'till lately, if they do not even at this time.

‡ Mr. Chancellor Furney, in his papers, whence this account is taken, fays, the original grant is in my cuftody.

the city, over thofe who had ferved the office of mayor.

The prefent arms of the city affigned by Sir Edward Bifh, garter principal king at arms, Auguft 14, 1652, are, *Or, three cheverons gules, between ten torteauxes* 3, 3, 3, *and* 1; which are now ufed upon the city-feal, and the feal of mayoralty. At the fame time he adorned the coat with two fupporters, viz. *On both the dexter and finifter fides, A lion rampant gules, each holding in his dexter gamb a broad-fword erect proper*; and added this creft, viz. *Out of a mural coronet iffuant a lion gardant gules, holding in his dexter gamb a broad-fword erect proper; in the finifter gamb a trowel, and ftanding upon a fcrole, with this motto,* FIDES INVICTA TRIUMPHAT. Three cheveronels, were the arms of the Clares, earls of Gloucefter, and 'tis faid that Gilbert, one of thofe earls, gave them to the town. The torteauxes are part of the arms of the fee of Worcefter, out of which this diocefe was taken.

Of the BIRTHS, DEATHS, *and* BURIALS *of eminent* PERSONS.

BENEDICT, who wrote the life of St. Dubricius, archbifhop of Caerleon, printed by Mr. Wharton, was a monk of St. Peter's abbey, and lived about the year 1120.

Ofbern, commonly called Ofbernus Claudianus, Ofbern of Gloucefter, flourifhed about the year 1140, and was alfo a monk of that abbey. He is faid to have been inftructed, from his tender years, by the beft mafters in eloquence, and in good arts; to have been a man more pure and elegant in the latin tongue than any perfon of his time. He was alfo fkilled in philofophy, and fo excellent a divine, that he was worthy to be compared with the antients. The abbey obtained great honour on account of him, who was truly great and illuftrious, and he inftructed the monks in learning. He fpent a great deal of time in writing books, which were efteemed the chief ornament to the abbey; and 'twas apparent from his productions, that he ufed the moft excellent philofophers and divines, both greek and latin. He was very much efteemed by abbat Hameline on account of his great learning, and was intimate with one Nicholas, who feems to have been afterwards abbat of St. Albans, whom he calls a man of found doctrine and excellent knowledge. Some of his works were wrote by way of dialogue, and fome of them in a continued ftile: of thefe he dedicated fome to Gilbert, bifhop of Hereford, who was his laft abbat; others to Hameline, who fucceeded him. King Henry the Eighth took all his writings from the abbey library, and placed them in the royal one at London; among which was one dedicated to Hameline, called *Panormia*, being a kind of vocabulary or dictionary.

Robert of Gloucefter, who received his name from being a monk of this place, flourifhed about 1263, and wrote a hiftory of Britain from Brutus to fome time in the reign of king Henry the Third, in the beft verfe his times would afford. It is printed in black letter by Mr. Hearne, in two volumes octavo, 1724; and as his language, on account of the great diftance between the time when he wrote and the prefent, is unintelligible to the readers of this age, without an interpreter; therefore the editor publifhed a gloffary to it.

John Raftel, D.D. who died about 1600; Richard Caple, M.A. who was buried September 21, 1646; and John Corbet, B.D. who died 26th of December, 1680, were natives of this city, and very remarkable in the times in which they lived.

King Arviragus, (mentioned p. 82,) died about the year of Chrift 74, in the 31ft year of his reign, and was buried in a temple here, which he had dedicated in honour of the emperor Claudius, and wherein he facrificed every month.

Gildas Cambrius, in the fame age with Martial, Horace, Silius, Statius, Stella, Juvenal, and feveral others, and but little inferior to any of them, feems to have been the fon of fome nobleman. Having been inftructed in greek and latin by the beft mafters, he became a great proficient in thofe languages, and was the moft excellent mathematician, rhetorician, hiftorian, and poet of the age. He flourifhed in the year 60, and died here with king Arviragus, to whom he was dear, and at whofe intreaty he wrote feveral books.

King Lucius, who was truely a good man, and commended by his people, died and was buried here, on the 3d day of December, about the 12th year of his government. A monk of the abbey beftowed thefe verfes on him inftead of an epitaph:

Lucius in tenebris prius indola qui coluifti,
Es merito celebris, ex quo baptifma fubifti.
Cæleftis medici merito curam meruifti,
Omine fælici lotus baptifmate Chrifti,
Prinne's Ufurp. v. 1. p. 38.

Concerning king Ofric, queen Kyneburg, queen Eadburg, and queen Eva, fee an account of the abbey of St Peter's.

Prince Ethelred and his princefs Alfled, fometimes called Æthelfleda, and Elfleda, the founders of St. Ofwald's priory, are reported to have been buried in the eaft porch of St. Peter's church; and afterwards, when the foundations were dug up, to make room for a new one, their bodies were found intire; and 'tis faid their looks were then as graceful as when alive. He died in 908; fhe in 920. Huntingdon made the following verfes in praife of this warlike lady:

O Elfleda potens, ô terror virgo virorum,
Victrix naturæ, nomine digna viri.
Tu quoque fplendidior fieres, natura puellam,
Te probitas fecit nomen habere viri,

Te mutare decet, fed folam, nomina fexus,
Tu regina potens, rexq; trophæa parans,
Jam nec Cæfarei tantum meruere triumphi.
Cæfare fplendidior, virgo, virago, vale.

Which Peck *, in his *Antiquities of Stanford,* thus tranflates :

O potent Elfleda! maid! men's terror!
You who did conquer nature's felf, worthy
The name of man! more beauteous nature form'd
A woman: But your valour fhall fecure
Man's higher name. For name you only need,
Not fex, to change; unconquerable queen,
King rather, who fuch trophies have obtain'd!
O virgin, and virago both, farewel!
No Cæfar yet fuch triumphs hath deferv'd
As you, than any of the Cæfars more renown'd.

King Athelftan died here 6° Kal. Nov. 940 or 941; but was buried at Malmefbury, Co. Wilts.

Matthias, brother of Jeffry Ridel, the king's chief juftice, who was abbat of Peterborough, died and was buried here about the year 1104 or 1105. Perhaps the ftone at the north-eaft end of the body of the cathedral church, lying upon the ground, on the fouth of Mr. Blackleech's monument, whereon was carved an abbat with his paftoral ftaff, and which was lately taken away, was defigned for his memorial.

Duke Robert Curtois, or Shorthofe, eldeft fon of king William the Firft, after a long imprifonment of twenty feven years, at Cardiff caftle, was honourably buried by the king's order, in the middle of the choir of the conventual church here, in the year 1134, and had a grave-ftone over him, upon which was a crofs, now lately taken away. Over the grave-ftone was his image in armour, carved in Irifh oak, lying at length, crofs legged, to denote his having been in the holy war, with a ducal coronet on him, and a wire-lattice over the whole to preferve it. This monument was made long fince he was buried, and continued intire 'till 1641, when the foldiers broke it in pieces; but Sir Humphry Tracy, of Stanway, in this county, bought the pieces, and laid them up 'till the reftoration, and then at his own charge caufed the tomb to be repaired and beautified; a noble reprefentation of which is publifhed in *Sandford's Genealogical Hiftory.* This duke was a confiderable benefactor to the abbey, and his brother king Henry the Firft gave large poffeffions to it on his account.

Richard Fitz Giflebert, a noble and amiable perfon, being killed by the Welch, was brought hither and buried 17° Kal. Maij, 1136.

Pain, a noble knight of great valour, being earneftly in purfuit of the Welch, was mortally wounded, and brought hither to be buried.

Geofry Falebote, a ftout and courageous knight, was killed by thofe who lay in ambufcade for the earl of Gloucefter, in his journey to Bath from this place; and being conveyed hither in September 1140, was here buried.

Aldred archbifhop of York, concerning whom fee St. Peter's abbey, is thought to have been buried in the cathedral, and the fhelf-monument on the fouth fide of the choir, is generally fuppofed to have been erected for him.

Ralph de Maydefton, bifhop of Hereford, refigned that fee in the year 1239, and retiring to St. Peter's abbey, took upon him the monaftic habit, and was buried in the abbey church. *Willis.*

On the north fide of the choir lies the unhappy king Edward the Second, who was very barbaroufly murdered at Berkeley caftle, September 22, 1327, and brought hither by the abbat of St. Peter's. The common tradition is, that he was drawn by ftags; for which reafon there are feveral paintings of them round the pillars at each end of his tomb. After his body had been viewed by feveral perfons who were appointed for that purpofe, tho' it was done by them only privately and fuperficially, he was folemnly received by the town and monafteries, and was decently, but privately, and without any funeral pomp **, buried by the abbey, to which he had been a great benefactor §. His fon king Edward the Third † erected a fine monument of alabafter with his portraiture on it, a crown on his head, a fceptre in his right hand, and a globe or mound in his left; and founded a chantry in the place where he was buried. There is a noble reprefentation of this monument in *Sandford's Genealogical Hiftory.* 'Tis faid that miracles ‡ were wrought for him; and that therefore king Richard the Second propofed to tranflate him to fome more honourable place: But of this ftory every one may believe his proportion. Wolftan, bifhop of Worcefter, kept the anniverfary ‖ of this king's death, perfonally at Gloucefter, at the defire of king Edward the Third.

The monument erected for the king was repaired in 1737 by Oriel college, who caufed this infcription [E. II. 1327] to be painted on the pillar at the eaft end, feven ftags on the eaft pillar, and fix ftags on the pillar at the weft end; inclofed it with iron rails, and put three plates on them. On that at the eaft end is, *Hoc fundatoris fui monumentum, fitu vetuftatis deformatum, inftaurari curaverunt Præpof. et Soc. Coll. Oriel, Oxon.* A. D. 1737. On the next, The arms of king Edward the Second, with a crown over them.

* There are fome variations in thefe verfes publifhed by Peck, and alfo by Lloyd, in his *Hiftory of Wales.* In the third line, inftead of *fieres,* they have it *fecit.* For *folam* in the fifth line, they have *folum*; and in the feventh line, Lloyd has *mirere triumphas,* inftead of *meruere triumphi.*

** It is affirmed in a MS. now in my cuftody, that the expences of this king's funeral amounted to no more than nineteen fhillings and fome odd pence.

§ MS. Chron.

† Barnes's life of this king.

‡ Fuller's Ch. Hift. l. 4, p. 110.

‖ MS. Frauc. Appendix to Thomas's Survey of Worcefter Cathedral, pp. 112, 113.

On

On the third, The arms of Oriel college. This repair coft the college forty pounds.

The following perfons, according to Leland, were buried in the abbey chapter houfe, and moft of them had infcriptions for them written on the walls.

Roger de Lacy, earl of Hereford.

Walter de Lacy *.

Roger, earl of Hereford.

Roger the fon of Milo, earl of Hereford, took upon him a religious habit in this abbey, and died in 1154.

Richard Strongbow, fon of Gilbert earl of Pembroke, who was inftrumental in fubduing Ireland, died upon the nones of April, in 1176.

Paganus de Cadurcis, or Chaworth, in the reign of king Henry the Third, who married Gundred, the daughter of William Brewere, a great baron of that time.

Adam de Cadurcis, or Chaworth.

Bernard of New Market, or Newmarch.

Philip de Foye, knight.

Hugh de Portu.

Elias Giffard.

The lady Strongbow, countefs of Pembroke, was buried in abbat Parker's chapel, where, in making a tomb for him, they found a crofs wrapped in a bull's hide.

Humphry de Bohun, earl of Hereford, Warwick, and Arundel, and one of the twelve who governed the realm in the time of king Henry the Third, lies on the fouth-fide of the cathedral, behind the choir, with his wife. Over them is now to be feen an antient ftone mural monument, with their particulars on it.

As to what is faid of king Edmund Ironfide's dying and being buried here, by Knighton; of Richard, the youngeft fon of king William the Firft, being buried here in 1080, by the *Memorial of Gloucefter*; of a tomb near the altar erected for Ifabel, queen to king Edward the Second, by Sir Robert Atkyns; much credit cannot be given to any of thefe relations.

Further accounts of burials and monumental infcriptions may be feen under the following heads, *Government and Officers*, *St. Peter's Abbey*, *Bifhops*, *Deans*, *&c.* and in the hiftory of the feveral parifh-churches within the city, to which the reader is referred.

Of the *PUBLIC SCHOOLS, CHARITIES, WORKHOUSE, &c.*

THERE was a grammar-fchool in old Smith-ftreet, on this account called the School-houfe-lane, given, as appears by the *Monafticon*, by king Henry the Second to the priory of Lanthony; the mafters whereof antiently received 40 *den. per* quarter, or 2 *fol.* for each child. But 11° H. 4. only 12 *den.* In 1535, this houfe lay void. The priory had let it for 13 *s.* 4 *d.* a year, and it is faid in *R. Cole's Roll* to have been fometime in the holding of Sir William Chaplain, the fchoolmafter, in the reign of Henry the Sixth. 'Tis very probable that one Haymo, a fecular prieft, whom Bale calls Haymo Gloceftrius, was mafter of this fchool about 1160, for he was a native of, and chief fchoolmafter at Gloucefter, and accounted the moft learned man of his time. Roger occurs rector of the fchools in Gloucefter, September 29, 1209. Andrew Horne, who was very ftudious in the antiquities of this place, and compiled an excellent work intituled, *The Chronicle of Glofter*, flourifhed in the reign of king Edward the Firft, and Bale expreffly fays he was a fcholar of this place.

The free grammar-fchool of St. Mary de Crypt, ftanding upon the weft part of St. Mary's church-yard, was, in purfuance of the laft will of alderman John Cook, dated May 11, 1528, erected by his widow Joan Cook, who is faid in an old book in the cuftody of the city, to have taken the ring and mantle after her hufband's death, and thereupon became a lady. She, on the 11th of January, 31° H. 8. by indenture of three parts, between herfelf, the mayor and burgeffes of Gloucefter, and the bailiffs and citizens of Worcefter, vefted in the faid mayor and burgeffes, her manor, meffuages and lands, &c. in Poddefmede, Hempftead, Elmore, Bageworth and Bentley, with the county of the faid town of Gloucefter; lands and tenements in Brockworth, Stonehoufe, Ebley, Oxlinch, Standyfh, Weftbury, and Claxhill, *Com. Glouc.* to provide, with the rents of Poddefmede, Hempftede, and Elmore, an honeft and well learned fchoolmafter, for this fchool, to be chofen by the mayor, recorder, and two fenior aldermen; the mafter to receive a yearly ftipend of ten pounds, if a prieft, and nine pounds, if a layman. The mayor, recorder, the two fenior aldermen, the two fheriffs, the town-clerk, the four ftewards, the fword-bearer, the four ferjeants at mace, and the five porters of the gates, covenant herein to furvey the fchool once every year between Eafter and Whitfuntide, and caufe the neceffary reparations to be made. For the trouble of doing which, the mayor is to have 4 *s.* the recorder 3 *s.* 4 *d.* each alderman 2 *s.* each fheriff 20 *d.* the town-clerk 16 *d.* each of the ftewards and the fword-bearer 12 *d.* every ferjeant 8 *d.* and each porter 4 *d.*

The rents of the lands and tenements in Gloucefter, Badgeworth, Bentham, and Brockworth are to pay to the poor people of the hofpital of

* He gave his lands at Dean to the monks of this abbey, and being founder of the church of St. Peter in Hereford, when that work was almoft finifhed, climbing up a ladder there, he fell down, and being killed by the fall, 6 Kal. Apr. 1084, was buried in the chapter-houfe at Gloucefter. And Emeline his wife gave to the church of Gloucefter for the health of his foul, five hides of land at Duntefbourne. His fon Walter was a monk of the abbey Dug. Bar. v. 1, p. 95.

St.

St. Bartholomew 3*s.* 4*d.* weekly in money, and the overplus to repair this fchool-houfe. The rents of the lands and tenements in Stonehoufe, Ebley, Oxlinch, Standifh, Weftbury, and Claxhill, to the yearly value of 5*l.* are to be laid out on the Weft-bridge and caufey, between Gloucefter and Over.

Alderman Lawrence Wilfhire, in 1611, gave 100*l.* for the eftablifhment of an ufher in the fchool; and George Townfend, efq; in 1683, gave two perpetual exhibitions for the maintenance of two fcholars at Pembroke college, in Oxford, for eight years, to be elected by the mayor, fix fenior aldermen, and the chief fchoolmafter.

The rents of the eftate given by lady Cook being greatly advanced, the mafter of the fchool now receives 30*l.* a year, and the ufher 16*l.* The bailiff, aldermen, and chamberlain of the city of Worcefter are appointed by the founder as truftees, to fee that the mayor and burgeffes of Gloucefter furvey the fchool, for which they have a fmall annuity; and if the latter at any time nenegleft to perform the duties of their truft, they forfeit 10*l.* to the corporation of Worcefter for every default.

The corporation of Worcefter have vifited the fchool feveral times, particularly on the 12th of September, 1728, Mr. Wefton, (the mayor) with four aldermen, &c. after twenty years abfence, made their vifitation, and infpected the accounts of what was given to this fchool, and St. Bartholomew's hofpital, by lady Cook.

Mr. William Maffinger, to whom with feveral other perfons many feoftments had been made by alderman John Cook, for the purpofes beforementioned, endeavoured to get all the lands and premiffes for his own ufe; but by a decree in chancery, made February 12, 5° E. 6. and exemplified the 7th of May following, Maffinger was obliged to deliver up to the corporation all the evidences, &c. belonging thereto.

MASTERS of CRYPT-SCHOOL.

John Diftele occurs Nov. 4, 1547, as do

Thomas Bowland 4° Ed. 6.

Nicholas Oldifworth, rector of St. Michael's, 6° E. 6.

Richard Hewis, 1° Mar. 1.

After this there was a vacancy for a confiderable time, feveral perfons affifting in this office.

Hugh Walker occurs 5° Mar. 1. and 17° Eliz.

Gregory Downehall, or Downer, 20° Eliz. 1576.

Edmund Cugley, 21° Eliz.

Alexander Belfhire, 23° Eliz.

Henry Aifgill, afterwards prebendary, (*See prebendaries*) occurs 25° and 27° Eliz.

William Grove, 31, 40° Eliz. I believe he refigned in 1598, when he made the city lecture. (*See St. Mary de Crypt.*)

—— Floyde, amoved Aug. 20, 9° Jac. 1.

John Bird occurs 4° Car. 1. amoved May 18, 1641, and thereupon

John Beedle, M. A. was elected the 25th of May following. See his character in A. Wood's *Hift. and Antiq. Univ. Oxon.* l. 2. Upon his removal

James Allen, M. A. ufher of the fchool, was elected in October, 1645.

John Cooper, confirmed in July, 1647.

Thomas Bevan, faid to be elected 1652, upon Cooper's refignation; but

Nicholas Tailer occurs May 18, in the fame year.

William Rawlins, B. A. elected July, 1653.

Francis Stedman, B. A. elected Aug. 1654.

Abraham Heague, ufher, elected October 1658, upon whofe death

John Grubb, M. A. was elected October, 1696, and lies buried in the middle chancel of St. Mary de Crypt, under a ftone with an * infcription upon it.

William King, elected May, 1697, and upon his death

Philip Collier, B. A. elected June 16, 1711; licenfed June 25, 1711, amoved May 12, 1719, and thereupon

Richard Furney, M. A. was elected, and upon his refignation

Daniel Bond, B. A. the ufher hereof, was elected March 25, 1724, and was alfo vicar of Leigh.

USHERS.

Edward Barwell, elected September 22, 1613, and occurs afterwards incumbent of the parifh-church adjoining.

Jonathan Bullocke, elected July 15, 1628, upon Barwell's refignation, and occurs afterwards incumbent of the parifh-church adjoining. He refigned September 18, 1633, whereupon

Robert Bird at the fame time became elected, and was amoved September 19, 1629.

A vacancy for fome time, 'till

John Corbet, B. A. was elected Feb. 8, 1640, and occurs afterwards incumbent of the parifh-church adjoining, and one of the city lecturers. See his character in A. Wood's *Hift. and Antiq. Univ. Oxon.*

John Allen, M. A. elected July 8, 1643.

Thomas Smith, elected June 8, 1648, and upon his refignation

Abraham Heague, elected March 24, 1652, and upon his being made mafter,

Ifaac Heague was elected October 10, 1656; afterwards rector of Huntley. He refigned, and

William Wood became elected Nov. 16, 1668.

Oliver Gregory, B. A. was elected March 26. 1670,

* H. S. I. Johannes Grubb, A. M. natus apud Acton Burnell, in agro Salopienfi, Anno Domini 1645. Cujus variam in linguis notitiam, et fœlicem in erudiendis pueris induftriam, grata adhuc memoriâ, teftatur Oxonium. Ibi enim, Ædi Chrifti initiatus, artes excoluit; puerofq; ad eafdem mox excolendas accurate formavit. Huc demum unanimi omnium confenfu accitus, eandem fufcepit provinciam; quam fœliciter adeo abfolvit, ut mihi optandum fit, nifi ut diutius nobis interfuiffet: Fuit enim propter feftivam ingenii fuavitatem, fimplicem morum candorem, præcipuam erga cognatos, benevolentiam omnibus, defideratiffimus. Obiit 2° die Aprilis, A. D. 1697, Ætatis fuæ 51.

1670, and being removed to be mafter of the college-fchool,

Thomas Tippett, October 3, 1673, was elected; afterwards rector of Knoll-Parva, co. Wilts, and prebendary of Sarum. He refigned to become ufher of the college-fchool, and thereupon

Thomas Merret was elected January 14, 26° Car. 2. He was likewife perpetual curate of Barnwood, and dying, was fucceeded by

Daniel Bond, B. A. elected March 3, 1708.

John Gegg was elected March 25, 1724, upon Bond's refignation.

Henry Church, upon Gegg's refignation, was elected June 19, 1727, and being inftituted rector of St. Michael's in this city, left this place.

James Comeline, upon Church's refignation, was elected March 25, 1733; and being inftituted vicar of Haresfield left this place.

Thomas Gardiner, upon Comeline's refignation, was elected June 24, 1737.

Charity-fchool and *Work-houfe.*

Timothy Nourfe, efq; was the founder of this charity, towards which he gave 100*l.* *per ann.* for ever, which has been applied to the fupport of it. In the firft feffion of parliament 1° *Annæ*, 1702, an act was paffed for incorporating the mayor, three aldermen, and twenty-four others, to be called the governors, deputy-governors, and guardians of the poor of the city of Gloucefter, for the better providing for, and fetting to work the poor of the faid city; which act was to take effect from the 7th day of April then next following.

Sometime after this, the corporation of the city granted to Mr. Francis Yate a leafe of part of the eaft-gate for the poor-fchool, and alfo the old horfe-pool there, at a fmall rent.

In the *Account of Charity-fchools in England*, in the years 1707, and 1709, particular mention is made of this having been opened at Gloucefter, with fubfcriptions fufficient for the fupport of fixty children, with a fair allowance for the mafter and miftrefs. And in that of 1711, 'tis faid, that eighty-five children were taught in this fchool, and that feventy boys were cloathed the laft chriftmas.

Alderman John Hyett died Feb. 27, 1711, and gave 100*l.* to this fchool, and ordered by his will, if his fon Jofeph fhould die before the age of twenty-one years, 1000*l.* more for building a new charity-fchool and work-houfe, and 400*l.* for a ftipend for the mafter. This Jofeph Hyett died in 1713, in the twenty-firft year of his age, and left a further fum of 1500*l.* for the fupport and maintenance of this charity.

Sir John Powell alfo gave 20*l.* Mr. William Allen 20*l.* and Mrs. Dorothy Cocks 20*l.* *per ann.* which are all applied to this ufe. And the corporation of the city, defirous of promoting a charity which promifed fo fair for the general good, granted a leafe of the New-Bear Inn, which was large and commodious, for forty-one years, to the governor and guardians, referving a chief-rent of 40*s.* *per ann.* renewable every fourteen years at a fine certain of 37*l.* 10*s.* for the erecting of a work-houfe for all the parifhes belonging to the city, the fitting up of which coft about 600*l.*

In the year 1727, an act was obtained for repealing part of the former act, and appointing a governor, a deputy-governor, a treafurer, and fix fpecial affiftants, who were to continue in their office for two years. The mayor, five fenior aldermen, the bifhop, the dean, the chancellor, the arch-deacon, the fub-dean, and the treafurer, all refpectively for the time being; and thirty-one perfons to be chofen out of the feveral parifhes in the city, and the precincts of the college, were to be, and to continue in their office for fix years, and with thofe before-mentioned, and fome few others fince dead, to be incorporated by the name of the *Governor and Guardians of the poor of the city of Gloucefter.*

But the powers of the governors and guardians were fo circumfcribed by the fore-mentioned acts, that, together with the intereft of the feveral fums that had been given to the charity, they could not raife money fufficient for the maintenance of the poor, on account of their great increafe, and the dearnefs of provifions; fo that they not only fpent fome of the principal money, but contracted a debt of 830*l.* 8*s.* 8*d.* and were obliged, about May, 1757, to fhut up the work-houfe, and fend the poor to their refpective parifhes. But in the year 1764, another act of parliament was procured, by which the mayor, the five fenior aldermen, the right reverend the bifhop, the reverend the dean, the worfhipful the chancellor, the reverend the archdeacon, and the reverend the fub-dean and treafurer of the cathedral church of Gloucefter for the time being; the furviving truftees of Mr. Nourfe's will; and fuch as have been, and fhall be elected to fucceed them; thirty-one perfons to be chofen out of the parifhes in the city, and precincts of the cathedral, together with fuch as fhall be elected guardians on account of their donations to the poor, fhall be one body politick and corporate, by the name aforefaid, with power to make bye-laws. The laft mentioned thirty one perfons to continue in their office only one year, unlefs re-elected.

Thefe guardians, or any nine or more of this corporation, fhall meet annually on the fecond Thurfday in June, or within feven days afterwards, and elect by vote out of themfelves, one governor, one deputy governor, one receiver or treafurer, and fix fpecial affiftants, who fhall continue in their office for one whole year, and until fuch time as others fhall be chofen to fucceed them.

The guardians are to afcertain what money will be neceffary for the maintenance of the poor, which muft be certified to the mayor, and levied by the churchwardens and overfeers of the poor of the refpective parifhes, &c. which fums may exceed by one third part what the refpective parifhes paid in any one year of the five laft preceeding the paſſing of this act. They are alſo empowered to aſcertain what further ſums of money are neceſſary to be raiſed by each pariſh, to diſcharge the expences of this act, and to pay the ſaid debt of 830*l.* 8*s.* 8*d.* and for replacing the principal money ſpent as aforeſaid, and alſo for erecting of lamps to inlighten the city from the 29th of September to the 21ſt of March annually.

Benefactors and *Benefactions.*

John Fawkener, alderman, and thrice mayor of this city, by his will, dated September 18, 1545, beſides 50*l.* bequeathed by him for the repairing the highways and bridges near this city, gave to the mayor and burgeſſes all his lands and tenements, which were very conſiderable here, and at Wotton and other places in this neighbourhood.

Sir Thomas Bell, beſides the 10*l.* *per ann.* and other charities and gifts, (ſee bridges) gave to the poor and priſons about the city, 6*l.* 10*s.* *per ann.*

Rowland Atkinſon, ſometime ſheriff of this city, by his will dated November 20, 1600, gave to the mayor and burgeſſes all his poſſeſſions in the city, which were eight houſes.

William Holliday, a native of this city, and afterwards an alderman of London, by his will, dated December 16, 1623, gave 500*l.* wherewith, by the direction of his relict, afterwards counteſs of Warwick, lands were purchaſed of the clear yearly value of 30*l*; which money is now expended in apprenticing out ſix boys yearly, according to the direction of the lord keeper in 1628.

Leonard Tarne, alderman of this city, by his will, dated November 3, 1632, gave 4*l.* a year iſſuing out of Monk-leighton, near this city, to be diſtributed to 40 poor people, half yearly.

Sarah Browne, by her will dated October 8, 1643, gave ſeveral houſes in this city, worth 20*l.* a year, for apprenticing out three boys, who are to have 4*l.* a piece.

John Powel, alderman of this city, December 13, 1649, gave 100*l.* with the intereſt of which one boy is annually placed out apprentice.

John Morris gave 10*l.* that 13*s.* 4*d.* as the intereſt of it, ſhould be yearly beſtowed on the poor.

Joan Goldſtone, by her will, dated September 8, 1578, gave 20*l.* to remain as a perpetual ſtock for the proviſion of fewel for the poor.

Dame Eleanor Fettiplace, in 1625, gave 40*l.* for a ſtock for them; and now 70*l.* is allowed for a ſtock to provide them with coal, at 10*s.* a ton.

The following ſums of money were given to the city, to be diſpoſed of as the wills and deeds of the donors direct, *viz.*

Thomas Glouceſter, eſq; in 1446, gave 500 marks.

Sir Thomas White, Lord mayor of London, in 1554, gave to twenty three places*, whereof Glouceſter is one, 100*l.* *per ann.* clear, to be lent for ten years to poor clothiers, and to continue in the ſame order of ſucceſſion for ever. Glouceſter began to receive it in 1581, ſo that 900*l.* has already been paid to this city at nine payments.

John Haydon, *alias* Holden, alderman, and one of the ſheriffs of London, deceaſing in the year of his office, 1583, gave to this city 100*l.* to be lent to poor young tradeſmen, at the rate of 3*l.* 6*s.* 8*d.* *per ann.* which was to be diſpoſed of for the relief of priſoners and poor people. *Stow.*

Gregory Wilſhire, 27° Eliz. gave 100*l.*

Thomas Poulton, in the year 1608, gave 60*l.*

Alderman Thomas Machen, in the year 1614, gave 100*l.*

Alderman Fettiplace gave 100*l.*

Mr. Giles Cox, in 1620, gave 100*l.*

Henry Ellis, in 1647, gave 50*l.*

John Langley, 1657, gave 20*l.*

Mr. Willis gave 10*l.*

Sarah Wright, in 1669, gave 10*l.*

Biſhop Frampton gave 20*l.*

Several donations were but for terms, and upon conditions, which have long ſince expired; particularly thoſe of Mr. Richard Pates, the recorder, Mr. Robert Pettifer, alderman Jaſper Clutterbuck, and alderman Thomas Pury.

Some are quite loſt, as Iſabel Wytherington's 2*l.* *per ann.* notwithſtanding ſeveral of the poſſeſſions did, for many generations before, belong to this corporation.

'Tis very probable that the city derived many of the poſſeſſions it now enjoys from the gifts of Robert Banks, and alderman William Jordan, in 1545; of Alice Barker, in 1562; of William Golſton, in 1569; of William Saunders, in 1570; of Agnes Nevowe, 37° Eliz. and ſome others. Theſe poſſeſſions, together with the rents of aſſize, langable or ground rents for purpreſtures or incroachments; what the corporation have purchaſed, and what have been granted to, and given them by the crown and other perſons, from time to time, with other accidental advantages and acquiſitions, have rendered them a very wealthy body; inſomuch that the revenues which are in the diſpoſal of the magiſtracy, including thoſe which ſupport the government of the city, and the charitable uſes, were eſtimated to be worth 60000*l.* more than half a century ago, and have, ſince that time, been very conſiderably improved.

* This donation of 100*l.* clear, and 4*l.* more to be paid on St. Bartholomew's day yearly, at Merchant-taylors hall in London, by the corporation of Briſtol, is to be diſpoſed of to the undermentioned places as they ſucceed each other in the following table:

1577 York
1578 Canterbury
1579 Reading
1580 Merchant Tayl.
1581 Glouceſter
1582 Worceſter
1583 Exeter
1584 Saliſbury
1585 Weſt Cheſter
1586 Norwich
1587 Southampton
1588 Lincoln
1589 Wincheſter
1590 Oxenford
1591 Hereford Eaſt
1592 Cambridge
1593 Shrewſbury
1594 Lynn
1595 Bath
1596 Derby
1597 Ipſwich
1598 Colcheſter
1599 New Caſtle.

Of Saint PETER's ABBEY, and the ABBATS, &c. of that MONASTERY.

WULPHERE, the firft chriftian king of Mercia, is faid to have begun, and Ethelred his brother and fucceffor, who was afterwards monk and abbat of Bardney, to have carried on, and finifhed, a monaftery here, to the honour of St. Peter, about the year of Chrift 680[a], 681[b], or 682[c], chiefly by the care of Ofric, fometimes called[d] Ofhere, Oftric, or Hoftric, his nephew, and at that time his viceroy of the Wiccij, but afterwards king of Northumberland. Ofric having received from the king[e] the vill of Gloucefter, with feveral lands, and a large fum of money, to[f] found and endow this monaftery, faithfully difcharged the truft repofed in him, and by the advice of Bofil, firft bifhop of Worcefter, taking in nuns[g], made his own fifter Kyneburg, or Kenburg, the wife[h] of Alred, king of Northumberland, the firft abbefs. Juft after her confecration, he vefted all the lands which he had received, with very great addition to them, in the monaftery, to which he alfo granted many confiderable privileges. Kyneburg continued in her office twenty-nine years; and dying, was buried in St. Petronille's chapel, where her brother Ofric, who died 729, was firft interred, but he was afterwards removed into that of Our Lady; and in abbat Parker's time, was laid under a fair monument of free-ftone, upon which were his arms, on the north fide of the high altar; at the foot of which againft the wall the following infcription is now remaining: *Ofricus Rex, primus fundator hujus Monafterii*, 681.

Eadburg[i], or Eilburg, who had been wife of Wolphere, king of Mercia, was confecrated to fucceed Kyneburg; and governing the nunnery prudently and religioufly for twenty-five years, was buried by Wilfrid, bifhop of Worcefter, next to her predeceffor. After her came

Eva, fometime wife of Ethelred, king of the Mercians; or of Wolphere, fon of king Penda; who, after fhe had increafed the income of the monaftery, and procured the confirmation of former donations in many fynods, died in the thirty-third[k] year of her government, *anno* 768[l]; and was buried next her predeceffor. With her died the office of abbefs; for afterwards, in the wars between king Egbert and the king of Mercia, the nuns were ravifhed and forced to depart, and the monaftery became defolate, and continued fo 'till[m] 821; when Beornulph, or Bernulph, king of Mercia, repaired it, and beftowed part of the poffeffions towards the maintenance of fecular priefts, whom he had here inftituted.

King Burgred, in the year[n] 862, confirmed to thefe the lands which the kings Ethelred, Ethelbald, Offa, and Kenwolf, and other perfons had given: and by the confent of his great council exempted the monaftery, with its appurtenances and dependents, from all fecular fervice. But in the year[o] 1022, king Canute, at the inftigation of Wolftan, bifhop of Worcefter, having turned out the feculars, made them give place to monks of the order of Saint Benedict.

The governor and inhabitants of Gloucefter were fo averfe to monks at firft, that Wolphin or Ulfine le Rue[p], or Lehue, who was then conful, or chief governor, and a lord of great puiffance, flew feven of them, not far from the town, in 1033; but the pope foon afterwards obliged him to attone for his offence by giving Churcham and Highnam for the maintenance of feven monks in Saint Peter's abbey. The eftablifhment of the

[a] Tanner's Not. Monaft. p. 137. [b] M. S. Chron. Rot. Cap. Collect. Cl. Wharton in Bibl. Lambeth. Leland Itin. V. 4. &c. [c] 681, 682, Cl. Willis Hift. of Mit. Parl. Abbeys, p. 110. [d] Dug. Bar. V. 1, p. 3. Leland's Collect. V. 1, p. 240.

[e] In MS. Frouc. V. 1, is king Æthelred's gift to Ofric in 671. In MS. 'tis faid king Ulpher or Wolpher, in 672, laid the foundation of the monaftery, and dying, left the finifhing thereof to his brother Æthelred, his fucceffor in the kingdom of Mercia, having appointed him to take care of that work. Leland in his Itinerary, V. 4, fays, that Ofric built it with licence. And he is ever reputed to be the founder of this great nunnery, and was efteemed as fuch, as appears by the infcription for him mentioned in this account. According to fome, there was a monaftery here before the nunnery erected by Ofric; for feveral fcholars upon the interdict made againft the Pelagians for their herefy, fled to the monaftery here; but 'tis likely the firft that was endowed here was founded by him.

[f] Rot. Cap. King Burgred's Charter in MS. Frouc. 1. Mon. Anglic. p. 108, 993.

[g] Dr. Tanner thinks it probable, that this monaftery at firft received religious of both fexes, under the government of an abbefs.

[h] And doubtlefs wife before that to one of the king's of Mercia; for abbat Malvern, in his account of the abbey, and Willis in Hift. Mit. Abb. p. 112, fay exprefsly, that the three queens which prefided over this nunnery, were queens of Mercia. Mon. Anglic. p. 108, 109, 933. Collect. Cl. Wharton.

[i] Mon. Angl. p. 109, 993.

[k] The *Memor of Glouc.* fays, fhe died in the 30th year of her government, which is agreeable to abbat Malvern's account.

[l] After the fhort continuance of 87 years, or of 88, according to Leland, V. 4, p. 6.

[m] Mon. Angl. V. 1, p. 993. Willis, p. 110. Bifhop Tanner fays it continued fo 50 years.

[n] MS. Frouc. Part 1. Autograph. in my cuftody, not 852 as is miftaken in Rot. Cap.

[o] Mon. Anglic. p. 992. Collect. Wharton. Willis, p. 110. Bifhop Tanner's Not. Mon. p. 537.

[p] Leland's Itin. Le Ride. Rot. Cap.

monks was not fully compleated 'till [q] Aldred, biſhop of Worceſter, afterwards archbiſhop of York, in 1058, pulling down the decayed old church, which ſtood near the infirmary, built a fine new one at ſome diſtance from it, nearer the walls of the town, dedicated it to St. Peter, and gave rules to the Benedictines. Aldred took from this church the manors of Lech, Odinton, Standiſh and Berton, and appropriated them to the church of York; but they were afterwards publickly reſtored to this monaſtery by archbiſhop Thomas, in the chapter-houſe at Glouceſter, in the year 1095, who then ſtriking his breaſt, blamed himſelf for having detained them ſo long.

ABBATS of SAINT PETER's.

Edric [r], who before was one of the ſecular prieſts, and upon the introduction of monks, took upon him their habit, was, by biſhop Wolſtan, appointed the firſt abbat in 1022. By his naming himſelf abbat in Eldenham, or Ealdanhame, which ſignifies old place, he ſeems to allude to that antient monaſtery pulled down by the biſhop; for the abbey was exceedingly decayed 'till Aldred erected a new one; and this of Aldred's was then expreſſly called Newminſter [or Monaſtery,] in order to diſtinguiſh it from the former building; or perhaps, when he ſo called himſelf, Aldred's foundation was not then fully eſtabliſhed. Edric preſiding over the abbey for thirty-ſeven years, died in 1058, when the church was endowed and fully eſtabliſhed by Aldred: and having [s] alienated ſeveral of the poſſeſſions of the abbey, and departing from it, was not buried [t] therein.

Wilſtan [u], a monk of Worceſter, kinſman [w] to biſhop Aldred, was the ſame year, by the king's leave, conſtituted abbat by biſhop [x] Aldred. He died in 1072, in his journey towards Jeruſalem, and was at length [y] buried under the yew-tree in the plot in the midſt of the cloiſters, becauſe he had waſted the goods and poſſeſſions of the monaſtery.

Serlo [z], or Serlus, a monk of Saint Michael's in Normandy, and chaplain to king William the Firſt, 4 kal. September, 1072, was, by the advice and mind of St. Oſmond, promoted by the king to the governance of this abbey, which at that time was in great decay, and was then reputed but of little eſteem. He was a perſon of a very eminent character, and by the indefatigable labours of himſelf and Odo, the cellarer, procured very great donations to the abbey. At his entrance into his office he found here not above three [a], ſome ſay two [b] monks of perfect age, and eight ſcholars, or youths; tho' at his death he left 100 monks in it. June 29, 1089, he began [c] the foundation of a new church, the firſt ſtone whereof was laid by Robert biſhop of Hereford; and being finiſhed, was dedicated with great ſolemnity on the ides of July, 1100, by Sampſon biſhop of Worceſter, Gundulf biſhop of Rocheſter, and Serenus, (called Henricus in the *Monaſticon*) biſhop of Bangor. In 1101 [d], or 1102 [e], the town with the abbey was burnt, and 'tis probable this church eſcaped better than that, which in 1088 [f], was burnt with the monaſtery. King William the Conqueror [g], in the twentieth year of his reign, keeping his chriſtmas at Glouceſter, royally repaired and increaſed this monaſtery, being very much decayed. And Serlo having obtained [h] from him and his two ſons, king William the Second, and Henry the Firſt, and other noblemen, freedoms, lands, liberties and confirmations of the grants to this abbey, made by their ſeveral patents, died [i] the 5th nones of March, 1104, in or about the 68th year of his age; and was buried under a fair marble tomb on the ſouth ſide of the preſbytery. His intimate friend, Godfrey, prior of Wincheſter, made the following verſes for him.

Eccleſiæ murus cecidit, Serlone cadente,
Virtutis gladius, buccina juſtitiæ;
Vera loquens, en non vanis ſermonibus utens,
Et quos corripuit; principibus placuit,
Judicium præceps; contrarius ordinis, error,
Et levitas morum, non placuere ſibi.
Tertius a Jano menſis, lux tertia menſis,
Cum nece ſuppreſſum, vita levavit eum.

A great deal is ſaid in praiſe of him by Malmeſbury, from whom Bale has taken his character. Cent. 13, p. 136.

Saint Arild the virgin, martyr'd at Kington, near Thornbury, at whoſe tomb 'tis ſaid many miracles were wrought, was tranſlated hither in his time. In 1100, Haraldus, lord of Ewyas, gave the church of S. Michael, and other poſſeſſions at Ewyas, for the eſtabliſhment of a priory there; but as the income thereof was inſufficient, and this abbey had, for ſome years, to their great charge, maintained a prior and one or two monks;

[q] Mon. Ang. V. 1, p. 993.
[r] Mon. Anglic. Wharton's Coll. Willis's Hiſt. of M. Abbies.
[s] MS. Chron. Glouc. in Bibl. Bodl.
[t] The following is a declaration under the hand-writing of "abbat Edric: "I Edric abbat of Ealdanhame do make known, "and declare by this writing under my hand, that I being compelled in my great neceſſity, did grant to a certain Starmacotto "the lands in Hatherly and Badgeworth, belonging to the church, "to hold for his life; which I did in conſideration of money lent "by him, amounting to 15*l.* with which I did redeem all the "other farms belonging to the monaſtery, from that great exaction throughout England, called Lord Gelt. Witneſſes hereunto are Wolſtan, archbiſhop of York, Leſſey, biſhop of Worceſter, Aglaff Earl, and the whole ſociety of the antient monaſtery, and Anna the abbeſs, and all the brethren of the monaſtery of St. Oſwald; and Wihiſide the chief magiſtrate, and "all the citizens of Glouceſter, and many more both Engliſh "men and Danes: Wherefore, if he who holds the land ſhall "any ways be incumbred in the ſame, let him make amends out "of his own; but let the land be diſcharged, and return again to "the monaſtery after his death".
[u] Mon. Anglic. [w] MS. Frouc. 2[d].
[x] Wharton. Willis. [y] MS. Chron. Glouc. in Bibl. Bodl. [z] Mon Anglic. Rot. Cap. Willis. Wharton.
[a] Leland's Collect. Malmeſbury. [b] Willis Mit. Abb. p. 113. [c] Ib. [d] Leland. Dunelm.
[e] A MS. Extract out of the book of Glouc. now in CCC. lib. Ox.
[f] Mon. Anglic. [g] Mon. Anglic. [h] MS. Frouc.
[i] Willis's Mitr. Abb.

in

in 1358 [k], the bifhop of St. David's, with the confent of his chapter, of Roger de la Warre, lord of Ewias, and of Walter de Monmouth, diffolved that priory, and united it to the abbey of Gloucefter.

Peter [l], the prior of the abbey, became abbat in the nones of Auguft, 1104. He encompaffed the [m] abbey with an excellent ftone-wall, by the affent and affiftance of king Henry the Firft, and greatly enriched the convent with a collection of valuable books. King Stephen [n] confirmed by his charter the donations made to the abbey; and this abbat, after feven years and a half's governance, died on the 16th of the kal. of July, or Auguft, 1113. Upon his death

William Godemon [o], or Godemor, the prior, was promoted to the abbey; and having obtained great donations to it, and a licence to appoint his fucceffor, refigned in 1130. Retiring to St. Paternum, in Wales, he died on the 3d nones of March, fays Willis; but according to Mr. Wharton, 3d ides of July, the year after his refignation. On the [p] 8th ides of March, or May 8, 1122 [q], when the monks were finging mafs, and the deacon began the gofpel, the tower was fet on fire by lightning, and the whole monaftery was burnt, fo that all the valuable things therein were deftroyed, except a few books, and three priefts veftments.

Walter de Lacy [r], brother to the founder, or according to fome, the principal benefactor to Lanthony in Wales, being of the blood-royal of England, was promoted by abbat Godemor, whofe chaplain he was, and received the benediction from Simon bifhop of Worcefter, on the 3d nones of Auguft, 1130. At the petition of himfelf and fome of the nobles, in 1138, king Stephen, by his charter, confirmed the donations made to this abbey. He died on the [s] 6th of the ides of February, 1139, and was buried by Reinaldus, abbat of Evefham, and Roger, abbat of Tewkefbury. Hugh Fitz-William [t], the Norman, whofe family afterwards affumed the firname of Kilpeck, in 1134, gave to the abbey the priory of Kilpeck, in Herefordfhire, dedicated to St. David. It ftood from the caftle [u] above a quarter of a mile.

Gilbert Foliot [w], or Folieth, or Folioth, fometime a Cluniac monk of Burgundy, being prebendary of Newington, in the cathedral of St. Paul's, London, received the benediction [x] from Robert bifhop of Hereford, on Whitfunday the 3d of the ides of June, 1139, or, as 'tis faid, was inftalled [y] on the 11th of the ides of June, 1139. Upon abbat Lacy's death, [z] two of the monks of this abbey were fent to Gilbert, who was defigned for abbat; and king Stephen having heard of his excellent probity, at the requeft of Milo, earl of Hereford, whofe kinfman Foliot was, granted the government of the abbey to Foliot. In 1148 [a], he was removed to the bifhoprick of Hereford; and thence he was tranflated to that of London, being a very learned man and a great writer, as may be feen in Bale and Godwin [b]. Upon Foliot's removal to Hereford,

Hameline, the fub-prior was elected the [c] 6th of the calends of October, 1148, and received the benediction from Simon bifhop of Worcefter, on the nones of December. This abbat went to Rome to defend the rights of his monaftery againft the archbifhop of York, who claimed the manors of Leck, Oddington, Standifh, and Barton, as pertaining to the archbifhoprick, tho' his predeceffor Thomas had reftored them to the abbey, after the time was expired for which they were mortgaged; and obtained fuch fuccefs in the affair, that the bifhops of Chichefter and Lincoln [d], to whom this difpute was referred by pope Eugenius, adjudged it on the behalf of the abbey, and king Stephen confirmed it; but in 1157, this abbey, for preventing any future controverfy, gave to the archbifhoprick of York, Oddington, Condicote, and Shurdington, with certain lands; and the archbifhop, with the affent of his chapter, and a general fynod, renounced all claim to the other particulars. Pope Alexander III, by his bull dated 4th ides of July, in or about the year 1164, confirmed [e] this agreement, and fays, The controverfy about this matter was agitated before his predeceffor Adrian, who appointed the bifhops of Salifbury and Bath to act as his delegates in this matter. He died on the [f] 6th of the ides of March, 1179; in whofe time very confiderable donations were made [g] to the abbey. On the 5th of the ides of May [h] the abbey was again burnt.

Thomas Carbonel [i], or Carbonach, prior of St. Cuthlack's, or Guthlac's, near Hereford, was inftalled the 15th of the cal. of October, 1179, and died the 21ft of July, 1205. The abbey and great part of the town was burnt in 1204. After him,

Henry Blont, or Blond, the prior, [k] received the benediction from Maugre bifhop of Worcefter, September 29, 1205; and was inftalled the 6th of the ides, or nones, of October. In 1222, he began to rebuild [l] the tower of the church, which fell down, and committed the management thereof to Helias the facrift. And the fame year, with the abbat of St. Albans, was [m] appointed a prefident of the chapter of the benedictines at

[k] MS. Frouc. [l] Willis's Hift. M. Abbies. Wharton. [m] Rot. Cap. [n] MS. Frouc. Vid. Appendix, N°. 11. [o] Collect. Wharton. Willis's Hift. Mitr. Abb. [p] Ib. Saxon Chron. [q] Gloucefter Book in CCC. Library Oxon. [r] MS. Frouc. 1. [s] Willis's Hift. Mit. Abb. [t] Mon. Anglic. V. 1. [u] Bifhop Tanner's Not. Mon. p. 175. [w] Wharton's Collect. Willis's Mit. Abb. Newcourt's Repert. Eccles. [x] Wharton's Collect. [y] Willis's Mit. Abb. [z] Cont. of Flor. Wigorn. [a] Wharton's Coll. Willis's Mitr. Abbies, p. 114, &c.

[b] It is faid that he was the firft bifhop that was tranflated from one bifhoprick to another in this kingdom.
[c] Wharton's Coll. Willis's M. A. p. 114, &c.
[d] MS. Frouc. 2[d] Rot. Cap. [e] Cl. Wilkins's Councils V. 2, p. 437. [f] Collect. Wharton. Cl. Willis's Mit. Abb. p. 114. [g] Mon. Anglic. [h] Collect. out of MS. book of Glouc. [i] Wharton's Collect. Willis's Mit. Abb. 114. [k] Collect. Wharton. [l] Willis's Mit. Abb. [m] Reinerus de Congreg. Nigror. Monachor. in Anglia.

Berrmondſey. The abbey was twice deſtroyed [n] by lightning during his government, viz. in 1214, and in 1223. He died the 10th of the kalends of September, 1224, and was ſucceeded by

Thomas de Bredone [o], or Breden, the prior, who received the benediction at Worceſter, October 7, 1224. This abbat [p] died in 1228.

Henry Foliot [q], or Foleth, or Folet, prior of the cell at Bromfield, ſucceeding, received the benediction from William de Blois, biſhop of Worceſter, in 1228. He was a great benefactor to the abbey, and built a handſome tower in 1237; two years after which he made an aqueduct to ſerve the convent with water; he likewiſe vaulted part of the church; and ſometime before his death began a new tower at the weſt end. In 1230 [r], or 1231 [s], he appointed twenty marks yearly out of the church of Newport, in Glamorganſhire, for the charity of the abbey, in French wine and waſtel. About 1236 [t], for 30 marks, he granted to the burgeſſes of the town, the free common for their cattle, between the bridge of Glouceſter and old Leden; and Common in Preſtham, and all the meadows of the abbat beyond Severn, on the weſt ſide, after the hay was carried off, except the meadows belonging to foreign manors. Ralph de Willington [u], and Olympias, his wife, having at their own charges built our lady's [w] chapel, in the church-yard of St. Peter's, for two foreign prieſts, and a clerk to attend them; and erected a houſe within the precincts of the abbey for their habitation, the abbey received lands to the yearly value of 8*l.* 7*s.* for their maintenance and ſupport, whereupon the abbat and convent, extolling their extraordinary liberality to the abbey, particularly in this gift, covenant with them to keep all the buildings in good repair, and allow the chaplains a ſufficient corrody; that every year on the day of Ralph's death this agreement ſhall be read before the brethren; and he, Olympias, and all their anceſtors and ſucceſſors, in a full chapter, ſhall be abſolved to be partakers of all the good works done in the abbey, and in the churches pertaining to them; that on the day of his death the ſervice ſhall be performed as fully as for a monk, and that yearly; and that this agreement might continue inviolable, the convent in full chapter pronounced the bleſſing of God to all thoſe that keep it; and his curſe, as far as they ſay lay in their power, to the violaters thereof. The abbey, under their common ſeal, confirmed and gave this agreement to Ralph; and Ralph ſealed and gave another part to the abbey, to be kept by them. Tho' this chapel [x], we are told, was finiſhed in 1227, yet the agreement concerning it was made by abbat Foliet and the convent. This abbat died on the ides of July, 1243, And

Walter de St. John [y], the prior, received the benediction at Baſinger, on the 4th of the nones of October, and dying the ſame year, upon the day whereon he was to have been inſtalled,

John de Felda [z], or De la Felde, the precentor, received the benediction Dec. 6, 1243, and was inſtalled on the 12th following. He finiſhed the weſt tower on the ſouth part of the front, and in 1246, pulled down the old refectory, and began a new one. In 1251 [a], the abbey became indebted to the value of 3000 marks. The biſhop of Worceſter, to whom they had applied for relief, excluded and forbade the reception of ſtrangers, and retrenched the hoſpitality of the abbey. The abbat died the 6th of the kalends of April, 1263, and was ſucceeded by his chaplain,

Reginald de Homme [b], or Hamme, who was inſtalled the ſame year on the Sunday after the feaſt of St. Peter and St. Paul. At his entrance he [c] found the abbey in debt 1500 marks, by loſſes and misfortunes, which he could not repay, tho' he was in ſome meaſure relieved by king Edward the Firſt [d], who, in 1272, took the abbey into his protection, and appointed a commiſſioner that might take care for the obſervance of his grant, and keep all perſons from damaging or moleſting the abbey. And afterwards, the ſame king rebuilt a gate on the ſouth ſide of the abbey, which is now called by his name, but before was ſtiled Lichgate. In 1264 [e], this abbat, together with the biſhop of Worceſter, procured a truce to be made between the barons that were in the town of Glouceſter, and prince Edward, the king's ſon, who had taken the caſtle from the barons. And in 1274, being proctor of the whole dioceſe of Worceſter, by ſpecial order from the pope, the biſhop of Worceſter being by infirmity detained at home, he was at the council of Lyons, and died on the ides of Sept. 1284. In 1283 [f], John Giffard, baron of Brimsfield, built Glouceſter college in Oxford for thirteen monks, whom he choſe out of this convent, to be improved in learning; and on the feaſt of St. John the evangeliſt, in the preſence,

[n] Mon. Anglic. [o] Collect. Wharton. Willis's Mit. Abbies, p. 114. [p] Ib. [q] Ib. [r] Collect. MS. Chron. [s] Annal. Wig. in Angl. Sacra.
[t] Orig. in Cuſt. City. [u] MS. Frouc. 2.
[w] In this century the appointment of particular prieſts to officiate at the Virgin's chapel began to take place in England.
[x] Annal. Wig. in Anglia Sacra. [y] Ib. Collect. Wharton. Willis's Account of Mit. Abb. 114. [z] Ib.
[a] MS. Frouc. 2d Part. Collect. Wharton. In the donation of the particulars given to Glouceſter abbey, in Manaſtic. Anglic. 'tis ſaid, That in 1260, John Deffeld purchaſed of Lawrence de Chandos, knight, 55 acres of arable land in Brockworth, and 40 acres of incloſure, and all his wood in Bockholt, which contained 300 acres; but probably he only contracted for theſe particulars, and did not pay for them, which made the abbey ſo much in debt at his death. For in MS. A. 5. is a deed of conveyance to abbat Reginald from the ſaid Sir Lawrence de Chandos, and moſt of the particulars of Brockworth and Bockholt, which he had granted to abbat John, and another deed to abbat Reginald, whereby he granted and confirmed all the lands, &c. which his predeceſſor had of the ſaid Sir Lawrence. In this MS. but before theſe two grants, are ſeveral deeds whereby the ſaid Sir Lawrence granted many particulars in Brockworth and Buckholt. And I ſuppoſe the ſeal and payment was not quite finiſhed before the grant and confirmation was made to this Reginald.
[b] Collect. Wharton. Willis's Mit. Abb. [c] Sir R. A.
[d] Prinne's Intol. Uſurp. V. 3, p. 126. [e] R. of Glouc. p. 343. [f] Mon. Anglic. V. 1, p. 541. Stevens's Addit. V. 1. p. 337, &c. Annal. Wig. in Ang. Sac. MS. Chron. Dr. Hutton's Antiq. Oxf. &c. &c.

fence, and agreeable to the will of Giffard, abbat Homme was introduced into it. Other monafteries of Benedictines afterwards partook of the benefit of this houfe; and their lodgings were called agreeable to their names. That part called Gloucefter lodgings, as appears by the arms of the abbey at the entrance thereof, ftill remains, and is the habitation of the provoft of this houfe, which has lately changed its name of Gloucefter college, afterwards Gloucefter-hall, into Worcefter college. This abbey was obliged to maintain three or four of their monks here, and allowed each of them 15 marks *per ann.* The church of Chipping-Norton[g], co. Oxon, was appropriated for their fuftenance. This Reginald de Hamme appears to be the firft abbat of this church, who was fummoned to parliament, and that was, for the firft time, according to Dugdale, 49° H. 3.

John Gamages[h], or de Gamages, or Gag, prior of St. Cuthlacks, a perfon very religious, and of an honourable family, upon de Homme's death, was inftalled on St. Andrew's day, 1284, and confirmed Nov. the 20th following. In 1303[i], abbat Gamages pulled down the old dormitory, and began a new one, which was finifhed by his fucceffor in 1313. On July 16, 34° Edw. 1.[k] in confideration of a fine paid to the king, he obtained a charter for regulating the vacancies of the abbey, by which the abbey was granted to the prior and convent, to be the keepers of it 'till the abbat elected had received the temporalties. For every vacancy, whether it continued four months or not, they were to pay 200 marks; and if it continued longer than that time, to pay according to that rate In 1298[l], on the morrow after St. Barnabas, William de Brok, a monk, afterwards prior of this abbey, was an inceptor in divinity, under the chancellor of Oxford, and was the firft Benedictine monk in England who took the degree of doctor in it. At his vefpers Lawrence Honfum, S.T.B. a monk of this place, was refpondent; and at his inception were the abbat, with his monks, priors, obedientiaries, clerks, efquires, and feveral noblemen, to the number of 100 in all; the abbats of Weftminfter, Redynge, Abendon, Evefham, Malmefbury, many priors and monks, with divers rewards and exercifes. All other prelates almoft of the whole province of Canterbury of this order, who were abfent, fent exercifes; and fo this inception was finifhed to the honour of this abbey, and of the whole order. About the feaft of St. Hillary[m], 1305, this abbat made a fumptuous feaft in the great hall in the court of the abbey, when the king's juftices fat at Gloucefter upon the inquifition of Traylbafton. There were 30 knights, the priors of Lanthony and St. Ofwald, with other ecclefiafticks, and many of the more honourable perfons of the whole county, at this entertainment, which was fo well managed, that the juftices and other barons prefent expreffed their higheft approbation of it. On Epiphany day[n], 1300, a fudden fire furrounded the monaftery, and confumed the cloifter, belfry, and the great chamber, with other buildings adjoining. This abbat having, by his frugal management[o], brought the abbey out of debt, and increafed their ftock of fheep to 10,000, after he had lived[p] fixty-two years a monk of the convent, over which he had prefided as abbat twenty-three, he died 15 kal. May, 1307, and was buried with great honour, by the bifhop of Worcefter, being attended by feveral abbats to his grave, without the choir near the door of the cloifters, where his brother Sir Richard Gamages had been interred.

John Thokey[q], or Toky, or Chokey, the fubprior, was elected May 1, 1307, received the benediction at Hartlebury, 8 kal. July, fays Willis, but fome MS. papers in my cuftody fay June, and that he was inftalled on the 29th of that month. In 1313[r], he was excommunicated for refifting the prior of Worcefter's vifitation in the vacancy of the fee; but an award being made concerning it, the bifhop of Worcefter, September 2, 1314, abfolved the abbey, and required the official of the archdeacon of Worcefter to publifh it. At or before 14° E. 2. as appears by the king's patent then granted, the abbey had licence to appropriate the church of Haitherope, to find chaplains in the charnel houfe built by Peter Fox, in the abbey church-yard. *(Bifhop Tanner's Not. Monaft.)* During his government[s], king Edward the Second being barbaroufly murdered at Berkeley caftle, this abbat fetched him in his chariot from the caftle, the abbats of Kingfwood, Briftol and Malmefbury being afraid to do it, and with his convent, folemnly robed, accompanied with a proceffion of the whole city, honourably received him; which afterwards proved fo fortunate to Gloucefter, fuch numbers flocking to fee and pay their devotions to his relicks, that a great part of the church was built out of the offerings made on that occafion. Our abbat, in 1318, rebuilt the fouth aile, and did feveral other benefactions; but at length growing old and infirm, he refigned in 1329, and died foon after. February 28, 2° E. 3.[t] the king, with the confent of parliament, in confideration of the expences which the abbey had been at in celebrating his father's funeral, granted, That upon every vacancy of the abbey, they fhould compound with the king at the rate of 100 marks for the fpace of a year; but that all knights fees holden of the abbey, efcheats and prefentations to their churches, which fhould fall in the time of the vacancy, fhould belong to the king. The prior, as prefident, and the convent, fhould keep

[g] MS. Frouc. [h] Collect. Wharton. Willis's Mit. Abb.
[i] Willis's Mit. Abb. p. 115. [k] MS. Frouc. 1.
[l] MS. Chron. Glouc. [m] Ib. [n] Antiq. Eccles. Brit. p. 291. [o] Sir R. A.

[p] Willis's Mit. Abb. Annal Wigorn. in Anglia Sacra, V. 1.
[q] Willis's Mit. Abb. p. 115. [r] MS. Frouc. 1
[s] Willis's Mit. Abb. p. 115. [t] MS. Frouc.

the

the abbey in fafe cuftody, 'till another perfon was admitted thereto. The efcheator, or the fheriff, upon a vacancy, to make only fimple feifin within the abbey, and fo to depart.

John Wigmore[u], or Wygmor, the prior, by the procurement of abbat Thokey, was promoted in 1329. He gave an exceeding rich, embroidered garment, to be worn on the feftival of the pentecoft. While he was prior, he rebuilt the great chamber of the abbat, near the garden of the infirmary. He alfo built[w] the great grange at Highnam from the foundation; the chamber of the abbat next the great hall, with a little hall adjoining to it, and a chapel. He was well fkilled in mechanicks, and delighted in other arts. He began St. Andrew's aile, which in fix years he finifhed in a beautiful manner, out of the oblations made at the tomb of king Edward the Second, which was fo frequented by perfons coming hither in devotion, that the city of Gloucefter was fcarce fufficient to receive them; and their offerings were fo great, that 'tis thought they would have been enough to have built the whole church. This abbat obtained[x] of the king, Oct. 3, 10° E. 3. a grant to the abbey of the hundred of Dudfton, co. Gloucefter, with all its emoluments and appurtenances, at the fee farm rent of 12 *l.* *per ann.* Dying, the 12th of the kalends of March, 1337, he was buried on the fouth fide, near the entrance of the choir, which he built, with a fquare ftone pulpit over the weft door, and which in the year 1718, was demolifhed to make room for the organ.

Adam de Staunton[y], the prior, fucceeded the fame year. He built the great vault of the choir, and the ftalls on the prior's fide of it, as alfo the vineyard-houfe, out of the oblations[z] made at the tomb of king Edward the Second, by his fon king Edward the Third, queen Philippa, prince Edward, and feveral of the nobility and gentry. The king gave a fhip of gold, and another fhip, which, at the entreaty of the abbat and convent, was redeemed at the price of 100 *l.* The prince offered a crofs of gold, having in its compofition a part of the great crofs, and a ruby. Thefe oblations muft have been of great value, for this abbat, notwithftanding his great expences in building, left 1000 marks in the treafury. In 1338[a], he was one of the two prefidents of the chapter of the Benedictines at Northampton. June 25, 19° Edw. 3. by exchange, he[b] obtained for the abbey the manor of King's-Barton, adjoining to Gloucefter, with feveral other particulars. And dying, in 1351, was buried at the altar of St. Thomas, which his brother, John de Staunton, had[c] rebuilt. February 20, 17° Edw. 3.[d] the moveables and immoveables of the abbey were valued at 287 *l.* 18 *s.* 7 *d.* and the members of the convent, July 28, 1348, were thirty-fix.

Thomas Horton, the facrift, fucceeded, being chofen by way of compromife. He received the benediction at Cheltenham, from the bifhop of Hereford, by leave of the bifhop of Worcefter, Dec. 4, 1351; and had the temporalties granted to him the 12th of the fame month. He adorned his church with abundance of veftments, and caufed the great altar, and the prefbbytery, to be made, together with St. Paul's aile, and the great hall wherein the parliament was holden in the year 1378, during the feffion of which, the king, and his whole court, were lodged in the abbey. In the refectory[e] there was treating concerning the laws of arms. The common hall was defigned for the lords in parliament, and there was a chamber, which for its elegance was antiently called the king's, appointed for the fecret council of the nobles: and in the chapter-houfe was the common council of parliament. After this abbat had governed twenty-fix years, being very aged and infirm, he refigned November 8, 1377; and dying feventeen weeks and three days afterwards, was buried under a flat ftone in the north part of the tranfept, or great crofs aile. Nov. 20, 1° R. 2. the king confirmed feveral charters of his progenitors to the abbey; and among the reft, that of king Edward the Third, concerning the vacancy of the abbey. 'Tis probable this was done to preferve good order in the proceedings before the enfuing election of the abbat; for the king, under his great feal, fent a writ to the barons of the exchequer, in the difpute about the fum of money due for the vacancy, prohibiting them to give any moleftation to the abbey, in any thing contrary to his charter.

John Boyfield[g], or de Boyfeld, the præcentor, was elected 6 kal. Dec. 1377, and received the benediction from the bifhop of Hereford, at Whytebourn, on Sunday before Chriftmas; was inftalled December 24, and had the temporalties reftored to him on the 31ft of the fame month. Mr. Wharton fays, he obtained from the pope the ufe of the pontificals for himfelf and fucceffors; but probably this was done by his fucceffor, Walter Froucefter. Dying on the 3d of the kalends of January, 1381, in the fourth year of his government, he was buried in St. Paul's aile, near abbat Horton. In 1380[h], there were fifty-four monks in this convent, with an abbat, and 200 officers or fervants; the yearly income was then 1700 marks. The revenue[i] of the abbey being much leffened by extraordinary inundations, peftilences, and other calamities, and being continually fre-

[u] Collect. Wharton. Willis's Hift. Mit. Abb.
[w] MS. Chron. [x] MS. Frouc.
[y] Collect. Wharton. Willis's Mit. Abb. [z] Willis's Mit. Abb. MS. Chron. Sir R. A. [a] Reinerus de Congreg. Nigror. Monachor.
[b] MS. Frouc.
[c] This altar is mentioned in MS. Frouc. 2, when David Dunning and Walter Heich were præpofiti Glouc. alfo when William Sumery and John Fitz Roger Symon were præpofiti thereof. So that this altar, in abbat Staunton's time, was but repaired.
[d] Orig. Papers. [e] MS. Chron. [f] MS. Frouc.
[g] Collect. Wharton. Willis's Mit. Abb.
[h] Original Papers now remaining.
[i] MS. Frouc.

of

quented by guefts, as well poor foreigners as thofe of this kingdom, the expences were fo very great as to require the appropriation of St. Mary de Lode to defray them.

Walter Froucefter[k], or Frouceftre, or Frouceftor, or Froncefter, the chamberlain, was elected in January, and inftalled the 14th of February, 1381. The abbey was afterwards [l] fued for not paying the 200 marks, according to the charter of king Edward the Firft, but it was determined that they were no longer due on account of the vacancy. He procured from pope [m] Urban, by the intereft of the duke of Gloucefter and others, a grant for himfelf and the abbats his fucceffors, of the mitre, ring, fandals, and dalmatic: Alfo, that he might give the folemn benediction at vefpers, matins and at table, fo that no bifhop or legate of the apoftolic fee were prefent. He alfo [n] obtained a difpenfation for eating of flefh in the abbey, from feptuagefima to quinquagefima Sunday in-inclufive. He made the [o] fumptuous and beautiful great cloifters, concerning which fee the account of the cathedral church. He took great care and pains to collect and tranfcribe the records belonging to this abbey. And dying in 1412, was buried in a chapel at the fouth-weft part of the choir, under the arch of the tower, where his gravestone now remains, which appears to have had his effigy, mitre, &c. on it in brafs, which are now torn off. There was an anniverfary kept [p] for him in the church of Chipping-Norton, co. Oxon, 'till the time of the diffolution; and fix cloth gowns were given to fix poor men, and fome other particulars were then yearly diftributed there, as well as in the churches of St. Mary de Lode, and of the Holy Trinity in Gloucefter. In his time [q] the number of monks was forty-five, with an abbat and two hundred officers or fervants, the income being the fame as in the time of his predeceffor.

Hugh de Morton[r], or Moreton, fucceeding, had the temporalties reftored to him May 27, 13° H. 4. on whofe death, which happened *ann.* 1420,

John Morwent[s], Marewent, or Marlwent, called erroneoufly by Camden, in his *Britannia*, Nicholas Marwent, chamberlain of the abbey, had the temporalties reftored to him July 14, 8° H. 5. He made the weft front, and erected the ftately porch and two pillars, one on each fide of the body of the church at the weft end; intending, if he had lived, to have made the whole body of like work. [t] Auguft 2, 7° H. 6. [u] a compofition was made between the abbey and the town, whereby the lane under the fouth wall of the abbey was granted to the bailiffs and burgeffes. Their ferjeants were impowered to carry their maces before the bailiffs in the abbey; and the bailiffs or their ferjeants might execute any of the king's writs, fummonfes, &c. within the abbey, except upon the abbat, monks, their domeftick fervants, or counfellors. March 2, 9° H. 6. [w] the king, before he travelled beyond the feas, came to this abbey, and made an oblation. May 10, 1437 [x], this abbat occurs as prolocutor for the religious, and exhibited for them a fchedule with certain particulars at the convocation: And dying in 1437, had for his fucceffor

Richard Boulars[y], or Boulers, or Bolers, or Butler, who, November 12, 16° H. 6. had the temporalties reftored to him. In 1440, he was offered the bifhoprick of Landaff, but refufed it. In 1444[z], being appointed by the king to go to Rome, and other places, where his attendance might be required for a confiderable time, the prior and convent granted him 400 *l. per ann.* out of the profits of the abbey, during his abfence. July 20, 25° H. 6, 1447[a], there was another compofition made between the abbey and the bailiffs of the town, by which *int. al.* the bailiffs and burgeffes were to have free common, and dig earth, in the Common Ham; and to have the ufe of the water of Fulbrook, at the upper north-gate; of the lane under the fouth wall of the abbey, and of the two water-mills at the weft-gate: And the abbey to enjoy the ftone wall within fifteen foot of land in breadth within it, from St. John's Church-yard to the blind-gate. After Michaelmas[b], 1450, Richard duke of York, then at variance with king Henry the Sixth, took this abbat, and fent him prifoner to the caftle of Ludlow; but the fame year[c] he was advanced to the fee of Hereford, which he held 'till his removal to Litchfield. The motto which he ufed when abbat, was, MEMENTO, MEMENTO; by fome thought prophetical, and interpreted, *Remember, remember, this abbey muft be diffolved*; but fays Dr. Fuller[d], I like the text better than the comment, and there is more humility in the motto than folidity in the interpretation. Bowlers[e], when bifhop of Litchfield, by his laft will, dated March 23, 1458, and proved on the 10th of April following, gave his books to the library of this abbey.

Thomas Sebroke[f], or Seabroke, being elected, after Boulars was advanced to the fee of Hereford, had the temporalties reftored to him February 16, 29° H. 6. 1450. He pulled down the old tower, and began the building of that ftately one in the

[k] Collect. Wharton. Willis's Mit. Abb. [l] MS. Frouc.
[m] Collect. Wharton. Willis's Mit. Abb. MS. Chron.
[n] MS. Chron. [o] Willis's Mit. Abb. Leland's Itin. In fome MS. Collections now in my cuftody, 'tis faid, abbat Frowcefter began the building of a neat cloifter, whofe cieling and ornamental workmanfhip are nowhere furpaffed. All the windows along the fouth cloifter are contrived for writing places for the ufe of the monaftery, and at the weft end of the north cloifter there are many neat wafhing places near the refectory, for the convenience of the monks before and after their repaft.
[p] MS. Malv. 2. [q] Orig. Paper. Scac. Cap.

[r] Collect. Wharton. Willis's Mit. Abb.
[s] Ib. MS. Chron.
[t] See Account of the Cathedral Church.
[u] An Antient Copy in the cuftody of the abbey.
[w] Scac. Cap. [x] Synod. Anglic. p. 65.
[y] Collect Wharton. Willis's Mit. Abb. [z] Scac. Cap.
[a] An Old Book in the cuftody of the city.
[b] Speed's Chron. in the year. [c] Willis's Mit. Abb.
[d] Ch. Hift. l. 6. p. 334.
[e] Willis's Survey of Litchfield, p. 390.
[f] Collect. Wharton. Willis's Mit. Abb. p. 117.

middle of the church; but he died before it was finifhed, having firft committed the care of it to Robert Tully, a monk of this abbey, who was afterwards bifhop of St. David's, as appears by the infcription yet remaining at the bottom of the choir, over the arch of the tower;

Hoc quod digeftum fpecularis opufque politum,
Tullij hæc ex onere Seabroke Abbate jubente.

which is thus rendered in the laft edition of Camden's *Britannia* :

This fabric which you fee, exact and neat,
The abbat charged the monk to make compleat.

On the fouth wall under the tower are his arms, viz. *Ermine, a cinquefoil fable.* His motto, FIAT VOLUNTAS DOMINI, fome perfons have interpreted to denote, *If this abbey muft be diffolved, the will of the Lord be done.* But the fame may be faid of this [h] as was of his predeceffor's. His name, motto and arms, which now remain on many bricks beyond the bifhop's throne, fhew that he paved the choir. He died in 1457, and was buried in a chapel at the fouth-weft end of the choir, where his effigy is placed at length, in white alabafter, in his *pontificalibus*. In or about abbat Seabroke's time, John Twynning, a monk of this abbey, built from the foundation the great inn, called the New Inn, in the upper north-gate ftreet, to the great profit and advantage of the abbey. This inn, according to tradition, was intended for the reception of pilgrims.

Richard Hanley [i], or Hauley, or Haulaces, received the temporalties March 11, 36° H. 6. He [k] began the rebuilding of our Lady's chapel at the eaft end of the church, and died in 1472.

William Ferley [l], or Farley, a monk of the abbey, was confirmed April 22, 1472, received the benediction April 23, and had the temporalties reftored to him the 1ft of May following. He finifhed the rebuilding of the chapel, which his predeceffor had begun; and 18° Edw. 4. [m] with the abbats of Malmefbury and Winchcombe, as deputies of the king, received the fealty of Thomas Compton, abbat of Cirencefter.

John Malverne [n], or Mulverne, had the temporalties reftored to him December 17, 14° H. 7. and died about Auguft [o] 13, 15° H. 7. In the time of the vacancy [p] after his death, the monks were at fuch variance, and committed fuch enormities, in making intereft for the abbacy, that the king, with his privy council, directed a mandate to the prior, as prefident of the abbey, commanding him to punifh all the offenders, and to keep the abbey in due order during the vacancy. The election to be examined according to law by the king's council. At length

Thomas Branche [q], or Braunche, a monk of the abbey, was elected Auguft 31, 1500; confirmed by Dr. Wodyngton [r], vicar-general of the bifhop of Worcefter; received the benediction September 15, and had the temporalties reftored to him October 19, following. He died July 1, 1510. After his death [s], as after his predeceffors, a like mandate was fent to the prior for the government of the monks, who, on the vacancy, had committed many diforders. July 9, the abbey obtained a *congé d' elire*, and thereupon

John Newton [t], alias Browne, D.D. the king's chaplain, (who, about the year 1478, took upon him the order of St. Benedict in this abbey, and was at the time of his election prior of St. Cuthlack's near Hereford) was elected on the 30th of July, 1510, confirmed the 22d of November, had the temporalties reftored to him on the 28th, and was inftalled December 6, following, notwithftanding the violent oppofition made againft his election, when there were forty-eight monks in the abbey and fixteen in the cell, by John Huntley, the cellarer, with fixteen monks of his fide, and their appeal againft it to the bifhop of Worcefter. In the year [u] 1512 and 1513, 5° H. 8. there were fuch great divifions and animofities between the town and abbey, on account of common, which was faid to be witholden from the town by the abbey and its tenants, that the townfmen, to near the number of two hundred, affembled themfelves, and wounded fome of the fervants of the abbey; therefore a letter was fent from the king's privy council on the behalf of the abbey, commanding the mayor, under the penalty of appearing at the ftar-chamber, of paying 100*l*. and of forfeiting the liberties of the town, to fupprefs thefe difturbers, and keep the town and abbey in quiet, 'till the difpute fhould be determined. October 27, 5° H. 8. [w] an agreement between the town and abbey having been firft made, and the mayor firft having fent a letter of complaint to the abbey, an award was made by the abbat of Winchcombe, the prior of Lanthony, and feveral others concerning the matter; but, it feems, this was infufficient, for in the time of his fucceffor, Feb. 6, 9° H. 8. a compofition was made between the abbey and the town about this affair; and the 20th of March, 10° H. 8. another award was made, relating to the tenants of the abbey at Maifmore. This abbat died January 15, 5° H. 8.

William Malvern [x], alias Parker, B.D. mafter of the work, called at his predeceffor's election [y], *Baccalaureus Opponens*, and alfo *Proponens*, was elected on the 4th of May, 1514; confirmed at Gloucefter on the 1ft of June following, and had the temporalties reftored to him on the 6th of Auguft, 1515. Upon the requeft of the univer-

h Fuller's Ch. Hift. l. 6, p. 334.
i Collect. Wharton. Willis's Mit. Abb.
k Willis's Mit. Abb.
l Collect. Wharton. Willis's Mit. Abb.
m MS. n Collect. Wharton. Willis's Mit. Abb.
o MS. Br. and N. p Ib.

q Collect. Wharton. Willis's Survey, and his Mit. Abb.
r MS. Br. and N. s Ibb.
t Willis's Mit. Abb. MS. Br. and N. Willis's Survey.
u An old book in the cuftody of the city. w Ib.
x Collect. Wharton. Willis's Survey, and Hift. of Mit. Abb.
y MS. N.

fity

fity of Oxford, he took the degree of Doctor in Divinity. In 1524[z], he compiled a compendious hiftory of this abbey, printed in the 2d volume of Robert of Gloucefter's *Chronicle*. In March, 1525, cardinal Wolfey, by his commiffary Dr. Allen, exercifed a legantine vifitation in the abbey, when their yearly revenues, according to common account, amounted to 1022*l.* 15*s.* 1*d. ob.* and the abbey acknowledged themfelves indebted to the cardinal in 40*l.* 17*s.* 6*d. q.* The clergy of the kingdom having incurred a *premunire* for acknowledging and receiving the cardinal's authority from Rome, 22° H. 8. they compounded with the king for a fine of 200,000*l.* of which this abbey paid 500*l.* as its proportion. This abbat adorned the fouth, or king Edward's gate, belonging to the abbey; enlarged the gate (demolifhed fince in the beginning of the year 1722) leading to the buildings which now conftitute the epifcopal palace; repaired, or rebuilt, great part of the palace, then the abbat's houfe; rebuilt, or repaired, the great houfe at Prinknerfh; built the tower at Barnwood, the neat veftry at the north end of the crofs aile; and erected a handfome chapel on the north fide of the choir, juft below the tomb of king Edward the Second, wherein is a ftately tomb erected for this abbat, and an altar monument, with his effigy in white marble, lying at full length on it, in his *pontificalibus*, with a mitre and paftoral ftaff, and his arms, which were, *Sable, a bordure engrailed or, charged with eight pellets, a buck paffant between three pheons of the fecond*; which arms were 'till lately remaining on the gates, &c. abovementioned. Some perfons have expounded this abbat's motto, MERSOS REATU SUSCITA, *Raife up thofe that are drowned in guiltinefs*, as prophetical, in relation to king Henry the Eighth's raifing the abbey into a bifhoprick; but Dr. Fuller gives the fame anfwer to this, as he does to the mottos of his predeceffors Boulars and Sebroke. In his time, [a] Ofberne, the cellarer, made a fquare tower north-weft of the churchyard, part of which is the gate leading to St. Mary de Lode's church; and repaired the old Ram oppofite St. John's church, in the upper north-gate-ftreet, over the door of which are the following lines, cut in wood, ftill remaining:

En ruinofa dom⁹ quōdā quā tūc renovavit
Monachus urban⁹ Ofburne John rite vocatus.

This abbat, Richard Skidmor, and other monks to the number of thirty-four, fubfcribed to the king's fupremacy, and he continued abbat 'till the diffolution, foon after which he died. I have been told that he was a younger brother of the family of the Parkers, of Hasfield, in the county of Gloucefter; and that after the diffolution, he retired to them, and there continued for the remainder of his life.

The whole number of abbats was thirty-two, and not thirty-three, as Sir Robert Atkyns makes them, by reckoning Malvern and Parker as two diftinct perfons, whereas, according to Cl. Wharton, and Anthony Wood, they are only different names for the fame man.

The abbey was furrendered the 2d of January[b], 31° H. 8. by Gabriel Moreton, the prior, and the monks, under the conventual feal, when 'twas valued at 1946*l.* 5*s.* 9*d. per ann.* according to Dugdale, but 1550*l.* 4*s.* 5*d. ob.* according to Speed. In another account [c] is the fame value which Speed mentions, and the clear yearly fum 1430*l.* 4*s.* 3*d.* exclufive of its cells, which are valued diftinctly. Out of thefe revenues the king's commiffioners affigned the following penfions: To * Gabriel Morton[d], the prior, 20*l.* which was alfo confirmed to him by patent, dated on the 10th of February following. To Edward Bennet, late receyvour, 20*l.* Thomas Kingfwood 13*l.* 6*s.* 8*d.* William Morwent, Edmund Wotton, John Wigmore, chamberer, Walter Standley, 10*l.* each. * Thomas Hartland, hofteler, * Humphry Barkeley, Richard Anfelm, kitchener, 8*l.* each. * William Newport, 6*l.* 13*s.* 4*d.* * William Augufteyn, 6*l.* Thomas Lee, profeffed and no prieft, * William Symes, alias Deane, 100 *fol.* each. Thofe before whofe names the afterifm is prefixed, continued unpreferred, and received their penfions in 1553; and at the fame time the following penfions were paid to others who were fometime monks here. To Thomas Saybroke, 13*l.* 6*s* 8*d.* John Terris, alias Clyfford, 10*l.* William Burford, 8*l.* Chriftopher Horton, 6*l.* There remained alfo 32*l.* 19*s.* 4*d.* in fees, and 69*l.* 13*s.* 4*d.* in annuities, charged on the revenues of the late abbey.

The arms of the Abbey were *Gules, two keys in faltire, furmounted by a fword in pale argent.*

Of the monks were, the abbat; the chief prior; the fecond, or fub-prior; the third prior; the cellarer; the fub-cellarer; the almoner, frequently called the almoner of Standifh; the fub-almoner; the præcentor; the facrift; the keeper of the hoftiliary; the chamberlain; the keeper of the infirmary; the keeper of the refectory; the mafter of the churches; the mafter or keeper of St. Mary's chapel; the monk of the vill or town; the kitchener; the mafter of the work; certain monks called *Scholares Oxon*, refiding in Gloucefter college there. All thefe had particular lands, rents, or profits given to, or affigned for, their feveral offices.

Of the monks were alfo, the chaplain of the abbey; the fuccentor; the fub-facrift; the third facrift; the chaplain of the abbat; the fub-chaplain; the batchelor opponent.

Other officers were, the chief fteward; the under fteward; the receiver general; the phyfician;

[z] M. S. Malvern, V. 1 and 2, wherein are contained feveral particulars following relating to him.
[a] Leland's Itin.
[b] Burnet's Hiftory of the Reformation.
[c] Steven's Suppl. to Mon. Anglic. p. 33. Notes ro Tanner's Not. Monaft. p. 137.
[d] Willis's Hift. Mit. Abb. and Addenda thereto.

the

the attorney of the abbey; the chief porter; the under porters; the fteward of Stanley priory; the fteward of Ewenny; the fteward of the facrift; the fteward of the mafter of the work; the fteward of the almoner; the fteward of the chamberlain; the fteward of the manor of Standifh; the clerk of the exchequer, or treafury, or of the cellarer, and regifter of the abbey; the auditor of the accounts of the abbey; the ferjeant at mace in Gloucefter; the mafter of the choirifters, organ, and the grammar-fchool; the plumber; the keeper of the pantry; the attorney for the bufinefs of the abbey in the king's exchequer; the taylor; the fteward of Hinton, Buckland, and Clifford; the keeper of the fealing-axe for marking their trees; the abbat's fecretary; the bailiff of the following places, *viz.* Barton-Regis, Matfon, Kylpeck, Froucefter, Brockthrop, Ampney, Barnwood, Wotton, Laberton, Upton, Eftington, Longford; the barker; the principal or chief fhepherd; feveral other fhepherds; feveral clerks of the abbey and abbot; the bailiff of Dudfton and King's-Barton; the valet of the brewhoufe; the boy, or helper of the brewhoufe; the valet of the vineyard at Over; the auditor of the accounts of the farmers of the lands belonging to the cellarer; the ferjeant, or valet, of the refectory; the valet of the horfes; the bailiff of Stanley St. Leonard's, Ruddle, Rudge, or Farley; the valet of the hoftiliar; the keeper, or woodward of Buckholt wood; the keeper of Bird wood; the bailiff of Standifh; the hayward of Portham, Poolmead, Oxelefowe and archdeacon's mead, or of all the hay meadows near Gloucefter; the woodward of Woolridge; the woodward of Boldonne; the woodward of Standifh; the collector of Wotton, Northlech, Churcham, Froucefter, Newport, Barnwood, Kylpeck, Linkenholt, Maifmore, Ampney, Ullenwike, Buckland, Highneham, Matfon, Brompton, Rudford, Duntfburne, Longford, Barton-Abbats.

Thus we fee how many different offices there were in one of thefe great monafteries, an account of whom and their refpective duties may be feen in *Fuller's Church Hiftory.*

Befide the priory of Ewias, and the priory of Kilpeck, this abbey had four other cells, which were fubordinate to it in feveral refpects, *viz.*

1. The priory of St. Cuthlack[a], or Guthlac, formerly confifting of a provoft and fecular canons, without Bifhopgate-ftreet, in the eaft fuburbs of the city of Hereford. It had a prior, præcentor[b], a fub-prior, and three monks; the ordering, placing, or amoving of whom was at the will of the abbat of St. Peter's. In 1101, this priory, with all the revenues belonging to the collegiate church, was given to the abbey, by Hugh de Lacy. The priory, dedicated to St. Peter, St. Paul, and St. Guthlac, valued, according to Speed and Dugdale, at 121 *l.* 3 *s.* 3 *d. ob.* or as in another account, 169 *l.* 19 *s.* 6 *d. ob.* was granted 34° H. 8. to John ap Rice.

2. The priory of Ewenny[c], or Gwenny, or Wenny, in Glamorganfhire. In 1141, Maurice of London gave lands and poffeffions to the abbey, for the eftablifhment of a priory there. It confifted of a prior and two monks, who were alfo at the difpofal of the abbat. The donations to it were confirmed by William archbifhop of Canterbury, in his metropolitical vifitation, November 3, 1384; and by king Henry the Eighth, May 5, in the 8th year of his reign. The abbey, in confequence of a letter from the king, on the 28th of Feb. 28° H. 8. granted this cell, with its appurtenances, except the advowfons and prefentations to churches, to Edward Carne, L. L. D. for ninety-nine years, at the yearly rent of 20 *l.* 10 *s.* and to maintain three monks there, during the life of Edmund Wotton, the prior; afterwards only two monks, one of whom fhould be prior. It was dedicated to St. Michael, and was valued at its diffolution at 59 *l.* 4 *s. clare,* or according to other accounts, 71 *l.* 6 *s.* 8 *d. ob.* or 78 *l.* 0 *s.* 8 *d.* and granted, 37° H. 8. to Edward Carn.

3. Stanley St. Leonard's[d], in the county of Gloucefter, a fmall monaftery of prior and canons, founded in the church of St. Leonard, by Roger de Berkeley, who, with the confent of Sabrith, or Sabrath, the prior, gave it to the abbey in 1146, as their cell for benedictines, wherein was a prior and two monks. king Henry the Eighth[e], in a letter to the abbey, dated on the 10th of June, in the 30th year of his reign, obferving that the number of monks in the abbey was diminifhed, defired that fuch as were in this cell might be recalled, and that the abbey would grant a leafe of the cell, for ninety-nine years, to Sir William Kingfton, knight; which was accordingly done[f] the 18th of July, at the yearly rent of 36 *l.* 13 *s.* 4 *d.* with fome few refervations. 'Twas dedicated to St. Leonard; and at its diffolution[g] was valued at 126 *l.* 0 *s.* 8 *d.* but clear of all deductions at 106 *l.* 17 *s.* The fcite, as parcel of Gloucefter abbey, was granted to Sir Anthony Kingfton.

4. Bromfield[h], in Shropfhire. In 1155, the canons hereof gave it to this abbey by the hands of Gilbert bifhop of Hereford; which donation was confirmed by Theobald, archbifhop of Canterbury. There was formerly a little college of prebendaries, or fecular canons, in the church of St. Mary, who were turned into Black, or Benedictine monks. It confifted of a prior and two monks. 'Twas valued at its diffolution at 78 *l.* 19 *s.* 4 *d.* but clear of deductions at 77 *l.* 18 *s.* 3 *d.* or as 'tis in[i] another account, but 67 *l.* 18 *s.* 3 *d.* It was granted to Charles Cox, 4° & 5° Ph. & M.

[a] Mon. Anglic. MS. Brown and Newton. MS. Malv. 2. Tanner's Not. Mon. p. 174. [b] MS. in the A. office.

[c] Mon. Ang. MS. Brown and Newton. MS. Malv. 1 and 2. Tanner's Not. Monaft. p. 713.

[d] Mon. Anglic. [e] MS. Malv. 2d. [f] Ib.

[g] Stevens's Supplement. Tanner's Not. Monaft.

[h] Mon. Anglic. Tanner's Not. Mon.

[i] MS. in the Augmentation Office.

The

The abbats of this place had alfo eight fumptuous houfes, *viz.*

1. The Vineyard[k], near the town, at the end of the weft caufey. 'Twas a large houfe, built by abbat Staunton, and moated round. It ftood pleafantly fituated on a rifing ground, beyond Over's bridge, near the banks of the Severn, in the parifh of St. Mary de Lode. The vineyard and park were given to the bifhoprick of Gloucefter at it's foundation, and again confirmed 6° E. 6. The bifhops of this fee frequently refided there before the great rebellion, when 'twas demolifhed. It was very much plundered in the Chriftmas holidays, 1641, by lord Stamford, as were all the neighbouring places thereabout, and all the writings taken thence.

2. Hartpury[l], four miles north-weft. This manor belonged to the monaftery 'till its diffolution, and was given to it by Offa, king of Mercia, in the time of Eva the abbefs. Walter Compton, efq;[m] died on the 26th of July, 7° Eliz. feized of the manor or demean of Hartpury, and of and in the capital meffuage there, called the abbat's place, and fifty yard lands belonging to the manor; all which he obtained from William Harbert, knight of the garter, by his deed, dated on the 20th of February, 4° E. 6.

3. Prinknerfh[n], called alfo Prinkeneffe, or Prinknafh, or Prynkenafsh, three miles eaft of Gloucefter. The abbey had a park here, and free warren in all their demean lands in this place, granted by king Edward the Third, on the 3d of December, *regni* 28° and confirmed by king Richard the Second, the 20th of November, *regni primo*. 'Tis reputed extraparochial, and adjoins to the parifh of Upton St. Leonard's. The manor, which belonged to St. Peter's abbey at its diffolution, was granted to Edward Bridges and Dorothy Praye, 36° H. 8. and the reverfion of the houfe and park, to Sir William Sandys and Thomas Spencer, 3° Jac. 1. It was foon after purchafed by Sir John Bridgman, chief Juftice of Chefter, and was fold out of that family, 1770.

4. Newnham[o], twelve miles fouth-weft. In this parifh[p] is a hamlet called Ruddle, where the abbey had a manor, lands, tythes, meffuages, a water-mill, a fifhery, and a paffage over Severn 'till its diffolution. Ralph Bluet[q], foon after the conqueft, gave Rodele to it. King William the Second,[r] at the petition of abbat Serlo, and of fome of his nobles, confirmed this gift in 1096; and 'twas confirmed again by king Henry the Firft, and others after him. That king expreffly gave and confirmed to it the manor of Rudele, to find lights to burn continually before the high altar of St. Peter's, for the foul of duke Robert Curthofe, his brother; and a fifhery in Severn as far as their lands go; a grove or wood there, called Sudrug, to do as they pleafe with it; and to the facrift, common for all his cattle thro' the whole foreft of Dean. Henry the Third, by his charter, dated at Newnham, confirmed this fifhery to the abbey as fully as Henry the Firft gave it.

5. Berkeley[s], about fifteen miles fouth-weft.

6. Thornbury[t], about twenty miles fouth-weft.

7. The Manor Place at Froucefter[u], where the abbey then had a lordfhip of 100 marks a year, and where was once a college of prebendaries: And

8. Bromfield Manor Place[w], near Ludlow, in Shropfhire.

In a leafe of the abbat's lands at Hyneham, is the following refervation: 'And upon reafonable fummons[x] by the abbat made to the leffee, when the plague fhall be at Gloucefter or Over, the abbat referves a convenient part of the manfion-houfe at Hyneham, for the refidence of himfelf and his men, during the continuance thereof, March 12, 7° H. 8.'

At Standifh[y], five miles fouth of this city, was a building called the Almery, erected for the ufe of the abbey, which continued poffeffed of it 'till the diffolution. This place gave denomination to the chief almoner of the abbey, who was generally called the almoner of Standifh. Beornulph[z], king of the Mercians, in 821, gave this manor to the monaftery, which archbifhop Aldred, to whom it was mortgaged, took away, and the archbifhops of York claimed it, as belonging to that fee; but archbifhop Thomas, in 1095, about thirty-nine years after it was taken away, in the monks chapter-houfe, in the prefence of abbat Serlo and many others, reftored it to the abbey, much blaming himfelf for having detained it fo long. And king William the Second[a], at the petition of abbat Serlo, and fome of his great men, confirmed it by charter to the abbey in 1096. However there were frequent difputes about this affair 'till it was finally concluded by abbat Hameline, who ended it in the manner already mentioned.

After it was in the entire poffeffion of the abbey, it foon became applied to charitable purpofes, at the admonition of Mauger, bifhop of Worcefter. Thomas Carbonel, the abbat, reftored to the ufe of the poor all this manor, with its appurtenances, except to the cellarer, the antient rent paid at the anniverfaries of the abbats, and a few other things; and to the abbat two marks yearly at Chriftmas, and two marks yearly at Eafter, for the abbat's private alms. The manor to be converted by no perfon to any other ufe, unlefs in great neceffity, and by common counfel of the whole convent. This agreement was made in the chapter, on St. Mary Magdalen's day, 1202. Witneffes were Mauger the faid bifhop, the abbat

[k] Leland's Itin. Willis Mit. Abb. 112. Old papers in the cuftody of the city.

[l] Leland's Itin. Willis's Mit. Abbies.

[m] An old book in folio, of Efcheator's accounts now in the Bodleian library, Oxon.

[n] Leland's Itin. Willis's Mitr. Abb.

[o] Leland's Itin. [p] MS. Malv. 1 and 2.

[q] Mon. Anglic. [r] Ib. and MS. Frouc.

[s] Leland's Itin. and Willis's Mit. Abb. [t] Ib. [u] Ib.

[w] Ib. [x] MS. Malv. 1. [y] Sir R. Atkyns. MS. Malv. 1 and 2.

[z] Mon. Anglic. [a] MS. Frouc. 1.

of Winchcombe, William de Werdon, archdeacon of Glouceſter, and others. A decree [b] was made by the biſhop of Worceſter, 1346, that the almoner of the abbey, out of this manor, ſhould pay for the poor a certain proportion weekly for bread, and ninety yards of woollen cloth yearly, at Chriſtmas, for thirty poor people. And if it appears at the biſhop of Worceſter's viſitation, that the almoner has been negligent in delivering, or the ſub-almoner in diſpoſing thereof, the abbey ſhall forfeit 5 *lib.* A writ was directed to John de Hampton, the king's eſcheator, in the counties of Glouceſter, Worceſter, Hereford, &c. 17° Edw. commanding him to reſtore again to the abbey the manor of Standiſh, notwithſtanding it was ſeized into the king's hands, becauſe the abbey had appropriated it to a certain charitable uſe without the king's leave.

In the year 1516 [c], abbat Malvern, alias Parker, agreed with the members of his monaſtery, That whereas the manor of Standiſh, being of the value of 16 *l.* *per ann.* at leaſt, with other ſmall alms, *viz.* thirteen frize coats to thirteen poor people, to be provided by the town monk; 2 *ſol.* which the abbey cellarer did yearly diſtribute to each of them; and a meſs called the abbat's diſh, worth 8 *d.* every week, uſed heretofore to be paid at the manor of Standiſh in money, and ſince that in bread; and afterwards the ſame was diſtributed within the abbey in corn, which occaſioned great inconveniences, therefore there ſhould be thenceforth eſtabliſhed a fraternity of thirteen men, called Peter's men, to be appointed by the abbat, in honour of the Holy Croſs, one of which ſhould be prior, and wear a black mantle, for diſtinction. The town monk ſhould provide for them yearly thirteen black cloth gowns, which ſhould be made cloſe before, and with cloſe ſleeves, and a mantle, allowing three yards of cloth for each gown and hood, the cloth being not under 20 *den.* per yard, beſide what is for the mantle. And each of them ſhould have 8 *den.* a week, and the prior 9 *den.* They ſhould wear continually a large hood, a great pair of beads, the arms of the monaſtery embroidered on their right ſhoulders, and a croſs of red and blue on their breaſts; all to be provided by the town monk. They ſhould diligently attend divine ſervice, and perform the duties required of them devoutly and decently. The ſub-prior of the abbey ſhould have the overſight and government of them: and towards the charge of all this, the cellarer ſhould pay 6 *l.* 13 *s.* 4 *d.* *per ann.* for their bread, beer and money, to the almoner; and the almoner ſhould pay all other charges out of the manor of Standiſh. And all thoſe ſums ſhould be paid to the ſub-almoner, or pay-maſter, a month before hand.

The abbat was ſummoned [d] to ſeveral parliaments, or great councils, in the reigns of king Henry the Third, Edward the Firſt, Edward the Second, and Edward the Third. And [e] was appointed in this laſt king's reign to be one of the perſons who ſhall conſtantly attend at thoſe aſſemblies.

This was one of the twenty-ſeven mitred abbies which were in this kingdom. It was under the viſitation of the biſhop of Worceſter, until the time of its diſſolution, by the pope's grant, upon an unjuſt accuſation of abbat Boyfield, and his convent. The laſt [f] viſitation that occurs, was made in the chapter-houſe here, by Hugh Latimer, biſhop of Worceſter, the 28th of January, 1537.

The abbat [g] uſed to be ſummoned to the provincial chapters. He held ſome of his poſſeſſions by barony, and therefore attended at parliament as a peer of the realm.

This abbey, and ſome of their tenants enjoyed ſeveral particular privileges, beſides thoſe before-mentioned, among which were, 1. The tythe of all the hunting (*totius venationis*) in the foreſt of Dean, by the grants of king Henry the Firſt, and Henry the Second.—2. The having of all ſturgeons taken in their waters, by the grants of king William the Firſt, and Henry the Firſt.—3. That no perſon ſhall fiſh in their fiſheries, nor take any game in any of their manors without their leave, by the grants of king Henry the Firſt, king Steph. and king Henry the Second.—4. That whatſoever, or whereſoever, any thing neceſſary ſhould be bought, the monks might paſs free from toll, by the grants of the kings Henry the Firſt and Second.—5. The abbat had a power of making five publick notaries, and inveſting them in their office by a pen, pen or quill-caſe, and paper.—6. The free

[b] MS. Frouc. 1.

[c] MS. Malv. 1.

[d] Particularly 49 H. 3. 3, 9, 12, 17, 18, 23, 25, 27, 30, 32, 34 Edw. 1. 2 to 7, 8, 9, 11, 12, 13, 14, 15, 16 to 20 Edw. 2. 1, 2, 3, 4, 5, 6, 7, 8, 9, 10, 11, 12, 13, 14, 15, 16, 18 to 21, 22, 23 to 29, 31, 32, 33, 34, 36 to 39, 40, 41, 42 to 44, 46, 47, 49, 50 Edw. 3. Theſe ſummons are alſo added to Mr. Stevens's Additions to Mon. Anglic. &c. 1 to 7, 8 to 11, 12 to 18, 20, 21, 23 Rich. 2. 1 to 3, 4, 5, 7, 8, 11, 12, 14 Hen. 4. 1 to 7, 8, 9 Hen. 5. 1 to 5, 7, 9 to 11, 13, 15, 18, 20, 23, 25, 27 to 29, 31, 33, 38 Hen. 6. 1, 2, 6, 12, 22, 23 Edw. 4. 19 Hen. 7. 1, 3, 6, 14, 23, 28 Hen. 8.

[e] Fuller ſaith, that 49 Hen. 3. ſixty-four abbats and thirty-ſix priors were called to parliament; but this number being too great, king Edward the Third reduced it to twenty-five abbats and two priors, to whom were afterwards added two abbats, ſo that there were twenty-nine in all, and no more, that ſtatedly and conſtantly enjoyed this privilege, *viz.* The abbat of Tewkeſbury, the prior of Coventry, the abbats of Waltham, Cirenceſter, St. John's at Colcheſter, Croiland, Shrewſbury, Selby, Bardney, St. Bennets of Hulme, Thorney, Hide, Winchelcomb, Battle, Reading, St. Mary's in York, Ramſey, Peterburg, St. Peter's in Glouceſter, Glaſtonbury, St. Edmund's-bury, St. Auſtin's in Canterbury, St. Albans, Weſtminſter, Abingdon, Eveſham, Malmeſbury, and Taviſtock, and the prior of St. John's of Jeruſalem, who was ſtiled *Primus Angilæ baro*, but it was with reſpect to the lay barons only, for he was the laſt of the ſpiritual ones. I have here ſet down the firſt twenty-four of theſe in the order they went to parliament 3 H. 8. Mr. Hearne thinks that they took place in the houſe of lords according to the ſeniority of their creation; but John Anſtis, eſq; Garter king of arms, is of opinion that ſome of the abbats, like the biſhops, had by virtue of their abbies a certain fixed precedency, and that others of them took place according to the priority of their creation. Many have aſſigned the firſt place to the abbat of St. Albans, becauſe Saint Alban was the firſt martyr in this kingdom. *Tanner's Not. Mon. fol. preface.*

[f] MS. Reg. Malvern.

[g] Stevens's Add. p. 178.

cuftoms, liberties, and quietances, which the abbey freely, honourably, in peace, fully and clearly enjoyed, were granted or confirmed to them by the kings Henry the Firft, Stephen, and Henry the Second.—7. All their lands and poffeffions were quit of carriage, tallage, fummage, paffage, pontage, conduct, and king's works; with foca, or focne, and faca, and toll, and theam, and infangetheof, and all the free cuftoms thereof, as formerly granted, by the kings Henry the Firft, Stephen, and Henry the Second.—All the goods and chattles *(pecunia)* were quit of all toll and cuftom by the grants of the kings Stephen, and Henry the Second.

Upon every new election of an abbat, the abbey was obliged to maintain one of the king's clerks whom he thought fit to name; and accordingly corrodies for their lives were granted to them. In the reigns of king Henry the Seventh, and king Henry the Eighth, the value of thofe corrodies or grants was 5 *l.* a year.

When the abbat was confirmed, and received his benediction, he generally made the facrift of the priory of Worcefter fome valuable prefent, ufually of coftly robes, or veftments, or of materials to make them. In the annals of Worcefter, in *Anglia Sacra*, 'tis faid, that in the year 1241, the facrift of Worcefter received the *Alb* and *Cap*, as well for Walter, which was not inftalled, as for John, which was.

Tho' the chief of the lands and poffeffions of this abbey were in the town and county of Gloucefter, yet there were feveral belonging to it in Buckinghamfhire, the city of London, Devonfhire, Glamorganfhire, Hampfhire, Herefordfhire, Middlefex, Oxfordfhire, Shropfhire, Warwickfhire, Wiltfhire, and Worcefterfhire.

'Tis faid in the notes to bifhop Tanner's *Not. Monaft.* preface, p. 15, That all the parliamentary abbats and priors had houfes in Weftminfter, London, or Southwark, to live in, whilft the parliament fat: And 'tis probable, that the abbat of this place then inhabited a houfe near Saint Martyn's Vintry, London; for Radulph Peverell gave to this abbey the church there, and all the lands which belonged to the prieft. King William the Second confirmed this grant in the time of abbat Serlo, and 'twas alfo confirmed by king Henry the Firft.

In the reign of king William the Conqueror, the poffeffions of the church of St. Peter, which lay in Gloucefterfhire, are fet down under the tenth head of the General Survey of that county, as may be feen in the copy of *Domefday*, printed in this book, p. 66.

At that time the church of St. Peter of Gloucefter held the manor of Bertune, with the adjacent members, Berneuude, Tuffelege, and Mereuuent, in Dudeftanes hundred; Froweceftre, in Blacelawes hundred; Boxewelle, in Grimboldeftowes hundred; Culne [Coln Rogers] in Brictwoldefberg hundred; Aldeforde, in Begebriges hundred; Bochelande, in Wideles hundred; Hinetune, in Tetboldeftanes hundred; Hamme [Highnam] and Preftetune, in Tolangebriges hundred; Ledene, in Botelewes hundred; Hamme and Mortune, [fuppofed to be Churcham and Linton] in Weftberies hundred; Omenie, in Gerfdunes hundred; and Duntefborne in Circeftre hundred.

Several particular benefactions to this abbey are publifhed in Sir William Dugdale's *Monafticon*, and have been tranflated by Sir Robert Atkyns, and inferted in his *Ancient and Prefent State of Glofterfhire*; whence, omitting fome redundancies, and making a few neceffary corrections, the following Account of Donations is taken. But there is a roll of Benefactions among the records of the dean and chapter of Gloucefter, placed in chronological order, down to the year 1263, in which many of the following particulars are omitted.

Donations to the Monaftery of St. Peter at Gloucefter.

Alre.

Ethelbald, king of the Mercians, gave to God and St. Peter of Gloucefter, and to the nuns there, twenty hides of land in a village called Alre.

Afpertone.

Robert Curtoife gave to God and St. Peter, and to the monks of that place, one hide of land in Herefordfhire, called Afpertone, in the tenth year of the reign of king William Rufus, in the twenty-fifth year of the prefidency of abbat Serlo.

Alweftone.

Walter the fheriff, gave to God and St. Peter at Gloucefter, and to the monks of that place, the church of St. Helene of Alweftone, with one yard land in the fame parifh, in the feventh year of king Henry the Firft, the abbey being at that time vacant by the death of Serlo.

Ablode and Paygrave.

King Henry the Firft gave to God and St. Peter at Gloucefter, and to the monks of the fame place, Ablode and the grove of Barton called Paygrave, in exchange for the place where now the tower of Gloucefter ftandeth, where was heretofore an orchard belonging to the monks. The fame king Henry, in the ninth year of his reign, when Peter was abbat, gave fix ridges of land behind Ablodes court. Alfo Radulph de Wylinton, and Olympias his wife, gave fix ridges of land behind Ablodes court, when Thomas Bredone was abbat, in the twelfth year of the reign of king Henry the Second, after the conqueft.

Amney.

In the year 1126. I Winebald of Balon, one of the greater barons of king Henry the Firft, after the conqueft, and Roger my fon, have granted to St. Peter of Gloucefter half an hide in Amney, which Thomas, an Englifhman, did hold, quit and difcharged from every thing which belongs to to the king, except the king's danegelt. And we likewife, I and my fon Roger, have granted the faid land to God and St. Peter, and to the brothers of Gloucefter, free and difcharged from any thing relating to us, except the king's danegelt. And I Winebald am a witnefs that this was done before the monks of Tewkefbury had the manor of Aurenell.

Bache.

Bernard of Newmarket gave to God and to St. Peter of Gloucefter, one hide of land called the Bache, lying in the parifh of Coverne. This was given in the time when Serlo was abbat.

Barton Abbats.

Aldred governor of Gloucefterfhire, gave to God and St. Peter of Gloucefter, and to the nuns there, an hundred hides of land, which are now called Barton Abbats. This was done when Eva was abbefs.

Berton [King's.]

In the nineteenth year of king Edward the Third after the conqueft, this king gave and granted to the monks of Gloucefter, the manor of King's Berton, with the fifhery in the ftanding pools within Minfterworth, and half the fifhery in Duny, at a rent in fee-farm, in exchange for the church of Wyrardfbury, in the time of Adam of Staunton being abbat.

Bernewood.

William the Conqueror king of England, gave to the monks of Gloucefter the manor of Bernewood, with all its appurtenances, in the time of Serlo being abbat.

Bery.

William gave Bery: In lieu of which, his brother Gotelin gave to the monks Selden in Devonfhire, whilft Serlo was abbat.

Beverftone.

Anfelme de Gorney gave to God and to St. Peter of Gloucefter, five quarters of acres of land in Beverftone, with the advowfon of the church of that place, in the time of John Gamage being abbat.

Bockholt.

In the year 1121, Helyas Giffard, and Ala his wife, and their fon Elias, granted to the monks of Gloucefter, by deed which they laid upon the altar, their land in Bockholt, the woods and the plains eftimated at half an hide and half a yard land, free from all fervices to the king, and difcharged of all other cuftoms, except danegelt to the king. This was executed whilft William was abbat.

In the year 1096, Helyas Giffard gave to the church of St. Peter of Gloucefter, a parcel of wood-ground with three cottages; which grant was confirmed by king William the Second, in the time of abbat Serlo.

Bokeland.

Kynred, king of the Mercians, gave the manor of Bokeland, when Edburg was abbefs.

Boytone. [Bitton.]

Helias Boy Giffard, for the foul's health of Berta his wife, and his anceftors, gave to the monks of St. Peter of Gloucefter, the church of St. Mary de Boyton, and the church of St. George de Orchefton, with the chapel of St. Andrew of Winterborn, with the lands, tithes, meadows, paftures, ways, paths, and whatfoever appertaineth to the faid churches, faving the tenure of the church of Finctenay. This was given in the time of abbat Hameline.

Walter Giffard, fon of Helias, granted and confirmed the church of Boyton to the monks of Gloucefter, with all its appurtenances, with half an hide of land in the fame vill, and the tithes of the whole vill, with a building for eight oxen, one beaft, and 122 fheep; and all the tithes of the vill, both of the demeane lands and of the tenant lands, and of all things of which good chriftians ought to pay tithes. This was in the time when Hameline was abbat.

Helias Giffard laid claim to the church of Boytone. Abbat Thomas Carbonell, for peace fake, granted him the church of Orthefton, with the chapel of Winterborne referving the church of Barton. The lord Gofeline bifhop of Salifbury, granted and confirmed to the convent of St. Peter of Gloucefter, the gift made by Helias Giffard and Walter his fon. John bifhop of Salifbury confirmed and ordered, by virtue of his epifcopal authority, that the church of Barton fhould pay 40*s.* a year to the monks of Gloucefter to keep hofpitality.

Brankamfeld.

Earl Bodehard, the king's lieutenant, gave to God and to St. Peter of Gloucefter, and to the nuns there, four meffuages in Brankamfeld, in the time when Kyneburg was abbefs.

Brockrup.

Adeliza, the wife of Roger de Ivrie, gave Brockrup, with the church thereof, to the church of St. Peter of Gloucefter, in the time of abbat Serlo.

Roger the firft, and Hugh his heir, gave to the church of St. Peter of Gloucefter, eight acres of land near to Brochthrop court, whilft Hameline was abbat.

Gilbert de Myners confirms the grant of thofe lands which Roger the firft gave to the church of St. Peter of Gloucefter, in Brockthrop, and in La Rugge, when Hameline was abbat.

Brockworth.

In the year 1260, John Deffeld, abbat, purchafed of Lawrence de Chandos, knight, fifty-five acres of arable land in Brockworth, and forty acres of inclofure; and all his wood in Bockholt, which contained 300 acres.

Bromfeld.

Bromfeld.

In the year 1155, the canons of Bromfeld gave their church and themfelves to St. Peter of Gloucefter, by the hand of Gilbert bifhop of Hereford, and became monks there. This gift was confirmed by Theobald archbifhop of York, in the time when Hameline was abbat.

Bromptone.

William the Conqueror gave to the church of St. Peter of Gloucefter, the manor of Bromptone, with a fifhery in Wye, and the land lying by the bank of Wye, whilft Serlo was abbat.

Burneham.

Robert confirmed the gift of his father Harald, and moreover gave the church of Burneham to the priory of Ewias, that a convent might be fettled there, which was agreed to, but never performed. He farther gave unto them the tithes of all his manors, of all things of which chriftians ought to pay tithes. Theobald, the archbifhop, confirmed it; John, bifhop of Salifbury, likewife confirmed it.

Caftle Godric.

William the Marfhal, earl of Pembroke, gave to the monks of Gloucefter, in pure alms, one water-mill, with the toll, cuftom, and grinding of the whole vill of Caftle Godric, except the grinding of the caftle itfelf, with the cuftom of all the vill of Hunfton, and with all the appurtenances belonging to the faid mill. This was given when Henry Folet was abbat.

Cerney.

Walter, the fheriff of Gloucefter, gave to the monks of St. Peter of Gloucefter, the church of Cerney, with the tithes thereof, which was confirmed by king Henry when Peter was abbat.

Celefworth.

William the Second, king of England, gave to the church of St. Peter of Gloucefter, two brekes of wood within his fee of Celefworth, with a grove, and fome fmall meads adjoining to them, in free alms. Witnefs William the chancellor, at Newnham, in the time of abbat Serlo.

King Henry his brother confirms to the monks Odo and Hugh, and to the whole convent of Gloucefter, two new plowed grounds, and the wood which grows in the midft of them, with the adjoining little meads, lying in his manor of Celefworth, in free alms, in fee, and as free and quit from all charges, as his brother William had given the fame.

Chefterton.

Roger de Oiley, fon of Nigel de Oiley, gave the tithes of Ceftretone to the monks of St. Peter of Gloucefter, when Serlo was abbat.

Churcham and Highnam.

A certain nobleman, by name Wulfin le Rue, at the time when the monks firft inhabited Gloucefter, unhappily killed fix prefbyters between Churcham and Gloucefter, who being confounded at that horrid crime, went to the pope to beg abfolution; his repentance was accepted, and he was abfolved, upon condition to maintain fix priefts, who fhould fing prayers for him. He returned home chearfully, and gave Chircham and Hynham, with the meadows, plains, woods and paftures extending to the river Severn, unto the church of St. Peter, upon this condition, that feven monks, inftead of feven priefts, fhould be for ever maintained, to pray to God on his behalf. This was when Edric was abbat.

King Edward the Third, after the conqueft, granted licence to the monks of Gloucefter to make a park in Churcham and Uppledene, in the time of John Wigmore abbat.

Clifford.

In the year 1099, Roger de Bulley, knight, gave Clifford to the church of St. Peter of Gloucefter, which was confirmed by king William, when Serlo was abbat.

Coberly.

The manor of Cuburley was given to the church of St. Peter of Gloucefter, when Edith was abbefs.

Coln Alwyns.

In the year 1217, Silvefter, bifhop of Worcefter, gave to the monks of St. Peter of Gloucefter, the church of Culne St. Ælwin to their own ufe, for the increafe of hofpitality, when Henry Blond was abbat. Athelred, governor of Gloucefterfhire, gave his lands to the fame church, that is, he gave fixty meffuages of his land lying in Culne St. Ælwins.

Colne Rogers.

In the year 1105, Roger of Gloucefter, knight, was grievoufly wounded at Waleyfon, and gave Colne on the hills to the monks of Gloucefter, for the good of his foul. It was called Culne Rogers, and the grant was confirmed by king Henry, when the abbey was vacant by the death of abbat Serlo.

Combe.

Bernard de Bafkervile, when he took upon him the habit of a monk, gave himfelf, and one hide of land in Cumbe, to the church of St. Peter at Gloucefter; Walter and Robert de Bafkervile confirmed the fame in the time of abbat Hameline.

Cranham.

Helias Giffard, fon of Helias the elder, and Ala his wife, when he became monk, gave Cranham to St. Peter, and to the monks of Gloucefter ferving God, in the time when Hameline was abbat.

Dene.

In the year 1080, Walter de Lacy gave to St. Peter of Gloucefter his lands in Dene; to which king William the Firft gave his confent, and confirmed the fame. It was done at Berkeley, firft making an offering to the Lord and to St. Peter. Walter, his fon, was then an infant, and Serlo was abbat.

Roger de Staunton gave to God and St. Peter of Gloucefter, the water-courfe of Dene and of Clinch, to be brought to the mill pond, in the

 feventh

feventh year of king Richard, and in the time when Thomas Breedone was abbat.

King Henry gave and confirmed to the monks of St. Peter of Gloucefter the tithe of all venifon which fhould be taken in the foreft of Gloucefterfhire. King Stephen confirmed it in the time of abbat Peter.

Duni.

Roger, earl of Hereford, gave half of the fifhery of Duny to God and the church of St. Peter of Gloucefter. King Henry the Second confirmed the grant, in the time when Hameline was abbat.

Roger de Staunton gave to the church of St. Peter of Gloucefter one yard-land called Duni, and a hufbandman with his land. Cecilia Talbot confirmed this with her own grant, in the time of abbat Hameline.

Duntefborn.

In the year 1100, Gilbert de Efkecot, with his wife, and fon Robert, gave to the church of St. Peter of Gloucefter, his lands which he had in Duntefborn, for the good of the foul of Walter de Lacy, and of his own foul, when Serlo was abbat.

In the year 1085, Walter, the founder of St. Peter of Hereford, dying on the 27th day of March, his body was honourably interred in the chapter-houfe of Gloucefter. His wife Ermeline then gave to the church the village of Duntefburn, confifting of five hides, for the redemption of the foul of her hufband: Serlo was then abbat.

Edmundefton.

In the year 1095, Odo, the fon of Gamaliel, gave to St. Peter of Gloucefter Plinctru in Devonfhire, for which Nicholas de la Parle gave Elmundefton in Warwickfhire. King William the Second confirmed it in the time of abbat Serlo.

Eftlech.

Eftlech [Martin] was given to the abbey of St. Peter by Walter de Cliffort, in exchange for the manor of Glafbury.

Ewenny.

In the year 1141, Maurice of London, the fon of William of London, gave to the church of St. Peter of Gloucefter, the church of St. Michael of Ewenny, and the church of St. Bridgid, with the chapel of Ugmore of Lanfey, and the church of St. Michael of Colvefton, with the lands, meadows, and all other things belonging to the fame, free and quit, in pure alms, on condition that there fhall be a convent of monks in that place. He moreover gave the church of Oftrenewe in Goer, and the church of Penbray, and the church of St. Ifmael, with the lands and tithes belonging to the fame; which was confirmed by Theobald archbifhop of Canterbury, when Gilbert was abbat.

Ewias.

In the year 1100, Herald, lord of Ewias, gave to the church of St. Peter of Gloucefter the church of St. Michael, with the chapel of St. Nicholas of the caftle, and the chapel of St. James of Ewias, and the chapel of St. Kaene, with the chapel of Caneros, in pure and perpetual alms, on condition that there fhall be always a convent at Ewias ferving God. He further granted the tithes of all corn, of venifon and honey, and of all things whereof good chriftians ought to pay tithes. He alfo granted the church of Foy, with one plow's tillage, and the tithes of the fifheries in Foy. He gave a water-mill, and the church of Hidred, with all its appurtenances, and the church of Alyngetone, and the church of Burnham. Moreover he gave the tithes of his demeans throughout all his lands, to their own ufe, and the tithes of all his mills, and of Eelles. Theobald, the archbifhop, confirmed this grant, which was in the time when Hameline was abbat.

Robert confirmed the gift of his father Herald, and moreover gave the church of Burnham to the priory of Ewias, that a convent might be fetled in that place; this was agreed, but not performed. He further gave the tithes of all his manors as fully as any chriftians ought to pay them. Theobald, archbifhop of Canterbury, confirmed this grant when Hameline was abbat.

Fairford.

Burgred, king of the Wixes, gave to God and to St Peter of Gloucefter, and to the nuns of that place, two hides of land in Fayreford, when Eva was abbefs.

Forde [in Temple Guiting.]

Robert, conful of Gloucefter, gave to God and to St. Peter of Gloucefter a water-mill in Forde, when William was abbat.

Framelode.

In the year 1126, Winebald of Balon, with the confent of Roger his fon, gave to the church of St. Peter of Gloucefter a water-mill in Framelode, and half an hide of land in Amney, which Thomas, an Englifhman, held free and quit from all charges except danegelt to the king.

Froncefire.

Raban, the Englifhman, Revenfwert, and a famous brother of king Beornulph, gave Fronceftre to God and the church of St. Peter of Gloucefter, in the time when the conons fecular poffeffed the monaftery.

In the year 1225, William de Bloys, bifhop of Worcefter, at the defire of John de Columna, cardinal of the church of Rome, gave to the church of St. Peter of Gloucefter the church of Froncefter, with the chapel of Nimpsfield, provided that a fufficient vicar be there affigned. This was in the time of abbat Breden.

Frythmore.

Walter Giffard gave to God and St. Peter of Gloucefter his fhare which he had in Frythmore. In the time when Thomas Carbonell was abbat, there was a treaty between the monks and the faid Walter Giffard, in which it was agreed, that two parts in three of all the land in Wylingwiche fhould remain to the monaftery, and that the third part,

part, and the advowfon of the church, and the manfion-houfe fhould belong to the faid Walter.

Gare.

Alexander de Cormell gave to the church of St. Peter of Gloucefter one water-mill in Gare, with all its appurtenances. King Henry the Second confirmed it, when Thomas Carbonel was abbat.

Glafebury.

In the year 1088, when Serlo was abbat, Bernard of Newmarket gave to the church of St. Peter of Gloucefter, Glafebury, with all its appurtenances, free and clear, and all the tithes of his demeans which he had in Brekeneyham, *viz.* of all corn, cattle, cheefe, venifon and honey; he alfo gave the church of great Covere, with all the tithes of that parifh, and the lands belonging to that church, and one hide called Bache; king William the Second confented to it, and confirmed it in the fecond year of his reign. This year, by means of the wars between the great men in England, the city of Gloucefter, and the church of St. Peter, were deftroyed.

Abbat Gilbert changed the manor of Glafebury with the lord Walter de Cliffard for the manor of Eftleche, whereby Walter had Glafebury, excepting the advowfon of the church, which was referved to the monks of Gloucefter, and the monks of Gloucefter had Eftleche, with its appurtenances, in the beft manner that the faid Walter ever enjoy'd the fame. This was confirmed by earl Roger, in the year 1144; it was in the fame year confirmed by king Stephen.

Gloucefter.

In the year 1109, Robert de Bafkeville, after his return from Jerufalem, gave to the church of St. Peter of Gloucefter one hide of land, without the walls of the city, where now is the orchard belonging to the monks. King Henry confirmed it when Peter was abbat.

In the year 1125, Adeliza, the fhreifeffe, mother of Walter of Gloucefter, gave to the church of St. Peter of Gloucefter her houfes and rents which fhe had in Gloucefter, to wit, fourteen tenements, as they are mentioned in a grant, made when William was abbat.

Guyting.

In the year 1090, Gunuld de Loges gave to the monks of Gloucefter, for the good of the foul of her hufband Jurie, two hides of land in Guiting; which was confirmed both by king William the Second, and by king Henry, in the time of abbat Serlo.

Hampton.

William Revel gave to the church of St. Peter of Gloucefter one hide of land in Hamptone, with the confent of Bernard of Newmarket. King Henry the firft confirmed it when Peter was abbat.

Hugh Talemach, when he took upon him the monks habit at Gloucefter, gave one moiety of the town of Hamptone, with the church thereof. His fon Peter confirmed it: King Henry the Second alfo confirmed it when Hameline was abbat.

Harsfield.

Roger earl of Hereford, when he became monk of Gloucefter, gave to the church 100 ferdingals of land in Herefordfhire; for which his brother Walter, conftable of Hereford, gave fix yard-lands in the time of Hameline, free and difcharged from all earthly fervice: he alfo gave two yard-lands againft Briftol highway, near the park.

Hartpury.

Offa, king of the Mercians, gave the manor of Hardpery to the church of St. Peter of Gloucefter, when Eva was abbefs.

King Henry the Firft gave to the monks of Gloucefter, the new plowed grounds in Hardpyrie, in the twenty-third year of his reign, when William was abbat.

Hereford.

King William the Firft granted and confirmed to the church of St. Peter of Hereford, fo many of the lands which Walter de Lacy had given to that church which he himfelf had built, as related to four plow's tillage, and ten vills with ten villaines, one villaine belonging to Stoke in Herefordfhire, one in Staunton in Shropfhire, one in Stoke in the fame county, one in Webley in Herefordfhire, one in Brick Marisfrome in the fame county; and five villaines and five villages in Gloucefterfhire, one in Guyting, one in Quennington, one in Stratone, one in Wyk in Duntefborn, and one in Ham. Walter de Lacy gave two parts of the tithes of thefe ten vills to the faid church of Hereford. Hugh his fon confirmed this grant; king Henry the Firft alfo confirmed it. Walter de Lacy likewife granted the church of St. Owen in Hereford, to which one tything and an houfe did belong, and gave the whole manfion-houfe. He commanded that all thefe lands fhould be made free for ever from all cuftoms. This was performed when Serlo was abbat.

In the year 1101, Hugh de Lacy gave to the monks of St. Peter of Gloucefter the church of St. Peter of Hereford, which his father had built from the ground, with the prebends, and whatfoever belonged to that church. Serlo was abbat at this time.

Heycot.

Robert de Beckesford gave to the monks of Gloucefter certain tithes in Heycote, in the time of abbat Peter.

Heythrope.

Ernulph de Hefding gave the church of Heythrope, Linkholt, and a water-mill, with the lands belonging to the prieft and the church of Kempfford, with the lands belonging to the prieft; and alfo all other lands, pafture grounds, and privileges which the monks in Gloucefter have in that place. Patrick of Chaworth, and Maud his wife, teftified and confirmed by their deed, all donations made by their children. Pagan, the fon of Patrick, of his own gift, granted that he and his heirs after him, fhall with his own workmen, and at

his

his own charges, mow and make the tithes of his demeans at Kempsford. King Henry the Firft confirmed this, and of his own gift, gave to the monks of Gloucefter four marks yearly out of the church of Kempsford, when Serlo was abbat.

Hide.

Helewife the widow of William de Ebroys, gave to God and the church of St. Peter of Gloucefter a piece of land called Hide, lying in Herefordfhire, which Walter de Lacy gave to her on marriage. King Henry the Firft confirmed the grant, when William was abbat.

Hinton.

In the year 981, Elfred, fifter of king Ethelred, gave Hynetone to the church of St. Peter of Gloucefter, to pray for her foul. She was then barren, and in a low condition; and when five men were required for the king's wars out of this fmall eftate, they could not be had; then did the priefts, who prefided in the church, go to her, and entreat her to fpeak to the king on their behalf, which fhe did on the nativity of our Lord, when the king was at a feaft, fhe fell down on her knees, and obtained that thofe lands fhould for ever after be quit and free from all charges.

In the year 1156, it was adjudged in the county court of Gloucefterfhire, that the manor of Hynetone being, time out of mind, free from all charges, therefore it ought to be free from and quit from fines for murther. This was done when Hameline was abbat.

Hope Maleyfel.

In the year 1102, William de Pomerey gave to the monks at Gloucefter the village called Bery in Devonfhire, for which his brother Gofline gave Seldene, for which we now have Hopemaleyfel, King Henry the Firft agreeing to it, and confirming it, when Serlo was abbat.

Horcot.

Patrick of Chaworth gave to the monks of St. Peter of Gloucefter, a water-mill in Horcote, in the time of abbat William.

Hyneledene.

In the year 1239, Richard de Wigmore gave to the church of St. Peter of Gloucefter his lands in Hyneledene, and one hide, with the groves, paftures, meadows, and all appurtenances which Jeoffry de le Dene did enjoy. This was done when Henry Folet was abbat.

Janefworth.

Earl Robert de Bertone gave twenty fhillings yearly out of his rents in Gloucefterfhire, to the church of St. Peter of Gloucefter, to wit, ten fhillings out of Janefworth, and ten fhillings out of Chedworth; in the time when Walter de Lacy was abbat.

Radulph de Zouch gave Janefworth to the church of St. Peter of Gloucefter, free and quit of all fervices. King Henry confirmed it when Gilbert was abbat: king Stephen alfo confirmed it.

Reginald Thucks gave to the church of St. Peter of Gloucefter, and to the monks ferving God, in pure and perpetual alms, his village of Janeworth, free and quit from all fervices and cuftoms which did any ways belong to him or his heirs, to be enjoyed by them in perpetual right of inheritance. King Stephen confirmed this when Walter de Lacy was abbat.

Kempsford.

Patrick of Chaworth, the fon of Patrick, gave to the church of St. Peter of Gloucefter, in pure alms, one water-mill, called Horcot, in the village of Kynemaresford, with the lands adjoining and belonging to the faid mill, and the tithes of the meadows of the faid village; king Henry the Firft confirming it in the time when William was abbat.

Patrick de Chaworth gave to the monks of Gloucefter three mills in Kynemeresford, which king William the Second confirmed in the time of abbat Serlo.

John bifhop of Worcefter decreed, and of his own free will confirmed unto abbat Breedone, and to the convent of St. Peter of Gloucefter, two fheaves of tithes of the church of Kynemeresforde, with the lands and the other appurtenances which they did hitherto enjoy, to hold for ever to their own proper ufes. The fame bifhop, John, did grant to the monks four marks of filver yearly, iffuing out of four yard-lands in Kynemeresforde, to be received by the vicar.

Keteringham.

Radulph, the fon of Walter, gave to the monks the tithes of Keteringham, and thirty acres of land. William de Curam gave the tithes of his demeans in the fame village, in the time when Serlo was abbat.

Kylpec.

In the year 1134, Hugh, the fon of William Norman, gave to God and to St. Peter, and to the monks of Gloucefter, the church of St. David of Kylpec, with the chapel of the bleffed Mary of the caftle, and all thefe churches and chapels, and the lands which did belong to them, and all tithes of all his lands, of corn, hay, flax, wool, cheefe, colts, calves, lambs, pigs, and of all other things of which chriftians ought to pay tithes. He granted alfo that the pigs of the prior might go intermixt with his, and eat the malt; moreover he granted the joint benefit of his woods for the ufe of the monaftery. This was done when Walter de Lacy was abbat.

Lancarvan.

Robert, the fon of Hamon, gave the church of St. Cadoc of Lancarvan to God and St. Peter of Gloucefter, and gave Penham with fifteen hides of land. King William the Firft confirmed it when Serlo was abbat.

Lech.

In the year 1094, on Palm Sunday, Thomas archbifhop of York reftored to the church of St. Peter of Gloucefter, Lech, Odington, Standifh and

and Barton, much blaming himſelf, and beating his breaſt that he had detained them ſo long. This was done when Serlo was abbat.

Littleton.

In the year 1096, Hugh of the Port was made monk at Wincheſter: he then gave to the church of St. Peter of Glouceſter, Littleton in Hampſhire, which was confirmed by king William the Second. Henry, ſon of Hugh of the Port, confirmed his father's gift: Adam of the Port likewiſe confirmed it in the time of abbat Serlo.

Lynkeholt.

Ernulph de Heſding gave Lynkeholt to God and St. Peter, on the day of the purification of the Virgin Mary, in the year 1081, at Saliſbury. King William the Firſt gave his conſent, and confirmed it in the time when Serlo was abbat.

St. Martin's, in London.

Radulph Peverell gave the church of St. Martin to the church of St. Peter of Glouceſter. Peverell alſo gave all the lands which belonged to the prieſt. King William the Second confirmed it when Serlo was abbat.

Mayſemore.

King Henry the Firſt, in the year 1101, gave to God and St. Peter of Glouceſter, the manor of Mayſemore, with all the woods and plains thereunto belonging, as fully as ever he held the ſame, with all things appertaining to the ſaid land. The king confirmed this when Serlo was abbat.

Newberg.

King William the Second being grievouſly ſick at Glouceſter, gave to God and to the church of St. Peter of Glouceſter the church of St. Gundeley of Newberg, with fifteen hides.

Nimpsfield.

In the year 1093, Euſtace de Berkeley reſtored Nimpsfield to God and St. Peter of Glouceſter, when Serlo was abbat.

King William the Firſt gave lands in Nimdeſfield to the church of St. Peter of Glouceſter, and to abbat Wulſtan, to hold in as full and free manner as ever it had been formerly; and as in the reign of king Edward his kinſman, with the privilege of hearing judicial cauſes in all places, and forbade all invaſions on their rights.

Northlech.

In the year 1220, king Henry, the ſon of king John, granted to the monks of St. Peter of Glouceſter the market of Northlech, with ſuit of court. This was granted on the feſtival of the apoſtles Peter and Paul, when Henry Blont was abbat.

Northwich.

King William the Conqueror gave to the church of St. Peter of Glouceſter the church of St. Peter of Northwich, which ſtands in the market place there. Thomas the archbiſhop confirmed the ſame to their own uſes, and deſired William biſhop of Norwich to confirm it likewiſe. This was done when Serlo was abbat. Walo of St. Peter gave the church of St. Peter, which ſtands in the market place at Norwich, and himſelf, to the church of St. Peter of Glouceſter, in the time of abbat Serlo.

Norton.

In the year 1126, Robert, ſon of Walter, and Aveline his wife, gave to God and St. Peter of Glouceſter the church of Norton, with the lands, tithes, and all other things belonging to the ſaid church, as fully as Emeline, the mother of Aveline, ſome years ſince had given the ſame, to be free, peaceable and quiet from all charges. King Henry the Firſt confirmed this grant in the time of abbat William.

William Briton, in the time when William was abbat, gave to the church of St. Peter of Glouceſter the church of Norton, with the five yard lands. King Henry the Firſt confirmed it.

Oleney.

Ranulph, earl of Cheſter, gave to God and to the monks of St. Peter of Glouceſter, forty ſhillings yearly rent of a water-mill in Oleney, which deſcended to him by right of inheritance. He alſo confirmed a former grant of a mill in Toddewell, which Alice, his ſiſter, had given for the good of the ſoul of her huſband, Richard, the ſon of Gilbert, when Hameline was abbat.

Oſelworth.

Roger de Berkeley gave the church of Oſelworth to the priory of Stanley; and the church of Cowelege, and the church of Erlingham, and the church of Slimbridge, and the church of Uleye, with the tithes and lands, and whatſoever did belong to it.

Over.

In the year 804, Ethelrick, ſon of king Ethelmund, with the conſent of a ſynod, upon an invitation to the ſynod, granted thirty meſſuages in Over to the church of St. Peter of Glouceſter, and confirmed the grant of his father in the time when the canons ſecular reſided there.

Paterne, (St.) in Wales.

In the year 1111, Gilbert, the ſon of Richard, one of the chief noblemen of England, gave to the church of St. Peter of Glouceſter the land and church of Paterne in Wales, and all its appurtenances, as it is bounded by the ſea and two rivers; and half of the great fiſhery which he had made, and the tithes of all things belonging to the demeanes of the caſtle of Penwedith.

Paſſage. (free)

John, earl of Moreton, confirms to the church of St. Peter of Glouceſter, and the church of the apoſtles Peter and Paul, and St. Guthlac of Hereford, and to the monks there ſerving God, that they, their men and ſervants, ſhall be for ever free and quit from all toll, paſſage, loaden horſes, carriages, driving ſwine, money and bridge money, throughout all his lands, to wit, Briſtol, Keyrdiffe, Newburg, and all other his lands, for all manner of their own proper goods which they ſhall either ſell or buy.

Paygrave.

Robert the conful of Gloucefter, confirmed the gift of Richard, the fon of Nigelle, of land in Paygrave, and four farendells of land in the orchard of the almoner; and he gave the water-mill of Ford, and all his tithes in Wotton, and fix acres of land by deed, when William was abbat.

Penycombe.

Agnes, the widow of Turftin of Flanders, and his fon Euftace, a knight, lord of Witteney, gave to the church of St. Peter of Gloucefter, one hide of land in Penycombe and Sudenehale, free and quit from all charges, when Reginald was abbat.

Petfwell.

In the year 1117, Wyfbert, of the king's houfhold, gave to the church of St. Peter of Gloucefter, for the good of the foul of his wife Hawife, his lands in Petfwell, and laid the grant on the altar; and in the fame chapter, Wybert reftored the land which the abbat Serlo had conveyed to him, near to the king's houfe where the barton is. This was done when William was abbat.

Quenington.

Hugh de Lacy gave to the church of St. Peter of Gloucefter the church of Quenington, and the church of Wyke, at the fame time when he gave ten vills and ten villains. Thomas bifhop of Worcefter confirmed the grant in the time of abbat Serlo.

Rodesford.

King William the Second gave Rodesford to the church of St. Peter of Gloucefter, when Serlo was abbat.

Ruddle.

Radulph Bluet gave Rodele [in Newnham] to God and St. Peter of Gloucefter, in pure and perpetual alms, which was confirmed by king William the Second, in the time of abbat Serlo.

King Henry the Firft gave to God and St. Peter of Gloucefter his manor of Rodele, [in Weftbury] with a wood and a fifhery, to find a light at the high altar, which fhould be continually burning for the good of the foul of Robert Curtoife, his brother, who was buried there in the time of abbat William.

Rugge.

In the year 1112, Thomas of St. Joanne gave to the church of St. Peter of Gloucefter his lands in Rugge, which lye in Standifh, in pure and perpetual alms, free and quit from gold, money, and all other fervices and things which belonged to the king. King Henry the Firft confirmed this grant when Peter was abbat.

Seldene.

Henry de Pomeray gave Seldene to the church of St. Peter of Gloucefter, referving to himfelf two fhillings as an acknowledgement. His heirs confirmed this grant, and releafed the two fhillings.

Sexlingham.

John, fon of Richard, gave to the church of St. Peter of Gloucefter the tithes of Sexlingham. Euftace, the fon of John, gave twenty fhillings yearly rent out of the fame vill, in the time of abbat Serlo.

Shotefhore.

Roger de Berkeley the elder, on the feftival of St. Sebaftian, was made a monk under the lord abbat Serlo. He reftored Shotefhore to God and St. Peter of Gloucefter, free and difcharged, as he had unjuftly witheld it. King William the Second confirmed it. This was done in the year 1091, 4° W. 2.

Slimbridge.

In the year 1224, there was a fuit between Thomas of Berkeley and the lord abbat of Breedon, and the convent of Gloucefter, concerning the church of Slimburgge; it was ended by this means, Thomas Berkeley gave the place of Lorlynge, with all its appurtenances, to the church of Stanley, from him and his heirs, and the lord abbat Thomas releafed to him the church of Slimbrugge.

Standifh.

Beornulph, king of the Mercians, in the year 821, gave to the church of St. Peter of Gloucefter fifteen hides of land in Standifh, under Ezimbury. He was flain in battle by king Egbrit, in the year 823, when the canons fecular refided there.

Stanley.

In the year 1146, Roger de Berkeley gave to God, and to the convent of St. Peter of Gloucefter, the church of St. Leonard Stanley, with all its appurtenances, with the confent of Sabrithus the prior, and of the brethren of that place, by the hands of lord Symon, bifhop of Worcefter. The fame Roger gave the church of Ozleworth to the priory of Stanley, and the church of Cowly, and the church of Arlingham, and the church of Slimbridge, and the church of Uley, with the tithes, lands, and all things belonging to the fame. This was done when Gilbert was abbat.

Robert de Berkeley, fon of Maurice, gave to the church of Stanley a mill in Cowly, and a meffuage with lands belonging to the mill. The fame Roger de Berkeley, in the year 1156, gave the church of Camme, with the appurtenances, to the church of St. Leonard Stanley. King Henry the Third confirmed it; it was alfo confirmed by John, bifhop of Worcefter. The fame Roger gave to the faid priory a grove called Fifacre, in the time of abbat Hameline.

Teynton.

Hugh, fon of Norman, gave to the priory of Kylpec the church of Teyntone, and the chapel of Sylva, with a yard-land, when Walter de Lacy was abbat. Maud of Teyntone gave to God and St. Peter of Gloucefter the church of Teyntone, to find lights in the church, and Radulph Avenel confirmed it with an hermitage in that fame place, and one villain with his family. Gilbert Foliot, bifhop of Hereford, confirmed it in the time of abbat Hameline.

Tolls.

Tolls.

The charter of William, earl of Gloucester, whereby he exempted the church of St. Peter of Gloucester, and their men, from payment of tolls in the vill of Bristol; and another charter of his, whereby they are exempted from payment of tolls in Bristol, Kardiff, Newburg, and all other his lands. He moreover exempted the church of St. Guthlac of Hereford from payment of any tolls throughout all his lands in Wales.

Treygosse.

Robert, earl of Gloucester, gave Treygosse to the church of St. Peter of Gloucester. The same Robert, earl of Gloucester, the king's son, gave to the monks of St. Peter of Gloucester, Treygos and Penhore, with other appurtenances. He moreover made them and their men, and also the priory of Ewenny, free from paying toll throughout his lands. This was done when Walter de Lacy was abbat.

Tuffely.

Osberne, bishop of Exeter, gave Tuffely to the church of St. Peter of Gloucester, when Serlo was abbat. King Henry the Second confirmed it by his charter, and that the grove of Tuffely should be free, and that nobody should commit waste there.

Tythes.

Wido of Flanders gave all his tithes, and the churches of all his lands, and the tithes of the fishing, and a place to land the fish, and to build an house for the fisher-man, for rhe conveniency of the fishing, near to his castle of Elys. He also gave the land called Mount St. Mary, and the wood called Gengod.

Willingwyke.

In the year 1167, when Hameline was abbat, Helias Giffard, the younger, and Berta, his mother, gave to God and St. Peter, eight libratas of land in Willingwyke, and the abbat restored to them Cranham, which his father gave to them when he was made monk. Helias, their son, confirmed the same. Berta, the wife of Helias Giffard, gave to the church of St. Peter of Gloucester, certain lands in Willingwyke, on which he had built at his own charges. This was done when Hameline was abbat.

Wynterburne.

In the year 1112, Robert Gernoun gave to the church of St. Peter of Gloucester the church of Wynterbourne, and the church of Laverstoke, and half the water-mill, and half the land which did belong to it. King Henry the First confirmed it when Peter was abbat.

Of the BISHOPRICK and BISHOPS.

GLOUCESTER was antiently the seat of a British bishop, whose title sometimes occurs in the synodal acts by the name of *Cluve*, or *Cluviensis*, derived from *Clevum*, or *Glevum*, or perhaps from *Gloyw*, the British name of the city.

We read in the *Memorial of Gloucester*, that a bishop and preachers were settled here in the year of Christ 189, by king Lucius, concerning whom it is agreed, that he was called *Lever Mawr*, or Great Light, tho' the learned differ as to the precise time when he lived, and to some particulars attributed to him. However we have the testimony of the learned bishop Usher, that this king built here *ecclesiam primæ sedis*, a church of the first seat. Some antient writers also affirm, that this was one of the archbishopricks erected by him in the place or seat of one of the arch-flamens, or heathen chief-priests; and that afterwards, on account of the extraordinary sanctity of St. David, this archbishoprick was translated to *Menevia*, which, in honour of that saint, was afterwards called St. David's.

Bishop Usher, Sir William Dugdale, and other laborious searchers into matters of antiquity, affirm, that Eldad, Eldadym, or Eldall, was bishop here about the year 489. This is the same person whom Rous calls Sanctus Aldatus, a prelate of remarkable courage, wisdom and virtue, whose name appears in an inscription now over the bishop's seat in the cathedcal, thus written:

EDEL DVX
ELDADVS EPS GLOVC:
ELDO MAJOR
A: 490.

It is said that Theonus, called also Cernus, succeeded Eldad, and that he was translated to London in the year 553.

There is no further account to be found of the antient bishops and their succession, because the bishoprick probably ended, according to the opinion of bishop Tanner, when the heathen Saxons overrun this country, about the year 570. In succeeding ages, when the Saxon kings were converted to christianity, Oswy, king of Northumberland, having subdued Mercia, erected the bishoprick of Litchfield in the year 657, when Gloucestershire was made subject to Dwina, first bishop of that diocese. But in the year 679, this vast bishoprick was divided into five smaller ones, by the decree of Theodore, archbishop of Canterbury, and out of it sprung the bishopricks of Litchfield,

field, Dorchefter, Leicefter, Hereford, and Worcefter, of which laft Bofil was the firft bifhop, and then Gloucefterfhire was a part of his diocefe.

A fuffragan bifhop was fixed at Gloucefter by act of parliament, in the year 1534; but even as early as 1273, Reginald occurs by that name, who was fubftituted by the bifhop of Lincoln to vifit the churches in Oxfordfhire; and probably other appointments to that office may have taken place fince that time.

After the diffolution of St. Peter's abbey, king Henry the Eighth obtained an act of parliament, under which he erected the city of Gloucefter, and the county of that city, and all the county of Gloucefter into a bifhoprick[a], with a dean and chapter, by the name of the diocefe of Gloucefter; and ordained that fuch part of the then vill and county of Briftol, as formerly was in the diocefe of Worcefter, fhould be from thenceforward in the diocefe of Gloucefter for ever.

The king's letters patents, dated the 3d of September, 1541, are printed in the Appendix, No. 7; and thofe for the endowment of the bifhoprick are alfo inferted in the Appendix, No. 8, where the particulars may be feen at large, of which the following is a fummary account.

In the letters of endowment it is ordered, that the abbat's lodgings, with the buildings, chapels, grounds and other premiffes; his ftable, and the garden at the end of the church-yard, all within the precincts of the abbey; the houfe called the wood-barton, two ftables, two flaughter-houfes, and a dog-kennel, in the parifh of St. Mary de Lode, are to be called the palace of the bifhop of Gloucefter.

The bifhoprick is endowed with the following manors, lands, rectories, tythes, advowfons, &c.

The manors of Maifmore, Brokethorp, Harfcomb, Prefton, Longford, Droifcourt, Rudge and Farley, and part of the manor of Laffington, in the county of Gloucefter; and thofe of Hope Malefhal, Dewchurch and Kilpeck, in the county of Hereford; and all the lands, profits, &c. in the fields of Brokethorp, Harefcomb, Prefton, and Brockworth.—The vineyard-houfe and park, containing fifteen acres and three roods; Porthammeadow, containing fixty-feven acres, and the firft fhoot of it; a moiety of the wood at Woolridge, and a moiety of the wood called Le Perch, containing fixteen acres, all in the parifh of St. Mary de Lode.

The rectories of Hartpury, Maifmore, Upton St. Leonard, Cam, Northleach, Kempsford, Welford, South Cerney, and Standifh, in Gloucefterfhire; and thofe of Dewchurch, Kilpeck, Glafbury, Devennock, Cowern and Ewias Harold, in the county of Hereford; and of Newport, in the county of Wenlock in Wales, [now Monmouthfhire.]

The tithes or portions of tithes in Standifh, Caldrop, Hardwick, Over-Oxlinch, Nether-Oxlinch, Little Runwike, Harfefield, Sall, Putley, Farley, Holyrood-Ampney, Aldefworth, Linton, and Shipton-Solers, in Gloucefterfhire; and in Devennock, Wentworth, Talgarth, Afh-Leomyfter, Ferm or Venne, Barn or Verne, Bunches or Burch, Strood and Lake, in the county of Hereford.

The following penfions, *viz.* 2*l.* 13*s.* 4*d.* out of Kempsford rectory; 1*l.* 6*s.* 8*d.* from Teynton; 9*s.* from Rendcombe; 1*l.* 6*s.* 8*d.* from Nympffield; and 1*l.* 6*s.* 8*d.* from Newport.

The advowfon, prefentation, and right of patronage of the vicarages of Hartpury, Maifemore, Upton St. Leonard, Cam, Northleach, Kempfford, Whelford or Welford, South Cerney, and Standifh, in the county of Gloucefter; of Dewchurch, Kilpeck, Glafbury, Devennock, Cowern, and Ewias Harold, in the county of Hereford; of Newport, in the county of Wenlock [Monmouthfhire]; of the chapels of Maifmore, Cam, and Stinchcomb, in Gloucefterfhire; and Piperton, in Herefordfhire. All which manors, lands, rectories, tithes, penfions, and right of prefentation belonged to the abbey of St. Peter at Gloucefter.

The bifhoprick is fubject to the following payments, *viz.*

	£.	S.	D.
To the king at his court of Augmentation, — — —	33	16	4
Bailiff of Maifmore, — — —	2	0	0
Woodward of Woolridge, — —	0	11	0
Woodward of the Perch, — —	0	6	8
Bailiff of Brookthrop and Hafcomb,	1	6	8
Bailiff of Prefton, — — —	0	11	8
Bailift of Longford, — — —	0	6	8
Bailiff of Rudge and Farley, —	0	8	4
Vicar of Cam, and to the chaplain of Stinchcombe, — —	13	6	8
Vicar of Standifh, — — —	15	5	0
Collector of the penfions of Kempsford, Teynton, Rendecombe, and Nimpsfield, —	0	13	4
Bailiff of Hope Malefhal, — —	0	14	1
Bailiff of Dewchurch, and Kilpeck,	1	6	8
Chancell[r] of Hereford, for procurations of Dewchurch & Kilpeck,	0	5	0
Archdeacon of Brecknock, for procurations and fynodals, —	0	2	2
Glafbury church, — — —	0	0	10
Devennock church, — — —	0	0	5
Farmer of the rectory of Devennock and Glafbury, for his livery, —	0	13	4
Vicar of York, for a portion of tithes out of Cowern rectory,	0	2	0
Collector of portions in Afh-Leomyfter, Ferm, Farm, Briches, Strode and Lake, — — —	0	3	4
Bailiff of Droifcourt, — — —	0	6	8

[a] He had, fays Sir Robert Atkyns, at the fame time an intention of erecting eighteen bifhopricks, tho' he actually founded but five, befides Weftminfter, which laft continued but few years. A greater number might very well have been expected, and the extent and populoufnefs of the nation requires it, and king Henry the Eighth might well have afforded it; for the conftant yearly revenues of the diffolved monafteries which came to the crown, were 140,000l. and the true yearly value muft be eftimated at ten times as much. p. 43, 44.

The

The bifhoprick has not fuffered much by alienations; but in the years 1647, 1648, and 1649, the following particulars were fold, *viz* the manor of Reculver, and other lands in Kent and elfewhere, belonging to the fees of Canterbury, Norwich, and Gloucefter, to John Blackwell, for 3382*l.* 7*s.* 6*d.*—Gloucefter palace and other lands, to Thomas Hodges, for 913*l.*—Meffuages in the manor of Longford, to W. Mollins, for 24*l.* 11*s.* 2*d.*—Maifemore, Prefton, Longford and Afhchurch, which laft belonged to the fee of Briftol, to alderman Fowke, for 3819*l.* 14*s.* 1*d.* —Droifcourt, in the county of Gloucefter, and Macknage, in that of Northampton, belonging to the fees of Winton and Gloucefter, to Robert Gale, for 176*l.* 10*s.*—The manor of Dewchurch, to Sylvanus Taylor, for 181*l.* 18*s.* 6*d.*—The manor of Hope Malefhall, to Robert Thayer, for 130*l.* 16*s.* 3*d.*—The manor of Rudge, to William Mollins, for 976*l.* 1*s.* 1*d.* The total of which fales amount to 9917*l.* 8*s.* 7*d.* but fuch of thofe lands as were granted to this bifhoprick at the foundation, reverted to the fee at the reftoration.

The value of the endowment, as it is now rated for firft fruits, is 315*l.* 7*s.* 1*d.* but the real value is eftimated at about 900*l.* a year.

The arms of the fee are, *Azure, two keys in faltire, or.*

There is only one archdeaconry in the diocefe, which is divided into ten deaneries, with their proper rural deans, *viz.*

1. Campden Deanery,

Containing the following Parifhes and Places.

Alderton,	Moreton Henmarfh,
Afhton Uunderhill,	Pebworth,
Afton Somervile,	Pinnock,
Afton Subedge,	Prefton on Stour,
Batsford,	Queinton,
Beckford,	Saintbury,
Bourton on the Hill,	Seifencot,
Buckland,	Shenington,
Chipping Campden,	Snowfhill,
Clifford Chambers,	Stanly Pont Larch *chapel.*
Cowhonibourn,	Stanway,
Didbrook,	Staunton,
Dorfington,	Toddenham,
Dumbleton,	Toddington,
Ebberton,	Wafhbourn (Great)
Hailes, *a chapel.*	Welford,
Hinton,	Wefton Subedge,
Kemerton,	Wefton upon Avon,
Lemington,	Wickham (Child's)
Marfton Sicca,	Willerfey,
Mickleton,	Wormington.

2. Cirencester Deanery.

Ampney Crucis,	Bagendon,
Ampney Mary,	Baunton,
Ampney Peter,	Chedworth,
Cirencefter,	Harnhill,
Coates,	North Cerney,
Coln Deans, or Dennis,	Northleach,
Coln Rogers,	Prefton,
Compton Abdale,	Rendcomb,
Daglingworth,	South Cerney,
Driffield,	Stowel,
Duntfborn Abbats,	Stratton,
Duntfborn Militis,	Siddington Mary,
Farmington,	Siddington Peter.
Hampnet,	

3. Dursley Deanery.

Berkeley,	Oldbury, *a chapel.*
Beverftone,	North Nibley,
Cam,	Olpen, *a chapel.*
Cowley,	Ozleworth.
Durfley,	Rockhampton,
Falfield, *a chapel.*	Slimbridge,
Frampton on Severn,	Stinchcomb, *a chapel.*
Hill, *chapel.*	Stone, *a chapel.*
Kingfcot, *a chapel.*	Thornbury,
Kingfwood,	Uley,
Lafborough,	Wottonunderedge.
Newington Bagpath,	

4. Fairford Deanery.

Aldefworth,	Hatherop,
Barnfley,	Kempsford,
Bibury,	Leachlade,
Coln Aldwins,	Marfton, *a chapel.*
Down Ampney,	Meyfey Hampton,
Eaftlech Martin,	Quenington,
Eaftlech Turville,	Southrop.
Fairford,	Winfon, *chapel.*

5. Forest Deanery.

Abenhall,	Lea, *a chapel.*
Ailberton, *a chapel.*	Lidney,
Alvington,	Longhope,
Awre,	Minfterworth,
Bicknor (Englifh)	Newent,
Blackeney, *a chapel.*	Newland, *a chapel.*
Blaifdon,	Newnham,
Breeme, *a chapel.*	Oxenhall,
Bromfborow,	Pauntley,
Bully, *a chapel.*	Prefton,
Churcham, *a chapel.*	Rudford,
Colford, *a chapel.*	Ruerdean, *a chapel.*
Dean Magna,	Staunton,
Dean Parva,	St. Briavel's, *a chapel.*
Dymock,	Tainton,
Flaxley,	Tibberton,
Hewelsfield, *a chapel.*	Tidenham, *a chapel.*
Huntley,	Upleaden,
Kempley,	Weftbury,
Lancaut, *a chapel.*	Woolafton.

6. Gloucester Deanery.

Arlingham,	Barnwood,
Afhleworth,	Brookthrop,

 Churchdown,

Churchdown,
Elmore,
Frethern,
Hardwick, *a chapel.*
Harſcombe,
Harsfield,
Hartpury,
Hempſtead,
Laſſington,
Longney,
Maiſemore,
Matſon,
Moreton Valence,
Norton,
Pitchcomb,
Quedgley,
Rundwick, *a chapel.*
Sandhurſt,
Saul, *a chapel.*
Standiſh,
Upton St. Leonard's
Whaddon,
Wheatenhurſt,
Witcomb Magna.

In the City and Liberties.

St. Aldate,
St. Bartholomew, *chapel.*
St. Catherine,
St. John Baptiſt,
St. Magdalen,
St. Mary de Cript,
St. Mary de Grace,
St. Mary de Lode,
St. Michael,
St. Nicholas,
St. Owen,
Trinity.

7. HAWKESBURY DEANERY.

Abſon, *a chapel.*
Acton Turville,
Alderley,
Badminton Great,
Badminton Little,
Bitton,
Boxwell,
Charfield,
Cold Aſhon,
Cromhall,
Deinton,
Didmarton,
Dodington,
Dyrham,
Frampton Cotterel,
Hanham, *a chapel.*
Hawkeſbury,
Horton,
Iron Acton,
Leiterton, *a chapel.*
Littleton, *a chapel.*
Marſhfield,
Oldbury on the Hill,
Oldland, *a chapel.*
Puclechurch,
Rangeworthy, *a chapel.*
Siſton,
Sodbury Chipping,
Sodbury Little,
Sodbury Old,
Titherington,
Tormarton,
Tortworth,
Treſham, *a chapel.*
Wapley,
Weſterleigh, *a chapel.*
Weſtonbirt,
Wickwar,
Yate.

8. STONEHOUSE DEANERY.

Avening,
Biſley,
Brimpsfield,
Chalford, *a chapel.*
Cherington,
Coleſbourn,
Cowley,
Cranham,
Cubberley,
Eaſtington,
Edgworth,
Elkſtone,
Frowceſter,
Horſley,
Minchin Hampton,
Miſerden,
Nimpsfield,
Painſwick,
Radmarton,
Rodborow, *a chapel.*
Saperton,
Shipton Moign,
Stanley St. Leonard,
Stanley Regis,
Stonehouſe,
Stroud,
Syde,
Tetbury,
Winſton,
Woodcheſter.

9. STOW DEANERY.

Addleſtrop,
Aſton Blank,
Barrington (Great)
Barrington (Little)
Bledington,
Bourton on the Water,
Broadwell,
Clapton, *a chapel.*
Compton (Little)
Condicot,
Farmcot, *a chapel.*
Guiting (Power)
Guiting (Temple)
Haſleton,
Hawling,
Longborow,
Naunton,
Notgrove,
Oddington,
Riſſington (Great)
Riſſington (Little)
Riſſington (Wick)
Seiſencot,
Salperton,
Sherbourn,
Shipton Oliffe,
Shipton Solers,
Slaughter (Upper)
Slaughter (Lower)
Sutton under Brayles,
Stow on the Would,
Swell (Upper)
Swell (Lower)
Turk Dean,
Weſtcote,
Widford,
Windruſh,
Yanworth, *a chapel.*

10. WINCHCOMB DEANERY.

Aſhchurch,
Badgworth,
Biſhop's Cleeve,
Brokworth,
Charleton Abbat's,
Charleton King's,
Cheltenham,
Dowdſwell,
Down Hatherly,
Elmſton,
Gretton, *a chapel.*
Leckhampton,
Oxenton,
Preſbury,
Seven Hampton,
Shipton Olive,
Shurdington,
Stoke Archer, *a chapel.*
Sudely,
Swindon,
Tewkeſbury,
Tredington,
Twining,
Walton Cardiff, *a chapel.*
Whittington,
Winchcomb,
Withington.
Wolſton,

PECULIARS *in this Dioceſe.*

The following churches are Peculiars, the juriſdiction of which is particularly laid down under the heads of the reſpective pariſhes, *viz.*

Bibury, with Aldeſworth, Barnſley and Winſon.

Cleeve, with Stoke-Archer.

Deerhurſt, with Boddington, Corſe, Forthampton, Hasfield, Leigh, Staverton and Tirley.

Wickham, or Wickwane, or Child's-Wickham.

Withington, with Dowdeſwell.

Before this biſhoprick was erected, the following places were in the dioceſe of York, *viz.* Churchdown, Laſſington, Norton, Compton-Abdale, Sainthurſt, Saint Catherine, in Glouceſter; and to theſe, perhaps, may be added Oddington and Witcombe-Magna.

The deanery of the Foreſt belonged to the biſhop of Hereford 'till this ſee was erected; but being part of the county of Glouceſter, the biſhop of Glouceſter, ſoon after the foundation, inſtituted, viſited, and performed many other epiſcopal functions therein; however the archdeacon of Hereford ſtill retains his juriſdiction in it, and under the biſhop of Glouceſter, viſits there in the ſummer every year, and receives the procurations; but the biſhop of Glouceſter's chancellor viſits the

the other half year. All the other deaneries in this diocese are under the jurisdiction of the archdeacon of Gloucester, together with the deanery of Bristol, and a few churches within the diocese of Worcester.

Bristol Deanery *contains*,

Almondesbury,	Mangotsfield,
Clifton,	Olveston, with Alveston.
Compton Greenville,	Saint George,
Elberton,	Stapleton,
Filton,	Stoke Giffard,
Henbury, with Aust.	Westbury,
Horfield,	Winterbourne.
Littleton,	

Bishop Cheiney certified to queen Elizabeth, in 1562, 'That at the foundation of the bishoprick of Bristol, the city and deanery of Bristol were appointed and limitted to the bishop of Bristol, and his successors, as they heretofore have alledged.' But yet no mention is made, in the charter of erection of the see of Bristol, that it shall have any part or parcel of the county of Gloucester.

The following churches are within the archdeaconry of Gloucester, tho' in the diocese of Worcester, *viz.* Blockley vicarage, and the rectories of Dailsford, Ditchfield, Evenlode, Iccombe, and Stratton upon the Foss.

This archdeaconry is valued at about 120*l.* *per annum.* In the twenty-sixth year of Henry the Eighth, the full value of it, distinct from the rectory of Dursley, was 64*l.* 10*s.*

The account of the archdeacons follows that of the deans and chancellors.

BISHOPS of Gloucester.

John Wakeman[a], (alias Wich) B.D. the last abbat of Tewkesbury, being the king's chaplain, was appointed September 3, 1541, to be the first bishop of this foundation, who accordingly was consecrated September the 25th, or according to Le Neve, the 20th, by the archbishop of Canterbury, assisted by the bishops of London and Westminster; and thereupon the pension of 266*l.* 13*s.* 4*d.* allowed him at the dissolution of his abbey, ceased. He was appointed to inspect the English translation of part of the New Testament; and dying at [b] Forthampton, in the co. of Gloucester, where he had an house and little chapel, in the beginning of November, 1549, was there buried. There is an effigy in memory of him, lying on a tomb behind the high altar at Tewkesbury, which he had provided while he was abbat. Upon bishop Wakeman's death, archbishop Cranmer sent a commission to prebendary Williams to be his commissary, to visit this church, and to be the keeper of the spiritualities of the city and diocese.

John Hooper, or Hoper, D.D. [c] an exemplary, zealous, pious and learned man, who in his younger years had been a monk of Cleeve, in Somersetshire, was nominated on the 15th of May, appointed bishop on the 3d of July, 1550, consecrated on the 8th of March following; and installed by proxy by archbishop Cranmer, assisted by the bishops of London and Rochester, the 22d of the same month. He was very active in the visitation of the diocese, then remarkably abounding with popery, and greatly promoted the reformation. With the consent of the dean and chapter, he surrendered the bishoprick of Gloucester to the king, the 26th of April, 1552, and, on the 12th of May, made a deed of gift of all the lands and annuities which he enjoyed by means of his bishoprick. Upon Dr. Heath's being deprived of the see of Worcester, by virtue of an act of parliament, by the king's letters patents, dated May the 20th, in the same year, the bishoprick of Gloucester was dissolved, and converted into an archdeaconry, dependent on Worcester, as it had been formerly; but the dignities of the dean and chapter thereof continued. The king then gave Dr. Hooper the bishoprick of Worcester, with power and authority to appoint all the prebendaries of both cathedrals. In September, another patent was granted him for the discharge of his first fruits. This year a letter was sent him for the surrender of the bishoprick of Worcester, in order that there might be a new collation, or presentation thereto: and on the 8th of December following, the bishopricks of Worcester and Gloucester were united into one, and thenceforth to be one diocese, as Bath and Wells, Litchfield and Coventry: the bishop to be called the bishop of Gloucester and Worcester, and was to live one year in Worcestershire, and the next in Gloucestershire; and to have the power of appointing archdeacons and prebendaries as before. To this bishop and his successors likewise were given a few manors, belonging to the bishoprick of Worcester, and all the lands, &c. granted to the bishoprick of Gloucester at its foundation, as fully as he had surrendered them to the king; which then extended to the clear yearly value of 100 marks, besides tenths and yearly rents. The tenths of the bishoprick formerly came to 136*l.* 10*s.* 5*d.* *ob.* but he was to pay only 66*l.* 13*s.* 4*d.* in lieu of them, and to be discharged of first fruits; and he and his successors to be for ever discharged of 26*l.* 13*s.* 4*d.* to be paid to Mr. John Taylor for keeping the register of the bishop of Gloucester. Some time after he was discharged of all his first fruits, and all persons were forbidden to demand a fee of him. But this union continued no longer than

[a] Willis's Survey of Glo. Cathedral. Memoriale Glouc. being a MS. Musæo Ashmoleano Oxon.
[b] Willis's Hist. M. Abbies.

[c] Willis's Survey of Gloucester Cathedral. Collier's Hist. Burnet's Ref. Fox's Martyrs. Strype's Cranmer. Thomas's Survey of Worc. Cath. Godwin de Praſul. and other Historians.

than the life of king Edward the Sixth, by whom it was granted. As bifhop Hooper had ftrenuoufly oppofed Gardiner and Bonner, they had a peculiar enmity againft him, and when the king died, it was refolved to make him the firft facrifice. Accordingly, on the 1ft of September, foon after queen Mary's acceffion to the crown, he was fent to prifon, by an order from the queen, [d] dated March 15, 1553-4, and on the 18th, his bifhoprick was declared void. January the 28th, 1554-5, [e] he was brought before Gardiner, bifhop of Winchefter, and feveral others, at St. Mary Overy's church, in Southwark, and there condemned as an heretick. In February, he was degraded of his priefthood [f] by bifhop Bonner, in Newgate, where he had been feverely ufed for feveral months; and afterwards fent from London to Gloucefter, where he had been moft active, to be burnt. After a journey of three days, attended by fix of the queen's guards, he was brought to this city, and lodged in the houfe of Robert Ingram, oppofite St. Nicholas church. Jenkins and Bond, the fheriffs, would have put him into the north-gate prifon, but were diffuaded from it by the queen's guards. He had one day's interval, and on Saturday, the 9th of February, being market-day, was led by the fheriffs, attended by the mayor, lord Chandois, Sir Edmund Bridges, Sir Anthony Kingfton, and others, from Ingram's houfe, to a place near the elm tree, without the gate, on the north-weft fide of the lower church-yard; where, not being permitted to fpeak to the people, who were about 7000, as he was going, nor at the place of execution; and refufing all offers of pardon, they chained him to a ftake, and burnt him with three fucceffive fires, made of green wood. The good man fupported himfelf, it is faid, with all imaginable firmnefs for above three quarters of an hour, and then expired, about the 60th year of his age. The queen fent an order, that perfons of reputation in the county fhould be called to affift the mayor and fheriffs on this occafion; and after the execution, a dinner was provided [g], at the expence of the corporation, for thofe who were ordered by the queen to attend at it.—Thus bigots in power have practifed every fpecies of cruelty, under pretence of ferving that religion, the fpirit of which is meeknefs and charity; and many men, otherwife thought of found judgment and integrity, have promoted thofe perfecuting meafures, which in fucceeding times have been condemned by the concurrent judgments of all.

James Brookes [h], D.D. fometime fellow of Corpus Chrifti College, and afterwards mafter of Baliol College, in Oxford, upon bifhop Hooper's deprivation, was elected March 26, 1554; had reftitution of the temporalties May the 8th; and was confecrated in the church of Saint Saviour, Southwark, the 1ft of April following. The commiffions he exercifed as delegate, or fub-delegate, againft archbifhop Cranmer, bifhop Ridley, bifhop Latimer; and in vifiting the univerfity of Oxford, prove him to have been a very zealous man in thofe times, who is obferved by Dr. Fuller to have fpent his fury moftly out of his diocefe. He died September the 7th, 1558, according to Le Neve, and was buried in a ftrong coffin, under abbat Parker's monument, without any infcription over him. It feems that he collated at firft to the prebends of this church, a privilege granted to his predeceffors. Upon his death, queen Mary iffued out a writ [i], dated the 25th day of October, for the keeping of the temporalties, to John Bowrfher, B.D. who was nominated to the bifhoprick; but the queen's death prevented his having it.

A vacancy for above three years.

Richard Cheiney, B.D. fometime of Pembroke-hall, in the univerfity of Cambridge; the archdeacon of Hereford, who oppofed tranfubftantiation in the year 1555, in convocation, and was deprived in the reign of queen Mary; but was afterwards rector of Maydefnorton, in the diocefe of Lincoln; of Bifhop's-Hampton, in that of Worcefter; prebendary of Weftminfter, and alfo of this church; was elected bifhop, March the 9th, 1561; the temporalties were reftored to him on the 15th of April, in the fame year; he was confecrated in the archbifhop's chapel at Lambeth, on the 19th; and in ten days after, had the bifhoprick of Briftol given to him to hold in *commendam* with it. He died April 25, 1579, according to Le Neve, and was buried near his predeceffor, under abbat Parker's monument, without any infcription.

A vacancy for above two years, the reafon of which, according to Mr. Strype, was that the queen might fatisfy her debt of 500*l.* owing to her for the tenths of the clergy out of the revenues of the fee.

John Bullingham, D.D. prebendary of Worcefter and Lincoln; fometime rector of Boxwell, and of Withington, in Gloucefterfhire, was elected on the 15th of Auguft, confirmed the 1ft of September, and confecrated on the 3d, 1581, by the archbifhop of Canterbury, affifted by the bifhops of London and Rochefter, in the chapel of Croydon. April 21, 1585, he was inftituted to the vicarage of Painfwick, in this county, which he held in *commendam* with his bifhoprick for fome time; as he did the bifhoprick of Briftol, from the time of his confecration 'till 1589, when Dr.

[d] Strype's Memorial.

[e] Ibid. Fox's Mart. Burnet's Reform. Wood's Athen. Ox. &c.

[f] Bifhop Hooper was degraded only of priefthood, and not of his epifcopal office; for it feems that the bifhop of London, and others of his perfuafion, did not think it neceffary to degrade him of any higher order; for they reputed him, and the other bifhops made in the reign of king Edward the Sixth, as nothing more than priefts.

[g] From an old book of orders and agreements belonging to the city.

[h] Willis's Survey of Glouc. Cath. Wood's Athen. Ox. &c.

[i] Rymer's Fœdera.

Fletcher was confecrated thereto; and that bifhoprick being taken from him, the rectory of Kilmington, *aliàs* Culmington, in the deanery of Carey, and diocefe of Wells, was conferred on him, in July, 1596. He died at Kenfington, May 20, 1598, and was buried in this cathedral, without any memorial; and, the fame year, he was fucceeded by

Godfrey Goldfborough, D.D. formerly fellow of Trinity college in Cambridge, archdeacon of Worcefter, fometime rector of Stockton, archdeacon of Salop, in the church of Litchfield, prebendary of London, Hereford, and Worcefter; who was elected the 2d of Auguft, and confecrated November the 12th, 1598, by the archbifhop of Caterbury, affifted by the bifhops of London, Litchfield and Coventry, and of Chichefter, at the archbifhop's palace at Lambeth; inftalled the 20th of December, and had licenfe to hold the prebend of Worcefter in *commendam* with it. He died on the 26th of May, 1604, at his palace at the Vineyard, and was buried in this cathedral, in a little chapel on the north fide of the lady's. Over his grave, according to his defire, there is an handfome altar monument erected for him by his executors, with his effigy in his epifcopal habit, and at the head of it this infcription in capitals:

IN OBITVM REVERENDI PRÆSVLIS GODFRIDI, QVONDAM GLOVCESTRIENSIS EPISCOPI, QVI XXVI MAII, MDCIV. EX HAC VITA MIGRAVIT.

Aureus, et fulvo nomen fortitus ab auro,
Hic Goldifburgus nunc requiefcit humo,
Scilicet orta folo pretiofa metalla parente,
In matrem redeunt inveterata fuam.

SEDIT ANNOS SEX.

Over it are the arms intended for thofe of the fame fee, *viz. Or, three cheverons gules*, the middle one charged with a mitre with labels *argent*, *impaled with his own arms*; *viz.* Quarterly, 1. *argent*, *a crofs flory fable*; 2. *argent*, *three cheverons*, *fable*: *in the middle a mullet*, *gules*: the 3d as the 2d, the 4th as the 1ft; a mirte for the creft.—After bifhop Goldfborough's death, William Tooker, or Tucker, D.D.[a] dean of Litchfield, was nominated by king James the Firft, to that fee; and the *congé d'elire*, or letter patent, iffued out[b] for his election; but it was revoked, tho' 'tis not faid on what account.

Thomas Ravis, D.D. rector of Bredon in Worcefterfhire, dean of Chrift-church in Oxford, a man of eminent learning, gravity, and approved prudence, was elected on the 17th of December, 1604, and confecrated the 19th of March following, at Lambeth, by the archbifhop of Canterbury, affifted by the bifhops of Durham and Chichefter. Whilft he was bifhop here[c] he was at a very confiderable expence in repairing his palace at Gloucefter, made feveral water-courfes there, and repaired the vineyard houfe. In 1607, he was tranflated to London, and fucceeded by

Henry Parry, D.D. dean of Chefter, who was confecrated by the archbifhop of Canterbury, affifted by the bifhops of London, Rochefter, and Chichefter, at Lambeth, July 12, 1607; and whilft he prefided here, made the pulpit in the body of the cathedral, at his own charge, and gave very liberally to the poor of this city. He was tranflated to Worcefter in the end of September, 1610.

Gyles Thompfon, D.D. fometime rector of Pembridge, in the county of Hereford, dean of Windfor, and canon of Hereford, was elected on the 15th of March, 1611, confirmed on the 9th of June, had reftitution of the temporalties on the 27th of the fame month, and was confecrated at Lambeth, by the archbifhop of Canterbury, affifted by the bifhops of Oxford, Ely, Bath and Wells, and Litchfield and Coventry; having liberty to hold his deanery in *commendam* only for one year. He never came into his diocefe, but died June 14, 1612, to the great grief of all that knew his piety or learning, after he had taken great pains, by the command of king James the Firft, in tranflating part of the New Teftament; and lies buried in a chapel on the north fide of Windfor collegiate church, where is on his monument the buft of a bifhop, and this infcription:

Individuæ Trinitati per omnia fecula gloria, per quam fui, ero. Hic fitus eft Ægidius Tomfon, hujus capellæ quondam decanus, cujus mens fincera, lingua docta, manus munda. Fuit Londini natus, educatus Oxoniæ, in collegio omnium bonorum indigentium eruditiffimorum amantiffimus femper vixit, cujus corpus quamvis mortalitas terræ fubjecit, illius tamen animam pietas cœlis inferuit. Hunc virum, moribus gravem, prudentiâ infignem, pietate fummum, hæc regia capella per annos 10 decanum habuit. Inde a fereniffimo rege Jacobo, in epifcopatum Glouceftr. commendatum, mors intempeftiva, anno decurfo, præfulem rapuit. Obijt 14 Junij Ann. Domini 1612, Ætatis fuæ 59.

On the right hand is the figure of time, over whofe head is an angel, holding a fcroll thus infcribed;

In memoria æterna erit juftus.

On the left hand, on a fcroll held by another angel:

Juftorum animæ in manu Dei funt.

His will was dated Feburary the 12th, 1605, and proved July the 7th, 1612.

Miles Smith, D.D. fucceeded, being elected July 15, 1612, and confecrated at Croydon, by the archbifhop of Canterbury, affifted by the bifhops of London, Litchfield and Coventry, and of Rochefter, on the 19th or 20th of September following. He was rector of Hartlebury and Upton-upon-Severn, in the county of Worcefter, prebendary of Exeter, and canon refidentiary of Hereford; was appointed by king James the Firft, May the 8th, 1610, one of the firft fellows of Chelfea-college, being a man of fuch eminent learning, as to occafion him to be called a walking library. He is faid to have difliked the hot proceedings of fome very zealous perfons, efpecially

[a] Epift. Cl. Willis ad me.
[b] Willis, Le Neve, Wood, &c. &c.
[c] Epift. Cl. Willis's ad me.

after doctor Laud was made dean: and having compofed the preface [d] that is now before our church bibles, and tranflated the four major and the twelve minor prophets, he died at his palace at Gloucefter on the 19th of October, 1624, much lamented by the poor of the city, to whom he had been very charitable, and was buried November the 9th, in the lady's chapel. Over his grave was laid a white ftone, without any infcription, and only his arms impaled with thofe of the fee.— Upon his death, Dr. John Prefton was offered the bifhoprick, but waved it on account of his lecture, which he preferred to it.

Godfrey Goodman, D.D. prebendary of Weftminfter, rector of Weft-Ildefley, in Berkfhire, and of Kemmerton in this diocefe, (the advowfon of which he gave to the corporation of Gloucefter) and dean of Rochefter, was elected on the 26th of November, confirmed March the 5th, confecrated the next day at Lambeth, by the archbifhop of Canterbury, affifted by the bifhops of Lincoln, London, Rochefter, and Landaff, and inftalled April the 4th following. He held in *commendam* with his bifhoprick his canonry of Windfor, and rectory of Weft-Ildefley. In 1640, he was fequeftrated [e] from the bifhoprick, firft committed to a purfuivant, and afterwards to a gate-houfe, on account of fome notions favouring the church of Rome, to which he was reconciled [f] before his death, which happened January the 19th, 1655, in St. Margaret's parifh, Weftminfter; in which parifh church he was [g] buried, near the font in the weft part, without any memorial.

A vacancy 'till after the reftoration.—John Hacket, D.D. [h] in 1660, was offered this bifhoprick, but refufed it, and the next year accepted that of Litchfield; whereupon

William Nicholfon, D.D. archdeacon of Brecknock, canon refidentiary of St. David's, vicar of Llandilovawr, in the county of Carmarthen; and afterwards rector of Bifhop's-Cleeve, in the county of Gloucefter, was elected on the 26th of November, 1660; confecrated in king Henry the Seventh's chapel at Weftminfter, by the archbifhop of York, affifted by the bifhops of Durham, Chichefter, Lincoln, and Peterborough, by commiffion from the archbifhop of Canterbury, January 6, 1660; inftalled the 11th of January, and had the temporalties reftored to him on the 5th of Feburary following. He, fays Mr. Wood, being a man of great erudition, prudent, modeft, and of a moderate mind, died Feburary the 5th, 1671; and was buried in a little chapel on the fouth fide of the lady's, where is a monument againft the eaft wall erected for him, with this infcription on it, compofed by his great friend Mr. Bull, afterwards the very learned and pious bifhop of St. David's:

Æternitati S. in fpe beatæ refurrectionis, hic reverendas exuvias depofuit Theologus infignis, epifcopus vere primitivus, Gulielmus Nicholfon. In agro Suffolciano natus, apud Magdalenfes educatus, obfidem regi et ecclefiæ afflictæ præftitam, ad fedem Glouceftrenfem merito promotus anno MDCLX. In concionibus frequens, in fcriptis nervofus, legenda fcribens, et faciens fcribenda, gravitas epifcopalis in fronte emicuit; pauperibus quotidiana charitate beneficus; comitate erga clerum et literatos admirandus. Gloriæ ac dierum fatur, in palatio fuo, ut vixit, pie deceffit, Feb. 5° anno Ætatis LXXXII. Dom. MDCLXXI.

Elizabetha conjux præivit in hoc facello, fepulta Apr. xx. An: Dom: MDCLXIII. Owenus Brigftock, de Lechdenny, in comitatu Caermarthen, armiger, prædictæ Elizabethæ nepos, hoc grati animi monumentum (executore recufante) propriis fumptibus erexit, ann. M.DC.LXXIX.

Over it his arms, impaled with thofe defigned for the fee of Gloucefter, *viz. Azure, a key argent, furmounted of another key, Or, for the fee. Azure, in chief three leopards heads cabofhed, gules; two bars ermin,* for his own arms. On the fame monument are likewife, 1. *Parted per pale counterchanged, Or and fable, three efcallops counterchanged of the field.* 2. *Or, a cheveron fable, between three ravens proper.*

John Prichard, or Prichet, D.D. vicar of St. Gyles's Cripplegate, London; rector of Harlington, in the county of Middlefex, and prebendary of Mora, in the church of St. Paul's; was elected on the 10th of October, 1672; confecrated at Lambeth by the archbifhop of Canterbury, affifted by the bifhops of London, Ely, Rochefter, and Chefter, November the 3d; and had the temporalties reftored to him the 29th of January following. He held the three preferments before-mentioned in *commendam* with his bifhoprick, and died January the 1ft, 1680; and was buried at Harlington, with this infcription on a copartment affixed to a pillar on the north fide near his grave, which was under the pulpit:

In memoriam Johannis Domini epifcopi Gloucefter, filii Walteri Pricket de prædio Cowlenfi, vulgo Cowley-hall, in agro Middlefexiæ, armigeri, qui e Katherina uxore, caftiffima fæmina, fex liberos progenuit, viz. Georgium, Wilhelmum, Walterum, Thomam, Johannem & Sufannam, quorum Johannes et Sufanna jam fuperfunt. Hoc loco minifterium facrum, et felici omine, exercuit, nec non Aliciæ Comitiffiæ Derbiæ, viduæ, aliquando a facris domefticis, dein in ædem fancti Andreæ Underfhaff, apud Londinenfes promovebatur; ubi paftoris boni fidelifque labores alacriter fuftinens, graffante jam inteftino & diro bello, regifque partibus depreffis, ipfe tum in regem, tum in ecclefiam pius, illinc depulfus eft, perque totum id tempus, quo Carolus Secundus rex in exilio erat, fidelis; ergo graviora paffus. Tandem reftaurato fideliter principe, in res fuas reftituebatur, inque prædictum poft epifcopatum inauguratus, cui Sacro-Sancto muneri ubi quum novem annos invigilaverat, obijt cal. Januarii ann. Dom. 1680; annoque Ætatis 75. Hocce fubtus roftrum monumentum fui quidem optimum, pro juffu fuo, corpus jacet fepultum.

Robert Frampton, D.D. [i] dean of this church, rector of Fontmill, in Dorfetfhire, born at Pimpern, in that county, was elected on the 28th of January, 1680; and confecrated [k] in the chapel of All-Souls college in Oxford, by the archbifhop of Canterbury, affifted by the bifhops of London, Rochefter, Ely, Exeter, and Lincoln, March the 27th, 1681; having licenfe to hold Fontmill in *commendam*. In 1684, he refigned Fontmill for Avening, in the county of Gloucefter; in 1685, he refigned Avening for Standifh vicarage in the fame county. And Feburary the 1ft, 1690, was

[d] Le Neve's Lives of proteftant archbifhops. A. Wood, &c. &c.
[e] Lord Clarendon's Hiftory.
[f] Walker's fufferings. Wood's Athen. Ox.
[g] Strype's Edition of Stowe's Survey of London.
[h] Willis's Survey of Cov. and Litchf. p. 894.
[i] Cl. Willis's Survey of Gloucefter Cathedral.
[k] Le Neve's lives of proteftant Archbifhops.

deprived,

deprived, for refufing the oaths then appointed. After his deprivation, he continued at Standifh, and, by connivance, had the profits thereof 'till he died; which was on the 25th of May, 1708. He is buried in the chancel of that church, within the communion rails, and had a black marble grave-ftone laid over him with this infcription on it:

Robertus Frampton Epifcopus Glouceftrenfis. Cætera quis nefcit. Obiit 8 Cal. Junii An. Ætatis fuæ 86, Confecrationis 28, Æræ Chriftianæ 1708.

His will was dated in Feburary, 1702, and proved in November, 1708, by which he bequeathed, amongft other things, 100*l.* for each of the following purpofes, to promote the gofpel in foreign parts; to deprived minifters; to poor fervitors in CCC. Oxford.

Edward Fowler, D.D. born at Wefterleigh, in Gloucefterfhire, prebendary of this church, rector of Northill, in the county of Bedford, and All-hallows, Breadftreet, London; upon bifhop Frampton's deprivation, was nominated, April the 23d, 1691; elected the 8th of June, confirmed the 2d, and confecrated the 5th of July, by the archbifhop of Canterbury, affifted by the bifhops of Winchefter, Salifbury, Worcefter, Briftol and Ely, in the church of St. Mary le Bow, London; holding his vicarage in *commendam* with his bifhoprick. He died at Chelfea, Auguft 26, 1714, and was buried in a vault, on the north fide of Hendon church-yard, near Hampftead, in Middlefex. Within the chancel is fet up a handfome marble copartment, with colums and arms at top, which bears this infcription:

To the pious memory of the Right Reverend Edward Fowler, late Lord Bifhop of Gloucefter; to which ftation he was advanced by king William, in the year 1691, for his known fteadinefs to the true intereft of the church of England, and of his country, in times of danger. He approved himfelf worthy of that dignity, by a faithful and diligent difcharge of his paftoral office; 'till difabled by age and bodily infirmities, he refted from his labours in the 82d year of his age, admitted to partake of his reward. He departed this life Auguft 26, 1714, and was interred in the grave of his firft wife, in this church; leaving behind him, in the excellent Treatifes, publifhed by himfelf, lafting monuments of learning, judgment, piety and chriftian temper of mind. He was twice married, firft to Ann, daughter of Arthur Bernardifton, of the Inner Temple, efq; one of the mafters of chancery. She departed this life December 19, 1696. He had by her three fons, Nathaniel, Edward, and Richard; and five daughters, Anne, Anne, Sufannah, Elizabeth, and Mary, furvived him. His fecond wife Elizabeth, who likewife furvived him, was Elizabeth, widow of the Reverend Dr. Ezekiah Burton, and daughter of Ralph Trevor, of London, merchant.

Underneath is as follows:

This monument was erected at the coft of Richard Fowler, LLB. the younger fon above-mentioned, who married Sufannah, daughter of John Pyke, of Downfey, in the Ifle of Purbeck, gent. by whom he had one daughter Anne, both which dying many years before him, were buried in this church, near his mother, and his father's youngeft fifter Sufanna, the firft wife of Mefhack Smith, A.M. then vicar of this church. The faid Richard Fowler died November 9, 1716, and did by his laft will direct his executors, viz. his brother Edward, and his fifter Sufanna, to caufe a vault to be made, which for want of rome in the church was made in the church-yard, at the weft corner of this wall, wherein is depofited his body, and into which are removed the remains of his wife and daughter, with thofe of his father and mother; all reft there together. An. Dom. 1717, in hope of a joyful refurrection.

His fucceffor was

Richard Willis, D.D. born at Bewdley, in Worcefterfhire, fometime fellow of All-Souls college, the king's chaplain, chaplain-general of the army; fub-preceptor to the duke of Gloucefter, prebendary of Weftminfter, and dean of Lincoln. He was elected December the 10th, 1714, confirmed January the 15th, confecrated January the 16th, in Lambeth chapel, by the bifhops of Salifbury, Litchfield and Coventry, and of Bangor, by commiffion from the archbifhop of Caterbury, and inftalled the 13th of April following; and had licence to hold his deanery in *commendam* with it: But was tranflated to the fee of Salifbury in 1721, and thence, in 1725, to Winchefter; where he was buried towards the fouth fide of the body of the church, and has a fine monument in marble erected for him againft the fouth wall, being at length, in a recumbent pofture, attired in his epifcopal habit, with the George hanging on his breaft, as prelate of the order of Saint George, and this infcription and character, which he very juftly deferved:

In Memoriam Reverendi admodum in Chrifto Patris RICHARDI WILLIS, Epifcopi Wintonienfis; viri ea morum fimplicitate, ea animi integritate, et verborum fide, ut qui illum optimè noverint, fi maximè æftimaverint, propenfiffimè dilexerint. Patriam, principem, et libertatem publicam, unicè amavit. Religionem interea vere chriftianam fanctiffime coluit, acerrime vindicavit. Nulla temporum varietate debilitari, aut frangi, potuit. In republica, in ecclefia, fidelis; conftans, et fui fimilis. Egregiis hifce virtutibus inftructus, in mediis, quos abundè meruit, honoribus feliciffimè confenuit; donec annorum plenus, obiit 10 die Augufti, Anno Domini 1734, Ætatis 71. JOHANNES WILLIS, armiger, filius ejus et Heres, pie memor pofuit.

John Wilcocks, D.D. born at Briftol, fometime fellow of Magdalen college in Oxford, upon bifhop Willis's tranflation to Salifbury, was elected November 25, 1721, confecrated December the 2d, inftalled the 22d of the fame month, and held a prebend of Weftminfter in *commendam* with his bifhoprick; but being tranflated to the fee of Rochefter, and having the deanery of Weftminfter along with it, he was fucceeded by

Elias Sydall, D.D. fometime fellow of Bennet, alias *Corpus Chrifti* college in Cambridge, and afterwards prebendary of Canterbury, who was tranflated hither from the bifhoprick of Saint David's November the 4th, 1731; being then alfo dean of Canterbury, which office, together with this bifhoprick, he held 'till his death, on December the 24th, 1737.

Martin Benfon, D.D, fucceeded, whofe character is admirably drawn in the following infcription, on a fine marble monument, erected for him in the cathedral at Gloucefter:

Reader be admonifhed by this marble, to imitate Martin Benfon, late bifhop of this diocefe. A rational piety raifed the views of this excellent man above the world, and formed his whole temper into a truly chriftian fpirit of refignation. An uncommon warmth of benevolence made it the bufinefs and pleafure of his life to go about doing good, by inftruction in righteoufnefs, and by works of charity. He watched the flock of Chrift as a faithful fhepherd, from a fenfe of his own duty, and a difinterefted concern for their common welfare: And he maintained the dignity of his authority, by the meeknefs with which he exercifed it. He felt a deep compaffion for the vicious; and fhewed it, even whilft he was expofing the folly and wickednefs of vice, with a ftrength and turn of language peculiar to himfelf. His reproofs being dictated by friendfhip, qualified by candour, and

delivered

delivered with a natural delicacy of manners, were fincere without roughnefs, and endearing without diffimulation. He was by conftitution liable to a depreffion of fpirits, but innocence of heart enlivened his mind, and his converfation, with a chearfulnefs that created a more affectionate regard for his fuperior worth, by rendering it more familiar and amiable. Under the moft acute pains of his laft illnefs he poffeffed his foul in patience, and with a firm truft in his redeemer, calmnly refigned his fpirit to the father of mercies.

That fuch an example might be perpetuated, Gabriel Hanger erected this monument in memory of his ever honoured friend.

Another decent monument is fixed by his executor againft the weft wall of the nave of this church, near the place of his interment; which, at the requeft of this amiable and good prelate, is as near the door as conveniently might be.

William Johnfon, D.D. fucceeded bifhop Benfon, and was tranflated from this fee to that of Worcefter, November the 9th, 1759, upon which

William Warburton, D.D. was elected. His writings fhew him to be a perfon of great learning, and he is the prefent bifhop of this diocefe.

Of the DEANERY, DEANS, CHAPTER, &c.

IN the charter of foundation of the bifhoprick of Gloucefter, the king eftablifhed a dean and fix prebendaries in the place of the abbats and monks, and endowed them by his letters patents, with

The Manors of Tuffley, Ablode, and Sainthurft, Barnwood and Croneham, Matfon, Wotton, Churcham, Rudford, Coln-Rogers, Ablington, Coln-Aldwyns, Eaftlech-Martin, alias Burthroppe, Cotes, Tyberton, Tayneton and Bulley, in the county of Gloucefter; Willingifwike and Monkhide, in the county of Hereford; Tregoffe and Pennon, in the county of Glamorgan; Linkynholt, Littleton, and Wallop, in the county of Southampton.

The White Hart inn in Holborn, together with the rent of eight fhillings, which ufed to be paid for the faid inn, or tenement, to the late monaftery of Carthufians, near the city of London.—The firft herbage of Meneham meadow, containing thirty-nine acres, and of Archdeacon's meadow, containing eighteen acres, both in the county of Gloucefter.—A moiety of the wood called Wolridge, containing by eftimation five hundred acres, and a moiety of the wood called Le Perch, containing by eftimation fixteen acres; both lying in the parifh of Saint Mary de Lode; Barnwood grove, containing ten acres; the wood called Buckholt, containing two hundred acres; the wood called Byrd-wood, containing one hundred acres; all lying in the county of Gloucefter; the wood called Weft-woods, in Lynkynholte, in the county of Southampton, containing fixty acres; the wood called Littleton-Coppice, in the faid county, containing forty-eight acres.

A fee-farm rent of 4*l*. a year out of the manor of Wallop, in the county of Southampton; and all the houfes, market, fairs, toll, and all profits whatfoever, lying or being in the city of Gloucefter, or fuburbs thereof, which belonged to the late monaftery of Saint Peter there.

The rectories of Barnwood, Brokethrop, Churcham, Colne-Alwyn, Fairford, and Eaftlech-Martyn, in the county of Gloucefter; of Saint Mary de Lode, and the rectory and church, or chapel of Gracelane, in the city of Gloucefter; the rectories and churches of Sherfton and Aldrington, in the county of Wilts; Great-Marlow, in the county of Bucks; Chippingnorton, in the county of Oxford; Lancarnan, Lantwit, Lamblethian, Lantriffam, Senmarke and Cardiffe, with the chapel of Saint Donats, in the county of Glamorgan.

Portions of tithes in Barton-Abbats, in the parifh of Saint Mary de Lode; and in Senebrug, both in the county of the city of Gloucefter; in Fairford, Upleaden, Hyneleaden, Ablode, Sainthurft, Wotton, Ewrendyefield, Kings-Furlong, and Innyfworth, in the county of Gloucefter; in Hilmerton, in the county of Wilts; and Okeborne, in the county of Bucks.

Penfions yearly to be taken out of the following rectories, &c. *viz.* 20*s*. out of St. John Baptift, and 13*s*. 4*d*. out of St. Nicholas, both in the city of Gloucefter; 10*s*. out of Mattifden, in the county of Gloucefter; 53*s*. 4*d*. out of Alcannynge, and 20*s*. out of Lydyard Tregoz, both in the county of Wilts; 4*l*. out of St. Peter de Mancroft, in the city of Norwich; 40*s*. out of St. Martin in Vintry, in the city of London; and 10*s*. to be paid by the guardians of Braze-nofe college, Oxon.

Advowfons, and rights of patronage, to the rectories of Mattifdon, Rudford, Coln-Rogers, Ablington and Taynton, in the county of Gloucefter; and Lynkynholte, in the county of Southampton;—And to the vicarages of Fairford, Brookthrop, Churcham, Lyncham and Colne-Alwyns, in the county of Gloucefter; of the Holy Trinity, in the city of Gloucefter; of Sherfton, and Aldrington, in the county of Wilts; of Great Marlow, in the county of Bucks: of Lantwitt, Lamblethian, Lantriffam, Penmarke, and Cardiffe, with the chapel of St. Donats, in the county of Glamorgan. The chapter prefent alfo to Chipping-Norton, in Oxfordfhire.

The dean and chapter are fubject to a rent-charge, at firft referved to the crown of 90*l*. 14*s*. *ob.* but which was granted away from it by king Charles the

the Second, and is now, or at least was lately, paid to a person of the name of Da Costa. They are also subject to other annual payments to the amount of 44*l.* 16*s.* 7*d.* *q.* which may be seen more particularly in the Charter of Endowment printed in the Appendix No. 9.

The manors of Linkynholt and Littleton, were given by the dean and chapter, under their common seal, to king Henry the Eighth, the 20th of May, 37° *regni*; and probably Wallop was granted to him about the same time, since which there have been but few alienations from the first endowment.

It was affirmed in parliament, June the 15th, 1641, that upon a survey of the lands, &c. of this deanery, 'it then appeared to have above twelve rectories of great value; about thirty vicarages; pensions, and portions of tythes; almost the third part of the houses of the city of Gloucester, of which the old rent was about 175*l.* besides the yearly revenues of eighteen goodly manors, divers other lands, tenements and hereditaments, manor-houses, and premisses; the old rent of assize of one of the eight manors, being 80*l.* a year.'

The dean's house seems to have belonged to the prior of the abbey; and it is said in an old book in the custody of the corporation, that on the 8th of July, 1648, a lease for seven years was granted of the deanery, by the mayor and burgesses, to Thomas Pury, jun. at 40*s.* *per ann.* in consideration of his having laid out 80*l.* to repair it.

The letters patent for the foundation of the deanery are printed in the Appendix No. 7; and the statutes of the cathedral, which are the same with those of Bristol, and other new foundations, are printed in the Appendix No. 28. They were compiled by Dr. Heath, then bishop of Worcester, in whose diocese Gloucestershire was, 'till erected into a distinct bishoprick; he was afterwards archbishop of York and lord chancellor of England; by Dr. Day, then bishop of Chichester; and archdeacon Cox, who was afterwards preceptor and almoner to king Edward the Sixth, chancellor of the university of Oxford, and dean of Christ-church, from whence he was removed to the deanery of Westminster. He was a great maintainer of the English liturgy and rights, at Frankfort, against Knox and the Puritans, when he was exiled in the reign of queen Mary; and was preferr'd by queen Elizabeth to the bishoprick of Ely.

The arms of the dean and chapter, appointed by Christoper Barker, esq; principal king at arms, March 28, 1542, are, *Azure, a fess Or, charged with three crosses formy, fitchy, of the first. In chief a canton gules charged with a demy rose with beams of the third, between two demy fleurs de lis of the first.*

DEANS of GLOUCESTER.

William Jenings, B.D. (the last prior of St. Oswald's, a monk of St. Peter's abbey) being the king's chaplain, was appointed the first dean by the charter of foundation, dated September 3, 1541. Whilst he was dean, he was incumbent of St. John's, in Gloucester, and of Swindon, Beverstone, and Cromhall, in this diocese. He died November the 4th, 1565, and was buried in the middle of the choir, opposite the choristers seat; and had a large stone laid over him, which was removed, in the year 1718, to the east cloister, before the old chapter-house door; at each corner of which stone his arms are engraved on a brass plate; *viz.* 1. *On a fess three roundels.* 2. *A bull's head caboshed.* 3. *On two bars six martlets.* 4. as the first. On another plate is the following inscription:

> Hic Gulielme jaces Jeninges, quem sex quater annos
> Edes decanum viderat ista suum.
> Milleni, a Christo, quinginti bisque triceni
> Et quinti, quarta luce Novembris, obis.
> Clarus avo fueras, clarus patre, clarus et ipse;
> Doctrina clarus, clarus et ingenio.
> Non tam pane tuo, quam Christi pane replesti
> Christicolas, ergo vivis et astra tenes.

John Man, A.M. master, or keeper, of St. Bartholomew's hospital in this city, warden of Merton college in Oxford, and prebendary of Bigleswade in Lincoln cathedral, being presented by queen Elizabeth on the 10th of December, was instituted by proxy, in the person of Mr. Walter Jones, February 2, 1565. It appears by the books in the custody of the register, that the queen granted him a dispensation that he might keep all his preferments, and receive all the profits of them, without being obliged to take any other degree, which is said to have been done, to enable him to perform an embassy the more honourably, on which the queen intended to send him. He died March the 18th, 1568, and was buried in the church of St. Anne, Aldersgate, London, without any memorial; and was succeeded by

Thomas Cooper, or Cowper, D.D. who was instituted on the 5th of July, 1569. He was removed to the bishoprick of Lincoln in 1570, and thence to Winchester in 1584.

Lawrence Humfry, or Humphrey, D.D. *regius professor* of divinity, and president of Magdalen college, in Oxford, was instituted on the 13th of March, 1570. In 1574, he occurs one of the ecclesiastical commissioners for the queen; as he does in 1576, to the archbishop of Canterbury, for metropolitical visitation. Being afterwards preferred to the deanery of Winchester, he was succeeded by

Anthony Rud, D.D. who was instituted the 10th of January, 1584; and on the 9th of June, 1594, was preferred to the bishoprick of St. David.

Griffith, or Jeffry, or Griffin, Lewis, D.D. rector of Kingsland, was installed the same year. In his will, dated February 5, 1606, and proved July the 16th, he desires to be buried in one of the cathedrals of Gloucester, Worcester, or Hereford, or Westminster abbey, in all which he was a dignitary;

and accordingly was interred in the cathedral church of Hereford, June the 6th, 1607; but there is no memorial of him.

Thomas Moreton, D. D. fucceed him on the 22d of June, 1607. In 1609, he was removed hence to the deanery of Winchefter; and thence, in 1616, to the bifhoprick of Chefter; thence alfo, in 1618, to the bifhoprick of Litchfield and Coventry; and laftly, was promoted to that of Durham in 1632.

Richard Field, D. D. chaplain to queen Elizabeth and king James the Firft, canon of Windfor, rector of Burg (or Borough) Clere, in Hampfhire, was promoted to this deanery in 1609. In the year 1610, the king appointed him one of the fellows of Chelfea college, who were a body of very eminent divines. He died on the 21ft of November, 1616, and was buried at Windfor, with this infcription on his grave-ftone:

Richardus Field hujus olim coll. canonicus, et ecclefiæ Glouceft. Decanus, vere Doctor Theologiæ, et author librorum V. *De ecclefia*; una cum Elizabetha Hariffia, fanctiffima et chariffima conjuge, ex qua fex reliquit filios, et filiam unicam; hic, fub communi marmore, expectant Chrifti reditum, qui felicitatem quam ingreffi funt adventu fuo perficiat ac confummet. Obierunt in Domino, hic, anno falutis 1616, Ætatis fuæ 55: hæc, anno falutis 1614, Ætatis fuæ 41.

Mr. A. Wood, in his *Athenæ*, tells us, that he was a principal maintainer of proteftancy, a powerful preacher, a profound fchool-man, and an exact difputant.

William Laud, D. D. fucceeded, and was inftalled December the 20th, 1616; promoted to the fee of St. David in 1621; thence removed to Bath and Wells, afterwards to London, thence to Canterbury, and was beheaded on the 10th of January, 1644.

Richard Senhoufe, D. D. fellow of St. John's college, in Cambridge, and chaplain to prince Charles, was inftalled the 13th of December, 1621, and, in 1624, was made bifhop of Carlifle; whereupon

Thomas Winniff, D. D. chaplain to the king, and fome time to prince Henry, and prince Charles, was inftalled November the 10th, 1624, and afterwards made dean of St. Paul's; and thence removed to the fee of London.

George Warburton, M. A. the king's chaplain, was inftalled on the 11th of June, 1631; but in Auguft following was removed to the deanery of Wells.

Accepted Frewen, D. D. the king's chaplain, prefident of Magdalen college, and vice-chancellor of Oxford, was inftalled September the 13th, 1631. In 1644, he was advanced to the bifhoprick of Litchfield and Coventry; and in 1660, was tranflated to the archbifhoprick of York.

William Brough, D. D. was nominated by the king Auguft the 17th, 1643, and inftalled the 20th of November, 1644. He died July the 5th, 1671, and was buried at Windfor, of which he had been one of the canons, with this fhort infcription on his grave-ftone:

Dr. William Brough, dean of Gloucefter, and prebendary of Windfor, was buried here.

Thomas Viner, D. D. prebendary of this cathedral, and canon of Windfor, was inftalled the 23d of July, 1671. He died April 11, 1673, and was buried in the lady's chapel in this cathedral, on the 18th, with the following infcription on his graveftone:

Thomas Viner, D. D. hujus ecclefiæ decanus, et Winforianæ prebendarius; illuftris genere, pietate in Deum, venuftate, ingenio, comitate, morum integritate vitæ illibatæ longe illuftrior, qui fummo amicorum luctu & mœrore deceffit, April. 11, A. D. 1673, Ætatis 44.

Robert Frampton, M. A. prebendary of this cathedral, was inftalled on the 6th of May, 1673, and promoted to the bifhoprick in 1680-1.

Thomas Marfhal, D. D. rector of Lincoln college in Oxford, a noted critic, and, according to Mr. Wood, every way worthy of his ftation in the church, was inftalled April the 30th, 1681; and dying, April 19, 1685, was buried in All-Saints church, in Oxford, with this epitaph:

P. M. S. Tho. Marfhal, S. T. D. quem in agro Leiceft. Barkbega genuit; Oxonium educavit; ex paftore mercator. Dordrect. Lincoln Collegium primo focium, deinde rectorem, fecit. Gloucefttriæ decanus impiger, concionibus potens, & creber pietate, infignis doctrina linguarum orientalium & occidentalium, aquila perfpicax, Ægyptiæ phænix unicus. Ex mufæo inftructiffimo academiæ libros in B. P. defideratos, collegio reliquos, et pecunias amplas, legavit: fui depofitum heic reliquit 18 Aprilis, 1685.

William Jane, D. D. *regius profeffor* of divinity in Oxford, prebendary of Exeter, was inftalled June the 6th, 1685; and dying at Chrift's-church college, in Oxford, where he was one of the canons, was buried in the cathedral there, without any memorial.

Knightley Chetwood, or Chetwode, D. D. archdeacon of York, rector of Rifington Magna, and Rifington Parva, in this diocefe, was inftalled the 6th of April, 1707. And dying about March, 1719, was buried at Tempsford, co. Bedford, (where he had an eftate) with this infcription:

Knightly Chetwoode, egregius fane et fingularis vir, ingenio adeò fublimi et venufto, adeo divinis et humanis literis exculto, ut nihil fupra. Ecclefiæ et patriæ amiciffimus, catholicæ fidei rigidus fervator. Immortalitatem adivit, annum exigens fexagefimum octavum, tertio nonas Aprilis, MDCCXX.

Τὸ θνητὸν τῦτο ἐνδύσηται ἀθανασίαν.

John Waugh, D. D. rector of St. Peter's, Cornhill, London, and prebendary of Lincoln, was inftituted Auguft the 4th, 1720, and inftalled on the morrow. In Auguft, 1723, he was made bifhop of Carlifle, and had his deanery in *commendam* 'till chriftmas following. In his time the common feal of the dean and chapter, which had been ufed all along from the foundation thereof, was altered, being the old picture of the Trinity, and a new one appointed to be ufed inftead of it. On the old one was reprefented an old man fitting under an arch, with a long beard and a great beam of light over his head, intended for God the Father: he had between his knees a crofs, with our Saviour on it, held by his hands at each of the crofs ends, defigned for God the Son; and a dove at the upper end of the crofs, intended for God the Holy Ghoft. Below were the arms of dean Jeninges, and on the fides the initial letters of his

his name, W. J.—Round it was SIGILLV COMVNE DECANI ET CAPITVLI ECCLESIÆ CATHEDRAL. SCTE ET INDIVIDVÆ TRINITAT. GLOU. The feal now made ufe of by the dean and chapter has the arms of the dean and chapter, and under them the arms of dean Waugh, *viz. On a chevron three roundlets*; and on the fides of his arms the initial letters of his name, I. W.

John Frankland, D. D. rector of St. Stephen's, Briftol, upon dean Waugh's promotion, was appointed to fucceed him; and left this deanery for that of Ely, and the mafterfhip of Sidney college, in Cambridge.

Peter Alix, D. D. rector of Caftle-Camps, in the county of Cambridge, upon Dr. Frankland's exchange, was promoted in the year 1729, and exchanged it for the deanery of Ely.

Daniel Newcombe, D. D. rector of Whimple in the county of Devon, upon Dr. Alix's exchange, was admitted in 1730.

Jofiah Tucker, D. D. fucceeded July 13, 1758, who was one of the prebendaries of Briftol, and rector of St. Stephen's in that city. He refigned his prebend, but holds the rectory, and is the prefent dean. Befide the great learning and abilities which diftinguifh him in his profeffion, he is eminent for his extenfive charity, and for his great knowledge in the true principles of trade and commerce, and other matters refpecting the police of a country.

CHANCELLORS, or VICARS GENERAL.

John Williams, LL. B. (afterwards LL. D.) and Richard Brown, LL. B. took upon them jointly the office of chancellor, on the 28th of November, 1541. How long they enjoyed it together does not appear; but probably it might be 'till about the year 1545, when a commiffion was granted to Hugh Whittington, LL. B. for exercifing a part of the vicar-general's office in fome deaneries of this diocefe, only during the bifhop's pleafure. This Williams, in king Henry the Eighth's reign, appears very zealous in the execution of the fix articles. In the next reign, he was a fudden convert to proteftantifm; and he began queen Mary's with depriving feveral clergymen of their livings for their marriage. In 1555, he condemned Henry Hicks, a carpenter or joiner of this city, to carry a faggot in Berkeley church, and in this cathedral; and delivered over to the fecular power Thomas Croker, a bricklayer, and Thomas Drowry, a blind boy, who were both burnt in May, 1556. It is affirmed, that in 1558, when the ecclefiaftical commiffioners appointed by queen Elizabeth were coming to Gloucefter, and dean Jeninges (with whom he dined that day) intreating him to meet the commiffioners, he declared he never would fee them, and was as good as his word, for he died on the fame day. He was fometime incumbent of the Holy Trinity in Gloucefter, of Rockhampton, Beverftone, Painfwick, Siddington St. Mary, Coln St. Dennis, and Welford, in this county; and a prebendary in Gloucefter cathedral.

After Dr. Williams's death, during the vacancy of this fee, Dr. Powel is mentioned as dean, who was then vicar-general to the archbifhop of Canterbury for this diocefe, and keeper of its fpiritualties, and was afterwards chancellor.

John Louth, LL. B. was advanced on the 4th of November, 1562, to continue during the bifhop's pleafure. And, November the 26th, 1565, was removed to give place to

Thomas Powel, LL. D. who was foon after promoted; but, January the 12th, 1570, the bifhop recalling his letters commiffional for this office, granted them to

Richard Green, LL. B. auditor, or commiffioner, to the bifhop in his court. He occurs a commiffioner for ecclefiaftical caufes, appointed by queen Elizabeth in 1574, 1575, and 1577. But about the beginning of the year 1576, was amoved in order to reftore

Dr. Powel, who occurs in this office April the 10th, 1576, as alfo a commiffioner for ecclefiaftical caufes, appointed by the queen. He feems to have been fometime vicar of Barrington Magna, and rector of Kemmerton. In 1579, he was fufpended by the queen's commiffioners from this office during his life, and excommunicated.

William Blackleach, LL. B. was promoted in 1581. In 1588, the bifhop recalled his commiffion; and on the 13th of March, in the fame year, granted it to Gilbert Borne, LL. B. yet Blackleach notwithftanding continued by force the exercife of this office. And refufing to withdraw from the confiftory court, the bifhop excommunicated him on the 8th of July. From this fentence he appealed to the archbifhop of Canterbury, and at length, by an injunction from the lord high chancellor, was reftored to his office by the bifhop on the 6th of October, 1590. After this, great animofities and contradictions continued between the bifhop and Blackleach, concerning their feveral jurifdictions, but nothing more material enfued.

John Seaman, LL. D. was promoted about the 2d of October, 1600; and Thomas Edwards, LL. D. occurs with him in this office Auguft the 10th, 1608; but upon what account it does not appear. He died in 1623, and was buried in the chancel of Painfwick, where there was a handfome monument of alabafter and black marble erected for him, with the following infcription:

Hic iacent Cineres Domini (fumme venerabilis) Johannis Seaman LL Doris Diocefeos Glouc^r Cancell: tum Virtutis, tum Fortunæ dotibus fpectatiffimi.

> Ingenio, ratione vigens, pietate, fideq;
> Vixit: at effractus corp're mille malis.
> Hæc patet ad cœlos via confopita fatigat
> Corda ftupor: fapiunt faucia corda Deum.
> Ille bonis merito charus, charum caput: acer
> Ille malis cenfor: iuftitiæq; tenax.

Pofuit chariffimæ olim nutricis: fidiffimæq; femper coniugis cura piiffima. Labores claufit annis Salutis, 1623, Ætatis 59.

William

William Sutton, M. A. (afterwards D. D.) was confirmed by the chapter July the 16th, 1623. In 1627, this office was granted by patent to him and Dr. Baber jointly and feverally; but foon after, articles were exhibited againft Sutton in the high commiffion court, and tho' he moved for a prohibition to ftop the proceedings, it was not granted, and he was deprived. *See Godolphin's Repert. Ecclef.*

Francis Baber, LL. D. was chancellor in the year 1631, as appears by the books in the office of the regifter. He died in 1669, and was buried in abbat Seabroke's chapel, at the weft end of which, againft a pillar, is a monument erected for him, with this infcription :

Hic fitus eft Vir dum Vixit Venerabilis, Francifcus Baber, Armiger, natus ex Antiqua Familia Baberienfi in Comitatu Somerfet, vtriufque Juris Dr. Cancellarius Diocefeôs Gloucestrienfis per triginta novem annos, quod munus integre executus mira cum omniū Laude Probabtus fuit tum litteris tum moribus. Vixit fuis Charus obijt omnibus defideratus Junij 17.

Anno { Domini 1669
Ætatis fuæ 69.

Elizabetha Conjux filia Jo: Adderley in Com. Midlefex Arm: Obijt 14 Jan :

Anno { Ætatis 63
Dom: 1673.

Over it were his arms, *Gules, a lion couchant in feffe, between fix crofs croflets, three in chief, and as many in bafe, Or.*

John Nicholfon, LL. D. (the bifhop's brother) was advanced in the beginning of July, 1669, and upon his death

Richard Parfons, LL. B. (afterwards LL. D.) was prefented on the 4th, confirmed on the 7th, and admitted on the 24th of April, 1677. He died in 1711, and was buried in the lady's chapel, and on the grave-ftone is the following infcription :

Rich. Parfons, DLL. fellow of the new college in Oxon, vicar of Dryfield, and chancellor of this diocefe, in which ftation he lived thirty-four years, diligent in the execution of his office, and eminent as well for hofpitality to ftrangers, as charity to the poor. He died June 12, 1711, aged 68.

Henry Penrice, LL. D. fucceeded him on the 18th of June, 1711. And in the year 1715, was advanced to be judge of the high court of admiralty, and to the honour of knighthood.

James Benfon, M. A. now LL. D. was appointed in the year 1752, and is the prefent chancellor of the diocefe.

Of the Archdeaconry and Archdeacons.

Archdeacons were antiently inferior to rural deans, and were originally appointed to infpect the diligence of deacons in the collecting and diftributing of alms; but by their perfonal attendance on bifhops, engroffed their favour, and gradually grew to be more confiderable than rural deans.

The places fubject to the archdeacon of this diocefe, are fet down in pp. 153, 154, 155. It remains only to obferve, that John Carpenter, bifhop of Worcefter, appropriated the rectory of Durfley to the archdeaconry of Gloucefter, in the year 1475, which rectory belonged to St. Peter's abbey, and was given in exchange for the archdeacon's houfe in Gloucefter.

Nicholas Wotton, LL. D. the king's chaplain, who was the laft archdeacon of Gloucefter in the church of Worcefter, was appointed archdeacon by the charter of foundation, September the 3d, 1541. About the fame time he was made dean of Canterbury, and in the year 1544, was alfo made dean of York, and then he refigned this archdeaconry.

Guy Eaton, B. D. was poffeffed of it about 1545; and in the year 1553, he left it, with his other preferments, and quitted the kingdom.

John Williams, LL. D. chancellor of the diocefe, and one of the prebendaries of this church, in queen Mary's reign, concerning whom fee chancellors, occurs September the 15th, 1554; but upon queen Elizabeth's acceffion to the crown

Guy Eaton was again made one of the prebendaries of this church, in the year 1559; but afterwards refigning,

George Savage, LL. B. rector of Saintbury in this county, was inftituted February the 1ft, 1574, by the chancellor, in the chapel of the church of Stow; having firft fworn, as appears by the book in the bifhop's regifter, to pay a yearly penfion of 25 *l.* to Guy Eaton, for his life. In 1575, he occurs commiffioner for ecclefiaftical caufes; and in the year 1580, the archbifhop of Canterbury made him his commiffioner for a metropolitical vifitation.

Robert Hill, B. D. was collated September the 1ft, 1602, who, it is fuppofed, either died about the year 1604, being rector of Tredington, in Warwickfhire, or quitted this office, for

Samuel Burton, M. A. rector of Long Marfton, or Marfton Sicca, in this county, occurs in 1606; and dying on the 14th of June, 1634, was buried at Long Marfton before-mentioned, and has this infcription on a brafs plate on his tomb, on the fouth fide of the chancel :

Cineres reverendi viri magiftri Sam. Burton fub hoc lapide quiefcunt, quem Staffordienfis ager eduxit, Ædes Chrifti, Oxon, in re literaria educavit, et academia novit theologum eruditum, quem incolæ hujus loci per 36 plus minus annos habuerunt doctum perfpicuum et affiduum præconem, pium etiam et pacificum rectorem; quem quinque Glouceftrienfes epifcopi probarunt occulum vigilantem; diocefis expertus fuit prudentem archidiaconum, comitatus peritum juftitiarium. Hic poft laborum 66 annos in ergaftulo humanæ carnis fortiter exantlatos et emenfos, terrena reliquit, et in Domino placidè obdormivit 14 Junii ann. poft Chriftum natum 1634.

Hugh Robinfon, D. D. canon of Wells, fucceeded him, who died April the 6th, 1755.

John Middleton was inftalled Auguft the 7th, 1660, having been prefented July the 19th to this dignity by the crown, to which it was lapfed after Dr. Robinfon's death. He was rector of Hanwell in Middlefex, where probably he was buried.

Edward Pope, M. A. was collated November the 2d, 1662, and was buried at Walton on the Hill, in the county of Surry, within the communion rails, with this epitaph on his grave-ftone :

Here is interred the body of Edward Pope, archdeacon of Gloucefter, and rector of this parifh; honoured for piety and pains in preaching and catechifing; learned in Hebrew, Greek, Latin, and the arts; beloved for his courteous demeanour to all perfons; charitable to blind and lame, to fick, to fore, to poor. Now rewarded piety, charity, and works of hofpitality, refteth here. Quod claudi potuit hic jacet. To eternize his memory this is here erected. He died the 26th of December, 1671.

John

John Gregory, M.A. was collated December the 31ſt, 1671, and dying December the 10th, 1678, was buried in the chancel of Hempſted church, near Glouceſter, with this inſcription upon him.

John Gregory ſecond rector of this church, and archdeacon of Glouceſter, died December 10, 1678, in the 50th year of his age.

Ἁμαρτωλῶν πρῶτος, ἁγίων ἐλαχιστότερος.

Thomas Hyde, M.A. was collated the 10th of December, and inſtalled the 12th of January, 1678. He died February the 12th, 1702, and was buried at Hanborough, near Oxford.

Robert Parſons, M.A. was inſtalled March the 10th, 1702, and dying July the 18th, 1714, was buried at Oddington, in this county, whereof he was rector.

Nathaniel Lye, D.D. prebendary of Briſtol, and rector of Kemmerton, in this county, was collated on the 29th of July, and inſtalled the 1ſt of Auguſt, 1714; being alſo one of the prebendaries of this cathedral. He died on the 31ſt of October, 1737, and was buried in St. Michael's church in this city, under the ſeats over againſt the pulpit, and has a ſmall monument againſt the north wall, with this inſcription:

Near this place is interred the body of NATHANIEL LYE, D.D. archdeacon and prebendary of GLOUCESTER, and rector of the pariſhes of KEMERTON, and DURSLEY, in this county. He married BRIDGET, the daughter of RICHARD GODDARD, of SWINDON, in the county of WILTS, Eſq; who alſo lyes buried here, by whom he left iſſue one daughter, now the wife of RICHARD SOUTHBY, of CARSWELL, in BERKSHIRE, Eſq; He died 31ſt of October, 1737, aged 89.

William Geekie, D.D. prebendary of Canterbury and of Allhallows, Barking, London, upon Dr. Lye's death, was admitted (by an option granted to the late archbiſhop of Canterbury upon biſhop Benſon's conſecration) on the 4th of November, 1737. Upon whoſe death,

Richard Hurd, B.D. now D.D. was collated Auguſt the 27th, 1767; and is the preſent archdeacon. He is the author of *Moral and Political Dialogues*, 8vo. and of ſeveral other writings which have been well received by the public.

Prebends and Prebendaries.

When the Norman monarchy was firſt ſettled, prebendaries and prieſts in England were not obliged to celebacy; and it was grown into a cuſtom, for eccleſiaſtical benefices to deſcend hereditarily to the next of blood, which occaſioned a great conteſt between the heirs of the prebends of the monaſtery of St. Peter and St. Paul at Shrewſbury, and the monks of the ſame place, who claimed the prebends after the death of the firſt prebendaries. *Camden, col.* 656.

Formerly lay-men might have been prebendaries of our cathedrals, except of thoſe erected by king Henry the Eighth. It is ſaid, that the duke of Somerſet, in the reign of king Edward the Sixth, had engroſſed to himſelf fifty prebends. But the laity are now excluded by the *act of uniformity*, made after the reſtoration of king Charles the Second, which requires the reading of the whole divine ſervice within two months after being admitted.

There are ſix prebends in this church, five of which are in the gift of the king, and one is annexed to the maſterſhip of Pembroke college in Oxford, by 12° *Annæ*, ſt. 2. c. 6. ſ. 7. None of the prebends are charged with the payment of firſt fruits or tenths. Though there are no fixed ſtalls kept here ſince the reſtoration, and the cuſtom is to inſtall the junior prebendary always in the ſixth, or loweſt ſtall, the ſeries ſeems to ſtand in the following order.

Firſt Stall.

Richard Browne, LL.B. the king's chaplain, was appointed at the foundation, September the 3d, 1541; and on the 2d of April, 1554, was deprived of his prebend, and the rectory of Great Riſington, in this county, becauſe he was married.

Robert Morwent, M.A. was thereupon collated by biſhop Brookes, on the 11th of June following; and dying Auguſt the 26th, 1558, was buried at Corpus Chriſti college in Oxford, where he was preſident.

John Woodward, M.A. was preſented on the 2d of September, inſtalled on the 10th, 1558, and reſigned in 1571.

Thomas Perry, or Pury, M.A. who afterwards took the degree of B.D. was inſtalled January the 30th, 1571, upon Woodward's reſignation. He was rector of Beverſtone, in this county, and reſigned his prebend about the year 1610.

Thomas Prior, M.A. afterwards B.D. and lecturer to the corporation of this city, was inſtalled the 21ſt of September, 1612. He was alſo curate of St. Nicholas, in this city, and rector of Cowley, and of Seiſincote, in the county of Glouceſter; and dying about Auguſt, 1632, was ſucceeded by

George Palmer, B.D. who was inſtalled on the 25th of October, 1632. He was ſequeſter'd from this dignity, and from his vicarage of Northall, in the county of Middleſex, in the year 1642, and was buried at Hays, near Uxbridge, September the 28th, 1658.

Walter Blandford, D.D. was preſented Auguſt the 6th, and inſtalled the 22d, 1660. In the year 1665, he was made biſhop of Oxford, and was ſucceeded by

Henry Savage, D.D. maſter of Baliol college in Oxford, who was inſtalled on the 12th of January, 1665. He died in January 1672, and was buried in Baliol college chapel, without any memorial.

Robert Frampton, M.A. was inſtalled on the 23d of July, 1672, who being made dean,

Nathaniel Hodges, M.A. was inſtalled on the 20th of May, 1673. He died the 28th of Auguſt, in the year 1700, and was buried in Norwich cathedral, where he was alſo a prebendary, with this inſcription on his grave-ſtone:

Reliquiæ Nath. Hodges, A.M. viri doctrina & ſapientia ornatiſſimi; probi & bene moralis, qui Ædis primum Chriſti apud

Oxonienſes ſocius, in eadem academia procuratoris, & moralis philoſophiæ prælectoris, officium ſumma cum laude præſtitit. Eccleſiæ tandem Norwicenſis, & Glouceſtrenſis, canonicus, cujus omnis religio quum vere cœleſtis fuit (virtus ſcilicet omnimodum animi Deo conjunxit) juſtitiam bonitatemque divinam imitando coluit pietatem non cavendo pius. Annos natus LXVI, denatus eſt Aug. XXVIII, anno Domini MDCC.

Benjamin King, M. A. afterwards D. D. ſucceeded, and was inſtalled on the 26th of September, 1700. He was ſometime vicar of All-Saints, in the town of Northampton, and of St. Mary de Lode in this city, on the ſouth ſide of the chancel of which church he was buried, but has no memorial.

Henry Galley, D. D. was inſtalled in 1728, and again, upon his being made prebendary of Norwich, alſo in 1731; to whom,

Edward Wilſon, A. M. ſucceeded September the 1ſt, 1769.

Second Stall.

Henry Willis, B. D. vicar of Toddington, in this county, was appointed at the foundation on the 3d of September, 1541, and was deprived of his prebend, of the rectory of Uly, and of the vicarage of Sherburn, in this county, the 2d of April, 1544, upon account of his marriage.

William Collynge, B. D. was thereupon preſented the ſame day; and collated by biſhop Brookes, June the 11th, 1554. Upon his death,

John Tomſon, B. D. was collated, October the 3d, 1556.

John Smith, LL. D. upon Tomſon's removal, was preſented by queen Elizabeth, 1559, and was alſo archdeacon of Landaff. Dying about February, or March, 1563-4, he was ſucceeded by

Robert Jones, in the year 1564, who reſigning in 1573, was alſo ſucceeded by

Richard Shippar, or Sheppard, M. A. inſtituted November the 26th, 1573. Probably, he was buried at Wantage, in Berkſhire, where he was vicar.

Elias Wrench, M. A. was inſtituted on the 22d of March, 1598, and afterwards rector of Laſſington, and of Rudford, both in Glouceſterſhire, which he held to the time of his death; which happening in 1633, he was buried in the cathedral, near the entrance into the choir, and had this inſcription on braſs over him; but the ſtone to which the braſs was fixed is now taken away. The ſtone ('tis probable) was removed ſome years paſt to the weſt cloiſter.

Hic quod reliquum eſt de corpore Eliæ Wrench hujus eccleſiæ per annos 34 prebendarii, Chriſtum morte ſuſcitaturum expectat.

Nuntius æterni verbi ſincerus Elias,
Æquo ſervavit tramite pacis iter.
Cœleſtem conſtante viam pietate ſecutus,
Speq; fideq; ratis, amplior ardet amor.

Obiit ætatis 71, Octo: 4to, anno ſalutis 1633.

John Engliſh, D. D. ſucceeded him here and in the rectory of Rudford. He was preſented the 4th of November, 1633, inſtalled the 22d of April following, and died before the reſtoration. At the eaſt end of the chancel of the church of Cheltenham, in this county, is the following epitaph, on a table of free-ſtone, for his wife and daughter:

The ſad memorial of John Engliſh, D[r]. in divinitie, to Jane, his moſt deare wife, daughter to the H[le]. Eliz[th]. Lady Sandys, baroneſſe de la Vine, comit. Southton, from whom he was divorced by eighteen months cloſe impriſonm[t]. which ſoon after cauſed her death, on Aug[st]. 8th, 1643: and to Marie, his 2[d] daughter, who deceaſed Oct[r]. 25 following.

John Engliſh S {acri / anctæ / empiternæ} V {erbi / eritatis / itæ} ſtudioſus.

J. E.

Thomas Warmſtry, D. D. rector of Minchin-Hampton, in this county, was preſented July the 27th, and inſtalled Auguſt the 19th, 1660; and dying October the 30th, 1665, being about ſixty years old, was buried in the cathedral of Worceſter, of which he was dean.

Memoriæ dicatum, Thomæ Warmſtrey, S. S. Theol. Dr. decani olim Wigorn. Strenuus hic eccleſ. Anglic. hyperaſpiſtes, pietatis æmulandæ, fidelitatis indelibatæ, Deo ſuum Cæſarique donavit. Cujus hoſpitalitatem ad majorum munificentiam compoſitam ſenſerunt pauperes, coluerunt peregrini, humanitatem ſtupuit quicquid humanum eſt, charitatem quicquid in homine divinum eſt Paulinum illum etiam etiamnum inculcat, Imitatores mei eſtote. 1 Cor. xi. 1.

Hujus poſthumæ concionis vixit ad exemplar, et ſublimato poſt ſæcula pulvere, redintegratum corporis ſumet amictum, iterum concionaturus vel in obſequium tui, vel in judicium viator. 30mo 8[bris] die deceſſit, anno ſalutis noſtræ 1665. Ætatis ſuæ circa ſexageſſimum.

Thomas Vyner, B. D. rector of Staunton, in this county, was inſtalled November the 20th, 1665, and being promoted to the deanery of this church,

Abraham Gregory, M. A. afterwards D. D. one of the king's chaplains, rector of Cowley, and vicar of Churcham, both in the county of Glouceſter, and præcentor of Landaff, was inſtalled July the 31ſt, 1671; and dying, was buried in the eaſt cloiſter of this cathedral, near the old chapter-houſe door, with this inſcription on his grave-ſtone:

Hic ad terram reverſum eſt quicquid Terreſtre fuit ABRAHAMI GREGORY, S. T. P. qui cathedralem hanc eccleſiam per 19 annos canonicus digniſſimus, eruditione ſumma ac moribus ſpectatiſſimis ornavit. Vir eximia ac minime fucata in Deum pietate, et invicta erga eccleſiam anglicanam (hinc illæ lacrymæ) conſtantia: Aſſiduam magis in paſtorali munere diligentiam, propenſiorem in egenos animum, apertiorem manum, ſinceriorem in colendis amicitiis fidem, in collegii hujuſce commodis promovendis impenſius ſtudium, ſtrictiorem erga omnes juſtitiam charitate melius temperatam, inter ſibi ſuperſtites vix reliquit: Talis cum eſſet, indigno huic ſæculo, tam immatura morte ereptum, minus mirabere ſed magis dolebis. Obiit Julij 29, anno Domini 1690, Ætatis ſuæ 47.

At the upper part of the ſtone are theſe arms. *Two bars, in chief a lion paſſant.*

John Newton, M. A. ſucceeding, was inſtalled on the 24th of September, 1690; and dying, was buried in the chancel of St. Nicholas's church in this city, on the ſouth ſide of which is a ſmall monument erected for him, with this inſcription:

Hic jacet R. vir JOHANNES NEWTON, A. M. eccleſiæ Anglicanæ preſbyter, olim aulæ de Clare, apud Cantabr. ſocius, et eccleſiæ S[ti] Martini apud Leiceſtrenſes, vicarius; deinde eccleſiæ cathedralis Glouceſt. prebendarius, et eccleſiæ de Taynton, in agro Glouc. rector digniſſimus. Vir, dum vixit, erga Deum pius, erga homines benevolus et beneficus: Amicus fidus, vicinus utilis et innocuus, paſtor ſedulus, maritus et pater amantiſſimus, et ſuis chariſſimus: Qui demum, LXXIII annorum pondere, variiſq; infirmitatibus gravatus, deſideratus obiit, Sept. XX, MDCCXI.

And

And theſe arms. *Argent, on a cheveron azure, three garbs Or*, impaling *per feſs ſable, and argent, three elephants heads with their proboſcides.*

Richard Blechindon, LL.D. the firſt provoſt of Worceſter college in Oxford, (called before Glouceſter hall) was inſtalled September the 28, 1711.

Joſeph Atwell, D.D. rector of Exeter college, Oxford, upon Dr. Blechindon's death, was admitted in the year 1736. He was alſo prebendary of York, and Southwell, and chancellor of Norwich, rector of Oddington, and vicar of Fairford, both in this county. He died in the year 1768, and was ſucceeded by

George Smythe, A.M. October 14, the ſame year; who reſigning,

John Sleech, A.M. was inſtituted Auguſt the 26th, 1769.

Third Stall.

John Rodley, B.D. was admitted at the foundation, the 3d of September, 1541; but dying, or being amoved ſoon after his nomination,

Thomas Kingſwood[a], who had been a monk of the abbey, occurs March the 28th, 1542. He died about Auguſt, 1559, and was buried in this cathedral, being then vicar of Churcham and rector of Taynton, in this county.

Richard Cheiney, B.D. was made prebendary in 1559, and was advanced to the biſhoprick in the year 1562.

Robert Johnſon, M.A. was inſtituted June the 3d, 1562, and died the ſame year, poſſeſſed alſo of Churcham vicarage, in this county.

Arthur Saule, M.A. ſometime fellow of Magdalen college in Oxford, and prebendary of Briſtol, was inſtituted on the 3d of June, 1562; and dying in 1585, poſſeſſed of this dignity, of a prebend in the church of Briſtol, of the prebend of Bedmynſter and Redclive in the church of Saliſbury; of the vicarage of Berkeley, and rectory of Deinton, in this county, was buried in Briſtol cathedral, near the ſteps to the communion table, with an inſcription on his grave-ſtone, in part defaced, as follows:

Here lyeth buried Arthur Sawle, ſometyme prebendary of this church, from his youth up zealous in the goſpel. In the days of hereſie he left his contry for confeſſing of the trueth. In this bleſſed tyme of her majeſty he did long preache the word ——— Paſſed the age of ——— years, he departed this miſerable world very conſtantly, yielding his body to the yerthe, from whence he came, and commytting his ſowle to God who gaue it; wyth whom he liveth everlaſtingly.

Lawrence Bridger, M.A. ſucceeded about the year 1586, and reſigning his ſtall five years before his death, was buried at Slimbridge, in this county, where the following inſcription is on his grave-ſtone:

Here lyeth the body of Lawrence Bridger, who was above 40 years rector of this pariſh. He was buried the 18th day of October 1630.

John Wood, M.A. afterwards B.D. was inſtalled November 23, 1625, and by his will, dated September the 6th, 1639, gave to the mayor and burgeſſes of Glouceſter, a yearly rent charge of 10*l.* 13*l.* 4*d.* for ever out of his lands in Dimmock, in this county, to pay 10*l.* of it to the miniſter of Alſtone in the pariſh of Overbury, in Worceſterſhire, for a lecture ſermon there, and to keep the remaining 13*s.* 4*d.* for their care and trouble.

Gilbert Oſborne, B.D. rector of Withington, in this county, was inſtalled March the 10th, 1639, and was buried at Withington, with this inſcription on his monument, on the ſouth ſide of the chancel.

M. S. viri reverendi Gilberti Oſborne, S. T. B. prebendarii eccleſiæ cathedralis Glouceſtr. necnon rectoris de Withington; qui cum in temporibus pluſquam difficillimis, egregium charitatis exemplar, grandeque fidei ſpecimen dediſſet, et in omnibus vitam ἄσπιλον ϗ ἀνεπίληπτον egiſſet; in beatorum conſortium lubens ſeceſſit. Anna, domini Richardi Oſborne, baronetti de Knocknam, Hiberniæ, filia, mœſtiſſima relicta, amoris erga defunctum conjugem, et mœſtitiæ pignus, hoc, lachrimis humidum, erexit marmor. Obijt Feb. 16, Ætatis 56, A. D. 1656.

Εἰς ἐμὲ ὁρῶν εὐσεβὴς ἔσω.

Diſce ab hoc uno eſſe mori beatum,
Vita cujus mors erat, et ſepultus
Prædicet; vivens, moriens, vocetur
Jure ſacerdos.
Norma vivebat pietatis; hoc ſtet
Marmor, ut poſtea, homines futuri
Sciverint, hæc peſſima ſecula ferre
Eccleſiaſtem.

Thomas Waſhbourne, M.A. (afterwards D.D.) rector of Dumbleton, in this county, was nominated to ſucceed Gilbert Oſborne in 1643, who reſigned. But his inſtallation being thought irregular, he was preſented again on the 23d of July, and inſtalled the 7th of Auguſt, 1660. Dying on the 6th of May, 1687, he was buried in the Lady's chapel in this cathedral, near the north wall; againſt which there is a ſmall monument for him with the following inſcription:

Chariſſimis necnon fraternis, immiſcet cineres, eheu! theologus vere chriſtianus, vere primitivus, Thomas Waſhbourne, S. T. P. eccl. cath. Glouc. per annos 44 prebendarius. Suum hoc humili titulo inſcribens monumentum, Primus peccatorum, minimus miniſtrorum Dei: Plenus dierum, liberorum, curarum, non ita (ſemper enim calcavit) divitiarum, anno ſalutis 1687, Ætatis 80, ſpiritum in manus creatoris tradidit, glorioſam in Chriſto expectans reſurrectionem.

At the top of the monument are theſe arms: *Argent, a feſs gules, charged with three cinque foils of the firſt, between ſix martlets of the ſecond.* Impaled with *Or, between two bars ſable, three croſſes fitchy of the firſt.*

Luke Beaulieu, B.D. on Dr. Waſhbourne's death, was inſtalled on the 21ſt of May, 1687. He died about the end of May, 1723, and was buried at Whitchurch, co. Oxon, where he was rector, as he was alſo prebendary of St. Paul's, London. His ſucceſſor was

Nathaniel Lye, D.D. archdeacon of Glouceſter; who taking this in exchange for a prebend of Briſtol, was inſtalled July the 3d, 1723; and upon his death

---

[a] Kingſwode, by his laſt will, dated Auguſt the 30th, 1559, deſires that his body may be buried in the cathedral, and among other things bequeathed to the maintenance of the weſt bridge 10l. to the poor of the Margarets 40s. to the poor of St. Bartholomews 5l. to the poor of the city 4l.

Samuel Salter, M. A. fucceeded him in the year 1737; and refigning,

Samuel Woolley, A. M. was inftituted February the 8th, 1744; who dying, was fucceeded by

Charles Bertie, A. M. November 28, 1764.

Fourth Stall.

James Vaughan, M. A. appointed at the foundation on the 3d of September, 1541. Upon his death, May 8, 1546,

John Williams, LL. D. chancellor of the diocefe, fucceeded him, and died in the year 1558.

Chriftopher Yaxley was probably the next in fucceffion; for he occurs in 1560. In his will dated February 26, 1569, he appoints to be buried at White-chapel in London, in the chancel of his parifh; having, three years before his death, refigned this dignity to

Griffith Williams, who was inftituted June the 16th, 1567.

William Shingleton, M. A. vicar of Thornbury in this county, upon the death of Mr. Williams, was inftituted December the 21ft, 1573, and occurs in the begining of the year 1594.

John Robinfon alfo occurs about the end of the year 1594.

Edward Muns, M. A. of Peter-houfe, Cambridge, was prefented July the 15th, 1597, and upon his refignation,

Edmund Bracegirdle, rector of Stowel, and vicar of Chedworth, in this county, was inftituted November the 13th, 1600, and died in 1601-2.

Peter Cocks, M. A. of Magdalen college, Oxon, rector of Cleeve, in this county, was inftituted in 1603, and in 1612, was buried at Cleeve.

Thomas Anian, M. A. afterwards D. D. and prefident of *Corpus Chrifti* college in Oxford, was prefented in 1612. In 1613, he refigned the rectory of Deinton, in this county, and dying, was buried on the 17th of July, 1632, in the cathedral of Canterbury, where he was prebendary; upon whofe death,

Gilbert Sheldon, B. D. was inftalled the 26th of February following; and being made bifhop of London, in 1660,

Richard Harwood, D. D. fon of Richard Harwood of this city, where he received his grammar learning, was inftalled on the 11th of November, 1660, and died in 1669, being rector of Wick Rifington, and of Rudford. He was buried at St. Michael's in this city, without any memorial.

William Wafhbourn, M. A. was inftalled May the 8th, 1669, and dying on the 28th of November, 1675, was buried in the Lady's chapel, by the north wall near his brother Dr. Wafhborne, and has a monument erected for him, with this infcription:

Sacrum memoriæ viri admodum reverendi, Gulielmi Wafhborne, A. M. eccl. cath. Glouc. digniffimi prebendarii, coll. Orielenfis, Oxon. focii et ornamenti. Qui poft vitam fumma cum animi erga Deum pietate, ecclefiam Anglicanam fidemque catholicam conftantia, amicos fidelitate, egenos minime mendicantes charitate, omnes candore, tranfactam; precibus magis quam morbis laborans, genibus flexis, Deo fpiritum emifit, Novemb. 28, ann. Ætatis 60, Salutis 1675.

Over it are thefe arms. *Argent, a fefs gules charged with three cinque foils of the firft, between fix martlets of the fecond; a mullet fable in chief, for difference.*

Edward Fowler, M. A. afterwards D. D. was inftalled February the 19th, 1675; and upon his being promoted to the bifhoprick,

Benjamin Barnet, M. A. afterwards D. D. was inftalled July the 19th, 1691; and dying, was buried at Plumfted, in Kent, where he had been vicar.

Robert Cook, M. A. rector of Little Wittenham, in the county of Berks, was inftalled on the 27th of November, 1707. He was alfo inftalled archdeacon of Oxford, April the 24th, 1724; and dying about the beginning of Auguft, following, was buried in the little chapel of Highnam, without any monument. He was fucceeded here by

Anthony Ellis, M. A. afterwards D. D. in the year 1724. He was incumbent of a church in the old jury London; vicar of Great Marlow, Bucks; and afterwards bifhop of St. Davids. He is buried near bifhop Benfon, and a neat fmall monument is erected to his memory againft the fouth wall, on the left hand of the great porch at the enterance of the church. To him fucceeded

Alexander Malet, A. M. February 26, 1761.

Fifth Stall.

Edward Bennet, a monk, and the receyver of of the abbey, was appointed at the foundation September 3, 1541. He died in the year 1546, being alfo vicar of Badgworth, in this county.

Richard Mounflow[a], the king's chaplain, and laft abbat of Winchcombe, in this county, was prefented November the 14th, 1546. Upon the diffolution of his abbey, a yearly penfion of [b] 140*l.* and forty loads of fire-wood out of Depewood were affigned him by the king's commiffioners 21ft December, 31° H. 8. and in 1553, occurs only with an abatement of 40*l.* on account of fome preferment from the king. He was fometime rector of Notgrove, in this county; a commiffioner to cardinal Pool, for vifiting the diocefe and chapter of Gloucefter, 1554, 1556, 1557; and dying in 1558, was probably buried in the cathedral, according to his will.

Walter Jones, M. A. afterwards D. D. archdeacon of Brecknock, and prebendary of Weftminfter, was prefented January the 15th, 1559. He was fometime rector of St. John's in this city, vicar of Painfwick, in Gloucefterfhire, and pre-

[a] A MS. now in my cuftody affirms, that his penfion was 140l. not 160l. as Mr. Willis fays, by patent dated the 21ft of January, 31° H. 8. Whilft he was lord abbat he was frequently called Ancelm, alias Mounflow, but after the diffolution of that abbey, he occurs only by the name of Mounflow.

[b] Richard Mounflowe, prieft and prebendary of Gloucefter, by his laft will dated the 13th of Auguft, and proved the 27th of the fame month, 1558, defires that his body may be buried in the cathedral there, and bequeaths to Mr. Turbet, parfon of Hafleton, his furred gown, to Mr. Alfyld, fchoolmafter, 20s. and his fecond gown, to the petty canons 40d. a piece, to every fingle man 20d. to every chorifter 8d.

centor

centor of Hereford; and dying in the year 573, was buried in that cathedral, without any memorial.

Thomas Philips, upon Dr. Jones's death, was inftituted July the 18th, 1573, and occurs in 1579.

Roger Green, rector of Dowdefwell, occurs in 1585, and upon his refignation,

Samuel Proctor, M.A. was inftituted Auguft the 3d, 1586, but he alfo refigning,

William Loe, M.A. afterwards D.D. the king's chaplain, and vicar of Churcham, in the county of Gloucefter, was inftituted on the 30th of September, 1602, and died at Pultney in Surry, in the year 1648.

Hugh Naifh, M.A. afterward D.D. was inftalled on the 10th of September, 1660; and upon his death, being rector of Harlaxton, in the county of Lincoln,

Afahel King, M.A. was inftalled April the 1ft, 1676, and died about two years afterwards, being rector of Deinton, in the county of Gloucefter.

Ralph Cudworth, D.D. was inftituted on the 22d, and inftalled the 25th of May, 1678, and was buried in Chrift college chapel, Cambridge; where is this infcription for him:

Here lyeth the body of Dr. Ralph Cudworth, late mafter of Chrift college; about thirty-four years Hebrew profeffor, and a prebendary of Gloucefter. He died June 26, 1688, in the 71ft year of his age.

Richard Duke, M.A. was inftalled on the 7th of July, 1688, and died in 1710. He was rector of Witney in Oxfordfhire, and chaplain in ordinary to queen Anne; and was fucceeded in his prebend, by

Chriftopher Baynes, M.A. rector of Farmington, who was inftalled March the 25th, 1711. He was buried in the chancel at Farmington, where is this infcription for him.

C. B. hujus ecclefiæ rector, obijt 23 die Septembris, Ann. Dom. 1718. Ætatis fuæ 53.

Matthew Pantling, D.D. mafter of Pembroke college in Oxford, was inftalled on the 18th of November, 1718. By virtue of the act of parliament before mentioned, and this being the firft ftall that became vacant after that act, it was therefore annexed to Pembroke college. He alfo fucceeded Mr. Baynes in the rectory of Colne-Rogers, in the county of Gloucefter.

John Ratcliff, B.D. afterwards D.D. on Dr. Pantling's death, fucceeded him in the places before mentioned in 1738.

Sixth Stall.

John Huntley, laft prior of Tanridge, in Surrey, was appointed at the foundation September the 3d, 1541.

Richard Ramfey, alias Hawling, M.A. rector of Shenington, in the county of Gloucefter, occurs in the year 1558, and was deprived in 1559.

Guy Eaton, or Heton, formerly chaplain to bifhop Hooper, and archdeacon of Gloucefter, was inftalled in the year 1559, and refigned in 1571. He was fometime vicar of Great Barrington, and rector of Horton, in this county; and upon his refignation,

John Angel, M.A. was inftituted the 28th of November, 1571. He was vicar of Wroughton, in Wilts; and dying in 1577, was fucceeded by

Anthony Higgins, who was inftituted June the 30th, 1577. He was fometime rector of Sutton under Brailes, and of Lechampton, and vicar of Campden, and of Painfwick in this county; and dying in 1578, was fucceeded by

Thomas Cooke, M.A. who was inftituted the 21ft of March, 1578; and upon his death

Robert Alfield, or Aufield, M.A. was inftituted February the 18th, 1579, who died in the year 1583, being rector of Bourton on the water, and of Barnfley, in this county.

Ralph Cooke, alias Eaton, occurs in the year 1585, and died in 1587, being rector of Kemmerton, and of Wick Rifington, in this county.

William Wingfield, rector of Buckland, in this county, was inftituted July the 5th, 1587.

Adrian Saravia, D.D. was prefented Auguft the 22d, 1591. He was afterwards made prebendary of Canterbury, and refigned this. Whereupon,

Henry Aifgill, M.A. was inftituted November the 19th, 1599. He died on the 18th of June, 1622, and was buried in the church-yard of Down Hatherly, in this county, with this infcription on his monument.

Hic jacet fepultus venerabilis vir Henricus Aifgill, ecclefiæ cathedr. Menevenfis cancellarius, Glouceftr. prebendarius, necnon hujus parochiæ vicarius, qui obijt in domino Junii 18, A. D. 1622.

Eft decus hic tumulo, non hic fe jactat Apelles,
Nam magnum jacet hic pauperis auxilium.
Se fua roftra carent, diferta hunc pulpita lugent,
Tam pius et conftans concionator erat.
Non fibi mors triftis, animo maturus et annis,
Fatalem falcem non timuit, petiit.
Nec tandem moritur, fed victa morte refurget,
Et fua, magna licet, gloria major erit.

Thomas Ifles, D.D. was inftituted on the 13th of July, 1622; and dying in 1649, was buried without any memorial, at Chrift church college in Oxford, where he was canon.

Robert Harris, M.A. was inftalled September the 24th, 1660.

Francis Jacob was admitted January the 17th, 1662.

Anthony Andrews, M.A. vicar of Standifh, in this county, was inftalled the 20th of November, 1665, and dying in the year 1678, was buried at Harsfield, in the county of Gloucefter, where he was vicar, under a ftone, juft without the rails of the altar, with this infcription:

Hic jacet Antonius Andrews, cler. qui obijt 4 die Septembris, 1678.

George Bull, M.A. rector of Siddington St. Mary, and vicar of Siddington St. Peter, in this county, was inftalled October the 9th, 1678. He was afterwards prefented to the degree of D. D. by the univerfity of Oxford, and being at length preferred to the fee of St. David's, refigned his prebend to his fon,

Robert Bull, B.A. who was inftalled on the 27th of December, 1705. He was afterwards rector of Tortworth, vicar of Churcham, in this county, and D. D.

Nathaniel Templeman, M.A. upon his death fucceeded him in 1729.

Thefe fix prefbyter prebendaries and canons have each of them a houfe alotted to him out of the monaftery; and yearly on the 30th of November one of them is chofen fub-dean, another the receiver, and a third the treafurer. The yearly falary of each of them is 20*l.* and by other accidental profits about 100*l.* more.

Befide a dean and fix prebendaries, king Henry the Eighth appointed fix minor-canons; out of whom were chofen, The precentor, the facrift, the deacon, and the fub-deacon. The king alfo appointed the chief fchool-mafter, the under fchool-mafter, or ufher; the organift, or mafter of the chorifters; fix lay-clerks, or finging men; eight chorifters, four alms men, two door-keepers, or virgerers; one butler, one cook, and one under cook.

The fix minor-canons, at the reftoration, were reduced to four; and have each of them a houfe, and a falary of 20*l.* *per annum.*

The fix lay-clerks, or finging men, have now each of them a houfe, and 10*l.* *per annum.*

The eight chorifters have each 5*l.* *per annum.*

As the great refectory is now quite demolifhed, and the ufes in which 'twas employ'd are laid afide, the places of butler, cook, and under cook have not been filled for feveral years. But, befide the offices before named, they now choofe an auditor, a chapter-clerk, and two fub-facrifts.

PRINCIPAL REGISTERS.

John Tayler, alias Barker, occurs foon after the foundation of the bifhoprick, and Auguft the 31ft, 1569.

Richard Hands[a], was appointed for fixty-one years on the 21ft of February, 12° Eliz. but he conveyed his right to

John Jones, who (as 'tis on his monument) was regifter to eight feveral bifhops of this diocefe, who muft have been the bifhops Cheiney, Bullingham, Goldfborough, Ravis, Parry, Tompfon, Smith, and Goodman. He died in 1630.

Henry Jones, and Edward (called alfo Gabriel) Goodman, held the office together, before

Owen Brigftock, and William Brigftock had a patent granted them the 29th of January, 1660, for their lives. Owen Brigftock dying, his fon William refigned; and thereupon

Richard Fowler, LL.B. fon of bifhop Fowler, had a patent granted him the 5th of April, and confirmed the 7th, 1698. Upon his refignation,

Thomas Stephens, efq; and Edward Stephens, his fon, had a grant of this office the 21ft of March, 1712, which was confirmed the 25th of March, 1713; and upon their deaths

William Mount was prefented to this office October 19, 1736. But the Reverend John Benfon, A.M. was admitted joint patentee with him in 1759; the furvivor to enjoy the whole. In 1770, Mr. Mount died, and left Mr. Benfon fole patentee; but in the fame year, Ralph Warburton Allen, efq; fon to the bifhop, was made joint patentee with him, and they now enjoy this office together.

The SCHOOL *of the* CATHEDRAL, *commonly called the* COLLEGE SCHOOL.

There was antiently a grammar-fchool in the abbey, and upon the foundation of the chapter, the abbey library was converted to a fchool. Elizabeth Wilfhire, widow, repaired it, and made it more convenient for that purpofe, which was gratefully expreffed in an infcription fet up in the year 1587, that remained for many years afterwards.

The mafter of this fchool has the yearly ftipend of 20*l.* and a houfe; and the ufher has 10*l.* a year and a houfe. Mr. Wheeler, in 1686, began the eftablifhing a library in it for the ufe of the fcholars, who alfo enjoy part of the common orchard of the abbey.

MASTERS.

Robert Aufield occurs 1558, 1563.

Tobias Sandford occurs 1576.

Thomas Waftel, or Waftal, occurs 1580.

Elias Wrench, M.A. occurs 1588, 1594.

William Loe.

Thomas Potter occurs 1605, 1610.

John Clark occurs 1612, 1613.

John Langley, M.A. admitted March 9, 1617, and occurs 1635.

Thomas Widdows occurs 1636, but he might then be an affiftant to Langley. For Mr. Walker, in his *Sufferings of the Clergy*, fays, that Thomas Widdows, A. M. was made mafter of this fchool in 1640, and was foon turned out for his loyalty.

William Ruffel lies buried in St. Michael's church in this city, where, upon a fmall monument is the following infcription:

Juftæ memoriæ Gulielmi Ruffel, fcholæ collegialis in hac civit. archididafculi; eruditione et pietate, necnon fingulari aptitudine ad pueros in iis inftituendos, infigniffimi: Cujus reliquiæ, non fine magno reip. literariæ damno, et communi, tam totius agri et civit. Glevenfis, quam uxoris, liberorum, et fcholarium, mœrore et planctu, hic reconduntur, Julii 9°, anno Ætat. 42, Salut. 1659. in fpe gloriofæ refurrectionis.

Benjamin Mafter, elected 1659.

John Gregory, elected April 9, 1660, occurs 1673. and

Oliver Gregory, M.A. elected Auguft 29, 1673.

---

[a] Hands, formerly regifter to the bifhop, lived an alderman of the city of Gloucefter only twenty-one days, dying of the plague on the 24th of Auguft, 35° Eliz. (1593).

Maurice

Maurice Wheeler, M. A. September 11, 1684, was afterwards prebendary of Milton manor, in the cathedral of Lincoln; and dying on the 6th of October, 1727, aged 79, being then rector of Thorp Mandevill, in the county of Northampton, was buried at Warpenham, in that county, of which alfo he had been rector.

Benjamin Newton, M. A. upon Wheeler's refignation, was appointed.

William Alexander, M. A. rector of Colefbourn, removed from the grammar-fchool at Cheltenham, was admitted September the 22d, 1718. He was vicar of Hartpury, and dying on the 1ft of May, 1742, was buried in the church of St. Mary de Crypt, when

Edward Sparkes, B. A. late ufher of this fchool, and fellow of Trinity college in Cambridge, fucceeded him, both in this fchool and the vicarage, and is the prefent mafter.

USHERS.

John Lightfoot occurs 1563, and was inftituted into Bifley vicarage June 11, 14° Eliz. 1572.

Francis Peerfon occurs 1576.

Francis Arnold occurs 1594.

Thomas Wood occurs 1605.

Thomas Loyd occurs 1607, 1610, and was inftituted into Harefcomb and Pitchcomb rectory October 31, 1612.

Chriftopher Prichard occurs 1612, 1613.

Daniel Williams, admitted October 14, 1618.

Thomas Daniel, elected October 8, 1621.

Gyles Workman, B. A. elected June 23, 1628.

Thomas Widdows, M. A. elected November 3, 1635.

Chriftopher Prior, B. A. elected November 13, 1635.

John Graile occurs 1635.

Richard Lovel, B. A. elected March 7, 1637.

William Collins occurs 1638.

William Elbridge, B. A. elected May 21, 1639, and was licenced to Cirencefter curacy March 29, 1644, and inftituted in Winfton rectory, 1648.

—— Batten, who refigned, whereupon

—— Bays was elected in 1659.

Abraham Gregory occurs 1661, and 1665.

Nathaniel Lye, M. A. admitted Auguft 7, 1671.

Thomas Trippet, LL.B. elected January 4, 1674, occurs 1679.

John Hilton, M. A. curate of St. Nicholas, but being inftituted into Stonehoufe vicarage March the 6th, 1707, refigned the fchool.

Henry Abbot, M. A. upon Hilton's refignation, was appointed. He was afterwards vicar of Longney.

Jeremiah Butt, ufher of the grammar-fchool at Cheltenham, was inftalled (or admitted) September 22, 1718; and being made vicar of Sherfton, in the county of Wilts, left this place.

Jofeph Gegg, B. A. upon Butt's refignation, was admitted in 1727.

Edward Sparkes, B. A. upon Gegg's amoval, was admitted in 1739.

John Palmer, B. A. upon Sparkes's refignation, was admitted in 1742.

Charles Bifhop, M. A. fucceeded John Palmer, and is the prefent ufher.

Of the CATHEDRAL CHURCH.

AN account has been already given of the original building, and gradual increafe of this noble edifice, which was the antient abbey-church of Saint Peter; but it will be convenient to recapitulate fome of the particulars.

Aldred, bifhop of Worcefter, pulled down the old church, which was decay'd, and building a fine new one, dedicated it to St. Peter in the year 1058, which was intirely burnt down in 1088. The next year abbat Serlo rebuilt it from the foundation. Several times afterwards it fuffered from fire, but perhaps was never totally deftroyed. Henry Foliot, the twelfth abbat, built a handfome tower in 1237, and vaulted part of the church; and fometime before his death, began a new tower at the weft end, on the fouth part of the front, which John de Felda, one of his fucceffors, finifhed.

But we muft date the origin of this noble edifice, in the form we now fee it, from the death of king Edward the Second, who was buried here, at whofe tomb fuch vaft offerings were made, as enabled the fucceeding abbats to raife a more magnificent pile. This they did at feveral times with the contribution and affiftance of the gentlemen in the neighbouring country, as the Cliffords, Throckmortons, Defpencers, Pauncefoots, Botelers of Sudely, and others, whofe arms, together with thofe who had formerly been friends to the abbey, were painted on the glafs windows for a memorial of their benefactions.

This great work was begun by abbat Thokey, who rebuilt the fouth aile in 1318, and his fucceffor John Wigmore rebuilt St. Andrew's, fuppofed to be the north tranfept or crofs aile. Adam de Staunton new vaulted the choir, and built the ftalls on the prior's fide, and his brother John rebuilt St. Thomas's altar. Thomas Horton fucceeding, made the high altar, and prefbytery, above the choir; and Walter Frowcefter, a fucceeding

abbat,

abbat, built the cloiſter, which is reputed the fineſt in England. John Morwent made the fine porch, and weſt end; Thomas Seabroke built the ſtately tower, and the abbats Richard Hanley and William Farley built the Lady's chapel.

Moſt of theſe abbats, with ſome others, lie under grave-ſtones in the church, which I ſhall take occaſion to ſpeak of hereafter.

The length of the cathedral from eaſt to weſt is 420 feet, and from north to ſouth 144 feet. The breadth of the body and ſide ailes 84 feet, which is the height of the vaulting of the choir; but that of the croſs aile is only 66 feet. The tower, which ſtands in the middle, is 222 feet.

At the diſſolution of the abbey, when this church was converted into a cathedral, it had the good fortune to be ſo intirely preſerved, that no conventual church in the kingdom, except that of Weſtminſter, eſcaped ſo well. But by the books and papers in the cuſtody of the biſhop's regiſter, it appears, that in the year 1576, it greatly wanted reparation, which being neglected from time to time, 'till the year 1616, when doctor Laud was appointed dean of it, there was ſcarcely a church in England ſo much in decay; therefore the doctor procured an act of the chapter, by which ſixty pounds a year were allowed for repairing it.

During the ſiege and civil wars, it ſuſtained leſs damage than could have been expected; but it was afterwards in danger of total deſtruction, from the plots and contrivances of ſome perſons, who are ſaid to have agreed amongſt themſelves for their ſeveral proportions of the plunder expected out of it.

In the year 1657, this church was granted to the mayor and burgeſſes of the city, at their own requeſt; and Oliver Cromwel, under his broad ſeal, gave them an exemplification of it; but it is probable that before this time they had intereſted themſelves in its preſervation; for Mr. Dorney, in his 10th ſpeech, about the year 1653, commends to the officers of the city then elected, *that they would, together with others, join their ſhoulders to hold up the ſtately fabrick of the college church, the great ornament of this city, which ſome do ſay is now in danger of falling.*

The Lady's Chapel has been uſed for early morning prayers, ever ſince the ſeats were brought hither from the choir, when that was beautified. At the eaſt end of it was a very fine lofty altar, to which there was an aſcent by three ſteps, whence the weſt end of the church might be ſeen without any thing to interrupt the view. Here is a large eaſt window, the glaſs of which was curiouſly painted, but the figures are now defaced. This chapel, on the ſouth ſide of which were three confeſſionals, as it is now certainly one of the largeſt in the kingdom, ſo at the diſſolution is ſaid to have been one of the richeſt, and a tradition goes that a great part of it was then gilt, and glorioufly ornamented. There were battlements upon it 'till they were pulled down in the civil wars.

Several eminent perſons have been buried in it. *viz.* Biſhop Goldeſborough in a little chapel on the north ſide. The inſcription for him is to be found in p. 157.

On a grave-ſtone alſo is the following epitaph:

Hic conditur quod reliquum eſt Heſteræ Goldſborough
Diſce viator verum ſi ſupra fidem
Hic jacet lectiſſima virgo mater matrona
Tribus expedita viris potita tribus
Civibus hic ſummis ſummo illo antiſtite
Eccleſiæ queis ſingulis apprime vixit chara
Rara in pietate modeſtia modeſtia pietas
Noſce quæ non videns videns non admireris
Munificentiam in pauperes ſine arrogantia
Non imitandam vivas dotes non æquendæ
Fœminæ octodenos liberoſque utriuſque
Tam numeroſi: Sexûs ſobolem ſine numero
Filios egregios filias tantum non matri pares
Hoſce felices unam feliciter Aviam
Inter amplexus omnium et pia vota omnium
In ſenectute ultimâ ſenectam non languidam
Et fidem ſpirantem & expirantem in fide
Serviit quæ Chriſto in Chriſto obdormientem.
An. 1622. Ætatis 80.

Biſhop Nicholſon's tomb is in a little chapel on the ſouth ſide. For the inſcription ſee p. 158.

In the ſame chapel is a raiſed monument of ſtone, and on one ſide of it a ſcroll on which is written,

O Lord into thy hands I commit my ſpirit.

On the other ſide a large coat of arms, and a man kneeling in a lawyer's gown, and over his head,

Miſericordias Domini in æternum cantabo.

And underneath,

Tho. Fitzwilliams late of this City, Eſq; departed this Life 26. November. A. D. 1579. whoſe body lyeth buried under this ſmall monument of Stone.

Robert Wiſe late of this City Gent. (now deceaſed) married with Elenor one of the Daughters of the ſaid Thomas Fitzwilliams, by whom he had three Sons and three Daughters, *viz.* Thomas, Urian, Dennis; Alice, Jane and Margaret; and the ſaid Robert Wiſe had alſo by a former Wife fifteen Sons and Daughters more, which in all were in Number one and twenty Sons and Daughters.

The ſaid Dennis Wiſe, one of the Aldermen of this City, being the twentieth Child of his ſaid Father, and ſole Survivor at this Time of all the reſt of his ſaid Brethren and Siſters; He did in An. Dom. 1648. repair and amend this antient ſmall Monument to the farther Continuance of the laudable Memory of the ſaid Thomas Fitzwilliams his Grandfather; and the rather, for that the Monument of the ſaid Robert Wiſe and the ſaid Elenor his Wife, being defac'd and ruinated by the diſſolving and taking down of the Pariſh Church of St. Ewens, without the South Gate of this City, in the late unhappy Wars and Diviſions of this Kingdom, in which Pariſh Church both the ſaid Robert and Elenor, with many more of their Children and Children's Children lieth buried.

O Lord into thy Hands I commend my Spirit, O God of Truth which haſt redeemed me, judge me not according to thy Righteouſneſs, but after thy great Mercy and pity.

Againſt the north wall of the lady's chapel is a magnificent white marble monument for judge Powel. For the inſcription ſee p. 119.

And againſt the ſame wall was a monument for major-general Lawrence Crawford, killed at the ſiege of Hereford, being commander of the Scotch army. He was buried here September the 5th, 1645. Mr. Willis obſerves, that the inſcription, which is printed in Le Neve, juſtifying the rebel cauſe, the monument was defaced, and intirely taken down after the reſtoration.

On

On dean Viner's grave-ſtone is an inſcription, as in p. 162.

Dr. Parſons, chancellor of the dioceſe, was buried in this chapel. The inſcription on his grave-ſtone is under his name p. 164.

Dr. Thomas Waſhbourne was alſo buried here, and againſt the north wall is a ſmall monument for him, with an inſcription as in p. 167.

Here is a monument alſo for his brother William Waſhbourne, A. M. See p. 168.

On a grave-ſtone is the following inſcription :

Hic jacet Jervaſius Smith, Art. Magiſter, et reverendi in Chriſto patris Milonis EPI. nuper Glouceſtrenſis, filius natu maximus.

Doctus et infœlix juvenis matriſque patriſque
Spes equidem votis maxima forte brevi
Cæpta ſub adverſis dubie matura juventus
Obtinuit buſtis juncta parenta ſuis.
Obiit 17 Januarii 1625. Ætatis ſuæ 31.

Againſt the ſouth wall of the Lady's chapel is the figure of a woman, in white marble, in a kneeling poſture, leaning her head on her hand, and underneath this inſcription :

Memoriæ ſacrum.

In obitum Margeriæ Clent, Jac. Clent, generoſi conjugis chariſſimæ, reverendique in Chriſto Patris Dom. Milonis Gloceſtrenſis Epiſcopi Filiarum alterius, quæ curſum in terris pie ac placide conſummavit 8 die April. A. D. 1623. ætatis ſuæ 21.

Obſequioſa viro fuit, obſequioſa Parenti,
Et patuit miſeris dextera, corque Deo.
Cætera continuos virtus rediviva per annos
Claruit ad celſum ſubſequiturque Polum.
Subſequiturque infans uteri ſub nocte reluctans
Nec potuit lucem viſere mors vetuit.

Tabellam hanc quaſi pignus amoris Brigida conjux Gulielmi Clent, nuper de hac Civitate Glevenſi poſuit in memoriam ejus, qui obiit Octob. 10. 1655.

On the oppoſite ſide is a monument of the ſiſter of the above perſon, bearing this inſcription:

Elizabetha Loquitur.
Conjugis effigiem ſculpſiſti in marmore conjux,
Sic me immortalem te ſtatuiſſe putas.
Sed Chriſtus fuerat viventi ſpeſque fideſque :
Sic me mortalem non ſinit eſſe Deus.
Jul. 4. A. D. 1622.

Pie ac Placide ad Dominum migravit Elizabetha Williams, Joannis Williams, armigeri conjux amantiſſima, Doctiſſimi reverendique in Chriſto Patris D. D. Milonis Glouceſt. Epiſcopi Filia natu minima. Annos nata XVII.

Hic jacet Carolus Sutton infans 7 dierum ſeptimus filius Wilhelmi Sutton, cancellarii dioc. Glouceſtr. qui extremum clauſit diem Junii 5. 1626.

Parve nec invideo ſine me puer ibis ad aſtra
Parve nec invideas lætus ad aſtra ſequar.

Sacred to the memory of Thomas Sutton, and alſo of William Sutton, Gent. whoſe bodies were buried Aug. 21. 1636.

Could youthful Vigor, ought that is in Man,
Have conquer'd Death, theſe had been victors then :
Could learned Art, or Parents Tears have given
Them longer Life, they had ſtill living been :
But God decrees ; 'tis not in human Power,
Longer to live than he hath ſet their hour.

Here reſteth the body of Ann, late wife to Iſaac Bromwich, of Framton, Eſq; ſole daughter of Edward Trotman, of this city, councellor of Law ; ſhe departed this life May 26, 1628.

Here lyeth the body of Thomas Varnam, of this city, Gent. who departed this life Nov. 24, 1634.

Sacrum Memoriæ Thomæ Dobbes, Generoſi, unius clericorum de Banco regis, qui de vita hac migravit, 21 Feb. An. ſalutis humanæ 1635.

Sat ſcio juſtificat nullum lex tradita Moſi
Nec mea me juſtum jura dedêre virum.
Unum Cauſidicum cœlis habeamus Ieſum.
Unus non multi ſunt ibi cauſidici,
Cauſidicus Chriſtus ; ſunt cauſidicique fideles
Cœlo, ſed ſummi ſanguine cauſidici.

Hic jacet Franciſca, Jacobi Clent, ex hac civitate gener. Gen. conjux.

Dum pario perii, partus enixa labore
Langueo, per dubias inde ſoluta moras
Chara meis vixi : morior natiſque viroque
Chara, quibus vivis mox rediviva fruar.
Obiit Julii 28, Anno ſalutis 1630. Ætatis 29.

Alſo here lyeth the body of William Clent, the ſon of James Clent, of this city, Gent. who departed this life Oct. 15, 1635.

Johannes Cholmleius mærens April 29, 1635.

Hic Audleia jacet conjux ſelecta Johannis
Cholmleii, lachrimis parcite ; terra gravis
Tantum corpus habet, cælum mens ſanior altum
Incolit, & Chriſtus cum redit illa redit.

Here lyeth the body of John Merro, who deceaſed March 23, 1636.

I once did ſing in this,
Now in the Choir of Bliſs.

Here lyeth Elizabeth, the wife of John Merro, who departed this life Nov. 13, 1615.

Here lyeth the body of Ann Maſſinger, who was wife and widow of Arthur Maſſinger, of this city, Gent. aged 52 years. She departed this life Oct. 21, 1636. Ætatis ſuæ 70.

Annæ filiæ Franc. Baber, LL. D. Corpuſculum hic jacet in ſpe pene triennis ; obiit ad Dominum Aprilis 3, 1639.

Francis, ſecond ſon of Francis Baber, Dr. of Laws, and Elizabeth his wife, departed this life Sept. 3, 1640, aged 22 years and 5 months : whoſe body reſteth under this ſtone in hopes of a future bleſſed reſurrection.

Exuviæ hic ponuntur Eliz. filiæ Franc. Baber, LL. doctoris, biennis & Bimeſtris quas anima depoſuit March 19, 1641.

Here lyeth the body of Arthur Brett, Eſq; Groom of the bedchamber unto King James ; who died July 2, 1642.

Here lyeth interred Mary Kenn, the daughter of George Kenn, Eſq; who departed this life May 22, in the year of our Lord 1649, being but Nine days old.

Here lyeth the body of Francis, ſon of George Watſon, of York, Gent. late Secretary to the honourable Col. Morgan, Governor of this City ; who departed this Life Oct. 3, A. D. 1646.

Here lyeth the body of Mary, the Daughter of Michael Straunge, Eſq; firſt Wife of Samuel Coxwell, Gent. and afterwards of James Kyrle, Eſq; who died Aug. 13, 1645.

Quem neque mœſta Calamitas, nec fallax
Rerum Terreſtrium adulatio elevaret, nec
Mortis horrenda facies exterritat.

Hic jacet Jacob. Clent, Gen. qui poſt 70 plus minus annos laborioſe pieque tranſactos, longo tamen fatigatus itinere immortalitatem anhelans placide occubuit An. nato Chriſto 1645, Sept. 5.

Depoſitum Jacobi Powel, generoſ. extincti 26 Nov. A. D. 1645, ætatis 31. hic inhumatur.
Sic ubi fata vocant nam ſic quoque fata vocabunt tendimus in tumulum.

Over it his arms. *Per pale, three lions rampant.*

An acroſtick for one William White, who died *An.* 1646.

W hat Man more valiant was than he that lies,
I ntombed here after his Victories :
L et ſuch as his undaunted Courage knew,
L ive to report, and witneſs what is true.
I n famous Berkeley Caſtle he was known
A s Governor, tho' aged but twenty-one :
M aintaining ſtill the Cauſe with much renown
W hich he at firſt for Right and Juſt did own.
H is Name and Houſe ſince conquering William's Days,
I s regiſtered, his Life's deſerving Praiſe :
T ill Death at Ragland Caſtle, by a Wound,
E nded his Days, that ſo he might be crown'd.
An. 1646.

Here lyes the body of Samuel Bridger, Gent. who departed this life upon the 21ſt day of July, An. 1650.

Receiver of this College Rents, he paid
His Debt to Nature, and beneath he's laid,
To reſt until his Summons to remove,
At the laſt Audit, to the Choir above,

Depofitum hic Ægidii Gilby, Stemmata quem decorant Integritas, candor: Invaletudo terens quem maceravit, fic corpore deficiens temnere mundana prædidifcit, requiem percipere æternam, difcubiat domino. Hunc Deus adducet cum domino: Vigila, vive memor Lethi.

Obiit 26 Septembris A. D. 1650, Ætatis 29.

Here lyeth the body of Frances, daughter of John Clent, of this city, Gent. fhe departed this life April 4, 1652.

Here lyeth the body of Henry Robins, of this city, Gent. he departed this life in the true faith, May 8, An. 1653.

Elizabeth, third daughter of Miles Clent, Gent. and of Dorothy, his dear wife; who departed this life Jan. 15, 1654.

Within this Urne an Infant nine Months old
Is laid in Duft, God takes his pureft Gold
Firft to himfelf, we all are but as Flowers
That fpring and grow, and fade in a few Hours.

This ftone belongeth unto William Hoar; he died Feb. 1654, aged 76.

O mortal Man that lives by Breath,
Confider thou muft come to death;
And after Death all muft appear,
Before God's Judgment Seat both far and near;
To give Account for what they've done,
Be fure of this there's none can fhun.
Then whilft thou liveft cry and call,
To Chrift thy Saviour to pardon all;
Left after Death it be too late,
To enter in at Peter's Gate.

Richardus filiolus Thomæ & Mariæ Browne, qui Aug. natus 6, obiit 3. annis 1654.

May 27, 1657. Hic jacet juxta fratrem Amia Browne, fex menfium Infantula. Heu quanto pro viribus fub pondere, fed eft qui faxum revolvet.

Quod terrenum Johannis Futter filii Henrici Futter, Londinenfis, Dec. 21, 1655.

Elizabetha, chara, modefta, cafta, pia conjux Tho. Harvey de Larford, generofi, hic jacet depofita 15 Dec. 1657.——— fic tamem alloquitur, poft fata Refurgam ——— pofuit cum lachrymis mœftiffimus maritus.

Hic jacet Henricus Shaftow, Gen. natus in vico de Bramley in Com. Surrey, denatus Glouceftriæ, fepultus 13 April. ætatis fuæ 8, Anno Salutis noftræ 1658. Ultima dies, prima quies.

Miles, the fecond fon of Miles Clent, of this city Gent. lyeth interred here; who died June 7, 1658.

No fooner peep'd i'th World, came out o'th Womb
Of my dear Mother, but hurried to my Tomb;
Death was my Harbinger, my Nurfe the Grave,
My Life no Life, till now my God I have,
And do enjoy: Farewel fond worldly Blifs
Your Joys to mine are a Parenthefis.

Reliquiæ Thomæ Browne, generofi, qui 2 die Martii, An. falutis 1662, Ætatis fuæ 45, obiit, hic funt depofitæ, fub fpe non dubiæ refurrectionis ad vitam die noviffimo.

Hic fuit veri microcofmus, amplis
Qui bonis cunctis placide pieque
Vixit, & tandem, domino vocante,
——— Exit ad illum.

Elizabeth, fole daughter of Thomas Harvey, Gent. firft wife to James Powell, and fecond wife to Edward Harvey, Efq; lies here depofited Feb. 1662.

Twice married, once buried, here lies,
Her Body, whofe fweet Soul above the Skies,
Immortallized doth reft with longing Eyes,
Expecting when the Body fhall arife;
That reunited they may fympathife,
In endlefs Joys to all Eternities.

Memoriæ facrum domini Johannis Vaulx, generofi epifc. Glouceftr. proregiftrarii, quod reliquum, hic inhumatur Dec. 9, 1663.

Corde vir hic patiens, vitâ probus, ore modeftus,
Moribus ingenuis ingeniofus erat.
Poftque moras longas, ac tædia multa,
Morte cadit corpus, cætera falva manent.

Here lyeth the body of Elizabeth, daughter of Arthur Meffenger, of this city, Gent. who departed this life A. D. 1665, ætatis fuæ 73.

Here lyeth John, the fon of Owen Brigftock, Efq; who died Sept. 17, 1665, aged near fix Years.

Uxor Georgii Wall, Rectoris de Hempfted, hic jacet cum priore conjuge Richard Marwood, hujus eccl. precentoris confepult: Dec. 23, 1665. In refurrectionem εις ἀγγελοι Luc. 20, 39.

In a chapel on the north fide of the Lady's, upon the upper part of the altar, were the following arms in two rows, *viz. Azure, a crofs Or.* —*Ermine, a crofs azure.*—*Checky, gules and Or, a cheveron vert within a bordure of the latter.*— France and England quarterly.—The Trinity reprefented by a triangle, with lines drawn from each angle to a point in the middle.—*A cheveron gules.*—*Vert, on a canton a rofe.*—*Or, a fefs azure, in chief three roundlets of the fecond.*—*Azure, a crofs Or.*—*Vert, a buck's head cabofhed gules.*—*Gules, a fefs company Or and azure* .—Throckmorton.— *Checky gules and argent, a cheveron ermine.*—*Gules, a fefs between fix mullets Or.*—Defpencer.—Edward the Confeffor.—The fee of London.—Quarterly 1ft and 4th England, 2d and 3d *Checky Or and azure.*—Montacute, earl of Sarum.—*Argent, a fleur de luce between three bulls heads cabofhed fable.* —*Azure, a cheveron gules, between three griffins heads erafed Or.*—*Parted per fefs indented Or and azure.* —Veel.—*Argent, on a crofs fable a leopard's head cabofhed.*—*Sable, a bordure and two bars argent.*— *Azure, a crofs Or.*—On the bricks in this chapel, *a fret.*—*A fefs between fix crofs croflets,* 3, 2, 1.

King James, during the time he was at Glouceſter, refided at the deanery, and in the afternoon of the next day after his arrival, touched one hundred and three perfons in the Lady's chapel for the king's evil. I mention this as an hiftorical fact, and not from any perfuafion of the efficacy of the royal touch, of which I leave every perfon to judge as may feem moft reafonable.

This chapel is thirty yards long, and about ten broad.

The Choir is one hundred and forty feet long. The high altar, to which there is an afcent of three fteps, has been lately very much repaired. On the north fide are four confeffionals, and on many of the bricks are the arms of king Edward the Confeffor, of the abbey, and of Bridges, quartered with others.

On the bifhop's feat it is thus written:

EDEL DVX
ELDADVS EP̄S GLOVC.
ELDO MAIOR
A : 490.

Over againft the bifhop's is the archdeacon's feat, where the mayor now fits on Sundays, which has no infcription over it. There are thirty-one ftalls on each fide, built in the time of the monaftery, very regular and lofty, with *Allelujah* written in gold letters on each of them.

The great Eaft Window, which is the largeft in England, was finely painted, but at this time the figures are not to be diftinguifhed. However now, or not long fince, the following arms remained in it; *Gules, a cheveron ermine between ten croffes*

croffes patee argent.—*Gules, a lion rampant, Or.*—Berkley.—Quarterly, 1ft and 4th, *Gules, a bend Or, and argent.* 2d and 3d, *Azure, five diamonds Or.*—*Gules, a cheveron between ten crofs croflets Or.*—*Gules, a fefs between fix crofs croflets, Or.*—Defpencer.—*Azure, on a chief two mullets Or.*—Montacute.—Earl of Clare.—Earl of Oxford.—*Argent, fix croffes fitchee on a chief between two mullets Or.*—Mortimer.—*Vairy gules and Or.*—*Fretty*, impaled with England.

In a little chapel on the fouth fide, on the bricks are thefe arms, *A cheveron charged with a rofe flower and two lillies, between five trees*, 2 and 3.—*A fret.*—Clare, earl of Gloucefter.—*Within a bordure charged with ten roundlets, a lion rampant.*—*A fefs between fix crofs croflets*, 3, 2 and 1.

On the north fide, even with the rails of the altar, is the effigy in free-ftone of Ofric king of Northumberland, with a crown on his head, and againft the wall is written,

Ofricus Rex primus fundator hujus Monafterii. 681.

Robert, the eldeft fon of William the Conqueror, and Richard, his youngeft fon, were both buried in this church. Richard died in the year 1080, Robert in 1134, who having been deprived of his lands and liberty by Henry the Firft, a cruel and tyrannical brother, and fhut up in a clofe prifon at Cardiff, after a confinement of twenty-fix years, being broke with grief and age, he refigned a miferable life for a long expected death; and his body being brought to this church, to which in his life time he had been a munificent benefactor, it was buried in the middle of the choir, where a monument was erected for him, which was lately moved into one of the little chapels on the north fide of the choir, where it ftill continues. See p. 126.

On the fouth fide is a fhelf monument for Aldred bifhop of Worcefter, who built the old church. His effigy is carved in free-ftone on the tomb; but whether, fays Mr. Willis, this was a cœnotaph I cannot fay.

On the north fide oppofite to bifhop Aldred's, between two pillars, is a monument for abbat Parker, in the time of whofe government the abbey was diffolved. His effigy, in his *Pontificalibus*, curioufly carved in white marble, is lying along on the tomb, which was provided for him in his life time, but he was not buried in this church. See p. 139.

Above the abbat's, between two other pillars, is the tomb of king Edward the Second, who having incurred the hatred of the nation, by his blind attachment to Piers Gavefton and the two Spencers, his favourites, was taken prifoner by an army which the queen, the prince, and the nobles raifed againft him, and confined in Berkely caftle, where he was murdered, whence his body was brought to Gloucefter, and buried in the choir of the abbey church His effigy curioufly cut in alabafter lies under a very elegant canopy of free-ftone. Further particulars are related in p. 126.

In a window oppofite to king Edward's tomb, the letters W. P. A. are painted on the glafs in many places; where alfo are to be feen the remains of the pictures of two bifhops, or mitred abbats, and two monks; and over one of the latter is written *S. T. Cant.* [*Sanctus Thomas Cantuar.*] and *E. R.* [*Edwardus Rex.*]

Abbat Staunton was buried under a grave-ftone before St. Thomas's altar.

Abbat Frowcefter was buried on the fouth fide of the choir, in a chapel at the lower end. See abbats.

On the fouth fide of the entrance to the choir, between two pillars, is the fine tomb of abbat Seabroke, on which is his effigy in white alabafter, in his *Pontificalibus*; but his tomb has been moved, and the part which at firft ftood to the eaft is now placed to the north.

A little to the fouth of the above, under an arch, are two effigies in free-ftone of Humphry Bohun, earl of Hereford, and his lady. He died 1367. and lies in armour.

Juft below the afcent into the choir, on each fide of it, was a fine ftone fkreen-work, erected by one of the abbats; and directly oppofite to the entrance of the choir was a large door and an arch over it, which had a chapel with a fine altar upon it, fupported by two pillars. Thefe were taken down in the year 1741, and there is now in the room a handfome fkreen of carved ftone-work, fupported by three arches, which ftand on fluted pillars four at each abutment. On a table in the middle of the fkreen is this infcription: MARTINUS EPISCOPUS FECIT AN. DOM. MDCCXLI. ET CONSECRAT^S. SVE VII^mo.

When the workmen were making the above alteration they found in the paffage three abbats, buried near the furface of the ground, in ftone coffins, in their *Pontificalibus*, part of their gloves and apparel remaining. And another ftone coffin, with a fword, a little pewter chalice, a ftaff and two fkulls in it, which, I fuppofe, belonged to Sir Nicholas Gamage and his wife, who were buried near their brother abbat Gamage, who was laid near the door opening to the cloifters; and probably this abbat was one of the three above mentioned, who were all of them buried again where they were found.

Before this alteration there were five other large grave-ftones found, to which brafs plates were fixed, long fince torn off, three of which belonged to fome of the abbats.

On the fouth fide of the choir, in the chapel belonging to the Boteler family, the letters I. B. are written on the north and fouth walls, the I paffing thro' the B, with a crown over them; and not many years fince here was a large efcutcheon in wood, on which were three golden cups, the family arms.

The

The altar is much defaced, on the upper part of which was the following infcription:

Hoc Baptista Tyrou Gloucestre fecit honore
Fac hunc ergo frui Celi fine fine decore;
Hic etiam cultor precibus memorare tuorum
Et Rex Celorum femper fit tutor eorum
Hoc Pater et flamen concordat jugiter Amen.

On a ftone at the weft end of the chapel it is written:

Kurie Eleifon Aie
Fratris Johis Tyrou.

On a ftone on the outfide wall, in black letter,

✠ Hic jacet Willhelmus Pippardus vicecomes Glouceftr.

On a brafs plate near the pulpit, in black letter,

Here lyeth under this Stone in the Mercy of God, the body of Henry Machen, late Alderman of the City of Gloftre, which died March 5, 1568,

Whofe Body and Soul we wifh as Love doth bynd
In Heaven with Chrift a Place to find.

Near it round a free-ftone,

Here lyeth ——— Daughter to Henry Machen, and firft married to Peter Romney, and laft Wife to Thomas Beft, who died May 7, 1587.

On another,

Gloriæ fundamentum Labor.

Here lyeth buried the body of Peter Gouch, Gent. firft Cuftomer in the Queen's Majefty's Port of Gloucefter; who deceafed Auguft 25, 1585. And Jane his Wife deceafed February 4, following.

In the great Crofs Aile, in St. Anthony's chapel, under the tower, is St. Anthony with his pig, and the bell painted on it. On the north fide of this aile is a handfome veftry, which feems to have been built by abbat Parker, fince his arms were placed on it, but now deftroyed.

Here is an antient grave-ftone, with the following infcription in Old Black character:

Hic jacet Robertus Stanford quondam ferviens hujus Monafterii, ac fpecialis ac munificus Benefactor ejufdem Monafterii, qui obiit viceffimo fecundo ———————————

Upon Stanford's grave-ftone is a little brafs plate with the following memorial for Mr. William Lifle, who has a monument erected for him.

Near this place lieth the body of William Lifle, Gent. who by his will gave fifty pounds a year for ever, in lands at Epney, in charity, to the parifhes of St. Nicholas in Glouc. and St. Werburgh in Briftol. He died Dec. 2, 1723, aged 25.

Next to Stanford's is a grave-ftone, round the verge of which it appears there have been feveral capital letters, long fince worn out. Perhaps this ftone belonged to one of the abbats Horton or Boyfield, who are faid to have been buried under a flat ftone in the north part of the tranfept, or crofs aile. Abbat Wigmore alfo was buried in that part called St. Andrew's aile, on the fouth fide next the choir.

At the eaft end of the north tranfept, near the door leading to the choir, was fome time fince a pedeftal, with a large image on it, and the following infcription, lately deftroy'd.—*Orate pro Anima Magiftri Johannis Schelton.*

In this aile were buried, Thomas Lane efq; fometime recorder of this city.—Charles Hyett, efq; fometime member of parliament for it.—Richard Corfley, fometime mayor, buried Sept. 2, 1742, *Ætat.* 77.

Againft the weft wall is a tomb, with this infcription,

Memento mori.

Vayne, Vanity, witnefs Solomon, all is but vayne. Richard, Guy, Giles, Thomas, Thomas, Kingfton, Peter, John, John, Anna, Margaret, Doroth. Eliz. Nanfan, Catherine, Joan. John Boyer had nine fons and feven daughters by his wife Ann Boyer. John Boyer departed this life the 28 day of January, A. D. 1615. Ann Boyer departed this life upon the firft day of December, An. 1613.

On a grave-ftone it is thus written in black letter,

Cum Fex cum Limus cum res viliffima fimus
Unde fuperbimus ad Terram Terra redimus.

Here lieth buried the body of John Smith, Alderman, and once mayor of this city, whofe foul doth reft in the Lord, and was feparated from the body July 18, 1586.

Here lieth buried Alice Woodward, widow, daughter to Thomas Winfore. She lived eighty odd years, departed this life June 5, and was buried the ninth of the fame month, 1593.

Here lyeth the body of John Long, Millard and Milwright, who departed this life April 16, 1596.

Here lyeth buried under this ftone Thomas Snead of the city of Gloucefter, Mercer, who deceafed October 10, Anno Dom. 1597.

On a brafs plate is the following,

Here lyeth interred the body of Lawrence Wilfire, Gent. fometime mayor of this city; by his vocation a clothier, wherein he did much good to the poor, and employed many poor people at work. He departed this life in the true faith of Chrift A. D. 1612.

Here lyeth the body of William Blackleach, Batchelor of the civil laws, Chancellor of this Diocefe, for the fpace of 25 years, Efq; who departed this life March 24, 1617. p. 343.

For the infcription on Henry Robins, efq; fee p. 119.

Here lyeth buried Thomas, the Son of William B——— in Glamorganfhire, near Cardiff, who died at fchole in this city, Oct. 15, in the year of Chrift 1613. ætatis 15.

Hic jacet Egidius Coxe, Generofus, qui 17 die Octobris A. D. 1620, et ætatis fuæ 55 obiit cœlebs, collatis prius per teftamentum tam in hanc ecclef. cathedralem quam ecclef. parochialem de Santhurft, ad inftituendam ibid. facram concionem, in egenos, vias publicas, aliofque pios ufus, quam in amicos et cognatos, opibus fuis ampliffimis.

Hic jacet corpus Gulielmi Lane, ex hac civitate, armiger. Obiit die 11 Martii, An. falutis 1620. ætatis ———

Alfo here lyeth the Body of Ellen, the Wife of William Lane, Efq; and afterwards Wife of Chriftopher Capell, and William Price, both Aldermen of this city; who departed this Life Dec. 16, An. 1652.

In the fouth great crofs aile is Mr. Richard Pates's monument, and infcription, which fee in p. 118.

Over the door leading into the chapel near the prefent chapter-houfe is *T. C.* [*Thomas Cantuarienfis*] and near this door was an oratory, not long fince demolifhed.

On a little chapel behind the confeffionals, are T. O. T. O. but the ragged ftaff which was alfo upon it is much defaced.

The nave or body of the church, in length 171 feet, in breadth 84, confifts of a middle aile, and two fide ailes, feparated from the middle by two rows of pillars, eight on each fide, feven of which, about feven yards in circumference each, are round, with four pillafters over them; the eighth was

was handsomely fluted by abbat Morwent, who built the west part of the church where these stand.

There were places for lamps in the third and fourth pillars on the north side; a handsome wooden chapel, or burying place, between the second and third pillars from the east end, on the same side; and a handsome pulpit with the letters H. G. 1609, erected by bishop Parry; but these are lately demolished.

Against the east wall, behind the wainscot, adjoining to which the dean and prebendaries had a seat, when the sermons were preached in the body of the church, was found in the year 1718 a fine old painting on oak, representing the general judgment. This picture is supposed to have lain there ever since the year 1541, and is now kept in the south cross aile. Opposite to the above mentioned seat were others erected for the mayor and corporation; but they are now all taken down. The little chapel, commonly called the mayor's, which was inclosed with a wall or skreen, is now also laid open. In this chapel was a grave-stone with an abbat carved on it, but the stone is removed.

In the south aile is the consistory court, railed in, on which are the arms of bishop Fowler, and chancellor Penrice.

Between the court and the great porch, against the south wall, is a neat little marble monument for doctor Ellys, (see p. 168) on which is the following inscription:

Near this place lies the body of Anthony Ellys, D.D. minister of the united parishes of St. Olaves Old Jury, and St. Martin's, Ironmonger-lane, in the city of London; 38 years prebendary in this church, 37 years consecrated bishop of St. David's, 28 Feb. 1753, who departed this life 17 Jan. 1761, aged 68 years. A person truly excellent, learned, just, benevolent, pious: To whose rare virtues and abilities adulation cannot add, envy cannot deservedly take from. He married Ann the eldest daughter of Sir Stephen Anderson, of Eyworth in the county of Bedford, Bar. whom he left with only one daughter, to lament the common loss of one of the best of mankind.

In a chapel at the upper end of the south aile, on a white marble table supported by two Ionic pillars, this inscription:

Siste viator & a me discito quam vanæ spes sint, quam fluxa hominum gaudia: Jacet heu Catherina mea uxorum scilicet lectissima, optima; tam venusta, tam casta, tam pia, ut nihil supra; si ætas, si forma deflenda sit, si corporis animique dotes, Luctui hic nullus erit modus; marmor hoc dicavit Gulielmus Pembruge, Gen. Memoriæ suavissimæ Conjugis, quæ fato defuncta est 15 Junii, An. Ætatis 24, salutis 1690.

Against the west wall of the body of the church, is the figure of a man to the waist, with a book in his hand, and round him, *I heard a voice from Heaven, saying unto me, Write, Blessed are the dead that die in the Lord.*

Underneath him on a tablet of black marble,

John Jones, Alderman, thrice Mayor of this City, Burgess of the Parliament at the Time of the Gunpowder-Treason; Register to eight several Bishops of this Diocese.

On a gravestone beneath,

Here lieth the Body of John Jones, Alderman, Esq; thrice Mayor of this City; who departed this Life June 1. in the sixth Year of the Reign of King Charles, 1630.

This monument which was originally inclosed in a skreen of wood, now taken down, was finished in the alderman's life time, who made some alteration in it.

Against the same wall is a marble monument for bishop Benson. But there is another elegant monument and inscription for him, as in p. 159.

On the north side of the nave, near the cross aile, inclosed with iron palisadoes, an elegant monument of white marble, with the effigies of a man and his wife lying at length; and at their feet this inscription:

To the happy Memory of Abraham Blackleach, Gent. Son of William Blackleach, Esq; a Man not only generally beloved in his Life, but deservedly endeared to Posterity by rare Examples of seldom pattern'd Piety, exercised in his Bounty to St. Paul's in London, to this Church, to the High-Ways about, and to the Poor of this City; who laying aside the vileness of Mortality, was admitted to the Glory of Eternity Nov. 30. 1639.——— Gertrude his Wife, Daughter of Ambrose Elton Esq; and Anne, Sister to Walter Lord Aston, hath erected this Monument as a Testimony of his same, and her Observance.

On a scroll, *All flesh is grass, and all the goodliness thereof is as the flower of the field*; Is. xl. 6.

Over all, these arms, *Barry of six, sable and Or.*

Near the above was a raised monument of stone, and the effigies of a man and woman kneeling before a desk, with their seven sons and six daughters, and this inscription:

Here lieth the Bodie of Thomas Machen Esq; late Alderman of the City of Gloucester, and thrice Mayor of the same; who departed this Life Oct. 18. 1614. in the 74th Year of his Age; and of Christian his Wife, with whom he liv'd in the State of Marriage 50 Years, and had Issue seven Sons and six Daughters; she departed this Life June 29. 1615. in the 70th Year of her Age.

Res redit, huc morimur, mors ultima linea Rerum.

Near this also on a copartment, against the wall,

In Charissimam memoriam Samuelis Browning, è Famil. de Cowley, Gen. qui obiit 3. Feb. 1676. Ætatis suæ 57. Juxta etiam defuncti jacent Liberi ejus tres per dilectissimam Uxorem Margaretam, filiam Gulielmi Selwyn de Matson, arm. *viz.* Margaret, Sam. Ann. Browning. In tenerrimâ Ætate mortui omnes.

Near the door leading into the cloisters, on a marble copartment affixed to the wall,

To the virtuous Memory of Anne, the most entirely beloving and beloved Wife of John Hilton, Clerk, Usher of the College School; who died Feb. 26. 1691-2. Ætatis An. 30.

Meek was her Temper, Modest was her Life;
A Chast and Humble Virgin, Loyal Wife:
Her Manners graceful, pregnant was her Wit,
Her Nature amiable, her Behaviour sweet:
Her Soul adorn'd with Dove-like Innocence,
To gain a heavenly Mansion hasted hence;
And bids surviving Walkers o'er her Grave,
Love the World less, and strive their Souls to save.

Eccles. vii. 36. Remember thy End and thou shalt never do amiss.

On the same wall, a monument of marble on a tablet, between two black twisted pillars this inscription:

M. S. Juxta obdormiscit in Christo Edwardus Wright, Medicinæ Doctor, vere christianus; quippe qui naturam investigans, naturæ Deum & agnovit & veneratus est: Vir doctus, pius, severe justus; qui ægris non funerandis sed sanandis nomen et famam conciliavit. Nec tam ægrotantium crumenis, quam bonæ inhiavit valetudini. Unde nulli inimicus, inimicum non habuit præter ignorantem. In egenos usque adeo fuit beneficus, ut concilium, opem, medicamina, liberaliter et gratis suppeditavit. Dum autem aliorum sedulo curavit salutem, propriam amisit; immatura nimirum morte præreptus tristissimum hic reliquit desiderium Julii 24, A. D. 1701, ætatis 36.

 Conjux

Conjux ſuperſtes Memoriæ viri optimi meriti hoc qualecunque Monumentum, amoris ergo, lugens mœrenſque poni curavit.

In the north aile, not far from the weſt end, was a painting of the twelve apoſtles, but this is deſtroyed. Underneath is an eſcutcheon containing the following rebus: The capital letter T, on the right of which a ſword pendant, piercing a heart, conjoined with the wing of a dove in the baſe of the ſhield; on the left ſide of the letter, a palm-branch joined to another wing. This rebus is in another part of the church, with ſeveral figures not now underſtood.

Againſt the north wall is a monument for Mrs. Lucy Stokes, (only daughter of doctor Harwood, a prebendary of this cathedral) *ob.* Jan. 11, 1732, *ætat.* 73.

Thomas Browne, eſq; ſometime mayor, was buried Nov. 15, 1730. *ætat.* 84.

A memorial for Edmund Gregory, ſometime mayor, *ob.* Sept. 23, 1720, *ætat.* 80.—Edward Machen, ſometime mayor, *ob.* 20 Sept. 1740, *ætat.* 61.

Againſt a pillar in the middle of the nave, on a copartment,

To the happy Memory of Thomas Batherne, the only Son of Richard Batherne of Penhow, in the County of Monmouth, Gentleman; he departed this Life Sept. 25. 1652, aged 22. leaving behind him his ſorrowful Mother, who out of her dear Affection to him, erected this Monument.

On a grave-ſtone beneath,

Here lieth the Body of Mary Batherne, the Wife of Richard Batherne of Penhow, in the County of Monmouth, Gent. who departed this Life March 29, 1665, aged 74.

Near abbat Seabroke's monument, againſt a pillar is an inſcription for Francis Baber, eſq; as in p. 164. but to that I ſhall add the following,

Elizabetha conjux, filia Johannis Adderley, in com. Middleſex, arm. obiit 14 Januarii, Ætatis 63, A. D. 1673.

On their grave-ſtones, on which are the family arms, *viz. On a feſs gules, three falcons heads eraſed,* are the following inſcriptions:

Corpus Franciſci Baber, Legum Doctoris, ſub hoc ſaxo eſt conditum Junii 21, 1669.

Hic jacet Elizabetha Baber, Januarii 14, A. D. 1673.

The renowned Whiſpering Place is a long gallery, extending from one ſide of the choir to the other, built in the form of an octagon, with three ſides taken off, as in the margin; and contrived ſo as not to darken the great eaſt window of the choir, behind which it ſtands.

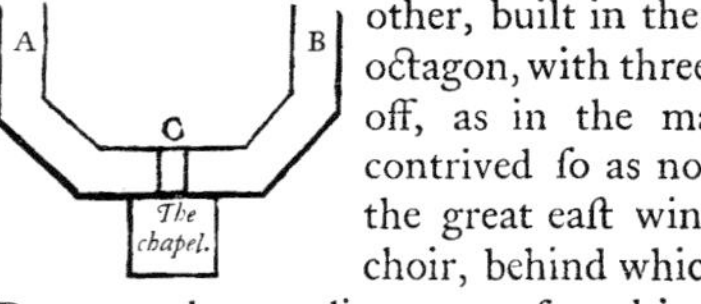

Between the two lines, repreſented in the figure, is the paſſage. If a perſon whiſper at A, every ſyllable may be heard diſtinctly at B, which is twenty-five yards diſtant, tho' the paſſage is open in the middle, and there are large openings in the wall for a door and window. C denotes a door into a chapel, which is in the outward wall.

Some impute this wonderful effect to the cloſe cement of the wall, which, as one intire ſtone, conveys the voice like a tube; others attribute it to the repercuſſion of the voice on the ſeveral angles; whilſt a third opinion is, that the chapel and open places contribute to the ſound; but lord Bacon gives his ſentiments of this matter as follows: "I ſuppoſe there is ſome vault or hallow, "or iſle behind the wall, and ſome paſſage to it "towards the farther end of that wall againſt "which you ſpeak, ſo as the voice of him that "ſpeaketh ſlideth along the wall, and then enter-"eth at ſome paſſage, and communicateth with "the air of the hollow; for it is preſerved ſome-"what by the plain wall; but that it is too weak "to give a ſound audible, 'till it has communi-"cated with the back air."

Moſt people are of opinion that this effect was not produced by the art and deſign of the builder, but was merely accidental, eſpecially as on ſurveying the outſide of the church, it may be ſeen, that two parts of the gallery were tacked on, merely as paſſages into a chapel erected there. In this chapel are the following arms upon bricks;—*England.*—*A Fret.*—*A feſs between ſix croſs croſslets,* 3, 2, 1.—*A lion rampant.* In the window over the weſt end, *Argent, a bend between two bendlets dancette gules.* At the eaſt end are the remains of an altar of unhewn ſtone, on each ſide of which the lord abbat and others were uſed, it is ſaid, to ſtand to ſee divine ſervice performed in the Lady's chapel, into which it looks.

In the middle of the whiſpering place are theſe verſes:

Doubt not but God, who ſits on high,
Thy ſecret Prayers can hear;
When a dead wall thus cunningly
Conveys ſoft whiſpers to the ear.

The great Cloiſters lie on the north ſide of the church, between the tranſept or croſs aile and weſt end. They were built by abbat Walter Frowceſter in the ſtile of King's college, Cambridge, and are ſo curious and beautiful as to be eſteemed the fineſt in England. They make a ſquare, one ſide of which is 150 feet long. The idea of the roof is taken from a walk of trees whoſe branching heads are curiouſly imitated in the arching.

In one of the windows was a draught of the old church, and ſeveral verſes intimating the original of the convent; but theſe were all deſtroyed in the civil wars.

In the eaſt cloiſter, in the wall at the ſouth end, is an old mural monument, without any inſcription, or arms, only a croſs cut on it; and near it is an old door, which led into a long room, perhaps the abbey workhouſe.

Not far from that, is a little door and ſtair-caſe leading to the abbey library, now uſed for the college-ſchool; and there is a large wainſcot door leading into the preſent college library, which was formerly the abbey chapter-houſe, where Leland informs us ſeveral perſons of great eminence have been buried, whoſe names, in the time of that great

great antiquary, were painted on the wall, near their grave-ftones, in black letter, as follow:

Hic jacet Rogerus, Comes de Hereford.
Hic jacet Richard Strongbowe, filius Gilberti comitis de Pembroke.
Hic jacet Gualterus de Lacy.
Hic jacet Philipus de Foye, Miles.
Hic jacet Bernardus de Novo Mercato.
Hic jacet Paganus de Cadurcis.

Thomas Pury, jun. efq; whofe arms are on the north fide of the eaft window, affifted by Mr. Sheppard, captain Heming and others, made this library at a great expence in the year 1648, and, as Sir Robert Atkyns has obferved, encouraged literature to affift reafon, in the midft of times deluded with imaginary infpiration. In 1656 this library was fettled upon the mayor and burgeffes, who made themfelves guardians of it; but Mr. Pury, Sir Matthew Hale, and the officers of the garrifon were the principal benefactors to it. It is above twenty-four yards long, and eleven wide within the walls. Mr. Wheeler began to ftock the library with books in the year 1686, but the collection is even now by much too fcanty.

Before the library door is buried William Lambe, fometime mayor, who died Oct. 21, 1705; and not far from him lies Mr. Abraham Rudhall, a very noted bell-founder of this city.

Here is a door that leads into the common orchard, where, or near to it, by the infirmary, ftood archbifhop Aldred's church, the fcite of which is called the grove, becaufe Mr. Wheeler, formerly mafter of the fchool, planted it with trees; fo that what Camden fays of the prefent cathedral being the fame which Aldred built, is a miftake.

On the bricks in the pavement are the following arms: *France and England quarterly.*—*A cheveron between three crofs croflets fitchy.*—*A fefs charged with a crefcent between fix crofs croflets.*—*Checky, a fefs fretty.*—Berkely.—*Within a bordure a lion rampant.*—*Three bendlets the middle one charged with an efcallop.*

In the North Cloifter, towards the weft end, is the lavatory, confifting of eight arches, and directly oppofite is the fudatory, or place to hang up towels, confifting of two arches.

In the Weft Cloifter, at the north end, is a door which led into the abbey refectory, or great hall, now a confiderable time fince demolifhed. About the middle is a door leading to the houfe now affigned to the dean, but formerly belonging to the chief prior of the abbey. At the fouth end is a little room where the glafs belonging to the church was kept, and where the glaziers did their work.

In the South Cloifter, on the north fide of it, are twenty diftinct places or feats, according to tradition, for the monks to write in, before the invention of printing. feveral perfons have been buried, and have grave-ftones and infcriptions on them here; and near the eaft end is an old mural monument without any infcription or arms, only a crofs and the letters W. B. on it.

The little cloifters feem to have been made by archbifhop Aldred, near the church which he built. Some part of them was pulled down in the civil wars.

The beautiful Tower, as bifhop Gibfon fays in his additions to Camden's *Britannia*, is fo neat and curious, that travellers have affirmed it to be one of the beft pieces of architecture in England. Abbat Seabroke, the firft defigner of it, dying, left it to be finifhed by Robert Tully, one of the monks of the abbey, which is intimated in two Latin lines written under the arch of the tower, as in p. 138. It is 222 feet high, fupported by a ftrong wall at each of the four corners, by a flender arch from the eaft to the weft fide, and a fmall pillar in the middle. It has a peal of eight large bells in it, fome of them very antient. In a loft under thefe is a very large one, weighing about 6500 pounds, with this infcription on it, ME FECIT FIERI MVNCVTVS NOMINE PETRI; whence fome have concluded that it was given by Peter, the fourth abbat, for between the words of the infcription are the arms of the abbey, with a coronet of four flowers de luce over them. The coronet may ferve to fhew that it was caft in the time of the dukes of Gloucefter. The diameter of this bell is five feet ten inches, and that of the ftar-hole in the arch but five feet, whence it may be concluded, that the bell was put into the tower before the arch under it, which is over the choir, was finifhed.

It is faid, that round about the choir are twelve chapels, fome over, fome under others, in memory of the twelve apoftles, whofe names they are affirmed to bear, and perhaps they are as follow: In the fouth paffage from the Lady's chapel one, one over it, and one under it; more wefterly in that paffage one, one over and one under it; in the north paffage from the Lady's chapel one, one over and one under it; going into the chapter-houfe one, one over and one under it. There were feveral other chapels difperfed over many parts of the church, particularly one in the Lady's chapel on the fouth fide, and one over it; one on the north fide, and one over it; one over the weft end of it, one over the door leading to the great fouth crofs aile, one under the tower on the fouth fide, one dedicated to St. Anthony on the north fide of it, one at the eaft end of the body of the church, taken down to make room for the organ, one for abbat Seabroke, one for king Edward the Second, and one for abbat Parker.

On the outfide of the body of the church are fix buttreffes, which fupport as many ftatues for principal benefactors to the abbey. The firft figure at the eaft end hath a fceptre in the left hand, and a church in the right, and under it a charter with three

three ſeals appendant to it upon his breaſt. The ſecond hath a ſceptre in the right hand, and in the left a church reſting on his breaſt. The others are much defaced.

Part of the buildings which belonged to the abbey are ſtill remaining. The infirmary is converted into a houſe for one of the prebendaries, and for others belonging to the church. There was a chapel in it dedicated to St. Bridget, and endowed in the time of Henry the Third.

The number of houſholders in the college precincts are not mentioned by Sir Robert Atkyns, but in the year 1743 they were fifty-one, and of inhabitants two hundred and twenty-ſeven. Out of theſe precincts two perſons are elected guardians of the workhouſe.

Sir Robert Atkyns was miſtaken in ſaying that there were inſcriptions in this church for the abbats Seabroke and Parker, and the biſhops Cheyney and Smith, as there were never any; nor any tomb, as he ſays, for queen Iſabel, wife of king Edward the Second, who was buried in the Grey Friars, London, and had nothing erected here to her memory. *Willis.*

In deſcribing the abbey church, I cannot but obſerve how perfectly it correſponds with the antient form of churches, which I find in a ſcarce and valuable book, intituled *The Fardle of Facions*, tranſlated into Engliſh by William Watreman, and printed in the year 1555, where it is ſaid, 'Their oratories temples, or places of praier '(whiche we calle churches) might not be built 'without the good will of the Biſhoppe of the 'Dioceſe. And when the Timbre was redy to 'be framed, and the foundacion digged: it be'hoved them to ſende for the Biſhoppe, to hal'low the firſte corner ſtone of the foundacion, 'and to make the ſigne of the croſſe therupon, 'and to laie it, and directe it juſte Eaſte and 'weſt. And then mighte the Maſons ſette up'on the reſte, but not afore. This Churche 'did thei uſe to builde, aftre the facion of a Croſſe, 'and not unlike the ſhape of a manne. The 'Chauncelle (in the whiche is conteined the highe 'Altare and the Quiere) directe fulle into the 'Eaſte, repreſenteth the heade. And therfore 'ought to be made ſomwhat rounde, and muche 'ſhorter then the Body of the Churche. And yet 'upon reſpecte that the heade is the place for the 'eyes, it ought to be of more lighte, and to bee 'ſeperate with a particion, in the ſteade of a necke, 'from the body of the Churche. This particion 'the Latine calleth Cancelli: and out of that 'cometh our terme Chauncelle. On eche ſide of 'this chauncelle peradventure (for ſo fitteth it 'beſte) ſhould ſtand a Turret; as it were for two 'ears. And in theſe the Belles to be hanged, to 'calle the people to Service, by daie and by night. 'Undre one of theſe Turrettes, is there commonly 'a vaulte, whoſe Doore openeth into the quiere. 'And in this are laid up, the hallowed veſſelles and 'ornamentes, and other utenſiles of the Church. 'we calle it a veſtrie. The other parte oughte to 'be fitted, that having as it ware on eche ſide an 'arme, the reſte maye reſemble the bodye with 'the fete ſtretched in breadthe, and in lengthe. 'On eche ſide of the bodye the pillers to ſtonde. 'Upon whoſe coronettes or heades the vaulte or 'rophe of the Churche maye reſte. And to the 'foote beneth, aulters to be joyned. Thoſe aulters 'to be orderly alway covered with two aulter 'clothes, and garniſhed with the croſſe of Chriſte, 'or ſome litle cofre of reliques. At eche ende a 'candelſticke: and a Booke towarde the middes. 'The walls to be parieted without, and within, 'and diverſly paineted. That thei alſo ſhould have 'in every pariſhe a faire rounde Stone, made ho'lowe, and fitte to holde water: in the whiche the 'water conſecrate for baptiſme, may be kept for 'the chriſtening of children. Upon the right 'hande of the highe aulter, that ther ſhould be 'an almorie, either cutte into the walle, or framed 'upon it: in the whiche thei woulde have the 'Sacrament of the Lordes bodye; the holy oyle 'for the ſicke, and Chriſmatorie, alwaie to be 'locked. Furthermore thei woulde that ther 'ſhould be a pulpite in the middes of the Churche, 'wherein the Prieſte may ſtonde upon Sondaies 'and holidayes, to teache the people thoſe thinges 'that it behoveth them to knowe. The Chaun'celle to ſerve only for the prieſtes, and clerkes. 'The reſt of the temporalle multitude to be in 'the body of the church. Seperate notwith'ſtonding, the men on the ryghte ſide, and the 'women, on the left. And eche of them to 'be ſobre and honeſte in apparelle and behav'our. Whatſoever is contrary to good facion 'or chriſtiane religion, with greate diligence to 'ſhoune it. It was the maner in the firſte churche, 'both amonge men and women to let their heare 'growe, to ſhewe out their naked ſkinne, and very 'litle or nothing to diffre in apparelle. Sainct 'Peter put firſt order, that Women ſhould cover 'their heades, and men rounde their heare, and 'either of them to go in ſeveralle and ſondry ap'parelle. Moreover that to every church, ſhould 'be laide out a Churchyarde of the Grounde ad'joyning, in the whiche all chriſten mennes bodies 'mighte indifferently be bewried. The ſame to be 'conſecrate, or halowed by the Biſhoppe, and to 'enjoye all the privilegies that the churche may 'enjoye.

'The funeralle for the deade, thei kepe not in 'every place ylike. Some mourne and kepe dirige 'and Maſſe ſeven daies continualle together, ſome 'ix. ſome xxx. or fourtye, ſome fivetie, and a Hun'dred, and other a whole yere, wrapped up in 'blacke. The counſeile of Toledo ordeined that 'the corps beinge firſte waſhed and then wrapped 'up in a ſhiete, ſhould be caried forthe with ſing'ing by menne of his owne condicion or ſorte, 'clerkes by clerkes, and lay menne of lay menne. 'And aftre what time the prieſt hath ſenſed the 'corps, throwen holy water uppon it, & ſaid cer'taine

'taine prayers, to laye it into the grave with the 'face upward, and the heade into the Weafte. 'Then to throwe in the earth again, and in token 'that there is a chriftian ther bewried, to fette 'up a croffe of wodde, garnifhed with yvie, cipres, 'or laurelle. Thefe be the orders and facions of 'the Chriftiane religon.

Notwithftanding I have inferted the above abftract, becaufe I thought fome of my readers might be pleafed to fee it, 'tis not my prefent purpofe to difcufs the point what form would be moft convenient for our churches, according to the prefent eftablifhed method of divine fervice. Wife men have differed in their judgment, and will ftill continue to differ, concerning modes of worfhip; and it is probable they will not better agree as to the moft eligible form for a place of worfhip; therefore I difmifs the fubject, without offering my opinion concerning it.

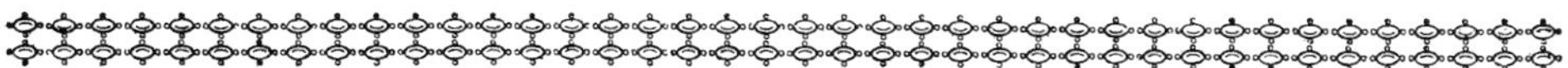

Of the feveral PARISHES within the City of GLOUCESTER.

St. ALDATE's.

THIS was a low fpired church, covered with fhingles. It confifted of one aile, and ftood not far from the city wall, near the upper North-gate, where the hall belonging to the fraternity of fmiths, &c. and other adjacent buildings now are. It was dedicated to Saint Aldate, Aldact, or Eldad, and was a rectory formerly belonging to the priory of Deorhurft, the prior of which was taxed at half a mark in this church 19° E. 1. The rectory was valued at 3*l.* 17*s.* 3*d.*

The commiffioners appointed to make a return of the value of livings 26° H. 8. certified as follows:

Rectoria Sancti Aldati valet clare in decimis et oblationibus, ultra 12 *denarios folutos pro Senagio,* 5 *folidos archidiacono pro procuratione,* 8 *den. epifcopo pro vifitatione,* 77 *fol.* 3 *den.*

In this church were a chantry, dedicated to St. Mary, a chantry or fraternity, dedicated to St. John, the light of St Katherine, and the light of the Holy Crofs.

In 1648, by an ordinance of parliament, this parifh was united to St. Michael's, and the church and its appurtenances were given to the corporation of the city, who made an order that the church-wardens of St. Michael's fhould take it down, and fell the materials, to defray the expence of building a brick wall round their own church-yard; accordingly, in 1653, St. Aldate's was demolifhed, and St. Michael's was repaired with part of the materials. But the ordinance of parliament being annulled at the reftoration, the parifhes became feparate.

Incumbents.

William occurs rector in the reign of H. 3.
Geffry att Birch, 31° E. 3.
Thomas Billey, 1424.
John Dayly, 1472.
John Keyble, or Kebul, fometime a gray frier, 1547.
Richard Burnel, fometime a chantry prieft of St. Ann's fervice in Saint Michael's, occurs curate 1551.
Ralph Salmon, curate of St. Owen's, 1562.
John Mery, fometime curate of St. Mary de Grace, occurs curate 1569, having been formerly a chantry-prieft of St. Mary's fervice, in the church of St. Mary de Lode.
Evan Williams, rector of St. Mary de Crypt, occurs in 1572.
Richard Taylers, B. A. rector of St. Michael's, 1576.
William Beft obtained the fequeftration, April 15, 1579, and was curate.
Nicholas Fayrere, alias Pitt, vicar of St. Owen's, obtained the fequeftration, and was curate June 11, 1580.
Richard Jones, curate of All Saints, occurs 1587.
William Evans, 1593.
Thomas Wood, rector of St. John's, 1594.
Richard Jones, curate of All Saints, 1594-5, 1599.
Robert Provis, alias Charlion, curate of St. John's, feems to have refigned the curacy of St. Katherine's for this, 1600, and occurs 1625.
Edward Williams, curate of All Saints, occurs 1628, 1635, being a minor-canon, and to that office he was again reftored by king C. 2.
Daniel Remington.
Benjamin Newton, A. M. is the prefent incumbent.

N. B. Thofe who are mentioned as curates of this church, or of any other in the city, were the only incumbents; for as the income of thofe livings are but fmall, they were generally held by fequeftration, and the incumbents of them were really no more than curates.

Benefactions.

Mrs. Elizabeth Aram, who was buried in the nave or body of the cathedral in 1741, by her will bequeathed 500*l.* to rebuild the church, and accordingly a chapel has been built, on or near the fpot where the church ftood; and the living was augmented by lot in the year 1746, and returned.

Sir Thomas Bell gave a houfe to the parifh towards keeping the church in repair, &c.

Mr. Daniel Lyfons gave 30*s. per ann.* to the poor for bread.

	Baptifms.				Burials.			
1759	males	7	females	3	males	5	females	3
1760	——	7	——	7	——	10	——	4
1761	——	8	——	9	——	2	——	1
1762	——	6	——	5	——	5	——	1
1763	——	6	——	7	——	8	——	2
1764	——	16	——	9	——	4	——	4
1765	——	10	——	5	——	5	——	5
1766	——	6	——	10	——	6	——	3
1767	——	5	——	11	——	4	——	5
1768	——	6	——	2	——	5	——	1
	Total	—	145		Total	—	83	

In the year 1562, there were 50 houfholders in this parifh; in 1712, there were 62 houfes and about 350 inhabitants, according to Sir Robert Atkyns; and in 1743, the exact number of houfholders were 92, of inhabitants 401.

			l.	*s.*	*d.*
Royal Aid in	1692,	——	302	8	0
Poll Tax —	1694,	——	090	5	0
Land Tax —	1694,	——	314	9	3
The fame in 1770, for St. Michael's, St. Aldate's, and St. Mary de Grace, at 3*s.* in the pound.			224	3	6

One guardian is chofen out of this parifh for the work-houfe, towards which it paid quarterly in 1770 10*l.* 10*s.* 6*d.* and 3*l.* 15*s.* 8*d.* towards the lamps.

ALL SAINTS, or ALL HALLOWS.

THIS was a fmall church confifting of one aile, with a chancel. At the time of the conqueft, the fee of Exeter had poffeffions in Gloucefter, as appears by Domefday book, where it is faid, "Ofbernus the bifhop holds the land "and manfions which Edmarus held. They pay "10*s.* with other cuftom." This church might probably be a part of thofe poffeffions, for Robert Chichefter, bifhop of Exeter, granted it as a chapel to the priory of Lanthony, which received a penfion of 2*s.* out of it, now paid to the crown. In the 19th year of king Edward the Firft, that priory was taxed eight marks in this church.

By an ordinance of parliament in 1648, this parifh was united to that of St. Mary de Crypt, and in the year 1664, bifhop Nicholfon not only united it to, but incorporated it with that parifh in all refpects, the church having been converted into the Tolfey, or place of public judicature, where the mayor and fheriffs hold their courts, &c. on which account the corporation pay 2*l.* 13*s.* towards repairing the church of St. Mary de Crypt, the minifter of which performs all the duties of the parifh prieft. See p. 89, under Tolfey.

In the valuation 26° H. 8. are the following particulars: *Rectoria Omnium Sanctorum valet clare in decimis et oblationibus, ultra* 12 *den. pro fenagio,* 2 *fol. penfionem priori et conventui Lanthoniæ,* 8 *den. epifcopo pro vifitatione,* 12 *fol. pro vino, cera, et pane, annuatim folutos,* 6*l.* 13*s.* 6*d. ob.*

There was a chantry dedicated to St. Mary, and another fervice called the feoffees fervice.

The lot fell on this parifh to augment the living with queen Ann's bounty, in the year 1739, but the governors would not allow of the augmentation on account of the union of the parifhes.

A part of the church has been converted into a chapel, for the ufe of the corporation; but the whole building hath been fince taken down and rebuilt, and now forms a large and commodious court for the adminiftration of public juftice; together with an elegant chamber over it, for the private bufinefs of the corporation; who now attend divine fervice at the cathedral church. On the front, in an efcutcheon, are the arms of the city cut in free-ftone.

	l.	*s.*	*d.*		*l.*	*s.*	*d.*
Firft fruits,	7	1	8	Pentecoftals,	0	0	6
Tenths, —	0	8	0	Synodals, —	0	1	0
Procurations,	0	5	0				

Incumbents and Patrons.

Robert occurs rector 29° E. 1.
John Benet, rector, 12° E. 3.
Thomas Watton, rector, exchanged with Roger Harry, for the vicarage of Brockworth, in 1371, and the faid Roger Harry was prefented July 10, 1371, by Simon the prior and the convent of Lanthony.
John Gregory, occurs rector 1° E. 4.
Thomas Monmouth, upon Gregory's refignation, was prefented by Henry Deane the prior, and the convent of Lanthony.
Thomas Woddeward, fometime rector of St. Mary de Crypt, prefented 1491, by the fame.
Chriftopher Woodwell occurs 34° H. 8.
John Henbury, occurs curate in 1562.
John Merrey, occurs curate 1572.
Richard Jones, fometime a minor-canon, occurs 1580, 1599.
John Johnfon, one of the minor-canons, 1600, 1619.
Philip Hofier, fometime curate of St. Mary de Crypt, and of St. John's, occurs curate 1622, 1625.
Edward Williams, fometime curate of St. Aldate's, 1628.
Thomas Thache, A. M. nominated by the corporation, but licenced by the bifhop.

Benefactions.

Mr. Richard Hoar, in 1607, gave a perpetual annuity of 2*l.* 13*s.* for the ufe of this parifh, which is what the corporation pay to St. Mary de Crypt.

Mr. Daniel Lyfons gave 20*s. per ann.* in bread to the poor.

The

The number of housholders in 1562, was 15. In Sir Robert Atkyns's account of housholders this parish is taken in with St. Mary de Crypt, and so cannot be distinguished; but in 1743, the housholders were 21, and the number of inhabitants 80.

St. JOHN BAPTIST.

THIS parish extends a little on the north side of the lower North-gate, and takes in all the lower North-gate street.

The church is a rectory, depending upon the benevolence of the parishioners. The lord chancellor is patron, but before the dissolution it belonged to the abbey of St. Peter, to which it had been confirmed by the kings Henry the First, and Stephen; and it was appropriated by abbat Hameline to the precentor, for maintaining the feast of St. Oswald. The church was taxed 19° E. 1. at ten marks, and the abbey received a yearly pension of 20*s.* out of it, which at the dissolution was granted to the dean and chapter.

The present church is a new building, on the west side of the street, just within the upper North-gate. The old church, affirmed to have been built by king Ethelstan, and taken down about forty years since, consisted of a large nave, and south aile of the same length, a chancel, a slender steeple at the west end of the aile, and a large porch on the north side. It was a stone building 80 feet long and 50 broad, the estimate of the charge of rebuilding of which was 2310*l.* and upwards. A brief was obtained for this purpose, and 435*l.* 8*s.* 10*d.* collected upon it, which being insufficient, a further sum was raised by taxation on the parishioners, and by private contributions from well disposed persons, for building the present church, the foundation of which was laid on the first day of June, 1732. The new church, which was first preached in on August 4, 1734, consists of three ailes, of which the middle one is the widest. The old steeple is left standing, with five bells in peal, and a saint's bell.

In the old church were the several chapels, chantries, and services following:

1. A chapel dedicated to St. Bridget, on account of which, and some other particulars, St. Peter's abbey was adjudged by the pope's delegates, in 1222, to pay 20*s.* *per ann.* to St. Oswald's priory.

2. A chapel dedicated to St. Thomas, wherein abbat Thokey, with the consent of the rector, in 1390, ordained, that the rectors of the church should say mass every week, and receive a certain corrody for that service of the sub-almoner of the abbey.

3. A chantry dedicated to St. Mary, several of the possessions of which, and of many others in Gloucester, were granted to Thomas Chamberlain, knight, and Richard Pates, esq;

4. A chantry dedicated to St. Ann.

5. A chantry dedicated to the Holy Rood, in the patronage of St. Peter's abbey. Richard Boyden, the last incumbent of it, was allowed a pension [a] of 4*l.* at its dissolution.

6. The light of St. Nicholas.

7. The light of St. Catherine, which Maud Browd, before the year 1393, endowed with certain lands near Alvingate.

'Tis also said that a chantry was erected in this church in 1340, and annexed to the church of the Holy Trinity, but whether it was either of the above it does not appear.

At the visitation of this church, 26° H. 8. the commissioners certified as follows: *Rectoria Sancti Johannis valet clare in decimis et oblationibus, ultra 20 sol. solutos abbati et conventui Glouc. pro quadam pensione annuali,* 12 *den. pro senagio,* 6*s.* 8*d. archidiacono pro procuratione,* 13 *den. episcopo pro visitatione,* 14*l.* 0*s.* 10*d. ob.*

By an order of parliament in 1648, Saint Katherine's being united to this parish, the perpetual patronage was granted to the mayor and burgesses. An annuity of 60*l.* and one of the prebendal houses were settled upon this rectory, and the incumbent was to pay first fruits and tenths according to the rate of 8*l.* a year; but the parishes became distinct at the restoration.

The living has been augmented by Mr. Hodges's legacy, and the queen's bounty; besides which, three pounds a year are left for the minister to read prayers on Wednesdays, and ten shillings for a sermon. There was no house for the minister 'till lately, but these donations will more particularly appear in the list of benefactions.

	l. s. d.		*l. s. d.*
First fruits,	14 : 0 : 10	Synodals,	0 : 2 : 0
Tenths,	01 : 8 : 01	Pentecostals,	0 : 1 : 2
Procurations,	00 : 6 : 08		

After the battle of Bosworth-field, in 1485, wherein king Richard the Third was slain, Francis viscount Lovel and the lord Stafford fled to this church for sanctuary.

[a] Having now first mentioned this pension of a chantry-priest, I shall here take occasion to observe, that tho' it may at first appear to have been a very trifling allowance to a clergyman for his maintenance; yet the matter will be seen in a very different light, if we compare the prices of things now, with what they were formerly; for which purpose Mr. Willis, in his first volume of his *History of Mitred Parliamentary Abbies*, p. 11, has produced an item from the farmer's account of the impropriation of Ravenston, in Buckinghamshire, with Christ Church college, Oxford, in the reign of king Henry the Eighth; wherein the farmer, by way of discount out of his rent, reckons only 1l. 6s. 8d. for the vicar's diet for the whole year; so that five pounds a year then, says the same author, would maintain any one in great honour and credit.

Robert

Incumbents and Patrons.

Edward Frowcefter, D. D. occurs rector 11° H. 7. being alfo rector of Clifford Chambers. He was afterwards preferred to the deanery of Hereford. William Malvern the abbat, and the convent of St. Peter's Gloucefter, Patrons.

William Jennings, B.D dean of Gloucefter, inftituted October 6, 1546, and refigned Auguft 30, 1547.

William Sheldon occurs 1547.

Hugh Whittington, LL. B. fometime rector of St. Mary de Crypt, occurs rector 1551, and was promoted to the vicarage of Staverton.

Walter Jones, on Whittington's refignation, was inftituted June 21, 1553.

Thomas Partridge, rector of Deinton, occurs curate in 1562, as does

Maurice Williams, curate of St. Katherine's, in 1569.

The church vacant in 1571.

Thomas Woodcock, afterwards rector of St. Mary de Crypt, 1572.

Thomas Richardfon, one of the minor-canons, fometime vicar of Kempley, and rector of Stratton, occurs curate 1580.

Thomas Wood, rector of Pinnock, inftituted Feb. 3, 1583.

Robert Provis, alias Charlion, fometime curate of St. Aldate's and St. Katherine's, obtained the fequeftration and was curate March 5, 1593.

Edward Kyfte, occurs 1628.

Philip Hofier, fometime curate of St. Mary de Crypt and All Saints, 1534.

——— Hinman, 1642.

——— Frier, 1642.

Thomas Jennings was prefented September 15, 1648.

Thomas Walnough, M. A. rector of St. Michael's, 1664.

Amos Jones, M. A. rector of St. Michael's, 1675, but refigned in 1677.

George Vernon, M. A. fucceed both to this and St. Michael's curacy, but was amoved from both in 1687.

John Abbat, M. A. rector of Witcomb, fupply'd the cure, and dying was buried in the veftry, at the eaft end of the north aile.

William Elliot, M. A. was prefented by the king, and inftituted June 27, 1733. He was alfo perpetual curate of Barn wood, and dying, was buried in the north aile of the church of St. Mary de Lode.

Daniel Remmington, B. A. upon Elliot's death, was prefented by the king, and inftituted, 1761.

Benjamin Newton, A. M. fucceeded, and is the prefent incumbent.

Monuments and Infcriptions.

Upon a large grave-ftone in grey marble, which was in the chancel before the old church was demolifhed, but now altered, or taken away, was a plate of brafs, on which the effigy of a man at length between two wives and feveral children, was engraven, and the following infcription, in old black character.

Here under buried John Semys lyeth,
Which had two wives, the firft Elizabeth,
And by her vi. foonnes, and daughters five;
Then aftur by Agnes, his fecund wive,
Eight foonnes, feven daughters, goddes plente,
The full numbre in all of fix and twentie.
He paffed to God in the moneth of Auguft,
The thoufand five hundred and fortie yere juft.
(24 Aug.)

Round the verge of the ftone, on the fouth fide,

Plaude poli patria, plaude et paradife colonum,
Aftri chorus plaudat, plaudat hic aftra petens;
Plaufus culmen opes; p'cul ite valete mag'ri,
Laus et fama, vale decor: caro putreat opto.

On the weft fide,

Scripta legas tumuli moritus nunc reperat hic qui
Laudis erat dignus, prudens, fapienfque, benignus.

On the north fide,

Mitis, item lenis, difcretus, largus egenis,
Hic quafi fundator, miferis fuit et miferator.
Plangit Conventus paftorem Religionis,
Regula tutorem: plangito, plange domus.

On the eaft fide,

Patria plange patrem, dominum vos plangite fui
Plange potens paup---------- natio plange fua.

On each of the four corners, without the infcription, was a fcroll with writing on it, but one of the braffes long fince torn off. On the others it is thus written:

Sifte gradus, Ora, Cogita, Reminifcere, Plora.
Sic redis in cineres, hujus es, et ejus es.
Gloria divicie fugiunt te, mors, manet et te.

Within the verge, at the fouth-weft corner, are the old arms of the city, and no other arms upon it.

Upon an antient ftone, engraved on brafs, the effigies of a man in armour, and a woman attired in her proper habit. The man has a fword by his fide, his fpurs on, and at his feet a greyhound couchant. There are alfo the following arms, and infcription: Quarterly. 1. *A cheveron.* 2. *a pile.* 3. *Checky, on a bend three lions paffant.* 4. *a crofs charged with a leopard's head cabofhed.*

John a Brigges, Gentilman, lyeth buryed here,
Sometyme of this contrey, Worfhipful Squyer,
The XIX day of April flefh and bone dyede he,
In the yere of grace M° CCCC four fcore and three.
And Agnes his Wife, good gentilwoman was fhe.
They ben retourned into erth, and fo fhall ye.
Of erth we were made and fourmed,
And into erth we be retourned.
Have this in mynd and parfite memorie,
Ye that liven here leiveth to dye;
And beholdeth here youre owne deftene,
For as ye ben now fomtyme were we.
Ihu wth thi moder Mary, maiden fre,
Have mercy on us for your grete pite.
God yeve them ioy and everlafting life
That prayen for John Brigges and Agnes his wife,
That our paynes leffed may be:
For cherite feith Pater nofter and Ave.

Not many years ago there was a griffin's head, which was their creft, above the effigies.

The following perfons, the firft feven of whom were mayors of the city, were buried here:

Thomas Rich, father of the pious founder of the blue-coat Hofpital, *ob.* July 1, 1607.

Thomas Adams *ob.* 1621.

Richard Smith, *ob.* July 1, 1637.

Edmund Collet.

William Ruffel, *ob.* January 14, 1681.

Giles Rodway, *ob.* September 2, 1729, aged 80.

Samuel Brown, *ob.* September 7, 1738.

Richard Keylock, fheriff, *ob.* 1636.

Richard Broad, fheriff, *ob.* 1670.

Richard Bofley, fheriff, *ob.* 1677.

Thomas Price, gent. *ob.* 1654.

Robert Lawrence, fon of Robert Lawrence of Sevenhampton, gent. *ob.* 1670.

Robert Nicholls, M. A. vicar of Sandhurft, *ob.* March 28, 1702.

Abel Wantner, who compiled a Hiftory of Gloucefterfhire, and publifhed propofals for printing it a little before his death. The manufcript is now in the Bodleian library at Oxford. He died July 8, 1714.

Benefactions.

Benefactions.

John Wyman, in 1556, gave a tenement between the two North-gates, for the reparation of the church.

Hugh Aphowel, gent. in 1558, gave two tenements in the lower North-gate ftreet, for the ufe of the parifh.

Alderman Thomas Semys, in 1662, gave the yearly rent of a ftable and garden in Oxbody-lane, part for a fermon yearly on the Sunday after the Purification of the Bleffed Virgin, and part for the ufe of the poor.

Alderman John Hayward, who died June 8, 1641, gave 20*l.* to ciel the chancel, and feveral tenements in St. Aldate's parifh, for the maintenance of two widows, allowing each 6*d.* a week, and a little houfe near the church-door.

Mr. Richard Keylock gave 3*l. per ann.* for prayers to be read in this parifh church weekly, which is now done on Wednefdays in the morning.

Sir Thomas Rich gave eight pieces of gilt plate, and a confiderable quantity of crimfon velvet and linen, for the fervice of the church.

Mr. Daniel Lyfons gave 30*s.* yearly for bread for the poor.

Mrs. Sarah Wright gave 10*s.* yearly for bread, and 16*s.* every fecond year to cloath poor widows and orphans.

Mr. John Cromwell gave two acres and a half of land lying in Corn-mead, Walham, and Windmill-field, the rent to be diftributed in coals to the poor of the parifh.

Benjamin Bathurft, and John Selwyn, efqrs. Mr. Richard Price, Mrs. Bridget Price, and feveral others, were great benefactors towards the erecting and ornamenting of the new church.

Mr. Samuel Pawling gave an inn, which lets at 13*l.* a year, to the minifter of this parifh for ever, out of which 40*s.* a year is paid to a parifh in Herefordfhire. He alfo gave a houfe in this parifh to provide cloth gowns for poor people.

Alderman Samuel Brown, whofe daughter Hefter had given 10*l.* that the intereft of it might be given to the poor in bread, gave alfo 10*s.* yearly for the fame purpofe; and 10*s.* yearly more to the two widows who dwell in alderman Haywood's houfes.

	Baptifms.		Burials.	
1759	males 12	females 7	males 4	females 6
1760	—— 17	—— 8	—— 16	—— 19
1761	—— 23	—— 14	—— 12	—— 9
1762	—— 12	—— 8	—— 8	—— 10
1763	—— 11	—— 9	—— 10	—— 14
1764	—— 13	—— 9	—— 12	—— 16
1765	—— 13	—— 8	—— 11	—— 15
1766	—— 10	—— 11	—— 10	—— 17
1767	—— 11	—— 7	—— 22	—— 16
1768	—— 10	—— 9	—— 10	—— 12
	Total — 222		Total — 249	

The number of houfholders in this parifh, in the year 1562, was 76; Sir Robert Atkyns's account, about 1712, is 103 houfes, and about 500 inhabitants; in 1743, there were 172 houfes, and 699 inhabitants.

This parifh paid quarterly 29*l.* 17*s.* 6*d.* to the workhoufe, and 12*l.* 2*s.* 4*d.* for lamps in 1770.

To the Royal Aid, in	1693, £.	91 : 04 : 00
Poll tax, —	1694,	47 : 09 : 00
Land tax, —	1694,	123 : 07 : 11
The fame, —	1670,	100 : 19 : 06

In this parifh ftands

SAINT MARGARET'S HOSPITAL.

This hofpital was built in honour of the fepulture of our Lord, and of St. Margaret. It was called *The Hofpital, or Houfe of the lepers of St. Sepulcher's and St. Margaret's*; alfo, *The lower Houfe of Dudftan.*

There were formerly houfes of this kind in moft cities and confiderable towns in England, Ireland, the Low Countries, Germany, &c. and no longer than a century or two ago, there was indeed too much occafion for them. It feems no difficult matter to account for the leprofy being fo rife formerly, and fo little known at prefent. That loathfome difeafe is occafioned by bad air, but more efpecially by unwholfome diet. The caufes of bad air are now in a great meafure removed among us, by cutting down our large forefts, draining our marfhes, and cultivating our lands; and it cannot be denied but we live better than our forefathers.

No longer ago than Cromwell's time, the leprofy was very common in Ireland. It was occafioned by the people's living fo much upon falmon and other fifh, which every river and brook abounded with, and the poor people had for catching. The Englifh getting poffeffion of the country, limited the ufe of fuch unwholfome food, and forbad it at a certain feafon of the year. They introduced the planting of coleworts, and other gardenftuff, in confequence of which the poor people were cured, and the many hofpitals expreffly built to receive the lepers are now gone to ruin.

I am told that formerly it was almoft a ftanding condition in the indentures of apprenticefhip at Gloucefter, that the fervant fhould not be obliged to eat falmon more than thrice a week; which was undoubtedly intended as a precaution againft this grievous diforder.

The founder of this hofpital and the time of its foundation are equally unknown. It confifted of a mafter or fupervifor, a prior, a chaplain, and brethren and fifters. Alured, bifhop of Worcefter, the king's chaplain, who, according to Mr. Willis, was enthronized April 13, 1158, granted to thefe lepers liberty to bury in their own churchyard, which evidences the foundation to have been of great antiquity.

The patronage of the houfe belonged to the abbey of St. Peter, which prefcribed rules for it;

 therefore,

therefore, when Thomas (perhaps Horton) was abbat, they called it *noftrum hofpitale apud Newlond*, our hofpital at Newlond; and it is fo called in a deed witneffed by the abbey's hundred, or court, held there; but the town of Gloucefter, foon after the diffolution of the abbey, had the fole government of it.

According to the certificate of the commiffioners appointed 37° H. 8. a copy of which is now among the city records, the yearly value of this hofpital was then 11 *l.* 8 *s.* 4 *d.* of which the brethren and fifters received 8 *l.* 12 *s.* the prieft had for his falary 2 *l.* and the out-rents, which came to 15 *s.* The goods, plate, ornaments, &c. belonging to it were valued at 24 *l.* 7 *s.* 6 *d.*

At a metropolitical vifitation held in St. Bartholomew's hofpital, November 8, 1580, John Fenner, *alias* Spring, being then governor, or fupervifor of the Margaret's hofpital, it appeared, that the foundation of the houfe, by which was meant the charter of the foundation, was delivered to Mr. Rumney, then deceafed, who had been mayor of the city in the year 1572, and was not returned; but that by the foundation *fix poor people were to be fed* [or maintained] *therein*; that John Povey, alias Shepherde, Alice Cooke, Katherine Bryan, William Sprynge, fon of the governor aforefaid; Agnes ——, and Grace Sprynge, *alias* Fenner, wife of the faid governor, were then maintained in it. But according to bifhop Cheiney's account of the diocefe in 1562, a reader and ten men were belonging to it. Since that time the number varied, 'till it was fixed, as it now is, to eight men, a reader, and fome other officers. Each of the poor perfons now receives 2 *s.* a week, and the remainder of the income is expended in fees and other charges.

On the S. W. fide of the hofpital ftands a fmall chapel, which, in the certificate above-mentioned, is faid to be a parifh church, at which prayers are read every Saturday morning.

At the eaft end were the prior's lodgings, upon the fite of the adjacent houfe. The old hall was converted into a barn the thirty-firft year of queen Elizabeth; and at the fiege of the city, in 1643, fome of the king's forces took up their quarters in the hofpital, which feems to have been then very much damaged.

Benefactors to the Hofpital.

Henry le Locker, Roger Toli, Maurice Niger, Henry le Mercer, Richard Eurgens, Luke Cornwaleys, Hugh de Winchcomb, *alias* Poucteley, John Tinctor [or Dyer], John Gofedike, John Ingolf, Roger de Bofco, Reniida Thurftan, Richard Fitz Ernys, all in the reign of king Henry the Third; Maurice Faber, Henry le Cnufer, William Bruyn, Thomas le Sporener, all in the reign of Edward the Firft; Simon de Alre, in Edward the Second's reign; John Walton, Peter Hardeley, both in the reign of Henry the Fifth; John Richemon, 32° H. 6. Thomas and Agnes Andreux, 38° H. 6. Elias Giffard, Aylgena de Bernwode, Richard de Pancefot, Helena de Wigorn, Henry de Hasfield, William de la Hakton, Richard de Afton, Richard de Hida, Henry Mercer, Philip de Kinemerefbury, Alexander de Telbrug, Simon de Elbrug, Anfelm Niger. Thefe laft are without date.

Mafters of the Hofpital.

Frier Lewin occurs, when John Simond and William de Cheltenham were Præpofiti Glouc. (probably in 1255.)
Helias occurs about 15° E. 1.
John de Dumbleton occurs 2° and 16° E. 2.
Edward Taverner 17° and 23° R. 2. and was formerly bailiff of the town.
Robert Burdon 3° and 4° H. 4.
Roger Balle 5° H. 4. being fometime bailiff of Gloucefter.
John Byeley 8° and 26° H. 6. being fometime bailiff of Gloucefter.
Richard Dalby, 9° H. 6. being fometime bailiff of Gloucefter.
Richard Manchefter, probably in king Henry the Sixth's reign.
Thomas Berfton, 32° and 35° H. 6.
John Afplyn, 4° E. 4.
John Hillery, 5° E. 4.
John Natton, 1497, being afterwards mayor of Gloucefter.
Ralph Halfey, 1518, being then alderman of Gloucefter.
Thomas Bell, jun. 26° and 27° H. 8. He, and all the fucceeding mafters enjoyed the office, after they had been fheriffs of the city, and before they were mayors.
Thomas Payne, 27° 28° H. 8.
Maurice Vaughan, 28° 29° H. 8.
John Uggons, 29° 30° H. 8.
Raphael Rawlins, 30, 31 H. 8.
Edmund Allen, 31, 32 H. 8.
Thomas Clouterbuck, 32, 33 H. 8.
Richard Edwards, 33, 34, H. 8.
John Raftel, 34, 35 H. 8.
Thomas Loveday, 35, 36 H. 8.
William Traheron, 36, 37 H. 8.
William Michel, 37, 38 H. 8.
John Sandford, 38 H. 8. 1 E. 6.
Thomas Pury, 1, 2 E. 6.
John Todd, 2, 3, 4 E. 6.
Robert Moreton, 4, 5 E. 6.
William Jenkins, 5, 6 E. 6.
William Bonde, 6 E. 6. 1. M. 1.
Thomas Maffinger, 1, 2 M. 1.
Lewis Leyfaunce, 2, 3 M. 1.
Edmund, or, as it is in fome accounts Hugh, Aphowel 3, 4 M. 1.
Henry Machyn, 4, 5 M. 1.
Robert Adams, 5, 6 M. 1.
Thomas Hide, 6 M. 1. 1 Eliz.
Laurence Singleton, 1, 2 Eliz.
John Woodward, 2, 3 Eliz.
Thomas Semys, 3, 4 Eliz.
Henry Kynge, 4, 5 Eliz.
Thomas Heath, 5, 6 Eliz. with whom the office expired; for the corporation having obtained St. Bartholomew's hofpital, 6 Eliz. the fame governors became thenceforth appointed for the Margaret's and Magdalen's alfo.

Priors.

Gilbert de Siffore occurs, when Hugh Siffor and Walter Kentwin were Præpofiti Glouc.
Walter occurs, when John Pain and Robert le Wife were Præpofiti Glouc. probably in 1269.
William de Slouhtre occurs, when Walter Sevare and Will. Wyghtfield were bailiffs of Gloucefter, probably in 1297.
William Confelard, 14 E. 3.
Walter de Dumbleton, occurs 14, 15 E. 3.
William ——, occurs 29 E. 3. I know not whether he was William Brouning, who occurs 44 E. 3. 4 R. 2.
Henry Palmer, 17 R. 2.
John Attewode, 3 H. 4.
John Aldeford, 11 H. 4.
Stephen Rich, 2, 5 H. 4. He obtained from the king, for himfelf and the brethren and fifters, a pardon for all offences committed before December 8, 1414.
John Cookes, or Cokes, or Cocks, 5, 6 H. 5.
Thomas Bokeland, occurs 2, 13 H. 6.
Richard Athelard, 19 H. 6.

John Morſe, 26 H. 6.
Richard Athelard, 32 H. 6.
John Fermor, 4, 5 E. 4.
Richard Paaſe, or Payſe, 5 H. 7.
Robert Clouterboke, 9 H. 7.

William Organ, huſbandman, was admitted a brother, and his wife Emmote, a ſiſter, of the hoſpital in 1518, by the mayor and all the burgeſſes of Glouceſter, with the maſter of the houſe: He was then by the ſame perſons advanced to the priorſhip, which he was to enjoy for his life, upon payment of 10l. yearly to the brethren and ſiſters, and employing the lands in huſbandry. In his time the grant of Helias Giffard (long enjoyed by the hoſpital) of the full carriage of one horſe-load of wood every day in the winter, and three waynloads every week in the ſummer, to be had from Brimpsfield wood, being detained by the king's officers; he, in behalf of himſelf and the hoſpital, petitioned the king that their right might be reſtored to them, but with what ſucceſs is uncertain. He occurs April 4, 11 H. 8.

Thomas Peers, or Perce, occurs 25, 38 H. 8.

Robert Hobbes, September 23, 6 E. 6.

Thomas Wilſe, of Dimmock, huſbandman, admitted a brother of the hoſpital October 24, 6 E. 6. was at the ſame time advanced by the maſter, with the conſent of the brethren and ſiſters, to the office of prior; but to admit no brother or ſiſter, without leave of the mayor and three of the eldeſt aldermen. The value of the goods belonging to the hoſpital then was 59l. 7s. 3d. 1 Mary 1. he occurs in the office; but the next year was diſpoſeſſed of it whether by reſignation or removal doth not appear. After him no other perſon occurs in this office; but a father and a matron are appointed for this houſe by the governors of the Bartholomew's hoſpital, where, as at the principal houſe, courts are occaſionally holden, and the poor people of the Margaret's are obliged to attend them.

In this pariſh alſo is

SAINT MARY MAGDALEN'S, or KING JAMES'S HOSPITAL.

This houſe is ſituate northward of St. Margaret's, and was therefore called the Upper Houſe, or Hoſpital of Dudeſtan. The priory of Lanthony is acknowledged as the founder, and uſed to ſupply it weekly with a certain quantity of bread.

This hoſpital, as appears by the *Monaſticon*, ſeems to have been in part ſuſtained with a moiety of the lordſhip of Bernyſtone, [Barrington,] in this county, which was given to the priory of Lanthony, by earl Milo, the conſtable, for thirteen lepers. It appears by a manuſcript now in C.C.C. college, Oxon, that the brethren received yearly to the value of 12*l.* 6*s.* 8*d.* for providing certain loaves, called the loaves of Dudeſtan, and for other neceſſaries, from the priory of Lanthony; to the monks of which the cure of this houſe was the uſual title for obtaining of holy orders.

It is ſaid in the regiſter book of Henry Deene, prior of Lanthony, that the poor people of this hoſpital aſſigned two loaves a day, a load of hay, and a tree for fewel yearly, with the paſturage of a cow, and ſome other lands, for the maintenance of their prieſt.

John Carrell, eſq; Richard Pate, and Edward Goſtroyke, gentlemen, were commiſſioners appointed by the king, 37° H. 8. who certified, That this hoſpital was founded for a maſter and certain poor people, who were to enjoy the income of all the lands, amounting to 3*l.* 6*s.* 8*d.* yearly. The goods, plate, and ornaments belonging to it were valued at 6*l.* 8*s.* 8*d.*

The priory of Lanthony being diſſolved, this hoſpital was ſo poor, and the buildings ſo miſerably decayed, that queen Elizabeth, December 4, in the 41ſt year of her reign, granted the patronage and power of placing a ſupervisor or governor over it, to the mayor and burgeſſes of Glouceſter, in conſideration of their rebuilding it, at which time there were only four perſons in it of the old foundation. And afterwards, on account of the great expence the corporation had been at in this building, king James the Firſt, in the 14th year of his reign, by his charter granted, That the hoſpital ſhould be under the government of the city, and that thenceforth it ſhould be called by his name: That whereas the kings of England paid an annual penſion of 13*l.* to this hoſpital, that penſion, with all the former gifts, grants, and lands, ſhould be applied for the maintenance of nineteen poor people and a miniſter.

In 1562, according to biſhop Cheiney's account of the dioceſe, there were then one reader and ſix poor people only maintained in it.

It appears by original writings in the cuſtody of the corporation, that an annuity of 20*l.* payable out of the manors of Newland and Ruredean, in the county of Glouceſter, was ſold to the mayor and burgeſſes in the year 1650, and at that time king James's penſion of 13*l.* before-mentioned was aſſigned to the hoſpital.

At ſome diſtance from the hoſpital, on the weſt ſide next the highway, is a neat chapel, which in the before-mentioned certificate is called a pariſh church; and there was a meſſuage near the hoſpital called the old parſonage houſe.

Priors.

Thomas Tully occurs 9 H. 7.

William Malvern, who died ſometime after the 25th of June, 1551.

Thomas Povey, *alias* Shepherd, who died between April and October, 1571.

John Fenner, *alias* Spring, was preſented by the queen, March 26, 15 Eliz. His will is dated June 13, 1603, and was proved in May following; on the back of which is an inventory of the houſhold goods, &c. which came to him as prior of the hoſpital, and are to remain to it for ever. Firſt, one cornewayne and one dungwayne, with one pair of iron-bound wheels.—Item two yokes for oxen and two iron ſtringes, one plow with a ſhear and coulter, one ſow, one cock with three hens.—Item, four braſſe potts, two great potts and two little potts.—Item, three braſſe pans and one braſſe kettle.—Item, one little braſſe poſnet.—Item, one pewter candleſtick.—Item, a challis or communion cup of ſilver.—Item, in the church, one table cloth and a ſurplis.

Alderman Thomas Machen, upon Fenner's death, was elected by the corporation, September 5, 1 J. 1. He placed thirteen perſons in the hoſpital, which he governed with great prudence, and gave to it the yearly ſum of 3l. 15s. for ever. No other prior occurs after him, but ever ſince this hoſpital has been ſubject to the ſame governors as the Margaret's, and the poor people attend the courts held at the Bartholomew's.

St. KATHERINE'S, *alias* St. OSWALD'S.

THIS pariſh is ſituate partly in the city, and partly in the liberties.—St. Oſwald, king of Northumberland in the year 634, a devout and religious prince, was killed by the Danes, and his relicks firſt carried to the abbey of Bardney, in Lincolnſhire;

Lincolnfhire; whence, upon the approach of the Danes afterwards to thofe parts, they were removed to this place, by Ethelred and the famous princefs Ethelfleda, who built a college here for fecular priefts, which was dedicated to the honour of St. Ofwald, and afterwards converted into a priory of regular canons, of which more particularly hereafter.

This priory had antiently a free chapel with a fpire fteeple, ftanding upon the bank of the old river Severn, dedicated to St. Katherine, which afterwards became the parifh church of which I am now about to give a further account.

Thurftan, archbifhop of York[a], pulled down the old church, which was very fpacious, built a new one at great expence, and enlarged and repaired St. Ofwald's tomb. He alfo granted to the heirs of the crown two thirds of the yearly income of the canonry, and appropriated the other fhare for the reparation of the church.

In the taxation made in the 19th year of king Edward the Firft, this church, with its chapels of Churchdown, Norton, Sainthurft and Compton, was valued at fixty marks. The rectory and advowfon of the above church and chapels belonged to the priory of St. Ofwald's 'till it was diffolved; when the king, on the 18th of November, 34° H. 8. granted all, except Sainthurft, to the dean and chapter of Briftol, who now pay 10*l.* a year to the curate of this parifh; befides which, the living was augmented with the queen's bounty in the year 1747.

By an ordinance of parliament in the year 1648, the parifh was united to St. John's, the church with its materials given to the corporation of the city, and in 1665, the roof and fome other parts of it were ufed in building the Barley-market-houfe, in the Eaft-gate-ftreet. This ordinance became null at the reftoration, and the parifh was again feparate, and is at prefent fupply'd by its own curate in the church of St. Mary de Lode; but they bury in their own church-yard.

There was a chantry in this church dedicated to St. Katherine, and another called the charnel fervice, which the commiffioners, in their certificate made 1. E. 6. fay, was founded, and its lands put in feoffement for a prieft, at the yearly penfion of 3*l.* 6*s.* 2*d.* and the value of its jewels, ornaments, and other goods, was 2*l.* 15*s.* 10*d.*

Pentecoftals, 0*l.* 0*s.* 9*d.*

Incumbents.

Nicholas Newland occurs in 1541.
Henry, or Harry Francomb, fometime of St. Bartholomew's hofpital, occurs in 1558, as doth
Thomas Waftal, fometime curate of St. Mary de Lode, and mafter of the college fchool, May 26, 1594.
Thomas Tomkins, vicar of St. Mary de Lode, in 1594.
Francis Arnold, before curate of St. Nicholas, but then of St. Mary de Crypt, occurs June 28, 1597.
Robert Charlion, *alias* Provis, feems to refign this curacy for that of St. Aldate's in 1599.
Giles Knowles occurs in 1600.
Barnabas Morrice, a minor canon, in 1605.
John Phelps, afterwards vicar of the Holy Trinity, occurs 1607.
——— Martrevis occurs 1616.
Richard Brodgate, 1622, 1635.
No curate in 1666.
George Evans, licenced July 24, 1674, occurs 1678, being alfo a minor canon.
John Price, vicar of St. Mary de Lode.
Daniel Bond, B. A. ufher of Crypt School, admitted in 1716.
Thomas Gardiner, M. A. licenced December 24, 1731.
John Warren, LL.D.
The Reverend Mr. Robert Rickards.
Hugh Price, A. M. is the prefent incumbent.

Monuments and Infcriptions.

In the church-yard is a raifed tomb with the following infcription:

Here lyeth old Mr. Richard Tully,
Who lived C and 3 years fully.
He did the fword of the city beare
Before the mayor Thirty-one yeare.
Four wives he had, and here they lye
All waiting Heaven's eternity.
He died -------- March, 1619.

There is a memorial for Mr. Bridges Patefhall, late owner of the adjacent priory, who died April 11, 1720, aged near 40.

Benefactors, &c.

Alderman Thomas Machen gave 24*s.* a year to twelve poor perfons of this parifh; and

Mr. Daniel Lyfons gave 40*s.* a year in bread for the poor.

The number of houfholders in 1562 was 102; about 1712, according to Sir Robert Atkyns, there were 100 houfes and about 500 inhabitants; but in 1743, there were 119 houfholds and 406 inhabitants.

The baptifms and burials of this parifh are regiftered at St. Mary de Lode, and included in the account of them there.

In this parifh is the fite of

The PRIORY of St. OSWALD.

This houfe ftood N.N.W. of St. Peter's abbey, upon the bank of the Severn, near the old key or wharf, which, on occafion of a difpute between the town and the priory, was removed. Some of the legendary writers report[b], that Merwald, viceroy of the weftern part of Mercia, and his wife Domneva, about the year 660, built a ftately monaftery here in honour of St. Ofwald, the king and martyr, which from the abundance of ornaments about it, was vulgarly called the golden one. But the better and more certain account, is that which has been juft touched on at the beginning of the fhort hiftory of the parifh of the fame name, taken from the Saxon Chronicle, and from bifhop Tanner's *Monafticon.* Thefe great authorities fay that Ethelred, earl of Mercia, and the famous Elfleda his princefs, tranflating the remains of St Ofwald from Bardney in Lincolnfhire, in the year 909, richly entombed him here, built a college in honour of that faint, and filled

[a] Godwin in Præful. in vit.——Dodefworth's Collections in the Bodleian Library.

[b] Leland's Collect. v. 2, p. 170. E libro Gotcelini de Vita S. Milburgæ.

it

it with prebendaries. In the wars with the Danes, the monks were driven away, and from that time it became a college of ſecular prieſts, and was accounted a free chapel royal, exempt from the juriſdiction of the archbiſhop of Canterbury, and the biſhop of Worceſter, and ſubject only to the archbiſhop of York.

Having refuſed to acknowledge the authority of the archbiſhop of Canterbury, in the year 1083, that prelate[b], for their contumacy, excommunicated the prior, and ſeveral of the principal officers, and ſent his mandate to the biſhop of the dioceſe to execute the ſentence publickly in all his churches, which he did with bells ringing, and lighted candles; but this diſpute was afterwards ſettled in favour of the college.

In the reign of king William the Second, according to biſhop Tanner, the ſecular prieſts were changed into canons regular of the order of St. Auguſtine, of which Leland gives the following account. A certain biſhop of Lincoln, who was alſo the chancellor, and highly in favour with the king, intreated the king to intercede with the archbiſhop of York for ſome lands in Lindſey and Moteham, which belonged to that ſee. The archbiſhop granted the king's requeſt, but on condition that this houſe, which was the king's free chapel, ſhould ever afterwards be appropriate to the ſee of York, which the king readily complied with. And this accounts for the churches under the patronage of St. Oſwald's, being in the dioceſe of York.

When the archbiſhop had got the houſe into his hands, he treated with the poſſeſſors of it about a new foundation of regular canons. Some of them complied, but others at firſt refuſed: however at length prevailing, he appropriated benefices to them, but reſerved ſeveral of their lands for the church of York. Geofry of Malmeſbury ſays that the archbiſhop drove out the poſſeſſors by force of hoſtility, but preſerved ſeveral of their lands, and beſtowed them upon his own monks.

Rudburn accounts[c] differently for this priory being appropriated to the church of York, and Sir William Dugdale agrees in part with both accounts, *viz.* that the king gave this houſe and the monaſtery of Selby, at his own charge, in ſatisfaction for the claim which the archbiſhop had in Lincoln and Lindſey.

After the king's grant had been confirmed by the popes[d] Honorius, Paſchal, Alexander, and Innocent, the priory again denied the juriſdiction of the ſee of Canterbury, whereupon the members of this priory, the clerks and officials of the ſee of York, were ſummoned to the viſitation of the archbiſhop of Canterbury, and not attending, were ſuſpended. They appealed to the pope, and Brompton and Hoveden both relate that the next year, a cardinal of the name of Hugezun, or Hugh, was diſpatched from Rome to ſettle the difference, which was done at a council at Wincheſter, where it was agreed that the archbiſhop of Canterbury ſhould quit his claim to this priory, being eſteemed the king's chapel, and ſhould abſolve thoſe whom before he had excommunicated.

At a provincial council held at Lambeth in 1280, archbiſhop Peckham[e] pronounced his ſentence againſt the prior and convent, by which he commanded, that no perſon ſhould preſume to ſell them any bread, wine, or victuals, for their ſuſtenance; to pay them any tithes; to buy any thing of them, or to have any commerce with them. It was alſo put under a like ſevere ſentence by Godfrey Giffard, biſhop of Worceſter, which was afterwards ratified by Robert Winchelſey, archbiſhop of Canterbury; but the king, by his writs, commanded theſe proud prelates to revoke their decrees; and the archbiſhop was afterwards attached to anſwer the prior in the king's bench, in the octaves of Candlemas, for excommunicating of him and his canons, to the contempt of the king, and prejudice of his majeſty, and in the damage of 200 *l.* to the priory. Notwithſtanding all this, the archbiſhop ſtill refuſed to abſolve the prior, therefore the king iſſued his mandate to the keeper of his ſpiritualties of that province to have him abſolved, which had its proper effect. Another mandate was ſent in November following to William de Geyneſborough[f], then biſhop of Worceſter, and his official, prohibiting them from exerciſing any eccleſiaſtical juriſdiction over the priory; and in 1318, a general prohibition was iſſued againſt making any kind of incroachments on its liberties and privileges, which put a ſtop to them intirely.

The donations to the priory were confirmed by the kings Henry the Firſt, and Richard the Second.

In the grant of the tenths of the clergy to the king, 2° H. 7. the prior is rated at 46 *ſol.* 4 *den. ob.* for temporalties. The priory was valued at the diſſolution at 90 *l.* 10 *s.* 2 *d. ob.*

The king, July 7, 31° H. 8. in conſideration of 100 *l.* and of former ſervices, granted to John Jennings, eſq; the ſite of the priory, with all its houſes and lands in the city and ſuburbs of Glouceſter, and ſome other particulars, at the twentieth part of a knight's-fee, and the yearly tenths of 1 *l.* 10 *s.* 4 *d.* Several other lands, tithes, &c. in Longford, Churchdown, Norton, Sainthurſt, Compton Abdale, and other parts of the county of Glouceſter, were granted to the biſhop and to the dean and chapter of Briſtol, upon the erecting of that ſee; and a fiſhery which had belonged to this priory, was granted to the chapter of Glouceſter, 38° H. 8.

[b] Thomas's Antiqu. Maj. Malvern, p. 47, 48.——Leland's Itin. v. 4, p. 78.

[c] Hiſt. Mon. Winton in Anglia Sacra.

[d] Mon. Anglic. v. 3, p. 131, 132, 143, 260.

[e] Brompton's Chronicle, p. 1000, 1007. Antiq. Eccleſ. Angl. in Vita.

[f] Prinne's Uſurpations.

The ſite of the priory afterwards deſcended to Agnes Wright, daughter of Joan Kemp, who was daughter of —— Jennings, ſon and heir of Sir John Jennings, who had the original grant before he was knighted. The huſband of Agnes Wright had livery granted him 5° *Mariæ*, and their ſon Richard had livery 17° Eliz. but it is now the property of the Reverend Mr. John Newton, who reſides here.

Moſt of the priory has been long ſince demoliſhed; but by the buildings yet remaining, it ſeems to have been a ſmall quadrangle, with a gate on the ſouth ſide, and another on the north, leading to the church adjoining.

Priors, collected out of the regiſter books of York and Worceſter, and other authorities.

Humphry, a man of eminent learning and piety, of the priory of Lanthony, was, in 1153, made the firſt prior after the introduction of regular canons, as we learn from Haguſtaldenſis, in his Continuation of Simon Dunelm.
William occurs when Geffry Cuttſtich and Walter Hoich were prepoſiti of Glouceſter.
Richard occurs in the reign of king Henry the Third.
Richard de Freynges occurs about 1260.
Richard de Buckampton or Buchampton was elected 1281.
Guydo died in 1289, and was ſucceeded by
Peter de Malbern, or Malburn, who reſigned 1301, and was ſucceeded by
Walter de Bingham, who reſigned alſo in 1310.
Humphrey Lavynton ſucceeded, and reſigned alſo in 1312.
John Ayſhwell ſucceeded, and reſigned the ſame year, to
Richard Kidderminſter, who was amoved in 1314, and
John Ayſhwell reſtored.
William Heved occurs 1352, as does
Thomas Duk 1398, and
John Players 1404, to whom
John Shiptyn, or de Shipton, ſucceeded in 1408.
John Sucley was elected 1433, as was
John Higins, canon of Wigmore co. Hereford, 1434, who reſigning, was ſucceeded by
John Mylis, canon of Cirenceſter, co. Glouceſter, collated by the archbiſhop of York, 1447.
Richard ——— occurs 1458.
John Beke, or Beche, was collated by the archbiſhop of York (*quamdiu nobis placuerit*) in 1464, but reſigning,
William Newland was collated, 1474.
Nicholas Fawkener, or Falkner, a canon of Lanthony, was collated by the archbiſhop of York, 1491. How long he continued doth not appear, nor does the election of
William Giffard, *alias* Jenings, who occurs June 24, 21° H. 8. and obtained from St. Peter's abbey a preſentation to the rectory of Rudford, Auguſt 4, 1533, with which he held the priory in *commendam* 'till 1536, when he reſigned that rectory. After his priory was diſſolved, he became a monk of St. Peter's, and in 1541, was made the firſt dean of the cathedral.

In this pariſh is the ſite of the monaſtery of

The WHITE FRIERS, or COLLEGE of CARMELITES.

This houſe ſtood without the lower North-gate, not far from Brook-ſtreet, towards the weſt end of the meadow which is ſtill called the friers ground.

According to Mr. Speed, from whom Sir Robert Atkyns takes his ſhort account, and to whom biſhop Tanner refers, it was founded by queen Eleanor, Sir Thomas Giffard, and Sir Thomas Berkeley; but ſome MS. collections of Mr. Stow make Sir Thomas Berkeley the ſole founder. William Giffard, archbiſhop of York[g], granted the friers leave to build an oratory in Brook-ſtreet, without Glouceſter, 15 kal. Feb. 1269. It was ſurrendered [h] July 28, 1538, to Richard, ſuffragan biſhop of Dover, in the preſence of the mayor and three of the aldermen, when it was ſaid to be but a ſmall houſe in decay. It had no rents, except 2*s.* a year for land on leaſe for twenty years. Thomas Knight, William Pleaſans, and Henry Birchwood, who were friers of it, had then permiſſion to change [i] their habits.

After it was diſſolved, the houſe, and two acres of land called Elmrow, belonging [k] to the friery, were granted July the 4th, 35° H. 8. to Richard Andrews, and Nicholas Temple, who ſold them ſoon after to Sir Thomas Bell, by whom the houſe and meadow adjacent, granted to Alexander and Daniel Perte, 7° E. 6. were applied towards the ſupport of St. Kimbro's, or Kineburg's hoſpital, of which hereafter. Other lands in the pariſh of Leigh, belonging to the friery, were granted to Sir Thomas Bell, 36° H. 8.

Great part of the friery ſeems to have been deſtroyed about the year 1567, yet in the reign of queen Elizabeth ſeveral of the buildings belonging to it remained, and the houſe of correction for the county of the city was appointed to be kept in ſome part of them. The laſt and total deſtruction of this houſe was reſerved for the time of the civil wars, when ſome of the materials were uſed in the fortification of the city. Some of the buildings, called the founder's lodgings, were converted into a barn, which proved very ſerviceable to the city at the ſiege.

The corporation have now the land whereon the friery ſtood, for which they pay yearly to the crown a quit rent of 1*s.* 3*d.*

Nicholas Cantelupe, or Cantelow, D.D. [l] but called from the place of his nativity and reſidence Nicholas of Glouceſter, was of the ſame family with a canonized biſhop of Hereford, and being a Carmelite, preſided over the convent of his order here. He was intimately and familiarly acquainted with Humphry the good duke of Glouceſter. Being choſen prior at Northampton, he continued there 'till his death, in 1441, leaving behind him ſeveral monuments of literature, in divinity and hiſtory.

David Boys, called ſometimes Boſchus, and Boethius, D. D. [m] a Carmelite here, viſited moſt of the foreign univerſities for improvement, and was alſo a familiar friend to duke Humphry. After he had been for ſome time governor of this monaſtery, he died in that office about 1450, or 1451, and was buried among his brethren here, having led a religious life, and left ſeveral learned works behind him.

[g] Biſhop Tanner's Notitia Monaſtica, p. 151.
[h] MS. in Cotton library.——[i] Ibid.
[k] It is ſo ſaid in a MS. wrote about 1653, which belonged to Thomas Pury, eſq; who was general receiver of Glouceſterſhire and Wiltſhire; but Sir Robert Atkyns ſays, p. 125, that Elmrow belonged to Studley priory, in Warwickſhire.
[l] Stevens's Supplement to the Monaſticon.——[m] Ibid.

St. MARY de CRYPT,

Called alfo *Chrift-Church*, and *St. Mary in the South.*

THIS is a handfome church fituate on the eaft fide of the South-gate ftreet, confifting of a low aile on each fide of the nave, a crofs aile, and a neat tower with eight fmall but very mufical bells in it; a chapel on each fide of the chancel, a large porch againft the fouth aile, and a fmaller one at the weft end. It feems to have received the name of Crypt, which fignifies a vault or charnel houfe, from the vaults under it, of which there are two; that under part of the fouth and middle chancel is thirteen yards long, ten broad, and about three deep; the other at the weft end, into which there is a defcent out of the ftreet, feems to be larger.

The rectory, now in the patronage of the lord chancellor, is worth, befides voluntary contributions, about 26*l.* a year, including the rent of three houfes, and money paid for fermons. It was given to the priory of Lanthony in 1137, by Robert Chichefter, bifhop of Exon, who built the church, together with all its profits, except a penfion of 20*s.* to the nunnery of Godftow, in the county of Oxford.

In the taxation of ecclefiaftical preferments made 19° E. 1. it is thus expreffed: *Rectoria Sanctæ Mariæ in auftro villæ Glouc. alias ecclefia Chrifti, valet clare in redditu una cum decimis et oblationibus ibidem per annum ultra* 6*s.* 8*d.* *folutos archidiacono pro procuratione*, 20*s.* *pro finagio*, 20*s.* *abbatiffæ de Godftow pro penfione*, 3*s.* *facriftæ Lanthoniæ pro quadam annua penfione*, 4*d.* *ob. coquinario Lanthon. pro capitali redditu*, 8*d.* *comiti Glouceftriæ pro longabulo*, 3*s.* 4*d.* *fenefcallis Glouceftriæ pro quodam quieto redditu*, 13*d.* *epifcopo pro vifitatione*, 14*l.* 6*s.* 6*d.*

The dean and chapter of Gloucefter now pay the rector 1*s.* 6*d.*

By an ordinance of parliament, All Saints and St. Owen's were united to this church, and one of the prebendal houfes, with an annuity of 80*l.* was fettled for the rectory; the rectory to pay for firft fruits and tenths according to the rate of 8*l.* a year; and the patronage was given to the corporation.

In this church were the following particulars:

1. A chantry, dedicated to St. Mary, to which Richard Manchefter was a great benefactor in 1454.
2. A chantry on the fouth part of the church, dedicated to St. John Baptift, to which Manchefter likewife contributed.
3. A chantry dedicated to St. Katherine, the lands of which lying in Lidney in Gloucefterfhire, and Ripple and Naunton in Worcefterfhire, were fold to Sir Thomas Bell, and Richard Duke, efq; Auguft 17, 2° E. 6.
4. A fraternity dedicated to St. Thomas.
5. An anniverfary, fome of the poffeffions of which were fold to the two laft mentioned perfons.
6. A yearly obit on September 13, for alderman John Cook, his father, mother, wife, and others, mentioned in the will of lady Cook, 1544, by whom it was founded.

Great part of the Black-Horfe inn was formerly the parfonage houfe, which is the only one now remaining to any of the parifhes in the city, and at this time it pays a confiderable chief-rent to the rector. There certainly were parfonage houfes antiently belonging to all thofe rectories or livings, the incumbents of which did not live in the religious houfes to which their churches were appropriated; Saint Mary de Grace, and the Holy Trinity had them, and the parfonage-houfes of All Saints, St. Aldate, St. Mary de Lode, and St. Michael, all occur in the old records. How they came to be loft does not appear; perhaps they might be taken away under pretence of concealed lands, or of forfeiture.

Upon feveral bricks now remaining in the church and chancel, are the following arms: *A fefs between fix crofs croflets.*—The arms of archbifhop Deene.—The arms of the Berkeley family.

Firft fruits,	£.14 : 7 : 1	Synodals, —	£.0 : 2 : 0
Tenths, —	1 : 8 : 9	Pentecoftals,	0 : 1 : 2
Procurations,	0 : 6 : 8		

Incumbents.

John Butterley occurs rector before 25° H. 3.
Alexander occurs in the fame reign, as do
Walter de Elbrugge in that of king Edward the Firft.
Simon Tangard, 14 E. 3.
William le Heyberare, 31 E. 3.
John Burgeys occurs rector in 1433.
Thomas Stuard, or Styward, 1455. He was afterwards batchelor of degrees, and had a grant of the perpetual curacy of Hempfted. He was inrolled in the obituary of the priory of Lanthony, where one of the canons officiated daily for him for two years, and having done good fervices to the priory, there was the fame yearly commemoration for him as for a canon.
Thomas Oldbury, rector of Rockhampton, in exchange with Stuard, was prefented 1468, by the prior and convent of Lanthony, who continued to prefent 'till John Tolfon, by their grant, prefented Thomas Young, as under.
William Frifer occurs rector 1472.
William Jones, 1 R. 3.
John Adam, 1492, and refigning,
Thomas Nuland was prefented in 1496.
Thomas Woodward, fometime rector of All Souls, dying,
Thomas Newman was prefented 1499.
Robert Stinchcomb, batchelor in degrees, occurs, 1528.
Thomas Greenwood, D. D. occurs rector 34 H. 8. and was alfo vicar of Standifh.
Thomas Young, M. A. inftituted March 1, 1542, by John Tolfon as above-mentioned.
Hugh Whittington, who refigned in 1548.
Henry Hawkes, inftituted 1548.
Evan Williams, inftituted 14 Eliz. by the queen.
Thomas Woodcocke, curate of St. John's, 1575. He was inftituted to Haresfield, March 1, 1577.
Alexander Borun, upon a vacancy, obtained the fequeftration, and was curate, 1579.
Thomas Difley, upon deprivation, was inftituted by queen Elizabeth in 1584.
Thomas Wrenche occurs curate in 1594.
Francis Arnold, before curate of St. Nicholas's, then of St. Katherine's, in 1597.
William Grove, M. A. fometime mafter of Crypt fchool, and the city lecturer, 1599; but being collated to Hartpury, in 1603,
Thomas Elliotts probably fucceeded, for he occurs in 1619.
Edward, or Edmund Barwell, ufher of Crypt-fchool, 1620.
Philip Hofyer, curate of All Saints, and St. John's, 1628.
Jonathan Bullock, M. A. 1632.
John Allibond, curate of St. Nicholas's, 1634.
John Maffinger, 1638.
John Corbet, ufher of Crypt-fchool, 1641.
Samuel Kenrick, M. A. 1648, Corporation patrons.

Clement

Clement Barkfdale, elected in 1657, by the fame.

William Jones, prefented in 1658, by the fame.

Edmund Hall, M. A. fometime rector of Great Rifington, inftituted in 1662, by king Charles the Second.

John Gregory, M. A. upon Hall's refignation, was inftituted in 1664. He was afterwards rector of Hempfted, and archdeacon of Gloucefter.

Richard Littleton, vicar of Longney, occurs curate in 1671.

Dennis Huntingdon was curate in 1675, and the fame year inftituted into the vicarage of Prefton.

Abraham Gregory, M. A. was inftituted 1675, and was afterwards a prebendary of Gloucefter cathedral. King C. 2. patron.

William Whittington, M. A. a minor-canon of the cathedral, and rector of Rudford, was inftituted, 1679, upon Gregory's refignation, and dying in 1684, was buried in the middle chancel, under a ftone with an infcription for him.

Matthew Yate, M. A. occurs 1697. He was inftituted into the rectory of Matfon, and dying June 5, 1717, aged 53, was buried under a tomb erected for him near the eaft end of the church-yard. Upon whofe death,

John Nourfe, M. A. was inftituted. King G. 1. patron.

Edward Robinfon Payne, M. A. upon Nourfe's ceffion, 1723. Same patron.

Edward Niccolls, M. A. upon Payne's being inftituted into the rectory of Cowling, in the deanery of Rochefter, was inftituted in 1733. G. 2. patron.

Richard Rogers, LL. B. is the prefent incumbent.

Monuments and Infcriptions.

In the fouth chancel, or St. Mary's chapel, againft the fouth wall, is a raifed tomb, on which are painted the old arms of the city, and *Argent, on a cheveron gules two bars gemels fable, between three hawk's-bells Or; on a chief of the fecond a lure, and two martlets of the firft.* Creft. *A dexter arm armed, holding a battle-ax erect, argent.* Upon the upper part of the tomb, in the old character,

The Tombe of Syr Thomas Bell, knight, and of dame Joane, his wyfe.

Lower on the tomb is a painting of Sir Thomas Bell, kneeling, in a fcarlet gown, with a chain of gold about his neck. Alfo his wife kneeling, with a fcutcheon of their arms between them, and the following infcription in black character.

Bereffe this lyfe, here lyeth under ftone
Syr Thomas Bell, whylom a knyght of fame;
Who lyuing here, gaue foode to many a one,
And eke behynde prouifion for the fame
Hathe lefte in ftore for euer to be hadd,
Amonge the pore that here in towne fhall dwell.
Off lyme and ftone an Almefhowfe hath he made
For fixe pore folkes, and buylt the fame full well,
Here in this ftreat faft by the foutherne yate:
And hath the fame with lyuelyhoode endewede,
That aye fhall laft, and neuer fhall abate.
Thriefe w[t] free uoyce eke hathe this towne allowde
This worthy man a mayors rome to wealde,
And thryefe him cald in parlement to fytt,
Forre wealthe of them in reft at home that dwelde.
And nowe hath deathe his worthy trayuayle quyte,
When he had runne of fowerfcore yeres the race
Whofe fpryte in May, as pleafyd GOD prefyxe,
The fyxe and twentie daye, and yere of grace.
A thowfand fyue hundred threfcore and fyxe,
This ayer fled into the heauenly fkye
Where he, God graunt, an euerlaftynge tyme
In ioye may lyue, and neuer more to dye.

Below on the outfide of the tomb,

Dame Joone Bell, the Wydowe of Syr Thomas Bell, knyght, hath caufid this tombe to be made, and fynifshed the fame, the xiiii day of Iune, in the yere of ower LORD GOD 1567.

Within the fame wall, a mural monument, the infcription and croffes on brafs torn off, fuppofed to be for the founder of this chapel.

John Cook, efq; who died September 14, 1529, with lady Joan Cook his wife, the pious founder of Crypt-fchool, were buried near St. John Baptift's altar. Their effigies and the infcription, which were on brafs, laid in a grey marble, are now torn off and loft.

A monument for Mr. Daniel Lyfons, with the following infcription.

Sifte viator, et paulo attentius imaginem meditare DANIELIS LYSONS, viri, ad cujus exemplar integri Chriftiani fimulachrum potes effingere: Fuit enim, inter mercatores juftus, inter literatos eruditus, inter doctores theologus, inter liberales munificus: Linguarum non folum Latinæ, fed Grecæ et Hebraicæ, exquifita cognitione infignis; et literarum, quam lucri amantior, ad facras literas fe totum applicuit, earumque plenitudinem adeo fubmiffe adoravit, ut raro aut nunquam, in mufeolo, nifi flexis genibus, facras paginas evolveret. In cumulandis opibus promptus, fed beneficus, et eleemofynis largiendis tam propenfus, ut quotannis, decimam partem redituum pauperibus erogaret. Tam flagranti fanctimonia vitam degit, quali alii e vivis difcedunt; tot tantifque claruit virtutibus, quot vel natura mortalis recipit, vel induftria perficit. Denique, animam lœtitia fpirituali repletam, et firmiter de divina mifericordia perfuafam, Deo reddidit, Decembris 13, 1681, Ætat. 38.

Againft the fame wall, a little to the right, is a handfome blue and white marble monument for John Snell, efq; who had been one of the members for the city, with the following infcription:

H. S. E. Johannes Snell, Armiger, honefta ftirpe natus; forma elegans & confpicuus; ingenio facundus & fuavis; moribus gravis & urbanus; vitæ integerrimus; fenatu celeberrimus; numerofa prole feliciffimus; conjugi præmerenti, et patriæ fimiliter orbatæ, defideratiffimus. Animam Deo reddit die Septembris IX, MDCCXXVI. Vixit annos XLIIII, menfes tres. Monumentum hoc, virtutibus viri optimi facrum, poni curavit uxor mœftiffima.

To the right of the above, a beautiful marble monument reprefenting Piety in a fitting pofture; before her a buft in high relief of Mrs. Dorothy Snell, and underneath, upon a table, the following infcription.

To the Memory of Dorothy Snell, Daughter of Charles and Elizabeth Yate, of Coulthorpe, in the County of Gloucefter. Born the 20th day of February 1709-10; Married May the 21ft, 1737, to Powell Snell, Efq; of Lower Guiting. She exchanged this Life for a better, on rhe 30th Day of March, 1746, furvived by two Sons and one Daughter. In her Conduct to her Parents, Hufband, and Children, obedient, faithful, affectionate; to her Friends, Neighbours, and all Mankind, fincere, benevolent, charitable. In Health, an engaging affability and innocent Chearfulnefs rendered her the Delight of all who knew her. In Sicknels, fhe fuftained a tedious and painful Diftemper, and felt the approaches of Death with a Refignation and Fortitude which Chriftian Piety could alone infpire. This Monument, in Gratitude to fo valuable a Wife, Powell Snell hath caufed to be erected.

Powell Snell, efq; of Lower Guiting, who died in the year 1770, is buried here, but as yet there is no monument erected for him.

Many perfons who have been mayors of the city are buried here, *viz.* John Cook, as above.

Thomas Pury, efq; (twice mayor) who died in April, 1580.

Lawrence Holliday, who died June 30, 1587.

Luke Garnons, efq; thrice mayor, who died February 12, 1614.

Richard Lane, who died 1667. His daughter Sarah Wright, gave feveral charities to the city.

Robert Payne, mayor, buried January 5, 1670.

William Hill, who died Auguft 29, 1636.

John Scriven, who died June 23, 1645.

Thomas Hill, who died in October, 1652.

Thomas Pury, who died Auguft 23, 1660.

John Ewins, who died April 30, 1696.

Thomas Longden, who died April 25, 1702.

Thomas

Thomas Snell.

Sir Samuel Eckly, knight, ſometime high ſheriff of this county, who died Auguſt 7, 1706.

Robert Payne, eſq; twice mayor and parliament man for the city, who died February 20, 1712, aged 82.

John Bell.

John Radway, who died May 17, 1736.

Many other perſons of note have alſo been buried here, *viz.*

James Kyrle, eſq; who died February 1, 1645. and Ann, his wife, who died September 19, 1642.

John Tomes, ſheriff, who died April 17, 1658, aged 37.

Anthony Nourſe, M. D. who died Aug. 14, 1659.

John Partridge, of Mitchel-Dean, gent. who died April 12, 1667.

Thomas Williams, eſq; bencher of the Inner Temple, who died 1667.

Sarah Gough, who died February 18, 1669.

John Bell, who died February 20, 1672.

John Purlewent, ſheriff, who died March 19, 1678. John his ſon died January 5, 1686.

Samuel Roſe, ſheriff, who died 1680.

William Alexander, M. A. maſter of the college-ſchool, and vicar of Hartpury, who died May 1, 1742.

Benefactions.

Mr. Walter Pury, in 1506, gave 20*s.* a year, half to the church, the remainder to ten poor widows.

Sir Thomas Bell gave 10*l.*

John Tunks gave 10*l.*

Mr. John Hill, gave 10*l.*

Mrs. Margaret Norton gave 80*l.*

Mrs. Sarah Wright gave two houſes.

Alice Whitfield gave 3*l.* a year for a term of years.

Philip Lewis gave 40*l.* to this pariſh and St. Owen's, and 10*l.* more to this.

Mrs. Eleanor Weaver gave 100*l.*

Mr. Joſias Randle 50*l.*

Mr. Samuel Burroughs 40*l.*

Mr. Daniel Lyſons gave 4*l.* 5*s.* yearly for ever, 2*l.* of which for two ſermons, the one on Good Friday, the other on Holy Thurſday; 2*l.* a year to the poor for bread on Good Friday; and 5*s.* for bread and wine at the ſacrament that day.

Alderman Robert Payne gave 1*l.* 3*s.* yearly to the poor of this pariſh and St. Owen's, for bread, and 6*s.* 8*d.* for reading prayers on Candlemas-day.

Mrs. Mary Shail, in 1734, gave 50*l.*

Mrs. Ann Pitt gave 10*l.* for a ſermon on Eaſter Monday.

And according to Sir Robert Atkyns, Mr. Richard Hoar gave 53*s.* yearly to the poor, of which my other accounts take no notice.

	Baptiſms.		Burials.	
	males	females	males	females
1759	5	7	10	12
1760	14	10	17	20
1761	14	10	28	11
1762	5	6	21	23
1763	12	12	22	23
1764	10	13	19	23
1765	11	9	35	37
1766	6	11	30	20
1767	5	16	27	28
1768	10	12	24	23
1769	21	11	23	21
Total	230		497	

N. B. The baptiſms and burials of the pariſh of All Saints are included in this account.

There were 71 houſholders in this pariſh in the year 1562; by Sir Robert Atkyns's account about 1710 there were 155 houſes and about 700 inhabitants, in this pariſh, and thoſe of All Saints and St. Owen's; but in the year 1743, there were in this pariſh, ſeparate from the other two, 109 houſholds, and 495 inhabitants.

The particulars of the free-ſchool have been already given p. 127.

		l.	*s.*	*d.*
The Royal Aid in	1692,	184	0	0
Poll Tax —	1694,	82	1	0
Land Tax —	1694,	272	2	0
The ſame in	1770,			

In 1770, this pariſh paid quarterly to the workhouſe 32*l.* 4*s.* 6*d.* and 19*l.* 19*s.* towards lamps.

The Friery, called the Black Friers, or the *Houſe*, or *College of Friers Preachers.*

This ſtood within the town, ſays Leland, not far from the caſtle-garth, or court-yard. It was founded by king Henry the Third and Stephen lord of Harneſhull, about the year 1239. King Edward the Third, in the 39th year of his reign, as we learn from biſhop Tanner, gave licence to the prior and brethren of this friery to enlarge their manſion-houſe.

A manuſcript in the Cotton library mentions the ſurrender of this monaſtery on the 28th of July, 1538, to Richard, (perhaps Richard Yngworth) ſuffragan biſhop of Dover, in the preſence of the mayor and three of the aldermen They had no rents, but their gardens were in leaſe for a long term of years. Thomas Bell then kept 300 men at work in the friery, for which reaſon the biſhop deſired he might continue in it.

John Rainolds, B.D. the prior; John Hooper, Richard Bylond, William Swan, afterwards rector of Shipton Solers; William Walton, Ralph Howel, or Powel, Thomas Mekins, afterwards curate of Upton St. Leonard's, and vicar of Aſhelworth, were the friers at the time of the ſurrender, and were permitted to change their habit.

The ſite of this friery, with ſome other lands, were granted to Sir Thomas Bell July the 12th, 31° H. 8. in conſideration of 240*l.* 5*s.* 4*d.* and ſoon afterwards this houſe was improved into a handſome manſion, called Bell's Place, where the manufacture of cap-making was carried on. From Bell it deſcended to one of his wife's rela-

 tions,

tions, married to Thomas Dennis, efq; whofe defcendents fold it to Mr. Samuel Cockerell, of whofe family Mr. John Bufh purchafed the capital building for a dwelling-houfe, in the year 1768.

Dr. Stukeley has given a draught of this priory in his *Itinera Curiofa*, as it ftood in 1721, and one of the plates in Buck's collection of the remains of Englifh religious houfes, is of this monaftery and of Lanthony together. A good part of the church is ftill remaining.

Upon a broken ftone dug up in 1716, was the effigy of a frier, and on another *Offa Johannis Bifeley*.

There were lately upon fome bricks in the floor of one of the houfes, made out of the ruins of the friery, the arms of archbifhop Dene, of the bifhoprick of Durham, of St. Peter's abbey, and *a bend cotifed, between fix trees*; and in a miffal found in the friery, in the year 1714, were the names of Walter Bowden, Agnes his wife, Richard Warminfter, John Brigge, Robert Durnel, and Julian his wife, who probably were benefactors to it. Thomas lord Berkeley, about the reign of Edward the Firft, relieved the brethren of this houfe very liberally out of his granaries.

There was formerly in this parifh, a priory of Black Canons, founded by king Athelftan, which feems to be different from the houfe of Dominicans, or Black Friers, juft fpoken of, for that order was not in being 'till fome hundreds of years after the time of Athelftan; but the accounts of thefe houfes are fo confufed, that there is not much to be learnt concerning the latter diftinct from the other.

In this parifh ftood alfo

The Grey Friers, or, *The Houfe or College of Friers Minors, or Francifcans.*

This houfe, according to the undoubted authority of Leland, ftood within the city, eaftward of the church of St. Mary de Crypt, and was founded by one of the lords of Berkeley. William Gerard gave the monks of this houfe a fupply of water from Matfon, or Robin-Hood's hill, the quantity of which, on account of a difpute between the friery and St. Peter's abbey, was fettled by Edward the Black Prince, in 1350.

Thomas lord Berkeley, about 35° E. 3. gave them fome adjacent lands and tenements; and it is faid in Dugdale's *Baronage*, that William, marquis of Berkeley, by his will, dated February 5, 1491, ordered that a frier fhould perpetually officiate for himfelf and relations in this houfe, towards the rebuilding of which, Leland fays, he gave 20*l*. We have it alfo on Dugdale's authority, that the lady of James lord Berkeley was buried in the choir of this monaftery, in the year 1452. She had been unjuftly imprifoned in the caftle of Gloucefter, by Margaret countefs of Shrewfbury, on account of fome violent contefts at law, which for a great number of years fubfifted between thofe two families, and there kept 'till fhe died, which was on Saturday before the feaft of St. Michael.

It is faid that this friery was in fome meafure under the direction of the warden of the Grey Friers in Lewinfmead, Briftol, but how far I cannot learn.

This houfe was furrendered July 28, 1538, to Richard, fuffragan bifhop of Dover, in the prefence of the mayor and three aldermen, when it was faid to be " a goodly houfe, much of it new builded, efpecially the church, choir, and dorture; the reft fmall lodgings ".

William Lightfoot, afterwards vicar of Tetbury, John Beacheley, or Berklay, Henry Tacket, George Cooper, and John Kebul, afterwards rector of St. Aldate's, friers of this houfe, were permitted to change their habit.

After the diffolution, the king, April 2, 33° H. 8. granted it with a clofe of pafture ground on the eaft fide, the church-yard, a garden in the fouthgate ftreet, and all other particulars belonging to the fcite of the monaftery, to Sir John Jennings, for twenty-one years, at 33*s*. a year, referving all the buildings to be thrown down and carried away, as he by his commiffioners fhall think fit; but the fame year he convey'd the fee to the fame perfon. From Jennings it paffed to Hugh Gethyn, and thro' feveral hands 'till Mr. Thomas Pury granted it, in 1630, to the corporation of the city.

Great damage was done to the buildings of this houfe at the fiege, by the king's artillery; but there are ftill confiderable remains of the monaftery; the walls of the church, which was large, are entire. It is now formed into three tenements, which, together with others, a bowling-green, orchard and gardens, all belonging to the faid monaftery, are now the property of Powell Snell, efq; who has a leafe of them from the corporation for a long term, at a fmall chief-rent.

Dr. Stukeley, in his *Itinera Curiofa*, has given a plate of this alfo, as it ftood Auguft 24, 1721, but he was miftaken in calling it the White Friers.

Mr. Juftice Powell, one of the judges of the king's bench, was a native of this city, and refided in this houfe, whofe folid judgment in the municipal laws, and moderation in behaviour, defervedly placed him on the bench of the higheft courts of judicature in the nation. He died in the year 1713, and was buried in the Lady's chapel, in the cathedral church, where is a magnificent monument for him, as in p. 119.

Littleworth, and fevaral of the South Hamlets lie in this parifh, but they will all be confidered at the conclufion of the account of the city, under Suburbs.

St. MARY de GRACE, or GRACE-LANE; called alfo *St. Mary in the Market*.

THIS church confifted of one aile, with a fpire fteeple, and ftood on the place now called the knap, where the herb and fifh market is kept, eaft of the fite of the king's board. It

is

is a rectory, but was antiently a chapel to the Holy Trinity. The abbey of St. Peter granted the oblations and profits of it to a chaplain, at the yearly rent of 10*s*.

In the valuation or certificate 19° E. 1. it is thus expressed: *Exitus Capellæ, viz. de decimis personalibus ad Pascha* 49 *sol.* 11 *den. oblationibus* 39 *sol. oblationibus ad imaginem Beatæ Mariæ ibidem* 4 *sol.* 4 *den. in purificationibus, anniversariis obsequiis, et aliis consimilibus* 22 *sol.* 10 *den. quæ omnia et singula curatus ibidem percipit pro salario suo, preter* 10 *sol. nomine cujusdam pensionis, annuatim solutos abbati. Valet clare* cxvi. *sol.* i. *den.*

The value of this living has been twice augmented by lot, with queen Ann's bounty, and returned.

This church was united to that of St. Michael by an ordinance of parliament in 1648, and the building was granted to the corporation in consideration of their keeping powder and ammunition for the defence of the city. In 1653, it was intirely taken down by order of the corporation, and part of the materials were used in repairing St. Michael's; but ever since the restoration, the parishes have been separate and distinct, though the inhabitants go to St. Michael's church, the minister of which is generally licenced to this curacy.

In this church was a chantry dedicated to St. Mary, and in Grace-lane a messuage called Grace-lane college, or priest's college, belonging to this chantry, which being purchased of the crown, at the dissolution, by Richard Pate, esq; he gave it to Corpus Christi college, in Oxford, towards the maintenance of a school and hospital at Cheltenham.

Incumbents.

John Hamelyn occurs in 1344.
John Playsted 1509, 1512, whose successor was
William Slekeborn, but the time of his admission does not appear.
John Fishpoole, presented May 25, 1531.
Richard Lawrens occurs in 1548.
John More in 1551 and 1552, afterwards vicar of Standish.
John Mery, or Merrie, sometime a chantry priest of St. Mary's service in St. Mary de Lode, occurs in 1556, afterwards curate of St. Aldate's.
Thomas Sebroke, sometime curate of the Holy Trinity, occurs in 1558.
Roger Stiche, one of the minor-canons, 1562. He had been reader of the gospel in the cathedral.
Thomas Leipse, 1569.
William Preston, in 1572, sometime curate of St. Michael's and St. Nicholas's.
William Fortie, vicar of Minsterworth, was licenced May 29, 1575, and occurs in 1576.
William Webster, vicar of St. Mary de Lode, occurs 1580.
Nicholas Dismyll, 1594.
Robert Hawerd, or Haverd, curate of St. Owen's, 1597, 1628.
William Hulett, curate of St. Owen's, 1634, 1635, minor canon, deprived with the other members of the cathedral.
John Palmer, A. M. is the present incumbent.

Benefactions.

Mr. Daniel Lysons gave 21 *s*. a year to the poor of this parish for bread.

The baptisms and burials are registered in the book at St. Michael's, and included in the account of them in that parish.

The number of housholders in this parish in 1562 was 29; about the year 1710, according to Sir Robert Atkyns, there were 42 houses, and 240 inhabitants; but in the year 1743, there were 45 houses, and only 137 inhabitants.

Before the workhouse was erected, this parish had paid 6*l*. towards the maintenance of the poor of other parishes, having none of its own; but in the year 1770 it paid quarterly to the workhouse 7*l*. 9*s*. 1*d*. and towards lamps 6*l*. 19*s*.

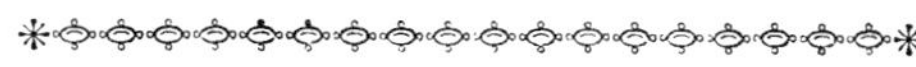

St. MARY de LODE;

Called also *St. Mary before the Gate of St. Peter's, St. Mary Broad-Gate,* and *St. Mary de Port.*

THE church is very old, but handsome, with two side ailes, and a vestry at the end of that on the south, and a cross aile at the end of that on the north. In the middle is a low square tower, with six bells, and it is said there was antiently a lofty spire upon it, which was demolished by a storm. The first name seems to have been given it on account of its situation, for the river Severn formerly ran near it.

Gilbert Foliot, when he was abbat of St. Peter's, with the advice and consent of his convent, assigned this church, with its chapels of St. Giles at Maisemore, St. Lawrence at Barnwood, and St. Leonard at Upton, to the maintenance of a light at the altar of St. Peter.

This vicarage was taxed at thirty marks 19° E. 1. John de Rodberow had a pension in it of twenty-three marks, the sacrist of St. Peter's had five, and the prior of Lanthony, in great tithes, two marks. The rector of this church had five shillings out of that of Matson. The portion of John de Rodberow was a share of the tithes, which for some time was reputed a distinct and independent rectory, enjoyed before him by William de Berners, to which the abbey presented. Reginald de Schipton resigned this portion on the 19th of February, 1301, and on the 15th of April following, it was annexed to the vicarage by the authority of the archbishop of Canterbury.

In 1304, by a composition between the vicar and the abbey, the former and his successors were granted a certain corrody, as formerly received, with a yearly pension of five marks, pay for one horse, and entertainment for himself, a chaplain, a deacon, and two clerks at the abbey table, on certain festivals. All persons belonging to the abbey, tho' parishioners, might be interred in the abbey church-yard; the vicar to have the first mass, and all oblations arising from it; and the abbey to pay no tithes for things privileged within the parish.

In 1313, the vicarage of this church was assigned, by the king's licence, for sustaining and repairing the Virgin Mary's chapel in the abbey.

Pope

Pope Urban the Sixth, and Boniface the Ninth alfo appropriated the revenues of this church, which were then forty marks, to the fervice of the abbey, and in 1394, the appropriation was acknowledged and ratified by the bifhop of Worcefter; and again, at a metropolitical vifitation, on the 3d of September, 1534.

In 1398, the abbey granted an annual penfion of 6*s.* 8*d.* for all epifcopal dues.

On the 3d of April, 1403, the bifhop of Worcefter, with the confent of the abbey, ordained, that inftead of all former penfions, &c. the vicar fhall have only the care of the vicarage, and enjoy a yearly penfion of 16*l.* with the vicarage houfe; the abbey to pay 26*s.* 8*d.* to the poor of the parifh; and, receiving all the oblations and profits arifing in the church, to provide at their charge what other chaplains fhall be neceffary, or ufed to be, in the church and the chapels belonging to it.

Some of thefe particulars are taken from abbat Fraucefter's regifter, which contains many things relating to this vicarage; the prefentation to which, together with the rectory, coming to the crown at the diffolution of the abbey, they were granted by king H. 8. to the dean and chapter at their foundation, who were appointed to pay the vicar 10*l.* 13*s.* 4*d.* In the year 1666, they paid him 53*l.* 13*s.* 4*d.* and continued fo to do for twenty-one years; but it appears by the bifhop's vifitation book, that fince the expiration of that term, they have paid only 40*l.* which, it is there faid, will be continued to a refident vicar; the privy tithes of part of the parifh, eafter offerings, and furplus fees may amount to 30*l.* more.

Certain portions of tithes, and a moiety of the wood at Woolridge and of another at Le Perche, all faid to be in this parifh, are alfo granted by the king to the dean and chapter, in their charter of endowment.

Lands in St. Mary de Lode, lately belonging to St. Peter's abbey, were granted to Richard Andrews and Nicholas Temple 35° H. 8.

The hermitage of Sendbridge, or Senbrugge, or Sondbrugge, or Sandbrug is in this parifh. The abbey of St. Peter granted it by the name of the chapel or hermitage of Sendbridge, with the oblations, &c. to Humphry Wilkins, clerk, September 29, 23° H. 8.

William Nottingham, efq; the king's attorney general, gave to St. Peter's abbey certain lands at Senbrugge, to maintain a chantry in the abbey for two monks.

In the ordinance of parliament 1648, for uniting certain churches in the city, this is wholly omitted; but in the year 1650, the corporation petitioned the parliament to unite the cathedral with this parifh, and to appoint a preaching minifter in the college church: And in 1654 they petitioned again that the cathedral might be made the parifh church, and that St. Mary's and St. Katherine's might be united with it.

There were in this church,

1. A chantry dedicated to St. Mary, whereof John Mery, the laft incumbent, obtained a penfion of 4*l.* Sir Thomas Bell, and Richard Duke, efq; purchafed certain poffeffions belonging to this chantry 2° E. 6. The houfes at the north-weft end of the church, adjoining to the church-yard, belonged to the chantry priefts.

2. A fraternity dedicated to the Holy Trinity, whereof William Taylor, the laft incumbent, obtained an annuity of 2*l.* 10*s.* I fuppofe this is the guild of which it is faid, the mafters were yearly elected by the corporation out of their own body.

This is a large parifh, and antiently was much larger than it is at prefent. Tuffley and Kingfholm, with fome part of Laffington, Longford, Twigworth, Down Hatherley, and Wotton, and other lands without the weft-gate are reputed to belong to it; and it is faid that Lawford's-gate, with forty-eight houfes on this fide of it, adjoining to the city of Briftol, alfo belonged to it, and had a proper officer affigned for receiving the dues, and for other neceffary purpofes. Lands in Stow on the Wold are likewife faid to have belonged to this parifh. The chapelries which were formerly dependent on it, are now become feparate and independent parifhes; and the hamlets juft mentioned will be confidered diftinctly under the title Suburbs.

Firft Fruits,	£ 10 : 13 : 4	Synodals,	£.0 : 4 : 0
Tenths, ——	1 : 1 : 4	Pentecoftals,	0 : 1 : 4
Procurations,	0 : 11 : 0		

Incumbents.

William de Chamberlayn, prefented March 29, 1302; and John de Briftol, prefented March 10, 1304; both by John Gamages the abbot, and convent of St. Peter's, patrons.

John Fyfch, inftituted February 6, 1389, and refigned Auguft 24, 1390; whereupon the abbey enjoyed the impropriation, the abbat being put into the poffeffion thereof. King R. 2. patron.

John Ofburne, LL. B. fucceeded next, and refigning upon his prefentation to the vicarage of Standifh,

George Teylowe, M. A. was prefented April 1, 1501, and upon his death,

Robert, and in fome accounts, Walter Walker, prefented October 7, 1507; and upon his death,

Thomas, and in other accounts, John Bodelych, was prefented September 8, 1508. John Bodelych was made keeper of the pantry of the abbey 1505; and the fame year Thomas Bodelych inftituted into Froucefter vicarage.

Thomas Barker fucceeded, and dying,

Thomas Greenow, LL. B. was prefented February 2, 1514, and upon his refignation,

Humphry Wilkins was prefented in March 1521.

N. B. The feven laft were prefented by the abbat and convent of St. Peter's.

John Jannys, or Yannes, fometime a ftipendiary prieft in this church, perhaps belonging to the guild of the Holy Trinity, occurs curate in 1542, 1543, as do

William Taylor, fometime of the Holy Trinity guild in this city, 1545.

Humphry Wilkinfon, vicar in 1545.

John Jannys, curate, deprived and degraded April 2, 1554, on account of marriage. On the 15th of October in the fame year, he was collated to Standifh; and in 1559 inftituted into Taynton.

William Taylor occurs as vicar April 16, 1556, then making his laft will.

Richard Warret, minor canon, and fometime rector of Shenington, occurs curate in 1562, being prefented to the vicarage November 27, 1563, which he held with the curacy of St. Nicholas, by the dean and chapter of Gloucefter.

Thomas Waftal, or Weftal, occurs curate in 1580, being afterwards curate of St. Katherine's.

William

William Webſter inſtituted January 18, 1580, upon a lapſe, and in the ſame year occurs curate of St. Mary de Grace. Upon his preſentation to this vicarage 'tis ſaid, *Stipendium vicariæ eſt admodum exiguum. Summa ſcilicet 10l. 13s. 4d. in pecuniis numeratis.* Queen Elizabeth patron.

Thomas Thomkins, minor canon, and curate of St. Katherine's, was inſtituted March 25, 1596, upon the reſignation, or, as other accounts ſay, the deprivation of Webſter. Dean and chapter of Glouceſter patron.

Peter Brooks, minor canon, inſtituted March 29, 1627, upon Thomkins's death, occurs in 1641. Being deprived of his minor canonry, he lived not to be reſtored with others of the cathedral.

Francis Hanſlape, M. A. inſtituted February 25, 1660, and was one of the minor canons. King Ch. 2. patron by a lapſe.

Thomas Waſhborne, D. D. inſtituted June 6, 1668, upon Hanſlape's reſignation. He was one of the prebendaries. vide p. 167. Dean and chapter of Glouceſter patrons.

John Deighton, minor canon, inſtituted December 5, 1670, upon Dr. Waſhborne's reſignation. He lies buried in the body of the cathedral, with this inſcription over him,

Johannes Deighton, Cler. obiit 17° Die Januarii,
MDCLXXXXV, Ætat. ſuæ 53.

John Price, B. A. inſtituted October 6, 1697. King William and queen Mary patrons, by a lapſe.

Benjamin King, D. D. one of the prebendaries, upon Price's death, was inſtituted November 15, 1716; and dying, was buried on the ſouth ſide of the chancel here, and as yet has no memorial over him. Dean and chapter of Glouceſter patrons.

William Tyndale, M. A. rector of Cotes, was inſtituted June 11, 1722, upon Doctor King's reſignation.

John Warren, LL. D.

Robert Rickards, M. A.

Hugh Price, M. A. is the preſent incumbent.

Monuments and Inſcriptions.

In the north wall of the chancel, oppoſite the outward door, is an antient mural tomb, with the effigy of a man lying on it, ſaid to have been erected in memory of Lucius, the firſt chriſtian king, who is reported to have been buried here. Collier's *Hiſtorical Dictionary*. This figure is attired like archbiſhop Aldred in the cathedral, and was probably intended for ſome benefactor to the church. The tomb was broken open in the time of the laſt civil war, in hopes of finding valuable treaſure, but the perſons engaged in this buſineſs were diſappointed.

In the croſs aile below the chancel are ſeveral antient ſtones, but the inſcriptions are moſtly gone. Upon the verge of one of them, in old Engliſh letters, may be read,

Orate pro anima dmni Philipi Hoggas - - - - - - - CCC - - - - - - - - picietur dn amen.

On the next ſtone is a croſs. Round the verge

Claudit^{r}. tuba Spenſer Ion ſic et ✕ Iohanna - - - - -

Part of both the above are covered with ſeats.

Almoſt at the weſt end of the ſouth aile, is a ſtone with a croſs at top, about the middle of it is this inſcription in old black letter:

Hic jacet Ioannes Benha quonda Herimita de Senbrige Cm' - - - - - - de - - - - -

Upon ſome bricks within the weſt door and in the ſouth aile, is written *Katherina Koke*, probably a benefactor to this church.

Benefactions.

Mr. Thomas Singleton, in 1656, gave 3*l.* a year to the poor for ever.

Edward Nourſe, eſq; gave 50*l.* to purchaſe land, the rent to be applied as follows, 10*s.* for a ſermon on the 25th of March yearly, the reſt for the poor.

George Coulſtance gave 20*s.* to be diſtributed yearly to the poor in Eaſter week.

Mrs. Alice Whitfield gave four tenements to the poor during the term of her leaſes, and 20*s.* a year for the poor on Holy Thurſday.

Mr. Daniel Lyſons gave 40*s.* a year, to be diſtributed to the poor in bread, one half on Chriſtmas day, the other on Good Friday.

Timothy Nourſe, eſq; in 1698, gave to this pariſh and that of St. Katherine 12*l.* 10*s.* a year for apprenticing of five boys; and gave alſo three gowns for three poor perſons, at the diſcretion of the miniſter of this pariſh, and the officers of both.

Mr. James Sayer, in 1712, gave 40*s.* a year to forty widows.

	Baptiſms.		Burials.	
	males	females	males	females
1759	26	26	38	22
1760	19	36	24	28
1761	26	31	16	23
1762	22	19	17	17
1763	25	30	24	19
1764	21	36	21	23
1765	42	36	36	60
1766	29	34	35	31
1767	40	30	36	35
1768	27	16	18	9
1769	28	30	23	17
Total	629		572	

In the year 1562, there were 156 houſholders in this pariſh; in 1712 there were about 106 houſes and 500 inhabitants, according to Sir Robert Atkyns, in that part of the pariſh which is within the city; and in 1743 the exact number of houſholds in the pariſh were 123, of inhabitants 482.

Land Tax in 1770, at 3*s.* in the pound, 45 : 6 : 8
The ſame for the college precincts, 64 : 11 : 4

Two guardians over the workhouſe are annually choſen out of this pariſh, towards the ſupport of which, in the above year, the pariſh and the precincts of the college paid 24*l.* 5*s.* 10*d.* a quarter, and 5*l.* 8*s.* towards lamps.

St. MICHAEL's.

THE church is large, conſiſting of two ailes of equal dimenſions, and a ſquare tower at the weſt end, with ſix bells in it. It was antiently part of the poſſeſſions of the ſee of Exeter. Peter, one of the biſhops of that ſee, ſold it with its chapel of St. Martin, to St. Peter's abbey, in the year 1285. At the diſſolution of the abbey, the patronage devolving to the crown, the lord chancellor is now patron. It is a rectory, worth about 15*l.* a year in tithes, beſides ſurplus fees and voluntary contributions. Robert Cole informs us, that the church of St. Martyn ftood where that of St. Michael now is.

The church and chapel were valued at feven marks 16° E. 1. and three years afterwards at nine; but in the fixth year of the next reign they were valued at ten marks. In the commiffioners certificate, 26° H. 8. it is thus expreffed, *Rectoria Sancti Michaelis valet in decimis et oblationibus, ultra 20 den. folutos epifcopo pro vifitatione,* 6*s.* 8*d. archidiacono pro procurationibus,* 2*s. pro finagio, et* 2 *den. fenefchallis villæ Gloucefriæ,* 21*l.* 5*s.* 9*d. ob.* The firft fruits of this rectory, which before the year 1624 were 21*l.* 5*s.* 9*d.* halfpenny, were then reduced by a decree of the barons of the exchequer, to 8*l.* 16*s.* 4*d.* on the appeal of Mr. Woodruffe, the rector.

In 1366, the parifhioners, who before were interred in the church-yard of the abbey, acquired the right of fepulture in their own, paying 20*s.* yearly to St. Peter's; but their church-yard having been confecrated without the approbation of the bifhop of Worcefter, was continued under an interdict 'till November 1368.

By an ordinance of parliament in 1646, the parifhes of St. Aldate and St. Mary de Grace were annexed to this, and 80*l.* a year with a prebendal houfe were fettled upon the rectory, the patronage of which was given to the mayor and burgeffes. This church being at that time much out of repair, both the others were taken down, and many of the materials ufed on St. Michael's in the year 1653, when it was under built with three new pillars. At the reftoration the parifhes became feparate, and have continued fo ever fince.

In this church were the following particulars. 1. A chantry dedicated to St. Ann, of which the fraternity of weavers were patrons, and Richard Burnell the laft incumbent. Lands in Nailfworth, in the parifh of Avening, belonged to it. 2. A chantry dedicated to St. John Baptift, whereof Stephen Pool, the laft incumbent, obtained a yearly penfion of 4*l.* 3. A chantry dedicated to St. Mary, of which Hugh Fifherpole, the laft incumbent, obtained a penfion of 4*l.* a year. 4. A fraternity of brethren and fifters, dedicated to St. John Baptift, who inhabited a houfe in the Eaft-gate ftreet, called Brethren-hall. 5. Our Lady's chapel. 6. The Rood light. 7. St. Katherine's light.

Here was alfo a very folemn anniverfary kept, and attended by the fheriffs and ftewards of the town, in memory of mafter Thomas Whytefeld, who ordained by his laft will that 30*s.* fhould be expended on it.

Abbat Malvern gave feveral rich veftments to the church in 1499, for eftablifhing a yearly obit on the 18th of July, for John Hertland, one of the monks of St. Peter's, and his parents.

In abbat Fraucefter's MS. a great deal is faid relating to this rectory, and there are now fome antient papers in the cheft on the fame fubject.

In a window of the north aile, eaft of the pulpit, is the following coat; *Gules, a crefcent between fix efcallops,* 3, 2, 1, *argent.* Near it another efcutcheon, the field *gules,* but the bearing not intelligible.

The eaft end of the fouth fide of this church was rebuilt in 1736.

Firft fruits,	£.8 : 16 : 4	Synodals, -	£.0 : 2 : 0
Tenths, —	0 : 17 : 8*ob.*	Pentecoftals,	0 : 1 : 4
Procurations,	0 : 6 : 8		

Incumbents.

John Nelm, M. A. was prefented by the mayor and burgeffes of Gloucefter in 1648.
Thomas Woolnough, M. A. inftituted 1664. Ch. 2. patron.
Amos Jones, M. A. 1675.
George Vernon, M. A. 1677.
Thomas Thache, M. A. 1687.
Samuel Lawrence, M. A. 1721.
Henry Church, M. A. 1727. The two laft were buried near the north door of the chancel.
Thomas Woore, M. A. 1732, buried near Mr. Lawrence.
John Palmer, M. A. 1741, who is the prefent incumbent.

Monuments and Infcriptions.

There are feveral monuments and memorials in this church, among others, for

John Webb, once mayor, who died Auguft 17, 1643.

John Nelme, fometime fheriff, who died May 9, 1645.

Enfign Jonathan Cracker, who died 1646.

William Ruffel, mafter of the college fchool, who died in 1659. See his infcription p. 170.

Alderman William Corfley, who died 1691.

John Hyett, efq; alderman and twice mayor, who died Feb. 27, 1711.

Mr. Jofeph Hyett, his fon, who died Jan. 22, 1713. For a further account of both thefe perfons, fee p. 129.

Of the Blue-Coat Hospital.

Sir Thomas Rich, of Sunning, in the county of Berks, baronet, who was a native of this city, by his laft will, dated May 16, 1666, gave to the mayor and burgeffes, his houfe, lying on the north fide of the Eaft-gate ftreet, and 6000*l.* to buy lands of the value of 300*l.* a year, or upwards, for the following ufes, *viz.* That 160*l.* be employed for the yearly maintenance of twenty boys with diet, lodging, wafhing, cloathing, and other neceffaries; their drefs to be blue coats and caps, according to the ufage of Chrift-church hofpital in London, none of whom to be admitted under ten years of age, nor to continue after the age of fixteen. That 20*l.* be for ever paid to an able fchoolmafter, to live in that houfe, and to teach the boys to write and read. That 60*l.* be paid for putting out fix of the poor boys apprentices. That 30*l.* be annually laid out in blue gowns, fhoes, ftockings, and linen cloth for ten men and ten women. That on St. Thomas's day annually, the corporation fhall meet and make up the accounts of this charity, and twenty nobles are allowed for their dinner. That after the above

above difpofitions are made, and neceffary repairs done to the houfe, if any money remains, to be given to young beginners, and maid fervants who have lived in any place faithfully for three years, and to decayed houfekeepers.

The corporation purchafed the manor of Awre and Blakeney with Sir Thomas Rich's money, worth about 200*l.* a year; which being infufficient for the above purpofes, feveral additions have been fince made to the charity.

Lady Napier's gift of 50*l.* to the city, was applied to it in 1715.

Mr. Amity Clutterbuck, who had been one of the twenty boys brought up in this hofpital, gave 1000*l.* to it in 1722.

Alderman Thomas Brown alfo gave 400*l.* to it.

Mr. Richard Elly, by his will in 1755, gave, after the deceafe of his fifter, 1000*l.* the one half to be applied to the benefit and improvement of this hofpital, the other half to the improvement of St. Bartholomew's, in this city. He alfo gave, after his fifter's deceafe, 200*l.* to the fociety for promoting chriftian knowledge; 200*l.* to the fociety for propagating the gofpel in foreign parts; and the refidue of his eftate, which is confiderable, to be difpofed of in charity, as his executors fhall think proper.

Benefactions.

Alderman John Fawkener, in 1545, gave 40*l.* to be lent out to fome of the poor tradefmen of this parifh.

Mr. William Drinkwater gave 40*s.* a year towards eftablifhing a lecture fermon.

Mrs. Margaret Cartwright gave 10*l.*

Edward Nourfe, efq; gave 50*l.* to buy land, 10*s.* of the produce whereof to be paid to the minifter for a fermon on Michaelmas day; the remainder to be given to the poor.

Alderman John Webb gave 20*s.* *per ann.*

Mr. Nicholas Webb gave 30*s.* *per ann.*

Mr. Henry Redvern, 20*s.* *per ann.* for a fermon on new-year's day.

Jofeph Horner, 4*l.* *per ann.*

Mr. Daniel Lyfons, 2*l.* *per ann.* in bread.

Mr. Thomas Barns gave 100*l.* in the year 1702, the intereft of which to be given to four poor widows for their lives.

Phillis Lewis, widow, gave 20*l.*

Mr. John Coulftance 20*s.* a year to the poor, and 20*s.* for the repair of the highways.

Mr. John Brown gave 10*l.* for a fermon yearly on Good Friday.

Mr. Charles Trippet, prebendary of Sarum, having given 200*l.* to the chamber of the city of Gloucefter, the place of his nativity, the corporation applied the intereft of that fum to the ufe of the minifter, for reading prayers in this church twice every day, which commenced at Michaelmas 1708. And

Mr. Francis Yate gave 200*l.* to be applyed to the fame ufe.

Mrs. Sarah Marden, in 1727, gave 10*l.* for the minifter to preach a fermon yearly, upon the funday of every Lent affize.

Mr. Giles Marden, in 1728, gave 11*l.* 10*s.* for a fermon yearly on the funday of the fummer affize.

Thomas Webb, efq; in 1734, gave 50*l.*

Mrs. Mary Shail gave 50*l.* the fame year.

Mr. Richard Elly dying in February 1755, gave by his laft will, immediately after his deceafe, to the rector for the time being, and his fucceffors for ever, a very good houfe and garden; and a good houfe to the parifh clerk, and his fucceffors for ever. He alfo gave the intereft of 500*l.* to be paid to the rector (except 20*s.* to the fexton) for reading divine fervice every Sunday morning in this church.

Part of this parifh is without the city, very feparately difperfed, and is called Barton St. Michael, to diftinguifh it from that part which is within the liberties of the city.

	Baptifms.		Burials.	
	males	females	males	females
1759	12	11	11	10
1760	10	9	10	12
1761	9	12	8	13
1762	10	10	7	14
1763	11	11	8	3
1764	9	10	9	13
1765	9	6	19	15
1766	13	13	9	15
1767	9	12	10	7
1768	10	15	7	4
1769	9	8	9	10
	Total — 228		Total — 223	

The number of houfholds in this parifh in the year 1562, was 106; about 1712, according to Sir Robert Atkyns, there were 105 houfes and near 600 inhabitants; in 1743 there were 137 houfholds, and 605 inhabitants.

St. NICHOLAS's.

THE church ftands on the north fide in the Weft-gate ftreet. It confifts of a handfome nave, with an aile on each fide of it, and a veftry at the eaft end of the north aile. At the weft end of the nave is a lofty fpire with fix bells, befide a faint's-bell. On the fpire is a mural coronet, whence it has been conjectured, that the church was built by king John, who had been earl of Gloucefter. It is dedicated to St. Nicholas, bifhop of the city of Myra, in Lycia.

The advowfon of the church was granted to Nicholas Ragnel, in the fourth year of the reign of king John; and William Coxnell held it as incumbent 5° H. 3. for the repairing of the Weftbridge.

King

King Henry the Third, at the requeft of his queen, gave it to St. Bartholomew's hofpital, in the 13th year of his reign; and pope Gregory, (perhaps the 11th of that name, 'tho it be not expreffly faid which of them) by his bull, confirmed it to the hofpital; but recites that it was given by a bifhop of Worcefter, with the confent of his chapter.

After the diffolution, it was granted with the faid hofpital, by queen Elizabeth, to the mayor and burgeffes of Gloucefter, fubject to a penfion of 13*s*. 4*d*. granted out of it to the dean and chapter, by their charter of foundation, being part of the revenues of the late diffolved abbey there.

This church was valued at 40 marks 19° E. 1. but the clear yearly value of it, in tythes and oblations, 26° H. 8. was 9*l*. 18*s*. The certificate runs thus: *Ecclefia Sancti Nicholai Glouc. valet clare in decimis et oblationibus per annum, ultra 2s. per annum folutos epifcopo Wigorniæ, 6s. 8d. pro procuratione archidiaconi Glouc. 13s. 4d. pro vifitatione epifcopi Glouc. juxta ratam cujuflibet tertii anni 40s. et 104s. fingulis diebus dominicis per totum annum inter pauperes et mulieres dicti hofpitalis* [St. Bartholomei] *diftribut. ratione appropriationis dictæ ecclefiæ ex fundatione Henrici 3. nuper regis Angliæ, 9l. 18s.* The voluntary contributions are worth about 50*l*. a year. This living has been twice chofen by lot to be augmented by queen Anne's bounty, and was returned. There is no parfonage-houfe, but the minifter has a lodging in Bartholomew hofpital.

The church of the Holy Trinity was united to this, by an ordinance of parliament in 1648, and an annuity of 80*l*. annexed to the curacy, with one of the prebendal houfes; the incumbent to pay firft fruits and tenths after the rate of 8*l*. a year. But the parifhes are now diftinct.

There were in this church the following particulars: 1. A chantry dedicated to St. Mary. 2. Another chantry dedicated to St. Katherine, at which a light was provided for William Sanford and Owen Windfor, by the prior of St. Bartholomew's. This William Sanford, about the middle of the reign of Henry the 3d, gave to that hofpital all his lands and poffeffions in and about the town of Gloucefter, for the honourable maintenance of a fecular prieft, to officiate daily in this church, and for providing 2*s*. weekly to be given to the poor of the hofpital. The prieft to have 20*s*. a year to buy him cloathes, and to receive his victuals and have his lodging in the hofpital more honourable than any of the brethren, next to the prior. 3 A chantry for one prieft, founded by the will of Thomas of Gloucefter, dated May 18, 1446. 4. An altar dedicated to St. Thomas, at which the prior, or one of the brethren of the faid hofpital, officiated for the fouls of Sanford and Windfor; and a light burning for them from fun-rifing to fun-fetting, at the high altar; and another taper burning before the crofs. 5. An obit on December 28, in memory of William Francomb, and Alice his wife, for which the faid Alice gave certain lands in 1491. In the reign of queen Elizabeth, the rent of the land was detained by the crown; but the churchwardens have received 6*s*. 8*d*. a year ever fince on that account.

Incumbents.

Hugh Fifhpoole, fometime a chantry-prieft of St. John's fervice in St. Michael's, was curate at his death.
John Henbury occurs in 1562.
Richard Warret, or Warrint, a minor canon, 1569.
William Prefton, 1583.
Henry Aifgill, M. A. 1587, one of the prebendaries.
Giles Randle, 1587.
John Ward, 1594, afterwards rector of Farmington.
Francis Arnold occurs Dec. 31, in the fame year.
Elias Wrench, B. A. 1597, afterwards a prebendary.
Evan Vaughan, B. A. 1609.
Thomas Prior, M. A. 1613, one of the prebendaries.
John Workman, 1622. On his tomb in the churchyard is this infcription:—In Memory of that pious worthy divine, Mr. John Workman, once minifter of this Parifh, who was buried the 12th of January, 1640, aged 50.
John Foordham occurs in 1628.
John Holford occurs in 1634. He lies buried in the chancel, and on the ftone is a memorial for him, his wife and feveral relations. Over the firft pillar on the north fide of the church, above the pulpit, upon a table is the following infcription: To the happy memory of John Holford, fometime minifter of this Parifh, who died Auguft 17, 1653.
Quid loquar, aut quorfum Lachrimæ, nec Carmina poffunt
Sat dare pro meritis, Ter venerande. Vale.
John Allibond, M. A. 1635.
Help-on-high Fox, M. A. was elected June 12, 1645. The corporation of Gloucefter patron.
Thomas Singleton, 1679.
John Hilton, 1686, afterwards vicar of Stonehoufe.
Benjamin Newton, M. A. 1708.
Samuel Gwinnet, LL B. 1735, who is the prefent curate.

Monuments and Infcriptions.

Amongft many others, here are monuments for
Nicholas Sankey, efq; who died in 1589.
John Walton, alderman, who died in 1626.
Walter Taynton, mercer, who died in 1646.
Robert Holford, who died in 1654.
William Window, gent. who died in 1659.
Jafper Clutterbuck, who died in 1659.
Robert Tuther, once mayor, who died in 1660,
William Singleton, efq; twice mayor, and member of parliament for the city, who died in 1667.
John Deighton, who died in 1676.
Thomas Lugg, alderman, who died in 1679.
John James Belveze, late French advocate at Montaubon in France, who died in 1708.
Richard Maffinger, once fheriff, who died 1721.
Richard Green, who died in 1729.
Thomas Ludlow, who died in 1734.

Benefactions.

Thomas Gutter, alias White, gave three houfes and a garden for the fupport of the fervice of the altar.

Alderman John Thorn, in 1617, gave 13*s*. 4*d*. yearly for a fermon on Afhwednefday, and 6*s*. 8*d*. to the poor.

John Window gave 50*s*. yearly, to be given in coals to the poor.

William Window gave 2*s*. a week to buy bread, and 20*s*. a year for a fermon on St. John's day.

Thomas

Thomas Singleton, of the city of London, mercer, in 1656, gave 5 *l.* for the repair of the church, and 3 *l.* to the poor, and 20 *s.* a year for a fermon on Good Friday.

Alderman John Woodward gave two houfes for a term of years.

Daniel Lyfons gave 2 *l.* a year for bread.

Elizabeth Morris gave 50 *l.* the intereft whereof to be diftributed among twenty houfekeepers.

Mrs. Weaver gave the intereft of 100 *l.* for five widows.

Richard Green gave the intereft of 50 *l.* to be diftributed in bread.

Thomas Whithenbury, in 1722, gave a piece of garden-ground to provide 40 *s.* for bread, and 10 *s.* for a fermon yearly.

Thomas Mee, in 1722, gave 50 *l.*

Jofeph Reeve gave 85 *l.*

William Lifle gave 25 *l.* a year. He is buried in the cathedral ; fee his memorial p. 176.

	Baptifms.		Burials.	
	males	females	males	females
1759	28	28	19	12
1760	26	24	40	27
1761	22	21	27	34
1762	24	23	12	24
1763	20	28	24	20
1764	22	29	20	34
1765	25	19	32	50
1766	16	25	25	38
1767	33	18	36	38
1768	18	24	29	23
1769	27	29	37	25
Total	529		626	

There were 146 houfholders in this parifh in the year 1562. Sir Robert Atkyns's account about the year 1710, is 196 houfes, and about 1000 inhabitants ; but in the year 1743 there were 282 houfes, and 1309 inhabitants.

To the Royal Aid, in 1692, £.	248	0	0
Poll tax, in 1694,	90	7	0
Land tax, in 1694,	341	6	0
The fame, in 1770, at 3 *s.*	274	13	0

In the year 1770, this parifh paid quarterly 52 *l.* 10 *s.* to the workhoufe, and 24 *l.* 15 *s.* 4 *d.* towards lamps.

In this parifh is

St. Bartholomew's Hospital.

This hofpital is fituate between the bridges on the north fide of the weft-gate ftreet. In an inquifition taken upon oath before William the prior of Lanthony, and William de Chiltenham, 30° E. 3. it is faid to owe its original to William Myparty, a burgefs of Gloucefter; who, when Nicholas Walred, clerk, began to build the weft bridge, in the reign of king H. 2. gave him a piece of land, whereon the hofpital now ftands, built a houfe upon it for the convenience of Walred and his workmen, and retiring to them himfelf, with feveral other perfons of both fexes, they all lived there together, in hermitical habit, under the government of a prieft, upon the charity of well difpofed perfons. But king H. 3. on the twenty fixth of June, in the thirteenth year of his reign, being at Gloucefter, gave them the church of St. Nicholas; and from that time the houfe was called the *Hofpital of St. Bartholomew the apoftle.* Soon after, the fame king, upon their petition, granted them liberty to choofe a prior; and on the 12th of September, in the forty ninth year of his reign, gave them fixteen ells of land in length, and five in breadth, to be taken out of the ftreet, for the enlargement of their chancel.

Leland fays this hofpital was founded by one of the bifhops of Worcefter, but by which of them is not known. Others attribute it to Bofil, the firft bifhop of that fee. However that be, it was found upon the inquifition mentioned at the beginning of this account, that after St. Nicholas's was granted to the hofpital, the bifhop of Worcefter claimed a right of vifiting it. According to bifhop Tanner, king E. 3. order'd the ftate of this hofpital to be furvey'd; and we learn from Mr. Prynne, in his *Animadverfions on Coke's Inftitutes,* that king R. 2. iffued out a commiffion for vifiting it. But on the nineteenth day of November, 9° H. 4. the king granted the prior and brethren a new charter, which is now in the cuftody of the corporation, and the tranflation of it may be feen in the Appendix. N°. 12.

The hofpital confifted of a mafter, or prior, or guardian, and three fellows, befides the poor people. Andrew Whitmay the mafter, John Henbury, John Harsfield, and Henry or Harry Francum, the three brethren, fubfcribed to the king's fupremacy, Sept. 4, 1534.

There was formerly a chapel in this hofpital, dedicated to St. Urfula. A chantry in Newent church-yard, dedicated to St. James and St. Anne, belonged alfo to this hofpital, 'till its diffolution.

In the fifth year of king Henry the feventh, this hofpital was valued at 23*l.* 7*s.* 6*d.* About the time of its diffolution, the accounts are exceedingly various. The profits were computed at 33*l.* 8*s.* 8*d.* clear of all reprifals 26° H. 8. The next year the whole rent was faid to be 74*l.* 0*s.* 1*d.* and the clear income 44 *l.* 7 *s.* 2 *d.* *ob.* which was increafed the year afterwards to 65 *l.* 7 *s.* 8 *d.* *ob.*

The commiffioners appointed 37° H. 8. certified, that this hofpital was founded for a mafter, who was to have a falary of 20 *l.* 5 *s.* 5 *d.* *q.* for five priefts, [perhaps the three brethren and two others to officiate here and at St. Nicholas's] whofe falary was 29 *l.* for thirty two poor people, who receive 30 *l.* 0 *s.* 3 *d.* and for finding a lamp and two tapers in the above church, at the yearly expence of 14 *s.* 6 *d.* Befides the above payments, there were 6 *l.* 15 *s.* 2 *d.* for out rents; 4 *l.* 8 *s.* 8 *d.* *ob.* for tenths; 1 *l.* 9 *s.* 8 *d.* fynodals and pentecoftals for the churches belonging to it ; and

2*l.* 13*s.* 4*d.* for fees. The value of the ornaments, plate, goods, &c. then belonging to it was 20*l.* 6*s.* 2*d.*

The commiffioners, 1° E. 6. certified, that the clear yearly value was 25*l.* 11*s.* 2*d.* and that the feveral poffeffions of the poor people belonging to the hofpital were worth 25*l.* 4*s.* 5*d.* I fuppofe before the outgoings were deducted. And that valuation being approved, 9 February, 3° E. 6. the mafters were to pay firft fruits to the crown accordingly for it. In archbifhop Sancroft's MS. Valor. it is 25*l.* 6*s.* 3*d.* *toto*, 4*l.* 10*s.* 11*d.* *ob. clare.* Thirty-four poor perfons were then in the hofpital. The full income of the lands belonging to it was 78*l.* 1*s.* 2*d.* when it was granted from the crown.

By the intereft of Mr. Pates, recorder of the city, queen Elizabeth, by letters patents, dated July 14, *regni* 6° granted this hofpital to the mayor and burgeffes of Gloucefter, with the patronage of the office of mafter, &c. when the fame fhould become void by the death of John Man, efq; and alfo the revenues of it, for the maintenance of a minifter, a phyfician, a furgeon, and forty poor people. This grant was obtained on condition that the mayor, &c. would releafe an antient annual penfion of 9*l.* 2*s.* paid by the crown to the hofpital, which was done on the 17th of the fame month. The mayor, &c. covenanted with the queen, that the whole clear yearly profits fhould be expended in the manner mentioned.

The hofpital was in a deplorable condition when it came into the hands of the corporation. The church was ruinous, and the houfe fo decay'd, that they rebuilt twenty-one chambers, and were at great expences in other repairs.

Soon after the corporation obtained the grant of this hofpital, they elected a prefident or provoft, a treafurer, two furveyors, two almoners, and two fcrutineers yearly, as they now continue to do, to manage the affairs of this hofpital, who have alfo the fuperintendency over thofe of St Margaret, and the Magdalen or king James's. The ftatutes for their government were compofed, it is faid, by archbifhop Laud, about the year 1636.

The queen's grant has fince been confirmed by act of parliament, which provides, that the bifhop of Gloucefter, or other ordinary of the diocefe, fhall freely vifit the hofpital every third year to fee if the above covenant be truly obferved.

In Leland's time there were fifty-two poor perfons in the hofpital; but 26° & 27° H. 8. there were only twenty-four. In Sternhold's and Man's mafterfhips were thirty-two, at four pence half penny or three farthings a week. Soon after the grant, it was increafed to fix-pence each. In the time of king Charles the firft, it came to two fhillings each, and then from time to time, additional chambers were added, fo that at prefent there are twenty-fix men and thirty women in fo many chambers, who receive two fhillings and fix-pence each weekly.

I have a large folio book of abftracts from the original grants to this hofpital, which exhibits the names of near a hundred benefactors to it.

Priors or Mafters.

Adam Garon, or de Garne, was the firft prior or mafter. About the time of his government, Ofbert Giffard gave lands in Brimpsfield for the maintenance of a chaplain, to officiate for himfelf and anceftors. A perpetual chaplain was appointed for Philip and Margery Apothecary. And Adam de Ardern gave a certain fum of money for eftablifhing a chantry in the hofpital.

John de Monumeta occurs in the reign of H. 3.

Adam Reyner.

John de Bofco.

William Abenhalle, or Abbehal occurs *temp.* E. 1.

John de Wode.

John de Oke, del Oks, or de Oka, occurs 29 E. 1. In 1318, a perpetual anniverfary was erected here for John Thormerton. This prior dying in 1326,

John de Bykenor was advanced to the priorfhip.

Nicholas Hardewyke occurs 5°, & 28° E. 3. William de Bohun earl of Northampton, July 15, 17° E. 3. gave to him and the hofpital the advowfon of the church of Newnham, and chapel of Little Dean, *co. Glouc.* And in 1374, a perpetual chantry was erected here for Ralph Baron.

Walter Gibbes occurs 36° E. 3.

John Bilmulle fucceeding, occurs 12° & 21° R. 2.

John Prentys fucceeded. He refigned in 1401, whereupon

John Arundel was elected the fame year.

Thomas Carpenter occurs 1°, & 6°. H. 5.

William Wirceftre occurs 2° H. 6. upon whofe refignation,

Stephen Myle fucceeded Mar. 8. 1425, and dying 1454,

William Sobbrory, called alfo John Sodbury, alias Holwey, was elected.

John Haffefeld was advanced July 12, 1476. He had a difpute with the prior of Lanthony about ten loaves which that priory had engaged to furnifh every day to the poor people of this hofpital, in confideration of 220 marks given to the faid priory, upon that condition, by Richard the prieft of Heytherleia, about the time of king H. 3. and which the priory had refufed or neglected to furnifh. The bifhop of Worcefter made a definitive fentence for the hofpital againft the priory Aug. 18, 1477; but the latter often failed in performance, and the prior and convent were feveral times fummoned and cited before different authorities, particularly 4° H. 7. by the archbifhop of Canterbury, to fhew caufe why they did not perform their covenant with Richard de Hatherley.

Richard Baker occurs 8°, & 11° H. 7.

Thomas Aphowel occurs 14° H. 7. About the time of his government, one Pauncefote is faid to have been a great benefactor. He was buried in the chapel of the hofpital. The raifed tomb, under an arch between the church and the little fouth aile, was probably erected for him.

Andrew Whitmay, fuppofed to be born at Wheatenhurft, occurs as prior 4° H. 8. He raifed the houfe, fubject before to the frequent inundations of the Severn, and built a handfome lodging for himfelf, in the windows of which the initial letters of his name are ftill remaining. He was archdeacon of St. David's, and a fuffragan bifhop of the diocefe of Worcefter. He fubfcribed to the king's fupremacy, and held the government of the hofpital till his death, about 1546.

Thomas Sternhold, efq; groom of the king's wardrobe, had the mafterfhip conferred upon him Sept. 25, 1° E. 6. for from the time of the diffolution the title of prior ceafed.

John Man, efq; was prefented to it Oct. 29, 3° E. 6. Upon queen Elizabeth's grant of the reverfion of this office to the corporation, he refigned it to them, who paid him a penfion of 38*l.* a year. He was inftituted to the deanery of this cathedral, and died 1568. See Deans.

Many lands and poffeffions in this city, and the counties of Gloucefter and Worcefter, belong to this hofpital. Among others are, the perpetual curacy of St. Nicholas; the perpetual curacy of Newnham; the perpetual curacy of Little Dean; the rectory of Kemmerton, given by bifhop Goodman, all in this county; and thirty pounds a year paid out of the improved rent of Bentham-farm, given to the corporation by lady Cook; fo that the whole revenues of the hofpital, according to bifhop Tanner, are about 500*l.* a year.

No perfon can be admitted into this, nor the hofpitals of St. Margaret, and Mary Magdalen, under the age of fifty two years, unlefs on account of fome irrecoverable infirmity. The governors hold a court, at leaft once a month, for thefe hofpitals, at which all the poor people attend.

St. OWEN's.

THE church, which ftood on the weft fide, a little without the South-gate, was burnt down by the citizens, with the reft of the fuburbs, at the fiege, after the meffengers from the city had returned their anfwer to the king's fummons, on the tenth of Auguft, 1643. It was founded by Walter the conftable of Gloucefter, and dedicated, and made parochial, by epifcopal authority.

In the year 1137, earl Milo gave it and its appurtenances to the priory of Lanthony. The appurtenances were, a chapel within the caftle; a fmall piece of land upon the bank of the Severn, to find a light to the faid chapel; all the offerings of the keepers of the tower of the caftle, and the barons refiding there; half the oblations of himfelf and family, if his chaplain was prefent, and the whole if abfent; St. Kyneburgh's chapel, and the whole parochial land of the conftable of the caftle, within the South-gate and without; and all the land which Roger de Tocheham and Richard the chaplain poffeffed within and without that gate. Earl Milo, at the fame time, gave to the faid priory feveral rural churches or chapels, particularly Hempfted, Elmore, and Quedgly, and many other things expreffly fet down in earl Milo's charter to the priory of Lanthony.

When Walter de Cantelupe was bifhop of Worcefter, the value of the feveral particulars belonging to this vicarage, was as follows; the alterage, fmall tythes, and other obventions of St. Owen's, 3*l.* 13*s.* 4*d.* the alterage, &c. of Hechamfted, 60*s.* and other tythes 21*s.* *i. e.* 4*l.* 1*s.* the alterage and fmall tythes of Quedreffe [Quedgley] and other obventions, four marks, and tythe of other lands, 5*s.* 9*d.* in all 2*l.* 19*s.* 1*d.* the fmall tythes of Elmore, and other obventions, five marks, other tythes 6*s.* 7*d.* and tythes of villainage 20*s.* in all 4*l.* 13*s.* 3*d.* So that one vill and three contiguous country cures, were ferved for 15*l.* 6*s.* 8*d.* which the bifhop ratified at the appointment of the vicarage.

The vicar complaining afterwards, to the prior and convent of Worcefter, who were guardians of the fpiritualties, that his vicarage was infufficient, and that if he was obliged to live upon it, the prior and convent of Lanthony were bound, by an antient agreement, to build an *habitacle* for him; it was agreed, that the vicar fhould have fix marks of filver, three and a half of which to be expended *in building a houfe* at Heyamftede, for the ufe of the vicarage of St. Owen's.

The vicarage was taxed at thirteen marks, 19° E. 1. The abbey of Lyra, in Normandy, had 20*s.* out of it; and in 1398, the pope appropriated it to the priory of Lanthony, which paid, by compofition with the bifhop of Worcefter, a penfion of 3*s.* 4*d.* for all epifcopal demands on account of this church, in which the prior and convent held their halimot court.

In this church were, 1. A gild dedicated to St. John Baptift, whereof Thomas Briftol was the laft incumbent. 2. A chantry dedicated to St. Mary, whereof Richard Stanley, the laft incumbent, upon its diffolution, obtained a penfion of 4*l.* a year. Sir Thomas Bell, and Richard Duke, efq; had a grant of feveral of the poffeffions belonging hereto, 2° E. 6. 3. An altar dedicated to St. Katherine. 4. The rood-light.

By an ordinance of parliament in 1646, this parifh was united to St. Mary de Crypt; but that being null, they are now feparate, notwithftanding the rector of St. Mary's parifh performs parochial duties, as curate, to the parifhioners of this. In the year 1740, bifhop Benfon procured 200*l.* of queen Anne's bounty to augment the vicarage. The church ftood on or near the place whereon a new meeting-houfe was erected in 1730. This parifh has one churchwarden and one overfeer.

For benefactions fee St. Mary de Crypt.

The number of houfholds in 1562, was 93. Sir Robert Atkyns joins this parifh with that of St. Mary de Crypt. In 1743, the exact number of houfholds was 65, of inhabitants 186. The baptifms and burials are included in the account of thofe of the laft mentioned parifh.

St. Owen's pays to the workhoufe quarterly 5*l.* 14*s.* 3*d.* and 2*l.* 14*s.* towards lamps.

In this parifh are Kyneburgh's Hofpital, and another charitable inftitution, called Mr. Hill's Houfe. And firft

Of KINEBURGH'S HOSPITAL.

We have already fhewn that the chapel of St. Kyneburg, as an appurtenant to the church of St. Owen, was given by earl Milo to the priory of Lanthony, at its foundation. It ftood on part of the town wall. Upon the diffolution of Lanthony, this chapel was fold by the crown to Thomas Bell, gent. Aug. 1, 34° H. 8. who being afterwards knighted, gave five tenements, which he built on part of the fite of the old chapel, and another chamber at the weft end of it, of antient building, with fome lands belonging to the late diffolved monafteries in this county, for the maintenance of fix poor people; and queen Elizabeth confirmed the donation in the forty-firft year of her reign. In the year 1608, Mr. Thomas Hobbes gave 2*l.* a year; and Mrs. Margaret Norton gave the intereft of 50*l.* to the poor people of this hofpital, each of whom now receives 1*s.* 6*d.* weekly, and fome money quarterly. The

government

government of this charity is vefted in the corporation.

A portion of the weft part of the old chapel, given by the founder for the poor people to perform their public devotions in, was granted, in the year 1671, to the fraternity of cordwainers, for their common hall. On the fouth-weft fide of it is a raifed ftone monument, whereon lies the effigy of a young lady, with a coronet on her head. The common tradition is, that it is the tomb of one Maud Kimbros, who is faid to have been drowned in a well on the north part of the chapel, where are vifible remains of a door, fuppofed to lead to that well.

Mr. Hill's Houfe, on the weft fide adjoining to the South-gate, was defigned for an almfhoufe by the proprietor, who had been thrice mayor of the city; and by his will, beqeathed 80*l.* to erect a houfe for the habitation of fix poor people of the fouth ward, which has been fince done by the corporation.

There were formerly feveral other almfhoufes belonging to the city. Mr. Pates's houfe, and alderman Thomas Semys's houfes occur in 1643. And it is faid that Mr. Richard Keylock erected two houfes for two poor people in St. John's parifh. But probably they were not endowed with revenues to fupport them, and fo falling to decay, they are now undiftinguifhable.

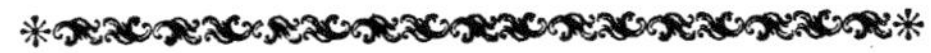

TRINITY.

THE church of the Holy Trinity ftood in the middle of the Weft-gate-ftreet, and confifted of one aile, with a beautiful tower at the weft end of it.

It was antiently a rectory, but in the year 1391, it became a vicarage, and was appropriated to St. Peter's abbey. The appropriation of this vicarage, with it's chapel of St. Mary de Grace, was ratified and confirmed by the bifhop of Worcefter, Oct. 14, 1394, and afterwards by other authorities. The dean and chapter of Gloucefter are patrons. The vicarage was augmented by lot, and returned, in the year 1743.

By an ordinance of parliament in 1648, this parifh was united to that of St. Nicholas, and the church granted to the corporation to be converted to a fchool-houfe, which was done accordingly, the bells, feats, and other particulars, being removed to the chapel of St. Bartholomew's hofpital, to Teynton, St. Nicholas's, and other places. At the reftoration, the ordinance was annulled, and the parifh became diftinct and feparate; but by a faculty, obtained in 1698, the church, which for a long time had been in a ruinous condition, was taken down, except part of the walls towards the weft end, which, with fome addition, were converted to a houfe for keeping the fire-engines, and other neceffaries for the ufe of the city. The beautiful tower was alfo fuffered to remain, becaufe, according to the notion of thofe times, it was of public ufe as well as ornament to the city; and beneath it a conduit was erected in 1702. But how fluctuating and uncertain are all human affairs! In a few years afterwards, this beautiful tower, and the more beautiful high crofs, were confidered as mere public nuifances, and accordingly were taken down by virtue of an act of 23° G. 2. and the materials purchafed and ufed in rebuilding the parifh church of Upton upon Severn.

"The *fite* of this church, Sir Robert Atkyns "obferves, is turned into a *market*; but the mar-"ket is fo well regulated, that it gives no dif-"turbance to the many worthy magiftrates of "this city who lye buried underneath."

In this church were the following particulars: 1. A chantry dedicated to the Holy Jefus, whereof Matthew Walker, the laft incumbent, upon its diffolution, obtained a penfion of 4*l.* a year. 2. A chantry dedicated to St. Mary, whereof George Cooper, the laft incumbent, obtained an annuity of 4*l.* 3. A fraternity dedicated to St. Thomas a Becket; for the augmentation of which, and finding a chaplain to officiate at the altar there, for his own foul, and for the fouls of all the faithful deceafed, Thomas Pope gave certain lands, rents and reverfions, by his will dated Sept. 18, 1400.

A houfe in Gore-lane, given by Richard Pate, efq; to Corpus Chrifti college, towards the maintenance of a fchool and hofpital at Cheltenham, was antiently called Trinity-college, where all the priefts of this church inhabited.

Firft fruits, £.	9 : 0 : 0	Synodals, - £.	0 : 1 : 0
Tenths, —	0 : 18 : 0	Pentecoftals,	0 : 1 : 0
Procurations,	0 : 5 : 0		

Richard Morwood, one of the minor-canons, was inftituted to the vicarage in 1617, and occurs in 1636. He was the laft incumbent of this church, and was buried in the fouth part of the tranfept of the cathedral, of which he was præcentor.

The minifter of St. Nicholas now performs moft of the parochial duties.

Benefactions.

Mr. Peach gave four houfes to four poor people, rent free.

Mr. Samuel Willet gave 10*l.* the intereft of which to buy bread for the poor.

Mrs. Mary Broad gave 40*s.* *per ann.* for the fame purpofe.

Mr. Daniel Lyfons gave 20*s.* *per ann.* for the fame ufe.

The baptifms and burials are included in thofe of the parifh of St. Nicholas.

The number of houfholds in this parifh in 1562, was 60; about 1710, according to Sir Robert

Robert Atkyns, there were 134 houfes, and about 600 inhabitants; but in 1743, there were 119 houfholds, and 491 inhabitants.

The Royal Aid in	1692,	£. 92 :	0 : 0
Poll Tax —	1694, —	43 :	13 : 0
Land Tax —	1694, -	121 :	4 : 0
The fame —	1771, -	101 :	17 : 6

In 1770, this parifh paid quarterly to the workhoufe 19*l.* 4*s.* 7*d.* and 12*l.* 11*s.* towards lamps.

SUBURBS.

THE fuburbs are not at prefent fo large as they were before the fiege, in the year 1643, when they were fet on fire by the governor, and are faid, in the petition of the mayor and burgeffes to parliament, for relief on that account, to have been a full third part of the city. They certified that two hundred forty and one houfes, befides barns, ftables, and out-buildings, were then burnt and deftroyed; and it appears by good evidence, that they even exceeded that number.

The houfes joined on both fides, almoft all the way from without the lower North-gate to St. Margaret's hofpital. On the weft fide were houfes from the gate to Feate-lane, which had feveral good buildings in it; and beyond that lane, and at the weft end of it, were many others.

There was a ftreet which led from the South-gate to Rignor's-ftile; and without the gate were houfes on both fides, called lower South-gate, and Sudbrook-ftreet; on the weft fide were St. Owen's lane, and Severn-ftreet. It is very certain that antiently there were houfes without the Weft-gate alfo; but Leland in his *Itinerary* takes no notice of them.

Within the liberties of the city, but without the walls, which extended no farther than the four gates, (of which the upper North-gate was one) on the eaft fide is Fullbrook, running from Morin's mill, under the North-gate, through the antient abbey, to which it was given by king W. 1. and after confirmed by charter in feveral fucceeding reigns. Many particulars concerning it are related in abbat Froucefter's manufcript.

Without the upper North-gate on the weft fide, was the caftle of Croydon, ftanding in Hairlane, otherwife Herlon, Harelane, and Boundlane, where the countefs of Stafford had lands; and where was a houfe called Dunning's Place, belonging to the abbey.

The lower North-gate belongs to the mayor's porter. It ftands on the fouth bank of the brook Wyver, which begins at the poftern, and runs beyond Alvingate into the Severn. All the land on each fide of it, without the gate, has been called Neulond, or Newland, for many ages paft, and extended nearly to St. Margaret's hofpital.

At the north end of the lower North-gate-ftreet ftood Alvingate, which was frequently repaired by the corporation, and had a particular porter belonging to it. This was probably deftroyed at the fiege. Juft without the gate was Kingefham or Kingefhome-ftreet, which occurs in 1269. A little diftant from the road, ftood a chapel dedicated to St. Thomas, and occurs in 1273. It was new built by Philip Monger, in 1454; and tho' long fince demolifhed, there is a houfe belonging to Bartholomew's hofpital, built on the fite of it, which is now called the Chapel houfe.

The place called Le Hurft in antient writings, was very probably a wood, about the time of the conqueft, as the name fignifies. It extended from Hairlane before-mentioned, to

Bridelane, called alfo Farther Harelane; and reached to the eaft corner of Wood-garden, and near Hangman's-pits, oppofite to the wall of the cathedral, next the orchard belonging to the prebendary of the third ftall.

Watering-ftreet, or Water-ftreet, commonly called Katherine-ftreet, was from

St. Ofwald's-ftreet, which was directly oppofite to the church of that name.

The White Friery is now intirely demolifhed. The ground on which it ftood is ftill called the Frier's-ground.

Featlane, Feetlane, Feytlane, or Featlone, is now alfo deftroy'd. It ftood northward of the above, and the archbifhop of York had tenements in it: Lady-croft, or Lendy-croft, which occurs in the reigns of H. 3. E. 1. and E. 2. was very near it.

Brook-ftreet, juft without the poftern-gate, extended to Morin's mill, given by John de Thormerton to the abbey 11° E. 2. which enjoy'd it till the diffolution. Afterwards Sir Thomas Bell being poffeffed of it, gave it with other things for the maintenance of Kimbro's hofpital. The greateft part of the fouth fide of this ftreet is in the parifh of St. Michael, the north fide is in that of St. Katherine. It was deftroyed at the fiege, but fome few of the houfes have been fince rebuilt.

Leland in his *Itinerary*, fpeaking of Gloucefter, obferves, *that there were divers pretty ftreets that now be clean decay'd, as St. Bride's-ftreet, and Silver-girdle-ftreet.* Several others occur in antient records, that have been long fince deftroy'd. Antiently the town extended northwards and fouthwards, with few buildings on the eaftern and weftern fides. The more noble part of it ftood where now the Kingfholm houfe is. It had handfome, fpacious ftreets of the following names: White-ftreet gave entrance into the town from the London road, thro' Pedmark's field; King's-ftreet led from Kingfholm to Gloucefter; Queen-ftreet, Silver-ftreet, Long-ftreet, towards Longford; Milk-ftreet; Caftle-ftreet, which led from the Old-Bear to the caftle. Befides thefe, there were fome others of lefs note. Many of thefe ftreets were very fubject to floods from the

 Severn,

Severn, which made the inhabitants defert them by degrees, to build on a higher and more fecure fituation.

Without the Eaft-gate, Barton-ftreet extended, with houfes joining almoft all the way on both fides, to a place called the World's-end; and on the north fide of it, near the gate, were many houfes along Gawdy-green. Part of it is within the liberties of the city, and part not. All within the liberties is in the parifh of St. Michael; and what is beyond them, lies in the parifhes of St. Michael, and St. Mary de Load. In the reign of king E. 1. there was, in the north part of this ftreet, a place called the King's ditch, and Law-day ditch, intended perhaps to feparate the liberties of the town from the county.

There were antiently two diftinct manors here, King's-barton and Abbat's-barton. The firft was fo called, becaufe it was a farm in the king's hands, to fubfift the caftle of Gloucefter. It was a confiderable manor, of which *Domefday book* gives the following account:

'In Bertune king Edward had nine hides, of 'which feven were in demean. And there were 'three plow tillages, and fourteen villeins, and 'ten bordars, with nine plow tillages. There 'were feven *fervi*. Two free men held two hides 'of this manor, and have there nine plow tillages. 'They cannot feparate themfelves nor the land 'from the manor. There is a mill of 4*s*. [value] 'King William's bailiff [*prepofitus*] added eight 'bordars, two mills, and one plow tillage. In 'king Edward's reign it paid 9*l*. 5*s*. and 3000 'loaves for the dogs. It now pays 20*l*. 20 cows, '20 hogs, and 16*s*. in lieu of the bread.

'Ældred the archbifhop claimed Brewere, one 'member of this manor. There are three yard 'lands and three men. Milo Crifpin holds it.

'Optune, another member, Aluui the fheriff 'claimed. There is one hide of land and four 'men. Hunfridus holds it.

'The fame Aluui claimed Merwen, a third 'member. There are three yard lands. Nigellus 'the phyfician holds it.

This manor continued in the crown 'till 2 H. 3. when Jeoffry Lucy was feized of it. Robert le Savage was feized of Barton-court 45° H. 3. Walter Wither held it 54° H. 3. John Mufgrofs was feized of this place 3° E. 1. Ralph de Walefworth held it 8° E. 1. The rent of the caftle, and the Bertone and Tyne of Gloucefter, which was 110*l*. a year, was fettled on queen Margaret, in part of her dower, 27° E. 1.

The abbey of Gloucefter was feized of the manor of Berton and of fix plow tillages, in the 17th year of the reign of king Edward the third, who, two years afterwards, by his charter dated June 25, granted to the abbey this manor with its appurtenances, and a pool at Minfterworth, a moiety of the pool at Dunye, with its appurtenances, and the privilege of having twigs out of the foreft of Dean to repair the pool, in fee for ever. The abbey to pay 48*l*. *per ann.* into the king's exchequer, for the advowfon of the church of Wyrardefbury, in the county of Bucks; but to be difcharged, out of the faid 48*l*. of a penfion of 5*l*. a year, which they ufed to pay to that church. This charter was confirmed by king Richard the fecond.

But Elizabeth, the widow of Thomas duke of Norfolk, and daughter of Richard earl of Arundel, was feized of the manor of King's-Barton 3° H. 6.

Robert Maell, and Cicely his wife, were feized of a mill, and of one acre and a half of arable land, and two acres of meadow in Barton near Gloucefter.

There was a houfe in the South-gate-ftreet, which, in a leafe from the priory of Lanthony, dated March 27, 47° E. 3. is faid to be in the liberty of the King's Barton.

Abbat's Barton was fo called, becaufe it belonged to St. Peter's abbey. Aldred, under-king of the Wicces, gave an hundred hides to this monaftery, when Eva was abbefs. In *Domefday book* it is faid,

'In the time of king Edward, Saint Peter of 'Gloweceftre held Bertune, in Dudeftanes hun-'dred, with its adjacent members, Berneuude, 'Tuffelege, Mereuuent. There are twenty-two 'hides, lefs one yard land. In demean nine plow 'tillages, and forty-two villeins, and twenty-one 'bordars, with forty-five plow tillages. There 'are twelve *fervi*, and a mill of 5*s*. and 120 acres 'of meadow, and a wood five furlongs long and 'three broad. It was worth 8*l*. and is now 'worth 24*l*. This manor was always exempt 'from geld, and from all royal fervice".

It has been already fhewn, under the account of abbat Hameline, that archbifhop Aldred took this manor, and fome other eftates from the monaftery, to repay himfelf the great expences he had been at in rebuilding the abbey, and that afterwards they were reftored by his fucceffor; from which time this manor continued in the poffeffion of the abbey 'till its diffolution; when it came to the crown. A leafe of the fite of it, with feveral lands belonging to it, was granted 31° H. 8. for twenty-one years, to John Ap-Rice, at the yearly rent of 14*l*. 4*s*. 4*d*. And the reverfions of all thefe, and many other lands here and elfewhere, were fold to the city[a] on the 11th of September, in the 34th year of the fame reign. But the crown refumed its claim, for the manor of Barton Abbat's was granted to Anne Fortefcue, widow of Sir Adrian Fortefcue, and to his heirs male, 5° Mariæ. And according to Sir Robert Atkyns, it did again *belong* to the crown, in the year 1608. But it is now the property of the corporation of the city of Gloucefter.

[a] Civ.

Lands

Lands in Barton Abbat's, and the firft feeding of the meadow called Pully-mead, and the tythes of the fame, lately belonging to the priory of Lanthony, were granted to Arthur Porter 32° H. 8.

A portion of tythes in St. Mary de Load, in Barton, formerly belonging to the abbey of Gloucefter, were granted to the chapter of Gloucefter, 33° H. 8. And other tythes in Barton Abbat's, formerly belonging to the priory of St Ofwald, were granted to John Fernham 22° Eliz.

The bord-lands, parcel of the manor of Barton-Abbat's, and other lands in the fame manor, were granted in truft, to Richard Andrews and Nicholas Temple 35° H. 8. And Robert Thornhill and Leonard Warcop had a grant of other lands there 38° H. 8.

Here is a fair on the 28th day of September, which ufed to be fo famous for large quantities of cheefe, as to fet the price of that article for the whole year, in all the neighbouring parts; but fince the factors [b] have made a practice of buying it up at the dairy-houfes, all the cheefe-fairs and markets in this country are funk to nothing; and that neceffary article of provifions advanced to more than double the price it bore about twenty or thirty years fince.

The manors of King's-barton and Abbat's-barton, by a long unity of poffeffion, are fo confufed with each other, as not to be every where diftinguifhed.

King James the firft, in the 8th year of his reign, granted the hundreds of Dudfton [c] and King's-barton to Sir William Cook, knight, for twenty-one years. The next year, the fame king granted them for ever to George and Thomas Whitmore, and —— Whitmore, efq; of Slaughter, fon of general Whitmore, who died in the year 1771, is the prefent proprietor of them.

The places in the hundreds of Dudfton and King's-barton are fet down p. 41, of which the following owe fuit and fervice to the court-leet of King's-barton. The hamlet of St. Michael, Barton-ftreet, Upton St. Leonard, Pitchcombe, Harefcombe, South-gate and Woolftrop, Sainthurft, Twigworth, Matfon, and Kingfholm.

In the year 1770, when the land-tax was at 3*s.* in the pound, Barton St. Michael paid 27*l.* 9*s.* Barton St. Mary 113*l.* 14*s.*

[b] The modern cheefe-factor is a dealer on his own ftock, and at his own rifque; it is therefore an abufe of the term to call him factor. He buys whole dairies together, which are carried from the farm-houfes to his warehoufe, and not a cheefe of them appears in the market, except what he rejects on account of fome imperfection. The dairy-man fells none of his beft cheefe from the dealer, unlefs he be tempted by an extravagant price, or induced by fome particular circumftance or connexion. Some factors are either in actual poffeffion, or in affurance of forty or fifty dairies each; how then can it be difficult to account, even in a time of plenty, for the exorbitant price of cheefe?

Our forefathers were of opinion that commerce in the great neceffaries of life fhould be reftrained, and provided laws to prevent a monopoly of them; but we have lately experienced the infufficiency of thofe laws. If it be neceffary in large cities and towns, that cheefe-mongers be provided with a fufficient ftock for the inhabitants of fuch places; yet no perfon I believe, will think it equally neceffary that the whole produce of the dairy be drawn into the dealers warehoufes, or fhut up in the cheefe-lofts, in order at length to pafs through their hands to the confumers. I infift not that the cheefe-factor and meal-man are unlawful dealers; but it is an error in the police to fuffer them to conduct their bufinefs after the prefent method.

[c] It is not abfolutely certain where Dudfton lay; but it was probably without the lower North-gate, beyond the New-land. It was alfo called Dudeftan, Dodeftan, &c. perhaps from the Saxon words *Dyd* dead, and *Stan* ftone. It might be the common burying place in the time of the Romans. Bertachia, from *Bergenne* a grave, is mentioned in antient writings, in the reign of E. 2. and might lie adjacent to Dudfton.

OF THE PARISHES IN Gloucefterfhire.

ABBENHALL.

THIS is a fmall parifh, full of little hills and dingles, within the hundred of St. Briavel's; twelve ftatute miles weft from Gloucefter, and three north from Newnham. It is bounded on the north-weft by Mitchel Dean, on the fouth-eaft by Flaxley, with Blaifdon to the north-eaftward, and Little Dean to the weftward of it.

The abbat of Flaxley had antiently a houfe here, whence the place obtained the name of Abbenhall. It was not particularly fpecified in *Domefday-book*, when the general furvey was made; and as late as the ninth year of king Edward the Firft, the fheriff, in his account of all the vills in the county of Gloucefter, returned Mitchel Deane, Parva Deane, and Abbenhalle as one vill.

The ftones in this parifh are of a rufty colour, with fhining particles of iron in their compofition. The greateft part of the land is pafturage, with a confiderable portion of commonable places, over-run with fern and bufhes.

There is a place called Gun's Mills, where was formerly an iron furnace, but the machinery is now converted to the ufe of a paper-mill, which is driven by a fine fpring of water rifing out of a rock in the foreft, on the fide of a hill juft above the mill. The foreft is extraparochial, wherefore I fhall take notice of the fpring in this place. It is called St. Anthony's Well. At the head, the water runs into a fquare bafon (with fteps on one fide) made for the purpofe of bathing. I have been told by people of credit and judgment in the neighbourhood, that bathing in this water is an infallible cure for the itch, and other cutaneous diforders; and a gentleman of Little Dean affured me, that his dogs were cured of the mange by being thrown into it two or three times. The water is extremely cold; but whether on that account only it is capable of producing thofe falutary effects, I fhall not determine.

Maynard Colchefter, of Weftbury, efq; has a good houfe here, called the Wildernefs, fituate on the brow of a hill, which gives it a very extenfive profpect.

Of the Manor and other Eftates.

The manor of Abbenhall belonged antiently to a family who took their name from this place. John de Abbenhalle was poffeffed of it when the fheriff made his return to the king's writ 9 E. 1. Ralph de Abbenhall died feized of it in the 29th year of the fame reign. John his fon and heir died feized of the manor, and of the advowfon of the church, 10 E. 2. Reginald his fon and next heir died feized of this manor 15 E. 3. Sir Ralph de Abbenhall, fon of Reginald, died feized of it, and of the cuftody of a wood in the foreft of

Dean 21 E. 3. ſince whoſe time I find no more of this name here. It is probable that the heireſs of this family married into that of the Talbots, for they quarter the arms of Abbenhall, *viz. Or, a feſs gules*, and had at that time great eſtates in the neighbourhood.

The Grenders were the next poſſeſſors of this eſtate; John Grender was ſeized thereof 5 H. 4. in which year, and alſo in the laſt of that reign, he was high ſheriff of this county. Robert his ſon died ſeized of this manor 26 H. 6. leaving Elizabeth his only daughter and heireſs, married to John Tiptot earl of Worceſter, who, after the death of his wife, held this eſtate by the courteſy of England during his life. He was a firm adherent to the houſe of York, and on the reſtoration of king Henry the Sixth, loſt his head on Tower-hill, and was buried in the Black Friers, London. He left no iſſue, wherefore the manor deſcended to John Grender, *alias* Greyndour, the next heir to the preceding Robert.

—— Walwyn (ſon of William Walwyn, who had been high ſheriff of Glouceſterſhire 10 H. 4.) married the daughter and heireſs of the laſt-mentioned John Grender, by whom he had the manor of Abbenhall, which deſcended to his ſon William Walwyn.

Thomas Baynham, of Clowerwall, married Alice, daughter and heireſs of William Walwyn, with whom he had this eſtate. Sir Chriſtopher Baynham, their ſon and heir, died ſeized of it 32 H. 8. His ſon, ſir George Baynham, died ſeized thereof 38 H. 8. whoſe ſon Chriſtopher had livery of this manor 3 E. 6. His ſon Thomas had alſo livery thereof 23 Eliz. and continued ſeized of it 6 Jac.

Marſhall Brydges, of Worceſterſhire, eſq; related to the family of the lord Chandois, was lord of this manor in the year 1711, but John Howell, eſq; is the preſent proprietor.

Of the other eſtates, the records ſhew, that Margaret the widow of —— Huntley died ſeized of lands within this manor, and of a rent iſſuing out of Little Dean 49 E. 3. Robert Pyrke died ſeized of lands in Abbenhall 9 Car. and left Richard his ſon fifteen years old.

Of the Church, &c.

The church is a rectory, in the Foreſt deanery, worth about 70*l.* a year. John Howell, eſq; is patron, and Mr. Hoſkyns is the preſent incumbent.

There are thirty acres of glebe, and all the lands are ſubject to tithe; but there is no parſonage houſe, and even the place where it ſtood is forgotten.

The church, dedicated to St. Michael, hath an aile on the ſouth ſide, which was rebuilt in 1749, and a ſmall tower at the weſt end, covered with tile.

Firſt fruits £.	6	6	8	Proc.&Syn. £.	0	6	6
Tenths —	0	12	8	Pentecoſtals -	0	1	4

Monuments and Inſcriptions.

On a flat ſtone of grey marble in the chancel, are memorials for Richard Pyrke, of Mitchel Dean, who died in 1609, and Johan his wife, daughter of John Aylway. And beneath are the effigies of Thomas and Robert their ſons; and of Duncombe Pyrke, ſecond ſon of Nathaniel Pyrke, eſq; who died in 1725.

Againſt the north wall is a monument, with theſe arms, *Party per pale, baron and femme*, 1. *Argent, a feſs ſable, charged with three mullets of the field.* 2. *Gules, a chevron between three eſtoiles Or.* And under, on a table of white marble, this inſcription:

Near unto lies interred the Body of Nath. Pyrke of Michel-deane, Eſq; who was deſcended of an ancient Family who had their chiefe Seat of Reſidence in this Neighbourhood ever ſince the Conqueſt. He married Mary the daughter of Duncombe Colcheſter, kn[t]. and by her had iſſue three ſons and two daughters. Thomas the eldeſt married Dorothy the daughter of Richard Yate, of Arlingham, eſq; Duncombe the ſecond married Elizabeth the daughter of William Guillam of Longſtone in the county of Hereford, eſq; and Jane married Rowles Walter ſon and heir of Thomas Walter of Stapleton in the county of Glouc. eſq; Nath. and Deborah died infants and *lies* interred near this place. He was a faithful ſubject to his prince, a good father to his children, charitable to the poor, and Iuſt in his dealings. He left behind him an inconſolable widdow, who erected this monument in remembrance of ſoe tender and loving a huſband. He died the 28th of October, 1715, in the ſixtyeth Year of his Age.

Alſo in Memory of Deborah the Mother of the ſaid Nath. Pyrke, and Wife of Thomas Pyrke, Eſq; She was a pious good chriſtian, and lies interred near this place. She died the 9th of February 1662. But Thomas Pyrke her Huſband, and Father of the ſaid Nath: lies buried in the Pariſh Church of Little Deane.

Alſo here lieth Dorothy the Daughter of Thomas Pyrke, eſq; grand-daughter of the ſaid Nath. She was buried Iune the 21ſt, 1715.

Alſo in Memory of Mary Pyrke, the Widow and Relict of the above-named Nathaniel Pyrke who departed this life the 22d of November Anno Dom. 1738. Ætatis 76. And of Nathl. Son of Duncombe and of Elizabeth Pyrke who died January the 10th 1748, aged 31 Years.

Taxes.					
	The Royal Aid in	1692, £.	163	14	0
	Poll-tax ——	1694, —	28	1	0
	Land-tax ——	1694, —	166	14	0
	The ſame, at 3*s.*	1770, —	50	0	0

When ſir Robert Atkyns compiled his account of Glouceſterſhire, there were, according to him, 22 houſes, and about 88 inhabitants in this pariſh, of whom 6 were freeholders; yearly births 3, and burials 3. But examining the regiſter, I find, that in ten years, beginning with 1700, the whole number of baptiſms was 24, and of burials 34: And that in the like period of time, beginning with the year 1760, the baptiſms were 37, and the burials 21. The inhabitants were then about 158, from which the ſituation appears to be very healthy, and that the people are increaſing.

ABSTON and WICK

IS a pariſh in the hundred of Pucklechurch, five miles weſt from Marſhfield, ſeven ſouth from Sodbury, ſeven eaſt from Briſtol, and ſeven north-weſt from Bath. It is bounded on the north by Puckle-

Pucklechurch, on the eaſt by Dointon and Cold Aſton, on the weſt by Siſton, and on the ſouth-eaſt by part of Somerſetſhire. The houſes lie chiefly under the weſt ſide of that ridge of hills which runs from north-eaſt to ſouth-weſt through the county.

The great poſt and turnpike-road from London to Briſtol leads through Wick, and there is beſide, a turnpike-road from Bath, by the monument on Lanſdown, which communicates with the Briſtol road at this place.

Abſton is probably a contraction of *Abbat's-town*; for this manor formerly belonged to the abbat of Glaſtonbury. *Wick* ſignifies a *hamlet* dependent on a place of better note; for in antient grants and charters of townſhips, after the name, it commonly follows, *cum ſuis berwicis*, which favours the above conjecture.

The pariſh conſiſts chiefly of good paſture and meadow ground. Three diſtinct ſtreams, *i.e.* the Filtham, riſing in Pucklechurch; a brook from Dyrham, and another from Tog-hill, empty themſelves into the river Boyd; and in the ſtreet at Wick, the old bridge having lately been taken down, a more commodious one of four arches hath been erected in its room, at the charge of the commiſſioners of the Briſtol turnpikes.

Between this pariſh and that of Dointon, is a deep, narrow glyn, formed by rocks of a ſtupendous height, riſing almoſt perpendicularly from the bottom, where the river Boyd runs. On the Dointon ſide are large fortifications and intrenchments oppoſed by others on the ſide of the glyn, in this pariſh. The ſtone of the rocks I am ſpeaking of, is of a compact texture, of which the inhabitants burn great quantities into excellent white lime. And there is in the neighbourhood, a blue kind of ſtone, which makes a brown lime, that hardens under water, and anſwers the purpoſe of foreign terras.

They dig coal in this pariſh, and burn large quantities of it into coak, for making of malt, and other purpoſes. Here is alſo lead ore, but the proprietors have not hitherto raiſed enough of it to anſwer the working. Belemnites, aſtroites, and ſerpentine ſtones are likewiſe found here, and ſome of the rocks have a ſparry ſubſtance upon them, which ſir Robert Atkyns calls rock-diamonds; but this ſpar is not ſo beautifully brilliant as that commonly called Briſtol ſtones, found in the rocks about Clifton.

This village deſervedly ſtands one of the foremoſt in the neighbourhood on account of its antiquities, as well as its natural productions. Sir Robert Atkyns, in the four laſt lines of his account of it, mentions, "that great quantities of Roman or Britiſh brick have been dug up in an adjacent field, where appear alſo the extended ruins of conſiderable buildings".

Since the publication of ſir Robert Atkyns's Hiſtory, other antiquities have been found in a field called Beach, in the hamlet of Wick, by people at plough, in the year 1743, who turned up with the ſoil a quantity of brick, very hard and ponderous, and much ſuperior in fineneſs to what we now make. Mr. Haynes, the proprietor of the ground, cauſed the ſurface, for a conſiderable ſpace, to be laid open, and preſently found that theſe were parts of a brick pillar. There were three foundations of ſuch pillars ſtanding in a line, each twenty-one inches ſquare. The intervals were thirteen inches. The third pillar ſtood againſt the middle of an abutment, or foundation of rough ſtone-work, meaſuring five feet and a half in front, which being carried on in the ſame direction with the pillars, about twenty-two inches, then ſpread itſelf outwards on each ſide in a concave ſweep.

Between the pillars, in beds of mortar, were parts of ſeveral urns of fine red pottery, but of different ſhapes and dimenſions, ſome pieces of wood burnt to a coal, a crooked ſacrificing knife, about ſix inches long, and the jaw bone of a ſheep or goat. And ſome time afterwards, the capital, or head of a pillar of freeſtone, about two feet ſquare, with the cornice, was turned up by the plough in the ſame field. From theſe remains, and from a great number of Roman coins found there, which are in Mr. Haynes's poſſeſſion, there can be no doubt of this having been a Roman work. For as the Romans had poſſeſſed themſelves of Bath, to which they gave the name of *Aqua Solis*, where they formed a ſtation; and had alſo made incurſions and conqueſts on the other ſide of the Severn, in the country of the Silures, it was neceſſary to preſerve a free intercourſe between thoſe places. The route by land from *Aqua Solis* to the paſſage over the Severn, leading to that country, lay in a ſtraight line through this pariſh; and from theſe fields where the ruins were found, is a full view of the country towards the paſſage, or *Trajectus* of Antoninus. This therefore was a proper ſituation for a garriſon, by which intelligence might be communicated from one ſtation to another.

The late Mr. Richard Haynes, who was lord of the manor, and reſided here, contended very ſtrongly that this was the *Abone* of Antoninus, which he endeavoured to make out by ſuppoſing miſtakes in the diſtances, and that the ſtations are tranſpoſed in Antoninus's *Itinerary*. But he was certainly miſtaken, as may be ſeen under Lidney, where the ſubject of the *Abone* is diſcuſſed more at large.

There is a field in this pariſh called the *Cheſtles*, or *Caſtles*, where are three large ſtones about five feet high from the ground, drawn thither from the cliffs below, and placed upright pretty near together, in a triangular form. They are without inſcriptions, but one of them having been taken down, at the foot of it were found ſome old coins, a circumſtance more eſpecially denoting them to be monumental; but to what age or people they are to be attributed, is not eaſy to determine.

determine. It is ſuppoſed, however, that they were placed there after the time of the Romans, as a memorial for ſome chiefs who fell in battle in this part of the country; and their number, and nearneſs to Dyrham, an adjoining village, lead me to conjecture that they ſtand for the three Britiſh princes whom Ceaulin the Saxon ſlew in a bloody battle, as mentioned under that place, in the year 577. But what could induce Mr. Donn to call theſe *druidical* ſtones, in his accurate map of the environs of the city of Briſtol, is to me unaccountable, ſince neither hiſtory nor tradition favours that notion.

I muſt not omit to mention a memorable battle fought in the time of the civil war, on the 5th of July, 1643. Lord Hopton, prince Maurice, and the earl of Carnarvon drew up the king's forces upon Tog-hill, part of which is in this pariſh, to engage the parliament's forces on Lanſdown, under the command of ſir William Waller. The fight laſted from two in the afternoon 'till one the next morning, when the latter quitted the field, leaving lighted matches on the hedges to ſecure their retreat. But an accident prevented the king's army from improving the victory, for their powder blew up and wounded many officers, among whom was lord Hopton himſelf. Sir Bevil Grenvil was mortally wounded, which occaſioned the titles of earl of Bath and viſcount Lanſdown being conferred on his ſon, by king Charles the Second, after the reſtoration. That earl built the monument on Lanſdown, on which is an inſcription, now much obliterated, but it may be ſeen in lord Clarendon's hiſtory of that war, giving ſome particulars of this battle.

Of the Manor and other Eſtates.

In *Domeſday-book* the manor of Abſton and Wick is not diſtinguiſhed by any particular name, but included in the account of the large pariſh of Pucklechurch, to which it belonged, and which was then held by the abbey of Glaſtonbury, having been given to it by king Edward the Confeſſor. But when king Richard the Firſt was priſoner at Vienna, the emperor Leopold obliged him to annex that abbey to the ſee of Bath and Wells, and to give that biſhoprick to Savaricus the emperor's kinſman. And in the year 1205, the monks of Glaſtonbury quitted their right in the manors of Pucklechurch, Abſton, and Weſterleigh, and in the patronage of ſeveral churches, to that biſhoprick, upon condition that Joceline the biſhop would reſtore to them the election of their own abbat.

The ſucceſſive biſhops of Bath and Wells held Abſton and Wick, without interruption, above two hundred and fifty years; but the records ſhew, that Hugh Dennis levied a fine thereof 11 H. 7. However this manor belonged to the ſame biſhoprick 37 H. 8. when the king purchaſed it, together with the advowſon of the rectory, and Friers wood in Abſton, of William, then biſhop of Bath and Wells; and granted it the ſame year to John Wintour, with all rights of court leet, and court of the manor, which have been kept in uſe to this time from the poſſeſſion of the Wintour family, under the ſtile, as ſpecified in the court rolls, of the court leet and court of the manor of Wick and Abſton.

Maurice Dennis died ſeized of this manor 5 Eliz. and was ſucceeded by Walter Dennis his brother and heir, who was at that time ſixty years old, as appears by the eſcheator's inquiſition.

Sir Edward Wintour was lord of this manor in the year 1608. Sir John Wintour, ſon of ſir Edward, granted it away 8 C. 1. and by divers meſne conveyances it was aſſigned to Mr. Thomas Haynes, in the year 1665.

Richard Haynes, eſq; ſon of Thomas, was lord of this manor when ſir Robert Atkyns compiled his Hiſtory. He was ſucceeded by his ſon Thomas Haynes, whoſe ſon, Richard Haynes, eſq; is the preſent proprietor. The anceſtors of this family, many generations paſt, were ſeized of Southmead in the pariſh of Weſtbury upon Trim, but after purchaſing Wick and Abſton in the laſt century, they have reſided here.

Lands in Nether Wyke and Over Wyke, which belonged to Cript hoſpital near Briſtol, and other lands which belonged to Weſtbury college, were all granted to ſir Ralph Sadler, 35 H. 8.

The hamlets in this pariſh are,

1. *Berdwic*, now written Wick.

2. *Holy Brook*, ſo called from a ſpring dedicated to the holy virgin.

3. *Churchley*, which obtained that name from an antient chapel, dedicated to St. Bartholomew, now intirely ruined. John de Button was ſeized of Churchley 7 E. 2. Robert Grinder was ſeized of it 22 H. 6. when it was reputed a manor; and ſir John Bar was ſeized of it 22 E. 4.

4. *Bridge-Yate*. 5. *Tog-hill*.

Of the Church, &c.

The church is in the deanery of Hawkeſbury. It is annexed to Pucklechurch. It pays 1*s.* 6*d.* for pentecoſtals.

All corn tithes are paid in kind, all others by *modus*. Sir Robert Atkyns mentions, "that the tithes of hay in Wyke did belong to the priory of Bradenſtoke in Wiltſhire," and that "theſe tithes were granted to the dean and chapter of Briſtol, 34 H. 8." But the grant he refers to, relates to Wick in Berkeley, and not to this pariſh.

The church, which is dedicated to St. James, ſtands in Abſton. It conſiſts of one aile, handſomely pewed, with a neat gallery at the weſt end, where the tower ſtands, adorned with pinnacles.

Clerk and patron the ſame as at Pucklechurch.

Monuments and Inſcriptions.

On a flat ſtone in the church. In a lozenge, *Party per pale, baron and femme,* 1. *Argent, on a feſs gules three bezants, between as many demy hinds azure,*

azure, for Haynes. 2. Obliterated. Beneath, this inſcription :

Here lyeth the body of Mrs. Mary Haines, the widdow and relict of Mr. Thomas Haynes of the city of Briſtol, lord of this mannor, who deceaſed the XVIII day of May, A. Dni. MDCCIX, aged LXXX years.

On another flat ſtone is an inſcription for Samuel Woodward, gent. who died July 2, 1648. Under, a ſcutcheon bearing three chevronels, but the colours, &c. are not expreſſed. And beneath the ſcutcheon, a memorial for Mrs. Mary Seede, widow, formerly wife of the ſaid Mr. Woodward. She died Sept. 14, 1695.

In the church-yard, on a head-ſtone,

Here lieth the body of Robert Collins of this pariſh, mathematician, who died the 21ſt of Jan. 1733, in the 62d year of his age.

On a flat ſtone, for Edward Strange, of Deinton, the following lines, which I have inſerted on account of their merit :

Vain king of Terrors, boaſt no more
Thine antient, wide extended pow'r ;
Each ſaint in life, with Chriſt his head,
Shall reign, when thou thyſelf art dead.

Benefactions.

Chriſtopher Cadle, by his will dated 1662, deviſed money to purchaſe lands, and erect a houſe for four poor people ; and a ground and houſe at Holy-Brook were provided and ſettled according to the will.

William Hart, clerk, has given 20*s.* yearly for two ſermons.

John Hathway hath given a rent-charge of 10*s.* yearly, to the uſe of poor houſekeepers.

Beloved Wilks, who died in the year 1727, left a part of his houſe in Wick, for the habitation of two clergymen's widows, to be choſen by the miniſters of Pucklechurch, Deinton, and Dyrham, with 10*l.* a year, and half a load of coal to each. With the overplus of his eſtate, a lad, to be choſen out of the above mentioned pariſhes, is to be maintained at the univerſity 'till he takes the degree of batchelor of arts. He has given 15*s.* a year to be ſpent at the annual meeting of the truſtees and widows.

Mr. Thomas Stephens, ſometime alderman of Briſtol, hath endowed two hoſpitals in Briſtol, with lands in this pariſh. And other lands have been purchaſed with Mr. Langton's money for the uſe of the poor of Dyrham and Deinton. See Dyrham.

In a ſeries of ten years from 1700 to 1709, both incluſive, there are regiſtered 76 baptiſms and 56 burials. In a like ſeries from 1760 to 1769, there are alſo regiſtered 92 baptiſms and 86 burials. About the year 1710, when ſir Robert Atkyns was compiling his hiſtory, it is ſaid this pariſh contained 50 families, and about 230 inhabitants, whereof 8 were freeholders. There are now (1772) about 400 inhabitants ; ſo that the people have conſiderably increaſed here ſince the beginning of this century.

ACTON, *or* IRON-ACTON,

LIES in the vale, the greater part of it in the hundred of Thornbury ; but the hamlet in this pariſh diſtinguiſhed by the additional name of *Ilger*, is in the hundred of Grumbald's-aſh. The church ſtands three miles W. from Chipping-Sodbury, ſeven ſouthward from Thornbury, nine north-eaſtward from Briſtol, and about twenty-nine ſouth-weſtward from Glouceſter.

The foreſt of Kingſwood extended over a large tract of land in this country, and the place of which I am writing is ſaid to have been much over-run with the oak-tree, whence it is ſuppoſed to derive its name ; for Acton, from the Saxon word Ac, is the ſame in ſignification with Oak-town. The great quantities of iron-cinders, lying about in ſeveral places, ſhew that here were formerly iron-works, which probably ceaſed for want of wood to carry them on, for here is ſtill great plenty of ore ; hence it has ſometimes been called *Iron-Acton*, to diſtinguiſh it from *Acton-Turville*, in the hundred of Grumbald's-aſh. There is alſo a coal-pit now in work. The pariſh conſiſts almoſt equally of paſturage and of arable ground. It lies on the verge of that country which is one vaſt continued bed of coal ; but I cannot learn that it is remarkable for any other natural productions beſide the foſſils already mentioned. The river Froome, riſing at Dodington, receives the brook Laden at this place, and runs to Briſtol, where it forms the key of that port.

Of the Manor and other Eſtates.

Before the Norman conqueſt this pariſh conſiſted of two manors. Sir Robert Atkyns erroneouſly prefixed an abſtract of the *Domeſday* account of Cold Aſton to this place, which he has adapted to it by writing the name *Actune*, inſtead of *Eſcetone*, as I read it in my copy of that record. And other writers, following him, have been equally miſtaken in ſaying that the church of St. Peter at Bath held this manor in the reigns of the confeſſor and conqueror. Sir Robert Atkyns has indeed, added a paraphraſtic account of ſome of the particulars of the manor of Actune from *Domeſday-book* ; but the following is a literal tranſlation, referring, by the figures at the end, to the page of this book where the *Domeſday* account is printed, in the language, and as nearly as could be done with common printing types, after the manner of the original.

'Hunfridus the chamberlain holds Actune in 'Bacheſtanes hundred. Heroldus a [free] man 'of Aluui of Hereford held it, who could go 'where he would. There are two hides and a 'half. In demean is one plow-tillage, and three 'villeins, and three bordars, with half a plow-'tillage. There are two *ſervi*, and a mill and a 'half of ſixty-four pence, and five acres of 'meadow. It is worth, and was worth 40 'ſhillings. *Domeſday-book*, p. 79.

Leland says, 'the erles of Heriford were once lords of Acton lordshippe.' John de Acton was probably descended from them, and took his surname from this place of his residence, according to the custom of early times. He was seized of the manor of Actune at the beginning of the reign of H. 3. and it appears by a record 15° E. 1. that he and his ancestors had enjoyed it time immemorial. His grandson John de Acton was seized of Iron-Acton, with court-leet, gallows and tumbrel 15° E. 1. which privileges were allowed him in a writ of *Quo warranto* brought against him that year. The statute of *Quo warranto*, in this, and some of the subsequent reigns, proved an excellent instrument by which to extort money from the subject; for the king being chief lord of many manors and possessions, of which the deeds, charters, and other evidences were frequently lost or destroyed in those days, by civil wars, length of time, or other casualties; it became a common practice, under colour of promoting the good purposes of that law, to put men upon the most rigorous proof of their right to their estates, in which if they failed by any accident, their lands were resumed by the crown, or very heavy fines exacted from the owners for permission to enjoy them. This accounts for the many writs of *Quo warranto* occasionally mentioned in the subsequent parts of this work.

John de Acton, son of the last mentioned John, was high-sheriff of Gloucestershire 4° E. 2. and dying seized of this manor in the eighth year of that reign, was succeeded by George de Acton; who forfeited his estate in the rebellion against king Edward the Second to expel the Spencers. Hugh le Despencer obtained a grant, and levied a fine of this manor 18° E. 2. but John de Acton, (son of George) was restored to all his father's lands 1° E. 3. being then under age.

Richard de Bellers held Iron-Acton 3° E. 3. probably in right of guardianship, for he was then also seized of the manor of Elkstone, which belonged to the Actons. The last mentioned John de Acton was knighted, and dying seized of those manors without issue, 17° E. 3. his cousin and heiress Maud, by marrying with sir Nicholas Poyntz, brought them into that name and family; for sir John Poyntz, son of sir Nicholas and Maud his wife, succeeded to those estates as heir to his mother.

This family of Poyntz, or Ponz, descended from Drogo, son of de Ponz, an antient family of Normandy. Three brothers, Walter, Drogo or Drew, and Richard, assisted the conqueror in his invasion of England. Walter, grandson of Drogo, resided at Clifford castle in Herefordshire, and thence took the name of Clifford; but the younger branch of Gloucestershire still retained the name of Poyntz.

Robert Poyntz held the manor of Iron-Acton of Hugh earl of Stafford, as of his manor of Thornbury, by one knight's-fee 10° R. 2. He married Catherine daughter and coheir of Thomas Fitz Nicholas, a branch of the Berkeley family.

Nicholas Poyntz, son of Robert, married, first, Elizabeth daughter of Henry Hassey of Sussex; and secondly Elizabeth daughter of sir Edward Mills of Harscombe, and dying 29° H. 6. was succeeded by

John Poyntz, his son by the second wife, who married Alice daughter of — Cox of Skynvraith, in Monmouthshire; and dying 5° E. 4. was also succeeded by his son

Sir Robert Poyntz, who married Margaret the natural daughter of Anthony Woodvil, earl of Rivers, and died in the year 1519.

Sir Anthony Poyntz, his son, married Elizabeth daughter and coheiress of sir William Hudfield of Devonshire.

Sir Nicholas Poyntz, son of sir Anthony, married Joan daughter of Thomas lord Berkeley, and dying seized of Iron-Acton 4° Mar. was succeeded by his son

Sir Nicholas Poyntz, who had to his first wife Anne daughter of sir Ralph Verney, of Penley in Hertfordshire; but she dying, he married, secondly, Margaret daughter of Henry earl of Derby.

Sir John Poyntz (son of the last sir Nicholas by his first wife) succeeded his father, and married Ursula daughter of John Sidenham, of Brampton in Somersetshire. He was seized of this manor in the year 1608. His son

Sir Robert Poyntz was made one of the knights of the Bath, at the coronation of king Charles the First. He wrote a treatise in vindication of monarchy, and dying in the year 1665, was buried with his ancestors in Acton church. He had two wives, but no male issue by the first. His second wife was Cicely daughter of Mr. Smith, by whom he had his son and successor,

Sir John Poyntz, who married Anne daughter of Mr. Cæsar of Hampshire. He died in the year 1680, and left Acton to his widow, of whom it was purchased by William Player, esq; after it had continued in the family near six hundred years; for it passed by descent from the Actons to the Poyntzs, who were very eminent in Gloucestershire, where they have many times served the office of high sheriff, as may be seen by the list in the former part of this book. The arms of Poyntz are, *Barry of eight, Or and gules.*

Sir Samuel Astry bought the manor of Iron-Acton of Mr. Player, and left the inheritance of it by will to his widow, who was afterwards married to Simon Harcourt, esq. It came afterwards to sir Philip Parker, from whom it descended to Walter Long, of South Wraxall, in the county of Wilts, esq; who is the present lord of the manor.

Mr. King is possessed of Acton-lodge, a considerable estate of the Poyntz's in this parish; and the late Mr. Liston, his uncle, used to hold a court-baron, as I am informed, but it was discontinued before his death.

Other

Other lands in Iron-Acton belonged to various perfons, of which the following account is drawn from the records. Thomas Brook and Joan his wife levied a fine of lands in Iron-Acton to Ralph Purceval and Edmund Pine 15° R. 2. He died 5° H. 5. feized of other lands here; and Joan his widow died 15° H. 6. feized alfo of three yard-lands, twelve acres of meadow, and ten acres of pafture in Iron-Acton.

Thomas Cheddre was feized of divers meffuages in Iron-Acton 21° H. 6. And Joan his daughter, widow of John Talbot vifcount Lifle, died feized of thofe lands 7° E. 4. and fir Humphry Talbot levied a fine of them 15° E. 4.

William earl marfhal and of Nottingham levied a fine of lands in Iron-Acton and Acton-Ilger to Edward Willoughby and Robert Legg 3° H. 7.

A meffuage in Iron-Acton belonged to the Magdalen hofpital in Briftol, and was granted to Edward Brain and John Marfh 37° H. 8.

HAMLETS. There are two hamlets in this parifh.

1. *Acton-Ilger*, which lies in the hundred of Grumbald's-afh, and has a diftinct tything-man. The cognomen was taken from Ilger or Algar, who held this as a manor in the reign of William the conqueror, as I find it in the record, of which the following is a tranflation:

'The bifhop of St. Laud [in Conftance] holds 'Actune in Bacheftanes hundred, and Ilgerus '[holds it] of him. There are two hides and a 'half. In demean is one plow-tillage; and four 'villeins and five bordars, and one *fervus*, and two '*ancillæ* with one plow-tillage and a half. There 'is[the] half [fhare of] a mill of fixteen pence, and 'ten acres of meadow, and one furlong of wood. 'It is worth and was worth 40*s*. Ebbi, a [free] 'man of Brictric the fon of Algar, held this 'manor. *Domefday-book*, p. 70.

This tything lies very much intermixed with Iron-Acton. Clofe to the church-yard weftward lies the parfonage, in Iron-Acton; and clofe to it alfo eaftward ftands an antient houfe called the old inn, which is in Acton-Ilger. It is obfervable that Iron-Acton and Acton-Ilger both lay in Bacheftanes hundred, as recorded in *Domefday-book*. But Thornbury hundred being erected fince that time, was taken out of the old hundreds of Bacheftanes and Edereftan, more efpecially where the lords of Thornbury had property.

Ofbert Giffard and Alice Mordack were feized of this manor 31° H. 3.

Maurice, fon of Thomas de Berkeley held Acton-Ilger 42° E. 3. and fir Thomas de Berkeley and Margaret his wife were feized of this manor 5° H. 5. Richard de Beauchamp earl of Warwick married Elizabeth the only daughter and heirefs of that fir Thomas de Berkeley, lord Berkeley, and in her right died feized of this manor 17° H. 6. Thomas Cheddre was feized of it 21°. H. 6. Joan one of his daughters, and widow of John Talbot vifcount Lifle, died feized hereof 7° E. 4. And Margaret countefs of Shrewfbury was feized of Acton-Ilger the fame year.

2. *Lateridge* or *Ladenridge*, fo called on account of its lying on a high ridge of land on the north-weft of the brook Laden, over which, a few years fince, a bridge was built at the expence of the county.

Of the Church, &c.

The church is a rectory, in the deanery of Hawkefbury, worth about 200*l*. a year. The patronage is in the dean and chapter of Chrift-church, Oxford. Jofeph Jane, B. D. is the prefent incumbent. Forty acres belong to the glebe. The church is dedicated to St. James. It hath a fouth-aile, and a tower at the weft end, remarkably large and maffy. It feems not to have been raifed nearly to the height intended, as may be concluded from the fmallnefs of the pinnacles, the fudden contraction of the upper ftory, and the difproportion of the height to the bulk. On the fouth fide of the chancel is a vault belonging to the manor-houfe, where fome of the family of Poyntz are buried.

Firft fruits, £.	16 : 10 : 0	Synodals, - £.	0 : 2 : 0
Tenths, —	1 : 13 : 0	Pentecoftals,	0 : 0 : 8
Procurations,	0 : 6 : 8		

Benefactions.

Mr. Humphry Brown of Briftol, merchant, has given 10*s*. yearly to the minifter, for a fermon on the feftival of St. John Baptift; and 40*s*. yearly to the poor, payable by the mayor of Briftol. He alfo gave a pulpit-cloth, cufhion, filver flaggon, and chalice. Mr. Edward Brinkworth gave 20*l*. to the poor. Mr. John Brinkworth gave 20*l*. Mr. John Mortimer, (who died in 1701) rector of this church, gave 20*l*. and Mr. Simon Sloper gave 10*l*. to the poor.

In the year 1761 the parifh paid to the poor 187*l*. 3*s*. 9*d*. and from that time the poor-tax hath been gradually encreafing, fo that in 1767 it came to 232*l*. 18*s*. 8*d*.

Iron-Acton.

Taxes.	The Royal Aid in	1692,	£.	119 : 0 : 0
	Poll-tax —	1694, —		27 : 13 : 0
	Land-tax —	1694, —		157 : 18 : 0
	The fame —	1770, —		105 : 13 : 6

Acton-Ilger.

Taxes.	The Royal Aid in	1692,	£.	25 : 13 : 4
	Poll-tax ——	1694, —		8 : 4 : 0
	Land-tax ——	1694, —		25 : 16 : 0
	The fame ——	1770, —		20 : 6 : 9

According to fir Robert Atkyns, when he compiled his account of this parifh, there were 60 houfes and about 240 inhabitants, whereof 24 were freeholders; the yearly births were 10, and the burials 8. But upon examining the parifh-regifter, I find that in a feries of ten years from 1700

1700 to 1709 both incluſive, there were regiſtered 112 baptiſms and 80 burials; and in a like ſeries from 1760 to 1769 incluſive, there were entered 205 baptiſms, and 115 burials: And upon a calculation that one in forty dies annually, the whole number of people will be found to be 460; ſo that the inhabitants are increaſing very faſt in this pariſh.

◇◇◇◇◇◇◇◇◇◇◇◇◇◇◇◇◇◇◇◇◇◇

ACTON-TURVILLE.

THIS is a ſmall village in the hill country, within the hundred of Grumbald's-aſh. It is bounded on the ſouth-eaſtward by Wiltſhire, and lies about five miles E. from Chipping-Sodbury, five N. from Marſhfield, and about twenty-eight S. from Glouceſter. The lands are chiefly arable, with ſome paſture. Conſiſtent with the etymology of the preceding pariſh, it may be ſuppoſed that the oak-tree grew ſo plentifully here as to give the place the name of Acton; but it received the additional name of Turville from the family of the Turbervilles, who were the antient lords of the manor.

In the middle of the place ſtands a ſmall ſtone building, remarkable not only for its antiquity, but for its having been a ſanctuary, as it is ſaid, dedicated to the virgin Mary, ſuppoſed to have been built by one of our Saxon kings. Churches were ſanctuaries very antiently in England The fifth law of king Ina enacted, that *If any one be guilty of a capital crime, and flee to the church, let him have his life; but let him make ſatisfaction, as right directs. If any one forfeit his hyde, and flee to the church, let his laſhes be forgiven him.* The clergy of the church to which the criminal fled were bound to provide victuals for him while in ſanctuary. He had liberty of going thirty paces from the church, and forty if it were a cathedral. All but clerks, here in England, who took the privilege of ſanctuary for greater crimes, were bound to ſwear that they would leave the kingdom, and not return without royal licence. After taking this oath, they were to go by the direct road to the next port, and embark by the firſt opportunity, and while they were in that road they were deemed to be in ſanctuary. But the reader may ſee more of theſe matters in the 13th page of this book.

Of the Manor and other Eſtates.

Among the particulars belonging to Ernulfus de Heſding, in the hundred of Grimboldeſtou in Glouceſterſhire, Achetone is one ſet down in the record, which may be thus tranſlated:

'The ſame Hernulfus holds Achetone. There 'are five hides taxed. Edricus held it. In de'mean are three plow-tillages; and four villeins, 'and three bordars, with four plow-tillages. 'There are fifteen acres of meadow. It is worth, 'and was worth 100*s*. *Domeſday-book*, p. 77.

Richard Turberville was ſeized of this manor 12° and 15° E. 1. and it had then obtained the name of Turberville, ſo that it muſt have been in that family ſoon after the conqueſt.

Richard earl of Arundel held Acton-Turberville 30° E. 1. John de la Rivere was ſeized thereof 8° E. 2. And it was held by knight-ſervice of Edward earl of Kent 4° E. 3. Sir John Drayton died ſeiſed of this manor 5° H. 5. and William St. Loe had livery thereof granted to him 2° Eliz.

The earl of Shrewſbury was lord of the manor in the year 1608. It came afterwards to Henry Cavendiſh, duke of Newcaſtle, who granted it to ſir John Top, from whom it deſcended to ſir John Top, late of Tormarton. He had two daughters, one of them married to —— Hungerford, eſq; whoſe ſon John Hungerford, of Dingley-hall in Northamptonſhire, eſq; is the preſent lord of the manor.

Richard Verney had livery of divers lands in this pariſh, 2° Eilz.

Of the Church, &c.

The church is a vicarage in the deanery of Hawkeſbury. It was united to Tormarton in the year 1344, and the rector of Tormarton had the preſentation, but it is now in the crown, by lapſe. The glebe lands are worth about 15*l*. a year, and the vicar has the ſmall tithes. Mrs. Adey of Old Sodbury is the impropriator. Philip Bliſs, M. A. incumbent.

The church is ſmall, with a low tower in the middle.

Firſt fruits, £	6 : 13 : 4	Synodals £.	0 : 2 : 0
Tenths, ——	13 : 4	Pentecoſtals,	0 : 0 : 10
Procurations -	6 : 8		

Taxes.	The Royal Aid in	1692, £.	42 : 17 : 4
	Poll-tax — —	1694, —	4 : 17 : 0
	Land-tax ——	1694, —	35 : 0 : 0
	The ſame, at 3*s*. --	1770, —	27 : 18 : 3

According to ſir Robert Atkyns, when he compiled his account of this pariſh, there were 20 houſes and about 80 inhabitants, and the yearly births were 2, and burials 2. About the year 1747 there were 85 inhabitants; and in a ſeries of ten years from 1760 to 1769 incluſive, the regiſtered baptiſms are 43, burials 20; ſo that population increaſes, and the number of ſouls is about 90.

◇◇◇◇◇◇◇◇◇◇◇◇◇◇◇◇◇◇◇◇◇◇

ADLESTROP, *or* ÆDELSTHORP,

IS a village in the hundred of Slaughter, pleaſantly ſituated on the gentle ſlope of a hill, with a ſouth aſpect; three miles north-eaſtward from Stow, ten S. E. from Campden, and twenty-eight N. E. from Glouceſter. It is bounded on the eaſt by Oxfordſhire, with the pariſh of Evenlode in Worceſterſhire, to the northward; and the river of of the ſame name divides it from Broadwell on the weſt, and Oddington on the ſouth. It was antiently written Eadleſthorp, Tadleſtrop, Tedeſtrop, and in ſome old writings Caſtlethorp; and it is ſaid that in the charter of Egwine, biſhop of Worceſter, who founded the abbey of Eveſham in the year 700, to which this manor belonged, the name is written Tiddleſtrop. The diverſity of writing the name occaſions ſome doubt as to the etymology of it; but it is the common received opinion, that as in the Anglo-Saxon language Æðel ſignifies a nobleman, and ðorp a village or habitation, it was ſo called becauſe it had been the place of reſidence of ſome noble Saxon; and that the others are corrupt modes of writing the ſame name. But as to Caſtlethorp, it was probably ſo called from a round fortification, ſuppoſed to be Daniſh, called Caſtlebarrow, upon Caſtleton-hill, near the boundaries of this pariſh.

Of the Manor and other Eſtates.

As the church of Eveſham was originally endowed with this manor, ſo at the time of the general ſurvey, in the reign of William the Firſt, it belonged to that abbey, as appears by the record, where, under Salemones hundred, it is thus ſaid:

'The ſame church [St. Mary of Eveſham] holds 'Tedeſtrop. There are ſeven hides. In demean 'are two plow-tillages; and ten villeins, and two 'bordars, with three plow-tillages. There are 'four *ſervi*, and one knight with two plow-til'lages. There is a little meadow. It was worth '4*l.* now 100*s.* *Domeſday-book*, p. 72.

The church of Eveſham continued in poſſeſſion of this manor 'till the time of the diſſolution of monaſteries. That abbey was dedicated to the Virgin Mary, and valued at 1268*l.* 9*s.* 9*d.*

After the diſſolution, the manor and the tithes were granted to ſir Thomas Leigh, 7° E. 6.

The anceſtors of this family aſſumed their name from the town of High-leigh in Cheſhire, where they were ſeated before the Norman invaſion. Collins deduces their pedigree, with many particulars, which, for want of room, are not admiſſible in this place, from Hamon, lord of the mediety of High-leigh, whoſe ſon William was father of Richard, who had for his ſon another Richard, who had a daughter Agnes.

This Agnes, by her ſecond huſband, William Venables of Bradwell, had iſſue John, who took the name of Leigh after his mother, but bore his father's arms, and died in 1322; leaving, by Ellen his wife, three ſons, John, Robert, and Peter; and according to ſome accounts, he had another ſon William by a ſecond wife.

Robert, the ſecond ſon, was of Adlington in Cheſhire, whoſe eldeſt ſon was ſir Robert Leigh, and his ſecond ſon ſir Peter Leigh, of Maxfield, who by his wife Margaret, daughter and heir of ſir Thomas Dangers, had a ſon ſir Peter Leigh, who was made a knight banneret, and was ſlain at the battle of Agincourt, 1415.

This ſir Peter Leigh, knight banneret, married Cecilie daughter of John del Hagh, and had by her a ſon John, and two daughters. John was eſcheator of Cheſhire in the reign of H. 6. and marrying Alice daughter and heir of Thomas Alcock, had three ſons, Roger, Richard, and John.

Richard the ſecond ſon left iſſue Roger, who had two ſons; William the eldeſt was ſeated at Wollington in Shropſhire, and at Ruſhall in Staffordſhire, but Thomas the younger brother of William was bred up under ſir Rowland Hill, a rich merchant and lord mayor of London, who having no child, gave him in marriage his favourite niece Alice Barker, on whoſe iſſue he entailed the greateſt part of his eſtate.

This Thomas Leigh was one of the ſheriffs of London in the year 1555, and lord mayor of that city at the death of queen Mary, and during his mayoralty was knighted. He had by his lady three ſons, Rowland, Thomas, and William; and four daughters. Thomas the ſecond ſon is the anceſtor of the preſent Edward Leigh, lord Leigh of Stoneley. William was father of lord Dunſmore, afterward raiſed by king C. 1. to the higher dignity of earl of Chicheſter, which title, for want of a male heir, became extinct at his death in the year 1653.

Rowland the eldeſt ſon was largely provided for at Longborough in this county, and other places, by ſir Rowland Hill his god-father. He married a daughter of ſir Richard Berkeley of Stoke-Gifford, by whom he had iſſue ſir William Leigh, who died in the year 1631, and was ſucceeded by his ſon William Leigh, eſq; of Adleſtrop, who dying in the year 1690, was ſucceeded by his ſon

Theophilus Leigh, eſq; who married a daughter of —— Craven. His ſecond wife was Mary daughter of James lord Chandois, by whom he had William Leigh, eſq; who was ſucceeded in this eſtate by his eldeſt ſon James Leigh, eſq; the preſent lord of the manor of Adleſtrop. He married Caroline the only daughter of his grace the late duke of Chandois. He hath greatly repaired and enlarged the old family ſeat, in the Gothick taſte, and reſides here. His arms are, *Gules, a croſs engrailed argent, a lozenge in the dexter chief of the ſecond.*

Of the Church, &c.

The church is a rectory, annexed to Broadwell, in the deanery of Stow. They are worth together about 350*l.* a year. Dr. Johnſon, who was rector of this church, built a parſonage-houſe in the year 1670, on which he expended 1500*l.* James Leigh, eſq; is patron; his brother, Mr. Thomas Leigh, incumbent.

The advowſon of the chapel of Adleſtrop was formerly in the abbat of Eveſham, who by an antient reſervation in the year 1450, received 6*l.* yearly of the rector, which is now paid to the patron. After the diſſolution of religious houſes, the advowſon of the chapel of Adleſtrop was granted to Richard Andrews, 37 H. 8. Two

 yard-

yard-lands belong to the glebe. The demeans pay no tithe of hay.

The church hath been twice rebuilt in the ſpace of a few years, owing to the unſkilfulneſs of the workmen employed in the firſt rebuilding. The inhabitants formerly buried at Broadwell, but in the year 1590, the anceſtors of Mr. Leigh gave land for a church-yard, and procured it to be conſecrated. In the chancel are memorials for ſeveral perſons of Mr. Leigh's family.

Benefactions.

Mr. Thomas Barker, who formerly reſided here, gave 20*l.* a year to the uſe of the poor.

Lady Turner, ſiſter of the preſent lord of the manor, by her will in the year 1770, amongſt other legacies of the ſame kind, gave 50*l.* to the poor of this place.

Taxes.			£.	s.	d.
	The Royal Aid in	1692, £.	79	11	4
	Poll-tax — —	1694, —	32	3	0
	Land-tax — -	1694, —	93	16	8
	The ſame - —	1770, —	57	3	9

When ſir Robert Atkyns compiled his hiſtory, there were 34 houſes, and about 200 inhabitants, which is nearly the preſent ſtate of this pariſh.

ALDERLEY,

IS a ſmall pariſh in the hundred of Grumbald's-aſh, ſeated on a riſing ground, yet ſheltered every way by the hills that ſurround it, except on the weſt and ſouth-weſt ſides; whence it commands a fine proſpect of the village of Kingſwood, and other parts of the vale. It lies three miles ſouth from Wotton-under-edge, eleven weſtward from Tetbury, and about twenty-two ſouthward from Glouceſter. It was antiently the utmoſt bounds of the foreſt of Kingſwood.

To inveſtigate the ſignification of the name is no leſs difficult than to fix, with certainty, the moſt antient and original manner of writing it. For ſome centuries back it hath been written Alderſley, and Alderleigh, differing very little from the modern orthography; all which ſeem to be compoſed of the Anglo-ſaxon words Ealdor or Aldor, older, and Ley, a paſture ground. But I offer this as a mere conjecture, as it may be objected, that more antiently, in *Domeſday-book*, the name is written *Alrelie*, which doth not favour this etymology.

Upon the hill, eaſtward and ſouth-eaſtward of the village, are found petrifications of ſeveral marine ſubſtances, as the oiſter and cockle, in great abundance; but this pariſh produces nothing remarkable, or rare, in the vegetable world.

It hath been matter of doubt with ſome perſons, how ſo many ſhell-fiſh, and other productions of the great deep, ſhould be intermixt with the materials of our higheſt hills, at ſuch a diſtance from the ſea; but it is now generally allowed to have been the effect of the univerſal deluge, and to furniſh the ſtrongeſt arguments for that great event that can be drawn from nature. This ſubject hath been largely handled by Dr. Woodward, Mr. Catcott, and other eminent perſons, to whoſe writings the curious are referred.

This pariſh is hilly, and the lands are pretty equally divided into paſture and arable. The ſoil is good, in ſome parts naturally, in others 'tis made ſo by cultivation, and the air is healthy. Two ſmall brooks bound the pariſh on the north and ſouth, and joining, are called in antient evidences the Avon, and run from this place to Berkeley.

The clothing buſineſs hath been ſettled here ſome hundreds of years ſince. Leland, in his Itinerary, calls Alderſley a clothing village; but that buſineſs hath lately been declining in the whole neighbourhood. The ſame author, among the memorable things taken notice of by him, informs us, that in the year 1225, a man of Adderlay, which I take to be intended for this place, feigned himſelf to be Chriſt, and for his moſt infamous preſumption was carried to Oxford, and there crucified.

But Alderley is moſt remarkable for being the birth place of that great and ſolid lawyer, ſir Matthew Hale, lord chief juſtice of the king's bench. He was (ſaith a learned author, who hath nearly thus drawn his character) a perſon eminent for his piety, learning, and juſtice. His piety was manifeſt by his excellent Private Contemplations, publiſhed at the importunity of others, and by his conſtant attendance on public divine ſervice on ſundays, from which he was not once abſent in thirty-ſix years. His learning is evident by his laborious works, ſome of which are depoſited in Lincoln's-inn library. His juſtice and integrity could never be warped by private intereſt, nor attachments, which often prove too powerful for human nature to withſtand. He lived in the time of the greateſt civil commotion this country ever knew, when envy and inveteracy ſullied the moſt reſpectable characters; yet he carried himſelf ſo uprightly as to be equally admired and eſteemed by all ranks and conditions of men. If Glouceſterſhire hath not produced ſo many eminent perſons as ſome other counties, yet this great man may well go for many, *Quantum inſtar in ipſo eſt!*

Of the Manor and other Eſtates.

Milo Criſpin held ſeveral eſtates in Glouceſterſhire at the time of the general ſurvey, for in *Domeſday-book* it is thus recorded:

'The ſame Milo [Criſpin] holds Alrelie 'in Grimboldeſtou hundred. Wigot held it. 'There is one hide. In demean are two plow-'tillages; and ſeven villeins, and five bordars, 'with ſeven plow-tillages. There are four *ſervi*, 'and a mill of 10*s.* [value,] and twelve acres 'of meadow. It is worth and was worth '100*s.*' *Domeſday-book*, p. 78.

Leland

Leland ſpeaking of this manor, ſays, 'the Chanſeys were ſumtyme lords of it, as in Edward the Third's days.' *Itin.* vol. 7. p. 90.

Robert Stanſhaw, eſq; was ſeized of the manor of Alderleigh 12 E. 4. Joan the widow of Robert Stanſhaw being married to John Bodiſaunt, they both joined in a fine of the manor and advowſon of Alderleigh, to Richard Becket and others 14 H. 7.

John Poyntz, ſon of ſir Robert Poyntz, and younger brother of ſir Anthony Poyntz of Acton, became lord of the manor of Alderley. He married Catherine, daughter of ſir Matthew Browne of Surrey, and dying 36 H. 8. was ſucceeded by his ſon

Matthew Poyntz, who married Winnifred, one of the daughters and coheirs of Henry Wild, of Camberwell. Robert Poyntz, his younger brother, was a learned author, and a great zealot for the Roman catholic religion.

Nicholas Poyntz, ſon of Matthew, was lord of this manor in the year 1608. He married Anne, daughter of ſir Maurice Berkeley, of Bruton in Somerſetſhire. From him it deſcended to his ſon

Robert Poyntz, who ſold it to one Mr. Rogers.

Mr. Barker, of Fairford, purchaſed this manor of Mr. Rogers, and conveyed it to ſir Matthew Hale, in exchange for Meiſey-Hampton.

Matthew Hale, eſq; deſcended from ſir Matthew Hale, lord chief juſtice of the king's bench, is the preſent proprietor of this manor, and hath a handſome ſeat near the church. His arms are, *Argent, a feſs ſable, in chief three mullets of the ſecond.* This family is of antient ſtanding in the county, and hath always been eſteemed for their probity and charity.

Of the Church, &c.

The church is a rectory, in the deanery of Hawkeſbury, worth 70*l.* a year. Mr. Hale is patron, Mr. Draper the incumbent.

The church is ſmall but neat, and hath a tower at the weſt end, with pinnacles, and an aile on the north ſide, and a ſmall aile on the north ſide of the chancel, belonging to Mr. Hale.

On the left of a window, in the ſouth wall of the church, is a ſmall effigy, with a crown on its head; and the figure of a biſhop, with his mitre, ſtands on the other ſide of the window, in the ſame wall. Theſe are ſuppoſed to repreſent the antient founders of the church; but tradition doth not ſay who they were.

Firſt fruits, £	11	4	6	Synodals, £.	0	1	0
Tenths, —	1	2	5	Pentecoſtals,	0	0	10
Procurations,	0	6	8				

Monuments and Inſcriptions.

Lord chief juſtice Hale was buried in the church-yard, for whom there is a neat monument of black and white marble, with this memorial:

Hic inhumatur corpus Mathæi Hale, militis, (Roberti Hale, et Ioannæ uxoris ejus, filii unici) nati in hâc parochia de Alderly 1° Nov. 1609, denati vero ibidem 25 Dec. 1676, Ætat. ſuæ 67.

There are alſo ſeveral other tombs and memorials for perſons of this family.

Taxes.					
The Royal Aid in	1692, £.	65	0	0
Poll-tax — —	1694, —	20	1	0
Land-tax ——	1694, —	72	12	0
The ſame, at 3*s.* —	1770, —	44	15	0

There are about 157 inhabitants in this pariſh.

ALDERTON *and* DIXTON.

ALDERTON is a pariſh in the upper part of the hundred of Tewkeſbury, and Dixton is a hamlet within it. Alderton lies ſeven miles eaſt of Tewkeſbury, four miles north-weſt from Winchcombe, and about fifteen north-eaſtward from Glouceſter. It ſeems to have been ſo called from the Saxon word Alᵭoꞃ, older, and the common termination ton, becauſe, in reſpect to Dixton, it is the more antient place. It is a ſmall village in the vale part of the county, conſiſting chiefly of rich tillage land, with ſome paſture, and affords nothing remarkable, except only, that on the top of Dixton hill, which ſtands ſingly in the vale, are intrenchments thrown up, not unlikely in the time of the Saxon wars.

It is mentioned by ſir Robert Atkyns, that 'near 'the weſt end of a wood belonging to Mr. Hig-'ford, a great quantity of wood and trees, from 'the top of a hill, parted and ſlipt away out of 'this county into Worceſterſhire.' But upon inquiry, I find that ſir Robert had been miſinformed in reſpect of the trees reſting in that county.

This pariſh is reputed to be within the juriſdiction of the honour of Glouceſter. A brook runs through it into the Carant below Beckford, and the turnpike-road from Tewkeſbury to London leads through the pariſh.

Of the Manor and other Eſtates.

In *Domeſday-book*, under the head *Terra Regis*, it is thus recorded:

'Dunning held ſix hides and a half in Aldri-'tone, and four hides and a half in Dridedone, 'and a thane held one hide in Hundeuuic. Hun-'fridus held theſe lands of the king, and he had 'there four plow-tillages in demean; and five 'villeins and eight bordars with three plow-til-'lages, and one radchenifter with one plow-'tillage, and one burgeſs in Wi'combe, and 'there were twelve acres of meadow. The whole 'was worth 11*l.* in the time of king Edward, 'and is now worth 6*l.* *Domeſday-book*, p. 68.

Brictric the ſon of Algar was a great thane, and held the manor of Tedekeſberie, in the reign of king Edward the confeſſor, and was the chief lord of this eſtate at Aldritone, and many others thereabout.

But the abbey of Winchcombe had an eſtate in this pariſh ſoon after the conqueſt, for among the poſſeſſions of that abbey in Greteſtanes hundred, it is thus recorded:

'The

'The fame church [St. Mary de Wincelcumbe] 'holds Aldritone, and a certain knight [holds it] 'of the abbat. There are two hides and a half, 'and two plow-tillages in demean; and one 'villein with one plow-tillage, and there may 'be three befides. There are four *fervi*. It was 'worth and is worth 30*s*. *Domefday-book*, p. 71.

Thus the record fhews that this place was then in fo rude a ftate, that lands fufficient for three plow-tillages were uncultivated; and immediately after, under Niwetone in the parifh of Afhchurch, it is faid, that fix other plow-tillages might be made there; fo that the country muft have been very thinly inhabited, to fuffer fo fine a part of it to remain neglected.

This manor antiently belonged to the Dickleftons, who took their name from Diclefton, or Dickleſton, or Dixton, the place of their refidence. William Dickleſton held the manors of Dickleſton and Aldrington in the reign of E. 3. John Dickleſton held the fame 12 H. 4. Margaret the widow of John Dickleſton, and Thomas their fon, were feized of the manor of Dickleſton, and of the advowfon of the church of Aldrington 6 H. 5. Sir John Dickleſton, brother to Thomas, fucceeded him, and died feized thereof 1 H. 6 leaving only female iffue. John Hugford, efq; married Elizabeth one of his daughters, and had with her the manor of Dickleſton.

The manor of Aldrington came afterwards into the family of the Tracies. Sir William Tracy, of Todington, was feized thereof in the reign of H. 7. William Tracy his fon died feized of Aldrington 20 H. 8. But this eftate did not remain long with the Tracies, for

John Hugford had livery of the manors of Dickfton and Alurinton 3 E. 6. and they have continued in the fame name ever fince, fo that the reverend Mr. Henry Higford is the prefent lord thereof.

The Higfords are a very antient family in Shropfhire, and were formerly called Hugford. Robert Hugford was controller to Thomas Beauchamp earl of Warwick, and much in his favour, which brought him out of Shropfhire, to fettle at Empfcot in Warwickfhire, which he purchafed of Richard Revel 9 H. 4. John Hugford, fon of Robert, married Elizabeth, daughter and coheirefs of fir John Dickleſton, and was fucceeded by his fon John, who married the daughter of Norman Wafhborn. Thomas Hugford, fon of the laft John, married Ifabel, daughter of fir Thomas Hungerford of Down-Ampney. William Hugford, fon of Thomas, married Margaret, daughter of —— Horgan of Selrin in Somerfetfhire, and dying 37 H. 8. was fucceeded by John Hugford his fon, who married Elizabeth, daughter of Edward Fetiplace of Befhefley in Berkfhire, and was fucceeded by his fon John, who married Dorothy, daughter of William Rogers of Dowdefwell, and was lord of this manor in the year 1608. William his fon (who wrote his name Higford) married Mary, daughter of John Meulx of the ifle of Wight, and had a fon John, born in the year 1607. James Higford was lord of this manor in the year 1712, who was fucceeded by his brother Henry, rector of this parifh; to whom fucceeded William, father of the late William Higford, M. D. who was fucceeded by his brother the reverend Mr. Henry Higford, the prefent rector of this parifh, and lord of the manors of Alderton and Dixton. His arms are, *Vert, on a chevron between three bucks heads cabofhed Or, as many mullets gules*. By this account it appears, that the manor of Dixton has continued in the fame family upwards of four hundred years, whereof it has been more than three hundred in the name of Hugford, or Higford.

William de Ditchford levied a fine of a moiety of lands in Aldrington, to Joan the widow of John Newington, and others, 5 E. 2.

Two meffuages in Aldrington and Dixton, formerly belonging to the abbey of Tewkefbury, were granted to Richard Gunter 36 H. 8.

HAMLET. Dickleſton, or Dixton, is a hamlet in this parifh, the fame, I apprehend, which in *Domefday-book* is written Dridedone, as in the beginning of this account. It ftands about a mile weftward from the church, on the fide of a hill, and was formerly called Caftle-hill, from the intrenchments there.

Mr. Higford has a large, handfome houfe here, built of ftone. In the hall windows are the following arms painted on the glafs, *viz.*

1. *Quarterly*, 1ft and 4th, Hugford as before, 2d and 3d, *Sable, a pile argent*. Thefe are impaled with, 1ft and 4th, *Argent, two chevrons gules*, for Fettiplace. 2d and 3d *quarterly*, 1ft and 4th, *Argent, three befants*. 2d and 3d, *Sable, a lion paffant argent*. And beneath is written HUGGEFORD and FETTIPLACE.

2. *Argent, two bars gules; in chief three cinquefoils fable, in the fefs point a mullet for difference*, for Denton;—impaled with, *quarterly of fix*, 1ft *Argent, a chevron between three etoiles of eight points fable*, for Mordaunt. 2d, *Gules, a crofs patonce Or*. 3d, *Or, an eagle difplayed argent*. 4th, *Argent, on a bend fable* the bearing obliterated. 5th, *Quarterly per pale indented, Or and gules, in the firft and fourth quarter a mullet of the fecond*. 6th, Mordaunt. Beneath the fcutcheon, in antient letters, DENTON and MORDAUNT.

3. *Quarterly*, 1ft and 4th, Hugford. 2d and 3d, *Sable, a pile argent*;—impaling, *quarterly*, 1ft and 4th, *Or, a greyhound courant fable, between three leopards heads cabofhed azure*, for Hennege; 2d and 3d, *Gules, three garbs Or*.

There is a chapel near the houfe dedicated to All Saints, but now difufed, and fallen to decay.

Of the Church, &c.

The church is a rectory, in the deanery of Campden, worth about 120*l*. a year. The reverend

reverend Mr. Henry Higford is patron and incumbent. The rectory pays 20*s.* yearly to the crown. In Willis's edition of *Ecton's Theſaurus* it is ſaid, *Abb. Tewkſbury* xx*s.* *Patrono* liii*s.* iv*d.* *Abb. Winchcomb* iv*s.* viii*d.*

The church is ſmall, and hath an aile on the ſouth ſide, and a low tower, with battlements, at the weſt end, and ſix bells in it. It is dedicated to St. Margaret. The Higfords arms are painted in the chancel window.

William Higford, eſq; a very ingenious poet, died 1657, and lies buried in the chancel. He had his education in the univerſity of Oxford, and left behind him a large manuſcript of *Inſtitutions* to his grandſon, which were epitomiſed and publiſhed by Clement Barkſdale.

The family of the Higfords are buried in the chancel, without any monuments or inſcriptions.

In the year 1373, this pariſh had a licence granted to bury *Villanos tantum apud Alerington, et quod rector habeat omnes oblationes funerales, pro quibus ſolvat* 2*s.* *ſacriſto de Winchcombe, in feſto Sti. Kenelmi, ſalva ſepultura mortuorum in villa Dixton abbat. Winchcombe.*

Firſt fruits, £. 22	2	9	Synodals, £. 0	2	0
Tenths, — 2	4	2	Pentecoſtals, 0	0	9
Procurations, 0	6	8			

Benefactions.

William Higford, eſq; in the reign of H. 8. gave 6*l.* 3*s.* 1*d.* yearly, charged on his eſtate, to repair the utenſils and ornaments of the church. The church-wardens, in memory of this charity, are to pay annually at Michaelmas, a couple of capons to the heirs of Mr. Higford. — Henry Tovey gave by will 40*s.* to the poor for ever. — John Page, in the year 1610, gave 12*l.* to the uſe of the poor for ever.

Taxes.					
The Royal Aid in	1692, £.	178	0	0
Poll-tax — —	1694, —	19	10	0
Land-tax ——	1694, —	95	4	0
——— at 3*s.* —	1770, —	49	19	0
——— for Dixton	1770, —	30	9	0

There are about 172 inhabitants in this pariſh.

A L D S W O R T H.

THIS pariſh lies in the Coteſwold country, on the turnpike-road from Bath, through Cirenceſter, to Oxford, ten miles north-eaſtward from Cirenceſter, ſeven ſouth-weſtward from Burford in Oxfordſhire, about twenty-three eaſt from Glouceſter, through Northleach, from which it is diſtant four miles. The houſes ſtand near together, on the north ſide of the turnpike-road, on a gentle riſing ground.

In *Domeſday-book* the name is written *Aldeſwrde*, and *Aldeſorde*, and comes either from Alꝺ, old, and ƿoꞃð, a village, ſtreet, croft, farm, court, or place; or elſe, the former part of the word is the name of ſome antient proprietor of the manor; and, in that ſenſe, it is the ſame as *Alde's* court, or place: For, as *villa* among the Romans implied the houſe of a nobleman, within his own eſtate, ſo did ʒueoꞃð, or worth, among the Saxons.

The lands are chiefly arable, with ſome paſture. This village affords nothing worthy the notice of the naturaliſt, or traveller; but the downs in the neighbourhood, part of which are in this pariſh, afford excellent ſport to thoſe that delight in hunting.

Of the Manor and other Eſtates.

In *Domeſday-book* it thus expreſſed:

'Elward the ſon of Reinbald holds Aldeſwrde 'in Becheberie hundred. Balchi held it. There 'are two hides taxed. In demean is one plow-'tillage; and four villeins, and two bordars, with 'two plow-tillages, and one *ſervus*. It was worth '40*s.* now 30*s.*' *Domeſday-book*, p. 71.

But the church of Glouceſter held a larger eſtate in this pariſh, for in the ſame record, under the head *Terra S. Petri de Glowec'.* in Begebriges hundred, it is ſaid:

'The ſame church holds Aldeſorde. There 'are eleven hides, and three plow-tillages in 'demean; and twenty-one villeins, and five 'bordars, and two *francigeni*, with fifteen plow-'tillages. There are ſix *ſervi*. It was worth '100*s.* now 8*l.*' *Domeſday-book*, p. 79.

This manor belonged to the abbey of Glouceſter 17 E. 3. It was in the crown in the year 1608; but James Lenox Dutton, eſq; who reſides at Sherborne in this county, is the preſent lord thereof.

Divers lands in Aldeſworth, with common for 300 ſheep, and a portion of tithes lately belonging to the abbey of Cirenceſter, were granted to Richard Andrews, and Nicholas Temple, in truſt for others, 34 H. 8.

William Coley died ſeized of a farm called Wall, in Aldſworth, with tithes of lamb and wool, 4 Mar. Eſcheator's inquiſition.

Of the Church, &c.

The church is in the peculiar of Bibury. The rectory, and advowſon of the vicarage, belonged to the monaſtery of Oſney, and were granted to the chapter of Oxford, 34 H. 8. who are the impropriators. There are about 250 acres of glebe. Portions of the tithe of Aldeſword, formerly belonging to the abbey of Glouceſter, were granted to the biſhoprick of Glouceſter 33 H. 8. and were confirmed by another grant 6 E. 6. The curacy is worth 20*l.* a year, beſides the tithe of cows and calves, Eaſter-offerings, garden-pence, and the rent of two little houſes. The impropriation pays 6*s.* 8*d.* a year to the crown.

The church is dedicated to St. Peter, and hath a handſome ſpire, which ſhews itſelf to advantage,

 ſtanding

ſtanding upon high ground. There are three cottages given to repair the church.

Taxes.					
The Royal Aid in	1692, £.	58	6	4
Poll-tax — —	1694, —	11	2	0
Land-tax ——	1694, —	75	7	0
The ſame at 3s. —	1770, —	56	7	3

About the year 1710, according to ſir Robert Atkyns, there were 30 houſes, and about 120 inhabitants in this pariſh; yearly births 4, burials 3. Upon examining the regiſter, I find that in ten years, from 1701 to 1710, there were entered 53 baptiſms, and 31 burials; and from 1760 to 1769 incluſive, there were 49 baptiſms, and 34 burials, ſo that population continues in the ſame ſtate nearly, as it was in the beginning of this century.

ALMONDSBURY.

THIS is a large pariſh, in the vale part of the county, conſiſting of four tithings, of which only the tithing of Almondſbury lies in the lower part of the hundred of Berkeley. The other three lie in other hundreds, as will be ſhewn hereafter. The church ſtands in the tithing of Almondſbury, eight miles north from Briſtol, ten weſt from Chipping-Sodbury, and twenty-nine ſouth-weſtward from Glouceſter.

It is ſaid to derive its name from Alcmond, a Weſt-Saxon prince, father of Egbert, the firſt ſole monarch of England, (who is ſuppoſed to be buried in the church;) and from a fortification of a rampire and double ditch, at Knole in this pariſh; for ſuch our anceſtors called *Burghs*, and we, by frequent uſe, have ſoftened the word into *borough* and *bury*.

This camp is ſituated upon the brow of a hill, next the Severn, ſo as to command an extenſive view of that river, and every thing paſſing upon it. 'Tis ſuppoſed to be Saxon, but no mention is made of it in the Chronicle, nor by any of the antient writers. Tradition will have it to be the work of Offa, king of the Mercians, whoſe coffin the common people think was dug out of a tumulus, at Over, in this pariſh, in the year 1650, but Florilegius affirms, that he was buried at Bedford, whoſe authority, in this matter, ought to be preferred to vulgar opinion. It is however related in Mr. Wantner's papers, that at the time and place above mentioned, there were found the intire bones of two men. One of the ſkeletons was of an uncommon ſize, incloſed in a vaſt ſtone coffin, ſo artificially cemented together, that the joint was not diſcernible. The ſtone that covered the coffin was very ponderous, of a greyiſh colour without, but reddiſh, and ſtudded with a ſhining ſparry ſubſtance within. Two coins were found in the coffin, one of which bore the impreſſion of a faulcon, as the writer expreſſeth himſelf; on the other was a head, which he ſuppoſes to be that of Claudius Cæſar, but makes no mention of any inſcription. I have no doubt as to the facts, but cannot determine, from the circumſtances related, to whom the remains belong. If to a Roman, why were the bones unburnt, and no inſcription cut on the ſtone? If to a Saxon, how ſhall we account for the Roman coins found in the ſepulchre itſelf? But this is certain, ſays the writer of thoſe papers, the bones were thoſe of a man, whoſe height exceeded the ordinary ſtature by more than three feet. The corps was buried ſitting, which Drexelius ſaith was the cuſtomary manner of burying kings and princes, as an emblem of eternity.

Knole, the antient ſeat of the family of Cheſter, ſtands upon the brow of a hill, about two miles from the Severn, ſurrounded by the fortifications already mentioned, from whence there is a moſt extenſive and agreeable proſpect, over the Severn, into Monmouthſhire.

In ſo large a pariſh the ſoils muſt be various; There is more paſture than arable land, and a great deal of marſhy ground towards the river Severn. The proprietors have given an account to the commiſſioners of ſewers, that 1342 acres are more particularly liable to be overflowed by that river. *See* p. 26.

Tockington marſh-lands lie in this tithing.

It is obſervable, that neither Camden, nor his learned editor, hath taken any notice of this place.

Of the Manor and other Eſtates.

In *Domeſday-book* it is ſaid, that two hides in Almodeſbury (as it is there written) did then belong to the manor of Berchelai. *Dom. B.* p. 68.

This eſtate continued the property of the lords of Berkeley, 'till Robert Fitz-Harding, in the year 1148, founded the abbey of St. Auguſtin in Briſtol, and endowed it, among other very conſiderable eſtates, with the manor of Almondſbury. The ſame abbey held Almondſbury, with court leet, 13 and 15 E. 1. and had a charter for fairs and markets, and free-warren within it. The fair to be on Whit-monday, and to continue for ſix days; the weekly market on wedneſday. Many of the charters of markets and fairs, in this and ſome of the ſubſequent reigns, were granted only with a view of aggrandiſing the ſeignorie of thoſe manors which belonged to very eminent proprietors, and this paſſage, *Quantum in nobis eſt*, was always inſerted in the original grant. So that when it came to be diſcuſſed afterwards, before the judges itinerant, at the general aſſizes, *Quo warranto* they were held, that is to ſay, what authority there was to ſupport them, if they were found convenient and neceſſary, they were ratified and continued; but on the contrary, if they were deemed unneceſſary and ſuperfluous, they were, by the power of the law then veſted in the judges, vacated and taken away.

This

This manor continued in the abbey of St. Auguſtin 'till that houſe was diſſolved. It was afterwards granted, with a reſervation of 8*l.* 10*s.* rent, to Miles Partrige, 36 H. 8. who conveyed it to Arthur Darcy 7 E. 6. Henry Darcy had livery of it 1 Eliz. and afterwards ſold it to Thomas Cheſter.

William Cheſter, father of Thomas, was a younger branch of the Cheſters of Huntingdonſhire, and gentleman of the horſe to the duke of Buckingham, who was beheaded in the year 1522. He married Jane, the daughter of John Wear, and was mayor of Briſtol 1539.

Thomas Cheſter, who purchaſed this manor, was alſo mayor of Briſtol 1569, and was ſucceeded in this eſtate by his ſon

William Cheſter, who married Catherine, the daughter of Richard Dennis, of Dyrham.

Thomas Cheſter was ſon and heir of William. He married, firſt, Elizabeth, daughter of John Backhouſe, of Swallow-field in Berkſhire; ſecondly, Elizabeth, daughter of ſir George Speke, of Somerſetſhire, and was ſeized of this manor in the year 1608. By his ſecond wife he had

Thomas Cheſter, his ſon and heir, who married Elizabeth, daughter of ſir John Howe, of Compton, and died 1686.

Thomas Cheſter, ſon of the laſt Thomas, married Anne, daughter of ſir Samuel Aſtry, of Henbury, and was ſucceeded in this eſtate by his ſon

Thomas Cheſter, born in the year 1696, who having repreſented this county in five ſucceſſive parliaments, died at Knole, Oct. 1, 1763, without iſſue, bequeathing his eſtate to the daughter and only child of his brother Richard Howe Cheſter; who marrying William Bromley, of —— in the county of Warwick, eſq; he, by virtue of the king's mandate to the earl marſhal of England, aſſumes the name and arms of Cheſter. Other particulars of the laſt mentioned Thomas Cheſter, eſq; are largely expreſſed in the well written memorial for him, printed in the courſe of this account. It remains only to be obſerved, that his relict is the preſent poſſeſſor of Almondſbury and Knole.

William de Gale held the manor of Knowl, of Brimpsfield caſtle, 7 E. 3. John St. Loe, eſq; was ſeized of it, and of Barton hundred, of the foreſt of Kingſwood, and of the fiſhing in Stapleton, 5 H. 6.

Thomas Hill died ſeized of lands in Almondſbury 6 Car. and left Edward his ſon fourteen years old.

TITHINGS and *HAMLETS.*

The other tithings are 1. *Over.* 2. *Hempton* and *Patchway.* 3. *Gaunt's Urcot.* of which in their order.

1. *Over* lies in the hundred of Langley and Swineſhead, about a mile and a half weſtward from the church, and has a diſtinct peace officer. What ſir Robert Atkyns ſays of Ethelric granting thirty meſſuages in Overe to St. Peter of Glouceſter, ſhould be underſtood of Over near that city, and not of this place.

This tithing is not expreſsly named in *Domeſday-book*, but it is probable that the following particulars relate to the tithings in this large pariſh.

'Roger the ſon of Ralph holds a manor in 'Sineſhoved hundred, which Seuuin the mayor 'of Briſtou held of king Edward, and he could 'go with his land wherever he pleaſed, and he 'gave no farm [rent] for it. There are three 'hides, and ſix plow-tillages in demean; and 'ſix villeins, and ſix bordars, with two plow-'tillages. There are three *ſervi*, and eight acres 'of meadow. It was worth 100*s.* and is now '[worth] 60*s.*

'Roger hath a manor of one hide of land in 'Sineſhovedes hundred, and he hath there two '*ſervi*. There was no perſon who could anſwer 'concerning this land.

'Walter hath one manor of one yard-land. 'It was worth 20*den.* and is now worth 2*s.*' *Domeſday-book*, p. 79.

Maurice de Gaunt died ſeized of Oure 14 H. 3. which afterwards came to Robert de Gourney, his ſiſter's ſon, who died ſeized of it in the fifty-third year of that reign. Anſelm de Gourney held Over 14 E. 1. and John de Gourney died ſeized thereof 19 E. 1. From him it went to John ap Adam, who had married Elizabeth, the daughter and heir of John de Gourney. Thomas ap Adam, his ſon, ſold it to Thomas lord Berkeley, and Margaret his wife, 4 E. 3.

Catherine, the widow of Thomas de Berkeley, of Beverſtone, was ſeized of the manor of Overe, and of the advowſon of the chantry 9 R. 2. in which family it continued to ſir William Berkeley, who was attainted of treaſon, and the manor of Over was granted to Thomas Brian, and his heirs male, 2 R. 3.

From Brian the manor was conveyed to John Poyntz, whoſe grand-daughter Alice married ſir Edward Berkeley, and brought this manor again into that family. John Berkeley, grandſon of ſir Edward, was ſeized of Over 1 H. 8. From him it paſſed in a lineal deſcent to John Berkeley, who had livery thereof 20 Eliz. and ſold the manor to

John Dowel, who was the ſon of James Dowel, a wealthy merchant of Briſtol. From him it paſſed in a lineal deſcent to John Bridges Baker Dowel, eſq; who died unmarried in the year 1743, and was buried in Almondſbury church, where there is a very handſome monument, and a memorial for him, and for ſeveral of his family, which is inſerted at the end of this account.

Mr. Dowel bequeathed his whole eſtate to the reverend Mr. Degge, who had travelled with him as a tutor; and Mr. Degge dying in the year 1766, this manor, with ſeveral other large eſtates in the county, devolved to his ſiſter Mrs. Wilmott, the preſent proprietor. The manor-houſe is large and

and handſome, with a park adjoining, in which are the traces of a large round camp, ſtill viſible.

Eaſter Compton is a ſmall hamlet in this tithing.

2. *Hempton* and *Patchway* lies in the hundred of Langley and Swineſhead, about a mile and a half diſtant ſouthward from the church. This tithing is not mentioned by name in *Domeſday-book*; but it is likely that the two ſmall eſtates diſcribed in that record, and placed at the head of this account, belonged to this tithing. However that may be, it appears by the records, that Margaret, the widow of Nicholas Stanſhaw, was ſeized of the manor of Hempton 14 H. 6. but Alice, the widow of William Chedder, held it in the 34th year of that reign. John Baker was ſeized of Hempton and Patchway 1608. Mrs. Wilmott has a good eſtate at Hempton; but Mr. Cheſter has the chief eſtate at Patchway.

Woodland is a hamlet in this tithing, where Mrs. Tace has a good houſe.

3. *Gaunt's Urcot*, ſo called from the family of Gaunt, lies in the hundred of Thornbury, near three meaſured miles eaſtward from the church. This is ſaid to be within the juriſdiction of the court of the honour of Glouceſter. In *Domeſday-book* it is thus expreſſed:

'The ſame biſhop [of St. Laud in Conſtance] 'holds Herdicote, in Langelie hundred, and Robert holds it of him. Cuulf held it in the time 'of king Edward. There are two hides taxed, 'and two plow-tillages in demean, and two bordars, and four *ſervi*, and four villeins, and ten 'acres of meadow, and a wood. It is worth and 'was worth 40*s*.' *Domeſday-book*, p. 71.

This manor antiently belonged to Gilbert de Gaunt, whoſe ſiſter's ſon and heir, Richard de Gourney, founded an hoſpital in his manor-houſe called Bilſwick, and gave this manor to it; which hoſpital being diſſolved, the manor of Gaunt's Urcot was granted to the city of Briſtol, for public uſes, 33 H. 8. and the mayor and commonalty of that city are the preſent lords of this manor. The Gaunt's hoſpital was originally founded for a hundred poor people. It ſtands within the liberties of the city of Briſtol, was refounded in the reign of queen Elizabeth, and now entertains the blue-coat-boys.

Within this manor is a farm called St. Swithin's chapel, ſurrounded with a moat. The body of the chapel and the chancel were lately ſtanding, but the croſs building which was at the weſt end, ſuppoſed to have been the prieſt's lodging, hath been long ſince taken down, and the foundation new built upon. The inhabitants hereabout talk of an abbey dedicated to St. Swithin, that ſtood not far from it, but there are no traces of it to be found. Mr. Edgar is the preſent proprietor of the farm

Brokenborow is a place within this tithing, where a chantry was erected in the ſame year as the abbey of St. Auguſtin was founded, and the patronage of it given to that abbey. John Harold was the laſt incumbent, and had a penſion of 4*l*. according to Mr. Willis. Lands lying in Almondſbury, formerly belonging to this chantry, were granted to Richard Moor, and Thomas Monford, 6 Jac. Brokenborow was a reputed manor, for William Turner, and Alice his wife, and her anceſtors, were found by an inquiſition, 9 H. 6. to have been ſeized, time out of mind, of the manor of Brokenborow, with the alternate preſentation to the chantry, which they ſettled on Thomas his younger ſon. This manor paſſed to Thomas Ivy, who was ſeized of it 4 H. 8. Thomas lord Berkeley had livery of it 24 H. 8. and Henry lord Berkeley ſold the fourth part of it to John Holliſter, and others, 6 Eliz.

Of the Church, &c.

The church is a vicarage, in the deanery of Briſtol, worth about 70*l*. a year. It is one of the diſcharged livings, valued in the king's books 40*l*. 13*s*. 10*d*. The biſhop of Briſtol is patron, Mr. Taſwell incumbent. The rectory, and advowſon of the vicarage of Almondſbury, belonged to the abbey of St. Auguſtin, in Briſtol, and that houſe being diſſolved, were granted to Paul, biſhop of Briſtol, and his ſucceſſors, 34 H. 8. In a ſurvey about that time, they were valued at 18*l*. 15*s*. *Willis*. This was the mother-church to Filton and Elberton.

The church is large, and handſome, with an aile on each ſide, of the ſame height and length with the body. It hath a ſpire in the middle, with croſs ailes on each ſide, and is dedicated to the virgin Mary. The church and ſpire are covered with lead. The chancel is handſomely wainſcotted ſix feet high, with an altar-piece of Dutch-oak, ornamented with fluted pillaſters and capitals of the Corinthian order, and enriched with carvings and inlaid work, by a good hand. The communion-table is of grey marble, about ſix feet long. In the ſteeple are eight bells, and a clock.

Monuments and Inſcriptions.

In the north croſs aile, upon a raiſed tomb, is the effigy, as it is ſuppoſed, of one of the abbats of St. Auguſtin, without any inſcription.

In the ſame aile, which belongs to the Cheſter family, againſt the wall, is a very elegant pyramidal monument of Egyptian marble. In front ſtands a beautiful female figure, in a looſe robe, leaning her arm on a vaſe, in whoſe countenance the paſſion of grief is excellently expreſt. Above, a drawn curtain diſcovers the arms of the deceaſed, *Gules, a lion paſſant ermine, between three lures argent*. In the feſs point a ſcutcheon of pretence, *Gules, on a feſs argent, a lion paſſant azure, between three boars heads couped Or*. Motto, POST FUNERA VIRTUS. And below, upon a large table, is the following inſcription:

To

To the Memory of Thomas Cheſter Eſq; and in Record of his Anceſtry.

Arthur Cheſter, Gent. was buried	June	17,	1603.
William Cheſter, Eſq; - - - - -	Oct.	13,	1607.
William Cheſter, Gent. - - - -	Oct.	18,	1638.
Thomas Cheſter, Eſq; - - - - -	Nov.	24,	1653.
Dominick Cheſter, Gent. - - - -	Mar.	19,	1669.
William Cheſter, Gent. - - - -	Oct.	6,	1675.
George Cheſter, Gent. - - - - -	Sept.	22,	1685.
Thomas Cheſter, Eſq; - - - - -	Feb.	26,	1686.
Thomas Cheſter, Eſq; - - - - -	Feb.	26,	1703.

The Succeſſion of this Lineage was cloſed in the Death of THOMAS CHESTER, Eſq; late of Knole, Son of the laſt recorded of this Name. He was by unanimous Suffrage of his County called up to be KNIGHT of the SHIRE in five ſucceſſive Parliaments; and on his own Part did the Honour that became him to their Choice, by the moſt inflexible Attachment to what he thought the true Intereſts of his Country. From theſe he could never be prevailed on to ſwerve, nor during ſo long a Service by one Vote, or conniving Abſence, to deſert, or diſappoint the Expectations of his Conſtituents.

His Country muſt long ago lament in Him the Loſs of a moſt upright and uſeful Magiſtrate. Juſtice was his conſtant Object, temper'd only with Compaſſion, as Occaſion called it forth; which his benevolent Heart would never ſuffer Him to eſtrange himſelf from; but never was he to be biaſſed by any ſiniſter View, or private Intereſt, from the Execution of his proper Duty.

Nor was He leſs amiable in his private Character, than reſpectable in his public; Under every Connection in which He ſtood, anſwering with his beſt Powers to its reſpective Duties, and ſuſtaining in Character, as in the different Scenes of Life they aroſe upon Him, the *Neighbour*, the *Friend*, the *Brother*, the *Huſband*, with no leſs Eſteem, Honour and Virtue —— than the MAGISTRATE and SENATOR: a Truth, which cannot better be evinced, than by the great and heart-impreſs'd Grief that not only attended his Loſs, but has faithfully adhered to his Memory; and which, as long as any Traces of it ſhall remain with Thoſe who had the Happineſs to know Him, will more than anſwer This, or any Other Record that can be given of Him.

His firſt Wife was the Right Honourable SARAH HENRIETTA, the only Daughter of HENRY Earl of SUFFOLK and BINDON, by PENELOPE, Daughter of the Earl of THOMOND, who was buried April 6, 1722. In 1735 He married MARY, the Widow of GEORGE GUINNET, Eſq; of Shurdington in this County, and Daughter and Heireſs of JEREMY ———— Eſq; of London.

He died on the 1ſt of October, 1763, and having no Iſſue, left his Eſtate to his Niece ELIZABETH LUCY CHESTER, Wife of WILLIAM BROMLEY CHESTER, Eſq; and only Child of his Brother RICHARD CHESTER, Eſq; who died on the 15th of July, 1760, and lies alſo near Him.

MARY CHESTER, his ſurviving Widow, deeply afflicted for his Loſs, and venerating his Memory and Virtues, took upon herſelf the Care and Direction of this Monument.

In the ſame aile are inſcriptions for others of this family, but nothing very obſervable in them.

In the ſouth croſs aile, upon a large raiſed tomb, lie the effigies, in full proportion, of a man in armour, with ſpurs on, and of a woman, in the dreſs of the age in which they lived. There is a canopy of ſtone-work over them, ſupported by ſix fluted pillars and two pillaſters, about five feet high; and againſt the wall, on a table, it is thus written, in capital letters:

HERE LYETH THE BODIES OF EDWARD VEELE ESQVIER WHO WAS BVRIED THE 9 OF SEP. 1577. AND OF KATHERINE HYS WYFE WHO DEPARTED THYS LYFE THE 7 OF NOVEM: 1575:

ΜΑΚΑΡΙΟΙ ΟΙ ΝΕΚΡΟΙ.

QVIS VIR ITA VIVAT VT NON VIDEAT MORTEM.

ALL FLESH YS GRASS.

Over all, on a ſcutcheon, *Argent, on a bend ſable, three calves Or*, for Veel, quartered with a great many other arms of families who have married with the Veels. This Edward was of the family of the Veels of Tortworth, who were ſometime lords of the manor of Over, in this pariſh.

In the ſame aile ſtands a very large pyramidal marble monument, with this inſcription:

To the Memory of JOHN BAKER DOWELL, Eſq; and ELIZABETH his Wife, whoſe Bodys are depoſited in a new Vault made for them under the middle Iſle of this Church; together with three of their Children that dyed Infants. The ſaid JOHN BAKER DOWELL, Eſq; was the Son of JOHN DOWELL, Eſq; Lord of the Mannour of *Over* in this Pariſh, by MARY his Wife, one of the four Daughters and Coheireſſes of Sir JOHN BAKER, Baronet, the laſt of his Family, Lord of the Mannours of *Siſſingherſte*, *Compton*, *Comden*, *Stone*, *Stapleherſte*, and *Blithcourt*, all in the County of *Kent*, and departed this Life the twentieth Day of October MDCCXXXVIII. The ſaid ELIZABETH DOWELL was the Daughter and ſole Heireſs of JOHN BROWNING of *Coley*, Eſq; by ELIZABETH his Wife, Siſter and Coheireſs of ROBERT BRIDGES of *Woodcheſter*, Eſq; both in the County of *Glouceſter*; and departed this Life the thirty-firſt Day of December MDCCXXV.

To his well-deſerving Parents, JOHN BRIDGES BAKER DOWELL, Eſq; cauſed this Monument to be erected.

The Family of the DOWELLS, Aunceſtors by the Father's Side of the ſaid JOHN BAKER DOWELL, Eſq; are depoſited in their Vault underneath this Monument. The Body of JOHN BRIDGES BAKER DOWELL, Eſq; who erected this Monument, and departed this Life March the XXXI. MDCCXXXXIIII, is alſo depoſited in the ſame Vault with his Parents.

Upon the Monument are the following arms: *Argent, within a bordure, a lion rampant, ſable*; for Dowell. —— *Quarterly*, 1ſt and 4th, Dowell, as before; 2d and 3d, *On a feſs ingrailed, three roſes, between as many lures*, (the colours not diſtinguiſhable) for Baker. Over all, on a ſcutcheon of pretence, *Argent, three bars wavy, azure*, for Browning. —— On a ſeparate ſcutcheon, the arms of Baker, as before.

On a ſtone in the church-yard is this inſcription:

Here lies alas! long to be lamented, BENJAMIN DOBINS, Gent. who left his Friends ſorrowing, Feb: 2, 1760. Aged 42.

The coſtly Marble may, perhaps, expreſs,
In lying Lines, th' Unworthy's Worthineſs:
Thy humble Stone ſhall this ſad Truth convey,
The beſt belov'd is ſooneſt call'd away.
Full ſhort, but full of Honour, was thy Span,
Thou tender Huſband, and thou honeſt Man.

Firſt fruits, £	20	0	0	Synodals, £.	0	1	0
Tenths, —	2	0	0	Pentecoſtals,	0	1	6
Procurations,	0	6	8				

Benefactions.

Lands of the yearly Value of 60*l.* are given to the church, and about 6*l.* yearly are given to the poor.

Almondſbury.

Taxes.	The Royal Aid in	1692,	£.	129	18	0
	Poll-tax — —	1694,	—	25	8	0
	Land-tax ——	1694,	—	103	8	0
	The ſame, at 3*s.* —	1770,	—	77	11	0

Over.

Taxes.	The Royal Aid in	1692,	£.	70	14	8
	Poll-tax — —	1694,	—	13	7	0
	Land-tax — -	1694,	—	62	12	0
	The ſame, at 3*s.*	1770,	—	52	3	0

Hempton and Patchway.

Taxes.	The Royal Aid in	1692,	£.	122	16	0
	Poll-tax — —	1694,	—	16	13	8
	Land-tax ——	1694,	—	152	4	0
	The ſame, at 3*s.* —	1770,	—	114	3	0

Gaunt's Urcot.

Taxes.					
The Royal Aid, in	1692, £.	45	12	0
Poll-tax — —	1694, —	9	1	0
Land-tax ——	1694, —	53	1	0
The ſame, at 3*s.* -	1770, —	40	1	9

According to ſir Robert Atkyns, when he publiſhed his account of this pariſh, there were 132 houſes, and about 530 inhabitants. The preſent ſtate of population was not received when this account went to the preſs, wherefore it muſt be given in the *Addenda.*

ALVESTON, *vulgarly* ALLISTON.

THIS pariſh lies in the vale, in the hundred of Langley and Swineſhead, eight miles and a half north-eaſt from Briſtol, two miles and a half ſouth-weſt from Thornbury, and about twenty-eight ſouthward from Glouceſter. It is bounded on the weſt by Almondſbury.

There is a ſteep deſcent as from a hill, on the ſide next the Severn. On the top is a large, round camp, called the *Old Abbey,* over-looking that river, but how it obtained the name is uncertain. There are many camps in this neighbourhood, and many engagements muſt have happened hereabout, in early times, betwixt our anceſtors and their enemies; for the effects of them are ſtill viſible in the barrows thrown up in different places. About a hundred years ago, ſeveral ſtone coffins were dug out of one of thoſe barrows, near the above fortifications, in which were the bones of the chief perſons, perhaps, who fell in ſome battle. There is an account, in the preceding pariſh, of ſtone coffins, with bones, having been taken out of a tumulus at Over. In ſhort, there are few pariſhes in this county that do not exhibit ſome veſtiges of camps and barrows, but hiſtory is ſilent concerning moſt of them.

The houſes in this village ſtand a mile diſtant from the church. A turnpike-road from Glouceſter to Briſtol, leads thro' the pariſh.

In *Domeſday-book* the name is written *Alweſtan,* and *Alveſtone.* It is now generally pronounced *Alliſton.* The etymology is difficult, and uncertain. If *Alfe's* town, or *Alve's* town, (as being the property of ſome perſon of that name) be not the true explanation, I cannot give a better.

Of the Manor and other Eſtates.

When William the Firſt cauſed a general inquiſition to be made concerning landed property, this place was ſhared between two proprietors, of which the record gives the following account:

'Earl Herald held Alweſtan, in Langelei hundred. There were ten hides. In demean is one plow-tillage; and twenty-three villeins, and five bordars, with twenty-two plow-tillages, and two *ſervi.* The ſteward [*prepoſitus*] added two plow-tillages, and five *ſervi* there. It paid 12*l.* by weight.' *Domeſday-book.* p. 67.

All the lands which were king Harold's, at the time of the conqueſt, William ſeized for his own, and accordingly we find the above in the liſt of the king's lands. The abbey of Bath was the other proprietor.

'Saint Peter of Bath held Alveſtone, in Langelei hundred. There are five hides. Three pay taxes, [but] two of them are exempt from tax, by the grant of king Edward and king William. In demean are two plow-tillages, and nine villeins, and ſix bordars, and a prieſt, and one radchenifter, with ten plow-tillages. There are ſeven *ſervi,* and meadow and wood for the ſupport of the manor. It was worth 100*s.* now 4*l.* The ſame church holds it now.' *Domeſday-book,* p. 71.

It doth not appear when this manor was alienated from the abbey of Bath, but it was in the crown in the reign of king H. 3. who reſerved his park in Alveſton when the foreſt of Kingſwood was diſafforeſted.

It ſoon after paſſed from the crown to the family of the Fitz-Warrens; for Fulk Fitz-Warren died ſeized thereof, and left it in dower to Conſtantia de Todeni, his widow, who was alſo ſeized of it, with court-leet, view of frank-pledge, and waifs, and alſo of the hundred of Langley, 15 E. 1. Fulk Fitz-Warren, ſon of Fulk, died ſeized of Alveſton 16 E. 2. having given it to Walter of Glouceſter, one of his ſons. This Walter was ſucceeded by his ſon Walter of Glouceſter, in Alveſton and Urcot, 14 E. 3. who ſettled them in remainder, after the death of Peter his ſon, on Peter Corbet, of Siſton, who had married his daughter. By virtue of which ſettlement, they came to Margaret, daughter and coheireſs of Peter Corbet, who was married to ſir Gilbert Dennis, and ſettled theſe manors on her huſband and his heirs, whereby they came into the family of Dennis.

Sir Gilbert Dennis died ſeized of the manors of Alveſton and Urcot, and of Langley hundred, 10 H. 5. from whom they paſſed, in a lineal deſcent, to Richard Dennis, who ſold them to Maurice Shepard 19 Eliz.

Richard Haughton married the daughter and heir of Maurice Shepard, and joined with his wife in the ſale of Alveſton, to Robert Webb, 22 Eliz.

Webb ſold it to Nicholas Veel, from whoſe grandſon, Nicholas, it paſſed by purchaſe to Edward Hill, eſq; who was lord of the manor in the year 1712. But Miſs Jefferis, ſiſter of the late Mr. Cann Jefferis, is the preſent proprietor thereof.

Walter the ſheriff gave one yard-land in Alveſton to the abbey of Glouceſter 7 H. 1.

William Wiryot, and Margaret his wife, held lands within the manor of Alveſton and Urcot, 2 R. 2.

HAM-

HAMLETS. 1. *Row Urcot,* which hath been often mentioned in the account of the defcent of the manor of Alvefton, is a hamlet containing fourteen houfes.

2. *Grovefend,* or *Grovening,* lies about three miles north-eaft from the church, and confifts of about feven families.

Of the Church, &c.

The church is in the deanery of Briftol, and is annexed to Olvefton, from whence it is diftant about three miles. The building is fmall, dedicated to St. Helen, and hath a low tower at the weft end.

Monuments and Infcriptions.

There are no monuments or infcriptions worthy particular notice. Colonel Thomas Veel, who died 1663, and Nicholas Veele, efq; who died 1703, lie buried in the chancel. And fome of doctor Clayton's defcendants are alfo buried there.

Taxes.					
The Royal Aid in	1692, £.	135	3	4
Poll-tax — —	1694, —	34	7	0
Land-tax ——	1694, —	214	16	0
The fame at 3s -	1770, —	162	3	0

About the year 1712, according to fir Robert Atkyns, there were 42 houfes in this parifh, and about 240 inhabitants, whereof 8 were freeholders. The yearly baptifms were 6, and burials 6. Having examined the parifh regifter, I find that in a feries of ten years, from 1760 to 1769 inclufive, there were enter'd 63 baptifms, and 44 burials; and the number of inhabitants are at this time about 198.

****

ALVINGTON,

IS a fmall parifh, in the hundred of Blidefloe, in the foreft-divifion of the county; nine miles fouth-eaft from Monmouth, fix north-eaft from Chepftow, and twenty-two fouth-weft from Gloucefter. It is bounded on the north-eaftward by Lidney, from which it is feparated by the brook Coln; on the fouth-weftward by Woollafton, and has the river Severn on the fouth-eaft of it.

Mr. Camden calls it *Aventone*; and fince *Avon*, or *Afon*, in the Britifh language fignifies a river, thinks it not improbable that it took its name from thence, becaufe it is ftretched along the banks of the Severn. He was alfo of opinion that this place was the *Abone* of Antoninus, as well on account of the refemblance of the names, as becaufe it lies exactly nine miles diftant from Caer Went, or the *Venta Silurum* of the Romans; which is the diftance *Abone* is faid to be from the laft mentioned place, in the fourteenth *Iter*.

But I fee no great refemblance between the names *Abo*, or, as fome will have it, *Abone*, and Alvington, as the latter ought to be, or at leaft has been written, for the laft five hundred years; and unlefs the learned hiftorian had a precedent in higher antiquity, I think he hath taken an unwarrantable liberty in deviating fo widely from that manner of writing it. As to the diftance from Caer Went, it may anfwer well enough; but that from *Abo* to the *Trajectus*, being nine miles according to the Itinerary, is very different from the true diftance between this place and Oldbury, the fuppofed *Trajectus*, which is not more than four miles at fartheft. Indeed there is a manifeft miftake in the *Iter*, as to the diftances, for at the beginning it is faid, *Ab Ifca Callevam m. p.* ciii, *fic*; from Caerleion to Calleva, one hundred and three miles, thus: and then the intermediate diftances between the various places are fet down, which make together only ninety-eight miles, *i. e.* five miles fhort of the grofs account.

But the greateft objection feems to be, that, fuppofing the *Abo* to have been fituated in the country of the Silures, (a people that gave the Romans more trouble than any of our countrymen) it muft have been well fortified, garrifoned, and fecured againft the attacks of fo hardy and active a people; and being in fo important a fituation, one might expect to find ruins of antient buildings, chequer'd pavements, hypocaufts, and fuch other works as have been difcovered in thofe places where the Romans had ftations; but none of all thefe have been found at Alvington; for which reafon, among others, I am of opinion that this was not the *Abo* of Antoninus; and that, if Mr. Camden had feen the ruins in Lidney park, two or three miles higher up the river, he would rather have fixed on that place for the Roman ftation in queftion. *See Lidney.*

Of the Manor and other Eftates.

In *Domefday-book* are many particulars of villages and lands on the foreft fide of the Severn, and in Wales, as it was then reputed to be, agreeable to the divifion of the two countries at that time; for antiently all on the north-weft of that river was called Wales; but afterwards the Wye became the boundary between them, according to Alexander Neckham:

Inde vagos Vaga Cambrenfes, hinc refpicit Anglos.

On this fide, Wye the Englifh views,
On that, the wandering Welch purfues.

Thofe villages and eftates are not defcribed by their refpective names, nor is this place any where mentioned therein; fo that it is impoffible to fhew whofe property it was at the time of the antient furvey. But the priory of Lanthony held the manor of Alvington, with markets and fairs, 49 H. 3. and had court-leet and waifs therein, 15 E. 1. which they proved in their anfwer to a writ of *Quo warranto* brought againft them that year; and the church of Lanthony were proprietors

of

of it, 'till that houſe was diſſolved; for tho' it appears by the records, that Edward Blount, and Margaret his wife, were ſeized of it, 4 R. 2. it was probably either in truſt, or by uſurpation; for the priory was ſeized of it again in the 18th and 19th years of the ſame reign.

At the diſſolution of monaſteries, this manor was veſted in the crown, and the ſite of it, with divers lands, was granted, 32 H. 8. to Arthur Porter, who was a conſiderable purchaſer of abbey-lands at that time.

But ſir William Herbert had a grant of the manor 4 E. 6. and certain tithes in Alvington were alſo granted to him in the firſt year of the ſame reign.

From him it paſſed thro' various hands, 'till it came to William Compton, eſq; who was lord of this manor in the year 1608.

It came afterwards into the name of Higford, for William Higford, of Dixton, eſq; was lord of the manor in the year 1712, and from him it hath paſſed, in regular deſcent, to the reverend Mr. Henry Higford, of the ſame place, who is the preſent proprietor, and hath a good eſtate here. *See Alderton and Dixton.*

Of the Church, &c.

The church is called the chapel of Alvington. It is in the deanery of the foreſt, and annexed to Woollaſton.

The church is ſmall, with a tower at the weſt end, and an aile on the ſouth ſide, belonging to the lord of the manor. John Higford, eſq; died in the year 1706, and was buried in this church.

Proc. and Syn. £. 0 1 6 Pentecoſt. £. 0 1 4

Taxes.	The Royal Aid in	1692, £.	89	4	0
	Poll-tax —— —	1694, —	17	18	0
	Land-tax ——	1694, —	83	8	0
	The ſame, at 3*s.* —	1770, —	61	13	0

The ſtate of population muſt be given in the *Addenda*, as it was not received early enough to be printed with the above.

AMNEY CRUCIS.

THIS pariſh lies in the hundred of Crowthorn and Minety, two miles diſtant eaſt from Cirenceſter, ſix north from Cricklade in Wiltſhire, and nineteen ſouth-eaſt from Glouceſter.

The name was antiently written *Omenie*, and *Omenel*, and afterwards *Amney*, which ſir Robert Atkyns derives from *amnis*, the Latin word for a river; but this etymology ſeems to be ſuggeſted by the modern, rather than by the antient manner of writing the name; however, as I have no better to offer, I ſhall govern myſelf by Horace's rule. The cognomen was given it on account of a large croſs erected in this pariſh, which ſerved to diſtinguiſh it from two other adjoining pariſhes of the ſame name. And becauſe our Saxon anceſtors called the croſs the Halig Rode, this pariſh hath ſometimes alſo been called Holy Rood Amney.

The turnpike-road from Cirenceſter to London, and another turnpike-road from Bath to Oxford, lead through this pariſh, which hath lately been incloſed, by act of parliament.

As the workmen were digging ſtone on the ſide of the laſt mentioned road, about two years ago, they found an earthen urn, containing burnt bones and aſhes, and ſome Roman coins of the latter empire. There was a ſmall ſilver coin of Honorius, with this inſcription round the head: D N HONORIVS P F AVG. On the reverſe: a Roman ſoldier holding a ſpear in one hand, and victory in the other; and round the figures, VIRTVS ROMANORVM. This Honorius was ſon of Theodoſius, whom he ſucceeded in the government of the weſtern part of the empire, when he was a boy of ten years old. When he grew up, he was active and diligent, and ſecured Britain againſt the ravages of Picts, Scots, and Saxons, but at laſt fell a victim to his ambitious views, and made a miſerable end, about the time of the expiration of the Roman empire in Britain.

Of the Manor and other Eſtates.

As the pariſhes of Amney Crucis, Amney St. Mary, and Down Amney were not diſtinguiſhed by different names in the antient ſurvey, it is impoſſible, with any certainty, to ſelect the particulars from *Domeſday-book*, proper to each place; therefore, reſpecting this pariſh, I have implicitly followed ſir Robert Atkyns.

'Turſtin the ſon of Rolf holds Omenie of the 'king. There are ſeven hides. Tovi held it of 'king Edward. In demean are three plow-tillages, and eight villeins, and a prieſt, with eight 'plow-tillages. There are eight *ſervi*. Of this 'eſtate Tovi held the land of two villeins, and a 'certain knight held the land of four villeins. 'Half a hide and four acres of meadow belonged 'to the church. It was worth 8*l.* now 6*l.* 'This Turſtin holds one hide there which Uluui 'held for a manor, and could go where he would. 'In demean are two plow-tillages, with one bor'dar. It was worth 40*s.*' *Domeſday-book*, p. 78.

Under *Terra Hunfridi Camerarii*, it is thus expreſſed:

'The ſame Hunfridus holds one hide in Ome'nie. Æluui held it for a manor of king Edward. 'In demean are two plow-tillages, and four *ſervi*, 'and one bordar, and a mill of 5*s.* rent. It is 'worth and was worth 25*s.*' *Domeſday-book*, p. 79.

'Baldwin holds of the king three yard-lands 'in Omenie, in Gerſdones hundred. Aluuin 'held it in the time of king Edward. There is 'one plow-tillage, with two bordars. It is worth 'and was worth 10*s.*' *Domeſday-book*, p. 79.

The

The abbey of Tewkesbury held one hide at Amney, which king H. 1. confirmed to it, reciting that it did belong to Humphry the cook, which, I apprehend, should have been Humphry the chamberlain. He also confirmed to it the church of Amney, which belonged to Robert the chamberlain. And it was seized of court-leet, waifs, and felons goods in Amney Holy-rood, by the grant of W. 2. which privileges were allowed in a writ of *Quo warranto*, 15 E. 1.

From this time the monks of Tewkesbury gradually improved their estate here, for Isabel, daughter of Gilbert de Clare, granted to them one messuage and one plow-tillage in Holy Rood Amney, 1 E. 2. And the abbat purchased seven other messuages, four cottages, two hundred twenty-six acres of arable, five acres of meadow, and a rent of ten pence half-penny in Amney, of John de Boteler, 20 E. 2.

The abbey of Tewkesbury continued seized of the manor and rectory of Amney Holy Rood, 'till by the dissolution of that house they were vested in the crown, by which they were granted to John Playdell, or Pleydell, of Westcot in Berkshire, in the fourth year of the reign of queen Elizabeth. He was descended from the Playdells, antiently of Coleshill, in Berkshire.

Robert Playdell, fourth son of John, and heir to him by the death of his elder brothers without issue, removed from Westcot to Holy Rood Amney, and was lord of the manor in 1608. He married Susanna, daughter of Edward Saunders, of Brixworth, in Northamptonshire, esq; and dying in 1642, was succeeded by his son and heir

John Playdell, who dying without issue, was succeeded by his brother

Robert Playdell, or Pleydell. He married Elizabeth, daughter of John Saunders, M. D. and dying in 1678, was also succeeded in this estate by his son and heir

Robert Pleydell, who married Sarah, daughter of Philip Sheppard, of Minchin-hampton, esq; by whom he had a son and two daughters. The son and one of the daughters dying without issue, the manor of Amney Crucis, and several large estates in other places, as well as in this parish and neighbourhood, descended to his youngest daughter Charlotte-Louisa; with whom they went, by marriage, in 1724, to the honourable John Dawnay, eldest son of Henry lord viscount Downe. In this name and family they continued, 'till about the year 1765, when John lord viscount Downe sold the manor and estate of Amney Crucis, amongst other particulars, to

Samuel Blackwell, esq; who is the present proprietor, and has a large estate in this parish, and several other parts of the county. He married Anne, eldest daughter of James Lenox Dutton, of Sherborne, esq; by whom he has issue several children. His arms are, *Argent, a greyhound courant sable, collared, compony, Or and gules; on a chief indented of the second, three besants.*

Hugh le Despencer had an estate in this parish, for Eubulo l'Estrange, and Aleria his wife, levied a fine thereof to him 18 E. 2. And divers messuages in Holy Rood Amney, in the tenure of Richard Bye, belonged to the priory of Bradenstoke, in Wiltshire, which was founded by Walter earl of Salisbury, for black canons, in the reign of king Stephen. It was dedicated to the blessed Virgin, and valued, at the dissolution, at 270*l.* 10*s.* 8*d.* yearly. These messuages were granted to James Gunter, and William Lewis, 37 H. 8.

An estate called the *Sheep-House*, &c. in Amney, which belonged to the abbey of Tewkesbury, was granted to James Woodford, and Thomas Ludwell, 2 Eliz.

Of the Church, &c.

The church is in the deanery of Cirencester. It is a vicarage, improved since the inclosing of the common fields in the year 1769, to about 70*l.* a year. The advowson of the vicarage formerly belonged to the nunnery of Clerkenwell, in Middlesex, and was granted to sir William Herbert, 4 E. 6. The lord chancellor has the presentation. William Sandeford, D. D. is the present incumbent.

I have shewn that the patronage of the church, and the impropriation, formerly belonged to the abbey of Tewkesbury, and were confirmed to that church by king H. 2. But part of the tithes and glebe belonged to the abbey of Gloucester, and, after the dissolution, were granted to the bishoprick, 33 H. 8. and confirmed 6 E. 6. Other tithes of corn and hay belonged to the abbey of Cirencester, and were granted to Peter Osborn, and others, 3 Eliz. The impropriation of the corn tithes was vested in the lord of the manor; but by the bill for inclosing the common fields in this parish, all the lands are exonerated from tithe, and the bishop, impropriator, and vicar had lands allotted to them in lieu thereof.

The bishop's allotment lies on beggar-hill.

The vicar's portion is 110 acres in the upper-field. He hath Easter-offerings, and surplus fees, as before.

The church is built in the form of a cross, with a tower at the west end. In the window at the east end, are the arms of the Clares, originally placed there by the abbey of Tewkesbury, in grateful remembrance of Isabel Clare, their benefactress.

Benefactions.

Robert Pleydell, esq; hath endowed a free-school for the educating, cloathing, and apprenticing of poor children in this parish, with 80*l.* a year, charged on *Ranbury-farm.* *See his epitaph.*

There are cottages of 50*s.* a year given to the use of the church. And four acres of arable land, newly inclosed, near Meurstals, to other charitable uses.

Monuments and Inſcriptions.

There is a free-ſtone monument in the north aile, upon which are the figures of a man and woman, and twelve children, without any inſcription; but by the coat of arms upon it, 'tis ſuppoſed to have been erected for one of the Lloyds, formerly owner of this manor, and anceſtor of the Lloyds, late lords of the manor of Wheatenhurſt, in this county.

In the chancel is a white marble monument, with this inſcription:

ROBERTUS PLEYDELL, ROBERTI juxta ſiti Filius Unicus, natus 23 Julij 1687. Mortuus eſt Mar. 22, 1719. En! Virum Sereniſſimæ Frontis, Mitiſſimi Ingenij, Optimarum Artium Studiis liberaliter eruditum, Prudentem, Pium, Juſtum, Abſtinentem: Qui *Filij*, *Fratris*, *Amici*, Officia omnia diligenter ſancteq; explevit.

Si ei etiam quæ *Maritum*, quæ *Patrem* decerent, experiri per Fata licuiſſet; Quàm Beata fuiſſet *Uxor! Progenies* quàm Proba! Quam autem Curam in *Suâ Prole* inſtituendâ impendi vetuit Deus, Eam omnem in *Alienâ* educandâ (Largo ad id negotij annuo ſumptu in omne ævum dato) Adhibuit, ſic feræ Poſteritatis factus Pater. O Quot ex illo *Pauperioris Juventutis* Seminario, Benevoli hujus Viri Munificentia extructo, in lætiora ſola quotannis transferantur, HUIC NOMINI Proſperitatem ſuam acceptam relaturi; et veluti illæ Arbores quas, animi recreandi gratiâ, Ipſe Suâ Manu ſerere ſolebat, *Præſenti* et *Futuris* Sæculis prodeſſe poſſint.

Vale Anima pura et candida, Sequere Patris Tui veſtigia Per obſcuram Mortis Umbram, Donec in æternam Lucem perveneris: Ubi ſtudio pari, et junctis precibus Orabis, Ut Pia Mater Charæq; Sorores Virtuti Tuæ gratulantes, Te in cœlum recepto, in Fide, in Innocentia, in Operibus bonis Perſeverent; Uſq; dum iſto Tuo dilectiſſimo Conſortio, Quod Vehementer deſiderant, In perpetuum Fruantur.

Under, upon the ſame monument:

He hath Endowed a CHARITY-SCHOOL in this Pariſh with a Rent charge of Eighty Pound per An. for ever, for the Yearly Apprenticing of Two Poor Boys or Girls, and for the Cloathing and Inſtructing in Writing, Reading, and in Chriſtian Knowledge as many more as the Reſidue of that Sum will be ſufficient for.

Againſt the ſouth wall of the chancel, is a marble table, with the following inſcription:

This *STONE* is erected to the *MEMORY* of S[r]. HENRY PLEYDELL DAWNAY, Baronett, Lord Viſcount DOWNE, Whoſe Remains lie buried at MEURS near WEZEL, on the Banks of the *LOWER RHINE*. He was Lord of the Bed Chamber to GEORGE the *third*, both when *KING* and *PRINCE* of *WALES*; was twice elected Knight of the Shire for the County of YORK; Colonel by Brevet; Colonel of the Southern Battalion of Militia of the Weſt Riding of the County of YORK; and Lieutenant Colonel of the *Twenty fifth* Regiment of Foot, which he Commanded at the Battle of MINDEN, *Auguſt* 1ſt 1759. And again at the Battle of CAMPEN, *Octob.* 16, 1760, where being Mortally wounded he died the *Ninth* of *December* following, in the *Thirty third* Year of his Age.

There is a handſome pyramidal marble monument, on the weſt wall of the north aile, for Anne, the wife of Robert Berkeley Freeman, gent. and near it, another for Thomas Powell, M. A. vicar of this pariſh, who died Dec. 29, 1764, aged 62.

Taxes.			£.	s.	d.
	The Royal Aid in	1692,	81	4	0
	Poll-tax — —	1694, —	36	1	0
	Land-tax ——	1694, —	62	16	0
	The ſame, at 3*s.* —	1770, —	48	1	6

About the year 1712, according to ſir Robert Atkyns, there were 100 houſes, and about 350 inhabitants in this pariſh, whereof 25 were freeholders. The yearly births were 8, and burials 7. Upon examining the pariſh regiſter, I find, that in a ſeries of ten years, from 1760 to 1769 incluſive, there were entered 103 baptiſms, and 76 burials; and there are now, by actual numeration, 357 inhabitants.

****

AMNEY St. MARY, *or* EASTBROOK.

THIS pariſh is ſituated in the hundred of Crowthorne and Minety, about three miles eaſtward from Cirenceſter, ſix north from Cricklade in Wiltſhire, and about twenty-one eaſtward from Glouceſter. The etymology of Eaſtbrook is eaſy, the principal part of the pariſh lying on the eaſt ſide of the brook which runs from Amney Crucis into the Thames or Iſis.

Ten or twelve houſes which belong to Amney Crucis lie intermixt with this pariſh, which is ſmall, and ſeems, in early times, to have been taken out of Amney Crucis. It conſiſts moſtly of meadow ground. The turnpike-road from Cirenceſter to London leads thro' this pariſh.

Of the Manor and other Eſtates.

In *Domeſday-book*, it is thus expreſt:

'Reinbaldus holds Omenie, in Gerſdones hun-'dred, of the king. Godric held it in the time 'of king Edward. There are four hides and one 'yard-land. In demean are two plow-tillages, 'and eight villeins, and one bordar, with ſix 'plow-tillages, and a prieſt. There are eight '*ſervi*, and two mills of 10*s.* and twenty acres 'of meadow. It was worth and is worth 100*s.*' *Domeſday-book*, p. 73.

This Reinbald, or Reimbald, or Rumbald, was dean of the college of Cirenceſter at that time, and had been chancellor of England in the reign of Edward the Confeſſor. There were two other ſmall eſtates, according to the record:

'Durand [of Glouceſter] holds one hide in 'Eſbroc, and one of his knights holds it of him. 'In demean is one plow-tillage, and one bordar, 'and one *ſervus*. It is worth and was worth '10*s.*' *Domeſday-book*, p. 76.

Humphry the chamberlain had alſo an eſtate here, for it is thus expreſt:

'The ſame Hunfry holds one virgate of land in 'Eſtbroce, and William holds it of him. Aluuine 'held it for a manor. There is one villein. It 'was worth and is worth 2*s.*' *Dom. Book*, p. 79.

It appears by an *Inſpeximus* of the grants to the abbey of Cirenceſter, that king H. 1. granted four hides and one yard-land in Amney to that church, which had formerly been the eſtate of Reimbald the prieſt. But the records ſhew alſo, that a manor in Eſtbrook belonged to Roger le Hore, 8 E. 1. which was probably that which Aluuine held. Other records ſhew, that Aſhbrook was held of Humphry de Bohun, earl of Hereford and Eſſex, and of Joan his wife, 46 E. 3.

But

But I do not underſtand this to be the manor granted to the abbey of Cirenceſter.

Sir Robert Atkyns hath not ſhewn to whom this manor was granted by the crown, after the diſſolution of the abbey; but John Partrige, eſq; was lord of it in the year 1608. It came afterwards into the family of the Pleydells, of Holy Rood Amney, for Robert Pleydell was lord of this manor in the year 1712; from which time, it hath paſſed in the ſame manner, and acknowledged the ſame proprietors as Holy Rood Amney, ſo that Samuel Blackwell, eſq; is the preſent lord of it.

Of the Church, &c.

The church is in the deanery of Cirenceſter. It is an impropriation. The tithes of hay and corn in Amney St. Mary, which formerly belonged to the abbey of Cirenceſter, were granted to Peter Oſborn, and others, 3 Eliz. but the tithes of the demeans were granted to John Playdel, 5 Eliz. The incumbent received 13*s.* 4*d.* of the impropriator, beſides about 8*l.* in privy tithes. But ſince the year 1769, when the common fields and commonable places in the pariſh were incloſed, lands have been allotted to the impropriator and to the vicar, and the whole pariſh is exonerated from tithe.

The living has been twice augmented by queen Anne's bounty. Mr. Blackwell is patron; William Sandeford, D. D. is the preſent incumbent.

The church is ſmall, without any ſteeple, and is dedicated to the virgin Mary.

Procurations, £. 0 6 8 Synodals, £. 0 2 0
Pentecoſtals, — 0 0 8

Taxes.					
The Royal Aid in	1692, £.	45	2	0
Poll-tax —— —	1694, —	8	10	0
Land-tax ——	1694, —	45	6	0
The ſame, at 3*s.* —	1770, —	25	8	1

About the year 1712, according to ſir Robert Atkyns, there were 20 houſes, and about 80 inhabitants in this pariſh, whereof 8 were freeholders. The yearly births 2, burials 2. But examining the pariſh regiſter, I find, that in a ſeries of ten years, from 1760 to 1769 incluſive, there are entered 38 baptiſms, and 17 burials, and the inhabitants being numbered, are found to be 118.

AMNEY St. PETER, *or* EASTINGTON,

LIES in the hundred of Crowthorne and Minety, four miles diſtant eaſt from Cirenceſter, ſix north from Cricklade in Wiltſhire, and twenty-one ſouth-eaſtward from Glouceſter. It is a ſmall pariſh, conſiſting chiefly of meadow and paſture land. Lying to the eaſtward of the other Amneys, occaſioned its being diſtinguiſhed by the name of Eaſtington.

Of the Manor and other Eſtates.

In *Domeſday-book*, in the account of lands belonging to the church of St. Peter of Glouceſter, it is thus expreſt:

'The brother of Reinbald holds two hides in 'Omenie, in Gerſdunes hundred. There are 'two plow-tillages, and five villeins with three 'plow-tillages, and four *ſervi*, and twenty-four 'acres of meadow, and a mill of 5*s.* rent. It 'was worth 40*s.* now ſcarce 20*s.*' *D. B.* p. 71.

'Hernulf [de Heſding] holds four hides and 'two virgates and a half of land in Omenie, in 'Gerſdones hundred. Elric and Godric held 'them for two manors. In demean are three 'plow-tillages, and ſeven villeins, and two bor-'dars, with two plow-tillages. There are four '*ſervi*. The whole was worth and is worth 6*l.*' *Domeſday-book*, p. 77.

In the account of the donations to the abbey of St. Peter at Glouceſter, p. 143, it is ſaid, that in the year 1126, Winebald de Balon, one of the great barons of the realm, and Roger his ſon, granted to that monaſtery half a hide in Amney, which Thomas an Engliſhman held, free from all payments, except the king's dane-gelt.

Now it will be difficult to prove that the above eſtates lay in this pariſh, and not in one of the others of the ſame name; but it is probable that the firſt and laſt of them did, becauſe the records ſhew, that in the ſeventeenth year of king E. 3. this manor, and the impropriation, belonged to the abbey of Glouceſter. And they continued to be a part of the poſſeſſions of that abbey 'till it was diſſolved. After the diſſolution, the manor and tithes were granted to Richard Knight, 1 Mariæ; and Robert Knight, his ſon and heir, had livery of the manor 15 Eliz.

From him it went to George Gaſcoign, eſq; who was lord thereof in the year 1608. And then paſſing to

Robert Pleydell, eſq; it hath ever ſince been the property of the owners of Amney Crucis, ſo that Samuel Blackwell, eſq; is the preſent lord of this manor.

Of the Church, &c.

The church is in the deanery of Cirenceſter. It is a curacy, in the gift of the biſhop of Glouceſter. In the thirteenth year of C. 1. it was inſtituted to as a vicarage. The reverend Mr. Thomas Smith is the preſent incumbent, who receives 1*l.* 6*s.* 8*d.* from the leſſee of the appropriation. There is no houſe for the miniſter. The living has been thrice augmented by the queen's bounty, with which, lands of 14*l.* 10*s.* a year have been purchaſed, in the pariſh of South Cerney.

A portion of tithes in Farley, near Amney, antiently belonging to the abbey of Glouceſter, was granted to the biſhoprick 33 H. 8. and it hath been already ſhewn, that other tithes in this pariſh, belonging to the ſame abbey, were granted to Richard Knight, 1 Mariæ.

Ranbury farm, which is given to ſupport the charity ſchool at Amney Crucis, Kingſton meadow, and moſt of the pariſh, pay no tithe.

The church is ſmall, without any ſteeple. It is dedicated to St. Peter. Two acres in each common field, in the pariſh of Amney St. Mary, and one acre in Mr. Trynder's piece, were given to repair the church, before the fields were incloſed.

Pentecoſtals, - - £. 0 0 6

Taxes.	The Royal Aid, in	1692,	£.	36	2	0
	Poll-tax — —	1694,	—	6	16	0
	Land-tax ——	1694,	—	36	3	6
	The ſame, at 3s. -	1770,	—	27	2	2

According to ſir Robert Atkyns, about the year 1710, there were 22 houſes, and about 100 inhabitants in this pariſh, of whom 10 were freeholders; yearly births 3, burials 2. Examining the pariſh regiſter, I find, that in a ſeries of ten years, from 1760 to 1769 incluſive, there were entered 39 baptiſms, and 22 burials; and the inhabitants are about 105.

****

ARLINGHAM.

THIS pariſh lies in the hundred of Berkeley, ten miles north-weſtward from Stroud, nine north from Durſley, and nine ſouth-weſtward from Glouceſter. It is peninſulated by the river Severn on the eaſt, weſt, and north ſides, and bounded by Frampton on the ſouth-eaſt. A turnpike-road leads from Stroud to a paſſage over the Severn, in this pariſh; but the paſſage-houſe is at Newnham, exactly oppoſite to Arlingham. The river, at high water, is about a mile over, or ſomething leſs. Perſons well acquainted with the river, ride, and drive a carriage over the ford at this place, at low water; but ſome have miſcarried in the attempt.

The name, reſolved into its parts, and compared with the alphabetical liſt of words for explaining the names of places, will be found to ſignify a village, or town, upon the meadows; the letter *l* ſerving only for the ſake of ſound. And this is exactly agreeable to the ſituation of the place, which lies in the upper level, and has 738 acres of land, more particularly ſubject to inundations from the Severn.

The air is made very unwholeſome by the copious humid exhalations from the river, and from the lands which are ſo frequently overflowed. This occaſions inveterate agues, and all thoſe topical diſorders incident to a low, damp ſituation, in which the poorer ſort of people, who live hard, have ſo manifeſtly the diſadvantage in point of health. In Holland, where agues are very frequent, ſuch as go abroad early in the morning, uſually fortify themſelves againſt the moiſt air, by taking a dram, and a cruſt of bread, a diſh of coffee, ſome gingerbread, or the like, which is thought to be a good method of preſervation.

Notwithſtanding the ſituation of this village upon the Severn, fiſh is not ſo commonly the food of its inhabitants as might be imagined, on account of the great price it uſually bears. Salmon, in the greateſt plenty of the ſeaſon, commonly ſells for three pence half penny or four pence a pound. I took ſome notice, about two years ago, of an eel, juſt taken, five feet ten inches long, and twenty-eight pounds weight, which a butcher was ſtripping at this village, and thought it a great curioſity; but ſeveral perſons informed me, that there was nothing extraordinary in it, as a man, then living in the place, had taken one which weighed ſix ſcore pounds. The fleſh of this animal was ſold to poor people at two pence a pound. It was very white, but of a ſtrong, naſty ſmell, and muſt be unwholeſome food.

There are no rare plants found here, but large quantities of wood are frequently dug out of the meadows next Frethorn, which, when dry, falls to pieces on touching it. This wood muſt have been carried thither at a very early period of time, when the ground was in a boggy ſtate, ſo as to ſuffer the logs to ſink down to the depth whence they are now taken.

There is a good proſpect over the Severn, from Barrow-hill, in this pariſh, ſo called, perhaps, from the reſemblance it bears to a large tumulus, or barrow.

Of the Manor and other Eſtates.

Arlingham was antiently a member of the great lordſhip of Berkeley. In the liſt of eſtates belonging to that lordſhip, entered in *Domeſday-book*, it is ſaid, that nine hides in Erlingham belong to Berchelai. Hence I conclude, there were other lands beſide the nine hides, which belonged to one or more freeholders at that time; and the ſubſequent records, taking early notice of various proprietors of manors in this pariſh, ſerve to juſtify the concluſion. The following particulars are drawn from the records:

Maurice lord Berkeley died ſeized of the manor of Erlingham 9 E. 1. and left it to ſir Robert Berkeley, his ſecond ſon; whoſe ſon and heir, John Berkeley, died ſeized thereof, 14 E. 2. leaving four daughters coheireſſes.

The abbat of St. Auguſtin in Briſtol was ſeized of the manor of Erlingham, with court-leet, and of lands called *Kern* and *Bethlea*, in Erlingham, 15 E. 1. and his right was allowed in a *Quo warranto* the ſame year.

Walter de Thornhall, in the right of Elizabeth his wife, was ſeized of the third part of the manor of Arlingham, and of a fiſhery in the Severn. They jointly levied a fine of their eſtate, and ſettled it on themſelves in fee-tail, the remainder on James, the ſon of Elizabeth by her former huſband, 29 E. 3.

Geoffery le Mareſchal held Erlingham 32 E. 3.

John At-Yate was ſeized of the manor of Erlingham, 41 E. 3. This is the ſame perſon who, by by the name of John de Yate, was aſſigned, with four others, to view and repair the banks and drains of the lands bordering on the Severn, betwixt Briſtol and Glouceſter, 33 E. 3.

Agnes, widow of ſir Thomas Bradeſtone, was poſſeſſed of a manor here, 43 E. 3. And Thomas Bradeſtone, grandſon of Thomas, died ſeized of it, 48 E. 3. and left Elizabeth his only daughter and heireſs, married to ſir Walter de la Pool.

Richard Seimour was probably a truſtee of the Bradeſtones, as he was ſeized of this manor, together with Stinchcombe and Horton, both belonging to the Bradeſtones, 2 H. 4. which ſoon after reverted to them again; for

Sir Walter de la Pool, and Elizabeth his wife, daughter and heireſs of Thomas Bradeſtone, were ſeized of one meſſuage and one yard-land in Erlingham, 12 H. 6. and ſir Edward Ingoldſthorp was ſeized of this manor, and of the other eſtates mentioned before, as belonging to the Bradeſtones, 35 H. 6. After this time, I find nothing more of that family in Arlingham.

I now return to the family of the Berkeleys, who were lords of the manor of Arlingham. Richard Beauchamp, earl of Warwick, married Elizabeth, the only child of Thomas lord Berkeley, with whom he had this manor, and died ſeized of Arlingham 17 H. 6. He had three daughters, of whom, Margaret, the eldeſt, married to John Talbot, the firſt earl of Saliſbury, died ſeized of Erlingham, 7 E. 4.

William marquis of Berkeley having no iſſue, and taking a diſlike to his brother Maurice, who ſhould have ſucceeded him, levied a fine of the manor of Arlingham, and of other lands in that pariſh, to Edward Willoughby, and Robert Legg, 3 H. 7. and granted them to the king and his heirs male, with remainder to the right heirs of the ſaid marquis; ſo that at the death of king E. 6. (who was the laſt male heir of king H. 7.) this manor reverted to Henry lord Berkeley, who had livery thereof 1 & 2 P. & M.

But there was another reputed manor in this pariſh, part of the poſſeſſions of the abbey of Flaxley, and after the diſſolution of that houſe, was granted to ſir Anthony Kingſton, 36 H. 8. and is mentioned in the grant to be of the clear yearly value of 5 *l.* 7 *s.* 8 *d.*

The manor of Arlingham came afterwards into the family of the Weſtwoods; for Robert Weſtwood, on the death of his father, had livery of it, 1 Eliz.

From them it paſſed to the family of the Yates, who came into England at the Norman conqueſt, and have reſided in Glouceſterſhire ever ſince. They had eſtates, ſoon after their coming, at Durſley, Flaxley, Cam, &c. and particularly at Arlingham, as appears by antient deeds, wherein —— de la Yate grants lands in Erlingham, in the reign of king John; and one of their anceſtors gave part of the ground on which the church is built, and the parſon, at this time, pays a yearly rent to the proprietor of the manor, in acknowledgement thereof.

John at Yate married Margaret, the youngeſt daughter of John Berkeley, (who died, as already obſerved, 14 E. 2.) and in her right became ſeized of an eſtate in Erlingham; and dying, was ſucceeded by his ſon John. He alſo left a ſon John, who died ſeized of the bailiwick of Abbenhall, in the foreſt of Dean, and of lands in Walmore, and Littlemore, in the pariſh of Weſtbury, and of lands in Durſley, Hatherley, and Arlingham, 41 E. 3. William Yate was his ſon, who had two ſons, Richard and Walter. Richard dying without iſſue, Walter ſucceeded his brother, and married Elizabeth, daughter of Thomas Wye, eſq; by whom he had a ſon Thomas Yate, whoſe ſon was Richard Yate, who had a ſon Richard, whoſe ſon Walter Yate was high-ſheriff of Glouceſterſhire in the year 1696.

Richard Yate ſucceeded Walter, and married Elizabeth, one of the daughters and coheireſſes of Thomas Price, eſq; mayor of Glouceſter, by whom he had two ſons, Charles and John; and three daughters, Elizabeth, Joyce, and Mary, the two laſt dying infants; which John ſettled at Colthorp, in the pariſh of Standiſh, in this county.

Charles Yate, ſon and heir of Richard, married Mary, daughter and coheireſs of — Hickes, eſq; by whom he had iſſue one only child, John, and died in the year 1738; whereby this manor and eſtate devolved to his ſon, who alſo dying unmarried in the year 1758, the male line of this antient family is extinct. The widow of Charles Yate, eſq; is the preſent proprietor of this manor, who hath a handſome houſe called the Court, with pleaſant gardens, and a park, and a large eſtate in this pariſh. The arms of Yate are, *Azure, a feſs Or, in chief two mullets of the ſecond.*

Of the other eſtates, the records ſhew, that Elianor, dutcheſs of Somerſet, married to Thomas lord Rouſe, was ſeized of lands in Arlingham, formerly belonging to Thomas lord Berkeley, 7 E. 4. Thomas Baker levied a fine of lands in Arlingham to John Eſterfield, John Walch, and others, 9 H. 7. And Thomas Pany, and Catherine his wife, levied a fine of lands in Arlingham, 16 H. 7. William Warner alſo levied a fine of lands in Arlingham, in the 17th year of the ſame reign. Lands in Arlingham which belonged to the abbey of St. Auguſtin in Briſtol, were granted to the dean and chapter of that place, 34 H. 8.

HAMLETS. 1. *Overton*, which lies a mile from the church.

2. *Milton End*, of two or three families.

Of the Church, &c.

The church is a vicarage, in the deanery of Glouceſter, worth 76 *l.* a year. Roger lord Berkeley gave this church to the priory of Leonard Stanley. The rectory and church of Arlingham were granted to ſir William Rider, 7 Jac. Mr. Bridgman

Bridgman hath lately fold the advowfon of the vicarage, and the impropriation, to Mrs. Elizabeth Rogers, who hath a good eftate in this parifh, purchafed of the family of Bycke. Mr. Davis is the prefent incumbent. The impropriation pays 15*l.* a year to the crown. The church is a long building, with a tower at the weft end, and fix mufical bells. It is dedicated to the virgin Mary. Lands let for 40*s.* a year are given to adorn the church.

Monuments and Infcriptions.

Againft the wall, between the body of the church and the chancel, ftands a grey marble monument, in the form of an obelifk, over which are the arms of Yate, with quarterings, pretty much defaced. The motto, QUO VIRTUS VOCAT. There is an urn in front, with feftoons, and other decorations, and a table beneath bears the following infcription :

Near this Place lyeth the Body of Charles Yate, Efq; who died the 11th of Nov. 1738, aged 46.

He was one of his Majefties Juftices of the Peace, likewife Deputy Lieutenant of this County : He difcharged with Juftice & Equity to all, and with Honour and Reputation to himfelf, the Offices of a Magiftrate and a Chriftian : His Authority might have made him refpected whilft alive ; but it was the peculiar fweetnefs and affability of his Manners, his great kindnefs and humanity to all, his agreeable Cheatfulnefs of Difpofition, annexed to a virtuous Mind, which could alone render him fo truly regretted when dead.

Againft the north wall of the church ftands another marble monument, with the coat armour of Yate, and motto, as before. In front, a female figure, kneeling, holds an anchor in her right hand, in her left a heart inflamed. Upon a table it is thus infcribed :

Here lyeth the body of John Yate, Efq; Lord of this Manor, the laft Heir Male of his Family, and only Son of Charles Yate, Efq; He was in the Commiffion of the peace, one of the Deputy Lieutenants of this County, and Deputy Conftable of St. Briavell's Caftle. Defcended from a long Race of worthy Anceftors, He improved his native Virtues with every amiable Qualification that gains the Love and Veneration of Mankind. A lively Senfe and uniform Practice of Religion, accompanied with Candor, Affability, and Sweetnefs of Temper, filled him with Joy and inward Satisfaction. Charity, Compaffion, and univerfal Benevolence, chiefly directed and difpofed of his ample Fortune. Of pureft Morals, of an irreproachable Life, of filial Affection, of Sincerity in Friendfhip, of true Honour, of Integrity of Heart, He was an uncommon Example. With this admirable Affemblage of Virtues, joined to a polite Tafte of Literature, the Scholar in him perfected the Gentleman, as the Chriftian perfected the man.

In the Flower of Youth, expecting, but not fearing Death, He willingly refigned his Soul to God on the 24th of May, 1758, aged 27. To whofe ever dear and honoured Memory, this Monument is erected by his moft truly affectionate and much afflicted mother, M. Y.

On flat ftones are memorials for Richard Yate, efq; who died Nov. 2, 1661, aged 78; for Colonel Richard Yate, who died June 17, 1701, aged 41; for his wife, Elizabeth, daughter of major Price, who died July 14, 1705, aged 40, and two of their daughters, Joyce and Mary, both infants ; and for Charles Yate, efq; who died Nov. 11, 1738, aged 46.

	£.	s.	d.		£.	s.	d.
Firft fruits,	19	7	2	Synodals,	0	2	0
Tenths, —	1	18	8	Pentecoftals,	0	0	7
Procurations,	0	6	8				

Benefactions.

Here is a free-fchool endowed with 40*l.* a year, of which the following infcription, on a table in the front of the fchool-houfe, exhibits the particulars :

John Yate, Efq; by Virtue of his Will, endowed this School, which charity was carried on by his parent, who furvived him. And in the year 1768, *fhe erected this building at her own Expence for the Benefit of the fame. And by the Authority that was invefted in her, fhe compleated the Endowment in her Life-Time.*

Thomas Lifton, merchant, has given 10*s.* a year to the poor, paid out of *Woolcroft*, in this parifh.

The inhabitants of Arlingham, in their turn with other parifhes, have a right of fending two perfons to a hofpital at Warwick, founded 13 Eliz. by Robert Dudley, earl of Leicefter, of the Berkeley family ; who founded the hofpital for twelve poor men hurt in the wars, and if no fuch, then Erlingham to have the benefit.

Taxes.			£.	s.	d.
	The Royal Aid in	1692,	188	4	0
	Poll-tax — —	1694, —	31	4	0
	Land-tax ——	1694, —	141	14	0
	The fame, at 3*s.* —	1770, —	107	18	6

According to fir Robert Atkyns, when he publifhed his account of this parifh, there were 80 houfes and about 400 inhabitants, of whom 25 were freeholders. The yearly births were 14, burials 11. But in a feries of ten years, from 1700 to 1709 inclufive, there appear to be entered in the parifh regifter 161 baptifms and 121 burials, and in a like feries, from 1760 to 1769, there were entered 116 baptifms and 110 burials. The number of inhabitants is 372, *i. e.* nearly in the proportion of 34 to 1 of the annual burials ; which fhews the declining ftate of population.

ASHCHURCH.

THIS parifh is fituate in the vale, in the lower part of the hundred of Tewkefbury, diftant two miles eaftward from the town which gives name to the hundred ; about feven weft from Winchcombe, and eleven northward from Gloucefter. It is bounded on the eaft by Teddington in Worcefterfhire, and by Beckford in this county ; on the weft by Tewkefbury ; on the north by the river Caran, or Carant ; and on the fouth by the parifhes of Cleeve and Tredington. It confifts of rich meadow and pafture, with a confiderable proportion of deep arable land. The turnpike-road from Tewkefbury to London leads thro' it ; before the gates were erected it was almoft impaffable.

This parifh was antiently, and ftill is, divided into tithings, or hamlets, diftinguifhed by the names of Eftone, or Effetone, Pamintonie, Fitentone, and Natone, fomething different in ortho-

graphy

graphy from the modern names. In the time of king Edward the Confeſſor, they were members of the great manor of Tewkeſbury. Eſtone was ſo called, becauſe it was ſituate in the eaſt part of the pariſh; and the pariſh obtained the name of Eſtchurch, or Eaſtchurch, becauſe the church lay eaſtward from the town of Tewkeſbury; but in proceſs of time, by a vicious pronunciation, the name hath been corrupted to Aſhchurch, as we now write it.

In the tithing of Northway and Newton there is a ſpring of purgative mineral water, which, about thirty years ago, the town of Tewkeſbury endeavoured to improve to its advantage. They erected a pump over the well, and ſome of the water was uſed medicinally; but it ſoon fell into neglect, as being too near to Cheltenham ſpaw to ſucceed at the ſame time. The properties of both waters are ſaid to be nearly alike.

Of the Manors and other Eſtates.

In the time of king Edward the Confeſſor, the lands in this pariſh were held by ſeveral tenants, under the great but unfortunate Brictric, the ſon of Algar, except only a ſmall portion which belonged to the church of Tewkeſbury. At the time of the conqueſt, they were taken from Brictric by W. 1. and given to his queen; and were afterwards poſſeſſed by the ſame proprietors who held the manor of Tewkeſbury, down to the reign of king E. 6. But the particulars will beſt appear under the heads of the ſeveral tithings.

TITHINGS and *HAMLETS.*

1. *Northway* and *Newton*. The records ſhew that William de Valentia was ſeized of this manor, by the gift of Robert de Pont de Larch, 36 H. 3. But it reverted afterwards to the lords of Tewkeſbury [a]. George duke of Clarence, in right of Iſabel his wife, daughter of Anne counteſs of Warwick, was ſeized of Northy, 18 E. 4. And Anne counteſs of Warwick levied a fine of this manor, and of all her eſtates, to the king, 3 H. 7.

The manor of Northy was granted to Robert earl of Leiceſter, and to John Morley, 23 Eliz. and afterwards in the ſame reign, Thomas Cox, of Cleeve, eſq; became the proprietor of it. His grandſon, ſir John Cox, had a ſon and daughter, to whom this eſtate deſcended, who dying without iſſue, it went, by the gift of the daughter, to her mother. She ſettled it on Elianor, niece of ſir John Cox, married to John Stafford, eſq; from whom it deſcended to his ſon Henry Stafford; from whoſe family it paſſed by purchaſe to Thomas Hayward, of Quedgley, eſq; who is the preſent lord of the manor of Northway and Newton.

Lands in Northy were granted to Francis Maurice, and Francis Philips, in truſt for ſir William Rider and others, 7 Jac.

2. *Pamington*, containing about 22 houſes. *Domeſday-book* ſhews that there were eight hides in Pamintonie, belonging to the manor of Tewkeſbury, in the reign of king Edward the Confeſſor.

King W. 2. granted court-leet, waifs, and felons goods in Pamington to the abbey of Tewkeſbury, which privileges were allowed them in a writ of *Quo warranto*, 15 E. 1. but yet notwithſtanding, the manor was afterwards in the lords of Tewkeſbury. George duke of Clarence was ſeized of it in right of Iſabel his wife. And Anne the great counteſs of Warwick, levied a fine of it to the king, 3 H. 7. This manor was granted from the crown to Anne Forteſcue, widow of ſir Adrian Forteſcue, and to the heirs male of ſir Adrian, 5 Mariæ. Lord Craven is the preſent owner of it.

3. *Fiddington*, containing about 20 houſes. It is ſaid in *Domeſday-book*, that there were ‘ſix hides ‘in Fitentone belonging to the manor of ‘Teodecheſberie. A radecheniſter held two hides ‘in Fitentone, now Bernard holds them.’

‘The underwritten lands belong to the church ‘of Teodecheſberie. In Fitentone two hides. ‘There is one villein, and two *coliberti*, with two ‘plow-tillages. It was worth and is worth 10*s*. ‘One of theſe hides was quit from tax.’ *Domeſday-book*, p. 68.

Fiddington, Aſhton in Clifford Chambers, and Porton, were held by knight's ſervice of Gilbert de Clare, earl of Glouceſter and Hertford, 8 E. 2. Roger de Acton held Fiddington 35 E. 3. But the lords of Tewkeſbury were afterwards proprietors of this manor, 'till Anne counteſs of Warwick levied a fine of it to king H. 7. in the third year of his reign. Sir Thomas Seimour obtained a grant of the manor of Fiddington, lately the earl of Warwick's, 1 E. 6. and this manor and other lands, were granted to John earl of Warwick, in exchange for Warwick-caſtle, 3 E. 6.

There was another manor in Fiddington, which belonged to the abbey of Tewkeſbury, from before the conqueſt, 'till that houſe was diſſolved. And this laſt mentioned manor was granted to Daniel Perte and Alexander Perte, 7 E. 6.

Robert Aſhton levied a fine of the manor of Fiddington to Henry Moody, 2 Mariæ. Thomas Cluterbuck, in right of his wife Elizabeth, died ſeized of the manor of Fiddington, 15 Car. Thomas Kemble, eſq; is the preſent lord of this manor.

The records ſhew that John Coal died ſeized of *Hall's Court* in Fiddington, 16 H. 8. And that James Gunter, and Anne his wife, levied a fine of lands in Fiddington, to Thomas Berew, and Margaret his wife, 1 Mariæ.

Natton lies in this tithing. *Domeſday-book* ſhews, that three hides and a half in Natone were

[a] What ſir Robert Atkyns hath ſaid of the abbeſs of Iſwis, of the knights Templers, and of John de Berkeley, being ſeized of this manor, was occaſioned by his having miſtaken ſeveral different places for this, on account of the reſemblance of name; as Newington Bagpath, Newington in Winchcombe, and the pariſh of Naunton.

held

held of the manor of Tewkefbury. The capital meffuage of Natton, with divers lands, meadows, and paftures in Natton, parcel of the poffeffions of the late monaftery of Tewkefbury, were granted to John Bellow, and Robert Biggot, 38 H. 8. *Stevens's App.* p. 9.

4. *Afton*, or *Afton upon Caran*, containing about 22 families. The manor, and capital meffuage and lands called Afhchurch, late belonging to Richard earl of Warwick, were granted to fir Ralph Fane, 1 E. 6. but they were afterwards in the crown, for other records fhew, that the manor and farm of Afhchurch were granted to William Hawtree, 7 E. 6. John Harrington had livery of this manor, 20 Eliz. Thomas Hughes, efq; was lord of it in the year 1608. But Afton is now the eftate of Henry Wakeman, of Beckford, efq; The manor court has been difcontinued time out of mind.

John Pullen and Alice his wife were feized of lands in Afton upon Carent, 1 R. 2. And John Karante was likewife feized of lands in Afton Karante, 6 R. 2. A meffuage called Caran's Place and Caran's Mill, in Afhchurch, was granted to Dorothy Darel, and to George Trefham, 36 H. 8. Lands in Afton upon Carent, which belonged to the alien priory of Belbeck, and afterwards to the college of Fotheringhay, were granted to fir Edward Lee, 1 E. 6.

Haman's Downs, (fo called from Robert Fitz-Haman, lord of Tewkefbury, and proprietor of a vaft eftate in this country) is a fmall hamlet in this parifh. Livery of the manor of Homefdown, and Nether Homefdown, was granted to Thomas Lane, 3 E. 6. Hamand Downs in Afhchurch, lately belonging to Thomas lord Seimour, were granted to Chriftopher Hatton, in exchange for lands in Hampfhire, 18 Eliz.

Each of the four tithings has a diftinct overfeer, tithing-man, and furveyor.

Of the Church, &c.

The church is a curacy, in the deanery of Winchcombe. John Parfons, efq; patron; the reverend Mr. John Dark is the prefent incumbent, who at vifitation is ftiled rector of Afhchurch.

Tithes in Afhchurch, Northway, Newton, Cardiff, Pamington, and Afhton, formerly belonging to the abbey of Tewkefbury, were granted to Thomas Stroud, Walter Earl, and James Paget, 36 H. 8.

The rectory of Afhchurch, and tithes of hay in Northy, and tithes in Afton upon Carent, were granted to Daniel Perte, and Alexander Perte, 7 E. 6. And other tithes in Afton upon Carent, which belonged to the abbey of Tewkefbury, were granted to Francis Maurice, and Francis Philips, in truft for fir William Rider, and others, 7 Jac.

Tithes of hay in the meadows called Tenants Meadow, and Pamington Doles, which belonged to the abbey of Tewkefbury, were granted to Roger Manners, efq; 18 Eliz.

The tithes which belonged to the college of Fotheringhay were granted to fir Richard Lee, 1 E. 6.

The impropriator of Northway and Newton pays 8*l.* a year to the curate. The living has been augmented by queen Anne's bounty, and Mr. William Ferrers, by his will, gave 5*l.* a year to the curate, who fhall ordinarily and weekly refide in the parifh, and preach; the payment of which is charged on his manor of Shellingthorpe, in Lincolnfhire. Mr. Scrimfhire has alfo given 12*l.* a year to the curate, charged on the impropriations of Tredington, and of Fiddington in this parifh, of which a more particular account may be feen under Tewkefbury. A fmall houfe, and a little piece of pafture ground belong to the curacy.

The church is large, with battlements on the fouth fide. It hath a large aile on the north fide, formerly called St. Thomas's chapel, and a handfome tower at the weft end, adorned with pinnacles and battlements, and fix fmall bells in it.

In one of the windows of the north aile are thefe arms, *Gules, three efchalop fhells argent.* —— *Gules, a chevron ermine.*

Pentecoftals, - - £. 0 1 3 *ob.*

There are two church-wardens for this parifh.

Benefactions.

A houfe, and the church-yard, and three ridges of land, worth 3*l.* a year, are given towards the repair of the church.

Mr. William Ferrers hath given 10*l.* a year to the poor, notwithftanding it is faid to be 5*l.* a year in the memorial for him.

Thomas Haynes, citizen of London, gave 40*s.* a year to the poor, or the profit of 50*l.* to be laid out in lands.

Charles Parfons, of Breedon, gent. by his will dated 1731, gave 20*s.* a year to the poor, charged on a ground called Butfham, and a little meadow called Kinfham, in Breedon.

Monuments and Infcriptions.

Againft the fouth wall is the effigy of William Ferrers, and round it written *Live well and dye never. Dye well and live ever.* Over the figure are his arms, *Or, on a bend gules, three horfefhoes of the field.* And beneath, upon a table, it is thus infcribed:

MEMORIÆ SACRVM.

William Ferrers, Citizen of London, fecond Sonn of Roger Ferrers of Fiddington, gent. had 3 wives, with whom hee lived 50 yeares moft lovingly: and by whom hee faw himfelf a happy Father and Grandfather. All his children died before him. Hee preferred many of his brothers, of his kindred, and of his cowntrymen, and left behind him feverall works of Piety As to the Poore of this place where hee was borne, to a Preacher in this Parifh, and to ye mending of ye Highwayes abowt Fiddington, to every one 5*l.* yearly for ever. Moreover hee gave 30*l.* yearly for ever towards a Free Schoole in Tewxbery; and 5*l.* p. annum to ye Poore of y^t^ place wth feverall guiftes to ye Poore and other pivs ufes in and abowt London. He likewife gave large Legacies both in landes & Monyes to his 3 grandchildren, brothers and kindred. Hee departed this lyfe ye 26th

ye 26th day of September 1625, & lyes buryed in Allhallowes Church in Lumbar-ſtreet London.

Thomas Ferrers his Brother & Part Executor with Love & Care built this ſmall Monument.

On a braſs plate, againſt the ſame wall, within a ſcutcheon, *five eſchalop ſhells*, no colours expreſt; and beneath, engraved in capitals,

MEMORIÆ ROBERTI BARKER, GENER. QVI PHTHISIS LABORANS & CVPIENS DISSOLVI, VOTI COMPOS FVIT 3^tio DIE MARTII ANNO DNI 1671. ÆTATIS VERO SVÆ 40.

Then follow ten lines of uncouth Engliſh verſification.

On a flat ſtone of white marble, in the chancel, *Party per pale*, 1. *A bend wavy*. 2. *A chevron between three griffons heads eraſed*. No colours expreſſed in the ſculpture. Under the ſcutcheon, a memorial for Thomas Smithend, of Tewkeſbury, who died in 1717; and for Paulina his wife, who died in 1735.

There is a memorial againſt the wall of the north aile, for George Banniſter, ſen. gent. who died in 1734, aged 57; and for Sarah his wife, who died in 1729, aged 56; and for Sarah and Edmund their infant children. And upon the ſtone are the following arms *Party per pale*, 1. *Argent, a croſs patonce ſable*. 2. *Gules, a feſs between three fleurs-de-lis Or*.

There is alſo a memorial, on a flat ſtone in the chancel, for Nicholas Steight, of Pamington, who died in 1763, aged 80, with his arms, *A feſs embattled between three lions rampant*.

Northway and Newton.

Taxes.	The Royal Aid in	1692, £.	185	16	0
	Poll-tax — —	1694, —	14	4	0
	Land-tax ——	1694, —	299	6	0
	The ſame, at 3*s*. -	1770, —	172	17	6

Pamington.

Taxes.	The Royal Aid in	1692, £.	82	10	0
	Poll-tax — —	1694, —	2	12	0
	Land-tax ——	1694, —	63	4	0
	The ſame, at 3*s*. -	1770, —	75	14	7

Fiddington and Natton.

Taxes.	The Royal Aid in	1692, £.	115	6	0
	Poll-tax — —	1694, —	8	10	0
	Land-tax ——	1694, —	139	16	0
	The ſame, at 3*s*. —	1770, —	105	10	7

Aſton upon Caran.

Taxes.	The Land-tax in	1694, £.	54	16	0
	The ſame, at 3*s*.	1770, —	41	7	7

According to ſir Robert Atkyns, about the year 1710, there were 77 houſes in this pariſh, and about 308 inhabitants, whereof 10 were freeholders. The yearly births 14, burials 13. But the following particulars are carefully extracted from the pariſh regiſter. In a ſeries of ten years, from 1700 to 1709 incluſive, there are entered 113 baptiſms and 94 burials. In a like ſeries from 1760 to 1769 incluſive, are 120 baptiſms and 108 burials. And there are about 436 inhabitants, ſo that the people have been increaſing in this pariſh ſince the beginning of this century.

ASHELWORTH,

IS a ſmall pariſh in the hundred of Berkeley, though diſtant ten or twelve miles from any other part of that hundred. This is one of the ſeveral inſtances, occaſionally to be taken notice of in the courſe of this work, of the unnatural and inconvenient allotment of pariſhes to hundreds, which, by their ſituation, they have no connexion with. As to Aſhelworth, this irregularity aroſe in very early times, when the pariſh was firſt made a member of the great lordſhip of Berkeley, whoſe tenants were obliged to attend at the court of that hundred. It is ſeven miles eaſt from Newent, ſeven ſouthward from Tewkeſbury, and five northward from Glouceſter; ſituate on the weſt ſide of a gentle riſing ground called Cookſhill, which joins to Corſe; is watered by the Severn, on the eaſt; bounded by Haſfield, on the north; and on the ſouth by the pariſh of Hartpury.

The lands are chiefly meadow and paſture, with much clay in their compoſition, very ſuitable to orcharding, for which the pariſh hath formerly been diſtinguiſhed; but it is far otherwiſe at preſent.

The plantations remaining are old and decayed, and the nature of the tenure, (being leaſehold under a fluctuating proprietor) is unfavourable to planting, and every kind of improvement. The cottages and farm-houſes are ſuch as might be expected, miſerable hovels, generally covered with ſtraw, and in ruinous condition. The courſe of huſbandry, for they have ſome tillage land, is three crops, *i. e.* wheat, beans, wheat, and then fallow.

Of the Manor and other Eſtates.

In *Domeſday-book* it is expreſt, that three hides in Eſceleuuorde belong to Berchelai; and they were part of that lordſhip in the time of king Edward the Confeſſor.

Robert Fitz-Harding founded the monaſtery of St. Auguſtine, in Briſtol, and endowed it with this manor, which continued in that abbey 'till it was diſſolved in the reign of king H. 8. and the lands and poſſeſſions belonging to it, among which were the manor, the rectory, and the advowſon of the vicarage of Aſhelworth, were granted to the biſhop of Briſtol, at the firſt erection of that ſee, 34 H. 8. Thomas Hayward, of Quedgley, eſq; is the preſent leſſee under the biſhop, of the manor and impropriation; and holds a court-leet here.

HAMLETS. There are places or hamlets in this pariſh, of the following names. — 1. *Longbridge.* — 2. *Knight's Green.* — 3. *Nupping-end.* —— 4. *White-end.* — 5. *High Croſs.* — 6. *Wickeridge.* — 7. *Mare-end.*

Of the Church, &c.

The church is a vicarage in the deanery of Glouceſter, worth 40*l.* a year. The biſhop of Briſtol is patron and impropriator, and Mr. Edwards is the preſent incumbent. The vicar, who has a ſmall portion of the great tithes, repairs one part of the chancel.

The church hath two ailes, and a chancel by the ſide of the greater chancel, with a ſpire ſteeple at the weſt end. It is dedicated to St. Andrew.

	£	s	d		£	s	d
Firſt fruits,	11	9	0	Synodals,	0	2	0
Tenths,	—	1	0 3	Pentecoſtals,	0	0	11
Procurations,	0	6	8				

Benefaction.

Lands in Hareſfield and Aſhelworth, of the value of about 14*l.* a year, are given to the uſe of the church and poor.

Taxes.			£	s	d
	The Royal Aid in	1692,	104	4	0
	Poll-tax — —	1694, —	19	0	0
	Land-tax — -	1694, —	88	18	0
	The ſame, at 3*s.*	1770, —	65	9	6

◇◇◇◇◇◇◇◇◇◇◇◇◇◇◇◇◇◇◇◇

ASTON-BLANK, *or* COLD ASTON,

IS a ſmall pariſh in the hundred of Bradley, five miles north from Northleach; ſix ſouthweſtward, upon the turnpike-road, from Stow; and twenty-two eaſtward, upon the ſame road, from Glouceſter.

Aſton, or *Eaſton*, is a name very commonly given to pariſhes and hamlets ſituated eaſtward from places which they have ſome relation to, or dependance upon. Sir Robert Atkyns's notion of its being derived from the aſh-trees growing here, is chimerical. The place lies on the eaſtern extremity of the hundred, and was therefore called *Eſtone*, as I find it written in the moſt antient record of the kingdom. Lying high, and much expoſed to the weather, gave riſe to the appellation of *Cold*; but I can render no account how it obtained the additional name of *Blank.* The air is good and healthy, and the lands are chiefly arable.

In the Camp-field, on the right hand of the road leading to Bourton on the Water, are intrenchments, now pretty much levelled, and a *tumulus*, or barrow, at a ſmall diſtance from them, which hath not been opened. I am informed that Roman coins have been found there, which indicate the works to be of that people; and probably ſerved as an advanced poſt to their ſtronger fortifications at Bourton.

Of the Manor and other Eſtates.

At the time of the general ſurvey, 'Drogo 'held ten hides in Eſtone, of the biſhop of Wor'ceſter. *Domeſday-book*, p. 70.

There is another pariſh, near Marſhfield, called Cold Aſton, or Cold Aſhton, which, on account of the ſimilarity of name, ſir Robert Atkyns hath confounded with this, to which the following extracts from the records undoubtedly belong, as they can have no relation to the other, becauſe the abbey of Bath held that manor from before the Norman conqueſt, 'till that houſe was diſſolved.

Walter Baſkervil was ſeized of Cold Aſton, and dying 16 John, left Ralph Fitz-Nicholas his heir; whoſe ſon Robert died ſeized of it 1 E. 1. Ralph de Pipard was his heir and ſucceſſor, whoſe ſon Robert Pipard died ſeized of Cold Aſton 3 E. 2. And John Pipard levied a fine of the manor of Cold Aſton 4 E. 2.

Edmund le Boteler married the heireſs of this family of Pipard, and had with her the manor of Cold Aſton, which he held, with free warren, 9 E. 2. James Boteler, his ſon, was created earl of Ormond, and was ſeized of this manor 2 E. 3. In this name and family it continued down to James Boteler earl of Ormond, who was created earl of Wiltſhire, and was ſeized of the manor of Cold Aſton 1 E. 4. but being attainted, the manor was forfeited to the crown, and was granted to ſir Walter Devereux, and to his heirs male, the ſame year.

Sir Walter Devereux had married Anne, daughter and heireſs of William lord Ferrers of Chartley, and for his eminent ſervices againſt the houſe of Lancaſter, was advanced to be lord Ferrers by king E. 4. but was afterwards ſlain in Boſworth field, fighting for king R. 3.

Following the fortune of the crown, the manor of Cold Aſton reverted to the Botelers, on the ſucceſs of king H. 7. Thomas earl of Ormond, the laſt of that name who was proprietor of this manor, left no iſſue male, whereby it deſcended to his two daughters. Anne, the eldeſt, was married to ſir George St. Leger, and ſurviving her huſband, ſhe and her ſiſter Margaret Boteler had livery of it, 7 H. 8. The lady Anne dying, 24 H. 8. livery of the manor was then granted to ſir John St. Leger, her ſon and heir.

John Carter, eſq; was lord of this manor in the year 1608, in whoſe name and family it continued above a hundred years; but lady Doily is the preſent proprietor of it.

Lands lying in Aſton Little, within the pariſh of Cold Aſton, formerly belonging to the priory of Weſtwood in Kent, were granted by the crown to Robert Acton and Charles Acton, 30 H. 8.

Little Aſton farm, now let for 160*l.* a year, was the property of George Townſend, eſq; which he gave to Pembroke college, in Oxford.

Of

Of the Church, &c.

The church is a vicarage, in the deanery of Stow. The lord Chancellor is patron. Mr. James is the prefent incumbent. Edmund Waller, efq; has the impropriation. The vicarage was worth about 30*l.* a year, but Mrs. Dorothy Vernon gave 200*l.* to augment the living, and a few years fince, queen Anne's bounty was obtained for it, and the money is laid out on lands in the parifh of Bourton on the Water. The vicar hath the tithes of hay, and the leffer tithes.

The priory of Malvern formerly prefented to this church, which priory was founded by Aldwin a monk, 11 W. 1. for Benedictine monks, and was valued at the diffolution at 98*l.* 10*s.* 9*d. ob.*

The church is dedicated to St. Mary, and hath a low tower, adorned with battlements, with five bells in it.

Monuments and Infcriptions.

There is a monument in the church againft the wall, over which are the following arms: *Party per pale, baron and femme.* 1. *Sable, two lions rampant combatant Or, armed and langued gules.* 2. *Or, two bendlets azure; between them in the dexter chief an efchalop gules,* for Tracy. Upon a table below, it is thus infcribed:

In Memoriam Cl. Viri Ægidij Carter, olim de Swell Inferiori in hoc Comitatu Armigeri, Qui probitate Morum, fide et pietate in divinis, necnon erga principem infignis, inter paucos piâ fenectute vitam claudens, Deceffit anno Ætatis fuæ octogefimo, vicefimo quarto die Martij Annoq; Dom. 1664.

Et præivit octo ante menfibus chariffima ejus uxor Elizabetha, honeftâ et fplendidâ familiâ de Tracy orta, quæ una cum illo fexaginta annos matrimonio vixit, uterq; cœleftis regni, ne rurfus feparentur, participes.

Gyles Carter was the eldeft Sonn of John Carter, of Nether Swell in the County of Gloucefter, Efq; his two Brethren being John Carter of Charlton-Abbats, and William Carter of Breefnorton, in Oxfordfhire. He married Elizabeth the Daughter of Sir Paul Tracy of Stanwell, & died without Iffue.

In the chancel is this memorial:

In Memory of Samuel the Son of Jofhua Elyott, Clerk, and Elizabeth his Wife, daughter unto Edward Aylworth of Aylworth, in the county of Gloucefter, efq; He died Aug. 1st, 1667. She died Ian. 17, 1672.

The Lord hath called Samuel hence,
Who Jofhua did fucceed.
He feafteth now on Joys divine,
Who here his Flock did feed.

Under the table is a fcutcheon, parted per pale, the baron's fide blank. On the finifter fide, *Argent, a fefs ingrailed, between fix billets gules,* for Aylworth.

Within the rails of the chancel, upon a flat ftone,

Bernard Winchcombe, Gent. Sub Centurion many Years, loyal to his King and Church, meekly fubmitted to Death, and came to this Place of Reft Feb. 16, 1683. Æt. 71.

Firft fruits, £.	6	12	9	Synodals, £.	0	2	0
Tenths, —	0	13	10	Pentecoftals,	0	0	9
Procurations,	0	6	8				

Benefaction.

Mr. Goddard Carter gave 5*l.* a year to teach children to read.

Taxes.			£.	s.	d.
	The Royal Aid in	1692, £.	56	0	0
	Poll-tax — —	1694, —	9	16	0
	Land-tax ——	1694, —	39	10	8
	The fame, at 3*s.* —	1770, —	33	3	0

About the year 1710, according to fir Robert Atkyns, there were 25 houfes and about 120 inhabitants, whereof 0 were freeholders, in this parifh; the yearly births 3, and burials 3. But examining the parifh regifter, I find that in a feries of ten years, from 1760 to 1769 inclufive, the baptifms were 45, the burials 34; and the inhabitants having been numbered are found to be 171, fo that population increafes in this place; and the proportion of fouls to the average number of yearly burials is as 50 to 1.

ASTON, *or* COLD ASTON,

IS a village in the hundred of Pucklechurch, bounded on the fouth by Somerfetfhire; three miles weft from Marfhfield, five north from Bath, five fouth-eaft from Sodbury, and thirty-four fouth from Gloucefter. That part of the village where the church ftands lies high, and much expofed to the violence of the winds. The great road from London, through Marfhfield to Briftol, leads thro' this place, at a fmall diftance from the church.

Sir Robert Atkyns's derivation of the name from the afh trees growing here, is not founded on fact. The place is not remarkable for that kind of tree, nor indeed is *Afhton* the proper name of it. The true and fignificant name is *Eafton,* or *Afton.* In *Domefday-book* it is written *Efcetone.* It was fo called from its fituation in the hundred of Pucklechurch, being the moft eafterly village in that hundred. The prenomen *Cold* was given it on account of its expofed fituation, and to diftinguifh it from Eafton near Briftol, and another Eafton in the neighbourhood of Bath.

The parifh is about three miles in length, and a mile and a half in breadth. It confifts principally of arable land, with fome pafture and woodland, but produces no remarkable plants nor foffils. Part of Lanfdown is in this parifh. Five fprings, *viz.* Hamefwell, Bridewell, Romewell, Clintonfwell, and another large fpring rifing in Monkwood, after joining their waters together, empty themfelves into the Avon; but none of them runs into the Boyd, as mentioned by fir Robert Atkyns.

The following account is taken literally from that learned hiftorian. About fourteen years fince, [*i. e.* 1698] in this parifh, as a perfon was plowing with oxen, one of the oxen faultered in a hole, which when the earth was removed from it, appeared like the tun of a chimney, through which feveral perfons have been let down, where they found a *cavity* in which one might walk above half a mile one way, and it is not known how far the other; and as they walked with candles,

candles, they obferved feveral fuch tunnels afcending towards the furface of the earth.

It is not faid what depth or what figure this cavity was of, particulars which might have given fome light as to the ufe of it. Being on the fpot, I was informed that the paffage was from north-eaft to fouth-weft, but the holes were all carefully ftopt up to prevent accidents, fo that I could not defcend to view the place myfelf.

Of the Manor and other Eftates.

The particulars of the manor and other eftates are as follow.

In *Domefday-book*, under the head *Terra Eccle' de Bade*, it is expreft after this manner:

'The fame church holds Efcetone, in Polcre-'cerce hundred. There are five hides, of which 'two are quit from geld, by the grant of king 'Edward and king William; but three are taxed. 'In demean is one plow-tillage, and three villeins, 'and three bordars, and one radchenifter, having 'amongft them three plow-tillages. There is one 'colibert, and a mill of fifty pence, and fix acres 'of meadow. It is worth and was worth 4*l.* *Domefday-book*, p. 71.

The abbey of Bath continued to enjoy this manor 'till that houfe was diffolved; fo that neither the Bafkervilles, nor any other of thofe perfons mentioned by fir Robert Atkyns as fucceffive lords of it, from the beginning of his account down to the 24th year of king H. 8. had the leaft property here. The truth is, all that we find in that gentleman's hiftory, concerning this manor, down to the thirty-ninth line of p. 229, relates to *Afton Blank*, fometimes alfo called Cold Afton, and was placed to this parifh by miftake. This confufion of names led fir Robert into another miftake of the fame nature, for in his lift of clerks and patrons of this church, four of them belong to Afton Blank.

This manor, with the manor of Tatwick, and feverai woods in Hamefwell, Tatwick, and Cold Afhton, and the advowfon of the church, were granted, after the diffolution of the abbey of Bath, to fir Walter Dennis, 32 H. 8.

John Stratford, efq; died feized of this manor 7 E. 6. and livery of it was granted to his fon Henry Stratford, who foon afterwards conveyed it to Mr. Pipwell, mayor and alderman of Briftol, who died about the 15th year of queen Elizabeth; and his fon Michael Pipwell had livery of the manor granted to him. John Pipwell, fon of Michael, was lord of it in 1608, and fold it to Mr. Gunning, mayor and alderman of Briftol.

From him it defcended to his fon fir Robert Gunning, who dying without iffue, it came to his fifter and heir. She was married to fir Thomas Langton, mayor and alderman of Briftol, whofe fon Thomas Langton, efq; was lord of this manor in 1712.

William Whittington, efq; is the prefent proprietor, and has a feat here. He is defcended from the Whittingtons of Pauntly, under which head are the arms and pedigree of that family.

HAMLET. *Hamefwell* is a hamlet in this parifh, formerly belonging to the prior of Bath, who had free warren therein 5 E. 1. It was afterwards the property of the Pipwells, and is now the feat of Mr. Whittington, who has a good houfe there.

Turner's Court is a handfome old houfe, which had antiently a confecrated chapel, now converted to prophane ufes. This feat formerly belonged to the Strouds, and by marriage became the property of Mr. Wyndham, of whom it was purchafed by M. Gunning, the prefent proprietor.

The records fhew that William Cheltenham was feized of lands in Abbot Efton 40 E. 3. Sir Robert Atkyns places this abftract under Abfton, but I apprehend it fhould ftand under this parifh, the true name of which is Eafton, and belonged to the abbat of Bath. The fame author was alfo miftaken in reprefenting Tatwick to be in this parifh, whereas it is in that of Swanfwick, in Somerfetfhire.

Of the Church, &c.

The church is in the deanery of Hawkefbury. The priory of Bath formerly prefented to it. It is a rectory, worth 120*l.* a year. Mr. Whittington is patron, Mr. Cafwell the prefent incumbent. The glebe is above a hundred acres.

The church, which hath an aile on the fouth fide, and a low tower at the weft end, is adorned with pinnacles and battlements. It has a flat roof, and was built by Thomas Key, rector thereof, and dean of Durham, who was buried in or near the chancel, where, on a brafs plate againft the wall, is the following infcription for him:

Egregius Rector Thomas cognomine Keius
Conditur hac celebri pertumulatus humo:
Qui totam hanc facram propriis ex fumptibus Ædem
Conftruxit, fummi motus Amore Dei.
Obfecro concedat tali pro munere fanctus
Trinus et unus ei celice Regne Deus.

The fame perfon built the prefent parfonage houfe in 1509, but it has the appearance of greater antiquity. There is a confeffionary in it, and it is faid, feven of the friars belonging to the abbey refided there. Sir Bevil Granville, who was mortally wounded at the battle of Lanfdown in the civil wars, was carried to the parfonage houfe of this place, and died there.

	£.	s.	d.		£.	s.	d.
Firft Fruits,	17	1	7	Synodals,	0	2	0
Tenths,	1	14	2	Pentecoftals,	0	0	1
Procurations,	0	6	8				

Benefaction.

There is a benefaction of 5*l.* a year, charged on the eftate of William Whittington, efq; to fupport a fchool; of which charity Mr. Whittington and the minifter are truftees.

Taxes.

Taxes.					
The Royal Aid in	1692, £.	129	12	0
Poll-tax ——	— 1694, —	30	15	0
Land-tax ——	1694, —	135	19	0
The fame, at 3*s*. —	1770, —	102	10	0

About the year 1710, according to fir Robert Atkyns, there were 33 houfes in this parifh, and about 142 inhabitants, whereof 4 were freeholders; yearly births 4, burials 3. But upon examining the parifh regifter, I find that in a feries of ten years, from 1700 to 1709 both inclufive, there were regiftered 43 baptifms and 31 burials; and in a like feries, from 1760 to 1769, were 73 baptifms and 55 burials; and by actual numeration, there are now 38 houfes and 213 inhabitants; fo that the people are increafing in this parifh, and the proportion of the living inhabitants to the average of yearly burials is nearly as 40 to 1.

****

ASTON SOMERVILE.

THIS parifh lies in the lower part of the hundred of Kiftfgate, four miles diftant fouth from Evefham in Worcefterfhire; feven north from Winchcombe, and twenty-four north-eaft from Gloucefter. It is fituated in the vale, about two miles weft from the Cotfwold-hills above Buckland, with Hinton to the north-weftward, Child's Wickham to the north-eaft, and Wormington to the fouthward of it.

Afton or *Eftune* is a relative name, given to this place from its fituation in the old hundred of Greteftan, and *Somervile* is the name of an antient proprietor of the manor, ferving to diftinguifh the parifh from two others of the fame name, in this neighbourhood.

Serpentine-ftones, Belemnites, petrifications of the nautulus, and of the cockle, with other foffil fubftances, are commonly plowed and dug up in the fields and other parts of the parifh, of which Mr. Reynalds, the late rector, fhewed me feveral curious fpecimens. And lately a falt-fpring broke out here, which in future time may be worked to advantage, but as yet lies neglected. A brook running from this place falls into the Avon, at Hampton, near Evefham.

Of the Manor and other Eftates.

In *Domefday-book* are the following particulars:
'The fame Hafcoit [Mufard] holds Eftune in 'Greteftan hundred. There are fix hides taxed. 'Ernefi held it. In demean are three plow-til-'lages, and twelve villeins with four plow-tillages, 'and nine *fervi* and *ancillæ*. There is a mill of '8*s*. [value] and twenty acres of meadow. It was 'worth and is worth 6*l*.' *Domefday-book*, p. 78.

The records fhew that fir John de Afton Somervile held the manor of Afton Somervile 35 H. 3. fo that this manor had obtained the name, and belonged to the family of Somervile foon after the Norman conqueft.

Ralph Mufard held the manor of Efton, 1 E. 1. and Mafculine Mufard, in truft for the abbat of Evefham, was feized of the manor of Afton Somervile, with the advowfon of the church, 31 E. 1. But the manor foon reverted to the family who had been the former proprietors; for William Somervile, fon of fir John Somervile, gave a hundred marks fine, and was admitted lord of the manor of Somervile Afton, with the advowfon of the church, 5 E. 2. and his fon fir William Somervile was feized of this manor 1 & 11 E. 3. They refided in a large houfe moated round, near the fouth fide of the church, which has been long fince demolifhed, and there are fcarcely any traces of it remaining.

Sir John Somervile, fon and heir of the laft fir William, was fucceeded by his fon Robert, high fheriff of this county in the year 1401. Thomas Somervile, a defcendant of Robert, married Joan, daughter and heir of John Alefbury, efq; of Edfton in Warwickfhire, and died 16 H. 7. and from that time the family refided in Warwickfhire.

Robert Somervile, fon of Thomas, married Mary, daughter of John Grevil, of Milcot, and dying 29 H. 8. was fucceeded by his fon John, who married Elizabeth, daughter of William Corbet; and dying 20 Eliz. was alfo fucceeded by his fon John Somervile, who was feduced by his confeffor to kill queen Elizabeth, and condemned for the attempt, in the twenty-fifth year of that reign, but was found ftrangled in Newgate before the time appointed for his execution.

Sir William Somervile, brother to John, married Elizabeth, daughter of fir Humphry Ferrers, of Tamworth caftle; and dying in 1616, this eftate defcended to his fon fir William Somervile, who married Cicely, daughter and coheir of fir John Shirley, of Isfield in Suffex. He died in 1628, and was fucceeded by his fon and heir William Somervile, who married Anne, daughter of Robert lord vifcount Tracy, of Todington. Robert Somervile was his fon and fucceffor, whofe fon William Somervile, efq; author of that well known and ingenious poem the *Chafe*, fold the reverfion of this eftate to the late lord Somervile, who became poffeffed of it in the year 1742. His lordfhip dying in 1765, was fucceeded in honour and eftate by his eldeft fon, now lord Somervile, the prefent owner of this manor.

Sir Walter de Somervile, an anceftor of this family, was of Norman extract, and came to England with the Conqueror. Roger de Somervile was fummoned as a baron to parliament, and died 1 E. 3. Sir Philip de Somervile, fon of Roger, was obliged by tenure to give a flitch of bacon in his hall at Wicknore in Staffordfhire, to all who had been married a year, and would make oath that they had not repented of their marriage. He died 29 E. 3. and with him the barony was extinct.

Of the Church, &c.

The church is a rectory, in the deanery of Campden. It was worth 80*l.* a year. The glebe was forty acres; but in the year 1746, the rectory was confiderably improved by inclofing the common fields and commonable places, when a rent-charge and a portion of land were fet apart for the rector in lieu of tithes, by the common concurrence of the bifhop, the lord of the manor, (the only freeholder) and the rector. It is valued at 9*l.* 3*s.* 4*d.* in the king's books. Lord Somervile is patron, Mr. William Somervile is the prefent incumbent. It antiently belonged to the abbey of Evefham, whereby the demeans of the manor paid no tithes; and there was a fmall impropriation, which belonged to the abbey of Winchcombe, granted to fir Thomas Seimour, 1 E. 6.

The church was rebuilt in 1688, with a tower at the weft end, adorned with pinnacles and battlements, and had four bells in it; but three being fplit, were fold fome time fince, and a church-clock, and a fmall library of books for the ufe of the rector, purchafed with the produce of them. Four fmall parcels of land were given to repair the church. In the chancel window are the Somerviles arms, *Argent, on a fefs between three annulets gules, as many leopards heads caboſhed Or.*

Monuments and Infcriptions.

On the fouth fide of the old church was an aile, where the Somerviles had a burying-place, and there is now, in a niche on that fide, a very antient figure, in ftone, of a knight in armour, as large as life, reprefenting one of that family, who lived about the time of king Edward the Third, as may be judged from the fculpture. This monument has been fhamefully violated by the country people, who at fheep-fhearing have been fuffered to whet their knives and fhears *againft old Somervile's nofe*, as they ufed to fay, fo that almoft half the face is whetted away.

In the chancel is a memorial for John Parry, A. M. rector of the church fifty-four years, who died in 1714; and for his wife Rebecca, daughter of Thomas Fullwood, gent. of an antient family in Warwickfhire. Over the tablet are their arms, *Baron and femme*, 1. *Argent, a fefs between three lozenges fable*, for Parry. 2. *A chevron between three mullets*, for Fullwood.

	£.	s.	d.		£.	s.	d.
Firft fruits,	9	3	4	Synodals,	0	2	0
Tenths, —	0	18	4	Pentecoftals,	0	0	7
Procurations,	0	6	8				

Taxes.			£.	s.	d.
	The Royal Aid in	1692,	104	6	0
	Poll-tax — —	1694, —	8	14	0
	Land-tax ——	1694, —	54	3	0
	The fame, at 3*s.* —	1770, —	38	19	9

According to fir Robert Atkyns, there were 12 houfes and about 60 inhabitants, whereof 4 were freeholders, in this parifh, when he compiled his account of it; yearly births 2, burials 1. But the parifh regifter fhews, that in a feries of ten years, from 1700 to 1709 inclufive, there were 18 baptifms and 18 burials; and in a like feries, from 1760 to 1769 inclufive, there are entered 15 baptifms and 10 burials, befides five or fix more from Clifford, and other places; and there are 51 inhabitants, fo that population appears to be decreafing.

ASTON SUBEDGE.

THIS parifh lies in the upper part of the hundred of Kiftfgate, fix miles fouth-eaftward from Evefham in Worcefterfhire, two northweftward from Campden, and thirty-one northeaft from Gloucefter. It derives its name from being fituated eaft from the neighbouring parifh of Wefton, and lying under the edge of a hill adjoining to Campden. The parifh confifts chiefly of arable lands, which were much in common field, 'till about three years ago they were inclofed by act of parliament. It produces no remarkable plants nor foffils.

Mr. Endymion Porter, fo much efteemed in the courts of king James and king Charles the Firft, was born in this parifh, and died in the year 1652.

Of the Manor and other Eftates.

'The church of St. Mary de Lanheie holds 'Eftune in Celfledeftorn hundred. Goda the 'countefs held it in the time of king Edward. 'There are four hides. In demean are three 'plow-tillages, and fix villeins, and one knight 'with three plow-tillages and a half. There are 'fix *fervi* and three *ancillæ*. It was worth 100*s.* 'and is now worth 4*l.*'[b] *Domefday-book*, p. 72.

Subfequent records fhew that Margaret de Cormeiles held Efton and Begfoure, 10 H. 3.

Sir Richard Stafford died feized of the manor of Afton-under-edge, and of the advowfon of the church, 4 R. 2. and Maud his widow was feized thereof, 1 H. 4. Edward earl of Stafford held Afton, 4 H. 4. Edward Stafford, bifhop of Exeter, was feized of the manor of Afhton-under-edge, 7 H. 5.

Sir Chriftopher Savage died feized of this manor 4 H. 8. and was fucceeded by Chriftopher his fon and heir, whofe fon Francis Savage had livery of it, 37 H. 8.

The manor was in the crown in the year 1608, and was afterwards purchafed by Richard Graves, efq; and by him fold to William Morgan, one of the fix clerks in chancery, who married the daughter of Richard Graves. Richard Morgan the grandfon of the faid William, by his will bearing date May 29, 1740, bequeathed this manor, and

[b] The abftracts from *Domefday-book* placed by fir Robert Atkyns to this parifh, certainly belong to *Afhchurch*. And what he fays of Ralph Mufard under this head, as well as under *Afton Blank*, fhould have been applied to *Afton Somervile*.

others

others in this county to Morgan Graves, of Mickleton, esq; whose son, Walwyn Graves, esq; is the present lord of the manor. *See Mickleton.*

The hundred court for the upper part of Kiftsgate hundred is held here by Mr. Graves, to whom the royalty of that extensive hundred descended with this manor. The common fines issuing out of each parish, specified in the grant of royalty, are paid by the lord to the crown.

Thomas Freeman and Joan his wife levied a fine of lands in Ashton-under-edge to Nicholas Cowley, 32 H. 6.

Of the Church, &c.

The church is a rectory, in the deanery of Campden, which was worth about 80*l.* a year; but is supposed to be much improved by the inclosing of the common fields a few years ago. It is valued in the king's books at 10*l.* 2*s.* 3½*d.* The reverend Mr. Feild is the present incumbent.

First fruits £.	10	2	3½	Synodals £.	0	1	0
Tenths —	1	0	2	Pentecost.	0	0	7
Procurations	0	3	0				

Benefaction.

Mr. Endymion Canning gave 20*l.* to the poor.

Taxes.					
The Royal Aid in 1692,		£.67	0	0
Poll-tax —	1694, —	10	0	8
Land-tax —	1694, —	39	0	0
The same, at 3*s.*	1770, —	30	0	0

According to sir Robert Atkyns, there were 24 houses, and about 104 inhabitants, whereof 10 were freeholders, in this parish; yearly births 4, burials 3. But in the last particular his account is erroneous, for in a series of ten years, from 1700 to 1709 inclusive, there are registered only 21 baptisms, and 7 burials. In the year 1751, there were 31 housholders, and 80 inhabitants; but the lands are now let into four farms, which made seven before the inclosing, and at this time (1773) there are only 20 housholders, and 63 inhabitants.

ASTON-UNDER-HILL, or ASHTON-UNDER-HILL.

ONE part of this parish lies in the hundred of Tibbleston, the other in the upper division of that of Tewkesbury. It is seven miles distant north-westward from Wichcombe, six north-east from Tewkesbury, five south from Evesham, and sixteen north-eastward from Gloucester.

It was antiently a member of the manor of Beckford, and was called *Estone*, (and by corruption *Aston*, and so in length of time deviating further from the true reading, *Ashton*) from its situation to the eastward of that place. The additional name has also a local meaning, too obvious to need an explanation.

The parish consists of a due proportion of pasture and arable land, with some wood-land. It hath lately been inclosed by act of parliament. Here is a spring of water pretty strongly impregnated with iron; but the parish produces no remarkable plants, and only a few fossils of the oister and muscle kinds.

Of the Manor and other Estates.

In *Domesday-book*, the account of this village stands under the title *Terra Regis*, and may be thus translated:

'Turbertus, a thane of earl Harold, held Estone 'in Tetboldestane hundred. There are eight 'hides, and four plow-tillages in demean, and 'ten villeins, and four bordars, with six plow-'tillages. There are eight *servi*, and three *ancillæ*.

'Of these two vills [*i.e.* Beceford and Estone] 'earl William made one manor, and they were 'not put to farm 'till Roger de Lurei let them for '30*l.* The same earl gave the tithe and the 'churches, with two villeins, and three virgates 'of land to the abbey of Cormeile.' *D. B.* p. 69.

Sir Robert Atkyns places here, by mistake, some abstracts from the early records concerning Aston Carant, in the parish of Ashchurch.

King Henry the Eighth granted this manor to sir Richard a Lee, who had two daughters coheiresses, who made a partition of their estates; and the manor of Beckford, of which Aston was a part, was sold to sir Richard Franklyn and Edward Wakeman. Sir Thomas Glover having purchased Franklyn's estate in Ashton-under-hill, he, with Mr. Wakeman, took a fresh grant of the manor from the crown, in the reign of king James the First, and afterwards by deed, reserving to himself and his heirs certain manerial rights over his own lands, conveyed all other manerial rights over the residue of the manor, to Mr. Wakeman. Henry Wakeman, of Beckford, esq; a descendant of that Mr. Wakeman, is the present lord of the manor, from whose son I received this account of the descent of it. *See Beckford.*

Of the Church, &c.

The church is in the deanery of Campden. It is an impropriation, annexed to Beckford. In the bishop's visitation-book it is stiled the chapel of Ashton, or Aston-under-hill. Joseph Biddle, M. A. is patron and incumbent. The impropriation pays 20*s.* a year to the crown.

The church hath a handsome tower, with pinnacles at the west end, and an aile on the north side.

Benefaction.

Mr. Endymion Canning gave 20*l.* to the poor.

Taxes.

Taxes.	The Royal Aid in 1692,	£. 57	16	0
	Poll-tax ——	1694, — 4	0	0
	Land-tax —	1694, — 47	17	0
	The same, at 3s.	1770, — 35	18	0

AVENING.

THIS parish lies in the hundred of Longtree, It is three miles south from Hampton, three north from Tetbury, nine west from Cirencester, and fourteen south from Gloucester. A bourn runs through the middle of it, westward and north-westward, towards Horsley and Woodchester, and so on 'till it falls into the Froome, or Stroud river, and is carried with it into the Severn. Hence the name of Avening, from *Afonig*, the British word for a bourn.

The parish consists chiefly of arable, with some wood lands and pasture ground. The clothing business furnishes employment for the lower class of the inhabitants.

Edward Sheppard, esq; has lately built a handsome house at Gatcombe in this parish, where he resides, and has a large estate, and a park, called Gatcombe-park, one part of which lies in this parish, and the other in Hampton.

The antiquities of this place consist of some *tumuli*, thrown up by the Danes or Saxons, or both, between whom there have certainly been various engagements hereabout, tho' history has not pointed out the precise spots where they happened. Two of those *tumuli*, called the *Barrow Tumps*, are not far from Mr. Sheppard's house, and I have been informed that an old sword was taken out of one of them, about twenty years ago. Two other *tumuli*, or barrows, lie on the road from this place to Hampton, with a stone placed on the top of each of them. The country people call them *Long-stone*, and *Tangle-stone*, and suppose them to bear the respective names of two generals who fell in battle in the Danish wars. They are undoubtedly monumental; the latter name seems to be no other than a corruption of *Angle's-stone*, *i.e.* the Englishman's stone, or monument; whilst that erected upon the other barrow obtained the present appellation on account of the form of it, and was probably a memorial for the Danish captain. But the reader will observe that *Long-stone* is in the parish of Hampton.

The timber-wood of this parish and neighbourhood is chiefly beech, intermixt with oak and ash. The beech wood is manufactured into gun-stocks, card-boards, and saddle-trees; and the refuse converted into charcoal, or used for common fire wood. But there is no scarce plant nor remarkable fossil found here.

Of the Manor and other Estates.

At the time of the general survey, soon after the Conquest, this manor belonged to the king, and accordingly in *Domesday-book* it stands under the title *Terra Regis*. It was a part of the large possessions of Brictric, who fell under the Conqueror's displeasure, as will be shewn more largely under Tewkesbury. After mentioning some other estates that formerly belonged to that unfortunate nobleman, it is expressed after this manner in the record:

'The same Brictric held Aveninge in Langetreu 'hundred: In the reign of king Edward there 'were ten hides, and eight plow-tillages in demean; 'and twenty-four villeins, and five bordars, and 'thirty *servi*, with sixteen plow-tillages. There 'were four mills of [the rent of] nineteen shil'lings and two-pence. The steward hath now 'added one mill of forty-pence. There is a wood 'two miles long, and half a mile broad. There is 'an hawk-aiery. It is worth 27*l*.' *D. B.* p. 69.

King William the First probably gave this manor to the nuns of the abbey of Caen in Normandy, not long after he gave them Hampton, for they were the antient proprietors of it, and enjoyed it 'till the suppression of alien monasteries, in the second year of the reign of king Henry the Fifth; after which it was given to the abbey of Sion, or Sheen in Middlesex, which was founded by that king for sixty nuns of the order of St. Bridget, thirteen priests, four deacons, and eight lay brethren. It was dedicated to St. Saviour, St. Mary, and St. Bridget, and was the richest nunnery in England, being valued at the dissolution at 1731*l*. 8*s*. 4½*d*. When king Henry the Seventh built his palace at Sheen, he gave it the name of Richmond, which it has retained ever since.

At the general dissolution of monasteries, Avening fell to the crown, and king Henry the Eighth, in the 34th year of his reign, granted it to Andrew lord Windsor, in exchange for the manor of Stanwell near Windsor, which had been in the family of the Windsors ever since the Norman conquest. Walter their ancestor assumed the name of Windsor on his being constituted constable of the castle of that place, in the reign of king Henry the First. William lord Windsor, son and heir of Andrew, had livery of this manor 35 H. 8. Thomas lord Windsor was proprietor of it in the year 1608. Thomas lord Windsor (grandson to the former by his eldest daughter married to Dixey Hickman) sold it to

Mr. Samuel Sheppard, who was succeeded by his son Philip Sheppard, of Hampton in this county, esq; from whom it descended to his son and heir Samuel Sheppard. Samuel Sheppard, son of the last Samuel, succeeded to this estate, whose son Samuel Sheppard, esq; dying in the year 1770, without male issue, this manor came to his only brother Edward Sheppard, esq; the present proprietor of it His arms are, *Ermine, on a chief sable three battle axes argent.*

As to other estates, the records shew, that John Hewet levied a fine of lands in Avening to William Webb, 1 E. 6. And some lands in Avening, which belonged to the abbey of Tewkesbury, were granted

granted by the crown to Daniel Pert and Alexander Pert, 7 E. 6. in truſt for other perſons.

TITHINGS and *HAMLETS*.

1. *Nailſworth*, about a mile and a half weſtward from the church, is a populous tithing containing upwards of 60 houſes. Catherine, the widow of Thomas Leach, was ſeized of the manor of Nailſworth 8 H. 5.

2. *Aſton*, ſo called on account of its being ſituated eaſtward from the church, is a conſiderable eſtate, formerly for many generations belonging to a family of the name of Driver. It came afterwards to Richard Breresford, eſq; and then by purchaſe to Mr. Matthew Sloper of Tetbury, who ſold it to Thomas Eſtcourt of Shipton, eſq; the preſent poſſeſſor.

Loſemore farm is a reputed manor. It was granted by king Henry the Eighth to Andrew lord Windſor. William lord Windſor had livery of it, 35 H. 8. It came afterwards into the Driver family, then to Mr. Richard Breresford; and was purchaſed by the before-mentioned Mr. Sloper, whoſe executors are the preſent proprietors.

Of the Church, &c.

The church is a rector y in the deanery of Stonehouſe, worth upwards of 200*l.* a year. There was formerly a chapel at Nailſworth, and another at Aſton. Edward Sheppard eſq; is patron, —— Saluſbury Heaton, A. M. the preſent incumbent. It is ſaid in chancellor Parſons's ſurvey of the dioceſe of Glouceſter, (a manuſcript in the Bodleyan library) that the rector pays 250*l.* to the patron, I ſuppoſe he means at his preſentation, but of this matter I have had no further information. Eight acres of meadow and paſture, and 123 acres of arable land, with ten cottages, belong to the glebe.

The abbeſs of Caen in Normandy formerly preſented to this church, as did the abbeſs of Sion in the year 1488.

The church ſtands on the ſide of a riſing piece of ground. It is built in the form of a croſs, with a low embattled tower in the middle, having five bells.

Dr. Frampton, rector of this church, was made biſhop of Glouceſter: and Dr. Bull, alſo rector of this church, was made biſhop of St. David's.

Firſt fruits, £	24	0	0	Synodals, £.	0	2	0
Tenths, —	2	8	0	Pentecoſtals,	0	1	3
Procurations,	0	6	8				

Monuments and Inſcriptions.

In the chancel,

Here lieth the Bodye of William Bvſhie Rector of the churche of Avening, who deceaſed the 1 of December Anno Dn. 1600.

Here reſteth the body of William Hall, rector of this church, who departed this life ye 9th day of Nov. 1683 Æt: 74.

Within the rails of the communion table,

Iohannes Swynfen, Staffordienſis, Sacræ Theologiæ Baccalaureus, hujus Eccleſiæ ob viginti et duos Annos Rector, Nat. Aug. 15, 1654. Denat. Apr. 29, 1728.

On the ſame ſtone is a memorial for Elizabeth his relict, who died Apr. 4, 1752, in her 82d year.

On a flat ſtone, at the top, *Party per chevron ſable and ermine, in chief two boar's heads couped Or*, and under, this inſcription:

Here lyeth the body of SAMUEL SANDFORD late of London, Merchant, who departed this life the ninth day of April, Anno Dom. 1710, in the ſixty eighth year of his age.

Againſt the ſouth wall of the chancel, a ſcutcheon, Quarterly, 1ſt and 4th, *Argent, a chevron between three mullets ſable.* 2d and 3d, *Gyronny of ſix pieces, Or and ſable, upon the firſt, three heads couped of the ſecond.* Under, on a marble table, this inſcription:

Id quod morti ceſſit Roberti Browne Pharmacopœi, de Oppido Stroud in agro Gloceſtrienſi, juxta exuvias Elizabethæ matris, Thomæ fratris, Chirurgi, Elizabethæ Clementis ſororis, Gulielmi Hall A. M. Avunculi, ſubtus jacet depoſitum. Die quinto Julii anno ætatis 59°, ære Chriſtianæ 1739°, Animam in manus Dei efflavit.

On the north ſide, a ſmall marble monument for George Fletcher, clothier, who died Apr. 6, 1762.

Againſt the wall, on a ſcutcheon, *Party per pale, baron and femme*, 1. *Party per pale indented argent and azure, two lions rampant combatant, counterchanged*, for Driver. 2. *Argent, a chevron ingrailed ſable, between three crabs gules*, and under, the following inſcription:

To the happy Memory of Iohn Driver Gent. who deceaſed Iune the 12th 1681, in the 85th year of his age. And alſo Elizabeth his wife, who deceaſed Ianu. 28th A° Dni 1675, aged 73 years, they having lived together 52 years. Reſurrectionem expectantes glorioſam.

On another monument againſt the wall, the arms of Driver, and this inſcription:

Carolus filius natu maximus Iohannis Driver Gent. obijt xx°. die Januarij Anno Domini 1636, Ætat. 5°.
Mattheus ejuſdem Johannis natu ſecundus, olim Colleg. Omnium Animarum in Oxon Socius, poſtea Conciliarius ad legem, obijt xxviii die Januarij Anno Dom. 1661, Ætat. 27.
Reſurrectionem corporum expectamus glorioſam.

In the ſouth aile, (which belonged to the Driver family) under an arch, the effigy of a man, at top theſe arms, *Party per pale, baron and femme*, 1. Driver, as before. 2. *Party per chevron, argent and gules, a creſcent counterchanged*, for Chapman. Under, on a table, this inſcription:

M. S. Iohannis Driver Gen. Iohannis Filij tertij, qui, mortuis Carolo et Mattheo fratribus, in paterna hæreditate ſatis ampla, (ſine cujuſquam invidia) ſucceſſit. Vir omnibus quibus notus erat deſideratiſſimus, utpote *Philoxenos Philagathos*, nemini inimicus, amicus amiciſſimus, demum in pauperes et egenos beneficentiæ exemplar illuſtriſſimum. Obijt nonis Ianuarij A. D. MDCLXXXVII, Ætatis LI. Beati miſericordes quoniam ipſi miſericordiam conſequentur.

Under the effigy it is thus written:

Hoc monumentum in honorem conjugis optimi de ſe meriti, ſuiq; immortalis in ipſum amoris qualecunque teſtimonium, propriis ſumptibus erexit Elizabetha vidua.

In the north aile or chapel is the figure of a man in freeſtone, in a kneeling poſture. Over his head, in a ſcutcheon, *Argent, on a croſs ſable a leopard's head caboſhed Or*, for Brydges, and under the figure this inſcription:

Here lyeth the Body of Henry Brydgis Efquier, fonn to Iohn Lord Chavndos Baron of Shevdley, who departed this Life the 24 day of Iannvari Anno Dom. 1615.

Againft the wall, the arms of Sandford, already blazoned, and this infcription:

In Memory of Sarah the wife of William Sandford of Stonehoufe, Gent. and daughter of Samuel Adams of this parifh, Cloth[r]. who died the 17th of February Anno Dom. 1722. She gave by confent of her hufband the houfes, garden, orchard, and a piece of pafture ground adjoining, lying and being in this parifh, at a place called the Crofs, then in the tenure and poffeffion of one John Harris, who doe hold it by Leafe for three lives, paying yearly twenty fhillings due at Chriftmas. And after that leafe fhall be expired, then the full profits for ever to be apply'd towards the education of poor children belonging to this tithing of Avening, as directed by deede of truft left with her hufband.

Againft the wall, in a fcutcheon, *Gules, a crofs Or, in the dexter canton an eagle difplay'd of the fecond.* Under, on a table, this infcription:

In memory of Richard Webb of this parifh Clothier, who died Aug. 16, 1712, aged 78. Alfo of Richard his fon who died June 11, 1748, aged 60 years.

Benefactions.

John Driver, efq; of Afton, gave the intereft of 50*l.* for ever to bind out poor children apprentices.

Mrs. Elizabeth Coxe gave the intereft of 150*l.* for ever, to be thus apply'd, *viz.* the intereft of 100*l.* to bind out poor children apprentices, and the intereft of 50*l.* to teach poor children to read, and to provide books for them.

Mr. Ambrofe Webb gave the intereft of 4*l.* and Mr. Burge of Afton, the intereft of 2*l.* to be diftributed in fmall bread every Chriftmas.

Mr. Samuel Sandford, late of London, gave the intereft of 200*l.* for ever, to teach fix poor boys to read their primer, and fay the catechifm, when they are to be cloathed and put away, and to be conftantly fucceeded by fix others.

Mr. Richard Cambridge, of London, merchant, gave the intereft of 20*l.* to be annually diftributed among the poor of that part of Nailfworth which lies in this parifh.

Taxes.					
The Royal Aid in	1692,	£. 128	11	4
Poll-tax — —	1694,	— 48	16	0
Land-tax — -	1694,	— 180	5	0
The fame, at 3*s.*	1770,	— 138	19	9

Sir Robert Atkyns, whofe Hiftory of Gloucefterfhire was publifhed in the year 1712, reckons 160 houfes, and about 600 inhabitants in this parifh, and fets down the yearly births at 16, and the burials at 15; but it appears by the parifh regifter, that in a feries of ten years, from 1706 to 1715, there were 179 baptifms and 127 burials; and in a like feries, from 1760 to 1769 inclufive, there were regifter'd 241 baptifms and 214 burials; and reckoning the proportion of the number of living inhabitants to the number of annual burials, as 40 to 1, which will be found to be a moderate computation in healthy fituations, the whole number of fouls in this parifh will then be 856. But this account, drawn from the parifh regifter, falls fhort of the true number of births and burials, for there are three diffenting meeting-houfes in the parifh and neighbourhood, at which fome of the inhabitants are buried, and at two of them there is adminiftration of baptifm. From thefe circumftances it appears that population is greatly increafed here fince the beginning of the laft century.

A W R E.

THIS parifh lies in the hundred of Blidefloe, in the foreft divifion, fituate on the north-weft bank of the Severn; four miles fouth-weftward from Newnham, feven fouthward from Mitchel-Dean, and fixteen fouth-weftward from Gloucefter. It is about four miles in length, and nearly as much in breadth, confifting of arable, pafture, and fome woodland. A rivulet feparates it on one fide from Newnham, and Linch-brook divides it on the other from the parifh of Lidney. It lies in the upper level.

The foil in many places is of a reddifh yellow, which gave occafion to the name, for *Aure* in the Britifh language fignifies yellow.

At this place the Severn is above two miles over, tho' a little higher not more than half fo wide. Oppofite the church, lies the bar of fands called the *Noofe*, which formerly rendered the navigation fo difficult, that nobody durft attempt it without a pilot. Upon the tide's firft approach to thefe fands, it foams and makes a hideous noife. The air is not very good, becaufe of the frequent irruption of the tides, which have fometimes flowed over the fea-wall three feet perpendicular.

There is a common near the river, called the *Old Warth*, above a mile long, and about half a mile broad.

This is an antient village, formerly much more confiderable than at prefent, for tradition will have it that there was once a large town of the name of Pomerton within it, of which there is fcarce any thing left but the name. *Domefday-book* mentions Pontune and Peritone, in Blitefla u hundred, to which it is faid earl William joined the manor of Neft. Now as Pirton and Nafs are contiguous to this parifh, it feems not unlikely that Pontone was fituated near them, and was very probably the fame with the above defolated town of Pomerton, with only a little variation in the name; but more of this matter under the tithing of Blakeney.

Thomas Sternhold, who verfified fome of the Pfalms, was a native of this place. It is faid that his pofterity turned papifts.

The names of Adeane, Bathern, Keddick, and Berkin are of great antiquity in this neighbourhood.

Of the Manor and other Eftates.

Awre was part of the antient demefnes of the crown. *Domefday-book* furnifhes the following particulars:

'King

'King Edward held Aure in Bliteſlau hundred. 'There are five hides, and in demean one plow-'tillage, and twelve villeins, and eight bordars, 'with fourteen plow-tillages. There is one *ſervus*, 'and a mill of 30*d.* and a ſalt-work of [the rent 'of] thirty ſeams of ſalt, and a church with one 'yard-land.

'This manor paid half a night's farm in the 'time of king Edward, and it does the ſame now.

'Half a hide of this manor lies waſte, and ſo 'pays only 12*l.* to the ſheriff, but nevertheleſs it 'pays all the farm.

'There are three members ſeparated from the 'manor, which were, and ought always to be 'within it, as the men of the county ſay, *i. e.* 'Peritone, Eteſlau, Bliteſlau. In theſe are ſeven 'hides, and in demean one plow-tillage, and 'twenty villeins, and three bordars, with thirteen 'plow-tillages, and two *ſervi*, and a fiſhery.

'Peritone is in fee to earl William. Roger de 'Berchelai holds Etelau. William the ſon of 'Baderon holds Bliteſlau. Aluui the ſheriff put 'theſe out of farm.' *Domeſday-book*, p. 67.

It appears by an inquiſition 4 E. 1. that the manor of Aure was in the crown in the reign of king Henry the Firſt. But there have been ſeveral diſtinct manors in this pariſh, of the ſame name, otherwiſe the records are contradictory. Henry de Bohun held Awre 1 John, and releaſed all his right therein to the king.

In the fifth year of the ſame reign, Walter de Awre had a grant of the manor of Awre for his life. This family took their name from the place, and continued poſſeſſed of a manor here 'till the end of the reign of Edward the Third.

Yet other records ſhew, that William earl of Saliſbury was ſeized of Awre 3 H. 3.

Richard Marſhal earl of Pembroke had a grant of the inheritance of the hundred of Awre 17 H. 3. by which it ſhould ſeem that this place gave name to a hundred, nevertheleſs I ſuppoſe it to have been no other than the hundred of Blideſlow, which was a member of the manor of Awre.

Philip Baderon was ſeized of Awre 6 E. 1. and of one yard-land in Awre 15 E. 1. and of one meſſuage and thirty acres of land 30 E. 1. John Baderon was ſeized of Awre, and of a fiſhery in the Severn, 6 E. 3.

In obedience to the king's writ, the ſheriff of Glouceſterſhire returned, that Thomas Berkeley, ſen. Maurice Berkeley, and Margaret Mortimer had the lordſhip of Awre, 9 E. 1. Roger de Mortimer earl of March died ſeized of Awre 11 E. 1. William de Valentia, and Joan his wife, and Maud de Mortimer were ſeized of the manor of Awre, and of the hundred of Blideſlowe, with return of writs, 15 E. 1. And their right was then allowed in a writ of *Quo warranto*. Upon the death of Maud de Mortimer, 29 E. 1. her eſtate in the manor deſcended to Edmond, ſon and heir of earl Roger her huſband; but he did not enjoy it long, for he died of a wound given him in battle againſt the Welch, 31 E. 1. whereupon Margaret his widow, a Spaniſh lady, near kinſ-woman to queen Elianor, was ſeized of Awre.

Sir Maurice, ſon of Thomas de Berkeley, held the manor of Awre, with its members, Etlowe and Blakeney, and the hundred of Blideſlow, 42 E. 3. and Elizabeth the widow of ſir Maurice Berkeley, was ſeized of all thoſe particulars, 13 R. 2. Sir Thomas de Berkeley, and Margaret his wife, were ſeized of them 5 H. 5. And Richard de Beauchamp earl of Warwick, in right of Elizabeth his wife, daughter and heir of Thomas lord Berkeley, died ſeized of Awre, Etloe, Blakeney, and the hundred of Blideſloe, 17 H. 6. leaving three daughters, of whom Elizabeth was married to George Neville lord Latimer, and carried this manor into that family. Richard Neville lord Latimer died ſeized of the manor of Awre and Purton 22 H. 8. and his ſon John lord Latimer had livery thereof the ſame year.

Sir Edward Wintour was lord of the manor of Awre in the year 1608.

Sir Thomas Rich, of Sunning in the county of Berks, baronet, among other things, gave 6000*l.* to the corporation of Glouceſter in truſt, to be laid out in lands, for the endowment and ſupport of the blue-coat hoſpital in that city; with which money they purchaſed the manor of Awre and Blakeney, worth about 200*l.* a year. *See* p. 198. The corporation are the preſent lords of this manor, and hold court leet here.

Of the other eſtates the records ſhew, that Walter de Awre held one yard-land and ſix acres in Awre, and a meadow called Hundins, and one yard-land called Haworth, 5 John. Robert de Awre held one meſſuage and one yard-land in Awre 19 E. 2.

Robert Badderon was ſeized of a fiſhery in Awre 36 E. 3.

John Sabin and others, for the abbey of Flaxley, were ſeized of one meſſuage, two plow-tillages, and a yearly rent of 100*s.* in Awre 10 R. 2.

Robert Badderon was ſeized of a tenement called Handomere in Awre 3 H. 4.

John Berew levied a fine of lands in Awre, Etloe, Blakeney, and St. Briavel's, and of a fiſhery in Severn, to ſir Alexander Baynham and others, 10 H. 7. Lands formerly belonging to the abbey of Flaxley, of the value of 4*l.* 4*s.* 11*d.* a year, were granted, by the name of the manor of Newnham, Awre, and Poulton, to ſir Anthony Kingſton 36 H. 8. of which grant I have a copy. Edward Berew died ſeized of lands in Awre, Etloe, Blakeney, Gatcomb, and Poulton, and of a woodwardſhip in the foreſt of Dean, 12 Eliz. and was ſucceeded by James his ſon.

TITHINGS and *HAMLETS.*

1. *Hagloe* is a tithing, about a mile from the church, not mentioned in *Domeſday-book.*

2. *Blideſlow*, or *Bliteſlau*, is another diſtinct tithing, which gives name to the hundred. It appears

appears by *Domeſday-book*, that this was a member of the manor of Awre at the time of the general ſurvey, and that it was then in the tenure of William the ſon of Baderon.

John Tiptot earl of Worceſter was ſeized of Blideſlow, 9 & 10 H. 6. He married Elizabeth, the only daughter of Robert Grender, lord of the manor of Abbenhall, in this county; which Robert Grender was ſeized of Blideſlow 22 H. 6. and his daughter the counteſs of Worceſter was alſo ſeized thereof 31 H. 6. After whom, this eſtate deſcended, like Abbenhall, to John Grender, and was carried by his daughter in marriage into the family of Walwyn. Thomas Baynham of Clowerwall marrying the heireſs of the Walwyns, became poſſeſſed of this eſtate; and their ſon ſir Chriſtopher Baynham died ſeized of it 32 H. 8. and was ſucceeded by his ſon ſir George Baynham, whoſe ſon Chriſtopher died ſeized of the manor of Blideſlow 5 Mariæ. Richard Baynham, his brother, had livery of it the ſame year; and Thomas Baynham, ſon of Chriſtopher, had alſo livery of this manor granted to him 16 Eliz. The Baynhams had antiently a ſeat here, which has long ſince been converted to a farm houſe. This is a reputed manor, belonging to Mr. Robert Boy.

3. *Etloe*, or *Eteſlau*, lying more than two miles from the church. It is now a diſtinct tithing, and is mentioned in the abſtract from *Domeſday-book*, at the beginning of the account of this pariſh, to be then a member of the manor of Awre. Patrick de Chaworth was ſeized of Etloe, which, according to ſir William Dugdale, was part of the barony of Kennesford, 11 E. 1. His daughter Maud was married to Henry, nephew to king Edward the Firſt, afterwards earl of Lancaſter. Henry his ſon ſucceeded him, and was afterwards created duke of Lancaſter. Richard Mortyn levied a fine of the manor of Etloe, and of other lands belonging to the dutchy of Lancaſter, to the king, 15 E. 4. to the uſe of Richard Mortyn for one month, the remainder to Elizabeth the queen, to the archbiſhop of Canterbury, and others. This manor was granted in truſt to the archbiſhop of Canterbury, and other great perſons, 3 H. 5. Etloe-dutchy is a reputed manor, the property of Charles Barrow, eſq.

The tithings of *Blideſlow*, *Etloe*, and *Hagloe*, (antiently written *Bliteſlau*, &c.) were probably ſo called from the antient barrows in thoſe tithings. It was uſual with the Romans, and with the northern nations after their example, to raiſe heaps of earth over the corps of thoſe that were ſlain in the field, when every ſoldier brought his turf, or turfs, to be placed together in the form of a little hill, as a memorial for the defunct. Thoſe *tumuli*, in different parts, have obtained different names, as barrows, and lawes, loes, or lows. The latter names are ſuppoſed to be derived from the old Britiſh word *Llehau*, which Dr. John Davis explains by *locare*, *collocare*: So that *lau* ſignifies a little hill made by art, and it is ſaid by ſir William Dugdale, in his Antiquities of Warwickſhire, that it is uſed in the ſame ſenſe by the Scots at this day.

4. *Blakeney*, a diſtinct tithing, lying more than two miles from the church. No mention is made of it in *Domeſday-book*, but it is now become the moſt conſiderable tithing in the pariſh, containing above fifty families. The earlieſt period in which this place is mentioned in the records is 8 R. 2. when Elianor de Haresfield was ſeized of one meſſuage and one plow-tillage in Blakeney. This hamlet has two yearly fairs, originally fixt on May-day and All-ſaints-day, for horned cattle and hogs; but ſince the alteration of the ſtyle, thoſe fairs are kept on the twelfth day of April, and the twelfth day of November. This place is diſtinguiſh'd in ſome maps and topographical books as a market-town, whoſe market is kept on wedneſdays, but at preſent it has none. The inhabitants of the tithing maintain two bridges over a trout-river, which runs from this place into the Severn at Bream's-pill, where pentagonal ſtones are found. It is probable that from theſe bridges Pontune took its name. And why may not that Pontune or Pomerton be the ſame place which is now called Blakeney, eſpecially as there is no hamlet of the name of Pontune or Pomerton in the pariſh or neighbourhood; and there are many inſtances of places loſing, by diſuſe, their antient names, and taking others in their room; thus, the antient name of Miſerden was Grenhamſtede, the preſent Batsford was Beceſhore, and the name of Strigoil gave place to that of Chepſtow.

At Blakeney is a chapel of eaſe, of which the particulars will be given under the account of the church of Awre, on which it is dependant.

5. *Hayes* is a reputed manor, the property of Mr. Savage.

6. *Gatcombe* is a place in this pariſh, ſituate on a little cove of the river Severn. A ſmall ſloop in the Iriſh trade, and ſome ſmall craft, are fitted out from, and belong to this place, which is ſaid to have been heretofore a port of conſiderable trade; but I confeſs, there ſeems to be little ground for ſuch a notion.

7. *Poulton-court* is a reputed manor in this pariſh. Sir Robert Atkyns obſerves, that Adeliza de l'Iſle, widow of Reginald de Dunſtanville, gave the lordſhip of Poulton to the abbey of Tewkeſbury, in the reign of king H. 1. but I apprehend this is to be underſtood of ſome other place of the name of Poulton; for the records ſhew that John de Willington held Poulton 12 E. 3. with ſeveral other eſtates in this county, particularly Frampton Cotterel, to which head the reader is referred for an account of the deſcent of this manor, which acknowledged the ſame proprietors with Frampton down to 20 H. 7. It was afterwards granted to Edward duke of Somerſet, upon whoſe attainder it reverted to the crown. Another grant was made of it to William Bridgman, and

Richard

Richard Wilfon, 5 Mariæ. And within a few years fince, it was the property of Samuel Blackwell, efq; who, about the year 1766, fold it to Mr. James Thomas, of Oatfield, the prefent proprietor. Sir William Poulton feems to have taken his name from this place, whofe eftate it was in the reign of king Henry the Fourth, by the marriage of an heirefs of the family of Wrath, defcended by the female line from the Willingtons. Here was antiently a chapel, long fince demolifhed.

Of the Church, &c.

The church is a vicarage in the Foreft deanery, worth 120*l.* a year, in the gift of the company of haberdafhers in London, but valued in the king's books at 10*l.* 5*s.*

Edmund de Mortimer and Margaret his wife were feized of the advowfon of Awre 32 E. 1. One of the lords of Berkeley gave the advowfon to the priory of Lanthony, and the monks of that houfe procured the tithes to be appropriated. The rectory of Awre and Purton, with certain tithes and fifheries in the Severn, late belonging to that priory, were granted to Thomas James, in truft for Thomas Erfkyn, vifcount Fenton, 5 Jac.

Mr. Hammond, who was of the company of haberdafhers, purchafed the great tithes, which pay 13*l.* 15*s.* 1 *d.* to the crown, and divided them between the vicarage of Awre and the curacy of Blakeney. The vicar of Awre has the vicarial tithes of both. Mr. John Sargeaunt is the prefent incumbent. The chancel of Awre is kept in repair out of the great tithes.

The minifter of Blakeney is ftiled the chaplain or affiftant preacher at the chapel of Blakeney. There is no houfe for the minifter, nor any chapel-yard at Blakeney. By Mr. Hammond's will both the minifters muft refide, and not be at any time abfent more than forty days.

The church of Awre is a large double building, fupported by pillars in the middle, with a handfome embattled tower at the weft end. It is dedicated to St. Andrew; but the chapel at Blakeney is dedicated to All Saints.

Two tenements in Awre, and a fmall parcel of land near the Severn, are given towards the repair of the church. The church houfe is affigned to the ufe of the poor.

Firft fruits, £.	10	10	0	Synodals, £.	0	2	0
Tenths, —	1	1	0	Pentecoftals,	0	1	4
Procurations,	0	6	8				

Taxes.					
The Royal Aid in	1692, £.	224	12	0
Poll-tax — —	1694, —	63	12	0
Land-tax ——	1694, —	232	8	0
The fame, at 3*s.* —	1770, —	171	3	0

According to fir Robert Atkyns, there were 139 houfes and about 700 inhabitants in this parifh, whereof 44 were freeholders; yearly births 20, burials 19. But his numbers are too high. In a feries of ten years, from 1700 to 1709 inclufive, there are regiftered 163 baptifms, and 173 burials. In a like feries, from 1760 to 1769, the baptifms are 247, and burials 236; whence it appears that the inhabitants have increafed fince the beginning of this century, notwithftanding the burials exceed the baptifms in the firft feries, occafioned by a great mortality in the year 1700. If we reckon the number of living inhabitants to bear a proportion to the annual burials, as 32 to 1, making allowance for the lefs healthy fituation of this parifh on the banks of the Severn, the prefent number of inhabitants will be 755.

BADGWORTH.

THIS parifh is fituated in the vale, in the hundred of Dudfton and King's-barton, three miles fouth-weftward from Cheltenham, twelve fouth from Tewkefbury, and feven north-eaftward from Gloucefter. The greateft part of the parifh is fine rich pafture ground, and the reft very good arable land; but there are no remarkable vegetables nor foffils, except a few petrifications of the bivalve kind, and of the *echinus marinus*, or fea-hedge-hog.

There is a fpring of mineral water at a place called Cold Pool, in the hamlet of Badgworth, the properties of which are nearly the fame with thofe of Cheltenham water.

It is alfo worthy obfervation, amongft the great works of nature, that in the year 1772, Prifcilla the wife of Thomas Bullock, the parifh clerk, was delivered of three boys, who are all living.

From the hill above Crickley, in this parifh, is a moft beautiful and extenfive profpect over the vale, not to be equalled in many parts of this kingdom.

As to the etymology of the name of this parifh, whether we confider the antient or modern way of writing it, there can be little certainty concerning it. It is conjectured, that the former part of the name carries in it that of fome antient proprietor; the latter part hath been already explained under Aldfworth.

Of the Manor and other Eftates.

From *Domefday-book* we learn the following particulars:

'The fame William [*i. e.* William de Owe] 'holds Beiewrde in Dudeftanes hundred. Aleftan 'held it. There are eight hides. In demean are 'fix plow-tillages, and twenty villeins, and fourteen bordars, with twenty-four plow-tillages. 'There are feventeen *fervi*, and a mill of 12*d.* '[rent.] a wood two miles long and one broad. 'It was worth 15*l.* and is now worth 13*l.*' *Domefday-book*, p. 73.

This William de Owe, or de Ewe, was earl of Ewe, in Normandy, and was rewarded by king William, with one hundred and fifteen manors in feveral parts of the kingdom, of which, eleven were in Gloucefterfhire, as may be feen by turning to the above page of this book. He took up arms againſt William the Second, in behalf of Robert Curthoiſe, the king's elder brother, and very much ravaged Glouceſterſhire; but was gained over to the king by large promiſes, and again proved treacherous to him. He was afterwards taken, and demanding to juſtify himſelf in a duel, was vanquiſhed, and impriſoned at Saliſbury, where he was caſtrated, and had his eyes put out, 9 W. 2. and all his eſtates were ſeized by the crown. He was accuſed of treaſon before the conſtable and marſhal of England, before whom the court of Chivalry was held. In this court, judgment was always given againſt the vanquiſh'd, whether appellant or defendant; for according to the law of arms, the accuſer being overcome, incurred the ſame puniſhment that the defendant ought to have done, if he had been vanquiſhed.

It is to be obſerved, that trial by duel was introduced here by the conqueror, and remained long after the reign of Henry the Third; yet this, as well as ordeal, was forbidden by the popes. The people were led to appeal to the firy trial and the teſt of arms, by the ſame abſurd notion which obtained in the dark ages that produced them, *that divine providence would miraculouſly interpoſe in favour of innocence.* Thus duelling, in certain caſes relative to war, became a due proceſs of law, and by degrees came into uſe to terminate little diſputes of every nature. And notwithſtanding this barbarous practice hath been long ſince forbidden by our laws, and condemned upon the principles of religion, morality, and good policy; yet, to the opprobrium of the Britiſh nation, it prevails at this day as much as ever. A deteſtation of this fooliſh, this wicked practice, hath carried me out of my line; but I return.

This manor was afterwards granted to Gilbert Marſhal, who was ſo called from his exerciſing the office of marſhal to the king. To him ſucceeded John his ſon, who had likewiſe John his ſon and heir, who dying without iſſue in the laſt year of king Richard the Firſt, was ſucceeded by his brother William earl of Pembroke, and hereditary marſhal. He died 3 H. 3. and was ſurvived by Iſabel his wife, the daughter and heireſs of Richard earl of Strigul or Strigoil, now called Chepſtow; ſhe had the manor of Badgworth in dower 3 H. 3. which, at her deceaſe, deſcended ſucceſſively to William, Richard, Gilbert, Walter, and Anſelm, ſons of William earl of Pembroke, who all dying without iſſue, left five ſiſters their heireſſes; Maud, married to Hugh Bigod earl of Norfolk, and afterwards to John de Warren earl of Surry; Joan, the ſecond daughter, married to Warin de Monchenſy; Iſabel, the third daughter, married to Gilbert de Clare earl of Glouceſter, and afterwards to Richard earl of Cornwal; Sibil, the fourth daughter, married to William de Ferrers earl of Derby; and Eve, the fifth and youngeſt daughter, was married to William de Braoſe.

The manor being divided among ſo many heireſſes will account for the great variety of owners at the ſame time, who, notwithſtanding they are generally ſaid in the records to hold Badgworth, were ſeized of a part of it only.

Thus the records ſhew, that Gilbert de Clare earl of Glouceſter and Hertford held it 8 E. 2.

Hugh de Audley the elder was ſeized of it in the ſame reign, but taking part with the barons againſt the king to expel the Spencers, was impriſoned, and his lands ſeized, and this manor was granted to Hugh le Diſpencer the younger 15 E. 2. but Iſolda, the widow of Hugh de Audley, was reſtored to the lands of her huſband 1 E. 3. Hugh de Audley earl of Glouceſter, and Margaret his wife were ſeized thereof 21 E. 3. as was ſir James de Audley, 9 R. 2. Sir Nicholas lord Audley died ſeized of a fourth part of the manor of Badgworth, 15 R. 2. John lord Audley died ſeized of one ſhare of this manor 10 H. 4. John, the ſon of ſir James Audley had livery of it 23 H. 8.

John Giffard of Brimpsfield, in right of Maud de Long Eſpee his wife, was ſeized of the manor of Badgworth, and obtained free warren therein 9 E. 1. He left two daughters his heireſſes, of whom, Elianor was married to —— le Strange, deſcended from Guy, ſon of the duke of Britain, who came into England in the reign of king Henry the Firſt, and obtained the name of Leſtrange becauſe he was a ſtranger. John le Strange, ſon of —— le Strange, was ſeized of a moiety of the manor of Badgworth, in right of his mother, 23 E. 3. and was ſucceeded by Fulk his eldeſt ſon, who left this eſtate to his brother John, who was alſo ſucceeded by Elizabeth his daughter and heir, married to Thomas Mowbray earl of Nottingham; after whoſe death, this moiety went to Ankaret her aunt and heir, daughter to John lord Strange of Blackmere, who was then married to ſir Richard Talbot; which ſir Richard had livery of all the lands that deſcended to her, 7 R. 2.[b] Gilbert Talbot died ſeized of it 7 H. 5.[c]

John Troutbeck and Margaret his wife levied a fine of a moiety of a moiety of Badgworth, to the uſe of themſelves in tail, the remainder to the heirs of Margaret, 23 H. 6. and ſir William Troutbeck held it in the thirty-eighth year of the ſame reign.

John earl of Shrewſbury was ſeized of this manor 38 H. 6. and of the ſame and of Hunthouſe 13 E. 4. Catherine counteſs of Shrewſbury was ſeized in dower of a moiety of the manor of Badgworth, and of a meſſuage called Hunt-thorns, 15 E. 4. Livery of this manor was granted to John Talbot and Margaret his wife, daughter of Adam Troutbeck of Mobberley in Cheſhire, and couſin and heir of ſir William Troutbeck, 3 H. 8. and John Talbot had alſo livery of it 7 Eliz.

Other records ſhew, that John Muſgroſe was ſeized of this manor 3 E. 1. and that John Calew levied a fine of lands in Badgworth to the uſe of

[b] Rot. Fin. 7 R. 2. m. 26.

[c] Eſch. 7 H. 5. n. 68.

John Maltravers the younger, 4 E. 3. and sir John Maltravers held this eftate 38 E. 3. I apprehend thefe records relate to Little Shurdington in Badgworth, which came afterwards to the Arundels, as did feveral other eftates in this county held by the Mufgrofes in the reign of king H. 3. and the three firft Edwards.

John lord Chandos died feized of Badgworth 4 Mariæ; and it appears by the efcheator's inquifition, that Edmund lord Chandos died feized of Badgworth, and of the grange and tenements in Badgworth called Crippits, worth 34*l.* 15*s.* 10*d. ob. per ann.* 15 Eliz. and that Giles Bridges his fon had livery thereof the fame year.

Mr. Gwinnet was lord of the manor of Badgworth in the year 1712. Mrs. Chefter is the prefent proprietor. *See Almondfbury.*

HAMLETS, &c. 1. *Badgworth*, where the church ftands, confifts of 20 houfes and 113 inhabitants.

2. *Little Shurdington*, above a mile from the church, is a hamlet of 13 houfes and 106 inhabitants. Roger Maltravers was feized of Little Shurdington in the manor of Badgworth, 25 E. 3. as was John Arundel of Arundel 9 H. 5. and John Fitz-Alan earl of Arundel was feized thereof 13 H. 6. It is now the property of Robert Lawrence, efq; who has an elegant feat called the *Greenway*, in this hamlet, and a fine eftate of rich pafture land round it. His arms are, *Argent, a crofs raguly gules.*

Mr. Edwards has alfo a good houfe and eftate here.

3. *Bentham*, is a large hamlet, confifting of 38 houfes and 160 inhabitants, near two miles from the church. Fulk Fitz-Warren held lands in Bentham of Thomas lord Berkeley of Brimpsfield, by the fervice of carrying a horn in Brimpsfield park, between the feafts of the Affumption and the nativity of the bleffed Virgin, whenever the king fhould hunt there, 23 E. 3. Fulk Fitz-Warren was alfo feized of this manor 1, 6, and 15 R. 2. which manor was held of Hugh, Thomas, and William, fucceffive earls of Stafford, by the fifth part of a knight's fee, 10, 16 & 22 R. 2. Edward earl of Stafford was feized of the manor of Bentham 4 H. 4. and Fulk Fitz-Warren was feized of the fame 9 H. 4. Fulk Fitz-Warren alfo held this manor, with divers knight's-fees thereto belonging, 8 H. 5. Sir John Berkeley held forty acres in Bentham 6 H. 6. Maurice Berkeley of Beverftone was feized of the manor of Bentham 38 & 39 H. 6. and 14 E. 4.

Hunt's-court is a capital meffuage in this hamlet. Sir Richard Haukeford and Anne his wife were feized of Hunt-court in Bentham 9 H. 6. and Elizabeth, one of his daughters and coheirs, was feized of the fame 12 H. 6. A fine was levied of the manor of Bentham called Hunt-court, to the ufe of William Bircher and Thomafia his wife, and to the heirs of their bodies, the remainder to the right heirs of William, 21 H. 6. Livery of the manor of Hunt's-Court was granted to William earl of Bath 20 Eliz. Mr Hinfon was the proprietor of it about the beginning of this century; it was afterwards fold to Charles Hyett, of Gloucefter, efq; whofe fecond fon Nicholas Hyett, efq; is the prefent owner of it. His arms are, *Argent, a lion rampant fable, a chief of the laft furmounted by another indented of the firft.*

4. *Little Witcombe*, containing 24 houfes and 117 inhabitants.

5. *Crickley*, is the name of an eftate belonging to William Prinne, of Charlton, efq; where was formerly a good houfe, now occupied by the tenant of the farm.

6. Part of *Great Shurdington*, containing 11 houfes, and 53 inhabitants. Mrs. Chefter has a good houfe and fine eftate here; and Thomas Randell, efq; has alfo a neat houfe here.

7. *Buckland's-place*, is an eftate which Richard Buckland granted to John Cook, alderman of Gloucefter, 3 H. 8.

Of the Church, &c.

The church is a vicarage in the deanery of Winchcombe, worth about 80*l.* a year. The manor of Badgworth, with the rectory and advowfon of the vicarage, belonged to the nunnery of Ufk in Monmouthfhire, and were granted to James Gunter and Walter Lewis 37 H. 8. Other tithes in Badgworth, belonging alfo to the fame nunnery, were granted to — Bergavenny, 34 H. 8. and again others were granted to John Fernham, 22 Eliz. That nunnery, at the diffolution, was valued at 69*l.* 9*s.* 8*d.* The priory of Chepftow, for black monks of the Cluniac order, had tithes and rents in Badgworth 7 R. 2.

The glebe-lands, formerly belonging to the nunnery of Ufk, are divided between Mrs. Tracy, daughter and heirefs of the late fir William Dodwell, and Mr. Burroughs; 1*l.* 6*s.* 8*d.* a year is paid out of them to the crown.

Jefus College in Oxford hath the greateft part of the impropriation, worth 130*l.* a year, for the maintenance of a fchool at Abergavenny. The college pays 16*l.* a year out of it to Chrift College in Cambridge, in lieu of tithes belonging to them. The rector of Oddington receives 5*l.* a year for great tithes in Great Shurdington. Mrs. Tracy is patronefs, the reverend Mr. John Baghot Delabere the prefent incumbent. The chapel of Shurdington is annexed to this church.

The church is dedicated to St. Mary. It hath a neat embattled tower at the weft end, fixty-nine feet high, with fix excellent bells in it, and a chapel on the north fide, dedicated to St. Margaret, who, according to the legends, was of noble birth, and being compelled by her parents to marry, efcaped from her hufband on the wedding night, in man's apparel, became a monk, and afterwards, by order of the monaftery, was made governor

vernor of a nunnery; one of the nuns of which place proving with child, it was concluded that St. Pelagius (for ſo St. Margaret called herſelf) was the father. Upon this ſhe was immured, and did not diſcover herſelf 'till juſt expiring, and after her death was found to be a chaſte virgin of the female ſex.

Firſt Fruits, £. 20	11	3	Synodals, £.	0	2	0
Tenths, — -- 2	1	1	Pentecoſtals,	0	1	0
Procurations, - 0	6	8				

Monuments and Inſcriptions.

There is a handſome monument in the church, with the following memorial:

Near this place is interr'd George Gwinnet Gough, who departed this life the 27th day of May, 1756, deſcended on his father's ſide from an antient family of the Gwinnets in North-Wales, who came to ſettle in this pariſh in the beginning of the reign of queen Elizabeth.

His afflicted mother, daughter of Jeremy Gough, of London, eſq; erected this monument in memory of her moſt beloved and truly worthy ſon.

There is alſo another handſome monument, whereon is inſcribed,

READER! Let this marble be a monitor to the Living, as well as a memorial of the Dead: And when thou readeſt the name of LYTTLETON LAWRENCE, Eſq; be inſtructed not to place thy confidence in the moſt perfect corporeal excellencies, which like his muſt undergo the deformity of corruption. And let his virtues excite thy imitation, particularly his parental affection, inflexible honeſty, and chriſtian benevolence, which, through a ſtedfaſt faith in thy Redeemer, will advance thee to a life immortal and full of glory.

He died the 5th day of April, 1740, aged 54.

Benefactions.

Mr. Stanſby, late vicar of Badgworth, left an eſtate, which lets at 14*l.* a year, for apprenticing of boys of this pariſh, Churchdown, and Cheltenham; whereof Badgworth is to receive 5*l.* a year, Churchdown 3*l.* and Cheltenham the remainder. The vicar of the pariſh for the time being is a truſtee to this charity, with power to end all diſputes that may ariſe concerning it.

Giles Cox, of Upton St. Leonard's, gent. gave 6*l.* a year in lands in that place, for the uſe of the poor of this pariſh.

William Mills, of this pariſh, gent. gave four nobles yearly, charged on lands in Little Witcomb, to the uſe of the poor.

Katherine Talbot, of Droitwich in the county of Worceſter, in the year 1698, gave 4*l.* a year, to be paid on the firſt day of May, to the uſe of the poor.

Lyttleton Lawrence, eſq; of this pariſh, gave a purple pulpit-cloth and cuſhion, with a cover of the ſame for the communion-table.

Benjamin Hyett, eſq; of Hunt-court in this pariſh, in the year 1757, gave the tapeſtry and two tables of the commandments at the altar; which tapeſtry was an altar-piece in the cathedral church of Glouceſter.

Taxes.					
The Royal Aid in	1692,	£. 306	1	4
Poll-tax — —	1694, —	36	18	0
Land-tax — -	1694, —	360	14	0
The ſame, at 3*s.*	1770, —	266	0	6

The ſtate of population given by ſir Robert Atkyns muſt have been very erroneous. He reckons Badgworth to contain 25 houſes, Bentham 24, Little Witcombe 26, part of Great Shurdington 8; which by miſtake in caſting up he makes 104 in all, and ſets the inhabitants down at 500, the yearly births 16, burials 15. —— At preſent there are 109 houſes, and 549 inhabitants. In a ſeries of ten years, from 1700 to 1709 incluſive, there are entered in the pariſh-regiſter 143 baptiſms and 106 burials; in a like ſeries, from 1760 to 1769, 213 baptiſms, and 160 burials. Comparing the numbers together, we find that population is greatly increaſed here ſince the beginning of this century, and that ſir Robert's eſtimate for the inhabitants was much too high. Perhaps 360 would have been near the truth, as I conclude from the average of yearly burials in the firſt ſeries, which bear a proportion in this place to the number of the living inhabitants as 1 to 34.

****

BADMINTON (GREAT,)

LIES in the upper diviſion of the hundred of Grumbald's-aſh. It is ſituate in the hill-country, on the confines next Wiltſhire, nine miles ſouth-weſtward from Tetbury, ſix north-eaſt from Chipping Sodbury, and twenty-eight ſouthward from Glouceſter. It is bounded on the north by Little Badminton, on the ſouth by Acton Turville, on the eaſt by Alderton in Wiltſhire, and on the weſt by Old Sodbury. The air is healthy, and the ſoil more ſuitable to corn than paſture. There is no river, nor ſtream of water running through it.

The etymology of the name is difficult and uncertain, wherefore I decline giving, as my own, an explanation of it. Some people, however, have conjectured, that it is compounded of two Anglo-Saxon words, beðan, to pray, and moiȝn, a monk; and ſo make it to ſignify the ſame as the prieſt's town; but the antient manner of writing it [Madminton] as it is in *Domeſday-book*, is an argument againſt that notion.

It hath been aſſerted of this village, as of Lindley in Leiceſterſhire, that no adder, ſnake, nor lizard hath ever been found in it, notwithſtanding they are frequent in the neighbouring places; but, as to Badminton at leaſt, this is a vulgar error, yet the inhabitants affirm, that thoſe animals were very rarely ſeen 'till within theſe few years. Here are found ſome foſſils of the oiſter and periwinkle kinds, and that round ſtone called the bullet-ſtone, which doctor Plot ſeemed ſo deſirous of examining into the nature of, had his intended journey thro' England, in ſearch of natural curioſities, taken place. In my viſit to this place I could not procure the ſight of one, nor any further account of it, than that it is a round ſtone of a very compact texture.

But

But that from which this village derives its greateſt conſequence, is the fine ſeat which has been the chief reſidence of the princely houſe of Beaufort, ever ſince the deſtruction of Ragland-caſtle in the great civil wars. It is called *Badminton-Houſe*, and was formerly the ſeat of the antient family of the Botelers. The front next the grand avenue has two wings; the centre conſiſting of three ſtories, of which the ſecond is ornamented with pillaſters and capitals of the Corinthian order. At the top of the Attic ſtory are the Beaufort arms, with ſupporters, well executed in freeſtone.

This noble ſtructure ſtands not far from the centre of a large tract of ground, incloſed by a wall about ten miles in circumference, within which are ſeveral diſtinct parks for red and fallow-deer, full of large and beautiful plantations of firs and other foreſt-trees.

The grand approach is through the park from Worceſter-lodge, which ſtands at the diſtance of two miles and three quarters from the houſe, and is itſelf a fine, lofty freeſtone building, with iron gates.

It was neceſſary to give ſome general account of this noble ſeat; but it would be difficult by words to convey a tolerable idea of the beautiful plantations belonging to it, which have been raiſed from time to time at a vaſt expence, and are continually improving under the direction of the preſent noble proprietor. Indeed this ſubject is more proper for the pencil and engraver. I ſhall however obſerve, for the information of thoſe who have ſeen them in their former ſtate, that the labyrinth, and all that profuſion of figures in box and yew, which came firſt into uſe in this country about the reign of William the Third, are taken away, and give place to the modern taſte, and leſs reſtrained method of planting.

Of the Manor and other Eſtates.

Domeſday-book, under the title *Terra Ernulfi de Heſding*, gives the following particulars:

'The ſame Hernulfus holds Madmintune in 'Grimboldeſtou hundred. There are four hides 'taxed. Edricus held it. In demean are two 'plow-tillages, and ſix villeins, and eight bordars, 'with a prieſt having thirteen plow-tillages. 'There are nine *ſervi*, and eight acres of meadow. 'It is worth and was worth 10 *l.*' *Dom. B.* p. 77.

Ralph Boteler died ſeized of Badminton and of the hundred of Grumbald's-aſh 3 E. 1. He was deſcended from Ralph Boteler, or *Radulphus Pincerna*, ſo called from his bearing the office of butler to Robert earl of Mellent and Leiceſter, in the reign of king Henry the Firſt.

Thomas Boteler, ſecond ſon of Ralph, and brother to William, ſucceeded in Badminton, which deſcended to his ſon ſir Thomas Boteler. He married a near relation of Edmund Fitz-Alan earl of Arundel, who taking part with the Spencers, was put to death at Hereford with many other adherents to the cauſe of the royal favourites.

Alan Boteler, ſon of ſir Thomas, had a ſon and heir ſir Alan, whoſe ſon Thomas was ſeized of this manor 41 E. 3. He was ſucceeded by his ſon ſir Ralph Boteler, whoſe ſon John was knighted, and had a ſon John; whoſe ſon Ralph died before his father. Sir John Boteler, ſon of Ralph, married Sylveſtra, daughter of ſir Anſelm Guyes, of Elmore, and died 5 E. 6. leaving a ſon William, who married Theophila, daughter of ſir John Newton, of Bar-Court. Nicholas Boteler, ſon of William, married Margaret, daughter of ſir John Young, and was lord of this manor in the year 1608. He left three ſons, John, Robert, and Alan.

Thomas Somerſet, third ſon of Edward earl of Worceſter, was created viſcount Somerſet of Caſhel in Ireland. He purchaſed this manor of Nicholas Boteler, the laſt proprietor of that family, and left an only daughter Elizabeth, who dying unmarried, gave it to Henry Somerſet, lord Herbert, afterwards duke of Beaufort. His grace the preſent duke of Beaufort is lord of this manor, and proprietor of the hundred of Grumbald's-aſh.

This noble duke derives his genealogy from Geoffry Plantagenet, earl of Anjou, ſon of Foulk, king of Jeruſalem, by Maud the empreſs his wife, daughter of Henry the Firſt king of England; being lineally deſcended from John of Gaunt, duke of Lancaſter, who cauſed all his natural children by Catherine the widow of ſir John Swinford, knight, who became afterwards his third wife, to be called Beaufort, from the caſtle of that name in the county of Anjou, the place of their nativity, and part of the inheritance of the houſe of Lancaſter. By the ſaid Catherine he had three ſons, John, Henry, and Thomas; and one daughter, Joan. Thomas was created earl of Dorſet, and afterwards duke of Exeter; Henry was made biſhop of Wincheſter, in the year 1405, alſo one of the cardinals, and lord chancellor of England; John the eldeſt was created earl of Somerſet 20 R. 2.

Which John died in the year 1410, and was buried in the cathedral at Canterbury; having married Margaret, ſiſter and coheir to Edmund Holland earl of Kent, by whom he had iſſue four ſons, Henry, John, Edmund, and Thomas; and two daughters, Joan, married firſt to James the Firſt king of Scotland, afterwards to ſir James Stuart, anceſtor to the preſent duke of Athol; and Margaret, married to Thomas Courtney, the ſixth earl of Devonſhire of his family. Henry the eldeſt ſon dying unmarried, left his inheritance to his brother

John, who ſucceeded him as third earl of Somerſet, and was created duke of Somerſet 1443. Dying the year following, he was buried at Winbourn-abbey in Dorſetſhire, leaving iſſue by Margaret his wife, daughter of ſir John Beauchamp, knight, an only daughter Margaret, married to Edmund of Hadham, called alſo Edmond Tudor, earl of Richmond, by whom ſhe was mother of king Henry the Seventh.

To him succeeded Edmund his next brother, who was earl of Mortein, or Moreton, in Normandy, of which he was made regent. He was created marquis of Dorſet in the year 1443, and duke of Somerſet 26 H. 6. He was ſlain in the battle of St. Albans in 1455, leaving iſſue by Eleanor, ſecond daughter and coheir to Richard Beauchamp earl of Warwick, four ſons, of whom hereafter, and five daughters, *viz.* 1. Eleanor, the ſecond wife of James Butler earl of Ormond and Wiltſhire; 2. Joan, firſt married to ſir Robert St. Lawrence, baron of Howth in Ireland, and ſecondly to ſir Richard Fry, kn^t^. 3. Anne, married to ſir William Paſton, of Paſton in Norfolk, kn^t^. 4. Margaret, married to Humphry Stafford earl of Stafford, and ſecondly to ſir Richard Darrel, kn^t^. by whom ſhe had a daughter Margaret, wedded to James Touchet lord Audley, anceſtor to the preſent earl of Caſtlehaven; and 5. Elizabeth, married to ſir Henry Lewis, kn^t^. — The ſons of Edmund the ſecond duke of Somerſet were Henry, Edmund, John, and Thomas.

Henry, the eldeſt ſon, had the title of earl of Moreton in his father's life-time. He was knight of the garter, and third duke of Somerſet, and gained great honour in the wars with France. He took the caſtle of Anjou by aſſault, and put 300 Scots to the ſword, and hanged all the French that were in it. Adhering to the houſe of Lancaſter, he was taken priſoner at the battle of Hexham, by John Nevil marquis of Montacute, and there beheaded, in the year 1463, leaving iſſue by Joan Hill, or de la Montaign, an only natural ſon of the name of Charles, who aſſumed the ſurname of Somerſet; whereby the honour devolved upon Edmund his next brother, who was taken priſoner and beheaded at the battle of Tewkeſbury in 1471, without iſſue; and John and Thomas, his third and fourth brothers, alſo dying without children, in them terminated the male iſſue of John of Gaunt.

Which Charles Somerſet being a perſon of great abilities, arrived to high honours and great employments. He was made privy counſellor to king Henry the Seventh, and admiral at ſea; created banneret, elected knight of the garter, and made captain of the guards; was ſent on ſeveral important embaſſies, and employed by the king on arduous affairs. He married Elizabeth, ſole daughter and heir to William Herbert earl of Huntingdon, lord Herbert of Ragland, Chepſtow, and Gower; and in her right bore the title of lord Herbert. He was advanced to the dignity of earl of Worceſter by patent, 5 H. 8. by reaſon of his noble deſcent, and near alliance to the king in blood, as the patent imports. And dying in the year 1526, was privately interred, agreeable to his will, in Beaufort chapel, in the church within the caſtle of Windſor, leaving iſſue by his firſt wife Elizabeth, Henry his heir and ſucceſſor. His ſecond wife was Elizabeth, daughter of Thomas Weſt lord De-la-War, by whom he had iſſue ſir Charles Somerſet, kn^t^. captain of the tower of Ryſebank, in the haven of Calais; and ſir George Somerſet, of Bedmundesfield in com. Suff. kn^t^.

Henry the ſecond earl of Worceſter, for his ſignal exploits in the wars of France, had been knighted, during his father's life-time, by Charles Brandon duke of Suffolk; and ſhortly after his father's death, was appointed one of the commiſſioners for concluding a peace with the French. He married Elizabeth, daughter to ſir Anthony Browne, kn^t^. and by her had iſſue four ſons, 1. William, his heir and ſucceſſor; 2. Thomas, who died in 1587, in the tower of London; 3. Sir Charles, who died in 1529; 4. Francis, ſlain in Muſſelborough-field by the Scots: Alſo four daughters, 1. Eleanor, married to ſir Edward Vaughan, of Tretour, in com. Brecon, kn^t^. 2. Lucy, to John Nevil lord Latimer; 3. Anne, to Thomas Percy earl of Northumberland; and 4. Jane, to ſir Edward Manſel, kn^t^. This earl Henry dying in the year 1549, was buried at Ragland.

Which William, the third earl, was knight of the garter, and one of the peers that ſat on the trial of Mary queen of Scots. He married Chriſtian, daughter to Edward North, lord North of Carthlege; by whom he had Edward his only ſon and heir; and two daughters, Elizabeth, married to William Windſor, eſq; youngeſt ſon of William lord Windſor; and Lucy, to Henry Herbert, eſq; ſon and heir of ſir Thomas Herbert, of Wyneſtone in com. Monmouth, kn^t^.

Edward, the fourth earl, was made maſter of the horſe to queen Elizabeth, being the beſt horſeman and tilter of the times, which were then the manlike and noble recreations of the court, and ſuch as caught the applauſe of men, and the commendation of the ladies. He continued in that office 'till the 13 J. 1. when he was appointed lord privy ſeal, of which he had afterwards a grant for life, with the fee of 1500*l.* a year. He was alſo knight of the garter, and dying in the year 1627-8, was buried in St. Mary's chapel at Windſor, leaving iſſue by Elizabeth, daughter of Francis earl of Huntingdon, eight ſons and ſeven daughters; *viz.* 1. William lord Herbert, who died unmarried in his father's life-time;—2. Henry lord Herbert;—3. Thomas, who having been ſent, with ſir Charles Percy, to notify to king James the demiſe of queen Elizabeth, and his majeſty's being proclaimed her ſucceſſor, was made knight of the Bath with prince Charles; who being afterwards king, in the ſecond year of his reign, promoted him to the dignity of viſcount Somerſet, of Caſhel in Ireland. He married Eleanor, daughter of David lord Barry, and viſcount Buttevant of Ireland, relict of Thomas Butler earl of Ormond, by whom he had iſſue only one daughter Elizabeth, who died unmarried. —4. Charles; and —5. Francis, both died infants;—6. Charles, made knight of the Bath, who

who married Elizabeth, the daughter and heir of ſir William Powel, of Lanpylt com. Monmouth, by whom he had three daughters, Elizabeth, Mary, and Frances.—7. Chriſtopher, who died young;—8. Sir Edward Somerſet, knight of the Bath, who married Bridget, daughter and heir of ſir William Whitmore, of Leighton com. Ceſtr. kn[t]. but died without iſſue. The daughters were, —1. Elizabeth, married to ſir Henry Guildford, of Hempſted-place in Kent;—2. Catherine, to William lord Petre, of Writtle;—3. Anne, to ſir Edward Winter, of Lidney in Glouceſterſhire, kn[t]. —4. Frances, to William Morgan, of Lanternan com. Monmouth, eſq;—5. Mary, who died an infant;—6. Blanch, married to Thomas lord Arundel, of Wardour; and —7. another Catherine, married to Thomas lord Windſor. He was ſucceeded by his eldeſt ſurviving ſon,

Henry, the fifth earl, who was created marquis of Worceſter, by patent, in the year 1642. He was a nobleman of great parts and ample fortune, which was much impaired by the large ſupplies of men and money ſpent in the royal cauſe, which he powerfully aſſerted during the whole courſe of the civil war, in the reign of King Charles the Firſt. He maintained his caſtle of Ragland, againſt the parliament, with a garriſon of 800 men, from 1642, to Aug. 19, 1646, without receiving any contribution from the country; and then yielded it to ſir Thomas Fairfax, who beſieged it in perſon, upon honourable terms; but the conditions of capitulation being baſely violated, the marquis was taken into the cuſtody of the parliament's black-rod, in which he died in December following, and was buried at Windſor. His caſtle, after the ſurrender of it, was demoliſhed, and all the timber in the three parks near the houſe ſold, to the amount of 100,000*l*. Add to this, as large a ſum at leaſt lent to the king, and the further expence of ſupporting the above-mentioned garriſon, and of raiſing and maintaining two ſeveral armies, commanded by his ſon Edward earl of Glamorgan, at his own expence, together with the ſequeſtration from 1646; and laſtly, the loſs of that whole eſtate, which was ſold by the parliament, amounting, as appears by that year's audit, to about 20,000*l*. a year, which was not reſtored 'till the year 1660; and then ſome judgment may be formed of the loſs ſuſtained by this noble family in the royal cauſe. His lordſhip married Anne, the only child of John lord Ruſſel, and by her had iſſue nine ſons and four daughters. 1. Edward lord Herbert, of whom hereafter; —2. lord John Somerſet, who married Mary, daughter of Thomas lord Arundel, of Wardour; —3. lord William, who died an infant;—4. lord Henry, who died unmarried;—5. lord Thomas, who died at Rome in 1676;—6. lord Charles died a canon of Cambray in Flanders;—7. 8. 9. lords Frederick, Francis, and James, all died young. His lordſhip's daughters were, —1. lady Elizabeth, who died an infant;—2. lady Anne died a nun;—3. lady Mary died unmarried;— 4. lady Elizabeth was wedded to Francis Brown viſcount Montague.

Edward Somerſet, lord Herbert, ſucceeded his father in the year 1646, to whom, in his father's life-time, the king had directed ſeveral letters by the title of earl of Glamorgan, which he uſually bore. He was a perſon very highly eſteemed by the king, who made him generaliſſimo of his armies, and granted him, by patent,[d] ſeveral very extraordinary priveleges, which the peers took ſo ill, that, on the 18th of Auguſt, 1660, they appointed a committee to take that patent into conſideration. Accordingly, on the 23d of the ſame month, they reported, that the marquis was willing to deliver it to his majeſty; and it was delivered up on the 3d of September following. His lordſhip ſtands in the honourable Mr. Walpole's liſt of royal and noble authors, for two pieces, the one intituled, *A Century of the Names* and

[d] The commiſſion ran as follows: —— 'Charles, by the 'grace of God, King of England, Scotland, France and Ireland, 'Defender of the Faith, &c. To our right truſty, and right 'well-beloved couſin, Edward Somerſet, alias Plantaginet, Lord 'Herbert, Baron Beaufort, of Caldicote, Griſmond, Chepſtow, 'Ragland and Gower, Earl of Glamorgan, ſon and heir ap-'parent of our entirely beloved couſin, Henry Earl and Marquis 'of Worceſter, greeting. Having had good and long experience 'of your proweſs, prudence, and fidelity, do make choice, and 'by theſe nominate and appoint you, our right truſty, and 'right well-beloved couſin, Edward Somerſet, &c. to be our 'Generaliſſimo of three armies, Engliſh, Iriſh, and Foreign, 'and Admiral of a fleet at ſea, with power to recommend your 'Lieutenant-general for our approbation, leaving all other 'officers to your own election and denomination, and accordingly 'to receive their commiſſion from you: willing and commanding 'them, and every of them, you to obey, as their General, and 'you to receive immeditate orders from ourſelf only. And 'leſt, through diſtance of place, we may be miſinformed, we 'will and command you to reply unto us, if any of our orders 'ſhould thwart, or hinder any of your deſigns for our ſervice. 'And there being neceſſary great ſums of money, to the carrying 'on ſo chargeable an employment, which we have not to furniſh 'you withal, we do by theſe empower you to contract with 'any of our loving ſubjects of England, Ireland, and 'Dominion of Wales, for wardſhips, cuſtoms, woods, or any 'our rights and prerogatives; we by theſe obliging our Selves, 'our Heirs and Succeſſors, to confirm and make good the ſame 'accordingly. And for perſons of generoſity, for whom Titles 'of Honour are moſt deſirable, we have entruſted you with 'ſeveral patents under our Great Seal of England, from a Mar-'quis to a Baronet, which we give you full power and authority 'to date, and diſpoſe of, without knowing our further pleaſure; 'ſo great is our truſt and confidence in you, as that, whatſoever 'you do contract for, or promiſe, we will make good the 'ſame accordingly, from the date of this our commiſſion for-'wards; which for the better ſatisfaction, we give you leave to 'give them, or any of them, copies thereof, atteſted under your 'hand and ſeal of arms. And for your own encouragement, 'and in token of our gratitude, we give and allow you hence-'forward ſuch fees, titles, preheminences, and privileges, as 'do, and may belong unto your place and command above-'mentioned, with promiſe of our dear daughter Elizabeth to 'your ſon Plantaginet in marriage, with three hundred thouſand 'pounds in dower or portion, moſt part whereof we acknow-'ledge ſpent and diſburſt by your father and you, in our ſervice; 'and the title of Duke of Somerſet to you and your heirs male 'for ever; and from henceforward to give the Garter to 'your Arms, and at your pleaſure to put on the George 'and Blue Ribbon: and for your greater honour, and in 'teſtimony of our reality, we have with our own hand affixed 'our Great Seal of England, unto theſe our commiſſion and 'letters, making them patents. Witneſs our ſelf at Oxford, 'the firſt day of April, in the twentieth year of our reign, and 'the year of our Lord one thouſand ſix hundred and forty-four.' *Collins's Peerage*, V. 1. p. 200. 4th Ed.

and Scantlings of ſuch Inventions, &c. the other, *Certamen Religioſum, or a Conference between King Charles* I. *and Henry late Marquis of Worceſter, concerning Religion.* This noble peer married, firſt, Elizabeth, daughter of ſir William Dormer, kn[t]. and ſiſter to Robert earl of Carnarvon, by whom he had iſſue, Henry lord Herbert, of whom hereafter; lady Anne, married to Henry Howard duke of Norfolk, anceſtor of the preſent duke of Norfolk; and lady Elizabeth, married to William Herbert, earl and marquis of Powis. He married, ſecondly, Margaret, daughter to Henry Obrien earl of Thomond, by whom he had iſſue a daughter Mary, who died an infant. His lordſhip departing this life April 3, 1667, was ſucceeded by

Henry his only ſon, who, on the reſtoration of king Charles the Second, was conſtituted lord lieutenant of Glouceſterſhire; and in 1672, lord preſident of the council in Wales, and lord lieutenant of the ſeveral counties in that principality; and of the county and city of Briſtol, having the ſame year been inſtalled one of the knights of the garter. He was, by letters patent dated Dec. 2, 1682, advanced to the title of duke of Beaufort, with remainder to the heirs male of his body. His grace exerted himſelf againſt the duke of Monmouth in 1685; and afterwards endeavoured to ſecure Briſtol againſt the adherents of the prince of Orange, upon whoſe elevation to the throne, refuſing to take the oaths, he lived in retirement 'till his death, in the 70th year of his age, 1699. His grace had iſſue by Mary his wife, daughter of Arthur lord Capel, and widow of Henry lord Beauchamp, five ſons, Henry, who died young; Charles, his ſucceſſor; another Henry, Edward, and Arthur; and four daughters, the ladies Elizabeth, Mary, Henrietta, and Anne. He was buried in Beaufort-chapel, before mentioned, where is the following inſcription for him.

Sub hoc Marmore conquieſcit, Armorum & Titulorum Satur, *Henricus Somerſet*, *Dux de Beaufort*, *Marcio & Comes de Vigorniâ*, *Baro Herbert de Chepſtow*, *Raglan & Gower*, è Nobiliſſimo ordine Pericellidis Eques. Excellenti Animo ac Virtute vir; qui ſingularis Prudentiæ Laudem, cum inſigni Juſtitiæ Gloria conjunxit; et illuſtriſſimæ ſuæ Familiæ non modo Fortunas a Perduellibus everſas in integrum reſtituit; ſed & Antiquos Honores feliciter amplificavit. Neque tamen Rei Privatæ ſtudio intentus, defuit Publicæ: Erat enim idem, regnante Carolo & Jacobo ſecundo Conſilii in Principatu Wallenſi Preſes; Comitatuum Civitatumq; Gloceſtriæ, Herefordiæ, Briſtolii, Monumethiæ, necnon totius Walliæ, Præfectus; Arcis de Briavil Caſtellanus, et Saltus de Dean Cuſtos Principalis, Civitatum inſuper Gloſceſtriæ & Herefordiæ; Municipiorumq; Malmſburii, Teuxburii & Andoveri Seneſcallus. Quin & utriſque Carolidum, quibus intemerata ſemper fide adheſit, a Camerâ & a Conſiliis ſanctioribus. Conjugem unicam atq; unicè dilectam habuit, Mariam Honoratiſſimi Arthuri Domini Capel Filiam natu maximam; ex quâ Progeniem ſatis numeroſam ſuſcepit, V. Filios, Henricum Dominum Herbert hic juxta ſepultum, Carolum de Vigornia Marchionem; Henricum & Edvardum præmaturâ morte abreptos; Arthuru m Dominum Sommerſet. IV. Filias, Elizabetham, tenera Ætate mortuam; Mariam Ormondiæ Duciſſam; Henriettam Dominam de Obrien; Annam Coventriæ Comitiſſam.

H. M.

Cariſſimo Viro Dominoq; poſuit Superſtes & mœrens Duciſſa: Cui, poſt Annos XLIII ſuaviter in Conjugio actos, triſte ſui deſiderium reliquit Senex Suptuagenarius Jan. xxi. A. D. MDCXCIX.

Charles the ſecond ſon, ſurviving his elder brother, was ſtiled marquis of Worceſter after his father was created duke of Beaufort. He married Rebecca, daughter of ſir Joſiah Child. Unhappily leaping out of his coach, to avoid the danger he was expoſed to by the horſes running down a ſteep hill, he received a violent bruiſe, and broke his thigh-bone, of which he died in the 38th year of his age, 1698, during his father's life-time; leaving iſſue three ſons, Henry, Charles, and John; and three daughters, lady Mary, and lady Elizabeth, who died infants; and lady Henrietta, married to Charles duke of Grafton. Lord Charles Somerſet died on his travels in 1710; and lord John died in the year 1704.

Henry the eldeſt ſon ſucceeded his grandfather as duke of Beaufort. In the year 1711-2, his grace was conſtituted captain of the band of penſioners, lord lieutenant of Hampſhire and Glouceſterſhire, and cities of Briſtol and Glouceſter, and counties of the ſame. He was inſtalled knight of the garter in 1713, and departing this life on the 24th of May the next year, left iſſue by his lady, daughter and coheir of the earl of Gainſborough, Henry marquis of Worceſter, born in 1707; lord John, who died ſoon after he was born; and lord Charles-Noel, born in 1709, of whom his mother died in child-bed the next day. His grace had a former wife, lady Mary, only daughter of Charles Sackville earl of Dorſet; and alſo a third wife, lady Mary, youngeſt daughter to Peregrine Oſborne duke of Leeds, but had no iſſue by either of them.

Henry his eldeſt ſon ſucceeded as third duke of Beaufort. He wedded Frances, only child of ſir James Scudamore, of Home-Lacy in Herefordſhire, baronet, and viſcount Scudamore in the kingdom of Ireland; from whom his grace was divorced in the year 1743-4, upon account of her incontinence. His grace died without iſſue in 1745-6, and was ſucceeded in dignity and eſtate by his brother

Charles-Noel Somerſet, fourth duke of Beaufort, who diſtinguiſhed himſelf in the ſenate by a ſteady oppoſition to unconſtitutional and corrupt meaſures, and endeared himſelf to mankind by his ſocial virtues. His grace married Elizabeth, daughter of John Berkeley, of Stoke-Giffard in Glouceſterſhire, eſq; and ſiſter of the late Norborne lord Botetourt, by whom he had iſſue Henry, now duke of Beaufort, born in the year 1744; and five daughters, *viz.* lady Anne, married to Charles earl of Northampton; lady Elizabeth, who died in 1760; lady Rachel, who died an infant; lady Henrietta, and lady Iſabella.

Henry, the fifth duke of Beaufort, having accompliſhed his ſtudies at Oxford, where he received the degree of LL. D. embarked in the year 1764, for his travels in foreign parts, whence he returned in 1766, and the ſame year married Elizabeth, daughter of the late admiral Boſcawen, and niece of the viſcount Falmouth, by whom he he hath iſſue, living, two ſons and a daughter. His grace's arms are, *Quarterly*, *France and England, within a bordure compone argent and azure.* Creſt, *On a wreath, a portcullis Or, nailed azure, chains pendent thereto of the firſt.* Supporters, on the dexter ſide, *A panther argent, ſpotted with various colours, fire iſſuing out of his mouth and ears proper, gorged with a collar and chain pendent Or*; on the ſiniſter ſide, *A wyverne vert, holding in his mouth a ſiniſter hand coupé at the wriſt proper.* Motto, MUTARE VEL TIMERE SPERNO.

Of the Church, &c.

The church is a vicarage in the deanery of Hawkeſbury, worth 13*l.* a year. It formerly belonged to the abbey of Perſhore. The duke of Beaufort is patron and impropriator. The living is further augmented by two donations from the late patron and his brother, making together 50*l.* a year.

The church joins to the houſe of the duke of Beaufort, and accommodation is made in it for the inhabitants of Little Badminton, in the pariſh of Hawkeſbury, who, by an agreement and order made in the year 1750, are to be for the future, as to eccleſiaſtical matters, under the miniſter of this pariſh.

The ſeat belonging to his grace the duke of Beaufort is an aile on the north ſide of the chancel, under which is the veſtry room. On the ſouth ſide is another aile, and under it the vault belonging to that noble family.

Monuments and Inſcriptions.

In the ſouth aile of the chancel is an elegant raiſed monument of white marble, with the following arms and inſcriptions: In a lozenge, *Party per pale, baron and femme*, 1. Beaufort as before. 2. *Gules, a lion rampant between three croſs-croſſlets fitchy, Or*, for Capel.

Mary Widow to HENRY Lord BEAUCHAMP Maryed HENRY Duke of BEAUFORT, & by him had theſe Children, ELIZABETH Buried att RAGLAN, HENRY att WINDSOR, EDWARD att RAGLAN, Another HENRY att RAGLAN, CHARLES Lord Marquis of WORCESTER att RAGLAN, Lord ARTHUR Somerſett Maryed MARY Daughter to S^r^. WILLIAM RUSSELL Barronett. MARY Maryed to IAMES Duke of ORMONDE. HENRIETTA Firſt Maryed to HENRY HORATIO Lord OBRIAN, now to HENRY Earle of SUFFOLK and BINDON. ANNE Maryed to THOMAS Earle of COVENTRY.

On the ſouth ſide:

MARY Eldeſt Daughter of ARTHUR Lord CAPELL Marryed Firſt to HENRY Lord BEAUCHAMP Son to WILLIAM Duke of Somerſett & by him had theſe Children: FRANCIS, Buried att HADHAM, MARY att BEDWIN, WILLIAM Duke of Somerſett att BEDWIN, ELIZABETH Counteſs of AILESBURY at AMPTHILL.

On the eaſt end the arms of Beaufort. On the weſt end:

The Moſt Noble MARY Dutcheſs of BEAUFORT Relict of ye Moſt Puiſant Prince HENRY Duke of BEAUFORT, Daughter to ye R^t^ Honble ARTHUR Lord CAPELL (who was murder'd by ye Rebells in ye year 1648) Departed this Life january the 7th 1714 In the 85th year of her Age.

There is a grey marble flat ſtone, inlaid with braſs, upon which are ingraved the figures of two knights; in a ſcutcheon, a lion rampant, and round the edge, in old black characters, *Radulphus Botiler, Miles dominus* * * *

Upon a braſs plate, fixed on a flat ſtone, *three lions rampant in a lozenge*, and this inſcription:

D. O. M.

Sub hoc lapide Reſuſcitationem Juſtorum præſtolantur exuviæ MARGARITÆ filiæ ſecundo-genitæ ARTHURI PROGER de Badmonton, Generoſi, Ancillæ honorariæ præcellentiſſimæ Heroinæ ELENÆ Comitiſſæ Ormondiæ et Oſſoriæ; Deſponſata fuit EDVARDO MOLLINEVX Vectenſi Armigero è clientela nobiliſs^i^ Dni THOMÆ Vicecomitis SOMERSET.
Sed deſtinatas vetuit nuptias
In-opinato fatum vulnere
SPONSO fido ſuperſtite:
Qui amantem deflens VIRGINEM
Hoc marmor atratus poſuit.
Obijt vi^to^ die menſis Auguſti anno reparationis humanæ MDCXXXV ætatis ſuæ XXVI.

On a blue ſtone:

Hic jacet Carolus Price, Illuſtriſſimo Domino Henrico Duci de Belleforti dum vixit a Secretis, Cui quinquaginta novem annorum ſpatio pervigili opera et induſtria in agendo Servum ſe præbuit perquam fidelem. Obijt ii^o^ die Februarij, Anno Domini 1703, Ætatis ſuæ 79. Requieſcat in Pace.

Firſt Fruits, £.	5	5	5	Synodals, £.	0	2	0
Tenths, — --	0	10	6	Pentecoſtals,	0	1	0
Procurations, -	0	8	8				

Benefactions.

Mary the firſt dutcheſs of Beaufort erected a handſome pile of building in Badminton ſtreet, the centre of which is a ſchool-houſe, and appointed a ſalary for a maſter, to teach the children of the pariſh to read and write. On each ſide of the ſchool are three almſhouſes, for three poor men and three poor women, with preference, it ſeems, to thoſe that have been ſervants in the family, who have 2*s.* 6*d.* a week each.

Taxes.					
The Royal Aid in	1692, £.	66	13	4
Poll-tax — —	1694, —	76	0	0
Land-tax ——	1694, —	78	1	4
The ſame, at 3*s.* —	1770, —	58	11	1

BADMINTON (LITTLE,)

IS a ſmall place in the upper diviſion of the hundred of Grumbald's-aſh, eight miles ſouthweſtward from Tetbury, ſix north-eaſt from Chipping Sodbury, and twenty-ſeven ſouthward from Glouceſter. It is bounded on the ſouth by Great Badminton. The greateſt part of it lies within the duke of Beaufort's park.

This was not a diſtinct vill at the time of the general ſurvey, wherefore no mention is made of it in *Domeſday-book*. It is now conſidered as a tithing belonging to the pariſh of Hawkeſbury. The air is healthy, and the ſoil more ſuitable to tillage than paſture; but the place furniſhes nothing remarkable in natural hiſtory.

Of the Manor and other Eſtates.

The manor formerly belonged to the abbey of Perſhore, after the diſſolution of which, it was granted to John Boteler, 37 H. 8. and hath ever ſince had the ſame proprietor as the manor of Great Badminton, ſo that his grace the duke of Beaufort is the preſent lord of it.

Richard Urdle levied a fine of lands in Little Badminton to the uſe of John Young and William Lypiat, 18 R. 2.

Of the Church, &c.

The church is in the deanery of Hawkeſbury, worth 5*l.* a year to the curate. It formerly belonged to the abbey of Perſhore. After the diſſolution, the chapel of Badminton Little, with tithes, were granted with the manor, as above, and have deſcended together down to the preſent time.

The chapel is gone to decay, and accommodation hath been made for the inhabitants, in the church of Great Badminton, ever ſince the year 1750, as already obſerved under that pariſh.

Pentecoſtals, - - - - £. 0 0 6 *ob.*

Taxes.	The Royal Aid in 1692, £.				
	Poll-tax — —	1694, —	1	12	0
	Land-tax — -	1694, —	32	8	0
	The ſame, at 3*s.*	1770, —	32	5	3

****

BAGENDON,

IS a ſmall village, about three miles and a half long, and one mile broad, ſituate in the hundred of Crowthorne and Minety, in the cotſwold country, three miles northward from Cirenceſter, nine ſouth-weſtward from Northleach, and fourteen ſouth-eaſtward from Glouceſter. The church and houſes, for the moſt part, ſtand in a narrow dale, through which a little rivulet runs, and falls into the Churn about a mile below the church.

A little ſouth-eaſtward of the church, in the fields, are two very conſiderable intrenchments fronting each other, one of which extends for above a quarter of a mile down to a place called Barrow's-bridge in this pariſh, with the rampire and graff intire in ſome parts; and two or three large barrows, (near which have been found ſeveral ſpear-heads and other warlike weapons) ſtand not far diſtant from them. Theſe bear inconteſtible evidence of ſome battle having been fought here.

Now whether this Barrow's-bridge be the ſame with Beꞃanbẏꞃiᵹ, mentioned in the Saxon Chronicle, where Cinric king of the Weſt-Saxons, and Ceaulin his ſon, fought a bloody battle againſt the Britons, with doubtful ſucceſs, in the year 556, is a matter worthy inquiry. Hiſtorians differ in opinion concerning this Beꞃanbẏꞃiᵹ; Dr. Howell fixing it at Banbury in Oxfordſhire, on account of the ſimilarity of the name, and antiquity of the place; but Mr. Camden thinks it improbable that the Saxons could carry their conqueſt ſo far as the borders of Northamptonſhire by that year; wherefore he gives the preference to Barbury-caſtle in Wiltſhire, as a place more likely on ſeveral accounts, ſuch as the large barrows and fortifications found there, the ſimilitude of names, and the courſe of the time of the Saxon victories. Theſe arguments, I think, are good againſt Banbury, whilſt they point out this place, in the ſtrongeſt manner, for the ſcene of that action: for, as to ſituation, it lies in the country where the Britons and Saxons had frequent ſkirmiſhes about that time; the fortifications and barrows ſhew that a battle was fought here; and laſtly, what two names can agree better in ſound than that mentioned in the Chronicle, and our Barrow's-bridge? As to the latter being derived either from a bear-herd's killing a woman at this place, or from its being the bearer's way from Billey, for the inhabitants to bury at Bibury, they ſeem to be ſilly conceits, not worth the trouble of confuting. But I would not determine too abſolutely in a matter of ſo uncertain a nature.

The kind of ſtone called Dagham-down ſtone is found in the fields of this pariſh, for the particulars of which ſee Daglingworth.

Of the Manor and other Eſtates.

Benwedene is a manor ſet down in *Domeſday-book*, as lying in the hundred of Cirenceſter. It is probably the ſame place which was afterwards called Bagendon. Of that manor it is thus recorded:

'The ſame Hugo [*i. e.* Hugo Laſne] holds 'Benwedene in Cireceſtre hundred, and Giſlebertus holds it of him. There are three hides 'taxed. Wluuard held it. In demean are three 'plow-tillages, and five villeins with three plow-'tillages, and ſix *ſervi*, and a mill of 10*s.* and 'eight acres of meadow. It is worth and was 'worth 4*l.*' *Domeſday-book*, p. 78.

This was a hamlet or portion of ſome adjoining pariſh at the time when the ſheriff of the county, in obedience to the king's writ, made a return of all the vills therein, 9 E. 1. for there is no mention in his return of any ſuch place as Bagendon, if my copy of it be perfect; and the preciſe time when it became a diſtinct pariſh is uncertain. However it is mentioned in a record of 4 E. 3. by which it appears that Richard de Bagendon and Agnes his wife levied a fine thereof to Reginald Pedewardine, to the uſe of themſelves and the heirs of their bodies. And a fine of the third part of this manor was levied 11 E. 3. by Richard ſon of Richard de Bagendon, which Lucy his widow then held in dower.

This manor was afterwards conveyed to Robert Plain and others 6 R. 2. for the uſe of the chantry of the holy Trinity, in the pariſh church of Cirenceſter.

Cirenceſter. Trinity-mill in this pariſh obtained that name becauſe it belonged to that chantry. And a ſpring of fine water is ſtill known by the name of Trinity-well for the ſame reaſon, to which many virtues are attributed, particularly that of curing ſore eyes.

After the diſſolution of chantries, the manor was granted to ſir John Thynn and Chriſtian his wife, 3 E. 6. and it hath continued in that family ever ſince, ſo that the lord viſcount Weymouth is the preſent lord of the manor. His lordſhip's arms are, *Barry of ten, Or and ſable.* Creſt, *On a wreath, a rein-deer Or.* Supporters, on the dexter-ſide, *A rein-deer Or, gorged with a plain collar ſable*; on the ſiniſter-ſide, *A lion gules.* Motto, J'AY BONNE CAUSE.—It is remarkable of his lordſhip's family, that their antient name was Botevile, deſcended of ſir Geofry Botevile, who came out of Poictou into England in the reign of king John, and ſettled at Stretton in Shropſhire. They loſt their original name in the reign of king Edward the Fourth, when John Botevile was firſt called *John of the Inne,* from his manſion in Stretton, and thence came the ſurname of Thynne, as it is now uſed. *Collins's Peerage,* V. 6. p. 257.

William Nottingham and Elizabeth his wife levied a fine of lands in Bagendon to the uſe of themſelves and the heirs of their bodies 20 H. 6.

Other lands in Bagendon belonged to the knights hoſpitallers of St. John of Jeruſalem, after whoſe diſſolution, they were granted to John Walter and Thomas Carpenter, 1 Mar.

Of the Church, &c.

The church is a rectory in the deanery of Cirenceſter, worth about 60*l.* a year. Lord viſcount Weymouth is patron, Mr. Timothy Meredith the preſent incumbent. John Young, chaplain to the chantry of St. Trinity and St. Mary, in the church of St. John Baptiſt in Cirenceſter, preſented to it in the year 1403.

About ſeventeen acres of meadow and paſture, and forty-ſeven of arable, belong to the glebe.

The church is ſmall, with a very low tower, and ſome painted glaſs in the windows, but nothing further worth notice in it.

Firſt fruits, £	8	4	4	Synodals, £.	0	1	0
Tenths, —	0	16	5	Pentecoſtals,	0	0	6
Procurations,	0	2	0				

Taxes.					
The Royal Aid in	1692, £.	21	11	4
Poll-tax — —	1694, —	5	8	0
Land-tax ——	1694, —	17	0	0
The ſame, at 3*s.* —	1770, —	12	15	0

Sir Robert Atkyns reckons 13 houſes and 60 inhabitants in this pariſh; yearly births 2, burials 2. I could not get a ſight of the regiſter-book in uſe at the time when he collected thoſe materials; but in a ſeries of ten years from 1760 to 1769, both incluſive, there are regiſtered 67 baptiſms, and 24 burials; and the inhabitants having been numbered, are found to be 139, which ſhews a very great increaſe in this pariſh ſince the beginning of the preſent century. And the proportion of the whole number of inhabitants to the average of annual burials is nearly as 58 to 1, which accounts for that increaſe from the great healthineſs of the place, hardly to be equalled.

BAGPATH.

See NEWINGTON-BAGPATH.

BARNSLEY.

THIS pariſh lies in the hundred of Britwel's-barrow, four miles north-eaſt from Cirenceſter, and eighteen miles eaſtward from Glouceſter. The turnpike-road from Cirenceſter to Oxford runs through it.

The antient name of this place is Barneſleis, as in *Domeſday-book.* Barnwell in Cambridgeſhire is explained by Mr. Campden to ſignify *the wells of children or barns; for young men and boys met there once a year upon St. John's eve, for wreſtling, and the like youthful exerciſes, and alſo to make merry with ſinging and other muſick.* And it is poſſible that Barnſley may have taken its name from young people aſſembling in like manner, for their diverſion, upon the *lays* or paſture-grounds of this place at ſtated periods.

The air is healthy, and the ſoil good. There are large quarries, on the north-eaſt ſide of the village adjoining to Bibury, where they raiſe a very excellent kind of white freeſtone, almoſt equal to that of Bath. The pits are fifty or ſixty feet deep, out of which they get the blocks of ſtone by means of a wheel and axis.

About twenty years ago, a vein of coal was found in one of thoſe pits, which gave hopes to the country of being ſupplied from thence at an eaſy rate, with that uſeful fuel, which came ſo expenſive to them by reaſon of long carriage; but thoſe hopes were ſoon fruſtrated, and the proprietor diſappointed. Indeed I am told that the matter was never examined into with that diligence and perſeverance which the importance of it required.

Miſs Perrot has an elegant houſe in this pariſh, built of freeſtone. It ſtands at a proper diſtance from the turnpike-road, with a park and plantations about it. The cielings are done by the beſt Italian maſters.

Of the Manor and other Eſtates.

At the time of the general ſurvey, the manor of Bibury, on which this of Barnſley depended, was the property of the church of Worceſter.

The

The paſſage in *Domeſday-book* relating to Barnſley may be thus tranſlated:

'Durandus holds three hides and one yard-land 'in Berneſleis [in Becheberie hundred] of the 'biſhop [of Worceſter] as a manor depending on 'Becheberie; and Eudo holds ſeven yard-lands 'there for a manor.' *Domeſday-book*, p. 70.

Under Bibury may be read other particulars from this record, which are in common to both pariſhes.

Not long after the conqueſt, this manor came into the family of the Fitz-Herberts. Peter Fitz-Herbert was ſeized of it in the reign of king Henry the Third, who married the third daughter and coheir of William de Braos baron of Brecknock, and dying 19 H. 3. was ſucceeded by his ſon, called *Herbertus fil' Petri*, whoſe brother Reginald ſucceeded him as heir, and died ſeized of this manor 14 E. 1. leaving John his ſon and heir, the laſt of that name who were owners of Barnſley; for

Hugh le Diſpencer the elder had a charter of free-warren in Barndeſly 28 E. 1. which manor he afterwards ſettled on his ſon Hugh le Diſpencer the younger, who being attainted of high treaſon, his eſtate was forfeited to the crown, and granted 1 E. 3. to Edmund earl of Kent, grandſon to king Edward the Firſt. He was ſucceeded by his brother John earl of Kent, who died ſeized thereof 26 E. 3. without iſſue; whereby this manor came to Joan his ſiſter and heir, commonly called the *Fair Maid of Kent*, at that time married to ſir Thomas Holland, who in her right was created earl of Kent by king Edward the Third, and died in the thirty-fourth year of that king's reign. She was afterwards married to the Black Prince, and by him was mother to king Richard the Second. It is very remarkable that ſhe had been twice married before, and twice divorced. She died in the ninth year of her ſon's reign, and the right of the manor of Barnſley deſcended to Thomas Holland earl of Kent, her ſon by her firſt huſband, who dying 20 R. 2. was ſucceeded by her ſon Thomas Holland earl of Kent and duke of Surry, beheaded at Cirenceſter 1 H. 4. as will be related more at large under that place. Leaving no iſſue, he was ſucceeded by his brother Edmund earl of Kent, who alſo died without iſſue. But this manor was held in dower fifty-eight years by Elizabeth, widow of the forementioned John earl of Kent, who died ſeized thereof 10 H. 4.

After her death the manor deſcended to Elianor Holland, ſiſter and coheir to the family of the Hollands. She was married to Roger Mortimer earl of March, whereby this eſtate was carried into that name and family; for Edmund Mortimer, their ſon and heir, died ſeized of it 3 H. 6. without iſſue; and Richard duke of York, ſon of Anne his ſiſter, and heir to the crown of England, became his heir. But this prince was ſlain at the battle of Wakefield in the laſt year of king Henry the Sixth, whereupon Cicely dutcheſs of York, his widow, had the grant of this manor the ſame year, and a confirmation of it 1 E. 4. She died in the year 1495, and king Henry the Seventh having married the heireſs of the houſe of York, became heir to this manor in right of his queen.

It was ſoon after granted to Thomas Moreton, upon whoſe death it deſcended to ſir Robert Moreton his ſon, who died ſeized of it 6 H. 8. William his ſon ſucceeded him, and died at thirteen years of age 14 H. 8. whereupon it came to his ſiſter Dorothy, married to Ralph Johnſon, who had livery of the manor of Barnſley granted to them 16 H. 8.

From them it paſſed by purchaſe to William Bourchier, eſq; ſon of Anthony Bourchier, and of Thomaſin, ſiſter of ſir Walter Wildmay, and daughter of ſir Miles Mildmay; which William married Suſan the daughter of —— Brown, and dying 6 Eliz. Thomas Bourchier, his ſon and heir, had livery of this eſtate granted to him the ſame year. He dying, left two daughters coheireſſes, whereof Anne was married to Thomas Rich, of North Cerney, eſq; but Walter Bourchier, brother to Thomas, ſucceeded in the manor of Barnſley, of which he had livery 4 Jac. He married Mary the daughter of — Brown, of Shingleton in Kent, and was lord of this manor in the year 1608. William Bourchier, his ſon and heir, married Martha, daughter of Randall Brereton, eſq; and was ſucceeded in this eſtate by his ſon Brereton Bourchier, eſq; who married firſt, Elizabeth, daughter and heireſs of Thomas Hulbert, of Corſham in Wiltſhire; ſecondly, Catherine the youngeſt daughter of James lord Chandois.

From the Bourchiers this eſtate went by marriage to Henry Perrot, eſq; who left two daughters coheireſſes, the younger of whom died unmarried in the year 1773, whereby the manor of Barnſley, and a large eſtate in this pariſh, became ſolely veſted in Mrs. Caſſandra Perrot, the ſurviving ſiſter. Her arms are, *Gules, three pears Or; on a chief argent, a demy lion rampant ſable.*

There were ſeveral lands in this pariſh belonging to the priory of Lanthony near Glouceſter, moſt of which, after the diſſolution of that priory, were granted to William earl of Southampton and his heirs male, 31 H. 8. And others of them were granted to John Pope 37 H. 8.

Of the Church, &c.

The church is a rectory within the peculiar of Bibury, worth about 140*l.* a year. Mrs. Perrot is patroneſs; Mr. Charles Coxwell the preſent incumbent. There were fifty acres of arable land belonging to the glebe, but they were exchanged for other lands, when the common fields were incloſed in the year 1762, and the glebe now conſiſts of about twenty computed acres, which are let for 16*l.* a year.

Humphry de Bohun, earl of Hereford and Eſſex, in right of Joan his wife, was ſeized of the advowſon of this church 46 E. 3. which paſſed in marriage, with Elianor one of their daughters,

to

to Thomas duke of Gloucefter; and Elianor furviving her hufband died feized of it 1 H. 4. from whom it defcended to Anne, one of her daughters and coheireffes, married to Edmond earl of Stafford, who, in her right, died feized of the advowfon of this church 4 H. 4.

The church hath an aile on the north fide, and a fmall tower at the weft end. It was built by fir Giles Tame, who alfo built the inn at this place for his own accommodation in the road from his houfe at Fairford to Rendcombe, where he was then building the parifh church of that place.

Firft fruits, £. 13 15 4 Tenths, £. 1 7 6 *ob.*

Monuments and Infcriptions.

In the chancel, againft the north wall, is a white marble monument with the following infcription:

Hic propè fitum eft quod mortale fuit *Elizabethæ* Uxoris præftantiffimæ *Breretonis Bourchier*, de *Barnefley* in Agro *Gloceftrienfi* Armigeri, filiæ unicæ *Thomæ Hulbert* de *Corfham*, in Agro *Wiltonienfi* Generofi & *Annæ* Uxoris ejus. Enixa gemellos Filiam primogenitam, (qui paucorum tantum dierum luce fruebantur, in partu, obitu, & fepulturâ pene individui:) decem deinde menfibus non penitus elapfis, magna imbecillitate corporis fracta, Obijt 2° Novembris Anno Salutis 1691°, Ætatis fuæ 22°.

Over this monument is a fcutcheon, *party per pale, baron and femme*, 1. *Azure, a chevron Or, between three martlets argent*; *a crefcent for difference*, for Bourchier. 2. *Sable, a crofs between four leopards heads flory, Or*, for Hulbert.

There is alfo a fmall marble monument for Sarah, widow of William Bourchier, M. A. late rector of Hatherop in this county; and daughter of Robert Brereton of Cirencefter, gent. with the Bourchiers arms, as before, impaling thofe of Brereton, *i. e. Barry of five pieces, argent and fable.* She died in 1762, aged 93.

Alfo a Latin memorial on a flat ftone for Richard Payne, M. A. rector of this church forty-two years, who died in 1739. And for Anne his wife, who died in 1742. Their arms are palewife, 1. *Azure, three befants*; *on a chief embattled argent, as many as in the field*, for Payne. 2. The arms of Perrot.

Benefaction.

Mr. William Wife of this place, who died in the year 1774, gave 25*l.* for a ftock for the ufe of the poor of this place for ever.

Taxes.					
The Royal Aid in	1692, £.	62	12	0
Poll-tax — —	1694, —	20	9	0
Land-tax ——	1694, —	71	4	11
The fame, at 3*s.* -	1770, —	45	0	0

At the beginning of this century, according to fir Robert Atkyns, there were 46 houfes and about 160 inhabitants in this parifh; births 4, burials 3. In a feries of ten years, from 1701 to 1710, there are regiftered 33 baptifms and 43 burials. In a like feries from 1760 to 1769 inclufive, are regiftered 68 baptifms and 56 burials; there are 54 families, and the number of inhabitants is increafed to 217, which is in the proportion of about 40 to 1 of the average number of annual burials.

****

BARNWOOD.

THIS is a fmall parifh in the united hundreds of Dudfton and King's-Barton. It lies in the vale country, one mile eaft from Gloucefter, upon the turnpike-road from that city to London; and confifts of rich pafture, with fome arable land. A fmall brook runs from Prinknafh thro' this place to Gloucefter.

The name of this village fhews that it was antiently over-run with wood, which indeed was the cafe with two or three other little hamlets adjoining to it, for *Wotton* is nothing more than the wood town, or woody town; and *Hucklecot* fignifies the high wood, from the Britifh *Ukel* high, and *coed* a wood.

The old Roman road from Gloucefter to Cirencefter runs through this place, but it is fo worn out and deftroyed as not to be difcoverable, by a flight obferver.

Of the Manor and other Eftates.

It hath been already fhewn from *Domefday-book*, p. 206, that the church of St. Peter of Gloucefter held Berneuude in Dudeftanes hundred, as a member of the manor of Bertune, in the reign of king Edward the Confeffor. *See alfo Domefday-book*, p. 71.

This manor, with all its appurtenances, was confirmed to the abbey of Gloucefter by William the Conqueror, when Serlo was abbat; and king Edward the Third granted to the abbey free-warren in all their demean lands at Bernewode, in the twenty-eighth year of his reign. In fome papers relating to the abbey, are the following particulars concerning this eftate in the feventeenth year of the laft mentioned reign. The abbey had then four carucates of land of 20*s. per ann.* each; two mills of 30*s.* 6*d. per ann.* and, as it is there expreffed, *relaxationem operum et cenfuum per ann.* 13*s.* 4*d.* the fum being 6*l.* 3*s.* 10*d.*

The abbey continued feized of this manor 'till the diffolution of religious foundations, when it was granted by king Henry the Eighth, in the thirty-third year of his reign, to the chapter of Gloucefter, by the charter of endowment, and is part of the revenues of the dean and chapter of that cathedral.

Of the Church, &c.

The church is a curacy in the deanery of Gloucefter, worth 35*l.* a year. The impropriation pays 12*l.* a year to the curate. The dean and chapter of Gloucefter are patrons and impropriators.

The church, which is dedicated to St. Lawrence, hath an aile on the north fide of the nave, and a

 handfome

handſome tower, with battlements, at the weſt end. It was built by abbat Parker, of St. Peter's in Glouceſter.

Synodals, £. 0 2 0 Pentecoſtals, £. 0 0 7

Taxes.					
The Royal Aid in	1692, £.	128	10	8
Poll-tax — —	1694, —	13	18	0
Land-tax ——	1694, —	129	19	0
The ſame, at 3s. -	1770, —	97	15	3

At the beginning of this century there were 40 houſes and 180 inhabitants in this pariſh, according to ſir Robert Atkyns. The yearly births were 7, and burials 5. In a ſeries of ten years from 1700 to 1709 incluſive, there were regiſtered baptiſms and burials. In a like ſeries, from 1760 to 1769, there were baptiſms and burials; and the preſent number of inhabitants is

BARRINGTON (GREAT.)

THE principal part of this pariſh lies in Glouceſterſhire, in the lower diviſion of the hundred of Slaughter; but there are twenty-three houſes in Berkſhire, and ſome lands are reputed to be in the county of Oxford. It is three miles weſt from Burford in Oxfordſhire, ſix eaſt from Northleach, and twenty-ſix eaſt from Glouceſter; bounded on the north by Bledington, on the ſouth by Little Barrington, and on the eaſt by Tainton in Oxfordſhire.

It gave denomination to the hundred of Bernitone, now compriſed in that of Slaughter, for that was the antient manner of writing the name of this place, as in *Domeſday-book*. If there had been ſome Saxon or other antient proprietor of the manor of the name of Bernard or Berni, the etymology would have been eaſy; but we have no account of the names of the proprietors in thoſe early times.

That part which belongs to Berkſhire is many miles diſtant from the body of that county. In the preſent ſtate of things, this diviſion of the pariſh is ſo unſuitable and inconvenient, that one is at firſt diſpoſed to think it originally directed by whim and caprice; but it may be far otherwiſe, for as there are ſeveral more inſtances of the ſame nature, in this county, and as the abolition of the feudal ſyſtem hath ſo materially altered many things concerning the internal government of our country, we have loſt ſight of the reaſon of ſome eſtabliſhments, under that ſyſtem, which are continued down to us. Having already touched upon thoſe irregularities in the introductory part of this work, I ſhall not repeat what is there ſaid of them, as the reader, by turning to the 45th page, may ſee the moſt probable conjectures upon them which I have any where met with.

Lady Talbot has a fine ſeat in this pariſh, upon an eaſy elevation on the north ſide of the river Windruſh, which winds its courſe thro' the meadows in a beautiful manner, about two hundred yards below the houſe. Her ladyſhip, according to her accuſtomed generoſity, hath given a plate of her ſeat, which will convey a better idea of it than verbal deſcription.

The houſe is in Glouceſterſhire, but part of the offices in Berkſhire.

The air of this place is reckoned healthy, and the ſoil good, but it produces no ſcarce plants nor foſſils. The river I have mentioned has very fine trout, and other fiſh of leſs conſequence. Here is alſo a quarry of freeſtone remarkable for its durableneſs, and therefore, it is ſaid, much of the ſtone hath been uſed in repairing of Weſtminſter abbey; and Blenheim-houſe was built with it.

The broad cloth manufacture hath been carried on here, but there is very little done at preſent.

Of the Manor and other Eſtates.

The *Domeſday* account of this village may be thus tranſlated:

'Tovi Wideneſa, a domeſtick ſervant (*huſcarle*) 'of earl Harold, held Bernitone. There are four 'hides. In demean are three plow-tillages, and 'ten villeins, and five bordars with five plow-tillages. There are four *ſervi*, and a mill of 5*s.* '[value.] It is worth 8*l.* and was worth 7*l.* 'Elſi de Ferendone holds it in farm of the king.

'Eilmer held four hides in Bernitone for a 'manor in the time of king Edward. There is 'one plow-tillage in demean, and ſeven villeins, 'and three bordars, with four plow-tillages. 'There are ſix *ſervi*, and a mill of 5*s.* It was 'worth 100*s.* now 60*s.* Godwin de Stantone 'holds it in farm of the king.' *Dom. Book*, p. 69.

This manor afterwards belonged to the priory of Lanthony near Glouceſter. The prior purchaſed a charter of free-warren in Berinthone, and ſeveral other manors, 21 E. 1.

At the diſſolution of that monaſtery it was veſted in the crown, and the manor, with the tithes of the demeans, were granted to John Gyeſe, anceſtor of ſir William Guyſe of Rendcombe, in exchange for Aſple-Gyeſe in Bedfordſhire, 32 H. 8.

It was afterwards purchaſed, with the fiſhery, free warren, and frank-pledge, by Richard Monnington, eſq; who levied a fine thereof 1 Mariæ.

He had an only child Anne, married to Reginald Bray, eſq; and ſo this eſtate came into that family, which continued in poſſeſſion of it near two hundred years. About the year 1734, it was purchaſed, together with the manor of Great Riſſington in this county, and thoſe of Tainton and Fifield in Oxfordſhire, of Reginald Morgan Bray, eſq; [e] in the name of the late lord chancellor Talbot,

[e] This family is of very antient extraction. Le ſeigneur de Bray, lord of Braie, or Bray, in Normandy, came into England with the Conqueror, of whom mention is made in the *Flores Hiſtoriarum* of Matthew Weſtminſter. Ralph de Braye, lord of Cumtone,

Talbot, but principally with a part of the fortune of the prefent Mary countefs Talbot, wife of William earl Talbot, lord fteward of his majefty's houfhold, and fole daughter and heirefs of Adam de Cardonnel, efq; fecretary at war in the reign of queen Anne. This purchafe was made in her ladyfhip's minority; but on her coming to age, about fix years afterwards, fhe fold her eftates in Hampfhire, Suffex, and Yorkfhire, and bought the whole of thofe four manors abovementioned, and her ladyfhip is the prefent proprietor of them. Her coat of arms is, *Gules, a lion rampant, within a border engrailed Or; a crefcent for difference.*—Supporters, *On either fide a talbot argent, collared with a double treffure flory counter flory gules.*—Motto, HUMANI NIHIL ALIENUM.

Other lands in Barrington belonged to the priory of Burton, and were granted to Edmund Hermor 35 H. 8.

Of the Church, &c.

The church is a vicarage in the deanery of Stow, worth 75*l.* a year. Lady Talbot is patronefs, and has the impropriation, which pays 6*l.* 6*s.* 8*d.* yearly to the crown. It formerly belonged to the priory of Lanthony.

The lady of the manor pays one acre of wheat, and another of barley, in lieu of tithe-corn of the demeans; and a modus in money for fheep and mills.

Mr. Bradley, fometime vicar of this parifh, built a vicarage-houfe, which ftood in Berkfhire; but that was exchanged, fome years ago, with lord Talbot, for another houfe which ftands in the fame county.

The church is dedicated to St. Peter. It is a handfome building, with a tower, adorned with battlements and pinnacles, at the weft end, and an aile on the north fide, which was the burying-place of the family of the Brays. There are fix bells.

Cumtone, was fheriff of the counties of Northampton, Southampton, Somerfet, Dorfet, Oxford, Leicefter, Bedford, and Bucks, in the reigns of John and Henry the Third. There was a fir James Bray of the county of Northampton, from whom the defcent of this family is regularly deduced in Vincent's book in the heralds office.

Thomas Bray was great grandfon of fir James; William was fon and heir of Thomas, and Edmund Bray, of Eton Bray, in the county of Bedford, was fon and heir of William. He had a fon Richard, who was privy-counfellor to king Henry the Sixth, and was buried in Worcefter cathedral. By his fecond wife he had iffue fir Reginald, and another fon, John.

Sir Reginald was receiver-general to fir Henry Stafford, who married Margaret countefs of Richmond, mother to king Henry the Seventh. When the duke of Buckingham had concerted, with Morton bifhop of Ely, the union of the houfes of York and Lancafter, by the marriage of the earl of Richmond with the princefs Elizabeth, fir Reginald, by the bifhop's recommendation, was employ'd to tranfact that affair with the countefs, and other principal perfons, which he manged with great dexterity and fuccefs.

King Henry was fo fenfible of his fervices, that he made him knight of the Bath at his coronation, and, in the firft year of his reign, appointed him joint chief juftice with lord Fitz-Walter, of all the forefts fouth of Trent, and to be one of the privy-council. He was afterwards appointed high treafurer, chofen knight of the garter, made chancellor of the dutchy of Lancafter, and high fteward of the Univerfity of Oxford; and he was alfo made a knight banneret. Thefe and many other honours and great emoluments are mentioned by our hiftorians to have been conferred upon him by the king, particularly by Hall, Hollinfhead, Anftis, and Afhmole. He died in the year 1503, without iffue, and was buried in the chapel at Windfor. He had a younger brother, John, who had three fons, Edmund, Edward, and Reginald.

Edmund, the eldeft fon, fucceeded to a large part of fir Reginald's eftate, and in 1530, had fummons to parliament as baron of Eton Bray. He married Jane, daughter and heir of fir Richard Haleighwell, who brought many great eftates into his family, and had iffue by her one fon, John, and fix daughters.

John lord Bray died without iffue, whereby his fix fifters became his coheireffes.

I return now to fir Edward Bray, fecond fon of John, who married Elizabeth, daughter and coheir of Henry Lovell, from whom he was divorced, and afterwards married Beatrice, daughter of Ralph Shirley, of Wiftenton in Suffex, by whom he had iffue two fons, Edward and Owen, and one daughter. She dying, he married Jane, daughter of fir Matthew Brown, of Betchworth caftle in Surry, (and widow of Francis Poyntz, efq;) by whom he had no iffue; which laft marriage was a very unfortunate one for his family; for dying, he gave all his fee-fimple lands to his wife Jane for life, with all his woods and underwoods, and willed that if his fon Edward interrupted her, fhe fhould have them in fee.

Sir Edward Bray fucceeded his father in the fettled eftates, but difagreeing with lady Jane, fhe fold all the lands in her power by her hufband's will, whereby the paternal eftate was greatly diminifhed. He married firft, Magdalene, daughter of fir Thomas Cotton, by whom he had iffue Reginald his fon and heir. He had alfo a fecond wife Mary, by whom he had three daughters. In the latter part of his life he refided at Shere in Surry, which has been the refidence of his defcendants ever fince.

Reginald Bray, efq; only fon of fir Edward, married a daughter of Richard Covert, of Hafcomb in Surry, efq; by whom he had three fons and one daughter.

Edward, his eldeft fon, married Jane, daughter of Edward Covert, of Twynham in Suffex, efq; by whom he had feven children; and by a fecond wife he had one daughter.

Edward, his eldeft fon and heir, married Sufanna, daughter of William Heath, of Pedinghoe, efq; by whom he had feven children.

Edward, the eldeft, married Frances, daughter of Morgan Randyll, of Chilworth in Surry, efq; by whom he had nine children; and by this marriage his defcendants have a claim of founder's kin at All Souls college, Oxford.

Randyll, his eldeft fon, dying without iffue, Edward, the fecond fon, became his father's heir. He married Anne, eldeft daughter of George Duncombe, rector of Shere, by whom he had four fons, of whom

George, his eldeft fon, fucceeded him, and entered into holy orders in the year 1752. — Edward, his fecond fon, was bred a furgeon, and was appointed furgeon to the thirty-fifth regiment of foot. — Charles, the third fon, died an infant. — William, the fourth fon, was bred an attorney, had an employment at the board of green cloth, and was afterwards appointed, by the lord fteward, clerk of the verge. He married Mary, daughter of Henry Stevens, of Wipley in Surry, gent. by whom he has iffue feveral children.

But the branch of this family to whom Barrington belonged, fprung from Reginald Bray, third fon of John, and youngeft nephew of the firft fir Reginald. This Reginald the nephew married Anne, daughter and heir of Richard Monnington, of Barrington, efq; and fettled there. He was fucceeded by Edmond his eldeft fon, who married Agnes, daughter and heir of Edmund Harman, of Taynton in Oxfordfhire, by whom he had Edmond his fon and heir, who married Dorothy, daughter of fir John Tracy, of Toddington. He was a captain in queen Elizabeth's time, of whom further mention is made under *Monuments and Infcriptions.*

Sir Giles, fon and heir of the laft Edmond, married Anne, daughter of Richard Chetwood, and was fucceeded by his fon and heir fir Edmond, who was an active royalift, and was forced to compound for 1191*l.* 15*s.* 9*d.* He died about 1684, and was fucceeded by Reginald his fon and heir, who alfo died in 1688. Edmond his fourth fon became his heir, and married Frances, daughter and coheir of fir John Morgan, of Lantarnam in Monmouthfhire, bart. with whom he had a great eftate. Reginald Morgan Bray was his eldeft fon and heir, who fold Barrington, as above related, and died without iffue.

Monuments

Monuments and Inſcriptions.

Lord chancellor Talbot is buried in the chancel without any memorial.

There is a handſome marble monument in the church, againſt the wall of the north aile, for captain Edmund Bray, with the figures of him and his wife well executed.

And in the ſame aile is a handſome freeſtone monument, without any inſcription. It repreſents a man in armour, lying at length, with his ſword girt on the right ſide, and is ſaid to be for another captain Edmund Bray, father of ſir Giles Bray, who had unhappily killed a man, and was pardoned by queen Elizabeth at Tilbury camp. He ever afterwards wore his ſword on the right ſide, and never uſed his right hand, in token of his true ſorrow, and ſincere repentance. The arms of the family are in a ſcutcheon over the monument, *viz. Argent, a chevron between three eagles legs erazed ſable.*

There is an inſcription for Reginald Bray, eſq; who died in the year 1692. And another for James Stephens, eſq; who married Barbara, daughter of Reginald Bray, eſq; and for James and John two of their children, who died young. The arms of Stephens, impaling thoſe of Bray, are on the monument, *viz. Per chevron, azure and argent, in chief two eagles diſplay'd Or.*

There is a memorial, on a flat ſtone in the chancel, for Philip Parſons, M. D. preſident of Hart-hall in Oxford, who died in 1653, with his arms, *Gules, two chevronels, in the dexter canton an eagle diſplay'd.*

Firſt fruits, £.	7	6	8	Synodals, £. 0	2	0
Tenths, —	0	14	8	Pentecoſtals, 0	1	1
Procurations,	0	6	8			

Benefactions.

The long cauſeway, between this pariſh and Little Barrington, was erected by Thomas Strong of London, freemaſon, who gave 5 *l.* the intereſt of which to be given to the poor on St. Thomas day.

William Matthews, of London, gave 5 *l.* the intereſt of which to be given to the poor at the ſame time. And

John Tailer hath given an annuity of 20 *s.* to the poor, charged on lands at Milton.

Taxes.					
The Royal Aid in	1692, £.	90	8	0
Poll-tax — —	1694, —	30	15	6
Land-tax ——	1694, —	65	12	0
The ſame, at 3 *s.* —	1770, —	47	13	3

N. B. The land-tax of Little Barrington is included in the above.

At the beginning of this century there were 43 houſes in this pariſh, whereof 28 were in Glouceſterſhire, and about 120 inhabitants in the ſame county. The yearly births were 6, burials 4. *Atkyns.*—But examining the regiſter, I find, that in a ſeries of ten years, from 1700 to 1709, there were 62 baptiſms and 57 burials. And in a like ſeries, from 1760 to 1769, the baptiſms were 109, the burials 55. And the number of inhabitants is about 393, which is in the proportion of 70 to 1 of the average number of annual burials.

Before I cloſe the account of this pariſh it is proper to obſerve, that lady Talbot's paternal coat of arms is *Argent, two chevronels azure, between three trefoils vert*; and that the arms deſcribed in the preceding page, are thoſe of the earl of Talbot, her ladyſhip's conſort.

BARRINGTON (LITTLE,)

IS a ſmall pariſh in the lower diviſion of the hundred of Slaughter, ſituate on the banks of the river Windruſh, mentioned in the preceding pariſh, three miles weſt from Burford in Oxfordſhire, and twenty-ſix eaſt from Glouceſter. The common fields were incloſed in the year 1760, and the rents much improved thereby.

Of the Manor and other Eſtates.

Domeſday-book, among the lands of William Gozenboded, gives the following particulars:

'The ſame William holds two hides in Berintone in Berintone hundred, and Radulfus holds 'them of him. Alwinus held them in the time 'of king Edward. In demean is one plow-tillage, 'and one *ſervus*, and a mill of 40 *d.* [rent] and 'ſix acres of meadow. It is worth and was 'worth 40 *s.*' *Domeſday-book*, p. 74.

'Walter the ſon of Roger holds Bernintone in 'Berninton hundred, of the king. There are 'eight hides. Turſtan and Eduui held them for 'two manors. In demean are four plow-tillages, 'and fourteen villeins, and a prieſt, and two bor'dars with nine plow-tillages. There are four'teen *ſervi*, and a mill of 10 *s.* [rent] and twenty 'acres of meadow. It is worth and was worth '8 *l.* *Domeſday-book*, p. 77.

The maſter of the knights-templers was ſeized of court-leet, waifs, and felons goods in Little Barrington, by the grant of king Henry the Third.

The prior of Lanthony held another manor in Little Barrington, which had been granted by Maud the Empreſs, 15 E. 1. and ſeveral privileges were allowed the ſame year in a writ of *Quo Warranto*.

One of theſe manors, probably the firſt, was held of William de Clinton earl of Huntingdon, 28 E. 3.

Other lands in Little Barrington belonged to the abbey of Bruern in Oxfordſhire, and were granted to Edward Powell, 36 H. 8.

This manor was the joint property of Thomas Smith, eſq; of London, and Mr. Joſeph Ellis of Ebley, in the year 1768; but ſince the death of the latter, his nephew Mr. Thomas Ellis hath purchaſed

purchased Mr. Smith's moiety, and is the present proprietor of the manor.

Of the Church, &c.

The church is a vicarage in the deanery of Stow, worth about 35 *l.* a year before the inclosing; which has considerably improved it. The priory of Lanthony near Gloucester had formerly the presentation to this church, which is now in the lord chancellor.

A portion of tithes formerly belonging to Lanthony priory, was granted to Lawrence Baskerville and William Blake, 3 Jac. The impropriator hath now an estate allotted him in lieu of tithes.

The church is dedicated to St. Mary, and has an aile on the north side, and a tower at the west end, adorned with battlements.

First Fruits, £.	4	19	1	Synodals, £.	0	1	0
Tenths, — --	0	9	11	Pentecostals,	0	0	4
Procurations, -	0	0	0				

Benefaction.

There is an estate in this parish, which now lets for 22 *l.* a year, for the repairs of the church, and relief of the poor.

This parish is rated in the public tax with Great Barrington.

At the beginning of this century, according to sir Robert Atkyns, there were 18 houses, and about 82 inhabitants in this parish. The yearly births 2, and burials 2. In a series of seven years, from 1761 to 1767 inclusive, there were register'd 22 baptisms, and 14 burials; and the present number of inhabitants is 124, exactly in the proportion of 62 to 1 of the average number of annual burials. A remarkable instance of salubrity.

BARTON near GLOUCESTER.

See SUBURBS of GLOUCESTER, p. 206.

BATSFORD.

PART of this parish is situated on the slope of a hill looking towards the east; the rest is in a vale. It lies in the upper division of the large hundred of Kiftesgate, four miles south-eastward from Campden, and six north from Stow in this county; eight west from Shipston in Worcestershire, and twenty-nine north-eastward from Gloucester. It is bounded by Blockley (a large detached parish in Worcestershire) on the west and north sides, and by Morton-in-marsh and Bourton-on-the-hill on the south, extending to a place where four counties meet, of which there is a particular account under Morton-in-marsh.

The parish is three miles in length and one in breadth; the air healthy, and the soil, for the most part, a fine loam.

The modern name implies an idea of the place being situated at the ford of some brook or river. The antient name of it was *Beceshore*, and signifies nearly the same, from *bec*, a stream of water; accordingly there is a small brook which runs into the Evenlode, which rises near this place.

The great Roman foss-road, from the north, runs through the parish, and so on to Cirencester, Bath, &c. and there is a small intrenchment, almost intire, supposed to have been thrown up by the Romans.

Of the Manor and other Estates.

Soon after the Norman conquest, Ansfrid de Comeliis was possessed of several good estates in Gloucestershire, of which this was one, described in the record in the following manner:

'The same Ansfrid holds Beceshore in Witelai 'hundred. Brismer held it. There are three 'hides. In demean are three plow-tillages, and 'ten villeins, with six plow-tillages, and sixteen '*servi*, and one man paying six *sochs*. It was 'worth 8 *l.* and is now worth 6 *l.* *Dom. B.* p. 78.

From Ansfrid it descended to his son and heir Richard de Cormeliis, who dying 23 H. 2. was succeeded by Walter his son, who left three daughters coheiresses, Margaret, Albreda, and Sybil; of whom, the first held Begsoure 10 H. 3.

But Hugh Giffard, a younger brother to Elias Giffard of Brimpsfield, marrying Sybil the youngest daughter, had the manor of Beckshore, with others, assigned to him for her share. He was made constable of the tower of London 20 H. 3. Walter de Giffard was their son and heir, who dying without issue, was succeeded by his brother Golefry, whose son Golefry, or Geofry Giffard, was seized of Beckshore, and purchased a charter of free warren therein, 9 E. 3.

From this time there is a large vacancy in the account of the descent of this manor; for we come next to John Croker, esq; who was lord of it in 1608. He left three daughters coheiresses, from whom were descended sir Christopher Hales, formerly of Coventry, —— Pye, of Farringdon, esq; and a family of the name of Barker, of Berkshire, who enjoyed this manor in the year 1712.

The manor of Batsford, and a great estate in the parish, is now the property of Thomas-Edwards Freeman, esq; descended from an antient family, justly esteemed in their country, which has long resided in this place. John Freeman was seated here in the reign of Henry the Seventh. Thomas Freeman was a descendant from him, whose son Richard Freeman married Margaret, daughter of —— Rutter, of Queinton, esq; He was succeeded by his son John, who married Anne, daughter of —— Croft, of Sutton; and was also succeeded by his son Richard Freeman, who married Elizabeth, daughter of sir Anthony Keck, one of the lords commissioners of the great seal, in the reign of king William the Third, by whom he had an only child Mary, of whom hereafter. His second wife was Anne, daughter and

 heir

heir of Richard Marſhall, eſq; of Sellaby, in the county of Durham.

He was made lord chief baron of the exchequer in Ireland, in the year 1706, and his eminent merit ſoon advanced him to be lord high chancellor, and to be one of the lords juſtices to govern that kingdom in the abſence of the lord lieutenant. Theſe great preferments were not his own ſeeking; his great prudence, integrity, and moderation claimed ſo high a ſtation. He died in Ireland in the year 1710, having continued in the poſſeſſion of thoſe high offices to the time of his death.

Richard Freeman, eſq; only ſon of the chancellor, by Anne Marſhall, his ſecond wife, ſucceeded his father in this and his other eſtates, and married Margaret-Elizabeth Sawyer, daughter of —— Sawyer, of Bedfordſhire, eſq; by whom he left no iſſue. Walter-Edwards Freeman, eſq; (ſon of Mary, only daughter of chancellor Freeman, married to Walter Edwards, of the county of Glouceſter, eſq;) ſucceeded his uncle in this and other eſtates, and dying unmarried, was ſucceeded by Thomas-Edwards Freeman, eſq; youngeſt ſon of the ſaid Mary, already mentioned to be the preſent lord of this manor. He married Elizabeth, daughter of Henry Reveley, of Newby-Wiſk, in the county of York, eſq; by whom he has living one ſon, Thomas, born in 1754. He gives two coats of arms quarterly. 1ſt and 4th, *Azure, three lozenges in feſs, Or.* 2d and 3d, *Party per bend ſiniſter, ermine and erminois, a lion rampant Or.*

Mr. Freeman has an elegant ſeat here, of which he has been pleaſed to give the annexed engraving.

Of the other eſtates, the records ſhew that Richard Thurgreen was ſeized of divers lands in Beckſhore, and left them to Joan his only child, married to Thomas Hoddington, who together levied a fine thereof to themſelves in ſpecial tail, the remainder to Thomas the ſon of Alexander de Beckford, 14 R. 2.

Lands called Monk-meadow, or Monken-meadow, in Batesford, belonged to the abbey of Tewkeſbury, and were granted to John Fernham 22 Eliz.

Of the Church, &c.

The church is a rectory in the deanery of Campden, worth 180*l.* a year, of which the glebe only is worth about 100*l.* This land was ſet out for the rector, when the pariſh was incloſed, in the reign of queen Elizabeth. Chriſt-Church college in Oxford is patron, the reverend Edward Smallwell, B. D. the preſent rector.

Richard Thurgreen was ſeized of the advowſon of this church, which deſcended from him in the ſame manner as the lands above mentioned, down to 14 R. 2.

The abbey of Winchcombe was poſſeſſed of tithes in Batesford, which, after the diſſolution, were granted to ſir Thomas Seimour, 1 E. 6.

This pariſh was under the peculiar juriſdiction of Blockley in Worceſterſhire, where they formerly buried; and the inhabitants ſtill pay mortuaries to the vicarage of that place.

All the lands in the pariſh are ſubject to tithe.

The church is ſmall, and was formerly called the chapel of Beckford.

Monuments and Inſcriptions.

There is a monument in the church to the memory of lord chancellor Freeman, his ſon Richard Freeman, eſq; and other branches of the family.

Another monument in memory of the reverend doctor Thomas Burton, prebendary of Durham, and late rector of this pariſh.

	£.	s.	d.		£.	s.	d.
Firſt fruits,	13	3	9	Synodals,	0	1	0
Tenths, —	1	6	7	Pentecoſtals,	0	0	5
Procurations,	0	2	0				

Benefaction.

In the year 1728, Mrs. Anne Freeman gave the intereſt of 100*l.* by will, for reading prayers, and doing other duties on particular faſts and feſtivals.

Taxes.			£.	s.	d.
	The Royal Aid in	1692,	108	4	0
	Poll-tax — —	1694, —	18	6	0
	Land-tax ——	1694, —	93	18	0
	The ſame, at 3*s.* -	1770, —	70	8	0

At the beginning of this century there were 11 houſes and about 80 inhabitants in this pariſh, of whom 6 were freeholders; yearly births 4, burials 2, *Atkyns.* In a ſeries of ten years, from 1760 to 1769 incluſive, there were regiſtered 14 baptiſms and 13 burials; and the number of inhabitants is 87.

****

B A U N T O N.

THIS is a ſmall village in the hundred of Crowthorn and Minety, one mile diſtant north from Cirenceſter, and ſixteen ſouth-eaſtward from Glouceſter. It is ſituated on the eaſt ſide of the river Churn, which runs to Cirenceſter.

The name of the place was antiently written *Baudintone*, and *Pennington*. The latter manner of writing it, more eſpecially carries with it an idea of its ſituation *at the top of the town*, *i. e.* of Cirenceſter; for *pen* or *ben*, in the Britiſh language, ſignifies the top of any thing; and indeed the place ſeems to have been formerly dependent on that town, where its inhabitants had formerly a right of ſepulture.

The place affords nothing obſervable in natural hiſtory. The common fields and commonable places were incloſed and divided, about the year 1768, to the great advantage of the proprietor. The air is healthy, and the ſoil chiefly employed in tillage.

Of the Manor and other Eſtates.

In *Domeſday-book* are the following particulars : 'Edric the ſon of Ketel holds Baudintone, in 'Cireceſtre hundred, of the king, which his father 'held in the time of king Edward. There are 'three hides and three yard-lands taxed. In de-'mean are two plow-tillages, and three villeins 'with one plow-tillage, and four *ſervi*, and fifteen 'arces of meadow. It is worth and was worth '60*s.*' *Domeſday-book*, p. 79.

'Goisfridus Orleteile holds of the king, in 'Baudintune, two hides and one yard-land, taxed. 'Bolli held them. It is not in demean ; but 'there are two villeins, and eight bordars, with 'three plow tillages. It is worth and was 'worth 40*s.* There are eight acres of meadow.' *Domeſday-book*, p. 76.

Sir Robert Atkyns, under this head, aſſerts, that the manor of Baudintone was held of Hugh de Audley earl of Glouceſter, and Margaret his wife, 21 E. 3. and that it was held of Humphry de Bohun earl of Hereford and Eſſex, and of Joan his wife, 46 E. 3. and of Hugh earl of Stafford, by half a fee, 10 R. 2. of Thomas earl of Stafford, the 16th, and of William his brother, 22 R. 2. But I am of opinion, that the ſeveral records referred to by theſe dates, relate not to this place, but to Boddington, in the hundred of Tewkeſbury, which was held as of the honour of Glouceſter, and is ſaid to be within the juriſdiction of the honour court at this time.

The abbey church of Cirenceſter was very early poſſeſſed of the manor of Baudintone, of which Robert Playne and others, for the uſe of that church, were ſeized 6 R. 2. and it continued to be part of the poſſeſſions of that abbey, 'till the diſſolution of it ; upon which event, the family of the Georges became lords of it. They had been long owners of an eſtate in this place, which came to them by the marriage of William George with Catherine, daughter and coheir of Robert de Pennington, 3 E. 2. and it continued in that family four hundred years.

Chriſtopher George married Anne, daughter of Robert Strange, of Cirenceſter. Robert George, his ſon, married Margaret, daughter of Edward Oldſworth, eſq; and was ſucceeded by John George, his brother, eminent for his loyalty in the great civil wars, and who ſerved in parliament as burgeſs of Cirenceſter, in the reigns of king Charles the Firſt, and king Charles the Second. He died in 1675, leaving an only daughter, married to Richard Whitmore, of Slaughter, eſq; but he ſettled the manor of Baunton on his nephews. William George, his ſurviving nephew, ſold it to Thomas Maſter, of Cirenceſter, eſq; about the end of the laſt century, whoſe deſcendant in a direct line, Thomas Maſter, of Cirenceſter, eſq; is the preſent lord of the manor. *See Cirenceſter.*

Of the other eſtates, the records ſhew, that John Pain of Baudinton, and Alice his wife, levied a fine of lands therein, to the uſe of themſelves in tail ſpecial, 11 E. 3.

William Nottingham levied a fine of lands in Baunton, to the uſe of himſelf in ſpecial tail, 20 H. 6.

Lands in Baunton, formerly belonging to the knights hoſpitallers, were granted to John Walters and Thomas Carpenter, 1 Mar.

Of the Church, &c.

The church is an impropriation, in the deanery of Cirenceſter, worth 10*l.* a year to the curate. It formerly belonged to the abbey of Cirenceſter. Thomas Maſter, eſq; is patron and impropriator ; Mr. Joſeph Chapman the preſent incumbent.

The church is ſmall, without a ſteeple. In the year 1625, Dr. Godfrey Goodman, then biſhop of Glouceſter, conſecrated the burying ground, at the requeſt of John George, eſq; before which time the inhabitants buried at Cirenceſter.

Pentecoſtals, — £. 0 0 4 *ob.*

Taxes.	The Royal Aid in	1692,	£. 17	4	8
	Poll-tax — —	1694, —	5	8	0
	Land-tax ——	1694, —	21	16	0
	The ſame, at 3*s.* —	1770, —	17	2	0

At the beginning of this century there were 18 houſes and about 70 inhabitants in this pariſh ; yearly births 2, burials 1. *Atkyns.* But examining the pariſh regiſter, I find, that in a ſeries of ten years, from 1700 to 1709 incluſive, there were 15 baptiſms and 7 burials ; and in a like ſeries, from 1760 to 1769, there are regiſtered 30 baptiſms and 21 burials ; and the number of inhabitants is 56.

BECKFORD.

THIS pariſh is ſituate in the vale. The greater part of it lies in the hundred of Tibbleſtone, but the tithing of Didcot is in the upper part of Tewkeſbury hundred. The pariſh is five miles diſtant north-weſt from Winchcombe, five north-eaſt from Tewkeſbury, and fifteen north from Glouceſter. It is about four miles in length, and as many in breadth ; bounded on the eaſt by Aſton-under-hill, on the weſt by Kemmerton, on the north by Overbury, in Worceſterſhire, and on the ſouth by Teddington, a detached pariſh belonging to the laſt mentioned county.

This pariſh was incloſed in the year 1773. Part of Breedon hill lies within it, on the ſide of which great numbers of Roman coins have been found, of which further mention will be made under Kemmerton.

The hundred of Tibbleſtone, antiently written Tetboldeſtane, derives its name from a ſtone in this pariſh, now ſtanding near the turnpike-road from Tewkeſbury to London.

The

The river Caran, or Carant, riſes here, and runs into the Avon near Tewkeſbury.

Of the Manor and other Eſtates.

Beckford is one of thoſe manors, placed in *Domeſday-book*, under the head *Terra Regis*, where it is expreſſed after this manner :

'Rotleſc, huſcarle of king Edward, held Beceford in Tetboldeſtane hundred. There were 'eleven hides, and three plow-tillages in demean, 'and thirty-four villeins, and ſeventeen bordars, 'having thirty plow-tillages. There are twelve '*ſervi*, and four *ancillæ*. Earl William gave three 'hides of this manor to Ansfridus de Cormeliis, 'in which were twelve villeins with five plow-'tillages.' *Domeſday-book*, p. 69.

'Turbertus, a thane of earl Herald, held Eſtone. 'There are eight hides, and four plow-tillages in 'demean, and ten villeins and four bordars with 'ſix plow-tillages. There are eight *ſervi*, and 'three *ancillæ*. Of theſe two villages earl William made one manor, and they were not put 'to farm 'till Roger de Lurei let them for 30*l*. 'The ſame earl gave the tithe and the churches, 'with two villeins, and three virgates of land, to 'the abbey of Cormeile.' *Domeſday-book*, p. 69.

Robert Fitz-Alan founded a priory of regular canons in this place, which was made a cell to the abbey of St. Martin and St. Barbara in Normandy. For the charters of grants relating thereto, ſee *Appendix*, N°. 28.

The priory was ſeized of the manor of Beckford, Aſton, and Grafton, 56 H. 3.

William de Beauchamp earl of Warwick was ſeized of a manor in Beckford, with free warren and court-leet, 15 E. 1. But I apprehend it muſt have been in truſt for the priory, for the prior of Beckford held the manor of Beckford, with court-leet and waifs, and his right was allowed the ſame year, in a writ of *Quo warranto*.

King Edward the Third, upon his wars with France, had the eſtates of all the priories in England, that were cells to monaſteries in France, granted to him in parliament 10 E. 3. (*i. e.* 1336.) whereupon he let out thoſe priories to farm, with all their lands and tenements. This priory was afterwards totally ſuppreſſed in the year 1414, 2 H. 5. (when all other alien monaſteries in England were ſuppreſſed by act of parliament) and the manor of Beckford, and the lands belonging to it, were granted to Eton college, by king Henry the Sixth, in the twenty-ſecond and twenty-third years of his reign ; and afterwards they were granted to the college of Fotheringhay, 2 E. 4. And in the firſt year of king Edward the Sixth, when all the religious endowments, which had eſcaped king Henry the Eighth, were taken away, the manor and park of Beckford, with the advowſon of the vicarage, together with the rectory and advowſon of the vicarage of Grafton, all which belonged to that college, were granted to ſir Richard Lee.

John Wakeman was lord of this manor in the year 1608 ; and Henry Wakeman, eſq; is the preſent lord thereof, and of the hundred of Tibbleſtone, of which he holds court-leet and court-baron at Beckford. He is deſcended from the antient family of the Wakemans, of Rippon in Yorkſhire. His arms are, *Vert, a ſaltire wavy ermine*. Mr. Wakeman has a very large, handſome ſeat near the church.

TITHINGS and *HAMLETS*

There are four tithings in this pariſh.

1. *Beckford.*

2. *Grafton.*

3. *Bengrove.* Adam de Ardeen held lands in Bengrave 56 H. 3. and Thomas Roberts died ſeized of lands in Bengrove 11 C. 1. which deſcended to Thomas his ſon.

4. *Didcot*, or *Didcot Paſtures*. Lands in Didcot formerly belonged to the abbey of Tewkeſbury, and were granted to Richard Tracy 36 H. 8.

Of the Church, &c.

The church is a vicarage, in the deanery of Campden. Joſeph Biddle, M. A. is the preſent patron and incumbent. The church and advowſon were given to the abbey of Cormeile by king H. 1. and having accompanied the manor, were granted, at the diſſolution of the college of Fotheringhay, to ſir Richard Lee. Mr. Wakeman, the impropriator, has the tithes of Beckford, Grafton, and Didcot ; and Mr. Morris has part of the tithes of Bengrove. The tithes of Bengrove pay 40*s*. a year to the crown.

The impropriator formerly paid the vicar eight quarters of wheat, four quarters of barley, ſix quarters of oats, and eight pounds in money yearly : but the bill for incloſing the common fields, &c. in the pariſh, empowered the commiſſioners to ſet out land for the vicar in lieu thereof. The vicarage was eſtimated at 80*l*. a year ; but it hath been lately much improved.

The church is dedicated to St. Barbara, (martyred in the reign of the emperor Maxentius) and hath a handſome high tower in the middle, with pinnacles, and a veſtry on the north ſide of the chancel.

Monuments and Inſcriptions.

Againſt the north wall of the chancel is a plain marble monument, with a ſcutcheon, on which are the arms of Wakeman impaling the following, *Argent, on a chevron between three lions heads erazed ſable, an eſtoile proper*, for Hall. Upon the table it is thus inſcribed :

D. O. M.

Mortale Spolium Richardi Wakeman Armig. Inſignibus genere et Pietate Parentibus Odoardo et Maria oriundi hoc tegit ſaxum. Qui Sacramento fideli ad extremam belli Aleam Strenuus dura perituri Regis ſecutus fata, domum tandem redux dixero an relegatus ? Recuſſis in Raſtra et Ligones armis (Romanorum conſulum exemplo) Gramineam facile colonis omnibus Fœlici rei ruſticanæ peritiâ Coronam præripuit.

Sed

Sed eheu! brevis paterni Agri hæres, prid. Kal. ſept. A°. a part. virg. CIↃ. DC. LXII. ex ipſâ Ætatis meridie præceps in occaſum ruit. Ægre perquam Extincti tulêre deſiderium Amici, Propinqui, Sorores, Fratres, Liberi, ſed omnium ægerrime Anna conjux mœrentiſſima, quæ perenni viri deſideratiſſimi, memoriæ Aureis hiſce inciſis marmori characteribus, (Pullam ipſa nunquam mutatura) Parentavit.

Spiritus ut Cœlum ſubeat novus Incola, numen
Primævâ ſupplex devenerare Fide.

On a blue ſtone, a ſcutcheon, party per feſs, baron and femme, 1. *Argent, a chevron ſable, between three hawthorn leaves proper*, for Thornton. 2. *Party per chevron, three lions paſſant, (no colours expreſſed)* for Lunn. And under, this inſcription:

En quo ſecundam D. Ieſu expectat epiphaniam, Pulchra, modeſta, chara, Elizabetha Thornton, quæ Parentes Lebbeum Lunn, eccleſiæ hujus Paſtorem, fideliſſimam uxoremq; ipſius Elizabetham, Et conjugem Robertum Thornton, A. M. de Staunton in agro Wigornienſi, triſtes reliquit, et infelices, Sept. 4° Anno Dom. 1706, Ætat. ſuæ 29.

	£.	s.	d.		£.	s.	d.
Firſt fruits	16	18	10	Synodals	0	4	0
Tenths —	1	13	8	Pentecoſt.	0	1	1
Procurations	0	6	8				

Benefaction.

The land called the Church Land, worth about 9*l*. a year, is given to the uſe of the poor.

Taxes.			£.	s.	d.
	The Royal Aid in	1692,	93	14	0
	Poll-tax ——	1694, —	28	2	0
	Land-tax ——	1694, —	130	12	0
	The ſame, at 3*s*.	1770, —	98	9	6

At the beginning of this century, there were 56 houſes, and about 250 inhabitants in this pariſh, whereof 10 were freeholders; yearly births 7, burials 5. *Atkyns*. But in a ſeries of ten years, from 1700 to 1709 incluſive, there are entered in the pariſh regiſter 84 baptiſms, and 60 burials. In a like ſeries, from 1760 to 1769, there are regiſtered 109 baptiſms, and 94 burials: So that the inhabitants being 403, are very much increaſed, and the average of annual burials, is to the whole number of living, nearly as 1 to 37.

BERKELEY

IS a very large pariſh, in the lower level of the Vale of Glouceſterſhire. It lies within the hundred of the ſame name, which took denomination from the town or borough of Berkeley, ſituate about the middle of the pariſh, five miles diſtant weſt from Durſley, ſeven north from Thornbury, and eighteen ſouth-weſtward from Glouceſter. The pariſh is bounded on the north-weſt by the great river Severn.

In *Domeſday-book* the name is written *Berchelai*, whereas the Saxons wrote it Beoꞃcenlau. It is ſuppoſed to have been ſo called from Beoꞃce, the beech-tree, becauſe it grew very plentifully there. Some perſons, however, may object to this etymology, ſince at preſent there is no beech wood in the pariſh; but it is evident that there was a wood in Berkeley, from an inquiſition taken by the king's eſcheator, 15 E. 2. wherein it is ſaid, *There are forty acres of high wood, the pannage of which is worth half a mark, and no more*. And furthur, to obviate the objection, it may be added, that there are many places which took denomination from antient woods, which being aſſarted, have no traces of them left but in the names of ſuch places only.

The town is one of thoſe antient boroughs, of which there were five in Glouceſterſhire in the time of king Edward the Firſt, (p. 43.) It is ſituated on the Avon, a ſmall river riſing in two heads at Boxwell and Kilcot, and receiving the contributions of two or three brooks in its courſe, falls into the Severn a little below the town, which, on this account, as I find it in Willis's *Notitia Parliamentaria*, hath been alſo called *Aveney*.

King Edward the Third granted to William lord Berkeley and his heirs, the privileges of a mintage for coining, and the return of writs within the town and hundred of Berkeley; ſo that no ſheriff, bailiff, or other of the king's officers, ſhould exerciſe any authority there; but thoſe privileges have been long ſince diſuſed, becauſe the expence of paſſing accounts in the exchequer exceeded the profits ariſing from them.

What the town was above two centuries back, may be ſeen by Leland's deſcription of it: 'The 'Towne of Berkeley,' ſays he, 'is no great 'Thinge, but it ſtandythe well, and in a very 'good Soyle. It hathe very muche occupied, and 'yet ſome what dothe, Clothinge. The churche 'ſtondithe on an Hille at the South Ende of the 'Towne. And the Caſtle ſtondithe at the South 'Weſt End of the Churche. It is no great 'Thinge. Divers Towres be in the Compaſe of 'it. The Warde of the firſt Gate is mitely 'ſtronge, and a Bridge over a Dyche to it. There 'is a ſqware Dongeon Towre in the Caſtle, *ſed* '*non ſtat in mole ægeſtæ Terræ*. There longe to 'Berkeley 4 Parks, 2 Chaces. Okely Parke hard 'by. Whitwike. New Parke. Hawlle Parke. 'Miche Wood Chace.' *Leland's Itin*. v. 7. p. 96.

The town is honoured by giving both name and title to the earls of Berkeley. I come now to treat of the preſent ſtate of it. It is called a borough, tho' it ſends no members to parliament, and has a mayor annually choſen at the court-leet, who has the tolls of the town, and wheelage of all goods landed from the veſſels in the river, at 2*d*. a load; but the authority and privilege of his office ſeem to extend no further. The borough conſiſts principally of one ſtreet of mean buildings, through which there is little or no travelling, the turnpike-road from Glouceſter to Briſtol running about a mile to the ſouth of it. Several old accounts mention the clothing trade having flouriſhed in this place, but it hath long ſince deſerted it, and is not ſucceeded by any other kind of manufacture. Tueſday is the day of the market, which is ſo little frequented that it ſcarcely deſerves to be called one. Since the alteration of the

ſtyle,

ſtyle, the fair, which uſed to be on the third, is held on the fourteenth of May, for hogs and other cattle.

It hath been obſerved that this borough gives name to one of the hundreds of the county, which is very large, conſiſting of thirty-three pariſhes and tithings, beſide the borough, (p. 40). There were 2064 able men returned out of the hundred, upon a general muſter taken 6 Jac. and ſoon after the new militia law took place, 30 G. 2. the hundred of Berkeley was appointed to raiſe 85 men for its proportion towards the county militia; which was found to be the twenty-ninth part of the whole number of able men, between the ages of eighteen and fifty, that were then reſident within it, and liable to that ſervice; ſo that the whole number upon the liſts muſt then be 2465. There were formerly twelve parks, and two chaces in this hundred: Caſtle-park, Whitley-park, New-park, Okely-park, Shepnaſh-park, Ham-park, Beverſtone-park, Hill-park, Ozleworth-park, Almondeſbury-park, Cromhall-park, and Uley-park: The two chaces were Micklewood and Redwood. This hundred is famous for producing the beſt cheeſe in the kingdom.

Berkeley-caſtle is one of the few buildings of that ſort which is ſtill preſerved from ruins. It is ſaid that Roger de Berkeley began it in the ſeventeenth year of king Henry the Firſt, and that it was finiſhed by Roger the Third, in the reign of king Stephen. It is certainly of very great antiquity, and received its preſent form from Robert Fitz-Harding, who repaired and enlarged it in the reign of king Henry the Second, when it was called the honour of Berkeley. Leland has given a ſhort deſcription of it in the preceding quotation; but a conſiderable part of it was beaten down ſince his time, in the great civil war of king Charles the Firſt. The annexed plate exhibits the ſouth-weſt view of it. The Hall in the caſtle is exceeding large, and very much admired for its antient ornaments; and on the left hand at the entrance is the ſtuffed ſkin of an animal, which the old women of the town and neighbourhood believe to be that of a monſtrous toad, found in the dungeon of the caſtle; but it appears to be a ſeal ſkin, or ſomething much like it.

King Edward the Second having been thought to ſhew too great favour to the Spencers, his queen and the prince of Wales headed a party againſt him, took him priſoner, and carried him from place to place, 'till at length he was brought to this caſtle, and murdered Sept. 22, 1327. On the road from Briſtol to Berkeley, the guard made the king walk on foot whilſt they rode, and otherwiſe uſed him with contempt and deriſion. Adam Orlton, biſhop of Hereford, is ſaid deſignedly to have promoted the king's death, by writing the following ſentence to his keeper:

Edvardum occidere nolite timere bonum eſt.

yet the ſenſe is ſo ambiguous, according to the ſtops in reading of it, as to bear a contrary meaning. It is thus tranſlated in the laſt edition of the *Britannia*, where the ambiguity is preſerved:

To ſeek to ſhed king Edward's blood
Refuſe to fear I think it good.

But the author of the Survey of the city of Worceſter pronounces the biſhop innocent of that heinous crime, by ſhewing that he was beyond ſea all the time of the unfortunate king's confinement in the caſtle.

As the pariſh is large, ſo the ſoils are various; but a red kind of earth or clay enters into the compoſition of moſt of them. There are ſome orchards that produce good cider. The oak thrives well here, but 'tis no where leſs cultivated. It is ſhocking to ſee almoſt all the trees wantonly lopt and headed for firing, a practice the more inexcuſable, as the foreſt-coal is rendered cheap by means of the navigation up the river.

There is plenty of iron ore in this pariſh, but not a ſufficiency of wood to work it. However, it appears by the great quantities of rich cinders which have been lately found at Peddington, and carried to the furnaces in the foreſt of Dean, that our anceſtors had iron-works here.

The lands lying near the Severn are very ſubject to floods from that river, which ſometimes do great damage. In a printed account of the dreadful effects of a great wind, which happened on the 26th of November, 1703, is the following paſſage: 'At Berkeley, the overflowing of the river Severn 'beat down and tore to pieces the ſea wall, 'whereby the waters flowed above a mile over one 'part of the pariſh, and did great damage to the 'land: It carried away one houſe which was by 'the ſea ſide, and a gentleman's ſtable, wherein 'was a horſe, into the next ground. Twenty-ſix 'ſheets of lead were blown off from the middle 'iſle of the church, and taken up all joined to'gether, as they were on the roof, the ſheets 'weighing three hundred and a half one with 'another.'

Thoſe who would ſee the long ſtory of the witch of Berkeley, may find it in *Haywood's Hiſtory.*

Of the Manor and other Eſtates.

There was an antient, famous nunnery in this place, in the time of the Saxons, to which this large manor belonged. Who was the founder of it, and when it was founded, are circumſtances equally unknown; but the following account of its diſſolution, taken from *Walter Mapes*, who lived above five hundred years ſince, is not unworthy the reader's peruſal:

Berkeley is a village near Severn, of the yearly value of five hundred pounds, in which was a nunnery govern'd by an abbeſs, that was both noble and beautifull. Earl Godwyn, a notable ſubtle man, not deſiring her but her's, as he paſſed by, left his nephew, a young, proper, handſome ſpark, (under pretence of being ſeized with ſickneſs) 'till he ſhould return back thither, and inſtructed him to counterfeit an indiſpoſition, 'till he had got all who came to viſit him, both lady abbeſs,

and

and as many of the nuns as he could, with child. And to carry on the intrigue more plausibly, and more effectually to obtain the favour of their visits, the earl furnished him with rings and girdles, that by those presents he might the more readily corrupt and gain their inclinations. There needed no great intreaty to perswade this young gallant to undertake an employment so amorous and pleasing. The way to destruction is easy, and quickly learnt; he seem'd wonderful cunning to himself, but all his cunning was but folly. In him were concentered all those accomplishments that might captivate foolish and unthinking virgins; beauty, wit, riches, and obliging mein: and he was mighty solicitous to have a private apartment to himself. The devil therefore expelled Pallas, and brought in Venus; and converted the church of our Saviour and his saints into an accursed pantheon, the temple into a stew, and the lambs into wolves. When many of them proved with child, and the youth began to languish, being overcome with the excess and variety of pleasure, he hasten'd home with the reports of his conquests (worthy to have the reward of iniquity) to his expecting lord. The earl immediately addresses the king, and acquaints him, that the abbess and the nuns were gotten with child, and had render'd themselves prostitutes to all comers; all which, upon inquisition, was found true. Upon the expulsion of the nuns, he begs Berkeley, and had it granted him by the king, and settled it upon his wife Gueda; but (as Domesday-book *hath it) she refused to eat any thing that came out of this manor, because of the destruction of the abbey: And therefore he bought Udecester for her maintenance, whilst she lived at Berkeley: Thus a conscientious mind can never relish ill gotten possessions.*

But the wickedness of this earl did not long prosper, for the large, fruitful isle, since known by the name of the Godwin Sands, being part of his possessions, was irrecoverably swallowed up in the sea; and it was not long after, that he and his whole family were banished out of the kingdom.

William the Norman, about this time, obtained the crown of England, and rewarded Roger, one of his own countrymen, with this manor, who therefore assumed the name of Roger de Berkeley.

It is one of the largest manors in England. In the time of Roger lord Dursley, who was also lord hereof, it paid a fee-farm rent to the king of 500*l.* 17*s.* 2*d.* The extent of it will appear by the following abstract from *Domesday-book.*

'In Berchelai king Edward had five hides, and 'in demean five plow-tillages, and twenty villeins, 'and five bordars with eleven plow-tillages, and 'nine *servi*, and two mills of 12*s.* rent. There 'are ten radchenisters having seven hides and 'seven plow-tillages. There is a market-town, 'where seventeen [free] men reside, and pay a 'tax in farm.

'These hamlets belong to Berchelai. In Hilla 'four hides; in Almintune four hides; in Hinetune four hides; in Camma six hides, and eleven 'other hides; in Gosintune four hides; in 'Dersilege three hides; in Couelege four hides; 'in Euuelege two hides; in Nimdesfelle three 'hides; in Uutune fifteen hides, and half a yard-'land; in Simondeshale half a hide; in Chingescote four hides and a half; in Beurestane ten 'hides; in Osleuuorde half a hide; in Almodes-'berie two hides; in Horefelle eight hides; in 'Westone seven hides; in Cromale two hides; 'in Erlingeham nine hides; in Esceleuuorde 'three hides. The above are members all belong-'ing to Berchelai.

'There were in these hamlets, in the time of 'king Edward, forty-nine plow-tillages and a half 'in demean, and two hundred and forty-two 'villeins, and one hundred and forty-two bordars 'with one hundred and twenty-six plow-tillages. 'There are one hundred and twenty-seven *servi.*

'There are nineteen free men, radchenisters, 'having forty-eight plow-tillages with their men. 'There are twenty-two *coliberti,* and fifteen '*ancillæ.* There are eight mills of 57*s.* 6*d.* [rent.]

'In this manor, two brothers, in the time of 'king Edward, held five hides in Cromhal, having 'in demean two plow-tillages, and six villeins, 'and five bordars having six plow-tillages. These 'two brothers might dispose of themselves, with 'their land, as they pleased, which was then 'worth 4*l.* now 3*l.* Earl William commended 'them to the steward of Berchelai, that he might 'have their service, as Roger says.

'For this manor, with all its appurtenances, 'Roger pays a farm [rent of] 170*l.* in weight, 'of lawful money.

'The same Roger hath (belonging to this 'manor) two hides in Hislinbruge, one hide at 'Claenhangare, one hide at Hirslege, [Hurst] 'seven hides at Neuetone, [Newington Bagpath]. 'There are in demean ten plow-tillages, and thir-'teen villeins, and twenty-one bordars with 'twenty-two plow-tillages. There are sixteen '*servi,* and a mill of 5*s.* The whole, in the time 'of king Edward, was worth 9*l.* now 11*l.* 10*s.*

'The same Roger holds five hides, the land of 'Bernard the priest. He hath there three plow-'tillages, and two villeins, and six bordars with 'five plow tillages. It was worth and is worth 60*s.*

'There are five hides in Nesse belonging to 'Berchelai, which earl William set apart to make 'a little castle, as Roger reports.' *Domesday-book,* p. 68.

The above particulars amount to the sum of one hundred and forty-four hides and a half, and there are two hundred and ninety-four plow-tillages and a half, a prodigious estate for one manor.

Roger de Berkeley, the proprietor of it, was a nobleman in the court of king William, who also held the manors of Coberley, Dodington, and Siston, in this county. He was a great benefactor to the priory of Stanley St. Leonard, and in the year 1091, became a shorn monk therein; and having no issue, this manor of Berkeley descended to William de Berkeley, his nephew and heir, who, in the year 1139, founded the monastery of of Kingſwood in Wiltſhire. William was ſucceeded by Roger de Berkeley, his ſon and heir, who was alſo baron of Durſley, and taking part with king Stephen againſt Henry the Second, was violently diſpoſſeſſed of his caſtle of Berkeley, by Walter, brother of Milo earl of Hereford, and his whole eſtate confiſcated.

King Henry had been aſſiſted, in thoſe wars, with great ſupplies of money, by Robert Fitz-Harding, a powerful man in thoſe times, (mayor and governor of Briſtol) whom, therefore, the king rewarded with a grant of the caſtle of Berkeley,[f] with the manor of Berthone, in the county of Glouceſter, as alſo 100*l.* a year in lands in Berkeley, and afterwards with the whole lordſhip of Berkeley, and Berkeley-herneſſe, thereunto belonging, of which Roger de Berkeley had been diveſted. He was ſurnamed Fitz-Harding, becauſe he was the ſon of Harding, mayor and governor of Briſtol, deſcended, according to Leland, from the kings of Denmark; which Harding accompanied William duke of Normandy into England, and was with him at that memorable battle againſt king Harold, at Haſtings. In *Domeſday-book* he is called Hardinc, where it is ſaid he held Witenhert, [now Whitenhurſt] in Glouceſterſhire, in mortgage of Brictric. Newland, abbat of St. Auguſtine's in Briſtol, wrote a pedigree of the Berkeley family, and proves that they are lineally deſcended from this Harding, who died at Briſtol, Nov. 6, 1115, 16 H. 1.

Robert Fitz-Harding, whom we ſhall now call Robert lord Berkeley, took his ſeat in the houſe of peers 1 H. 2. Roger, the former lord of this place, at the interceſſion of friends, was reſtored to the barony of Durſley; but he bore a violent hatred againſt Robert lord Berkeley, for depriving him of his inheritance, until the king interpoſed, and in the preſence of many noblemen made a counter-match in the two families; that is, between Maurice, ſon of the lord Berkeley, and Alice, daughter of the lord Durſley; and between the heir of the lord Durſley, and Helena, daughter of the lord Berkeley; and by the original writings, ſtill extant in the family, it appears, that Alice was to have 20*l.* a year in land, of the fee of Berkeley, for her dower; and Helena, the manor of Siſton for hers; whereupon all right in the barony of Berkeley was voluntarily releaſed by the lord Durſley. This Robert lord Berkeley founded the abbey of St. Auguſtine's in Briſtol, and dying in the year 1170-71, was buried in the quire thereof. Being ſtiled *canonicus*, he is ſuppoſed to have been a canon in that abbey, whoſe yearly revenues, at the diſſolution, were valued at 767*l.* 15*s.* 3*d.* and are the preſent maintenance of the biſhop and prebendaries of Briſtol. He married Eva, daughter of Godiva, ſiſter to William the conqueror. She founded a religious houſe called the Magdalen's, near Briſtol, and was prioreſs thereof. By her he had iſſue five ſons, Henry, Maurice, Robert, Nicholas, and Thomas; and two daughters, Helena, of whom already, and Aldena, married to Kingſcot of Kingſcot. But Henry dying young,

Maurice de Berkeley, the ſecond ſon, ſucceeded his father, and gave a fine of 1000 marks to the king, for a confirmation of his title to Berkeley and Berkeley-Herneſſe. He was the firſt of them who dwelt at Berkeley. He fortified the caſtle, and founded two hoſpitals, one at Lorwing, between Berkeley and Durſley, and that at Longbridge, to the north of Berkeley, dedicated to the holy Trinity. By his wife Alice, daughter of lord Durſley, he had iſſue ſix ſons, Robert, Thomas, Maurice, William, Henry, and Richard. The two laſt accompanying William king of Scotland into that country, when he returned from being a priſoner in England, became the anceſtors of many eminent families in Scotland, France, and Ireland. He had alſo an only daughter, married to —— Giffard. And dying, according to abbat Newland, in the year 1190, was interred in the church of Brentford, com. Middleſex, towards the building of which he had been a great benefactor.

Robert his eldeſt ſon ſucceeded his father, and 3 R. 1. gave the king 1000*l.* for livery of his inheritance. And again 1 John, he paid 60 marks for a confirmation[g] thereof, and for a charter of fairs in his manor of Berkeley. The king had oppreſt his ſubjects with large demands for the renewal of charters, for eſcuage, and other ſervices, wherefore this lord, with others, took up arms againſt him. He made his peace[h] 15 John; yet two years afterwards fell again from his duty, and with others, invited Lewis, the French king's ſon, into England, and ſwore allegiance to him, for which this lord was excommunicated by the pope, and his caſtle of Berkeley, and all his lands ſeized,[i] and the profits of the ſame ordered for the maintenance of the caſtle of Briſtol. But 18 John, he obtained letters of ſafe conduct to come to the king, then at Berkeley-caſtle; where, upon his ſubmiſſion, he got a grant of his manor of Came, in the county of Glouceſter, for the ſupport of Juliana his wife, daughter of William de Pontlarch, and niece to the great earl of Pembroke, earl marſhal of England, and afterwards protector to king H. 3. at whoſe acceſſion to the crown, in 1216, lord Robert, for a fine of [k]966*l.* 13*s.* 4*d.* was reſtored[l] to all his lands, except the caſtle and town of Berkeley. He was a great benefactor to St. Auguſtine's at Briſtol, Bradenſtoke in Wilts, Stanley priory in Glouceſterſhire, as alſo to the canons of Hereford, and built the hoſpital of St. Catherine's, at Bedminſter near Briſtol. He had two wives, (the latter was Luci, who afterwards married Hugh de Gournay)

[f] Ex Autographo, in Caſtro de Berkeley.
[g] Rot. pip. 3 R. 1. Glouc. [h] Rot. fin. 15 J. m. 5.
[i] Clauſ. 18 Joh. m. 4, & 9.
[l] Clauſ. 1 H. 3. m. 1. & m. 12.
[k] Rot. pip. 1 H. 3. Salop.

but

but died without iſſue by either, 1219, and was buried in a monk's cowl, in the north aile of St. Auguſtine's abbey aforeſaid.

Whereupon, Thomas his brother and heir had livery of his lands, and afterwards had reſtitution of Berkeley-caſtle 8 H. 3. He was as remarkable as his father for piety and benefactions to the church, and departing this life Nov. 29, 1243, was buried in the ſouth aile of St. Auguſtine's abbey; leaving iſſue by Joan, daughter of Ralph de Somery, lord of Campden, in com. Glouc. ſix ſons, Maurice, Thomas, Robert, Henry, William, and Richard; alſo a daughter Margaret, wife of ſir Anſelme Baſſet, of Baſſet's-court, in Uley, Glouceſterſhire.

Maurice the eldeſt ſon ſucceeded his father, and paying 100*l.* for his relief, had livery of his inheritance. He accompanied his father[m] in the wars of France, and 41 H. 3. was in that expedition with prince Edward againſt the Welch. In 42, 43, 44, and 47 H. 3. he was ſummoned[n] to attend the king againſt the magnanimous Llewellyn ap Gryffyth, prince of Wales, then in arms. He married Iſabel, daughter of [o]Maurice de Creoun (a great baron in Lincolnſhire) by Iſabel his wife, ſiſter to William de Valence, earl of Pembroke, uterine ſiſter and brother to king Henry the Third; notwithſtanding which, this lord afterwards adhered to the rebellious barons, for which his lands were ſeized; but the king having a reſpect for the lady Iſabel, whom he calls his beloved niece, [p]aſſigned the manors of Herietſham and Tottesclyffe for her maintenance. However this lord obtained pardon 55 H. 3. He died ſeized of the barony of Berkeley, which he held by the ſervice of three knight's fees, April 4, 1281, having given divers lands in Berkeley, Bevington, Wolgaſton, and Erlingham to the abbey of St. Auguſtine's in Briſtol, in the north aile of which he was buried. He had iſſue by his ſaid wife, Maurice, (ſlain at Ingſt, in a tournament whilſt his father was living) Thomas, and Robert; and according to ſome accounts, one daughter Maud. He was ſucceeded by

Thomas, the ſecond, but eldeſt ſurviving ſon, a very wiſe and provident perſon, keeping exact accounts with all his bailiffs and ſtewards. He had two hundred attendants in his family, of knights, eſquires, yeomen, grooms, and pages, beſide huſbandmen. The wages of an eſquire was three-pence half-penny a day, a horſe and two ſuits of furred cloaths were provided for him, and three half-pence a day was given for a boy to wait on him. This lord, in obedience to the king's ſummons, appeared, at different times, at [q]Worceſter, at [r]Montgomery, at [s]Shrewſbury, and at Glouceſter, to oppoſe the Welch; and for thoſe ſervices had a ſpecial [t]grant for hunting with his own dogs in the king's foreſt of Mendip, and the chace of Kingſwood, and was acquitted of an [u]hundred marks, the then relief of his barony. In ſhort, he was in moſt of the battles fought in Wales, Scotland, and France, during the reign of king Edward the Firſt; and in the twenty-fourth year of that king's reign, was one of the commiſſioners to treat of peace between England and France; and the next year was made [w]conſtable of England. He was ſent ambaſſador to Rome, 35 E. 1. with Dr. Gayneſburg, biſhop of Worceſter, about affairs in France, and his two ſons accompanied him. He went into the field twenty-eight ſeveral times, and being taken priſoner at the fatal battle of Bannockburne, paid a large [x]fine for his redemption. He was a benefactor to the canons of St. Auguſtine's in Briſtol, where he was buried; to the monks of Kingſwood, and to the Bartholomews, and Minorites at Glouceſter, as appears by antient books in the caſtle at Berkeley. Dying in the year 1321, he left iſſue by Jane his wife, daughter of William de Ferrers earl of Derby, three ſons, Maurice, John, of Wymundham in com. Leic. and James, who was rector of Slimbridge, and, in the year 1326, conſecrated biſhop of Exeter: he had alſo two daughters, Iſabel and Margaret, who both died unmarried. He was ſucceeded by his eldeſt ſon,

Maurice, who in his father's life time, on June 23, 23 E. 1. had ſummons to parliament as lord Berkeley of Berkeley-caſtle. He delighted from his youth in military actions, and was in ſeveral tournaments held at Worceſter, Dunſtable, Stamford, Blythe, and Wincheſter. He had been many years in the wars with his father in Scotland and Wales, and, in 1312, was made [y]governor of Glouceſter, and in 1314, [z]governor of the town and caſtle of Berwick upon Tweed, and the next year was appointed juſtice of South Wales, and had the cuſtody of all the caſtles there. The year following he raiſed 1000 foot in thoſe parts, 200 more out of the foreſt of Dean, and 100 out of Gowerland in Wales, for the king's ſervice in the north; and in 1319 he was made [a]ſteward of the dutchy of Aquitaine. In 1321 he joined with the earl of Lancaſter and other barons againſt the two Spencers, laid waſte their eſtates, and took from the father 28,000 ſheep, 2,200 beaſts, 2,000 ſwine, &c. 40 tuns of wine, and 600 muttons in the larder; from the ſon they carried off 60 breeding mares, and 1,000 beaſts, beſide their young. The Spencers were baniſhed by an act of the enſuing parliament, but were recalled, within a year, by the ſame authority, and their opponents declared traitors. This lord Berkeley [b]neglecting, upon ſpecial ſummons, to ſubmit to the king, his caſtles and lands were ſeized, and he was afterwards ſent priſoner to Wallingford-caſtle, where,

[m] Rot. pip. 28 H. 3. Glouc. [n] Clauſ. 42, 43, 44 & 47 H. 3. in dorſa. [o] [p] Clauſ. 48 H. 3. in dorſ. m. 4.
[q] Rot. Scutag. de ann. 5 & 10 E. 1. [r] [s] Rot. Wall. 10 E. 1. in dorſ. [t] Pat. 11 E. 1. m. 23. [u] Clauſ. 12 E. 1. m. 10.
[w] Rymer, tom. 4. p. 783. [x] Compot. Ballivi de Wotton, de ann. 10 E. 2. in caſtro de Berkeley. [y] Pat. 6 E. 2. p. 1. m. 24.
[z] Rot. Scoc. 8 E. 2. m. 4. [a] Rot. Vaſc. 13 E. 2. m. 12.
[b] Clauſ. 15 E. 2. in dorſ.

according to Walſingham, he died on May 31, 1326, and was buried in St. Auguſtine's abbey, Briſtol. He built a friery at Holmes, an iſland in the Severn. He married two wives, 1. Eve, daughter of Eudo la Zouch, lord Zouch; 2. Iſabel, daughter of Gilbert de Clare, earl of Glouceſter, who died without iſſue by him; but he left iſſue by his firſt wife, 1. ſir Thomas, who ſucceeded him; 2. ſir Maurice, from whom the Berkeleys of Stoke Giffard, and lord Berkeley of Stratton, with their ſeveral deſcendants; 3. John, from whom the Berkeleys of Shropſhire are deſcended; 4. Eudo, rector of Llanbeder, com. Caernarvon; 5. Peter, a dignitary in the church of Wells; alſo a daughter Iſabel, married to Robert lord Clifford, and afterwards to Thomas lord Muſgrave.

Sir Thomas, ſecond lord Berkeley, ſucceeded his father. He had joined the earl of Lancaſter and his followers, in oppoſing the Spencers, and was firſt committed to the tower of London, whence he eſcaped; but being retaken, was ſent to Berkhamſted caſtle, and afterwards to Pevenſey in Suſſex. On the queen and prince of Wales's returning from France, with a great force, the ſcene was changed, and this lord was ſet at liberty, and his caſtle of Berkeley delivered up to him, whereof Hugh le Deſpencer the younger had poſſeſſed himſelf. The queen's party having afterwards made the king priſoner, Nov. 16, 1326, he was received by this lord Berkeley, according to Leland, by indenture from Henry Plantagenet, earl of Lancaſter, having an [c]allowance of 5*l. per diem* for his expences. But he was not long entruſted with the care of him, for being thought to treat him with too much lenity, he was commanded to deliver the king, [d]together with the caſtle, to John lord Maltravers and ſir Thomas Gournay, and thereupon he retired to Bradley, one of his manorhouſes. But the king being barbarouſly murdered, as already related, he was indicted as acceſſary thereto, yet, upon tryal, was honourably acquitted by the jury, and afterwards by the parliament. He had livery of his lands 1 E. 3. and was the ſame year in commiſſion with John Maltravers the younger, as principal guardians of the peace in com. Glouc. Wilts, Oxon, Berks, Southampton, Somerſet, Dorſet, and Hereford. He was in all the wars againſt the Scots, and 19 E. 3. was made warden of the king's foreſts on the ſouth of Trent; and was with the king at the famous battle of Creſſy, 20 E. 3. and the ſame year appeared at the ſiege of Calais, with ſix knights, thirty-two eſquires, thirty archers on horſeback, and two hundred on foot, of his own retinue. On Sept. 19, 1356, he was one of the chief commanders at the battle of Poictiers, where the Engliſh obtained immortal honour, and he there took ſo many priſoners, that out of their ranſoms he rebuilt Beverſtone-caſtle, in Glouceſterſhire, the lordſhip of which he purchaſed, together with that of Over in Almondeſbury, about the fifth year of the king's reign. In his domeſtic retinue, he had no leſs than twelve knights, and ſometimes more, who took wages, with two ſervants and a page each; and twenty-four eſquires, who had each a man and a page. He kept the demeans of ſixty or eighty manors in his hands, and had in all about 300 in family, beſides bailiffs, hinds, &c. He ſheared at Beverſtone, with the eſtates thereabout, 5775 ſheep, and a minute account of all his concerns was exactly regiſtered. He gave lands to the [e]church of Portbury, and fifty other acres of land, and 40*s.* rent in Portbury, to a chapel there, for prieſts to ſay maſſes for his anceſtors, himſelf, and his ſucceſſors; and founded a chantry in the chapel of Newport, near Berkeley, another at Syde, one in the chapel at Wortley, a fourth in the chapel at Cambridge, another at Over, all in the county of Glouceſter; another in the chapel of St. Catherine Pulle, near Briſtol, one in the abbey of St. Auguſtine at Briſtol, and another chantry at Worceſter; and gave lands to the chantry of Sheppardine in Hull, and an annual rent of 3*l.* 6*s.* 8*d.* to a [f]prieſt to ſing for the ſoul of his wife Margaret, in St. Auſtin's church, Briſtol, and the like rent to another prieſt to ſing for her in Keinſham monaſtery, com. Somerſet. He married firſt, Margaret, fourth daughter to Roger Mortimer earl of March, by whom he had iſſue, ſir Maurice, Thomas, Roger, and Alphonſus; and Joan, married to ſir Reginald Cobham, kn^t^. His ſecond wife was Catherine, daughter of ſir John Clivedon, of Charfield in the county of Glouceſter, widow of ſir Peter le Veel, of Tortworth, in the ſaid county, kn^t^. by whom he had iſſue, Thomas, Maurice, Edmund, and John, the anceſtor of the Berkeleys of Beteſham, in Hampſhire. She long ſurvived her huſband, and founded a free-ſchool and chantry in Wotton-under-edge, and the chantry of St. Andrew in Berkeley church. This lord died Oct. 27, 1361, and was buried in Berkeley church; leaving ſir Maurice, by his firſt wife, his heir.

Which ſir Maurice, third lord Berkeley, in 1336, being then ſeven years old, went with his father into Scotland, and was there knighted; next year he married Elizabeth, daughter of Hugh le Deſpencer, and four years afterwards went a voyage to Granada in Spain, and continued abroad about five years. He attended the Black Prince into Gaſcoigne, and on Sept. 19, 1356, received ſeveral wounds in the battle of Poictiers, of which he was never cured, but did not die 'till [g]June 8, 1367; leaving iſſue by his ſaid wife, four ſons, *viz.* Thomas, his ſucceſſor; ſir James, married to the daughter and heir of ſir John Bloet, with whom he had the manor of Ragland, and other eſtates in Monmouthſhire and Glouceſterſhire; ſir John;

[c] Clauſ. 1 E. 3. p. 1. m. 1 & 3.
[d] Plac. Cor. in Parl. 4 E. 3. n. 16.
[e] Ex Autog. apud Berkeley.
[f] Ex compot. apud Berkeley, 38 E. 3.
[g] Eſch. 42 E. 3.

and

and Maurice; alſo three daughters, Catherine, Agnes, and Elizabeth.

Thomas ſucceeded his father, and was the fourth lord Berkeley. This lord let out moſt of his lands at a yearly rent, which at this time began to be cuſtomary all over England. In [h]1378, 2 R. 2. he was employ'd by ſea and land in the wars with France and Spain; ſerved in France and Britanny the two ſucceeding years, and afterwards in Scotland. In 10 R. 2. he entertained the king at Berkeley-caſtle; and being preſent at Flint-caſtle in [i]1399, when the king reſigned, he teſtified it, in the king's preſence, in the tower of London; and on the meeting of the three eſtates in parliament, a biſhop, abbat, earl, baron and knight, being the repreſentatives choſen to pronounce his majeſty's depoſition, he was the baron appointed for that purpoſe. In 5 H. 4. he was made admiral of the king's fleets, from the mouth of the Thames to the weſt and ſouth, and ſworn of the king's privy council, in open parliament. He [k]burnt fifteen ſail of French ſhips in Milford-haven, part of the fleet ſent to the aſſiſtance of Owen Glendourdwy, and took fourteen more, on board of which were the ſeneſchal of France, and eight officers of note, whom he made priſoners. In 6 and 7 H. 4. he was chief commander in the Welch wars, and engineer at the ſiege of Lampader-vaur in Pembrokeſhire. In ſhort, he was not only a great ſoldier, but was diſtinguiſhed as a lover of learning. John Trevifa, the famous vicar of Berkeley, celebrated by Bale for his learning and eloquence, tranſlated the Old and New Teſtaments into Engliſh, at the requeſt of this lord Berkeley. His lordſhip married Margaret, daughter and heir to Gerard Warren lord Liſle, by Alice, daughter and heir to Henry lord Teys; and departing this life July 13, 1416, was buried near his lady, (who died before him) in the church of Wotton-under-edge, leaving iſſue by her only one child Elizabeth, wedded to Richard Beauchamp earl of Warwick, who, in right of his wife, died ſeized of many manors and eſtates in Glouceſterſhire, as may be ſeen under their reſpective heads.

His lordſhip dying without iſſue male, his nephew James, ſon and heir of ſir James de Berkeley, his lordſhip's brother, became his heir, and was the fifth lord Berkeley; for by virtue of a ſpecial entail and fine, he enjoy'd the caſtle and lordſhip of Berkeley, with other lordſhips mentioned in the ſaid fine; but not without great interruptions and diſturbance [l]from Richard Beauchamp earl of Warwick, who had married the only daughter of the laſt lord Berkeley. Between theſe two great perſons and their poſterity was a law-ſuit for the Berkeley eſtate, which laſted one hundred and ninety-two years, and was carried on with uncommon violence; during which, Berkeley-caſtle was beſieged and defended many times with great forces on each ſide. The weight of power and intereſt was ſo great againſt lord Berkeley, that he thought it prudent to give a thouſand marks to Humphry duke of Glouceſter for his patronage. He married firſt, a daughter of Humphry Stafford of Hooke, in com. Dorſet, by whom he had no iſſue. 2. Iſabel, widow of Henry, ſon and heir of William lord Ferrers of Groby, and ſecond daughter of Thomas Mowbray, firſt duke of Norfolk; by whom he had iſſue, four ſons, William; Maurice; James; and Thomas, from whom deſcended the Berkeleys of Herefordſhire, and Worceſterſhire; and three daughters, [m]Elizabeth, Iſabel, and Alice. Which Iſabel lady Berkeley died in priſon in the caſtle of Glouceſter, (ſee p. 194.) His lordſhip married, to his third wife, Joan, daughter of John Talbot, earl of Shrewſbury, by whom he had no iſſue; and dying in 1463, was buried in an alabaſter tomb, in a chapel which he built on the ſouth ſide of the high altar, in the pariſh church of Berkeley.

William his eldeſt ſon, ſixth lord Berkeley, was knighted at Calais in 1438; and, after the death of his father, defended himſelf in the ſuit at law carried on againſt him by Thomas Talbot viſcount Liſle, whom he afterwards killed in a fight, as related under the pariſh of Nibley. In 21 E. 4. he was [n]advanced to the honour of viſcount Berkeley, and ſoon after had a grant of 100 marks *per annum* for life; and 1483 was [o]created earl of Nottingham, a dignity enjoyed by his maternal anceſtors the Mowbrays, extinct dukes of Norfolk. When the earl of Richmond acceded to the crown, in 1485, he was [p]appointed earl marſhal of England, with limitation to the heirs male of his body, with a fee of 20*l. per annum*; and, in the fourth year of that reign, was further [q]advanced to the dignity of marquis of Berkeley. He married 1. Elizabeth, daughter of Reginald Weſt, lord la Warre, from whom he was divorced without iſſue by her. 2. Jane, widow of ſir William Willoughby, kn[t]. and daughter of ſir Thomas Strangeways, kn[t]. by whom he had iſſue Thomas and Catherine, who died young. 3. Anne, daughter of John Fiennes, lord Dacre of the ſouth; but he died, without iſſue by her, in the year 1491-2, and lies buried in the church of the friers Auguſtins, near Broad-ſtreet, London.

[h] Rot. Franc. 2 R. 2. m. 18. [i] Walſ. in eodem anno.
[k] Walſ. in eodem anno. [l] Ex vet. ſcript. apud Berkeley.
[m] She was married to Thomas Burdet, of Arrow, in the county of Warwick, eſq; who incurred the diſpleaſure of king Edward the Fourth, by his attachment to the duke of Clarence, that prince's brother; and hearing that the king, hunting in his park at Arrow, had killed a white buck which he valued, paſſionately exclaimed, that *he wiſhed the deer, horns and all, in the belly of the perſon who adviſed his majeſty to that action*; for which he was convicted of high treaſon, and ſuffered death 17 E. 4. tho' that upright judge, ſir John Markham, oppoſed the judgment.
[n] Cart. ab ann. 19, uſq; 22 E. 4. n. 6 [o] Cart. 1 R. 3. m. 1.
[p] Pat. 1 H. 7. p. 5. [q] Cart. de ann. 4 H. 7.

Maurice, his brother, ſhould have ſucceeded to the paternal eſtate, and title of baron of Berkeley; (and, in that caſe, he would have been the ſeventh, according to the before recited ſummons) but the marquis his brother, having taken exception at his conduct, ſettled the caſtle of Berkeley, to which the barony is appendant, with thoſe lands and lordſhips which were the body of that antient barony, upon king Henry the Seventh, and his iſſue male, in failure of which, to revert to the right heirs of the marquis. But Maurice, by diſcreet management, obtained poſſeſſion of his ſhare of the eſtate that devolved to him in right of his mother Iſabel Mowbray. He married Iſabel, daughter of Philip Mead, eſq; deſcended from the Meads of Wraxhall, in Somerſetſhire, by whom he had iſſue three ſons, Maurice, his ſucceſſor; Thomas, who ſucceeded Maurice; and James; and one daughter, Joyce, married to William Aſtley, eſq; He reſided chiefly at Yate, in Glouceſterſhire, and dying in the year 1506, was ſucceeded by

Maurice his ſon and heir, who ſhould have been eighth lord Berkeley. He was made knight of the Bath, at the coronation of king Henry the Eighth, and, in the 7th and 8th years of that king's reign, was high ſheriff of Glouceſterſhire; in the laſt of which he was alſo conſtituted lieutenant of the caſtle of Calais, and captain of fifty men at arms. In the 14th year of that reign, he was [r] ſummoned to parliament as a baron, and, the enſuing year, was ſent into France with the army under the command of Charles Brandon duke of Suffolk. He married Catherine, daughter of ſir William Berkeley, of Stoke-Giffard, kn[t]. but died at Calais, 1523, without iſſue by her, and was ſucceeded by his brother Thomas.

Which Thomas, ninth lord Berkeley, had a command in the Engliſh army at the battle of Flodden, in 1519, and, for his ſignal ſervice there, received the honour of knighthood from Thomas Howard earl of Surrey, the general. He was made conſtable of Berkeley-caſtle [s] 24 H. 8. which was then in the crown, and died the ſame year. He married 1. Eleanor, widow of John Ingleby, eſq; and daughter of ſir Marmaduke Conſtable, of Yorkſhire, kn[t]. by whom he had no iſſue. 2. Cecilie, widow of Richard Rowden, in the county of Glouceſter, eſq; by whom he had [t] two ſons, Thomas, his heir; and Maurice.

Which Thomas, tenth lord Berkeley, married 1. Mary daughter of George Haſtings, firſt earl of Huntingdon, but by her had no iſſue. 2. Anne, daughter of ſir John Savage, of Frodſham, in Cheſhire, kn[t]. by whom he had Henry, a poſthumous ſon and heir; alſo a daughter Elizabeth, (afterwards married to Thomas Butler, tenth earl of Ormond) ſcarce three quarters of a year old when his lordſhip deceaſed. He was buried at Stone, where he died, in his journey from his houſe at Yate in Glouceſterſhire, towards London, on Sept. 19, 1534. It is ſaid that Maurice, this lord's brother, bore a great enmity to his ſiſter-in-law the lady dowager, and came, with ſeveral companions, one night to deſtroy her deer, and intended afterwards to ſet fire to a hay-rick that ſtood near the houſe, with deſign to burn the houſe; but another party of deer-ſtealers happening to be in the park at the ſame time, who had fled to the hay-rick to hide themſelves, they frightened one another, and ſo the miſchief was prevented.

Which Henry, the eleventh lord Berkeley, ſucceeded his father. King Edward the Sixth dying, who was the laſt male heir of king Henry the Seventh, he obtained livery of Berkeley-caſtle, and of all thoſe lordſhips ſettled on that king by William marquis of Berkeley, before mentioned, by ſpecial warrant from the queen, 1 & 2 Phil. & Mar. before he was at full age, at the old rent, which was 687*l.* 5*s.* *per annum*, not accounting the parks and chaſes thereunto belonging. His lordſhip thereupon repoſſeſſing the old barony of his anceſtors, was ſummoned by writ to parliament 4 & 5 Phil. & Mar. and there placed according to the antient precedence. He was much embroiled in law-ſuits upon the old title of heir general and heir ſpecial; for queen Elizabeth had granted ſeveral of thoſe lands, forfeited by the deſcendants of lord Liſle, to the earls of Warwick and Leiceſter; who, by great power, and by corruption of juries, and other groſs means, ſaith ſir Robert Atkyns, maintained a long chargeable ſuit againſt him, which at laſt was ended by a reference 7 Jac. after having continued 192 years. The earl of Leiceſter, continues the ſame author, pretended at firſt a great kindneſs to lord Berkeley, and acknowledged the honour to be deſcended from his family, and deſired that he might ſend an herald to examine the pedigree, and take a ſurvey of his records, and antient writings; and this herald was bribed, by the earl of Leiceſter, to ſteal away the moſt material evidences which concerned the lord Berkeley's eſtate. His lordſhip was appointed lord lieutenant of the county of Glouceſter [u] 1. Jac. There is an anecdote of this lord,

[r] Ex Autograph. apud Berkeley. [s] Pat. 24 H. 8. p. 2.

[t] Collins's Peerage, v. 3. p. 460.

[u] His lordſhip's commiſſion ſhews that he enjoyed the utmoſt confidence of his prince, who inveſted him with greater powers than, by the laws of this country, any king could give: The commiſſion runs thus: ' James, by the grace of God, king of ' England, Scotland, France, and Ireland, defender of the faith, ' &c. To our right truſty, and well beloved Henry lord Berkeley, ' greeting. Know ye, that for the great and ſingular truſt and ' confidence we have in your approved fidelity, wiſdom, and ' circumſpection, we have aſſigned, made, conſtituted, and or' dained, and by theſe preſents do aſſign, make, conſtitute, and ' ordain you to be our lieutenant within our county of Glouceſter, ' and city of Glouc. and county of the ſame city, and in all ' other corporate and privileged places, within the limits or pre' cincts of the ſaid county of Glouc. and city of Glouc. and either ' of them, as well within liberties as without: And do, by theſe ' preſents, give full power and authority unto you, that you from ' time to time may levy, gather, and call together *all and ſingular* ' *our ſubjects, of what eſtate, degree, or dignity, they or any of* ' *them be*, dwelling or inhabiting within our ſaid county and city, ' or county of the ſame city, and within all other places corporate and

lord, that queen Elizabeth having offered a hundred marks for a lute, his lordſhip out bid her, and bought it. His firſt wife was Catherine, third daughter of Henry Howard earl of Surry, by whom he had iſſue two ſons, Thomas, and [w] Ferdinand: Thomas married Elizabeth Carey, only child of ſir George Carey, kn[t]. afterwards lord Hunſdon, by whom he left iſſue George and Theophila, and died before his father. Ferdinand died at Yate in Glouceſterſhire, and was there buried. He had alſo, by the ſaid Catherine, four daughters, of whom, Mary was married to John Zouch, eſq; ſon and heir to ſir John Zouch, of Codnore in com. Derby, kn[t]. and Frances was married to George Shirley, of Aſtwell, in com. Northampton, eſq; afterwards created a baronet, and anceſtor of the preſent earl Ferrers. Lord Berkeley had to his ſecond wife, Jane, youngeſt daughter of ſir Michael Stanhope, and widow of ſir Roger Townſend, by whom he had no iſſue. He died in the year 1613, and was buried in the family vault, in the chancel at Berkeley, where is a monument and inſcription for him.

George, only ſon of the ſaid Thomas, ſucceeded his grandfather Henry as twelfth lord Berkeley, according to the ſummons of 23 E. 1. He was made knight of the Bath, at the creation of Charles prince of Wales, on Nov. 4, 1616. The following inſcription, on a monument erected to his memory in Cranford church, in Middleſex, recites his character, marriage, and iſſue.

Here lyeth the body of GEORGE Lord BERKLEY, Baron of Berkley, Mowbray, Seagrave, and Bruce, and Knight of the Bath, who departed this life the 10th day of Auguſt, A. D. 1658. He married ELIZABETH, ſecond daughter and coheir of Sir MICHAEL STANHOPE, of Sudbury in the county of Suffolk, Kn[t]. by whom he had iſſue CHARLES, ELIZABETH, and GEORGE. CHARLES, drowned in his paſſage to France, Jan. 27, 1641. ELIZABETH married to EDWARD COOK, Eſq; grand child and heir to Sir EDWARD COOK, Kn[t]. ſometime Lord Chief Juſtice of both Benches. She died Novemb. the 9th, A. D. 1661, and lieth buried at Higham in Norfolk; and GEORGE Lord Berkley now living: This deceaſed Lord, beſides the nobility of his birth, and the experience he acquired by foreign travels, was very eminent for the great candour and ingenuity of his diſpoſition, his ſingular bounty and affability towards his inferiours, and his readineſs (had it been in his power) to have obliged all mankind.

George, the only ſurviving ſon of the laſt lord George, became, at the death of his father, thirteenth lord Berkeley, and was advanced to the dignity of viſcount Durſley, and earl of Berkeley, Sept. 11, 31 C. 2. 1679. His lordſhip made a preſent to Sion-college of a valuable library, collected by ſir Robert Coke, upon which the governors of that college preſented his lordſhip with their addreſs of thanks. When king James the Second withdrew himſelf, on Dec. 10, this earl was one of thoſe peers who met at Guildhall, and ſubſcribed a declaration, 'That they would 'aſſiſt his highneſs the prince of Orange in ob-'taining a free parliament, &c.' and at the acceſſion of king William and queen Mary, was appointed one of their privy-council; and on July 27, 1689, conſtituted Cuſtos Rotulorum of the county of Surry. This noble peer departing this life, was buried at Cranford in Middleſex, where a monument is erected to his memory, with this inſcription:

Here lyeth the body of GEORGE Earl of Berkeley, Viſcount Durſley, Baron of Berkeley, Mowbray, Seagrave, and Bruce, who had the honour to be a Privy-counſellor to K. CHARLES the II. and K. JAMES; eminent for his affability, charity, and generoſity. He married ELIZABETH, one of the coheireſſes of JOHN MASSINGBEARD, Eſq; of the family of the MASSINGBEARDS in Lincolnſhire. He departed this life the 14th of October, 1698, Ætat. 71. in hopes of a bleſſed reſurrection; for the merciful ſhall obtain mercy.

By the lady Elizabeth, his wife, he had two ſons, and ſix daughters; 1. Charles, who ſucceeded him in honour and eſtate; 2. George, inſtalled one of the prebendaries of Weſtminſter, June 13, 1687, who married Jane, daughter of George Cole, of the county of Devon, eſq; 3. Elizabeth, wedded to William Smith, of the Inner Temple, eſq; 4. Theophila, married firſt to ſir Kingſmill Lucy, of Bloxburn, in com. Hertford, bar[t]. and ſecondly to the pious and learned Robert Nelſon, of London, eſq; 5. Arabella, ſecond wife to William Pulteney, eſq; 6. Mary, married to Ford lord Grey, of Werk, afterwards earl of Tankerville. 7. Henrietta, who died unmarried; 8. Arethuſa, ſecond wife to Charles Boyle, lord Clifford of Laneſborough.

Charles, ſecond earl of Berkeley, was made one of the knights of the Bath, at the coronation of King Charles the Second, and, in 1679 and 1681,

'and privileged, within the limits and precincts of the ſame 'counties, and of either of them, as well within liberties as 'without, mete and apt for the wars, and them to train, array, 'and put in a readineſs; and them alſo, and every of them, after 'their abilities, degrees, and faculties, well and ſufficiently to 'cauſe to be armed and weaponed, and to take the muſters of 'them from time to time, in places moſt mete for that purpoſe, 'after your good diſcretion: And alſo, the ſame our ſubjects ſo 'arrayed, trained, and armed, as well men of arms, as other 'horſemen, archers, and footmen, of all kinds and degrees, 'mete and apt for the wars, to conduct and lead, as well againſt 'all and ſingular our enemies, alſo againſt all and ſingular rebels, 'traytors, and other offenders, and their adherents, againſt us, 'our crown and dignity, within our ſaid county and city, and 'county of the ſaid city, and all other places corporate and pri-'vileged, within the limits and precincts of the ſame counties, 'as well within liberties as without, from time to time, as often 'as need ſhall require, by your diſcretion; and with the ſaid 'enemies, traytors, and rebels to fight, and them to invade, reſiſt, 'repreſs, and ſubdue, ſlay, kill, and put to execution of death, 'by all ways and means, by your ſaid good diſcretion: And to 'do, fulfil, and execute all and ſingular other things which ſhall 'be requiſite for the levying and government of our ſaid ſubjects, 'for the conſervation of our perſon and peace, ſo by you, in form 'aforeſaid, levyed and to be led: *And to do, execute, and uſe againſt 'enemies, traytors, rebels, and ſuch other like offenders, and their 'adherents, as neceſſity ſhall require, by your diſcretion, the law called 'the Marſhal Law, according to the Law Marſhal:* And of ſuch 'offenders apprehended, or brought in ſubjection, to ſave whom 'you ſhall think good to be ſaved, *and to ſlay, deſtroy, and put to 'execution of death ſuch and as many of them as you ſhall think mete, 'by your good diſcretion, to be put to death.* And farther, our will 'and pleaſure is, and by theſe preſents we do give unto you full 'power and authority, that in caſe any invaſion of enemies, 'inſurrection, rebellion, riots, routs, or unlawful aſſemblies, *or 'any like offences* ſhall happen to be moved in any place of this our 'realm, out of the limits of this our commiſſion; that then, and 'as often as you ſhall perceive any ſuch miſdemeanour to ariſe, 'you, with all the power you can make, ſhall, with all diligence, 'repair to the place where any ſuch invaſion, unlawful aſſembly, 'or inſurrection ſhall happen to be made, *to ſubdue, repreſs, and 'reform the ſame, as well by battle or other kind of force, as otherwiſe, 'by the laws of our realm, and the Law Marſhal, according to your 'diſcretion.'* &c. &c.

[w] Collins's Peerage, v. 3. p. 461. Ferdinand is not mentioned upon his lordſhip's monument. See *Monuments and Inſcriptions.*

was returned to parliament for the city of Gloucester. On the acceſſion of king William and queen Mary, he was called up, by writ, to the houſe of peers, (his father then living) and took his ſeat as baron Berkeley of Berkeley, on July 11, 1689; and the ſame year relieved the earl of Pembroke, in quality of envoy extraordinary and plenipotentiary to the ſtates of Holland. On May 25, 1694, he was conſtituted lord lieutenant of the county of Glouceſter; and, in the year 1699, was appointed one of the lords juſtices of the kingdom of Ireland. On June 7, 1702, his lordſhip was appointed conſtable of the caſtle of St. Briavel, in the foreſt of Dean, and lord lieutenant and Cuſtos Rotulorum of the counties of Glouceſter and Surry. His lordſhip died at Berkeley-caſtle, Sept. 24, 1710, and was interred, in the family vault, in Berkeley church, where is an inſcription for him, inſerted towards the end of the account of this pariſh. His lordſhip married Elizabeth, daughter of Baptiſt Noel viſcount Campden, by whom he had iſſue four ſons, and three daughters; 1. Charles, lord viſcount Durſley, who died of the ſmall-pox in May 1699; 2. James, third earl of Berkeley; 3. Henry, who, in his youth, was page of honour to queen Anne; and, in the year 1717, was appointed firſt commiſſioner for executing the office of maſter of the horſe, and conſtituted colonel of the 4th regiment of foot; and, in 1719, was appointed colonel of the 2d troop of grenadier guards. He was elected one of the knights of the ſhire for the county of Glouceſter, in three ſucceeding parliaments, and died at Bath, in May 1736, leaving iſſue by Mary, only daughter to Henry Cornwall, of Bredwardine-caſtle, in Herefordſhire, eſq; two ſons, Henry, and Lionel-Spenſer Berkeley; and three daughters, Mary, Elizabeth, and Iſabella-Bernardina. 4. George Berkeley, fourth and youngeſt ſon, who ſerved in two parliaments for the port of Dover, married Henrietta, daughter of ſir Henry Hobart, bar^t. and died, in 1746, without iſſue. 5. Lady Mary; 6. lady Elizabeth; 7. lady Penelope.

James, third earl of Berkeley, ſucceeded his father in the year 1710, and was the ſame year conſtituted lord lieutenant of the county of Glouceſter, and city of Briſtol, warden of the foreſt of Dean, and high ſteward of the city of Glouceſter. During the reign of queen Anne, he had diſtinguiſhed himſelf in many gallant actions at ſea, under ſir George Rooke, and ſir Cloudſley Shovel, and was made vice-admiral of the blue in 1707-8, and vice-admiral of the white in 1709. In the life-time of his father, 1704, he was called, by writ, to the houſe of peers, by the title of lord Durſley; and, at the acceſſion of George the Firſt, was appointed one of the lords of the bed-chamber. On March 18, 1717-18, he was conſtituted firſt lord commiſſioner of the admiralty, which office he held all that reign, being likewiſe vice-admiral of Great Britain, &c. and, in 1718, was inſtalled a knight of the moſt noble order of the garter. In 1727, he was appointed lord lieutenant of the counties of Lincoln, Glouceſter, and [x] Surry, and of the cities and counties of Glouceſter and Briſtol; conſtable of the caſtle of St. Briavel, and keeper of the foreſt of Dean; alſo vice-admiral of Great Britain, &c. His lordſhip married the lady Louiſe Lennox, eldeſt daughter to Charles firſt duke of Richmond, by whom he had iſſue one ſon, Auguſtus, born on Feb. 18, 1715-16; and a daughter lady Elizabeth, married to Anthony Henly, of the Grange, in the county of Southampton, eſq; His lordſhip dying, was buried at Berkeley, and on a plate upon his coffin was the following inſcription:

The Moſt Noble and Puiſſant James Earl of Berkeley, Viſcount Durſley, Baron Berkeley of Berkeley-Caſtle, Moubray, Seagrave, and Breaus of Gower, Vice-Admiral of Great Britain, Lord Lieutenant of the County of Glouceſter, and Cities and Counties of Briſtol and Glouceſter; Cuſtos Rotulorum of the Counties of Glouceſter and Surry, Warden of the Foreſt of Dean in the County of Glouceſter, and Conſtable of the Caſtle of St. Briavel's in the Foreſt of Dean, one of His Majeſty's Moſt Honourable Privy Council, and Knight of the Moſt Noble Order of the Garter, died September 2, 1736, at Aubigny in France, aged 54 Years.

Auguſtus, fourth earl of Berkeley, upon his father's death, ſucceeded him in honour and eſtate. In 1737 he was conſtituted lord lieutenant and Cuſtos Rotulorum of the county of Glouceſter, and preſented to a company of the ſecond regiment of foot guards, with the rank of colonel. In 1739 he was nominated one of the knights of the moſt antient order of the Thiſtle, or St. Andrew; and, in 1745, was made colonel of one of the regiments raiſed to go againſt the Scotch and Engliſh rebels. His lordſhip married, on May 7, 1744, Elizabeth, daughter of Henry Drax, of Charborough in Dorſetſhire, and of Ellerton-abbey in Yorkſhire, eſq; and by her, who, in July 1745, was appointed one of the ladies of the bed-chamber to her royal highneſs Auguſta, princeſs of Wales, had iſſue, 1. Frederick-Auguſtus, now earl of Berkeley, born May 24, 1745. 2. James, born in 1747, and died the ſame year. 3, 4, 5. Ladies Louiſa, Elizabeth, and Frances, all born July 28, 1748, and lived to be chriſtened, but died ſoon after. 6. Lady Georgina-Auguſta, born Sept. 18, 1749. 7. Lady Elizabeth, born in December 1750, and, on May 10, 1767, married to the honourable Mr. Craven, brother to lord Craven. 8. George-Cranfield, born Aug. 10, 1753. His lordſhip departed this life on Jan. 9, 1755, and was ſucceeded in honour and eſtate by his ſon

Frederick-Auguſtus, the preſent and fifth earl of Berkeley, and the twenty-firſt in deſcent from Harding the royal Dane. His lordſhip was conſtituted lord lieutenant and Cuſtos Rotulorum of the county of Glouceſter, and of the cities of Briſtol and Glouceſter, conſtable of the caſtle of

[x] Bill. ſignat. 1 Geo. 2.

St.

St. Briavel, and warden of the foreft of Dean, July 2, 1766; and, on Aug. 19 following, was chofen high fteward of the city of Gloucefter; and is colonel of the militia of the county of Gloucefter, and of the cities of Briftol and Gloucefter.

His lordfhip's TITLES are, Earl of Berkeley, Vifcount Durfley, Baron Berkeley of Berkeley-caftle, Mowbray, [the name of a family] Seagrave, [the name of a family] and Breaus of Gower [the name of a family] in Glamorganfhire. The creations are already recited.

ARMS. *Gules, a chevron between ten croffes pattee, fix above and four below, argent.* But, by intermarriages, his lordfhip has a right of quartering the following coats, *Bloet*, *Brotherton*, *Mowbray*, *Breaus*, *Seagrave*, *Chancombes*, *Longefpey*, *Albeney*, *Fitz-Allen*, *Blundeville*, *Warren*, *Plantagenet*, *Marfhall*, *Strongbow*, *Murchard*, *Mead*, *Read*, and *Stanhope*. CREST. *On a wreath, a mitre gules, garnifhed Or, charged with the paternal coat.* SUPPORTERS. *Two lions argent, the finifter having a ducal crown, and plain collar and chain, Or.* MOTTO. DIEU AVEC NOUS.

Having traced the defcent of the manor down to the prefent time, I come now to treat of the

TITHINGS and *HAMLETS*.

There are feven very confiderable tithings in this parifh.

1. The *Borough*, which has been mentioned at the beginning of this account. Mr. Wefton has a handfome houfe in it, and a good eftate in the parifh. Lands in the town of Berkeley, which belonged to the chantry of St. Andrew, whereof Thomas Chefter was the laft incumbent, and had a penfion of 5 *l.* were granted to William Herick and Arthur Ingram, 5 Jac. and four acres in Short Grove, belonging to the fame chantry, were granted, the fame year, to Edward Newport and John Crompton.

Lands in Berkeley and Beenham did belong to the archbifhop of Canterbury, and were granted to Robert earl of Leicefter, and John Morley, in exchange for lands in Montgomery, 23 Eliz. There are two conftables belonging to the borough.

2. *Ham*, in which are included *Ham*, *Clapton*, *Bevington*, *Whitley-park*, *Peddington*, and *New-park*. Thomas Berkeley held the manor of Ham 15 E. 2. Thomas de Berkeley was feized of the manor of Ham 6 R. 2. and Catherine his wife was feized of two meffuages, eight acres of arable, two acres of meadow, one acre of wood, and a yearly rent of 7 *s.* in Ham, for St. Andrew's chantry in Berkeley, 7 R. 2. The earl of Berkeley now receives from the crown, 5 *s.* a year for St. Andrew's chantry.

As to other eftates, befides the manor, the records fhew, that John Sergeant was feized of lands in Ham, 30, 36, & 47 E. 3. And John Fitz-Nichol (one of the Berkeley family) was feized of Wikeftow in Ham, 49 E. 3. John Kendal was feized of Avenfcot, [in Alkington tithing] and of the manors of Peddington, and Wyke [in the tithing of Alkington] in the parifh of Berkeley, and was attainted of high treafon, in the beginning of the reign of Henry the Seventh, and thofe eftates were granted to William Treefree, 4 H. 7. to hold at pleafure. The fame were granted to John Pate and John Dingle during pleafure, 2 H. 8. and afterwards to John Dingle, and the heirs of his body, paying a brace of greyhounds, whenever the king fhould come within two miles of that place, 10 H. 8. He died 33 H. 8. and John Dingle, his fon, had livery of them the fame year. Thomas Hickes, efq; has a handfome houfe at Peddington, and a good eftate in this tithing. Ham has a diftinct tithingman.

3. *Hinton*, *i. e.* the old town, from *hen*, in the Britifh language, which fignifies old. This tithing includes *Sanager*, lying along the river; antiently written *Seven-hangar*, perhaps a corruption of *Severn-hen-gaer*, *i. e.* the old wall of the Severn, or fea-wall. Sanager gave name to an antient family, whofe property it was, and who refided there; a defcendant of that name and family is ftill living, but the eftate, by a late purchafe, is now lord Berkeley's. Part of *Halmore* lies alfo in this tithing. Hinton has a diftinct tithingman.

4. *Alkington*, including *Swanley*, *Woodford*, *Rugbag*, *Micklewood-chafe*, *Wike*, and *Newport*; which laft lies in the road between Gloucefter and Briftol, and has in it two or three inns of good accommodation. The name of this tithing was antiently written Almintune, as may be feen in the *Domefday* account of the parifh of Berkeley. Maurice de Berkeley held this manor 9 E. 1. Margaret countefs of Shrewfbury was feized of the manor of Alkintone 7 E. 2. Thomas de Berkeley held the manor of Alkintone, and granted one quarter of beans, and three ells and a half of woollen cloth yearly, to Ady Tilly, for his life, 17 E. 2. Thomas de Berkeley held the manor of Alkinton 6 R. 2. and ever fince that time, it has defcended with the barony of Berkeley.

Befide the manor, the records fhew that John Sergeant, (mentioned under Ham) was feized of lands in Alkinton, 30, 36, & [y] 46 E. 3. Margaret, the widow of Nicholas Stanfhaw, held Wike, 14 H. 6. Thomas de Berkeley had a grant of a fair in Newport, 22 E. 3. There was a chantry in St. Maurice's chapel, at Newport, founded by Thomas lord Berkeley, 17 E. 3. of which John Baker was the laft incumbent; who, according to Mr. Willis, had a penfion, after the diffolution, of 6 *l.* a year. A meffuage in Swanley, late belonging to the above chantry, was granted to

[y] I have followed fir Robert Atkyns in the date of this record; but I apprehend it fhould be 47 E. 3. as it ftands in Ham, and occurs afterwards in the account of Stone.

Robert earl of Leicefter, 23 Eliz. There is a proper tithingman to this divifion.

5. *Stone.* This place is inferted in alphabetical order, among the parifhes.

6. *Hamfallow*, in which are *Wanfwell*, *Wannifwell*, or *Wanfel*; part of *Halmore*; and *Hamfallow*. Wanfwell was probably fo called from the Britifh word *gwaun*, a meadow. Thorp of Wanfwell held his lands to guard a tower in Berkeley-caftle, called Thorp's-tower, which was built in the reign of king Edward the Third. Thomas Thorp died feized of the manor of Wanfwell, 17 H. 8. Thomas his fon had livery thereof 29 H. 8. and Nicholas Thorp had livery of it 1 Eliz. William Butler died feized of this manor without iffue, 10 Eliz. whereby it defcended to Anne, his fifter and heir. Here is a tithingman.

7. *Bradftone.* Thomas de Bradftone, (a perfon of eminence, fee p. 87) was feized of the manor of Bradftone 34 E. 3. which defcended to his fon Thomas, who held this manor 48 E. 3. Richard Seimour was probably a truftee of the Bradftones, for he was feized of the manor of Bradftone 2 H. 4. but Ela, widow of Thomas Bradftone, was feized thereof, 11 H. 4. Sir Walter de la Pool, and Elizabeth his wife, daughter and heirefs of Thomas Bradftone, were feized of the manor of Bradftone 12 H. 6. and fir Edward Inglefthorp (or Ingoldfthorp) was feized thereof, and of Arlingham, Stinchcombe, and Horton, belonging to the Bradftones, 35 H. 6. There was formerly a chantry at Bradftone, the lands belonging to which were granted to Lewis Williams, by king Edward the Sixth. Bradftone has a tithingman.

Sir William Stourton, of Stourton, held the manor of Veelham, near Berkeley, 17 E. 4. and Robert Grinder, efq; was feized of Stubmarfh-park, in the hundred of Berkeley, 22 H. 6.

Of the Church, &c.

The church is a vicarage in the deanery of Durfley, worth about 170*l.* a year; of which the earl of Berkeley is patron, and Mr. Auguftus-Thomas Hupfman incumbent.

The rectories of Berkeley and Hinton, which belonged to St. Auftin's abbey, at Briftol, were granted to the dean and chapter of Briftol, together with the advowfon of the vicarages, 34 H. 8. But, in virtue of an act of parliament, they were given, by that body, to the late George lord Berkeley, in exchange for the rectory of St. Michael's, in Sutton Bennington, in Nottinghamfhire. The vicar is intituled to a mortuary of 10*s.* from the executor of every perfon of this parifh dying worth 40*l.*

Maurice de Berkeley founded an hofpital at Longbridge, in the tithing of Ham, (p. 272) where was a chapel dedicated to the holy Trinity; yearly tenths 1*l.* 15*s.* 10*d.* *ob.* But the eftate, with which it was endowed, is now part of the impropriation.

There was a chantry in this church, dedicated to St. Andrew, founded by the lady of Thomas lord Berkeley; and another chantry, dedicated to our Lady, to which Thomas, fecond lord Berkeley, gave lands in Hamme, 17 E. 3. for an anniverfary for his father, for his wife, and himfelf, after his deceafe. *Collins's Peerage*, v. 1. p. 451.

The church, dedicated to St. Mary, is large and handfome, confifting of the nave and two ailes, with a large chancel. On the fouth fide of the chancel is a chapel and vault, belonging to the earl of Berkeley; and on the north fide is the veftry room. The tower, with fix bells in it, is newly built, and ftands diftinctly from the church, at the other end of the church-yard, where probably the old church ftood.

There was antiently a nunnery in this place, of which the particulars are given in the account of the manor.

Monuments and Infcriptions.

In the body of the church, inclofed with iron rails, is a very antient raifed tomb, with the figures, in alabafter, of a man in armour, at full length, and a woman by his fide, defigned for Thomas lord Berkeley, and his lady. His lordfhip died in 1361. At that time the family had no particular burying place here; but three generations afterwards, James lord Berkeley built the chapel and vault on the fouth fide of the chancel.

Under an arch in the wall, between the faid chapel and the chancel, upon a raifed tomb of white marble, (ornamented on the fide, with figures in compartments, of the virgin Mary, St. Peter, St. Chriftopher, and other figures of foldiers, and ecclefiafticks, fome of them bearing fcutcheons of the Berkeley arms upon their breafts) is the effigy, in white marble, of James the fifth lord Berkeley, lying along in full proportion, with his coat armour upon his breaft, who died in 1463, and was buried in this chapel. And at his left hand is the figure of a youth, defigned for Thomas his grandfon, bearing alfo the family arms upon his breaft, and a label of three points, to fhew that he was the eldeft fon.

At the eaft end, upon a raifed tomb, are the figures, in alabafter, of lord Henry Berkeley and his lady; his feet refting againft a mitre, the family creft, and over their heads are the Berkeley arms, with twelve quarterings, and this infcription in capital letters:

HERE LYETH THE BODY OF SIR HENRY BERKELEY KNIGHT, LORD BERKELEY, MOWBRAY, SEAGRAVE, AND BRUCE. LORD LIEVTENANT OF THE COVNTY OF GLOVC. WHO DEPARTED THIS LIFE THE 26 DAY OF NOVEMBER IN THE YEARE OF OVR LORD GOD 1613, BEING THE DAY THAT HE ACCOMPLISHED THE AGE OF FOWERSCORE YEARES. HE FIRST MARIED, KATHERINE, SISTER TO THOMAS HOWARD, DUKE OF NORFOLKE, BY WHOM HE HAD YSSVE, THOMAS, MARY, AND FRANCES, THOMAS BEINGE A KNIGHT OF THE BATHE, MARIED ELIZABETH, ONELY DAVGHTER AND HEIRE UNTO SIR GEORGE CAREY KNIGHT LORD HVNSDON. MARY THE ELDEST DAVGHTER WAS MARIED UNTO SIR IOHN ZOVCHE KNIGHT: AND FRANCES THE SECOND DAVGHTER, WAS MARIED VNTO SIR GEORGE SHIRLEY BARONET.

HE

He secondly maried Iane the Widowe of Sir Roger Townsend Knight, yet livinge, by whom he had no issve.

Againſt the ſouth wall, in a ſcutcheon, baron and femme, 1. Berkeley. 2. *Topaz, fretty ruby, a canton ermine*, for Noel, and under, upon a black marble table, this inſcription :

H. S. E.
CAROLUS Comes de Berkeley, Vice Comes Durſley,
Baro BERKELEY de Berkeley Caſt. Mowbray, Seagrave,
Et Bruce, E Nobiliſſimo ordine Balnei Eques.
Vir, ad genus quod ſpectat, & Proavos, uſquequaq; Nobilis,
Et longo, ſi quis alius, Procerum ſtemmate Editus ;
Munijs etiam tam illuſtri ſtirpe dignis Inſignitus.
Siquidem, à Gulielm: III°. ad ordines fœderati Belgij
Ablegatus & Plenipotentiarius Extraordinarius.
Rebus, non Britanniæ tantum, ſed totius ferè Europæ
(Tunc temporis preſertim arduis) per annos V. incubuit.
Quàm felici Diligentiâ, Fide quàm intemeratâ
Ex illo diſcas, Lector, quod, Superſtite Patre
In magnatum ordinem adſciſci meruerit.
Fuit à Sanctioribus conſilijs & Regi Guliel: & Annæ Reginæ,
E proregibus Hiberniæ Secundus,
Comitatuum Civitatumq; Gloceſt: & Briſt: Locum-tenens.
Surriæ & Gloceſt: Cuſtos Rot: urbis Gloceſt: magnus
Seneſcallus, Arcis Sancti de Briavell Caſtellanus,
Gardianus Foreſtæ de Dean.
Deniq; ad Turcarum primùm, deinde ad Roman: Imperatorem
Cum Legatus Extraordinarius deſignatus Eſſet,
Quo minus has etiam ornaret provincias,
Obſtitit adverſa Corporis valetudo.
Sed reſtat ad huc, præ quo ſordeſcunt cætera,
Honos verus, ſtabilis, & vel morti cedere neſcius,
Quòd veritatem Evangelicam ſeriò amplexus ;
Erga Deum pius, Erga pauperes munificus,
Adverſùs omnes Æquus & Benevolus,
In Chriſto jam placidè obdormivit,
Cum eodem olim regnaturus unà.
Natus VIII°. April: MDCXLIX, denatus
XXIV°. Septem: MDCCX, Ætat: Suæ LXII.

Againſt the ſouth wall, is this memorial, in capital letters.

To the perpetval Memory of the most vertvovs and prvdent Lady Elizabeth lady Berkeley the Widdowe of S[r]. Thomas Berkeley Knight, Sonne and Heire of Henry lord Berkeley : George lord Berkeley her onely Sonne, hath in this Chapple of his Ancestors in a dvtifvll acknowledgement of her piovs life and death, consecrated this inscription for a memoriall of her vertve : who leaft this life at her hovse at Cranford in the covnty of Middlesex, the 23[d] Day of April Anno Domini 1635.
Where, accordinge to the direction of her will, shee lieth bvried.

In the chancel are ſeveral memorials for the Weſtons, deſcended from a knightly family, of Weſton-hall in Shropſhire, with their arms, *An eagle diſplay'd*, the blazon not expreſt. —— for the Hoptons of Berkeley and Cam, with their arms, *Gules, a lion rampant between nine croſſes croſlets fitchy, Or.* ——for Richard Saffyn, M. A. vicar of Berkeley, who died in 1690, with his arms, *three eſtoils iſſuing out of as many creſcents.* ——for Mr. Henry Head, vicar of Berkeley, and one of the prebendaries of Briſtol, who died in 1728, with his arms, field ſuppoſed, *Azure, a chevron ermine, between three unicorns heads caboſh'd.* ——for the Nelmes's of Breadſtone, with their arms, *three elm trees.*

In the body of the church, upon a braſs, fixt on a grey marble flat ſtone, is the figure of a man in a looſe robe, holding a heart upon his breaſt, inſcribed with mcy, and round the edge of the ſtone, in antient characters :

✠ Hic jacet corpus Willielmi Freme . . . . . . cujus anime propicietur deus, et animarum omnium fidelium defunctorum parentum et . . . . ſuorum Amen. Contende intrare per anguſtam portam.

Againſt the wall of the ſouth aile of the church, a memorial for Thomas Hickes, of Peddington, who died in 1746, with his arms, *Gules, a chevron wavy, between three fleurs-de-lis, Or.*

Upon flat ſtones in the church, are memorials for ſeveral perſons of the name of Jaye, who came from Darking in Surry, but deſcended from an antient family of that name in Hampſhire. The bearings on the ſcutcheons are, *Three leopards heads crown'd with a ducal coronet.* The blazon not expreſſed.

Firſt fruits, £.	32	14	8	Synodals, £.	0	3	0
Tenths, —	3	5	6	Pentecoſtals,	0	2	6
Procurations,	0	6	8				

Benefactions.

Mr. John Atwood, of Berkeley, gave a meadow called Longbridge, lying in Ham, to the poor of the borough, worth 10*l.* 10*s.* a year.

Mr. Thomas Machin, of this pariſh, in 1630, gave a ground near Parkham-meadow, of the yearly rent of 3*l.* 10*s.* to the poor.

Mr. John Mallet, of this pariſh, in 1639, gave a ground near Prior's-wood, of the yearly value of 5*l.* 10*s.* to the poor.

The bridewell-houſe, and the town-houſe, of the yearly value together of 7*l.* 10*s.* were given to the poor by an unknown benefactor, and have been enjoy'd time immemorial.

The tithing-barn of Ham is charged with the annual payment of 7*s.* to the poor.

Mr. Thomas Bayley, of this pariſh, charged a ground in Halmer, called Stunings, with the payment of 15*s.* a year to the poor.

Richard Everett, of this pariſh, gave the intereſt of 10*l.* for ever, to the poor houſe-keepers of Ham.

Samuel Thurner, M. B. of Magdalen Hall, Oxon, in 1696, gave lands in Thornbury and Rockhampton, let together at 16*l.* 5*s.* a year, for teaching twenty-ſix boys of Berkeley town to read, write, &c.

John Smith, M. A. of Magdalen College, Oxon, in 1717, gave a ſum of money, which, with 40*l.* given by the right honourable the counteſs dowager of Berkeley, was laid out in lands in this pariſh, worth 10*l.* 10*s.* a year, for teaching twelve boys to read and write.

Thomas Hopton, eſq; in 1718, gave 1*l.* 10*s.* a year to the miniſter of this pariſh, for a ſermon on Good Friday, and another on November 5 ; and 2*l.* 10*s.* a year to the poor in bread, charged on his eſtate at Littleton upon Severn.

Mrs. Bridget Vick, in 1724, gave a ground in Hinton, called the Tining, of 3*l.* a year, to be diſtributed in bread to the poor.

Thomas Pearce, in 1728, charged his eſtate in Wick with the payment of 12*s.* a year, to be given, at Chriſtmas, to ſix poor men of Alkington tithing.

Mrs. Elizabeth Beaven, in 1728, gave 120*l.* which her executor laid out in lands, and, purſuant to her will, charged an eſtate called the Acktrees, near Berkeley heath, with the payment of 3*l.* a year to the miniſter, for reading prayers, and 3*l.* a year to be given to the poor in bread.

Sir Robert Atkyns mentions the following donations, which I have otherwiſe no account of: Thomas Baldwin gave 6*l.* a year, to be diſtributed to ſix poor widows at Eaſter.—Mary Hort gave a tenement to the poor.—Mr. Boucher gave another to the ſame uſe.——The borough of Berkeley has purchaſed a ground called Prieſt's-Croft, lying in Ham, for the benefit of the poor.

Borough of Berkeley.

			£.	s.	d.
Taxes.	The Royal Aid in	1692, £.	22	0	0
	Poll-tax — —	1694, —	33	12	0
	Land-tax ——	1694, —	14	8	8
	The ſame, at 3*s.* —	1770, —	11	2	0

Ham and Hamfallow.

			£.	s.	d.
Taxes.	The Royal Aid in	1692, £.	506	0	0
	Poll-tax — —	1694, —	55	17	0
	Land-tax ——	1694, —	478	9	8
	——— at 3*s.* (Ham)	1770, —	232	6	9
	——— (Hamfallow)	———	122	14	9

Alkington.

			£.	s.	d.
Taxes.	The Royal Aid in	1692, £.	152	8	0
	Poll-tax — —	1694, —	28	10	0
	Land-tax ——	1694, —	213	9	0
	The ſame, at 3*s.* -	1770, —	158	9	6

Bradſtone.

			£.	s.	d.
Taxes.	The Royal Aid in	1692, £.	34	4	0
	Poll-tax — —	1694, —	8	12	0
	Land-tax — -	1694, —	41	2	0
	The ſame, at 3*s.*	1770, —	30	18	0

Stone. See *Stone* as a pariſh.

Hinton.

			£.	s.	d.
Taxes.	The Royal Aid in	1692, £.	107	12	0
	Poll-tax — —	1694, —	16	2	0
	Land-tax ——	1694, —	106	12	0
	The ſame, at 3*s.* —	1770, —	79	19	0

At the beginning of this century, according to ſir Robert Atkyns, there were 500 houſes in this pariſh, and about 2500 inhabitants, whereof 140 were freeholders; yearly births 67, burials 58. And I underſtand the tithing of Stone is not included in theſe particulars, except as to births and burials. But certainly ſir Robert's eſtimate was too high; for in a ſeries of ten years, from 1700 to 1709 incluſive, there appear to be entered in the pariſh regiſter 473 baptiſms, and 399 burials; and from 1760 to 1769 incluſive, 531 baptiſms, and 502 burials. By which it appears that the inhabitants have increaſed during the laſt ſeventy years, and are now about 1854 in number, which is nearly in the proportion of 35 to 1 of the annual burials.

BEVERSTONE.

THIS pariſh lies in the upper diviſion of the hundred of Berkeley, in a healthy country, upon the Cotſwold hills, ſcarce two miles north-weſtward from Tetbury, five from Minchin-hampton, and twenty ſouthward from Glouceſter. The land is chiefly arable, with ſome good paſturage, but no meadow ground.

Leland ſays *there is a quarre of good ſtone at Beverſtane, unde nomen, ex conjectura*; but ſir Robert Atkyns goes ſtill further, in pronouncing that *it was antiently called Bureſtan, from the blue ſtones found in this place.* The name, in *Domeſday-book*, is written *Beureſtan*; and tho' the termination, in the Saxon language, ſignifies ſtone, yet the whole word, taken together, is ſo difficult and abſtruſe, that I confeſs myſelf totally ignorant of its original and ſignification.

There are conſiderable remains of an antient caſtle in this place, ſaid to have been originally built in the time of the Saxon heptarchy; but by whom is not certainly known. Godwin earl of Kent, in the time of Edward the Confeſſor, having offended the king by refuſing to puniſh the chief actors of a diſorder which happened in Canterbury, without their being firſt brought to trial; the king called an aſſembly of all the nobility at Glouceſter, that the matter might be debated; but Godwin and his ſons, inſtead of appearing there, raiſed a great force, and took up their quarters at Beverſtan; and ſome accounts expreſſly ſay, that they ſeized the caſtle, which ſhews it to be of older ſtanding than the Norman conqueſt. Maurice lord Berkeley repaired and fortified this caſtle in the reign of king Henry the Third, and Thomas lord Berkeley afterwards greatly beautified and enlarged it, by the ſpoils and ranſom of priſoners which he took at the battle of Poictiers, in the reign of king Edward the Third. It was built ſquare, moated on all ſides, and had a tower at every corner; but a great part of the caſtle having been deſtroyed by fire, there is only one of the towers now remaining. The dining room was where a part of the farm-houſe now ſtands, as appears by the remains of a magnificent window, adjoining to the eaſtern part of the caſtle, and the noble fire-place yet remaining.

It was garriſoned by the king's forces in the great civil war, and attacked by colonel Maſſey, with three hundred foot and fourſcore horſe, without ſucceſs; but afterwards, the governor, captain

captain Oglethorpe, being taken priſoner, and carried to Glouceſter, by the parliament's party, colonel Maſſey learnt from him where the caſtle might be attacked with the greateſt advantage; and advancing with a body of horſe and foot before it, ſummoned it to ſurrender. The lieutenant, who had the command, immediately complyed, tho', it was thought, he might have held it with eaſe. The garriſon, leaving their arms, ammunition, and baggage, had liberty to retire where they pleaſed. Of ſo great ſimplicity was the king's officer, as to aſk where was the next deſtination of the parliament's forces, expreſſing his fears, if the garriſon ſhould go to Malmeſbury, of their being taken a ſecond time; and going there, it happened to them as they apprehended, the next day after their arrival.

This place had antiently a market and fair, as appears by the ſubſequent account of the manor, but they have been long ſince diſuſed.

Of the Manor and other Eſtates.

This manor was antiently parcel of the manor of Berkeley, and belonged to the nunnery there: And, at the time of the general ſurvey, there were ten hides in Beureſtan belonging to Berkeley. *See Berkeley.*

King Henry the Second gave the manor of Beverſtan to Robert Fitz-Harding, anceſtor of the Berkeley family, who ſettled it on Robert his ſecond ſon, in marriage with Alice, the daughter and heireſs of Robert de Gant, and of Alice, the daughter of William Paganell; which Robert de Gant was ſon of Gilbert de Gant, who came into England with William the conqueror, and had married Alice, the daughter of Hugh de Montfort. His wife being thus deſcended, Robert de Berkeley obtained, by that marriage, the great lordſhip of Were, in com. Somerſet, whence he took the name of Robert de Were. He founded the hoſpital of St. Mark at Billeſwike, near Briſtol, and left iſſue a ſon named [z]Maurice, and a daughter [a]Eva, wedded to Thomas de Harpetre.

Which Maurice aſſumed the name of de Gant from his mother, on account of her great inheritance. In 17 John, taking part with the rebellious barons, his lands were ſeized, and given to Philip de Albini, whereupon he addreſſed himſelf to the king, to make his peace. And 11 H. 3. having fortified his caſtle of Beverſtan without licence, he went again to the king to excuſe himſelf for ſo doing, and obtained a confirmation thereof. Having no iſſue, he gave to the king his lordſhips of Weſton, Beverſtan, and Albricton, and died 14 H. 3. The bulk of his inheritance came to the iſſue of Eva, his ſiſter, whoſe ſon Robert, ſome time after, aſſumed the ſurname of Gournay, and, 15 H. 3. had livery of the manor of Paulet, and other lands in Somerſetſhire, and of all his lands in [b]Glouceſterſhire, excepting Beverſtan, Weſton, Radewic, Oure, and Albricton; which however, he not long after obtained of the king.

Which Robert Gournay, ſon and heir of the ſaid Eva de Berkeley, whoſe barony conſiſted of no leſs than twenty-two knights-fees, died ſeized of Beverſtan 53 H. 3. and was ſucceeded in this eſtate by his ſon Anſelm, whoſe ſon John Gournay dying ſeized of it 19 E. 1. left his only daughter and heir Elizabeth, married to John ap Adam, who both joined in a fine, and ſettled this manor, and the advowſon of the church, and the manors of King's-Weſton, and Pirton in Churchdown, on the joint heirs of their bodies, the remainder on the heirs of Elizabeth, 25 E. 1. Which John and Elizabeth purchaſed a charter of free-warren in Beverſtan, and a weekly market on Monday, and a fair to begin on the [c]eve of the aſſumption of our Lady, and to continue for three days.

Thomas ap Adam, ſon of John, ſold this manor and caſtle, and the manor of Over, to Thomas lord Berkeley 4 E. 3. who died ſeized thereof 35 E. 3. and Catherine his widow died alſo ſeized of it 9 R. 2.

Sir John La Warr, in right of Elizabeth his wife, widow of Thomas de Berkeley, was ſeized thereof 22 R. 2.

Sir John Berkeley was poſſeſſed of this manor, and of Beverſton-caſtle, and of the advowſon of the church, 6 H. 6. and Maurice Berkeley of Beverſton, was alſo ſeized of the caſtle and manor 38 H. 6. Sir William Berkeley died ſeized of the manor 5 E. 6. and the next year livery was granted to ſir John Berkeley his ſon, who died ſeized of it 20 Eliz. and the ſame year livery was granted to ſir John Berkeley, his ſon and heir, who alienated this manor to ſir John Pointz; but it ſoon went out of that name, for ſir John ſold this manor, and that of Hill, to Henry Fleetwood, eſq; who was lord of them in the year 1608.

In a few years afterwards, this manor was purchaſed by ſir Michael Hicks, from whom it deſcended to his heir ſir Henry Hicks, whoſe ſon Michael Hicks, eſq; died ſeized thereof in the year 1764; and Michael Hicks, an infant ſon of Howe Hicks, of Witcombe, in this county, eſq; is the preſent lord of the manor. His arms and pedigree are inſerted under *Witcombe.*

Of the Church, &c.

The church is a rectory, in the deanery of Durſley, worth about 240*l.* a year. The abbey of Glouceſter was formerly patron; but the preſentation is now in the crown, and Mr. Selwyn is the preſent incumbent. The chapel of Kingſcot is annexed to this church.

One hundred and eight acres of arable in Beverſtone, thirty-two in Kingſcot, and thirty-five acres of incloſure, in both pariſhes, belong to the glebe.

[z][a] Rot. fin. 17 Johan.

[b] Rot. fin. 16 H. 3. m. 3.

[c] Dugd. Bar.

The

The church is ſmall, dedicated to St. Mary, with an aile on the ſouth ſide, and a croſs aile on the north, belonging to the lord of the manor, and a ſtrong tower, with pinnacles, at the weſt end.

Monuments and Inſcriptions.

Againſt the wall, in the chancel, is the following inſcription.

A° 1604. Ætat. 69. Epicedium Katherinæ Pury.

Quæ defuncta jacet ſaxo tumulata ſub illo
Bis Cathara, haud ficto nomine, dicta fuit.
Nomen utrumque ſonat mundam, puram, piamq;
Et verę, nomen quod referebat, erat.
Nam puram puro degebat pectore vitam;
Pura fuit mundo, nunc mage pura Deo.

There are memorials for Richard Hall, rector of this pariſh, who died June 30, 1638; for another Richard Hall, rector, who died in 1684; and for Andrew Needham, alſo rector of Beverſtone, who died in 1710.

	£.	s.	d.		£.	s.	d.
Firſt fruits,	30	0	0	Synodals,	0	2	0
Tenths, —	3	0	0	Pentecoſtals,	0	0	8
Procurations,	0	6	8				

Taxes.			£.	s.	d.
	The Royal Aid in	1692,	80	1	0
	Poll-tax —— —	1694,	18	0	0
	Land-tax ——	1694,	86	16	0
	The ſame, at 3*s.* —	1770,	64	4	0

At the beginning of this century there were 34 houſes and about 164 inhabitants, whereof three were freeholders, in this pariſh; yearly births 5, burials 4. *Atkyns.* But upon examination, I find, that in a ſeries of ten years, ending with 1768, there were entered in the pariſh regiſter 57 baptiſms, and 44 burials; and the exact number of inhabitants is 144, which is nearly in the proportion of 33 to 1 of the annual burials: Whence one may be induced to think the place unhealthy, notwithſtanding it lies in an open part of the country; but I am informed that it is really otherwiſe, and that the late dilapidation of cottages hath driven many of the younger people out of the pariſh, to which alone the decreaſe of inhabitants ought to be attributed.

****

B I B U R Y.

THIS is a pariſh of conſiderable extent, in the cotſwold part of the country, ſix miles ſouth from Northleach, ſeven north-eaſtward from Cirenceſter, and nineteen eaſtward from Glouceſter. The tithing of Winſon is in the hundred of Bradley, but all the reſt of the pariſh lies in the hundred of Britwelſbarrow.

The name of this place, antiently written *Becheberie*, and *Begeberie*, ſeems to have been given it on account of the ſituation of the village upon the river; for bece or beke ſignifies a ſtream or river, and beɼıe a flat piece of ground. The latter part of the name, if referred to the place where the church ſtands, agrees well enough with the ſituation; but ſome of the houſes ſtand on the ſide of an eminence. Here the river Coln riſes in ſo copious a manner as to drive a mill at a ſmall diſtance from the head of the ſpring.

The turnpike-road from Cirenceſter to Oxford leads through this place, and where it croſſed the river, the water was broad and deep, and being near the ſpring, ſo remarkably cold, as frequently to injure cattle, which, heated with travelling, paſſed through it; wherefore a bridge was erected by ſubſcription a few years ago, to obviate thoſe inconveniencies.

This place gave name to the hundred of Becheberie, now ſwallowed up in that of Britwelſbarrow. The pariſh hath lately been incloſed, and great part of thoſe lands which lay in downs are now converted to tillage.

Eſtcourt Creſwell, eſq; hath a large eſtate and a good houſe here, of which his generoſity hath furniſhed the annexed beautiful copper-plate.

Of the Manor and other Eſtates.

In the *Domeſday* account of the lands belonging to the church of Worceſter, it is expreſſed after the following manner:

'The ſame church held Becheberie in Becheberie 'hundred. There are twenty-one hides. In de'mean are four plow-tillages, and nineteen villeins 'and two bordars with eleven plow-tillages. 'There are three radchenіſters having four hides 'and four plow-tillages, and a prieſt having three 'hides, and, with his, four plow-tillages. There 'are eleven *ſervi* and *ancillæ*, and two mills of 17*s.* '[rent,] and ten acres of meadow. Durand holds 'three hides and one yard-land in Berneſleis of 'the biſhop, as a manor dependent on this manor; 'and Eudo holds ſeven yard-lands there for a 'manor.

'In theſe are five plow-tillages in demean, and 'twelve villeins with ſix plow-tillages. There 'are twelve *ſervi*. The whole manor, in the time 'of king Edward, was worth, and now alſo is 'worth 18*l.*

'The ſame church holds Aicote, and Ailric 'holds it of her. It lies in Begeberie. There is 'one hide. In demean are two plow-tillages, and 'two villeins and four bordars with two plow'tillages. There are two *ſervi*, and eight acres of 'meadow, and a mill of 64*d.* It was worth 20*s.* 'now 30*s.* *Domeſday-book*, p. 70.

The latter is ſuppoſed to be the manor afterwards given to the priory of Oſney. But the biſhop of Worceſter was ſeized of a manor called the manor of Bibury, with court-leet and free-warren, 15 E. 1. which privileges were allowed to him in a writ of *Quo warranto* brought againſt him the ſame year. In a MS. taxation of the temporalties of the ſee of Worceſter, in the time of Edward the Firſt,, which I found in the Cotton library, [*Tiberius*, C. F. 76.] are the following particulars:

particulars: *Item apud Bibur' de reditu assis.* 4*l. et* 3 *caruc. terræ, et valet caruc.* 30*s. et* 1 *columbarium quod valet* 7*s. et* 1 *molendinum aquaticum quod valet* 2 *marc. dim. et de placitis et perquisitis* 30*s. Summa* 12*l.* 4*s.* A survey having been made of this manor, 26 H. 8. it was then valued at 10*l.* 14*s.* a year.

The see of Worcester continued in possession of this manor 'till it was alienated therefrom, 3 E. 6. when it was granted to John Dudley earl of Warwick, afterwards duke of Northumberland, which is the reason that one part of Bibury is now, for distinction sake, called Bibury Northumberland.

It appears, by the evidences belonging to this estate, that John Harrington was soon after possessed of this manor, which he alienated to sir William Sherrington, who sold it, by virtue of the king's licence, dated June 23, 6 E. 6. to William earl of Pembroke, *in perpetuum*. The earl procures a licence from the crown, dated nine days after the former, and alienates it to Hugh Westwood. But, after the attainder of the duke of Northumberland, different people coming into favour, and the queen reversing many things done by king Edward, this manor was granted to John Walters and Thomas Carpenter, 1 Mariæ. However, William Westwood, esq; was lord of it in the year 1608.

Sir Thomas Sackville bought Bibury of Hugh Westwood, (who was probably son of the above mentioned William) and built the mansion-house, according to the date over the porch, in the year 1623. He married Barbara, daughter of sir John Hungerford, of Down Amney, by whom he had issue two sons, John and Richard, and two daughters. John Sackville succeeded his father, but dying unmarried, this estate came to his brother Richard, who had two sons, John and Henry. John succeeded his father, but having no issue, left his estate to Henry. Which Henry left issue, by his first and second marriage, two daughters coheiresses, Elizabeth and Catherine, the latter of whom died unmarried; but Elizabeth, the elder, was wedded to Edmond Warneford, esq; by whom she had an only child Anne Warneford, married to Thomas Estcourt Cresswell, of Pinkney in the county of Wilts, esq; and by him had issue only one son, Estcourt Cresswell, esq; who, in the year 1768, was chosen one of the representatives in parliament for the borough of Cirencester, and is the present lord of the manor of Bibury. His arms may be seen at the foot of the plate of his seat.

The other manor of Bibury, with the rectory and advowson, formerly belonged to the priory of Osney, wherefore it was called Bibury Osney, and was granted to the chapter of Oxford 34 H. 8.

TITHINGS and *HAMLETS.*

1. *Bibury*, which contains 59 families, and 307 inhabitants, and is divided into two tithings, *Bibury Osney*, and *Bibury Northumberland*, as already observed.

2. *Ablington*, containing 22 families and 91 inhabitants. The reverend Mr. Charles Coxwell has a seat and a good estate here. He is descended from an antient family formerly residing in Cirencester, who having large possessions in the town, occasioned a certain street to be called by their family name. His arms are, *Argent, a bend wavy between six cocks gules.*

Ralph de Willington and Olimpias his wife purchased a moiety of the manor of Ablington, 9 Joh. John de Willington had a charter of free-warren in Ablington and other manors, 3 E. 2. and died seized hereof 12 E. 3. Sir Ralph de Willington died seized of this manor 22 E. 3. and livery thereof was granted to his son Henry the next year; whose son sir John de Willington had seizin of it 2 R. 2. He had a son Ralph, whose wife Joan survived him, and was afterwards married to Thomas West, whom also she survived, and held the manor of Ablington 6 H. 4. The last Ralph Willington had two sons, Ralph and John, who died without issue, and a daughter Joan, married to John Wrath, by whom she had a son John Wrath, who dying, without issue, seized of this manor, 13 H. 4. left his two sisters coheiresses, of whom, Elizabeth was married to sir William Poulton, and Isabel was the widow of William Beaumont.

Sir William Poulton and Elizabeth his wife levied a fine of the sixth part of the manor of Ablington, to the use of themselves in special taille; the remainder to John, the son of sir William, in taille general; the remainder to the right heirs of Isabel, widow of William Beaumont. They dying without issue, the estate came to Isabel Beaumont, who had issue John and Isabel. John died without issue, whereby his sister became seized, who dying unmarried 2 H. 6. the estate descended to her next kinsman and heir sir Thomas Beaumont, who died seized 29 H. 6. and was succeeded by his son sir William Beaumont, in some records stiled William Beaumont, esq; who died 32 H. 6. and was succeeded by Philip Beaumont his brother, who died 13 E. 4.

Hugh Beaumont and Elizabeth his wife, and John Basset and Elizabeth his wife, levied a fine of this manor to Richard bishop of Durham and divers great persons, among whom was sir Giles d'Aubeny, 16 H. 7. Giles lord d'Aubeny died seized thereof 6 H. 8. and livery of it was granted the same year to Henry lord d'Aubeny his son. This manor was afterwards granted to Edward duke of Somerset, and, after his attainder, it was granted to James Basset, 4 Mariæ, and again confirmed to Arthur Basset, 7 Eliz. The succession to this manor is the same with Frampton Cotterell, Sainthurst, Westonbirt, and Poulton in Awre.

Lands in this place, which had been formerly given for finding lamps in the church of Bibury, were granted to sir William Rider, 7 Jac.

3. *Arlington*, which consists of 55 families and 255 inhabitants. This manor is expressly

 mentioned

mentioned in *Domeſday-book*, which gives the following particulars :

'Chenvichelle, one of king Edward's thanes, 'held Alvredintune. There were five hides, and 'four plow-tillages in demean, and twelve villeins 'and one bordar with ſix plow-tillages, and ſixteen '*ſervi* and *ancillæ*, and two mills of 20*s*. [rent.] 'A wood one mile long, and half a mile broad. 'Of theſe two manors [*i.e.* Cedeorde and Alvredin-'tune] the ſteward paid what he pleaſed in the 'time of king Edward. They now pay 40*l*. of 'white money, of which 20 in ora. Earl Roger 'held them. *Domeſday-book*, p. 69.

Gilbert de Clare, earl of Glouceſter and Hertford, held Alurington 1 E. 2. Alice, widow of John de Pembrige, held it 7 E. 3. in which year Roger Norman levied a fine, and ſettled this manor on himſelf for life, the remainder on Roger his ſon in taille. Roger Norman had a charter of free-warren in Alurington 19 E. 3. and died ſeized thereof 23 E. 3. leaving Giles his couſin and heir, who was ſeized of Alurington, near Cirenceſter, 36 E. 3. but William Clareſhull was ſeized of this manor the following year; Edward earl of Stafford held it 4 H. 4. and Richard de Beauchamp and Iſabel his wife were ſeized hereof 2 H. 5. The manor afterwards belonged to the priory of Oſney, and was granted to John Barrington, 1 E. 6. purſuant to the will of king H. 8.

4. *Winſon*, where are 24 families and 127 inhabitants. This tithing lies in Bradley hundred, about three miles from the church, and has a chapel of eaſe dedicated to St. Michael, with a yard conſecrated for ſepulture in the year 1738. Mr. Creſlwell is patron. The manor belongs to Dr. Doiley. Mr. Howſe has a good eſtate here.

Note. Aldeſworth, Barnſley, and Winſon appear at the court-leet of the lord of the manor of Bibury. The other lords hold courts-baron.

Of the Church, &c.

The church is a vicarage, worth about 400*l*. a year. John Pagan, biſhop of Worceſter, appropriated the tithes of Bibury to the monaſtery of [d] Oſney, near Oxford, in the year 1130, which monaſtery hath preſented to this church. Mr. Creſſwell is patron and impropriator. The reverend Mr. Somerville, nephew of the late lord Somerville, is the preſent incumbent. He bears the ſame arms with his lordſhip, *viz. Azure, three mullets Or, accompanied with ſeven croſſes croſlets fitchy ſable, three in chief, one in feſs, two in flank, and the laſt in baſe.*

The vicarage-houſe, which is a very good one, was built by Dr. Vannam, the vicar, great grandfather to the preſent incumbent, about the beginning of this century.

At the incloſing of the common fields, about the year 1769, the pariſh was exonerated from tithe, and the impropriator and miniſter had lands allotted to them in lieu thereof.

This church is a peculiar, with juriſdiction over thoſe of Aldeſworth, Barnſley, and the chapel of Winſon. What the rights of this peculiar were, had been a ſubject of diſpute ever ſince the foundation of the ſee of Glouceſter, but it was agreed, between Dr. Benſon, late biſhop of Glouceſter, and Mrs. Warneford, then lady of the manor, to lay all evidence relating to it before the dean of the arches, and to enter into reciprocal engagements to abide by his award; which award was made Mar. 26, 1741. But the agreement became void at the death of that prelate; and the matters in controverſy, reſpecting the peculiar, are in the ſame ſtate as before. The lord of the manor doth not allow, to the biſhop of the dioceſe, a right of viſitation; he appoints his own official and chancellor, who hath the *probat.* of wills, and the grant of licences for marriage, to thoſe within the limits of the peculiar.

Peculiars took their riſe from the conſtitutions of Lanfranc archbiſhop of Canterbury, in the 11th century, who exempted all the pariſh prieſts of thoſe places where he was the lord or patron, in any dioceſe, from the juriſdiction of the biſhop.

The church is large and handſome, conſiſting of a nave and two ailes, with a tower at the weſt end, in which are ſix muſical bells. It is dedicated to St. Mary. The chancel belongs to the impropriator.

There was a coloſſal figure of St. Chriſtopher painted againſt the wall of this church, in purſuance of an opinion that prevailed in the ages of ignorance and ſuperſtition, that whoſoever had ſeen the image of that ſaint, ſhould not die of ſudden or accidental death; whence, ſays the author of the French Hiſtorical Dictionary, 'he is 'repreſented of a prodigious ſize, carrying the 'infant Jeſus upon his ſhoulders, and placed at 'the gates of cathedrals, and at the entrance of 'churches, that every body may ſee him the more 'eaſily.' Accordingly this figure was oppoſite to the entrance at the ſouth door of the church; but it hath lately been covered with white-waſh, and nothing remains to be ſeen but the two following lines, incorrectly written in antient characters, under the figure.

Xpofori ſcī ſpeciem quicunque tuetur,
Illo nanque die nullo langore gravetur.

Which may be thus engliſhed :

Saint Chriſtopher's fair figure who ſhall view,
Faintneſs nor feebleneſs that day ſhall rue.

Monuments and Inſcriptions.

In the north aile, againſt the pillar behind the pulpit, is this inſcription :

[d] This monaſtery was firſt founded at Oxford, for ſecular canons, by Robert d'Oily, but tranſlated to Oſney in the year 1129, and the canons then became regulars of the order of St. Auguſtine. It was dedicated to the virgin Mary, and was valued at the diſſolution, at 775*l*. 18*s*. 6*d*. yearly. Upon the erection of the biſhoprick of Oxford, by king H. 8. the ſee was placed at Oſney, but ſoon after, in 1546, it was removed to Chriſt-Church.

SACRÆ

SACRÆ MEMORIÆ VIRI VERE REVERENDI BENJAMINI WYNNINGTON, ART. MAG. HVIVS ECCLESIÆ VICARIJ, QVI VITAM HANC MORTALEM IN ÆTERNAM COMMVTAVIT IVL. 28, 1673.

Proh Dolor! invictæ Mortis jacet ille Trivmphvs,
Qvi vivvs nullo victvs ab hoſte ſvit.
Ecce Miniſter erat Chriſti perdoctvs, amatvs,
Eccleſiæ veræ Gloria, Fama, Decvs.
Vt Dixit Vixit,
Et Moriendo Vivit.
Nec non officio fama decvſq; ſvo.

Mr. Wynnington was a very laborious miniſter, of whom it is ſaid, that after he had preached an hour by the glaſs, he would turn it, aſſuring the congregation, that he meant to continue in his ſermon *only one hour longer*. And it is added, that during the ſecond hour of the ſermon, Mr. Sackville, then lord of the manor, uſually retired from church to ſmoak his pipe, but always returned in time to receive the benediction.

There is an elegant pyramidal monument of Syena marble, againſt the north wall of the chancel, with theſe arms in a lozenge, *Party per feſs embattled, argent and ſable, ſix croſſes patee counterchanged*, for Warneford. On an eſcutcheon of pretence, *Quarterly*, 1ſt and 4th *Or*, 2d and 3d *gules, over all a bend vaire*, for Sackville. A ſmall white marble table bears the following inſcription:

Near this place lieth interred the body of Elizabeth Warneford, relict of Edmond Warneford, eſq; She was eldeſt daughter of Henry Sackeville, eſq; late of this place. She departed this life the 15th of May, 1756, to the inexpreſſible grief of her family and acquaintance, aged 67. She was a perſon of diſtinguiſhed piety and virtue, and moſt exemplary in her life and converſation.

Pſ. xxxiv. v. 19. *Great are the troubles of the righteous, but the Lord delivereth him out of all.*

Oppoſite to the above, there is a ſmall but elegant monument, of the ſame kind of marble, with the arms of Sackville, and this inſcription:

Near this place lieth interred the body of Katherine Sackville, youngeſt daughter of Henry Sackville, eſq; late of this place, who departed this life Sept. 13, 1760, aged 68. She was a perſon of a truly religious and good life, which was diſtinguiſhed by a conſtant performance of the offices of friendſhip, piety, and charity.

Againſt a pillar in the church are two ſmall marble monuments, whereon are the arms of Coxwell, and the following inſcriptions:

Underneath lieth the body of John Coxwell, eſq; late of Ablington in this pariſh, who died greatly lamented, Aug. 13, 1754, aged 56 years. He left behind him a widow (who cauſed this to be erected) and eleven children. He was a loving huſband, a tender father, a kind maſter, and a bountiful friend to the poor. *Prov.* x. 7. *The memory of the juſt is bleſſed.*

Near this place lieth the body of Mrs. Mary Coxwell, relict of John Coxwell, eſq; of Ablington. She died March 15, 1767, aged 54. Her conſcientious and exemplary diſcharge of all ſocial and religious duties, made her no leſs deſervedly eſteemed in her life time, than regretted at her death, by all her relations and acquaintance.

In the body of the church is a memorial, upon a flat ſtone, for Thomas Baker, A.M. late vicar of this pariſh, and one of his majeſty's juſtices of the peace for this county, who died Nov. 8, 1755. His arms, *Azure, a feſs Or, charged with three cinquefoils gules, between as many ſwans heads erazed of the ſecond, gorged with ducal coronets of the firſt.*

Upon flat ſtones, in the chancel, are the following memorials:

John Vannam, D. D. vicar of Bibury, died July the 13th, 1721, aged 84.

Eliz[a]. Hickes, daughter of Dr. Vannam, and wife of Rob[t]. Hickes, eſq; of Comb in y[e] county of Glouceſter, died July y[e] 30th, 1720, aged 44.

George Vannam, M. A. Rector of Buſcot, Berks, died Nov. y[e] 27th, 1716, aged 37.

Benefactions.

There is a charitable inſtitution here, called Jeſus Almſhouſe, founded by Hugh Weſtwood, for a maſter and three brethren. The maſter receives eighteen-pence a week, and the brethren ſixteen-pence each; and they have beſides a load of wood yearly, and a coat, with a plate of ſilver, whereon are engraven the arms and initial letters of the name of the founder. There are governors appointed to this charity, of which the preſent lord of the manor, the miniſter, and church-wardens are of the number.

John Smyther, of Arlington, gave 10*l.* the intereſt of which to be beſtowed upon four poor widows of this pariſh.—The firſt mention of the diſtribution of this charity is in the year 1682.

Mr. William Forder, of Amney Crucis, by his will dated Mar. 30, 35 C. 2. gave 5*l.* to the pariſh church of Bibury, to remain as a ſtock for ever.

— Tawny, (probably of this pariſh) in 1685, bequeathed, after the expiration of one life, 50*l.* as a ſtock for the uſe of the poor.

Mrs. Katherine Sackville, by her will, left 100*l.* for the uſe of the poor; the intereſt of it to be diſtributed annually, at the diſcretion of the miniſter and church-wardens.

Bibury.

			£.	s.	d.
Taxes.	The Royal Aid in	1692, £.	48	12	0
	Poll-tax — —	1694, —	23	1	0
	Land-tax —	1694, —	46	4	0
	The ſame, at 3*s.* —	1770, —	34	13	0

Ablington.

			£.	s.	d.
Taxes.	The Royal Aid in	1692, £.	48	11	10
	Poll-tax — —	1694, —	9	0	0
	Land-tax —	1694, —	34	1	0
	The ſame, at 3*s.* —	1770, —	25	10	9

Arlington.

			£.	s.	d.
Taxes.	The Royal Aid in	1692, £.	48	11	10
	Poll-tax — —	1694, —	15	3	0
	Land-tax — -	1694, —	41	5	5
	The ſame, at 3*s.*	1770, —	30	12	6

Winſon.

			£.	s.	d.
Taxes.	The Royal Aid in	1692, £.	39	1	2
	Poll-tax — —	1694, —	6	12	0
	Land-tax —	1694, —	20	17	6
	The ſame, at 3*s.* -	1770, —	23	11	8

At the beginning of this century, according to ſir Robert Atkyns, there were 100 houſes and about 500 inhabitants in this pariſh, whereof 16 were freeholders; yearly births 17, burials 13. But

But it appears by the pariſh regiſter, that in a ſeries of ten years, from 1714 to 1723 incluſive, there were 145 baptiſms and 110 burials; and in a like ſeries, from 1760 to 1769, 194 baptiſms and 156 burials; and there are, at preſent, 160 families and 780 inhabitants. So that population hath very much encreaſed in this century; and the number of living inhabitants is, to the average of annual burials, exactly as 50 to 1, which ſhews the place to be very healthy.

BICKNOR (ENGLISH,)

LIES in the hundred of St. Briavel, in the Foreſt diviſion of the county, three miles diſtant north from Colford, five eaſtward from Monmouth, and twenty-two weſtward from Glouceſter.

It is ſituated upon the bank of the river Wye, whence it was called *Bicanofre*, from Bec, a river, and Oppe, which ſignifies upon. It is diſtinguiſhed, as above, from another pariſh on the oppoſite ſide of the ſame river, called *Welch Bicknor*, becauſe all on the other ſide was formerly reputed to be in Wales.

This village, like moſt others in the foreſt of Dean, produceth coal and iron ore. It conſiſts of rich meadow and paſture ground, with very little arable. A ſmall rill, called *Eaſtpitch-brook*, riſes in the pariſh, and empties itſelf into the Wye.

Of the Manor and other Eſtates.

This manor, ſoon after the Conqueſt, was held by William the ſon of Norman, for in *Domeſday-book* it is thus expreſt:

'The ſame William [*i. e.* ſon of Norman] holds 'Bicanofre in Weſtberie hundred. Morganan 'held it in the time of king Edward. There is 'half a hide, and in demean half a plow-tillage, 'with ſix bordars. It was worth 5*s.* and is now 'worth 10*s.* *Domeſday-book*, p. 74.

One of the bailiwicks of the foreſt was denominated from this place, and William Aminell held it 8 and 20 H. 3.

William de Muſgros was ſeized of the manor of Bicknor 15 E. 1. and Cicely de Muſgros held the ſame, as appears by the records, in the 15th and 29th years of the ſame reign.

Richard Talbot, of Goderick-caſtle in Herefordſhire, in right of Elizabeth his wife, one of the ſiſters and heirs of John Comin of Badenaugh, of the royal blood of Scotland, was ſeized of the manor and advowſon of Bicknor, and levied a fine thereof to the uſe of himſelf in taille, 12 E. 3.

This manor, ſoon after, came into the family of Ferrers, of whom, John lord Ferrers de Chartley, in right of Elizabeth his wife, the widow of Fulk le Strange, and daughter of Ralph de Stafford, was ſeized of it, and died 41 E. 3. Which Elizabeth was afterwards married to Reginald lord Cobham, and died ſeized of this manor 49 E. 3. Robert lord Ferrers of Chartley, ſon of ſir John, ſucceeded his father in this eſtate, and marrying Margaret, daughter of Edward lord Spencer, died ſeized of Bicknor Engliſh, 1 H. 5. leaving Edmond lord Ferrers of Chartley their ſon and heir, who died ſeized of Tainton and of this manor, with the office of woodwardſhip in the foreſt of Dean, 14 H. 6. William lord Ferrers, ſon of Edmond, had livery of the manor preſently after his father's death, and dying 28 H. 6. left an only daughter Anne, married to Walter d'Evereux, eſq; who afterwards, in her right, became lord Ferrers of Chartley. Elizabeth the widow of William lord Ferrers levied a fine of the manor of Bicknor, to Thomas archbiſhop of Canterbury, and to many other great men, 32 H. 6. By this account it appears, that the manor of Bicknor continued in the name of Ferrers about one hundred and twenty years.

The manor ſoon after came to William Wallein, or Walwyn, proprietor of Abbenhall, who died ſeized thereof 11 E. 4.

Sir John Luterell had livery of the manor of Bicknor 1 Eliz. and the earl of Clanricard was ſeized of it in the year 1608. It afterwards came to Benedict Hall, of Highmeadow, eſq; from whom it deſcended to lord viſcount Gage, the preſent lord of the manor. For his lordſhip's arms, &c. ſee *Newland*.

Alexander Carent was ſeized of lands in Bicknor 5 E. 3. and John his ſon and heir held the ſame 6 R. 2.

Edward Tomkyns Machen, eſq; has a good houſe and eſtate in this pariſh. He is deſcended of an antient family which has long reſided in this county. Thomas Machen, his anceſtor, was thrice mayor of the city of Glouceſter, who died in 1614, and lies buried in the body of Glouceſter cathedral, as mentioned p. 177.

The family of the Wyrrals, which has been ſeated here ſeveral generations paſt, is of great antiquity. Matthew Wyrral was high ſheriff of this county in 1259. John Wyrral, a deſcendant from him, died 33 E. 3. and left William Wyrral his ſon and ſucceſſor, who died alſo 38 E. 3. John Wyrral, ſon of William, had a wife of the name of Maud, and died in the reign of Richard the Second; and John Wyrral, ſon of the laſt John, died in the reign of Henry the Sixth, leaving Jenkyn Wyrral his ſon, who married Margaret, daughter of —— Machen, of St. Briavel's. He died 7 E. 4. and was buried in the church-yard of Newland, concerning whoſe epitaph there have been very frequent miſtakes. John Wyrral, ſon of Jenkyn, married the daughter of —— Price, by whom he had a ſon William, who wedded Anne, daughter and heireſs of John Aſhurſt. John Wyrral, ſon of William, married Iſabel, daughter and heireſs of Robert Motton, and had a ſon William, whoſe ſon William Wyrral married Maud,

Maud, daughter of Thomas Baynham, of Clowerwall, and died in the reign of king Henry the Eighth. George Wyrral, son of the last William, married Bridget, daughter of George Wintour, of Churcham, and William his son married Catherine, daughter of Michael Chadwell, of Chipping-Norton in Oxfordshire. George Wyrral, son of William, married Mary, only daughter of Dennis Compton, and had a son William, who married Anne Kyrle. Jephtha Wyrral, son of William, married Martha, daughter of Thomas Pury, of Tainton, and George his son possessed a good house and estate in the parish of Bicknor, at the beginning of this century. The arms of this family are, *Gules, a chevron Or, between three crosses croslets argent, in chief a lion passant of the third.*

Of the Church, &c.

The church is a rectory in the forest deanery, worth about 130*l.* a year. Mr. Jones is patron; Mr. Meredith the present incumbent.

The church is dedicated to the virgin Mary. It is a large one, with two side ailes, a low embattled tower at the west end, and a small chapel on each side of the chancel, one belonging to the family of Machen, the other to that of Wyrral, where they bury.

	£.	s.	d.		£.	s.	d.
First Fruits,	13	6	8	Synodals,	0	2	0
Tenths, — --	1	6	8	Pentecostals,	0	1	4
Procurations, -	0	9	8				

Benefactions.

There are six or seven acres of land, and two acres of wood given to the use of the poor; who have also 5*s.* given them in bread annually, on Christmas-day.

Taxes.			£.	s.	d.
The Royal Aid in	1692,		87	12	0
Poll-tax — —	1694,	—	28	7	0
Land-tax ——	1694,	—	146	4	0
The same, at 3*s.* —	1770,	—	107	8	9

At the beginning of this century there were 60 houses and about 300 inhabitants, whereof 19 were freeholders; yearly births 12, burials 10. *Atkyns.* But the people are now encreased to near 500.

****

BISLEY.

THIS large parish lies in the hundred of Bisley, to which it gives name. The church is about three miles east from Stroud, nine westward from Cirencester, four north from Minchin-hampton, and ten southward from Gloucester.

Bisley has a weekly market on Thursdays, now little frequented, for the town is most unfavourably situated for a market, being of very difficult access, by reason of the deep bottoms which environ it every way; but it has two yearly fairs, for cattle, &c. which are considerable, *viz.* one upon St. George's day, the other upon All-saints day, granted by king James the Second.

There are two small brooks which run through the parish into Stroud river. The greater part of the parish is high ground, consisting mostly of arable and woodland, with extensive wastes, on which are several populous villages, inhabited chiefly by poor people employ'd in the clothing manufacture. But it is probable that it was formerly much more woody than at present, and that its name is compounded of *bois*, a wood, and leaz, a pasture. Leaving this etymology to stand or fall as reason and better judgments may determine, I proceed to give a short description of such places in this parish as more particularly deserve notice.

In the woodland part, on the northern border, lies a small sequestered glyn or valley, called *Timbercomb-bottom*, noted for its singular situation, being intirely separated from the rest of the world by thick surrounding woods, which make it not easily accessible, nor is it to be seen 'till you enter into it. It is an estate belonging to Mr. Smart.

Chalford-bottom is a deep and narrow valley, about a mile in length, lying partly in Minchin-hampton, but the greater part, being on the north side of the river which runs to Stroud, is in this parish. On the curious traveller's first approach, it presents at once a very striking and respectable appearance, consisting of a great number of well-built houses, equal to a little town, lying very contiguous, but not joined together. These are intermixt with rows of tenters, along the side of the hill, on which the cloth is stretched in the process of making. This variety of landscape is uncommonly pleasing, and so great and surprising is the acclivity where some of the buildings stand, that in different approaches to the same house, you ascend to the lowest story, and descend to the highest. In this bottom are eight fulling-mills, and here, and in the villages above the hill, called the *Linches*, within the parish, great numbers of people, employed in the different branches of the woollen manufacture, reside. But the trade has lately been very much on the decline.

Chalford is likewise noted for the petrifying quality of a remarkably clear spring of water, issuing, by several apertures, out of the north side of the hill next to Minchin-hampton. Its effects are seen on various substances lying in its course, such as moss, and small pieces of wood; but they are particularly observable on the axis and other parts of a mill-wheel, on which the water is continually dropping, so that in the course of a year, it forms incrustations nearly half an inch thick, not much unlike pieces of manna. Falling into cavities, it forms *stalactites*, and large petrified masses in various uncommon shapes, pieces of which are occasionally taken out and reserved as curiosities.

The inhabitants of Chalford and its vicinities are estimated at near two thousand, who are above two miles distant from the parish church; wherefore

fore a neat chapel was erected there some years ago, for their accommodation, in which they had sermons on sundays, and the officiating minister was supported by subscription. But for a year or two past, the contributions have failed, either from the lessened abilities of the inhabitants, thro' the decline of trade, or from some other cause, and there has been no regular service since.

Sir Robert Atkyns asserts, but I know not upon what authority, that the first clothing-mill in these parts was erected in *Todgmore*, or *Todesmore-bottom*, in this parish; and that the famous Roger Bacon, commonly called friar Bacon, (an eminent mathematician and philosopher for the age he lived in, and thence reputed a conjurer by the vulgar) was born there; and that he was educated at St. Mary's chapel in Chalford, now St. Mary's mill. This is a house belonging to Mr. Thomas-Fry Clark, in which is a room said to have been friar Bacon's study. But Dr. Cave and other biographers make Ilchester in Somersetshire to be the place of that great man's nativity. He died in 1284.

Of the Manor and other Estates.

In *Domesday-book* it is thus expressed:

'Earl Hugh holds Biselege in Bileleie hundred, 'and Robert holds it of him. There are eight 'hides. In demean are four plow-tillages, and 'twenty villeins, and twenty-eight bordars with 'twenty plow-tillages. There are six *servi*, and 'four *ancillæ*. There are two priests, and eight 'radchenisters having ten plow-tillages, and 'twenty-three other men paying [a rent of] 44*s*. 'and two sextaries of honey. There are five mills 'of 16*s*. value, and a wood of 20*s*. and eleven 'burgages in Gloucester yielding 66*d*. It was 'worth 24*l*. and is now worth 20*l*. *D. B.* p. 73.

It appears that this manor was afterwards in the crown 'till the time of king Edward the First, when it came, by marriage, to the Mortimers, a great and noble family, descended from Roger de Mortimer, who was general to William duke of Normandy, and, twelve years before the conquest of England, obtained a glorious victory for him against Odo, brother to the French king.

Ralph de Mortimer (probably the son of Roger) was one of the Conqueror's chief commanders in his expedition against England, and afterwards subdued and took prisoner Edrick earl of Shrewsbury, (who, in the marches of Wales, stood out against the Conqueror,) and was rewarded with his vast estate.

His son and heir Hugh was a great enemy to king Henry the Second, and incited Roger earl of Hereford to fortify his castle of Gloucester, and other his strong holds, as he had his own, against the king; but the earl of Hereford returning to his duty, Mortimer's three castles were at the same time besieged, and he forced to yield. His other turbulent actions shew him to have been of a proud and haughty spirit. He died 31 H. 2.

Roger his son and heir, who performed considerable exploits, especially against the Welsh, had for his second wife, Isabel, sister and heir to Hugh de Ferrers, upon whose death, 6 Joh. Roger gave 300 marks, and a horse for the great saddle, whereupon he had livery of the lordships of Leachlade and Lagebery in Gloucestershire, part of the inheritance of his said wife, who founded a nunnery at Leachlade, and was buried there. This Roger died 17 Joh.

Hugh Mortimer, his son by his first wife, succeeded him, who being firm to the king's interest against his rebellious barons, attended the king with all his armed power at Cirencester, according to summons, the year before his father's death, 16 Joh. and was well rewarded by that king. He married Annora, the daughter of William de Braose, by whom he had lands in Cherleton and Chiriton, and died without issue 11 H. 3.

Ralph Mortimer, half brother to Hugh, and son of the last Roger by his second wife, succeeded, and paying 100*l*. for relief, had livery of all his lands in Gloucestershire and elsewhere, excepting Leachlade. He was a great warrior, and built several castles upon his lands next Wales, and was so much in favour with the Welch, that prince Llewellin gave him his daughter Gladuse Duy in marriage, with large possessions. He died 30 H. 3.

Roger, his son and heir, had livery of all his lands (his mother's jointure excepted) upon paying 2000 marks, 31 H. 3. For some time he suffer'd greatly in his estate, by firmly adhering to king Henry the Third, against his rebellious barons; and was afterwards the chief occasion of their total defeat at the battle of Evesham, which victory was much owing to the forces raised by him, after he had been the sole occasion of delivering prince Edward, taken prisoner at the battle of Lewes. At this battle of Evesham, he commanded the third part of the prince's army, as the prince himself and the duke of Gloucester did the other two; whereby, assaulting the rebels on each side, they gained a glorious victory, recovering the captive king; for all which faithful services, this great earl was well rewarded. He married Maud, daughter and coheir of William de Braose, and, after other considerable services, died 10 E. 1.

Edmond, son of the last Roger, with other barons of the marches, encountered and slew in battle, Leoline prince of Wales, 10 E. 1. He married Margaret, a Spanish lady, kinswoman to queen Elianor, with whom he had great estates bestowed on him, among which was the manor of Bisley, and two parts of the advowson of the church, whereof he died seized 31 E. 1.

Roger Mortimer was son and heir of Edmond, upon whose departing without leave from the king's army in Scotland, 34 E. 1. the sheriffs of Gloucestershire, &c. were commanded to seize his lands, but they were restored the next year. In 18 E. 2. he was imprisoned for his rebellious practices, and his lands given to the Spencers: He escaped efcaped into France, and returned and dethroned king Edward the Second, and obtains not his own only, but much of the Spencers eftate, among which were the caftle and manor of Hawley, with the chafes of Malvern and Corfe, in the counties of Worcefter and Gloucefter. He had a grant of one meffuage, 10 librats of land, and rents in Bifley, which lately belonged to Hugh le Difpencer, 1 E. 3. and obtained for Jeffery his third fon, the manors of Leachlade and Sodington; but his wicked practices and infolent pride brought him to the gallows, 4 E. 3.

Edmond his eldeft fon (not earl of March) married Elizabeth, daughter of Bartholomew lord Badlefmere, and died the year after his father, 5 E. 3. leaving Roger his fon, then three years of age, heir to the remains of his eftate, who obtained a reverfal of his grandfather's fentence, 26 E. 3. and fo recovered the title of earl of March, and the whole eftate; moft of which had been given to William de Montacute earl of Salifbury. Elizabeth Badlefmere, afterwards married to Henry Spencer, dying 33 E. 3. he had livery of her lands, (being her heir) and died himfelf, feized of Byfelege and Winfton, 34 E. 3.

Edmond Mortimer earl of March, &c. was his fon and heir, by Philippa, daughter to William earl of Montacute. He married Philippa, daughter to Lionel duke of Clarence, (whence the Mortimers had juft title afterwards to the crown.) He did great fervices, efpecially in Ireland, where he was deputy, and where he died 5 R. 2. This Edmond was alfo heir, by his wife, to the third part of the earldom of Gloucefter; for his wife was the daughter of Elizabeth, heirefs to William de Burgh, who was heir to John de Burgh earl of Ulfter, who had married the third fifter and coheir of Gilbert de Clare.

Roger Mortimer was his fon and heir, born 48 E. 3. one of whofe godfathers was Thomas Horton abbat of Gloucefter. He was made lieutenant of Ireland 5 R. 2. and was declared, in parliament, heir apparent to the crown, in the ninth year of that reign. He married Elianor, daughter to Thomas Holland earl of Kent, and neice to king Richard the Second; and was flain in Ireland 22 R. 2. dying feized of the manor of Bifley, and of two parts of the church.

Edmond was his fon and heir, then fix years of age, and the laft earl of March of this family. He was taken prifoner by Owen Glendourdwy prince of Wales, and afterwards married his daughter. His fecond wife was Anne, daughter of Edmond earl of Stafford; but he died without iffue 3 H. 6. feized of the manors of Bifley, Barnfley, Leachlade, Miferden, Charleton, Winfton, Brimpsfield, and Over-Siddington.

Richard duke of York was fon and heir of Anne, who was fifter and heir of Edmond Mortimer the laft earl of March, and fucceeded him in the manor of Bifley, and in the reft of his great eftates. He was flain in the battle of Wakefield, attempting to recover his right to the crown of England. And the manor and hundred of Bifley were granted to his widow, Cicely dutchefs of York, for her life, 38 H. 6. which was confirmed to her 1 E. 4. and fhe died 10 H. 7. By this account it appears, that the manor of Bifley had continued in the name of the Mortimers 180 years, and then, by defcent from their heir female, was united to the crown.

Edward the Fourth, king of England, was fon and heir of Richard duke of York, whereby the manor of Bifley came to the crown.

Richard the Third grants the manors of Bifley, Tunly, and Swagefwick to fir William Nottingham, all which were held of the honour of Hereford.

The manor of Bifley foon after reverted to the crown, and, with the advowfon of the vicarage, was granted to fir Miles Mildmay, 3 E. 6.

The manor was again in the crown in the year 1608, and was granted, by king James the Firft, to the marquis of Rockingham, who granted it over to Thomas Mafter, D. D. and mafter of the Temple; whofe heir fold it to fir Robert Atkyns of Saperton, from whom it was purchafed by Thomas Stephens, efq; whofe fon John Stephens, of Upper Lypiat, efq; is the prefent lord of the manor. His arms are, *Per chevron, azure and argent, two falcons difplay'd Or.*

Peter Corbete was feized of two parts of the hundred of Bifelegh; Theobald de Verdune held a fourth part, and Richard de Bifelegh held the other fourth part, 15 E. 1. The hundred of Bifley was granted to fir Thomas Seimour 1 E. 6. who was afterwards attainted of treafon, and fir Miles Mildmay became proprietor of it; and then it was granted to Robert Davis, 2 Eliz. and was again conveyed to Thomas Perry, in the ninth year of the fame reign. It became afterwards the property of fir Robert Atkyns of Saperton, and is one of the feven hundreds now in difpute between the earl of Bathurft and Mr. Chamberlayne. *See Cirencefter.*

Humphry de Bohun, earl of Effex and Hereford, purchafed lands in Bifley of John de Walerond, the fon of John, 39 H. 3.

William Mansfield (perhaps the fame with William Manfell, mentioned in the records relating to Lypiat) held one vineyard, fixteen acres of land, [or fix acres of land, as fir Robert Atkyns, whom I have followed in this particular, has it in another place, p. 32.] and three acres of wood in Bifley, 18 E. 2.—From this record that learned hiftorian hath undertaken to prove the improbability of there having ever been any vineyards in Gloucefterfhire, otherwife than apple-orchards. But I have already given my fentiments on this matter, which the reader may fee in the note p. 25, where that gentleman's argument is quoted at large.

TITHINGS and *HAMLETS*.

There are nine tithings in this parifh, *viz.*

1. *Bifley,*

1. *Bifley*, of which already, with two conftables.

2. *Avenage*, where is nothing remarkable.

3. *Bidfield*. Owen de Roderick was feized of Bidfield in the reign of king Edward the Third, but being attainted for rebellion, Bidfield was granted to Mary Herney, widow of William Herney, 47 E. 3. This manor afterwards belonged to Thomas Butler and Maud his wife; but upon their furrender, it was granted to John Baker for life, 5 E. 4. and was again granted to Thomas Gilbert, for his life, in the twelfth year, and again to Edward Pye, for his life, in the fixteenth year of that reign. Bidfield in Bifley, and many other eftates, were granted to Thomas Hennage and the lord Willoughby, in confideration of lands in other places, 2 E. 6. Sir Anthony Grey had livery of this manor 4 Eliz. and Bidfield-farm, in the tenure of fir Anthony Kingftone, was granted to Arthur lord Grey 9 Eliz. Bidfield now belongs to John Stephens, of Upper Lypiat, efq;

4. *Buffage*.

5. *Chalford*. Thomas Mull and William Mull were feized of Chalford 2 E. 4.

6. *Ockeridge*. George Rawleigh, efq; died feized of lands in Okerinch and Avenafh 37 H. 8. and Simon Raleigh, his fon, had livery thereof the fame year. Lands in Okerinch in Bifleigh, which had belonged to the abbey of Cirencefter, were granted to Thomas Stroud, Walter Earl, and James Paget 36 H. 8.

7. *Steanbridge*, of which there is nothing obfervable.

8. *Troham*, or *Trougham*, generally called *Druffham*. This place is mentioned in *Domefday-book*, where it is faid,

'The fame earl [Hugh] held there [*i. e.* in 'Bifelege] one hide at Troham. Levenod held it 'of king Edward, and could go where he pleafed. 'This land was taxed. There were four bordars 'with one plow-tillage, and four acres of meadow. 'It was worth 20*s*. The fame earl held half a 'hide there, which Roger de Laci challenged to 'belong to Egefuurde, as the county witneffeth. 'It is worth 10*s*. and paid tax.' *Dom. B.* p. 73.

William Compton died feized of the manor of Trougham 38 H. 8. livery of which was granted to Walter Compton, his fon, the fame year. Mr. Smart has a good houfe and eftate in this tithing, which hath been long enjoyed by his anceftors; and Mr. Turner has alfo a good houfe and eftate here.

This place is remarkable for quarries of good tile, from which the vale country is fupply'd at five fhillings a thoufand, or twenty-five fhillings the waggon-load. Should the navigation to Stroud take place, it is probable this article may be of confiderable confequence.

9. *Tunley* and *Daneway*. Thefe places confift chiefly of woodland, with fome tillage and pafture ground, in deep hollows, and little glyns of difficult accefs. It has been fuppofed that the Danes harboured themfelves in the latter of thefe places, when this country was fo terribly infefted with them; and fo it became diftinguifhed with their name, from its being a chief place of their refort. John Clifford held one meffuage and one plow-tillage in Daneway 20 R. 2. Mr. Hancock has a good old houfe, and a good eftate at Daneway. His anceftors, from about the reign of queen Elizabeth, have carefully tranfmitted to him the fafhionable houfhold furniture of their times, and an intire fuit of man's apparel, not the worfe for wear, which he prudently preferves as real curiofities, and many people refort to fee them.

Of the Church, &c.

The church is a vicarage, in the deanery of Stonehoufe, worth 150*l*. a year, of which the lord Chancellor is patron, and Mr. Phillips the prefent incumbent.

The tithes of this parifh, and of Stroud (for the parifh of Stroud was formerly annexed to this church) were divided into three portions, whereof two were appropriated to two prebends of Weftbury-college in this county; the other, which was the firft in order, was appropriated to the prebend of the college of Stoke, near Clare in Suffolk. The rectory of thefe three prebends, as alfo a wood called Hawkley-wood, in Bifley, which alfo belonged to the prebend of Stoke, were granted to Lawrence Bafkervil and William Blake, fcrivener, 3 Jac. Thefe tithes are vefted in the earl of Coventry, and are worth about 400*l*. a year.

The tithe of all tithe-corn and hay belonging to the impropriation, and all the tithes of lamb and wool, and oblations, offerings, and all privy tithes were appointed to the vicar, by an antient endowment made by Reginald bifhop of Worcefter, in the year 1360; befides which, the full tithes of the glebe-land of the impropriation belong to the vicar.

There was formerly a chantry in this church, the revenue whereof was granted to Walter Compton 2 E. 6. but the chantry-houfe in Bifley, and lands which had belonged to the chantry of St. Mary in Weftbury, were granted to Francis Maurice and Francis Philips, in truft for Anthony Cope and others, 10 Jac.

The church is large and lofty, confifting of the nave and two ailes, with a high fpire at the weft end, and fix bells in the tower. The church hath lately been new feated in a neat manner, and makes a good appearance. It is dedicated to All Saints, and is faid to have been built by one of the Mortimers.

Monuments and Infcriptions.

In the fouth aile is the figure in ftone of a knight templer, well preferved, reported by tradition to have been the founder of the church.

Near the nave of the church, upon brafs, fixed on a grey marble flat ftone, is engraved the figure of a woman, and on the right and left below, a reprefentation of fix fons and fix daughters, with this infcription in old black characters.

Pray for the foule of Kateryn Sewell late the Wyf of Thomas Sewell, whiche Kateryn deceffed the viii day of Ianuary, the yere of o[r] Lord M v[c]xv. on whofe foule Ihu haue mercy amen. ——*This family lived at Ferrie's-Court, near Upper Lypiat.*

Againft the eaft wall of the chancel is a monument, with an infcription for Thomas Freame, of Lypiat, efq; who died in 1659, and his arms, *viz.* 1. *Azure, a crofs flory gules, between eight ears of ripe wheat, ftalked and pendent, proper.* 2. *A fefs between three birds.* And oppofite to it is a handfome monument, and memorial in Latin, for William Freame his fon, with his effigy, holding a book in his hand. He died in 1696.

Againft the fouth wall of the chancel are feveral memorials for the Jaynes, of this parifh, with thefe arms, *viz.* 1. *Gules, a chief vaire, argent and azure, impaling* 2. *On a chevron, between three eagles heads erafed Or, three trefoils fable.*

Againft the fouth wall, is a marble monument, with the arms of Stephens, as before, and this infcription:

Underneath this Monument are depofited the Remains of Thomas Stephens, Efq; Barrifter at Law, Steward of the Sheriff's Court, and Deputy Town-Clerk of the City of Briftol, younger Son of Thomas Stephens of Over Lupiatt, Efq; who in feveral Parliaments ferved as Knight of the Shire for this County, and was Lord of the Manor. His great Candour and Benevolence juftly intituled him to the Efteem of all that knew him, and he was not only an Ornament to his Profeffion, but alfo to the worthy and antient Family from whence he defcended. He died greatly lamented the 7th Day of December in the Year 1745, aged 46 Years.

In the nave of the church, a monument for John Mills, gent. who died in 1718, and Efther his wife who died in 1701, with thefe arms, *Ermine, two faltires in pale fable.*

A memorial for Scholaftica Sevill, wife of William Sevill of Chalford; with thefe arms, *viz. Argent, upon a bend fable, three eagles difplay'd Or.*

Againft the fouth wall of the nave, very high, is erected a handfome monument of white marble, with the family arms, *Argent, a chevron between three pheons heads fable*; and upon the table it is thus written:

In the North Ifle of this Church, near the Remains of a much-beloved Wife, Father and Mother, lie thofe of Thomas Smart, Efq; of *Grays* in this Parifh; who having, with Integrity, and the moft endearing Goodnature and Chearfulnefs, difcharged all the Offices of this Life, exchanged it for Immortality on the 26th of December, in the Year of our Lord 1746, and in the 63[d] Year of his Age.

There alfo lie the Bodies of his Sons William and Thomas, the former died in his Infancy, the latter on the 25th of April, 1752, aged 44.

This Monument, with the higheft Senfe of Affection, Gratitude and Duty, was erected to their Memory, by their furviving Son and Brother Richard Smart, Efq;

The above-mentioned Thomas Smart, Efq; had Iffue likewife another Son, of the Name of Richard, elder Brother to the faid William, Thomas and Richard, who died very young, and lies buried at Duntifborne Roufe.

Firft fruits, £	19	10	5	Synodals, £.	0	2	0
Tenths, —	1	19	0	Pentecoftals,	0	2	0
Procurations,	1	0	0				

Benefactions.

There is an eftate leafed out by feoffees upon lives, at the rent of 38*l.* a year, clear of all taxes; thus difpofed of, 2*l.* is paid to the parifh clerk, 10*l.* to a fchool-mafter, for teaching fixteen boys; the remainder of the income is apply'd to the ufe of the church; and, upon the removal of a life, the fine is applied to the fame ufe. The donor of this charity is not known.

Mr. John Taylor, in 1732, left an eftate which lets at 25*l.* a year, of which the fchool-mafter receives 8*l.* for teaching eight boys, and the remainder is applied to the clothing of them.

Mr. Thomas Butler, clothier, in 1688, gave 1*l.* 10*s.* a year for a fermon, and for bread to the poor.

Mr. Walter Ridler, clothier, in 1697, gave 300*l.*

Mrs. Jane Ridler, in 1714, gave 300*l.*

Mrs. Mary Ridler, in 1715, gave the intereft of 100*l.* provided the parifh fhould apply the produce of the two foregoing donations to the teaching of children to read.

Mr. Samuel Allen gave a houfe and orchard at King's-Stanley, and a ground at Calfway, let at 4*l.* 6*s.* a year, to clothe five poor widows.

Mr. Thomas Rogers, Blackwell-hall factor, in 1723, gave 25*l.*

Charles Coxe, efq; of Lower Lypiat, in 1729, gave 10*l.*

Thomas Radcliffe, of Gloucefter, efq; in 1732, gave 9*l.*

The reverend Mr. Richard Butler, vicar of Arlingham, gave 20*s.* a year in bread, and 10*s.* for a fermon on Eafter-monday.

Mrs. Mary Bafton gave 80*l.* afterwards laid out in land of the yearly value of 3*l.* 4*s.* for the ufe of the poor.

Taxes.					
The Royal Aid in	1692, £.	170	16	0
Poll-tax — —	1694, —	87	9	0
Land-tax ——	1694, —	201	19	0
The fame, at 3*s.* -	1770, —	150	11	6

The regifter of this parifh commences as early as 1547, 2 E. 6. and has been well kept from that time to the prefent. In particular, it was regularly kept from 1640 to 1660, during the civil war and *interregnum*, by Mr. Britton the minifter, an uncommon inftance in thofe days. The medium of burials for the years 1548 and 1549 was 18 yearly, and of chriftnings 37, (more than double the burials) which fhews the parifh to have been very healthy in thofe days; and the number of deaths fhews that it was not very thinly inhabited; as fuppofing 1 in 55 to die yearly, which, confidering the healthinefs of the place, feems not an undue proportion, there would be near 1000 inhabitants. At that time, there is reafon to fuppofe, they had fome little of the clothing manufacture in the parifh.

For ten years, form 1701 to 1710 inclufively, the average of burials is 58, of chriftnings 85. From 1761 to 1765 inclufively, the medium of burials is 81, of chriſtnings 127; and during the ſubſequent five years, which are given diſtinct, as the inhabitants were more unhealthy from an epidemic fever prevailing, the burials are 116, the chriſtnings 121, and the medium of burials for the whole ten years is 99, of chriſtnings 124.

Hence it may be obſerved, that the inhabitants have gradually increaſed to the preſent time, and the burials have alſo increaſed more than the baptiſms; which latter circumſtance may be attributed to various cauſes, as the acceſſion of people from other parts, to a growing manufacture, as it has been 'till within a few years; the poor people's incommodious way of life in cloſe and crouded habitations; but eſpecially the general intemperance of manufacturing people, their wants, neceſſities, and reduced manner of living when paſt their labour, as few of them make any proviſion for ſickneſs or old age; and a hard ſeaſon, with the want of accommodations they formerly enjoyed, carries many of them off.

In the regiſter, many ages are recorded from 70 to 80, ſeveral betwixt 80 and 90, a few above 90, but none of 100 for many years paſt, tho' it is a very healthy air.

There is an Independent meeting-houſe near Chalford, and another belonging to a ſmall ſociety of Baptiſts, in the ſame neighbourhood, at each of which ſome perſons are occaſionally buried; but it is apprehended, not ten yearly at both. In calculating the number of inhabitants in the pariſh, which cannot be exactly aſcertained, theſe muſt be taken into the account: And allowing one in forty-five to die yearly, which is probably near the truth, they are 4905.

BITTON

IS a pariſh of very large extent, in the hundred of Langley and Swineſhead. The church is about ſix miles eaſt from the city of Briſtol, ſeven weſt from Bath, and thirty-eight ſouth-weſtward from Glouceſter. It is bounded on the eaſt by a corner of Somerſetſhire, from which it is ſeparated by the brook Swinford; on the weſt by St. George's, on the north by Abſton and Siſton, and on the ſouth by the river Avon, which parts it from Keynſham in Somerſetſhire.

The river Boyd runs through and gives name to the pariſh, which hath been variouſly written in different ages, as *Betune* in *Domeſday-book*, *Button* in other antient records, and latterly *Bitton*, as it ſtands at the head of this account, all which are ſuppoſed to be contractions of, or corrupt modes of writing, *Boyd-town*, *i. e.* the town upon the river Boyd.

Langley and Swineſhead were antiently two diſtinct hundreds, of which the latter has been thought to take its name from the brook Swinford; but I apprehend that to be a miſtake. For ſince in *Domeſday-book* the name is written *Sineſhoved*, and *Suinheve*, which I underſtand to ſignify Sine's or Suin's houſe, from the Saxon ƿoꝼe a houſe, (whence our word *hovel*) it is probable that the hundred was denominated from the houſe of one *Sine*, or *Swain*, (for that record is not very accurate in orthography) who, in the Saxon times, might be the chief perſon of the hundred; and reſiding near the place where the road croſſed the water, by parity of reaſoning, the paſſage was alſo called Sine's-ford, or Swinford, after his name, which, in time, was applied to the whole river.

The pariſh, or the greater part of it, lies in that tract of ground formerly called the foreſt of Kingſwood, which was diſafforeſted, according to ſome accounts, in the reign of king Henry the Third. It is beautifully varied with eaſy elevations, and ſome bolder riſing grounds, which form a very agreeable landſcape, as ſeen from ſeveral points of view. The ſoil is rich and fertile, conſiſting chiefly of loam, intermixt with different proportions of ſand, and in ſome parts a little clay. The greater part is meadow and paſture, with ſome arable, both in common field and incloſures.

Great quantities of coal are dug in this pariſh, out of pits which are fifty yards deep, and ſome of them more. Here is alſo plenty of iron-ore, and rich cinders of the ſame metal, for ſmelting of which a furnace hath lately been erected, where they uſe coke inſtead of charcoal. The ſerpentine-ſtone, and many petrifications of the bivalve kind, are not uncommon in the fields and quarries. But upon the ſtricteſt inquiry, I cannot find that the ſoil produceth any rare vegetable. There is, however, a ſpring of purging mineral water near Comb-brook, which paſſing over a bed of iron-ore, carries with it ſome of the finer particles, and depoſits them in its courſe. The water of Gold-well, in the turnpike-road from Bath to Briſtol, is reckoned very fine and pure. There is a pump erected, and a can chained to it, for the uſe of travellers, to drink as they go along.

Several manufactures are carried on here, which deſerve particular notice. The braſs-mills are large works for making utenſils and thin plates of that metal. There are alſo machines for rolling and ſplitting of iron, for grinding of logwood, &c. and a pin-manufacture, though yet in its infancy, furniſhes employment for a conſiderable number of hands.

At Upton in this pariſh, a large ſtone coffin was lately found by people at plow in the field, containing a very perfect ſkeleton; but there were no coins, warlike inſtrument, nor other thing tending to diſcover whoſe bones they were. And human bones have been found ſeveral times, juſt within the ſurface of the ground, in a meadow called Siddenham, where a ſkirmiſh happened in the duke of Monmouth's rebellion.

The antiquities of this pariſh conſiſt of old foundations of buildings, found in the tithing of Hanham, and the remains of camps and fortifications,

fortifications, which have not without reaſon been attributed to the Romans; for Tacitus informs us, that in the emperor Claudius's time, P. Oſtorius, prætor of Britain, ſubdued the *Iceni* and the *Cangi*, and planted ſeveral garriſons upon or near the *Antona*, generally ſuppoſed to be the Avon, which ſeems to have been the boundary of the country of the *Cangi* in theſe parts. As a confirmation of this opinion, we find their name ſtill remaining in the compoſition of the names of ſeveral places in the north of Wiltſhire and Somerſetſhire, as Cannington, Cannings, Wincaunton, ſometimes called Cangton, and to mention but one inſtance more, Keynſham or Kaynſham, directly oppoſite to Hanham, on the other ſide of the river.

Theſe remains of antiquity induced the late Doctor Gale, in his Commentary upon Antoninus's *Itinerary*, to ſuppoſe that Hanham is really the place of the Roman ſtation *Abone* therein mentioned, and that it ought to have been placed after the *Trajectus*, whereas it ſtands before it, in the fourteenth *Iter*; for then would the diſtance be ſix computed miles from *Abone* to *Aqua Solis*, or Bath, as ſet down by Antoninus, from the preceding ſtation to that city. Thus, by tranſpoſing the order of the ſtations, the diſtances in the *Itinerary* come near the truth; but preſerving the order, there muſt be ſome miſtake in the diſtances. The late Mr. Haynes of Wick, upon principles ſimilar to the foregoing, fixed upon a ſpot in the pariſh of Abſton for the ſite of the Roman ſtation in queſtion.

Theſe conjectures are ingenious, but not altogether ſatisfactory to thoſe who know that the diſtances in the *Itinerary* are erroneous in other inſtances. In the thirteenth *Iter* it is ſet down, from *Durocornovium*, or Cirenceſter, to *Spinæ*, fifteen miles; whereas, if we are not miſtaken as to the ſituation of thoſe ſtations, which I believe is univerſally allowed, the real diſtance between them is more than double. If therefore there is ſo great a miſtake in our copies of the *Itinerary*, reſpecting the diſtance in the laſt mentioned inſtance, why may not that be the caſe alſo as to the *Abone* and the *Trajectus*? and then we ſhall have reaſon to think they are placed in their natural order, as I ſhall endeavour to ſhew when the ſubject is reſumed under Lidney.

Having briefly touched on the antiquities and natural hiſtory of the place, I ſhall juſt mention a particular cuſtom which formerly prevailed, and is not, even now, wholly laid aſide. There are three meadows which are common after the hay of the firſt crop is taken off. The proprietors of three eſtates break thoſe meadows in the following manner: One of them turns into the firſt a white bull, another into the ſecond a black boar, and the remaining proprietor puts a black ſtone-horſe into the third meadow; after which, thoſe who have a right of common drive in their ſtock immediately. What could give riſe to this cuſtom may be matter of ſpeculation; but I conjecture, that the ſame reaſon that obliged the parſon of many pariſhes to keep a bull for the uſe of his pariſhioners, might alſo oblige the abbat of Keynſham, to whom the meadows formerly belonged, to provide a male of each of the beforementioned ſpecies for the uſe of the pariſh where the meadows lie; and the obligation continued in force on the poſſeſſors, after the diſſolution of monaſteries.

Barr's-Court in this pariſh, taken notice of by Mr. Camden and other topographers, as a fine ſeat in the foreſt of Kingſwood, is now moſtly taken down, and the remainder gone much to ruin.

I come now to treat

Of the Manor and other Eſtates.

Bitton is part of the antient demeſnes of the crown. In *Domeſday-book* it is thus recorded:

'There were thirty-ſix hides at farm in Betune, 'in Suinheve hundred, with its two members 'Wapelei and Wintreborne, in the time of king 'Edward. In demean were five plow-tillages, and 'forty-one villeins and twenty-nine bordars with 'forty-five plow-tillages. There are eighteen '*ſervi*, with one mill.

'In the time of king Edward this manor paid 'a farm of one night, and it does the ſame now.' *Domeſday-book*, p. 67.

The paying a night's farm was finding a night's entertainment for the court in thoſe reigns, agreeable to the explanation of that expreſſion, p. 80.

'Dons [one of the king's thanes] holds Betone 'of the king, and he held it in the time of king 'Edward. There are two hides, one of which 'paid tax, the other belonged to the church. In 'demean are two plow-tillages, and five villeins, 'and two bordars with five plow-tillages. There 'are four *ſervi*, and ten acres of meadow. It was 'worth 6 *l.* and is now worth 3 *l.*' *Dom. B.* p. 80.

There are records of the following dates, which ſhew who were the ſucceſſive proprietors of this manor, *viz.* Adam d'Amavil was ſeized of the manor of Button by the grant of king H. 2. and his ſon Robert d'Amavil died ſeized of it, with a right to markets, 11 H. 3. A ſon of that Robert married Petronella de Vinon, who ſurviving her huſband, was ſeized of this manor 45 H. 3. and married Richard de la Moor, who purchaſed a charter in Button in the 53d year of that reign. Adam d'Amavil, ſon of Petronella, died ſeized of this manor 15 E. 1. and leaving no iſſue, his two ſiſters became his heirs, the one being married to Richard de la Moor, ſon of the former, who, in her right, was ſeized of the manor of Eldeland in Bitton; Amabel, the other ſiſter, was married to David le Blount, the ſon of David, who, in her right, was ſeized of the manor of Button, by the ſurrender of Petronella de Vinon, 15 E. 1. which David and Amabel were alſo ſeized thereof, 21 and 32 E. 1.

David le Blount, their ſon, died ſeized of the manor 17 E. 2. and was ſucceeded by his ſon Richard,

Richard, who held it in the twentieth year of that reign; and dying without iſſue, the manor of Button was poſſeſſed by his brother Edmond, who married one Agnes, and died ſeized thereof 36 E. 3. Edmond Blount, their elder ſon, and Margaret his wife, held this manor, and one meſſuage and half a yard-land in Button, 4 R. 2. William Blount was ſeized thereof 22 R. 2. and Iſabel his daughter and heireſs held the ſame 4 H. 4. and dying unmarried, the manor came to her next kinſman Robert Blount, who was ſeized of it 9 H. 4. and he and his tenants had a right to heath, wood, and coal in Kingſwood chaſe.

John Blount, ſon of Robert, married one Willona, and died ſeized of Button, Oldland, Weſt-Hanham, Swinford, and Beach 26 H. 6. and Wentlin his widow (perhaps the ſame with Willona) being endowed with Button, died ſeized thereof 32 H. 6. Edmond Blount, eſq; ſon of John, died alſo ſeized of this manor 8 E. 4. as did his ſon Simon, 16 E. 4.

Margaret, the daughter and heireſs of Simon Blount, was married to ſir John Barr, who, in her right, was ſeized of the manors of Button, Oldland, Eaſt-Hannam, Weſt-Hannam, and Upton 22 E. 4. and left Joan, his only daughter and heireſs, married to ſir Thomas Newton, who, in her right, became ſeized of the aforeſaid manors, and of Barr's-Court, which took its name from ſir John Barr.

The family of the Newtons is derived from Howel ap Grono, lord of Newton in Rouſe. Cradock ap Howel ap Grono, was ſon of Howel ap Grono. Sir William Cradock, ſon of Cradock ap Howel, married Jane, daughter of ſir Mathew Wogan, and lies buried at Newton. William Cradock, ſon of ſir William, married Catherine, daughter and heireſs of ſir William de la Meer, of Rickſton. John Cradock, ſon of William, married Joan, daughter of ſir John Elider, by whom he had a ſon Robert, who married Margery, daughter of Nicholas Sherborn. John Cradock, ſon of Robert, married Neſt, daughter of ſir Peter Ruſſel, and had a ſon John, who married Margaret, daughter of Howel Meythe, of Caſtle-Ordin, and Fountain-gate. Sir Richard Cradock, ſon of the laſt John, was Chief Juſtice of England: He married Emma, daughter and coheireſs of ſir Thomas Perret, of Iſlington, *and dwelled or was born* (ſays Leland) *at Tre-newith*, [*i.e.* New Town] *in Powiſland, and ſo was called* [Newton] *after that place.*

Sir John Newton, his ſon, married Iſabel, daughter and heireſs of ſir John Chedder. Sir Thomas Newton was brother to ſir John, and ſon of ſir Richard the Chief Juſtice: He married Joan, daughter and heireſs of ſir John Barr, by whom Barr's-Court, and the manor of Bitton, and other manors came into the family of Newton, 22 E. 4. as before related.

Thomas Newton, ſon of ſir Thomas, married Margaret, daughter of ſir Edmond George, of Wraxwell in Somerſetſhire; and had a ſon ſir John Newton, who married Margery, daughter of ſir Anthony Pointz. Sir Henry Newton, ſon of ſir John, married Katherine, daughter of ſir Thomas Paſton, and had a ſon ſir Theodore Newton, who married Penelope, daughter of ſir John Rodney, of Rodney-Stoke in Somerſetſhire. He was lord of the manor of Bitton in the year 1608. His ſon ſir John Newton, baronet, married Grace, daughter of —— Stone, and dying without iſſue, lies buried in the cathedral of Briſtol. He was the laſt of the Newtons of Barr's-Court, and gave this eſtate to ſir John Newton of Lincolnſhire, on whom he entailed the baronetage. Barr's-Court, and a very large eſtate in the pariſh of Bitton, is now the property of Michael Newton, of Lincolnſhire, eſq.

An eſtate, by the name of the manor of Bitton, was granted to Robert Fitz-Harding, afterwards lord of Berkeley, by king Henry the Second; and various records ſhew that the Berkeley family was afterwards ſeized of ſuch manor. Maurice lord Berkeley died ſeized of the manor of Bitton 15 H. 8. and Thomas lord Berkeley, his brother and heir, had livery granted to him the 16th, and died ſeized thereof 24 H. 8. Thomas his ſon died ſeized of this manor 26 H. 8. and was ſucceeded by his ſon Henry lord Berkeley, an infant, who had livery granted to him 3 Mariæ.

The records ſhew that William Pigot held lands in Button 14 H. 3. Sir John Tracy and others were ſeized of lands in Button and Upton 37 E. 3. The abbey of Keynſham held lands and rents in Button, Weſt-Hanham, Upton, and Oldland, which were purchaſed in the name of John Becket and others, in truſt for the abbey, 10 R. 2.

Highfield is now the chief houſe in the pariſh, and, together with a good eſtate, is the property of Doctor Drummond.

TITHINGS and *HAMLETS.*

There are four tithings in this pariſh, *viz.*

1. *Bitton*, of which already.

2. *Hanham*, a place whoſe name vouches for its antiquity, for *hen*, in the Britiſh language, ſignifies antient. The late learned doctor Gale interprets it, either as a contraction of *Avonham*, *a ham or manſion at Abone*, or elſe conſiders it as a ſmall variation from *Henham*, *an antient ham or ſtation.* I have taken notice, at the beginning of this account, of what is moſt obſervable in this tithing, wherefore little more need be ſaid of it. But with reſpect to the manor, it ſtands, in *Domeſday-book*, among the lands of Ernulf de Heſding, recorded as follows, *viz.*

'The ſame Hernulf holds Hanun in Sineſhovedes hundred, and Humbaldus holds it of 'him. Edric held it. There is half a hide. In 'demean are two plow-tillages, with eight 'bordars,

'bordars, and four *fervi*. It is worth, and was 'worth 40*s*.' *Domefday-book*, p. 77.

John de Button held Hannam 7 E. 2. and William de la Green held Weft Hannam of the honour of Gloucefter 4 E. 3. Robert Grinder, efq; was feized of the manor of Hannam, with woods in the foreft of Kingfwood belonging to the faid manor, 22 H. 6. and Joan his widow held the fame 24 H. 6. William Join and his wife levied a fine of lands in Weft Hannam, Down Hannam, and Oldland to Andrew Windfor 12 H. 7.

Handclif-wood in Weft Hannam, which belonged to the abbey of Keynfham, was granted to Thomas Bridges, efq; 6 E. 6.

The manor of Hannam-Abbats, which belonged to the abbey of Keynfham, was granted to Rowland Hayward 2 Mariæ; but the lands belonging to Hanclif-wood, which were formerly in the poffeffion of the faid abbey, were granted to John Fernham 19 Eliz.

The manor-houfe in Hannam, called the Grange, belonged to the priory of Farley in Wiltfhire, and was granted to Roger Langsford and Chriftopher Martin 17 Eliz. This is now the eftate of Charles Bragge, efq.

Henry Crefwicke, efq; has a good houfe and a good eftate here, called Hanham-Abbats, becaufe it antiently belonged to the abbat of Keynfham. It was formerly the feat of the Baffets. His anceftors held a court here. His arms are thus blazoned in the laft heralds vifitation of the county, *viz. Or, a lion rampant within a bordure fable befanty.*

Mr. Kedgwin Webley of London, a defcendant of the Webleys of the Mead, in the parifh of Tiddenham, purchafed a very handfome, pleafant feat, and a large eftate in this tithing, formerly belonging to Thomas Trye, efq; which is now in the poffeffion of Mrs. Frances Parry, widow of David Parry, of Noyadd in the county of Cardigan, efq; and only child of Mr. Webley.

There were formerly two machines in this tithing, for raifing water for the ufe of the city of Briftol, taken notice of in fome books, but they were removed in the year 1720.

There is a chapel of eafe at Hanham, clofe to Mr. Crefwicke's houfe, where divine fervice is performed every Sunday, and it has a right of fepulture; but Hanham is not reputed a feparate parifh, as mentioned by fir Robert Atkyns.

3. *Oldland* is another large tithing, diftinctly mentioned in *Domefday-book*, after this manner:

'The bifhop of Execeftre holds Aldelande in 'Sinefhovedes hundred. Aluui held it. He was 'one of earl Harold's [free] men, and could go 'wherever he pleafed. There are two hides, one 'of which pays tax, the other does not. In de'mean are two plow-tillages, and one villein, and 'fix bordars with one plow-tillage. There are 'two *fervi*, and ten acres of meadow. It was then 'worth 4*l*. and is now worth 20*s*.' *D. B.* p. 70.

It is probable, that after the death of the bifhop, this manor was in the crown, and that it was granted, with Button, by king Henry the Second, to Adam d'Amavil. It paffed, by the marriage of one of the coheireffes of the d'Amavils, to Richard de la More, who died feized of Eldeland, which he held by the fervice of half a knight's fee 20 E. 1. and was fucceeded by his fon Thomas de la More, who had 20*l*. a year in land, and was made a knight by king Edward the Firft. He lived in the court of king Edward the Second, and wrote a hiftory of the life and death of that king, which is now extant. Stephen de la More held Oldland in Button 2 E. 3. and Walter de la More poffeffed the manors of Oldland and Upton, and a hundred acres of Kingfwood foreft, 14 E. 3. and John de la More, his fon, was feized of the manor of Oldland in the 23d year of the fame reign.

Cicely, the widow of Nicholas de Berkeley, was feized of Oldland, 16 R. 2. Sir John Denrofe held the manor of Oldland, and forty acres of arable and pafture there, within the manor of Button, of Roger Mermion 20 R. 2. and John Denrofe was feized of the manor of Oldland, and of a tenement there called Mermions, 7 H. 5. John Chefbrook and Joan his wife levied a fine of one moiety of the manor of Oldland in Bitton, and of the hundred, to the ufe of Thomas Wikes, 2 H. 6. Thomas Wikes, fon of Thomas, died feized of the manor of Oldland 13 E. 4. which afterwards defcended to Richard Wikes, who died 5 Mariæ, and livery thereof was granted to his coufin and heir Robert Wikes the fame year.

Wefton's-court was fo called after the name of fome perfons of eminence, who were the proprietors of it. Nicholas de Wefton was heretofore feized of it, and John Wefton was alfo feized of Wefton's-court in Oldland in the reign of king Henry the Sixth. It is now the eftate of Mrs. Blake.

There is alfo a chapel of eafe at Oldland, where they bury. The benefactions to Hanham, Oldland, and Bitton ftand together at the end of this account.

4. *Upton*, or *Upton-Cheney*. The parfonage of Upton belonged to the prebend of the church of Sarum 10 R. 2.

Beach and *Swinford* are alfo hamlets in this parifh.

Barr's-court, Hanham, Oldland, Upton-Cheney, and Beach are within the jurifdiction of the honour of Gloucefter.

The manerial rights of this parifh are in difpute between feveral claimants.

Of the Church, &c.

The church is a vicarage in the deanery of Hawkefbury, worth about 200*l*. a year. The prebendary of Bitton in Salifbury cathedral, in right of his prebend, is patron; Mr. Charles Elwes is the prefent incumbent.

The impropriation belongs to the fame prebend, and is in leafe to Thomas-Edwards Freeman, of Batsford, efq.

The church is dedicated to St. Mary. It is lofty and in good repair, and has a very handſome embattled tower at the weſt end, with Gothick ornaments and pinnacles, and ſix bells in it. There is a large chantry-chapel on the north ſide, adjoining to the church, built by ſir John Barr, which is now the burying-place of the Newton family.

Monuments and Inſcriptions.

There is a ſmall monument againſt the north wall of the chancel, with this inſcription:

MEMORIÆ SACRVM IOH: SEYMOR MILITIS COMIT: GLOVCES: Qui non minus Illuſtris animi dotibus excelluit, quam præilluſtri et nobili ortu claruit. Mortem obijt nouembris 17mo. Anno Epoche Chriſtianæ 1663.

Si moueat virtus Lachrymas, defuncta, Viator,
Siſtas, officij ſic memoratq; tui.
Se pietas fato præbet Crucianda ſuperbo.
At quamuis Jaceat non quaſi vita, tamen
In te certabant Virtus et nobilis ortus
Quis prior: Heu! fato ceſſit utrumq; tuo.
Dum vigeat Phœbi Laurus, dum viuida virtus,
Vives, non norunt hæc monumenta mori.
Tu bene vixiſti, uita an felicior eſſes
An obitu, fieri Queſtio jure poteſt.
Sic uixit Patriæ lumen, ſic occidit, eheu!
Fallimur, in Cœlo jam noua ſtella micat.
Vivito ut incluſus vixit modo nobilis Heros,
Certa licet fuerit ut Amica venit.

Age peripatetice Dum intuearis Cineres defuncti mort... en facel... breui fortaſſis tuæ.

On the ſtone are theſe arms: *Gules, two wings conjoined in feſſe Or.*

Againſt the wall of the chapel is a white marble monument, and this inſcription:

Here lieth the Body of Sir IOHN NEWTON, Bar[t]. thrice Burgeſs of Parliament. A moſt loving Huſband, careful Father, & faithful Friend. Pious, Iuſt, Prudent, Charitable, Valiant, & belov'd of all. He was born Ivne y[e] 9th A. D. 1626, being the Son of THOMAS NEWTON of Gunwarby in the County of Lincoln, Eſq; and died May 31st A. D. 1699. He married Mary the daughter of S[r] IERVASE EYER of Ramton in the County of Nottingham K[t]. They liv'd happily all their Time together w[ch] was 55 Years, by whom he had Iſſue four Sons & thirteen Daughters. This Monument was erected at the Charge of his youngeſt Son Gervas Newton, Eſq.

Over the table are theſe arms, Quarterly, 1ſt and 4th, *Argent, on a chevron azure three garbs Or.* The arms of Ulſter in a canton, for Newton. 2d and 3d, *Sable, two thigh-bones in ſaltire argent.*

Under the table, *Per pale*, 1ſt. Newton as before. 2d *Argent, on a chevron ſable three quatrefoils Or.* for Eyer.

Near the above, a ſmall marble monument, with this inſcription:

ELIZABETH STRINGER obijt triceſimo primo die Iulij Anno Dom. 1694.

SEQVIMVR
QVAMVIS NON PASSIBVS ÆQVIS.

Upon a ſcutcheon, *Per pale*, 1ſt. *Per chevron ſable and Or, three eagles diſplay'd counterchanged.* 2d. *Sable, two thigh-bones in ſaltire argent.*

There are ſeveral memorials in the church for the families of Creſwicke, Weare, Parker, Jones, &c. but there is nothing in them deſerving particular notice.

There were two antient ſtatues of ſtone lying at length, but for whom they were deſigned is unknown. *Atkyns.* They are now taken away.

Firſt Fruits, £.	18	14	10	Synodals, £.	0	2	0
Tenths, — --	1	17	6	Pentecoſtals,	0	0	2
Procurations, -	0	6	8				

Benefactions.

To Bitton. Mr. Freeman has given, for four ſermons every year, 40*s.* for ever; and 10*s.* a year to the poor.——Mr. Seed has given 40*s.* Mr. Shewring of Briſtol 1*l.* 6*s.* 4*d.* Mr. Gully of Briſtol 9*s.* Mrs. Badcock 7*s.* and Mr. Davis 2*s.* all to the poor, annually for ever.

To Oldland. Mr. Arthur Farmer of Briſtol gave 6*l.* a year for a ſermon on every firſt Sunday in the month.—Mr. Robert Kitchen 10*s.* a year for a ſermon on Good Friday, and 10*s.* to the poor for ever.—Mrs. Elizabeth Warn gave 40*s.* for four ſermons, and 40*s.* to the poor, annually for ever.—Mr. Thomas Woodward gave 20*s.* to the poor, as often as any rate ſhall be made at Oldland for their relief.

At Hanham. Mrs. Parry gives annually, to ſixteen poor widows, 5*s.* each, on St. Thomas' day, which was left by one of the Tryes.

Bitton.

Taxes.	The Royal Aid in	1692, £.	180	12	0
	Poll-tax — —	1694, —	46	17	0
	Land-tax ——	1694, —	202	3	4
	The ſame, at 3*s.* —	1770, —	151	11	3

Hanham.

Taxes.	The Royal Aid in	1692, £.	89	6	0
	Poll-tax —— —	1694, —	21	11	0
	Land-tax ——	1694, —	77	6	0
	The ſame — —	1770, —			

Oldland.

Taxes.	The Royal Aid in	1692, £.	89	6	0
	Poll-tax — —	1694, —	27	0	0
	Land-tax ——	1694, —	116	15	6
	The ſame at 3*s.* --	1770, —	87	12	0

At the beginning of this century, according to ſir Robert Atkyns, there were 320 houſes and about 1150 inhabitants in this pariſh, whereof 37 were freeholders; yearly births 56, burials 46. But it appears by the pariſh regiſter, that in a ſeries of ten years, from 1700 to 1709, there were 633 baptiſms and 432 burials; and in a like ſeries, from 1760 to 1769, 1116 baptiſms, and 998 burials; and the inhabitants having been exactly numbered in the year 1767, were found to be 4634. There are religious ſectaries who have diſtinct burying places, and are ſuppoſed to bury about 9 or 10 every year, and taking theſe into the account, the average number of annual burials will be 109.8; ſo that about 1 in 42 dies every year, which ſhews it to be a healthy ſituation, and that the inhabitants have more than doubled their number within the laſt ſeventy years. Sir

Robert

Robert Atkyns's eſtimate of the inhabitants was greatly too low, as will appear by multiplying the average number of annual burials in the firſt ſeries, *i. e.* 43.2 by 42, which will give 1814 for the number of inhabitants at that time.

BLAISDON.

THIS is a ſmall pariſh in the hundred of Weſtbury, in the foreſt diviſion, three miles diſtant eaſt from Mitchel-Dean, four north from Newnham, and eight weſtward from Glouceſter.

Before the Norman conqueſt, our kings had granted ſeveral parcels of land, part of the foreſt, by the names of *Denes*, *i. e.* woody places; which afterwards received ſome addition, as *Mitchel-Dene*, *Little-Dene*, *Rure-Dene*, and laſtly *Blethes-Dene*, or *Bleches-Dene*, which was the antient name of this place, having one of the firſt proprietors of it for the *pre-nomen*, to diſtinguiſh it from the reſt. The pariſh conſiſts moſtly of paſture and woodlands. A ſmall rill, called Natſwood-brook, runs through it to Weſtbury, and empties itſelf into the Severn.

This was not erected into a pariſh in the time of king Edward the Firſt, for in the ninth year of that reign, the ſheriff, in his return of all the vills in Glouceſterſhire, mentions Longhope *cum Hamletto de Bletcheſden*; whence it appears that it was then appendant to Longhope.

Of the Manor and other Eſtates.

Domeſday-book makes no diſtinct mention of this place; but there are records of the following dates which ſhew who were the proprietors of it: William de Muſgroſe was ſeized of Bleteſden 49 H. 3. as was Ralph de Abbenhall 29 E. 1. Jeffry le Mareſcal held Blecheſden, and the advowſon of the church, 32 E. 3. and in the 46th year of the ſame reign, this manor was held of Humphry de Bohun earl of Hereford and Eſſex, and of Joan his wife.

This manor was afterwards called Blaiſdon, and was granted to the abbey of Flaxley, and upon the diſſolution of that abbey, it was granted to ſir Anthony Kingſton 36 H. 8. William Kingſton and Mr. Ayleway were lords of it in the year 1608. Mr. Wade was lord of the manor at the beginning of the preſent century, and it ſtill continues in the ſame family. The arms of Wade are, *Azure, a croſs moline between four eſchallops Or.*

Of the Church, &c.

The church is a rectory, in the Foreſt deanery, worth 50*l.* a year. Mr. Hayle and Mrs. Wade are patrons, and preſent alternately.

The church hath a low tower at the weſt end, with battlements.

	£	s.	d.		£	s.	d.
Firſt fruits,	5	7	4	Proc. & Syn.	0	6	6
Tenths,	—	0	10	8 Pentecoſtals,	0	1	6

Taxes.			£	s.	d.
	The Royal Aid in	1692,	49	4	0
	Poll-tax — —	1694,	12	0	0
	Land-tax ——	1694,	51	10	4
	The ſame, at 3*s.* -	1770,	38	9	10

At the beginning of this century there were 40 houſes and about 180 inhabitants in this pariſh, yearly births 5, burials 4. But the number of inhabitants is now decreaſed to 137.

BLEDINGTON.

THIS pariſh lies in the upper diviſion of the hundred of Slaughter, four miles ſouth-eaſtward from Stow, five weſt from Chipping-Norton in Oxfordſhire, and twenty-nine eaſtward from Glouceſter. It is bounded on the eaſtward by the river Evenlode, which divides it from Oxfordſhire. The ſoil is generally good, conſiſting of meadow, paſture, and arable.

The common-fields have lately been incloſed by virtue of an act of parliament, which directs that the Far-heath and the cow-commons do remain unincloſed, to be enjoyed, in a commonable manner, by the proprietors of lands there, in proportion to their rights and properties therein, except the dean and chapter of Oxford, who are excluded. By this act alſo, a portion of furze or heath-ground, not exceeding ſix acres, in the Home-heath, is veſted in the church-wardens and overſeers of the poor, in truſt for raiſing furze for the benefit of the poor pariſhioners.

Of the Manor and other Eſtates.

In the *Domeſday* account of lands belonging to the abbey-church of Winchcomb, it is thus expreſt: 'The ſame church [of St. Mary de Wincelcumbe] holds Bladintun [in Salemones hundred.] 'There are ſeven hides. In demean are two plow-'tillages, and eight villeins, and four bordars with 'five plow-tillages, and eight *ſervi* and two *ancillæ*. 'There is a mill of 5*s.* [rent,] and thirty acres of 'meadow. It was worth 4*l.* and is now worth '3*l.*' *Domeſday-book*, p. 71.

The abbey procured this manor to be diſcharged from the hundred-court 8 H. 3. and purchaſed a charter of free-warren in Bladington, and divers other manors, in the 35th year of that reign, which privilege was allowed to the abbey in a writ of *Quo warranto* 15 E. 1.

The abbey of Winchcomb aſſigned the manor of Bladinton to the church of St. Ebrulph at Utica in Normandy, 12 E. 2. and afterwards, upon the ſeizure of foreign monaſteries, it was granted to the church of Eveſham; and upon the diſſolution of that abbey, it was granted to ſir Thomas Leigh 7 E. 6. from whom it deſcended down to the preſent time in like manner with Addleſtrop, and is now

now the property of the heir of James Leigh, efq; lately deceafed.

Of the Church, &c.

The church is in the deanery of Stow. It is an impropriation belonging to Chrift-church in Oxford. Lands in Bledington, with the rectory and advowfon of the vicarage, which belonged to the abbey of Winchcomb, were granted to the chapter of Oxford 38 H. 8. The dean and chapter of Oxford are patrons, and Mr. Henry Brown is the prefent incumbent. The impropriation pays to the curate 20*l.* a year, and the act for inclofing directs the commiffioners to lay out lands of the value of 4*l.* a year, as an augmentation of the vicarage; but before this time it had been augmented with two donations of 200*l.* each, and queen Anne's bounty, with which an eftate was purchafed in Werndydyr in Radnorfhire.

The impropriation is worth about 200*l.* a year, and is in leafe to Ambrofe Reddall, efq; of Stonehoufe in this county.

The Upper Oar and the Lower Oar, and fome other lands adjoining, were tithe-free before the inclofing act, by virtue of which the dean and chapter had one feventh of fuch lands as were fubject to tithe allowed them in lieu thereof.

There was a charge of 20*s.* a year on Bledington, to find neceffaries for mafs at Winchcomb-abbey, which was confirmed by the pope, by the archbifhop, and by the bifhop of Worcefter.

The church is dedicated to St. Leonard. It hath an aile on the fouth fide, and a tower at the weft end.

	£.	s.	d.		£.	s.	d.
Firft fruits,	6	13	4	Synodals,	0	2	0
Tenths, —	0	13	4	Pentecoftals,	0	0	10
Procurations,	0	6	8				

Taxes.			£.	s.	d.
	The Royal Aid in	1692,	115	6	0
	Poll-tax — —	1694, —	23	7	0
	Land-tax — -	1694, —	62	14	0
	The fame, at 3*s.*	1770, —	49	16	3

At the beginning of this century there were 53 houfes and about 260 inhabitants in this parifh; yearly births 8, burials 6. *Atkyns.* There are now only 251 inhabitants.

BODINGTON.

THE hamlets of Bodington and Barrow in this parifh, lie in the lower divifion of the hundred of Tewkefbury; but Heydon and Withybridge are in the lower divifion of the hundred of Weftminfter. The parifh is fituated in the vale part of the county, about five miles fouthward from Tewkefbury, four weftward from Cheltenham, and fix north-eaftward from Gloucefter. The turnpike-road between the two laft mentioned places is carried through it. The river from Cheltenham alfo runs through it, and empties itfelf into the Severn near the Haw-paffage.

It is probable, that in very early ages, here was a houfe of fuch confequence as to give denomination to the place, for *Bodington* (from the Britifh word *bod* a manfion) fignifies a capital houfe or manfion in the town upon the water, agreeable to a former explanation of the feveral parts of the name. Leland fays, *Ther is at Bodington a fair manor place and a park.* The park is now a farm, and the manor houfe is occupied by the farmer.

There is a little fugar-loaf hill in the hamlet of Barrow, which, from its refemblance to a *tumulus*, gave name to the hamlet. From the top of this hill, in a clear day, is a diftinct view of thirty-fix parifh churches, a circumftance arifing from the fituation of the hill in the middle of a large extent of flat country. However improbable this may feem, it is neverthelefs ftrictly true, as I am affured by a gentleman of veracity living in the parifh.

At Barrow, and at Moredon in the hamlet of Heydon, are feveral fprings of faline purgative water, brackifh and difagreeable to the tafte, which have been often ufed with a medicinal view by the country people.

The parifh confifts of rich meadow and pafture land, with about one hundred and twenty acres of coppice wood; and there is a common lot-meadow, of about a hundred acres, called Bodington-moor. Bodington is within the jurifdiction of the court of the honour of Gloucefter.

Of the Manor and other Eftates.

'Three hides in Botintone belong to this 'manor. [Tedekefberie.] Girard holds them, and 'he hath there two plow-tillages, and four vil'leins with three plow-tillages; and there are 'three *fervi*, and a mill of 8*s.* [rent] and eight 'acres of meadow. [This eftate] is worth and 'was worth 40*s.*' *Domefday-book*, p. 68.

But it appears, by the fame record, that there were two hides at Botingtune, part of the lands belonging to the church of St. Peter at Weftminfter, and in the hundred of Derheft, which Wluui, one of the king's thanes, held in the time of king Edward the Confeffor, but which Girard held at the time of the furvey, after the Conqueft. Thefe particulars ftand under the head *Terra S. Petri Weftmon.* p. 72.

This manor was granted to Robert Mufgrofe 38 H. 3. and was held of the earl of Gloucefter and Hertford, as of the honour of Gloucefter, by one knight's fee, 47 H. 3. and 8 E. 2. John de Bures held it 24 E. 3. and the next year John de Holloway was feized of it.

Robert lord Ferrers of Chartley died feized of Bodington 1 H. 5. and left Edmond lord Ferrers his fon and heir, by Margaret his wife, daughter of Edward lord Spencer, who died feized thereof 14 H. 6.

The Beauchamps were foon after proprietors of this manor, for Richard lord Beauchamp died feized ſeized of Bodington 18 H. 7. and left three daughters his heireſſes; Elizabeth, married to Robert Willoughby, lord Brook, whereby a third part of the manor deſcended to Edward lord Willoughby, their ſon and heir, who left two daughters, Anne and Blanch, of whom the latter was married to Francis Dawtry, who had livery of a moiety of the third part of the manor 25 H. 8. Anne, the ſecond daughter and heireſs of Richard lord Beauchamp, was married to Richard Liggon: Margaret, the third and youngeſt daughter, was married to —— Reed, who left their third part to Richard Reed their ſon and heir, 4 H. 8. whoſe ſon, John Reed, had livery of the ſcite of the manor 9 Eliz.

Livery of the manor of Bodington, Barrow and Heydon, was granted to Oliver St. John 15 Eliz. and it was afterwards purchaſed by lord Craven, who ſold it to Mr. Lock. Matthew Lock, eſq; was the proprietor of it at the beginning of this century, and Mrs. Lock is the preſent lady of the monor, and holds a court-baron here.

As to other eſtates in Bodington, the records ſhew, that Hugh Muſtel held one meſſuage and eighty acres of land in Botinton 19 E. 2. And Hugh Muſtel and Elizabeth his wife levied a fine of lands in Bodington to the uſe of themſelves in taille, the remainder to Philip Boteler, the ſon of ſir Thomas le Boteler, 7 E. 3. and they levied another fine of lands in Bodington to the uſe of themſelves in taille, the remainder to Thomas, the ſon of ſir Thomas le Boteler, in taille, the remainder to Alan le Boteler, brother of Thomas, 19 E. 3.

TITHINGS and *HAMLETS.*

1. *Bodington* and *Barrow,* to which there is one tithingman. Barrow is weſtward from the church.

2. *Heydon* and *Withy-bridge,* eaſtward from the church. Theſe lie in the lower part of Weſtminſter hundred, and have one tithingman. The manor of Heydon antiently belonged to the abbey of Weſtminſter. John Browning was ſeized of the manor of Heydon, under the abbat, 3 H. 5. This manor was part of the poſſeſſions of the ſame church in its ſeveral viciſſitudes. Thus it was granted afreſh to the church of Weſtminſter 34 H. 8. was reſtored to the abbey of Weſtminſter 4 Mariæ; and again returned to the church of Weſtminſter 2 Eliz. John Partrige, eſq; held it under that church in the year 1608. It is now the eſtate of the right honourable William Dowdeſwell, eſq; as leſſee under the dean and chapter.

Butler's-Court, in Withy-bridge, is a reputed manor, belonging to lord Craven, who has a very conſiderable eſtate in Heydon and Withy-bridge.

Hugh Muſtel held forty-eight acres of land in Heydon 19 E. 2. William de Rodbearg held two meſſuages and two plow-tillages in Lye and Heydon 3 R. 2. William Nottingham, and Elizabeth his wife, levied a fine of lands in Heydon to the uſe of themſelves in taille 20 H. 6. and ſir William Nottingham, their ſon, was ſeized thereof 1. R. 3.

Of the Church, &c.

The church is within the peculiar of Deerhurſt, and is annexed to Staverton. It is an impropriation, without any endowment to the curate. Some lands, and the tithes of Barrow, belonged to the monaſtery of Thornton in Lincolnſhire, founded in the year 1139, for black canons, by William earl of Almebarle; which lands and tithes were granted to John Fernham 19 Eliz.

The rectory of Bodington belonged to the abbey of Tewkeſbury, and was granted to Francis Philips and Richard Moor, in truſt for Richard Bourk, earl of Clanricard, 6 Jac.

The impropriation belonged to Mr. Brown, from whom it paſſed to Mr. Wells, who ſold it to Mr. Thomas Arkell the preſent proprietor, and patron of the living. The reverend Mr. John Kipling is the incumbent.

The advowſon of the vicarage, and chapel of Bodington and Staverton were granted to Thomas Gatwick and Anſelm Lamb 5 Mariæ.

The church, dedicated to St. Mary Magdalen, is ſmall, with a low tower at the weſt end. The church-yard was conſecrated in the year 1469, with the conſent of the abbat of Tewkeſbury.

Pentecoſtals, — £. 0 0 7 *ob.*

Benefaction.

Three acres and a half in Dead-furlong and Stapleton-field are given to the church and poor.

Bodington.

Taxes.	The Royal Aid in	1692, £.	64	4	0
	Poll-tax —— —	1694, —	8	2	0
	Land-tax ——	1694, —	28	11	0
	The ſame, at 3*s.* —	1770, —	22	12	3

Heydon and Withy-Bridge.

Taxes.	The Royal Aid in	1692, £.	79	13	0
	Poll-tax — —	1694, —	11	16	0
	Land-tax ——	1694, —	61	12	0
	The ſame, at 3*s.* —	1770, —	46	10	1

There were, at the beginning of this century, 40 houſes and about 180 inhabitants, whereof 4 were freeholders, in this pariſh; yearly births 6, burials 5. *Atkyns.* In ten years, from 1700 to 1709 both incluſive, there are entered 65 baptiſms and 49 burials; and in eight years, from 1760 to 1767 incluſive, there are 46 baptiſms and 25 burials; and the number of inhabitants is 95; ſo that population is on the decline.

BOURTON *on the* HILL.

ONE part of this pariſh lies in the upper diviſion of the hundred of Tewkeſbury, the other in the upper diviſion of the hundred of Weſtminſter, and conſequently the pariſh is under the authority of two conſtables. It is five miles diſtant northward from Stow, five ſouth from Campden, and thirty north-eaſt from Glouceſter. It is about five miles long and one broad.

The houſes are ſituated on the ſide of a hill facing the eaſt, whence there is a fine proſpect over Morton-in-marſh, to the borders of Oxfordſhire. This ſituation gave riſe to the name of the village, for *Bourton* is a contraction of *Bourgtown*, from the Anglo-Saxon Beorg, which ſignifies a *hill*, a *fort*, or *caſtle*. The lands are moſtly arable and ſheep lays. There are two ſprings in this pariſh, one running eaſtward into the Thames, the other, by a contrary courſe, into the Severn. The turnpike-road from Worceſter to London paſſes through the village.

Of the Manors and other Eſtates.

There are two diſtinct manors. *Domeſday-book* ſhews that eight hides in Bortune belonged to the church of St. Peter at Weſtminſter, as part of the manor of Derheſt. Wluui (a radchenifter, or free man) held two hides at Bortune in the time of king Edward, which Girard held at the time of the ſurvey, in the Conqueror's reign. *See* p. 72.

Robert Fitz-Hamon ſacrilegiouſly took this manor from the abbey of Weſtminſter, in the reign of William the Second, and it was injuſtly detained 'till the reign of Henry the Second, when Lawrence the twenty-fifth abbat of Weſtminſter recovered it by a ſuit at law.

The abbat of Weſtminſter was ſeized of the manor of Bourton 15 E. 1. After the diſſolution of the abbey, and the erection of the ſee of Weſtminſter, the manor was granted to the chapter of that church 34 H. 8. The monaſtery being reſtored to its former eſtate by queen Mary, this manor was regranted to the abbey and convent of Weſtminſter in the fourth year of her reign. Another revolution taking place ſoon after, it was confirmed to the chapter of Weſtminſter 2 Eliz. The manor is held by leaſe under the church of Weſtminſter, by William Bateſon, eſq; who is lord thereof, and has a good ſeat and large eſtate in this pariſh. He married Suſannah, youngeſt daughter of Edmund Pytts, late of Kyre in the county of Worceſter, eſq; deceaſed, ſometime one of the repreſentatives of that county in parliament. His arms are, *Argent, three bat's wings erected ſable, 2 and 1. On a chief gules, a lion paſſant gardant of the firſt.*

His anceſtor was eminent for his loyalty in the time of the great civil wars, and was ſequeſter'd, and compounded for 700*l.* and his grandfather was high ſheriff of Glouceſterſhire in the year 1710.

The other manor lies in Tewkeſbury hundred. Walter de Burgton was ſeized of Burgton 15 E. 3. Joan the widow of John de Wincheſter was ſeized of this manor 36 E. 3. and John Rouſe and others were alſo ſeized of it in the 49th year of the ſame reign. Gilbert de Stonour, ſon of Robert de Stonour, held Bourton 3 H. 5. Thomas lord Wentworth married Margaret, daughter and heir of Anne Forteſcue, and with her had the manor of Bourton, and lands in Condicot, of which he died ſeized 5 E. 6. and livery of the eſtate was granted the ſame year to Thomas lord Wentworth his ſon.

The manor paſſed from the Wentworths to ſir Nicholas Overbury. He married Mary, daughter of Giles Palmer, of Ilmington in Warwickſhire, by whom he had ſir Thomas Overbury, who was born in this pariſh. He was one of the judges of the marches of Wales, and was poiſoned in the tower in the year 1613, by the malicious contrivance of the counteſs of Somerſet, of which murder ſhe and her huſband were afterwards convicted. Sir Thomas left this eſtate to his nephew ſir Thomas Overbury, who publiſhed the trial of Joan Perry and her two ſons, John and Richard, for the ſuppoſed murder of Mr. William Harriſon, in the year 1676, who afterwards appeared. Of this ſtrange affair there is a further account under Campden. This laſt ſir Thomas died at Adminton in the pariſh of Queinton, and lies buried in that church.

Alexander Popham, eſq; purchaſed this manor of the truſtees of ſir Thomas Overbury in the year 1680, after whoſe death it came to Edward Popham, his ſon and heir; ſoon after which it paſſed out of that name, and is now the property of William Bateſon, eſq.

Of the other eſtates the records ſhew, that Samuel de Bourton was ſeized of lands in Bourton 2 H. 3. and John Rouſe and others were ſeized of lands in Bourton 49 E. 3. Edward de Stoure, or Stonour, held lands in Burgton 5 R. 2.

—— Head, of the county of Berks, eſq; has a very handſome modern built houſe, with pleaſant gardens, in this pariſh, in right of his wife, daughter and ſole heireſs of Dr. Harward.

Of the Church, &c.

The church is a rectory, in the deanery of Campden, worth about 300*l.* a year. Thomas Kemble, eſq; is patron, Mr. Matthew Bloxam the preſent incumbent. Morton-in-marſh is annexed to it.

Tithes of the pariſh of Bourton on the Hill belonged to the abbey of Tewkeſbury 'till the diſſolution of that abbey, and were afterwards granted to William Duncan and Thomas Eſcourt 2 Eliz. A conſiderable part of the tithes of Morton-in-marſh is appropriated, and belongs to Mr. Bateſon.

This pariſh and Morton-in-marſh were formerly within the peculiar of Blockley in Worceſterſhire, and mortuaries are ſtill paid to the vicar of that church, with whom the rector of Bourton compounded for the liberty of burial in the year 1542.

The church is large, with two ailes, and a tower at the weſt end. It is dedicated to St. Lawrence.

Monuments

Monuments and Inſcriptions.

In the ſouth aile, on a blue marble table, is this memorial:

Near this Place is interred the Body of Brilliana, Wife of Alexander Popham, of this Pariſh, Eſq; Alſo that of her third Daughter Letitia Popham. B. P. died Sept. 12, 1688; L. P. died Oct. 11, 1738. ——— Over, in a lozenge, *Argent, on a chief gules, two ſtags heads caboſhed Or.* for Popham.

On a white marble monument,

In Memory of Kemp Harward, Doctor in phyſick, who died Jan. 15, 1743, aged 66 years; and of Altham Harward, who died Feb. 20, 1733, aged 20 years. This Monument is erected by Lucy Harward, as the laſt and only remaining Teſtimony of filial Duty and Regard to her Father, and affectionate Remembrance of her Brother. ——— The arms on it are, *Checky, Or and azure, on a bend gules two eagles diſplay'd argent.*

A white marble monument, thus inſcribed:

In Memory of Robert Devereux Bateſon, Eſq; Son of William Bateſon, Eſq; of this pariſh. He married Anne, ſecond Daughter of Allen Cliffe, of Mathon in the County of Worceſter, Eſq; by whom he left Iſſue two Sons, William and Robert, and one Daughter Anne. He died the 23d Day of October, 1736, in the 45th Year of his Age. This Monument was erected to his Memory by his equally loving and beloved Wife, Anne Bateſon. ——On it are theſe arms, 1ſt and 4th, Bateſon, as before; 2d and 3d, *Argent, a feſs gules, charged with a creſcent of the field. In chief three roundlets,* the colour not diſtinguiſhable, for Cliffe.

Firſt Fruits, £. 14	0	0	Synodals, £.	0	1	0
Tenths, — -- 1	8	0	Pentecoſtals,	0	0	6
Procurations, - 0	6	8				

The Part in Weſtminſter Hundred.

Taxes.	The Royal Aid in	1692, £.	84	10	0
	Poll-tax — —	1694, —	17	14	8
	Land-tax ——	1694, —	52	12	0
	The ſame, at 3*s.* —	1770, —	39	9	0

The Part in Tewkeſbury Hundred.

Taxes.	The Royal Aid in	1692, £.	25	8	0
	Poll-tax — —	1694, —	8	14	0
	Land-tax ——	1694, —	18	8	0
	The ſame at 3*s.* --	1770, —	13	16	0

It is ſaid there were 60 houſes in this pariſh at the beginning of the preſent century, and 250 inhabitants, whereof 11 were freeholders; yearly births 8, burials 6. *Atkyns.* But the true ſtate of population is as follows. In ten years, from 1700 to 1709 both incluſive, are regiſtered 67 baptiſms and 50 burials; and, from 1760 to 1769 incluſive, 75 baptiſms and 58 burials, and there are 269 inhabitants. Hence it may be obſerved, that about one in forty-ſix dies every year, which ſhews the healthineſs of the air; yet the inhabitants have increaſed very ſlowly, which muſt be attributed to frequent emigrations.

BOURTON *on the* WATER.

THIS pariſh lies in the lower diviſion of the hundred of Slaughter, four miles diſtant ſouth-weſtward from Stow, eight north-weſt from Burford in Oxfordſhire, ſix north-eaſtward from Northleach, and twenty-four eaſtward, inclining to the north, from Glouceſter.

This village is ſituate about a quarter of a mile ſouth-eaſt from the Roman foſs, in a fertile vale, ſurrounded by hills at a pleaſing diſtance, and is watered by a river which riſes a little above it, and, as it enters the village, forms itſelf into an elegant ſerpentine canal about thirty feet wide, flowing, with an agreeable rapidity, about the depth of fourteen or fifteen inches. Many of the houſes are ranged into a ſtreet, tho' ſomewhat irregularly, on each ſide of this natural canal, the banks of which being well gravelled, and very rarely overflow'd, afford a delightful walk. The river is remarkable for fine trout, eel, and crayfiſh. In the centre of the place is a handſome freeſtone bridge of three arches, built in 1756, beſide which there are ſeveral wood bridges for foot paſſengers, at ſuch diſtances as to render the communication perfectly commodious. There is a good raiſed road carried through the place; but it is to be regretted, that ſome of the beſt houſes are not arranged in the ſtreet, which would have made a great addition to the agreeable appearance of this handſome village.

Nature has been laviſh with her favours to this place, and with a little more of the aſſiſtance of her younger ſiſter, Art, it might vie in beauty and elegance with any Dutch village. Many topographers have made no mention of it, and none have done it juſtice; for tho' it has not a market, here are ſhops for the ſupply of goods, and the more neceſſary kinds of trades are carried on as in a market town; and there is reaſon to believe, that it has been much larger and more populous than at preſent, for there are many foundations ſtill viſible, which are undoubtedly the ruins of houſes, as may be concluded from the aſhes of wood and coal that are found about them.

Adjoining to the village, and within the pariſh, is a large quadrangular Roman camp, incloſing about ſixty acres, now divided into twenty fields. The veſtiges of it are moſt perfect to the north-eaſt, where, at a gap in the rampart, a court-leet is held twice a year, for the liberty of Salemaneſbury, the antient name of a hundred now included in that of Slaughter. After calling over the jury, they adjourn to ſome other place to finiſh the buſineſs.

There can be no doubt of the camp being Roman, as many of the coins of that nation have been, and ſtill are, frequently found about it; and a gold ſignet was lately found, weighing near an ounce. The ring-part is ſo very ſmall, that it could not be intended for the finger. The impreſſion on the ſignet is a Roman ſoldier ſitting upon a tripod, with a ſpear in his left hand, holding a victory in the right, and the Roman eagle ſtanding at his feet. Round part of the camp, a paved aqueduct was diſcovered not long ſince, by people who were ſinking a well; and human bones have been often taken up in digging the foundations for walls.

Petrifications of various kinds of ſhell-fiſh are very commonly found in the quarries on Bourton-hill

hill. The moſt remarkable among them is of a ſpiral form, with the contortions ſeparate and diſtinct, in the manner of a cork-ſcrew. It weighs above a pound; but I know not what name to call it by.

It is uncertain what was the name of this place in the time of the Romans, but queſtionleſs it received its preſent appellation from our Saxon anceſtors, on account of the camp or fortification, which they called Beoɲʒ, as I have obſerved elſewhere, and ſo came the name *Burgtone*, as it is written in ſome antient grants.

Three conſiderable brooks meet in this pariſh, one from Guiting, another from Slaughter, and a third from Swell. Theſe are joined below by a brook from Sherbourn, and run in one courſe to Windruſh, from whence the river is called the *Windruſh*, and running to Burford and Witney, empties itſelf into the Thames.

Of the Manor and other Eſtates.

Amongſt the particulars of the eſtates belonging to the abbey church of St. Mary of Eveſham, recorded in *Domeſday-book*, it is expreſs'd after this manner:

'The ſame church holds Bortune, in Salemones 'hundred. There are ten hides. In demean are 'ſix plow-tillages, and ſixteen villeins, and eight 'bordars, and two free men with ſeven plow-'tillages. There is a prieſt with half a plow-'tillage. It was worth 8*l.*' but is now worth '12*l.*' *Domeſday-book*, p. 72.

The abbey of Eveſham purchaſed a charter of free-warren in this place 35 H. 3.

At the diſſolution of abbies this manor came to the crown, and was granted to Edmond lord Chandos 4 Eliz. who died ſeized thereof 15 Eliz. and livery was granted the ſame year to Giles lord Chandos, his ſon. He died in the 44th year of that reign, and was ſucceeded by Grey lord Chandos, his ſon, who was ſeized of this manor in the year 1608, and ſold it to ſir Thomas Edmonds, treaſurer of the houſhold, and privy counſellor to king Charles the Firſt. He left Iſabella, his daughter and coheireſs, married to Henry lord de la Ware, who, in her right, was ſeized of this manor. John lord de la Ware, grandſon to Henry, ſold it to Charles Trinder, eſq; from whom it paſſed to Mr. Boddingham, and from him to Mr. Church, then to Mr. Partridge, and laſtly to Samuel Ingram, eſq; who is the preſent lord of the manor. For his arms ſee *Coln St. Aldwin's*.

Sir Robert Atkyns mentions, that Walter de Burgton, John Rouſe, Edward de Stoure, (or Stonor) and others, were at different times ſeized of Burgton; but this is rather to be underſtood of one of the manors in the preceding pariſh, and not of this, which the abbey of Eveſham continued to poſſeſs 'till that houſe was diſſolved.

Six acres of meadow in Bourton on the Water, lately belonging to the abbey of Eveſham, were granted to ſir Philip Hobbey 37 H. 8.

There is a very handſome modern houſe, built by William Moore, eſq; who married Miſs Collet, daughter of Mr. Collet, late of this place, by whom he had a good eſtate in the pariſh; but he died about the year 1771, without iſſue, and his widow, Mrs. Moore, is the preſent proprietor.

HAMLET. *Nethercot* is a hamlet in this pariſh. It was held of the honour of Wallingford, by Edmond earl of Cornwall 28 E. 1. It was afterwards the eſtate of the abbey of Eveſham, and was granted to William Lloyd and Thomas Parker, in truſt for others, 10 Jac. and is now the property of Mr. Palmer of Bourton.

Of the Church, &c.

The church is a rectory, in the deanery of Stow, worth about 500*l.* a year. The advowſon of the rectory of this church belonged to the priory of Kirkham in Yorkſhire, founded by Walter Eſpee, for monks of the order of St. Auſtin, in the year 1122. At the diſſolution of religious houſes it was veſted in the crown, by which it was granted to ſir Chriſtopher Hatton 21 Eliz.

The reverend Mr. Richard Vernon was the late patron and incumbent. He was ſurvived by his ſiſter Mrs. Dorothy Vernon, who dying unmarried in the year 1764, bequeathed the advowſon of this church to the warden and fellows of All Souls college in Oxford, for ever; who are to preſent perſons qualified according to the directions of her will. The reverend Mr. William Vernon is the preſent incumbent.

The pariſhes of Clapton and Lower Slaughter are annexed to this church; but they are now reputed ſeparate pariſhes, and have their diſtinct officers and rates to taxes.

The rector hath only the third part of the tithes of corn and hay in Bourton and Clapton, but he hath the whole of all other tithes in thoſe places, and the whole tithes of corn and hay in Slaughter.

Thirty acres of meadow, and eighty-five of arable belong to the glebe. The parſonage-houſe is large and well built.

Anthony Palmer, author of a book intituled the *Goſpel New Creature*, was rector of this church in the time of the great civil wars. He was of ſtrong Calviniſtical principles, and firmly adhered to the intereſt of the parliament during thoſe troubles.

The church hath an aile on the ſouth ſide. It is a very antient building, as appears more particularly from the form of the tower, which ſtands between the chancel and the body of the church, and has a roof like a dwelling houſe, with parapet walls inſtead of battlements. The aile was lately rebuilt in the modern taſte, when a ſtone coffin was diſcovered, without any inſcription. In the tower are ſix bells, with a clock and chimes. The church, tower, and chancel are 120 feet long, and 21 feet broad. The aile is 25 feet broad. It is called Clapton-aile, becauſe the inhabitants of that place once ſat there.

There

There was a chantry in this church dedicated to the Virgin Mary, whereof Nicholas Saunders was the laſt incumbent, and retired with a penſion of 3*l.* 6*s.* 8*d.* *Willis.*

Monuments and Inſcriptions.

There is a handſome pyramidal monument of marble againſt the north wall of the chancel, with this inſcription :

In Hoc Cancello contumulantur Reliquiæ
Revdi viri *GEORGII VERNON*, A. M.
Hujuſce Paroch: nec non de *SARSDEN* in Com. Ox.
Rectoris vere pij.
Et *ELISABETHÆ* Viduæ plurimum Mœrentis
Non longo tamen intervallo ſejunctæ.
Ille enim Obijt 17 Dec. 1720, Æt. 83.
Illa 1°. Aprilis 1724, Æt. 80.
Propè jacent duo Filij
THOMAS Infans deceſſit Sep. 10, 1670.
RICHARDUS LL. B. hujus Paroch: poſt Patrem Rector,
Indigentiæ tacitè munificus
Obijt Feb: 18, 1752, Æt. 78.
Hoc in cariſſimorum Memoriam
DOROTHEA VERNON P. P.

At top are theſe arms, *Party per pale*, 1. *Or*, *on a feſs vert three garbs of the field*, for Vernon. 2. *Argent*, *a chevron ſable charged with three maſcles of the firſt*, *between as many pellets each charged with a martlet of the field.*

On the table of a freeſtone monument, againſt the ſouth wall of the church,

IN MEMORY OF ANTHONY COLLETT, Gent. who lies att the Entrance of ye ſeat. His Charity and Zeal for his Religion ſurvives in a Donation of Ten Pounds yearly, for the Inſtruction of twelve poor Boys in the Principles of the Church of England, who Deceas'd in 1719.——At top are theſe arms, *Sable*, *on a chevron*, *between three hinds argent*, *as many annulets Or.*

Firſt fruits, £. 27	2	8	Synodals, £.	0	2	0
Tenths, — 2	14	3	Pentecoſtals,	0	1	1
Procurations, 0	6	8				

Benefaction.

Mr. Anthony Collett gave 10*l.* a year to eſtabliſh a ſchool for teaching twelve poor boys to read, write, and ſay the catechiſm.

Taxes.					
The Royal Aid in	1692, £.	138	0	8
Poll-tax — —	1694, —	50	12	8
Land-tax — -	1694, —	112	0	4
The ſame, at 3*s.*	1770, —	87	19	6

At the beginning of this century, it is ſaid, there were 70 houſes and about 350 inhabitants in this pariſh, whereof 35 were freeholders; annual births 11, burials 8. *Atkyns.* But it is very difficult to give the true ſtate of their population; for ſome of the people of Clapton and Slaughter bury here, and are entered in the pariſh regiſter. Beſides, here is a large congregation of diſſenters, ſome of whom bury at the church, and are regiſtered, others at the meeting-houſe, and are not regiſtered. It appears, however, that from 1700 to 1709 incluſive, there were regiſtered 129 baptiſms and 93 burials; and that from 1760 to 1769, there were 194 baptiſms and 98 burials; and there are about 500 inhabitants. The great diſproportion between the baptiſms and burials ſhews a defect in the regiſter. The inhabitants have increaſed during this century.

BOXWELL *and* LEIGHTERTON.

THIS is a ſmall pariſh, about four miles long from eaſt to weſt, and two broad from north to ſouth. It lies in the hundred of Grumbaldſaſh, ſix miles weſt from Tetbury, four eaſt of Wotton-under-edge, and twenty ſouth from Glouceſter. The ſoil is adapted to tillage and the feeding of ſheep, which are ſecure from the bane, or rot, in every part of the pariſh, and may amount in number, *communibus annis*, to between two and three thouſand.

The village of Boxwell, where the church and houſes are, lies at the top of a little glyn or dale, about half a mile from the turnpike-road from Glouceſter to Bath; and ſeen from ſeveral points of view, appears extremely rural and picturеſque. It is watered by a rill which riſes in the pariſh, and runs through it; and is covered, at an agreeable diſtance, by a hanging wood on one ſide of it; a ſituation particularly eligible in the ſummer ſeaſon, and the ſurrounding hills ſecure it from the bleak and cold winds of the winter.

Leland informs us that there was antiently a nunnery in this place, which ſeems to be extremely well adapted by nature to the peaceful habitation of the religious in early ages; but that houſe was deſtroyed by the Danes.

Boxewelle was the manner of writing the name, as it ſtands upon record ſeven hundred years ago. It is ſuppoſed to have been ſo called from a plentiful ſpring riſing out of a rocky hill, in a ſmall free warren, covered with about ſixteen acres of box-wood, the moſt conſiderable of that kind in England, except Boxhill in Surry. Upon this ſuppoſition, the box-trees muſt have grown here a long time, and this remarkable wood ſtill continues in a flouriſhing ſtate.

Several medicinal and poiſonous plants grow in this warren, as the deadly nightſhade, hemlock, henbane, wild thyme, dwarf elder, marjoram, and ſome others. A conſiderable number of petrifications, commonly, but erroniouſly, ſuppoſed to be of the cockle fiſh, to which indeed it has ſome reſemblance, are found in the hill; and with them the ſerpentine or ſnake ſtones. The latter are ſo called from their likeneſs to a ſerpent cloſely coiled up, with the tail part in the middle; not that they really had their origin from that ſpecies of reptile, which is not only unlikely, but impoſſible; for in that caſe, the head would ſometimes be found perfect in the ſtone, which never happens; and yet that part is full as likely to be turned into ſtone as the body. But the truth is, there are no petrifications of the fleſhy parts of land animals, nor of fiſh, that I ever heard of, except the teſtaceous kinds. And theſe ſtones are generally, if not always accompanied in the beds where they lie, with petrifications of ſhell fiſh ; wherefore it is moſt likely that theſe are marine ſubſtances, and a ſpecies of ſhell fiſh alſo.

There is a large *tumulus* at Leighterton called *Weſt-barrow*, which was opened by Mr. Matthew Huntley, great grandfather of the preſent Mr. Huntley of Boxwell, in which he found three vaults arched over like ovens, and at the entrance of each, an earthen urn, wherein were many aſhes and men's bones imperfectly burnt and broken ; but the ſculls and thigh-bones were whole.

The rill I have mentioned is conſidered as one of the heads of the Berkeley Avon. It produces ſmall trout and crayfiſh at Boxwell. About half a mile from its ſource it joins another little brook from Laſborough, and uniting their waters with a ſtream from Kilcot, take their courſe to Stone and Berkeley, and empty themſelves into the Severn.

Of the Manor and other Eſtates.

'The church of St. Peter of Gloweceſtre holds 'Boxewelle in Grimboldeſtowes hundred. There 'are five hides. In demean are two plow-tillages, 'and twelve villeins, and one radcheniſter, having 'twelve plow-tillages. There are eight *ſervi*, and 'a mill of 5*s.* [rent.] It was worth 70*s.* but is 'now worth 100*s.*' *Domeſday-book*, p. 71.

The abbey of Glouceſter held the manor of Boxwell 17 E. 3. The manor and advowſon of the pariſh and church, with the eſtates at Boxwell, have been many generations in the family of the Huntleys, before the diſſolution of the abbey, partly in fee, and partly by leaſe under that church. John Huntley, of Standiſh, eſq; granted to his ſon Henry Huntley, upon his marriage with Elizabeth, daughter of William Throckmorton, eſq; all his lands, meſſuages, and rights in the manor of Boxwell, 34 H. 8. He then recites a grant of lands and rights in the ſaid manor, and other places, from the abbat and convent of St. Peter's at Glouceſter, dated 24 H. 8. to the ſaid John Huntley for 90 years, ſubject to a yearly payment of 40*l.* 18*s.* 3*d.* which leaſe he alſo ſettles upon his ſon Henry. So that the manor ſeems to have been a joint property between them and the abbey, 'till the diſſolution.

A moiety of lands in Boxwell, Laterton, and Waſt in Hawkeſbury, which antiently belonged to the abbey of Glouceſter, was granted by the crown to Arthur Swayne and William Bennett 41 Eliz. who ſold it to ſir Walter Raleigh in 1601 ; but reverting to the crown upon his attainder, it was granted to Peter Vanlore and William Blake 3 Jac. who ſold it to George Huntley in 1612, as appears by evidences in the poſſeſſion of the reverend Mr. Richard Huntley, who is the preſent lord of this manor, and reſides at Boxwell, where he has a good houſe and pleaſant gardens. His arms are, *Argent, on a chevron between three ſtags heads erazed ſable, as many bugle horns ſtringed of the firſt.*

John Huntley of Standiſh, who lived in the reign of king Henry the Eighth, was ſon of John Huntley, of Rid in Glouceſterſhire, or of Hadnock in Monmouthſhire, and married Alice, daughter of Edward Langley, by whom he had Henry Huntley of Boxwell. Henry, who was brother to George Huntley of Froceſter, married Elizabeth, daughter of William Throckmorton ; and ſurviving her, had to his ſecond wife, Anne, daughter of John Rufford. George Huntley was his ſon and heir, who married Conſtance, daughter and coheireſs of Edward Ferris, by whom he had John Huntley, who married Frances, daughter of ſir John Conway ; but he had a ſecond wife whoſe name was Vaughan. John Huntley was ſon and heir of the laſt John, whoſe ſon Matthew Huntley ſucceeded him in the manor of Boxwell, who was alſo ſucceeded by Richard Huntley, father of the reverend Mr. Richard Huntley, the preſent lord of the manor, as already mentioned.

Mrs. Woodward has a very good houſe here. She is ſiſter to Mr. Huntley. Beſide this and the manor-houſe, there are only ſix others in Boxwell, and no freeholder but the lord of the manor.

HAMLET. Leighterton is ſomething more than a meaſured mile ſouth-eaſt from Boxwell. There are 25 houſes and 120 inhabitants. Leighterinton was held of Humphry de Bohun earl of Hereford and Eſſex, and of Joan his wife, 46 E. 3. and Robert Stanſhaw, eſq; was ſeized of the manor of Leighterton 12 E. 4. The reverend Mr. Richard Huntley is the preſent proprietor of it. This hamlet is rated in payments with Boxwell. It lies high, and in a dry ſummer the inhabitants are much diſtreſſed for water.

Here is a ſmall chapel, with an embattled tower at the weſt end, the patronage of which is veſted in Mr. Huntley.

Mr. Stephens, who married Mr. Huntley's eldeſt ſiſter, has a good houſe in this hamlet, where he reſides.

Of the Church, &c.

The church is a rectory, in the deanery of Hawkeſbury, worth about 140*l.* a year. The reverend Mr. Richard Huntley is patron and incumbent. The advowſon of the rectory of Boxwell belonged to the priory of Walſingham in Norfolk, founded by Jeffrey de Faverches, for black canons, in the reign of king William the conqueror. This advowſon was granted, after the diſſolution, to William Grew and Anthony Forſter 6 Eliz. The abbey of Glouceſter preſented to this church in the year 1541.

About twenty acres in each common field belong to the glebe.

The church is ſmall, with a low ſpire in the middle, and a narrow aile on the north ſide. Several of the family of the Huntleys lie buried under flat ſtones in the chancel ; but there is no remarkable inſcription.

Firſt fruits, £. 23	4	8	Synodals, £.	0	1	8
Tenths, — 2	6	5	Pentecoſtals,	0	0	4
Procurations, 0	5	0				

Benefaction.

Three acres of land in the north field are given toward the repairing of Leighterton chapel.

Taxes.					
The Royal Aid in	1692, £.	73	6	8
Poll-tax — —	1694, —	24	7	0
Land-tax ——	1694, —	63	10	6
The ſame, at 3s. -	1770, —	49	10	9

There were 26 houſes and about 104 inhabitants in this pariſh, whereof 5 were freeholders, at the beginning of this century; yearly births 2, burials 1. *Atkyns.* In a ſeries of eight years, from 1761 to 1767 incluſive, there were regiſtered at Boxwell 11 baptiſms and 6 burials; at Leighterton 31 baptiſms and 19 burials; in all 42 baptiſms and 25 burials; and there are 175 inhabitants. Here we ſee a conſiderable increaſe in the number of inhabitants, of whom only 1 dies in about 54 every year, which ſhews the place to be very healthy. This is further confirmed by the following obſervation: Mr. Wykes Huntley died in the year 1726, who was the third incumbent that had not ſung maſs there.

St. BRIAVEL's.

THIS pariſh lies in the foreſt diviſion of the county, in the hundred of St. Briavel's, to which it gives name, about ſeven miles north from Chepſtow in Monmouthſhire, four ſouth from Colford, and twenty-three weſt from Glouceſter. It is of a middle ſize, about fourteen miles in compaſs, and bounded for three miles on the weſt by the river Wye, which divides it from Monmouthſhire. To the account already given of this river, it ſhould be added, that there is great plenty of elvers taken in it, by means of hair ſieves, every ſpring, which ſome writers have ſuppoſed to be peculiar to the rivers of Somerſetſhire.

It was antiently called Brulais, and reputed to be part of the pariſh of Newland; but I cannot ſo much as gueſs at the meaning of the name, or what gave occaſion to it.

The ſoil is much inclined to clay, and the pariſh lies on very high ground, yet 'tis plentifully ſupply'd with wells and ſprings of water. Three conſiderable brooks, Markſbrook, Woodwards-brook, and Aylesmore-brook riſe here, of which the firſt runs into the Wye, the others empty themſelves into the Severn.

From the church to Bickſwear is a ſteep deſcent, almoſt covered with large blocks of limeſtone, of a grey colour, cloſe grain, and ſhining grit, like the rocks of St. Vincent in Clifton. About a third part of their bulk riſes above the ſurface of the ground, which may be ſaid to be ſtudded with them, as they ſtand ſingly, and make a very odd appearance.

There is a ſtone ſet on end in a piece of ground called *Cloſetuft*, ten feet high above the ſurface, ſix feet broad, and five thick. It is probably a monumental ſtone of the antient Britons, but this is mere conjecture, as there is no inſcription or other thing whatever to direct the judgment concerning it. But the moſt conſiderable remains of antiquity in theſe parts, are thoſe of the caſtle of St. Briavel's, taken notice of by Mr. Camden, and other writers of Engliſh antiquities. The caſtle is environed on every ſide by the lands of this pariſh, but as it is extraparochial, and particularly connected with the foreſt of Dean, it was thought proper to conſider it under that head, p. 31. Where alſo I have endeavoured to give a ſuccinct account of the mine-law court, the court for trying all perſonal actions ariſing within the hundred, &c. which have their peculiar rights and juriſdictions.

The pariſh joins to the foreſt of Dean, in which the inhabitants have a right of common of paſture and common of eſtovers; and they have alſo common of wood and of paſture in Hudnolls, confirmed to them by an act of parliament 20 C. 2.

They have a cuſtom of diſtributing yearly upon Whitſunday, after divine ſervice, pieces of bread and cheeſe to the congregation at church, to defray the expence of which, every houſholder in the pariſh pays a penny to the churchwardens; and this is ſaid to be for the liberty of cutting and taking the wood in Hudnolls. The tradition is, that the privilege was obtained of ſome earl of Hereford, then lord of the foreſt of Dean, at the inſtance of his lady, upon the ſame hard terms that lady Godiva obtained the privileges for the citizens of Coventry.

Brockwear, upon the river Wye, lies partly in this pariſh, and partly in that of Hewelsfield. The tide flows up to this place, and hither the corn, and other products of the country lying upon that river (which is navigable to Glaſebury in Radnorſhire) are brought down in barges, and put on board larger veſſels of about ſixty tons burthen, and carried down the Severn, to Briſtol and other markets.

The great road from Roſs in Herefordſhire, through Colford to Auſt paſſage over the Severn, and ſo to Briſtol, leads through this village.

Of the Manor and other Eſtates.

There is no mention of this place in *Domeſday-book*; but the following account is extracted from other records.

Jeffry Wither held the town of St. Briavel's, with twelve acres of land, and a bailiwick in the foreſt of Dean, 20 Joh. which had been held by his anceſtors.

William de Leſebroke held St. Briavel's in the foreſt of Dean 45 H. 3. and Walter Wither was ſeized of it in the 54th year of the ſame reign.

The

The manors of Newland and St. Briavel's were found to be in the crown by an inquisition 4 E. 1. and paid 33 *l.* a year.

There was a grant of fairs and markets in this town 2 E. 2. and Hugh le Dispencer the younger had a grant of the manor of St. Briavel's, with fairs and markets, 12 E. 2. William de Staure held St. Briavel's 17 E. 2. Robert de Aure held St Briavel's 19 E. 2.

King Henry the Fourth settled St. Briavel's castle, and the town, on John duke of Bedford, his third son, in the first year of his reign, who died seized thereof 14 H. 6. Henry de Aure was seized of St. Briavel's 3 H. 4.

Richard Nevil earl of Warwick, and Anne his wife, were seized of the castle and manor of St. Briavel's, and levied a fine of them to the use of themselves in taille, the remainder to the right heirs of Richard Beauchamp, late earl of Warwick, 6 E. 4. And the same countess afterwards levied a fine of the manor and castle to the use of king Henry the Seventh, in the third year of his reign.

This manor was in the crown in the year 1608, but the earl of Berkeley is the present lord thereof. It was formerly holden by Henry the first duke of Beaufort, whose dutchess dowager parted with it to the Berkeley family.

The Hatheways were antiently possessors of lands in St. Briavel's, and have given their name to a manor within this parish. Ralph Hatheway died seized of lands in St. Briavel's, and in Horeston in the forest of Dean, 10 E. 2. and William Hatheway his son had livery of those lands granted to him the same year. Thomas Hatheway, son of William, died seized of one messuage and forty acres of land in St. Briavel's 5 R. 2.

John Tiptot earl of Worcester was seized of Hatheway's tenement in St. Briavel's 9, 10, and 38 H. 6. The manor of Hatheway's afterwards came to the Baynhams. John Berne levied a fine of lands in St. Briavel's, and of a fishery in the Severn, to sir Alexander Baynham and others 10 H. 7. Thomas Baynham, son of Christopher, had livery of the manor of Hatheway's 20 Eliz. This antient manor, together with a good estate in this parish, is now the property of Charles Wyndham, of Clowerwall, esq.

The abbey of Grace de Dieu [a] in Monmouthshire had two plow-tillages and common of pasture in St. Briavel's, Hermitor, and Penyardwood, 11 H. 3.. The tenants of this manor were admitted to their estates by the constable of the castle 'till that time, when it was ordered, that they should not be admitted for the future, 'till they had compounded for their fines with the king. William Warren died seized of this estate 14 Eliz. It is a manor and grange, called *Stow Grange*, of which Mr. Kedgwin Hoskins, of Clowerwall, is the present proprietor.

William de Staure held one messuage and twelve acres of land, with the castle of St. Briavel's, 2 E. 2. Sir John de Wysham, and Joan his wife, levied a fine of lands in St. Briavel's and Newland, to the use of themselves in taille, the remainder to John de Bures, son of Andrew de Bures, 20 E. 3. William Warren held lands in St. Briavel's 38 E. 3. John Stephens was seized of ten acres, and of 12*s.* rent in St. Briavel's, and of a bailiwick in the forest of Dean, 9 R. 2. William Warren was seized of lands in St. Briavel's, and of a bailiwick in the forest of Dean 7 H. 5. William Baker and his wife levied a fine of lands in St. Briavel's to the use of Thomas Baker 12 H. 7.

There were other lands in St. Briavel's and Redmore's Grove, which belonged to the priory of Lanthony, and were granted to Arthur Porter 32 H. 8.

Bickswear is an antient seat in this parish, upon the banks of the river Wye. The bishop of Landaff was seized of Bickswear 13 E. 2. The abbey of Tintern [b] in Monmouthshire was seized of Bickswear 19 E. 2. This is the estate of major James Rooke, son of the late James Rooke, esq; who had it in right of Joan his wife, the only daughter of Tracy Catchmay, esq. He was son to major general Rooke, of a Kentish family, and married, to his first wife, the countess dowager of Derwentwater, and mother of the unfortunate earl of Derwentwater. The Catchmays, residing for many years in this place, have been of great reputation in this county.

Aylesmore house and estate is the joint property of Mr. Prosser, in right of his wife Frances, and of Miss Elianora Bond, the two daughters and coheiresses of Mr. Richard Bond.

The reverend Mr. James Davies has a good house and estate here and in other places.

Mr. William Gough has a good house and estate at Willsbury in this parish, and in Hewelsfield and Woollaston. He is of an antient family, of British extraction, long resident in this part of the country. Their ancestor, sir Matthew Gough, or Goche, served, with great reputation, in the wars of France, and was slain upon London-bridge by the Kentish rebels, 28 H. 6. William Gough, his descendant, died seized of a capital messuage in Woollaston 5 E. 6. His son William married —— daughter of Mr. Madocke of Wibden, by whom he had George Goughe. He married Mary, one of the three daughters and coheiresses of William Warren of St. Briavel's, and with her had a manor and capital messuage in Hewelsfield. He had issue by Mary his wife, two sons, William

[a] This was a Cistertian priory, founded by John de Monemuth in the year 1233, dedicated to the Virgin Mary, and valued, at the dissolution, at 19*l.* 4*s.* 4*d.*

[b] This abbey was founded by Walter de Clare in 1131, for monks of the Cistertian order, and was valued, at the dissolution, at 256*l.* 11*s.* 6*d.*

who

who ſucceeded him in Hewelsfield; and Warren Goughe, who ſettled at Willſbury. Warren Goughe was one of the verderors of the foreſt of Dean 10 C. He married Dorothy, the daughter of Mr. Barrow of Bream, by whom he had two ſons, Richard and James. Richard married Joice, the daughter of George Kingſtone of Flaxley, and had one ſon William, who married, firſt, Anne, only child of ſir John Douglas, who fell at the battle of Worceſter, 1651; his ſecond wife was Mary, one of the daughters of ſir Nicholas Throckmorton. By his firſt wife he had a ſon Charles Gough, who married Elizabeth, daughter and heireſs of William Smart of Woollaſton, upon the iſſue of which marriage he ſettled his eſtate at Willſbury; and William Gough, the eldeſt ſon of Charles by the ſaid Elizabeth, is the preſent poſſeſſor of Willſbury. In the year 1717, he married Katherine, the only daughter, and at length heireſs of Chriſtopher Portrey, eſq; the grandſon, and heir by his mother, to Morgan Aubrey, of Yniſkedwin, in the county of Brecknock, eſq; where James Gough, eſq; the eldeſt ſurviving ſon, and heir apparent of the ſaid William Gough, now reſides, and has taken the name of Aubrey, which is that of his mother's anceſtors. The arms of Gough are, *Azure, three boars heads couped argent.*

Thomas Foley, of Stoke in Herefordſhire, eſq; ſometime member of parliament for Droitwich, has a good eſtate in this pariſh.

Of the Church, &c.

The church is a vicarage in the Foreſt deanery, annexed to Lidney. It is an impropriation belonging to the dean and chapter of Hereford. The rectorial tithes are in leaſe to Mr. James of Sully, and are worth about 60*l.* a year. There is no vicarage houſe nor glebe, except the church-yard.

The church is dedicated to the Virgin Mary. It is built in the form of a croſs, with a low tower in the middle.

There was a chantry in this church dedicated to the Virgin Mary, whereof Richard Fletcher was the laſt incumbent, and retired with a penſion of 4*l.*

Monuments and Inſcriptions.

There is a handſome monument in the chancel, with the figure of a man and woman in a cumbent poſture, and upon a compartment under them are three children. Two corinthian pillars ſupport a pediment, upon which the figures of Faith, Hope, and Charity are relieved; and upon a ſhield are the arms of Warren, *viz. Checky Or and azure.* There is no inſcription, but the monument was erected to the memory of William Warren and Mariana Catchmay, his wife, from whom the family of James of Sully is deſcended, by Margaret, one of the daughters of that William Warren. He was buried in the church-yard 14 Eliz. by appointment of his will.

Warren Gough, grandſon of the above William Warren, was buried in the ſame grave in 1636, and a handſome tomb, with the arms of Gough, was erected over him.

Several of the families of Whittington, Bond, and Byrkin are buried in the church; and ſeveral of the Catchmays, and of the James's of Sully, or Soilwell, lie in the chancel.

Proc. & Syn. £. 0 6 4 Pentecoſt. £. 0 1 4

Benefactions.

Sir William Whittington gave 3*l.* yearly to put out an apprentice, 3*l.* a year to the poor, 1*l.* 6*s.* 8*d.* for four quarterly ſermons, and 20*s.* a year for adorning the church, for ever.

John Gunning, eſq; gave 5*l.* a year, Mr. William Hoſkins 20*s.* a year, and Mr. John Broban 40*s.* a year, all for the uſe of the poor.

Taxes.					
The Royal Aid in	1692,	£. 159	10	8
Poll-tax — —	1694,	— 32	4	0
Land-tax ——	1694,	— 239	6	8
The ſame, at 3*s.* —	1770,	— 181	10	10

At the beginning of this century there were 80 houſes and about 400 inhabitants in this pariſh, whereof 20 were freeholders; yearly births 14, burials 12. *Atkyns.* In a ſeries of eight years, from 1760 to 1767 incluſive, there are entered in the pariſh regiſter 90 baptiſms and 85 burials. The houſes and cottages are 122, and the preſent number of inhabitants 766; by which it appears that one in 72 dies every year; a proof of the uncommon healthineſs of the place, and longevity of the inhabitants. In the year 1767, five perſons died, whoſe ages put together amounted to 450 years. Thomas Evans and Sarah his wife were two of thoſe perſons, who were born in the pariſh, and having lived in it, in the married ſtate, upwards of 77 years, died within nine days of each other. They have often declared that neither of them was ever blooded, nor had taken phyſic.

BRIMPSFIELD.

THIS pariſh lies in the hundred of Rapſgate, about ſix miles ſouth from Cheltenham, five north-eaſt from Biſley, and ſeven ſouth-eaſt from Glouceſter.

It is ſituate on the brow of that ridge of hills which runs through the county, whence there is a moſt beautiful and extenſive proſpect over the vale and the foreſt, with the lofty mountains in Monmouthſhire on one hand, and the blue hills of Malvern in Worceſterſhire on the other, to terminate the view.

Brimpsfield is a corruption of *Brimesfeld* as it is written in the antient records. It is compounded of bpyme, famous, and ƿelð, the open country.

Here was formerly a caſtle, with four towers, of conſiderable ſtrength. There is no certain account in hiſtory when or by whom it was built; but as the building of caſtles was the prevailing taſte about the reign of king Stephen, its original may be dated as high as that time at leaſt. It was demoliſhed in the barons wars, and there is nothing to be ſeen of it, except ſome traces of the foundation.

Here was alſo an antient monaſtery, of the value of 78 *l.* 19 *s.* 4 *d.* but being a cell to the abbey of St. Stephen de Fonteney in Normandy, as an alien priory, it was diſſolved by act of parliament 2 H. 5. and the lands belonging to it were granted to the college of Windſor, by king Edward the Fourth. *Appendix*, N°. 29. The priory is ſuppoſed to have been an elegant building, as there were windows of poliſhed marble dug up where it ſtood, about the beginning of this century.

In the reign of king Edward the Third, the duke of Clarence was lord of the manor. He purchaſed a charter for a weekly market on Tueſday, and a yearly fair on the eve of the feaſt of *Corpus Chriſti*, both of which have been long ſince diſcontinued. The market and fairs were held upon a part of the town called Haywick; and the men of that place being killed, it was afterwards, upon that occaſion, called *Manleſs-town*, which is the name of a hamlet in the pariſh at this time.

The head of the Stroud river riſes here, and the turnpike-road from Glouceſter to Cirenceſter, which is the *Irminſtreet* of the Romans, extends along the ſide of the pariſh, and divides it from Cowley.

Of the Manor and other Eſtates.

Under the title of lands belonging to Oſbern Gifard, in *Domeſday-book*, it is expreſſed after this manner :

'The ſame Oſbern holds Brimesfelde in Reſpi- 'get hundred. There are nine hides taxed. Duns 'held it of earl Harold. There are three plow- 'tillages in demean, and ſixteen villeins, and ſix 'bordars, and a prieſt, with twelve plow-tillages. 'There are eight *ſervi*, and four *ancillæ*, and two 'mills of 64 *d.* [rent.] In Glouceſter are five 'burgages of 2 *s.* It is worth and was worth '12 *l.* *Domeſday-book*, p. 77.

This Oſbern Gifard, or Giffard, was deſcended from count Giffard, a great nobleman of Normandy. William earl of Arques, uncle to the Conqueror, attempted to gain the dukedom of Normandy to himſelf, during the duke's minority; but count Giffard, who was general for the young duke, fought him, and obtained a complete victory. Oſbern attended the Conqueror in the invaſion of England, and for his ſervices was rewarded with this and three other manors in Glouceſterſhire.

Elias Giffard, ſon of Oſbern, gave lands and woods in Bockholt, in this pariſh, to the abbey of Glouceſter, about the year 1100. Elias his ſon was a monk in Glouceſter abbey, and gave to that church the manor of Croneham, the church of St. Mary at Bitton, the church of St. George at Orcheſton, and the chapel of St. Andrew at Winterborn. Elias, grandſon to the laſt Elias, died 2 R. 1. and was ſucceeded by Thomas Giffard, and after him another Elias Giffard, who took part with the rebellious barons againſt king John, who ſeized his lands in the 18th year of his reign, and granted them to Bartholomew Peeche. But they were reſtored to Giffard again, in the beginning of the reign of king Henry the Third, and he died in the 33d year of that reign.

John his ſon and heir ſucceeded him. He was made governor of St. Briavel's caſtle, and warden of the foreſt of Dean, 47 H. 3. He married Maud Longeſpee, widow of William Longeſpee, ſon of William earl of Saliſbury, and daughter and heir to Walter de Clifford, and carried her to his caſtle of Brimpsfield. She makes complaint to the king, and afterwards deſiſts from her complaint, but paid a fine of 300 marks for marrying without licence. He purchaſed a charter of free-warren in the manors of Badgworth, Stonehouſe, Rockhampton, Stoke-Giffard, and Tetbury, and in divers manors in other counties, 9 E. 1. He founded Glouceſter-hall in Oxford 11 E. 1. for twelve monks choſen out of the abbey of Glouceſter; but afterwards, other monaſteries of the order of St. Benedict contributing to the enlargement of the buildings, with the conſent of the founder and of the abbat of Glouceſter, partook of the benefit of that foundation. He died at Bitton 27 E. 1. and was buried at Malmeſbury, having been ſummoned as a baron to parliament from the 23d year of that reign to his death.

He was ſucceeded by his ſon John Giffard, called *John the Rich*, who took part with the barons againſt the Spencers, and therefore king Edward the Second, in his march from Cirenceſter to Worceſter, ſent ſoldiers to demoliſh his caſtle at Brimpsfield. He was afterwards taken priſoner at the battle of Burroughbridge, and ſent to Glouceſter to be executed as a traytor.

Upon his attainder, the caſtle and manor of Brimpsfield were granted to Hugh le Diſpencer the elder, with remainder to Hugh the younger, 15 E. 2. but the ſcene of affairs changing, all the lands, lately belonging to John Giffard, were granted to John Maltravers 1 E. 3. as a reward for murdering the late king. He procured a confirmation of the manor from John de Callew, the heir of the Giffards, who levied a fine, and acknowledged the right of John Maltravers 4 E. 3. He was ſoon after convicted of high miſdemenors, and his eſtate ſeized.

The cuſtody of the caſtle and manor of Brimpsfield was granted for life to Maurice Berkeley, ſecond ſon of Maurice lord Berkeley, 14 E. 3. upon whoſe death, 22 E. 3. the king granted the manor and caſtle to his third ſon Lionel de Antwerp, duke of Clarence, to whom ſir John Maltravers levied a fine thereof 26 E. 3.

Edmund

Edmund de Mortimer, earl of March and Ulfter, married Philippa, daughter and heir of Lionel duke of Clarence, whereby he was intituled to the manor of Brimpsfield, which, from this time, acknowledged the fame proprietors as that of Bifley, (to which the reader is referred) 'till they both came to the crown, by the death of Cicely dutchefs of York, 10 H. 7. Brimpsfield was then fettled by king Henry the Eighth, on queen Catherine.

In the firft year of king Edward the Sixth, this manor and park, and lands called *Hafel-hanger*, [probably from the Britifh *hen-gaer, i.e.* an old wall or fortification,] were granted to fir John Bridges, afterwards lord Chandos, who died feized thereof 4 Mariæ. Livery of the manor and park of Brimpsfield was granted the fame year to his fon Edmond lord Chandos, who died feized thereof 16 Eliz. and was fucceeded in honour and this eftate by Giles lord Chandos his fon and heir. He died feized thereof 36 Eliz. and left two daughters coheireffes; Elizabeth, married to fir John Kenida; and Catherine, married to Francis lord Ruffel of Thornhagh.

From thefe the manor was transferred to Miles Sandys, of Latimers in Buckinghamfhire, fifth fon of William Sandys, and younger brother of Edwin Sandys archbifhop of York. He was feized of this manor in the year 1608, and was high fheriff of Gloucefterfhire in the year 1625. He died feized of the manor of Brimpsfield 17 Car. Sir Edwin Sandys,[c] his fecond fon, (his elder brother, fir George, dying without iffue) fucceeded to this eftate. William was the eldeft fon of fir Edwin, and for his prodigality was called *Golden Sandys*. He died without iffue, but fold this manor to his uncle, fir William Sandys of Miferden. Miles Sandys, fon of William of Miferden, fucceeded to this eftate, and was high fheriff of the county 30 C. 2. From him it went to William Sandys, of Miferden, efq; fon of Miles, who fold it, and it is now the property of lord Edgecumbe, who holds a court-leet here. The old manfion houfe is gone to ruin, and the park turned into a farm. His lordfhip's arms are, *Gules, on a bend ermines, cotoifed Or, three boars heads couped argent.* CREST. *On a wreath Or and gules, a boar paffant argent, about the neck, a chaplet of oak-leaves vert, fructed proper.* SUPPORTERS. *On each fide, a greyhound argent, guttée de poix, collar'd dovetail double gules.* MOTTO. AU PLAYSIRE FORT DE DIEU.

HAMLETS. 1. *Caudle-green* is a hamlet in this parifh, eaftward of the church.

2. *Manlefs-town*, already mentioned, is the name of another hamlet, if a place may be fo called which has no houfe in it.

3. *Birdlip*, fo much of it as lies on the fouth fide of the road, is in this parifh, the reft in Cowley.

Of the Church, &c.

The church is a rectory, in the deanery of Stonehoufe, worth about 80*l.* a year. Lord Edgecumbe is patron, the reverend Dr. White the prefent incumbent.

There are thirty acres of arable, and feven of pafture belonging to the glebe.

The church is fmall, with a low tower in the middle.

	£.				£.		
Firft fruits,	9	11	11	Synodals,	0	2	0
Tenths, —	0	19	1	Pentecoftals,	0	0	7
Procurations,	0	6	8				

Benefaction.

The intereft of 20*l.* given by feveral benefactors, is diftributed annually at Eafter, among the fecond poor of this parifh.

Taxes.			£.		
The Royal Aid in	1692,	£.	96	9	4
Poll-tax — —	1694,	—	13	19	0
Land-tax ——	1694,	—	90	17	0
The fame at 3*s.* --	1770,	—	50	12	0

At the beginning of this century there were 52 houfes and 200 inhabitants in this parifh, whereof 10 were freeholders; yearly births 7, burials 7. *Atkyns.* Since that time population has increafed. The average of annual births is 8, of burials 5; the prefent number of houfes 63, of inhabitants 283; fo that, in this healthy fituation, about one in fifty-fix dies annually.

BROADWELL.

THIS parifh lies in the upper divifion of the hundred of Slaughter, about two miles diftant northward from Stow-on-the-Wold, eight fouth from Campden, and twenty-fix north-eaftward from Gloucefter.

The name is derived from the large fpring which rifes in this place near the manor-houfe, and runs into the Evenlode, and fo into the Thames.

The lands are chiefly arable, with a little pafture.

Of the Manor and other Eftates.

In *Domefday-book* it is recorded after this manner: 'The fame church [St. Mary of Evefham] holds 'Bradewelle in Salemones hundred. There are 'ten hides. There are fix plow-tillages in de'mean; and thirteen *fervi*, and twenty-five vil'leins, and eight bordars, and one free-man, and 'a prieft, having between them all twelve plow'tillages. In Glouuecefter there are four bur'gages, and in Wincelcombe one, paying 27*d.* 'The whole was worth 8*l.* but is now worth 12*l.*' *Domefday-book*, p. 72.

In fir Robert Atkyns's abftract from *Domefday-book*, Bradewelle is faid to have been held by the

[c] Pedigree of this family in the poffeffion of *William Bayntun*, efq.

church

church of St. Mary of Wincelcumbe, in the reign of king William the Conqueror. But that was a miſtake, which, I apprehend, he was led into by an imperfect copy of that record; for I have myſelf ſeen a copy thereof, in which the head or title XII. *Terra S. Marie de Eveſham*, and the accounts of Malgereſberie, Tedeſtrop, and Bortune were omitted; whereby the manors of Bradewelle, Svelle, Willerſei, Weſtune, Stoch, and Hedecote, which all belonged to the laſt mentioned abbey, ſeemed to be the property of that of Wincelcumbe, whoſe eſtates are placed immediately before thoſe of the church of Eveſham in order. And I am the rather induced to account for the miſtake in this manner, becauſe the learned hiſtorian has fallen into the ſame error with reſpect to the five other manors above mentioned alſo. This matter will be clearly underſtood by inſpecting the printed copy of *Domeſday* at p. 71 and 72.

The abbey of Eveſham purchaſed a charter of free-warren in Bradwell, and divers other manors, 35 H. 3.

The maſter of the knights-templers was ſeized of court-leet, waifs, and felons goods in Bradwell, by the grant of king Henry the Third, which privileges were allowed, in a writ of *Quo warranto*, 15 E. 1. Thomas de Beauchamp earl of Warwick, and others, held Bradwell 24 E. 3. William de Clinton earl of Huntingdon died ſeized of the manor of Bradwell 28 E. 3. But notwithſtanding I find theſe records applied to this pariſh by ſir Robert Atkyns, there is reaſon to believe that they ſhould be referred to ſome other of the name of Bradwell; for this manor continued in the poſſeſſion of the abbey of Eveſham 'till the diſſolution of that houſe.

It is probable that Richard Andrews had a grant of this manor, and the advowſon of the church, from the crown, ſoon after the diſſolution; for he and Urſula his wife levied a fine of Bradwell, and of the advowſon of the church, to the uſe of Thomas Baſkerville and Anne his wife 6 E. 6.

— Ligon died ſeized of this manor 9 Eliz. and livery of it was granted the ſame year to Richard Ligon his ſon and heir.

Elianor Talbot, widow, was poſſeſſed of it in the year 1608, ſoon after which it was purchaſed by Mr. Hodges. Danvers Hodges, eſq; was lord of it at the beginning of this century; and Henry Danvers Doughty Hodges, eſq; is the preſent proprietor of it, and has a handſome ſeat here, built on the ſcite of the old houſe, by Dr. Chamberlayne, late dean of Briſtol, who married a daughter of the late Mr. Hodges. His arms are, *Argent, three creſcents ſable. In a canton a coronet*

The meadow called Burybradnam in Broadwell, belonged to the abbey of Eveſham, and was granted to ſir Philip Hobbey 37 H. 8.

Of the Church, &c.

The church is a rectory in the deanery of Stow. Adleſtrop is annexed to it, and both together are worth about 350*l.* a year. The advowſon, and great part of the tithes antiently belonged to the abbey of Eveſham. The abbat and convent preſented to this church in 1402. They granted all their tithes, except of their demeans, whilſt in their own hands, to the incumbent, in the year 1450, reſerving in all 6*l.* yearly; which rent is now paid out of the rectory to the patron. The heir of the late James Leigh, eſq; is patron; the reverend Mr. Leigh the preſent incumbent.

The church hath an aile on the ſouth ſide, and a tower at the weſt end. There is a chapel in the aile, belonging to Mr. Hodges, where ſeveral of that name lie buried, and there is an antient monument erected to their memory. There is another handſome monument in the aile, in memory of Herbert Weſton, eſq; who died in 1635.

Firſt Fruits, £. 23	11	8	Synodals, £. 0	1	6
Tenths, — -- 2	7	2	Pentecoſtals, 0	0	6
Procurations, - 0	6	8			

Benefactions.

Three little houſes, a piece of meadow ground, and ſome land in the field are given for repairing the church.

Taxes.			£.	s.	d.
	The Royal Aid in	1692, £.	116	14	0
	Poll-tax — —	1694, —	15	8	8
	Land-tax — -	1694, —	87	1	0
	The ſame, at 3*s.*	1770, —	67	2	0

At the beginning of this century there were 30 houſes and about 126 inhabitants in this pariſh, whereof 15 were freeholders; yearly births 5, burials 4. *Atkyns.* But the inhabitants are nearly doubled ſince that time, being in number 245.

BROCKWORTH.

THIS pariſh is ſituate in the vale part of the county, in the upper diviſion of the hundred of Dudſton and King's-barton; ſix miles diſtant ſouth from Cheltenham, five north from Painſwick, and four eaſt from Glouceſter. It lies on the antient Roman way called the *Irminſtreet*, ſome traces of which may ſtill be diſcovered hereabout, where the ſand and ſtone of the old road, being cut through by the long uſe of carriages, appear, in the banks on the ſides of it, diſtinctly from the natural ſoil.

Cooper's-hill, in this pariſh, is taken notice of by ſir Robert Atkyns, as being the place of reſidence of John Theyer, a learned antiquary, and a firm loyaliſt to king Charles the Firſt. He had the advantage of the library of the priory of Lanthony near Glouceſter, which his grandfather, who had married the ſiſter of Richard Hart, the laſt prior, had procured into the family. Theyer died in the year 1673, and left eight hundred manuſcripts, which were purchaſed by king Charles the Second for the library at St. James's. In

In the antient record the name of this place is written *Brocowardinge*, which ſignifies *Broco's place*, from the Anglo-Saxon ƿorð, or ƿeorð, already explained under Aldeſworth.

The pariſh is ſmall, conſiſting of rich arable and paſture ground. A brook runs through it in its courſe to the Severn, by Sandhurſt.

Of the Manors and other Eſtates.

In *Domeſday-book* it is thus written :

'Hugo Laſne holds Brocowardinge in Dudeſtan 'hundred of the king. There are five hides. 'Turchil held it of king Edward. In demean are 'two plow-tillages, and eight villeins, and ſix 'bordars, and a prieſt, and two free men, and a 'ſteward, who have between them all fifteen plow-'tillages. There are four *ſervi*, and a mill of 2*s*. '[rent;] a wood one mile long, and half a mile 'broad. It was worth 6*l.* now [only] 100*s*.' *Domeſday-book*, p. 77.

The greateſt part of this pariſh was in the poſſeſſion of the Chandos's before the reign of king John; which king, in his charter of confirmation to the priory of Lanthony, recites the particulars given to the canons of that houſe, among which are the following: The church of Brockewordin given by Robert de Chandos, with half a hide of land and a houſe on the weſt ſide of the church-yard; and the land called Norbroc in Brockwordyn, and two new-plowed grounds which Richard de Brockwordyn gave unto them; and half a yard-land which was Aldred's; and whatſoever was given by Roger de Chandos the younger in Brockwordyn, and the lands in Brockwordyn which the canons had in exchange for Kyneceſtre. *Appendix*, N°. 19.

The priory of Lanthony had free warren in Brockworth 15 & 21 E. 1. and enjoyed this manor 'till that houſe was diſſolved. After the diſſolution, the manor and appurtenances, together with the tithes of the demeans, were granted to John Gyes, eſq; in exchange for Aſple Gyes in Bedfordſhire, and for Widdington in Oxfordſhire 32 H. 8. and have continued in that family ever ſince, ſo that ſir William Gyſe, Baronet, is the preſent lord of this manor, and has a large eſtate in the pariſh; for an account of whoſe family and arms, ſee *Rendcombe*.

The abbey of Glouceſter was ſeized of another manor in this pariſh. John Deffeld, the abbat, purchaſed of ſir Lawrence de Chandos fifty-five acres of arable land, and ſeveral houſes in Brockworth, and forty acres of incloſure, and all his wood in Bockholt, containing 300 acres, 44 H. 3. which particulars were afterwards conveyed to Reginald de Hamme, who was the next ſucceeding abbat. See p. 134.

Walter of Glouceſter and Hawiſe his wife held the manor of Brockworth of the abbey of Glouceſter at half a knight's-fee, and the manor of Elbrugge, 5 E. 2. *Eſc. ſub anno.*

Henry Brockworth was ſeized of Brockworth, it is ſuppoſed as tenant to the abbey of Glouceſter, 22 E. 3. The abbey of Glouceſter was ſeized of it 49 E. 3. At the diſſolution of that abbey, the biſhoprick of Glouceſter was erected, and endowed with the manor of Droiſcourt in this pariſh, which belonged to St. Peter's abbey.

Henry le Drogue was ſeized of one yard-land in Brockworth, and was attainted of felony 28 E. 1.

HAMLETS. 1. *Cooper's-hill*, of which already.

2. *Elbrug.* Walter of Glouceſter held the manor of Elbrugg 5 E. 2. Sir Robert de la Mere and Maud his wife were ſeized of this manor 5 R. 2. Leonard Pool, eſq; of Saperton, died ſeized of the manor of Elbridge 30 H. 8. and livery thereof was granted the ſame year to his ſon Giles.

Of the Church, &c.

The church is a vicarage in the deanery of Winchcombe, worth about 20*l*. a year. The rectory belonged to the priory of Lanthony, and was granted to Robert earl of Leiceſter, in exchange for other lands, 16 Eliz. Sir William Gyſe is patron and impropriator.

The church is dedicated to St. George. It has a low tower between the body of the church and the chancel.

Monuments and Inſcriptions.

There is a handſome marble monument in the chancel for ſir Chriſtopher Gyſe, baronet, erected by his ſon ſir John Gyſe. He died in the year 1670, having been a great promoter of the recovery of the hundred of Dudſton and King's-barton from the city of Glouceſter to the county at large. Dudſton and King's-barton were formerly two diſtinct hundreds in the county of Glouceſter, but had been made part of the In-county, and appurtenant to the city of Glouceſter.

	£.	s.	d.		£.	s.	d.
Firſt fruits,	6	17	0	Synodals,	0	2	0
Tenths, —	0	13	8*ob*.	Pentecoſtals,	0	11	0*ob*.
Procurations,	0	6	8				

Taxes.		£.	s.	d.
The Royal Aid in	1692,	106	5	4
Poll-tax — —	1694, —	14	5	0
Land-tax ——	1694, —	111	16	0
The ſame, at 3*s*. -	1770, —	83	17	0

About the year 1710 there were 50 houſes and about 200 inhabitants, whereof 10 were freeholders; yearly births 8, burials 6. *Atkyns*. But in a ſeries of ten years from 1760 to 1769 incluſive, there were 84 baptiſms and 60 burials; and the preſent number of inhabitants is 253; ſo that they bury one in forty-two every year.

****

BROMSBOROW,

LIES in the hundred of Botloe, in the foreſt diviſion of the county, four miles diſtant ſouth from Ledbury in Herefordſhire, five north from Newent, and twelve northward from Glouceſter. One part of it extends to the top of Malvern-hill; and the Glinch, a ſmall brook, runs from hence into the river Leden. The whole pariſh is ſandy ground.

Lambard was miſtaken in the geography of this place, who repreſents it as ſtanding upon the river Severn, from which, in reality, it is diſtant eight or ten miles, being nearer the Wye than the Severn. He calls it *a town which Ethelfleda, ſiſter of Edward, and doughter of Ethred kinge of Mercia builded* 913. *It is famous amonges hyſtoriens for a victorie that Adelſtan had theare over Anlaf kinge of Irland, which gatheringe an army of Scottes and Danes, came againſt Atthelſtane with* 615 *ſhippes, whom Adelſtane metinge at this place, overthrew, ſo that he reigned ever after peaceably. Of this victorie the Saxons made a Pamphlet or Ryme, which begynneth,* Ædelſtean cyninȝ, *&c.* Lambard's Eng. and Wales, p. 26.

The name ſeems to be compoſed of Bꞃyme, A. S. *famous*, and beꞃȝ, *a town*, or beoꞃȝ, *a caſtle, hill*, or *fortification*.

Of the Manor and other Eſtates.

Domeſday-book gives the following account of this manor:

'The ſame Radulfus [de Todeni] holds Brunmeberge in Botelau hundred. There are five hides. Earl Herald held it. In demean is one plow-tillage, and eleven villeins, and eight bordars, with fourteen plow-tillages. There is one *ſervus*. A wood two miles long and one broad. It was worth 8*l.* now 100*s.*' *Domeſday-book*, p. 76.

The manor of Bromſborough was granted to Roger de Toni 6 Joh. John de Penrys was ſeized of Bromſborow 15 E. 1. William de Whitefeld had free warren in Bromeſborow 14 E. 2. Thomas de Beauchamp, earl of Warwick, was ſeized of the manor of Bromberghe 2 H. 4.

This manor afterwards belonged to the Bromwicks, deſcended from Wido de Bromwick, who reſided at a place of that name in Warwickſhire, 15 H. 2. and Henry de Caſtle-Bromwick was grandſon to Wido. A younger branch of this family ſettled here in the reign of king Richard the Second, and ſir John Bromwich and Catherine his wife levied a fine of the manor and advowſon of Bromſborough, to the uſe of themſelves in ſpecial tailie, 10 R. 2. and that family continued here 'till the ſeventeenth century.

This manor afterwards came to the Yates. Walter Yate, eſq; was lord of it at the beginning of this century. He died without iſſue male, whereby John Yate, of Arlingham, eſq; his nephew, became poſſeſſed of this eſtate, and died unmarried.

Robert Dobyns, eſq; on the death of the above John, aſſumed the name and arms of Yate, and took all the eſtates of Walter Yate, in purſuance of his will. He was high-ſheriff of this county in 1765, but died before the expiration of that year; leaving two ſons and four daughters, by his wife Elizabeth, the daughter of Richard Gorges, of Eye, in the county of Hereford, eſq. Robert-Gorges-Dobyns Yate, eſq; eldeſt ſon of Robert Dobyns, is the preſent lord of this manor, and proprietor of the eſtates of the ſaid Walter Yate. He hath a very handſome, new-built ſeat, called *Bromſborough Place*, and a good eſtate in this pariſh. His arms are, Quarterly, 1. *Azure, a feſs Or, in chief two mullets of the ſecond*, for Yate. 2. *Azure, a chevron between three annulets Or*, for Dobyns. 3. *Gules, a chevron between ten croſſes pattée, ſix above and four below, argent*, for Berkeley. 4. *Gules, a ſtag's head caboſhed Or*, for . MOTTO. QUO VIRTUS VOCAT.

John Hawkeſlow and his wife levied a fine of lands in Bromſborough, to the uſe of John Machin and his wife, 13 H. 7. Mrs. Nanfan, widow of John Nanfan, eſq; has a good houſe called *Brownſend*, and a good eſtate in this pariſh. The *Grove-houſe* and eſtate is the property of Mr. William Brooke.

HAMLET. Woodend is a ſmall hamlet in this pariſh, conſiſting of two houſes.

Of the Church, &c.

The church is a rectory in the foreſt deanery, worth 140*l.* a year. Robert-Gorges-Dobyns Yate, eſq; is patron; the reverend Mr. Hayward the preſent incumbent.

The glebe conſiſts of about ſixty acres.

The church hath a ſmall tower at the weſt end; it is dedicated to the Virgin Mary.

Monument and Inſcription.

There is an inſcription in the chancel for Ricius Yate, eſq; a branch of the Arlingham family, who married Catherine, daughter of Thomas Wall, of Lintridge, eſq. He died in 1690. Beneath is this apoſtrophe:

Nunc Amice ſpectator, et quantillum contra Mortem valeant iſta mortalia, Opes, Robur, Ingenium, ſerio nec ſero meditere.

Firſt Fruits, £.	7	15	0	Synodals, £.	0	2	0
Tenths, — --	0	15	6	Pentecoſtals,	0	1	4
Procurations, -	0	7	6				

Benefactions.

Two cottages, a garden, and five acres of arable land in one piece, one acre called Church-meadow, another called Gooſeacre, a piece of arable in Brookman's-field, another piece in a field called Mugles, another piece at Woodend-ſtreet, and another piece intermixt with Mr. Yate's land, are given for the uſe of the church.

Mrs. Catherine Yate gave 40*l.* a year, and Walter Yate, eſq; gave 30*l.* a year, to the poor of this pariſh.

Taxes.			£.	s.	d.
	The Royal Aid in	1692, £.	74	8	0
	Poll-tax — —	1694, —	23	11	0
	Land-tax ——	1694, —	82	8	4
	The ſame, at 3*s.* —	1770, —	61	16	3

At the beginning of this century there were 20 houſes and about 80 inhabitants in this pariſh, whereof 7 were freeholders; yearly births 3, burials 2. *Atkyns.* In the year 1770 there were 138 inhabitants.

BROCKRUP,

BROCKRUP, *or* BROCKTHORP.

THIS pariſh lies in the hundred of Dudſton and King's-barton, ſix miles diſtant north from Stroud, three weſt from Painſwick, and four ſouth-eaſt from Glouceſter. It is a ſmall pariſh, conſiſting almoſt intirely of paſture land.

Doꞃp, ðꞃep, or ðꞃop, in the Anglo-Saxon, ſignifies a *ſtreet*, or *village*. This place, as I conjecture, was the property of ſome perſon, in the Saxon times, whoſe name it bears; and it might be either *Bros*, *Broc*, or *Bruc*, as it is differently written in the records; but I know no authority for writing it, as I have ſeen it, *Brookrup*.

I find nothing of ſingular note here; but Corbet relates a circumſtance that happened to the parliament's troops at this place, which I ſhall juſt mention.

'Two thouſand men of the king's forces, after 'the ſiege of Glouceſter, marching from Tewkeſ- 'bury to Painſwick, the governor Maſſie ſallied 'out of Glouceſter with two hundred muſketiers, 'and a hundred horſe, and marched to the top of 'Brockthorp-hill, there to expect the enemy, 'whom he found divided into three bodies, and 'himſelf born down by the multitude; for whilſt 'two parties faced him, the third ſtole down a 'hollow lane, and had almoſt ſurrounded him 'unawares, by the negligence of the ſcouts; ſo that 'our whole body was brought into great danger, 'driven by a ſudden and confuſed retreat, and the 'governor himſelf left deeply engaged: Yet moſt 'of our men got off, being preſerved by the gal- 'lantry of a few reſolved men, that ſtood in the 'breach; and of them captain George Maſſie 'ſtriving to retard the purſuit, grappled with three 'together, hand to hand, received a very ſore 'wound in the head, and was happily reſcued by 'a ſerjeant of the company. Of ours, two lieu- 'tenants and ſixteen private ſoldiers were taken 'priſoners; the reſt in diſorder ran down a ſteep, 'through a rough and narrow lane, and recovered 'a houſe at the foot of the hill, where a party was 'left to make good the retreat, and the enemy 'durſt not purſue; by which means all the bottom 'was preſerved from ſpoil.' *Military Government of Glouceſter.*

Of the Manor and other Eſtates.

This eſtate ſtands under the title *Terra Regis*, in *Domeſday-book*, where it is ſaid,

'In Broſtrop Aluric held three virgates of land. 'He had here two plow-tillages and one villein, 'three bordars and four *ſervi*. Theſe five eſtates '[Herſefel, Athelai, Sanher, Herſecome, and 'Broſtrop] earl Herald took away after the death 'of king Edward; and Roger de Lurei put them 'to farm for 46*l.* 13*s.* 4*d.*' *Dom. Book*, p. 67.

Adeline, the widow of Roger de Ivori, gave this manor to the abbey of Glouceſter 1103, and king Stephen confirmed it by his grant, wherein ſhe is called Adeline de Ibreo, occaſioned by tranſlating the name Ivori into Latin. She was daughter of Hugh de Grantmaiſnil.

Elias Giffard and Ala his wife, and their ſon Elias, granted to the monks of Glouceſter, by deed, which they laid upon the altar, all their land in Bruckrup, eſtimated at half a hide, and half a yard-land, free from all cuſtoms, except dane-gelt due to the king, 21 H. 1.

Roger the Firſt, and Hugh his heir, gave to the church of St. Peter at Glouceſter eight acres of land near to Brockrup-court, whilſt Hameline was abbat; which grant was confirmed by Gilbert de Myners, about the end of the reign of king Stephen.

The abbey of Glouceſter was ſeized of the manor of Brockrup 17 E. 3. which was held of Humphry de Bohun, earl of Hereford and Eſſex, and of Joan his wife, 46 E. 3. and continued in poſſeſſion of it 'till that houſe was diſſolved. After the diſſolution of the abbey, the manor of Brockrup was granted to the biſhoprick of Glouceſter 33 H. 8. and was confirmed to it 6 E. 6. to which it now belongs.

Roger le Rus was ſeized of three yard-lands in Bruckrup, which belonged to the Bertune of Glouceſter, 22 E. 1. There were lands and a portion of tithes in this pariſh, which belonged to the priory of Lanthony. The lands were granted to Richard Andrews and Nicholas Temple, in truſt for others, 35 H. 8. The tithes were granted to ſir William Ryder 17 Jac.

Of the Church, &c.

The church is a vicarage in the deanery of Glouceſter, worth about 55*l.* a year. The dean and chapter of Glouceſter are patrons; the reverend Mr. John Newton incumbent. This living has been augmented with queen Anne's bounty, and a legacy bequeathed by one Mr. Hodges.

The impropriation belongs to the dean and chapter of Glouceſter, worth about 50*l.* a year. It pays 1*l.* 13*s.* 4*d.* a year to the vicar, and ſixteen throw of wheat, ſixteen throw of beans, and thirteen buſhels and a half of peaſe. In the taxation of eccleſiaſtical preferments, 19 E. 1. 'tis ſaid, *Eccleſ. de Brockthorp 2 marc.*

The church is dedicated to St. Swithin. It is ſmall, with a little, low, embattled tower at the weſt end.

Firſt fruits, *l.*	7	17	6	Synodals, *l.*	0	2	0
Tenths, —	0	15	9	Pentecoſtals	0	0	4*ob.*
Procurations,	0	0	0				

Benefaction.

Forty ſhillings a year are allotted to this pariſh out of the charity of Mr. Cox of Sandhurſt.

Taxes.					
The Royal Aid in	1692, £.	93	12	0
Poll-tax —	1694, —	6	4	0
Land-tax ——	1694, —	103	4	0
The ſame at 3*s.*	1770, —	77	18	0

In the year 1562, there were 16 houſholders in this pariſh.—At the beginning of this century there

there were 40 houſes and 200 inhabitants, whereof 5 were freeholders; yearly births 5, burials 4. *Atkyns.* But there are now only 107 inhabitants, ſo that population declines.

BUCKLAND.

THIS pariſh lies in the lower diviſion of the hundred of Kiftſgate, five miles diſtant weſt from Campden, ſix ſouth from Eveſham, and twenty-three eaſtward from Glouceſter.

The church and houſes are ſituate on an eaſy acclivity, at the foot of the great ridge of hills which parts the vale from the cotſwold country, with an aſpect towards the weſt. The pariſh conſiſts of good arable, paſture, and wood-lands.

The village obtained its name from the tenure of the land by a deed in writing, which was antiently called *Bocland*: So other land, which was not held by writing, was called *Folcland*, as having no other evidence than the teſtimony of the folk or people. See p. 65.

Kynred, king of the Mercians, gave the manor of Bocland to the monaſtery of Glouceſter, when Edburg was abbat. *Domeſday-book* gives the following particulars:

'The ſame church [St. Peter of Glowec.] holds 'Bocheland in Wideles hundred. There are ten 'hides. In demean are three plow-tillages, and 'twenty-two villeins, and ſix bordars, with twelve 'plow-tillages. There are eight *ſervi*, and ten 'acres of meadow. It was worth 3*l.* but is now 'worth 9*l.*' *Domeſday-book*, p. 71.

The abbey of Glouceſter held this manor 17 E. 3. and continued poſſeſſed of it 'till the diſſolution. It was then granted to ſir Richard Greſham, lord mayor of London, in exchange for lands in Yorkſhire, 38 H. 8. Sir John Thynne married, to his firſt wife, Chriſtian, daughter of ſir Richard Greſham,[d] and ſiſter and heir to ſir Thomas Greſham, who founded and endowed Greſham-college, and built the Royal Exchange in London; with whom he had the manor of Buckland, which has ever ſince continued in that family. Livery of this manor was granted to John Thynne, ſon of ſir John, 22 Eliz. James Thynne, eſq; was lord of it, and left it to his nephew Thomas Thynne, eſq; ſon of Henry. Lord viſcount Weymouth is the preſent lord of this manor, and has a ſeat near the church, and a large eſtate in this pariſh. His lordſhip's arms, &c. are given under *Bagendon.*

HAMLET. *Laverton*, a tithing in this pariſh, lies about a mile from the church. It has always acknowledged the ſame proprietor as Buckland. There was a chapel in this hamlet, which is now converted into a poor-houſe.

Of the Church, &c.

The church is a rectory, in the deanery of Campden, worth 150*l.* a year. The abbat and convent of Glouceſter were patrons, and preſented to it in the year 1515. Lord Weymouth is patron, the reverend Mr. John Martin incumbent.

The tithes of Buckland and Laverton belonged to the abbey of Winchcombe, and were granted to ſir Thomas Seymour 1 E. 6. The rector hath one part of the corn-tithes, and lord Weymouth the other part. The demeans pay no tithes. Mr. James Thynne, in the year 1704, gave a piece of land in the field, called *Hallier's quarter*, containing forty-one lands, to the rector and his ſucceſſors, and diſcharged the ſame from tithe, in compenſation for the loſs which the rectory might ſuſtain, by reaſon of his having incloſed ſome tillage-lands, which paid tithe to the rector, and converted them to paſture.

The church, which hath an aile on the north ſide, is covered with lead. It has a handſome embattled tower at the weſt end, with ſix bells, a clock, and a ſet of chimes in it. In the eaſt window of the chancel are three compartments of painted glaſs. The ſubject ſeems to be a repreſentation of a manor-court. The abbat of Glouceſter, who was lord of the manor, is diſtinguiſhed by his mitre, and attended by ſeveral religious perſons in monkiſh habits; and the ſteward is known by his purſe hanging at his girdle. In the ſouth window are the arms of the abbey, *Azure, a ſword in pale, pointing downwards, pomeled and hilted Or, between two keys in ſaltire of the ſecond.*

The parſonage houſe is a good one, built about the beginning of the ſixteenth century. The hall is large and lofty. There are two pannels of painted glaſs in one window, well preſerved. In a ſhield is a tun or caſk, with a graft or branch of an apple-tree iſſuing out of it, deſigned as a rebus for the name, as it is written below in antient characters, *Willm Grafton, rector*, who probably built the houſe. There are alſo the ſame arms with thoſe in the window of the church, and ſeveral labels inſcribed *In noie Ihu*, i. e. *In nomine Jeſu.*

Monuments and Inſcriptions.

There is a handſome marble monument againſt the ſouth wall of the chancel, with this inſcription:

Here lyeth the body of JAMES THYNNE, Eſq; Son of Sir HENRY FREDERICK THYNNE, Bar. and MARY Daughter of the Lord Keeper COVENTRYE. A Man of Exemplary Vertue and Charity, beloved and valued by his Equals, bleſt and pray'd for by the Poor. After ſome Legacies to his Relations, his whole large Perſonal Eſtate he bequeathed to pioús uſes, and his Lands to his Nephew THOMAS THYNNE, who erected this Monument in gratitude to his Memory. He dyed March 15th 1708-9, Aged 66.

Over the table are theſe arms, Quarterly, 1ſt and 4th, *Barry of ten pieces Or and ſable.* 2d and 3d, *Argent, a lion rampant gules.*

[d] Sir Robert Atkyns's accounts of this intermarriage, under Buckland and Kempsford, are inconſiſtent. I have followed Collins's Peerage, vol. 6. p. 261.

On

On a raifed tomb, in the church-yard, is this infcription :

Coll. BERNARD GRANVILLE Son to Bernard Granville, Efq; and Grandfon to Sir Bevill Granville who was killed in Lanfdown Fight, lyes here interred. He departed the fifty third year of his Age, on the eighth of December, 1723.——There is a fcutcheon on the tomb, *Party per pale*, 1. *Three clarions*. 2. Obliterated. —— The tomb was inclofed with rails, but now tomb and all are fallen to decay.

Firft fruits £.29	6	8	Synodals £. 0	2	0
Tenths — 2	18	8	Pentecoftals 0	1	1*ob*.
Procurations 0	6	8			

Benefactions.

Mr. James Thynne erected and endowed a free fchool at Laverton in this parifh, for reading, writing, and arithmetick. The mafter is appointed by the feoffees. He receives 20*l*. a year, and has a houfe, which is kept in repair for him. This fchool, with that at Campden of this gentleman's foundation, is fupported by an eftate at Staunton in this county, vefted in feoffees, and now lets at 100*l*. a year.

Mr. Maltby, formerly rector of this parifh, who died in the year 1630, gave 200*l*. to the ufe of the poor.

Taxes.					
The Royal Aid in	1692, £.	167	16	0
Poll-tax —	1692, —	31	15	0
Land-tax —	1694, —	160	4	0
The fame, at 3*s*.	1770, —	112	14	6*ob*.

At the beginning of this century there were 50 houfes and 250 inhabitants in this parifh, whereof three were freeholders ; yearly births 7, burials 6. *Atkyns*. But it appears by the parifh regifter, that in a feries of ten years, from 1700 to 1709 inclufive, there were 71 baptifms and 49 burials ; and in a like feries, from 1760 to 1769, there were 100 baptifms and 57 burials ; and there are now about 316 inhabitants. So that population is increafing in this parifh, where the proportion of the inhabitants to the average of annual burials, is as 55 to 1.

B U L L Y.

THIS parifh lies in the foreft divifion of the county, within the hundred of the dutchy of Lancafter, feven miles diftant eaftward from Mitchel-Dean, feven fouthward from Newent, and five weftward from Gloucefter. It is a very fmall parifh, confifting of good pafture and arable land.

Of the Manor and other Eftates.

'Walter Baliftarius holds of the king Bulelege 'in Weftberie hundred. There are four hides 'taxed. Tovi held it of king Edward. In de'mean are two plow-tillages, and four villeins and 'fix bordars with four plow-tillages. There are 'four *fervi*, and ten acres of meadow. In Glowec. 'one burgage paid 18*d*. It was worth 60*s*. and 'is now worth 40*s*.' *Domefday-book*, p. 77.

It does not appear who was the immediate fucceffor to the above Walter; but Juliana, Annabel, Joan, and Lucy de Mufgrofe levied a fine of lands in Bully and Ludefcot, to the ufe of Walter de Mufgrofe, 43 H. 3. William de Mufgrofe was feized of Bullelegh 49 H. 3. John de Monemuthe was feized thereof 9 E. 1. Roger de Mortimer, earl of March, held the manor of Bully 34 E. 3.

John Elliford held Bully by the fourth part of a knight's-fee, of Roger de Mortimer, 22 R. 2. Ifabella, his widow, furvived him, and was married to Richard de la Moor, whom fhe likewife furvived, and died feized of the manor of Bully 9 H. 5. John Elliford was feized thereof 3 H. 6. John Milborn, efq; and Elizabeth his wife, were feized of the manor of Bully 15 H. 6.

Mr. Morgan, Mr. Burgefs, and Mr. Webb were joint lords of this manor when fir Robert Atkyns compiled his account of it. Nicholas Hyett, efq; is the prefent lord of it. See his arms under *Hunt's-court* in *Badgworth*.

Of the Church, &c.

The church is confidered as a chapel to Churcham, in the deanery of the foreft. The dean and chapter of Gloucefter are impropriators. The fmall tithes are worth about 5*l*. a year.

The church is a plain building.

Pentecoftals, ——	£. 0	0	2 *ob*
Land-tax, at 3*s*. 1770,	£. 37	2	3

At the beginning of this century there were 20 houfes and about 85 inhabitants in this parifh, whereof 4 were freeholders ; yearly births 3, burials 3. *Atkyns*. But there are at prefent only 51 inhabitants.

C A M.

THIS parifh lies in the vale, in the hundred of Berkeley, one mile north from Durfley, five eaft from Berkeley, and fourteen fouth-weftward from Gloucefter. Some part of the turnpike-road from Durfley to Berkeley runs through it.

Here are no antiquities whatever. The foil is various ; in the lower part of the parifh it is rich, and produces fome excellent cyder, and as good corn and cheefe as any in the famous hundred of Berkeley.

The river, which runs through the village, rifes at Owlpen or Ewlpen, and paffing by Durfley, where it is confiderably augmented by the water of that place, takes its courfe through this parifh, and Slimbridge, and empties itfelf into the Severn at Frampton-pill. It feeds no kind of fifh except eels, on account of the great quantity of dye-ftuff thrown into it. The courfe of it is crooked, like an arch or bow, wherefore it was called the *Cam*, which, in the Britifh language, fignifies *crooked* ; and the village took its name from the river.

The poor are employ'd in the clothing bufinefs, by mafters at Durfley and Uley; but about thirty years ago, there were three or four confiderable clothiers refiding in this parifh, who are fince dead, or have declined bufinefs.

Great numbers of petrifications of the bivalve kind are found at Newnham-quarry, in the road from hence to Berkeley.

Stinchcombe antiently belonged to this parifh.

Of the Manor and other Eftates.

At the time of the Conqueft, this was a member, or Berewick, of the great lordfhip of Berkeley, of which, the whole account from *Domefday-book* is inferted among the particulars of that place and lordfhip. There were then, it is faid, 'in Camma 'fix hides, and eleven other hides.' p. 271.

Other records, of the following dates, fhew the fucceffive lords of this manor.

John Berkeley, and Maurice his fon, were feized of the manor of Cam, with free warren, 36 H. 3. and Maurice Berkeley died feized of it 9 E. 1.

Ralph de Cam was feized thereof 16 E. 1. But as it was common, in early times, to call a part by the name of the whole, it is moft likely that this was only a manor within the manor of Cam; for Thomas de Berkeley was feized of Cam 15 E. 2. & 18 E. 3. and Thomas lord Berkeley held it 35 E. 3. Maurice, fon of Thomas lord Berkeley, was feized thereof 42 E. 3. Thomas Berkeley held the fame 6 R. 2. as did Catherine his wife, in the 9th year of that reign. Sir Thomas de Berkeley, and Margaret his wife, were feized of the manor of Cam 5 H. 5. Sir John Berkeley held the fame 6 H. 6. and Richard Beauchamp, earl of Warwick, in right of Elizabeth his wife, daughter and heir of Thomas lord Berkeley, died feized of Cam 17 H. 6. Sir Maurice Berkeley of Beverftone was feized of this manor 38 & 39 H. 6. & 14 E. 4.

During the time of the laft mentioned dates, and for a long time afterwards, there were great commotions and law-fuits about the lordfhip of Berkeley, as already related, wherefore the records, during part of that difpute, are imperfect as to this manor, and fome others belonging to the Berkeley family.

William lord Berkeley, created earl-marfhal and earl of Nottingham, and Anne his wife, levied a fine of this manor to the ufe of king Henry the Seventh and his heirs male, 3 H. 7. whofe heirs male ending at the death of king Edward the Sixth, livery of Cam was granted to Henry lord Berkeley 1 Mar. and the prefent earl of Berkeley is the lord of this manor.

Edmund Baffet held one meffuage, fixty acres of land, and three acres of meadow in Cam 4 E. 2. John Serjeant was feized of lands in Cam 30 E. 3. William Warner levied a fine of lands in Cam, to the ufe of William Harding, 18 H. 7.

Upthorp, *Afhmead's*, and *Hockerhill* are places in Upper-Cam; *Til's-down*, *Clinger*, and *Bower's-lye* are in Lower-Cam.

Lorrenge-farm was given, by Thomas lord Berkeley, in the reign of king Henry the Third, to the priory of Leonard-Stanley, of which the abbat of Gloucefter had the patronage; and the monks of that abbey procured it to be confidered as belonging to the parifh of Stanley; and it has been ever fince, and ftill is, affeffed to the relief of the poor of that parifh, whereas the land-tax of the farm goes in aid of the parifh of Cam.

Of the Church, &c.

The church is a vicarage, in the deanery of Durfley. Roger lord Berkeley gave this church, with its appurtenances, to the priory of Stanley St. Leonard, in the year 1146, and gave the patronage of that priory to the abbey of St. Peter at Gloucefter.

After the diffolution of the abbey of Gloucefter, the rectory and advowfon of the vicarage, and the chapel, were granted to the bifhop of Gloucefter and his fucceffors, 33 H. 8. and confirmed 6 E. 6. So that the bifhop of Gloucefter is patron and impropriator. The bifhop pays to the vicar, out of the impropriation, 60*l.* a year in money, which was fo fettled in the year 1660. The glebe and houfe are worth about 10*l.* a year. The impropriation is in leafe to Mr. Matthew Eftcourt.

The church, dedicated to St. George, confifts of the nave, and an aile on each fide. It has a large, high, embattled tower, with five bells, at the weft end. The ftatue of St. George, carved in wood, ftood in the porch of the church, and was taken from thence by a clothier, and carried, in his waggon, to Colebrook, in the road to London, which gave name to the George-inn in that place. *Atkyns.*

The church is called *Beatæ Mariæ de Cam*, in fome old deeds in the reigns of Henry the Fourth, and Henry the Fifth.

Firft fruits £	6	13	4	Synodals £	0	2	0
Tenths —	0	13	4	Pentecoftals	0	0	7*ob.*
Procurations	0	6	8				

There is a meeting-houfe of proteftant diffenters at this place, endowed with 20*l.* a year.

Benefactions.

There are feveral fmall tenements, and little parcels of land, given to the poor. The church-houfe, and a ground called the Almfhoufe-hay, and fome other fmall tenements, are given to the ufe of the church.

Mr. Throgmorton Trotman, a native of this place, and merchant in London, in the year 1663, gave 30*l.* a year, to be paid by the company of haberdafhers in London, for the ufe of the poor.

Mr. Chriftopher Woodward, of Briftol, granted a rent-charge of 20*s.* a year on lands in Henbury, half for a fermon on new-year's day, and half to the poor.

Mr.

Mr. Richard Hicks of Cam, by his will, in 1710, gave 120*l.* for the uſe of the poor, with which, and the intereſt thereof, making together 200*l.* two cloſes, in the pariſh of Berkeley, have been purchaſed, worth 10*l.* a year.

Mr. Edward Trotman, and his ſiſters Elianor and Margaret, by their deed in 1727, gave 10*l.* a year for ever; 6*l.* whereof for ſix poor widows, and the remaining 4*l.* to be diſtributed in bread to the poor.

Mrs. Frances Hopton of Cam, in the year 1737, left an eſtate of 50*l.* a year, to found a free-ſchool, for the educating and clothing of ten boys and ten girls of this pariſh, 'till they are fourteen years old. There is a houſe for the maſter and miſtreſs.

Taxes.					
	The Royal Aid in	1692, £.	277	6	0
	Poll-tax — —	1694, —	42	9	0
	Land-tax ——	1694, —	246	15	0
	The ſame, at 3*s.*	1770, —	231	6	0

At the beginning of this century, there were 150 houſes and about 800 inhabitants in this pariſh, whereof 30 were freeholders; yearly births 18, burials 16. *Atkyns.* The average of baptiſms entered in the pariſh regiſter for ſeven years, is now 23, of burials 21; and by a ſurvey of the inhabitants in the year 1767, they were found to be 1070. There are ſome baptiſed at the meeting-houſe, but few buried there; ſo that the proportion of the inhabitants to the annual burials, is nearly as 50 to 1; which ſhews it to be a very healthy place, conſidering the ſituation of it in the vale.

CAMPDEN

LIES in the lower part of the hundred of Kiftſgate, about twenty miles diſtant eaſt from Tewkeſbury, ten north from Stow, and twenty-eight north-eaſtward from Glouceſter; ſeated in a pleaſant, fertile bottom, ſurrounded with hills and hanging woods. A ſmall brook runs from hence into the Stour, and ſo into the Avon, a mile below Stratford.

It is ſometimes called *Chipping-Campden*, to diſtinguiſh it from *Broad Campden*, a hamlet in the ſame pariſh. The *prænomen* denotes it to be a market-town, from the Saxon Cyppan, *to traffick.* For the other part of the name, Camp, in the ſame language, ſignifies a *fight*, or *battle*; and den, a *woody place in a valley.* Agreeably to this etymology, there is a tradition, that a great battle was fought in the hamlet of Barrington, between the Mercians and Weſt-Saxons; and there is a bridge in that place ſtill called Battle-bridge. The camp of the Mercians is ſaid to have been at Willerſey, adjoining to this pariſh, and that of the Saxons upon Meen-hill, about three miles off. See *Mickleton*.

The town of Campden, as John Caſtor aſſerts, is alſo famous in antiquity for being the place of congreſs of all the kings of the Saxon heptarchy, who met here in the year 689, to conſult of making war and peace with the Britons. It might, at that time, be a place of conſiderable note. At preſent, it conſiſts of one long ſtreet, with a market-houſe in the middle, built by ſir Baptiſt Hicks, viſcount Campden, whoſe arms are on the north ſide of it. The market is held on Wedneſday.

The town is an antient borough and corporation, but ſends no members to parliament. The burgeſſes obtained their preſent charter 3 Jac. by which they are made a body corporate and politic, and have a common ſeal. The corporation conſiſts of fourteen capital burgeſſes, (out of whom two bailiffs are choſen annually, on the Wedneſday before Michaelmas,) and twelve inferior burgeſſes. They elect a ſteward, who is to be a perſon learned in the law, and is amovable at pleaſure.

There is a court of record, every fourth Friday in the year, before the bailiffs and ſteward of the borough, or his deputy, where they hold pleas of treſpaſs, of debt, contract, fraud, on the caſe, and all perſonal actions ariſing within the borough, its liberties and precincts, not exceeding the value of 6*l.* 13*s.* 4*d.* And they have two ſerjeants, with ſilver maces, to execute proceſſes.

The corporation has power of making laws reſpecting the borough, and of inflicting penalties by fine and amerciament. The capital burgeſſes fill up vacancies in the common council out of the burgeſſes.

There are four annual fairs, *i.e.* on St. Andrew's day, Aſh-wedneſday, St. George's day, and St. James's day. The profits of the two former belong to the corporation; of the two latter to the lord of the manor.—See the charter of incorporation, *Appendix*, No. 27.

Mr. Robert Dover, who lived in the reign of king James the Firſt, became a very popular man in this country, by his hoſpitality and generoſity. He inſtituted an annual meeting for the practice of all ſorts of manly exerciſes, and diſtributed prizes to ſuch as excelled in them. Theſe exerciſes and their patron are the ſubject of a ſmall collection of verſes, intituled *Annalia Dubrenſia*, written by the beſt poets of that age. And there is ſtill a meeting of young people upon Dover's-hill, about a mile from Campden, every Thurſday in Whitſun-week. See p. 24.

Sir Baptiſt Hicks, the firſt viſcount Campden, built a noble houſe near the church, the outſide of which coſt 29,000*l.* and in the lanthorn, on the top of the houſe, he ordered lights to be ſet up in dark nights for the benefit of travellers. This houſe was, without any great reaſon, burnt down by the king's party in the great civil war, leſt it ſhould be made a garriſon by the parliament.

Of the Manor and other Eſtates.

In *Domeſday-book* it is expreſſed after this manner: 'The ſame earl [Hugh] holds Campedene in 'Witelai hundred. Earl Harold held it. There 'are fifteen hides taxed. In demean are ſix plow-

'tillages,

'tillages, and fifty villeins, and eight bordars, with 'twenty-one plow-tillages. There are twelve '*fervi*, and two mills of 6*s*. 2*d*. and two *ancillæ*. 'It was worth 30*l*. now only 20*l*.' *D. B.* p. 73.

The records of the following dates fhew the defcent of the manor. Guinar Briton was feized of all Campden 1 Joh. The archbifhop of Canterbury was feized of Campden 6 Joh. Sir Ralph de Somery, a great baron, whofe daughter Joan was married to Thomas lord Berkeley, died feized of Campden 1 H. 3. Roger, earl of Chefter and Lincoln, was feized of Campden, with markets and fairs, 2 H. 3.

One Serlo died feized of the manor of Campden, and Agatha the wife of Henry ——, and Juliana the wife of William de Stratton, were his fifters and coheireffes. They and their hufbands affign the manor of Campden to Anne the widow of Serlo, who had then married Hugh de Stratton, 4 H. 3.

Roger de Somery held Campden and Segleigh, and had a grant of free warren and markets 31 H. 3. & 1 E. 1. But a charter was granted to Hugh de Grundenel, and other burgeffes of Campden, 35 H. 3. and there was another grant, the fame year, to thefe burgeffes, to be exempted from tolls in markets and fairs.

Ralph Cromwell and partners held Campden 1 E. 1. John Strangeways was feized thereof 4 E. 1. John de Ludloe, and Ifabel his wife, held a moiety of the manor of Campden; and lady Mabel de Sudely held a fourth part of the faid manor, and Ralph, fon of Ralph de Cromwell, held the other fourth part, by the grant of John le Strange, 15 E. 1. John de Ludloe held Campden 23 E. 1.

Gilbert de Clare, earl of Gloucefter and Hertford, was lord of Campden, and had the advowfon of the chapel of St. Catherine, of which he died feized 24 E. 1. and Joan his widow held it 35 E. 1. It was held of the earldom of Chefter, as the eighth part of a knight's fee. Gilbert de Clare, earl of Gloucefter, fon of the forementioned Gilbert, died feized of Campden, and of the advowfon of the church, 8 E. 2.

The manor of Campden, with the advowfon of the chapel, were held of Hugh de Audley earl of Gloucefter, and Margaret his wife, 21 E. 3. William de Ludloe was feized of a moiety of the manor of Campden 23 E. 3. Richard de Stafford was feized of Campden, and had a grant of a fair therein 34 E. 3. Thomas de Ludloe held the manor of Campden, with the advowfon of the chapel of St. Catherine, 50 E. 3. Sir Richard Stafford died feized of a moiety of the manor of Campden, and the advowfon of the church, 4 R. 2. Thomas de Ludloe, of Campden, held Campden 16 R. 2. Maud, the widow of fir Richard Stafford, was feized of the manor of Campden 1 H. 4.

William Grevile, of Campden, was feized of Campden 3 H. 4. Edmund Ludloe held Campden 11 H. 4. Edward Stafford, bifhop of Exeter, was feized thereof 7 H. 5. Thomas Stafford, efq; was feized of a moiety of the manor of Campden, with the advowfon of the chapel, 4 H. 6.

Margaret, the widow of fir Baldwin Strange, was feized of Ludloe's, within the manor of Campden, 10 H. 6. by which it appears, that the eftate held by the Ludloes, called Campden in fome of the above records, was a part of the manor, or a manor within the manor of Campden. William Molvneux, efq; was feized of the manor of Chipping Campden 6 E. 4. Sir John Burgh held a manor of the name of Campden 11 E. 4. and John Molyneux, efq; held Chipping Campden 13 E. 4.

The manor of Campden, and the advowfon of the chapel of St. Catherine, defcended to Cicely, the wife of —— Fitzherbert: Her fecond hufband was John Joflyn, who, with his wife, levied a fine of them to the ufe of Thomas Molineux and others 8 H. 7. Euftace Fitzherbert was Cicely's fon and heir, who died feized thereof 9 H. 8.

Sir John Ruffel died feized of the manor of Chipping Campden 4 Mar. and was fucceeded by fir Thomas Ruffel, his fon and heir. This manor afterwards came to the crown, and was granted, by queen Elizabeth, to fir Thomas Smith, whofe anceftor was an alderman of Worcefter. Anthony Smith, efq; was lord of this manor in the year 1608.

It was purchafed, foon after, by fir Baptift Hicks, who was created vifcount Campden 4 C. 1.

Edward lord Noel having married Juliana, eldeft daughter and coheir of Baptift vifcount Campden, obtained a grant of that honour to himfelf and his heirs male, on failure of male iffue of the faid vifcount Campden, at whofe death he fucceeded to the title, and to the manor of Campden. Mary, the other daughter, was married, firft, to fir Charles Morifon, of Caifhobery in Hertfordfhire, and afterwards to fir John Couper, of Winburn in Dorfetfhire. This Edward vifcount Campden was active in the royal caufe, at the breaking out of the civil war, and dying at Oxford, 1643, was carried to Campden, and lies buried there, under a fumptuous monument erected over him by his lady. He left iffue, by the above lady, two fons, Baptift and Henry; and two daughters, Elizabeth, married to fir Erafmus de la Fountain; and Penelope, to John vifcount Chaworth.

Baptift vifcount Campden fucceeded his father in title and eftate. He raifed and maintained, at his own coft, a troop of horfe, and a company of foot, for the fervice of king Charles the Firft, and paid, to the fequeftrators, 9,000*l*. compofition for his eftate, befides 150*l*. a year, fettled on the minifters of the times. He married firft, Anne Fielding, fecond daughter to William earl of Denbigh, by whom he had three children, who died in their infancy; fecondly, Anne daughter of fir Robert Lovet, widow of Edward earl of Bath, by whom he had one fon ftill-born. His third wife was Hefter, one of the four daughters and coheireffes of Thomas lord Wotton, by whom

he

he had two ſons, Edward and Henry; and four daughters, Mary, afterwards counteſs of Northampton; Juliana, wife of William lord Allington; Heſter, who died an infant; and Elizabeth, married to Charles earl of Berkeley. His fourth wife was Elizabeth Bertie, eldeſt daughter of Montague earl of Lindſey, by whom he had ſix ſons, Lindſey, Baptiſt, John, James, and two ſtill-born; and three daughters, Catherine, married to John earl of Rutland; Bridget, and Martha-Penelope. His lordſhip dying in 1682, was buried at Exton in Rutlandſhire.

Edward Noel, who was advanced to the degree of a baron, by the title of lord Noel of Titchfield, in his father's life-time, 33 C. 2. ſucceeded his father at his death, and was created earl of Gainſborough the ſame year. He married lady Elizabeth, eldeſt daughter and coheir of Thomas-Wriotheſley, earl of Northampton, by whom he had iſſue Wriotheſley-Baptiſt, his ſucceſſor, and four daughters; lady Frances, married to Simon lord Digby; lady Jane, married to William lord Digby, brother and heir to the ſaid Simon lord Digby; lady Elizabeth, married to Richard Norton, eſq; and lady Juliana, who died unmarried.

Wriotheſley-Baptiſt, ſecond earl of Gainſborough, married Catherine, eldeſt daughter of Fulke Grevile, fifth lord Brooke, and departing this life in 1690, left iſſue only two daughters; lady Elizabeth, married to Henry Bentinck, firſt duke of Portland; and lady Rachael, wedded to Henry Somerſet, ſecond duke of Beaufort.—On his lordſhip's failing of iſſue male, the honours, and this eſtate, deſcended to Baptiſt Noel, ſon of Baptiſt, ſecond ſon of Baptiſt viſcount Campden, by his fourth wife, Elizabeth, daughter of the earl of Lindſey.

Which Baptiſt, third earl of Gainſborough, having married lady Dorothy Manners, ſecond daughter of John, firſt duke of Rutland, died of the ſmall pox in 1714, leaving iſſue three ſons, Baptiſt, his ſucceſſor; John, and James who died unmarried; and three daughters, lady Catherine; lady Suſannah, married to Anthony earl of Shafteſbury; and lady Mary, who died young.

Baptiſt, the eldeſt ſon, ſucceeded as fourth earl of Gainſborough. He married Miſs Elizabeth Chapman, by whom he had iſſue three ſons, Baptiſt, his ſucceſſor; Henry, now earl of Gainſborough; and Charles, who died young; and nine daughters, lady Elizabeth; lady Jane, married to Gerrard-Anne Edwards, of Welham in Leiceſterſhire, eſq; lady Juliana, wedded to George Edwards, lord Carbery; lady Penelope, who died young; lady Anne; lady Lucy, married to Horatio Mann, eſq; lady Mary; lady Suſannah; and lady Sophia. His lordſhip died March 21, 1750-51, and was ſucceeded by his eldeſt ſon,

Baptiſt, fifth earl of Gainſborough, who being on his travels, died a batchelor at Geneva, in 1759; upon which, his only ſurviving brother,

Henry, born in 1743, became the ſixth earl of Gainſborough, and is the preſent lord of the manor of Campden.

His lordſhip's titles are Earl of Gainſborough, Viſcount Campden of Campden, Baron Noel of Ridlington, Baron Hicks of Ilmington, Baron Noel of Titchfield, and Baronet. ARMS. *Or, fretty gules; a canton ermine.* CREST. *On a wreath, a buck at graze argent, attired Or.* SUPPORTERS. *Two bulls argent, armed, maned, and ungued ſable.* MOTTO. TOUT BIEN OU RIEN.

Mr. William Harriſon, ſteward to this family, was ſuppoſed to be murdered in 1676, and three perſons were executed for the murder; but he returned to Campden about two years afterwards, and ſir Thomas Overbury [e] publiſhed an account of that myſterious affair.

HAMLETS. 1. *Barrington*, in which the church ſtands. Henry Stapleton, gentleman, was ſeized of a virgate of land, a barn, and a cloſe

[e] The following is the ſubſtance of ſir Thomas Overbury's account.

Mr. William Harriſon went from Campden to Charringworth, about three miles off, to receive his lady's rents, and not returning at his uſual time, his wife ſent their ſervant, John Perry, to ſee for him; and neither of them returning that night, Mr. Harriſon's ſon went in ſearch of them, and found Perry, who ſaid his maſter was not at Charringworth. Soon after they were informed that a hat, band, and comb had been found by a poor woman leaſing in the field, which proved to be Mr. Harriſon's; and as the band was bloody, and the hat cut, he was ſuppoſed to be murdered. Search was made for the body, but in vain. Suſpicion ariſing againſt Perry, he was examined by a magiſtrate, and tho' nothing appeared againſt him, was kept in cuſtody for ſeveral days. It was ſaid, however, that he told ſome perſons that a tinker had killed his maſter; and others, that a gentleman's ſervant had done it. And being taken before the magiſtrate again, he affirmed that his mother and brother had robbed his maſter and killed him, and that it was a matter previouſly agreed upon between him and them, relating a great variety of probable circumſtances concerning the murder, ſuch as where they had thrown the body, &c.

Joan and Richard Perry, the mother and brother, were apprehended and examined, who both denied the charge; but John ſtill perſiſted that he had ſpoke the truth; however, the body could not be found any where.

It is remarkable, that returning from the juſtice's, Richard Perry, who walked a good diſtance behind John, pulling a handkerchief out of his pocket, dropped a piece of inkle, with a reeve-knot at one end. This being ſhewed to John, he declared it was the ſtring his brother ſtrangled his maſter with.

At the next lent aſſizes, they were tryed upon an indictment for the ſuppoſed murder, and pleaded not guilty; but they were all convicted upon John's confeſſion before the magiſtrate, and a few days after, were brought to the place of execution on Broadway-hill, in ſight of Campden. The mother and Richard were firſt executed, profeſſing their innocence, and beſeeching John to declare what he knew. But he, with a dogged, ſullen carriage, told the people he was not obliged to confeſs to them; yet immediately before his death, ſaid, he knew nothing of his maſter's death, nor what became of him; but they were all executed, and John was hanged in chains.

Execution thus done upon thoſe unhappy wretches, it muſt ſtrike the reader with horror and amazement to be informed that the ſame Mr. Harriſon returned to Campden, about two years afterwards, alive and well, and gave an account of his having been taken away, by three perſons on horſeback, as he was returning from Charringworth: They travelled by night 'till they came to Deal, where he was put on board a ſhip, and after being at ſea about ſix weeks, he, and others in the ſame condition, were landed in the Turkiſh dominions, and diſpoſed of to different perſons. It was his lot to be choſen by an old phyſician, who died in ſomething more than a year afterwards. From thence he eſcaped by a ſhip that was bound to Portugal, and ſo returned to England, where he was received by his wife and family as one riſen from the dead.

formerly belonging to the chantry of St. Catherine, ſituate in Byrrington in the pariſh of Campden, which Thomas Smythe purchaſed of him, and died ſeized thereof 41 Eliz. as appears by the eſcheator's inquiſition in that year.

2. *Weſtington* and *Comb*. Henry de Faunton was ſeized of the manor of Weſtington 7 E. 2. Robert Cotel was ſeized of the manor of Combe, and Alice, his wife, ſurviving him, had the third part of this manor aſſigned to her in dower, 9 E. 3. Adam de Hermington held the manor of Comb near Campden, 16 E. 3. Combe-grange, *alias* Combe, in the pariſh of Campden, formerly belonging to the abbey of Bordeſley, was granted, by the crown, to Thomas Smyth and Katherine his wife, to be held by the ſervice of one fortieth part of a knight's fee, 7 E. 6.

3. *Broad Campden*. Here was formerly a chapel, which was afterwards turned into a barn. Sir Chriſtopher Savage died ſeized of the manors of Broad Campden, Burington, and Weſtington 4 H. 8. and livery of theſe manors was granted to Chriſtopher Savage, his ſon, 12 H. 8. Thomas Boner[f] purchaſed a moiety of the manor of Campden, and of divers other lands in Campden, Buryngton, and Weſtington, of Chriſtopher Savage 37 H. 8. and ſold the ſame to Thomas Smyth. A meſſuage in Broad Campden, formerly belonging to the abbey of Tewkeſbury, was granted to James Gunter and William Lewis 37 H. 8. James Gunter, and Anne his wife, levied a fine of the manor of Broad Campden, to the uſe of ſir Roger Cholmondeley, lord chief-baron of the court of exchequer, 1 E. 6. and Roger Cholmondeley levied a fine of the ſame, to William Waſhborn, 5 Mariæ. Three yard-lands,[f] and two cloſes, and divers other lands in Broad Campden, late belonging to the chantry of St. Trinity in the church of Campden, were granted, by king Edward the Sixth, to Henry Stapleton, 3 E. 6. which he ſold to Thomas Smyth the ſame year.

Of the other eſtates in this pariſh the records give the following account. Henry de Erdington held lands in Barew and Campden by the eighth part of a knight's fee, 5 E. 1. and Ralph de Cromwell held lands in Barew and Campden, in right of his wife, by the ſervice of a fourth part of a knight's fee, 5 E. 1.

Sir Edward Berſtead levied a fine of the third part of lands in Campden, Weſtington, Muckleton, Pebworth, and Olington, to the uſe of Lewis Grevil 4 H. 4. William Milner, and Margaret his wife, levied a fine of lands in Campden, to the uſe of John Marſhal 5 E. 4. Sir William Compton died ſeized of thirty meſſuages and ſeventy acres in Campden 20 H. 8.

A mill, and lands in Campden, which belonged to the nunnery of Cockhill[g] in Worceſterſhire, were granted to Nicholas Forteſcue and Catherine Forteſcue, and to the heirs male of Nicholas, 34 H. 8.

Of the Church, &c.

The church is a vicarage, in the deanery of Campden, worth about 300*l*. a year, in the patronage of the earl of Gainſborough. Mr. Weſton is the preſent incumbent.

The abbat of Cheſter was ſeized of the advowſon of the church of Campden 15 E. 1.

The rectory of Campden belonged formerly to the nunnery of St. Warburg in Cheſter, which ſaint was daughter of Wolpher, king of Mercia. It was granted to the chapter of Cheſter 33 H. 8. And the church and rectory were granted to Lawrence Baſkervil and William Blake 3 Jac.

The impropriation formerly belonged to the abbey of Welbeck, and is now veſted in the earl of Gainſborough.

Sir Baptiſt Hicks purchaſed the impropriation of Winfrith in Dorſetſhire, worth, at that time, about 100*l*. a year, which was afterwards annexed to the vicarage of Campden, by Edward lord Nöel.

The church is large and beautiful. The nave is ſixty feet high, with an aile on each ſide, and a very handſome tower, thirty-five yards high, beſides the battlements and twelve pinnacles. The church and ſide ailes are fifty-ſeven feet broad, and the length of the whole building is one hundred and thirty feet. There are alſo two handſome chapels and a ſpacious chancel, in the leaſt window of which are the arms of ſir Baptiſt Hicks, curiouſly painted, ſix feet in height. There is a peal of eight bells, and a ſet of chimes in the tower. The church is dedicated to St. James.

The church is ſuppoſed to have been built about the beginning of the reign of king Richard the Second. There is a grey marble flat ſtone in the church for Mr. William Grevel, who died in 1401, 2 H. 4. on which he and his wife are repreſented on a braſs plate, ſtanding in two niches, embelliſhed with pinnacles, which correſpond exactly with the fine Gothic carved work over the great door, and belfry window, at the weſt ſide of the tower. From this circumſtance ſome perſons have ſuppoſed that he built the tower; and the legend in the window, over the door of the north aile, to *pray for the ſouls, &c.* and the many mullets, part of his arms, diſperſed over the windows, ſhew him to have contributed, at leaſt, towards the building or repairing of that aile. The floor of the nave was formerly adorned with very curious plated marble flat ſtones; but they are now covered with large pews to ſit in.

There was formerly a great deal of curious painted glaſs, of which only a few fragments remain.

There were four chantries in this church, *i. e.* 1. Stratford's, or St. Catherine's firſt chantry,

f Eſcheator's inquiſition, 42 Eliz.

g This nunnery was founded by Iſabel counteſs of Warwick, in the year 1260; and valued, at the diſſolution, at 34*l*. 15*s*. 11*d*. yearly.

whereof

whereof Daniel Tibot was the laſt incumbent, and had a penſion, in 1553, of 5*l.* 2. St. Catherine's ſecond chantry, of which Chriſtopher Baxter, the laſt incumbent, received a penſion of 5*l.* 3. A chantry called *God's Service*, dedicated to the holy Trinity, whereof Thomas Mortiboys, the laſt incumbent, received a penſion of 5*l.* 4. St. Mary's, *alias* Bernard's chantry, of which Robert Joy was the laſt incumbent, and received a penſion of 5*l.*

Divers lands in Campden, formerly belonging to the holy Trinity chantry, and St. Mary's, were granted to ſir William Ryder and others 7 Jac.

Monuments and Inſcriptions.

On a marble graveſtone, nine feet long and five broad, are the effigies, in braſs, of Mr. Grevel and his wife, five feet four inches in length, and the following inſcription, on a fillet of braſs, round the margin of the ſtone :

Hic jacet Wilelmus Grevel de Campedene quondam Civis London & flos Mcator lanar. tocius Anglie qui obijt pmo die menſe Octobris An dm Millmo CCCC°. pmo. Hic jacet Mariona vxor predicti Wilielmi que obijt Decimo die menſis Septembris Anno dni Millmo CCC°. LXXX. VI°. Quor. aiabs ppicietur Deus Amen.

On the north ſide of the chancel, within the communion rails, is a curious ſtone monument for Thomas Smith, eſq; with the effigies of himſelf, his two wives, and thirteen children, very finely carved, and on it this inſcription :

HIC IACET SEPVLTVS, VIR VERVS CHRISTIANVS, THOMAS SMITH ARMIGER. QVONDAM MANERII DE CAMPDEN DOMINVS. A PVERITIA SVA AVLICVS. QVI SVO TEMPORE FVIT. E CONSILIIS REGIS, MARCHIE WALLIE, BISQ. VICECOMES COMITATVS GLOCESTRIE, AC IVSTITIARIVS PACIS EIVSDEM COMITATVS, VSQ. AD EXTREMVM ÆTATIS, QVI HABVIT DVAS VXORES, PRIMAM ELIZABETHAM FILIAM ET HEREDEM EVSTATII FITZHARBERT ARMIGERI; SECVDAM KATHERINAM FILIAM GEORGII THROKMARTON MILITIS. CVM FILIIS ET FILIABVS VT HIC PATET ; QVI OBIIT DIE . . . . AN°. DOM. 1593.

On the north ſide of the north chapel is a large altar monument for Mr. Robert Lilly, (uncle to the famous William Lilly, the aſtrologer) and at the eaſt end, on a blue ſtone tablet fixed in the wall, is the following inſcription, now ſcarce legible :

Mag^{ster} Robertus Lillius Sonante tubâ reſurget ultima. Vir Summe pius probus ac facundus; Quem peperit Leiceſtrenſis, nutriuit Alma Mater Cantabrigia, fidelem demum Paſtorem ſenſit grex hic miſcellus. Undiquâque dum vixit fœlix, niſi quod Calculi dolores acutiſſimi Autumnũ vitæ fecerant valetudinarium, et (impedito ultra XX^{ti}. dies totio) prorſus afflictiſſimum; Qui tandem, exantlatis XX^{ti}. annorũ hic loci laboribus, Tribus, optimæ ſpei, liberis, funeri ſe ſentiens Superſtitem, duas dulciſſimas quas præmiſiſſet, filias cælo Sequutus eſt: Naturæ conceſſit XXI^{mo}. die octobris 1636, et ætatis Suæ 54to.

Exiguum hoc perpetui amoris monumentum, Amantiſſima pariter ac mœſtiſſima conjux Honora Lilly lugens poſuit.

Againſt the north wall of the chapel is a neat monument, thus inſcribed :

Lege Spectator & luge. Hoc enim ſub lapide in pulverem percolatur, vir ſummo ingenio & pietate Gulielmus Bartholomew A. M. è Coll: Trin: Cantabr: Primitias annorum & Miniſterij, Edvardo Vicecomiti Campden, clariſſimo Heroi, fæliciter dicavit: cui in ædibus Brookianis è ſacris fuit. Mox in hujus Eccleſiæ vicarium ſuccenturiatus, viginti quatuor per annos, negotio animarum incubuit, omnium cum amore, laude, admiratione. Orator eximius, Malleus ſectoriarum Orthodoxæ religionis Eccleſiæ Anglicanæ, partium Carolinarum (peſſimis licet temporibus) intrepidus aſſertor : Moriens, Eodem in tumulo, quo Suſannam filiolam olim condiderat, mortalitatis ſuæ exuvias voluit recondi. Obijt Illa Sept. 3^{d}. An°. Dom: 1642. Ætatis Suæ 3. Obijt Ille Octo: 11°: An°. Dom: 1660. Ætatis Suæ 56°.

Sanctis exilium mundus, ſua patria cœlum :
Qui moritur Chriſto, non perit, ille redit.

Upon a flat blue ſtone are the arms of Hicks, and this inſcription :

H. S. E.
Dnũs Henricus Hyckes,
Collegij SS: Trinitatis apud Oxonienſes Alumnus,
Gradu Magiſtri in Artibus ibidem inſignitus,
Eccleſiæ Parochialis { de Stretton Rector, de Campden Vicarius.
Utriuſq; per annos tantum non quinquaginta
Paſtor fidelis ;
Eccleſiæ Anglicanæ verè Apoſtolicæ
Filius Orthodoxus,
Et contra omnes Adverſarios,
Tam Pſeudo Catholicos quam nuperos Novatores,
Intrepidus Vindex.
Hic etiam reconditæ ſunt Reliquiæ
Mariæ,
Dni Gulielmi Bartholomew,
Hujus Eccleſiæ olim Vicarii,
Et exploratæ in Regem fidelitatis Viri,
Filiæ,
Et predicti Henrici Conjugis.
Diem Supremum obijt { Illa Dec. 23rd. A. D. 1701. Ætat. 62. Ille Ian. 17th. A. D. 1708. Ætat. 78.

In the middle of the ſouth chapel ſtands a moſt magnificent monument of black and white marble, with the effigies of ſir Baptiſt Hicks and his lady lying upon it: The top of it is ſupported by twelve columns of Egyptian marble, and on the north ſide is the following inſcription, in gold capitals :

TO THE MEMORIE OF HER DEARE, & DECEASED HUSBAND BAPTIST LORD HICKS, VISCOUNT CAMPDEN. BORNE OF A WORTHY FAMILY IN THE CITIE OF LONDON; WHO BY THE BLESSING OF GOD ON HIS INGENIOUS ENDEAVORS, AROSE TO AN AMPLE ESTATE, & TO THE FORESAID DEGREES OF HONOUR: AND OUT OF THOSE BLESSINGS, DISPOSED TO CHARITALE USES, IN HIS LIFETIME, A LARGE PORTION, TO THE VALUE OF 10000l. WHO LIVED RELIGIOUSLY, VERTUOUSLY & GENEROUSLY, TO THE AGE OF 78 YEARES: AND DIED OCTO: 18: 1629.

ELIZABETH VISCOUNTESSE CAMPDEN,
HIS DEARE CONSORT, BORNE OF THE FAMILY OF THE MAYS, LIVED HIS WIFE IN ALL PEACE & CONTENTMENT, THE SPACE OF 45. YEARES, LEAVING ISSUE BY HER SAID LORD & HUSBAND TWO DAUGHTERS, IULIANA MARRIED TO EDWARD LORD NOEL, NOW VISCOUNT CAMPDEN, AND MARY MARIED TO Sr. CHARLES MORISON Knt. AND BARONETT, HATH PIOUSLY AND CAREFULLY CAUSED THIS MONUMENT TO BE ERECTED AS A TESTIMONIE OF THEIR MUTUALL LOVE, WHERE BOTH THEIR BODIES MAY REST TOGETHER, IN EXPECTATION OF A JOYFULL RESURRECTION.

On the ſouth ſide it is thus inſcribed :

AD TERRAM CAMPDENICAM.
CAMPDENA FOELIX, POSSIDES LARGAS OPES CORPVS PATRONI, QVÆ RECONDIS OPTIMI; DOMINVM POTENTEM PRÆDIIS, ET QVI ADDIDIT ISTIS HONORVM FLOSCVLOS TERRIS NOVOS. DOMINO SEPVLCHRAM PREBEAS; ILLE ÆDIBVS DECORAVIT AMPLIS, HORTVLIS NITIDIS AGRVM TVVM, NEC ÆDEM NEGLIGI EST PASSVS DEI, SED INDIGENTES FORTE SVSTINVIT PIA. VIVO VOLVPTAS, MORTVO FAC SIS QVIES. HIC ET PVDICAM, QVÆ SOCIA VITÆ FVIT, TENES MATRONAM: CORPVS HOC GEMINVM FOVE RESVSCITANDVM, ET CONTEGAS ALMO SINV.

On a beautiful marble monument, fixed in the wall, at the eaſt end of the north chapel, a half length figure, of admirable workmanſhip, and under it this inſcription :

The Moſt Exquiſite Model of Nature's beſt Workmanſhip,
Y^{e}. Richeſt Magazin of all Divine and Moral Vertues,
PENELOPE NOEL.
Having added to the Nobilitie of her Birth a brighter Shyne of true Nobleneſſe ye Exemplarie ſweetneſſe of her Converſation, her Contempt of earthly vanities, And her Zealous affection towards Heaven, after 22 Yeares Devotions commended her Virgin Soule into the hands of its true Brydgroome JESUS CHRIST,

Christ, May 17. A°. 1633. Over whofe pretious Duft here referved her fad Parents, Edward L^d. Noel Vifc. Campden, And the Lady Iulian his Wife dropt their Teares, and Erected this Marble to the Deare Memorie of their unvaluable loffe.

Superata tellus Sidera donat.

On the fouth fide of the fame chapel ftands a very ftately monument of black and white marble, with the effigies of lord and lady Noel, larger than life, ftanding in a niche, in their fhrouds ; and upon two folding doors, on each fide of them, are the following infcriptions:

This Monument is Erected to preferve The Memory and Pourtrait of the Right Honorable Sir Edward Noel Vicount Campden, Baron Noel of Ridlington, and Hicks of Ilmington: A Lord of Heroik high parts & Prefence; He was Knight Banneret in the Wars of Ireland being Young: And then Created Baronet Anno 1611. He was afterwards made Baron of Ridlington. The other Titles came unto him By Right of Dame Iuliana his Wife, Who ftands Collaterall to him in this Monument: A Lady of Extraordinary great Endowments both of Virtue, and Fortune. This Goodly Lord Died at Oxford at the beginning of the late Fatal Civil Wars, whither he went to Serve & Affift his Souverain Prince Charles the Firft: And fo was Exalted to the Kingdome of Glory 8°. Martij. 1642.

The Lady Iuliana Eldeft Daughter, and Coheire (of that Mirror of his time) S^r. Baptift Hicks Vicount Campden, She was Married To that Noble Lord Who is here Engraven by her, By whom She had Baptift Lord Vicount Campden now living (Who is Bleffed with a Numerous & Gallant Iffue) Henry her fecond Son Died a Prifoner For his Loyalty to his Prince. Her Eldeft Daughter Elizabeth was Married To Iohn Vicount Chaworth. Mary her Second Daughter To the very Noble Knight S^r. Erafmus De la Fontaine. Penelope Her Youngeft Daughter Died a Maid. This Excellent Lady for the Pious, and Unparallell'd affections She retained to the Memory of her Deceafed Lord Caufed this Stately Monument To be Erected in her life time in September, Anno Dom. 1664. [h]

Firft fruits £.	20	6	8	Synodals £.	0	2	0
Tenths —	2	0	8	Pentecoftals	0	1	10
Procurations	0	6	8				

Benefactions.

Mr. John Fereby, *alias* Verby, founded a grammar-fchool in this town, in the year 1487, and endowed it with a moiety of the manor of Lynham in Oxfordfhire, and with a large clofe called Fines-clofe ; but by the ill management of the feoffees, this eftate was fold, and another at Barton-on-the-Heath, in Warwickfhire, was purchafed with the money, which was fettled, by a decree in chancery, 1627, in a certain number of feoffees, for the maintenance of a fchool-mafter and ufher, and now lets at 80*l.* a year, of which the mafter has 40*l.* the ufher 20*l.* The effigy of the founder is fet up in the fchool.

James Thynne, efq; of Buckland, gave 1000*l.* for the founding of a charity-fchool for thirty girls, to be cloathed every year whilft they continue in the fchool; and appointed 10*l.* a year to the miftrefs. This charity is fupported by an eftate at Staunton, near Campden.

George Townfend, efq; gave 4*l.* a year, to teach a certain number of poor children to read.

Sir Baptift Hicks, in the year 1612, founded an almfhoufe for fix poor men and fix women, and endowed it with 3*s.* 4*d.* weekly to each perfon, with a black gown, a hat, and a ton of coals yearly ; each perfon having two handfome rooms and a garden. He likewife gave, by his laft will, 500*l.* for a ftock to fet the poor at work.

Mr. William Freeman, of London, in 1642, gave 2*s.* a week, for ever, to be given in bread to the poor.

Mr. Robert Tainton, of London, gave 50*l.* Mr. William Blakely, in 1672, gave 50*l.* and Edward lord Noel, in 1674, gave 40*l.* the intereft of which feveral fums is directed to be diftributed weekly in bread to the poor for ever.

Mr. John Ballard, a phyfician of Wefton-Subedge, in the year 1678, gave 100*l.* to the ufe of the poor.

Mr. Endymion Canning, of Brook in Rutlandfhire, who died in 1683, by his will gave 100*l.* the intereft of which to be diftributed weekly in bread to the poor of Campden and Barrington for ever; and another 100*l.* to be added to the town-ftock, and to be difpofed of by the feoffees of the charities in this town, and their fucceffors, for ever.

Mr. William Yate, in 1690, gave one dozen of bread weekly to the poor.

There have been other benefactions of a lefs permanent nature. Sir Baptift Hicks gave a pulpit-cloth and cufhion, of gold tiffue ; a brafs faulcon ; two communion cups, and two falvers, double gilt ; and one of the bells in the tower, which coft 66*l.* He expended 200*l.* on the roof of the chancel, repaired the fouth chapel, built a wall round the church-yard, at the expence of 150*l.* and built the market-houfe, which coft 90*l.* in the year 1624. Mr. William Blakely, in 1665, gave the third bell ; and Mr. Thomas Ballard, in 1682, gave the chimes. James Thynne, efq; gave the gallery for the children of his fchool to fit in. And John Savage, efq; in 1734, gave 100*l.* to erect an altar-piece, and 10*l.* to be given to the poor in bread.

[h] In a manufcript lent me by a friend, wherein are many particulars relating to the church of Campden, I find the following very pertinent reflections.

'I have often lamented,' fays the writer, 'the facrilegious fpoil and deftruction of the venerable monuments of our great and good anceftors, by men in power and office; men, fometimes, of liberal education, who know, or at leaft ought to know, that there is a refpect due to the dead; that the memory of the righteous ought to be had in everlafting remembrance; and that even the heathens themfelves have looked upon the violation of the monuments of the dead with the utmoft deteftation and abhorrence. And yet, alas! neither greatnefs of birth, true patriotifm, valour, munificence, nor other qualifications and indowments whatever, have been fufficient to protect the monuments of our anceftors from violence. By my intereft, a fine old monument in Campden church was preferved, which would have fallen a facrifice to the lucre of an iron grate that incompaffed it, the fale of which would have put a few pounds in the fpoiler's pocket. I remember feveral old monuments for perfons of merit, which have been demolifhed, and laid afide as rubbifh, to make room for new ones, for perfons who very little deferve a memorial. Among the monuments of antiquity now remaining, none decline fo faft as the old ftones with brafs plates. The plates fall a prey to petty church-robbers, whofe behaviour is countenanced by the bad example of great ones, or negligence of their fuperiors; fo that in another century, unlefs greater care be taken, but very few of thofe monuments will be found remaining.'——Thefe reflections are applicable to other places befides Campden.

Chipping Campden.

Taxes.	The Royal Aid in 1692, £.	44	12	0
	Poll-tax —— 1694, —	86	0	0
	Land-tax —— 1694, —	71	0	0
	The ſame, at 3*s.* 1770, —	56	5	0

Broad Campden.

Taxes.	The Royal Aid in 1692, £.	75	18	0
	Poll-tax — 1694, —	20	17	0
	Land-tax —— 1694, —	50	8	2
	The ſame at 3*s.* 1770, —	43	16	1*ob.*

Barrington.

Taxes.	The Royal Aid in 1692, £.	68	2	0
	Poll-tax —— 1694, —	16	4	0
	Land-tax —— 1694, —	61	8	0
	The ſame, at 3*s.* 1770, —	49	1	0

Weſtington and *Comb.*

Taxes.	The Royal Aid in 1692, £.	80	6	0
	Poll-tax —— 1694, —	12	10	0
	Land-tax —— 1694, —	64	0	0
	The ſame, at 3*s.* 1770, —	48	7	6

At the beginning of this century there were 391 houſes and about 1618 inhabitants in this pariſh, whereof 61 were freeholders; yearly births 48, burials 45. *Atkyns.* In a ſeries of ten years, from 1700 to 1709 incluſive, the average number of annual baptiſms entered in the pariſh regiſter, was of burials . And, from 1760 to 1769, the average of baptiſms was , and of burials , including the diſſenters. And the whole number of inhabitants is about . So that the proportion between the living and the annual burials is nearly as 45 to 1; which ſhews the place to be healthy.

CERNEY, (NORTH.)

THIS pariſh lies in the hundred of Rapſgate, in the coteſwold country, four miles north from Cirenceſter, ſeven ſouth-weſt from Northleach, and fourteen eaſtward from Glouceſter.

It is ſituate upon the river *Churn*, whence it took its name, for *Cern-ey* ſignifies the *Churn-water*. This pariſh conſiſts moſtly of arable land, with ſome meadow and paſture. Cirenceſter races are run upon Cerney-down, which is eſteemed a very fine two mile courſe, as well for running as for the ſpectators.

There is a camp in Cerney-field, of conſiderable extent; and about ſeventy years ago, there was an urn of blue glaſs dug up in Calmſden-field, in this pariſh, full of burnt bones and aſhes.

Of the Manors and other Eſtates.

'Saint Oſwald [of Glouuec.] held in Cernei, in 'Reſpigete hundred, one manor of four hides, in 'the time of king Edward. The ſame ſaint holds 'it ſtill, and has two plow-tillages in demean, 'and ſix villeins, and two bordars, with five plow-'tillages. There is one *ſervus*, and a mill of 7*s.* '[rent] and two acres of meadow. It was then 'worth 100*s.* and is now worth 4*l.*' *Domeſday-book*, p. 70.

'Giſlebert [the ſon of Turold] holds Cernei in 'Reſpiget hundred. There are ſeven hides. Elaf 'and his brother, two thanes, held it for two 'manors, and could go where they pleaſed. In 'demean are four plow-tillages, and ſeven villeins, 'and ſix bordars, with five plow-tillages. There 'are ſix *ſervi*, and a mill of 8*s.* [rent] and ſix 'acres of meadow; a wood two quarters [of a 'mile] long, and one broad. Four knights 'belonging to Giſlebert, with their men, have 'ſeven plow-tillages, and a mill of 8*s.* [rent] The 'whole, in the time of king Edward, was worth '14*l.* and is now worth 12*l.*' *Ibidem*, p. 76.

The above Giſlebert took part with Robert Curtoiſe againſt king William the Second, wherefore his eſtates in England were ſeized. He was alſo lord of Rendcombe, which manor was granted to Robert Fitz-Hamon, and went, with Mabel his daughter, to Robert Mellent, and ſo deſcended to the ſeveral earls of Glouceſter down to the Staffords, who were lords of the manors of Rendcombe and Cerney; wherefore I conjecture, that upon Giſlebert's defection, this manor was granted, with Rendcombe, to Robert Fitz-Hamon, and deſcended together, 'till the attainder of Humphry earl of Stafford, after he was killed in the battle of Northampton, 38 H. 6. But the records are imperfect, as to Cerney, for a great part of the above time.

Hugh earl of Stafford held lands in Cerney, with the advowſon of the church, at the time of his death, at Rhodes, in his return from a pilgrimage to Jeruſalem, which happened 9 R. 2. as appears by an inquiſition of the following year. Thomas earl of Stafford died ſeized of them 16 R. 2. Edward earl of Stafford was ſeized of the manor of North Cerney, and of the advowſon of the church, 4 H. 4.

Edward Stafford, duke of Buckingham, was ſeized of the manors of North Cerney and Woodmancot, when he was attainted and executed, 14 H. 8. whereby they came to the crown, and the advowſon of the church, and the manor of Woodmancot were granted to ſir Richard Cornwall, and his heirs male, the ſame year.

The manor of North Cerney was granted to Henry lord Stafford 2 Mar. He died in 1558, and livery of the manors of North Cerney and Woodmancot was granted to Edward lord Stafford, his ſon and heir, 13 Eliz.

John Partridge, eſq; was ſeized of North Cerney in the year 1608. Three perſons, Mr. Combs, and two gentlemen of the name of Oatridge, were afterwards joint owners of it, who ſold it to the earl of Bathurſt, the preſent lord of the manor.

Robert de Mara purchaſed lands in North Cerney, of Jordan his brother, 1 Joh. Henry the

 ſon

ſon of Gerald, purchaſed, by exchange, lands in Cerney, of William de Alneto, 11 Joh. John Dunſen was ſeized of lands in this place 30 H. 3. John Weſtby, and Margaret his wife, levied a fine of lands in North Cerney, Calmſden, and Woodmancot, to the uſe of William Tracy and others, 19 H. 7.

Thomas Tyndale, eſq; has a good houſe and a good eſtate in this pariſh, which he purchaſed of the late Mr. Pickering Rich. His arms are, *Argent, a feſs gules, between three garbs ſable.*

HAMLETS. 1. *Woodmancot*, about two miles north-weſtward from the church. William de Marre, of Ryndecumbe, releaſed to the convent of Lacok, for ſeventeen pounds ſterling, all his rights in the manor of Wodemancote, except the view of frankpledge of the earl of Glouceſter, to be made twice a year at Rindecumbe. Conſtantia de Lega gave to God and the bleſſed Mary, all the manor of Wudemanecote, to make an abbey at Lacok, and afterwards, in the reign of king Henry the Third, acknowledged, before the king's juſtices, that two carucates of land, with their appurtenances in Wodemancote, were the right of the convent of Lacok.

The foregoing is taken from *Stevens's Supplement to the Monaſticon*, (Appendix, N°. 448.) where are many other particulars of lands in Wodemancote, ſaid to be granted to the monaſtery of Lacok; but as the county is not mentioned, and as there are many places of that name in other parts, beſides three in Glouceſterſhire, it cannot be aſcertained to which of thoſe places the lands belonged.

Thomas the ſon of Otto, and Beatrix his wife, were ſeized of the manor of Woodmancot 2 E. 1. Gilbert de Clare, earl of Glouceſter and Hertford, was ſeized of the manors of Woodmancot and Calmſden, with court-leet, 15 E. 1. Warine the ſon of Warine was ſeized of the manor of Woodmancot 16 E. 3. John Blount held Woodmancot and Calmſden, in North Cerney, 22 H. 6. and Wentlyn, his widow, was ſeized thereof 32 H. 6.

2. *Calmſden*, which was held by the earl of Glouceſter and John Blount, as above mentioned. Alice Burley held a third part of the manor of Calmondeſden in dower, and John Burley, her ſon, and Iſabel, his wife, levied a fine of the other two parts, to the uſe of themſelves, 4 H. 4. Richard, the ſon of Roger de Calmſden, gave divers lands to the knights templers, which afterwards came to the knights hoſpitallers of Jeruſalem. Conſtantia de Lega, widow, gave to the nuns of Lacok 25*s.* yearly rent in Calemundeſden, which the knights hoſpitallers uſed to pay her. *Stevens*, as above. Mabilia, Robert, and William de Mara gave to the knights hoſpitallers all their demeans in Calmſden. After the diſſolution of religious foundations, ſuch of the above lands as belonged to the knights hoſpitallers of Jeruſalem, were granted to Thomas lord Seimour; after whoſe attainder they reverted to the crown, and were again granted to Catherine Buckler, widow, and to Richard Buckler and Catherine his wife, 7 E. 6.

There was a manor in Calmſden which belonged to the archbiſhop of York 14 E. 3. and was granted to ſir Thomas Chamberlain 6 E. 6. But the tithes of the archbiſhop's demeans belonged to the monaſtery of St. Oſwald in Glouceſter, and were granted to the chapter of Briſtol 34 H. 8. Sir William Gyſe claims the manors of Woodmancot and Calmſden.

There was formerly a chapel in each of theſe hamlets, but they have been long ſince demoliſhed.

Of the Church, &c.

The church is a rectory, in the deanery of Cirenceſter, worth 300*l.* a year. Gilbert de Clare, earl of Glouceſter and Hertford, was ſeized of the advowſon of Cerney 8 E. 2. The advowſon was in diſpute between the late ſir John Gyſe, and the executors of the late Charles Coxe, eſq; which ended in an agreement to convey both their rights to Univerſity-college, Oxford. The reverend Thomas C. Coxe is the preſent incumbent, and one of the repreſentatives of the clergy in the houſe of convocation.

Ninety-ſix acres of arable, and between twenty and thirty of paſture, belong to the glebe.

The church is handſomely pewed, and hath two croſs ailes and a low tower. There was a ſtatue of a prieſt in his robes, in a niche in the ſouth wall of the chancel, ſuppoſed to be for the founder of the church, but it is now taken away.

There is a piece of ground given to adorn the church, which lets for 22*s.* a year.

Monuments and Inſcriptions.

On the table of a handſome monument, in the ſouth aile, is this inſcription:

Here lyeth y[e] Body of Tho: Rich, Eſq; one of y[e] M[rs] of y[e] High Court of Chauncery, who married Anne one of y[e] daught. & Coheires of Tho: Bourchiere of Barneſley Eſq[ir]: by whom he had Ten Sonnes, Tho: Will: Edw: Sam: Jo: Robt: Ewſtace: Hen: Antho: & Cha: & Five daught[rs]: Bridget, who marryed Jo: How, Baronet, Suſan who married Edw: Bathurſt Baro: Mary who married Giles Dowle, Gent. & Anne & Anne who died younge. Who departed y[s] life the 27th of Octo. 1647.—— At top are theſe arms, Quarterly, 1ſt and 4th, *Per pale, ſable and gules, a croſs botonny fitchy, between four fleurs de lis Or*, for Rich. 2d and 3d, Bourchier, as before under *Barnſley*.

On another monument, in the ſame aile, is a memorial for Thomas Rich, gent. who died in 1704-5, and Suſannah his wife, daughter of Edward Nott, of Bradon, with their arms, *i. e.* 1ſt, Rich, as before, impaling, *Azure, on a bend between three leopards heads caboſhed Or, as many martlets gules*, for Nott.

Firſt fruits £.	21	10	5*ob.*	Synodals £.	0	2	0
Tenths —	2	3	0*ob.*	Pentecoſtals	0	1	6
Procurations	0	6	8				

Taxes.				
The Royal Aid in 1692, £.		91	13	2
Poll-tax —	1694, —	13	1	0
Land-tax —	1694, —	59	1	4
The ſame, at 3*s.*	1770, —	62	3	0

There

There were 42 houfes and about 190 inhabitants in this parifh, whereof 16 were freeholders; yearly births 6, burials 5. *Atkyns.* Examining the parifh regifter, I find, that in a feries of ten years, from 1700 to 1709 inclufive, there were 58 baptifms and 43 burials; and in the fame number of years, from 1760 to 1769, both inclufive, there were 99 baptifms and 82 burials. And the number of inhabitants is 384, fomething more than 46 to 1 of the average of the annual burials.

CERNEY, (SOUTH.)

THIS parifh lies in the hundred of Crowthorn and Minety, four miles fouth from Cirencefter, four north-weftward from Cricklade in Wiltfhire, and twenty-one fouth-eaftward from Gloucefter. The river Churn runs through it, and empties itfelf into the Thames at Cricklade. The parifh confifts chiefly of meadow and pafture, with fome rich arable. The meadows are greatly improved by turning the river water over them in the winter feafon, which invigorates the foil, and infures a plentiful crop every year, without manure; which I mention, becaufe the method is not generally ufed, nor even heard of in many parts of the kingdom.

The name is explained under the preceding parifh, and more largely under *Cirencefter*.

Of the Manors and other Eftates.

In *Domefday-book* are the following particulars: 'Walter [the fon of Roger] holds Cernei in 'Gerfdones hundred. There are fourteen hides, 'and one yard-land. Archbifhop Stigand held it. 'In demean are two plow-tillages, and twenty-'five villeins, and a prieft, and nine bordars, with 'ten plow-tillages. There are four *fervi*, and a 'hundred acres of meadow, and there were three 'mills of 30*s*. [rent.] It was worth 16*l*. and is 'now worth 12*l*.'

'This manor was claimed by the church of St. 'Mary of Abendone, but all the county teftified 'that Stigand the archbifhop held it ten years 'when king Edward was living. Earl William 'gave this manor to Roger the fheriff, father of 'Walter.' *Domefday-book*, p. 77.

'Radulf [de Todeni] holds Omenie and Cerney 'in Gerfdones hundred, and Roger holds them of 'him. There are four hides. Four thanes held 'them for four manors, and they could go where 'they would. In demean are ten plow-tillages, 'and one villein, and nineteen bordars. There 'are twenty-one *fervi*, and a mill of 5*s*. and thirty 'acres of meadow. It was worth 10*l*. and is 'now worth 6*l*.' *Domefday-book*, p. 76.

There are, at prefent, three manors in this parifh, whereof the largeft belonged to the barons of St. Amand. Guy de St. Amand was poffeffed of eftates in South Cerney, Wick, and Cirencefter, which came to William St. Amand, and were purchafed of him by Almarick de St. Amand, governor of St. Briavel's caftle, and warden of the foreft of Dean. Ralph de St. Amand, fon of Almarick, married Afceline, one of the heireffes of Robert d'Aubeny, baron of Caynho in Bedfordfhire, and dying 30 H. 3. was fucceeded by his fon Almarick de St. Amand, who died feized of South Cerney 14 E. 1. Guy, his fon and heir, left no iffue, but Lucia, his wife, furviving him, was endowed with a third part of the manor of South Cerney.

Almarick de St. Amand, brother of Guy, was the next heir, and was fummoned as a baron to parliament 28 E. 1. but he dying without iffue, was fucceeded by John de St. Amand, his brother, who was educated in the civil law. He was alfo fummoned as a baron to parliament 2 E. 2. and died feized of South Cerney and Cerney Wick 20 E. 2. Almarick de St. Amand was fon and heir to John. He and his wife Joan levied a fine of the manor of South Cerney to the ufe of themfelves and the heirs of their bodies, the remainder to the right heirs of Almarick, 4 E. 3. He was conftituted juftice of Ireland 31 E. 3. and was made knight of the Bath in 1400. He died 4 H. 4. leaving two daughters, Elianor, by Ida his firft wife, and Ida, by Elianor his fecond wife.

Elianor, his eldeft daughter, was married to Gerhard Braybrook. They left three daughters, whereof Elizabeth, the eldeft, was married to William Beauchamp, fon of Walter Beauchamp of Powyk, and grandfon to John lord Beauchamp. He was created lord St. Amand, and fummoned to parliament 27 H. 6. and died 35 H. 6. But it does not appear that he was poffefs'd of this manor; for Richard de Beauchamp, earl of Warwick, died feized of South Cerney 17 H. 6.

The above Richard de Beauchamp had three daughters, of whom Elizabeth, the youngeft, was married to George Nevile, lord Latimer. Richard lord Latimer, grandfon and heir of George, died feized of the manor of South Cerney and Cerney Wike 22 H. 8. and livery thereof was granted the fame year to John lord Latimer, his fon, who died 34 H. 8. He left a fon John, who had livery granted to him the next year. He married lady Lucy, daughter to Henry earl of Worcefter, and died 20 Eliz. leaving four daughters coheireffes, who had livery granted to them the fame year. Lucy, the third daughter, was married to fir William Cornwallis, who, in her right, was feized of this manor in the year 1608. Thus it appears that the chief manor of South Cerney and Cerney Wike continued, by defcent, in the fame family above four hundred years.

Afterwards it came to fir Nevil Pool, who fold it to fir Edward Atkyns, from whom it defcended to fir Robert Atkyns; and he fettled it on his fon fir Robert Atkyns, who fold away the greateft part to divers freeholders, and the remaining part was vefted in Mr. John Jones.

Richard

Richard Jones, esq; was his son, whose trustees sold it in chancery to Henry Cook, Edward Dewe, and John Jones, in survivorship. Dewe dying, Cook and Jones conveyed their rights to their respective sons, and William Cook, son of Henry, purchased of Richard Jones, son of John, his share of the manor. He died, and left it by will to his mother, Amy Cook, who is the present proprietor, and holds court-leet, but there are no copyholders belonging to the manor.

The priory of Lanthony near Gloucester was seized of another manor in this parish, and had court-leet and waifs 15 E. 1. Upon the dissolution of religions foundations, this manor was granted to William earl of Southampton and his heirs male 31 H. 8. The same manor, and the tithes of the demeans, were granted to William Fitz-Williams and Arthur Hilton 7 E. 6. who conveyed it to George Carlton the following year; and he sold it, in 1556, to Francis Wye. Another Francis Wye gave it to his niece Isabel, wife of William Gower, esq; in 1653; whose son John Gower sold it to John Jones, esq; in 1677: His grandson John Jones, esq; is the present lord of this manor, who has a good house and large estate in this parish, and in other parts of the county. His arms are, *Ermine, a chevron humetty sable*. The above manor is free from tithes.

The third manor was granted by the crown to the dean and chapter of Bristol, and is now in lease to Thomas Bush, esq; who has a good house and good estate here, and in other parts. He holds a court-baron, but no court-leet. His arms are, *Argent, a horse rampant sable, in chief three crosses pattee gules*.

Of the other estates the records shew, that Philip de Ferlege gave all his lands in Cerne to the priory of Bradenstoke. *Dugd. Bar.* Lands in Cerney Wike belonged to the priory of Ferley in Wiltshire, and were granted to Alexander Staples and John Lovel 16 Eliz.

Halstone-bridge is half in Cerney and half in Chelworth in the parish of Cricklade, and each parish supports its respective part. Halstone-farm is wholly in Chelworth.

Of the Church, &c.

The church is a vicarage, in the deanery of Cirencester, worth 130*l.* a year. Walter, the sheriff of Gloucester, son of earl Roger, gave the church of Cerney, with the tithes thereof, to the monks of St. Peter's at Gloucester, in the reign of king Henry the First. The bishop of Worcester appropriated this church to the abbey of Gloucester, and settled the allowance to the vicar, in the year 1327. After the dissolution of religious foundations, the rectory and advowson of the vicarage were granted to the bishop of Gloucester, by the charter of foundation of that see. The bishop of Gloucester is patron and impropriator; and the reverend Mr. Anselm Jones the present incumbent. The impropriators, ever since the reign of king Charles the Second, have augmented the living with 11*l.* a year.

The chapel of Halstone, formerly called *Cerney Milonis*, was annexed to this church. *Atkyns.*

The church consists of the nave and one aile, with a handsome spire steeple, and five bells, at the west end. It is dedicated to All Saints. No monument of note.

Here was a custom, which prevailed 'till lately, of strewing coarse hay and rushes over the floor of the church, which is called *Juncare*; and the lands which were subject to provide those materials, now pay a certain sum of money annually, in lieu thereof.

	£.	s.	d.		£.	s.	d.
First fruits	6	16	8	Synodals	0	2	0
Tenths —	0	13	8	Pentecostals	0	1	6
Procurations	0	6	8				

Benefaction.

—— Cutts gave a yard-land and five acres, being together about thirty acres, and six small tenements, all worth 28*l.* a year, to the use of the church, the poor, and the repair of the highways. There is no account when the donation was made; but it must have been several ages since, if tradition may be credited, that a very antient flat stone in the church-yard, with half-length figures of a man and woman, is for the donor and his wife.

			£.	s.	d.
Taxes.	The Royal Aid in	1692,	219	15	9
	Poll-tax — —	1694, —	42	16	0
	Land-tax ——	1694, —	176	0	0
	The same, at 3*s.*	1770, —	124	17	9

At the beginning of this century there were 120 houses and about 500 inhabitants in this parish, whereof 60 were freeholders; yearly births 15, burials 14. *Atkyns.* But by the entries in the parish register, it appears, that in ten years, from 1731 to 1740, both inclusive, there were 188 baptisms and 105 burials; and in the same number of years, beginning at 1760, there were 215 baptisms and 161 burials. The present number of houses is 247, and of inhabitants 806; so that population is considerably increased, and about 1 in 50 dies every year.

****

CHARFIELD.

THIS is a small parish in the upper division of the hundred of Grumbaldsash, six miles distant north from Chipping-Sodbury, three miles west from Wotton-under-edge, and twenty-three south-west from Gloucester.

It is very difficult to fix the etymology of the name, if sir Robert Atkyns was not right in his conjecture, that it was so called from being the *field* where *Cerdic* or *Cirdic* obtained a victory over the Britons.

Tafarn-bath,

Tafarn-bath, corruptly from *bâch*, confifting of a little ale-houfe and another cottage, at the crofs-ing of the two roads on the borders of this parifh, claims our notice for its antiquity. The name is Britifh, and fignifies a *little ale-houfe*, which fhews that there was a houfe of entertainment there, as long fince as it was ufual to give Britifh names to places in this country.

The greateft part of the parifh is pafture, with fome arable. It is feparated from Kingfwood by a fmall brook, which runs down to Berkeley.

Of the Manor and other Eftates.

'Gozelinus Brito holds Cirvelde, in Bacheftanes 'hundred, of the king. Elfelt held it of king 'Edward. There are three hides. In demean are 'two plow-tillages, and four villeins, and feven 'bordars, with four plow-tillages. There are 'four *fervi*, and a mill of 10*s*. [rent] and eight 'acres of meadow; a wood half a mile in length 'and breadth. It was worth 4*l*. and is now 'worth 40*s*.' *Domefday-book*, p. 79.

The Mayfeys, or Maffeys, were lords of Charfield in the reign of king Henry the Third. John de Mayfey granted this manor to Robert le Veel, who was feized thereof, and of court-leet and free warren, 15 E. 1. This record implies fome re-conveyance, and fhews that Charfield did more antiently belong to the Veels. Sir Peter, fon of fir Peter le Veel, married Cicely, daughter and heir of John Mayfey, (or Maffey, as he is called elfe-where) with whom he had the manor of Charfield 4 E. 3. and held the fame 17 E. 3.

Sir John Berkeley, fon of fir Thomas Berkeley, by Catherine, daughter of fir John Clivedon of Charfield, knight, and widow of fir Peter le Veel of Tortworth, was feized of the manor of Charfield 6 H. 6. But John Veel was feized of it 36 H. 6.

Sir Maurice Berkeley of Beverftone held Charfield 38 & 39 H. 6. and 14 E. 4.

Robert Stanfhaw, efq; was feized of this manor 12 E. 4. and John Stanfhaw, and Humphry his brother, levied a fine of lands in this parifh 12 H. 7.

William Berkeley was feized of this manor in the reign of king Richard the Third, and granted it to fir Thomas Brugge and his heirs male, in taille, 1 R. 3.

This manor, foon after, paffed to the Throckmortons of Tortworth. Thomas Morgen levied a fine of lands in Charfield, Huntingfeild, and Oldbury, to the ufe of Thomas Throckmorton 3 Mar. and upon his death, livery of the manor, and of a moiety of the advowfon, was granted to Thomas Throckmorton, his fon, 9 Eliz. Sir William Throckmorton was lord of it in 1608. It paffed afterwards into the name and family of Hicks, and is now the property of lieutenant colonel Brome, of the royal regiment of artillery. Colonel Brome's arms are, *Sable, three fwans Or, a crefcent for difference.*

The manor of Charfield was held of the honour of Gloucefter 21 E. 3.—10, 16, & 22 R. 2. and 4 H. 4. by one knight's fee; and it is now reputed to be within the jurifdiction of the court of that honour.

Of the Church, &c.

The church is a rectory, in the deanery of Hawkefbury, worth 150*l*. a year. Mr. Richard Tyndale[1] is patron and incumbent. The rector hath 20*l*. a year out of Micklewood-chace, and no lands in the parifh are free from tithe.

The church confifts of the nave, and an aile on the north fide, with a low tower at the weft end.

Firft fruits £	10	1	2	Synodals £.	0	2	0
Tenths —	1	0	1*qr*.	Pentecoftals	0	0	10
Procurations	0	6	8				

Benefactions.

Joan Burton hath long fince given 20*l*. to the poor. The widow Pierce gave 24*s*. a year, to charitable ufes, of which 10*s*. is for a fermon. And there is a rent of 6*s*. 8*d*. a year charged on —— Jocham's houfe, towards the repair of the church.

Taxes.					
The Royal Aid in	1692,	£. 100	12	0
Poll-tax — —	1694, —	15	18	0
Land-tax ——	1694, —	133	10	0
The fame, at 3*s*.	1770, —	104	0	7*ob*.

There were 30 houfes and about 145 inhabitants in this parifh, whereof 10 were freeholders, when fir Robert Atkyns compiled his Hiftory; yearly births 5, burials 4. *Atkyns*. In the courfe of ten years from 1759, there are regiftered 48 baptifms and 42 burials, and the inhabitants are upwards of 200; fo that the number of living is to the annual burials, nearly as 50 to 1.

CHARLTON ABBAT's

IS a very little parifh in the lower part of Kiftfgate hundred, five miles diftant north-eaft from Cheltenham, two fouthward from Winchcombe, and thirteen north-eaft from Gloucefter.

Charlton, from the Saxon ceorl, fignifies the *country-man's town*; and being part of the poffeffions of the abbey of Winchcombe, occafioned the additional name, to diftinguifh it from another Charlton in this neighbourhood.

A rivulet rifes in this parifh, whofe head is called Tinning-Well, and running directly north, empties itfelf into the Severn. Another fpring, rifing near it, runs fouthward into the Thames.

Of the Manor and other Eftates.

'The church of St. Mary of Wincelcumbe 'holds Cerletone in Greteftanes hundred. There

[1] Mr. Tyndale's family came into Gloucefterfhire about the time of king Edward the Fourth, and, for fome time, paffed by the name of Hitchens, to avoid the refentment of party, having been concerned in the difputes between the houfes of York and Lancafter; but when thofe difputes were ended, they re-affumed their proper name. *For their arms, fee North Cerney.*

'are two hides free and quit [from tax.] In 'demean is one plow-tillage, and four villeins, 'and two bordars, with four plow-tillages. There 'are ſix *ſervi*, and a mill of 20*d.* [rent] and two 'acres of meadow. It is worth and was worth '20*s.*'. *Domeſday-book*, p. 71.

The abbat of Winchcombe purchaſed a charter of free warren in Charleton 35 H. 3. which privilege was allowed him in a writ of *Quo warranto*, 15 E. 1. And the church of Winchcombe continued in poſſeſſion of this manor 'till the diſſolution of that houſe.

After the diſſolution, it was granted by the crown to Henry Tracy of Toddington, 7 E. 6. ſoon after which, it was purchaſed by John Carter, eſq; whoſe deſcendant Eſtcourt Carter, eſq; ſon of Cornelius, a younger ſon of John Carter, ſon of another John, who was the ſon of the firſt purchaſer, is the preſent lord of the manor, and has a good eſtate here and in Oxfordſhire. His arms are blazoned under *Aſton Blank*.

Of the Church, &c.

The church is in the deanery of Winchcombe. It is an impropriation, ſubject to the payment of 10*l.* a year to the curate. There is no ſettled incumbent; but divine ſervice is performed once a fortnight, by ſome neighbouring clergyman. Mr. Aylworth left 800*l.* to purchaſe land for the augmentation of Charlton Abbats, Cold Salperton, Sevenhampton, and Compton Abdale, out of which the curate of this church receives about five guineas a year. There was an attempt to procure the queen's bounty, but the income being now improved to upwards of 10*l.* a year, the truſtees would not allow it.

The tithes of this pariſh belonged to the abbey of Winchcombe, and were granted to ſir Thomas Seimour 1 E. 6. after whoſe attainder, they were again granted by the crown to John Huſſey and John Haward 20 Eliz. The impropriation is now the property of Edward Carter, eſq. The demeans of the manor are tithe free.

The church is ſmall and very ruinous. The inhabitants bury at Winchcombe, except thoſe who bury in the church.

Taxes.			£.	s.	d.
	The Royal Aid in	1692,	53	10	0
	Poll-tax ——	1694, —	8	11	0
	Land-tax ——	1694, —	34	16	0
	The ſame, at 3*s.*	1770, —	24	9	10*ob.*

At the beginning of this century there were 13 houſes and about 60 inhabitants, whereof 3 were freeholders. *Atkyns*. There are now 12 houſes and 63 inhabitants.

CHARLTON KING's

LIES in the hundred of Cheltenham, one mile diſtant eaſtward from the town of that name, ſeven ſouth from Winchcombe, and eleven eaſt from Glouceſter.

Charlton is explained under the preceding pariſh, from which this is properly diſtinguiſhed by the additional name of *King's*, becauſe at the Norman conqueſt it was part of the demeans of the crown.

This pariſh conſiſts of rich paſture and arable, with ſome woodland. It is watered by three brooks which unite here, and drive ſeveral corn-mills; and is very advantagiouſly ſituated under the Lechampton hills, which ſecure it from the eaſterly winds.

Of the Manors and other Eſtates.

As this was a member of the great manor of Cheltenham, at the time of the conqueſt, it was included in the general account of that manor in *Domeſday-book*. In the ſubſequent records, we find a manor deſcribed by the name of Aſhley, *alias* Charlton King's, as tho' thoſe two names were really and ſtrictly proper to the ſame place; whereas the manor of Aſhley doth not comprehend the whole of Charlton, but is a manor holden of, and lying within the manor of Cheltenham; and Charlton, and Bafford in Charlton, are parcels of the ſame manor of Cheltenham, diſtinct from, and far more extenſive than Aſhley.

Charles prince of Wales, afterwards king Charles the Firſt, was lord of the manor of Charlton. James-Lenox Dutton, eſq; is the preſent lord of this manor.

Walter de Eſheley took his name from the manor of Aſheley in this pariſh, and was ſeized of part of Charlton 30 H. 3. Petronella Mareſchal held the manor of King's Charlton 54 H. 3. but this is to be underſtood of Aſhley only, which was given her in free marriage by Walter de Eſheley.

This manor belonged afterwards, for many deſcents, to the family of the Grevils, who enjoyed ſeveral eſtates in the pariſh of Cheltenham, and other parts of Glouceſterſhire. Thomas Rawlins and his wife levied a fine of lands in Charlton, Gineton, Preſbury, and Cheltenham, to William Grevil and William Baynham, 9 H. 7. Francis Grevil levied a fine of Charlton King's, *alias* Aſhley, 3 E. 6. Giles Grevil and Arthur Parker were owners of this manor in the year 1608.

The manor of Aſhley, *alias* Charlton King's, came afterwards to Mr. Edward Mitchel. It is now the property of William Prinn, eſq; who has a good houſe and a good eſtate in this pariſh. His arms are, *Or, a feſs engrailed between three eſcallops azure*,

Mr. Whithorn has alſo a good houſe and good eſtate in this pariſh.

Of the other eſtates the records ſhew, that Richard Forſter levied a fine of a moiety of lands in Charlton and Ham, to John Walſh and others, 12 H. 7.

HAMLET. *Ham* is a hamlet in this pariſh, about half a mile from the church. Richard Grevil levied a fine of the manor of Ham, and of lands

lands in Charlton King's, 3 E. 6. Ralph and Richard Goderick levied a fine of lands in Ham and Norfield, to Robert Bidle 3 E. 6.

An act of parliament was paſſed 1 C. 1. intitled, *An Act for the ſettling and confirming copyhold eſtates, and cuſtoms of the tenants in baſe tenure, of the manor of Cheltenham, com. Glouc. and of the manor of Aſhley, otherwiſe Charlton King's, in the ſaid county, being holden of the ſaid manor of Cheltenham, according to an agreement thereof made between the King's Moſt Excellent Majeſty, being then Prince of Wales, Duke of York, and Earl of Cheſter, lord of the ſaid manor of Cheltenham, and Giles Grevile, eſq; lord of the ſaid manor of Aſhley, and the ſaid copyholders of the ſaid ſeveral manors:* The ſubſtance of which act is given under *Cheltenham.*

Of the Church, &c.

The church is in the deanery of Winchombe. It was antiently a chapel to the church of Cheltenham, of which the rectory, formerly belonging to the abbey of Cirenceſter, was granted by the crown to ſir William Rider 7 Jac. It is an impropriation belonging to the earl of Eſſex. The curate is nominated by Jeſus college Oxford, and approved by the heir of ſir Baptiſt Hicks, exactly in the ſame manner, and under the ſame limitations preſcribed for Cheltenham. He receives 35 *l.* a year out of the impropriation. Mr. Bedwell is the preſent incumbent. Here is no houſe for the miniſter.

The church is dedicated to St. Mary. It is a flat building, with an aile on the ſouth ſide. It has a handſome ſquare embattled tower with pinnacles, and ſix bells in it, ſtanding in the middle, and there are two chapels on the north and ſouth ſides of the tower, making together the form of a croſs.

Monuments and Inſcriptions.

There is a neat pyramidal marble monument in the north chapel, with this inſcription.

HEREUNDER lye the Remains of Mrs. ELIZABETH PRINN, late the Wife of *William Prinn*, Eſq; and eldeſt Daughter of *Thomas Ridler*, late of *Edgworth*, in the County of *Gloceſter*, Eſq; who departed this Life *March* 5th, 1771, aged 51 Years. ALSO of Mrs. ELIZABETH HUNT, Daughter of the above named *William Prinn*, and *Elizabeth Prinn*, who was Married to *Dodington Hunt*, of the Inner Temple, *London*, Eſq; and departed this Life *Auguſt* 10th, 1772, aged 24 Years and Six Months. ——— At bottom are theſe arms, *Or, a feſs ingrailed between three eſcallops azure*, for Prinn.

In the chancel there is the following inſcription upon an oval braſs plate:

SAMUEL COOPER of this Pariſh, Gent. died the 13th of *May*, 1743; who by Will gave to the Truſtees under mentioned, and to their Succeſſors his Truſtees for ever, the Rents of his Grounds in the ſame Pariſh, called *Cutham Butts*, and *Battle Downs*; for buying Books, and teaching *ſix poor Children* of this Pariſh to read two years, at the End of which Time *ſix* others, to be choſen by the ſaid Truſtees, with the Privity of the Church-wardens. The Overplus to provide Fuel, and cloath *ſix aged or infirm poor Perſons* not receiving *Alms* of the Pariſh. Truſtees, Robert Gale, ſen^r. Edm^d. Welſh, Edwd. Gale, Gent. ——— At botton, on a ſcutcheon, *Vert, a tortoiſe palewiſe proper.*

Againſt the north wall of the chancel is a memorial for ſeveral of the family of Brereton, and theſe arms, *Quarterly*, 1ſt and 4th, *Argent, two bars ſable.* 2d and 3d, *Sable, a bend argent, charged with three lozenges of the field.*

There is an inſcription upon a ſtone in the church for Winifrid, wife of James Ingram, and at top are her arms, *A croſs lozengy between four roſes.* The colours not expreſſed.

There is a tomb in the church-yard, with a memorial for Mrs. Margaret Rich, daughter of Ed. Rich, of Dowdeſwell, eſq; buried Sept. 2, 1692. And the arms of Rich, (as under *North Cerney*) impaling, *A chevron charged with three ſtags heads caboſhed, between as many lozenges.* No colours expreſſed.

Pentecoſtals 9*d. ob.*

Benefactions.

There are lands of the value of 12 *l.* a year given for the repair of the church, and for the relief of the poor. Mr. Alexander Packer gave 100 *l.* to the poor. And ſmall donations from ſeveral perſons amount to 70 *l.* which is made a ſtock for the uſe of the poor.

For Mr. Cooper's donation for teaching poor children of this pariſh to read, and for buying fuel for poor families, ſee *Inſcriptions.*

Taxes.						
The Royal Aid in	1692,	£.	189	14	0
Poll-tax —	1694,	—	46	5	0
Land-tax —	1694,	—	208	9	3 ob.
The ſame, at 3 *s.*	1770,	—	156	8	5

According to ſir Robert Atkyns, when he compiled his *Hiſtory*, there were 102 houſes in this pariſh, and about 550 inhabitants, whereof 60 were freeholders; yearly births 16, burials 15. But it appears by the pariſh regiſter, that in ten years from 1700, there were 125 baptiſms and 153 burials, but in four of thoſe years there was a great mortality in the pariſh, which carried off 88 perſons, being about 40 more than died in four common years. In ten years, from 1760, there were 147 baptiſms, and 107 burials; ſo that the annual average of burials is 10.7, and the number of inhabitants is about 458. From the ſtate of the pariſh regiſter, it ſeems that ſir Robert Atkyns's eſtimate of the inhabitants was too high; and from a compariſon of the baptiſms in thoſe diſtant periods, it may be concluded, that population is rather increaſing here.

CHEDWORTH.

THIS pariſh lies in the coteſwold country, in the hundred of Rapſgate, four miles ſouth-weſt from Northleach, ſeven northward from Cirenceſter, and about ſixteen eaſtward from Glouceſter.

Ceo ſignifies the *brow* or *deſcent of a place,* and pop𝔡 *a village,* which is exactly deſcriptive of the preſent ſituation of the houſes in this pariſh, moſt of which ſtand on the declivity of two hills, facing each

each other, with the river Coln running between them, in its courſe to Coln Deans, Coln Rogers, Coln Aldwins, and Fairford, a little below which it empties itſelf into the Thames.

This place gives the title of baron to the Right Honourable Henry-Frederick How, third lord Chedworth, whoſe father, John How, was created baron of Chedworth in the county of Glouceſter, by letters patent, dated May 12, 1741.

John Chedworth, biſhop of Lincoln in the year 1471, is ſuppoſed to have been a native of this place.

Of the Manor and other Eſtates.

What is advanced by ſome writers, that *Burgred king of Mercia, about the year* 854, *gave fifteen hides in Chedanwyrd on the hills to the monaſtery of Glouceſter, whilſt Gaffe was abbeſs thereof*, ſeems to be a miſtake: For Eva, the laſt abbeſs of that monaſtery, died in 768; and afterwards, in the wars between king Egbert and the Mercians, the nuns abandoned the monaſtery, which became deſolate, and ſo continued 'till the year 821. Beornulph king of Mercia then repaired it, and beſtowed part of its former poſſeſſions for the maintenance of ſecular prieſts, whom he had placed there. And king Burgred, in the year 862, confirmed to them the lands which had been given them. See p. 131.

This manor ſtands under the title *Terra Regis*, in *Domeſday-book*, and, at the time of the Norman conqueſt, was part of the demeans of the crown.

'Wlward held Cedeorde in Reſpiet hundred. 'There were fifteen hides including the wood, the 'plain, and the meadow; and ſeven plow-tillages 'in demean, in the time of king Edward; and 'ſixteen villeins, and three bordars, with ſix plow-'tillages, and three mills of 14*s.* 2*d.* and the toll 'of the ſalt which came to the [king's] hall. The 'ſheriff added eight villeins and three bordars, 'having four plow-tillages.'

'Of theſe two manors [Cedeorde and Alvredin-'tvne] the ſtewards paid what they pleaſed in the 'time of king Edward. They now pay 40*l.* of 'white money, of which twenty is in *ora.* Earl 'Roger held it.' *Domeſday-book*, p. 69.

Earl Roger was ſtiled Roger de Bellemont, and was earl of Mellent. He ſettled this manor on Henry de Newburg, a younger ſon, who was afterwards created earl of Warwick by king William the Second, and died ſeized of Chedworth 23 H. 1. He was ſucceeded by his ſon Roger earl of Warwick, who married Gundred, daughter of earl Warren, and died 18 Steph.

William earl of Warwick, ſon and heir of Roger, dying 30 H. 2. without iſſue, was ſucceeded in title and eſtate by Walerond his brother, who married Margaret, daughter of Humphry de Bohun, earl of Hereford. His ſecond wife was Alice, daughter of John de Hercourt; which Alice, upon the death of her huſband 6 Joh. had Chedworth aſſigned to her in dower.

Henry earl of Warwick, ſon of Walerond, died ſeized of the manor of Chedworth 13 H. 3. Thomas earl of Warwick, his ſon, married Ela, ſecond daughter of William Long Eſpee, earl of Saliſbury, natural ſon to king Henry the Second, by Fair Roſamond, and died without iſſue 26 H. 3. Ela, his widow, was ſeized of the third part of the manor of Chedworth in dower 36 H. 3.

John de Pleſſets, or Placetis, married Margery, ſiſter and heir to Thomas earl of Warwick. He was in great favour with king Henry the Third, who made the match, and obliged the lady to ſettle her whole eſtate on him for life, altho' ſhe ſhould have no children by him. He held two parts of the manor of Chedworth in right of his wife, 27 H. 3. and afterwards had the title of earl of Warwick; but ſhe having no iſſue, the manor deſcended to the Beauchamps. For Walerond, the before mentioned earl of Warwick, beſides his ſon Henry, had a daughter Alice, or Eliſia, married to William Manduit de Hanſlape, the king's chamberlain. They had iſſue William and Iſabel. William Manduit, in right of his mother, upon failure of the former line, was created earl of Warwick; but he died 52 H. 3. without iſſue, whereby his ſiſter Iſabel became his heireſs. She was married to William Beauchamp.

William de Beauchamp, earl of Warwick, ſon of the laſt William, by his wife Iſabel Manduit, died ſeized of the whole manor of Chedworth 52 H. 3. of which the third part had been reſigned to him by Ela, the widow of Thomas earl of Warwick.

At this time the manor began to be divided, for Patrick de Chaworth, the fourth of that name, marrying Maud, daughter of the above William Beauchamp, had with her the third part of it, of which he died ſeized 11 E. 1. And Henry earl of Lancaſter marrying Maud de Chaworth, his daughter and heir, was ſeized, in her right, of the third part of the manor of Chedworth 1 E. 3. which deſcending to Henry duke of Lancaſter, was given, with the manor of Kempsford, and other lands, to Newark hoſpital at Leiceſter, which he had founded.

But William de Beauchamp, earl of Warwick, ſon of the before mentioned William, died ſeized of the reſidue of the manor of Chedworth 26 E. 1. and was ſucceeded by Guy earl of Warwick, his ſon and heir, who was twenty-ſix years old at his father's death. Guy was ſeized of the manor of Chedworth, which he held of the king *in capite*, by one knight's fee, and had in demean 200 acres of arable land, worth 2*d.* an acre, and not more, becauſe it was hill country land; eight acres of meadow, worth 1*s.* 6*d.* an acre; and 200 acres of wood, the underwood of which was worth 30*s.* and not more, becauſe it was common. This abſtract from the eſcheator's inquiſition ſerves to ſhew the value of land at that time. He died 9 E. 2. and left Thomas earl of Warwick his ſon and heir, then only two years old; who married Catherine, daughter of Roger lord Mortimer, and died of the plague at Calais, ſeized of Chedworth,

Chedworth, 43 E. 3. He was ſucceeded by Thomas de Beauchamp, earl of Warwick, his ſurviving ſon and heir. He had taken up arms againſt king Richard the Second, and was attainted, and his eſtates forfeited, whereupon this manor was granted to John Montacute, earl of Saliſbury; who afterwards endeavouring to reſtore the ſame king, and being taken priſoner at Cirenceſter, and there beheaded by the townſmen, 1 H. 4. this eſtate was reſtored to Thomas de Beauchamp, who died ſeized of Chedworth 2 H. 4.

Richard de Beauchamp, earl of Warwick, ſucceeded Thomas his father, and married Iſabel, the only ſurviving heireſs of the Diſpencers, who were heirs to the Clares earls of Glouceſter, and died ſeized of Chedworth 17 H. 6. Henry his ſon was created duke of Warwick, and died ſeized of this manor 23 H. 6. He left Anne, his only daughter and heireſs, an infant, who dying ſoon after, the inheritance came to Anne, ſiſter to Henry duke of Warwick; but the manor was aſſigned to Cicely dutcheſs of Warwick, his widow, in dower, 25 H. 6. This laſt Anne married Richard Nevil, earl of Saliſbury, who, in her right, was alſo earl of Warwick, and was often called the Make-King, from his great power and influence, in the reign of king Henry the Sixth. He was ſlain in Barnet field, fighting againſt king Edward the Fourth. Anne, his widow, had two daughters by him, coheireſſes to her vaſt eſtate; and becauſe ſhe had taken part in the deſigns of her late huſband, her eſtate was taken from her by an act of parliament 14 E. 4. and was ſettled on her two daughters, of whom Iſabel, the elder, was married to George duke of Clarence, brother to the king; and Anne, her ſiſter, was married to Richard, duke of Glouceſter, afterwards king Richard the Third.

George duke of Clarence, in right of Iſabel his wife, died ſeized of the manor of Chedworth 18 E. 4. and left Edward Plantagenet, the laſt heir male of that line, his ſon and heir; who by court contrivances, was attainted and beheaded, 15 H. 7.

King Henry the Seventh pretending the injuſtice of diveſting Anne dutcheſs of Warwick of her large inheritance, procured another act of parliament, in the beginning of his reign, to re-inſtate her, and then artfully prevailed with her to ſettle that great inheritance on him and his heirs, to the diſinheriſon of the iſſue of her own daughters, after this manor had been in the ſame family, by lineal deſcent, nearly five hundred years.

The manor of Chedworth continued in the crown till it was granted to John Dudley, earl of Warwick, afterwards duke of Northumberland, 1 E. 6. He being attainted 1 Mar. the manor reverted to the crown, and was granted to ſir Edward Unton. Sir John Tracy was lord of the manor of Chedworth in the year 1608.

This manor went afterwards to ſir Richard How, of Compton; from whom it deſcended to John How, eſq; of Stowell, ſometime one of the knights of the ſhire for the county of Wilts, who in 1741, was created baron of Chedworth; and lord Chedworth, who reſides at Stowell, in this county, is the preſent lord of the manor.

The other part of the manor of Chedworth, which had been given by Henry duke of Lancaſter to the hoſpital at Leiceſter, continued in the poſſeſſion of that hoſpital 'till the general diſſolution of religious foundations. Theſe lands were called *Dean-lands*, becauſe the dean and chapter of Leiceſter were intruſted with them for the uſe of the hoſpital, and were granted to John earl of Warwick 2 E. 6. upon whoſe attainder they were again granted to Erſkin earl of Marr, 1 Jac.

John Atwood was ſeized of a tenement in Chedworth called Woodland, 3 H. 4. And Thomas Mines levied a fine of lands in Chedworth to Simon Hercourt and others 23 H. 7.

Of the Church, &c.

The church is a vicarage, in the deanery of Cirenceſter, worth about 70*l.* a year. It is in the gift of Queen's college, Oxford. The reverend Mr. Rawys is the preſent incumbent. The advowſon was given by William Fitz-Oſborn, earl of Hereford, ſoon after the conqueſt, to the abbey of Lyra in Normandy. Afterwards William de Beauchamp, earl of Warwick, granted the advowſon to the abbey of Eveſham 2 E. 1. And the advowſon and impropriation both belonged to the priory of Bethleem at Sheen in Surry, who preſented in the year 1489. The impropriation was given by Hugh Weſtwood, eſq; towards the maintenance of a free grammar-ſchool at Northleach. The impropriation pays 16*s.* 2*d.* a year to the crown.

The vicar hath a third part of all tithes, twelve acres of paſture in eight cloſes, two yard-lands and a half of arable land, 150 ſheep-paſtures, and three half acres of land on a hill, where was a chapel dedicated to St. John. The chapel has been long ſince demoliſhed, and there are aſh-trees growing on the ſpot, which bear the name of *St. John's Aſhes*, and are to be ſeen at a great diſtance.

The vicarage-houſe is a very good one, built by the preſent incumbent.

The church hath a low tower, with five bells, at the weſt end.

Monuments and Inſcriptions.

In antient characters, againſt one of the buttreſſes of the church, is this inſcription:

Hic jacet in tumba Ricard Sely & . . . . . Uxīs ſue qui obiit 12 die menſis Mayi An dm 1461 cu aie ppciet d.

In the chancel:

GALFRIDVS WALL, A.M. hujus Eccleſiæ circiter Annos LXI Vicarius, Obijt Maij 25, Anno Dom. MDCCXLIII. Ætat. LXXXVIII.

Firſt fruits £.	7	8	4	Synodals £.	0	2	0
Tenths —	0	14	10	Pentecoſtals	0	1	10
Procurations	0	6	8				

Benefactions.

Lands were given for the repair of the church, and for the relief of the poor, in the reign of king Richard the Second. In the year 1691, they were leaſed out for ninety nine years, in two parcels, one at 30*s.* the other at 24*s.* a year. The lands are now worth 10*l.* a year. There are alſo ſix cottages given to the ſame uſes.

Taxes.			£.	s.	d.
	The Royal Aid in	1692,	92	15	2
	Poll-tax ——	1694, —	28	19	0
	Land-tax ——	1694, —	54	4	0
	The ſame, at 3*s.*	1770, —	57	3	0

At the beginning of this century, according to ſir Robert Atkyns, there were 150 houſes, and about 500 inhabitants in this pariſh, whereof almoſt 40 were freeholders; yearly births 13, burials 11. But it appears by the regiſter, that in ten years, from 1700, there were 153 baptiſms, and 110 burials; and in the ſame number of years, from 1760, the baptiſms were 234, and the burials 168. There are now 181 families, and 787 inhabitants. And the proportion of the living to the average number of perſons buried annually, is nearly as 47 to 1.

The following particulars came to hand not 'till after the former part of this account was printed, which prevented their being inſerted in the uſual place.——About the year 1760, a perſon ſinking a ditch, diſcovered a Roman bath, at Liſtercomb-bottom in this pariſh. It was ſupported by pillars of brick, round and ſquare alternately, of about nine or ten inches diameter, and the floor was alſo of brick. All the bricks were mark'd ARVIRI in Roman capitals, about two inches long, which I read, A ROMANIS VIRIBVS. There was a ſpring, and a ciſtern to receive the water; and many other things in the bath, which the perſon deſtroy'd, and could give but little account of. He uſed moſt of the bricks in building an oven, but the late doctor Shaw had a perfect one, which is preſerved amongſt his curioſities. This place lies about two miles on the north-weſt ſide of the Roman *Foſs*, and very probably there was a ſummer ſtation of that people at Chedworth. On the hill, a little above the bath, is a large *tumulus*, which had a huge, rough ſtone ſet upright on the top of it, ſuppoſed to be raiſed by the Britons or Saxons. Not long ſince, ſome of the farmers removed the ſtone with a double team of oxen, and ſo expoſed great quantities of human bones lying near the top of the barrow.

****

CHELTENHAM

IS a market-town within the hundred of its own name. It lies ten miles eaſt from Glouceſter, fifteen north from Cirenceſter, nine ſouth from Tewkeſbury, and a hundred weſt from London; from all which places there are turnpike roads leading to this town. The market is on Thurſday.

Chylt, or Cylt, in the Anglo-Saxon language, ſignifies clay. Some, however, have ſuppoſed *Chilt* to be the proper name of the brook that riſes at Dowdeſwell, and runs by this town, which they think took denomination from it; but I know not upon what grounds that ſuppoſition is founded. In ſhort, little can be ſaid with certainty of the derivation of the name of this place; but according to the firſt acceptation of the word Cylt, it ſignifies *a village* or *town of clay*; perhaps ſo called from the buildings being firſt made of earth or clay, before our Saxon anceſtors had learnt the art of brick-making; for it is pretty generally allowed, that after the Romans left Britain, that art and many others were loſt. But the Saxons had opportunities of improvement during the reign of king Alfred, who ſent for builders and artificers of almoſt every kind, from countries where they were more ſkilful.

The town conſiſts of one handſome ſtreet, near a mile long. The buildings are chiefly of brick. It is ſituated on the border of a fine fertile vale, about two miles from Cleeve, Preſbury, and Leckhampton hills, which join the Coteſwolds, and forming a kind of ſemi-circle, defend the town from thoſe cold blaſts which proceed from the eaſtern quarter.

As the pariſh is large, the ſoils are various: On the eaſt is a very looſe, white ſand, weſtward a ſtrong clay, ſouthward a fine rich loam, and in other parts a mixture of loam and ſand. The air is healthy, and the water not ſo hard, nor ſo fully charged with calcareous earth, as Dr. Lucas has repreſented it; for the inhabitants, and all who viſit them, uſe it for every common purpoſe, notwithſtanding they might have the brook water with little trouble.

Here is no manufacture carried on, but the women and children of the poorer ſort ſpin woollen yarn, for the clothiers about Stroud.

On an eaſy aſcent, about half a mile ſouthward of the church, in a loamy ſoil, riſes the Cheltenham *Spaw*, which firſt drew the public attention about the year 1740. What led to the diſcovery of its virtues, was an obſervation made by ſeveral perſons, that flocks of pidgeons reſorted to the ſpring, to eat a white ſalt, caſually made from the water by the heat of the ſun. And it had alſo been obſerved, that in hard, froſty weather, when other ſprings were frozen, this water continued fluid. Upon trial, it was found to be cathartic. It then roſe in a ſlow, obſcure ſpring, and ran upon the ſurface of a paſture ground. Mr. Maſon became the proprietor of it, by purchaſing the field in the year 1718, and firſt made a well, and erected a ſhed over it. In the year 1738, Mr. Henry Skillicorne purchaſed the premiſſes, built a dome over the well, and erected a large handſome room for the convenience of company. About this time, Dr. Short, who was

was then ſearching after all the mineral waters in the kingdom, viſited this place, and made experiments on the water, which are publiſhed in his *Eſſay towards an experimental Hiſtory of Mineral Waters.* Many other eminent phyſicians have alſo, at various times, examined and recommended it, which eſtabliſhed its reputation, and brought it into uſe.

The late ingenious Dr. Lucas *found it pretty clear, colorleſs, but not the moſt perfectly bright. It had hardly any remarkable ſmell, and taſted ſaline, bitteriſh, and ſlightly vitriolic. It may be rather ranked among the diſagreeable, then the agreeable to the palate.* Eſſay on Waters, Part 2.

Dr. Rutty concludes, not only from his experiments made with this water, but alſo from the experience of thoſe who have uſed it, that it gives a keen appetite, is ſucceſsful in the gravel, effectual in ſcorbutic humours, and will cure old ſcorbutic ulcers, even in the legs, tho' of twenty years ſtanding; is a remedy in eryſipelaſes, ſtrumous inflammations of the eyes, and thoſe tormenting pains of the hips and lumber muſcles which proceed from a lodgment of hot ſcorbutic ſalts; and that it is, at leaſt, of equal efficacy with the Alford waters, in bilious cholics, and other diſorders of the *primæ viæ.*

Dr. Short gives it the preference to all waters of the ſame kind yet diſcovered in England, and indeed, excepting Stoke water, it carries the greateſt proportion of ſalt in the ſame volume.

I ſhall conclude my account of it, in the words of Dr. Lucas, taken from his Eſſay already quoted. *In obſtinate obſtructions and ſcurvies, in cold phlegmatic conſtitutions, thoſe [waters] impregnated with iron muſt be, as experience ſhews them, the moſt effectual. Of theſe it is very remarkable, that purging with them is rarely, if ever, attended with any degree of dejection: for while the ſalts diſſolved in the waters purge, the mineral ſpirit, charged with iron, warms and invigorates the whole frame. In theſe the peaſants commit extraordinary exceſs, without feeling any ſenſible ill effect. I have ſeen old men drink Cheltenham water by the quart, without number or rule. Upon enquiring their intention and method, they have anſwered, they had drank them on ſuch days and holidays for upwards of thirty years. They ſaid they had no diſorders; but they reckoned it wholeſome to clean their bodies, and they had no rule, but to drink 'till the water paſſed clean through them. Yet I have not been able to diſcover any ill effects from this ſtrange practice.*

Pleaſant gravel walks lead from the town to the ſpaw, where, between rows of elms, that give a moſt delightful ſhade, is a walk more ſpacious than the reſt, upwards of two hundred yards long, and twenty foot broad. At convenient diſtances from the town, are many agreeable airings upon the hills, which afford extenſive views of the vale below.

Here are aſſemblies and public breakfaſtings, as at other places of like reſort. The ſeaſon is from May to October, but there is moſt company in the months of June, July, Auguſt, and part of September.

Of the Manor and other Eſtates.

In *Domeſday-book* this manor ſtands under the title *Terra Regis,* where it is thus recorded: 'King Edward held Chintenham. There were 'eight hides and a half. Reinbald holds one 'hide and a half which belongs to the church[k]. 'There were three plow-tillages in demean; and 'twenty villeins, and ten bordars, and ſeven *ſervi,* 'with eighteen plow-tillages. The prieſts [have] 'two plow-tillages. There are two mills of 11*s.* 'and 8*d.* King William's ſteward added to this 'manor two bordars, and four villeins, and 'three mills, of which two are the king's, the 'third is the ſteward's; and there is one plow-'tillage more. In the time of king Edward it 'paid 9*l.* and 5*s.* and three thouſand loaves for 'the dogs. It now pays 20*l.* and 20 cows, and 20 'hogs, and 16*s.* inſtead of the bread.' *D. B.* p. 67.

The town of Cheltenham belonged to Henry de Bohun earl of Hereford 1 John. who exchanged it with that king for other lands; and king Henry the Third granted the manor and hundred to William Long Eſpee, earl of Saliſbury, in the third year of his reign; who died poſſeſſed thereof, and was ſucceeded by his ſon William earl of Saliſbury, who had his eſtates ſeized for going out of the kingdom without the king's licenſe.

This manor was granted in dower to queen Elianor, daughter of the earl of Provence, 27 H. 3. and according to the records, the biſhop of Hereford was ſeized of it in the thirty-firſt year of the ſame reign.

The abbey of Fiſchamp in Normandy purchaſed the manors of Cheltham and Sclaugtre, and the hundreds of Cheltham and Salemaneſberie, with free warren, by exchange of lands in Winchelſea and Rye in Suſſex, 36 H. 3. and their right to thoſe and other great privileges which they enjoyed therein, was allowed 15 E. 1. And they obtained the king's licenſe to ſell thoſe manors and hundreds the 18th year of the ſame reign.

John Limel died ſeized of this manor 2 E. 2. which I apprehend he held by leaſe only. It afterwards belonged to the priory of Montburg in Normandy; but the lands of alien monaſteries being veſted in the crown, by act of parliament, 2 H. 5. the manor and hundred of Cheltenham were granted to the nunnery of Syon in Middleſex; and for the further confirmation of the title, Maud, the abbeſs of that houſe, levied a fine thereof 22 H. 6. and they had another confirmation 1 E. 4. In the fourth year of the ſame reign, ſir Maurice Berkeley of Beverſtone held the ſame, as it is ſuppoſed, by leaſe from the abbeſs

[k] Reimbald was dean of the collegiate church of Cirenceſter.

of

of Syon; for that nunnery was poffeffed of the manor of Cheltenham at the time of its diffolution, when it came to the crown. Charles prince of Wales, afterwards king Charles the Firft, was lord of it.

James-Lenox Dutton, efq; is the prefent proprietor of this manor, which came into the Dutton family by grant from the crown.

There was a court of pleas, called the three weeks court, held by the fteward of the manor, for the recovery of debts of any amount; but this court hath been long difufed. By an act of parliament 1 C. 1. it is enacted, that the defcent of the cuftomary lands fhall be from thenceforth in fee fimple, according to the rules of common law; faving only, that if any copyholder of the faid manor, fhall dye without iffue male, having daughters, the eldeft daughter fhall inherit folely, as the eldeft fon ought to do by the courfe of the common law; and that if any of the faid cuftomary lands or tenements ought, according to the courfe of the common law, to defcend to any fifters, aunts, or female coufins, in every fuch cafe, the eldeft fifter, aunt, or female coufin, fhall inherit the fame lands and tenements folely and alone.

Of the other eftates, the records fhew that John Cheltenham died feized of lands in Cheltenham near Arle, 33 E. 3.

The abbey of Cirencefter were owners of a mill and other lands in Cheltenham when that houfe was diffolved, which particulars were granted to Peter Ofborn 3 Eliz. and were probably thofe mentioned in *Domefday-book* to be held by Reimbald, or the two plow-tillages which occur afterwards in the abftract quoted from that record.

Here are five fairs held on the following days, *i.e.* on the fecond Thurfday in April.—Holy Thurfday.—St. James's day *O. S.*—Second Thurfday in September.—Third Thurfday in December.

HAMLETS. There are five hamlets in this parifh, befides the town, *viz.* 1. *Arle.*—2. *Alfton.*—3. *Weftal.*—4. *Naunton.*—5. *Sandford*; of which in their order.

1. *Arle* lies about a mile from the town, down an eafy defcent. On the fouth fide of the road leading from Cheltenham to this place, on the left hand, is a fpring of purging water, rifing perpendicularly in the middle of a ditch, filled up with fludge and weeds, where the common water ouzes, and runs into and mixes with it, wherefore no juft eftimate can be made of the quantity of its fixt parts. However, according to Dr. Short, *it contains nitre and alcaline earth. The falt is full as bitter and purging as that of the laft.* [i. e. *the Hyde water. See Prefbury.*] *This water is neither fo clear, pleafant, nor brifk as the other, becaufe of its mixture with the ditch-water. Its falt is alfo much different, being not calcarious, but the fame with Aftrope, both in colour and cryftals.*

Arle-court antiently belonged to a family that took their name from this place; and from them this eftate came to the Grevils, by the marriage of Robert Grevil, brother of judge Grevil, with the daughter and coheirefs of John Arles. One of the female heirs of the Grevils carried it by marriage into the family of Liggon; and in like manner it came to fir Fleetwood Dormer, by the marriage of one of the Liggons. Judge Dormer was the proprietor of this eftate fome time fince the beginning of this century, who was fucceeded therein by Mrs. Catherine Dormer, lately deceafed. The honourable Mr. John Yorke, (brother to the late earl of Hardwick) who married the only daughter of Reginald Lyggon, of Maddersfield in Worcefterfhire, efq; is the prefent proprietor. There is a tithingman to this hamlet.

2. *Alfton*, of which there is nothing obfervable, except that it hath a tithingman diftinct from the other hamlets.

3. *Weftal.* Thomas Phillips was feized of Arle-Weftal, Cheltenham-Arle, and Hardhurft 6 E. 4.

4. *Naunton*, from *Nant*, which in the Britifh language fignifies a *valley*, and fometimes a *brook.* Francis Grevil levied a fine of lands in Naunton and Cheltenham, to the ufe of Thomas Barret and John Willis, 3 E. 6. Sir Henry Capel and Anne his wife levied a fine of lands in Naunton and Alfton, to John Ilk and Richard Horwood, 3 Mar.

5. *Sandford*, fo called from the fandy foil, and the ford or paffage over the brook. Thomas Dingley and Philippa his wife were feized of the manor of Sandford, and of lands in Cheltenham. George Barret married their only daughter Elizabeth, who jointly fued out livery of thofe lands 9 H. 8. One tithingman ferves for Weftal, Naunton, and Sandford.

Of the Church, &c.

The church is in the deanery of Winchcombe. It is an impropriation formerly belonging to the nunnery of Syon, but immediately before the diffolution of monafteries, it belonged to the abbey of Cirencefter, and was granted to fir William Rider 7 Jac. A portion of the tithes belonged to the nunnery of Ufk in Monmouthfhire, which tithes were granted to John Fernham 22 Eliz. The impropriation is now the property of the earl of Effex. Jefus College in Oxford recommends three of its own fellows to the heir of fir Baptift Hicks, anceftor of the prefent earl of Gainfborough, who chufes one, to be the parfon, and prefents him to the bifhop. The minifter is only a ftipendiary, receiving 35*l.* a year of the impropriator.

The college derive their title from fir Baptift Hicks, and by agreement between them, the incumbent muft not continue longer than fix years. The minifter has furplice fees. Here is no parfonage houfe.

The church is built in the form of a crofs. It has a high fpire in the middle, with a ring of eight mufical bells, and a fet of chimes. There is an aile

aile on each ſide of the church. The gallery at the weſt end was built by Mrs. Anne Norwood, in the year 1628; the other was erected by the ſubſcription of the inhabitants.

Here is a lecture ſermon, by ſubſcription, in the afternoon.

Monuments and Inſcriptions.

There is a handſome marble cenotaph in the chancel, with this inſcription:

In Memory of BAPTIST SMART, M.D. late of this Place, who after a long and painful Illneſs, departed this Life at the Hot-Wells, Briſtol, Decem[r]. 20th 1772, in the 63[d] Year of his Age, and lies interred at Clifton.——At bottom are his arms, *Argent, a chevron between three pheons heads ſable.* On a ſcutcheon of pretence, *Quarterly, Ermine and azure, a croſs Or.*

In the chapel at the eaſt end of the north aile, on the table of a freeſtone monument,

Hic juxta ſita eſt
CATHARINA
Fleetwoodi Dormer Equitis Aurati Sponſa,
Johannis Lygon de Arle-Court Armigeri,
Ex Elizabethâ Uxore Filia,
Utriuſq; Parentis Hæres unica,
Cujus Familia in Agro Wigornienſi
Per trecentos et amplius annos
Floruit, et adhuc fœliciter floret:
A tanto licet Genere oriunda, Nobiliq; nupta,
Stirpem, tamen et Conjugem,
Utroſq; antea illuſtres,
Morum Sanctitate Illuſtriores reddidit;
Maritum ſi non Patrem, Hæredem ſcripſit;
Hæc illum moriens amplo Patrimonio,
Ille hanc amiſſam, hoc Monumento decoravit.
Deceſſit Feb. 3.
Anno { Ætatis 72. / Domini 1678.

Johannes Lygon ſupradictus obijt 1644. Filius unicus Ricardi Lygon de Maddersfield Arm: ex ſecundis nuptijs cum Margaretâ Filiâ Joh: Talbott Militis, ex Stirpe Comitum Salopiæ, Affinis etiam fuit Baronibus de Berkeley Caſtro, aliiſq; Proceribus, et per Vxores ſuas Hæredibus quorum Inſignia ſupernè depinguntur.

On the upper part of the monument are theſe arms, *Per pale,* 1. *Azure,* 10 *billets Or,* 4, 3, 2, 1; *on a chief of the ſecond a demy lion rampant ſable,* for Dormer. 2. *Argent, two lions paſſant gardant in pale gules.* The arms alluded to in the inſcription are in fifteen quarterings, of the families of *Lyggon, Bracey, Maders-field, Harefleet, Decors, Gifford, Beauchamp, Abtot, Uffleet, Furnival, Luftot, Verdon, Grevile, Arie,* and *Southiey.*

There is a memorial upon a flat ſtone for William Grevil, one of the judges of the common pleas, who died in the year 1512.

Procurations £.	0	6	8	Synodals £.	0	2	0
Pentecoſtals	0	1	3 *ob.*				

Benefactions.

In the year 1574, Mr. Richard Pates, of Glouceſter, founded a ſchool and an hoſpital here. He endowed the ſchool with 16*l.* a year for the maſter, and 4*l.* for the uſher. The maſter has a houſe to live in. Mr. Pates gave the lands to ſupport theſe charities to *Corpus Chriſti* college in Oxford, who nominate the maſter and uſher, and the biſhop of the dioceſe approves. From the ſchool, an exhibitioner goes to Pembroke college, for eight years, with 10*l. per Ann.* given by Mr. Townſend. To the hoſpital, Mr. Pates's heirs nominate three men and three women, with a ſtipend of 12*d.* each weekly, 4*d.* quarterly; and 16*s.* yearly for a coat for each of the men, and a gown for each of the women. They have alſo 2*d.* weekly each, from another donor.

Mr. Townſend hath founded another ſchool, and endowed it with 4*l.* a year to the maſter, and hath left 5*l.* a year for apprenticing out lads of this pariſh.

Lady Caple hath alſo founded a ſchool, with a ſalary of 8*l.* a year to the maſter.

Thomas George, in the year 1620, gave by his will 3*s.* 4*d.* a year to the poor, and the ſame ſum to the miniſter for a ſermon, the payment of which is charged on lands now belonging to Mr. Robert Cox.

John Wallwyn, by his will in 1627, gave 2*l.* 10*s.* a year for ever to the poor of this town, charged on the manor of Swindon.

In 1667, divers charities aſſigned for the benefit of the poor, and for putting out apprentices, were laid out in the purchaſe of lands called the poors grounds, at that time worth 8*l.* 5*s.* a year; but they are now let at the improved rent of 18*l. per annum.*

In the year 1704, the reverend William Stanſby, vicar of Badgworth, left an eſtate at Badgworth, which lets at 14*l.* a year, for apprenticing boys, of which that pariſh is to have 5*l.* Churchdown 3*l.* and Cheltenham the overplus.

The following are donations of a leſs permanent nature. In the year 1603, Lodovick Packer, gent. gave the third bell.—In 1721, lord viſcount Gage gave a fire-engine, and the ſame year ſir John Dutton, baronet, gave another.—1738, Edmund Smith, ſurgeon, gave a large, handſome braſs ſconce for the church.—1741, Norborne Berkeley, eſq; gave a crimſon velvet pulpit-cloth and cuſhion.

Cheltenham.

				£.	s.	d.
Taxes.	The Royal Aid in	1692, £.		145	13	0
	Poll-tax —	1694,	—	130	19	0
	Land-tax —	1694,	—	226	7	0
	The ſame, at 3*s.*	1770,	—	171	0	9

Arle.

				£.	s.	d.
Taxes.	The Royal Aid in	1692, £.		78	12	0
	Poll-tax ——	1694,	—	17	6	0
	Land-tax ——	1694,	—	77	4	4
	The ſame, at 3*s.*	1770,	—	57	18	3

According to an account publiſhed in the year 1712, there were 321 houſes in this pariſh, and about 1500 inhabitants, whereof 200 were free-holders; the yearly births 48, burials 44; which appear to be the true numbers for the baptiſms and burials upon the pariſh regiſter, on an average of ten years beginning at 1703. And in a like ſeries of years, from 1760 to 1769 incluſive, the births were 455, and the burials 368, or 45 baptiſms and 37 burials, nearly, upon an average every year; and the inhabitants are about 1433. Hence it appears that population decreaſes, and that one in about 39 dies every year.

CHERINGTON.

THIS pariſh is ſituated in the country adjoining to the Coteſwolds, and lies in the hundred of Longtree, about three miles diſtant north from Tetbury, three ſouth-eaſtward from Minchin-Hampton, and ſixteen ſouthward from Glouceſter.

Sir Robert Atkyns aſſerts that the name *is derived from Kinning, that is King's town*; but there is not, in my opinion, the leaſt ſhadow of probability on his ſide. In *Domeſday-book* it is written *Cerintone*, where the *C* had undoubtedly a hard ſound. And as Ceꞃꞃe in the Anglo-Saxon language ſignifies *bent* or *crooked*, and inꝫ a *meadow*, or *place of water*; ſome perſons have thought that the name implies a town upon a crooked ſtream of water; for here is a ſmall brook which runs in a winding courſe from hence to Avening, and Stroud, where it joins another river, a little below the town. It is by means of this water, that the preſent undertakers of the Stroud navigation purpoſe to join their canal with the Thames at Cricklade, if they ſhould ſucceed to their wiſhes, in the firſt ſtep to Stroud.

In the great civil war, ſo fatal to many families of eminence and diſtinction, John lord Stuart, ſecond brother to the duke of Richmond, ſir John Smith, the colonels Sandys, Scot, and Manning, all eminent perſons on the part of the king, were ſlain on the downs in this pariſh, in an engagement which happened between lord Hopton and ſir William Waller, when the parliament's forces, under the latter, obtained the victory on the 29th of March, 1644.

Petrifications of the bivalve kind, as of the oiſter, and muſcle, are often found in the fields and ſtone-quarries, in this pariſh and its neighbourhood.

Of the Manor and other Eſtates.

This was one of the eighty-eight manors beſtowed upon Miles Criſpin, by the conqueror, for his aſſiſtance in the expedition againſt England.

'Milo [Criſpin] holds Cerintone in Langetreu 'hundred, and Goisfrid holds it of him. Haminc 'held it of king Edward. There are two hides 'taxed. In demean are three plow-tillages, and 'three villeins, and eight bordars with three plow-'tillages and a half. There are twelve *ſervi*, and 'a mill of 30*d.* [rent] and four acres of meadow. 'It is worth and was worth 4*l.*' *D. B.* p. 78.

This Miles Criſpin married Maud, daughter and heir to Robert D'Oiley, and died 7 H. 1. without iſſue. The manor was afterwards held by the priory of Lanthony, of Edward earl of Cornwall, as of the honour of Wallingford 15 & 28 E. 1.

But Peter de la More, or de la Mere, was ſeized of this manor 20 E. 1. and Robert de la More was alſo ſeized of it 2 E. 2. About this time ſir Robert Atkyns ſuppoſed that the Balacotes and the Mortimers held this manor; but their eſtate lay in Charlton in Tetbury, which he had miſtaken for Cherington.

Beatrix le Boteler was ſeized of the manor of Cherington 32 E. 3. Elianor le Boteler held the ſame 46 E. 3.

It came again into the poſſeſſion of the De la Mores, for ſir Robert de la More and Maud his wife were ſeized of this manor 5 R. 2. and Maud ſurviving him, was ſeized thereof 6 H. 4.

Sir Walter Beauchamp was ſeized of the manor and church of Cherington 9 H. 6. and ſir William Beauchamp of St. Amand, a baron, died ſeized of the ſame 35 H. 6.

This manor paſſed afterwards to the Baintons. Sir Edward Bainton was ſeized thereof in right of Iſabel his wife. She ſurviving him, was married to John Stump, and died ſeized of the manor 10 Eliz. and livery was granted the ſame year to Henry Baynton her ſon and heir. It paſſed from this family into that of the name of Stephens.

Thomas Stephens, eſq; was lord of this manor in the year 1608. Edward Stephens, eſq; was lord of it when ſir Robert Atkyns compiled his Hiſtory. It went afterwards to ſir John Turner, baronet; who ſold it to —— Smith, eſq; of London, who is the preſent lord of the manor of Cherington, and has a very good eſtate in the pariſh.

This manor is holden of the honour of Ewelm. The ſeat of Ewelm, lying a ſmall diſtance from Benſon in Oxfordſhire, was built by William de la Pole, duke of Suffolk, whoſe grandſon, John earl of Lincoln, being engaged in a conſpiracy againſt king Henry the Seventh, his eſtate was confiſcated; and king Henry the Eighth, with the addition of ſome neighbouring manors, made an honour of it; and among theſe manors was Wallingford, which had a long time belonged to the dukes of Cornwall, of whom, it has been obſerved, the manor of Cherington was holden.

Lands in Cherington belonged to the rich nunnery of Benedictines at Godſtow, in Oxfordſhire, and were granted to John Smyth and Richard Duffield 6 Eliz.

HAMLET. 1. *Weſtrip* is a ſmall hamlet in this pariſh.

Of the Church, &c.

The church is a rectory in the deanery of Stonehouſe, worth about 130*l.* a year. Mr. Smith is patron, the reverend Samuel Lyſons, M. A. the preſent incumbent.

There were 61 acres in the weſt field, and 59 acres in the eaſt field, belonging to the glebe, before the incloſing, at which time the rector had 330 acres of land allotted to him in lieu of tithe.

The church is dedicated to St. Nicholas. It has a croſs aile on the ſouth ſide, belonging to the lord of the manor, and a low embattled tower at the weſt end.

Monuments

Monuments and Inſcriptions.

In the chancel are the following memorials:

M. S.

Viri Reverendi D. Joſephi Trapp, A. M. Ædis Chriſti Oxon. olim Alumni, & hujus Eccleſiæ per Annos 37 Rectoris Vigilantiſſimi. Cujus (licet obſcuro in loco poſitus fuerit) dignæ ſunt Virtutes quæ poſteris traduntur. Eximia erga Deum Pietas; In Uxorem Liberoſq; Affectus propenſiſſimus; Munificentiâ in Pauperes, pœne quam par fuit, effuſior; In Amicos Fides & Obſequium; In Univerſos Benevolentia. Ingenio fuit vividus & perſpicax; Eruditione non mediocriter inſtructus; Summè humilis interim & modeſtus. In Congreſſibus comis, humanus, facilis; Sciſmaticis omne genus infenſus; Diſciplinæ Fideiq; Eccleſiæ Anglicanæ Tenax. Hoc tamen vitio vertimus Viro cætera laudatiſſimo, (Ignoſcendum illud quidem ſed Doctis & Piis heu! nimium ſolenne) Quod Animarum ſolummodo ſanitati invigilaverit, de ſano Corpore parum ſolicitus. Obijt Sept. 23d, Anno Dom. 1698, Ætat. ſuæ 61.

Mariæ, Theophili Quintin, Viri Reverendi Eccleſiæ Briſtolienſis Præbendarii, Tockenhamenſis vero in agro Wilton, Rectoris, Filiæ natu minimæ,
Quæ fuit
Vultu a Natura ad Modeſtiam compoſito,
Ingenio facili ſed reconditiori,
Virtutum omnium, præſertim Chriſtianarum, eximium et Ornamentum et Exemplar.
Temporis frugi, in Nummis erogandis perquam liberalis;
In Verbis ſolummodo parca.
In S. Scriptoribus verſatiſſima,
In Precibus Publicis privatiſq; dubium frequentior an flagrantior.
Eccliæ Anglicanæ Fidem & Diſciplinam ſemper coluit.
Vita illibata, ſancta, vere virginea.
Mortem deniq; ex confluentibus (ut ſolet) minacem, teterrimam, gravem,
Patientia tulit, Spe amplexa, et Immortalitati deceſſit,
Ætatis ſuæ 34, Nati Chriſti 1695.

Firſt fruits £	13	0	0	Synodals £.	0	2	0
Tenths —	1	6	0	Pentecoſtals	0	0	6
Procurations	0	6	8				

Benefactions.

The church-houſe, with ſix acres of land in each field, twenty ſheep-paſtures, and two beaſt-paſtures, were given to repair the church. And one Mr. Cox gave 5 *l.* to the poor.

Taxes.				
The Royal Aid in	1692, £.	49	14	0
Poll-tax — —	1694, —	3	17	0
Land-tax ——	1694, —	50	12	0
The ſame, at 3 *s.*	1770, —	37	19	3

According to ſir Robert Atkyns, there were 30 houſes and about 120 inhabitants in this pariſh, whereof 6 were freeholders; yearly births 5, burials 4. But it appears by the pariſh regiſter, that in ten years, from the year 1700, there were 37 baptiſms, and 33 burials; and that in the ſame number of years, beginning with 1760, there were regiſtered 51 baptiſms, of whom 30 were males, and 54 burials. At this time the exact number of houſholders is 78, and of inhabitants 158. But during the latter period, there were two years of great mortality in the pariſh, which carried off 17 more than the greateſt number of burials in any other two years during that period; and making a deduction on that account, the average number of annual burials will be 3. 7; which is in proportion to the whole number of inhabitants nearly as 1 to 43.

CHURCH-DOWN

IS a pariſh in the hundred of King's-barton, ſituated in the vale part of the county, ſix miles diſtant weſt from Cheltenham, nine ſouth from Tewkeſbury, and four eaſt from Glouceſter.

The church ſtands at the top of a ſteep ſugar-loaf hill, whence there is a very extenſive proſpect over the vale, particularly up as high as Worceſter. There is a ſilly tradition in this part of the country, that the church was begun to be built on a more convenient and acceſſible ſpot of ground, but that the materials uſed in the day, were conſtantly taken away at night, and carried to the top of the hill; which was conſidered as a ſupernatural intimation that the church ſhould be built there. The pariſh takes its name from the ſituation of the church upon the hill or down. It is vulgarly called *Choſen*, and few of the common people know the proper name of it.

The ſoil is rich, and the pariſh conſiſts chiefly of paſture, but with a good portion of arable. A ſmall brook runs from hence, and empties itſelf into the Severn at Sainthurſt.

John Harmar, the famous Greek profeſſor in Oxford, was born in this pariſh. He died in 1670.

Of the Manor and other Eſtates.

In *Domeſday-book*, this manor ſtands under the title *Terra Thome Archiep'i*, the eſtate of Archbiſhop Thomas; and it is thus recorded:

'Stigand the archbiſhop [of Canterbury] held 'Circeſdune. There were fifteen hides and a half, 'and two plow-tillages in demean, and eighteen 'villeins, and five bordars, and ſeven radecheniſters 'with thirty plow-tillages. There was a wood 'half a mile long, and three quarters broad. It 'was then worth 13 *l.* [*i. e.* when Stigand held the 'manor;] and is now worth 12 *l.* Afterwards follow the particulars of Hochilicote and Nortune, and then it is ſaid 'Archbiſhop Thomas now holds 'theſe three manors.' *Domeſday-book*, p. 69.

Thomas was archbiſhop of York; he was found by inquiſition to be ſeized of this manor 7 Joh. And a *Quo warranto* was brought againſt him, as againſt almoſt every other proprietor of lands, 15 E. 1. to ſet forth the privileges of this manor.

The temporalties of the archbiſhop of York were extended 14 E. 3. amongſt which was the manor of Church-Down; but it was afterwards reſtored, and continued in the archbiſhoprick till it was granted to ſir Thomas Chamberlain 6 E. 6. and hath ever ſince continued in that family. Sir John Chamberlain was lord of this manor in 1608; Edmund Chamberlain, eſq; died ſeized of it in the year 1774, and the reverend Mr. John Chamberlain, is the preſent lord of the manor. *For his arms, &c. ſee Maugerſbury.*

The principal eſtate in Church-Down, late belonging to Henry Window, eſq; is now the property of Mr. Richard Rogers, of Glouceſter.

John de Oldney, and Agnes his wife, levied a fine of lands in Church-Down, Nokey, and Hucklecot, to the uſe of themſelves in taille, 3 E. 3.

TITHINGS and HAMLETS.

1. *Church-Down*, of which already.

2. *Hucklecot*,

2. *Huckelcot*, antiently written *Hochilicote*, and *Uchelgoed*. The name is compounded of two Britiſh words *Uchel*, lofty, and *coed* a wood. Here was a large wood at the time of the conqueſt; and not only in this place, but in ſeveral of the neighbouring villages there was a great deal of woodland, as the very names of Bernewood, or Barnwood, Wotton [*i. e. wood-town*] and Sainthurſt, import.—This is a diſtinct tithing from Church-Down, and maintains its own poor.

It was alſo a diſtinct manor at the time of the general ſurvey, tho' under the ſame proprietor with Church-Down.

'The ſame Stigand held Hochilicote. There 'were four hides, and in demean two plow-'tillages, and eleven villeins, and five bordars with 'eleven plow-tillages. There is a mill of 32*d.* '[rent,] and a wood one mile long, and half a 'mile broad. It was then, and is now, worth 4*l.*' *Domeſday-book* p. 69.

When this record was made, the manor was held by Thomas archbiſhop of York, and continued in the ſee of York, 'till it was granted to ſir Thomas Chamberlain 6 E. 6. It has deſcended in the ſame manner, and ever had, and ſtill continues to have, the ſame proprietor with Church-Down.

The abbey of Eveſham had an eſtate in Hudlecot and Bartram, which has been called a manor, and was granted to Philip Hobby, eſq; 34 H. 8. and paſſed afterwards to —— Hanks, from whom it deſcended to Robert Hanks, who had livery thereof 1 Eliz.

The priory of St. Oſwald in Glouceſter had other lands in Hucklecot, called the *New Houſe*, which were granted to John Fernham and John Doddington 17 Eliz.

Sir William Strachan, baronet, has a good houſe here, which he holds by leaſe of Samuel Hayward, eſq. Sir William married one of the daughters and coheireſſes of —— Popham, of the Lodge, near Tewkeſbury, eſq.

The reverend Mr. Rogers, of Glouceſter, to whoſe family I am greatly indebted for ſome papers relating to that city, has a good houſe and eſtate here. His arms are *Argent, a chevron ſable, between three bucks courant Or.*

3. *Pirton* or *Parton*, and *Elmbridge*. This is a hamlet, but not a diſtinct tithing. There is another hamlet of the name of Pirton, in the pariſh of Lidney, which has occaſioned ſome confuſion and miſtake in the accounts which ſir Robert Atkyns gives of them. He has applied the ſame records to both places. Thus he ſays, *John de Badeham and Elizabeth, his wife, levied a fine of the manor of Periton to John de Knovil, to the uſe of themſelves, and the heirs of their bodies, the remainder to the heirs of Elizabeth* 25 *E.* 1. *In the ſame year, another fine was levied by John Ap Adam and Elizabeth, his wife, to the uſe of themſelves, in tale ſpecial.* And further on, *Maurice, ſon of Thomas de Berkeley, held Piriton* 42 *E.* 3. Upon which I obſerve, that John de Badeham and John Ap Adam, is the ſame identical perſon; for Badeham is a corruption of Ap Adam, and therefore the ſuppoſed two fines are one and the ſame, levied by the ſame perſon. And I am of opinion that Pirton, the property of Ap Adam, and afterwards of Maurice Berkeley, lay not in this pariſh, but in Lidney, where the Gournays, Ap Adams, and Berkeleys, (all deſcendants from Fitz-Harding, the great anceſtor of the Berkeley family) had other very conſiderable poſſeſſions, about the times of the dates above-mentioned.

But to return to Pirton in Church-Down. This manor belonged to the priory of St. Oſwald in Glouceſter, and was probably given to it in very early times. Upon the diſſolution of that houſe, it was granted to ſir John Jennings 37 H. 8. who had obtained the grant of the ſite of the priory before he was knighted. From him it deſcended to —— Jennings, ſon of ſir John, who dying without iſſue 5 Mar. it deſcended to John Wighte, or Wright, in right of Agnes his wife, who was daughter and heireſs to Joan the wife of Robert Kemp, which Joan was daughter of the laſt mentioned —— Jennings, ſon of ſir John Jennings. John Wighte and Agnes, his wife, had livery of this manor the ſame year. And Richard Wighte their ſon, died ſeized of the manor of Perton, *alias* Parton, as I find it written in the Eſcheator's inquiſition, 43 Eliz. and deviſed it in truſt, to be ſold, to raiſe portions for his children. Lord Craven is the preſent lord of this manor. This is not a diſtinct tithing. William Singleton, eſq; has a good eſtate at Parton.

4. *Brickhampton*. This is a reputed manor. The prior of Glouceſter was ſeized of Trithampton 19 E. 1. which I mention, not as being certain that this manor is the Trithampton of the record, but becauſe I find it thus expreſs'd by ſir Robert Atkyns. John Sage granted 100 ſolidatas of land in Brickhampton, to the abbey of Hayles, 6 E. 2.

This manor belonged to ſir Robert Atkyns of Saperton, at the beginning of this century; and is now the joint property of the reverend Mr. Chamberlain and Mr. Hoard.

5. *Noke*. John de Oldney and Agnes, his wife, levied a fine of lands in Nokey 3 E. 3. John de Wiſham was ſeized of Noketon 6 E. 3. This is now the eſtate of Samuel Hayward, eſq;

Of the Church, &c.

This church is an impropriation in the deanery of Glouceſter. It was a chapel to St. Catherine's, *alias* St. Oſwald's, in Glouceſter 19 E. 1 & 2 H. 7. The rectories, with the advowſon of the vicarages of Church-Den and Hucklecot, belonged to the priory of St. Oſwald's at Glouceſter, and were granted to the dean and chapter of Briſtol 34 H. 8. who are the patrons and impropriators. The leſſee of the impropriation pays the curate 20*l.* a year.

year. The reverend Mr. Evans is the prefent incumbent. The living has been augmented with queen Anne's bounty, added to a donation of 200*l.* given by Mrs. Urfula Taylor, which makes it now worth about 50*l.* a year.

The church confifts of the nave and an aile on the fouth fide, with a tower and five bells at the weft end.

Monuments and Infcriptions.

Here are no very remarkable monuments. Againft the fouth wall of the chancel is this infcription.

Here lyes Sir Robert Auften, Bar^t^. of Hall Place, near Dartford in Kent, of an antient Family. He was honeft and generous. He died September the 20th, 1743, in the 43^d^ year of his age. His arms are on a fcutcheon, *Or, a chevron gules, between three lions paws erazed and erected fable.* The arms of Ulfter.

On a tomb in the church-yard, is the following infcription, with four lines out of Horace. Ode 3. lib. II.

Hoc Sepulchro in diem refurrectionis reconditur corpus Dni Iohis Brown fen. hujus Paroch. qui ex hac vita migravit 21°. Feb. Anno Dni 1689, Ætatis fuæ 72°.

Omnes eôdem cogimur, omnium
Verfatur urna; feriùs, ocyùs
Sors exitura, & nos in æternum
Exilium impofitura cymbæ.

On another fide of the tomb:

Hic etiam acquiefcunt corpora Catharinæ, Annæ, & Henrici, natorum dni Iohis Brown, fen. & Catharinæ uxoris ejus. Catharina humata erat Martii 28°; Anna, Junii 20°; Henricus, Julii 15°; tres eodem Anno, 1683.

There is a memorial upon two flat ftones under the fouth wall of the church, for Henry Windowe, efq; who died in 1745-6, aged 63; and for Sarah his wife, who died in 1759, aged 60.——Mr. Windowe's arms are engraven on the ftone, *i. e. Azure, a fefs raguly between three lions paws erazed and erected Or.*

Pentecoftals 6*d.*

Benefactions.

Mr. Cox of Sandhurft gave 50*l.* a year to the poor of feveral parifhes, of which thofe of this parifh, not receiving alms, have 6*l.* 13*s.* 4*d.* ——Blount, gentlewoman, gave five acres of pafture ground, inclofed in Hatherly meadow, for fuch poor labourers and widows of this parifh as receive no alms. Richard Holford, gent. gave four almfhoufes, with three acres and a half of arable land, and one acre of pafture, for the ufe of four poor widows of this parifh. William Stanfby, gent. gave 3*l.* a year for apprenticing out poor boys. And Jeremiah Mitchell, gent. gave 24*s.* a year to provide bread and wine for nine monthly facraments.

Henry Windowe, efq; late of this parifh, gave an eftate in Badgworth, now let for 28*l.* a year, for the endowment of two charity-fchools; the one for inftructing all poor boys and girls of this parifh, and of Badgworth, upwards of fix years of age, in reading and writing, under a mafter; the other for inftructing younger boys to read, and girls to read, knit, &c. under a miftrefs. And he gave two houfes in this parifh, for the mafter and miftrefs to live in.

Taxes.			£.	s.	d.
	The Royal Aid in	1692,	321	5	4
	Poll-tax ——	1694, —	18	15	0
	Land-tax ——	1694, —	279	16	0
	The fame, at 3*s.*	1770, —	69	8	3

According to fir Robert Atkyns, there were 100 houfes and about 400 inhabitants in this parifh, whereof 20 were freeholders; yearly births 10, burials 8. But it appears by the parifh regifter, that the average of annual burials, in ten years from 1700, was 7, of baptifms 13.1. And in the like number of years, from 1760, the average of baptifms was 16.8, of burials 13.2. The prefent number of houfholders is exactly 131, of inhabitants 630. Thefe numbers fhew that the place is remarkably healthy for a vale-fituation, as only one in 47.8, upon an average, dies every year; and that population increafes very confiderably.

****

CHURCHAM

LIES in the foreft divifion, in the hundred of Weftbury, eight miles eaft from Mitchel-Dean, feven north-eaft from Newnham, and five north-weftward from Gloucefter. There are three hamlets belonging to it, which lie in a different hundred.

Hamme was the antient name of it, as we find it written in *Domefday-book.* But there was another *Hamme* mentioned in the fame record, which lay contiguous to the firft. The vicinity of two places of the fame name occafioned confufion, wherefore it was requifite to diftinguifh them. The parifh church lay in the *Hamme* of which I am now treating, and was therefore called *Churcham.* The other *Hamme* lay higher up, on the banks of the Severn, wherefore it obtained the name of *Highnam.* This diftinction had taken place 9 E. 1. for in that year, the fheriff returned Chircham to be a vill in the hundred of Weftbury, but Highnam was one of the vills in the hundred of Dudfton.

Of the Manors and other Eftates.

Wolphin, or Ulfine le Rue, or Lehue, was conful or governor of Gloucefter in the fifth year of the reign of king Canute. He was alfo lord of the two manors of Hamme. At the inftigation of Wolftan bifhop of Worcefter, king Canute turned out the fecular priefts from the abbey of of Gloucefter, and placed monks of the order of St. Benedict in their ftead; but this le Rue was fo averfe to the monks, that he flew feven of them, not far from the town, in the year 1033, or, according to another account, in 1048. The pope afterwards obliged him to attone for his offence, by giving thofe manors for the maintenance of feven monks in St. Peter's abbey. I fhall now treat of them diſtinctly. *Domeſday-book* gives the following account of Churcham:

'The ſame church [of St. Peter of Glowec'.] 'holds Hamme and Mortune, in Weſtberies hun-'dred. There are five hides in wood and in plain. 'In demean are two plow-tillages, and ſeven 'villeins, and two bordars, with ſix plow-tillages. '[There is] a wood one mile long and one broad. 'The church had veniſon in three parks there, 'in the time of king Edward, and ſo ſhe hath in 'the time of king William. It was worth 20 *ſol.* 'and is now worth 40 *ſol.*' *Domeſday-book*, p. 71.

The ſheriff returned, that the abbey of Glouceſter was ſeized of this manor 9 E. 1. and free warren therein was allowed to the abbat in a writ of *Quo Warranto* 15 E. 1. The ſame abbey had a grant of eighty acres and ſixty perches of land in Churcham 6 E. 3. to make a park there.

This manor continued in the abbey 'till the diſſolution of religious foundations. The manor of Churcham, with the rectory, and advowſon of the vicarage, as alſo a wood in Churcham, called Byrdewood, containing by eſtimation one hundred acres, were granted to the dean and chapter of Glouceſter 33 H. 8. Charles Barrow, eſq; one of the repreſentatives of the city of Glouceſter, and James Money, eſq; are leſſees of the manor, under the dean and chapter. *For Mr. Barrow's arms, ſee* Minſterworth.

Of the other eſtates the records ſhew, that Edward Barrow died ſeized of lands in Churcham 12 Eliz. and James, his ſon and heir, had livery of them the ſame year.

TITHINGS and *HAMLETS.*

There are three hamlets in this pariſh, *Highnam*, *Linton*, and *Over*, which lie in the hundred of Dudſton and King's-Barton, and together make one tithing, and maintain their poor jointly, but diſtinctly from Churcham. They were antiently within the hundred of Tolangbrige, which is now compriſed in Dudſton and King's-Barton.

1. *Highnam* is two miles diſtant from Glouceſter. Of this manor it is thus recorded:

'The church [of St. Peter of Glowec'.] holds 'Hamme in Tolangebriges hundred. There are 'ſeven hides. In demean are three plow-tillages, 'and twenty-two villeins, and four bordars, with 'ſeven plow-tillages. There are eight *ſervi*, and 'thirty acres of meadow, and wood ſufficient for 'the manor. It was worth 40 *ſol.* but is now 'worth 4*l.*' *Domeſday-book*, p. 71.

In the leaſe of this manor, granted by the abbat of Glouceſter 7 H. 8. part of the manſion-houſe is reſerved for the abbat and his men, if the plague or peſtilence ſhould be in Glouceſter or Over.

This eſtate continued in the poſſeſſion of the abbey of Glouceſter 'till that houſe was diſſolved, wherefore all the demean lands are tithe free. The manors of Highnam and Over, and divers meſſuages and lands, with the tithes thereof, lying in Churcham, all formerly belonging to the abbey of Glouceſter, were granted to John Arnold of Monmouthſhire, eſq; 33 H. 8. at whoſe death, livery of the manor of Highnam was granted to his ſon, ſir Nicholas Arnold, 37 H. 8. He married Margaret, daughter of ſir William Dennys of Dyrham, and was ſucceeded by Rowland Arnold, his ſon, who married Mary, daughter of John Brydges, lord Chandois, and left an only daughter and heireſs, wedded to Thomas Lucy, ſon of ſir Thomas Lucy, of Charlcot in Warwickſhire.

Thomas Lucy likewiſe left an only daughter, married to ſir William Cook, deſcended from the family of the Cooks of Giddy-hall in Eſſex. By this marriage, ſir William Cook had the manor of Highnam, of which he died ſeized in 1618. Sir Robert Cook was ſon and heir of ſir William. He married Dorothy daughter of ſir Miles Fleetwood, of Aldwincle in Northamptonſhire. William Cook, ſon of ſir Robert, ſucceeded him, and married Anne, daughter of Dennis Rowls, of Devonſhire. He was high ſheriff of Glouceſterſhire in 1663, and ſerved in ſeveral parliaments for the city of Glouceſter. Dennis Cook, eſq; eldeſt ſon of William, married Mary, ſiſter of the lord Scudamore of Herefordſhire; but dying before his father without iſſue, his brother Edward Cook, eſq; ſucceeded to the eſtate. He married Mary, daughter of Roger Newborough, of Somerſetſhire. William Cook, eſq; was his ſon and heir, but dying unmarried, his brother Dennis ſucceeded to this eſtate; and he dying without male iſſue, the eſtate devolved to his two ſiſters, agreeably to their father's will. The elder was married to Reynon Jones, of Naſs, in this county, eſq; and the younger to Henry Guiſe, of the city of Glouceſter, eſq; whoſe ſon John Guiſe, eſq; is the preſent poſſeſſor. He has a beautiful ſeat at Highnam with large gardens, fiſh-ponds, and a very extenſive park. It commands a proſpect of the city of Glouceſter, and of the vale. The public is indebted to his generoſity for the plate annexed. Mr. Guiſe's arms are, *Gules, ſeven lozenges vaire*, 3, 3, 1, *on a canton Or, a mullet of ſix points pierced ſable. A creſcent for diſtinction.*

The lord of the manor of Highnam claims a very ſingular right, of turning two horſes into the mowing graſs of a large meadow near the city of Glouceſter, called Wollam, from St. George's day 'till the whole is cut down.

2. *Linton*, but antiently *Lilton*, and *Lylton*. The tithes of this place, and the parſonage of Aldeſworth, formerly belonging to the abbey of Glouceſter, were granted to the biſhoprick of Glouceſter 33 H. 8.

3. *Over*. This hamlet lies on the banks of the Severn, oppoſite to the city of Glouceſter, with which it has a communication by bridges over the ſeveral branches of that river. Over-bridge is the loweſt on the Severn, and is maintained at the public expence of the county.

In ſir Robert Atkyns's account of Over in Almondſbury, is the following particular, which ſeems

ſeems to belong to this place. In the year 804 Ethelrick, ſon of king Ethelmund, at the requeſt of a ſynod held at Glouceſter, wherein he was preſent, granted thirty meſſuages in Overe to the church of St. Peter in Glouceſter, and confirmed the grant of his father, in the time when the canons ſecular reſided there. But there ſeems to be a miſtake in the date of this account, for it does not appear that the ſecular canons were then ſettled at Glouceſter. Lands lying in Over, which formerly belonged to the abbey of Glouceſter, were granted to Edward duke of Somerſet 1 E. 6.

Mr. Guiſe holds court-leet and court baron for Highnam, Linton, and Over.

Of the Church, &c.

The church is a vicarage, in the Foreſt deanery, worth about 80*l.* a year. The dean and chapter of Glouceſter are patrons and impropriators; the reverend Mr. Edward Sparkes the preſent incumbent. The chapel of Bully is annexed to it.

The church conſiſts of the nave only, with a ſpire ſteeple at the weſt end. It is dedicated to St. Andrew There is a chapel at Highnam, built by the family of the Cooks, ſome of whom are buried there, without any memorial. Their arms are, *Or, a chevron checky gules and azure, between three cinquefoils of the laſt.*

Monuments and Inſcriptions.

There is an inſcription in the church, in memory of John Arnold, eſq; and Elizabeth his wife. He died in 1546. Another inſcription for Edward Oldiſworth, eſq; and of Tacy his wife, daughter of Arthur Porter, eſq. and granddaughter of John Arnold, eſq. Mr. Oldiſworth died in 1570. In the chancel is an inſcription for John Brown, eſq; alderman of Glouceſter, and leſſee of this manor, who died in 1639. And another inſcription for Mr. John Harris, ſon of John Harris, an alderman of Glouceſter, and leſſee of this manor. He died in 1680.

Firſt fruits	£. 20	5	0	Synodals	£. 0	7	8
Tenths	— 2	0	6	Pentecoſtals	0	2	0
Procurations and							

Benefactions.

There are four houſes and five acres of land ſettled for the benefit of four poor women. Mr. Cox has given an annuity of 6*l.* 13*s.* 4*d.* to the poor. Mr. Blount has alſo given five acres to the uſe of the poor.

Churcham.

Taxes.					
	The Royal Aid in	1692,	£. 115	8	0
	Poll-tax — —	1694, —	14	9	0
	Land-tax ——	1694, —	127	2	0
	The ſame, at 3*s.*	1770, —	95	3	0

Highnam, Linton, and Over.

Taxes.					
	The Royal Aid in	1692,	£. 144	1	4
	Poll-tax —	1694, —	32	0	0
	Land-tax —	1694, —	168	14	0
	The ſame, at 3*s.*	1770, —	126	9	0

There were 77 houſes and about 340 inhabitants in this pariſh, whereof 18 were freeholders, yearly births 15, burials 13, according to ſir Robert Atkyns, when he compiled his account of it. But having examined the pariſh regiſter, it appears, that in ten years, from 1700 to 1709, both incluſive, there were 118 baptiſms and 76 burials; ſo that the average about that time was very ſhort of ſir Robert's numbers. In the ſame number of years, from 1760 to 1769, both incluſive, there were regiſtered 143 baptiſms, and 78 burials, which ſomewhat exceed thoſe in the former period; and the inhabitants are at preſent about 309. From the great diſproportion between the baptiſms and burials, I judge, that many of the natives who are baptiſed here, ſettle elſewhere. This indeed might be expected from the ſituation of the pariſh ſo near to the city of Glouceſter. Beſides it lies near the river Severn, the great navigation upon which takes all perſons concerned in it from home, and is a great means of changing their ſettlements.

CIRENCESTER.

1. *Of the Situation, Name, Extent, Antiquities, &c.*

CIRENCESTER is a market and borough town, ſituate in Lat. 51° 13′ 30″ Long. 90 miles weſt from London. It is thirty-ſix miles diſtant eaſtward from Briſtol, and thirty-three from Bath; thirty-four weſtward from Oxford, ſeventeen ſouth-eaſt from Glouceſter, and ſeven north-weſt from Cricklade in Wiltſhire.

The pariſh, conſiſting of a due proportion of meadow and paſture, arable and woodland, is about four miles and a half long, and two and a half broad.

The town is ſituated on the borders of the Coteſwold country, in the ſouth-eaſt part of the county, where three great Roman roads meet, the *Foſs*, the *Irminſtreet*, and the *Ikenild-way*. It ſtands on the river *Ceri*, or *Cori*, or *Corin*[l], which we now call the *Churn*, and takes its name from that river[m]; for the Britons called it *Caer-Ceri*[n], and *Caer-Cori*[o]; in whoſe language *caer*, which in its genuine ſenſe ſhould be tranſlated a *wall*, or *fortreſs*, came at length, when uſed in the compoſition

[l] Dr. Howell's Hiſtory of the World, Part 4, p. 171.—*Coryn* in the Britiſh language ſignifies the *top*, and is very properly apply'd to this river, becauſe it is the higheſt ſource of the Thames.

[m] Eorum vero [i. e. *Dobunorum*] prima civitas fuit *Corinium*, à *Corino* fluvio vicino ſic appellata. Britannicè dicta eſt *Cair Keri*, vel rectius *Cori*. Saxonicè autem *Churnceſtre*: deinde et *Cirenceſter*: at nunc, ablata media vocabuli parte, *Ciceſtre*. Hic ingens vis numiſmatum imaginibus Cæſarum, lege Britannis impoſita, ſignatorum reperiuntur. Paucis ab hinc annis ibidem erutæ inter mœniorum rudera tabulæ Ro. literis inſcriptæ. *Lelandi Itin.* v. 9, p. 32, ſub verbo *Dobuni*.

[n] Aſſer de Reb. Geſt. Ælfredi, p. 35, Ed. Wiſe.

[o] Lambard's Deſcription of England.

ſition of the names of places, to ſignify a *walled* or *fortified town*.

The Roman name of this place was framed from the Britiſh; Ptolomy calls it *Corinium*, Antoninus *Duro-Cornovium*, probably from *dwr*, the Britiſh word for *water*. The latter name ſeems to be moſt expreſſive, yet both ſignify the town upon the water or river *Corin*.

The Anglo-Saxons, either from the Britiſh, or from the Roman name, called the town Coꞃneceaꞅꞇꞃe, Cuꞃmneceaꞅꞇꞃe[p], Cyꞃenceaꞅꞇꞃe; upon which I ſhall once more obſerve, that ceaꞅꞇꞃe is nothing more than a tranſlation of the Britiſh word *caer* into the Saxon language. The name of the town, as it is now written, ſtands at the head of this account, but the preſent common appellation is *Ciſeter*.

On a near approach to the town, there is a gentle deſcent every way, except from the ſouth. The air is ſo remarkably pure and ſalubrious, that a phyſician, who ſettled here about forty years ſince, after ſtaying a time ſufficient, as he thought, to make trial of his ſucceſs, pronounced it impoſſible for one of his profeſſion to ſubſiſt on the practice the town and its neighbourhood afforded. The water is ſufficiently pure and pleaſant, riſing in a fine gravel, about fourteen or fifteen feet below the ſurface, and almoſt every houſe has a pump.

The town conſiſts of eleven ſtreets, beſides lanes and alleys. *Dyer-ſtreet*, but more antiently *Chipping-ſtreet*, ſo called becauſe the market is held in it, is that by which you enter the town from London and Oxford. From the round ſtone at the bottom of it to the other extremity, at the croſſing of the four principal ſtreets, it meaſures 549 yards.—*Cricklade-ſtreet* is ſo called becauſe it leads to the antient town whoſe name it bears. From a ſtone which marks the limits of the borough on that ſide, at the bottom of the ſtreet, to the other extremity, it meaſures 360 yards.—*Caſtle-ſtreet*, which name was given it from its leading to the antient caſtle, is that by which you enter the town from Briſtol and Bath, and is 274 yards long.—*Goſditch-ſtreet*, leading from the middle of the town northward to the firſt bridge towards Glouceſter, is in length 180 yards. —*Dollar-ſtreet*, or in old writings, *Le Foſſe*, commencing at the firſt bridge, and extending to the ſecond, on the ſame road, is 190 yards long.—*St. Lawrence-ſtreet*, or *Glouceſter-ſtreet*, was ſo called becauſe the church of St. Lawrence ſtood in it, and becauſe it leads to Glouceſter. This ſtreet is 427 yards long.—*Cecily-ſtreet*, or *Cecily-hill*, took its name from the church of St. Cecilia ſtanding in it. From Groomſtole-bridge, where this ſtreet begins, to the end of it, leading to Minchin-hampton, it is 190 yards.—*Black-jack-ſtreet*, which leads from Groomſtole-bridge, and ſeems like a continuation of the laſt mentioned ſtreet, is in length 300 yards.——*Silver-ſtreet*, making the communication between Black-jack-ſtreet and Caſtle-ſtreet, is in length only 75 yards. —*Thomas-ſtreet* had its appellation from an hoſpital ſtanding in it, dedicated to the ſaint of that name, and, extending from Groomſtole-bridge to the bottom of Dollar-ſtreet, is 227 yards long.—*Coxwell-ſtreet* was ſo called from the name of a perſon of conſiderable property who lived in it; but the more antient name is *Abbat-ſtreet*, which was given it becauſe it led to the abbey. This ſtreet is 221 yards long.—*Shoe-lane*, (ſo called from the ſhoe-makers ſettling there) the *Butter-row*, and the *Butcher-row*, lie parallel to each other on the weſt ſide of the corn-market, whence the two latter lead to the high-croſs, and are 33 yards long.—Beſides theſe, there are *Sheep-ſtreet-lane*, on the ſouth-weſt ſide of the town; *Spital-gate-lane*, corruptly called *Spiringate-lane*, on the north ſide of it; *Leauſe-lane* on the ſouth-eaſt, and the *Law-ditch-lane* on the weſt ſide of it.

Coming into the town from Glouceſter, a great part of the ſtreet is a hollow way, in ſome places five feet deep, where a portion of the Churn water runs, and empties itſelf into one of the arms of that river at the ſecond bridge. There is a tradition that the river antiently ran through the middle of the town, which is ſtrengthened by a paſſage in Leland, who ſays, *Be lykehod yn times paſt Guttes were made that Partes of Churne Streame might cum thorow the Cyte, and ſo to returne to theyr great Bottom.* Itin. v. 5, p. 61. And not many years ſince, as the workmen were digging a vault under the ſtreet, near where the four principal ſtreets meet, at about the depth of ſix feet under the ſurface, they found ſtones ſet up edge-ways, like thoſe commonly placed in a water-courſe, for people to ſtep on. This circumſtance, I think, puts the matter out of doubt, that antiently the water ran through the town by the high croſs, and ſo down Cricklade-ſtreet, and at length joined the main river at Watermore.

There is a great deal of travelling through this place from the northern to the weſtern parts of England, and from Bath and Briſtol to London, through Oxford and Abingdon. Two ſtage-coaches paſs thro' it to London, and a third in its courſe between Bath and Oxford; which, with a great number of heavy carriages that keep their regular ſtages, open a communication between this place and Monmouthſhire, South Wales, Hereford, Glouceſter, Worceſter, Warwick, Coventry, Leiceſter, Nottingham, the Weſt, and many other places; a circumſtance ſo favourable to trade, that, next to Glouceſter, this is eſteemed the principal market-town in the county.

It has two weekly markets, on Monday and Friday. The firſt, for grain and all ſorts of commodities, is very much frequented; the other is chiefly for wool, butchers-meat, and poultry. The wool-market was once very conſiderable, 'till the dealers in that article began to travel the country, and buy their wool at the farm-houſes, which at length had this effect, that inſtead of thirty or forty waggon-

[p] Lambard, p. 259.

waggon-loads, which uſed to be brought hither every market-day, there has been, for ſome time, ſcarcely any ſent to market; and the Boothall, where the wool was uſually depoſited, is now taken down.

Frequent oppoſitions in the borough, in chooſing their repreſentatives in parliament, have made the poor inhabitants more licentious, and leſs induſtrious, than they formerly were. Theſe circumſtances are unfavourable to manufactures, and generally prevent them from riſing to any degree of eminence. The cloathing buſineſs flouriſhed here, according to Leland, in the reign of king Henry the Eighth; but at preſent little is done in that manufacture.

The heavy edge-tools of this place are in great reputation, eſpecially thoſe knives which curriers uſe in ſhaving leather, and which find a market all over Europe and America. Wool-combing is on the decline. Carpet-making hath been lately introduced; and there are a few cheneys, harrateens, and light ſtuffs manufactured. But ſtocking frame-knitting, which was ſet on foot about forty years ſince, lies at the laſt gaſp, under many diſadvantages, and is only kept from expiring by the cordial influence of a very large eſtate, which was charitably intended to promote ſome conſiderable manufacture here. The principal buſineſs is woolſtapling and yarn-making, for which the town is well ſituated, near the cloathing country.

This is called an antient city, and, according to the opinion of ſome perſons, of ſo high antiquity as to have been built by the Britons, before the Roman invaſion. But that the Britons had then any cities or towns, in the ſenſe we now underſtand thoſe terms, is a notion very contrary to the teſtimony of antient authors, of the greateſt credit as to that matter. Cæſar indeed, in his book *De Bello Gallico*, ſpeaks of their towns, but he tells us what they were; *Oppidum autem Britanni vocant, quum ſilvas impeditas vallo atque foſſa munierunt:* The Britons call that a town, when they have ſurrounded and fenced about their thickeſt woods with a bank and a ditch. And Xiphilin ſpeaking of the *Mæatæ*, or inhabitants of the now moſt northern counties of England, aſſerts, that they had neither *walls* nor *cities*; what paſſed under the name of cities in Britain, being, according to Strabo, no other than *groves*. Theſe authorities will ſtand their ground againſt the fond conceits and looſe conjectures of later writers; and upon this ground I ſhall venture to ſay that Cirenceſter was built by the Romans. The preciſe time of its foundation I do not pretend to aſcertain, but I apprehend it might be very ſoon after they had eſtabliſhed themſelves in Britain. Three great roads meeting at this place, rendered it the moſt deſirable ſituation for a town that can be conceived, and no doubt that circumſtance induced them to make choice of it.

Being the metropolis of the large province of the *Dobuni*, it was called *Corinium Dobunorum*, and became a very eminent ſtation for the Roman armies. Antoninus places it at the diſtance of fourteen miles from *Glevum*, or Glouceſter, in the thirteenth *Iter* from *Iſca*, now Caerleon in Monmouthſhire, to *Calleva*, which Dr. Gale will have to be Henly, the *Calleva Attrebatum*, or chief city of the *Attrebatii*, whilſt others give that honour to Wallingford in Berkſhire.

According to Brompton, and ſeveral other antient writers, this city lay in the province of Wiccia. The antient city wall was more than two miles in circumference. It was intire in the reign of king Henry the Fourth, but muſt have been razed ſoon after. Leland traced it quite round in king Henry the Eighth's time, but even then there were but few veſtiges of it remaining;

. . . . *Sic omnia fatis*
In pejus ruere, ac retro ſublapſa referri. Virg.

He tells us, that 'A man may yet, walking on 'the bank of Churne, evidently perceyve the cumpace of foundation of towers ſumtyme ſtanding 'in the waul. And nere to the place wher the 'right goodly clothing mylle was ſet up a late by 'the abbate, was broken down the ruine of an old 'tower, toward making of the mylle waulles, in 'the which place was fownd a quadrate ſtone 'fawllen down afore, but broken *in aliquot fruſtra*, 'wherein was a Romain inſcription, of the which, 'one ſcantly letterd that ſaw yt, told me, that he 'might perceyve PONT. MAX. Among divers *nu-miſmata* fownd frequently there, Diocleſian's be 'moſt faireſt; but I cannot adfirme the inſcription 'to have bene dedicate onto hym. In the middes 'of the old town, in a medow, was found a flore '*de teſſellis verſicoloribus*, and by the town *noſtris temporibus* was fownd a broken ſhank bone of a 'horſe, the mouth cloſed with a pegge; the which 'taken owt, a ſhepard found yt fillid *nummis argenteis*. In the ſowth-ſouth-weſt ſide of the waul be 'lykelyhod hath bene a caſtel, or ſum other great 'building, the hilles and diches yet remayne. The 'place is now a waren for conys, and therin hath 'be fownd mennes bones *inſolitæ magnitudinis*, 'alſo to ſepulchres *ex ſecto lapide*. In one was a 'round veſſel of leade covered, and in it aſhes and 'peaces of bones.' *Leland's Itin.* v. 5, p. 65.

Dr. Stukeley viſited this place in the year 1723, and fancied that he could even then trace the old city wall quite round the town. But antiquities give way to modern improvements, and all that remains of it, at preſent, lies on the eaſt and ſouth-eaſt ſides, about half a mile in length, covered with earth and rubbiſh fourteen or fifteen feet high. A ſmall part being uncovered in 1774, it was found to be eight feet thick, built with hewn ſtone, ſtrongly cemented with lime and gravel.

A little within the old city wall, is a pretty large tract of ground called the *Leauſes*, now converted to garden-ground and corn-fields, where, for many ages paſt, have been found antient carvings, inſcriptions, and teſſellated pavements, with great abundance of Roman coins, rings, and intaglio's, which have been long ſince loſt or diſperſed. From theſe circumſtances, together with the name, Dr. Stukeley, with good reaſon, ſuppoſed the *Leauſes* to have been the Roman *Prætorium*, for *llys*, in the Britiſh language, ſignifies a *court*.

Several authors have barely mentioned theſe antiquities, but they have not tranſmitted down to us a catalogue of the coins, nor given us ſo many particulars as the ſubject deſerved: I ſhall, however, collect from them what has been written, and then ſubjoin my own particular obſervations.

Leland has left us no more than what is quoted in the preceding page.

Sir Robert Atkyns follows next in order. 'Here,' ſays that gentleman, in his account of Cirenceſter, 'are often dug up, in old foundations, 'a great many and great variety of ancient Roman 'coins. There was accidentally diſcovered, in a 'meadow near the town, an ancient building 'under ground. It was 50 foot long and 40 'broad, and about 4 foot high; ſupported by 100 'brick pillars; inlaid very curiouſly with teſſeraick work, with ſtones of divers colours, little 'bigger than dice: It is ſuppoſed to have been a 'bathing-place of the Romans.' This is all ſir Robert ſays, from whoſe account the reader will not very readily underſtand what part was ſo curiouſly inlaid; whether the pillars, the whole building, or (as it is moſt likely) the pavement only.

Then comes Doctor Stukeley, who has not complimented the good people of Cirenceſter on account of their taſte for works of antiquity. 'Large quantities of carved ſtones,' ſays he 'are 'carried off yearly in carts [meaning from the Leauſes] 'to mend the highways, beſides what 'are uſeful in building. A fine moſaic pavement 'was dug up here in September 1723, with many 'coins. I bought a little head, which had been 'broken off from a baſſo-relievo, and ſeems by 'the tiara, of a very odd ſhape, like fortification-'work, to have been the genius of a city, or ſome 'of the *Deæ Matres* which are in the old inſcrip-'tions, ſuch like in Gruter, p. 92. The gardener 'told me he had lately found a little braſs image, 'I ſuppoſe one of the *Lares*; but upon a dili-'gent ſcrutiny, his children had played it away. 'Mr. Richard Biſhop, owner of the garden, on 'a hillock near his houſe, dug up a vault ſixteen 'feet long, and twelve broad, ſupported with 'ſquare pillars of Roman brick, three feet and a 'half high, and on it a ſtrong floor of terras. 'There are now ſeveral more vaults near it, on 'which grow cherry-trees, like the hanging 'gardens of Babylon. I ſuppoſe theſe the foun-'dations of a temple, for in the ſame place they 'found ſeveral ſtones of the ſhafts of pillars, ſix 'feet long, and baſes of ſtone near as big in 'compaſs as his ſummer houſe adjoining, as he 'expreſſed himſelf; theſe, with cornices very 'handſomely moulded, and carved with mo-'dillions and the like ornaments, were converted 'into ſwines-troughs. Some of the ſtones of the 'baſes were faſtened together with cramps of 'iron, ſo that they were forced to employ horſes 'to draw them aſunder, and they now lie before 'the door of his houſe as a pavement. Capitals 'of theſe pillars were likewiſe found, and a 'crooked cramp of iron, ten or twelve feet long, 'which probably was for the architraves of a 'circular portico. A moſaic pavement near it, 'and intire, is now the floor of his privy vault.

'Sometimes,' continues the doctor, 'they dig 'up little ſtones as big as a ſhilling, with ſtamps 'on them. I conjecture they are counterfeit dies 'to caſt money in. We ſaw a monumental in-'ſcription' [ſee the margin] 'upon a ſtone of 'Mr. Iſaac Tibbot's, 'in Caſtle-ſtreet, in 'very large letters, 'four inches long[s]. 'It was found at a 'place half a mile 'weſt of the town, 'upon the north ſide 'of the Foſs-road, 'called the Querns, 'from the quarries 'of ſtone there-'abouts. Five ſuch 'ſtones lay flat-wiſe upon two walls, in a row, 'end to end, and underneath were the corpſes of 'that family, as we may ſuppoſe. He keeps 'Julia Caſta's ſkull in his ſummer-houſe, but 'people have ſtole all her teeth out for amulets 'againſt the ague. Another of the ſtones ſerves 'for a table in his garden; 'tis handſomely 'ſquared, five feet long, and three and a half 'broad, without any inſcription. Another is laid 'for a bridge over a channel near the croſs in 'Caſtle-ſtreet. There were but two of them 'which had inſcriptions; the other inſcription 'periſhed, being unluckily expoſed to the wet in 'a froſty ſeaſon, probably of the huſband. Several 'urns have been found thereabouts, being a 'common burying-place. I ſuppoſe them buried 'here after Chriſtianity.' *Stukeley's Itineraria Curioſa.*

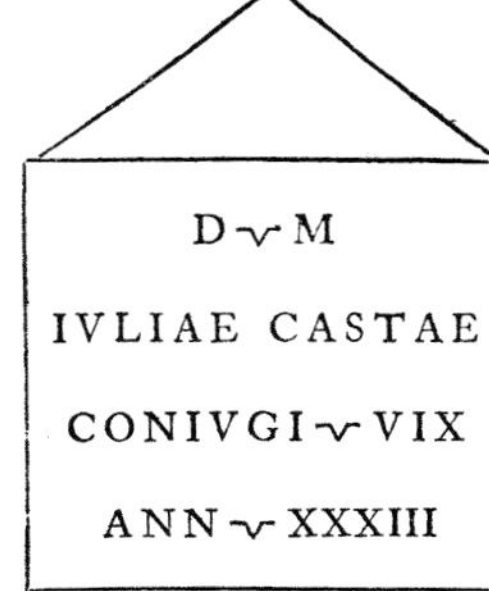

When we compare theſe accounts together, it ſeems probable that the antient building mentioned by ſir Robert Atkyns (and which ſeems to be the ſame that, according to a manuſcript which I have ſeen, was opened in 1683) was in part dug up and deſtroyed by the gardener, in Dr. Stukeley's time. What remained of it being afterwards covered over with earth, was again opened in 1780. The opening was made about ſixteen yards from a wich-elm, growing in the S. W. wall of the garden. About three feet and a half below the ſurface, the workmen came to a very ſmooth floor of terras, which they found to extend about twelve

twelve feet further north-eaftward, where it was broken down and deftroyed. And finking deeper there, they came to another floor of terras, four feet five inches below the furface of the firft, and running all the way under it; for they prefently difcovered that there was a large cavity between them, and that the upper floor was fupported by rows of brick pillars, which ftood upon that beneath. Clearing the earth away from off the fecond, or laft mentioned floor, they came to a wall of hewn ftone, rifing within about two feet of the furface of the ground, at the diftance of fifteen feet from the broken edge of the upper terras, which latter, it was evident, had originally extended to this wall. Here feems to have been the boundary of the works on the north-eaft fide. Soon afterwards they came to another upright wall on the fouth-eaft fide, which joined to, and made a right angle with the former. Thefe appear to be the north-eaft and fouth-eaft walls of a vault, whofe dimenfions are not certainly known, as the other two walls are deftroyed. In each wall were obferved five maffy ftones, forming the crown of an arch, the cavity of which lay almoft intirely below the top of the fecond terras. In order to examine thefe arches, a fmall part of the under floor was beat up along the fides of the walls, and at the depth of thirty-four inches, there was a third ftrong floor of terras, running under the fecond, the fpace between being filled with rough ftones, thrown together in a promifcuous manner. This laft ferved as a floor to the arches, which had nothing in them but rubbifh, and at bottom a bed of wood-afhes about two inches thick.

A large hole was made through the fouth-eaft wall, about eight feet from the angle where the two walls join. This wall was found to be forty inches thick, yet it was only a partition; for on the fouth-eaft fide of it was another vault, with floors and brick pillars, on the fame level, and exactly correfponding with thofe in the firft-mentioned vault, but in a more imperfect ftate.

The ground was then carefully opened from the furface, on the fouth-eaft fide of the partition wall, about twelve feet from the angle where the two walls join, and at the depth of three or four feet, there were found vaft quantities of flat bricks, of different fizes, like thofe ufed in the conftruction of the firft-mentioned vault, intermixt with broken funnels and other rubbifh, but the vaulting had been totally deftroy'd. However, the greater part of the partition wall remained, and twenty feet diftant from the north-eaft end of it, was an opening three feet wide, with fquare quoins, but its height is not known, as the top was broken down. This aperture ferved for a communication between the two vaults, and having an arch on each fide, exactly at correfponding diftances, (about four feet) feems to indicate a regular building, and makes it probable that this wall was divided into two equal parts by it, and confequently that the whole extended forty-three feet. The arches are all upon the fame level, and of like dimenfions, thirty-five inches wide, and thirty-feven from the crown to the floor, and therefore too low for door-ways.

The great ftrength and ftability of the vaulting are remarkable: The two lower floors of terras, with the bed of ftones between them, were defigned by the architect as a firm bafis to fupport the brick pillars, and the maffy floor that lay upon them. The upper floor of each vault is fourteen inches thick; the pillars thirty-nine inches high, and eight inches and a quarter fquare, made of courfes of entire bricks of the fame fuperficial dimenfions, and about an inch and three quarters thick, except that each pillar has a large brick of eleven inches fquare for its bafe, and another of the fame fize by way of capital. They ftand in rows fifteen inches afunder, and are covered with wide bricks at top twenty three inches fquare, upon which the terras is laid. What now remains of the upper floor in the firft mentioned vault, is fupported by twenty-two pillars only, arranged in feven rows one way, and fix the other; and where the pillars are deficient, the gardener has taken care to fupport the floor with timber.

The under part of this floor, (which, as already obferved, confifts of broad bricks) and all the pillars, are very much burnt, fo that but few of the latter are perfect, occafioned in fome meafure, perhaps, by the force of long continued fires; but I apprehend they have fuffered much injury alfo by other accidents, fuch as knocking off pieces from the fides and angles with iron inftruments ufed in ftirring the fire, and placing the fewel, which muft fometimes have happened unavoidably. There were found difperfed all over the fecond floor, which I fhall now call the hearth, a very confiderable quantity of wood afhes, intermixed with coals, and confolidated into a hard mafs, by length of time and natural humidity; whence it appears fufficiently evident, that fires have been kept burning uniformly all over the hearth, to heat the floor above, but not for the purpofe of a bathing-place, as fir Robert Atkyns conjectured, whofe opinion I had adopted before I faw the ruins. And ftill lefs probable is Dr. Stukeley's opinion, that 'thefe are the foundations of a temple;' but they appear very evidently, to me at leaft, to be the remains of two Hypocaufts.

It may be obferved, from the dimenfions of the pillars, and the diftance by meafurement which they ftand from each other, that in a fpace of 50 feet long and 40 broad, as the building formerly difcovered is faid to have been when intire, there muft have been near four times the number of them mentioned by fir Robert Atkyns; yet as he does not pretend to have feen them, and as no great accuracy can be expected from hearfay accounts, I have not the leaft doubt but thefe are the

the remains of the ſame building taken notice of by the two laſt mentioned authors.

Hypocauſts, (from the Greek, υποκαιω, to *burn under*) were a kind of large, ſubterraneous ovens, which the Romans made uſe of for warming their houſes. Palladio, the great Italian architect, gives a ſhort account of them. *The antients*, ſays he, *made a fire in a ſmall ſubterraneous vault, from which many funnels of various ſizes were carried to the ſeveral rooms in the houſe, and the heat aſcended in them in the ſame manner as it is found to paſs through the narrow neck of an alembic, one end of which, tho' very diſtant from the fire, is not leſs warm than the part neareſt to it. Thus, the heat ſo equably diffuſes itſelf into all parts, that it fills the whole houſe. This is not the caſe with chimney-hearths, near which if you ſtand, you are ſcalded; if at a diſtance, you are chilled; but where theſe pipes are carried, a mild air diffuſes itſelf around. Theſe funnels which conveyed the heat had not open mouths, ſo they did not emit flame nor ſmoak, but only a hot vapour, and perpetual warmth. A ſmall fire in the vault, provided it were continual, was ſufficient. At the mouth of the vault they dreſſed their victuals. Pots and veſſels were placed on every ſide in the walls, full of hot water, to keep their victuals warm; a very great advantage without expence, liable to no danger, no filth, nor ſmoak, and free from a thouſand inconveniencies which accompany other kinds of fires*[t].

Hence it appears, that the hypocauſts of antient Rome, as deſcribed by Palladio, were ſomething different from thoſe which have been found here. For as this country is much colder than Italy, ſo the Romans in Britain found it convenient, in this cold country, to make their hypocauſts immediately under their parlours and lower rooms; and both their vaults and fires were larger than thoſe in uſe at Rome. But, probably, in all other reſpects they were alike. Many fragments of earthen funnels have been found among the ruins of our Hypocauſts, and one piece has the cavity intire, of an oblong form, ſix inches by four; and in ſeveral parts of the partition wall, particularly in the large ſtones of the arches, are a great many holes, in which were fixt, and are ſtill to be ſeen, the ends of iron hooks or ſtaples, [as may be ſuppoſed,] to ſupport the earthen funnels, and lead them to the upper rooms, in the manner deſcribed by this author. The mouths of both Hypocauſts, where they were ſupply'd with fewel, which were probably on the north-weſt and ſouth-eaſt ſides, are both deſtroy'd.

The editor, from repeated inſpection of theſe ruins, being enabled to give a more perfect account of them than he had ever ſeen, could not reſiſt the pleaſure which he promiſed himſelf of obliging the public with it; and therefore, ſince the original publication of his work in 1779, he has printed this additional ſheet, to be fixed in his books in the room of the leaf paged 345, 346, which contained the old account, and is now to be cancelled. [March 6, 1782.]

Fragments of Roman pottery, and ſmall cubical ſtones of different colours, which are undoubtedly the ruins of ſome teſſellated pavement, are continually found in theſe gardens; but the upper floors of the Hypocauſts do not appear to have been teſſellated. A portion of a large pillar, and the capital of a pillaſter of the Corinthian order, which were formerly dug up there, among other ornamental parts of buildings, and perhaps the very pieces mentioned by Dr. Stukeley, are now in good preſervation, in Mr. Buſh's garden in Cirenceſter: The ſhaft of the pillar, when intire, muſt have been ten or twelve feet long, independent of the capital and other members.

There was a fine figure of Apollo, in braſs, about the height of eighteen inches, found in the ſame gardens about forty years ſince, and is now in the Bodleian Library at Oxford, by the favour of Mr. Maſter, who preſented it to the univerſity. And a ſmall altar, about ſeven inches high, was thrown up among the rubbiſh a few years ſince, but there is no inſcription on it. This is now in Mr. Buſh's poſſeſſion, and was probably the portable altar of ſome poor man, uſed only in the offering of incenſe, or ſalt flour, ſuch as Camden mentions in his account of Lancaſhire, adding, that the Romans raiſed altars not only to their Gods, but out of a ſervile flattery, to their Emperors likewiſe, under the impious title of *Numini Majeſtatique eorum*. At theſe they fell on their knees and worſhiped, theſe they embraced and prayed to, before theſe they took their oaths,

[t] Veteres in *ſubterraneo* fornice non magno, cujus extrema pars extra domum muro terminabatur, unum ignem incendebant. Ab hoc canales plurimi, variæ magnitudinis, intimis fabricæ parietibus incluſi, ut hodie aquarum et ſentinarum fiſtulæ, ad ſummam contignationem permeabant. His ſingulis nares erant ad os fornicis domus parietibus adjunctum, per quas calor inter parietes aſcendens, ad oecos, triclinia, tablina manabat, et ad omnia loca quibus calorem procurare vellent. Quemadmodum vim ignis per canaliculos quoſdam alembicum penetrare videmus: ubi ignis quidem longiſſime diſtat ab ore vitri, quod tamen non minus calet, quam illa vaſis pars, quam ignis proxime calefacit. Calor ille adeo æquabiliter in omnes partes ſe diffudit, ut totum habitaculum impleret. Non ita camini, quibus ſi propius ſtes, æſtuas; ſi longius, friges. Illic vero aer mitiſſimus ſe circumfudit; ut cameram, cui caminus in adverſo muri latere collocatus eſt, accenſus ignis paulatim et leniter tepefacit. Canales illi qui calorem diſpenſabant, patulas fauces non habuerunt; quare nec flammam nec fumum, ſed calidum tantum vaporem, et perpetuum teporem emiſerunt. Ignis in fornice parvulus, modo continuus, locis adeo occluſis, vaporandis ſuffecit. Ad os fornicis edulia parabant. Quaquaverſum in muro vaſa et ollæ collocatæ ſunt, aquis ferventibus repletæ, quæ dapes calidas ſervarent.

Commodum ſine ſumptu maximum! nullo periculo, nullis ſordibus, non fumo turbatum; mille incommodis ſolutum, quæ reliqua focorum genera comitantur. Non illic fumariolis, ignitabulis, vel thermocliniis, tot malorum cauſis, opus fuit: non variis inſtrumentis ad frigus domandum, et fovenda calore corpora. Sed in ſingulis cameris per omne ſpatium æqualis tepor et molliſſimus aer ſe diffudit. Canales plus minus calebant, ut ratio temporum poſtulabat. Peritiſſimi enim in calore moderando veteres fuerunt; uſi lenis auræ refrigeratione, qualem organorum folles ſpirant, quæ non minus ſuavis et placida eſt, quam illa acuta eſt, vehemens, et fæda, quam fabrorum folles ejectant.

Si divites et principes viri, qui ædes ſibi ædificant, exemplo adeo commodo uterentur, rem facerent digniſſimam; quam omnes amplecterentur, et quæ minore cum ſumptu innumeris ærumnis nos expediret. *Palladio de Focis Veterum, in fine libri cui titulus Antiquitates Urbis Romæ. Ital. & Lat. Oxonii*, 1709, *8vo.*

Not underſtanding Italian, the editor, from neceſſity, quotes the Latin tranſlation of Palladio.

and to be ſhort, in theſe and their ſacrifices the whole of their religion conſiſted; ſo that thoſe among them who had no altar, were ſuppoſed to have no religion, and to acknowledge no deity.

There is alſo a monumental ſtone, now placed in a building in the garden belonging to Siddington houſe, which was dug up, about fourteen or fifteen years ſince, at Watermore common, juſt without the city wall. It has a pediment at top, with a creſcent in low relief, and the following inſcription:

D M
P VICANAE
P VITALIS
CONIVX [t]

Lying by the ſtone was an urn, with aſhes and bones half burnt. This ſtone may be referred to the ſame age with that taken notice of by Dr. Stukeley.

There was alſo a glaſs urn, of a green colour, dug up, about fifteen years ago, in Kingſmead, which lies about half a mile from the town, on the ſide of the *Irminſtreet*. This urn, which contained many aſhes and pieces of burnt bones, was placed in a ſtone, chiſſelled out in a hollow form proper to receive it, and a flat ſtone covered the top. All theſe were depoſited in the midſt of a piece of ground about twenty feet ſquare, incloſed with a ſtone wall which lay below the ſurface of the ground. The relicks were further ſecured by a pavement ſpringing from the wall on every ſide, and riſing in the middle over the urn, in the form of a very obtuſe cone. This was undoubtedly Roman, but unaccompanied with coins, unleſs the workmen concealed them on the firſt diſcovery.

About the ſame time, a large ſtone coffin was dug up on the ſide of the road leading to Tetbury, not a quarter of a mile from the town. A human ſkeleton was found within it, with the ſcull between the legs, and a ſword lying on the right ſide of it.

On the eaſt ſide of the town, lies *Tor-barrow-hill*, which is undoubtedly a *tumulus*, as the name ſignifies. This muſt certainly be the hill ſaid to ſtand in Colton's-field, near Cirenceſter, and of which there is a ſtrange account[u] in a paper printed by William Budden, 1685, and preſerved in the Bodleian Library, among Dr. Rawlinſon's papers.

Weſtward of the town alſo, a little within lord Bathurſt's park, is a large round mount of earth, thrown up to the height of about twenty feet, according to tradition, by Godrum the Dane, who is called Gurmundus in the Britiſh annals; whence, by vulgar corruption, the place hath obtained the name of *Griſmund's-tower*, and *Chriſtmas-tower*. There was probably a wooden watch-tower erected on it, according to the cuſtom of the Danes, the better to explore the country, and to guard againſt a ſudden ſurpriſe from the enemy. Upon opening the mount, about fifteen years ago, ſeveral large earthen veſſels, full of aſhes and burnt bones, were found in it, and the earth and ſtones very much burnt for a great ſpace in one part of it. But that a leaden veſſel, with ſome aſhes and bones of an uncommon ſize have been found *on* the mount, I have read no where but in Buſching's Geography. Indeed Leland ſpeaks of ſuch a veſſel, with aſhes and pieces of bones, having been found where the caſtle ſtood, which Buſching miſtook for this tower. Who were the proprietors of theſe bones, and what bodies theſe aſhes are a part of, are queſtions above the reach of antiquariſm; but it is probable that they belonged to ſome perſons of eminence among the Danes, who fell in battle againſt the Saxons and Britons in theſe parts.

What gave riſe to the practice of burning the dead is uncertain: ſome have conjectured that it was to avoid a viſible degeneration into worms, and to leave a laſting portion of their compoſition after death; whilſt others have thought it an expedient to eſcape the malice of enemies. But whatever was the occaſion, the practice is of great antiquity. Homer has given many beautiful deſcriptions of the funeral obſequies of Patroclus, Achilles, Hector, and other chiefs among the Greeks and Trojans. At firſt they burnt the bodies of thoſe only who were moſt eminent among them, but denied that honour to ſuch as had laid violent hands on themſelves, or had betrayed their country, becauſe they conceived them enemies to the gods. The funeral pile was compoſed of roſemary, larynx, yew, cypreſs, and fir, by

[t] *Conjux* (for *Conjugis*) is the true reading on the ſtone. But this muſt have been a miſtake in the ſtone-cutter, who might be an ignorant man, as many of them were, making frequent blunders by omitting letters, and ſometimes adding others; more particularly when they were not immediately overſeen by the perſon whoſe office it was to direct them. There are many inſtances of omiſſions and redundancies in antient coins and inſcriptions; thus we often find COS for CONS, or CONSVL; IDEA IOVIS for DEA IOVIS, IDEA PALATINA for DEA PALATINA, &c. &c. More of this may be ſeen in Mr. *Hearne's Diſſertation on the Stunsfield Teſſellated Pavement*, at the beginning of the 8th Vol. of *Leland's Itinerary*.

[u] The ſtory is to the following effect: Two men digging a gravel-pit at the foot of this hill, having ſunk four yards deep, diſcovered an entrance into the hill, where they found ſeveral rooms with their furniture, which being touched, crumbled to duſt. In one of them were ſeveral images and urns, ſome with aſhes, others full of coins, with Latin inſcriptions on them. Entering another, they were ſurprized at ſeeing the figure of a man in armour, having a truncheon in its hand, and a light, in a glaſs like a lamp, burning before it. At their firſt approach, the image made an effort to ſtrike, ſo at the ſecond ſtep, but with greater force; but at the third it ſtruck a violent blow, which broke the glaſs to pieces, and extinguiſhed the light. Having a lanthorn, they had juſt time to obſerve, that on the left hand [I ſuppoſe of the figure] lay two heads embalmed, with long beards, and the ſkin looking like parchment, when hearing a hollow noiſe like a groan, they haſtily quitted thoſe dark appartments, and immediately the earth fell in, and buried all the curioſities.——— Camden was informed by credible perſons, that at the ſuppreſſion of monaſteries, there was found a lamp burning in the vault of that little chapel wherein Conſtantius Chlorus was thought to be buried. Lazius, ſays that antiquarian, tells us, that the antients had an art of diſſolving gold into a fat liquor, and of preparing it ſo that it would continue burning in the ſepulchres for many ages. *Camden*, v. 2, col. 880, in his account of York city.

by which, being trees of perpetual verdure, it has been thought they intended to convey fome hints of a refurrection.

The Romans adopted the practice from the Greeks, and fo it came into ufe among the Celtæ in the weftern world. In Britain, urn-burial was not confined to the Romans, for we learn from Pomponius that the druids ufed to burn and bury; and it is affirmed, that Bellinus, brother to the Britifh king Brennus, was burnt. Cæfar fays that burning was practifed in Gaul; and fince we learn from Tacitus, that the Britons were foon brought to build temples, to wear the gown, and ftudy the Roman laws and language, it is no improbable conjecture, that they foon alfo conformed to their cuftoms in burial.

The Saxons, Jutes, and Angles came from parts where burning was antiently practifed, and the Germans, from whom they defcended, ufed it, as Tacitus affirms.

In Denmark and Norway many urns have been found, very different from thofe of the Romans, as may be feen in Wormius; whence it fhould feem, that the Danes very antiently burned the dead; indeed Frotho the Great made a law, that princes and great commanders fhould be committed to the fire, tho' the common fort had grave-interment. It was alfo the cuftom of thofe people to diftinguifh the remains of the moft noble among them, by placing large ftones in circles about them.

The urns we find are neither uniform in figure, nor of one capacity; the largeft contain about three gallons, fome not much above half that meafure. Some have handles, ears, and long necks, but moft are of a circular form; many are red, fome black, fome covered with brick or tile, and fome have earthen covers adapted to them, whilft great numbers have no covering, but the earth preffed into them. Some have lachrimatories, or tear-bottles, attending them, either as facred to the *Manes* of the deceafed, or paffionate expreffions of their furviving friends, who, with hired tears, folemnized their obfequies.

Where we find D. M. [*Diis Manibus*] we commonly meet with *Pateræ*, and veffels of libation, upon old fepulchral monuments. An urn preferved by cardinal Farnefe contained the heads of feveral gods and goddeffes, an ape of agate, a grafs-hopper, an elephant of amber, a cryftal ball, three glaffes, two fpoons, and other things, which probably the deceafed took pleafure in; and in fome urns we find money, rings, darts, and pieces of broken armour. It has been conjectured, that the money was intended as a fee for old Charon; but whatever was the defign, the putting coins in urns, and the prefent practice of burying money in the foundations of noble buildings, are laudable means of chronological difcovery, and pofterity will applaud them.

As the time is uncertain when the practice of burning the dead began, fo is that of its ceafing alfo. Macrobius affirms that it was difufed in his days. In Minutius's time, it was objected againft the Chriftians, that tho' they did not hefitate, for the caufe of religion, to give their bodies to be burnt when alive, yet they condemned[w] the practice of burning after death; fo that we may conclude with great certainty, that it ceafed about the time of the converfion to chriftianity; and as the Romans confeffedly practifed it after they poffeffed Britain, the urns we find here are generally attributed to them, or to the Britons romanifed. But to return from this digreffion to my former fubject.

There was a Roman teffellated pavement found in a garden in Dyer-ftreet, belonging to a houfe the property of Mr. Jofeph Small; another was lately difcovered in digging a cellar in Mr. Cripps's houfe, belonging formerly to the family of the Georges; and another was found, a few years ago, in digging the vault under the fhambles at the Boothall; and without doubt many more are left for future ages to difcover. Thefe probably belonged to the halls or principal rooms of fome great officers under the *prætor*, or chief magiftrate that governed the town. The teffellated pavements were of two orders. Thofe of the nobler kind, which had ufually the figure of Apollo, or fome other deity upon them, were called *Megalographia*, in contradiftinction to the other fort of them, on which were reprefentations of moft inferior beings. This fort was ftiled *Ropographia*. But what thofe were, of which I have juft been fpeaking, is uncertain, as there is no drawing of them, and the works themfelves are deftroy'd, to the regret of the lovers of antiquity.

The coins that have been found here are chiefly thofe of Antoninus, Dioclefian, and Conftantine.

Three Roman confular ways meet at this place, the great *Fofs-way*, the *Irminftreet*, and the *Acman-ftreet*.

The *Fofs* comes from Scotland, and enters this county from Warwickfhire, by Lemington. It paffeth thro' Moreton-henmarfh and Stow, by Bourton on the Water, and Northleach, and croffing the river Coln at a place called Fofs-bridge, leads directly to Cirencefter.

The *Acmanftreet-way*, but fometimes called the *Ickenild-way*[x], croffeth Oxfordfhire, and coming to Broadwell-grove, where it is very high and perfect, enters this county at the parifh of Eaftleach, and joins the great *Fofs-way* about a mile north-eaft of Cirencefter. Four miles and a half weftward of

[w] Execrantur rogos, et damnant ignium fepulturam. *Minut. Fel.* p. 97.

[x] 'The *Ickenild-way* pafs'd not far from it, [Witney] on the 'right Hand in its Courfe to Cirencefter, where all the four *great* '*Ways* crofs'd.' *Difcourfe concerning fome Antiquities found in Yorkfhire*, publifhed at the end of Vol. I. of *Leland's Itin.* p. 119.—The *Fofs*, on the weft of Cirencefter, ar far as Bath, is by fome writers called the *Acmanftreet-way*, and thus Leland makes the number of the Roman ways meeting here, to be *four*.

the

the town, it leaves the turnpike-road, at a place called *Jacuments-bottom*, but more truly *Acman's-bottom*, and enters Wiltshire near Kemble, in its straight course to Bath, the Accmanneſceaſteꝛ of the Saxons.

Another of the great Roman ways, supposed by some to be the *Irminstreet*, leads from Caerleon in Monmouthshire, through Gloucester and this place, to Cricklade, and so on to Southampton[y]. Mercury was thought to preside over the highways, and the Germans worshipped him by the name of *Irmunsul*, whence, according to Mr. Camden, this Roman way derives its name.

The notion which some have entertained of these roads having been thrown up by one Mulmutius, long before the birth of Christ, is now generally exploded. Isidore's testimony, that *highways were made almost all over the world by the Romans*, in which they employ'd the soldiery and the people, that they might not grow factious by too much ease, goes a great way in determining to whom they ought to be attributed; but further, there are antient records, which say, that *In the days of Honorius and Arcadius there were made in Britain certain highways from sea to sea*. And here it may be proper to observe, that we derive the custom of placing mile-stones on our turnpike-roads from the Romans, for at the end of every mile, along their great roads, pillars were erected by the emperors, with figures cut in them to signify the number of miles. Hence Sidonius Apolonius,

Antiquus tibi nec teratur agger,
Cujus per spatium satis vetustis
Nomen Cæsareum viret columnis.

Nor let the antient causey be defac'd,
Where, in old pillars, Cæsar's name's exprefs'd.

By the sides of them were also the graves and monuments of famous men, to put the traveller in mind of his own mortality; whence arose that usual apostrophe, *Siste Viator*, in monumental inscriptions.

The learned antiquary before mentioned, in his account of Radnorshire, has shewn, that large heaps of stones, confusedly piled up together, are common in Wales, Scotland, Ireland, in the north, and probably in other parts of England, and are called by the British name *Karneu*, *Karned-heu*, and *Kairn*, which he understands to be a primitive word, signifying a *heap of stones*. He is of opinion, that most of them were intended for memorials of the dead, not only because he observed, near the summit of one of them, a rude stone monument in the form of a coffer or chest, but also, because it was antiently the custom to throw up large heaps of stones for sepulchral monuments, and in later times, more particularly over the graves of malefactors: What led me to this observation, is a piece of ground on the south-west side of the town, just without the old city wall, which goes by the name of the *Querns*, or *Kairns*, full of such large heaps of stones, but now, in length of time, covered with herbage. Large monumental stones have been dug up there, as already taken notice of from Dr. Stukeley, who concluded from thence, that the Querns was the common burying-place of the antient city of Cirencester; but, notwithstanding the name, I am far from thinking those heaps of stones are so many funeral piles, but rather, that they are heaps of rubbish, made by digging for stone to raise the city wall, or some other large buildings.

I must not, however, leave the Querns, without first taking notice of a plot within it, of an elliptical form, called the *Bull-ring*, the longest diameter of which is sixty-three yards, the other forty-six. Round it is a mound or wall of earth, thrown up to the height of about twenty feet, sloped on the inside with so much exactness as to manifest the hand of care and design; and I am of opinion, that there were originally rows of seats, or steps, one below the other, from top to bottom; but time has much defaced them. There are two avenues to this area, (east and west) and on the north side also is another strait approach, between two stone walls, lately discovered by people digging for stone. It is directed to the centre of the area, and about thirty inches wide between the walls, which were designed to keep up the high bank of earth on each side. Probably this is a Roman theatre, or else one of those places where antiently people met at the *Gurimawrs*[z], which were held in spacious places, inclosed with earthen banks, having room sufficient for thousands of people within. But tradition is silent as to the use of it; nor do I find the place itself taken notice of any where in history. Mr. Camden mentions one something like it in Westmoreland, called *King Arthur's Round Table*, which he thinks might possibly be a justing-place.

[y] In an essay concerning the four great Roman ways, at the end of the 6th Vol. of Leland's Itinerary, I find Mr. Camden quoted for his observation, (p. 240) that 'Several towns lye on 'and near the last mentioned causeway, that retain the word '*Sarn* in their names, as *Sharncote* and *South Sarney*, between 'Crecklade and Cirencester, and *North Sarney* about two miles 'above the latter upon the river Churn, and *Sharnton* about three 'miles from Gloucester. All which have taken their appellations 'from the British word *Sarn*, which imports *stratum*, or '*pavimentum*, and in Wales we have such an one called *Sarn* '*Helen* to this day.' But I differ in opinion from that learned antiquary, respecting the names of the above places, for the following reasons: The *C* in those names had originally a hard sound, as the same letter in *Corneceastre*, *Curineceastre*, also had; for I apprehend that the name of the town and of the villages had one common source, that is, *Corin*, or *Churn*, the name of the river on which both the *Cerneys* are situated: *Cerney*, therefore, is only a small deviation from *Churn-ey*, i. e. *the water Churn*. And as to *Sharncote*, which is adjoining to South Cerney, on the contrary side of it from the Roman road, I suppose it to be nothing more than *Cerney-coed*, so called from the British word *coed*, which signifies *wood*, as having been antiently a woody place.

[z] *Guiredd*, in the British language, signifies *truth*, and *mawr*, *great*; so that the word may signify the *scriptures*, or *great truths*. It is generally agreed that these circular places have been appropriated to religious purposes, and probably some parts of the scripture history were usually represented in them, for the instruction of the people.

2. *Of Military Affairs, and other memorable Events.*

This town hath feen many great events and memorable tranfactions. From Orofius's manner of expreffing himfelf, one might be induced to think it a place of note in the time of Julius Cæfar. The third battle, fays he, which that general had with the *Bryttas, was near the river which men call the Temefe, near thofe fords which are called Wallingford; after which, not only all the inhabitants of* Cyrnceaftre *fubmitted, but the whole ifland.*

Some fay the emperor Conftantine was crowned king of the Britons here, whilft others infift that York has a better claim to that honour; however it is certain, that Cirencefter was a very confiderable place in that emperor's time.

Under the Heptarchy, it lay within the kingdom of Mercia, which, as it appears by Ethelwerd, was divided from that of the Weft Saxons by the river Avon; but in the year 577, this city was won from the Britons of Mercia, who had 'till then defended themfelves in thefe parts with great bravery againft the Weft Saxons, by whom they were totally routed that year at Deopham, [Dyrham] under two of their leaders, Cuthwin and Ceaulin. Three Britifh princes, Commeail, Condidan, and Fariemeiol were flain in battle, and the cities of Cirencefter, Gloucefter, and Bath fell into the hands of the enemy; and foon after, Cirencefter was made a frontier garrifon againft the Mercians.

About fifty years afterwards, *anno* 628, Penda, king of Mercia, endeavoured to recover this place from the Weft Saxons, and meeting Cynegils and Cwichelm, (the king and his fon) near Cirencefter, with great forces on both fides, a bloody battle enfued; when, according to Huntingdon, both armies having abjured flight, they were parted only by the darknefs of the night; and this engagement not being much in favour of either party, they made peace the next morning, which continued but for a fhort time. The Weft Saxons, however, remained mafters of Cirencefter, 'till Peada, the firft chriftian king of Mercia, and fon of Penda, retook it from them in the year 656.

From that time, either no very interefting tranfactions happened here, for a fpace of two hundred years, or our hiftorians have taken no notice of them. But in the year 879, the Danes, under their leader Godrum, having been routed by king Alfred at Ethandun in Wiltfhire, furrendered their caftle in that neighbourhood, and made peace with the king, on condition that they might have leave to quit the kingdom; and accordingly they came immediately from Chippenham to Cirencefter[a], and remaining here one whole year, went afterwards to the eaftern parts of the kingdom. This Godrum, or Gothrum, is probably the fame that Polydore Virgil and others call Gormon and Gurmond, an African tyrant.

It is mentioned in the Britifh Annals, that the fame Gurmundus, after befieging this city a long time in vain, at laft ordered wild-fire and combuftible matter to be tied to the legs of fparrows, and letting them fly, they lighted on the houfes and fet them on fire, by which ftratagem he took the city; whence Giraldus calls it the *City of Sparrows*. Alexander Neccham, from the fame annals, writes of it thus:

> *Urbs vires experta tuas, Gurmunde, per annos*
> *Septem.* . . . . . .

> A city that experienc'd Gurmund's power
> For feven long years.

But it fhould be remembered, that poets are not always good hiftorians; nor is there the leaft reafon to believe that Gurmund, if he be the fame with Affer's Godrum, was longer here than one year, unlefs we fuppofe it to be before his convention with king Alfred.

The next memorable thing taken notice of to have happened here, was in the year 1020, when king Knute, after his return from Denmark, held a general council of the kingdom, at Eafter, in this town, in which Ethelwold was outlawed.

Here was a caftle on the fouth-weft fide of the town, and tho' I have not been able to difcover when nor by whom it was built, our hiftories give us a more certain account of its deftruction; for in the year 1142, the town having been made a garrifon for Matilda the emprefs, againft king Stephen, he came fo fuddenly and unexpectedly upon the caftle, as to furprife and burn it. However it was foon afterwards rebuilt, and held out againft the king by the earl of Leicefter's conftable, who at length furrendered it, to procure better terms for his mafter on his fubmiffion. This caftle was garrifoned by the barons who took up arms againft king Henry the Third; but that king foon recovered it, and caufed it to be immediately demolifhed.

When the barons took up arms againft king John, in the 16th year of his reign, the royal army was drawn together at this place; and again, upon a like occafion, this was the rendezvous for the army which king Edward the Second affembled, to crufh the confederacy formed by the earl of Lancafter and the lords of the marches, againft Hugh le Defpencer the king's favourite.

But this place is more remarkable for the fuppreffion of the rebellion raifed by the dukes of Aumerle, Surry, and Exeter, and the earls of Gloucefter and Salifbury, and their adherents, in the 1ft year of king Henry the Fourth. This fignal fervice was effected by the bravery and conduct of the mayor, as he is called in our hiftories, and about 400 of the townfmen only. Thofe noblemen had formed a confpiracy to feize and affaffinate the king, at a tournament at Oxford, to which he was invited. The plot was committed to writing, and each confpirator had a copy, figned and fealed by all the confederates. Afterwards, Aumerle being at dinner with his father the duke of York, the latter obferv'd a paper in his fon's bofom, feized it, and reading the contents, order'd his horfes to be

[a] Afferii Annales Rerum geftarum Ælfredi Magni. p. 35

be faddled immediately. Sufpecting his father's intention, Aumerle rode full fpeed to the king at Windfor, and difcovering the confpiracy, obtained pardon before the duke arrived. The other confpirators fufpecting themfelves difcovered, raifed a numerous army to furprife the king at Windfor. But Henry having alfo affembled 20,000 men, marched to give them battle, which fo difcouraged them, that they retreated to Cirencefter, and encamped without the gates. The chiefs quartered in the town, but the mayor perceiving that the gates and avenues were unguarded, affembled 400 men in the night, feized the gates, and attack'd the four noblemen in their quarters. The duke of Surry, and earl of Salifbury were taken, and beheaded on the fpot; but the duke of Exeter, and the earl of Gloucefter, efcaped by the tops of the houfes to the camp, which the foldiers had abandoned, and fled; imagining, from the noife and tumult of fighting in the town, which had been fet on fire by the rebel party, that a detachment of the king's troops had entered it. The duke of Exeter and earl of Gloucefter were taken fome time after, and loft their heads in the fequel. The heads of Surry and Salifbury were fent to London, their bodies having been buried in the abbey; but the head of the latter was reftored, and his body removed to Buftlefham, now Bifham in Berkfhire, where he had founded a priory for canons of the order of St. Auftin, dedicated to Chrift Jefus and the virgin Mary, valued at the diffolution at 327*l.* 4*s.* 6*d.*

The king, for this great fervice done him by the men of Cirencefter, granted them all the rebels goods, and four does in feafon out of his foreft of Bredon, and one hogfhead of wine out of his port of Briftol. And to the women, he granted fix bucks in right feafon, and one hogfhead of wine out of the fame port. See *Appendix*, N°. 1. Afterwards, in the 4th year of his reign, the fame king granted to the town, a court of Staple for merchandize, erecting a corporation of a mayor and two conftables, and others the commonalty, for the encouragement of trade, by the execution of the *Statute Merchant*. But this charter, after a long fuit in the Exchequer, was decreed to be cancelled, 37 Eliz.

All thefe events fhew the town to have been large, and of great account, in the times of which I have been fpeaking; but even in later ages, it has been the fcene of remarkable tranfactions; for here, as I find it in *Corbet's Hiftory of the Military Government of Gloucefter*, was the firft forcible oppofition to king Charles the Firft, in the year 1641, by infulting lord Chandois, then lieutenant of the county, who was at that time executing the commiffion of array. The rabble encompaffed him, and forced him to fign a paper, promifing that he would no more attempt to put it in execution. His lordfhip efcaped unhurt in his perfon, but his coach was cut in pieces.

This place was garrifoned, foon after, by the parliament's forces, and about the firft of January, 1642, was threatened to be ftormed by the main ftrength of the king's army, which came before it; but after ftaying two days, withdrew to wait for a reinforcement of horfe and artillery, and returned again on the 30th of the fame month, under the command of prince Rupert, who affaulted the town on the 2d of February, of which action the following is a fhort account, drawn from one publifhed by his highnefs's chaplain. The prince had two eighteen pounders, and four field-pieces; and a mortar-piece to throw granades. Proper difpofitions being made, the attack began at an inclofure between Mr. Poole's houfe (now the fite of lord Bathurft's houfe) and that of the Barton. The affailants being twice reinforced, beat the townfmen from the hedge, to the garden wall of the Barton. Mean while, a ftrong body, under general Wilmot and colonel Uffer, attack'd and burnt the Barton houfe, whence the townfmen were driven, and afterwards purfued by 500 of colonel Kirk's men, to the firft turnpike, (a kind of barricado) by Cicely hill. Lord Wentworth, who had the command of the right wing of the army, was to have fallen to the fouthward, on the right hand of the mount, now called Grifmund's Tower; but being mifled on the left hand of it, was flanked by a battery of two fix pounders, erected on the mount, and annoyed by the mufquettry from a high wall before them; which thinking it difficult to force, they drew to the left, into the lane leading to Cicely-hill, and joining colonel Kirk's men there, entered the barricado, or turnpike, together. Colonel Scrimfour, with a party of horfe, then pufhed into the town, and drove all before them. Colonel Fettiplace, who was the governor, captain Warneford, and Mr. George, one of the members for the borough, with many others, were taken prifoners in the town, and together with fuch of the fugitives as were taken in their flight, were fecured in the church. Great numbers of arms were found in the houfes, and drawn out of the river, to the amount of upwards of 3000, for this place had been a magazine for the country.

This town was afterwards made quarters, fometimes for the king's army, at others for that of the parliament. After the fiege of Gloucefter was raifed, the earl of Effex beat up the king's quarters here, and drove fir Nicholas Crifp and colonel Spencer, with their two regiments of horfe, out of the town. In this action he took 400 horfe, and 30 cart-loads of provifions, which was a feafonable fupply to his army.

Here alfo was the firft bloodfhed in the laft revolution, in the year 1688, when lord Lovelace, being on his march to join the prince of Orange with a party of horfe, was attacked by captain Lorange of the county militia, animated by the duke of Beaufort, who was a zealous man for king James. The captain was proprietor of Haymes in this county, and tho' both he and his fon loft their lives at that time, his men overpowered lord Lovelace, took him, and carried him prifoner to Gloucefter jail, having flain fome unfortunate gentlemen at the fame time.

The

The fummer affize for the county was held here, by lord chief juftice Scroggs and fir Robert Atkyns, on account of a peftilentical diforder being at Gloucefter, in the year 1679.

3. *Of the antient and prefent State of the Hundred of Cirencefter, and its Subdivifions; of the Borough, the Manor, and other Eftates.*

This place very antiently gave denomination to a hundred, which, at different times, was more or lefs extenfive. Soon after the conqueft, as we find in *Domefday-book*, it included the following places, *viz. Achelie, Benwedene, Circeftre, Duntefborne, Hunlafefed, Nortcote, Penneberie, Preftetune, Stratone, Sudintone, Torentune, Turfberie.*

In the ninth year of the reign of king Edward the Firft, the fheriff of the county returned, that in the hundred of Cirencefter are the underwritten vills, *viz. Baudinton, Cirencefter, Cotes, Daglinworth, Down Ampney, Dryfeild, Duntefburne, Hampton Moyfey, Prefton, Sodington, South Cerney, Upampney.*

By comparing the two accounts, it is obfervable, that Cotes is a new name, and ftands, in the fheriff's return, in the room of Hunlafefed, Torentune, and Turfberie, as we find them fet down in *Domefday-book*. Achelie, Nortcote, and Penneberie, fpecified in the *Domefday* account, are not mentioned by the fheriff, becaufe, at that time, they were confidered as members only of fome of the vills fet down in his return. Daglinworth, in the latter account, is fubftituted for Stratone in *Domefday*, which latter is not fet down as a vill in the above-mentioned fheriff's return; whereas the former is no where to be found in the general furvey; I conclude, therefore, that both thofe places, efpecially as they join together, were, 'till fome time after the fheriff's return, reputed to be one vill or parifh only, which took denomination, at firft from Stratton, but afterwards from Daglingworth, 'till it came to be divided into two parifhes. It is alfo remarkable, that both the Ampneys, Dryfeild, and Hampton Moyfey, which in *Domefday-book* are placed in Gerfdon hundred, are returned by the fheriff as belonging to that of Cirencefter.

Afterwards, another very material alteration took place in this hundred. In the fourth year of the reign of king Henry the Fourth, the town was erected into a kind of corporation, and two conftables placed over it, whereby it became a diftinct jurifdiction. The out-parifhes, with Minety, were fevered from it, and held a feparate *Torn* or court, which for diftinction was probably called *The Out Torn and Minety*, but now vulgarly, and as I conceive corruptly, *Crowthorne and Minety*. The hundred was the property of the abbat, who chofe rather to have the people of his houfe under the jurifdiction of the conftable of the *Out-Torn*, than fubject to the officers of the borough, or *In-Torn*, which alone retained the name of the hundred of Cirencefter. Thus the abbey and all its precincts and offices became diftinct from the borough, and have continued fo ever fince.

From that time the hundred and the borough have been commenfurate.

The borough is divided into feven wards, *i. e.* Dyer-ward, Cricklade-ward, Caftle-ward, Gofditch-ward, Dollar-ward, St. Lawrence-ward, and Inftrip-ward. To each ward two wardfmen, or petty conftables, are annually appointed at the leet; where alfo two high conftables are appointed, whofe authority extends over the hundred and borough.

This borough fent reprefentatives to a great council 11 E. 3. and by the grant of queen Elizabeth, in the thirteenth year of her reign, it fends two members to parliament. At firft, only the free burgeffes were electors, but on the occafion of a contefted election, in the reign of king James the Firft, it was determined, that the inhabitants houfholders, not receiving alms, fhould make the election; but the houfe of commons, Nov. 4, 1690, refolved, *That the inhabitants of the borough of Cirencefter, being inmates, have no right to vote in electing burgeffes to ferve in parliament*; and by their refolution of Dec. 1, 1709, *the inhabitants of the Abbey, the Emery, and the Spiringate-lane have not a right to vote in fuch election.* The number of electors is between fix and feven hundred.

A Lift of the Burgeffes who have ferved in Parliament for this Borough.

1571, Gabriel Blike, efq; Thomas Poole, gent.
1572, Thomas Powle, Thomas Strange, gent.
1585, Tho. Poole, junr. efq; Will. Eftcourt, gen.
1586, Charles Danvers, efq; Geo. Mafters, gent.
1588. Charles Danvers, efq; Geo. Mafters, gent.
1592, Oliver St. John, Henry Ferrys, gent.
1596, James Wroughton, efq; Hen. Powle.
1601, Rich. Browne, efq; Rich. George, efq.
1603, Rich. Marten, efq; Arnold Oldifworth, efq.
Edw. Jones, kt. in Marten's place, and
Anth. Mannye, kt. in Jones's place, decd.
1614, Lord Newborough, Tho. Rowe.
1620, Tho. Roe, knight, Tho. Nicholas, efq.
1623, William Mafters, kt. Hen. Pool, efq.
1625, Miles Sandys, kt. Hen. Pool, efq.
1625, Nevill Pool, kt. John George, efq.
1628, Giles Eftcourt, kt. & bart. John George, efq.
1640, Hen. Pool, efq; John George, efq.
1641, Theobald Gorges, kt. John George, efq. In their places, Thomas Fairfax, kt. Nath. Rich, efq.
1653, The Little Parliament. No boroughs fent reprefentatives.
1654, John Stone, of Friday-ftreet, London, efq.
1656, John Stone, efq; of Weftminfter.
1658-9, John Stone, efq; Rich. Southby, efq.
Thefe three laft were the Common Wealth Parliaments.
1660, Rich. Honour, John George.
This was called the Convention Parliament.
1661, Rich. Honour, John George.
1678, Hen. Powle, Sir Rob. Atkyns.
1680, Hen. Powle, Sir Rob. Atkyns.
1680-1, Hen. Powle, Sir Rob. Atkyns.
1685, Tho. Mafter, Earl of Newburgh.
1688, Tho. Mafter, John Howe.
1689, John Howe, Rich. Howe.
1695, John Howe, Rich. Howe.
1698, Hen. Ireton, Charles Coxe.
1700, Char. Coxe, James Thynne.
1701, Char. Coxe, William Mafter.
1702, Char. Coxe, William Mafter.
1705, Allen Bathurft, Hen. Ireton.
1707, Allen Bathurft, Hen. Ireton.
1708, Allen Bathurft, Charles Coxe.
1710, Charles Coxe, Thomas Mafter.
1713, Tho. Mafter, Benj. Bathurft.
1714, Tho. Mafter, Benj. Bathurft.
1722, Tho. Mafter, Benj. Bathurft.
1727, Tho. Mafter, Peter Bathurft.

1734, Tho.

1734,	Tho. Maſter,	William Wodehouſe.
1741,	Tho. Maſter,	Henry Bathurſt.
1747,	Thomas Maſter,	Henry Bathurſt.

But Thomas Maſter dying in 1748, John Coxe was elected.

1754,	John Dawney,	Benjamin Bathurſt.
1761,	John Dawney,	James Whitſhed.
1768,	James Whitſhed,	Eſtcourt Creſſwell.
1775,	James Whitſhed,	Samuel Blackwell.

The arms of the town are, *A Phœnix in Flames*, alluding to its having riſen out of the aſhes of the antient city, as the young phœnix is ſaid to proceed from the aſhes of the old one.

Cirenceſter gives the title of baron to William duke of Portland, whoſe anceſtor, by letters patent dated Apr. 9, 1689, was created [b]baron of Cirenceſter, viſcount Woodſtock, and earl of Portland.

Richardus Corinienſis was ſo called becauſe he was born here. He was a monk of Weſtminſter, and is famous for collecting an Itinerary, in the 14th century, of Roman Britain, from ſome remains of records drawn up between the years 138 and 170, by the authority of a Roman general, ſuppoſed to have been *Lollius Urbicus*, governor of Britain under Antoninus Pius; which work was a long time loſt to his native country. Mr. Bertram, an Engliſh gentleman, diſcovered the manuſcript at Copenhagen, in 1747. A copy having been tranſmitted to the late Dr. Stukeley, he publiſhed a tranſlation of the Itinerary, part with a comment, in 1757, and in the ſubſequent year the whole work was printed at Copenhagen, and a few copies ſent to England as preſents.

Here are three fairs in the year, *viz.* on Eaſter-Tueſday, July 18, and Nov. 8. The two cloth-fairs mentioned by ſir Robert Atkyns, one in the week before Palm-Sunday, the other in the week before the feaſt of St. Bartholomew, are both diſcontinued.

The property of the hundred deſcended with the principal manor, which is next to be conſidered.

The manor of Cirenceſter is of the antient demeans of the crown, of which *Domeſday-book* gives the following particulars:

'King Edward had five hides of land in 'Cireceſtre hundred. There are five plow-til-'lages in demean, and thirty-one villeins, with 'ten plow-tillages. There are thirteen *ſervi*, and 'ten bordars, and three mills of 30*s.* ſome mea-'dow, and two woods of 50*s.* And there are two 'free men who have two plow-tillages. The 'queen hath the wool of all the ſheep. In the 'time of king Edward, this manor paid three 'buſhels [*modios*] and a half of corn for bread, 'three buſhels [*modios*] of barley, and ſix ſextaries 'and a half of honey, and 9*l.* 5*s.* and 3000 loaves 'for the dogs. It now pays 20*l.* 5*s.* and twenty 'cows, and twenty hogs, and 16*s.* inſtead of the 'loaves, and 20*s.* for the new market, of which 'St. Mary hath the third penny.' *D. Book*, p. 67.

The church of St. Mary held two hides in the hundred, which will be taken notice of in its proper place; and there were two other manors in the vill, thus particularized in the record;

'A free man held two hides of land in Cireceſtre, 'and paid 20*s.* and did ſervice to the ſheriff 'throughout all England. Earl William put this 'land out of farm, and gave it to one of his men.'

'William the ſon of Baderon held two hides in 'Cireceſtre, and Hugh holds them of him. There 'is one plow-tillage in demean, and one villein 'and a half, and four bordars, with one plow-'tillage. There are two *ſervi*. It was worth 100*s.* 'now 70*s.* Aluui held this land.' *D. B.* p. 73.

It is impoſſible, at preſent, to diſtinguiſh between the two laſt manors with any degree of preciſion; but I conjecture that the firſt of the three continued in the crown 'till it was granted, with the juriſdiction of the ſeven hundreds, by king Richard the Firſt, to the abbat and convent of Cirenceſter. Sir Robert Atkyns is imperfect in his account of theſe manors and their appendages; which is the more remarkable, as he himſelf claimed to be the proprietor of ſome of them. I will give the beſt account I can of them, from the materials in my poſſeſſion.

When the townſmen of Cirenceſter ſuppreſſed the rebellion againſt king Henry the Fourth, they petitioned the king to be incorporated; whereupon the king directed his writ to the eſcheator, to inquire what damage others might ſuſtain if he ſhould comply with their requeſt. The eſcheator returned the king's writ, the petition, and the inquiſition, which he had taken at Glouceſter, 4 H. 4. into the court of chancery, where they were exemplified, and whence I have extracted the following particulars: 'The jurors ſay, that the 'town of Cirenceſter and the town of Mynety, 'with the appurtenances, make and are the manor 'of Cirenceſter, and were ſo in the time of king 'Richard the Firſt. That the church of St. Mary 'of Cirenceſter is of the foundation of king Henry 'the Firſt, and within his patronage. That king 'Richard the Firſt gave to God, and the church 'of St. Mary of Cirenceſter, his whole manor of 'Cirenceſter, with all and ſingular the appurte-'nances, and with the town of Mynetie, which is 'a member of the ſaid manor, and with the ſeven 'hundreds to the ſame manor, and to his farm 'belonging, and with all other the appurtenances, 'to be holden of the ſaid king and his ſucceſſors 'for ever, at the rent of 30*l.* a year, with [c]Soca, 'Saca, Thol, Them, Infangtheof, and Outfang-'theof, Hamſoca, and Girthbriche, Blodewite, 'Murder, Foreſtall, Flemsfleet, Ordeal, and Oreſt, 'within time and without, and in all places and 'with all cauſes which may be. And that the 'rent of aſſize of the ſaid manor of Cirenceſter 'is 143*l.* 4*s.* 8*d.* yearly, payable to the abbat. 'And that the ſaid ſeven hundreds are but as one 'hundred, and time out of man's memory have

[b] Collins's Peerage, Vol. 2, p. 139. Edit. 1768.

[c] The explanation of theſe terms may be ſeen in the Appendix, N°. 29.

 'been

'been ufed as one hundred before the making the 'aforefaid deed, and belonging to the faid manor 'of Cirencefter, and are holden at the town of 'Cirencefter, from three weeks to three weeks, in 'a certain houfe called the Tolfede[d], fituate in the 'middle of the faid town. That the manor of 'Cirencefter is the antient demean of the crown, 'and that to the faid manor belong two free te-'nants, William Erchbald and the holder of the 'court, and that all other tenants to the faid 'manor, in the aforefaid town of Cirencefter and 'Mynetie belonging, hold all their lands and 'tenements according to the cuftom of the manor 'of Cirencefter.'

Hence it is evident that this is the fame manor with that mentioned in *Domefday-book* to have been held by king Edward; which, with the hundred of Cirencefter, the feven hundreds, and other particulars granted to the abbey of Cirencefter, were part of the poffeffions of that abbey 'till it was diffolved. Yet, according to fir Robert Atkyns, Ela, countefs of Warwick, held the hundreds of Cirencefter and Briftwoles Borough 11 E. 1. and the abbefs of Lacock in Wiltfhire was feized of the hundred of Cirencefter 12 E. 1. But 15 E. 1. the king's writ of *Quo warranto* was iffued againft the abbat of Cirencefter, for the liberties of the feven hundreds, and his claim was allowed. At the diffolution of the monaftery, all thefe particulars reverted to the crown.

The hundred of Cirencefter, Crother', Brightwaldes barrowe, Refpegete, Bradley, Langtre, and Myntye, and the feven hundreds of Cirencefter, were afterwards granted to fir Thomas Seymour, lord Seymour of Sudley, as I find it recited in a fubfequent grant of them to fir Anthony Kingftone, 6 E. 6. of which I have an office copy.

Sir John Danvers died feized of the manor 37 Eliz. and was fucceeded by his fon, Henry Danvers earl of Danby, who built a large houfe on the weft fide of the town, and made the famous phyfic-garden, for the public ufe of the univerfity of Oxford. The manor and hundred were afterwards fold to Henry Poole, whofe fon and heir fir William Poole, in 1645, affigned them, with their appurtenances, and levied a fine thereof to the lady Poole, his mother, (in lieu of dower) for her life, and after her death, to her daughter Anne Poole, and her heirs; which Anne was married to James earl of Newburgh, and previoufly thereto, and in confideration thereof, fhe releafed to him the manor, borough, and town of Cirencefter, with their appurtenances and franchifes, to the ufe of him and his heirs. Charles was his heir. He married Frances ——, who furvived him, to whom he left the premiffes in fee. She fold them, in the year 1695, to fir Benjamin Bathurft, father of the Earl of Bathurft[e], the prefent proprietor; between whom and Mr. Chamberlayne there is a difpute concerning the right to the feven hundreds. His

[d] The lower part of the Tolfede, or Tolfey, is now converted into a grocer's fhop, in the Butter-row, and the rooms over it are part of a dwelling houfe.

[e] His Lordfhip's anceftors were feated at a place called Bathurft, in Suffex, not far from Battle-abbey, of which they were difpoffeffed, and their caftle demolifhed, in the troublefome times of the difpute between the houfes of York and Lancafter.

Lawrence Bathurft was feated at Cranebrook in Kent, within three miles diftance of the antient feat; and held lands at Staplehurft in the fame county, befide his paternal eftates at Cranebrook and Canterbury. He left iffue three fons, Edward, anceftor to the Earl of Bathurft; Robert, of Horfemanden in Kent; and John, who had lands in Staplehurft, by his father's gift.

Edward, the eldeft fon of Lawrence Bathurft, was feated at Staplehurft, and among other children, had

Launcelot Bathurft, alderman of London, who, in the beginning of the reign of queen Elizabeth, was poffeffed of the manor of Franks, in the county of Kent. He married Judith, daughter of Richard Randolph, of London, by whom he had iffue four fons and three daughters, Randolph, Launcelot, Edward, and George Bathurft; Elizabeth, married to John Brown, efq; Mary, wedded to Edmund Pefhall, efq; and Sufan, efpoufed to Robert Owen, efq. From the eldeft fon, Randolph Bathurft, the family at Franks defcended, now extinct in the male line.

George Bathurft, youngeft fon of the faid Launcelot, in the year 1610, married Elizabeth Villiers, daughter and coheir of Edward Villiers, of Howthorp, in com. Northampton, defcended from an anceftor of George Villiers duke of Buckingham, and had with her the faid manor of Howthorp, where he fettled, and had iffue twelve fons and four daughters. Several of the fons died in the fervice of king Charles the Firft, during the civil war. Thofe who furvived were Ralph, Villiers, Henry, Mofes, and fir Benjamin. Ralph was educated at Trinity-college in Oxford, for a divine, but during the civil war ftudied phyfic, and was employed as a phyfician in the navy. At the reftoration, refuming his former function, he became fellow of the Royal Society, prefident of Trinity-college, and one of the king's chaplains; and on June 28, 1670, was inftalled dean of Wells. He died on the 14th of June, 1704, and was buried in the chapel of Trinity-college, which he built at his own expence, and was highly efteemed for his learning.——Villiers Bathurft was judge-advocate of the navy, in the reigns of king Charles the Second, and king William and queen Mary, and died in the fame poft in the reign of queen Anne.——Henry was attorney-general of Munfter, and recorder of Cork and Kinfale; but he and Mofes dying without iffue, their eftates defcended to their younger brother,

Sir Benjamin Bathurft, who, in the reign of king Charles the Second, was elected governor of the Royal African Company, under his Royal Highnefs James duke of York; alfo governor of the Eaft India Company, in the years 1688, 1689. He was afterwards treafurer of the houfhold to the princefs Anne of Denmark, on the eftablifhment of it, and was appointed cofferer when fhe acceded to the crown. Sir Benjamin died Aug. 27, 1704, and was buried at Pauler's Pury in Northamptonfhire, leaving iffue, by Frances his wife, daughter of fir Allen Apfley, of Apfley in Suffex, knight, three fons, Allen, Peter, and Benjamin; and one daughter, Anne, wedded to Henry Pye, of Farringdon in Berkfhire, efq.

Allen, the eldeft fon of fir Benjamin Bathurft, ferved in parliament for the borough of Cirencefter, from the year 1705, 'till queen Anne, in confideration of his own great merit, and the long fervices of his father, was pleafed to advance him to the dignity of a peer of Great Britain, by letters patent dated Dec. 31, 1711. In the year 1742, his lordfhip was fworn one of the privy council, and the fame day appointed captain of the band of gentlemen penfioners, but refigned his office in 1744. In 1757, he was conftituted treafurer to his prefent majefty, then prince of Wales, at whofe acceffion to the throne, he was continued in the lift of privy counfellors, but declined accepting of any employment, on account of his great age. His lordfhip married Catherine, daughter and heir of fir Peter Apfley, fon and heir of fir Allen beforementioned, by whom he had iffue four fons and five daughters. Her ladyfhip died in the year 1768, aged 79, and was buried in a vault in Cirencefter church.—Benjamin, the eldeft fon, born Aug. 12, 1711, married Elizabeth, fecond daughter to Charles lord Bruce. He was chofen one of the knights of the fhire for the county of Gloucefter, in the 8th parliament of Great Britain, and was alfo chofen one of the members for the borough of Cirencefter, in the year 1754. He died without iffue Jan. 23, 1767; and his lady died Nov. 11, 1771, and both are buried at Siddington St. Peter.——Henry Bathurft, his lordfhip's fecond fon, applying himfelf to the ftudy of the law, foon became eminent in his profeffion, and was fucceffively appointed folicitor-general and attorney-general to Frederick prince of Wales. On the 2d of May, 1754, he was made a ferjeant at

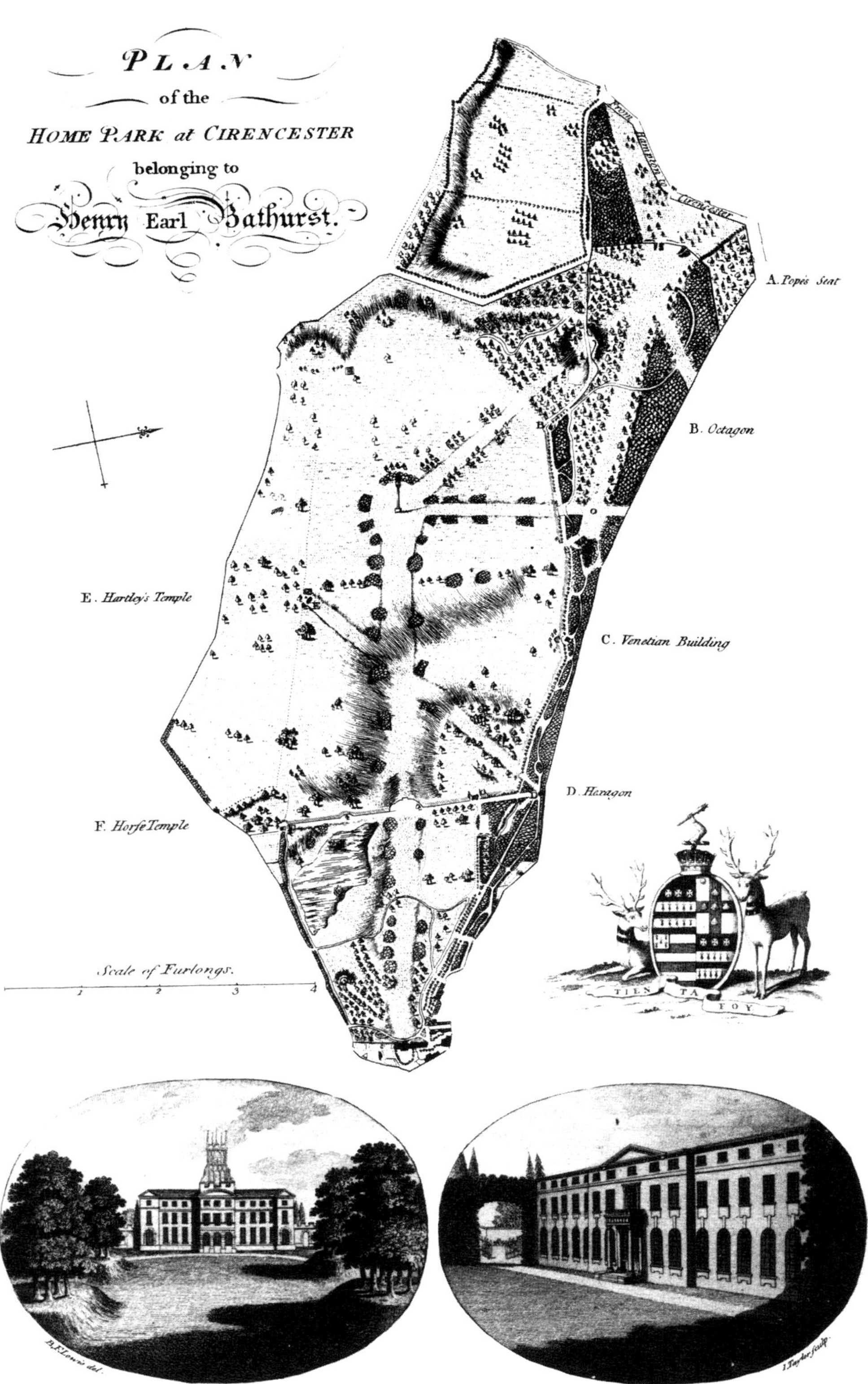

Views of the House at Cirencester.

His lordſhip holds courts for the hundred of Cirenceſter in the borough; and thoſe for the ſeven hundreds are held by Thomas Horde, eſq; and the reverend Mr. Chamberlayne, within their reſpective juriſdictions.

Soon after his lordſhip was poſſeſſed of the above eſtate, by the death of his father, he purchaſed a large one, adjoining to it, of ſir Robert Atkyns; and taking down the old houſe, built the preſent manſion upon the ſite of it. It has a free-ſtone front next the town, but a high wall, lined with ever-greens, prevents the view on that ſide.

This ſeat is diſtinguiſhed by its extenſive and elegant plantations. The park is well ſtock'd with deer. The entrance to it is at a lodge on the north ſide of the houſe, by a ſpacious gravel-walk, lined on each ſide with a row of ſtately elms. At a ſmall diſtance from the entrance, to the left, is an oblique proſpect of the north-weſt front of the houſe, with a fine ſweep of lawn before it, and a grove of lofty trees on either ſide. Turning to the right, the walk divides; one branch of it leads to the terras, the other runs by the ſide of it, in a ſerpentine direction, above a mile in length, finely arched and ſhaded by the plantation through which it paſſes. At ſuitable diſtances it communicates with the terras, where are ſeveral buildings and benches for the convenience of reſting and proſpect. At the end of the ſerpentine walk is a ſmall building, called *Pope's Seat*, perhaps becauſe that great genius frequently retired thither, when he viſited his noble friend at Cirenceſter. There is a lawn before it, to the centre of which eight viſtas are directed, which terminate with the proſpect of neighbouring churches, and other agreeable objects. One of thoſe objects is a fine lofty column in the midſt of the deer-park, on which is placed the ſtatue of queen Anne, larger than life. This pillar is near a mile diſtant from the houſe, behind which ſtands the beautiful tower of the pariſh church of Cirenceſter, ſo directly in the centre of it, with their fronts parallel to each other, that an obſerver at the pillar might be eaſily induced to believe the tower to be a part of his lordſhip's houſe, were it not of a different colour.

The terras is ſheltered on the north-eaſt by a thick plantation of wood, with a moſt agreeable border, or lining, of ſhrubs and evergreens. It commands a diſtant proſpect of the north of Wiltſhire, and terminates at a handſome octagonal building, about a mile from the houſe. In the middle of the terras is a large pair of gates, for a communication between the deer and lodge-parks. At theſe gates is ſeen a large lake of water, a little to the right of the houſe, which looks like a part of a conſiderable river; but 'tis only a pleaſing deception, for nature hath dealt her favours to this place with ſo ſparing a hand as to that element, that there is not perhaps a perennial ſpring to be found within it. This agreeable effect is produced by planting clumps of trees to conceal the extremities of the lake, which is one of the numberleſs inſtances of that fine taſte, every where to be ſeen in the diſpoſition of this place, all laid out and perfected in the manner we now ſee it, in the life-time, and by the particular directions of the noble proprietor. The eye is no where offended with the appearance of bare walls, nor can it judge of the extent of the park, as the country about it is taken into view, over foſſees and concealed boundaries made for that purpoſe, where they have the beſt effect.

Adjoining to the deer-park weſtward, are the lodge-park, and Oakley Woods, particularly meriting the traveller's attention. Of theſe I have attempted a ſhort deſcription under the tithing of Oakley. I now return to Cirenceſter.

As to the other eſtates in Cirenceſter, mentioned in *Domeſday-book* to be held by lay-men, it is impoſſible for me to give a diſtinct account of the deſcent of them; but I apprehend a part was granted to the abbey-church, of which hereafter, and a part paſſed in the following manner.

Ralph Cuſron was ſeized of twenty acres in Cirenceſter 3 H. 3. and Jeffry de Erchebald, whom I take to be a deſcendant of the free man mentioned in *Domeſday-book*, held an eſtate in Cirenceſter 36 H. 3. William Erchbald, a deſcendant of the ſaid Jeffry, was found to be a free tenant here, by the eſcheator's inquiſition, 4 H. 4. Philip Smith and Agnes his wife levied a fine of lands in Cirenceſter and Cheſterton, to the uſe of ſir Giles

at law, and one of the juſtices of the court of common pleas; 'till when, by ſucceſſive re-elections, he had ſat in parliament for the borough of Cirenceſter from the year 1735. In 1770, he was appointed one of the lords commiſſioners of the great ſeal; and his majeſty was alſo pleaſed to advance him to the dignity of a baron, by the title of baron Apſley, on the 22d day of January, 1771; having on the 12th day of the ſame month, appointed him to the important office of lord high chancellor of Great Britain; which office he continues to diſcharge with great abilities and honour. His lordſhip married Anne, daughter and heir of —— James, eſq; who dying without iſſue, he wedded, ſecondly, Tryphena, daughter of Thomas Scawen, of Maidwell, in Northamptonſhire, by whom he has iſſue two ſons and three daughters.—John Bathurſt, third ſon of Allen earl of Bathurſt, reſides at Saperton in this county, and remains unmarried.—Allen, the fourth ſon, was fellow of New-college, Oxford, and rector of Beverſtone and Saperton in this county. He died unmarried, in the year 1768. —— His lordſhip's five daughters were 1. Frances, married firſt to William Woodhouſe, eſq; who died knight of the ſhire for Norfolk, May 31, 1735; ſecondly, to James Whitſhed, of Hampton Court in Middleſex, eſq; one of the preſent repreſentatives of this borough. —— 2. Catharine, married to Henry-Reginald Courtney, eſq; brother to ſir William Courtney, bar^t^. afterwards created viſcount Courtney. — 3. Jane, married to John Buller, of Morvall, in Cornwall, eſq; and knight in parliament for that county. —— 4. Leonora, married to colonel Edward Urmſtone, of the firſt regiment of foot-guards, now a major-general. —— And 5. Anne, married to the reverend James Benſon, LL. D. the preſent chancellor of the dioceſe of Glouceſter.

In conſideration of his lordſhip's great merits, his majeſty was pleaſed to advance him to the dignity of an earl, by the title of Earl of Bathurſt, of Bathurſt in Suſſex, by letters patents dated Aug. 12, 1772.

His lordſhip's arms are, *Sable, two bars ermine, in chief three croſſes pattee Or.* CREST. *On a wreath, a dexter arm in mail embowed, holding a club with ſpikes, all proper.* SUPPORTERS. *Two ſtags argent, each gorged with a collar gemel ermine.* MOTTO. TIEN TA FOY.

Bruges,

Bruges, 17 H. 7. and ſir Edward Seymour, ſon of Edward duke of Somerſet and the lady Catharine his wife, levied a fine of lands in Cirenceſter, to the uſe of the king, 7 E. 6. Thoſe lands are now divided between a great number of proprietors.

TITHINGS and *HAMLETS.*

There are five tithings, or hamlets, in this pariſh, all in the hundred of the *Out-Torn*, or *Crowthorne and Minety*, of the following names, *viz.* 1. *Spital-gate*, now vulgarly and corruptly called *Spiringate-tithing*. 2. *Wiggold*. 3. *Cheſterton*. 4. *Barton*. 5. *Oakley*.

1. *Spital-gate* tithing lies on the north and eaſt ſides of the town. The abbey of Cirenceſter had its *hoſpitium*, for the entertainment of ſtrangers; and the entrance to that part of the abbey was called the *Spital-gate*. This gate gave denomination to the tithing in which it ſtands, and to an adjoining farm. There are other lands in this tithing, called the *Almery-farm*, from the *almery* of the abbey, to which it belonged. The *Almery-gate* is alſo ſtanding. Both theſe farms were granted to Richard Maſter 6 Eliz. and are now the property of Thomas Maſter, eſq; who has a fine ſeat, with handſome gardens in this tithing, built on, or near, the ſite of the antient abbey, and therefore called the *Abbey-Houſe*, of which more may be ſeen in the account of the abbey.

2. *Wiggold* lies on the north-eaſt of the town, beyond the forementioned tithing. John Biſſet, chief foreſter of England, died ſeized of Wiggold 25 H. 3. His wife Alice ſurvived him, and held Wiggold in dower. After her death, the manor deſcended to his four daughters; Margaret, married to Richard de Rivers; Ela, Iſabel, and Edith; which laſt was called Edith lady of Wiggold. Roger Normand purchaſed a charter of free-warren in this manor 9 E. 3. which was confirmed 15 R. 2. William Boys and others held lands in Wiggold and Cirenceſter 32 E. 3. Sir William Nottingham was ſeized of this manor 1 R. 3. and William Pole and Anne his wife levied a fine of it to George Prater 3 E. 6. Mr. Talbot and Mr. Grey were proprietors of it in the year 1711, but Mr. Talbot and Mr. Townſend are the preſent lords of this manor. The tithes of Wiggold, belonging formerly to the abbey of Cirenceſter, were granted to Thomas Erſkyn, viſcount Fenton, 5 Jac. but Thomas Maſter, eſq; is the preſent impropriator. The tithe of hay, and all privy tithes, belong to the miniſter of the pariſh.

3. *Cheſterton*, ſituate on the ſouth and ſouth-eaſt ſides of the borough, the name of which has in it a kind of evidence of its antiquity; for the Saxon Ceaſtre, (and ſo our *Cheſter*,) comes plainly from the Roman *Caſtrum*; and Mr. Burton has obſerved, that the name is given to ſuch places only where the Romans built their *Caſtra*. But the antiquities found in this tithing have already been largely ſpoken of in the former part of this account, under the name of the Leauſes, which lie within it; to which the reader is referred.

Jeffry Langley was ſeized of Cheſterton 2 E. 1. Edmond Langley held this manor of Henry earl of Lancaſter, by the third part of a knight's fee, 2 E. 3. John Langley was ſeized of it 38 & 39 H. 6. Iſabel, the widow of Walter Langley, held this manor 14 E. 4. It afterwards deſcended to William Arundel, as heir to his father, 20 Eliz. and he had livery granted to him the ſame year.

Robert D'Oiley, ſon of Nigel, gave the tithes of Cheſterton to the monks of St. Peter of Glouceſter, when Serlo was abbat. Sir John Nelthorp is the preſent impropriator. The tithe of hay and privy tithes belong to the miniſter, as in Wiggold.

The earl of Bathurſt, Thomas Maſter, eſq; and the reverend Mr. Thomas Coxe, have very conſiderable eſtates in this tithing.

4. *Barton-tithing* includes a conſiderable tract of land on the weſt ſide of the town, beſide the Barton-farm; which great farm belonged to the abbey of Cirenceſter, and was granted to Richard Berners 36 H. 8. and livery of it was granted to Gerard Croker 15 Eliz. It was veſted in ſir Richard Onſlow, ſpeaker of the houſe of commons, during part of queen Anne's reign, who ſold it to Allen Bathurſt, eſq; now earl of Bathurſt, the preſent poſſeſſor, whoſe deer park lies in this tithing.

5. *Oakley-tithing* lies further weſtward of the town. Of this place *Domeſday-book* gives the following account:

'Roger de Laci holds Achelie. There is one 'hide and a half. Leuuinus held it, now Girard 'holds it of Roger. There are two plow-tillages 'in demean, and two villeins, with a prieſt, having 'two plow-tillages and a half. There are nine '*ſervi*. It was worth 4*l.* now 3*l.*' *D. B.* p. 75.

'Giſlebert the ſon of Turold holds one hide in 'Achelie of the king, and Oſulf holds it of him. 'Keneuuard held it in the time of king Edward. 'There are two plow-tillages in demean, and three 'bordars, and ſix *ſervi*. It was worth 40*s.* now '[only] 30*s.*' *Domeſday-book*, p. 76.

'Turſtin the ſon of Rolf holds one hide in 'Achelie. Brictric held it for a manor of king 'Edward. There is one plow-tillage in demean, 'and three villeins with three plow-tillages. There 'are ſix *ſervi*, and four acres of meadow. It was 'worth and is now worth 50*s.* Girvius holds it 'of Turſtin.' p. 78. Thus far *Domeſday-book*.

In the exemplification of the charter of king Henry the Firſt to the church of Cirenceſter, it is thus expreſſed: 'I have alſo granted a water-'courſe, and the wood called Acley, with the 'foreſt, and all its lands, and I retain to myſelf 'nothing out of the wood beſides my hunting; 'and the abbat may not plow up [or aſſart] any 'part of it.'

This eſtate was part of the poſſeſſions of the abbey 'till its diſſolution. Sir Thomas Seymour, uncle to king Edward the Sixth, obtained a grant of

PLAN of OAKLEY GREAT PARK belonging to
Henry Earl Bathurst.

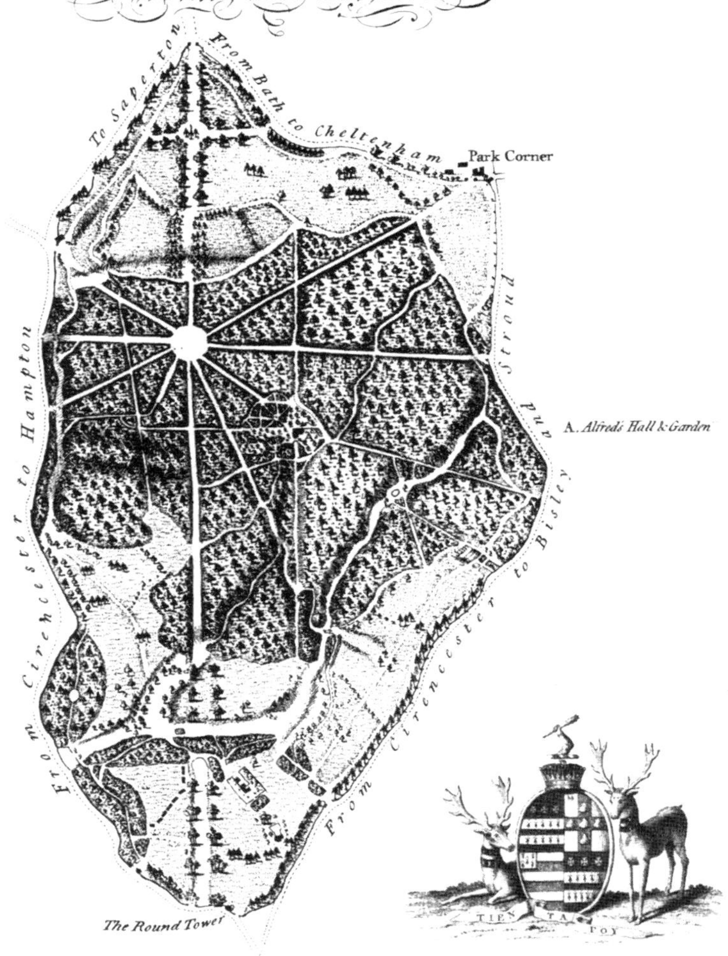

Scale of Furlongs.

B. F. Lewis del. I. Taylor sculp

Views of Alfreds Hall

of Oakley woods, in the firſt year of that king's reign; but he being attainted, they were granted to John duke of Northumberland 6 E. 6. after whoſe attainder, they reverted to the crown, and were again granted, 2 Eliz. to ſir Thomas Parry, who died ſeized thereof 6 Eliz. and his ſon had livery granted him the ſame year. The laſt mentioned family ſold them to ſir John Danvers, who was poſſeſſed of them 37 Eliz. at the time of his death. They were afterwards purchaſed by ſir Henry Pool, whoſe ſon, ſir William Pool, ſold them to ſir Robert Atkyns of Saperton, of whom they were bought by the earl of Bathurſt, the preſent proprietor of them, and of the whole of this extenſive tithing.

The truffle is a vegetable production found in ſufficient abundance in Oakley woods.

Theſe woods deſerve our particular notice. Near the middle of them, on a riſing ground, is the point from which, like ſo many *radii*, ten cuts or ridings iſſue. The largeſt, about fifty yards wide, has the lofty tower of Cirenceſter to terminate the view; others, directed to neighbouring country churches, clumps of trees, and various diſtant objects, produce an admirable effect. Concealed as it were in the wood, ſtands Alfred's-hall, a building that has the ſemblance of great antiquity, with a bowling-green, and many beautiful lawns and agreeable walks about it. Over the door oppoſite to the ſouth entrance, on the inſide, is the following inſcription, in the Saxon character and language:

Ðiꞅ iꞅ ꝥ ꝼꞃẏþe ꝥ Ælꝼꞃeꝺ cynninᵹ ⁊ ᵹẏðꞃun cẏnninᵹ ⁊ ealleꞅ anᵹelcẏnneꞅ ƿiꞇan. ⁊ ealꞅeo ðeoꝺ þe on eaꞅꞇenᵹlum be oþ ealle ᵹecƿꝺen habbaþ ⁊ miꝺ aþum ᵹeꝼæꝼeꞅꞇnoꝺ ꝼoꞃ hi ꞅelꝼe ⁊ ꝼoꞃ heoꞃa ᵹinᵹꞃan. ᵹe ꝼoꞃ ᵹeboꞃene ᵹe ꝼoꞃ unᵹeboꞃene ðe ᵹoꝺeꞅ milꞇꞅe ꞃecce oþþe uꞃe;

Æꞃeꞅꞇ ẏmb uꞃe lanꝺᵹemæꞃa up on ꞇemeꞅe ⁊ ðonne up on liᵹan ⁊ anꝺlanᵹ liᵹan oþ hiꞃe æƿẏlm ðonne on ᵹeꞃihꞇe ꞇo beꝺanꝼoꞃꝺa ðon up on uꞅan oþ ƿæꞇlinᵹaꞅꞇꞃæꞇ;

Over the ſouth door is the following Latin tranſlation:

FOEDUS quod Ælfredus & Gythrunus reges, omnes Angli ſapientes, & quicunq; Angliam incolebant orientalem, ferierunt; & non ſolum de ſeipſis, verum etiam de natis ſuis, ac nondum in lucem editis, quotquot miſericordiæ divinæ aut regiæ velint eſſe participes jurejurando ſanxerunt.

Primò ditionis noſtræ fines ad Thameſin evehuntur, inde ad Leam uſq; ad fontem ejus; tum rectà ad Bedfordiam, ac deniq; per Uſam ad viam Vetelingianam.

Behind this building is a ruin, with a ſtone over the chimney-piece, on which, in antient characters relieved on the ſtone, is this inſcription:

IN · MEM · ALFREDI·
REG · RESTAVR:
ANO · DO · 1085.

It would have been inexcuſable in the topographer to have paſſed by ſo curious a place without notice; but the hiſtorian would have been equally culpable, who ſhould not have informed the reader, that this building is an excellent imitation of antiquity. The name, the inſcription, and the writing over the doors, of the convention between the good king and his pagan enemies, were probably all ſuggeſted by the ſimilarity of *Achelie*, the antient name of this place, to *Æcglea*[f], where king Alfred reſted with his army, the night before he attacked the Daniſh camp at Ethandun, and at length forced their leader Godrum, or Guthrum, or Gormund, to make ſuch convention.

Windſor, Richmond, and Stow have been ſung by their reſpective bards; ſo the park and woods of this place are the ſubject of a ſhort deſcriptive poem, by Mr. Edward Stephens, not wholly deſtitute of ſentiment.

Of the Abbey.

King Henry the Firſt built the abbey church, which he began in the year 1117, and compleatly finiſhed it in fourteen years. This church was dedicated to St. Mary and St. James. But before the conqueſt, here was a rich college of prebendaries, ſays Leland, *but of what Saxon's foundation no man can tell.* It was antiently endowed with lands and poſſeſſions, of which *Domeſday-book* gives the following account:

'The church of Cireceſtre holds of the king 'two hides in Cireceſtre hundred in elemoſinage, 'and held them of king Edward quit from all 'cuſtom. There are ſix acres of meadow. This 'is now, and was then worth 40*s*.' *D. B.* p. 73.

And further in the ſame book, in the regiſter of lands belonging to Roger de Laci, at Wiche, now Painſwick, in Biſley hundred, it is alſo recorded, that 'Saint Mary of Cireceſtre holds one 'vill (as I read it) and part of a wood in this 'eſtate. King William granted it to her. It is 'worth 10*s*.' p. 75.

Reinbaldus, a prieſt, and a very eminent perſon of his time, was dean of this collegiate church. He was alſo chancellor to king Edward the confeſſor, and, as ſuch, ſet his hand to witneſs the charter of privileges granted by that king to the abbey of Weſtminſter[g]. Beſide his eccleſiaſtical and other preferments, he held in this county four hides in Amney, ſeven in Driffield, one in North-

[f] Diluculo ſequenti illuceſcente, rex inde caſtra commovens, venit ad locum qui dicitur *Æcglea*, et ibi una nocte caſtrametatus eſt. Inde, ſequenti mane illuceſcente, vexilla commovens, ad locum qui dicitur *Ethandun* venit; et contra univerſum paganorum exercitum, cum denſa teſtudine, atrociter belligerans, animoſeque diu perſiſtens, divino nutu tandem victoria potitus, &c. *Aſſerius de Rebus Geſtis Ælfredi.* Editio T. Wiſe. p. 34.

[g] For many of theſe particulars ſee *Leland's Itin.* v. 2, p. 22. and v. 5, p. 62.

cote, and eight in Preston, and in other counties very considerable estates, which, at his death, devolved to the crown.

King Henry having placed regular canons in the abbey church, and obtained pope Innocent's licence, and the consent and approbation of the archbishops, bishops, princes, and barons of the kingdom, as I find it expressed in the exemplification of his charter, (*Appendix*, N°. 13.) endowed it, among other things, with all Reinbald's estates. And king Richard the First further increased its revenues, in the 9th year of his reign, by annexing to it the jurisdiction of the seven hundreds, as will appear by the exemplification of that king's charter, 4 H. 4. an abstract of which is given in the account of the manor and hundreds, to which the reader is referred. And king John, in the first year of his reign, confirmed all these grants to the abbey by his charter, which see also in the *Appendix*, N°. 14.

There was a rent of 30*l.* a year reserved out of the manor of Cirencester, and the seven hundreds, to be paid into the exchequer at Michaelmas, which was settled, by king Edward the First, on queen Margaret, as part of her dower. This rent was afterwards granted to Edmond de Woodstock, the king's brother, 13 E. 2. and again, 1 E. 3. to Edmond earl of Kent, who was beheaded at Winchester. And John earl of Kent was seized of the same rent 26 E. 3.

The lands of William of Cirencester, in Minety, were granted to this monastery 5 Joh. and a new farm was granted to it in the 17th year of the same reign.

The abbat of Cirencester held Crinclewood, containing thirty acres, 9 E. 2. And Walter Wrilock and others granted two messuages, one toft, twenty-six acres, a yard-land, four acres of meadow, with other particulars, to the abbey, 13 E. 2. William Erchebald and others, for the church of Cirencester, were seized of seventeen messuages and twenty acres in Cirencester, 16 R. 2.

This monastery obtained a grant of a fair 17 Joh. and it had another grant of fairs in the town of Cirencester 37 H. 3. and of markets there, and in the seven hundreds, 42 H. 3.

I have already observed, in the account of the manor, &c. that a writ of *Quo warranto* was brought against the abbat, for the hundreds, 15 E. 1. So there was another large and strict inquisition issued against him 1 H. 4. for usurping divers privileges in the towns of Cirencester and Minety, and in the seven hundreds. But I apprehend these were mostly vexatious proceedings, to extort money from the subject for new grants; which were thought necessary in those times, when by casualties in the civil wars, or otherwise, any of the possessor's deeds and evidences happened to be lost or destroyed.

The extent of the abbat's jurisdiction in the manor court of Hatherop, was particularly specified, and mutually settled and agreed, by a composition between Hugh the abbat, and convent of Cirencester, and Wymark the prioress and the convent of Laycock, to whom that manor belonged; which composition is preserved in the *Appendix to Stevens's Supplement to the Monasticon*, N°. 445.

There was a deed made in the year 1305, between the abbat of Cirencester and John de Latton, an ancestor of a family of that name at Kingston Bagpaze, in Berkshire. This deed is taken notice of by sir Robert Atkyns, as remarkable for the abbat's concessions to the other party; and as there is a translation of it in sir Robert's book, I have also inserted a copy of that translation in the *Appendix*, N°. 29.

The following is a List of the Abbats, from Mr. Willis's History of the Mitred Parliamentary Abbies.

1. Serlo, the fourth dean of Salisbury, was made the first abbat after the foundation, *anno* 1117. He died *anno* 1147, and was succeeded by

2. Andrew, who died *anno* 1176, and had for his successor,

3. Adam, prior of Bardney. He died *anno* 1183, and

4. Robert, canon of Cirencester, succeeded; who dying the same year, the convent elected another

5. Robert for their abbat; upon whose death, which happened *anno* 1187,

6. Richard, prior of St. Gregory's, Canterbury, succeeded. He died *anno* 1213; in which year,

7. Alexander Nequam, *alias* Neccham, was made abbat. He was a very learned man, and greatly renowned for his skill in poetry, and all sorts of literature. See an account of him in Leland, and Bale *de Scriptoribus*. Weever says he was buried in St. Alban's abbey, tho', with better authority, other historians mention his interment in the cloysters of the cathedral church at Worcester, with this epitaph:

Ecclypsim patitur sapientia, sol sepelitur,
Qui dum vivebat studii genus omne vigebat.
Solvitur in cineres Neccham. *Cui si foret hæres*
In terris unus, minus esset flebile funus.

The year after his death, which happened *anno* 1227, or, as in Willis, 1217,

8. Walter, or, as some records have it, Richard, was elected abbat. He died 1230, whereupon

9. Hugh de Bampton, *alias* Bathon, who is elsewhere called Henry, succeeded. He died *anno* 1238, and was succeeded by

10. Roger de Rodmarton. He died *anno* 1266, and was succeeded by

11. Henry de Munden, to whose election the king consented Oct. 10, 1266. I don't find when he died, but *anno* 1281,

12. Henry de Hamptonel was made abbat. He died Nov. 2, 1307, eleven days after which,

13. Adam Brokenbury was elected abbat; but his election was vacated 'till the 3d of December, at which time he obtained a confirmation of it. He died *anno* 1319, and was succeeded by

14. Richard de Charleton, on whose resignation, *anno* 1334,

15. William Hereward was admitted abbat. He died Apr. 25, 1352, and was succeeded by

16. Ralph de Estcote, who dying *anno* 1357, was succeeded by

17. William de Marteley, or Martelege. He died *anno* 1361, and was succeeded by

18. William de Dinton, who dying *anno* 1363, was succeeded by

19. Nicholas de Ameney, who dying *anno* 1394, was succeeded by

20. John Lekhampton. His successor was

21. William Best, *anno* 1416. He procured to himself and successors, the use of the mitre and pontificals, and dying 1429,

22. William Wotton obtained the benediction, Mar. 5, 1429. On his death, 1440,

23. John Taunton was consecrated abbat the same year, and dying *anno* 1445, had for his successor,

24. William George, who received the benediction April 10, 1445, at Pershore. He died *anno* 1461, whereupon

25. John Solbury, or Sadbury, received the benediction at Alnchurch, Oct. 13, 1461. I find not when he died, but *anno* 1478,

26. Thomas Compton occurs abbat. He died Oct. 11, 1481, and was succeeded by

27. Richard Clyve, elected Oct. 25, and confirmed Nov. 5, 1481. He was succeeded 1488, by

28. Thomas

28. Thomas Aſton, confirmed abbat, in the biſhop of Worceſter's chapel in the Strand, London, October 22, 1488. He reſigned *anno* 1504, and was ſucceeded by

29. John Hakeborne, or Haukebourne, who was confirmed abbat December 7, 1504; of whom Anthony a Wood tells us, that in the year 1500, being then prior of St. Mary's college in Oxford, he commenced Batchelor of Divinity, and afterwards Doctor, and dying about the year 1522, was ſucceeded by

30. John Blake, the laſt abbat. In the year 1534, he ſubſcribed to the king's ſupremacy, with Richard Ciceter, prior, Will. Cerney, and other monks of his houſe, in number ſixteen.

This abbey was ſurrendered to the commiſſioners on the 29th of December, 1539, 31 H. 8. according to Mr. Willis's emendations, inſerted after the index, in his *Hiſtory of Parliamentary Mitred Abbies*; where I find the following account of the penſions aſſigned to the abbat and the religious of this monaſtery. 'John Blake, late 'abbat, 250*l*. Richard Woodwall, late prior, '13*l*. 6*s*. 8*d*. William Warbot, late cellerer, 8*l*. 'William Philips, vicar of the pariſh church of 'Circeſter, *nihil*; *declaratur in pede*. Thomas 'Fiſher, Thomas Hedde, John Ruſſel, John 'Walle, William More, Richard Bolle, John 'Straunge, Thomas Logger, Anthony Chilcoke, 'Henry Hawks, James Plebeien, William Smyth, '6*l*. 13*s*. 4*d*. each. Richard Lane, 5*l*. 6*s*. 6*d*. '——Memorandum, That William Philippes 'abovenamed, is aſſigned to the Vicarage & Cure 'of the Pariſh of Circeſter, with the hole Tithes 'of Woolle, Lambe, Hey, Oblations, Alterages 'and all other Profitts bilonging to the ſame 'Churche: The Tithes of the Domayne-Lands, 'latelie being in Occupation of the late Abbot and 'Convent there, only excepted. Yeldinge, ther-'fore, unto the King's Majeſtie, in Conſideration, 'the ſame Vicar ſhall be charged with the finding 'of three Preiſts beſydes hymſelf to myniſter there, 'alſo ſhall finde Wyne and Wax at his propre 'Coſts and Charges Yerely, 53*s*. 4*d*. And ſo the 'ſaid Vicar ſhall have a reaſonable Living and a 'convenyant Portion of the Profitts of the ſaid 'Churche, the Quantitie of the Cure there Duelie 'conſidered.'

Robert Southwell.	John London.
Edward Carne.	Rychard Poulet.
Ric. Gwent.	Will. Berners.

This was a mitred abbey. The abbat was ſummoned to parliament 43 H. 3. but had not a ſtated ſeat there 'till William Beſt obtained the mitre, and a ſeat among the barons, for himſelf and ſucceſſors, in the year 1416. The abbey was valued, at the time of its diſſolution, at 1051*l*. 7*s*. 1*d.ob*. as I find it in Stevens's Supplement to the Monaſticon.

The abbat had the privilege of coinage. I have ſeen a braſs piece, ſomething ſmaller than a copper halfpenny, which was found in the year 1772, in Mr. Maſter's garden. On one ſide was a coronet, charged with *three rams heads*, (part of the arms of the abbey) and round it this inſcription, AVE MARIA · GRACIA · PLEN · On the reverſe, *a croſs flory between four fleurs de lis*; and round the quarters the letters ·G· ·A· ·G· ·A· for *George, Abbas*. From which it appears, that it was coined between the years 1445 and 1461, during which time William George was abbat.

Leland, who had ſeen the abbey church, ſays, *The Eſt part of the Chirch ſhewith to be of a very old building. The Weſt part, from the Tranſeptum*, [the great croſs aile] *is but new Work to ſpeke of*. The whole fabric was probably demoliſhed ſoon after the ſurrender, and the materials were ſo totally removed, that the preciſe place where it ſtood was ſoon forgotten; but there are two gates, the *Spital-gate* and the *Almery-gate*, belonging to the abbey buildings, and the abbey barn, ſtill remaining. Mr. Willis conjectures that the abbey ſtood on the north ſide of the pariſh church, which was, no doubt, ſays he, ſet within part of the abbey cemitery. He has given the following dimenſions of the abbey church, from William of Worceſter's MS. in Bennet-college, Cambridge. *viz*.

The length of the great church contains 140 ſteppys, the breadth of the nave of the church 41 ſteppys, with two ailes; or 24 yards. The chapel of the bleſſed Mary on the ſouth part of the church contains 41 yards, with an aile adjoining. The breadth of the ſaid antient chapel contains 21 graſſus, with the antient aile. The length of the cloiſter 52 graſſus. The length of the chapter-houſe 14 yards and 10 yards in breadth.——The graſſus, or ſtep, is about two feet.

In the Body of the [abbey] *Chirch*, ſays Leland, *in a Sepulchre Croſſe of white Marble is this* [inſcription,] *Hic jacet Rembaldus Preſbyter quondam hujus Eccleſiæ Decanus* [*& Tempore Edwardi Regis Angliæ Cancellarius*[h].] *Ther ly 2 Noblemen of S. Amandes buried withyn the Preſbyterie of Cirenceſtre Abbay Church. And there is buried the Hart of Sentia, Wife to Richard King of* [the] *Romains, and Erle of Cornwalle*. Sir Robert Atkyns was greatly miſtaken in repreſenting theſe particulars as being in the preſent pariſh church, inſtead of the abbey church.

The arms of the abbey were, *Gules, on a chevron argent three rams heads caboſhed ſable, attired Or*.

The ſite of the abbey was granted, Aug. 19, 1 E. 6. to Thomas lord Seymour, with lands in fifteen ſhires, to be held *in capite* by the ſervice of one knight's-fee, paying 1*l*. 1*s*. 8*d*.[i] But on his attainder it reverted to the crown, and was afterwards granted to Richard Maſter, 6 Eliz. and is now the property of Thomas Maſter, eſq;[k] who has an elegant houſe and gardens on the ſite of the abbey, and a large eſtate adjoining.

One

[h] Leland's Itin. v. 5, p. 62.

[i] Stevens's Supplement to the Monaſticon, from Fuller's Hiſtory of Abbies, p. 364.

[k] Richard Maſter of Cirenceſter, anceſtor to the preſent poſſeſſor, was deſcended from the family of Maſter in Kent. He was phyſician to queen Elizabeth, and married Elizabeth daughter of——Tunnely of Lincolnſhire.

George Maſter, eſq; ſon of Richard, married Bridget, daughter and heireſs of John Cornwall, of Marlborough in Wiltſhire.

Sir

One hundred fifty two meſſuages lying in the town of Cirenceſter, and which formerly belonged to the abbey, were granted to John Polland and William Birt 36 H. 8. St. Mary's-Mill (at the firſt bridge, now taken down) and Barton-Mill, formerly belonging to the abbey, were granted to James Woodford and Thomas Woodford 2 Eliz. Bridgbury-farm in Cirenceſter, alſo belonging to the abbey, was granted to Percival Bowes and John Moſier 10 Eliz.

Thus far of the *town* and *abbey*. The regiſter and other books belonging to the abbey, which might have given further light into the antient affairs of this place, are ſuppoſed to be loſt. Doctor Tanner had not ſeen them, and the editor of this account, after diligent inquiry, has not been able to get the leaſt information concerning them.

Of the Church, &c.

The church is in the deanery of Cirenceſter. The biſhop of the dioceſe is patron of the curacy, which, with various augmentations and perquiſites, is now of conſiderable value. The particulars of the ſeveral donations to it ſtand under the head *Benefactions.*

The rectory of Cirenceſter, and the advowſon of the vicarage, were granted to ſir Thomas Treſham and George Treſham 5 E. 6. But William Bourchier, of Barnſley, eſq; died ſeized of the rectory in the beginning of the reign of queen Elizabeth, and livery thereof was granted to his ſon Thomas Bourchier the ſame year. The impropriations of Cheſterton and Wiggold are already taken notice of under thoſe tithings.

A portion of tithes called Archebalds, formerly belonging to the abbey of Cirenceſter, were granted to Francis Philips and Richard Moor 6 Jac.

There have been three pariſh churches in this town, one dedicated to St. Cecilia, which was intirely down in Leland's time; the church of St. Lawrence is ſtill ſtanding, but now converted into ſmall tenements. The third is the preſent pariſh church, dedicated to St. John the evangeliſt. It is a large and beautiful building, conſiſting of the nave, two large ailes, and five chapels. The roof is ſupported by two rows of ſtone pillars, very handſomely fluted. There are five pillars and two pillaſters in each row. The length of the nave is 77 feet, and the breadth of the church, including the two ailes, 74 feet. Over the pillars are the buſts of ſeveral benefactors to the church, with proper ſcutcheons, arms, and devices. The firſt two (one in each row) next the chancel, are for Thomas Ruthal, biſhop of Durham, with the arms of his ſee impaling his own paternal coat. He was a native of Cirenceſter, and was conſecrated biſhop of Durham 1 H. 8.——The next figure in each row, repreſents John Hakebourne, twenty-ninth abbat of Cirenceſter; one ſcutcheon bears the arms of his abbey; on the other is *a mitre pierced with a croſier*, to ſhew that his abbey was a mitred one; and upon both are I. H. the initial letters of his name.——The arms over the third pillar, in one row, *Quarterly* 1ſt. and 4th. *two lioncels paſſant*; 2d. and 3d. *a chevron.* On the other, *a wyvern in combat with a lion*, a creſcent for diſtinction.——Over the fourth pillar on one ſide, R. R; on the other row, *a croſs moline* between the letters I. P.——Over a fifth pillar are the letters H. G. and the ſcutcheon oppoſite to it has *three greyhounds palewiſe courant.* ——The arms of the town ſtand near the top of the fourth pillar; and other devices, among which are the crown of thorns and inſtruments of crucifixion, are arranged over the arches.

Theſe circumſtances ſhew that the nave of the church, and probably all weſtward, including the tower, was rebuilt when John Hakebourne was abbat, *viz.* between the years 1504 and 1522. But the original church was built long before, for there are monumental inſcriptions ſtill remaining, of dates almoſt a hundred years prior to abbat Hakebourne's government. The arms of biſhop Ruthal, placed among thoſe of the benefactors to this church, is ſo ſtrong a circumſtance of his having contributed to the rebuilding of it, that I cannot aſſent to Leland, who ſays, he *promiſid much, but preventid with Deth gave nothing.*

The windows were very curiouſly painted, but they have ſuffered from bigots and bungling workmen. Thoſe on the ſouth ſide are beſt preſerved, and of thoſe the great one on the right of the entrance is moſt intire. This conſiſts of three ranges of figures, of four compartments each. The principal figures in the uppermoſt, are three of the antient fathers of the church, and the Pope. They ſtand in the following order, 1ſt. *St. Auguſtine*, 2d. *St. Jerom*, 3d. *the Pope*, 4th. *St. Ambroſe*. The names of the fathers are written beneath; but the Pope is diſtinguiſhed only by his *tiara*, or tripple crown. Under St. Auguſtine, in the ſame compartment, is a figure kneeling, with a ſcroll round his head, whereon is written *Sc's Auguſtinus*[1] *ora pro nobis*. His name, *Willm'*

Sir William Maſter, ſon of George, married Alice, daughter of Edward Eſtcourt, of Saliſbury, eſq. He was high ſheriff of Glouceſterſhire 3 Car. 1, 1627, and was a perſon of great worth and loyalty. He ſerved in parliament for the borough of Cirenceſter, and lies buried in the church of that place.

Thomas Maſter, eſq; ſon of ſir William, married Elizabeth, ſiſter of ſir Thomas Dyke, of Suſſex. He died 1680, and lies buried near his father in Cirenceſter church. He alſo ſerved in parliament for that borough.

Thomas Maſter, ſon of Thomas, married Elizabeth, daughter and heireſs of John Driver, of Aſton, and has likewiſe ſerved in parliament for the ſaid borough.

Thomas Maſter, ſon of the laſt Thomas, married Joan, daughter and heireſs of Jaſper Chapman, of Stratton, eſq; who before his death gave this eſtate to his ſon,

Thomas Maſter, eſq; who married Elizabeth, daughter and heireſs of ſir Thomas Cann, bar[t]. and dying the latter end of May, 1749, left iſſue by the ſaid Elizabeth, two ſons, Thomas and Richard, and one daughter Elizabeth.

Thomas Maſter, ſon of the laſt Thomas and Elizabeth, the preſent proprietor of the abbey eſtate, married Mary, daughter of James-Lenox Dutton, of Sherbourn in this county, eſq. His arms are, *Gules, a lion rampant gardent, his tail double Or, holding in his paws a roſe Argent.*

[1] Not *Sc'e Auguſtine*, which I obſerve, leſt the reader ſhould think the above an error of the preſs.

Hampton,

Hampton, ſtands at foot, to ſhew that he was the donor of this light, or compartment of the window. There are alſo figures at the feet of the other fathers, with their names thus written, *Iohes Hampton & ux ei'*; *Willm' Okyn & Iohana ux. eiuſd*; *Will. Colſburn Bower & Alicia Iohana*. Theſe gave the reſpective compartments in which they are placed.——The principal figures in the ſecond range are, 1ſt. *St. Catherine*, 2d. *St. Margaret*, 3d. *St. Dorothy*, 4th. defaced. They have all ſcrolls round them, upon which portions of ſcripture, in Latin, are written in old character; and the donor of each compartment is placed, with his name, under the principal figure.——The figures in the four lights of the lower range are, *Sc's ...... de Beu'laco*; *Johes de Bev'laco*; *Will Eberaco*; *....s Oſmund de Sarr'* with ſcrolls and paſſages of ſcripture round them. In the ſmall lights, at the top of the window, are various figures and repreſentations, as of the trinity in a triangular form, as commonly expreſs'd; of the virgin mother, &c. &c.

In the window on the other ſide of the ſouth door, are written on the glaſs the names of the benefactors to the lights wherein they ſtand, *viz. Ioh'es Rowthale M'garet & Alic' ux.* in one compartment, *Iohanes Langele*[1] in another, and *Iohana Whyt* in a third; and round the head of the latter, in a ſcroll, *Sc'a Batildis ora pro nobis*; which ſaint is the principal figure above in this compartment. There is a large figure in each of the other lights, over the perſons above-mentioned, but their names do not appear. In the other windows, on the ſame ſide of the church, are figures of canonized ſaints, with portions of ſcripture, in Latin, upon ſcrolls round them; but a deſcription of every particular would be too minute and tedious.

There is a gallery or ſcreen-work at the entrance of the choir, upon which a handſome organ was erected in the year 1683, and has been ſeveral times ſince repaired and enlarged at a great expence.

The chapels were built at different times, and are the following:

1. *Jeſus-chapel*, built of Iriſh oak, at the eaſt end of the ſouth aile. It is 12 feet long, and 9 broad. Round the top of it are ſeveral coats of arms belonging to the families of benefactors to the church and poor; as, 1. Bathurſt, 2. Maſter, 3. Monox, 4. Atkyns, 5. Cox, 6. Coxwell, 7. Smyth impaling Maſter, 8. *Or, a feſs between three wolves heads eraſed ſable*, for How of Guiting.

2. *St. John's*, on the ſouth ſide of the choir, is 34 feet long, and 24 broad.

3. *St. Catherine's*, on the north ſide of the choir, is 34 feet long, and 13 broad. The roof is curiouſly arched with ſtone, and ornamented with arms, knots, and devices; among others, 1. *Quarterly, France and England*. 2. *Three oſtrich's feathers iſſuing out of a ducal coronet*. 3. *A roſe enſigned with a coronet*. 4. The letters I. H. ſeveral times repeated, for John Hakebourne, as already mentioned. This chapel was roofed in abbat Hakebourne's time, principally at the expence of himſelf and biſhop Ruthall. The effigy in ſtone of Richard Oſmund, with a purſe at his girdle, lay under an arch in the wall of this chapel, with his head upon a pillow, but now is injudiciouſly placed upright againſt the wall. He is ſuppoſed to have been the founder of it. The figure of St. Catherine, as large as life, with her wheel and ſeveral votaries at her feet, is rudely painted on the ſouth wall, and 'till lately has been covered with white waſh.

4. *St. Mary's*, formerly endowed with great revenues. It ſtands on the north ſide of St. Catherine's, and is 74 feet long, and 21 broad.

5. *Trinity-chapel*, on the north ſide of the north aile. The glaſs windows of this chapel were very beautiful. In the eaſt window were the figures of Peter king of Caſtile, Richard duke of York, Thomas duke of Surry, Richard earl of Saliſbury, and of ſir John Jeneville, who was buried here; but thoſe figures are now defaced. In the wall at the eaſt end are the arms of benefactors. 1. *Gules, a chevron between three mullets Or*. 2. *Argent, on a bend gules three martlets Or*. 3. *Gules, two bars Or, in chief two ſtags heads caboſhed of the ſecond*. 4. *Argent, on a bend gules three cinquefoils Or*. 5. *Gules, a chevron between ten croſſes pattee argent*. 6. Obliterated. 7. *Argent, a feſs between three croſſes pattee ſable*. 8. *Sable, a croſs argent*. 9. *Gules, three couples-cloſes argent*. 10. *Checky Or and gules, a feſs ermine*, for Roe. 11. *Argent, a chevron between three creſcents Or*. 12. *Nebule Or and gules*. 13. *Argent, a chief indented ſable*. 14. *Sable, ſix doves argent*. 15. *Argent, a bend Or, in chief a label*. 16. *Ermine, on a croſs gules five martlets Or*. 17. *Checky Or and ſable, a chief argent gutty gules*. 18. *Argent, fretty gules*. 19. *Gules, fretty argent, a canton of the ſecond in the dexter chief*.— In a niche, at the eaſt end of this chapel without, are the effigies in ſtone of the virgin Mary, and the infant Jeſus in her arms.

The tower ſtands at the weſt end of the church. It is 134 feet high, well proportioned and beautiful, with pinnacles and battlements. On the dexter ſide of the weſt door are the arms of Cirenceſter abbey; on the other ſide, *Quarterly, France and England*. There is a peal of twelve bells in this tower, which no place in the kingdom can boaſt of, except London. In the ſouth-weſt angle of the tower, in a niche, is the figure of St. John, as large as life, to whom the church is dedicated; and in the north-weſt angle ſtands another figure.

There is a very curious repreſentation in the north wall, at the top of the church, of a *Whitſon-Ale*, with the lord and lady, in high relief, and the ſteward, purſe-bearer, and all the mock officers which attend that kind of merry-making, almoſt peculiar to this country. See pp. 23, 24.

The ſouth porch is a fine Gothic ſtructure facing the market-place, thirty-eight feet in

[1] He was lord of the manor of Siddington Peter, of which he died ſeized 39 H. 6.

 front,

front, and fifty high. It is ornamented with curious pinnacles and battlements of hollow work, and with a great variety of carved reprefentations of dragons, beafts, and other figures, very neatly finifhed. In twelve niches in the front, formerly ftood the twelve apoftles; but the rigorous principles of the times, about the latter end of the reign of king Charles the Firft, would not permit them to remain. Over this porch is the town-hall, now ufed on parifh meetings, and other large affemblies of the inhabitants; but formerly the general Seffions of the county hath been kept in it; on which account, I apprehend, the figure of Juftice, ftanding over the door of the ftairs leading to the hall, was firft placed there. Alice Avening, aunt to bifhop Ruthall by the mother's fide, gave 100 marks towards the building of the porch, and his mother, and other parifhioners, contributed to the finifhing of it.

There were feveral chantries and religious offices eftablifhed in this church, viz.

1. The chantry of St. Mary.
2. The chantry of Jefus.
3. The chantry of St. Chriftopher, whereof Thomas Edmonds was the laft chaplain, and had a penfion, after the diffolution, of 4*l. Willis.* The lands belonging to thefe three chantries, were granted to fir Oliver Cromwell 5 Jac.
4. The chantry of the Holy Trinity, whereof William Painter was the laft incumbent, and had a penfion of 4*l. Willis.* The lands belonging to it were granted to —— Skevington, in the reign of Edward the Sixth.
5. The fervice of the Holy Trinity, of which Thomas Marfhall was the laft incumbent, and had a penfion of 5*l. Willis.*
6. The chantry of St. Catherine.
7. The office of St. Thomas the Martyr, founded by fir William Nottingham, whereof Thomas Neal was the laft chaplain.
8. The chantry of St. Anthony.
9. The chantry founded by John Jones.
10. The fervice of St. John.
11. Robert Richard's chantry, whereof William Wilfon was the laft incumbent, and had a penfion of 4*l. Willis.*
12. Alice Avening's chantry, whereof Henry Jones was the laft chaplain, and had a penfion of 5*l. Willis.* Her name is now in the window of St. Catherine's chapel.
13. The Fraternity of St. Catherine, and
14. The Fraternity of St. John Baptift.

Monuments and Infcriptions.

On a flat ftone, engraved on brafs, in the fouth aile, are the effigies of a man and woman. On labels proceeding from their mouths,

Mercy God of my mifdeede. — Lady help at my moft neede.

On a brafs plate under their feet,

Reyfe gracious Ihu to endles lyfe at thy grete dome where all fchall Apere Hughe Norys Groc' & Iohan hys wyf nowe dede in grave & beryed here yo' p'yers defyryng There Soules for chere the x day of Iuly the yere our lord god M°CCCCCXXIX.—— *The above verfes are engraved on the plate in a continued form, like profe.*

In the paffage before the chapels are the effigies of a man and woman engraved on a brafs plate, and this infcription in old characters:

Orate pro aiabus Willi Nottingham et Criftine uxoris ejus qui quidem Willms obiit xxi° die menfis Nouembris Anno d'ni Millmo CCCC° XXVII°. Et predict. Criftina obiit iiij° die Iulij A°. Dni M° CCCC° XXXIIIJ°. q°r. aiab' p'piciet. deus Amen.—— *Clofe by, on another ftone (lately removed) was written,*

Munde vale tibi ve, fugiens me dum fequerer te,
Tu fequeris modo me, munde vale tibi ve.

Under the figure of an ecclefiaftic, engraven on brafs, it is thus written:

Orate pro anima dni Radulphi Parfons quondam capellani p'petue cantarie Ste trinitatis in hac ecclefia fundate, qui obiit xxix° die augufti a° dni M CCCC lxxviii Cuj. aie p'piciet' deus Amen.

Near the above, upon a flat ftone,

Cum Ianâ Uxore, Radulphus Willet,
In dandis Confiliis Sapiens,
In expediendis negotiis Promptus,
In componendis Litibus Prudens,
Et in omnibus animi motibus
Æqualiter temperandis
Supra modum fœlix,
Hic fepultus eft.
Ob. { Hic } Aug. 23, 1692 } Annorum { 67.
{ Illa } Sept. 8, 1679 } { 49.

On a flat ftone before the chancel, *Azure, a lion rampant argent, in chief three efcalops of the fecond.* And this memorial:

Near this place are interred the Remains of Mr. James Clutterbuck, Born Oct. 11, 1673. Dyed June 30, 1722, and Sufanna (Daughter of John and Sufanna Willett) his Wife. She was born Iune 11, 1671, Dyed Febry 4, 1757.

Edward	their Sons born	Mar. 1, 1689	dyed	Apr. 17, 1728.
John		Oct. 8, 1697		Nov. 27, 1699.
John		Jan. 21, 1700		July 2, 1701.
Mary	their Daughr.	Jan. 1, 1711		Jan. 11, 1711.

Againft the wall, at the weft end of the church,

Hic prope fitum eft
quod mortale fuit Thomæ Deacon,
Opidani utilis et amati,
Viri quidem fcientis,
Nec non munere erga Deum et homines Fungentis,
Multum deploratus obijt
4°. Augti. Anno { Salutis 1661,
{ Ætatis 46.
Illi
(poft annos circiter Viginti novem
purâ et fanctâ Viduitate elapfos)
Acceffernnt exuviæ Margeriæ
ejufdem Thomæ Deacon
Vxoris præftantiffimæ.
Hanc mortalitatem exuit
19no Maij Anno { Salutis 1690,
{ Ætatis 74.

Upon a flat ftone near the belfry, thefe arms, *A crofs cotoifed between four lions rampant, in chief three rofes.* And under, this memorial:

Underneath are depofited the Remains of THOMAS DEACON, of Elmftree, in the Parifh of Tetbury, Gent. And likewife of ANNE his fecond Daughter. The Father departed this Life Sept. ye 30th 1723, aged 78 Years. The Daughter ye 19th of Dec. following, aged 36 Years.
They with the other Relations here interr'd all dying in a well grounded Hope of a joyful Refurrection.

Againft the north wall, on a plain table of white marble:

This Marble is placed here in memory of Mr. JOHN GASTRELL,
Who died the 18th day of Iune, 1767, in his 45th Year,
And is buried in the North Weft Corner
Of the Church-Yard of *St. Mary le Strand* in the County of *Middx.*
He was a Native of this Town;
And after a liberal Education in *Winchefter* School,
Served an Apprenticefhip in the Parifh of *St. Mary le Strand,*
Where he was foon after admitted to a fhare of the Bufynefs,
And by diligence, fweetnefs of manners, & an unblemifht conduct,
Obtained

Obtained the good will of all ranks of People,
Acquired a decent Fortune,
And bequeathed it to his Relations & Friends
With a clear Head & benevolent Heart.
His Father RICHARD GASTRELL *Gent.*
Discharged the office of *Steward* of the Manor of *Cirencester*
For many Years,
With proper dignity, much judgment, & great candour;
Was eminent & justly esteemed as an *Attorney & Conveyancer*,
And remarkable for being more attentive
To the advantage of his numerous Clients,
Than to the rewards which his skill & success
Entitled him to expect or demand.
He departed this Life the 27th day of February, 1736,
Aged 57,
And lieth interred in the Parish Church of *Crudwell*
In the County of *Wilts.*

Against the south wall of the south aile, on a small marble table, *Gules, a lion rampant regardant Or.* And under, it is thus written:

Non procul hinc repositum est quod fuit mortale Bridgidiæ, JACOBI SMALL Filiæ natu maximæ, Inter Laudandas Laude nonnulla dignæ: Matrimonio conjuncta fuit JACOBO PENRY, de Abersenny in Agro Breconiensi Clerico, Cui peperit Annam Filiolam, in eodem Sepulchro contentam.

Obt. { Hæc } Decimo
{ Illa } Die Sept. Anno Dom. 1735,
Vicesimo quarto.

Upon a small brass plate, in the south aile,

HERE LYETH bvried ye Body of HODGKINSON PAINE, Clothier, who died ye 3d of Feb. 1642.

The Poore's Supplie his life & calling grac't
'till warre's made rent & PAINE from poore displac't.
But what made poore vnfortunate PAINE blest,
by warre they lost their PAINE, yet found noe rest,
Hee loosing quiet by Warre yet gained ease,
by it PAINE's life began, and paine did cease;
And from ye troubles here him God did sever,
by death to life, by Warre* to peace for ever.

* He was killed at the taking of Cirencester in the Civil War.

And under, on a plate,

Here lieth the body of Elizabeth Paine deceased the 8th day of Ianuary An. Do. 1668.

One was our thought One life wee sought
One rest wee both jntended
Our bodies haue To sleepe one graue
Our soules to God ascended.

In Jesus chapel is a handsome marble monument, with three busts at top. 1. of Mr. William Georges, with his arms, *Argent, a fess gules between three faulcons with their wings display'd azure, beak'd and bell'd Or.*—2. *Gules, three fleurs de lis Or, on a chief argent a lion of the first.*— 3. *Party per fess Or and argent, a lion rampant gules,* for Powell. On the table this inscription:

To the Lasting Remembrance
of
WILLIAM GEORGES, Esq;
This Monument was erected
by
REBECCA his *Relict.*
Who being afterwards married to
THOMAS POWELL, Esq;
Ordered that his Memory also should be
Herein transmitted to Posterity.
WILLIAM GEORGES, Esq;
Was underneath interred, Iune the 18th 1707,
In the 81st Year of his Age.
By his Body was deposited That of
THOMAS POWELL, Esq; Sept. the 13th 1718,
In the 67th Year of his Age.
To their Remains were added Those of
REBECCA,
Nov. ye 8th 1722, in ye 80th Year of her Age:
Whose Bequest, out of ye Estate devised to her by W. G. did, at Lady-Day, 1728, amount to 2400*l.* and 200*l.* a year, for Erecting & Endowing a Charity-School, or Schools, in this Town. The other Pious and Charitable Gifts of R. P. and also of W. G. & T. P. are recorded in ye Catalogue of Benefactions to this Parish.

In St. John's Chapel is an elegant raised monument of black and white marble. Over an arch are, *Parted per pale baron and femme,* 1. *Argent, on a chevron sable between three oak leaves proper as many besants; on a chief gules a sea mew between two anchors erected of the first,* for Monox. 2. *Argent, on a bend sable three pears Or, in the chief point a trefoil,* for Perry. Under the arch are the figures of a man and woman kneeling, with their respective arms over their heads, as above, and between them a table, with the following inscription in gold capital letters:

MEMORIÆ SACRVM GEORGIJ MONOX ARMIG. CIRENCESTRIÆ NATI, QVI (POST PLVRIMOS ANNOS IN MERCANDIZIS LABORIOSE & PRVDENTER PERIMPLEVERAT) AD GRADVM & DIGNITATEM OFFICIJ VICECOMITIS LONDINENSIS VNANIMI OPTIMATVM CONSENSV, FVIT VOCATVS. MAGNAS DENARIORVM SVMMAS SEPARALIB' LOCIS IN PIOS VSVS LEGAVIT; & VT SINGVLAREM AMOREM QVO NATALE SOLVM VIVVS AMAVIT FVTVRIS SÆCVLIS MANIFESTARET, CENTVM LIBRAS IN PECVNIIS NVMERATIS, & TENEMENTA ANNVI VALORIS VIGINTI LIBRARVM PRO MELIORI HVIVS VILLÆ PAVPERVM SVSTENTACIONE, & LECTVRA HAC ECCLESIA SINGVLIS MENSIBVS PRÆDICANDA IN PERPETVVM ASSIGNAVIT. Maria vxor mœstissima (ex qua solas duas filias superstites suscepit) Viro Charissimo, pietatis, amoris, et obseruantiæ ergò posuit.

OBIJT 26° DIE IVNIJ ANNO SALVTIS 1638, ÆTATIS SVÆ (68.) *Dies mortis æternæ vitæ natalis est.*

Under are the figures of the two daughters, one of them with the arms as on the dexter side abovementioned; the other, *Baron and femme,* 1. *Vert, a chevron undy between three griphons rampant Or.* 2. Monox, as above.

In the chancel, before the steps which lead to the altar, is a memorial [J. H. 1753. C. H. 1733.] for Joseph Harrison, M. A. the late vicar of this church, and Catherine his wife; the brevity of which, without an explanation, would soon defeat the intention of it. Close by it, on another table of white marble, is written,

Sr. THOMAS HARRISON, Knt.
Chamberlain of the City of London,
youngest Son of Joseph Harrison Clerk,
late Minister of this Parish,
died the 2d of January 1765, aged 64.
Dame DOROTHEA HARRISON, Relict of
Sir Thomas Harrison, died Jany. 8th 1773, aged 71.

On a flat stone,

M. S.
Rogeri Burgoyne
M. D.
Qui post
Prudentem, piam, prosperam
Facultatis Medicæ
(Annos circitèr Viginti)
Administrationem,
tandem,
Debilitato Corpore,
Subitâ sed non improvisâ morte
Occubuit,
Decembris 21mo,
1674,
Ætatis suæ 46.

At top, *Parted per pale baron and femme,* 1. *A chevron between three talbots, on a chief embattled three martlets.* 2. *Six roundlets,* 3, 2, 1, *on a chief a lion passant.*

On a small marble monument this inscription:

In Memory of
EDWARD WILBRAHAM, Woolstapler,
who departed this Life the 10th of Octor. 1771,
aged 60 Years.
Also of *MARY* his first Wife,
who died the 14th of April, 1753, Aged 57.

On

On the table of a neat monument againſt the ſouth wall,

H. S. E.
Juxta cariſſimum Fratrem,
Vix ipſe fratri ſuperſtes,
Samuel Selfe, Johann. et Eliz.
Filius natu maximus.
Cui nihil unquam amicis deſideratum
Preter Etatem diuturniorem.
Dolemus ut Homines,
Ut Chriſtiani lætamur.
Optimis quippe conditionibus natus,
Annum agens viceſimum,
Cœlo maturus,
Vitam æterna caducam
Feliter permutavit
D. Feb. 5. A. S. 1759.

M. S.
Egregii Juvenis
RADULPH. WILLET SELFE,
Ioannis et Elizabethæ Selfe Fil. ſecund.
Vultu honeſto,
Pectore generoſo,
Moribus placidiſſimis;
Carus Parentibus,
Carus Præceptoribus,
Virtute quam annis maturior.
Diem obiit ſupremum
XI Kal. Feb.
M DCC LVIII.
Vale Anima dulciſſima!

Near this Place lies
The Body of John Selfe, Clothier,
Who was a moſt kind and affectionate Huſband,
An indulgent and good Father,
A good Maſter and a faithful Friend.
He departed this Life on the 28th of Jan.
In the Year of our Lord 1763,
And in the 56th Year of his Age.
E. S. died July ye 29th, 1766, aged 49 Years.

At bottom, *Ermine, three chevronels gules; on a ſcutcheon of pretence, barry of twelve pieces ſable and argent, on a chief of the ſecond three lioncels rampant of the firſt,* for Willet.

Againſt the ſame wall is a neat marble monument, with this inſcription:

Near this place reſteth the Body of
M^{rs}. ELIZABETH CRIPPS, Wife of M^{r}. JOHN CRIPPS Junr.
who departed this Life Feby. 3^{d} 1758, Aged 41 Years.
Alſo of Edward their Son who died Feb. 9, 1758,
Aged 9 Years.
And alſo John & Henry their Sons, both Born $Decem^{r}$. 3^{d},
And both died the 10th of y^{e} ſame Month, in the Year 1743.
To theſe are added
the Remains of the above named M^{r}. JOHN CRIPPS,
who died the 7th day of May, 1771, aged 49 Years.

A ſtone, with the following inſcriptions, lay where Mr. Harriſon's is placed: *viz.*

H. S.
Thomas Carles, Art. M^{r}.
De Cirenceſter Paſtor } Digniſs.
De Barnſley Rector }
Vtriuſq; Ornamentum,
Mortuus Triſte Deſiderium.
Vir
Integritate vitæ,
Suavitate morum,
Ingenii Dotibus,
Concionandi venuſtate
Adeo inſignis,
Vt non ſine ingenti
Totius Diocæſeos luctu
Deceſſerit,
Oct. 7, Ann. $Æt^{s}$. 50,
Dom. 1675.

H. R. J. P.
Depoſitum Subditi fidelis Eccleſiæ Anglicanæ,
Filij morigeri et Artis Chirurgiæ peritiſſimi,
Gulielmi Freame, Generoſi,
Qui obijt Oct. 24° Ann. Dom. 1678, Ætat. 58.
Siſte Viator,
Mortuus Loquor,
Audi;
Morte meâ cecidi,
Chriſti virtute Reſurgam:
Ergo et tu.

In St. Catherine's chapel, under two figures engraved on braſs, is this inſcription in capitals:

MR. IOHN GUNTER AND ALICE HIS WIFE, BEING FULL AS OF YEARES SO OF BOVNTY AND CHARITY, ARE GATHERED TO THEIR FATHERS IN PEACE. SHEE WAS HERE BVRYED 18° MARTIJ A^{o}. DNI 1626 AGED 86 YEARES. HEE WAS BVRYED AT KYNTBURY IN THE COUNTY OF BERKS WITH THE LIKE MONVMENT 2do IANUARIJ A^{o}. DNI 1624 AGED 89 YEARES. IO^{s}. PLATT AR. $EORUND^{m}$. GENER ET $EXEC^{r}$. HOC POSVIT.

A flat ſtone, *On a bend ermine three leopards heads caboſhed,* (the colours not expreſſed) and underneath this inſcription:

Hic requieſcit
Ærumnarum portu et meta Salutis
quicquid terreſtre fuit
Thomæ Kemble, Gen.
Cujus anima
Ad Superos evolavit
14 Cal. Aug.
Anno { Ætat. Suæ 71,
Æræ Chriſtianæ 1710.
Anne Kemble, Daughter of Anthony Kemble, was buried the 14th day of Dec. 1733.
William Kemble, Gent. obiit June 22^{d}. 1745.

In the ſame chapel were the two following memorials:

Sub hoc tumulo requieſcunt corpora Iohanis Avening et Alicie uxoris ejus qui obierunt xiiii die Aprilis anno Dni 1501.
——*Alice Avening founded a chantry in this church.*

Pray for the ſouls of Iohn George, eſq; and Alice his wife, who were buried here, which Iohn deceſſid the 8th day of October 1556. And the ſaid Alice deceſſid the 3d day of May 1557, and had four ſons and eight daughters. —— *He was lord of the manor of Baunton.*

Under a free-ſtone arch, in St. Mary's chapel, are the effigies of a man in the habit of a lawyer, and of a woman in the genteel dreſs of her time, lying along, with their hands in a praying poſture. On a table this memorial:

Here *lyeth* the bodies of Humfry Bridges and Elizabeth his wife. He dyed the 17 of April 1598. Shee dyed the 6 of Iuly 1620. They had both ſonnes and $daught^{s}$. He gaue 40*s.* yeerly for ever to the poore of this towne. Shee gave 6 habitations for 6 poore widdowes with 6*s.* weekly for ever.

Over the figure of a young man kneeling at the head,

$Humfrid^{s}$. Fil. ſen. de Medio Templo obijt 2° Decemb. 1610.

Over a like figure kneeling at the feet,

Anthon. Fil. jun. de Medio Templo obijt 2° Aug. 1617.

At bottom are the figures in minature of one ſon and eight daughters, with books in their hands. The whole monument is in good preſervation, with iron palliſadoes round it.

Againſt the ſouth wall is an elegant white marble monument for ſir William Maſter. He is repreſented in a cumbent poſture, leaning on his left elbow, and over him, on a table, this inſcription:

Quos Deus conjunxit ſeparat tantum
non repudiat Mors.
MEMORIÆ SACRUM
Fidiſſimi ſerui dei et Regis ſubditi
Patriæque amantiſſimi ſuæ,
GULIELMI MASTER apud Corinios
Equitis Aurati;
Qui Martyrem Regem mœrens Martyr
Semimortuus vixit diu;
Citius dominum ſecutus, ni morbo paralytico
Reſtitiſſet firma fides
Reſtituendi Regis Inſigniſſimi,
Caroli Secundi;
Vtcunq; apud Vigorniam, fuſi.
Voti tandem, ac vaticinij compos factus,
Tantiq; pignoris, Juſtorum reſurrectionis,
Vitam mortalem exuit; imortali deo
Cœlitum choro gratias acturus.
Anno Dom: 1661 (Ætatis 61) Mens: Mart: die 3.
He married Alice one of y^{e} $daught^{rs}$. of S^{r}. Edw: Eſtcowrt of Newnton in y^{e} county of Wiltes K^{t}. by whome he had iſſue 6 Sonns and 6 daught: A Lady highly eminent both for her partes and pietie who haveing by y^{e} bleſſing of God paſſed through y^{e} troubles of an inteſtine warr, & liued to ſee her Children bred up, reſigned her Soule to God, whoſe body lyes here interred waiting for ye reſurrection of ye Iuſt. Sept. 5: 1660.

Under

Under his figure are four other tables, with inscriptions. Upon the firft is written,

M. S.
Elizabethæ Uxoris Thomæ Mafter,
Thomæ Filii,
Quæ
(Variolarum morbo contracto)
Proximè a puerperio obiens,
Unà cum infantulo
Hic jacet Sepulta:
Ob nativam comitatem,
Ingenij Elegantiam,
Singularem modeftiam,
Omnefq; alias, quæ femina, uxore,
Aut Matrem exornant virtutes
Maxime deflenda: præfertī Conjugi,
Cui, in Solatium tanti doloris,
Et ad Supplendas amicitiæ vices
(a fato Solum diffolvendæ)
Infantes duos Tho: et Elizab.
Chariffima Amoris Pignora
Legavit A. D. 1691, Æt. 26.

Upon the fecond,

Hic fubtus Depofitum eft
Quicquid mortale fuit
ELIZ. MASTER, THO. & ELIZ. filiæ,
Immortalem fi requiras partem,
Ad patriam Cœleftem redijt,
Itineris terreni maculis
Quam minimùm inquinata:
In qua Ingenij Elegantia, Geftus
Suavis, Compofitus, Decorus,
Omnes deniq; enituere virtutes,
Quibus indoles optima
Ad pietatem, prudentiam,
Et Mores pudicos Formata,
Inftrui et Ornari poffit,
Adeo ut licet Ætas fit imperfecta,
Vita tamen illi perfecta.
Obijt Aug. 15 A° Dom. 1705 Æ. 16.

Upon the third,

M. S.
ELIZ. MASTER, Tho: Mafter Arm. viduæ,
Et THO: DYKE de Horeham
In Agro Suffexiæ Arm. Filiæ,
Quæ fe
Morum elegantiæ, Integritatis puræ,
Temperantiæ, & Modeftiæ feveræ,
Candoris eximij, & Pietatis fînceræ,
Omnibus imitandū Exemplum præbuit.
His Animi dotibus acceffit
Valetudo ad Extremam
Senectutem Integra:
Quæ fi tibi contingant Lector,
Summam hujus Vitæ
Fælicitatem Confequeris,
Et Futuræ Gloriam expectes.
Obijt Ian: 28: A°: Dom: 1703-4. Æ. 83.

Upon the fourth,

P. H. M.
Filius Unicus
In memoriam Patris Optimi,
THOMÆ MASTER Armigeri,
In quo,
Morū gravitas, humanitate condita,
Animus piè liberalis,
Indoles verè generofa,
Quicquid demū aut Virū probū,
Aut ornatū decebat,
Summè emicuit.
Virtutes has imitare Lector,
Ut fias Deo et hominibus charus.
Obijt A. D. 1680, Æt. 56.

At the entrance of St. Mary's chapel, againft the wall, on a brafs plate, is the effigy of an old man in a gown, with a taylor's fhears over his head, and a dog at his feet. At bottom,

In Lent by will a fermon hee deuifed
And yerely precher with a noble prifed
Seuen nobles hee did geue ye poore for to defend
And 80*l*. to xvi men did lend
In Cicefter Burford Abington & Tetburie
Euer to be to them a ftocke Yerrly.
Phillip Marner who died in the yeare 1587.

In Trinity chapel are feveral very antient flat ftones of grey marble, with infcriptions on brafs. Upon one of them is the figure of a gentleman, with a lady on each fide of him, and this memorial:

Hic fepeliuntur Willms Prelatte Armiger fpecialiffim' benefactor huj' Capelle Agnes nup' uxor Iohannis Martyn et Iohana filia et heres Ricardi de Cobyndon Relicta Iohannis Twynyho de Cayforde in Comitatu Soms. Armigeri uxores ip'ius Willi qui quidē Willms Prelatte obiit in vigilia Afcencionis d'nice XXVI° die maij Anno d'ni M° CCCC° lxij°. quor' p'piciet de' ā.

On another ftone, inlaid with brafs (whereon are the effigies of a man and woman, and fourteen children) was this infcription, part of which is torn off:

Hic jacet Robertus Pagge cum Margareta fibi fponfa prole fecunda
Vicinis gratus fuerat mercator amatus
Pacificus plenis manibus fubventor egenis
Ecclefiifq; viis ornator et hiis reparator
Mill C quater ..... quater et anno fed Aprilis
Octava luce mortem pertranfiit ipfe
Celi folamen De' illi conferat Amen.

On a label, iffuing out of the woman's mouth, is

That to the Trinite for us pray fynge or rede.

Another ftone. On brafs are engraven the figures of a man, his two wives, and eight children, with this infcription:

Orate pro aīabus Iohannis Benett .... et Agnetis uxor' fuarum qui quidem Iohannes obiit decimo nono die menfis Iulii Anno Domini Millimo CCCC° nonagefimo feptimo quor animabus ....

Over his firft wife's head is written,

Spiritus fci de' miferere nobis.

Over his head,

Sācta Trinitas unus Deus miferere nobis.

Over his other wife's head (now torn off) was written,

Fili redemptor mundi miferere nobis.

On the brafs plate of another ftone are reprefentations of a man and his four wives, two on each fide, and on the brafs, round the edge of the ftone, in old characters,

Hic jacent Reginaldus Spycer quondam m'cator ifti' ville qui obiit IX° die Iulij Anno dni Mill'mo CCCC° xlij° et Margareta Iuliana Margareta ac Iohna uxores ej' quor' aiab' p'picietur d's Amen.

On another brafs plate is the effigy of a man in armour, with fpurs on, and a fword girt to his fide, in the pomel of which are thefe arms, *A pile, over all a chevron*. Round the ftone, on brafs, it was written, but now imperfect,

Hic jacet Richardus Dixton Armiger qui obiit die fancti Laurencii martyris Anno dni M CCCC xxxviii° cujus anime propicietur de' Amen.

On a plain marble table againft the north wall,

In remembrance
of Mr. William Turner, late of this place:
and of Catharine, (for more than fifty-fix years)
his entirely beloved wife.
He was the youngeft fon of the reverend John Turner
of Somerford Keynes in the county of Wilts:
and died the 21st of Auguft 1769, aged feventy-fix years.
She was the fecond daughter of the reverend Jofeph Harrifon,
more than fixty-three years minifter of this parifh:
and died four months after her hufband,
and of the fame age.
They were a very humane and exemplary pair:
acknowledged THE MOST HIGH in every difpenfation:
and kept through life the ferious thought of death.

In the fouth porch, againft the wall, is the following modeft memorial:

Under your Feet lyeth the Body of William Cletherow, Gent. an humble Penitent, who thoughte himfelfe unworthy of the loweft Place in the Houfe of God. He departed this Life the 8th day of November 1680.

In the church-yard, on a handsome raised tomb,

Huic Tumulo mandati sunt Cineres
Ioannis Adye Generosi
Filii Edvardi & Esteræ Adye
Quorum exuviæ juxta requiescunt,
innocui, probi, bonis Literis imbuti,
Turbamq; fugientis.
Obiit 26° Martii A. D. 1745 Ætatis suæ 68.
Hic etiam sepulta est Maria
Ioannis Adye uxor chariffima
Et Edvardi Foyle de Somerford Keyns in Agro Wiltoniensi Arm.
Filia valde deploranda:
De vitâ excessit 24° Februarii A. D. 1724 Ætatis suæ 43.
Idem quoque Tumulus continet
Quicquid mortale fuit Mariæ Ainge [Generosi
Uxoris Ricardi Ainge de Lechlade in Comitatu Gloucestriensi
Et Ioannis Adye sororis non indignæ
Obiit 30° Maii A. D. 1744 Ætatis suæ 71.

On the north side of the tomb,

Consanguineorum Affiniumq; juxta Exuvias
voluerunt et suas jacere
Richmundus Day
de Civitate Bristoliensi Mercator eximius
Vir Iustitiæ pertinax, fidusq; Ecclesiæ Anglicanæ Discipulus
Et Maria Conjux ejus dilectissima
Unicaq; Ricardi & Mariæ Ainge
et nequaquam impar Filia.
Hos Animo, Pietate, Morumq; Suavitate pares
Annis plusquam quadraginta
domesticas Virtutes exercendo
et Amore mutuo peractis
Mors eodem fere Tempore corripuit:
Uxor a vitâ decessit 29° Iunii A. D. 1758 Ætatis suæ 63.
Maritus 19° Augusti A. D. 1758 Ætatis suæ 70.
Hunc Tumulum
Parentibus indulgentissimis Consanguineisq; sacrum
Filius, Nepos, jussit extrui
1759.

The arms of Adye are, *Azure, a fess dancetty between three cherubims display'd Or.*—Ainge. *Azure, a chevron ermine between three crosses formy argent.*—Day. *Ermine, on a chief indented azure two eaglets display'd Or.*

Benefactions.

Doctor William Clarke, late dean of Winchester, having devised certain lands and tithes in the parish of Tillingham, in the county of Essex, in trust among other things, to augment ten small ecclesiastical benefices with 30*l.* *per ann.* each for ever; and Dr. Henry Compton, bishop of London, and the dean and chapter of St. Paul's, having the nomination of six of those benefices, declared they would assign this charity to such market-towns as would settle an equal revenue on their minister. And the inhabitants of the town of Cirencester, with the assistance of others, having raised the sum of 619*l.* 11*s.* 8*d.* by free contribution, and with 600*l.* of the said money purchased an annuity for their minister of 30*l.* a year, charged on the tithing of Oakley, in this parish; the said trustees then appointed Cirencester to be one of those benefices so to be augmented, by an instrument dated Jan. 17, 1698. But by a deficiency in the profits of the trust estate, from inundations and other accidents, the annual payments to the respective ministers, from the first commencement in 1699, have often fallen under, tho' sometimes exceeded 15*l.* a year. The surplus of the money (19*l.* 11*s.* 8*d.*) was given to the minister towards defraying his expences in settling the augmentation. The principal contributors to this laudable benefaction were, sir Robert Atkyns jun. knight, who gave 100*l.* Thomas Master, esq; 100*l.* Mrs. Bridget Smith, a daughter of sir William Master, knight, 100*l.* Mrs. Winifred Master, 50*l.* Mrs. Anne Williams, 43*l.* Sir Benjamin Bathurst, knight, 20*l.* Sir Jonathan Raymond, knight, 20*l.* Sir Richard Onslow, baronet, 10*l.* Sir Richard Howe, baronet, 10*l.* John Willet, clothier, 20*l.* Bernard Ballinger, 20*l.* John Coxe, clerk, rector of North Cerney, 10*l.* Ralph Willet, clerk, rector of Stratton, 10*l.* Robert Brereton, gent. 10*l.* Other contributions were from 5*l.* to 10*s.* each.

'Till about this time there was no vicarage-house. The inhabitants first purchased a lease of the present house; afterwards William George, esq; gave the quit-rent of it, and in the year 1708, Mrs. Rebecca George, his widow, gave the fee of it for ever.

For Sermons, Prayers, and Catechizing.

1587, Philip Marner gave 6*s.* 8*d.* for ever, for a sermon on the first Friday in clear Lent.

1607, Sir Giles Fettiplace gave an annuity of 20*s.* out of lands in Eastington; half for a sermon on the 5th of November, and half for ringing on the same day, and for mending the ropes.

John Coxwell, esq; gave 20*s.* a year for two sermons in Christmas tide and Lent.

1618, Jeffry Bath, bailiff of the town, gave 6*s.* 8*d.* for a sermon on Ascention-day.

1637, Sir Thomas Roe, of Cranford in Middlesex, gave 2*l.* for a sermon or prayers on the 13th of September, for ever.

1639, George Monox, esq; gave 8*l.* *per ann.* for a sermon on the first Wednesday in every month.

1681, Mrs. Mapson, a native of the town, gave 10*s.* for a sermon on St. Andrew's day.

1695, John Master, M. D. gave 200*l.* one half of the income of which to the minister for ever, for reading morning prayers; the other half to poor house-keepers not receiving alms.

Mrs. Rebecca Powell gave 10*l.* a year to the minister, for catechizing the children, and for expounding the catechism; and 2*l.* a year to provide candles necessary for that service.

Mrs. Hannah Ashwell gave 10*l.* the interest whereof for a sermon on the 30th of January for ever; but the principal money is now lost. She also gave 10*l.* more, the interest of which to be divided between the minister and parish clerk, for a psalm, with *Gloria Patri*, to be sung every Monday at morning prayers.

Nicholas Edwards gave to the minister the interest of 5*l.* for ever.

To the Church, &c. and for Educating and Apprenticing poor Children.

The large, handsome gallery, on the north side of the church, was built at the expence of the Right Honourable the Earl of Bathurst. That at the entrance of St. Catherine's chapel was erected by sir Anthony Hungerford.

The organ was purchased with the contributions of the inhabitants of the town and neighbourhood.

The two large silver flaggons, used at the communion, were given by Edward Dixon, esq; in the year 1434; William George, esq; and his wife, gave the two plates for collecting the offerings; Mr. John Adye gave the gilt strainer for the chalice; and Mrs. Bridget Smith, and others (whose names are either forgotten, or who chose to conceal them) furnished the remainder of the noble service of plate with which this church is accommodated.

The best bible and common prayer book were given by Thomas Powell, esq; and his wife; and the marble font was presented by the female inhabitants of the town.

For the ornamenting and repairing of the church, there is a revenue of 67*l.* 9*s.* 4*d.* a year, arising chiefly from houses lying within the town, and a close in the tithing of Chesterton, given by John Jones, and other benefactors, whose names have not been transmitted down to us; about 22*l.* of which is laid out in repairs, and the remainder expended in salaries, except 4*l.* paid to the minister, and 8*l.* to the master of the free Grammar School, as directed by a decree in chancery 1 Jac. 1.

The Grammar School was built and founded by bishop Ruthall. The master has a good house kept in repair for him, and besides the 8*l.* a year before-mentioned, queen Mary endowed the school with 20*l.* a year out of the exchequer, which bounty was afterwards confirmed by queen Elizabeth.

The Blue School, for cloathing and educating twenty boys and twenty girls, with provision for teaching younger children in quarterly schools, out of it, was set up in 1714, by the general beneficence of the inhabitants and their friends. But Thomas Powell, esq; and Rebecca his wife, were the principal benefactors. In the year 1718 he endowed it with 15*l.* a year, part of an annuity for 99 years, paid out of the exchequer; and a moiety of the profits of Maskelyne's Ham in Cricklade. And the court of chancery, in the year 1737, appropriated 20*l.* a year, out of the estates bequeathed to Mrs. Powell for erecting and endowing a charity school or schools in this parish, for the support of this school; and in 1744, appointed the produce of 562*l.* 7*s.* 6*d.* to be paid yearly for the benefit of this school, as a provisional supply, after the expiration of the annuity out of the exchequer.

The Yellow School was erected and endowed by virtue of the will of Mrs. Rebecca Powell, who died in the year 1722, and left an estate for that purpose. A school-house was purchased and fitted up at the expence of near 1200*l.* but some difficulties arising about carrying the will into execution, the court of chancery, upon application to it, decreed that 212*l.* 8*s.* *per annum* be apply'd to the cloathing, maintaining, teaching to write and cast accounts, and bringing up twenty boys in the art of stocking-frame knitting. Twenty girls are also cloathed every year, and are taught to read, and to spin worsted.

Sir Thomas Roe gave a rent-charge of 25*l.* a year out of lands at Mouswell in this county, 40*s.* of which for a sermon, as already mentioned, the rest to put out poor children of this parish apprentices, on the 13th of September annually; and once in three or four years, a boy out of the parish of Rendcombe, if presented.

Mr. Thomas Perry gave 100*l.* and his son Mr. Timothy Perry gave 12*l.* which sums were laid out in the purchase of a freehold estate in the parish of Upton St. Leonard in this county.

Richard George, esq; gave a rent-charge of 3*l.* a year, out of a house in Gloucester-street; William Forder, late of Amney Crucis, gave 20*l.* Thomas Powell, esq; gave 40*l.* James Clutterbuck, late citizen of Exeter, gave 100*l.* James Shewell, silkman, gave

gave 10*l.* and Mrs. Elizabeth Edwards, in 1726, gave 100*l.* the annual produce of all which to be apply'd to the putting out poor children apprentices.

Hoſpitals and Almſhouſes.

King Henry the Firſt founded St. John's Hoſpital, for three poor men and three poor women, who receive 1*s.* 8*d.* each weekly.

St. Lawrence's Hoſpital was founded by Edith, lady of Wiggold, in this pariſh, for a maſter, with a ſalary of about 40*s.* a year, and two poor women, who have 12*d.* a piece weekly.

St. Thomas's Hoſpital was erected by ſir William Nottingham, who lived in the reign of king Henry the Fourth, and endowed it with a rent-charge of 6*l.* 18*s.* 8*d.* *per annum*, out of an eſtate in the pariſh of Thornbury, which is divided between four poor weavers.

In the year 1620, Mrs. Elizabeth Bridges gave an Almſhouſe in Dollar-ſtreet for ſix poor widows, and 1*s.* a piece weekly for ever.

William George, eſq; and Rebecca his wife, in the year 1702, gave ſix tenements and gardens in Leauſe-lane, for ſix poor widows; and aſſigned two other tenements in Cricklade-ſtreet, one charged with 6*l.* a year to buy garments for the widows, and what remains of the produce of them to keep the houſes in repair.

Thomas Powell, eſq; gave a moiety of the rent of Maſkelyne's Ham to the ſame widows; and Rebecca his widow gave them 20*s.* a year each, to buy them firing.

John Morſe gave two dwellings in Glouceſter-ſtreet for two poor widows.

To be given or lent in Money to the Poor.

In the year 1587, Philip Marner gave 20*l.* and in 1613, Henry Hill gave 30*l.* to be lent to tradeſmen without intereſt.

The ſame Philip Marner gave a rent-charge of 3*l.* 13*s.* 4*d.* on a houſe in Abbat-ſtreet; Alice Avening, in 1498, gave a houſe in Dollar-ſtreet, of 40*s.* a year; John Weobley, the ſame year, gave a houſe, ſince exchanged for an annuity of 1*l.* 6*s.* 8*d.* charged on the Greyhound inn; William Hooper, in 1605, gave a houſe in Little Silver-ſtreet, of 2*l.* 4*s.* rent; Jeffry Bathe, in 1618, gave, out of a houſe in Cricklade-ſtreet, 1*l.* 13*s.* 4*d.* John Chandler, in 1632, gave a houſe in Cicely-ſtreet of 2*l.* a year; Mr. Humphry Bridges gave a houſe in Cricklade-ſtreet, of 2*l.* a year; George Monox, eſq; in 1639, gave five houſes in this town, now let at 23*l.* 10*s.* the produce of which (except 8*l.* a year for a monthly ſermon, and 6*s.* 8*d.* to be ſpent) to be given in money to the poor. John Pathe, butcher, in 1641, gave a rent-charge of 4*l.* on a houſe in Dollar-ſtreet, half to decayed butchers and half to the other poor. Rowland Freeman, in 1658, gave a rent-charge of 40*s.* on a houſe and land now incorporated with the earl of Bathurſt's park. Theſe rents were all given to the uſe of the poor.

The following ſums were alſo given that the annual intereſt of them may be apply'd to the ſame uſe.

In 1625, Samuel Coxwell, gent. gave 50*l.* 1639, George Monox, eſq; gave 100*l.* 1645, Sir Henry Pratt, of London, baronet, gave 100*l.* William Blomer, of Hatherop, gent. gave 40*l.* Mrs. Chambers gave 50*l.* Others, in ſmall contributions, gave 53*l.* Which ſums were all laid out in the purchaſe of land in South Cerney, except 20*l.* part of Mr. Blomer's gift, with 10*l.* of which a houſe in Glouceſter-ſtreet was purchaſed for the poor.

Thomas Damſel gave 100*l.* In 1620, a man who had a lottery here 40*l.* Mr. Thomas Shermore, of London, 20*l.* Mr. John Stone 20*l.* Robert George, eſq; 10*l.* The heirs of Robert Strange, eſq; 10*l.* Mr. Edward Pratt, jun. 10*l.* 1606, Thomas Smith 20*l.* 1615, John May, of Amney St. Mary, 10*l.* Robert Stech, butcher, 10*l.* Edward Church 20*l.* 1669, Lady Atkynſon, of Stowel, 10*l.* 1679, John Oates, clothier, 10*l.* 1680, William Kerby, of London, ſalter, 10*l.* John Coxwell, eſq; 100*l.* The reverend Mr. William Maſter 50*l.* 1706, Mrs. Winifred Maſter 60*l.* Other benefactions, in ſmaller ſums, amounted to 22*l.* 10*s.* Mrs. Elizabeth Edwards gave 30*l.* and four tenements in Caſtle-ſtreet, (which were ſold for 60*l.* about the year 1729) the intereſt to be diſtributed yearly among four poor families. But theſe ſums, with 100*l.* before mentioned to have been given by her for apprenticing children, were laid out in the purchaſe of the church-yard.

The following charities are to provide cloathing for the poor.

In 1642, ſir Anthony Hungerford gave Weſt-Mead in Amney Crucis. Thomas Perry, ſenior, in 1673, gave 20*l.* Edward King, in 1692, gave a rent-charge of 2*l.* 9*s.* on two houſes in Coxwell-ſtreet. Anne Peters gave 20*l.* Nicholas Edwards 40*l.* Sarah Humphris 10*l.* and Frances Peek 5*l.*

The intereſt of the following donations is to be annually given to the poor in bread.

Mrs. Mary Chambers, daughter of Mr. Monox, gave 50*l.* Mr. Fettiplace 20*l.* Nicholas Edwards 10*l.* Elizabeth, his widow, 5*l.* and Iſaac Tibbet, her father, 20*l.*

The large Engine for extinguiſhing fire was given by ſir Benjamin Bathurſt. That of a more modern conſtruction, built by Newſham, was preſented to the town by the two repreſentatives, the Honourable Mr. Henry Bathurſt, (now Lord Apſley, and Lord High Chancellor of Great Britain) and Thomas Maſter, eſq. The ſmall one was purchaſed by the inhabitants of the town.

Dyer-ward.

Taxes.				
The Royal Aid in	1692, £.	87	7	0
Poll-tax — —	1694, —	62	12	0
Land-tax ——	1694, —	169	14	0
The ſame, at 3*s.*	1770, —	132	6	1*ob.*

Cricklade-ward.

Taxes.				
The Royal Aid in	1692, £.	35	9	8
Poll-tax —	1694, —	23	6	0
Land-tax —	1694, —	84	6	0
The ſame, at 3*s.*	1770, —	62	16	1

Caſtle-ward.

Taxes.				
The Royal Aid in	1692, £.	20	4	0
Poll-tax ——	1694, —	15	17	0
Land-tax ——	1694, —	63	19	0
The ſame, at 3*s.*	1770, —	45	14	0

Goſditch-Ward.

Taxes.				
The Royal Aid in	1692, £.	57	10	8
Poll-tax ——	1694, —	36	15	0
Land-tax ——	1694, —	103	3	0
The ſame, at 3*s.*	1770, —	79	4	0

Dollar-Ward.

Taxes.				
The Royal Aid in	1692, £.	38	9	0
Poll-tax —	1694, —	39	1	0
Land-tax ——	1694, —	97	0	0
The ſame at 3*s.*	1770, —	65	18	0

St. Lawrence-Ward.

Taxes.				
The Royal Aid in	1692, £.	14	19	8
Poll-tax ——	1694, —	12	17	0
Land-tax ——	1694, —	40	12	0
The ſame, at 3*s.*	1770, —	27	0	0

Inſtrip-Ward.

Taxes.				
The Royal Aid in	1692, £.	5	1	4
Poll-tax ——	1694, —	4	19	0
Land-tax ——	1694, —	16	12	0
The ſame, at 3*s.*	1770, —	10	2	10*ob.*

Spittlegate.

Taxes.				
The Royal Aid in	1692, £.	44	18	8
Poll-tax ——	1694, —	8	2	0
Land-tax ——	1694, —	72	18	0
The ſame, at 3*s.*	1770, —	49	10	6

Wiggold.

Taxes.				
The Royal Aid in	1692, £.	15	0	0
Poll-tax ——	1694, —	0	16	0
Land-tax ——	1694, —	20	0	0
The ſame, at 3*s.*	1770, —	15	0	0

Cheſterton.

Taxes.				
The Royal Aid in	1692, £.	21	11	4
Poll-tax ——	1694, —	0	0	0
Land-tax ——	1694, —	47	12	0
The ſame, at 3*s.*	1770, —	35	14	0

Barton.

Taxes.				
The Royal Aid in	1692, £.	45	5	4
Poll-tax ——	1694, —	0	6	8
Land-tax ——	1694, —	62	15	6
The ſame, at 3*s.*	1770, —	45	10	6

Oakley

Oakley.

Taxes.	The Royal Aid in 1692, £.	52	12	0
	Poll-tax —— 1694,—	0	16	0
	Land-tax —— 1694,—	28	0	0
	The fame, at 3*s.* 1770,—	21	0	0

I come now to give the ftate of population. According to fir Robert Atkyns, when he compiled his account of this parifh, there were near 800 houfes, and about 4000 inhabitants, whereof above 100 were freeholders; yearly births 103, burials 87. But thefe numbers are too high; for having examined the regifter, I find, that in ten years, beginning with 1700, which includes the time mentioned in his account, there were 933 baptifms, and 821 burials. During this period the diffenters (except the quakers, of whom there were but few) buried in the church-yard, and were duly regiftered; and allowing 3 births and 2 burials to the quakers, the annual number, upon an average, will be 96.3 baptifms, and 84.1 burials. In a like feries of ten years, beginning with 1760, there are regiftered 774 baptifms, and 775 burials; but during this time the diffenters in general are not regiftered; and allowing for them 14 baptifms and 10 burials annually, the prefent ftate of the account will be 88.4 baptifms, and 87.5 burials.

After the fmall-pox had left the town in the year 1741, the inhabitants were found to be 3797; and after a vifitation of the fame kind in 1758, the people were numbered at 3458; but in 1775, an exact account having been taken, the whole number of houfholders was 838, and of inhabitants 3878, fomething more than four perfons and a half to a houfe. The increafe of inhabitants when the burials fo nearly equal the births, muft be attributed to the afflux of people from other places: wherefore the burials, as they now ftand, are improper for making an eftimate of the healthinefs of the place. For, had the people rifen to the prefent number, without fuch adventitious affiftance, it is eafy to prove, that the burials would have been fewer in proportion. Suppofe ten in a year ought to be deducted on that account, the number of inhabitants to the average of annual burials will be as 50 to 1. This is a proof of what was advanced of the healthinefs of the place, confidered as a town, where intemperance and diforder are more prevalent than in country villages.

CLAPTON

IS a fmall parifh, in the lower divifion of the hundred of Slaughter, five miles fouth-weftward from Stow, five north-eaftward from Northleach, and twenty-three eaftward from Gloucefter. It is fituated upon an eminence to the weft, above Bourton-on-the-Water. The etymology of the name is uncertain: and the parifh affords nothing worthy the attention of the naturalift or antiquary.

Of the Manor and other Eftates.

In the lift of the manors belonging to William Goizenboded, in Ceolflede hundred, it is thus recorded:

'The fame William holds Cloptune. A houfhold fervant (*hufcarle*) held it in the time of king Edward. There are ten hides. In demean are three plow-tillages, and twelve villeins, and four bordars, and one radchenifter, with nine plow-tillages. In Wicelcombe one burgage. It was worth 8*l.* and is now worth 100*s.* *D. B.* p. 74.

The abbey of Evefham purchafed a charter of free warren in Clopton and divers other manors 35 H. 3. But Roger de Quincy, earl of Winchefter, was feized of Clopton 55 H. 3. and a charter of free warren in Clapton was granted to Richard Clapton 56 H. 3. I have retained the extracts from the records of the two laft dates, becaufe I found them in fir Robert Atkyns's account; but they may poffibly relate to fome other place of the fame name.

Alan la Zouch, baron of Afhley, died feized of Clapton 7 E. 2. leaving three daughters coheireffes, from whom the manor went to the family of the Bruggs.

Richard de Brugg was feized of Clapton, and having been in rebellion againft king Edward the Second, his whole eftate was forfeited, and feized into the king's hands, but it was reftored to him again 1 E. 3. Edward Brugg was feized thereof 15 H. 6. as was fir John Brugg 11 E. 4.

Mr. Woodman is the prefent lord of this manor. It was formerly part of the manor of Bourton-on-the-Water.

Lands in Clapton, called Clerk's and Smith's Mill, and divers other lands and meffuages, formerly belonging to the abbey of Evefham, were granted to Michael Afhfield 32 H. 8.

John Dolphin, efq; has lately purchafed a good eftate in this parifh, but he refides at Eyeford in this county, late the eftate of William Wanley, efq.

Of the Church, &c.

The church is in the deanery of Stow. It is a chapel of eafe to Bourton-on-the-Water. The church is dedicated to St. James. It was built, together with the chancel, about 1670.

Taxes.	The Royal Aid in 1692, £.	46	0	0
	Poll-tax —— 1694,—	15	18	6
	Land-tax —— 1694,—	39	11	0
	The fame, at 3*s.* 1770,—	30	19	6

There were 18 houfes and about 80 inhabitants in this parifh when fir Robert Atkyns compiled his account of it; but the inhabitants are increafed fince that time to 112. Part of them bury and are regiftered at the mother church, and part here, fo that no ufeful information can be derived from the regifter.

CLEEVE.

CLEEVE, *or* BISHOP's-CLEEVE,

LIES in the hundred of its own name, about four miles north from Cheltenham, five ſouth from Tewkeſbury, and eleven north-eaſtward from Glouceſter. It is bounded on the north by Woolſton, from which it is ſeparated by a brook, called the Tirle in the chronicles of Worceſter, that runs into the Carrant; on the ſouth by Preſbury; on the eaſt by Poſtlip-warren, in the pariſh of Winchcombe; and on the weſt by Tredington.

It is a very large pariſh, conſiſting of ſeveral tithings and hamlets, more than five miles in length, and nearly of the ſame breadth; part of it lying in the vale, and part extending over the great ridge of hills which divides the vale from the Coteſwold country. This ſituation on the ſide of the hill very probably gave occaſion to the name; for Clif, in the Anglo Saxon language, ſignifies a *high rock*, or *ſteep aſcent*. It is ſometimes called Biſhop's-Cleeve, (having been antiently the property of the biſhop of Worceſter) to diſtinguiſh it from Prior's-Cleeve, and from Cleeve in the pariſh of Weſtbury, in this county.

The lands, in the vale part, conſiſt chiefly of rich arable, with a mixture of good meadow and paſture.

I have had frequent occaſions to mention the many camps, intrenchments, and fortifications found in various parts of the Coteſwold country, but more eſpecially on the verge of thoſe hills next the vale; ſituations which ſeem to have been choſen on two accounts, as being leſs liable to ſurpriſe or attack, and commanding a large extent of country below, where the oppoſite party could do nothing without being obſerved. On the edge of Cleeve-hill, commonly called *Cleeve-cloud*, is a large double intrenchment called the *Camps*, extending 350 yards along the ſummit of the rock, in the form of a creſcent, and inacceſſible on every ſide but the front. The name of *Cleeve-cloud* ſeems to have been given to the edge of this hill on account of its bold and lofty appearance, when viewed from the vale below; for from the foot of it, to the top of the rock where the camp ſtands, (tho' little more than half a meaſured mile) there is an aſcent of 630 feet perpendicular. Upon Nottingham-hill, (a part of the ſame range, ſo called) in the hamlet of Gotherington, are other very conſiderable lines of fortifications and intrenchments; and in the middle between theſe two incampments, which are about a mile diſtant from each other, are four large *tumuli*, or barrows, one of which was lately opened, and found to contain a great quantity of human bones, broken and crumbled into very ſmall pieces, and ſurrounded with a particularly ſoft and fine kind of mould. Hence it may be concluded, that ſome bloody engagement formerly happened here. It will not be expected of me to point out the exact time when, nor the people by whom theſe works were raiſed, ſince our once miſerable country has been a ſcene of bloodſhed and deſolation for many hundreds of years together, and but few of the military tranſactions of early ages are recorded in hiſtory. If they were raiſed by the Romans, ſome of the coins of that people would probably have been found thereabout; but I hear of no ſuch thing. They are therefore ſuppoſed to be Saxon, raiſed ſome time about the ſeventh century, when the Weſt-Saxons were continually at war with the Mercians.

About the mid-way between Cleeve and Gotherington, is a ſpring of ſaline purging water, not unlike that in the neighbouring pariſh of Preſbury. And the inhabitants of this part of the country have been agreeably amuſed with the expectation of coal being to be found in Long-Wood in this pariſh. The proprietor is now ſearching for that uſeful foſſil, in which I wiſh him ſucceſs for his own ſake, and for the general good of the neighbourhood. I come now to treat

Of the Manors and other Eſtates.

In *Domeſday-book* are the following particulars, under the title *Terra Eccl'e de Wireceſtre*:

'The ſame church held Clive in Tedboldeſtan 'hundred. There are thirty hides. In demean 'are three plow-tillages, and ſixteen villeins, and 'nineteen bordars, with ſixteen plow-tillages. 'There are eight *ſervi*, and one Moor. [*Afrus*.] 'There is a prieſt who hath one hide and two 'plow-tillages, and a radchenister having one hide 'and two plow-tillages. There is a little wood. 'Durandus the ſheriff holds of the church ſix 'hides of land of this manor in Surham, Ra'dulphus four hides in Sapletone, Turſtinus the 'ſon of Rolf ſix hides in Godrinton. In theſe 'lands are eight plow-tillages in demean, and 'twenty-two villeins, and ſeven bordars, with 'thirteen plow-tillages. There are twenty *ſervi*, 'and three Moors, [*Afri*,] and a mill of 12 *den*. '[rent,] and a little meadow. Bernardus and 'Raynaldus hold ſeven hides of the ſame land in 'Stoches, and they would do no ſervice for St. 'Mary. [*i. e.* the church of Worceſter.] The 'whole manor, in the time of king Edward, was 'worth 36*l.* and it is now worth 26*l.* in the 'whole. Ulſtanus the biſhop holds this manor.' *Domeſday-book*, p. 70.

Thus it appears that part of Salperton formerly belonged to the manor of Cleeve. Surham, (now Southam,) Godrinton, and Stoke are tithings in this pariſh, of which hereafter.

The manor of Cleeve was ſettled in jointure on queen Elianor 27 H. 3. Humphry de Bohun, earl of Hereford and Eſſex, was ſeized of Cleeve and Clifborn 3 E. 1. but he held it, moſt likely, under the biſhop of Worceſter; for in the 15th year of the ſame reign the biſhop was ſeized of this manor, and divers privileges were allowed him in a writ of *Quo Warranto*.

In a taxation of the temporalties of the fee of Worcefter in the laft mentioned reign, as I find it in a manufcript in the Cotton library, it is thus expreft: *Item, At Clyvam the rents of affize* 8 *l.* —— *carucates of land, and each carucate is worth* 20 *s. and a dove-houfe worth* 6 *s. and a water-mill worth* 30 *s. and the pleas and perquifites of the court* 30 *s. In the whole* 13 *l.* 6 *s.* In the furvey taken of this manor 26 H. 8. it was valued at 55 *l.* 10 *s.* 9 *d.*

This manor was refumed by the crown 1 Eliz.[m] together with the manors of Bredon, Bifhop's-Wyke, Henbury, and Knight-Wyke, in the counties of Gloucefter and Worcefter, part of the poffeffions of the fee of Worcefter; in lieu of which the queen, in the 4th year of her reign, granted to Dr. Edwin Sandys, then bifhop of Worcefter, the impropriations of Bifhampton, Church-Lench, and Elmely, and the tenths of the bifhoprick and of the archdeaconry of Worcefter.

The manor of Cleeve, formerly belonging to the bifhoprick of Worcefter, was granted to Peter Vanlore, merchant, 2 Jac. who was lord of it in the year 1608. John Bridges was lord of this manor at the beginning of the prefent century. It paffed afterwards to Thomas Hayward, efq; and from him to William Strachan, LL. D. whofe fon fir William Strachan, baronet, fold it lately to Mr. Thorneloe and Mr. Lilly, of Worcefter, the prefent proprietors.

Of the other eftates, the records fhew, that lands in Cleeve, which belonged to the abbey of Tewkefbury, and were in the tenure of Roger Fowler, were granted to Richard Gunter 36 H. 8. Thomas Bullen and Margaret his wife levied a fine of lands in Cleeve, Gotherinton, and Woodmancot to the ufe of Richard Southwell, 1 E. 6.

Lands called Bufhcomb-wood, in Cleeve, formerly belonging to the bifhop of Worcefter, were granted to Chriftopher Hatton 18 Eliz. which eftate is now the property of Mr. Branch of Gloucefter.

A meffuage in Cleeve, formerly belonging to the chantry of St. Mary in Weftbury-upon-Trim, was granted to Anthony Cope 10 Jac.

TITHINGS and *HAMLETS.*

1. *Southam,* fo called becaufe it lies fouthward of the church. This is a large tithing, wherein Thomas-Baghot De-la-Bere, efq; has a feat, and a very fine eftate. The houfe is one of the greateft curiofities in the county. It is a low building, in the ftile of the age of Henry the Fourth, or thenabout. The hall is floored with painted bricks, brought from Hayles-abbey foon after the diffolution of that houfe. There are many curious devices upon them of different kinds, containing the names, and rebuffes of the names, of the abbats Ford and Melton. There are alfo great numbers of fcutcheons, with arms, among which are the following: 1. *France and England quarterly.* 2. *Or, an eagle difplay'd fable,* for Richard duke of Cornwall, as king of the Romans, the founder of Hayles-abbey. 3. *Quarterly,* 1ft and 4th, *Azure, a bend argent, cotoifed Or, between fix martlets of the laft,* for De-la-Bere; 2d and 3d, *Gules, a fret argent,* for Huddlefton. &c. &c. The bricks are in exceeding good prefervation, and are valuable remains of the abbey to which they belonged. There are alfo in this houfe many very antient paintings of eminent perfons, particularly a whole length figure of king Edward the Sixth, done upon oak, which is very much admired; but fome of the pieces are injured by time.

There are two manors in this tithing, both defcribed in the records by one common name, which I fhall endavour to diftinguifh in their defcent.

Six hides in Surham, part of the manor of Clive, were held of the church of Worcefter by Durand the fheriff, at the time of the general furvey. Southam was confirmed to the abbey of Tewkefbury 1 H. 3. Humphry de Bohun, earl of Hereford and Effex, held this manor of the bifhop of Worcefter 3, 27, & 30 E. 1. in which laft year it was feized by the crown. Elias de Iccumb held the manor of Southam 5 E. 3. and Humphry de Bohun, earl of Hereford, and William de Bohun, earl of Nottingham held Southam 37 & 47 E. 3. refpectively The manor of Southam was granted to Ralph Butler, for life, 16 H. 6. and a fine was levied thereof, and of other lands belonging to the dutchy of Lancafter, to the ufe of Elizabeth, queen to king Edward the Fourth, and to the ufe of the archbifhop of Canterbury and other great men, 15 E. 4. This manor and many others were granted to Henry Stafford duke of Buckingham[n], as heir of blood to Humphry de Bohun earl of Hereford, 1 R. 3. who was beheaded the fame year. A wood called Queen's-wood in Southam, and the manor of Southam belonging to the dutchy of Lancafter, were granted to Robert earl of Salifbury 5 Jac. And he fold all his manor, lands, and intereft in Southam, (except fome lands before granted by copy of court roll) to Richard De-la-Bere, of Lincoln's-Inn, efq; the following year.

Thomas Baghot De-la-Bere[o], efq; is the prefent lord of this manor, whofe arms are blazoned in the former part of this account.

Cockbury

[m] Willis's Survey of Worcefter Cathedral. [n] Dugdale's Bar.

[o] His anceftor, fir Richard Dalabar, came into England with king William the Conqueror. Sir John Dalabar, fon of fir Richard, lived in the reign of king William the Second. He married Joan, daughter and heirefs of Stephen de Heven, lord of Heven. Sir Stephen Dalabar, fon of fir John, married Mabel, one of the daughters of Brian, lord of Brompton in Shropfhire. Sir Simon Dalabar, fon of fir Stephen, married Sibil, daughter of fir Henry Pembridge. Richard Dalabar, efq; fon of fir Simon, married Sibil, daughter of fir Robert Harley. He affigned a rent-charge to Sibil his wife 3 E. 2.

Sir Richard Dalabar, fon of Richard, married Margaret, daughter of fir William Gammage, lord of Rogiad in Monmouthfhire. He lived 20 E. 2. and fucceeded to the eftate of Alan lord Pluganet, as next heir of the whole blood. He was prefent at the glorious battle of Creffy, 20 E. 3. where he acquired great honour by refcuing Edward the Black Prince, then in imminent danger, and was by him, for this great fervice, prefented with the prefent creft to the family arms, which is *Five oftrich feathers iffuing out of a ducal coronet.* Tho' Crefts are now confidered as mere ornaments, they were formerly greater marks of honour than

Cockbury is a farm in this tithing, belonging to Edward Rogers, efq; held of Mr. De-la-Bere's manor.

Peter Fitz-Herbert[p] obtained a charter of free warren throughout all his lands in the hundred of Cleeve 12 H. 3. and Reginald the fon of Peter was feized of the manor of Southam 14 E. 1. John Fitz-Herbert, and Reginald Fitz-Herbert, were fucceffively feized of Southam 22 & 26 E. 3. Thomas Dinley, in right of Philippa his wife, died feized of the manor of Southam 9 H. 8. and left an only daughter Elizabeth, married to George Barret, to whom livery of this manor was granted the fame year. William Emundefham was lord of the manor of Southam, and left Elizabeth his daughter and heirefs, married to Roger Bodenham, of Dewchurch in Herefordfhire. Roger died feized of Southam 2 E. 6. Richard Baker had livery of the manor of Southam 1 Eliz. And the reverend Mr. Richard Rogers has the manor in Southam and Brockhampton, late Baker's. His arms are, *Argent, a mullet fable, on a chief gules a fleur de lis Or.*

The records alfo fhew, that William Stokes was feized of Fletchard's-croft in Southam 5 H. 6.

Brockhampton, or *Brockington*, is a hamlet in this tithing.

Haymes is a manor within the tithing of Southam, which continued in the name and family of Lorange for about four hundred years, from the reign of king Edward the Second. It was purchafed by ferjeant Goodinge, who was *Cuftos Brevium* of the court of Queen's-bench, in the reign of queen Anne. It came afterwards to fir William Strachan, a baronet of Nova Scotia, who a few years fince built a very handfome feat here, upon an eminence, commanding a delightful profpect over the vale of Evefham, terminated by Malvern and Abberley hills, in the county of Worcefter. This feat was lately fold to fome perfons of Worcefter. Sir William married one of the daughters and coheireffes of Edward Popham, efq; of the Lodge, near Tewkefbury in this county, by whom he has no iffue.

2. *Gotherington*, which lies north-eaftward of the church. Almerick de St. Amand was feized of the manor of Gotherington 4 E. 2. Hugh le Defpencer and Elizabeth his wife, the relict of Giles Badlefmere, were feized of Gotherington and Stoke-Archer 23 E. 3. The manor of Gotherington and other lands belonged to the abbey of St. Auguftine in Briftol, and were granted to the dean and chapter of Briftol 34 H. 8. Another manor in Gotherington, formerly belonging to the abbey of Tewkefbury, was granted to Anne Fortefcue, widow of fir Adrian Fortefcue, and to the heirs male of fir Adrian, 5 Mar. Lord Craven is the prefent lord of this manor.

3. *Stoke-Archer*, now commonly, but improperly, written *Stoke-Orchard*. This tithing lies fouth-weftward of the church, in two different hundreds; the greater part in the hundred of Cleeve, the other in the lower divifion of the hundred of Tewkefbury. It took the name of *Archer* from a family furnamed *le Archer*, who held a manor in this tithing by the fervice of providing a man, with bow and arrows, at their own charge, to attend the king's army forty days when it marched againft the Welch. It had not obtained that name at the time of the general furvey, as may be feen by the following abftract.

'In Stoches Hermer' and Aluuinus held three 'hides, lefs one yard-land. Now Bernard holds 'them of the king, and has there one plow-tillage 'in demean, and four acres of meadow. It was 'worth 60*s*. and is now worth 40*s*. Thofe who 'held thefe lands in the time of king Edward, 'were both themfelves and the lands under the 'government of Brictric.' *Domefday-book*, p. 68.

The above is the part in the hundred of Tewkefbury.

The abftract from *Domefday-book* which fir Robert Atkyns, by miftake, placed under this head, belongs to Lark-Stoke. He was alfo miftaken in faying, as from the record, that it was held by the church of Winchelcumbe, whereas the eftate therein defcribed was held by the church of Evefham.

The following abftract relates to that part of this hamlet which lies in the hundred of Cleeve.

'Bernard and Raynald held feven hides in 'Stoches, and they would do no fervice for St. 'Mary.' *Domefday-book*, p. 70.

I fhall endeavour to trace the defcent of thefe eftates diftinctly.

Thomas Berkeley of Coberley was feized of that part of Archer-Stoke which lies in the hundred of Cleeve, 25 E. 3. Henry de Berkeley held the

than coats of arms, being only worn by heroes of great valour, and principal commanders, that they might be the better diftinguifhed in an engagement, and thereby enabled to rally their men. Sir John Dalabar, fon of fir Richard, lived 39 E. 3. He married Agnes, daughter of fir Pain Turbervil, who dying before his father, fhe was grandaughter and coheir to fir Gilbert Turbervil. Sir Richard Dalabar, fon of fir John, lived 46 E. 3.

Sir Alan Dalabar, fon of fir Richard, married the daughter and heir of Waldron Bafon, lord of Kilpetheg, and of Haflebury in Dorfetfhire. Sir Richard Dalabar, fon of fir Alan, married Margaret, daughter of fir William Abrahal.

Sir Kynard Dalabar was fon of fir Richard. Sir Richard Dalabar was fon of fir Kynard: He lived in the reign of king H. 6. Sir Kynard Dalabar, fon of fir Richard, married Joan, the eldeft daughter and coheirefs of fir Thomas de Barry. Sir Richard Dalabar, fon of fir Kynard, married Elizabeth, daughter of —— Norris, ferjeant of the hall to king Henry the Seventh.

George Delabar, fon of fir Richard, married Sybil, daughter to Thomas Walwen, efq. John Delabar, fon of George, married Sybil, daughter of John Scudamore, of Homelacy in Herefordfhire. Kynard Delabar, fon of John, married Blanch, daughter to —— Spencer. Kynard Delabar, fon of Kynard, married Joan, daughter of John Hales, of Coventry, efq. John De-la-Bere, fon of the laft Kynard, married Anne, daughter of John Stephens, of Lypiat. He was high fheriff 3 W. 3. 1690. Kynard De-la-Bere, fon of John, married Hefter, one of the daughters and coheireffes of John Neal, of Dean, in the county of Bedford, efq; and was fucceeded in this eftate by his nephew William Baghot De-la-Bere, of Prefbury, efq; who was fon of Anne, eldeft fifter and heirefs of Kynard De-la-bere. He married Hefter, daughter of Thomas Stephens, of Lypiat, efq; and his eldeft fon and heir, Thomas Baghot De-la-Bere, efq; is the prefent lord of this manor, as already mentioned.

[p] Cart. 12 H. 3. m. 7.

fame

same 26 E. 3. Joan the widow of William de Whittington, and formerly the wife of Thomas Berkeley of Coberley, held the manor of Stoke-Archer 46 E. 3. Thomas Berkeley of Coberley was seized of the manor of Stoke-Archer 6 H. 4. and left an only daughter Alice, who carried this estate into the family of the Brugges, by her marriage with sir Thomas Brugge, whom she survived, and was afterwards married to John Browning[q]; and surviving him also, she died seized in dower of this manor 2 H. 5. Giles Brugge, or Bruges, her son, was seized of this manor 6 E. 4. Sir Giles Brydges died seized thereof 3 H. 8. and livery was granted to his son sir John Brydges 16 H. 8. John lord Chandois died seized of the manor of Archer-Stoke 4 Mar. and livery thereof was granted to his son Edmond lord Chandois the same year. He died seized thereof 15 Eliz. and livery was granted to his son Giles lord Chandois the same year.

Of that part of Stoke-Archer which lies in the hundred of Tewkesbury, the following account is drawn from the records.

John, son of Robert de Stokes, was seized of Stoke and Gotherington 38 H. 3. Nicholas le Archer held two plow-tillages in Stoke 15 E. 1. by the service of providing a man, with bow and arrows, to attend the king's army forty days when it marched against the Welch. Edmond Archer held Stoke-Archer 7 E. 2. It was held of Gilbert de Clare, earl of Gloucester and Hertford, 8 E. 2. Elianor the widow of Henry le Dispencer was seized of the hamlet of Archer-Stoke 11 E. 3. Jeffry le Archer held the manor of Archer-Stoke 24 E. 3. and Cicely his widow was seized of it the same year.

John Arundel of Arundel held Archerds 9 H. 5. John Fitz-Alan, earl of Arundel, died seized of Archerds 13 H. 6. Elianor the widow of sir Walter Hungerford, late wife of sir Richard Poynings, and formerly wife of sir John Arundel, died seized of the manor of Archerds 33 H. 6. Nicholas Madesden, esq; was seized of Archer-Stoke 14 H. 6. and Robert Madesden held the same 36 H. 6. George duke of Clarence, in right of Isabel his wife, was seized of Archer-Stoke 13 E. 4. Anne, sister and heir of Henry duke of Warwick, made an assignment of the manor of Stoke-Archer to the king and his heirs male 3 H. 7. Thomas earl of Arundel died seized of the manor of Archerds 16 H. 8. and livery was granted to his son William earl of Arundel the same year, who died seized thereof 35 H. 8. and livery was also granted to his son Henry earl of Arundel 36 H. 8. The manor of Stoke-Archer, lately Warwick's and Spencer's lands, was granted to John Hall and Henry Sheldon 37 H. 8. John Hall died seized thereof 2 E. 6. and livery was granted to his son Francis 3 Mariæ.

The manor of Stoke-Archer is now the property of Mrs. Rogers, widow of the late Richard Rogers, of Dowdeswell, esq.

There is a chapel of ease in this hamlet.

4. *Woodmancot* lies south-eastward of the church, where Mr. James Cocks has a good house and estate.

Of the Church, &c.

The church is in the deanery of Winchcombe. It is a rectory worth 500*l.* a year. The reverend Mr. Reid is patron and incumbent. It is a peculiar, exempt from the archdeacon's visitation, but subject to the bishop's triennially. The rector exercises archidiaconal jurisdiction, proves wills, and grants administration. It was a prebend to the college of Westbury, who placed a vicar here.

Godfrey Giffard, bishop of Worcester, in the 13th century, obtained this rectory for his life by a bull from the pope. The bishops of Worcester were patrons, 'till the bishop conveyed away the advowson to Thomas Seymour lord Sudely, by whose attainder it came to the crown, and was afterwards granted, with the advowson of the chapel of Stoke-Archer, to sir Christopher Hatton 21 Eliz.

John Parkhurst was rector of this church, and was made bishop of Norwich in 1560.

John Cleymand was president of Magdalen-college in Oxford; and upon his removal to be the first president of Corpus Christi-college, because the latter was of less value, he was presented to this rectory; wherefore he gave a scholar's place in Brazen-nose-college for a native of this parish, 1548.

Dr. Nicholson, bishop of Gloucester, had also been rector of this church.

The church is very large, dedicated to St. Michael the archangel. It hath an aile on the north side, two on the south, a handsome tower, with pinnacles, in the middle, and a cross aile on each side. In the year 1696, the spire fell down, and the present tower was rebuilt, without a steeple, in the year 1700, at the expence of 770*l.*

There were four chantries in this church, dedicated to St. Nicholas, to St. Catherine, to All Saints, and to St. Mary.

Monuments and Inscriptions.

Under a handsome arch, in the wall of a chapel on the south side of the church, lies the effigy in stone of a man in antient armour, girt with his sword, and a large shield on his left arm. His legs are crossed, like a knight templer, with spurs on, and his feet rest on a dog. Tradition will have it to be for Gilbert the Bold.

There is also the figure of a military person upon a brass plate fixt on a stone in the chancel, with his arms, *three piles*, and this inscription in old character:

. . . . armiger qui obiit undecimo die mensis Iulij M°. CCC°. LXX°. quinto Cujus aiæ p'picietur deus amen.

In the south aile of the church, against the wall, is an elegant monument of black and white marble, erected to the memory of Richard De-la-Bere, esq; by his widow, daughter and heir to — Newman.

[q] Collins's Peerage, V. 2. p. 244, 245.

It

It confifts of two compartments. The lower contains a table defigned for an infcription, which has not yet been put upon it. Over the table are two fcutcheons. On the dexter fide are the arms of De-la-Bere; on the finifter, *Azure, a fefs undy between fix dolphins nayant,* 3 & 3, *argent,* for Newman. All round are the arms of feveral families with whom the De-la-Beres have intermarried. In the middle of the upper compartment is a large fcutcheon with eight quarterings. 1. De-la-Bere. 2. *Gules, a chief counter compony Or and azure, over all a bend argent.* 3. *Azure, a lion rampant between eight croffes croflets argent.* 4. *Gules, on a chief argent three martlets fable.* 5. *Paly of fix argent and fable, four bars gules,* for De Barry. 6. *Barry of fix Or and azure, over all a bend gules,* for Pembridge. 7. Newman, as before. 8. *Argent, a bend voided gules, in chief a rofe.* This monument is inriched with marble pillars of the Corinthian order, and with pyramids whofe bafes are ornamented with emblematical figures. Before it, upon a large raifed tomb, are the effigies in white marble, of a man and woman, lying along in full proportion, both in rich dreffes, defigned for Richard De-la-Bere, efq; and his wife. He died in 1635. Near this, on another raifed tomb, is the figure of a lady lying along, with an ermine mantle covering her head, and hanging down to her elbows; but it has no infcription. The whole is inclofed with iron palifadoes, and in good prefervation.

Againft the fouth wall in the chancel is this infcription.

H. S. E. Edmundus Bedingfield ex Æde Chrifti in Univerfitate Oxon'fi olim Alumnus et Socius. Ecclefiæ hujus Parochialis Rector. Vir clarus ingenio; In Divinis Scripturis eruditus. Ecclefiæ Anglicanæ et fidei Orthodoxæ Affertor ftrenuus; Et in extremis Ecclefiæ miferiis ei maxime fidus: Concionator etiam ad ultimum Affiduus. In cujus memoriam optimo Marito Mœftiffima Conjux hoc Monumentum pofuit. Obijt Feb: 14° Anno Æræ Chriftianæ 1695. Sub Anno Ætatis fuæ 55. Duas habuit Uxores quæ juxta fitæ funt.—On a fcutcheon thefe arms, *Ermine, an eagle difplay'd gules.*

Near the above:—Maria Chetwind Ex Agro Staffordienfi Ob. Mar. 31mo 1674.—Arms, *Azure, a chevron between three mullets Or.*

On the other fide of Dr. Bedingfield's monument: Catherina Norwood hujufce Comitatus Ob. Nov. 14to 1711.—Arms, *Ermine, a crofs ingrailed gules.*

On a plain table of black marble:

In Memoriam Ianæ nuper Uxoris Iohannis Reed de Mitton Armigeri, filiæ et Cohæredis Georgij Huntley de Frocefter Equitis Aurati. Richardus Reed de Lugwardine in Comit. Herefordienfi Armiger ex mandato ultimo Eleanoræ Uxoris fuæ, filiæ et hæredis prediɛtorum Iohannis et Ianæ pofuit, Quæ Iana obijt in Puerperio die An° Dni 16—— She died in 1630.

On a blue ftone in the chancel, the two following infcriptions:

Hic jacet Iohannes Cocks nuper Commenfalis Collegij Pembrochiæ Oxon. Filius natu maximus Iohannis Cocks de Woodmancoat in hâc Parochiâ Generofi: Optime Spei Iuvenis. Natus xv Kal. Aprilis Anno Dni MDCCIV. Denatus Idibus Decemb. Anno Dni MDCCXXIV.—Arms, *Sable, a chevron between three ftags horns with the fcalps argent.*

In Memory of John Cocks Senr. of Woodman Coat in this Parifh Gent. who departed this life the 7th day of April in the year 1729 aged 60 years. And of Mary his beloved Wife who died Sept. the 25th 1746, in the 74th year of her Age. Mors Ianua Vitæ.

On a flat blue ftone:

H. S. I. Gulielmus Curwen Artium Magifter Et Ecclefiæ hujus Parochialis Rector. Ecclefiæ etiam Anglicanæ et Fidei orthodoxæ Affertor ftrenuus. Obiit Vir defideratus 24to Die Martii Anno Dom. 1708, Ætat. 62.—Arms, *fretty, a chief.* no colours expreffed.

On another flat ftone:

H. S. E. IACOBUS UVEDADE A. M. Hujus Ecclefiæ Rector digniffimus. Sacræ Scripturæ Pro fumma fua Doctrina Fidus Interpres. Concionator gravis et difertus, eximia erga Deum Pietate, Benevolentia erga Omnes prope fingulari, tanta erga Pauperes Charitate ut Domus ejus *Pandoxeion* videretur. Obijt 27 die Martij Anno Dom. 1737 Ætatis 54.—Arms, *Baron and femme,* 1. *A crofs moline.* 2. *Checky, on a chief a rofe.* No colours expreft.

On a blue ftone in the chancel:

Robertus Stubbe filius Edmundi Stubbe apud Huntingfield in agro Suffolcienfi S. T. P. nec non ita pridem hujus Ecclefiæ Rector qui obiit 1° die Menfis Maij 1665, fub hoc marmore expectat fecundum Xti Adventum.—Arms, *On a bend, three buckles between three pheons heads.*

Firft fruits, £. 84 6 8 Tenths, £. 8 8 8

Hamlet of Cleeve.

Taxes.		£.	s.	d.
	The Royal Aid in 1692, £.	134	15	0
	Poll-tax —— 1694,—	25	16	0
	Land-tax —— 1694,—	87	12	0
	The fame, at 3*s.* 1770,—	66	10	6

Southam.

Taxes.		£.	s.	d.
	The Royal Aid in 1692, £.	134	15	0
	Poll-tax —— 1694,—	18	18	0
	Land-tax —— 1694,—	88	12	0
	The fame, at 3*s.* 1770,—	66	9	0

Gotherington.

Taxes.		£.	s.	d.
	The Royal Aid in 1692, £.	134	15	0
	Poll-tax —— 1694,—	13	18	0
	Land-tax —— 1694,—	73	0	0
	The fame, at 3*s.* 1770,—	54	15	0

Stoke-Archer.

Taxes.		£.	s.	d.
	The Royal Aid in 1692, £.	67	9	0
	Poll-tax —— 1694,—	6	0	0
	Land-tax —— 1694,—	46	4	0
	The fame, at 3*s.* 1770,—	34	5	10 2*q*

Woodmancot.

Taxes.		£.	s.	d.
	The Royal Aid in 1692, £.	67	19	0
	Poll-tax —— 1694,—	12	8	0
	Land-tax —— 1694,—	47	7	0
	The fame, at 3*s.* 1770,—	35	4	1 2*q*

A charter was obtained 25 H. 6. to exempt this town from taxes and fifteenths for two years, on account of the great lofs which the inhabitants fuftained by fire.

According to fir Robert Atkyns, there were 175 houfes and about 875 inhabitants in this parifh, whereof 30 were freeholders; yearly births 27, burials 25. But having examined the parifh regifter, I find, that in ten years beginning with 1700, there were 314 baptifms, and 206 burials. The average annually being very different from fir Robert's numbers. And in ten years beginning with 1760, the baptifms were 306, and the burials 242. The prefent number of houfes is 295, of inhabitants 1252; fo that the proportion between

 the

the average number of annual burials, and the whole number of inhabitants is nearly as 1 to 52. Here is a burying ground belonging to the Quakers.

CLIFFORD CHAMBERS.

THIS parifh is fituated in the vale, on the fouth fide of the river Stower, on the borders of the north-eaft part of the county. It lies in the upper divifion of Tewkefbury hundred, ten miles diftant north from Campden, one fouth-weft-ward from Stratford upon Avon, in Warwickfhire, and thirty north-eaftward from Gloucefter.

The name is compounded of the Saxon word Clyf, a fteep and rocky place; and *ford* a paffage over a river; exactly defcriptive of the fituation. And as Afton Somerville, Coln Rogers, and feveral other places in this county, took the *cognomen* from their refpective proprietors; fo, by analogy, I fuppofe that Chambers was the name of fome owner of this manor, tho' not mentioned in the fubfequent records, and that it was added to diftinguifh this parifh from Rhyan Clifford, in the county of Warwick, which lies at a fmall diftance from it, on the oppofite fide of the Stower.

The parifh confifts chiefly of meadow and pafture lands, with fome arable; but produces no rare plants, foffils, nor mineral waters; nor are there any remains of antiquity within it; wherefore I proceed to give the defcent

Of the Manor and other Eftates.

Under the particulars of the manor of Tewkefbury, in *Domefday-book*, it is thus expreffed:

'Seven hides in Clifort belong to the fame 'manor. There are three plow-tillages in demean, 'and fourteen villeins with five plow-tillages, and 'a mill of 12*s.* [rent] and two acres of meadow. 'There are thirteen *fervi* and *ancillæ*, and there is 'a church, and a prieft with one plow-tillage. 'It was worth 8*l.* now 6*l.* The queen gave this 'land to Roger de Bufli, and it was taxed for four 'hides in [the manor of] Tedechefberie.' *Dom. Book*, p. 68.

In the year 1099, the above Roger de Bufli, then called Roger de Bulley, gave the manor and advowfon of Clifford to the church of St. Peter of Gloucefter, whofe grant king William the Second confirmed when Serlo was abbat.

The abbey of St. Peter at Gloucefter was feized of Clifford 17 E. 3. and continued poffeffed of it 'till the diffolution of that houfe.

What is mentioned by fir Robert Atkyns, of Gilbert de Clare being feized of this manor, 15 E. 1. muft relate only to Ailfton, a hamlet in this parifh, of which he died feized 7 E. 2. as appears by the efcheator's inquifition of the following year.

The manor of Clifford Chambers, formerly belonging to the abbey of Gloucefter, was granted to Charles Rainsford 4 Eliz. Hercules Rainsford, his fon and heir, died feized of it in 1583, and was fucceeded by his fon fir Henry Rainsford, who died feized thereof in 1622. Henry Rainsford, efq; was fon and heir of fir Henry. His eftate was fequeftered in the great civil wars, for the part he took with the king, and he compounded for 900 *l.*

The laft Henry Rainsford fold the manor &c. to Job Dighton, efq; in the year 1649. He was fucceeded by his fon Henry Dighton, efq; who died in 1686, and was fucceeded by his fon Richard Dighton. Francis-Keyt Dighton was fon and heir of Richard. His fon Lifter Dighton, efq; is the prefent lord of this manor, and has a large eftate here, with a good houfe and pleafant gardens, fituate on the river Stower. His arms are, Quarterly, 1 & 4, *Argent, a lion paffant between three croffes formy fitchy gules.* 2 & 3, *Gules, a chevron between three kites heads erazed Or*, for Keyt.

The poor of the city of Coventry have a confiderable eftate in this parifh, lying between Clifford-bridge and Stratford.

HAMLETS. There are two hamlets in this parifh.

1. *Ailfton*, or *Alefton*. Part of this hamlet lies in the parifh of Atherfton, in Warwickfhire. At prefent there is no houfe in that part which lies in Clifford. This eftate was held of Gilbert de Clare, earl of Gloucefter, at the time of his death, 7 E. 2. as appears by the efcheator's inqufition of the following year.

2. *Wincot*, fo called from Wenric, lord of it in the time of Edward the confeffor. Only part of this hamlet lies in the parifh of Clifford, and that part was antiently appurtenant to the large manor of Tewkefbury, as appears by *Domefday-book*, where, among the particulars belonging to that manor, it is thus expreffed.

'A thane held three hides in Wenecote. The 'queen gave this land to Rainald the chaplain. 'There are three villeins with half a plow-tillage. 'It was worth 40*s.*' *Domefday-book*, p. 68.

The other part of the hamlet is in the parifh of Queinton, and lay in the old hundred of Witelai, (now comprized in that of Kiftfgate) as we learn from the record: See Queinton.

Of the Church, &c.

The church is a rectory in the deanery of Campden, worth about 100*l.* a year. Lifter Dighton, efq; is patron; Mr. John Martyn the prefent incumbent. The abbey of Gloucefter were formerly patrons of this church.

The rector has the tithe of two yard-lands in that part of the hamlet of Ailfton which lies in the parifh of Atherftone, in Warwickfhire, and intirely out of the diocefe of Gloucefter.

The church is dedicated to St. Helen. It has a handfome tower, with pinnacles and battlements at the weft end.

Monuments and Inſcriptions.

On a tomb in the manor ſeat, in old character:

Here lyeth Buryed the Boddy of Hercules Rainsford Eſquier Lord of this mannor of Clifford who marryd Elizabethe Parry Daughter of Robert Parry eſquier by whome havynge Iſſue too Sonnes and on Daughter died the ſecond daye of Auguſt An° DM'. 1583. and in the yeare of his age 39.———Over it are theſe arms, *Argent, a croſs ſable*, for Rainsford; impaling, *Argent, three boars heads caboſhed ſable*, for Parry.

On a flat ſtone, at the foot of the ſteps leading to the altar, is the figure of a woman in braſs, and this inſcription:

Under this ſtone lyeth the Body of Elizabeth Daughter of Hercules Rainsford of Clifford in the County of Gloc: Eſquire, maried to Edward Marrowe Sonne and Heire of Samuell Marrowe of Barkſwell in the County of Warwick Eſq. w[h] Elizabeth deceaſed the 29 of Octob' 1601.———On another piece of braſs, a ſcutcheon, Baron and femme, 1. *Argent, a feſs engrailed ſable between three maids heads couped proper*, for Marrowe; impaling 2. Rainsford, as before.

On the north ſide of the chancel is a handſome monument, with the figures of a man and his wife kneeling, and between them this inſcription:

Sir Henry Rainsford of Clifford in the County of Gloc'. Knight (Sonne of Hercules Rainsford, Eſq;) Died the 27th of Ianuary 1622. in the yeare of his age 46: He married Ann Daughter and Co-Heire of Sr Henry Goodere of Polſworth in the County of War: Kni. wth whom he lived 27 yeares and had iſſu 3 ſons. Williã Died: Henry married Elianor Daughter and Co Heire of Robert Boſwell of Combe in ye County of Southamp' Eſq. & Francis.

Beneath the monument:

Henrico (hue charũ caput) Herculis Fi Rainsfordi Eq. Aur: hujuſq; dum vixit villæ Dno: Ingentis animi viro, nec ideo prudentis aut mitis minus. Ad honeſta quæcunq; nato, ad meliora regreſſo, fratri chariſſimo & (quod pulchrius) amico. Cum lectiſſima & luctuoſiſſima conjuge ejus eorumq; duobus filiis patrizantibus Henricus Guliel: Fi: Gooderus tanti vix damni & doloris Superſtes, dum Suis et Suorum lachrymis indulget,

Merentiſſimè
Mærentiſſimus P L
Nec minus exultat in memoria & exemplo

Tantæ { Charitatis / Induſtriæ / Pietatis } cujus Teſtis { Uxor, familia, amicorum conſenſus / Patria, patriæ Colonia Virginia / Deus.

Nec ſibi exoptat aliud Monumentum aut meliorem famam quam quod tantarum virtutum teſtis ſit
Henricus Gooderus.

There is a ſcutcheon with fifteen quarterings, the firſt is Rainsford, as before. 2 & 3, *Azure an eagle diſplay'd*. 4. *Sable, on a chief three lozenges Gules*. 5. *Argent, an eagle diſplay'd gules*. 6. *Azure, a chevron ermine between three ſtags Or*. 7. *Argent, a chief indented azure*. 8. *Per pale Or and argent, a chevron ermine*. 9. *Gules, on a chevron argent between three garbs Or, a cinquefoil of the laſt*. 10. *Azure, a chevron between three cinquefoils gules*. 11. *Argent, a chevron ingrailed between three eſcallops ſable*. 12. *Vaire, Gules and argent, on a bend ſable three boars heads couped argent*. 13. *Or, three bears heads muzzled erazed ſable*. 14. *Argent, three bendlets azure; on a canton ſable, a lion paſſant Or*. 15. *Or, three couple cloſes braced argent; on a chief gules, three plates*. Motto, TOVS IOVRS LOYALL.

Benefactions.

Hugh Caſnel, clerk, gave four tenements in Stratford in Warwickſhire, for the benefit of the poor. Thomas Jackſon of this place, gave 100*l.* to endow a free-ſchool, and 50*l.* to the poor; and his executors gave 50*l.* more, which money was laid out on a rent-charge of 10*l.* a year, on lands in Tiddington and Alveſton in Warwickſhire, 7*l.* 10*s.* of which is appropriated to the ſchool, the remainder diſtributed in bread to the poor. The church-houſe, worth 6*l.* a year, was built by the inhabitants for the uſe of the poor.

Taxes.			£.		
The Royal Aid in	1692;		141	4	0
Poll-tax	—	1694, —	26	14	0
Land-tax	—	1694, —	188	0	0
The ſame, at 3*s.*		1770, —	127	17	0

According to ſir Robert Atkyns, there were 76 houſes and about 320 inhabitants in this pariſh, whereof four were freeholders; yearly births 11, burials 9. But he was far from being accurate in the two laſt particulars; for it appears by the regiſter, that in ten years, from 1700 to 1709 both incluſive, there were only 79 baptiſms and 62 burials. In the ſame number of years, from 1760 to 1769 incluſive, the baptiſms were 70, and the burials 39. Several cottages have been taken down during the laſt century, ſo that there remain only 51 tenements; and the number of inhabitants is about 249; the proportion between the average of annual burials and the number of inhabitants being nearly as 1 to 60, which ſhews the place to be very healthy.

◇◇◇◇◇◇◇◇◇◇◇◇◇◇◇◇◇◇◇◇

CLIFTON,

ONE of the moſt agreeable villages in the kingdom, lies in the hundred of King's-Barton. It is ſituated on the ſouth and ſouth-weſt of a *cliff*, or hill, (whence its name) about thirty-ſix miles ſouthward from Glouceſter, and one mile weſtward from the city of Briſtol, over which it commands a very pleaſing proſpect.

Some of the houſes grace the ſummit of the hill, but moſt of them lie at a ſmall diſtance lower down, upon a ſlope, near the banks of the river Avon, which divides this pariſh from Somerſetſhire[r]. The well-cultivated lands in that county, riſing gradually for four or five miles from the verge of the river, to the top of Dundery-hill, preſent themſelves towards the village in a very beautiful landſkape. And what very much enriches it, is the view of the ſhips and boats continually paſſing before the eye, up and down, upon every returning tide.

A little weſtward of the houſes, nature diſplays herſelf in a bolder manner. Rocks riſe from the very edge of the water on both ſides of the river, almoſt perpendicularly, near two hundred feet high. They are, in ſome places, bare and craggy; in others, beautifully covered with ſhrubs and hanging coppice wood.

Theſe rocks extend over a large ſpace of country on each ſide of the river; and the *ſtrata* of which they are compoſed all lie in the ſame direction, dipping

[r] The following are the metes and bounds of the pariſh, deſcribed in an old book in the church. From the paſſage of Rownham, by the river Avon, to the chapel of St. Vincent, and from thence, by the river aforeſaid, to Wallcam-ſlade, and from thence to a place called the Hawthorn, and from thence to a certain ſtone called the Mere-ſtone, lying between the chapel of St. Lambert and the royal way; and from thence, by the aforeſaid way, to Smock-acre, from thence to the White-ſtile, and then to Dedyſtone-ſtile, and thence to the Lime-kilns, and then by the river Avon to the paſſage aforeſaid.

dipping towards the ſouth, making an angle of about fifteen or twenty degrees with the horizon. Thoſe on one ſide of the river ſo perfectly correſpond in every reſpect with the oppoſite, that people, in all ages, ſeem to have concurred in this general opinion, that they have ſome time or other united in the ſame body; but various are the notions concerning the cauſe of their ſeparation.

In early times, when the nature of things was leſs attended to and leſs underſtood, it was uſual to attribute ſuch events as could not otherwiſe be accounted for, to an extraordinary interpoſition of divine power, which we call miracle. This gave riſe to the following ſtory. There was a chapel on the top of theſe rocks, long ſince demoliſhed, dedicated to St. Vincent, who was a native of Spain, and ſuffered martyrdom about the year 305. And once upon a time, I know not when, but before the port of Briſtol was ſettled in the river Frome, a diſpute is ſaid to have ariſen, whether a place called Say-Mills was not a more convenient port than another which was propoſed, ſeveral large ſhips having been built in that place. One Goram, a hermit, becauſe his hermitage lay on the ſide of the brook Trim, which ran down to Say-Mills, contended for that port; but the diſpute was determined in favour of the river Frome, by St. Vincent's cleaving thoſe rocks aſunder, thereby giving paſſage to the river, in honour of the chapel that was ſo built and dedicated to him.

Some ſuppoſe the rock to have been ſplit by an earthquake; but it is oppoſed to this opinion, that then the *ſtrata* would have been diſordered by the riſing and convulſions of the earth, and not have lain, as we now ſee them, exactly in the ſame direction on both ſides of the river.

The moſt rational opinion concerning this event ſeems to be, that the deep and narrow channel, in which the Avon runs, was made at the Deluge. The impetuous torrent of waters not finding vent faſt enough, at going off, through the vale a little to the ſouth, burſt a paſſage this way, and waſhed the channel of the river when the earth was in a ſoft and yielding ſtate. And that the ſoft, ſtony matter, through which the waters then made their way, have ſince petrified into thoſe vaſt rocks, the dividing of which is otherwiſe ſo difficult to account for.

Giant's-Hole is a vaſt cavern, half way down St. Vincent's rocks, deſcribed in William of Worceſter's manuſcript, in Bennet-college library, Cambridge. It is ſuppoſed to have been an old hermitage, and originally to have communicated with the ſurface near the chapel. There is alſo a place called *Jack's-Hole*, in the ſame rocks.

The river Avon empties itſelf into the eſtuary of the Severn at Kingroad, ſeven or eight miles below Clifton. The tide riſes in it to the height of thirty feet and upwards, upon which the merchant-ſhips ride into the port of Briſtol.

There are antient fortifications and intrenchments upon Clifton-hill, where a wind-mill now ſtands; and coins of the later Roman emperors have been frequently found about the camp. Other intrenchments ſtand oppoſite to them, on the Somerſetſhire ſide of the Avon. They are all ſuppoſed to be the works of the Roman ſoldiers under Oſtorius, who cauſed fortifications to be raiſed in many places along that river, above and below Briſtol; for which reaſon, probably, the Britons gave the name of *Caer Oder*, i. e. *Caſtrum Oſtorij*, to that city.

This camp on Clifton-hill is neceſſarily of a circular form, taking the ſhape of the hill, with a double ditch, and *aggera*. The ſpot was choſen with the greateſt military judgment, being the higheſt ground about this part of the country. It ſtands on the banks of the Avon, with a *vadum* acroſs at low water, to paſs to the camp on the Somerſetſhire ſide. It ſeems to be the firſt of a chain of forts[a] conſtructed by that warlike people, to command the Severn, and the country bordering upon it; and to ſecure the paſſage over that river at Oldbury, which was undoubtedly the *Trajectus* of Antoninus.

That paſſage was of the higheſt importance to the Romans, as it preſerved a communication between their ſtations at *Iſca*, *Venta Silurum*, and *Abone*, on the north ſide of that river, and *Aqua Solis* and other ſtations, on the ſouth ſide of it.

Tho' it was a long march from *Aqua Solis*, or Bath, to that paſſage, the camps on Sodbury-hill and Horton-hill, about the mid-way, were thought ſufficient to protect that road; but ſo great was their attention to ſecure the *Trajectus*, that, in a ſhorter diſtance of ground, they conſtructed no leſs than ſeven camps of obſervation in the line from Clifton to Oldbury. Two of them are about four miles diſtant each from Clifton, one a little to the right, on Bury-hill, in the pariſh of Winterbourn; the other to the left, on Blaiſe-hill, in the pariſh of Henbury; and a little further, on Comb-hill and King's-Weſton-hill, are two others, which ſurvey the Severn. From Blaiſe-hill to the camp at Almondſbury is about five miles, and from thence to another called Old-Abbey, at Alveſton, four miles; which latter is about the ſame diſtance from the *Trajectus* at Oldbury.

Their great care to ſecure the paſſage at the *Trajectus*, from the country of the *Silures*, on the other ſide of the Severn, is no leſs apparent. For, from the *Abone*, which I would fix at Aylberton, in the pariſh of Lidney, is a deep intrenchment and *agger*, all the way down to the river, almoſt oppoſite to the *Trajectus*.

All theſe camps are ſituated upon high ground, that one might look upon the others, and be ſeen by them; and that the ſoldiers might the better deſcry the enemy, and being within ſight, might alarm their diſtant friends of approaching danger.

[a] Mr. Barrett of Briſtol, a perſon of great learning and judgment, who is writing the Hiſtory and Antiquities of that city, favoured me with an account of theſe camps, having particularly traced and examined them himſelf.

And

And ſo extenſive and beautiful is the proſpect from the camp at Clifton particularly, that it is the reſort of the gentry at the Hot Wells and Clifton every fine day.

Before I quit this ſubject, I muſt obſerve, that beſide the camps on Sodbury and Horton hills, ſuppoſed for the purpoſe of protecting the road from *Aqua Solis* to the *Trajectus*, there were two poſts occupied by the Romans on the ſides of that road; one at Wick, about eight miles from Bath, the other at Cromhall, about ſeven miles from Oldbury. That they were Roman works, will appear from the circumſtanees related under the reſpective places.

The excellent proſpects from various parts of Clifton, and the fine air, have induced many gentlemen to build and reſide there.

Matthew Brickdale, ſometime a repreſentative in parliament for the city of Briſtol, Samuel Worrall, Iſaac Elton, John Freeman, Henry Hobhouſe, —— Hibbs, and John Vaughan, eſq[rs]. have very handſome modern houſes, with freeſtone fronts and proper offices, upon Clifton-hill. Mr. Goldney has a handſome houſe here, with fine gardens, a grotto of ſhell-work, and a canal with fountains, ſupply'd with water by a fire-engine.

Sir William Draper has alſo a very handſome ſeat upon the hill. As you face the front, there ſtands at a diſtance before it, on the right hand, a free-ſtone obeliſk, with this inſcription on the baſe:

GVLIELMO PITT, COMITI DE CHATHAM,
Hoc Amicitiæ privatæ Teſtimonium,
Simul et Honoris publici Monumentum,
Poſuit Gulielmus Draper.

On the left, to anſwer the obeliſk, is a Cenotaph, conſiſting of a raiſed tomb, ſupporting a large vaſe, with an urn at top, well executed in freeſtone. Engraven on the ſide of the vaſe, are the following elegant verſes:

SISTE GRADUM, SI QUA EST *BRITONUM* TIBI CURA, VIATOR,
SISTE GRADUM; VACUO RECOLAS INSCRIPTA SEPULCHRO
TRISTIA FATA VIRUM, QUOS BELLICUS ARDOR *EÖUM*
PROH DOLOR! HAUD UNQUAM REDITUROS, MISIT AD ORBEM:
NEC TIBI SIT LUGERE PUDOR, SI FORTE TUORUM
NOMINA NOTA LEGAS, SED CUM TERRAQUE MARIQUE
INVICTOS HEROUM ANIMOS, ET FACTA REVOLVES,
SI PATRIÆ TE TANGIT AMOR, SI FAMA *BRITANNUM*,
PARCE TRIUMPHALES LACHRIMIS ASPERGERE LAUROS.
QUIN SI *ASIÆ* PENETRARE SINUS, ATQUE ULTIMA *GANGIS*
PANDERE CLAUSTRA PARES, *INDOSQUE* LACESSERE BELLO,
EX HIS VIRTUTEM DISCAS, VERUMQUE LABOREM;
FORTUNAM EX ALIIS. ————

And beneath, on a table,

S A C R E D
To the Memory of thoſe departed Warriors
of the ſeventy ninth Regiment,
By whoſe Valour, Diſcipline, and Perſeverance,
The French Land Forces in Aſia
were firſt withſtood and repulſed;
The Commerce of Great Britain preſerved;
Her Settlements reſcued from impending Deſtruction.
The memorable Defence of M A D R A S S,
The deciſive Battle of W A N D E W A S H,
Twelve ſtrong and important Fortreſſes,
Three ſuperb Capitals,
A R C O T, P O N D I C H E R R Y, M A N I L L A,
And the P H I L I P P I N E I S L A N D S,
Are laſting Monuments of their Military Glory.
Their generous Treatment
of a vanquiſhed Enemy
Exhibits an illuſtrious Example
of true Fortitude and Moderation,
worthy of being tranſmitted
To lateſt Poſterity;
That future Generations may know
H U M A N I T Y is the Characteriſtic
of B R I T I S H C O N Q U E R O R S.

The ſides of the table are inſcribed with the names of the officers of the ſeventy-ninth regiment who fell in Aſia:

Field Officers; *C. Brereton, I. Moore.* — Captains; *Knuttall, Stewart, Wingfield, Delaval, Chiſholm, Cheſhyre, Upfield, Strahan, Muir, Moore.* —— Lieutenants; *Whaley, G. Browne, Hopkins, Robinſon, T. Browne, Le Grand, Winchelſea, Roſton, Campbell, Fryer, Turner, Richbell, Bouchier, Buſteed, Hardwick.* — Enſigns; *Collins, Vaſiette, La Tour, Horler, Mac Mahon.* —— Surgeons; *Smith, Atherton.*

At the ends of the tomb, in ſmall oval tables, it is thus written:

Siege of Madraſs raiſed, Feb. 17, 1759.
Conjeveram taken by Storm, April 13, 1759.
Battle of Wandewaſh gained, Jan. 22, 1760.
Arcot recovered, Feb. 10, 1760.
Carical taken, April 5, 1760.
The Lines of Pondicherry ſtormed, Sept. 10, 1760.
Pondicherry ſurrendered, Jan. 16, 1761.
Manilla taken by Storm, Oct. 6. 1762.

Every attempt to perpetuate the memory of heroes who have nobly fallen in the ſervice of their country, muſt be highly grateful to the lovers of it. It is the only tribute we can pay to their merit. It is a grateful acknowledgment to thoſe who were engaged in the ſame glorious, but hazardous enterprizes, and more fortunately ſurvived them. I have, therefore, furthered the deſign ſo worthily conceived by ſir William Draper; and am perſuaded, that this page of my book will be read with pleaſure, when other parts of it lie neglected.

From the bottom of theſe famous rocks of St. Vincent, iſſues the Briſtol Hot-well water, deſervedly eſteemed for its efficacy in a variety of diſorders. The ſpring is very plentiful. It is the property of the ſociety of merchants of Briſtol. It riſes near the bed of the Avon, the ſalt water of which uſually breaks in upon it at very high ſpring-tides; and therefore, they are then obliged to leave off pumping, a few hours in the day.

Various experiments have been made upon this water, to diſcover its diſtinguiſhing properties. The heat of a cold ſpring in that neighbourhood is fifty degrees in Fahrenheit's thermometer; that of the new warm well of the merchants near Briſtol, ſixty-eight degrees; Mallow-water in Ireland, ſixty-eight degrees; the water of this well at Clifton, ſeventy-ſix; warm milk from the cow, eighty-nine; the Hot-bath at Bath, 114; the Croſs-bath there, 107 degrees. By the niceſt experiments, the heat of the Clifton Hot-well water is ſcarcely ever found to vary. the taſte of it, at the ſpring, is particularly ſoft and milky,

 and

and very grateful to the ftomach; yet it leaves a fort of ftypticity, or drynefs, upon the palate. It curdles with foap; with oil of tartar, it gives a bluifh white cloud, and white fediment; fpirit of fal-ammoniac whitens it; galls do not turn it purple, but it turns green with fyrup of violets; and makes a confiderable ebullition with acids.

The fire feparates from it a white matter on the fides of the veffels, and a chalky fcum. Dr. Shebeare got fifty-fix grains from a gallon, by a gentle fand-heat. The tafte of the fediment is brackifh, bitter in the throat, and makes an ebullition with acids. The falt feparated from the terreftrial matter is white, confifting, according to the doctor, of octagonal cryftals, interfperfed with cubical ones; but the nitrous feem to preponderate. Diluted with oil of vitriol, it gives a genuine fpirit of falt; and all appearances fhew, that it is of the neutral kind, confifting of marine falt and calcarious nitre. The earth feparated from the falt, and dried, ferments with acids, and by calcination becomes lime. The proportion of earth to the falt, in one experiment, was as 15 to 11; in another, as 13 to 11; thus the calcarious matter exceeding the faline, the water is rather fweetening and aftringent, than purgative; as, on the contrary, where the falts predominate, as in Cheltenham and other waters, thefe prove purgative. It has this peculiar property, that it keeps good for many years, having been carried feveral voyages to Guinea, and has yet been fweet and good.

It differs greatly from the Bath water, being lighter, has no ferruginous parts, lefs marine falt, and the heat of it is not fo great. The Bath water is powerfully attenuant and laxative, corroborating and heating; whereas this is incraffating, aftringent, cooling, and fuccefsfully prefcribed in inflammations, hectics, coughs, hemorrhages, hemoptoe, dyfentery, immoderate fluxes, and the fcurvy with heat. It was firft ufed for external ulcers, and many of the fcrophulous and cancerous kinds have been very unexpectedly cured by daily wafhing and fomenting the part with it, and at the fame time drinking the water.

Internally, it ftrengthens the ftomach, promotes appetite, affifts digeftion, corrects acrimony, and immoderate fecretions and difcharges. Randolph attributes its virtues to a mineral air impregnating the water, and obferves, that it cures a diabetes fometimes in three weeks, fometimes not in as many months; and yet, by care and perfeverance, makes a perfect cure at laft. It cures a hectic fever, ftops the fpitting of blood, and is of great fervice in obftinate coughs and obftructions in the lungs; fo that a great part of thofe whom confumptions have carried off, might probably have been faved by it, had they applied in time.

Some perfons are of opinion, that the true fource of the virtues of this water is the great rocks of lime-ftone through which it runs; and endeavour to fhew, that lime-water gives the virtues to common water which this water poffeffes. Without difputing the fact, it muft be acknowledged, that this is not a very philofophic way of reafoning; however, the doctors Keir and Rutty are of that opinion; to whom, and to the other writers on this fubject, I refer the reader for further fatisfaction.

The houfe at the wells was built by fubfcription. The feafon is from May to September. There is mufic in the rooms, and public breakfafting, affemblies, and other amufements ufual at fuch places.

The beauties of nature on the banks of the Avon invite to the healthy exercife of walking; and the numbers of fhips and veffels continually paffing in view, to and from the port of Briftol, with every tide, awaken the fancy to a train of agreeable ideas, various as the objects from which they arife.

For thofe who cannot walk, or who prefer riding, there is the fineft opportunity in the world. The downs are near and fpacious, with delightful profpects; and the air is fo excellent, that Clifton is efteemed the *Montpelier of England.*

The fituation of Clifton is peculiarly advantageous for excurfions of another nature. Parties are frequently going in pleafure-boats, attended with mufic, down the river to Kingroad. For the firft two miles the Avon runs in a very deep channel, between rough and craggy rocks, romantic beyond defcription. The cliffs project in a manner aftonifhing, and many of them, covered with fhrubs, tufts of grafs, tall plants, and little trees, have the appearance of hanging woods, fcarcely any where to be equalled; and the winding of the river between them beautifuly diverfifies the fcene.

Clifton, however, with all its advantages, cannot boaft of fertility of foil. The herbage is fhort and poor, and the rocks on Durdham-down, near it, in many places appear above the furface of the ground. The ftone of thefe rocks is very heavy and compact, harder than moft marbles, of which it is a fpecies, and bears a good polifh. It is full of fhining particles, when broken; and not only the rock, but the earth itfelf about Clifton and Durdham-downs, is much intermixt with mundic and metallic fubftances.

The ftone, in this part of the country, is rich in iron ore, which when broken from it, is of various colours, redifh, crimfon, brown, and yellow; fome like fpar, only heavier and tranfparent; others like emery, and there is a fort in pieces, beautifully ftreaked, and rifing in the appearance of little bubbles, which the druggifts call the blood-ftone.

In the fields near Clifton is a kind of hollow ftone, the cavities of which contain fpar and cryftal, in clufters of various forms. The common people confound thefe fubftances by the general name of cryftal; but they are neverthelefs of diftinct kinds, and different in themfelves. The latter is clear and bright, cuts glafs, and fuffers no change in the fire, except it be very violent; whereas fpar breaks,

breaks, when tryed on glafs, and put into the fire, prefently calcines to lime; *aqua fortis* alfo corrodes it, but takes no effect on cryftal. The fhoots of fpar are triangular, or pentangular; but thofe of cryftal are hexagonal, and terminate in a point.

This cryftal is the true Briftol-ftone, held by lapidaries in good eftimation, before the invention of pafte, and is found in great plenty in this neighbourhood. The cryftals about Clifton refemble table-diamonds, and fome of them rofe-diamonds; and the largeft, when feparated, are about the fize of a hazle-nut. Moft commonly, the fhoots of the pureft fort grow upon a thin coat of redifh ferruginous matter, which fpreads itfelf over a kind of cruft or bed of fouler cryftal, about half an inch thick, of the appearance of allum. They are of every tincture between a vivid red and a ftate perfectly colourlefs. There are alfo various fhades of yellow, and of brown, down to almoft black, which are very brilliant, and of a hardnefs exceeding all the reft.

In the fame rocks are veins of lead-ore, intermixed with a brown ftone, of the nature of calamine, which is not uncommon in thefe parts. And there are feveral forts of ochre of different fhades, from a deep red to a light lemon-colour, but they are never found except about the lumps of iron-ore, from which they originate.

Cryftals, like other ftones, are undoubtedly generated by the agency of water; and in this part of the country, it muft of neceffity be from rain; as there is no fpring near the places where they are found. In many parts, the furface of the ground is fo firm and compact, that water does not eafily penetrate. Now if cryftals were found in quantities under fuch places, it would deftroy this hypothefis; but the cafe is otherwife, for very few if any are found in fuch places. In other parts, the earth and materials under the furface of it are loofe and fpungy, and on breaking them away, a great number of exceeding fmall tracks and channels may be perceived, through which the water makes its way from the furface. In following thefe, there are always found vaft quantities of cryftals, in the cracks and cavities of the iron-ore which lies underneath. And as this is the cafe without exception, can there be any doubt of the cryftals originating from water? The different colours of them are owing to the materials through which the water paffes before petrification; for invariably, where it is ftrained through the red ochre found among the iron-ore, they are ftrongly tinged with that colour; if through yellow ochre, they are yellow; but if it paffes through earth, fand, or other matter that gives no colour to water, then the cryftal is colourlefs.

Mr. Owen has publifhed obfervations refpecting the natural hiftory of the country about Briftol, in which he attempts to fhew that it is particularly difpofed to petrifaction; and that even the ftone-duft on Clifton-hill, moiftened by rain, cements into a body of ftone again. But he was deceived in fancying that the incruftations which he had obferved on fome ftones lying on the fides of the road, were formed as above; when it is certain, that thofe ftones were taken out of the pit with the incruftations upon them.

Clifton is alfo famous for its vegetable productions. The following is a catalogue of rare plants found in this parifh.

Afplenium [Linnei] *five Ceterach.* Spleenwort, or Miltwaft. Gerhard's Herbal, p. 978.—Parkinfon's *Theatrum*, p. 1046.—Ray, p. 118.

Afparagus Paluftris, [*Officinalis,* Linn.] Marfh Afparagus, flowering in autumn. Park. 454.—Gerh. p. 947.—Ray, p. 267. Below Cook's-folly, in the meadows.

Cardamine pumila, Bellidis folio. Tower Muftard, with daify leaves. Ray, p. 294.—Parkhurft, p. 834. Daify-leaved Lady's-Smock. Parkh. p. 828, fig. 6.—Hill's Herbal, p. 247.—Ray, p. 300. Flowering in May. On the wall behind the old Hot-well houfe, and on St. Vincent's rocks.

Cardamine impatiens. The leffer, hairy, impatient Lady's Smock. Flowering in April.—Hill, p. 247.—Ray, p. 299. In moift places.

Carduus tomentofus Anglicus. Englifh woolly-feeded Thiftle; flowering in July. Parkh. 978. In barren fields.

Campanula rotundioribus imis foliis Alpina. The leffer Mountain Bell-flower, with the lower leaves round; flowering in July and Auguft. Ray, p. 277. On Durdham-down.

Cochlearia maritima. [*Cochlearia Anglica,* Linn.] Sea Scurvy Grafs. Along the banks of the Avon, from Briftol to St. Vincent's rocks, and beyond.

Fœniculum. Under Giant's-hole in St. Vincent's rocks, by the water fide.

Geranium hæmatodes, Linn. The bloody Cranefbill; flowering from May to July. Park. Parad. 229.—Ray, 360. On St. Vincent's rocks.

Glaux maritima minor. Sea Milkwort, or Black Saltwort; flowering and feeding at the end of fummer. Park. 1283.—Ray's *Indiculus.* Meadow by Wapping. Rope-walk next the water.

Gramen Caninum nodofum duobus nodis, majori femper fuperimpofito minori. Below Briftol, in the meadows on the north of the river by the ferry. Ray's *Ind.* Dubious.

Hyacinthus autumnalis minor. [*Scilla autumnalis,* Linn.] The leffer autumnal Star Hyacinth; flowering in the beginning of September, before the leaves appear. Park. Parad. 132,—Ray, 373. On the very brow of St. Vincent's rocks, near the lime-kiln.

Hypericum elegantiffimum non ramofum, folio lato. Elegant imperforate St. John's Wort; flowering in July and Auguft. Park. 576, fig. 2.—Ray, p. 243. On St. Vincent's rocks, below the turnpike.

Hemionitis minor. The leffer Mule's Fern. Park. 1047. In a cave on St. Vincent's rocks. This plant, after having been kept in a pot two years, changed its form into a jagged Hartfhorn.

Hippofelinum,

Hipposelinum, seu Smyrnium vulgare. Common Alexanders. In May. Park. 930. St. Vincent's rocks, near Giant's-hole.

Laver. At low-water mark, on the south side of the Hot-well house.

Nasturtium sylvestre Osyridis folio. [Quere, if not *Lepidium ruderale*, Linn.] Narrow-leaved wild Cresse. Park. 829. Flowering in June. Ray, p. 303. In the rope-walk, near Lime-kiln-lane, glass-house.

Nasturtiolum montanum annuum, tenuissime divisum. [*Lepidum petreum*, Linn.] Finely cut annual Mountain Cresse. On St. Vincent's rocks, in the road to Giant's-hole; flowering in the beginning of April, and somewhat later on the northern part of the rocks. Ray 304.

Orchis. [*Ophris muscifera*, Linn.] Fly Orchis. About fifty yards below the new Hot-well house, near the water side, and half way up the hill; flowering in the middle of May.

Orchis apifera. [*Ophris Myodes apifera*, Linn.] The Bee Orchis. In the road from the back door of the old Hot-well, up the rocks to Clifton, in great plenty, flowering about the middle of June. There are also some on the hill at the back side of the new Hot-well. They may be taken up and transplanted for gardens about November, when their first leaves appear.

Orchis spiralis alba odorata. Tripple Lady's Traces. Ray's *Synopsis*, p. 378. Lesser sweet Ladies Traces. Park. 1354. On St. Vincent's rocks.

Peucedanum minus. [*Sesebi pumilum*, Linn.] Rock Parsley, or Sow Fennel; flowering and feeding in July and August. Park. 880. — Ray, p. 217. On St. Vincent's rocks; just above the Hot-well house; and on the edges of the cliffs, about twenty yards below the weather-cock pole.

Potentella verna, [Linn.] Cinquefoil. Ray. St. Vincent's rocks, near the weather-cock pole.

Ruta muraria. Wall Rue. On all the walls about Bristol.

Rubea sylvestris aspera. [*Rubea Anglica*, Linn.] Wild rough Madder; flowering in July. Park. 274. On St. Vincent's rocks.

Sedum minus è rupe S. Vincentii. [*Sedum rupertre*, Linn.] Small Sengreen, or Stone Crop of St. Vincent's rock; flowering in June. Ray, 270, On the north side of St. Vincent's rocks, and in the road to Giant's-hole.

Sedum minus, circinato folio. Small white flowered Stone Crop. Ray, p. 271. On the walls about Clifton; flowering in July.

Sisimbrium murale, [Linn.] Barreliensis, p. 421, tab. 131. St. Vincent's rocks; about the distance of two stones-cast from the new Hot-well house, on the rocks between the foot path and high water mark. Flowering in June.

Tragopogon purpureo cæruleum porrifolio. Ray, p. 172. In the meadows beyond St. Vincent's rocks, under Cook's-folly.

Trifolium maritimum, [Linn.] *Anonis procumbens maritim.* Ray, p. 332. Rest Harrow. With the above.

Veronica spicata minor. Small spiked Speedwell. In October and November. On the north brow of St. Vincent's rocks; and in the road to Giant's-hole and Jack's-hole, at the end of the down.

Vicia minima præcox Parisiensium. In the spring or May. On St. Vincent's rocks.

Mr. Henry Jones, author of Kew-Gardens, &c. about the year 1767, celebrated this village in a poem of two cantos, intitled CLIFTON [1]. In the second canto, he pays his devoirs to King's-Weston, Stoke-Giffard, and other neighbouring villas.

Of

[1] This poem has a considerable degree of merit, tho' in some parts a little obscure. Such of my readers who have not seen it, may be pleased with the following extract from it.

CLIFTON, rich source of *Heliconian* stream!
Thou teeming topic! and thou lofty theme!
Where art, where nature leads the soul along,
And taste and commerce crown the copious song;
Where vast variety the heart expands,
And giving grandeur opens wide her hands;
With nature's noblest gifts regales the soul,
Each part a paradise—a heaven the whole!
Where health, where vigour quaffs the winnow'd air,
And drives far off the ugly fiend, *Despair*.
My muse, O CLIFTON! would thy summits climb,
And hand thy beauties down to latest time;
To ages yet unborn thy charms display,
In numbers lasting as the lamp of day;
Would *Inspiration* prompt my proud desire,
The song and subject should at once expire.
How epic wonders here the soul delight!
There, distant beauties strain th' impassion'd sight;
See rocks coeval with the world arise,
Whose cloud-swept groves seem waving in the skies;
By ages furrow'd deep, with time plow'd mein,
With adverse frowns, with fractur'd foreheads seen,
Whilst *Neptune* rolls his rapid tides between.
See *Wealth* quick flying in the freighted gale,
See East, see West expand th' impatient sail;
Here earth, here ocean, mountains, rocks unite
And in harmonious discord give delight;
There, princely piles in classic taste exprefs'd
In *Grecian* garb, in *Roman* grandeur dress'd,
A line of palaces o'erlook the town,
That with a jealous pride the prospect crown:
On different heights they stand in stately strife,
Like rank and dignity in moral life:
In various climax court th' attracted eyes,
The objects changing as the structures rise:
From pile to pile a prospect new appears,
And now the hills, and now the river cheers.
See num'rous ships with sudden glance shoot by,
The sails and streamers only strike the eye:
Between th' embracing banks, for ever green,
They seem to move on land, their bulk unseen;
By glad propitious gales impatient blown,
With rapid speed and motion not their own.
See next a * steeple on yon hill appear,
Yon distant hill, the *Proteus* of the year;
From whose oft-changing look, the watchful swain,
Foretells the weather, and avoids the rain.
The blue ætherial hills see last uprise,
In azure robe to meet the bending skies.
Here pendent gardens with rich fruits appear,
The rip'ning bounty of the lavish year.
The temple rais'd above the group see sway,
And all th' extended various views survey.
Divine ambition in the choice is found,
Nay taste itself mark'd out the sacred ground;
With holy pride the lofty seat to shew,
And reign exulting o'er the world below;
Where some on others look with scornful phlegm,
Whilst others look with equal scorn on them;
With mole-hill malice dash the cup of life,
An inch in difference makes the mountain strife:

* The steeple on *Dundry-hill*.

Of the Manors and other Eſtates.

It appears by *Domeſday-book*, that Clifton was part of the antient demeans of the crown, and a member of the manor of Weſtberie, (as it was then written) in which the king had thirty hides of land; and that it continued a member of that manor during the firſt four years of the Conqueror's reign. But afterwards, according to the record, ſix hides in Chire, ten in Cliftone, eight in Noent and Chingeſtune, and one in Ladenent, were taken from the manor of Weſtberie, and held by three proprietors; namely, the abbey of

From proud compariſon we quaff our all,
That ſource of human ſweets, or human gall:
At which the reſtleſs ſoul impatient pants,
Begets her anguiſh, and creates her wants.
Oh frantic fallacy! oh brain-ſick need!
Shall thy ſleek beaver make my boſom bleed?
Thy better buckled belt make me repine,
Or if thy nails be cloſer cut than mine?
Shall I my lips with inward anguiſh bite,
If thy black kitten's tail be tipt with white?
Or if thy leeks than mine ſhould greener grow,
And make thy fancied bliſs, my REAL woe?
Envy in courts and cottages will dwell,
Nay climb to heaven itſelf, tho' born in hell:
In every living boſom lurks this peſt,
But reigns unrival'd in the human breaſt;
On reaſon's throne uſurps a thorny part,
And plants a thouſand daggers in the heart.

THE moral here and natural world we ſee,
In wiſe gradation, and in juſt degree:
Where all conſtructed for one ſyſtem's ſake,
A happy, heterogeneous proſpect make:
Where reaſon's ſcale from claſs to claſs can fall,
And meaſure equal bounty dealt to all;
Each lot can juſtly prize, in fortune's wheel,
But not from what we have, but what we feel.

FROM moral ſtrains, let my glad numbers ſoar,
And yon coincidence with ſpeed explore:
Where ſtrong extremes produce a ſtriking taſte,
A *Gothic* building by a *Greek* embrac'd:
In contraſt kind, the feaſted eye to fill,
And mark the ſummit of the ſocial hill:
Where *Goldney* acts the meek, the moral part,
And daily works new miracles of art.
Where he like *Moſes* makes the water flow,
His gold the rock obeys, but not his blow:
His gold, that conquers nature's hardeſt laws,
And fountains from the rocky centre draws:
His well-ſpent gold a two-fold tranſport gives,
The garden gladdens, and the labourer lives.
Such toils refreſh at once the heart and head,
Give taſte a banquet, and the ruſtic bread:
Make nature wonder at her thin-wove maſk,
And truth ſurvey her own tranſparent taſk.
The maſter's pleaſure with th' improvement grows,
In all the rapture, that a parent knows:
When wiſe diſcretion weighs th' unerring coin,
And makes his pleaſure with his prudence join.
Then ſweet ambition bids the heart begin,
For genius feels a paradiſe within:
And tho' at firſt her taſk may ſeem too hard,
Th' accompliſh'd wonder is its own reward.
Then fancy triumphs, when by judgment led,
And wears the well-earn'd wreath around her head:
Without a bluſh her own bright work ſurveys,
Improves the rapture, and enjoys the praiſe:
A new creation lifts th' admiring lid,
Here nature looks abroad, here art lies hid:
O'er the grand form her mantle meek ſhe flings,
But ornaments are arbitrary things:
Yet even there ſhould fancy never ſtray
From nature's path, or ſeek a wiſer way;
Art is but nature in her beſt array.
With ſimple elegance ſhe ſmiling ſtands,
In blameleſs garb, put on by *Goldney's* hands.
Him genius taught the taſteful eye to cheer,
With ſober judgment whiſpering in his ear:
As wiſe diſcretion rules the realms of wit,
The happy medium here, he happy hit;
Where each bright incident performs its part,
With inward rapture melts the maſter's heart;
And each congenial gueſt with joy invades
The fountains, grottos, and the clear caſcades;
The tall parterres that lift the comely face,
And yield at once ſuch majeſty and grace,
With ev'ry growing beauty in its place.
A minor *Stow* on *Clifton's* crown we find,
In *Epic* meekneſs, like its maſter's mind.

HERE buildings boaſt a robe, tho' rich yet chaſte,
The robe of judgment, and of ripen'd taſte:
Convenience here is mix'd with manly grace,
Yet ornament but holds the ſecond place.
To human frames theſe ſtructures ſeem akin,
With aſpect fair, while reaſon rules within.
Theſe domes diſcretion decks, and fancy cheers,
Palladio's ſtile in *Patty's* plans appears:
Himſelf a maſter with the firſt to ſtand,
For *Clifton* owes her beauties to his hand.

HENCE to the vale, by mountain rocks ſecur'd,
By nature's own immortal hand immur'd,
The vale, where ſkreen'd *Avona* ſinks and ſwells,
That warping leads me to the hallow'd *Wells*,
I wander joyful, with unbounded glee,
From all I raptur'd hear, and raptur'd ſee:
To where ſweet health her far-ſought balm beſtows,
And beauty with re-kindled fervor glows.
Above this fountain of ſupreme delight,
Two ponderous rocks ſurpriſe and pleaſe the ſight:
With bending brows of nearer terms they treat,
Thro' countleſs ages eſſay'd oft to meet;
With grey addreſs the tedious courtſhip con,
And wiſh the aerial arch would make them one.
The nuptial bridge* ſublime their brows would join,
Whilſt *Europe* wonder'd at the work divine.
Blenheim ſhould bluſh, tho' high her concave ſwells,
Nay *Venice* veil her bonnet to the *Wells*:
Her proud *Rialto* ſhould no more appear,
But *France* and *Italy* come crowding here;
Can then ambition ſleep when GLORY calls,
The MUSE herſelf ſhall help to raiſe the walls;
With *Orphean* ſounds the work divine advance,
And make the willing ſtones in order dance;
Expand the joy-touch'd heart, enlarge the mind,
And *Lacy* leave one wonder more behind:
The groves on high their frequent nod beſtow,
And earth and water give conſent below;
Whilſt ART ſtands ready with impatient hands,
But gold, demurring gold forbids the bans:
That ſcrupulous wight, whom lock'd-up ſouls adore,
He liſtens not alas! to am'rous lore,
Who many a noble match hath marr'd before.

THE walks ſee full, ſee health diſcloſe her hive,
Whilſt all the neighbouring objects ſeem alive;
See bounty there her healing ſtore unlocks,
Breathes all her vital veins, her genial rocks,
Diſtill'd by nature in her richeſt cell,
Where health ſits brooding, and her offspring dwell;
With heaven in council deep, for mortal weal,
Where angels blend the balm, and bid it heal;
There love and beauty revel in the tide,
There grace and vigour wanton at their ſide;
That with more luſtre make glad beauty glow,
Than all the diamonds orient realms beſtow;
The cheek to vermil, and relume the eye,
And make diſeaſe, that pallid fantom, fly
From all its windings in the nerves and limbs,
When thro' the laxed tubes he lazy ſwims,
The ſizy, creeping, tardy, torpid flood,
That long in heſitating lakes hath ſtood,
With loaded bane to blaſt the balmy blood,
With pining atrophy, and ſpitting gore,
And all the waſtings of the vital ſtore;
With diabetes and its irkſome train,
And life-conſuming dews, and mental pain.
Here health expels diſeaſe, that deep-hid mole,
Winds up the body, and lets looſe the ſoul,
Calls virtue home, with health, in exile ſtill,
Revives th' affections, and awakes the will,
Bids love and friendſhip in the boſom play,
And drives each dark diſſocial cloud away. &c. &c.

* *James Lacy*, eſq; the deſigner of *Ranelagh-houſe*, was conſulted on the project of building a bridge of one arch from rock to rock, over the river *Avon*. A gentleman, whoſe name I have forgot, bequeathed 1000*l.* towards this work; which, had it been perfected, would have been the nobleſt bridge of one arch in the world.

Cormeile, Oſborne, and William the ſon of Richard. This is not a literal tranſlation of the paſſage in *Domeſday-book*, but will be found to agree with it in ſubſtance. *See* p. 67.

Theſe three were originally joint proprietors of thoſe eſtates, which were ſome time afterwards divided. The abbey of Cormeile was an alien priory; and as ſuch, all the lands belonging to it, in England, were veſted in the crown by act of parliament 2 H. 5.

The ſhares of the other proprietors ſeem to have deſcended diſtinctly by the general name of Clifton, according to the records of the following dates; which records ſhew, that Lettice the daughter of Nicholas purchaſed Clifton of Joan her ſiſter, who was married to Nicholas de la Hay, 8 Joh.

Richard de Clare, earl of Glouceſter and Hertford, was ſeized of Clifton 47 H. 3. John de St. Lando held Clifton, with free warren, 20 E. 3. Sir Edward le Diſpencer and Elizabeth his wife, daughter and heir of Bartholomew Burghurſt, were ſeized of the manor of Clifton 49 E. 3. in which year he died.

Sir John Chidiock held this manor 14 R. 2. John Rache and Joan his wife levied a fine of the third part of the manor and advowſon of Clifton to ſir John Moigne 15 R. 2. Sir John Botreaux and Elizabeth his wife were ſeized of the manor of Clifton, held of the honour of Glouceſter, 18 R. 2. Richard Seimour held this manor 2 H. 4. John Rache was ſeized of the ſame 11 H. 4. probably the ſame third part of which John Rache and Joan his wife levied a fine to ſir John Moigne, as above.

Richard de Beauchamp and Iſabel his wife held the manor of Clifton 2 H. 5. Sir John Chidiock was ſeized thereof 3 H. 5. Nicholas Seimour held this manor 2 H. 6. Elianor the widow of ſir John Chidiock, or Chadock, was ſeized of the manor of Clifton 12 H. 6. John lord Zouch was alſo ſeized of this manor, and being attainted 1 H. 7. his eſtate was forfeited, and this manor was granted the ſame year to ſir William Willoughby and his heirs male.

All the property which the crown had in the manor of Clifton, formerly belonging to the abbey of Cormeile, was granted to ſir Rafe Sadleir 35 H. 8. And, according to ſir Robert Atkyns, Ralph Sadler, eſq; was lord of the manor in the year 1608.

It is morally impoſſible that the whole manor ſhould change maſters ſo often as mentioned by the records of the foregoing dates; or that there ſhould be ſo many diſtinct manors in this pariſh, as there are different owners in and about the ſame age; wherefore, to obviate every difficulty, and to account for the confuſion in the deſcent of the manor, I ſuppoſe it to have been divided and ſubdivided, perhaps by the marriage of coheireſſes; and the parts to have been often ſold, or demiſed for terms of ſhort duration; and that each paſſed by the general name of *the manor of Clifton*; of which ſimilar inſtances are not wanting in other places.

The merchants adventurers of the city of Briſtol are owners of one part of this manor; the other, which antiently belonged to ſir Rafe Sadleir, is the property of Mr. Ruſs, and Mrs. Adams's family of Briſtol.

Of the Church, &c.

The church is an impropriation, in the deanery of Briſtol. It has been augmented with queen Anne's bounty, ſo that the preſent real value is about 100*l.* a year. Mr. John Taylor is patron and incumbent. The miniſter has no tithes. His income ariſes chiefly from the voluntary contribution of the pariſhioners. There is a chapel alſo in the pariſh, but no proviſion for repairing the building; nor endowment for the miniſter, beſide the voluntary contributions of the company reſorting to the Hot-wells, amounting uſually to about ſixty guineas.

The impropriation of Clifton was given, by John Carpenter, biſhop of Worceſter, to the college of Weſtbury upon Trim. It was lately veſted in Mr. Hodges, and is now the property of his daughter, Mrs. Hamly.

The church has a new building added to it, and is handſomely pewed.

Procurations £. 0	0	8	Pentecoſt. 0	0	6 *ob.*
Synodals	0	1	0		

Monuments and Inſcriptions.

Againſt the north wall of the chancel is a ſmall marble monument, with this inſcription:

Hic Sepultus jacet JOHANNES HAMILTON Vicecomitis de BINNING filius, Comitis de HADINTON nepos, Matrem habuit RACHAELEM, GEORGIJ BAILLIE de JERVISWOOD, Armigeri, Filiam ſecundam. Puer optimæ ſpei, et miro ſupra Annos ingenio prædītus, Deliciæ Parentum, Propinquorum, Omnium. Haud Formam præſtantiorem Terra tulit: Haud cœlum excepit pulchriorem animam. Obijt anno ætatis IV: Æræ Chriſtianæ MDCCXXX.—— Arms, *Quarterly*, 1ſt & 4th, *Gules, on a chevron between three cinquefoils argent, a buckle between two roundlets azure, all within a bordure Or charged with eight thiſtles proper.* 2d & 3d, *Argent, a feſs undy between three roſes gules.*

In the church, is a monument thus inſcribed:

In this Church are depoſited the Remains of ROBERT DINWIDDIE, Eſq; formerly Governor of Virginia, who deceaſed July 27, 1770, in the 78th Year of his Age. The Annals of that Country will teſtify with what Judgment, Activity, and Zeal, He exerted himſelf in the Publick Cauſe, when the whole North American Continent was involved in a French and Indian War. His Rectitude of Conduct in his Government, and Integrity in other publick Employments, add a Luſtre to his Character, which was revered while he lived, and will be held in Eſtimation whilſt his Name ſurvives. His more private Virtues, and the amiable ſocial Qualities he poſſeſſed, were the Happineſs of his numerous Friends and Relations, many of whom ſhared his Bounty, all lament his Loſs. As his happy Diſpoſitions for domeſtic Life were beſt known to his affectionate Wife and Daughters, They have erected this Monument to the Memory of his Conjugal and Paternal Love, which they will ever cheriſh and revere with that Piety and Tenderneſs he ſo greatly merited.

Farewell bleſt Shade! no more with Grief oppreſt,
Propitious Angels guide thee to thy Reſt.

On another marble monument, this inſcription:

To the Memory of Mrs. ELIZABETH BLENMAN, (Wife of WILLIAM BLENMAN, Eſq; of the Iſland of Barbadoes, and one of the Daughters of JOSEPH DOTIN, Eſq;

Eſq; of the ſaid Iſland) who died in this Village on the 10th Auguſt 1763, in the 36th Year of her Age & the 15th of her Marriage, leaving Four Sons & Two Daughters. A WOMAN uniformly and without Oſtentation actuated by the great Principles of VIRTUE and RELIGION ; moderate in her Deſires & Enjoyments ; by Prudence and a well diſpoſed Mind ſecured from Temptation or Surprize. Tenderneſs and Benevolence were ſeen in her pleaſing Countenance ; an amiable Simplicity of Manners in her Deportment ; and both ſhewed the conſtant Influence of TRUTH and INNOCENCE. Quick to diſcover & acknowledge Merit, yet Indulgent to the Failings of Humanity, She contemplated with Delight the Excellencies of her Friends, and ſaw with Candour their Defects. Inſenſible of her own Worth, She viewed with partial Eyes Her HUSBAND ; and gave him the warm and active Affection of a Heart which knew no Joy or Intereſt unconnected with *His*. Let this Monument record *Her* Virtues, *His* Gratitude and Love. —— Arms, *Gules, two lions paſſant in pale Or.*

On another marble monument is the following inſcription :

Near to this Monument lies interr'd the Body of Lieut. Col. ALEXANDER TENNENT of *Handarwood* in *Edinburgh-Shire*. In whom Courage, Honour, Probity, joined with the mildeſt Temper and gentleſt Manners, were equally conſpicuous. His Strength being waſted by Wounds received in the Service of his Country, at Minden, Warburg, & Campen, he died at the Hot Wells Sept. the 17th 1763, Aged 40. —— Arms, *Argent, within a bordure two creſcents in feſs azure, in chief a boar's head couped Or.*

There are likewiſe inſcriptions for Margaret Minſhul, who died in 1732 ; for Mary Davis, who died in 1758 ; for Miſs Mariamne Eyre ; and for Margaret Stirling, who died in 1761.

Benefactions.

Mr. Ailiff Green gave 20*l.* towards adorning the church ; 16*l.* for communion plate ; and in 1690 he gave 20*s.* yearly for a ſermon on Good Friday, and 20*s.* yearly for the poor in bread on that day. Mr. David Roynon gave 10*l.* Cornelius Davis, in 1703, gave 5*l.* John Wakeman, in 1716, gave 5*l.* Charles Jones, in 1737, gave 20*l.* John Gwynne 5*l.* and Anthony Oliver gave 60*l.* the intereſt of which ſums to be given in bread to the poor every year, except one guinea, out of Oliver's, for a ſermon on the 25th of June. And Mrs. Katherine Freeman gave the intereſt of 20*l.* to buy coals for the poor.

Taxes.					
	The Royal Aid in	1692, £.	63	9	4
	Poll-tax ——	1694, —	35	18	0
	Land-tax ——	1694, —	151	12	0
	The ſame, at 3*s.*	1770, —	116	11	0

According to ſir Robert Atkyns, when he compiled his account of this pariſh, there were 90 houſes, and about 450 inhabitants, whereof 10 were freeholders ; yearly births 14, burials 12. The reſort to the Hot-wells, ſince that time, has greatly increaſed population, and conſequently the number of baptiſms and burials ; for in ten years, beginning with 1760, the average of annual baptiſms is 36.2, of burials, 49.3 ; and the inhabitants, excluſive of lodgers, are about 1367. It is obſervable that the burials greatly exceed the baptiſms, occaſioned by the interment at Clifton of ſuch perſons as, coming to the wells for the recovery of their health, have died there. Of ſuch there have been, for ſome time paſt, about 19 in a year, upon an average. This reduces the annual burials of the ſettled inhabitants to 30.3 ; nearly in the proportion of 1 to 45 of the whole number of the living.

COLESBOURN,

IS in the hundred of Rapſgate, ſix miles diſtant ſouth-eaſtward from Cheltenham, nine north-weſtward from Cirenceſter, and eleven eaſtward from Glouceſter.

It is a little retired village, about a mile eaſtward of the road from Cirenceſter to Cheltenham. It lies in a narrow valley, through which the river Churn paſſes to Cirenceſter, and takes its name from that river ; for *Coleſbourn*, with a ſmall allowance for corruption in long and vulgar uſe, is the ſame with *Corinſbourn* ; *i. e.* the river *Corin*, or *Churn*, upon which the village ſtands.

Here the Lyde, or Wyde, a ſmall brook riſing in Withington, falls into the Churn, and helps to ſtore it with plenty of ſmall trout and cray-fiſh.

Rapſgate, or *Reſpigete*, is a hamlet in this pariſh, which gives name to the hundred : And *Coleſbourn-pen*, ſo called, from *pen* the head or top of any thing, is a ſpot of high ground, ſeen at a very conſiderable diſtance in this part of the county.

The pariſh conſiſts chiefly of arable land, with ſome wood, and a little paſture-ground ; but affords nothing worthy the traveller's notice, except that in the north field there are the remains of an antient encampment.

Of the Manor and other Eſtates.

In the regiſter of lands held by the church of Worceſter, *Domeſday-book* gives the following account :

' The ſame church [*i.e.* St. Mary of Worceſter] ' held Coleſborne, in Reſpigete hundred, and ' Suein held it of her, and he could not depart ' [from this eſtate.] There are eight hides taxed. ' Walter the brother of Roger holds it of the ' church. In demean is one plow-tillage, and ' eighteen villeins, and two bordars with five ' plow-tillages. There are two *ſervi*, and three ' acres of meadow, and two mills of 7*s.* 6*d.* [rent.] ' It was then worth 8*l.* now 4*l.*' *Dom.B.* p.70.

But the ſame record gives account of other eſtates in Coleſbourn, which belonged to the manors of Withington and Elkſtone, under which pariſhes the particulars may be ſeen.

This manor was alienated from the church of Worceſter, and became veſted in the priory of Lanthony, which purchaſed a charter of free warren therein 21 E. 1. and continued in poſſeſſion thereof till that houſe was diſſolved.

The manor of Coleſbourn, which had belonged to the priory of Lanthony, was granted to Thomas Reeve and others 6 Eliz. William Higgs, eſq; was lord of this manor in the year 1608, in whoſe family it continued for ſeveral generations. It

was

was afterwards purchaſed by Mr. Sheppard of Hampton, whoſe ſon Philip Sheppard, eſq; was lord of the manor at the beginning of this century; and John Sheppard, eſq; a deſcendant from him, lately ſold it to Francis Eyre, eſq; who is the preſent lord of the manor. The arms of Eyre, as I find them on a monument in Clifton-church, *Argent, on a chevron ſable three quatrefoils Or.*

There is an antient farm-houſe, with a chapel adjoining to it, called the *Priory.*

Of the Church, &c.

The church is a rectory, in the deanery of Stonehouſe, worth about 45*l.* a year. Mr. Eyre is patron, Mr. Millechamp the preſent incumbent. The priory of Lanthony formerly preſented to it.

Milo, conſtable of Glouceſter, gave two parts of the tithes of Coleſbourn Sampſon, and two parts of the tithes of Elias Leholt of Coleſbourn, to the priory of Lanthony, in the year 1137; ſo that the rector hath only one third part of the tithes.

The advowſon of the rectory, of which the earl of Arundel was poſſeſſed, was granted to George and John Huntley 6 Eliz. A portion of tithes, and divers ſheep-paſtures, which belonged to the priory of Lanthony, were granted to John Arundel 38 H. 8.

The church is dedicated to St. James. It is ſmall, in form of a croſs, with a low embattled tower at the weſt end. The north aile belongs to the lord of the manor, the other to the pariſh.

Firſt fruits £.	5	6	3½	Synodals £.	0	2	0
Tenths —	0	10	8½	Pentecoſtals	0	0	8
Procurations	0	6	8				

Benefactions.

There are four acres of land given to the uſe of the church; and the miniſter has a ſmall portion of land, by an agreement on incloſing ſome part of the pariſh, for which he is to find bell-ropes.

Taxes.					
	The Royal Aid in	1692, £.	39	19	2
	Poll-tax ——	1694, —	13	3	0
	Land-tax ——	1694, —	38	14	0
	The ſame, at 3*s.*	1770, —	33	3	9

According to ſir Robert Atkyns, there were 30 houſes and about 120 inhabitants in this pariſh, whereof 6 were freeholders; yearly births 3, burials 2. But by the regiſter, from May 6, 1759, to May 8, 1769, there were 76 baptiſms; and from Jan. 2, 1759, to Feb. 19, 1769, 44 burials. The families are 48, and the inhabitants being number'd, are exactly 254; ſo that the average of annual burials, to the whole number of people, is as 1 to 57.7; which ſhews the place to be very healthy.

COLFORD.

See NEWLAND.

COLN St. ALWIN's.

THIS pariſh lies in the hundred of Britwel's-barrow, nine miles diſtant north-eaſtward from Cirenceſter, five north-weſtward from Leach-lade, and twenty-three eaſtward from Glouceſter.

The river *Coln*, increaſed by the Bibury water, runs reluctantly through this pariſh, with a ſlow ſtream; and the trout grows in it to a good ſize, whereas at Bibury 'tis always light and ſlender. The pariſh takes its name from the river, and from *St. Alwin*, to whom, it is ſuppoſed, the church was originally dedicated. He was tutor to Charles the Great, and famous for his great ſkill in diſputation.

This is a pretty little village. The lands riſe in a bold manner on each ſide the Coln, and the church and houſes are ſeen pleaſantly ſituated on the north-eaſt ſide, overlooking the river, the ſtone-bridge upon which is part repaired by this pariſh, and part by Quenington.

The *Ikenild-way*, a Roman road, leading from Oxfordſhire through this pariſh to Cirenceſter, is ſtill viſible in a high ridge in many parts of it. It paſſes through a corner of Poulton in Wiltſhire, at an eminence about ſix miles from Cirenceſter, and croſſes another road where a tall aſh tree grew; which tree was particularly convenient as a land-mark and token to travellers; and hence that place obtained the name of *Ready-token.*

The pariſh hath lately been incloſed by act of parliament.

Of the Manors and other Eſtates.

Athelred, governor of Glouceſterſhire, gave ſixty meſſuages of his land, lying in Culne St. Ælwin's, to the monks of St. Peter of Glouceſter. See p. 145. And the manor was held by the ſame church ſoon after the Conqueſt, as appears by *Domeſday-book.*

'The church [of St. Peter at Glouceſter] holds 'Culne. There are four hides. In demean are 'three plow-tillages, and eleven villeins, and ſeven 'bordars, with twelve plow-tillages. There are 'four *ſervi.* It was worth 6*l.* now 8*l.* Two 'mills paid a rent of 25*s.*' *Domeſday-book*, p. 71.

The abbey of Glouceſter reſerved for rent 100 ſheep, or 9*l.* 3*s.* 4*d.* a year, at the election of their ſteward. They were ſeized of this manor 17 E. 3. and continued proprietors of it 'till the diſſolution; after which it was made a part of the endowment of the dean and chapter of Glouceſter, 33 H. 8. who are the preſent owners.

Thomas Ingram, eſq; and others, are leſſees of this manor under the dean and chapter of Glouceſter. Mr. Ingram has a good houſe near the church, where he reſides. His arms are, *Azure, a chevron between three lions paſſant gardant Or.*

HAMLET. *Williamſtrip* is a hamlet and manor in this pariſh, about half a mile eaſtward of the church. John de Handelo levied a fine of this manor 4 E. 3. and was ſucceeded therein by his ſon Richard, whoſe wife Iſabel, by virtue of a

ſettlement

fettlement, enjoyed it 'till her death 35 E. 3. Edmond de Handelo, grandfon of Richard, dying without iffue 49 E. 3. left a great eftate to his two fifters; of whom Margery the eldeft, firft married to Gilbert Chateline, and afterwards to John de Appleby, had this manor.

From their time I find no account of the proprietors, 'till Henry Powle, efq; became poffeffed of it. He was fpeaker of the houfe of commons, mafter of the rolls, and one of the privy council to king Charles the Second, and king William the Third. From this family the manor of Williamftrip went, by the marriage of his only daughter and heirefs, to Henry Ireton, efq. It afterwards paffed to Brooke Forrefter, and then to Humphry-Mackworth Praed, who fold it to Samuel Blackwell, efq; one of the reprefentatives in parliament for the borough of Cirencefter, who is the prefent lord of the manor. He has a very handfome feat and large eftate here, and in other parts of the county. For his arms, &c. fee p. 229.

Of the Church, &c.

The church is a vicarage, in the deanery of Fairford, now worth about 60*l.* a year. It has been augmented by queen Anne's bounty. Sylvefter bifhop of Worcefter, in the year 1217, gave the impropriation of this church to the abbey of Gloucefter, for the increafe of hofpitality, when Henry Blond was abbat. And the impropriation and the advowfon of the vicarage were granted to the dean and chapter of Gloucefter, by their charter of foundation. At this time there is no incumbent, by reafon of the deceafe of the late Mr. Fifield, 1775. The vicar has 20*l.* a year out of the impropriation, and at the late inclofing of the parifh, lands were allotted to him in lieu of tithe.

Catland-houfe was given by the abbey of Gloucefter for the purpofe of a church-houfe.

The church confifts of the nave only. It is dedicated to St. John Baptift. The tower ftands on the fouth fide, and there is a large gallery at the weft end, built by the donations of Henry Powle and his brother William, in 1646. The tower was built by abbat Gamages, as appears by the initial letters of his name, I. G. over the door on the eaft fide, and his arms, *a crofs*, which ftand a little above. On the fouth fide, on the battlements, are the arms of the Clares earls of Gloucefter, *Topaz, three chevronels ruby.* And on the weft fide are the arms of St. Peter's abbey, Gloucefter, and of the prince of Wales.

Monuments and Infcriptions.

There is a freeftone monument in the chancel, with the figures of a man and woman kneeling, in one compartment, and fix children in another. It was defigned for George Fettiplace, efq; as appears by a fcutcheon of his arms, *viz. Quarterly,* 1ft, *Gules, a chevron argent.* 2d, *Three roundlets,* 3d, *A lion rampant,* 4th as 1ft. He was one of the judges of South Wales in the reign of queen Elizabeth, and died of the plague in 1578.

On a flat ftone in the chancel :

Here lies the Body of Thomas Church, efq; (fon of Thomas Church, of Tunftall in Shropfhire, and of Theophila Fettiplace his wife, youngeft daughter of Giles Fettiplace, of this place, efq;) He departed this Life at the Bath, the 15th day of March, 1734, aged 31.

On a flat ftone, inlaid with white marble :

Here lyeth the Body of Henry Poole, Efquire, who died Anno Dom. 1643. ——— Arms, *A lion rampant.*

There is an infcription for Mr. John Lambert, who died in 1716; with his arms, *A chevron between three lambs.*

	£.	s.	d.		£.	s.	d.
Firft fruits	8	19	5	Synodals	0	2	0
Tenths —	0	17	11½	Pentecoftals	0	0	10
Procurations	0	6	8				

Benefactions.

Mrs. Catherine Ireton has given 10*l.* a year to the poor of this parifh ; and there is a fmall donation from another perfon.

Taxes.			£.	s.	d.
	The Royal Aid in	1692,	65	12	0
	Poll-tax ——	1694,—	18	13	0
	Land-tax ——	1694,—	72	11	0
	The fame, at 3*s.*	1770,—	56	14	1½

According to fir Robert Atkyns, there were 53 houfes and about 300 inhabitants in this parifh, whereof 7 were freeholders ; yearly births 7, burials 6. The parifh regifter being very ill kept, can give no light into the ftate of population; but it is certain that the place is very healthy. There are 80 families, and 392 people, of which 48 inhabit Williamftrip.

COLN St. DENNIS

IS a fmall village in the upper divifion of the hundred of Deerhurft, in the Cotefwold country, fituate on the eaft fide of the *Fofs-road* leading from Cirencefter to Stow, a little mile below Fofs-bridge; bounded on the weft by Chedworth, on the fouth by Coln Rogers; having Hamnet on the north, and Northleach on the eaft of it. It is feven miles north of Cirencefter, three fouth of Northleach, and twenty eaft of Gloucefter.

It takes its name from the river *Coln,* which runs through it, and is diftinguifhed from *Coln Rogers* by the additional name, derived from the abbey of *St. Dennis* in Normandy, to which it antiently belonged.

The houfes ftand in a little comb, or bottom. The parifh confifts principally of arable land, with fome meadow and pafture on the fides of the river; but it has nothing remarkable to engage the attention of the naturalift.

Of the Manor and other Eftates.

The following is all that is mentioned of this manor in *Domefday-book.* ' In Derheft hundred ' the church of St. Dennis holds five hides in Colne ' and Caldecote.' *D. B.* p. 72.

 This

This manor was appropriated to the uſe of the priory of Deerhurſt, which was a cell to the abbey of St. Dennis in France; and the monks, by their intereſt, procured it to be annexed to the hundred of Deerhurſt, tho' it lies many miles diſtant from any other part of it.

The alien priories, of which Deerhurſt was one, being diſſolved, this manor was granted to the abbey of Tewkeſbury 7 E. 4. and afterwards, at the general diſſolution of religious foundations, the manor of Coln Deans, and lands in Caldecot, were granted to William Sharrington 34 H. 8.

Livery of the manors of Coln Deans and Calcot, *alias* Caldecot, with the advowſon of the church, was granted to Robert Weſtwood 1 Eliz.

The manor came afterwards to Thomas Maſter, eſq; of Cirenceſter, who ſold it, and Mr. Dorrel, of Oxfordſhire, is the preſent proprietor of it.

HAMLET. *Caldecot*, now *Calcot*, is a hamlet in this pariſh. Humphry Bohun was ſeized of the manor of Caldecot 3 E. 1. and Gilbert Gamage and Lettice his wife were ſeized of it 6 R. 2. from whom it deſcended to Roger their ſon and heir.

Of the Church, &c.

The church is a rectory in the deanery of Cirenceſter, worth about 140*l.* a year. The reverend Mr. John Hughes is patron and incumbent.

Two parts of the tithes of Caldecot were granted to the priory of Lanthony, by Milo conſtable of Glouceſter, in the year 1137.

The church is ſmall, without battlements, and has a low tower in the middle, in which are five bells.

The church-houſe and a barn, four acres and three-quarters in each common field, ten ſheep-paſtures, and a dwelling-houſe called the Maple, have been given at ſeveral times for the repair of the church.

There are memorials for John Hughes, who died in 1726; for Charles Hughes, M. A. who died 1742; and for Andrew Hughes, M. A. who died in 1756, all rectors of this church; but there are no family arms.

Firſt fruits £	10	19	4½	Synodals £.	0	2	0
Tenths —	0	19	11¼	Pentecoſtals	0	0	8
Procurations	0	6	8				

Taxes.	The Royal Aid in 1692, £.	40	4	0
	Poll-tax —— 1694, —	7	4	0
	Land-tax —— 1694, —	30	12	0
	The ſame, at 3*s.* 1770, —	27	9	0

At the beginning of this century, according to ſir Robert Atkyns, there were 16 houſes and 80 inhabitants in this pariſh, whereof 6 were freeholders; yearly births 2, burials 2. But in ten years, beginning with 1760, there are regiſtered 41 baptiſms and 29 burials; and the number of families is 26, of inhabitants 112; ſo that about one in 39 dies every year.

COLN ROGERS

IS a ſmall pariſh in the hundred of Bradley, three miles ſouth from Northleach, ſeven north-eaſt from Cirenceſter, and twenty-one miles eaſt from Glouceſter. It was ſo called from its ſituation on the river *Coln*, and from Roger of Glouceſter, its antient poſſeſſor. But in the grant of king Stephen to the abbey of Glouceſter, it is called *Coln St. Andrew*, becauſe the church is dedicated to that ſaint.

The village ſtands in a little dale. The lands are chiefly arable, with a little paſture near the river.

Of the Manor and other Eſtates.

Roger of Glouceſter, knight, being dangerouſly wounded at Walliſon, gave the manor of Coln Rogers, *alias* Coln on the Hills, to the monks of Glouceſter, in the year 1105, to pray for his ſoul; and the grant was confirmed by king Henry, when the abbey was vacant by the death of Serlo.

The abbey of Glouceſter was ſeized of the manor of Coln Rogers 17 E. 3. and continued poſſeſſed of it 'till the diſſolution; when it was granted to the dean and chapter of Glouceſter 33 H. 8. who are the preſent lords of it.

Alexander Colſton, eſq; is leſſee under the dean and chapter.

Pindrop, or *Pendrop*, from *pen*, the *top*, and ꝺoꞃp, a *dwelling*, ſo called from its ſituation above the village, is a conſiderable farm in this pariſh, the property of Thomas Cotton, eſq; a banker in London, who has a good houſe here.

Of the Church, &c.

The church is a rectory in the deanery of Cirenceſter, worth about 100*l.* a year. The dean and chapter of Glouceſter are patrons. The living is now vacant.

Twenty-four acres in each common field belong to the glebe.

The demeans of the lord of the manor pay only the twentieth part in lieu of tithes.

The church is ſmall, dedicated to St. Andrew, and contains nothing worth notice. It has a tower at the weſt end, with three bells in it. Two acres in each common field, called the *Church-land*, are given to find bell-ropes.

Firſt fruits £.	7	0	5	Synodals £.	0	2	0
Tenths —	0	14	0½	Pentecoſtals	0	0	0
Procurations	0	6	8				

Taxes.	The Royal Aid in 1692, £.	39	1	2
	Poll-tax —— 1694, —	9	1	8
	Land-tax —— 1694, —	20	14	0
	The ſame, at 3*s.* 1770, —	23	11	8¼

At the beginning of this century, there were 18 houſes in this pariſh, and about 70 inhabitants, whereof 3 were freeholders; yearly births 2, burials 2. But on an average of ten years, from 1760, the annual baptiſms are 4.2, burials 3; and the

the number of families is 26, of inhabitants exactly 125. So that the annual burials are to the whole number of inhabitants, nearly as 1 to 42.

COMPTON ABDALE

IS a ſmall pariſh in the hundred of Bradley, in the Coteſwold country, eleven miles north from Cirenceſter, four north-weſtward from Northleach, and ſixteen eaſt from Glouceſter.

The village takes its name from the ſituation of the church and houſes in a little comb or valley, for *combe* in the Anglo Saxon, ſignifies a narrow *valley*; but the greater part of the pariſh lies upon the hills. It conſiſts principally of arable land, with a conſiderable ſhare of wood, and a little paſture on the banks of the Coln, a branch of which runs through it. But what moſt diſtinguiſhes it, is the bold appearance of lord Chedworth's plantations, which ſtand on a high part of the Coteſwold.

Of the Manor and other Eſtates.

Domeſday-book gives the following account of this manor:

'Stigand archbiſhop [of York] held Cuntune 'in Bradelege hundred. There were nine hides. 'There are two plow-tillages, and five acres of 'meadow, and twenty-two villeins, and five bor'dars, with eleven plow-tillages. There are five '*ſervi*, and a mill of 5*s*. In the time of king 'Edward it was worth 9*l.* now 7*l.* Thomas 'archbiſhop [of York] holds it. A free man of 'Roger de Lurei holds one manor of three hides 'belonging to this manor. The archbiſhop 'claims it.' *Domeſday-book*, p. 70.

The temporalties of the archbiſhop of York were extended 14 E. 3. of which this manor was a part.

Thomas Lane held the capital meſſuage of Compton Abdale, under the archbiſhop of York, and died ſeized thereof 37 H. 8. leaving Thomas his ſon eighteen years old. This manor was taken from the archbiſhop of York, and granted to ſir Thomas Chamberlain 6 E. 6.

It was afterwards purchaſed by ſir Richard Grubham, of Wiſhford, in Wiltſhire, who was lord of it in 1608; and dying without iſſue in 1629, left this and many other great eſtates to his nephew John How, eſq; from whom it deſcended, like Chedworth and Stowell, down to lord Chedworth, who is the preſent lord of the manor; an account of whoſe family and arms is inſerted under Stowell, where his lordſhip reſides.

William Docket and Elizabeth his wife levied a fine of lands in Compton-Abdale, to the uſe of Edmund Tame 19 H. 7.

Of the Church, &c.

The church is a curacy, in the deanery of Cirenceſter. The rectory of Compton-Abdale, and the advowſon of the vicarage, belonged to the priory of St. Oſwald in Glouceſter; and after the diſſolution of that houſe, were granted to the church of Briſtol 34 H. 8. The dean and chapter of Briſtol are the appropriators and patrons, and pay the incumbent 10*l.* a year. The curacy has been twice augmented; firſt by a donation from the late Mr. Aylworth, and by queen Anne's bounty, in the year 1737; and again in 1760, by donations from Alexander Colſton, eſq; (as executor of the late Edward Colſton, eſq;) and Charles Page, M. A. the preſent incumbent, and by the queen's bounty.

The church is very ſmall, dedicated to St. Oſwald, and has nothing in it worth notice.

Procurations £.	0	6	8	Pentecoſt. £.	0	0	6
Synodals	0	2	0				

Taxes.					
	The Royal Aid in	1692, £.	53	15	0
	Poll-tax — —	1694, —	3	0	0
	Land-tax ——	1694, —	48	0	8
	The ſame, at 3*s*.	1770, —	32	4	1¼

According to ſir Robert Atkyns, there were 30 houſes and about 130 inhabitans in this pariſh, whereof 4 were freeholders; yearly births 4, burials 3. In ten years, beginning with 1760, there were regiſtered 34 baptiſms, and 28 burials, and the inhabitants are at preſent 130 in number.

COMPTON GREENFIELD.

THIS pariſh lies in the hundred of Henbury, ſix miles north-weſt from Briſtol, nine ſouth-weſtward from Thornbury, and thirty-three ſouth-weſtward from Glouceſter.

It is bounded on every ſide by the pariſhes of Almondſbury and Henbury, except a ſmall portion on the weſt, where the river Severn is its boundary. The former part of the name is explained under the preceding head; the latter was given it with great propriety, becauſe the pariſh conſiſts almoſt wholly of meadow and paſture land, and to diſtinguiſh it from Eaſter Compton in Almondſbury.

The turnpike-road from Briſtol to Auſt-paſſage leads along the north-eaſt ſide of it, near the church.

Tho' this little village affords but few materials to enrich a hiſtory, and is diſtinguiſhed by neither foſſils, camps, nor antient coins, yet it may be deſervedly ranked among the happieſt claſs for its vegetable productions, I mean its excellent paſturage.

Of the Manor and other Eſtates.

It appears by *Domeſday-book*, that at the time of the general ſurvey this was a member of the large manor of Hueſberie, [now Weſtbury] in Bernintreu hundred; and that Giſlebert the ſon of Turold then held three hides and a half in Contone, as it is written in that record.

This manor was granted to Ralph, ſon of Ralph Bloet, 18 Joh. but it was in the Berkeley family

as

as early as 28 E. 3. and in the 30th year of that reign, Maurice Berkeley and Joan his wife levied a fine of it to the uſe of themſelves in taille, the remainder to Thomas the brother of Maurice, and Catherine his wife, which latter died ſeized of Compton Greenvill, and of two parts of the advowſon of the chapel, 9 R. 2. It was afterwards held by Thomas de Beauchamp 2 H. 4. by ſir Thomas Brooke 5 H. 5. by ſir John Berkeley, with the advowſon of the chapel, 6 H. 6. by Thomas Chedre 26 H. 6. and by ſir Maurice Berkeley of Beverſtone 38 & 39 H. 6. and 14 E. 4.

Sir William Berkeley of Stoke Giffard was ſeized of this manor in the beginning of the reign of king Richard the Third, but taking up arms in favour of that king, he was attainted after the battle of Boſworth-field, his eſtates ſeized, and the manor of Compton was granted to Thomas Brugge 1 H. 7. But the Berkeleys were ſoon reſtored to their eſtate. Sir William Berkeley of Beverſtone died ſeized of Compton Greenfield 5 E. 6. whoſe grandſon, John Berkeley, ſold it to Thomas Mallet, eſq; who died 22 Eliz. and left a ſon John twelve years old.

Patrick Young was lord of this manor in 1608. Sir Thomas Cann, knighted by king James the Second in the laſt year of his reign, was lord of the manor at the beginning of this century. He had two ſons, Robert and William. Robert ſucceeded to the title of baronet, on the death of his couſin ſir William Cann, but dying unmarried, was ſucceeded in title and eſtate by his brother ſir William Cann, who had iſſue one ſon Robert. He had alſo a daughter Elizabeth, married to —— Jefferies of Briſtol, to whoſe iſſue, the male line failing at the death of the late ſir Robert Cann, in 1765, this eſtate is devolved. Henry Lyppingcott, eſq; married Miſs Jefferies, and, in her right, is the preſent lord of this manor. *See Weſtbury.*

John Newton and Joan his wife levied a fine of lands in Compton Greenfield, to the uſe of themſelves in taille, 8 H. 5. and their ſon and heir John Newton ſold them to William More, and levied a fine of them 28 H. 6.

Of the Church, &c.

The church is a rectory in the deanery of Briſtol, worth 100*l.* a year, of which the glebe is worth upwards of 40*l.* Henry Lyppingcott, eſq; is patron, Mr. New the preſent incumbent.

The church, tho' ſmall, is very antient, as appears by the ſtile of the arch of the door at the ſouth entrance. In the 13th century it was ſtiled *capella de Contone*, at which time Weſtbury was probably the mother church. There is a low tower at the weſt end, but neither monument, inſcription, nor coat of arms in the church.

Taxes.			£.	s.	d.
	The Royal Aid in	1692,	169	8	0
	Poll-tax ——	1694, —	18	17	0
	Land-tax ——	1694, —	196	2	6
	The ſame, at 3*s.*	1770, —	142	12	0

At the beginning of this century there were 5 houſes and about 20 inhabitants, whereof 2 were freeholders; yearly births 4, burials 3. Here are now 6 houſes and 37 inhabitants. The diſproportion of the baptiſms and burials to the number of inhabitants, is occaſioned by the people of Almondſbury and Henbury ſometimes baptiſing and burying here, for convenience.

COMPTON, (LITTLE.)

THIS pariſh is ſituate in the upper diviſion of the hundred of Deerhurſt, five miles diſtant north-eaſt from Stow, eight ſouth-eaſt from Campden, and thirty-one north-eaſt from Glouceſter. The former part of the name has been already explained; the addition of *Little* ſerves to diſtinguiſh it from the adjoining pariſh of Long-Compton, in Warwickſhire.

The village lies under the weſt ſide of a hill, which ſecures it from the cold eaſterly winds. It is bounded on the north by Warwickſhire, on the eaſt, weſt, and ſouth, by Oxfordſhire; and has the convenience of the turnpike-road from Worceſter to London running through it. A conſiderable part of the pariſh is uninclofed. There is a common about two miles in length, and in ſome places above half a mile broad, of very good land, and exceedingly improvable.

There is a point of land in this pariſh which extends to a place where a pedeſtal is erected, with a ſun-dial on the top, and inſcriptions on the four ſides, to denote the joining of four counties where it ſtands; *i.e.* thoſe of Glouceſter, Worceſter, Warwick, and Oxford. This is occaſioned by the pariſh of Evenlode, which is a disjoined member of Worceſterſhire, running up to the ſouth ſide of the pedeſtal or pillar, (of which there is a more particular account under Morton-hen-marſh.) But the ſpot where the pillar is erected, is near twenty miles diſtant from the continent of Worceſterſhire.

Of the Manor and other Eſtates.

Domeſday-book ſays only thus much of the manor:

'The church of St. Dennis holds twelve hides 'in Contone in Derheſt hundred.' *D. B.* p. 72.

This manor was appropriated to the uſe of the priory of Deerhurſt, which was a cell to the abbey of St. Dennis in Normandy. But after the ſuppreſſion of alien priories, this and other eſtates, formerly belonging to the ſame priory, were granted by king Edward the Fourth to the abbey of Tewkeſbury, in whoſe poſſeſſion they continued 'till the diſſolution of that houſe. The manor of Little Compton was granted to ſir Thomas Pope 38 H. 8.

John Todmere died ſeized thereof 20 Eliz. and left Elizabeth his only daughter and heireſs married to ſir Robert Cotton, who in her right had livery granted him in the year 1608.

It

It afterwards paffed by purchafe to Dr. William Juxton. He had been dean of Worcefter, bifhop of the fees of Hereford and London, and at length obtained the metropolitical fee of Canterbury. In 1635 he was made lord treafurer, by the intereft of Dr. Laud, which giving difguft to many of the nobility, he was obliged to refign that office in 1641. In the year 1649, he attended king Charles the Firft on the fcaffold, at the time of his execution, and afterwards retired to his manor of Little Compton. But at the Reftoration he was promoted to the metropolitical chair of Canterbury, in which dignity he died in the year 1663, aged 81, and was buried in St. John's College Oxford, to which he had been a generous benefactor.

William Juxton fucceeded his uncle Dr. Juxton in this eftate, and was created a baronet Dec. 22, 12 C. 2. He was high fheriff of the county in 1676; and was fucceeded in title and eftate by his fon fir William Juxton, who died in 1739, without iffue, whereby the title was extinct. His lady furviving him, was afterwards married to lord Fane, and is the prefent proprietor of Little Compton, where fhe has a good houfe, and refides there fome part of the year.

John Mufgrofe was feized of lands in Little Contone 3 E. 1. Robert Ferrers of Chartley was feized of lands in Compton 1 H. 5. Sir Edward Ferrers de Chartley held four marks rent in Little Compton 14 H. 6.

Of the Church, &c.

The church is a curacy, in the deanery of Stow. The appropriation and advowfon of the vicarage belonged to the abbey of Tewkefbury, and were granted to the chapter of Oxford 38 H. 8. They pay 22*l.* and Dr. South has given 10*l.* a year to the curate. Mr. Baker is the prefent incumbent. About the year 1771, the college gave 200*l.* arifing from an eftate given them by Dr. Stratford, to augment the living; but the money is not yet laid out on land. The appropriation is in leafe to Mr. John Davis, and Mr. Richard Jordan.

The church is dedicated to St. Dennis, and hath a tower on the fouth fide.

Monuments and Infcriptions.

On a flat ftone in the chancel:

Under this Stone lieth interred the Body of Sir William Juxton, late of this Parifh, Knight and Baronet, who died the 3d Day of Feb. 1739, in the 79th Year of his Age. He was the eldeft Son of Sir William Juxton, Knight and Bart. alfo deceafed, who intermarried with Elizabeth a Daughter of Sir John Walter of Sarfden in the County of Oxford Bart. alfo deceafed. Sir William Juxton the Son intermarried with Sufanna Marriott, youngeft Daughter of John Marriott late of Stufton, in the County of Suffolk, Efq; deceafed, but has left no iffue, whereby the title is extinct.

On another flat ftone:

Mortale Thomæ Juxton Armigeri, qui Cœlum petijt 28° Febr. Anno Domini 1643.

Procurations 7*s.* 8*d.* Synodals 2*s.* Pentecoft. 7½*d.*

Benefaction.

Archbifhop Juxton gave the intereft of 100*l.* to the poor, which is paid by lady Fane.

Taxes.					
The Royal Aid in	1692,	£.	66	0	0
Poll-tax —	1694,	—	25	12	0
Land-tax —	1694,	—	58	9	0
The fame, at 3*s.*	1770,	—	52	15	3

At the beginning of this century there were 35 houfes in this parifh, and about 180 inhabitants, whereof 6 were freeholders; yearly births 5, burials 4. *Atkyns.* But examining the parifh regifter, I find that in ten years, beginning with 1700, there are entered 40 baptifms and 36 burials; and in a like feries from 1760, there are entered 80 baptifms, and 53 burials. The prefent number of inhabitants is exactly 242, nearly in proportion to the annual burials as 47 to 1; which fhews the place to be healthy.

CONDICOT.

THIS parifh lies partly in the hundred of Kiftfgate, and partly in that of Slaughter. It is three miles diftant north-weftward from Stow, feven eaftward from Winchcombe, and twenty-five north-eaftward from Gloucefter.

It is a fmall parifh, confifting chiefly of arable land. I conjecture that formerly it was overgrown with wood, from the termination of the name, which comes from *coed*, a *wood*, in the Britifh language.

Of the Manor and other Eftates.

This little parifh was divided among feveral proprietors at the time of the general furvey. That part of it which lay in the old hundred of Salemanefberie (now Slaughter) was a hamlet belonging to Oddington, and was then held by Thomas archbifhop of York. His predeceffor, Aldred, had taken a mortgage of this and other eftates, of the abbey of St. Peter at Gloucefter, to fecure the payment of fome money he had expended on that abbey, of which more may be feen p. 133, 141. See alfo the *Domefday* account of Oddington. In the fame record are the following particulars:

'The church of Wireceftre holds two hides in 'Condicote [in Tedboldeftan hundred] and Ofbern 'holds them of the bifhop. It was and is worth 40*s.*

'Ofbern holds one hide and a half in Condicot 'in Witelai hundred, of Durand [de Gloueceftre] 'It is and was worth 20*s.*

'William Froiffelew holds half a hide in Connicote in Witelai hundred, which paid tax. 'There was one plow-tillage and four *fervi.* 'It was worth 20*s.* now 3*s.* Brittric held it in 'the time of king Edward'. *D. B.* p. 70, 77, 74.

The principal manor and eftate in this place, were held by the archbifhop of York 6 E. 6. in which year they were granted to ſir Thomas Chamberlain. But the records mention other eſtates by the general name of Condicote. Thus Hugh de Condicote gave half a hide of land in Condicote, to the knights-templars, who were ſeized of court-leet, waifs, and felons goods in their lands there, by the grant of king Henry the Third; and their claim to thoſe privileges was allow'd 15 E. 1. and they were poſſeſſed of this eſtate 2 E. 3.

The manor of Condicote, or rather a manor in Condicote, was held by William de Clinton earl of Huntingdon, 28 E. 3. by Edward de Stonore, 5 R. 2. and by Gilbert ſon of Robert de Stonore, 3 H. 5.

Mr. Machin was lord of this manor in the year 1608. Mr. Cox was the proprietor of it at the beginning of this century, but Mr. Haſlam is the preſent owner.

A meſſuage in Condicote called *Nun-heys*, becauſe it formerly belonged to the nunnery of Cokehill in Worceſterſhire, and from *hai*, a *hedge*, *park*, or *incloſure*, was granted, after the diſſolution of religious foundations, to Nicholas Forteſcue and Catherine Forteſcue 34 H. 8. Thomas lord Wentworth married Margaret daughter and heir of Anne Forteſcue, and with her had this meſſuage, which on his death, 5 E. 6. deſcended to Thomas lord Wentworth his ſon.

Hinſwick is a conſiderable eſtate, part lying in this pariſh, and part in that of Breedon in Worceſterſhire. Lands in this place belonged to the abbey of Bruern in Oxfordſhire, as appears by the charter of king John, confirming the donations to that abbey, *De fœodo Willielmi filii Bernardi unam hidam in Hunchewic*. Chart. *ann. regni* 6°.

Leland ſpeaks of a water, 'riſing at Kenſdale 'in Coteſwald, and [running] thens to Hinch-'wike, wherabout yt rennith undre the grounde; 'thens to Swelle village by Stow; from Swelle to 'Slaughter and ſo into Bourton Water.' *Itin.* v. 5. p. 1.

Of the Church, &c.

The church is a rectory in the deanery of Stow, worth 70*l.* a year. It was formerly within the peculiar of Blockley. Mr. Haſlam is patron; Mr. Baker the preſent incumbent.

Ninety-eight acres of arable land, and five acres of paſture, belong to the glebe. The tithes belonged to the abbey of Winchcombe, and were granted to ſir Thomas Seimour 1 E. 6. No lands in the pariſh are tithe free.

The church is ſmall, dedicated to St. Nicholas.

	£.				£.		
Firſt fruits	7	0	10½	Synodals	0	0	0
Tenths —	0	14	1¼	Pentecoſtals	0	0	3½
Procurations	0	6	0				

In Slaughter Hundred.

Taxes.		£.	s.	d.
The Royal Aid in	1692,	12	18	8
Poll-tax ——	1694, —	2	15	0
Land-tax ——	1694, —	6	12	0
The ſame, at 3*s.*	1770, —	5	1	3

In Kiftſgate Hundred.

Taxes.		£.	s.	d.
The Royal Aid in	1692,	26	2	0
Poll-tax — —	1694, —	2	12	0
Land-tax ——	1694, —	20	2	0
The ſame, at 3*s.*	1770, —	15	6	0

At the beginning of this century there were 18 houſes, and about 80 inhabitants in this pariſh, whereof 7 were freeholders. There are now 105 inhabitants.

C O R S E.

THIS pariſh lies in the lower diviſion of the hundred of Weſtminſter, on the north-weſt ſide of the river Severn. It is ſix miles diſtant eaſt from Newent, nine ſouth-weſt from Tewkeſbury, and five and a half north-weſt from Glouceſter. It is three miles and a half long and two broad, bounded on the eaſt by the river *Laden* or *Leaden*; and the waters of Howbrook, which run through this pariſh, after joining another little rivulet called Collier's-brook, empty themſelves into that river.

There is a large tract of paſture-ground called the Lawn, of which the greater part, about 1200 acres, is in this pariſh, the remainder in that of Eldersfield in Worceſterſhire. Two turnpike-roads, one from Glouceſter to Worceſter, the other to Ledbury, are carried over it. The fine verdure with which it is cloathed, makes this part of the journey particularly agreeable in the ſpring and ſummer ſeaſons. It is a fine plain, about three miles long, with a beautiful ſlope, like a lofty terrace, running on the eaſt ſide for a good part of the way. This piece of ground is common to the pariſhioners, who depend much on depaſturing large flocks of ſheep upon it; but it often proves fatal to them, for in a wet ſeaſon it is ſo rotting, that ſcarce a ſheep ſurvives. This fine tract of ground might be greatly improved, and rendered more healthy; but there is an inſuperable obſtacle,—it belongs to the church of Weſtminſter.

There is a ſmall and very fragrant ſort of wild thyme growing about the ant-hills on the Lawn.

Mr. Pennant, among his many beautiful deſcriptions of places in Scotland, mentions the *Carſe*, or rich plains of Gowrie; and it remains a doubt with me, whether the pariſh of Corſe was denominated from the Lawn I have been ſpeaking of, or whether it was ſo called from the Britiſh word *Cors*, a marſh or bog; as formerly it was much covered with wood, and conſequently more rotten and boggy then at preſent; for the records mention Corſe-foreſt, Corſe-chaſe, Corſe-wood; but now there is no ſuch thing in the pariſh.

The huſbandry of this country, for many miles round, is in an unimproved ſtate. The farmers leave much to nature, and tho' there is plenty of *marle* in the pariſh, particularly at Horridge, I cannot find that they ever uſed it as a manure.

The

The ſoil is ſtrong, and the Herefordſhire method of planting fruit-trees in the incloſures of tillage land prevails in this place, where they make ſome pretty good cyder. The elm is the chief timber-tree, but the oak grows very well; and I obſerved that in the pariſhes of Hasfield, Tirley, and all the way to Tewkeſbury, the tenants have topped almoſt every oak-tree, that they may be afterwards, of right, intitled to the lop. This is an injury of a public as well as of a private nature, and I ſpeak of it as the more unpardonable in this part of the country, where coal comes at an eaſy rate down the Severn.

Of the Manor and other Eſtates.

Corſe is not mentioned in *Domeſday-book*, but it appears by later records that there was a foreſt or chaſe there; and that Richard de Clare earl of Glouceſter and Hertford held Cors-foreſt and Cors-court 47 H. 3. and Joan his widow held Cors-chaſe 35 E. 1. and that Gilbert de Clare died ſeized of the ſame chaſe and court 7 E. 2. leaving three ſiſters coheireſſes.

Elianor the eldeſt ſiſter was married to Hugh le Deſpencer the younger, who in her right was ſeized of the manor and chaſe of Cors. He was beheaded, and Roger Mortimer procured a grant thereof to himſelf and his heirs 1 E. 3. But Roger being attainted and executed, this manor and chaſe were ſoon after reſtored to Hugh, the ſon of the laſt Hugh le Deſpencer, who died ſeized of them 23 E. 3. and was ſucceeded by Edward le Deſpencer his nephew. He died ſeized of the manor and chaſe of Cors 49 E. 3. and was ſucceeded by Thomas his ſon and heir, who was attainted and beheaded 1 H. 4.

This manor and chaſe were held by Richard Deſpencer his ſon and heir, who dying without iſſue, left two ſiſters his coheireſſes, of whom Elizabeth died young. Iſabel ſucceeding to this eſtate, carried it in marriage to Richard Beauchamp, lord Bergavenny. He died 17 H. 6. leaving John Throgmorton one of his executors, who died ſeized of this manor and chaſe 13 E. 4.

Cors-court was held by Philip Throgmorton 5 H. 8. and by his ſon William 28 H. 8. whoſe ſon Thomas ſucceeded him; and another Thomas Throgmorton, eſq; was lord of it in the year 1608. It paſſed afterwards into the family and name of Dowdeſwell, for Richard Dowdeſwell, eſq; was lord thereof at the beginning of this century, and the right honourable William Dowdeſwell, eſq; who had been chancellor of the exchequer, and one of his majeſty's moſt honourable privy council, (which important ſtations he had filled with great abilities and integrity) died ſeized thereof in the year 1775. His arms are, *Or, a feſs undy between ſix billets ſable.*

The manor of Corſe-Lawn antiently belonged to the abbey of Weſtminſter. It was granted to the chapter of Weſtminſter 34 H. 8. and being confirmed 2 Eliz. now continues in that church.

HAMLET. Horridge is a hamlet in this pariſh. Lands called *Horredge*, in Corſe, formerly belonged to the Benedictine priory of the leſſer Malvern, in Worceſterſhire; and after the diſſolution of religious foundations, were granted to Henry Leigh 37 H. 8.

Stainbridge is another place in this pariſh.

Robert Widecomb and Emma his wife levied a fine of lands in Corſe to the uſe of the heirs of Emma 16 H. 6. Chriſtopher Raſtal died ſeized of lands in Corſe 6 Eliz. and Thomas Raſtal his ſon had livery the ſame year.

Of the Church, &c.

The church is within the peculiar of Deerhurſt. It is a vicarage endowed with the tithes, worth about 70*l.* a year. The lord chancellor is patron, the reverend Mr. Robert Gegg, the preſent incumbent. The patronage was formerly in the priory of Deerhurſt, and afterwards transferred to the abbey of Tewkeſbury. About fifteen acres belong to the glebe.

The church is dedicated to St. Margaret. It is ſmall, with a ſpire ſteeple at the weſt end.

Firſt fruits	£. 6	2	9½	Pentecoſt.	£. 0	0	4½
Tenths —	0	10	3½				

There is a quakers burying-ground adjoining to the church-yard.

Benefactions.

Three tenements are given for the repair of the church, for the communion, and for the benefit of the poor, now let at 7*l.* 10*s.* a year. One of them is a houſe in Horridge, called St. Margaret's-place, another, a houſe with lands in Stainbridge, and there is a third undeſcribed.

Taxes.					
	The Royal Aid in	1692, £.	42	2	0
	Poll-tax ——	1694, —	17	1	0
	Land-tax ——	1694, —	54	14	0
	The ſame, at 3*s.*	1770, —	39	14	8¼

There were 65 houſes, and about 300 inhabitants in this pariſh, whereof 20 were freeholders, at the beginning of this century; yearly births 9, burials 9. *Atkyns.* But it appears that in ten years, beginning with 1700, there were 69 baptiſms, and 65 burials entered in the pariſh regiſter; whereof 12 of the latter were quakers. And in the ſame number of years, beginning with 1760, there were 97 baptiſms, and 53 burials, in which number the quakers are not included; and the inhabitants in 1771, were exactly 253. So that population is nearly in the ſame ſtate as it was ſeventy years ago.

COTES, *or* COATS.

THIS pariſh lies in the Coteſwold country, in the hundred of Crowthorn and Minety, three miles weſt from Cirenceſter, ſeven north-eaſtward from Tetbury, ſeven eaſt from Minchin-hampton, and eighteen ſouth-eaſtward from Glouceſter. This

This name was unknown at the time of the general ſurvey, *temp.* W. 1. In *Domeſday-book* the pariſh is deſcribed by the names of Hunlafeſed, Turſberie, and Torentune; but in the ſheriff's return of all the vills in the hundred of Cirenceſter, 9 E. 1. theſe were omitted, and the general name of Cotes occurs in their ſtead.

Sir Robert Atkyns was of opinion, that it received its name from being ſeated among the *Cotts* in *Coteſwold*; but it was more probably from the Britiſh word *coed*, a *wood*, becauſe here was one of thoſe great woods which are ſuppoſed to have extended over almoſt all the country from this place to Stow, and to have given the name of *Coteſwold* to a large extent of ground upon the hills of Glouceſterſhire. *Wold*, from the Saxon pealo, ſignifies the ſame as *coed*; ſo that there is a redundancy in the name of *Coteſwold*, of which there are inſtances in the appellations of other places. The preſent ſtate of the country about Cotes ſerves to confirm the etymology; for there are ſtill two large woods, at Hailey, and Oakley, adjoining to this pariſh, the latter of which was granted by the crown to the abbat of Cirenceſter, on condition that it ſhould not be aſſarted; a reſtriction which has preſerved it to our time, otherwiſe it might have fared as moſt of the antient wood-lands have done.

There is a ſtrong camp, with a double ditch, in the hamlet of Trewſbury, called *Trewſbury caſtle*. It was probably a Roman camp of obſervation, lying a little to the north of the *Acman-ſtreet-way*, which led from *Corinium* to *Aqua Solis*, (now Cirenceſter and Bath) two eminent Roman ſtations. The Romans had another poſt about a mile and a half farther weſtward, on the ſame ſide of that road, where a great many coins and other veſtiges of that people have been found, as related under Rodmarton.

The head of the Thames or Iſis, poetically deſcribed by the learned Camden, is commonly reputed to be in this pariſh; but the well ſo called, does not overflow in the ſummer, unleſs in very wet ſeaſons, and there is no conſtant ſtream in the place. Indeed if this were perennial, it would not be the higheſt ſource of that river, as I have ſhewn more largely at p. 48.

This village lies high and open, and is remarkably healthy, as appears by the ſtate of population at the end of this account. The women and children are employ'd in ſpinning woollen-yarn.

Of the Manor and other Eſtates.

Gilbert de Clare was ſeized of the manors of Cotes and Trewſbury, with court-leet, 15 E. 1. They came afterwards into a family of the name of Vernon. Richard Vernon ſold them to ſir William Nottingham, who died ſeized of them 2 R. 3. without iſſue, leaving them to his widow for her life, the remainder to truſtees. Richard Poole married Elizabeth, widow of ſir William Nottingham, and purchaſed the reverſion of the inheritance of the truſtees, 7 H. 7. Sir Leonard Poole was ſon and heir of Richard, and dying 30 H. 8. was ſucceeded by his ſon ſir Giles, who died in 1588. Sir Henry Poole, ſon of ſir Giles, died in the year 1616, leaving ſir Henry Poole his ſon and heir; whoſe ſon ſir William was ſucceeded by his ſon ſir Henry, the laſt male heir of his family. He ſold the manor, &c. to ſir Robert Atkyns of Saperton, about the year 1660, who dying in 1709, was ſucceeded by his ſon ſir Robert Atkyns, who alſo died in 1711. Mr. Atkyns is the preſent lord of the manor.

This pariſh is reputed to be within the juriſdiction of the court of the honour of Glouceſter. It conſiſts almoſt intirely of arable land.

HAMLETS. 1. *Hunlafeſed*, i. e. *Hunlafe's ſed*, or *ſeat*, ſo called from the name of the Saxon proprietor. It is now called *Hullaſed*. The particulars whereof are thus ſet down in *Domeſday-book*:

'Elmar poſſeſſed Hunlafeſed in Cireceſtre hun-'dred, in which were three hides and a half. The 'biſhop of Baieux held it. It is now in the 'king's hands. In demean is one plow-tillage, 'and four villeins, and four bordars, with three 'plow-tillages. It was worth 4*l.* now 50*s.*' *Domeſday-book*, p. 68.

The abbeſs of Romſey had the advowſon of a chapel, and was poſſeſſed of lands in this place, 36 H. 6. The chapel is now ſtanding, and retains the name, but it is converted to a barn.

2. *Trewſbury*, but antiently *Turſberie*, was probably ſo called from *traws*, *ſloping*, and *berg*, a *camp*, or *fortification*. *Domeſday-book* gives the following account of this eſtate:

'The ſame Giſlebert [the ſon of Turold] holds 'half a hide in Turſberie, in Cireceſtre hundred, 'and Oſuuard holds it of him. Aluuard held it. 'In demean is one plow-tillage. It was worth '10*s.* now 15*s.*' *Domeſday-book*, p. 76.

3. *Torleton* is a hamlet, part of which lies in Rodmarton, and part in this pariſh. Torleton in Cotes lies a mile weſtward from the church, and contains ſixteen families. In *Domeſday-book* it is thus deſcribed:

'Radulfus Pagenel holds Torentune in Cire-'ceſtre hundred, and Radulfus holds it of him. 'There are four hides and a half taxed. Merle-'ſuen held it. In demean are three plow-tillages, 'and ten villeins, and one bordar with three 'plow-tillages. There are ten *ſervi*. It was worth '10*l.* now 100*s.*' *Domeſday-book*, p. 75.

Of the other eſtates, the records ſhew, that William Golding and Joan his wife levied a fine of lands in Cotes, to the uſe of themſelves for life, the remainder to William Panton and Joan his wife, daughter of William Golding, 23 H. 6. William Lewelline and Joan his wife levied a fine of lands in Cotes to William Nottingham, 7 E. 4. The royalty of the hamlets is veſted in the lord of the manor of Cotes.

Of

Of the Church, &c.

The church is a rectory in the deanery of Cirencester, worth 200*l.* a year. Mr. Atkyns is patron, Mr. Chaunler the present incumbent.

Three acres of pasture land, adjoining to the parsonage house, eighty-two acres in the common fields, 170 sheep-pastures in Cotes, and 200 in Torleton, belong to the rector. *Parish Register.*

The tithes of the demeans belonged to the abbey of Cirencester, and were so adjudged in the year 1463; and afterwards, Richard Peachy, rector of this church, by indenture dated in 1486, quitted claim to the tithes of the demeans to Richard Clyve, abbat of Cirencester, Richard Vernon being then lord of the manor.

The church is large, dedicated to St. Matthew. It has a handsome well-built tower at the west end, with two bells in it. On the north side of the church is a small chapel, which, by tradition, was built by the Nottinghams for a burying-place.

Under a void niche, on the west side of the tower, is an inscription engraven in antient characters, in the stone, mistaken by sir Robert Atkyns; and which cannot be better explained than by the following abstract from the curious register of the parish of Rodmarton, in the year 1636, where it is thus written: 'In the windowe of the south 'isle, adjoining to the chancel, was a little picture 'in the glasse, of one praying in the habit of a 'minister, *cum baculo pastorali*; and under-written '*Richardus Exall*, which was broken by children. 'Perhaps he was at the charge of that window. 'There is also upon the west side of Cotes tower, 'in stones, *Orate p' animab' Richardi Wiat, et* '*Richardi de Rodm'ton*; It may bee it was this 'Richard which did joyne with the person of 'Cotes to build that tower.'

Mr. Tyndale, late rector, caused this device to be placed over the door of the parsonage-house. A large rose, handsomely carved in freestone, and *Under the Rose,* (alluding to that saying) in Roman capitals, NE GRY QUIDEM FORAS; by which he meant to caution his friends against tale-bearing. I found something like this in the parlour of the parsonage-house at Buckland. To intimate that conversation in chearful societies should not be betray'd, there is a large gilt rose in the middle of the ceiling, over the place for the dining-table, and round it, in gold letters, *Qui Dicta vel Facta Foras eliminat, eliminetur. i.e.* Let him that divulges what is said or done here, be kick'd out of doors. It was the antient custom at sympofiac meetings, or merry-makings, to wear chaplets of roses about the head, which gave rise to the phrase of *speaking under the rose.*

Thomas Master, of the family of that name now residing at the abbey in Cirencester, was rector of Cotes, and a great scholar. He published several learned pieces, and assisted the lord Herbert of Cherbury in composing his *History of king Henry the Eighth.* He died in 1643, and lies buried in the chapel of New College Oxford.

Monuments and Inscriptions.

On a flat stone in the chancel, is an acrostic for Ales Marshefield, the letters of whose name appear on the margin of the stone, but the verses are very imperfect.

On another stone, in capitals:

Gulielmus Mounsteven
Annos 25 sedvlvs Hvjvs
Ecclesiæ Rector
per Afflictiones ad cœlum ornatus
Illuc adijt 17th Janvarij Ano 1677.
Cujus hic reponuntur cineres
beatæ resurrectionis spe.

On a small brass plate:

Elias Carteret Rect^r. of y^s. Parish died Decem^r. 30th, 1720, Aged 68.——Arms, *Argent, a fess lozengy.*

First fruits £.	9	6	8	Synodals £.	0	2	0
Tenths —	0	18	8	Pentecostals	0	0	8
Procurations	0	6	8				

Benefactions.

Elias Carteret, by will, gave the interest of 10*l.* to be distributed to the poor at Christmas.—Mr. Tyndale, late rector, gave the interest of 10*l.* to be distributed to the poor at the same time.

Taxes.			£.		
The Royal Aid in	1692,		48	13	4
Poll-tax ——	1694,	—	4	19	0
Land-tax ——	1694,	—	52	8	0
The same, at 3*s.*	1770,	—	39	5	9

At the beginning of this century, according to sir Robert Atkyns, there were 26 houses in this parish, and about 120 inhabitants, whereof 5 were freeholders; yearly births 3, burials 2. On an average of ten years, beginning with 1760, the annual baptisms are 4.4, burials 2. The present number of families is 40, of inhabitants exactly 200; by which it appears that only 1 in 100 dies every year, a proof of the astonishing healthiness of the place.

COW HONIBORN.

THIS district, or hamlet, lies in the upper division of Kiftsgate hundred; four miles distant east from Evesham in Worcestershire, five north from Campden, and thirty north-east from Gloucester.

The corrupt manner of writing the modern names of places often misleads in judging of their derivation. If Honiborn has any determinate signification, it is a very different one from that of Heniberge, the old name of this place, as I find it written in *Domesday-book.* The antient name seems to be composed of ƿæn, Saxon, *stone,* and beoꞃᵹ, a *camp* or *fortification*; or of *hen,* British, *old,* and beoꞃᵹ, as before. Sir Robert Atkyns omits the *Domesday* account of this place, and overlooking the antient name, says nothing of its derivation; but he observes of the prenomen *Cow,* that it was so called from the number of cows kept there, and to distinguish it from Church-Honiborn in the neighbourhood.

This little place confifts principally of pafture land, with fome good arable. Two fmall brooks, from Wefton-Subedge, and Afton-Subedge, run through it into the Avon.

Of the Manor and other Eftates.

In *Domefday-book* are the following particulars: 'The fame church [St. Mary of Wincelcumbe] 'holds Heniberge in Celflede hundred. There 'are ten hides, of which two are in demean and 'eight in fervice. In demean are five plow-tillages, 'and fifteen villeins, with five plow-tillages. 'There are nine *fervi*, and three *ancillæ*. It was 'worth 6*l.* now 8*l.*' *Domefday-book*, p. 71.

The right of free warren in this place was allowed to the abbey of Winchcombe in a *Quo Warranto* 15 E. 1. and that houfe continued poffeffed of the manor 'till it was diffolved; after which the manor was granted to lord Burley and John Fortefcue, efq; 33 Eliz. and was purchafed by fir Edward Grevil, of Milcot in Warwickfhire, in the 36th year of that reign, who was lord of it in 1608. The manor feems now to be in the crown, from whom the inhabitants have taken long leafes.

What fir Robert Atkyns mentions of William Strupes being feized of Honiborn 10 E. 1. cannot relate to this place, unlefs it means that he held it under the church of Winchcombe.

Of the Church, &c.

The church of this place ftands in Church-Honiborn in Worcefterfhire. Here was a chapel formerly belonging to the deanery of Campden; but it has been long fince converted into a poor-houfe.

Tithes of hay in Cow Honiborn, formerly belonging to the abbey of Evefham, were granted to John Green and Ralph Hall, 7 E. 6. Other tithes in Honiborn, which belonged to the abbey of Winchcombe, were granted to fir Thomas Seimour 1 E. 6.

Mr. Williams has the impropriation and the advowfon of the vicarage.

Pentecoftals 3*d.*

Taxes.					
The Royal Aid in	1692, £.	115	14	0
Poll-tax ——	1694, —	20	18	0
Land-tax ——	1694, —	114	0	0
The fame, at 3*s.*	1770, —	84	0	0

There were 39 houfes and about 156 inhabitants in this place, whereof 15 were freeholders, when fir Robert Atkyns compiled his Hiftory; yearly births 6, burials 5. And there are now 40 families, and about the fame number of inhabitants.

COWLEY

IS a parifh in the hundred of Rapfgate, in the Cotefwold country, five miles fouth from Cheltenham, nine north-weftward from Cirencefter, and nine eaft from Gloucefter.

The village lies moftly in a narrow glyn, through which the river Churn runs, with hanging woods to the fouth of it, and the rifing lands of Coberley to the north.

Sir Robert Atkyns fuppofes the name to fignify a pafture-ground where cows are kept. This opinion is fupported by the teftimony of the inhabitants, who fay, that within the memory of man the lands were moftly employed in breeding large herds of cattle. But they are at prefent chiefly in tillage, with a due proportion of pafture, and about 100 acres of wood.

Of the Manor and other Eftates.

In *Domefday-book* are the following particulars, omitted by fir Robert Atkyns:

'The church of St. Mary of Perfore holds 'Kvlege in Refpigete hundred. There are five 'hides taxed. In demean are two plow-tillages, 'and fourteen villeins, and one bordar, with feven 'plow-tillages. There are five *fervi*, and a mill 'of 50*d.* and fix acres of meadow, and a wood 'three-quarters of a mile long, and one broad. 'It is worth 100*s.*' *Domefday-book*, p. 72.

The manor continued in the abbey of Perfhore 'till the diffolution, when it was granted to the church of Weftminfter, 34 H. 8. and confirmed 2 Eliz. Henry Bret, efq; was leffee of the manor at the beginning of the prefent century. He was paffionately fond of ringing, and continually travelling about the country with a company of ringers, at a vaft expence, diffipated a plentiful fortune. George Hawker, efq; is the prefent leffee of the manor.

Richard de Brudelep gave two acres of land in Cowley to the brethren of St. Bartholomew's hofpital, Gloucefter.

HAMLETS. 1. *Stockwell*, lying one mile from the church. A fmall ftream rifes here, and falls into the Churn at Cockleford.

2. *Birdlip*, fo much of it only as lies on the north fide of the road from Cirencefter to Gloucefter, is in this parifh.

Of the Church, &c.

The church is a rectory, in the deanery of Stonehoufe, worth 180*l.* a year; the lord chancellor is patron, the reverend Dr. John Brickinden the prefent incumbent.

The church is a fmall building, dedicated to St. Mary, with a neat embattled tower at the weft end, in which are fix mufical bells, the gift of Henry Bret, efq.

Under a niche, in the north wall of the chancel, is the figure of a man lying along, with a lion couchant at his feet. No other monument worth notice.

	£.	s.	d.		£.	s.	d.
Firft fruits	9	1	$10\frac{1}{2}$	Synodals	0	2	0
Tenths —	0	18	$2\frac{1}{4}$	Pentecoftals	0	0	7
Procurations	0	6	8				

Taxes.					
The Royal Aid in	1692, £.	41	19	10
Poll-tax ——	1694, —	8	1	0
Land-tax ——	1694, —	38	0	6
The fame, at 3*s.*	1770, —	30	1	$6\frac{3}{4}$

At

At the beginning of this century there were 39 houſes in this pariſh, and about 160 inhabitants, whereof 4 were freeholders; yearly births 5, burials 5. *Atkyns.* In ten years, beginning with 1760, there are regiſtered 80 baptiſms and 60 burials, and the inhabitants are 268.

****

COWLEY, *or* COALEY,

IS a pariſh in the hundred of Berkeley, ſix miles north-eaſtward from Berkeley, three north from Durſley, and twelve ſouth from Glouceſter. It lies under the north ſides of Uley and Nimpsfield hills, and conſiſts chiefly of good paſture land.

Cowley's-Pick is a ſugar-loaf hill in this pariſh, whence there is an extenſive proſpect over the vale. A ſmall brook runs from hence into the Severn, near Slimbridge.

The public roads here are the worſt that can be conceived; and the poor labouring people are ſo abandoned to naſtineſs, that they throw every thing within a yard or two of their doors, where the filth makes a putrid ſtench, to the injury of their own health, and the annoyance of travellers, if any come among them. The better houſes are gone to ruin, and there is not a gentleman reſident in the pariſh; but this is not peculiar to Cowley.

Of the Manor and other Eſtates.

It appears by *Domeſday-book*, that four hides in Couelege belonged to the honour of Berchelai. And the manor of Cowley has been held by the Berkeley family, and the owners of Berkeley-caſtle, down to the preſent earl of Berkeley, who is lord of this manor.

Richard de Coueley held divers lands in this pariſh in the reign of king Henry the Second. John de Coueley, a deſcendant from him, held one meſſuage, eighty acres of arable, eight acres of meadow, nine acres of paſture, and ten acres of wood, of the king, as of the manor of Berkeley, *Ratione rebellionis manerij de Berkeley*, by the fourth part of a knight's fee. *Eſcheator's Inquiſition* 18 E. 2. And this eſtate continued in the ſame name and family down to 7 H. 5. when it deſcended to daughters.

William Coryet held lands and tenements in Coueley of the king in *capite*, as of the manor of Berkeley, 18 E. 2. *Eſcheator's Inquiſition.*

John Clifford de Daneway was ſeized of 15*s.* rent iſſuing out of a tenement in Cowley 21 R. 2.

Thomas lord Berkeley died ſeized of a tenement called Canon's-court, in Cowley, 5. H 5. and Richard de Beauchamp earl of Warwick died ſeized of it 17 H. 6.

William Warner levied a fine of lands in this pariſh to the uſe of William Harding 18 H. 7. and another fine of other lands to the uſe of John Jones 22 H. 7.

James de Covel gave to St. Bartholomew's hoſpital, in Glouceſter, the meadow of Willewood, with its appurtenances, 44 H. 3.—Robert de Benecumb gave to the ſame hoſpital his land in Boſeley, and one acre and a half in Cliffield, in this pariſh. *Gwydewell-brook* and *Illebrook* occur in the laſt mentioned record; and *Hathmer's-mill*, and *Athemere's-field*, *temp.* H. 3.

Roger de Berkeley gave to the church of Stanley a mill in Cowley, and a meſſuage, and lands belonging to the mill. And Thomas lord Berkeley gave lands in Cowley to St. Bartholomew's hoſpital, Glouceſter, that the *obit* of Maurice his father, and Iſabel his mother, ſhould be kept in full choir. *Magn. cartul. apud Berkeley, fol.* 293.

Of the Church, &c.

The church is a vicarage in the deanery of Durſley, worth 60*l.* a year; the lord chancellor is patron, Mr Hornage the preſent incumbent.

The impropriation was given by Roger de Berkeley to the abbey of Glouceſter, and continued in that houſe 'till the diſſolution of religious foundations, when it paſſed through a variety of hands till it came to the Brownings, who were leſſees of it, and purchaſed the inheritance 14 J. 1.

The impropriation was lately purchaſed of the Brownings by Mr. John Minett, the preſent owner.

Forty-five acres of arable, and thirteen acres of paſture, belong to the glebe.

The church is dedicated to St. Bartholomew, and conſiſts of the nave, and an aile on the north ſide. It has a handſome tower, with pinnacles, at the weſt end, and five bells in it.

	£						
Firſt fruits	8	2	0	Synodals £.	0	2	0
Tenths —	0	16	$2\frac{1}{2}$	Pentecoſtals	0	0	$7\frac{1}{2}$
Procurations	0	6	8				

There are ſeveral memorials in the chancel for the family of Browning, which was of good account, and formerly reſident here.

Benefactions.

Mr. Woodward of Briſtol gave 20*s.* a year to the poor.—Mr. Browning gave 12*s.* rent, two acres of meadow, four of paſture, and four tenements, which are veſted in twelve feoffees for the benefit of the poor.

Taxes.			£.		
The Royal Aid in	1692,		234	8	0
Poll-tax ——	1694,	—	39	19	0
Land-tax ——	1694,	—	245	4	0
The ſame, at 3*s.*	1770,	—	177	3	0

At the beginning of this century, there were 120 houſes in this pariſh, and about 500 inhabitants, whereof 12 were freeholders; yearly births 14, burials 11. *Atkyns.* But examining the pariſh regiſter, I find that in ten years, beginning with 1700, there were 160 baptiſms, and 103 burials; and in a like number of years, beginning with 1760, there were entered 245 baptiſms, and 175 burials. And the preſent number of inhabitants is 598, nearly in the proportion of 35 to 1 of the average of the annual burials.

CRANHAM.

CRANHAM.

THIS parifh lies in the hundred of Rapfgate, eight miles fouthward from Cheltenham, twelve miles north-weftward from Cirencefter, and fix fouth-eaftward from Gloucefter.

Suppofing the name to be derived from *Croen*, Britifh, *rugged*, and *ham* a *village*, it is particularly well adapted to this place, which is remarkably uneven, with many fteep and rugged hills covered with beech wood. But towards Painfwick, there is a fine fpacious opening, which communicates with the vale.

The large beech wood is ufually converted into gun-ftocks for Birmingham, and the wafte and fmaller wood into charcoal.

Tho' the peculiar fituation and other diftinguifhing marks of each parifh are generally noticed under its refpective head; yet as the parifhes lie difperfed thro' this work according to alphabetical arrangement, it may be fometimes neceffary, in order to convey to the reader a more competent idea of the face of a country, to take a fhort view of a larger diftrict. If it were poffible that the eye could be raifed above the horizon, fo as at once to comprehend this, and the adjoining parifhes of Brimpsfield, Side, Miferden, Edgworth, and Bifley, it would be highly delighted with the multiform appearance of hills and dales, woods and paftures, little fields and turgid rifing grounds, watered by fo many rills and limpid ftreams, meandring in a thoufand different forms. The little glyns and dales are fo deep and narrow, that the fun's enlivening rays never fall on them for months together; yet every fpot is cultivated with unremitting labour, and rewards the induftrious hand with plentiful crops of corn and pafture. There are landfcapes which have more of the *Great* and *Wonderful*; but few more truly picturefque, or of greater variety than this would be. The vaftly different foils and afpects, if diligently examined, would probably furnifh a confiderable lift of curious natural productions, of which fome are mentioned under Miferden, tho' it is apprehended many have efcaped notice.

Of the Manor and other Eftates.

There is no place taken notice of in *Domefday-book* of the name of Cranham, nor any thing like it, in Gloucefterfhire. And as Brimpsfield, by the account given of it in that record, feems to have been of much greater extent and confequence than at prefent, being taxed at nine hides, Cranham, adjoining to it, was probably included in that account. Accordingly we find that the Giffards, who were lords of Brimpsfield, were alfo owners of Cranham when it was firft mentioned in the records by that name. Helias, or Elias Giffard, gave Croneham to the abbey of Gloucefter, of which he was a monk, when Hameline was abbat. Elias Giffard, fon of that Elias, in the year 1167, gave eight librats of land in Willingwike in Herefordfhire to the monks of Gloucefter, in exchange for this manor. But the manor of Cranham foon reverted to the abbey, which continued poffeffed of it 'till the diffolution, when a confiderable part was granted, by the name of a manor, to the dean and chapter of Gloucefter, 33 H. 8.

The other part of the manor, with two mills, lately belonging to Catherine queen of England, was granted to John Bridges, afterwards lord Chandos, 1 E. 6. Edward lord Chandos died feized of this manor 15 Eliz. and Giles lord Chandos his fon had livery of it the fame year.

It was foon after purchafed by fir William Sandys, who died 17 C. 1. leaving William his grandfon and heir, whofe grandfon, William Sandys, was lord of the manor at the beginning of this century. It went afterwards, by purchafe, to lord Edgcumbe, who is the prefent lord of it. For his lordfhip's arms, fee *Brimpsfield*.

Climperwell is a confiderable eftate in this parifh, the property of Samuel Hayward, of Wallfworth-Hall, efq.

Lands in Cranham, which belonged to the abbey of Cirencefter, were granted to Richard Andrews and Nicholas Temple, in truft, 35 H. 8.

Of the Church, &c.

The church is a rectory, in the deanery of Stonehoufe, worth about 50*l*. a year. Lord Edgcumbe is patron, Mr. Wallbank the prefent incumbent. The rector receives 1*l*. 18*s*. a year out of *Tibboth-farm*.

The church ftands on the fide of a very fteep afcent, and is dedicated to St. James. It hath an aile on the fouth fide, and a tower at the weft end.

Firft fruits £.	6	4	7	Synodals £.	0	2	0
Tenths —	0	12	8	Pentecoftals	0	0	10

Taxes.					
The Royal Aid in	1692, £.	39	10	4
Poll-tax — —	1694, —	0	9	5
Land-tax ——	1694, —	64	0	0
The fame, at 3*s*.	1770, —	30	1	9

At the beginning of this century, there were 43 houfes and 170 inhabitants in this parifh, whereof 9 were freeholders; yearly births 7, burials 5. *Atkyns*. But examining the parifh regifter, I find that in ten years, beginning with 1700, there were 71 baptifms, and 37 burials; and in a like number of years, beginning with 1760, there were 77 baptifms, and 36 burials; and the number of inhabitants is nearly the fame as feventy years ago.

CROMHALL.

THIS parifh lies in the vale, in the hundred of Berkeley, about feven miles diftant fouth from the town of that name, fix fouth-weft from Wotton-under-edge, and twenty-three fouth from Gloucefter.

The

The name is of doubtful original. It is probable that the old road from *Aqua Solis*, or Bath, to the *Trajectus* at Oldbury, and ſo on to the Roman ſtations in Monmouthſhire, led through this pariſh, or perhaps a little to the ſouthward of it; for there are the remains of a ſtrong encampment in Cromhall-park, where it may be ſuppoſed the ſoldiers were poſted to protect that road. That this was a Roman work is pretty certain, from ſome coins which have been found, and from a teſſellated pavement ſometime ſince diſcovered there, about eighteen feet long, and fifteen broad, compoſed of ſmall cubical bricks, or ſtones, of various colours, and ſet together with a ſtrong cement, in a very curious order and regularity. The above camp lies at a convenient diſtance from two others for obſervation, on Sodbury and Horton hills, a little eaſtward of the ſame line of road, which probably led through Pucklechurch and Weſterleigh, and was guarded between Bath and thoſe places, by a lodgment of ſoldiers at Wick, of which veſtiges have alſo been lately diſcovered.

St. Auguſtine, by the aſſiſtance of Ethelbert king of Kent, called a council of Saxon and Britiſh biſhops to confer on matters of religion. At that time Bangor in Wales was a famous ſeminary of learning, ſome of the monks of which place came hither to conſult an holy anchorite, who had a cell upon a hill in this pariſh, whence it is called *Anchorite-hill*, where the ruins of his cell are ſtill to be ſeen.

Cromhall-heath is a large common of pretty good land, permitted to remain in the unimproved ſtate of nature, like many other fine tracks of ground in this part of the county, to the great injury of the community.

The foſſil productions of this village are pit-coal, and white-lay ſtone. Of the former there is great plenty; but the works have relaxed for ſome time. The latter is common to many other neighbouring pariſhes. It burns to an excellent kind of white, ſtrong lime, in making of which ſome of the labouring inhabitants are employed, whilſt the women and children ſpin wollen-yarn for the clothiers about Wotton-under-edge.

There was formerly a fair for cattle, and a variety of goods, held here on St. Andrew's day; but it has long ſince fallen into neglect and diſuſe.

Of the Manors and other Eſtates.

Before and after the conqueſt, Cromhall was a member of the great manor of Berkeley, for in *Domeſday-book* it is thus expreſſed:

'Two brothers held five hides in Cromhal in 'that manor [*i. e.* Berchelai] in the time of king 'Edward. In demean are two plow-tillages, and 'ſix villeins, and five bordars having ſix plow-til-'lages. Thoſe two brothers might do what they 'pleaſed with themſelves and their land. It was 'then worth 4*l.* now 3*l.* Earl William commit-'ted them to the care of the ſteward of Berchelai, 'that he might have their ſervice, as Roger ſays.'

And in another place in the ſame record, it is ſaid, 'Two hides in Cromale belong to Berchelai.' *Domeſday-book*, p. 68.

Robert lord Berkeley, in the year 1148, gave one of thoſe manors to the monaſtery of St. Auguſtine in Briſtol, wherefore it was called *Cromhall-Abbats*. The abbey had free-warren and court-leet therein 13 & 15 E. 1. and continued in poſſeſſion of this manor 'till the diſſolution. It was afterwards granted to Paul, biſhop of Briſtol, and his ſucceſſors, on the eſtabliſhment of the ſee of Briſtol, 34 H. 8. and now is in that church; but it was ſold to Richard Kirrington and Roger Cook, for 568*l.* 0*s.* 2*d.* in the year 1649.

There is another manor in this pariſh, called *Cromhall-Ligon*, becauſe it formerly belonged to the Ligons.

William de Wantone levied a fine of the fourth part of the manor of Cromhall, and of the advowſon, 18 E. 2. and a perſon of the ſame name levied another fine thereof 11 E. 3.

Sir John Berkeley of Beverſtone died ſeized of the manor of Cromhall 6 H. 6. out of which family it went by purchaſe to the Ligons; and livery of the manor of Cromhall and Redgrove was granted to Richard Ligon, 9 Eliz. but ſir William Throgmorton was lord of the manor in 1608.

It was ſoon afterwards purchaſed by ſir Robert Ducie, from whom it deſcended to lord Ducie, the preſent owner of this manor; whoſe deſcent and arms are given under Woodcheſter, his lordſhip's reſidence.

Sir William Ducie obtained a licence for incloſing Cromhall-park in the year 1661.

John Newton of Briſtol, and Joan his wife, levied a fine of lands in Cromhall 8 H. 8.

Woodend is a place in this pariſh, where the late Mr. Matthews, who had been ſteward to the earl of Berkeley, built a large handſome houſe, which coſt him many thouſand pounds.

Of the Church, &c.

The church is a rectory, in the deanery of Hawkeſbury, worth upwards of 200*l.* a year; of which Oriel college has the advowſon; and the reverend doctor Penny is the preſent incumbent.

About fifty acres of land belong to the glebe; and a ground called *Didnam's-Place*, containing ſix acres, part in Wickwar, and part in this pariſh, is given to repair the church.

The church is dedicated to St. Andrew. It conſiſts of the nave and a ſouth aile, in which was an antient ſtone monument, conſiſting of the figure of a man lying croſs-legged, intended, as ſuppoſed, for one of the Ligons. But it was lately built in the ſouth wall, to ſave the pariſh three-pence in materials for the repair.

Firſt fruits £.	16	19	2	Synodals	0	2	0
Tenths —	1	12	11	Pentecoſt.	0	1	0
Procurations	0	6	0				

 There

There is a Latin memorial for Nicholas Hickes, B.D. who had been rector of Charfield, and a prebendary in the church of Chichester, who died in 1710. His arms are, *Gules, a fess undy between three fleurs-de-lis Or.* And another for Robert Webb of Abbat's-side, in this parish, who died in 1731; and for Lucia his wife, daughter of Robert Allen of Woodend; and for Robert their eldest son, who died in 1762. Their arms, *Sable, three eschallops in bend argent.*

Taxes.						
	The Royal Aid in	1692,	£. 123	14	0
	Poll-tax —	1694, —	42	0	0
	Land-tax —	1694, —	151	0	0
	The same, at 3*s.*	1770, —	112	8	11¼

There were 73 houses in this parish, and about 360 inhabitants, at the beginning of this century, whereof 34 were freeholders; yearly births 12, burials 11. *Atkyns.* There are now about 316 inhabitants.

CUBBERLY, *or* COBERLEY.

THE greater part of this parish lies in the hundred of Rapsgate, but some part of it is in Bradley hundred. It is four miles south from Cheltenham, ten north-westward from Cirencester, and nine east from Gloucester; and is bounded on the south by Cowley.

These two parishes have something of the appearance of a bason, with a piece broken off one side to the bottom; for to the north, west, and south, the lands extend up the sides of the hills which divide the Coteswold from the Vale, and so form the top of a little valley, with an opening to the east.

From *Crickley-hill*, which lies partly in this parish, there is a most astonishing prospect of the country towards Gloucester; and there is another very extensive view from the top of *Pinswell*, (a hamlet in Coberley) as far as the city of Worcester on one hand, and almost to Marlborough in Wiltshire on the other, which places are above sixty miles asunder.

The river Churn rises here, at a place called the *Seven Wells*, within a small distance of the road from Gloucester to Oxford. This is deservedly considered as the head of the Thames, being the highest source of that river. The united waters of these springs are so copious as to drive a corn-mill a little below. The Churn runs through Colesbourn, Rendcombe, North Cerney, and so on to Cirencester.

Coberley, from the British word *Cop*, signifies the top of the pasture, and I am told that within the memory of some of the inhabitants, the whole parish was in lays or pasture; but now the greater part is converted to tillage. This etymology is from conjecture; but Leland was certainly mistaken, who calls in *Cowberley*, as he says, shortly for *Cow Berkeley*; for Coberleie was the name of it in the reign of king Edward the Confessor, before the Berkeleys had any property here, as appears by the following record.

Of the Manor and other Estates.

'Roger de Berchelai holds Coberleie in Respigete 'hundred. There are ten hides. Dena, a thane 'of king Edward, held it. In demean are two 'plow-tillages, and nineteen villeins, and four 'bordars with five plow-tillages. There are four '*servi*, and five acres of meadow; a wood three-'quarters of a mile long, and half a mile broad. 'It was worth 7*l.* now 8*l.*' *Domesday-book*, p. 75.

The manor, says sir Robert Atkyns, did afterwards pass to Robert Waleran, but he was most probably mistaken; for there were two manors or estates in this parish, at the time of the general survey. And it is observable, that in those times the records often describe several manors in the same parish by one general name. These estates lay in different hundreds, and continued in different proprietors for a long time. Sir Robert's inattention to those distinctions occasioned the mistake. There is therefore the strongest reason to believe, that the principal manor continued in the uninterrupted possession of the Berkeley family 'till it was carried out of it by the marriage of an heiress.

The records shew that sir Thomas de Berkeley held the manor of Cubberly 8 E. 3. and that Thomas Berkeley his son held it 25 E. 3. and died seized thereof 6 H. 4. leaving Alice, his only daughter and heiress, married to sir John Brugg, who had issue by her two sons, Giles and Edward. Alice surviving her husband, was married to Thomas Browning, whom she also survived, and held this manor in jointure at the time of her death 2 H. 5. Sir Giles Brugg, or Bruges, was her son and heir; who married Catherine, daughter of James Clifford, of Frampton, esq; and relict of Anselm Gyse, of Elmore in this county, esq; and died seized of the manor of Coberley 6 E. 4. Thomas Brydges was his son and heir; who married Florence, daughter of William Darrel, and was succeeded by his son sir Giles Brydges, who married Isabel, daughter of Thomas Baynham, and died seized of the manor of Coberley 3 H. 8. leaving John his son nine years old. He had livery of this manor granted to him 16 H. 8. and married Elizabeth, daughter of Edward lord Grey of Wilton. He was created lord Chandos of Sudley 1 Mar. and died in the 4th year of the same reign, leaving Edmund lord Chandos his son and heir, who had livery of the manor of Coberley the same year. He married Dorothy, daughter and coheir of Edmond lord Bray, and died 15 Eliz. Giles lord Chandos, his son, had livery of the manor the same year. He married Frances, daughter of Edward earl of Lincoln, and died 36 Eliz. leaving two daughters coheiresses. Frances his widow held Coberley in jointure, and was seized thereof in 1608.

This

This manor was ſoon after purchaſed by the Duttons of Sherbourn. John Dutton gave it in marriage with his daughter Lucy, to ſir Thomas Pope, earl of Down. It was again purchaſed, about the middle of the laſt century, by the Caſtleman family. Jonathan Caſtleman, eſq; in the year 1720, ſold the manor of Coberley for 40000*l.* to John How, eſq; father of John firſt lord Chedworth; and Henry-Frederick lord Chedworth is the preſent lord of this manor.

HAMLETS. 1. *Lower Coberley*, as before.

2. *Pinſwell*, ſometimes called *Upper Coberley*, conſiſting of only two houſes. It lies in the hundred of Bradley, and was a member of the manor of Northleach, as appears by *Domeſday-book*. It has contributed to the relief of the poor of that pariſh, and ſtill pays land-tax in aid of Eaſtington there. The name of *Pinſwell*, from *pen* the *top*, and *well*, a *ſpring of water*, is exactly deſcriptive of its ſituation on the top of a high hill above the reſt of the village; a perennial ſpring riſing on the brow of the hill, runs down a ſteep deſcent, and joins the Churn water at the manor-houſe of Coberley. This eſtate is deſcribed in *Domeſday-book*, under the head *Terra Thome Archiep'i, viz.*

'In Culberlege in Bradelege hundred is one 'hide belonging to this manor [*i.e.* Lecce, which 'we now call Northleach.] The hide at Culberlege 'is worth 20*s.*' *Domeſday-book*, p. 70.

The manor of Coberley, then called *Turpindeſwelle*, corruptly for *Tre-pindeſwelle*, [i.e. *Pinſwell-place*] was given to the nunnery of Glouceſter when Eva or Edytha was abbeſs, who died in 768. In 1058 it was taken from the abbey of Glouceſter by Aldred archbiſhop of York, as being a member of the manor of Lecce, to reimburſe him his expences in rebuilding the abbey; but it was reſtored to that houſe by Thomas archbiſhop of York, in 1094, ſoon after the general ſurvey.

Robert Waleran died ſeized of the manor of Coberley 1 E. 1. He left no iſſue, and was ſucceeded by his nephew Robert. John Waleran, and Robert Waleran with Iſabel his wife, were ſeized of 4*l.* rent in Coberley 2 E. 2. but John Limel held the manor the ſame year.

Though the above perſons are ſaid to be ſeized of the manor of Coberley, yet it muſt be underſtood only of Pinſwell, or Upper Coberley, which they held under the abbey of Glouceſter.

The abbey of Glouceſter was ſeized of lands, and of a portion of tithes, in Coberley, 17 E. 3.

It does not appear to whom Pinſwell was granted at the diſſolution of Glouceſter abbey. But it is probable that it paſſed into lay hands, together with the manor of Northleach, of which it was a member. One of the Duttons of Sherbourn purchaſed the manor of lower Coberley, and John Dutton gave it in marriage with his daughter Lucy, to Thomas earl of Down. It is likely that this eſtate went with the other manor, for ſince that time they have had the ſame proprietors.

Of the Church, &c.

The church is a rectory, in the deanery of Stonehouſe, worth 200*l.* a year. Lord Chedworth is patron, the reverend Mr. John Arnold the preſent incumbent.

The rector preſented to a chantry in the church of Beauvale in Nottinghamſhire in the year 1401.

The patronage of this church belonged to the priory of Little Malvern in Worceſterſhire.

There was a chantry in the church dedicated to the virgin Mary, founded by Thomas Berkeley in the year 1340, of which William Williams was the laſt incumbent. This chantry was granted to ſir John Brydges 1 E. 6.

The church is an antient building, dedicated to St. Giles, with a ſmall aile on the ſouth ſide, and a ſtrong tower at the weſt end, with three bells in it.

There is a tradition that there was a chapel at Pinſwell, and foundations of buildings have lately been dug up there, on the ſpot where the chapel is ſaid to have ſtood.

Firſt fruits £	10	0	0	Synodals	0	2	0
Tenths —	1	0	0	Pentecoſtals	0	1	7
Procurations	0	6	8				

In the chancel is the figure of a knight in armour, lying on his back, girt with a ſword, and his legs acroſs, with a lion at his feet: Oppoſite is the figure of a lady, in the dreſs of the age of Edward the Third. Under a niche in the north wall, is the figure of a man in net armour, holding his eſcutcheon before him, but the arms are utterly deſtroyed: And under an arch in the ſouth wall, is an antient female figure, lying along in full proportion; but no account can be given of the perſons they were intended for.

Taxes.			£.		
The Royal Aid in	1692,	£.	51	4	4
Poll-tax ——	1694,	—	22	7	0
Land-tax ——	1694,	—	52	12	0
The ſame, at 3*s.*	1770,	—	33	17	4

At the beginning of this century, there were 14 houſes and about 80 inhabitants in this pariſh, whereof 3 were freeholders; yearly births 3, burials 2. *Atkyns.* But in ten years, from 1764, the average of annual baptiſms was 2.8, of burials 1.8; and the preſent number of families is 27, of inhabitants exactly 178. But no fair concluſion concerning the healthineſs of the place, can be drawn from the above numbers, ſince ſome of the inhabitants have buried at the neighbouring pariſh of Cowley.

DAGLINGWORTH

LIES in the hundred of Crowthorne and Minety, in the Coteſwold country, three miles north-weſtward from Cirenceſter, ſix eaſt from Biſley, and fifteen ſouth-eaſtward from Glouceſter.

The name ſeems to be derived from the Saxon ꝺiᵹel, *hidden*, and ƿeoꞃð, a *village*; the greater part of the houſes ſtanding in a narrow dale, not eaſily

eaſily ſeen from the great road, which lies a little to the eaſt of it.

A ſmall ſtream, riſing in Dunteſbourn, runs through the village to Stratton, and falls into the Churn at Cirenceſter. And the *Irminſtreet*, a great Roman road, leading from Cirenceſter to Glouceſter, paſſes thro' the pariſh. It is thrown up very broad and high, and notwithſtanding it is much injured by the injudicious management of ſurveyors, yet it ſtill remains very viſible for many miles together. I have given the derivation of the name of this road, agreeably to Camden, under Cirenceſter: But it has ſince occurred to me, that the name is of Saxon original; for Heꞃe in that language ſignifies *an army*, and Heꞃeman *a ſoldier*. So that *Irminſtreet* is nothing more than the expreſſion *via militaris* tranſlated into the Saxon language; and ſignifies the *ſoldier's road*, as having been made by the Roman ſoldiers, who were occaſionally employed that way.

The Romans had an advanced poſt in this village, as appears by the ruins of ſome foundations, and a teſſellated pavement, diſcovered in a ground called *Cave-Cloſe*, about a century ago.

On the eaſt ſide of this Roman way, on a large down, is found a kind of ſtone peculiar to this place, and the neighbouring pariſhes of Stratton and Bagendon. It is called the *Dagham-down-ſtone*. It lies juſt under the ſod, on a bed of black mould, unmixed with any other kind of ſtone. It is of a cloſe whitiſh grit, very hard, and endures all weathers. The ſtones riſe ſingly, of infinite ſhapes and uncommon figures, occaſioned by a number of circular perforations, from one inch to three or four inches diameter; which ſeem to have been made by a kind of fermentation in the ſtony matter, whilſt in a ſoft ſtate; for the ſurface of the hollow part is as ſmooth as if cut with a ſharp inſtrument. They are ſhaped like various kinds of animals, human ſculls, bones, and other irregular figures, much eaſier conceived than deſcribed; and are carried to great diſtances to ornament grottos, bridges, and ruſtic buildings, in which they have an effect vaſtly ſuperior to any work of art.

And on the ſame down, there is another curious kind of ſtone lying near the ſurface. It riſes ſometimes three or four feet ſquare, is of a whitiſh grit, hard as marble, full of petrified ſhells, and bears a good poliſh.

Of the Manor and other Eſtates.

In *Domeſday-book* this place is not mentioned, being probably conſidered at the time of the ſurvey, as a part of the manor of Stratton; but in the ſheriff's return of all the vills in the hundred of Cirenceſter 9 E. 1. Daglingworth is expreſſly mentioned, and Stratton omitted, whence it ſeems probable, that 'till that time at leaſt they were one pariſh.

This manor was held by Ralph Bloet in the reign of king Henry the Second, and by another Ralph Bloet, who had a grant of free-warren in Daglingworth 9 E. 3. Sir John Bloet, ſon of Ralph, died ſeized of this manor, leaving Elizabeth his only daughter and heireſs, who by her marriage with ſir James de Berkeley, carried this manor into that name and family, in which it continued down to 44 Eliz. when Henry lord Berkeley ſold it to ſir Henry Poole for 1320*l*. From the Pooles it paſſed to ſir Robert Atkyns of Saperton, who was lord of it at the beginning of this century, out of whoſe family it went by purchaſe to the earl of Bathurſt, whoſe ſon the preſent earl of Bathurſt is lord of the manor.

Of the other eſtates, the records ſhew, that William Boiſe and others held lands in Daglingworth 32 H. 3. William Nottingham and Elizabeth his wife levied a fine of lands in Daglingworth to the uſe of themſelves in ſpecial taille 20 H. 6.

Of the Church, &c.

The church is a rectory, in the deanery of Cirenceſter, worth about 80 *l*. a year, the lord chancellor is patron, Mr. Chapman the preſent incumbent.

The abbeſs of Godſtow in Oxfordſhire preſented to this church in the year 1499.

Seventy-three acres of arable land in the common fields belong to the glebe.

The church is ſmall, dedicated to the Holy Croſs, and has a ſtrong tower at the weſt end.

Firſt fruits £.	8	6	3	Synodals £.	0	2	0
Tenths —	0	16	7½	Pentecoſtals	0	0	6
Procurations	0	6	8				

Taxes.					
The Royal Aid in	1692, £.	28	16	0
Poll-tax ——	1694, —	5	6	0
Land-tax ——	1694, —	21	12	0
The ſame, at 3*s*.	1770, —	16	4	0

At the beginning of this century, there were 31 houſes in this pariſh, and about 138 inhabitants, whereof 7 were freeholders; yearly births 4, burials 3. But in ten years, beginning with 1700, there are entered in the pariſh regiſter 48 baptiſms, and 18 burials; and in a like ſeries, beginning with 1760, there are entered 46 baptiſms, and 41 burials, and the preſent number of inhabitants is 184, nearly as 45 to 1 of the annual burials.

DEAN, *or* MITCHEL DEAN,

LIES in the hundred of St. Briavel, (but antiently in Weſtbury hundred) in the foreſt-diviſion of the county, ſeven miles diſtant ſouth from Newent, five north from Newnham, and twelve weſt from Glouceſter.

Agreeably to the name, this place is ſituated in a little low valley, between two hills, with the foreſt of Dean on the weſt and ſouth-weſt of it. It is a little market-town, conſiſting of one very narrow, crooked ſtreet, of ordinary low buildings. The market is held on Monday, and pretty well fre-

frequented; for the convenience of which a new market-houſe hath been lately built by the lord of the manor. Here is a fair on Eaſter-monday, and another on the 10th of October.

The town had formerly ſome ſhare in the cloathing-trade, which gave way to that of pin-making, and this hath long ſince left it, (for want of proper ſpirit in the manufacturers) to be foſtered under abler managers at Glouceſter: ſo that at preſent, having no ſupport from manufactures, and but little from travelling, tho' the turnpike-road from Glouceſter to Monmouth leads through it, the town is evidently in decline.

In this place, and in many others about the foreſt, large quantities of rich cinders have been found, from which our anceſtors, for want of more powerful engines, could not extract the iron.

Of the Manor and other Eſtates.

'William the ſon of Norman holds two hides, 'two yard-lands and a half in Dene. Three 'thanes, Godric, Elric, and Ernui held theſe lands 'in the time of king Edward. There are three 'plow-tillages in demean, and thirty-eight bordars 'have ſeven plow-tillages and a half, three of 'which pay 8*s*. It was worth 33*s*. now 44*s*. 'King Edward exempted theſe lands from tax, 'for the preſervation of the foreſt.' *D. B.* p. 74.

The regular canons of Southwick in Hampſhire were ſeized of lands in Dean, and had a charter of liberties therein 1 Joh. and a grant of another part of Dean in the 5th year of that reign, the reſt remaining in the king's hands.

This manor, and a bailiwick in the foreſt, were held by William de Dean 47 H. 3. and by Henry de Dean 20 E. 1. John Abbenhall was ſeized of the manor of Michel-Dean, and of one meſſuage, and 140 acres of land, 10 E. 2. and William de Dean held Great Dean, St. Briavel's-caſtle, and four acres of aſſart-land in Bradell, 12 E. 2. and Reginald de Abbenhall had a grant of markets and fairs in Great Dean 2 E. 3.

John Tiptot, earl of Worceſter, had this manor in marriage with Elizabeth Grender, and held it till his death; but leaving no iſſue by her, it reverted to the Grenders, and went out of that name to the Walwyns, by the marriage of an heireſs. It was afterwards carried out of the name of Walwyn, by an heireſs to the Baynhams; and deſcended like Abbenhall, down to Chriſtopher Baynham, who had livery of this manor 3 E. 6. He dying 5 Mar. livery was granted the ſame year to his brother Richard; as it was to Robert Baynham 9 Eliz. and to Joſeph Baynham 14 Eliz. And Thomas Baynham had livery of the fourth part of the manor of Mitchel-Dean, and of the third part of the advowſon of the rectory, 20 Eliz.

It afterwards became the property of ſir Robert Woodruffe; but Maynard Colcheſter, of Weſtbury, eſq; is the preſent lord of the manor.

Walter de Laci gave his lands in Dene to the abbey of Glouceſter, which gift the king confirmed 14 W. 1. Roger de Staunton gave the water-courſe of Dene and of Clinch to the ſaid abbey, 7 R. 1. And the abbey held lands in Dean of Edward earl of March 3 H. 6.

The inhabitants of Dean had right of eſtovers and paſturage in the foreſt of Dean 7 H. 3.

Of the Church, &c.

The church is a rectory, in the deanery of the foreſt, worth 50*l*. a year. Mr. Colcheſter is patron, Mr. John Harris the preſent incumbent. There is no land tithe-free.

The church hath two ailes, and a handſome ſpire at the weſt-end, with eight bells. It is dedicated to St. Michael, whence the town is called Mitchel-Dean. There was a ſmall chantry, dedicated to the holy Trinity, whereof Henry Hooper was the laſt incumbent.

Five ſmall parcels of land, and ſome cottages, are given for the repair of the church, and for the uſe of the poor.

Firſt fruits £.	10	16	0	Proc.&Syn. £.	0	2	6
Tenths —	1	1	7¼	Pentecoſtals	0	2	0

Taxes.	The Royal Aid in 1692, £.	86	18	0
	Poll-tax —— 1694, —	30	7	0
	Land-tax —— 1694, —	87	5	10
	The ſame, at 3*s*. 1770, —	63	15	0

At the beginning of this century, there were 120 houſes and about 600 inhabitants in this pariſh, whereof 20 were freeholders; yearly births 19, burials 18. *Atkyns*. But the above numbers are incorrectly taken, for in ten years, beginning with 1700, I counted from the regiſter 225 baptiſms, and 150 burials; and in ten years, from 1760, 188 baptiſms, and 143 burials; and there are now 590 inhabitants.

****

DEAN (LITTLE.)

THIS is a pariſh in the hundred of St. Briavel, in the foreſt of Dean, three miles ſouth from Mitchel-Dean, two north from Newnham, and twelve weſtward from Glouceſter.

It abounds with excellent coal and iron ore, and great quantities of very rich iron cinders have been dug here. The labouring inhabitants are employ'd in mining, and in a ſmall nail manufacture. Here is a market-houſe without a market. On Whit-monday, and on the 26th of November, are two fairs for pedlery.

This village affords very little matter for the entertainment of the curious. If it were not an offence to quote a writer profeſſedly in the parliament's intereſt in the reign of king Charles the Firſt, I would mention from Corbet a melancholy tranſaction which happened here. Governor Maſſy (of whom the reader may ſee more under Glouceſter) ſent a party of horſe to alarm a little garriſon at this place, whilſt he fell upon Weſtbury himſelf. This party ſurpriſed and took about twenty of the king's men; and alſo ſurrounded colonel

colonel Congreve, governor of Newnham, and one captain Wigmore, with a few private ſoldiers, who were in ſome houſes. They had accepted quarter, and were ready to ſurrender, when one of the company from the houſes killed a trooper, which ſo enraged the reſt, that they broke in upon them, and put them all to the ſword. Congreve died with theſe words, *Lord, receive my ſoul*: but Wigmore uttered nothing but the bittereſt execrations: upon which Corbet makes a remark of the extreme contrariety in the ſpirits of men, even under the ſtroke of death.

Mr. Pyrke has a good houſe and eſtate here. Thomas Pyrke, eſq; the late owner of them, married Dorothy, daughter of Richard Yate, of Arlingham, eſq; by whom he had two ſons and a daughter; and ſurviving them, he bequeathed this eſtate to —— Watkyns, deſcended, by the mother's ſide, from a brother of the ſaid Thomas Pyrke, who aſſumes the name of Pyrke and reſides at this place. See inſcriptions at Abbenhall, for the family arms.

Of the Manor and other Eſtates.

There is no diſtinct account of this manor in *Domeſday-book*, becauſe it was taken out of Great Dean, or Mitchel-Dean, ſince the compilation of that record. William de Dean (of whom already under Mitchel-Dean) died 12 E. 2. ſeized of Dean, which he held in *capite*, paying 10*s.* a year to the conſtable of St. Briavel's caſtle, and ſerving the king in his army in the counties of Glouceſter, Hereford, and Worceſter, three days at his own expence. *Eſch.* The manor afterwards came to the Grenders, and deſcended preciſely like the manor of Mitchel-Dean to Maynard Colcheſter, eſq; who is the preſent lord of this manor.

Sir Anthony Kingſton had a grant of an eſtate by the name of a manor in Little Dean 36 H. 8. valued at that time at 14*l.* 2*s.* 2*d.* Richard Brain, eſq; died ſeized of lands in Little Dean 15 Eliz.

Of the Church, &c.

The church is an impropriation in the foreſt deanery, belonging to St. Bartholomew's hoſpital, Glouceſter. The corporation of that city are patrons, Mr. Webb is the preſent incumbent. It is uſually joined in the ſame preſentation with Newnham. The incumbent has a leaſe of the impropriation, out of which he pays 8*l.* a year for the uſe of the hoſpital, the reſt being allowed to him as curate.

The church is dedicated to St. Ethelbert. It has a double roof, ſupported by pillars in the middle. There was a chantry erected 13 H. 4. dedicated to the holy Trinity. George Pomefrey, the laſt incumbent, retired with a penſion of 4*l.* And the lands of this chantry were granted to William Herick and Arthur Ingram 5 Jac.

Procurat. and Synodals 1*s.* 0*d.* Pentecoſt. 1*s.* 4*d.*

Monument and Inſcription.

On the ſouth ſide of the chancel,

Vanus honor tituli, nec opum poſſeſſio certa;
Virtus ſola decus, mens bona divitiæ.
O quicunque domum cupias nomenq; tueri,
Nomen amare pius divi domumq; Dei.

H. S. E. Tho: Pyrke, Armiger, qui uſque adeo in verbis fidem, in vitâ ſobrietatem, et, in hoc comitatu Juſticiarius, pacem publicam conſervavit, ut tandem ævi ſatur, An. Ætat. LXXII April ix. A. D. MDCCII. in pace deceſſit. Uxore Debora tribuſq; filiis diu antea præmiſſis, et in eccleſia de Abbenhall, una cum primagenitorum ſtirpe, ſepultis, ejus memoriæ Nathaniel filius hæreſq; hoc monumentum gratus parentavit.

Taxes.			£.	s.	d.
	The Royal Aid in	1692,	60	4	0
	Poll-tax ——	1694, —	29	0	0
	Land-tax ——	1694, —	73	5	3
	The ſame, at 3*s.*	1770, —	53	5	0

At the beginning of this century, according to ſir Robert Atkyns, there were 70 houſes, and about 320 inhabitants in this pariſh, whereof 8 were freeholders; yearly births 10, burials 9. But I find that in ten years, beginning with 1714, there were 146 baptiſms, and 115 burials; and in the ſame number of years, beginning with 1761, the baptiſms were 144, the burials 106. And the inhabitants are now about 423.

DEERHURST, *or* DERHURST.

PART of this pariſh (the tithing of Derhurſt) lies in the hundred of its own name, three miles diſtant ſouth from Tewkeſbury, and eight north from Glouceſter.

The pariſh is bounded by the Severn for two miles on the weſt, and lying moſtly flat and low, is extremely ſubject to floods from that river. In 1770, the flood roſe to the top of the firſt floor of moſt of the houſes in the village, and ſo continued many days together; but it was much higher in ſome parts of the pariſh. The roads are almoſt impaſſable in the winter.

It appears from *Domeſday-book*, that there was a large wood in Derhurſt, that in part gave denomination to the place; for the name is compoſed of *Dwr*, Britiſh, *water*, and Ƿeȝꞅꞇ, Saxon, *a wood*, and ſignifies *the wood by the water*. This explanation agrees preciſely with the ſituation, and is much preferable to that which accounts for the former part of the name, by ſuppoſing that deer formerly harboured there, which notion probably took riſe from the more modern manner of writing it.

Common occurrences are improper for hiſtory, becauſe unintereſting; and the marvellous and wonderful are to be admitted with caution. Finding the following ſtory in ſir Robert Atkyns, is my only reaſon for giving it a place in this account. The ſtory is, that a ſerpent of a prodigious bigneſs was a great grievance to all the country about Derhurſt, by poiſoning the inhabitants and killing their cattle. The inhabitants petitioned the king, and a proclamation was iſſued out, that whoſoever ſhould kill the ſerpent ſhould enjoy an eſtate on Walton-hill in this pariſh, which then belonged to the crown. One John Smith, a labourer, engaged in the enterprize, and ſucceeded: For having put a quantity of milk in a place to which the ſerpent reſorted, he gorged

the

the whole, agreeable to expectation, and lay down to sleep in the sun, with his scales ruffled up. Seeing him in that situation, Smith advanced, and striking between the scales with his axe, took off his head. The family of the Smiths enjoyed the estate, when sir Robert compiled this account, and Mr. Lane, who married a widow of that family, had then the axe in his possession.

There is a small island here, called the Eight, made by the dividing of the waters of the Severn, which some writers have taken for the Olanige, or Alney, where Edmund Ironside and Canute the Dane fought in single combat for the kingdom; but the isle of Alney, near Gloucester, was most probably the scene of that famous engagement.

Derhurst common is remarkable for its great extent, and for being frequently overflowed with water. It begins at the church-yard, and goes round a good part of the parish, about four miles in length, joining the Leigh common. A few years ago the inhabitants of the Leigh dug a deep ditch across, to divide the parishes, whereupon an action was brought against them; and on trial, the right of common being a manerial right, under the manor of Plaistow, which includes both parishes, a verdict with damages passed against them. If I am not mistaken, a commission of sewers, for the improvement of estates liable to be overflowed by the Severn from Gloucester upwards, was issued in the last king's reign; which, if carried into execution, might make this a most valuable piece of ground, and greatly improve many other estates in this part of the country.

Here is an antient bridge, which obtained the name of *Gildable-bridge*, from certain tolls and customs having been formerly paid at it. 'Tis part repaired by Norton, and part by Derhurst. And here was a fair held on Holy-rood day, now totally disused.

But more observable for antiquity is the priory which stood in this place, which Bede mentions to be a famous monastery in his time. It is said to have been built about the year 715, of which Leland gives the following account from a manuscript he had seen in Tewkesbury abbey. Almarick, brother to Odo and Dodo, great noblemen of Mercia, was buried in a small chapel at Deorhurste, which had been a royal palace; where, in the wall over the door, it was written, *Hanc aulam Dodo dux consecrari fecit in ecclesiam, ad honorem beatæ Mariæ Virginis, ob amorem fratris sui Almarici:* i.e. Duke Dodo, for the affection he bore to his brother Almarick, caused this palace to be consecrated into a church, to the honour of the blessed Virgin Mary. *Itin.* v. 6. And in the year 1675, there was an old stone dug up here in Mr. Powell's orchard, with this inscription: *Odda dux jussit hanc aulam regiam construi, atq; dedicari in honorem S. Trinitatis pro anima Germani sui Elfrici, quæ de hoc loco assumpta erat. Ealdredus vero episcopus qui eandem dedicavit* ii *idibus April.* xiv° *autem anno S.*[u] *regni Eadwardi regis Anglorum.* That is, Duke Odda commanded this royal palace to be built, and to be dedicated to the Holy Trinity, for the soul of his cousin (or brother) Elfrick, which was parted from his body in this place. But Ealdred was the bishop who consecrated it, on the second of the ides of April, in the 14th year of the reign of the holy king Edward.

To reconcile these accounts, we must suppose that Almarick and Elfrick are only accidental variations in the name of the same person. The dedication to the virgin Mary mentioned in the first account, refers to the original consecration. But the Danes ravaging and destroying the monastery, it continued in a low condition for many years; 'till Edward the Confessor caused it to be rebuilt and consecrated in the year 1056; and the latter account must relate to the second consecration. He also endowed the priory with the advowsons of Derhurst, Woolstone, Prestone, and Compton, and made it an alien priory, subject to the abbey of St. Dennis at Paris; all which William the Conqueror confirmed[w] in the year 1069. But William of Malmesbury tells us, that in his time this house was only an empty monument of antiquity. Leland says, *The olde Priory stode est from Severn a bow shotte, and north of the town. There remayne yet dyverse names of streates, as Fisschar-streate, and others. But the buildings of them are gone*; to which I must add, that many ruins of old foundations have been found, which shew the place was formerly much larger than at present.

St. Alphege, archbishop of Canterbury, about the year 960, was a private monk in this monastery.

King Richard the Second found some pretence for seizing into his hands all the manors and lands belonging to this priory, and John de Beauchamp of Holt obtained a grant of them 11 R. 2.

By the statute of 2 H. 5. all the possessions of alien priories were vested in the crown, except of such as were conventual. This house therefore was not within that statute. But king Henry the Sixth having wars with France, it was not thought fit to permit the abbey of St. Dennis to have the patronage of this cell, and the right of presenting the prior; he therefore by his[x] charter makes it a priory denizen 1 H. 6. and grants them power to elect their own prior; but gave the patronage of the monastery to the abbey of Tewkesbury. Hugh Magason was the last prior alien.

King Henry the Sixth, in the nineteenth year of his reign, founded Eaton-college, and dissolving the monastery of Derhurst, gave most of their lands to that college, the rest to Tewkesbury abbey, which occasioned great law-suits between the college and the abbey, that were not finally determined till Henry the Seventh's reign; when it was settled, that Goldcliff-priory and lands should go to the college, and Derhurst to the abbey of Tewkesbury. John Bromsgrove was the last prior, and had a pension of 13*l.* 6*s* 8*d.*

[u] *S.* should be placed after *regni*.

[w] Appendix N°. 32.

[x] Ibid. N°. 33.

King

King Edward the Fourth being willing to abrogate the acts of king Henry the Sixth, who was of the Lancaſtrian line, takes away thoſe lands from Eaton-college, 17° *regni*, and beſtows them on the college of Fotheringhay in Northamptonſhire, which was founded by Edward duke of York, of his own family, in the year 1415; which lands were afterwards regranted to the college of Eaton by king Henry the Eighth.

Lands in Derhurſt, and the ſcite of the priory, which lately belonged to the abbey of Tewkeſbury, were granted to Giles Throgmorton, in conſideration of the manor of White Waltone, and other lands in Berkſhire, 34 H. 8. and Thomas Throgmorton had livery of them 12 Eliz. The ſcite of this antient priory is exempt from tithes, and is now the property of the earl of Coventry, who is alſo viſcount Deerhurſt. His lordſhip's arms are *Sable, a feſs ermine between three creſcents Or.* SUPPORTERS, *Two eagles, wings expanded, argent, member'd and beaked Or.* MOTTO, CANDIDE ET CONSTANTER.

Of the Manors and other Eſtates.

'The church of St. Peter at Weſtminſter holds 'Derheſt in Derheſt hundred. There are fifty-'nine hides. There were five hides in the chief 'manor in the time of king Edward. There are 'three plow-tillages and twenty villeins, and eight 'bordars with ten plow-tillages. There are ſix '*ſervi*, and ſixty acres of meadow; a wood two 'miles long, and half a mile broad. It is worth 'and was worth 10*l*.' *Domeſday-book*, p. 72.

But it is ſuppoſed that the above fifty-nine hides include other manors which were held of this, and are expreſſly mentioned in the record to be *ad hoc manerium Berewicci*, members belonging to this manor; and are as follow: Herdduuic, Bortune, Teodecham, Sudtune, in which were twenty-five hides. And there were beſides ſmaller eſtates held by Radechenifters, or free men, who notwithſtanding they were free, did, in the time of king Edward, plow, harrow, reap and mow at all the lord's work[y]; which eſtates lay in Almundeſtan, Telinge, Wicfeld, Toteham, Botingtune, Bortune, Chinemertune, Giningtune, Tereige, Trinleie, Hasfelde, Lemingtune, and Montune.

'The whole manor in the time of king Edward 'paid a farm of 41*l*. and eight ſextaries of honey 'of the king's meaſure. It is now worth 40*l*. of 'which 26*l*. belong to the manor, and 14*l*. to the '[free] men.' *Domeſday-book*, p. 72.

This lordſhip was taken by the Conqueror[z] from the abbey of Perſhore, and given to the church of Weſtminſter; and Robert Fitz-Haman (ſometimes erroneouſly ſtiled earl of Glouceſter) took it again from the abbey of Weſtminſter, with all their poſſeſſions in Glouceſterſhire; which abbat Lawrence recovered by a law-ſuit in the reign of king Henry the Second. The abbat of Weſtminſter was ſeized of the hundred of Derhurſt 15 E. 1. and held the manor of Derhurſt, with the hamlets of Hardwick, Walton, Corſe, Trinelly, and Haurick, [Tyrley and Haw] 27 E. 1. At the diſſolution of religious foundations, this manor was veſted in the crown, and granted to the dean and chapter of Weſtminſter 34 H. 8. but was reſumed, and granted to the convent of Weſtminſter 4 Mar. and again regranted, and confirmed to the church of Weſtminſter 2 Eliz. who are the preſent proprietors.

HAMLETS. 1. *Apperley*, where Mr. Capel Payne has a good eſtate, lately belonging to the Lanes. The manor of Apperley antiently belonged to the abbey of Weſtminſter, upon the diſſolution of which, it was granted to the dean and chapter of that church, 34 H. 8. and confirmed 2 Eliz.—There is ſaid to be another manor in Apperley, of which Edward Brugg was ſeized 10 H. 4. Edward Brugg, eſq; held 30 meſſuages in Trinly, and one capital meſſuage called Aperly-place, 200 acres of land, 30 acres of meadow, and 100 acres of paſture in Derhurſt, 15 H. 6. The manor of Apperley was held by John Throgmorton 13 E. 4. by Philip Throgmorton 5 H. 8. by William Throgmorton 28 H. 8. and livery thereof was granted to Thomas Throgmorton 12 Eliz.—Lands in Apperley, late Warwick's and Spencer's lands, were granted to James Gunter and William Lewis 37 H. 8.

2. *Wightfield*. Eduui, a free man, held one hide in Wicfeld of the manor of Derheſt in the time of king Edward, which Walterius Pontherius held at the time of the general ſurvey. *D. B.* Gilbert le Diſpencer was ſeized of two meſſuages, 400 acres of land, &c. in Wightfield and Apperley, 5 R. 2. John Caſſey, lord chief baron of the exchequer, died ſeized of this manor 1 H. 4. as did Robert Caſſey, eſq; 1 E. 6. and Henry Caſſey his ſon, 38 Eliz. Powell Snell, eſq; is the preſent lord of this manor, and owner of the eſtate in Wightfield, but holds no court.

3. *Walton*. This manor antiently belonged to the abbey of Weſtminſter, and, with others, was granted to the dean and chapter of Weſtminſter 34 H. 8. and confirmed 2 Eliz. William Nottingham and Elizabeth his wife levied a fine of lands in Walton by Derhurſt 20 H. 6. Lands in Derhurſt-Walton, which lately belonged to the abbey of Tewkeſbury, were granted to James Gunter and William Lewis 37 H. 8. Sir Henry Caple and Anne his wife levied a fine of lands in Walton 3 Mar.

The manor of *Hardwick* by Derhurſt was alſo antiently in the abbey of Weſtminſter, and after the diſſolution was granted to that church.

Theſe three hamlets lie in the lower part of Weſtminſter hundred.

The repreſentative of the late William Dowdeſwell, eſq; of Pull-court, as leſſee under the dean and chapter of Weſtminſter, is lord of the manor of Plaiſtow; and at that court, all the places in the lower diviſion of Weſtminſter hundred owe ſuit and ſervice.

[y] See the whole account in the original language p. 72.

[z] Leland.

Of

Of the Church, &c.

Derhurſt is a peculiar, and the mother of the following churches; Corſe, Forthampton, Hasfield, the Leigh, Staverton, Bodington, and Tirley, which had no right of ſepulture 'till they obtained it of the priors of Derhurſt. Theſe, with their mother church, claim to be viſited at Derhurſt, as probably they were heretofore ſerved by monks of the priory, whom the archdeacon viſited there. It is a curacy, formerly in the gift of the impropriator; but the biſhop hath appointed the curate for many years paſt. Here is no houſe nor glebe for the incumbent, who receives 6*l.* 13*s.* 4*d.* from the impropriator, which a few years ſince was all the income; but it hath lately been twice augmented by the queen's bounty, and the pariſhioners have undertaken to make the whole 20*l.* a year. It was a laudable act in the people, ſo far as it extends, but ineffectual to any good purpoſe; for the clergy, like other men, have need of meat, drink, and cloathing, which this pitiful income cannot ſupply. Hence the church of Derhurſt has ſervice performed in it once in four, five, or ſix weeks, at uncertain times; and hence alſo the greater part of the inhabitants of this large pariſh, either frequent alehouſes on the Sunday, idle about, or lie, like ſwine, in the lanes and public highways, for want of a miniſter to teach them their duty; to the great injury of the cauſe of religion, and to the general depravity of morals. I diſlike the invidious reflections thrown out by Spelman, Stevens, and others, againſt the Reformation; but in all caſes ſimilar to the above, I ſincerely wiſh to ſee the Reformation reformed, and am ſure the clergy will heartily join me. —The prior of Derhuſt was ſeized of the advowſon of this church 5 H. 3.

Livery of the rectory of Derhurſt was granted to Thomas Throgmorton 12 Eliz.

The impropriation, worth 150*l.* a year, belongs to Powell Snell, eſq; whoſe father purchaſed it of the family of Fermor.

The church conſiſts of a lofty nave, with two ſide ailes. The chancel is higher than the church, with a large aile on each ſide, all covered with lead. There was a handſome ſpire at the weſt end, which was blown down in 1666, inſtead of which, there is now a ſmall tower with pinnacles, and five muſical bells in it. There is a ſmall place at the upper end of the ſouth aile, called Petty France, with a door, through which the prior uſed to come out of his houſe into the church. There are ſome remains of painted glaſs in the windows, with the figures of St. Agatha, St. Catherine, &c. Upon the whole the church is a good figure, but kept in a miſerable filthy condition. The church-yard contains about an acre of ground.

Proc. and Syn. 13*s.* 4*d.* Pentecoſt. 1*s.* 8*d.*

Monuments and Inſcriptions.

In the north aile is the following inſcription upon braſs, round a grey marble ſtone:

Hic jacet Iohēs Caſſy miles quondam capitalis Baro Sc'c'ij dnī Regis qui obijt xxiij° die Mar. Anno dnī M° CCCC° Et Alicia uxor ejus quor' animab' p'picietur Deus.——The figures of a man and woman are engraven in braſs on the ſtone, and very perfect. Over the man's head, *Argent, a chevron between three eagles heads eraſed gules,* for Caſſey. At his feet, *three lioncels paſſant in pale.* The arms over the woman's head are torn off.

In the north aile, is a memorial for William Lane, eſq; of Apperley, who died in 1755, and theſe arms, *Party per pale argent and gules, three ſaltires counterchanged; a mullet for difference.*

On a flat ſtone in the chancel, is a memorial for Peter Fermor, ſecond ſon of Henry Fermor, of Tuſmore in Oxfordſhire, eſq; who died in 1691, with his arms, *A feſs between three wiverns heads eraſed; a creſcent for difference.*

There are ſeveral memorials for the Powells, the Mortimers, &c. but nothing worthy notice.

Benefactions.

Thomas Halker gave 20*l.* to the poor. And there is a rent of 40*s.* a year given to the poor, charged on an eſtate at Walton. Mr. Snell pays 20*s.* a year towards putting poor boys out apprentices. And there are about twelve acres of land, which let for 5*l.* 12*s.* a year, to repair the church.

Derhurſt and Walton.

Taxes.					
The Royal Aid in	1692,	£.	52	4	4
Poll-tax —	1694,	—	7	0	0
Land-tax —	1694,	—	73	4	0
The ſame, at 3*s.*	1770,	—	55	7	7½

Apperley and Wightfield.

Taxes.					
The Royal Aid in	1692,	£.	143	4	0
Poll-tax ——	1694,	—	30	13	0
Land-tax ——	1694,	—	249	8	0
The ſame, at 3*s.*	1770,	—	187	8	1½

According to ſir Robert Atkyns, when he compiled his account of this pariſh, there were 100 houſes, and about 620 inhabitants, whereof 20 were freeholders; yearly births 18, burials 16 Having examined the pariſh regiſter, I find that in ten years, beginning with 1700, the baptiſms were 172, burials 121; and in a like ſeries, beginning with 1760, the baptiſms were 166, burials 153. But the regiſter appears to be very ill kept, and no certain deduction can be made from it. The inhabitants are now about 530.

DEINTON, *or* DOINTON,

IS a ſmall pariſh, at preſent in the hundred of Langley and Swineſhead, but it lay antiently in that of Pucklechurch. It is bounded on the eaſt by Dyrham, on the weſt by Bitton, on the north by Abſton, and on the ſouth by Langridge and Lanſdown in Somerſetſhire; eight miles diſtant eaſt from Briſtol, about ſeven north-eaſt from Bath, four weſt from Marſhfield, and thirty-three ſouthward from Glouceſter.

It was antiently called Didington; a little brook runs thro' it into the Boyd, and ſo into the Avon.

The Boyd runs between this pariſh and Abſton, in a very deep channel, between rocks of a prodigious height, riſing almoſt perpendicularly from the bottom; and on each ſide are fortifications and intrenchments, raiſed, it is ſuppoſed, with a view to preſerve a communication between *Aqua Solis* and *Trajectus*, two antient Roman ſtations, already mentioned more largely under Cromhall, Clifton, and other places.

This little pariſh is within the juriſdiction of the court of the honour of Glouceſter. It is pleaſantly ſituated under Lanſdown. It produces no rare plants, but there are ſome veins of lead ore, which are not rich enough to defray the expence of working. The ſtone of the rocks abovementioned makes an excellent, white, ſtrong lime.

The women and children are employed in ſpinning woollen yarn.

Of the Manor and other Eſtates.

'The ſame biſhop [*i. e.* the biſhop of Conſtance] 'held Didintone in Polcrecerce hundred, and 'Robert held it of him. Aluuard a thane of 'king Edward held it. There are five hides taxed. 'In demean are three plow-tillages and fourteen 'villeins, and eight bordars with eight plow-'tillages. There are ten *ſervi*, and two mills of '10*s.* and 10*d.* and two men of 5*s.* and twelve 'acres of meadow, a wood half a mile long, and 'half a mile broad. It is worth and was worth '8*l.*' *Domeſday-book*, p. 70.

The family of the Deintons took their name from this place, and held the manor for ſeveral generations, of the Clares, earls of Glouceſter. Thomas de Deinton ſold the manor and advowſon of the church to John de Tracy, and levied a fine thereof 6 E. 1. and John de Tracy, ſon of the former, proved his right to courts leet and waifs in this manor, in a *Quo warranto* 15 E. 1. The manor continued in the name of Tracy 300 years, and was ſold out of that family to Mr. Arthur Player and others, in the reign of queen Elizabeth.

Robert Langton, eſq; was lord of this manor at the beginning of this century, and Joſeph Langton, eſq; is the preſent lord of it.

But there was an antient manor called the Bury, which belonged alſo to the Tracies, afterwards to the Stills, and is now, by purchaſe, the property of Mr. Hillman.

The lodge-houſe in Tracy-park, which for many generations belonged to the Ridleys, is the property of Mr. Frankham.

John Stanſhaw and Humphry Stanſhaw his brother, levied a fine of lands in Deinton to William Fream, 12 H. 7.

Of the Church, &c.

The church is a rectory, in the deanery of Hawkeſbury, worth 130*l.* a year, of which the lord chancellor is patron; the reverend Mr. Thomas Coker the preſent incumbent.

Eighty acres belong to the glebe. Tracy-park pays a mark yearly in lieu of tithes; all other places pay full tithes.

There was antiently a free chapel belonging to the manor-houſe, dedicated to the virgin Mary; and Mr. Hillman pays an audit to the crown of 5*s.* 4*d.* for the ſite of it.

The church is ſmall, with an aile on the north ſide, a handſome gallery at the weſt end, and an embattled tower with five bells in it. It is dedicated to the holy Trinity. The preſent rector rebuilt the chancel about the year 1768.

Monument and Inſcription.

There is a handſome monument in the church, of white marble, with the following inſcription:

M. S. Elizabethæ Langton, filiæ Edwardi Bridges de Cainſham, in Com. Somerſet. Arm. uxoris Johannis Langton, de Deinton, in Com. Gloceſt. Gen. a cujus morte Vidua vixit annos ultra quadraginta, ut Charitati in Pauperes, Benignitati in ſuos, Pietati in Deum, Curis ſoluta, ſeſe devoveret. Ob. Ann. Ætat. 83°, Salutis 1702-3. Sancta Matrona ſuas exuvias juxta illuſtrium Majorum Cineres in Eccleſia de Cainſham recondi juſſit: Sed cum inter multifaria numeroſæ familiæ Marmora in anguſtis iſtius Cancellis Monumento defuerit locus, in hujus Parochiæ Eccleſiâ (in qua longam bonis operibus peragendis viduitatem conſumpſit) Carolus Symes & Amy Meredith, Nepotes et Executores, Marmor hoc gratitudinis ergo poſuerunt.——

Arms, *Quarterly, ſable and Or, over all a bend argent,* for Langton.

Firſt fruits £. 14	11	2	Synodals	0	2	0
Tenths — 1	9	1½	Pentecoſtals	0	0	8
Procurations 0	5	0				

Benefactions.

There is a rent charge of 6*s.* a year on an eſtate in Deinton belonging to Mr. Walker, for the uſe of the poor. John Langton, of Deinton, eſq; in the year 1660, gave 20*l.* with which a piece of ground was purchaſed in this pariſh for the poor. Mr. William Langton, rector of Dyrham, in 1668, ſettled 200*l.* in truſt for educating and apprenticing out poor children of this pariſh.

Taxes.					
The Royal Aid in	1692,	£. 112	16	8
Poll-tax ——	1694,	— 18	9	0
Land-tax ——	1694,	— 168	16	0
The ſame, at 3*s.*	1770,	— 121	10	0

At the beginning of this century, according to ſir Robert Atkyns, there were 48 houſes and about 200 inhabitants in this pariſh, whereof 8 were freeholders; yearly births 6, burials 6. But in ten years, beginning with 1700, I counted from the pariſh regiſter 83 baptiſms, and 41 burials; and in a like ſeries, beginning with 1760, the baptiſms were 110, and the burials 79. And there are now about 340 inhabitants, nearly in the proportion of 44 to 1 of the average of annual burials.

DIDBROOK

IS a ſmall pariſh in the lower diviſion of Kiftſgate hundred, three miles diſtant northward from Winchcombe, nine ſouth-weſt from Campden, and eighteen north-eaſtward from Glouceſter.

This little village is pleaſantly ſituated under the ſouth-weſt ſide of the ridge of hills which divide

divide the vale from the Cotefwold country. It confifts of excellent arable and pafture-land, but there is nothing more to recommend it to our notcie. A little rivulet runs from hence into the Avon near Evefham; and as *Diddan* in the Britifh language fignifies *pleafant*, it is probable that the place took its name from its fituation upon this *pleafant brook* or ftream of water.

Of the Manor and other Eftates.

This manor formerly belonged to the abbey of Hayles, which continued in poffeffion of it 'till the diffolution of religious foundations, when it paffed by grant into the name and family of Tracy, in which it has remained ever fince; lord vifcount Tracy of Todington, being the prefent proprietor of it.

TITHING. *Cofcomb* is a tithing in this parifh, fituate in a little dale on the brow of the hill, facing the vale towards Tewkefbury. It formerly belonged to the abbey of Hayles, at the diffolution of which houfe, the capital meffuage of Coftombe, *alias* Coftom, in Didbrook, among other particulars, was affigned to Stephen Segar, the laft abbat of Hayles, 'till he fhould be otherwife provided for. But the fame meffuage, by the name of the Abbat's-Lodging, was granted to Robert Acton 32 H. 8. Anthony Dafton died feized thereof 20 Eliz. as did another Anthony Dafton 12 C. 1. leaving Richard his fon 12 years old.

This eftate belonged to the late Mr. Juftice Tracy, who built a handfome feat here, commanding an extenfive profpect over the vale of Evefham. His grandfon Robert Tracy, efq; dying without iffue, it came to the prefent owner, Robert Pratt, efq; reprefentative in parliament of the borough of Horfham in Suffex. Here are two houfes in this tithing; and there was formerly a fmall chapel, now converted to prophane ufes.

Wormington-grange is a place in this parifh. William Fravellcfworth held Little Wormington 33 E. 3. Wormington-farm, which belonged to the abbey of Hayles, was granted to Robert Acton 32 H. 8. Lands in Wormington, formerly belonging to the fame abbey, were granted to fir Richard Grefham, in exchange for lands in Yorkfhire, 38 H. 8. Lands called Hayles-clofe in Wormington, were granted to Henry Ruffel and Charles Brockton 2 Mariæ.

Of the Church, &c.

The church is a vicarage in the deanery of Campden, of which lord vifcount Tracy is patron; the Honourable John Tracy, D.D. the prefent incumbent. It was formerly appropriated to the abbey of Hayles. The advowfon of the rectory and vicarage of Didbrook was granted to fir Edward Seimour 1 E. 6. and afterwards to John Dudley and John Afcough 18 Eliz. The impropriation belongs to lord vifcount Tracy, and pays four marks yearly to the vicar.

In the year 1738, this vicarage, the rectory of Pinnock, and the chapel of Hayles were confolidated into one prefentation, by the concurrence of the bifhop, the patron, and incumbent.

The church is fuppofed to be dedicated to St. George, from the picture of that faint in armour being in the window near the belfry. It has an embattled tower, and four bells, at the weft end.

In the chancel window, painted on the glafs, is the head of an old man, and this infcription was under it: *Orate p' aia Will'i Whytchyrche qui hoc templum fundavit cum cancello.* And under, thefe arms, *Argent, a lion rampant gules, in a bordure charged with four befants.* But the latter part of the writing is now deftroyed. This William Whytchurch was abbat of Hayles in 1470, and lies buried here in a ftone coffin. The church was polluted by bloodfhed in 1472.

Firft fruits £.	8	0	0	Synodals £.	0	1	0
Tenths —	0	16	0	Pentecoftals	0	0	6½
Procurations	0	6	8				

Monument and Infcription.

Againft the eaft wall of the chancel, is a marble monument of good workmanfhip, with this infcription:

Near this place
Lies interred the Body
Of the Honourable ROBERT TRACY, Efq[r].
Son of the Right Honourable ROBERT late
Lord Vifcount TRACY of Todington.
He was a Judge twenty-fix Years
In the Courts of Weftminfter,
But being ftruck with the Palfy
in the Year 1726, Refigned a Commiffion
which he had fo long executed
with the greateft Knowledge,
Moderation, and Integrity,
To the Honour
of his Prince,
and the univerfal Satisfaction
of his fellow Subjects.
Obijt 11 Sept. Anno 1735.
Ætat. 80.
Benefacere magis quam confpici.

Taxes.					
The Royal Aid in	1692, £.	102	7	8
Poll-tax ——	1694, —	6	10	0
Land-tax ——	1694, —	56	1	0
The fame, at 3*s.*	1770, —	39	1	3

At the beginning of this century there were 20 houfes in this parifh, and about 100 inhabitants, whereof 7 were freeholders; yearly births 3, burials 3. *Atkyns.* There are now 17 houfes, and the inhabitants fall fomething fhort of the above mentioned number. The births and burials are regiftered with Hayles and Pinnock.

DIDMARTON

LIES in the upper divifion of the hundred of Grumbaldfafh, fix miles weftward from Tetbury, twenty eaftward from the city of Briftol, and twenty-three fouthward from Gloucefter.

It is fituated in the hill country, and bounded on the fouth fide by Wiltfhire. This feems to account

account for *merton*, the latter part of its name, which ſignifies *a boundary town*, from mepc, Saxon, *a boundary*; but I am totally ignorant of the meaning of the former part of it.

The turnpike-road from Oxford, thro' Cirenceſter, to Bath and Briſtol, leads through this village, where are two or three little inns for the accommodation of travellers.

The antient family of the Codringtons had a large ſeat near the church, which, with the eſtate belonging to it, is now gone out of that family, and there is only one wing and part of the front left ſtanding.

The pariſh conſiſts chiefly of arable land, and has nothing in it to engage the attention of the naturaliſt or antiquary.

Of the Manor and other Eſtates.

'Durand of Glowec' holds Dedmertone in 'Grimboldeſtou hundred, and Anſchitil holds it 'of him. There are three hides taxed. Leuuin 'held it of earl Herald. In demean are three 'plow-tillages, and eight bordars with one plow-'tillage, and four *ſervi*, and ſix acres of meadow. 'It was worth 30*s.* now 40*s.*' *D. B.* p. 76.

Otnell de Siward was ſon of the above Anſchitil, who was called Anſchitil of the wood. This Otnell granted two hides in Dudmarton to his uncle Elias; and the manor continued ſeveral generations in the family of the Sywards. It paſſed afterwards to the Roſtons, for William Roſton held the manor of Didmarton of the honour of Hereford 10 H. 4. Their name was afterwards varied to Wroughton, and from them this manor paſſed to the Seacoles.

Richard Seacole, eſq; died ſeized of Didmarton, and left two daughters Griſle and Anne, coheireſſes, of whom the former had livery of the manor and advowſon 13 Eliz. Anne being married to Simon Codrington of Codrington, carried this manor into that name and family, from which it paſſed by purchaſe to the late duke of Beaufort, father of the preſent duke, who is the lord of this manor.

Of the other eſtates, the records and evidences ſhew that Oſwald, who founded the monaſtery of Perſhore in Worceſterſhire, in the year 604, gave ſeveral tenements in Dydimeretune to that monaſtery, which king Edgar confirmed to it; and thoſe lands, after the diſſolution of monaſteries, were granted to Chriſtopher Smith and Thomas Wharton 2 Mar.

John Joy died ſeized of one meſſuage and one yard-land in Dudmarton 19 R. 2.

Of the Church, &c.

The church is a rectory, in the deanery of Hawkeſbury, worth 50*l.* a year, of which the duke of Beaufort is patron. Henry Dennis had livery of the advowſon 4 Eliz. In the year 1735, this church was united in one preſentation with that of Oldbury upon the hill. The rectory pays 2*s.* a year to the lord of the manor of Hawkeſbury, which manor formerly belonged to the abbey of Perſhore.

Fifty-two acres of land belong to the glebe.

The church is built in the form of an L, becauſe the name of St. Lawrence, to whom it is dedicated, begins with that letter. It is ſmall, with a wooden turret, in which is a clock. There are no monuments nor inſcriptions worthy notice.

Firſt fruits £. 8	0	0	Synodals £. 0	2	0
Tenths — 0	16	0	Pentecoſtals 0	0	5
Procurations					

Taxes.	The Royal Aid in	1692, £.	24	0	0
	Poll-tax — —	1694, —	13	9	0
	Land-tax ——	1694, —	24	0	0
	The ſame, at 3*s.*	1770, —	14	10	6

When ſir Robert Atkyns compiled his account of this pariſh, there were 11 houſes, and 56 inhabitants, whereof 3 were freeholders; yearly births 2, burials 1. There are at preſent 17 families, and 72 inhabitants; and in ſixteen years, beginning with 1760, the burials have been 20; ſo that the proportion of annual burials to the whole inhabitants, is as 1 to 58, which ſhews the place to be remarkably healthy.

DIMMOCK.

THIS pariſh lies in the hundred of Botloe, in the foreſt diviſion, almoſt at the extremity of the county next Herefordſhire; eleven miles north from Mitchel-Dean, thirteen weſt from Tewkeſbury, and ſeventeen north-weſt from Glouceſter.

It is a large pariſh, ſituated in the vale, and but little frequented by travellers, wherefore the roads are exceedingly deep and founderous. Sir Robert Atkyns ſuppoſes that antiently it was covered with wood, and that the name may be reſolved into two Saxon words, Dim, *obſcure*, and Aac, *oak*; as if it was ſo called on account of the place being *darkened with oaks*. If the reader ſhould diſlike this etymology, he may take a conjecture of my own, or reject both at pleaſure. I ſuppoſe the name to be originally Britiſh, and to be corrupted from *Ty-Môch*, which ſignifies the *ſwineherd's houſe*, and being the firſt that was built in the place, gave name to it; as Newent took its name from a new inn which was the firſt houſe in that place, built there for the convenience of travellers.

As it lies in the neighbourhood of Herefordſhire, ſo the people here, like the inhabitants of that fine county, cultivate orcharding, and make a rich kind of cyder and perry. And it is very remarkable, that it was from the Ryelands in this pariſh, that king Edward took the ſheep which he preſented to the Spaniſh monarch, from the breed of which we are now ſupplied with wool for our fineſt manufactures.

It is watered by the river Leden, which paſſes by and gives name to the town of Ledbury in Herefordſhire, about ſix miles north of this village, and

and empties itſelf into the Severn near Glouceſter. Dimmock has more paſture than arable land. The oak-tree delights in a deep ſoil, and grows with uncommon vigour here. There are two large woods of oak, and great numbers of fine trees lie diſperſed in the meadows and paſture grounds. The arable-lands are planted with fruit-trees, with large intervals between the rows; and there are ſeveral thouſand hogſheads of cyder and perry made in this pariſh in a good year.

Cyder being a principal object, they give great attention to the culture of fruit-trees, ſtirring the earth about the roots of them when the fields lie fallow; but the foul appearance of their corn fields manifeſts a want of ſkill, or of induſtry, in that department. They know nothing of watering their meadows, as practiſed about Cirenceſter, and are negligent in draining the wet lands, both which would make prodigious improvements. However the ſoil is ſo exceedingly rich, that this, and two or three of the adjoining pariſhes, may vye with any diſtrict of the ſame extent in the county.

When the fruit-trees are in full bloſſom, the appearance of this plantation from ſome elevated ſpot is inconceivably fine. It has been compared to a garden overſpread with flowers; but the utmoſt ſtretch of verbal deſcription would produce an idea very inadequate to the beauty of this flowry landſcape.

Dimmock was formerly privileged with markets and fairs, which were let to farm to the inhabitants 10 H. 3. according to the records. And to add to its conſequence, it is ſaid that one of the Bohuns, earls of Hereford, built a caſtle here; but there are no veſtiges remaining, except the caſtle-rock and the caſtle-tump. The tump is a round mount on the borders of the pariſh next Newent, thrown up by hands, with an area at top, by much too ſmall for a building of any great ſtrength. The market failing from difficulty of acceſs, or other diſadvantages in ſituation, many houſes were deſerted and fell to ruin, of which the antient foundations have been found in the fields above a quarter of a mile from the church, with old paved cauſeys, &c. There is a place near the church called the *Back of St. Clement's*; and the *Butcher's-row*, or *Butcher's-lane*, occurs in the court-rolls of the manor; whence it appears that the town was formerly much larger than the village is at preſent.

Dimmock was ever remarkable for hoſpitality. The lords of the manors, and other proprietors of the beſt eſtates, (and there have been, and ſtill are, very conſiderable land-holders here) uſed to reſide in the pariſh, and their houſes were open to all comers; and tho' ſome have now left it, yet the ſame convivial old Engliſh ſpirit remains with this generous, hoſpitable people.

Roger Dimmock, a Dominican frier, and D.D. at Oxford, was a native of this place, and a perſon of ſuch ſingular learning, that the univerſity choſe him for their diſputant againſt Wickliff's doctrines. He flouriſhed in 1390. And Robert Burhill, a profound and judicious ſcholar, and editor of many learned works, was alſo a native of this pariſh. He aſſiſted ſir Walter Raleigh in writing the *Hiſtory of the World*, and died in 1641.

Of the Manor and other Eſtates.

This manor is part of the antient demeſnes of the crown, the privileges [a] whereof are briefly mentioned pp. 66, 67. In *Domeſday-book* are the following particulars:

'King Edward held Dimoch in Botelau hun-'dred. There were twenty hides, and two plow-'tillages in demean, and forty-two villeins, and ten 'bordars, and eleven free men [*coliberti*] having 'forty-one plow-tillages. There is a prieſt having 'twelve acres, and four radecheniſters with four 'plow-tillages. There is a wood three miles long 'and one broad.

'The ſheriff paid what he pleaſed for this 'manor in the time of king Edward.

'King William held it in his demeſnes four 'years. Earl William and his ſon Roger had it 'afterwards, the men of the county know not 'how. It now pays 21 *l.*' *Domeſday-book*, p. 69.

Roger and his two brothers dying without iſſue male, the manor of Dimmock came to Roger earl of Hereford, who gave the demeans thereof, and half the wood, to the abbey of Flaxley which he had founded. But he and his four brothers, Walter, Mahel, Henry, and William, dying without iſſue, their inheritance came to their three ſiſters, of whom Margery the eldeſt was married to Humphry de Bohun, who, in right of his wife, had the manor of Dimmock, of which Humphry their ſon died ſeized 33 H. 2. Henry de Bohun, ſon of Humphry, was created earl of Hereford 1 Joh. and had the *Tertium Denarium Comitatûs* granted to him, in conſideration that he had releaſed all his right in Dimmock to the king, the ſame year.

[a] In the reign of king H. 6. the ſheriff of the county would have charged the freeholders of Dimmock with contribution to defray the wages of the knights of the ſhire, which occaſioned the following writ:

'Henry, by the grace of God, king of England, and France, 'and lord of Ireland, to all and ſingular ſheriffs, mayors, bailiffs, 'conſtables, officers, and other our liege people, as well within 'liberties as without, to whom theſe preſents ſhall come, greeting: 'Whereas by the antient and approved cuſtom of our realm of 'England, the inhabitants and tenants of the antient demeſnes of 'the crown of England were wont, throughout the ſaid kingdom, 'to be excuſed from tolls, and the expences of knights of the 'ſhires who come to our parliaments, and to the parliaments of our 'progenitors formerly kings of England. And whereas it ap-'pears by the certificate of our treaſurer and chancellor, tranſ-'mitted into our chancery by our command, and which is ſtill 'remaining on the files of our chancery, that the inhabitants and 'tenants of the town of Dimmock in the county of Glouceſter 'are of the antient demeſnes of the crown: We therefore com-'mand, that in purſuance to the cuſtom aforeſaid, you acquit 'and diſcharge them from the payment of toll, and from con-'tribution towards the expences of the knights of the ſhire which 'ſhall come to our parliaments, or to the parliaments of any 'of our heirs.

Witneſs ourſelf at Weſtminſter, 12 Jul. in the twelfth year of our reign.

The king granted Dimmock to Walter de Clifford the younger, brother to Fair Rofamond, who died feized thereof, with markets, fairs, a wood, and other appurtenances 6 H. 3. And it appears by the account of Walter de Burg that this manor paid yearly to the king 63*l.* 12*s.* 8*d.* 23 H. 3.

Morgan de Kerlynn held this manor 30 H. 3. and the king granted it to Ela countefs of Warwick, after the death of her hufband, for her better fupport, 36 H. 3. But fhe furrendered it afterwards, for William de Grandifon proved his right to courts leet and free warren in Dimmock, in a writ of *Quo warranto* 15 E. 1. He had been a domeftic fervant to Edmond earl of Lancafter, and was fummoned as a peer to parliament. He married Sybil, younger daughter and coheirefs of John de Tregoz, with whom he had a large eftate, particularly Lydiard in Wiltfhire, which from his wife's family was called Lydiard-Tregoz, the feat of the prefent lord vifcount Bolingbroke.

Peter Grandifon, fon of William, died feized of Dimmock 32 E. 3. as did John de Grandifon, brother to Peter, 43 E. 3. to whom fir Thomas Grandifon his nephew fucceeded, and died without iffue 49 E. 3.

The manor now became divided among feveral owners. Sir Roger de Beauchamp was feized of a rent iffuing out of it, and Catherine widow of Robert Todenham held the 4th part of it 7 R. 2. Margaret the widow of fir Thomas Grandifon died feized of the third part of it 18 R. 2.

Two parts of the manor of Dimmock were held by Richard Ryhale 9 H. 4. a part by John Phelepot, efq; 13 H. 4. a fourth part by another Richard Ryhale 3 H. 5. a part by Elizabeth widow of William Ryhale 7 H. 6. a part by Richard de Montacute 8 H. 6. George Breinton, Thomas Leightfoot, Thomas Barton, and Thomas Smith were lords of Dimmock 8 H. 6. and Richard Ryhale held the manor of Dimmock 11 H. 6.

Befide the principal manor, there were two others in Dimmock, and there is no diftinction made between them in the records, which accounts for the unufual fluctuation of property, as it may feem, in the principal manor.

Richard Pointz and John Langley transfer the poffeffion of the manor of Dimmock to fir Walter Devereux 26 H. 6. Richard Oldcaftle had a right in the manor 31 H. 6. Four parts of the manor of Dimmock were granted to fir Walter Devereux and Elizabeth his wife 32 H. 6. The manor continued in the Devereuxes, lords Ferrers, during the reigns of E. 4. H. 7. and H. 8.

Letitia countefs of Leicefter was feized of this manor 23 Eliz. Giles Forfter, efq; was lord of it in the year 1608. Edward-Pye Chamberlain was proprietor of it in 1712, and another gentleman of the fame name fold it to Mrs. Anne Cam, who is the prefent lady of the manor, and has a handfome feat called the Bois, and above 1000*l.* a year in this parifh, but fhe refides in London. Her arms are,

Mr. Chamberlain's arms are, *Gules, an efcutcheon between eight mullets argent.*

Mune was antiently a manor within the manor of Dimmock. It was granted to William de Gammage 1 Joh. whofe fon Jeffery de Gammage dying 37 H. 3. left Elizabeth his only daughter and heir, married firft to John Penbrug, and afterwards to Walter Pedewardin, who proved their right to free warren and other privileges in the manor of Mune in a *Quo warranto* 15 E. 1. John Penbrugg, fon and heir to Elizabeth by her firft hufband, held this manor 29 E. 1. as did Edward his brother 34 E. 1. and William de Penbrugg 11 E. 2. & 16 E. 3. Henry Penbrugg held Gammage-hall 36 E. 3. as did John Penbrugg 50 E. 3. and Sybil his widow, married afterwards to Ralph de Staunton, died feized of it in dower 9 R. 2. Walter Penbrugg died feized of the manor of Gammage-hall, and left Elizabeth his only daughter and heirefs, married to fir Rowland Moreton, who died 1 Mar. and left Richard Moreton his fon and heir.

Thomas Wenman died feized of the Old Grange of Dimmock, and of Dimmock Little, *alias* Gammage-hall, 1582, and left Richard his fon nineteen years old. William Wintour died feized of the manor, rectory, and advowfon of Dimmock Little, 1627, of which his fon Giles, who married Alice Caerwardine, widow, died feized in 1629, leaving a fon William four years old. Wenman Winniat, efq; was lord of the manor of Little Dimmock at the beginning of this century. The manor place of Gammage-Hall hath lately been purchafed by Mr. Richard Hall, but the manerial rights are referved by the reverend Mr. Winniat, (a direct defcendant of Wenman Winniat, efq;) who has a very good eftate here. His arms (as on a family monument in the church) are, *Sable, on a fefs argent, between three anchors Or, a dragon gules.* The old Grange and new Grange, having belonged to the abbey of Flaxley, are exempt from tithes.

It hath been already obferved, that the abbey of Flaxley had a grant of the demefnes of the manor of Dimmock, which in procefs of time were reputed a manor; and after the diffolution of religious foundations, were granted as fuch to fir Anthony Kingfton. Sir John Lutterel had livery of Dimmock demefnes granted to him 1 Eliz.

Other records fhew, that John Handborough and Maud his wife levied a fine of lands in Ketford in Dimmock 36 H. 6. and that John Garrine levied a fine of lands in Dimmock 2 E. 4.

The eftate belonging to the White-houfe is the rectory, formerly the property of Mr. Wintour. It is worth about 500*l.* a year, and now belongs to Mifs Lambert, a minor.

Mr. Lambert has the Lintrige, which belonged to Mr. Wall, and a good eftate in this parifh.

John Cam, of Hereford, M. D. has a large eftate here, of which the Pounds is the chief, and has long been in his family.

Mr.

Mr. Richard Hill, of the Pithouſe, has a very good eſtate here. The caſtle-rock and the caſtle-tump-houſe are both Mr. Hill's. The houſe called the Callow is Mr. Yate's, and another called the Green-houſe belongs to Mr. Hankins. Mr. James Cooper has alſo a good eſtate here. There are many other freehold eſtates in the pariſh, not here particularly mentioned; beſides eſtates of inheritance to a great amount, held according to the cuſtom of the manor.

HAMLETS. There are three hamlets in this large pariſh, which all meet in the church-yard; and it is remarkable that the families are buried in that part of it belonging to the reſpective diviſions in which they lived.

1. *Ledington,* (lying on the river Leden) in which there is a tithingman. The account from *Domeſday-book* which ſir Robert Atkyns placed to this tithing, belongs to the pariſh of Upleaden.

2. *Ryeland,* (ſo called, becauſe being a ſandy ſoil, it was formerly thought unfit to be planted with any thing but rye) in which are two tithingmen, one belonging to the tithing of the ſame name, the other to Ockington, in this hamlet. The manor of Rye was held by Robert Attgreen and Maud his wife for their lives, of Henry duke of Lancaſter, 14 E. 3. This manor was granted to the archbiſhop of Canterbury and ſeveral other great perſons in truſt 3 H. 5. And the manor, late parcel of the dutchy of Lancaſter, was granted to Charles earl of Devonſhire 1 Jac.

3. *Woodend,* which has a diſtinct tithingman.

Of the Church, &c.

The church is a vicarage, in the foreſt deanery, worth 60*l.* a year, paid out of the impropriation. Miſs Lambert is patroneſs; Mr. Hayward the preſent incumbent. The church and advowſon were granted to the abbey of Cormeille in Normandy, by the king, 56 H. 3.

The impropriation, worth 500*l.* a year, belongs (as before obſerved) to Miſs Lambert, a minor. It pays 40*s.* a year to the crown.

The church is built in the form of a croſs. It is dedicated to the virgin Mary, and has a low tower at the weſt end, and a ſmall wooden ſpire.

There was a chantry in the church, dedicated to the virgin Mary, whereof John Wood was the laſt incumbent. A paſture ground, late belonging to it, at Scanborough-bridge, and lands called Portlands, were granted to ſir William Ryder 7 Jac.

A houſe and orchard in Dimmock, which belonged to the chantry of the Holy Trinity in Stow, were granted to ſir Anthony Cope 10 Jac.

Monuments and Inſcriptions.

In the church and chancel are monuments with the following inſcriptions, *viz.*

Juxta hoc Marmor Johannes Winniat, Gener. Vir pius et probus, Liberalis in omnes, Pauperibus largâ manu beneficus, Exuvias Depoſuit 15 Octob. 1670.

Stay, paſſenger, and reverence the Duſt
Of a good Neighbour, peaceable and juſt,
Who freely treated both ye Rich & Poore,
Neither went ſad or empty from his Doore:
So y[t] his Bounty will preſerue his Fame
Did not ye Tombe record his pretious Name.

Richardus Wynniat, Filius Pietatis ergo poſuit.—Arms as before.

Here lyes interred the body of Robert Wintour of the Inner Temple Gent. ſon of William Wintour of Dymock, Eſq; (the laſt of the heirs male deſcended from that antient and honourable family) who departed this life the 22[d] day of February 1718, aged 61 years, and was a good benefactor to the poor of this pariſh.———Arms, *Sable, a feſs ermine.*

On a flat ſtone is a memorial for Edward Pye of Boyce, eſq; who died in 1692, aged 80.———Arms, *Ermine, a bend lozengy.*

A memorial for Thomas Rokebye, Gent. of the antient family of the Rokebyes of Morton-Slaningford in Yorkſhire, who died in 1723.———Arms, *A chevron between three rooks.*

On a raiſed tomb, a memorial for James Machen, ſen. who died in 1760.———Arms, *Gules, a feſs vaire between three pelicans heads erazed Or.*

There is a handſome monument in the church-yard, incloſed with iron paliſadoes; and upon the vaſe are ſeveral memorials for the family of the Cams, of whom William Cam, eſq; died in 1767, aged 85; and John Cam, his ſon, died the ſame year, aged 32 years. No arms.

A memorial on a raiſed tomb for Robert Hall, who died in 1711,———Arms, *Argent, a chevron between three talbots heads erazed ſable.*

Firſt fruits £.	9	13	8	Proc. & Syn. £. 0	13	2
Tenths —	0	19	4½	Pentecoſtals 0	1	0

Benefactions.

In 1650, William Skinner of Ledbury, L. D. gave 4*s.* a year to the poor, out of Fair-tree eſtate. In 1717, Robert Wintour gave 30*l.* for clothing twenty poor people. In 1719, William Weal gave 5*l.* a year to the poor for ever. In 1734, William Hooper gave 3*l.* a year towards maintaining a charity ſchool, and 10*s.* a year to the miniſter. William Wall of Lintridge, gave three tenements in Dimmock, now demoliſhed. Thomas Murrel gave the intereſt of 10*l.* to ten poor widows.

Taxes.			£.	s.	d.
	The Royal Aid in	1692,	299	8	0
	Poll-tax ——	1694, —	65	17	0
	Land-tax ——	1694, —	414	13	0
	The ſame, at 3*s.*	1770, —	310	19	0

When ſir Robert Atkyns compiled his account of this pariſh, there were 250 houſes, and about 1000 inhabitants, whereof 40 were freeholders; yearly births 28, burials 27. Having examined the pariſh regiſter, I find that, beginning with the year 1700, the average of baptiſms is 26, of burials 19; and that in ſeven years, beginning with 1768, the average of baptiſms is 34, of burials 26; and the number of inhabitants is now about 1116, which is nearly in the proportion of 43 to 1 of the annual burials.

DODINGTON

LIES in the lower diviſion of the hundred of Grumbaldſaſh, ten miles north of Bath, thirteen eaſt from Briſtol, and thirty ſouthward from Glouceſter.

It

It is ſituated on the verge of the vale, and ſecured from the bleak eaſterly winds by the high lands of Tormarton, with old Sodbury hill to the north of it.

Sir William Codrington has a ſeat here, ſeen through a viſta, at the diſtance of about five or ſix hundred yards to the right from the road which leads from Glouceſter to Bath. Tho' the houſe is not in the modern taſte, it is large and handſome. There are two very beautiful pieces of water, one above the other, in the front, with the fineſt lawn about it that can be conceived, interſperced with venerable oaks and other foreſt trees, riſing to the view from the houſe in a moſt exquiſite landſcape.

The ſpring which ſupplies thoſe pieces of water riſes juſt above, and is the head of the river Froome, which runs to Briſtol Back, ſo called from bec, Saxon, *a river*; where the key of that port was dug in the year 1247. Before that time, Briſtol key, or port, was near St. Mary-port-ſtreet, which was ſo called upon that account.

The Romans left veſtiges behind them of their preſence in this village; for Leland (*Itin.* v. 6.) relates, that ſeveral earthen pots (I ſuppoſe what we now call urns) very finely flouriſhed in the Roman times, were dug out of the ground in Dodington field, in one of which were Roman coins; and further, that there was a glaſs containing bones, found in a ſepulchre in the highway by the church; but omits to ſay when theſe things were diſcovered.

The *Orchis Apifera*, or Bee Orchis, with other ſpecies of that plant, is found growing in this pariſh. And the *Circæa*, or Inchanter's Nightſhade, grows plentifully here.

This pariſh is within the juriſdiction of the court of the honour of Glouceſter.

Of the Manor and other Eſtates.

'Roger de Berchelai holds Dodintone in 'Hedredeſtan hundred. There are three hides, 'and two parts of half a hide. Aluuin held it in 'the time of king Edward. In demean is one 'plow-tillage, and ſeven villeins, and four bordars 'with four plow-tillages. There are four *ſervi*, 'and ten acres of meadow. It is worth and was 'worth 3 *l*.' *Domeſday-book*, p. 75.

'The biſhop of St. Laud in Conſtance holds 'Dodintone in Edredeſtan hundred, and Roger 'holds it of him. Ulnod held it in the time of 'king Edward. There is one hide and a half, and 'the third part of half a hide. In demean is one 'plow-tillage, and four villeins, and one bordar 'with one plow-tillage. There are three *ſervi*. 'It is worth and was worth 30 *s*.' *D. B.* p. 71.

Thus it appears that in the time of king Edward the Confeſſor, Dodington was held by two different proprietors, who were both diſpoſſeſſed of their eſtates ſoon after the conqueſt. Part of it was given to Roger de Berkeley, who was alſo tenant of the other part under the biſhop. But that family ſoon became poſſeſſed of the whole in their own right, which they held of the honour of Glouceſter, as appears by the records of 47 H. 3. 21 E. 3. and 4 H. 4. It was held by William de Berkeley 5 E. 3. by John Berkeley of Durſley 19 & 22 E. 3. by ſir Nicholas Berkeley, his ſon, together with one meſſuage and two yard-lands in the ſame place, 6 R. 2.

Maud, widow of Robert de Cantelupe, and daughter and ſurviving heir of ſir John de Berkeley, was ſeized of this manor 4 H. 4. as was Margaret the widow of ſir John Blacket 8 H. 5. Richard Chedder had married the daughter and heireſs of Robert de Cantelupe, by whom he had a daughter and heireſs married to Thomas Wekys, who in her right was ſeized of Dodington 13 E. 4. John Wekys, ſon of Thomas, married Maud, daughter of Walter Langley of Siddington Langley, and was ſucceeded by his ſon Edward, who married Elizabeth, daughter of Robert Norton. Nicholas Wekys, ſon of Edward, married Elizabeth daughter of ſir Robert Pointz, and died ſeized of Dodington 5 Mar. John Wekys, ſon of Nicholas, married a daughter of ſir Thomas Danvers, of Dancy in Wiltſhire, and dying before his father, livery of the manor of Dodington was granted to Robert Wekys, ſon of John, 5 Mar. He built the large houſe at Dodington, and afterwards ſold the eſtate to Giles Codrington.

Giles Codrington was deſcended from Robert Codrington of Didmarton. Thomas Codrington, a younger ſon of Robert, married Elizabeth daughter of ſir Robert Pointz, by whom he had Ambroſe Codrington, who married Mary, daughter and heireſs of Lawrence Teſt, and died 6 H. 6. Francis Codrington, ſon and heir of Ambroſe, married Margaret, daughter and heir of —— Stripman. Giles Codrington, ſon of Francis, was the purchaſer of Dodington, and married Elizabeth, daughter of Arthur Porter. His ſon Richard Codrington married Joyce, daughter of John Burlace; and Samuel Codrington, ſon of Richard, married Elizabeth, daughter of Thomas Stephens of Sodbury. Thomas Codrington, ſon of Samuel, married Heſter, daughter of —— Plummer, and dying in 1675, was ſucceeded by Samuel Codrington his ſon and heir, who ſold the manor of Dodington to his kinſman Chriſtopher Codrington, ſon of Chriſtopher, who gained a large eſtate in the Weſt-Indies. He died governor of the Leeward Iſlands, and diſpoſed of large ſums of money in charity. By his will, dated Feb. 22, 1702, he gave 10,000 *l*. to All-Souls College in Oxford, of which he was a fellow; 6000 *l*. part thereof, was to build a library, the remainder for books, and he gave his own valuable library to furniſh it. He alſo ſettled a large revenue for propagating the Chriſtian knowledge in foreign parts.

He left the manor of Dodington to his kinſman William Codrington, who was created a baronet by patent, whoſe ſon ſir William Codrington, baronet, is the preſent lord of this manor. His arms are, *Argent, a feſs ſable between three lions paſſant gules.*

A ſmall

A ſmall manor, with the rectory of Dodington, belonged to the abbey of Keynſham in Somerſetſhire, and after its diſſolution, was granted to ſir Richard Long 30 H. 8.

Other lands in Dodington belonged to the priory of Black Canons at Bradenſtoke in Wiltſhire, and were granted to John Wiley and John Scudamore 37 H. 8.

Amicia la Walſh was ſeized of one meſſuage and one yard-land in Dodington and Oldbury 18 E. 2. Anthony Walſh died ſeized of lands in Dodingt n 4 Eliz. leaving Nicholas Walſh of Olveſton his brother and heir.

John Stanſhaw, eſq; was ſeized of lands in Dodington 12 E. 4. and John and Humphry, his ſons, levied a fine of them 12 H. 7.

John Cotherington and Alice his wife levied a fine of lands in Dodington 49 H. 6.

Of the Church, &c.

The church is a rectory, in the deanery of Hawkeſbury, worth about 100*l.* a year. Sir William Codrington is patron; Mr. Bliſs the preſent incumbent. The abbat of Glouceſter was patron in the year 1500.

The church is ſmall, dedicated to the virgin Mary, with a low tower at the weſt end; and there is a vault under the chancel, which is the burying-place of the Codrington family.

Firſt fruits £.	5	6	8	Synodals £.	0	2	0
Tenths —	0	10	7½	Pentecoſtals	0	1	0
Procurations							

Monuments and Inſcriptions.

There is a ſmall monument in the chancel, with this inſcription :

P. M. Quod Reliquum eſt Ioannæ filiæ Ricardi Codrington, Gen[t]. uxoris Chariſſimæ Ieremiæ Horler Rectoris de Sodbury Parva, quæ obiit tertio die Martii Anno Dom. 1721.

Depoſitum etiam Ieremiæ Horler prædict. qui obiit primo die Martii 1723-4.

Reliquiæ etiam Richardi Codrington A. M. hujus Eccleſiæ Rectoris. Obiit 1° Feb. 1732.——At bottom, *Per pale*, 1. *Azure, three ſquirrels argent.* 2. Codrington.

Againſt the ſouth wall in the chancel :

P. M. Roberti Greenaldi hujus Eccleſiæ Paſtoris an. 38, qui obiit 8° die Ian. 1660. Æt: 83.

Præco pacis erat viridis Greenaldus Oliva,
Quo muto, liquidum dant ſua facta, ſonum ;
Vir pietate probus, vivax virtutis imago,
Lucis evangelicæ ſtella, tabella, fuit.

On a flat ſtone in the church :

Here Lyeth the Body of Mrs Dorothy Chapman, Siſter to the Honorable William Codrington, Eſq[r]; who Departed this Life Ivne the 25 Ann. Dom. 1712.——Arms, *Per pale, baron and femme*, 1. *Quarterly* 1ſt and 4th, Codrington; 2d and 3d, *Or, on a bend argent three roſes gules, in chief a dexter hand.* 2. *On a chevron between three boars heads couped, a ſtar of ſix points.*

Taxes.					
The Royal Aid in	1692, £.	88	14	8
Poll-tax ——	1694, —	13	3	0
Land-tax ——	1694, —	104	12	8
The ſame, at 3*s.*	1770, —	72	18	6

There were 14 houſes and about 56 inhabitants in this pariſh, at the beginning of this century, according to ſir Robert Atkyns. There are now about 98 inhabitants.

DORSINGTON

LIES in the upper diviſion of the hundred of Kiftſgate, ſeven miles diſtant north-eaſt from Eveſham in Worceſterſhire, four weſt from Stratford upon Avon in Warwickſhire, and thirty-one north-eaſt from Glouceſter.

Sir Robert Atkyns derives the name *from* Dorſum, *Latin for the back*; *this place being ſituated*, ſays he, *on the back or ridge of an hill.* But ſir Robert's etymology is not founded on fact, for Dorſington lies in a flat vale country, at a conſiderable diſtance from any hill.

Great part of the pariſh is common field. The roads are very bad, and as ſtone is ſcarce, the few houſes in this village are either brick or wattled.

Of the Manor and other Eſtates.

'Roger de Belmont holds Dorſintune in Ceolfled 'hundred, and Robert holds it of him. There 'are ten hides. Saxi held it. In demean are three 'plow-tillages, and eight villeins with five plow-'tillages, and ſix *ſervi*. It was worth 8*l.* It is 'now worth 100*s.*' *Domeſday-book*, p. 75.

From Roger de Belmont this eſtate deſcended through the ſeveral generations of the earls of Warwick, preciſely as it is related of the manor of Chedworth, 'till it came to Thomas de Beauchamp, who died ſeized of Dorſington 2 H. 4.

But the Draytons held this manor of the earls of Warwick; for Baldwin de Drayton and Alice his wife levied a fine of Dorſington, and ſettled it on their ſon John de Drayton, 18 R 2. And William Drayton, eſq; died ſeized of the manor of Great Dorſington 5 E. 4. as did Richard Drayton 19 E. 4.

William Watſon had livery of this manor 15 Eliz. from whom it paſſed afterwards to George Shirley, eſq; who was lord of it in the year 1608.

Thomas Rawlins, ſerjeant at law, was afterwards lord of this manor, who was ſucceeded by his ſon Thomas; and Thomas Rawlins, eſq; a deſcendant from them, is the preſent lord of the manor of Dorſington, which comprehends the whole pariſh, except Braggington-farm.

Alice the widow of Thomas Paynel died ſeized of nine meſſuages, and two plow-tillages in Little Dorſington 16 H. 6.

Of the Church, &c.

The church is a rectory, in the deanery of Campden, worth 105*l.* a year. Thomas Rawlins, eſq; is patron; Mr. Martyn the preſent incumbent.

Three yard-lands belong to the glebe, with nine cow-paſtures, 60 ſheep-paſtures, ſix horſe-paſtures, and paſture for a colt in the commons.

The church was rebuilt with brick in the year 1758, having been burnt down with ſome part of the village.

Firſt fruits £.	12	19	2	Synodals £.	0	1	0
Tenths —	1	5	11	Pentecoſtals	0	0	7½
Procurations							

Taxes.				
The Royal Aid in 1692, £.		90	8	0
Poll-tax ——	1694, —	11	6	8
Land-tax ——	1694, —	50	0	0
The fame, at 3*s.*	1770, —	37	10	0

When fir Robert Atkyns compiled his account of this parifh, there were 20 houfes, and about 100 inhabitants, whereof 3 were freeholders; yearly births 3, burials 3. In ten years, beginning with 1760, there were regiftered 20 baptifms, and 23 burials; and there are 17 houfes, and about 90 inhabitants.

DOWDESWELL

LIES in the hundred of Bradley, five miles diftant eaftward from Cheltenham, feven fouth from Winchcombe, and twelve north-eaft from Gloucefter.

It is fituated in a fine part of the Cotefwold country; for tho' Pegglefworth lies fo high as to be efteemed one of the loftieft fpots in the Cotefwold, and Cold-Comfort was undoubtedly fo called from its expofed fituation; yet there is a very confiderable proportion of pafture-ground in the parifh. The farmers in this country manage their land very judicioufly. If they have too little pafture to carry a good ftock of cattle, they fupply the deficiency with faintfoin, which ufually lafts in pretty good heart ten or twelve years. Their practice is then to pare off and burn about half an inch of the furface of the ground, with the roots of the grafs, and plow in the afhes, upon which they have generally an excellent crop of wheat or turnips. The paring and burning coft from fifteen to twenty fhillings the acre. In thefe particulars, I mean not to confine myfelf to Dowdefwell only, as they are applicable to a confiderable extent of country in its neighbourhood.

The turnpike-road from Gloucefter to Oxford leads thro' the parifh, and there is a good inn for accommodation, at a place antiently called Anneford, now Andiford, and Andover's-ford; from *An*, the name of the little rivulet which croffes the road there.

Mrs. Tracy, daughter of the late fir William Dodwell, and relict of the late Thomas Tracy, efq; fometime a reprefentative in parliament for the county of Gloucefter, has a handfome feat and park at Sandiwell in this parifh, of which fhe has obliged the editor and the public with the plate annexed. The houfe was built by Mr. Brett. In removing the old houfe there, and digging drains for the convenience of the new one, feveral lead coffins were found, fuppofed to have contained perfons of confiderable note. The bodies lay north and fouth, but it has never been difcovered whofe they were. This parifh hath certainly been the fcene of feveral military actions, as appears from the camps which ftill remain vifible; and one of them upon Dowdefwell-hill, called the Caftles, is fuppofed to be Roman.

William Rogers, efq; has a pleafant feat in this place, and a large eftate; and Mr. Van Notten, a merchant in London, has the large houfe and eftate formerly belonging to the family of Rich.

Of the Manors and other Eftates.

Dowdefwell was antiently appurtenant to the large manor of Withington, which at the time of the general furvey, belonged to the church of Worcefter; when 'Robert held four hides and a 'half in Dodefuuelle and Peclefurde of that church.' *Domefday-book*, p. 70.

King Henry the Third granted the manor of Lower Dowdefwelle, Pegfworth, and Aniford, afterwards called Aniford-Temple, with courts leet, waifs, and felons goods, to the knights templers, who proved their right to them in a *Quo warranto* 15 E. 1. But William de Dowdefwell brought an affize againft them for the manor of Dowdefwell 3 E. 1. After the fuppreffion of the order of knights templers, thofe lands were granted to the college of Weftbury near Briftol: And the manor of Dowdefwell, and the hamlets of Oldbury, Pegfworth, and Aniford were held of William de Clinton, earl of Huntingdon, as of his manor of Guiting-Temple, 28 E. 3. Upon the diffolution of Weftbury college, they were granted to fir Raufe Sadleir, and were held of the manor of Guiting-Temple.

William Rogers, efq; was lord of the manor of Lower Dowdefwell in the year 1608; but a perfon of the fame name prefented to the church in the year 1575. William Rogers died feized of the manor and advowfon of Dowdefwell, held of the manor of Guiting, 17 Car. leaving Daniel his fon feven years old. William Rogers, a mafter in chancery, fucceeded to this manor, and gave it by will to his nephew John Rogers, clerk, who likewife gave it by will to his nephew William Rogers, efq; the prefent proprietor. His arms are, *Argent, a mullet fable, on a chief gules a fleur-de-lis Or.*

Records of the following dates, efpecially the latter of them, relate to the manor of Upper Dowdefwell; but in thofe of early dates, it is difficult to diftinguifh between the two manors.

Edward Croupes was feized of the manor of Dowdefwell 35 E. 3. William Gernoon and Elizabeth his wife levied a fine of lands in Dowdefwell and Peglefworth 11 E. 6. and another fine 13 H. 6. and William died feized thereof 19 E. 4.

This manor was foon after purchafed by Edmond Tame, to whofe ufe a fine thereof was levied by Ralph Lutham 20 H. 7. Sir Edmond Tame died feized thereof 26 H. 8. and livery was granted the fame year to Edmond Tame, his fon.

From the Tames it paffed to Nicholas Abbington, from whom it came through four generations down to John Abbington of Dowdefwell, efq; who was fequeftered in the great rebellion, and compounded for 364*l.*

Lionel Rich, efq; fon of fir Edward Rich, was poffeffed of it at the beginning of this century; from whom it paffed to his fon Baily Rich, efq; whofe

whoſe ſon Edward-Gilbert Rich had a daughter Mary, married to Robert Lawrence, of Shurdington, eſq; and dying without male iſſue, this eſtate went by entail to her couſin Thomas Rich, who ſold it, about the year 1774, to Mr. Van Notten of London, the preſent proprietor.

HAMLETS. Sandiwell and *Andiford* are hamlets in this pariſh, both held of Richard de Clare earl of Glouceſter and Hertford 47 H. 3. Henry Brett, eſq; ſold Sandiwell in Lower Dowdeſwell to lord Conway, from whoſe ſon, the earl of Hertford, it went by purchaſe to the late Thomas Tracy, eſq; and is now the property of his widow Mrs. Tracy, before-mentioned.

William de Dowdeſwell gave his demean, and two virgates and a half of land in Anneford, to the knights templers. *Dugd. Mon.*

Peggleſworth-farm is an eſtate of about 200*l.* a year, belonging to Mr. Wade.

There are records which ſhew that John Handborough, and Thomas Bruges and Maud his wife, levied a fine of the third part of lands in Dowdeſwell 36 H. 6. And that William Garrine and Elizabeth his wife levied a fine of lands therein 2 E. 4.

Of the Church, &c.

The church is a rectory, in the deanery of Winchcombe, worth about 200*l.* a year. Mr. Rogers is patron; Mr. John Arnold the preſent incumbent.

The church is in the form of a croſs, with a ſmall ſpire in the middle. The ſpire was built in 1577, by Mr. Rogers, Mr. Abbington, and others.

Firſt fruits £. 13	6	8	Synodals £.	
Tenths — 1	6	8	Pentecoſtals	
Procurations				

Monuments and Inſcriptions.

The moſt antient is the effigy of a man engraven on braſs, which has been miſtaken for an abbat of Hayles. The figure is not repreſented in the dreſs of an eccleſiaſtick, but in a long robe ſemée with mullets and fleurs-de-lis, which denote him to be of the family of Rogers.

On the table of a monument in the chancel:

To the Memory of William Rogers of Sandiwell in this pariſh of Dowdeſwell, Gen. who departed this Life ij° Ian. 1663, in ye 67 Y[r] of his Age.

In hope to reſalute his Soul here lies
This ſleeping Body, now Death's Sacrifice
Death & the Grave graunts the Conjunction
Of both by Chriſt his Reſurrection.
Noe more than Earthe can Earthe make Man inherit
But Heaven's a Guift of Grace not gained by Meritt.
Reader be confident noe Good Son dies
But, as the Day's Sun, only Setts to riſe.

To the Memory of Eliz. Rogers, Widow, late Wife of W. Rogers of Sandiwell Gent. decd. 22 Iuly 1670.

A happy Change, for now ſhee's paſt to reſt
From Sorrows here to a Kingdome euer bleſt.

On another table, againſt the wall:

Parcite Cælicolæ lachrymis, hi morte quieſcunt.
Funebris hæc requies funera mortis erit.
Vincula diſſolvit Chriſtus, Domino remeantur
Conſortes: thalamis ſic redière ſuis.

Vpon the death of William Rogers Gent. buried here Iune 2[d] 1649. And of Hellen his Wife, interred February the firſt 1648.

Weepe not, bleſt quire, theſe reſt in death, theyr fall
Is not ſoe much theyrs, as death's funerall:
Chriſt hath diſſolud our nuptiall bond, yet wee
In him our head now reunited bee.

On the table of a handſome marble monument in the chancel, with a buſt, under a pediment ſupported by two Corinthian pillars, is this inſcription:

Hic prope jacet GULIELMUS ROGERS, Armiger, Magiſtrorum Curiæ Cancellariæ nuper primus. Obijt nono Die Aprilis, anno Domini 1734, Etat. ſuæ 76.

Chriſtianæ Religionis veritatem firmiter credens,
Omnem Superſtitionem vehementer abhorrens,
Dei Unitatem Religioſe Colens,
Chriſti Redemptionem ſtrenue expectans,
Iuſtum et Honeſtum Utili anteferens.

Againſt the wall of the ſouth croſs aile:

In Memory of Edward Rich, of Upper Dowdeſwell, Eſquire, Bencher and Barriſter at Law of the Honourable Society of Lincoln's Inne, who deceaſed the 5th Day of February, A[no] D[ni] 1680, Aged 78 Years.

Mary, Wife of Lionel Rich, Eſq; Buried 7th Feb. 1734, Aged 69 Y[rs].

Lionel Rich, Eſq; Buried 26th April 1736 Ag[d]. 71 Y[rs].

At top, *Baron and femme,* 1. *Per pale, Sable and gules, over all a croſs botonny fitchy between four fleurs-de-lis Or,* for Rich. 2. *Argent, on a chevron azure three ſtags heads caboſhed Or between as many lozenges ſable.*

In the ſame aile:

In Memory of BAILY RICH, eldeſt Son of LIONEL RICH, of Upper Dowdeſwell, Eſq; he Married the Only Daughter and Heir of JOHN GILBERT, of Swindon in the County of Wilts, Gent. by whom he had one Son Born 15th Feb. 1688, Buried 18th April 1723.

Elizabeth, Daughter of Edw[d] Gilbert Rich, Eſq[r]. and Mary his Wife, Born 18th Aug[st] 1740. Buried 19th April 1741.

Here likewiſe are repoſed the Remains of MARY his Daughter, the beloved Wife of ROBERT LAWRENCE, Eſq[r]. Whoſe Mind was a ſweet Aſſemblage of every ſocial and benevolent Affection, eminently diſplay'd by the warm Exertions of Friendſhip; the endearing Sympathy of Connubial Love; and by Meekneſs & Humility, & the regular Practice of all thoſe Duties which are the Reſult of a truly Chriſtian Faith. Thus fitted for a better State, ſhe calmly reſigned her Soul into the Hands of her Bleſſed Redeemer, on the 21st Day of Jan. in the Year of our Lord 1761, Aged 22.

Elizabeth their Daughter died an Infant.

At top are theſe arms, *Baron and femme,* 1. Rich, as before. 2. *Azure, on a chevron argent three roundlets gules,* for Gilbert.

Taxes.					
	The Royal Aid in 1692, £.	138	14	0
	Poll-tax —— 1694, —	32	7	0
	Land-tax —— 1694, —	133	14	0
	The ſame, at 3*s.* 1770, —	87	0	6½

There were 25 houſes and about 120 inhabitants in this pariſh, when ſir Robert Atkyns compiled his account of it; yearly births 3, burials 3. And there are now 34 families, and 199 inhabitants.

DOWN-AMNEY

LIES in the hundred of Crowthorn and Minety, two miles north from Cricklade in Wiltſhire, ſix ſouth-eaſtward from Cirenceſter, and twenty-two ſouth-eaſtward from Glouceſter.

It is ſo called, becauſe it lies *down* the river which runs from the other Amneys, and empties itſelf into the Thames at Eiſey. It is a flat country, and very ſubject to floods from thoſe rivers. The ſoil is very rich, with leſs paſture than arable land.

It

It is obfervable, that part of the large manor houfe lies in Wiltfhire, part in Gloucefterfhire, and that a line drawn acrofs the kitchen divides the counties. The church exhibits what is further remarkable in this little parifh, wherefore I pafs to the particulars

Of the Manor and other Eftates.

'Ednod held Omenel in Gerfdon hundred in 'the time of king Edward. There were fifteen 'hides taxed, of which king Edward remitted the 'tax of five hides, as the county fays, and after- 'wards Ednod paid for ten hides. There are in 'this manor four plow-tillages in demean, and a 'prieft, and nineteen villeins, and three bordars, 'with ten plow-tillages. There are twelve *fervi*. 'This manor belonged to the bifhop of Baieux, 'and was worth 20*l*. It now pays a farm rent 'of 26*l*. to the king.' *Domefday-book*, p. 69.

This record ftands under the title *Terra Regis.*

'Radulf [de Todeni] holds Omenie and Cernei 'in Gerfdones hundred, and Roger holds them of 'him. There are four hides. Four thanes held 'them for four manors, and they could go where 'they pleafed. In demean are ten plow-tillages, 'and one villein, and one bordar. There are 'twenty-one *fervi*, and a mill of 5*s*. rent, and 'thirty acres of meadow. It was worth 10*l*. 'now 6*l*.' *Domefday-book*, p. 76.

As there are four parifhes in the fame hundred of the name of Amney, it is very difficult to apply the accounts from *Domefday-book* to the refpective parifhes, becaufe the manors are in nowife diftinguifhed in that record. And, feeing no reafon to the contrary, I have followed fir Robert Atkyns in placing the above abftracts to the parifh of Down-Amney. If the eftate in Amney, mentioned in the fecond abftract, belong to this parifh, it is probably that which the fubfequent records mention by the name of Wike, and belonged afterwards to the abbey of Cirencefter. The firft eftate was feized by the Conqueror, and was granted by king Henry the Second, to Alice, daughter of William de Caffey; but Edmond Crouchback, earl of Lancafter, was afterwards feized of it, and 55 H. 3. granted the manor of Down-Amney to Nicholas de Valers, (afterwards written Vilers, or Villers) probably the fame perfon with fir Nicholas de Villers, who in 1268 was in the holy war, and relinquifhing his paternal coat of arms, *viz. Sable, three cinquefoils argent*; affumed *The crofs of St. George, charged with five efcallop fhells*, being the antient badge of the croifes. The faid Nicholas proved his right to view of frankpledge within the manor of Down-Amney 15 E. 1.

William Cufons held one meffuage and one plow-tillage called Wike in Down-Amney 7 E. 3. Sir William de Cufons died feized of the manor of Down-Amney, and of the lands in Wike 19 E. 3. John de Handelo died feized of the manor of Wike 20 E. 3. as did Edward de Handelo 32 E. 3. Peter de Cufons and Margaret his wife levied a fine of the manor of Down-Amney 35 E. 3.

Sir Thomas Hungerford (who was the firft ftanding fpeaker of the houfe of commons, 51 E. 3.) purchafed a charter of free warren in Down-Amney 8 R. 2. He married Joan, daughter and coheir of fir Edmond Huffey, and was fucceeded by his fon and heir fir Walter Hungerford, lord high treafurer of England, and baron Hungerford. He married Catherine, one of the daughters and coheireffes of Thomas Peverel, and died 27 H. 6. leaving two fons, Robert and Edmond, of whom the latter married Margaret, daughter and heir of Edward Burnel, and died feized of this manor, and of Wike near Hampton-Meyfey, 2 R. 3. Sir John Hungerford his fon and heir died feized of Down-Amney 16 H. 8. as did fir Anthony Hungerford, fon of fir John, 1 Eliz. He was fucceeded in this manor by John Hungerford, his fon, whofe fon fir John Hungerford married Mary, the daughter of fir Richard Berkeley, and died 10 Car. Sir Anthony Hungerford, his fon and heir, left Bridget his only furviving daughter and heirefs, who being married to Edmond Dunch, efq; carried this manor into that name and family.

Hungerford Dunch fucceeded his father Edmond, and was fucceeded in this manor by his fon Edmond Dunch, who married the daughter of colonel Godfrey, and was lord of the manor at the beginning of this century. It paffed afterwards by purchafe to James Craggs, efq; fecretary of ftate, whofe two furviving daughters and coheireffes were married, the one to lord Clare, the other to Mr. Elliot, who are the prefent lords of this manor.

William Golding and Joan his wife levied a fine of lands in Down-Amney 23 H. 6. as did William Lewellyn and Joan his wife 7 E. 4. A ground called Le Wike, and two other meffuages, belonged to the abbey of Cirencefter, and were granted to fir Anthony Hungerford 32 H. 8.

Of the Church, &c.

The church is a vicarage, in the deanery of Fairford, and fince the augmentation, by the gifts of Dr. Godolphin and Mr. Wells, which procured the queen's bounty, it is worth about 60*l*. a year.

King Edward the Firft gave the church of Down-Amney to the knights templers. The patronage and impropriation belonged afterwards to the abbey of Cirencefter, and were granted to Chrift-church college, Oxford, 38 H. 8. where they remain. Mr. Smith is the prefent incumbent. The manor pays 25*l*. to the vicar, and every yard-land 5*s*.

The church, dedicated to All Saints, is built in the form of a crofs, with a handfome fpire, and five bells, at the weft end.

Firft fruits £	10	5	8	Synodals £	0	2	0
Tenths —	1	0	7	Pentecoftals	0	1	6
Procurations	0	6	8				

Monuments

Monuments and Inſcriptions.

On the north ſide of the chancel, under an arch in the wall, is a fine marble tomb in the form of a coffin, with a croſs engraven on it, the top of which is incircled with a wreath of olive. It has no inſcription, but it is ſuppoſed to be for one of the antient patrons of the church.

In the ſouth croſs aile, are two very antient monuments under an arch in the wall. One is the figure of a woman in freeſtone, lying along, with her hands in a ſupplicating poſture. This is very much defaced and broken. The other is that of a man in black marble, well executed, and in good preſervation, lying along in compleat armour; his legs are croſſed, with his right hand on the hilt of his ſword, as if about to draw it, and on the left arm a large ſhield, bearing *Five eſcallops on a croſs of St. George*. Theſe are the arms of Villers, and without doubt, the figure was intended to repreſent Nicholas de Villers, who had been in the holy war, and was lord of this manor in the reign of king Edward the Firſt, as before mentioned.

There is a noble monument of marble againſt the wall of the north croſs aile, with a pediment ſupported by two Ionic pillars. Under the pediment are the figures of two knights in armour, kneeling and facing each other, with books upon a deſk before them. Under the figures are two tables of black marble, on which are the following inſcriptions: On the dexter table,

MORS MIHI LVCRVM.

IN THIS CHAPELL LIETH THE BODY OF S[r]. IOH. HVNGERFORD, KNIGHT, (LINEALLY DESCENDED FROM WALTER LORD HVNGERFORD, KNIGHT, OF THE NOBLE ORDER OF THE GARTER) WHO WAS HON[ble] IN HIS LIFE, SERVICEABLE TO HIS KING AND COVNTRY, LIBERALL TO HIS FRIENDS, CHARITABLE & COVRTEOVS TO ALL. HEE FIRST MARRIED MARY THE DAVGHTER OF S[r]. RICHARD BARKLY, KNIGHT, BY WHOM HEE HAD THREE SONNES & FOWER DAVGHTERS; AND AFTERWARDS ANNA THE DAVGHTER OF EDWARD GODDARD, ESQ. HEE DIED THE XVIII DAY OF MARCH IN THE LXIX YEARE OF HIS AGE. ANO R. R. CAROLI DECIMO, ANOQ. DNI 1634.

On the ſiniſter ſide,

CHRISTVS MIHI VITA.

S[r]. ANTHONY HVNGERFORD, KNIGHT, NOW LIVING (ELDEST SONNE TO THIS S[r]. IOHN HVNGERFORD, KNIGHT) WAS FIRST MARRIED TO ELIZ. LVCY, DAVGHT[r]. OF S[r]. TH. LVCY, KNIGHT, BY WHOM HEE HAD TWO DAVGHTERS, (ONE DIED YONG, BRIDGET SVRVIVED & WAS MARRIED TO EDMVND DVNCH, ESQ.) AND AFTERWARDS Y[e] SAID S[r]. ANTHONY MARRIED IANE EARNLY, DAVGHTER TO MICHAEL EARNLY, ESQ. BY SVSAN HVNGERFORD, DAVGHTER & ONE OF Y[e] COHEIRES OF S[r]. WALTER HVNGERFORD OF FARLEY, KNIGHT: HEE ERECTED THIS MONVMENT IN Y[e] LIIth YEARE OF HIS AGE, FOR Y[e] HONOVR OF HIS DEARE FATHER, & IN REMEMBRANCE OF HIS OWNE MORTALITY. SEPT. XXX. ANO R. R. CAROLI XIII. ANO DNI 1637.

Over the figures are the following arms on different ſcutcheons, *viz.* on the dexter ſide, 1. *Gules, a chevron ermine between ten croſſes patee Or.* 2. *Gules, a chevron vaire between three creſcents Or.* 3. *Sable, two bars ermine, in chief three plates*, for Hungerford. 4. *Gules, three fiſhes hauriant between eight croſſes croſslets Or.* 5. ——— *on a bend ſable three eaglets diſplay'd Or.* In the middle of the pediment is a ſcutcheon with twenty quarterings.

On a braſs plate, againſt the ſouth wall,

Chriſtus eſt reſurrectio mortuorum.

HIC IACET MARIA DOMINA HVNGERFORD, NVPER VXOR IOHANNIS HVNGERFORD DE DOWNE-AMPNEY, MILITIS, (FILIAQVE RICHARDI BARKLEY, MILITIS, QVI A MAVRICIO DOMINO BARKLEY, PER DOMINAM ISABELLAM VXOREM EIVS, FILIAM RICHARDI PLANTAGINET COMITIS CORNVBIÆ AC REGIS ROMANORVM, FILII IOHANNIS REGIS ANGLIÆ, LINEALITER DESCENDEBAT) QVÆ FVIT VERÆ PIETATIS RARVM EXEMPLVM, BONARVM LITERARVM VALDE STVDIOSA, EXQVISITÆ PVDICITIÆ OBSERVANTISSIMA, MARITO SVO CHARA, ET AMANTISSIMA LIBERIS, COGNATIS ET AMICIS SVIS PLENA CHARITATIS ET BONORVM OPERVM: VIXIT CVM MARITO SVO CONIVNCTISSIME QVADRAGINTA ET QVATVOR ANNOS: APOSTEMA IN PECTORE VITAM EIVS FINIVIT DECIMO OCTAVO DIE IVLIJ, VESPERI CIRCA HORAM SEPTIMAM, ANNO ÆTATIS SVÆ SEXAGESIMO QVINTO, ANNOQVE DOMINI, COMPVTATIONE ANGLIÆ, 1628. { Sicut vita, Finis ita. Viuit poſt Funera virtus.

VLTIMVM OFFICIJ ET AMORIS MEI ERGA EANDEM MARIAM DOMINAM HVNGERFORD, ET VERVM TESTIMONIVM.

WILLIELMVS PLATT.

On a ſtone at the north end of the ſame aile,

HERE LYETH IOHN SECOND SONNE OF S[r]. IOHN HVNGERFORD, KNIGHT, WHO WAS BVRIED THE 5 DAY OF MARCH ANO DOM. 1643. WHO AMONGST OTHERS OF HIS PIOVS WORKS LEFT THIS HIS ENSVING EPITAPH.

MY SAD DAIES ENDED HERE I LIE,
THAT IS MY BODI WRAPD IN EARTH,
MY SPIRIT IS ASCENDED HIGH,
AND RESTS WITH HIM THAT GAVE IT BIRTH.
TO THIS MUST ALL MANKIND BE DRIVEN,
EARTH MUST TO EARTH, THE SOVLE TO HEAVEN.

And under, on the ſame ſtone,

THIS MONVMENT I FIX VNTO THE WALL
IN MEMORY OF HIM WHO GAVE ME ALL.
HIS NAME I SERVE, I LOVE, I HONOVR STIL
WITH BODY, MIND, & WITH A REDY WIL.

ANTHONY PREDY.

Benefaction.

John Kingſton gave 20*l.* one half to the church, the other to the poor.

Taxes.					
The Royal Aid in	1692, £.	173	3	0
Poll-tax ——	1694, —	17	8	0
Land-tax ——	1694, —	106	2	0
The ſame, at 3*s.*	1770, —	79	10	9

At the beginning of this century there were 36 houſes in this pariſh, and about 180 inhabitants, whereof 3 were freeholders; but the inhabitants are now increaſed to about 248.

DOWN-HATHERLEY.

THIS pariſh lies in the hundred of Dudſton and King's-Barton, ſix miles diſtant ſouth from Tewkeſbury, ſix weſtward from Cheltenham, and four north-eaſtward from Glouceſter.

It is a ſmall pariſh in the vale, conſiſting chiefly of rich paſture ground. A ſmall brook from Badgworth runs through it, and falls into the Severn near Sandhurſt. The roads are ſo exceedingly deep and miry in the winter, as to deter the curious traveller from viſiting it, and indeed there is nothing worthy his notice.

Of the Manor and other Eſtates.

At the general ſurvey, it was found that Edmar, a thane, had held three manors in Dudeſtan hundred, of which Athelai was one, and that he could give or ſell his land to whomſoever he pleaſed. But *Domeſday-book* mentions that earl Harold took away thoſe lands, with ſome others, after the death of king Edward; and accordingly they ſtand in record under the title *Terra Regis*, with other lands which the Conqueror ſeized for his own

 property,

property, as formerly belonging to Harold. See *Domesday-book*, p. 67.

It is uncertain how long this manor continued in the crown; but Robert Musgross died seized of Down-Hatherley 38 H. 3. as did his son John 3 E. 1. and Roger, son of Roger de Burghull, held it 31 E. 1.

It afterwards passed to the Willingtons, for John de Willington died seized of this manor 4 E. 2. and Ralph his son, and others, held it by one knight's fee, of the manor of Brimpsfield 1 E. 3.

Sir Thomas Brook and Joan his wife levied a fine of it 12 R. 2. and sir Thomas Brook, their son, died seized thereof 5 H. 5. as did the widow of the last sir Thomas 15 H. 6.

Fulk Grevil, second son of sir Edward Grevil, married Elizabeth, the surviving grandaughter and heir of Robert Willoughby, lord Brook, whereby the manor of Down-Hatherley came to the Grevils. This Elizabeth had two sisters, coheiresses. Anne died unmarried; Blanch was married to sir Francis Daintry, who, in her right, was seized of a third part of this manor; and by the death of Anne, had also livery of the moiety of her third part; but Blanch also dying without issue, the intire manor came to Elizabeth the wife of Fulk Grevil, who surviving his wife, died seized thereof 1 Eliz. and Fulk his son had livery 4 Eliz.

From the Grevils it passed to the Norwoods. Livery of the manor was granted to Nicholas Norwood, 14 Eliz. and Richard Norwood was lord of it in 1608. Mr. Gwinnet was proprietor of it about the beginning of this century; but Mrs. Chester is the present lady of the manor.

The records of the following dates shew, that Robert de Sauvage held lands in Down-Hatherley, 44 H. 3. as did John Attyate 41 E. 3. Fifty-five acres in Down-Hatherley were held by sir John Berkeley 6 H. 6. and by sir Maurice Berkeley of Beverstone 38 & 39 H. 6. and 19 E. 4.

Mr. Gibbs has a handsome house, and a good estate in this parish.

Of the Church, &c.

The church is in the deanery of Winchcombe. It is a vicarage endowed, worth about 100*l.* a year. The lord chancellor is patron; Mr. Barry is the present incumbent. It belonged to St. Oswald's in Gloucester 33 E. 1. and the priory of Usk hath presented to it; and so did the abbey of Gloucester in the year 1500.

The church is small, with a strong embattled tower at the west end. It is dedicated to Corpus Christi. The inscription upon a tomb in the church-yard for Henry Aisgill, vicar of this church, chancellor of St. David's, and a prebendary of Gloucester, is inserted p. 169.

First fruits £.	8	14	4	Synodals £.	0	1	0
Tenths —	0	17	5½	Pentecostals	0	0	1¼
Procurations							

Benefactions.

William Drinkwater gave 40*s.* yearly to a preacher in Gloucester, and 10*s.* yearly to the poor of this parish. There is a house, and four acres of land, worth 50*s.* yearly, given to the use of the poor.

Taxes.					
The Royal Aid in	1692, £.	64	4	0
Poll-tax — —	1694, —	8	19	0
Land-tax ——	1694, —	82	14	0
The same, at 3*s.*	1770, —			

At the beginning of this century, there were 20 houses in this parish, and about 100 inhabitants, whereof 6 were freeholders. *Atkyns.* The number of inhabitants is much the same as seventy years ago.

DRIFFIELD

IS a small parish in the hundred of Crowthorne and Minety, four miles south-eastward from Cirencester, three north-westward from Cricklade in Wiltshire, and twenty-one south-eastward from Gloucester. The parish is bounded by Latton in Wiltshire, and by the turnpike-road from Cirencester to Cricklade on the south and west. It is a strong soil, and requires judicious management; for in the winter, an infinite number of small springs break out, and spreading over the surface of the ground, infallibly destroy the crops of corn, if not carried off by proper drains.

The name was probably taken from two Saxon words, ꝺꞃoꞅ, *dirty*, and ꝼelꝺ, *an open country*; for a great part of this parish lies low and springy. The river from the upper Amneys runs thro' it to Down-Amney, by means of which the farmers water their meadow grounds. Something of this practice has been mentioned under South Cerney, but without sufficiently describing it. I will therefore take this opportunity of making a few short observations on that head.

A level is first taken from the highest part of the river, to see if the water may be carried over the highest ground in the meadow, allowing a fall of three or four inches for current in about 300 yards. A shallow trench, about four or five feet wide, (according to the size of the meadow, and quantity of water required) is then cut from the upper part of the river through the highest ground, taking care to preserve a current, and first paring off the turf to lay uppermost on each side of the trench. This is called the grand carry. From the sides of which, smaller cuts must be made, if required, with breaches in their banks, to let the water into little trenches (which must be carried up to those breaches) made by turning up the turf on one side, like the furrow of a plow; and in the sides of each of these small cuts, there must be a sufficient number of broken places to let out the water, so that by this management it may

may be evenly diftributed, and continually running over every part of the meadow. Laftly, from the loweft part there muft be a cut or drain, to convey the water into the loweft courfe of the river, fo that the meadow may be perfectly drained at pleafure, and no water left to ftagnate. A bay muft be erected acrofs the river, to turn a fufficient quantity of water into the grand carry, and fometimes there may be occafion for bays in the large carries, to diftribute the water properly into the fmaller ones. In this bufinefs there are three principal objects, 1. That the water be carried over every part of the meadow if poffible. 2. That it be kept every where brifkly running, but fo as not to cover the tops of the grafs, if it can be avoided; becaufe ftraining thro' the grafs, it depofits the matter which makes the manure. 3. That the drains be fo contrived as to clear the loweft places from water.

This operation is generally performed at the beginning of the winter, and the water kept running over the meadows 'till about the beginning of March, when it is drawn off, and the fmaller carries are levelled by turning the fod into the places whence it was originally taken. The running water, during the winter, keeps the froft from nipping the blade, and vegetation is fo much the ftronger and earlier in the fpring, that it is ufual to feed off the firft crop, and afterwards give the ground a watering for two or three days, about the beginning of May, and then hayne it for cutting.

If this fhort account of the method of drowning meadows be not fufficiently explicit to be underftood by fuch as are not acquainted with it, for whofe ufe it is intended, it will be worth their time and expence to make a journey of five hundred miles to get further information.

The abbat of Cirencefter had a country-houfe in this parifh, on the fcite of which ftands the prefent manor houfe, near the church, the feat of lord Coleraine.

Of the Manor and other Eftates.

'Reinbald the prieft holds Drifelle. Elaf held 'it of earl Tofti[b]. There are feven hides. There 'are fifteen *fervi*, and a mill of 5*s*. rent, and 'twenty acres of meadow. It is worth and was 'worth 8*l*.' *Domefday-book*, p. 73.

Reinbald, or Rumbald, granted this manor, and the advowfon of the church, to the college of Cirencefter, of which he was dean; and they continued in the abbey of that place from its firft foundation 'till its diffolution. The manor was then granted to Humphry Brown and George Brown, in exchange for lands in Waltham in Effex, 37 H. 8. Sir Humphry Brown died feized thereof 4 Eliz. and left four coheireffes. Roger Townfend, who married the eldeft, had livery of the fourth part of the manor, in right of his wife, 5 Eliz. One of the coheireffes dying foon after, livery of the third part of the manor was granted to Mary Brown, coheirefs of fir Humphry, 9 Eliz. and livery of another third part was granted to Chriftiana Brown, coheirefs of fir Humphry, 14 Eliz.

Thomas Wilford, efq; was lord of the manor in 1608. It was afterwards purchafed by John Hanger, a Turkey merchant. George Hanger, efq; defcended from the faid John, had two fons, George and John. George, the eldeft fon, was knighted by king William for his fteady attachment to the religion and laws of his country. He married Anne, daughter and coheir of fir John Beale, of Farmingham in the county of Kent, baronet; by whom he had four fons, George, John, Gabriel, and William; and four daughters, Anne, Delicia, Jane, and Mary. Gabriel furviving his elder brothers, fucceeded to the paternal eftate, and was created baron Coleraine, of Coleraine in the county of Londonderry, in the year 1761. His lordfhip married Elizabeth, daughter and heir of Richard Bond, of Cowbury in the county of Hereford, efq; by whom he had iffue three fons, John, William, and George; and one daughter, Anne. His lordfhip died in the year 1773, and is fucceeded in title and eftate by his eldeft fon John lord Coleraine, the prefent lord of this manor, and proprietor of all the lands in the parifh. His lordfhip's arms are, *Ermine, a griffin rampant fegreant, parted per fefs topaz and fapphire.* SUPPORTERS. *Two griffins fegreant.* MOTTO. ARTES HONORABIT.

Of the Church, &c.

The church is a vicarage, in the deanery of Cirencefter, endowed with all the tithes, and worth about 90*l*. a year. Lord Coleraine and Thomas Smith, efq; are patrons, and prefent alternately; Thomas Bray, D.D. is the prefent incumbent.

Twelve acres inclofed, and twenty-four acres in the common-fields belong to the glebe.

The late lord Coleraine took down the old church, and rebuilt it. The prefent church, dedicated to St. Mary, is a very neat building, well pewed, with a handfome altar-piece, and a fmall tower at the weft end, in which are three bells.

[b] This Tofti, or Tofti, was earl of Northumberland, and brother to king Harold. He is reprefented by the archdeacon of Huntingdon as one of the moft inhuman wretches that ever exifted. Taking a jealous antipathy to his brother Harold for being fo well in king Edward's favour, he hafted to Hereford, where his brother had made vaft preparations to entertain the king, and murdering many of the fervants, put a leg, an arm, or head, into each of the veffels of liquor defigned for the entertainment, fending the king word, *That he had made ample provifion for pickled meats, but his majefty might bring other forts with him.* For this horrid villainy he was banifhed. But his implacable fpirit fought every method of revenge againft his brother: At length, when Harold came to the crown, by the death of king Edward, Tofti engaged the king of Norway to invade England in conjunction with him. And having united their fleets, they failed up the Humber, and fhortly after ranfacked York. But Harold meeting them with an army at Stanford-bridge, gave them battle (wherefore it was afterwards called Battle-bridge) and obtained the victory; in which fight Tofti and the Norwegian were both killed.

Firſt fruits £.	8	2	4½	Synodals £.	0	2	0
Tenths —	0	16	2¾	Pentecoſtals	0	0	8
Procurations	0	6	8				

John Blake, the laſt abbat of Cirenceſter, lay buried in the old church, without any inſcription; and the memorials for all thoſe perſons who were buried before the building of the new one, were taken down, and have not been replaced.

Taxes.					
The Royal Aid in	1692, £.	58	18	0
Poll-tax —	1694, —	18	16	0
Land-tax —	1694, —	56	2	0
The ſame, at 3 *s.*	1770, —	42	1	6

At the beginning of this century there were 25 houſes in this pariſh, and about 120 inhabitants, whereof 4 were freeholders; yearly births 4, burials 3. *Atkyns.* Here are now only 21 houſes, but the inhabitants are increaſed to 137.

DUMBLETON.

THIS pariſh lies in the lower diviſion of the hundred of Kiftſgate, ſix miles diſtant ſouthward from Eveſham in Worceſterſhire, four north from Winchcombe, and eighteen north-eaſtward from Glouceſter.

The brook Iſbourn runs through it from Winchcombe, in its courſe to the Avon.

It is ſituated in the vale, on the north-eaſt ſide of a fertile little hill, to which this pariſh gives name, though the greater part of the hill lies in the pariſhes of Beckford and Waſhbourn. On the ſide of it riſes a little ſpring of medicinal water, whoſe properties have been found to be very much like the waters of Aſtrop-wells.

No gentleman's family is reſident at Dumbleton, and part of the manſion houſe, the ſeat of the late ſir Robert Cocks, has lately been taken down, to reduce it to a farm houſe.

Many gentlemen's ſeats in this county are totally deſerted, and falling to ruin; and too many others, in compliance with the taſte of the preſent age, are left by the owners for the greater part of the year, to partake more largely of the pleaſures of the metropolis, and other places of public entertainment. This cuſtom is fraught with many great evils; firſt to the poor inhabitants, whoſe pinching neceſſities were formerly relieved by a prudent hoſpitality, and whoſe morals might improve from the good example of their betters reſiding among them. But gentlemen themſelves pay dearly for their diverſions. How many ſquander what better œconomy would lay up for their children! How many ſpend their fortunes before they come to the poſſeſſion of them! To this cuſtom we owe that luxury and extravagance which pervade all ranks and degrees of people; that *cacoethes ludendi* which has ſpread itſelf over the land; that general depravity of morals which bids defiance to our laws, and endangers the ſtate. This obſervation aroſe from reading an inſcription in the pariſh church here, where hoſpitality and reſidence in the country are mentioned with commendation. And tho' the remark is not in the leaſt applicable to Dumbleton, the manor-houſe becoming void by the death of the whole family; yet it ſtands under this head with ſome propriety, that is, to avoid particular application.

Of the Manor and other Eſtates.

King Athelſtan, in the year 931, gave Swinford, and Sanford, and Dumelton, in the county of Glouceſter, to the abbey of Abingdon, when Cinath was abbat. *Stevens's Supp. to the Monaſt.* v. 1. p. 507. But it appears that there was a diſpute ſoon afterwards, about the right to this manor; for Wulfric Spot, an earl of Mercia, gave it to Elfric, archbiſhop of Canterbury, in the year 1004, from which ſee it had been witheld, as alledged, by the church of Abingdon; but that church held it at the time of the general ſurvey, as appears by the record.

'The church of St. Mary of Abendune holds 'Dubentone in Greteſtan hundred. There are 'ſeven hides and a half. In demean are four 'plow-tillages, and thirteen villeins, and eight 'bordars, with eight plow-tillages. There are ſix '*ſervi*, and a mill of 6*s.* rent. In the time of 'king Edward it was worth 12*l.* now 9*l.* This 'manor paid tax in the time of king Edward.' *Domeſday-book*, p. 72.

But there was then another eſtate in this pariſh of ſmaller value, of which the following are particulars:

'William Goizenboded holds one hide in Dun'bentune in Greteſtan hundred. Sauuin held it 'in the time of king Edward, and could go 'where he would. It was worth 20*s.* now 12*s.*' *Domeſday-book*, p. 74.

The abbey of Abingdon held this manor 'till that houſe was diſſolved; and the abbat proved his right to free warren and other privileges 15 E. 1.

The manor and advowſon of Dumbleton, after the diſſolution of abbeys, were granted to Thomas lord Audley, and to ſir Thomas Pope, in exchange for the manor of Layer-Marney in Eſſex, 34 H. 8. and the manor was confirmed to ſir Thomas Pope 36 H. 8.

Edmond Hutchins, eſq; was afterwards lord of this manor. He married Dorothy, daughter of Thomas Cocks of Cleeve, who was a younger branch of a family of that name of Cocks-Hall in Kent, and lived in the reign of king Henry the Eighth. This Edmond Hutchins, by his will, gave his eſtate to Dorothy his wife, whereby it came into her family. She was afterwards married to ſir Charles Percye; but leaving no iſſue by him, Charles Cocks, her brother, ſucceeded to this eſtate, and ſir Richard Cocks, baronet, ſecond ſon of Richard Cocks, of Caſtle-ditch in Herefordſhire, eſq; and grandſon of Thomas Cocks of of Cleeve, fucceeded his relation, Charles Cocks, in the manor of Dumbleton. He married Sufanna, daughter of Ambrofe Elton, of the Hafle in Herefordfhire, efq; and was created a baronet in 1666. Richard Cocks, efq; eldeft fon of fir Richard, married Mary, daughter of fir Robert Cook of Highnam, and died before his father.

Sir Richard Cocks, fon and heir of Richard, married Frances, daughter of Richard Nevell, of Bickingbeer in Berkfhire, efq; and was elected knight of the fhire in three fucceffive parliaments in the reign of king William the Third. He married fecondly Mary, daughter of William Bethell, of Swindon in Yorkfhire, efq; but died without iffue by either wife. He was fucceeded in title and eftate by his brother Robert Cocks, D.D. who married Mrs. Anne Fulks, of Oxford, by whom he had feveral fons and daughters; and dying in the year 1735-6, was fucceeded by his fourth fon Robert. Sir Robert Cocks married Elizabeth, daughter of James Cholmeley, of Eafton in the county of Lincoln, efq; by whom he had iffue feveral fons and daughters. He died by a fall from his horfe, in the year 1765, and leaving no male iffue, the title is extinct, and the eftate devolved to Charles Cocks, efq; of Caftle-ditch in Herefordfhire, the prefent proprietor.

John Dafton was feized of lands in Dumbleton 6 E. 4. probably the fame which William Goizenboded held at the general furvey, and which afterwards, in refpect to the large eftate held by the abbey, was called Littleton. Anthony Dafton levied a fine of lands in Dumbleton 1 E. 6. Another Anthony Dafton died feized of lands in Dumbleton, called Littleton's-fields, 12 C. 1. and left Richard his fon twelve years old.

A meadow in Dumbleton, called Dockham, belonged to the abbey of Gloucefter, and was granted to Clement Throckmorton, and Alexander Avening, 37 H. 8. And a portion of tithes in Dumbleton belonged to the abbey of Evefham, and was granted to fir Thomas Seymour 1 E. 6.

Of the Church, &c.

The church is a rectory, in the deanery of Campden, worth 200*l.* a year. The lord of the manor is patron; the reverend John-Baghot De-la-Bere is the prefent incumbent.

Part of the parifh is an impropriation, belonging to Trinity college in Oxford, worth 10*l.* a year, to which the rector pays 10*s.* a year. The parifh has a claim to a fellowfhip in that college.

Three little clofes, and about feventy acres of arable, belong to the glebe.

The church is dedicated to St. Peter. It has an aile on the fouth fide, and a crofs aile on the north fide, which formerly belonged to the Daftons, where feveral of them lie buried. It has a tower at the weft end, with fix bells.

The lord of the manor repairs the church. Jefus college, Oxford, repairs the north aile.

Firft fruits	£18	16	6	Synodals	£0	2	0
Tenths —	1	17	8	Pentecoftals	0	0	10½
Procurations	0	6	8				

Monuments and Infcriptions.

In the north crofs aile, upon a flat ftone, under the figures of a man and woman in brafs, is this infcription in old characters:

Orate p' aīabus Willi Dafton filii Iohīs Dafton et Annæ uxoris ejus qui quidem Willīus obiit anno dni Millimo CCCC° XIII° quor. aiab[s]. p'picietur deus.

Round a very antient flat ftone, in old French, and capital letters, partly Saxon:

ROBERT DASTYN FVNDVR: D...... .... DEV · DEL : ALME EYT MERCI : +:

Round another,

MARGERIE DASTYN .... GIST ISI DEV DEL ALME ....

Againft the north wall of the chancel, is a monument with the figures of a man and woman kneeling, and this infcription:

Here lye the Bodies of S[r]. Charles Percye, Knight, 3[d] Sonne of the Earle of Northvmb. and of Dame Dorothy his Wife, the Davghter of Thomas Cocks of Cleeve Efq; and of Anne their Davghter. S[r]. Charles was bvried the 9th Day of Ivly, Ano Dōni 1628; Dame Dorothy the 28th of Ivne, Ano Dōni 1646. ——Over the figures, in a fcutcheon, Quarterly 1ft and 4th, *Or, a lion rampant azure.* 2d and 3d. *Gules, three lucies, or pikes, hauriant,* for Lucy; the arms born by Percy earl of Northumberland. Between the figures, in a fcutcheon, *Baron and femme,* 1. The above. 2. *Sable, a chevron between three ftags horns with the fcalps argent,* for Cocks.

On another monument, with the arms of Cocks:

Memoriæ Sacrum

Caroli Cocks, Arm. Filij Quarti Thomæ Cocks, de Cleeve in Agro Glouceftrienfi, Armigeri, Qui obijt decimo quinto die Augufti, anno Ætatis fuæ octogeffimo tertio, annoq; Dni MDCLIV.

Richardus Cocks, Bar[tus]. Nepos ejufdem Caroli, et cui maximam hereditatis fuæ partem legavit Carolus, hoc Monumentum, amoris et gratitudinis ergo extruxit.

On the table of a handfome marble monument,

In Memory of S[r]. Richard Cocks, Bar: and of Dame Sufanna his Wife: He was the 2[d] Son of Richard Cocks, of Caftle-Ditch in the County of Hereford, Efq; and of Iudith his Wife, Daughter and Coheir of Iohn Elliott, Efq[r]. She was the 5th Daughter of Ambrofe Elton, of the Hafle in the County of Hereford, Efq; and of Ann his Wife, Daughter of S[r]. Edward Afton, of Tixall in the County of Stafford. He, in his younger Days, accompanied his Unkle Chriftopher Cocks, (Who was honoured by King Iames the Firft with a public Character) into Mufcovy, and after his return, he retired into the Country, and was concerned with no Publick matters more then the offices of Juftice of the Peace and Highfheriffe. She was a Lady diftinguifhed by very great ornaments of Mind and Body, the vifible remains of which continued with her to her laft hour. They kept good Hofpitality, loved their Tenants and Neighbours, and on all occafions did them all the fervice they could. He liv'd peaceably with them, and kept them in peace one with another. She healed their difeafes, and cured their fores. He was a great fufferer for his love to the Royal Family, and for his zeale for the Laws, and for the eftablifhed Religion of his Country. They were indulgent Parents, good to their Servants, and charitable to the Poor. They gave their Children good fortunes and liberal education. They had three Sons, Richard, Charles, and Iohn: and two Daughters, Iudith and Elizabeth. But Iohn the younger, and Elizabeth the relict of S[r]. Iohn Fuft, of Hill in this County, Bar: only furvived them. She, out of a juft remembrance and gratitude to fo good Parents, and believeing the memory of them would be grateful to their Neighbours, ordered her brother Iohn Cocks to erect this Monument for them. He died September 16, A.D. 1684, aged 82. She died March 10th A. D. 1689, aged 84. ——Arms, *Baron and femme,* 1. Cocks, 2. *Paly of fix Or and gules, over all on a bend fable three mullets of the firft,* for Elliott.

On a plain marble table,

To the happy Memory of M[rs]. Dorothy Cocks. She died the 29th Day of October, 1714, in the 58th Year of her Age, & lies

 inter'd

inter'd in ye Chancel, near the Communion Table. She was Eldeſt Child of Richard Cocks, Eſq^r^. & of Mary his Wife, the youngeſt daughter of S^r^. Robert Cooke, of Hynam, by his firſt Wife; her Father and her Mother both died when ſhe was about 14 years old. She was of a middle ſtature, endowed with great ornaments of Body, & with far greater of the mind. She was a woman of a very good and compaſſionate nature, of a great underſtanding, & made a very good uſe of it. She choſe rather to be a Mother to her younger Siſters, then to be engaged in another family; & by her care and good inſtructions ſhe helped to breed them up in piety & religion, and other neceſſary knowledge. Envy itſelf can't charge her with an unbecoming action or expreſſion in her whole life. She was a woman of great piety, patience, and humanity: She ſpent great part of her life in her devotions & prayers for herſelf, her friends, and country. She bore a tedious ſickneſs, and other misfortunes that attended her infirm body, with all chearfulnes & reſignation: ſhe made uſe of her time & fortune, not only to ſerve her friends and relations, but even ſtrangers, that were diſtreſſed: therefore S^r^. Richard Cocks, her Eldeſt brother, out of a gratefull remembrance of theſe virtues, has choſe rather to ſet up this true and juſt Epitaph then a magnificent Monument, with an intention to make her family bluſh when they deviate from ſuch a preſident; and that they & others may imitate her Example in this world, & be happy wth her in ye next.

Sic Vovet R. C.

In the ſouth aile, on the table of a very neat monument of white marble:

Elizabeth, Wife of S^r^. Robert Cocks, Bar^t^. and Daughter of James Cholmeley, Eſq; of Eaſton in the County of Lincoln, with three of her Children, Charles, Ann, & Catherine, were carried ſucceſſively by the ſame fatal Sickneſs, a Fever and Sore throat, to the Grave, in a few Days. A moſt excellent and amiable Mother. The two youngeſt in the brighteſt dawn of Hope, the Eldeſt in the ſweeteſt bloom of Virtue, growing up like the faireſt Flowers, like the faireſt Flowers were cut down. This Place where they ſleep is marked out by the unfeigned grief of a Huſband, mixt with the Tears and unflattering Praiſe of Surviving Friends: Unhappy in being Survivors, unleſs they tread in the ſame blameleſs Steps: Happy, could they, by keeping her in Remembrance, reach the ſame ſhining Heights of Lovelineſs, Virtue, and Religion.

Charles	died	Jan. 21	aged	3 Years
Ann		Jan. 28		8 Years
Elizabeth		Jan. 30		39 Years
Catherine	A. D. 1749	Feb. 7		16 Years.

Alſo

Three other Children,

Chubb	died	April 3^d^, 1735,	aged	1 Year 8 Months
Elizabeth		July 2^d^, 1738,		9 Months
Robert		Sept. 27, 1740,		10 Years.

Another, with this device, a lilly, the ſtem broken near the flower, in alluſion to the following inſcription:

To the Memory of Miſs Dor^y^. Cocks, the youngeſt and only ſurviving Child of S^r^. Robt. Cocks, of Dumbleton, Bar^t^. who died April 24th, 1767, aged 18 Years, much lamented by all who knew her. A fair Flower cut off in the Bloom of Life, amiable in her Perſon, ſenſible and prudent in all her Actions, untainted with the Follies and Diſſipation of the Age in which ſhe lived.

This little Monument, in Teſtimony of her great Love and Affection, is erected by her Aunt, M^rs^. Sarah Cocks.

Benefactions.

Mrs. Dorothy Cocks, by her will, gave 40*s*. a year for teaching children to read. And Mr. Richard Cocks, by his will, in 1728, gave an eſtate in Tainton, worth 21 *l*. a year, part for putting a poor boy out apprentice, the remainder to be given to the poor of this pariſh not receiving alms.

Taxes.				
The Royal Aid in	1692,	£. 312	5	0
Poll-tax ——	1694, —	24	2	0
Land-tax ——	1694, —	170	1	0
The ſame, at 3*s*.	1770, —	120	1	6

There were 46 houſes, and about 200 inhabitants in this pariſh, whereof three were freeholders; yearly births 5, burials 4. *Atkyns*. And there are now about the ſame number of inhabitants.

DUNTESBOURN ABBATS

LIES five miles north-eaſtward from Cirenceſter, ten ſouthward from Cheltenham, and twelve ſouth-eaſtward from Glouceſter. Part of it is in the hundred of Crowthorne and Minety, and the other part in that of Rapſgate.

This is ſometimes called Upper Dunteſbourn. It conſiſts moſtly of arable land, and lies on the ſouth-weſt ſide of the *Irminſtreet*, a Roman road, already deſcribed under Daglingworth, and other places.

A ſmall *bourn*, or brook, riſes in this pariſh, and joins the Churn at Cirenceſter. It is moſt likely that the manor was very antiently the property of one *Dun*, or *Dunt*, whoſe name, with the genitive or poſſeſſive ending, *Dunte's*, is very diſcernible in that of the pariſh. *Abbats*, the cognomen, was afterwards given it for a like reaſon, becauſe it was the property of the abbat of Glouceſter, and ſerved to diſtinguiſh it from the other Dunteſbourns.

Of the Manor and other Eſtates.

'The wife of Walter de Laci, by the licence 'of king William, gave the manor of Dunteſborne 'in Cireceſtre hundred, conſiſting of five hides, 'to ſaint Peter [the abbey of Glouceſter] for the '[good of the] ſoul of her huſband. In demean 'are three plow-tillages, and eight villeins, with 'five plow-tillages. There are ſixteen *ſervi*, and 'a mill of 2*s*. rent. It is worth 4*l*.' *D. B.* p. 71.

'Ansfrid de Cormeille holds one hide in Tanteſ'borne in Cireceſtre hundred. Elmer held it for 'a manor, and could go where he would. In 'demean is one plow-tillage, and one villein, and 'two bordars, and five *ancillæ*. It was worth '40*s*. and is now worth 20*s*.' *D. B.* p. 78.

In the year 1100, Gilbert de Eſkecot gave lands in Dunteſbourn to Glouceſter monaſtery, to pray for the ſoul of Walter de Laci.

Odo de Mara granted to Jordan, the ſon of Iſaac of Cirenceſter, lands in Dunteſbourn, 1 Joh.

Over Dunteſbourn was held of Humphry de Bohun, earl of Hereford and Eſſex, and of Joan his wife, 46 E. 3.

This manor was held by the abbey of Glouceſter till that houſe was diſſolved, and was granted afterwards to William Morgan and James Dolle 5 Mar. James Dolle died ſeized of it 42 Eliz. and left Anthony Dolle his ſon and heir 40 years old. Mr. Edward Dolle was lord of the manor in the year 1608. The earl of Radnor is the preſent lord of the manor. For his arms, ſee *Pucklechurch*.

Richard Murdac gave one hide in Dunteſburn to the priory of Lanthony, which was confirmed 1 Joh. Lands in Bockham in Dunteſbourn were granted to Richard Andrews and Nicholas Temple 35 H. 8. which formerly belonged to the priory of Lanthony near Glouceſter; and two meſſuages and lands in Dunteſburn, formerly belonging to the ſame priory, were granted to Richard Andrews and George Hiſley 36 H. 8.

HAM-

HAMLET. *Duntefbourn-Lyre* is a hamlet in this parifh, fo called, becaufe it was the property of the abbey of Lyre, or de Lira, in Normandy. This hamlet lies in the hundred of Rapfgate.

'The church of St. Mary of Lire holds 'Tantefborne in Refpiget hundred. There is 'one hide and one yard-land. In demean is one 'plow-tillage, and two bordars. It is worth and 'was worth 20*s*. Roger de Laci gave this land 'to that church. Edmer held it in the time of 'king Edward.' *Domefday-book*, p. 72.

'Roger de Laci holds Tantefborne in Ref-'pigete hundred, and Giflebert holds it of him. 'Keneuuard, a thane of king Edward, held it, and 'could go where he would. There are two hides. 'In demean is one plow-tillage, and two villeins, 'and two bordars with one plow-tillage and a 'half. There are two *fervi*. It is and was worth '40*s*.' *Domefday-book*, p. 75.

'Ansfrid de Cormeille holds two yard-lands 'and a half in Dantefborne in Refpigete hundred, 'and Bernard holds them of him. Elmer held 'them for a manor, and could go where he would. 'There is one bordar. It is worth and was 'worth 40*s*. Ansfrid had the above of Walter 'de Laci when he took his niece. *D. B.* p. 78.

'Chetel holds three yard-lands and a half in 'Dantefborne in Refpiget hundred, and he held 'them in the time of king Edward. There is one 'plow-tillage, and two bordars, and two *fervi*. 'It was worth 10*s*. and is now worth 15*s*.' *Domefday-book*, p. 79.

Nutebean-farm, in Duntefbourn-Lyre, belonged to the abbey of Cirencefter, and was granted to William Sherington 34 H. 8. Thomas Pleydall was feized of the fcite of the manor of Duntef-bourn-Lyre, and of a capital meffuage called Nutbeame-farm, *alias* Nutbeane in Duntefbourn-Lyre, of which he levied a fine 32 Eliz. to the ufe of John Pleydall and his heirs in fee taille.

Of the Church, &c.

The church is a rectory, in the deanery of Cirencefter, worth 90*l*. a year. The advowfon of the rectory of Over Duntefbourn was granted to Efme Stewart, lord Aubeny 8 Jac.

The advowfon of the rectory is in truft for the ufe of the reverend Mr. Jofeph Chapman's children. Mr. Chapman himfelf is the prefent incumbent.

No lands in the parifh are tithe free. By an agreement made between the bifhop of the diocefe and the rector, in the year 1681, the latter is to pay 20*s*. a year to the poor on Palm-funday, in lieu of a calf, and other entertainment, formerly given to the parifhioners on that day. And the poor of this parifh are intitled to a fourth fhare of the rent of Bull-bank clofe, given by the will of Mr. Thomas Muggleton, to be diftributed to them on Good-friday.

The church is fmall, dedicated to St. Peter.

Firft fruits £.	13	0	0	Synodals £.	0	2	0
Tenths —	1	6	0	Pentecoftals	0	0	9
Procurations	0	6	8				

Duntefbourn Abbats.

			£.	s.	d.
Taxes.	The Royal Aid in	1692, £.	15	0	0
	Poll-tax ——	1694, —	3	11	0
	Land-tax ——	1694, —	10	6	0
	The fame, at 3*s*.	1770, —	7	13	0

Duntefbourn-Lyre.

			£.	s.	d.
Taxes.	The Royal Aid in	1692, £.	15	8	6
	Poll-tax ——	1694, —	3	0	0
	Land-tax ——	1694, —	9	0	0
	The fame, at 3*s*.	1770, —	11	18	3

There were 42 houfes and about 180 inhabitants in this parifh, whereof 12 were freeholders; yearly births 4, burials 3. *Atkyns*. But it appears by the regifter, that in ten years, beginning with 1700, there were 55 baptifms, and 30 burials; and in the fame number of years, beginning with 1760, the baptifms were 43, burials 26; and the inhabitants are 176; almoft 68 to 1 of the annual burials.

DUNTESBOURN ROUS.

THIS parifh lies in the hundred of Crowthorn and Minety, one mile lower on the Bourn, and nearer to Cirencefter, than Duntefbourn Abbats, wherefore it is fometimes called *Lower Duntefbourn*. And becaufe the knightly family of the Roufes were antiently proprietors of it, their name was added for the cognomen, and fome-times their title, as *Duntefbourn Militis*, in contra-diftinction to *Duntefbourn Abbatis*, the preceding parifh, where the reft is fufficiently explained.

A fmall brook parts this parifh from Edgworth, and runs into the Froom river, which goes to Stroud. The lands are chiefly arable.

Of the Manors and other Eftates.

'William de Ow holds Duntefborne in Cire-'ceftre hundred. Aleftan held it in the time of 'king Edward. There are five hides and a half 'taxed. In demean are two plow-tillages, and fix 'villeins, and four bordars with five plow-tillages 'and a half. There are feven *fervi*, and a mill of '8*s*. Radulf holds this manor of William, and 'pays tax; but he witholds the tax of three hides. 'A foreigner [*francigena*] holds half a hide of 'this land, and has one plow-tillage there with 'his men. The whole in the time of king 'Edward was worth 10*l*. and is now worth 8*l*.' *Domefday-book*, p. 73.

'Durand the fheriff holds two hides in Duntef-'borne in Cireceftre hundred, and Radulf holds 'them of him. Wluuard held them for a manor 'of king Edward. In demean are two plow-'tillages, and three villeins, and one bordar with 'one plow-tillage. There are four *fervi*, and 'two acres of meadow. It is worth and was 'worth 40*s*.' *Domefday-book*, p. 76.

Soon after the Norman conqueft, this manor became the property of John Rufus. This is the fame ſame name with le Rous and le Rus. They were ſo called from having red hair, as the Blonds or Blounts obtained their name from having white hair, and a fair complexion. Roger le Rous held one yard-land in Dunteſburn 22 E. 1. as did John le Rous in the reign of king Edward the Second, when he was attainted for rebellion; but his lands were reſtored 1 E. 3.

This manor afterwards paſſed into the family of Mull. Thomas Mull and William Mull were attainted 2 E. 4. and the manor granted by the crown to Thomas Herbert and to his heirs male 2 & 5 E. 4. which Thomas dying without male heirs, the manor was granted to ſir Richard Beauchamp 14 E. 4. It was afterwards purchaſed by Dr. Fox, biſhop of Wincheſter, in the reign of king Henry the Seventh, and by him ſettled on Corpus Chriſti College in Oxford, which was founded by him; and it now belongs to that college.

HAMLET. *Pinbury* is a hamlet, lying part in this pariſh, and part in that of Edgworth. It is an antient manor, and has a park ſituated on high ground, with a camp in the midſt, whence it obtained the above name, which is compoſed of *pen*, the *top*, and beoƿȝ, a *camp* or *fortification*. There was a large manor-houſe in the park, where a branch of the Atkyns family reſided; but the park is converted to a coney-warren, the houſe gone to decay, and ſome of it taken down. There was alſo an antient chapel in this hamlet, with ſeveral houſes, of which the old foundations are ſtill to be ſeen. In *Domeſday-book* we read thus of the manor:

'The church of the nuns of the holy Trinity 'of Cadom holds Penneberie in Cireceſtre hundred 'of the king. There are three hides. In demean 'are three plow-tillages, and eight villeins, and 'one artificier [*faber*] with three plow-tillages. 'There are nine *ſervi*, and a mill of 40*d.* rent. 'It was worth and is now worth 4*l.*' *D. B.* p. 72.

The abbeſs of Caen proved her right to court leet and free warren in Pendebury, in a *Quo warranto*, 15 E. 1.

After the ſuppreſſion of foreign monaſteries, the manor was granted to the nuns of Sion in Middleſex; and after the general diſſolution of religious foundations, it was again granted, with Avening, Hampton, &c. to Andrew lord Windſor, in exchange for Stanway, &c. in Middleſex, 34 H. 8. who dying, his ſon had livery thereof 35 H. 8. Sir Henry Pool purchaſed it of lord Windſor. Sir Henry Pool, grandſon of that ſir Henry, ſold it to ſir Robert Atkyns of Saperton; and the children of Edward Atkyns, eſq; who are minors, are the preſent owners of Pinbury. The greater part of the park lies in this pariſh.

Of the Church, &c.

The church is a rectory, in the deanery of Cirenceſter, worth about 100*l.* a year. Dr. Robert Morwent bought the advowſon, and gave it to Corpus Chriſti college in Oxford, in the year 1557, who are patrons; and Mr. Finden is the preſent incumbent. The rector pays 13*s.* 4*d.* yearly to the crown, which was a rent formerly paid to the knights of St. John of Jeruſalem.

The church is ſmall. There is a vault under the chancel belonging to the rector, with ſtairs into the church, ſuppoſed to have been uſed in confeſſion.

Two acres of land in each field are given towards the repair of the church.

	£	s	d		£	s	d
Firſt fruits	8	14	7	Synodals	0	2	0
Tenths —	0	17	5½	Pentecoſtals	0	0	10
Procurations		6	8				

Taxes.			£	s	d
	The Royal Aid in	1692,	40	12	0
	Poll-tax ——	1694, —	19	0	0
	Land-tax ——	1694, —	30	10	0
	The ſame, at 3*s.*	1770, —	22	17	6

When ſir Robert Atkyns compiled his account of this pariſh, there were, according to him, 13 houſes, and about 60 inhabitants, whereof three were freeholders; yearly births 1, burials 1. There are now 72 inhabitants.

DURSLEY.

THIS pariſh lies in the hundred of Berkeley, five miles eaſt from the town of that name, four north from Wotton-under-edge, and fifteen ſouthward from Glouceſter. The pariſh is not large, but the market-town within it merits particular conſideration.

The town of Durſley is ſituated under the north ſide of a ſteep hill, covered with a fine hanging beech wood. It is one of the five antient boroughs in Glouceſterſhire, and was returned ſo to be by the ſheriff of the county, in the ninth year of the reign of king Edward the Firſt; and in that reign the criminals of this place were tried and executed at Berkeley.

Under the antient conſtitution of the borough, there was a chief officer (the *Præpoſitus*) appointed over it, and there is now a bailiff elected annually at the manor court, out of the better rank of people in the borough, who is honoured by the attendance of the principal inhabitants, with accuſtomed ceremonies. This officer formerly collected the king's rents, and perhaps executed ſome proceſſes within the borough. He now examines into the ſufficiency of weights and meaſures, but his authority ſeems to extend no further; though we are told by topographers, that the borough is governed by a bailiff and four conſtables.

Here was an antient caſtle, and the ruins of its foundations are ſtill viſible in a garden not a quarter of a mile north-weſtward of the town. The fields adjoining are ſtill called *the Caſtle-fields*. The caſtle belonged to the antient family of the Berkeleys, and falling to decay, was taken down, and part of of the materials uſed in building the manor-houſe at Dodington, by Robert Wekys, who was lord of both the manors of Durſley and Dodington 5 Mariæ. Our hiſtorians ſay very little about it, but Leland obſerves, that it had a good moat, or in his own words, *a metely good dyche*, round it; and that it was chiefly built of *a towſe ſtone, full of pores and holes lyke a pumice*.

There are no papers, that I can find, which give any further light into the antient ſtate of this place, wherefore I proceed to a ſhort account of its preſent condition. It is a little town, not much frequented by travellers, conſiſting of two narrow ſtreets, forming ſomething like the figure of the letter T. But beſide theſe two ſtreets, there is a large hamlet without the borough, containing more houſes than either of them. Leland calls the town *a praty clothinge towne*, ſo that if we reckon from his time, it has enjoyed the clothing trade between two and three hundred years, which hath inriched ſome individuals, and is the preſent ſupport of the place. The buſineſs of making cards for the clothiers has been long ſettled here, and employs a pretty many hands.

There is a handſome market-houſe, of free-ſtone, in the middle of the town, built about the year 1738, with the ſtatue of queen Anne in a niche at the eaſt end, and the arms of the lord of the manor in the front. But what confers great honour on the town, is the earls of Berkeley taking their title of viſcount from it; and the eldeſt ſon is ſtiled lord Durſley.

The weekly market is on Thurſday, and pretty well frequented; but this part of the country is chiefly ſupply'd with grain and flour from Cirenceſter, Glouceſter, and Tetbury; for the neighbourhood of Durſley, next the Severn, runs greatly on dairy, and produces the beſt ſort of Glouceſterſhire cheeſe. The fairs are on the 6th of May, and the 4th of December.

On the ſouth-eaſt ſide of the church-yard are many ſprings, which riſe perpendicularly out of the ground like boiling water, in ſo copious a manner, that they drive a fulling-mill at about a hundred yards diſtance below. At their riſe, they cover a fine, level, gravelly bottom, for the ſpace of about fifteen feet ſquare, with near two feet depth of water, wherefore the inhabitants call the place the *Broad Well*; but in old writings concerning property thereabout, the name is *Ewelm*. This is a Saxon word, [epylm] uſually tranſlated by *Origo Fontis*, the head of the ſpring. It is conjectured, that this remarkable water gave name to the town, for in the Britiſh language *Dwr* ſignifies *water*, and *ley*, *lege*, *lega*, are common terminations, denoting *paſture ground*. The *ſ* in the name was added to make the ſound more agreeable.

There is a curious foſſil ſubſtance found in great plenty in this pariſh, which Leland calls Towſe ſtone. It lies in one intire bed or *ſtratum*, and is ſo ſoft as to be cut out in pieces or blocks of any ſize or ſhape; but when it has been dried in the ſun and air, is extremely hard and durable. The walls of Berkeley-caſtle, and thoſe of the church of Durſley, are built in part with this ſtone, and tho' the caſtle walls have ſtood above ſix hundred years, the ſtone remains as ſound as ever.

One thing more, perhaps, recommends itſelf to our notice, on account of its antiquity. It is a place called the *Hermitage*, at the top of the hill near Nibley park, where an anchoret is ſaid to have ſpent his days. I fancy very few in this age will chuſe his ſituation, or practice the auſterities of thoſe rigorous devotees, who thought an extreme mortification of the body quicked the exerciſe of religion, and added fervor to devotion.

Mr. Phelps, Mr. Wallington, and Mr. Stiff have good houſes in the town. Mr. John Purnell has a good houſe and eſtate at King's-hill, on the weſt ſide of it; and another Mr. John Purnell has a beautiful houſe, on an elevated ſituation, at a place called the New Mills, on the eaſt ſide, where Mr. Tippets has alſo a good houſe.

Edward Fox, biſhop of Hereford in 1535, was a native of this place, and very active in promoting the divorce of king Henry the Eighth from queen Catherine.

Of the Manors and other Eſtates.

At the time of the general ſurvey, in the reign of William the Firſt, Derſilege (*i.e.* three hides in Derſilege) being a member of the honour of Berkeley, was given by the Conqueror to Roger de Berkeley, as appears more fully under Berkeley. Roger de Berkeley, founder of the monaſtery of Kingſwood, was certified, upon an aid for marrying the king's daughter, to hold one hide in Durſley, of the old feoffment, 12 H. 2. And upon levying ſcutage to carry on war againſt Scotland, it was certified that ſix knights fees and a half were held of the honour of Durſley 13 Joh. Henry de Berkeley proved his right to certain privileges in his manor of Durſley in a *Quo warranto* 15 E. 1.

John de Berkeley of Durſley and his wife levied a fine of the manor of Durſley 5 E. 3. and were in poſſeſſion thereof 22 E. 3. and John Atyate, of the Berkeley family, died ſeized of it 41 E. 3. Sir Nicholas Berkeley and Cecily his wife were ſeized thereof 2 R. 2. About this time the manor went out of the name of Berkeley, by the marriage of Maud, daughter and ſurviving heir of John de Berkeley, to Robert de Cantelupe, who ſurvived her huſband, and held the manor of Durſley 4 H. 4. Richard Chedder married the daughter and heireſs of Robert de Cantelupe, by whom he had a daughter and heireſs, married to Thomas Wekys, who, in right of his wife, died ſeized of the manor of Durſley 13 E. 4.

This manor continued ſeveral generations in the name and family of Wekys, for Nicholas Wekys died ſeized of it 5 Mar. and left Robert Wekys his grandſon and heir, (by his ſon Nicholas) who had livery thereof the ſame year, and ſold it to the Eſtcourt family 9 Eliz.

Sir Thomas Eſtcourt was lord of it in 1608, from whom it deſcended in a direct line to Walter Eſtcourt of Laſborough, eſq; who was ſucceeded by Thomas Eſtcourt of Shipton-Moigne, eſq. He dying unmarried, was alſo ſucceeded by his brother Edmond, of Burton-Hill, near Malmeſbury, in the county of Wilts, eſq; who dying without iſſue male, bequeathed his large eſtate to Thomas Eſtcourt, eſq; (ſon of the late Mr. Eſtcourt of Cam) the preſent lord of this manor. His arms are, *Ermine, on a chief indented gules three eſtoiles Or.*

But the deſcent of the manor ſeems to have been interrupted in the turbulent reigns of Henry the Sixth and Edward the Fourth; for the records ſhew that Richard de Beauchamp, earl of Warwick, who had married Elizabeth, heireſs of the Berkeley family, held the manor 17 H. 6. Sir Maurice Berkeley of Beverſtone, died ſeized of Durſley and Woodmancot 38 H. 6. And Margaret counteſs of Shrewſbury, daughter of the above Richard de Beauchamp, died ſeized of this manor 7 E. 4.

Richard Forſter, and John Moor and his wife, levied a fine of lands in Durſley to the uſe of John Walch 1 & 6 H. 7. George Dennis, late of Tetbury, and Agnes his wife, levied a fine of lands in Durſley and Woodmancot to William Auſtin jun. and others 17 H. 7.

TITHING. Woodmancot is a hamlet and tithing in this pariſh, eaſtward of, and adjoining to, the borough. The village lies under the ſide of a hill covered with wood, which gave name to the tithing. A tithing in the pariſh of North Nibley lies within the manor of Woodmancot.

Robert de Swineborn held the manor of Woodmancot near Durſley 19 E. 2. Sir John Berkeley was ſeized of the manor of Woodmancot, with the hamlets of Nibley, 6 H. 6. Sir Maurice Berkeley of Beverſtone died ſeized of it 38 H. 6. as did Maurice his ſon 14 E. 4. William Berkeley, ſon of the laſt Maurice, taking up arms againſt Richard the Third, was attainted, and his lands ſeized, and the manor of Woodmancot was granted to ſir Thomas Brugge, and his heirs male 1 R. 3. But king Henry the Seventh reſtored him to his eſtate. Sir Edward Berkeley, ſon of William, married Alice, daughter and heir of Robert Poyntz, who ſurviving him, held Woodmancot in jointure, and died ſeized thereof 1 H. 8. She was ſucceeded by her grandſon John Berkeley, whoſe father Thomas died before the ſaid Alice. Sir William Berkeley ſucceeded to John, and died ſeized of Woodmancot 5 E. 6. and his ſon John had livery thereof the following year. The manor came afterwards to Mr. John Arundel, but Mr. Phelps of Durſley is the preſent lord of the manor. His arms are, *Argent, a lion rampant ſable between ſix croſſes croſſlets fitchy gules.*

Tilſdown is a place in this pariſh.

Of the Church, &c.

The church is a rectory, in the deanery of Durſley, worth 80*l.* a year. John Carpenter, biſhop of Worceſter, appropriated the rectory of Durſley to the archdeaconry of Glouceſter, in the year 1475; which rectory belonged to St. Peter's abbey, and was given in exchange for the archdeacon's houſe in Glouceſter, and has continued annexed to the archdeaconry ever ſince.

The church, which is dedicated to the holy Trinity, is large, with an aile on each ſide of the nave, and a handſome tower at the weſt end, with ſix bells and a ſet of chimes. The altar-piece is neatly wainſcotted, and railed in.

There was a chantry in the north aile, dedicated to the virgin Mary, whereof Richard Breic was the laſt incumbent, and retired with a penſion of 5*l.* a year. There was another chantry in the ſouth aile, dedicated to St. James, founded by one Tanner. And againſt the ſouth wall, under a canopy ſupported by pillars, is the effigy in ſtone of a naked perſon, lying along, ſuppoſed to be deſigned for Mr. Tanner, who probably built that aile.

Firſt fruits £.10	14	4½	Synodals £.0	2	0
Tenths — 1	1	5¼	Pentecoſtals 0	1	0
Procurations 0	6	8			

Monuments and Inſcriptions.

In the chancel on a marble table:

H. S. E. Thomas Purnell de Kingſhill armiger, Vir ingenio admodum humanus, moribus gravis, vitæ integerrimus. Qui cum Patriæ diu inſervìſſet, amicis pariter ac familiaribus carus. Annis tandem et honore gravis, animam Deo reddidit die Octob. 29° A. D. 1729° Ætatis ſuæ 72°.

Non procul ab hoc Marmore jacet Filius natu minimus Nathaniel optimæ ſpei adoleſcentulus. Obijt 10 Octob. 1718 Anno Ætatis 17°.

Et Anna uxor Thomæ Purnell Armigeri, quæ hanc vitam deceſſit viceſimo die Feb. 1745. Ætatis ſuæ octogeſimo anno.

Et Gulielmus Purnell Generoſus, filius prædicti Thomæ ſecundus. Qui poſtquam inter Rutenos honeſto mercatoris officio intentus, Patriæ ſuæ diu inſerviſſet, commodo peregre reverſus, in placido apud Tilſdown receſſu, vitam conſummavit 24° die Octob. A. D. 1751, Æ. 57.———Arms, Baron and femme, 1. *Argent, on a feſs ſable between three lozenges gules as many cinquefoils of the field,* 2. *Sable, on a bend argent three roſes gules. In chief a fleur.de-lis of the ſecond.*

There are ſeveral other monuments, obſervable only for the family arms, *viz.*

For Samuel Clarke, mercer, and ſeveral of his family.——— Arms, *Argent, on a bend gules between two torteauxes three ſwans of the field.*

For William Plomer of Briſtol.———*A chevron between three lions heads erazed Or.*

For John Phelps, and for his ſon John De-la-Field Phelps, who was in the commiſſion of the peace, and ſerved the office of high ſheriff of this county in 1761.——*Argent, a lion rampant ſable, between ſix croſſes croſlets fitchy gules.*

For Henry Ady, and his family.——Baron and femme, 1. *Or on a bend ſable, three leopards heads caboſhed of the field.* 2. *Gules, a feſs between three creſcents Or.*

For William Tippets.———*Or, on a chevron between three dolphins ſable as many croſſes patee of the firſt.*

For Charles Wallington, vicar of Frampton.——*Barry undy of ſix argent and ſable, on a chief gules a ſaltire Or.* Impaling Purnel as before.

Benefactions.

The church-houſe, and a piece of land called the Torch-acre, and two tenements at the Broadwell, (the latter given by Mr. Hugh Smith) are for repairing the church. Mr. Spilman gave a rent charge of 4*l.* a year for ever, on an eſtate at Standiſh, for the poor. And ſir Thomas Eſtcourt, in in 1642, gave the profits of a moiety of tenements at Tetbury, now ſettled at 10*l.* a year, to the poor. Mr. Henry Stubs gave 10*s.* a year in books. Mr. Throgmorton Trotman, by his will in 1663, gave 15*l.* a year to be paid by the company of Haberdaſhers in London, for a weekly lecture on Thurſdays.—In 1703, John Arundel of Durſley gave the rent of an acre of land in Cam, for buying books, and teaching poor children to read. And Mrs. Anne Purnell, in 1759, gave 100*l.* to be laid out in land, out of the profits of which 10*s.* a year to the officiating miniſter for a ſermon on Good-friday; the remainder for buying books, and teaching children to read; ſhe alſo gave 60*l.* to buy land, 10*s.* of the profits of which for another ſermon on New-year's-day; the remainder to be given to forty poor widows.—About the year 1736, Joſeph Twemblo, a diſſenting miniſter, gave a houſe in Durſley, fitted up like a meeting-houſe, to be employ'd as a ſchool-houſe, and for the diſſenting miniſter of Cam to repeat his ſermons in occaſionally; and Joſiah Sheppard of London gave 100*l.* with which a piece of land called Withybears, in Berkeley, was purchaſed, to endow this ſchool. And Mary Twemblo, and others, gave afterwards 260*l.* with which lands in Hamfallow, in the pariſh of Berkeley, were purchaſed. Out of the rents of theſe lands the maſter to have 12*l.* a year, and 20*s.* a year for coals; for which he is to teach forty boys to read and write, and to ſay the ſhorter Aſſembly's catechiſm. The remainder of the rents to keep the houſe in repair, and buy books.

Taxes.						
	The Royal Aid in	1692,	£. 95	14	0
	Poll-tax — —	1694,	— 50	1	0
	Land-tax ——	1694,	— 124	9	3
	The ſame, at 3*s.*	1770,	— 87	15	0

At the beginning of this century, there were 600 houſes and about 2500 inhabitants in this pariſh, whereof 40 were freeholders; yearly births 42, burials 38. *Atkyns.* But ſir Robert's eſtimate was too high, for notwithſtanding there is reaſon to believe the inhabitants are not decreaſed ſince that time; they are now only about 2000.

DURHAM *or* DYRHAM.

THIS pariſh lies in the hundred of Grumbald's-aſh, four miles weſt from Marſhfield, five ſouth from Chipping-Sodbury, eight northward from Bath, and thirty-one ſouthward from Glouceſter.

The village is ſecured from the cold eaſterly winds by an hill, and the high lands about Littleton and Cold Aſton, which bound the pariſh on that ſide. It is plentifully ſupply'd with water from ſprings which riſe at the foot of the hill, and forming a brook, empty themſelves into the Boyd. It is conjectured that from theſe ſprings the pariſh obtained the name of Durham, i. e. *Dwr*, Britiſh, *water*, and *ham*, *a village*; yet I am not ignorant that in ſome of the chronicles it occurs by the name of *Deorham*.

It is remarkable in antiquity for a bloody battle which was fought here between the Britons and Saxons, about the year 577. The latter, under Cuthwin and Ceaulin, vanquiſhed the Britons, and ſlew three of their princes, Commeaile, Condidan, and Fariemeiol; in conſequence whereof, the cities of Cirenceſter, Glouceſter, and Bath, with the country round them, ſurrendered to the conquerors. And upon Henton-hill is a large camp of a ſingle intrenchment, but imperfect on the ſouth-weſt ſide, incloſing near twenty acres of ground, which the Saxons are ſuppoſed to have occupied.

This village is diſtinguiſhed by the fine ſeat of William Blathwayt, eſq; built by his grandfather after a deſign of the ingenious Mr. Talmen, in 1698. There is a plan of this houſe, and an elevation, in Campbell's *Vitruvius Britannicus*. The principal ſtory is large and convenient, with a variety of very good apartments. The garden front extends one hundred and thirty feet. The firſt ſtory is intirely ruſticated, and the coins to the cornice. In the ſecond ſtory, the windows are dreſt with alternate pediments, over which are attic windows; and the front finiſhes with a handſome cornice and baluſtrade, adorned with trophies and vaſes of an excellent choice.

There is a park adjoining to the gardens; but the curious water-works, which were made at a great expence, are much neglected and going to decay. From this ſeat there are very agreeable proſpects weſtward, over the foreſt of Kingſwood, and the city of Briſtol.

Of the Manor and other Eſtates.

'William the ſon of Widon holds Dirham in 'Grimboldeſtou hundred of the king. Aluric 'held it in the time of king Edward. There are 'ſeven hides taxed. In demean is one plow-'tillage, and thirteen villeins, and thirteen bordars 'with two plow-tillages. There are eight *ſervi* 'and *ancillæ*, and three mills of 15*s.* rent, and ſix 'acres of meadow. It was worth 12*l.* now '[only] 8*l.*

'The ſame William held three hides of this manor, 'with which Durand the ſheriff had endowed 'St. Mary of Perſhore, by the king's order; which '[hides] earl William had given to Turſtin the ſon 'of Rolf with this manor.' *Domeſday-book*, p. 74.

This manor was ſoon after transferred to the barons of Newmarch, who were deſcended from Bernerd de Newmarch, (*de Novo Mercatu*,) who came in with the Conqueror. Henry de Newmarch, ſon of William, was ſeized hereof and left it to James his brother, who died 17 Joh. leaving Iſabel and Hawiſe his coheireſſes.

John Ruſſel of Berkſhire purchaſed the wardſhip of thoſe daughters, and married Iſabel the eldeſt

eldeſt of them to his ſon Ralph Ruſſel, who, in right of his wife, was ſeized of Durham. Ralph Ruſſel, by deed, gave this manor in marriage with his daughter Maud, to Robert Walerand, who was governor of St. Briavel's-caſtle, and warden of the foreſt of Dean, and four times high ſheriff of this county in the reign of H. 3. He died 1 E. 1. and ſhe ſoon after, both without iſſue; whereby this manor went to William Ruſſel, her elder brother, who by his wife Jane, daughter of Robert Peverell, had iſſue Theobald Ruſſel, anceſtor by his ſecond wife to the preſent duke of Bedford. By his firſt wife, daughter and coheir of Ralph de Gorges, a baron in parliament *temp.* E. 3. he had three ſons, of whom Theobald the youngeſt aſſumed the name and arms of Gorges, viz. *Lozengy Or and Gules*, and is anceſtor of the Gorges of Wraxall. The above William Ruſſel was ſucceeded by his ſon William, who died ſeized of Dyrham 4 E. 2. Ralph Ruſſel was ſeized of this manor 30 E. 3. and ſir Maurice Ruſſel died ſeized of it 2 H. 4. Sir Maurice left two daughters Margaret and Iſabel, the firſt married to ſir Gilbert Dennys, knight; who, with ſir John Drayton and Iſabel his wife, the other daughter of ſir Maurice, (married before to ſir John St. Loe) were jointly ſeized of the manor of Dyrham 3 H 5. But ſir Maurice by a ſecond wife, had a ſon Thomas, whoſe only child was named Margery, and died without iſſue; this Thomas and Margery were ſeized of one yard-land called Barn-place, and of one meſſuage and one yard-land called Saleſbury's, in Dyrham, 10 H. 6. But the manor and other lands never came into the poſſeſſion of Thomas, having been ſettled in truſt by ſir Maurice, to pay the portions of his daughters.

Sir John Drayton ſold his moiety to ſir Gilbert Dennys, who died ſeized of the intire manor 10 H. 5. Maurice Dennys was ſon of ſir Gilbert; ſir Walter Dennys ſon of Maurice, and ſir William Dennys[c] ſon of ſir Walter. Sir Walter Dennys, ſon and heir of ſir William, was the next and laſt poſſeſſor of Dyrham of that family; for he, joining with his eldeſt ſon Richard, ſold the manor in the thirteenth year of queen Elizabeth, to George Wynter, eſq; brother to ſir William Wynter, of Lydney in the foreſt of Dean.

[c] This ſir William Dennys, and his lady Anne, daughter of Maurice lord Berkeley, with ſome others, founded a Gild in the church of Durham, in the year 1520. The method of its foundation, and the ſtatutes, are ſtill preſerv'd, and are here inſerted, to ſhew the nature of Gilds in general.

Memorandum, In the year of our Lord 1520, October the firſt, in the twelfth year of king Henry the Eighth, ſir William Dennys, knight, dame Anne his wife, Robert Llen, parſon of the church of Durham, Thomas Llen and William Were, who were ſervants to the ſaid ſir William and dame Anne, founded firſt a prieſt to ſing maſs dayly within the pariſh church of Dyrham, within the chapel of St. Dennys, to pray for the founders of the ſaid maſs, and for all them that will become brothers and ſiſters, or any thing helping for the maintenance of the ſaid fraternity or gild.

Item, The ſaid prieſt ſhall, ere he begin his maſs, pray in general for the good ſtate of the founders, and brothers and ſiſters, and for all benefactors to the ſaid gild.

Item, The prieſt, at his coming to the ſavetory, ſhall ſay for the ſouls of the ſaid founders, brethren and ſiſters, which be dead, *De Profundis*.

Item, The proctor of the ſaid gild, for the time being, ſhall cauſe 4 ſolemn dirges and maſſes, according to note, to be ſung at 4 times within the year; which times ſhall appear, following theſe words, *Let us pray*.

Item, The dirge and maſs to be kept upon St. Dennys eve, and the maſs upon the day, which ſhall be the ninth day of October.

Item, The ſecond dirge and maſs to be kept the eighth and ninth days of January.

Item, The third dirge and maſs to be kept the twenty-ninth and thirtieth days of March.

Item, The fourth dirge and maſs to be kept the twenty-ſeventh and twenty-eighth days of June.

Item, The ſaid prieſt, before he goeth to the quarter maſs, ſhall pray for the ſtate of the founders, brothers and ſiſters, and for the ſouls of them that be dead, generally or eſpecially, as he hath time.

Item, The proctor of the ſaid gild, ſhall cauſe at every quarter of the year, to be at the ſolemn maſs, the parſon of the church, or his prieſt in his abſence, with 4 other honeſt prieſts, to help to ſing the dirge, and to ſing maſs on the morrow.

Item, The proctor of the ſaid gild, ſhall, of the ſtock of the ſaid gild, pay every prieſt for his coming, and for his devout doing 6*d.* and to the ringers 4*d.*

Item, Such perſons as ſhall be named and choſen to be proctors of the ſaid gild, ſhall be every year named and choſen the firſt day of February.

Item, The ſaid proctors ſhall make the account every year upon the firſt day of February.

Item, The ſaid proctors ſhall make their account upon the ſaid day, within the church of Dyrham, within the Trinity chapel, and to lay down the money of their collection upon the altar there.

Item, The account ſhall be made before the lord of the lordſhip, or the lord's bayliff in his abſence; the parſon of the church, or his prieſt in his abſence, and 2 of the elder brethren within the pariſh, and all the brethren within the ſaid pariſh, if they will be at it.

Item, At the account, the old proctors, before they be diſcharged, ſhall name to the ſaid lord, or to his bayliff, the parſon or his prieſt, ſuch as ſhall take the account, 6 perſons; of which 6, the ſaid lord or his bayliff, the parſon or his prieſt, that taketh the accounts, ſhall name two to be collectors; and there openly the ſaid lord or bayliff, parſon or prieſt which taketh the account, ſhall deliver the ſaid money to the new proctors.

Memorandum, That William Were hath given to St. Dennys chapel, a challice of ſilver.

Memorandum, That where ſir William Dennys, and dame Anne his wife, and Robert Llen parſon of the church of Dyrham, Thomas Llen and William Were, having conſtituted and ordained a prieſt to ſing dayly in St. Dennys's chapel, within the church of Dyrham, for the maintenance of the ſaid prieſt, ſir William Dennys hath promiſed to give to the proctors and their ſucceſſors of the gild of St. Dennys, for the aforeſaid maintenance of the ſaid prieſt, 16 kine.

Item, The ſaid dame Anne, by the licence of the ſaid ſir William her huſband, hath promiſed to give 8 kine.

Item, Robert Llen, parſon of the aforeſaid church, hath promiſed to give 100 ſheep.

Item, Thomas Llen, 50 ſheep.

Item, William Were, in oxen and kine, 16.

Item, There is let to John Ford of Pucclechurch, 8 kine of St. Nicholas Stock, paying by the year for every cow 22*d.*

Item, In like manner let to Humphry Llen of St. Nicholas Stock, 4 kine.

Item, To John Ward of St. Nicholas Stock, 4 kine.

Item, The proctors of St. Dennys gild ſhall pay quarterly to the prieſt that ſingeth in the ſaid chapel, for his ſalary, 33*s.* 4*d.*

Item, The proctors ſhall receive the money for the payment of the ſaid prieſt as followeth :

	s.	*d.*
Of ſir William Dennys quarterly, 'till the ſaid 16 kine be delivered to the proctors of the ſaid gild, for the time being,	6	8
Of dame Anne Dennys, — —	3	4
Of Mr. Robert Llen, parſon of the ſaid church,	6	8
Of Thomas Llen, — —	3	4
Of William Were, —	6	8
Of John Ford, — —	3	4
Of Humphry Llen, —	1	8
Of John Ward, — —	1	8
	33	4

Memorandum, The ſaid prieſt ſhall find himſelf, for to ſing at the ſaid altar, bread, wine and wax.

Many were the brethren and ſiſters of this gild, who were prevailed upon to contribute towards its maintenance, which perſons lived in 50 ſeveral pariſhes at leaſt, in Briſtol, Bath, Somerſetſhire, and Glouceſterſhire, and might amount in number to 300 perſons. The uſual pay from each perſon was 10 or 20*d.* quarterly.

John Wynter, ſon of George, had livery of the manor 23 Eliz. He accompanied ſir Francis Drake in his famous voyage round the world, as his vice-admiral, and married the daughter of ſir William Bruen of Dorſetſhire. Sir George Wynter, ſon and heir of John, married Mary, daughter of Edward Rogers, of Cannington in Somerſetſhire, eſq; and dying in 1638, left John Wynter his ſon and heir then ſixteen years old. He married Frances, daughter and coheireſs of Thomas Gerard of Trent, in the county of Somerſet, eſq; deſcended from the Gerards of Lancaſhire. He died ſeized of Dyrham in 1668, leaving an only ſurviving daughter Mary, married to William Blathwayte, eſq; whoſe family came out of Cumberland. This gentleman's knowledge in modern languages, and his early and ſteady application to buſineſs, advanced him to ſeveral public and profitable employments. He was ſecretary at war, and ſecretary of ſtate to king William during his abode in Holland and Flanders; and was one of the commiſſioners for trade and plantations, and clerk of the privy council in the reigns of king Charles, king James, king William, and queen Anne. He was lord of the manor of Dyrham at the beginning of this century, and his grandſon William Blathwayte, eſq; is the preſent lord of this manor. His arms are, *Or, two bends ingrailed ſable.*

Walter Gaſelin held three plow-tillages in Dyrham 7 E. 3.

HAMLET. *Hinton* is a hamlet in this pariſh, about a mile from the church. The name ſignifies the *old town*, from *Hen*, Britiſh, *old.* The manor antiently belonged to the family of De la Rivere, ſometimes written *de Ripariis.* Sir John Tracy and others were ſeized of it in truſt for Richard de la Rivere 37 E. 3. and Thomas de la Rivere, ſon of Richard, was ſeized of it 48 E 3. The heir of De la Rivere ſold the manor to the Ruſſels, lords of Dyrham; and the ſeveral proprietors of the manor of Dyrham, have been alſo lords of the manor of Hinton ever ſince.

Sir Gilbert Dennys and ſir John Drayton, who had married the two coheireſſes of ſir Maurice Ruſſel, joined in the ſale of part of the lands of Hinton, to Nicholas Stanſhaw, who was ſeized thereof 3 H. 5. Margaret the widow of Nicholas died ſeized of thoſe lands 14 H. 6. The heir of Stanſhaw ſold them to Mr. Thomas White, who granted them to the mayor and corporation of Briſtol, for public uſes, 32 H. 8. and they are ſtill veſted in the corporation of that city, and the profits thereof are faithfully diſpoſed of to the intended uſes.

Of the Church, &c.

The church is a rectory, in the deanery of Hawkeſbury, worth about 150*l.* a year. Mr. Blathwayte is patron; Mr. Peter Grand the preſent incumbent. Eighty acres belong to the glebe.

The church is not large, but very neat. It is dedicated to St. Peter.

	£.	s.	d.		£.	s.	d.
Firſt fruits	14	12	4	Synodals	0	2	0
Tenths —	1	9	3	Pentecoſtals	0	1	6
Procurations	0	6	8				

Monuments and Inſcriptions.

There is a flat ſtone, with a large repreſentation of a man and woman, for Maurice Ruſſel, who died in 1401, and Iſabel his wife, and under it the following monkiſh verſes:

Miles privatus vita jacet hic tumulatus
Sub petra ſtratus Maurice Ruſſel vocitatus
Iſabel ſponſa fuit hujus militis iſta
Quæ jacet abſconſa ſub marmoreo modo alto
Cœli ſolamen, Trinitas, his conferat Amen.
Qui fuit eſt et erit. Concita morte perît.

At the upper end of the ſouth aile, is a very handſome freeſtone monument. The figures of a man in armour, and a woman on his right hand, large as life, lie under a canopy, ſupported by five fluted pillars, with Corinthian capitals; and four ſons and ſeven daughters are repreſented kneeling, with their hands in a ſupplicating poſture. On a table is this inſcription:

Georgio Wynter armigero (qui animam efflavit xxix° die Novembris Ano Dni 1581) Anna Wynter uxor pia, charo conjugi hoc monumentum poſuit: ſtatuens cum et ipſa, dei juſſu, vitæ hujus ſtationem peregerit, hic ivxta mariti funus ſuum quoque reponi: ut quibus vivis unus erat animus, eiſdem et mortuis unus eſſet corporum quieſcendi locus, ſub ſpe futuræ reſurrectionis.

Round the baſe of the monument, theſe verſes:

Mole ſub hac placidam capiunt en Membra Georgii
Wynteri requiem, dures perſæpe labores
Qui ſolida in Terra, qui flućti vagantibus undis,
Et pace innocua, ſimul et pugnacibus armis,
Suſtinuit Patriæ, dum publica Munia geſſit.
Anna fuit quondam hæc illi fidiſſima conjux;
Undenas Thalami ſoboles tulit iſta, viriles
Quatuor, et ſeptem generoſo ſtemmate natas.

In a ſcutcheon are, 1. *Sable, a feſs ermine, a creſcent for difference*, for Wynter. Impaling 2. *Quarterly* 1ſt *and* 4th, *Sable, on a feſs between three bugle horns argent a boitling ſtock Or, with a boitle gules*, for Brain. 2d *and* 3d not underſtood.

There is alſo the following memorial:

M. S. Gulielmi Langton A. M. hujus Eccleſiæ Paſtoris nuper vigilantiſſimi. De grege ſuo multiſq; alijs optime merentis. Qui quum ad uſus cum Pietatis tum Charitatis 800l. non minus dediſſet, poſt laudabilis vitæ (annorum ſcil. 59) ſtadium ad patriam cæleſtem evocatus. Quod mortale in eo fuit, hoc in pulvere deponendum curavit. Obijt. Aug 7, ſepultus 17, 1668.

Munde vale, valeant ſub cælo ſingula, Chriſtus
Solus juſtitiæ Sol, mihi ſola ſalus.
Non animam relevat morituri copia rerum;
Exulat hæc rerum copia; Chriſte veni.
Quos mihi parca manus, largos congeſtit acervos
Hos alijs larga mente, manuq; dedi.
Cede Lues, Medicina Quies, mors ultimus hoſtis
Vincitur; e Chriſti funere Victor eo.

Amoris & Gratitudinis ergo poſuit Johannes Meridith Armiger.

Benefactions.

Mr. William Langton, formerly rector of this pariſh, left by his will, 600*l.* to be laid out in lands, the income of which to be employed in teaching children to read, and putting them out apprentices. Dyrham to have two thirds of this charity, and Deinton the other. And Mr. Peter Grand, the preſent rector, deſirous of promoting this laudable deſign, built a ſchool-houſe in Dyrham, at his own expence, about the year 1770.

			£.	s.	d.
Taxes.	The Royal Aid in	1692,	191	12	0
	Poll-tax ——	1694,	27	3	0
	Land-tax ——	1694,	195	10	8
	The ſame, at 3*s.*	1770,	154	3	1½

At the beginning of this century, there were 60 houses in this parish, and about 270 inhabitants, whereof 6 were freeholders; yearly births 7, burials 6. *Atkyns*. But in ten years, beginning with 1700, there are registered 88 baptisms, and 52 burials; and in a like series, beginning with 1759, there are registered 109 baptisms, and 74 burials, and the present number of houses is 70, of inhabitants 350; by which it appears that 1 in 47.3 dies every year.

EASINGTON *or* EASTINGTON.

THIS parish lies in the vale, in the hundred of Whitston, six miles westward from Stroud, six north from Dursley, and ten south from Gloucester.

It consists mostly of pasture, as the soil is rich, but in some parts it is much inclined to clay. The river Froom runs through it, and divides the tithing of Eastington from that of Alkerton.

In the latter tithing, there is a spring of water of a cathartic property, which, upon examination, is found to contain a large portion of salts, like those extracted from the Epsom water, some calcareous earth, and a little sea salt.

The name of Eastington, or any thing like it, is not to be found in *Domesday-book*. It is probable, therefore, that Eastington was a member of Frampton, when the survey for that record was made; but in process of time, acquiring parochial rights, it became a distinct and independent parish. Upon this ground the etymology is easy, for the village was very properly called *Eastington*, i.e. *the east town upon the water*, because it lay on the east of the parish of Frampton, upon the river. And accordingly we find, that the names of *Norton*, *Weston*, *Siddington*, *Sutton*, have been given to many places for similar reasons.

At Framiload, which is a hamlet lying part in this parish and part in Morton Valence, there is a passage over the Severn, leading from this country to the upper part of the forest of Dean, and so on to Herefordshire. The passage-house lies on the south-east side of the river, which at this place is near a mile over at high water. Here the navigable canal from Stroud is intended to fall into the Severn, if the bill for making it, now depending in parliament, should pass into a law.

The clothing business extends itself in the line from Stroud to this parish, which enjoys some share of it, chiefly in the fine way; but the parish produces nothing curious or uncommon in the fossil and vegetable kingdoms.

The handsome manor-house near the church is going to ruin, and has for many years been occupied only as a farm-house.

Of the Manors and other Estates.

Winebald de Balun, son of Drogo de Balun, together with his brothers Hameline and Wyonoc, came into England with William the First. Winebald had obtained the manor of Easington 2 W. 2. He gave a mill in Framelode to the abbey of Gloucester, in the year 1126, and was at that time stiled one of the great barons of the realm. Roger succeeds his father Winebald, and was succeeded by Hameline de Balun, one of the same family; whose son John de Balun levied a fine of this manor 11 H. 3. Sir John de Balon, or Balun, son of John, was the next possessor. He joined with Simon Montfort and other barons against the king, and, in conjunction with sir John Giffard of Brimpsfield, took Gloucester-castle by stratagem in 1264, as already related, p. 107; but he afterwards obtained the king's pardon, and the manor descended next to Isolda de Balun, married first to her kinsman Walter de Balun, by whom she had no issue; secondly, to Hugh de Audley the elder, who purchased a charter of free warren in Easington 12 E. 2. She survived her second husband, and died seized of this manor 11 E. 3. Hugh de Audley, their son, succeeded to this estate, and married Margaret, second sister and one of the coheiresses of Gilbert de Clare, earl of Gloucester, and widow of Piers de Gaveston, the favourite of king Edward the Second. This Hugh de Audely died 21 E. 3. leaving Margaret his only daughter and heiress, married to Ralph lord Stafford, who died 46 E. 3.

Hugh earl of Stafford, their son and heir, died at Rhodes, in his return from a pilgrimage to Jerusalem, seized of Easington 9 R. 2. as appears by an inquisition taken the following year. He settled the manors of Easington, Haresfield, and a moiety of the manor of Alkerton, on Hugh Stafford his younger son, who married Elizabeth, daughter and heir of Bartholomew lord Bourcher, and was summoned to parliament as lord Bourcher 12 H. 4. He died without issue 9 H. 5. whereby the manor of Easington came to his nephew Humphry earl of Stafford, who was son of Edmond, elder brother to the lord Bourcher. He was created duke of Buckingham in the succeeding reign, and died seized of this estate 38 H. 6. He was succeeded by his grandson Henry duke of Buckingham, son of Humphry earl of Stafford, who had been slain at the battle of St. Albans, four years before his father's death. This Henry took up arms against king Richard the Third, and was beheaded at Salisbury; but Edward his son and heir was restored to his father's honours and estates, by king Henry the Seventh. He began the magnificent castle at Thornbury, which he did not live to finish, being attainted and beheaded 13 H. 8. and the same year the manor of Easington was granted to Thomas Heneage and Catherine his wife for life. Henry, son and heir of Edward, had this manor restored to him 23 H. 8. and his son Edward lord Stafford sold it to Edward Stephens 15 Eliz.

The family of Stephens are of antient standing in this county. Ralph son of Stephen, and William

William his brother, were joint high fheriffs of Gloucefterfhire four years, beginning 18 H. 2. and William Stephens was high fheriff 22 H. 2. and fo continued thirteen years together.

Henry Stephens of Eafington, married the daughter of —— Lug, of Herefordfhire; and Edward Stephens, his fon, the purchafer of this manor, married Joan, daughter of Edward Fowler of Stonehoufe. He died in 1587, and was fucceeded by his fon Richard Stephens, efq; who married, firft, Margaret, daughter of Edward St. Loe, of Kingfton in Wiltfhire, efq; and furviving her, he married, fecondly, Anne Kerry, widow, one of the daughters and coheireffes of John Stone of London, and died 41 Eliz.

Thomas Stephens, third fon of Edward, and brother of Richard, was attorney to prince Henry and prince Charles, and by Elizabeth his wife, daughter and coheirefs of John Stone of London, had three fons; Edward, the eldeft, anceftor to the Stephens's at Sodbury; John, anceftor to the family of that name at Lypiat; and Nathaniel, the third fon, anceftor to the Stephens's, formerly of Cherington. But to proceed with the defcendants of Richard Stephens.

Nathaniel, fon of the faid Richard Stephens of Eafington, married Catherine, daughter of Robert Beall, of Prior's Marfton in Warwickfhire, efq; and dying in 1660, was fucceeded by his fon Richard, who married Anne, eldeft daughter of fir Hugh Cholmeley, of Whitby in Yorkfhire, bart. and died in 1678. Nathaniel Stephens, fon of the laft Richard, married Elizabeth, daughter of fir Francis Pemberton, who had been lord chief juftice of both benches. This Nathaniel ferved the office of high fheriff of this county in 1698, and was lord of the manor of Eafington at the beginning of the prefent century. Richard Stephens, efq; died feized thereof in the year 1775, and is fucceeded by his brother Robert Stephens, who refides at Chavenage, and is the prefent proprietor of this manor, and of the hundred of Whitfton, and holds courts for both. His arms are, *Party per chevron, azure and argent, in chief two eagles with wings elevated Or.*

Winebald de Balun gave a mill in Framelode to the abbey of Gloucefter in 1126. Walter the prior of Lanthony purchafed a mill at Hamelaw, now Framelode, of Arnold the miller 8 Joh. Simon de Framilode was feized of lands in this place *temp.* H. 3. The abbey of Winchcombe granted a fifhery in the Severn, near Framilode, to the abbey of Gloucefter, in exchange for 4*l.* yearly rent out of the manor of Northleach 14 E. 2. and the abbey of Gloucefter was feized thereof 17 E. 3. and of two water-mills in Framilode 6 H. 8.

A meffuage and the ferry at Framilode's paffage, late the duke of Buckingham's, were granted to Ambrofe Shelton 22 H. 8. A mill and lands in Eafington, late the duke of Buckingham's, were granted to fir Thomas Seimour 1 E. 6. upon whofe attainder they were granted to John earl of Warwick, afterwards duke of Northumberland, 3 E. 6. He being likewife attainted and beheaded, the mill and lands, then in the tenure of Walter Clutterbuck, were granted to William Britton 2 Mariæ.

HAMLET. *Alkerton* is a hamlet and tithing in this parifh, taken notice of in the beginning of this account for its medicinal water. The manor is thus defcribed in *Domefday-book.*

'Edric the fon of Chetel holds Alcrintone in 'Blacheleu hundred. His father held it in the 'time of king Edward. There are four hides and 'a half taxed. In demean is one plow-tillage, 'and fix villeins, and four bordars with eight 'plow-tillages. There are three *fervi*, and a mill 'of 10*s.* and ten acres of meadow; a wood one 'mile long, and half a mile broad. It is worth 'and was worth 3*l.*' *Domefday-book*, p. 80.

William Walton was feized of this manor, with affize of bread and ale, 31 E. 1. and 5 E. 2. The manor afterwards came to the Staffords, and defcended like Eafington down to Mr. Robert Stephens, the prefent lord thereof.

But there were two manors in this tithing, as appears by the efcheator's inquifition, 41 Eliz. where it is faid that Richard Stephens died feized of Eftington and Alkerton, late the duke of Buckingham's, held *in capite*; and of the manor of Alkerton, alias Amycourt, part of the poffeffions of Robert Bradftone, efq; held by free foccage of the honour of Hereford, paying 6*s.* 8*d.* a year.

There are particular places in this parifh of the names of *Nupend, Weftend, Millend, Churchend*, and *Naffend.*

Of the Church, &c.

The church is a rectory, in the deanery of Stonehoufe, worth 140*l.* a year. Mr. Stephens is patron and incumbent.

Winebald de Balun, in 1088, gave the tithes of Eafington to the monks of Bermondfey in Surry. The advowfon of the rectory of Eafington was granted to the Benedictine nunnery of Clerkenwell in London, and after the diffolution, was granted to fir William Herbert 4 E. 6. The rector pays 20*s.* a year to the vicar of Frocefter, in lieu of a portion of tithes in Alkerton.

Sixteen acres of arable, forty of pafture, and fome meadow, belong to the glebe.

The church is dedicated to St. Michael, and confifts of two ailes, with a low tower at the weft end. There was a chantry called the chantry of Alkerton, in this church, dedicated to Thomas Becket and St. Catherine, to which the prior of Stanley St. Leonard prefented. And there was an inhibition in 1339, that the parifhioners at Alkerton fhould not hear divine fervice in any other church than that of Eaftington.

Doctor Richard Capel, once rector of this church, was fon of Chriftopher Capel, alderman of Gloucefter, who was born at Hoo Capel in Herefordfhire. The doctor was eminent for his learning,

learning, and refufing to read the *book of fports*, on the Lord's-day, in 1633, was obliged to refign his parfonage, and practiced phyfic at Pitchcombe, near Stroud. He was chofen one of the affembly of divines, but never fat among them. He publifhed feveral religious books, and died in the year 1656.

Firft fruits £. 39	14	9	Synodals £. 0	2	0
Tenths — 3	5	$5\frac{3}{4}$	Pentecoftals 0	0	9
Procurations	6	8			

Here are feveral monuments for the family of Stephens; but as the particulars of their marriages are fully fhewn in the account of that family, it is unneceffary to infert the infcriptions at large.

Taxes.					
The Royal Aid in	1692, £.	137	6	8
Poll-tax ——	1694, —	46	8	0
Land-tax ——	1694, —	230	12	0
The fame, at 3*s.*	1770, —	175	13	6

According to fir Robert Atkyns, at the beginning of this century there were 100 houfes in this parifh, and about 450 inhabitants, whereof 11 were freeholders; yearly births 15, burials 14. But population has increafed fince that time, fo that the number of fouls is now about 767.

EASTLEACH-MARTIN

IS a fmall parifh in the hundred of Britwell's-Barrow, eight miles fouth-eaft from Northleach, three north from Leachlade, and twenty-feven eaftward from Gloucefter.

The air is healthy, and the foil well adapted to tillage; but there is good pafture-land on the fide of the river *Lech*, upon which this village is fituated, and from which it takes its name.

In *Domefday-book* there are four villages all bearing the name of *Lecce*, and denominated from the river upon which they lie. But they were afterwards diftinguifhed in the following manner. The river runs fouth-eaftward, and the firft, becaufe the moft northerly of thofe villages, was called *Northleach*, now a market town. For a fimilar reafon, the moft foutherly of them, dropping the name of the river, was called *Southrop*; and the two others, becaufe fituated more eaftward than Northleach, obtained the name of *Eaftleach*. But further to diftinguifh the two latter, the one was called *Eaftleach-Martin*, from the name of the faint to whom its church was dedicated; the other received the additional name of *Turville*, for the reafon affigned in its proper place. But this parifh is fometimes called *Buthrop*.

Of the Manor and other Eftates.

'Drogo the fon of Ponz holds Lece in Bricftu-'oldes hundred. There are ten hides taxed. 'Cola held it. In demean are four plow-tillages, 'and fifteen villeins, and four bordars, with nine 'plow-tillages. There are nine *fervi*, and a mill 'of 10*s.* and ten acres of meadow. It was worth '8*l.* now 10*l.*' *Domefday-book*, p. 77.

This manor, foon after the conqueft, belonged to the priory of Great Malvern in Worcefterfhire. But it did not long continue in that houfe, for Walter de Clifford became poffeffed of it, and gave it to the abbey of Gloucefter, in exchange for the manor of Glafebury; and the grant was confirmed by king Stephen in 1144. The abbey of Gloucefter was fezied of the manor of Eaftleach St. Martin 17 E. 3. and continued in poffeffion of it 'till the diffolution, when it was granted to the dean and chapter of Gloucefter, who are the prefent lords of the manor.

Mr. Slade Nafh is leffee under the dean and chapter, by purchafe from the truftees of the late Viner Small, efq; deceafed, and pays 1*l.* 6*s.* 8*d.* a year to the crown.

HAMLETS. 1. *Fifield.* 2. *Coat*, which from its name feems to have been woodland.

Of the Church, &c.

The church is a rectory, in the deanery of Fairford, worth about 160*l.* a year; the lord chancellor is patron; Mr. James Parfons is the prefent incumbent.

The church is fmall, dedicated to St. Martin, and has a fmall aile on the north fide, and a tower at the weft end, in which are three bells.

The parfonage-houfe was built by Dr. Smith, canon of Chrift-church, and rector of this church.

Rowland Searchfield S. T. B. fellow of St. John's college, Cambridge, was rector of this church, and afterwards bifhop of Briftol. He died in 1622, and lies buried in Briftol cathedral.

Firft fruits £. 10	0	0	Synodals £. 0	2	0
Tenths — 1	0	0	Pentecoftals 0	0	6
Procurations 0	6	8			

Benefaction.

Dr. Smith gave 50*l.* to the poor, the intereft of which to be diftributed by the rector to five poor houfekeepers.

Taxes.					
The Royal Aid in	1692, £.	65	12	2
Poll-tax ——	1694, —	7	5	0
Land-tax ——	1694, —	60	0	0
The fame, at 3*s.*	1770, —	45	0	0

When fir Robert Atkyns compiled his account of this parifh, there were 30 houfes, and 120 inhabitants, whereof five were freeholders; yearly births 3, burials 2. But fince that time, the inhabitants are increafed to the number of 313.

EASTLEACH-TURVILLE.

THIS parifh lies in the hundred of Britwell's-Barrow, in the Cotefwold country, feven miles fouth-eaftward from Northleach, four north from Leachlade, and twenty-eight eaft from Gloucefter.

It

It is ſituated upon the river *Lech*, which divides it from Eaſtleach-Martin. This part of the country lying high and open, enjoys a healthy air. The ſoil is rather ſtony, but ſweet, and well adapted to tillage; and a great part of the pariſh, conſiſting formerly of ſheep-lays and common fields, has been lately incloſed by act of parliament.

There is a well of water in Church-lane of a cathartic property; and the common well water will turn meat, when waſhed in it, as red as if it had been cured with ſalt-petre.

The Roman road called the *Ikenild-way* enters this pariſh from Oxfordſhire. It is hereabout pretty perfect, and paſſing weſtward through Coln St. Alwin's and Amney, joins the *Foſs* at Cirenceſter.

The etymology of *Eaſtleach* is given under Eaſtleach-Martin. Sir Robert Atkyns ſpeaking of this pariſh, ſays, *The name is taken from its ſtanding on the eaſt ſide of the river Lech, and from the tower of the church.* But he was totally miſtaken as to the firſt particular; for the pariſh lies on the *weſt*, not on the *eaſt* ſide of that river. The addition of *Turville* was probably taken from a family of the name of *Turberville*, or *Turville*, who reſided and had poſſeſſions in this county about the time of king Henry the Third, and king Edward the Firſt[d]. It was intended to diſtinguiſh this place from the other *Eaſtleach*, as *Acton-Turville* was ſo called to diſtinguiſh it from two other neighbouring places of the name of *Acton*. But it muſt be acknowledged that I ſpeak from conjecture, as by the defect in the records concerning this manor, about the time above mentioned, we are deprived of poſitive evidence.

Of the Manor and other Eſtates.

'The ſame Roger [de Laci] holds Lecce in 'Brictwoldeſberg hundred, and William holds it 'of him. There are five hides. Alduin held it 'in the time of king Edward. In demean are two 'plow-tillages, and twelve villeins, and one bordar, 'with five plow-tillages. There are five *ſervi*, 'and eight acres of meadow. It is worth and was 'worth 6*l*.' *Domeſday-book*, p. 75.

A *Quo warranto* was brought againſt Gilbert de Clare earl of Glouceſter, to ſet forth by what right he held courts leet in this pariſh, and his claim was allowed 15 E. 1. The manor was held by one knight's fee of Gilbert de Clare, the laſt earl of Glouceſter of that name, who was ſlain at the battle of Bannockſbourne in Scotland, in 1314. It was likewiſe held of Hugh de Audley and Margaret his wife, ſiſter and one of the coheireſſes of the laſt Gilbert de Clare, 21 E. 3. and of the earls of Stafford, deſcended from Hugh de Audley, by one knight's fee, 10, 16, & 22 R. 2. and 4 H. 4.

Sir Edmond Tame died ſeized of this manor 26 H. 8. as did Edmond Tame his ſon, without iſſue, 36 H. 8. He left three ſiſters his coheireſſes; Margaret, married to Humphry Stafford; Alice, married to ſir Thomas Verney; and Iſabel, the wife of Lewis Watkin, who all had livery 37 H. 8. Sir Thomas Verney was ſucceeded by Richard Verney his ſon, whoſe ſon George Verney died ſeized of Eaſtleach-Turville 16 Eliz.

The meſne lords of this manor were as follow. Theobald de Verdune died ſeized of Eaſtleach-Turville 10 E. 3. as did Richard de Wideſlade 29 E. 3. and Mary the widow of William Herney 7 H. 4. Edward Leverſegge died ſeized of this manor, and Elizabeth his widow died ſeized of 140 acres in Eaſtleach 1 H. 6. Robert Leverſegge died ſeized of the manor 4 E. 4. and was ſucceeded by his ſon William Leverſegge, whoſe ſon Robert Leverſegge died ſeized of the manor of Eaſtleach-Turville 6 E. 6. and livery was granted to his ſon William Leverſegge the following year.

William Blomer was lord of this manor in the year 1608; but ſir John Webb, baronet, is the preſent proprietor. For his arms, ſee *Hatherop*.

There were other lands, reputed to be a manor, which belonged to the Ciſtercian abbey of Bruern in Oxfordſhire, founded by Nicholas Baſſet in 1147. Lands in Eaſtleach, late belonging to the abbey of Bruern, were granted to John Dodington and John Jackſon 2 Eliz. This eſtate was afterwards purchaſed by Richard Keeble, (deſcended from ſir Henry Keeble, lord mayor of London in 1510) in whoſe family it continued down to Richard Keeble, the proprietor of it at the beginning of this century, and the ſixth in lineal deſcent of the ſame chriſtian name. It is now annexed to the principal manor by purchaſe, and is the property of ſir John Webb.

Thomas Oddington levied a fine of lands in Eaſtleach-Turville 14 H. 7. and John Wright and his wife levied a like fine the ſame year. Sir Walter Dennis and Agnes his wife levied a fine of lands in Eaſtleach 15 H. 7.

Of the Church, &c.

The church is a curacy in the deanery of Fairford. The dean and chapter of Glouceſter are patrons and impropriators, Mr. Price is the preſent incumbent, who has been preſented to the living of Coln Rogers, ſince the account of that pariſh was printed off.

In the year 1500, the impropriation belonged to the priory of Derhurſt, and afterwards to the abbey of Glouceſter. It is now the property of the dean and chapter of Glouceſter, and pays 30*l.* a year to the curate, in conſequence of the biſhop's injunction.

Eighty-two acres belong to the glebe.

The church, dedicated to St. Andrew, is very ſmall, with an aile on the north ſide, and a low tower at the weſt end, in which are two bells. This church and that of Eaſtleach-Martin lie at but little more than a hundred yards diſtance from each other, the former on the weſt, the latter on the eaſt bank of the little river Lech, which ſeparates the pariſhes.

[d] See p. 216.

Proc. 10*s.* Syn. 2*s.* Pentecoft. 1*s.*

Benefaction.

Mr. Thomas Hows has given 20*s.* a year to the poor.

Taxes.					
The Royal Aid in	1692, £.	58	6	4
Poll-tax — —	1694, —	10	3	0
Land-tax ——	1694, —	72	7	0
The fame, at 3*s.*	1770, —	53	17	0

When fir Robert Atkyns compiled his account, at the beginning of this century, there were, according to him, 60 houfes, and about 200 inhabitants in this parifh, whereof 10 were freeholders; yearly births 5, burials 4. Since which time the inhabitants are increafed to near 400.

EBBERTON, *or* EBBRINGTON,

LIES in the hundred of Kiftefgate, two miles diftant north-eaft from Campden, eleven fouth-weft from Evefham in Worcefterfhire, and thirty-three north-eaftward from Gloucefter.

It lies on an eafy afcent north-weftward from Blockley. The manor houfe is agreeably fituated on an eminence clofe by the church. It is large, and, tho' not a modern building, may be ranked among the handfomeft country feats of the laft age. The foil is very fertile, and the air remarkably falubrious, as appears by the ftate of population at the clofe of this account.

The name is of uncertain original. Some have fancied it to be a contraction of *Egbert's town*, as if the village had been a part of the demean lands of that king. Others have fuppofed the denomination to be taken from the dedication of the church to St. Edburg. But the name of Ebberton, or Ebbrington, is not to be found in that part of *Domefday-book* relating to Gloucefterfhire; and if the particulars of this manor are not omitted in that record, they muft be given under fome other name. Accordingly I find *Briftentune* in the old hundred of Witelai, (now comprized in that of Kiftefgate) which I apprehend was then the name of this parifh, efpecially as Cheuringaurde, now Charingworth, was held, at the time of the conqueft, by the fame proprietor.

Of the Manor and other Eftates.

'William Goizenboded holds Briftentune in 'Witelai hundred. Brifmar held it. There are 'ten hides. In demean are four plow-tillages, and 'eighteen villeins, and four bordars, with four-'teen plow-tillages. There are eight *fervi*, and 'three *ancillæ*, and two mills of 15*s.* [rent.] It 'was worth 12*l.* and is now worth 7*l.*' *D.B.* p.74.

This manor had obtained the name of Ebberton, and was held of Roger de Quincie, earl of Winchefter, 55 H. 3. Ernald de Bofco, who founded the abbey of Bittlefden in Buckinghamfhire in the year 1147, was feized of it, and his family held it for feveral generations. Another Ernald de Bofco died poffeffed of this manor 4 E. 1. and John de Boyfe, his fon, in a *Quo warranto* brought againft him, proved his right to courts leet and waifs therein 15 E. 1. About this time the manor went out of that family, for Alan de Zouch, grandfon and heir of the earl of Winchefter, died feized of Ebberton 7 E. 2. leaving three daughters coheireffes.

It afterwards paffed to the Corbets, for Roger Corbet had a grant of free warren in Ebberton and Coate 6 E. 3. Sir Robert Corbet died feized of Ebberton and Hidcote 2 H. 4. as did another fir Robert Corbet 5 H. 5.

Sir John Fortefcue, lord chancellor of England in the reign of king Henry the Sixth, purchafed the manor of Ebbrington, *alias* Ebberton; and upon his attainder, 7 E. 4. it was granted to fir John Brug, who died feized of it 11 E. 4. But it was afterwards reftored to the Fortefcue family, and Matthew lord Fortefcue, a direct defcendant from lord chancellor[e] Fortefcue, is the prefent lord of this manor, and holds a court leet here.

Cateflade is a manor appurtenant to, and dependant on, the manor of Ebberton, notwithftanding it lies within the parifh of Guiting-Power, where fome further account of it will be given.

One plow-tillage in Ebberton, with the advowfon of the church, was granted to the abbey of Bittlefden 1 R. 2.

TITHINGS and *HAMLETS.*

1. *Ebberton,* of which already.

2. *Charingworth,* of which *Domefday-book* gives the following account.

[e] Martin Fortefcue, efq; fon and heir of John Fortefcue, lord chancellor of England, (by Elizabeth his wife, daughter of fir Miles Stapleton) married Elizabeth, daughter and heir of Richard Deynfell, of Filleigh in com. Devon, efq; and had iffue two fons, John and William. John married Jaquetta, eldeft daughter of Ralph St. Leger, efq; by whom he had iffue Bartholomew, whofe fon and heir, Hugh Fortefcue, married Elizabeth, eldeft daughter of fir John Chichefter, of Raleigh in com. Devon, and had by her John Fortefcue, efq; which John married a daughter of fir John Specot, knight, by whom he had iffue Hugh Fortefcue, his fon and heir. This Hugh, by his wife, daughter of fir Samuel Rolle, had iffue colonel Robert Fortefcue, who died without iffue; and Arthur Fortefcue, efq; who married a daughter of ——— Elford, efq; and had iffue by her four fons, of whom Hugh Fortefcue, of Filleigh, efq; the eldeft, married Bridget, fole daughter and heir of Hugh Bofcawen, of Tregothnan in Cornwall, by Margaret his wife, fifth daughter, and at length coheir of Theophilus Clinton, earl of Lincoln; by whom he had iffue Hugh, Theophilus, Margaret, and Bridget. He married fecondly, Lucy, daughter of Matthew lord Aylmer, by whom he had Matthew, Charles, who died at fchool, and one daughter Lucy, married to George Lyttelton, afterwards lord Lyttelton.

The barony of Clinton being in abeyance, king George I. conferred it on the faid Hugh Fortefcue, efq; fon of Hugh and Bridget, in the year 1721; and in 1746, he was created lord Fortefcue, baron of Caftle-hill in com. Devon, and earl of Clinton; with limitation of the barony to Matthew his half brother. His lordfhip dying unmarried, the title of Clinton devolved on his fifter Margaret; and his faid brother Matthew fucceeded to the barony, and is the prefent lord Fortefcue. His lordfhip married, in 1752, Anne, fecond daughter of John Campbell, efq; one of the lords commiffioners of the treafury, and by her ladyfhip hath iffue feveral children. His lordfhip's arms are, *Azure, a bend ingrailed argent, cotifed Or.* CREST, *A plain fhield argent.* SUPPORTERS, *Two greyhounds argent, each with a ducal collar and line gules.* MOTTO, FORTE SCVTVM SALVS DVCVM.

'Radulph de Todeni holds Cheuringaurde in 'Witelai hundred, and Roger holds it of him. 'There are ten hides. Brifmar held it. In demean 'are three plow-tillages, and thirteen villeins, and 'one radchenifter with fix plow-tillages, and nine '*fervi* and *ancillæ*. It was worth 8*l.* and is now 'worth 6*l.*' *Domefday-book*, p. 75.

Edward Burnel died feized of this manor 9 E. 2. Gilbert Chaftelyne purchafed a charter of free warren in Charingworth 29 E. 3. Richard Stafford died feized of the manor 4 R. 2. as did Maud his widow 1 H. 4. and Richard Turftan 1 H. 5. The manor paffed afterwards to the Grevils, who had confiderable poffeffions in this part of the county. John Grevil died feized thereof 23 H. 6. as did another John Grevil 1 E. 6. and Edward Grevil, his fon, had livery the following year. Lewis Grevil had alfo livery of this manor 1 Eliz.

The late Mr. John Barnfley had a houfe and good eftate in this tithing.

3. *Hidcoat Bois*, alias *Cote*. 'The church of 'St. Mary of Evefham holds Hedecote in Widelei 'hundred. There are three hides. In demean 'is one plow-tillage, and two *fervi*, and the wives 'of four villeins lately deceafed have one plow-'tillage. It is worth and was worth 20*s.*' *Domefday-book*, p. 72.

The family of Keyt has refided in this parifh about four hundred years. Sir John Keyt was created a baronet in 1660, in reward of his loyalty to king Charles the Firft, for whom he raifed a troop of horfe at his own charge. There are feveral monuments and infcriptions in the church, fhewing the alliances and other particulars of this family. Sir William Keyt married the daughter of fir Francis Coventry, fon of the lord Keeper Coventry, and died in 1702. Sir William Keyt, fon of William Keyt, efq; married in 1710, Anne, the daughter of William vifcount Tracy, by whom he had iffue Thomas-Charles, who fucceeded to the baronetage, and dying without iffue, was fucceeded by his brother Robert, the prefent baronet. The laft mentioned fir William Keyt, being in his houfe at Norton in this parifh, when it was burnt down, voluntarily perifhed in the flames, in the year 1741. Soon after his death, the fcite of the houfe, together with the eftate, was fold to the late fir Dudley Ryder, lord chief juftice of England, whofe fon, Nathaniel Ryder, efq; is the prefent proprietor of Hidcoat Bois.

Of the Church, &c.

The church is a vicarage, in the deanery of Campden, worth about 30*l.* a year. The crown is patron, Mr. Jacob Mould the prefent incumbent.

The advowfon of the church was granted to the abbey of Bittlefden 1 R. 2. And after the diffolution of that abbey, the rectory and church of Ebrington were granted to Anthony Bonner and George Bonner 4 Jac. Tithes in Charingworth, which belonged to the abbey of Winchcombe, were granted to fir Thomas Seimour 1 E. 6. and the earl of Gainfborough pays 8*l.* a year for thofe tithes.

There is no glebe-land. Sir William Keyt gave 10*l.* a year to augment the vicarage, which fum is included in the above mentioned value.

The church is large and handfome. The eaft window of the chancel is ornamented with painted glafs, in pretty good prefervation, wherein are feveral coats of arms, as *Sable, a fefs ermine between three crefcents Or*, for Coventry. *France and England, quarterly*. The arms of Keyt, &c. Upon two wreaths is written, *Beati qui lugent.— Beati Pauperes.* And towards the bottom are two hiftorical pieces, the one, Jofeph telling his dream to his father and brothers; the other reprefents him flying from the temptations of Potiphar's wife. In a tower at the weft end, are fix mufical bells.

Monuments and Infcriptions.

Againft the north wall of the chancel is a large monument for lord chancellor Fortefcue, with his effigy, in fcarlet robes, lying on a raifed tomb ornamented with fcutcheons of coat armour. On a table is the following infcription:

In fœlicem et immortalem memoriam Clariffimi viri Dni IOHANNIS FORTESCVTI militis, grandævi, Angliæ judicis primarij, et proceffu temporis fub HENRICO VI^to^ Rege, et EDWARDO principe, Summi Cancellarij, Conciliarij Regis Prudentiffimi, Legum Angliæ peritiffimi, nec non earundem hyperafpiftis fortiffimi; qui corporis exuvias, lætam refurrectionem expectantes, hic depofuit.

Marmoreum hoc Monumentum pofitum eft Anno Dni MDCLXXVII, Voto et expenfis ROBERTI FORTESCVTI, Armig. ejufdem familiæ hæredis, nuper defuncti.

Angligenas intra Cancellos juris et æqui
  Qui tenuit, cineres jam tenet vrna viri:
Lex viva ille fuit, patriæ lux fplendida legis.
  FORTE bonis SCVTVM, fontibus at fcutica.
Clarus erat titulis, clarus majoribus, arte
  Clarus, virtute aft clarior emicuit.
Jam micat in tenebris veluti carbunculus orbi,
  Nam virtus radios non dare tanta nequit.
Vivit adhuc FORTESCVTVS laudatus in ævum;
  Vivet et in LEGVM LAVDIBVS ille fuis.

To perpetuate the memory of that learned and excellent Man, Chancellor Fortefcue, this Monument was repaired by his Defcendant Matthew Lord Fortefcue, in the year 1765.

On the table of another monument, as follows:

D. O. M.

IN MEMORIA ÆTERNA ERIT IVSTVS.

DEPOSITVM GVLIELMI KEYT, ARMIGERI, HOC SVB MARMORE PRÆSTOLATUR, IESUS DONEC SVVS, TVBÆ CLANGORE, EXURGERE, & CORRVPTIONEM INCORRVPTIONEM INDVERE IVSSERIT.

Comitatus Wigornienfis vicecomitis officio functus eft. Familiâ fuit fatis antiquâ, ut quæ per tricentos plus minus annos villæ hujus primatum obtinuit. Duxit in vxorem Eglantinam Riley, E qua duos filios, Iohannem & Gulielmum, totidemq; fufcepit filias, Annam nempe et Elizabetham.

Infigniter erat pius: habuitq; erga pauperes (vici prefertim hujus) *Splagchna Oiktirmoon*, utpote qui decem vaccarum uberibus diftentis lac, a decimo die Maij ufq; ad primum Novembris, in perpetuum ipforum alimentum mifericors legavit.

Amicis iucundiffimus, cunctis gratiffimus, optimus fenex fenio confectus, (fummo bonorum omnium luctu ac defiderio) mortalitatem cum perennitate placide commutavit Idibus Octobris, anno Verbi incarnati 1632. Ætatis fuæ 78.

Io: Keyt filius MŒSTISSIMVS chariffimo parenti *Mnemofynon* hoc pietatis ergo pofuit.

This monument is ornamented with coats of the family arms, *viz. Azure, a chevron between three kites heads erazed Or*, for Keyt; impaling, *Or, a chevron between three croffes patee fitchy fable*. Alfo Keyt impaling, *Quarterly*, 1ft *and* 4th, *Gules, three pikes hauriant proper*, for Lucy. 2d *and* 3d, *Argent, a bend vert between a mullet in chief and an annulet in bafe gules.*

There

There are alſo the following memorials :

Memoriæ Sacrum Ioannis Keyt, armigeri, Gulielmi filij primogeniti, qui reclinavit annoſum in hoc pulvere depoſitum. Conſortem tori fideliſſimam, prudentem, providam, et pudicam, Thomæ Porter, generoſi, filiam duxit Janam, quæ chariſſima reliquit conjugi pignora, ſeptem filios et quinque filias. Primo Wigornia, poſtea Glouceſtria vidit vice-comitem, paciq; præpoſitum. Regis, reipublicæ, religionis ergo, dux, vice-comes, Irenarchus. Bellum fortiter, pacem ſuaviter geſſit, coluitq; Nobilis ingenij, vitæ intemeratæ. Pietatis in Deum, fidelitatis in principem, charitatis in proximum, Exemplar æmulandum. Communi procerum populiq; jacturâ fato ſuccubuit, Aprilis 25°, Anno Salvatoris 1660, Ætatis 76. Ioannes Keyt, Baronettus, filius, mœrens poſuit.

DOMINVS IOANNES KEYT, IO: FIL: GVIL: NEP: BARONETVS (QVI NVPERIS MOTIBVS EX PARTE REGIS PROPRIJS SVMPTIBVS HIPPARCHVS FVIT) EX MARGARETA, GVIL: TAYLER, ARMIG: HÆREDE, SOBOLEM SVSCEPIT D. GVIL: KEYT BARONETVM, IOANNEM, THOMAM, ET FRANCISCVM FILIOS : ELIZABETHAM VXOREM IO: TALBOT, DE LACOCK, EQ: AVR: MARGARETAM VXOREM IO: PACKINGTON, FIL: ET HÆREDIS IO: PACKINGTON, BARONETI.
DIEM OBIJT ILLE 26 DIE AUG. A. D. MDCLXII. DIEM OBIJT ILLA 28 DIE IVN. A. D. MDCLXIX.

H. S. E. Cl. V. Gulielmus Keyt, Baronettus, qui uxorem duxit Elizabetham Honorabilis Franciſci Coventrye filiam, et Honoratiſſimi Thomæ Baronis Coventrye, Magni Sigilli Cuſtodis, Neptem : Ex qua ſuſcepit quatuor filios, Iohannem, Anonymum, Gulielmum, Thomam, (quibus omnibus ſuperſtes fuit) filiasq; duas, Margaretam et Dorotheam. Pauperibus et Operarijs indies benevolum ; Regibus etiam exulantibus ſemper fidelem ; hujus eccleſiæ paſtoribus (quibus annuatim ſolvendas decem legavit libras) in perpetuum ſe exhibuit munificum. Mortiferum quo laboravit morbum animo vere Chriſtiano perpeſſus, tandem placide obdormivit S. Andreæ feſto, Chriſti Incarnati MDCCII° Anno, Ætatis ſuæ ſupra LX^m^ VI^tum^.

H. S. E. D^s^ Thomas Keyt, D^ni^ Gulielmi Keyt Baronetti, et D^nae^ Elizabethæ Uxoris ejus, Hon^bilis^ D^ni^ Franciſci Coventrij Armigeri filiæ natu maximæ, filius natu minimus : Summâ in parentes obſervantia nulli ſecundus, Cœlibum pudicitiam colentium facile primus ; moribus adeo caſtus, et pudore integer, ſeculo licet corruptiſſimo, ut ab incontinentiæ ſuſpicione abeſſet. Natus XIV Cal. Sept. MDCLXXII. Denatus IV Cal. Iun. MDCCII. Qui rem familiarem dilectiſſimo fratrino Franciſco Keyt tabellis teſtamentarijs legavit.

Fratrum, altero haud ita pridem defuncto, familiæ cladem et luctum renovavit Mors præmatura alterius, viz. Wilhelmi Keyt (2) Baronetti, D^ni^ Wilhelmi Keyt (1) Armigeri, filij natu tertij, et, ſi Deus annuiſſet, Hæredis futuri : Qui ex generis thalamiq; Conſorte fideliſſimâ, meritoq; dilectiſſimâ, Agnete, D^ni^ Iohannis Clopton, de Clopton Equitis Aurati, filia primogenitâ, poſtquam ſeptem procreaſſet filios, Wilhelmum, Coventreium, Thomam, Gilbertum, Iohannem, Franciſcum, et Haſtingium ; et tres filias, Elizabetham, Barbaram, et Margaretam ; ab omnibus deploratus hinc emigravit, feſti Omnium Sanctorum Vigiliâ, ad participandam Sanctorum Sortem, Anno poſt Chriſtum natum MDCCII°, Ætatis ſuæ XXXIV°.

Here lyes the Body of Alice Keyt, Daughter of S^r^. William Spencer, of Yardington in the county of Oxford, Baronet, and of Conſtance his Wife, ye Daughter of S^r^. Thomas Lucy, of Charlecott in the county of Warwick ; which ſaid Alice was the late Wife of Francis Keyt of Hithcoat Eſq; & deceaſed ye 29th of May in the year 1687. A Lady dignifyed not only by her birth, but, beſides her other Vertues, for her Love and Fidelity to her Huſband. —— *This is upon a large blue ſtone, on which are the arms of* Keyt *and* Spencer *impaled.*

Mortis exuvias in hunc tumulum recondidit, certâ ſpe reſurgendi ad vitam immortalem, Matrona pientiſſima Maria Gualteri Dayrell de Abendonia in Agro Bercheriæ Armigeri filia : Que fauſte et feliciter bis nupta fuit, primum, Reverendo Iohanni Morris, S. T. D. Ædis Chriſti apud Oxonienſes Canonico, et linguæ Ebrææ profeſſori Regio : Deinde, rei militaris peritiſſimo Duci Thomæ Keyt, de Wolford-Magnâ, in comitatu Warwici Armigero. Nullam poſt ſe reliquit ſobolem, Nomen vero melius et multo perennius quam quod habere poterat a filijs et filiabus. Poſtquam annos plus minus ſeptuaginta, pudice, ſancte, pie, peregiſſet, terrenum depoſuit Tabernaculum, nono Kalendas Novembris, Anno Æræ Chriſtianæ MDCLXXXI.

Memoriæ Sacrum Thomæ Keyt de Wolford Armigeri, Iohannis Filij natu minoris, Cognatis et Neceſſarijs amiciſſimi, Ægrotis et Egenis munificentiſſimi, Omnibus humaniſſimi, Fato defuncti V^to^ Idus Ianuarias, Anno Salutis MDCCI^mo^. Wilhelmus Keyt Armiger, quem Hæredem ex Aſſe inſtituit, Lapidem hunc ſepulchralem poſuit.

Firſt fruits £.	9	0	0	Synodals £.	0	2	0
Tenths —	0	18	11¼	Pentecoſtals	0	1	0½
Procurations	0	6	8				

Benefactions.

William Keyt, eſq; gave the milk of ten cows, for ſix ſummer months, as expreſſed in the memorial for him, to the poor of this pariſh, one cow's milk to two families. And the rent of a little meadow in Blockley, a detached pariſh in Worceſterſhire, is given for the repair of part of the church furniture.

Taxes.					
The Royal Aid in	1692,	£. 285	0	0
Poll-tax ——	1694, —	22	17	0
Land-tax ——	1694, —	184	4	0
The ſame, at 3s.	1770, —	71	0	0

When ſir Robert Atkyns compiled his account of this pariſh, about the year 1710, there were, according to him, 74 houſes, and 341 inhabitants, of whom 10 were freeholders; yearly births 15, burials 15. But from an accurate examination of the pariſh regiſter, it appears, that in ten years, beginning with 1700, the baptiſms were 139, burials 87; and in a like ſeries of years, beginning with 1761, the baptiſms were 164, the burials 76; and there are now 94 houſes, and 469 inhabitants. So that about one in every ſixty-one of the inhabitants dies every year.

EDGWORTH.

THIS is a ſmall pariſh in the hundred of Biſley, in the Coteſwold country, ſix miles north-weſt from Cirenceſter, three north-eaſtward from Biſley, and twelve ſouth-eaſtward from Glouceſter.

The ſituation of the village on the ſide of a hill, gave riſe to the name, which is compoſed of two Saxon words, Ecge, the ſharp ſide of a thing, and peorð, a village.

It hath been already obſerved, under Cranham, that the face of the country hereabout is exceedingly uneven, with much beech wood growing on the ſteep acclivities. The bottoms are generally paſture; but the greater part of this pariſh is arable land. A ſmall brook runs through it into the river Froom.

Part of Pinbury-park lies in this pariſh, the reſt in Dunteſbourn Rous.

Of the Manor and other Eſtates.

'Roger de Laci holds Egeſworde in Biſelege 'hundred. There is one hide and a half taxed. 'Eluuin held it. In demean are four plow-'tillages, and four villeins, and three bordars with 'two plow-tillages. There are two free men 'with two plow-tillages. There are fifteen *ſervi*, 'and a mill of 30*d.* and two acres of meadow. 'A wood one mile long, and half a mile broad. 'It is worth and was worth 6*l.*' *D. B.* p. 75.

'Earl

'Earl Hugh holds half a hide at Egeiſuurde, 'which Roger de Laci claims, as the county 'witneſſeth. It was worth 10*s*. and pays tax.' *Domeſday-book*, p. 73.

Audomar de Valencia, earl of Pembroke, ſon of William de Valencia, who was half brother, by the mother, to king H. 3. was ſeized of Edgworth. Mary his third wife had two parts of the village in dower, and died ſeized thereof 17 E. 2. Thomas de Eggeworth held the third part of the vill of Eggeworth of the ſaid earl, as of the manor of Paynſwyke, by half a knight's fee, 17 E. 2. *Eſch*.

Walter Helvin died ſeized of this manor 16 E. 3. as did Robert de Aſton the 23d, and John Coaffe 36 E. 3. when it was held of the manor of Painſwick. The manor ſoon after paſſed to the Raleighs. Thomas Raleigh died ſeized of the manor of Edgworth, which he held by half a knight's fee, of Richard lord Talbot and Anchoret his wife, 21 R. 2. Thomas Raleigh, his ſon and heir, died ſeized of this manor 6 H. 4. as did Walter Raleigh, ſon and heir of Thomas, 8 H. 5. William Rawleigh and Elizabeth his wife levied a fine of the manor and advowſon of Edgworth 28 H. 6. of which William died ſeized in the reign of king Edward the Fourth. Sir Edward Rawleigh, ſon of William, died poſſeſſed of this manor 5 H. 8. and George Rawleigh died ſeized of it, and of the advowſon of Edgworth 37 H. 8. which were held by ſoccage of ſir Henry Jerningham, as of the manor of Painſwick. Sir George Rawleigh and Edward his ſon ſold the manor to ſir Henry Pool of Saperton, 44 Eliz. who was lord of it in the year 1608, and died in 1616. Out of this name and family it paſſed not long after. Nathaniel Ridler, eſq; was lord of the manor at the beginning of this century. From him it deſcended to Thomas Ridler, eſq; who left three daughters, coheireſſes, 1. Elizabeth, married to William Prinn, of Charlton-King's, eſq; 2. Anne, the preſent lady of the manor; 3. Barbara, married to the reverend Mr. Richard Brereton. The arms of Ridler are, *Argent, a bull paſſant gules*.

John Mandevil was ſeized of lands in Edgworth and Painſwick 34 E. 3. John Timbrel levied a fine of lands in this pariſh 24 H. 7. A tenement and water-mill here belonged to the abbey of Glouceſter 2 H. 8.

Of the Church, &c.

The church is a rectory, in the deanery of Stonehouſe, worth 100*l*. a year. The reverend Mr. Richard Brereton, in right of his wife, is patron and incumbent.

Sixteen acres of paſture, twenty-one acres of arable in the north field, and eighteen acres in the ſouth field, belong to the glebe.

The church is dedicated to St. Mary, and has a tower at the weſt end.

Firſt fruits £.	8	0	0	Synodals £.	0	2	0
Tenths —	0	16	0	Pentecoſtals	0	0	7
Procurations	0	6	8				

Taxes.				
The Royal Aid in 1692, £.	46	0	8
Poll-tax —— 1694, —	8	4	0
Land-tax —— 1694, —	30	12	0
The ſame, at 3*s*. 1770, —	25	13	0

When ſir Robert Atkyns compiled his account of this pariſh, there were 24 houſes, and about 120 inhabitants, whereof 4 were freeholders; yearly births 3, burials 2. There are now only 106 inhabitants.

ELBERTON

LIES in the lower diviſion of the hundred of Berkeley, eleven miles north from Briſtol, ten north-weſt from Chipping-Sodbury, and twenty-eight ſouth-weſtward from Glouceſter. It is ſituated in the lower part of the vale, on the eaſt ſide of the Severn, where the river is two miles over. And tho' the greater part of the houſes ſtand upwards of a mile from it, the inhabitants are ſubject to agues, and diſorders particularly incident to countries ſituate upon large rivers; yet in a leſs degree than ſome of their neighbours in the marſhes.

There is a ſmall camp, with a ſingle ditch, on the hill eaſtward of the village, peculiarly well adapted to obſerve every thing paſſing on the river, with a full view of the country on the other ſide of it. It was probably thrown up by the Romans, to preſerve a communication between the *Trajectus* at Oldbury, and the country about the Briſtol Avon.

In *Domeſday-book* the name is written Eldbertone, which ſignifies the *old barton*, or *farm*.

Of the Manor and other Eſtates.

It appears by the abſtract from the above mentioned record, given under Berkeley, that five hides in this place belonged to the manor of Berkeley; and went with that manor, by the gift of king Henry the Second, to Robert Fitz-Harding.

He ſettled this manor on his ſecond ſon Robert, in marriage with Alice de Gaunt. Robert and Alice had iſſue Maurice, and a daughter Eva[f], married to Thomas Harpetre, deſcended from Gouel de Percheval, ſometimes called Gouel de Yvery, ſirnamed *Lupus*, who attended the Conqueror in the invaſion of England, and was rewarded with ſeveral manors, among others, with that of Weſt Harpetre in the county of Somerſet. Maurice, by his deed, bearing date at Portſmouth, gave[g] to the king, then paſſing into Britany, his lordſhips of Weſton, Beverſtone, and Albricton, and died[f] without iſſue the ſame year. But it is probable that he did not diſpoſe of the inheritance; for the greateſt part thereof went to the iſſue of his ſiſter Eva, whoſe ſon Robert aſſumed the ſurname of Gournay, and 15 H. 3. had livery of all his[h] lands in Somerſetſhire and Glouceſterſhire, except Beverſtan, Weſton, Rudewic, Oure,

[f] Rot fin. 17 Joh. [g] Dugdale ſub tit. Gaunt. [h] Rot. fin. 16 H. 3. m. 3. Collins's Peerage, V. 3, p. 441.

and Albricton; which, however, he not long after obtained of the king.

John Tropyn[i] died feized of the manor of Aylbrigton *juxta* Olvifton, by the fervice of the tenth part of a knight's fee, 11 E. 2. Sir John Walfh died feized of Elberton 38 H. 8. And Maurice Walfh, his fon and heir, who married Bridged Vawfe, had livery thereof the fame year.

George Smith, efq; was lord of this manor in 1608. It paffed afterwards to fir Thomas Cann of Stoke-Bifhop, and from him to Cann Jefferis, efq; who dying without iffue, it went by the marriage of his fifter, to Henry Lyppingcott, efq; who is the prefent lord of the manor. See *Stoke-Bifhop*.

Lands in Ailberton belonged to the monaftery of St. Auguftine at Briftol, and at the diffolution, were granted as[k] part of the endowment of the bifhoprick of Briftol, 34 H. 8.

Lands called Prieftcroft in Aleberton, *alias* Elberton, were granted to Edward Sallus 3 Jac.

Mr. Goldney has a good houfe and eftate in this place, which formerly belonged to the Browns, and afterwards to lord Vaughan.

Of the Church, &c.

The church is a vicarage, in the deanery of Briftol, worth about 60*l.* a year. The rectory and advowfon of Allberton, formerly belonging to St. Auguftine's monaftery at Briftol, were granted at the diffolution, to Paul, bifhop of Briftol[l], and his fucceffors for ever, 34 H. 8. The bifhop of Briftol is patron; the rev. Mr. Camplin incumbent. In the year 1767, the church of Elberton was confolidated with that of Olvefton.

The bifhop of Briftol has given the impropriation to the curate of Horfield.

The church confifts of a nave, and an aile on each fide, with a fpire in the middle; and hath a very large church-yard. From both ailes, are fquare holes cut through the pillars which fupport the roof, in a direction to the altar, that the congregation might the more conveniently fee the prieft elevate the hoft, in time of mafs.

Monuments and Infcriptions.

There is a large ftone coffin in the fouth crofs aile, in which 'tis fuppofed one of the Walfhes lies buried.

There is a flat ftone in the body of the church, with a plate of brafs, and this infcription:

Here lyeth the Body of Jofeph Fricker jun[r]. Son of Jofeph Fricker of Tockington. Qui obijt Aug. 27 Anno 1707.—Then follow three verfes, *viz.* Job. xiv, 1. in Hebrew; Ephef. v, 14. in Greek; Ecclef. xii, 1. in Latin.
Memento Creatoris fui in Diebus Electionum fuarum.

Procurations 1*s.*

Benefaction.

Mr. John Hicks of this parifh, gave by will 50*l.* the intereft of which to be thus difpofed of; 10*s.* to the minifter for a fermon; the reft to the fecond poor in bread and beef.

Taxes.					
The Royal Aid in	1692, £.	108	4	0
Poll-tax ——	1694, —	9	19	4
Land-tax ——	1694, —	110	1	0
The fame, at 3*s.*	1770, —	82	10	9

There were 26 houfes, and about 104 inhabitants in this parifh, whereof 4 were freeholders; yearly births 4, burials 3. *Atkyns.* In ten years, beginning with 1700, I counted upon the parifh regifter 36 baptifms, and 33 burials; and in other ten years, beginning with 1760, 18 baptifms, and 37 burials. From which I judge they have baptized chiefly at fome other church. The inhabitants are now about 122.

ELKSTONE

IS a fmall parifh in the hundred of Rapfgate, in the Cotefwold country, eight miles northweftward from Cirencefter, feven fouth from Cheltenham, and ten eaft from Gloucefter.

The turnpike-road from Cirencefter to Cheltenham leads through it. The parifh confifts chiefly of a ftone-brafh arable land, with a little pafture. The greater part of it lies bleak, and much expofed to the wind from every quarter, which fo impedes vegetation, that the harveft is later here than in any other part of the county.

Here is a quarry of very excellent ftone to endure the weather. It cuts eafy at firft, but hardens in the air, and is very durable. And I am inclined to think that the place took its name from the fhallow ftony foil; for the antient name is Elcheftane, perhaps from *El*, a *place*, and *ftane*, *ftone*, i.e. *the ftony place.*

Of the Manor and other Eftates.

'Ansfrid de Cormeliis holds Elcheftane in 'Refpigete hundred. Two Leuuini [perfons of 'the name of Leuuinus] held it for two manors. 'There are four hides and a half; and in Colefborne 'one hide and a half. Eluuinus held it for a 'manor, and thefe three thanes could go where 'they pleafed. In demean are two plow-tillages, 'and five villeins, and two bordars, with three 'plow-tillages and a half. There are four *fervi*, 'and ten acres of meadow; a wood half a mile 'long, and two quarters broad.'

'One knight holds a moiety of this manor 'of Ansfrid, and has two plow-tillages there, 'and five villeins, and two bordars, with three 'plow-tillages; and another knight holds Colef-'burne of him, and has half a plow-tillage 'there, and two villeins, and two bordars, with 'one plow-tillage, and a mill of 50*d.* This '[manor] was worth 8*l.* now 7*l.* and 10*s.*' *Domefday-book*, p. 78.

The manor of Elkftone was granted to John le Brun 50 H. 3. and John his fon was feized thereof 31 E. 1. John de Acton was feized of this manor 8 E. 2. And George de Acton having forfeited his

[i] Efch. fub anno. [k] Willis's Thefaurus. [l] Ibid.

his lands by rebellion, Hugh Muftel became poffeffed of Elkeftone, of which he died feized 19 E. 2. Richard de Bellers held the manor 3 E. 3. but it could only be in truft for fir John de Acton, then under age, who had been reftored to all his father's lands 1 E. 3. He died without iffue 17 E. 3. leaving his coufin Maud his heir. She was married to Nicholas Poyntz, whofe fon and heir, fir John Pointz, was feized of this manor 1 & 6 R. 2. and it continued many generations in his family.

James Huntly was lord of this manor in the year 1608; but lord Craven is the prefent proprietor. His lordfhip's arms are, *Argent, a fefs between fix crofs croflets fitchy gules.* CREST. *On a chapeau gules, turned up ermine, a griphon of the* 2d. *beaked Or.* SUPPORTERS. *Two griphons ermine.* MOTTO. VIRTUS IN ACTIONE CONSISTIT.

HAMLETS. 1. *Cockleford*, lying about a mile north-weftward from the church. In this hamlet, in the road from Cirencefter to Cheltenham, lies *Cockleford-hill*, well known to travellers for the difficulty of the afcent, and badnefs of the road.

2. *Combend*, fo called from its lying at the top of a *comb*, or little *valley*, about a mile eaftward of the church. Thomas Eftcourt died feized of the manor or farm of Colefcombe, *alias* Combefend, *alias* Combefcottle 41 Eliz. which, with the manor of Winfton, he had fettled on his fon Thomas, who married Mary, the daughter of William Savage. *Efch.* This eftate paffed afterwards to the Hortons. Thomas Horton, efq; died feized of it at the beginning of this century; after whom, William Blanch, efq; became poffeffed of it, who dying without iffue, in the year 1766, bequeathed all his eftates to his wife, during her life, and after her death, to Mr. James Rogers of Gloucefter, and his heirs. Mr. Samuel Walbank of London, wine-merchant, married Mrs. Blanch, and holds this eftate in right of his wife.

Of the Church, &c.

The church is a rectory, in the deanery of Stonehoufe, worth 100*l.* a year; lord Craven is patron, the reverend Mr. Lloyd the prefent incumbent.

The church, dedicated to St. John the Evangelift, is fmall and neat, with a handfome tower at the weft end, and four bells.

Fifty-one acres of inclofed ground, and fifty acres in the common-fields belong to the glebe.

	£	s	d		£	s	d
Firft fruits	12	9	2	Synodals	0	2	0
Tenths —	1	4	11	Pentecoft.	0	0	3
Procurations	0	6	8				

Taxes.		£	s	d
The Royal Aid in	1692,	70	0	0
Poll-tax ——	1694, —	6	12	0
Land-tax ——	1694, —	59	9	0
The fame, at 3*s.*	1770, —	45	18	7½

At the beginning of this century there were 35 houfes in this parifh, and about 160 inhabitants, whereof 4 were freeholders; yearly births 6, burials 5. *Atkyns.* In ten years, beginning with 1760, there are regiftered 71 baptifms, and 32 burials. The prefent number of houfes is 40, of inhabitants 178.

ELMORE.

THIS parifh lies in the hundred of Dudfton and King's Barton, eight miles north-weft from Stroud, five north-eaftward from Newnham, and four fouth-weftward from Gloucefter.

Elmor, from the Britifh *Allmor*, fo likewife *Armor*, fignifies *a low fituation near the fea*, or fome *great river*; and the name was given with great propriety to this parifh, which is almoft peninfulated (if I may fo exprefs myfelf) by the Severn, and often fuffers confiderable damage from the overflowing of that river. But the notion of its being fo called from the great number of *eels* taken in the *moors*, is puerile and vulgar.

The channel of the river winding here, and being fo much narrower than it is a few miles below, caufes the fpring-tides to come in with a very great head, fometimes eight or ten feet high.

The boundaries of the parifh are remarkably confufed and irregular. It is natural to fuppofe that the Severn would have been the boundary between fuch places as lie on the oppofite fides of it; but here is an exception; for there are fome lands at a place called *Elmore's Back*, on this fide the river, which belong to the parifh of Minfterworth.

They have fome tillage land in common-field, but the greater part is pafturage; for the foil being rich, and fubject to floods, is improper for tillage. The air is not remarkably unwholefome for the fituation; but the inhabitants fuffer the topical diforders generally incident to places lying on large rivers and ftagnated water.

A rock, called *Stone-Bench*, runs acrofs the Severn here, but the water is feldom low enough to make it fordable. Here is alfo a place of deep water, called *Groundlefs-Pit*, (made by the floods breaking the fea-wall) commonly, tho' erroneoufly, faid to have no bottom.

Thefe are the chief particulars which diftinguifh this parifh; but Leland fpeaks of another, in the Third Vol. of his *Itinerary*, publifhed by Hearne. *Mr. Gyfe*, faith he, *hath at his manor of Elmore in Glocestrefhir, Okes, the rootes whereof be converted into hard ftones within the ground.* From this account the reader may fuppofe, that the trunks and branches above the ground remained in their natural ftate, at leaft, if they did not retain the power of vegetation. I have made fome inquiry as to the fact, and find that there is no fuch thing at prefent, nor any tradition of what he mentions. I never heard of an inftance of the roots of a live tree, nor indeed of any tree, petrifying in the place where it grew; and it is extraordinary that the learned and judicious antiquary fhould be fo much impofed impoſed on as to believe and report this incredible ſtory.

Sir William Guiſe has a large, handſome ſeat here, ſtanding on an eminence, with a chapel in it, and good offices and gardens; but he reſides at Rendcombe.

Of the Manor and other Eſtates.

The pariſh or manor of Elmore is not mention'd in *Domeſday-book*, but at the time when that record was compiled, it muſt have paſſed by ſome other name, or was conſidered as a part only of another pariſh. However, it ſoon afterwards acquired the preſent name, for it is expreſſly mentioned in a regiſter book of the priory of Lanthony, near Glouceſter, that Hubert de Burgo[m], earl of Kent, and juſtice of England, by his deed, gave to the ſaid priory tithe of lampreys, and all fiſh, taken in his gurges of Elmore. *Teſte* Richard, biſhop of Chicheſter, the king's chancellor.

John de Burgh, ſon of Hubert, by his wife Margaret, daughter of William, king of Scotland, held the manor of Elmore, with free warren, 44 H. 3. the year in which his mother died.

Nicholas de Gyſe, ſon of Robert, of the family of Gyſe of Aſple-Gyſe, or Gowiz, in Bedfordſhire, married a near relation of John de Burgh, and had with her the manor of Elmore, by the gift of the ſaid John, and aſſumed the arms of De Burgh in honour of that family. Aunſelme de Gyſe, ſon of Nicholas, had a freſh grant of the manor of Elmore, with its appurtenances, from John de Burgo, 2 E. 1. at the yearly rent of a clove-gilliflower, and proved his right to free warren, in a *Quo warranto*, 15 E. 1.

John de Gyſe, knight, by his deed dated at Elmore, on the feaſt of St. Vincent, 31 E. 3. grants the manor of Elmore, and the pool there, to William Haybarare, chaplain, Robert le Little of Coveley, clerk, and Richard Stout of Heyhamſtude. And the king gave licence to thoſe three perſons to grant the ſame manor, with the appurtenances, valued at 12*l.* a year, to the priory of Lanthony near Glouceſter, for the uſes therein mentioned, which they did by their deed 32 E. 3.

A re-feoffement was made, by William, the prior, and the convent of Lanthony, to John de Gyſe, knight, of their manor of Elmore, for his life, dated Apr. 5, 32 E. 3. and they engage to pay him 20*l.* a year for his life; and that he ſhall have twelve yards of the ſuit of the principal clerks; alſo one robe for his eſquire, of the ſuit of the eſquires of the prior; and one robe of the ſuit of the free tenants, for his chamberlain. And they alſo engage to celebrate one canon perpetually for the ſouls of his father and mother, of himſelf, and of the lady Joan his wife; and that they ſhall have a ſolemn anniverſary, with maſs, and the office of the dead, for ever.

But it is probable that the inheritance of the manor did not paſs by the above grant to the priory, for Anſelm Gyſe died ſeized of Elmore 13 H. 4. as did his ſon Reginald 8 H. 5. And from them it deſcended to ſir William Guiſe, bar[t]. the preſent lord of the manor, whoſe arms are given under *Rendcombe*, the place of his reſidence.

This manor was held of Humphry de Bohun, earl of Hereford and Eſſex, and of Joan his wife, as of the honour of Hereford, 32 & 46 E. 3. and of Henry lord Stafford, as of the ſame honour, 5 Mariæ.

By an inquiſition 23 E. 1. it was found, that the king was ſeized of four tenements in this pariſh, and the priory of Lanthony was ſeized of two; which latter, after the diſſolution of the priory, were granted to William Doddington 7 Eliz.

The abbey of Glouceſter held lands in Elmore, which were granted, at the diſſolution, to Joan Cook, widow, 31 H. 8.

Of the Church, &c.

The church is a curacy, in the deanery of Glouceſter. It is an impropriation belonging to ſir William Guiſe, who allows the curate the privy tithes and a houſe. The curacy was augmented by lot in 1746. Sir William Guiſe is patron, Mr. Cheſter the preſent incumbent.

In the year 1137, Milo conſtable of Glouceſter gave the tithes of Elmore to the priory of Lanthony, and two years afterwards, he gave a meadow in Elmore to the ſame houſe, all which the priory enjoyed 'till it was diſſolved.

The church, dedicated to St. Bartholomew, is a double building, ſupported by pillars in the middle, and has an embattled tower, with five bells, at the weſt end.

Pentecoſtals, - - - 6*d.*

Monuments and Inſcriptions.

On the top of a raiſed tomb, in the ſouth chancel, is a rude engraving of the figure of a man, and round the edge, in old characters,

Hic jacet Johēs Gyſe et Alicia uxor ejus qui quidem Iohannes feliciter obijt in . . . . Mileſimo cccc lxxix quōr animabus propicietur Deus Amen.

On a black marble monument, this inſcription:

This for the Worthy Memory of S[r]. William Guyſe, who deceaſed Sept. 19, 1642. And of William his eldeſt Son by his firſt Wife, Margaret, Daughter to Chriſtopher Kenn, Eſq; who marryed Cicelia, Daughter to John Dennis of Puckle-Church, Eſq; by whom he had 4 Sons and 3 Daughters. Hee deceaſed Auguſt 26, 1653. —— Arms, *Quarterly*, 1ſt *and* 4th, Guiſe; 2. *Gules, a feſs between ſix billets Or*; 3. *Sable, a feſs between three martlets argent.*

[m] The chronicles of his time are full of the praiſe of this man, who was looked upon by the people as the *father of his country.* Having offended king H. 3. he took ſanctuary in the chapel of Boiſars, which the king hearing, ſent one Canecumbe, with three hundred men, to apprehend him. A ſmith being called to ſet a pair of gyves, or fetters, upon his legs, aſked who he was; and when he underſtood him to be Hubert de Burgh, *What*, ſaith he, *Shall I fetter him that hath ſo often delivered this kingdom from enemies? Whatever may be the conſequence, I will never do it.*

On

On another monument,

In Memory of William Guiſe, Eſq; of the City of Glouceſter. He was the eldeſt Son of Major Henry Guiſe of Winterbourn in this County, and Grandſon of William Guiſe, Eſq; of this Pariſh. He departed yᵉ Life Auguſt the 28th 1716, in the 68th Year of his Age, and lyeth here interr'd with William his 4th Son.

Alſo Dorothea his Wife departed this Life Iune the 12th 1738, aged 76. A Lady remarkable for her ſtrict Piety, diffuſive Charity, and engaging Courteouſneſs of Behaviour, flowing from the trueſt Sentiments of Religion, Goodneſs, and Humanity. She was the only Daughter of John Snell, eſq; Lord of the Manor of Uffeton in the County of Warwick; which Manor, with Lands to the Value of near a Thouſand Pounds a Year, he gave by Will to ſupport the Intereſt of Epiſcopacy in Scotland. But this Application of his intended Benefaction being defeated by the Union, a decree was obtained in the High Court of Chancery for ſettling the Eſtate on Baliol College in Oxford for ever, to maintain, ſupport, and educate certain ſcholars to be ſent thither by the Univerſity of Glaſgow, allowing to each Fifty Pounds a Year, for ten Years. Only eight partake at preſent of theſe Exhibitions, though the Eſtate may be deemed capable of ſupporting a greater Number.

She had Iſſue three Sons and one Daughter. John, the eldeſt, died aged 21 Years. He was a Gentleman of a very extraordinary Genius, and eminently ſtudious, having in that early Time of Life acquired a perfect Knowledge of all the polite Languages, antient and modern. William, the ſecond Son, died aged 12 Years. Henry, the third Son, is ſtill living, and cauſed this Inſcription; & Theodoſia, the Daughter, was married to Dennis Cook of Highnam, eſq; and lies interred in Highnam Chapel.— Arms. 1ſt Guiſe, impaling 2d. *Quarterly gules and azure, over all a croſs flory Or*, for Snell.

On a flat ſtone,

Here lieth the Body of Henry Guiſe, eſq; of the City of Glouceſter (youngeſt Son of William Guiſe, eſq; who lies interred in this Chancel) a Gentleman in his private Converſation, well known for his engaging Affability, in Public for his ſtrict Adminiſtration of Juſtice. He died much lamented, the 23d of October 1749, aged 51.——Arms. Quarterly, 1ſt and 4th Guiſe, 2d and 3d Snell. On a ſcutcheon of pretence, *Or, a chevron checky gules and azure between three cinquefoils of the laſt*, for Cook.

There is a large vault or burying-place in the church-yard, for ſir William Guiſe's family, incloſed with paliſadoes, and covered with a pyramidal roof, ſupported by arches ſpringing from each corner.

Benefaction.

Three pounds a year, part of the large benefaction of the late Mr. Cox of Upton St. Leonard, to ſeveral places, is aſſigned to the poor of this pariſh.

Taxes.		£.	s.	d.
The Royal Aid in	1692,	81	5	4
Poll-tax — —	1694,—	18	3	0
Land-tax ——	1694,—	97	16	0
The ſame, at 3s.	1770,—	73	7	0

In the year 1562, there were only 36 houſholders in this pariſh; but according to ſir Robert Atkyns, about the beginning of this century, there were 70 houſes, and about 300 inhabitants, whereof 10 were freeholders; yearly births 8, burials 7. And there is now about the ſame number of inhabitants.

ELMSTON

IS a ſmall pariſh in the vale, lying part in the lower diviſion of Weſtminſter hundred, and part in the lower diviſion of Derhurſt hundred, five miles ſouth-eaſt from Tewkeſbury, four northweſt from Cheltenham, and eight northward from Glouceſter.

The pariſh conſiſts principally of good arable, with ſome paſture land. The little river Swilyate runs through it, down to Tewkeſbury, where it empties itſelf into the Severn.

In old records the name is written *Almundeſtan*, *Aylmundeſtan*, and *Aylmundſton*, but why it was ſo called is uncertain.

Of the Manors and other Eſtates.

In *Domeſday-book*, Elmſton is ſet down as a member of the large manor of Derhurſt, then belonging to the abbey of Weſtminſter, where it is ſaid, 'Brictric held one hide at Almundeſtan. 'Reimbald holds it.' *Domeſday-book*, p. 72.

Robert Fitz-Haman took the manor from the abbey of Weſtminſter in the reign of king William the Second; but Lawrence the 25th abbat recovered it by a ſuit at law, in the reign of king Henry the ſecond, and it continued in poſſeſſion of the abbey 'till its diſſolution; when it was granted to the dean and chapter of Weſtminſter, who are the preſent lords of the manor. The church ſtands in Elmſton, but there is no houſe in this part of the pariſh.

TITHING and *HAMLETS.*

1. *Uckington* is a tithing and manor in this pariſh, lying in the lower diviſion of Derhurſt hundred. It has its own proper conſtable, with a tithingman under him for the pariſh of Staverton, which is a member of this manor. The ſoil of part of this hamlet is a very looſe ſand, but it bears good crops of corn.

In *Domeſday-book*, under the title *Terra Sci Dyoniſii Pariſii*, it is ſaid, 'The church of St. 'Dennis holds five hides in Hochinton, in Derheſt 'hundred.' *Domeſday-book*, p. 72.

The priory of Derhurſt, which was a cell to the abbey of St. Dennis, was ſeized of Hochington 56 H. 3. The earl of Oxford was lord of the manor at the beginning of this century; from whoſe heirs it was purchaſed by Mr. Rogers of Dowdeſwell, about ſixty years ago; and Mrs. Rogers, widow of the late John Rogers, eſq; is the preſent proprietor, and holds a court leet for her manor at Uckington, where the inhabitants of Staverton attend. For her arms, *ſee Dowdeſwell.*

Mr. Thomas Buckle had a good eſtate in this tithing, at the beginning of the preſent century, which is now the property of his grandſon Mr. John Buckle. His arms are, *A chevron between three annulets.*

This tithing is joined with Staverton in the payment of taxes.

2. *Hardwick* is a hamlet and manor in this pariſh, and lies in the lower part of Weſtminſter hundred. It is generally called *Elmſton-Hardwick*, to diſtinguiſh it from the pariſh of Hardwick, near Glouceſter. It conſiſted of five hides, and was a member of Derhurſt, as appears by *Domeſday-book*, p. 72.

Henry Eden and Margaret his wife levied a fine of Elmſton-Hardwick, to John Seaborn and John

Chilkel, 21 H. 7. Maurice lord Berkeley died ſeized of it 15 H. 8. as did Thomas lord Berkeley, his brother, in the 24th year of the ſame reign, whoſe ſon Thomas lord Berkeley had livery of it the ſame year. Livery of this manor was alſo granted to Richard Ligon 9 Eliz.

Richard Dowdeſwell, of Pool-court in Worceſterſhire, eſq; was lord of the manor at the beginning of this century; as was the late right honourable William Dowdeſwell, eſq; at the time of his death, in 1775. *See Corſe.*

Of the Church, &c.

The church is a vicarage, in the deanery of Winchcombe, worth 40*l.* a year. The lord chancellor is patron; Mr. Freeman is the preſent incumbent.

The impropriation, worth 170*l.* a year, formerly belonged to the abbey of Tewkeſbury, but now it is veſted in Jeſus college, Oxford, and Mrs. Cheſter is leſſee under the college.

Tithes of corn and hay in Elmondeſton belonged to the abbey of Tewkeſbury, and were granted to Anthony Cope 10 Jac.

The church is large, with an aile on the ſouth ſide, and a handſome embattled tower at the weſt end.

Lands worth 2*l.* 12*s.* a year are given to repair the church.

Taxes.					
The Royal Aid in	1692, £.	79	13	0
Poll-tax ——	1694, —	5	8	0
Land-tax ——	1694, —	72	9	4
The ſame, at 3*s.*	1770, —	54	18	1½

At the beginning of this century, according to ſir Robert Atkyns, there were 35 houſes in this pariſh, and about 150 inhabitants, whereof 6 were freeholders; yearly births 5, burials 4. The preſent number of inhabitants is 144.

FAIRFORD.

THIS pariſh is of a middle ſize. It lies in the hundred of Britwell's-barrow, four miles diſtant weſt from Leachlade, eight eaſt from Cirenceſter, and twenty-three ſouth-eaſtward from Glouceſter.

It is a flat part of the country, affording very little variety. A fine gravel lies near the ſurface, which makes it dry and healthy. The arable lands produce good corn, and the meadow and paſture ground, of which there is a due proportion, is rich and luxuriant. The river Coln runs thro' it.

I know it has been ſaid, that the place takes its name from the *Fair Ford* that was there before the bridge was built over the river. It is difficult to remove opinions that have been commonly received, and uncontroverted; and tho' I am well convinced of that not being the true etymology, it may not be eaſy to ſatisfy others; but I ſubmit my ſentiments to the candour of competent judges. The antient and proper name is *Fareforde*, where *fare* does not ſignify *fair*, or *beautiful*, but a *paſſage*, in which ſenſe we even now ſometimes uſe it; and is derived from the Saxon verb ꝼaꝛan, to *go*, to *paſs*. The name was ſuggeſted by, and is deſcriptive of, the ſituation of the place, and ſignifies the *paſſage* at the *ford*. The river produces excellent trout, and empties itſelf into the Thames a little below.

The pariſh includes a little town, conſiſting of two ſtreets, with a market, tho' not much frequented, on Thurſdays; and two fairs, held, ſince the ſtyle was altered, on May 14, and Nov. 12, for cattle and pedlery. Another fair, ſaid to have been formerly held on the 18th of July, is now diſcontinued. The turnpike-road from Cirenceſter to London leading through it, there are two or three inns for the accommodation of travellers. But the town is moſt diſtinguiſhed by the handſome ſeat belonging to Mrs. Lamb, and by the fine painted glaſs windows of the pariſh church. The earl of Hilſborough was born in the manor houſe, on which account his lordſhip has done the place the honour of taking the title of viſcount from it.

Mrs. Lamb's ſeat ſtands about a quarter of a mile above the town. It is a good houſe, with a deer-park, and gardens well laid out, and kept in proper order. There is a viſta from the north front, terminated by an obeliſk about a mile from the houſe. A fine plantation ſtretches along the eaſt bank of the Coln, with pleaſant ſerpentine walks, and openings from ſeveral ſeats and buildings, to take in views of the Wiltſhire hills and other diſtant objects.

The houſe was built by Mr. Barker, grandfather to the preſent proprietor, but modernized and much improved by the late Mr. Lamb. Dr. Parſons relates, that at the building of it, many urns and medals were found, the former broken by the workmen in digging, without ſaying what the medals were. And as this happened in the Doctor's time, I rely upon his authority. Sir Robert Atkyns took his account from Dr. Parſons's *Collections*, and enlarged the ſenſe, in ſaying, that medals and urns were *often* dug up; and our topographical writers have followed him. But upon ſtrict inquiry, I am aſſured, that none have been found here, except the above. Theſe valuables were moſt probably concealed, previouſly to a ſkirmiſh which happened hereabout, not unlikely in the time of the civil wars between the Yorkiſts and Lancaſtrians, tho' our hiſtorians have not taken notice of it. Yet, that there was an engagement is certain, from two *tumuli*, little more than half a mile from the houſe, which having been opened about the end of the laſt century, were found to contain many human ſculls and bones of the ſlain. But there is no veſtige of an encampment in the pariſh.

Of the Manor and other Eſtates.

King William the Firſt having ſeized this manor into his own hands, it ſtands under the title

Terra

Terra Regis in *Domesday-book*, which gives the following particulars :

'Brictric held Fareforde in Bristoldesberg hundred. There were twenty-one hides in the time of king Edward, and fifty-six villeins, and nine bordars, with thirty plow-tillages. There is a priest who held one virgate of land of the manor, and three mills of 32 *s.* 6 *d.* There are now only thirteen hides, and one yard-land. Queen Maud held this manor, and Hunphry paid her 38 *l.* and 10 *s.* by tale. The queen gave four hides of the land of this manor to John the chamberlain. There are two plow-tillages, and nine villeins, and four bordars, with four plow-tillages. There are fourteen *servi*, who pay 9 *l.* for their farm. The queen also gave Baldwin three hides and three virgates of the same land, and he has there two plow-tillages, and five *servi*, and one free man, who has one plow-tillage, and two bordars. It is worth 4 *l.* Those who held these two estates in the time of king Edward, could not withdraw themselves from the chief of the manor.' *Domesday-book*, p. 69.

It is uncertain who had the first grant of it from the crown; but Philip of Worcester was seized of Fairford 5 Joh. as was George de Sunevil the following year.

The manor and town of Fairford belonged to Richard de Clare, earl of Gloucester and Hertford, 47 H. 3. and Gilbert de Clare proved his right in a *Quo warranto*, to markets, fairs, and a court leet therein, 15 E. 1.

Gilbert de Clare, earl of Gloucester, died seized of this manor 7 E. 2. and left no surviving issue. Hugh le Dispencer the younger married Elianor, eldest sister and coheiress to the last earl, and with her had the manor of Fairford. Hugh le Dispencer, their son, succeeded, but died without issue; whereby Edward Dispencer, son to Edward, who was brother of the last Hugh, became possessed of this manor, of which he died seized 49 E. 3. He left Thomas Dispencer his son, who was attainted and executed for treason 1 H. 4. Richard was son of Thomas. He died before he was fourteen years old, and left two sisters; Elizabeth, who died in her infancy, and Isabel, married first to Richard Beauchamp, lord Bergavenny, and secondly to Richard Beauchamp, earl of Warwick. And the manor continued in the Beauchamp family, 'till king Henry the Seventh prevailed upon Anne, the great heiress thereof, and widow of Richard Nevil, the great earl of Warwick, to convey it to him and his heirs male, in the third year of his reign.

John Tame, a merchant of London, purchased the manor of the king, and levied a fine thereof 13 H. 7. He married Alice, daughter of Mr. Twiniho, and died seized of Fairford 15 H. 7. Sir Edmond Tame, his son, succeeded him, and married Agnes, daughter of sir Edward Grevil. He was three times high sheriff of the county of Gloucester, and died 26 H. 8. Edmond Tame, son and heir of sir Edmond, married Catherine, daughter of sir William Dennis. He was twice high sheriff of this county, and died without issue 36 H. 8. His wife surviving him, held Fairford in jointure. She was afterwards married to sir Walter Buckle, who procured an additional grant of the manor of Fairford, and of all the lands in this parish, then lately belonging to the earl of Warwick, and formerly to the Dispencers, 38 H. 8. The last mentioned Edmond Tame left three sisters, coheiresses; Margaret, married to sir Humphry Stafford; Alice, married to sir Thomas Verney; and Isabel, the wife of Lewis Watkin. They and their descendants sold the manor to sir Henry Unton and John Croke, from whom it was purchased by the Tracys. Sir John Tracy was lord of the manor in the year 1608.

Andrew Barker, esq; purchased the manor of the Tracys, and was succeeded therein by his son Samuel Barker, who was high sheriff of this county in the year 1691. He married the daughter of Mr. Hubbard of London, and left two infant daughters, coheiresses. One died unmarried; Esther, the surviving daughter, was married to James Lamb, of Hackney, in the county of Middlesex, esq. He died without issue in the year 1761, and his widow is the present lady of the manor. The arms of Barker, are, *Argent, five escallops in cross Or.*

Sir Walter Dennis and Agnes his wife levied a fine of lands in Fairford 15 H. 7.

Leland says, sir Edmund Tame of Fairford came out of the house of Tame of Stowel. He takes frequent occasion to speak handsomely of the family; and says, *Fairford never florished afore the Cumming of the Tames onto it.* Sir Edmond Tame had to his second wife, Elizabeth, sister to John Morgan, of Monmouthshire, who was a colonel in the reign of king Henry the Seventh. This alliance induced the colonel to purchase an estate in Fairford, and to reside there, and was the occasion that Edmond has been a frequent Christian name in the family.

Edmond Morgan was the son of John. He had likewise a son Edmond, who married Margaret, daughter of —— Sadler of Purton. Walter Morgan, son of the last Edmond, married Elizabeth, daughter of —— Betterton of Fairford; and had issue Edmond, who married Mary, daughter and heiress of Robert Savory, of Hannington, a family which continued in that place from the time of king John, 'till towards the end of the last century; and then the estate was carried, by the above marriage, into the name and family of Morgan. The last Edmond Morgan had a son Edmond, who was an officer in the king's army at the time of the great rebellion. He married Mary, daughter of Edward Pleydell, of Cricklade, esq; by whom he had a numerous issue, among whom were Robert and James, both proprietors of estates at Fairford. Edmond Morgan was son of Robert, and Charles the only son of Edmond. He died in the year 1754, leaving two sons, 1. Robert,

now

now a captain of a ſhip in the ſervice of the Eaſt-India company, who married a daughter of captain White, of Devonſhire. 2. Charles-Tyrrel Morgan, an eminent barriſter, who married Britannia, daughter of John Raymond, of London, eſq. Mr. Charles Morgan had alſo four daughters. Their arms are, *Sable, a chevron between three ſpears heads argent.*

The houſe and eſtate in Fairford which belonged to this family, have lately been purchaſed by Mr. Raymond.

TITHINGS. 1. The *Borough*, which has its proper conſtable.

2. *Eaſt End*, which has a tithingman.

3. *Milltown End*, which has alſo a tithingman.

Of the Church, &c.

The church is in the deanery of Fairford. It is a vicarage worth about 150*l.* a year. The preſentation is in the dean and chapter of Glouceſter. Mr. Evans is the preſent incumbent.

Part of the advowſon of the church of Fairford was granted to Matthew de Winterborn, 18 Joh. The parſonage belonged afterwards to the abbey of Tewkeſbury, and upon the diſſolution of that houſe, was granted to the chapter of Glouceſter 33 H. 8.

The impropriation, worth 300*l.* a year, is in leaſe to Mr. Oldiſworth. All the corn tithes belong to it; the vicar hath all other tithes. When the commonable places in the pariſh were incloſed, about five or ſix years ago, the vicar had allotted to him, in lieu of what he before enjoyed, about half an acre of orcharding near his houſe; 4*a.* 1*r.* 9*p.* in the Moor, and 4*a.* 2*r.* in Prieſt Hurſt, both pieces of meadow ground; and 19*a.* 39*p.* of arable land.

The church is a large and beautiful building, 125 feet long, and 55 broad. It conſiſts of a ſpacious body, and two proportionable ailes, very handſomely paved in chequers of blue and white ſtone, and neatly pewed. It has a handſome tower in the middle, ornamented with pinnacles, and ſeveral ſcutcheons of coat armour. On the ſouth ſide is *Checky, bearing a chevron.* On the eaſt ſide, *three chevronels*, for Clare, earl of Glouceſter. There are three chancels and a veſtry. That on the north belongs to the lord of the manor, the middle to the impropriator, and the ſouth chancel to the vicar. The middle chancel is fitted up with ſtalls like the choir of ſome cathedrals. In the ſouth porch of the church are the arms of Tame, *Argent, a dragon combatant vert with a lion rampant Azure, crowned proper.*

A View of Fairford Church from the E.S.E. Entrance of the Church Yard.

John Tame having taken a ſhip bound for Rome, in which was a large quantity of very curious painted glaſs, built this church in the year 1493, for the ſake of placing the glaſs in it, and dedicated it to the virgin Mary. The figures were deſigned by that eminent maſter, Albert Durer, to whom the greateſt improvements in painting on glaſs are attributed. There are ſome curious pieces of perſpective. The colours are very lively, and ſome of the figures ſo well finiſhed, that ſir Anthony Vandyke affirmed, that the pencil could not exceed them.

There are twenty-eight windows, exhibiting the following ſubjects:

Firſt window. The ſerpent tempting Eve; God appearing to Moſes in the fiery buſh; the angel conducting Joſhua to war; Gideon's fleece; the queen of Sheba trying Solomon's wiſdom, and offering him preſents.

2d. The ſalutation of Zacharias and Elizabeth; the birth of John the Baptiſt; Mary viſiting Elizabeth; Joſeph and Mary contracted.

3d. The angel Gabriel's ſalutation of Mary, *Ave Maria plena* [*gratiæ*] *dominus te*[*cum*]; the birth of our Saviour; the Epiphany, or the wiſe men offering him preſents; the purification of the virgin mother; the circumciſion of our Saviour, and

and Simeon receiving him in the temple, with an infide view of the temple.

4th. Jofeph and Mary flying to Egypt; the affumption of the virgin Mary; Chrift difputing with the doctors in the temple.

5th.? Advent, *viz.* Our Saviour riding to Jerufalem; Zacheus; the multitude crying *Hofanna*, and finging, *Gloria, laus, et honor tibi fit.* Our Saviour praying in the garden; Judas going to betray him; Pilate and the high prieft fitting in judgment againft him; their fcourging him, and compelling him to bear his crofs; in the upper part of the window, he is crucified between two thieves.

6th. Jofeph of Arimathea and Nichodemus taking down the body, and placing it in the fepulchre; a reprefentation of the wonderful darknefs; St. Michael and his angels fighting the dragon and the fallen angels, with Belzebub looking through a fiery grate.

7th. The burial of our Saviour; the angel that rolled away the ftone, &c. with perfpective views of buildings in the garden; the transfiguration; Mofes and Elias; St. Peter, James, and John, with their three tabernacles; Jefus appearing to his mother, with this falutation, *Salve fancta parens.*

8th. Chrift appearing to two difciples going to Emmaus, and afterwards to the twelve apoftles.

9th. Jefus appearing to his difciples fifhing in the fea of Tiberias; the miraculous draught of fifhes; his afcenfion into heaven from the mount of Olives; the holy ghoft defcending on his difciples in the likenefs of a dove.

10th. In four compartments, 1. Peter, with a fcroll round his head, on which is written, *Credo in deum patrem omnipotentem, creatorem celi et terræ.* 2. St. Andrew, *Et in Jefum Chriftum filium ejus unicum dominum noftrum.* 3. St. James, *Qui conceptus eft de fpiritu fancto natus ex Maria virgine.* 4. St. John, *Paffus fub Pontio Pilato crucifixus mortuus et fepultus.*

11th. 1. St. Thomas, *Defcendit ad inferna tertio die refurrexit a mortuis.* 2. St. James, *Afcendit ad celos fedit ad dexteram dei patris omnipotentis.* 3. St. Philip, *Inde venturus iudicare vivos et mortuos.* 4. St. Bartholomew, *Credo in fpiritum fanctum.*

12th. 1. St. Matthias, *Sanctam ecclefiam catholicam fanct'um communionem.* 2. St. Simon, *Remiffionem peccatorum.* 3. St. Jude, *Carnis refurrectionem.* 4. St. Matthew, *Et vitam eternam. Amen.*

13th. The primitive fathers, St. Jerom, St. Gregory, St. Ambrofe, and St. Auguftin.

14th. King David fitting in judgment againft the Amalakite for flaying Saul.

15th. Is the great weft window, reprefenting the day of judgment. In the upper part, Chrift fits on the rainbow, incompaffed with cherubims. Below, St. Michael weighs a wicked perfon in one fcale, againft a good one in the other, and tho' a devil endeavours to turn the fcale, the good outweighs the bad. The dead are rifing out of their graves. From the mouth of an angel, receiving a faint into heaven, proceeds a label, on which is written, *Omnis fpe-s lauda d'um.* St. Peter, with the key, lets the bleffed into heaven, who, having paffed him, are cloathed in white, and have crowns of glory. In another part, is a reprefentation of hell, and the great devil, with red and white teeth, three eyes, fcaly legs and face. There is Dives praying for a drop of water, to cool his tongue; and Lazarus is placed in contraft among the bleffed, in Abraham's bofom; with many other devices, agreeable to the grofs ideas of the defigner. This window is of high eftimation.

16th. A little broken. Solomon determining the live child to the harlot; Midas king of Phrygia, with afs's ears; the ftory of Sampfon, Delilah, and the Philiftines; Jewifh fenators; and a piece of glafs faid to reprefent rubies and diamonds.

17th. The four evangelifts, with their fymbols. In the three next windows are the twelve prophets, with fcrolls round their heads, whereon are written the following felect parts of their prophefies.

18th. Hofea, *O tua mors ero tua* [not exact] c. xiii. 14. Amos, *Qui edificat in cælum afcenfione.* c. ix. 6. Malachi, - - - *udam ad vos judicio, et ero teftis velox.* c. iii. 5. Joel, *In valle Jofephat judicabit omnes gentes.* c. iii. 2.

19th. Zephaniah, *Invocabuntur omnes eum, & fervient ei.* c. iii. 9. Micah, *Eum odium habueris dimitte.* Ezekiel, *O v'am vos de fepulchris veftris pop'le meus.* c. xxxvii. 12. Obadiah, *Et erit reg'um d'ni amen.* v. 21.

20th. Jeremiah, *Datorem invocabitis qui fecit & indidit Jelos.* David, *Deus dixit, en filius meus es tu, ego hodie genui te.* Pf. ii. 7. Ifaiah, *Ecce virgo concipiet & pariet filium.* vii. 14. Zechariah, *Sufcitabo filios tuos.* ix. 13.

The remaining eight windows are in the body of the church. In the four on the north fide, are the perfecutors of the church, with devils over their heads, *viz.*

21ft. Domitian, Trajan, and Adrian.

22d. Antonine, Nero, and Marcus Aurelius.

23d. Herod, Severus, and Maximinus.

24th. Decius, Annanias, and Caleb.

25th, 26th, 27th, and 28th, (on the fouth fide) exhibit twelve antient worthies, preservers of the church, *viz.* Philippus, Valerianus, &c. with angels over them.

In the hiftorical pieces, are reprefented many other figures and circumftances not mentioned in this fhort account, but which are very proper appendages to the main fubjects. The whole was very happily preferved from the fury of men of an intemperate zeal in the great rebellion, by the care of Mr. Oldifworth, the impropriator, and others; not by turning the figures upfide down, as fome fuppofe, (for they never minded which end was upwards, if they were but images and paintings) but by fecuring the glafs in fome private place, 'till the reftoration, when it was put up again.

Monuments and Infcriptions.

In the north aile is a raifed monument, with the figures of a man and woman lying along on the

the top, for Roger Ligon, esq; and his wife, who had two husbands before she was married to him; first, Edmond Tame, esq; and secondly, sir Walter Buckle, privy counsellor to queen Elizabeth, who all lie buried in the church.

On a large flat stone of grey marble, are the figures of sir Edmond Tame, and his two wives, on brass plates; and upon plates of brass round the edge, it is thus written in antient black characters,

✠ Of youre charite pray for the soule of Edmond Tame knyght here under buried which decessid the first day of October in the yere of oure lord god a thousand ccccxxxiiij and for the soule of Agnes his first Wife which decessid the xxvi day of Iuly an° . . . . es & all xpēn soules Ihū have mercy Amen. ——On the dexter side, at top, are the arms of Tame, as before. On the sinister side, the same coat, impaling, *Sable, on a cross within a bordure ingrailed Or, five pellets*, for Grevil.

Under an arch, between the north and middle chancels, there is a very large, handsome tomb of grey marble, polish'd, and in excellent preservation, for John Tame, esq; who built the church. The effigies of him and his wife are engraved on brass plates at top, and this writing stands at their feet:

For Ihūs loue pray for me: I may not pray nowe pray ye:
With a pater noster & an ave: That my paynys relessyd may be.

Round the verge of the top stone,

✠ Orate pro animabus Johīs Tame Armigeri et Alicie uxoris eius qui quidem Johēs obiit octauo die Mensis Maij anno dnī Milesimo quingentesimo et anno Regni Regis Henrici sept'i sextodecimo. Et predicta Alicia obiit vicesimo die Mensis Decembris anno Domini Millimo cccc° septuagesimo primo quorum aīabus propicietur dē. For Ihūs loue pray for me I may not pray now pray ye With a pater noster ande ave That my paynys relessyd may be. —— The tomb is ornamented at top and round the sides with several scutcheons of his arms, as before, and those of his wife, *viz. A chevron between three birds*, the species not distinguishable.

In the middle chancel are several memorials for the antient family of Oldisworth, among which are the two following:

Depositum AUSTINI OLDISWORTH prosapiâ veteri, utroq; nomine, oriundi: Viri inter Ecclesiæ Anglicanæ Fautores, inter Rei antiquariæ Studiosos, intra Affines, Cives, Amicos, et Familiares suos, diu multumq; desiderati. Obijt 27° die Augusti, Anno Salutis 1717, Ætatis Climacterico.

Sacrum Reliquiis
Venerabilis Viri
IACOBI OLDISWORTH,
Cujus
In Deo colendo Pietatem,
In curandis animis Diligentiam,
In Parochiali Regimine Authoritatem,
In Eleemosynis largiendis Fidem,
In OEconomiâ ordinandâ Prudentiam,
In Hospitiis celebrandis Alacritatem,
In Ecclesiis ornandis Munificentiam,
In omni demum vitæ stadio & Colore,
Integras Virtutes, moresq; castos & verè Christianos,
Tota hæc Vicinia,
Et ora omnium quibus innotuit,
Palam clamant, abundèq; testantur;
Dum in Posteros efferunt,
(Quod Historiam potius quam Epitaphium desideret)
Rarum et memorabile Exemplar.
Obijt tercio die Septembris MDCCXXII°.
Ætat. LXXXII°.

In a scutcheon at top are the family arms, *viz. Gules, on a fess argent three lioncels passant gardant purpure. A crescent for difference.*

On an oval marble table,

Near to this place lyeth the body of the Lady Bridget Tracy, Wife to the Right Honble the Lord Tracy, she was buried ye fifth of November, 1632. She was a Lady of excellent natural Parts, she understood ye Latin tongue & other useful parts of Learning; but that wch excells all, she was truly pious & charitable. Here also lyeth buryed her Eldest Daughter Marial, who was married to S^r^. William Poole of Saperton. Her youngest Daughter was Marryed to William Somervile, Esq; whose youngest son, M^r^. Benjamin, was a very beautiful Person and an excellent Scholar, for which he was most entirely beloved of his Mother. She bred him vp at Eaton School, and from thence removed him to Oxford, where he dyed in the nineteenth year of his age, and was buryed here by his Grandmother Tracy, December 3, 1686.
This Monument was erected by the Honble Mrs Somervile, to the worthy Memory of her most dear Mother, Sister, and Son. ———At bottom, Tracy impaling *Argent, a chevron between three escallops sable.*

Against the south wall of the chancel, without,

In Memory of
CHARLES MORGAN, Gent. of this Parish,
who departed this Life the 18th Day of August, 1754,
In the fortieth Year of his Age.
He was the only surviving Descendant
of a very antient Family,
Whose Virtues, together with their Possessions, he inherited.
By the uniform and unaffected Practice of the one,
As well as by a liberal Use of the other,
He truly merited and universally obtained
The distinguishing Characters
Of a faithful Friend, a good Neighbour, and a worthy honest Man.
Also of Elizabeth his Wife,
Who exchanged this Life for a better
The 12th Day of October, 1772, Aged 58 Years.
She succeeded her Consort in the Care and Education
of a numerous Family of Children,
A Charge which she most affectionately undertook,
And happily liv'd to accomplish:
And at her Departure, she left them,
As the best Rule of their future Conduct,
The amiable Pattern of her own Life and Manners.
In grateful Testimony of so much maternal Excellence,
They here unite their common Tribute of filial Regard and Veneration,
To the best of Mothers.

	£.	s.	d.		£.	s.	d.
First fruits	13	11	4	Synodals	0	6	8
Tenths —	1	7	1½	Pentecostals	0	1	6
Procurations	0	6	8				

Benefactions.

Lands called Church Lands, of the yearly value of 30*l.* are given for the repair of the church, the almshouse, and highways.

Thomas Morgan of Fairford, by his will, dated Nov. 20, 1632, gave the interest of 100*l.* to be distributed to the poor on Good-friday.

The lady Mico, of London, (sister to Elizabeth, wife of Andrew Barker, esq;) gave 400*l.* with which lands in Leachlade were purchased, and the rents are applied as she directed, to bind out four boys apprentices annually, out of the parish of Fairford. She likewise gave two dozen of bread to be distributed to the poor every Sunday; and the donation is secured by a rent charge on a meadow in Meysey-Hampton, called Settle Thorn.

The widow Cull, by her will, dated May 5, 1674, gave 20*l.* to the poor; and Morgan Emmetts gave 5*l.*

Mr. Smith of London, gave 30*s.* a year for teaching poor children to read, charged on his estate at Fairford, now the property of Mr. Raymond.

Andrew Barker, esq; gave 100*l.* for paving and seating the body of the church, which sum was apply'd to that purpose in 1703.

The honourable Mrs. Farmor, (daughter of lord Lemster, and grandaughter of Andrew Barker, esq;) by her will, gave 1000*l.* (now laid out in the purchase of an estate at Chasely in Worcestershire, which

which lets for 52*l.* a year,) for the maintenance of an afternoon lecture every Sunday, in the pariſh church; out of the profits of which eſtate, 1*l.* 5*s.* beſides one fifth of the remainder, after ſuch deduction, to be paid to a ſchool-maſter for teaching 20 poor children to read and write. And about the year 1738, a large, handſome ſchool-houſe was built. The nomination of the lecturer, ſchool-maſter, and ſcholars, is veſted in Mrs. Lamb, as heir of Samuel Barker, eſq. Mrs. Farmor likewiſe gave 200*l.* which was expended about the year 1725, in purchaſing the wire lattices, placed on the outſide of the church windows, to preſerve the glaſs from accidents.

William Butcher of this pariſh, who died June 17, 1715, gave the intereſt of 40*l.* to be diſtributed weekly to the poor in bread. But this money, with 30*l.* of the Good-friday's money, was apply'd in purchaſing a peſt-houſe; and the overſeers pay the intereſt of both ſums, for the uſe of the poor.

The reverend Mr. Huntingdon, in 1738, gave the intereſt of 10*l.* to be diſtributed to the poor in bread, on the anniverſary of his funeral, Aug. 12.

Mr. Robert Jenner, in 1770, gave 10*l.* the intereſt whereof to be diſtributed annually to five poor widows.

Alexander Colſton, eſq; who died in 1775, gave the intereſt of 100*l.* to the poor.

Elizabeth, relict of Andrew Barker, gave the large ſilver communion flaggon, and one ſilver paten, on both which are the family arms.

Thomas Delves, eſq; gave one large branch candleſtick; and William Butcher gave the other.

Taxes.					
	The Royal Aid in	1692, £.	145	15	8
	Poll-tax ——	1694, —	35	16	0
	Land-tax ——	1694, —	150	11	1
	The ſame, at 3*s.*	1770, —	112	14	0

At the beginning of the preſent century, there were 143 houſes, and about 660 inhabitants in this pariſh, whereof 18 were freeholders; yearly births 20, burials 14. *Atkyns.* The inhabitants are now increaſed to about 1200.

FARMINGTON

IS a ſmall pariſh, in the hundred of Bradley, in the Coteſwold country, two miles northward from Northleach, eight weſtward from Burford in Oxfordſhire, and twenty-one eaſt from Glouceſter.

About ſeven hundred years ago, the name of this place was *Tormentone.* It was afterwards variouſly written in the records, according to the different judgment of perſons in office; as, *Thormenton, Thormarton*; which come ſo near to *Tormarton*, the name of another pariſh in this county, that, if ſome miſtakes have happened in the application of particulars, it will be the more excuſable. The modern name of this pariſh is *Farmington*, but I am totally ignorant of its ſignification.

The face of this part of the country is turgid, uneven, and almoſt wholly deſtitute of plantations, in which laſt particular, there is certainly great room for improvement. The ſoil produces very good corn, to which the greater part is appropriated; and the farmers give much attention to the breed of their ſheep, for which they are deſervedly famous.

Norbury-camp, mentioned by ſir Robert Atkyns, and others, as being in Farmington, lies in the hamlet of Eaſtington, in the pariſh of Northleach, where the particulars of it are given.

The turnpike-road from Glouceſter to Oxford paſſes thro' this pariſh; and a ſtream from a ſpring, which riſes here, empties itſelf into the Windruſh, below Sherbourn.

Of the Manor and other Eſtates.

This is ſet down as part of the large manor of Lecce, [now Northleach] in *Domeſday-book*, where it is ſaid, 'There are two plow-tillages in demean 'at Tormentone, and twenty-five villeins, with 'twelve plow-tillages, and four *ſervi.*' *D.B.* p. 70.

Thomas de Blachamp and William Haſtings were ſeized of the manor of Thormenton, which they held by the ſervice of one knight's fee, 5 E. 1. and Peter de Staunton held the manor 16 E. 1. About this time it paſſed to the St. Phileberts; for Benedict Blakenham had licence to alienate one plow-tillage, and the advowſon of the chapel, to Henry de St. Philebert, 26 E. 1. John de St. Philebert, ſon of Henry, ſucceeded, and held the manor, with free warren, 14 E. 2. and died ſeized thereof 7 E. 3. leaving ſir John de St. Philebert, his ſon and heir, who levied a fine, and ſold the manor and advowſon of Thormenton, for 200 marks, to William de Eddington, biſhop of Wincheſter, 25 E. 3. The biſhop gave this manor to the Auguſtin priory of Bonhommes, at Edington in Wiltſhire, which he founded in 1352. It was dedicated to St. James, St. Catherine, and All Saints, and valued at the diſſolution at 521*l.* 12*s.* 0½*d.*

After the diſſolution of the priory, the manor and advowſon of Thormarton were granted to Michael Aſhfield 32 H. 8. who dying the ſame year, livery was granted to his ſon Robert 4 Mar. Robert Aſhfield, eſq; was lord of the manor in 1608, and ſold it to ſir Rice Jones, whoſe deſcendant, ſir Henry Jones, diſtinguiſhed himſelf in the wars in Flanders, and was ſlain there, leaving an only daughter and heireſs, married to the earl of Scarborough, who, in her right, was lord of the manor about the beginning of this century. Of him it was purchaſed by Edmond Waller, eſq; whoſe ſon Edmond Waller, eſq; is the preſent lord of the manor. His arms are, *Azure, on a bend ſable cotized argent, three walnut leaves Or.*

The following records ſeem to belong to Farmington, tho' ſir Robert Atkyns has placed them under Tormarton, where the Phileberts hadno concern.

William de Haſtings levied a fine of lands in Tormarton [it ſhould be Tormentone] to Benedict Blakenham and Julian, or Joan, his wife, 1 E. 1. John

John de St. Philebert levied a fine of lands in Tormarton to Roger de Afperley, and Juliana his wife; and they reconvey Juliana's right of dower to John de St. Philebert, referving a rent of 20*l.* for her life, 5 E. 3. Thomas Hungerford, and others, were feized of 14*s.* rent, iffuing out of two meffuages and two yard-lands in Tormarton, in truft for the priory of Bonhommes, at Edington in Wiltfhire, 16 R. 2.

Of the Church, &c.

The church is a rectory, in the deanery of Cirencefter, worth 120*l.* a year; Edmond Waller, efq; is patron, Mr. Binam the prefent incumbent.

The church, dedicated to St. Peter, is a fmall building, neatly pewed, with a low tower at the weft end, in which are three bells. The inhabitants of this parifh formerly buried at Northleach.

Firft fruits £.	16	5	4	Synodals £.	0	2	0
Tenths —	1	12	6½	Pentecoft.	0	0	8
Procurations	0	6	8				

Monument and Infcription.

On a flat blue ftone in the chancel,

MARIAM juxta Uxorem,
IOHANNES EYKYN, LL. B.
Iftius Ecclefiæ Rector,
Diem hic expectat
Supremum.
Tu vero Lector Vigila
Ne Dies tremendus ille
Tibi fuperveniat
Inopinanti.

I. E. } ob. { Jul. 27°, 1734, } AN. { 63.
M. E. } ob. { Nov. 24, 1729, } AN. { 68.

Taxes.					
The Royal Aid in	1692, £.	53	18	10
Poll-tax ——	1694, —	6	9	0
Land-tax ——	1694, —	57	7	0
The fame, at 3*s.*	1770, —	33	3	0

At the beginning of the prefent century, according to fir Robert Atkyns, there were 25 houfes in this parifh, and about 100 inhabitants, whereof 3 were freeholders; yearly births 3, burials 3. The prefent number of houfes is 38, of inhabitants exactly 195.

FILTON *and* HAY.

THIS is a fmall parifh, in the lower divifion of the hundred of Berkeley, four miles north from Briftol, eight fouth from Thornbury, and thirty fouth-weftward from Gloucefter.

The turnpike-road from Gloucefter to Briftol leads through it, and one of the heads of the river *Trim*, or *Trin*, rifes in it, and runs to Weftbury. The name is fuppofed to be compounded of *fell*, *rocky*, *ftony*; and *ton*, a common termination.

Of the Manor and other Eftates.

At the time of the general furvey, in the reign of king William the Firft, this was a part of Horfelle, (now written Horfield) wherefore there is no account of the manor in *Domefday-book*, under the name by which it is known at prefent. But Robert Fitz-Harding having given the other part of Horfelle to St. Auguftin's monaftery at Briftol, this began to be diftinguifhed from it, by the name of Felleton, and Filton.

Sir Thomas Fitz-Nichols, defcended from the above Robert Fitz-Harding, died feized of this manor 16 R. 2. and was fucceeded by his fon, Thomas Fitz-Nichols, who died 6 H. 5. leaving two daughters coheireffes; of whom, Elianor, the elder, was married to John Browning, of Haresfield; whereby John Browning, fon of John, became feized of this manor 8 H. 5.

But it was probably a moiety of the manor only, becaufe the records fhew, that the manor of Filton, which I fuppofe to be the other moiety, was held by the Blounts, about the time of the above dates. Edward Blount and Margaret his wife were feized of it 4 R. 2. and Wenteline, widow of John Blount, died feized of the fame, and of Bitton, 32 H. 6.

Thomas Mallet, efq; died feized of this manor 22 Eliz. and left John, his fon, twelve years old at his father's death. Mr. Pope was late lord of this manor.

Robert Fitz-Harding gave fix meffuages in this parifh to the abbey of St. Auguftin's in Briftol, wherefore the abbat would have them confidered as parcel of the manor of Horfield; and accordingly his claim to a court leet in Horfield and Filton was allowed, in a writ of *Quo warranto*, 15 E. 1. After the diffolution of that abbey, thefe lands in Filton were granted, with the manor of Horfield, to the bifhoprick of Briftol, 34 H. 8. and they now belong to that bifhoprick. Thefe lands were afterwards deemed a manor, for in Willis's edition of *Ecton's Thefaurus*, it is faid, the manors of Horfield and Filton were fold out of the bifhoprick, to Thomas Andrews, for 1256*l.* 14*s.* in the year 1649.

HAMLET. *Hay* is a hamlet in this parifh. John Newton, burgefs of Briftol, and Joan his wife, levied a fine of lands in Le Hay, near Filton, to the ufe of themfelves in fpecial taille; and John Newton, fon of John, levied a fine of the fame lands, to the ufe of William Moor, 28 H. 6. Henry Strangeways and Catherine his wife levied a fine of lands in Filton and Herry-Stoke 16 H. 7.

A meadow in this parifh belonged to the Magdalen hofpital in Briftol, and was granted to John Bellowe and John Bloxolme 37 H. 8.

Of the Church, &c.

The church is a rectory, in the deanery of Briftol, worth about 80*l.* a year. The lord of the manor is patron, and Mr. Davis the prefent incumbent. This is one of the fmall livings augmented by Mr. Colfton's donation.

The rectory and advowfon of the vicarage of Filton antiently belonged to the abbey of St. Auguftin's in Briftol, and after the diffolution of that abbey, were granted to the bifhop of Briftol, 34 H. 8. But I underftand by the word rectory,

rectory, in this place, nothing more than the tithes of the ſix meſſuages which belonged to that abbey, as already obſerved.

The church, dedicated to St. Peter, is ſmall, with a little aile on each ſide of the nave, and a low tower, with five bells, at the weſt end, which had a ſpire, blown down about ninety years ſince.

Firſt fruits £.7 0 0 Procurations £.0 3 4
Tenths — 0 14 0

Taxes.					
The Royal Aid in	1692, £.	84	4	0
Poll-tax ——	1694, —	9	13	8
Land-tax ——	1694, —	94	0	0
The ſame, at 3*s*.	1770, —	70	18	0

At the beginning of this century, there were 20 houſes, and about 80 inhabitants in this pariſh, whereof 6 were freeholders; yearly births 2, burials 2. *Atkyns*. There are now about 125 inhabitants.

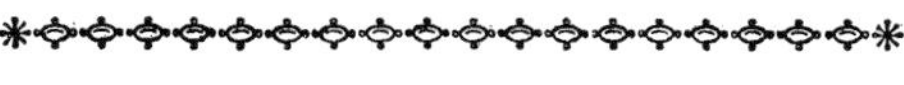

FLAXLEY

IS a pariſh of no great extent, in the hundred of St. Briavel's, in the foreſt diviſion of the county, two miles diſtant ſouth-eaſt from Mitchel-Dean, three north from Newnham, and ten ſouth-weſtward from Glouceſter. The name was antiently written *Flaxlyn*, which comes from *glyn*, *a valley*; and agrees with the ſituation of the place. The pariſh conſiſts chiefly of paſture and woodlands The manufacture of the place is iron, for making of which there is a furnace and forges.

An abbey was founded here, by Roger, the ſecond earl of Hereford, in the reign of king Henry the Firſt, for monks of the Ciſtertian order,[n] who were Benedictines reformed. The founding of which ſeems to have been occaſioned by an accident which happened to the earl's brother, who was killed by an arrow in hunting, in the very place where the abbey was afterwards built, as Leland found it related in a table hung up in the abbey church. King Henry the Second, whilſt duke of Normandy, gave the monks of this place a charter, confirming to them their lands and poſſeſſions; and afterwards, when king of England, he gave them another; both which charters are inſerted in the *Appendix* N°. 15 and 16. In the former, ſome particulars omitted in ſir Robert Atkyns's tranſlation are ſupply'd. In the latter, it is obſervable, that the abbat and his conventuals are called *the monks of Dene*; whereby it appears, that Flaxley was at that time appurtenant to Dene, and not a diſtinct pariſh; and the lands, at this time, lie very confuſed and intermixt with thoſe of Little-Dean, and with the woods of the foreſt.

The abbey was ſituated in the valley of Caſtiard, a name at preſent unknown to the pariſhioners. It was under the juriſdiction of the biſhop of Hereford,[o] by whom the abbats were conſecrated.

[n] It has been already ſhewn, (p. 11) by what means lands, formerly belonging to the Ciſtertian monaſteries, and ſome others, became exempt from tithes; and it is well known that ever ſince the diſſolution of the houſes to which they belonged, they have been privileged with the ſame exemption. But Mr. Stevens has given a very extraordinary opinion reſpecting ſuch lands, in the ſecond volume of his *Supplement to the Monaſticon*, which deſerves to be taken notice of. It is on the ſtate of the caſe of the owners and inheritors of certain lands within the lordſhip of Bernoldſwick, by them and their anceſtors purchaſed from king Henry the Eighth.

He ſtates, that thoſe lands were given to the Ciſtertian abbey of Kirkſtall, before the Lateran council, and were of their own manure and tillage. And that by the ſaid Lateran council it was declared, that the lands poſſeſſed by the Ciſtertians, before the holding of that council, ſhould pay no tithes.

Now comes the opinion, which Mr. Stevens produces to determine the preſent right of exemption from tithes. His words are theſe:

'In fine, it has been reſolved, by council learned in the law, 'that the land purchaſed in fee of king Henry the VIIIth, and 'occupied by the owners of the inheritance, being of the Ciſtercian order, and given to the abbey before the Lateran council, 'as this of Bernoldſwick was, ought to be free by law, whilſt it 'continues in the occupation of any owner of the inheritance, 'but when it is in leaſe or farm, the privilege does not extend to 'the farmer or tenant, and ſo they ought to pay.'

How happy is it for the proprietors of ſuch lands that the opinion or *reſolution* of Mr. Stevens's learned council does not conſtitute a law. I have elſewhere expreſs'd my diſapprobation of matters being ſo ſettled at the Reformation, as not to make better proviſion out of appropriations, for ſome of the parochial clergy. But, as things now are, it would be the higheſt injuſtice to take away thoſe exemptions, eſpecially from eſtates which have paſſed by purchaſe through ſeveral hands, and valuable conſiderations have been paid on account of them.

Mr. Stevens was no friend to the Reformation, as appears from ſeveral exceptionable paſſages collected from ſir Henry Spelman's *Hiſtory of Sacrilege*, and other ſources. Having ſhewn that king Henry the Eighth granted the ſcite of Rufford monaſtery, in Nottinghamſhire, and all its lordſhips, to the earl of Shrewſbury, he ſays, 'From the aforeſaid earl of Shrewſbury, this eſtate came by the 'females (the male line being extinct) to the family of the 'Saviles, the laſt of which line alſo was the famous viſcount, 'then earl, and laſtly marquis of Halifax, in the reign of king 'Charles and king James the Second; where we ſee the bane of 'thoſe church-lands attending both thoſe great families, quite 'extinguiſhed in ſo ſhort a time; I mean that line of the Saviles, 'for I know there are ſtill others of other branches.' And again, after ſhewing that Ralph Rowlet the elder, had a grant from king Henry the Eighth of the manor of Byſhemead, which belonged to the abbey of that place, in Bedfordſhire, he proceeds with the deſcent of the manor to Ralph his ſon and heir, who died without iſſue; and then concludes, 'Thus the family was extinct in the 'firſt heir that took poſſeſſion of this land dedicated to God.'

There is nothing in which men ſo much diſagree as in their notions of religion; nor is there any eſtabliſhment but may gain a degree of reſpect from habit and education. This makes reformation difficultly effected; for the ſmalleſt changes from eſtabliſhed principles and forms diſguſt vulgar minds. Nay we ſee that ſome perſons of learning cannot part from what they have been taught to venerate without great reluctance, tho' the ſeeming loſs ſhould be real gain. Hence they remonſtrate and complain; but ſurely the zeal of theſe men has carried them too far, in repreſenting the want of iſſue in one family, and a decline in fortune in another, (for that is alledged by them in ſome inſtances) as the judgment of God, particularly ſent to puniſh ſuch perſons as have not acted agreeably to their peculiar mode of thinking, by purchaſing lands which formerly belonged to diſſolved monaſteries; whereas they are nothing more than common events, which have happened to all ſorts of people, and are daily brought about in all countries, under every kind of eſtabliſhment.

[o] This appears from ſeveral entries in the regiſter books of the biſhops of that dioceſe, particularly in the following years, 1288 fol. 53; 1314, fol. 189; 1372, fol. 11; 1426, fol. 107; 1509, fol. 45. The following is extracted from the regiſter book of biſhop Courtenay:

6 Julii 1372, Apud Sugwas Dnūs Richardus Payto monaſterii de Flaxley Heref[d] Dioceſ. electus abbas. Fuit per dnūm intra miſſarum ſolennia benedictus, et profeſſionem in ſcriptis fecit ſub hac forma verborum. Ego Richardus eccleſiæ ſuæ monaſterii de Flaxley Heref. dioceſ. electus abbas, profiteor ſanctæ Hereford eccleſiæ tibique Patri Willīmo, ejuſdemque eccleſiæ epiſcopo, tuiſque ſucceſſoribus in ea canonice ſubſtituendis, canonicam in omnibus obedientiam et ſubjectionem. Et idem abbas ſubſequenter crucem ſubſcripſit talem, ✛ jure / ſalvo ✛ ordine / noſtro — additis in verbis, ſalvo jure ordine noſtro. Preſentibus dominis Tho: Peyto, Thoma de Breynton, et Hugone Frene, vicariis chori eccleſiæ cathedralis Hereford. et aliis.

It was dedicated to the virgin Mary, and valued at the diſſolution at 112*l.* 3*s.* 1*d.* a year, as I find it ſet down in a table of the value of all the monaſteries in England, taken from a manuſcript in the Cotton library. Thomas Ware was the laſt abbat, who retired, after the diſſolution of his houſe, to Tame in Oxfordſhire, where he died in the year 1546. The abbey church is ſo totally demoliſhed, that it can only be gueſſed where it ſtood.

Of the Manor and other Eſtates.

In *Domeſday-book*, this manor is included in the general account of Dene. It was given to the abbey at the foundation of it, by Roger, earl of Hereford. The abbat had a grant of an iron forge, and of two oaks every week out of the foreſt of Dean, for the maintenance of the forge, of king Henry the Second. But the taking of the two oaks was very deſtructive to the foreſt, wherefore the monks had a wood granted to them inſtead thereof, 42 H. 3.

This manor, with the wood, continued in the poſſeſſion of the abbey 'till the diſſolution; and was afterwards granted to ſir William Kingſton, who died ſeized thereof 32 H. 8. and livery was granted to ſir Anthony Kingſton, ſon of ſir William, the ſame year; who, by his deed, conveyed it to the king, and in the 36th year of the ſame reign, the king, by his letters patent, regranted to him the ſcite of the late abbey or monaſtery of Flaxley, and all the church, bell-houſe, and church-yard of the ſame, and all the houſes, buildings, rivers, pools, lands, grounds and ſoils of the ſame, as well within as without the ſaid ſcite; and alſo all other the manors and granges of Flaxley houſe, &c. &c.

William Kingſton, eſq; was lord of the manor in the year 1608, ſoon after which it paſſed to Abraham Clarke, eſq; who died ſeized of it in 1683.

From him the manor went to his relation, William Bovey, eſq; who dying in 1692, his widow enjoy'd it; after whom it paſſed to Thomas Crawley, eſq; who aſſumed the name and arms of Bovey. He married a daughter of —— Lloyd, by whom he had iſſue ſeveral children, and dying in the year 1775, poſſeſſed of a large eſtate in this pariſh, was ſucceeded by his ſon Thomas-Crawley Bovey, eſq; the preſent lord of the manor. The arms of Bovey are, *Ermine, on a bend gules and ſable, between two martlets of the latter, three gutties d'Or.*

The manor houſe is that wherein the abbat formerly lived, with ſome addition to it. Notwithſtanding it is a long, low building, of two ſtories, it has a handſome and venerable appearance.

Richard Brain, eſq; died ſeized of lands in Flaxley 15 Eliz. and left Thomas, his grandſon, twenty years old at his grandfather's death.

Of the Church, &c.

The church is a curacy, in the deanery of the foreſt. The lord of the manor is patron, Mr. Crawley is the preſent incumbent. The church was formerly appropriated to the abbey of Flaxley. The impropriation belongs to Mr. Bovey, who pays 8*l.* a year out of it to the curate; who beſides has the intereſt of 1200*l.* left by Mrs. Bovey, to improve the curacy. The church is very ſmall. It was rebuilt by Mrs. Pope.

Monuments and Inſcriptions.

There is the following memorial on an old monument in the chancel:

On George Kingſton, Gent. who was buried Mar. 4 1644
Vixi dum vellem, moriebar tempore grato,
Et ſic vita mihi, mors quoque grata fuit.
Kings have ſtones on them when they die,
And here Kingſtone under a ſtone doth lie.
Thus prince, nor peer, nor any mortal wight,
Can ſhun Death's dart; Death ſtill will have his right.
O then bethink to what you all muſt truſt
At laſt to die, & come to Judgment juſt.

On the table of a handſome monument,

Hic dormit Abrahamus Clarke, Armiger, beatam reſurrectionem expectans. In omni vita modeſtus ac ſobrius, Juſtitiæ, Equitatis, cultor eximius. Summa in amicos fide, veraque in Deum pietate, conſpicuus. Egenorum fautor ac patronus, Orphanorum pater. Liberalitatem exercere maluit quam oſtentare. Alios munificentiæ teſtes preter Deum ægre admiſit. Satis Ei magnum ad virtutem incitamentum, rectæ factorum conſcientiæ. Obiit Decem. 5, A. D. 1683, Ætat. 61.

On another,

M. S. Gulielmi Bovey Armig. qui fide et fama ornatiſſimus; non fui parcus, non appetens alieni; nemini notus ex injuria, E beneficentia innumeris. Maximam vitæ partem feliciter tranſegit; tandem vero, cum mole corporis obeſiſſimi anima nimium opreſſa, ſuſpiraret, graviter et gemeret, ut liberiorem ſui copiam haberet; Deo miſerante, ad Superos migravit lætiſſime, Aug. 26, A. D. 1692, Æt. 35. H. M. Catharina conjux fidiſſima M. P.

Benefactions.

Abraham Clarke, eſq; gave 60*l.* to the poor. William Bovey, eſq; gave 100*l.* to the ſame uſe. The widow Conſtance gave 20*s.* a year to the poor. Mrs. Bovey gave 1200*l.* to augment the curacy; and left 600*l.* more, now laid out in lands by truſtees; two thirds for apprenticing children of the pariſh; the remainder for buying religious books for the poor of this pariſh, and of Little-Dean.

Taxes.						
	The Royal Aid in	1692,	£. 112	0	0
	Poll-tax ——	1694, —	20	11	0
	Land-tax ——	1694, —	156	13	0
	The ſame, at 3*s.*	1770, —	115	10	9

When ſir Robert Atkyns compiled his account of this pariſh, there were, according to him, 40 houſes, and about 200 inhabitants, whereof 4 were freeholders; yearly births 5, burials 4. There are now about 196 inhabitants.

FORTHAMPTON.

THIS is a ſmall pariſh, in the lower diviſion of Tewkeſbury hundred, three miles weſt from Tewkeſbury, and eight north from Glouceſter.

It is bounded on the north ſide by Worceſterſhire, and has the river Severn running on the eaſt of it, for about half a mile. In the road from this

this place to Tewkeſbury, is a paſſage over that river, called the Lower Load.

The pariſh conſiſts chiefly of rich paſture ground. Dr. York, biſhop of St David's, has repaired the roads in this pariſh, at a great expence, which before were exceedingly bad. The oak delights in a deep ſoil, and flouriſhes here; but the tenants have committed intolerable waſte, by polling the trees, that they may afterwards take the lop. This is the leſs excuſable, as coals, brought down the river from Shropſhire and Staffordſhire, are very reaſonable.

Of the Manor and other Eſtates.

This manor was in the crown at the time of general ſurvey. Among the particulars of the large manor of Tewkeſbury, in *Domeſday-book*, it is thus recorded :

' In Fortemeltone nine hides belonged to this ' manor [of Teodekeſberie.] There are two plow- ' tillages in demean, and twenty plow-tillages are ' ſhared among the villeins and bordars, and ſix ' among the *ſervi* and *ancillæ*. There is a wood. ' It was worth 10*l.* in the time of king Edward, ' now [only] 8*l* Earl William held theſe two ' eſtates [*i.e.* Hanlege and Fortemeltone] and they ' paid tax in behalf of Tewkeſbury.' *D. B.* p. 68.

King Henry the Second gave to the abbey of Tewkeſbury the vill of Ferthelmenton, which was held of the honour of Robert Fitz-Hamon; and the abbey had court leet, waifs, and felons goods therein, which were allowed them, in a writ of *Quo warranto*, 15 E. 1.

The manor continued in the poſſeſſion of the abbey 'till its diſſolution. And the manor-houſe of Forthampton, and certain lands there, were granted to Giles Harper 33 H. 8. The manor was afterwards granted to Robert, earl of Saliſbury, 5 Jac. Charles Dowdeſwell, eſq; was lord of the manor at the beginning of this century. His ſucceſſor, Charles Dowdeſwell, eſq; ſold it to Samuel Clarke, eſq; and he ſold it to Dr. Iſaac Maddox, late lord biſhop of Worceſter. His lordſhip left iſſue one only daughter, who, after his death, was married to the honourable Dr. James Yorke, now lord biſhop of St. David's, who in right of his wife, is the preſent lord of this manor, and proprietor of a large eſtate in this pariſh, where he has a handſome ſeat. His lordſhip's arms are, *Argent, a ſaltire azure, with a bezant in the center.*

Mr. Hayward has a good houſe and eſtate in this pariſh.

A portion of tithes in Forthampton and Buſhley, with a paſture ground called Oxley, lately belonging to the abbey of Tewkeſbury, were granted to Edward lord Clinton 1 E. 6. The cloſe called Oxley was granted to Roger Dowdeſwell 7 Jac.

HAMLETS. 1. *Swaily.* Edward earl of Stafford held Swaily, 4 H. 4.

Down-end is another hamlet.

Of the Church, &c.

The church is a curacy, within the peculiar of Derhurſt, value 13*l.* 6*s.* 8*d.* paid by the impropriator. The lord of the manor is patron and impropriator. The impropriation formerly belonged to the abbey of Tewkeſbury.

The church is dedicated to St. Mary. It is a large building, and ſtands on a riſing ground, with a ſtrong tower, and five bells, at the weſt end.

Pentecoſtals - - - $9\frac{1}{2}$*d.*

Monuments and Inſcriptions.

On a marble monument in the chancel,

Hic infra reconduntur Cineres Notabilis Viri Caroli Dowdeſwell, ex hac Parochia Armigeri. Filius erat Richardi Dowdeſwell, nuper de Pool-Court in Comitatu Wigorn. Armigeri, natu maximus. Vir probitate et induſtria inſignis, quippe qui paternas opes laudabili modo ampliavit. Duos filios, Carolum ſcilicet et Richardum, et tres filias, Margaretam, Georgio Smith, Armigero, de North Nibley in hoc Comitatu, nuptam; Elizabetham, Gualtero Yates, de Bromſberowe, in Com. prædict. Armigero, deſponſatam; et Annam adhuc Virginem, ſuperſtites reliquit, ex Elizabethâ filia Tim. Coles, de Hatfield in Comitatu Hereford. Armigeri, ſuſceptos. Annos vixit ſeptuaginta et duos, et tandem, divitiarum et deliciarum hujus mundi ſatur, melioribus politus obiit 21° die Octobris, Anno Chriſti 1706. ——— Arms, *Baron and femme*, 1. *Or, a feſs undy between ſix billets ſable*, for Dowdeſwell. 2. *Gules, on a feſs Or three bars gemels of the firſt, between three leopards heads erazed of the ſecond*, for Coles.

On a flat ſtone in the church,

H. S. E. Hopewellus Hayward, Gen. probitate et induſtria inſignis. Obijt 20 die Ian. Anno Dom. 1722, Ætatis 76.

Hic quoque jacet Eliz[a]. Hayward, ejus uxor, ſeptem Liberorum Mater. Qualis erat, ſupremus ille dies indicabit, in quo omnes a Deo Laudem accipient. Ob. 26° Feb. 1728, Æt. 50. ——— Arms, *Baron and femme*, 1. *On a bend three fleurs de lis, in chief a lion paſſant.* 2. *A croſs patonce.*

There are alſo other memorials for the family of the Dowdeſwells, for the Haywards, and for Alice, the wife of Richard Betts, and daughter of John Colles, eſq; who died in 1694.

Taxes.					
	The Royal Aid in	1692,	£. 205	18	0
	Poll-tax — —	1694, —	32	13	0
	Land-tax ——	1694, —	125	16	8
	The ſame, at 3*s.*	1770, —	96	11	3

At the beginning of this century, there were 40 houſes, and about 160 inhabitants in this pariſh, whereof 8 were freeholders; yearly births 6, burials 6. *Atkyns.* Since which time the inhabitants are increaſed to about 208.

FRAMPTON

IS a village in the hundred of Whitſton, in the vale part of the county; bounded on the north by the river Severn, on the ſouth-weſt by Slimbridge, on the north-eaſt by Whitminſter, and on the north-weſt by Arlingham. It is ten miles ſouth-weſt from Glouceſter, eight weſtward from Stroud, ſeven north of Durſley, and five ſouth from Newnham, acroſs the Severn. The pariſh conſiſts of rich paſture, meadow, and ſome arable land, with gravel in many places little more than a foot below the ſurface. The water riſes almoſt to the top of the gravel, ſo that the houſes have no cellaring.

The

The Stroud river, whoſe name I ſuppoſe to be the *Froom*, riſes at Brimpsfield; paſſes by, and gives name to Frampton, a hamlet in the pariſh of Saperton; runs to Froomhill or Froomill, near Stroud, and ſo on to Froombridge in this pariſh; and at length empties itſelf into the Severn at Framilode, *i. e. the emptying of the Froom*; for *lode* comes from laꝺian, which in the Saxon language, ſignifies *to empty*. Theſe circumſtances ſeem to prove that *Froom* is the true name of the river, which it has communicated to this village, for *Frampton* ſignifies *the town upon the Froom*. It is generally called *Frampton upon Severn*, to diſtinguiſh it from another Frampton, near Briſtol. What ſir Robert Atkyns ſays of the Berkeley river bounding this pariſh on the ſouth, is ſo great a miſtake, that it is in no part within ſeveral miles of it.

The turnpike-road to the paſſages over the Severn, at Framilode and Arlingham, leads thro' this village, which is one of the handſomeſt and pleaſanteſt in the county. It conſiſts chiefly of one ſtreet; and tho' the houſes are not all joined together, after the manner of our market-towns, yet they ſtand in two ſtraight rows, parallel to each other, with the ſpace of about one hundred and fifty yards between them.

The piece of ground, or ſtreet, between the rows of houſes, was formerly called *Roſamond's-Green*, from the name of an unfortunate lady of the family of the Cliffords, whoſe ſtory is pretty well known.

On the ſouth ſide, about the middle of this vaſt ſtreet, is an elegant free-ſtone houſe, with large offices and gardens, ſuitable to the fortune and dignity of a nobleman. This was the ſeat of the late Richard Clutterbuck, eſq; deceaſed. It is built on the very ſcite of the antient family manſion of the Cliffords. To this gentleman the neighbourhood is indebted for the improved ſtate of the pariſh. The green I have been ſpeaking of, is a flat piece of ground, and 'till lately was generally overflowed with water in the winter, and conſequently very rotten. The road was almoſt impaſſable, and the inhabitants extremely ſubject to agues. But he made underground drains to carry off the water, and threw up a fine, ſtraight, gravelly road, through the middle of the lawn, which contributes to give the place that beautiful appearance, for which it is ſo deſervedly admired. And ſince the drains have been made, the people are as free from the ague, as the inhabitants of any part of the vale.

At Froombridge in this pariſh, hath been lately erected one of the largeſt and compleateſt works in the kingdom, for making of iron and ſteel wire, uſed in this and ſome of the neighbouring counties, more eſpecially in the manufacture of cards for the clothing buſineſs. From this work alſo that valuable branch of our commerce, the Newfoundland fiſhery, is partly ſupply'd with ſteel wire for fiſh-hooks, to a very conſiderable amount annually. And at this place alſo there is a braſs-work lately erected.

Of the Manor and other Eſtates.

'Drogo the ſon of Ponz holds Frantone of the 'king. There are ten hides taxed. Erneſi held it. 'There are three plow-tillages in demean, and 'ten villeins, and eight bordars, with ſix plow-'tillages. There are nine *ſervi*, and a mill of 10*s*. '[value] and ten acres of meadow, a wood one 'mile long and three furlongs broad, one burgage 'in Glouceſter of 6*d*. [value]. It is worth and 'was worth 100*s*. Roger de Laci holds unjuſtly 'one hide of this manor.' *Domeſday-book*, p. 77.

Ponz was a noble Norman, whoſe three ſons, Walter, Drogo, and Richard, attended king William in his invaſion of England. Drogo died ſeized of this manor without iſſue 20 W. 1. and was ſucceeded by his brother Richard, who had large revenues in Wales, and was a great benefactor to the priory of Malvern in Worceſterſhire. He had two ſons, Simon and Walter, which latter being ſeated at Clifford in Herefordſhire, took the ſurname of Clifford, and had this manor of Frampton ſettled upon him.[p] He had iſſue two ſons, Walter and Richard, and two daughters, whereof Roſamond, the younger, was the famous miſtreſs to Henry the Second,[q] and mother to William Long Eſpee, earl of Saliſbury. The manor of Frampton was ſettled on Richard, the younger ſon, who had livery of it 2 R. 1. He married Lettice, daughter of William de Albaniaco, of Camber.

Sir Hugh Clifford, ſon of Richard, ſucceeded him in this manor, and died ſeized thereof, with markets and fairs, 38 H. 3. Sir John Clifford was his ſon and heir, and died ſeized of Frampton 27 E. 1. He had a ſon Richard, and two daughters, who died before him, whereby[r] Iſabel, his only

[p] He gave a mill in Frampton, and a meadow adjoining to it, called Lecton, to the nuns of Godſtow in Oxfordſhire, to pray for the ſouls of Margaret his wife, and Roſamond his daughter.

[q] She died at Woodſtock, in a ſpacious and large appartment which king Henry the Second cauſed to be made for her, with great art, like a labyrinth, on purpoſe to ſecure her from the violence of queen Eleanor, who neverthelefs, if we believe the common report, found out the paſſage, and poiſoned her. But John Brompton and Henry Knighton tell us, that ſhe died a natural death, ſoon after ſhe had been incloſed in the ſaid apartment. And the ſame thing is alſo aſſerted by Ranulph Higden. She was buried in the choir of the nunnery of Godſtow, and it is ſaid the following epitaph was placed upon her tomb:

Hic jacet in tumba Roſa mundi, non Roſa munda;
Non redolet, ſed olet, quæ redolere ſolet.

But Higden and Knighton have both of them *quod* for *quæ* in the laſt line.

[r] Thus it appears that the manor went out of the name of the Cliffords by the marriage of this Iſabel; but the capital meſſuage and divers lands in Frampton remained in a younger branch of that name, who in a lineal deſcent are ſeized of part of them at this preſent time, as may be ſeen by the following pedigree: Henry Clifford (brother of ſir Hugh, who was grandfather of Iſabel) was living 12 E. 1. and held an eſtate in Frampton. William Clifford, ſon of Henry, had to his ſecond wife, Catherine, daughter of Ralph de St. Maur. William Clifford his ſon died 15 E. 2. John, ſon of William, was conſtituted warden of the foreſt of Bradon in Wiltſhire, 1 H. 4. Here is a deficiency in the pedigree. Henry Clifford, ſon of James, was high ſheriff of Glouceſterſhire 27 H. 6. James Clifford, ſon of Henry, was buried

only ſurviving daughter, became his ſole heir. She was married to Robert Fitz-Pain, ſteward of the king's houſhold, who died ſeized of Frampton 9 E. 2. This manor was held of Thomas de Berkeley by the ſervice of 22 marks yearly. At this time there were 420 acres of arable land, let at 6*d.* an acre; 50 acres of meadow, at 2*s.* 6*d.* 30 acres of paſture, at 6*d.* and 40 acres of oak wood, the herbage of which was worth half a mark. There were 15 free tenants, who paid 8*l.* 4*s.* rent of aſſize. There were 6 yard-lands in villeinage, at 20*s.* a yard-land; and the pleas of the court were worth half a mark. *Eſcheator's Book.*

Robert, ſon and heir of Robert Fitz-Pain, left an only daughter Iſabel, married to ſir John Chidiock, who had iſſue another ſir John Chidiock, who, in right of his mother, had the manor of Frampton. He married Elianor, daughter of ſir John Fitz-Warren, by whom he had a ſon John Chidiock, who married Catherine, daughter of ſir Ralph Lumley, and left only daughters coheireſſes.

Catherine, one of the coheireſſes, was married to ſir John Arundel, of Llanhern in Cornwall, and afterwards to Roger Lukenore, and dying ſeized of the manor of Frampton 19 E. 4. was ſucceeded by ſir Thomas Arundel, her ſon, whoſe ſon and heir, ſir John Arundel, died ſeized of this manor 5 Mariæ. His ſon, John Arundel, eſq; had livery of it the ſame year, whoſe ſon John was ſeized of the manor of Frampton-upon-Severn in the year 1608, and afterwards ſold it to ſir Humphry Hook, alderman of Briſtol.

Sir Heel Hook is ſaid to be the preſent lord of this manor, but Mr. Stephens holds the court baron.

Of the other eſtates, the records ſhew, that William de Lucy held lands in Frampton 1 H. 3. Sir Hugh Clifford purchaſed lands in Frampton on Severn of Walter de Clifford 33 H. 3. The knights templers were ſeized of lands in Frampton upon Severn 2 E. 1. A fine was levied of lands in Frampton to Robert Iſham and others 14 H. 7.

Here is a fair kept on the 3d of February, called Frying-pan fair.

The pariſhioners have a right of common of paſture in Slimbridge-Wharfe; and have alſo a common containing about 120 acres, called Egrove.

Of the Church, &c.

The church is in the deanery of Durſley. It is a vicarage, worth upwards of 60*l.* a year, having been doubly augmented with the queen's bounty. Mr. Wicks is patron and impropriator. Here is no parſonage houſe.

The rectory and the advowſon of the vicarage did belong to the Cliffords. Being forfeited to the crown by attainder, they were granted to Edward Couper, and Valentine Fairweather, 7 E. 6.

The vicar hath one third of all tithes, and the impropriator the other two. Chancellor Parſons, who made his collections at the beginning of this century, ſays, '*the impropriation formerly paid* 18*s. per ann. to the pariſh clerk, but* [the payment] *has been detained for twenty years laſt paſt. There was alſo* 20*s. to the hayward, in lieu of an acre called the hayward's mead, by the lord of the manor, but detained for theſe twenty years*'. The impropriation is worth about 70*l.* a year. The preſentation formerly belonged to the abbey of Cirenceſter.

The church is a neat one, conſiſting of two ailes, and a chapel on each ſide of the chancel, with a handſome gallery, and a pinnacled tower, in which are ſix bells, at the weſt end. The middle chancel belongs to the vicar, the two ſide chancels, or chapels, to the impropriator.

	£.				£.		
Firſt fruits	7	11	0	Synodals	0	2	0
Tenths	0	16	0	Pentecoſtals	0	0	8
Procurations	0	6	8				

Monuments and Inſcriptions.

In the north wall of the chancel, in a niche, is the figure of a knight, lying along in full proportion, croſs-legged, with ſpurs on, a ſhield on his left arm, and a dog at his feet. Near it, in another niche, is the figure of a lady. They are both in free-ſtone, perfectly intire, and are ſuppoſed to repreſent ſome of the Cliffords.

On an old ſtone in the chancel:

Hic jacet humatum corpus Elizabethæ Clifford, quæ obijt viceſimo quarto die menſis Septembris anno Dni millimo cccc° lxvi. Sub eodem vero lapide jacet corpus Iohannis Clifford qui obijt . . . . Maij anno Dni millimo cccclxxxvii° quorum animabus propitietur Deus Amen.

Within the rails in the chancel, an antient ſtone, the inſcription much obliterated in the ſecond line; but I read the whole thus:

HERE LIETH THE BODY OF WALTER WIAT PREACHER AND VICARE OF THIS CHR϶HE DECESED THE 30 DEY OF SEPTEMBER ANNO DOMINI 1578 ANNOQVE REGNI REGINÆ ELISABETH VICESIMO.

In the north aile, on black marble,

In Memoriam Iohis Clifford, Gen. Maſculorum antiquiſſimi Nominis Cliffordiorum, infra hanc Parochiam, ultimi, qui obijt XXVII die Octob. Ano Dni 1684, hoc erigitur.

buried, with his wife, in the ſouth chancel of Frampton church, 1468, as appears by an inſcription there. Henry was ſon of James, and married Anne, daughter of Thomas Baynham, which Anne was afterwards married to William Try, of Hardwick, eſq. James Clifford, ſon of Henry, married Anne, ſiſter and one of the coheireſſes of Thomas Harewell, eſq. She was afterwards married to Nicholas Wickes. Henry, ſon of James, married Mabel, daughter of ſir John Welche, and died in the year 1558. He had four ſiſters, *viz.* Margaret, married to Robert Bradſtone of Winterbourn; Frances, married to Edward Barrow of Field-Court; Haviſe, to Matthew Madox of Lidney; and Alice, married to Anſelm Guiſe of Elmore. James Clifford, ſon of Henry, married Dorothy, daughter of Charles Fox of Bramhill, in Shropſhire, eſq. William Clifford, fourth brother of James, married Joan, daughter of Thomas Beard of Saul, in Glouceſterſhire. Henry was third ſon and ſurviving heir of William. James Clifford, of Swindon in this county, who had for his ſecond wife, Blanch, daughter of Thomas Hopkins of Howelfield, or Hewelsfield, in this county, was ſeized of an eſtate in Frampton in 1608. John Clifford, ſon of James, married Mary, daughter of William Shepard of Horſley, and left only three daughters, *i. e.* Mary, married to Nathaniel Clutterbuck of Eaſtington; Roſamond, married firſt to Edward Haynes of Frampton, ſecondly, to John Simmons, and thirdly, to Zachariah Wintle; and Elizabeth, married to Gilbert Tripet of Aure.

The late Richard Clutterbuck, eſq; a deſcendant of the above Nathaniel, built a fine ſeat in this pariſh. He died in 1775, and his two ſiſters ſucceeded to this eſtate.

Againſt the wall, on a white marble monument,

Anna Wade, filia natu tertia Iohannis Dunch, de Puiſy in comitatu BERKS, Armigeri, ANNÆq; uxoris, ex MAIJORUM apud Hamptonienſes Domo, Familijs ambabus Religione pariter ac Generis Splendore conſpicuis, Digna Propago; Conjux merito chariſſima THOMÆ WADE, Agri hujus Oppidiq; Generoſo, cui quatuor peperit Liberos (uno eodemque ſuaui Filiolo ſuperſtite) Rei domeſticæ ſtrenue perita, nec minus in Rebus Dei aſſidua. Filia, Soror, Uxor, Mater, Domina, Vicina, Amica, Fœminarum lectiſſimis annumeranda. Luce a Partu ſexta, ardente Febri correpta, Ardentiori adhuc Amore in patientia chari REDEMPTORIS Brachia ſanctam expiravit Animam. Menſis Julij die XUII Ano Æræ Chriſtianæ MDCLXXXVII Ætatis XXX. Chariſſimæ uxoris M. S. M. P. Thomas Wade. —— Arms, at top, *Party per pale Baron and Femme*, 1. *Azure, a ſaltire between four fleurs de lis Or, charged with five eſcallops of the firſt*, for Wade. 2. *Sable, a chevron between three caſtles argent*, for Dunch.

On a blue ſtone,

Qd mortale fuit Saræ nuper ux. Willi Clutterbucke Gen. et filiæ Iohis Wade Ar. ſub hac petra repoſitum eſt. Quæ obijt 25° die Iunij Anno Ætatis ſuæ 28, Salutis 1685. —— Arms, *Baron and Femme*, 1. *Quarterly* 1ſt *and* 4th, *Azure, a lion rampant argent, in chief three eſcallops of the laſt*, for Clutterbuck; 2d *and* 3d, *Checky Or and azure, on a bend gules three lions rampant of the firſt*, for Clifford. 2. Wade, as before.

In the north aile, behind the pulpit, on a handſome white marble monument:

M. P. S. Gulielmi Clutterbuck, hujus Parochiæ Generoſi, qui 15° Febr. Anno Æræ Chriſtianæ MDCCXXVII. ex hac vitâ deceſſit, Annos 67 natus. N^lis^ Clutterbuck, de Naſtend, in Parochiâ Eaſtingtoniæ in hoc Agro, Generoſi, Filius, ex Maria Uxore, Ioannis Clifford, hujus Parochiæ, Generoſi, maxima natu Filiâ, quam una cum alijs Hæredem pater reliquerat.

Quæ Pietas, quæ priſca Fides meruiſſe putantur,
Hæc Eadem huic merito ſunt referenda Viro.
Omnibus ex æquo Dolor eſt queis cognitus; Ullum
Nec lugere alio pluſve minuſve decet.
Quis Pauper Patrem ſibi non deplorat ademptum?
Quæ Vidua amiſſum non dolitura Virum?
Oppreſſis Vindex, queis fraus innixa Patronus,
Et Lite implicitis Conciliator erat;
Iuſtitiæ Cultor, Veri rigiduſq; Satelles:
Hæc Super Emicuit, Religionis Amor.
Quas evitaſti Vivus, nunc accipe Laudes,
Optime Vir, ceſſent et Monumenta loqui.
Dignius Hæc referent qui Patre et Matre Carentes,
Alterum experti, te claruere Patrem.

Arms, at top, *Quarterly* 1ſt *and* 4th, Clutterbuck; 2d *and* 3d, Clifford, as before.

On a tomb in the ſouth aile,

Here lyeth the body of the Right Worſhipfull Henry Clifford Eſq; who deceaſed 4th of June 1558, & the Body of Mabel his wife, one of the daughters of Ser IHON WELCHE, Knight, who deceaſed in Septr. 1592. & the Body of Anne Watſon daughter of the ſaide Henry & Mabele, at the proper charg of Weliam Watſone Gentelemane 1595.

On a braſs plate,

Inter Cliffordorum cineres hic jacet Edrus Haynes, unus Atturnat. Cur. de Com. Banco, in cujus memor. Roſamunda (filia Iohis Clifford) mœſtiſſima ſua relicta hoc poſuit. Ob. 11° Junij 1668.

Taxes.					
The Royal Aid in	1692,	£. 138	0	0
Poll-tax ——	1694,	— 27	13	0
Land-tax ——	1694,	— 184	0	0
The ſame, at 3*s*.	1770,	— 138	0	0

Bricks uſed to ſell at this place for 6*s*. 6*d*. a thouſand; but they are now advanced to 8*s*.

When ſir Robert Atkyns wrote his Hiſtory, there were ſaid to be 100 houſes in this pariſh, and about 500 inhabitants, whereof 26 were freeholders; yearly births 14, burials 13. In a ſeries of ten years, from 1710 to 1719, both incluſive, there are regiſter'd 139 baptiſms, and 104 burials. In a like ſeries of ten years, from 1760 to 1769, both incluſive, are regiſter'd 182 baptiſms, and 135 burials; which ſhews that the inhabitants of this pariſh have increaſed very conſiderably, ſince the date of the firſt ſeries; and they are now about 600.

FRAMPTON COTTEREL.

THIS pariſh lies in the hundred of Langley and Swineſhead, five miles diſtant ſouth-weſtward from Sodbury, ſeven miles ſouth from Thornbury, and about thirty miles ſouthward from Glouceſter.

It is ſo called from the river *Froom*, which runs through it, in its courſe to Briſtol, where it makes the key of that port; and from the family of the *Cotels*, who were antiently lords of the manor.

The pariſh conſiſts chiefly of meadow and paſture ground, with ſome arable land. The ſtone is of a rediſh brown grit, and ſeems to have a ſmall proportion of iron in it.

Here is a conſiderable manufacture of felt hats, which employs a pretty many hands.

The pariſh is ſaid to be within the juriſdiction of the court of the honour of Glouceſter.

Of the Manor and other Eſtates.

'Walter Baliſtarius holds Frantone, in Langelie 'hundred. There are five hides taxed. Aleſtan 'held it of Boſcombe. In demean is one plow-'tillage, and ten villeins, and eleven bordars, with 'five plow-tillages. There are five *ſervi*, and two 'mills of 5*s*. [rent]. And there is a church, 'which was not [in the time of king Edward.] 'It was worth 8*l*. now [only] 3*l*.' *D. B.* p. 77.

This manor belonged to the family of the Cotels ſoon after the Norman conqueſt. John Cotel, the laſt of that family, died ſeized of it 29 H. 3. before which the pariſh had obtained the name of *Frampton Cotel*.

Robert Walerond was ſeized of Frampton Cotel, and purchaſed a charter of free warren 41 H. 3. His wife Maud held it in dower, and proved her right to markets, fairs, and free warren, in a *Quo warranto*, 15 E. 1. John Walerond, and Robert Walerond, and Iſabel his wife, were ſeized of this manor 2 E. 2.

John de Willington held this manor of the honour of Wallingford 12 E. 2. and died ſeized thereof 12 E. 3. as did ſir Ralph de Willington, his ſon, 22 E. 3. whoſe ſon Henry, had livery thereof the following year. Sir John de Willington, ſon of Henry, had ſeizin of this manor, and of the advowſon of the church, 2 R. 2. and Ralph de Willington, ſon of ſir John, died ſeized thereof 6 R. 2. Joan his widow had the third part of the manor aſſigned to her in dower 8 R. 2. and having married Thomas Weſt, whom ſhe alſo ſurvived, died 6 H. 4. Ralph de Willington, ſon of Ralph and the ſaid Joan, died ſeized of the other two parts of this manor 19 R. 2. and was ſucceeded by his brother John, who died ſeized of this manor, and of the advowſon of the church 20 R. 2. leaving no no iſſue; whereby his ſiſter Joan became his heir. She carried this eſtate, by her marriage, to John Wrath, and John Wrath, their ſon, dying without iſſue 13 H. 4. left his two ſiſters his heirs; of whom, Elizabeth was married to ſir William Poulton, and Iſabel was the widow of William Beaumont.

Sir William Poulton and Elizabeth his wife levied a fine of the moiety of the manor of Frampton 14 H. 4. They dying without iſſue, the whole manor was veſted in Iſabel Beaumont. She had iſſue John and Iſabel, who both dying without iſſue, were ſucceeded by ſir Thomas Beaumont, who died ſeized of this eſtate 29 H. 6. as did his ſon William Beaumont 32 H. 6. and Philip Beaumont, brother of William, 13 E. 4.

Hugh Beaumont and Elizabeth his wife, John Baſſet and Elizabeth his wife, John Beaumont, clerk, John Chicheſter and Margaret his wife, and John Croker and Anne his wife, by ſeveral fines levied 16, 18, & 20 H. 7. convey the manor and advowſon of Frampton Cotel, to king Henry the Seventh.

The manor was afterwards granted to Giles lord D'Aubeny, who dying 6 H. 8. his ſon, Henry lord D'Aubeny, had livery thereof the ſame year. The manor again reverted to the crown, and was granted to Edward duke of Somerſet, who being attainted, John Baſſet obtained a grant of it 4 Mariæ, which was confirmed to Arthur Baſſet 7 Eliz.

The manor was afterwards purchaſed by the Players. William Player, eſq; was lord of the manor at the beginning of this century, as was his ſon, Thomas Player, eſq; in the year 1736. Charles Bragge, eſq; is the preſent lord of the manor.

Sir John Seymour had a large houſe, with a park, and a good eſtate in this pariſh, from whom they went by purchaſe to Henry Symes, eſq; and were carried, by the marriage of his daughter Jane, to Edward Biſs, eſq; and then paſſed out of that name, by the marriage of his daughter, to Gabriel Hale, eſq; who was the owner of them when ſir Robert Atkyns compiled his account of this pariſh; but they are now the property of William Southwell, eſq.

John de Acton and Sybil his wife were ſeized of a mill and eighty acres in Frampton Cotel 6 E. 2. Walter Gacelyn died ſeized of one meſſuage and two plow-tillages in Frampton Cotel 7 E. 2. as did Walter his ſon 7 E. 3. and William, ſon of the laſt Walter, 20 E. 3.

Jeffry Stowel and Matthew Stowel were both ſeized of lands in Frampton 37 E. 3. William Forſter levied a fine of a moiety of lands in Frampton Cotel, to John Walſh and others 12 H. 7.

TITHING and *HAMLET*.

Wickwick is a tithing in this pariſh, about two miles from the church, from which an antient family reſiding here, took their name.

The manors of Magnesfield and Wickwick were granted by king Henry the Eighth, to ſir John Seymour, who died ſeized of them 27 H. 8. and was ſucceeded by his ſon, ſir Edward Seymour. The manor of Wickwick came afterwards to the Kemyſes, and then to the Browns. This manor, with a large eſtate in the tithing, was lately the property of Francis Brown, eſq; deceaſed, who leaving two daughters coheireſſes, one of them was married to —— Daubony, eſq; of the city of Briſtol, who, in her right, has a moiety of the manor and eſtate. His arms are, *Gules, four fuſils in feſs argent*.

Of the Church, &c.

The church is a rectory, in the deanery of Hawkeſbury, worth about 130*l*. a year. The patrons are, the duke of Beaufort, (as heir to the late lord Botetourt) Mr. Southwell, and Mr. Jacob; whoſe ſhares being unequal, an agreement was made in the year 1765, to preſent in the following order, *viz*. 1. The duke of Beaufort. 2 and 3. Mr. Southwell. 4. Mr. Jacob. 5. The duke of Beaufort. 6 and 7. Mr. Southwell. 8. Mr. Jacob. 9. Mr. Southwell. Mr. Philip Bliſs is the preſent incumbent.

A portion of tithes in Frampton belonged to the abbey of Winchcombe, and were granted to ſir Thomas Seimour 1 E. 6.

Fifty acres belong to the glebe.

The church is dedicated to St. Peter and St. Paul. It hath an aile on the ſouth ſide, and a tower, with ſix bells, at the weſt end; and the effigies of thoſe ſaints, of the virgin Mary, and of ſome king, ſtand in niches, on the ſides under the battlements.

	£.			
Firſt fruits £.	11	16	0	Synodals £.
Tenths —	1	3	7¼	Pentecoſtals
Procurations				

Monuments and Inſcriptions.

In the ſouth aile, are the following:

Reader, thou treadeſt on the Sacred Aſhes of IOHN SYMES, Eſq[r] who in the late unhappy times of Rebellion was forc't (for his ſignal Loyalty to his Prince) to leave his former Habitation at POVNDISFORD in the Pariſh of PITMINSTER, in the County of SOMERSET, and to ſeek a Repoſe for his old Age in this Pariſh. He was a man greatly renowned for Wiſedome, Iuſtice, Integrity, & Sobriety, which Talents he did not hide in a Napkin, but religiouſly exerciſed in the whole conduct of his Life, eſpecially in the Government of the County wherein he bore all the Honourable Offices incident to a Country Gentleman, as Knight of the Shire (elected *Nemine contradicente*) for the Parliament held at Weſtminſter in the 21th Yeare of King Iames, High Sheriffe, Deputy Lieutenant for many Yeares, & Iuſtice of the Peace for 40 yeares and upward. And as he was careful and ſolicitous to diſcharge his Duty to God, his Sovereigne, & his Country, ſo God was pleaſed to beſtow on him ſeveral Badges (Alſo) of his ſpeciall favour, as Length of dayes, accompanyed with a moſt healthy Conſtitution of Body for above 80 yeares, and of his Mind to the laſt. As alſo a numerous Poſterity, even of Children and Children's Children, to the number of 100 & upwards, deſcended of his Loynes (by his only wife AMY the Daughter of THOMAS HORNER, of *Cloved* in the County of Somerſet, Eſq[r]. And when he was full of Days and of Honour, having lived 88 yeares 7 months and 17 dayes, and ſeene the ſafe returne of his Prince to his Crown & Kingdomes, after a long & horrible exile, & thereby the flouriſhing Condition both of Church & State, having finiſhed his work on earth, he cheerfully reſigned his Soule to God that gave it, the 21th day of October Anno Domini 1661, in full aſſurance of a joyfull Reſurrection.——

This memorial is on a braſs plate. At top are theſe arms, viz. 1. *Azure, three eſcallops in pale Or*, for Symes, impaling 2. *Sable, three talbots argent*, for Horner.

HERE

HERE LYETH THE BODY OF ANNE SYMES, WIDOW AND RELICT OF HARRY SYMES, ESQ. WHO DEPARTED THIS LIFE ON THE 25th DAY OF MAY ANNO DOMINI 1686. SHE WAS THE DAUGHTER OF Sr JOHN SEYMOUR FORMERLY OF THIS PARISH, BY DAME ANNE HIS FIRST WIFE, THE DAUGHTER OF WILLIAM POULET, OF COTTLES IN THE COUNTY OF WILTS, ESQ. SON OF MY LORD GILES POULET, FOURTH SON OF WILLIAM POULET, MARQUIS OF WINCHESTER, AND LORD HIGH TREASURER OF ENGLAND.
GREAT WAS HER BIRTH, GREATER WERE HER VIRTUES; THE BEST OF WIVES, THE BEST OF MOTHERS, THE BEST OF WOMEN.

Arms, In a lozenge, 1. Symes, impaling, 2. *Gules, two pinions conjoined in lure Or*, for Seymour.

Here lyeth the Body of Mrs. Iſabella Player, Daughter of William and Siſter of Thomas Player, Eſq. the preſent Lord of this Manor, who departed this Life the 16th Day of June, 1736. ——Arms, *Gules, a feſs Or, in chief two mullets argent.*

In the ſame aile, are memorials for ſeveral perſons of the name of Kemys, with theſe arms, *Vert, on a chevron argent three pheons heads ſable.*

Frampton Cotterel.

Taxes.	The Royal Aid in	1692, £.	123	8	0
	Poll-tax ——	1694, —	43	19	0
	Land-tax ——	1694, —	140	0	0
	The ſame, at 3*s*.	1770, —	84	3	3

Wickwick.

Taxes.	The Royal Aid in	1692, £.	12	18	0
	Poll-tax ——	1694, —	6	18	0
	Land-tax ——	1694, —	20	18	0
	The ſame, at 3*s*.	1770, —	22	1	0

At the beginning of this century, there were 56 houſes, and about 300 inhabitants in this pariſh, whereof 20 were freeholders; yearly births 9, burials 8. *Atkyns.* The inhabitants are now increaſed to 393.

FRETHORN

IS a ſmall pariſh in the hundred of Whitſtone, three miles ſouth-eaſtward from Newnham, ſix northward from Durſley, and nine ſouthward from Glouceſter.

It is bounded on the weſt by the river Severn, with Frampton on the ſouth, Arlingham to the north, and Saul to the eaſt of it.

The lands are chiefly in meadow and paſture. The air is unwholeſome, and the inhabitants are ſubject to the ague.

Frith comes from *Fretum*, a ſtreight or narrow paſſage of the ſea; and *hurn* ſignifies a *corner*.

It is ſaid, the inhabitants of this pariſh claim the privilege of being toll-free in all markets, and have free paſſage over the Severn. Fair Roſamond, miſtreſs to king Henry the Second, was born in a large houſe in this pariſh, which ſtood on the bank of the Severn. It was originally built by an anceſtor of the Clifford family, and was remarkable for a noble ſtair-caſe, and two chimney-pieces, one of them bearing the Cliffords arms, and 1598; which is ſuppoſed to be the date when it was rebuilt by James Clifford, eſq; one of the gentlemen of the privy chamber to queen Elizabeth. This houſe was taken down about twenty years ago.

Of the Manor and other Eſtates.

'Turſtin the ſon of Rolf holds Fridorne in 'Blachelaue hundred. Auti held it. There are 'three hides taxed. There is one plow-tillage in 'demean, and three villeins, and three bordars, 'with two plow-tillages, and one *ſervus*. It was 'worth 60*s*. now [only] 30*s*.' *Dom. Book*, p. 78.

Nicholas Veel held Frethern, Coteworth, and Eſton 9 E. 2. Jeffry de Frethern held one meſſuage and one plow-tillage in Frethern 14 E. 2. John de Frethern was ſeized of the manor of Frethern 27 E. 3.

James Clifford, eſq; was lord of the manor in the year 1608. William Bayly, eſq; was afterwards the proprietor of it, whoſe family ſold it to John Yate, of Arlingham, eſq; and Robert-Gorges-Dobyns Yate, eſq; is the preſent lord of the manor, and reſides at Bromſborough in this county.

Of the Church, &c.

The church is a rectory, in Glouceſter deanery, worth about 50*l*. a year. Mr. Yate is patron, Mr. Davis the preſent incumbent.

Forty-four ridges of land belong to the glebe.

The church is dedicated to St. Mary. It is a ſmall building, with a wooden tower, at the weſt end.

There are ſeveral memorials in the chancel for the family of the Baylys, with their arms, *viz. Gules, a ſcutcheon of pretence per pale argent and azure.* Within the communion rails, is this verſe,

Hic Thomæ Wotton Proles tumulo jacet Anna.
Dum veniet Chriſtus, ſufficit iſta domus.

Firſt fruits £.	5	6	8	Synodals £.	0	2	0
Tenths —	0	10	8	Pentecoſt.	0	0	8
Procurations	0	5	0				

Benefaction.

Mrs. Dorothy Bayly left an eſtate of 40*l*. a year to improve the living, after the death of Mrs. Price.

Taxes.	The Royal Aid in	1692, £.	92	0	0
	Poll-tax —	1694, —	20	19	0
	Land-tax —	1694, —	143	7	4
	The ſame, at 3*s*.	1770, —	34	19	6

There were, at the beginning of this century, 25 houſes, and about 125 inhabitants in this pariſh, of whom 7 were freeholders; yearly births 8, burials 8. *Atkyns.* There are now 96 inhabitants.

****

FROCESTER

IS a ſmall pariſh in the hundred of Whitſtone, four miles north-eaſt from Durſley, five weſt from Stroud, and eleven ſouth-weſt from Glouceſter. It is bounded on the north by Eaſington, on the ſouth by Nympsfield, with Cowley and Cam to the weſt, and Leonard Stanley to the eaſt of it.

It lies in the vale, on a declivity facing the north, with a large hanging beech-wood on the ſide towards Nympsfield, down which the turnpike-road leads from Bath to Glouceſter. The ſoil is rich and good, and the air tolerably healthy.

A ſmall

A ſmall brook runs down to Cowley, and ſo into the Severn. It is ſaid the houſes formerly ſtood near the church, in the lower part of the pariſh, but were burnt down ; and afterwards, for the conveniency of a drier ſpot, the inhabitants built them where they now ſtand. There are about 207 acres of common field, lying in ſix different fields; but the greateſt part of the pariſh is rich paſture. It is not remarkable for any uncommon natural productions.

The name is differently written, as *Froweceſtre, Frouceſtre, Fronceſter*; but I apprehend the latter form aroſe by miſtaking the letter *u* for *n*, which in old writings are much alike. This gave riſe to the notion of its being ſo called, becauſe it was a frontier caſtle.

The abbats of Glouceſter had a ſumptuous houſe in this village; and it is ſaid, that formerly here was a college of prebendaries.

This village was honoured with a viſit from queen Elizabeth, who lay a night at the manor houſe, as appears by an entry in the pariſh regiſter, as follows : *Hoc anno* 1574° *die feſto Laurentij martyris Sereniſſima Regina n'ra Elizabetha hoc n'rm oppidatum acceſſit et inviſit, in eoq; in Ædibus Georgii Huntleij, armigeri, comiter, benigneq; et ſum'a cum humanitate tractantis, p'noctavit, indeq; Barkleyum Caſtellum conceſſit. i. e.* On the day of the feaſt of St. Lawrence, in this year, 1574, our moſt ſerene queen Elizabeth came into this our town, and lodged in it that night, at the ſeat of George Huntley, eſq; by whom ſhe was elegantly and ſplendidly entertained ; and afterwards ſhe went to Berkeley caſtle.

Of the Manor and other Eſtates.

In the general ſurvey, ſoon after the conqueſt, under the head *Terra S. Petri de Glowec'*, it is thus recorded :

'The ſame church held Froweceſtre in Blace-'lawes hundred. There are five hides. In demean 'are four plow-tillages, and eight villeins, and 'ſeven bordars, with ſeven plow-tillages. There 'are three *ſervi*, and ten acres of meadow, and a 'wood three furlongs long, and two broad. It 'was worth 4*l.* now worth 8*l.*' *Dom. B.* p. 71.

This manor continued in the abbey of Glouceſter 'till its diſſolution. After the diſſolution of monaſteries, this manor, and the advowſon of the vicarage, were granted to Edward duke of Somerſet, 1 E. 6. and notwithſtanding his attainder, theſe and other particulars were confirmed to his widow, in ſatisfaction of all claim of dower, 3 Mar. The manor of Froceſter, and divers lands which had been granted before to the ſaid duke, were again granted to Chriſtopher Hatton, 17 Eliz.

Sir William Doddington, of Bremer in Hampſhire, was lord of this manor in the year 1608. He left only daughters, of whom Anne, the ſurviving heir, was married to Robert Grevile, lord Brook, whereby his lordſhip was intituled to this manor. The earl Brooke[e] and earl of Warwick is the preſent lord of the manor of Froceſter.

The ſcite of the manor houſe, with divers lands, and the rectory and advowſon of the vicarage, were granted to Giles Huntley, 1 Mar. They afterwards deſcended to ſir George Huntley, who came by a violent end in the park.

[e] It is ſaid this family is of Norman extraction. The name was antiently written Graville, or Grevill, and ſometimes Grevel. William Grevill died ſeized of the manors of Inglethwait and Awldtoftes in Yorkſhire, 1294. John Grevill died before 33 E. 3. and was ſucceeded by his ſon William, who was ſeated at Campden in Glouceſterſhire, and lent king R. 2. three hundred marks. William was his ſon and heir, who purchaſed the manor of Milcot in Warwickſhire, in the year 1398. He was buried in the church of St. Mary in Campden, to the repair of which he gave 100 marks, and 200*l.* for four chaplains to ſay maſs in that church for his ſoul, for ten years following. He was ſucceeded by his ſon John, who reſided at Campden, and married, firſt, Sibil, daughter and heir of ſir Robert Corbet; ſecondly, Joyce, daughter of ſir Walter Cokeſey, knt. by whom he had iſſue John, his ſon and heir, who reſided at Charlton Regis, com. Glouc. and who had the manor of Milcot 28 H. 6. He died in the year 1480, after having the honour of knighthood conferred on him, and ſerving in five parliaments for Glouceſterſhire. Thomas was his only ſon, who aſſumed the ſurname of Cokeſey. At the coronation of king H. 7. he was created knight of the Bath, and afterwards was made a knight Banneret. He died without iſſue, whereby the inheritance of the Cokeſeys reverted to that family; but the eſtates he had from the Grevills went to John Grevill, a deſcendant of Lodowick, ſecond ſon to William Grevill of Campden. Which John was one of the juſtices for the goal-delivery at Warwick 15 H. 7. He had iſſue, by his wife Jane, daughter of ſir Humphry Forſter, two ſons, Edward and Robert. Edward was knighted for his valiant behaviour in the engagement called the *Battle of the Spurs*, from the ſwiftneſs of the French in running away, 5 H 8. He was one of the knights appointed to attend the king and queen to the conference with Francis I. the French king, 12 H. 8. He obtained the wardſhip of Elizabeth, one of the daughters, and at laſt ſole heir of Edward Willoughby, the only ſon of Robert lord Brooke. He married Anne, daughter of John Denton, by whom he had iſſue four ſons, John, Fulke, Thomas, and Edward. The two laſt died without iſſue, and the elder branch, from John, became extinct in the fourth deſcent from him. Fulke, the ſecond ſon, married Elizabeth, his father's ward, one of the greateſt heireſſes in England, by whom he had three ſons, Fulke, Robert, and Edward; and four daughters. Fulke, the eldeſt, was ſucceeded by his ſon Fulke, who was advanced to the dignity of a baron, by the title of lord Brooke, with limitation of that honour, in default of heirs male of his own body, to his kinſman Robert Grevile ; which ſaid Fulke lord Brooke dying unmarried, he was ſucceeded in honour and eſtates by the ſaid Robert, ſecond lord Brooke, who married lady Catherine Ruſſel, eldeſt daughter to Francis earl of Bedford, by whom he had five ſons, Francis, Robert, Edward, Algernon, (the two laſt dying batchelors) and Fulke. Francis ſucceeded his father, but died unmarried ; whereby Robert became the fourth lord Brooke. He married Anne, daughter to John Doddington, eſq; by whom he had ſix ſons, who all died young, and two daughters. He died at Bath, in 1676, and was ſucceeded in honour and eſtate by Fulke, his youngeſt brother. This Fulke, fifth lord Brooke, married Sarah, daughter of ſir Samuel Daſhwood, alderman of London, by whom he had iſſue four ſons, Francis, Algernon, Doddington, and Robert; and ſeven daughters. He died in 1710, and Francis, the eldeſt ſon, died eleven days before his father, having married lady Anne Wilmot, eldeſt daughter and coheir of John earl of Rocheſter, by whom he had iſſue two ſons, Fulke and William, and two daughters.

Fulke, the eldeſt ſon, ſucceeded his grandfather as lord Brooke, but died at Univerſity-college, Oxford, in 1710-11, and was ſucceeded by his brother William.

Which William, ſeventh lord Brooke, married Mary, ſecond daughter and coheir of the honourable Henry Thynne, eſq; by whom he had three ſons, William, Fulke, and Francis. The two former died infants, and William lord Brooke, their father, died in 1727.

Francis, the third and only ſurviving ſon, ſucceeded to his father as eighth lord Brooke, when but eight years old. In the year 1746, he was created earl Brooke by king George the Second ; and the title of earl of Warwick being extinct, by the death of Edward Rich, earl of Warwick and Holland, in 1759, his majeſty was pleaſed to add the dignity of earl of Warwick to his lordſhip's other titles, the ſame year. His lordſhip married Elizabeth, daughter to the lord Archibald Hamilton, by whom he hath iſſue three ſons and four daughters. ARMS, *Sable, on a croſs within a border ingrailed Or, five pellets.* CREST, *In a ducal coronet gules, a ſwan with wings expanded argent, beaked ſable.* SUPPORTERS, *Two ſwans argent, beaked and membered ſable, and ducally gorged gules.* MOTTO, VIX EA NOSTRA VOCO.

Sir Robert Ducie purchaſed of the Huntleys the court-houſe, and a large eſtate belonging to it, now the property of lord Ducie.

Sir Robert Atkyns was miſtaken in repreſenting his lordſhip's park as being any part of it in this pariſh.

A mill in Froceſter, lately belonging to the abbey of Glouceſter, was granted to William Rameſden and Edward Hobbey 37 H. 8.

Of the Church, &c.

The church is in the deanery of Stonehouſe. It is a vicarage worth 50*l.* a year. The advowſon was given to the abbey of Glouceſter by William de Blois, biſhop of Worceſter, in the year 1225, when Thomas de Bredone was abbat. Lord Ducie is patron and impropriator; Mr. Hayward is the preſent incumbent.

The demean lands are tithe free, as having belonged to the abbey of Glouceſter.

The church, dedicated to St. Peter, hath an aile on the ſouth ſide, and a large ſpire in the middle, in which are ſix bells. There is a ſmall chancel on the north ſide of the large one, which formerly was the burying place of the Huntleys, and now belongs to the earl of Warwick. In the chancel is an antient monument, ſuppoſed to be for the founder. There is a ſmall farm in Cowley, and a rent-charge of 9*s.* 4*d.* both given to keep the church in repair, which is very antient, and ſtanding upwards of a mile from the houſes, divine ſervice is performed at a chapel, and not in the church, except at funerals; for they bury there. The chapel is built on lord Warwick's land.

Proc. 6*s.* 8*d.* Syn. 2*s.* Pentecoſt. 4*d.*

Taxes.	The Royal Aid in	1692, £.	125	18	8
	Poll-tax ——	1694, —	16	7	0
	Land-tax ——	1694, —	142	2	0
	The ſame, at 3*s.*	1770, —	107	18	1½

According to ſir Robert Atkyns, there were 61 houſes, and about 250 inhabitants in this pariſh, whereof 7 were freeholders; yearly births 8, burials 7. But I find that in a ſeries of ten years, from 1700 to 1709 incluſive, there were regiſtered 107 baptiſms, and 61 burials; and in a like ſeries, from 1760 to 1769, there were 103 baptiſms, and 63 burials; and the preſent number of inhabitants is 262.

St. GEORGE'S.

THIS is a newly erected pariſh. It lies in the hundred of King's Barton, about thirty-ſix miles ſouth from the city of Glouceſter. It is bounded[t] on the eaſt by Bitton, on the weſt by the out-pariſh of St. Philip and Jacob, on the north by Stapleton and Mangotsfield, and on the ſouth by the river Avon. The weſtern extremity is diſtant three quarters of a mile from [u]Laford's-Gate, in the city of Briſtol; and its greateſt length from eaſt to weſt is two miles and a quarter.

It was part of the out-pariſh of St. Philip and Jacob, but an act of parliament paſſed for erecting it into a diſtinct pariſh 24 G. 2. By that act, all rates made for the relief of the poor, for the repair of the highways, and all taxes granted, or to be granted, by parliament or otherwiſe, are to be made upon the inhabitants of St. Philip's and St. George's, jointly and in common; and the workhouſe in the old pariſh is to be for the common uſe of both. The orders of juſtices of the peace, relating to the poor, are to be made and directed as before the making of the ſaid act for erecting the ſaid pariſh; but the church-rates are to be ſeparate. There are two petty conſtables appointed annually for this pariſh, at the hundred-court.

Before this ſeparation, the whole of the out-pariſh of St. Philip and Jacob was called *Eaſton*, becauſe it lay eaſtward of the city of Briſtol; but more antiently, the name of it was *Bertune*. It was part of the antient demeſnes of the crown, as appears by *Domeſday-book*, and gave denomination to the hundred of *Barton Regis*.

The greater part of the pariſh lies within the boundaries of the foreſt, or chaſe, of [w]Kingſwood, and is one of thoſe places (all ſituated in the neighbourhood

[t] The boundaries of the pariſh are ſettled to be from a bridge at the foot of Lawrence-hill, called Lawrence-bridge, along the lane ſouthward, called Barton-hill-lane; thence, in a direct line, along Little Marſh-lane; thence by a little ſtream of water which runs from the ſaid lane into King's-pill; and thence along by the King's-pill to the river Avon, and along up the ſide of that river to the utmoſt extent and boundary of the old pariſh of St. Philip and Jacob on that ſide thereof. From St. Lawrence-bridge aforeſaid, weſtward to Dod-lane; along this lane northward to Gane-bridge, in the road leading from Briſtol to Glouceſter, and ſo on to Comb-brook, and thence to the utmoſt boundaries of the old pariſh, eaſtward to the river Avon. Act, 24 G. 2.

[u] It is generally written *Lawford's Gate*; but that erroneous manner of writing it deſtroys the idea which the true name conveys. The caſtle of Briſtol was built by Robert Mellent, or Fitz-Roy, conſul and earl of Glouceſter. He was lord of the manor and hundred of Bertune, wherefore this gate was called *Laford's-Gate*, *i. e.* the *Lord's-Gate*, from the Anglo Saxon *Hlaford*, which ſignifies *Lord*. This gate has lately been taken down.

[w] The following are the bounds of Kingſwood Chaſe, copied from a ſurvey taken by order of government, May 26, 1652, and communicated by a learned friend, for the ſatisfaction of the curious.——— Kingſwood was bounded by divers incloſed lands ſhewed to the ſurveyors by antient inhabitants within the bordering pariſhes, beginning near a ſtone in the high road called Dungel's-croſs, ſo to Roe-yate northwards, by ſeveral incloſed lands, to the manor houſe and ground called Ridgway, unto a gate called Longland's-gate, abutted on the north by ſaid Ridgway-houſe, on to Bullibroke, aud along the foot of the new pools to Rublay's-yate-lane; thence abutted on the eaſt by Longwalls, next Mangotsfield pariſh, along to Erford's-lane, ſo down Bromley's-heath unto Brimble-gate, and thence returning towards the ſouth, ſurrounding the ſaid heath, paſſing along by Player's manſion houſe and grounds called Cleave's-hill; thence ſouth-eaſtward to Downing's-green, thence northward to Sodbury-gate and road; thence eaſtward, ſurrounding the ſaid green, unto Weſterley-gate; thence unto grounds called Charnock's, and into Mangotsfield-bottom unto Siſton's-brook, and along it ſouthward, returning down Mangotsfield-bottom, unto the highway, or road, from Dungel's-croſs, abutted by Siſton's-common; and thence unto Grimſbury-lane, above Mr. Woodward's houſe; thence winding weſtward by Grimſbury-hill, and along Cock-rode-hill down eaſtward by Workman's-green, and thence ſouthward unto the highway towards Mr. Newton's houſe and manor; thence paſſing unto Herring-lane end, and over the hill called Martin's-

neighbourhood of each other) whence the city of Briſtol is ſupply'd with its coal, which is ſo excellent, for its durable quality, that the very cinders will burn over and over again, 'till they are wholly reduced to vapour and aſhes.

Some of the coal-pits are of a prodigious depth. That at Two-mile-hill[x], belonging to his grace the duke of Beaufort, is 107 fathom deep. At this and many others they uſe a fire-engine, to draw out the water which flows in upon the miners, and would prevent their working.

There are the ſame kinds of foſſils found here which are particularly mentioned in Bitton, and are common to all the coal-lands in Kingſwood; but upon diligent inquiry, I cannot find that there is any thing curious or uncommon in the vegetable ſyſtem. However, I ſhould not omit to mention a flat ſtone that was found, not long ſince, near the ſide of the Avon, in this pariſh, about nine inches long and ſix broad, which had ſo beautiful an impreſſion of a very large ſpecies of the fern plant (native of America) on one ſide of it, that it looked more like the work of a maſterly engraver than the production of nature. I ſaw it in the cabinet of a curious naturaliſt, and very worthy gentleman, in the city of Briſtol. He ſhewed me, at the ſame time alſo, a ſparry incruſtation, which had almoſt filled up a pipe made of boards, of which the cavity was about four or five inches ſquare. This pipe, if I miſtake not, had ſerved for the conveyance of water to ſome of the copper-works here, 'till the ſtony matter filled up the cavity, except a ſmall hole in the middle, and rendered it uſeleſs. The grain of the wood, and the marks of the ſaw, were ſo perfectly impreſt on the incruſtation, that the eye could not diſtinguiſh it from a piece of ſawed timber.

This village is not wholly deſtitute of antiquities. On a hill, within a few yards of the turnpike-gate leading down to Crew's-hole, there is a ſmall dwelling-houſe, which in former ages was a Romiſh chapel, dedicated to St. Anthony; and it retains the name of St. Anthony's chapel to this day. In the highway, about two hundred yards weſtward of the church, ſtood *Don John's Croſs*, which was a round freeſtone column, ſupported by an octangular baſe. The upper part of the column, and the croſs at top, were probably deſtroyed by the parliament's party in the great civil war, who demoliſhed every thing of that ſort. When the church was built, it was removed, and the baſe is now depoſited at the door of an adjacent houſe. It is very uncertain what event this was intended to preſerve the memory of; but tradition ſays, that here the corpſe of one *Don John*, a noble Spaniard, reſted in its way to the place of its interment. If there be any foundation for this ſtory, it might be ſhipped for Spain, from the port of Briſtol.

Here are two copper-works, and a glaſs-houſe for the manufacture of bottles. But the principal production of art is a curious hydraulic machine, erected upon the river Avon, and invented and conſtructed by the late ingenious mechanic and mathematician, Mr. John Padmore, for throwing water into a reſervoir, for the uſe of the city of Briſtol. The reſervoir is at a little diſtance, on the top of a hill, whence, by ſubterraneous pipes, the water is conveyed to the city. There were formerly two machines for the ſame purpoſe, at Hanham-mills, in the pariſh of Bitton, but they were taken down in the year 1720.

There is a turnpike-road from Bath to Briſtol leading through this pariſh; and another from Briſtol to London, by way of Marſhfield.

Some of the ſubſequent records concern the whole hamlet of Eaſton, and conſequently have a relation, as well to the preſent out-pariſh of St. Philip and Jacob, as to St. George's; but as they could not properly be divided, they are placed here, and referred to from St. Philip's.

Martin's-horſe-hill, unto Cadbury's-bottom; thence ſouthward up Jeffery's-hill into the road-way from Briſtol to Bath, then north up the ſaid road to the door of H. Stone, where we croſs the ſaid road; thence ſouth along by ſome houſes, and weſtward along by Proffer's-gate unto Cadimore-brook, unto Hanham's-lanes, and over Jeffery's-hill, and along down Conham's-hill to the lower end of Strode-brook, ſo to Deanridge-lands, rounding them to the river Avon; thence turning ſhort about to the north-weſt by Harris-hill, unto the north-eaſt of the ſaid hill, near to the Bath road; ſo along weſtward by the dean and chapter's lands 'till we come over-againſt Sims's ſmith-ſhop and Dungel's-croſs, whence we ſet out. Total of acres of the whole chaſe were 3432 and 2 Roods. ——— There were formerly 1500 or 2000 head of deer in the chaſe, but there have been none for upwards of ſeventy years paſt.

[x] In the year 1735, three men and a boy lay ten days and nineteen hours in a dark cavern, in the midſt of a coal-pit near Two-mile-hill, in this pariſh, thirty-nine fathom under ground, environed with water, and on the brink of a precipice ſixteen fathom perpendicular. As theſe perſons were wedging out coals, on the 7th of November, a prodigious torrent of water burſt on a ſudden out of a vein, and put out all the lights; the people were ſtruck with the utmoſt conſternation, and knew not which way to take, but crawling on their hands and knees from place to place to avoid the water, they providentially got to a riſing ground, where creeping up higher and higher, as the water roſe, at length reached a hollow place, whence coals had been dug, and there continued. In their way, they found a bit of beef and a cruſt of bread, together about a quarter of a pound, which they divided equally, and eat. It was for ſome time very eaſy to get water, but the water ſinking, it became more and more difficult, 'till at length, not being able to obtain it, they were forced to drink their own urine, and to chew ſome chips which they cut from a baſket; but loſing their knife, even this miſerable expedient failed them, and one endeavoured to eat his ſhoe. They were almoſt ſuffocated with heat, and with the nauſeous fumes that aroſe from their bodies, and continued without any other ſuſtenance 'till the 17th, when their friends, after ſeveral ineffectual attempts, let down a large quantity of burning coals, which diſſipated the black vapour; and the water being gone off in a great meaſure, five men ventured down, and calling out, were ſurpriſed to find them alive and able to anſwer. The eldeſt, about ſixty years old, was delirious, and all of them very weak, and for ſome time intirely blind. They were taken out, and having received ſome refreſhment, walked to their homes, to the great aſtoniſhment of a vaſt croud of people aſſembled from all parts. The men did not apprehend they had been above five days under ground. At the water's firſt burſting in upon them, there were four other boys in the mine, but being at the *Tip of the work*, ran to the rope, crying to be pulled up, and notwithſtanding it was done with as much expedition as poſſible, yet the water was at the heels of the laſt boy, who, as the other three were hawling up, caught hold of the feet of one of his companions, and all got ſafe out.

Of the Manor and other Eſtates.

Under the head *Terra Regis*, in *Domeſday-book*, it is thus expreſſed:

'In Bertune at Briſtou were ſix hides. In de-'mean were three plow-tillages, and twenty-two 'villeins, and twenty-five bordars, with twenty-'five plow-tillages. There were ten *ſervi*, and 'eighteen free men [*coliberti*] having fourteen 'plow-tillages. There were two mills of 27*s*. '[rent.] When Roger received this manor of the 'king, he found there two hides, and two plow-'tillages in demean, and ſeventeen villeins, and 'twenty-four bordars, with twenty-one plow-'tillages. There were four *ſervi*, and thirteen 'free men with three plow-tillages.

'In Manegodesfelle, one member of this manor, 'are ſix cows in demean.

'The church of Briſtou holds three hides of 'this land, and has one plow-tillage there.

'A radecheniſter holds one hide, and has one 'plow-tillage, and four bordars with one plow-'tillage.

'This manor and Briſtou pay 110 marks of 'ſilver to the king. The burgeſſes ſay, that biſhop 'G. [Goisfrid] has thirty-three marks of ſilver, 'and one mark of gold, beſides the king's farm.' *Domeſday-book*, p. 68.

The manor and hundred of Bertune have been generally held by perſons of great eminence. It appears by the fines regiſtered 3 H. 3. that Richard earl of Glouceſter had been ſeized of Bertune near Briſtol, of Finchwood, and Keynſham-chaſe. And his ſon, Gilbert earl of Glouceſter, was afterwards ſeized of them. Bertune near Briſtol was granted to queen Iſabel, in part of her dower, 11 E. 2. The manor of Bertune was granted, in part of dower, to queen Philippa, 4 E. 3. and afterwards to queen Catherine.

The manor of Bertune, and the hundred, and the advowſon of the hoſpital of St. Lawrence, within the ſaid hundred, belonged to Edward duke of York, grandſon to king Edward the Third, who was ſlain at Agincourt, and died without iſſue. His brother, Richard earl of Cambridge, having been attainted and executed, this manor reverted to the crown, and was granted to Humphry duke of Glouceſter, and to his heirs male, 3 H. 5. He and Elianor his wife levied a fine thereof to the uſe of themſelves in taille, the remainder to the king, 14 H. 6. and the duke made a leaſe of this manor and hundred to Ralph Butler and John Beauchamp, for their lives.

Henry Beauchamp, duke of Warwick, had a grant of the manor and hundred to him and his heirs, in reverſion, after the death of the duke of Glouceſter; but the duke of Warwick dying 25 H. 6. the year before the duke of Glouceſter, the eſtate came to Anne, an infant daughter and heir of the duke of Warwick, who dying 27 H. 6. the manor and hundred went to Anne, ſiſter to the duke of Warwick, who was married to Richard Nevil, the *Make-king*, afterwards earl of Warwick in her right. They join in levying a fine of this eſtate to the uſe of themſelves and the heirs of their bodies, the remainder to Richard Beauchamp, afterwards earl of Warwick.

Iſabel, one of the daughters and coheirs of Richard Nevil earl of Warwick, and Anne his wife, was married to George duke of Clarence, brother to king Edward the Fourth; and by virtue of an act of parliament which deprived the mother, he, in right of his wife, held the manor and hundred of Bertune, of which he died ſeized 17 E. 4.[y] But Anne counteſs of Warwick was afterwards reſtored to her right, with a ſiniſter deſign, by that covetuous monarch king Henry the Seventh; for ſhe was obliged to paſs away this manor, and many others, to the king, as frequently obſerved in the courſe of this work, 3 H. 7.

The manor and hundred, and two mills, called French-Mills, were granted, by king Henry the Eighth, to his laſt queen Catherine, in part of her dower. She died 2 E. 6. and preſently afterwards the manor was granted to ſir Thomas Arundel, the duke of Somerſet's favourite, who was attainted and executed with the duke, 5 E. 6. for conſpiring the death of John duke of Northumberland, and other privy counſellors.

The manor and hundred were again granted by the crown to William earl of Pembroke, in conſideration of 8000*l*. 7 E. 6. Maurice Dennis died ſeized of the manor and hundred of Berton 5 Eliz. and left Walter Dennis, his brother and heir, then ſixty years old.

This manor and hundred were ſoon after purchaſed by Thomas Cheſter, of Knole, eſq; and from him it has deſcended, down to the preſent time, in the ſame manner with Almondeſbury in this county, to which the reader is referred.

The lords of this manor have conſtantly held courts leet and hundred courts for the manor and hundred.

Beſide the manor, the records give the following particulars of other eſtates in this pariſh, and ſuch parts of its neighbourhood as cannot, perhaps, at this time, be diſtinguiſhed therefrom. Thomas de Amenel, in right of his manor of Bitton, had tack of ſwine in Briſtol-Bertune and Finchwood 7 H. 3 Roger Corbet was ſeized of lands in Bertune by Briſtol 18 E. 1. John de Saltmarſh was ſeized of twenty acres of wood in Kingſwood-chaſe 14 E. 2. William Corbet was ſeized of fourteen acres of land in Bertune near Briſtol 2 R. 2. Sir William Rodney died ſeized of ſeveral tenements in Berton and in Briſtol 6 E. 4. Roger Kemys, a lunatick, held a tenement, called Girdelars, 21 E. 4. A meadow in Berton near Briſtol, which had belonged to St. Mary Magda-

[y] Sir John Pelham, Thomas archbiſhop of Canterbury, and the biſhop of Durham had a releaſe from the king, and for his heirs and ſucceſſors, of all his right in the manor and hundred of Berton near Briſtol, in com. Glouc. which they had by grant of Edmund duke of York, by the king's authority. Pat. 13 H. 4. p. 2, m. 15.

len's hoſpital in that city, was granted, after the diſſolution of religious foundations, to Henry Brain and John March, 37 H. 8. The lords commiſſioners to examine the king's revenues throughout England, made a return 6 E. 6. that the ranger of Kingſwood and Fillwood had a yearly ſalary of 11*l.* 8*s.* 1*d.*

The hoſpital of St. Lawrence, for lepers, which ſtood within the bounds of this pariſh, was granted, at the diſſolution, to ſir Raufe Sadleir, knight. A piece of ground, about ſix acres, which belonged to that hoſpital, lying on the north ſide of the chapel of St. Lawrence, is exempt from tithe. Sir William Dugdale, in his *Monaſticon*, places this hoſpital in Somerſetſhire, by miſtake.

Blackſworth, or *Blackenſworde*, is a manor conſiſting of detached lands in ſeveral pariſhes. The greater part is in this, and ſome, particularly the paſſage over the river Avon at Rownham, in the pariſh of Clifton. The monaſtery of St. Auguſtin in Briſtol was endowed with this manor by the founder, Robert Fitz-Harding. It is now the property of the dean and chapter of Briſtol, and is in leaſe to Thomas Tyndale, of the Fort, eſq.

Of the Church, &c.

The church is a vicarage, worth 150*l.* a year, under the juriſdiction of the biſhop of Briſtol and of the archdeacon of Glouceſter; the mayor and corporation of the city of Briſtol are patrons, the reverend Mr. Hart is the preſent incumbent.

Dr. Butler, biſhop of Durham, gave 400*l.* towards endowing the church: And the late Thomas Cheſter, eſq; gave two acres, one rood, and ſix perches of land, bounded on the weſt by Don John's Croſs, (as recited in the act of parliament) for the ſcite of the church and cœmetery. Beſides theſe, other donations, to a large amount, were contributed by various perſons, for the augmentation of the vicarage; and, together with what was procured from the governors of queen Anne's bounty, were laid out, by the commiſſioners, in the purchaſe of ſeveral lands in this pariſh, to the value of between 70 and 80*l.* a year. There is a very good new houſe for the reſidence of the incumbent.

The church is a very neat, tho' plain building, ſeventy feet long by ſixty broad, conſiſting of the nave and two ailes, ſupported by two rows of handſome freeſtone pillars. The chancel is very ſmall, with a Venetian window over the communion table. At the weſt end is a large ſquare tower, ſeventy-two feet high, with two bells.

The building was begun in the year 1752. The mayor of Briſtol, attended by the reſt of the commiſſioners, went in proceſſion, on the 3d of March, from the Lamb inn to the ſpot of ground upon which the church was to be erected, where the mayor laid the firſt foundation ſtone, with this inſcription:

Templum hoc,
Dei Opt. Max. Glorie
et Hominum indies peccantium ſaluti
Sacrum,
Erigi voluit Pietas publica.
Abſit tamen
quod inter ignota Nomina
Reverendi admodum in Chriſto Patris
Ioſephi Butler,
nuper Briſtolienſis Epiſcopi,
Lateat nomen:
D. D. D. 400*l.*
Iam tum ad Dunelmenſes migraturus.

Regnante Georgio Secundo,
Iuſto, Clementi, Forti,
Angularem hunc lapidem
5 Non. Mart. A. D. 1752, S. N.
Poſuit
David Peloquin, Briſtolie Prætor.

Several pieces of coin, incloſed in lead, being laid on the ſame ſtone, the whole was covered with a proper ſheet of lead, and then another ſtone laid thereon, with the following inſcription:

Domine Deus noſter!

Aperti ſint Oculi tui nocte dieque ſuper domum hanc; Orationes populi tui, quodcunque oraverint in loco iſto, exaudias; in Loco Habitaculi tui in Cœlis exaudias; et cum exaudieris, propitius eſto! 1 *Reg. c.* 8, *v.* 29, 30.

The church was conſecrated Sept. 6, 1756, and was called St. George's. A revel is conſtantly kept on the anniverſary of the church's conſecration, in pious commemoration of the divine goodneſs, in cauſing this fabrick, at a great expence, to be founded and endowed, for the accommodation of the inhabitants in their weekly attendance on divine worſhip: Which revel is moſt devoutly celebrated by great numbers of the pariſhioners, and others, in the adjacent ale-houſes, with all the ſolemnities of an old pagan feſtival; that is, drunkenneſs, gluttony, riot, debauchery, curſing and ſwearing, ſcolding and fighting, fiddling and dancing, Bacchanalian ſongs, and midnight impurities.

What induced the truly worthy perſons concerned in this good work to give the church the name of St. George's,[z] is to me unaccountable, as that ſaint is not to be found in the calendar of the church of England, ſince the reformation.

Firſt fruits £.	Synodals £.
Tenths —	Pentecoſtals
Procurations	

Benefactions.

[z] The following extraordinary ſtory of St. George, as it is related in an antient manuſcript feſtival, written about the time of king Henry the Sixth, and in the poſſeſſion of a particular friend, may ſerve as a ſpecimen of our language, of the credulity of the people, and of the ſtate of religion at that time: and tho' a legendary tale, may afford ſome entertainment to the reader.

De fō Stī Georgij. [*Of the feaſt of St. George.*]

GODE men & wymen ſuche a day &c. ze ſhull haue the feeſt of Seynt George the whiche day ze ſhull come to chyrche ī the worſhyp of God & of his hooly martyr Seynt George. that bouzte hys day ful der for we redē ī h^{s} lyf th^{t} th^{r} was an orrybul dragō byſyd' a cyte th^{t} was called Syrene of the whych dragō mē of the cyte wer ſo aferd th^{t} by coūſel of th^{t} kyng uche day th^{y} zyuē hym aſheep & chyld for to ete for he ſhulde not com īto th^{e} cyte to ete hē. thēne whē all the chyldrē of the cyte wer etē. for encheſō th^{t} th^{e} kyng zaf hē th^{t} coūſel th^{y} conſt'ynede hym th^{t} had but oon dawzt^{r} for to zeve hur to the dragō as th^{y} had zevē her chyldrē byfore thēne the kyng for fere of the pepul wepyng & gret ſorow makyng delyv'ed hē hys dowgt^{r} in her beſte aray. & th^{y} ſettē hur in the place thē as they wer woned to ſette her chyldrē to abyde the dragō & a ſheep w^{t} hur. but thene by the ordynāce of God Seynt George coom rydyng that wey. & whē he ſyz the aray of the maydē he thouzte wel th^{t} hoe ſhulde be a

Benefactions.

The late Mr. Paul Fiſher, of Clifton, left, by his will, the intereſt of 300*l.* for ever to the vicar of St. George's for the time being, for reading prayers on Wedneſdays, Fridays, and ſaints-days, for preaching a ſermon on Good-friday and Chriſtmas-day, and for adminiſtering a monthly ſacrament.

Of the donations formerly left to the poor of St. Philip's pariſh, amounting to 16*l.* a year, the church-wardens of this pariſh receive a third part, which they diſtribute in bread to the poor.

The donations, formerly given to the old pariſh for repairing the highways, are not divided; particulars of which are given under St. Philip's.

St. George's and St. Philip's, and the out Part of the Pariſh of St. James.

Taxes.	The Royal Aid in	1692, £.	198	4	0
	Poll-tax ——	1694, —	138	13	0
	Land-tax ——	1694, —	568	4	0
	The ſame, at 3*s.*	1770, —	426	0	0

In a ſeries of ten years, beginning with 1760, there are regiſtered 1145 baptiſms, and 499 burials. But the burials give no light reſpecting population, becauſe many of the pariſhioners are every year interred at the neighbouring pariſhes, eſpecially at St. Philip's, where moſt of their anceſtors lie; which accounts for the great diſproportion between the numbers of baptiſms and burials here. There are about 700 houſes in this pariſh, and if we eſtimate the whole number of inhabitants to be to the average of annual baptiſms in the proportion of 30 to 1, which is the proportion commonly found in like ſituations, the number of people will then be 3435; *i.e.* nearly five to a houſe.

GUITING-POWER.

THIS pariſh is ſituated in the Coteſwold country, in the lower part of the hundred of Kifteſgate, ſix miles diſtant weſt from Stow, ſix eaſtward from Winchcombe, and nineteen north-eaſt from Glouceſter.

It is generally called *Lower-Guiting*, from its ſituation lower down the river, to diſtinguiſh it from another Guiting, lying nearer to the ſource of that river.

It is a fine, open, ſporting country, with bold riſing grounds, conſiſting chiefly of ſheep-walks, and arable lands; but there are ſome woodlands and meadow grounds. Petrifications of the cockle, the muſcle, and the *echenites* are found in plenty, particularly in and about the manor of Guiting Grange; and the water of a ſtream near the village is of a ſtrong incruſting quality. The little river is the head of the Windruſh, and abounds with ſmall trout and excellent eels.

Powell Snell, eſq; has a large eſtate called the *Grange*, in this pariſh, with a handſome ſeat, where he reſides.

Of the Manors and other Eſtates.

Under the head *Terra Willi Goizenboded*, in *Domeſday-book*, are the following particulars:

'The ſame William holds Getinge in Holeford 'hundred. King Edward held it, and permitted 'Aluuin his ſheriff to hold it for his life, but he 'did not give it to him, as the county witneſſeth. 'After Aluuin's death, king William gave his '[Aluuin's] wife and land to one Richard a young 'man. Now William, ſucceſſor to Richard, holds 'the land in the ſame manner. There are ten

wōmō of gt worſhyp & aſked hur why hoe ſtode th'r wt ſo moornyng chere. thene onſwered hoe & ſayde. gentul knygt wel may I moorne & be of heve cher tht ā akyng' dowztr & now am ſet her to be an orrybul dragon' p'ye tht etē all the chyldrē of ths cyte. & for all they bē etē now mot I be etē alſo. for my fadr gaf hē that coūſel. & th'fore gentul knyzt go hēn' faſte & ſave thy ſelf leſt he leſe the as he wol me. Damyſel q' George tht wer gte ſhame to me tht am a knyzt wel arayed zyf I ſhulde fle & thu tht art a wōmō abyde. thēne wt thys word anoō the orybul worme putte up hys hed ſpyttyng fyr owt of hs mowth & p'fered batel to George. thēne made George a c'ſſe byfore hym & rood at hym wt hys ſpere wt ſuche a mygte tht he bar down the dragō to the yrthe. thēne bad he the damyſel tye hir gurdul abowt hs nekke & lede hym aftr hur into the cyte. thēne the dragō ſued hur forth as ht had ben a gētul hownd mekely wtout any myſdoyng. but whē the pepul of the cyte ſyz the dragō come they flowen uche mon īto hujue for ferde. thēne George called the pepul ageyn & bad hē not be aferd. for zyf they woldē beleue ī Crſt & take C'ſtēdome he wold ſlen hym byfore hem anoō & ſo delyverē hē of hē enimy. thēne wer they all ſo glad tht twenty 1000 of mē wtowtē wymē & chyldrē wer fulwed anoō fyrſt the kyng & al hys howſhold wt hym. And thēne he ſlowz the dragō & bad hem tye to hym oxon & drawe hym owt of the cyte tht the ſavor of hym ſhulde not greve hem. & then he bad the kyng bylde church' faſt in uche cornel of the lond & be luſty to here godd' ſervyſe & do honor to all mē of hooly chyrche & evermoore have minde & cōpaſſion of all that wer nedy & pore. thēne whē George had don ths & trned all the lond to cryſtē feyth. he herde how the emporor Dyoclicyn dude mony c'ſtē men to dethe. thēne gode he to hym & booldly repreved hym of hys curſed doyng. thēne the emp'ror anoon commanded to do hym into p'ſon & legge hym thr uprygt & amylſtoon on hys breſte & ſo to preſte hym to dethe. But whē he was ſēved ſo. p'yed god of helpe. & anoō god kept hym ſo tht he felde noo harm in noo party of hys body. but whē the empō herde th'ofe he bad make a wheel & ſettē ht ful of hoks ī tht oon ſude & ſwerd' poynt' ſtyked ī an oth' wheel ageynſt th't. & ſette George ī the myddul & ſo turnd the wheel' for to have alto raſed hys body on eyther ſyde. but when he was in ths turmentry he p'yde C'ſt of ſokē & he was holpen anoō. thēne aft' he was put ī a hoot lyme cullē & cloſed th'in to have be brend. but God of hs mygt turned the heete īto coolde & ſo he lay th'e thre day' & thre nygtus. & whē he had leyn th'e ſo longe tht thy wōde he had be brend alto clene powd'. thēne was he foūdē lygte & mery & thonkyng god. thēne aft whē he was fat & ſet byfore the emp'ō. he rep'ued hym of hys falſe godd' & ſeyde th't they wer but fynd' & wtowtē mygt & falſe at nede. thēne was the empō to bette hys mowth wt ſton' tyl ht was alto poned. & thēne he made to bete hys body wt dryed boole ſenowus tyl the fleſh fel fro the boon' & hs bowell' mygtē be ſeyn. & zet aft' that thy madē hym to drynke venym tht was maad ſtrong for the noons to have puyſoned hym anoō to deth. but when George had made a ſyyne of the croſſe on hit he drank ht wtowtē any greef. ſo tht for wōder th'of the mon tht made the puyſon anon tūed to the feyth of C'ſt & anoō aft' was doō to deth for C'ſt' ſake. thēne ī the nyzt aft' as George was in p'ſon p'yyng to God byſyly. God coō to hym wt a gr lygt & bad hym be of good comfort. for on the moraw he ſhulde make an ende of hys paſſyon & come to hym into the joye tht ev' ſhall laſte. and when he had don he ſette a c'wne of gold on hys hed and gaf hym hys bleſſyng & ſteyz into hevē. thēne on the morow for he would not do ſacryfyſe to the emp'ō falſe godd' he made to ſmyte of hys hed & ſo he paſſed to God. & when the emp'ō wolde have go to hys palis the leyt fyre brende hym & al hys frind'. In a ſtory of Antyago ht is writē tht whē c'ſtē men byſegeden jeruſalem a feyr yong knygt appered to a pryſt & ſayde that he was Seynt George & was ledar of cryſtē men & thē he covenāded wt hym tht he wolde be wt hē at ſawtyng of the wallus. but whē the c'ſtē men coome to the wall' of jeruſalem. the Sareſen' wer ſo ſtrong wtin tht the c'ſtē men durſtē not clymbe upon her ladder' thēne coō Seynt George clothed in whyte & a reed croſſe on hs breſte & gode up a laddā & bad the c'ſtē mē come aft' hym. & ſo wt help of ſeynt George thy wōnē the town & ſlowē all the Saraſen' that wer fownd, &c.

'hides

'hides, of which nine pay tax. In demean are 'four plow-tillages, and four villeins, and three 'foreigners, and two radchenifters, and a prieft, 'with two bordars, who have between them all, 'five plow-tillages; and the *fervi* and *ancillæ* 'have eleven [plow-tillages] and two mills of 14*s*. 'There are five falt-pits, which yield twenty feams 'of falt. Two houfes in Winchcombe pay 11*s*. 4*d*. 'It was worth 16*l*. now 6*l*.' *Domefday-book*, p. 74.

The mafter of the knights templers, in a writ of *Quo warranto* brought againft him, proved his right to court leet, waifs, and felons goods in Guiting-Poers, by a grant 53 H. 3.

Two virgates of land, each of 3*s*. rent, were given to the knights templers by Roger de Waittevil. *Dug*.

This manor, Farmcot, Cateflade and Caldecot, were held of Roger de Quincy, earl of Winchefter, 55 H. 3. and afterwards of Alan la Zouche, baron of Afhley, who was grandfon and heir to the faid earl, by one of his coheireffes; which Alan died 7 E. 2. and left coheireffes.

Roger Corbet died 7 E. 2. feized of four knights fees and a half, and of one third part of a knight's fee, in Ebrington, Hudecote, Clopton, Farnecote, Catteflade *parva*, Gytinge, and Teynton; which he held of Alan Szouche, and they were worth 48*l*. 6*s*. 8*d*. *Efch*.

Adam de Hermington died feized of the manor of Nether-Guiting 16 E. 3. and fir John Butler died feized of the manors of Nether-Guiting and of Whitbridge 17 E. 4.

This manor came afterwards to the Horwoods. William Horwood was feized of it, and obtained a grant of the impropriation 35 H. 8. which latter formerly belonged to the knights templers. He died 37 H. 8. and left two coheireffes; Anne, who was afterwards married to Ambrofe Dudley; and Margaret, who was married to Thomas Throgmorton. They had livery granted to them 3 Mar. And livery of one moiety of the manor, and of the rectory and advowfon, was granted to Thomas Horwood 15 Eliz.

Henry Stratford, efq; was lord of this manor in the year 1608. Sir James Howe married one of the coheireffes of the heir of Henry Stratford, and was lord of the manor when fir Robert Atkyns compiled his account of it. But it did not continue long afterwards in that family, for David Hughes, efq; was lord of it in the year 1726. He was fucceeded by David his fon, who dying unmarried in the year 1753, bequeathed his eftate to his three fifters, of whom the eldeft was married to Thomas Vernon, of the city of Gloucefter, efq; deceafed, by whom fhe has one fon; the fecond to Mr. William Smart, of Winchcombe, apothecary, deceafed; and the youngeft to John Holland, of Mickleton in this county, gentleman, by whom fhe had feveral children. Mr. Vernon and Mr. Holland are the prefent lords of the manor, and hold a court baron; but Guiting-Power, Catflade, and Farmcot owe fuit and fervice to the court leet at Ebbrington, held by lord Fortefcue. The manor of Guiting-Power pays 9*l*. 19*s*. a year to William Wyndham, of Halling, efq.

But there was another manor of Guiting at the time of the general furvey.

'The wife of Geri de Loges holds of the king 'four hides in Getinge, in Holiforde hundred. 'Three thanes, Gulvert, Tovi, and Turber held 'them for three manors, and paid tax. In demean 'is one plow-tillage, and one villein, with half a 'plow-tillage. It was worth 40*s*. now 20*s*.' *Domefday-book*, p. 79.

It is impoffible at this time to trace the defcent of thefe lands diftinctly from the former; only the records fhew, that Gunuld de Loges, the widow of Jurie or Geri de Loges, gave two hides of land in Guiting to the monaftery of Gloucefter, to pray for the foul of her hufband.

William de Ebroicis and Maud his wife, formerly the wife of —— de Trevel, levied a fine of lands in Guiting to the ufe of Maud for her life, with feveral remainders, 5 E. 1.

TITHINGS and *HAMLETS*.

1. *Farmcot*, but antiently, and perhaps more rightly, *Fernecote*; from *fern*, and the Britifh word *coed*, a *wood*; for there is a large wood which gave occafion to the name. This hamlet, lying near three miles from the church, is divided from the body of the parifh by the intervention of lands in Guiting-Temple. It is an antient manor, thus defcribed in the furvey:

'William Goizenboded holds Fernecote. 'Aluuinus held it. There are three hides taxed. 'In demean are two plow-tillages, and four villeins, 'with four plow-tillages, and thirteen among the '*fervi* and *ancillæ*. Goisfrid holds it of William. 'It was worth 10*l*. now 3*l*.' *Domefday-book*, p. 74.

Roger Corbet died feized of lands in Farnecote, &c. which he held of Alan Szouche 7 E. 2. John Benne died feized of this manor 16 E. 3. as did fir Robert Corbet 5 H. 5. having affigned it to Joan his widow in dower. John Grevil married Sybil, the daughter of fir Robert Corbet, and in the life time of the faid Joan, entered upon the lands which fhe held in dower, for which he had the king's pardon[a] 8 H. 5. John Grevil died feized of Farmcot 23 H. 6. as did fir John Lineham 19 E. 4.

This eftate foon afterwards came into the family of the Stratfords, who have continued to enjoy it to the prefent age; but that antient family falling to decay, this manor and eftate were fold to Robert Tracy, efq; grandfon to the late Mr. Juftice Tracy; who dying without iffue, bequeathed it to Robert Pratt, efq; reprefentative in the laft parliament for Horfham in Suffex.

The large wood is the property of George Pitt, efq; reprefentative in parliament for the county of Dorfet.

On a piece of ground called the Langet, ftood a fmall preceptory, belonging to the commandery at Quenington in this county, to which the great tithes belonged. King Henry the Eighth fold

[a] Pat. 8 H. 5. m. 14.

ſold the great tithes to biſhop Fox, who gave them to Chriſt-Church college in Oxford. The preceptory and the Langet were granted to Richard Andrews and Leonard Chamberlain of Hayles, 34 H. 8. and afterwards purchaſed of them by Mr. John Stratford, at that time owner of the reſt of Farmcot. Other lands in Farmcot, which belonged to the abbey of Hayles, were granted to William marquis of Northampton, 5 E. 6.

Here is a chapel of eaſe, where divine ſervice is performed once every kalendar month, by the miniſter of Lower-Guiting.

This tithing has its own conſtable, and pays all rates, except the poor's rate, diſtinctly.

2. *Caldicot* is another hamlet, but it is not known by that name at preſent. When *Domeſday-book* was compiled, this hamlet lay in a different hundred from the reſt of the pariſh, according to the following entry :

'William Goizenboded holds Callicote in Sale-'maneſberie hundred, and Rannulf [holds it] of 'him. Aluuin held it in the time of king Edward. 'There are three hides taxed. In demean are 'three plow-tillages, and eight among the *ſervi* 'and *ancillæ*. It was worth 60*s*. now [only] 40*s*.' *Domeſday-book*, p. 74.

The lands of this place are now called the Weſt Field, about a mile from the church, divided from the other lands of the pariſh, by thoſe of Naunton and Halling. This eſtate belonged to the family of Aylworth, which became extinct in the preſent age. It is now the property of Henry Blagg, of the county of Nottingham, eſq.

3. *Caſtlet*, antiently written *Cateſlat*, and *Cateſlade*, is another hamlet, of which it is thus recorded:

'William Goizenboded holds Cateſlat. Aluuin 'held it. There are two hides taxed. In demean 'are two plow-tillages, and four *ſervi*, and a mill 'of 5*s*. It was worth 40*s*. now only 10*s*.' *Domeſday-book*, p. 74.

This manor, tho' within the pariſh of Guiting, is a member of the manor of Ebbrington. It conſiſts of a capital meſſuage and a corn-mill. David Hughes, eſq; lately deceaſed, died ſeized of this manor. Chriſt-Church college in Oxford has the great tithes; but the vicar has tithe of hay, ſome pieces of ground excepted. Cateſlat has a diſtinct conſtable. It is exempted from ſtatute-labour, but in all other reſpects, it joins in payments with the pariſh at large.

4. *The Grange*. This is an independent manor, and pays an annual rent to the crown. It was a grange belonging to the abbey of Bruern, and tho' it does not appear when theſe lands were granted to that houſe, it was certainly not before the reign of king John.

Three fourths of the great tithes of this manor are paid to Chriſt-Church college, Oxford; the remainder to the truſtees of the charities left by George Townſend, eſq.

Within this manor is a plot of ground, in the midſt of an arable incloſure, where the foundations of a chapel are viſible, of which, however there is no written account. It is ſuppoſed to have been the burying-place of the inhabitants of the Grange, and to have been dedicated to the Holy Trinity, as the ford thro' the adjacent brook is even now called Trinity ford, and probably gave name to the old hundred of Holeford, *i.e. holy ford*, in which it lay. The piece of ground between thoſe ruins and the Grange-houſe, ſtill retains the name of the Bier-way-piece. Add to this, that the plot of ground where the foundations are ſeen belongs to the vicar.

Lands in Nether-Guiting, formerly belonging to the abbey of Bruern, were granted to Anthony Stringer and John Williams 34 H. 8. This manor and eſtate were the property of William Gardiner, eſq; at the beginning of this century, and were purchaſed of Mr. Gardiner, about fifty years ſince, by John Snell, of the city of Glouceſter, eſq; who marrying Anna-Maria, daughter and ſole heireſs of Robert Huntingdon, D.D.[b] ſometime biſhop of Raphoe, by Mary his wife, ſiſter to the late ſir John Powell, knight, one of the juſtices of the court of queen's bench, had by that marriage ſeveral ſons, of whom the late Powell Snell, eſq; was the eldeſt. He incloſed the antient grange within a park ſtock'd with deer. In the year 1737, he married Dorothy, one of the coheireſſes of Charles Yate, of Colthrop, in this county, eſq; by whom he had iſſue Powell, John, Charles, and Dorothy. And ſurviving her, married ſecondly, Suſannah, ſecond daughter of Benjamin Bathurſt, of Lidney, in this county, eſq; but by her had no iſſue. He died in the year 1767, and is ſucceeded in this and other eſtates, by his eldeſt and only ſurviving ſon, Powell Snell, eſq; who reſides here. His arms are, *Quarterly, gules and azure, over all a croſs flory Or.*

Of the Church, &c.

The church is a vicarage, in the deanery of Stow, worth 52*l*. a year. Thomas Vernon, eſq; and Mr. David-Hughes Holland are patrons; Mr. King the preſent incumbent. The impropriation belonged to the abbey of Bruern, in Oxfordſhire.

The church, dedicated to St. Michael, is a very antient fabrick. The door-way of it, and the arch between the church and chancel, are thought to be of Saxon workmanſhip. It hath a well built embattled tower at the weſt end.

First fruits	£. 14 19 7	Proc. & Syn.	£. 0 7 8
Tenths	— 1 9 11½	Pentecoſtals	0 0 7½

[b] He was eſteemed the beſt ſkilled in the oriental languages of any in his time, and being chaplain to the Engliſh factory at Aleppo, made the tour of the holy land, where he purchaſed a very valuable collection of oriental manuſcripts, which are now in the Bodleian library, in Oxford.

Benefactions.

Benefactions.

George Townſhend, eſq; gave a portion of tithes in this pariſh, to be applied in apprenticing out poor children; one of this pariſh to be taken in rotation with ſome others. Two acres of land are given to repair the church. And one Compere gave 100*l.* the intereſt of which to be laid out in bread for the poor.

Guiting.

			£.	s.	d.
Taxes.	The Royal Aid in	1692, £.	71	9	0
	Poll-tax ——	1694, —	19	5	0
	Land-tax ——	1694, —	78	6	8
	The ſame, at 3*s.*	1770, —	51	17	3¾

Farmcot.

			£.	s.	d.
Taxes.	The Royal Aid in	1692, £.	65	14	0
	Poll-tax —	1694, —	2	11	0
	Land-tax —	1694, —	50	0	0
	The ſame, at 3*s.*	1770, —	35	1	0

At the beginning of this century, there were 62 houſes, and about 300 inhabitants in this pariſh, whereof 10 were freeholders; yearly births 9, burials 8. *Atkyns.* At preſent, the baptiſms, on an average of ſeven years, are 12, burials 7; the number of houſes 82, and of inhabitants 375. Hence it appears, that the proportion of annual burials, to the whole number of inhabitants, is nearly as 1 to 53; which ſhews the place to be very healthy.

GUITING-TEMPLE.

THIS pariſh lies on the Coteſwold hills, in the lower part of Kifteſgate hundred, ſeven miles north-weſtward from Stow, five eaſtward from Winchcombe, and twenty north-eaſt from Glouceſter.

It was called *Temple-Guiting*, becauſe the knights templers had great property here. It is now generally called *Upper-Guiting*, and formerly, in old writings, *Over-Guiting*, becauſe ſituated above the adjoining pariſh of Guiting-Power.

It is of a middle ſize, conſiſting moſtly of arable land, with ſome paſture and woodland, and two large commons, on which great numbers of cattle are depaſtured.

It is a fine country for hunting, abounds with game, and enjoys a very healthy air, as appears by the ſtate of population at the end of this account.

The honourable and reverend George Talbot, D.D. third ſon of Charles lord Talbot, late high chancellor of Great Britain, reſides in the hamlet of Barton, in this pariſh. And Mrs. Jane Allen reſides at Guiting. She is deſcended, on the mother's ſide, from the very antient family of Puſey, of Puſey, in the county of Berks, which flouriſhed there in the time of king Canute the Dane. She is poſſeſſed of that famous Charter-Horn, of which Mr. Pegge gives ſome account in a work intitled *Archæologia*, publiſhed in the year 1775. This horn is ornamented with ſilver gilt rims, and a broad ſilver ring in the middle, and neatly mounted on hound's feet, which ſupport the whole. It was produced in court before lord chancellor Jefferies, in the reign of king James the Second, and proved from the inſcription upon it, and other admiſſible evidence, to be the identical horn, by which, as by a charter, king Canute conveyed the manor of Puſey to the family of that name, about 700 years before. It appears to have been originally a hunting horn, but as a hound's head, of ſilver gilt, is made to ſcrew in, as a ſtopper, at the ſmall end, it is ſuppoſed to have been alſo a drinking horn.

Of the Manor and other Eſtates.

The account of this manor, in *Domeſday-book*, ſtands under the head *Terra Rogerij de Laci*, and may be thus tranſlated :

'The ſame Roger holds Getinge in Holeford 'hundred. There are ten hides taxed, beſides 'the lord's, which is not taxed. Brictric held it, 'who was one of king Edward's thanes. In de'mean are five plow-tillages, and twenty-five vil'leins, and a prieſt, and ſeven radcheniſters, with 'eighteen plow-tillages. There are eighteen among 'the *ſervi* and *ancillæ*, and three mills of 24*s.* and a 'ſalt-pit of 20*s.* and twelve ſeams of ſalt, and in 'Wincelcombe three burgages of 32*d.* and two 'burgages in Glouueceſter of 10*d.* From wood 'and paſture forty hens. It is worth and was 'worth 10*l.*' *Domeſday-book*, p. 75.

Walter de Laci, father of the above Roger, was a great ſoldier, and very much in favour with the Conqueror; and this Roger had one hundred and ſixteen manors given him, of which twenty were in Glouceſterſhire. Taking part with Robert Curthoiſe, the elder brother, againſt king William the Second, his poſſeſſions were taken from him, and given to Hugh de Laci, his younger brother, who founded the priory of Lanthony.

Hugh de Laci left no ſurviving iſſue, whereby his inheritance deſcended to Gilbert, ſon of Emme, his ſiſter and ſurviving heireſs; which Gilbert aſſumed the name of Laci. He gave twelve hides and one virgate[c] of land, with his demeſnes in Guiting, and five burgages in Winchcombe, to the knights templers, of which order he afterwards profeſt himſelf.

Hugh de Laci, who diſtinguiſhed himſelf in the wars in Ireland, was ſon and heir of Gilbert, and died ſeized of the manor of Temple-Guiting 31 H. 2. Walter de Laci, ſon of Hugh, ſucceeded him, in whom, and his deſcendants, the manor of Guiting continued 'till the death of Alice, daughter and heireſs of Henry de Laci, the laſt earl of Lincoln of that name. The knights templers held of Alice counteſs of Lincoln, the manor of Great Guiting, called Temple-Guiting, with all its members, and the advowſon of the church, 17 E. 2. She died 22 E. 3.

From the Lacies, the manor of Temple-Guiting went to William de Clinton, earl of Huntingdon,

6 C who

[c] Dugdale.

who held this manor, together with the hamlets of Kynton and Bereton, in Temple-Guiting, jointly with his wife Julian, daughter and heir of ſir Thomas de Leybourn, and widow of John lord Haſtings of Bergavenny; and died ſeized thereof 28 E. 3. Julian ſurviving him, died ſeized thereof 41 E. 3. They leaving no iſſue, the manor deſcended to ſir John de Clinton, (ſon of John, the elder brother of the before-mentioned William earl of Huntington) who died ſeized thereof [d] 22 R. 2. He married Idonea, eldeſt daughter of Jeffery lord Say, and at length coheir to her brother William lord Say, and had by her, ſir William Clinton, his heir, who married Elizabeth, daughter of ſir William Deincourt, knight; but dying in the life time of his father, left iſſue William, his heir, who ſucceeded his grandfather. This William, fifth lord Clinton, bore the title of lord Say, to which he was heir by his grandmother Idonea, and was a very great warrior. He died 10 H. 6. and John Clinton, his ſon and heir, ſucceeded him; but it does not appear that he had any property in this manor, unleſs he was the ſame perſon deſcribed in the records by the name of John Clinton, of Clinton and Say, who levied a fine of lands in Over-Guiting 2 R. 3.

The manor of Temple-Guiting was ſoon after purchaſed by Dr. Richard Fox, biſhop of Wincheſter, who gave it to Corpus Chriſti college in Oxford, which he had founded: The preſident and fellows of which college are the preſent lords of the manor, and keep a court leet.

It is on record, that the knights templers purchaſed a charter of free warren, and of court leet, waifs, and felons goods in Guiting, Barton, Kyngton, Holford, and Weſton, 53 H. 3. and that their right was allowed, in a writ of *Quo warranto*, 15 E. 1. This ſeems incongruous with the preceding account of the deſcent of the manor, from before that time 'till long afterwards, in the family of the Lacies; but the difficulty immediately vaniſhes, if we conſider them as meſne lords under that family, which was really the caſe, as expreſſly mentioned by the record of 17 E. 2. But tho' they were not the chief lords, their lands and poſſeſſions in this pariſh were very conſiderable. Upon the ſuppreſſion of their order, in the reign of king Edward the Second, their lands in Guiting, and in almoſt all other places, were given to the knights hoſpitallers; and after the general diſſolution of religious foundations, the rectory and advowſon of the vicarage, and lands in Temple-Guiting, lately belonging to the knights hoſpitallers of Jeruſalem, were granted to the dean and chapter of Oxford 38 H. 8.

Of ſome other eſtates, the records ſhew, that Robert de Brives died ſeized of lands in Guiting-Temple 53 H. 3. Walter de Laci gave lands in this pariſh to the abbey of Glouceſter, which abbey was ſeized of one meſſuage, one plow-tillage, and ſix yard lands in Temple-Guiting 32 E. 1. The abbey had alſo a grant of four marks rent, out of a meſſuage and one yard land, 33 E. 3.

HAMLETS. 1. *Guiting*, containing 28 houſes, and 177 inhabitants.

2. *Ford*, containing 17 houſes, and 80 inhabitants. Robert conſul of Glouceſter gave to the monaſtery of Glouceſter a water-mill in Ford, when William was abbat. Here was formerly a chapel of eaſe, long ſince converted to ſecular uſes. This hamlet pays to the church and poor of Guiting, but it is a conſtablewick annexed to Pinnock, to which it is rated for ſtatute labour. Lord Tracy is lord of the manor.

3. *Kyneton*, which has 16 houſes, and 84 inhabitants. Thomas Cook and Juliana his wife, and John Collet, levied a fine of lands in Kyneton 3 E. 6. One of the large commons within the pariſh is appropriated to the uſe of this hamlet.

4. *Barton*, containing 7 houſes, and 44 inhabitants. Livery of the manor of Barton was granted to Maurice Rodney 1 Eliz.

5. *Hyde-farm*. This is ſituated between Guiting and Ford; but tho' its ſituation ſeems to intitle it to be taken notice of in this pariſh, yet it pays neither to the church nor poor of Guiting, and is within the conſtablewick of Pinnock. And I conjecture, that Pinnock, Ford, and Hyde, conſtituted that diſtrict which is called *Pinnockſhire* in ſome antient writings.

Beſides the above, there are ſome ſcattered tenements, which make the whole number of houſes 75, of inhabitants 428.

Of the Church, &c.

The church is a curacy, in the deanery of Stow, and in the gift of Chriſt Church college, Oxford. Mr. King is the preſent incumbent.

The tithes and church revenues of this pariſh are appropriated, and veſted in the dean and chapter of Oxford, and the manor and temporal revenues belong to Corpus Chriſti college. Tho' both are of a conſiderable value, yet the allowance to the curate is only 20 *l.* a year; upon which ſir Robert Atkyns has obſerved, that it would be an advantage to both the colleges, and juſtice to the church, to improve the curacy; for then there might be a competent proviſion for a member of their own ſociety, and the colleges might preſent alternately.

The church is dedicated to St. Mary. By the generoſity of Dr. Talbot, the late miniſter, and the concurrence of the inhabitants, this church has been beautified in a more elegant manner than is often ſeen in village churches. The chancel is ſmall, but ornamented with a handſome altar-piece, and the windows are of antient painted glaſs. The church is newly pewed and glazed throughout, and the walls and cieling are of ſtucco. There is a handſome ſquare tower at the weſt end, with four bells.

Proc. 6 *s.* 8 *d.* Syn. 2 *s.* Pentecoſt. 9½ *d.*

Taxes.

[d] Eſch. 22 R. 2.

Taxes.					
The Royal Aid in	1692, £.	144	14	8
Poll-tax ——	1694, —	21	12	0
Land-tax ——	1694, —	60	18	0
The ſame, at 3*s.*	1770, —	43	1	0

At the beginning of this century, there were 45 houſes and about 191 inhabitants in this pariſh, whereof 8 were freeholders; yearly births 7, burials 6. *Atkyns.* The average of annual baptiſms at preſent is 16, of burials 8; the exact number of houſes 75, of inhabitants 428; which ſhews that the place is very healthy; the proportion of annual burials, to the whole number of inhabitants, being exactly as 1 to 53.5.

****

HAMPNET

IS a ſmall pariſh in the hundred of Bradley, one mile north-weſtward from Northleach, and eighteen eaſt from Glouceſter.

It is ſituated in the Coteſwold country, with a healthy air, and a light ſoil, chiefly employ'd in tillage. A little rivulet riſes here, and runs to Northleach in its way to Leachlade, where it empties itſelf into the Thames. It is called the *Lech,* (*i.e.* in the Britiſh language, a *ſtone*) from the petrifying quality of its water, which incruſts wood and other ſubſtances lying in its courre with ſtony matter.

The name of this village was antiently written *Hantone,* but there being two other pariſhes in Glouceſterſhire of the ſame name, both much larger than this, the diminutive termination was added for diſtinction, and it was then called *Hamptonet,* which, by vulgar uſe, was ſoon contracted to *Hampnet.*

Of the Manor and other Eſtates.

The earlieſt account we have of this manor is in *Domeſday-book,* where it is thus recorded:

'Roger de Lurei holds Hantone in Bradelege 'hundred. There are ten hides. Arch-biſhop 'Eldred held it, to whom king Edward gave two 'of thoſe ten hides quit [from tax] as they ſay. 'In demean are three plow-tillages, and ten 'villeins, with a prieſt, and one bordar, with five 'plow-tillages. There are eleven *ſervi,* and ten 'burgages in Winchcombe pay 65*d.* It was 'worth 8*l.* now [only] 6*l.*' *Domeſday-book,* p. 75.

The manor of Hampton was held of Roger Mortimer, earl of March, 34 E. 3. Edward de Mortimer, earl of March and Ulſter, was ſeized of a rent out of Hamptonet, near Northleach, which was then conſidered as a member of Biſley, 5 R. 2. Richard Hercourt, and Agnes his wife, levied a fine of the manor and advowſon of Hampnet 23 H. 7.

This manor, and that of Stowel, have had the ſame owners for many generations. Edmond Horn was ſeized of Hampnet 1 E. 6. and levied two fines of the manor and advowſon of Stowel, one the ſame year, the other 4 E. 6. He died 2 Mariæ, and left an only daughter and heir, married to Anthony Bourne, who, in her right, had livery of Hampnet the ſame year.

The manor paſſed afterwards to Henry Atkinſon, of Stowel, eſq; who was lord of it in 1608. Sir Henry Atkinſon, the laſt male heir of his family, dying without iſſue, gave this manor to William earl of Strafford, grandſon to ſir William Wentworth, who had married Anne, the eldeſt ſiſter of the before-mentioned Henry Atkinſon. John How, eſq; purchaſed the manor of the earl of Strafford, and lord Chedworth is the preſent lord of the manor of Hampnet. See *Stowel.*

Of the other eſtates in this pariſh, the records ſhew, that John Hanborow, and Thomas Bruges and Maud his wife, levied a fine of the third part of certain lands in Hampnet 36 H. 6. Alſo William Garine, and Elizabeth his wife, levied a fine of lands in Hampnet 2 E. 4.

Of the Church, &c.

The church is a rectory, in the deanery of Cirenceſter, worth 160*l.* a year. Lord Chedworth is patron, Mr. Hawker is the preſent incumbent.

The church of Stowel was annexed to Hampnet by the conſent of the biſhop and patron in 1660. There are about fifty acres of glebe.

The church, dedicated to St. Matthew, is ſmall, with a tower at the weſt end, but there is nothing in it worthy notice. It is, however, remarkable, that a woman has for many years officiated as clerk of the pariſh.

Firſt fruits £	10	0	0	Synodals £.	0	2	0
Tenths —	1	0	0	Pentecoſt.	0	0	6
Procurations	0	6	8				

Taxes.				
The Royal Aid in	1692, £.	39	1	0
Poll-tax ——	1694, —	6	11	0
Land-tax ——	1694, —	35	16	0
The ſame, at 3*s.*	1770, —	24	4	6

There were 14 houſes in this pariſh, at the beginning of this century, and about 60 inhabitants, whereof 4 were freeholders; yearly births 2, burials 1. *Atkyns.* There are now the ſame number of houſes, and 78 inhabitants.

HAMPTON.

THIS pariſh lies in the hundred of Longtree, three miles diſtant ſouth from Stroud, ſix north from Tetbury, ten weſt from Cirenceſter, and twelve ſouth-eaſtward from Glouceſter.

The name is compoſed of *Ham,* a *village,* and *ton,* a common termination. The manor antiently belonged to the nuns of Caen in Normandy, wherefore it was called *Minchen-Hampton,* from the Saxon word Mynchen, a *nun,* in order to diſtinguiſh it from another pariſh of the name of *Hampton* in this county. It is alſo called *Hampton-Road,* becauſe it lies on the great road from the ſouth-eaſt country to the paſſage over the Severn.

The

The greater part of the pariſh lies high and healthy. It conſiſts moſtly of arable lands, a large common, and ſome beech woods.

On the north eaſt ſide of the town, are ſeveral fortifications and rampires, thrown up at the time when the Danes ravaged this part of the country; and a great battle was fought thereabout, between Wolphang the Saxon, and Uffa the Dane, as related by one of our antient hiſtorians, wherein the latter was routed; and the place has ever ſince borne the name of *Woeful Dane's Bottom*, or rather, *Uffa Dane's Bottom*, in memory of that event. There are alſo very large intrenchments on the weſt ſide of the town, made probably about the ſame time, to check the incurtions of thoſe terrible robbers.

Within the pariſh, is a little town of the ſame name, with a market on Tueſdays, and two fairs in the year, *viz.* one held on Trinity-Monday, the other on the 29th of October. The abbeſs of Caen purchaſed a grant of markets and fairs here, in the fifty-third year of the reign of king Henry the Third; but the charter was renewed in 1541. The town conſiſts of four ſtreets, in the form of a croſs, with three market-houſes, one of which was built in the year 1700, for ſtoring of wool and yarn, in expectation of eſtabliſhing a great mart for thoſe commodities, as the town is well ſituated for that purpoſe in a great clothing country; but it ſeems not to have fully anſwered the deſign.

In the pariſh, not in the town, the clothing buſineſs is carried on in a very extenſive manner, where it has been ſeated for ſeveral ages, and will probably continue; for the many brooks and ſtreams of water on the north and weſt ſides of the pariſh, are particularly neceſſary for driving the fulling-mills uſed in that buſineſs.

Here was formerly a furnace for making of iron, and the place where it ſtood is now called the *Iron-mills*.

Amberley is a large tract of common of paſture, on the weſt ſide of the town, conſiſting of about a thouſand acres, given to the pariſh, according to tradition, by dame Alice Hampton, who lies buried in the church. In this common are quarries of very fine freeſtone, and weather ſtone.

So much of Chalford as lies on the ſouth ſide of the river, is within the boundaries of this pariſh; and notwithſtanding ſome account has been given of it under Biſley, it is neceſſary in this place to take notice of the petrifying quality of a remarkably clear ſpring of water, iſſuing from ſeveral apertures, out of the north ſide of the hill facing the bottom. The petrifying effects of this water are ſeen on various ſubſtances, lying in the courſe of the ſtream, ſuch as moſs, and ſmall pieces of wood; but they are particularly obſervable on the axis and other parts of a mill-wheel, on which the water is continually dropping; ſo that in the courſe of a year, it forms incruſtations nearly half an inch thick, not much unlike pieces of manna. Falling into cavities, it forms *ſtalactites*, and large petrified maſſes, in various uncommon ſhapes, pieces of which are preſerved as curioſities.

St. Mary's-Mill, in this pariſh, was formerly a chapel, famous for a room in it called Friar Bacon's Study, becauſe Roger Bacon is ſaid to have been educated there. He died in 1284, and was the greateſt mathematician and philoſopher of the dark and ignorant age in which he lived. His ſkill in thoſe ſciences was ſo much ſuperior to that of all others, that he was caſt into priſon, on ſuſpicion of having communication with the devil; and, it is ſaid, was indicted for bringing the ſun, moon, and ſtars down to the end of a long ſtick. Hence it ſeems probable that he had ſome knowledge of optical glaſſes; for what elſe can that *long ſtick* be, than ſome kind of teleſcope.

Mr. Sheppard has a very good houſe cloſe by the church, and a park adjoining, with plantations of beech wood, particularly large and fine.

Of the Manor and other Eſtates.

Sir Robert Atkyns, giving an account of the antient proprietors of this manor, has appropriated ſome records to this place, which really belong to others. Thus, the manor of Hantone which the Conqueror gave to Roger de Lurei, (whom ſir Robert calls de Ivory) lay at that time in the hundred of Bradley, as appears by *Domeſday-book*; and tho' he has applied that account to Minchin-Hampton, yet it can belong to no other place than Hampnet in Bradley hundred. He alſo mentions, under this head, another manor of Hantone, in Biſley hundred, whereas there was no ſuch manor there. The particulars he ſpecifies, ſhould have been applied to Hampton-Meyſey, which at the time of the general ſurvey, lay in Gerſdones, not in Biſley hundred, according to the fore-mentioned record. The following account is proper to this manor:

'The church of the Holy Trinity of the nuns 'of Caen holds Hantone in Langetreu hundred. 'Goda the counteſs held it in the time of king 'Edward. There are eight hides. In demean 'are five plow-tillages, and thirty-two villeins, 'and ten bordars, with twenty-four plow-tillages. 'There is a prieſt, and ten *ſervi*, and eight mills 'of 45*s*. [rent] and twenty acres of meadow; a 'wood two miles long, and half a mile broad. 'It is worth 28*l*.' *Domeſday-book*, p. 72.

The nuns of Caen in Normandy purchaſed a grant of markets and fairs in Hampton 53 H. 3. and the abbeſs proved her right to court leet and free warren in Hampton, in a writ of *Quo warranto* brought againſt her, 15 E. 1.

The nuns of Caen enjoy'd this manor 'till the reign of king Henry the Fifth, when all the eſtates in England belonging to alien monaſteries were taken from them. And that king having founded a ſtately nunnery at Syon in Middleſex, as already mentioned under Avening, endowed it with many

great

great eftates, and among others, with the manor of Hampton. The nuns of Syon obtained a confirmation of this eftate 1 E. 4. to be held after the death of the dutchefs of Suffolk, who had a grant of it for her life.

After the final diffolution of religious foundations, this manor was granted to Andrew lord Windfor, in exchange for the manor of Stanwell in Middlefex, and other lands near Hampton-court, 34 H. 8. fince which time it has had the fame proprietors with that of Avening, where they are particularly fet down. Edward Sheppard, efq; is the prefent lord of the manor.

Sir Robert Atkyns obferves, that the manor of Hampton was held of Richard de Clare, earl of Gloucefter and Hertford, 47 H. 3. but this muft be underftood of Meyfey-Hampton, and not of Minchin-Hampton, where he had placed it by miftake.

In the account of donations to St. Peter's abbey at Gloucefter, taken from fir William Dugdale's *Monafticon*, it is faid, that William Revel gave to the church of St. Peter at Gloucefter, one hide of land in Hamptone, with the confent of Bernard of Newmarket, which king Henry the Firft confirmed to the abbey, when Peter was abbat. And that Hugh Talemach, when he took the monk's habit at Gloucefter, gave one moiety of the town of Hamptone, with the church thereof, which his fon Peter confirmed; as did afterwards king Henry the Second, when Hameline was abbat. But it is not certain that thefe particulars belong to Minchin-Hampton, nor does it appear that Gloucefter abbey ever prefented to this church.

Several lands in Muneching-Hampton were given to the monaftery of Malmefbury, about the time of king Henry the Second. And the records fhew, that the following perfons had eftates in this parifh.

Peter de la Mere was feized of Minchin-Hampton, with free warren, 20 E. 1. This could not be the chief manor, but was probably the fame eftate of which Robert de la Mare died feized 2 E. 2. confifting of one meffuage, and fixty acres of land[f], for which he paid to the abbefs of Caen 13*s*. 4*d*. and to the abbat of Malmefbury 40*s*. yearly; and left Peter de la Mare his fon and heir, who was feized of the fame eftate 12 E. 2.

Here it may be proper to obferve, that in the fubfequent account, notwithftanding the records mention feveral perfons who were feized of the manor; yet they muft either be mefne lords only, or the expreffion muft be underftood in a qualified fenfe, to fignifiy fome confiderable eftate, or reputed manor, and not the principal one, which was held by the religious 'till the reformation. Thus it is faid, Edmond de Pinkney held this manor 4 E. 3. Thomas de Rodborough was feized of the manors of Minchin-Hampton and Havenpen 8 E. 3. William Ballecot held Hampton 20 E. 3. Sir John Maltravers and Agnes his wife levied a fine of lands in Minchen-Hampton 30 E. 3. and John Maltravers the elder was feized of one plow-tillage, twelve acres of meadow, and 100*s*. rent, with one knight's fee in Muchin-Hampton 31 E. 3. Sir John Maltravers held the fame 38 E. 3. John Berdolf de Wermefe was feized of Nalefworth, held of the manor of Munchin-Hampton, 45 E. 3. Agnes, widow of John Maltravers the elder, held the manor of Muchin-Hampton 49 E. 3.

Sir John de Arundel was feized of the manor of Hampton 3 R. 2. Sir John de la Mere and Maud his wife were alfo feized of the manor in Minchin-Hampton, held of the honour of Wallingford, 5 R. 2. Roger Gulden levied a fine of lands in Minching-Hampton to John Pearl and others 14 R. 2. Hugh Rodborough held the manor of Redewike, and lands in Sencle, within the manor of Muchin-Hampton, 17 R. 2. Thomas duke of Gloucefter was feized of lands in Muchin-Hampton and Rodborough 21 R. 2. John Pentour and Agnes his wife levied a fine of lands in Hampton and Rodborough 22 R. 2. Reignald Cobham the elder, of Sternbrugh, held Minchin-Hampton 4 H. 4. as did his widow 6 H. 4. Welleline, widow of fir John Roches, was feized of the manor of Muchen-Hampton 12 H. 4. Sir John Philips held the fame 3 H. 5. John Fry, fon and heir of John Fry, levied a fine of lands in Minching-Hampton and Rodborough, to the ufe of John Moody, efq; 4 E. 4.

Delamere manor, *alias* Lambert's, near Minchin-Hampton, was granted to George Nevil, efq; and his heirs males 2 R. 3. Henry Hammerfton levied a fine of lands in Minching-Hampton 10 H. 7. John Hyet alfo levied a fine of lands in Hampton and Avening, to William Webb, 1 E. 6.

The manors and advowfons of Hampton, Avening, Pinbury, &c. which lately belonged to the nunnery of Syon in Middlefex, were granted to Henry earl of Northampton, William lord Howard, and Nicholas Barnfley, 10 Jac.

HAMLETS, and places of diftinct names.

1. The *Box*. William de Lafboroke held La Box and La Planch 45 H. 3. and William de Staure held eight acres in Box 17 E. 2. Box and Longford were held of Humphry de Bohun, earl of Hereford and Effex, and of Joan his wife, 46 E. 3.
2. *Hawcombe*.
3. The *Iron Mills*.
4. *Longford's Burley*.
5. *Hide*.
6. *Wall's Quar*.
7. *Brimfcombe*.
8. The *Knap*.
9. The *Golden Valley*.
10. *Cowcombe*. Three tofts, two yard-lands, two acres of meadow, and twenty of pafture in Colcombe, near Hampton, which belonged to William Mull, *alias* Mill, attainted of treafon, were granted to Thomas Herbert and his heirs males in *taille* 5 E. 4.
11. *Forwood*.

[f] Efcheator's inquifition of that year.

Of the Church, &c.

The church is a rectory, in the deanery of Stonehouſe, worth about 400*l.* a year. Edward Sheppard, eſq; is patron; Doctor White is the preſent incumbent.

The pariſh of Rodborough is annexed to this rectory. The abbeſs of Caen in Normandy has preſented to this church; as did Agnes abbeſs of Syon, in the year 1538.

Gilbert Bourn was rector of this church in the year 1551, and was conſecrated biſhop of Wells in 1554.

Anthony Lapthorn was preſented to this rectory in the year 1612, of whom there is this anecdote. Being chaplain in ordinary to king James, he was preſent one day when the king and ſome of the nobility were at bowls, the archbiſhop of Canterbury and others ſtanding by. The king laid a bowl cloſe to the jack, which the nobleman who bowled next ſtruck away, on which his majeſty, falling into a paſſion, ſwore at a terrible rate. The archbiſhop taking no notice of it, Lapthorn boldly expreſt himſelf as follows: The king ſwears, and the nobles will ſwear. If the nobles ſwear, the commons will ſwear. What a ſwearing kingdom then ſhall we have! And for you, my lord archbiſhop, who have the immediate charge of his majeſty's ſoul, to hear him take God's ſacred name in vain, and to have never a word for his ſake, I will ſay to you, as one Paul ſaid to Annanias, *Thou painted wall, God will ſmite thee.* Which reproof wrought ſo great a reformation in the court, that if the king heard any perſon ſwear, he would reprove him, and ſay Lapthorn was coming.

The church is dedicated to the holy Trinity. It is built in the form of a croſs, with two ſide ailes. It had formerly a ſpire in the middle, but half of it was taken down, and the remainder ornamented with pinnacles and battlements; of which Dr. Frampton, biſhop of Glouceſter, who had viſited the holy land, uſed to ſay, that it greatly reſembled the pillar erected in memory of Abſalom, ſon of king David.

There was a chantry in the church, dedicated to the virgin Mary. Richard Gravener, the laſt incumbent, received a penſion of 5*l.* in 1553.

Firſt fruits £41	12	4	Synodals £	0	2	0
Tenths —	4	3	4	Pentecoſtals	0	1	4
Procurations	0	6	8				

Monuments and Inſcriptions.

The moſt antient are the effigies of a man and woman lying in two niches in the wall of the ſouth aile. The man is girt with a ſword, and has a large ſhield on his left arm, charged, in the firſt quarter, with an eagle diſplay'd. His feet reſt on a lion. This was intended for one Anſloe, who is ſaid to have built the aile.

In the north aile, engraven on braſs plates, and fixed on a flat ſtone, are the effigies of a man and his wife in ſhrouds, and this inſcription:

Of yor charite pray for the ſoules of Iohn Hampton gentleman, Elyn his wife, & all their Children, ſpecially for the ſoule of Dame Alice Hampton his daughter, whiche was right beneficial to this church & p'riſh. Whiche Iohn deceſſed in the yere of o'r lord MCCCCCLVI. on whoſe ſoules Ihu have mercy, Amen.

In the chancel,

PIÆ MEMORIÆ IEREMIÆ BVCKE, ARMIG. QVI CVM 35 SOLES ENVMERAVERAT, FATO CORREPTVS PRÆPROPERO, DIE DOMINICO ANTE NATIVITATEM CHRISTI, VITAM CVM MORTE COMMVTAVIT. MOESTISSIMA CONIVX URSVLA BVCKE HOC MARMOR ERIGI CVRAVIT.

I Intomb'd here lies a pillar of the ſtate;
E Each good man's friend, to th' Poor compaſſionate;
R Religion's patron, juſt men's ſure defence;
E Evil men's terror, guard of innocence:
M Matchleſs for virtues which ſtill ſhine moſt bright:
I Impartially to all he gave their right.
A Alas! that few to heart do truly lay
H How righteous men from earth depart away.

B By's death we looſe, but he much gaine acquires,
V Vnto his body reſt: His ſoule aſpires
C Coeleſtial manſions, where he God on high
K Knowes and enjoyes to all eternity.

Arms, *Per feſs nebule, argent and ſable, three bucks horns counterchanged, the ſcalps Or.*

Mr. Buck died in 1653. There is alſo a memorial for his ſon, Jeremiah Buck, who died in 1668, and for others of that family.

Within the communion rails:

Hic juxta ſitus eſt PHILIPPVS, filius unicus GEORGII de RIDPATH, Cognomen ducens a Baronia de RIDPATH, in Scotia, Patrimonium Avitum. Iuvenis erat ſummæ Spei, Supra Ætatem doctus, Acri Ingenio, indole optima, Aliiſque Eximijs animi Dotibus præditus. Sanitatis ergo, Parentum conſenſu, ac Medicorum Conſilio, e LONDINO rus ſe contulit, at in itinere GLOCESTRIAM verſus, 3° idibus Iulij 1705, repentino dolore in tergo correptus, Poſtridio ſummo mane, hac in Urbe, remedijs fruſtra tentatis, Animam piam ac puram, placide Deo reddidit, ineunte viceſimo ſecundo Ætatis Anno. Omnibus cum quibus Conſuetudinem habuit, Deſiderium ſui non mediocre reliquit. — Arms, at top, *Argent, a chevron ingrailed between three wolves heads erazed gules.*

On a handſome marble monument,

Haud procul hinc Tumulo jacet PHILIPPUS SHEPPARD, Armiger, hujus Eccleſiæ et Manerii, æque ac illius de Avening Patronus idem et Dominus. Fideli erga Regem animo, ac in Vicinos perquam benevolo. (Per annos quinquaginta et amplius) Irenarchæ munus arduum rogatus ſuſcepit, adminiſtrando ornavit; Patriæ Salutis ergo et Conſcientiæ Cauſâ, in Biennio tantum Iacobi 2^{d} conſtanti animo detrectavit: Parentis, Mariti, Magiſtratûs, Heri, ſingulis ipſe perfunctus Officiis cum Curâ, Studioq; maximo, Exemplum Poſteris optimum reliquit. Regi, Reipublicæ, et Eccleſiæ Anglicanæ obſequentiſſimus; plus æque pene ſobrius, pacificus, pius. Uxores duxit binas, Amantes viciſſim ac amatas; 1^{mam} Elizabetham, Gamalielis Capell, Militis, Filiam, ex qua tres Liberos adhuc Superſtites ſuſcepit, Samuelem, Philippum, Saram, præter Mariam et Elizabetham, olim in Cœlos hinc receptas. 2^{dam} Franciſcam, viduam, Prænobili Domino Gulielmo Domino Vicecomiti Downs olim nuptam. Rerum et Dierum plenus, nullius Morbi, nullius Ægritudinis, extremæ Senectutis tantum pondere laborans, lubens tandem hic Requiem aſſecutus eſt, Anno Domini 1713, Ætatis 82.

Hic juxta quoque ſita eſt Elizabetha Sheppard, prædictis Philippo Neptis, Samueli Filia. Virgo modeſta, humilis, pudica; nec minus facili Comitate Morum vere amabilis: Heu! tamen immatura Morte, quatriduum ante Avum abrepta, Anno Ætatis 30mo. Patri ac Filiæ Chariſſimis, Majora Meritis, Hoc qualecunq; Amoris et Obſervantiæ Monumentum, Samuel Sheppard, Philippi Fortunæ et Virtutis Hæres, *Mnemoſynes* ergo poni curavit.

There are ſeveral other memorials in the chancel, for this family, *viz.* for Samuel Sheppard, eſq; who died in 1724; and for Anne his wife, who died in 1734; with their arms, 1. Sheppard, impaling 2. *Or, a croſs quarterly quartered gules and ſable, in the firſt quarter an eagle diſplayed of the laſt,* for Webb.—For Philip Sheppard, M.A. rector of this

this pariſh forty-nine years, who died in 1768; and for Mary his wife, who died in 1753. No arms. —For Francis, Rebecca, and Thomas Sheppard, and Sarah Day, widow, (ſons and daughters of Samuel Sheppard, eſq;) who died reſpectively, in 1741, 1741, 1757, and 1764.—And there is a neat, tho' ſmall monument, for Samuel Sheppard, eſq; who died in 1770.

There is a ſhort memorial, without arms, for Robert-Saluſbury Heaton, M. A. rector of this pariſh and of Avening, who died in 1774.—And in the north aile are memorials for George Small, eſq; who died in 1704; and for John Small, eſq; who died in 1725. He married Elizabeth, one of the daughters and heirs of John Overy, of Greenville, com. Oxon. gent. On a ſcutcheon are theſe arms, *Sable, on a bend argent three roſes gules; in the ſiniſter chief a cheſs-rook of the ſecond*, for Small.

In the body of the church is a memorial for John Iles, of Chalford, eſq; many years in the commiſſion of the peace for this county, with his arms, *Argent, a feſs ingrailed ſable, in chief three fleurs de lis of the ſecond.*

Engraven on a large braſs plate, fixed on the end of a tomb in the church-yard, is the following memorial for the late profeſſor Bradley, who was worthy of a better monument:

H. S. I. Jacobus Bradley, S. T. P. Regalium Societatum Londini, Lutetiæ Pariſiorum, Berolini, et Petropoli Sodalis; Aſtronomus Regius, et Aſtronomiæ apud Oxonienſes Profeſſor Savilianus. Vir in rerum Phyſicarum Scientia excolenda, præcipue vero, in penitiſſimis arcanis indagandis, tam felici Diligentia, et ſagaci Ingenio, ut quotquot ubique gentium iiſdem honeſtiſſimis Studiis navabant operam, illi omnes libenter aſſurgerent: tam ſingulari interim modeſtia, ut, qua eſſet apud graviſſimos Iudices exiſtimatione, ipſe ſolus ignoraſſe videretur. Diſceſſit iii Id. Iul. A. D. MDCCLXII. Ætatis LXX.

Benefactions.

Samuel Sheppard, eſq; built an alms-houſe here, for eight poor people, but it has no endowment.

In 1698, Mrs. Urſula Tooke gave twenty acres of land in Weſt-field, and 80*l.* in money, the produce of which ſhe has thus diſpoſed of; 8*l.* a year for the ſchooling of ſix boys; 5*l.* a year to be given to four poor people; and 2*l.* a year for the truſtees, for their care. Each charity to be benefited or abated proportionably, on an increaſe or decreaſe of rent.

Mr. Henry King gave 250*l.* with which lands in the pariſh of Randwick, and a piece of ground called Sloven's-acre, in Hide, have been purchaſed, the produce of which to be applied in teaching eight boys to read and write.

Mr. William Webb, of Hocomb, has given five ſhifts, or 15*s.* in money, annually for ever, for five poor widows, ſecured on Hilbore's-mead, in this pariſh.

Mrs. Sarah Webb, of Giddinap, gave 300*l.* the intereſt of which to provide twelve brown cloth, or ſerge gowns, and twelve ſhifts, to be given to twelve antient maidens, or widows, of this pariſh, on the 3d of January, for ever.

Mr. William Vick, of Briſtol, gave the intereſt of 300*l.* for ever, to be diſtributed annually as follows; 1*l.* 1*s.* to the miniſter for prayers and a ſermon; 1*l.* 1*s.* to be ſpent by the veſtry at the Talbot, whilſt it continues a publick houſe; 10*s.* to the clerk; 10*s.* to the ringers; 2*s.* 6*d.* to the ſexton; and the reſt to be diſtributed by the clerk to the poor in bread. This donation, as it is expreſſed in Vick's will, is to commemorate our happy deliverer king William, and the ſecurity of our civil and religious rights by the revolution.

For the particulars of the endowment of the ſchool at St. Loe, and for other charities relating only to Rodborough tithing, ſee *Rodborough*.

Taxes.					
The Royal Aid in	1692, £.	99	15	4
Poll-tax ——	1694, —	71	16	0
Land-tax ——	1694, —	225	8	8
The ſame, at 3*s.*	1770, —	150	3	3

At the beginning of this century, there were 377 houſes in this pariſh, and about 1800 inhabitants, whereof 60 were freeholders; yearly births 33, burials 31. *Atkyns.* But ſince that time, population is very much increaſed, and it is computed that, excluſive of Rodborough, there are now not leſs than 4000 inhabitants.

HARDWICK

LIES in the hundred of Whitſtone, in a deep vale country near the Severn; ſeven miles north from Stroud, and four weſt from Glouceſter. The name is probably from *Hardd*, Britiſh, *ſplendid*, and *wic*, a *village*.

The ſoil is a ſtrong clay, therefore more proper for paſture than tillage; yet they have ſome arable land: And here, and almoſt in every part of this vale, they make excellent cheeſe, and ſtout cyder.

Of the Manor and other Eſtates.

This pariſh was probably a member of the large manor of Standiſh, when king William the Firſt cauſed the kingdom to be ſurveyed; wherefore *Domeſday-book* makes no diſtinct mention of it. The manor of Hardwick was antiently held of the earls of Glouceſter and Hertford. Petronella de la Mere was ſeized of Hardenwick 47 H. 3. John Kenn died ſeized of Hardwick 6 H. 4. as did Robert Kenn 31 H. 6.

John Trye was high ſheriff of Glouceſterſhire 27 H. 6. He married Elizabeth, daughter and heireſs of Almery Boteler, *a Park*, of Hardwick-court, and had that eſtate in right of his wife. The manor and eſtate of Hardwick and Hardwick-court continued in the Tryes[g], 'till it was purchaſed of

[g] This family was eminent in Glouceſterſhire for many generations. Their *originall deſcent & Name is from a Towne beyound the Seas called Trye*, (as I find it written on a monument for William Trye, eſq; in the family chapel at Hardwick) whence their anceſtor came into England about ſix hundred years ago.

Rawlin Trye married Margaret, daughter and heir of Thomas Berkeley,

of them by the late lord chancellor Hardwick, when he was attorney-general. And when his majeſty king George the Second was pleaſed to create him a baron of Great Britain, in 1733, and afterwards to advance him to the dignity of an earl, in 1754, his lordſhip took both thoſe titles from this place. His lordſhip died[h] in the year 1764, and was ſucceeded by Philip his eldeſt ſon, the preſent earl of Hardwick, and lord of this manor.

The abbey of Glouceſter had divers lands and poſſeſſions in this pariſh. Certain lands in Hardwick which belonged to that abbey, were granted to Edward duke of Somerſet, 1 E. 6.

HAMLETS. 1. *Rudge* and *Farley*, lying in the lower part of the pariſh, near Elmore church. The manor of Farleigh and de la Rugge was part of the poſſeſſions of St. Peter's abbey at Glouceſter 17 E. 3. After the diſſolution of that houſe, this manor, and a portion of tithes and glebe, were granted to the biſhop of Glouceſter 6 E. 6. and are now part of the endowment of the ſee of Glouceſter.

2. *Field-Court.* The name was antiently written *Feld*, and *La Feld*. Feld was held of William de Clinton, earl of Huntingdon 28 E. 3. It is an antient ſeat which has been long in the family of the Berows, or Barrows. Edward Berow died ſeized of Field-court 12 Eliz. and left James Berow, his ſon, twenty-eight years old. Mr. Thomas Barrow died poſſeſſed of this eſtate in the year 1736; whoſe only daughter, Elianor, carried it, by her marriage, to the rev. Mr. Thomas Savage, eldeſt ſon and heir of George Savage, of Broadway, in the county of Worceſter, eſq; by whoſe death, in 1760, it deſcended to his only ſurviving ſon and heir, George Savage, eſq; the preſent proprietor of this eſtate, and of the manor of Blakeney in the pariſh of Awre. His arms are, *Argent, ſix lioncels rampant ſable*, 3, 2, 1.

The conſtable of Hardwick has juriſdiction in the hamlet of Colthrop in the pariſh of Standiſh.

Of the Church, &c.

The church is a vicarage, in the deanery of Glouceſter, annexed to Standiſh, and worth to the vicar about 30*l.* a year. The tithes in Hardwick, and ſome lands called the Rugge, were given to the abbey of Glouceſter by Thomas de St. John, and after the diſſolution of the abbey, were granted to the biſhop of Glouceſter 33 H. 8. and were confirmed 1 E. 6.

Berkeley, with whom he had the manor of Alkington in Berkeley, in the reign of king Richard the Second; and was ſucceeded by his ſon John, who was alſo ſucceeded by his ſon William. John Trye was ſon of William. He married Elizabeth, daughter and heireſs of Almery Boteler, *a Park*, of Hardwick court, and had that eſtate in right of his wife. He was high ſheriff of Glouceſterſhire 27 H. 6. William Trye, ſon of John, married Anne, daughter of Thomas Baynham, and widow of Henry Clifford, of Frampton upon Severn, according to ſome accounts; but it appears by a monument in Hardwick church, that William Trye, eſq; lord of the manor of Hardwick, ſon of John Trye, eſq; lived in the time of king Edward the Fourth, and married Iſabella, daughter of James lord Berkeley, of Berkeley-caſtle. Edward Trye, ſon of William, married Sybil, daughter and coheir of ſir Simon Milborn of Herefordſhire, and widow of ſir Thomas Monington, and was ſucceeded by his ſon John Trye, who married Elizabeth, one of the coheirs of Charles Brandon, knight, duke of Suffolk, and died in the year 1579, as appears by a memorial for him. John Trye, ſon of John, married firſt, Margaret, daughter of ſir William Skipwith of Herefordſhire; ſecondly, Alice, ſiſter of ſir James Crofts. William Trye, ſon of the laſt John, married Mary, daughter of ſir Edward Tyrrell, of Thornton in Buckinghamſhire, and died in 1609. From this marriage all his deſcendants have a claim of kindred to the founder of All-Souls college in Oxford, whereby they will have a better chance of a fellowſhip in that college, than others who are not of the founder's kindred.

William Trye was ſon of William, and married Anne —— deſcended from the family of ſir Francis Vincent, of Stoke in the county of Surry, knight, and by her had eight ſons and ſix daughters. John, William, and Henry, the three eldeſt ſons, died without iſſue. Thomas, the fourth ſon, married Anne, eldeſt daughter of Richard Jones, of Hanham, eſq; and died before his father; whereby William, ſon of Thomas, was heir to his grandfather. He married Mary Horne, one of the coheireſſes of Thomas Horne, of Horncaſtle in Yorkſhire, eſq; and died poſſeſſed of the manors of Hardwick and Haresfield in the year 1717. He was ſucceeded by Thomas, his ſon and heir, who married Mary, daughter of Thomas Norwood, of Leckhampton, eſq; and was alſo ſucceeded by his ſon William Trye, late of Sudgrove in the pariſh of Miſerden, eſq; deceaſed, whoſe ſon Thomas Trye is now living. Arms, *Or, a bend azure.*

[h] On the day following his death, there appeared a ſhort account of his lordſhip, his offices and promotions, with his character. He ſtudied the law in the Middle-temple, with ſuch ſucceſs, that at 29 years of age he attained the office of ſolicitor-general; and the ſame year, 1720, received the honour of knighthood. In 1723-4, he was conſtituted attorney-general, and held that office 'till Oct. 31, 1733, when, having firſt received the degree of ſerjeant at law, his majeſty was pleaſed to conſtitute him lord chief juſtice of the court of king's bench, the ſame day; and to create him a baron of Great Britain, on the 23d of November following. On Feb. 21, 1736-7, his lordſhip had the great ſeal delivered to him; and in the years 1740, 1743, and 1745, he was nominated one of the lords juſtices for the adminiſtration of government during his majeſty's abſence from the kingdom, as he was alſo ſeveral times afterwards. In 1746, he was appointed lord high ſteward of England, for the tryals of the earls of Kilmarnock and Cromartie, and lord Balmerino; and again in 1747, for the tryal of lord Lovat. His majeſty, in conſideration of his long and eminent ſervices, was pleaſed to advance him to the titles of viſcount Royſton, and earl of Hardwick, by letters patent, bearing date Apr. 2, 1754. He reſigned the great ſeal in November 1756, and departed this life March 6, 1764.

The reputation with which he filled the ſeat of judicature in the king's bench could only be equalled by that with which he afterwards diſcharged the office of lord high chancellor; and it is no ſmall evidence of the abilities and integrity with which he preſided in the court of chancery, that, during the ſpace of near twenty years, in which he ſat there, (a period longer than any of his predeceſſors ſince lord chancellor Egerton) only three of his decrees were appealed from, and thoſe afterwards confirmed by the houſe of lords. His talents as a ſpeaker in the ſenate, as well as on the bench, have left too ſtrong an impreſſion to need being dilated upon; and thoſe, as a writer, were ſuch as might be expected from one who had early diſtinguiſhed himſelf in that character in the *Spectator*. In his public character, wiſdom, experience, probity, temper, candor, and moderation were ſo happily united, that his death, as public affairs were then ſituated, was reckoned a loſs to his country as unſeaſonable as important. And his private virtues, learning, and amiableneſs of manners were as much eſteemed and admired by thoſe who had the honour and happineſs of his acquaintance, as his ſuperior abilities were by the nation in general.

His lordſhip married Margaret, one of the daughters of Charles Cocks, of the city of Worceſter, eſq; (by Mary his wife, eldeſt ſiſter of John lord Somers) and by her ladyſhip, who died on Sept. 19, 1761, had iſſue five ſons and two daughters. 1. Philip, now earl of Hardwick. 2. Charles, who filled the offices of ſolicitor-general and attorney-general, and is now deceaſed. 3. Joſeph, knight of the Bath, and ambaſſador to the States General. 4. John, clerk of the crown, &c. 5. James, now biſhop of St. David's. And two daughters, 1. Lady Elizabeth, married to lord Anſon. 2. Lady Margaret, wedded to Gilbert Heathcote, eſq.

ARMS, *Argent, a ſaltire azure, with a bezant in the center.* CREST, *On a wreath of the colours, a lion's head erazed proper, collared gules, charged with a bezant.* SUPPORTERS, *On the dexter ſide, a lion gardant Or, collared gules, charged with a bezant. Siniſter ſide, a ſtag proper, attired and unguled Or, and collared in like manner.* MOTTO, NEC CVPIAS NEC METVAS.

The

The glebe is worth about 15*l.* a year.

The church confifts of the nave, and an aile on the fouth fide, with an embattled tower at the weft end. On fome old bricks in the floor, is written in a circular form, *Ave Maria g. p.* for *gratiæ plena*; and on others, a crofs between four martlets.

Pentecoftals - - - 9½*d.*

Monuments and Infcriptions.

In the eaft end of the fouth aile are many monuments for the Tryes, with their arms and quarterings, all in a ruinous condition. That part of the pedigree of this family which differs from fir Robert Atkyns's, is drawn from the infcriptions. The following are the moft obfervable:

Here lieth ye Body of William Trye ye Elder Efq^r Lord of ye Mannor of Hardwicke, who married Mary, fecond Daughter to Sr Edward Tyrrell, of Thorneton in the County of Buckingham, Knight, & died the 13th Day of March, Anno Dni 1609.

Here lyeth interred the Body of William Trye, Efq^r; Lord of ye Mannor of Hardwicke and Harsfeild, nobly defcended by his Aunceftors & by their matching in fundrie Noble Families. The laft was with one of ye Coheireffes of Sr Charles Brandon, Duke of Suffolk, K^t of ye moft Noble Order of ye Garter.

He had by his vertuous and charitable Wife M^ris Anne Trye fourteen Children defcended of ye Family of Sr Fran. Vincent Baronet of Stoke in ye County of Surrey. He died one Tuefday at Night the 20th Day of Decemb^r. An^o Dni 1681 aged aboute 84 Years.

His originall defcent & Name is from a Towne beyond the Seas called Trye, from whence his Aunceftor came into England about five Hundred Years fince.

Dux Militaris Thomas Trye
Filius Gul: Trye de Hardwicke Armig.
Suis Comitatuiq; Glouenfi charus,
Regi et Ecclefie Fidelis,
Utriufq; Inimicis Formidabilis;
Poft quadraginta Annorum Militiam,
Hic tandem Arma et Exuvias depofuit;
Corona triumphali Emeritorum,
Ultra omnia Secula,
Apud Cœlicolos decorandus.
obiit 16 Feb. 1670.

In cujus Memoriam, Anna, dilectiffima ejus Conjux, trium Filiarum ac Coheredum Ricardi Iones de Hanham in agro Glevenfi Armigeri natu maxima, Monumentum hoc mœrens extruxit.

In the chancels are feveral memorials for the Strattons of this parifh, with their coat armour, *viz. Argent, on a crofs fable five bezants.*

Taxes.					
The Royal Aid in	1692,	£. 138	17	4
Poll-tax — —	1694, —	36	5	8
Land-tax ——	1694, —	216	4	0
The fame, at 3*s.*	1770, —	162	2	0

At the beginning of this century, there were 70 houfes in this parifh, and 280 inhabitants, whereof 20 were freeholders; yearly births 7, burials 6. *Atkyns.* I have not been able to procure the exact number of fouls at prefent in this parifh, but by eftimation they are about 250.

HARESCOMB, *or* HARSCOMB,

IS a fmall parifh, lying in the united hundreds of Dudfton and King's-barton, five miles diftant north from Stroud, one from Painfwick, and five fouth from Gloucefter. It confifts of good pafture, with fome arable.

Of the Manor and other Eftates.

It is expreffly mentioned in *Domefday-book*, that Edmar, one of the king's thanes, could either give or fell his three manors of Herfefel, Athelai, and Sanher, to whomfoever he would; and it follows immediately after,

'In Herfecome, Wiflet held three virgates of 'land as free as Edmer. He had two plow-tillages 'there, and two bordars, and five *fervi*, and 'meadow [proportionable] to the plow-lands'.

This fhort account of Herfecome is fucceeded by the particulars of Brookthrop, already given under that head; then follows a paffage in the record more difhonourable to Harold and William than any I have found in that part of it relating to Gloucefterfhire. It is there faid, that 'Earl 'Herald took away thofe five eftates after the 'death of king Edward, and Roger de Lurei put 'them to farm for 46*l.* 13*s.* 4*d.*' *i.e.* for the ufe of king William. Thefe were the lands which the owners held fo freely that they might give or fell them as they pleafed; and if they had incurred a premunire, fo as to forfeit their title, it would undoubtedly have been mentioned, as in the cafe immediately following: 'Uluuard held half a 'hide of king Edward free [from rent] in the fame 'hundred, near to the city [of Gloucefter;] but 'earl William gave this to his cook, for Uluuard 'was outlawed.' But no outlawry, no crime, is pretended againft Edmar and Wiflet; yet Harold firft deprived them of their right, and William, far from reftoring their property, as juftice required, took poffeffion of it himfelf, upon the ufurper's title.

Roger le Rus, or le Roufe, died feized of Harfcomb 22 E. 1. John Roufe was feized of one meffuage and half a yard-land in Harfcomb 19 E. 2. Joan the widow of William Bokeland died feized of this manor 35 H. 3. which I conjecture fhe had in dower from one of the Roufes, a former hufband, as it foon reverted to that family; for Thomas Roufe was feized of the manor of Hafcomb, and of a tenement called the Orchard, 48 H. 3. and 1 R. 2.

William Mull, (perhaps a fon of fir Edward Mills, who lived at Harfcomb) was afterwards lord of this manor; and being attainted, his eftate was forfeited, and granted to Thomas Herbert, and to his heirs males, 2 E. 4. which Thomas dying without male iffue, the manor, and one toft, and one yard-land called Organs, were granted to fir Richard Beauchamp, and his heirs, 14 E. 4.

In the charter of endowment of the bifhoprick of Gloucefter, it is recited, that the manor of Hafecomb lately belonged to the abbey of Gloucefter. And, by that charter, it was granted to the bifhoprick, 33 H. 8.

The abbat of Gloucefter was poffeffed of lands in this parifh, which were granted to the bifhoprick of Gloucefter 33 H. 8 and were confirmed 6 E. 6.

Of the Church, &c.

The church is a rectory, in the deanery of Gloucefter, to which Pitchcombe is annexed, worth together about 60*l.* a year. Mr. Purnell is patron; Mr. Rice Jones the preſent incumbent. Fourteen acres belong to the glebe.

Tithes in Harſcomb, with the advowſon, which belonged to the abbey of Glouceſter, were granted to the biſhoprick 33 H. 8. and again confirmed 6 E. 6. Other tithes in Haſcomb, which belonged to the priory of Lanthony, were granted to ſir William Rider 7 Jac. The priory of Lanthony received a penſion of 5*s.* yearly of the rector.

The church, dedicated to St. John Baptiſt, is ſmall, with only a ſmall turret.

	£.	s.	d.		£.	s.	d.
Firſt fruits	9	18	1½	Synodals	0	2	0
Tenths —	0	19	9¾	Pentecoſtals	0	0	5
Procurations							

Taxes.		£.	s.	d.
The Royal Aid in	1692,	37	18	8
Poll-tax ——	1694, —	5	10	0
Land-tax ——	1694, —	94	15	0
The ſame, at 3*s.*	1770, —	74	5	0

At the beginning of this century, there were 14 houſes, and about 60 inhabitants in this pariſh, whereof 6 were freeholders; yearly births 2, burials 1. *Atkyns.* There are now 74 inhabitants.

HARESFIELD.

THIS pariſh lies in the hundred of Whitſtone, in the vale country, five miles northweſt from Stroud, and ſix ſouth from Glouceſter.

It is a very rich part of the country, ſituated beneath a ridge of hills, ſheltering it from the bleak eaſterly winds. The pariſh is pretty extenſive. Moſt of it is in paſturage and orcharding, and produces cheeſe and cyder of the beſt qualities.

From a hill called Broadbridge-green in this pariſh, is a very fine proſpect over the vale, for many miles above and below, with the waving woods and riſing lands of the foreſt of Dean in the front, on the oppoſite ſide of the Severn.

Of the Manor and other Eſtates.

At the time of the general ſurvey, this pariſh lay in two hundreds, as appears from the following extracts from *Domeſday-book*:

'Edmar, a thane, had three manors in Dudeſtan 'hundred, Herſefel, Athelai, and Sanher. He 'might give or ſell his land to whom he pleaſed. 'This eſtate was taxed at two hides. There were 'eight plow-tillages in demean, and four villeins, 'and four bordars, and thirty *ſervi*, with five 'plow-tillages, and meadow proportionable to the 'plowed-land. *Domeſday-book*, p. 67.

Of that part which lay in Whitſtone hundred it is ſaid, 'Durand of Glouceſter, holds ſeven 'hides taxed, in Herſefeld in Witeſtan hundred. 'Godrick and Edric, two brothers, held them for 'two manors, and could go where they would. 'There are three plow-tillages in demean, and 'nine villeins, and eleven bordars, with nine plow-'tillages. There are four *ſervi*, and five potters 'pay 44*d.* There is a wood half a mile long, 'and three furlongs broad. It was worth and is 'worth 6*l.* *Domeſday-book*[1], p. 77.

In the reign of king Stephen, this manor belonged to Milo the great earl of Hereford, ſon of Walter, conſtable of England. He married Sybil, daughter and coheireſs of Bernard de Newmarch, lord of Brecknock, by Neſta, daughter of Griffith ap Llewellin, prince of Wales, by whom he had five ſons and three daughters. This manor deſcended to Roger, his eldeſt ſon, who dying without iſſue, Walter the conſtable, of Hereford, was his brother and heir. He gave to the monks of Glouceſter, when Hameline was abbat, ſix yard-lands in Haresfield, and two yard-lands againſt Briſtol high-way, near the park, in exchange for a hundred fardingals of land in Herefordſhire. He and his brothers dying without iſſue male, this manor deſcended to Margery, his eldeſt daughter, married to Humphry de Bohun, whoſe heirs, in her right, were afterwards earls of Hereford, and ſucceeding owners of this manor.

Humphry de Bohun, great grandſon of Humphry and of Margery the heireſs, ſettled this manor on ſir John de Bohun, his eldeſt ſon by Maud de Avenbury, his ſecond wife. This ſir John took part with the rebellious barons againſt king Henry the Third, but made his peace in the 53d year of the king's reign. He proved his right to view of frank-pledge and free warren in this manor, in a writ of *Quo warranto*, 15 E. 1. and died in the 20th year of that reign; as did his ſon George de Bohun, 10 E. 2. and Humphry de Bohun 46 E. 3.

This manor came afterwards to the Staffords, by marriage with a deſcendant from the Bohuns, earls of Hereford. Humphry Stafford, duke of Buckingham, died ſeized of Haresfield 38 H. 6. as did Edward duke of Buckingham, who was attainted and beheaded 13 H. 8. whereby it came to the crown.

Lord Coke, in the fourth part of his *Inſtitutes*, ſays, the office of conſtable of England was of inheritance, by the tenure of the manors of Haresfield, Newland, and Whitenhurſt, by grand Serjeanty. This office became forfeited to the crown by the attainder of the duke of Buckingham, and ſince that time, both in reſpect of the amplitude of the authority, in war and peace, and of the charge, it was never granted to any ſubject, but now of late *hac vice*.

This manor was granted to ſir Anthony Kingſton 4 E. 6. from whoſe family it paſſed to the Jerninghams. Sir Henry Jerningham died ſeized of it 20 Eliz. and Henry Jerningham, his ſon, was the proprietor of it in the year 1608. Out

[1] Sir Robert Atkyns mentions, as from *Domeſday-book*, that "*Eight hides in Haresfield did belong to the manor of Berchelai in the reign of king William the Conqueror.*" But this is a miſtake, occaſioned by his reading *Haresfield* for *Horfelle* in that record.

of this name and family it paſſed to the Tryes. William Trye of Hardwick died ſeized of this manor in 1717, and was ſucceeded therein by his ſon and heir, Thomas Trye, who ſold the manors of Haresfield and Hardwick to ſir Philip Yorke, attorney-general, afterwards earl of Hardwick. His lordſhip's eldeſt ſon, Philip earl of Hardwick, is the preſent lord of this manor, and has a very large eſtate here. For his lordſhip's arms, &c. ſee *Hardwick*.

The records which mention the following particulars, either cannot relate to the manor of which I have been treating, or elſe the perſons mentioned therein muſt have been tenants under the Staffords. Anchoret, the widow of ſir Richard Talbot, was ſeized of the manor of Haresfield 1 H. 5. Alice, the widow of John Browning, held the ſame 2 H. 5. and John earl of Shrewſbury died ſeized of it 38 H. 6. I have given theſe a place in the account of this pariſh, becauſe I found them in ſir Robert Atkyns, and they may poſſibly relate to it. But what he ſays of Giles Bruges being ſeized of the manor of Haresfield, 6 E. 4. muſt be underſtood of Hasfield.

Beſide the manor, the records mention other proprietors of eſtates in this pariſh. The priory of Lanthony was poſſeſſed of lands in Haresfield, ſome of which were granted to Arthur Porter 32 H. 8. And a manor in Haresfield lately belonging to Lanthony (for the religious affected to call their eſtates by that name) was granted to Richard Andrews and Nicholas Temple, in truſt, 35 H. 8. The inn called the George, in Haresfield, lately belonging to Lanthony, was granted to William Partridge 5 Eliz.

The lay proprietors were the following: William de Littlecot died ſeized of lands in Haresfield 1 H. 3. Reginald Fitz-Herbet died ſeized of lands in this pariſh 14 E. 1. and was ſucceeded by his ſon John Fitz-Reignald. Matthew Fitz-Herbert, a deſcendant from them, levied a fine of lands in Haresfield, with various remainders, 14 E. 3. and died ſeized of thoſe lands 30 E. 3. as did Edward St. John of Scopham, and Joan his wife, 6 R. 2. William Mull was ſeized of one toft and one yard-land in Haresfield, called Henbarrows, and being attainted, the lands were forfeited to the crown, and granted to ſir Richard Beauchamp 14 E. 4. Chriſtopher Raſtal died ſeized of land in Haresfield 16 Eliz. leaving Thomas, his ſon, thirty years old.

Mr. Samuel Niblet, of the city of Glouceſter, is poſſeſſed of eſtates to the amount of near a thouſand pounds a year in this pariſh, and of the houſe formerly belonging to the family of Rogers.

The handſome houſe, formerly the Warners, and afterwards Mr. Trye's, is now the property of Mrs. Longford, deſcended by her mother from the Tryes.

The late Mr. Smith's houſe and eſtate are the property of the earl of Hardwick.

HAMLETS. 1. *Hareſcomb*, which is diſtinct from the pariſh of that name.

2. *Park-End*. Mr. Rogers had a good houſe and eſtate in this hamlet, now the property of Mr. Bearcroft, and Mr. Jones, in right of their wives, who are the daughters and coheirs of Mr. Rogers. Sir Almarick Boteler was ſeized of the manor of Park-End (hence ſometimes called *Almarick a Park*) and of one furlong of land called Beaurepeire, in Harsfield, 20 R. 2. John Kenn died ſeized of fifty acres of arable, ſix acres of meadow, and twenty-four of paſture, in Haresfield and Hardwick, 16 H. 6. Robert Kenn, eſq; was lord of Beaurepeire in Haresfield 31 H. 6.

Of the Church, &c.

The church is a vicarage, in the deanery of Glouceſter, worth 80*l.* a year. The earl of Hardwick is patron; Mr. James Comelyne is the preſent incumbent.

The rectory and church of Haresfield, lately belonging to the priory of Lanthony, were granted to Lawrence Baſkervil and William Blake, ſcrivener, 3 Jac. The earl of Hardwick has the impropriation, which pays 9*l.* 18*s.* 8*d.* a year to the crown.

Ten acres of meadow, and ten acres of arable land belong to the glebe. The vicarage houſe is a very good one, with handſome gardens, and a fiſh-pond.

The church conſiſts of the nave, with two chancels, one beyond the other. The fartheſt belongs to the vicar, the other to the impropriator. At the weſt end is a ſpire, with five bells and a clock.

	£.				£.		
Firſt fruits	17	0	0	Synodals	0	2	0
Tenths —	1	4	0	Pentecoſtals	0	1	0
Procurations	0	6	8				

Monuments and Inſcriptions.

In the chancel are the effigies, in ſtone, of a man and a woman lying along, without any device or memorial.

There are many memorials for the family of Rogers, out of which I have ſelected the following:

M. S.
Cum de Mortuis
Nec omnia tacere fas ſit
Nec omnia effundere;
Sciant Poſteri,
Iohannem Rogers, Generoſum,
non ſolum multis Ingenii
Dotibus, iiſq; eximiis,
Verum etiam, et Animæ
Virtutibus quamplurimis
Exornatum claruiſſe.
Qui ergo Omnium Amorem,
Dum adhuc in vivis eſſet,
Facillime attraxit;
Idem Luctum Omnium Funebrem
Cum Fato cederet, Iure merito
excitavit.
Vixit ille Annos 58.
Obiit Anno 1698.

M. S.
Dominæ Mariæ Rogers,
Hic juxta ſepultæ;
Feminæ, ſi qua alia,
merito celebrandæ;
Non tamen ob paucas Virtutes,
Quod facile eſt Infirmioribus,
Si modo velint;
Sed ob plurimas, fere omnes,
Eaſq; præclariſſimas.
Quas, ut a Majoribus receperat
Sancte obſervandas,
Ita Poſteris omnibus, Exemplo ſuo
Illuſtriores factas,
reliquit obſervandas.
Vixit illa Annos 56.
Obiit Anno 1697.

Over the monument, in a ſcutcheon, 1. Rogers, (as given under Dowdeſwell) impaling, 2. *Gules, three lioncels rampant argent*, for Pauncefoot.

P. M. S.

P. M. S.

To the Memory of Iohn Rogers, eldeſt Son of Iohn Rogers, Gent. & Mary his Wife, daughter of Poole Pauncefote of Newent, eſq; who was born the 9th of Auguſt 1672, and died Aug. 19, 1683. A Lad of rare Piety, Beauty, Docibility, Wit, and Good Nature.

Of gentle Blood, his Parents only Treaſure,
Theyr laſting Sorrow, & theyr vaniſh'd Pleaſure,
Adorn'd with Features, Vertues, Wit, & Grace,
A large Proviſion for ſo ſhort a Race.
More mod'rate Gifts might have prolong'd his Date;
Too early fitted for a better State.
But knowing Heav'n his Home, to ſhun Delay
He leapt o'er Age, & took the ſhorteſt Way.

There are ſeveral memorials in the chancel, for the Poultons, with their arms, *viz. On a feſs, between three mullets, as many roundlets.*

Benefactions.

Mr. Samuel Poulton, and Mrs. Anne his wife, gave 40*l.* each; and Mrs. Elizabeth Poulton, his ſecond wife, gave 20*l.* the produce of which ſums, together with 5*l.* a year given by Thomas Teekle, in the year 1675, to be employ'd to the uſe of the poor. The rev. Mr. Longford gave 50*l.* for apprenticing out poor children with the intereſt of it. Mr. John Rogers gave the church clock; and Stars-mead houſe for the pariſh clerk to live in, for ringing the great bell every morning and evening from Nov. 1, to Feb. 2, for ever. Mrs. Anne Poulton, ſen. gave a ſilver plate, and Mrs. Elizabeth Poulton gave a ſilver flaggon, for the communion ſervice. Mrs. Mary Capel gave 20*l.* for teaching poor children to read; and Mr. Daniel Niblet, about the year 1773, by will, left 100*l.* for the ſame laudable purpoſe; with the intereſt of which ſums, greatly aſſiſted by the annual contribution of Mr. Samuel Niblet, a charity-ſchool is eſtabliſhed for teaching ten children to read and write.

Taxes.					
The Royal Aid in	1692, £.	137	15	4
Poll-tax ——	1694, —	27	1	0
Land-tax ——	1694, —	238	14	0
The ſame, at 3*s.*	1770, —	179	0	6

At the beginning of this century, there were 120 houſes in this pariſh, and about 500 inhabitants, whereof 10 were freeholders; yearly births 14, burials 12. *Atkyns.* The inhabitants are ſuppoſed to be now about the ſame number.

****

HARNHILL

IS a ſmall pariſh in the hundred of Crowthorne and Minety, three miles eaſt from Cirenceſter, and twenty ſouth-eaſtward from Glouceſter.

It was antiently called *Harehille*, and *Harnhull.* It lies on the edge of a vale, and conſiſts of a due proportion of paſture and arable land. The ſoil is ſtrong, and the air healthy; but in this little village there is nothing very remarkable.

Of the Manor and other Eſtates.

'Radulf de Todeni holds Harehille in Gerſdones 'hundred, and Roger holds it of him. There are 'five hides. Elric, Aluuin, and Aluric held it for 'three manors.' *Domeſday-book*, p. 76.

William de Harnhull died ſeized of the manor of Harnhull, with the advowſon of the church, 17 E. 2. which manor was held of Humphry de Bohun, earl of Hereford and Eſſex, and of Joan his wife, 46 E. 3.

Edward de Stonor died ſeized thereof 5 R. 2. as did John, his ſon and heir, 13 R. 2. He was ſucceeded by Robert de Stonor, whoſe ſon Gilbert died ſeized of this manor 3 H. 5.

From this family, it went to the Tames. Sir Edmond Tame died ſeized of Harnhill 26 H. 8. as did Edmond his ſon 36 H. 8. leaving three daughters coheireſſes, married, as related under Fairford; who, with their huſbands, had livery of this manor 37 H. 8.

Thomas Aubury, eſq; was lord of this manor in the year 1608; but Thomas Smith, eſq; who reſides in Oxfordſhire, is the preſent lord of the manor of Harnhill, and has a good houſe (now occupied by the tenant of the farm) and a good eſtate in this pariſh. His arms are, *Per pale, ermine and erminois, over all an eagle diſplay'd ſable, member'd gules, arm'd and langued azure.*

Of the Church, &c.

The church is a rectory, in the deanery of Cirenceſter, worth about 45*l.* a year. Mr. Smith is patron; Dr. Bray is the preſent incumbent. There are no lands tithe free.

The church is dedicated to St. Michael, and hath a ſmall ſpire at the weſt end.

	£.						
Firſt fruits	5	16	3	Synodals £.	0	2	0
Tenths —	0	11	$7\frac{1}{2}$	Pentecoſt.	0	0	6
Procurations	0	3	4				

Taxes.					
The Royal Aid in	1692, £.	24	16	0
Poll-tax —	1694, —	4	12	0
Land-tax —	1694, —	23	18	3
The ſame, at 3*s.*	1770, —	17	8	9

At the beginning of this century, there were 20 houſes, and about 80 inhabitants in this pariſh, whereof 3 were freeholders; yearly birth 2, burials 2. *Atkyns.* But it appears by the pariſh regiſter, that in ten years, from 1700, to 1709 incluſive, there were 29 baptiſms, and 16 burials; and from 1760, to 1769, there were 24 baptiſms, and 17 burials; and the inhabitants are now exactly 89. So that 1 in 52 dies annually.

HARTPURY.

THIS pariſh lies in the united hundreds of Dudſton and King's Barton, ſix miles eaſtward from Newent, nine ſouth-weſt from Tewkeſbury, and four north-weſt from Glouceſter. It conſiſts of rich meadow and paſture, with ſome very good arable land. The low grounds are exceedingly liable to floods from the Leden, and from a brook which runs from Tiberton.

This

This village is not diſtinguiſhed by antiquities, the curious productions of nature or art, nor any remarkable tranſactions: only, *en paſſant*, it may be obſerved, that in the great civil war, colonel Maſſy placed a garriſon in the manor houſe, after the ſiege of Glouceſter, to ſecure Corſe-lawn, and to oppoſe colonel Myn, of the king's party, who lay at Newent, Highleden, and Taynton.

Hardeper, *Hardepery*, and *Hartpury*, are variations of the ſame name, whoſe ſignification is uncertain. The vulgar notion of its ariſing from *harts*, or red deer, frequenting the place, is to me very unſatisfactory; for how does that account for *pere*, or *pery*. If the name of the brook from Tiberton were the *Deper*, the etymology would be eaſy; for rejecting the aſpirate, *Ar-Deper*, and *Ar-Depery* would denote the ſituation of the village *Upon the Deper*; but this is all conjecture. The name ſeems to have been given it ſome time ſince the conqueſt; for though it is affirmed that Offa, king of Mercia, gave the manor of Hardepery to the church of St. Peter at Glouceſter, when Eva was abbeſs, who died in the 33d year of her government, *anno* 768, it does not appear to have been given by that very name, but the contrary is moſt probable; for in *Domeſday-book* no ſuch name can be found, the place being there called *Merewent*; and part of the pariſh is diſtinguiſhed by the name of *Morewent* to this day.

Of the Manor and other Eſtates.

When *Domeſday-book* was compiled, Merewent was a member of the manor of Bertune, under the account of which, at p. 206, is a tranſlation of that record, which includes the particulars of this pariſh. The manor at that time was part of the poſſeſſions of the abbey of Glouceſter. King Henry the Firſt confirmed to the monks of Glouceſter the aſſart lands, or new plowed grounds in Hardeper, 23° *regni*, which were granted to them by William earl of Glouceſter. He alſo, by his charter, gave to Glouceſter abbey free warren in all their lands beyond Severn, and the abbey's right for Hardepirie, in particular, was allowed 15 E. 1. by which it appears, that the place had then obtained its preſent name.

The abbats of St. Peter's at Glouceſter continued in poſſeſſion of this manor, and of a very large eſtate here, 'till that houſe was diſſolved.

Walter Compton, eſq; died July 26, 7 Eliz. ſeized of the manor of Hartpury, and of the capital meſſuage there, called the *Abbat's-Place*, and of fifty yard-lands belonging thereto, all which he had by the grant of William Herbert, knight of the garter, dated Feb. 20, 4 E. 6. *Eſch. ſub anno.*

The above Walter Compton was deſcended from the Comptons in Wiltſhire. From him the manor paſſed, thro' ſeveral generations, down to ſir William Compton, baronet, who was lord of it at the beginning of this century. He was ſucceeded by his ſon, ſir William Compton, baronet, who had iſſue three ſons and three daughters. One ſon died an infant. William, the eldeſt, ſucceeded to the title and eſtate, but dying without iſſue, his brother, ſir Walter Compton, baronet, ſucceeded him. Which ſir Walter Compton deceaſing in the year 1773, without iſſue, this manor and eſtate devolved on his two ſurviving ſiſters, Catherine and Jane; Helen, the third ſiſter, being then dead. Catherine was married to Edward Bearcroft, of Droitwich in the county of Worceſter, eſq; and died in the year 1775, without iſſue alſo; Jane is married to John Berkeley, of the city of Worceſter, eſq; who, in her right, is the preſent lord of the manor of Hartpury.

HAMLETS. 1. *Morewent-end.* William de Morewent, (who took his name from this place, where he had a conſiderable eſtate) gave twenty acres of wood for ever to the poor, which therefore bore the name of *William's Wood*; but the wood was deſtroy'd in the reign of king Charles the Firſt, and is now in waſte.

2. *Moor-end*, where is a common by the ſide of the Leden.

3. *Corſe-end.*

4. *Blackwell's-end.*

5. *Lamper's-end.*

6. *Butter's-end.*

Of the Church, &c.

The church is a vicarage, in the deanery of Glouceſter, worth 80*l.* a year. The biſhop of Glouceſter is patron; Mr. Sparks is the preſent incumbent.

The great tithes were appropriated to the abbey of Glouceſter, and were granted to the biſhoprick of Glouceſter 33 H. 8. and confirmed 6 E. 6.

The church, dedicated to St. Mary, conſiſts of the nave, with a tower at the weſt end, on which are the Comptons arms, *viz. Sable, a lion paſſant gardant Or, between three helmets cloſe proper.* The church is out of repair, and in a filthy condition.

	£	s	d		£	s	d
Firſt fruits	16	9	5	Synodals	0	2	0
Tenths —	1	12	7½	Pentecoſtals	0	0	6
Procurations	0	6	8				

Monuments and Inſcriptions.

This was not the common burying-place of the Compton family, ſo that there are but few memorials for them; but within the communion rails, on braſs, is the following:

Here lye y[e] Bodys of Willi. Compton Eſq[r]. Lord of y[e] Manor of Hartpvry, & Elinor his Wife, Daught. of S[r] Iohn Mevx, K[t]. She died Anno 1631. He died Anno 1641. to whoſe Memory their dear Daughter Dame Elinor Button Wife of S[r] Robert Button Baro[nt] here put this Monument.——Arms, 1. Compton, impaling 2. *Paly of ſix, in chief three croſſes paty*, for Meux.

There is a memorial for Walter Compton, eſq; who died in 1627.

Benefactions.

Lands in this pariſh, given to the poor by a perſon unknown, now let at about 8*l.* a year. Mr. Anthony Jelſe gave 50*l.* with which lands in Longney have been purchaſed for the uſe of the

 poor,

poor. Beſides theſe, 3*l.* 10*s.* a year, part of Mr. Cox's charity, is allotted to this pariſh. And I find a memorandum in biſhop Benſon's book, that lady Button left 100*l.* to the poor, which, at the time when that entry was made, is ſaid to have been in Mr. Jones's hands.

Taxes.					
The Royal Aid in	1692, £.	238	13	4
Poll-tax ——	1694, —	43	18	0
Land-tax ——	1694, —	303	14	0
The ſame, at 3*s.*	1770, —	226	10	0

At the beginning of this century, there were 60 houſes in this pariſh, and about 300 inhabitants, whereof 10 were freeholders; yearly births 10, burials 9. *Atkyns.* There are now about the ſame number of inhabitants.

HASFIELD.

THIS pariſh lies in the lower diviſion of Weſtminſter hundred, ſix miles diſtant eaſt from Newent, five ſouth from Tewkeſbury, and ſix north from Glouceſter.

It is ſituated on the north-weſt ſide of the Severn, and conſiſts of rich meadow and paſture. About a thouſand acres of meadow ground, lying along the ſide of the river, are in common part of the year. But there are only 125 acres of arable land in all the pariſh.

Of the Manor and other Eſtates.

'Brictric held one hide and a half at Hasfelde, 'of the church of Weſtminſter, in the time of 'king Edward. Turſtin the ſon of Rolf now 'holds it.' *Domeſday-book*, p. 72.

The above could not be the manor, for king Henry the Third gave that to Richard Pauncefot, in the thirty-third year of his reign, whoſe family had been eminent in this county, and flouriſhed in Wiltſhire in the time of king William the Firſt. Grimbald Pauncefot, ſon of Richard, proved his right to privileges in this manor, in a writ of *Quo warranto*, 15 E. 1. and dying 8 E. 2. left Almarick his brother and heir. John Pauncefot died ſeized of this manor 3 H. 5. and was ſucceeded by his ſon, ſir John Pauncefot, who was ſeveral times high ſheriff of Glouceſterſhire. Livery of the manor of Hasfield was granted to John Pauncefot, ſon of Nicholas, 1 Eliz.

Paul Tracy, eſq; was lord of this manor in the year 1608. Sir Humphry Tracy ſold it to Mr. John Parker, about the year 1655, and John Parker, eſq; a deſcendant from him, is the preſent lord of this manor, and has a good eſtate in the pariſh. His coat armour, as I find it in the laſt herald's viſitation, is, *Sable, a buck trippant argent between three pheons Or.* But he now uſes the following: *Sable, a feſs argent charged with a buck's head caboſhed and two pellets of the field, between three pheons Or.*

Edward Bruges of Lone, brother of ſir Giles Bruges of Coberley, died 15 H. 6. ſeized of four meſſuages, and eight acres of land, and a tenement called Underhills, conſiſting of thirteen acres of arable, and of eight acres of meadow and paſture; which eſtate is called the manor of Hasfeld in the eſcheator's inquiſition of that year. By another, taken at Glouceſter 15 Eliz. it was found, that Edmund lord Chandois died ſeized of the manor of Harsfield; but this was not the manor which had been ſo long enjoy'd by the Pauncefoots.

The eſtate held by the church of Weſtminſter at the time of the conqueſt, was ſometime afterwards called a manor. At the diſſolution of religious foundations, it was veſted in the crown, and granted to the dean and chapter of Weſtminſter 34 H. 8. but reſumed, and granted to the abbat and convent of Weſtminſter 4 Mar. and again regranted to the chapter 2 Eliz. The right of the church of Weſtminſter to the manor of Hasfield was tried 33 C. 2. when it appeared from the court-rolls, as early as 8 E. 2. that the manor was then held of the heirs of William Ruſſel, and not of the church of Weſtminſter, by the ſervice or rent of a ſparrow-hawk yearly.

Thomas Throckmorton levied a fine of lands in Hasfield to John Webb, 1 E. 6.

Wickeridge is a hamlet in this pariſh.

Of the Church, &c.

The church is a rectory, within the peculiar of Derhurſt, worth about 130*l.* a year. John Parker, eſq; is patron; Mr. Parker is the preſent incumbent. The rector pays 20*s.* yearly to the crown.

Thirteen acres of meadow, and ſome arable, belong to the glebe.

A portion of tithes in Hasfield, formerly belonging to the monaſtery of Derhurſt, was granted to Francis Philips and Richard Moor 1 Eliz. and another portion, likewiſe belonging to the ſame convent, was granted to Richard Hill and William James 13 Eliz. Theſe tithes afterwards belonged to the Browns, and, by purchaſe, are now the property of Nicholas Hyett, of the city of Glouceſter, eſq; who pays a fee-farm rent of 3*l.* a year to the crown.

The church, dedicated to St. Mary, is pleaſantly ſituated on a riſing ground. It is twenty-eight yards long, with a ſtrong embattled tower at the weſt end. In the windows were the following coats, 1. *Gules, ſix plates*, 3, 2, 1.—2. Pauncefoot. —3. *Or, a lion rampant gules ſemeé with croſs croſlets.* —4. Bridges.

Firſt fruits £. 13	6	8	Pentecoſtals £.	0	0	5¼
Tenths —	1	6	8			

Benefactions.

There are about ſeven acres of meadow and paſture ground given for the uſe of the church and poor. And Lawrence Gilbert gave 5*s.* a year for the repair of the church, charged on a piece of ground called Benjamin's-Croft, in Hasfield.

Taxes.					
The Royal Aid in	1692, £.	84	3	0
Poll-tax ——	1694, —	30	7	0
Land-tax ——	1694, —	140	13	0
The ſame, at 3*s.*	1770, —	106	4	6¾

At

At the beginning of this century, there were 48 houſes, and about 200 inhabitants in this pariſh, whereof 6 were freeholders; yearly births 6, burials 6. *Atkyns.* But it appears by the regiſter, that in ten years, from 1700, there were 53 baptiſms, and 50 burials; and in a like period, from 1760, the baptiſms were 51, burials 67; and the preſent number of inhabitants is 175.

HASLETON

IS a ſmall pariſh in the hundred of Bradley, three miles north-weſtward from Northleach, nine ſouth-eaſtward from Winchcombe, and ſeventeen eaſt from Glouceſter.

It is ſituated high on the Coteſwolds, with a fine healthy air. The country hereabout is almoſt deſtitute of trees, and ſo much expoſed to the winds from every quarter, that vegetation is not a little retarded. The ſoil is generally light and ſtony, and moſtly in tillage; yet agriculture is lately ſo much improved in this open, I had almoſt ſaid naked region, that the farmers obtain good crops of corn, and feed and fat great numbers of ſheep, and ſome black cattle; and many of them keep a little dairy beſides. This pariſh hath lately been incloſed, and it is hoped that, as well for profit as ornament, planting of beech, aſh, and fir, which ſuit the ſoil, may take place with other improvements.

Of the Manor and other Eſtates.

'Sigar de Cioches holds Haſedene in Bradelege 'hundred. Goda the counteſs held it. There 'are ten hides. King William granted three of 'them free from tax, as the county affirms. There 'are three plow-tillages in demean, and fourteen 'villeins, and a prieſt, with ten plow-tillages; and 'there are ſix *ſervi*. It was worth 8*l.* now 7*l.*' *Domeſday-book*, p. 79.

This manor was given to the abbey of Winchcombe, by Robert Gyves, 35 H. 3. and the abbat proved his right to free warren therein 15 E. 1. It continued in poſſeſſion of the abbey 'till the general diſſolution, and was granted to Thomas Culpeper the younger, and to his heirs males, 33 H. 8. reſerving a rent of 16*l.* 8*s.* 4*d.* Notwithſtanding this, Richard Tracy obtained a grant of the manor of Haſleton, and Haſleton-grove, lately belonging to the abbey of Winchcombe, 36 H. 8. However, Thomas Culpeper died ſeized of the manor 1 Eliz. when livery was granted to Alexander Culpeper, his ſon; and ſir Anthony Culpeper was lord of it in the year 1608.

Mr. Serjeant Wyat, of Kent, was afterwards lord of the manor of Haſleton; as was Mr. Serjeant Banniſter, of Turk Dean, at the beginning of this century. Edmund Waller, eſq; is the preſent lord of this manor, and of Farmington.

HAMLET. Yanworth is a hamlet in this pariſh, from which it is ſeparated by the pariſh of Hampnet.

'Sigar de Cioches holds Ieneurde in Bradelege 'hundred. Goda held it. There are five hides, 'of which three are exempted from tax by king 'William, as Sigar's man ſays. There are three 'plow-tillages in demean, and fourteen villeins, 'and two bordars, with ſeven plow-tillages. 'There are ſeven *ſervi*, and a mill of 40*d.* [rent] 'a wood three furlongs long, and two broad. It 'was worth 7*l.* now 6*l.*' *Domeſday-book*, p. 79.

Radulph de Zouch gave Janeſworth [*i.e.* his property therein] to the church of St. Peter of Glouceſter, free and quit from all ſervices. And Reginald Thucks gave to the ſame church, his village of Janeworth [*i.e.* his ſhare of it] in perpetual right of inheritance, free and quit from all ſervices and cuſtoms. Earl Robert de Bertone gave to the ſame church 10*s.* rent out of Janeſworth, in the time when Walter de Lacy was abbat. And king Stephen and king Henry the Second, confirmed theſe grants to the abbey. See p. 148.

John de Ganeworth, or Yanworth, was abbat of Winchcombe 31 H. 3. and probably he procured this manor from the abbey of Glouceſter to his own houſe, either by purchaſe or exchange; for in the proceedings of a *Quo warranto*, the abbat of Winchcombe proved his right to privileges in Yanworth, 15 E. 1. and the manor continued in that houſe 'till it was diſſolved.

After the diſſolution of the abbey of Winchcombe, the manor of Yanworth was granted to Thomas Culpeper 35 H. 8. as that of Haſleton had been, and was enjoy'd by that family. But other records mention, that the manor of Yanworth, a quarry of ſtones, and the church-houſe, lately belonging to the abbey of Winchcombe, were granted to Thomas Stroud, Walter Earl, and James Paget, 36 H. 8. And that Henry earl of Arundel had the manors of Haſleton and Yanworth, for they were granted to Edward earl of Bedford, 8 Jac. and in his grant they are mentioned to have been lately the earl of Arundel's. Theſe ſeeming inconſiſtencies may be reconciled, by conſidering that, as Yanworth was given in ſeveral portions to the abbey, ſo in all probability, each grant had relation only to one of thoſe eſtates, all different from each other, tho' all deſcribed by the name of Yanworth. Lord Chedworth is the preſent lord of the manor of Yanworth, which deſcended to him from his anceſtor, ſir Richard How of Compton.

Edward Horn levied a fine of lands in this hamlet 1 E. 6.

This place has a chapel of eaſe, dedicated to St. Michael, with an aile on the north ſide, and an embattled tower at the weſt end. The inhabitants antiently buried at Haſleton, but are now buried at this chapel. The biſhop of Worceſter, in 1366, made a decree between the abbat of Winchcombe and the rector of Haſleton, concerning the ſettling of a chaplain at Yanworth.

Of the Church, &c.

The church is a rectory, in the deanery of Stow, worth about 110*l.* a year. The lord chancellor is patron; Mr. Rawlins is the preſent incumbent. At the incloſing of the pariſh, the rector had lands allotted to him in lieu of tithes.

The abbey of Winchcombe preſented to this church in the reign of king Richard the Firſt. The advowſon of the rectory and vicarage of Haſleton belonged to the abbey of Hayles, and was granted to ſir Thomas Seimour 1 E. 6.

The church, dedicated to St. Andrew, is ſmall, with a low tower at the weſt end.

Firſt fruits £.19	5	5	Synodals	£.0	2	0
Tenths — 1	18	6½	Pentecoſtals	0	0	6½
Procurations 0	6	8				

Haſleton.

		£.	s.	d.
Taxes.	The Royal Aid in 1692, £.	39	1	0
	Poll-tax —— 1694, —	2	11	0
	Land-tax —— 1694, —	33	6	0
	The ſame, at 3*s.* 1770, —	24	4	6

Yanworth.

		£.	s.	d.
Taxes.	The Royal Aid in 1692, £.	39	1	0
	Poll-tax — — 1694, —	5	12	0
	Land-tax —— 1694, —	41	8	0
	The ſame, at 3*s.* 1770, —	24	4	5¼

At the beginning of this century, there were ſaid to be 25 houſes, and about 100 inhabitants in this pariſh, whereof 3 were freeholders; yearly births 2, burials 2. The preſent number of families in Haſleton is 14; of inhabitants 77. And at Yanworth the inhabitants are 84, ſo that the whole number of ſouls is 161.

HATHEROP.

THIS pariſh lies in the hundred of Britwell's-barrow, ſeven miles diſtant ſouth-eaſt from Northleach, ten eaſtward from Cirenceſter, and twenty-four ſouth-eaſtward from Glouceſter.

Sir Robert Atkyns ſays, *The Name is derived from Throp, which in the Saxon Language ſignifies an Habitation, and Heither, becauſe it lies lower on the River than Bouthrop, which lies higher.* As I profeſs not to underſtand the latter part of this ſentence, I ſhall paſs it over without further remark, and give my own opinion of the derivation of the name, which was antiently written *Hetrope*, and *Etherope*. The village is ſituated upon an eminence, but particularly above Quenington, an adjoining pariſh, which lies in a little narrow valley to the ſouthward; and it was undoubtedly this high ſituation that gave occaſion to the name; for Ꞃeah, in the Anglo-Saxon, ſignifies *high*, and Ꝺꞃop, a *village*.

There are two camps in this pariſh, one about a mile to the north-weſt of the Roman *Ikenild-way*; the other near the ſide of that antient road, at a place now called *Aſton-Barrow*. The latter is thought to be that which was antiently called *Brictwoldeſberg*, and gave name to the hundred, now corruptly written *Britwell's-barrow*.

Sir John Webb has a noble old houſe here, but not making it his conſtant reſidence, 'tis too much neglected, and the offices and gardens are falling to ruin. About the year 1773, ſir John exerted a very laudable ſpirit, in ſearching ſeveral places in this pariſh for coal, with uncommon perſeverance; but his ſucceſs was not equal to the wiſhes of the country, nor to his own expectations. It is ſaid that the workmen found ſome detached pieces of coal, but no continued ſtratum. It is ſaid alſo, that they drew up a quantity of aſhes from the depth of a hundred feet. If this be true, it ſeems utterly unaccountable how they ſhould be lodged there.

Of the Manors and other Eſtates.

There were antiently two diſtinct manors in this pariſh, of which the following was the moſt conſiderable:

'Ernulf de Heſding holds Etherope in Brict-'uoldeſberg hundred. There are ſeven hides. 'Uluuard held it. There are ſix plow-tillages in 'demean, and twenty-three villeins with ten plow-'tillages. There are twelve *ſervi*, and a mill of '15*s.* It was worth 8*l.* now 12*l.*' *D. B.* p. 77.

Ernulf de Heſding gave the church of Heythrope, and a water-mill, with the lands belonging to the prieſt, in the ſame place, to the monks of Glouceſter, when Serlo was abbat; which particulars were confirmed to them by king Henry the Firſt, and king Stephen, p. 147.

This Ernulf de Heſding was alſo lord of the manor of Kempsford, in this county, which he conveyed to Patrick de Chaworth, in the reign of William the Firſt; and probably this manor paſſed to the Chaworths at the ſame time; and came to Walter, grandſon of Walter de Ewrus, earl of Roſchar, by his marriage with Sybilla de Chaworth. He gave lands in Hatherop to the priory of Bradenſtoke in Wiltſhire, which was of his foundation, and he and his wife lie buried near the choir of that monaſtery.

Patrick his eldeſt ſon, created earl of Saliſbury by the empreſs Maud, was ſlain in a quarrel by Guy de Lozinnian 13 H. 2. His ſon and heir, William earl of Saliſbury, married Alianore de Vitrei, daughter of Tirrel de Mainers, by whom he had Ela, his only daughter and heireſs, married to William Longeſpee, natural ſon to king Henry the Second, by Fair Roſamond.

She ſurvived her huſband, and founded a nunnery at Lacock in Wiltſhire, of which ſhe herſelf was abbeſs, and endowed it with the manor of Hatherop, with the advowſon of the church, and with the hundred of Briteſwold Barrow; which endowment was confirmed by her ſon, William de Longeſpey, and by king Henry the Third. She died in the year 1300, having founded the church at Rewley near Oxford, and was buried before the high

high altar there, as appears by an inſcription on a ſtone dug up in the year 1705. This manor continued in the nunnery of Lacock 'till its diſſolution.

The other manor is thus deſcribed:

'Roger de Laci holds Hetrope in Brictwoldeſberg 'hundred, and William holds it of him. There 'are two hides. Duning held it in the time of 'king Edward. There are two plow-tillages, 'and three villeins, and three bordars, with one 'plow-tillage. There are ſix *ſervi*. It is worth 'and was worth 100*s*.' *Domeſday-book*, p. 75.

Eubulo le Strange, and Aleria his wife, levied a fine of this manor to Hugh le Diſpencer 18 E. 2. and Theobald de Verdon died ſeized thereof 10 E. 3.

Hugh le Diſpencer conſtituted John de Handelo governor of St. Briavel's caſtle, and warden of the foreſt of Dean, in the year 1299, which John levied a fine of the manor of Hatherop, with ſeveral remainders, in the year 1325, and was ſeized of it in 1340. His ſon Richard married Iſabel, daughter of Almarick de St. Amand, and died before his father, but Iſabel held Hatherop in jointure, and died ſeized of it in 1355. Edmond, ſon of Richard, was heir to John his grandfather, and died ſeized of a great eſtate in Kent, and other counties, and of the manors of Hatherop, Wike, and Williamſtrip, in Glouceſterſhire, leaving two ſiſters his coheireſſes. Margaret, the eldeſt, was married, firſt to Gilbert Chaſtelain, or Chateline, and afterwards to John Appleby; and Elizabeth, the other ſiſter, was married to Edmond de la Pool. But the above-mentioned lands, lying in Glouceſterſhire, were aſſigned to Margaret, whereby John Appleby, in her right, was lord of this manor.

This is an abſtract from the records, as I find them applied to Hatherop by ſir Robert Atkyns; but it may be obſerved, that in the deſcent of the manor of Williamſtrip, he makes Edmond de Handelo grandſon of Richard. In all other reſpects the accounts are conſiſtent.

It will be proper now to paſs to the manor poſſeſſed by the nunnery of Lacock.

After the diſſolution of that houſe, their manor and eſtate at Hatherop, and lands in this pariſh which had been veſted in the priory of Bradenſtoke, were granted to ſir William Sherington 2 E. 6.

About this time, both the manors in Hatherop were enjoy'd by the ſame proprietor, and ſo continuing, the diſtinction was loſt by unity of poſſeſſion.

John Blomer, deſcended from the antient family of the Blomers in Weſtmoreland, had livery of the manor of Hatherop 1 Eliz. William Blomer was lord of it in the year 1608. John Blomer, ſon of William, married Frances, daughter of Anthony viſcount Montacute, by whom he had three ſons and three daughters, who all died without iſſue, except Mary, the youngeſt, who was married, firſt to Richard Draycott, of Painſly in the county of Stafford, eſq; and afterwards to ſir John Webb, of Canford in the county of Dorſet, baronet. Her iſſue by her firſt huſband left no children, whereby ſir John Webb, ſon and heir, by her, of ſir John Webb, ſucceeded to this manor and eſtate; and ſir John Webb, baronet, grandſon of the laſt mentioned ſir John, is the preſent lord of this manor. His arms are, *Gules, a croſs between four muſcovy ducks Or*.

John Tame and Edmond Tame levied a fine of lands in this pariſh 13 H. 7. And ſir Walter Dennis and Agnes his wife levied a fine of the ſame lands 15 H. 7.

Of the Church, &c.

The church is a rectory, in the deanery of Fairford, worth about 160*l*. a year. Sir John Webb is patron; Dr. William Sandford is the preſent incumbent. There were about 100 acres of land belonging to the glebe. But the pariſh hath lately been incloſed by act of parliament, and the rector hath other lands allotted to him in lieu of tithe.

The church, dedicated to St. Nicholas, conſiſts of the nave only, with a tower between that and the chancel, in which are ſix bells.

Firſt fruits £.	10	0	0	Synodals £.	0	2	0
Tenths —	1	0	0	Pentecoſtals	0	1	6
Procurations	0	6	8				

Monuments and Inſcriptions.

In the chancel are ſeveral monuments and memorials for the Blomers, among which the following is moſt obſervable:

To the Pious Memory of IOHN BLOMER Eſq[r] ſixth ſon to WILLIAM BLOMER of HATHEROPE in the County of Glouceſter Esq & of FRANCES his Wife, Daughter to ANTHONY VISCOVNT MONTACVTE, by whom he had Iſſue three ſons, IOHN, WILLIAM and ANTHONY, which laſt died in the 19th year of his age, and three daughters, CATHERINE, FRANCES, who died Infants, and MARY, who firſt Marryed RICHARD DRAYCOTT of PAINSLY in the County of STAFFORD Eſq[r] and afterwards S[r] IOHN WEBBE of Canford, in the County of DORSET BARONET. Theſe were all Branches of IOHN & FRANCES BLOMER, who were both Inſtances of ſingular Piety & Goodneſſe the one continually promoting the Peace of the Neighbourhood: the other ſtill ſeconding of him in all Chriſtian Virtues, which ſhining moſt conſpicuouſly in her throw the three ſeveral Conditions of her Life, when Maid, Wife, Widow; gave a true Glory and Luſter to her high Birth.——Arms, *Baron and femme*, 1. *Gules, on an eſcutcheon of pretence argent a lion rampant of the firſt, within a bordure of the ſecond*, for Blomer; impaling, 2. *On a bend three lions rampant*. This blazon is agreeable to the laſt herald's viſitation of the county; but the colours are not expreſſed on the monument.

On another monument is a memorial for John and William Blomer, eſq[rs]; ſons of the above John, who died batchelors in 1685 and 1686, reſpectively.

On a black marble ſtone is a memorial for lady Mary Webb, daughter of the above John Blomer, who died in 1709.

In the chancel, on a flat ſtone, is a memorial for John Bradley, rector of Hatherop, &c. who died in 1741, with his arms, *Gules, a feſs between three buckles argent*.

Benefactions.

Sir Henry Blomer gave 100*l*. for the uſe of the church and poor: And there are, beſides, a few donations to the poor, now regularly diſtributed in bread and money by ſir John Webb.

Taxes.					
The Royal Aid in	1692, £.	65	12	0
Poll-tax ——	1694,—	18	10	0
Land-tax ——	1694,—	101	11	0
The fame, at 3*s*.	1770,—	77	19	3

At the beginning of this century, there were 30 houfes in this parifh, and about 150 inhabitants, whereof 6 were freeholders; yearly births 3, burials 3. *Atkyns*. The inhabitants are now increafed to 204.

HAWKESBURY.

THIS parifh lies in the upper divifion of the hundred of Grumbald's-afh, four miles diftant north from Sodbury, four north-eaft from Wickwar, and twenty-five fouth from Gloucefter. Two turnpike-roads, one from Gloucefter to Bath, the other from Oxford to Bath and Briftol, lead through it.

Part of it lies upon the hills, in a fine, healthy, open country, moftly corn fields; and part on the weft fide, beneath the great ridge which feparates the upland, or Cotefwold country, from the vale.

The name was antiently written *Havochefberie*, *i. e. Havoche's-hill*, or *camp*, according to the explanation of *berie*, already given. But of this Havoche hiftory gives no account.

Petrifications of the bivalve kind are common in the upper part of the parifh. Two little brooks rife here, and empty themfelves into the Berkeley river.

Gilbert Ironfide, bifhop of Briftol, is faid to have been born here in the year 1588.

Of the Manor and other Eftates.

'The church of St. Mary of Perfore holds 'Havochefberie in Grimboldeftou hundred. There 'are feventeen hides. In demean are five plow-'tillages, and eighteen villeins, and twenty-five 'bordars, with fifteen plow-tillages. There are 'two *fervi*, and feven free-men [*coliberti*.] Three 'mills of 19*s*. 2*d*. [rent] and ten acres of meadow. 'A wood two miles long, and one broad. It 'was worth 16*l*. now 10*l*.' *Domefday-book*, p. 72.

The abbey of Perfhore had a grant of markets, fairs, free warren, and court leet in Hawkefbury 37 H. 3. which they pleaded in a *Quo warranto* brought againft them 15 E. 1. and their claim was allowed.

William Wafp and others were feized of the manor of Hawkefbury, and of twelve meffuages, one toft, three plow-tillages, nine acres of meadow, three acres of wood, and a yearly rent of 7*s*. 2*d*. in Hawkefbury and Hildefley, in truft for the abbey of Perfhore, 15 R. 2. at which time the abbey was feized of the town of Hawkefbury in their own hands.

At the diffolution of this abbey, the manor of Hawkefbury was granted to John Butler. And lands in Kilcot, Trefham and Seddlewood, and a wood in Hawkefbury, Stoke, &c. lately belonging to the abbey of Perfhore, were granted to the fame John Butler 37 H. 8. who died feized thereof 5 E. 6. After whom, Sylveftra, his widow, held the manor in jointure, and died 7 Eliz. William Butler, fon and heir of fir John, had livery of the manor the fame year, as alfo of Hilfley, Kilcot, Trefham, Seddlewood, Upton, and Gufton. Nicholas Butler, efq; was lord of the manor of Hawkefbury in the year 1608.

The manor paffed from the Butlers to the Crews, and from them to the family of the prefent owner, fir Banks Jenkinfon, boronet, who is lord of the manor of Hawkefbury. His arms are, *Azure, on a fefs undy argent a crofs paty Gules; in chief two eftoiles Or*. The manor-houfe having been uninhabited for fome time, is gone to decay.

John le Fifher was feized of a reputed manor in Hawkefbury 19 E. 3. which was held by John Doily in the 33d year of that reign. William Cheltenham held lands in Hawkefbury 33 E. 3. as did Thomas Beverftone 48 E 3. Richard Urdle levied a fine of lands in Hawkefbury 18 R. 2. Robert Stanfhaw was feized of lands in Hawkefbury, Hilfley, Kilcot, and Trefham 12 E. 4. And John Stanfhaw, and Humphry his brother, levied a fine of lands in Hawkefbury and Trefham 12 H. 7.

Lands in Ingftone, in Hawkefbury, which belonged to the knights templers, and afterwards to the knights hofpitallers of St. John of Jerufalem; and lands and a fulling-mill in Dilton, in Hawkefbury, formerly belonging to the priory of Bonhommes, at Eddington in Wiltfhire, were granted to Richard Andrews and Nicholas Temple, in truft, 35 H. 8.

TITHINGS. 1. *Hilfley*. This is a very confiderable village, and has a diftinct tithingman.

'Turftin the fon of Rolf holds Hildeflei in 'Grimboldeftou hundred, and Bernard holds it 'of him. There is one hide. Aluric held it. In 'demean are two plow-tillages, and five half vil-'leins, and feven bordars, with two plow-tillages. 'There are eight *fervi*, and three mills of 18*s*. 'rent, and eight acres of meadow. It was worth '40*s*. but is now worth 60*s*.' *Domefday-book*, p. 78.

Robert Lynet held Hildfley of William Ruffel, whofe heir he was, and he held one meffuage, a fmall wood, and certain lands at Brodecroft of the abbey of Perfhore, at the rent of 4*s*. a year, 9 E. 2. *Efch*. William Cheltenham held lands in Hildfley in truft for the abbey of Perfhore 40 E. 3. & 19 R. 2. The manor of Hilfley belonged to the Cofyns for feveral generations, and paffed out of their name, by the marriage of an heirefs, to Mr. Tipping of Oxfordfhire. It is now vefted in Matthew Hale, of Alderley, efq.

Here was a chapel dedicated to St. Giles, now converted into tenements for the poor. Sir Thomas de Berkeley and Margaret his wife were feized of the advowfon of the chapel of Hildfly 5 H. 5. of which William, earl marfhal, levied a fine

fine 3 H. 7. And there was a chantry in this chapel 40 E. 3. of which Thomas Swetheman was the laft incumbent, and received a penfion of 5 *l.* in the year 1553.

2. *Trefham, i.e.* the *village place*. Thomas Kennet and Margaret his wife levied a fine of lands in Trefham and Hull 21 E. 3. This manor belongs to Mr. Hale. Here is likewife a chapel of eafe, with divine fervice once a month.

3. *Kilcot*, perhaps from the Britifh *Cyll*, the hazle-tree, or *Cil*, out of fight, and *coed* a wood. Maud de Evers was feized of the manor of Kilcot, with free warren, 15 E. 1. John Bodifant, and Joan his wife, who had been the widow of Robert Stanfhaw, levied a fine of lands in Kilcot, Hildefley, and Trefham, 14 H. 7. The manor of Kilcot belonged to the late Samuel Barker, of Fairford, efq; deceafed, and is now the property of William Springett, efq.

4. *Settlewood*. This eftate was late Mr. Workman's. It now belongs to Mr. Timothy Thomas, of Uley. Trefham, Kilcot, and Settlewood are united in one tithing.

5. *Upton*. This is a large tithing, fituated upon the hill. John Cotherington and Alice his wife levied a fine of lands in Hawkefbury Upton 49 H. 6. in which year that king recovered the crown for a fhort time. This manor belongs now to fir Banks Jenkinfon, baronet.

6. *Waft*. The abbat and convent of Perfhore granted a licence 47 E. 3. to Thomas Beverfton clerk, and John Godwell, to give their manor and lands of Waaft, in the manor of Hawkefbury, to the abbey of Gloucefter, on condition that the latter do grant to the abbat of Perfhore and his fucceffors 6 *s.* 8 *d.* out of thofe lands on the death of every abbat of Gloucefter. And accordingly Beverfton and Godwell gave the fame manor, with the advowfon of the chapel, to the abbey of Gloucefter, by their deed executed at Standifh 49 E. 3. The chapel of le Waft, with all tithes and appurtenances, were granted to Francis Moris and Michael Cole 12 Jac. The manor of Waft belonged afterwards to Robert Cotherington, of Didmarton, efq; and is now the property of the duke of Beaufort.

A moiety of lands in Waft, which antiently belonged to the abbey of Gloucefter, was granted to Arthur Swayne and William Bennet 41 Eliz. See *Boxwell*.

7. *Little Badminton*, belonging alfo to the duke of Beaufort.

Of the Church, &c.

The church is a vicarage, in the deanery of Hawkefbury, to which it gives name. It is worth about 80 *l.* a year. Sir Banks Jenkinfon is patron; Mr. Potter Cole is the prefent incumbent. The vicar's income, for the chapels of Trefham and Little Badminton, arifes from certain eftates there, out of which he receives in the proportion of 6*d.* to the pound of their refpective rents. At prefent, Little Badminton pays 19 *s.* Trefham 7 *l.* 1 *s.* 6 *d.*

The chapel of Little Badminton was taken down in the year 1750, by the confent of the bifhop, &c. and the inhabitants have feats in the church of Great Badminton, who, as to ecclefiaftical concerns, are made fubject to the vicar of that church. The fcite of the chapel, and the yard, which may be ftill ufed for fepulture, is to be kept well fenced round by the duke of Beaufort.

The vicar of Hawkefbury receives mortuaries from Alderley, which parifh ftill repairs a part of the church-yard wall at Hawkefbury.

The impropriation formerly belonged to the abbey of Perfhore. The tithes in Hawkefbury and Hawkefbury Upton, lately belonging to that abbey, were granted to John Butler 37 H. 8. The impropriation of this large parifh is now divided between the duke of Beaufort, fir Banks Jenkinfon, and other perfons.

The church is large, and adorned with battlements. It has a fouth aile, the upper end of which belongs to fir Abraham-Ifaac Elton, and a lofty embattled tower at the weft end. It was formerly faid to be the mother of feven daughters, or chapels of eafe, within her jurifdiction. A licence was obtained to fet up a gild, or fraternity, in this parifh, dedicated to the virgin Mary, and to purchafe land of 10 *l.* a year for its endowment, 30 H. 6.

Firft fruits £.	18	9	8	Synodals £.	0	2	0
Tenths —	1	16	11¾	Pentecoftals	0	2	0
Procurations	0	6	8				

Monuments and Infcriptions.

On a handfome marble tomb in the church,

Dedicated to the Memory of Edward Cofyn, Efq; late of Hillefley in this Parifh, Lord of the Mannor of Charley in the County of Leicefter, who departed this Life the 20 day of Feb. *Anno Dni* 1689 *Ætatis fuæ* 88. Who marryed Frances eldeft Daught[r]. of William Trye, Efq; of Hardwick in this County. *Then follow four indifferent lines of verfification, and as many words in the Hebrew character.* The tomb is ornamented with coats of arms, *viz.* 1. *Argent, a chevron ermine between three wolves heads erazed fable*, for Cofyn; impaling, 2. Trye.

There is a handfome monument againft the wall in the chancel, finifhing with an obelifk of Siena marble, with the family arms at top, and other ornaments; and on the vafe is the following infcription:

In Memory of S[r] Robert Jenkinfon, Bar[t] who departed this Life Aug[st] 8th in the year of our Lord 1766 and in the 46th of his Age. He was the eldeft Son of S[r] Robert Banks Jenkinfon Bar[t] by Catharine his Wife, third Daughter of S[r] Robert Dafhwood of North Brook in the County of Oxford Bar[t]. He married Mary the Daughter of S[r] Jonathan Cope, Bar[t] but left no iffue, yet let his Name be preferved to Pofterity, for his filial Piety, his conjugal Love, and fraternal Affection, and all thofe virtues which beft adorn the honeft Englifh Gentleman and fincere Chriftian. Fortified with thefe he bore with Patience a long and painful Illnefs 'till he refigned his foul with faith and Confidence into the Hand of his Creator. Difdain not, Reader, what, from too high a Veneration for more glaring and oftentatious Characters, thou mayeft be taught to think a very humble Encomium; for remember, that Purity of Life and Integrity of Manners will receive the greateft Praife at the laft Day, from him who is the fupreme Judge of all Virtue and Merit, and who alone can affign them their due Reward.

There

There are alſo, on other monuments, the following memorials and coats of arms :

Sacred to the Memory of Harry Cole, Son of the Rev[d] Mr. Potter Cole, and Sarah his Wife, who departed this Life June the 12th 1756, aged 15 years. Alſo of Elizabeth Cole their Daughter, who died March the 16th 1762, aged 23 years. Alſo of Frances Cole their Daughter, who died May the 15th 1768, aged 16 years.——Arms, 1. *Argent, a bull within a bordure ſable, charged with eight bezants,* for Cole ; impaling, 2. *Gules, a chevron ermine between three pheons heads argent,* for Arnold.

Erected to the Memory of Matthew Symonds of this Pariſh, Gent. and Elizabeth his Wife. He left iſſue only one Daughter Barbara married to William Mountjoy jun. of Biddleſton in the County of Wilts, Gent. He died June y[e] 3[d] 1719 Æt. 65. She died Nov. y[e] 2[d] 1719 Æt. 63.——Arms, *Argent, a bend ingrailed azure between two granades proper,* for Symonds.

Sacred to the Memory of Mary, Wife of Mr. John Jobbins, who was buried May 24, 1754, aged 53. Alſo of John Jobbins, their ſon, who was buried June 2, 1743, aged 19. Alſo of Mary Jobbins, their Daughter, who was buried Apr. 13, 1752, aged 24. ——Arms, *Argent, on a croſs engrailed gules a roſe of the field between four pheons heads azure.*

Benefactions.

Mr. Richard Thynne, by his will, in 1704, gave lands called the Lance, in this pariſh ; and Daniel Belſire, gent. by his deed in 1733, gave 30*s.* a year for ever, charged on lands called Hawkeſbury Barns; both to the relief of the poor. Mr. Daniel Walker, by his will in 1734, gave 100*l.* with which lands called Burs Buſh, in the pariſh of Yate, were purchaſed, the produce of which to be laid out in the education of poor children of this pariſh.

Hawkeſbury,

			£.	s.	d.
Taxes.	The Poll-tax —	1694, £.	18	12	0
	Land-tax —	1694, —	130	14	8
	The ſame at 3*s.*	1770, —	100	7	8¼

Hilſley

			£.	s.	d.
Taxes.	The Poll-tax —	1694, £.	12	15	0
	Land-tax —	1694, —	71	16	0
	The ſame at 3*s.*	1770, —	50	3	9¾

Treſham, Kilcot, and Settlewood.

			£.	s.	d.
Taxes.	The Poll-tax —	1694, £.	14	2	0
	Land-tax —	1694, —	84	8	4
	The ſame at 3*s.*	1770, —	66	18	6

Upton.

			£.	s.	d.
Taxes.	The Poll-tax —	1694, £.	10	10	0
	Land-tax —	1694, —	47	10	8
	The ſame at 3*s.*	1770, —	37	0	11¼

In all.

			£.	s.	d.
Taxes.	The Royal Aid in	1692, £.	358	14	8
	Poll-tax ——	1694, —	55	19	0
	Land-tax ——	1694, —	234	9	8
	The ſame, at 3*s.*	1770, —	254	10	11¼

At the beginning of this century, there were 150 houſes in this pariſh, and about 598 inhabitants, whereof 25 were freeholders; yearly births 25, burials 22. *Atkyns.* But it appears by the regiſter, that in ten years, beginning with 1700, the baptiſms were 280, burials 206. And in a like period, beginning with 1760, there were 302 baptiſms, and 196 burials. And the inhabitants are now about 896. By which it ſeems that ſir Robert Atkyns's numbers for families and inhabitants were too low; ſince the average of the annual burials, is to the number of ſouls, nearly as 1 to 45.

****

HAWLING

IS a pariſh in the lower diviſion of Kiftſgate hundred, in the Coteſwold country, ſix miles north-weſtward from Northleach, ſix ſouth-eaſt from Winchcombe, and ſeventeen north-eaſtward from Glouceſter. The turnpike-road from Stow to Glouceſter leads through it.

This village, which lies in an open champain country, is ſaid to be one of the higheſt places on the Coteſwolds, and is remarkable for its healthy air, ſound ſheep, and ſweet mutton. Huſbandry is the chief employment of the male inhabitants, but the women and children ſpin woollen yarn for the clothiers. The common fields in this pariſh, containing 977 acres, were incloſed by act of parliament in the year 1756.

Of the Manor and other Eſtates.

'Sigar de Cioches holds Hallinge, in Holiforde 'hundred, of the king. Goda the counteſs held 'it. There are ten hides taxed. In demean are 'three plow-tillages, and twenty villeins, and five 'bordars, with nine plow-tillages. There are ſix '*ſervi*, and three *ancillæ*. There is a wood. It 'was worth 7*l.* now 8*l.*' *Domeſday-book*, p. 79.

This manor was given to the abbey of Winchcombe by Robert Gyves 35 H. 3. and the abbat proved his right to free warren, in a *Quo warranto*, 15 E. 1. The ſame abbey enjoy'd the manor 'till that houſe was diſſolved, when the manor of Hallynge, *alias* Hawlynge, was granted by the crown to William Whorwode, eſq; in conſideration of 791*l.* 6*s.* 8*d.* 36 H. 8. He died the following year, leaving two daughters coheireſſes, of whom, Anne was married to Ambroſe Dudley, and had livery of the manor 37 H. 8. and Margaret was married to Thomas Throckmorton, who had livery granted to them 3 Mariæ. Livery of one moiety of the manor was granted to Thomas Horwood 15 Eliz.

Henry Stratford, eſq; was lord of the manor in 1608, and died in 1649. Henry Stratford, his ſon, died in 1671; and Richard Stratford, eſq; lord of the manors of Guiting and Hawling, died in the year 1692. Henrietta, one of the ſiſters and coheireſſes of Richard Stratford, was married to William Wyndham, eſq; (younger ſon of ſir Wadham Wyndham) who, in her right, was lord of the manor at the beginning of this century; and William Wyndham, eſq; is the preſent lord of the manor of Hawling. His arms are, *Azure, a chevron between three lions heads erazed Or.*

HAMLET. *Rowell*, or *Roell*, is accounted extraparochial, but being contiguous to Hawling, I have

I have placed it in the manner of a hamlet. It is an antient manor thus defcribed in *Domefday-book:*

'The church of St. Ebrulf holds Rawelle in 'Holeford hundred of the king. Wluuard held it in 'the time of king Edward. There are ten hides. 'In demean are four plow-tillages, and fixteen 'villeins, and two bordars, with fix plow-tillages. 'There are three *fervi*. It is worth and was 'worth 10*l*. This manor never paid tax.' *Domefday-book*, p. 72.

The church of St. Ebrulf in Normandy was feized of the manor and church of Rowel, and of two plow-tillages, 56 H. 3.

At the fuppreffion of alien monafteries, this manor was granted to the abbey of Winchcombe, which continued poffeffed of it 'till the diffolution, when it was granted, together with the tithes, to fir Ralph Sadleyr, 1 E. 6. Livery of the manor of Rowel was granted to Brian Carter, and Mary his wife, daughter of fir Philip Hobbey, 1 Eliz.

The manor came afterwards to lord Chandos. Chriftopher Montacute, efq; was lord of it at the beginning of this century, and Mr. Montague is the prefent lord of the manor.

Here was a chapel of eafe, now demolifhed.

Of the Church, &c.

The church is a rectory, in the deanery of Stow, worth 69*l*. a year. Mr. Wyndham is patron; Mr. Lawrence is the prefent incumbent.

When the common fields were inclofed in 1756, the rector quitted claim to all tithes, &c. in confideration of receiving 25*s*. yearly, in money, for every yard-land; the whole to be reckoned at 30 yard-lands. He likewife gave up his glebe land, confifting of 63 acres, in confideration of 10*s*. a year for every acre, to be paid to him and his fucceffors, by the lord of the manor, in the great porch of the parifh church of Hawling.

A compofition was made, April 13, 1464, between the abbat of Winchcombe, and Hugh Ward, rector of Halling, by which the abbat's lands in Halling and Rowell were exempted from tithes; the abbat agreeing to pay the rector 30*s*. a year in lieu thereof, and for his duty at Rowell.

The abbey of Winchcombe prefented to this church in 1313. After the diffolution of that houfe, the advowfon of the rectory and vicarage, and the tithes of Hawling and Rowell, were granted to fir Thomas Seimour 1 E. 6.

The demeans of the manor pay 13*s*. 4*d*. in lieu of tithes.

The church, dedicated to St. Luke, is fmall, with a low embattled tower, and three bells, at the weft end. A houfe and orchard, and thirteen acres of land, in three pieces, are given for the repair of the church.

	£.	s.	d.		£.	s.	d.
Firft fruits	10	18	8	Proc. & Syn.	0	3	6
Tenths —	1	1	10½	Pentecoftals	0	0	6½

Monument and Infcription.

In the chancel is the following memorial:

M. S.
Richardi Stratford, Arm.
De Hawling & Guiting
Toparcha.
Juvenis Moribus fuaviffimis,
Omnibufq; Dotibus, & Animi & Corporis,
Supra Coævos fuos illuftris.
Qui, quatuor Annis in Academia Oxon
feliciter pofitis,
Spem Viri egregii omnibus fecit;
Nec fefelliffet, nifi illum Febris
Vota
Deo, Ecclefiæ, Patriæ
nuncupata
Rediturum Præripuiffet,
An° { Ætat. 22,
Dom. 1692.

Arms, *Barry of eight argent and azure, over all a lion rampant gules*, for Stratford; agreeable to the herald's laft vifitation of the county. But the Stratfords of Guiting bore, *Gules, a fefs humetty Or, between three treffels argent.*

Hawling.

			£.	s.	d.
Taxes.	The Royal Aid in	1692, £.	68	6	0
	Poll-tax ——	1694, —	8	0	0
	Land-tax ——	1694, —	51	13	0
	The fame, at 3*s*.	1770, —	36	7	7½

Rowell.

			£.	s.	d.
Taxes.	The Royal Aid in	1692, £.	47	5	0
	Poll-tax — —	1694, —	1	1	0
	Land-tax ——	1694, —	29	4	0
	The fame, at 3*s*.	1770, —	20	13	3

At the beginning of this century, there were 21 houfes, and about 100 inhabitants in this parifh, whereof 3 were freeholders; yearly births 2, burials 2. *Atkyns*. There are now about 132 inhabitants.

HAYLES.

THIS parifh is fituated in the lower divifion of the hundred of Kiftfgate, at the foot of that range of hills which divides the Cotefwold from the vale part of the county, running from north-eaft to fouth-weft nearly the whole length of it. It ftands two miles diftant north-eaft from Winchcombe, ten eaft from Tewkefbury, and feventeen north-eaft from Gloucefter. A fmall brook runs from this place into the Avon at Evefham in Worcefterfhire.

Sir Robert Atkyns fays, It is fo called from *haly*, which is Saxon for *holy*: and indeed if this name had been given it after the founding of its monaftery, the refidence of fo many holy men, or of any other religious houfe prior to that foundation, there might have been fome reafon for this conjecture; but *Heile* being the antient name of the place long before any religious houfe was here founded, this etymology will fail. *Hail*, or *heile*, antiently, as well as at prefent, fignified *ftrong, healthy*; and *lei, ley*, or *lie* in the Saxon language fignifies a *pafture ground*; fo that this place was probably fo called from the ftrength and fertility of the foil, for which the piece of ground wherein the church ftands, in particular, is now very remarkable. Befides pafture, here are woodlands, and fome rich arable lands; but this parifh furnishes nothing remarkable in the fossil or vegetable kingdoms.

Of the Manor and other Estates.

'William Leuric holds Heile in the hundred of 'Greteſtan. Osgot held it in the time of king 'Edward. There are eleven hides. In demean 'are three plow-tillages, and nine villeins, and 'eleven bordars, with eight plow-tillages. There 'were twelve *servi*, whom William made free. 'There is a mill of 10*s.* [rent] and a wood one 'mile long, and half a mile broad. It was worth '12*l.* [but] now [only] 8*l.* This manor pays 'tax.' *Domesday-book*, p. 74.

A considerable part of this manor was granted to the abbey of saint Ebrulph in Normandy. Jeoffrey de Luci was seized of it 6 John, and the 17th year of the same reign, he granted part of the lands to Robert de Maci. John de Julin was also seized of it 3 H. 3. and 10 H. 3. it came to the crown, when the inhabitants of the parish were discharged from the hundred of Winchcombe. King Henry the Third granted it to his brother, Richard earl of Cornwall, king of the Romans, who, in the year 1246, founded a monastery in this place, and endowed it with this manor.

Adam le Hunt also granted twenty solidates of land in Hayles, and one messuage, one toft, and three acres of meadow in Sudely, to the abbey of Hayles, 13 E. 2. See accounts of other grants to this abbey under Didbrook, Pinnock, Churchdown, Sudely, Guiting-Power, Longborough, Todington, and other parishes. For the charter of the endowment of the abbey, see N°. 17, in the *Appendix*.

This abbey was surrendered to the king's commissioners, Dec. 31, 1539, by Stephen Sagar, the last abbat, and not Whaley[k], as mentioned by sir Robert Atkyns; and was valued at 357*l.* 7*s.* 8*d.ob.* *per annum*.

After the dissolution, the scite of the monastery, and the greater part of the manor, (probably Hayles-wood, Pinnock's-wood, and Hayles-park) containing 500 acres, value 65*l.* 14*s.* 8*d.* were granted to sir Thomas Seymour, in fee, Aug. 19, 1 E. 6. He being attainted of high treason, and afterwards beheaded, the scite of the monastery, and the rest of the lands, were granted to William marquis of Northampton, June 12, 4 E. 6. The marquis, on the 16th of June, in the same year, leased it to one Hodgkins, for twenty-one years, at 159*l.* 16*s.* It seems afterwards to have been in the crown, for queen Elizabeth, July 18, in the 7th year of her reign, leased it again to Hodgkins for twenty-one years at the same money. Hodgkins had three sons, but he bequeathed this estate to his daughter, who married William Hobby, esq; of whose family this manor and estate was purchased by John lord viscount Tracy, whose descendant, Thomas-Charles lord viscount Tracy, is the present proprietor, and resides at Todington in this county.

Hayles-wood, containing 102 acres, which formerly belonged to the abbey of Tewkesbury, was granted to Robert earl of Salisbury, 5 Jac. Lord viscount Tracy is the present possessor, and pays an annual rent out of it to the present earl of Salisbury.

A meadow which belonged to the marquis of Northampton, and formerly to the abbey, called Browning's, was granted to Henry Browning and Charles Brockton, 2 Mariæ.

Other lands in this parish, formerly belonging to the abbey, were granted to Theophilus Adams and Richard Adams, 25 Eliz.

An inn and divers houses, formerly granted to the marquis of Northampton, which, before the dissolution, belonged to the abbey, were granted to sir Thomas Smith and Edward Lascelles, 2 Jac.

Of the ABBEY.

In the year 1246, Richard earl of Cornwall, in performance of a vow which he made when he was in great danger at sea, on his return from Gascony[l], erected a monastery in this place, and brought hither twenty monks, of the Cistercian order, from Beaulieu in Hampshire[m]. These monks chose one from among themselves to be abbat, whom the earl invested with the abbey, and all things belonging to it. On the 5th day of November, 1251, being the year in which the church, dormitory, cloisters, and refectory were finished, the earl procured this church of Hayles, which he had built at a vast expence, to be dedicated, with great pomp and solemnity, to the virgin Mary, and to All Saints, by the bishop of Worcester; the king, the queen, and above three hundred persons of quality being present on the occasion. Thirteen bishops celebrated mass on the day of dedication, each at a separate altar, the bishop of Lincoln officiating at the high altar. This grand company was all entertained together, upon a sunday, with a noble and magnificent

[k] Sir Robert Atkyns says, 'Abbot Whaley was the last Abbot, 'who, *in hopes of a Pension*, surrendered it to King Henry the 'Eighth.' This is assigning no very *laudable* motive for the abbat's resignation. But why this reflection; what had he done? He gave up all the dignity and state, the authority and power, attendant on his office, for a private station; and this, probably, not by choice, but in obedience to that authority which he could not withstand. Certain writers, however, have endeavoured to blacken the characters of many that appear to have been merely passive in the first steps to the Reformation. Stevens says of Thomas Kampswell, the last prior of Worcester, that 'He was 'one of those poor spirited creatures, who, either out of fear, or 'some worse consideration, surrendered their monasteries to king 'Henry VIII. at the general dissolution; by which means he procured to himself a good pension of 133*l.* 6*s.* 8*d.* as the reward 'of his treachery and sacrilege. Death was the penalty for 'refusing to submit, and a plentiful support for an idle or vicious 'life the recompence for complying: How few are there that can 'bravely face the terrors of the former, and withstand the temp'tations of the latter.' —— True, very true, Mr. Stevens, You and I are happy in not having been put to the trial, or we ourselves might have shrunk at the sight of the gallows.

[l] Prout in mari voverat, quando a Gasconia rediens, in mari suborta tempestate, periclitabatur, vix portum attingens in Cornubia. *Matt. Paris.*

[m] Leland's Itinerary. Tanner's Notitia Monastica. Sir William Dugdale has it *de Bello-loco*; but sir Robert Atkyns, Beaulieu, in France.

dinner,

dinner, worthy of themſelves and of the occaſion: But the religious dined upon a vaſt variety of fiſh, at a ſeparate table. An eminent writer, ſpeaking of this affair, delivers himſelf to the following purpoſe. 'If I ſhould endeavour fully to deſcribe the 'magnificence of that entertainment, every one 'would conclude that I exceeded the truth; and 'leſt I ſhould write a falſity, I will relate what I 'had from Matthew Paris. The earl aſſured him, 'for an undoubted truth, that, reckoning all 'charges, he had expended 10000 marks on the 'building of that church, adding theſe memorable 'and commendable words, "That he wiſhed to "God that all the money which he had laid out "on the caſtle of Wallingford had been expended "ſo wiſely, and to ſo good purpoſe as this."

The abbey church and moſt of the buildings were burnt down in the year 1271, and the damage was eſtimated at 8000 marks.

This was a mitred abbey. Stevens, in his *Monaſticon*, gives a liſt of abbats, &c. ſummoned to parliament, from the clauſe rolls in the tower, by which it appears, that the abbats of this houſe, and of Hales-Owen in Shropſhire, were uſually ſummoned together; but neither of them in the year 1294, as ſir Robert Atkyns affirms, in which there were only two ſummonſes extant.

The abbat and convent paid an annual rent of 16*l.* 16*s.* 10*d.ob.* for Pinnockſhire, 27 E. 1. which rent was, the ſame year, ſettled by the king on queen Margaret, as part of her dower.

In the annals of this monaſtery is recorded the hiſtory of the founding of a ſmall one, of monks of the order of Bon-hommes, or Good-men[n], the ſubſtance of which is as follows. Edmund earl of Cornwall, as yet a boy, being with his father in Germany, and ſeeing a large, cloſe, golden vial, full of relicks of the precious blood of our Lord, which had been ſent as a great preſent to Charlemain, from Greece, he prevailed to have a conſiderable part given him, which he brought into England with him, and carried to the monaſtery of Hayles, and laid it up in the abbey church there, both the convents of Hayles and Winchcombe attending; Edmund himſelf, who was preſent for his devotion, carrying the veſſel in ſolemn proceſſion. This precious relick he divided, and leaving one part at Hayles, gave the other to the monaſtery of Aſhridge in Buckinghamſhire, which he himſelf had built. — At the diſſolution of Hayles monaſtery, this precious blood is ſaid to have been diſcovered to be the blood of a duck, or perhaps ſome other animal, which was weekly renewed. Of this it was affirmed, that a man being in mortal ſin, and not abſolved, could not ſee the blood; but as ſoon as he was abſolved, he might plainly diſcern it. The prieſt ſhewed it in a cabinet of cryſtal richly adorned, both ſides whereof ſeemed alike, yet one ſide of the cryſtal was much thicker than the other; and until the penitent had paid for as many maſſes as the prieſt thought fit, the thicker ſide of the cryſtal was preſented towards him, through which nothing could be ſeen; but having paid to the prieſt's ſatisfaction, the thin and more tranſparent ſide of the cryſtal was preſented, and then, to his great joy, he might diſcern the blood. This impoſture had been practiſed for many ages, and greatly enriched the monaſtery.

The following account of the penſions aſſigned to the religious at the ſurrender, is taken literally from Willis's Hiſtory of Abbies, *viz.* '*Stephen* '*Sagar*, late Abbot ther, 100*l.* and alſo to have of 'the Kyngs Majeſtie the Capital Meſſuage or 'Manſion-Houſe callyd *Coſtombe*, alias *Coſton*, 'within the Pariſh of *Didbroke* in the Countie 'aforeſaid, with the Stable ther, and oon Cloſe 'nere therunto adjoyning; and the furſt Veſture 'oone lytle Mede adjoyning unto a Grove callyd '*Coſtcombe*-Grove, with the lytle Garden; and the 'Courte ther duringe the natural Liff of the ſame '*Stephen*, untill the ſeid *Stephen* be promoted by 'the King's Majeſtie to ſome Benefyce or Benefyces to the Some aboveſeid, and further to have 'fortye Lodes of Fyreword and Houſebote ſufficient out of the Kings Majeſties Woods callyd '*Hayles* Wood by th' Aſſignement out of the Receyvor of his Highneſs Court of Augment within 'the ſeid Countie, (or his ſufficient Deputy for the 'tyme byinge.) *John Dawſon*, B. D. late Prior, '*Philipp Brode*, B. D. 8*l.* each; *Richard Eddon*, 'B.D. *Roger Rede*, B.D. 7*l.* each; *John Silveſter* 'Kychynner, *Thomas Farr* Cellerer 6*l.* 6*s.* 8*d.* each; '*Will Choo* ſenyor, *John Griffith*, 6*l.* each; *Tho.* '*Hopkyns*, *Richard Dawnſer* Sub Prior, 106*s.* 8*d.* '*Reginolde Lane*, *Adam Tyler*, *Will. Netherton*, '*Richard Woodward*, *Will. Holidaye*, *Tho. Reede*, '100*s.* each; *Elye Dugdel*, *John Hatt*, *Chriſtofer* '*Hodgeſon*, 53*s.* 4*d.* each; *John Holme* 40*s.* *Richard* '*Dene* 26*s.* 8*d.*'

The abbat's houſe was a large, handſome building. John lord viſcount Tracy died there, *anno* 1686, but was buried at Todington, ſince which time it has not been the reſidence of any of his family. It is now ſo far fallen to decay, as to be habitable for a few poor perſons only. Long ſince ſir Robert Atkyns publiſhed his hiſtory, the arms of the founder were in the hall window, and round them, in old characters, RICARD' PLANTAGENET SEMPER AUGUSTUS FUNDATOR NOSTER. The arms, and other painted glaſs of the windows of this houſe, have lately been put up in the hall windows at Todington; and a noble old chimney-piece from hence is alſo put up in the great hall there, by the preſent lord Tracy.

What now remains of the old abbey is ſituated in a rich paſture ground, of five or ſix acres. The north-weſt ſide of the cloiſter, in length about thirty-five yards, is tolerably intire; in the roof of which are the following arms: Quarterly, 1ſt and 4th, *Five fuſils in feſs.* 2d and 3d, *Barry of ſix, a bend over all.* — Quarterly, 1ſt and 4th, *Sable, a lion paſſant gardant Or between three helmets argent*, for Compton earl of Northampton. 2d and

[n] Stevens's *Monaſticon*, Vol. 2. p. 277.

and 3d, *A chevron within a bordure charged with roundlets.* — Quarterly, 1ſt and 4th, *Gules, fretty argent.* 2d and 3d, *Two bars,* impaling *A lion rampant.* — *A chain with a ſhack-bolt at each end between three mitres,* which are ſuppoſed to be the arms of the abbey.

The outer walls of the other three ſides of the cloiſters are in part ſtanding. There are three or four doors leading out of the north-eaſt ſide to the place where the church ſtood, of which nothing remains, except part of the foundation.

Round the area are four or five habitations, formed from the outer buildings of the old monaſtery, as appears by the arches of the windows and doors, now walled up.

The inn, already mentioned to have been granted to the marquis of Northampton, is ſtill remaining. It is a large old building near the abbey houſe, formerly uſed for the reception of pilgrims and devout perſons viſiting the monaſtery; and has been kept open, as an inn, ever ſince the reformation, 'till very lately.

Upon a large ſtone, lying in a heap near the abbey houſe, I obſerved a device in a ſcutcheon, expreſſed in the following manner: A mitre pierced with a croſier in pale; on the dexter ſide, the letter A; on the ſiniſter, the letter M ſtanding over a tun; intended for a kind of rebus on the name of *Melton*, one of the abbats. In the floor of the hall at *Southam Houſe* are a great many painted bricks, taken from this place, and carried thither when the abbey houſe belonged to Mr. Hobby, who was related to the De-la-Bere family. Upon ſome of them is the ſame rebus, and upon others, the name of *Ford* ſeveral times expreſſed within a wreathe; and there are the arms of benefactors to the abbey upon others, as deſcribed under the account of that houſe, in the pariſh of Cleeve.

The inhabitants ſay there is a ſubterraneous paſſage from this place to Coſcomb, which was called the Abbat's-lodging. One Freeman of Didbrook, in this neighbourhood, declared to an old man at the abbey houſe, that he went ſo far in it 'till he came to a pair of iron gates, which ſtopt him from proceeding; that the top is handſomely arched with ſtone, and in the walls are niches, or ſeats, all along: The mouth, or opening, he ſaid, was in the orchard near the houſe; but Freeman is dead, and nobody could ſhew it me, yet the people give intire credit to his relation.

Richard[o] earl of Cornwall, king of the Romans, and brother to Henry the Third, died at the caſtle of Berkhamſted, April 2, 1272. His heart was buried in the church of the friars minors in Oxford, and his body at Hayles. His wife, who died 1261, was buried here; and Edmund, their ſon, earl of Cornwall, was interred in this church *anno* 1300. His funeral was performed with great ſolemnity, king Edward the Firſt, and a great number of the nobility attending; ſo that this abbey church contained the aſhes of a king, a queen, and their ſon.

Viewing the venerable remains of theſe once noble buildings, where the aſhes of ſo many eminent perſons lie ſcattered and undiſtinguiſhed amongſt the ruins, 'tis not eaſy to avoid reflecting on the tranſitory nature of riches, power, titles, honours, which ſo much engage the attention of the buſy world, and which all muſt ſhortly leave behind.

Sir Robert Atkyns ſpeaks of Alexander de Hales[p], whence it might be inferred that he had ſome connexion with this place: And Camden, in his *Britannia*, ſays, 'this place is famous for its 'great ſcholar, Alexander de Hales;' but as it is generally agreed that he died in the year 1245, he certainly could have no relation to this monaſtery, which was not founded 'till the year following. The truth is, this great ſchoolman was of Hales-Owen in Shropſhire.

In the reign of king Henry the Fourth, a battle was fought on Braham-moor, in the north of England, between the earl of Northumberland, and other rebels, and ſir Thomas Rokeſby, ſheriff of Yorkſhire, on the part of the king; the firſt were routed, and the abbat of Hales being then taken

---

[o] He was a powerful prince in his time, and a religious perſon; valiant in war, and of great reſolution and conduct. In Aquitain he behaved with wonderful courage, and had equal ſucceſs. He forced the Saracens to a truce in the Holy Land; refuſed the kingdom of Apulia, when offered him by the pope; quieted ſeveral tumults in England; and being choſen king of the Romans in 1257, was crowned at Aix la Chapelle; but this got him no great reputation, for, according to a common verſe, he is ſuppoſed to have bought this honour:

Nummus ait pro me nubit Cornubia Romæ.
Cornwall to Rome almighty money joyn'd.

For, before that time, we are told by a cotemporary writer, that he was ſo famous a monied man, as to be able to ſpend 100 marks a day for ten years together. This is the ſubſtance of Camden, col. 27.

[p] He went to France, and ſtudied ſchool divinity and canon law in the academy at Paris, in both which he became ſo very famous, as to be commonly called *Doctor Irrefragabilis.* He flouriſhed about 1230, and having entered himſelf in the order of Franciſcans, died at Paris, Aug. 27, 1245. — Cave's *Hiſtoria Literaria*, p. 714. — He lies buried in the midſt of the body of the church of the Cordeliers in Paris. Near the ſteps aſcending to the choir is a monument of black marble, raiſed about two feet from the ground, with this inſcription in yellow letters:

R. P.
Alexandri de Hales,
Doctoris irrefragabilis, quondam
Sanctorum Thomæ Aquinatis et
Bonaventuræ preceptoris.

EPITAPHIUM.

Clauditur hoc ſaxo famam ſortitus abunde;
Gloria doctorum, decus et flos philoſophorum:
Auctor ſcriptorum, vir Alexander, variorum;
Norma modernorum, fons vera lux aliorum;
Inclytus Anglorum fuit Archilevita, ſed horum
Spretor cunctorum, frater collega minorum,
Factus egenorum, fit doctor primus eorum.

Obijt A. D. MCCXLV. Calend. Sept. 12.

Si quis honos meritis, ſi qui virtute coluntur;
Hunc animo profer, hunc venerare patrem.

Reverendiſſimus pater Benignus a Genua, totius ordinis ſancti Franciſci miniſter generalis, pro ſua in ſanctum doctorem pietate, et religionis zelo, hoc monumentum erigi curavit, A. D. 1622, Martij 25.

in

in armour againſt the king, was hanged for his defection. The biſhop of Bangor was taken at the ſame time, but his life was ſpared, becauſe he was found in his ordinary habit. Notwithſtanding this ſtory is admitted here, it is moſt probable that the unfortunate abbat belonged to Hales-Owen, as in many inſtances theſe two places are not properly diſtinguiſhed in hiſtory.

In the ſupplementary part of Mr. Willis's *Hiſtory of Abbies*, after the index to the ſecond volume, under Hayles, at p. 10. is the following note; 'This abbey, tho' ſurrounded with Glouceſterſhire, 'and at a diſtance from any part of Wiltſhire, is 'reputed in Wiltſhire.'—This is a miſtake, for it was always reputed in Glouceſterſhire. However, this blunder, I think, ſhould not be charged on Mr. Willis, which I preſume was the printer's, who ſhould have placed the note under the account of the abbey of Kingſwood, immediately following, of which the obſervation is juſt.

Of the Church, &c.

The church is in the deanery of Campden. In the year 1738, by the conſent of the biſhop, the patron, and the incumbent, the rectory of Pinnock, the vicarage of Didbrook, and the donative of Hayles were conſolidated into one preſentment. Lord Tracy is patron and impropriator; and his lordſhip's brother, the honourable John Tracy, D. D. warden of All Souls college in Oxford, is the preſent incumbent of theſe conſolidated churches, which are worth, *comm. ann.* about 120*l.* a year.

The curacy of Hayles was augmented by lot, with queen Anne's bounty, in the year 1738, as the vicarage of Didbrook had been two years before.

The rectory, chapel, and tithes of Hayles, formerly belonging to the abbey, were granted to John Dudley and John Aſcough, 18 Eliz.

Godfrey Giffard, biſhop of Worceſter, in the year 1270, endowed[q] the vicarage of Hayles with ten marks yearly, (a ſum equal in value, at that time, to 100*l.* of our preſent money) to be paid by the abbat and convent, in two equal portions, with the allowance of offerings, and a houſe and garden.

The church is a mean ſtructure, with a ſmall wooden tower. It was built by William Hobby, eſq; who was buried in it Mar. 17, 1603, aged 103, but there is no memorial for him. In the churchyard is a memorial upon a grave-ſtone, placed over the remains of John Langley, eſq; (ſon of Philip Langley of Mangotsfield) who married a daughter of John lord Tracy.

Taxes.			£.	s.	d.
The Royal Aid in	1692,	£.	133	14	0
Poll-tax ——	1694,	—	7	12	0
Land-tax ——	1694,	—	121	14	0
The ſame, at 3*s.*	1770,	—	85	13	9¾

At the beginning of this century, there were 18 houſes and 80 inhabitants in this pariſh, whereof 3 were freeholders; yearly births 2, burials 2. *Atkyns.* The baptiſms and burials in Didbrook and Pinnock are regiſtered at Hayles, without diſtinguiſhing what belongs to each place; wherefore nothing can be concluded from them. On an average of ſeven years, the baptiſms are 7, the burials 4. The houſes at preſent at Hayles are 16, and the inhabitants 90.

HEMPSTED

IS a ſmall pariſh in the united hundreds of Dudſton and King's-barton, diſtant about a mile ſouth-weſt from Glouceſter, upon the turnpike-road from that city to Briſtol.

The name of it has been variouſly written in different ages, as *Hechaneſtede*, about ſeven hundred years ago; afterwards *Hey-Hamſteed*, and by contraction, *Hampſtead*, and *Hempſted*, as we now uſe it. I apprehend the firſt form is moſt agreeable to the original orthography, and ſignifies *Hechane's-town*; for *ſted*, or *ſtadt*, is a *town* or *ſtation*.

This village is bounded on the north by the river Severn. It conſiſts of rich paſturage and orcharding, and produces excellent cheeſe and cyder. Daniel Lyſons, eſq; a phyſician, has a very handſome houſe and a large eſtate in this place, with plantations of trees that run up to the great road, whence it is ſeen at an agreeable diſtance.

Of the Manor and other Eſtates.

'Edric Lang, a thane of earl Herald's, held 'Hechaneſtede in Dodeſtan hundred. There were 'five hides, and in demean three plow-tillages, 'and ſix villeins, and eight bordars, with ſix plow-'tillages. There are ſix *ſervi*, and half a fiſhery. 'Earl William held this manor in demean, and it 'was not in farm; but now the ſheriff has let it 'at 60*s.* a year.' *Domeſday-book*, p. 69.

[q] The endowment runs thus: *Univerſis et ſingulis Chriſti fidelibus, ad quos preſens ſcriptura pervenerit, Godfridus, permiſſione divina, Wigorn. epiſcopus, ſalutem in Domino ſempiternam. Cum ſacrorum ſtatuta canonum, per quæ genus humanum regitur in terris, vias prælatorum ad diſponendas in eccleſia Dei, tam de regimine quam regentium vita, ſuo periodo ordinent et diſponant; quædam inter cætera ipſorum ſtatuta vicarios in eccleſiis parochialibus reſidere conſtringunt; nos eis de vitæ neceſſariis, et de bonis eccleſiæ, cui vitas regunt, præſunt, competenter providere compellunt: hinc eſt quod nos, conſiderata animarum curâ eccleſiæ parochialis de Hales, Wigorn. dioceſeos, quam religioſi viri abbas et conventus monaſterii de Hales, ordin. Premonſtrenſis, in proprios uſus obtinent, et onera curæ eidem, tam in temporalibus quam in ſpiritualibus; ſtatuimus et definimus ut in dicta eccleſia perpetuus ſit vicarius, nobis per dictos religioſos preſentandus, qui de animarum curâ nobis reſpondeat, et obediat ut ſubditus, et noſtris ſucceſſoribus in futurum; cui, de dictorum religioſorum conſenſu, expreſſo nomine vicariæ, decem marcas ſterlingorum, ſingulis annis, de camera dict. abbatis, per duos anni terminos, portione dimidia et equali, ſcilicet, quinque marcas in feſto ſancti Michaelis, et reſiduas quinque marcas in paſchali dominicæ reſurrectionis, fideliter perſolvi præcipimus et ordinamus. Inſuper, aſſignamus eidem vicario demenſum et manſum, cum edificiis, cum horto et gardino, quæ vicarius habere conſuevit, ad habitandum; cum herbagio cæmeterii, et oblationibus; et eidem religioſi, de ſuis ſtipendiis, preſbyterum alium ſecundarium invenient, apud Didbrooke, in eadem eccleſia miniſtrantem, et omnia onera ordinaria et extraordinaria, qualitercunque fuerint, impoſita ſuſtinebunt abbas et conventus. In cujus rei teſtimonium has literas noſtras patentes fieri fecimus, et ſigillo noſtro communi. Dat. apud Hanbury, in Salſo Mariſco, 10 cal. Octob. anno gratiæ 1270; pontificat. vero noſtri anno ſecundo finiente.* Regiſt. Wigorn.

This manor was given to the priory of Lanthony by Milo earl of Hereford, in the year 1136. The prior's claim to court leet and felons goods was allowed, in a *Quo warranto*, 15 E. 1. and in the 21ft year of the fame reign, he purchafed a charter of free warren in Hey-Hempftead and Podgmead. The manor continued in the poffeffion of the priory of Lanthony 'till that houfe was diffolved; and was then granted, together with a fifhery in the Severn, to Thomas Atkyns and Margaret his wife, 37 H. 8. Sir Robert Atkyns of Saperton was lord of the manor at the beginning of this century. Daniel Lyfons, efq; died feized of it in the year 1773, and was fucceeded by his fon, Daniel Lyfons, efq; who is the prefent lord of the manor. His arms are, *Gules, a chief argent, on the lower part thereof a cloud, the fun's refplendent rays iffuing thereout proper.*

Certain lands and tithes in Hempfted, with a fifhery in the Severn, lately belonging to the priory of Lanthony, were granted to Arthur Porter 32 H. 8.

HAMLET. Rea is a hamlet, lying about half a mile from the church.

Podgmead is a tithe free farm of confiderable value, in this parifh, formerly belonging to the priory of Lanthony. The fcite of the manor of Poddefmead, and feveral other lands, in confideration of 266*l.* 6*s.* 8*d.* were granted to Joan Coke, 31 H. 8. to be held by the tenth part of a knight's fee, paying 30*s.* yearly to the crown. Podgmead came afterwards to Mr. Hofkins, who granted it to the corporation of the city of Gloucefter, on condition that they fhould conftantly renew to the next heir male of his family, a leafe for thirty-one years, at a certain referved rent, on the payment of a fmall fine.

Of the Church, &c.

The church is a rectory, in the deanery of Gloucefter, worth about 90*l.* a year. The hon. Mr. Howard, who married Mifs Scudamore, is patron in her right; Mr. Taylor is the prefent incumbent. It was formerly a chapel belonging to St. Owen's in Gloucefter.

In the year 1137, earl Milo gave the tithes of this church to the priory of Lanthony. Small tithes in Hampftead, lately belonging to the priory of Lanthony, were granted to fir Chriftopher Hatton, 24 Eliz.

John lord Scudamore, in the year 1662, fettled on the minifter the vicarage houfe, garden, and orchard, the parfonage clofe and barn, and a parcel of meadow ground in Hempfted-moor, with his tithes, &c. in Hempfted, which particulars he had purchafed of Henry Powle, efq; of Williamftrip in this county, as appears by a conveyance, dated Jan. 17, 13 C. 2. To the above he added the church-yard of Lanthony priory, and all the tithes of his demeans there. Thefe particulars were fettled by act of parliament. He likewife built the prefent parfonage houfe, at the expence of 700*l.* over the door of which is written, in gold letters,

Whoe'er doth dwell within this door,
Thank God for vifcount Scudamore.

The church, dedicated to St. Swithin, ftands on a rifing ground, whence there is an extenfive profpect over the vale, and has a tower between the nave and the chancel.

	£				£		
Firft fruits	8	0	0	Synodals	0	1	0
Tenths —	0	16	0	*Annuapenfio regi*	2	0	0
Procurations	0	1	0				

Monuments and Infcriptions.

Againft the north wall of the chancel is a brafs plate, with the following infcription in black character:

Nere this place lyeth buryed the bodyes of Nicholas Porter, Henry, Roger, and Nicholas jun^r. Cecilly and Bridgid, fonnes and daughters to Arthur Porter, Efquy^r. and Alys his Wife, An^o M v^c xlviii. On whofe foules Ihu have m'cy.——Over, on a fcutcheon, *Baron and femme*, 1. Quarterly, 1ft and 4th, *Gules, five martins wings in faltire argent*, for Porter. 2. . . . . . *three helmets clofe fable, tipt Or.* 3. *Argent, three bars fable, over all as many cart ropes Or.* —— 2. Quarterly, 1ft and 4th, *Gules, a chevron ermine between three pheons heads Or*, for Arnold. 2d and 3d, *Sable, a chevron Or between three lures argent.*

In the chancel,

Here lieth Elenor the wife of Richard Atkins Efquior and daughter of Thomas Marfhe of Warefleie in the countie of Huntington Efquior, who died the 3 of Aprile An^o Dn^i 1594.

Hir godli life hir bleffed deathe
Hir hope and confolation
Were fignes to us and feales to her
Of joyful refurrection.

Againft the north wall of the chancel is a very handfome raifed monument, for Richard Atkyns, chief juftice of South Wales, with his effigy, in judge's robes, lying thereon. A flat ftone near it bears this infcription:

Here lyeth buried the body of Richard Atkins of Tuflay Efquior waighting for the refurrection of glory, and was buried the 3 day of November ano 1610.

Benefactions.

Sylvanus Lyfons, efq; left an eftate of about 300*l.* a year, after his widow's death, which happened in 1750, charged with the payment of 20*l.* a year each to nine clergymens widows of this diocefe, (the Foreft deanery excepted;) 2*l.* 2*s.* for a fermon in Hempfted church; and 5*l.* for an entertainment on Afcenfion-day. If any overplus remains, it is to go to the rector of Hempfted. Five feoffees (three clergymen and two laymen) are appointed to the management of the charity.

Mrs. Harris of Abergavenny, fifter to Sylvanus Lyfons, efq; left 1000*l.* now laid out in the purchafe of an eftate at Upton St. Leonard's, the rents to be apply'd as follows: 20*s.* for an anniverfary fermon on the 27th of June, which was the day of her death; 5*s.* to provide bread and wine for a facrament, and 2*s.* 6*d.* to the clerk; and the fame at Whaddon. Four widows are to be clothed on that day. What remains of the rent to be employed in putting out boys apprentices, two of this parifh for one of Whaddon. If the boys are not apprenticed, then the money to be expended in clothing poor men.

Taxes.

Taxes.					
	The Royal Aid in 1692, £.	64	13	4
	Poll-tax —— 1694, —	26	14	0
	Land-tax —— 1694, —	82	16	0
	The ſame, at 3*s*. 1770, —	62	2	0

At the beginning of this century, there were 30 houſes in this pariſh, and about 140 inhabitants, whereof 8 were freeholders; yearly births 4, burials 4. *Atkyns*. The inhabitants are now about 129; ſo that population is on the decline.

HENBURY.

THIS is an extenſive pariſh, lying at the weſtern extremity of the county, part of it in the hundred of its own name, and part in the hundred of Berkeley; five miles diſtant northward from Briſtol, and thirty-five ſouth-weſtward from Glouceſter. It is bounded on the eaſt by Almondeſbury and part of Weſtbury, on the weſt by the Avon, on the north by the Severn, and on the ſouth by Clifton and part of Weſtbury.

The name ſufficiently evinces the antiquity of the village. It is compoſed of *hen*, Britiſh, *old*, and *berg*, a *camp*, or *fortification*; and ſignifies emphatically the *old camp*, for there were more *bergs*, or *camps*, than one in this place, and its neighbourhood, when the name was firſt given it.

Lord Clifford has a fine ſeat at King's Weſton, in this pariſh, enriched with plantations, and beautiful lawns and paſture grounds. It lies at the diſtance of about two miles from the Severn, which appears from thence like a large arm of the ocean, with ſhips generally lying at anchor in Kingroad, either bound to or from the port of Briſtol. From a little hill, not far from the houſe, the proſpect is exquiſitely beautiful, and uncommonly extenſive, commanding the country on the Briſtol channel, from Pembrokeſhire on one ſide, and Somerſetſhire on the other, almoſt up to the city of Glouceſter, with the Welch mountains, at a vaſt diſtance, for an evaneſcent ground. Turning ſouthward, the view is leſs extenſive, but not leſs agreeable, over a rich cultivated country, interſperſed with villas, on the Glouceſterſhire ſide of the Avon, as far as the city of Briſtol. Mr. Jones, in his CLIFTON, ſlightly touches on the beauties of this ſeat:

KING'S WESTON there, delightful various ſcene!
The muſe enjoys, and reigns a raptur'd queen,
With throbbing boſom, and extatic eye,
O'er all the ſubject, ocean, hills, and ſky,
The faint perſpective, and the dying view,
The boundleſs plan to juſt proportion true,
Where each bright beauty ſpreads its tints abroad
In all the ſplendors of thy pencil, *Claude!*
Where parts on parts reflect a lucid ray,
That all the luſtre of the whole diſplay;
Where harmony her happy order ſhews,
In all the art that on the canvaſs glows;
The plaſtic picture ſtrikes th' aſtoniſh'd mind,
The ſhips in proſpect, and the hills behind;
The woods, the mountains at due diſtance riſe,
In perfect uniſon with ſea and ſkies:
There light and ſhade their wond'rous ſtrength impart,
There nature ſeems to take the hint from art.
The vale incult, by random robe ſee grac'd,
With SOUTHWELL ſoaring to the mark of taſte;
Whoſe claſſic eye each erring ſtroke ſhall ſcan,
Reform the model, and improve the plan;
To ſimple majeſty reduce the pile,
And bid diſcretion through the garden ſmile;
Make truth and unity in all combine,
And taſte and judgment crown the clear deſign;
Unnumber'd beauties thence attract the ſoul,
That ſeem expanded to the diſtant pole;
The outline endleſs, charms th' inſatiate eyes,
Within that trait ten thouſand beauties riſe,
With incidents above *Salvator*'s hand,
Of ocean, air, of foreſt, ſky, and land.

From this ſhort viſit to King's Weſton, we return to the village of Henbury; where, not far diſtant from the church, ſtands Blaſe-hill, of a ſugar-loaf form, whoſe ſides are covered with a fine wood. It is ſo called from an old chapel formerly erected upon it, ſaid to have been dedicated to St. Blaſius, biſhop of St. Sebaſte, and patron of the wool-combers. On the ſummit of this hill are ſtrong lines of fortification, which were very probably the *old camp* that gave name to the village.

About the year 1766, in digging the foundation of a pleaſure houſe on the top of this hill, ſome braſs coins of Veſpaſian, Antoninus, Conſtantine, Conſtantius, Tetricus, and others of the later empire, were found, with a few ſilver ones, chiefly of Gordianus. The moſt curious of them all was a large braſs medal, with a very fine head of Fauſtina, and a female figure, holding an infant in one hand, on the reverſe; whence, and from the inſcription, FERTILITAS, it is ſuppoſed to have been ſtruck upon the occaſion of that empreſs's lying-in. But theſe remains were only the gleanings of a fuller harveſt, which happened in the year 1707, when many coins, and other Roman antiquities were found there, as we are told in general by ſir Robert Atkyns. Then, alſo, the foundation of the old chapel was dug up, and a vault diſcovered, ten yards long, and ſix broad, wherein were many human bodies, with the ſculls intire, and teeth white.

Beſides this camp, there are two others, one on King's-Weſton-hill, the other on the ſummit of Comb-hill, both ſuppoſed to be Roman.

Blaſe-caſtle, which is the name of the pleaſure-houſe above-mentioned, is elegantly finiſhed in the Gothic ſtile, at a very conſiderable expence, by Thomas Farr, eſq; the preſent chief magiſtrate of the city of Briſtol, who has a good houſe and a large eſtate in this village. From this caſtle is a moſt delightful proſpect of the country round it, with the windings of the Avon, the beautiful riſing incloſures on the ſide of Dundery-hill, the more diſtant country of Glamorganſhire, Monmouthſhire, and the waving woods of Dean-foreſt on the oppoſite ſide of the Severn, with the mountains in Wales to cloſe the landſkape.

Here FARR with inbred rapture may reſort,
And ſee his ſhips glad ſailing into port,
With *Indian* treaſures on the current ride,
To crown the proſpect, and enrich the tide:
What nameleſs raptures muſt his joys renew,
With growing taſte at once, and wealth, in view;

The

The harbour, ſhips, the ſea, the mountains ſhine,
With inſtant luſtre, and with ray divine;
Lo, SOUTHWELL's landſkip, happy FARR, is thine!
There on the right a *Roman* camp we find,
Left by the lords and maſters of mankind;
Where coins and medals narrative are found;
Thoſe ſtory'd regiſters from under ground,
A moral lecture to the mind convey;
The *Latian* glories, in their laſt decay,
May mad ambition's frantic boaſt deride,
And human vanity, and human pride.
From hence kind nature opens wide her arms,
Her pictures raviſh, and her proſpect charms;
From hence the fated ſoul forbids the ſight,
O'ercome, and fill'd with ſurfeits of delight.
Where erſt the *Roman* eagles wav'd in air,
Behold a peaceful growing pile appear,
For friendly banquet, in a *Gothic* guiſe,
From forth the center of the camp ariſe;
Which ſhall each ſenſe with each regale ſupply,
But feaſt for ever the inſatiate eye;
Thence down a vegetable arch we ſtray,
A growing gallery, with winding way,
Where lovely labyrinths in mazes run
To the ſweet ruſtic lawn where we begun:
There FARR with willing heart can frequent blend
The connoiſſeur, the merchant, and the friend;
At the rich genial board in each can ſhine,
And make his converſe lively as his wine;
His three years toil with happy eye may view,
And joyful gueſs what three years more can do.
His lov'd LUCINDA in her orb can charm,
Her ſmile can gladden, and her muſic warm;
From forth the anſwering keys her fingers call
The ſoul of harmony, that joy of all;
Her meaſures, like her mind, are fill'd with grace,
In ſounds you hear, you ſee it in her face.

Jones's CLIFTON.

Here, with the poet, we take leave of Blaiſe-hill, and obſerve, that Mr. Sampſon, and Mr. Miller have very good houſes in the midſt of the village, and good eſtates in the pariſh.

Henbury, Clifton, Redland, Kingſdown, Stapleton, and Winterbourn are to Briſtol, what Iſlington, Hempſtead, Bow, and other circumjacent villages are to London; an agreeable retreat from the noiſe and hurry of a buſy life, and they mark the taſte and opulence of a trading people.

This large pariſh conſiſts chiefly of paſture and meadow ground, with ſome arable and woodland, and there are ſome marſhy grounds next the Severn.

The following plants, among others of leſs note, are found here, *viz.*

Aſparagus Paluſtris, [*Officinalis* Linnei] Marſh Aſparagus; flowering in autumn. Park. 454. Gerh. p. 947. Found in Maidenham, or Madam-meadow, in Lawrence-Weſton.

Naſturtiolum Montanum annuum tenuiſſime diviſum, [*Lepidum petreum* Linnei] Finely cut annual Mountain Creſs; flowering in the ſpring, on the low rocks over-againſt Goram's-chair. Ray, 304.

Polygonum minus. Small Knot-graſs. Park. 446, ſect. 4. On the ſhore of the Severn, about Weſton.

The *Entrochus*, a petrification of the worm, or grub claſs, from one to three inches long, compoſed of ſeveral joints, with *radii* on each diſk, and perforated through the middle, is ſometimes found at King's Weſton.

In this pariſh are two ferries over the Severn. The uppermoſt, or *Old Paſſage*, is in the tithing of Auſt, thirteen miles on a turnpike-road from Briſtol: There the river is above two miles over, and the oppoſite houſe is at Beachley, in the pariſh of Tidenham in this county. The other ferry, called the *New-Paſſage*, is at Redwick, about three miles further down the river, and eleven miles diſtant from Briſtol. There the water is about three miles over; and the oppoſite paſſage-houſe is at a place called the *Black Rock*, near St. Pierre's in Monmouthſhire. See obſervations on theſe paſſages, p. 47.

Of the Manors and other Eſtates.

Sir Robert Atkyns, attempting to give an account of this manor from *Domeſday-book*, has intermixed with it ſome particulars of that of Sodbury, which commence in the fourth line, and run on to the end of his account. In the detail of the large manor of Weſtbury, in Bernintreu hundred, which, before and after the conqueſt, belonged to the church of St. Mary of Worceſter, it is thus recorded: 'Theſe members, Henberie, 'Redeuuiche, Stoche, Giete, belong to this manor. 'In theſe are nine plow-tillages in demean, and 'twenty-ſeven villeins, and twenty-two bordars, 'with twenty-ſix plow-tillages. There are twenty '*ſervi*, and two *ancillæ*, and twenty free men, '[*coliberti*] with ten plow-tillages, and a mill of '20*d.*' *Domeſday-book*, p. 70.

The biſhop of Worceſter proved his right to court leet and free warren in Henbury, in a *Quo warranto* brought againſt him 15 E. 1.

In an antient taxation of the manor, found in the Cottonian library, it is ſaid, The lord biſhop of Worceſter has at Henbury in the Salt-marſh 40*l.* in rent of aſſize; and five carucates of land, worth two marks each; and a dove-houſe, worth 6*s.* 8*d.* and in pleas and perquiſites of the court, twelve marks; and a water-mill, with ſome other income, worth 100*s.* In all 60*l.* *Tiberius*, C. x. E. 76.—In another ſurvey of the manor, 26 H. 8. it was valued at 71*l.* 12*s.* 9*d.* *per annum.*

Henbury continued in the ſee of Worceſter from before the conqueſt, 'till Dr. Heath alienated this manor, and that of Stoke-Biſhop, with the advowſon of the vicarage of Henbury, to the crown, in the year 1547, in exchange for ſome other manors and eſtates in Herefordſhire and Worceſterſhire.

King Edward the Sixth, by letters patents, 30 Jun. 1° *regni*, grants the manors of Biſhop's Stoke and Henbury in Salt-Marſh, and the hundred of Henbury, with the advowſon of the vicarage of the pariſh church of Henbury, late parcel of the poſſeſſions of the biſhop of Worceſter, to ſir Rafe Sadleir, and his heirs. Sir Thomas Sadleir, ſon of Rafe, was owner of theſe eſtates 32 Eliz. and left one ſon, Rafe Sadleir, eſq; who had no iſſue, and

and one daughter Gertrude, married to ſir Walter Aſton, of Tixal in Staffordſhire.

Walter lord Aſton, their ſon and heir, ſold the manor and hundred of Henbury, with the advowſon of the vicarage of Henbury, and the manor of Weſtbury Bryan, *alias* Weſtbury upon Trim, lately belonging to the college of Weſtbury, to Thomas Yate and Gregory Gearing, 20 May, 1675; from whom they paſſed by purchaſe to ſir Samuel Aſtry, of Henbury, in 1680.

By the death of ſir Samuel Aſtry, the manor and hundred of Henbury, &c. deſcended to his three ſurviving daughters and coheireſſes; Elizabeth, married to ſir John Smyth, baronet; Diana, the wife of Richard Orlebar, eſq; and Arabella, the lady of Charles-William earl of Suffolk, whom ſhe ſurvived. And dying without iſſue, ſhe left her third part to ſir John Smyth, baronet; whoſe ſon, ſir John Smyth, ſold a moiety of that third to the heirs of Edward Colſton, eſq; who had purchaſed the third part late Mr. Orlebar's. A moiety was then in ſir John Smyth, whoſe three ſiſters and coheireſſes ſold it to ſir Jarrit Smith, baronet, who married Florence, one of the ſaid coheireſſes. The other moiety deſcended to the two daughters and coheirs of Thomas Edwards, eſq; one of whom was married to Francis lord Middleton; the other was wedded to Alexander Ready, eſq; who afterwards took the name of Colſton, and died in the year 1775. So that ſir Jarrit Smith is the preſent owner of one moiety of the manor and hundred of Henbury, &c. and the honourable Thomas Willoughby, ſecond ſon of the late lord Middleton, and Alexander Colſton, eſq; at the time of his death, were proprietors of the other moiety. Sir Jarrit Smith bears for his arms, *Gules, on a chevron between three cinquefoils argent, as many leopards faces ſable.*

TITHINGS and HAMLETS.

1. *King's Weſton,* where lord Clifford has a fine ſeat, as mentioned in the introductory part of the account of this pariſh. This tithing received its name from being the king's antient demeſnes, and lying fartheſt weſtward of any part of Berkeley hundred, of which it is a member, tho' far detached from the continent of that hundred.

It is thus mentioned in *Domeſday*: 'Seven 'hides and one virgate in Weſtone belong to 'Berchelai.' King Henry the Second granted the lordſhip of Berkeley, and Berkeley herneſſe, *i.e.* the diſtrict of Berkeley, to Robert Fitz-Harding, who ſettled this manor and that of Beverſtone, on Robert his ſecond ſon. From that time the manor of King's Weſton and that of Beverſtone deſcended to the ſame proprietors, as related under the account of the latter, down to 9 R. 2. when Catherine, the widow of Thomas lord Berkeley, died ſeized of both, after having married, to her ſecond huſband, ſir John de Throp, who was poſſeſſed of King's Weſton 11 R. 2.

Sir Maurice Berkeley held this manor 2 H. 4. and was ſucceeded by ſir John Berkeley, his heir, who enjoy'd it 6 H. 6. From him it deſcended to ſir Maurice Berkeley of Beverſtone, who dying 38 H. 6. was ſucceeded by ſir Maurice Berkeley of Uley, who was ſeized of this manor 4 E. 4. His ſon and heir, ſir William Berkeley, taking part with king Richard the Third, his eſtate was ſeized by king Henry the Seventh, and the manor of King's Weſton was granted to Jaſper duke of Bedford, and to the heirs males of his body. But the king granted the reverſion, after the duke of Bedford's entail, to ſir William Berkeley, the former owner, 4 H. 7.

Sir John Berkeley, ſon of ſir William, ſucceeding his father, died ſeized of King's Weſton 37 H. 8. and left Richard, his ſon, who had livery 6 E. 6. and deceaſing the ſame year, was ſucceeded by his couſin John Berkeley, ſon of ſir William Berkeley, who was younger brother of ſir John Berkeley.

Sir William Berkeley, ſon of ſir John, ſold this manor to ſir William Wintour 12 Eliz. And ſir Edward Wintour was ſeized of it 8 Jac. From the Wintours it paſſed by purchaſe to Humphry Hook, alderman of Briſtol, whoſe ſon ſir Humphry Hook conveyed it, in the year 1679, to ſir Robert Southwell, a gentleman of great abilities and worth, deſcended from an antient family, ſeated at a place of the ſame name; whence they removed to Woodriſing, where, and in other parts of Norfolk, they enjoy'd large eſtates.

Richard Southwell was eminent in the reign of king Henry the Eighth, and was by that king conſtituted one of the overſeers of his laſt will.

Robert Southwell, eſq; married Helena, daughter of major Robert Gore, by whom he had ſir Robert Southwell, the purchaſer of King's Weſton.

Sir Robert Southwell married Elizabeth, eldeſt daughter of ſir Edward Dering, of Surrenden-Dering in Kent, baronet, and had iſſue by her ſix children. He died in the year 1702, and was ſucceeded by his ſon and heir, Edward Southwell, eſq;

Which Edward Southwell entered early on buſineſs, under the conduct of his father, and, like him, deſervedly filled ſeveral offices of the greateſt eminence in the kingdom of Ireland. He married firſt, the lady Elizabeth Cromwell, daughter and heireſs of the earl of Ardglaſs, by whom he had iſſue Edward, who ſucceeded him; and Robert, Thomas, and Elizabeth, who died in their infancy. But this lady deceaſing in 1709, he married, ſecondly, Anne Blathwayte, by whom he had iſſue one ſon, William Southwell.

Edward Southwell, the father, dying in the year 1730, was ſucceeded by his ſon and heir, the right honourable Edward Southwell, who married Catherine Watſon, daughter of Edward lord Sondes, and had iſſue by her one ſon Edward, and one daughter Catherine. He ſerved in three ſucceſſive parliaments for the city of Briſtol, and died in the year 1755.

Edward Southwell ſucceeded his father, and having been choſen one of the repreſentatives of this county in three ſucceſſive parliaments, which important truſt he diſcharged with great ability and independency, was ſummoned by writ to the houſe of peers in 1776, by the title of baron Clifford, of Clifford in Glouceſterſhire. This title had been for ſome time in abeyance, to which he had a claim as being lineally deſcended by his mother from Robert lord Clifford, who was firſt ſummoned to parliament 28 E. 1. This Edward lord Clifford married Sophia, daughter of Samuel Campbell, eſq; of Mount Campbell in the county of Leitrim, in the kingdom of Ireland, and dying ſeized of King's Weſton in 1777, left iſſue by his lady, who ſurvives him, four ſons, *viz.* Edward, now lord Clifford, born in 1767; Robert-Campbell, born in 1770; Henry, and John, which two laſt are deceaſed: Alſo five daughters, *viz.* Mary, Katherine, Sophia, Elizabeth, and Henrietta, all living. His lordſhip bears two coats, Quarterly, 1ſt and 4th, *Argent, three cinquefoils gules, each charged with five annulets Or*, for Southwell. 2d and 3d, *Checky Or and azure, a feſs gules*, for Clifford. CREST. *A demy goat argent, eared and gorged with a ducal coronet, and charged with three annulets in bend gules.* SUPPORTERS. On the dexter ſide, *A wivern gules*; on the ſiniſter, *A monkey proper.* MOTTO. LE ROY LE VEUT.

The monumental inſcriptions in the cloſe of this account exhibit many intereſting particulars of his lordſhip's family, to which, for brevity ſake, the reader is referred.

Thomas Mallet, eſq; died ſeized of lands in King's Weſton and Lawrence-Weſton 22 Eliz. and left John his ſon twelve years old.

There was formerly a chapel of eaſe in this place, but it is now intirely demoliſhed. The rectory and advowſon of the vicarage of King's Weſton belonged to the abbey of St. Auguſtin's in Briſtol, and were granted to the biſhoprick of Briſtol 34 H. 8.

Bewy's-croſs, of which there are ſtill remains, ſtood near the ſide of the Severn. It was formerly held in high eſtimation by ſeamen, who paid their devotions to it on their ſafe landing.

2. *Lawrence-Weſton*, ſo called, becauſe the hoſpital of St. Lawrence near Briſtol had lands there. Nicholas de Caldecot levied a fine of the manor of St. Lawrence Weſton, to the uſe of John Bradley, and Iſabel his wife, 12 E. 2. which John and Iſabel levied a fine of lands in Weſton St. Lawrence, Charleton, and Thredland, (*i.e.* The Redland) to John de Weſtbury, and to the uſe of themſelves for life, the remainder to Walter, Robert, and Thomas, brothers of John, in ſucceſſive fee taile, 5 E. 3. Sir William Berkeley died ſeized of this manor 5 E. 6. and John his ſon and heir had livery thereof 6 E. 6. Henry Lewis, eſq; was ſeized of this manor in the reign of king James the Firſt, and was ſucceeded therein by his ſon George, who died 10 C. and left William his ſon and heir, then ſeven years old. Six acres in Biſhop's Moor, and other meſſuages and lands in Weſton St. Lawrence, lately belonging to the Magdalen hoſpital in Briſtol, were granted to John Bellowe and John Bloxholme 37 H. 8. as appears by a copy of the grant B. 2, *Appendix to Stevens's Supplement* to the *Monaſticon*. Here was alſo a chapel of eaſe, now demoliſhed.

3. *Redwick*, which lies along the Severn, five miles from the pariſh church. I have already ſhewn from *Domeſday-book* that this was a member of the large manor of Weſtbury, and that the New Paſſage over the Severn is in this tithing. Maurice de Gaunt died ſeized of the manor of Redwick, with markets and fairs, 6 H. 3. as did Robert de Gourney 53 H. 3. whoſe ſon Anſelm was ſucceeded by John de Gourney, whoſe only daughter, Elizabeth, was married to John Ap Adam, (ſometimes called John de Badenham) which John and Elizabeth levied a fine of the manors of Redwick and Northwick 25 E. 1. John de Knovill held theſe manors 13 E. 2. and Alice his widow died ſeized of Redwick 28 E. 3. Sir John Walſh died ſeized of the manors of Redwick and Northwick 38 H. 8. of which livery was granted to his ſon, Maurice Walſh, the ſame year; and Nicholas Walſh died ſeized of them, and of Camer's Place 20 Eliz. and Henry Walſh, his ſon, obtained livery thereof in that year.

Reginald de Botreaux and Iſabel his wife levied a fine of lands in Redwick 4 E. 3. William Stoke and Iſabel his wife levied a fine of lands in Redwick and Northwick, and of a fiſhery called Cheſyll-pill, to the uſe of Robert Pointz 49 H. 6. Richard Beke levied a fine of lands in Redwick and Gronen-down-hill, to Edward Veel, 1 Mar.

4. *Northwick.* The records concerning this hamlet are ſet down with Redwick. It remains to obſerve that here is a chapel of eaſe.

5. *Auſt.* This tithing was antiently called Auſtre Clive, becauſe it is ſituated on the ſouth cliff of the river Severn.

There is great plenty of alabaſter in the rocks all along the ſhore at this place, and I have ſeen a grinding tooth of ſome animal, nearly as big as a man's fiſt, taken out of theſe rocks. Here I expected to have found great plenty and variety of petrifications, as others have done; but was diſappointed, after a diligent examination.

Walter Mapes relates a memorable tranſaction at this place. *Edward the Elder*, ſays he, *lay at Auſt Clive, and Leoline prince of Wales at Betherſley*, [Beachley] *on the oppoſite ſhore. When the latter refuſed to come acroſs the Severn, to a conference with the king, Edward paſſed over to Leoline; who knowing the king, threw his royal robes upon the ground, which he had prepared to ſit in judgment with, and leaping breaſt high into the water, embracing the boat, ſaid, 'Moſt wiſe king, your humility has conquered my 'pride,*

'*pride, and your wisdom triumphed over my folly.* '*Mount upon that neck which I have foolishly exalted* '*against you, so shall you enter into that country* '*which your goodness has this day made your own.*' *And so, taking him upon his shoulders, he made him sit upon his robes, and joining hands did him homage.*

Domesday-book says, 'Turstin the son of Rolf 'holds five hides in Austreclive of the land of this 'manor,' *i.e.* of the manor of Huesberie. William Russel held the manor of Aust 4 E. 2. and Roger de Acton was seized thereof 35 E. 3. John Kemish, esq; and Margaret his wife, and Stephen Hatfield and Isabel his wife, levied a fine of one moiety of the manor of Aust to the use of sir Maurice Berkeley of Uley, 15 R. 2. And sir Thomas Brook and Joan his wife levied a fine of the other moiety of that manor, and of lands in Coats near Aust, 15 R. 2. Sir Thomas Brook died seized of the manor 5 H. 5. and Joan his widow died seized thereof, and of Coats near Aust, which she held in dower, 15 H. 6. It is probable that she had married sir John Stradling, for he and Joan his wife held the third part of the manor of Aust, in right of dower 13 H. 6. Thomas Chedder was seized of the manor of Aust and of Coates 21 H. 6. and John Kemish held Aust 16 E. 4. The manor of Aust belonged afterwards to the Dennises of Durham, and passed to the Capels. Sir Giles Capel married Isabel, one of the daughters and heirs of Richard Newton, esq; son of sir John Newton, and died seized of Aust 3 Mar. and was succeeded by his son sir Henry Capel, who dying without issue, Edward Capel his brother had livery 5 Mar. Sir Edward Capel, with Humphry Capel, and Roger Capel, esqrs. sold this manor to John Browning, out of whose family it went by purchase to sir Samuel Astry, in the year 1652. Sir Samuel devised it to dame Elizabeth his widow, who gave all her estates between her three surviving daughters, and upon a partition, this manor fell to the youngest daughter, Arabella countess of Suffolk, who devised it to sir John Smith, baronet. His son, sir John Smith, dying in 1741, without issue, devised his estate to his three surviving sisters and coheirs, who, in 1750, sold this manor to sir Jarrit Smyth, baronet, who sold it to the reverend Staunton Degge, late of Over, and Mrs. Wilmot is the present lady of this manor.

Livery of Aust-passage, *alias* Haman Hay, was granted to Elizabeth Randoll 15 Eliz. It was purchased by sir Samuel Astry, and has since passed like the manor of Aust. There is a neat chapel in this tithing. See *Inscriptions* and *Benefactions*.

6. *Stowick*, which lies in the marshy part, along the banks of the Severn. The low grounds near the river were antiently called *Salt Marsh*. John de Stoner died seized of lands in Salt Marsh 9 E. 2. as did his son John de Stoner 28 E. 3. and Edward son of the last John 5 R. 2. and John son of Edward 13 R. 2. Sir Ralph Stoner held the same lands 18 R. 2. and Gilbert de Stoner, son of Robert, died seized of the same 3 H. 5. Sir Edward Seimour, son of Edward duke of Somerset, and lady Catherine his wife, levied a fine of lands in Salt Marsh 1 E. 6.

7. *Aylminton*, alias *Elminton*. Four hides in Almintune belonged to the lordship of Berkeley at the time of the general survey. John Musgrose was seized of this manor 3 E. 1. John Blount held the manor of Aylminton in Henbury 22 H. 6. as did Wentlyn his widow 32 H. 6. and Edward Blount, esq; and Simon his son and heir were seized of it respectively 8 & 16 E. 4. Sir John Smyth was lord of this manor, whose coheirs sold it in the year 1749, to sir Jarrit Smyth, baronet, who is the present lord of the manor of Aylminton.

Of the Church, &c.

The church is a vicarage, in the deanery of Bristol, worth about 80*l.* a year. The presentation to the vicarage is alternate in the heirs of sir John Smyth, baronet, and the heirs of Thomas Edwards, esq; Mr. Gardiner is the present incumbent. The church was appropriated to the see of Worcester, and the advowson of the vicarage was in that bishoprick before the reign of king Edward the Sixth.

The church is dedicated to St. Mary. It consists of the nave and two ailes, with a handsome altar-piece railed in, and a large tower at the west end, containing six bells and a clock. Lands worth 60*l.* a year are given to keep it in repair.

First fruits £.30	0	0	Synodals £.	
Tenths —	3	0	0	Pentecostals
Procurations				

Monuments and Inscriptions.

On the left of the communion table, as you front it, there is a large monument of white marble, ornamented with the family coat of arms, and inscribed with the following memorial:

Here lyeth
The Body of Sr. ROBERT SOUTHWELL
of *Kings-Weston* in the County of Glocestr. Knt
He was eldest Son of ROBERT SOUTHWELL of *Kinsale*
in *Ireland*, Esq; and of HELENA the daughter
of Major ROBERT GORE.
He was born at Ballyn Varwick on the River of *Bandon*
near Kinsale the 31st Decembr 1635.
He came for his Education into *England* in 1650,
And spent his younger years at *Queen's Colledge*
in *Oxford*, in *Lincoln's Inne*, and in Travel abroad.
He was by King CHARLES the 2d made one of the *Clerks*
of his most Honble *Privy Council* in Septr. 1664.
He married ELIZABETH eldest daughter of Sr. EDWARD DERING
of *Surrenden Dering* in *Kent* Bart.
by whom he had issue 6 Children.
He was employ'd in several foreign Negotiations,
First in quality of *Envoy* with powers to mediate a Peace
between *Spain* and *Portugal*, proving happily
Instrumental in giving a period to that War,
Which had continued 28 years without intermission.
He was sent a second time to the Court of *Portugal*
in Quality of *Envoy Extraordinary*,
Afterwards with the like Character to the Governour of *Flanders*
the Conde de Monterey in 1672;
And with the same Commission to the Elector
of *Brandenburgh* at *Berlin* in 1680, attending in his way
the Prince of *Orange* at the *Hague*, by whose Counsels
that Negotiation was to be directed.
After his return he retired from publick Businesse,
Living at Kings-Weston 'till King WILLIAM

was

was advanc'd to the Throne.
He was then by his *Majeſty* made *Principal Secretary of State* for *Ireland*, and attended him in his Expedition in 1690 for the Reduction of that Kingdom, holding the ſaid Office 'till his death.
He had ſerved in three Parliaments, And was 5 times Choſen *Preſident* of the *Royal Society*.
He dyed at Kings-Weſton the 11th day of Sept. 1702, Aged 66 Years.

On the north ſide of the chancel is a very ſuperb marble monument, with this inſcription on the pyramidal part, in gold letters;

To the Memory of
EDWARD SOUTHWELL, Eſq;
who after leaving the Univerſity of *Oxford*,
was Early enter'd into Buſineſs,
under the Conduct of his Father Sr ROBERT,
who then attended KING WILLIAM into *Ireland*
as Principal Secretary of State of that KINGDOM,
In which Employment he ſucceeded his Father,
and Continued in it to his Death.
His Skill and Experience in Buſineſs
recommended Him to four PRINCES ſucceſſively,
whom he attended as Clerk of the Councill.
He was thrice Ioint Commiſſioner of the Privy Seal,
twice chief ſecretary to the LORD Lieutenant of *Ireland*.
Clerk of the Crown in *Ireland*, & Vice Admiral of *Munſter*.
In theſe ſeveral Stations
He improved his Family Eſtate with Integrity and Induſtry.
He was helpful to all Mankind, & affectionate to his family.
He enjoyed life with Chearfulneſs and Innocence,
and bore a moſt long and Painful ſickneſs,
with patience, firmneſs, & Reſignation.
He was born 4th Septr. 1671 & died 4th Decber 1730.

On the vaſe of the ſame monument,

Here Lieth the Right Honble the Lady ELIZABETH Sole Daughter and Heireſs of VERE ESSEX CROMWELL Baron of *Oakham*, *Viſcount Lekale*, and Earl of *Ardglaſs*, by CATHERINE HAMILTON. ſhe was Tenth Deſcendant from THOMAS CROMWELL, Firſt Baron of *Oakham* and Earl of *Eſſex*, Vicar General and Chief Promoter of the Reformation in the Reign of HENRY 8th. She was born 3d December 1674, Married to EDWARD SOUTHWELL Eſq; 29th October 1704, and died 31st March 1709, Leaving Iſſue EDWARD, ROBERT, THOMAS, and ELIZABETH, the three laſt died in their Infancy. She was a Lady diſtinguiſh'd by a Superior Genius and Underſtanding, and her Affection to her Huſband and Family. Her Charity, and the Reſolution with which She bore her laſt Illneſs and Foreſaw Her Death, are ever to be Remembred to Her honour, and to be recommended to the Imitation of Poſterity.

Here alſo Lieth ANN, the daughter of WILLIAM BLATHWAYT, Eſq; by ANN WYNTER, of *Dyrham* in ye County of *Glouceſter*, a Lady of Singular Virtue and merit, who died much lamented 1st Iuly, 1717, Aged 27, a year after Her marriage with EDWARD SOUTHWELL, Eſq. leaving one Son WILLIAM SOUTHWELL.

At the bottom are two ſcutcheons, the firſt bears the arms of Southwell, with a ſcutcheon of pretence, *Quarterly Or and azure, four lions paſſant counterchanged*, for Cromwell. The ſecond is *Baron and femme*, 1. Southwell. 2. *Or, two bendlets ingrailed ſable*, for Blathwayt.

On the other ſide of the communion table, upon the table of a very handſome monument, in gold letters,

To the Memory of
The Right Honble Edward Southwell,
Son of Edward Southwell, & Lady Elizabeth Cromwell,
Born 17 June 1705:
He married, 21 Augt. 1729,
Katherine Watſon, Daughter of Edward Lord Sondes,
Son of Lewis Earl of Rockingham.
Their Children were
Edward, born 6 Iune, 1738,
Katherine, born 10 Decr. 1739, ſhe died 17 Mar. 1748,
And is buried near her Father,
Who exchanged this Life for a better 16 Mar. 1755.

He was choſen Member of Parliament for the City of Briſtol in the Year 1739, & rechoſen for the ſame Place the two following Parliaments; in the diſcharge of which Truſt, His Conduct was uninfluenced by the Temptations of Ambition, Avarice, or Popularity: equally true to his King & his Country, & ever ſteady to what he thought Right. In private Life He was Iuſt, Charitable, Benevolent, Friendly. A tender affectionate Huſband, & Father; A kind Landlord & Maſter; and, what comprehends all civil and moral Virtues, a ſincere and pious Chriſtian.

Againſt the north wall of the chancel,

ELIZABETH, Eldeſt Daughter of Sr. EDWARD DERING, of Surrenden-Dering in Kent, Baronet (one of the Lords Comrs. of His Majtys Treaſury) and of Dame MARY his Wife, Lyes Here Interred. SHE dyed in London on the 13th of Ianry 1681, in the 33d year of her age, And was here depoſited (in hopes of a bleſſed Reſurrection) on the 26th Day of the ſame Month. SHE was married on the 26th Day of Ianuary, 1664, to Sr ROBERT SOVTHWELL, Knt. then one of the Clerks attending his Matie King CHARLES the ſecond, in His Moſt Honble privy Councell. They had Iſſue RUPERT, EDWARD, HELENA, ELIZABETH, MARY, (who died an Infant) and KATHERINE. RUPERT, who was born in London, the 21st of May, 1670, and dyed there on the eighth of May, 1678, lyes here now alſo Interred. Such a SONNE and ſuch a WIFE, deſerve ſomething more durable than Marble, to the Memory of their Virtues. SHE had all the Perfections of Beauty, Behaviour, and Underſtanding that could adorn this Life; And all the inward Bleſſings of Virtue and Piety which might Intitle Her to a Better. The Boy was in his Years only a Child, ſo that none had ſo much hopes of what He might be, as of Diſpaire that He was not intended for this world.

To the Memory of Both (who lived too Short for thoſe They left behind) the afflicted Huſband and Father, Sr. ROBERT SOUTHWELL, of Kings Weſton in the County of Glouceſter, Kt. Erects this Stone.

On a ſcutcheon, *Parted per pale*, 1. Southwell. 2. *Or, a ſaltire ſable*, for Dering.

In the chapel at Auſt,

In the Vault underneath is depoſited all that was mortal of Sr. SAMVEL ASTRY, Knt. Coroner & Attorney of ye King's Bench from the 29th year of King CHARLES ye 2d, & ſo continued to ye 3d year of Queen ANNE; Deſcended from ye Antient Equeſtrian family of Aſtry in ye County of Bedford, & Lord of this Manor. He married ELIZABETH, only daughter & heireſs of GEORGE MORSE, of Henbury in this County, Gent. by whom he had two Sons, LVKE, & St. IOHN; & four daughters, ELIZABETH, DIANA, ANNE, & ARABELLA. He died ye 22d day of September, 1704, in ye 73d year of his Age. Which ſaid ELIZABETH, in memory of her dear Huſband, erected this as a monument of her love & griefe.

Alſo LVKE ASTRY, Eſq; Son as aboveſaid, who died ye 7th of May, An: Dom. 1701, in ye 28th year of his Age.

Arms, *Argent, three bars azure, on a chief gules three beſants.*

Againſt the ſouth wall of the chancel, at Henbury,

H. S. E.
Iuvenis, tum genere tum virtutibus Spectabilis,
SANCTUS-JOHANNES ASTRY, Armiger,
Utroq; a nomine ornatus,
Utriuſq; Simul Ornamentum.
Quippe
Familiæ de ASTRY, apud WOODEND in agro BEDFORDIENSI ſera ſoboles,
Stemmate gaudens ab antiquitatem haud ignoto,
Uxore Ducta de Stirpe St. JOHN, de Bletſho, nobili.
Filius alter, unicus Superſtes [HENBURY, Arm.
SAMUELIS ASTRY, ex ELIZABETHA, filia et herede GEORGII MORSE, de
Qui quidem SAMUEL titulo Equeſtri donatus,
Si merita ſpectes, omni titulo Major,
Per XL circiter annos continuos
Clerici Coronæ munus arduum nec inhoneſtum,
Summa fide pariter ac ſolertia, obivit.
JUVENIS Hic, patre dignus,
Gentilitios, quotquot ſunt, honores proprios fecit
Ob paternas virtutes clarus, etiam ſine ijs clariſſimus;
Animo benigno, moribus ingenuis pollebat ſine æmulo ſuis,
Egregiæ Vir humanitatis, Juſtitiæ alias Inauditæ:
Erga pauperes liberalem, erga omnes benevolum:
Proſequebantur Omnes amore vivum, morientem deſiderio.
Obijt die XXI NOVEMB. Anno { Salutis Noſtræ M.D.C.C.XII. / Ætatis ſuæ XXXVII.
Cujus Memoriæ ſacrum eſſe voluit hoc Marmor
Soror natu minima,
ARABELLA ASTRY,
Sororum amantiſſima, hæredum Mœſtiſſima.

Againſt the ſouth wall of the chancel,

Sacred to the Memory
Of ANNE SMYTH,
Eldeſt Daughter of Sr. JOHN SMYTH, Baronet,
Of LONG ASHTON, in the County of Somerſet.
She lived a conſpicuous Example
of all Chriſtian Virtues.
Her Piety was without Hypocriſy,
Her Charity without Oſtentation,
And her Hoſpitality without Extravagance.
Such was her amiable Diſpoſition,
And ſuch her unbounded Beneficence,
That ſhe was alike reſpected and beloved

By

By the Rich and Poor.
Her Liberality still remains
In her pious Bequests
To the Parish of LONG ASHTON
And to the Parish of HENBURY.
She left respectively the Sum of Ten Pounds for ever.
Obijt December 21st, 1760, Ætat. 68.

Arms, the same with sir Jarrit Smyth's, already emblazoned.

In the south aile,

To the Memory of EDWARD SAMPSON, of Henbury, Gent. who departed this Life ye 1st of Feb. 1695, Aged 45 Years. He was second Son of JOHN SAMPSON of Charlton, in this Parish, Gent. He spent his younger Years at Nevis, and other the Western Islands, where he resided as a Factor, until the Death of his elder Brother, JOHN SAMPSON, of the Inner Temple, London, Esq; and then returned to England, and married MARY, sole Daughter and Heiress of EDWd. LONG, of Olveston in this County, Gent. SHE dyed ye 14th of Apr. 1716, Aged 66 Years, and lyeth here interr'd. THEY had Issue 3 Children, MARTHA, JOHN, & MARY. MARY dyed an Infant. MARTHA submitted to inexorable Fate ye 24th of June, in the Year of our Lord 1710, & of her Age the 25th.

Here lyes a Virgin, virtuous, fair, & good,
Whom Grace and Nature might be understood
All their Perfections frankly to have joyn'd
To beautify in Body and in Mind.
To spoil this lovely Piece Death vainly strove;
Unveil'd of Flesh, She brighter shines above.

Arms, at bottom, *Sable, a cross flory Or, between four escallops argent*, for Sampson; impaling, *Sable, a lion rampant azure, between six crosses croslets argent*, for Long.

In the north aile, on a handsome monument,

Near this Tablet are intomb'd the Remains of JOHN SAMPSON, Esq; (Son of EDWARD SAMPSON, of this Parish, Gent.) who departed this Life on the twenty-first of December 1753, in the 66th Year of his Age. After the usual Time dedicated to his Studies, at the College of St. JOHN in OXFORD, He was affianced in Marriage to MARY, Daughter and Coheiress of NICHOLAS HICKES, Esq; Alderman of the City of Bristol; by whom he had Issue four Sons and two Daughters; none of whom survived the Period of Minority, except JOHN, who deceased at the Age of twenty-eight: And EDWARD, who in Remembrance of an indulgent Father, erected this Monument.

Plain is the Tale unvaried Life affords,
And such an artless narrative records.
Yet think not all of human glory springs
From Camps, from Senates, or the Pow'r of Kings.
True Wisdom oft avoids the Pomp of State,
Serene, collected, in an humbler Fate.
There too fair deeds & Joys unmixt are known,
While Virtue seeks no Trophies but her own.

At bottom are these arms, Quarterly, 1st and 4th, *Argent, a cross flory between four escallops sable*; 2d and 3d, *Gules, a fess undy between three fleurs de lis Or*.

Note, There is a memorial for *John Sampson*, of Charlton in Henbury, Gent. who died in 1732, with *these* arms, *Gules, three swords in fess, hilted Or*.

On a flat stone,

Here lyeth the Body of CHRISTOPHER COLE, of Charlton, Esq; who deceased the 11th day of May, anno dom. MDCLXXXXIX, aged LXXVI years. He had VI children, Christopher, and Charles, Mary, Bridget, Ann, and Elizabeth, of whom Ann is the alone survivor, maryed to Richd Haynes, of Abston in this County, Esq.

Hee was exquisitely verst in or Laws & Constitution, exerting his Knowledge to ye honor of his PRINCE, and benefit of his COUNTRY, no less studious of Right and Equity then skilful in distributing Justice, not regarding his privat, so much as the publick good, whereby he discharged ye office of a true JUSTICIAR.

Hee was devout towards God, & remarkable among Men for an antient Freedom & Integrity of Mind, protecting ye innocent, punishing and repressing ye injurious, acting by perswasion & mildness rather then by extremity and force, composing differences and promoting peace, whereby hee discharged ye duty of a true CHRISTIAN.

Arms. *Baron and femme*, 1. *Ermine, a bull within a bordure ingrailed sable charged with* 12 *roundlets*. 2. *Within a bordure a pomegranate*.

Against the wall of the south aile,

To the Memory of Christopher Cole, Gent. Son of James Cole of Bristol, Merchant, Who gave the Residue of his Estate, amounting to near One Thousand Pounds, for the better Maintenance and Increase of the poor Boys Belonging to the Free-School of this Parish. He deceased ye 21st March, 1736, aged about Seventy, and lies interred near this Monument.

Arms, *Per pale Or and argent, over all a bull sable; on a chief of the third three bezants.*

Against the same wall,

Ex adverso hujusce Loci
(Prospiciens ipse Sibi Sepulchrum)
Exuvias suas deponi voluit
Robertus Sandford Armiger:
Patre quidem Cive Bristoliensi,
Proavis de Sandford Hall in Agro Salopiensi oriundus.
Improles obiens,
Quas accepit a Suis Opes
(Auctiores ipsius Industria redditas)
Testamentum condens, ita dispertivit,
Ut dum liberalem se in suos præstaret,
Utilitatis publicæ non immemor extaret.
Beneficentiæ Monumenta rogas?
En, qui testentur Paræciæ istius Incolæ,
Quippe quibus mille et sexcentas Libras legavit.
Quum fuisset jamdiu in Negotiis versatus,
Otio tandem aliquantisper ut frueretur,
(Suo dentibus item Annis, et uberiori Reditu)
Bathoniæ Secessum quæsivit:
Ubi, Annum agens sexagesimum tertium,
Arthritide correptus, decessit 29 Jan: 1756.

On a pyramid are these arms, *Baron and femme*, 1st *Per chevron sable and ermine in chief two boars heads couped Or*. 2d, *Azure, a bend between three leopards faces Or*.

Benefactions.

In the year 1623, Mr. Anthony Edwards of King's Weston erected a free-school in this parish, and endowed it with 80*l*. a year, of which the master is to have thirty marks yearly, and the usher twenty; and there is a house for each. The remainder of the revenue to be employ'd in maintaining blue-coat boys at the school. To this charity Mr. Christopher Cole made a considerable addition, as already exprest in the memorial for him. There are now about ten or twelve boys cloathed and maintained in this school.

Robert Sandford, esq; in the year 1759, gave 1500*l*. to establish a school to teach poor children to read and write; and a further sum of 100*l*. out of the income of which the minister is to give 20*s*. a year in bread to the poor, and the residue is appointed for two sermons, on Good-friday and St. Thomas day, for ever.

In 1760, Mrs. Anne Smith gave 10*l*. a year out of Redcliff meads, for teaching poor girls to read, knit, and sew.

Mr. William Burroughs gave 20*s*. a year out of an estate, late Hort's, in King's Weston, for a sermon on Trinity-sunday. Mr. William Cotterill gave 10*s*. out of Baker's-leaze, for a sermon on Good-friday for ever. Mrs. Grace Jayne, in 1728, gave 20*s*. a year to the poor of Lawrence-Weston, charged on her lands in that tithing. And Mrs. Mary White gave 20*l*. the income of which to be given in bread to the second poor.

Lady Elizabeth Astry, in the year 1707, settled 20*l*. a year to have divine service performed at the chapel of Aust every sunday; and John Baker gave 10*s*. a year for ever to the vicar of Henbury, for a sermon at Aust chapel on the anniversary of St. John the evangelist. And 20*s*. a year to the poor of that tithing, charged on his estate there.

Henbury.

Taxes.		£.	s.	d.
The Royal Aid in	1692,	66	10	0
Poll-tax — —	1694,	34	10	0
Land-tax ——	1694,	120	2	0
The ſame, at 3*s.*	1770,	90	1	6

King's Weſton.

Taxes.		£.	s.	d.
The Royal Aid in	1692,	106	12	0
Poll-tax ——	1694,	17	6	0
Land-tax ——	1694,	124	0	0
The ſame, at 3*s.*	1770,	93	0	0

Lawrence-Weſton.

Taxes.		£.	s.	d.
The Royal Aid in	1692,	135	8	0
Poll-tax ——	1694,	13	6	0
Land-tax ——	1694,	150	5	4
The ſame, at 3*s.*	1770,	113	9	0

Redwick and Northwick.

Taxes.		£.	s.	d.
The Royal Aid in	1692,	169	8	0
Poll-tax ——	1694,	16	11	0
Land-tax —	1694,	165	0	0
The ſame at 3*s.*	1770,	123	4	0

Auſt.

Taxes.		£.	s.	d.
The Royal Aid in	1692,	125	3	0
Poll-tax —	1694,	16	10	0
Land-tax —	1694,	77	0	0
The ſame at 3*s.*	1770,	57	15	0

Stowick.

Taxes.		£.	s.	d.
The Royal Aid in	1692,	339	4	0
Poll-tax ——	1694,	29	2	0
Land-tax ——	1694,	313	0	0
The ſame, at 3*s.*	1770,	234	15	0

Charlton.

Taxes.		£.	s.	d.
The Royal Aid in	1692,	96	4	0
Poll-tax —	1694,	49	18	0
Land-tax —	1694,	95	4	0
The ſame, at 3*s.*	1770,	71	3	0

In all.

Taxes.		£.	s.	d.
The Royal Aid in	1692,	1040	9	0
Poll-tax — —	1694,	177	3	0
Land-tax —	1694,	1044	11	4
The ſame at 3*s.*	1770,	783	7	6

At the beginning of this century, there were 218 houſes, and about 880 inhabitants in this pariſh, whereof 150 were freeholders; yearly births 27, burials 26. *Atkyns.* But ſince that time population hath very much increaſed, and tho' I could not obtain the exact number of inhabitants, they are now eſtimated to be at leaſt 1200.

HEWELSFIELD

IS a ſmall pariſh in the hundred of St. Briavel's, ſix miles diſtant north-eaſt from Chepſtow in Monmouthſhire, ſeven ſouth from Colford, and twenty-four ſouth-weſtward from Glouceſter.

It is ſituated on high ground, in the foreſt of Dean, and enjoys a healthy air and a variety of ſoil. It was conſidered as a part of Lidney 9 E. 1. when the ſheriff made a return of all the hundreds and vills in the county of Glouceſter.

The inhabitants claim the privileges of the dutchy of Lancaſter, to which they pay a certain ſum annually; and they have common of paſture and of wood in Harthill.

The name has been variouſly written in different ages, as *Huwaldesfield* in the time of king Edward the Firſt, *Huerſfielde*, *Huelſfielde*, and *Huetſfield* about the reign of queen Elizabeth, and, in the latter ages, as it ſtands at the head of this account. It has been ſuggeſted, that it was occaſioned by ſome general (I ſuppoſe either Briton or Saxon) of the name of *Huer*, or *Huel*, or perhaps *Huwald*, very antiently obtaining a victory upon this ſpot; becauſe, it is ſaid, the names of places ending in *field* have commonly been given them upon ſuch an occaſion. But if this opinion ſhould have any weight as to other places, it cannot be applied in the preſent caſe; for the name of this place does not appear to be *Huwaldsfield*, but *Hiwoldeſtone*, about the time of the conqueſt; and dividing it into *Hiwolde's Town*, it becomes eaſy and intelligible to every body.

Of the Manor and other Eſtates.

What I have aſſerted concerning the orthography of the name will be juſtified by the following extract from the antient ſurvey, where, among the eſtates belonging to William the ſon of Baderon, it is thus recorded:

'The ſame William holds Hiwoldeſtone in 'Ledenei hundred. Ulfeg held it in the time of 'king Edward. There are three hides. By the 'king's order this eſtate is in the foreſt. It is 'worth 30*s.*' *Domeſday-book*, p. 74.

Walter Wither was ſeized of Hawaldsfield 54 H. 3. John de Monemuta was afterwards ſeized of this eſtate, and gave lands in this pariſh, called the Vineyard, and a meadow called the Vineyard-meadow, together with 100*s.* rent, to the hoſpital of the holy Trinity in Monmouth, which he had founded. *Dugd. Monaſt.* And it appears by an inquiſition taken 4 E. 1. that Hualdesfield had eſcheated from John de Monemuta to the crown, and that the king had then given it to the abbat of Tintern in free alms.

The abbey of Tintern held this manor 'till that houſe was diſſolved.

By an inquiſition taken at Wotton-underedge, Feb. 4, 4 E. 6. after the death of Henry earl of Worceſter, it appears that he died, Nov. 26, 1549, ſeized of Hewelfield, and of 82 meſſuages, three mills, 1000 acres of plowed land, 70 of meadow, 1000 of paſture, 600 of wood, 500 of heath and turf, and 20*l.* 8*s.* rent in Brockwere, Wolveſton, Almington, Alveſton, Hewelsfield, and Modeſgate; with the fiſheries in the Wye called Plomwere, Aſhwere, Ithelſwere, and Walwere; and the rectory of Walwere, and advowſon and vicarage of the ſame; the manor of Tiddenham, and divers meſſuages, lands and tenements in Strote, Widden,

Widden, Biſten, Betteſley, and Sudbury, all in the county of Glouceſter. The duke of Beaufort is the preſent lord of the manor.

John Calmer and Joan his wife levied a fine of lands in Hueldfield, to John Maddox, ſen. and to John Maddox, jun. 21 H. 7.

Thomas Symonds, of Pengethly in Hereford-ſhire, eſq; has a good houſe and eſtate in this pariſh, which his anceſtor, Robert Symonds, purchaſed of the daughters and coheirs of ſir Nicholas Throckmorton, who held the ſame in right of his wife, Alice, one of the daughters and coheireſſes of Richard Gough, ſon of William Gough, eldeſt ſon of George Gough of Hewelſ-field, whoſe ſeat and eſtate it had been.

James Rooke, of Bickſwear, eſq; eldeſt ſon to major-general Hayman Rooke, deſcended from a family of long ſtanding in the county of Kent, died about the year 1771, ſeized of good eſtates in this pariſh and in Woollaſton, in right of his wife, Jane, only daughter of Tracy Catchmay, eſq; ſon and heir of ſir William Catchmay, by Eleanor his wife, the other daughter and coheireſs of the above-named Richard Gough. And James Rooke, eſq; a major in his majeſty's forces, ſucceeds his father in thoſe eſtates.

Of the Church, &c.

The church is a vicarage, in the Foreſt deanery, annexed to Lidney, the incumbent of which hath all the tithes of this pariſh, great and ſmall, worth 40*l.* a year.

The church is a ſmall building, dedicated to St. Mary Magdalen, with the tower in the middle, and a ſmall aile on the north ſide.

Procurations 1*s.* 6*d.* Penteceoſtals 1*s.* 4*d.*

Benefactions.

One acre in Clay-hill, a quarter of an acre in the old orchard, an acre in the old leaze, an acre in Platnedge, half an acre in Widdon's, a quarter of an acre called Jackſtries, three acres called Church-mead, a piece called the Harp, a garden about a quarter of an acre, an acre at Bremel's-ford, an acre in the Rye-fields, and the church-houſe and garden at Brockſwear, are given to the uſe of the poor ; —two ſmall pieces of ground, about half an acre, for keeping the church-porch in repair; and Mrs. Williams gave 20*s.* a year for eight poor widows, 10*s.* a year to adorn the church, and 5*s.* a year for a ſermon on Good-friday.

Taxes.					
The Royal Aid in	1692,	£.	67	12	0
Poll-tax ——	1694,	—	17	3	0
Land-tax ——	1694,	—	69	0	0
The ſame, at 3*s.*	1770,	—	50	5	0

There were 40 houſes, and about 200 inhabitants, of whom 10 were freeholders, at the beginning of this century ; yearly births 7, burials 6. *Atkyns.* In eight years, beginning with 1760, the baptiſms were 36, and burials 37 ; the houſes are 54, and inhabitants 253 : So that the average of annual burials is to the whole number of inhabitants as 1 to 54.6.

H I L L

IS a ſmall pariſh in the hundred of Berkeley, three miles diſtant ſouth-weſtward from Berkeley, four north from Thornbury, and twenty-two ſouth-weſtward from Glouceſter.

It was called *Hull*, or *Hill*, from the elevated ſituation of part of the pariſh towards the eaſt.

The ſeat of ſir John Fuſt, baronet, is pleaſantly ſituated on the ſide of that acclivity, with the river Severn in front, at the diſtance of about two miles to the weſt ; of which river, and of the high lands and pendent woods of the foreſt of Dean on the other ſide, it commands an uninterrupted and moſt agreeable proſpect for many miles.

This place was formerly dependent on Berkeley, which it even now acknowledges, by paying one ſhilling a year towards the great bell-rope, and the like ſum towards the wall of the church-yard there.

Of the Manor and other Eſtates.

Four hides in Hill belonged to the great lordſhip of Berkeley at the time of the general ſurvey, as appears by the account of the members of that lordſhip. This manor was granted to Robert Fitz-Harding, anceſtor of the Berkeley family.

Maurice lord Berkeley gave the manors of Hill and Nimpsfield to his brother Nicholas, and died 1 R. 1. William Berkeley, ſon of Roger, died ſeized of Hull 46 H. 3. John Fitz-Nicholas was lord of this manor 9 E. 1. His family name was Berkeley, but being the ſon of Nicholas, he took the name of Fitz-Nicholas. Nicholas Berkeley, ſon of Ralph, held this manor in the 15th year of the ſame reign, when a *Quo Warranto* was brought againſt him to ſet forth his right to privileges, and his claim was then allowed.

John Fitz-Nichols died ſeized of Hull 15 E. 2. John Fitz-Nichols, ſon of John, died ſeized of the manor of Hull 29 E. 3. Sir Thomas Fitz-Nichols held this manor, and two plow-tillages, and a yearly rent of 20*s.* in Hull, 7 R. 2. and ſir Thomas Fitz-Nichols died ſeized of this manor 6 H. 5. Catherine, one of his daughters and coheirs, was married to Robert Pointz, eſq; by which marriage this manor was carried into the family of Pointz. Elianor, the other daughter and coheir, was married to John Browning, eſq.

Sir Nicholas Pointz died ſeized of Hill 4 Mar. and it continued in that name and family 'till ſir John Pointz ſold it, in the reign of queen Elizabeth.

The family of the name of Pointz, or Pontz, is ſaid to have come into England with William the Norman, or ſoon after. The eldeſt branch of that family ſettled at Sutton in Dorſetſhire, and the male line ending with one Nicholas Pontz, his lands paſſed, by heirs general, to the New-borows and Fitz-James's. *Leland.*

Henry Fleetwood was lord of the manor of Hill in the year 1608 ; ſoon after which it paſſed by purchaſe to Richard Fuſt, of the city of London, eſq.

eſq. His ſon, ſir Edward Fuſt, married Bridget, daughter of ſir Thomas Denton, of Hillerſden in Buckinghamſhire. He was created a baronet Aug 21, 14 C. 2. and was ſucceeded by his ſon, ſir John Fuſt, who married Elizabeth, daughter of ſir Richard Cocks of Dumbleton, and was high ſheriff of this county 27 C. 2. Sir Edward Fuſt, his ſon, married Anne, daughter of Thomas Stephens, of Lypiat, eſq; his ſecond wife was Elizabeth, daughter of William Mohun, of Portiſhead in Somerſetſhire; his third wife was Catherine, daughter of Francis Mohun, of Fleet in the county of Dorſet, eſq; and he took to his fourth wife, Suſanna, daughter of Richard Cocks, eſq; of Dumbleton. By his ſecond wife he had ſir Edward Fuſt, who ſucceeded to the title and eſtate, but dying without male iſſue, they devolved to his brother Francis, eldeſt ſon of ſir Edward by his third wife; which ſir Francis, in the year 1724, married Fanny, daughter of Nicholas Tooker, of the city of Briſtol, merchant, by whom he had eight ſons and four daughters. Sir Francis died in the year 1769, and was ſucceeded by his ſon, ſir John Fuſt, baronet, who married Miſs Philippa Hamilton, and is the preſent lord of this manor. His arms are, *Argent, upon a chevron between three hedge bills erected ſable, as many mullets of the field.*

By records of the following dates it appears, that Adam le Waleys died ſeized of one meſſuage and one yard-land in Hull 9 E. 2. Robert Wither granted one yard-land, twenty-nine acres of arable, and a yearly rent of 13*s.* 6*d.* in Hull, Berkeley, and Bevington, to the abbey of Kingſwood, 2 E. 2. which were granted, after the diſſolution of the abbey, to ſir Nicholas Pointz, 31 H. 8.

William Martel held three yard-lands and 20*s.* rent iſſuing out of Hull, 14 E. 2. John de Hull held lands in this pariſh 16 E. 3. as did Gilbert Tynden 24 E. 3. and John Sergeant 30 & 36 E. 3. Thomas Kennet and Margaret his wife levied a fine of lands in Hull 21 E. 3, as did Richard Forſter, to John Walſh and others, 12 H. 7. Richard Tyladam died ſeized of lands in Hill 34 Eliz. and left two daughters coheireſſes.

HAMLETS. 1. *Nupdown.* 2. *Woodend.*

Of the Church, &c.

The church is a donative, in the deanery of Durſley, worth 30*l.* a year, in the gift of ſir John Fuſt.

The tithes of hay in Hill and Ham, which belonged to the abbey of St. Auguſtin's in Briſtol, were granted to the dean and chapter of Briſtol 34 H. 8. to whom the impropriation now belongs.

The church is dedicated to St. Michael. There is a ſmall chancel on the ſouth ſide, built by ſir Edward Fuſt, and ſince uſed as the burying place of the family. Over the door, within the church, is the following inſcription:

To drain this pariſh from its during flood;
To model and repair this houſe of God;
Are patterns good I ſet to future time.
Free profit yours; ye coſt & labour mine.

Sir Francis Fuſt, Baronet, lord of this manor, for the benefit of its inhabitants, at his own expence, planned, built and erected, in the year 1750, the great ſewer at Hill-pill, next the river, called the *Imperial Draught*, and the two others above it. He alſo, in 1759, new modelled and repaired this church. All the coſts and materials for all the ſaid works are a gift from him freely to this pariſh, for the uſe above. Let thoſe of ability ſtrive to do good.

Pentecoſtals - - - 10½*d.*

Monuments and Inſcriptions.

On the tablet of a ſmall monument,

Piæ Memoriæ Venerab. Viri Lancelotti Law, S S. T. B. Pietatis Patientiæ et Temperantiæ egregij Exemplaris. Qui eodem Scloppo qvo avivm petebat vitam incavte amiſit. ſvam. Dec. 7, 1650.

Mors tibi Tormenti fuit ictu Prima, Secunda
Ut ſine Tormento ſit tibi vita necis.
Bombardæ ſonitu Præſens ablata, Futura
Ut ſit cum ſonitu reddita vita Tubæ.
Sic ſubito miſerâ privatus vulnere vitâ
Gaudium ad æternum per breve nullus iter.

On a flat ſtone,

In Memory of the Reverend Mr. William Pritchard, A. M. Rector of Corringham in the County of Eſſex, and more than 36 Years Miniſter of this Pariſh, who died the 14th Day of May, A. D. 1743, in the 63d Year of his Age. —— Arms, *Ermine, a lion rampant.*

Benefaction.

Heſter Mallet, of the pariſh of Rockhampton, has given a cloſe in Hill, called the Poor's-leaze, the rent of which to be divided between the poor of Hill and of Rockhampton.

			£.	s.	d.
Taxes.	The Royal Aid in	1692,	114	4	0
	Poll-tax ——	1694, —	25	12	0
	Land-tax ——	1694, —	185	9	0
	The ſame, at 3*s.*	1770, —	139	2	3

At the beginning of this century, there were 40 houſes, and about 200 inhabitants in this pariſh, whereof 5 were freeholders; yearly births 6, burials 5. *Atkyns.* If this account may be depended on, population has been much on the decline ſince that period. In ſeven years, beginning with 1766, there are entered 17 baptiſms and 27 burials, in the pariſh regiſter, which has been very ill kept. The houſes in Hill are 32, and the preſent number of inhabitants exactly 146.

HINTON

IS a ſmall pariſh in the hundred of Tibbleſtone, three miles ſouth from Eveſham in Worceſterſhire, eight weſt from Campden, and twenty-three north-eaſtward from Glouceſter.

The pariſh lies in a rich vale country, and conſiſts almoſt intirely of paſture land, whence it is ſometimes called *Hinton on the Green.*

A little river, which comes from Wormington, runs by this village, and falls into the Avon at Hampton, near Eveſham.

Of the Manor and other Eſtates.

In the year 981, Elfrede, ſiſter of king Ethelred, gave Hynetune to the church of St. Peter at Glouceſter, to pray for her ſoul; and the king, at her requeſt, exempted it from all ſecular charges.

Under

Under the head *Terra S. Petri de Glowec'* in *Domeſday-book*, is is thus recorded :

'The ſame church holds Hinetune in Tetboldeſ- 'tanes hundred. There are fifteen hides. In 'demean are two plow-tillages, and thirty villeins, 'and ſeven bordars, with ſixteen plow-tillages. 'There are eleven *ſervi*, and one foreigner. It 'was worth 3*l.* now 10*l.* This manor is free 'from tax, and from attendance on any court but 'that of the church.' *Domeſday-book*, p. 71.

The abbey of Glouceſter was ſeized of the manor of Hinton, with markets, fairs, court leet, and free warren, and their right was allowed in a *Quo warranto*, 15 E. 1.

In the year 1156, it was adjudged in the county court of Glouceſterſhire, that the manor of Hinetune being time out of mind free from all charges, therefore it ought to be free from fines for murder.

The abbey continued in poſſeſſion of this manor 'till the general diſſolution, when it came to the crown, and was granted, with the advowſon of the church, to ſir Edward Worth 36 H. 8. Thomas Barners was afterwards ſeized of the manor, and left an only daughter and heireſs married to Thomas Baker, who was ſeized of it in right of his wife; and ſir Thomas Baker was lord of the manor in 1608.

The manor came afterwards to ſir John Hanmer, who ſold it to ſir Robert Jaſon. His widow held it in jointure, and was afterwards married to ſir Chriſtopher Aires; and ſurviving him, was married, thirdly, to David Warren, eſq; who, in her right, was lord of the manor at the beginning of the preſent century.

About the year 1739, Joſeph Swayne, of Briſtol, eſq; married the widow of a ſucceeding ſir Robert Jaſon, and became poſſeſſed of the manor of Hinton, which he ſold, together with the Jaſon eſtate, to the reverend Dr. Stephens, who bequeathed it to his brother Philip Stephens, eſq; the preſent lord of the manor.

Of the Church, &c.

The church is a rectory, in the deanery of Campden, worth 120*l.* a year. Philip Stephens, eſq; is patron, and the rev. Mr. Stephens is the preſent incumbent.

The impropriation formerly belonged to the abbey of Glouceſter. The biſhop of Glouceſter has two thirds of the great tithes.

Four acres of meadow, eight of paſture, and one third of the great tithes belong to the rector.

The church, dedicated to St. Peter, conſiſts of the nave only, and has a handſome embattled tower, with five bells, at the weſt end.

In the year 1740, an old grave-ſtone being removed, the following mutilated inſcription was found on the under ſide:

Hic . . . . . etur Corpus Dni Will'mi Halfordiæ quondam Abbatis de Bordeſleya, qui feliciter obijt XII Die Sept'bris Anno Dni Milleſimo . . . .

Firſt fruits £.	8	13	11	Synodals £.	0	2	0
Tenths —	0	17	4½	Pentecoſt.	0	0	11½
Procurations	0	6	8				

Taxes.		£.	s.	d.
The Royal Aid in	1692,	90	16	0
Poll-tax ——	1694, —	13	11	0
Land-tax ——	1694, —	77	16	8
The ſame, at 3*s.*	1770, —	57	8	6½

At the beginning of this century, there were 25 houſes in this pariſh, and about 100 inhabitants, whereof 4 were freeholders; yearly births 3, burials 3. *Atkyns.* The preſent number of inhabitants is 105.

HORFIELD

IS a ſmall pariſh in the hundred of Berkeley, two miles north from Briſtol, nine ſouth from Thornbury, and thirty-four ſouth from Glouceſter. It conſiſts moſtly of rich paſture land.

One of the heads of the little river *Trin*, or *Trim*, riſes in the north weſt part of this pariſh, and runs down to Weſtbury, (from this brook called *Weſtbury upon Trim*) and thence into the Avon, about three miles below Briſtol.

Of the Manor and other Eſtates.

When *Domeſday-book* was compiled, this was a member of the great lordſhip of Berkeley, as may be ſeen in the copy of that record, p. 68.

Robert Fitz-Harding, the firſt lord Berkeley of his family, gave the manor of Horfelle to the abbey of St. Auguſtine's in Briſtol, which he himſelf had founded. And the abbat's claim to court leet in this manor was allowed in a *Quo warranto*, 15 E. 1.

At the diſſolution of religious foundations, the manor and rectory were granted to the biſhoprick of Briſtol 34 H. 8. And the biſhop of Briſtol is the preſent lord of this manor.

Roger, the ſon of Roger, was ſeized of eight acres of arable in Horfield 3. E. 2.

Of the Church, &c.

The church is an impropriation, in the dioceſe and deanery of Briſtol, formerly worth only 8*l.* a year to the curate. But in the year 1718, it was augmented by the queen's bounty, and the joint donations of Edward Colſton, and Thomas Edwards, eſq[rs]. The biſhop of Briſtol is patron and impropriator.

The church is a ſmall building, with a low pinnacled tower at the weſt end, and affords nothing worthy of obſervation.

Taxes.		£.	s.	d.
The Royal Aid in	1692,	84	14	0
Poll-tax — —	1694, —	10	4	0
Land-tax ——	1694, —	74	4	0
The ſame, at 3*s.*	1770, —	56	6	10½

At the beginning of this century, there were 26 houſes in this pariſh, and about 100 inhabitants, whereof 8 were freeholders; yearly births 3, burials 2. *Atkyns.* There are now about 125 inhabitants.

HORSLEY.

THIS pariſh is in the hundred of Longtree, three miles diſtant ſouth-weſt from Hampton, four north from Tetbury, and fourteen ſouth from Glouceſter. It is bounded on the eaſt by Avening, on the weſt by Nimpsfield, on the north by Woodcheſter, and on the ſouth-weſt by Beverſtone. Here is a market on Saturday, now almoſt diſuſed.

The name ſignifies a woody place. It is derived from Ƿẏꞃꞅꞇ, a Saxon word for *wood*; and *lei*, contracted from leᵹa, a *place*; and the preſent condition of the pariſh juſtifies the propriety of the name, for a conſiderable part of it is ſtill in woodland.

There are in this pariſh, more eſpecially where ſome of the houſes are built, ſeveral dingles and narrow bottoms, with hanging woods, and verdant ſteeps, which give it a romantic appearance, not eaſily to be deſcribed. By the highway, towards the top of that part where the houſes are, next to Avening, I obſerved two or three ſmall ſprings, ouzing out of the ſide of the bank, pretty ſtrongly tinged with iron mine.

The cloathing buſineſs hath encouraged great numbers of families to ſettle here, but that manufacture declining of late, the poor are very burthenſome, for want of employment; but much of their wretched condition is owing to idleneſs and bad habits.

Of the Manor and other Eſtates.

'The church of St. Martin of Troars holds 'Horſelei[t] in Langetrew hundred, by the gift of 'king William. Goda, ſiſter to king Edward, 'held it. There are ten hides. There are four 'plow-tillages in demean, and ſix villeins, and 'five bordars, with ſix plow-tillages, and one 'radcheniſter. And there is a houſe in Glouue'ceſtre of 6*d.* [rent]. There is a mill of 50*d.* 'It was worth 12*l.* and is now worth 14*l.*' *Domeſday-book*, p. 73.

It appears by the eſcheator's inquiſition, taken 1 R. 2. that this manor was exchanged with the prior of Bruton[u] for lands in Normandy belonging to that priory, 45 E. 3.

After the diſſolution of religious foundations, the manor of Horſley, with lands called Crainmere, were granted to ſir Thomas Seimour 33 H. 8. and after his attainder, ſir Walter Dennis had a grant of it 7 E. 6.

Richard Stephens died ſeized of this manor 41 Eliz. as appears by the eſcheator's inquiſition the ſame year; where it is ſaid that this Richard ſettled Chavenydge-farm on his wife Anne, one of the daughters of John Stone, haberdaſher of London, 35 Eliz. This manor and eſtate have continued ever ſince in the ſame name and family. The reverend Mr. Robert Stephens, of Chavenage, is the preſent proprietor of them. His arms, and ſome account of his family, may be ſeen under *Eaſington*. Chavenage hath been variouſly written, as *Chavenydge*, *Thevenage*, *&c.* and may be ſo called from its ſituation on the borders of the pariſh of Avening, *q. d. Aven-edge*.

Sir Walter Dennis was ſeized of lands in Horſley and Thevenage 28 H. 8.

TITHINGS. 1. *Tichmor-end.* 2. *Nup-end.* 3. *Barton-end.* 4. *Nailſworth.*

Of the Church, &c.

The church is a vicarage, in the deanery of Stonehouſe. The rectory was antiently appropriated to the priory of Bruton. In the year 1380, the biſhop of Worceſter, at the requeſt of the prior, appointed twelve marks a year to be paid to the vicar of Horſley, by the ſaid priory, as appears by the antient regiſter of that dioceſe; and the vicar now receives 8*l.* a year of the impropriator. In the year 1733, the vicarage was augmented by the benefaction of Paul Caſtleman, eſq; and queen Anne's bounty, which, together, make the preſent value about 45*l.* a year, beſides a houſe called Rockneſs, lately purchaſed for the vicar. Lord chancellor is patron.

The rectory coming to the crown at the diſſolution, was granted to ſir Walter Hungerford 6 Eliz. It is now the property of Mr. John Selfe, and is worth about 80*l.* a year. The prior of Bruton had a ſeat here, of which little more than the gate-way remains. There was alſo near the church, a building called the chapel, now reduced to ruins.

The church is large, with an aile on the ſouth ſide, and a handſome tower at the weſt end, adorned with pinnacles and battlements. It is dedicated to St. Martin. There is alſo a ſmall aile on the north ſide, called St. George's chapel.

	£	s.	d.		£	s.	d.
Firſt fruits	7	11	9	Synodals	0	2	0
Tenths —	0	5	1½	Pentecoſtals	0	0	7
Procurations	0	6	8				

Benefactions.

The reverend Mr. Henry Stubs gave 20*l.* the intereſt of which to be laid out in New Teſtaments for the poor.

Mr. Walter Chambers, in the year 1714, gave 10*l.* the intereſt of which to buy bread for the poor.

Mr. Edward Webb gave 200*l.* to the charity ſchool in this pariſh.

[t] Sir William Dugdale, by miſtake, makes this Horſley to be in Eſſex. Tom. i. p. 604. Tom. ii. p. 1002.—Hurſt in the pariſh of Berkeley is written *Hirſtlege* in *Domeſday-book*, which occaſioned ſir Robert Atkyns, by a like miſtake, to place an account of that large farm to this pariſh of Horſley.

[u] The priory of Bruton in Somerſetſhire was founded in the year 1005, by Aldgar earl of Cornwall, for Benedictine monks, who were afterwards changed to Black Canons. It was valued at the diſſolution at 480*l.* 17*s.* 2*d.*

Taxes,

Taxes.					
	The Royal Aid in 1692, £.	125	14	0
	Poll-tax — — 1694, —	37	0	0
	Land-tax — 1694, —	160	17	6
	The ſame at 3*s.* 1770, —	120	7	4½

According to ſir Robert Atkyns, when he compiled his hiſtory, there were 300 houſes, and about 1200 inhabitants in this pariſh, of whom 18 were freeholders; yearly births 22, burials 20. But from an examination of the pariſh regiſter, it appears that in a ſeries of ten years, from 1718, where the regiſter begins, to 1727 incluſive, there were 296 baptiſms, and 248 burials. And in a like ſeries, from 1760, to 1769 incluſive, there were 423 baptiſms, and 414 burials. Upon which it is to be obſerved that the inhabitants have increaſed greatly between theſe two periods of time; but we cannot make any tolerable judgment of the number of them from the burials, becauſe there are in this pariſh and neighbourhood three meeting houſes, of different denominations, at two of which they adminiſter baptiſm, and there is ſepulture at all of them.

HORTON.

THIS pariſh lies in the hundred of Grumbald's-aſh, two miles diſtant north-eaſt from Chipping Sodbury, four ſouth-eaſt from Wickwar, and about twenty-ſeven ſouthward from Glouceſter.

About half the pariſh lies in the vale, and conſiſts of paſturage, with an extenſive common; the other part is ſituated on the ſide of a hill, and on a lofty plain above, where the ſoil is lighter, but produces good corn. On the brow of the hill facing to the weſt, there are the intrenchments of a camp, called the *Caſtles*, overlooking the vale country to a very conſiderable extent. The camp is of a ſquare form, ſuppoſed to be Roman, but I cannot learn that either coins or inſtruments have been found near it, by which it may be determined of a certainty to what people it belonged.

Mr. Paſton has a large, antient ſeat, cloſe to the church, where his anceſtors have reſided ever ſince the year 1710, upon their manſion-houſe at Appleton, in the county of Norfolk, being intirely burnt down in the year 1708.

Of the Manor and other Eſtates.

'Robert de Todeni holds Horedone in Grimboldeſtou hundred. There are ten hides taxed. Ulf held it. In demean are three plow-tillages, and eleven villeins, and eight bordars, with eight plow-tillages. There are ſeven *ſervi*, and a mill of 6*s.* and twenty acres of meadow; a wood two miles long, and one broad. It was worth 12*l.* now 7*l.*' *Domeſday-book*, p. 76.

Richard de Abbingdon was lord of this manor 9 E. 1.

William Kayleway and Alice his wife levied a fine of the manor of Horton to the uſe of themſelves for life, the remainder to the heirs of Alice in ſpecial taille, the remainder to the right heirs of Thomas de Bradeſtone, 19 E. 3.

Thomas de Bradeſton died ſeized of Horton 34 E. 3. as did Agnes his widow 43 E. 3. and Thomas Bradeſton his ſon 48 E. 3. Ela the widow of Thomas de Bradeſton died ſeized of the manor of Horton 11 H. 4.

Thomas Burton and William his ſon levied a fine of Horton to the uſe of Thomas Burton, ſon of William, in ſpecial taille.

This manor afterwards paſſed to William Knight, eſq; prothonotary of the Common Pleas, who built the large manor houſe. Edward Paſton, eſq; was lord of the manor in the year 1608, and Clement Paſton, eſq; is the preſent lord of the manor of Horton.

But there were two reputed manors in this pariſh; for Agnes, who had been the wife of Hubert de Ria, and Henry her ſon, gave the manor of Hortun to the church of Saliſbury, in the time of Richard Powr, biſhop of that ſee; and it was annexed to a prebend of the ſame, of which Ralph de York was prebendary; who ſet forth his claim to free warren and court leet within the manor of Horton, in his anſwer to a writ of *Quo warranto* brought againſt him 15 E. 1. and his claim was allowed. The ſame manor continued in that prebend 'till king Edward the Sixth granted it to Edward duke of Somerſet, who being attainted, it was afterwards granted to Clement Paſton, eſq; and the manor and prebend of Horton, and the advowſon of the rectory, were again granted and confirmed 1 Mar. This manor was formerly known by the name of Horwood. The manerial rights of the whole pariſh now belong to Mr. Paſton, whoſe deſcent and arms are exhibited under *Monumental Inſcriptions*.

Sir Walter de la Pool, and Elizabeth his wife, were ſeized of *Draycot's Place*, in Horton 12 H. 6. William earl marſhal and earl of Nottingham, levied a fine of lands in Horton 3 H. 7. Certain lands in Horton, called *Frayres-hay*, which belonged to the commandery of the knights-templers at Quenington, were granted to John Bellowe 38 H. 8.

Of the Church, &c.

The church is a rectory, in the deanery of Hawkeſbury, worth about 130*l.* a year, having the great and ſmall tithes of the whole pariſh, except of Horwood eſtate, called the demeſnes, for which a modus of 2*l.* 13*s.* 4*d.* is paid in lieu of all tithes, as I was informed by the late Mr. Paſton, who ſold the right of preſentation ſome years ſince for three lives, to John Unwin, of Took's Court, London. Mr. Edward Draper is the preſent incumbent. Thirty acres belong to the glebe.

The church is dedicated to St. James. It hath an aile on the north ſide, which Mr. Paſton repairs,

repairs, on account of Horwood eſtate, and a tower with a clock at the weſt end. An acre in Caſtle-field, an acre and a half in the Inn-field, and 6*d.* each from two houſes, are given for repairing the church.

Firſt fruits £.	16	0	0	Synodals £.	0	2	0
Tenths —	1	12	0	Pentecoſtals			
Procurations	0	6	8				

Monuments and Inſcriptions.

In the north aile, the upper part of which is the burying-place of the Paſton family, are ſeveral very handſome marble monuments, with the following inſcriptions, arms, &c.

D. O. M. ✢ B. M. V.
Cineres
Gulielmi Paſton et Mariæ uxoris
Hac Ædicula commiſcentur.
Hic in agro Norfolcienſi, ex antiquo et præclaro Genere,
Obijt 24° Martij 1673.
Illa Iacobi Lawſon Armigeri filia, in Eboracenſi
Comitatu, Stirpe non minus celebri, Obijt 23° Sept. 1679.
In quibus, vera in Deum Pietas, in Proximum Charitas,
In alterutrum fidiſſimus Amor refulſit.
Necnon
Trium Conjugalis Amoris Pignorum,
Quorum Gulielmus, 14 annum agens,
Maximæ Spei juvenis, mortem eheu ſubijt Iunij 5° 1677.
Sub hoc Marmore
Deponuntur Exuviæ Franciſcæ Paſton,
Iohannis Paſton Armigeri uxoris,
Henrici Titchborn Baronetti, et Mariæ Arundell
Uxoris filiæ, Natalibus ab utroq; latere nobiliſſimis;
Quæ pietate, ingenio, prudentia, forma, in adverſis
Fortitudine et animi conſtantia ſexum ſuperavit;
Et poſtquam 18 annos Conjugis Amantiſſimæ et Matris
Chariſſimæ omnibus exemplum præbuiſſet, infelici
Puerperio 10° Aprilis 1712 abijt, non obijt. Vivit
Etenim in Progenie Illuſtriſſima.
Præſens gaudium, Abſens Amicorum et mariti gemitus,
Qui Pietatis et Amoris ergo
Hoc Monumentum mœſtiſſimus poſuit.
O Deus quot bona
parvula Æde conduntur.
ut requieſcant
Tu Lector de Profundis.

Arms, 1. *Argent, ſix fleurs de lis azure,* 3, 2, 1, for Paſton. Impaling 2. *Argent, a chevron between three martlets ſable.*

✢

Beneath this Stone reſteth the Body of the Honble Ann Paſton, Daughter of the Right Honble Charles Calvert Baron Baltimore of the Kingdom of Ireland. She was Wife to Edward Somerſet of Pauntly Court in the County of Glouceſter Eſq; & after his Dece[s]. Married John Paſton of Horton Court in the ſaid County Eſq; She having punctually perform. all the Duties of a moſt Loving Wife, a tender Mother, & faithful Friend in the Care ſhe took of her laſt Huſband's Children by his firſt Wife her Dear Friend who lies intered by her, Ended her life by a moſt tedious and Painfull Sickneſs (Suffered with the greateſt Courage & Patience) on ye tenth of February MDCCXXXI.
Cujus Animæ Propitietur Deus.

Arms, 1. Paſton, impaling 2. *Paly of ſix Or and ſable, over all a bend counterchanged.* — MOTTO, DE MIEULX JE PENSE EN MIEULX. — SUPPORTERS, On the dexter ſide, *A bear muzzled, collared, and chained Or:* On the ſiniſter, *An oſtrich proper, with a horſeſhoe in its beak Or.* — CREST, *A griphon with wings elevated Or.*

✢
D. O. M.

Hoc Tumulo conduntur Exuviæ JOHANNIS PASTON, olim de Appleton in Agro Norfol: nuper de Horton in Com: Glouc. Armigeri. De numeroſa Prole, quam ex Prima Conjuge, Franciſca Henrici Titchbourne de Titchbourne in Com: Hant: Baronetti Filia ſuſcepit, tres duntaxat Natos, Gulielmum, Clementem, & Jacobum, duaſq; Filias, Mariam ſcil[t]. & Franciſcam, ſuperſtites reliquit. Alteris Nuptiis Annæ Calvert, Caroli Baronis de Baltimore, & demum Catharinæ Nathanielis Boſtock de Wixhal in Agro Salop: Armigeri Filiæ (quam mœſtam reliquit Viduam) Conjunctus fuit. Poſt Vitam Deo vere piam, Sponſis fidelem, Amicis ſuavem et benignam, Proli autem maxime deſideratam, Diem obijt ſupremum poſtridie Nonas Octob. Anno Salutis 1737, Ætatis 68.
Cujus Animæ propitietur Deus.

Arms, Supporters, &c. as on the laſt.

✢

Sacred to the memory of WILLIAM PASTON, late of *Horton*, Eſq[r].

A Mind enrich'd by Nature and by Art,
With what could pleaſe and intereſt every Heart;
In upper Life, by all who ſaw, approv'd,
In lower Life, by all who knew him, lov'd;
No Epitaph his Virtues need proclaim,
His Actions ever will endear his Name:
An upright, Generous, open hearted Friend,
HORTON, deplore thy Loſs! lament his End!

He was twice Married. His firſt Wife was MARY, Daughter of JOHN COURTENAY of *Molland* in the *County* of *Devon*, Eſq[r]. one of the Coheireſſes of her Brother JOHN COURTENAY of the ſame Place, Eſq[r]. She died Oct[r]. the 29th A. D. 1747. His ſecond Wife was MARY, Daughter of GILES CHICHESTER of *Arlington* in the *County* of *Devon*, Eſq[r] who as a grateful Memory, in Teſtimony of her ſincere love & affection, cauſed this Monument to be erected to the deceaſed.

By his firſt Wife he had Iſſue one Daughter ANNA MARIA, married to George the only Son of S[r]. ROBERT THROCKMORTON, of *Weſt-Underwood* in the *County* of *Bucks*, Bart.

By his ſecond & ſurviving Wife he had no Iſſue.

He died January the 11th Anno { Dom. 1769, Ætatis ſuæ 69.

REQUIESCAT IN PACE.

Arms, 1. Paſton, impaling 2. *Checky Or and gules, a chief vaire.* On a ſcutcheon of pretence, *Or, three roundlets gules, in chief a label of three points of the ſecond.* Supporters and Motto as before.

Taxes.					
The Royal Aid in	1692, £.	152	0	0
Poll-tax ——	1694, —	20	17	0
Land-tax ——	1694, —	222	15	2
The ſame, at 3*s.*	1770, —	174	2	0

At the beginning of this century, there were 80 houſes, and about 120 inhabitants in this pariſh, whereof 6 were freeholders; yearly births 8, burials 7. *Atkyns.* The inhabitants are now about 332.

HUNTLEY.

THIS pariſh lies in the hundred of the dutchy of Lancaſter, in the Foreſt diviſion, five miles north eaſt from Dean, eleven eaſt from Roſs in Herefordſhire, and ſeven weſt from Glouceſter.

The pariſh conſiſts of good arable and paſture land. Part of Yartleton-hill lies within it, and is eſteemed the higheſt ground in the Foreſt diviſion. It affords plenty of iron ore, intermixt with ſhining particles of a white and yellow colour, vulgarly ſuppoſed to be ſilver and gold, but I never heard that either of thoſe precious metals have been extracted from the ore.

In the great civil war, the parliament had a garriſon in this place, which captain Davis betrayed into the hands of ſir John Wintour.

The great turnpike-road from Glouceſter to Hereford leads through this village.

Of the Manor and other Eſtates.

'William the ſon of Baderon holds Huntelei 'in Botelau hundred. Aluuin held it of Eldred 'the archbiſhop [of York,] and could go where 'he would. There are two hides. In demean is 'one plow-tillage, and four villeins, and ſix 'bordars, with three plow-tillages. There is one '*ſervus.* A wood two miles long, and one broad. 'It was worth 40*s.* now 30*s.*' *Dom. B.* p. 73.

Reginald

Reginald de Gray purchased a charter of free warren in Hunteley, and all his lands in Gloucestershire, 53 H. 3. Robert Sapye, or de Sapy, was lord of Huntley, with free warren, 9 & 11 E. 1. and died seized thereof 20 E. 2.

Richard lord Talbot, of Goderick-castle in Herefordshire, (whose anceftor, Richard Talbot, came into England with the Conqueror) married Elizabeth, one of the daughters and coheiresses of John Comyn, of Badenagh, of the blood royal of Scotland, and with her had the manor of Huntley, of which he died seized 30 E. 3. Elizabeth, his widow, survived him, but dying soon after, this manor descended to Gilbert lord Talbot, son of Richard, who died seized of Huntley and Longhope 10 R. 2 leaving Richard lord Talbot his son and heir, who died seized of Huntley, Longhope, Leigh, and Lidney 20 R. 2. Gilbert lord Talbot, son of Richard, on the death of his mother, had livery of a fourth part of this manor 1 H. 5. *Dugd. Bar.* He died seized of the above-mentioned manors, and of a moiety of the manor of Badgworth, and of a third part of those of Painswick, Moreton-Valence, and Whaddon, 7 H. 5. leaving Ankaret, or Anchoret, his only daughter and heiress, who dying at the age of four years, 9 H. 5. John lord Talbot, brother of Gilbert, and uncle to Anchoret, so famous for his victories in France, as to be esteemed the Achilles of England, was her heir. He was created earl of Shrewsbury 20 H. 6. and was slain[w] by a cannon shot, at the siege of Chastillon in France, July 20, 31 H. 6. and died seized of the before-mentioned manors which had belonged to his father and brother. He was succeeded in title and estate by his son and heir, John, second earl of Shrewsbury, who took part with the house of Lancaster, and was slain at the battle of Northampton, July 10, 1460.

John, third earl of Shrewsbury, died seized of all the before-mentioned manors 13 E. 4. Catherine, his widow, survived him, and had this manor assigned her in part of dower 15 E. 4.

George, fourth earl of Shrewsbury, son of the last John, died 30 H. 8. and was succeeded by his son Francis, fifth earl of Shrewsbury, who had livery of this manor the same year, and dying 32 Eliz. was succeeded by Gilbert his son, the sixth earl of Shrewsbury, who died seized of Huntley, and other manors in Gloucestershire, 14 Jac. leaving three daughters coheiresses.

Elizabeth, his second daughter, was married to Henry earl of Kent, who had for her share the manor of Huntley, and other estates in Gloucestershire, which must have been settled on him and his heirs, otherwise they would have descended to the issue of Gilbert earl of Shrewsbury; for the above Henry earl of Kent dying without issue in 1630, the manor of Huntley came to Anthony Grey, the next heir male of his family, who died seized of it, leaving Henry earl of Kent his son and heir. He died in the year 1644, and was succeeded in honour and estate by Anthony his son and heir. Henry duke of Kent, son of Anthony, was lord of the manor at the beginning of this century.

The manor came not long afterwards to John Hopkyns Probyn, esq; and Edmund Probyn, esq; is the present lord of the manor of Huntley, and resides at Newland. His arms are, *Ermine, on a fess gules a lion passant Or.*

Thomas Rawlings and his wife levied a fine of lands in Huntley to William Baynham 8 H. 7.

Of the Church, &c.

The church is a rectory, in the Forest deanery, worth about 60*l.* a year. Mr. Morse is patron and incumbent.

Wienochus de Monemut gave the chapel of Huntley to the monks of the church built by him in his castle of Monmouth, which was a cell to the abbey of St. Florence de Salurmo. *Dugd. Mon.*

The church, dedicated to St. John Baptist, has a tower at the west end, and a small chancel.

The church house, and some lands, worth together about 4*l.* a year, are vested in feoffees, and the produce distributed to the second poor.

First fruits £.	7	5	10	Proc. & Syn. £.	0	6	6
Tenths —	0	14	10	Pentecostals	0	1	6

Taxes.					
The Royal Aid in	1692, £.	48	0	0
Poll-tax —	1694, —	13	5	0
Land-tax —	1694, —	59	18	0
The same, at 3*s.*	1770, —	42	7	6

At the beginning of this century, there were 54 houses in this parish, and about 240 inhabitants, whereof 9 were freeholders; yearly births 7, burials 6. *Atkyns.* There are now about 269 inhabitants.

****

ICOMBE

IS a tithing and hamlet in Icombe, of which the chapel and the greater part of the place is in Worcestershire; but the hamlet of Icombe lies in the hundred of Slaughter, and constitutes a part of the county of Gloucester. It is distant two miles south-eastward from Stow, ten northward from Northleach, and twenty-six north-eastward from Gloucester.

It had been long accounted extraparochial, and not subject to the orders of the magistrate touching the

[w] When the body of the earl of Shrewsbury, the Achilles of England, was found, after the battle of Chastillon upon Dordon, by his herald, who had worn his coat of arms, he kissed the body, and broke out into the following dutiful expressions: *Alas! is it you? I pray God pardon all your misdoings. I have been your officer of arms forty years or more, 'tis time I should surrender it to you.* And while the tears trickled plentifully down his face, he disrobed himself of his coat of arms, and threw it over his master's body, which was the accustomed rite performed heretofore at funerals. *Collins, from Anstis.*

the maintenance of the poor, &c. But on a late trial in the court of king's bench, it was adjudged to be a vill to all intents and purpoſes, a conſtable having been always appointed for it by the lord of the hundred and leet of Slaughter.

The name, contrary to vulgar uſage, ſhould be written with one [C] only. It is the ſame in ſound and ſignification with the Britiſh *Ycwm*, i.e. *the valley*, and is deſcriptive of the ſituation of the place, in a fine valley, on the ſide of the river Evenlode, which ſeparates it from Worceſterſhire.

Of the Manor and other Eſtates.

At the time of the general ſurvey, Icombe in Glouceſterſhire included a much larger diſtrict than the hamlet ſo called at preſent; for there were then three manors of the name of Icombe, two of which have ſince exchanged it for that of Weſtcot. The third is thus deſcribed in the record:

'Durand of Glowec' holds Iccumbe, and Walter 'holds it of him. There are two hides taxed. 'Turſtan held it. In demean are two plow-'tillages, and two villeins, and two bordars with 'one plow-tillage, and ſix between the *ſervi* and '*ancillæ*. It was worth 30*s.* now 40*s.*' *D.B.* p. 76.

In obedience to the king's writ, the high ſheriff of Glouceſterſhire returned the names of all the vills within the ſaid county, by which it appears that the fourth part of the vill of Icombe was in the hundred of Salmoneſburye, and that Thomas de Icombe was lord of the ſame fourth part 9 E. 1. Several different manors paſſing by the ſame name in the records occaſions confuſion, and renders it impoſſible to diſtinguiſh one from the others. I have therefore ſet down the ſubſequent records as I find them in ſir Robert Atkyns's account, notwithſtanding ſome of them may be miſapplied.

Elias de Icombe died ſeized of Icombe 5 E. 3. John earl of Kent was ſeized of it 26 E. 3. and Thomas de Beauchamp, earl of Warwick, held Combe near Stow (probably Combe-Baſkerville, in Weſtcot) 2 H. 4. Elizabeth, widow of John earl of Kent, held the manor of Icombe in part of dower, and died ſeized thereof 12 H. 4.

Robert Whitney died ſeized of Icombe 33 H. 8. and Robert, his ſon, had livery granted to him 37 H. 8. as had James Whitney, ſon of the laſt Robert, 9 Eliz.

The eſtate, conſiſting of the hamlet of Icombe, came afterwards to colonel William Cope, of the family of the Copes of Oxfordſhire and Berkſhire. He was ſucceeded by his ſon and heir colonel Henry Cope, who held it at the beginning of this century. Mr. Hopton and Mr. Gregory are the preſent proprietors of it. The large manſion-houſe of the Copes is now in decay, and occupied by one of the farmers.

Sir Robert Atkyns, with diffidence, appropriates the following particulars to this place, which, however, have no relation to Icombe in Glouceſterſhire. *viz.* Certain lands therein, and the advowſon of the rectories of Icombe and Sodbury were reputed a manor, and did belong to the monaſtery of Worceſter, and after its diſſolution, were granted to the dean and chapter of Worceſter 33 H. 8. The manor of Icombe, and a yearly rent of 8*l.* formerly belonging to the biſhoprick of Worceſter, were granted to the chapter of Windſor 1 E. 6. Another record mentions the manor of Icombe, lately belonging to the priory of Worceſter, to have been granted to the chapter of Worceſter 6 Jac.

The inhabitants of this hamlet have the uſe of one aile in Icombe chapel, which lies in Worceſterſhire, but is within the deanery of Stow.

Taxes.					
The Royal Aid in	1692, £.	50	4	0
Poll-tax ——	1694, —	0	10	0
Land-tax ——	1694, —	50	0	0
The ſame, at 3*s.*	1770, —	38	6	3

There are now only two farm-houſes in this hamlet.

KEMERTON.

THIS pariſh lies in the lower diviſion of the hundred of Tewkeſbury, four miles diſtant north-eaſtward from the town of that name, ſeven north-weſtward from Winchcombe, and fourteen northward from Glouceſter.

It is ſituated in the vale of Eveſham, with Beckford to the eaſt, Overbury and Breedon in Worceſterſhire to the north and weſt, and Tredington to the ſouth of it; and is reputed to be within the juriſdiction of the court of the honour of Glouceſter.

The name is variouſly written, as *Caneberton*, *Chenemertone*, and *Chinemertune*, and is of uncertain derivation. It may ſignify either the *chief farm*, from *chen*, or *kyn*, which is augmentative, and *berton*, a *farm*; or the *town* at the *great* or *ſtrong camp*, from *chen*, as before, *beorg*, a *camp*, and *ton* a common termination; or it is reſolvable into the Britiſh word *Cwmru*, and *ton*, that is, the *Briton's town*.

Breedon-hill, celebrated by Drayton for its proud ſituation in the boſom of the vale, not far from the Avon, is remarkable for its fine paſturage, and fertile corn fields. And as part of it lies in this pariſh, it is proper to take notice of the camp on the top, which appears to be Roman, from the many coins that have been found there, of which a country-man gave me the four following:

1. IMP. CARAVSIVS P. F. AVG. *Reverſe*, a female figure, with an olive branch in her hand. *Legend*, PAX AVG.

2. IMP. MAXENTIVS P. F. AVG. *Reverſe*, a ſoldier ſitting in a temple. *Legend*, CONSERV. VRB. SVAE.

3. MAGNENTIVS P. F. AVG. *Reverſe*, a ſoldier holding a ſtandard in his left hand, and in the right a victory, crowning him with laurel. *Legend*, FELICITAS REIPVBL.

4. Imp. licinivs p. f. avg. *Reverse*, a foldier. *Legend*, obliterated.

On the brow of the hill, near the camp, ftands a ftone of a prodigious magnitude, which the people of that neighbourhood call *Benbury-ftone*, placed there, without doubt, to commemorate fome fignal event; but time has totally defeated the intention, and left us no part of its hiftory befide the name, which fignifies the *ftone at the top of the hill*, or *head of the camp*.

The curious natural productions of this village confift of foffil fhells, particularly of the mufcle kind; and I am informed that the *aftroites* have been found in fome parts of the parifh.

Mr. Parfons has a very good houfe here, where he refides.

Of the Manor and other Eftates.

Domefday-book, reciting the particulars of the large manor of Tewkefbury, has this paffage:

'Brictric the fon of Algar held this manor in 'the time of king Edward. He had in his time 'the fubfequent eftates of other thanes under his 'authority:

'Let held eight hides in Chenemertone, and they 'were a manor. Now Girard holds them, and has 'three plow-tillages there, and fourteen villeins, 'with four plow-tillages. There are eight *fervi*, 'and three mills of 15*s*. [rent]. It was worth 8*l*. 'now 6*l*.' *Domefday-book*, p. 68.

'Leuuinus held half a hide at Chinemertune, 'which Girard now holds.' and which was appurtenant to the manor of Derherft.

'Eluuinus held half a hide at Chinemertune, 'which Baldwin the abbat holds.'

'Befide thefe, Girard the chamberlain holds 'eight hides in Chenemertune, and three hides in 'Botingtune, which always paid tax, and did 'other fervices in Derhefte hundred; but after 'Girard had them, they neither paid tax nor did 'fervice.' *Domefday-book*, p. 72.

The manor of Kemerton was held of the Clares and their fucceffors, earls of Gloucefter. William, fon of Gerald, was feized of Kenemerton, with markets, 2 H. 3. Robert Mufgrofe died feized thereof 38 H. 3. as did John Mufgrofe 3 E. 1. and Robert Mufgrofe 9 E. 1. leaving Hawife his only daughter and heir, then married to fir William Mortimer, a younger fon of Roger earl of March, who in her right had livery of the manor 10 E. 1. But it feems fhe was twice married, for fome authors mention her as the wife of John de Ferrers, baron of Chartley.

The manor of Kemerton belonged afterwards to Thomas earl of Arundel, whofe fifter and coheirefs, Joan, carried it in marriage to William de Beauchamp, lord Bergavenny, who dying 12 H. 4. fhe furviving him, was feized thereof at the time of her deceafe 14 H. 6.

Richard de Beauchamp, earl of Warwick, fon and heir of William and of Joan, left Henry, afterwards duke of Warwick, his fon and heir, who dying at twenty-two years of age, and leaving an infant daughter, who furvived him but a fhort time, his fifter Anne became his heir; but Cecily, his widow, held this manor for life, in part of her dower. The faid Anne was married to Richard Nevil, earl of Salifbury and of Warwick, by whom fhe had two daughters. Ifabel, the eldeft, was married to George duke of Clarence, brother to king Edward the Fourth. By virtue of an act of parliament which deprived the mother, he, in right of his wife, died feized of this manor 17 E. 4. But Anne countefs of Warwick was afterwards reftored to her right, with a finifter defign, by king Henry the Seventh, to whom fhe was obliged to pafs away this manor, and her other great eftates, 3 H. 7. and died foon after.

Sir Robert Willoughby, lord Brook, married Elizabeth, one of the daughters and coheireffes of fir Richard Beauchamp, by Elizabeth, daughter of fir Humphry Stafford. She furvived him, and died feized of Kemerton 6 H. 8. and livery thereof was granted to Edward Willoughby, their fon and heir, the fame year. He left three daughters coheireffes; Elizabeth, married to Fulk Grevil; Anne, who died unmarried; and Blanch, married to fir Francis Dautry. Anne, the fecond fifter, dying foon after, livery of a moiety of a third part of the manor of Kemerton was granted to Francis Dautry and Blanch his wife, 25 H. 8.

The manor of Kemerton was afterwards granted to Thomas Hewes and Margaret his wife, and to their heirs in fpecial taille, 4 Mar.

Livery of the manor of Kemerton was granted to Richard Ligon 9 Eliz. Sir Arnold Ligon and Thomas Hewes, efq; were lords of this manor in 1608. John Parfons, efq; was lord of the manor at the beginning of this century, and dying in 1721, was fucceeded by his fon, John Parfons. He died in 1759, and was fucceeded by his fon, John Parfons, efq; the prefent lord of this manor. His arms are, *Azure, a chevron ermine between three trefoils argent.*

Afton upon Carant is a tithing in the parifh of Afhchurch, but is within the conftablewick, and part of the tithing within the manor of Kemerton.

Of the Church, &c.

The church is a rectory, in the deanery of Campden, worth about 300*l*. a year. The corporation of the city of Gloucefter are patrons; the rev. Mr. Godfrey Goodman is the prefent incumbent.

Godfrey Goodman, bifhop of Gloucefter, May 8, 1638, granted the advowfon of the church of Kemerton to the mayor and burgeffes of the city of Gloucefter, who reconveyed the fame to the bifhop for his life.

On the vacancy of the rectory, the corporation of Gloucefter are to enquire of the corporation of Ruthyn in Denbighfhire for a relation of bifhop Goodman's, to be prefented to this living. If there

there ſhould be none, then the living to go to a ſon of the mayor of Glouceſter, or of the ſenior alderman.

The rector, on the ſealing of his preſentation, pays 10*l.* for a dinner at St. Bartholomew's hoſpital in Glouceſter, to which the biſhop muſt be invited. He likewiſe pays two quarters of wheat yearly, to the treaſurer of that hoſpital, for the poor people there, in the week before Eaſter.

Alicia de Bello Campo preſented to this church in the reign of king Edward the Third.

The church is large, with an aile on each ſide, and a low pinnacled tower at the weſt end, in which are ſix very muſical bells.

	£.	s.	d.		£.	s.	d.
Firſt fruits	17	13	0	Synodals	0	2	0
Tenths —	1	15	3½	Pentecoſtals	0	1	0½
Procurations	0	6	8				

Benefaction.

Archbiſhop Juxton gave 200*l.* to the poor of this place, 100*l.* of which money has been laid out in the purchaſe of lands in Morton Henmarſh.

Taxes.			£.	s.	d.
	The Royal Aid in	1692,	186	18	0
	Poll-tax —	1694, —	28	13	0
	Land-tax —	1694, —	66	10	0
	The ſame at 3*s.*	1770, —	50	11	9

At the beginning of the preſent century, there were 36 houſes in this pariſh, and about 150 inhabitants, whereof 6 were freeholders; yearly births 4, burials 4. *Atkyns.* The inhabitants are now about 225.

KEMPLEY.

THIS pariſh lies in the hundred of Botloe, in the foreſt diviſion of the county, five miles north-weſt from Newent, ſix ſouthward from Ledbury in Herefordſhire, and fifteen north-weſtward from Glouceſter.

It is of a middle ſize, bounded on the north by Dimmock, on the ſouth by Oxenhall, on the eaſt by Pauntley, and hath Herefordſhire on the weſt. It poſſeſſes an agreeable variety of ground, with eaſy ſlopes, and bolder acclivities, which however riſe not into hills. Something more than half the pariſh conſiſts of meadow, paſture, and orcharding; the reſt is arable and woodland, where the oak grows with uncommon vigour.

Here the arable lands are planted with rows of fruit-trees, with large intervals between; for the ſoil of theſe parts produces a rich and pleaſant cider, which is a principal object with the farmer. What has been ſaid of Dimmock is equally applicable to Kempley. Theſe places, with Preſton and Oxenhall, make a diſtrict of rich country, in the neighbourhood of Herefordſhire, with which the produce is nearly the ſame, and the methods of cultivation ſimilar to thoſe in uſe in that fine county, as mentioned under Dimmock.

Stonehouſe, in this pariſh, is a ſeat of the antient family of the Pindars, where they reſided at the beginning of the preſent century; but it hath long ſince been occupied by the tenant of the principal farm. Indeed the founderous and impaſſible condition of the public roads, in the winter, is an inſuperable objection to a gentleman's reſidence.

The air is ſaid to be pure and healthy; and it is remarked, in Dr. Parſons's account of this village, that no native had ever been known to have either gout or ſtone; and that no perſon had died in Mr. Pindar's houſe within the memory of man, notwithſtanding there were near fifteen or twenty in family great part of the time, to the year 1703. Perhaps cider, which is here the common liquor, may be a preſervative from the above-mentioned diſorders.

Of the Manor and other Eſtates.

'Roger de Laci holds Chenepelei in Botelau 'hundred of the king. Edric and Luric held it 'for two manors, in the time of king Edward, 'and could go where they would. There are 'three hides. In demean are three plow-tillages, 'and ten villeins, and ſeven bordars, with twelve 'plow-tillages. There are ſeven *ſervi*. It was 'worth 4*l.* now 100*s.*' *Domeſday-book*, p. 74.

Henry de Grey held the manor of Kempley in the reign of Richard the Firſt. John de Grey, ſecond ſon of Henry, was ſeized of it 9 E. 1. and was ſucceeded in this eſtate by his ſon Reginald, who died 1 E. 2. leaving John de Grey[x], his ſon, forty years old. John died 17 E. 2.[x] ſeized of Kempeley, which he held in *capite* by the ſervice of half a knight's fee, and left Henry de Grey, his ſon and heir, who died ſeized of this manor 16 E. 3.[y] Richard Grey held the manor of Kempley 22 R. 2.

John Abrahall, eſq; was ſeized of the manor of Kempley 3 E. 4. William Pigot died ſeized of it 7 E. 6. leaving Edward his ſon forty years old, who had livery granted to him the ſame year. Henry Pigot, ſon of Edward, left Anne, his only daughter and heireſs, married to Henry Finch, who, in her right, was ſeized of Kempley in the year 1608, and died in 1631. Francis Finch, ſon and heir of Henry, married Jane, daughter of Dr. Thornborough, biſhop of Worceſter, and left John Finch his ſon and heir.

The manor was ſoon afterwards purchaſed by ſir Thomas How, of the family of that name at Compton. And from him it paſſed, in the ſame manner, to Reginald Pindar, eſq; who was lord of the manor when ſir Robert Atkyns compiled his account of it. Thomas Pindar, eſq; died in 1722, and Reginald-Pindar Lygon, of Maddersfield in Worceſterſhire, eſq; is the preſent lord of the manor. His arms are, *Argent, two lions paſſant gardant in pale gules.*

The prior and brethren of St. Bartholomew's hoſpital in Glouceſter had lands in this pariſh very anciently,

[x] Eſcheat. ſub annis.

[y] Dugd. Bar.

antiently, for there is ſtill in being a leaſe from them, to Ralph Dragun and Emma his wife, of all their land in Kenepeleya, which Henry Hythenard ſometime held of them, at the rent of three cranocs [half quarters] of wheat, and two quarters of oats.

Of the Church, &c.

The church is a vicarage, in the Foreſt deanery, worth about 60*l.* a year. The dean and chapter of Hereford, as guardians of the hoſpital of Ledbury, are patrons; Mr. Bourn is the preſent incumbent.

The vicar has the great tithes, except of Prior's-court, which is ſubject to the repair of the chancel, and is held under the hoſpital of Ledbury.

The church is ſmall, with a ſmall ſpire at the weſt end, in which are three bells. The churchyard is near an acre of ground, and intirely planted with apple trees.

Firſt fruits £	5	6	8	Proc. & Syn. £.	0	6	6
Tenths —	0	10	7½	Pentecoſtals -	0	1	6

Monuments and Inſcriptions.

In the chancel is the following inſcription:

P. M. S.
Macte Marmor,
Eloquere,
Nec taceas cineres Henrici Finch, Armigeri, hic eſſe
Reconditos.
Sitq; tibi non ingratum Munus Fidelitatis ſuæ Symbolum
In { Principem / Patriam / Amicos } Exſtare.
Efferto Vivis, Poſteris Annuntia, Temporibuſq; propalato
Futuris,
Quam
Sincerus Numinis Cultor,
Sedulus Veritatis Indagator,
Candidus Æquitatis Diſpenſator,
Acerbus Fraudis Exoſor,
Beneficus Paupertatis Suſtentator,
Studioſus Hoſpitii Propugnator,
Vixit Occiditq;
{ Deo / Ecclefiæ / Amicis / Optimis / Proximis / Omnibus } Fuiſſe { Supplicem, / Morigerum, / Charum, / Jucundum, / Familiarem, / Comem.
Bis octo annorum luſtra in Viuis peregiſſe,
Et
Supremam non metuiſſe ſed exoptaſſe horam:
Illumq;
Votum ſuum, precibus & ſuſpiriis uſq; adeo expetitum,
22° Auguſti E cœlorum gremio accipuiſſe,
An° Sui Ieſu MDCXXXI.
Porro, non ſine Piaculo Conticeſcas,
Annam, ex non obſcura Pigotorum Proſapia, fideliſſimam
Conſortem, hic lateri eius dormientem adiacere;
Quorum
Socialis Amor morte non finitur,
Sed unitur.
Hanc
Unicum Marito peperiſſe Filium, quem amabant unice,
Qui { Amoris / Obſequij / Pietatis } Ergo,
In P. Parentum M.
Hæc
Non ſine Lacrymis
Dicauit,
Æ. C.
M D C XXXIII.

Arms, *Quarterly of ſix,* 1. *Argent, a chevron engrailed between three gryphons paſſant ſable,* for Finch. 2. *Sable, three pickaxes argent,* for Pigot. 3. *Gules, three lioncels in pale argent.* 4. *Argent, within a bordure engrailed three pikes hauriant ſable.* 5. *Party per bend and per feſs indented argent and ſable, four hunting horns counterchanged.* 6. as 1ſt.

On a very handſome white marble monument,

Near this Place
lyeth Interred

THOMAS PYNDAR, Eſq; who dyed May the 18th, Anno { Dom. 1722, Ætat. 60.

ELIZABETH PYNDAR dyed Jan^ry ye 10th, 1759, Ætat. 92.

REGINALD PYNDAR, Eſq; only Son of THO. PYNDAR and ELIZABETH his Wife, who dyed July the 10th, Anno { Dom. 1721, Ætat. 33.

As their Memorials have one Stone,
So were their Hearts intirely one;
Whoſe Virtues could this Stone relate,
Or couldſt thou, Reader, imitate,
This Stone all others would excell
In ſpeaking, Thou in doing well.

Arms, on the dexter ſide of the monument, 1. *Argent, a chevron between three lions heads erazed Or,* impaling 2. *Two piles, on a chief a lion paſſant.* On the ſiniſter ſide, 1. as before, impaling 2. *Two lioncels paſſant in pale.*

Benefactions.

Mrs. Pindar left 2*l.* 2*s.* a year for a monthly ſacrament. And Joan Wotton gave a rent charge of 10*s.* a year for the uſe of the poor.

Taxes.					
The Royal Aid in	1692,	£. 78	14	0
Poll-tax ——	1694, —	28	1	0
Land-tax ——	1694, —	74	12	0
The ſame, at 3*s.*	1770, —	55	19	3

At the beginning of this century there were 40 houſes in this pariſh, and about 180 inhabitants, whereof 10 were freeholders; yearly births 5, burials 5. *Atkyns.* The preſent number of families is 45, of inhabitants exactly 257.

KEMPSFORD

IS a pariſh of a middle ſize, in the hundred of Britwel's-Barrow, four miles ſouth-weſtward from Leachlade, nine eaſtward from Cirenceſter, and twenty-five ſouth-eaſtward from Glouceſter.

The river Coln enters this pariſh on the north ſide, from Fairford, and running through it, falls into the Thames, which, at this place, is a boundary between Glouceſterſhire and Wiltſhire.

The name was antiently written *Chenemeresford. Chene,* or *Kyn,* is of extenſive ſignification, as *ſtrenuous, bold, valiant*; and in compoſition, *great, principal, chief*; *mer* ſignifies the *ſea,* or ſome *large water,* and *mere* is alſo a *boundary*: The name therefore ſignifies the *Ford of the principal river,* or *great boundary,* as the Thames may be very properly called in this part of the country.

Some topographers have taken this for the ford through which Ethelmund, general of the Wiccian army, paſſed to give battle to Werſtan earl of Wiltſhire; but by Higden's account of that tranſaction, who ſays, *Ethelmund leaving his own territories, marched out as far as the ford Chimeresford,* it appears that this could not be the place; for all Glouceſterſhire lay in Wiccia. Beſides, it is moſt probable, from other circumſtances, that it

 was

was at Cummerford, near Calne in Wiltſhire, for near that place are remains of large intrenchments, which ſeem to put the matter out of doubt.

About half the pariſh is rich meadow and paſture, and the other part very good arable land; but it affords nothing curious in natural hiſtory.

Henry duke of Lancaſter reſided here in the reign of king Edward the Third, where his only ſon came to an unfortunate end, which determined the duke to leave the place; and his horſe caſting a ſhoe at his departure, the inhabitants nailed it to the church door, where it remains as a memorial of that event at this day.

The family of the Thynnes have alſo honoured this village with their reſidence for many ſucceſſive generations, one of whom built the antient manor houſe near the church, which was very large and handſome, but is now uninhabited, and in a very ruinous condition.

Of the Manor and other Eſtates.

'Hernulf de Heſding holds Chenemeresforde 'in Brictuoldeſberg hundred. There are twenty-'one hides taxed. Oſgot held it of earl Herald. 'In demean are ſix plow-tillages, and thirty-eight 'villeins, and nine bordars, and one radcheniſter, 'with eighteen plow-tillages. There are fourteen '*ſervi*, and four mills of 40*s.* and 40*d.* rent, and '9*l.* from the meadows beſide the paſture of the 'cattle, and from the ſheep-fold 120 weight of 'cheeſe. In Glouuec' ſeven burgeſſes paying 2*s.* 'In the time of king Edward it was worth 30*l.* 'now 66*l.* 6*s.* 8*d.*' *Domeſday-book*, p. 77.

This manor was the head of an antient barony, called the barony of Kenemeresford or Kenesford; and Hannington, and a moiety of Ingleſham, both lying in Wiltſhire, and Etloe in Awre, were members of it.

About the end of the reign of king William the Firſt, Ernulf de Heſding conveyed this manor to Patrick de Chaworth, who was one of the *Cadurci* in France, and therefore ſometimes called *de Cadurcis*. Which Patrick granted three water-mills in Kynemeresford to the abbey of Glouceſter 20 W. 1. and the grant was confirmed by William Rufus. Patrick, his ſon, gave a water-mill called Horcote, with the lands adjoining, and the tithes of the meadows of the ſaid village, to the ſame monaſtery, when William was abbat. He paid 6*l.* upon levying of ſcutage for the redemption of the king out of captivity 6 R. 1.

Pain de Chaworth, ſon and heir of the laſt Patrick, married Gundred, daughter and heir of William de la Fert, and was buried in the chapter houſe of the abbey of Glouceſter. Patrick the Third, ſon of Pain, being under age at his father's death, paid 500*l.* for his own wardſhip and marriage, 23 H. 3. He married Hawiſe, daughter and heir of Thomas de London, lord of Ogmore and Kidwelly in Wales, and obtained a grant of markets and fairs in Kempsford 28 H. 3. and died ſeized of Radene, and of the *barony of Kenesford*, 42 H. 3. His ſon Pain being then only thirteen years of age, his mother purchaſed his wardſhip at 1000 marks. Pain, with his two brothers, attended prince Edward in the Holy Land 54 H. 3. and died without iſſue 7 E. 1.

Patrick the Fourth, brother to the laſt Pain, ſucceeding him, married Iſabel, daughter of William de Beauchamp, earl of Warwick, and died 11 E. 1. leaving Maud his only daughter and heireſs. Iſabel, his widow, ſurviving him, held the manor of Kempsford in dower. She being ſoon after married to Hugh le Deſpencer, without the king's licence, this manor was ſeized by the crown, and granted to Ela counteſs of Warwick 15 E. 1. but Iſabel was reſtored upon payment of 2000 marks. After the death of Iſabel, the manor came to Maud, her daughter by her former huſband: She was married to Henry, afterwards earl of Lancaſter, nephew to king Edward the Firſt, who joined with his elder brother, Thomas earl of Lancaſter, and other barons, againſt king Edward the Second, to expel the Spencers. Thomas earl of Lancaſter was taken priſoner, and beheaded at Pontefract for treaſon, and Kempsford, with all the other eſtates of Henry, was ſeized by the crown 15 E. 2. and granted to Roger Boyfield the ſame year. Upon the dethroning of king Edward the Second, Henry ſucceeded to his brother's honour, and had reſtitution of this manor, of which he died ſeized 19 E. 3. leaving Henry, his ſon and heir, afterwards created duke of Lancaſter. He reſided ſome time at Kempſford, but taking a diſlike to the place, on account of the unfortunate death of his only ſon; he granted the manor of Kynemersford, one third of Chedworth, Hanendon [Hannington in Wiltſhire] a moiety of Ingleſham, and other lands, to the collegiate church of St. Mary the Leſs in the caſtle of Leiceſter, for the maintenance of a hoſpital there, called Newark, or New-work, of which he was the founder, 28 E. 3. The dean and college of Leiceſter purchaſed a grant of free warren in Kynemeresford and Chedworth 30 E. 3. and continued poſſeſſed of this manor 'till the general diſſolution of religious foundations.

King Edward the Sixth, in the third year of his reign, granted this manor to ſir John Thynne, (deſcended from ſir Geoffery Botevile, as mentioned under Bagendon) a very eminent perſon, who was at the battle of Muſſelburgh, and was knighted in the camp before Roxburgh in Scotland, by the duke of Somerſet, to whom he was ſecretary, and received the Scotch lion as an addition to his arms. He built a noble manſion at Longleate in Wiltſhire, ſaid to be the firſt well built houſe in England, which was finiſhed in the year 1579, at the expence of 8016*l.* 13*s.* 8*d.* beſides the timber and ſtone, which were his own. He married, firſt, Chriſtian, daughter of ſir Richard Greſham, lord mayor of London, and ſiſter and heir to ſir Thomas Greſham, who founded and endowed Greſham college, and built the Royal Exchange in London, with whom, it is ſaid, he had eſtates to the amount of 2000*l.* a year, and by by her had iſſue three ſons and eight daughters. His ſecond wife was Dorothy, daughter of ſir William Wroughton, by whom he had five ſons, and dying May 21, 1580, was buried at Deverel-Langbridge in Wiltſhire.

Sir John Thynne, eldeſt ſon of ſir John, by his firſt wife, had livery of this manor on the death of his father, and married Joan, daughter of ſir Rowland Hayward, with whom he had Caus-caſtle, the manor of Stretton-hall in Shropſhire, and other lands to the value of 1000*l.* a year. He was knighted by king James the Firſt, May 11, 1603, and died in 1606, according to ſir Robert Atkyns, (but Nov. 21, 1604, according to Collins) and was ſucceeded by his eldeſt ſon,

Sir Thomas Thynne, who was lord of this manor in 1608. He married, firſt, Mary, daughter of George Touchet, lord Audley; and ſecondly, Katherine Howard, grandaughter of Thomas viſcount Bindon, by whom he had three ſons and one daughter, and died in 1639.

Sir Henry-Frederick Thynne, ſecond ſon of ſir Thomas, had this manor given him by his father. He married Mary, one of the daughters of Thomas firſt lord Coventry, and was created a baronet July 15, 1641, by king Charles the Firſt, in whoſe cauſe he was a great ſufferer, being obliged to pay 3554*l.* compoſition, beſides ſettling lands of the value of 200*l* a year, as the ſequeſtrators directed. He died in 1680, and was ſucceeded by his eldeſt ſon,

Sir Thomas Thynne, created baron Thynne of Warminſter, and viſcount Weymouth, in 1682. By the death of his uncle, ſir James Thynne, without iſſue, and of his couſin Thomas Thynne, eſq; who was murdered by the procurement of the Count Conningſmarke, he ſucceeded to their great eſtates. He married lady Frances Finch, eldeſt daughter of Heneage, ſecond earl of Winchelſea, and died in 1714.

Thomas, ſecond viſcount Weymouth, great nephew to the above Thomas, ſucceeded him in honour and eſtate. He married, to his ſecond wife, lady Louiſa, daughter of John earl of Granville, and died in 1741, leaving

Thomas, third viſcount Weymouth, his ſon and heir, who ſold this manor to Gabriel Hanger, afterwards lord Coleraine, whoſe widow is the preſent lady of the manor of Kempsford.

HAMLETS. 1. *Dunville.*

2. *Horcote.* Richard Forſter levied a fine of a moiety of lands in Horcote 12 H. 7.

3. *Welford.* What ſir Robert Atkyns has ſaid concerning this hamlet, relates to the pariſh of Welford.

Of the Church, &c.

The church is a vicarage, in the deanery of Fairford, worth 230*l.* a year. The biſhop of Glouceſter is patron; Mr. Price is the preſent incumbent.

Ernulf de Heſding gave the advowſon of this church to the abbey of Glouceſter, and the grant was confirmed by king Henry the Firſt. The abbey had likewiſe the impropriation of Welford, which, together with the advowſon, was granted to the biſhoprick of Glouceſter 33 H. 8. and confirmed 6 E. 6.

The church is large and handſome, with a lofty well built tower in the middle, in which are ſix muſical bells. At the four corners of the tower, within, are theſe arms. 1. *Three chevronels,* for Clare earl of Glouceſter. 2. *A Gauntlet within a bordure.* 3. *A croſs flory.* 4. *Three lions in pale, in chief a label of three points,* for Henry duke of Lancaſter.

Firſt fruits £	19	0	0	Synodals £	0	2	0
Tenths —	1	18	0	Pentecoſtals	0	1	6
Procurations	0	6	8				

Monuments and Inſcriptions.

In the chancel, on a large grey marble ſtone, inlaid with braſs, are the effigies of a man, his wife, and four children; and round the edge is the following inſcription, in old characters:

Off youre charite pray for the ſoule of Walt. Hichman here buryd which deceſſid the xxvij day of September the xiii yere of the reign of kyng Henry the viij Anno dni Millmo CCCCC° XXI°. And for the ſoule of Criſtyan his Wyffe which had to gedd' iiij ſonnes vz Thoms Iohn Robert & Iohn On whoſe ſoules & all Xp'en ſoul' ihu haue mercy AMEN.

Within the communion rails, on a blue ſtone,

Here lyeth expecting an happy reſurrection the body of S[r] Henry Fredericke Thynne K[t] & Bar[tt]. deſcended in a right line from Geofery Boteuile, who came into England Genr[l] of an Army of Poicteuins to aſſiſt king Iohn againſt his Barons. he was sonne of S[r] Thomas Thynne and M[rs] Katherine Howard, Grandaughter of Thomas Visc[t] Bindon, & married Mary one of the daughters of Tho[s] Lr[d] Couentry Lr[d] Keeper of y[e] great Seale of England, & by her had issue three ſonnes & two daughters, all now liuing, viz. Thomas, now Visc[t] Weymouth, Iames, & Henry Fredericke, Mary married to Rich[d] Howe Eſq[r]. & Katherine to S[r] Iohn Lowther of Lowther Bar[t]. He was A man of Excellent parts, Greate loyalty to his Prince, a conſtant aſſertor of y[e] Church of England in the Worſt of times, Kinde and obliging to his family & friends, & dyed March y[e] 6th 1680 aged 66 yeares and 5 days.

The memory of y[e] iuſt is bleſſed.

Arms, at top, *Barry of ten Or and ſable,* for Thynne, impaling *Sable, a feſs ermine between three creſcents Or,* for Coventry.

Benefactions.

In the year 1709, Thomas viſcount Weymouth ſettled 20*l.* a year on the vicar, and founded a charity ſchool in this place, endowing it with 10*l.* a year for the maſter. The money for both charities is paid out of the manors of Weobley and Roſs in Herefordſhire. The ſchool houſe was erected by the inhabitants in 1750, upon a piece of ground given for that purpoſe by lord Weymouth.

There is a ſmall benefaction of eighteen hay cocks, worth 16*s.* a year, for the repair of the church.

Taxes.			£.	s.	d.
	The Royal Aid in	1692,	364	9	0
	Poll-tax — —	1694, —	52	2	0
	Land-tax —	1694, —	263	13	0
	The ſame at 3*s.*	1770, —	197	14	0

At the beginning of this century, there were 66 houſes in this pariſh, and about 340 inhabitants, whereof 9 were freeholders; yearly births 9, burials

burials 6. *Atkyns.* The preſent number of houſes is 104, of families 106, and of inhabitants 493.

KINGSCOT.

THIS is a ſmall pariſh in the hundred of Berkeley, five miles diſtant north-weſt from Tetbury, ſix north-eaſt from Wotton-under-edge, and ſixteen ſouth from Glouceſter.

It appears by *Domeſday-book* that *Chingeſcote* was part of the antient demeſnes of the crown; and it is probable, from the preſent ſtate of the pariſh, which conſiſts principally of woods and of arable lands, and from the name it bears, that it was formerly much overgrown with wood, for *Chingeſcote* ſignifies the *King's Wood.*

The inhabitants have a tradition, that there was once a city here, of the name of *King Cheſter*, which, however may be a miſtake, if underſtood agreeably to their notion of a city; but as tradition has generally ſomething of truth for its foundation, it ſerves, at leaſt, to ſhew that this village has been antiently diſtinguiſhed by camps or ſome eminent buildings. And accordingly it appears that there was a Roman ſtation at a place called the *Cheſtles*, not only from the name of it, which ſeems to have ſomething of a military ſignification, as if it were the ſame with *caſtle*, from *caſtellum* a *fort* or *town*; but alſo from the remains of a teſſelated pavement, and great numbers of Roman coins which have been found there, in plowing the fields at different times: A large ſtatue of ſtone, and other remains of antiquity, have alſo been turned up by the plow in the ſame field. I ſaw many of the coins, and ſome of the dice-like pieces that compoſed the pavement, which were of brick of different colours, in the poſſeſſion of Mr. Brooks of this place. There was alſo an antient *Fibula Veſtiaria*, of braſs, curiouſly chequered on the back part with red and blue enamel, found in the ſame field in the year 1691, as mentioned in the late editions of the *Britannia*, with ſome deſcription of the manner of uſing it. Had a perſon of judgment been preſent when theſe things were diſcovered, many curious particulars might have been preſerved, which were either unnoticed, or deſtroy'd by the plow-man.

I ſuppoſe the *Cheſtles* to have been the *King Cheſter* above-mentioned, and the *greater camp* referred to by the name of a little village in this neighbourhood, called *Laſborough*, but more truly and antiently written *Leſſeberge*, which ſignifies the *ſmaller camp*, or *fortification.*

Of the Manor and other Eſtates.

This manor, at the time of the general ſurvey, was a member of the lordſhip of Berkeley, belonging to which there were 'in Chingeſcote four 'hides and a half.' *D. B.* p. 68. It was given to Roger de Berkeley, by king William the Firſt, and afterwards taken from another Roger de Berkeley, by king Henry the Second, and given to Robert Fitz-Harding; whoſe daughter Aldeva was married to Nigell de Kingeſcote, and had this manor for her portion.

But the records ſhew, that Anſelm de Gournay was ſeized of Kingſcot 14 E. 1. Nigell de Kingeſcote died ſeized of one meſſuage and one carucate of land in Kingeſcote, worth 60*s.* 19 E. 2. which he held of Thomas de Berkeley by the ſervice of one ſixth part of a knight's fee. William the ſon of Nigell being a minor at his father's death, the eſtate was in the cuſtody of Maurice de Berkeley, ſon of Thomas; who engaging in the barons wars, the king ſeized Kingſcote and other eſtates, and put them in the cuſtody of Robert de Aſton, on account of Maurice's rebellion. *Eſch.* 19 E. 2.

Richard Beauchamp, earl of Warwick, died ſeized of Kingſcot 17 H. 6. which was at the time of the violent law ſuits and outrages which happened about the lordſhip of Berkeley, as mentioned p. 275. And Margaret counteſs of Shrewſbury was ſeized of the manor of Kingſcot 7 E. 4. William earl of Nottingham, and earl marſhal, (afterwards marquis of Berkeley) levied a fine of lands in Kingſcot 3 H. 7.

Anthony Kingſcot, eſq; was lord of this manor in the year 1608, and died in 1654. Nigell Kingſcot, eſq; died unmarried in the year 1774, and left this manor, and a large eſtate in this pariſh and other places, to his nephew Robert Kingſcot, eſq; ſon of Robert, brother of the ſaid Nigell, who is the preſent lord of the manor of Kingſcot, and has an antient ſeat cloſe by the church. His coat of arms, and many particulars of his family, are given under *Monumental Inſcriptions.*

HAMLETS. 1. *Binley.* William Mauduit forfeited his lands in Beley for treaſon 1 E. 1.

2. *Hailecot.*

3. *Smith's-Shop*, lying on the great turnpike-road from Glouceſter to Bath.

Of the Church, &c.

This is a chapel in the deanery of Durſley, annexed to Beverſtone. The manor lands pay a modus in lieu of tithe of hay.

The chapel, dedicated to St. John the Evangeliſt, is ſmall, with a low tower at the weſt end, in which are five bells.

Pentecoſtals - 6½*d.*

Monuments and Inſcriptions.

On a raiſed tomb in the church-yard,

Here lyeth the Body of Troylus Kingſcote Gent. who did Service as a Comander for the Prince of Orange 40 yeares; and being 80 yeares old, ended this Life upon the 10th Day of September, Anno Dni 1656.

In the church-yard is a triangular pyramidal monument, on the baſes of which are three marble tables, bearing the following inſcriptions: On the firſt table,

Nigellus

Nigellus de Kingſcote,
Arthuri ab Antiquis Britannis orti Filius,
Aldevam, Rob[tl] Fitz-harding Natam
Duxit Uxorem.
Hujus Rob[ti] Danor. Rex Avus erat,
Evaq; (Gulielmi illius Normanni Neptis)
Uxor.
Sedem *Kingſcotienſem* cum Manerio
Hic Nigellus cum Aldevâ illâ
Dotem,
Terram de Combâ
(Meritorũ in Matildam Imperatr[cem] gratiâ)
Donatum accepit.
Hanc Sedem, tum ipſe tum poſteri
Ornarunt vivi;
Mortuos autem (maxima ex parte)
Eccleſia hæc cum Cœmeterio ſervat.
Antonius Kingſcote (Ar.) primus,
(Ne Majorum cineres violaret,)
Hoc Cœmeterium deſignavit, Locum
Quo ſe & ſuos
Abrum ſcil't Filium & Willum Nepotem,
Sepeliendos fore voluit.

On the ſecond table,

Domus hujus non pauci
Arma geſtarunt, nec inglorij.
Hoc Pictonum & Agincortij Arva,
Hoc idem Mauritius Auraſinis Princeps
Teſtati ſunt.
Omnes ad Unum
Contra quamcunq; Tyrannidis Speciem,
Tam in Sacris quam in Civilibus,
Strenue & ſemper certaverunt.
Gulielmus Kingſcote (Ar.)
(ab Arthuro Viceſimus primus,
Muneribus Magiſtratus, Amici, Patris,
Summa cum Laude functus)
obijt,
Omnibus niſi ſibi immature,
Menſe Octobris,
Anno { Dni MDCCVI°: Ætatis XL.

On the third table,

Huic Genitus,
Vir cariſſimus omnibus quibus notus fuit,
Gulielmus, deceſſit
Ann. Dom. 1731,
Ætat: 41.
Poſt Patrem
Ad hanc properabant Sedem
Antonius,
Annum agens viceſimum,
Et Henricus,
Qui undeviceſimum nondum compleret,
Ann[s]: Dom:
1740,
1746.
De quibus merito tradendum,
Quod Illorum Spes maxima fuit omnibus,
Adeo profecerunt,
Hic Prudentiâ Juris civilis,
Ille quippe Satellitum Præfectus,
Rebus militaribus.

Arms, *Quarterly*, 1. *Gules, a mullet pierced Or*. 2, 3, & 4. *Argent, three eſcallops ſable*.

Benefactions.

The widow of Mr. Troylus Kingſcot gave 30*l*. as a ſtock for the uſe of the poor. And William Wellſteed, in 1699, gave 20*l*. the intereſt of which to be diſtributed to the ſecond poor.

Taxes.					
The Royal Aid in	1692,	£. 65	2	0
Poll-tax —	1694, —	13	4	0
Land-tax —	1694, —	78	13	4
The ſame at 3*s*.	1770, —	56	16	9

There were 40 houſes in this pariſh, and about 180 inhabitants, whereof 12 were freeholders, at the beginning of this century; yearly births 4, burials 3. *Atkyns*. There are now 134 inhabitants.

LANTHONY.

THIS place lies in the united hundreds of Dudſton and King's-barton, adjoining to the ſouth ſide of the city of Glouceſter, and is accounted one of the ſouth hamlets. It is extra-parochial, and obtained its name from the famous monaſtery of Lanthony that ſtood there, of whoſe original and foundation the following is a ſhort account.

At Ewias, in the north part of Monmouthſhire, is a ſolitary place, among woods, rocks and vallies, where St. David, biſhop of Menevia in Pembrokeſhire, (which from him obtained the preſent name of St. David's) built a ſmall chapel and cell, in the ſixth century, and lived many years retired from the world, by the ſide of the brook Hotheni; which place, from the name of the biſhop, and of the little river, the Britons called *Llandeuui Nanthotheni*; that is, the church of David on the brook Hotheni, and in proceſs of time, the name was corrupted to *Lanthony*.

After the death of St. David, this place was deſolate and uninhabited. But in the year 1103, Hugh de Laci, an Engliſh nobleman, going a hunting that way, with many knights, gentlemen, and attendants, was led into that valley, and one of thoſe knights, of the name of William, admiring the ſolitude, and ſeeing a chapel already built, took a reſolution to forſake the world, and devote himſelf to an hermetical life there. And having lived ſome years in that manner, he became ſo famous for his auſterity and holineſs, that Erneſi, who was chaplain to queen Maud, and a perſon of conſiderable account in the court of king Henry I. took a journey to viſit him; and being highly pleaſed with his holy converſation, and place of retirement, became his aſſociate.

Theſe two holy men having ſpent ſome time together, mutually encouraging and ſtrengthening each other in pious habits, Hugh de Laci took them into his ſpecial protection and favour, and enabled them to build a ſmall church, which was conſecrated by Urban, biſhop of Landaff, and Rameline, biſhop of Hereford, *anno* 1108, and dedicated to St. John Baptiſt, the patron of the hermits. The ſame perſon granted them ſome of his large farms for their maintenance; but they, preferring little before too much, accepted what they thought juſt neceſſary, and peremptorily refuſed the reſt.

Having found ſo good a benefactor, they began afterwards to think of taking others into their holy ſociety, which William was averſe to at firſt, but at length yielded to the perſuaſions of Erneſi. And with the advice and approbation of Anſelm, archbiſhop of Canterbury, a monaſtery was founded of the order of the canons regular of St. Auſtin; which order they choſe, becauſe thoſe canons were ſatisfied with the moſt moderate ſubſiſtence, were moſt eſteemed for their charity, and wore the moſt decent habit without affectation of ſanctity.

They now invite divers perſons, fearing God, out of the eminent convents of Moreton, the holy Trinity at London, and Colcheſter, to be brethren at Lanthony, and being thus increaſed to the number of forty or more, chooſe Erneſi for their firſt prior. The ſtrict rules, and ſolemn devotion which he kept up in his monaſtery, made the great men of the kingdom, and even the king and queen themſelves, deſirous of the prayers of this holy congregation; and hence the monks found many benefactors, who conferred more lands and revenues on them than they would receive.

Robert de Beton ſucceeded upon the death of Erniſius, and ſome time afterwards was tranſlated to the biſhoprick of Hereford.

Robert de Braci ſucceeded him. In his time the convent was much infeſted and ravaged by the Welch, whereupon, applying to the biſhop of Hereford for advice and protection, the biſhop reſigned his palace to them, and maintained them at his own charge for two years, (ſome few only excepted, who would not leave the place of their converſion and profeſſion.) But the inteſtine diſturbances continuing in that part of the nation, the biſhop applies to Milo earl of Hereford, the king's conſtable, on behalf of the diſtreſſed monks of Lanthony, reminding him of his father's devotion, who lay buried in their monaſtery; and ſo prevailed with the earl, that he gave them a place near Glouceſter, called the *Hide*, where they built a church and monaſtery. This place they called *Lanthony*, from their former ſeat, and this was the original of the place of which I am to give an account. The church was conſecrated by Simon, biſhop of Worceſter, and Robert, biſhop of Hereford, *anno* 1136, and dedicated to St. Mary the virgin. From this time, the following perſons were priors:

William of Wycombe, who had been chaplain to Robert biſhop of Hereford, occurs prior in 1137. He was a man of profound learning, and had publiſhed in writing *The whole Tyranny and malicious Proceedings of Milo earl of Hereford, who for ſome time violently perſecuted the church and church men, for which he was puniſhed with excommunication.* This made him odious to Roger earl of Hereford, the patron of the monaſtery; and beſides, he was diſliked by the monks of his own houſe, on account of his great auſterity; wherefore he reſigned his government, and retired with one canon to Freme, for the remainder of his life.

Clement, the ſub-prior, being choſen in his room, governed the monaſtery for many years.

Roger de Norwich, ſub-prior, ſucceeded next. He preſided in 1178, and was ſucceeded by

Geffry de Henelawe, a clerk of great fame, who had lived in the ſervice of Robert Hardingh, at Briſtol, and was much celebrated for his ſkill in phyſic. He was preferred to the ſee of St. David's in the year 1203, whereupon

Matthew was elected to this dignity, who, in the year 1214, was made abbat of Bardney, in the county of Lincoln.

John occurs prior *anno* 1218, and dying in 1240,

Godfrey ſucceeded him, and reſigning in the year 1251,

Everard was elected prior. After him,

Martin; and then

Roger de Godeſtre; and after him

Walter, in the year 1285; and

John de Chaundos, *anno* 1289. To whom, I judge, (ſays Mr. Willis) ſucceeded

Stephen; and to him,

Philip, by ſome called Peter; then

David, whoſe ſucceſſor was

Thomas de Glouceſter. He reſigned in 1301, and was followed by one

John, occuring *anno* 1310. After him are found

Simon Brockworthe,

Edward St. John, and

William Cheritone,. Then ſucceeded

William de Penebury, and

Tho: Elinham, who preſided *anno* 1415.

Henry Dean, who preſided here in the time of king Edward the Fourth. He was firſt made biſhop of Bangor, and afterwards, in 1502, archbiſhop of Canterbury.

Edward Foreſt ſucceeding, governed in 1513, and had, it is preſumed, for his ſucceſſor,

Richard Hempſted, whom A. Wood calls Hart. He, with William Nottingham, and twenty-one others, ſubſcribed to the king's ſupremacy, Sep. 2, 1534, and on May 10, 1539, with the like number of monks, ſigned the ſurrender, and had a penſion of 100 *l. per ann.*

This monaſtery was valued at the diſſolution at 748 *l.* 0 *s.* 11½ *d.*; but according to ſir William Dugdale, at 648 *l.* 19 *s.* 11 *d.* At firſt, this was only a cell to the former monaſtery in Monmouthſhire, and was ſo confirmed by king John, who was a conſiderable benefactor to it, and made them large grants of land by charter, confirmed to them 18 E. 2. But king Edward the Fourth, in the twentieth year of his reign, united theſe two monaſteries of Lanthony by his charter, making this near Glouceſter the principal, and obliging theſe monks to maintain only a reſidentiary prior and four canons in the old priory to ſay maſſes, which prior was removable at will; and thus the monaſtery of Lanthony in Monmouthſhire became a cell to this near Glouceſter.

In the year 1553, there remained 20 *l.* 6 *s.* 8 *d.* in annuities, and the following penſions, *viz.* To Will. Henlowe, John Ambros, David Matthew, *alias* Kempe, 8 *l.* each. John Kellom, Will. Worceſter, George Dean, Richard Weſtbury, Will. Abington, Will. Barrington, 6 *l.* each. John Hempſted, Maurice Berkley, Will. Byford, Will. Preſbury, 4 *l.* each. *Willis.*

Many deſcendants of the great family of Bohun, earls of Hereford, and lords of Brecknock, were buried in the church of this monaſtery, *viz.*

Margery

Margery de Bohun, eldeſt daughter of Milo earl of Hereford, and patroneſs of this monaſtery. She was married to the lord Humphry de Bohun, ſteward to king Henry the Firſt, and died in 1187. —Humphry de Bohun, the fourth of that name, (ſon of Margery) and Elianor his wife.—Henry Bohun the Good, earl of Hereford, and Maud his wife, daughter of the earl of Ewe, and Alice her daughter.—Humphry de Bohun, the fifth of that name, who died in 1275, and Maud de Avenbury his wife.—The aſhes of all theſe great perſons, and many more, lie buried in the ruins of Lanthony; and it is to be lamented, that the noble tombs deſigned to preſerve their memory, were ruined and deſtroyed ſoon after the diſſolution. Of the monaſtery itſelf there are very few remains, beſides a large gateway, upon which are the arms of the noble family of the Bohuns, who were great benefactors to the priory.

The ſcite of this monaſtery, and the adjoining lands, were granted to ſir Arthur Porter 32 H. 8. and Thomas Porter had livery of this eſtate 1 Eliz. who dying in the 40th year of that reign, left Arthur Porter, his ſon, then thirty years old, on whom he had ſettled the capital meſſuage or ſcite of the late priory of Lanthony, with lands in Hempſted, as expreſſed in the inquiſition after his death, taken by the king's eſcheator the ſame year. But ſir Robert Atkyns has it, that Thomas Porter left an only daughter, married to ſir John Scudamore, anceſtor to lord viſcount Scudamore, of Ham Lacy in Herefordſhire, who was the proprietor of this eſtate when ſir Robert drew up the account of it. The honourable Charles Howard the younger, in right of his wife Frances Fitzroy Scudamore, is the preſent proprietor of Lanthony, and patron of the vicarage of Hempſted.

This hamlet, at the diſſolution of monaſteries, was exempted from the payment of tithes, as having been the demeſne lands of the priory of Lanthony. But John lord Scudamore, in the year 1662, generouſly annexed all the tithes of Lanthony to the rectory of Hempſted, which was confirmed by act of parliament, and has improved that rectory to a very conſiderable amount.

A ground called Long Madely, and other lands belonging to the priory of Lanthony, were granted to the city of Glouceſter 34 H. 8. Other lands called Madely, belonging to the ſaid priory, were granted, the ſame year, to Thomas Bell.

Richard the prieſt of Hatherleya, about the time of king Henry the Third, gave to the priory of Lanthony by Glouceſter 220 marks, that they ſhould every day give ten loaves, called the loaves of Dudeſtan, to the poor of St. Bartholomew's hoſpital, which were to be of the ſame corn, weight, and quantity as the loaves were which the brethren of the upper hoſpital of Dudeſtan received of them, or ſixpence in lieu thereof.

Anne, widow of Thomas earl of Stafford, and daughter of Thomas of Woodſtock, duke of Glouceſter, by will dated 16 Oct. 17 H. 6. bequeathed 100 marks, and 20*l.* yearly for twenty years, to this church, where ſhe was buried.

For the ſeveral grants and confirmations to this priory, ſee *Appendix*, N°s. 18, 19, 20, 21.

LASBOROUGH.

THIS is a ſmall pariſh, in the hundred of Longtree, in the Coteſwold country, five miles eaſt from Wotton-underedge, five weſt from Tetbury, and nineteen ſouth from Glouceſter. The lands are chiefly in tillage, and produce very good crops of corn.

A ſmall ſtream riſes here, and after joining another from Boxwell, runs down to Berkeley, and afterwards into the Severn.

Leſſeberge, the antient name of this place, ſignifies the *ſmaller camp*, or *fortification*, ſo called in reſpect to ſome larger work in the neighbourhood, which, from its vicinity, I conjecture to be the *Cheſtles*, in the pariſh of Kingſcot, where was a Roman lodgment, upon which this *ſmaller poſt*, or *Leſſe-berge*, depended.

A few years ſince a monumental ſtone was turned up by the plow, in Bowldown-field in this pariſh, with the following inſcription, communicated to me by Mr. James Dallaway, then reſident at Briſtol. There is no date of the year upon the ſtone, but by the two firſt letters, which are to be read *Diis Manibus*, it appears to have been before the eſtabliſhment of chriſtianity in this country, and conſequently is of great antiquity. The three firſt letters of the ſecond line are ſuppoſed to be the initials of the perſon's name, and ICENA denotes her to be one of the people called *Iceni*, who inhabited Norfolk, Suffolk, and Cambridgeſhire. One letter, if not more, is broken off from her age, which might be either XXIIII, XXXIIII, or LXIIII. There were ſeveral ſtones, with inſcriptions of the ſame kind, found at Cirenceſter, as mentioned in the account of that antient place. The memorials are ſuppoſed to be for perſons who died when the Romans were in theſe parts, tho' the time cannot be preciſely determined, for want of dates.

Of the Manor and other Eſtates.

In *Domeſday-book* this manor is thus deſcribed: 'Hugo Maminot holds Leſſeberge in Langetrew hundred of Giſlebert biſhop of Liſiaux. 'Leuuinus held it. There are five hides. In 'demean is one plow-tillage, and five villeins, and 'a prieſt, with two plow-tillages. There are ſeven '*ſervi*. It was worth 10*l.* now 50*s.*' *D.B.*p.73.

The manor antiently belonged to a family that took their name from the place, for William de Laſſeburge died ſeized of it 45 H. 3.

William

William de Dene died ſeized of Laſſebergh, which he held of Hugo le Deſpencer by the ſervice of one knight's fee, 12 E. 2. *Eſcheat.*

John Baſſet had a confirmation of a grant of free warren in Laſſeburge 28 E. 3. and died ſeized of the manor 36 E. 3. John Baſſet, ſon of John, died ſeized of the manor of Laſſeburge, and of the advowſon of the church, 7 R. 2. as did John Baſſet, ſon of the laſt John, 21 R. 2. leaving Margaret, his daughter and heireſs, married to Walter Brown, who, in her right, became ſeized of Laſborough.

Thomas Perry levied a fine of the manor of Laſborough 5 Mariæ, and Thomas, his ſon, had livery granted to him 7 Eliz.

The manor afterwards came to the Eſtcourts. Walter Eſtcourt, eſq; was lord of the manor when ſir Robert Atkyns compiled his account of it. It came next to Thomas Eſtcourt, whoſe only brother, Edmund, ſucceeded him, and left one daughter, Anna-Maria, married to Thomas Earl, of Malmeſbury, eſq; ſince deceaſed; but he bequeathed the bulk of his large fortune to Thomas Eſtcourt, eſq; ſon of Matthew Eſtcourt, of Cam, in this county, who is the preſent lord of this manor, and has a large old houſe here, and a park adjoining, of conſiderable extent, part of which lies in the pariſh of Newington Bagpath.

Lands in this pariſh belonged to St. Catherine's chantry in Campden, and were granted to ſir William Ryder 7 Jac.

Of the Church, &c.

The church is a rectory, in the deanery of Durſley, worth about 60*l.* a year, in the gift of Thomas Eſtcourt, eſq. It is a free chapel, but takes inſtitution from the biſhop of Glouceſter. The chapel and the rector's houſe are incloſed in the park.

Firſt fruits £. 8	0	0	Synodals £. 0	2	0
Tenths — 0	16	0	Pentecoſtals 0	0	6½
Procurations 0	3	4			

Taxes.				
The Royal Aid in 1692,	£. 64	11	4
Poll-tax —— 1694, —	2	15	0
Land-tax —— 1694, —	63	0	0
It is now taxed jointly with Weſton-Birt.			

There are only three houſes in the pariſh.

****

LASSINGTON.

THIS is a ſmall pariſh, in the hundred of Dudſton and King's-barton, eight miles ſouth from Tewkeſbury, eight eaſtward from Newent, and about two miles north-weſtward from Glouceſter.

The pariſh lies on a point of land between the Severn and Leaden, and conſiſts principally of rich meadow and paſture, with ſome very good arable land. Part of the village lies on a riſing ground, on the bank of the Severn, from which ſituation it moſt probably took its name, which in *Domeſday-book* is written *Leſſedune*, and ſignifies the *ſmaller hill*, as it might with propriety be called, in compariſon of *Circeſdune*, on the other ſide of Glouceſter, which then belonged to the ſame proprietor.

On the ſide of the hill, in this pariſh, are found little ſtar ſtones, called *aſtroites*, of a greyiſh colour, and formed by nature of a very curious pentangular ſhape. They are from one to three inches in length, with a ſtar-like appearance at the ends, ſtriated from the center to the circumference. They break uniformly into *lamina*, about the thickneſs of a halfpenny, in a tranſverſe direction, as tho' at ſo many joints, for which reaſon they have been ſuppoſed to be a petrification of ſome marine animal; but the more general opinion is, that they are a ſpecies of coral. When put into vinegar, it is ſaid they have a motion for a conſiderable time; but I don't affirm this from my own knowledge, having never made the experiment.

Part of Laſſington is in the pariſh of St. Mary de Lode, in Glouceſter.

Of the Manor and other Eſtates.

'Ulchetel held Leſſedune in Langebrige hun-'dred, a manor of two hides. Now Roger holds 'it of Thomas the archbiſhop [of York]. This 'eſtate pays tax. In demean is one plow-tillage, 'and five villeins, and two bordars, with three 'plow-tillages. There are three *ſervi*, and twenty 'acres of meadow. It was worth 40*s.* now 30*s.*' *Domeſday-book*, p. 70.

The family of Muchegros, or Muſgroſe, was very antiently ſeized of lands in this pariſh, for it appears from the deeds and evidences belonging to St. Bartholomew's hoſpital in Glouceſter, that Walter de Muchegros gave to the brethren and ſiſters of that hoſpital, two cranocs [eight buſhels] of oats, payable at Michaelmas for ever, out of his barn at Laſſedune. William de Muſegroſe died ſeized of Leſſendun 49 H. 3. John Monemothe died ſeized of Laſſingdon 9 E. 1. according to ſir Robert Atkyns; but in the ſheriff's return of all the vills in this county, the ſame year, it is ſaid, *Laſſingdon, et ejuſd. ville eſt d'na Abbatia de Helyon.* Walter Helvin died ſeized of the manor of Laſſingdon 16 E. 3. John Cooffe, or Coaffe, or Cove, held Laſſington 32 E. 3. and was that year found to be an ideot, and died 36 E. 3. John Pyrie, parſon of Staunton next Cors, Thomas de Beverſtone, and John Godwell, who probably had a claim to the manor in right of their wives, as heirs of Cooffe, had livery granted to them 37 E. 3. and obtained a licence from the king, to grant a third part of the manor of Laſſyndon, with all the lands and appurtenances thereto belonging, and a third part of the advowſon of the church, to the abbey of Glouceſter.

The manor came ſoon afterwards to Thomas Raleigh, who died ſeized thereof 21 R. 2. as did his ſon, Thomas Raleigh, 6 H. 4. and was ſucceeded

ceeded by his ſon, Walter Raleigh, who died 8 H. 5. Edward Bromfleet and Joan his wife, daughter of William Raleigh, levied a fine of the manor of Laſſington to the uſe of themſelves in ſpecial taille, 5 H. 6. William Raleigh, eſq; and Elizabeth his wife, and John Oldney, and Idonea his wife, levied a fine of a moiety of this manor to the uſe of Edward Bromfleet for his life, the remainder to William Raleigh, and his heirs, 28 H. 6.

Sir John Scudemore was ſeized of this manor; but being attainted for treaſon, in the beginning of the reign of Edward the Fourth, the manor came to the crown, and was granted to ſir Richard Herbert, and his heirs males, 4 E. 4. It afterwards belonged to William Whorwood, eſq; lord of the manor of Hawling, who dying 37 H. 8. left two daughters, whereof Anne was married to Ambroſe Dudley, Margaret, the other daughter, was married to Thomas Throgmorton, who, with Margaret his wife, had livery of a moiety of the manor 3 Mariæ.

Edward Cook, of Highnam, eſq; was lord of this manor when ſir Robert Atkyns compiled his account of it, and his family had been for ſome time poſſeſſed of it. William Cook was ſon and heir of Edward, and dying unmarried, was ſucceeded by his brother Dennis, who leaving no male iſſue, the manor came to his two ſiſters. One of them was married to Roynon Jones, eſq; the other to Henry Guiſe, eſq; whoſe ſon, John Guiſe, of Highnam, eſq; purchaſed Mr. Jones's moiety, and is the preſent lord of this manor.

That part of Laſſington which lies in the pariſh of St. Mary de Lode, belonged to the abbey of Glouceſter, by the gift of John Pyrie, &c. as before related, and was granted to the biſhoprick of Glouceſter 33 H. 8. and confirmed 6 E. 6.

Of the Church, &c.

The church is a rectory, in the deanery of Glouceſter, worth about 32 *l.* a year. John Guiſe, eſq; has two turns in the preſentation, and the biſhop of Glouceſter has the third. Mr. Philips is the preſent incumbent.

Eight acres belong to the glebe.

The rectory formerly belonged to St. Auguſtin's abbey, and it now pays 8 *s.* to the dean and chapter of Briſtol. It appears by the viſitation of the archbiſhop of York, in 1618, that this church was a peculiar.

In the taxation of eccleſiaſtical preferments 19 E. 1. it is ſaid, *Porcio prioris S. Oſwaldi in Eccleſ. de Laſſyndon* 8 *s.*

The church is a ſmall building, with a low mean tower at the weſt end.

Firſt fruits	£ 6	10	0	Synodals	£			
Tenths —	0	13	0	Pentecoſtals	0	0	3	
Procurations								

Taxes.				
The Royal Aid in 1692,	£. 35	1	4
Poll-tax —— 1694, —	4	19	0
Land-tax —— 1694, —	25	15	0
The ſame, at 3 *s.* 1770, —	21	5	0

In the year 1562, there were 10 houſholders in this pariſh. When ſir Robert Atkyns compiled his account of it, there were 10 houſes, and about 45 inhabitants, whereof 4 were freeholders; yearly births 1, burials 1. But the preſent number of ſouls is only 33.

The LEA.

ONE part of this place lies in the hundred of St. Briavel's, in Glouceſterſhire, the other part is in Herefordſhire. It is diſtant two miles north from Mitchel-Dean, ſix ſouth from Newent, and twelve weſt from Glouceſter. The church lies about a quarter of a mile on the left hand of the great road from Glouceſter to Hereford.

Of the Manor and other Eſtates.

'The biſhop of Conſtance holds Lega, in 'Letberge hundred, and Robert holds it of him. 'Algar held it in the time of king Edward. There 'is one hide taxed, and two plow-tillages in 'demean, and three bordars, and two *ſervi*, with 'one plow-tillage. It is worth and was worth '20 *s.*' *Domeſday-book*, p. 71.

Richard Talbot had a grant of the manor of Lea, (or Leigh, as it is ſometimes called) with a weekly market on Wedneſday, and a yearly fair on St. Bartholomew's day, 21 E. 3. Richard Talbot, of Caſtle Richard, died ſeized of the manor 43 E. 3. as did ſir Gilbert Talbot 20 R. 2. John Talbot, the great earl of Shrewſbury, held it at his death 31 H. 6. and was ſucceeded in this eſtate by his ſon, John Talbot, ſecond earl of Shrewſbury, who was ſlain at the battle of Northampton 38 H. 6.

John Throckmorton died ſeized of this eſtate 13 E 4. and Philip Throckmorton died 5 H. 8. ſeized of 30 meſſuages, and land in Lea, of which William Throckmorton, his ſon, had livery the ſame year. Richard Hameline was lord of this manor in 1608. Maynard Colcheſter, eſq; was lord of it at the beginning of this century, and Maynard Colcheſter, of Weſtbury, eſq; a deſcendant from him, is the preſent proprietor.

Thomas de Bruge and Elizabeth his wife levied a fine of lands in Lea, and in the bailiwick of Dean, to the uſe of themſelves in ſpecial taille, the remainder to Richard Curle, 5 R. 2.

Of the Church, &c.

The church is a curacy, in the Foreſt deanery, annexed to Linton in Herefordſhire. The ſmall tithes only belong to the curate. It has been augmented with the queen's bounty. Mr. Weſtphaling is patron. The biſhop of Hereford has the impropriation.

The church is dedicated to St. John Baptiſt. It is a handſome building, with a double roof, ſupported by pillars in the middle. It has a

 handſome

handſome ſpire at the weſt end, and a ſmall chancel by the ſide of the greater.

Proc. & Syn. 6*d*. Pentecoſt. 1*s*. 4*d*.

Taxes.					
The Royal Aid in	1692,	£.	22	10	0
Poll-tax ——	1694,	—	3	16	0
Land-tax ——	1694,	—	26	14	0
The ſame, at 3*s*.	1770,	—	12	1	6

In that part of Lea which lies in this county, there were 20 houſes, and about 80 inhabitants, whereof 3 were freeholders, at the beginning of the preſent century; yearly births 2, burials 2. *Atkyns*. There are now about 96 inhabitants.

LEACHLADE.

THIS pariſh lies in the hundred of Britwell's-barrow, ſix miles diſtant weſt from Farringdon in Berkſhire, about nine ſouth from Burford in Oxfordſhire, twelve eaſt from Cirenceſter, and twenty-nine, thro' the laſt-mentioned town, from the city of Glouceſter.

It conſiſts of rich meadow and paſture-ground, with ſome arable land. There is a ſmall market-town of its own name, ſeated within it, whoſe market on the Tueſday is at preſent but little frequented.

The river Thames waters it on the ſouth and eaſt ſides, and divides it from Wiltſhire and Berkſhire. The *Lech* alſo, one of the little rivers from the Coteſwold country, directs its courſe thro' the north ſide of the pariſh, which takes the one half of its name from that river, and the other from the old Saxon word, labian, *to empty*, becauſe here the *Lech* empties itſelf into the *Thames*.

The laſt-mentioned river is navigable at this place for barges of forty or fifty tons burthen, but the want of water one part of the year, and long continued floods at other times, render the navigation extremely uncertain, and notwithſtanding it leads to the metropolis, 'tis not ſo beneficial to the town as might be ſuppoſed, becauſe it cannot be depended on for the general conveyance.

The junction of this river with the Severn has been long talked of, but the execution of that project, on a good plan, is rather to be wiſhed than expected. A late application to parliament on behalf of the Stroud-water canal, brought this ſcheme anew into contemplation, and the country was ſlightly ſurveyed in the year 1775, in order to extend the canal from Sroud to Cricklade, where the Thames is firſt navigable; but what purpoſe can ſuch a junction anſwer, unleſs the navigation of that river were improved?

The great road from London to Cirenceſter, and other places weſtward in that line, leads through the town of Leachlade, and is very much travelled. That part of it which was formerly obſtructed by floods, about a mile eaſtward of the town, is now ſo much raiſed and improved, that travellers may paſs commodiouſly at any time. Mr. Buſching, in his Geography, pretends to have found traces of a Roman way from this town to Cirenceſter, but I am convinced that none but himſelf ever dreamt of any ſuch thing. The Roman road, which was the great one in uſe for about a thouſand years after the Romans left Britain, from the weſt of Glouceſterſhire, and part of South-Wales to London, led through Cirenceſter, and Cricklade, and ſo to Wallingford; and it was not 'till after king Henry V. built a bridge at Abingdon, and the roads were greatly repaired thereabout, that this through Leachlade was much frequented; and then the towns of Cricklade and Wallingford, which before drew great advantages from travelling, began to decline.

Here are two fairs in the year, one on the 10th of Auguſt, for horſes and other cattle; the other on the 9th of September, chiefly for cheeſe, and great quantities are brought hither, but nothing like ſo much as formerly. The latter is held in a meadow, near the bridge which belonged to a ſmall priory in this place, dedicated to St. John, wherefore 'tis called *St. John's-bridge fair*; and the bridge, which ſtands over the Thames, is repaired by the lands formerly belonging to the priory.

This priory was founded by Richard earl of Cornwall and Senchia his wife, and confirmed by king Henry III. who gave to the brethren there the hermitage of Lovebury, in the foreſt of Whichwoode, on condition that they ſhould provide a chaplain to celebrate maſs daily in the ſaid hermitage. It was dedicated to St. John Baptiſt. King Edward IV. in the 12th year of his reign, granted the patronage and advowſon of it to his mother Cicely, dutcheſs of York, with licence to change it into a chantry of three perpetual chaplains, to celebrate divine offices daily at the altar of our lady, in the church of Lechelade, who ſhould be a body corporate, and have power to purchaſe land, and have a common ſeal. By the ſame deed, the king granted liberty to John Twynnihoo of Cirenceſter, to found another chantry at the altar of St. Blaſe, in the ſame church, for one perpetual chaplain, to whom the fore-mentioned three were allowed to grant a yearly rent of ten marks. In the reign of king Henry the Seventh, Underwood, dean of Wallingford, procured two of the three prieſts to be removed thither. John Lece, the laſt incumbent of Blaiſe chantry, had a penſion of 5*l*. in the year 1553.

Of the Manor and other Eſtates.

The following particulars are extracted from the public records:

'Henry de Fereres holds Lecelade in Brictuoldeſ-'berg hundred. Siward a baron held it. There 'were fifteen hides, which paid tax in the time 'of king Edward, but that king granted that ſix 'hides ſhould be quit from tax, as all the county 'witneſſeth, and he that keeps the ſeal. There

are

'are four plow-tillages in demean, and twenty-'nine villeins, and ten bordars, and one ftranger 'holds the land of one villein. They have among 'them all fixteen plow-tillages. There are thir-'teen *fervi*, and three mills of 30*s*. and a fifhery 'of one hundred and feventy-five eels; from the 'meadows 7*l*. 7*s*. befides hay for the cattle. In 'Wicelcumbe two burgages pay 16*d*. and one in 'Gloucefter without affeffment. In the time of 'king Edward the whole manor was worth 20*l*. 'and fo it is now likewife.' *Domefday-book*, p. 77.

In our antient books is the following fabulous account of the defcent of Siward. The daughter and heirefs of a great earl, of the royal blood of Denmark, walking in a wild foreft, was ravifhed by a bear, and bore a fon with ears like a bear. This fon of a bear fucceeded his mother in the earldom, and was father of Siward, who quits Denmark, and arrives in England, where he is kindly received by king Edward the Confeffor; and upon a quarrel with Tofti earl of Huntingdon, he flew him, and carried his head to the king, who in reward gave him the earldom of Huntingdon and Northumberland, and made him governor of the northern counties, which were much infefted by the Danes.

The above Henry de Fereres, or de Ferrariis, was fon of Guicheline de Ferriers in Normandy. His chief feat was at Tutbury in Staffordfhire. He was fucceeded by his fon Robert de Ferrers, who was created earl of Derby 3 Steph. and died the year following, leaving Robert his fon and heir. William de Ferrers, fon and heir to the laft Robert, married Margaret, daughter and heir of William Peverel of Nottingham, by whom he had two fons; Robert, the eldeft, who fucceeded him in the earldom of Derby, and Walcheline, his younger fon, who had the manor of Leachlade. Hugh Ferrers, his fon and heir, dying without iffue, left Ifabel his fifter and heir, married to Roger Mortimer, progenitot of the earls of March, and grandfon of Ralph de Mortimer, who came in with William the Conqueror, and behaved with great courage in the battle of Haftings. She doing her fealty, had livery of the manor of Leachlade 6 John. It is probable that fhe was married a fecond time to Peter Fitzherbert, for he obtained[z] a licence to erect a gate on the caufeway at Leachlade-bridge, *com. Glouc.* before the hofpital there founded by him; and dying 19 H. 3. Ifabella his wife had livery[a] of the lands of her inheritance, particularly of the manor of Leachlade. She is faid to have founded a nunnery at Leachlade, but of that houfe I find no farther particulars.

This manor came to the crown, and was granted by the king to his brother Richard earl of Cornwall, king of the Romans, and to Senchia his wife, and the heirs of their bodies, 36 H. 3.

Edmund earl of Cornwall, fon of Richard, was feized of it 4 & 15 E. 1. and dying 28 E. 1. without iffue, the manor of Leachlade reverted to the crown, and was granted, by king Edward the Firft, to Richard Talbot the younger, and Elizabeth his wife; which Richard was fon of Richard Talbot, who had married Joan, one of the daughters and coheirs of Hugh de Mortimer.

But upon the revolution of public affairs, in the turbulent reign of king Edward II. this manor was granted to Hugh le Difpencer the younger, who being foon after attainted and executed, it was again granted, 1 E. 3. to Edmond of Woodftock, earl of Kent, fecond fon of king Edward the Firft; and he being attainted and executed at Winchefter 4 E. 3. the manor was granted to Jeffry de Mortimer, and the heirs of his body, the remainder to Roger Mortimer and his heirs.

John earl of Kent, fon of Edmond, being reftored, died feized of this manor 26 E. 3. But Elizabeth, the widow of John earl of Kent, and daughter of the duke of Juliers, held this manor in dower, and had a confirmation of fairs and markets in Leachlade 18 & 22 R. 2. and died feized of this eftate the 10th, or according to fome accounts 12 H. 4.

After her death, the manor of Leachlade defcended to her hufband's heir, who was Edmond Mortimer, earl of March, fon of Elianor Holland, fifter and heir to John the laft earl of Kent, by her hufband Roger Mortimer, earl of March. Edmond Mortimer, earl of March, died feized of the manor of Leachlade 3 H. 6. leaving Joan, one of his fifters and coheirs, then the widow of fir John Grey, who died feized of it, and of the advowfon of the church 4 H. 6. This manor was granted to Cicely dutchefs of York, for life, 38 H. 6. and again confirmed 1 E. 4. She died 10 H. 7.

The manor and town of Leachlade were afterwards made part of the dower of Catherine, queen to king Henry the Eighth; and after her death, they were granted to Dennis Toppes and Dorothy his wife 4 E. 6. in exchange for the manor of Rockholts, and other manors in Norfolk, referving a rent of 27*l*. 4*s*. 3*d*. to the crown.

The manor and town of Leachlade were granted to Robert Bathurft, efq; 4 Jac. Robert Bathurft, fon of Robert, died under age, feized thereof 3 C. and left Edward Bathurft his brother and heir, thirteen years old. Edward Dadge, efq; was feized of this manor, (by what means I cannot learn) and gave it to fir Edward Bathurft, baronet, who died feized thereof in 1674. He was a perfon of great loyalty to king Charles the Firft, and paid a compofition of 720*l*. for his fequeftered eftate. Lawrence Bathurft, efq; fon of fir Edward, died in 1670, and left two daughters coheireffes; one married to Mr. Coxeter, the other to Mr. John Greening, whofe defcendants fold the manor in moieties to different perfons, and it paffed, fo divided, to fir Jacob Wheate, baronet, and Mr. Pullen, who were lords of the manor in the year 1774, when fir Jacob purchafing Mr. Pullen's moiety, became the fole proprietor. His arms are *Vert, a fefs dancetty Or, in chief three garbs of the fecond. In a canton the arms of Ulfter.*

The

[z] Cart. 12 H. 3. m. 2.

[a] Cart. 25 H. 3. m. 2.

The records ſhew that Thomas de Cliene purchaſed lands in Lechelade of Robert de Clinterton and Emme his wife, 20 H. 3. Robert Hayſheet and Petronella his wife levied a fine of lands in Lechelade to the uſe of Robert de Bradneſton and Alice his wife 51 H. 3. John de Waſre and Iſabel his wife levied a fine of lands in Lechelade to the uſe of Simon Withers 52 H. 3. The abbey of Hayles was ſeized of lands in Lechelade 29 E. 1. and Adam le Hunt granted two meſſuages here to that abbey 13 E. 2. Robert de Franklin held one meſſuage, one water-mill, and one yardland 10 E. 2.

The farm called the Priory, which formerly belonged to the college of Wallingford, was granted to Dennis Toppes 14 Eliz. and the lands formerly belonging to the priory of St. John in this place, were granted to Thomas Toppes 20 Eliz.

Mr. Charles Loder, Mr. Robert Loder, and Mr. Richard Ainge, have good houſes in the town of Leachlade, and good eſtates; and Mr. Day has a good eſtate at Clay-Hill, which he purchaſed of the Bathurſt family. The arms of Day and Ainge are emblazoned p. 366; thoſe of Loder are, *Or, ſix annulets ſable.*

Of the Church, &c.

The church is a vicarage, in the deanery of Fairford, worth about 300*l.* a year. Sir Jacob Wheate is patron; Mr. Wheate is the preſent incumbent. The patronage and impropriation formerly belonged to the priory of St. John Baptiſt in this place.

Lawrence Bathurſt, eſq; ſon of ſir Edward Bathurſt, endowed the vicarage with the tithes of his whole eſtate, by his will dated Sept. 16, 1670, which hath improved the vicarage above 150*l.* a year. There is no glebe.

The church is dedicated to St. Lawrence. It is large and handſome, with double ailes, ſupported by two rows of fluted pillars, and has a handſome ſpire, with five bells. It was new built, with the aſſiſtance of the priory and inhabitants, by Conrade Ney, who was vicar in the reign of king Henry the Seventh.

There was a priory or hoſpital, and ſeveral chantries here, of which ſome account has been already given.

Firſt fruits £	12	13	3½	Synodals £.	0	2	0
Tenths —	1	5	4	Pentecoſt.	0	1	6
Procurations	0	6	8				

Monuments and Inſcriptions.

On a handſome marble monument in the chancel,

Near this place lie the Remains of Mrs Anne Simons, whoſe Life compleated the true Character of the Gentlewoman, the Friend, and the Chriſtian. She was ſincere in her Friendſhip, affable and candid in her Converſation, pious in her Devotion, liberal and ſecret in her Charity. Her acquaintance have loſt a real Friend, the Poor a daily and conſtant Benefactreſs. She lived to a good old Age, and tho' ſhe declined gradually thro' the Weakneſs and Infirmity of Body, yet ſhe retained a chearful Temper and Vivacity of Spirits to the laſt. *She is gone to receive the Reward of her Virtue, and has left her Friends to imitate her Example.* She died the 24th of September 1769, aged 76.——Arms, in a lozenge, *Or, a bend ingrailed vert, between two roſes gules.*

Within the communion rails is a memorial for ſir Edward Bathurſt, baronet, with his arms, impaling *a chevron between three greyhounds courant,* ſuppoſed for his ſecond wife, whoſe name was Morris. There are alſo memorials for ſeveral other perſons of his family; and for ſeveral of the Coxeters, (deſcended in the female line from Lawrence Bathurſt, eſq;) with their arms, *Argent, a chevron between three fighting cocks heads erazed, gules.* As alſo for the Bamptons, with their arms, *Checky, on a chief three garbs.*

Benefactions.

In 1586, Nicholas Rainton, gent. gave 4*l.* a year to repair the church. In 1599, Edward Dadge, eſq; by his will, gave 5*l.* a year to the poor. In 1602, William Blomer, eſq; and his heirs, &c. were compelled by law, to deliver to the vicar and church-wardens, five buſhels of wheat, and five of barley, given by two maiden ſiſters, for the uſe of the poor for ever, out of the profits of Dolemead. In 1703, Mr. Richard Wellman gave 10*s.* a year out of Pidgeon-houſe cloſe, to be given to the poor in bread. In 1720, Francis Loder, gent. gave the intereſt of 100*l.* to orphans or widows, natives of the pariſh. In 1721, Robert Loder, gent. gave 20*s.* a year in bread to the poor. In 1725, Mr. Richard Ainge gave 20*s.* a year to be diſpoſed of in like manner. Mrs. Simons, by her will, gave the intereſt of 200*l.* to the poor. Mrs. Loder has alſo given the intereſt of a conſiderable ſum to widows and orphans. And ſeveral pious perſons have given plate, &c. for the communion table, and a branch for the church.

Taxes.	The Royal Aid in 1692,	£.	221	11	2
	Poll-tax — — 1694,	—	81	8	0
	Land-tax — 1694,	—	438	3	9½
	The ſame at 3*s.* 1770,	—	326	5	6¾

At the beginning of this century, there were 157 houſes, and about 500 inhabitants in this pariſh, whereof 35 were freeholders; yearly births 15, burials 12. *Atkyns.* There are now 925 inhabitants.

LECHAMPTON.

THIS pariſh lies in the hundred of Cheltenham, three miles diſtant ſouth from the town of that name, twelve north-weſtward from Cirenceſter, and eight eaſtward from Glouceſter.

About half the pariſh lies in dairy farms, in the vale of Glouceſter, the other part ſtretches eaſtward over a ſtupendous ridge of hills, whence there is a large proſpect over the vale and the river Severn, above and below the city of Glouceſter. It probably takes the former part of its name from the vaſt rock of ſtone, on the brow of the hill, for *Lech*, in the Britiſh language, ſignifies *ſtone*; and ſerves to diſtinguiſh this pariſh from ſeveral other places of the name of Hampton, in Glouceſterſhire.

Of

Of the Manor and other Eſtates.

'William Leuric holds Lechantone in Chilteham 'hundred of the king. Oſgot held it in the time 'of king Edward. There are three hides taxed. 'In demean are two plow-tillages, and two villeins, 'and eight bordars with one plow-tillage. There 'are four *ſervi*, a wood one furlong long, and one 'broad. It is worth and was worth 40*s*.' *D. B.* p. 74.

But there was then another manor, according to the record.

'Brictric holds four hides in Lechametone in 'Chiltenham hundred of the king, and pays tax. 'He held two hides, and Ordric held the other 'two in the time of king Edward. King William, 'as he was going into Normandy, granted both 'eſtates to Brictric. He has one plow-tillage in 'demean, and nine bordars, with three plow-'tillages, and two *ſervi*, and one *ancill.* There 'is a wood half a mile long, and half a mile broad. 'It is worth 30*s*.' *Domeſday-book*, p. 79.

Adam le Diſpencer, ſon of Triſtram, was ſeized of this manor, and had a grant of fairs, markets, and free warren 37 H. 3. which he pleaded in a *Quo warranto* brought againſt him 15 E. 1. and his plea was allowed. The ſame grant was alſo allowed 16 Jac. and the original is now in the cuſtody of Mr. Norwood, the preſent poſſeſſor of this manor.

This manor was held by grand ſerjeanty of the king, by performing the ſervice of ſteward at the great feſtivals of Chriſtmas, Eaſter, and Whitſuntide, as appears by a record 23 E. 1. Walter de Munemuth held it 30 E. 1. and John Limell died ſeized of it, and of the advowſon of the church, 2 E. 2.

It ſoon after came to the Giffards, for ſir John Giffard died ſeized of it 3 E. 3. and it continued ſeveral generations in that name and family; but after the death of John Giffard, the laſt heir male, this manor paſſed by the marriage of Elianor, one of his daughters and coheirs, to [b] John Norwood, in whoſe family it has continued ever ſince, and Henry Norwood, eſq; is the preſent lord of the manor of Lechampton. His arms are, *Ermine, a croſs ingrailed gules.*

Robert Preſbury held lands in Lechampton 18 E. 2. Sir John Berkeley was ſeized of ſeventy acres of land in this place, held of the manor of Cheltenham 6 H. 6. as was ſir Maurice Berkeley of Beverſtone 38 & 39 H. 6. and 14 E. 4. William Golding and Joan his wife levied a fine of lands in Lechampton to the uſe of themſelves for life, the remainder to William Panton and to Joan his wife, daughter of William Golding.

Of the Church, &c.

The church is a rectory, in the deanery of Winchcombe, worth about 140*l*. a year. Mr. Norwood is patron, and Mr. Draper the preſent incumbent. The advowſon, and one of the manors

[b] This family is deſcended from the Norwoods of Kent. Jordan Norwood, of the iſle of Shepey, flouriſhed in the reign of king Henry the Second, and lies buried in Minſter church, with many of his poſterity, and his monument is ſtill remaining. He was ſeized of the manor of Northwood, to which one hundred burgeſſes of the city of Canterbury owed ſuit and ſervice in the reign of king Edward the Confeſſor.

Stephen Norwood, ſon of John, reſided near Shepey, at Norwood-Chaſtners, ſo called from the abundance of cheſnut trees growing there.

Sir Roger de Norwood, ſon of Stephen, was ſeized of the manor of Shorne in Kent, 54 H. 3. He diſdaining to hold his lands by the lazy tenure of *Gavelkind*, changed it for the more active one of knight's-ſervice, in the 14th year of king Henry the Third. He married Bonafilia, ſiſter and heir of John de Wantham of Shorn, with whom he had that manor, and dying 13 E. 1. was ſucceeded by his ſon and heir ſir John de Norwood, who married Joan, ſiſter and heireſs to Giles lord Badleſmere. He was high ſheriff of Kent 20, 21, 23, 24, & 28 E. 1. and was ſummoned to parliament in ſeveral years of that reign, particularly in the 22d, and 6 & 9 E. 2.

His ſon, ſir John de Norwood, married Agnes, daughter and coheireſs of William Grantſon, deſcended from William de Grantſon, who had married Sibele, daughter and coheireſs of John lord Tregoz; which John died 12 E. 2.

Sir Roger Norwood, ſon of the laſt ſir John, married Julian, the daughter, or ſiſter, of Geffrid lord Say. He was one of the conſervators of the peace for the county of Kent 34 E. 3. Sir John de Norwood, eldeſt ſon of this Roger, married Joan, daughter and one of the coheireſſes of Robert Hert, of Feverſham, eſq. His name occurs in the ſummons to parliament 43 & 47 E. 3. but not the name of Roger, as mentioned by ſir Robert Atkyns.

William de Norwood, ſecond ſon of ſir John, ſucceeded his father, Roger, his elder brother, dying unmarried. John de Norwood was ſon and heir of William, and died without iſſue. James de Norwood, next brother to the laſt William, and third ſon of the laſt ſir John, married Margaret, daughter and coheireſs of Robert Gralle, of Gralle in the county of Suffolk, by whom he had iſſue John de Norwood, eſq; who married Margaret, daughter of John Martin, eſq.

James de Norwood, his ſon and heir, married Jane Clinton, as appears upon her tomb in the church of Milton. His ſon and heir, John de Norwood, eſq; was lieutenant of the Tower of London, and conſtable of Queenborough. By Elizabeth his wife, daughter and coheireſs of Miles of Elton, ſon of ſir John of Elton, he had the manor of Gilling; and dying 4 H. 7. lies buried at Milton. John de Norwood, eſq; married Elizabeth, daughter and coheireſs of Thomas Fragenhall, eſq. He died 12 H. 7. leaving only three daughters.

John Norwood, couſin and heir male of the laſt John, married Elianor, daughter and coheireſs of John Giffard, with whom he had the manor of Lechampton, and died in 1509.

Roger Norwood of Lechampton, ſon of John, married Alice, daughter of ſir John Butler of Badminton. Ralph Norwood, ſon of Roger, married Jane Knight of Shrewſbury. Henry Norwood, ſon of Ralph, married Catherine, daughter of ſir Robert Throgmorton, of Coughton in Warwickſhire. William Norwood, ſon of Henry, married Elizabeth, daughter of William Ligon, of Madersfield in Worceſterſhire. Richard Norwood, ſon of William, married Elizabeth, daughter of Nicholas Steward, LL. D. and died without iſſue. Francis Norwood, his brother, and ſecond ſon of William, married Judith, daughter of Timothy Gates, rector of Cleeve. He died in 1682.

Henry Norwood, ſon of a younger brother of Richard, purchaſed Lechampton of Francis; and having diſtinguiſhed himſelf for his loyalty in the civil wars, was made governor of Tangier by king Charles the Second, and ſerved in parliament for the city of Glouceſter. This colonel Henry Norwood underwent great variety of fortune. He was one of the company, in a voyage, who were reduced to the laſt extremity for want of victuals. They caſt lots to determine which of them ſhould be killed to be a morſel for the reſt, and he on whom the lot fell was directed to go into the hold of the ſhip to prepare himſelf. Their ravenous hunger compelled them to follow him in a ſhort time, where they found him dead; and notwithſtanding the accident, they greedily fell to, and made a hearty meal of the carcaſe. The remains were buried handſomely.

Colonel Norwood died in 1689, and by will returned the eſtate to the family of Francis Norwood. Richard Norwood, William, and Thomas, ſons of Francis. ſucceeded to it in order, and the reverend Thomas Norwood, eighth ſon of Francis, was the owner of Lechampton at the beginning of this century. Charles Norwood poſſeſſed it afterwards, and Henry Norwood, eſq; is the preſent lord of the manor.

By this pedigree it appears, that the family of the Norwoods have a right to quarter the ſeveral coats of arms of Tregoz, Wantham, Badleſmere, Grandiſon, Hert, Gralle, Elton, and Giffard.

formerly belonged to the abbey of Fiſchamp in Normandy; and a portion of tithes in Lechampton, formerly belonging to the nunnery of Uſk in Monmouthſhire, was granted to John Fernham 22 Eliz. which tithes, worth 3 *l.* a year, now belong to the impropriator of Cheltenham. Mr. Norwood has the tithes of one tithing, worth 10 *l.* a year.

Ten acres of paſture, and ſome arable, belong to the glebe.

The church hath a handſome ſpire, with ſix bells, in the middle, and an aile on the ſouth ſide, the eaſt end of which aile is the burying-place of the lord of the manor.

Firſt fruits £.	18	13	4	Synodals £.	0	2	0
Tenths —	1	17	4	Pentecoſtals	0	0	6
Procurations	0	6	8				

Monuments and Inſcriptions.

There is a raiſed tomb under the arch between the nave and the aile, upon which are the figures in ſtone of a man and woman lying along. The man is in armour, with a large ſhield over his left arm, is girt with a ſword, and has ſpurs on, his feet reſting on a lion. Theſe figures are ſuppoſed to repreſent ſome of the Giffards, who were lords of the manor. The woman's dreſs is about the age of Henry the Fourth.

Upon a braſs plate againſt the wall, is the following memorial:

ELIZABETHA NORWOOD, VXOR GVLIELMI NORWOOD ARMIGERI, CVI PEPERIT NOVEM FILIOS FILIAS DVAS. ANNOS NATA 50: APRILIS 16, ANO DNI 1598. PIE ET FELICITER EXPIRAVIT IN CHRISTO.

Scilicet undena vixi quæ prole beata,
Uno non potui funere tota mori.
Liberior totum mihi vita excurrit in orbem,
Cœlum anima teneo, poſteritate ſolum.
Si tellure poloq; fruar diviſa, neceſſe eſt
Dufunctum nullo me periiſſe loco.

Arms, In a ſhield, 1. Norwood, impaling 2. Liggon.

Againſt the eaſt wall,

M. S.

Franciſci Norwood, Armigeri, ex antiquâ in agro Cantiano familiâ oriundi, cujus Majores conjugiis aliiſq; contractibus hic ſedem fixerunt. Ille cum ſola et chariſſima conjuge Iuditha, Annos 38 conjugales implevit; ex qua novem filios et totidem filias ſuſcepit, quorum 16 ad maturitatem perduxit, et patrimoniis amplis honeſtavit. Tandem annorum et vitæ ſatur, cum 42 Annos Dominus hujus Manerii, ſummo cum vicinorum amore, vixit, eorum deſiderio et luctu obijt Martij 8, Anno Ætatis 82, Domini 1682.

There are other memorials for the Norwoods, and one for Robert Jones, rector of the pariſh, but they contain nothing intereſting.

Taxes.					
The Royal Aid in	1692,	£. 84	14	0
Poll-tax ——	1694, —	17	18	0
Land-tax ——	1694, —	96	8	0
The ſame at 3 *s.*	1770, —	70	13	0

At the beginning of this century, there were 30 houſes, and about 120 inhabitants in this pariſh, whereof 5 were freeholders; yearly births 4, burials 3. *Atkyns.* There are now 142 inhabitants.

The LEIGH, *or* LYE,

IS a ſmall pariſh in the vale of Glouceſter, lying partly in the hundred of Derhurſt, and partly in the lower diviſion of that of Weſtminſter. It is ſix miles diſtant weſtward from Cheltenham, four ſouth from Tewkeſbury, and ſix north from Glouceſter.

It is ſituated in a flat country, very ſubject to floods from the Severn, particularly a large tract of rich paſture ground, which lies in common between the inhabitants of this pariſh and thoſe of Derhurſt. A few years ago the people of the Lye dug a large trench acroſs that common, to divide their part from Derhurſt; but they were obliged, by a ſuit at law, to open the communication again.

The name is written *Lalege* in the antient record, with the prepoſitive article, after the Norman manner; and *Lege*, properly ſignifies the *place*[c]. It was uſual with our Saxon anceſtors to give this name to a ſeat or capital manſion, which later generations have converted into *lye*. But *ley*, and *lay* ſometimes ſignify alſo a paſture ground. Perhaps the prior of St Dennis, or ſome other perſon of eminence, had a ſeat here in early times, called *La lege*, which afterwards gave name to the whole pariſh.

This place is remarkable for nothing in natural hiſtory, but for a large quantity of dwarf elder growing here.

Of the Manor and other Eſtates.

'The church of St. Dennis of Paris holds one 'hide in Lalege, in Derheſt hundred.' *D. B.* p. 72.

Gilbert de Kynerdeſley granted the manor of Lye, with all his lands in Staverton, Heydon, Hawe, and Turley, to Joan de Rodborough, lady of Notgrove, 7 E. 3. William de Redbeargh held Lye, and two meſſuages, and two plow-tillages in Lye and Heydon 3 R. 2. John de Redbearghe died ſeized of the manor of Lye 7 R. 2. as did John Browning 3 H. 5. to whom ſucceeded Richard Browning, who dying without iſſue, Cicely Browning was his ſiſter and heir: She was married to ſir Guy Whitington, who, in her right, had Notgrove, Lye, and Rodborough. Richard Whitington, ſecond ſon of ſir Guy, by Cicely his wife, had this manor ſettled on him. Thomas Whitington, eſq; who married Margery, daughter of William Needham, died ſeized of the manor of Leigh, 38 H. 8. and left ſix daughters coheireſſes, by which means it went out of this name.

Richard Brown, eſq; died ſeized of this manor 15 Eliz. and Thomas Brown, his grandſon and heir, had livery granted him 17 Eliz. William Riddale, eſq; was lord of it in the year 1608.

Lord Tracy afterwards purchaſed this manor, and ſold it to Stephen Cook, eſq; to whom ſuc-

[c] Recentiores verterunt *lege*, quod *locum* latine ſignificat, in *le* & *ley*. Leland's Itin. v. 9, p. 68. Comment. in Cygneam Cantionem.

ceeded

ceeded Thomas Cook, who dying unmarried, bequeathed his eftate to his fifter, wife of —— Dalton, efq; by whom fhe had one daughter, married to Edmund Probyn, of Newland, in this county, efq; who, in her right, is the prefent lord of this manor.

HAMLET. *Evington* is a hamlet in this parifh, but it lies in the lower divifion of Weftminfter hundred, of which manor the late right honourable William Dowdefwell, efq; died feized in the year 1775. Half the mill-houfe is in this hamlet, and the other part in the parifh of Bodington.

Lands in this parifh formerly belonging to the White Friers in Gloucefter, were granted to Thomas Bell 36 H. 8. And tithes in Lye antiently belonging to the priory of Derhurft, and afterwards to the abbey of Tewkefbury, were granted to Richard Pate 16 Eliz.

Of the Church, &c.

The church is a vicarage, within the peculiar of Derhurft, worth about 60*l.* a year. The lord chancellor is patron, and Mr. John Chefter the prefent incumbent.

The impropriation belonged to the priory of Derhurft in 1379, and is now vefted in *Corpus Chrifti* college in Oxford. It pays 11*l.* 10*s.* yearly to the crown.

The church is fmall, with a fmall crofs aile on the fouth fide, and a low embattled tower at the weft end. It is dedicated to St. James, according to bifhop Benfon's book.

Firft fruits	£.7	16	3	Synodals £.0	2	0
Tenths —	0	15	$7\frac{1}{2}$	Pentecoftals 0	0	$5\frac{1}{2}$
Procurations	0	6	8			

Benefactions.

Mrs. Loach, widow, gave 20*s.* yearly to the poor, and a tenement and fome land are given to the fame ufe. But there are lands in this parifh worth 70*l.* a year, vefted in C. C. C. Oxford, for the maintenance of a free fchool, and other charitable ufes, in Cheltenham, as fpecified under that parifh.

Taxes.					
The Royal Aid in	1692,	£. 33	11	0
Poll-tax —	1694, —	2	1	0
Land-tax —	1694, —	37	12	0
The fame at 3*s.*	1770, —	28	16	$1\frac{1}{2}$

At the beginning of this century, there were 40 houfes in this parifh, and about 160 inhabitants, whereof 10 were freeholders; yearly births 3, burials 3. *Atkyns.* The inhabitants are now increafed to about 245.

****

LEMINGTON

IS a fmall parifh, in the upper divifion of the hundred of Tewkefbury, five miles diftant fouth-eaft from Campden, five fouth-weft from Shipfton upon Stoure in Worcefterfhire, and thirty-three north-eaft from Gloucefter.

The greater part is pafture, with a confiderable tract of ground in common, over-grown with furze, fern, and hawthorn bufhes, and capable of great improvement.

The parifh lies on the verge or extreme limit of the county, next to Oxfordfhire, wherefore, like the town of the fame name in Hampfhire, it was antiently called *Limentone*, and fince altered to *Lemington*, from *Limes*, a *boundary*; but it has another title to its name, on account of the great Roman *Fofs-way* entering Gloucefterfhire at this place, for the fame Latin word fignifies alfo a *great broad way*. It is called Lower Lemington, to diftinguifh it from Lemington, a hamlet in the parifh of Toddenham. Before Mr. Camden's time, many Roman coins were plowed up here, and fome have been found fince, for which reafon it is thought that the Romans had a fmall poft or ftation at this place.

Of the Manor and other Eftates.

The church of Tewkefbury held twenty-four hides of land in Gloucefterfhire, which were taxed only as twenty, in the time of king Edward the Confeffor, of which eftate the record fhews, that 'There were three hides in Limentone. There 'were two plow-tillages, and eight villeins, with 'four plow-tillages, and fix *fervi*, and one bordar. 'It was worth 60*s.* now 40*s.*' *Dom. Book*, p. 68.

The abbey of Tewkefbury had court leet, waifs, and felons goods in Lemington, by the grant of king William the Second, which were allowed 15 E. 1. And the abbey continued in poffeffion of this manor 'till that houfe was diffolved. The manor was afterwards granted to Ambrofe Smith 18 Eliz. and paffed to fir William Juxton, who was lord of it at the beginning of this century. Lady Fane, who was the relict of fir William Juxton, and afterwards married to lord vifcount Fane, is the prefent lady of this manor.

Of the Church, &c.

The church is a curacy, in the deanery of Campden, value 10*l.* from the impropriation, befides the income of about fourteen acres of land, purchafed with queen Anne's bounty, and other money, raifed in 1737, to augment the living. The impropriation belongs to lady Fane, who is patronefs of the curacy, and Mr. Baker is the prefent incumbent. It was formerly reputed a rectory, worth 50*l.* a year. The church is fmall.

Pentecoftals - - - - - 6*d.*

Monument and Infcription.

On a plate of brafs, fixed to a blue ftone in the chancel, is the following memorial:

HERE LYE THE BODIES OF CHARLES GREVILL AND PETER GREVILL, ESQVIORS, WHOE WERE NATVRAL BRETHREN AND LATE PATRONES OF THIS CHAPPELL. THEY WERE BROVGHT VP AND LIVED TOGETHER IN A VERTVOVS AND PIOVS COVRSE, AND TAKING TRVE CONTENT AND COMFORT ONE IN THE OTHER, LEDD SINGLE LIVES AND DIED BATCHELLORS ANNO DNI 1736.——Over the infcription, is a large fcutcheon, with

with the Grevills arms, *Sable, a croſs and bordure engrailed Or, pelletty*, and twenty-four quarterings. The Grevills of this place ſprung from Lodovick Grevill, of Drayton in Worceſterſhire, anceſtor of the preſent earl Brooke, and earl of Warwick; and were allied to the Grevills of Campden.

Benefaction.

There is a charity of 200*l.* given to the poor, one half of which is laid out in the purchaſe of land.

Taxes.					
The Royal Aid in	1692, £.	53	0	0
Poll-tax —	1694, —	2	2	0
Land-tax —	1694, —	30	0	0
The ſame, at 3*s.*	1770, —	22	10	0

At the beginning of this century, there were 7 houſes, and about 36 inhabitants in this pariſh, whereof 2 were freeholders. *Atkyns.* In ten years, beginning with 1700, the baptiſms were 10, the burials 6; and in the ſame number of years, beginning with 1760, the baptiſms were 20, the burials 8; and the preſent inhabitants are in number 59, which ſhews the place to be remarkably healthy.

L I D N E Y.

THIS pariſh lies in the hundred of Blideſlow, in the Foreſt diviſion, ten miles ſouth-eaſt from Monmouth, eight north-eaſt from Chepſtow, and twenty ſouth-weſt from Glouceſter. The turnpike-road from that city, thro' Newnham to Chepſtow, and ſo on to Cardiff, Swanſea, and Milford-haven, is carried thro' it.

It probably took its name from being ſituated upon a broad part of the river Severn, for *Llydan*, in the Britiſh language, ſignifies *broad*, and the termination *ey* denotes a watry ſituation. Conſiſtent with this explanation of the name, the river is here between two and three miles over, and it was formerly much broader. Lidney antiently gave name to a hundred; for in *Domeſday-book* Aluredeſtone, Ledenei, Hiwoldeſtone, and W[illegible]gheiete, are mentioned as places within the hundred of Ledenei; but in the reign of king Edward the Firſt, there was no hundred of that name.

Lidney Park, the reſidence of Thomas Bathurſt, eſq; is a handſome ſeat, about a mile weſt of the church, with large gardens and offices, and very extenſive woods adjoining; of which ſeat that gentleman has obliged the public and the editor with the engraving annexed. It ſtands on the north-weſt ſide of the Severn, at about a mile and a half diſtance, and commands a large view of that river, of the ſeat of ſir John Fuſt, at Hill; of the town of Thornbury, and other places on the oppoſite ſide of the Severn; which, eſpecially from the height behind the houſe, make a rich and beautiful landſcape.

The pariſh is of great extent, conſiſting of rich meadow and paſture land, with ſome arable, and a large proportion of woodland. It is well watered on the eaſt by Linch-brook, dividing it from Awre; by Newarne-brook, running thro' the middle of it; and by Woodward's-brook, which is a boundary weſtward between this pariſh and Alvington, where it obtains the name of the Coln. All theſe riſe in the foreſt of Dean, and empty themſelves into the Severn.

The *New Grounds* here are a tract of above a thouſand acres of land next the river. In theſe, vegetation is quick and luxuriant, and cattle depaſturing on them improve uncommonly faſt: Horſes particularly are ſent in the ſpring from places at a great diſtance, to take the benefit of reſt, and of the ſalubrious food of the ſalt marſh. I cannot learn for a certainty when the waters firſt deſerted theſe grounds, but it muſt have been at the ſame time that a like event happened at Slimbridge, on the other ſide of the river; and ſince a ſuit at law was commenced in the reign of king Charles the Firſt, againſt lord Berkeley, to obtain the new grounds in the laſt mentioned pariſh for the crown, it muſt have been before that time.

That the tide in the Seven ſhould abate of its former height and power, and confine itſelf within a narrower channel, ſo as to leave dry this large tract of land, which it once overflowed, is an operation in nature not to be accounted for by all our philoſophy. Whatever was the cauſe, I am inclined to think the event was not ſudden, but gradual and progreſſive; and that even the old meadows here, which lie higher and further up, are acquiſitions from the river, tho' of longer ſtanding. And I am the rather diſpoſed to think ſo, from a tradition which the inhabitants have ſtill among them, that the tide in its uſual courſe formerly came up to a bank of earth called the Turret, juſt without the church-yard; and that a large ſhip was built near the place where there is now a ſpring of fine water, called the Turret-well.

Theſe are changes in the terraqueous globe, brought about in a long courſe of time, which however happen ſeldomer in this country than in moſt others.

To what hath been ſaid of the ſoil of the pariſh, and produce of the ground on the ſurface, ſhould be added, that below it are inexhauſtible treaſures of iron ore and cinders, pit-coal, red and yellow ochre, lime-ſtone, and other foſſils; and Mr. Bathurſt has a large furnace for ſmelting the iron ore, and ſeveral forges for manufacturing of iron.

The *Aſteria Columnaris*, a pentangular ſtone about the thickneſs of a large gooſe-quill, with a ſtar of five rays at each end, is commonly to be found at Pirton-paſſage; and ſeveral other curious ſubſtances, particularly (if I miſtake not) the grinders of an elephant, have been found at the ſame place.

Not far above Mr. Bathurſt's houſe, there is a cavern in the wood, called the *Scowls*, the entrance to which is between very long unwrought ſtones, ſerving as pillars to ſupport a rocky roof, on which

ſeveral

feveral large trees are now growing. The fpace within is about fixteen or eighteen feet broad, and nine or ten deep, and beautifully lined with mofs, which grows fpontaneoufly to the thicknefs of two or three inches. Tradition is intirely filent as to this place, and no traveller has taken notice of it. Perhaps it is nothing more than an old mine.

Upon the fummit of a little hill, in that part of Mr. Bathurft's park which lies contigious to Ailberton, are the remains of a large encampment, with foundations of many antient buildings; among which are the ruins of a Roman hypocauft, or bath, of an oval form. The longeft diameter is about feventeen feet, the other feven, as near as I could judge by my walking-ftick, with which I meafured it. Below the furface of the ground, the walls are intire; and part of a very ftrong terras, about fix inches thick, which ferved for the floor, is ftill remaining. A little weftward of this bath was a teffellated pavement, now intirely broken and deftroy'd; but great quantities of fquare bits of ftone and brick, like dice, which compofed it, lie fcattered all about. An old man informed me, that he had feen a part of this pavement, in a piece about a foot fquare. There have been alfo great quantities of Roman coins found in this place, and carried away; yet they ftill lie fo plentifully amongft the rubbifh, that a gentleman told me, he never failed to find fome of them after a fhower of rain; and I have myfelf found many pieces of urns and fine pottery. There were two ftatues in ftone of human figures, dug out of the ruins, and are now placed on the fide near the fummit of the hill.

This place is admirably fituated for defence; the approach to it is by a fteep afcent every way; and a fine ftream of water runs on the north fide of it, juft at the foot of the hill. It was not fufficiently, if at all, known to our learned Camden; yet every circumftance inclines me to think it the fcite of the *Abone* of Antoninus. In the former part of this work, I have flightly mentioned the prevailing opinions concerning the fituation of that Roman ftation. I fhall now briefly enter into a further difcuffion of them.

Mr. Camden fixes the *Abone* at Alvington, as well on account of the refemblance of the names, as becaufe the latter is nine miles from Caer Went, the *Venta Silurum* of the Romans; which is the exact diftance fet down in the *Itinerary* from that ftation to the *Abone*. But it has been objected that Alvington lies only about four miles from the *Trajectus*, which our learned antiquary fixes at Oldbury, whereas from *Abone* to the *Trajectus* fhould be nine miles, according to the *Itinerary*; wherefore, if the diftances in the *Itinerary* are right, either Oldbury cannot be the *Trajectus*, or Alvington is not the *Abone*. But it is pretty generally agreed, that the *Trajectus* was at Oldbury.

The learned Dr. Gale, in his Commentary on the *Itinerary*, fuppofing Antoninus's diftances to be right, thinks the ftations are tranfpofed by carelefs tranfcribers; and placing *Abone* after *Trajectus*, makes the former to have been at Hanham, in the parifh of Bitton, where are many old ruins and foundations of antient buildings; and the diftance from thence to Bath agrees with that fet down in the *Itinerary*, from the preceding ftation to *Aqua Solis*. The doctor interprets the name of Hanham, either as a contraction of *Avonham*, a *ham* or *ftation* at *Abone*; or confiders it as a fmall variation from *Henham*, an *antient ham*, or *ftation*.

Thus, by tranfpofing the order of the ftations, he thinks to accommodate the diftances fomething better to the *Itinerary*. But, had that been the cafe, it is a bad expedient to correct one error by committing another. The miftake feems more likely to be in the diftances than in mifplacing the ftations. The former are evidently wrong, as may be proved by the *Itinerary* itfelf. In the fourteenth *Iter*, from *Ifca* to *Calleva*, the diftance is faid to be 103 miles; but cafting up all the fpaces between the feveral ftations, the fum falls fhort by five miles of that number. So in the thirteenth *Iter*, from *Ifca* to *Calleva*, through *Clevum* and *Durocornovium*, *i.e.* Gloucefter and Cirencefter, it is faid to be 109 miles; whereas the fum of all the diftances between the intermediate ftations is only 90. In this journey, it is fet down from Gloucefter to Cirencefter 14 miles, which agrees exactly with the old computation; and from the latter to *Spinæ*, *i.e.* Speenham-land, (adjoining to Newbury) 15 miles. But every body knows that it is twice as far between the two laft mentioned ftations, as from Gloucefter to Cirencefter. Here then is a very great miftake in diftances, yet I believe nobody will contend, that Speenham-land is not the fcite of the Roman *Spinæ*.

Thefe circumftances confidered, will probably fo far eftablifh the order of the ftations as they ftand in the *Itinerary*, that no perfon may hereafter attempt to break it, merely to fupport the exactnefs of the diftances; fince it has been proved, that, in refpect to the latter, the *Itinerary* is inconfiftent with itfelf, in the very journey that mentions the ftation in queftion.

I am now to offer the reafons which induce me to fix on this place for the fcite of the *Abone*, in preference to Alvington and Hanham.

It was neceffary for the Romans, having conquered the country, to fortifiy their feveral ftations; and it is evident they did fo, from the ruins and fortifications found in almoft every place where they had them. In thofe places alfo, are found the remains of baths and teffellated pavements, with coins and other veftiges of that people. But none of all thefe have been found at Alvington, wherefore I think it cannot have been the *Abone*. As to Hanham, there is no doubt but the Romans made a lodgment there, as well as at many other places on the fides of the Avon; but neither can that have been the *Abone*, which we are to look for somewhere between *Venta Silurum* and the *Trajectus*. And since Ailberton is distinguished with every mark of antiquity, not only in the instances already taken notice of, but in the very name itself, which is evidently Ald-beorg-ton, *i.e.* the *town of the old camp* or *fortification*, I think we need go no further for the *Abone*. It stands at the proper distance from Caer Went, on one hand, but from hence, across the river to Oldbury, (if Antoninus did not make some allowance for the zig-zag manner of sailing) is not more than five or six miles. As to the distance from Oldbury, the supposed *Trajectus*, to *Aqua Solis*, there is undoubtedly a mistake in the *Itinerary*, which I know not how to rectify; only, if instead of VI. we read XI. for the distance, it will come nearer the truth, and exactly make good the deficiency in the sum of the distances in the *Iter* from *Isca* to *Calleva*. But these matters I submit to better judges, who may depend on the facts I have related, admitting or rejecting the argument as they see occasion.

Of the Manors and other Estates.

The following particulars stand in the antient survey, under the head *Terra Willi filii Baderon*.

'The same William [the son of Baderon] holds 'Ledenei in Ledenei hundred. Alfer held it in 'the reign of king Edward. There are six hides 'taxed. In demean are two plow-tillages, and 'three villeins, and five bordars, with two plow-'tillages. There are three *servi*, and a mill of 5*s*. '[rent,] and twenty acres of meadow, and half a 'fishery in Waie; a wood one mile long, and half 'a mile broad. It was worth 4*l*. now 40*s*.' *Domesday-book*, p. 74.

But there was then another manor, as we learn from the same record, wherein it is said:

'Earl William made a manor in Lindenee, in 'Blitesllau hundred, of four estates which he took 'from the lords thereof. Three hides from the 'manor of the bishop of Hereford; six hides from 'the manor set apart for the sustenance of the 'monks of Pershore, where were six villeins, with 'four plow-tillages. He took three hides and a 'half from two [d] thanes. There are in demean 'three plow-tillages, and eight bordars, and a mill 'of 40*s*. [rent,] a wood a mile long, and half a 'mile broad. It paid 7*l*. in the whole.' *Domesday-book*, p. 69.

Thus it appears, that there were two manors in this parish of the names of Ledenei, and Lindenee, which I take to be only an accidental variation from inaccuracy in writing, of which there are many more instances in the records. The principal manor was in the Beauchamp family for a long course of time; the other belonged to the Talbots.

Henry earl of Warwick, son of Walerond earl of Warwick, married Margery, coheiress of Henry D'Oiley, and died seized of the manor of Lidney, and of an iron forge in his woods there, and of other forges in the forest of Dean [e] 13 H. 3. His son Thomas de Newburg, earl of Warwick, succeeded him. He married Ela, second daughter of William Longespee, earl of Salisbury, natural son of king Henry the Second by Fair Rosamond, and died without issue 26 H. 3. John de Placetis married Mary, or Margaret, sister and heir to Thomas earl of Warwick. He was in great favour with king Henry the Second, who made the match, and obliged the lady to settle her whole estate on him for life, although she should have no children by him. He took the title of earl of Warwick, and died seized of Lidney 47 H. 3. But Mary, or Margeret, his wife, having no issue, the inheritance of the family went to the issue of her aunt Alice, daughter to Walerond earl of Warwick, who had been married to William Manduit, baron of Hanslape in Buckinghamshire, and by him left a son and a daughter, [f] William Manduit and Isabel. William, in right of his mother, was created earl of Warwick, but died 52 H. 3. without issue; whereby his sister Isabel, who was married to William Beauchamp, became his heiress. This William de Beauchamp died seized of Lidney [g] 52 H. 3. and was succeeded by his son William de Beauchamp, earl of Warwick, who died seized of this manor 26 E. 1. Guy de Beauchamp, earl of Warwick, was his son and heir. He died seized of a purparty of Lyden, held of the king in *capite*, appurtenant to his earldom, [h] 9 E. 2. And there were one hundred acres of underwood, worth (says the record) 1 *d. per* acre *per ann.* because it was in the royal forest.

Thomas, son and heir of Guy, was only two years old at his father's death. He was one of the chief commanders, who, under the Black Prince, led up the van of the English army at the battle of Cressy; and fought so long at that of Poictiers, that his hand was galled with the exercise of his sword and battle-ax. He married Catherine, daughter of Roger lord Mortimer, and died of the plague at Calais, seized of Lidney, 43 E. 3. and was succeeded by Thomas de Beauchamp, earl of Warwick, his surviving son and heir, who married Margaret, daughter to William lord Ferrers of Groby. He had taken up arms against king Richard the Second, and was attainted, and his estates forfeited, whereupon this manor was

[d] There were two orders of thanes: The royal thanes were the great feudatories, or nobility, of the kingdom, who held of the king in chief by knight-service, and were equivalent to the barons, as they were called, after the establishment of the Normans. The other thanes were sub feudatories, not honorary; the same whom the Normans called Vavasors, which word occurs in *Domesday* as a synonymy with *liberi homines regis*; but it grew out of use after the reign of king Henry the Fourth.

[e] Sir Robert Atkyns has it 17 H. 3. but it is the 13th in Collins's Peerage, V. 5. p. 206; and 1229 V. 5. p. 58. and sir Robert has it so himself under Chedworth and Dorsington.

[f] Collins's Peerage, V. 5, p. 207.

[g] 54 H. 3. in Collins.

[h] Sir Robert Atkyns has it 18 E. 2. in this place, but 9 E. 2. under Chedworth and Pirton, which agrees with the Escheator's book.

granted

granted to John Montacute, earl of Salifbury; who afterwards endeavouring to reftore the fame king, and being taken prifoner at Cirencefter, and there beheaded by the townfmen, 1 H. 4. as related more largely under that head, this eftate was reftored to Thomas de Beauchamp, 2 H. 4. who died feized of Lidney the fame year.

Richard de Beauchamp, earl of Warwick, fucceeded Thomas his father, and married, firft, Elizabeth, daughter and heirefs of Thomas lord Berkeley, vifcount Lifle, by whom he had three daughters: fecondly, Ifabel, the only furviving heirefs of the Difpencers, who were heirs to the Clares earls of Gloucefter, and died feized of Lidney 17 H. 6. Henry, his fon, was created duke of Warwick, and died feized of this manor 23 H. 6. He left Anne, his only daughter and heirefs, an infant; who dying foon after, the inheritance came to Anne, his fifter; but the manor was affigned to Cicely dutchefs of Warwick, his widow, in dower, 25 H. 6. This laft Anne was married to Richard Nevil, earl of Salifbury, who, in her right, was alfo earl of Warwick. He was famous for his great power, and was often called the *ftout earl of Warwick*, and the *king-maker*; for king Henry the Sixth and king Edward the Fourth held the crown by turns, as this earl favoured the fide; but he was at laft flain in Barnet-field, in which battle king Edward fecured the crown to himfelf. Anne, his widow, had two daughters by him, coheireffes to her vaft eftate; and becaufe fhe had taken part in the defigns of her late hufband, her eftate was taken from her by an act of parliament 14 E. 4. and fettled on her two daughters, of whom, Ifabel, the eldeft, was married to George duke of Clarence, brother to the king, and Anne, her fifter, to Richard duke of Gloucefter, afterwards king Richard the Third.

George duke of Clarence was drowned in a butt of Malmefey-wine, feized of Lidney, 18 E. 4. his brother, Richard duke of Gloucefter, moft inhumanly affifting at the execution. His children were Edward Plantagenet, earl of Warwick, attainted by court contrivances, and beheaded 15 H. 7. and Margaret countefs of Salifbury, beheaded 33 H. 8.

King Henry the Seventh pretending the injuftice of divefting Anne dutchefs of Warwick of her inheritance, procured another act in the beginning of his reign, to reinftate her, and then artfully prevailed with her to fettle that great inheritance on him and his heirs, to the difinherifon of the iffue of her own daughters; and accordingly fhe levied a fine of Lidney and many other manors to the king, 3 H. 7.

This manor continued in the crown 'till it was granted, by the defcription of late Warwick and Spencer's lands, to fir Thomas Seymour, 1 E. 6. but upon his attainder, it reverted to the crown, and was afterwards granted, by queen Elizabeth, to fir William Wintour,[i] vice admiral of England; who, with great valour and fuccefs, oppofed the famous Spanifh Armada, and was well rewarded by that queen. He built a ftately houfe at Lidney, called the *White Crofs*, which was begun in 1588.

Sir Edward Wintour, fon of fir William, fucceeded him, who married Anne, daughter of Edward earl of Worcefter. Sir John Wintour, fon and heir of fir Edward, was eminent for his loyalty to king Charles the Firft, throughout the whole civil war. He fortified his houfe at Lidney, and made it almoft inacceffible, to oppofe the garrifon at Gloucefter. At length he was put to flight, and, if you will believe a wonderful ftory, made a wonderful efcape, by leaping down from the rocks at Tiddenham (mentioned in Dr. Parfon's M S. to be near 200 yards high) into the river, which has given the name of *Wintour's Leap* to a place there. But tho' it may be true that he efcaped by taking the water, it is neverthelefs impoffible to be as related. The *White Crofs* houfe was afterwards demolifhed, and turned into buildings for an iron furnace. Sir Charles Wintour, fon of fir John, fucceeded to the manor of Lidney. He married one of the daughters and coheireffes of —— Napper, efq; who furvived him, and was owner of this manor when fir Robert Atkyns publifhed his Hiftory of Gloucefterfhire.

Of the other manor, the following account is extracted from the records: William Hatheway died feized thereof 10 H. 2. and was fucceeded by Ralph Hatheway his fon. Walter Wither died feized thereof 54 H. 3. William Buttler held Lidney and Peritune mills, and a bailiwick in the foreft of Dean 13 E. 1. He died the fame year, and left Perine, his only daughter and heirefs, married to Gilbert lord Talbot, who, in right of his wife, died feized of Lidney 20 E. 3. Richard lord Talbot died feized of Lidney, Huntley, Longhope, and Leigh 20 R. 2. Gilbert lord Talbot, his fon, fucceeded, and died feized of thofe manors, and a moiety of Badgworth, with a third part of the manors of Painfwick, Morton Valence, and Whaddon 7 H. 5. He left Ankoret, his only daughter and heirefs, but fhe dying at four years of age, John lord Talbot, her uncle, (fo famous for his victories in France as to be efteemed the Achilles of England) was her heir. He was created earl of Shrewfbury 20 H. 6. and being flain at the fiege of Chaftillon in France, by a cannon bullet, died feized of the manor of Lidney, &c. 31 H. 6. and was fucceeded by John earl of Shrewfbury, his fon and heir, who engaging on the part of the Lancaftrians, was killed in the

[i] There were three diftinct admirals of England 'till the reign of king Edward the Firft; one was admiral of the north, whofe ftation was at Yarmouth; another was admiral of the fouth, whofe ftation was at Portfmouth; the third was admiral of the weft, and kept his ftation at Plymouth; but king Edward joining the two admiralties of the fouth and weft under one perfon, king Henry the Fourth conftituted only one admiral for all England.

battle of Northampton 38 H. 6. He was succeeded by John his fon, the third earl of Shrewfbury, who married Catherine, daughter of Humphry Stafford, duke of Buckingham, and died 13 E. 4. as appears by the efcheator's book of that year, n. 52. From this time I have no account of the defcent of this manor, feparate from the firft; wherefore I conclude that the diftinction was loft by unity of poffeffion, and that both were afterwards enjoyed as one manor.

The manor of Lidney was purchafed of the Wintour family by Benjamin Bathurft, efq; third fon of fir Benjamin Bathurft, baronet, and uncle to the prefent earl of Bathurft. He married Finetta, daughter and heirefs of Henry Poole, of Kemble in the county of Wilts, efq; by whom he had iffue, 1. Thomas, of whom hereafter: 2. Poole, fometime commander of a company of foot in his majefty's fervice; who, in 1776, married Anne, one of the daughters and coheireffes of —— Hafketh, of the city of Salifbury, efq. 3. Anne, the eldeft daughter, married to Charles Bragge, of Mangotsfield in this county, efq; by whom he hath iffue two fons and one daughter: 4. Sufannah, the fecond daughter, married to Powell Snell, of Guiting-Grange in this county, efq. 5. Finetta, who died unmarried; and 6. Catherine, now unmarried. The faid Benjamin Bathurft married, fecondly, Elizabeth, daughter of the reverend Dr. Broderick, one of the prebendaries of Weftminfter, and rector of Mixbury in the county of Oxford; by whom he hath a numerous iffue. He died on Nov. 5, 1767, in the 76th year of his age, having reprefented the borough of Cirencefter in three parliaments, the city of Gloucefter in four, and the borough of Monmouth in two.

Thomas Bathurft, efq; the eldeft fon and heir of Benjamin Bathurft, married Anne, daughter and fole heirefs of fir William Fazakerly, of Totteridge in Hertfordfhire, and is the prefent lord of this manor. His arms, and a large account of his family, are given under Cirencefter, to which the reader is referred.

Of the other eftates in Lidney, the records fhew, that Bogo de Knovil died feized of affart lands at Gravenhull and Zerkeley, near Lidney, 12 E. 3. but this particular feems to belong more efpecially to the foreft of Dean. John Charburghe died feized of lands in Lidney and Aileberton 49 E. 3. Lands called Newton Myne, in Lidney, formerly belonging to the priory of Lanthony, were granted to John Marfh and John Turpine 2 Eliz. Other lands called Palewell Myne, in Lidney, formerly belonging to the priory of Lanthony, were granted to Anthony Collins and George Woodnet 26 Eliz. In the tithing of Lidney are 48 families, and 246 inhabitants.

TITHINGS and *HAMLETS.*

1. *Ailberton.* This tithing lies about a mile weft from the church, and confifts of 49 families, and 231 inhabitants. William Harpetre died feized of the manor of Halberton 12 H. 2. William Harpetre, fon of William, was his heir. He had committed many trefpaffes in the foreft of Dean, for which his lands were feized; but compounding for 100 marks, was reftored to his eftate 22 H. 2. Robert Harpetre was his fon and heir, who dying was fucceeded by John Harpetre. He died without iffue, whereby his fifter became fole heirefs, according to fir Robert Atkyns, and being married to Anfelm Gournay, was fucceeded in the manor of Aileberton by Robert Gournay their fon and heir, who died feized thereof 53 H. 3. But this feems to be a miftake; for Thomas Harpetre, brother of John, fucceeded to this eftate, and married Eva[k], daughter of Robert de Berkeley, who affumed the name of de Were, from the great lordfhip of Were in Somerfetfhire. They had iffue Robert, who fometime after affumed the name of Gournay, and had livery, 15 H. 3. of part of the poffeffions of Maurice de Gaunt, his uncle, and of all his lands in Gloucefterfhire, except Beverftan, Wefton, Radewic, Oure, and Albricton, which however, he not long after obtained of the king, and died 53 H. 3. He was fucceeded by his fon Anfelm, whofe fon John Gournay died 19 E. 1. and left Elizabeth, his only daughter and heirefs, married to John ap Adam, or, as he is fometimes called, de Badenham, who had iffue Thomas ap Adam.

Sir Robert Atkyns's account of the defcent of this manor breaks off at 53 H. 3. probably from fome defect in the records he had confulted; but he fays, it came afterwards to the family of the Berkeleys, *by the marriage of an heirefs.* ' It is however moft probable, that it defcended from Robert Gournay, together with the manors of King's Wefton and Beverftone, down to Thomas ap Adam; and like them was *fold* by him into the Berkeley family. Sir Maurice Berkeley purchafed King's Wefton of fir Thomas ap Adam 4 E. 3. which defcended thro' feveral generations to fir Maurice Berkeley of Uley, who died feized of that manor and of Aileberton 4 E. 4. Sir William Berkeley fucceeded his father in this eftate; but taking part with king Richard the Third, his eftates were feized by king Henry the Seventh, and granted to Jafper duke of Bedford in the firft year of that reign. Robert Woodroffe died feized of Aileberton 15 Car. and left Thomas his fon and heir feventeen years old. Thomas Bathurft, efq; is lord of this manor.

Sir Thomas Brook and Joan his wife levied a fine of lands in Aileberton 15 R. 2. Le Sterts and Goldgrove in Ailberton, and divers woods in Ailberton and Alvington, formerly belonging to the priory of Lanthony, were granted to William Wintour 32 H. 8. Here is a chapel of eafe, with a fmall tower at the weft end.

2. *Pirton*, or *Purton*, is a tithing three miles fouthward of the church, confifting of 8 families, and 44 inhabitants. Befides what is mentioned of

[k] Rot. Fin. 17 Joh.

of this manor in the abſtract from *Domeſday-book*, under Naſs, there are a few particulars relating to it that could not be ſeparated from the account of Awre, of which, according to that record, it was antiently a member, and a fief belonging to William de Ow.

Robert Gournay held Pereton 53 H. 3. John de Badeham, or ap Adam, and Elizabeth his wife, levied a fine of the manor of Peritone to John de Knovil, to the uſe of themſelves and the heirs of their bodies, the remainder to the heirs of Elizabeth, [k] 25 E. 1. Guy de Beauchamp, earl of Warwick, died ſeized of Peretone and Purton 9 E. 2. Maurice, ſon of Thomas de Berkeley, held Piriton [l] 42 E. 3. Thomas de Beauchamp, earl of Warwick, died ſeized of Peritone 2 H. 4. Thomas de Berkeley and Margaret his wife were ſeized of Purton 5 H. 5. Robert Goodrick and Edith his wife levied a fine of the manor of Purton 5 Mar. What ſir Robert Atkyns ſays here of lands in Purton belonging to St. Oſwald's in Glouceſter, ſhould be apply'd to Pirton in Churchdown. This manor is now the property of Thomas Bathurſt, eſq. Purton-paſſage over the Severn is in this hamlet, concerning which there are ſome uſeful obſervations at p. 47.

3. *Naſs*. This hamlet lies about two miles ſouth-eaſtward from the church, conſiſting of 6 families and 35 inhabitants. *Domeſday-book* gives the following account of it :

'Earl Herald held Neſt in Bliteſlau hundred. 'There were five hides, and in demean one plow-'tillage, and ten villeins, and two bordars, with 'nine plow-tillages. It was not put to farm in 'the time of king Edward. But earl William 'joined it to two other manors, that is to ſay, 'Pontune and Peritune. In theſe were nine hides, 'and two plow-tillages in demean, and fifteen 'villeins, and two bordars, and two *ſervi*, with 'nine plow-tillages. There is a fiſhery. The 'ſteward lately increaſed Pontune by one plow-'tillage. Peritune is in the king's farm. They 'pay 11 *lib*. in the whole.' *Domeſday-book*, p. 69.

Robert Grinder, eſq; was ſeized of Naſſe and Hurſt 22 H. 6. Sir John Barr died ſeized thereof 22 E. 4. John Baynham died ſeized of Naſſe 20 H. 8. and livery of it was granted to William his ſon 26 H. 8. in which family it continued to the reign of queen Elizabeth; and from that time it has been in the family of Roynon Jones, eſq; who is the preſent lord of this manor, and has a good eſtate and a ſeat here. He is ſon of the late William Jones, eſq; by Cholmley his wife, daughter of ſir John D'Oyley, baronet, of Cheſſel-Hampton in Oxfordſhire. His arms are, *Argent, a lion rampant gules*.

4. *Alliſton*, two miles north-eaſtward from the church, conſiſting of 24 houſes and 105 inhabitants. Of this tithing it is thus recorded :

'William de Ow holds Aluredeſtone in Ledenei 'hundred. Bondi held it in the time of king 'Edward. There are three hides taxed, no lands in 'demean, but five villeins and three bordars have 'three plow-tillages. There is a fiſhery of 12 *d*. '[rent] and ten acres of meadow; a wood half a 'mile long, and half a mile broad. It was worth '20 *s*. now 30 *s*. Henry de Fereriis claimed it 'becauſe Bondi held it; but Ralph de Limeſi alſo 'held it, who was predeceſſor to William. The 'ſame William holds two hides there which are 'taxed, and there are two villeins, with two plow-'tillages. Ulnod held them, and they are now 'and were then worth 10 *s*.' *Domeſday-book*, p. 73.

There was a caſtle at Alliſton in the reign of king William the conqueror, who made Gwarine de Meez, of the houſe of Lorrain, governor of it, and gave him Aleſtune to defend the marches againſt the Welch. But whether this laſt particular be true of Alliſton in Lidney, or of Olveſton in the hundred of Langley and Swineſhead, may admit of ſome doubt. Sir Robert Atkyns applies it to both places, of which however it cannot be equally true. But as this was ſituated in the marches which Gwarine was to defend, and as the record mentions a diſpute between two perſons concerning their right to this eſtate; it is probable the king afterwards put an end to the controverſy, by giving the manor to Gwarine de Meez. This Gwarine married Millet, one of the daughters of Pain Peverel, lord of Whitington in Shropſhire, who had declared, that whoſoever behaved himſelf with the greateſt courage at tilts, at the caſtle of Peake in Derbyſhire, ſhould wed his daughter; whereupon Gwarine meets at the place, and having there vanquiſhed a ſon of the king of Scotland, and a baron of Burgoyne, gained her for his wife.

Fulk, the ſon of Gwarine, ſucceeded him, of whom there is this remarkable anecdote. Playing at cheſs with king John, the king broke his head with the cheſs-board; but Fulk returned the blow, and almoſt killed the king. He was ſucceeded by his ſon Fulk, who was ſlain at the battle of Lewes, 48 H. 3. This family obtained the name of Fitz-Warine, from Gwarine their anceſtor, who came into England with the Conqueror.

5. *Soilwell*, or *Sully*, is a hamlet in Alliſton. Edward duke of York was ſeized of the manor of Sully 3 H. 5. Edward James, eſq; died ſeized of Sully, *alias* Soilwell-houſe, and Radmore 4 C. 1. He married Eleanor, daughter of John Powell, of Preſton, eſq; and left Thomas, his ſon, one year

[k] Sir Robert Atkyns has it 25 E. 3. But this is a miſtake, as appears by his account of Beverſtone, King's Weſton, Churchdown, &c.

[l] There is another hamlet of the name of Pirton in the pariſh of Churchdown, in this county, which occaſioned ſir Robert Atkyns, by miſtake, to apply this record and ſome others to that hamlet, whereas they belong to Pirton in this pariſh. There are alſo ſome other miſtakes in ſir Robert Atkyns, which are taken notice of under Churchdown.

and eight months old. William James, esq; was proprietor of this estate at the beginning of this century; but Soilwell-house and estate became afterwards the property of Mr. Richard Williams, by purchase from the family of the James's. Mr. Williams has now sold it to John Townsend, of Chiswick in the county of Middlesex, esq; the present proprietor.

6. *Hurst* is a hamlet in Alliston, about a mile eastward from the church. This was antiently a wood, or woody place, and took its name from the Saxon Ƿeorꞇ, *a wood*. Mrs. Morgan, relict of Probert Morgan, esq; eldest son of Richard Morgan, esq; by Elianor his wife, daughter of Henry Probert, of the Ar-goed in the county of Monmouth, esq; has a seat here.

7. *Newarne*. This hamlet lies about half a mile eastward from the church, and is part in the tithing of Lidney, and part in Alliston. Mrs. Lewis, daughter of Richard Morgan, of Hurst, esq; has a handsome house here.

8. *Rodleys* is a house and estate belonging to Mr. Edward Jones.

Of the Church, &c.

The church is a vicarage, in the Forest deanery, worth about 260*l*. a year. The dean and chapter of Hereford are patrons and impropriators; the reverend Mr. Evans, one of the canons of Hereford, is the present incumbent. The abbey of Lyra in Normandy formerly had the impropriation. Ailberton, St. Briavel's, and Hewelsfield are chapels annexed to this church.

The glebe at Ailberton lets at 2*l*. 15*s*. a year, but there is no glebe at Lidney.

The church is large, with an aile on each side, supported by two rows of pillars, and it has a very handsome spire at the west end. A small chancel on the north side of the great one, and a vault within the rails of the great chancel belong to the lord of the manor.

There was a chantry in this church, endowed by John Chardbrough and Julian his wife, 49 E. 3. whereof John Cook, the last incumbent, retired with a pension of 5*l*.

First fruits £. 24	6	8	Proc. & Syn. £. 0	9	8		
Tenths — 2	8	8	Pentecostals 0	1	4		

Monument and Inscription.

Mr. serjeant Powlet, recorder of the city of Bristol, and one of the justices of South Wales, died in 1703, and was buried in this church, but I find no memorial for him.

On a flat stone in the church,

Underneath this Stone lies buried the Body of Roynon Jones, of Nass, Esq; who died July the 26th A. D. 1732, Aged 69. ——Arms, 1. Jones, as before, impaling 2. *Or, a chevron checky gules and azure, between three cinquefoils of the last*, for Cooke.

Benefactions.

There is an almshouse of four rooms for the use of the poor.

Mr. Dunning of Purton, by his will dated 1625, gave 20*s*. a year to the poor. Mr. Morgan of Hurst, in 1660, gave 40*s*. a year, half to the poor, the other half for two sermons.

By indenture dated June 8, 1680, Christopher Willowby, of Bishopston, esq; gave 16*l*. a year, charged on the tithes of Clent, in the parish of Milton-Abbats in Wiltshire; of which 4*l*. a year each to be given to two poor old women, natives of Ailberton, for their lives; as often as one dies another to be chosen in her stead; 4*l*. 10*s*. to be equally divided between four poor persons of the same place; 10*s*. to each church-warden; 10*s*. to the parish clerk; 20*s*. to the minister for a sermon, and 20*s*. more for his trouble in keeping a register of the distribution of this charity, for want of which the whole to go to Bishopston.

Taxes.			£.	s.	d.
The Royal Aid in	1692,		224	12	0
Poll-tax ——	1694,	—	83	10	0
Land-tax ——	1694,	—	477	7	0
The same, at 3*s*.	1770,	—	236	12	9

According to sir Robert Atkyns, when he compiled his account of this parish, there were 153 houses, and about 700 inhabitants, whereof 24 were freeholders; annual births 28, burials 26. But examining the parish register, I find, that in ten years, beginning with 1700, there were 249 baptisms, and 251 burials; and in ten years, beginning with 1760, the baptisms were 196, and the burials 170; and the present number of inhabitants is 661. Upon comparing these numbers it will appear, that the people have decreased here this last century; that they were more healthy during the latter period of ten years, than in the former; and that the average proportion of burials to the whole number of souls is nearly as 1 to 39.

LITTLETON

IS a small parish in the hundred of Grumbald's-Ash, two miles distant north-westward from Marshfield, six south-west from Sodbury, and thirty-one south from Gloucester.

This was formerly a tithing in Tormarton, in respect to which it was a *little town*; but it is now a distinct parish. It is called *West Littleton*, to distinguish it from another Littleton, not far distant, in Wiltshire. The lands in this parish are chiefly arable.

Of the Manor and other Estates.

At the time of the general survey, this manor was not distinguished in the record from Tormarton.

Richard de Clare, earl of Gloucester and Hertford, was seized of the manor of Littleton 47 H. 3. It afterwards went to the family of De la Riviere, and from them to the Willingtons, and from them to the St. Loes. Whilst it remained in these

these families, it had the same owner with the manor of Tormarton.

George earl of Shrewsbury had married Elizabeth the widow of sir William St. Loe, captain of the guard to queen Elizabeth, the most distinguished lady of her time, for the beauty of her person and endowments of her mind, who had the inheritance of this manor, whereby the earl was seized of Littleton in her right, in the year 1608. They joined in conveying this manor to her son, William Cavendish, earl of Devonshire, who sold it to Mr. Willoughby, and others, by which means the manor was divided amongst divers freeholders.

Of the Church, &c.

The church is in the deanery of Hawkesbury, and is annexed to Tormarton. It is worth about 50*l.* a year.

The church is small, with a little low spire in the middle.

Taxes.		£.		
The Royal Aid in	1692,			
Poll-tax ——	1694,—	8	15	0
Land-tax ——	1694,—	47	13	6
The same, at 3*s.*	1770,—	37	12	3¾

At the beginning of this century there were 11 houses and 44 inhabitants in this parish, whereof 6 were freeholders; yearly births 1, burials 1. *Atkyns.* The present number of inhabitants is 67.

LITTLETON upon SEVERN.

THIS parish lies in the hundred of Langley and Swineshead, three miles south-westward from Thornbury, ten north-westward from Chipping-Sodbury, and twenty-six south-westward from Gloucester.

It consists chiefly of meadow and pasture, with some arable land, and is bounded on the west and north-west by the Severn.

Of the Manor and other Estates.

'The church of St. Mary of Malmesberie holds 'Liteltone in Langelei hundred. There are five 'hides, of which two and a half pay tax, the 'others are quit. In demean are two plow-'tillages, and thirteen villeins, and two bordars, 'with eight plow-tillages. There is a church 'and a priest, and thirty acres of meadow. It 'was worth 60*s.* but it is now worth 100*s.*' *Domesday-book*, p. 71.

A *Quo Warranto* was brought against the abbat of Malmesbury to set forth his right to court-leet in Littleton. He pleaded a grant from king Edward the Second, before the conquest, and his claim was allowed. The manor continued in the abbey of Malmesbury 'till the dissolution, and was granted, with the tithes of the demeans, to sir Richard Long, reserving a rent to the crown of 18*l.* 4*s.* 4*d.* 33 H. 8.

The manor was soon after purchased by Richard Hampden, who died seized of it 4 E. 6. and livery was granted to Edmond Hampden, son of Richard, 5 E. 6.

Edward Filton, esq; was lord of the manor in the year 1608; as was Mr. Hopton at the beginning of this century, and Mr. is the present lord of the manor.

HAMLET. *Stock* is a hamlet in this parish, of which there is a distinct account in *Domesday-book*:

'The bishop of Constance [in Normandy] holds 'Estoch in Sineshoved hundred, and Tetbald holds 'it of him. Eldred held it of earl Harold, and 'could go where he pleased. There are two hides, 'one taxed, the other not. There is one plow-'tillage in demean, and two villeins, and one 'bordar, with one plow-tillage. There are six '*servi*, and five acres of meadow. It was worth '40*s.* now 20*s.*' *Domesday-book*, p. 70.

Sir Robert Atkyns, or some person for him, by mistake, appropriated an abstract of the above account both to Stoke-Bishop in Westbury, and to this hamlet, which are distinct places.

Richard Foster levied a fine of a moiety of lands in Stoke to John Walsh 12 H. 7.

Of the Church, &c.

The church is a rectory, in the deanery of Bristol, worth about 45*l.* a year. Mr. Willoughby is patron, and Mr. Johns the present incumbent. The abbey of Malmesbury had the advowson.

The church is small, with a nave and a little north aile, and a small tower covered with tiles, and two bells in it.

First fruits £.	11	4	8	Synodals £.	0	2	0
Tenths —	1	2	9½	Pentecostals	0	0	6
Procurations	0	6	8				

Taxes.		£.		
The Royal Aid in	1692,	100	2	8
Poll-tax ——	1694,—	8	7	4
Land-tax ——	1694,—	71	0	0
The same at 3*s.*	1770,—	53	5	0

At the beginning of this century there were 18 houses and about 80 inhabitants in this parish, whereof 8 were freeholders; yearly births 2, burials 2. *Atkyns.* The inhabitants are now about 84.

LONGBOROUGH.

THIS parish lies in the upper part of Kiftsgate hundred, three miles distant north from Stow, seven south from Campden, and twenty-five east from Gloucester.

It is situated on an easy declivity facing the east, and commands a pleasant view of part of Oxfordshire, and some detached parts of Worcestershire and Warwickshire. Two turnpike-roads lead through the parish, one from Stow to Worcester, the

the other from Bath and Briſtol, thro' Cirenceſter, to Harford-bridge in Warwickſhire, and ſo on northwards.

The greater part of the pariſh is arable land, which furniſhes huſbandry buſineſs for the men, whilſt the women and girls employ themſelves in winding of ſilk for the throwſters at Blockley.

The name of the village was antiently written *Langeberge*, which was undoubtedly given it from the long form of a camp thrown up here, not far from the Roman *Foſs-way*, which paſſes by the village.

Of the Manors and other Eſtates.

One manor in this pariſh is part of the antient demeſnes of the crown, as appears by the following extract:

'King Edward held Langeberge in Cheſteſiat 'hundred, with Mene, a member thereof, in each 'of which were eight hides. There are three 'plow-tillages in demean, and ten villeins, and 'four bordars, with ſix plow-tillages, and a mill 'of 5*s.* and ſix *ſervi*, and a meadow of 10*s.* rent. 'In the time of king Edward the ſheriff paid for 'the farm what it yielded. It now pays 15*l.* with 'two hundreds which the ſheriff added to it.' *Domeſday-book*, p. 67.

But one part of this pariſh lay in Witelai hundred.

'Earl Moriton holds Langeberge in Witelai 'hundred. Tovi held it in the time of king 'Edward. There are two hides. In demean are 'two plow-tillages, and three villeins, and one 'bordar, with one plow-tillage, and four *ſervi*. It 'was worth 4*l.* now 40*s.* and pays tax.' *Ib.* p. 73.

'Hunfrid the chamberlain holds Langeberge in 'Witelai hundred of the king. There are four 'hides taxed. Elſtan, Blacheman, Edric, and 'Alric held it for four manors, and could go where 'they would. In demean were four plow-tillages, 'and three villeins, and five bordars, with three 'plow-tillages. There are nine *ſervi*. It was 'worth 16*l.* now 100*s.*' *Ibid.* p. 78.

Two of theſe manors were afterwards confuſed and united. Richard earl of Cornwall, king of the Romans, and brother to king Henry III. had a grant of the manor of Longborough. He founded the abbey of Hayles in the year 1246, and endowed it with this manor. A *Quo Warranto* was brought againſt the abbat, 15 E. 1. to ſhew by what right he held a court leet, and challenged waifs and felons goods, and his claim was allowed. The manor was held of the honour of Wallingford, and continued in poſſeſſion of the abbey of Hayles 'till the diſſolution.

The manor was granted to Rowland Hill and Thomas Leigh 1 Mar. Livery of it was granted to Rowland Leigh 15 Eliz. whoſe deſcendants have enjoyed it to the preſent time, and the heir of James Leigh, late of Addleſtrop, eſq; deceaſed, is the preſent lord of the manor.

Of the other eſtates the records ſhew, that William de Montacute was ſeized of lands in Longborough, and granted them to William Forho, reſerving to himſelf the advowſon, 16 H. 3. William de Bruſe held one meſſuage and ſix yard-lands in Longburg 15 E. 1. John de la Crane was ſeized of one meſſuage and one yard-land in Langeberge the ſame year. William de Cheſter and Alice his wife levied a fine of lands in Longborow to the uſe of themſelves for life, the remainder to John their ſon, 13 E. 2. Thomas Cole and others were ſeized of one meſſuage and one yard-land, in truſt for the abbey of Hayles, 15 R. 2. Lands in Longborough, which belonged to the abbey of Bruerne in Oxfordſhire, were granted to Edmond Hermas 35 H. 8.

HAMLET. Banksfee, or *Southfield*, is a hamlet and diſtinct manor, lying part in this pariſh and part in Condicot. It is ſometimes alſo called Longburrowe in the writings and evidences reſpecting it, and is undoubtedly one of thoſe manors called *Langeberge* in *Domeſday-book.* It is ſuppoſed afterwards to have received the name of *Blanck's-fee*, now ſomewhat changed to *Bank's-fee*, from Richard le Blanck, who was ſeized of one meſſuage and three plow-tillages here 15 E. 1. The college of Weſtbury upon Trim was ſeized of this manor, and continued in the poſſeſſion of it 'till the diſſolution of monaſteries. It was granted to ſir Ralph Sadleir 35 H. 8. William Freeman died ſeized thereof 20 Eliz. and livery was granted to his ſon Thomas the ſame year. John Talbott, of Longfere in the county of Salop, was in poſſeſſion of this manor 43 Eliz. as appears by evidences in the hands of the preſent poſſeſſor. In the year 1686, it was ſold to ſir Charles Shuckborough, baronet, in whoſe family it remained 'till 1753, when it paſſed, by purchaſe, to John Scott, eſq; who has built a handſome houſe on the ſcite of the old manor houſe, which he calls *Banksfee-Houſe.* He is in the commiſſion of the peace for the counties of Middleſex and Glouceſter, and has conſiderable eſtates in both counties. He is deſcended from an antient family in Scotland, and married Jane, daughter of Edward Wilſon, of Didlington in Norfolk, eſq; by whom he has one ſon and two daughters, John, Charlotte, and Catherine. His arms are, *Per pale indented argent and ſable, a ſaltire counterchanged.*

Here was antiently a chapel in this hamlet, dedicated to St. Edmond; but it is now wholly demoliſhed.

Of the Church, &c.

The church is a vicarage, in the deanery of Stow, worth about 50*l.* a year. The impropriation was in the abbey of Hayles from its firſt endowment in the year 1251.

Richard Pennehey was ſeized of the advowſon of this church 15 E. 1. The rectory and the advowſon of the vicarage were granted to ſir Rowland

Rowland Hill and Thomas Leigh 1 Mariæ. The heir of the late James Leigh, esq; presents for two turns, and the earl of Guildford one. Mr. Leigh is the present incumbent.

The vicarage was endowed in the year 1326, in the time of Thomas Cobham, bishop of Worcester, (called the good clerk) by the abbat of Hayles, with the tithe of sixteen yard-lands, then the fee of Richard de Hodington, and all privy tithes, except lamb and wool. And if the portion of the vicar, by reason of barrenness, or any other occasion, should not amount to 10*l. per ann.* by the oath of the vicar, the abbat and convent were to make it up to that amount. The demean lands pay no tithes.

A portion of tithes in this parish, which belonged to the abbey of Winchcombe, was granted to sir Thomas Seimour 1 E. 6. Other tithes, which belonged to Hayles abbey, were granted to Theophilus Adams and Richard Adams 25 Eliz.

The church is dedicated to St. James. It has an aile on the south side, and a handsome tower, with pinnacles. There is the effigy of a man in armour in the aile, without arms or inscription; and a handsome monument of black and white marble, with the effigies of sir William Leigh and his lady. He died in 1631.

First fruits £. 5	15	0	Proc. & Syn. £. 0	9	0
Tenths — 0	11	6	Pentecostals - 0	1	0½

Taxes.				
The Royal Aid in 1692, £.	153	6	0
Poll-tax —— 1694, —	13	18	0
Land-tax —— 1694, —	148	3	4
The same, at 3*s.* 1770, —	87	2	6

At the beginning of this century there were 80 houses in this parish, and about 400 inhabitants, whereof 15 were freeholders; yearly births 12, burials 11. *Atkyns.* There are now exactly 82 houses, and 389 inhabitants.

LONG HOPE.

THIS parish lies in the hundred of the Dutchy of Lancaster, three miles north-east from Mitchel-Dean, and nine west from Gloucester.

It is situated in a bottom, which gave occasion to the name; for *Hope* is a *valley*, says lord Coke, in the first part of his *Institutes.* It was called *Long Hope* to distinguish it from *Mansel-Hope*, not far distant from it, in Herefordshire. The greater part of the parish is arable land, with some wood-land and pasture ground.

Part of *Yartleton-Hill* lies in this parish, and part in several others. Annually, on the first day of May, there is a custom of assembling in bodies on the top of that hill, from the several parishes, to fight for the possession of it, upon which account it is sometimes called *May-Hill.* What gave rise to this custom I cannot with any certainty learn; but some are of opinion that it is a relick of the antient *Campus Martius*, which was an annual assembly of the people upon May-day, when they confederated together to defend the kingdom against all foreigners and enemies, as mentioned in the laws of Edward the Confessor.

There is a remarkable instance of longevity in the person of Thomas Bright, who was a native of this parish, and died here in the year 1708, one hundred and twenty-four years old, as appears by the inscription for him, on his grave-stone.

Of the Manor and other Estates.

'William the son of Baderon holds Hope in 'Westberie hundred. Forne and Ulfeg held it of 'king Edward. There were five hides taxed, and 'those thanes might go where they would. There 'are two plow-tillages in demean, and twelve vil-'leins, and one bordar, with twelve plow-tillages. 'There are three *servi*, and a mill of 17*d.* It 'was worth 8*l.* now 100*s.*' *Domesday-book*, p. 74.

William the son of Baderon was succeeded by Withenock his son, who took the name of Monmouth from his father's government. Baderon was son and heir of Withenock, and Gilbert was son and heir of Baderon. John de Monemuta was son and heir of Gilbert, and was made governor of St. Briavel's castle 18 H. 3. He died seized of the manor of Long Hope 40 H. 3. and having no male issue, gave the inheritance of all his lands to prince Edward, eldest son to king Henry the Third.

This manor was soon after granted to Gilbert Talbot, one of the justices itinerant for the county of Hereford, and governor of the castle of Monmouth. He married Gwenthlian, daughter of Rhese ap Griffith, prince of South Wales, and died seized of Rodleigh, and of Long Hope 2 E. 1. but the wife of John de Monemuta the younger held the latter some time in dower. Gilbert Talbot, son of Richard, son of Gilbert, died seized of Long Hope and Huntley [m] 10 R. 2. as did Richard, son of Gilbert, 20 R. 2. Gilbert, son of the last Richard, on the death of his mother, had livery of the fourth part of the said manors 1 H. 5. and John, brother and heir to Gilbert, died seized of the same 31 H. 6.

This manor continued long in the family of the Talbots, and had a succession of the same owners as the manor of Huntley. Edmund Probyn, of Newland, esq; is the present lord of both the said manors.

John Sabin and others were seized of one messuage and sixty acres of land in Long Hope and Huntley, in trust for the abbey of Flaxley, 10 R. 2.

Of the Church, &c.

The church is a vicarage endowed. It lies in the Forest deanery, and is worth about 250*l.* a year. Mr. David Jones is patron and incumbent.

[m] Dugdale's Baronage.

Robert de Chandos, who came into England at the Norman invaſion, gave the advowſon of the church of Hope to the abbey of Lyra in Normandy. The impropriation belonged afterwards to the priory of St. Mary and St. Florence in Monmouth. After the ſuppreſſion of monaſteries, the impropriation was veſted in the Nourſes, and deſcended to Mr. Nourſe Yate, who reſtored it to the vicarage in the year 1701.

The church is built in the form of a croſs. It has a ſpire and five bells at the weſt end. The chancel was rebuilt, and the church repaired in 1771.

Firſt fruits £. 9	7	11½	Proc. & Syn. £. 0	7	8
Tenths — 0	18	9½	Pentecoſtals - 0	1	6

Monuments and Inſcriptions.

There is a memorial in the chancel for Thomas Maſter, gent. who died in 1682, with the arms of the family of the ſame name reſiding at Cirenceſter. There are alſo ſeveral memorials, on flat ſtones, for the Yates of this pariſh, with the arms of the Yates of Arlingham; and for Yate Bromwich, clerk, vicar of the pariſh, and patron of the living, who died in 1774; with his arms, *i. e. Or, a lion rampant ſable, gutty of the field*; impaling, 2. Yate.

On a ſtone in the church-yard is this inſcription,

Here reſteth the Body of Thomas Bright, who departed this Life October 28th Anº 1708, Ætatis ſuæ 124.

His Patience was by long Affliction try'd ;
In ſtedfaſt Faith and Hope he liv'd and dy'd.

Benefactions.

John Palmer, gent. gave one meſſuage and fifteen acres of land in Long Hope, in the reign of king Richard the Second. John Bodenham gave other lands in the reign of Henry the Fifth, as did John Appleby, gent. in that of Henry the Sixth. Richard Elly, of Mitchel-Dean, gave a meſſuage and lands in Long Hope, in the reign of Henry the Seventh; and about the ſame time, Walter Giffard, *alias* Pekks, gave a tenement in Mitchel-Dean, and lands in Long Hope; and other lands were given to this pariſh, by Thomas Bond, in the ſame reign. John Gwin gave lands alſo in the reign of king Henry the Eighth. All theſe donations are for the purpoſe of repairing the pariſh church, and for the relief of the poor.

In the year 1675, Mr. Thomas Nourſe charged the impropriation with 5*l.* a year for ever to buy clothes for the poor; and 5*l.* for binding out one apprentice yearly. In the year 1701, Mr. Nourſe Yate endowed the vicarage with the impropriation, ſubject to the ſaid charities of 10*l.* a year.

Taxes.	The Royal Aid in 1692,	£. 106	4	0
	Poll-tax — 1694,	— 40	13	0
	Land-tax — 1694,	— 154	10	0
	The ſame, at 3*s.* 1770,	— 99	15	0

At the beginning of this century there were 100 houſes, and about 500 inhabitants in this pariſh, whereof 36 were freeholders; yearly births 13, burials 11. *Atkyns.* The preſent number of inhabitants is about 470.

LONGNEY.

THIS pariſh lies in the hundred of Whitſtone, ſeven miles north-weſt from Stroud, three eaſt from Newnham, and ſeven ſouth-weſtward from Glouceſter.

Sir Robert Atkyns aſſerts, that *it has been formerly called Long-Iſland, which gives*, ſays he, *the derivation of that name.* But no inſtance has occurred to me of the place being ſo called; and it could not be ſo, without the greateſt impropriety, as neither the pariſh, nor any part of it, is ſo much as peninſulated. The name ſeems to be compounded of Lanȝ, *long*, or *along*, and Ea, *water*, (the letter *n* ſerving only to facilitate pronunciation) and it is perfectly deſcriptive of the ſituation of the place, which ſtretches along the ſouth-eaſt ſide of the river Severn, and conſiſts of rich meadow and paſture grounds, with orcharding, and ſome arable land. This ſituation ſubjects the inhabitants to the topical diſorders incident to ſuch places.

I have had frequent occaſions of mentioning the cheeſe made in theſe parts with the commendation it deſerves; and with pleaſure I take this opportunity of recommending a particular ſort of cyder, of good ſtrength, colour, and excellent flavour, made in this pariſh and its neighbourhood, from an apple which, being originally cultivated here, is called the *Longney Ruſſet.* This village furniſhes nothing further remarkable in natural hiſtory, and is intirely deſtitute of antiquities.

Of the Manor and other Eſtates.

In *Domeſday-book* it is thus recorded:

'Elſi holds Langenei in Witeſtan hundred of 'the king, and he held it in the time of king 'Edward. There are five hides taxed. In demean 'are two plow-tillages, and ſix villeins, and twelve 'bordars, with nine plow-tillages. There are 'four *ſervi*, and ten acres of meadow, and a 'fiſhery. It was worth 100*s.* now 60*s.*' p. 79.

Soon after the Norman conqueſt, this manor was given to the monaſtery of Great Malvern in Worceſterſhire, by one Oſbert, or Oſburt, who in the charter is called *Oſburt fil. Pontii*; and it was confirmed by king Henry the Firſt to that monaſtery, which was founded by Aldwin an hermit, in the year 1085, and endowed by king William the Conqueror, and the before-mentioned king Henry. That monaſtery pleaded their right to court-leet, free warren, and felons goods in this manor, in a *Quo warranto* brought againſt them, 15 E. 1. and their claim was allowed.

The manor continued in the poſſeſſion of the monks of Malvern 'till the diſſolution, after which it it paſſed into lay-hands. Sir William Bond was lord of it in the year 1608.

Henry Smith, eſq;[n] a very charitable perſon, dying in the year 1627, his truſtees, purſuant to the directions of his will, purchaſed ſeveral eſtates, and amongſt others the manor of Longney, with the demean lands, and the rectory and parſonage, the income of which to be diſpoſed of in charities. And the manor, &c. ſtill continue veſted in ſuch truſtees, who hold a court leet here.

The demean lands and parſonage of Longney, with the quit-rents of the manor, are allotted to pay the following ſums annually, *viz.* to

	£.		
Bath-Eaſton, co. Somerſet -	10	0	0
Newton St. Loe, ſame county, -	30	0	0
Stanton-Priors, ſame county, -	10	0	0
Chippenham, co. Wilts, - - -	10	0	0
Calne, ſame county, - - - -	10	0	0
Chedeſton, co. Suffolk, - - -	10	0	0
Chipping-Barnet, co. Herts, -	10	0	0
King's Langley, ſame county, -	5	0	0
Chriſt Church, co. Surry, - - -	10	0	0
Horne, ſame county, - - - -	3	0	0
Streatham, ſame county, - - -	4	0	0
St. Thomas, Southwark, - - -	6	0	0
Northill, co. Bedford, - - - -	4	0	0
Odiam, co. Hants, - - - -	10	0	0
Ormſkirk, co. Lancaſter, - - -	9	0	0
Perſhore, co. Worceſter, - - -	50	0	0
St. Sepulchre, London, - - -	10	0	0
St. Olave, Old Jewry, - - - -	10	0	0
St. Vedaſt, Pater-noſter lane, -	10	0	0
St. Giles, Cripplegate, - - - -	10	0	0
St. Martin in the fields, - - -	12	0	0
Radnor, in Wales, - - - - -	5	0	0
Warbleton, co. Suſſex, - - - -	8	0	0

Of the other eſtates, the records ſhew, that William Mull, or Mills, who had eſtates in Hareſfield, Duntiſbourn-Rouſe, and Harſcombe, was ſeized of ten acres of meadow, ten of paſture, and ſix acres of wood in this pariſh; but being attainted 2 E. 4. his eſtates were ſeized by the crown, and granted to ſir Thomas Herbert and his heirs male; and were afterwards granted to ſir Richard Beauchamp, 14 E. 4.

Of the Church, &c.

The church is a vicarage, in the deanery of Glouceſter, worth about 50*l.* a year. The lord chancellor is patron, and Mr. Joſeph Cheſter is the preſent incumbent. The advowſon formerly belonged to the priory of Malvern.

The impropriation is veſted in Mr. Smith's truſtees. About 80 acres, called Sten-Meadow, are tithe-free.

The truſtees to Mr. Smith's charity have an eſtate in Suſſex, the income of which they divide amongſt the poor clergy; and Longney being a ſmall living, they ſometimes give the vicar a ſhare, as they do at preſent 10*l.* a year; but both the ſum and the continuance of it are intirely at their diſcretion.

The church, dedicated to St. Lawrence, hath a ſmall chapel on the ſouth ſide of the chancel, belonging to the manor. It has a handſome embattled tower on the ſouth ſide, with five bells in it. There are neither monuments nor memorials worthy notice; but it is ſaid that the founder of the church lies buried under a niche in the wall, on the north ſide of the chancel.

	£.				£.		
Firſt fruits	12	13	4	Synodals	0	2	0
Tenths —	1	5	4	Pentecoſtals	0	1	2
Procurations	0	6	8				

Benefactions.

Sir Edmond Pounce has charged the impropriation with the payment of fixteen buſhels of wheat to the poor on St. Lawrence's day. And ſix pounds yearly are charged on Mitchel's lands to the uſe of the poor. *Atkyns.*

---

[n] The following ſhort account of that very extraordinary man may be acceptable to my readers. The vulgar ſtory concerning him is, that he was a beggar, followed by a remarkable dog, whence he is often in Surry called Dog-Smith; and that he was whipped through ſeveral pariſhes in that county as a vagrant. But all this ſeems to be fiction. There was a reſpectable family of the Smiths, who had a manor and a conſiderable eſtate at Wandſworth in Surry, 11 Eliz. which they enjoy'd 'till about the year 1664; and as he was born and buried there, according to Mr. Aubrey, it is probable, tho' not abſolutely certain, that he was one of that family; and there is a monument for him in Wandſworth church. At length he became a citizen of London, of the falters company, tho' it is ſuppoſed he was a ſilverſmith; and having a very large real and perſonal eſtate, veſted the whole of it, in the year 1620, in truſtees, for the relief of poor priſoners, hurt and maimed ſoldiers, portions for poor maids on their marriage, ſetting up of poor apprentices, repairing of highways, and loſſes ſuſtained by fire, ſhipwreck, or otherwiſe; or ſuch other charitable uſes as he ſhould by deed or will direct, or as his truſtees, their heirs or aſſigns ſhould think moſt meet and convenient; reſerving 500*l.* *per ann.* for his own uſe during his life.

Afterwards, by deed-poll, dated Jan. 26, 1626, he ordered that his perſonal eſtate ſhould be laid out in purchaſing lands, to be ſettled to the ſame uſes; and directed, that the ſums allotted by him or his truſtees to any pariſh, be diſtributed by the churchwardens and overſeers, for the relief of the aged, poor or infirm people, married perſons having more children born in lawful wedlock than their labours can maintain, poor orphans, ſuch poor people as keep themſelves and families to labour, and put out their children apprentices at the age of fifteen; but by no means for the relief of perſons given to exceſſive drinking, whoremongers, common ſwearers, pilferers, or otherwiſe notoriouſly ſcandalous; nor to any that have been incorrigible or diſobedient to thoſe whoſe ſervants they have been, nor to any vagrants having no conſtant dwelling, nor to any that receive inmates to dwell in the houſe with them, or that have not inhabited in ſuch pariſh five years before the making of ſuch diſtribution, or, being able, refuſe to work, labour, and take pains.

He afterwards made his will, by which he gave ſome few legacies, but left the bulk of his eſtate to the diſpoſal of his truſtees, and died in January 1627.

Beſides Longney, there are ſeveral conſiderable eſtates in Suſſex, Kent, Hants, London, Middleſex, and Leiceſterſhire, given by Mr. Smith, or purchaſed with his money, and veſted in the truſtees to this well-directed charity, who, in the year 1772, when this account was communicated to me by William Bray, eſq; were the following noblemen and gentlemen, *viz.*

The earl of Aſhburnham,
The right honourable lord George Germaine,
Lord Onſlow,
Lord Pelham,
The right honourable George Onſlow, of Ember-Court in Surry, eſq;
Sir Francis Vincent, baronet,
Peter Burrell, of Beckenham in Kent, eſq;
General George Howard, of Stoke-Place, near Windſor,
George Onſlow, of Ockham in Surry, eſq;
Thomas Scawen, of Carſhalton in Surry, eſq;
Robert Scawen, of Ryegate in Surry, eſq;
Henry Talbot, of Chart-Park in Surry, eſq;
Abraham Tucker, of Betchworth-Caſtle in Surry, eſq;
George Woodroffe, of Poyle in Surry, eſq;

Mr.

Mr. Smith's truftees allow 8 *l.* a year to the poor of this parifh, not out of the manor of Longney, as mentioned by fir Robert Atkyns, but out of an eftate at Longftock in Hampfhire.

Taxes.					
	The Royal Aid in 1692, £.	137	6	8
	Poll-tax — — 1694, —	11	0	0
	Land-tax —— 1694, -	117	17	0
	The fame, at 3 *s.* 1770, —	90	5	3

At the beginning of this century there were 60 houfes, and about 260 inhabitants in this parifh, whereof 12 were freeholders; yearly births 6, burials 4. *Atkyns.* The inhabitants are now about 217.

MANGOTSFIELD.

THIS parifh lies in the hundred of King's-Barton, near Briftol, four miles diftant north-eaft from that city, feven fouth-weft from Chipping-Sodbury, and thirty-two fouth-weftward from Gloucefter.

It derives its name, fays fir Robert Atkyns, *from Mane, a Saxon general, who gained a victory in this place over the Britons.* But with due deference to that gentleman, this feems not altogether fatiffactory; for who has read of any fuch general gaining a victory here? Befides, fir Robert's notion that *the names of parifhes which terminate in* field *are moft commonly derived from a general having obtained a victory in fuch places*, as delivered by him in his account of Hewelsfield, is ill founded and erroneous.

In *Domefday-book* the name is written *Manegodesfelle*, as I conceive, from *maen*, Britifh, *ftone*, *goed*, or *coed*, in the fame language, a *wood*, and *felle*, a *hill*, or *common*, in which fenfe it is ftill ufed in the north of England; the whole, therefore, taken together, fignifies a *ftony place in the wood upon a hill.* And this explanation agrees with the fituation and antient condition of the place; for tho' the woods are now affarted, it muft formerly have been woody, as lying in Kingfwood-chafe; and on the hill, at Downend in this parifh, is one of the fineft rocks of ftone in the county. It rifes in very large fuperficial dimenfions, and fo evenly bedded as to be fit for pavements, without the leaft labour to fmooth the furface. Thefe circumftances feem to confirm the etymology.

There are few or no antiquities here, except a fmall camp of obfervation, at a place called *Bury-hill*, with a deep fofs, and high *agger*, thrown up, as fuppofed, by the Romans under Oftorius. And there is another of the fame kind, not far from it, in the parifh of Winterbourn.

Leland, in the fixth volume of his *Itinerary*, calls the village *Magatesfeld* and *Magnusfeld*, but he was not very accurate in writing the names of places, which he commonly did as they were pronounced upon the fpot. Speaking of a ruin which he found here, he fays, *It was ons withowte fayle a nunnery. Parte of the Cloyfter ftandithe yet.* But the ruin has been long fince deftroy'd, and we know nothing more of the nunnery than what he fays of it.

This village is one of thofe places in the neighbourhood of the city of Briftol, which abound with a very lafting kind of coal, already mentioned in the accounts of Bitton and St. George's.

Mangotsfield is reputed to be within the jurifdiction of the court of the honour of Gloucefter, now held at Thornbury.

Of the Manors and other Eftates.

The abftract from *Domefday-book* concerning the large manor of Bertune, of which Manegodesfelle was a member, ftands in the account of the parifh of St. George in Kingfwood.

One manor in Mangotsfield belonged to the Blounts of Bitton, whofe arms are cut in ftone on the church porch, *i.e. Argent, two bars azure, over all an efcarbuncle of eight rays gules, promette and florette Or.*

This manor was purchafed by William Player, efq; in whofe family it continued for feveral generations. It is now the property of Charles Bragge, efq; who married Anne, the eldeft daughter of Benjamin Bathurft, late of Lidney-Park in this county, efq; deceafed, by whom he hath iffue two fons, Charles and William; and one daughter, Anne. He has a handfome feat at *Cleeve-Hill*, in this parifh. His arms are, *Or, a chevron between three buffalos fable.*

Another manor, held of the honour of Gloucefter, antiently belonged to the Putots, whom fir Robert Atkyns calls Piccots. William de Putot died feized of it 15 H. 3. He built a chapel in his manor houfe at Manegodesfeld, and had a fpecial grant[o] of a free chantry in that chapel.

[o] This grant is inferted in Stevens's *Supplement to the Monafticon*, as follows:

Conceffio facta W. de Putot *de libera Cantaria habenda in Capella Curiæ de* Manegodesfeld.

NOTUM fit omnibus Chrifti fidelibus, præfens fcriptum vifuris vel audituris, quod *P.* Abbas *Theok.* & ejufdem loci Conventus, Magifter *Stephanus de Thorneburia* & *Dd.* tunc Decanus *Briftoll*, Rectores Ecclefiæ Beati *Petri* juxta Caftrum *Briftoll* & Capellæ villæ de *Manegodesfeld* ad ipfam pertinentis, concefferunt pure & liberaliter, quantum in ipfis eft, Domino *Willielmo de Putot* tunc Vic. *Gloucefrtiæ* & hæredibus fuis liberam Cantariam fuam ad opus fuum & totius familiæ fuæ & Hofpitum fuorum in Capella quam de confenfu omnium prædictorum conftruxit in Curia fua in *Manegodesfeld*, & quod Capellanus dictæ Capellæ in Curia, fivè continue refidens five abfens, habeat omnes obventiones & oblationes ipfius Capellæ, præterquam in Die Natalis Domini, & Pafchæ & fefti Sancti *Athelberti*, quod eft feftum Capellæ de villa. Quibus diebus dictus *W. de Putot*, & familia fua, & Hofpites qui præfentes fuerint & potentes, audiant divina in præfata Capella villæ. Et fi forte aliquæ obventiones dictis diebus in dicta Capella Curiæ evenerint, Matrici Ecclefiæ reddantur; falvis ipfi matrici Ecclefiæ omnibus Decimis majoribus & minoribus de Curia, & fibi legatis. Nullus autem Parochianorum admittatur in dicta Capella in Curia in præjudicium matricis Ecclefiæ, nifi fit de famila vel Hofpitibus Curiæ, ad aliqua Ecclefiaftica Sacramenta, nec aliquid tangens jus parochiale circa ipfos exerceatur a Capellano Capellæ de Curia fine confenfu Capellani Matricis Ecclefiæ, vel Capellani Capellæ de Villa. Et hoc fi noluerit Capellanus Curiæ, qui fi continua refidentia fuerit ibidem, facinus, matrici Ecclefiæ præftabit juramentum fidelitatis. In cujus rei robur & teftimonium prædictus Abbas & Conventus & prædicti Rectores Ecclefiæ Sancti *Petri* & prædictus *W. de Putot* tunc Vicecomes *Gloucefrtiæ* huic fcripto figilla fua appofuerunt. Hiis teftibus, *Radulpho de Wilet*, *Roberto de Turvile*, & *M. A.*

He

He was high ſheriff of Glouceſterſhire for ſeveral years. Lord Berkeley was ſeized of it afterwards, and granted it to Philip Langley, eſq; 9 Jac. 1. It was again ſold, in the year 1665, to John Meredith, eſq; who planted a large vineyard in this place, and was ſucceeded in the manor by his ſon John Meredith, who was lord of it at the beginning of this century. Mr. William Meredith ſold it to Edward Colſton, eſq; and it is now in jointure to the widow of the late Mr. Francis Colſton.

Ruggeway, or *Ridgway*, is alſo a diſtinct manor, lying part in this pariſh, and part in that of Stapleton. Nicholas Barſtable held Ruggeway within the manor of Bertune 13 H. 4. Edward earl of Hertford was owner of it 31 H. 8. It belonged to Matthew Smyth, of Long Aſhton in com. Somerſet, in the reign of queen Elizabeth, and is now the property of ſir Jarrit Smyth, bar[t]. by purchaſe of the coheireſſes of the late ſir John Smyth, baronet.

Edward Andrews, eſq; has a handſome ſeat in this pariſh, called *Hill-houſe*

HAMLETS. 1. *Downend* is a populous hamlet, already taken notice of on account of its quarries of excellent paving ſtone.

2. *Morend*, in which the before-mentioned camp is ſituated.

Of the Church, &c.

The church is a perpetual curacy, in the deanery of Briſtol, ſaid in Ecton to be about 20*l*. a year clear value; but it was augmented, in the year 1720, by the donations of Edward Colſton and John Dowel, eſq[rs]. and by queen Anne's bounty; and a ſecond time, in 1758, by contribution of the principal inhabitants, and by the queen's bounty. It was originally only a chapel of eaſe to St. Peter's church in Briſtol, and belonged to St. James's monaſtery there. The rectory and advowſon were granted to John Brain 35 H. 8. and paſſed afterwards to Mr. Dowel, and then to Mr. Wolly and others, who ſold to the ſeveral proprietors of lands the tithes of their reſpective eſtates. Mrs. Wilmot is patroneſs, and Mr. Chriſtopher Haines is the preſent incumbent.

The church is dedicated to St. James. It conſiſts of the nave, two ailes, and a chancel, with a ſpire ſteeple on the ſouth ſide, in which are ſix bells and a clock. There is a ſmall chancel on the north ſide of the great one, which is the burying-place of ſeveral of the family of the Merediths. Here are two effigies in ſtone, at full length, and well preſerved, ſuppoſed to be deſigned for ſome of the family of the Blounts, who had great property here, and in the neighbouring pariſh of Bitton.

Taxes.			£.	s.	d.
	The Royal Aid in	1692,	127	18	8
	Poll-tax ——	1694,—	27	15	0
	Land-tax ——	1694,—	184	17	0
	The ſame, at 3*s*.	1770,—	118	4	0

At the beginning of the preſent century there were 150 houſes, and about 750 inhabitants in this pariſh, whereof 24 were freeholders; yearly births 17, burials 15. *Atkyns.* But at that time the regiſter was very ill kept. In ten years, beginning at 1760, the baptiſms were 623, and the burials 372. And the preſent number of inhabitants is ſomething above 2000. By which it appears that the proportion of annual burials is to the number of inhabitants about as 1 to 51, and that the ſituation is very healthy.

MARSHFIELD.

THIS pariſh conſtitutes the upper diviſion of the hundred of Thornbury. It lies ſeven miles north-eaſtward from Bath, ſeven ſouth-eaſtward from Chipping-Sodbury, twelve and a half eaſt from Briſtol, thirty-five ſouth from Glouceſter, and one hundred and three weſt from London.

It is ſituated on high ground, with a fine healthy air, and bounded on the ſouth by a brook which divides it from Somerſetſhire; on the eaſt by the pariſh of Wraxal, in Wiltſhire; on the weſt by the village of Cold Aſton; and on the north by Sherill's-brook, which ſeparates it from Littleton. The greater part is a light ſoil, better adapted to corn than paſture, and there are ſome wood-lands which produce good oak, aſh, and elm, but no beech wood.

The town of Marſhfield ſtands near the middle of the pariſh, and conſiſts chiefly of one ſtreet, near a mile long, through which a turnpike-road leads from London to Briſtol. The buſineſs of making malt to ſupply the cities of Bath and Briſtol was formerly very great here, for which the town is conveniently ſituated in a corn country; and tho' it has been for ſome time declining, yet it is ſtill pretty conſiderable.

The market, which is but little frequented, except in the malting ſeaſon, is held on Tueſday; and there are two fairs in the year, on the 24th of May, and the 24th of October, for which privileges their charter was renewed in the reign of king James the Firſt.

The town has a bailiff for its chief officer, choſen annually at the court-baron. He is attended occaſionally by a ſerjeant at mace, and other officers, to examine the weights and meaſures, which ſeems to be the proper duty of his office; but he always acts as a peace officer in the abſence of the conſtable; and it is ſaid that he has authority to commit to priſon for certain offences, but no ſuch thing is remembered to have been done by any of the preſent inhabitants. There are three tithings in the pariſh, with their diſtinct peace officers. The borough, as it is called, and the pariſh are reputed to be within the juriſdiction of the honour of Glouceſter.

An extenſive down of fine paſture (which is common to the freeholders) lies a little eaſtward of the

the borough, where are viſible traces of intrenchments, and not far diſtant from them, five *tumuli*, or barrows, bearing teſtimony of a battle having been fought there. The people call the largeſt of them *Oſwald's Tump*, and have a tradition among them that the engagement was between Oſwald king of the Northumbrians, and Peuda king of the Mercians, wherein the latter proved victorious. It is probable, that upon the credit of this tradition ſir Robert Atkyns framed the etymology of the name of the town, which he aſſerts *is called Marſhfield from the Mercians, who gained a great victory over the Weſt Saxons near this place.* But the battle between Oſwald king of Northumberland, and Peuda king of Mercia, wherein the former was killed, really happened at a place called Maſerfeld, which being ſomething like Marſhfield occaſioned the miſtake. Oſwald's body was cruelly expoſed by his enemy upon a croſs, which, it is ſaid, occaſioned the place to be afterwards called Oſweſtre, in Britiſh *Croix Oſwald*, now a town in Shropſhire.

Our chronicles make no mention of any battle happening in this place, (tho' the barrows may be conſidered as an inconteſtible proof of it) wherefore we are totally in the dark as to the parties between whom, and the time when it happened.

There are three ſtones, near a place called the *Rocks*, to mark the limits of the counties of Glouceſter, Wilts, and Somerſet, where they meet in a point. One of thoſe ſtones ſtands in the pariſh of Marſhfield, which borders upon the two laſt mentioned counties; and I am inclined to think that this circumſtance gave occaſion to the name of the pariſh, for Meaꞃc, in the Anglo Saxon language, ſignifies a *limit*, or *boundary*. So Rodmarton, Didmarton, Tormarton, are names of villages all bordering on Wiltſhire, and are ſuppoſed to take their origin from the ſame circumſtance of ſituation, and to have the ſame Saxon word in their compoſition. Yet I am not ignorant that ſome would have the name derived from *Mars*, the god of war; whilſt others ſuppoſe that the true reading is *Marysfield*, from the dedication of the church to the virgin *Mary*; but the manner of writing it in *Domeſday* is unfavourable to theſe chymerical notions.

Of the Manor and other Eſtates.

This place is arranged in *Domeſday-book* under the title *Terra Regis*, and is conſequently part of the antient demeans of the crown.

'Queen Eddit held Meresfelde in Edredeſtane 'hundred. There are fourteen hides, and in de'mean five plow-tillages, and thirty-ſix villeins, 'and thirteen bordars, with thirteen plow-tillages. 'There are eighteen *ſervi*. A prieſt hath one of 'thoſe hides. In the time of king Edward it paid '35*l.* but it now pays 47*l.*' *Dom. Book*, p. 68.

Soon after the Norman conqueſt, this manor was given to the biſhoprick of Wells, and afterwards alienated, by John de Villula, biſhop of that dioceſe, who firſt aſſumed the title of biſhop of Bath, to the monaſtery of Bath in the year 1106. But it is probable they had only a term in it, for it paſſed afterwards to the earl of Glouceſter. William, the ſecond earl of Glouceſter, gave the manor of Marſhfield, with the hundred, to the abbey of Keynſham in Somerſetſhire, which he had founded for black canons, and amply endowed.

The abbat of Keynſham purchaſed a charter of markets and fairs, free warren, and other privileges, 50 H. 3. and a *Quo Warranto* iſſuing againſt him 15 E. 1. he pleaded this charter, and his plea was allowed; as it was in another *Quo Warranto* 2 R. 2. The abbat had a confirmation of markets, fairs, and other privileges, 2, 3, & 4 E. 4. and the manor continued in that abbey 'till it was diſſolved.

King Henry the Eighth granted a leaſe of this manor to ſir Anthony Kingſton, for ſix years, at 80*l.* rent; and lord Willoughby and ſir Thomas Henage obtained a grant of the inheritance, in exchange for lands in Lincolnſhire, 2 E. 6. Lord Willoughby conveyed the manor to the duke of Somerſet, by whoſe attainder it reverted to the crown.

King Edward the Sixth then granted a leaſe thereof, for thirty-nine years, at 80*l.* yearly rent, to ſir Henry Sydney. After which queen Elizabeth granted the fee to Thomas Ratcliffe, earl of Suſſex, and lord chamberlain, for his good ſervice againſt the rebels in the north. The earl ſold the manor to John Gorſlet, John Chambers, Nicholas Webb, and Thomas Cripps, which laſt died 43 Eliz. ſeized of Eggleſcombe's-wood, and divers meſſuages, lands, tenements, and of a certain annual ſum of money, called Port-rent and Burrowe-downe-rent, as appears by the eſcheator's inquiſition taken the following year. But much the greateſt ſhare of the eſtate was purchaſed by Gorſlet.

William Gorſlet, eſq; was lord of this manor in the year 1608, from whom it deſcended to John Harrington, of Kelſton in Somerſetſhire, eſq; whoſe mother was the daughter and heireſs of Mr. Gorſlet. From the Harringtons it paſſed by purchaſe, and is veſted in ſir William Codrington, baronet, the preſent lord of the manor.

William Att-Green was ſeized of four meſſuages and two yard-lands in Marſhfield, in truſt for the abbey of Keynſham, 19 E. 2. Sir John Tracy and others were ſeized of lands in this place 37 E. 3. William Gibbs and others were alſo ſeized of two meſſuages in Marſhfield, in truſt for the abbey of Keynſham, 21 R. 2.

TITHINGS and *HAMLETS*.

Beſide the borough, there are the eaſt, ſouth, and weſt tithings, with their proper officers. The hamlets are,

1. *Weſtonton*, formerly called *Old Marſhfield*, or *Little Marſhfield*. It has been a diſtinct pariſh, called St. Pancras, according to ſir Robert Atkyns; and a well in this hamlet ſtill bears the name of that ſaint.

The

The other hamlets made another diſtinct pariſh, under the denomination of St. Nicholas's pariſh.

2. *Okeford.* William de la Green held lands in Okeford and Upton, within the manor of Marſhfield, 4 E. 3. John Jacob, eſq; deſcended from the family of the Nortons in Wiltſhire, was lord of this manor at the beginning of this century, from whom it deſcended to Miſs Jacob, who has a handſome ſeat called the *Rocks*, near this place.

3. *Ayford.*

4. *Aſhwick.* Mr. William Webb was lord of the manor of Aſhwick, and proprietor of a good houſe and eſtate there, all which are now the property of Mr. Iſaac-Webb Hardwick.

5. *Bicks.* This manor formerly belonged to the Criſps, afterwards to ſir William Deans, and is now the property of Miſs Oland.

The manor of *Meers* in Marſhfield belonged formerly to the earls of Stafford. It was forfeited to the crown by the attainder of the duke of Buckingham, and granted to Henry lord Stafford, and to Urſula his wife, 2 Mar. and the ſame family now receives chief rents of ſeveral perſons in this place.

Of the Church, &c.

The church is a vicarage, in the deanery of Hawkeſbury, worth upwards of 200*l.* a year, including the ſeveral donations for its augmentation, before which it was valued at 50*l.* only.

In the reign of king Richard the Second, the impropriation and the advowſon belonged to the abbey of Keynſham; they were afterwards veſted in the abbey of Tewkeſbury, and coming to the crown at the diſſolution, queen Mary, 2° *regni*, gave them both, in exchange for the manor of Steepinglee, and other manors in Bedfordſhire and Eſſex, to New College in Oxford, who are patrons, and Mr. Michell is the preſent incumbent. The impropriation is worth about 300*l.* a year, and now in leaſe to Mr. Merryweather.

The vicarage was augmented in the year 1725, with a donation of 200*l.* by ſir William Perkins, and the queen's bounty.

The church is dedicated to St. Mary. It is a handſome building, conſiſting of the nave and an aile on each ſide, and a lofty tower, with pinnacles, at the weſt end, which, from its elevated ſituation, is ſeen at a great diſtance.

There were two chantries in this church: Jeſus chantry, of which Henry Neal was the laſt incumbent; and St. Clement's chantry, of which Robert Savage was the laſt incumbent, each of whom enjoyed a penſion of 1*l.* 10*s.* in the year 1553.

In the year 1529, Thomas Parker, who was chancellor and vicar general to Jeronimus de Ghinucciis, or de Nugutiis, an Italian, biſhop of Worceſter, at the requeſt of John Goſſelat the bailiff, and lord of the vill of Marysfield, (as it is called in a certain antient writing) and the greater part of the community of the ſame vill, eſtabliſhed a gild in this church, with rules or ſtatutes for the government of all that ſhould enter into that fraternity. More of the nature of theſe gilds may be ſeen under Dyrham. The ſame Thomas Parker new built the vicarage houſe, but that was taken down, and a very handſome one built on the ſcite of it, by Mr. Carey, the vicar, about the year 1734.

Firſt fruits £.29	4	8		Synodals £.0	2	0
Tenths — 2	18	5½		Pentecoſtals 0	1	0
Procurations 0	6	8				

Monuments and Inſcriptions.

There is nothing very curious under this head, what I have taken notice of being chiefly for the ſake of family arms, and charitable donations; except, indeed, the following quaint epitaph. Over it, in a ſcutcheon, is *a lion rampant*.

Life is the Day of Grace, and Death the Night;
Live well, who knows when he ſhall looſe the Light,
Soe did the tenant of this tombe, for hee
Made haſt to purchaſe Immortalitie.
Death finding him receaving Cuſtomes, lookes
Tymes Records, ſumde his Days, and croſſd the Bookes,
And now the Cuſtomers from Cuſtomes free,
He paid to Nature what her Duties bee.
Scarce had hee ranne ovt halfe his race of life,
When Heaven and Earth to have him were at Strife:
Whoſe active Sovle wore ovte his fleſh ſoe nigh,
Twas time ſhe ſhovld the tired corps lay by.
To bad men death is ſad; when good men dy
It is their Birth to ioyes eternitie:
Iudg then, what he did looſe who loſt but breath,
Liv'd to die well, and dyed A MEREDETH.

Non tam vita quam mortalitas finita.

On a marble monument,

Interred near this place lieth the Body of Dioniſia Long, Widow of Calthorp Long of Whaddon in the County of Wilts, Eſq. and Daughter of John Harrington of Kelſton in the County of Somerſet, Eſq. who departed this Life Dec. the 4th, 1744, Aged 86.—— Arms, *Baron and femme*, 1. *Sable, a lion rampant between ſix croſſes pattee argent, two voiders ermine*, for Long. 2. *Sable, a fret argent*, for Harrington.

On another marble table,

Near this Place lyeth interred the Body of IOHN GOSTLETT, Eſq. who departed this Life Ianvary the 24th MDCXCII. in the LXVIIth Year of his Age. —— Arms, *Gules, a chevron engraild ermine between three pheons heads Or.*

Againſt the ſouth wall are memorials for ſeveral of the Webbs of Aſhwick, with theſe arms, *Quarterly*, 1 & 4. *Or, on a bend ingrailed gules three croſſes croſlets fitchy argent.* 2 & 3. *Per pale gules and argent, a croſs patonce between four mullets counterchanged.*

In the north aile,

Here lyeth the Body of Elizabeth Gibbes, Relict of Alderman Henry Gibbes of the City of Briſtol Merchant, & eldeſt Daughter of John Harrington, Eſq; of Kelſton in the County of Somerſet, who departed this Life the 12th of October Anno Domini 1723, aged 67 Years. —— Arms, *Baron and femme*, 1. Harrington, as before. 2. *Argent, three poll-axes ſable*, 2 & 1, for Gibbes.

Againſt a pillar near the chancel,

This Monument is erected in Memory of Mr. Benjamin Viner of the City of Briſtol Merchant deceaſed, whoſe Body lies interred under a black Marble near this Place, leaving by Will 100*l.* to the Poor of this Pariſh, the Intereſt thereof to be given them half yearly on the 10th of March and the 10th of September for ever. The ſaid Sum was placed out on Government Security in New South-Sea Annuities in the Year 1748, in the Name of the Rev. Mr. John Carey, Vicar of this Pariſh.——Arms, *Azure, a bend Or, upon a chief argent two crows.*

Near

Near this place refteth the Body of Mr. Thomas Fecknaham, late vicar of this Parifh, who departed this Life the 2[d] Day of April An° Dom. 1704.

Si Labor terret, merces invitet.

Arms, *Sable, a chevron argent.*

Near this Place refteth the Body of IOHN BEARPACKER of the City of Briftol, Merchant, who departed this Life the 27th Day of Nov. 1715, aged 60 Years. Who gave One Hundred Pounds, the Profit thereof to be laid out yearly on ten Coats to be given to ten poor Men of this Parifh not receiving Alms, on every New-Years Day for ever. —— Arms, *Azure, a lion paffant between three croffes pattee fitchy.*

Benefactions.

The donations to the vicarage are fpecified under the account of the church.

John Harrington left 6*l.* a year, and the reverend Mr. Kennings 20*s.* a year for teaching children to read. Mrs. Dionifia Long gave an eftate of 29*l.* a year in Frampton Cotterel, and another of 26*l.* a year in Iron Acton, both purchafed in the year 1731, and 900*l.* in South-Sea Annuities, with which a fchool is endowed, and twenty boys have their clothing and education. But out of the income of thefe eftates, fix poor widows are to be paid 6*l.* a year each. The bifhop of the diocefe is a truftee.

Mr. Elias Crifpe, alderman of London, gave 4*l.* a year, paid out of Salter's-Hall, for eight fermons. He alfo founded an almfhoufe, confifting of a chapel, with a fpire in the middle, and eight dwellings for as many poor men and women, and endowed it with 26*l.* 13*s.* 4*d.* a year; which income fir Nicholas Crifpe afterwards enlarged by a donation of 100*l.* fo that the poor people now receive 1*s.* 6*d.* a week each. It appears by an infcription on the almfhoufe, that it was built in the year 1619.

Mr. Gunning, of Briftol, gave 5*l.* a year to the poor, and a piece of land has been purchafed with 150*l.* given at feveral times to the fame ufe.

Mr. Willis, killed at Gibraltar about eighty years ago, gave 25*l.* to be a ftock for the poor for ever.

Taxes.					
The Royal Aid in	1692,	£. 372	12	0
Poll-tax ——	1694,	—109	10	0
Land-tax ——	1694,	—394	4	0
The fame at 3*s.*	1770,	—219	0	0

At the beginning of this century there were 150 houfes, and about 800 inhabitants in this parifh, whereof 30 were freeholders; yearly births 29, burials 24. *Atkyns.* In ten years, beginning with 1760, the baptifms, exclufive of the diffenters, were 343, the burials, including all, 303; and the prefent number of inhabitants is about 1237.

MARSTON, *or* MARSTON SICCA.

THIS parifh lies in the upper divifion of the hundred of Kiftefgate, fix miles fouth-weft from Stratford upon Avon in Warwickfhire, fix north from Campden, and thirty-four north-eaft from Gloucefter.

It lies in a flat vale country, yet the greater part of the parifh is arable land. Antiently the name was written *Mereftone*, which I fuppofe to fignify the *marfhy town*, or *watry town*, for the parifh is very fubject to floods in the winter. This etymology is rendered more probable by confidering that there are feveral *Marftons* in Warwickfhire and Wiltfhire, which, as well as the place under confideration, lie in flat countries fubject to floods. The addition of *Sicca*, or *Dry*, tho' of an oppofite meaning, and incongruous to the former part of the name, is not unaptly apply'd to this place; for notwithftanding its fuperabundance of water in the winter, it is frequently very much diftreffed for want of it in dry feafons, and having no fpring in the parifh, the inhabitants are then obliged to drive their cattle to the Avon: What water they ufe for culinary purpofes, they commonly ftrain through fieves, to cleanfe it from myriads of infects with which it abounds in the fummer months. It is alfo called *Long Marfton*, from the length of the village, and becaufe the greater part of the houfes ftand in a row on the fide of the road.

The only curiofity in the village is a roafting-jack, in the poffeffion of Mr. Tomms, faid to be the fame which king Charles was fet to wind up, when he appeared as fervant to Mrs. Lane. It is not curious in itfelf, but only as it is connected in ftory with that prince.

Of the Manor and other Eftates.

'The church of S. Mary of Coventreu holds 'Mereftone in Celfleode hundred. There are ten 'hides, and three plow-tillages in demean, and 'fifteen villeins, and three bordars, with twelve 'plow-tillages. There are fix *fervi*, and a meadow 'worth 10*s.* It was worth 8*l.* now 100*s.*' *Domefday-book*, p. 72.

The eftate mentioned in the record to have been held by Hugh de Grentemaifnor, and apply'd to this parifh by fir Robert Atkyns, lies in Broad Marfton, in the parifh of Pebworth.

The prior of Coventry purchafed a charter for court leet, gallows, and tumbrel in this manor, in the reign of king Henry the Third, and pleaded this charter in a *Quo Warranto* brought againft him 15 E. 1. and his claim was allowed. It appears that the abbey of Winchcombe had a manor in Marfton at the fame time, for the abbey purchafed a charter of free warren in Merfton 35 H. 3. and bought the advowfon of the church in the fame reign. He was feized of the manor of Marfton, with free warren, 15 E. 1. at which time a *Quo Warranto* was alfo brought againft that abbat. But foon after, the whole manor was vefted in the abbey of Winchcombe, and fo continued 'till the diffolution.

It was granted to Robert earl of Leicefter 8 Eliz. and the lands were foon afterwards fold amongft feveral of the inhabitants, but the royalty of the manor was vefted in Ralph Sheldon, efq; in the year 1608, from whom it deſcends to William Sheldon, eſq; the preſent lord of this manor. His arms, as they are blazoned in the heralds laſt viſitation of this county, are, *Sable, a feſs Or between three drakes argent, a mullet for difference.*

The records ſhew, that Lettice the daughter of Nicholas purchaſed lands in Marſton, of Joan her ſiſter, who was married to Richard de la Hay, 8 Joh. Henry Cooper purchaſed lands in Dry Marſton, when they were divided, in the reign of queen Elizabeth, and left them to Thomas his ſon, who died ſeized thereof 9 Car. leaving Henry his ſon two years old.

Of the Church, &c.

The church is a rectory, in the deanery of Campden, of which Mr. Loggin is patron and incumbent. The pariſh has been lately incloſed, and lands allotted to the rectory in lieu of tithes, whereby the living, which before was worth about 145*l.* a year, is greatly improved. About 120 acres of paſture were the antient demean, and are tithe free.

The church is dedicated to St. James. It is a ſmall one, with a low tower. There is an inſcription for Mr. Samuel Burton, archdeacon of this dioceſe, which the reader may ſee at p. 164.

Firſt fruits £. 17	10	0	Synodals £. 0	1	0
Tenths — 1	15	0	Pentecoſt. 0	0	9½
Procurations 0	2	6			

Benefactions.

Mr. William Cooper, who died in 1643, gave 300*l.* to erect a ſchool in this pariſh, for the education of twenty-four boys, who are taught to read and write; *i. e.* out of Long Marſton eight, Pebworth ſix, Queinton four, Welford four, Dorſington two; which money purchaſed a houſe and cloſe in this pariſh, and a houſe and lands in Chipping-Norton in Oxfordſhire, let at 25*l.* a year.

Mr. Robert Loggin, who died in the year 1700, gave 40*l.* to the poor of this pariſh, and 10*l.* to the poor of Cow-Honeybourn.

Taxes.				
The Royal Aid in 1692,	£. 141	0	0
Poll-tax — — 1694,	— 29	10	0
Land-tax —— 1694,	— 116	14	0
The ſame, at 3*s.* 1770,	— 86	15	6

At the beginning of this century there were 40 houſes, and about 190 inhabitants in this pariſh, whereof 21 were freeholders; yearly births 6, burials 5. *Atkyns.* But ſir Robert's account was not accurate, for in ten years, beginning with 1700, the baptiſms were 70, and the burials 46; and in a like period, beginning with 1760, the baptiſms were 67, and the burials 42; and the preſent number of inhabitants is 199, which is in the proportion of ſomething more than 47 to 1 of the annual burials.

MATSON.

THIS pariſh lies in the hundred of Dudſton and King's-barton, ten miles diſtant ſouthweſtward from Cheltenham, ſeven north from Stroud, and three ſouth-eaſtward from Glouceſter.

It is very pleaſantly ſituated on the ſlope of a ſugar-loaf-hill, called Robin Hood's hill, which ſtands in the midſt of the vale, and tho' the aſcent is near a mile to the top of it, the ſoil is every where rich and fertile, and produces an excellent kind of herbage.

From before the Norman conqueſt, and for many ages afterwards, making and forging of iron was the principal employment of the town of Glouceſter, and the ore was fetched from this hill, where it is ſaid to be found in great plenty. The city of Glouceſter is ſupplied with their beſt water from ſprings that riſe on the ſide of it; and it appears by antient writings, that an aqueduct was carried from hence to that city, above four hundred years ago; for one William Gerard having granted the monks of the Grey Friers in Glouceſter a ſupply of water from this place, a diſpute aroſe between that houſe and St. Peter's abbey concerning the quantity the former was to receive, which was ſettled by Edward the Black Prince, in the year 1357.

The water of one of thoſe ſprings running over a bed of iron ore, diſſolves ſome of the finer particles, and is reputed to poſſeſs chalybeate properties.

The name of Matſon does not occur in *Domeſday-book*, nor does it appear by what name this village was known, when that record was compiled. About the reign of king Henry the Third, it was variouſly written, as *Matteſdune*, and *Mateſdone*; and afterwards *Matiſnoll*, *Mateſden*, and now as at the head of this account.

Of the Manors and other Eſtates.

The manor of Matſen was held of Humphry de Bohun and Joan his wife 46 E. 3. William de Gardinis was lord of Matteſdon in the reign of king Edward the Firſt.

William Nottingham, eſq; the king's attorney-general, by his deed, dated Aug. 13, 10 E. 4. gave the manor of Matteſdon to the abbey of Glouceſter, for the erecting of a chantry in the abbey, to be ſupplied by two of their own monks; and a family of the name of Robins, alias Botcher, were for ſeveral generations ſucceſſive tenants under the abbey. After the diſſolution, the manor was granted to the chapter of Glouceſter 33 H. 8.

There is another manor in this pariſh, for the records ſhew, that William Gerard de Mateſden, and Catherine his wife, levied a fine of the manor of Matteſden, and of lands in Cugley in the pariſh of Newent, to the uſe of themſelves in ſpecial taille, 8 E. 2.

The manor-houſe of Matteſdon, and all the buildings, orchards, gardens, and all the paſture

 and

and arable lands, formerly appurtenant to the houſe, being parcel of the land that belonged to the priory of Lanthony, were granted, by the crown, to the mayor and burgeſſes of Glouceſter, Sept. 11, 34 H. 8. And the mayor and burgeſſes, with the king's licence, ſold the ſame to Thomas Lane, eſq; Dec. 10, 35 H. 8.

Richard Pate was ſeized of Matſon in the reign of king Edward the Sixth. Richard Liggon had livery of it 9 Eliz. ſoon after which it was convey'd to the Selwyns.

William Selwyn was governor of Jamaica. He had three ſons; John, of whom hereafter; Charles, who died without iſſue; and Henry, who married Ruth Compton, daughter of Anthony Compton of Gainſlow, near Berwick upon Tweed, eſq; and by her had iſſue two ſons, Charles-Jaſper, and William; and ſeven daughters, Albinia lady Boſton, Catharine Wilkes, Mary, Charlotte, Frances, Hannah, (deceaſed,) and Louiſa.

Charles-Jaſper, the elder ſon, married Elizabeth, daughter of Mr. Coxeter, of Bampton in Oxfordſhire, and by her hath three ſons and three daughters.

William, the ſecond ſon, is an eminent barriſter at law. He married Frances-Elizabeth, daughter of Dr. John Dod, of Woodford in Eſſex, and by her hath iſſue two ſons, George and Thomas, and two daughters.

I return now to John the eldeſt ſon of governor Selwyn. He married Mary, daughter of major-general Farrington, of Chiſlehurſt in Kent, by whom he had iſſue two ſons, John, and George-Auguſtus; and one daughter Albinia, married to the honourable Thomas Townſhend, lately deceaſed, and by him had iſſue three ſons, Thomas, Charles, and Henry; and two daughters, Albinia, married to George lord Middleton; and Mary. Thomas Townſhend, the eldeſt ſon, married Elizabeth Powys, and by her hath iſſue four ſons and two daughters. Charles, the ſecond ſon, died unmarried. Henry, the third ſon, was a lieutenant-colonel of the firſt regiment of the foot-guards, and was killed at Wilhelmſtahl, in the year 1762.

John Selwyn, ſon of John, died unmarried in the year 1751, whereby

George-Auguſtus, the ſecond ſon, ſucceeded his brother, and is the preſent lord of this manor, and has a handſome ſeat near the church, and a large eſtate here. He has repreſented the city of Glouceſter in five ſucceſſive parliaments, and is now one of the repreſentatives for that city. His arms are, *Argent, on a bend ſable, cotized azure, three annulets, within a bordure ingrailed gules.*

Of the Church, &c.

The church is a rectory, in the deanery of Glouceſter, worth about 25*l.* a year, beſides the augmentation it has received by Mr. Hodges's legacy, and the queen's bounty. There is no houſe for the incumbent.

Ernulph the ſon of Ralph gave the church of Matteſdone to the abbey of Glouceſter, and Simon biſhop of Worceſter confirmed the grant. The advowſon of the rectory of Mattiſdon, late belonging to the abbey of Glouceſter, (not to the priory of Lanthony, as in ſir Robert Atkyns) was granted to the chapter of Glouceſter 34 H. 8. And the dean and chapter of Glouceſter are patrons.

The church is ſmall and neat, with the following inſcription over the door: *This Church rebuilt at the ſole Expence of Albinia Selwyn, Relict of his Excellency Major-General Selwyn, A. D.* 1739.

Firſt fruits	£. 3	16	$3\frac{1}{2}$	Synodals	£. 0	1	0
Tenths	— 0	7	$7\frac{3}{4}$	Pentecoſtals	0	0	$2\frac{1}{2}$

Monuments and Inſcriptions.

Againſt the ſouth wall,

Memoriæ Sacrum Gulielmi, Theophili, et Jaſperi, Filiorum Gulielmi Selwyn, Arm. et Margaretæ Uxoris ejus, qui uno eodemque fatali Morbo correpti, Fato ceſſere immaturo, Gulielmus, Parentum primogenitus, quinquennium pene expletus 7mo Die Auguſti Ano 1649 obijt. Theophilus triennium, Jaſperus Menſem Ætatis undecimum, peragentes, parum in Morte ſeparati occubuere, hic 27° ille 29° Die Septembris Ano 1655.

On a tomb in the church-yard,

Memoriæ Sacrum Viri admodum colendiſſimi Gulielmi Selwyn, de Matiſdon Armigeri, Civitatis Glouc. ſpecialis è Regis Mandato Aldermanni, nec non Prætoris digniſſimi; Tam Civitatis quam Comitatus Glouenſis per multos Annos Pacis Cuſtodis celeberrimi. Qui (poſt Annos juveniles Studiis Artibuſq; Academicis, maturiores et Deo et Principi Pietate heu nimis cito elapſos) poſt longam Paralyxin cruciat.. miſer.. ſubita Paryxiſmate (ſibi in Salutem, Patriæ in Damnum) ereptus. Animam Cœlis, his Urnis (quæ ſui Pars minima erant) Cineres commiſit, (Hoc Monumentum Pientiſſima et Deo et Conjugi erexit Uxor, Metam felicem ambiens eandem) Maij octavo, Anno Ætatis 56, Salutis 1679.

On a blue ſtone in the chancel, for a gentleman of the ſame family, who was killed in a duel,

Sacrum Memoriæ Edvardi, Gulielmi Selwyn Arm. filij natu maximi, Viri, cum Corporis forma, tum etiam Mentis dotibus, Præſtantiſſimi; Rationis Acumine, Memoriæ Firmitate, Eruditione non dicendi Copia, Morum Suavitate, Cœtaneorum cuipiam haud facile poſtponendi. Duxit in Uxorem Ioannam Filiam Iohannis Browning de Coaley Arm. qua cum per aliquot annos vitam agens feliciſſimam, nondum tamen, Proh dolor! ſuſcepta prole, ipſo adhuc Iuventutis flore, crudeli fato extinctus, ad plures conceſſit 3 Idibus April. 1673, et Ætatis ſuæ 23.

Sub tumulo jacet hoc funeſta cæde peremptus,
Quem Socii rapuit ſanguinolenta manus:
Heu Pietas, heu priſca Fides, ſic jungere Dextras,
Sic colere et ſanctæ Nomen Amicitiæ.
At Tu qui Lector fidum tibi queris amicum,
Doctus ab exemplis, ne ſociere Malo.

At the weſt end of the church,

In Memory of Henry Selwyn, Eſq; who died Sept. 1734, aged 45, and of M^rs. Ruth Selwyn, his Widow, one of the Daughters of Anthony Compton of Gainſlow, near Berwick upon Tweed, Eſq; who died the 3^d Day of May, 1761, aged 63. And alſo of two of their Daughters, Albinia Lady Boſton, who died the 2^d of April 1769, aged 49; and Hannah Selwyn, who died the 15th of November, 1756, aged 31.

Taxes.	The Royal Aid in 1692,	£. 30	1	4
	Poll-tax —— 1694,	— 5	14	0
	Land-tax —. 1694,	— 50	4	0
	The ſame at 3*s.* 1770,	— 37	13	0

In the year 1562, there were only 7 houſholders in this pariſh. At the beginning of the preſent century, there were 9 houſes, and about 50 inhabitants, whereof 3 were freeholders; yearly births 1, burials 1. *Atkyns.* The preſent number of inhabitants is 45.

MAYSEMORE

MAYSEMORE

IS a parifh in the hundred of Dudfton and King's-barton, feven miles fouth-eaft from Newent, eight fouth-weftward from Tewkefbury, and two north-weft from Gloucefter.

It confifts chiefly of rich meadow and pafture land. The turnpike road from Gloucefter to Worcefter, and to Ledbury, leads through it; and there is a bridge over the Severn at a place called the Lower Lode, which is repaired at the expence of this parifh. Upon Mayfemore bridge there formerly ftood a crofs, with this infcription :

In honore Dni nri Ihu Crifti qui nobis crucifixus erat. Ceofie croz fift Willm fiz Anketill de Lilton, Et Cifeoli Willm fiz Anketill comenza pont de Mazemore. That is, *For the honour of the lord Jefus Chrift, who was crucified for us, William the fon of Anketill made this crofs, and the fame William the fon of Anketill began the bridge of Mayfemore.*

Of the Manor and other Eftates.

The name of this manor is not to be found in *Domefday-book*, for when that record was compiled, this was part of the parifh of St. Mary de Lode.

King Henry the Firft gave this manor, then called Ablode, and the grove of Barton, called Paygrave, to the abbey of Gloucefter, *ad victum Monachorum*, in exchange for an orchard in Gloucefter, which belonged to the monks of that abbey; and in the year 1101, granted the abbey free warren therein, which was allowed 15 E. 1. It continued in that houfe 'till the diffolution, and upon erecting the fee of Gloucefter, was granted to the bifhoprick 33 H. 8. as appears by the endowment. It was confirmed 6 E. 6. and the bifhop of Gloucefter is lord of the manor.

Henry Bawn and others were feized of two meffuages and one yard-land in Mayfemore and Leghterton, in truft for the abbey of Gloucefter, 11 R. 2. John Trimmes and others were feized of two meffuages, twenty acres of arable, eight acres of meadow, and two acres of wood in Mayfemore, one toft in Gloucefter, and one acre in Alemore 15 R. 2.

A portion of tithes, and common in Pully-mead in Mayfemore, formerly belonging to the abbey of Gloucefter, were granted to Arthur Porter 32 H. 8.

HAMLET. Overton is a fmall hamlet in this parifh, of which there is nothing remarkable.

Of the Church, &c.

The church is a curacy, in the deanery of Gloucefter. The bifhop has the impropriation, and his leffee provides a minifter with the bifhop's approbation, to whom he pays 12*l.* a year. This curacy has been twice augmented, in the years 1719, and 1733, by donations from their lordfhips the bifhops of Winchefter and Gloucefter, and by a legacy left by Mr. Hodges, and the queen's bounty; fo that it is now worth 60*l.* a year. The church formerly belonged to St. Mary before the abbey gate. Abbat Gilbert Foliot granted it to the light of the altar of St. Peter, at the intreaty of the whole convent.

The church, which is dedicated to St. Giles, has a handfome embattled tower at the weft end, with five bells.

Synodals £ 0 1 0 Pentecoftals £ 0 1 0

Monuments and Infcriptions.

Near the chancel,

Infra repofiti fuere Cineres Francifci Wheeler, de Mayfemore, Generofi, et Gilberti filii ejus primogeniti : hVnC (anno ætatis 39) dies XIX noVeMbrIs PatreM Vero In ætatis sVæ LXXi DIes XVII aprILIs eXtInXti. Quorum Gratia Relicta Francifci chariffima hoc Marmor pofuit in Memoriam. Cujus etiam quod mortale fubtumulatum eft die 27 Maij An° 1630. Dimitte jam oculos Lector, tibi cave et confule, ora et abi. —— Arms, *Or, a chevron between three leopards heads caboſhed fable.*

By the pulpit,

Hic jacet Robertus Willoughby, filius Thomæ Willoughby de Bore Place in Comitatu Cantij Armigeri et Katherinæ filiæ Percivalli Hart in dict. Comitatu Militis, Collegij Magdalenfis olim Socius, in artibus Magifter, nec non Medicinæ Baccalaureus, qui mortem obijt 25 Aug. Ann. Salutis 1641.———Arms, *Or, fretty azure.*

Againft the chancel, in the church-yard,

M. S. In Spe beatæ refurectionis, Quod Mortale fuit hic depofuit Rob. Carpenter, gen. Vir, (fi quis alius) fpectatiffima fide, morum integritate, Quem Liberi Parentem vere benignum, Ecclefia Anglicana genuinum Filium, Omnes Defideratiffimum habuere. Hunc inter Vitæ tedia duobus annis plus minus colluctantem inveterata Phtyfis (vel invito Efculapio) corripuit in Cœlum xvi Junij Anno Ætatis 43, Domini 1675. Hoc quale Robertus filius natu maximus in perpetuum obfervantiæ Monumentum L. M. Q. P.———Arms, *Paly of fix argent and gules, a chevron azure charged with three croffes croflets bottony Or.*

Benefactions.

Mr. Francis Wheeler, arch-deacon of Salop, who died in 1675, and was buried here, gave 50*s.* for a fermon on New-years-day, paid by the minifter and bailiffs of Bridgnorth, and fecured by lands near that town. He alfo gave bread monthly to the poor, which charity is fecured by an acre of land in Wickham meadow. Mrs. Grace Wheeler, his widow, has given the like charity; and Mr. Edmond Ready has given bread to the poor.

Taxes.				
The Royal Aid in 1692, £.	113	5	4
Poll-tax —— 1694, —	21	12	0
Land-tax —— 1694, —	152	12	0
The fame, at 3*s.* 1770, —	114	9	0

In the year 1562, there were 36 houfholders in this parifh. At the beginning of this century, there were 44 houfes, and about 200 inhabitants, whereof 6 were freeholders; yearly births 6, and burials 6. The inhabitints are now 210.

MEYSEY-HAMPTON.

PART of this parifh lies in Wiltfhire, but the greater part is in the hundred of Crowthorne and Minety, in Gloucefterfhire, and antiently lay in Gerfdones hundred. The church ftands fix miles diftant weft from Leachlade, fix eaft eaſt from Cirenceſter, and twenty-three (by the road through the laſt-mentioned town) ſouth-eaſtward from Glouceſter.

It conſiſts of rich meadow and paſture, and very good arable land. It is bounded in part by the river Thames on the ſouth ſide, and by the road from Cirenceſter to London on the north.

The name of Hampton has been already explained. The prenomen was taken from the family of the Meyſies, who were antiently owners of this manor, and ſerved to diſtinguiſh it from two or three other places in this county of the ſame name.

Of the Manor and other Eſtates.

The *Domeſday* account belonging to this pariſh, was miſapplied by ſir Robert Atkyns to Minchin Hampton. It may be thus tranſlated:

'Earl Roger holds Hantone in Gerſdones hun-'dred, and Turold, nephew to Wiget, holds it of 'him. Leueric held it. There are five hides. 'There is one plow-tillage in demean, and four 'villeins, and two bordars, and a prieſt, and two 'other men, who have among them all two plow-'tillages and a half. There are ſix *ſervi*. It was 'worth 8 *l.* now [only] 3 *l.*' *Domeſday-book*, p. 73.

This manor was held of the honour of Glouceſter, and the pariſh is now within the juriſdiction of the court of that honour. The maſter of the knights-templers had court-leet, waifs, and felons goods, by the grant of king Henry the Third, which were allow'd in a *Quo warranto* brought againſt him 15 E. 1.

Robert de Meyſie was lord of this manor, and high ſheriff of the county, in the year 1255, whoſe ſon William ſucceed him, and left John Meyſie his ſon and heir. Robert Meyſie, kinſman to John, was ſeized of Marſton Meyſie in the ſame pariſh, and agreed to pay John 12 *d.* yearly, that the tenants of Marſton Meyſie ſhould pay ſuit of court to the manor of Hampton Meyſie only twice a year, 43 H. 3. The ſame John de Meyſie left Eve, or Elianor, an only daughter and heireſs, married to Nicholas de St. Maur, who, in her right, died ſeized of the manor of Hampton Meyſey, and the advowſon of the church, 11 E. 2. *Eſch.*

Richard Seymour, ſon of Nicholas, died ſeized of this manor 2 H. 4. and was ſucceeded by his ſon Richard, who had an only daughter and heireſs Alice, with whom this eſtate paſſed by her marriage to William lord Zouch.

William Zouch died ſeized of Meyſey-Hampton 23 H. 8. leaving Frances, his only daughter and heireſs, married to William Sanders, who levied a fine thereof to Edmond lord Chandos 4 Mar. Sir John Hungerford was lord of this manor in the year 1608. It was afterwards the property of ſir Matthew Hale, from whom it paſſed in exchange for Alderley, to Mr. Barker of Fairford, whoſe deſcendant, Mrs. Lambe, is the preſent lady of this manor, and keeps a court leet.

HAMLET. *Marſton* is a very large hamlet and tithing, lying in Wiltſhire, on the north ſide of the Thames, and had its name from its low and marſhy ſituation. The biſhop of Saliſbury is lord of this manor. For the convenience of the inhabitants, who are at a conſiderable diſtance from the church, there is a neat chapel of eaſe built in this hamlet, dedicated to St. James. The rector of Meyſey-Hampton is patron. It has been augmented by the queen's bounty. The intereſt of 70 *l.* is left for the education and apprenticing of poor children of this hamlet.

Of the Church, &c.

The church is a rectory, in the deanery of Fairford, worth about 300 *l.* a year, in the gift of Corpus Chriſti College in Oxford. The reverend William Camplin, clerk, is the preſent incumbent. Livery of the advowſon was granted to Giles Bridges, lord Chandos, 15 Eliz.

The glebe conſiſts of about 80 acres of arable, and 25 acres of meadow and paſture. No lands are exempt from tithe.

The church, dedicated to St. Mary, is built in the form of a croſs, with a tower in the middle, in which are ſix bells.

Firſt fruits £. 20	17	2	Synodals £. 0	2	0
Tenths — 2	1	8½	Pentecoſt. 0	1	6
Procurations 0	6	8			

Monuments and Inſcriptions.

There is a very large monument in the chancel, with the buſts of a man and his two wives. Under his buſt is this inſcription:

Stay, mortall, ſtay : and looke uppon
The language of A ſpeakeing ſtone ;
Nor wonder is't that he ſhould giue
Speech to A ſtone, who bade men liue ;
When nature bid them dye : 'tis hee
By whome I liue ; not he by mee.
This ſaid ; I may againe be dumbe
I'ue ſpoke enough to tell whoſe Tombe
This is : & thou mayeſt greeueing knowe
That none but VAVLX can lye below.

Hoc monumētū, quo melius apud poſteros patris dilectiſſimi uigeat memoria, non ſine lachrim: fieri fec: fil^s. natu max^s. Fr^s: Vavlx.

Over his firſt wife's head is written,

Here reſteth the body of Editha Iinner, who the 18th day of Au. 1617, being called to the Ioyes of A better world lefte behind her IX ſonnes and III daughters, all of them the pledges of that coniugal loue that was betweene herſelfe and her ſuruiuinge huſband, who was [*then over his buſt it follows*] that famous practitioner in Phyſicke & Chirurgery IAMES VAVLX, Eſquier, who deceaſed March 24th 1626 to the generall loſſe of the whole countrey & the priuate greefe of all his Freindes, more particularly of his moſt ſorrowfull then wife who was [*over his ſecond wife's buſt it follows*] Philip Horton, daughter of William Horton, of Staunton in the County of Worceſt. Eſq^r. who in greife & heauineſs partinge with her deereſt conſort is left behind to cheriſh ye hopes of three ſonnes now liuing, one daughter being called to heauen before her father.——Arms, over him, *Quarterly*, 1ſt & 4th, *Argent, a bend checky Or and gules*, for Vaulx. 2d & 3d, *Sable, a pelican argent vulned proper.* Over his firſt wife's head, *Three cups*, for Jenner. Over his ſecond wife, *Quarterly*, 1ſt, *Sable, three bendlets ingrailed*, for Horton. The other quarters are obliterated.

Doctor Vaulx's reputation was ſo great, that it is ſaid king James the Firſt ſent for him to court, to make him his phyſician; but aſking the doctor how he had acquired his knowledge in the healing art, whether from reading, or by obſervation and practice,

and

and being anſwered, by practice, his majeſty replied, *Then by my ſaul thou haſt killed mony a mon; thou ſhalt never practiſe upon me,* and ſo diſmiſs'd him.

In the ſouth croſs aile,

These ſtones erected for ye Memorie of Margaret Griſwald thvs doe teſtifie

A Margret, a Pearle of Price, lies here
Well born, well bred, embalmd in happie name
An Vnion right pretiovs and deare
Her Worth did fvlly eqvalize her name
This bleſſed Spark of that pvre flame above
Did ſhine moſt brightly in faith Hope and love
In peerleſſe bliſſe above the ſtares ſhes placed
Earth hath her tombe, heavens have her ſovle embraced.

Note, She was wife of Edward Griſwald, Gent. and died at Marſton June 23, 1625, whither ſhe went for doctor Vaulx's advice.——Arms, *A feſs between two greyhounds courant.*

Benefactions.

In the year 1650, Richard Samway, rector of the pariſh, gave 10*l.* the intereſt to be equally diſtributed every year between the poor of Meyſey Hampton, and thoſe of Marſton; and in the year 1712, John Beall, D.D. then rector, gave the like ſum to the ſame uſe. In 1706, Anne Forſhew gave 5*l.* In 1715, Thomas Gegg gave 5*l.* In 1721, John Forſhew gave 5*l.* the intereſt of which ſums to be given to the poor of this place. And John Kireheval, D.D. rector of this pariſh, gave 60*l.* each to Meyſey Hampton and Marſton, the intereſt to be expended in the ſchooling and apprenticing out of poor children; and in 1756, John Jenner gave 20*l.* to the former, and 10*l.* to the latter, for the uſe of their poor.

Taxes.						
	The Royal Aid in	1692,	£. 75	0	0
	Poll-tax —	1694, —	20	5	0
	Land-tax —	1694, —	64	4	0
	The ſame, at 3*s.*	1770, —	48	3	0

At the beginning of this century, there were 83 houſes, and about 360 inhabitants in the whole pariſh, whereof 14 were freeholders in the Glouceſterſhire part; yearly births 8, burials 8. *Atkyns.* In the year 1776, there were 54 houſes, and 265 inhabitants in the Glouceſterſhire part; and the ſouls in the hamlet of Marſton are computed to be at leaſt 200.

MICKLETON.

THIS pariſh lies in the upper diviſion of the hundred of Kifteſgate, ſeven miles diſtant eaſt from Eveſham in Worceſterſhire, five north from Campden, and thirty-one north-eaſtward from Glouceſter.

It is ſituated in the vale part of the county, and conſiſts wholly of rich paſture land. The name ſignifies the *great town,* from the old word *mickle,* or *muckle,* which is ſtill uſed for *great* in Scotland, tho' now obſolete in this part of our iſland. And it was very properly ſo called, for whilſt the neighbouring pariſhes conſiſted of three or four, and ſome of five or ſix hides of land, it appears by *Domeſday,* that there were no leſs than fourteen in Mickleton, independent of the hamlets of Clopton and Hidcote.

Meen-hill, ſtanding between this pariſh and Queinton, is no leſs beautiful on account of the richneſs of its verdure, than conſpicuous from its ſituation in the midſt of the vale. Part of it lies in this pariſh, and part in Queinton, under which head more may be read in its commendation from the good old poet Drayton, as well as ſome account of the camp on its top, and of the battle ſaid to have been fought there.

Giles Widows, and Thomas his brother, were natives of this place, and zealous friends to the royal cauſe in the great civil war. The former diſtinguiſhed himſelf as a clergyman, by his loyal ſermons, preached at Oxford, whilſt that city was garriſoned by king Charles the Firſt. He died in 1645. Thomas was ſucceſſively maſter of the ſchools at Glouceſter, Woodſtock, and Northleach, and author of a ſatyrical piece intituled, The *Juſt Devil of Woodſtock,* giving an account of the frightful apparition that diſturbed the parliament commiſſioners in the ſale of the king's lands. He died in 1655.

That great and eminent lawyer, ſir Anthony Keck, was alſo born here, in 1630, and was conſtituted one of the lords commiſſioners of the great ſeal of England, in 1688. At his death, he left a large eſtate to his ſon Francis Keck, of Great Tewe in Oxfordſhire, eſq; which is ſtill enjoy'd by his deſcendants.

But not leſs eminent for learning than either of the forementioned perſons, was Mr. Richard Graves, lord of this manor, who died in the year 1729. With great diligence he employ'd the latter part of his life time to inveſtigate, and to give an hiſtorical account of the antiquities of the country in this neighbourhood; but his papers were never publiſhed, and the editor of the preſent work greatly regrets the misfortune of not being able to avail himſelf of them.

Of the Manor and other Eſtates.

This manor was in the crown in the year 960, in the reign of king Edgar. Æthelmere, or Ailmer, earl of Devonſhire, gave it, with the advowſon of the church, to the abbey of Eynſham in Oxfordſhire, which he founded in the year 1005, for monks of the Benedictine order. In *Domeſday* it is thus recorded:

'The church of Egleſham holds Muceltude in 'Celfledetorn hundred. There are fourteen hides, 'and five plow-tillages in demean, and twenty 'villeins, and eight bordars, with ten plow-tillages. 'There are eight *ſervi,* and two *ancillæ,* and 'twenty-four meaſures of ſalt from Wich. It is 'worth and was worth 10*l.* The ſame church 'held it in the time of king Edward.' *D. B.* p. 72.

The abbat of Eynſham pleaded his right to court leet and free warren, in the proceedings on a writ of *Quo warranto* brought againſt him, 15 E. 1. and his claim was then allowed, as it was again 34 E. 3.

By the diſſolution of the abbey, the manor came to the crown, and it was not alienated 'till queen Elizabeth

Elizabeth, in the year 1591, granted it to Richard Lukenore, and others, in truſt for John lord Lumley, who, in the year 1597, ſold it to Edward Fiſher, eſq; who died ſeized of it in 1627. Sir Edward Fiſher, his ſon, ſucceeded him, whoſe ſon, Edward Fiſher, eſq; ſold this eſtate, in the year 1656, to Richard Graves, eſq; who alſo purchaſed the manors of Weſton-Subedge, Aſton-Subedge, and the royalty of the hundred of Kifteſgate.

Richard Graves, eſq; dying in 1669, was ſucceeded by his ſon and heir Samuel Graves, who died in 1708. His ſon, Richard Graves, eſq; ſucceeded him, and was father of Morgan Graves, eſq; who died about the year 1771, and was ſucceeded by his ſon and heir Walwyn Graves, eſq; the preſent lord of this manor, and of thoſe of Weſton-Subedge, and Aſton-Subedge, and of the royalty of the hundred of Kifteſgate. His arms are, *Gules, an eagle diſplay'd Or*, as I find them, with many quarterings, on the monuments for this family, in the church of Mickleton. He has a good houſe, and a large eſtate here, and in other parts of this county, and elſewhere.

The earl of Coventry has alſo a good eſtate in this pariſh.

John de Vall was ſeized of lands in Mickleton 36 E. 3. as were William Grevil of Campden 3 H. 4. and ſir John Burge 11 E. 4. William Dalby and his wife levied a fine of lands in Mickleton 11 H. 7.

TITHINGS and *HAMLETS*.

1. *Hidcote* is a tithing in this pariſh, diſtinguiſhed by the additional name of *Bateram*, from another Hidcote in the pariſh of Ebrington. In *Domeſday* it is thus recorded :

'The church of Wincelcumbe holds Hidicote 'in Celflede hundred. There are two hides free, 'and one plow-tillage in demean, with one *ſervus*. 'It is worth and was worth 40*s*.' *D. B.* p. 71.

This eſtate was afterwards veſted in the priory of Bradenſtoke in Wiltſhire, and at the diſſolution of that houſe, was granted by the crown to John Wyley and John Scudamore 37 H. 8. The manor now belongs to Thomas Edwards Freeman, of Batsford, in this county, eſq.

2. *Clopton* is another tithing. 'William Goizenboded holds Cloptune in Ceolflede hundred. A 'houſe-carle held it in the time of king Edward. 'There are ten hides, and three plow-tillages in 'demean, and twelve villeins, and four bordars, 'and one radecheniſter, with nine plow-tillages. 'In Wicelcumbe there is one burgage [belonging 'to it.] It was worth 8*l.* now 100*s*.' *D. B.* p. 74.

This manor was given to the priory of Bonhommes at Eddington in Wiltſhire, and was granted by the crown to Michael Aſhfield 32 H. 8. It afterwards paſſed to the family of the Overburies, then to Thomas Rowney, of Oxfordſhire, eſq; and was given by a deſcendant from him to the honourable Mr. Noel, who is the preſent lord of the manor, and proprietor of a conſiderable eſtate in this place.

Of the Church, &c.

The church is a vicarage, in the deanery of Campden, worth 80*l.* a year. The lord chancellor is patron, and Mr. Benjamin Feild is the preſent incumbent.

The rectory belonged to the abbey of Eynſham, and was granted to Roger Mannors, eſq; 18 Eliz. and now belongs to the honourable Mr. Noel, who has all the great tithes ; and the vicar hath all the vicarial tithes. Tithes in Mickleton and Hedecot belonged to the abbey of Winchcombe, and were granted to ſir Thomas Seymour 1 E. 6.

Twenty-eight acres belong to the glebe.

The church is very handſomely pewed. It conſiſts of a nave and two ſide ailes, with a large chancel, and a gallery at the weſt end, and a ſpire ſteeple in the middle, with ſix bells.

In the window of the north aile, are ſeveral ſcutcheons with the family arms of Graves, impaling thoſe of Bates and Swan ; alſo France and England quarterly. In two compartments, it is thus written in the Saxon character :

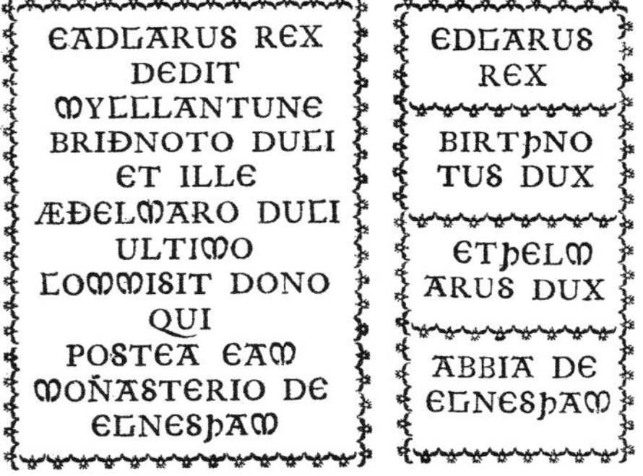

EADGARUS REX
DEDIT
MYCLLANTUNE
BRIDNOTO DUCI
ET ILLE
ÆDELMARO DUCI
ULTIMO
COMMISIT DONO
QUI
POSTEA EAM
MONASTERIO DE
EGNESHAM
EDGARUS
REX
BIRTHNO
TUS DUX
ETHELM
ARUS DUX
ABBIA DE
EGNESHAM

First fruits £.9 14 3 Synodals £.0 2 0
Tenths — 0 19 $5\frac{1}{4}$ Pentecoſtals 0 0 $11\frac{1}{2}$
Procurations 0 9 0

Monuments and Inſcriptions.

In the chancel is this inſcription,

M M. S. Subter aut prope hunc lapidem reconduntur Heroum vere nobilium et colendiſſimorum Exuviæ Edwardi Fiſher Armigeri ; qui uxorem duxit Aviciam filiam digniſſimam digniſſimi illius Richardi Thornhill de Bromly in Comitatu Cantiano Armigeri.

Edvardi Fiſher Militis, cui uxor erat Deo et hominibus chara Domina Maria filia primogenita eminentiſſimi viri, Armis literiſq; clari, Thomæ Chaloneri Militis, Auguſtiſſimo Principi Henrico Gubernatoris ; Dominorum hujus Manerij ex prænobili et antiquiſſima ſtirpe Fiſherorum de Fiſherwick ſuper Trentam in Comitatu Staffordiæ oriundum E. F. Arm. H. MMT. Po. An. Dom. 1659.———Over the inſcription, is a large ſcutcheon with twelve quarterings, 1ſt, *Gules, three demy lions Or, a chief of the ſecond*, for Fiſher, 2d, *Argent, on a feſs ingrailed azure three croſſes patty Or.* 3d, *Azure, three eagles diſplay'd Or.* 4th, *Ermine, five chevronels gules, on a canton of the ſecond, a lion paſſant Or.* 5th, *Barry of ten pieces argent and gules, within a bordure azure charged with eight martlets Or.* 6th, *Vaire, a pale ſable.* 7th, *Argent, three croſſes lozengy gules.* 8th, *Barry of ten pieces argent and gules, over all a lion rampant ſable.* 9th, *Argent, three horſeſhoes ſable.* 10th, *Quarterly*, 1ſt, *and* 4th, *Gules*, 2d, *and* 3d, *Vaire Or and Vert, Over all a lion rampant argent.* 11th, *Argent, a feſs Vaire Or and gules between three eagles diſplay'd of the laſt.* 12th, *Paly of ſix, argent and gules, a bend Vaire Vert and Or.* The ſame arms are painted on the glaſs, with this motto, VIGILET QVI VINCET.——On the

the dexter side of the table are the Fishers arms, impaling, *Azure, four bars argent, on a chief of the second a castle with three towers Or. Over all a bend of the first*, for Thornhill. On the sinister side, Fisher, impaling many arms quarterly.

Over their grave is a railed marble tomb, and against the Fishers arms at the head is written, Qui obiit 16 Sept. 1627, to be understood of Edward the father; and against his wife's arms, Quæ obiit 3 Julij, 1604.——Against sir Edward Fishers arms, at the feet, Qui obiit 29 Dec. 1654, and against his lady's, Quæ obiit 8 Nov. 1642.

On the table of another monument,

To the Memory of John Graves of Beamesley in Yorksh. Gent. of the Family of Grave of Heyton in that County, who mar[d] the d[r] & h[r] of Menseir. He died at Lond. 1616, aged near 103, & was bur. at S. Martin's, Ludgate.

Rich. Graves s. of I. Cit[n] of Lond. who by Frances d[r]. of Will. Gurney Esq; had Issue 4 sons & 5 d[rs]. He died 1626 æt. 54 & was bur. at S[t]. Martin's Ludgate.

Rich. Graves s. & h[r]. of R. L[d] of the Royalty of the Hundred of Kiftesgate & of the Man[rs] of Micklet[n]. Aston, & Weston in this County; for many years one of the Benchers, & at length Reader, of Lincoln' Inn; Who by two Wives had Issue 19 Child. viz. by Eln[r]. d[r]. & h[r]. of Th. Bates Gent. 6 sons, & 9 d[rs]. & by Eliz. d[r]. of Io. Robinson Esq[r]. 4 d[rs]. He died 1669 æt. 59. Eln[r]. 1656 æt. 39. & Eliz. 1713. æt. 96. And he, & Eliz. were bur. at Clarkenwell; & Eln[r] at Richmond.

Sam. Graves, s. & h[r]. of R. L[d] of this Man[r]. who by Suf. d[r]. & coh[r]. of Capt. Ri. Swann, & Dor. Danvers his Wife, s. of Capt. Ri. Swan, sen. by Damaris d[r]. & coh[r]. of Capt. Andr. Shilling; had Issue 6. sons, & 3 d[rs]. He died 1708. æt. 59. & she, 1719. æt. 68. & were both bur. here.

Rich. Graves, s. & h[r]. of S. who mar[d]. Eliz. d[r]. & coh[r]. of Capt. Th. Morgan, by Eliz. d[r]. & Coh[r]. of Ia. Brayne Gent. caused this Monument to be here erected in 1721. Who also hath had 3. sons bur. here, viz. Rich[d]. who died 1710. Sam[l]. 1712. & Sam[l]. a Twin, 1719. all in their infancy.

Over the memorial in a large scutcheon are the following arms in six quarterings. 1. Graves, as before. 2. *Vert, two greyhounds courant argent, on a chief Or three fleurs de lis gules*, for Menseir. 3. *Sable, a fess ingrailed argent between three dexter hands couped at the wrist Or*, for Bates. 4. *Azure, a chevron ermine between three swans argent*, for Swan. 5. *Sable, on a bend argent three mullets of the field*, for Shilling. 6. Graves. On the sides of the table are ten different scutcheons with bearings, six of them as last emblazoned; the other four are as follow, 1. *Argent, a cross engrailed, and voided, between four estoiles of six points gules.* 2. *Sable, a chevron between three pheons heads argent*, for Morgan. 3. *Vert, on a chevron between three stags Or, as many roses gules*, for Robinson. 4. *Ermine, on a bend gules three martlets Or, winged Vert*, for Danvers. And under the inscription table are, *Quarterly*, the arms of Graves, Menseir, Swan, and Shilling; and on a scutcheon of pretence, *Quarterly* 1st *and* 4th, Morgan, 2d *and* 3d, *Argent, on a pale gules three leopards heads of the field, in the dexter chief an annulet.*

Against the north wall of the north aile, on the table of an elegant monument of white marble, it is thus written:

Subtus Requiescit
RICARDUS GRAVES, Armiger, Hujusce Maneij Dominus,
Vir, si quis alius, Desideratissimus.
Qui eximias animi Dotes mirâ Indolis suavitate temperans,
Tam charus omnibus vixit, quam effusâ erat erga omnes Benevo-
Liberos Tenerrimo Affectu, [lentia;
Amicos inconcussâ fide semper prosecutus.
Inter hæc, otij literarij studiis efflorescens,
Ruris secessum Historiarum varietate eleganter distinxit: [grinis,
Non vero, ut Doctis sepe contingit nullibi nisi in Patriâ sua Pere-
Cum res Græcas Romanasq; penitus perspectas haberet,
Nostras fastidiose prætermisit.
His profecto unice deditus, in vestigandis
Acerrimam operam navavit,
Dilucidandis omnem adhibuit diligentiam.
Antiquitates demum Loci vicinitate commendatas,
Propriis illustrare Scriptis Occepærat;
Inchoati operis Gloriam adeptus,
Consummati famâ, Mortis interventu, privatus.
Uxorem duxit ELIZABETHAM filiam et coheredem
THOMÆ MORGAN, Armigeri,
Ex qua
Quatuor Filios Duasq; Filias Superstites reliquit,
Quarum una (proh Dolor!) Subtus Paterno Lateri adhæret.
Obiit ille decimo septimo Septembris Anno Domini 1729. Æt. 53.
Ne tantas Patris virtutes nescirent Posteri
Hoc Monumentum Posuit
MORGAN GRAVES, Arm.
Filius natu maximus.

Under the table are the arms, Quarterly, of Graves and Morgan.

In the same aile, round a well wrought marble urn,

To the Memory of Danvers Graves, Esq; Chief Agent to the hon[ble] E. India Company in Persia, whereby he greatly distinguished himself by his Resolution and fidelity during the Commotions in that Kingdom, and died at Gambroon MDCCLII.

On a blue stone,

Here lyeth the Body of Captain Richard Swan, who had made six Voyages to the East Indies, and departed this life 30 Iune, 1676, Ætatis suæ 59.——Arms, Swan as before.

Here lyeth the Body of Mrs. Dorothy Swan, Relict of Captain Richard Swan, who died 15 January, 1688.——Arms, Danvers as before.

On another urn, in the chancel,

UTRECIÆ SMITH,
Puellæ simplici, innocuæ,
eleganti,
R. G.
Unâ actæ memor pueritiæ,
Lugens posuit
M. DCCXLIV.

There is a memorial for Alice Keyt, placed, by mistake, to the account of Ebberton.

Benefactions.

In the year 1513, Richard Porter of Campden, gent. gave a messuage and yard-land in Mickleton, and a close in Overton, now worth 60*l*. a year; which income, by a decree in chancery, is first to repair the church, then 20*l*. a year to be paid to the master of a free-school, and the remainder, if there should be any, to go to the poor.

In 1612, at the inclosing of the fields, thirty-three acres of land, called Horestone, were laid out by the land-owners, for the poor.

In 1623, Mr. Thomas Perks of this place, charged his four meadows next Long Marston-way, with 20*s*. a year to the poor.

In 1678, Mrs. Dorothy Swan charged Tyms's close with the payment of 40*s*. a year, 10*s*. of which to the minister for a sermon on Christmas-day, the rest to be given in bread to the poor.

Mickleton.

Taxes.	The Royal Aid in	1692,	£. 433	14	0
	Poll-tax ——	1694, —	43	2	8
	Land-tax ——	1694, —	326	12	0
	The same, at 3*s*.	1770, —	245	14	0

Hidcote.

Taxes.	The Royal Aid in	1692,	£. 70	6	0
	Poll-tax ——	1694, —	2	16	0
	Land-tax ——	1694, —	59	2	0
	The same, at 3*s*.	1770, —	43	13	0

At the beginning of this century, there were 83 houses in this parish, and about 375 inhabitants, whereof 54 were freeholders; yearly births 10, burials 8. *Atkyns.* But by the parish register it appears that in ten years, beginning with 1700, the baptisms were 73, and the burials 63; which is widely different from sir Robert's account. Also in the same number of years, beginning with 1760, the baptisms were 106, and the burials 97. And in the year 1773, there were 68 housholders, and only 231 inhabitants. This account is more unfavourable to population than any I have found throughout the county, yet I have great reason to think

think the numbers are accurately taken, as I counted the names upon the regifter myfelf; and the minifter gave me the number of fouls in his parifh. The whole parifh is in dairy and grazing, in which fewer hands are employ'd than in tillage.

MINETY.

THE church lies fix miles diftant weftward from Cricklade in Wiltfhire, fix eaftward from Malmefbury, and twenty-five fouth-eaftward from Gloucefter. The parifh church, the parfonage, the vicarage houfe, and a very fmall hamlet, called Wiltfhire-row, lie in the hundred of Malmefbury in Wiltfhire; the reft, and far the greater part of the parifh, lies in the hundred of Crowthorne and Minety in Gloucefterfhire. But the whole parifh is detached from the body of this county, and totally invironed by Wiltfhire.

This place in part gives name to the hundred of Crowthorne and Minety. What Crowthorne, the other part, fignifies, will be the fubject of immediate inquiry. When king Henry the Fourth came to the crown, all thofe places now lying in this hundred were comprifed in that of Cirencefter, there being then no fuch hundred as Crowthorne and Minety, which was erected foon afterwards upon the following occafion. The townfmen of Cirencefter having fuppreffed a dangerous rebellion in the firft year of that reign, the king, at their requeft, granted them a Statute-Merchant, and other privileges, particularly that the town fhould from thence-forward be a feparate hundred, and hold a diftinct torn, or court. And all thofe villages which 'till then belonged to the hundred of Cirencefter, together with Minety, which was part of the manor of Cirencefter, and the precincts of the abbey, were erected into a new hundred, and a diftinct torn, or court, was held for them. The court held within the town was called the hundred of Cirencefter, and fo for fome time was the other, but it was neceffary to diftinguifh them. The *In-torn*, or hundred within the town, retained the old name, whilft the new torn, or court, held without it, received the appellation of *Th' Out-torn and Minety*; and in procefs of time has been corrupted, by vulgar fpeakers and ignorant writers, to the unmeaning name of Crowthorne and Minety. Thus, the proper and fignificant name being loft, the new one was fuppofed to be taken from a place within the diftrict, and fome very fagacious perfon fixing on a thorn-bufh in Stratton field, declared it to be the place in queftion. The folution was eafy, and fuited the vulgar. The notion was inconfiderately adopted upon the credit of tradition, and it has for fome time appeared in hiftory.

The names of feveral other hundreds are as ftrangely corrupted as this. I fhall inftance one only. It was antiently and properly written *Grimboldeftow*, i.e. *Grimbold's-place*; but at length the original fignification was loft, and, for a courfe of five hundred years, it has been written nearly as we now write it, *Grumbald's Afh*; and I have no doubt but there are many perfons who pretend to know the very tree which gave name to that hundred. But I return from this digreffion to the parifh of Minety.

Some part of it was full of wood in its antient ftate, as appears by king John's confirmation of former grants to the abbey of Cirencefter, wherein he referves his foreft of Minchey, which I apprehend to be what we now call Bredon.

Minety is fituated in a vale, and confifts chiefly of rich pafture land, fome wood land, and very little arable. Here they make very good cheefe, as they do alfo in moft parts of North Wiltfhire, with which this parifh is intermixt. But the moft uncommon and remarkable of its natural productions is a kind of fibrous talky fubftance, white, opake, and laminated, called by fome the *Silver Mica*, by others the *Fibrous Plaifter-ftone*. It is found in many parts of the parifh, at the depth of nine or ten feet from the furface. There is alfo a fpring of purging water, formerly much recommended by phyficians, and drank by great numbers of people; but fince fo many fprings at other places have been frequented, it has funk into neglect, and is at prefent very little regarded.

Should bufinefs or curiofity lead a ftranger into this country, I advife him to make his vifit in the fummer, leaft he be either drowned, or ftifled in the mire; for here *Swill-brook* overflows its banks, and fills the road (through which travellers muft pafs) with water from three to eight feet in depth, and notwithftanding fome have loft their lives, and many others are endangered every year, there is no order taken to carry off the water, nor to raife the road; fo infenfible, from habit, are thefe people to inconvenience and danger.

Of the Manor and other Eftates.

In the reign of king Richard the Firft, the town of Cirencefter, and the town of Minchey or Minety, with the appurtenances, made and were the manor of Cirencefter, as it is expreffly mentioned in an inquifition taken 1 H. 4. in order to difcover the particulars of that manor. And it is very probable, that at the time of the general furvey, Minety was included in the account of the manor of Cirencefter, wherefore we find no mention of this place in *Domefday*.

King Richard the Firft, in the ninth year of his reign, granted the manor of Cirencefter to the abbey of that place, including fo much of the town of Minchey as lay in Gloucefterfhire, and which was a member and barton of that manor; but he referved his foreft of Minchey, as already taken notice of. Another part of Minchey or Mynety, which lay in Wiltfhire, belonged then to the abbey of Malmefbury. John de Cannings held Minety of the abbey of Cirencefter, 20 E. 3.

After

After the diſſolution of abbies, this manor was granted to Edward Bridges and Dorothy Praye 36 H. 8. Sir Edmond Bridges, lord Chandos, knight of the garter, died ſeized of Minety 15 Eliz. and livery of it was granted to Giles lord Chandos, his ſon and heir, the ſame year. Grey lord Chandos was lord of this manor in the year 1608. The reverſion of the manor of Minety was granted to ſir William Sandys, and Thomas Spencer, 3 Jac. Lord Rivers is the preſent lord of the manor, and keeps a court leet here. *See Sudely.*

Adam de Periton purchaſed lands in Minety of Hugh de Peverell 33 H. 3. Other lands in Minety, which belonged to the priory of Lanthony, were granted to William earl of Southampton, and to his heirs male, 31 H. 8. The ſame were afterwards granted to Richard Andrews and Nicholas Temple, in truſt, in the thirty-fifth year of that reign, and were again granted to John Pope 36 H. 8. Lands in Minety, and the tithes of the demeans which belonged to the ſame priory, were granted to William Fitz-Williams and Arthur Hilton 7 E. 6.

There are ſeveral eſtates of inheritance in this pariſh, held of the lord by copy of court-roll, after the cuſtom of the manor, which can neither be alienated nor incumbered but by ſurrender in court.

Of the Church, &c.

The church is a vicarage, in the dioceſe of Sarum, worth about 90*l.* a year. The archdeacon of North Wiltſhire is patron, and Mr. Brickenden is the preſent incumbent. The impropriation belongs to the ſame archdeacon.

The church ſtands in Wiltſhire, and therefore does not properly fall under conſideration; yet as the greater part of the pariſh lies in Glouceſterſhire, I ſhall give ſome account of it. It is dedicated to St. Leonard, and conſiſts of the nave, and an aile on the north ſide, and has a low embattled tower, with pinnacles, and a ring of ſix bells at the weſt end. Round the canopy over the pulpit is written in capitals, FIDES EX AVDITV, AVDITVS AVTEM PER VERBVM DEI. ROM. 10, 17.

Monuments and Inſcriptions.

The moſt antient monument is a braſs plate fixed in the wall of the aile, and divided into two compartments by a pillar engraved in the middle. On the dexter ſide of it, are engraven the effigies and names of Nicholas Powlett, and Ames Powlett, his ſon, kneeling; and over the father's head are his arms, *Sable, three ſwords in pile, the points in baſe argent, pomels and hilts Or.* The creſt ſtands ſeparate on one ſide of the arms, *A dexter arm embowed, brandiſhing a broad ſword, all proper*; and the motto on a label on the other ſide, GARDES LA FOY. On the ſiniſter ſide of the pillar, facing them, are the figures of Mary Powlett, his wife, and Elizabeth, Mary, and Edith, their daughters, kneeling, with the wife's family arms, *Sable, two bars ermine, in chief three plates, a creſcent for difference,* for Hungerford; with the creſt on one ſide, *A garb erected between two ſickles proper.* And on the other ſide, *Three ſickles braced in a triangle.* I take this Nicholas Powlett to be the ſecond ſon of ſir Hugh Poulett, who died in the reign of queen Elizabeth, and was anceſtor to the preſent earl Poulet.

Upon a marble table in the chancel, it is thus written:

Near this place lyeth the body of CHARLES PLEYDELL of Minty, the youngeſt Son of Sr CHARLES PLEYDELL of Midg-Hall, K^{t}. in the County of Wilts, who died the 15th Day of June 1704, Aged 76.

Lyeth alſo near this place the body of ARABELLA his Wife, the youngeſt daughter of Sr ROBERT LOVET of Lyſcomb in the County of Bucks, who died the 24th day of June, 1704, Aged 72.

This Marble was erected to their Memories by Wm PLEYDELL, Vicar of Wotton-Baſſet in the County of Wilts, their Son and Heir.——Arms, at the top of the monument, *Per pale, baron and femme,* 1. *Argent, a bend gules gutty d'Or, between two Corniſh choughs proper, a chief counter compony Or and ſable.* 2. *Argent, three wolves paſſant in pale ſable, langued gules.*

There is alſo a monument and memorial for ſome of the deſcendants from Charles Pleydell; a memorial for Joſeph Not, who died in 1705; and another, upon a flat ſtone, for Godfrey Jenkinſon, vicar of this place, who died the ſame year.

William Penn, anceſtor to ſir William Penn, the admiral, and to the preſent proprietor of Penſylvania, died in the year 1591, and was buried in this chancel. *Atkyns.* But I could find no memorial for him.

			£.	s.	d.
Taxes.	The Royal Aid in	1692,	£. 205	2	0
	Poll-tax ——	1694, —	28	2	0
	Land-tax ——	1694, —	201	17	0
	The ſame, at 3*s.*	1770, —	150	18	0

At the beginning of this century, there were 96 houſes, and about 480 inhabitants in the Glouceſterſhire part, whereof 32 were freeholders. In Wiltſhire-row were 9 houſes, and about 40 inhabitants, whereof 4 were freeholders; yearly births 12, and burials 10. *Atkyns.* There are only 5 houſes at preſent in Wiltſhire-row, yet the inhabitants in general are computed to be about the ſame number as above. The freeholders, however, fall ſhort of the number mentioned by ſir Robert Atkyns. It is ſuppoſed he included the copyholders of inheritance.

MINSTERWORTH.

THIS pariſh lies in the hundred of the Dutchy of Lancaſter, in the Foreſt diviſion, ſix miles north-eaſt from Newnham, ſeven eaſt from Mitchel-Dean, and three ſouth-weſt from Glouceſter. It extends near three miles in length, and conſiſts of rich meadow and paſture, with ſome arable land, and has a very large common lying on the ſouth ſide of it next the Severn.

The turnpike-road from Glouceſter to Newnham runs through it, by the ſide of the river, which has a bold ſhore, finely wooded, and breaks upon the view in a very agreeable manner, in the courſe of the road between thoſe places.

It is almoft fingularly circumftanced, in not being limited by the Severn, as other parifhes are that lie on the banks of that large river, but ftretching over it, has fome of its lands intermixed with Elmore parifh, on the oppofite fide, at a place called Elmore's Back. How a divifion fo unnatural and extraordinary could originally take place, is difficult to conceive, unlefs the abbey of Gloucefter having lands in Elmore, by its influence procured them to be allotted to the parifh of Minfterworth, where they had larger poffeffions.

Part of this parifh lay formerly in the hundred of Weftbury, and part in that of Langebrige, now included in Dudfton and King's-barton; but when the Dutchy hundred was firft erected, this parifh and Bully were taken out of the hundred of Weftbury, which at that time had fome other places added to it by way of compenfation, as appears by comparing thofe which lay in that hundred when *Domefday* was compiled, with thofe of which it confifted fome ages afterwards.

Of the Manor and other Eftates.

'The church of St. Peter of Glowec' holds 'Hamme and Mortune in Wefberies hundred. 'There are five hides in wood and in plain, and 'two plow-tillages in demean, and feven villeins, 'and two bordars, with fix plow-tillages; a wood 'one mile long, and one broad. The church had 'venifon in three parks in the time of king 'Edward, and fo fhe hath in the time of king 'William. It was worth 20*s*. now 40*s*.' *D.B.* p. 71.

The reader may poffible be furprized, that in the above abftract from the record, Minfterworth is not fo much as mentioned. The reafon is, that there was then no place fo called. Its original name was Mortune, which fignifies *the town or place upon the great water*, from *Mor*, Britifh, *the fea*, or fome *very large river*. This is perfectly defcriptive of the fituation of Minfterworth. And that Mortune could be no other, I am induced to believe for the following reafons.

All the other places in Weftbury hundred are expreflly mentioned in that record by their prefent names, or by fuch as, varying but little from the prefent, cannot be miftaken, *viz*. Neunham, Staure, Hope, Bicanofre, Dene, Bulelege, and Rodele. Befide thefe, the manor of Hamme and Mortune lay in the fame hundred. Now Hamme muft be either Hampton, a place at prefent fo called in this parifh, or elfe Churcham, the next adjoining parifh. And as Hamme and Mortune were originally joined in one manor, where is the latter fo likely to be fituated as adjoining to the former? Befides, we find the very name ftill fubfifting in that of the hamlet of *Morcote*, in Minfterworth; for what is *Morcote* but a contraction of *Mortune-cote*. Here the Severn frequently overflows its banks, and makes a kind of fea, by laying the ham or common under water, which corroborates the foregoing arguments that the antient name of Minfterworth was Mortune; for the names of places are moftly defcriptive of their fituations, or expreffive of fome accidents attending them.

This Mortune was afterwards called Minfterworth, becaufe it belonged to the minfter or abbey of Gloucefter; which alteration in the name took place fometime before the reign of king John, for the records mention, that Henry de Bohun was created earl of Hereford in the firft year of that king's reign, and had the *Tertium Denarium Comitatûs* granted to him, in confideration that he had releafed all his right in his lands in Dimmock, Minfterworth, and Rodley, to the king, the fame year.

The records, and other evidences of the following dates, fhew to whom this manor defcended down to the prefent time. Simon de Montfort, earl of Leicefter, was feized of Minfterworth 43 H. 3.

Walter de Stukeley, the fheriff of Gloucefterfhire, being commanded by the king's writ to return into the exchequer the names of all the cities, boroughs, and vills in every hundred in his faid county, certified that Henry de Lancafter was lord of Mynfterworth and Rodley, in the hundred of Weftbury, 9 E. 1. Edmond earl of Lancafter, the king's brother, was feized of the fame, and his right to court-leet and free warren therein was allowed in the proceedings on a writ of *Quo warranto* 15 E. 1. He gave this manor and that of Rodley, or Rodele, to William Grandifon, brother and heir to Otho de Grandifon, who was fummoned as a peer to parliament 27 E. 1. This William had been a domeftic fervant to the earl, and thefe manors were given to him and his heirs male in reward for his fervices.

On default of the male heirs of William Grandifon, this manor reverted to the houfe of Lancafter, and accordingly we find that Henry duke of Lancafter died feized of it 35 E. 3. He left two daughters, of whom Maud, the eldeft, was married to William duke of Bavaria, and furviving her hufband, died feized of this manor 36 E. 3. John de Gaunt, duke of Lancafter, married Blanch, the younger daughter, who together levied a fine of Minfterworth, Rodley, and Tiberton, to the ufe of themfelves in fpecial taille 39 E. 3.

Sir Fulk Bourcher, lord Fitz-Warren, died feized of it 19 E. 4.

The manor of Minfterworth, late belonging to the dutchy of Lancafter, was granted to the archbifhop of York, and feveral other great perfons, in truft, 3 H. 5. and was afterwards held by feveral leafes granted from the crown to various perfons at yearly rents, 'till the fame was granted in fee to Salter and Williams, 7 Jac. 1. under an annual rent of 20 *l*. 6 *s*. 11$\frac{3}{4}$ *d*. Mr. Pury was lord of it about the middle of the laft century, whofe heir, about the year 1704, fold it to Mr. Thomas Burgeffe. From his heir it paffed by purchafe to Mr. Cook of Highnam, whofe only daughter and heir fold it to Charles Barrow, efq; who is the prefent lord of this manor, and has a handfome ſome ſeat here, called *Hygrove*, commanding an extenſive proſpect over the vale on the eaſt ſide of the river Severn. He is the heir male of the Barrows, otherwiſe Berrows, of Field-Court and Awre in this county, and one of the repreſentatives of the city of Glouceſter, for which he has ſat in five ſucceſſive parliaments. His arms are, *Argent, three bears heads erazed ſable, muzzled Or, a chief azure*, as I find them on a monument in Quedgley church.

There are ſome copyhold eſtates of inheritance in this pariſh, held according to the cuſtom of the manor, which cuſtom is, that if a tenant die without male heir, and leave more daughters than one, ſuch eſtate goes to the eldeſt of them, as at Cheltenham, and ſome other places.

In this manor, and at Rodley in the pariſh of Weſtbury, acknowledgments are paid to the lord for fiſhing in the river Severn, ſome of which were antiently called *Prid-gavel*, from the old word *Gavel*, a rent, and *Pride*, the name of a kind of wicker'd putt, or pouchin, which is laid in the water to catch the fiſh. So that Prid-gavel ſeems not to have the leaſt relation to Lampreys, as ſir Robert Atkyns, and ſome others, after him, have fancied.

There is a conſiderable eſtate in this pariſh called Hatheways, from Ralph Hatheway, who was ſeized thereof by the title of a manor 5 E. 2. The records 14 E. 2. mention Henry Caſy, and 15 E. 2. Walter Helvin, as being each of them ſeized of a manor in this pariſh; but they were not diſtinct manors. The fact is, that here, as in many other places, the owners of eſtates having little tenements erected on ſeveral detached parcels of their lands, granted ſome on leaſes for lives, and ſold others abſolutely, reſerving ſmall chief-rents, and thereby dignified their eſtates with the titles of manors, or reputed manors, tho' they had no copyhold tenants, which are neceſſarily incident to courts baron.

Bogo Goſeline was ſeized of a rent of 7*l*. 9*s*. in Minſterworth 13 E. 2.

Thomas Sayvill and Catherine his wife levied a fine of lands in Minſterworth to John Wordrof and others 16 R. 2. John Elis de Fiſhley and Margaret his wife levied a fine of lands in Minſterworth to the uſe of themſelves in fee taille, the remainder to Alice their daughter, 7 H. 4. Roger Gregg and Alice his wife levied a fine of lands in Minſterworth to the uſe of John Dabernoon, and to the right heirs of Alice 7 H. 6.

Lands formerly belonging to the abbey of Glouceſter, were granted to Thomas Reeves and Chriſtopher Bullet 5 Mariæ. But the meſſuage called Leedſwood Houſe, which ſir Robert Atkyns, by miſtake, repreſented as lying in this pariſh, is in Yorkſhire, tho' inſerted in the forementioned grant to Reeves and Bullet.

HAMLETS. 1. *Morcote*, or *Boyfield*, is a hamlet and manor, or at leaſt a reputed manor, in this pariſh. The names are nearly ſynonimous. The Britons called it by the former, from *Coed*, Br. *a wood*, becauſe it was a woody place, which, after the conqueſt, the Normans tranſlated by *Bois*, a word of the ſame ſignification in their language; and thence came *Boiville*, and *Boyfield* as it was afterwards written. At the time of the general ſurvey, Morcote lay in a different hundred from Minſterworth, as appears by the following extract:

'William the ſon of Norman holds Morcote 'in Langebrige hundred. Ulfegh held it in the 'time of king Edward. There is one hide, and 'in demean one plow-tillage, with two bordars. 'It was worth 8*s*. now 10*s*. This eſtate doth 'not pay tax.' *Domeſday-book*, p. 74.

If by Langebrige in the record, which gave name to the hundred, is meant the long bridge at Glouceſter, of which I think there can be no doubt, then Nicholas Walred, clerk, was not the firſt builder of a bridge there, as it is ſaid, in the reign of king Henry the Second, but only built that bridge anew.

Richard Veel was ſeized of Morcot 16 E. 3. John Boteler of the Park held the manors of the Park and of Morcot 36 E. 3. John Kenn was ſeized of both manors 6 H. 4. and another John Kenn died ſeized of one meſſuage and one plow-tillage in Morecot 16 H. 6. which deſcended to his ſon Robert Kenn, eſq; who was poſſeſſed of them 31 H. 6.

This eſtate was afterwards purchaſed by Thomas Elmbridge, who died 27 H. 7. and was ſucceeded by John his ſon and heir, and he dying without iſſue 17 H. 8. ſir John Danet, who had married Anne his ſiſter and heir, had livery of Morecot the ſame year. John Danet, ſon of ſir John, ſold this manor to Thomas Atkyns, of Tufleigh, eſq; and Thomas Hoard, eſq; who married a coheireſs of that family, and the reverend Mr. John Chamberlayne of Maugerſbury, deſcended from the other coheireſs, are the preſent proprietors, and have a good eſtate in this place.

2. *Hampton*, lies in the middle part of the pariſh, adjoining to the great ham or common. It is not a manor, but having antiently a diſtinct name, intitles it to our notice. Roger Boyfield was ſeized of one meſſuage and one yard-land in Hampton, parcel of the manor of Minſterworth, 15 E. 2. It is probable that this Roger Boyfield, or de Boyfield, took his name from the place of his reſidence in the hamlet of Boyfield, according to the cuſtom of early times.

3. *Dunny*, lies in the lower part of the pariſh. It is not called by any particular name in *Domeſday*; but the following abſtract ſeems to relate to it:

'William Goizenboded holds half a hide of 'land, and half a fiſhery in Weſtberie hundred. 'Alwin the ſheriff held this eſtate, and gave it to 'his wife. It belonged to the king's farm in 'Weſtberie.' *Domeſday-book*, p. 74.

Roger de Staunton gave a yard-land called Duni, in Minſterworth, and a huſbandman with his

his land, to Glouceſter abbey, when Hameline was abbat. Roger earl of Hereford gave half the fiſhery of Duny to the ſame church, which king Henry the Second confirmed; and king Edward the Third granted to the monks of that church the other half of that fiſhery, with the fiſhery in the ſtanding pools within Minſterworth, at a fee farm rent, in exchange for the church of Wyrardſbury, when Adam Staunton was abbat, 18 E. 3. as appears by an *Inſpeximus* and confirmation of thoſe grants 1 R. 2. And theſe fiſheries were afterwards granted with the manor 7 Jac.

Of the Church, &c.

The church is a vicarage, in the Foreſt deanery, to which the king's auditor pays 10*l*. a year, and the impropriator four loads of hay. It has been augmented by the queen's bounty, and is now worth 30*l*. a year. The biſhop of Briſtol is patron, and Mr. Draper the preſent incumbent.

Thomas Foliot was poſſeſſed of the church of Minſterworth 45 H. 3. and Nicholas le Bath was ſeized of the advowſon 5 E. 2. The rectory was appropriated to St. Oſwald's priory in Glouceſter 22 R. 2. and the rectory and advowſon of the vicarage belonged afterwards to the monaſtery of Boileau in Hampſhire, and were granted to the biſhoprick of Briſtol 34 H. 8. and the impropriation is now in leaſe from the biſhop of Briſtol to Mr. Joſeph Brown, for three lives.

The parſon was to have tithe of all the fiſh in the pools on the Severn within this pariſh, and he enjoy'd the ſame in Dunny and Minſterworth 15 E. 2.

The church is dedicated to St. Mary. It is a double building, ſupported by pillars in the middle. It had a ſpire, which was deſtroy'd, and the bells melted by lighting in the year 1702, and now it has a low tower at the weſt end.

Firſt fruits £.	10	13	4	Proc. & Syn. £.	0	9	6
Tenths —	1	1	4	Pentecoſtals	0	1	4

Benefactions.

Mr. John Hyett, citizen of London, who had been a poor boy of this pariſh, has given by his laſt will, dated Sep. 5, 1719, 20*l*. to 'prentice out a poor boy here every ſecond year, in the choice of whom a preference is to be given to the names of Hyett and Phelps.

In the year 1763, Suſanna Crump, widow, in her life time, ſettled an annuity of 4*l*. a year for a ſchool-miſtreſs, to teach ten poor children of this pariſh to read. Joſeph Wintle of Glouceſter, gave 20*l*. to be laid out in land, which hath been done in this pariſh, the rent whereof is to be expended in bread, and given yearly to twenty poor houſekeepers in this pariſh, on Chriſtmas Eve.

Taxes.					
The Royal Aid in	1692, £.	193	16	0
Poll-tax — —	1694, —	15	17	0
Land-tax ——	1694, —	170	0	0
The ſame, at 3*s*.	1770, —	120	15	0

At the beginning of this century, there were 60 houſes, and about 300 inhabitants in this pariſh, whereof 10 were freeholders; yearly births 10, burials 7. *Atkyns*. The houſes are now between 60 and 70, and the inhabitants about 300; but the pariſh was formerly more populous, and had upwards of 100 houſes in it, as appears by a yearly payment to the lord of 2*d*. for every houſe, and for every meeſe-place where a houſe formerly ſtood, which payment is called Smoak-ſilver.

MISERDEN, *or* MUSARDEN.

THIS pariſh lies in the hundred of Biſley, diſtant about two miles and a half north-eaſt from the town of that name, ſeven and a half north-weſt from Cirenceſter, and nine ſouth-eaſtward from Glouceſter. It is bounded on the ſouth-eaſt by Winſtone and Dunteſbourne, from which it is ſeparated by the brook Froome; on the ſouth by Edgworth, with Biſley on the weſt, Painſwick and Cranham on the north-weſt, and Brimpsfield and Side on the north and north-eaſt of it.

The village lies two miles ſouth-weſtward of the *Irminſtreet*, one of the Roman conſular ways. It is ſituated on the declivity of a hill, fronting northward, which makes it extremely bleak in the winter; but the cold, clear air braces the muſcles, and contributes to the health and longevity of the inhabitants. It is nevertheleſs better ſuited to hypochondriacal than conſumptive habits.

Here is a park about ſeven miles in circumference, full of fine beech-wood. It is watered by the Froome, which receives a ſupply at this place, from a confluence of little ſtreams running from Brimpsfield and Winſtone, that abound with ſmall trout and cray fiſh. The uninclosed part of the park reſembles a foreſt. It is a fine receſs for game, wild fowl, and many ſorts of ſinging birds; particularly here are ſeen two birds which are rare in this country, the French pye, and a water-fowl of a fierce nature, whoſe name I am not acquainted with. The enthuſiaſtic lover of nature, walking in the flowery glades of this retreat, might fancy himſelf in the primeval groves of our firſt progenitors.

Seated in a valley in this park is a mount of a circular form, now overgrown with trees. It is the ſcite of an antient caſtle, built in the reign of king John, by Ralph Muſard, one of the great barons of the realm, and lord of this manor. It is called *Caſtle-hill*, and the piece of ground below it, *Caſtle-meadow*. Part of the moat which incompaſſed the building is ſtill to be ſeen, and large hewn ſtones were dug up, and an apartment diſcovered beneath the rubbiſh, on this mount, a few years ago, but of no great extent; for the materials of the caſtle had been removed, according to tradition, and appropriated to the building of the preſent manor-houſe. The ſcite of the caſtle is moſt

moſt romanticly encompaſſed with adjacent woods and hills; and upon that ſpot a little hermitage might be erected, which would have the accompanyments of bubbling waters, impenetrable ſhade, and the various notes of the feathered tribes to heighten the idea of ſolitude and retirement.

The latter part of the name of the village was ſuggeſted by the ſituation of the caſtle, for *den*, ſignifies a dale, a glyn, a deep valley, or woody place. The former part of the name is that of a family who held the manor, from the conqueſt 'till the reign of king Edward the Firſt; but the village was not called *Muſarden*, but *Grenhamſtede*, 'till ſome time after it was the reſidence of that family, as appears by *Domeſday-book*.

Hazlehouſe is the ſeat of William Mills, eſq; who ſerved the office of high ſheriff of this county in the year 1756. At *Hazlehouſe-yate*, now called the *Camp*, are ſeveral barrows, one of which was opened about forty years ago, and the ſkulls and ſkeletons of eight bodies found lying in order in a vault beneath, which was then decently cloſed up again. There is another of thoſe barrows in the weſt field, near the Glouceſter road, which a few years ſince was found to contain human bones, and an urn, ſuppoſed to be Roman.

The face of this country is very uneven. The lands are moſtly arable, and bear good crops. About 300 acres lie in downs and common-fields. Wild thyme grows in great plenty, and the various ſpecies of the *Orchis* are found here. Much of the beech-wood in this pariſh and neighbourhood, of which there is great abundance, is converted into gun-ſtocks for Birmingham market, and of ſome they make charcoal. Here is a very good and durable ſort of tiles for covering houſes, which are ſold at 5*s*. a thouſand; but the difficulty of the roads is a great obſtacle to the ſale of them.

The clothing buſineſs is carried on very extenſively in the adjoining places to the ſouthward and weſtward, but there are only two clothiers in this pariſh, by whom the women and children are chiefly employ'd in ſpinning woollen yarn.

Of the Manor and other Eſtates.

The following is a tranſlation of the antient record reſpecting the manor:

'The ſame Haſcoit [Muſard] holds Grenham-'ſtede in Biſelege hundred. There is one hide 'taxed. Erneſi held it. In demean are three 'plow-tillages, and eight villeins, and five bordars, 'and a prieſt, and one radcheniſter. They have 'between them nine plow-tillages. There are 'ten *ſervi*, and eight acres of meadow, a wood a 'mile long, and half a mile broad. It was 'worth 100*s*. and is now worth 7*l*.' *Domeſday-book*, p. 78.

This Haſcoit Muſard attended the conqueror in his expedition againſt England, as appears by Scriven's liſt, and was rewarded with great eſtates in the counties of Berks, Oxford, Derby, Warwick, and Glouceſter; but the principal ſeat being at Muſarden, thoſe eſtates were in that reſpect all comprehended in the expreſſion *Baronia de Muſarden*, as appears by ſeveral records in after ages. Sir William Dugdage ſpeaks of him as being eminent for his piety and virtue, and ſays he at length became a monk in the monaſtery of Ely. His arms were to be ſeen in the windows of the pariſh church of Tamworth, *Gules, a lion rampant argent, crowned Or*.

Richard Muſard was ſon and heir of Haſcoit, and Haſcoit the ſecond was ſon and heir of Richard, and had fifteen knights's fees 12 H. 2. He died 33 H. 2. and was ſucceeded by Ralph his ſon and heir, who was ſheriff of Glouceſterſhire from the 17 Joh. to 9 H. 3. He married Iſabel the widow of John de Nevill, without the king's licence, and paid a hundred marks for his tranſgreſſion. He was a baron, and built the caſtle as before obſerved, and dying 14 H. 3. was ſucceeded by Robert his ſon, who entering upon his lands without ſueing forth livery, his caſtle of Muſarden and all his lands were ſeized into the king's hands, but were ſhortly after reſtored upon compoſition. He died without iſſue, when Ralph Muſard, his brother, was a minor, in ward to Jeffrey Deſpencer, who paid 500 marks to the crown for his wardſhip. Ralph had livery of his lands 31 H. 3. and died 49 H. 3. Ralph, ſon of the laſt Ralph, died 1 E. 1. and was ſucceeded by John Muſard, who had livery of the manor of Muſarden 15 E. 1. and died two years afterwards. Nicholas Muſard, uncle to John, and youngeſt brother of Ralph, had livery of this manor 17 E. 1. and died without iſſue 29 E. 1. whereby ſir Ralph Freſcheville, ſon of Amicia, his elder ſiſter, then dead, and Margaret his ſiſter then living, and Joan, (wife of William de Chelardiſton) the daughter and heireſs of Iſabel, his third ſiſter, then dead, were his heirs, and had livery of the manor of Muſarden granted to them 29 E. 1.

This manor ſoon after came to Hugh le Diſpencer the younger, who being attainted in the turbulent reign of king Edward the Second, it was granted to Edmond of Woodſtock, earl of Kent, youngeſt ſon of king Edward the Firſt, who being alſo attainted, and beheaded at Wincheſter in the beginning of the reign of Edward the Third, it was granted to Geoffry Mortimer, ſon of Roger Mortimer, earl of March. This earl was alſo executed at Smithfield the ſame year, his ſons attainted by parliament, and the ſons of Edmond of Woodſtock reſtored in blood. John, ſon of Edmond of Woodſtock, died ſeized of Muſarden 26 E. 3. which Elizabeth, his widow, held in dower 'till her death, 12 H. 4.

Joan, commonly called the *Fair Maid of Kent*, was ſiſter and heir to John. She was married to ſir Thomas Holland, who in her right was created earl of Kent. Elianor, ſiſter and coheireſs of the Hollands, was married to Roger earl of March, in the reign of king Edward the Third, and

Edmond Mortimer was their fon and heir; but he dying without iffue, the manor of Mufarden, or Miferden, defcended to Anne, fifter and coheirefs of Edmond, who was married to Richard duke of York, heir to the crown of England; whereby this manor defcended to his fon, king Edward the Fourth, and continued in the crown 'till the latter end of the reign of king Henry the Eighth.

The manor and park of Miferden were granted to fir Anthony Kingfton[n] 38 H. 8. in whofe family they continued down to William Kingfton, efq; who was lord of the manor in the year 1608. He fold it to Henry Jernegan the younger, fon and heir of Henry Jernegan the elder, of Coffey in the county of Norfolk, efq; of whom it was purchafed by fir William Sandys[o], of Fladbury in Worcefterfhire, and hath defcended thro' feveral collateral branches, down to Samuel Sandys, efq; the prefent lord of the manor.

The manor-houfe ftands upon an eminence in the park, which is a collection of hills. The beft front is on the fide next the garden to the fouth-eaft. The court and offices ftand to the north-weft. It is feen for many miles round, except to the fouth-weft, where the hills are a little above it. There are many handfome apartments in it, particularly the dining-room, with a large chimney-piece ornamented with the Sandy's arms. The ftory of Jephthah is well executed in tapeftry, and the old furniture, remaining in the drawing room, befpeaks the tafte and grandeur of its former inhabitants. In the hall was a compleat fuit of armour. In the garden are many yew-trees of an extraordinary fize and fhape.

[n] Sir William Kingfton, fon of fir Anthony, was provoft-marfhal in the reign of king Edward the Sixth. He feems to have been a man divefted of common humanity, and his name is preferved in hiftory to be execrated for his infamous, fportive cruelty. He ordered the mayor of Bodmin to erect a ftrong and lofty gallows in the market-place, and after feafting with him in a familiar manner, caufed him to be trufs'd up on it to experience its ftrength and firmnefs. A miller who had been concerned in fome infurrection in the fame country, flying from his houfe, his man pretended to be the mafter, wherefore fir William caufed him to be executed, faying, *he could do his mafter no better fervice than to be hanged for him*. This was the behaviour of him to whom the king had intrufted the adminiftration of juftice, and who for the fake of a joke, condemned and executed the innocent for the guilty.

[o] This antient family is defcended from William Sandes of Rottenby-caftle in the parifh of St. Bees in Cumberland, whofe fon William married the daughter of ——— Bonham; and had iffue William Sandes, who married Margaret, daughter and heir of William Rawfon, of the county of York, and coufin and heir to ——— Rawlinfon, abbat of Furnes in Lancafhire; and a daughter Margaret, married to Richard Bray, a privy counfellor to king Henry the Sixth.

Which laft William Sandys had iffue three fons, George, who married the daughter of ——— Curwin; William, and Oliver.

George had iffue William Sandys, who married Margaret, daughter of John Dixon, by which marriage the antient houfes of Roos and Sandys were united. They had iffue fix fons, and two daughters; George, flain at Muffelborough field, in 1547; William, who married the daughter of ——— Strickland, of Weftmoreland; Edwin, who was arch-bifhop of York; from whom the prefent lord Sandys of Omberfley in the county of Worcefter is defcended; Chriftopher; Miles, from whom the laft lord Sandys was defcended; and Anthony. Archbifhop Sandys was an excellent man, and fuffered a years imprifonment on account of his attachment to the reformed religion, in the reign of queen Mary. He was vice-chancellor of Cambridge, where, in the time of trouble, moft of his former acquaintance deferted him. After his enlargement from prifon, he went abroad, whence he returned at the death of queen Mary, and was made fucceffively bifhop of Worcefter, of London, and archbifhop of York, by queen Elizabeth. His fon, fir Edwin Sandys, was a perfon of great learning and abilities; and George Sandys, the bifhop's youngeft fon, was a moft ingenious gentleman, whofe book of travels and poetical writings are well known and much efteemed.

Myles Sandys, the fifth fon of the faid William and Margaret, was of Lattimer's, *alias* Iflehamftead, in the county of Bucks. He married Hefter, the daughter of William Clifton, of Barrington in Somerfetfhire, and had four fons, George, who was knighted, but died without iffue; Edwin, who was alfo knighted; William, who was alfo knighted; and Henry. He had alfo three daughters.

Sir Edwin Sandys, the fecond fon, married Elizabeth, fifter and heir of William lord Sandys, by whom he had three fons and fix daughters. William, who for his prodigality was called *Golden Sandys*. He was lord of the manor of Brimpsfield, which he fold to his uncle, fir William Sandys, hereafter mentioned, and died without iffue; Myles, who died unmarried; Henry, afterwards lord Sandys of the Vine, in the county of Southampton. The daughters were Bridget, Mary, Dorothy, Amy, Jane, and Hefter.

Sir William Sandys, third fon of the faid Myles Sandys, married Margaret, daughter and heir of Walter Culpepper, of Hanburrough in the county of Oxford, efq; by whom he had iffue 1. fir Myles Sandys, who had Brimpsfield park and eftate fettled on him on his marriage with Mary, the daughter of fir John Hanbury, of Kelmarfh in the county of Southampton. He died before his father, and was buried at Miferden. 2. William, who fettled in Kent, and was called *Water-work Sandys*, from his tafte in improvements of that kind. 3. Thomas, who died unmarried. They had alfo five daughters.

Sir Myles Sandys of Brimpsfield had iffue three fons, 1. William Sandys of Miferden, who married Elizabeth, daughter of Stephen Soames, of Haydon in the county of Effex. 2. Edward Sandys of Brimpsfield, efq; of whom hereafter; 3. Myles Sandys, who died unmarried. And one daughter Mary.

William Sandys, the eldeft fon of fir Myles, died in 1649, leaving iffue two fons, Myles Sandys, who married Mary, daughter of Stephen Soames, of Thurloe in the county of Suffolk, efq; William, who took to wife Philadelphica Uphill, of Hanwell-Rumford in the county of Effex. And one daughter Mary, who died a nun in France.

Myles Sandys, fon of William, had iffue by his faid wife Mary, two fons, William Sandys of Miferden, and Myles, who died unmarried in 1706.

Which William Sandys married Barbara, the daughter of fir William Kerle, of Herefordfhire, and dying without iffue, was buried at Miferden in 1712. He fold the manors of Brimpsfield and Cranham to his coufin Windfor Sandys the elder, as alfo Cranham and Winfton woods. He left the reverfion of Miferden and Winfton, fubject to his mother's and wife's jointures, to his coufin and heir at law, Windfor Sandys the elder, and his heirs.

I return now to Edward Sandys, the fecond fon of fir Myles Sandys of Brimpsfield. He married Hefter, the daughter of Fulke Walwin, of Much Marcle in the county of Hereford, by whom he had iffue, 1. Myles Sandys, who left two daughters, who died unmarried; 2. Edward Sandys, who died without iffue. 3. Windfor Sandys of Brimpsfield park. 4. Robert Sandys, who died unmarried; 5. Hanbury Sandys; and fix daughters, Mary, Anne, Hefter, Frances, Dorothy, and Martha.

Windfor Sandys, the third fon, married firft, mifs Aubery, by whom he had iffue Aubery Sandys, who died an infant: Secondly, Alice, the daughter of Matthew Lock, of Boddington in the county of Gloucefter, efq; by whom he had iffue three fons, 1. Windfor Sandys. 2. William Sandys, afterwards a captain. 3. Myles Sandys, of the Middle Temple, efq; who married and died without iffue. Windfor Sandys, the father, died and was buried at Miferden in 1729, and was fucceeded by his fon and heir

Windfor Sandys, who was high fheriff of Gloucefterfhire in 1725, and ferved that office with great fplendor again in 1745. He married Elizabeth, the only furviving daughter and at length heir of Richard Browne, of Gonthrop in the county of Nottingham, and of Iflington in the county of Middlefex, efq; and became poffeffed of the manors of Miferden park and Winfton, and dying in 1754, was buried in the family vault at Miferden. He left iffue five children, *i.e.* 1. Browne Sandys, who died unmarried in 1761; 2. Samuel Sandys, the prefent proprietor of Miferden and Winfton; 3. Catherine, married to William Bayntun, of Gray's Inn, efq; F. A. S. 4. Anne; and 5. Mary.

Mr. Sandys's arms are, *Or, a fefs dancetty between three crofs croflets fitchy gules; a crefcent within an annulet for difference.*

And

And notwithſtanding the whole now wears the melancholy aſpect of deſertion and decay, yet few gentlemen's ſeats have more natural advantages.

In the hamlet of Miſerden there are 39 houſes, and 166 inhabitants.

HAMLETS. 1. *Wiſhanger.* This hamlet is ſituated a mile north-weſt of Miſerden. Aſculf Muſard, of Muſarden, gave Wiſhanger, then called Riſeanger, to the knights-templers, from whom it went to the knights hoſpitallers of St. John of Jeruſalem; after whoſe diſſolution, it was granted to ſir Thomas Palmer, 6 E. 6. and upon his attainder, it was granted to William lord Howard, 1 Mar. Chriſtopher Bumpſted levied a fine of the manor of Wiſhanger to John Brown 4 Mar. very ſoon after which it came into the family of the Partridges. The principal houſe in this hamlet is the manſion and uſual reſidence of that family, who have enjoy'd this eſtate ever ſince, and have poſſeſſed many large eſtates in this county. Mr. John Partridge is the preſent owner thereof. His arms are, *Checky, argent and ſable, on a bend gules three eſcallops Or. Honeycombe* is the name of a good houſe in this hamlet, belonging to the reverend Mr. Mills, the preſent rector. There is a ſmall valley in this hamlet, called the *City*, where are ſeveral cottages. On the oppoſite ſide of the valley is the *Camp*, where are ten houſes. The whole number of houſes in this hamlet is 22, and of inhabitants 91.

2. *Sudgrove*, i.e. *Southgrove*, is ſituated on the ſouth-weſt of the village. There are two good houſes built of hewn ſtone; one of them was the ſeat of the Warnefords, a knightly family, of which the reverend F. Warneford, LLD. now living at Sevenhampton in the county of Wilts, is the repreſentative. This houſe, with the remaining lands belonging to it, was lately purchaſed by Mr. John Mills. The other is a more modern building, firſt erected by the reverend Mr. Durſton, then rector of Miſerden; and afterwards purchaſed and augmented by Mr. Temple, who ſold it to the late William Trye, eſq; of the family of the Tryes of Hardwick. His ſon, Mr. Thomas Trye, diſpoſed of this laſt patrimony of a once reſpectable, tho' now declined houſe, to John Selfe, late of Cirenceſter, eſq; who, from its pleaſant ſituation for proſpect, agreeable gardens, and plantations, has made it the place of his reſidence. Milo conſtable of Glouceſter, gave the tithes of Sutgrove-Reſtald to the church of Lanthony. In this hamlet are 24 houſes, and 103 inhabitants.

3. The *Slad*, or *Slade*, from the Saxon word Slaԁe, *a ſlip of ground.* There are ſeveral places of this name in Glouceſterſhire, all ſituated on the ſlopes of hills. The ſprings collecting on the ſides of ſuch hills looſen the earth, and frequently by their force drive whole acres of ground into the vallies beneath, a remarkable inſtance of which happened lately at the Throp in the pariſh of Stroud. Hence the name *Slade*. This hamlet lies three miles north-weſt of the village of Miſerden, towards Painſwick. It contains 26 houſes, and 117 inhabitants.

Of the Church, &c.

The church is a rectory, in the deanery of Stonehouſe, worth 140*l.* a year. Samuel Sandys, eſq; is patron, the reverend Mr. Giles Mills is the preſent incumbent. There are ninety acres of glebe, of which forty-four lie in common field.

The church is dedicated to St. Andrew, on whoſe anniverſary the feaſt is kept. It hath a tower at the weſt end, with one large bell. There are two croſs ailes; that on the ſouth ſide, with its vault, was built by the late Mr. Temple, and now belongs to Mr. Selfe. The north aile was erected by William Mills, of Hazlehouſe, eſq; and the preſent rector.

The parſonage-houſe was repaired, if not wholly built, by William Wolley, a former rector, the initial letters of whoſe name are on a ſun-dial thus (W 1665 W).

Monuments and Inſcriptions.

On the ſouth ſide of the chancel, ſeparated by a wire lattice, is a fine monument of alabaſter, whereon lie the effigies of ſir William Sandys and his lady, moſt curiouſly wrought, with their creſts at their feet. Sir William is in compleat armour, finely gilt; and his lady very richly dreſſed with point and bracelets, according to the high taſte of thoſe times; with their ten children kneeling round the ſeveral ſides of the tomb, which is decorated with ſcutcheons of arms. At the head of the tomb againſt the wall, upon a black marble, is the following inſcription in gold letters:

Here Lyeth the Bodie of S[r] Will[m] Sandys of Muſarden in the Countie of Glouc[r] Knight. He departed this Life Mar 2. 1640 Aged 77. And Dame Margaret his Wife, Daughter and Heire of Walter Culpepper of Hanborough in the County of Oxon Eſquire, and ſhe departed this Life June 13, 1644. Aged 64 Haveinge Iſſue five Sons & five Daughters

Here's in this Cabanet Earth's richeſt Treaſure
A pair unparalell'd, & therefore Reader,
Expect not Phraſes in ſad Elegyes,
To clawe thy Fancy but to thaw thine Eyes.
See here that Wealth, Bloud, Honour, Power, muſt
Return the owners to their Mother Duſt.
Vertue embalms them ſtill, with Chriſt they be
Thay chang'd the Rome, but not their Company.

This monument was made for ſir William in his life time. The whole is exquiſitely finiſhed and finely preſerved. It was executed in Italy, at the expence of 1000*l. from two paintings of him and his lady, done by ſir Cornelius Johnſon, which are now in the manor-houſe.*

Within the rails of the communion table, is a raiſed tomb decorated with arms, and the effigy in ſtone of a man in armour, with this memorial:

Here lyeth the Body of William Kingſton of Miſarden Eſquier, Sonne & Heire to Anthony Kingſton Eſquier who married Mary Daughter to John Waſhborne of Wichenford in the County of Worceſter, Eſquier, the which William Kingſton was Faithful to his Prince, and Loving to his Country, departed this Life the 12th day of December 1614 Ætatis 39.——The arms are, 1. *Azure, a croſs Or, between four leopards faces argent*, for Kingſton; impaling 2. *Argent, on a feſs gules three roſes of the firſt, between ſix martlets of the ſecond*, for Waſhbourne.

Near the above, on the north ſide, a ſtone monument with the effigies of a man and woman kneeling,

kneeling, and four children, with their arms, *Checky argent and ſable, on a bend gules three eſcallops Or.* And the following inſcription:

Here Lyeth the Body of Anthony Partridge of Wiſhanger Eſq[r] Son of Robert Partridge Eſq[r] who married Alice, Daughter of Timothy Cartwright Gent. by whom he had iſſue 5 Sons & 1 Daughter, who departed this Life the 25th day of March A D 1625. Aged 57.——The arms of Cartwright, *Or, a feſs embattled between three cart wheels ſable, a martlet for diſtinction.*

On a flat ſtone,

Henry Partridge Gent[n]. only ſon of Thomas & Heſter Partridge of Wiſhanger in this pariſh Gent. departed this Life 17 Aug[t]. A. D. 1730. aged 36 Y[rs].

Longior Vita diuturna Calamitas.

If Youth, or Health, or Friends could Life aſſure,
I, in the midſt of them had been ſecure,
They all uncertain are, you'l find by me,
Nothing more certain than Eternity.

A flat ſtone,

Mr. John Durſton, Interred here, was born at Ripple, Worceſterſhire, educated at Wincheſter, elected into New Coll: Oxon, preſented by that Coll: to the Rectory of Alton, Wilts. Rector likewiſe of this Church above 40 years, died 29th Feb: 1727 Æ. 82.

All words are vain
Where none can reach the worth.

At the foot of the ſteps of the altar is a flat ſtone, with a patriarchal croſs, within a bordure of alabaſter. It has no inſcription, but was probably intended for one of the Muſards.

A flat ſtone at the entrance of the chancel, at top, *Per feſs crenelle ſable and argent, ſix croſſes patty counterchanged,* and this inſcription:

In Memoriam Thom. Warneford Civis London filii natu maximi Tho. Warneford Generoſi de Sutgrove. Poſuit Hen: Warneford Conſanguineus et Heres ex teſtamento. Ob: 9. Jan. A. D. 1717 Æ. 63.

In Mr. Mills's aile, a handſome marble monument, with the family arms, *Barry of ten, argent and Or, ſix eſcutcheons gules,* 3, 2, 1; and this inſcription:

M S
Gulielmi Mills de Haſelhouſe
et Saræ uxoris ejus.
ille Vir probus et honeſtus
Omnibus carus
Morte correptus fuit Anno 1724
Ætatis 68.
Ipſa Vidua plorans, Mater
Pia et Benigna, tandem
efflavit animam Anno
1761, Ætatis 91.

Item Eliz[ae] Uxoris
Gulielmi Mills
de Haſelhouſe Armigeri
quæ ob Caſtitatem
Sanctitatem & Pietatem
eximiè illuſtris ex
hâc Vitâ in Spem melioris
diſceſſit Anno 1746
Ætatis 48.

In the church-yard is a memorial for Anthony Ockhold and Tacy his wife, 1605. The Ockholds were once freeholders of note in this pariſh, as were the Clements, and many others, who are now melancholy tho' common inſtances of the fluctuation of property. The event however, is an incitement to frugality and induſtry; for generally, property flies from the indolent and profligate, to be cheriſhed and improved by the diligence of the induſtrious. The Ockholds arms are, *Vaire, argent and ſable, on a pale gules three leopards faces Or.*

Firſt fruits £.	8	13	4	Synodals £.	0	2	0
Tenths —	0	17	4	Pentecoſtals	0	0	7
Procurations	0	6	8				

Benefaction.

Thomas Muggleton, who lies buried in the church-yard 1659, gave by his will to the poor of this pariſh, (with others) 15*s* yearly, charged on lands in Duntiſbourn Abbats.

Land-tax at 3*s*. in 1770, £ 50 4 0

About the year 1712, the poor-tax amounted to 2*s*. in the pound, and at this time (1773) it is advanced to 5*s*. in the pound.

According to ſir Robert Atkyns, there were 54 houſes, and about 250 inhabitants in this pariſh, whereof 20 were freeholders; yearly births 9, burials 6. But in ſeven years, from 1766 to 1772, both incluſive, it appears that there have been entered in the pariſh regiſter 80 baptiſms, and 68 burials. And the people having been numbered in 1762, they were found to be 112 families, and 460 inhabitants, who occupied 105 houſes. Alſo by an account taken in 1767, the number of ſouls was 451; and by the laſt account taken in 1773, there were 111 houſes, and 477 inhabitants, of whom 16 were freeholders.

From theſe *data* it appears, that the average of annual baptiſms is 11.3, and of burials 9.7; that the average of perſons to each houſe is 4.3; and that the proportion of annual burials to the whole number of inhabitants is nearly as 1 to 49, which ſhews the place to be healthy.

MORTON-HENMARSH.

THIS ſmall pariſh lies in the upper diviſion of Weſtminſter hundred, four miles diſtant north from Stow, five ſouth-eaſt from Campden, and twenty-nine north-eaſt from Glouceſter.

It lies in the vale, with a ridge of hills on the weſt of it, whence the water flows down upon the low lands in a wet ſeaſon, and cannot readily paſs off again; wherefore it was called Mortune, from *Moor*, a *marſh*, or *tract of low ground. Henmarſh*, *i.e.* the *old marſh*, is almoſt of the ſame ſignification, but of much later ſtanding than the former name. Indeed ſome perſons write *Morton in the Marſh*, and for aught I know, with equal propriety. But *Henmarſh* may be, as ſir Robert Atkyns ſeems to think, from *Hen*, *old*, and meaɲc, a *limit*, or *boundary*, for there is one corner of this pariſh, about two miles eaſt of the village, which borders on three other counties; and on that ſpot ſtands a handſome ſtone pedeſtal, about twelve feet high, with a dial at top, and an inſcription to inform travellers that *This is the four Shires Stone.* Oxfordſhire lies on the eaſt, Glouceſterſhire on the weſt, Warwickſhire on the north, and Worceſterſhire on the ſouth, which happens by Evenlode, a detached part of the laſt mentioned county, running up to this point.

The Roman *Foſs* leads from Cirenceſter thro this place northwards, and the great road from Worceſter to London croſſes it here, where are two pretty good inns to accommodate travellers. The greater part of the houſes are arranged on the ſides of the *Foſs*, and about the middle of the village ſtands a public building upon pillars, which gives

gives it ſomething of the air of a market-town. Indeed it had formerly a charter for a market and fair, which it enjoy'd with other privileges a long time; and not more that two centuries back, when many parts of the country were viſited with the plague, a market was kept here, and was at that time pretty much frequented.

The abbats of Weſtminſter, who were lords of this manor, have ſeveral times endeavoured, by various ways, to encourage the increaſe of inhabitants, and to raiſe this place into greater eminence. In the reign of king Henry the Fourth, the abbat procured a charter to exempt the burgeſſes, as they were then called, from paying toll in the ſeveral counties of Glouceſter, Oxford, Warwick, and Worceſter; and granted them their burgages in fee, paying a ſmall fine upon alienation. They had alſo a grant of courts for pleas of debt, and for the trial of ſome criminal actions.

What immediate effect theſe privileges had, does not appear, but as large plants require room for a vigorous growth, ſo it is probable that this place lay too near the neighbouring market-towns to become anywiſe conſiderable; for Morton, in its preſent ſtate, is no more than a pretty little village, where the women and children are employ'd in ſpinning of linen yarn for coarſe ſewing threads, cheeſe cloth, and linſeys.

As the place lies upon the *Foſs*, it was natural, on my viſit, to inquire after Roman antiquities, when the account in Dr. Parſons's manuſcript was confirmed by the inhabitants, that about a mile further northwards, in the fields, at a place called *Dorn*, great quantities of Roman coins have been formerly found. And not far from thence, but in this pariſh, are two conſiderable barrows; whence it ſeems probable, that there has been a ſmall poſt or ſtation at or near that place.

Of the Manor and other Eſtates.

Notwithſtanding ſir Robert Atkyns has appropriated to this place a large extract from *Domeſday*, concerning Moreton, (as he has it) in Celfledeſtern hundred, yet thoſe particulars have not the leaſt relation to any Morton whatever, but really belong to Nortune, or Norton, in the pariſh of Weſton-Subedge, as may be ſeen by referring to the printed copy of the record, at p. 78. And what the ſame learned author aſſerts, of this manor belonging to the family of the Cormeiles, is equally erroneous. Indeed this place does not appear to have been a diſtinct manor at the time of the general ſurvey, but as it was antiently part of the pariſh of Bourton on the Hill, ſo it ſeems to belong to the eight hides which the church of Weſtminſter had there, dependent on the large manor of Derhurſt.

Domeſday ſpecifies the number of hides in each place, belonging to that extenſive manor, and declares that, 'Certain radchenisters held part of 'thoſe lands of the church of Weſtminſter, in the 'time of king Edward, and tho' they were free 'men, yet they plowed, harrowed, reaped, and 'mowed at the lord's work;' and that 'Elfrid held 'half a hide at Montune, and holds the ſame;' *i.e.* he held it when the inquiſition was taken. This Montune is ſuppoſed to be the ſame with the pariſh of Morton, for the Saxon ƿ may have been miſtaken for the letter n, to which it bears ſome reſemblance.

The abbey of Weſtminſter purchaſed a charter for a market in this place in the eleventh year, and another charter for a fair, in the fifty-third year of the reign of king Henry the Third.

The learned author to whoſe labours I am ſo greatly indebted, obſerves, that William de Barking, the thirtieth abbat of Weſtminſter, new built the village of Moreton, of which the profits were aſſigned to obſerve an anniverſary for him, and the overplus to the benefit of the convent. And further, that he purchaſed the manor-houſe, and half the foreſt of Moreton, and two plow-tillages of aſſart land, and the caſtle of Moreton Foliot, with a moiety of that manor, and gave them to the convent of Weſtminſter. But he undoubtedly meant Richard de Barking, who was the twenty-ſecond abbat of Weſtminſter, according to Mr. Willis's liſt, in whoſe epitaph mention is made of ſome of theſe particulars.

At the diſſolution of the abbey, the manor was granted to the dean and chapter of Weſtminſter 34 H. 8. Queen Mary regranted it to the abbey, which ſhe had reſtored, 4 Mariæ, but it was again confirmed to the dean and chapter 2 Eliz.

William Bateſon, eſq; is leſſee of the manor, under the dean and chapter, and holds a court-leet here.

Richard Dalby and his wife levied a fine of lands in Moreton-Henmarſh 9 H. 7. Mr. Creſſwick has a large eſtate in this pariſh.

Of the Church, &c.

The church is in the deanery of Campden. It is a chapel of eaſe to Bourton on the Hill, and has the ſame incumbent.

There is no glebe-land. Bourton-farm is tithe free, but the reſt of the pariſh is tithable, and pays 53*l.* 11*s.* yearly for compoſition.

The church is dedicated to St. David. In the year 1512, pope Julius granted right of ſepulture to this pariſh, the inhabitants of which formerly buried at Blockley in Worceſterſhire.

Pentecoſtals - - - - 6*d.*

Benefactions.

A cloſe called Greenhill was given towards the repair of the church. Mr. Cook, a rector of Bourton, gave 40*s.* yearly to put out an apprentice, as the money ſhould grow ſufficient. Several perſons have alſo given ſmall ſums, amounting in the whole to 60*l.* to be a ſtock for the poor.

Land-tax at 3*s.* 1770, £ 42 9 0

At the beginning of this century, there were 120 houſes, and about 526 inhabitants in this

 pariſh,

parifh, whereof 30 were freeholders; yearly births 18, burials 16. *Atkyns.* But this was not the true average ftate of the regifter, for in ten years, beginning with 1700, the baptifms were 157, and the burials 120. And in a like period, beginning with 1760, the baptifms were 212, and the burials 131; and the prefent number of inhabitants is 579; fo that they are to the average of annual burials nearly as 44 to 1.

MORETON VALENCE.

THIS parifh lies in the vale, in the hundred of Whitftone, eight miles north from Durfley, four weft from Painfwick, and fix fouthward from Gloucefter.

It is laid out in dairy-farms, with fome orcharding, and produces good cheefe and ftout cyder; but it is fubject to inundations from its flat and low fituation.

Mortune was the antient name of the village, and fignifies the *town upon the water*, as already explained under Minfterworth, and might very properly be given to this place which is wafhed on the fouth by the river Froome, and on the weft by the Severn. It received the addition of *Valence* from a family of that name, who were earls of Pembroke, and lords of this manor in the reigns of Edward the Firft and Edward the Second.

Antient foundations of hewn ftones have been found in a piece of ground near the church, which appears to have been moated round, and is fuppofed to have been the fcite of the manfion-houfe of the Valences, or fome of their fucceffors, lords of this manor.

Of the Manor and other Eftates.

'Durand of Glowec' holds Mortune in Witeftan 'hundred. There are three hides taxed. Auti 'held it. In demean is one plow-tillage, and 'four villeins, and fix bordars, with three plow-'tillages and a half. There are four *fervi*, and 'twenty acres of meadow. It was worth 4*l.* now '40*s.*' *Domefday-book*, p. 77.

Robert de Pont de Larch, or Pont de l' Arch, was feized of this manor 30 H. 3. and gave it, together with feveral others, to William de Valencia, afterwards created earl of Pembroke, who was fon of Hugh le Brun, by Ifabel widow of king John, and uterine brother to king Henry the Third, by whom this grant was confirmed 36 *regni*. He married Joan, daughter of Gwarine de Monte Canifio, or Montchenfy, a great baron, (in that age efteemed the Craffus of England, the bequefts in his will amounting to above 200,000 marks) and afterwards heirefs to William her brother. He was flain by the French at Bayonne, feized of Moreton and Whaddon 23 E. 1. and was fucceeded in honour and eftate by

Audomar de Valencia, his fecond and furviving fon, who was killed in France 17 E. 2. on account of the part he had taken in the death of the earl of Lancafter, and left no iffue, whereby his three fifters became his coheireffes. Joan, the youngeft, was married to John Comyn of Badenagh, fon of John Comyn, one of the competitors for the crown of Scotland. They left only daughters, of whom Elizabeth was married to Richard Talbot of Goderick Caftle, anceftor to the earls of Shrewfbury, who, in her right, was feized of a third part of this manor 20 E. 2. and died 30 E. 3.

John earl of Shrewfbury, and Thomas vifcount Lifle, joined in levying a fine of the manor of Moreton to fir Richard Bingham, and others, 9 E. 4.

Elizabeth countefs of Shrewfbury died feized of Moreton Valence 11 H. 8. and Arthur Plantagenet and Elizabeth his wife had livery granted them the fame year.

The manor foon after came to the crown, and was granted to Thomas Cromwell, earl of Effex, and after his attainder, to fir William Kingfton 32 H. 8. who dying the fame year, livery was granted to fir Anthony Kingfton his fon and heir.

The manor was afterwards purchafed by the Jerninghams of Norfolk. Henry Jerningham, efq; was lord of it in the year 1608. Sir Ralph Dutton was proprietor of this manor when fir Robert Atkyns compiled his account of it. James Lenox Dutton, efq; died in the year 1776, and James Dutton, efq; his eldeft furviving fon and heir, is the prefent lord of the manor of Moreton Valence, and has a good houfe on Gab's-hill, which commands an extenfive profpect. For his arms, fee *Sherborne*.

Audomar de Valencia granted two acres and a half in Moreton to the abbey of Gloucefter 10 E. 2. Lands in Moreton Valence, lately belonging to the abbey of Gloucefter, were granted to Edward duke of Somerfet 1 E. 6.

HAMLETS. 1. *Horfe-Marley*, in the upper part of the parifh.

2. *Little Moreton.*

3. *Epney*, which extends down to the Severn. Lands in this place were granted to fir William Kingfton.

4. Part of *Framilode.*

Of the Church, &c.

The church is a curacy, in the deanery of Gloucefter, worth 50*l.* a year. It has been augmented by the queen's bounty. The impropriation, worth 75*l.* a year, belongs to one of the prebendaries of Hereford, whofe leffee is patron, and pays the curate 15*l.* a year; Mr. Jones is the prefent incumbent. Twenty-four acres of meadow and pafture, and eight acres of arable, belong to the glebe.

The church, dedicated to St. Stephen, has a large aile on the fouth fide, and a high embattled tower at the weft end. Over the church door is a reprefentation of St. Michael fighting with the dragon, very rudely carved in ftone.

First

Firſt fruits £. 14	5	0	Synodals £. 0	2	0
Tenths — 1	8	7	Pentecoſt. 0	1	3
Procurations 0	6	8			

Benefactions.

Several ſmall parcels of land, worth about 6*l.* a year, are given for the repair of the church. William How gave 20*s.* a year, charged on a piece of ground called Stack's-Bridge, to buy coals in winter for ſuch poor as do not receive alms. The church houſe, worth 50*s.* a year, belongs to the poor. Sir Edmund Penne, lord of the manor of Longney, gave a donation of bread to the poor, for which a compoſition of 20*s.* a year was formerly paid, but neither the money nor bread has been paid for more than eighty years paſt.

Taxes.					
The Royal Aid in	1692,	£. 80	1	8
Poll-tax — —	1694, —	10	10	0
Land-tax ——	1694, —	131	14	0
The ſame, at 3*s.*	1770, —	99	16	6

At the beginning of this century, there were 30 houſes in this pariſh, and about 150 inhabitants, whereof 8 were freeholders; yearly births 5, burials 3. *Atkyns.* The preſent number of families is 38, of inhabitants exactly 169.

NAUNTON

LIES partly in the hundred of Slaughter, and partly in that of Bradley. It is ſituated ſix miles ſouth-weſtward from Stow, ſeven ſouth-eaſt from Winchcombe, and nineteen eaſt from Glouceſter, and the turnpike-road from Stow to Glouceſter runs through the pariſh near four miles in length. The greater part of the pariſh is arable land. It has a little brook running thro' it from Guiting, which empties itſelf into the Windruſh, and ſerves as a nurſery to ſupply that river with trout, for which it is ſo deſervedly famous.

The preſent name of the village is ſo corrupted and altered from its original purity, by vulgar uſe, as not to bear the leaſt reſemblance to the antient and ſignificant appellation. It was written *Niwetone* in *Domeſday-book*, and was ſo called, becauſe ſomething later cultivated or inhabited than the other villages in the neighbourhood, in compariſon with which it was a *New town.* It was afterwards written *Niuenton*, *Newinton*, and ſometimes *Newinton in Cottſwold*, probably to diſtinguiſh it from *Newinton* (now called *Naunton*) in the pariſh of Winchcombe, and *Newinton*, or *Newton* in Aſhchurch.

The pariſh is of a middling ſize, ſituated in a fine open country, but has neither curious foſſils, rare plants, nor other uncommon natural productions to diſtinguiſh it; and the only cuſtom proper to the place ſeems to be, that of breaking a common called *Naunton-downs*, on the fourteenth day of May, for depaſturing milch-cows, young heifers, and cow-calves only. Antiquities are matters of accident and curioſity, and tho' Naunton has none of them to boaſt of, yet it enjoys one bleſſing in a very eminent degree, which may well compenſate for all its deficiencies. Whether from its open ſituation among the downs, free from woods, and far diſtant from marſhy lands and large waters; or occaſioned by what other cauſe I know not, but certain it is, that it enjoys a fine healthy air, ſcarcely to be equalled, not to be exceeded, by any ſpot in the kingdom.

Dr. Percival, in his curious inquiries concerning population, and the healthineſs of many places in and about Lancaſhire, finds, that at a village called Eſtham, one in thirty-five of the inhabitants dies in a year; at Cokey, one in forty-four; at Royſton, one in fifty-two; at Edale, one in fifty-nine; and at Hale, which is the healthieſt place of all the examples he produces, one dies annually out of ſixty-nine: And the reſult of my own inquiries through this county is nearly the ſame. But how much more healthy than any of thoſe is the pariſh of Naunton, where, from the moſt authentic particulars given at the cloſe of this account, it appears, that not one in a hundred dies in a year! The inhabitants are farmers and huſbandmen, living remote from any market-town, and there is not a public houſe in the village.

Of the Manor and other Eſtates.

There were antiently three manors in this pariſh, reckoning Ayleworth for one.

'Roger de Olgi holds Niwetone in Salemaneſberie hundred of Oſbern the ſon of Richard. 'There are five hides taxed. Turſtan held it. In 'demean are two plow-tillages, and eight villeins, 'with four plow-tillages and a half. It is worth '3*l.*' *Domeſday-book*, p. 76.

'Cvenild the monk holds nine hides in Niwetone in Salemaneſberie hundred of the king, four 'of which pay tax. Eſlmer held them for a manor. 'In demean are four plow-tillages, and ſeven villeins, with five plow-tillages: And he has now 'one plow-tillage, and a mill of 5*s.* and thirteen 'among the *ſervi* and *ancillæ*. It was worth 8*l.* 'now 5*l.*' *Domeſday-book*, p. 79.

In tracing the deſcent of the manor, ſir Robert Atkyns has fallen into the groſſeſt errors, by mingling and confounding the records, and appropriating to this pariſh the particulars which relate to Naunton in Winchcombe. He applies the ſame abſtract from *Domeſday-book* to both places, which ſerves to ſhew that this manor, or one of theſe manors, was held by the abbey of Winchcombe; and then aſſerts, that *this manor continued in the abbey of Winchcombe until its final diſſolution*; that *a leaſe of lands in Naunton, lately belonging to Winchcombe abbey, was granted to Henry Tracy* 36 *H.* 8. that *another grant was made to Henry Tracy and Elizabeth his wife* 7 *E.* 6. and laſtly, that *the tithes in Naunton did formerly belong to the abbey of Winchcombe, and were granted to ſir Thomas*

Thomas Seymour 1 *E.* 6. Whereas it does not appear that the abbey of Winchcombe ever had any property in this pariſh, nor had the Tracies any 'till by purchaſe within a few years paſt. In ſhort, the above particulars ſhould have been applied to the hamlet of Naunton in Winchcombe.

King Edward the Firſt commanded his ſheriff of Glouceſterſhire to make a return of all the vills, &c. in the ſaid county, with the ſeveral proprietors of them; and the ſheriff returned, that the prior of St. Oſwald in Glouceſter, and the prior of the Leſſer Malvern were lords of Neweton in the hundred of Salmoneſburye, 9 E. 1.

Giles Venfield and John Collet were joint lords of the manor in the year 1608, ſince which it has been divided between ſeveral freeholders. The late William Moore, eſq; by his marriage with the heireſs of Mr. Collet, claimed this manor; Powell Snell, eſq; alſo claims it, who now pays a fee-farm rent for it to the crown; and Thomas Stone has ſome pretentions to it; but no court has been held within memory.

John lord Clinton, John Smith, and William Warburton, levied a fine of lands in Naunton to John Twineho and John Underhill 1 R. 3. The capital meſſuage of Naunton was granted to John Baile who died 1 E. 6. and Thomas Baile, ſon of John, had livery thereof the ſame year. Robert Aſhton levied a fine of the manor of Naunton to Henry Moody 2 Mar.

HAMLETS. 1. *Ayleworth*, ſituated about a mile from the church. It lies in the hundred of Bradley, and gave name to a family who reſided here from the time of the conqueſt 'till the beginning of the preſent century. In *Domeſday-book* it is thus recorded:

'William Goizenboded holds Ailewrde in Salemaneſberie hundred. Aluuin held it in the time 'of king Edward. There is one hide taxed, and 'one plow-tillage in demean, and two *ſervi*. It 'was worth 6*s.* now 3*s.*' p. 74.

'Giſlebert the ſon of Turold holds Elewrde in 'Salemaneſberie hundred, and Walter holds it of 'him. Aluuin held it. There are four hides 'taxed, and two plow-tillages in demean, and 'three villeins with two plow-tillages, and ſix 'between the *ſervi* and *ancillæ*. It is and was 'worth 40*s.*' p. 76.

The ſubſequent records ſhew, that Petronella de la Mere died ſeized of Elworth 47 E. 3. Gilbert de Clare, earl of Glouceſter, proved his right to court leet and other privileges in this manor, and in Harford, in a *Quo warranto* brought againſt him 15 E. 1. At the diſſolution of religious houſes, this manor belonged to the priory of St. Oſwald in Glouceſter, and was granted to Richard Andrews and Nicholas Temple, in truſt, 35 H. 8. But there was a farm in Ayleworth which belonged to the priory of Lanthony, and was granted to Vincent Calmudee and Richard Calmudee, 6 Eliz. Other lands in Ayleworth, and a grove, belonged formerly to the chantry of St. Mary in Weſtbury, and were granted to Anthony Cope 10 Jac.

Richard Ayleworth had livery of the manor and capital meſſuage of Ayleworth, with lands lately belonging to St. Oſwald's priory; and of a farm called De Lantone, 9 Eliz. But John Ayleworth was ſeized of lands in Naunton, Calcut, and Ayleworth, as early as 16 E. 4. Joſhua Ayleworth, the laſt of this family, died in 1718, as did his widow the following year, aged ninety, as appears by the pariſh regiſter, and both were buried in the church, without any memorial. The manor and eſtate of Ayleworth were purchaſed by —— Herring, eſq; but Henry Blagg, of the county of Nottingham, is the preſent lord of the manor.

2. *Harford.* 'Giſlebert the ſon of Turold 'holds Hurford in Salemaneſberie hundred. Alfer 'held it. There is one hide taxed, and two plow-'tillages in demean, and four villeins, and one 'bordar, with two plow-tillages, and two *ſervi*, 'and a mill of 5*s.* It is worth and was worth 40*s.*' *Domeſday-book*, p. 76.

William de Clinton, earl of Huntingdon, was ſeized of the manor of Harford 28 E. 3. as was Richard the ſon of John Browning 2 H. 4. and the priory of Lanthony had lands in Harford and Ayleworth 13 H. 4. William Moore, eſq; died ſeized of Harford, in right of his wife, about the year 1771.

Lower Harford is an eſtate belonging to Corpus Chriſti College in Oxford, now in leaſe to Mrs. Tracy, relict of Thomas Tracy, eſq; deceaſed, and heireſs of the late ſir William Dodwell.

Bayle-farm is unworthily diſtinguiſhed by ſir Robert Atkyns as a hamlet. It was ſo called from a family of that name, to whom it belonged, and from whom it went afterwards to the Ayleworths, and is now called *Round-hill farm.*

Of the Church, &c.

The church is a rectory, in the deanery of Stow, worth about 250*l.* a year. The biſhop of Worceſter is patron; Mr. Anſelm Jones the preſent incumbent. The whole pariſh is ſubject to tithes, and two yard-lands belong to the glebe.

The church is dedicated to St. Andrew. It is a handſome building, with a neat tower adorned with pinnacles and battlements. It has a ſmall aile on the north ſide, which belonged to the Ayleworths, ſeveral of whom are buried there, but without any memorials. The whole church was formerly ornamented with painted glaſs, but time and miſchievous hands have in a great meaſure deſtroy'd it. In the ſouth window, near the pulpit, is a large figure of a ſaint, [*Scs Philippus*] and in a ſcroll round his head,

Inde venturus ut iudicaret vivos & mortuos;

at his feet a man and woman praying, and under,

Orate p' bono ſtatu . . . . . bayle . . . .

On the next pane, round a ſaint's head, is written,

Credo in ſpiritũ ſanctũ ſanctam eccleſiã catholicã;

at

at his feet a man and woman praying, and under,

Orate p' bono . . . . ayleworth et elſabeth . . . . . .

then at the bottom of the next pane, where are ſeveral figures in a praying poſture, it follows,

eius et ōniū fidelū defunctor'

In the ſouth window of the chancel is the figure of Chriſt, round whoſe head it is written,

aſcēdit ad celos ſedit ad dexteram dei patris ōipotentis ;

and near it, St. John Baptiſt, with this mutilated legend in a ſcroll round his head,

. . . . . . eſt de ſpiritu ſancto in eremam.

In the north window are the figures of St. Catherine, with her wheel, and St. Stephen, in very good preſervation.

Firſt fruits £.16	13	4½	Synodals £.0	2	0
Tenths — 1	13	4½	Pentecoſtals 0	0	11½
Procurations 0	6	8			

Monuments and Inſcriptions.

On a ſmall braſs plate, againſt the north wall of the chancel,

Clemens Barkſdalius artium magiſter evangelii miniſter quotidie orans, quotidie moriens, iubet te viator cœleſtem cogitare patriam IX*b*. XXIII. MDCLXX. ÆTAT LXI.

On another plate, againſt the ſame wall,

In Memoriam Caroli Barkſdale Cl. F. hic depoſiti Jan. 1. 82. æt. 30. Clementis propeinhumati Jun. 1. 68. æt. 24. Mariæ virginis annorum 33 Deo redditæ Lond. ad S. Brig. 77. Gulielmi Oxon ſepulti. Hos Liberos ſuos (Ioanne et Charletono relictis) ex Maria Charletona conjuge pia (pridem defuncta et Winch. juxta matrem condita) præmiſit Cl. P. mœſtus Ipſe ſenex annorum 75 Chriſtum expectat. Fiat voluntas Dei P. P. An. Dom. 1685.

Yong man lay to thy heart this ſacred Truth
Remember thy Creator in thy Yovth
Old man if piovs do not thy death fear
Having Good hopes of better things ſo near.

On another braſs plate, againſt the ſame wall,

Epitaphivm in Ioſephvm Hanxman hvivs Eccleſiæ rector qvi migravit ex hac vita primo die Avgvſti 1632.

Hic iacet in tvmvlo veri paſtoris imago
Os verbum vitæ mos verbi deniq; vita.
Perpende Lector.
Heere lies the Paterne of a trew Diuine
His word and life were one would ſoe were thine.

On a marble table, within the communion rails,

Near this Place lieth the Body of Ambroſe Oldys, Son of William Oldys, D. D. formerly V. of Adderbury in the County of Oxford, who for his Loyalty to his King, and Zeal for the eſtabliſhed Church (tho' a Clergyman) was barbarouſly murthered by the Rebels in the year 1645; whoſe unſhaken Loyalty to the Crown and conſtant Adherance to the eſtabliſhed Religion was nevertheleſs perfectly imitated by his Son: But with better Fortune, for after he had eſcaped many and eminent Dangers, as well by Sea, as in Battles fought for the Honour and Service of the King and Country, (to which he frequently with undaunted Courage expoſed himſelf) he ended his Days in Peace and Quiet, at his Houſe called Harford in this pariſh, which at his Death he left to his Siſter Cecilia Goad, who out of Gratitude to the Memory of ſo good a Man, and ſo kind a Brother, cauſed this Monument to be erected. Obijt 2do Die Maij Anno { Dom: 1710 / Ætatis ſuæ 77.

At top, *Azure, a chevron argent between three garbs Or.*

Benefactions.

An acre of hay-ground, and an acre of tillage-land in the eaſt upper-end field, and one acre of tillage in the weſt common field, in the lower end of this pariſh; and one acre of meadow-ground in the Brook-furlong, in the pariſh of Upper Slaughter; together with the yearly rent of 8*s.* charged on an eſtate at Harford in this pariſh, are given for the repair of the church. And Thomas Freeman, of this pariſh, yeoman, in the year 1746, gave 30*s.* yearly to teach poor children to read.

Taxes.			£.	s.	d.
The Royal Aid in	1692,		79	11	4
Poll-tax —	1694,	—	22	13	0
Land-tax —	1694,	—	63	19	0
The ſame, at 3*s.*	1770,	—	47	16	1½

At the beginning of this century, there were 34 houſes, and about 140 inhabitants in this pariſh, whereof 16 were freeholders; yearly births 5, burials 4. *Atkyns.* The old pariſh regiſter being loſt, I could not collect the numbers of the baptiſms and burials for ten years beginning with 1700, in my uſual manner; but in ten years, commencing with 1760, the baptiſms were 51, the burials 22; and in the year 1767, there were 52 houſes, and 257 inhabitants, who were increaſed to 288 in the year 1776.

NEWENT.

THIS pariſh lies in the hundred of Botloe, eight miles north-eaſtward from Mitchel-Dean, thirteen weſtward from Tewkeſbury, and ten north-weſtward from Glouceſter.

It is ſituated in the north-weſt part of the county, upon the borders of Herefordſhire. It is a large pariſh, extending full ſeven miles from eaſt to weſt, and about ſix from north to ſouth. By much the greater part of it lies in paſturage and orcharding, for the ſoil is very deep and good, and better ſuited to paſture than corn. The roads in this part of the country are ſo intolerable, that the writer of this account found it neceſſary to deſert his horſe, and to travel with a guide on foot from one village to another.

A rill, or brook, called the *Ell*, runs through the north part of it, and after driving ſeveral mills, empties itſelf into the Leden.

Leland and others ſay, the name of this place ſignifies the *New Inn*, and that it was given it becauſe very antiently an inn was erected here for the convenience of travellers paſſing between England and Wales, which was then the only houſe in the place, but others being afterwards added, it increaſed gradually to the ſize of a town.

The town once conſiſted of nine ſtreets and lanes, which are thus enumerated in a ſmall manuſcript, intitled *Fragmenta Newentenſia*, kindly communicated to me by Mr. Foley, the reſident miniſter of the place.

1. *New Street*, or *Upper Town*, or *Altus Vicus*, ſo called in the time of king Henry the Fifth, extending from Ellbridge to Peacock's brook.

2. *Lewall-ſtreet*, from Peacock's brook to the market-place.

3. *Church-ſtreet*, from the market-houſe, along by the church, to the turnings where the right hand way leading towards Glouceſter is called *Old Church-ſtreet*, or the *Bartholomew's*, and the left hand way, *Curryar's-lane*.

4. *Lux-lane*, from Lewall-ſtreet ſouthward, as far as the houſes are contiguous.

5. *Colford-ſtreet*, from Lux-lane ſouthward, to the croſs way that leads from Glouceſter to Bowlſdon, comprehending the green leading towards Colford, in the foreſt of Dean. This is ſaid to be within the perambulation of the foreſt.

6. *Lift-bridge-lane*, leading from the ſouth end of Lux-lane weſtward, over the bridge towards Bridge-field.

7. *Berry-Bar.*

8. *The Horſe-fair.*

9. *Park-lane*, leading from the rock, by the crown, eaſtward to the parks. But ſeveral of theſe lanes have at this time no houſes in them.

It appears that iron has been made in or near the town, before large bellows were driven by water, ſo as more perfectly to extract the metal from the ore, for here vaſt quantities of rich iron cinders have been dug, and ſmelted over again at a furnace in this pariſh, not many years ago, tho' the furnace has been for ſome time out of blaſt. In digging for thoſe cinders, the workmen found ſeveral coins of Julius Cæſar, Nerva, Veſpaſian, &c. and ſome pieces of fine Roman pottery, now all diſperſed or deſtroy'd.

The town had a charter for a market, and two fairs, as early as the reign of king Henry the Third, which was renewed in the reign of king Henry the Eighth. And king James the Firſt granted it a new one, to hold two additional fairs, ſo that it has now four in the year, *viz.* on the Wedneſday before Eaſter, the Wedneſday before Whitſunday, on the firſt day of Auguſt, and on the Friday next after the 8th day of September. The market was originally on Tueſday, but it is now held on Friday.

The town had formerly a bailiff for its chief officer, mentioned in an antient deed concerning half a yard-land, called *Totteland* in Newent, granted by Nicholas ſon of John de Camma, to the abbey of Cormeille and to the ſaid bailiff, to which Reginald de Acle, then ſheriff of Glouceſterſhire, was one of the witneſſes, in the reign of king Henry the Third. William White, who lived towards the end of the ſeventeenth century, was the laſt bailiff.

There was a ſmall priory here, for ſome time dependent on the abbey of Cormeille in Normandy, and the court-houſe adjoining to the church-yard, ſtands on the ſcite of the priory-houſe.

As the priory muſt have contributed to the growth and increaſe of the town, by procuring grants of a market, fairs, and other privileges for it, and by the company it drew thither, ſo the loſs of that houſe was very probably felt by it, at the diſſolution of alien priories. But this country, formerly ſo remarkable for old Engliſh hoſpitality, has ſuſtained a greater loſs in the courſe of the preſent century, by the general and too faſhionable deſertion of the manor and other houſes by their owners.

Newent, at preſent, is a ſmall market town, very irregularly built, and tho' there are a few pretty good houſes, the greater part are mean buildings, and ſome covered with thatch at the entrance into the town. It has no manufacture, except a little frame-knitting, nor trade, but with the neighbouring villages for common neceſſaries. The market, which is held on Fridays, is of neceſſity ſmall; for the bad condition of the roads makes it almoſt impoſſible for carriages to reach it, except on the ſide next Glouceſter, where there is a turnpike-road very ill repaired. Here was formerly a little clothing, and the place where a cloth-mill ſtood is ſtill called the Tuck-mill pool, but the trade is intirely loſt.

Of the Manors and other Eſtates.

In *Domeſday* it is thus recorded:

'The church of St. Mary of Cormelies holds 'Noent in Boteſlau hundred. King Edward held 'it. There are ſix hides which did not pay tax. 'Earl Roger gave it to this church for the good of 'his father's ſoul by the conſent of king William. 'In demean are three plow-tillages, and nine 'villeins, and nine bordars, with twelve plow-'tillages. There is a ſteward having one villein 'and a half, and five bordars. They have amongſt 'them all five plow-tillages, and a mill of 20*d.* '[rent.] There are two *ſervi*, and two mills of '6*s.* and 8*d.* [rent,] and in wood 30*d.* Durand 'holds one hide of this land of the abbat, and he 'has there one plow-tillage, and five bordars, and 'two *ſervi*, with two plow-tillages. There are 'two parks, [or incloſures] which the king hath 'ſeized. All the manor was worth 4*l.* in the 'time of king Edward, it is now worth 100*s.* 'Durand's hide is worth 12*s.* William the ſon 'of Baderon holds one yard-land by force.' *Domeſday-book*, p. 72.

This manor was afterwards confirmed to the abbey of Cormeille, by king Henry the Firſt, by pope Alexander the Third, and by king Henry the Second. *See Appendix*, N°s. 22, & 23.

The ſame abbey purchaſed two ſeveral grants of fairs and markets, with other privileges, in Newent, 10 & 37 H. 3. which were allowed in a writ of *Quo warranto* 15 E. 1.

King Edward the Third, during his wars with France, ſeized this manor into his hands; and king Richard the Second, in the 5th year of his reign, granted it to ſir John Devereux, and Margaret his wife, and to John and Joan his children, to hold during the war, at the rent of 126*l.* 13*s.* 4*d.* which rent was remitted 9 R. 2. But when the college of Fotheringhay, in Northamptonſhire, was founded by king Henry the Fourth and Edward duke of York, that king, by virtue of an act of parliament, granted to the ſaid college all the manors, with their appurtenances, that belonged to the priory of Newent, which was ſubject to the abbey of Cormeille; and at the ſuppreſſion of alien priories, this grant was confirmed by a ſtatute 2 H. 5. After

After the general diſſolution of religious foundations, the manor of Newent, and a wood called Yarkledon, were granted to ſir Richard Lee 1 E. 6. Sir Nicholas Arnold was afterwards lord of it, and ſold it to ſir William Wintour, upon which occaſion he punningly ſaid, *There had been fair weather for ſome time, but now Winter was come.* Sir Edward Wintour ſucceeded his father in this manor, and from him it deſcended to his ſon ſir John Wintour.

Mr. Thomas Foley purchaſed it of ſir John Wintour, and was ſucceeded therein by his ſon Paul Foley, eſq; whoſe ſon Thomas Foley was the next poſſeſſor; and Thomas lord Foley, grandſon of the laſt mentioned Thomas, is the preſent lord of this manor. He was created a baron by patent, May 20, 1776, and took his ſeat in the houſe of peers, on the 22d day of the ſame month. His lordſhip's arms are, *Argent, a feſs within a bordure ingrailed between three cinquefoils ſable.*

TITHINGS and *HAMLETS.*

Beſides the town, this large pariſh contains five tithings, diviſions, or holy waters.

1. *Compton.* Compton-houſe was formerly called *Walden's Court.* This houſe, with a good eſtate belonging to it, was the property of Reginald Bray, eſq; out of whoſe family it was ſold to Mr. Edward Rogers, who left two daughters coheireſſes, one married to Edward Bearcroft, eſq; an eminent barriſter; the other to Mr. Charles Jones, who, in right of their wives, are proprietors thereof.

Carſwell is an antient manor in this tithing, thus deſcribed in *Domeſday*: 'Roger de Laci holds 'Craſowel in Botelau hundred, and Odo holds it 'of him. Ulfel held it in the time of king 'Edward, and could go wherever he would. There 'is one hide and one yard-land, and in demean 'one plow-tillage, and three villeins, and one 'bordar, with three plow-tillages. It is worth 'and was worth 20*s*.' p. 75. This eſtate, which was formerly the Pauncefoots, now belongs to Mr. Bromley and Mr. Smith.

The *Waters End*, or the *Scarre*, formerly called *Atherlord's Place*, which was Mr. Dobyns's, is now the property of Mr. Sergeant.

The *Hays* is an antient place in this tithing. 'Ansfrid de Cormeliis holds one hide [in] Hege, 'which [with other lands] he had of Walter de 'Laci, as a portion with his niece.' *Dom. B.* p. 78. This formerly belonged to the Walls, and is now the eſtate of Mr. Pritchard.

2. *Maulſwick*, in which are comprehended *Okely-Clifford*, *Okely-Pritchard*, and *Okely-Grandiſon.* Theſe are not always diſtinguiſhed in the records. Philippa the widow of Henry Maſham died ſeized of Okely 8 H. 4. Elizabeth the widow of Robert Lovell died ſeized of Okely-Grandiſon 16 H. 6. Sir James Ormond (ſon of James earl of Ormond) and Amice his wife levied a fine of it 23 H. 6. and the latter died ſeized of this eſtate in the 35th year of that reign. James earl of Wiltſhire was ſeized of it 1 E. 4. John Roberts and his wife levied a fine of the manor of Okely-court 23 H. 7. The manor of Okely-Grandiſon belonged to Thomas duke of Norfolk, who being attainted, it was granted to Paul Withepool and others, as a ſecurity for money borrowed, 36 H. 8. Thomas Brook, eſq; died ſeized of Okely-Grandiſon, without iſſue, 38 H. 8. and Joan Arrowſmith, his ſiſter and heir, had livery thereof 1 E. 6. Mr. Rogers was lord of the manor of Okely, and proprietor of a good eſtate in this place, at the beginning of the preſent century, which are now come to Mr. Bearcroft and Mr. Jones, in right of their wives, who were the daughters and coheirs of the late Mr. Rogers. There was formerly a chapel in the manor-houſe.

Okely-Pritchard is the eſtate of George Smith, eſq.

3. *Cugley.* William Gerand of Matiſden, and Catherine his wife, levied a fine of lands in Cugley 8 E. 2.

Mr. Chin has a good houſe and eſtate in this tithing, called the Moat, formerly belonging to the Woodwards.

In the common, at the foot of Yartleton-hill, part of which lies in this tithing, there was formerly a glaſs-houſe, and the place where it ſtood it is ſtill called the *Glaſs-houſe.* Near the top of the ſame hill is *Crocket's Hole*, ſo called, becauſe one Crocket and his companion Horne uſed to hide themſelves there, in the perſecuting reign of queen Mary. Horne was taken, and burnt in the yard belonging to the priory-houſe in Newent, which is not mentioned in *Fox's Acts and Monuments.* His ſtory is briefly thus, as related by Horne's ſon, who had it from his mother. Horne was a papiſt and a man of parts, and meeting with ſeveral proteſtants who had aſſembled near the ſide of Yartleton-wood to diſcourſe on religious ſubjects, at length became a proſelyte, and refuſed to go to maſs; for which he was taken before the biſhop, in his conſiſtory court at Glouceſter, and committed to ſome priſon within the verge of the college. But eſcaping from it in the night, he returned home, and lay concealed in various manners; at laſt, his wife being with child was delivered, and an entertainment made at the baptizing of the child, when the mother deſired a cutting of ſome meat, (probably what ſhe knew her huſband loved) which having received, ſhe laid it by: This being obſerved by the midwife, created a ſuſpicion, whereupon ſhe procured an officer to ſearch for poor Horne, whom they found concealed under a veſſel with the head out. He was immediately carried to his trial, condemned, and led to the place of execution, ſinging the 146th pſalm, where he ſuffered with great Chriſtian fortitude. Horne was ſo well beloved by his neighbours, and his execution ſo much execrated, that when the news was but whiſper'd of queen

Mary's

Mary's death, the women, (men not daring to appear) took the prieſt that ſupply'd the church upon a horſe, with his face towards the tail, and leading him thro' the town, ſent him away. *Fragment. Newentenſia.*

About the year 1665, one Fairfax, a diſbanded ſoldier, adviſed by Lilly the aſtrologer, came down from London, and opened this hole, in hopes of diſcovering great riches therein, which drew many people thither. Some of them went into the hole, and told incredible things concerning it; at laſt, one Witcombe going in drunk, and dying there, put an end to all further examination.

4. *Boulesdon*, or *Boldeſdon*. John Atwood had one meſſuage and ſix acres of land in Bouleſdon, and being attainted of felony, his lands were ſeized by the king 29 E. 1. Thomas Boulſdon died ſeized of this manor 14 E. 4. whoſe family took their name from this place, where they enjoy'd a conſiderable eſtate for ſeveral generations. Thomas Porter, eſq; had livery of this manor 1 Eliz. Walter Nourſe was lord of it at the beginning of this century; but it is now the property of lord Foley. The manor houſe is down. From a place called the Caſtle-mount, there is a good proſpect over the vale. *Woeful-hill* in this tithing, is a place where it is ſaid criminals were formerly executed.

5. *Kilcot*, perhaps from the Britiſh *Cyll Coed*, a *hazle-wood*. This place is taken notice of in *Domeſday*. 'Ansfrid de Cormeliis holds one hide '[in] Chilcot, which he had of Walter de Laci, 'in marriage with his niece.' p. 78.

Robert de Muſgroſe died ſeized of Kilecot 38 H. 3. Bogo de Knovil had a grant of free warren in Kilcot 13 E. 1. and Bogo his ſon died ſeized of this manor 12 E. 3. Sir John de Verdune levied a fine of it to ſir Richard Pembrooke, who granted the ſame to Thomas Moine 37 E. 3. and Beatreaux the wife of Richard Burly died ſeized of it 16 R. 2. This manor lately belonged to Walter Nourſe, eſq; and is now the property of Mr. Lewis, who holds a court leet here.

There was formerly a chapel in this tithing, ſuppoſed to have been dedicated to St. Hillary, becauſe the ground where it ſtood lying high, is ſtill called *St. Tilly's Nap*, near Ghoſtly or Gorſtly common.

Of the Church, &c.

The church is in the Foreſt deanery. It is a vicarage endowed. Lord Foley is patron, and Doctor Foley is the preſent incumbent.

The rectory belonged to the college of Fotheringhay, and after the general diſſolution of religious foundations, was granted to ſir Richard Lee, 1 E. 6. It afterwards came to ſir John Wintour, who ſold it to Edward Warcup, eſq; who, in the year 1665, ſold it to Paul Foley, eſq. His grandſon, Thomas Foley, eſq; endowed the vicarage, which makes it a very valuable living, worth about 350*l.* a year. The rectory pays 10*s.* a year to the crown.

Dr. John Craiſter, who died vicar of this church in the year 1737, by his will, gave his library to the ſucceeding vicars.

The church is dedicated to St. Mary. It is large, and neatly pewed, and the roof is ſupported without pillars. It has a ſpire ſteeple over the porch, with ſix bells and a ſet of chimes in it, and a ſmall chancel on the ſide of the great one. The ſteeple is 153 feet high from the ground, the top of which was blown down in 1662; and the whole roof of the body of the church fell down on Sunday after evening ſervice, Jan. 18, 1673, but no perſon was hurt by the fall. The inhabitants did for ſome time commemorate this accident, by obſerving that day with thankſgiving for their deliverance. Under one of the pillars was found a tomb ſtone, with this inſcription: *Hic jacet W^s de capella monac. Corder. cuj^s aie p'pic' D^s*; and a gilt altar-piece was taken out of the wall. Theſe circumſtances ſhew that the church has been thrice built.

There were two chantries in this church, one dedicated to St. James and St. Anne, whereof Philip Wyat was the laſt incumbent, and had a penſion of 4*l.* The other was dedicated to St. Mary, of which William Brook was the laſt incumbent.

Lands in Newent, formerly belonging to theſe chantries, were granted to Ralph Dobbins and others, 3 Jac. And a tenement called the Porch-houſe, and Culford in Newent, late belonging to St. Mary's chantry, were granted to Robert earl of Leiceſter, and John Morley, 24 Eliz.

All Yartleton-wood, except Jordan's grove, and a few other lands are tithe free.

Firſt fruits £. 23	0	0	Proc. & Syn. £. 0	11	8
Tenths — 2	6	0	Pentecoſtals 0	1	4

Monuments and Inſcriptions.

The moſt antient monument in the church is a very fine alabaſter tomb, without *inſignia*, on which are lying the effigies of a man in armour, with his lady by his ſide, deſigned, it is ſuppoſed, for a lord Grandiſon.

On a braſs plate fixt to a grey marble ſtone, in the ſouth chancel,

Of yor charity pray for the ſoul of Roger Porter eſquyer wch Roger deceaſyd ye xv day of April ye yeare of o^r Lord God 1523. On whoſe ſoul Ihu haue mercy. Amen.

Againſt the wall,

H. P. I. Walterus Nourſe e Medio Templo Armiger (habilis Advocatus peritus Irenarcha, Virtute denique privatâ et publicâ multis nominibus deſiderandus) cum Conſorte ſuâ amabili Mariâ, Edvardi Engeham de Gunſtone in Agro Cant. Militis, Filia. Ille obijt 13° Nov. 1652. Hæc 19° Aug^ti 1636. Walterum et Mariam reliquere Liberos.——Arms, *Gules, a feſs between two chevronels argent*, for Nourſe; impaling, *Argent, a chevron between three pellets, on a chief gules a lion paſſant Or*, for Engeham.

On another table, in gold letters,

M. S. Chariſſ. Parentum Gualteri Nourſe Arm. necnon Mariæ conjugis fidiſſimæ, quæ ſacrificio veſpertinæ orationis divinum placando numen diem clauſit; quippe autiphona (Deus in adjutorium intende) et glorificationis hymno voce prolata, Subitaneo apoplexiæ ictu, genibus proſtrata, oculis manibuſq; leuatis, occubuit Nov. VIII An: MDCLXXIII ÆT LXIII. At non ex improviſo, Deo nimirum proximo, ſibi ipſi ſemper vacans, ſemper occupata, mortiq; ſeu verius immortalitati ſemper tempeſtiva.

tiva. MNEMOSUNON hoc exiguum, pietatis ergo, moerens filius Timotheus Nourſe, ejuſdem fidei, ejuſdem ſpei, ejuſdem charitatis, et nunc ejuſdem tumuli particeps, vivus vovit: Idemque, hemiplegia quatriduana hydropi diutino ſuperveniente, moriens Jul. XXI MDCXCIX uxori chariſſimæ Luciæ R.D. Ric. Harwood Præb. Glocest. fil. erigendum mandavit.

I. P. R. M.

Idem Timotheus Nourſe ex Reditibus terrarum in hac parochia domo manſionali Southerns adjacentium L. libras annuas ab hæredibus poſt uxoris obitum in perpetuum ſolvendas, nec non terras in . . . . ad valorem . . . . . . librarum per annum D. Epiſcop. et Decani Glocest. aliorumq; fidei commiſſariorum adminiſtrationi in ſucceſſione perpetua concreditas, ſive ad promovendam pauperum induſtriam, ſive ad eorum inopiam ſublevandam, teſtamento legavit. Hæc pietatis opera (Chriſtiane lector) hominis genium tibi ſatis indicant, ingenium ſcripta; in utroq; non indigni, quem cum laude imiteris; vel, ſi majora placent, abſque invidia exuperes. —— Arms, Nourſe, impaling, *Azure, a chevron ermine between three martlets argent.*

South chancel,

In Memory of Chriſtopher Woodward, of the Moat, Gent. buried July 19, 1731. —— Arms, *Azure, a pale between two eagles diſplay'd argent.*

Chriſtopherus Woodward Generoſus Mortalitati valedixit 3° die Apr. Anno Dom. 1699° Ætat. 70°.

Urna tenet cineres, Animam Deus, Inclyta Fama
Conſeruat Nomen. Quid perijſſe putes?

Hic etiam jacet quicquid terrenum eſt ejus filii natu minimi Chriſtopheri Woodward, Generoſi, qui cum ob ſummam humanitatem et miram Comitatem, admodum dilectus vixiſſet, diem obijt ſupremum 3° Ian. A D. 1710, Ætat. 50.

Me, ſcio, viciſti, Mors, duraq; in Orbe triumphas,
At ſurgam mortem Morſq; videbo tuam.

At top are theſe Arms, *Azure, a pale between two eagles diſplay'd argent*, for Woodward; impaling, *Argent, on a bend azure three bucks heads caboſhed Or*, for Stanley.

Againſt the wall of the great chancel,

P. M. S. William Rogers of Okle Gent. was born ye 15th of April 1640 & Dyed the 19th of Iuly 1690 leaving Iſſue three Daughters. He erected two Almes Houſes, gave Three Pounds per Annũ to the Poor for ever, was a Rewarder of Virtue, a Reprover of Vice, and a Reproacher of Vanity, a Servant to his Neighbour, & a truſty Guardian.

The Herſes Tombs and Cenotaphs They ſhew
Of the Great Dead are Monuments of Snow:
His Fame and Life (Moſt holy wiſe and Juſt)
Shall ever ſtick to's Name, embalme his Duſt:
The Feare of God, the Love of Men, a Friend
Lies here, the Pattern of a happy End.
His Bounty to this Pariſh, Church, and Poore
Was Great; This modeſt Poſtſcript tells no more.
Poſuit Frater I. R.

The arms on this monument are, 1. Rogers, (ſee Dowdeſwell) impaling, 2. *Sable, a feſs between ſix fleurs de lis argent*, for Hooke.

Johannes Bourne, nuper de Sutton Bourne in Agro Somerſetenſe Armiger, tam Artibus Ingenuiis quam Moribus honeſtis eximie memorabilis: Manſuetudine, Humilitate, et Temperantia, Pietate erga Deum, Iuſtitia et Charitate in Proximum, valde Inſignis: In Faucibus Necis, ſe nec ægrotare, nec Dolore cruciari hilariter profitens. Prope Conſortem Dorotheam fidiſſimam (E ſtirpe antiqua Godfreydorum, in Agro Cantii oriundam) Cumque prole natu quarta Benedicta, hic reponitur XXXI° die Menſis Auguſti Anno Dni 1708 Ætat. 88°. —— Arms, 1. *Sable, a chevron per pale Or and argent, between three griphons heads erazed of the laſt*, for Bourne; impaling, 2. *A chevron between three pelicans heads erazed*, for Godfrey.

There are alſo memorials for ſeveral other perſons, with their family arms, *viz.* for Miles Beale, gent. with his arms, *Or, on a chevron ſable between three griphons heads erazed gules, as many mullets argent.* For Francis Singleton, vicar of Newent, who died in 1642, bearing, *Argent, a chevron between three roundlets ſable.* For Stephen Skinner, who died in 1715, aged 80; and for another Stephen Skinner of London, merchant, who died in 1729, aged 72; bearing, *Sable, a chevron Or, between three griphons heads erazed argent.* For Nathaniel Spicer, late of Stardens, gent. who died in 1740; arms, *Per feſs embattled, three lions rampant.* For Elizabeth Draper, wife of Samuel Draper, gent. of this pariſh, who died in 1758; arms, *Bendy of eight pieces, vert and gules, over all three fleurs de lis Or.* For Edward Rogers, eſq; who died in 1763, with his arms, impaling, *Azure, three bucks trippant Or*, for Green.

Benefactions.

Walter Nourſe, eſq; gave 40*s.* yearly to apprentice out a poor child. Mr. Timothy Nourſe, his ſon, gave 120*l.* a year to charitable uſes, out of which the pariſh of Newent receives 12*l.* 10*s.*

Giles Nanfan, eſq; and Randal Dobyns, gave an almſhouſe, conſiſting of eight dwellings, with gardens, for the poor. And William Rogers gave two other almſhouſes, and 3*l.* a year out of lands in Kilcot, to apprentice out poor boys. William Heath gave lands in Boulſdon, worth 40*s.* a year, and Thomas Pace gave a cloſe and a barn in Kilcot, worth 30*s.* a year; John Dobyns gave a rent-charge of 10*s.* a year, out of a houſe in Newent, and Thomas Chedworth charged his lands in Compton tithing with 6*s.* a year, all to the uſe of the poor. Mr. Thomas Bower gave 20*l.* for the ſame uſe, which was laid out on lands in Boulſdon field. Beſide theſe charities, which are of a permanent nature, there have been the following donations to the poor:

Paul Pauncefoot, eſq; and his daughter Elizabeth, gave 30*l.* William Pauncefoot 12*l.* 10*s.* Alderman Colwal, of London, 20*l.* Richard Wallwyn 20*l.* Richard Rogers, gent. 10*l.* John Rogers, of Haresfield, gent. 10*l.* Dorothy Green 10*l.* Thomas Careleſs 10*l.* Thomas Avenant 20*l.*

Here is a charity-ſchool for teaching children to read and write.

Taxes.			£.	s.	d.
	The Royal Aid in	1692,	296	4	0
	Poll-tax ——	1694,	139	12	0
	Land-tax ——	1694,	459	16	0
	The ſame at 3*s.*	1770,	360	12	0

In the year 1676, there were in the town and pariſh 943 inhabitants, of ſixteen years old and upwards, and about 1570 ſouls in the whole. About the beginning of the preſent century, according to ſir Robert Atkyns, there were 270 houſes, and about 1100 inhabitants, whereof 93 were freeholders; yearly births 38, burials 37. But ſir Robert's numbers were probably too low. On an average of ſeven years, beginning with 1761, the annual baptiſms were 58, and the burials 39; and the inhabitants are at preſent about 1560.

There is the following entry in the pariſh regiſter. A. D. 1602, Feb. 24, Anne Wilſon, widow, mother of John Wilſon, buried, aged 115.

NEWINGTON BAGPATH

IS a ſmall pariſh in the hundred of Berkeley, four miles eaſtward from Wotton-underedge, ſix weſt from Tetbury, and ſeventeen ſouth from Glouceſter. It is full of little hills and ſteep acclivities, and the lands are moſtly employ'd in tillage. The houſes ſtand at the head of a very narrow comb, or valley, which extends weſtward to Ozleworth, Alderley, and Kingſwood, gradually opening itſelf 'till it joins the great vale a little below the laſt mentioned place. It has Simondſhall, (a tithing in the large pariſh of Wotton) to the north, Kingſcot to the eaſt, and Boxwell and Laſborough to the ſouth and ſouth-eaſtward of it. The church ſtands at a diſtance from the houſes, which is ſaid to have been occaſioned by a diſpute between the joint patrons; and becauſe neither of them would ſuffer it to be built near to the other's manſion houſe, they agreed that it ſhould ſtand about the midway between them.

The antient name of this place is *Neuetone*, which was given it from its being later inhabited or cultivated than ſome of the neighbouring villages. In order to diſtinguiſh it from ſeveral other places of the ſame name, the addition of *Bagpath* was afterwards made, and taken probably from a family of the name of *Bagpaze*, who might have property here ſometime between the Norman conqueſt and the reign of king Edward the Firſt; but as this is a matter unſupported by poſitive proof, it muſt reſt ſolely on conjecture.

Of the Manor and other Eſtates.

When *Domeſday-book* was compiled, this manor was a member of the great lordſhip of Berkeley; for under the particulars of that manor, it is there ſaid, 'Roger has ſeven hides at Neuetone of the 'land of this manor.'

What ſir Robert Atkyns ſays of its being held of the honour of Hereford, is moſt probably a miſtake. It was a member of the lordſhip of Berkeley before the conqueſt, and it has continued to be ſo ever ſince.

John, ſon of William de Berkeley, was lord of Newenton in Berkeley hundred (as appears by the ſheriff's return of all the vills in the county, with their ſeveral proprietors) 9 E. 1. John de Berkeley, of Durſley, and Hawiſe his wife, levied a fine of this manor 5 E. 3. Sir Nicholas Berkeley was ſeized of Newington 2 R. 2. and was living 6 R. 2.

The manor ſoon after paſſed to the Wekys's, deſcended from an heireſs of the Berkeley family, as may be ſeen under Dodington. John Wekys died ſeized of Newington, leaving Edward his ſon and heir, who likewiſe died ſeized of this manor 6 H. 8. and livery was granted to Nicholas Wekys, ſon of Edward, the ſame year. He died 5 Mariæ, and was ſucceeded by Robert Wekys, his grandſon and heir, who was likewiſe lord of the manors of Dodington and Durſley, both which he ſold in the reign of queen Elizabeth; and it is probable that he ſold this about the ſame time, for ſir Thomas Low was lord of the manor in the year 1608. Edward Webb was proprietor of it at the beginning of this century. It ſoon after paſſed to Nigel Kingſcot, eſq; whoſe nephew —— Kingſcot, eſq; is the preſent lord of this manor.

HAMLET. Bagpath, lying half a mile from the church. Sir Robert Pointz, died ſeized of this eſtate 12 H. 8. and was ſucceeded by ſir Anthony his ſon and heir, whoſe ſon, ſir Nicholas, died ſeized thereof 4 Mariæ, and livery was then granted to Nicholas Pointz, ſon of ſir Nicholas. Mr. Edward Webb was proprietor of it at the beginning of this century, and it is now veſted in Mr. Kingſcot.

Calcot, or *Caldecot*, is a farm in this pariſh, formerly the demeans of the abbey of Kingſwood. It was granted to ſir Nicholas Pointz 31 H. 8. and from his family paſſed to the Eſtcourts. Thomas Eſtcourt, of Shipton Moyne, eſq; is the preſent proprietor.

A moiety of lands in Bagpath, and in Bemerton and Sedworth near Bagpath, formerly belonging to the abbey of Glouceſter, was granted to ſir Walter Rawleigh, and upon his attainder, to Peter Vanlore, merchant, and William Blake, ſcrivener, 3 Jac.

Of the Church, &c.

The church is a rectory, in the deanery of Durſley, worth 120*l.* a year. Mr. Cliffold is the preſent incumbent. In 1503, the rector of this church was diſcharged from keeping a curate at Olepen, which is a chapel annexed to this church. The abbey of Glouceſter had the patronage of the rectory, in the year 1512.

The church is dedicated to St. Bartholomew, and has a large tower at the weſt end.

Firſt fruits £. 14	0	0	Synodals £. 0	2	0
Tenths — 1	8	0	Pentecoſt. 0	0	5
Procurations 0	6	8			

Taxes.					
	The Royal Aid in	1692,	£. 68	12	0
	Poll-tax — —	1694, —	11	8	0
	Land-tax ——	1694, —	74	4	0
	The ſame, at 3*s.*	1770, —	51	3	0

At the beginning of this century, there were 27 houſes in this pariſh, and about 120 inhabitants, whereof 6 were freeholders; yearly births 3, burials 3. *Atkyns.* The inhabitants are now increaſed to 354.

NEWLAND.

THIS pariſh is ſituated within the perambulation of the foreſt of Dean, and is bounded on the weſt by the river Wye. It is the largeſt pariſh in the county, with great variety of ſoil and of produce. It abounds with iron ore and ochre, and with a kind of coal that burns freely, and

and makes a ſtronger fire than the Kingſwood coal, but is not ſo laſting.

Newland was originally taken out of the foreſt, and granted away by the crown. When it became private property, it was then firſt aſſarted and cultivated, which gave occaſion to the name of *Nova Terra*, as it is called in antient records, and to that by which it is at preſent known. But this event had not taken place when *Domeſday* was compiled, as there is no mention of Newland in that record, but the name occurs in others as early as the reign of king Henry the Third.

The face of this country is full of little hills and vallies, intermixt with ſwells and ſlopes that form an infinite and pleaſing variety. The village of Newland lies on the ſide of one of thoſe vallies, not to be ſeen at any great diſtance, and conſequently has not the advantage of extenſive proſpect, but is nevertheleſs one of the handſomeſt villages in the county. It is the reſidence of ſeveral perſons of conſiderable fortune, whoſe houſes are ſuitable to their condition in life. They are not arranged in a ſtraight line, but form part of a ſquare, with the church and church-yard, which are both very large and handſome, ſituated where the area would be, if the ſquare were compleat. This may ſerve to give a general notion of the place, but the deſcription is not exact and perfect, as it may be ſuppoſed that many houſes lie out of this order, in a country village, where the figure of the whole could not to be attended to when the houſes were erected.

Highmeadow, the ſeat of lord viſcount Gage, lies about half a mile eaſtward from the village. The houſe is large and handſome, built in the form of the letter H, and from its elevated ſituation, commands a bird's-eye view of the village, and of the beautiful lawns and groves on the other ſide of the valley, at a very agreeable diſtance. Were his lordſhip poſſeſſed of the whole landſcape, he could not wiſh to diſplace a ſingle object; yet the proſpect might be improved by the addition of water, which it wants to make it compleat. Part of this ſeat is ſaid to ſtand in this pariſh, and part in that of Staunton.

There are ſeveral good houſes and pleaſant gardens in the village of Newland, of which the ſeat of Edmund Probyn, eſq; is the principal. He has a large eſtate in this pariſh, and in ſeveral other parts of the county.

The reverend Mr. Ball, the preſent incumbent of Newland, is poſſeſſed of a curioſity that deſerves to be mentioned. It is the cradle of king Henry V. who was born at Monmouth. The whole is made of oak, and the part where the infant lay is an oblong cheſt, open at top, with an iron ring at the head, and another at the feet, by which it hangs upon hooks fixt in two upright pieces, ſtrongly morticed in a frame which lies upon the floor. Thus ſuſpended, the cradle is eaſily put in motion. Each of the upright pieces is ornamented at top with the figure of a dove, gilt, and tolerably executed.

There is an iron-furnace in this pariſh, and two copper-works at a place called Red-Brook, but they have the copper ore from Cornwall, and other parts.

Of the Manor and other Eſtates.

The records ſhew, that John de Kinerdſley died ſeized of Newland in the foreſt of Dean 39 H. 3. and was ſucceeded by his ſon Hugh, who was attainted of treaſon, and his lands ſeized into the king's hands. The manor of *Nova Terra* was found to be in the crown by an inquiſition 4 E. 1. but it was granted to Richard Harine and his heirs the following year.

Sir John ap Howel was afterwards ſeized of the manor, which he forfeited by rebellion againſt king Edward the Second, but it was reſtored to him 15 E. 3. William Baynham levied a fine of it 6 E. 6. after which it eſcheated to the king, and the manor is now veſted in the crown.

But there was a reputed manor, or ſome eſtate dignified with the title of a manor, in this pariſh, formerly belonging to the abbey of Flaxley, which was granted, with the manor of Ruredean, to ſir Anthony Kingſton 36 H. 8.

Of the other eſtates the records ſhew, that ſir John de Wyſham and Joan his wife levied two fines of lands in Newland and St. Briavel's 20 & 30 E. 3. Joan the widow of Robert Grinder was ſeized of the patronage of a chantry in the church of Newland, and of one meſſuage, three tofts, and 200 acres of land 24 H. 6. James Bell died ſeized of two meſſuages, and three parcels of meadow, a piece of paſture called Tyllo's Hill, and twenty-four acres of arable land in Hymeade, in Newland, and of a cloſe in Aſhrydge, in the pariſh of Staunton, 43 Eliz. *Eſch.*

Wye-Seal is an eſtate in Newland, belonging to the dean and chapter of Hereford, and is exempt from tithes.

TITHINGS and *HAMLETS.*

1. *Clowerwall*, antiently called *Wellington*, and afterwards *Clowerwall*, and *Clearwell*, from a fine tranſparent ſpring of water riſing in this tithing. It antiently belonged to the Joyces, from whom it went to the family of the Grinders or Grendours. Robert Grendour died ſeized of Clowerwall 22 H. 6. and was ſucceeded by his ſon John. Alice Grendour, daughter and heireſs of John, was married to William Walwyn of Herefordſhire.

William Walwyn, ſon of William and Alice, married Elizabeth, daughter of William Lanks, by whom he had an only daughter and heireſs Alice, who, by her marriage, carried this eſtate to Thomas ap Enion, alias Baynham, who was high ſheriff of Glouceſterſhire 18 E. 4. But he had a former wife, Margaret, daughter of Richard Hoddy, a judge in one of his majeſty's courts.

Sir Chriſtopher Baynham, of Clowerwall, ſon of Thomas by the ſaid Alice, married Joan, daughter of Thomas Morgan of Monmouthſhire, and

and was high ſheriff of Glouceſterſhire 3 & 9 H. 8. He was ſucceeded by his ſon ſir George Baynham, who married to his firſt wife a daughter of ſir William Kingſton, whom he ſurvived; ſecondly, Cicely, daughter of ſir John Gage. He was high ſheriff of Glouceſterſhire 36 H. 8. and dying 38 H. 8. his ſon Chriſtopher had livery of this manor 3 E. 6. Thomas Baynham, ſon of Chriſtopher, married Mary, daughter of ſir William Wintour, of Lidney. He was high ſheriff of Glouceſterſhire 25 Eliz. and again in the laſt year of the ſame reign.

Sir William Throckmorton of Tortworth, baronet, married Cicely, daughter and coheireſs of Thomas Baynham, with whom he had Clowerwall.

This eſtate was afterwards veſted in Francis Wyndham, eſq; deſcended from the antient family of that name in Somerſetſhire, and paſſed from him to Thomas Wyndham, eſq; whoſe ſon, Charles Wyndham, eſq; is the preſent proprietor of Clowerwall, where he has a very handſome houſe, built by his father in the Gothic ſtile, and a park, with a large eſtate, and fine plantations. In the year 1762, he married Eleanor, the ſecond daughter of James Rooke, of Bickſwear, eſq; by Jane his wife, daughter of Tracy Catchmay, eſq; of the ſame place, and by her hath iſſue one ſon. His arms are, *Azure, a chevron between three lions heads crazed Or.*

2. *Colford.* This is a tithing, and a ſmall market town, on the turnpike-road from Glouceſter to Monmouth, about four miles diſtant eaſtward from the latter. King James the Firſt granted it a market to be held on Friday, and two fairs annually, one on the 9th, now held on the 20th of June, for wool; the other on the 24th of November, for cheeſe, &c. The market houſe was built by contribution, in the year 1679, towards which king Charles the Second gave forty pounds.

King Offa's dyke paſſes thro', and I am inclined to think gave name to this tithing, which from *Claudh Offa*, by a ſtrange and unaccountable corruption, is now pronounced *Covert*, but written as at the beginning of this account.

Corbet, in his *Military Government*, relates, that before the ſiege of Glouceſter happened, the forces raiſed by the earl of Worceſter, and his ſon, lord Herbert, attacked a regiment of the parliament's party under colonel Berrowe, at this place, which had been made a kind of looſe garriſon for the defence of the foreſt. 'Here the Welch fell on,' ſays he, 'but their officers, with ſtrange fury, 'drove our party before them, which was borne 'down by their multitudes, yet with a greater loſs 'on their part. Divers officers were ſlain, and 'with the reſt their commander in chief, ſir 'Richard Lawdy, major-general of South Wales. 'Of ours few were ſlain, but lieutenant-colonel 'Winter, and ſome inferior officers, with about 'forty private ſoldiers taken priſoners.' p. 26.

There is a chapel of eaſe in this town, of which the biſhop of Glouceſter is patron. The chapel was deſtroy'd in the civil wars, and remained in ruins 'till it was repaired about the year 1704, and queen Anne gave 300 *l.* out of the ſale of wood in the foreſt of Dean, to endow it, which ſum hath purchaſed a houſe and lands in Whitchurch and Ganerew, in Herefordſhire, now let at 18 *l.* a year. And the truſtees of the queen's bounty have given a further ſum of 200 *l.* to augment the curacy, which is not yet laid out on land. There is no houſe for the curate.

3. *Bream.* This tithing lies four miles diſtant from the church. The name ſignifies *ſharp, ſevere,* (from bpemma, Sax. to *rage* or *fume,*) and it is uſed in that ſenſe by Spencer in the following line,

Comes the breme *winter with chamfred brows.*

And perhaps the name was given to this place from its expoſed ſituation. Here is a chapel of eaſe.

Bream's-Lodge, is a large handſome houſe, late belonging to Mr. Barrow Lawrence, deceaſed. It ſtands part in this tithing, and part in that of Ailberton. He died about the year 1773, ſeized of a good eſtate here, and in the adjoining pariſh of St. Briavel's, as well as in Ailberton, with an extenſive warren in the laſt mentioned place, called Prior's Meen, (becauſe it formerly belonged to the priory of Lanthony) whence there is a very extenſive view of the vale of Glouceſterſhire, from Frampton downwards, to the extremity of the county at Kingroad; and a diſtant proſpect of the counties of Worceſter, Wilts, Somerſet, Monmouth, Brecon, Radnor, and Hereford. He was ſon of Anthony Lawrence, gent. of the Shurdington family, by Mary his wife, the only daughter of James Barrow, gent. (whoſe family long reſided at the ſame place) by Beata his wife, only ſiſter and heireſs of Mr. ſerjeant Powlet, once recorder of the city of Briſtol, and one of the juſtices of South Wales, who reſided at Bream's-Lodge many years, 'till the time of his death in 1703.

Paſtors-Hill in this tithing, is the houſe and eſtate of Mr. William Gough the younger, great grandſon of the late William Gough of Willſbury, by Mary his laſt wife; which eſtate was given to him by James Gough, gent. younger ſon of Warren Gough of Willſbury. Which James Gough, by his laſt will, dated Sep. 7, 1676, deviſed to truſtees an eſtate at Stroate, in the pariſh of Tiddenham, to pay five ſhillings to an able divine, for every Sunday that he ſhall read prayers and preach once in the day in the chapel of Bream. On every default, the five ſhillings to be laid out in repairing the chapel, or given to the poor. And if the ſaid eſtate ſhould exceed 13 *l.* yearly, the overplus to be given to the poor of this tithing. Mr. ſerjeant Powlet added 2 *s.* 6 *d.* weekly to this donation, and ſubjected his lands in Ailberton to the payment thereof.

Mary the widow of the above James Gough, by her will, gave 50 *l.* the intereſt to be paid for ever to a poor woman, to teach the children of this tithing to read.

4. *Le Baily*, formerly the eftate of John Tiptot, or Tiptoft, earl of Worcefter, and afterwards of the Talbots, earls of Shrewfbury. There is nothing worthy notice in this tithing.

Of the Church, &c.

The church is a vicarage, in the Foreft deanery, worth about 90*l.* a year. The bifhop of Landaff is patron, and Mr. Peregrine Ball is the prefent incumbent. The tithes of all the affart lands in the foreft were granted to the church of Newland 34 E. 1. and the great tithes of this church were appropriated to the bifhoprick of Landaff in the year 1399. The glebe and great tithes of this parifh are worth about 200*l.* a year.

The church is dedicated to All Saints. It is very large for a country village, with a gallery, and a handfome tower at the weft end, adorned with pinnacles, and furnifh'd with a clock. The church-yard is alfo large, with handfome walks acrofs, gravelled and kept in good order.

There was a chantry erected in this church, and endowed with 12*l.* a year by Robert Grendour and Joan his wife 24 H. 6. There were alfo feveral other chantries, one dedicated to St. Mary, whereof George Wadham was the laft incumbent, and enjoy'd a penfion of 4*l.* a year in 1553. The lands belonging to it were granted to fir Oliver Cromwell 5 Jac. and to Francis Philips and Richard Moor 6 Jac. Another was called king Edward's chantry, whereof Edward Brior was the laft incumbent, and received a penfion of 4*l.* a year. There was alfo Newland chantry, fome of the lands belonging to which were granted to Lewis Williams 1 E. 6. and others were granted the fame year to Robert Lea. Edward Sowice was a chantry prieft here, and enjoy'd a penfion, at the fame time with the above, of 4*l.* a year. *Willis.*

Firft fruits £. 15	7	0	Proc. & Syn. £. 0	9	8
Tenths — 1	10	8	Pentecoftals 0	1	4

Monuments and Infcriptions.

In the chancel, againft the wall,

Vnder this Stone interr'd doth lie
The mirrour of true Charitie :
To God his Friends & Country dear
The poor's Supporter far & near.
His days hee Spent in peace & Quiet
He never gaue himfelfe to riot
A Vertue Strange in thofe his days
When it was fcorn'd, & Vice had praife
Hee lived long, and did Surviue
Fully the Years of Seventy Five
And at the laft expir'd his date
April the 8th (16) 68.
Chriftopher Bond Gent.

His arms, as in Hewelsfield.

In the window of the north aile is an antient figure in ftone, lying along, but it is not known for whom it was defigned.

Againft the wall,

This Monument is Erected by IOHN HALL, Efq; in Memory of his deceafed & moft deare Uncle HENRY HALL, Gent. fecond fon of WILLIAM HALL of Highmeadow of the Parifh of Newland in the County of Gloucefter, Efq; onely Brother of BENEDICT HALL, Efq; He departed this life Ianuary 1644. was buried at Rolfton parifh Church in the County of Hereford who in teftimony of his great Love & Charitie left Fortie Pounds a year as a Rent charge in perpetuitie, to be paid half yearely & equally to be diftributed between the poore of the refpectiue parifhes of Newland & Staunton in the County of Gloucefter Charged by IOHN HALL Efq; Second Son of BENEDICT HALL Efq; late deceafed, Godfon & Sole Executor unto his Uncle HENRY HALL, upon certain Lands tenements & Hereditaments Called, & Known by the name of Trepenkennet in the parifh of St. Wenard's in the County of Hereford, now duely paid & Soe to continue to the Ufes of the faid Parifhes for ever.——Arms, *On a chevron between three talbots heads erazed an eftoile of fix points*, for Hall.

On the table of a very handfome marble monument,

To the Pious Memorie of
BENEDICT HALL
late of *Highmeado* in the Countie of
Gloucefter Efq; who lyeth here inter'd.
He departed this life April 16th 1668
Aged 78 Years.
Alfo to the like Memorie of ANNE HALL
Wife of the faid BENEDICT and Daughter
of Sr EDWARD WINTER of Lidnie Kt. and
the Lady ANNE SOMERSET third Daughter
of EDWARD Earl of *Worcefter*, Wife to the faid
BENEDICT, who died at *Cambray* in *Artois*.
She dyed the 10th of *March* 1675
This Monument is Erected by HENRY
BENEDICT HALL Eldeft Sonn of the faid
BENEDICT and the faid ANNE Ao. Do.
The Afsd H. Bencts lies here } MDCLXXXIIII { Alfo his Eldeft Son Benct
Non Mors fejungat quos Chriftus junxit Amore.
Here Alfo is Interred the Body of the Right
Honble the *Lady Vifcountefs* GAGE who died the
25 Day of *July* 1749. She was the only Daughter of
BENEDICT HALL of *High Meadow Efq*; And Wife
of THOMAS *Lord Vifcount* GAGE, who died
the 21 Day of *December* 1754. And lies buried
with his Anceftors at *Firle* in *Suffex*.

At bottom, 1ft, Hall as before; impaling 2d, *A fefs ermine, in chief a crefcent.*

On another monument,

In Memory of George Bond Efqr; of Redbrook and Mary his Wife, whofe Characters are an Honour to yr families. He departed this Life Janry the 11th 1731 Aged 89, She died June ye 23d 1715 Aged 60.—— At the top of this monument are the family arms, *Argent, on a chevron fable between three demy lions gules as many hunting horns Or, ftringed of the third.* — There are memorials for others of the fame name and family.

Here is alfo a memorial for George Morgan of Court-Bleathing, in the county of Monmouth, efq; who died in 1770, aged 72 years; and this diftich :

Say more I need not, and fay lefs who can;
Here lies the gen'rous, humane, honeft man.

In a chapel on the fouth fide of the chancel, which was founded by fir John Joyce of Clowerwall, and which belongs to the proprietor of that eftate, there is a very large monument, with the following infcription :

In this Chancel lye many of the Families of BAYNHAM, THROGMORTON, &c. And of WYNDHAM, near this Monument.

Francis Wyndham died Sepr 23d 1716 aged 46
and his Wife Mercy Wyndham died Mar 26 1719 aged 44
and their Son John Wyndham died Feb 12th 1724 aged 24
Jane Wyndham died Sept. 27th 1723 aged 35
Jane Wyndham died July 31st 1719 aged 6 Months
Thos Wyndham junr died May 29th 1751 Aged 31
Thos Wyndham fenr died Decr 4th 1752 aged 66
And his Wife Anne Wyndham died June 1st 1753 aged 52

Eleanor, Wife of Charles Wyndham died September 25th 1768 Aged 27 Years.

There is a chantry chapel on the fouth fide of the church, founded by fir John Joyce, and at the entrance to it a raifed tomb, ornamented with fcutcheons round it, and on the top are the figures of fir John in armour, and his lady by his fide.

 Within

Within the chapel, on a marble table, is this inſcription:

In Memory of William Probyn of Newland Gent. and Elizabeth his Wife. He was Son & heir of Edmund Probyn of Newland Gent. by Mary his Wife ye Daught^r^ of Thos Symonds of Clewerwall Gen^t^. And Grand Son & heir of Iohn Probyn of Newland Gen^t^. by Mary his Wife one of ye Daughters of Chriſt^pr^ Hall of High Meadow Eſq^r^. He died ye 11th day of Feb^ry^ 1702 Aged 86 and lyes buried in ye Middle Iſle of this Church. She was the Eldeſt Daughter of Edmund Bond of Walford in ye County of Hereford Gen^t^ had Iſſue by her 2^d^ Huſband Five Daughters Mary Sarah Hannah Frances & Blanch and two Sons Edmund Probyn now of ye Middle Temple London Barriſter att Law and William Probyn A Captain of one of his Majeſtyes Ships of War. She Died ye 19th day of Dec^ber^ 1714 Aged 70 And lyes buried in this Chancel.

Here is a noble marble monument, with a buſt well executed, and beneath, this inſcription:

Sacred to the Memory of
Sr EDMUND PROBYN, Kn^t^.
Lord chief Baron of his Majeſty's court of Exchequer
who died the 17th Day of May 1742.
DAME ELIZABETH PROBYN
The Widow and Relict of Sr EDMUND PROBYN the
Daughter of Sr JOHN BLENCOWE Kn^t^ one of the
Juſtices of the Court of Common Pleas at Weſtminſter
Died the 22^d^ Day of October 1749
And at her particular Deſire was buried in this Chancel
Near the Remains of her deceaſed Huſband.

Arms at top, *Ermine, on a feſs gules a lion paſſant Or.*

And cloſe by the laſt,

In Memory of WILLIAM HOPKINS of *London* Merchant, who died the 12 Day of April 1763, Aged 59. And of SARAH his Wife, Daughter of WALTER WILLIAMS of *Dingeſtowe* in the County of Monmouth, Eſq; who died the 14 Day of Feb. 1749, Aged 48.——— Arms, *Quarterly,* 1ſt *and* 4th, *Sable, on a chevron between three piſtols Or as many roſes gules.* 2d *and* 3d, *Ermine, on a feſs gules a lion paſſant argent, in the dexter canton of the ſecond a mullet pierced Or.*

There is a raiſed tomb in the church-yard, and upon it the figure of a man in full proportion, with a horn hanging at his right ſide, and a falchion at his left, his feet reſting on his faithful dog. Round the ſides of the tomb is this inſcription in old characters:

Here : lythe : Ion : Wyrall : Forſter : of : Fee : the : Whych : dyſeſyd : on : the : VIII : day : of : September : in : y^e^ : Yeare : of : oure : Lorde : M. CCCC. LVII. on : hys : Soule : God : have : Mercy : Amen :

Benefactions.

Mr. William Jones, a Hamborough merchant, founded a large hoſpital in this pariſh, conſiſting of ſixteen tenements for as many women and children, and endowed it with a rent-charge on lands in the county of Kent, to the amount of 2*s.* a week to each of the poor people, and a new gown yearly. He alſo founded a lectureſhip here, and endowed it with a rent-charge on lands in the ſaid county, of one hundred marks yearly, paid by the company of haberdaſhers in London, who chooſe the lecturer out of three clergymen returned to them by the pariſhioners. The lecturer has a houſe, orchard, and a cloſe of ground at Newland, worth about 20*l.* a year. He is chaplain to the hoſpital. Mr. James Birt is the preſent lecturer.

In the year 1633, Mr. Edward Bell, of Writtle in Eſſex, founded a grammar-ſchool here, and gave a ſchool-room, with a houſe and garden for the maſter, with a ſalary of 10*l.* a year. He alſo gave eight almſ-houſes and gardens for eight poor people of this pariſh, and 20*s.* a year to each, and left 40*s.* a year to repair the buildings, with the payment of which ſums he charged his eſtate; in lieu whereof his ſon Edward Bell, gent. granted the ſaid houſes and gardens, and other lands in this pariſh, then worth 20*l.* a year. And Mr. John Whitſton, alderman of Briſtol, afterwards, by his will, left a further ſum of 10*l.* a year to the maſter, and 12*l.* a year to the poor of Clowerwall, payable out of houſes in Briſtol.

George Bond of Wyeſeal, gent. and Chriſtopher Bond of Redbrook, gent. gave a meadow by the ſide of the Wye, then let at 5*l.* a year, 20*s.* of which to keep the church clean and repair the clock; the reſt to the eight almſ-people. And Mr. Bromwich has given 24*s.* yearly to the ſame poor people. William Hopkins of London, gent. charged his eſtate at Stow Grange with 40*s.* a year for ever to the poor.

For Mr. Hall's benefaction, ſee the inſcription.

With monies ariſing out of the above donations, and ſome others at preſent not well known, an eſtate has been purchaſed at Awre in this county, worth 30*l.* a year, for the uſe of the poor of this pariſh.

Newland.

			£.	s.	d.
Taxes.	The Royal Aid in	1692,	133	12	0
	Poll-tax —	1694, —	56	17	0
	Land-tax —	1694, —	216	12	0
	The ſame, at 3*s.*	1770, —	127	14	0

Clowerwall.

			£.	s.	d.
Taxes.	The Royal Aid in	1692,	165	14	0
	Poll-tax —	1694, —	42	6	0
	Land-tax —	1694, —	198	16	0
	The ſame, at 3*s.*	1770, —	147	0	0

Colford.

			£.	s.	d.
Taxes.	The Royal Aid in	1692,	143	2	0
	Poll-tax ——	1694, —	52	10	0
	Land-tax ——	1694, —	190	16	0
	The ſame, at 3*s.*	1770, —	138	15	0

Bream.

			£.	s.	d.
Taxes.	The Royal Aid in	1692,	63	4	0
	Poll-tax ——	1694, —	23	13	0
	Land-tax —	1694, —	88	4	0
	The ſame, at 3*s.*	1770, —	63	0	0

Le Baily.

			£.	s.	d.
Taxes.	The Royal Aid in	1692,	43	0	0
	Poll-tax ——	1694, —	5	7	0
	Land-tax ——	1694, —	19	14	7
	The ſame, at 3*s.*	1770, —	12	15	0

At the beginning of this century, according to ſir Robert Atkyns, there were 480 houſes, and about 2200 inhabitants in this pariſh, whereof 150 were freeholders; yearly births 48, burials 47. But the people are pretty much increaſed ſince that time, ſo that the preſent number of ſouls is about 2997. At the raiſing of the militia in the year 1760, one man was taken out of every 29 upon the liſts throughout the county, and this pariſh then found fifteen men for its proportion.

NEWN

NEWNHAM.

THIS is a market town, in the hundred of Weſtbury, in the Foreſt diviſion, ſixteen miles diſtant north from Chepſtow, ten eaſt from Colford, five ſouth-eaſt from Mitchel-Dean, and ten ſouth-weſtward from Glouceſter. It lies fourteen miles from the mouth of the river Wye, and ſixteen from Kingroad, where the Briſtol Avon empties itſelf into the Severn.

It is pleaſantly ſituated on an eminence along the weſt ſide of the Severn, which is here ſomething leſs than a mile over at high water; and, by means of that river, has a conſtant communication with London by ſhips of about 160 tons burthen. Here is a very ſafe paſſage or ferry over the river for horſes and carriages, and a ford paſſable at low water, the reſort to which, before ferries were eſtabliſhed, was moſt probably the original occaſion of the building of the town.

At this place was the firſt fortification erected on the weſt ſide of the Severn againſt the Welch. And Strongbow earl of Chepſtow, after having made very conſiderable conqueſts in Ireland, being commanded by king Henry the Second to appear before him, obeyed the royal mandate, and met the king at this town; wherefore we may ſuppoſe it to have been a place of good ſecurity at that time. Indeed here was antiently a caſtle, as appears by ſeveral grants of lands in Newnham to the prior and brethren of St. Bartholomew's hoſpital at Glouceſter, wherein the lands are deſcribed as lying next the caſtle and caſtle-ditch, on the one part, and extending to Staure's-mill on the other.

This town had ſome ſhare in the military tranſactions in the reign of king Charles the Firſt. Corbet, who wrote of thoſe affairs, profeſſedly favoured the parliament's intereſt, and gives an account that the royaliſts garriſoned Newnham, where colonel Congreve was governor, who was taken and killed at Little Dean, as I have related under that head. And that immediately afterwards, colonel Maſſie, governor of Glouceſter, came to this place, where ſir John Winter's forces kept garriſon in the church, and had a pretty ſtrong fortification adjoining. Maſſie poſſeſſed himſelf of the town without oppoſition, and drew up two pieces of cannon within piſtol-ſhot of the works, under cover of a blind of faggots; and having made every thing ready for a ſtorm, the king's party deſired a parley, but Maſſie inſiſted on their immediate ſurrender. In the interim, the king's troops deſerting the works, fled into the church, and were ſo cloſely purſued that the aſſailants entered along with them. 'Then' ſays Corbet, 'they cry'd for quarter, when in the very 'point of victory, a diſaſter had like to befall us; 'a barrel of gunpowder was fired in the church, 'undoubtedly for the purpoſe, and was conceived 'to be done by one Tipper, a moſt virulent papiſt, 'and ſir John Winter's ſervant, deſpairing of his 'redemption, being a priſoner before, and having 'falſified his engagements. This powder-blaſt 'blew many out of the church, and ſorely ſinged 'a great number, but killed none. The ſoldiers 'enraged, fell upon them, and in the heat of 'blood ſlew near twenty, amongſt others this 'Tipper. All the reſt had quarter for their lives, '(ſave one Butler, an Iriſh rebel, who was knock'd 'down by a common ſoldier) and an hundred 'priſoners taken. The ſervice was performed 'without the loſs of a man on our ſide.' *Corbet's Military Government of Glouceſter.*

Mention is made of *High-ſtreet*, *Horman-lane*, and *Shop-row*, as the names of places in grants of land in the borough, 15 E. 3. But the town at preſent conſiſts chiefly of one ſtreet, and is diſtant about a mile from the foreſt of Dean, to which there is an immediate aſcent, and a ſpacious road from the river: The lands are perfectly dry and healthy, and the inhabitants are not ſubject to agues and other diſorders, from noxious vapours and exhalations, as thoſe commonly are who live in low countries, near great rivers. It was an antient borough, of which, in the time of king Edward the Firſt, the ſheriff returned only five in the county, Briſtol, Glouceſter, Berkeley, Durſley, and Newnham; and it was governed by a mayor and burgeſſes. The ſword of ſtate, given to them with their charter by king John, and ſtill preſerved to be ſhewn in teſtimony of their former greatneſs and better condition, is of ſteel, finely poliſhed, and ornamented with curious workmanſhip. Its whole length is ſix feet, and the length of the blade four feet four inches, on which is this inſcription: *Iohn Morſe being Maier, this Sord did repaier*, 1584. Having loſt their charter, they ſtill continue, by preſcriptive right, to elect a mayor annually on the Monday after St. Hillary; but neither the mayor nor aldermen, of whom there are ſix, have any authority over the town, which is governed by two beams, or conſtables.

There are two fairs in the year, on the 11th of June, and the 18th of October, for cattle, horſes, and ſheep; and the market is held on Friday, but it is not much uſed, for the town is daily well ſupply'd, at an eaſy rate, with variety of the beſt proviſions of every kind from the neighbouring villages in the foreſt.

Tho' the town is extremely well ſituated upon a fine river, where ſhips of burthen may ſafely come to anchor, yet its trade has been very inconſiderable, and almoſt wholly confined to the exportation of oak bark to Ireland, 'till a few years ago, when Mr. Robert Pyrke, merchant there, built a commodious quay on the ſide of the river, with cranes and ſtore-houſes, for the convenience of ſhipping and landing all ſorts of goods; and from that time the manufacturers at Birmingham and other places have brought great quantities in barges down the river to this town, where they are ſhipped in veſſels from one to two hundred tons burthen, and carried to London.

And

And of late, many ſhips of large burthen have been built here. This ſeems to be an auſpicious beginning, which time and induſtry may improve to the great advantage of the town, eſpecially as it lies in a country full of an excellent kind of coal, which is brought hither on horſes backs, from the pits two or three miles off in the foreſt of Dean, to be ſent to other places by water, and may prove an inexhauſtible fund of wealth. Beſides, the foreſt and all the country hereabout is famous for fine ſtyre, and other prime ſorts of cyder, which liquor finds a ready market here, and is become a very conſiderable article of commerce to London and Ireland.

Sir Edward Manſell, in the reign of king Charles the Firſt, erected here the firſt glaſs-houſe in England, which was work'd with ſtone-coal, the foundation of which ſtill remains. The glaſs manufacture has been diſcontinued a long time, but there is lately a very conſiderable verdigris-work ſet up in its room, and carried on with a laudable ſpirit, and the trade of ſhip-building is much incouraged; from all which circumſtances, Newnham bids fair to be a flouriſhing little town, and is already much improved in its buildings. Roynon Jones, eſq; and Mr. Robert Pyrke, merchant, reſide in two of the principal houſes, very pleaſantly ſituated upon the river. A turnpike-road from Glouceſter leads through the town, and ſo to Chepſtow and South Wales.

Of the Manor and other Eſtates.

The town of Newnham was diſtinct from the manor, but they are both called Newnham in the records, which is the reaſon that ſo many different families ſeem to have been poſſeſſed of the manor; whereas the fact is, that the records ſometimes ſpeak of the town, and ſometimes of the manor, in the ſame terms, tho' they were different and diſtinct eſtates. The manor was given by king Canute, in the year 1018, to the Benedictine abbey of Perſhore in Worceſterſhire; and the town was given, with twenty-four other vills, by Leofric earl of Mercia, to an abbey of black monks which he had founded in Coventry, in the year 1050. How long they continued in poſſeſſion of theſe eſtates, I cannot preciſely tell, but the manor was in lay hands in the reign of the Conqueror, as appears by the following extract:

'William the ſon of Baderon holds Neuneham. 'There is one hide, and three villeins, and three 'bordars paying 20 *ſol.* This land pays no tax. 'There is a wood two furlongs long, and one 'broad.' *Domeſday-book*, p. 74.

This manor was afterwards enjoy'd by the Bohuns earls of Hereford and Eſſex, together with the manors of Haresfield and Whitenhurſt, by the tenure of which they held the great office of Conſtable of England, by grand ſerjeanty, as of inheritance. And that office was afterwards of right in the line of the Staffords, and dukes of Buckingham, as heirs general to them, and deſcended to Edward duke of Buckingham, who was attainted of treaſon 13 H. 8. whereby it was forfeited to the crown; and ſince that time, both in reſpect of the amplitude of the authority, in war and in peace, and of the charge, it hath never been granted to any ſubject, but now of late *hac vice. Coke's Inſtitutes*, part 4.

Henry de Bohun, earl of Hereford, releaſed all his right in Newnham to king John, in the firſt year of his reign. The manor was granted to William earl of Saliſbury 2 H. 3. who died ſeized of it the 10th, as did Thomas Foliot 45 H. 3. It was in the crown 4 E. 1. and yielded 10*l.* a year, as appears by an inquiſition of that date. Walter de Stukeley was ſheriff of the county of Glouceſter 9 E. 1. in which year he returned into the king's exchequer, that the king was then lord of the borough of Newnham.

Roger de Mortimer held this manor 11 E. 1. and Walter le Marſhal was ſeized of it in the 21ſt year of that reign, when he was convicted and attainted of felony, whereby the manor eſcheated to the crown. It was afterwards granted to Thomas earl of Norfolk and the heirs of his body 4 E. 3. and was again granted to William Bohun and the heirs of his body 6 E. 3. in which grant it was mentioned to have lately belonged to Thomas earl of Norfolk. William de Bohun, earl of Northampton, and Elizabeth his wife, levied a fine of the manor of Newnham to the archbiſhop of Canterbury and others, to the uſe of themſelves in taille ſpecial, the remainder to the king and his heirs, 20 E. 3. Humphry de Bohun earl of Hereford and Eſſex, and Joan his wife, were ſeized of the manor of Newnham 46 E. 3.

Thomas duke of Glouceſter, the youngeſt ſon of king Edward the Third, marrying Eleanor, the daughter and coheireſs of Humphry de Bohun, became poſſeſſed of the earldoms of Hereford, Eſſex, and Northampton, and was conſtable of England. He, in right of Eleanor his wife, was ſeized of the manor of Newnham, of Calcot-caſtle and Newton 21 R. 2.

Upon the diſſolution of the abbey of Flaxley, an eſtate called the manor of Newnham, late belonging to that abbey, was granted to ſir Anthony Kingſton 36 H. 8.

The manor of Newnham was afterwards granted to Henry lord Stafford and Urſula his wife 2 Mar. Edward lord Stafford, ſon of Henry, died ſeized thereof 2 Jac. and left Edward lord Stafford his ſon and heir, thirty years old at his father's death. This laſt Edward had a ſon of his own name, who died before him, and left one ſon Henry, and a daughter Mary. Henry died unmarried in 1637, whereby his ſiſter Mary became ſole heireſs. She was married to ſir William Howard, younger ſon to Thomas earl of Arundel and Surrey, who, in her right, was ſeized of the manor of Newnham. He aſſumed the name of Stafford, on account of his wife's being heir to ſo great a family, and was created viſcount Stafford by king Charles the

the Firft, but was attainted upon account of the popifh plot, and beheaded in 1678. Henry, their fon, was created earl of Stafford 4 Jac. and fucceeded to this manor. The earl of Effingham is the prefent lord of the manor of Newnham, and holds a court leet for the manor and borough once a year. His lordfhip's arms are, Quarterly, 1. *Gules, in the middle of a bend between fix crofs croflets fitchy argent, a fhield Or, therein a demi lion rampant (pierced through the mouth with an arrow) within a double treffure counterflory gules,* being an augmentation for the victory at Flodden, for Howard. 2. *Gules, three lions paffant paleways Or, a label in chief of three points argent,* for Brotherton. 3. *Checky Or and azure,* for Warren, earl of Surry. 4. *Gules, a lion rampant argent, armed and langued azure,* for Moubray, duke of Norfolk.

The records fhew, that William Bleith and Joan his wife were feized of one meffuage and fix acres of land in Newnham 34 E. 1. William Marfhal levied a fine of a fifhery in Newnham and Rudle 16 H. 7. and Jeffry Griffith and Joan his wife levied a fine of lands in Newnham 21 H. 7.

HAMLETS. 1. *Ruddle.* Ralph Bluet, foon after the conqueft, gave this manor of Rodele, and a fifhery, to the abbey of Gloucefter, which king William the Second confirmed in the year 1096, at the petition of abbat Serlo, and fome of his nobles. And king Henry the Firft gave and confirmed the manor of Rudele to the abbey, to find lights to burn continually before the high altar of St. Peter's, for the foul of duke Robert Curthoife, his brother. He alfo granted and confirmed to them a fifhery in the Severn as far as their lands extended, and a grove or wood there, called Sudrug, to do as they pleafed with it; and to the facrift of the abbey, common for all his cattle through the whole foreft of Dean. And Henry the Third, by his charter dated at Newnham, confirmed this fifhery to the abbey, as fully as Henry the Firft gave it.

The manor continued in the poffeffion of the abbey of Gloucefter 'till the diffolution, and was then granted to William earl of Pembroke 7 E. 6. who fold it to fir Giles Pool 4 Mar. It is now the property of Roynon Jones, of Nafs in the parifh of Lidney, efq; who hath lately built a handfome houfe, very pleafantly fituated at Hayhill in this hamlet, and annually holds a court leet for this manor.

2. *Stairs,* antiently written *Staure,* of which *Domefday* makes the following mention: 'William 'the fon of Baderon holds Staure in Weftberie 'hundred. Ulfeg held it in the time of king 'Edward. It was worth 10*s.* now 5*s.* There is 'one hide which doth not pay tax.' p. 74. William de Staure died feized of one meffuage, forty-feven acres of arable, three acres of meadow, and 3*s.* rent at Staure, in the manor of Rodley, as of the fee of Henry de Lancafter, by the fervice of paying 3*s.* 4*d.* a year, and doing fuit at the court of the faid Henry, 2 E. 2. *Efch.* William Morwent, efq; had formerly a good houfe here, now fallen to decay.

Cockfhoot, Bleythe's Court, and *Hill-houfe,* are unworthily diftinguifh'd by fir Robert Atkyns as feparate hamlets.

Of the Church, &c.

The church is an impropriation belonging to the corporation of Gloucefter, as truftees of Bartholomew's hofpital, who let the impropriation to the curate on leafe for 8*l.* a year, and a falmon to the mayor, tho' it is of much greater value; and this and Little Dean are in the fame prefentation. Mr. John Webb is the prefent incumbent.

William de Bohun gave the advowfon and impropriation of this church to the prior and brethren of St. Bartholomew's hofpital 25 July, 17 E. 3.

The church is dedicated to St. Peter. The piece of ground where the church ftands was given to the mayor and burgeffes of Newnham, by Humphry de Bohun, earl of Hereford, paying 4*d.* yearly to the fee of Rome, to pray for his foul. The church-yard is bounded by the Severn; but the old church ftood at a place called Nab's End, and being undermined by the river, was obliged to be taken down.

Procurations £. 0 7 8 Pentecoftals £. 0 2 0
Synodals — 0 2 0

Monuments and Infcriptions.

On a fmall monument in the chancel,

P. M. Johannis Aram Generofi de Newnham et Mariæ Conjugis dilectiffimæ, marmor hoc erexit officii pignus et Amoris, Thomas Aram Generofus, filius natu maximus. Diem claufit ultimum Ille 9° Decembris 1673, Hæc 10° Octobris 1664.

Quid loquar: aut quorfum lachrymæ, nec carmina poffunt
Sat dare pro meritis. . . . .
What needs there many Words, all's faid in this:
A loving pair lodge here, expecting bliffe.

On a tomb in the church-yard, for a fea-faring perfon,

In Memory of Mr. Thomas Yerbury of ye City of Gloucefter, who departed y^s^ Life Nov^br^ 18th A. D. 1759, Aged 67.

From ev'ry bluftrous Storm of Life,
And that worft Storm, domeftick Strife,
Which fhipwrecks all our focial Joys,
And ev'ry worldly Blifs deftroys;
I luck'ly am arrived at laft,
And fafe in Port my Anchor's caft;
Where fhelter'd by the blifsful Shore,
Nought fhall difturb, or vex me more;
But Joys ferene, & calmeft Peace,
Which Chrift beftows, fhall never ceafe.

Benefaction.

Mr. James Jocham, late of the city of Briftol, deceafed, by his will, in 1764, gave 1000*l.* after the deceafe of his fon James, the intereft of which to be applied to the clothing of fifteen poor boys of the parifh of Newnham yearly for ever; and if any thing fhould remain, he directs it to be given to poor lying-in women of the fame parifh. James, the fon, is fince dead, and the charity is applied according to the donor's will.

Taxes.					
The Royal Aid in	1692,	£. 118	4	0
Poll-tax ——	1694,	— 79	12	0
Land-tax ——	1694,	— 171	13	4
The ſame, at 3*s.*	1770,	— 132	19	9

At the beginning of this century, according to ſir Robert Atkyns, there were 90 houſes, and about 400 inhabitants in this pariſh, whereof 40 were freeholders; yearly births 18, burials 18. But by the pariſh regiſter it appears, that in ten years, beginning with 1701, the average of annual baptiſms was 15.6, and that of the annual burials 12.1. And in a like ſeries, beginning with 1761, the average of annual baptiſms is 17.7, and of burials 10.5; which ſhews that the place continued nearly in the ſame ſtate as to population for the laſt ſixty years; but I am informed that the inhabitants now amount to the number of a thouſand at leaſt.

N I B L E Y.

THIS pariſh lies in the hundred of Berkeley, two miles diſtant north-weſtward from Wotton-underedge, three ſouth-weſtward from Durſley, and eighteen ſouth from Glouceſter.

It is ſometimes called North-Nibley, to diſtinguiſh it from Nibley, a hamlet in Weſterleigh. Some part of it ſhoots up eaſtward over the hills between Wotton-underedge and Durſley, to the diſtance of near three miles from the church; and between thoſe hills there is a long and narrow dingle, gradually opening towards the weſt, called Waterley-Bottom, from a rivulet running down it. The ſteep ſides of the hills in this part of the country are covered with beautiful hanging woods, in which the beech predominates; and the little combs between them, of which there are many, are richly cultivated in ſmall incloſures of paſture grounds, interſperſed with here and there a cottage or a little dairy farm. This variety of objects and of ſituation is very picturesque, and the different lights and ſhades they produce have a moſt agreeable effect.

The other part of the pariſh lies in the vale, and conſiſts of rich paſture ground, with very little arable. The lands are in dairy farms, and produce excellent cheeſe. The dairy buſineſs is unfavourable to population, yet the inhabitants are pretty numerous, and are chiefly employ'd in rug-making, and in the clothing buſineſs.

Leland ſpeaks of a camp here, but I apprehend that which he meant lies in the pariſh of Wotton-underedge.

But what more particularly diſtinguſhes this village in hiſtory, is the engagement that happened between William lord Berkeley and Thomas viſcount Liſle. The quarrel aroſe in the following manner: Thomas fourth lord Berkeley, left Elizabeth, an only daughter and heireſs, married to Richard Beauchamp, earl of Warwick; but by a ſpecial entail and fine, ſettled the caſtle and lordſhip of Berkeley, with its appurtenances, on his nephew James, the next heir male of his family. This ſettlement produced a law-ſuit between James fifth lord Berkeley, and Richard Beauchamp, earl of Warwick, who, in right of his wife, claimed the Berkeley eſtate, and violently ſeized Nibley and ſeveral other manors into his own hands. He and his poſterity kept poſſeſſion of this manor one hundred and ninety-two years, for which ſpace of time the law-ſuit was carried on with unprecedented violence. During the continuance of this ſuit, Thomas Talbot, viſcount Liſle, deſcended from the before mentioned Elizabeth, ſent a letter with a chalenge[p] to William ſixth lord Berkeley, wherein he deſired him to fix a time and place for deciding their title by the ſword. The lord Berkeley, by his anſwer[p], appointed the next morning for the time, and Nibley-green for the place

[p] Lord Liſle's challenge was as follows:

'*William*, called Lord *Berkeley*, I marveill ye come not forth with all your Carts of Gunnes, Bowes, with oder Ordinance, that ye ſet forward to come to my Mannor of *Wotton*, to bete it down upon my Head. I let you witt, ye ſhall not nede to come ſo nye, for I truſt to God to mete you nere home, with *Engliſh* Men of my own Nation, and Neighbours. Whereas ye by ſubtle Craft have blowin about in divers Places of *England*, That I ſhould entend to bring in *Welchmen* for to deſtroy and hurt my own Nation and Cuntry. I lete the wit, I never was ſo diſpoſed, nere never will be. And to the Proof hereof I requyre thee of Knighthood and of Manhood, to appoint a Day to mete me half way, there to try between God and our two Hands, all our Quarrel and Title of Right, for to eſchew the ſheddinge of Chriſtian Mannis Bloud, or elſe at the ſame Day bring the uttermoſt of thy Power, and I ſhall mete thee. An Anſwer of this by Writing, as ye will abide by, according to the Honor and Ordre of Knighthood.

'*Thomas Tabot* the Vicount *Liſle.*'

[q] To this challenge, Lord Berkeley returned the following anſwer:

'*Thomas Talbot*, otherwiſe called Vicount *Liſle*, not long contenued in that Name, but a new found thing brought out of ſtrang Countrys; I marveil greatly of thy ſtrange and lewd Wrytinge, made I ſuppoſe by thy falſe untrue Counſel, that thou haſt with thee, *Hugh Mull* and *Holt*; as for *Hugh Mull*, it is not unknown to all the worſhipful learned Men of this Realm how he is attaynt of falſenes, and raiſinge of the King's Records; and as for the falſe miſchevous *Holt*, what his Rull hath be to the Diſtruction of the King's lege Pepull in my Lordſhip of *Berkeley*, as well to the Hurt of their Bodies as the Loſs of their Goods, againſt God's Law, Conſcience and all Reaſon; it is openly known, ſo that every worſhipful Man ſhould refuſe to have them in his Fellowſhip. And alſo of his own free Will, undeſired of me, before worſhipful and ſufficient Witnes, was ſworne on a Maſſe-Booke, that he ſhould never be againſt me in no matter that I had adoe, and eſpecially in that untrue Title that ye clayme, which ye hold my Lyvelode with wrong. And where thou requireſt me of Knighthood that I ſhould appoint a Day, and mete thee in the myd way betwene my Mannor of *Wooton* and my Caſtle of *Berkeley*, there to try betwixt God and our two Hands all our Quarrels and Title of Right, for to eſchew the ſhedings of Chriſten Mens Blood, or els the ſame Day to bring the utermoſt of my Powere, and thou would mete mee. As for the determining betwixt our two Hands, of thy untrue Claime, and my Title and Right of my Land and true Inheritance, thou wotteſt right well there is no ſuch Determination of Land in this Relme uſed. And I aſcertayne thee, that my Lyvelode, as well my Mannor of *Wotton*, as my Caſtle of *Berkeley*, be entayled to me by Fyne of Record in the King's Courts, by the Adviſe of all the Judges of this Lond in that Days beinge. And if it were ſo, that this matter might be determined by thy Hands and myne, the King our Soveraigne Lord and his Laws not offended, thou ſhouldeſt not ſoe ſoone deſire, but I would as ſoon anſwere thee in every Point that belongeth to a Knight: For thou art, God I take to record, in a falſe Quarrel, and I in a true Deffence and Title. And where thou deſireſt and requireſt me of Knighthood and of Manhood to appoint a Day, and that I ſhould be there with all

'the

place of action, and both parties meeting on the 20th of March, 1470, 10 E. 4. with their respective followers, amounting in the whole to about 1000 men, a furious engagement ensued, wherein about 150 men were slain, in which number was lord Lisle himself, being shot in the mouth with an arrow by one James Hiatte, of the forest of Dean. Lord Berkeley, after his victory, hastened to Wotton, where the lady Lisle resided, who being then big with her first child, miscarried through the fright. His lordship rifled the house, and carried away some of the furniture, and many deeds and evidences which concerned the lord Lisle's own estate, and they remain to this day preserved in Berkeley castle. Government was at that time prevented from taking cognizance of this violent outrage, by the civil wars which raged in the kingdom during great part of the turbulent reign of Edward the Fourth.

Nicholas Smyth, esq; has a large estate here, and a very handsome seat, built about the year 1763, by his father, George Smyth, esq; upon the scite of an old mansion house, which had been long in his family. His arms are, *Sable, on a chevron engrailed between six crosses patty fitchy Or, three fleurs de lis argent, each charged on the top with a plate.*

John Smyth of Nibley, ancestor to the present proprietor, was very eminent for his great assiduity in collecting every kind of information respecting this county and its inhabitants. He wrote the genealogical history of the Berkeley family, in three folio manuscripts, which sir William Dugdale abridged, and published in his *Baronage of England.* In three other folio manuscripts, he has registered, with great exactness, the names of the lords of manors in the county, in the year 1608, the number of men in each parish able to bear arms, with their names, age, stature, professions, armour, and weapons. The sums each land-holder paid to subsidies granted in a certain year are set down in another manuscript. He likewise committed to writing a very particular account of the customs of the several manors in the hundred of Berkeley, and the pedigrees of their respective lords. These, and some other manuscripts which cost him forty years in compiling, are now in the possession of Nicholas Smyth, esq; the fifth from him in lineal descent.

Of the Manor and other Estates.

As this place is not mentioned by name in *Domesday-book*, it was probably included, at the time of the general survey, in the accounts of the manors of Wotton and Dursley; and part of the parish is now within the manor of Woodmancot, in the parish of Dursley.

King Henry the Second gave this manor to Robert Fitz-Harding, ancestor of the earls of Berkeley, in whose family it continued 'till they were violently dispossessed of it, as before related. Lord Lisle was lord of this manor in 1608. But the great law-suit concerning the Berkeley estate being determined 7 Jac. after 192 years continuance, the earl of Berkeley obtained possession, and the present earl of Berkeley is lord of the manor.

The prior of Lanthony's claim to free warren in Nebele was allowed in the proceedings on a writ of *Quo warranto* 15 E. 1. Roger Bavent was seized of lands in Nebele 47 E. 3. William lord Berkeley, earl marshal and earl of Nottingham, levied a fine of lands in Nibley 3 H. 7. John Stanshaw and Humphry his brother joined in levying a fine of lands in North Nibley 12 H. 7. Lands in Nibley, formerly belonging to the abbey of Kingswood, were granted to Drew Drewry and Edward Downing 16 Eliz. and Edward Downing and John Walker had a grant of lands belonging to the same abbey 21 Eliz. The knights hospitallers had formerly lands in Nibley, which were granted to Edward Sallus and William Blake, scrivener, 3 Jac.

HAMLETS, and places of distinct names in this parish, are, 1. *Church-end.* 2. *Fortoy.* 3. *Mill-end.* 4. *Whor-end* 5. *Smart's Green.* 6. *Waterleigh.* 7. *Ridemisse.* 8. *Swinny.* 9. *Wooderlin.* 10. *Great* and *Little Green.* 11. *South-end.*

Of the Church, &c.

The church is an impropriation, in the deanery of Dursley, worth about 50 *l.* a year. Christ Church college, Oxford, has the patronage and impropriation; Mr. Hayward is the present incumbent. The vicar receives 20 *l.* a year out of the impropriation, and the living has been augmented with the queen's bounty. This was formerly a chapel united to Wotton-underedge, and belonged to the abbey of Tewkesbury.

The church, dedicated to St. Martin, or as some say, to St. Andrew, has an aile on the south side, a low embattled tower at the west end, with five bells, and a small spire for a saint's bell, between the chancel and the body of the church. Here was formerly a chantry, dedicated to the virgin Mary.

Pentecostals - - - 10 *d.*

Benefactions.

Thomas Pearce of Gloucester, by will, Sep. 25, 1685, gave 30 *s. per ann.* out of a tenement in

' the Power I could make, and that thou would mete me half ' way. I will thou understand: I will not bring the tenth part ' that I can make, and I will appoint a short Day to ease thy ' malicious Heart, and thy false Counsel that is with thee: Fail ' not to morrow to be at *Nibly Green* at eight or nyne of the ' Clock, and I will not fail, with God's Might and Grace, to ' meet thee at the same Place, the which standeth in the Borders ' of the Lyvelods that thou keepest untruly, redy to answere thee ' in all things, that I trust to God it shall be shewed on thee and ' thine to great Shame and Disworship. And remember thy self ' and thy false Counsel have refused to abide the Rule of the grete ' Lords of this Lond, which by my Will should have determined ' this Matter, by thy Evidences and myne. And therefore I ' vouch God to record, and all the Company of Heaven, that this ' Fact and the shedding of Christen Mens Bloud, which shall be ' betwixt us two and our Fellowships, if any hap to be, doth ' grow of thy Quarrel and not of me; but in my Defence, and ' in escheweing of Reproache, and only through thy malicious ' and mischevous Purpose, and of thy false Counsel, and of thy ' own simple Discretion; and keep thy Day, and the Truth ' shall be shewed by the Mercy of God.

' *William* Lord of *Berkeley*.'

Nibley to be thus diſtributed; 12*s.* for a ſermon on Jan. 10, 3*s.* to the clerk for ringing the bell, the remainder to the poor. There have been ſeveral other donations to the poor in money, which are now loſt.

Taxes.					
The Royal Aid in	1692, £.	127	14	8
Poll-tax ——	1694, —	50	1	0
Land-tax ——	1694, —	197	9	4
The ſame, at 3*s.*	1770, —	154	15	9

At the beginning of this century, according to ſir Robert Atkyns, there were 200 houſes, and about 1000 inhabitants in this pariſh, whereof 34 were freeholders; yearly births 26, burials 24. The people are now increaſed to upwards of 1700.

NIMPSFIELD.

THIS pariſh lies in the hundred of Berkeley, four miles north-eaſt from Durſley, four ſouth-weſt from Minchin-Hampton, and about fourteen ſouth from Glouceſter.

The greater part of the pariſh is uneven ground, with a conſiderable proportion of woodland. The turnpike-road from Bath to Glouceſter leads down Nimpsfield-hill, which is very ſteep and woody. Colonel Maſſie, famous for his memorable defence of Glouceſter againſt king Charles the Firſt, being diſguſted at ſome of the parliament's proceedings, deſerted their party, and about the year 1659, formed a deſign of ſeizing on Glouceſter, in which however he was diſappointed, and forced to take refuge in a little houſe near Simonſhall. There he was ſeized by a party of horſe, who mounted him before one of the troopers, and carried him towards Glouceſter; but in going down the ſteep part of Nimpsfield-hill, Maſſie tumbled himſelf and the trooper from the horſe, and being a ſtout man, and his guards a little intoxicated, made his eſcape under favour of a dark tempeſtuous night.

Of the Manor and other Eſtates.

At the time of the general ſurvey, this was a *berewic* or member of the extenſive lordſhip of Berkeley, belonging to which there were then 'In Nimdesfelle three hides.' *Dom. Book*, p. 68.

This eſtate, like Berkeley, deſcended from Roger de Berkeley, who held it *temp.* W. 1. to his nephew Roger, whom king Henry the Second diſpoſſeſſed of his whole eſtate, for joining with his competitor Stephen. The caſtle and lordſhip of Berkeley, of which this was a member, were granted to Robert Fitz-Harding, who therefore aſſumed the name of Berkeley. He gave Nimpsfield to Nicholas his fourth ſon, whoſe poſterity took the name of Fitz-Nichols. Nicholas Berkeley, or Fitz-Nichols, ſon of Ralph, held tenements in Hull and Nyndesfeld of the king in *capite*, by the ſervice of half a knight's fee: At Nyndesfeld he had 100 acres of arable land, at 2*d. per* acre; 3 acres of paſture, at 1*s. per* acre; and a wood worth 2*s. per ann.* as appears by the eſcheator's inquiſition after his death. His claim to free warren was allowed in a writ of *Quo warranto* 15 E. 1. and he died ſeized of the above particulars 6 E. 2. leaving John, his ſon and heir, twenty-two years old. John Fitz-Nichols, ſon of Nicholas, died ſeized of this manor 15 E. 2. and John his ſon died ſeized of Nimdesfield, and of the advowſon of the chantry of Kinley 29 E. 3. Sir Thomas Fitz-Nichols, ſon of the laſt John, was lord of this manor at the time of his death, 7 R. 2. Sir Thomas Fitz-Nichols, ſon of ſir Thomas, died ſeized of the manor of Nimpsfield, and of the advowſon of the chantry at Kinley 6 H. 5. leaving two daughters coheireſſes; Catherine, married to Robert Pointz, eſq; and Elianor, married to John Browning, eſq. The ſame John Browning, ſon of John, was ſeized of a moiety of the manor of Nimpsfield, and of the advowſon of the chantry at Kinley 8 H. 5. which he ſoon after conveyed to Robert Pointz, eſq.

Sir Edmond Tame of Fairford purchaſed this manor, and dying 26 H. 8. was ſucceeded by Edmond his ſon and heir, who died without iſſue 36 H. 8. leaving three [r] ſiſters coheireſſes. Margaret, the eldeſt, was married to Humphry Stafford; Alice to Thomas Verney; and Iſabel, the youngeſt, was the wife of Lewis Watkin, who all had livery 37 H. 8.

In the partition of the eſtates between the ſiſters, this monor was ſettled on ſir Thomas Verney, 1 E. 6. Richard Verney, ſon of ſir Thomas, had livery 1 Eliz. as had George Verney, ſon of Richard, in the 14th, and died in the 16th year of the ſame reign, leaving ſir Richard Verney his ſon and heir, who was lord of this manor in 1608.

The manor ſoon after paſſed to the Bridgmans, and John Bridgman, of Prinknaſh, eſq; was lord of it at the beginning of this century. Lord Ducie is the preſent lord of the manor.

HAMLETS. 1. *Kynley.* Here was an antient priory, dedicated to the bleſſed Virgin, and incorporated by the name of warden and brethren, to which the manor of Kynley belonged. This manor was ſeized by William the Firſt, and reſtored to the priory by William the Second, 1093. Here was alſo a chantry chapel, dedicated to St. Anthony, whoſe figure was painted at the eaſt end of the chapel, with a great boar by his ſide. And

[r] Sir Robert Atkyns, in ſome places, calls them daughters of Edmond Tame, in others, his ſiſters, and in one place his coheireſſes, without further explanation. That they were his ſiſters, not his daughters, will appear from what Leland ſays, who, after taking frequent occaſion to ſpeak handſomely of the family, obſerves, that 'Syr Edmunde Tame of Fairford up by 'Crekelade cam oute of the houſe of Tame of Stowel. Tame 'that is now at Fairford hath be maried a XII yere and hath no 'childe. Wherefore belikelihod Syr Humfre Stafford, Sun to 'old Staford of Northamptonſhire, is like to have the landes of 'Tame of Fairforde, for he maried his Siſter, and ſo the name 'of the Tames is like fore to decay.' *Leland's Itin.* V. 6. p. 16.

hither, it is ſaid, the Weſt Britons uſually came once a year to offer oblations for their ſins. In the year 1542, Edmond Tame preſented to this chantry James Ruthbone, or Ratterbone, who was the laſt incumbent, and had a penſion of 6*l*. The priory, tho' converted to a dwelling houſe, is ſtill charged with the payment of Tenths.

After the diſſolution of religious foundations, the manor of Kynley was granted to William Stump, eſq; who died ſeized thereof 6 E. 6. and livery was granted to ſir James Stump, his ſon and heir, the following year.

The chantry lands of this place have been the ſubject of long contentious law-ſuits between ſir Thomas Throckmorton of Tortworth, and ſir Henry Winſton of Standiſh.

2. *Tinkley* is another hamlet, of which there is nothing remarkable.

Aldred, governor of Glouceſterſhire, gave three tenements in Nimpsfield to the abbey of Glouceſter. King William the Firſt gave lands in Nindesfelle to the ſame abbey, to be held as freely as in the reign of king Edward his kinſman, with the privilege of hearing and determining judicial cauſes.

John Gifford de Nymdesfeld died 7 E. 2. ſeized of lands and tenements in Nymdesfeld, which he held of the king in *capite* by the ſervice of two pounds of pepper. *Eſch. ſub anno.*

Of the Church, &c.

The church is a rectory, in the deanery of Stonehouſe, worth about 60*l*. a year. Lord chancellor is patron, and Mr. Hayward is the preſent incumbent. Frocefter is the mother church, where the inhabitants baptized and buried in 1185. The chapel of Nympsfield, and the advowſon of the church of Frocefter, were given to the abbey of Glouceſter, by William de Blois, biſhop of Worceſter, at the requeſt of John de Columna, cardinal of Rome, in the year 1225.

The church is dedicated to St. Margaret, and has a tower at the weſt end, adorned with pinnacles and battlements, in which are two bells.

	£.	s.	d.		£.	s.	d.
Firſt fruits	11	5	0½	Synodals	0	2	0
Tenths —	1	2	6¼	Pentecoſtals	0	0	7
Procurations	0	6	8				

Taxes.		£.	s.	d.
The Royal Aid in	1692,	67	8	0
Poll-tax — —	1694, —	10	0	0
Land-tax ——	1694, —	54	5	8
The ſame, at 3*s*.	1770, —	41	19	9

At the beginning of this century, there were 56 houſes in this pariſh, and about 250 inhabitants, whereof 18 were freeholders; yearly births 7, burials 6. *Atkyns*. But examining the pariſh regiſter, I find that in ten years, beginning with 1700, there were 112 baptiſms, and 57 burials; and in the ſame number of years, beginning with 1760, the baptiſms were 137, burials 107, and the inhabitants are now about 497.

NORTH HAMLETS.

THESE hamlets, conſiſting of very rich meadow and paſture lands, lie in the hundred of Dudſton and King's-barton, and join to the north ſide of the city of Glouceſter.

1. The *Vineyard*. It lies in the pariſh of St. Mary de Lode, on a fine elevation, upon the ſide of the Severn, beyond Over's bridge from Glouceſter, and commands a very agreeable proſpect of the city, the river, and the rich meadows adjoining. Induced by ſo fine a ſituation, abbat Staunton built a large houſe here, and moated it round, which was afterwards one of the country houſes belonging to the abbats of St. Peter's at Glouceſter. This excited an emulation in the prior of Lanthony, who ſoon after built a rival houſe, and called it *Newark*, on a little hill on the other ſide of the Severn. The Vineyard and park were given to the biſhoprick of Glouceſter, by its charter of foundation, and were confirmed 6 E. 6. And here the biſhops frequently reſided, 'till the houſe was demoliſhed in the great civil war.

2. *Walham-Mead*, *Portham-Mead*, and many other rich meadows lying between the Weſtgate-bridge at Glouceſter, and Over-bridge, make another diviſion of the North Hamlets. The river Severn dividing its waters, incloſes many of thoſe meadows, and forms the iſland which our Saxon anceſtors called Olanige, and we *Alney*, famous for the ſingle combat fought in the year 1016, between Edmund Ironſide, king of England, and Canute the Dane, to decide the fate of the kingdom. The ſtory is told in all our hiſtories of thoſe times, that having fought for ſome time without much advantage on either ſide, the combatants made peace, and agreed to divide the kingdom between them; but Edmund dying ſoon after, the Dane ſeized the whole. Some of theſe meadows are extraparochial, others are in the pariſhes of St. Mary de Lode and St. Catherine, and belong to various proprietors. The prior of Lanthony held the meadow of Preſtenham, containing 40 acres, (lying under the caſtle of Glouceſter) in exchange for Southmead. He likewiſe held the meadow of Walham without Glouceſter, and Madley's-land, 49 H. 3. The town of Glouceſter held Preſtenham and Southmead 54 H. 3. Portham-Mead belonged to the abbey of Glouceſter, and was granted, after the diſſolution of that houſe, to John Arnold, 33 H. 8.

3. The *Caſtle of Glouceſter*, and divers adjoining meſſuages and lands, are extraparochial, and lie cloſe to the city of Glouceſter. Theſe three hamlets are jointly rated to the public taxes.

Taxes.		£.	s.	d.
The Royal Aid in	1692,	35	4	0
Poll-tax ——	1694, —	4	18	0
Land-tax —	1694, —	54	16	0
The ſame, at 3*s*.	1770, —	42	3	0

4. *Longford*, lies in the pariſhes of St. Catherine and St. Mary de Lode. John Muſgros was ſeized of Longford 3 E. 1. as was Cecilia de Muſgros 29 E. 1. John Read had livery of the manor of Longford 9 Eliz. and Oliver St. John had livery thereof 18 Eliz.

Lands in Longford belonged to the Auguſtin nunnery of Dartford in Kent, founded by king Edward the Third, in 1373. After the diſſolution, theſe lands were granted to Thomas Babington 35 H. 8. Tithes in Longford belonged to the priory of St. Oſwald in Glouceſter, and were granted to the dean and chapter of Briſtol 34 H. 8. A meſſuage in Longford, formerly belonging to the ſame priory, was granted to John Fernham and John Doddington 17 Eliz. Other tithes in this hamlet, which belonged to the ſame houſe, were granted to John Fernham 22 Eliz. Tithes in Longford and Wotton, which belonged to the priory of Lanthony, were granted to ſir William Rider 7 Jac. 1. Longford is now divided among ſeveral freeholders.

Taxes.			
The Royal Aid in 1692,	£. 89	18	8
Poll-tax —— 1694, —	7	6	0
Land-tax —— 1694, —	126	1	4
The ſame, at 3 *s*. 1770, —	94	11	0

5. *Twigworth*, which lies in the pariſh of St. Catherine in Glouceſter. This hamlet was granted to Cuthbert de Rivers 18 Joh. Robert le Savage held one yard-land in Twigworth at the yearly rent of 5 *s*. and by the ſervice of carrying the king's writs to the ſheriff at his own charges 5 H. 3. Robert le Savage and Maud his wife were ſeized of one yard-land in Twigworth 35 & 44 H. 3. John de Akerly was ſeized of twenty acres of arable, and ſix acres of meadow in Twigworth 2 E. 2. This manor afterwards belonged to the Beauchamps, and by marriage came to the Grevils. Fulk Grevil had livery thereof 4 Eliz. It is now divided among ſeveral proprietors, but the greateſt part belongs to Samuel Hayward, eſq. The chapel of Twigworth was ſeized into the king's hands 4 E. 3. The tithes of Twigworth belonged to the priory of St. Oſwald, and were granted to the biſhoprick of Briſtol 34 H. 8. This hamlet has its proper officers.

Taxes.			
The Royal Aid in 1692,	£. 45	14	8
Poll-tax —— 1694, —	4	9	0
Land-tax —— 1694, —	51	12	0
The ſame, at 3 *s*. 1770, —	33	10	6

6. *Kingſholm*, in the pariſh of St. Mary de Lode. William de Alba Mara was ſeized of two plow-tillages in Kingſholm in the reign of king Henry the Third; which king granted Kingſholm, then valued at 8 *l*. a year, to Robert le Savage, to be held by the ſervice of door keeper of the king's pantry. From him it deſcended to his ſon Robert le Savage, who granted it to John d'Aubeny 32 E. 1. John d'Aubeny, ſon of John, was ſeized of it 6 E. 3. and dying 19 E. 3. Cicely his widow continued in poſſeſſion. John Boteler of the Park held the manor of Kingſholm 36 E. 3. John ſon and heir of Elizabeth Giffard held it 16 R. 2. John d'Aubeny and Cicely his wife and Elias de Godeley held it 18 R. 2. Nicholas Maddeſdon, eſq; was ſeized of the manor of Kingſholm, and of three acres in Twigworth and Walham, 14 H. 6. This manor came afterwards to the Beauchamps. Sir Richard Beauchamp died ſeized thereof, and left Elizabeth his daughter and heireſs married to ſir Robert Willoughby, lord Brooke. They had three grand-daughters their coheireſſes. Anne Willoughby, one of the ſiſters, died ſeized of a third part 25 H. 8. whereupon Francis Daughtry and Blanch his wife, another of the coheireſſes, had livery of a moiety of her third part the ſame year. Thomas Thorp died ſeized of part of this manor 17 H. 8. and Thomas his ſon had livery thereof 29 H. 8. Rowland Arnold, eſq; died ſeized of the manor of Kingſholm, and left Dorothy, his only daughter and heireſs, married to Thomas Luci, who, in her right, had livery of the manor 15 Eliz. The hamlet is now divided among ſeveral proprietors.

John Dingbull was ſeized of lands in Kingſholm and Twigworth 15 H. 6. Chriſtopher Throckmorton, and Richard Buckland and Elianor his wife levied a fine of lands in Kingſholm to William Henſhaw and Alice his wife 21 H. 7. Tithes of corn and hay in Kingſholm belonged to the priory of St. Oſwald, and were granted to John Fernham 22 Eliz. This diviſion has its proper officers.

Taxes.			
The Royal Aid in 1692,	£. 28	0	0
Poll-tax — — 1694, —	1	4	0
Land-tax —— 1694, -	31	6	0
The ſame, at 3 *s*. 1770, —	25	17	6

7. *Wotton*, joining to the north gate of the city of Glouceſter, lies in the pariſh of St. Mary de Lode. 'William Froiſſelew holds Uletone, in 'Dudeſtan hundred, of the king. Goderic held it. 'There are two hides. In demean are three plow-'tillages, and four bordars, and four *ſervi*. It 'was worth 30*s*. and is now worth 60*s*.' *D. B.* p. 74.

Henry Bleichdein was ſeized of lands in Wotton for the uſe of the friers preachers in Glouceſter 19 E. 1. The prior of St. Oſwald's in Glouceſter was ſeized of 11 *s*. 8*d*. yearly rent iſſuing out of Wotton 33 E. 1. Lands in Wotton, formerly belonging to St. Oſwald's priory, were granted to Thomas Gatwick and Anſelm Lamb 5 Mar. Other lands and tithes in Emſworth in Wotton, lately belonging to the ſame houſe, were granted to John Hercy and John Edwards 20 Eliz. The reverend Mr. Brereton has a good houſe here, which was formerly the property of Mr. Horton.

Taxes.			
The Royal Aid in 1692,	£. 66	6	8
Poll-tax —— 1694, —	3	16	0
Land-tax —— 1694, —	80	0	0
The ſame, at 3 *s*. 1770, —	60	0	0

NORTH-

NORTHLEACH.

THIS pariſh lies in the hundred of Bradley, in the Coteſwold country, ten miles diſtant northward from Cirenceſter, nine weſtward from Burford in Oxfordſhire, and twenty eaſt from Glouceſter.

The ſoil is generally light and ſtony, but produces pretty good crops of corn. Plenty of petrifications, particularly of the cockle and ſtar fiſh, are found here, and in ſome parts there is very good free-ſtone.

The little river *Lech*, which riſes in the neighbouring pariſh of Hamnet, runs through and gives name to this place, as well as to ſome others lying in its courſe. In *Domeſday* there are four manors of the name of *Lecce*, or *Lece*, which in ſubſequent records are thus diſtinguiſhed. The moſt ſoutherly of them dropped the name of *Lece*, and was called *Southrop*. This place, from its ſituation, was called *Northleach*; and the two remaining villages, which lie eaſtward, received the apellation of *Eaſtleach*.

There is a ſmall market town within this pariſh, of the ſame name. It lies about half a mile on the eaſt ſide of the Roman *Foſs-way*, in a little valley, and was formerly a thriving place, where ſeveral clothiers and merchants of the ſtaple reſided, about two centuries ago. King Henry the Third, in the year 1220, granted to the monks of St. Peter's at Glouceſter, two yearly fairs, on the feaſts of St. Peter and St. Paul; and the abbey had a confirmation of markets and fairs in Northleach 5 H. 3. Here was a public market for wool and cloth, and ſome of the buildings for ſtowing of thoſe commodities are now ſtanding, with a ſpacious area in the middle, and galleries round for a communication. One part of thoſe buildings is now the Lamb inn. The other parts, no longer employ'd according to the original intention, ſerve for barns and receptacles of lumber.

From the remains of thoſe buildings, and from ſeveral memorials in the church for clothiers, and for reſpectable perſons, denominated wool-men, and merchants of the ſtaple, who died about 300 years ago, it appears that this was formerly one of the principal clothing towns in the county. It was conveniently ſituated for buying the raw materials, in a country abounding with ſheep; but on the other hand, it is deſtitute of water ſufficient for driving the machinery uſed in that trade, and this natural diſadvantage is alone ſufficient to account for the loſs of the manufacture. The town ſoon felt that loſs, and ſeems to have been declining ever ſince. Many houſes are fallen down, many uninhabited, and the greater part of the reſt are going faſt to decay. And there are not quite ſeven hundred inhabitants in the whole pariſh.

There is a free grammar-ſchool in this town, nobly endowed by Hugh Weſtwood, eſq; who, by his will, gave the impropriation of Chedworth for its maintenance. By a decree in chancery 4 Jac. the patronage of the ſchool is veſted in Queen's college, Oxford. The maſter has 80*l.* a year, and a houſe, and the uſher 40*l.* a year. It has been commonly reported, that Mr. Weſtwood being reduced in the latter part of his life, requeſted of his truſtees to be appointed maſter of his own ſchool, but was refuſed. From a regard to truth, and to prevent the further propagation of this groundleſs ſtory, I aſſure the public, that this eſtabliſhment did not take place 'till three years after Mr. Weſtwood's death; and it is wonderful how ſuch a tale could be firſt ſet a going.

There are two conſtables for the town, and an officer called a bailiff, annually appointed at the lord's court, whoſe office is only to collect the tolls which belong to the town, and to let and receive the rents of the town eſtate. The market is held on Wedneſday, and here are three fairs in the year, *viz.* on the Wedneſday before the 23d of April, on the third Wedneſday in May, and on the Wedneſday before the 29th of September.

The turnpike-road from South Wales, through Glouceſter and Oxford to London, paſſes through this town, and is pretty much frequented.

There is a very large camp, with a double *agger*, called *Norbury*, in the hamlet of Eaſtington in this pariſh, which ſome have ſuppoſed to be Roman, from its lying near the *Foſs-way*, but I have never heard that any Roman coins have been found there. It incloſes an area of about eighty acres; but is not every where perfect, having been levelled and deſtroy'd in ſome parts by the huſbandman.

Of the Manor and other Eſtates.

Before the conqueſt, the church of St. Peter at Glouceſter held divers lands in this place, by the gift of Athelred, king of England.

In *Domeſday-book*, under the title *Terra Thome Archie'pi*, it is thus recorded:

'St. Peter of Glouuec' held Lecce in Bradelege 'hundred, and Eldred archbiſhop [of York] held 'it with the abbey. There were twenty-four 'hides. In demean are four plow-tillages, and 'thirty-three villeins, and ſixteen bordars, with 'thirty plow-tillages. There are four *ſervi*, and 'two mills of 7*s.* 4*d.* [rent.]

'Stanuuelle adjoins to this manor. There are 'two plow-tillages in demean, and five villeins, 'with five plow-tillages, and a mill of 40*d.* and 'four *ſervi*, and two *ancillæ*; and in Culberlege 'is one hide belonging to this manor.

'Of the land of this manor, Walter the ſon of 'Pontz holds one manor of twelve hides, which 'lay in the ſame manor in the time of king 'Edward. There are two plow-tillages in demean 'at Tormentone, and twenty-five villeins, with 'twelve plow-tillages, and four *ſervi*.

'The whole manor in the time of king Edward 'was worth 18*l.* Thomas archbiſhop [of York] 'put it to farm for twenty-ſeven hides. The hide 'at Culberlege is worth 20*s.*

'That

'That which Walter [the fon of Pontz] holds 'is worth 14*l*. Archbifhop Thomas claims it.' *Domefday-book*, p. 70.

To make the above extract more intelligible, the reader will obferve, that the monaftery of St. Peter at Gloucefter had run greatly to ruin, when Aldred, bifhop of Worcefter, afterwards archbifhop of York, taking it in hand, pulled down the old church, and built a new one at his own expence. And to reimburfe him, the abbat gave him poffeffion of the manors of Lecce, Otintune, Stanedis, and Bertune, which were appropriated to the archbifhoprick of York. This is what is meant in the record by Eldred holding this manor with the abbey. Archbifhop Thomas fucceeded Aldred, and claimed all thofe manors at the time of the general furvey, yet he afterwards reftored them to the abbey, expreffing contrition for having detained them fo long; however the fucceeding archbifhops renewed their claim, and the difpute between the fee of York and the abbey was not finally determined 'till the year 1157, as particularly fet forth at p. 133. From that time the manor of Northleach, and the rectory and the advowfon of the vicarage, continued in the abbey of Gloucefter 'till its diffolution, when the manor was granted to lay hands. Sir Ralph Dutton was lord of the manor of Northleach at the beginning of this century, and it continued in his family 'till it was given, about the year 1769, by the will of John Dutton, eldeft fon of James-Lenox Dutton, of Sherbourn, efq; to the reverend Mr. Rice, who is the prefent lord of the manor.

The abbey of Winchcombe granted a fifhery in the Severn, near Framilode, to the abbey of Gloucefter, in exchange for 4*l*. yearly rent iffuing out of the manor of Northleach 14 E. 2. The prior of Lanthony was feized of lands in Northleach 13 H. 4. John Purlewyn and Anne his wife, daughter and heir of John Doding, levied a fine of lands in Northleach to William Midwinter 2 R. 3. Richard Hercourt and Agnes his wife levied a fine of lands in this parifh to Simon Hercourt 23 H. 7. Lands in Northleach, and the inn called the Crown, formerly belonging to the priory of Lanthony, were granted to fir Baptift Hickes 7 Jac.

TITHING. *Eaftington* lies on the eaft fide of the town, agreeable to its name. It comprehends the greater part of the land in the parifh, maintains its own poor, and pays taxes independently of Northleach. Here was formerly a chapel dedicated to Mary Magdalen, now demolifhed; but the chapel yard belongs to the vicar.

John Balue was feized of the manor of Eaftenton 3 E. 1.

Pinfwell, in Cubberly, is the hide of land mentioned in *Domefday* as belonging to the manor of Lecce. It is now charged to the land-tax jointly with Eaftington, and has paid to the relief of the poor of this tithing.

Of the Church, &c.

The church is a vicarage, in the deanery of Cirencefter, worth about 70*l*. a year. The bifhop of Gloucefter is patron; the rev. Thomas Hodfon is the prefent incumbent, and mafter of the free-fchool. The rectory and advowfon were granted to the bifhoprick of Gloucefter 33 H. 8. and the grant was confirmed 6 E. 6.

The church lies in the tithing of Eaftington. It is a large, handfome building, dedicated to St. Peter, and confifts of the nave and two ailes, with a chapel on each fide of the chancel, and a ftrong well built tower, with fix bells, at the weft end. The porch at the fouth entrance is remarkably handfome. The chancel belongs to the impropriator, the north chapel to the parifh, and the fouth chapel to the lord of the manor. There was a chantry in this church, dedicated to St. Mary, whereof Henry Bridge was the laft incumbent, and enjoy'd a penfion of 3*l*. 6*s*. 8*d*. in the year 1553. *Willis*.

The roof of the nave was confiderably raifed at the expence of John Forty, a wealthy clothier of this town, who died in 1458, and lies buried in the middle aile. William Bicknell built the fouth chapel, in the year 1489, and he and his wife lie buried there.

	£.				£.		
Firft fruits	10	19	0¾	Synodals	0	2	0
Tenths —	1	1	11	Pentecoft.	0	1	8
Procurations	0	6	8				

Monuments and Infcriptions.

There are feveral antient grey marble ftones, with effigies and memorials engraven on brafs, now moftly imperfect; but I thought proper to give fome account of the remains of them. Upon one in the chancel, is the figure of a man kneeling, with uplifted hands. Over him was another figure, now torn off. Proceeding from his mouth, it is thus written in old characters:

O regina Poli mediatrix efto Lawnder Willi.
O numen celi Lawnder miferere Willi.

On plates round the margin of the ftone,

Man In what ftate that euer thou be * Timor mortis fhoulde truble the * For when thou leeft wenyft veniet te * Mors fuperare . . . . * So thy graue grauis . . . . * Ergo mortis memorare.

In the fouth chapel, a man and his wife, with eight fons and feven daughters, and beneath, the reprefentation of a wool-pack, and a fheep couchant. Round the verge,

John Taylour and Ioone hys . . . . a Thoufand CCCC And Ioone his Wyfe . . . . The zeere of Owre lord God A Thoufād CCCC ōn whois foulis Ihū haue Mcy Amen.

On another ftone, (the brafs now torn off) was written,

Pray for the foulis of Wylliam Bicknell & Margt his Wyfe which of theyr charity caufed to be made this chappel & all theyr Childrens foulis the which Willm deceffyd the XXVI day of December the yere of our Lord MCCCCC & the faid Margt deceffyd the VI day of May in the yere of our Lord MCCCCXCIII On whois foulis Ihū haue Mcy Amen.

In

In the ſame chapel,

In Memoriam
Ioannis Parker
Cognatis et Amicis
Flendus, Pauperibuſque;
Vir Matriſque Patriſque
Priſco ſanguine clarus.
Vir infirmus et Annis
Fractus, ſed tamen acer
Libertatis avitæ
Vindex; uſque Piorum
Mirans fœdera Regum
Nos immanibus Anglos
Abſolventia vinc'lis.
Vir vultuque Manuque, &
Puro pectore (Nam vox
Hæſit faucibus) unum
Chriſtum Nomen adorans.
Obiit 18 die Octob.
Anno Dnī 1692,
Ætat: ſuæ 78.

Arms, 1. Parker, as under Hasfield, impaling, 2. *Three fuſils in feſs*, ſuppoſed for Freeman.

Alſo, on a braſs plate,

M i Frend the earthli Shrine that is interred here
A heavenly ſaint belongeth to that livde here forti yere
W hereof twice ten and three ſhe livde a vertuoſe maid
D uring the reſt a loiall wife one huſbands joyfull Aid
P arent of Children ten, whereof ſix her ſurvived
A daughter deare and dutifull to Parents whyleſt ſhe livde
R egarding as her own her huſband's kiſt and kin
K nown to the poor a frutefull frend, a foe to fraude and ſin.
E ſteemed where ſhe dwelt a neighbour good to all
R eſpecting carefully her charge that nought to waſte might fall
T hen viſited at laſt ſhe fixt her health in Chriſte
H olding moſt firmly in none elſe ſalvation did conſiſt
O f former deeds miſdone repenting pardon craved
M oſt reſolute by Xte's blood ſhe was for ever ſaved
A nd when the inſtant came that ſhe diſſolvd muſt be
S weet Ieſu take my ſoul ſhe cried I yeld it up to thee
Thus did ſhe live and dye to live for evermore
Belovd of men and bleſt of God, his name be praisd therefore
The fourth day of March, and in the yere of Grace
Five hundred thrice LXXX and fower in childbed hent her race.

On another, in the ſame aile,

Pray for the ſoules of Robt Serche and Anne hys Wyfe whych Robt deceſſed the xx day of Ianever the yere of our Lord MV^c and oon On whoſe ſowlys Ihu haue Mercy Amen. *At the four corners*, Ihu mercy, lady help.

In the north chapel, engraven on braſs on a flat ſtone, are the figures of two men, and a woman between them, ſtanding under Gothic arches richly ornamented, and at their feet is this memorial:

Hic jacent Thomas Fortey Wolman, Wills Soors Taylour, & Agnes ux . . corund . . q . . . quidē Thomas obiit p'mo die decemb. A° Dni M°CCCC°XA Wills obiit . . die . . . A° Dni M°CCCC° xx° Agnes obiit . . . die . . . A° Dni M°CCCC° . .

Round the verge of the ſtone,

Sub pede morte jacens Thomas Fortey § Et ſua ſponſa placens ſibi conſociatur . . . . Mercator dignus iuſtus ueraxq; benignus § noſcitur in ſignis non gaudens Ipe malignis § Eccleſiarum ſuarumq; viarum ſit Reparator § Criſte ſuarum ſis miſerator § Mille quater Centum quater & ſeptem Monumentum primo dat. Flamen Deceni Ihe hūc beat . . . .

In the middle aile is a large figure, ſtanding on a wool-pack and ſheep, and at his feet,

Reſpice quid prodeſt preſen^s temporis evum
Omne quod eſt nichil preter amare deum

Moſt of the braſſes which were round the ſtone are now gone. At each corner are the letters I. F. for John Fortey.

On another ſtone near it, the figure in braſs of a man and woman ſtanding on wool-packs, &c. and the following inſcription round the verge,

Farewell my Frendes the tyde abideth no man § I am departed from hence and ſo ſhall ye § But in this Paſſage the beſt Songe that I can § Is requiem eternam now Ihu graunte it me § When I haue ended all myn aduerſitie § Graunte me in Paradiſe to haue a manſion § That ſhed thy blode for my redemption. *The braſs which had the date is gone.*

Benefactions.

Hugh Weſtwood, eſq; gave the impropriaton of Chedworth, and a meſſuage and tenement, and two yard-lands and a half, 1 Eliz. then worth 120*l.* a year, to maintain a free grammar ſchool; and the inhabitants of the town purchaſed a ſchool-houſe for the maſter.

William King, 23 H. 8. gave ſome houſes in the town, then worth 53*s.* 4*d.* a year, to furniſh a ſtock to ſet up poor tradeſmen. Richard Hart gave 6*l.* Thomas Weſtmacott 20*l.* John Miller 10*l.* and his ſon John Miller 10*l.* William Edgley 10*l.* Thomas Patſhall, clerk, gave 3*l.* R. Weſtmacott gave 50*s.* John Dutton, of Sherbourn, eſq; gave 20*l.* all which ſums were to remain as a ſtock for the poor, but have been laid out on houſes for them. Joſhua Aylworth gave the intereſt of 100*l.* to the poor. And Simon Hughes, late rector of Hamnet, gave 10*s.* a year for a ſermon on Good-friday, and 10*s.* in bread for ever.

John Parker, eſq; in 1692, gave 10*s.* for a ſermon on St. Luke's-day, and 10*s.* to the poor in bread for ever. And Mrs. Mary Parker, and Mrs. Eliz. Emes, daughters of John Parker, gave the cuſhion and pulpit cloth, a large gilt flaggon, and a large gilt ſalver, and chalice, to the church. Mrs. Mary Parker gave 50*l.* to be diſtributed to the poor immediately after her deceaſe.

Thomas Dutton, by his will, gave 100*l.* to found an almſhouſe for ſix poor perſons for ever; and William Dutton, eſq; gave the great houſe in Northleach for ever, and 200*l.* to be lent to tradeſmen at 4*l.* a year, the income to be given to the ſick poor. Thomas Force gave 10*l.* to put the bells in three quarter wheels. Edward Carter, gent. gave 50*l.* to the uſe of the town, and James Thynne, eſq; gave 100*l.* to the poor. George Townſend gave 12*s.* a week in bread, 4*l.* a year to teach poor boys to read and write, and 5*l.* a year to put a poor boy out an apprentice.

Northleach.

Land-tax at 3*s.* 1770, £. 12 2 3

Eaſtington and Pinſwell.

Land-tax at 3*s.* 1770, £. 78 7 9¾

At the beginning of this century, according to ſir Robert Atkyns, there were 200 houſes, and about 900 inhabitants in this pariſh, whereof 34 were freeholders; yearly births 23, burials 21. The preſent number of families in the whole pariſh is 149, of inhabitants 683, by actual numeration; which ſhews the declining ſtate of the town.

N O R T O N

IS a ſmall pariſh in the hundred of Dudſton and King's-barton, ſix miles diſtant ſouth from Tewkeſbury, ſeven weſt from Cheltenham, and four north from Glouceſter, from whence the turnpike-road leads through this pariſh to Tewkeſbury.

It is ſituated on the eaſt bank of the Severn, and conſiſts chiefly of rich meadow and paſture, with a ſmall portion of arable land. Wainload-hill ſtretches along the river, and lies part of it in this pariſh, from the top of which there is an extenſive and very agreeable proſpect of the rich circumjacent country.

Norton, i.e. *North Town*, was ſo called from its relative ſituation to Glouceſter.

Of the Manors and other Eſtates.

'Stigand [archbiſhop of Canterbury] held Nortune. There were five hides and a half. In demean were two plow-tillages, and fifteen villeins, with fifteen plow-tillages, and four *ſervi*, and a mill of 22*d*. It was then and is now worth 4*l*. Thomas archbiſhop [of York] now holds theſe three manors [*i.e.* Circeſdune, Hochilicote, and Nortune]. Walchelin the nephew of the biſhop of Winton holds Nortune of him.' *Domeſday-book*, p. 69.

This manor was afterwards divided into two, which were held of the honour of Glouceſter, and were diſtinguiſhed from each other by the names of Biſhop's Norton, and Prior's Norton. Biſhop's Norton was ſo called becauſe it was the eſtate of the archbiſhop of York. Jeffery Giffard, archbiſhop of York, held the manor of Biſhop's Norton 7 E. 1. It continued in the archbiſhoprick of York 'till the Reformation, and was granted to ſir Thomas Chamberlain 6 E. 6. William Whitmore, of Lower Slaughter, eſq; was lord of the manor at the beginning of this century, and —— Whitmore, eſq; ſon of the late general Whitmore, is the preſent lord of the manor. His arms are, *Vert, fretty Or*.

The other manor was called Prior's Norton, becauſe it belonged to the priory of St. Oſwald in Glouceſter, and continued in that houſe 'till the general diſſolution of religious foundations. It was granted, with the chapel called St. John's, and a portion of tithes, to John Bloxholm, 36 H. 8. John Read had livery of the manor granted to him 9 Eliz. as had Oliver St. John in the eighteenth year of the ſame reign. The manor came afterwards to Mrs. Prince, daughter to lord viſcount Scudamore, who was the proprietor of it at the beginning of this century. It is now veſted in the honourable Charles Howard the younger, in right of his wife Frances-Fitz-Roy Scudamore, daughter and heireſs of colonel Fitz-Roy Scudamore.

William Britton gave five virgates of land in Norton to the abbey of Glouceſter, and the grant was confirmed by king Henry the Firſt. Nicholas Chamberlain and Agnes his wife were ſeized of lands in Norton 29 E. 1. John le Brun was ſeized of lands in Norton 31 E. 1. and a ſeat and eſtate here continued in the family of the Browns down to the beginning of the preſent century, when they were ſold to Daniel Lyſons, of Hempſted, eſq; of whoſe family they were purchaſed, and William Singleton, eſq; is the preſent proprietor.

A wood in Norton, called Prior's Wood, was granted to Thomas Bell, 36 H. 8.

Of the Church, &c.

The church is an impropriation, in the deanery of Glouceſter, but belonging to the dean and chapter of Briſtol, who have the patronage of the curacy, and pay the incumbent 20*l*. a year.

Elmelina gave the advowſon of Norton to the abbey of Glouceſter, and the grant was confirmed by her grandſon Robert, ſon of Walter, and by Avelin his wife, in the year 1126.

The rectory and advowſon of the vicarage of Norton belonged to the priory of St. Oſwald, and were granted to the dean and chapter of Briſtol 34 H. 8.

The church is ſmall, but has a handſome embattled tower at the weſt end.

Pentecoſtals - - - - 7*d*.

			£.	s.	d.
Taxes.	The Royal Aid in	1692,	156	17	4
	Poll-tax ——	1694, —	23	18	0
	Land-tax ——	1694, —	115	18	0
	The ſame, at 3*s*.	1770, —	86	18	6

In the year 1562, there were 31 houſholders in this pariſh: At the beginning of the preſent century, according to ſir Robert Atkyns, there were 62 houſes, and 300 inhabitants, whereof 17 were freeholders; yearly births 6, burials 5. But the people are now decreaſed to about 240.

NOTGROVE

IS a pariſh in the hundred of Bradley, about ſeven miles ſouth-weſtward from Stow, four north-weſtward from Northleach, and ſeventeen north-eaſtward from Glouceſter.

It lies high in the Coteſwold, in a fine open country for the chaſe, with many bold acclivities without hills, and little bottoms between them that cannot be called vallies. It enjoys a fine healthy air, and the ſoil, tho' light and ſtony, produces pretty good crops of corn, from the late improved method of huſbandry, and feeding large flocks of ſheep, to the breed and management of which the farmers hereabout give great attention. Here are ſome downs, and a little paſture beſide, but no meadow lands.

The name of the place was antiently written *Nategraue*, from the Saxon ᵹꞃæꝼ, a *grove* or *cave*; ſo it may either ſignify a *grove of nut-trees*, agreeable to ſir Robert Atkyns's opinion; or it may be reſolved into *Nate's Grove*, upon the ſuppoſition that *Nate* was the name of the antient proprietor of the place.

Of the Manor and other Eſtates.

Sir Robert Atkyns repreſents this place as lying in the old hundred of Witelai, and as dependent on on the manor of Condicote, but he was certainly miſtaken in both particulars; and was probably led into thoſe errors by the account of Condicote being intermixt with the particulars of the manor of Withington, in that copy of *Domeſday* which he uſed; and this I believe to have been the caſe, as I have myſelf ſeen the very ſame interpollation in another copy of that record.

Domeſday recites, that 'the church of Wireceſtre 'holds Widindune in Wacreſcumbe hundred, con-'ſiſting of thirty hides.' And after ennumerating many other particulars, it is ſaid, 'Schelinus holds 'five hides of the land of this manor in Nategraue.' p. 70. So that Schelinus was under-tenant to the biſhop of Worceſter; and the manor continued in the biſhoprick of Worceſter 'till the Reformation; but had been held ſucceſſively by the Rodboroughs, Brownings, and Whitingtons, as meſne lords under the biſhop, from the time of Edward the Third down to the Reformation.

John Browning, who is ſometimes ſtiled lord of Natgrove, married Agnes, ſiſter and heir of William de Rodborough, lord of the manor of Rodborough. Richard Browning, their ſon, was ſeized of lands in Notgrove 2 H. 4. and died 21 H. 4. Richard Tame and Margaret his wife levied a fine of lands in Notgrove to John Tame and others, 9 E. 4. Richard Pole and Elizabeth his wife and Thomas Kepel levied a fine of lands in Notgrove 14 H. 7.

After the Reformation, this manor was granted to the Whitingtons. John Whitington, deſcended from the family of that name at Pauntley, was lord of it in the year 1608. It came afterwards to ſir Clement Clerk, and was purchaſed by Nathaniel Pyrke, of Mitchel-Dean, eſq; about the beginning of this century. He died in 1715, and Thomas Pyrke, of Little-Dean, eſq; his eldeſt ſon and heir, was lord of the manor in the year 1750. He married Dorothy, daughter of Richard Yate, of Arlingham, eſq; by whom he had iſſue two ſons and a daughter, who all dying before him, he bequeathed this manor, and the houſe and eſtate at Little-Dean, to Joſeph Watts (deſcended by his mother's ſide from a brother of Thomas Pyrke) who now aſſumes the name of Pyrke, and is the preſent lord of the manor of Notgrove.

Of the Church, &c.

The church is a rectory, in the deanery of Stow, worth 200*l.* a year. Lord chancellor is patron, and Mr. Gough is the preſent incumbent.

Four yard-lands belong to the glebe.

Guy de Beauchamp, earl of Warwick, was ſeized of the advowſon of Notgrove 9 E. 2. Thomas de Beauchamp, earl of Warwick, levied a fine of the advowſon, to the uſe of himſelf for life, with ſeveral remainders, 35 E. 3. Richard Nevil, earl of Warwick, and Anne his wife, levied a fine of the fourth part of the advowſon to the uſe of themſelves in ſpecial taille, 6 E. 4. Anne counteſs of Warwick afterwards levied a fine of this advowſon to the uſe of king Henry the Seventh, and it has continued in the crown ever ſince.

The church is dedicated to St. Bartholomew, and has a low ſpire, with three bells, at the weſt end, and a croſs aile on the north ſide.

Firſt fruits £.	15	6	8	Proc. & Syn. £.	0	5	4
Tenths —	1	10	8	Pentecoſtals	0	0	4½

Monuments and Inſcriptions.

Againſt the ſouth wall of the chancel, is the effigy in ſtone of a man in armour, lying along, intended, as ſuppoſed, for John Whitington, of Pauntley, eſq; and beneath him another figure in a long robe, ſuppoſed to be for William Whitington, his ſon by a ſecond wife. There are three ſcutcheons over them, of which that on the dexter ſide is, *Per pale*, 1. *A feſs checky, in chief a mullet*, for John Whitington. 2. *Quarterly* 1 & 4. *A lion rampant*, for Pool. 2. *A feſs dancetty*, for Solers. 3. *On a bend four roundlets.*—The middle ſcutcheon bears, 1. Whitington. 2. *Argent, a chevron ermine between three eſcallops*, for Milbourne. The ſiniſter ſcutcheon bears Whitington, with a mullet for difference.

Under a niche, on the north ſide of the chancel, is the figure of a lady, ſuppoſed to be for one of the Whitingtons, lying along, in the faſhionable dreſs of her time, with no other memorial than the date, 1630.

In the north croſs aile is a very antient freeſtone figure, in a long robe, and in the churchyard are two other ſuch antient figures in ſtone, lying along in full proportion, concerning which I find the following ſtrange ſtory in Dr. Parſons's MS. About the year 1650, ſome of the pariſhioners removed one of thoſe ſtones, which was hollow, to make a trough for the cattle to drink out of; but there was ſuch a lowing and diſturbance amongſt them the day and night following, as ſtruck the people with terror and amazement, and cauſed them to bring back the ſtone to its former place, and then all was quiet again. This was atteſted by the miniſter of the pariſh, and ſeveral of his neighbours of good credit, in the year 1680.

Taxes.	The Royal Aid in 1692, £.	53	4	0
	Poll-tax —— 1694, —	15	0	0
	Land-tax —— 1694, —	40	5	0
	The ſame, at 3*s.* 1770, —	33	4	8¼

When ſir Robert Atkyns compiled his account of this pariſh, there were 33 houſes, and about 150 inhabitants, whereof 5 were freeholders; yearly births 5, burials 4. But ſince that time population is very much increaſed, and the preſent number of ſouls is exactly 218.

ODDINGTON.

THIS pariſh lies in the hundred of Slaughter, two miles diſtant eaſt from Stow, ſix ſouthweſtward from Chipping-Norton in Oxfordſhire, and twenty-ſeven north-eaſtward from Glouceſter.

Otintune

Otintune is the antient manner of writing the name, which ſeems eaſily and naturally reſolvable into *Otin-tune* i.e. the *Town of Otin*, or *Odin*, ſome very antient proprietor, long before the conqueſt.

Part of the village lies on the ſlope of a hill, and part in a fine valley, on the eaſt bank of the river Evenlode, which ſeparates it from Oxfordſhire. It conſiſts of about nine hundred acres of land, pretty equally divided into paſture and tillage. The air is remarkably healthy, as appears by the account of burials in the pariſh regiſter. In the year 1734, there was not one perſon buried, tho' the pariſh conſiſted of about eighty families; and only three very antient people died in the year 1773.

The herb *Colchicum*, or Meadow Saffron, grows plentifully in the meadows; and the *Juncus Floridus*, or Flowering Ruſh, is found on the weſt ſide of the river Evenlode, near Addleſtrop-bridge. Alſo between that place and the pariſh of Dailſford, grows a great quantity of the *Nymphæa Major Lutea*, or the Greater Water Lilly, bearing a yellow flower.

Crayle Crayle, eſq; has an eſtate, and a handſome ſeat in this pariſh, (formerly belonging to the late judge Talbot) where, in the ſummer months, he uſually reſides.

Of the Manor and other Eſtates.

'Eldred archbiſhop [of York] held Otintune 'in Salmanſberie hundred, with its hamlet Condicote. There were ten hides, and two plow-'tillages in demean, and ſixteen villeins, and two 'radecheniſters, and four bordars, with fourteen 'plow-tillages. This eſtate never paid tax. It 'was worth 6*l.* in the time of king Edward, and 'is now worth 10*l.* Thomas archbiſhop [of 'York] holds it. St. Peter of Glouueceſtre had 'it in demean 'till king William came into Eng-'land.' *Domeſday-book*, p. 69.

For the better underſtanding the *Domeſday* account, it is neceſſary to obſerve, that archbiſhop Eldred, or Aldred, had been at great expence in repairing the abbey of St. Peter at Glouceſter, and this manor, and thoſe of Lecce, Stanedis, and Bertune, were mortgaged to him, and put into his poſſeſſion, to ſecure the payment of his money.

Archbiſhop Thomas, ſucceſſor to Aldred, reſtored the mortgaged manors to the abbey, and expreſſed great penitence that he had ſo long and ſo unjuſtly detained them, from which it may be ſuppoſed that the mortgage had been then paid; yet notwithſtanding, the ſucceeding archbiſhop claimed all thoſe manors, and abbat Hameline found himſelf obliged to compromiſe matters with the archbiſhop, by making him an abſolute grant of Oddington, in the year 1157, from which time this manor continued in the poſſeſſion of the ſee of York 'till the general Reformation. Ottington was then taken from the archbiſhoprick, and given to ſir Thomas Chamberlain 6 E. 6.

Thomas Chamberlain, eſq; a deſcendant from ſir Thomas Chamberlain of Preſbury, by Anne his third wife, was lord of this manor in the year 1608; and another Thomas Chamberlain, eſq; poſſeſſed it at the beginning of this century.

The manor came afterwards to Charles Coxe, eſq; deſcended, by his mother, from this family of the Chamberlaynes; from whom it paſſed by purchaſe to Nathaniel Piggot, eſq; who is the preſent lord of this manor, and has a large eſtate in the pariſh; but he uſually reſides in Yorkſhire.

Of the Church, &c.

The church is a rectory, in the deanery of Stow, worth about 190*l.* a year. The precentor of York cathedral is patron, and Mr. Joſeph Mellar is the preſent incumbent.

The parſonage houſe was built by Dr. Parſons, arch-deacon of the dioceſe, and ſometime rector of this church. One yard-land belongs to the glebe, and a meadow called Fowl-moor, which is inſtead of tithe of the meadow grounds.

The church is dedicated to St. Nicholas, and ſtands at a conſiderable diſtance from the houſes. It has two ailes, a large chancel, and a handſome embattled tower on the ſouth ſide. The windows of the church and chancel were formerly ornamented with painted glaſs, which the rigid anti-papal principles, prevailing in the latter part of the reign of king Charles the Firſt, would not ſuffer to remain undemoliſhed.

Firſt fruits £. 21	6	8	Synodals £. 0	2	0
Tenths — 2	2	8½	Pentecoſtals 0	0	7½
Procurations 0	6	8			

Monuments and Inſcriptions.

There is a monument in the chancel, with the following inſcription:

Here lieth the Body of Thomas Chamberlayne Eſquire, deſcended from the Earls of Tankreville, High Chamberlains of Normandy. He was 3[d] Son of Sir Thomas Chamberlayne of Preſtbury in the County of Glouceſter, Kn[t]. Embaſſador from H. 8. Edw. 6. Q. Mary and Q. Eliza. to the Queen of Hungary, to y[e] King of Sweden, to the King of Portugal, and to Philip the 2[d] King of Spaine. He married Margarett Daugh[r] and Heir of Edw. Badghott of Preſtbury aforeſaid, gent. who alſo lies here interred. By her he left 5 Sons Thomas, John, Leonard, George, and Edward, and 5 Daughters, Anne, Margarett, Mary, Francis, and Elizabeth. He died the 4th of December, 1640, aged 72. ——Arms at top, *Gules, an eſcutcheon argent, within an orle of eight ſtars Or.*

Near the above, on two plain ſtones,

Here lieth the Body of Thomas Chamberlayne, born in December 1599, died the 17th of May 1689, eldeſt Son of Thomas Chamberlayne, buried hereby.

Here lieth the Body of Katherine only Daughter of Thomas Brent, Eſq[r] and only Wife of Thomas Chamberlayne, here nere interred. She was born in 1610, married 1630, and died the 26th October 1685.

Within the communion rails, on a plain ſtone,

Hen: Mar: Talbot Died Sept[r] 8th, 1747. [*She was the ſecond wife of the late judge Talbot, (ſecond ſon of the lord chancellor Talbot) and daughter of ſir Matthew Decker.*]

Taxes.			£.	s.	d.
The Royal Aid in	1692,		137	14	7
Poll-tax —	1694,	—	36	7	0
Land-tax —	1694,	—	86	3	0
The ſame, at 3*s.*	1770,	—	68	7	9

According to ſir Robert Atkyns, when he compiled the account of this pariſh, there were about

60 houfes, and 250 inhabitants, whereof 30 were freeholders; yearly births 8, burials 7. But the people are fince increafed to 338.

OLDBURY *on the* HILL,

IS a fmall parifh in the upper divifion of the hundred of Grumbald's-afh. It lies on the north fide of the turnpike-road from Cirencefter to Briftol, in an open champaign country, about fix miles fouth-weftward from Tetbury, twenty north-eaftward from Briftol, and twenty-three fouth from Gloucefter. The air is efteemed to be very healthy, and the lands are moftly in tillage.

Some barrows remain to fhew that this place has formerly been the fcene of war and bloodfhed; but I find no camp, intrenchment, or fortification in the parifh, nor can I learn that any thing of the kind is remembered here. *Aldeberie*, however, the old name, feems to indicate that here was antiently fome place of defence, tho' the work itfelf is now totally demolifhed, and there is not fo much as a tradition of its former exiftence.

The parifh is generally called *Oldbury on the Hill*, to diftinguifh it from *Oldbury on the Severn*, a tithing in Thornbury.

The *Biftort*, or *Snake Weed*, is a curious plant found in this parifh, in a ground belonging to Mr. Watts.

Of the Manor and other Eftates.

'Hernulf de Hefding holds Aldeberie in Grim-'boldeftou hundred. There are five hides taxed. 'Edric held it. In demean are three plow-tillages, 'and four villeins, with four plow-tillages; and 'there are nine *fervi*, and one *francigena*, having 'one plow-tillage. There are fix acres of meadow. 'It is worth and was worth 10*l.*' *Dom. Book*, p. 77.

Nicholas Burdon died feized of this manor, with free warren, 36 H. 3. leaving Nicholas his fon, who died feized of Aldebury 29 E. 1. and another Nicholas Burdon died feized thereof 17 E. 3. Edward Burdon, fon of the laft Nicholas, was feized of Oldbury at the time of his death 36 E. 3. and was fucceeded by John his fon and heir, whofe widow, Joan, died feized of the manor of Oldbury 7 H. 4.

From the Burdons the manor paffed to the Thorps. Henry Thorp, efq; was feized of it, and left it in jointure to Cecilia his widow, who died feized thereof 10 H. 5. Ralph Thorp, fon and heir of Henry, and Amice his wife, levied a fine of the manor and advowfon of Oldbury, to the ufe of themfelves in fpecial taille, 2 H. 6. William Thorp, fon and heir of Ralph, died feized thereof 25 H. 6. Ralph Thorp, fon of William, died feized of this manor 2 E. 4. and John Thorp had livery thereof 4 E. 4. whofe fon, William Thorp, fucceeded him, and was found by inquifition to be an ideot. Thomafin Thorp, fifter to William, was married to Thomas Clifford, who left Thomas Clifford, their fon and heir. He was twenty-eight years old at the time of the death of his uncle, William Thorp, whofe heir he was in right of his mother Thomafin. He had livery of the manor of Oldbury 1 H. 8. and was fucceeded by William his fon, who died feized of this manor 26 H. 8. Henry Clifford, fon and heir of William and Elizabeth Clifford, had livery 28 H. 8. and he and Elizabeth his wife levied a fine of the manor and advowfon of Oldbury to Hugh Dennis 4 Mar. Livery of the manor and advowfon was granted to Henry Dennis 4 Eliz. after whofe death it was granted to another Henry Dennis 14 Eliz. John Dennis, efq; was lord of this manor in the year 1608, and the two coheireffes of William Dennis, of Pucklechurch, efq; were proprietors of the manor, and patrons of the rectory, at the beginning of this century. His grace the duke of Beaufort is the prefent lord of the manor.

Amice le Walfh was feized of one meffuage and one plow-tillage in Oldbury and Dodington 18 E. 2.

Of the Church, &c.

The church is a rectory, in the deanery of Hawkefbury, worth about 90*l.* a year. His grace the duke of Beaufort is patron, and Mr. Cook is the prefent incumbent. This church was united in one prefentation with that of Didmarton, in the year 1735.

The church, dedicated to Arild the virgin, confifts of the nave only. It is decently pewed, and has two bells, in a low embattled tower, at the weft end.

	£	s	d		£	s	d
Firft fruits	16	0	0	Synodals	0	1	0
Tenths —	1	12	0	Pentecoft.	0	0	5
Procurations							

Benefaction.

Nicholas Iddols, in the year 1687, gave 50*l.* for the ufe of the poor of Oldbury and Didmarton, with which money land has been fince purchafed to their ufe in the parifh of Luckington.

Land-tax at 3*s.* in 1770, £.28 19 0

At the beginning of this century, there were 16 houfes in this parifh, and about 80 inhabitants, whereof 3 were freeholders; yearly births 2, burials 2. *Atkyns.* The regifter being very ill kept, gives but little light as to the falubrity of the place; but the people are greatly increafed within the laft fixty or feventy years, and are at prefent exactly 232.

OLDBURY *upon* SEVERN.

SEE THORNBURY.

OLEPEN, *vulgarly* OLDPEN,

IS a ſmall pariſh in the hundred of Berkeley, three miles diſtant eaſt from Durſley, five ſouth-weſtward from Minchin Hampton, and about fifteen ſouth from Glouceſter.

It is a kind of gloomy retreat. The church and houſes lie diſperſedly at the top of a deep and narrow combe, almoſt environed by ſteep hills, covered with hanging beech woods, and forming a kind of amphitheatre, except to the weſt, where there is an opening towards the adjoining pariſh of Uley.

This ſituation undoubtedley gave riſe to the name, which I find variouſly written, as *Olepenne*, and *Ullepenne*, (and latterly, tho' very corruptly, *Oldpen*) which ſignifies the *Top of Uley*, from the Britiſh word *Pen*, the *head* or *top* of any thing.

Sir Robert Atkyns was miſtaken in ſaying, *This place is ſo called from the family of the Oldpens, who antiently lived here, and whoſe coat of arms were owls*; for the fact was the reverſe, as will appear from the ſlighteſt attention to the family name, which was more antiently written *De Olepenne*, and not as he produces it. The herald gave the arms for a rebus on the name, but he was ignorant perhaps, that *Ole*, or *Ulle*, did not mean the bird of night, but was really a word of two ſyllables, and only a different manner of writing *Uley*, of which this place was probably once a part; for there is no mention of *Olepenne* in *Domeſday*, nor in any other record that I have ſeen earlier than the reign of king Edward the Firſt.

The pariſh conſiſts almoſt wholly of paſture land, and ſeveral ſprings riſing here, form a brook, which runs down to Uley and Durſley, and ſo, with the waters of thoſe places, into the Severn. There is no manufacture carried on here, but the inhabitants are employ'd by the clothiers at Uley, in the different branches of their manufacture.

Of the Manor and other Eſtates.

It is recited in the eſcheator's inquiſition, taken 4 E. 2. that John de Olepenne granted one meſſuage and half a yard-land in Olepenne to Edmond Baſſet; and the ſame John de Olepenne occurs as a benefactor to St. Bartholomew's hoſpital in Glouceſter 18 E. 2. Bartholomew de Ullepenne occurs about the ſame time in the liſt of benefactors to the abbey of Glouceſter. Theſe were then lords of the manor of Olepenne, which continued in the family of the ſame name 'till it came to John Daunt, by his marriage with Margery, the daughter and heireſs of Robert Oulepen. He died 13 H. 8. and Thomas Daunt,[a] eſq; a deſcendant from him, is the preſent lord of this manor, and

[a] The family of Daunt is very antient, and formerly of conſiderable eminence both in England and Ireland. The following pedigree is authenticated by Peers Mauduit, Windſor herald of arms, and by William Hawkins, Ulſter king at arms of all Ireland.

Nicholas Daunt, ſon of Simon, married Alice, daughter of ——— Tracy, by whom he had a ſon Nicholas, who was living 24 H. 6. He married Alice, daughter and heir of Walter Jurden of Camme, and left two ſons, Nicholas and John. John married Anne, daughter of ſir Robert Stowell, of Somerſetſhire, by whom he had three ſons, John, Thomas, and Stephen; and three daughters, Margaret, Maud, and Alice. He was a perſon attached to the Lancaſtrian family, and of conſiderable power, as may be gathered from the following letter, written in the year 1471, by Edward prince of Wales, ſon to king Henry the Sixth.

By the Prince.

Truſty and welbeloued wee greete yowe well acquaintinge yowe that this day wee bee arriued att Waymoth in ſefety bleſſed bee our lorde And att our landinge wee haue knowledge that Edwarde Earle of March the Kings greate Rebell our Enemy approcheth him in Armes towards the Kinges highnes whiche Edward wee purpoſe with Gods grace to encounter in all haſte poſſible. Wherefore wee hartely pray yowe and in the Kinges name charge yowe that yowe incontinent after the ſighte heerof come to vs wherſoeuer wee bee, with all ſuch felloſhippe as yowe canne make in your moſte defenſible Aray, as our truſt is that yee will doe. Written at Waymoth aforeſaide the XIII day of Aprill. Moreouer wee will that yowe charge the Bayliffe of Me . . . . Pavton to make all the people there to come in their beſte aray to vs in all haſte and that the ſayd Bayly bring with him the rent for our Lady day laſte paſte, and hee nor the tenants fayle not as yee intend to haue our fauor EDWARD.

To our truſty and welbeloued John Daunt.

John Daunt, ſon and heir of John, married Margery, the daughter and heireſs of Robert Oulepen, eſq; in whoſe right he became ſeized of this manor. They had iſſue five ſons, Chriſtopher, John, George, Robert, and William; and two daughters, Jane, and Alice.

Chriſtopher Daunt, ſon of John, married Anne, daughter of Giles Baſſet, of Yewley, eſq; by whom he had three ſons, Thomas, William, and Giles; and one daughter, Faith.

Thomas Daunt, the eldeſt ſon, married Alice, daughter of William Throgmorton, of Tortworth, eſq; and had iſſue five ſons, Henry, Thomas, Giles, William, and John; and four daughters, Mary, Elizabeth, Joyce, and Florence.

Henry, the eldeſt ſon, married Dorothy, daughter of Giles Huſſey, of Motcombe in Somerſetſhire, and left Frances, his only daughter and heireſs, married to John Bridgman, of Nimpsfield, eſq.

Thomas Daunt, ſecond ſon of Thomas, upon the death of Henry his elder brother without male iſſue, ſucceeded to this manor and eſtate. He married Mary, daughter of Brian Jones of Glamorganſhire, by whom he had Thomas, his only ſon and heir, and one daughter, Margaret.

Thomas Daunt, ſon of Thomas, married Katherine, daughter of John Clayton, of the county of Cheſter, and had iſſue four ſons, Thomas, John, Achilles, and George, who continued the family; and four daughters, Frances, Katherine, Mary, and Elizabeth.

Thomas Daunt, the eldeſt ſon and heir, married Elizabeth, daughter of ſir Gabriel Lowe, of Newark in the pariſh of Ozleworth, and left Anne, his only daughter and heireſs, who was married to Thomas Webb of Stone, in this county, and died in childbed, without iſſue; whereupon

George Daunt, youngeſt brother of the laſt Thomas, and next male heir of the family, ſucceeded to this manor and eſtate. He married Martha, daughter of major Henry Turner, of Bandon Bridge, in the county of Corke, in Ireland, by whom he left iſſue two ſons, Thomas, his ſucceſſor, and Henry, who ſettled in Ireland, and married Anne, daughter of Thomas Knolles of Killehegh, in the county of Cork, and by her had iſſue five ſons, Thomas, George, Henry, Achilles, and John, and one daughter Martha.

Thomas Daunt, eldeſt ſon of George, ſucceeded to the manor of Olepen, and married Elizabeth, daughter of George Singe, *alias* Millington, of Bandon Bridge, clerk. They had iſſue two ſons, twins, Thomas and Achilles, born in 1702; and four daughters, Martha, Hannah, Elizabeth, and Mildred.

Thomas Daunt, eſq; eldeſt ſon and heir of Thomas and Elizabeth, is the preſent lord of the manor of Olepen.

In the roll of the above pedigree are depicted the arms of the families with whom the Daunts have inter-married, viz. *Gules, a croſs lozengy argent*, for Stowell. — Olepenne, as afterwards. — *Ermine, on a canton gules a mullet pierced Or*, for Baſſet.—*Gules, on a chevron argent three bars gemels ſable*, for Throgmorton. — *Barry of ſix, ermine and gules*, for Huſſey.—*Sable, ten bezants* 4, 3, 2, 1, *on a chief argent a lion paſſant of the firſt*, for Bridgman.—*Gules, three lions rampant gardant argent, on a canton Or, a fret ſable*, for Jones. —*Argent, a ſaltire between four martlets gules*, for Clayton.—*Ermine, on a bend ingrailed azure three cinquefoils Or*, for Lowe.— *Per feſs, ſable and ermine, a pale counterchanged*; *on the ſable parts three mill inks Or*, for Turner. — *Ermine, on a chief ſable two boars heads caboſhed Or*, for Knolles. — *Quarterly* 1ſt *and* 4th, *Azure, three mill-ſtones argent, each charged with a mill ink ſable.* 2d *and* 3d, *Argent, an eagle with two heads diſplay'd ſable*, for Singe, *alias* Millington.

reſides

refides here. His arms are, *Argent, a chevron fable between three Cornifh choughs heads erazed proper.* But he quarters the arms of the family of de Olepenne, viz. *Sable, a chevron between three owls argent.*

Edmond Baffet of Uley died 4 E. 2. feized of one meffuage and half a yard-land in Olepenne, which he held of John Olepenne by the fervice of 6*d.* a year.

There was a place called Schefcombe in this parifh, as appears by a deed of fale of lands there, from Henry de Olepenne to the brethren of St. Bartholomew's in Gloucefter, in the reign of king Henry the Third. And the mayor and corporation of Gloucefter have thofe lands, as patrons of the Bartholomew's.

Of the Church, &c.

It is a chapel in the deanery of Durfley, annexed to Newington Bagpath. The chapel is very fmall, and has a low fpire at the weft end.

Pentecoftals - - - 10*d.*

Taxes.			£.	s.	d.
	The Royal Aid in	1692,	29	12	0
	Poll-tax ——	1694,—	8	9	0
	Land-tax ——	1694,—	37	14	0
	The fame, at 3*s.*	1770,—	30	3	0

At the beginning of this century, there were 28 houfes in this parifh, and about 140 inhabitants, whereof 4 were freeholders; yearly births 4, burials 4. *Atkyns.* There are now 196 inhabitants.

OLVESTON.

THIS parifh lies in the hundred of Langley and Swinefhead, ten miles diftant north from Briftol, three fouth-weft from Thornbury, and twenty-feven fouth-weftward from Gloucefter.

It is fituated in the vale, and confifts of rich meadow, pafture, and marfhy land, with fome orcharding, and a fmall proportion of arable.

The *Vervain,* or *Herba Sacra,* grows fpontaneoufly and plentifully in the upper part of this parifh, which herb has been very much celebrated of late, in the writings of John Morley, efq; as a fpecific for that dreadful diforder the King's Evil.

This and the adjoining parifh of Alvefton are not diftinguifhable by their names in *Domefday,* which made fir Robert Atkyns place the extracts from that record, relating to both, under Alvefton, and I have been led into the fame miftake in following him. They were, without doubt, originally one parifh, but in procefs of time became two diftinct manors, whofe common name *Alwefton,* or *Alvefton,* (i. e. *Alwy's-town*) fhews whofe property they were. When property was divided, and they were afterwards enjoy'd by different perfons, future ages thought proper to diftinguifh thefe places by a fmall diverfity, which affects only the firft letter of their names, and this was then called *Olvefton.*

There is a very high ftrong wall in this village, inclofing feveral acres of ground, which is the fcite of the antient feat of the Dennifes, who had confiderable property here, and fome ruins of that feat are ftill remaining.

Of the Manor and other Eftates.

In *Domefday* it is thus recorded:

'Saint Peter of Bath held Alveftone in Langelei 'hundred. There are five hides, of which three 'pay tax, and two do not pay, by the grant of 'king Edward and king William. There are two 'plow-tillages in demean, and nine villeins, and 'fix bordars, and a prieft, and one radchenifter, 'with ten plow-tillages. There are feven *fervi,* 'and meadow and wood fufficient for the manor. 'It was worth 100*s.* now 4*l.* The fame church 'holds it ftill.' *Domefday-book,* p. 71.

The prieft, mentioned in the record, fhews that the above particulars belong to this parifh, and not to that now called Alvefton, becaufe here was the mother church, to which that of Alvefton is only a chapel of eafe. And confequently fir Robert Atkyns was miftaken in faying that William the Conqueror gave the manor of Alefton (meaning this manor) to Guarine de Meez, whereas it was moft probably Allifton in Lidney, for reafons affigned under that head.

The manor of Olvefton, and the rectory and advowfon of the vicarage, were part of the poffeffions of the abbey of Bath 'till the diffolution. The manor was then granted to fir Ralph Sadleyr 1 E. 6.

But there was an eftate dignified with the title of a manor, called Alvefton and Berwick, of which Roger Crook was feized 1 E. 3. and Robert Green de Briftol was feized of Olvefton and of Berwick's tenement 27 E. 3.

Edward lord Stafford, duke of Buckingham, was feized of a manor here, which by his attainder came to the crown, and was granted to Thomas Henage and Catherine his wife, for life, 23 H. 8. Sir John Walfh died feized of Olvefton 38 H. 8. and left Maurice his fon, thirty years old, who had livery granted to him the fame year. Nicholas Walfh, fon of Maurice, died feized thereof 20 Eliz. whofe fon Henry had livery granted to him the fame year.

The manor of Olvefton came by purchafe to fir Robert Cann, who was fucceeded by his younger fon fir Thomas Cann.

Sir Thomas left two fons, of whom Robert, the elder, came to the title of baronet, on the death of his coufin fir William Cann. William, the fecond fon, was town clerk of Briftol, and fucceeded to the title and eftate of his brother, who died unmarried. Which fir William Cann had iffue one fon Robert; and one daughter Elizabeth, married to Mr. Jefferies of Briftol, by whom fhe had one fon Cann Jefferies, and one daughter.

Sir

Sir Robert Cann ſucceeded his father, and having married the daughter of —— Churchman, eſq; died without iſſue in the year 1765, whereby the title is extinct. The eſtate deſcended to his nephew Cann Jefferies, eſq; who dying unmarried, it came to his ſiſter, married to Henry Lyppingcott, eſq; who, in her right, is lord of this manor.

Roger Crook was ſeized of ſix *librats* of land in Olveſton, for the uſe of the biſhop of Bath, 16 E. 2. Sir Hugh Stafford was ſeized of thirty-ſix acres of land in Olveſton 1 H. 6. John Parmiter and Richard Forſter levied a fine each of lands in Olveſton 12 H. 7.

HAMLETS. Tockington is a very conſiderable hamlet, of which it is thus recorded :

'Wlgar, one of king Edward's thanes, held 'Tochintune in Langenei hundred. There were 'eight hides, and five plow-tillages in demean, and 'twenty villeins, and twelve bordars, and ten '*ſervi*, with twenty plow-tillages. This manor 'did not pay farm in the time of king Edward, 'but he lived upon it whoſe property it was. 'Earl William held it in demean, and the ſteward 'added one plow-tillage, and a mill of 8 *d.* It 'now pays 24 *lib.* of white money, of which 20 *lib.* 'are in *Ora*.' *Domeſday-book*, p. 69.

Sir Nicholas Ponz, or Pointz, lord of Corey Mallet in Somerſetſhire, was lord of this manor in the reign of king Henry the Third, as appears by a grant from him of a yard-land in Tockinton, to Clement Parmiter and his heirs, whoſe poſterity enjoy'd that eſtate, with a handſome ſeat in this place, down to the preſent century, but it is now the property of Mr. Caſmajor.

Nicholas Pointz died ſeized of Tockinton 5 E. 2. which he held of Gilbert de Clare, earl of Glouceſter, for one knight's fee, and left Hugh Pointz his ſon, eighteen years old. *Eſch.* This manor continued in the Pointz's for many generations, 'till Alice, the heireſs of the family, carried it by her marriage, to ſir Edward Berkeley, and dying 1 H. 8. it paſſed into that name and family. John Lawford, eſq; was lord of this manor at the beginning of this century. A daughter of the Lawfords married Mr. Goodyer, and afterwards Mr. Rayner, who ſurvived her, and ſold the manor to the reverend Mr. Degge, whoſe ſiſter, Mrs. Wilmott, is the preſent lady of the manor.

Hugh de Kilpeck was ſeized of one plow-tillage in Tockington, and left two daughters coheireſſes; Iſabel, married to William Walter, and Joan, married to Philip Marmion; and thoſe lands were aſſigned to Iſabel for her ſhare 42 H. 3. John Newton, burgeſs of Briſtol, and Joan his wife, levied a fine of lands in Tockington, to the uſe of themſelves in ſpecial taille, 8 H. 5. There was a free chapel in this place, belonging to the abbey of St. Auguſtin's in Briſtol, whereof Richard Berry was the laſt incumbent, and enjoyed a penſion of 2 *l.* 17 *s.* in the year 1553. It was in the tenure of —— Partridge, at the diſſolution of that abbey, and was granted to ſir Arthur Darcy 7 E. 6.

There are two fairs held annually at Tockington, one on the 9th of May, the other on the 6th of December, for cattle, &c.

Ingſt is another hamlet. There are alſo places of the following names in this pariſh, *viz. Hazel, Freeze-wood, Shipcombe, Old Down, Haw,* the *Holm, Walning, Gredige, Pilnend, Akely, Woodhouſe, Ridgeway,* and *Cote,* which laſt not having been rated to the land-tax, ſometime after the eſtabliſhment thereof, the commiſſioners ordered it to be aſſeſſed in aid of Thornbury, and it ſtill pays that tax in conformity with ſuch order.

Elizabeth Harriſon, widow, late wife of Thomas Stanſhaw, and daughter and heir of Alice, daughter of James lord Berkeley, levied a fine of lands in Coat, to the uſe of John Walſh, 13 H. 7.

Of the Church, &c.

The church is a vicarage, in the deanery of Briſtol, to which Alveſton is annexed, worth together about 200 *l.* a year. The dean and chapter of Briſtol are patrons, and John Camplin, M. A. præcentor of the church of Briſtol, is the preſent incumbent.

Walter the ſheriff gave the church of St. Helen's in Alveſton to the monaſtery of St. Peter of Glouceſter 7 H. 1. The church of Olveſton was appropriated to the priory of Bath 8 E. 2.

The rectories of Hampton, Alweſton and Forde, late belonging to the monaſtery of Bath, and the patronage of the vicarages, were granted to the dean and chapter of Briſtol 34 H. 8. And the impropriation ſtill belongs to the church of Briſtol, and is now in leaſe to —Willoughby, eſq.

A portion of tithes in Tockington, formerly belonging to the college of Fotheringhay in Northamptonſhire, was granted to Francis Barnham and Martin Barnham 11 Eliz.

The church is dedicated to St. Mary, and has a low pinnacled tower in the middle, with ſix large bells. The ſpire which ſtood upon it was thrown down by lightning, in the year 1603. The chancel is handſomely wainſcotted with Dutch oak, and the altar-piece and communion table are incloſed with circular paliſadoes, all in a very pretty taſte.

There was a chantry in this church, and a ſchool, of which ſir John Berkeley had the advowſon 6 H. 6.

Firſt fruits £. 24	0	0	Synodals £. 0	2	0
Tenths — 2	8	0	Pentecoſtals 0	1	0
Procurations 0	10	0			

Monuments and Inſcriptions.

There is a grey marble ſtone againſt the wall of one of the arches which ſupport the tower, with plates of braſs, on which are engraven the figures of two men kneeling, upon whoſe ſurcoats are the arms of Dennis, with thoſe of Gorges, Ruſſel, and Milborn, in quarterings. From the mouth

mouth of him on the dexter ſide proceeds a label, on which is written,

Unicus et trinus bone Ihū ſis Nobis Ihūs :

From the other's mouth,

In Trinitate p'fecta ſit nobis requies et et'na vita.

Between them, on a ſcroll,

Miſeremini n'ri miſeremini noſtri ſaltem vos filii et amici noſtri quia Manus domini tetigit nos :

And under, it is thus written,

Her lyeth buryed in ye midd of the quere Morys denys eſquyer ſonne and heire of Sr Gylbert denys knyght lorde of the Mano^r of Alueſton & of the Maner of Irdecote & alſo Sr Walter denys knyght ſonne and heire to the ſeid Morys denys eſquyer ye whiche Sr Walter denys deceſſed the firſt day of the Moneth of Septembre in the xxi yere of the reigne of kyng henry the vii whoſe ſoules Ihū p'don amē.

All ye that this rede and ſee of yor charite ſeye for their ſoules a pater noſter and an ave.

On a blue ſtone in the north aile,

Depoſitum
Reverendi Hugonis Waterman
A. M. qui Nuperrime de Olveſton
et Elberton Vicarius erat
Nequaquam indignus;
Filius Reverendi Hugonis Waterman
A. M. Præbendarij de Briſtoll.
Quorum Sumptibus de integro
Extructa fuit totalis, exceptâ
Culinâ, hujus Parochiæ
Vicaria Domus.
Obijt Anno { Domini 1741, Ætatis 45.

Benefactions.

A meſſuage, garden, and orchard; two cloſes called the Hayes, one cloſe called the Hilland, as alſo a ſmith's ſhop, houſe, and garden, and another houſe; alſo a paddock in Tockington, and another in Woodhouſe, together with other lands in this pariſh, in all worth 17*l.* a year, were left to feoffees by Jenkin Kite, to repair the church.

George Moſs gave a rent-charge of 10*s.* on the New Leaſes, for a ſermon; as did another perſon the like rent-charge on Gayner's Leaſe for another ſermon.

John Hancock, of Ingſt, gave 20*s.* a year by will to the poor, charged on a tenement in Bedminſter. In 1717, Martha Baker, of Auſt, gave a rent-charge of 40*s.* a year; and in 1719, John Mapſon, of Tockington, charged his lands in Tockington with 40*s.* a year, each for the uſe of the poor; and in 1722, Edward Wade, of Woodhouſe, gave 15*s.* a year out of a ground, to be diſtributed to the poor in bread on Good Friday.

Olveſton.

Taxes.	The Royal Aid in	1692, £.	206	4	4
	Poll-tax —	1694, —	25	14	0
	Land-tax —	1694, —	171	18	8
	The ſame, at 3*s.*	1770, —	129	14	0

Tockington.

Taxes.	The Royal Aid in	1692, £.	277	6	8
	Poll-tax ——	1694, —	52	13	0
	Land-tax ——	1694, —	422	0	0
	The ſame, at 3*s.*	1770, —	319	19	0

When ſir Robert Atkyns compiled his account of this pariſh, there were 50 houſes, and about 240 inhabitants, whereof 20 were freeholders; yearly births 8, burials 8. In ten years, beginning with 1760, the average of annual baptiſms was 19.9, of burials 15.3, and the preſent number of ſouls is 593; ſo that about one in thirty-eight dies in a year. In 1742, the inhabitants were 588; and it is remarkable that only one perſon, (a woman upwards of eighty years old) was buried from Feb. 20, 1751, to March 21, 1753.

OXENHALL.

THIS pariſh lies in the vale, in the hundred of Botloe, one mile north-weſt from Newent, eight north from Dean, and eleven northweſtward from Glouceſter.

It is by no means a flat country. The lands lie dry and healthy, in very beautiful ſlopes and ſwells; and the ſoil, which is a rich, ſandy loam, inclining in ſome places to clay, produces the great neceſſaries of life in perfection and abundance. This pariſh, and thoſe of Dimmock, Kempley, Preſton, and Pauntly, make as fine a diſtrict of country as any in the county of Glouceſter, but it is not, perhaps, equally well cultivated. The roads cannot be commended at any time, but in the winter they are almoſt impaſſible.

The arable lands, which conſtitute the greater part of the pariſh, are interſected with rows of fruit-trees, whoſe bloſſoms, in the ſpring, are captivating to the ſenſes, and from whoſe fruit, in the autumn, the farmer derives no inconſiderable profit.

The church and tower are chiefly built with a red kind of ſand ſtone, very hard and durable, if kept dry. This ſtone lies in one intire *ſtratum*, and may be dug on the ſpot, of any ſize or ſhape at pleaſure. It is ponderous, and full of ſhining particles, which I take to be iron: About fifty years ago, upwards of twenty tons of that metal were caſt weekly at a furnace here, which has been out of blaſt for ſome time.

Among other vegetable productions, the following plants, *viz.* Hoarhound, Wood-Wax, Wild Sorrel, Fox-Glove, and Daffodil, grow plentifully here.

A ſtream called Ellbrook riſes in Herefordſhire, and after running through this pariſh, and Newent, falls into the Leden, near Leden-court.

Of the Manor and other Eſtates.

'Roger de Laci holds Horſenehal in Botelau 'hundred. Turchil held it of earl Herald, and 'could go where he would. There are three hides. 'In demean are two plow-tillages, and five villeins, 'and three bordars, with five plow-tillages. There 'are two *ſervi*, and in Glouceſter three burgages 'of 15*d.* It is worth and was worth 40*s.*' *Domeſday-book*, pp. 74, 75.

William de Ebroecis, or de Evers, obtained a charter of free warren in Oxenhall 36 H. 3. His ſon, William de Evers, ſucceeded him, and Maud, widow of the laſt mentioned William, held lands within

within this manor in dower, and her right to free warren was allowed in the proceedings on a writ of *Quo warranto* 15 E. 1.

William de Grandison was lord of the manors of Oxenhall and Dimmock 9 E. 1. as appears by the sheriff's return of all the vills in the county, with their respective lords, the same year. He was summoned as a baron to parliament, and married Sybil, younger daughter and coheiress of John de Tregoz, with whom he had the manor of Lydiard-Tregoz in Wiltshire.

The manor came afterwards by marriage to the earls of Ormond. Sir James Ormond, son of James earl of Ormond, and Amice the wife of sir James, levied a fine of this manor, and of Okely Grandison in Newent, to the use of themselves in taille, the remainder to the right heirs of Amice, 23 H. 6.

James earl of Wiltshire was seized of the manor at the time of his attainder 1 E. 4. and the manor and advowson were granted to sir Walter Devereux and his heirs male the same year.

The manor afterwards reverted to the crown, and was granted to the duke of Northumberland, upon whose attainder it came again to the crown, and was mortgaged, as security for money borrowed, to Paul Withepole, and other citizens of London, 36 H. 8.

Thomas Brook, esq; died seized of the manor 38 H. 8 whereby Joan his sister, the widow of — Arrowsmith, became his heir, and had livery granted to her 1 E. 6. William Pigot, esq; died seized of Oxenhall and Kempley 7 E. 6. leaving Edward his son, forty years old, who had livery of those manors the same year. Henry Pigot, son of Edward, left Anne, his only daughter and heiress, married to Henry Finch, esq; who, in her right, was seized of this manor in the year 1608, and died in 1631. Francis Finch, only son and heir of Henry, married Jane, daughter of Dr. Thornborough, bishop of Worcester, and left John Finch his son and heir; but Mr. Foley was lord of the manor at the beginning of this century, and it is now the property of lord Foley.

Of the Church, &c.

The church is a vicarage, in the Forest deanery, worth about 15*l.* a year. The patronage was formerly in the impropriator, but the living has been held by licence from the bishop ever since the year 1636. Mr. Serjeant is the present incumbent. An acre of land, and twenty marks yearly, were decreed to the curate by the court of exchequer 15 C. 1. and the impropriator still continues to pay him 13*l.* 6*s.* 8*d.* a year.

The impropriation formerly belonged to the preceptory of Dinmore in Herefordshire, which was a cell to the priory of St. John of Jerusalem. It is now the property of Maynard Colchester, of Westbury, esq.

The church is small, with a spire at the west end.

First fruits £.	9	12	11	Proc. & Syn. £.	0	9	2
Tenths —	0	19	3	Pentecostals -	0	1	4

Taxes.	The Royal Aid in 1692, £.		79	10	0
	Poll-tax — —	1694, —	16	14	0
	Land-tax —	1694, —	23	13	0
	The same, at 3*s.*	1770, —	69	3	0

At the beginning of this century, there were 46 houses in this parish, and about 200 inhabitants, whereof 8 were freeholders; yearly births 6, burials 6. *Atkyns*. The present number of families is 46, of inhabitants exactly 202.

OXINTON

IS a small parish in the lower division of the hundred of Tewkesbury, about four miles distant eastward from the town of that name, five westward from Winchcombe, and twelve northward from Gloucester.

Part of it lies in the vale, and part stretches over one of those hills that bound the Coteswolds. The soil is good in general, but sheep depasturing on any part of the parish are very subject to the rot. The village consists only of one or two ordinary farm houses, and a few mean cottages.

Of the Manor and other Estates.

'In the time of king Edward there were five 'hides and a country-seat [*aula*] at Oxendone 'belonging to Teodekesberie. There are five 'plow-tillages in demean, and five villeins, and 'two radchenisters, having seven plow-tillages, 'and twelve among the *servi* and *ancillæ*. There 'are twenty-four acres of meadow. At Wince-'combe three burgages pay 40*d.* The whole is 'worth and was worth 8*l.*' *Dom. Book*, p. 68.

John de la Hay held the manor very antiently. Sir Ralph de la Hay and Eustachia his wife held the manor early in the reign of king Henry the Third, as appears by an agreement made between them and Peter the abbat of Tewkesbury concerning tithes, and other things; which agreement is inserted in Stevens's *Supplement to the Monasticon*, Vol. 2. *Appendix*, p. 205. He was seized of this manor 30 H. 3.

William Totchett was lord of the manor of Oxendon 9 E. 1. as appears by the sheriff's return made the same year; and a fine of the manor of Oxindon was levied to his use by Roger de Moreton and Isabel his wife 27 E. 1. He had a confirmation of free warren in this and other manors granted him in the 28th, and was summoned as a baron to parliament in the 34th year of the same reign, and died soon after, without issue. William Tuchet, son of Nicholas, was his heir. In the escheator's inquisition, taken after the death of Gilbert de Clare, earl of Gloucester, it is said, that William Tuchet held half a knight's fee in Oxindon and Aston (upon Carant) of the said Gilbert, worth 15*l.* a year, 8 E. 2. Taking part with the earl of Lancaster, in his endeavours to expel the Spencers, he was made prisoner at the battle of Burrowbridge, and hanged at York as a rebel,

rebel 15 E. 2. The manor thereupon was ſeized into the king's hands, and granted to Hugh le Diſpencer the younger, the ſame year.

This Hugh being afterwards attainted, the manor was granted to Bartholomew Badleſmere, (heir to the former Touchets) who was hanged at Canterbury for rebellion 2 E. 3. notwithſtanding which, Giles Badleſmere, ſon of Bartholomew, ſucceeded in this manor. He was ſummoned as a peer to parliament 9 E. 3. and died ſeized of Oxinton 12 E. 3. leaving four ſiſters, his coheireſſes; Maud, was married to John de Vere, earl of Oxford; Elizabeth, to William de Bohun, earl of Northampton; Margaret, to Sir John Tibitot; and Margery, to Willial lord Roos.

In the partition of the eſtates, this manor was aſſigned to ſir John Tibitot, who was ſummoned as a baron to parliament 9 E. 3. and died 41 E. 3. Robert lord Tibitot, ſon of John, ſucceeded him in the manor of Oxindon. He married Margaret, daughter of William Deincourt, and died 46 E. 3. leaving three daughters, his coheireſſes, who were granted in ward to Richard le Scroop, lord treaſurer of England. Margaret, the eldeſt daughter, was married to Roger le Scroop, eldeſt ſon of Richard le Scroop, whereby the manor of Oxenton came into that name and family, in which it continued down to the beginning of the preſent century.

Sir Stephen le Scroop and Milleſent his wife levied a fine of the manor of Oxenton 3 R. 2. Sir John Scroop died ſeized of this manor 8 H. 8. and Richard Scroop, his ſon, had livery thereof 17 H. 8. George Scroop had livery of this manor granted to him 15 Eliz. John Scroop, eſq; was lord of it in the year 1608, as was Charles Scroop, eſq; at the beginning of this century. Edmund Lechmere, eſq; is the preſent lord of this manor, and holds a court here.

There was another eſtate in this pariſh, entered in *Domeſday-book* among the lands belonging to the church of St. Dennis at Paris. 'Five hides in 'Olſendone belong to the ſame manor [Derheſt].' p. 72. Accordingly it appears by the terrier of the priory of Derhurſt, that the prior had twelve ox-tillages of land in Oxendon, and 4*l*. 12*s*. 2*d*. rents of aſſize, and 4*l*. 4*s*. 4*d*. from his villeins.

It does not appear to whom the above eſtate was granted at the general diſſolution, but it is probable that it became the property of the lay lord of the manor of Oxinton.

John de la Hay purchaſed lands in Oxendon of Ralph de la Hay and Euſtachia his wife 30 H. 3. and his claim to free warren was allowed in a *Quo warranto* 15 E. 1. A houſe and lands in Oxendon were granted to ſir Chriſtopher Hatton 24 Eliz.

Of the Church, &c.

The church is a curacy, in the deanery of Winchcombe. The earl of Coventry is patron and impropriator; Mr. Roberts is the preſent incumbent. The living was augmented with the queen's bounty, in the year 1746, and the curate receives 6*l*. a year out of the impropriation.

The rectory of Oxenton, and lands called Parſon's, with the tithes of Kemp, lately belonging to the abbey of Tewkeſbury, were granted to James Gunter and Walter Lewis, in truſt, 37 H. 8. Other tithes in Oxenton, lately belonging to the ſame abbey, were granted to Thomas Stroud, Walter Earl, and James Paget, 36 H. 8.

There is no glebe, nor houſe for the curate.

The church is ſmall, and has a ſmall tower at the weſt end.

Pentecoſtals - 6½*d*.

Taxes.						
The Royal Aid in	1692,	£.	107	7	0
Poll-tax —	1694,	—	9	1	0
Land-tax —	1694,	—	104	9	0
The ſame, at 3*s*.	1770,	—	75	14	7½

When ſir Robert Atkyns compiled his Hiſtory, there were 30 houſes in this pariſh, and about 120 inhabitants, whereof 4 were freeholders; yearly births 4, burials 4. The inhabitants are ſomething increaſed ſince that time.

****

OZLEWORTH

IS a ſmall pariſh in the hundred of Berkeley, about two miles eaſtward from Wotton-underedge, three ſouth-eaſtward from Durſley, and about eighteen ſouth from Glouceſter.

It is ſituated on the verge of the hill country, with large woods adjoining, and is moſt remarkable for the number of foxes killed in one year, in the reign of queen Elizabeth, which amounted to two hundred and thirty-one.

Of the Manor and other Eſtates.

Ozleworth was a *berewic*, or member, belonging to the manor of Berkeley, at the time of the general ſurvey, as appears by *Domeſday-book*, where it is ſaid, that 'half a hide in Oſleuuorde belongs 'to Berchelai.' p. 68.

The manor was afterwards granted by the Berkeley family to St. Auguſtin's abbey in Briſtol, whoſe claim to a court leet was allowed 15 E. 1. The abbey of Kingſwood in Wiltſhire was ſeized of Ozleworth 12 H. 4. and continued poſſeſſed of it 'till the general diſſolution of religious foundations, when it was granted to ſir Nicholas Pointz 31 H. 8. whoſe family were before ſeized of it as tenants under the abbey of Kingſwood, for ſir Robert Pointz, grandfather of Nicholas, died ſeized of the manor of Ozleworth 12 H. 8. Sir Nicholas Pointz, above mentioned, died 4 Mar. Nicholas Pointz, ſon of ſir Nicholas, had livery of the manor granted to him the ſame year, and ſold it to ſir Thomas Rivet, alderman of London, of whom it was purchaſed by ſir Gabriel Low, likewiſe alderman of London.

Sir Thomas Low, ſon of ſir Gabriel, was lord of this manor in the year 1608, and ſir Gabriel Low,

Low, ſon of ſir Thomas, died ſeized thereof in 1704. Timothy Low, eſq; ſon of ſir Gabriel, was lord of this manor when ſir Robert Atkyns compiled his Hiſtory. The late James Clutterbuck, eſq; who died in the latter part of the year 1776, was lord of the manor, and proprietor of a good eſtate in the pariſh, where he had a handſome ſeat called *Newark*, originally built by ſir Nicholas Pointz, out of the ruins of Kingſwood abbey, but repaired and greatly improved by its ſeveral ſucceſſive proprietors. The houſe ſtands on high ground, and commands an extenſive and very agreeable proſpect. The arms of Clutterbuck are, *Azure, a lion rampant argent, in chief three eſcallops of the laſt.*

Of the Church, &c.

The church is a rectory, in the deanery of Durſley, worth about 60*l.* a year, of which the late James Clutterbuck, eſq; was patron.

Roger lord Berkeley gave this church to the priory of Stanley St. Leonard, which was a cell to the abbey of Glouceſter, and the patronage was veſted in that abbey 2 H. 8.

The rectory pays 6*s.* 8*d.* a year to the crown.

The church is dedicated to St. Nicholas, and has a round tower, with a wooden ſpire in the middle.

Firſt fruits £. 6	10	5	Synodals £. 0	1	0
Tenths — 0	13	0½	Pentecoſtals 0	0	11½
Procurations 0	1	0			

Taxes.					
	The Royal Aid in 1692,	£. 44	4	0
	Poll-tax — — 1694,—	8	4	0
	Land-tax —— 1694, -	42	4	8
	The ſame, at 3*s.* 1770,—			

When ſir Robert Atkyns compiled his account of this pariſh, there were 17 houſes, and about 70 inhabitants, whereof 5 were freeholders; yearly births 2, burials 2. The people are increaſed ſince that time, and are now about 80 in number.

PAINSWICK.

THIS pariſh lies in the hundred of Biſley, four miles north-weſt from the town of that name, four north from Stroud, and ſix ſouth from Glouceſter.

At the time of the general ſurvey, the name of it was ſimply *Wiche*. About the reign of king John, it received the addition of *Pain*, from Pain Fitz-John, who was then lord of the manor; but ſir Robert Atkyns ſays, it had been called *Michaelſwick* before that time, of which, however, I have found no inſtance in the records.

The pariſh produces no very curious or uncommon plants or foſſils, except a very fine kind of white freeſtone may be ſo eſteemed. The ſoils are ſuch as are moſt commonly found in a country full of hills and uneven ground, with little bourns and meadows between them, and well cultivated paſture grounds and arable fields on the higher ſituations. Here is alſo a very large proportion of woodland, conſiſting almoſt intirely of beech.

There is a ſmall market town, about the middle of the pariſh, of the ſame name, very irregularly built, with ſhort ſtreets and frequent turnings, but pleaſantly ſituated on the ſouth ſide of the acclivity of the great hill *Sponebed*. It has two fairs in the year, one held on Whit-Tueſday, the other on the 19th of September, for ſheep and horned cattle; beſides a very large fair, or great market, for ſheep, on the Tueſday before All-Saints-day, according to the old ſtyle. The market is held on Tueſday, by a royal charter firſt granted 17 E. 2. and afterwards renewed in 1627. But the town is ſo environed with hills on every ſide, as not to be eaſily acceſſible to loaded carriages, and it is ſo nearly ſituated to Glouceſter and Stroud, that the market is very little frequented.

There is an antient fortification of double intrenchments upon the top of *Sponebed-hill*, about a mile above the town, called *Caſtle-Godwin*, and *Kimſbery-Caſtle*; of which it is obſervable, that the word *caſtle*, in the latter name, is redundant, as being fully expreſſed by *bery*, (from the Saxon beoрз) a *camp*, or *fortification*. It is a ſquare camp, incloſing about three acres of ground, and has ſome advanced works belonging to it. Several Roman coins have been found there at different times, and not above thirty years ago, a ſword, and ſome heads of ſpears were taken up, but ſo corroded with ruſt as hardly to hold together. It commands an extenſive proſpect over the vale and the Severn, from Newnham, below Glouceſter, as far as the city of Worceſter, which the eye can eaſily diſtinguiſh in a fair day. Theſe circumſtances put the matter out of doubt that this was one of the *Caſtra Exploratoria* of the Romans. I ſuppoſe it to have been occupied by earl Godwin, (from its bearing his name, and from other circumſtances related under Beverſtone) in that inſurrection, in the reign of king Edward the Conſeſſor, to expel all foreigners out of the kingdom, of whom the nation was very jealous, and whom the king, who then lay at Glouceſter, was thought to favour too much.

King Charles's army occupied this poſt after quitting the ſiege of Glouceſter; and there is a tradition, that the king, ſitting on a ſtone near the camp, was aſked by one of the young princes, *When they ſhould go home?* To which his majeſty anſwered, a little diſconſolately, that *He had no home to go to.*

The clothing manufacture has been long eſtabliſhed in theſe parts, by which many have acquired large fortunes. It is ſtill conſidered as a lucrative and genteel employment, capable of any extenſion; and it certainly deſerves the greateſt encouragement, becauſe it furniſhes labour for the poor of both ſexes, and all ages, who derive from it the neceſſaries and comforts of life; and the

air

air of this pariſh, which is remarkably ſalubrious, gives them a great ſhare of health to enjoy them.

The principal houſes in the pariſh are,

1. The *Lodge*, or manor-houſe, which is a large and handſome ſeat belonging to ſir James Jerningham, baronet, who keeps it in repair; but it has not been the reſidence of any of his family for many years.

2. The ſeat of Benjamin Hyett, eſq; ſituate a little above the town. It is an elegant houſe, with offices, finiſhed by his late uncle, who called it *Buenos Ayres*.

3. *Paradiſe*, a handſome ſeat, the property and reſidence of Charles Sheppard, eſq.

4. A very handſome, new-built houſe in the town, the reſidence of John Gardner, eſq.

The turnpike-road leads through the town from Stroud to Glouceſter.

Of the Manor and other Eſtates.

The following record was over-looked by ſir Robert Atkyns:

'Roger de Laci holds Wiche in Biſelege hundred. One hide there pays tax. Erneſi held it. 'There is one plow-tillage in demean, and twenty-five villeins, and ſixteen bordars, and a prieſt, 'and three radcheniſters, having amongſt them 'all fifty-two plow-tillages. There are eleven '*ſervi*, and four mills of 24*ſol.* and a wood five 'miles long, and two broad. It was worth 20*l.* 'now 24*l.* The thane himſelf could go where 'he would. St. Mary of Cireceſtre holds one vill '[or the land of one villein] and part of a wood, 'which king William granted to her, worth 10*s.*' *Domeſday-book*, p. 75.

The above Roger de Laci, taking part with Robert Curthoiſe, had his poſſeſſions taken from him by king William the Second, who gave them to Hugh de Laci, his younger brother. Hugh left no ſurviving iſſue, whereby his inheritance deſcended to Gilbert, ſon of Emme, his ſiſter and ſurviving heireſs, which Gilbert aſſumed the name of Laci. Hugh de Laci was ſon and heir of Gilbert, and died 31 H. 2. about which time this eſtate went out of the name of Lacy.

Robert and Ivo, or John, were two potent Normans, who came into England with king William the Conqueror. John married the daughter and ſole heireſs of William Tyſon, lord of Alnwicke in Northumberland. His ſon was Euſtace Fitz-John, who married Beatrix, a great inheritrix, and by her had iſſue William Fitz-John, who took the name of Veſci, one of his mother's titles. Pain Fitz-John, ſays ſir Robert Atkyns, younger brother of Euſtace Fitz-John, and ſecond ſon of Ivo, was ſlain by the Welch 1 Joh. But ſir Robert was probably miſtaken, for it was 133 years from the conqueſt to 1 Joh. and it is not likely that the ſon of that Ivo, who came into England with the Conqueror, ſhould ſurvive 'till that time. It is ſufficient, however, for our preſent purpoſe, that ſome Pain Fitz-John then died ſeized of the manor of Painſwick, which from him took its name.

Pain Fitz-John left two daughters, Cicely, married to Roger the ſon of Milo of Glouceſter; and Agnes, married to William de Monte Caniſio, or Monchenſy, who was ſeized of this manor in right of his wife; and William Fitz-Warine de Monchenſy pleaded his right of privileges in Painſwick, in a writ of *Quo warranto* brought againſt him, and his claim was allowed 15 E. 1.

Dioniſia de Monchenſy, daughter of William Fitz-Warine, and widow of Hugh de Vere, died ſeized of this manor 7 E. 2. and was ſucceeded by Joan the ſiſter, and at length heireſs of the aforeſaid William Fitz-Warine de Monchenſy; which Joan was married to William de Valentia, of the family of Luſignia, in Poictiers in France, and half brother, by the mother, to king Henry the Third.

Audomar de Valentia, earl of Pembroke, third ſon of William, after the death of his brothers, became heir to his father, and purchaſed a charter for a weekly market in Painſwick, to be held on Tueſday, and a yearly fair on the eve of the nativity of the virgin Mary, 17 E. 2. and dying the ſame year, his three ſiſters were his coheireſſes. Joan, the youngeſt, was married to John Comyn, of Badenagh in Scotland, ſon of John Comyn, one of the competitors for that kingdom. They left only daughters coheireſſes.

Elizabeth, one of thoſe daughters, was married to Richard Talbot, of Goderick-caſtle in Herefordſhire, whereby the Talbots were poſſeſſed of the manor of Painſwick, which continued a long time in that family. This Elizabeth was taken by the two De Spencers,[t] and confined by them near a twelve-month, during which ſhe was compelled by threats to paſs this manor to the eldeſt of them, and his heirs. But on the change of affairs, the ſame Richard Talbot and Elizabeth his wife levied a fine of the manor of Painſwick, to the uſe of themſelves in ſpecial taille, 12 E. 3.

John Talbot, earl of Shrewſbury, was lord of this manor, and held a court on the 21ſt of April 1 H. 4. to which he came, and by the advice and conſent of his homage, made ſeveral alterations in the cuſtoms of the manor, very much to the advantage of the tenants.

From the proceedings of this court,[u] we learn the original of the widows free bench in copyhold

[t] Dugdale's Baronage.

[u] The following proceedings at this court contain ſeveral curious particulars, and ſhew the nature of ſome things which length of time has made obſcure.

Com. Glouc'. THE courte holden at Painſwicke the xxi[th] of Aprille, *Anno Dom.* 1400, at which courte came lord John Talbot, earle of Shrewſbury, his owne p'ſon, with S[r] William Mill, knighte, his receaver by patent, Giles Abridges, eſquire, and Thomas Abridges his ſonne, and their ſtewards and ſurveiours jointlie by patent together, to the ſaid lord Talbot, of Paineſwick, Whaddon, and Morton. And the ſaid lord Talbot declared at the ſaid courte, certayne Articles as hereafter enſeweth,

hold eſtates. It was a voluntary gift of the lord, to which, however, the widows had ſome claim, founded on the principles of common juſtice and humanity; for it ſeems reaſonable that the lord

THE firſt Article was, That hee had been beyond the ſea, in the kings warrs, and at that tyme he had xvj^{n} men out of the lordſhipp of Painſwicke, of the which there were a xj. married men ſlaine, whereby the widdows cryed on the ſaid lord Talbott, not onely for looſing their huſbands, but alſoe for looſing their holdings, and ſome of them were his bandmen.

THE ſecond Article contayneth, how the ſaid lord Talbot was diſpoſed to let his demeanes unto his cuſtomary tenants, with all the herbage, and pawnadge, and tacke of piggs, of the common hills and paſture of arable lands, both to the whole yards, half yards, farnedells, and Mundies grounds.

THE third Article conteyneth, how the ſaid lord Talbot willed to ev'y widdowe in the ſaid lordſhippe, for their good will, their herriots to the nexte of their kynne, according to the praiſemente as they were prayſed at, and alſoe waved and ſtrayed goods, payeing the prayſement thereof to the takers thereof.

THE fourth Article conteyneth, how he would dimiſſe himſelfe from mans reepe, wifes reepe, and childs reepe, from the burgages and cottages which were builded out of his demeanes in the newe ſtreet of Painſwicke.

THE vth Article conteyneth, how that he would lett out his arrable lands, reſerving two meadows for his horſes and deare, that is to ſay, Whaddon meadow, and Band Meaddow.

THE ſixth Article conteyneth, whether the tennents would have the tenure of Damſells into their cuſtome or noo.

THE vijth Article conteyneth, how that he would knowe how many freeholders there were in the lordſhippe of Painſwicke.

THE viijth is touching the iiij. warrants of conyes.

UPPON the which Articles there were choſen at the court xx^{ti} men to make anſwer. There were choiſen xij^{e} out of the homadge of his cuſtomary tennents which be whole yards, half yards, ferendels and Mundies; and of the towne of Painſwicke were choiſen viij. men, which bee burgeſſers, curtaleg^{rs} and cottagers; and of the which twenty men were choiſen iij. out of the homadg of Edge, that is to ſay, Willm King, Thomas Caſcell, and Robt Tonley; iij. out of the homage of Strowde, the which were Willm Ward, Willm Browne, and Willm Jordeyne; iij. out of the homage of Sheppiſcombe, which were John Wether the elder, Willm Mynſterworth, and John Bonhill of the Beach; iij. of the homage of Sponebed, which were Willm Sponebedd, Willm Meriman, and Thomas Sawcome; and viij. of the towne of Painſwicke, that is to ſay, Willm Squawe, Willm Pytt, John Caſtle, Thomas Collins, Willm Chamber, Robert Frompton, Willm Scott, and Thomas Shawe; the which inqueſt being impannelled, the ſaid lord Talbot gave them charge to bring in an anſwer to the ſaid articles.

FIRST concerning the widdowes eſtate, whether they ſhould hold their liveing and marry as ofte as they were widdowes.

FOR the ſecond Article, what they would bring in, and make in ready money for yearelie rent, for his herbage of his common hills, and waſte grounde, & pawnadge of his woods, and tacke of piggs, and to ſett yard, halfeyard, ferendells and Mundies through the whole lordſhippe by equal porc'ons, & what value and ſome they would bring him in for the ſame.

THE third, the heriots geven to the widdowes, alſoe concerning waived goods and ſtrayed goods.

THE fourth, concerning the dimiſſing himſelfe from mans reepe, wiefes reepe, & childes reepe.

THE fifth, concerning the ſetting out of his arrable lande to his tennents, both in the towne and country, and the ſaid inqueſte ſhould bringe in what every man would give for an acre. Alſoe, likewiſe that the ſaid inqueſte ſhould bring in an anſwere of all the other Articles.

The Anſwere of the ſaid inqueſte given to the ſaid lord Talbot, concerning the ſaid Articles, as hereafter followeth.

TOUCHINGE to the firſte, the ſaid inqueſte doe agree, that the widdowes ſhall breake their olde cuſtome, and that they ſhould have their liveings dureing their life, and marry with whom they liſte. And the ſaid lord Talbot agreed to the ſame, and enrolled it in the courte and cuſtome.

AS concerning the ſeconde, touching herbage & pawnadge, tacke of piggs, of the common hills, & paſture of arrable land, the ſaid inqueſte broughte in x *lib.* overed in the rent of aſſiſſe, every man to his porc'on, to the which the ſaid lord Talbot agreed, and enrolled it into his cuſtome booke.

AS concerning the herriotts geven to the widdowes at the praiſement thereof, Alſoe wayved goods & ſtrayed goods, the ſaid inqueſte brought in, that the ſaid widdows ſhould have it according as the lords will was.

THE ſaid inqueſte brought in their anſwere concerning the reepes, that they ſhould be dimiſſed, by reaſon the ſaid lord gave up his houſholde.

THE anſwere of the arrable land, the ſaid inqueſte brought in, that every man ſhould have a porcon, the beſte lands at xij^{d} the acre, the ſecond for viij^{d} the acre, the third for vj^{d}, the fourth for iiij^{d} the acre, & ſome for ij^{d} the acre, all which demaines was ſett, ſaveing xiij. acres lyeing in Duddeſcombe in the Culverhouſe-hill. And at the laſte came one Willm Jourdayne & tooke the ſaid xiij. acres of land of the ſaid lord for xij^{d} by yeare, with a Culverhouſe decayed, payeing for the ſame ij^{d} by yeare; and iiij. acres of barren lande lyeing in Huddinalls Hill, for the ſaid iiij. acres came William Tonley, & tooke it of the lord for j^{d} an acre by the yeare. And in a litle ſpace every man made a copie of his porc'on, & the ſaid lord ſealed them.

TOUCHING the Damſells land, the ſaid inqueſte brought in, that ev'y man ſhould hold it according to the cuſtome, as other tennants doe, payeing theire rente & reliefe and noe other cuſtome to the lord. And there were halfe yarde lands in Shepeſcombe, the which the ſaid lord Talbot diminiſhed at the ſaid courte, one called Chrochen, and the other Jones. Out of Chrochen the ſaid lord bated xij. acres, lyeing in the parke, and out of Jones viij. acres. And the lord ceaſſed Chroche land at ij^{s} by yeare, and Jones lands at viij^{d} by yeare, and graunted to them to be cuſtomary holders in their comen as other, both for the batement of the ſaid lande. That is to ſay, xij. acres out of Chrochen, which lyeth in the parke in Cockſhoute launde, and viij. acres out of Jones, lyeing in the ſaid parke in Buſhie launde. And for having of the ſaid lande into the Parke, the ſaide lord covenanted at the ſame tyme to pay to the kinge at ev'y taſke vj^{s}.

THE ſaid inqueſte brought in for freeholders the p'or of Lanthonye, certayne tenements geven by the ſaid lord Talbot of late to the houſe of Swayneforde, conteyning v. yard land with ij. watter mills. The amin^{r} of the monaſterie of Ste Peters in Glouc^{r}. payeing to the lords kitchen yearely at the feaſte of our Lord God, one mutton ſheepe, Pigs lands, Delameeres lands in Sheppeſcombe, John Robins lands, Roſes lands, otherwiſe called Damſells, the which the ſaid lord had in his hands at that tyme already of late, the feoffees of the lands of our lady, ſince in the church of Paineſwicke, and Henry Hoynes for Withers lands.

THE ſaid inqueſte broughte in at the ſaid courte, for their anſwere, concerning the iiij. warrants, that ev'y homadge ſhould have one, as hereafter followeth, that is to ſay, Duddeſcombe and the ij. Frethes in the homadge of Stroude; the homadge of Edge, Arnegrove, and Highgrove; in Sponebed, Kynſbury with Hawking hill; the fourth in Longridge and Nettlebeds in Shepeſcombe. And the ſaid inqueſte deſired the ſaid lorde to ceaſſe the rente what ev'y tithing ſhould pay for their warrants. And the ſaid lord graunted that ev'y tithing ſhould pay yearelie iij^{s} iiij^{d} doeyng his neighbour noe harme. And the ſaid iiij. homadges to increaſe conies, ſoe that they doe not hurte their arrable lands or corne.

AND at the ſame courte the ſaid lord Talbot dimiſſed his iij. weekes courte and comytted it to ij. courts in the yeare onelie for Payneſwicke, and dimiſſed Whaddon & Morton. And that noe man of the ſaid tennents ſhould ſewe another in any courte but in Payneſwickes courte, ſaveing in the high courte above, and in the marches of Wales.

FURTHERMORE the ſaid lord commaunded his tennants to keepe his cuſtome every man in his behalfe, and that noe ſheriffe nor bayley arrant nor noe other out officers ſhould ſerve any writte or warrant on any of the ſaid tennents without the good-will of the ſteward there for the tyme being.

ATT the ſame courte came Dane William Sponebed amner of the monaſtery of Ste Peters in Glou^{r} and James Mille of Ebworth being farmer there, and agreed with the ſaid lord for ij^{s} by the yeare for the mutton ſheepe and to releaſe the iij. weekes courte. And alſoe the ſaid Dane William Sponebed and James Mille deſired the ſaid lord at the ſaid courte to have a copie out of the ſame courte roll, and the lord graunted them, and the ſaid Dane William Sponebed wroughte it out with his owne hand.

MOREOVER the ſaid lord willed his tennants that if any man came to clayme any lands in the lordſhip of Payneſwicke, that he or they that ſoe claymeth ſhould have a courte loking, payeing for the ſame ij^{s} and enter the ſame, and that there ſhould be choiſen xij. men, iij. out of ev'y homadge. And if the matter were in the towne, that then they ſhould choiſe viij. men out of the towne, and one out of ev'y homadge, and the inqueſte ſoe choiſen ſhould goe into an howſe and ſhould not come forth of the ſaid howſe untill they had brought in their verdict of the ſame before the ſteward for the time being, whoe had righte to the ſaid land.

FURTHERMORE if any of the tennants make a forſeite for lacke of reparac'ons that every tenente ſoe offending ſhall pay a double relieffe and enter into his former eſtate againe; and if any refuſe to pay the ſaid relieffe, then it ſhall be lawefull for his nexte heire to enter into the ſaide grounds payeing the ſaid relieffe. And like manner if any of the ſaid tennents be attainted for feloneye, or for any other cauſe, his nexte a kynne ſhall enter upon the grounde, payeing to the lord the aforeſaid double reliefe.

ſhould

ſhould provide for the widows of ſuch men as held eſtates for their lives, and were killed in the wars, in his cauſe.

Sir John Talbot and Margaret his wife levied a fine of this manor to the uſe of themſelves in ſpecial taille, the remainder to the right heirs of ſir John, 20 H. 6. John Talbot, the great earl of Shrewſbury, died ſeized thereof, and of a tenement called Damſels-land, 31 H. 6. It was afterwards ſettled on John viſcount Liſle, a younger branch of the earl of Shrewſbury, by Margaret, eldeſt daughter of Richard Beauchamp, earl of Warwick, and of Elizabeth, the great heireſs of Thomas lord Berkeley. John earl of Shrewſbury and Thomas viſcount Liſle levied a fine of this manor 9 E. 4. After the death of the ſaid Thomas viſcount Liſle, it was granted to Margaret his widow for life, 11 E. 4. Elizabeth Courtney, counteſs of Devonſhire, died ſeized of this manor 21 H. 7. Sir Arthur Plantagenet and Elizabeth his wife, couſin and heir of the counteſs of Devonſhire, had livery thereof granted them 11 H. 8.

The manor afterwards came to the crown, and was granted to Thomas Cromwell, earl of Eſſex, upon whoſe attainder it was granted to George earl of Shrewſbury 30 H. 8. And it was again granted by the crown, with Sponebed, and lands in Theſcomb, Stroud-end, and Horſwarly near Painſwick, to ſir William Kingſton 32 H. 8. who died ſeized thereof the ſame year, and ſir Anthony Kingſton, his ſon and heir, had livery upon his father's death, and levied a fine of this manor to ſir Nicholas Pointz 5 E. 6.

The manor afterwards paſſed to the Jerninghams, of Coſſey in Norfolk. Henry Jerningham had livery of it 15 Eliz. and conveyed this manor to his ſon Henry Jerningham, eſq; who was lord of it in the year 1608. John Jerningham was ſon and heir of Henry. Sir Francis Jerningham was proprietor of it at the beginning of this century, from whom it has deſcended, through ſeveral generations, to ſir James Jerningham, baronet, who is the preſent lord of the manor, and proprietor of a large eſtate in this pariſh. His arms are, *Argent, three buckles gules.* But in the laſt herald's ſurvey, I find them, *Argent, three bucks trippant gules.*

TITHINGS and *HAMLETS.*

1. The tithing of *Edge*, alias *Rudge*.
2. Tithing of *Sponebed*.
3. Tithing of *Shepſcombe*. In the reign of king Edward the Sixth, there were ſeveral inſurrections in the weſt, and other parts of the kingdom. At that time ſir Anthony Kingſton was knight-marſhal, and lord of the manor of Painſwick. He cauſed a gallows for the inſurgents to be erected upon Shepſcombe-green, and made a priſon in Painſwick to ſecure all ſorts of offenders : And ſuppoſing they might be uſeful to poſterity, he alſo gave three eſtates in his lordſhip, ſince called *Gallows-lands*, one always to maintain the gallows, a ſecond to keep two ladders in readineſs, and the third to provide halters; and that nothing in ſo neceſſary a buſineſs might be wanting, provided that the tithingman of Shepſcombe ſhould be hangman, and that he ſhould enjoy an acre of land in that tithing for his ſervice. I find this account in Mr. Wantner's *Collections*, in the Bodleian library. There are many people now living who remember the gallows, and the tithingman for the time being ſtill enjoys a piece of ground there called *Hangman's Acre*; but in this reſpect his office is a *ſine-cure*.
4. *Stroud-end* tithing.

Beſide theſe, there are places in the pariſh of the following names, the *Slad*, *Steanbridge*, *Wick-ſtreet*, *Halcomb*, and many others.

Many cuſtomary tenants hold of the manor of Painſwick, whoſe cuſtoms, as ſettled by the court of chancery 11 Jac. are as follow :

1. The tenants hold by copy of court-roll, *ſibi & ſuis*; whereby they have an eſtate of inheritance, which may be alienated by ſurrender to the ſteward in court, in the preſence of two cuſtomary tenants. Upon every deſcent, the lord to have one year's rent, and an heriot, if the lands are heriotable; but upon ſurrenders, the fine to be ſeven years rent.
2. After the death of a tenant, his wife, if he had any, ſhall be admitted to her free bench during her life, paying one penny.
3. If a tenant has ſeveral ſons, and the eldeſt die leaving iſſue, ſuch iſſue ſhall inherit as next heir to the grandfather. And if a tenant die, leaving ſeveral daughters only, and as many yards or half yards of land as daughters, then every daughter ſhall have a yard or half yard land; and the like order is obſerved with tenements.
4. No ſheriff, &c. to ſerve any proceſs upon any perſon within this liberty, unleſs it be with a commandment, or *ſubpæna*. There are many other articles of leſs conſequence, which are here omitted.

The records ſhew, that the prior of Lanthony had an eſtate in this pariſh, which has been called a manor. After the diſſolution of the priory, it was ſold to Arthur Porter, eſq; and has been ſince ſold and divided amongſt ſeveral freeholders.

Walter Wilton and Iſabel his wife recovered lands in Painſwicke againſt Oſbert Giffard 28 E. 1. John Mandevil was ſeized of lands in Paineſwick and Edgworth 34 E. 3. And Robert Hill and his wife levied a fine of lands in Painſwick and Edgworth 1 H 7. A meſſuage and lands in Painſwick, called Combe-houſe, lately belonging to the priory of Lanthony, were granted to Richard Andrews and Nicholas Temple, in truſt, 35 H. 8.

Ebworth is a conſiderable eſtate in this pariſh. Walter le Bret was ſeized of lands and tenements in Ebworth, worth 40*s.* yearly, in truſt for the abbat of Glouceſter 31 E. 1. The abbey of Glouceſter was ſeized of the manor of Ebworth 17 E. 3. Ebworth-farm is now the property of

Of

Of the Church, &c.

The church is a vicarage, in the deanery of Stonehouſe, worth about 200*l.* a year. The vicar is elective by all the payers in the pariſh. Mr. Moſely is the preſent incumbent.

The rectory of Wyche was given by Hugh de Laci, and confirmed by earl Roger to the priory of Lanthony, as appears by king John's confirmation of grants to that priory, in the Appendix N°. 19. But ſir Robert Atkyns mentions it to have been annexed to that priory 21 R. 2. The impropriation is now veſted in ſeveral proprietors.

A rent of 21*l.* 4*s.* 8*d.* reſerved out of the rectory, and divers lands in Painſwick, were granted to Francis Maurice and Francis Philips 9 Jac.

The advowſon of the vicarage of Painſwicke, which belonged to the priory of Lanthony, was granted, at the diſſolution, to Thomas lord Seimour, and upon his attainder, it was again granted to ſir Chriſtopher Hatton 21 Eliz. William Newport, nephew and heir to the lord keeper Hatton, ſold it to ſir Henry Winſton, of whom it was purchaſed, in the names of truſtees, for the inhabitants of the pariſh.

There is a large glebe belonging to the vicarage, worth 60*l.* a year. The demeans of the manor pay no tithes, becauſe the vicar hath Bangrove-mead in lieu of them.

The church conſiſts of a nave, with two ailes, and three galleries; and there are three chancels, of which, that next the communion rails, extending to the altar-piece, belongs to the vicar; another, between the vicar's and the nave, is appendant to one portion of the rectory; and a third, on the north ſide, was formerly a chantry chapel, of which William Corbuſt was the laſt incumbent, and had a penſion of 5*l.* 10*s.* This belongs to the lord of the manor.

The ſouth aile is built in the modern taſte, ſupported by Doric pillars, with capitals. The grand entrance into the church is at a portico on the ſouth ſide, of the Ionic order. The north aile is a Gothic building, decorated with battlements, under which iſſue four antique water-ſpouts, repreſenting ſo many evil demons flying away from the ſound of the bells, according to ſome received notions in former days, when it was cuſtomary to ſprinkle them with holy water at their being firſt placed in the tower, to give them a power of repelling evil ſpirits by their ſound. And if agreeable and muſical tones have any effect on a diſtempered mind, the ten bells in this tower have as much merit as any peal in the kingdom.

The altar-piece is of freeſtone, of the Ionic order, given by the late Benjamin Hyett, eſq; and executed by John Bryan, of this place, in the year 1743.

The tower ſtands at the weſt end, with a handſome ſteeple on it, fifty-eight yards high from the ground.

The church-yard is laid out in handſome gravel walks, with yew-trees on each ſide, cut into the form of cones, and is the place of reſort for the ladies and the polite inhabitants of the town in fair weather.

Firſt fruits £. 14	15	$1\frac{1}{2}$	Synodals £. 0	2	0
Tenths — 1	9	$6\frac{1}{4}$	Pentecoſtals 0	2	0
Procurations 0	6	8			

Monuments and Inſcriptions.

There are no very antient monuments in this church. The moſt antient was a grey marble tomb, againſt the wall of the north chancel, for ſir William Kingſton, with his effigy and an inſcription on braſs fixt in the wall; but his figure is intirely gone, and the braſſes are ſtolen away. And to mingle and confuſe one thing with another, there are now the effigies of doctor Seaman and his lady, placed on ſir William's tomb. They are in a praying poſture, with a deſk between them; he in a doctor of laws gown, and a ſhield, with their arms lying by, *viz. Baron and femme*, 1. *Gules, three bears heads couped argent.* 2. *Argent, on a bend between two lions rampant ſable, three aſcallops of the field*, for Norton. The doctor's monument, with a memorial, was placed in the chancel, and taken down to make room for the new altar-piece, ſee p. 163.

There are ſeveral memorials on flat ſtones for the Jerninghams, in this chancel, containing very little more than their names.

In the vicar's chancel,

Hic jacet ſepultum Corpus Reverendi Georgij Dorwood, hujus Eccleſiæ nuper Vicarius, cujus Anima hinc emigravit 2do Die Decembris Anno Domini 1685-6. Ætatis 70.

Strict was his Life, his Doctrine ſound, his Care
More to convert the Soul than pleaſe the Ear.
A Watchman true, whoſe peaceful Soul now bleſt;
Crown'd in a Moment with eternal Reſt.

Nehe. Dorwood, e filijs Georgij Dorwood hujus Eccleſiæ Vicarij, qui Carnem tabe conſumptam depoſuit 11° Nov. An° Salutis 1702°, Ætatis 45°. *No arms.*

Againſt the ſouth wall,

In Memory of Jonathan Caſtleman, Eſq[r]. who was a Perſon of ſtrict Probity, extenſive Charity, primitive Piety. He died Anno Ætatis 77 Dom. 1738.——Arms, *Azure, on a mount in baſe proper, a caſtle triple towered Or.*

In the body of the church,

In Memory of Charles Hyett, Eſq; a Repreſentative in Parliament for the City of Glouceſter in the Reign of King George the Firſt, and Conſtable of Glouceſter Caſtle, who died the 17th of February, 1738.——Arms, *Argent, a lion rampant ſable, a chief indented of the ſecond.* On a ſcutcheon of pretence the arms of Webb, *viz. Or, a croſs quarterly quartered, gules and ſable, in the firſt quarter an eagle diſplay'd of the laſt. N. B.* In the heralds laſt viſitation of the county, the arms of Hyett of Lydney, Weſtbury, and Glouceſter are thus emblazoned, *viz. Argent, a lion rampant ſable, a chief of the laſt ſurmounted by another indented of the firſt.*

Againſt the tower, on a marble monument,

In Memory of
Anne ſecond Wife of Littleton Lawrence Eſq[r]. Daughter of Henry Townſend of this Pariſh, Clothier, and Elizabeth his Wife.
To the irreparable Loſs of her Huſband and Family;
To the great affliction of her Neighbours and Acquaintance,
to whom her amiable Virtues and excellent Goodneſs
rendered her ever dear;
And to the ſorrowful ſighing of the Poor, to whom
Her liberal Hand was ever open;
She exchanged this mortal Life for an eternal and heavenly one,
Sept. 1st 1729, aged 31 Years.
Margaret her infant Daughter lieth here buried with her.
She left behind her two Sons, William and Robert, and four
Daughters, Anne, Elizabeth, Eleanor and Margaret.

Arms, Baron and femme, 1. *Argent, a croſs raguly gules*, for Lawrence. 2. *Azure, a chevron ermine between three aſcallops argent*, for Townſend.

There

There are alſo ſeveral memorials for Edmund Webb, and others of his family, with their arms; for Henry Townſend, and others of that name, with their arms; for George Wick, gent. and Anne his wife, with theſe arms, *Gules, a chevron between three wicks (or gates) Or*; for Nathaniel Adams, and Anne his wife, with their arms, *viz.* 1. *Gules, on a bend Or three trefoils ſable*, for Adams, impaling, 2. *Sable, a lion paſſant argent*, for Taylor.

Againſt the north wall of the church, without, are ſeveral memorials for the Maſſingers, formerly of Glouceſter, whoſe arms are, *Argent, a chevron gules between three helmets ſable.*

There is a burying-place in the church-yard, incloſed with handſome iron paliſadoes, with tombs and memorials for Mr. Daniel Gardner, of this pariſh, clothier, and others of his family.

And there are two or three tombs with memorials for the Pools, with their arms, *Azure, ſemy of fleurs de lis Or, a lion rampant argent.* And upon another tomb, on the ſouth ſide of the church, are memorials for John Edwards and his wife, and Mary their daughter, wife of Richard Pulton, apothecary, with the arms of Pulton, *viz. Argent, on a feſs azure, between three mullets ſable, as many bezants.*

Benefactions.

Here is a free-ſchool, endowed with lands in the pariſh of Haresfield, worth 20*l.* a year, for teaching twenty poor children to read and write; towards the purchaſe of which lands, Mr. Giles Smith gave 200*l.* Mr. Samuel Cole 50*l.* Mrs. Elizabeth Townſend 50*l.* Mr. Caſtleman 10*l.* John Downs, the vicar, Thomas Rawlins, clerk, William Palling, ſen. Edmund Wick, William Capel, John Palling, and Mary Shipton 20*l.* each; Luke Gardner 10*l.* and John Twining and Nathaniel Adams 5*l.* each.

Mr. Richard Cliflold, in the year 1683, gave 10*s.* a year to the poor. Mr. Samuel Webb, in 1687, and Mr. Stephen Gardner, in 1695, and Mrs. Mary Shipton, in 1753, gave the intereſt of 10*l.* each to the uſe of the poor. In 1722, Mr. William Hill, of Cirenceſter, gave a large ſilver flaggon and plate, worth 40*l.* for the communion ſervice; and Mr. Joſeph Hilman gave a ſilver baſon for the font.

Taxes.						
	The Royal Aid in	1692,	£. 241	14	8
	Poll-tax —	1694,	— 88	14	0
	Land-tax —	1694,	— 396	13	8
	The ſame, at 3*s.*	1770,	— 298	16	9¼

In ten years, beginning with 1652, I counted from the pariſh regiſter 309 baptiſms, and 180 burials. At the beginning of the preſent century, according to ſir Robert Atkyns, the annual baptiſms were 50, burials 47; and in ten years, beginning with 1760, I find, by actual numeration, that the baptiſms were 629, and the burials 583, which numbers, at diſtant periods, ſhew the gradual increaſe of population. When the militia was firſt raiſed by the new law, in the year 1758, there were 16 men choſen by ballot out of this pariſh, which was the twenty-ninth part of the whole number upon the liſt; and the preſent number of ſouls is about 3300.

PAUNTLEY.

THIS pariſh lies in the hundred of Botloe, in the Foreſt diviſion, four miles diſtant northward from Newent, and ten north-weſtward from Glouceſter. It is bounded by Upleden and Oxenhall on the ſouth, by Kempley and Dimmock on the weſt, and the river Leden ſeparates it, on the north and eaſt quarters, from Worceſterſhire.

The face of the country, throughout the whole pariſh, is full of ſwells, and ſlopes, and little vallies; whence it obtained the name of *Pantelie*, from *Pant*, Britiſh, *a valley.*

The upper part of the pariſh is a ſandy ſoil, which the antient inhabitants conſtantly planted with *Rye*, from a ſuppoſition that it was not capable of producing any other ſort of grain, and ſo called it the *Ryelands*, which name it ſtill retains. The other part is inclined to clay, and has obtained the name of the *Wheatlands*, for a ſimilar reaſon.

The Ryelands have uſually been depaſtured by a ſmall ſpecies of ſheep, with fine wool, and fleſh of a ſweet and delicious flavour, much ſought after by perſons of taſte and fortune. The common weight of a leg of one of thoſe animals, well fatted, is about four pounds.

Theſe lands now produce pretty good crops of wheat, and other grain, but they ſeem to require a better cultivation; for in ſome fine pieces of land I have ſeen as much fern as corn. The farmers plant a few turnips, which they pull for the ſheep and horned cattle. Near to theſe ſandy fields, are beds of clay and marle, but they never uſe either of them for manure. They neither water their meadows, nor drain their wet lands as they ought: In ſhort, nature is bountiful, but judgment and induſtry are wanting.

A ſpring of water, of a brackiſh taſte, and very ſtrong purging quality, riſes out of a ſwampy place by the ſide of the Leden; and flocks of pidgeons reſort thither to eat the ſalt made by evaporation from the water.

As cyder is a principal object with the farmer, the apple-tree is cultivated here, and in the neighbouring pariſhes, with an attention which ſeldom fails of being amply rewarded.

Of the Manor and other Eſtates.

'Ansfrid de Cormeliis holds one hide and a 'half in Pantelie, and one hide in Chilcot, and 'one hide in Chitiford, and one hide in Hege; 'in the whole four hides and a half. Ulfel, and 'Eluuard, and Wiga, held them for four manors. 'One hide and a half is free from tax. There 'are two plow-tillages in demean, and seven 'villeins, and three bordars, with seven plow-'tillages. There are two *servi*, and a mill of '7*s*. 6*d*. It was worth 3*l*. 10*s*. now 4*l*. They 'who held these lands could go where they would.

'Ansfrid had the above written estates, and 'Winestan, and Tantesborne, of Walter de Laci, 'when he married his niece. But he holds his 'other lands of the king.' *Domesday-book*, p. 78.

Walter de Pauntelye died seized of an estate called Pauntelye, leaving Margery, his daughter and heiress, married to John de Solers. Walter de Solers, son of Margery, was seized of Pauntelye 32 H. 3. in which year his mother, then the wife of Richard de Sutton, released to him all her right. Thomas de Solers, son of Walter, was succeeded by his son, John de Solers, who died seized of Paunteleye, which he held of the heir of the countess of Lincoln, as of the honour of Clifford, by the service of one knight's fee 4 E. 2. as appears by the escheator's inquisition of that year. Maud de Solers, daughter and heir of John de Solers-Hope, in Herefordshire, was married to William de Witinton, or de Vyteinton, and brought this estate into his family.

But tho' the above was a large estate, it seems not to have been the manor, for the sheriff returned, that William de Whytington was lord of the vill of Paunteley 9 E. 1. He died 12 E. 1. and another William Witinton, son of William, by the before-mentioned inquisition taken 4 E. 2. was found to be the next heir of John, son of Thomas de Solers, being then twenty-four years old; and in him the manor and estates seem to have been united. Sir William de Whitington, son of William, married Joan, daughter and heiress of Robert Linet. He levied a fine of the manor of Pauntley to the use of himself for life, the remainder to William his son, and Joan the wife of William, and daughter of William Mansel, and their heirs, 4 E. 3. and died seized of Pauntley in the fifth year of that reign. Sir William Whitington, son of sir William, died seized of Pauntley 33 E. 3.

Another William de Whitington, son of sir William, married Catherine, sister and heir of John de Staunton, and died seized of Pauntley 22 R. 2. which he held of Roger de Mortimer earl of March, as of the honour of Clifford-Castle. Robert de Whitington, son and heir of William, was high sheriff of the county 3 & 8 H. 4. Richard de Whitington, younger brother of Robert, was thrice lord mayor of London, and a great benefactor to that city.

Sir Guy de Whitington, son and heir of Robert, married Cicely, sister and heiress of Richard Browning, mesne lord of Notgrove, and lord of Lye and Rodborough. He was high sheriff of Gloucestershire 6 & 12 H. 6. and died seized of the manors of Notgrove, Lye, Rodborough, and Pauntley, 20 H. 6.

Robert Whitington, son of sir Guy, died before his father, 15 H. 6. leaving Robert his son, who was heir to his grandfather sir Guy; but he died under age, in ward to the king, and was succeeded by his brother and heir William Whitington, who married Elizabeth, the aunt and coheiress of sir Edmond Arundel, and died seized of Pauntley 11 E. 4. John Whitington, son and heir of William, married first, the daughter of Richard le Croft; secondly, Elizabeth, daughter and coheiress of Simon Milbourn, and by her had William Whitington, on whom he settled the manor of Notgrove. Thomas Whitington, son and heir of John by his first wife, married Margery, daughter of sir William Needham, and died seized of the manor of Pauntley in the year 1546, 38 H. 8. leaving six daughters his coheiresses; Blanch, married to John St. Aubin; Anne, to Brice Berkeley; Jane, to Roger Bodenham; Margaret, to Thomas Throgmorton; Alice, to —— Nanfan; and Elizabeth, married to sir Giles Pool of Saperton, who, in right of his wife, died seized of this manor in the year 1588. Sir Henry Pool, son of sir Giles, was lord of it in the year 1608, and died in 1616.

The manor came afterwards to Henry Somerset, esq; whose son, Edward-Maria Somerset, was lord of it at the beginning of this century. Henry Scudamore, of Canons-bridge, near Hereford, esq; is the present lord of the manor, by purchase from lady Somerset.

The large manor house at Pauntley-court is taken down, having been long since deserted by its owners.

The house and estate called Holend, formerly belonging to Henry Cruys, and the White House estate, which belonged to the Atwoods, are now the property of Mr. Scudamore.

Of the Church, &c.

The church is a vicarage, in the Forest deanery, worth 13*l*. 6*s*. 8*d*. from the impropriator, beside the privy tithes. The impropriator was patron, but there has been no presentation for many years, and the vicarage is now held by licence from the bishop.

The impropriation belongs to the lord of the manor, who pays 2*s*. 6*d*. out of it to the crown. The rectory and advowson of the vicarage of Pauntley, which formerly belonged to the abbey of Cormeile in Normandy, and afterwards to the college of Fotheringhay, were granted to sir Richard Lee 1 E. 6.

The church is dedicated to St. John the Evangelist, and has a low tower at the west end, with three bells. There was a chantry in this church, dedicated to St. George, of which Hugh Dowslins was the last incumbent, and had a pension of 3*l*. 6*s*. 8*d*. *Willis*.

Proc. & Syn £.0 1 8 Pentecost. £.0 1 4

Mon-

Monuments and Inſcriptions.

There is a braſs plate fixt to the wall of the ſouth chancel, with this inſcription in old characters :

Here lyeth Elizabeth late Wyff of S[r] Gyles Pole, knyght, oon of the Doughters and Sixe Coheires of Thomas Whyttyngton Eſquyer, deceſſyd, whiche Elizabeth paſſyd from this tranſytory Lyff y[e] xviii[th] day of Septēber in the yere of ō Lord God M V[c] xliij. on whoſe ſoule god have Mcy.

On a flat ſtone, within the communion rails,

Hic jacent Exuviæ mortales Philippi Petre, mutui Pœtreorum apud Eaſt-Saxones ornamenti, quorum ex Sanguine deduct. ſimul Fide, brevi quidem conſummatus, Sed longiora Tempora virtutibus Literiſque permenſus, in Affinium ædibus, huic Templo vicinis, præcoci fato conceſſit: Cui nuper Hominibus pergrato, jam Cœlitibus, ut pie ſperamus, accepto, hoc impar illius meritis, et Amori ſuo, monumentum poſuerunt Edoardus & Anna Somerſet, hujus Parochiæ Toparchæ. OB. VI: ID. FeB. A. D. MDCCIV Æt. xxxiv.

R. I. P.

Arms. *Gules, a bend Or between two eſcallops ſable.*

On an old raiſed tomb in the church-yard,

To the Memory of Poole Pauncefoote, of Carſwalls, Eſqr. Juſtice of the Peace of the Quorum, who married Elianor, the Daughter to William Rogers of Dodſwell Gent. by whom he had 1 Son & 3 daughters, William, Elianor, Mary, & Elizabeth; he was born at Newent upon St. Thomas day 1612, & died full of honour, wiſdom, and virtue, 13 April, 1687, leaving to his family the benefit of his providence and good example.

The old man's miſſing, whither is he gone ?
Sure on no law ſuit of his own ;
His leaſe is out, not ſhort'ned by the prayers
Of injur'd neighbours, or expecting heirs.
We wept his loſſe half blind, to whom we owe
The good we ſay, the goodneſs that we ſhow.
Take friendſhip, learning, prudence, piety,
Wealth, beauty, kindneſs, equanimity,
You have a looking glaſs made of his duſt,
And aſhes, for to dreſs the great & juſt.

On another,

Here lyeth in aſſurance of a glorious reſurrection the body of William Pauncefoote, of Carſewells, Eſqr. who lived a true Chriſtian, a good Subject, a loving Huſband, a kind Parent, a faithful friend, & a good example; he was born April 5, 1645, & having the comfortable memory of a well led life, he beheld Death without dread, & the grave without fear, & embrac'd both as neceſſary guides to endleſs glory, March 28, 1691. He left William, Henry, Grimbald, John, Elianor, Elizabeth, & Anne, All of probity, beauty, and hopes.

Dear Children all I pray take ſome
Advices from your Father's tomb :
Still pray to God, & give him praiſe
For all you have; walk in his ways,
Be humble, juſt, to ev'ry one,
Give to the poor, ſave for your own,
And do your beſt one for the other,
Then ev'ry Child's an elder Brother.

Taxes.			£.	s.	d.
	The Royal Aid in	1692,	87	4	0
	Poll-tax —	1694, —	21	3	0
	Land-tax —	1694, —	113	16	0
	The ſame, at 3*s.*	1770, —	85	1	0

At the beginning of this century, there were 30 houſes in this pariſh, and about 115 inhabitants, whereof 6 were freeholders; yearly births 3, burials 3. *Atkyns.* The inhabitants are now reduced to 87.

PEBWORTH

LIES in a fine vale, in the upper diviſion of the hundred of Kiftſgate, ſeven miles diſtant north-eaſt from Eveſham in Worceſterſhire, five northward from Campden, and thirty north-eaſtward from Glouceſter.

Who that *Pebe* was, whoſe name is tranſmitted down to us in that of this village, and what age he lived in, are matters of which hiſtory is totally ſilent, and perhaps it little concerns us to know.

The whole pariſh conſiſts of 2960 acres, pretty equally divided into paſture and arable, and a good part lies in common fields. It is deſtitute of antiquities, and yields nothing remarkable either in the foſſil or vegetable kingdoms. The moſt curious of its natural productions conſiſt of fine graſs and corn, which the rich ſoil produces very plentifully.

It lies on the northern limits of the county, and on the verge of the pariſh, in the hamlet of Ullington, ſtands an elm-tree, where Glouceſterſhire, Worceſterſhire, and Warwickſhire meet in a point. The little brook Nolcham runs from Mickleton, through Pebworth, in its courſe to the Avon. The houſes are built chiefly of wattling, ſome of brick, and fewer of ſtone; but there is not a good houſe in the village, nor any thing elſe, that I could either ſee or hear of, to diſtinguiſh it.

Of the Manors and other Eſtates.

'William Goizenboded holds Pebeworde, in 'Ceolflede hundred, of the king. Vluiet and 'Uluuard held it in the time of king Edward for 'two manors. There are ſix hides, and one yard-'land. In demean is one plow-tillage, and one 'bordar, and one *ſervus*. It was worth 7*l.* now '4*l.* 10*s.*' *Domeſday-book*, p. 74.

'Hugo de Grentemaiſnil holds Pebeworde, in 'Ceolflede hundred. There are two hides, and 'one yard-land. Two thanes held it for two 'manors. There are three plow-tillages, and one 'villein, and one bordar, and ſeven *ſervi.*' p. 77.

The manor of Pebworth was held of Roger de Quincy, earl of Wincheſter, 55 H. 3. It ſometime belonged to the Grevills of Campden. William Grevil was ſeized of Pebworth, and died in 1401. Sir Richard Vernham died ſeized of the manor, and left Elizabeth, his only daughter, married to John Vampage the elder. They joined in levying a fine of the manor to the uſe of themſelves in ſpecial taille, 26 H. 6.

The manor came afterwards to the Forteſcues, heirs of lord chancellor Forteſcue. Hugh Forteſcue, eſq; was lord of it in 1608, as was another Hugh Forteſcue, at the beginning of this century. Matthew lord Forteſcue is the preſent lord of this manor, whoſe pedigree and arms are inſerted under Ebberton.

John Rouſe, ſon and heir of John Rouſe de Rageley, was ſeized of a yearly rent of 100*s.* in Pebworth, 20 R. 2. Chriſtian Rouſe, widow of John, and William Rouſe, ſon of Robert, and grandſon of the ſaid Chriſtian, were ſeized of ſeven yard-lands, and of Marſton-wood in Pebworth, 8 H. 6. Thomas Saunders and Elizabeth his wife, ſiſter and heir of Edward Ipewell, levied a fine of lands in Pebworth and Broad Marſton 15 H. 7.

Another

Another manor in Pebworth belonged to the abbey of Eveſham in Worceſterſhire, and after the diſſolution of that houſe, was granted to Thomas Cromwell, earl of Eſſex, upon whoſe attainder it was again granted to Richard Farmer, 36 H. 8. Thomas Andrews obtained from the crown a reverſionary grant of this manor, after the death of ſir Thomas Andrews, 4 Eliz. It was again granted to John Fernham in the 18th year of the ſame reign. Robert Martyn, eſq; is the preſent lord of this manor, and reſides here.

This eſtate pays an audit to the crown, and acknowledges a dependance on the Dutchy of Lancaſter, and therefore the inhabitants claim to be toll-free throughout the kingdom.

HAMLETS. 1. *Broad Marſton*, about a mile eaſtward from the church. This hamlet lies very flat and low, and is commonly overflowed in the winter, for which reaſon it was called *Mereſtune*, i.e. *Marſh-town*. The prenomen *Broad* is of later date, and was probably given it in contradiſtinction to the adjoining pariſh of *Long Marſton*.

Domeſday mentions this manor, and ſays 'Hugo 'de Grentemaiſnil holds Mereſtune in Ceolflede 'hundred. There are two hides.' p. 77.

Sir Alan Buſhel was lord of this manor, and dying in the year 1245, was buried in Pebworth church. Richard Buſhel, ſon of ſir Alan, married Idonea, daughter of ſir John Cantilupe, of Smithfield in Warwickſhire, and was ſucceeded by Richard his ſon and heir, who married Elianor, daughter and heireſs of Clement Muſard. Roger Buſhel, ſon of Richard, married Eve, daughter of Jeffery d'Abitot, of Redmarley in Worceſterſhire. Richard Buſhel, ſon of Roger, married Emme, daughter of Hugh Ernold, of Glouceſterſhire, and had a ſon Richard, who married Katherine, daughter and coheireſs of ſir William Saltmarſh. Robert Buſhel, ſon of the laſt Richard, married Margaret, daughter of Thomas Hugford, of Edmedſcot in Warwickſhire, and had a ſon Edmond, who married Elizabeth, daughter of Thomas Blount, of Granden. Thomas Buſhel, ſon of Edmond, married Anne, daughter of John Normid, of Broadway, and had a ſon Edward, who married Dorothy, daughter of Thomas Andrews, of Winwick in Northamptonſhire, and died before his father; but left a ſon Thomas, who ſucceeded his grandfather in the manor of Broad Marſton, and married Elizabeth, daughter of Thomas Winter, of Ardington in Warwickſhire. Thomas Buſhel, ſon and heir of the laſt Thomas, married Margaret, ſiſter of Edward Grent, of Milcot in Warwickſhire; and the manor of Broad Marſton continued in his deſcendants, 'till it paſſed to the earl of Saliſbury. James earl of Saliſbury is the preſent lord of this manor.

Lands in Broad Marſton belonged to the abbey of Eveſham, and were granted to William Sheldon and Francis Sheldon 35 H. 8.

2. *Ullington* lies weſtward from the church, and conſiſts of three families. Here was formerly a chapel, the remains of which are ſtill to be ſeen.

3. *Winekton.* 'William Goizenboded holds 'Wenitone in Ceolflede hundred. A thane held 'it in the time of king Edward. There are five 'hides. In demean are two plow-tillages, and 'two villeins; and one *francigena* holds one hide 'and a half, with one plow-tillage. Earl Algar 'joined this manor to Pebeuuorde. It was worth '10*s.* now 40*s.*' *Domeſday-book*, p. 74.

The preſent inhabitants of the pariſh know nothing of the hamlet of Winekton, or Wenitone. Indeed it might not have been within the pariſh, tho' a member of the manor of Pebworth.

Of the Church, &c.

The church is a vicarage, in the deanery of Campden, worth 24*l.* a year. The earl of Saliſbury is patron and impropriator; and Mr. Mould is the preſent incumbent. The impropriation is worth 131*l.* 12*s.* 6*d.* a year, and is ſubject to the annual payment of 14*l.* 16*s.* 8*d.* to the vicar.

Richard, the ſon of Roger de Fredvill gave the church of Pebworth to the Benedictine priory of Alceſter in Warwickſhire, founded by Ralph Butler, in the year 1140, and valued at the diſſolution at 101*l.* 14*s.* He alſo gave a water mill in this place to the Ciſtercian abbey of St. Mary, at Combe in Warwickſhire, which was founded by Richard de Camville, in the year 1150, and valued at the diſſolution at 343*l.* 0*s.* 5*d.* a year. The rectory and church of Pebworth were granted to Lawrence Baſkervill, and William Blake, ſcrivener, 3 Jac.

The church is dedicated to St. Peter, and conſiſts of two ailes, with a tower, and five bells at the weſt end.

Firſt fruits £. 10	12	0	Synodals £. 0	2	0
Tenths — 1	1	1½	Pentecoſtals 0	0	8½
Procurations 0	6	8			

Benefaction.

Lady Finch, a former impropriatrix, gave 24*l.* for the benefit of the poor.

			£.	s.	d.
Taxes.	The Royal Aid in	1692,	374	14	0
	Poll-tax — —	1694,	34	12	0
	Land-tax ——	1694,	163	10	7
	The ſame, at 3*s.*	1770,	132	5	7½

At the beginning of this century, there were 95 houſes in this pariſh, and about 400 inhabitants, whereof 20 were freeholders; yearly births 10, burials 9. *Atkyns.* But ſir Robert Atkyns's numbers were not accurately taken, for in ten years, beginning with 1700, there are entered in the regiſter 133 baptiſms, and 58 burials; and in the ſame number of years, beginning with 1760, the baptiſms were 143, burials 96. The preſent number of families is 104, of inhabitants exactly 436; and the average of annual burials is to the whole number of ſouls, nearly as 1 to 45.4.

St. PHILIP

St. PHILIP's *and* St. JACOB's.

THE diftrict of which I am to give fome account, is only fo much of this parifh as lies in the hundred of King's-barton near Briftol, moft commonly called *Barton Regis*, to diftinguifh it from the hundred of King's-barton, near Gloucefter.

This diftrict is bounded on the eaft by St. George's, lately taken out of this parifh; and on the weft by Laford's gate, and the city of Briftol. It extends about three quarters of a mile eaftward of that gate, a great part of it confifting of feveral ftreets of good houfes, like the city; which were moft of them built in the laft century, occafioned by the refort of confiderable numbers of French and Flemings, who came over to carry on a manufacture of woollen-ftuffs. Not being allowed to fettle within the city, they took up their refidence as near to it as poffible, at a place juft without Laford's gate, where they continued many years; but at length the ftuff trade declining, this part of the parifh is now occupied by tradefmen of every denomination.

Kingfwood foreft antiently extended weftward very near to Laford's gate, and was much larger than the chafe defcribed in the perambulation under the account of the parifh of St. George's. At the diftance of a few yards from this gate, there is now a houfe of public refort, known by the fign of the *Forefter*, or *Green Man*; which, it is faid, was either itfelf a lodge, or ftands on the fcite of the lodge where a keeper refided, who had an adjacent gate of the foreft under his care, and received a penny a piece from travellers paffing through it, at two feafons of the year, to the fairs at Briftol. One of thofe keepers was buried in St. Philip's church; and round the verge of his grave-ftone, placed within the rails which inclofe the communion-table, is this infcription, THOMAS PVTLEY SVMTIMS KEPER OF THE QVEANNE FOREST DEPARTED THE LAST DAY OF OCTOR ANO DOMIN. 1596. And upon the fame ftone, are very rudely fketched the outlines of a bow and arrow, or rather crofs-bow, and of the keeper's faithful dog.

The city of Briftol following the laudable example of the metropolis, pulled down Laford's gate in the year 1767, to give a free current to the air, fo neceffary to health, and to prevent fuch accidents as had frequently happened there by the continual interruption of paffengers, and the unavoidable intermixture of carriages, horfes, and foot travellers, in fo long and narrow an entrance. At that time the curious antient carved figures with which the gate was ornamented, were taken away, and Mr. Reeve placed them at his country-feat a little without the city, at Briflington in Somerfetfhire. They formerly belonged to the caftle of Briftol, as appears by a paffage extracted from the annals of that caftle, lately found among a collection of antient papers, records, and other curious particulars, difcovered in a room belonging to the parifh church of St. Mary Redcliff in Briftol, and fuppofed to have been there depofited by the order of the great Mr. Canning, who was fix times mayor of that city, *viz.* in the years 1372, 1373, 1375, 1381, 1385, and 1389. The paffage alluded to is as follows:

'Allwarde, a Saxon fkyll'd Carveller in Stone 'and Woude. He lyved in the reygne of Eldred: 'He carvelled the worke of ye Caftle & ye Imageries 'whyen they ftoude yn faid Chapel of Alle [and] 'Coernicus, wardens of the Caftle yn daies of 'Yore. Robt of Glowefter removed them to y^e^ 'Walle of the Inwarde Tower, from whence the 'prefent Lorde Warden has tane them: Mafter 'Canynge fayne wowlde have the fame to be in 'his Cabynette, but my Lords entente is to place 'them at ye Gate of ye Caftle or owtfide of y^e^ 'Walls as a goodlie Specktalle for Menne to bee-'houlde and in fothe goodelie Specktalle thei have 'beeing feated & couronued in Roabes of Eftate '& paramented. Ne are enfayrer [inferior] 'Carvel then thofe of our Daies, of durable Stone 'and ye Depicture of the Faces ftill remayneynge 'bie means of theyre beeinge Keepen from the 'Wnwer [weather].'

The above feems not to have been written by Mr. Canning, as it fpeaks of him in the third perfon. I cannot anfwer for its being correctly copied, as I never had accefs to the original, but I give it exactly as I received it from my friend at Briftol. Alle is faid to have been warden of the caftle in the year 915, and Coernicus was his fucceffor.

In this diftrict there are feveral large works carried on by the wealthy citizens, fuch as iron-founderies, glafs-houfes for making crown glafs, and glafs bottles; a work for making of white lead, one for fmelting lead ore, and particularly a very large one at Baptift-mills for tranfmuting of copper into brafs. Formerly brafs kettles and other utenfils have been made there, chiefly, in its firft inftitution, by Germans; but that part of the bufinefs is now performed at the battery mills in the parifhes of Sifton, Bitton, and elfewhere.

The veftiges of an old chapel, dedicated to St. Lawrence, are to be feen adjacent to the high road on Lawrence-hill, and there is a field contiguous to it, with which it had been endowed, and is now exempt from tithes. I have taken notice of this piece of ground, and of the hofpital of St. Lawrence, under St. George's parifh, and am not abfolutely certain to which head thefe particulars belong; but they lay in the out-part of this parifh, before St. George's was taken from it.

The records, alfo, relating to this diftrict, are inferted under the head of St. George's, becaufe both were called the out-parifh of St. Philip's and Jacob's 'till the year 1756, when St. George's was erected into a diftinct parifh, and the records could not be properly feparated.

This diſtrict is very populous; but the account of baptiſms and burials is neceſſarily omitted, as they are intermixt in the regiſter with thoſe belonging to the inner part of the pariſh.

The pariſh church lies within the city of Briſtol, and not in Glouceſterſhire, wherefore an account of it is not to be expected in this work; but an office copy of the endowment of the vicarage falling into my hands, I have ſubjoined it as follows:

Clifford, Fol. 75. } *Donatio Vicariæ Sancti Iacobi Briſtoll.*

TENORE preſentium noverint univerſi quod nos Ricardus, Permiſſione divina, Wygorn. Epiſcopus, ſcrutato Regiſtro bonæ Memoriæ Domini Henrici Wakefield, nuper Wygornien. Epiſcopi, Prædeceſſoris noſtri, Ordinationem Vicariæ Eccleſiæ Sanctorum Philippi & Iacobi Briſtoll. noſtræ Dioces. invenimus in eodem contineri; cujus Ordinationis Tenor ſequitur & eſt talis.

NOVERINT univerſi quod cum nos Henricus, Permiſſione divina, Wigornien. Epiſcopus, Eccleſiam Paroch. Philippi & Iacobi Briſtoll. noſtræ Wigornien. Dioces. Religioſis Viris, dilectis in Chriſto Filijs, Abbati & Conventui Monaſterij beatæ Mariæ de Teukeſbury, & eorum Monaſterio antedict. & ipſorum Prioratui ſancti Iacobi Briſtoll. Dioces. memorate, ex Cauſis veris, ſufficient. & legitimis, de Conſenſu & Aſſenſu dilectorum Filiorum Prioris & Capituli Eccleſiæ noſtræ Wigorn. ac aliorum quorum Conſenſus requiritur in hac Parte, ſervatis omnibus de Jure requiſitis, canonice univerimus, appropriaverimus, ac in ipſorum proprios Uſus conceſſerimus, perpetuo poſidendam, Salva pro Suſtentatione perpetui Vicarij in dicta Eccleſia, unde ſuſtentari valeat, ac Onera ſibi incumbentia ſupportare, de Fructibus et Proventibus dictæ Eccleſiæ congruā Portionē. Nos ſubſequenter ad Ordinationem dictæ Vicariæ, & Aſſignationem Portionum ipſius, de Conſenſu & Voluntate dictorum Abbatis & Conventus de Teukeſbury, necnon Prioris Prioratus ſancti Iacobi ſupradict. expreſs. procedimus in hunc Modum. IN PRIMIS, quod Hugo Hope, Preſbiter, nunc primo preſentatus ad Vicariam illam, habeat unum Manſum competenter pro Statu ſuo edificatum, Sumptibus dictorum Abbatis & Conventus Monaſterij de Teukeſbury et Expenſis, et extunc manutenend. et ſuſtentand. per dictum Hugonem & Succeſſores ſuos de ipſorum Portione. ITEM, quod idem Hugo et Succeſſores ſui Vicarij, qui pro Tempore fuerint et erunt in futurum, percipient & habebunt annuatim de eiſdem Abbate et Conventu, de *Frucibus* et Proventibus ipſius Eccleſiæ Apoſtolorum Philippi et Iacobi, duodecim Marcas Argenti ad duos Anni Terminos, videlicet, Feſta Michaelis & Annunciationis Dominice, per equales Portiones, per Manus Prioris Prioratus ſive Cellæ Sancti Jacobi prædict. fideliter perſolvend. Conceſſerunt etiam dicti Religioſi, quod ad Solutionem dictæ Pecuniæ, *quotiens* ceſſatum fuerit per nos, in ipſius Solutione, & Succeſſores noſtros, noſtroſq; Offic. Sede plena, necnon Cuſtodem Spiritualitatis ſeu Adminiſtrationem Spiritualium, Sede vacante, per Sequeſtrationes Fructuum et Proventuum dictæ Eccleſiæ Philippi et Iacobi, & Subtractionem eorum, compelli valeant; & ad hoc ſe ſubmiſerunt expreſſe. Omnia vero, Decimas, Proventus, et Emolumenta ejuſdem Eccleſiæ, Religioſi Viri Abbas et Conventus antedicti, et eorum Prior Prioratus Sancti Iacobi memorati, integraliter percipient & habebunt; et Obvenientia ad Manus Vicarij ipſius Eccleſiæ, de Proventibus hujuſmodi *qualitercumq.* dictus Vicarius eiſdem Religioſis ſeu Priori prædicto fideliter perſolvet, et liberabit abſq. Diminutione ſeu Retentione aliquali. Et Vicar. dictæ Eccleſiæ eidem in Divinis Officijs deſerviet honeſte, prout decet, necnon Curam & Regimen Animarum Parochianorum ipſius geret, et eidem intendet ut tenetur. Alia vero Onera, tam ordinaria quam extraordinaria, eidem Eccleſiæ incumbentia, dicti Religioſi Viri Abbas et Conventus Teukeſbur. et Prior ipſorum Prioratus Sancti Iacobi prædict. ſubibunt ſuis Sumptibus et Expenſis. Quam quidem Ordinationem, attentis Emolumentis ipſius Eccleſiæ, et ponderatis ponderand. in hac Parte, congruam et ſufficientem atq. juſtam reputantes & conſpicientes, eam habere volumus et decernimus Robur perpetue Firmitatis. IN QUORUM omnium Teſtimonium Sigillum noſtrum fecimus hijs apponi. Dat. in Manerio noſtro de Bredon, decimo Die Menſis Octobr. Anno Domini Millmo CCC^mo nonageſimo quarto, Et noſtræ Conſecrationis Anno nono. Et ſubſequenter inter cætera, in Parliamento excellentiſſimi in Chriſto Principis et Domini noſtri, Domini Henrici, Dei Gratia Regis Angliæ & Franciæ illuſtris, quarto celebrato apud Weſtmon. Anno Regni ſui quarto, Statuta & ſalubriter ordinata, quoddam Statutum inſpeximus in hæc Verba. ITEM ordinez eſt et eſtabliez q' leſtatut de lappropriations des eſgliſes & lenduement des Vicaries en ycelle fait lan quinziſme le Roy Richard Seconde ſoit fermement tenuz & gardez & mis endue execution. Et ſi aſcune eſgliſe ſoit appropriez par la Licence du dit Roy Richard ou de Roy noſtre ſeignour qor eſt puis le dit an quinziſme countre le dit Statut q' ſoit duement reformez ſolonc le fait de dit eſtatut perentre cy & le feſte de Paſq. Prochein avenir. Et ſi tiel reformacion ne ce face depuiz le temps ſuiſdit q' les appropriacions & Licence ent faitz ſoient voidez & detout repellez & annullez per toutz jours forſpris leſgliſe de Hadynham en la Diociſe de Ely. Tenor vero Statuti dicti Regis Ricardi ſecundi, de quo ſupra fit Mentio, ſequitur in hijs Verbis. ITEM purce pluſours Damages & diſeaſes ſont ſouent evenuz & veignent de jour en autre as p'rochiens de diverſez lieux par les Appropriations des benefices des meſmes lieux accordez eſt et aſſentiez que Cheſcune Licence deſore affaire en la Chancellarie daſcune eſgliſe p'rochiel ſoit expreſſement contenuz & compris q' le Dioceſan del lieu en appropriation de tieux eſgliſes ordeignes une covenable Somme dargent deſtre paiez & diſtributz annuelment des fructz & profitz des meſmes les Eſgliſes par ceux qaveront les ditz Eſgliſes en propre oeps & par lour Succeſſours as poures p'rochiens des ditz Eſgliſes en aide de lour vivre & ſuſtenance a touz jours.

NOS igitur, Religioſorum Virorum Abbatis et Conventus ac Prioratus Sancti Iacobi prædictorum indempnitati, proſpicere & Statutum memoratum ut tenemus oportuno Tempore exequi cupientes, aſſignamus, et Tenore preſentium ordinamus, quod Religioſi prædicti, ne Penam ſeu Periculum dicti Statuti incurrant, de Fructibus & Obventionibus Eccleſiæ parochialis prædictæ decreto ſingulis Annis imperpetuum Summam ſex Solidorum & octo Denariorum Argenti, in Feſto Natalis Domini, pauperibus parochianis Eccleſiæ prædictæ in Augmentum Suſtentationis eorundem diſtribuant, ſeu diſtribui faciant & perſolvi; quam quidem Summam, attentis Exilitate dictæ parochialis Eccleſiæ, et alijs nonnullis gravibus Oneribus que eiſdem Religioſis incumbunt, ſic taxamus, ac tanquam competentem & congruam limitamus Teſtimonio præſentium, quas Sigillo noſtro fecimus communiri. Dat. in Palatio noſtro Wigorn. tertio Decimo Die Menſis Aprilis, Anno Domini, Milleſimo quadringenteſimo tertio, Et noſtræ Tranſlationis Anno ſecundo.

Exam[d] by Rich[d] Clarke D. Reg[r].

PINNOCK.

THIS pariſh lies in the lower diviſion of Kiftſgate hundred, at the foot of that range of hills which divides the vale from the Coteſwold, about two miles north-eaſtward from Winchcombe, ten eaſt from Tewkeſbury, and ſeventeen north-eaſt from Glouceſter.

The name is written *Pignocſire* in *Domeſday*. It ſeems to carry in it that of ſome Saxon proprietor, and to ſignify nothing more than *Pignoc's Portion*, or *Eſtate*; from the Saxon word Scipe, a *Portion* or *Diviſion*.

Whether Pinnockſhire enjoyed any particular privileges and immunities, is now difficult to determine. But it is thus taken notice of among the counties of England, in ſome verſes concerning their properties, inſerted in Leland's *Itinerary*, Vol. 5, p. 26.

—— Pynnokſhire is not to prayſe:
A man may go it in to dayes.

Pinnock, Ford, and Hyde, in Guiting-Temple, make one conſtablewick, and ſeem to have conſtituted the diſtrict of Pinnockſhire; but the poet, on the ſuppoſition that he meant to make the perambulation of the circumference two days journey, has greatly magnified its dimenſions, for the ſake of his rhime, ſince it is no more than a man could walk in three hours.

Of the Manor and other Eſtates.

'Alwold holds Pignocſire, in Holeford hundred, 'of the king. He held it in the time of king 'Edward. There are four hides, one of which 'did not pay tax. In demean are four plow-'tillages, and eleven villeins, and five bordars, 'with

'with four plow-tillages. There are eight *servi*, 'and a mill of 30*d*. In Wicelcumbe is one burgage yielding 8 *d*. A wood half a mile long, and 'one furlong broad. It is worth and was worth '4*l*.' *Domesday-book*, p. 79.

The abbey of St. Averel held Pinnockshire 56 H. 3. And the abbey of Hayles was seized of court leet, waifs, and felons goods in Pinnockshire 15 E. 1.

After the dissolution, it is probable that this manor descended like that of Hayles, 'till it was purchased by lord Tracy, whose descendant, Thomas-Charles viscount Tracy, is the present lord of it, and resides at Todington.

Of the Church, &c.

The church is a rectory, in the deanery of Campden, worth about 30*l*. a year. Pinnock, Didbrook, and Hayles, were consolidated into one presentation, in the year 1738. Lord Tracy is patron, and the honourable Dr. John Tracy is the present incumbent.

The advowson formerly belonged to the abbey of Hayles, and was granted to sir Thomas Seymour, Aug. 19, 1 E. 6.

There is no house for the rector, and the church has been demolished many years.

First fruits £. 3	13	4	Proc. & Syn. £. 0	1	0
Tenths — 0	7	4	Pentecostals - 0	0	6½

Taxes.				
The Royal Aid in 1692,	£. 54	0	0
Poll-tax — — 1694, —	3	9	0
Land-tax —— 1694, -	27	12	6
The same, at 3*s*. 1770, —	21	19	3½

At the beginning of this century, according to sir Robert Atkyns, there were 2 houses, and about 24 inhabitants in this parish, whereof 2 were freeholders; yearly births 1, burials 1. There are now 25 inhabitants. The baptisms and burials are intermixed with those of Hayles and Didbrook, without distinction, and are given together under the account of Hayles.

PITCHCOMBE

IS a very small parish, in the hundred of Dudston and King's-barton, two miles south-westward from Painswick, five northward from Stroud, and five south-eastward from Gloucester.

The village is situate in a *combe*, or *valley*, agreeable to the signification of its name, with a pleasant aspect towards the south, and has a small stream running through it from Painswick, which empties itself into the Froome below Stroud. It consists of rich pasture, but is not distinguished by any curious productions of nature or art.

Of the Manor and other Estates.

This place is not mentioned in *Domesday*, wherefore it could not be a distinct manor at the time when that record was compiled; but was probably included in the account of Haresfield and Hascomb.

Osbern Giffard and Alice Mordack held Pitchcombe 31 H. 3.

In the extract out of the pipe office, formerly sent to the sheriffs of the city of Gloucester, for levying certain sums due to the crown, it is said, *De Osberto Gifford de firma de Pinchcomb* 5*s*. and in Mr. Pury's account, drawn up about the year 1653, it is said, *Feoda firma de Pikelescumb concess. Osberto Gifford anno* 15 H. 3. *sub annuali redditu* 5 *s*.

Walter de Bruht released to Gloucester abbey, and to the almoner of Standish, a messuage, lands, and one hundred acres of wood in Pychenecomb, 31 E. 1. and Gilbert de Maysinton gave two messuages and lands in Pynchenecombe to Gloucester abbey, the same year.

The abbey of Gloucester had free warren in all their demean lands in Pychenecombe 28 E. 3. and the manor continued in the abbey 'till the dissolution; but was held from time to time by various persons, either as tenants or trustees for the abbey. Thus we find that Robert de Mandevil died 22 E. 3. and Isabel his widow 30 E. 3. seized of this manor. Joan the widow of William Bokeland held it at the time of her death, 35 E. 3. and Robert de Wolverton died seized thereof, 44 E. 3.

After the general dissolution of religious houses, this manor, a messuage and lands in this parish, and a wood called Pitchcombe-wood, were granted to Richard Andrews and Nicholas Temple, in trust, 35 H. 8. Thomas Porter, knight, died July 2, 40 Eliz. seized of the scite and capital messuage of the manor of Pitchcombe, which (with many other lands) he had settled in jointure on Anne his daughter in law, to be enjoy'd after his decease. This estate was then held of the queen, by the 20th part of a knight's fee, and was of the clear yearly value of 3*l*. 10*s*. 8*d*.

John Throckmorton, esq; was lord of the manor in 1608, as was Thomas Stephens, of Lypiat, esq; at the beginning of the present century, and John Stephens, of Lypiat, esq; is the present lord of it.

Walter de Wilton and Isabel his wife recovered lands against Osbert Giffard 28 E. 1. Walter survived his wife, and died seized of one plow-tillage, and of a yearly rent of 22*s*. issuing out of Pitchencombe, 17 E. 2. Another Walter de Wilton died seized of the same plow-tillage and rent 1 R. 2. Richard More of Picket, and Elizabeth his wife, were seized of seven messuages, 180 acres of land, eight acres of meadow, and ten acres of wood, and of the advowson of the church of Pychencombe, 11 H. 6.

Of the Church, &c.

The church is a rectory, in the deanery of Gloucester, united with Harescombe, and together worth about 60*l*. a year. Mr. Purnel is patron, and Mr. Rice Jones is the present incumbent. The parsonage house is at Harescombe.

Bene-

Benefactions.

Mr. Daniel Cliffold has given 20*s.* yearly to the minifter, and the like fum to the poor.

Taxes.					
The Royal Aid in	1692,	£.	15	16	0
Poll-tax ——	1694,—		4	13	0
Land-tax ——	1694,—		21	12	0
The fame, at 3*s.*	1770,—		16	4	0

At the beginning of this century, according to fir Robert Atkyns, there were 20 houfes in this parifh, and about 80 inhabitants, whereof 6 were freeholders; yearly births 2, burials 2. The prefent number of inhabitants is about 90.

PRESBURY.

THIS parifh lies in the hundred of Derhurft, about two miles northward from Cheltenham, feven fouthward from Tewkefbury, and about eleven north-eaftward from Gloucefter.

Part of it is in the vale, and confifts of rich pafturage, with a fmall proportion of tillage; and part ftretches up the weftern fide of that range of hills which feparates the Vale from the Cotefwold. The river Swilyate rifes out of Prefbury-hill, and paffing by Swindon, Elmftone, and Tredington, empties itfelf into the Upper Avon, a little below Tewkefbury.

This was formerly a market town; for king Henry the Third, at the inftance of Peter, bifhop of Hereford, who was lord of the manor, granted it a charter of a weekly market on Tuefday, and a yearly fair, to begin on the eve of the feaft of St. Peter *ad vincula*, and to continue for three days. And thefe privileges were confirmed in the 14th and 19th years of the reign of king Richard the Second. It may be fuppofed that the market was not very large, but fuch as it was, it muft have fuffered greatly by a conflagration which happened in the reign of king Henry the Seventh, and reduced the town to afhes. Some efforts were made to recover the market in the fucceeding reign, according to Leland, who then vifited this place, and fays, *It is now made a Market Toune againe a 20 Yeres fyns.* How long it continued to be confidered as fuch, does not appear, but I apprehend not a great while afterwards. It was too near to Winchcombe and Cheltenham to flourifh together, and lofing the patronage of the bifhop of Hereford, from whom the manor was taken at the Reformation, the town foon fell into the condition of a country village, and has continued fo ever fince.

A fine, clear fpring of faline purging water rifes at a place called *Hyde*, in this parifh, on an eftate belonging to lord Craven; and about the year 1750, when the Cheltenham Spaw was in the meridian of its reputation, doctor Linden analyzed the Hyde water, and wrote an Experimental Differtation on its nature, contents, and virtues; wherein he compares it with, and gives it the preference to, the Cheltenham waters, 'which 'have undoubtedly' fays he, 'manifefted them- 'felves to be of excellent virtues; but as the Hyde 'Spaw is of the very fame nature, (and perhaps 'the mother-fpring) and contains at leaft four 'grains of falt more in each quart, (which is a 'confiderable increafe) it is but juft to prefer 'them before the Cheltenham waters, &c.' The pamphlet was intended to bring Hyde waters into general ufe; falts were extracted from them, and advertifed to be fold at the Spaw warehoufes, and fhops; and fome conveniencies for bathing were made at the place, and lodgings provided for the reception of patients; but the doctor was miftaken in fome particulars, his treatife was ill written, and failed in the defign.

This place hath had fome fhare in antient military tranfactions. Prefbury fignifies the *Priefts camp*, not that the camp here was made by religious men, but the manor in which it lay took its prefent name from its becoming the property of the church of Hereford. Whether the camp is Saxon or Roman is uncertain.

But to come nearer to our own time. In the laft century, during the great civil war, colonel Maffie, governor of Gloucefter, placed a garrifon of one hundred and fifty foot in a ftrong houfe in this village, to protect the market of that city. It ferved alfo to preferve a communication between the parliament's garrifons at Gloucefter and Warwick, and to check the king's in Sudely-caftle. *Corbet.*

Hewlets is an antient feat, lying one part in this parifh, the other in Cheltenham. It commands an extenfive profpect over the vale towards the river Severn, and is the property of Thomas Baghott, efq; whofe family has refided in this village upwards of four hundred years.

Sebaftian Benefield, Margaret profeffor in Oxford, was a native of this place, and rector of Meyfey Hampton, where he died in the year 1630.

Of the Manors and other Eftates.

Under the title *Terra Eccle de Hereford*, in *Domefday*, it is thus recorded:

'The bifhop of Hereford holds Prefteberie in 'Chilteham hundred. There are thirty hides. 'In demean are three plow-tillages, and eighteen 'villeins, and five bordars, with nine plow-tillages. 'There is a prieft, and one radchenifter with two 'plow-tillages, and one burgage in Wicelcumbe 'paying 18*d.* and eleven [plow-tillages] among 'the *fervi* and *ancillæ*. There are twenty acres 'of meadow, and a wood one mile long, and 'half a mile broad.

'Sevenhantone is a vill adjoining to this manor, '[but] without the hundred. And twenty hides 'out of the thirty abovementioned, are in that 'place; and there are two plow-tillages, and 'twenty-one villeins, with eleven plow-tillages. 'There are three free men having feven plow- 'tillages with their men.

'Durand holds three of thofe twenty hides of 'the bifhop.

'The

'The whole manor, in the time of king Edward, 'was worth 12*l.* now 16*l.*

'Robert bifhop of the fame city [Hereford] 'holds this manor.' *Domefday-book*, p. 70.

Soon after the Norman conqueft, the earls of Gloucefter, by ufurpation, poffeffed themfelves of this manor; but Gilbert de Clare reftored it again to the bifhoprick of Hereford. Peter, bifhop of that fee, purchafed a charter of free warren, court leet, and a yearly fair in Prefbury 25 H. 3. and the claim to thofe privileges was allowed in a writ of *Quo warranto* 15 E. 1. The bifhoprick had a further confirmation of thofe privileges 14 R. 2. and had an additional grant of fairs and markets in the 19th year of the fame reign.

This manor continued in the bifhoprick of Hereford 'till the reformation, after which, fir Thomas Chamberlain, anceftor to the family of that name at Maugerfbury, and eminent for his many embaffies in four fucceeding reigns, obtained a long leafe of this manor, and refided here.

The fcite of the manor, and lands called Middle Breach, were granted to Robert earl of Leicefter, 16 Eliz. The fcite was again granted by the crown to Henry Chilman and Robert Knight, 3 Jac.

Reginald Nicholas, a fervant to fir John Chamberlayne, fon of fir Thomas, purchafed a grant of the reverfion of this manor, and fupplanting his mafter, was lord of it in 1608. Lord Craven is the prefent lord of the manor, and holds a court leet.

The priory of Lanthony had lands in Prefbury, and free warren in them, 15 E. 1. and the tithes were appropriated to that monaftery 21 R. 2. This eftate was reputed a manor, and was granted, with the advowfon of the vicarage, to Thomas Gatwick and Anfelme Lamb 5 Mar. The fame rectory, church, and tithes, then in the tenure of George Badget, *alias* Badger, were granted to Francis Philips and Richard Moor, 6 Jac. William Baghott, efq; was lord of this manor, and proprietor of a good eftate here, at the beginning of this century, which are now the property of Thomas-Baghott De-la-Bere, of Southam, in the parifh of Cleeve, efq.

Robert Prefbury was feized of lands in Prefbury 18 E. 2. Thomas Rawlins and his wife levied a fine of lands in Prefbury, Gineton, Charleton, and Cheltenham 9 H. 7. Lands called le Brook, lately belonging to the priory of Lanthony, were granted to Cicely Pickerel 4 Eliz. Other lands called Haywood's Plots were granted to fir Edward Warner the fame year. Lands in Prefbury, belonging to the bifhop of Hereford, were granted to Chriftopher Hatton 18 Eliz.

Mr. Caple has a good eftate in this parifh, and elfewhere, and a good houfe near the church.

HAMLET. *Overton* is a fmall hamlet, lying a little eaftward of the church, on a rifing ground towards the bottom of the hill. The name is defcriptive of its fituation.

Of the Church, &c.

The church is a vicarage, in the deanery of Winchcombe, worth about 80*l.* a year. Thomas-Baghott De-la-Bere, efq; is patron and impropriator, and the reverend Kinard Baghott is the prefent incumbent.

There are certain lands called the *Barton Demeans*, once the property of the bifhop of Hereford, two thirds of the great tithes of which belong to the dean and chapter of Hereford, the remainder to the impropriator. There are alfo other lands called *Farm Lands*, originally belonging to the priory of Lanthony, of which the impropriator has the tithes. All other tithes of the parifh, great and fmall, are equally divided between the impropriator and the vicar.

Mortuaries are due to the impropriator and vicar, according to the worth of the parifhioners, at the time of their death.

The church, dedicated to St. Mary, has a large aile on the north fide, and a fmaller one on the fouth, with a ftrong embattled tower at the weft end. The windows were formerly ornamented with variety of paintings and infcriptions on the glafs, all which are now defaced except the letters I. W. which ftill remain in feveral places, and are the initial letters of the name of John Wich, prior of Lanthony.

	£.	s.	d.		£.	s.	d.
Firft fruits	11	0	0	Synodals	0	2	0
Tenths —	1	2	0	Pentecoftals	0	0	7½
Procurations	0	6	8				

Monuments and Infcriptions.

In the chancel is the following infcription:

In Memory of
WILLIAM BAGHOTT Efq. and ANN his Wife
daughter of JOHN DELABERE
of Southam Efq;
He } died { Nov. 8, 1725 } Aged { 70 } years.
She } died { Oct. 31, 1739 } Aged { 77 } years.
They had Iffue Seven Sons and Eight Daughters
the Survivors of whom in Gratitude
and Refpect to their Parents
erected this Monument.

Arms, at top, *Per pale baron and femme*, 1. *Ermine, on a bend gules three eagles difplay'd Or*, for Baghott. 2. *Azure, a bend argent, cotoifed Or, between fix martlets of the laft*, for De-la-Bere.

On the left hand of the pulpit,

Near this Place lyeth the Body of Chriftopher Caple, Gent. He died the 15th of May 1740 aged 71. Where alfo lieth Sarah his Wife. She died the 6th of Auguft 1733 aged 68.

Alfo near this place are interred William and Sarah Caple Son and Daughter of the above.

He } died { 12 June 1733 } aged { 34.
She } died { 28 Nov. 1717 } aged { 21.

Arms, *Per pale baron and femme*, 1. *Checky Or and azure, on a fefs gules three lozenges argent*, for Caple. 2. *Checky argent and gules, a lion rampant Or*, for Pocock.

Benefactions.

The church-houfe, worth 40*s.* a year, and a ground called Culver Breach, worth 7*l.* a year, were purchafed with the parifh money for the benefit of the poor.

Taxes.			£.	s.	d.
The Royal Aid in	1692,		178	15	0
Poll-tax ——	1694,	—	42	11	0
Land-tax ——	1694,	—	123	18	0
The fame, at 3*s.*	1770,	—	90	4	0

At the beginning of this century, there were 100 houfes in this parifh, and about 445 inhabitants, whereof 40 were freeholders; yearly births 14, burials 11. *Atkyns.* And the inhabitants are now between 4 and 500.

PRESCOT

IS an extraparochial place, in the upper part of Tewkefbury hundred, fix miles eaftward from Tewkefbury, two weftward from Winchcombe, five north from Cheltenham, and fixteen north-eaftward from Gloucefter.

The little river *Tirle* wafhes the north part of Prefcot, and after dividing Cleeve from Woolfton, falls into the Carrant.

This place was covered with wood in its antient ftate, and belonged to the monks of Tewkefbury, wherefore it was called *Prieft Coed*, and by contraction *Prefcot*, that is, the *Prieft's wood*. In the progrefs of cultivation, thofe woods were affarted, and the greater part of the place now lies in pafture lands.

Of the Manor and other Eftates.

Domefday has not taken notice of it by its prefent name, which very probably it had not obtained when that record was compiled; but the abbey of Tewkefbury had a grant of courts leet, waifs, and felons goods in Prefcot, from king William the Second, which was proved, and allowed, in the proceedings on a writ of *Quo warranto* brought againft the abbat, 15 E. 1.

It was the conftant practice of the monks every where to feparate and diftinguifh their property from that of the laity, and to hold their eftates as unconnectedly as poffible. Hence we fee that where they held lands in fee, they commonly obtained the privileges of courts leet, and free warren; and in many inftances, efpecially where they had no concern in the church affairs of the parifh to which their eftates belonged, they procured a total feparation, and fo their lands became extraparochial, as in the prefent cafe.

This manor continued in the abbey of Tewkefbury 'till the diffolution, when it was granted, together with a wood called Prefcot Coppice, and the tithes, to Walter Compton, 36 H. 8. John Tracy, of Stanway, efq; was proprietor of it at the beginning of this century, and John Tracy, efq; is the prefent lord of the manor.

Taxes.			£.	s.	d.
	The Royal Aid in	1692,	92	12	0
	Poll-tax ——	1694,—	2	12	0
	Land-tax ——	1694,—	47	16	0
	The fame, at 3*s.*	1770,—	35	17	0

At the beginning of this century, according to fir Robert Atkyns, there were 12 houfes, and about 50 inhabitants, whereof 3 were freeholders. There are now 9 houfes, of which only 6 are inhabited; and the people are decreafed to 31.

PRESTON.

THIS parifh lies in the hundred of Crowthorne and Minety, about a mile and a half fouth-eaftward from Cirencefter, fix north-weftward from Cricklade in Wiltfhire, and about nineteen fouth-eaftward from Gloucefter.

Prefton is evidently *Prieft's town*, for the manor antiently belonged to Reinbald the prieft, who was chancellor to king Edward the Confeffor.

The lands are chiefly arable, with fome pafture, and very rich meadows on the fide of the river Churn, which are occafionally covered with water, by means of trenches cut from that river, and drained again at pleafure, whereby vegetation is furprizingly ftrong and early; and thefe works may very well ferve for a pattern to fuch as are unacquainted with this branch of hufbandry. A large meadow, (upwards of a hundred acres) called Kingfmead, lies one part of it in this parifh, the other, and by far the greater, in the parifh of Cirencefter, and is in common to both places after the firft vefture is taken off.

This parifh is bounded to the weftward by the *Irminftreet*, one of the Roman ways paffing thro' Cirencefter; and at the diftance of two miles from the town, but in this parifh, there ftands an antient, rude ftone, about four feet high, lately painted and mark'd as a mile ftone. This is vulgarly called *Hangman's Stone*, becaufe, it is faid, a fellow refting a fheep thereon, (which he had ftolen, and tied its legs together for the convenience of carrying it) was there ftrangled, by the animal's getting its legs round his neck in ftruggling. But this does not account for the ftone's being placed there, and confidering the common propenfity of inventing ftories to obviate names and things not generally underftood, I have fometimes been of opinion that all this is fiction, and that the right name of the ftone is *Hereman-ftone*, fo called, like the Roman way upon which it ftands, from *Hereman*, a *foldier*; and that the ftone is an antient monument for fome military perfon.

Of the Manor and other Eftates.

Under the title *Terra Renbaldi Pr'b'i* in *Domefday-book*, it is thus recorded:

'The fame Rainbald holds Preftetune in Cirecaeftre hundred. Elaf held it in the time of king 'Edward. There are eight hides taxed befide 'the demean. In demean are four plow-tillages, 'and feven villeins, and fix bordars, with fix plow-'tillages. There are nine *fervi*, and twelve acres 'of meadow. It is worth and was worth 8*l.* The 'fame Elaf could go where he would.' *D. B.* p. 73.

'Hunfridus the chamberlain holds one hide in 'Preftitune in Cirecaeftre hundred. Æluuin held 'it for a manor. In demean is one plow-tillage, 'and two *fervi*, and three bordars, with one plow-'tillage. It is and was worth 30*s.* He who held 'it could go where he would.' *Dom. Book*, p. 79.

King

King Henry the Firſt having built the abbey of Cirenceſter, endowed it, among other things, with the eſtates that had before belonged to Reinbald the prieſt, dean of the collegiate church of Cirenceſter; by which means this manor came into the poſſeſſion of the abbey, and ſo continued 'till the diſſolution of religious foundations.

The manor of Preſton, with the advowſon of the vicarage, and the tithes in Northcote, were granted to John Pope 37 H. 8. All which came afterwards to the family of the Maſters of Cirenceſter. William Maſter, eſq; was lord of Preſton in the year 1608, and Thomas Maſter, eſq; deſcended from him, is the preſent lord of the manor.

One meſſuage, and half a yard-land in Preſton and Northcote, belonged to the hoſpital of St. John Baptiſt in Cirenceſter 33 E. 1.

HAMLET. *Northcote* is a hamlet and an antient manor, thus deſcribed in *Domeſday-book:*

'The ſame Rainbald holds one hide in Nortcote 'in Cireceſtre hundred. Godric held it in the 'time of king Edward. In demean is one plow-'tillage, and two villeins, and two bordars, with 'two plow-tillages. There are ſix *ſervi*. It is 'worth 40*s*. This thane could go where he 'would.' *Domeſday-book*, p. 73.

'Hunfridus the chamberlain holds one hide in 'Norcote in Cireceſtre hundred. Eluuard held it 'for a manor. In demean are two plow-tillages, 'and two bordars, with half a plow-tillage. It 'is worth and was worth 40*s*. William held 'theſe two eſtates [Preſtitune and Norcote] of 'Humphry. They who held them could go where 'they pleaſed.' *Domeſday-book*, p. 79.

Gilbert de Clare, earl of Glouceſter and Hertford, had his right to court leet in Northcote, allowed in a writ of *Quo warranto* brought againſt him 15 E. 1.

Anſelm de Gournay held two knights fees in Sodinton and Northcote, value 63*l*. 6*s*. 8*d*. of Gilbert de Clare earl of Glouceſter 8 E. 2. as appears by the eſcheator's inquiſition taken after the death of the ſaid Gilbert.

Hugh le Diſpencer and Elizabeth his wife, the widow of Giles de Badleſmere, were ſeized of Churncote and Northcote 23 E. 3.

John Coaffe, or Cove, who was found by inquiſition to be an ideot 32 E. 3. died ſeized of this manor and Laſſington 36 E. 3.

Thomas Raleigh died ſeized of Northcote 21 R. 2. and was ſucceeded by Thomas his ſon, who died ſeized of it 6 H. 4. Walter Raleigh, ſon and heir of the laſt Thomas, had livery of the manor, and died 8 H. 5. Edward Rawleigh died ſeized thereof 5 H. 8. George Rawleigh, eſq; died 37 H. 8. ſeized of Northcote and of lands in Preſton, leaving Simon his ſon twenty-two years old, and Leonard a brother, who had a ſon Thomas

Henry Willoughby had livery of the manor granted to him 4 Eliz. The eſtate was afterwards divided, and part of it belonged to Thomas Maſter, of Cirenceſter, eſq; about the beginning of this century, whoſe deſcendant, Thomas Maſter, eſq; is the preſent proprietor. The other part was veſted in William George, of Cirenceſter, eſq; whoſe widow, the late Mrs. Rebecca Powell, gave it, with other lands, for the ſupport of the yellow ſchool in Cirenceſter, and it now lets for 152*l*. a year.

Of the Church, &c.

The church is a vicarage, in the deanery of Cirenceſter, worth about 150*l*. a year. Thomas Maſter, eſq; is patron and impropriator; and the reverend Mr. Daubeny is the preſent incumbent.

Seventeen acres of meadow and paſture, and fifty of arable, belonged to the glebe, before the common fields were incloſed by act of parliament about the year 1771, when lands were laid out for the impropriator and vicar, in lieu of tithe.

Two ſmall parcels of land, and a rent charge of 3*s*. are given for the uſe of the communion.

The church is dedicated to All Saints. It is ſmall, with a chapel on the north and another on the ſouth ſide, and a low ſtone tower at the weſt end, in which are four bells.

Firſt fruits	£.9	1	$4\frac{1}{2}$	Synodals £.			
Tenths —	0	19	$8\frac{3}{4}$	Pentecoſt.	0	0	10
Procurations	0	2	0				

Taxes.			£.	s.	d.
The Royal Aid in	1692,	£.	58	18	0
Poll-tax —	1694,	—	8	13	0
Land-tax —	1694,	—	56	6	6
The ſame, at 3*s*.	1770,	—	42	9	9

At the beginning of the preſent century, there were 17 houſes, and about 70 inhabitants in this pariſh, whereof 9 were freeholders; yearly births 2, burials 2. *Atkyns*. The houſes are now increaſed to 35, and the people to 171, by tale.

PRESTON

IS a ſmall pariſh, belonging to the hundred of Dudſton and King's-Barton, but ſeparated from it by the intervention of Botloe hundred. It lies upon the river Leden, at the north-weſtern extremity of the county, towards Herefordſhire, about three miles ſouthward from Ledbury, fourteen weſt from Tewkeſbury, and ſeventeen north-weſt from Glouceſter.

This manor antiently belonged to the monks of St. Peter's at Glouceſter, which accounts for the name.

The Herefordſhire method of planting orchards pervails in this and the neighbouring pariſhes, where they make excellent cyder, already obſerved in the accounts of Dimmock, Kempley, Oxenhall, and Pauntley.

Of the Manor and other Eſtates.

'The ſame church [St. Peter of Gloweceſtre] 'holds Preſtetune in Tolangebriges hundred. 'There are two hides. In demean are two plow-'tillages, and eight villeins, and four bordars, with 'eight

'eight plow-tillages. There are four *ſervi*. It 'was worth 30*s*. now 4*l*. *Domeſday-book*, p. 71.

The abbey of Glouceſter was ſeized of the manor of Preſton, with free warren, 15 E. 1. and continued poſſeſſed of the manor, advowſon, and tithes, 'till the diſſolution, when they were granted to the biſhop of Glouceſter 33 H. 8. and confirmed 6 E. 6. The biſhop of Glouceſter is the preſent lord of the manor.

Of the Church, &c.

The church is a vicarage, in the deanery of the Foreſt, worth about 40*l*. a year. The vicarage houſe and glebe are let for 11*l*. The biſhop of Glouceſter is patron.

The church is ſmall, with a low wooden tower at the weſt end.

Firſt fruits	£. 7	6	8	Proc. & Syn. £. 0	6	6
Tenths	— 0	14	8	Pentecoſtals	0	1	4

Taxes:				
The Royal Aid in 1692,	£. 56	9	4
Poll-tax —— 1694, —	3	0	0
Land-tax — 1694, —	39	7	8
The ſame, at 3*s*. 1770, —	29	10	9

At the beginning of this century, there were 13 houſes in the pariſh, and about 60 inhabitants, whereof 2 were freeholders; yearly births 2, burials 2. *Atkyns*. At preſent there are only 10 houſes, and about 40 inhabitants.

PRESTON *upon* STOUR.

THIS pariſh lies in the upper part of Derhurſt hundred, at the northern extremity of the county towards Warwickſhire, about two miles diſtant ſouthward from Stratford upon Avon, nine north from Campden, and twenty-nine north-eaſtward from Glouceſter. The village is ſituated upon the river Stour, and the manor antiently belonged to the monks of Derhurſt, wherefore it was called Preſton [*i.e. Prieſt-town*] upon Stour, to diſtinguiſh it from two other pariſhes of the name of Preſton in this county.

The pariſh is about two miles long, and one broad. It is divided into two hamlets (Preſton and Alſcot) by the river Stour, which runs thro' it, and falls into the upper Avon about two miles below.

There is a handſome ſeat at Alſcot, which belonged to the late James Weſt, eſq. The houſe is of freeſtone, in the Gothic taſte, and ſtands about half a mile to the left of the road leading from Oxford to Stratford, in the midſt of a park of excellent paſturage. The river Stour meanders before it, through a ſerpentine channel,

—— boaſting as he flows of growing fame,
And wond'rous beauties on his banks diſplay'd —
Of Alſcot's ſwelling lawns, and fretted ſpires,
Of faireſt model, Gothic or Chineſe. [w]

At this place I ſaw a natural curioſity. It was the ſkulls of two ſtags, with their horns ſo entangled by the animals fighting in the park when alive, that they could never diſengage themſelves, and ſo periſhed with hunger. They now remain not to be ſeparated by human force, without cutting or breaking ſome part of them.

Of the Manor and other Eſtates.

'The church of St. Dennis at Paris holds ten 'hides in Preſton in Derheſt hundred.' *D. B.* p. 72.

It appears by the terrier of the lands of the priory of Derhurſt, which was a cell to the abbey of St. Dennis, that the prior had the patronage of the church of Preſton, and two plow-tillages, worth 18*s*. a year, and 4*l*. 13*s*. 6*d*. from his plowmen and rents of aſſize, and 17*s*. from his villeins. At the diſſolution of alien priories, this eſtate was given to the abbey of Tewkeſbury by king Henry the Sixth, and confirmed to that abbey 7 E. 4.

After the diſſolution of the abbey of Tewkeſbury, the manor of Preſton, two mills, a meſſuage called the Miller's-houſe, and the fiſhery, were granted to the viſcount Liſle 37 H. 8. The manor was afterwards purchaſed by —— Hunks, who died ſeized thereof 1 Eliz. when livery was granted to Robert Hunks, his ſon and heir. Thomas Hunckes, ſon of Robert, had livery of the manor, rectory, and advowſon, granted to him in the latter part of the reign of queen Elizabeth. Sir Hugh Brawne was lord of the manor in the year 1608. From him it deſcended to his ſon ſir Richard Brawne, who died ſeized of it in 1650.

Thomas Marriot, eſq; married one of the daughters and coheireſſes of ſir Richard Brawne, and in her right, became lord of the manors of Preſton and Alſcot, which, at his death, deſcended to John Marriot, his ſon and heir, who was lord of them when ſir Robert Atkyns wrote his Hiſtory, about the year 1710. The late James Weſt, of Alſcot, eſq; was lord of this manor at the time of his death, in the year 1772.

William Dalby and his wife levied a fine of lands in Preſton upon Stour and Alſcot 11 H. 7.

HAMLET. *Alſcot* is a hamlet ſeparated from the reſt of the pariſh and county by the river Stour. Here was an antient chapel, now wholly demoliſhed, out of the ruins of which Alſcot houſe is ſaid to have riſen.

William Fravileſworth died ſeized of Little Wormington and Alveſcot 33 E. 3. William Wilicotes held the manor of Alveſcot upon Stour, and had a grant of free warren, 2 H. 4. Sir William Biſhopſhort was ſeized of it in the reign of king Henry the Fifth, and reſided there. It is probable that he left Joan and Margaret his daughters and coheireſſes; for William Wickham and Joan his wife, and ſir William Fennes and Margaret his wife, levied ſeparate fines of the manor of Wilecot, and of lands in Alveſcot, to the uſe of themſelves for life, 31 H. 6.

Thomas Conyers, eſq; levied a fine of the manor of Alveſcot, to William Broom and William Cobcot, 37 H. 6. William Cateſby had livery of this

[w] Jago's *Edgehill*, a Poem.

this manor 9 Eliz. It ſoon after paſſed to ſir Hugh Brawne, and deſcended, like Preſton, to the late James Weſt, eſq; who was lord of the manor at the time of his death, in the year 1772.

Of the Church, &c.

The church is a curacy, in the deanery of Campden, worth about 8 *l.* a year. The lord of the manor is patron and impropriator; Mr. Green is the preſent incumbent. The impropriation pays 8 *l.* a year to Chriſt-church college, Oxford.

The church, dedicated to St. Mary, ſtands on a riſing ground. It is ſmall, but neatly fitted up within. The windows are of painted glaſs, put up, at a great expence, by the late Mr. Weſt; but the ſubjects are uncommon for a church. The eaſt window conſiſts of two compartments. One ſeems to repreſent the univerſal dominion of *Death*, who is the chief figure in front, with *Des Dœts B.* written at his feet; a young man lies proſtrate behind him; and a military perſon appears on the right, juſt falling backwards, and cloſe by him a female figure leaning on the point of a ſword. On the left, another figure of death driving a carriage, as coachman, attended by three women on foot, and the devil appears behind. In the other compartment, the principal figure is a young man, with an olive-branch in his hand, and behind him ſits a young woman aſleep. Two figures, with each a ſtandard, one inſcribed *Ermoet*, the other *Arbeit*, walk before a carriage drawn by unicorns, and a woman ſits on the fore-part of it, holding an olive-branch, whilſt three other female figures attend on foot.

Firſt fruits £	8	13	4	Synodals £.	0	2	0
Tenths —	0	17	4	Pentecoſt.	0	0	7½
Procurations	0	6	8				

Monument and Inſcription.

A ſtone in the chancel bears this inſcription:

Hic jacet Rich. Brawne miles, filius Hugonis Brawne militis, hujus manerij Ds et eccleſiæ patronus. Vixit annos 56. Obijt 30 Sept. 1650.

Taxes.					
The Royal Aid in	1692, £.	87	14	0
Poll-tax ——	1694, —	30	7	0
Land-tax ——	1694, —	96	10	0
The ſame, at 3 *s.*	1770, —	70	7	6

When ſir Robert Atkyns compiled his account of this pariſh, there were 45 houſes, and about 200 inhabitants, whereof 9 were freeholders; yearly births 7, burials 6.

PRINKNASH

IS a ſmall extraparochial place, adjoining to Upton St. Leonard's, in the hundred of Dudſton and King's-barton, diſtant about three miles eaſt from the city of Glouceſter.

The whole eſtate conſiſts of one hundred and ninety acres of meadow and paſture land, and thirty-ſeven of arable. It belonged antiently to the abbats of St. Peter's at Glouceſter, who had a handſome country ſeat, and a park there.

King Edward the Third granted to the abbey of Glouceſter free warren in all their demean lands in this place, in the 28th year of his reign, which privilege was confirmed 1 R. 2. and by the intereſt of the abbat, the place became extraparochial.

This eſtate continued in the abbey of Glouceſter 'till the general diſſolution of monaſteries, and was granted, under limitations, to Edward Bridges and Dorothy Praye, 36 H. 8. and the reverſion of the houſe and park was granted to ſir William Sandys and Thomas Spencer 3 Jac.

The eſtate was ſoon afterwards purchaſed by ſir John Bridgman, chief juſtice of Cheſter, deſcended from an antient family who reſided at Little Dean in this county. John Bridgman, eſq; was lord of the manor of Prinknaſh, when ſir Robert Atkyns compiled his *Antient and preſent State of Glouceſterſhire*, and it deſcended to Henry-Toy Bridgman, eſq; of whom it was purchaſed, about the year 1770, by —— Howell, eſq; the preſent proprietor, who reſides there.

This ſeat has lately been very much improved by the preſent proprietor. It is ſituated on an eminence, from whence there is an agreeable proſpect of the city of Glouceſter, and a more extenſive one of the fine country round about it. There was a room in the houſe conſecrated for a chapel, in the year 1629, and dedicated to St. Peter.

Taxes.					
The Royal Aid in	1692, £.	9	0	0
Poll-tax — —	1694, —	9	5	0
Land-tax ——	1694, -	10	0	0
The ſame, at 3 *s.*	1770, —	7	10	0

****

PUCKLECHURCH.

THIS pariſh lies in the hundred of its own name, ſeven miles weſt from Marſhfield, ſeven eaſt from Briſtol, five ſouth from Chipping-Sodbury, and thirty-four ſouth-weſtward from Glouceſter.

It is about three miles in length, and two in breadth; bounded by Durham on the eaſt, Siſton on the weſt, by Weſterleigh on the north, and by Abſton and Wick on the ſouth. It enjoys a fine healthy air, being pleaſantly ſituated on an eaſy elevation in the vale. The brook *Filtham* divides it from Durham, but the Boyd does not touch on its borders, as ſome topographers have affirmed.

The name of the village was antiently written *Pulcrecerce*, and ſignifies the ſtately and magnificent church, which was given it, moſt probably, from its agreeable ſituation, and the beauty of that building. Camden calls it *Villa Regia*, becauſe it had been the reſidence of ſome of the Saxon kings; and there is a houſe now ſtanding on a rising ground, in the way to Durham, said to be built on the very scite of the palace of Edmund king of the West Saxons, which by the ruins in hillocks still remaining, seems to have been of large extent.

It was customary, in early ages, to celebrate yearly the feast of St. Augustin, who first preached the gospel to the Anglo-Saxons; and as the above king Edmund was solemnizing this feast at his palace here, in the year 946, he took notice of one Leolf, a notorious robber, who, notwithstanding he had been banished for his villainies, had the assurance to seat himself at one of the tables in the hall, where the king was at dinner. This villain attacked Leon, the king's sewer, (who endeavoured to apprehend him) with a naked dagger, which the king seeing, flew upon Leolf himself, and in the scuffle was stabbed in the breast, so that he expired upon the body of his murderer; but the villain made his escape in the confusion, as the guests were drunk when the fray happened. And it is said, the king's remains were deposited in the abbey of Glastonbury.

There was formerly a weekly market held here on Wednesday, now long since disused, and perhaps never much used; but it appears by the antient court papers, that the tenants have been amerced for not coming to the mercat here, for buying and selling elsewhere, for usury, for taking the first tonsure to the prejudice of the lord, for sueing a tenant of the lord's court by the king's writ, for conversing with those who had the leprosy, for marrying without the lord's licence, &c. all which serve to shew the great power which the lords of some manors exercised over their tenants, under the feudal system.

The antient roads from London and Oxford to Bristol passed through this place, and a turnpike-road from Christian Malford in Wiltshire, has lately been carried through it to Mangotsfield near Bristol.

There are also some vestiges remaining of an antient road leading from Bath, the *Aqua Solis* of the Romans, to the *Trajectus* at Oldbury; but it has been long since disused, and stopt up in many places, since that over the hills has been opened.

This parish consists chiefly of pasture ground, but, below the surface, it is full of a very bituminous kind of coal, which all the country abounds with, from Toghill and Lansdown westward, as far as the city of Bristol; and most of the poor inhabitants are employ'd in the coal-mines, and in a small manufacture of felt-hats carried on here, and in some of the neighbouring villages. Here are quarries also of a coarse kind of black marble, used for chimney-pieces and grave-stones; and plenty of marle, which in some places would be highly valued, but the use of it is here intirely neglected. The waters of *Holy-well* and St. *Bridget's-well* in this parish, were formerly in repute for curing sore eyes, and for their virtues in diet-drinks; but they really possess no others than are common to pure spring water in general.

Of the Manor and other Estates.

King Edmund coming to an untimely end at this place, as already related, was buried in the abbey of Glastonbury, wherefore this manor was afterwards bestowed on that house, to sing masses for the repose of his soul; and accordingly in the book of the general survey, I find it thus recorded:

'Saint Mary of Glastingeberie holds Pulcrecerce 'in Pulcrecerce hundred. There are twenty hides. 'In demean are six plow-tillages, and twenty-'three villeins, and eight bordars, with eighteen 'plow-tillages. There are ten *servi*, and six men 'pay ninety bars of iron, and in Gloucester is 'one burgage paying 5*d.* and two free men [*coli-'berti*] paying 34*d.* and there are three foreigners '[*fracig.*] and two mills of 100*d.* [rent]. There 'are sixty acres of meadow, and a wood half a 'mile long, and half a mile broad. It was worth '20*l.* and is now worth 30*l.*' *Dom. Book*, p. 71.

At that time the manor was much more extensive than it is at present, and included Westerleigh, and Abston and Wick. Under the latter of these parishes, it has been shewn, that the monks of Glastonbury quitted their right to this large manor, and to the advowson of the church, to Joceline the bishop of Bath and Wells, 7 Joh. on condition that he would restore to them the election of their own abbat.

A good part of this parish, when it was so extensive, (probably the hamlet of Wick) was within the forest of Kingswood, and the bishop of Bath procured it to be disaforested 12 H. 3. The bishop also purchased a charter of free warren in Pucklechurch, 41 H. 3.

The hundred and manor of Pucklechurch remained annexed to the see of Bath and Wells, 'till king Edward the Sixth, in the second year of his reign, took them, with the manor of Westerleigh, and others, by exchange, and granted the management of the former to sir Nicholas Pointz; but as they produced no profits, the king's commissioners recommended the letting of them on a small annual rent. They were, however, by letters patent, bearing date the 25th of June, in the seventh year of his reign, granted to William earl of Pembroke, to hold to the said earl, his heirs and assigns, of the king *in capite*, with an exception only of the lands called Pucklechurch park; from whom they passed by sale to sir Maurice Dennys, knight; and from him to the family of Codrington, who sold them to another branch of the Dennises. From them Mr. William Hallidaie purchased them, and with his daughter they went in marriage to Edward Hungerford, of Corsham in Wilts, esq. From this family they passed with an heiress, to Robert Sutton, lord Lexington, whose only daughter carried them to John Manners, duke of Rutland; from whom, in 1717, they were transferred by purchase to sir Edward Bouverie, of Longford-castle in Wilts, baronet; and from him, by devise, to his brother Jacob viscount Folkstone, grandfather of the earl

of

of Radnor,* the present possessor of the hundred and manor of Pucklechurch.

William de Cheltenham was seized of lands in Pucclechurch, 16, 33, & 40 E. 3. William Gatelin died seized of lands in Pucclechurch 20 E. 3. Sir John Bar died seized of lands in Pucclechurch 22 E. 4. Richard Forster, and Thomas Moor and his wife levied a fine of lands in Pucclechurch 1 & 6 H. 7. Giles Cotherington died seized of the capital messuage and other lands in Pucclechurch 20 Eliz. of which messuage livery was granted, the same year, to his son Richard; and of the lands to Francis, another of his sons.

A capital house and estate at Pucclechurch, formerly belonging to William Dennis, esq; is now the property of John-Hugh Smyth, esq; (eldest son of sir Jarrit Smyth, bart.) in right of Elizabeth his wife, daughter and sole heiress of Henry Woolnough, esq; who purchased them of Mrs. Mary Butler, eldest daughter and coheir of William Dennis, esq. There is a large scutcheon, in the front of this house, with the following arms carved in stone: *Quarterly of eight.* 1. *Gules, a bend ingrailed azure, between three leopards faces Or, jessant fleurs de lis of the second,* for Dennis. —2. *Or, within a bordure . . . . . . a raven proper,* for Corbet.—3. *Argent, on a chief gules three besants,* for Russel.—4. *Or, five fusils in fess azure,* for Pennington.—5. *Lozengy Or and azure, a chevron gules,* for Gorges.—6. *Argent, on a bend gules three martlets Or, winged vert,* for Danvers.—7. *Two bars, on a chief three stags heads caboshed.*—8. *Ermine, three roses gules,* 2 & 1, for Still.

Of the Church, &c.

The church is a vicarage, in the deanery of Hawkesbury, worth upwards of 200*l.* a year, including the churches of Westerleigh and Abston. Ralph Ergam, bishop of Bath, gave the advowson and impropriation to the chapter of Wells, in the year 1388; and the dean and chapter of that church are patrons and impropriators, and the reverend Walter Swayne is the present incumbent.

Fifty acres belong to the glebe.

The church, dedicated to St. Thomas the martyr, is situate on an eminence, and seen at a great distance, It has an aile on the north side, and a tower at the west end, with pinnacles.

First fruits £.	15	0	0	Synodals £.	0	2	0
Tenths —	1	10	0	Pentecostals	0	1	0
Procurations	0	8	0				

Monuments and Inscriptions.

In a niche on the north side of the aile, is an antient figure of a man, in a recumbent posture; and in another niche, on the south side, is that of a woman; both without inscriptions, but are supposed to represent some of the family of the Dennis's, who have been of long standing, and of whom there have been more high sheriffs in this county than of any other name.

On a large stone, with a brass on it,

Hic jacet Hugo Dennis armig[r] qui obijt 17 Sepr 1559. Et Katharina uxor ejus quæ obijt 15 April, A.D. 1583. Requiemini.

On a monument in the north aile,

In Memoriam Iohanis Dennis Armigeri, primogeniti et heredis Henrici Dennis Armigeri, qui 26 die Junij, Anno Domini 1638, ex hac vita decessit, postquam ex uxore sua Margaretâ, Dni. Georgij Speake, de Whightackington in comitatu Somerset.

* This family (whose name has been variously written, De la Bouverie, Des Bouveries, Des Bouverie, but now established by act of parliament Bouverie) is of antient and honourable extraction in the Low Countries, and quartered, with their own original arms, those of Melun and Wallincourt, more of which may be seen in Collins's Peerage, V. 6, p. 413. Ed. 1768. whence the following short account is extracted.

The first of this name who appears to be settled in England was Lawrence Des Bouveries, a younger son of Le Sieur Des Bouveries, of the Chateau de Bouverie, near Lisle in Flanders. He fled on account of religion to Franckfort on the Maine, where he married his wife Barbara, and coming with her to England, settled at Canterbury. By her he had five sons, Edward, John, Jacob, Valentine, and Samuel; and three daughters, Leah, Elizabeth, and Jane.

Edward Des Bouveries married Mary, daughter of Jasper de Fourneftraux, by Mary Tiberkin, whose father was burnt in Germany for the protestant religion. He had by her one son, Edward Des Bouverie, and three daughters.

This Edward Des Bouverie was born in Nov. 1621, and being an eminent Turkey merchant, acquired a very ample fortune. He was knighted by king James II. and died in 1694. He married Anne, daughter of Jacob Forterye of London, merchant, by whom he had seven sons, and four daughters.

William, the eldest son, was created a baronet Feb. 19, 1713-14. He married first, Mary, daughter of James Edwards, of London, esq; and by her had a son Edward, who died young. His second wife was Anne, daughter and sole heir of David Urry, of London, esq; by whom he had several children, whereof only the following survived him, *viz.* sir Edward, his successor; Jacob, successor to his brother; Christopher, who died unmarried; Jane, wedded to John-Allen Pusey, of Pusey, in Berks, esq; and Anne, who died unmarried.

Sir Edward Des Bouverie, baronet, succeeded his father. He married Mary, daughter of John Smith, of Beaufort-buildings in London, esq; and died without issue.

He was succeeded in dignity and estate by his only surviving brother, sir Jacob Bouverie, baronet, who by letters patent, dated June 29, 1747, was created lord Longford, baron of Longford, in the county of Wilts, and viscount Folkstone, of Folkstone in the county of Kent. His lordship was twice married; first to Mary, daughter and sole heir of Bartholomew Clarke, of Hardingstone, in the county of Northampton, esq; and secondly, to the honourable Elizabeth Marsham, eldest daughter of Robert lord Romney. By the first lady he had several children, who died young, besides two sons, and four daughters, who survived him, *viz.* William, (the late earl of Radnor) the honourable Edward Bouverie, married (1764) to Harriot, only daughter of the late sir Everard Fawkener, kn[t]. Anne, married (1761) to the honourable and reverend George Talbot, third surviving son to William lord Talbot, lord high chancellor of Great Britain; Mary, wedded to Anthony Ashley, earl of Shaftesbury; Charlotte, and Harriot. His lordship, (who by his second lady had two sons, Jacob, who died an infant; and Philip, born Oct. 8, 1746) departed this life Feb. 17, 1761; and was succeeded in honours and estate by his eldest son

William, then viscount Folkstone. His lordship married first, Harriot, only child of sir Mark-Stuart Pleydell, of Coleshill, baronet, by whom he had issue one son named Jacob; secondly, Rebecca, daughter of John Alleyne, of Barbadoes, esq; by whom he had issue four sons, *viz.* William-Henry, Bartholomew, Younge, who died an infant, and Edward; and two daughters, who also died infants. He married thirdly, Anne, relict of Anthony Duncombe, lord Feversham. By letters patent, dated Sept. 25, 1765, his lordship was advanced to the higher dignity of earl of the county of Radnor, with the additional honour of baron Pleydell-Bouverie, of Coleshill in the county of Berks; and dying in the year 1776, was succeeded in honour and estate by his eldest son Jacob, now earl of Radnor.

The arms of this noble earl are, *Quarterly, first* and *fourth, Party per fess Or and argent, an eagle display'd with two heads sable,* being the arms of Bouverie by English grant; *second* and *third, Gules, a bend vaire;* the original arms of Des Bouverie, as certified from the herald's office at Brussels. — The Crest. *On a wreath, a demi-eagle display'd with two heads, sable; beaked and ducally gorged Or, and charged on the breast with a cross croslet argent.*— Supporters. *On each side, an eagle regardant sable; gorged with a ducal coronet Or, and charged on the breast with a cross croslet argent.* —Motto. PATRIA CARA, CARIOR LIBERTAS. Chief Seat. At Longford-castle in Wiltshire, three miles from Salisbury.

Equitis

Equitis Balnei, e filiabus anâ, duos accepit filios, Johannem ſcilicet et Henricum: E quibus Johannes Dennis de Pucklechurch (alias Pulcherchurch) in com. Gloceſtriæ, Arm. duxit Mariam, Nathanielis Still, de Hutton in Comitatu Somerſet Arm. filiarum et coheredum unam; ex quâ tres accepit filios et filiam unam, viz. Henricum, Johannem, Gulielmum, et Margaretam.

Hoc quod eſt pulchri Templum eſt pulchrius.

Arms, at top, *Baron and femme*, 1. *Gules, a bend azure between three leopards faces Or, jeſſent fleurs de lis of the ſecond*, for Dennis. 2. *Ermine, three roſes gules*, for Still. — At bottom, two coats, 1. Dennis, as before, impaling, 2. *Argent, two bars azure, over all an eagle diſplay'd with two heads ſable*, for Speake.

Upon a blue ſtone,

HIC JACET IOHANNES DENNIS DE PVCKLECHVRCH IN COMITATV GLOVCESTRIÆ ARMIGER QVI OBIIT 3 DIE MAIJ ANO DNI 1660 ÆTATIS 44.

Ædibus his ſacris generoſus clauditur hoſpes,
Nominis illius laus, generiſq; decus.
Scilicet aſſiduus cultor poſt fata ſacrato
Qua potuit ſaltem nollet abeſſe loco.
Altera pars templum tenet hoc, pars altera cœlum,
Et ſane hoſpitiis utraq; grata ſuis;
Nam neutra excipitur nimirum gratis honorem,
Hæc addit Templo, reddit at illa Deo.

On a monument againſt the eaſt wall,

M. S.

Gulielmi Dennis, Armigeri, ob Ingenij facilitatem, inconcuſſam Amicitiæ fidem, indeſeſſumq; Charitatis ſtudium Deſideratiſſimi; Qui obiit 28 die Aug. anno Dom. 1701, Ætatis 56, Duas filias reliquens, antiqui generis et nominis ſuperſtites.

Et Mariæ Dennis, ejuſdem Gulielmi Chariſſimæ Genetricis, Nath. Still, de Hutton in Agro Somerſet Armigeri, Filiæ et Cohæredis: Quæ, annis et virtutibus plena, ex hac luce migravit 18° die Aug. A. D. 1698.

Et Johannis Dennis, Filij Gulielmi et Dorotheæ, quem vix ſemeſtrem immatura mors corripuit 30° die Julij, A. D. 1687:

Monumentum Hoc

Dorothea Filia D^i Iohannis Cottoni de Cunnington in Agro Huntington Baronetti, et Dorotheæ unigenitæ & hæredis Edmundi Anderſon de Eyworth in Com. Bedfordiæ Arm. Vidua, Nurus, et Mater mœrens poſuit.

On a flat ſtone in the church, for a perſon famous for curing wounds by ſympathy,

Here lyeth the Body of Charles Ridley of this Pariſh, Gent. who departed this Life the 10th Day of Auguſt, Anno Domini 1690, aged 54 Years.

The flouriſhing Panaces of our Sphere,
That cured others, itſelf lies withered here,
By Blaſt of Death, againſt whoſe force no art
Can either medicine, or help impart.
Reader, tis cuſtom, not neceſſity,
On Marble here preſents itſelf to thee,
For him, whoſe laſting fame will live alone
Beyond the Pow'r of verſe, or ſtrength of ſtone:
Each bleeding wound with crimſon tears will be
The Eternizer of his memory.

On a monument againſt the north wall,

Near this monument lies the body of Thomas Ridley, late of this Pariſh, Gent. ſon of John Ridley, late of Shrivenham in the County of Berks, Gent. who died the 6th Day of June, 1714. Alſo the body of Mary, Daughter of the above named John Ridley, who departed this life the 5th Day of April, 1688. And alſo the body of Sarah Ridley, another of the daughters of the ſaid John Ridley, and ſiſter of the ſaid Thomas Ridley, who departed this life the 14th day of Sept. A. D. 1726.

Reader, this Marble claims, as tribute due
To the dear Memory of ſacred duſt,
A ſigh at leaſt, if not a tear or two:
The Good lie here, the Pious and the Juſt.

Arms, *Argent, a bull paſſant gules, horned and hoofed Or.*

In the body of the church, on braſs,

Johannes Wickham, Gen. cum bene vixiſſet hic latere voluit; ingenio optimo, liberato, animoq; candido, clarus ſeculiq; dignus. Febris in meandris parum vagus devius. In cœlum migrabat, corpus morti triumphatum, animam Deo triumphantem, reddit et victor et victus. Præiit non periit, reſurget, Ætatis ſuæ 48. Abſit gloria niſi in cruce Domini. Obijt 13 Martij 1669.

Benefactions.

Mr. Prig gave 20*l.* to buy communion plate.

Mr. William Hart, clerk, gave 20*s.* yearly for two ſermons.

Henry Berrow, vicar of this church, gave 500*l.* to truſtees for teaching twenty poor children to read and write. With this money the truſtees purchaſed land in the pariſh of Rangeworthy, which lets at 24*l.* a year; a fifth part whereof having been ſettled by the donor, under the ſame truſt, for the better ſupport of the charity ſchool in the pariſh of Abſton and Wick.

Taxes.					
The Royal Aid in	1692, £.	164	4	0
Poll-tax —	1694, —	34	19	0
Land-tax —	1694, —	176	4	9
The ſame, at 3*s.*	1770, —	129	16	$7\frac{1}{2}$

According to ſir Robert Atkyns, when he compiled his account of this pariſh, there were 60 houſes, and about 250 inhabitants, whereof 8 were freeholders; yearly births 9, burials 8. But upon examination of the pariſh regiſter, I find that in a ſeries of ten years, from 1700 to 1709, incluſive, there were 118 baptiſms, and 76 burials. In a like ſeries of ten years, from 1760 to 1769, incluſive, there were 129 baptiſms, and 84 burials. And by a careful reckoning of a gentleman in the pariſh, in the year 1772, there appear'd to be 72 houſes, 92 families, and about 460 inhabitants. The proportion between the annual burials and the inhabitants, is nearly as 1 to 55, which ſhews that the place is remarkably healthy.

QUEDGLEY

IS a ſmall pariſh, in the hundred of Whitſtone, ſeven miles north-weſt from Stroud, ſix north-eaſtward from Newnham, and about three ſouthward from Glouceſter.

It conſiſts principally of rich meadow and paſture land, with orcharding. The turnpike-road from Glouceſter to Briſtol leads through it, and it is bounded on the weſt by the river Severn.

Of the Manor and other Eſtates.

No ſuch name as Quedgley occurs in *Domeſday-book*; it may therefore be ſuppoſed, that it was included in the account of ſome neighbouring and more conſiderable pariſh, at the time when that record was compiled.

Margaret de Bohun gave twenty quarter acres in Quedgley to the priory of Lanthony, and the grant was confirmed 1 Joh. The prior proved his right to court leet and waifs in Quedgley, in the proceedings on a writ of *Quo warranto* brought againſt him 15 E. 1. and he purchaſed a charter of free warren there, in the 21ſt year of the ſame reign. The manor continued in that houſe 'till the diſſolution, after which it was granted to Arthur Porter, 32 H. 8.

Sir William Dodington purchaſed it, and had a grant of common of paſture, and of lands in Quedgley, lately belonging to the priory of Lanthony, 7 Eliz. He was lord of the manor in the year 1608, and built the parſonage houſe. He

was

was fucceeded by William Dodington, efq; his fon and heir, who murdered his mother by running her through the body with his fword; wherefore the manor came to his two nieces, coheireffes, one of whom was married to Thomas Hobbey, efq; the other to lord Brooke, who, in her right, was lord of the manor and patron of the church. The manor belonged to Mrs. Anne Chapman about the beginning of this century; and it came, not long after, to Thomas Whorwood, efq; who was proprietor of it about the year 1738, from whom it was purchafed, and Robert-Gorges-Dobyns Yate, of Bromfborow, efq; is the prefent lord of the manor, and proprietor of a good eftate in the parifh. His arms are given under Bromfborow.

The knights templers were feized of lands in Quedgley 2 E. 3.

John Hanborow, and Thomas Bruges and Maud his wife, levied a fine of the third part of lands in Quedgley, 2 E. 4. and John Garrine and Elizabeth his wife levied a fine of lands in Quedgley the fame year. Another fine of lands in Quedgley was levied by William Bruges and Alice his wife, 21 H. 7. Lands called Rogers, in Quedgley, were granted to John Arnold 33 H. 8.

Netheruge, was a confiderable place in this parifh; for John the prior, and the convent of Lanthony, on the 8th of June, 8 H. 5. granted to James le Walfhe, or Waleys, fon and heir of Giles le Walfhe, their lands in Netheruge in Quedgley, to be held by the fervice of one knight's fee, paying 100*s.* for a relief, and fubject to the yearly payment of one pound of pepper at Michaelmas, and doing fuit twice in the year at the priory court at Lanthony. William le Walfhe, fon and heir of another James le Walfhe, on the eve of St. Matthew, 1511, after having done homage to Edmond Foreft, the prior, and paid 100*s.* for a relief, was admitted a free tenant of the land called Netheruge, by the fervice of one knight's fee.

Of the Church, &c.

The church is a curacy, in the deanery of Gloucefter, worth 60*l.* a year. The duke of Manchefter is patron, and Mr. Palmer is the prefent incumbent.

Earl Milo gave all the tithes of this church to the priory of Lanthony, in the year 1137, and the priory continued poffeffed of them 'till the diffolution. Lord Brooke, anceftor to the prefent patron, created a truft to certain perfons for leafing the great tithes to the curate, and they accordingly granted him a leafe for 70 years. Before this grant, the incumbent had only the privy tithes, and a fmall piece of glebe. The great tithes are fubject to the payment of a fee farm rent of 12*l.* a year to the crown.

The church is dedicated to St. James, and has a handfome fpire on the fouth fide, in which are five bells, and a clock.

Synodals £. 0 2 0 Pentecoftals £. 0 0 7

Monuments and Infcriptions.

Againft the fouth wall of the chancel is a brafs plate, with the following infcription in old characters:

Nere this place lyeth buryed y[e] bodies of Fredefwid Porter & Mary Porter doughters to Arthur Porter Efquyer, and Alys his Wyffe, An° M° U[c] xxxij on whofe foules & all criften Ihu haue mercy amē.——Arms, *the fame as at Hempfted.*

Againft the fouth wall of the north chancel, is an old freeftone monument, with this infcription in capitals:

Here lyethe Rychard Berow efqvyer decefed the 22 of March 1562, Gravnfather to Iamis Berow: and Elizabeth wife of Iamis Berow Efqvyer Nevy to the feid Richard and Davter of Edmond Foxe of Lvdford Efqvyer decefed the 9 of October 1584 by whom Iamis had Yffue Edmond Ihon Ihamis Dorety Mabel Frayncis.

In the fouth aile,

M. S. Richardi Berrow filij Edmondi Berrow Armigeri & Eleonoræ uxoris ejus natu minimi, viri fine fuco pii, fine fraude probi, in omnes candidi facilifq; Qui vitam (immortalē illam) anhelans Anno Iefu fui 1651, Ætatis 35, Conjugij 11, Monumentum hoc dilecta Conjux Angeletta (obfervantiæ et amoris ergo) mœrens pofuit.

Præivit Ricardus fequetur Angeletta.

Refurgemus ambo, et erimus ut Angeli. *Matt.* XXII. 30.

At top, Baron and femme, 1. *Argent, three bears heads couped fable, a chief*————. 2. *Argent, a lion paffant between three crofs croflets fitchy gules.*

In the fame aile, on a marble table,

In Memory of Margaret Relict of Thomas Barrow, of the Hayes in the Parifh of Awre, in the County of Gloucefter, Efquire, Daughter of John Knight, of the City of Briftol, Merchant. She was firft married to John Pope of the fame City, Merchant, and died the 24th of September, in the year of our Lord 1717, aged 72 years.

Near this Place lyeth interred Amie the Wife of Thomas Barrow, of Field Court, Efquire, Daughter of William Hayward, of Woolftrop in this Parifh Efquire. She died the 12th of June, in the year of our Lord 1730, aged 52 years.

Here alfo lyeth the Body of the faid Thomas Barrow, of Field Court, Efq[r] Son of the above-mentioned Thomas and Margaret Barrow. He died the 16th of April, in the year of our Lord 1736, aged 58 years.

Here alfo lyeth the Body of the Rev[d] Thomas Savage, Clerk, eldeft Son and Heir of George Savage, of Broadway, in the County of Worcefter, Efq; who married Elianor, the only Daughter and Heir of the faid Thomas Barrow and Amie his Wife, and died 24th April 1760, aged 60 years.

And alfo Thomas-Barrow Savage, and Martha, two of their Children, who died in their Infancy.

On another monument,

M. S. Gulielmi Heyward, Armig. et Eleanoræ uxoris optimæ, Filiæ Richardi Rogers de Dowdefwell, Gen: Qui animâ, corpore, et pulvere demum conjunctiffimi, virtutum omnium juxta œmuli multis nominibus claruerunt. Fide in Deum firmâ, Studio in liberis educandis prudentiffimo, eximia in rebus gerendis peritia, benignitate in proximos, Remotos, omnes, fœliciffimi uterque; Amicitiæ fanctioris femper tenaciffimi, tam bonos omnes charos habuerunt, quam ipfi omnibus chariffimi; Quod patuit non folum quoad in vivis effent, Sed in Exequiis utriufque celebrandis, Quorum Alteram Ap[l]. 18, An. 1684 Ætat. 33, Alterum Iul. 19, An. 1696, Ætatis 49, vita defunctos,

Innumeri melioris notæ e vicinia
Magno cum planctu nec minori pompa
deduxerunt.
Ex fuperftite Sobole Thoma Elizabetha Anna
Gulielmus primogenitus
M. P.

Arms, at top, *Baron and femme*, 1. *Argent, on a bend fable three fleurs de lis Or; on a chief of the fecond a lion paffant of the third*, for Hayward. 2. Rogers, as under Dowdefwell.

On a flat ftone, within the communion rails,

M. S.
Iohannis Makepeace
Hujus Ecclefiæ per 50 annos paftoris feduli,
Viri vere pacifici,
Simplicitatis innati et antiquæ fidei,

Suis deſiderati,
Vicinis chari,
Bonis omnibus grati:
Qui Anno Dni 1712 Ætatis ſuæ 80°
Febre correptus
Die 5° Septembris Animam Cælo
Et 7° Corpus humo reddidit.

Taxes.						
The Royal Aid in	1692,	£.	74	16	0
Poll-tax	—	1694, —	11	2	0
Land-tax	—	1694, —	104	8	0
The ſame, at 3*s.*	1770,	—	78	6	0

At the beginning of this century, according to ſir Robert Atkyns, there were 34 houſes in the pariſh, and about 170 inhabitants, whereof 5 were freeholders; yearly births 6, burials 5. The preſent number of families is 33, and of inhabitants exactly 166.

QUEINTON.

THIS pariſh lies in the Vale, in the upper part of Kiftſgate hundred, about ſix miles diſtant ſouth from Stratford upon Avon in Warwickſhire, five north from Campden, and twenty eight north-eaſt from Glouceſter.

It is about three miles long, and two broad, conſiſting of good paſture and rich arable land; and the common fields have lately been incloſed by act of parliament.

The etymology of Queinton, as applied to this place, is very doubtful. Sir Robert Atkyns aſſerts, that *this town is ſo called from belonging to a nunnery*; *for* Queen (he ſhould have ſaid Ɖpen) *in the Saxon language ſignifies a woman.* But he has not ſhewn when it was that the manor belonged to a nunnery. If that was ever the caſe, it muſt have been prior to the reign of king Edward the Confeſſor, for then, as well as in the Conqueror's reign, the manor of Quenintune, in Ceolflede hundred, was in lay hands.

Meen-hill ſtands particularly conſpicuous, in the midſt of the vale, one part in this pariſh, the other in Mickleton. Upon the top of this hill is a very large camp, of double intrenchments, ſuppoſed to have been thrown up and occupied by the Weſt Saxons, about the time when the engagement happened between them and the Mercians, at Barrington, near Campden. And the hill itſelf is thought to derive its name from that army, the greater part of which was compoſed of the *Iceni Magni*, a people that inhabited Hampſhire, and were deſcended from the Gauls who dwelt on the river Mayne, and were there called *Ceno Manni*. Theſe people left their name to many places in Hampſhire, as Meanſborow, Meanſtoke, Eaſt-Mean, Weſt-Mean; and ſo in like manner to this hill.

There were two ſtones lately found within the camp, about a foot each in diameter, one convex, the other concave, and a hole through the center of both; whence I conclude they were uſed for grinding corn, and left there perhaps by the army that occupied the camp; but the iron that ſerved to turn the upper ſtone could not be found, as in all probability the ruſt had totally conſumed it in the long ſeries of time of its lying there.

Mr. Drayton has celebrated this hill in his well-known *Poly-Olbion*, where, to check the inſolence and pride of Breedon-hill, he makes the vale addreſs him in the following antiquated alexandrines:

Of all the hills I know, let Mein thy pattern bee,
Who though his ſite bee ſuch as ſeems to equal thee,
And deſtitute of nought that Arden him can yeeld,
Nor of the 'ſpecial grace of many a goodly field;
Nor of deer Clifford's ſeat, (the place of health and ſport)
Which many a time hath been the muſe's quiet port:
Yet brags not he of that, nor of himſelf eſteems
The more for his faire ſite; but richer than he ſeemes,
Clad in a gown of graſſe, ſo ſoft and wondrous warm
As him the ſummer's heat, nor winter's cold can harme.

And the poet does no more than juſtice to this diſtinguiſhed ſpot, which is exceedingly fertile and beautiful. By *Clifford's ſeat*, he meant a handſome ſeat at Clifford Chambers, an adjoining village, then the reſidence of the Rainsfords.

There is no kind of manufacture carried on at Queinton, but the women and children are chiefly employ'd in ſpinning linen-yarn.

Of the Manor and other Eſtates.

The following is a literal tranſlation from *Domeſday-book*, under the title of *the lands of Hugh de Grentemaiſnil*:

'The ſame Hugh holds Quenintune in Ceol-'flede hundred. There are two hides. A thane 'held them. In demean are two plow-tillages, 'and five villeins, and one bordar, with three 'plow-tillages. There are four *ſervi*, and one '*ancilla*. They [*i. e.* Pebeworde, Mereſtune, and 'this Quenintune] were worth 7*l.* now 4*l.*'

'The ſame Hugh holds Quenintune, and Roger 'holds it of him. There are twelve hides. Bald-'win held it in the time of king Edward. In 'demean are three plow-tillages, and ſeventeen 'villeins, and two bordars, with nine plow-tillages. 'There are ſix *ſervi*. It was worth 7*l.* now 6*l.*' *Domeſday-book*, p. 77.

Thus it appears that there were two manors in Queinton at the time of the ſurvey. Robert Marmion attended the duke of Normandy in his conqueſt of England, and was well rewarded by him with the caſtle of Tamworth in Staffordſhire, in which place the nuns of the abbey of Poleſworth had great poſſeſſions. He had alſo the manor of Queinton given to him. This Robert was ſucceeded by Robert his ſon. Another Robert, ſon of the laſt, was the next heir; he was juſtice itinerant in Warwickſhire, and died 2 H. 3. He had two ſons by different wives, both named Robert; the youngeſt ſucceeded him in the manor of Queinton. He married Amice, the daughter of Jernegan Fitz-Hugh, and joined with the rebellious barons againſt king Henry the Third.

This

This Robert Marmion took away the abbey of Polesworth from the nuns of that place, and drove them to Oldbury. But when Marmion was in bed at Tamworth, ſays the legendary ſtory about that matter, Saint Edyth, to whom the abbey was dedicated, appeared to him with her croſier, and told him, that unleſs he reſtored the abbey to the nuns, he ſhould have an evil death, and go to hell; and then ſtriking him on the ſide with the croſier, ſhe vaniſhed. Upon which, under great anxiety, he confeſſed to a prieſt, reſtored the abbey immediately, and was well.

He left iſſue William, who married Lora, the daughter and heir of Roeſe de Dover. John Marmion was ſon and heir of William. He obtained a charter of free warren in Over Queinton and Nether Queinton, 20 E. 1. and died 16 E. 2. but he gave this manor to his ſon John, and his wife Elizabeth, ten years before his death, and ſo, ſays the record, *Nichil tenet in balliva mea. Eſch.* He married Maud, the daughter of the lord Furnival, and left John his ſon and heir, who held Queinton of the earl of Lancaſter by one knight's fee, and died 9 E. 3.

Robert, ſon and heir of the laſt John, died without iſſue, leaving two ſiſters; Joan, married to ſir John Burnack, and Avice, married to ſir John Grey of Rotherfield. Robert ſettled the manor of Queinton on the ſaid ſir John Grey and his wife Avice, and the heirs of their bodies, on condition that their iſſue ſhould take the name of Marmion.

Maud the widow of John Marmion levied a fine of the manor of Queinton to the uſe of herſelf for life, the remainder to John de Grey of Roderfield and Avice his wife in ſpecial taille, the remainder to John de Burnack and Joan his wife in ſpecial taille, 14 E. 3.

Sir John Grey died ſeized of Queinton 33 E. 3. and was ſucceeded by John his ſon, who in obſervance of the marriage ſettlement, aſſumed the name of Marmion. But he dying without iſſue, it went to Robert Marmion his brother; who married Lora, one of the daughters and coheireſſes of Herbert de St. Quintine, and left Elizabeth, an only daughter and heireſs, married to ſir Henry Fitz-Hugh, whom ſhe ſurvived, and died ſeized of the manor of Queinton 6 H. 6.

Sir William Fitz-Hugh, ſon of ſir Henry, and Margaret his wife, levied a fine of the manor of Queinton 8 H. 6. Sir John Burg died ſeized thereof 11 E. 4. and ſome time afterwards the manor was veſted in Magdalen college, Oxford, to which it ſtill belongs.

Of the other eſtates the records ſhew, that Thomas Andrews and Catherine his wife levied a fine of lands in Queinton to Edmond Dalby 1 E. 6.

The editor of the *Magna Britannia* ſays, Here was once a preceptory of the knights templers; but that is a miſtake, which was occaſioned by confounding this pariſh with that of Quenington, near Fairford, where the *knights hoſpitallers* had a preceptory.

HAMLETS. There are ſix hamlets in this pariſh.

1. *Upper Queinton.* There was formerly a conſiderable family in this hamlet, of the name of Rutter, which have ſeverely felt the viciſſitudes of fortune, and are now reduced. Michael Rutter of Queinton paid 300 *l.* compoſition for his eſtate, on account of the part he took with the king in the great civil wars. Some part of this hamlet claims to be toll free, as belonging to the dutchy of Lancaſter.

2. *Lower Queinton,* of which there is nothing further obſervable, except that the church ſtands in this hamlet.

3. *Adminton,* or *Adderminton,* or more antiently *Edelminton.* Among the lands belonging to the abbey of Winchcombe, in *Domeſday-book,* are the following particulars, which ſir Robert Atkyns overlook'd:

'The ſame church [of Wincelcumbe] holds 'Edelmintone in Celflede hundred. There are 'three hides and a half. In demean are two 'plow-tillages, and thirteen villeins, with ſix plow-'tillages. There are four *ſervi,* and two *ancillæ.* 'It was worth 4 *l.* now 3 *l.*' *Domeſday-book,* p. 71.

The abbey purchaſed a charter of free warren in Adelminton 35 H. 3. which privilege was allowed in a writ of *Quo warranto* 15 E. 1. The abbat of Winchcombe aſſigned this manor to the abbey of St. Ebrulf in Normandy 12 E. 2. but it reverted to the monks of Winchcombe, who were the proprietors of this manor 'till their houſe was diſſolved. Tithes in Adelminton, which belonged to that abbey, were granted to ſir Thomas Seimour 1 E. 6. The manor and chapel of Adminton, and lands called Wind-Cerney, &c. formerly belonging to the abbey of Winchcombe, were granted to William Brent, *alias* Burſton, 7 E. 6. Earl Brooke is the preſent lord of this manor, and has a large houſe here.

John Whitchurch granted ten librats of land in Adelminton to the abbey of Eveſham, 6 E. 2.

4. *Radbrook.* John de Hirford died ſeized of Radbrook, and of lands in Over Queinton and Nether Queinton, 15 E. 3. Sir William Clopton died ſeized of Radbrook 7 H. 5. Roger Lingen, eſq; was ſeized of an eſtate in Radbrook, which was ſequeſtered in the great rebellion, and reſtored for a compoſition of 283 *l.* Robert Burton, eſq; whoſe family name was Lingen, is the proprietor of this eſtate, and has a good houſe here. He aſſumed the name of Burton from his mother, who was ſole heireſs of a family of that name in Shropſhire, as appears by a memorial for her in Queinton church. His arms are blazoned under *Monuments and Inſcriptions.*

John Riland, ſon of Richard Riland of Radbrook, was fellow of Magdalen college Oxford, archdeacon of Coventry, and rector of Birmingham in Warwickſhire. He was an orthodox divine, and

and publiſhed ſeveral religious diſcourſes; and was buried in Birmingham church 1672.

5. *Wincot*, ſo called becauſe Wenric was lord of it. Part of this hamlet is in Clifford Chambers, and part in this pariſh. The latter lay in the old hundred of Witelai, now comprized in that of Kiftſgate, as appears by the following extract:

'William the chamberlain holds Wenecote in 'Witelai hundred. Wenric held it in the time 'king Edward. There are three hides. In demean 'are three plow-tillages, and two villeins, and two 'bordars, with one plow-tillage. There are four '*ſervi*. It is worth and was worth 4*l*. This 'manor is taxed.' *Domeſday-book*, p. 74.

Richard Wincote levied a fine of this manor 9 H. 7. George Throgmorton died ſeized of it 6 E. 6. and Robert his ſon had livery thereof the following year. Livery of one part of Wincot, but of which it is not ſaid in the record, was granted to William Barnes 9 Eliz. This manor and eſtate belonged afterwards to Mr. Robert Loggin, late chancellor of the dioceſe of Sarum; but they are now, by purchaſe, the property of Robert Burton, eſq; of Radbrook, abovementioned. There is only one houſe in this hamlet, which, as well as the land, is in two pariſhes; one part in Clifford, the other in Queinton.

6. *Mæon*, or *Meen*, whoſe etymology is given in the former part of this pariſh. This was antiently a member of the manor of Longborough, as appears by the *Domeſday* account of that manor. King John granted this manor to William de Gamaſh. John de Pembroke held two parts of the manor of Meen, and Walter de Pedwardine held the third part, and their claim was allow'd in a *Quo warranto* 15 E. 1. This manor afterwards came to the Grevills. William Grevill of Campden was ſeized thereof, as a member of the manor of Milecot in Warwickſhire, 3 H. 4. John Grevill died ſeized thereof 1 E. 6. and livery was granted to Edward Grevill, ſon of John, 2 E. 6. Lewis Grevill, of Weſton upon Avon and Milcot, had livery of this manor granted to him 1 Eliz. It is now the eſtate of Mr. Noel.

Of the Church, &c.

The church is a vicarage, in the deanery of Campden, worth about 90*l*. a year, before the pariſh was incloſed by parliamentary authority in 1772; but it is conſiderably improved by incloſing. Robert Marmion gave the advowſon of the church of Queinton to the nuns of Poleſworth 4 Steph. to whom the tithes were appropriated 12 R. 2. At the diſſolution of religious foundations, the rectory and advowſon of the vicarage of Queinton, late belonging to the nunnery of Poleſworth, were granted to the dean and chapter of Worceſter 33 H. 8. and were again confirmed to the church of Worceſter 6 Jac. The dean and chapter of Worceſter are patrons, and Mr. Taylor is the preſent incumbent.

Ninety-eight acres of arable land, and five of meadow, belonged to the glebe before the incloſing; but the vicar hath other lands ſet out by the commiſſioners in lieu of tithe; and he receives beſides, from the impropriator, four quarters of wheat, four of barley, and 45*l*. in money.

The church is large, with an aile on each ſide of the nave, and a handſome ſpire at the weſt end, with ſix bells; and according to biſhop Benſon's book, it is dedicated to Saint Swithin. There is a gallery at the weſt end of the church.

Firſt fruits £.	18	13	0	Synodals £.	0	2	0
Tenths —	1	17	4	Pentecoſt.	0	1	1½
Procurations	0	6	8				

Monuments and Inſcriptions.

On a very handſome tomb of grey marble, inlaid with braſs, and now in a perfect ſtate, is engraven the figure of a woman, with a label round her head, and on it in old characters:

Complaceat tibi dne ut eripias me. Dne ad adiuuandũ me reſpice.

On the dexter ſide at top, *Argent, two bars gules, fretty Or*, for Clopton. On the ſiniſter ſide, *Gules, a feſs argent between ſix pears Or*. Dexter at bottom, the firſt mentioned coat impaling the ſecond. Siniſter, as the firſt coat with the addition of a canton.

✠ Chriſte nepos Annæ Clopton miſerere Iohẽ
Quæ tibi ſacrata clauditur hic vidua
Milite defuncto ſponſo pro te Ihu fuit iſta
Larga libens miſeris prodiga et hoſpitibus
Sic ven'abilibus templis ſic fudit egenis
Mitteret ut celis quas ſequeretur opes
Pro tantis meritis ſibi dones regna beata
Nec premat urna rogi: ſed beat aula dei.

At the foot is this memorandum: T. Lingen Ar. reparavit Anno 1739.

In the church is the following memorial,

Sacred
To the Happy Memory of
ANN the Loving and Beloved Wife of
Thomas Lingen of Radbrook
In this Pariſh Eſq^r^.
Only Daughter
And at Length Sole Heir of
Robert Burton of Longner Hall
In the County of Salop Eſq^r^.
A Family of great Antiquity;
Being Poſſeſſors of Longner
In the Time of Edward ye IV.
And before that ſeated at Burton
In the ſaid County.
She was a Perſon truly excelling
In every Relation of Life
A Dutiful Daughter; a Tender Mother;
An Affectionate Wife;
She had Iſſue twelve Children, of whom
Robert, Thomas, Henry;
Ann, Eliz^th^. Frances, Blanch, and Rachel,
Survive her;
And doe with her Diſconſolate Huſband
Bemoan their Irreparable Loſs.
She died May 23^d^ 1737
In the 35th Year of her Age.

Arms, *Baron and femme*; on the dexter ſide, *Quarterly* 1ſt and 4th, *Barry of ſix Or and azure, over all on a bend gules three roſes* . . . . for Lingen. 2. *Argent, two bars gules, fretty Or*, for Clopton. 3. *Gules, a bend ermine*. On the ſiniſter ſide, *Quarterly azure and purpure, over all a croſs engrailed Or between four roſes* . . . . for Burton.

There is a memorial for Thomas Lingen, eſq; who died in 1742, and for ſeveral of the chidren of Thomas and Anne Lingen.

On

On a ſmall marble monument in the chancel,

To the pious Memory of the Rev. Robert Loggin Chancellor of Sarum, and Vicar of Adderbury, who departed this Life Nov. 22, 1728, in the 66th Year of his Age. M[rs] Joyce Loggin cauſed this Stone to be erected.

In the chancel,

In Memory of the worthy, pious, and benevolent Mr. Michael Corbett, of Upper Queinton, who departed this Life March the 27th, 1763, Aged 70 Years. Who did, by his Will and Teſtament, give to three Truſtees the Sum of 100*l.* to be by them laid out in Land, or ſet out on good Security, and the Rents, Intereſt, and Profits thereof to be by the Truſtees diſtributed amongſt the Poor of Upper and Lower Queinton, yearly and every Year for ever.

Sir Thomas Overbury, of Bourton on the Hill, was buried in this church in 1680. And there is a raiſed tomb in the church, with the figure of a man in armour, for Thomas le Rous, who was buried here in 1499. He was a deſcendant of the le Rouſes, an eminent family, who reſided at Ragley in Warwickſhire.

Benefactions.

There is a donation to the church of 3 *l.* a year in land; but the donor is careleſſly forgotten.

Mrs. Davis gave 100*l.* to the poor. And Mr. Michael Corbet gave 100*l.* to the ſame uſe, in 1763.

Queinton.

Taxes.					
The Royal Aid in	1692,	£. 478	6	8
Poll-tax ——	1694, —	35	9	8
Land-tax ——	1694, —	346	7	0
The ſame, at 3*s.*	1770, —	190	13	9

Adminton.

Taxes.				
The Royal Aid in	1692,	£. 120	14	0
Poll-tax ——	1694, —	10	8	8
Land-tax —	1694, —	96	7	0
The ſame, at 3*s.*	1770, —	72	5	3

There were 120 houſes, and about 500 inhabitants in this pariſh, whereof 32 were freeholders; yearly births 15, burials 13. *Atkyns.* But having examined the regiſter, I find, that in ten years, beginning with 1700, there were 129 baptiſms, and 98 burials; and in the ſame number of years, beginning with 1760, the baptiſms were 221, the burials 103; and the inhabitants are now about 547.

The vicinity of Lark Stoke to this pariſh occaſioned ſir Robert Atkyns to ſubjoin an account of it to Queinton; and as it eſcaped my notice 'till it was too late to inſert it under the proper letter, I muſt place it here in like manner.

LARK STOKE.

THIS place is a hamlet in the pariſh of Ilmington, or Illmingdon, in Warwickſhire, but the hamlet itſelf lies in Glouceſterſhire.

It is mentioned as a diſtinct manor in the antient ſurvey, of which the following is a tranſlation:

'The ſame church [St. Mary of Eveſham] holds 'Stoch in Widelei hundred. There are two hides, 'and one plow-tillage in demean, and ſeven 'villeins, and two bordars, with two plow-tillages. 'There is one *ſervus.* It is and was worth 40*s.*' *Domeſday-book*, p. 72

The manor antiently belonged to the family of the Biſhopſtones. John de Biſhopſdon died ſeized of Lark Stoke, with free warren therein, 13 E. 2. Sir William Biſhopſtone levied a fine of this manor to the uſe of divers perſons for life, the remainder to himſelf, and the heirs of his body by Philippa his wife, 11 H. 7. John de Vall was ſeized of lands in Larkſtoke and Queinton 36 E. 3.

This eſtate was afterwards in the poſſeſſion of the Brents, who were ſeized of it when ſir Robert Atkyns compiled his account of Glouceſterſhire, in which he has fallen into ſeveral miſtakes concerning it, and has placed the abſtract from *Domeſday* under Stoke Archer, in the pariſh of Cleeve.

Lark Stoke has been lately purchaſed by John Hart, eſq; who is the preſent lord of the manor, and proprietor of a good eſtate there.

Taxes.				
The Royal Aid in	1692,	£. 63	18	0
Poll-tax ——	1694, —	10	1	4
Land-tax ——	1694, —	111	12	0
The ſame, at 3*s.*	1770, —	56	16	0½

QUENINGTON.

THIS pariſh lies in the hundred of Britwell's-barrow, about two miles northward from Fairford, five north-weſtward from Leachlade, eight north-eaſtward from Cirenceſter, and twenty-ſix, through the laſt mentioned town, from Glouceſter.

The greater part of the pariſh conſiſts of arable land, but there is a conſiderable proportion of good meadow and paſture on the banks of the Coln, which bounds it on the eaſt and ſouth-eaſt ſides next to Hatherop and Fairford.

Quenington ſeems to be nothing more than a different manner of writing *Coln-ing-ton*, or *Conington*, for the letter *l* is dropt in pronunciation. It is deſcriptive of the ſituation of the village, and ſignifies the *town upon the river Coln.*

The knights hoſpitallers of St. John of Jeruſalem had a preceptory here, ſurrounded with a moat, now in a good meaſure filled up; but part of the antient building, with a croſs at the top of it, and an old gateway on the eaſt ſide, which belonged to it, are yet remaining, and conſtitute the *Court*, or manor houſe, occupied by the tenant of the principal farm.

The church and the principal houſes are ſituated on the bourn, where is a mill for making of writing paper, which furniſhes employment for a few hands; but the bulk of the people are engaged in huſbandry buſineſs.

Of the Manor and other Eſtates.

'Roger de Laci holds Quenintone in Brictwoldeſberg hundred. There are eight hides. 'Three free men, Dodo, and another Dodo, and 'Aluuold held it for three manors, and could go 'where they pleaſed, and paid tax. There are 'three

'three plow-tillages in demean, and twenty villeins, 'and ſeven bordars, and a prieſt, and a bailiff. 'They have among them all twelve plow-tillages; 'and two radchenifters, with one plow-tillage. 'There are twelve *ſervi*, and two mills of 20*s*. '[rent,] and ten acres of meadow. There is a 'burgage in Glouceſter which pays four ſhoes, '[*ſoccos*,] and a ſmith [*faber*] paying 2*s*. It was 'worth 8*l*. now 10*l*.' *Domeſday-book*, p. 75.

Walter de Laci came into England with William the Firſt, and by him was rewarded with this and many other manors in Glouceſterſhire. His ſon Roger de Laci ſucceeding him, was lord of this manor, and of nineteen others in Glouceſterſhire, when *Domeſday* was compiled.

Agnes Laci, William de Poictou, and the counteſs Cecilia, founded a preceptory for the knights-hoſpitallers in this place, and endowed it with their lands here. And Mabilia, the wife of William de Mara, and Robert de Mara,[y] gave them their demeans in Camſden, belonging to Quenington. And William de Lega[y] alſo gave many lands and tenements belonging to Quenington, to the knights of the ſame preceptory.

The prior of the hoſpital of St. John of Jeruſalem, reſiding in England, was ſeized of the manor of Quenington 9 E. 1. as appears by the ſheriff's liſt of all the vills in the county, with their reſpective lords, returned into the exchequer in that year.

The preceptory at Quenington, lately belonging to the knights hoſpitallers of St. John at Jeruſalem, was granted to ſir Anthony Kingſton, 37 H. 8.

William Kingſton, eſq; was lord of the manor in the year 1608, from whom it paſſed, thro' ſeveral hands, 'till it came into the poſſeſſion of Henry Powle, eſq; whoſe only daughter and heireſs Catherine, carried it by marriage to Henry Ireton, eſq; who, in her right, was lord of the manor when ſir Robert Atkyns compiled his account of it. Brooke Forreſter, eſq; was afterwards lord of it, from whom it paſſed to Humphry-Mackworth Praed, eſq; who ſold it to Samuel Blackwell, of Williamſtrip, eſq; the preſent lord of the manor.

Court-farm belonged to the preceptory of St. John at Jeruſalem, and is therefore tithe free. It is now the property of the lord of the manor.

Of the Church, &c.

The church is a rectory, in the deanery of Fairford, worth about 140*l*. a year. Samuel Blackwell, eſq; is patron, and the reverend Mr. Rice is the preſent incumbent. The rector pays 13*s*. 4*d*. a year to the patron.

Walter de Lacy, (or according to ſome, Hugh de Lacy) gave the church of Quenington, a yard land, and the tithes of the vill, to the abbey of St. Peter at Glouceſter, and the grant was confirmed by king Stephen, at the requeſt of Walter de Lacy, abbat of Glouceſter, in the year 1138.

Ninety-two acres of arable, and twenty-ſix acres of paſture, belong to the glebe.

The church is an antient, low building. It had formerly a ſpire between the nave and chancel, as appears by a part ſtill remaining. There is a rude carving in ſtone, over the north door, of Chriſt treading the devil under his feet, with the figures of three perſons in a praying poſture. Over the ſouth door is the repreſentation of God the father, God the ſon, and the beaſts mentioned in the Revelations, executed in the ſame groſs, unworthy manner.

	£	s	d		£	s	d
Firſt fruits	7	18	2	Synodals	0	2	0
Tenths —	0	15	10	Pentecoſt.	0	1	6
Procurations	0	6	8				

Monuments and Inſcriptions.

Upon flat ſtones, within the communion rails, are the following memorials:

Here lyeth ye body of ye R[t] Honble Henry Powle Eſq Maſter of ye Rolls: one of the Iudges delegates of ye Admiralty and of his Majeſties moſt Honble privey Councell who departed this life the 21 of november 1692, Ætatis 63.

Regi & regno fideliſſimus,
Æqui rectiq; arbiter integerrimus,
Pius, probus, temperans, prudens,
Virtutum omnium
Exemplar magnum.

Arms, at top, *Azure, a feſs ermine between three lions rampant Or, a creſcent for difference*, for Powle.

Here lieth Elizabeth the wife of Henry Powle Eſq[r]: and Davghter of Richard Lord Newport of high Ercall who departed this life 28 Ivly 1672.

Cui pudor et conjugij Fides,
Mores, ingenium, veraq; pietas;
Qvando ullam invenient parem?

At top, *Baron and femme*, 1. Powle. 2. *A chevron between three leopards heads caboſhed.*

Here lies HENRY IRETON, of Williamſtripp in y[e] County of Gloſter, Eſq. only Son of HENRY IRETON, of Adderborough in y[e] County of Nottingham, Eſq.

Who by the Great Probity & Equality of his Mind, together wth y[e] Love of his Country, w[ch] he Shewed in y[e] Various Turns of our Affairs, had Rendered himſelf not only a worthy Example of All the Virtues of a Private Life, but had Gained ſuch an Intereſt in his Country as to be Choſen a Member of ſeveral Parliaments. And ſo Conſiderable a Share in y[e] Favor of his Prince, as to be L[t]. Colonel of y[e] Dragoon Guards, Firſt Equerry & Gentleman of y[e] Horſe to K. W[m]. y[e] 3[d].

Having Long Acquired an Unuſual Command of his Appetites & Paſſions, from y[e] Natural Force of his Reaſon, & y[e] Motives of y[e] Chriſtian Religion; He departed This Life y[e] 14[th] of Dec. 1711, in y[e] 60[th] Year of his Age, w[th]out Reluctance or Grief, but for Leaving a Moſt Tender & Diſconſolate Wife, who Thus Tranſmits ſo Exemplary a Character to the World.

She was the only Daughter and Heireſs of the R[t]. Hon[ble] HENRY POWLE, Eſq. Maſter of the Rolls, Speaker of the Houſe of Commons, &c.

At top, *Baron and femme*, 1. *Ermine, a bend voided gules*, for Ireton. On an eſcutcheon of pretence the arms of Powle. 2. Powle, as before.

Here Lies
M[rs]. CATHARINE IRETON
Sole Daughter & Heireſs
of y[e] R[t]. Hon[ble] HENRY POWLE, Eſq[r] Maſter of y[e] Rolls, &c.
And Relict
of HENRY IRETON, of Williamſtrip in y[e] County of Glouc[tr] Eſq.
She was
Good Natured w[th]out weakneſs,
Chearful w[th]out Levity,
And Pious w[th]out Oſtentation;
A moſt Faithful & tender Wife,
A kind Relation & Friend,
An Affable & Courteous Neighbour,
A Bounteful Miſtreſs,
And a Liberal Benefactor to y[e] Poor,
Eſpecially at Her Death;
Leaving ten pounds yearly to the uſe of y[e] Poor
of this Pariſh;
And y[e] like yearly Sum to y[e] uſe of y[e] Poor
of COLN St. ALDWINS.
She departed this Life
Oct. 25: 1714.

Taxes.

[y] Dugdale's Monaſticon.

Taxes.					
The Royal Aid in	1692,	£. 65	12	0
Poll-tax ——	1694, —	11	2	0
Land-tax ——	1694, —	65	12	0
The ſame, at 3*s.*	1770, —	49	9	0

There were 30 houſes in this pariſh, and about 120 inhabitants, whereof 18 were freeholders; yearly births 4, burials 4. *Atkyns.* The preſent number of families is 54, of inhabitants exactly 267.

RANDWICK

IS a ſmall pariſh, in the hundred of Whitſton, about three miles diſtant north-weſtward from Stroud, three ſouth-weſtward from Painſwick, and about eight ſouthward from Glouceſter.

Randwick, from the Saxon ꞃenꝺan, to *divide*, and ƿic, a *ſtreet*, *hamlet*, or *ſmall village*, ſignifies a *hamlet ſeparated from the mother pariſh*. And the ſilence of the antient ſurvey concerning this place, is a ſufficient indication that it was formerly included in the account of ſome neighbouring manor, and I think none ſo likely as Standiſh, whoſe church is even at this time the mother church to Randwick.

The village lies on the ſouth-eaſt acclivity of a hill, that riſes with a pretty ſteep aſcent above the church, to a moderate height. The hill is lined with freeſtone, and ſeveral ſprings iſſue from the ſides of it. The ſituation, for air, water, and expoſure, is extremely advantageous and pleaſant.

Randwick-aſh, on the ridge or ſummit of the hill, is a noted land-mark, from which there is an extenſive proſpect to the ſouth-weſt, of the lower part of the vale of Glouceſterſhire, and the river Severn, with part of the Briſtol-channel and Somerſetſhire; and a view, directly weſt, of the foreſt of Dean, and of the Welch mountains in the back ground. To the eaſt is ſeen the country called the *Bottoms*, that is, the narrow vallies of Painſwick, Stroud, Woodcheſter, or Nailſworth; and the towns of Stroud and Painſwick, with the neighbouring hills.

At this place an annual revel is kept on the Monday after Low Sunday, probably the wake of the church, attended with much irregularity and intemperance, and many ridiculous circumſtances in the choice of a *Mayor*, who is yearly elected on that day, from amongſt the meaneſt of the people. They plead the preſcriptive right of antient cuſtom for the licence of the day, and the authority of the magiſtrate is not able to ſuppreſs it.

The whole pariſh is not eſtimated at more than 500*l. per ann.* but is very populous, chiefly inhabited by poor people employ'd in the woollen manufacture, and the rates for the relief of the poor have amounted, of late years, to 80*l. communibus annis.*

Of the Manor and other Eſtates.

Little can be ſaid of a place of which ſcarce any thing is recorded; but it appears that William ap Adam died ſeized of Randwick 18 H. 6. Thomas Whiſton and Anne his wife levied a fine of the manor to Thomas Mills 4 Mariæ. And Mr. Mitchel was the proprietor of it at the beginning of this century.

Of the Church, &c.

The church is a perpetual curacy, in the deanery of Glouceſter, to which the vicar of Standiſh preſents, and pays the curate 8*l.* 8*s.* a year. The living has been augmented by the queen's bounty, in the year 1719, and by another benefaction of 200*l.* in the year 1733.

The church is dedicated to St. John. It was very ſmall, but a new aile was added to it about fifty years ago, and the profits of the ſeat-places were intended, by the contributors to the building, to be applied to the ſupport of an afternoon lecturer on Sundays; which, with the augmentation, a ſubſcription for the lecture, an allowance from the vicar of Standiſh in lieu of ſmall tithes, and the ſurplice-fees, make up 60*l.* a year, or upwards.

John Cook, Thomas Framilode, and John Cugley, lords of one moiety of the manor of Randwick, by their deed dated 37 H. 6. granted to Thomas Hort, Thomas Holder, and fourteen other perſons, a piece of ground, ſixty-five feet in length, and thirty-five in breadth, in truſt for them, to build a houſe to the honour of God, the bleſſed Virgin Mother, and All Saints, in the church of Randwick. How it was endowed I cannot find. There remains now only a decay'd old houſe, called the *Church-houſe*, inhabited by poor people.

The tithes and ſome glebe land belonged to the abbey of Glouceſter, and were granted to the biſhoprick of Glouceſter 33 H. 8. and confirmed 6 E. 6.

The pariſh pays 3*s.* 4*d.* a year to be exempt from contributing to the repair of the mother church of Standiſh, which pariſh pays 10*d.* a year to be exempt from relieving the poor of Randwick.

Pentecoſtals - - - 8½*d.*

Benefactions.

Here is a charity ſchool, in which forty children of the pooreſt of the inhabitants are taught to read, and have bibles when they quit the ſchool. It has been well inſpected and conducted, and is of great uſe in this poor place, where numbers of children would otherwiſe be deprived of all inſtruction. It is endowed with lands worth 11*l.* a year, and a houſe has been built for the maſter; but the ſchool has been chiefly ſupported by ſmall donations and legacies, and for many years by the benefactions of the truly honourable lady Betty Germaine, and for ſome years paſt by the generoſity of John Elliot, eſq; late of London, now of Binfield, Berks, and of Bridgend in the pariſh of Stonehouſe, in this county.

Mr. Chandler left 150*l.* to purchaſe land, the produce of which is given one third to the miniſter, and the reſt to the poor. A paſture ground in

Hayward's

Hayward's field in Stonehouſe, is charged with the payment of 30*s.* yearly to the miniſter, and 30*s.* to the poor; and another eſtate in the ſame pariſh is charged with the payment of 2*s.* 6*d.* yearly to the miniſter, and the like ſum to the poor.

Taxes.			£.	s.	d.
	The Royal Aid in	1692,	43	10	8
	Poll-tax — —	1694, —	0	18	0
	Land-tax ——	1694, —	70	13	3
	The ſame, at 3*s.*	1770, —	53	4	7½

At the beginning of this century, there were 80 houſes, and about 400 inhabitants in this pariſh, whereof 10 were freeholders; yearly births 15, burials 16. *Atkyns.* The average of baptiſms, for five years preceding 1767, was 30, of which 9 belonged to neighbouring pariſhes; of burials 14, of which 3 were not inhabitants of this pariſh. For ſome time ſubſequent to 1766, the proportion of the burials to the baptiſms has been greater, from the ſmall pox being epidemical, and other cauſes; but in 1776 the births were 37, the burials 18. And according to an exact account taken a few years ſince, there were 140 houſes, and 650 inhabitants. From theſe particulars it appears to be a healthy and prolific place, ſtill increaſing in population.

RANGEWORTHY

IS a ſmall pariſh, in the hundred of Thornbury, about five miles ſouth-eaſt from the town of that name, three ſouth-weſt from Wickwar, and about twenty-five ſouthward from Glouceſter.

The name of this pariſh took its origin from circumſtances ſimilar to thoſe of Randwick, and was moſt probably derived from the Saxon ꞃenðan, to *divide*, and peoꞃðiȝ, a *habitation*, or *village*; and was ſo called becauſe it was ſeparated from ſome larger place, of which it had been antiently a member. *Domeſday* taking no notice of it, ſhews that it was not a diſtinct manor when that record was compiled, but was probably taken out of Thornbury, tho' it has ſince acquired manerial rights, and is now become a diſtinct pariſh.

Rangeworthy is reputed to be within the juriſdiction of the honour of Glouceſter. It conſiſts almoſt wholly of paſture land, with a pretty large common of a ſtrong ſoil, overgrown with fern, where a coal-pit has lately been opened. This part of the vale is ſuſceptible of very conſiderable improvement.

Of the Manor and other Eſtates.

This manor was held of Hugh de Audley, earl of Glouceſter, and Margaret his wife, 21 E. 3. John Talbot, viſcount Liſle, in right of Margaret his mother, deſcended from Warine Gerard lord Liſle, was ſeized of this manor; and Joan, his widow, one of the daughters and coheireſſes of Thomas Chedder, of Chedder in Somerſetſhire, held it in dower, and died ſeized thereof 7 E. 4. Elizabeth Courteney, counteſs of Devonſhire, died ſeized of Raingworthy, Nethercot, and Kingſton Liſle, 11 H. 8. Sir Arthur Plantagenet and Elizabeth his wife, heireſs to the counteſs of Devonſhire, had livery of the above mentioned manors the ſame year.

The manor of Rangeworthy was veſted in Robert Hale, eſq; in the year 1608, and Matthew Hale, eſq; was the proprietor of it at the beginning of this century. John de la Field Phelps, eſq; was lord of the manor at the time of his death, in the year 1771. His ſon and heir, John de la Field Phelps, is a minor. The arms of Phelps are, *Argent, a lion rampant ſable between ſix croſſes croſlets fitchy gules.*

Sir Thomas Brook died ſeized of lands in Raingworth 5 H. 5. and Joan his widow held them in dower, and died ſeized of one meſſuage, one plow-tillage, ten acres of meadow, and twenty acres of wood in Raingworthy, 15 H. 6.

Of the Church, &c.

The church is a curacy, in the deanery of Hawkeſbury, worth about 16*l.* a year; and in the gift of the vicar of Thornbury. Chriſt Church college in Oxford has the impropriation.

The church is a ſmall building, dedicated to the holy Trinity, and has a low tower at the weſt end.

Pentecoſtals - - - - 6*d.*

Benefactions.

The curate receives 6*s.* 8*d.* for a ſermon on Trinity Monday; and an eſtate worth 27*l.* a year has been given by an unknown benefactor, the rent of which is received by the overſeer of Rangeworthy, who pays 7*l.* to the curate, and the remainder is appropriated to the uſe of the poor. A cottage, worth about 18*s.* a year, has been given half to the curate, and the other half to the poor.

Land-tax at 3*s.* 1770, £. 29 10 3

When ſir Robert Atkyns compiled his account of this place, there were 30 houſes, and about 150 inhabitants, whereof 6 were freeholders; yearly births 7, burials 7. The people are now decreaſed to 120.

RENDCOMBE.

THIS pariſh lies in the hundred of Rapſgate, ſix miles northward from Cirenceſter, ſix ſouth-weſtward from Northleach, and about fourteen ſouth-eaſtward from Glouceſter.

It conſiſts chiefly of arable land, with ſome woodland and paſturage. The river Churn runs through it, and abounds with ſmall trout and minnows.

Rendcombe, more antiently *Rindecome*, is a peculiar ſituation. It is moated almoſt round by nature, with a very narrow *combe*, or valley, agreeable

agreeable to the signification of the name; for Ryng, in the Saxon language, is a *circle*. Within this ring or circle, which does not encompass the whole, but only a large portion of the parish, the ground lies high and lofty, and at the south-west extremity stands the village of Rendcombe.

Here sir William Guise has a noble seat, with a park, sheltered on the north and east quarters by a fine grove of lofty trees, and open for prospect to the south and west; where the river Churn glides along reluctantly, at the foot of a fine slope, not two hundred yards from the house. It is only of late that this antient family has resided here; and there cannot be a more healthy situation, with an open country round about, for the rational and gentleman-like exercises of riding and hunting. They formerly resided at Elmore and Brockworth, in the vale part of the county.

Of the Manor and other Estates.

There were two distinct manors in Rendcombe, as appears by the antient survey.

'Gislebert the son of Turold holds Rindecome 'in Respiget hundred. There are five hides taxed. 'Aluric held it. In demean is one plow-tillage, 'and three villeins, and seven bordars, with three 'plow-tillages. There are seven *servi*, and one 'foreigner [*francigena*] holds the land of two 'villeins, and a mill of 8*s*. and four acres of 'meadow. It was worth 7*l*. now 100*s*.

'The same Gislebert holds Rindecumbe in 'Respiget hundred, and Walter [holds it] of him. 'There are three hides taxed. In demean are 'two plow-tillages, and four villeins, and three 'bordars, with two plow-tillages. There are six '*servi*, and a mill of 5*s*. and three acres of meadow. 'It is worth and was worth 6*l*.' *Dom. Book*, p. 76.

This Gislebert, the son of Turold, taking part with Robert Curthoise, against king William the Second, in their contest for the crown, his estates in England were seized, and this manor, with the honour of Gloucester, and many other great estates belonging to the crown, were granted to Robert Fitz-Haman, or Hayman, of whom, and of many others herein after-mentioned, I have treated more largely in the accounts of the *Honour*, and of the *Earls of Gloucester*, p. 91, *& seq.*

Mabel, or Sibil, eldest daughter of Robert Fitz-Haman, carried this manor, by her marriage, to Robert Melhent, or Fitz-Roy, natural son of king Henry the First, who was created earl of Gloucester by his father, and dying in the year 1147, left William, his eldest son and heir. William had a daughter Amice, married to Richard de Clare, earl of Hertford, who, in her right, died seized of this manor 8 Joh.

Gilbert de Clare, son of Richard and Amice, was the first earl of Gloucester and Hertford jointly, and died at Penros in Brittany, seized of the manor of Rendcombe, 14 H. 3. Richard de Clare, eldest son and heir of Gilbert, succeeded to this manor, and died 46 H. 3. Gilbert de Clare was son and heir of Richard. His right to court leet in Rendcombe and Rendcombe Over, was allowed in the proceedings on a writ of *Quo warranto*, brought against him 15 E. 1. and he died in the 24th year of the same reign, leaving this manor in jointure to Joan de Acres, his second wife, daughter to king Edward the first, who died seized of it in 1307, the 35th and last year of her father's reign. Gilbert de Clare, son of Gilbert and Joan his wife, was the next possessor. He was slain at the battle of Bannocksburne, in Scotland, 7 E. 2. having no issue, and was found by the escheator's inquisition taken the next year, to have been seized of the manor of Ryndecombe, which he held of John de la Mare by the service of 2*s*. a year; of the advowson of the church, worth 100*s*. of 100 acres of arable land, worth 12*s*. 6*d*. *per ann.* of four acres and a half of meadow, worth 18*d*. *per* acre; of pasture worth 2*s*. and his free tenants paid him 41*s*. 10*d*.

Upon the partition of his estates between his three sisters and coheiresses, this manor fell to Margaret, then the wife of Piers Gaveston, but married afterwards to Hugh de Audley, who was created earl of Gloucester, and died 21 E. 3. Margaret, his only daughter and heiress, was married to Ralph lord Stafford, who, in her right, died seized of this manor 46 E. 3. and was succeeded by his son, Hugh earl of Stafford, who died at Rhodes 9 R. 2. in his return from a pilgrimage to Jerusalem, as appears by the escheator's inquisition taken the following year. Thomas earl of Stafford, son of Hugh, married Anne, daughter of Thomas of Woodstock, duke of Gloucester, by Eleanor his wife, eldest daughter and coheiress of Humphry de Bohun, earl of Hereford; but died before the marriage was consummated, 16 R. 2. seized of the manors of Rendcombe, North Cerney, and Thornbury, and was succeeded by his brother William, who died unmarried 18 R. 2. Edmond earl of Stafford was heir to his two brothers, Thomas, and William, and by special licence from the king, married Anne, widow of the former, with whom he had the manor of Wheatenhurst, *alias* Whitminster. He was killed at the battle of Shrewsbury, July 12, 1403, 4 H. 4. Humphry earl of Stafford, son and heir of Edmond, married Anne, daughter of Ralph Nevil, earl of Westmoreland, and was created duke of Buckingham 23 H. 6. He was slain at the battle of Northampton, in the 38th year of the same reign, at which time he was seized of the manors of Eastington, North Cerney, Rendcombe, Wheatenhurst, and Thornbury. He was attainted by parliament, after his death, whereby Rendcombe came to the crown, when it had continued near 400 years in the same family, from the grant of king William the Second to Robert Fitz-Haman, down to the death of Humphry duke of Buckingham.

King Edward the Fourth, after the duke of Buckingham's attainder, granted this manor to Richard Nevil, the great earl of Warwick, commonly called the *Make King*, who fell a victim to his

his own ambitious deſigns, for he was ſlain at the battle of Barnet, April 14, 1471, in attempting to depoſe king Edward the Fourth, whom he had before advanced to the throne, and was attainted in his turn; ſo that this manor came again to the crown.

John Tame, a wealthy merchant, obtained a grant of it, and purchaſed the manor of Fairford of king Henry the Seventh. He was ſucceeded by his ſon ſir Edmond Tame, whoſe ſon Edmond dying without iſſue 36 H. 8. his eſtates came to his three ſiſters, of whom Margaret, the eldeſt, was married to ſir Humphry Stafford, and they had livery of this manor the ſame year. See other particulars under Fairford.

The manor of Rendcombe, formerly the duke of Buckingham's, was granted to Henry lord Stafford, and to the lady Urſula his wife, 2 Mar. and Edward lord Stafford had livery thereof 13 Eliz.

From the Staffords this manor paſſed by purchaſe to ſir Richard Berkeley, whoſe widow, Elianor, was ſeized of it in the year 1608, and dying in 1629, it deſcended to ſir Maurice Berkeley, ſon and heir of ſir Richard. His eſtate was ſequeſtered by the parliament in the great civil wars, for which he paid 1372*l.* compoſition. Sir Chriſtopher Gyſe ſoon afterwards purchaſed Rendcombe from the Berkeley family, and ſir William Guiſe,[z] baronet, is the preſent lord of this manor. His arms are, *Gules, ſeven lozenges vair*, 3, 3, 1; *on a canton Or, a mullet pierced ſable.*

Robert de Mara purchaſed lands in Rendcombe of Jordan his brother 1 Joh. Lands in Rendcombe and Calmſden belonged to the abbey of Tewkeſbury, and were granted to Thomas Stroud, Walter Earl, and James Paget 36 H. 8.

Thomas Rich died ſeized of Green's and Upner's farms in Rendcombe, and was ſucceeded by William his ſon, who likewiſe died ſeized of them 15 Car. leaving Thomas his ſon ſeven years old.

Mariſden, in this pariſh, has been eſteemed a diſtinct manor, and is ſo called in the records. The manor of Mariſden, in Rendcombe, belonged to the Ciſtercian abbey of Bruern in Oxfordſhire, and was granted to ſir John Berkeley 28 H. 8. who dying ſeized thereof 37 H. 8. Richard Berkeley, his ſon, had livery of it 6 E. 6. It now belongs to ſir William Guiſe.

Eycot, (from the Britiſh *Y coed*, the *wood*) is a conſiderable eſtate in this pariſh; but it was formerly a member of the manor of Bibury, as appears by the following tranſlation from *Domeſday:*

'The church of St. Mary of Worceſter holds 'Aicote in Reſpigete hundred, and Ailric holds it 'of her. It lies in Begeberie. There is one hide. 'In demean are two plow-tillages, and two villeins; 'and four bordars, with two plow-tillages. There 'are two *ſervi*, and eight acres of meadow, and 'a mill of 64*d.* It was worth 20*s.* now 30*s.* 'Ordric holds it of the biſhop.' *Dom. Book*, p. 70.

Thomas de Berton died ſeized of the manor of Eycot, held of the manor of Bibury 49 E. 3. John Penger died ſeized thereof 7 H. 4. Catherine War 6 H. 6. granted the manor of Eycot, lying in Rendcombe, North Cerney, and Woodmancot in North Cerney, to Richard Beauchamp, earl of Warwick, and others; and they, two years afterwards, granted the ſame to the abbey of Winchcombe. Sir William Guiſe is the preſent proprietor of this eſtate.

Of the Church, &c.

The church is a rectory, in the deanery of Cirenceſter, worth about 130*l.* a year; Mr. Warner is patron, and the reverend Mr. Shellard is the preſent incumbent.

The lords of the manor were patrons of the church until the attainder of Humphry duke of Buckingham, after which the advowſon was granted to ſir Richard Cornwall, and his heirs males, 1 H. 7.

The church, dedicated to St. Peter, is a handſome ſtructure, conſiſting of the nave, and an aile on the ſouth ſide, with two chancels, and has a ſquare tower at the weſt end. Whether it was

[z] This antient family has been poſſeſſed of eſtates in Glouceſterſhire ever ſince about the year 1262, when Nicholas de Gyſe, ſon of Robert, of the family of Gyſe of Aſple-Gyſe, or Gowiz, in Bedfordſhire, married a near relation of John de Burgh, ſon of Hubert de Burgh, earl of Kent, and with her had the manor of Elmore in this county, by the gift of her relation John de Burgh, out of reſpect to whom, Nicholas aſſumed the arms of de Burgh, which have ever ſince been born by this family.

Sir Aunſelme de Gyſe, ſon of Nicholas, died 23 E. 1. John de Gyſe, was ſon and heir of ſir Aunſelme, and had a ſon John de Gyſe, who was living 32 E. 3. Sir Anſelme Gyſe, ſon of the laſt John, died 13 H. 4. and Reginald Gyſe, his ſon, died 8 H. 5.

John Gyſe, ſon of Reginald, married the daughter and heir of —— Wiſtam, and reſided at Aſple-Gyſe in Bedfordſhire, which place took the latter part of its name from his family. Sir John Gyſe, of Aſple-Gyſe, ſon of John, married Agnes, or Alice, daughter of —— Berkeley, and dying in the year 1479, was ſucceeded by John Gyſe, of Elmore, eſq; who had a grant of the manor of Brockworth in this county from king Henry the Eighth, 32 *regni*, in exchange for the manors of Widdington in Oxfordſhire, and Aſple-Gyſe in Bedfordſhire. He married the daughter of lord Grey of Wilton, and dying 4 Mariæ, left Anſelme his eldeſt ſon and heir forty-ſix years old; which Anſelme dying without iſſue 5 Eliz. was ſucceeded by his brother William Gyſe, who married Mary, the daughter of William Ratſey of Colmore. John Gyſe, ſon and heir of William, married Jane, daughter of Richard Pauncefoot of Hasfield, and was ſucceeded by his ſon ſir William Gyſe, who married to his firſt wife, Margaret, daughter of Chriſtopher Kenn, of Somerſetſhire, and after ſerving the office of high ſheriff of Glouceſterſhire, in the year 1608, died in 1642. William Gyſe, eldeſt ſon of ſir William by Margaret his firſt wife, married Cicely, daughter of John Dennis of Pucklechurch. He reſided at Brockworth, and was high ſheriff of Glouceſterſhire in the year 1647, and dying in 1653, was buried at Elmore.

Sir Chriſtopher Gyſe, ſon and heir of William, purchaſed the manor of Rendcombe of the Berkeley family, and was created a baronet by king Charles the Second, in the year 1661. He married Elizabeth, daughter of ſir Lawrence Waſhington, of Gaiſden in Wiltſhire, and dying in 1670, was buried at Brockworth. Sir John Guiſe, ſon of ſir Chriſtopher, married Elizabeth, daughter of John How, of Compton, eſq; and ſerved in ſeveral parliaments as knight of the ſhire for this county. Sir John Guiſe, ſon and heir of ſir John, married firſt, —— daughter of ſir Nathaniel Napper of Dorſetſhire, by whom he had one ſon, John; ſecondly, Anne, one of the daughters and coheirs of ſir Francis Ruſſel, of Strenſham in Worceſterſhire, baronet, but by her had no iſſue. He repreſented the county of Glouceſter in ſeveral parliaments, and died about the year 1732. Sir John Guiſe, only ſon of ſir John, married Jane, the daughter of —— Saunders, of Mungwell in the county of Oxford, eſq; by whom he had iſſue two ſons and two daughters. Sir William Guiſe, ſecond and only ſurviving ſon of ſir John, is the preſent lord of the manors of Brockworth, Elmore, and Rendcombe, and one of the preſent repreſentatives of this county in parliament.

built by fir Giles, or by fir Edmond Tame, is not agreed, but all accounts allow that it was built by one of that family; and E. T. the initials of the latter perfon's name are in the window of the fouth chancel. There is a crucifix ftill remaining intire on the eaft wall of the chancel, having remarkably efcaped the obfervation of the parliament's party in the great civil wars, who deftroy'd every thing they found of that kind.

Firft fruits £.	13	6	8	Synodals £.			
Tenths —	1	6	8	Pentecoft.	0	0	8
Procurations	0	6	8				

Monuments and Infcriptions.

At the eaft end of the fouth chancel, which belongs to the lord of the manor, is a large pyramid of black and white marble, intended as a monument for the late fir John Guife and his lady, but the infcription is not yet engraved.

Clofe to the above, round the verge of a tomb, it is thus to be read, in capital letters relieved on the marble,

Here lyeth Elenor Iermye firft married to Robert Roe, efq; & fecondly to S[r] Ry: Berkeley Knt. Dyed: 17: March: 1629.

There is a fcutcheon at the head of the tomb, bearing, [*Argent*] *a lion rampant* [*gules*] *a crefcent for difference*, fuppofed for Jermye. At the other end, Baron and femme, 1. *Checky, a fefs ermine.* 2. *A maunch.* In the front are two large fcutcheons; one fhews the marriage of Roe with Jermye, *viz.* Baron and femme, 1. . . . . . *a chevron between three trefoils* . . . . . . for Roe. 2. Quarterly 1ft and 4th, Jermye. 2d and 3d, [*Argent*] *a bend between fix martlets* [*fable*] fuppofed for Tempeft. The fecond fcutcheon denotes the fecond marriage, *viz.* Baron and femme, 1. [*Gules*] *a chevron ermine between ten croffes paty* [*argent*] for Berkeley, with quarterings. 2. Jermye, with quarterings as before.

Againft the eaft wall of the rector's chancel, are two handfome monuments, with the following infcriptions:

In Memory of Robert Berkeley, Efq; who died Febr. y[e] 2[d] 1690 Aged 76 years. And Rebecca his Wife, who died Auguft y[e] 16th 1707 Aged 83 Years. This Monument was erected by their moft Dutifull and moft Obfequious Daughter Rebecca Berkeley.

This is followed by the underwritten poor verfification,

Robert, that always was both good and iuft;
Of high defcent, years fince return'd to duft:
Who on his God at home, and Church did call;
Was ever Loyal, and Epifcopal.
The beft of Hufbands; and fo loving was
That he to Fathers been a pattern has.
And now prepared for her long repofe,
His Wife Rebecca by his fide lies clofe:
A tender Mother, of a Godlike mind;
Was to her Children all, and neighbours kind:
A pious dame, ftill ready to fulfill
Her God's, and her obligeing Hufband's will.
Thrice happy fouls, They never can mifs reft,
Who ftriving here each other to love beft,
Were then with peace, and now in heav'n are bleft.

Arms, *Baron and femme*, 1. *Gules, a chevron ermine between ten croffes patty argent*, for Berkeley. 2. *Azure, on a crofs fable five befants.*

Near to this place lies interr'd the Body of *JANE* Daught[r] of *ROBERT BERKELEY* of Rendcombe Efq[r] by *REBECCA* his Wife, Defcended from an Antient and Noble Family. She was of a Meek Temper, and obliging Behaviour, Dutiful to her Parents, Pious and Exemplary in her life and Converfation, & a true Daught: of the Church of England. In Short She was free from all the Modifh Vices, and Failings of her Sex and Age; and Endued with all thofe Virtues and Graces that could render her Life charming & defirable on Earth, or could qualify and difpofe her for the Rewards of Heaven. She died in the 19th Year of her Age, Anno Dom. 1672. This monument was erected by REBECCA her eldeft fifter, out of her tender Love and Affection.——Arms, Berkeley as above.

Benefaction.

Sir Thomas Roe gave an eftate of 25*l.* a year, to the parifh of Cirencefter, for putting out apprentices, &c. but ordered that a boy out of this parifh fhould receive the benefit once in three or four years, if prefented to the truftees at Cirencefter.

Taxes.						
The Royal Aid in	1692,	£.	65	1	8
Poll-tax —	1694,	—	31	1	0
Land-tax —	1694,	—	72	8	0
The fame, at 3*s.*	1770,	—	40	8	$4\frac{3}{4}$

About the year 1710, there were 21 houfes, and 120 inhabitants, whereof 3 were freeholders; yearly births 3, burials 3. *Atkyns.* The prefent number of families is 23, and of inhabitants 139.

RISINGTON (GREAT.)

THIS parifh lies in the lower divifion of the hundred of Slaughter, feven miles fouth from Stow, five north-eaftward from Northleach, and about twenty-five eaft from Gloucefter.

It is bounded by part of Oxfordfhire on the eaft, by the river Windrufh on the weft, by the other Rifingtons to the north, and by part of Great Barrington to the fouthward of it. It confifts of rich meadow and pafture on the fide next the river, with very good arable land in the higher fituations.

It is fometimes called Broad Rifington. *Rifedone*, *Rifedune*, and *Rifendune*, which are the feveral manners in which the name was antiently written, fignify that the village lies on the fide of a rifing ground, which is exactly the fituation of it, with an agreeable profpect of the vale beneath, through which the river Windrufh flows, in its courfe to Burford and Witney.

Of the Manor and other Eftates.

'Rotbert de Todeni holds Rifedone in Salemanefberie hundred. Ulf held it. There are 'thirteen hides taxed. In demean are three plow-'tillages, and twenty-three villeins, and fix bor-'dars, with ten plow-tillages. There are eight 'among the *fervi* and *ancillæ*, and a mill of 10*s.* 'and one burgage in Glouuceft' of 3*d.* [rent.] 'It was worth 12*l.* now 10*l.*' *Dom. Book*, p. 76.

The above mentioned Robert de Todeni died feized of the manors of Rifendone, Horedone, Saperton, and Frampton, in the year 1088, and was fucceeded by William his fon and heir, who took the name of de Albini, with the addition of Breto, to diftinguifh himfelf from William de Albini, chief butler of the realm.

The manor did not continue long in the family of Todeni, for Alard le Fleming was feized of it and of Saperton in the reign of king John, and both thofe manors continued in his defcendants down to the reign of king Richard the Second. Henry le Fleming, fon of Alard, died 5 H. 3. and was fucceeded by John le Fleming, his fon and heir, who was high fheriff of Gloucefterfhire

31 H. 3.

31 H. 3. and dying without iffue, was fucceeded by his kinfman Alard le Fleming, whofe widow Anne was afterwards married to Henry de la Lay. A *Quo warranto* was brought againft them for marrying without the king's licence, but the writ was difcharged, on producing a licence from king Henry the Third.

The laft Alard le Fleming left two daughters, coheireffes; Anne, (or as fhe is called in the efcheator's inquifition, Florence,) the eldeft, was married to William de Infula, or de Lifle; and Joan, the other daughter, was married to Henry Hoefe, or Huffey. Which faid William and Henry were jointly feized of the manor of Great Rifindon in right of their wives, as appears by the fheriff's return of all the vills in the county with their refpective lords, made in obedience to the king's writ, 9 E. 1. From this time they and their defcendants held this manor and that of Saperton jointly, for many fucceffive generations.

William de Infula, or de Lifle died 3 E. 2. feized of a moiety of the manor of Great Rofindon in right of Florentia his wife, and left William, his fon and heir by his faid wife, twenty-eight years old, (*Efch.*) who alfo died feized of the fame moiety 19 E. 3. His fon, Walter de Lifle, with Joan his wife, levied a fine of a moiety of the manor of Broad Rifington to the ufe of themfelves in fpecial taille; remainder to fir Henry Hoefe in taille, remainder to Elizabeth, the daughter of fir Henry, 21 E. 3. and died 31 E. 3. as did Joan his widow, in the forty-ninth year of the fame reign, feized of the fame moiety in dower. William de Lifle, fon of Walter, was feized thereof, with a moiety of the advowfon of the church, 51 E. 3. and dying 8 R. 2. was fucceeded by John Lifle, efq; his fon and heir.

I now return to Henry Hoefe, or de Huffey, who had married Joan, one of the coheireffes of Alard le Fleming, and in her right, was feized of a moiety of this manor 9 E. 1. He was feveral times fummoned to parliament among the barons in the reigns of E. 1. and E. 2. and died feized of [a moiety of] the manor of Rufyndon 6 E. 3. *Dugd.* Sir Henry Huffey, his fon and heir, levied a fine of a moiety of the manor and advowfon of Broad Rifington to the ufe of himfelf for life; the remainder to Henry his fon, and to Elizabeth, the daughter of John de Bohun, in fpecial taille; remainder to Richard, brother of Henry, in taille; remainder to Elizabeth, the daughter of Henry, in taille; remainder to John de Huntingfield, and his heirs, 21 E. 3. and died 7 R. 2. Anchoret, his widow, was feized of two acres of land in Rifington, and of a moiety of the manor of Saperton, in dower, at the time of her death, 13 R. 2.

The manor came afterwards to the Grevils. John Grevil died feized thereof 23 H. 6. and his fon, John Grevil, and Joan his wife, levied a fine of it 14 H. 7. William lord Sandys and Margaret his wife were feized of the manor of Broad Rifington. He died 32 H. 8. and livery was granted the fame year to Thomas lord Sandys, his fon; upon whofe death, William lord Sandys, fon of Thomas, had livery of the manor granted to him 9 Eliz.

About this time the manor came to the Brays of Great Barrington. Edmund Bray, efq; was lord of the manor in the year 1608, and it continued in his family 'till it was purchafed of Reginald-Morgan Bray, efq; about the year 1734, by lord chancellor Talbot, for the ufe, and with part of the fortune, of Mary, daughter and heirefs of Adam de Cardonnel, efq; now countefs Talbot, who is the prefent lady of the manor. Her ladyfhip's paternal arms are, *Argent, two chevronels azure, between three trefoils vert.*

Lands in Broad Rifington belonged to the Ciftercian abbey of Bruern in Oxfordfhire; and fir John Lovel and others were feized of one meffuage, one plow-tillage, 3*s.* yearly rent, and half a yard-land in Rifington, in truft for that abbey, 16 R. 2. Thefe lands, after the diffolution of the abbey of Bruern, were granted to Thomas Reeve and George Cotton 1 Mariæ.

A tenement and lands in Great Rifington belonged to a houfe of the knights hofpitallers of St. John at Jerufalem in Burford, and were granted to Edmond Hermon 35 H. 8. The advowfon of the church belonged to the fame knights, but was excepted in this grant to Edmond Hermon.

Richard Gilpyn and Alice his wife levied a fine of lands in Rifington Great 19 R. 2. Thomas de Lee and Joan his wife levied a fine of lands in Broad Rifington to the ufe of themfelves 20 R. 2. Lands in Broad Rifington belonged to fir William Berkeley, upon whofe attainder they were granted to Jafper duke of Bedford 1 H. 7. and John Walters and Thomas Carpenter obtained another grant of them 1 Mariæ.

Of the Church, &c.

The church is a rectory, in the deanery of Stow, worth 250*l.* a year. Lady Talbot is patronefs, and the reverend Richard Hayes, M.A. is the prefent incumbent.

Henry le Fleming levied a fine of the advowfon of Rifington to the ufe of Alice, widow of John le Fleming, 51 H. 3.

Four yard lands and a half belong to the glebe.

Knightly Chetwood, D.D. and dean of Gloucefter, who was prefented to this rectory in the year 1686, built the parfonage houfe for the benefit of his fucceffors; but it has been greatly improved by Mr. Upton and Mr. Hayes, the late and prefent incumbents.

The church, dedicated to St. John Baptift, is large, and built in the form of a crofs, with a ftrong low tower in the middle, in which are fix bells, and a gallery at the weft end. In three niches in the wall of the fouth porch, are the figures of our Saviour on the crofs, and one of his difciples on each fide of him; and in the chancel is a place formerly ufed for auricular confeffion.

Firft fruits £.22	2	$0\frac{3}{4}$	Synodals £.0	2	0		
Tenths —	2	4	$0\frac{1}{2}$	Pentecoft. 0	1	$1\frac{1}{2}$	
Procurations	0	6	8				

Benefactions.

Joan Bernard, (wife of John Bernard, gent. who was buried in the chancel 1621) gave 20*l.* the intereft to be diftributed to the poor. A perfon unknown gave 12*l.* to the fame ufe. Lady Jane Bray, of Shilton in Berkfhire, gave 20*s.* a year to buy clothing for the poor. And the rev. Mr. Webb, rector of this church, in the year 1739, gave 50*l.* the intereft of which to be expended in educating fix poor children of this parifh. There is a piece of ground fubject to provide bell-ropes.

Taxes.					
The Royal Aid in	1692, £.	138	2	0
Poll-tax ——	1694, —	30	1	4
Land-tax ——	1694, —	112	14	3
The fame, at 3*s.*	1770, —	79	9	3

When fir Robert Atkyns compiled his account of this parifh, there were 75 houfes, and about 277 inhabitants, whereof 36 were freeholders; yearly births 8, burials 7. In ten years, beginning with 1760, the baptifms were 74, burials 37, and the number of inhabitants is now about 252, which fhews the place to be very healthy.

Rifington (Little,) *or* Rifington Baffet.

THIS parifh lies in the lower divifion of the hundred of Slaughter, four miles fouth from Stow, fix north-eaftward from Northleach, and about twenty-five eaft from Gloucefter.

It is bounded on the fouth by Great Rifington, on the north by Wick Rifington, on the eaft by Weftcot, and on the weft by Bourton on the Water.

The name has been already explained under the preceding parifh; but the cognomen was given it from the family of the *Baffets*, to whom the manor antiently belonged.

Moft of the lands lie in a valley on the banks of the Windrufh, but the village itfelf is feated on a pleafant flope, with a fine afpect to the fouth-weft.

Of the Manor and other Eftates.

'Roger de Laci holds Rifedune in Salemanef-'berie hundred, and Hugh holds it of him. 'There are eight hides taxed. Aluuard, and 'Afchill, and Aluuard, and Uluui, held it for four 'manors. In demean are feven plow-tillages, and 'four villeins, with two plow-tillages. There 'are twelve *fervi*, and two *ancillæ*. There is a 'mill of 10*s.* It is worth and was worth 7*l.* and '10*s.*' *Domefday-book*, p. 75.

Roger de Laci taking part with Robert Curthoife againft king William the Second, his eftates were feized by the latter, and given to Hugh de Laci, his younger brother, who leaving no furviving iffue, they paffed to Gilbert, fon of his fifter Emme, who afterwards affumed the name of Lacy.

Soon after this time, Ralph Baflet, chief jufticiar of England, purchafed, among other large eftates, the manor of Little Rifington, which he gave to Gilbert a younger fon. Thomas Baffet, fon and heir of Gilbert, was juftice itinerant for Gloucefterfhire, and married Alice, the daughter of — Dunftanvil. Gilbert Baffet, fon and heir of Thomas, married Egeline, daughter of —— Courtney; and vefting the knights templers with lands in this parifh, he died 7 Joh. leaving an only daughter and heirefs, married to Richard de Comvil.

Robert de Briwes, or Brus, was poffeffed of the manor 53 H. 3. and died feized of it 4 E. 1. Robert Burnel, bifhop of Bath and Wells, the next lord of this manor, purchafed a charter of free warren 9 E. 1. and dying in the 21ft year of that reign, was fucceeded by Philip Burnel, his nephew and heir. The family of Burnel is defcended from fir Robert Burnel, who came into England with the Conqueror, and died in the laft year of that reign. His heirs fettled at Acton Burnel in Staffordfhire, where they had a caftle, which was honoured by an affembly of parliament in the reign of Edward the Firft; and the famous ftatute of Acton Burnel, fo often mentioned by our hiftorians, was fo called from being enacted at that place. The above mentioned Philip Burnel married Maud, the daughter of Richard earl of Arundel, and dying 22 E. 1. was fucceeded by Edward his fon and heir, who came of age 1 E. 2. and had then livery of his lands. He was fummoned as a baron to parliament 5 E. 2. and died without iffue in the 9th year of the fame reign, feized of the manor of Little Rifyndon, which he held jointly with Alina, or Aliva, his wife, of the king *in capite*, as of the honour of Wallingford, by the fervice of half a knight's fee. The manor then paid 10*l.* a year to the abbefs and convent of Godftow, as appears by the efcheator's inquifition, which found that Maud, his fifter, the wife of John Lovell, was his heir; but the manor was affigned to Aliva, the widow of Edward lord Burnel, in dower.

John de Handelo married Maud, fifter and heir of Edward lord Burnel, and widow of John lord Lovell; and they joined in levying a fine of this manor to the ufe of themfelves for life, the remainder to Nicholas their fon, 17 E. 3. John de Handelo, after the deceafe of his wife, held this eftate by the courtefy of England 'till his death 20 E. 3. Nicholas de Handelo had livery of the manor on the death of his father, and affumed the name of Burnel from his mother. He was fummoned as a baron to parliament 24 E. 3. and dying 6 R. 2. left fir Hugh lord Burnel his fon and heir, who married Joyce, daughter and heirefs of fir John Botetourt. He was one of the lords that received the refignation of the crown from king Richard the Second, and died 8 H. 5. feized of the manor of Rifindon Baffet, and other great eftates. Edward Burnel, only fon of fir Hugh, married Alice, daughter of the lord Strange, and died in the lifetime of his father, leaving three daughters, coheireffes to their grandfather; Joyce,

 married

married to Thomas Erdington; Margery to Edmond Hungerford; and Catherine, afterwards married to fir John Ratcliffe.

The heirs male of Nicholas, fon of Maud Burnel, by John de Handelo, being thus extinct, the manor reverted to the heir of Maud by her firft hufband, John lord Lovel, who was William lord Lovel, her great grandfon. He died feized of this manor 33 H. 6. and was fucceeded by John his fon, who married Joan, fifter of William vifcount Beaumont, and died 4 E. 4. Francis lord Lovel, fon of John, married Anne, daughter of Henry lord Fitz-Hugh. He was very much in favour with king Richard the Third, and equally hated by the people. Of him, and two others, Catefby, and Ratfby, the following diftich was commonly repeated:

The *Cat*, the *Rat*, and *Lovel* the *Dog*,
Rule all England under the *Hog*.

It fared with him, as it has often done with favourites exercifing undue influence over their fovereign, for he was attainted 1 H. 7. for divers mifdemeanors, and fled out of the kingdom; but returning, was flain near Newark 3 H. 7. leaving no iffue. His two fifters, Joan, married to fir Brian Stapleton, and Fridifwid, married to fir Edward Norris, could not inherit, on account of their brother's attainder, wherefore this manor came to the crown.

It was afterwards granted to Thomas duke of Norfolk, by whofe attainder it came again to the crown, and was granted to Paul Withepool and other citizens of London, as fecurity for money borrowed, 36 H. 8. John Fettiplace, efq; was lord of the manor in the year 1608. It was afterwards purchafed by feven perfons, who held it in common, and is now divided among feveral freeholders, and held of the honour of Ewe Elm in Oxfordfhire.

There was a manor, or at leaft a reputed manor in this parifh, which belonged to the Benedictine nunnery of Godftow in Oxfordfhire, and was granted, after the diffolution of religious foundations, to Richard Andrews and Leonard Chamberlain, 34 H. 8. The knights templers were feized of lands in this parifh 2 E. 3. Certain lands in Little Rifington belonged to the Ciftercian abbey of Bruern in Oxfordfhire, and were granted to Thomas Reeve and George Cotton 1 Mar.

Of the Church, &c.

The church is a rectory, in the deanery of Stow, worth 145 *l.* a year; the lord chancellor is patron, and the reverend John Dachair, D.D. is the prefent incumbent.

There was formerly a compofition between the rector of this church and the abbey of Ofney concerning tithes. An acre of furze, an acre of arable, and half an acre of pafture belong to the church-wardens.

The church, dedicated to St. Peter, has a fmall aile on the north fide, and a tower, with one bell.

Firft fruits £.	10	10	7½	Synodals £.	0	2	0
Tenths —	1	3	0¾	Pentecoftals	0	0	8
Procurations	0	6	8				

Taxes.	The Royal Aid in	1692,	£. 93	16	0
	Poll-tax ——	1694, —	22	15	0
	Land-tax ——	1694, —	62	13	0
	The fame, at 3 *s.*	1770, —	48	16	0

At the beginning of this century, there were 30 houfes, and about 170 inhabitants in this parifh, whereof 16 were freeholders; yearly births 6, burials 5. *Atkyns.* The people are fomething increafed fince the above period, and are now about 176 in number.

RISINGTON (WICK)

IS a fmall parifh, in the lower divifion of the hundred of Slaughter, three miles fouth from Stow, fix north-eaftward from Northleach, and about twenty-five eaftward from Gloucefter.

It lies on the flope of an eafy hill, which bounds a pleafant little valley to the fouthward of it. This part of the country being at a great diftance from any coal mines, has induced feveral gentlemen to bore, and fink pits in their eftates in fearch of that neceffary foffil, and particularly the late Mr. Dickenfon perfevered for three years in experiments of that nature. The attempt was laudable, but the bufinefs terminated in difappointment to himfelf and the whole neighbourhood. This gentleman built a handfome houfe that gives dignity to the eftate, and ornaments the village. It is called *Wick-Hill,* and ftands at a fmall diftance from the turnpike-road from Stow to Burford, commanding a moft agreeable profpect of the valley, and particularly of the pleafant village of Bourton on the Water.

The foil of this parifh is very fertile, and the lands pretty equally divided between arable and pafture, but the village feems to have nothing more to diftinguifh it, befide the particulars already mentioned.

Of the Manor and other Eftates.

The following record was overlooked by fir Robert Atkyns:

'Rotbert de Olgi holds Rifendvne in Salemanef-'berie hundred. There are ten hides taxed. 'Siuuard held four plow-tillages in demean, and 'twelve villeins, and two bordars, with five plow-'tillages. There are eight *fervi,* and two mills 'of 20 *s.* It was worth 10 *l.* now 8 *l.*' *D.B.* p.76.

Robert de Briwes was feized of the manors of Little Rifington and Rifington Wyke 53 H. 3. and died 4 E. 1. at which time he was likewife feized of the church of Wike Rifindon. The fheriff returned that the abbat of Evefham and William Lucy were lords of Wyke in Salmonefburye hundred 9 E. 1. Thomas Spencer and Walter de Burghton were feized of it, probably in truft, truſt, 5 E. 3. for it was afterwards veſted in the Lucies, and ſir Thomas Luci died ſeized of Riſindon Wike 3 H. 5. as did William Luci, eſq; 6 E. 4.

The manor paſſed ſome time afterwards to the Stratfords. John Stratford died ſeized of Riſindon Wike 7 E. 6. and livery was granted the ſame year to Henry Stratford, his couſin and heir. George Stratford was lord of this manor in the year 1608, in whoſe family it continued for more than a century afterwards; Mr. Coxe, by purchaſe after the death of Mr. Dickinſon, is the preſent lord of the manor, and proprietor of Wick-Hill.

John Rouſe and others were ſeized of lands in Wike Riſindon 49 E. 3.

Of the Church, &c.

The church is a rectory, in the deanery of Stow, worth about 150*l.* a year. The lord chancellor is patron, and Mr. Woodroffe is the preſent incumbent.

Robert le Bruſe, or de Briwes, was ſeized of this church 4 E. 1. as was Edward Burnel 9 E. 2. at which time the inquiſition found that the advowſon was worth 202*s.* Sir Hugh Burnel was ſeized of the ſame advowſon 8 H. 5. and the biſhop of Bath and Wells, lord Hungerford, and Thomas duke of Norfolk have likewiſe preſented.

The church is dedicated to St. Peter, and has a tower at the weſt end, which was built by —— Wakefield, who lies buried in the chancel.

Firſt fruits £.	16	2	6	Proc. & Syn. £.	0	3	6
Tenths —	1	12	3	Pentecoſtals -	0	0	9½

Benefactions.

A meadow called Clerk's Mead, which lets for 5*l.* a year, is charged with the annual payment of 13*s.* 4*d.* to the clerk, and the remainder of the produce is given for the repair of the church, or for ſuch other purpoſes as the majority of the pariſh ſhall think proper. Richard Winchin has given 10*s.* a year to the poor, charged on an acre in Vitock's-Ham.

Taxes.					
The Royal Aid in	1692,	£.	68	8	0
Poll-tax ——	1694,	—	16	14	0
Land-tax —	1694,	—	52	0	0
The ſame, at 3*s.*	1770,	—	40	16	3

At the beginning of the preſent century, there were 26 houſes, and about 120 inhabitants in this pariſh, whereof 13 were freeholders; yearly births 4, burials 4. *Atkyns.* The people are now increaſed to 182.

ROCKHAMPTON

LIES in the vale, in the hundred of Langley and Swineſhead, about two miles north from Thornbury, five ſouth from Berkeley, and twenty-two ſouthward, inclining to the weſt, from the city of Glouceſter.

The ſoil is rich, and moſtly in paſturage, but the parts next the river Severn, which bounds the pariſh on the weſt, are ſubject to inundations, which ſometimes do conſiderable damage. A ſmall ſtream riſes here, and empties itſelf into the Severn, at Shepardine.

Of the Manor and other Eſtates.

'Oſbern Gifard holds Rochemtune, in Langeleie 'hundred, of the king. There are three hides 'taxed. Dunne held it in the time of king Ed'ward. In demean are two plow-tillages, and 'ſix villeins, and ſeven bordars, with three plow'tillages. There are five *ſervi*, and twenty acres 'of meadow, and a ſalt-pit at Wich [paying] 'four ſeams of ſalt, a wood one mile long, and 'half a mile broad. It is worth 6*l.*' *Domeſday-book*, p. 76.

The above Oſbern Gifard, or Giffard, was a noble Norman, who attended king William the Firſt in his invaſion of England, and for his ſervices, was rewarded with the manors of Rochemtune, Stoche, Brimesfelde, and Aldeberie, in this county.

John Giffard of Brimpsfield purchaſed a charter of free warren in the manors of Badgworth, Stonehouſe, Rockhampton, Stoke-Giffard, and Tetbury, in this county, as already related under Brimpſfield, 9 E. 1. and his claim to court leet and waifs in Rockhampton was allowed, in a *Quo warranto* brought againſt him in the 15th year of that reign. He was ſucceeded by his ſon John Giffard, the laſt of that name, (commonly called *John the Rich*) who taking part with the barons againſt the Spencers, his caſtle of Brimpsfield was demoliſhed, his lands ſeized, and he himſelf being made priſoner at the battle of Burroughbridge, was attainted and executed at Glouceſter as a traitor. The manor was thereupon granted to Hugh le Diſpencer the younger, 17 E. 2. But after the depoſition and murder of king Edward the Second, this manor and Brimpsfield were granted to John Maltravers, for his ſervice in that bloody affair, and to him John de Callew, heir to the Giffards by a daughter, releaſed all his right. This manor was taken from John Maltravers, on account of his being convicted of divers miſdemeanors, and the inheritance of it was granted to Maurice, ſecond ſon of Maurice lord Berkeley, 11 E. 3. but John Maltravers having found means to make his peace with the king, was reſtored to this eſtate, of which he died ſeized, together with the advowſon of the church, 38 E. 3.

The manor neverthleſs reverted to the Berkeleys, in conſequence of the above grant to Maurice Berkeley, and continued in his family 'till ſir William Berkeley fled beyond ſea, after the battle of Boſworth-field, and was attainted 1 H. 7. for his attachment to king Richard the Third; whereupon the manors of Rockhampton and Sheppardine, with many others, were granted to Jaſper duke of Bedford, and his heirs male, the ſame year.

But

But ſir William Berkeley being afterwards received into the king's favour, obtained a reverſionary grant of this, and many of his other eſtates, after the duke of Bedford's entail, 4 H. 7. and upon the death of that nobleman, without iſſue, 11 H. 7. came again into poſſeſſion of them, and died in the 16th year of the ſame reign. Richard Berkeley of Stoke-Giffard, ſon of ſir William, died ſeized of Rockhampton 5 H. 8. leaving John, his eldeſt ſon and heir, three years old, who likewiſe held this manor at the time of his death, in the 37th year of that reign. Richard Berkeley, ſon and heir of ſir John, had livery of the manors of Stoke-Giffard and Rockhampton 6 E. 6. and died 2 Jac. 1.

This manor came afterwards to the Willoughbies. Henry Willoughby had livery of it 4 Eliz. Edward Hill of Alveſton was proprietor of it at the beginning of this century, and Mr. Pinfold and Mr. Hoſkyns are the preſent lords of the manor.

William Warine held lands in Rockhampton 38 E. 3. William Warren of St. Briavel's, a deſcendant from him, held lands in Rockhampton, of which he died ſeized 14 Eliz. and Warren Goughe, his grandſon, had livery thereof in the 21ſt year of the ſame reign, and together with Dorothy his wife, levied a fine of lands in Rockhampton and Shepardine, in Michaelmas term 12 C. 1.

William Goughe of Woollaſton died ſeized of lands in Rockhampton 5 E. 6. and was ſucceeded by his grandſon George Goughe, ſon of William, who was then ſixteen years old, and had livery of his lands 21 Eliz. as appears by the Ouſter le Mayne ſued out in that year. It may not be improper to take notice that the family name is *Goughe*, or *Gough*, not *Goffe*, as ſir Robert Atkyns has it, which is pronounced *Gove*, and ſignifies *a blackſmith* in the Britiſh language. A gentleman of this family being ſo unfortunate as to have his name written *Goffe*, agreeable to the Engliſh orthography, had a good eſtate given away from him, through the inadvertency of the writer.

John Wither was ſeized of lands in this pariſh, which he left to Margaret his daughter and heireſs, married to Thomas Seger, and died 36 Eliz. Two tenements in Rockhampton belonged to the abbey of Hayles, and were granted to Theophilus Adams and Robert Adams 25 Eliz.

HAMLETS. 1. *Rockhampton*, of which already.

2. *Newton.* Philip Jones died ſeized of two meſſuages, and divers lands in Newton in Rockington, *alias* Rockhampton, Mar. 23, 41 Eliz. and left John Jones, his ſon and heir, eighteen years old. *Eſch.*

3. *Shepardine*, lying three miles weſtward from the church, on the bank of the Severn, and conſiſting principally of marſh-land. Here was once a chapel, in which Thomas lord Berkeley founded a chantry 25 E. 3. It has long been converted to profane uſes, but ſtill retains the name of Shepardine chapel. And at this place there was formerly a paſſage over the Severn, but it is now wholly diſuſed.

Of the Church, &c.

The church is a rectory, in the deanery of Durſley, worth about 100*l.* a year. Mr. Jenner is patron, and the reverend Henry Jenner, M.A. is the preſent incumbent.

Eighteen acres in ſeveral grounds, and eight acres and a half of meadow, belong to the glebe, as ſatisfaction for all tithes in the meadow. Seventy acres of land in the common field are tithe free.

The church, dedicated to St. Oſwald, is ſmall, and has a tower at the weſt end, in which are three bells.

	£.	s.	d.		£.	s.	d.
Firſt fruits	15	0	0	Synodals	0	2	0
Tenths —	1	1	0	Pentecoſtals	0	0	7½
Procurations	0	6	8				

Benefactions.

Richard Berkeley, of Stoke-Giffard, 8 H. 7. gave a houſe and lands, worth 2*l.* a year, for repairing the church. Mabel Mallet gave 12*s.* a year to be diſtributed to the poor on the feaſt of the Nativity. And William Webb has given the intereſt of 5*l.* to the ſame uſe.

Taxes.			£.	s.	d.
The Royal Aid in	1692,		119	19	4
Poll-tax —	1694,	—	14	5	0
Land-tax —	1694,	—	112	9	8
The ſame, at 3*s.*	1770,	—	83	12	9

At the beginning of this century, there were 26 houſes, and about 120 inhabitants in the pariſh, whereof 6 were freeholders; yearly births 4, burials 4. *Atkyns.* But it appears from the regiſter, that in ten years, beginning with 1700, there were 48 baptiſms, and 29 burials; and in the ſame number of years, beginning with 1760, there are entered 38 baptiſms, and 35 burials. The number of houſes is 22, of inhabitants about 122.

RODBOROUGH.

THIS pariſh lies in the hundred of Longtree, about three miles weſtward from Minchin-Hampton, one ſouthward from Stroud, and ten ſouth-eaſtward from Glouceſter. The lands are pretty equally divided into paſture and arable, and a ſmall brook, riſing at Avening and Horſley, runs through it, and falls into the Froome at Dudbridge, a little below Stroud.

It ſtretches along the north and weſt ſides of a lofty hill, at the top of which the Coteſwold-country commences, whence the great road leads through Hampton, and ſo down this hill to both the paſſages over the Severn next below Glouceſter; on which account Hampton is ſometimes called

called *Hampton-Road*; and Rodborough, which was once a part of that pariſh, and is ſtill in ſome meaſure dependent on it, derives the former part of its name from the ſame *Road*, but the latter part was taken from the *Berg*, or *Camp*, by which the road is carried.

The beautiful villa or ſeat of ſir Oneſiphorus Paul, baronet, called *Hill-houſe*, erected a few years ago by his late father, is ſituated on an eminence in this pariſh, with a pleaſant proſpect of the river which runs from Nailſworth, of the village of Woodcheſter, and of the populous country towards Stroud and Painſwick. This gentleman's father, the late ſir Oneſiphorus Paul, was appointed high ſheriff of Glouceſterſhire, and knighted, in the year 1760, and on the 3d of September, 1762, was created a baronet of Great Britain.

Near the ſummit of Rodborough-hill, facing the weſt, ſtands the *Fort*, a pleaſure-houſe, built ſcarce twenty years ago, after the manner of a caſtle, by George Hawker, eſq; the preſent proprietor. From this place there is a moſt agreeable proſpect of the river Severn, and part of the vale through which it paſſes. There is a large tract of rich country in the fore ground of the landſcape, interſperſed with good houſes, gardens, and highly cultivated plantations and incloſures; and theſe are improved with the beautiful colouring of clothes on the tenters, accompanied with a variety of other objects peculiar to a clothing country. Here the fancy glows, and agreeable ideas riſe of the benefits and extenſiveneſs of trade and manufactures, which flouriſh moſt in free countries; and of the affluence and riches which are at once incitements to, and the rewards of integrity and induſtry.

Mr. James Winchcombe, an eminent clothier, has built a good houſe at a place called *Bownham's*, ſituate on the brow of the hill northward, where he enjoys a fine healthy air, and a pleaſant proſpect of a well inhabited valley, extending ſeveral miles along the Stroud river from the Golden Valley in Chalford, and gradually opening as it approaches the vale below Stroud.

I have not heard of any very curious natural productions at preſent exiſting in this pariſh; but Richard Clutterbuck, born here in the year 1638, was a perſon of extraordinary endowments. Mr. Timothy Nourſe ſaw him in the year 1698, and relates the following particulars, which I have in his own hand writing. At three years old, this perſon enjoy'd only ſuch a portion of ſight as enabled him to diſcern a difference between white and black, and at twelve he was totally dark, and ſo continued to his death; notwithſtanding which he walked up and down all the uneven ground in the neighbourhood, (and no ground can be more uneven) without a guide. He could tell when an hour-glaſs was run out by his hearing, which was ſo acute as to diſcover the loweſt whiſper in an adjacent room. He was a curious mechanic, and made oatmeal-mills, and pepper-mills, and could make a wheel for a cloth-mill with great advantage. He took a watch in pieces and mended it, and made a handſome chain for his own watch. He made violins, baſs-viols, and citterns, and a ſet of virginals with double jacks, and other improvements which were of his own invention; and play'd on each of thoſe inſtruments. He taught muſic according to a ſcale of his own forming, and cut his notes upon pieces of wood. He ran a race of two hundred yards length, after being turned three times round, in many difficult circumſtances, and could not be deceived. Theſe are ſome of the particulars of this extraordinary man, whom Dr. Plott takes notice of amongſt his curioſities, in his Natural Hiſtory of Staffordſhire.

Sir Leonard Holiday, lord mayor of London in the year 1605, was a native of this place.

Of the Manor and other Eſtates.

Rodborough is not to be found in *Domeſday*, but is included in the account of Hampton. It belonged antiently to a family who took their name from it, of whom Thomas de Rodburg was lord of the manor of Lye, as well as Rodborough, and high ſheriff of Glouceſterſhire 1 & 4 E. 3. William de Rodborough, ſon and heir of Thomas, ſucceeded him in his eſtates, and dying without iſſue 10 R. 2. Agnes his ſiſter, married to John Browning, meſne lord of Notgrove, was his heir, and had livery of them the ſame year. Richard Browning, ſon and heir of John and Agnes, dying alſo without iſſue 21 H. 4. the manor of Rodborough deſcended to Cicely his ſiſter, married to ſir Guy de Whitington of Pauntley, who died ſeized of the manors of Notgrove, Lye, and Rodborough, in right of his wife, 20 H. 6. Thomas Whitington, the fifth in lineal deſcent from ſir Guy, died ſeized of this manor 38 H. 8. leaving ſix daughters coheireſſes, whereby it paſſed out of the name of Whitington.

Philip Sheppard, of Hampton, eſq; ſon of Samuel Sheppard, died ſeized of it in the year 1713, and Edward Sheppard, of Hampton, eſq; a direct deſcendant from him, is the preſent lord of this manor. See his arms, &c. under Avening.

Of the other eſtates, the records ſhew, that Roger Gulden levied a fine of lands in Rodborough and Minchin Hampton to John de Pearle and others 14 R. 2. John Pentour and Agnes his wife levied a fine of lands in Rodborough and Hampton to their own uſe 22 R. 2. John Frye, ſon and heir of John Frye, levied a fine in like manner of lands in Minchin Hampton and Rodborough to John Moody, eſq; 4 E. 4. and he alſo levied another fine of lands in Rodborough and Rookſmore to William Elland 7 H. 7. Lands in Rodborough belonged to the nunnery of Sion in Middleſex, and were granted to Andrew lord Windſor 34 H. 8. Thomas Rogers of Wotton-Baſſet was ſeized of lands in Rodborough by deſcent from his mother 15 Eliz. and he had a poſthumous ſon, Thomas.

There are places of the following names in this pariſh, beſide thoſe already mentioned, *viz.* *Dudbridge*, *Walbridge*, *Froomill*, *Spilman's-Court*, *Rookſmore*, and *Lightpill*.

Of the Church, &c.

The church lies in the deanery of Stonehouſe, and is a chapel of eaſe to Minchin Hampton, to which it is annexed. The rector of Hampton, by a decree in chancery in the reign of king James the Firſt, is obliged to provide a curate to officiate in this chapel.

Here is a lecture every Sunday morning, endowed with lands, which at preſent yield 56*l.* a year, and are ſpecified under the account of *Benefactions*. Brazen Noſe college, Oxford, has the appointment of the lecturer, who is generally one of the fellows of that college. Of late years, the rector of Hampton, by agreement, has provided a curate to ſerve the church, and preach the lecture.

The church is dedicated to St. Mary Magdalen. It has an aile on the ſouth ſide, and a pinnacled tower at the weſt end. The pariſh acknowledges Hampton for the mother church, by the payment of 6*s.* 8*d.* a year towards the repairs of it.

Pentecoſtals - - 6*d.*

Monuments and Inſcriptions.

Againſt the north wall is the following inſcription:

HERE BENEATH DOTH LYE INTERRED THE BODY OF MICHAEL STRINGER, WHO DEPARTED THIS LIFE MARCH 1, 1603: AND ALSO THE BODY OF IOANE HIS WIFE, WHO DECEASED FEBRVARY 3, 1645.

HIC VNA VRNA DVOS HABET, VNA HABET OſſA DVORVM
VNA FIDES CHRISTI VITA DVOBVS ERAT.

ONE HEART WE HAD, ONE LIFE WE LED,
ONE DEATH WE BOTH DESIRED;
ONE GRAVE WE HAVE, OVR BODIES BED;
OVR SOVLS TO GOD RETIRED.
R. S.

At the eaſt end of the church is a monument for Doctor Stanfield, the greatly reſpected lecturer of this pariſh, and rector of Woodcheſter, who left behind him a great reputation, and whoſe memory is ſtill revered in theſe parts. Under his influence and direction, the clothiers of this pariſh and neighbouring bottoms, by their contributions in cloth and money, intirely clothed the regiment raiſed by ſir John Guiſe, at the revolution in 1688. On the monument is the following inſcription:

Hic ſubtus jacet
Jacobus Stanfield A. M. hujuſce Eccl^ae Prælector, Vicinæq; Woodcheſtriæ Paſtor fidelis, Theologus nulli Secundus, Catechiſtes ſui temporis facile Princeps, Et Genio et Literis Ornatiſſimus: Qui licet ad annum Ætatis nonageſimum pene pervixiſſet, Morte tamen nimis immatura præreptus, Utpote qui ſui Memoriam laboribus extendunt His nulla Mors non repentina. Obijt Dec. 25°.

Under this place lies James Stanfield A. M. A faithful Preacher of God's Word in this and the neighbouring Church of Woodcheſter. A Man of rare Wit and uncommon Learning. A profound Divine. An incomparable Catechiſt, & a moſt excellent Phyſician: Who, tho' he lived to a great Age, may very juſtly be ſaid to have died too ſoon; ſince his death muſt always be untimely whoſe pious Labours make his Life a Bleſſing and his Memory Great. Died Dec. 25, 1722.———No arms.

Near the above, on a ſeparate table,

The Reverend Mr. James Stanfield had Iſſue one Son and three Daughters. James his Son died at Borneo in the Eaſt Indies in his 3d Voyage. Elizabeth his Daughter died October 29, 1724. Mary his daughter died Nov. 14, 1707. Anne his Daughter died Nov. 12, 1725. Theſe three laſt named lye buried near this Place.

On a ſmall, but neat marble monument in the chancel,

Beneath this Monument lie the Remains of Samuel Hawker, Eſquire, one of his Majeſty's Juſtices of the Peace, who died 15th Septr. 1760, aged 67. Alſo of Mary his Wife, who died 14th Jany 1738, aged 34.—— Arms, *Sable, a feſs Or between three hawks argent.*

On a neat monument againſt the ſouth wall,

This Monument is erected
in Memory of Thomas Baylis of Newmills
in the Pariſh of Stroud, Clothier,
who departed this Life the 31st of March
1754, Aged 67.
Alſo of Jane his firſt Wife, Daughter of
Sidham (†) Pain of this Pariſh, who was buried
the 16th of June 1721, Aged 38.
Alſo of Elizabeth his laſt Wife, Daughter
of Daniel Window of Brimſcombe Clothier,
who departed this Life the 30th of Novem^r
1742, Aged 46.
And alſo of five of his Children who were
all interred in this Place.
Jehovah depauperat et ditat
deprimit etiam extollit.

(†) *It ſhould be* Sidenham.

There are inſcriptions in the chancel for Mr. Daniel Chance, clothier, who died in 1715; and for his ſon, and many of his family; but no arms.

On a tomb in the church-yard, incloſed with paliſadoes,

Beneath are depoſited the remains of *Mary*, Relict of JOHN LANGLEY, of Lambeth in the County of Surrey, Gent. and Daughter of THOMAS ROBERTS of this Pariſh Clothier. She departed this Life June the 3d, 1755, in the 22d Year of her Age.

Alſo of Rebecca, Wife of Bicknel Coney, of the City of London, Gent. and Daughter of Thos Roberts aforeſaid. She died Nov. 28, 1760, aged 29.

Here alſo are depoſited the Remains of Sarah Daughter of Thomas Roberts, who departed this Life Feb. the 21st A. D. 1743, aged 15 Years.

In Memory of Thomas Roberts of this Pariſh Clothier, who departed this Life May the 2d 1766 aged 68 Years.———Arms, *Baron and femme*, 1. *Ermine, on a pile gules a lion paſſant Or*, 2. *Argent, on a bend ſable three horſe-ſhoes Or.*

On another tomb,

To the Memory of Thomas Roberts, jun^r. who departed this Life the 22d Day of Nov. 1766, aged 29 Years. A moſt dutiful Son and ſincere Friend; the Loſs of whom is regretted by all that knew him: But the greateſt Affliction to his diſconſolate Mother.

There are alſo inſcriptions on other tombs for Giles Pinfold, who died in 1681; for Joſeph his ſon, who died in 1686; for another Joſeph Pinfold, who died in 1756; and for John Pinfold, who died in 1765; with their arms, *A chevron between three doves.*

Benefactions.

William de Notelyn, and William de Rodborough, gave lands in Biſley called Boerats, Hanſteeds, and Florens, in the reign of king Richard the Second; Hugh de Notelyn of Rookſmore gave lands in King's Stanley in the year 1398; Edmund de Rodborough gave lands called Dunyards and Hanſteeds in the year 1432; and Margery Brimſcomb gave other lands in Biſley in the year 1436; all which were for the maintenance of divine ſervice in the chapel of Rodborough, and for repairing the ſaid chapel. And by a decree in chancery, 2 Jac. 1. certain lands called Dunyards, Hanſteeds, Amberley, and Biſham, and

and a wood called Rodborough-wood, lying and being in the pariſhes of Biſley, King's Stanley, Hampton, and Rodborough, were veſted in feoffees for the above purpoſes, 5*l.* a year for repairing the chapel, the remainder for a lecture every Sunday morning.

Thomas Halliday, clothier, gave 100*l.* for ever for teaching three poor boys to read and write, &c.

Nathaniel Cliffold, merchant, gave 20*l.* Michael Halliday, clothier, 5*l.* Nathaniel Beard 10*l.* Henry King, clothier, 250*l.* Richard Cambridge, of London, merchant, 20*l.* all to the uſe of the poor; and Thomas Camm, merchant, gave 50*s.* a year, charged on Rigley-Stile ground, near Glouceſter, to be diſtributed to the poor at Chriſtmas.

Note, there is the tithing of Rodborough, in the pariſh of Minchin Hampton, to which the following benefactions properly belong, *viz.* Mr. Nathaniel Cambridge, Hamborough merchant, who died in 1697, gave 1000*l.* for educating poor boys of Woodcheſter and Rodborough, in reading, writing, and accounts; with which money Saintloe-farm, in the tithing of Rodborough, was purchaſed, and a free ſchool has been eſtabliſhed at Saintloe.

Mr. John Yeats, of Hampton, clothier, and Mr. Benjamin Cambridge, gave 100*l.* each, which ſums are laid out on lands in King's Stanley, for the uſe of the ſame ſchool. And Mr. Richard Cambridge of London, gave 100*l.* to the children of Saintloe ſchool, to be employ'd as his truſtees may think fit.

Taxes.					
The Royal Aid in	1692,	£. 99	9	4
Poll-tax ——	1694,—	58	12	0
Land-tax ——	1694,—	172	8	2
The ſame, at 3*s.*	1770,—	89	15	6¼
For Rodborough tithing,		44	17	9

When ſir Robert Atkyns compiled his account of this pariſh, there were, according to him, 160 houſes, and about 750 inhabitants, whereof 20 were freeholders; yearly births 26, burials 34. But the two laſt particulars are very injudiciouſly given, and differ widely from the average numbers of baptiſms and burials. In the year 1756, the burials were 27, and the whole number of ſouls 1481.

RODMARTON.

THIS pariſh lies in the hundred of Longtree, ſomething more than five miles weſt from Cirenceſter, and above four miles eaſtward inclining to the north from Tetbury, fifteen miles ſouth from Glouceſter, and about eight north from Malmeſbury in Wiltſhire. It is ſituate in a fine, healthy, open country, on the north-weſt ſide of the Roman way leading from Cirenceſter to Bath, which ſeparates it from part of Wiltſhire.

The pariſh conſiſts moſtly of arable land, is totally without wood land, and ſeems almoſt peculiarly unfortunate in having no continual brook or ſtream of water running through it. It is ſuppoſed to have derived its name from its lying on the Roman way, and being on one ſide a boundary of the county; for *mer*, contracted from *merc*, ſignifies a boundary; ſo that *Rod-mar-ton*, (or *Red-mer-tone*, which is the antient manner of writing the name) ſignifies *a boundary town upon the road.*

It is a place of conſiderable antiquity, as appears by a teſſellated pavement diſcovered by ſome people at plow, in the year 1636; and Mr. Yate, who was a learned and judicious perſon, and at that time rector of the church, has entered it on record in the pariſh regiſter, from which the following paſſage is literally taken: *Hoc anno* [1636] *in agris in loco* Hocberry *vocato, dum ſulcos aratro ducunt, diſcooperta ſunt teſſellat. pavimenta, tegulæ quibus ferrei clavi infixi ſubrutæ, nummi quoque ænei Antonini et Valentiniani Imp. Incolæ mihi dixerunt, ſe æneos et argenteos nummos ſepius ibidem reperiſſe, neſcientes quid rei eſſent: A patribus autem audiviſſe,* Rodmarton *ab illo loco tranſlatam olim ubi nunc eſt poſitam eſſe. Aparet autem ſtationem aliquam* Romanorum *ibidem aliquando fuiſſe.* Which may be thus tranſlated: This year [1636] in a field called *Hocberry*, as the people were at plow, the plow-ſhare turning up ſome tiles, diſcovered a teſſellated pavement, and they found alſo ſome braſs coins of the emperors Antoninus and Valentinian. The inhabitants told me that they had oftentimes found braſs and ſilver coins, but did not know what they were, and that they had heard their anceſtors ſay, that Rodmarton was formerly removed from that place to where it now ſtands. However, it appears that there was once a Roman ſtation there.

It ſeems this pavement was covered with ſlates, and perhaps other rubbiſh, with a view to its preſervation; for ſince coverings of the ſame kind have been found upon ſeveral other teſſellated pavements, it ſeems not to be a matter of mere chance or accident, but a cautionary method taken by the Romans themſelves when they left this iſland, upon a proſpect of their return hither again.

About the year 366, the Picts and Scots had broke in upon the Roman territories, and committed innumerable outrages, inſomuch that Theodoſius was ſent over hither to prevent a general inſurrection and revolt, as it was feared that the Britons were not a little diſpoſed to join the enemy. And this place lying upon the Roman way, at a convenient diſtance from *Corinium*, now Cirenceſter, which was a place of ſtrength, and of great conſequence to the Romans, they placed a garriſon here, to give early notice of the approach of any formidable body of the enemy, and to curb the inſolence of ſuch ſmall parties of them as ſhould ſtraggle in their way. This is conſiſtent with their practice in other places of leſs note, where teſſellated pavements have been found,

found, and which are ſuppoſed to have belonged to the houſe of ſome principal officer of the garriſon.

The Roman generals, amongſt their other baggage, uſed to carry about with them a quantity of *lapilli*, or *teſſellæ*, made of bricks or tiles, not much bigger than dice, ſufficient to pave the place where they ſet the *Prætorium*, or general's tent, or at leaſt ſome part of it, which is particularly related of Julius Cæſar, by Suetonius, in his Life of that general. And we learn from Salmaſius, in his Commentary on Suetonius, and from Pliny, in his Natural Hiſtory, that ſuch of theſe as were made of ſmall ſquare marbles, of various natural colours, were called *Lithoſtrata*; but if of ſmall bricks, artificially tinged with colours, they were diſtinguiſhed by different names, as *Pavimenta Teſſellata*, or *Opus Muſivum*. But it is ſaid that they had all one common name, *Aſarota*, from their not being to be ſwept, but wiped with a ſponge.

What figures were repreſented on the pavement I have been ſpeaking of is uncertain, as it is intirely deſtroy'd, and the regiſter gives no further particulars.

Of the Manors and other Eſtates.

In *Domeſday-book* are the following particulars: 'Hugo Maminot holds Redmertone in Langetrew hundred of Giſlebert biſhop of Liſieux, [in 'Normandy,] and he holds it of the king. There 'are two hides. In demean are two plow-tillages, 'and one villein, and two bordars, and a prieſt, 'with one plow-tillage. There are two *ſervi*. It 'was worth 4 *l.* and is now worth 3 *l.* Leuuinus 'held it of king Edward.' *Domeſday-book*, p. 73.

But in the ſame record it is written, 'Oſward 'holds of the king Redmertone in Langetreu 'hundred. There are three yard-lands taxed. 'He held the ſame in the reign of king Edward. 'There is one plow-tillage. It was worth 20 *ſol.* 'now 10 *ſol.*' *Ibid.* p. 79.

This Oſward was one of the king's thanes, whoſe eſtate was the ſmaller of the two at that time in Redmertone, but it is not poſſible to ſhew the deſcent of them diſtinctly from each other. All that can be done, is to ſet down the few records relating to this diviſion of the pariſh, in the order of time wherein they were made.

This manor was held of the honour of Glouceſter, by one knight's fee, 47 H. 3. The ſheriff returned that John Maltravers, the abbat of Kingſwood, John Bardone, Stephen de Chiltham, and Peter de la Mare were lords of the vill of Rodmerton 9 E. 1. Peter de Braoſe, or Breuſe, purchaſed a charter of free warren in Rodmerton 29 E. 1. and dying 5 E. 2. left Thomas, his ſon and heir, ten years old. Thomas de Berton died ſeized of Rodmerton 49 E. 3. as did John Langley, of Rodmerton and Torleton 10 H. 4. William Fitz-Warren was ſeized of the manor and advowſon of Rodmarton, and of lands in Torleton, and levied a fine of the ſame to ſir Ralph Boteler and John Edwards, and to the heirs of John, 19 H. 6.

Robert Cox was lord of this manor in the year 1608; ſir Walter Long was proprietor of it in the year 1710; but Charles Coxe, of Kemble in the county of Wilts, eſq; is the preſent lord of it. His arms are, *Sable, a chevron between three harts attires, each fixt to its proper ſcalp, argent.*

Lands in Rodmerton did belong to the abbey of Cirenceſter, and were granted to John Pope, 37 H. 8.

HAMLETS. 1. *Culkerton.* There were three ſmall eſtates in this hamlet at the time of the general ſurvey. Of one it is ſaid, 'The ſame 'William [de Owe] holds Culcortorne, and Her- 'bert holds it of him. Scireuold held it in the 'reign of king Edward. There are three yard- 'lands and five acres. In demean is one plow- 'tillage, and three *ſervi*. It is worth and was 'worth 35 *ſol.* Radulphus de Limeſi held this 'land; but it was never Aleſtan's.' *D. B.* p. 73.

The particulars of another are recorded as follow: 'The ſame Durand [de Glowec'] holds 'Culcortone, and Roger Ivri holds it of him. 'There are two hides, and two yard-lands and an 'half. Grim held it. There are two plow-tillages 'in demean, and ſix villeins, with three plow- 'tillages. It is worth and was worth 4 *lib.*' *Domeſday-book*, p. 76.

The third eſtate is thus deſcribed: 'The ſame 'Roger [de Lueri] holds Culcortone. Aluric held 'it, and Anſchitil held it of him. There is one 'hide and a half. In demean are two plow- 'tillages, and four *ſervi*. It was worth 20 *ſol.* 'but it is now worth 30 *ſol.*' *Dom. Book*, p. 75.

This manor belonged to the knights templers, who purchaſed a charter for court leet, waifs, and felons goods in the reign of king Henry the Third, and their claim to theſe privileges was allowed 15 E. 1. Culkerton was held of William de Clinton earl of Huntingdon 28 E. 3 It afterwards came to the Monoxes. Richard Monox died ſeized thereof 5 Mariæ. His ſon Thomas Monox, had livery granted to him the ſame year. Sir William Webb was lord of this manor in the year 1608. Charles Coxe of Lypiat, was lord of it about 1710, and his grandſon, Charles Coxe, of Kemble, eſq; is the preſent proprietor.

Adam de Smethelie granted one meſſuage, and one yard-land in Culkerton, to the abbey of Kingſwood, 5 E. 2.

Milo, conſtable of Glouceſter, gave the tithes of Culkerton to the church of Lanthony, in the year 1137.

2. *Haſleden.* The greater part of this hamlet is in Rodmarton, the reſt in Cherington. It contains only one farm-houſe. Here are two large *tumuli*, or barrows, that have never, that I know of, been opened. In *Domeſday-book* it is thus recorded: 'The ſame Roger [de Lueri] holds 'Haſedene in Langetrewes hundred. There are 'three hides and three yard-lands taxed. Elnoc 'held

'held it in the reign of king Edward. There are 'four plow-tillages in demean, and ſeven half 'villeins, and one bordar, with three plow-tillages, 'and ſeventeen *ſervi*, and half a mill of 30*d.* and 'fifteen acres of meadow. One Roger held this 'manor of the biſhop of Baieux for 16*l.* After- 'wards the biſhop gave it to the ſame Roger with 'the farm.' *Domeſday-book*, p. 75.

Reginald de St. Waleric, whoſe family name was taken from the port of St. Valerick in Normandy, and whoſe anceſtors came over with the conqueror, was lord of Haſleden about the year 1140. Having been diſſeized of this manor for rebellion againſt king Stephen, he recovered it again, and built a monaſtery for Benedictine monks at this place; but the monks removed hence, for want of water, to Tetbury, where they were not likely to be much better ſupply'd. Thence afterwards they moved, for want of wood, to Kingſwood, where they continued 'till that abbey was diſſolved. The abbey of Kingſwood held Haſleden grange and Culkerton 12 H. 4.

The abbey barn at Haſleden is ſtill remaining, within the eaſt porch of which is this inſcription: ANNO DNI: M°CC°XC°: HENRICI: ABATIS: XIX°: FUIT: ISTUM: CONSTRUCT. *i.e.* This was built in the year of our Lord 1290, and in the 19th year of Henry the abbat.

The abbat of Kingſwood paid a yearly penſion of two pounds for lands at Culkerton and Haſeldene, to the prior of Lanthony, ſeveral receipts for which are mentioned in the prior's regiſters.

It is remarkable that the inhabitants of this hamlet have no ſeat-place in either of the churches of Rodmarton or Cherington, wherein it lies; but it is ſaid they have a ſeat at Kingſwood.

This large farm or grange is now the property of lord Ducie.

3. *Torleton.* Part of this hamlet lies in the pariſh of Cotes. At the time of the general ſurvey, this hamlet lay in the hundred of Cirenceſter. In *Domeſday-book* it is expreſſed after this manner: 'William de Ow holds one hide in 'Tornentone, in Cireceſtre hundred, and Herbert 'holds it of him. Leuric held it in the reign of 'king Edward, and he might go where he pleaſed. 'There is one plow-tillage in demean, and four '*ſervi*. It was worth 40 *ſol.* It is worth 20 *ſol.*' *Domeſday-book*, p. 73.

John Langley was ſeized of one meſſuage and one plow-tillage in Torleton 18 E. 2. This is now a corps to a prebend of the church of Saliſbury. John Ebden, D.D. a prebendary in that church, was owner of this manor in the year 1608. John Coxe, eſq; is the preſent leſſee, and it has been in that name for many generations. Here is a chapel, but divine ſervice is diſcontinued.

Tithes in Torleton, with the chapel, lately belonging to the Benedictine nunnery at Rumſey in Hampſhire, founded by king Edgar in the year 907, were granted to Giles Pool 34 H. 8.

Of the Church, &c.

The church is in the deanery of Stonehouſe. It is a rectory worth 200*l.* a year. Samuel Lyſons, A.M. is the preſent patron and incumbent. It formerly belonged to the abbey of Oſney in Oxfordſhire. Mr. Yate, a rector of this pariſh, in the year 1641, recovered the tithes of Torleton, having proved it to have been a member of Rodmarton in the 14th year of king Edward the Third.

A yard-land in each field belongs to the glebe.

The church hath two ailes, and a ſpire in the middle. In the north aile were formerly the arms of the family of the Wyes, and the name of Allen in a window of the ſouth aile; whence it ſeems probable that ſome perſons of theſe families either built, or were large contributers towards the building of the reſpective ailes.

Firſt fruits £.	18	1	3	Synodals £.	0	2	0
Tenths —	1	6	1½	Pentecoſtals	0	0	10
Procurations	0	6	8				

Monuments and Inſcriptions.

Upon a grey marble ſtone in the chancel, is the effigy of a man in braſs, in the antient dreſs of a lawyer, and this inſcription:

Hic jacet Johēs Edward q°ndam dns Manerij de Rodmarton & verus patronus ejuſdem. Famoſus Apprentici[s] in lege p'itus. qui obijt die Januarij. A° Dni M°CCCC. lxi. cui[s] aīe p'p'icietur de[s] amen.

On the ſame ſtone, engraved on braſs,

Hic jacet Stephanus Collier A.M. nuper hujus Eccleſiæ Rector. Obijt decimo die menſis Auguſti anno Domini 1722, annoque Ætatis ſuæ 79.

In the chancel,

Iob[s] Yate Lon. ex vico Baſinglane paræc. Aldermariæ, renat[s] 24 Julij 1594. Coll. Em. Cantab. olim ſoc. S. Th. B. inductus in hanc eccleſ. veſp'ijs Dominicæ in albis 1628, mortalitatem exuit . . . .

Nudus Iob rediens ut venerat, ecce, receſſit
Rodmerton quondam qui tibi paſtor erat.
Is, quia quæ ſolitus nequit ex ambone monere,
Clamat et e tumulo prædicat iſta ſuo.
Mors tua, mors Chriſti, fraus mundi, gloria cœli,
Et dolor inferni ſunt meditanda tibi.
Truſt not the world, remember death,
And often think of hell;
Think often on the great reward
For thoſe that do live well.
Repent, amend, then truſt in Chriſt,
Soe thou in peace ſhalt die,
And reſt in bliſs, and riſe with joy,
And reign eternally.

Note, this monument was put up many years before Mr. Yate's death, as I find by a memorandum which he made himſelf in the regiſter. i.e. Menſe Decembri hujus anni mortalitatis memor, ipſe mihi poſui tale monumentum in Cancello. He died Jan. 13, 1668.

Within the rails in the chancel, on a blue ſtone,

H. S. E.

Reverendus Vir Sawyerus Smith hujus Eccleſiæ Rector Obijt 17° Aprilis Anno ſalutis 1756 Ætatis ſuæ 39.

In the ſouth aile, againſt the wall, is a handſome marble monument, with this inſcription:

Near this place lie the Remains of the Reverend John Coxe M.A. Rector of North Cerney in this county, and of this pariſh. He was what his holy Profeſſion called upon him to perſwade others to be. The duties he conſtantly taught he as conſtantly tranſcribed into his own practice, and was therefore an eminent example of all thoſe virtues that ought to be endearing to mankind (which was the chief view) that he knew well pleaſing to his God. Reader, if thou canſt be prevailed upon to learn from him how to live, thou wilt ſecure to thyſelf the ineſtimable bleſſing of dying the death of the Righteous. He died on the 14th of February, in the year of our Lord 1730, and the 75th of his age.——Arms, at top, *Sable, a chevron between three bucks attires with the ſcalps argent.*

In the north aile are ſeveral flat ſtones over the family of the Coxes. On one of them,

Here lyeth the body of Mary the daughter of John Coxe, Gent. dec[d]. and wife of George White, Gent. who departed this life the 12th Day of November, 1693.

Heavens grant it to the world no ill preſage,
Here lyes intomb'd the Phœnix of her age;
The beſt of wives, friends, neighbours, children, mothers:
That liv'd leſſe to her ſelfe then God and others.

Benefaction.

Henry Smith, of London, eſq; gave 5*l.* yearly, charged on Tolerſcomb-farm in Suſſex, for the benefit of the poor, and for apprenticing out the poor children of the hamlet of Culkerton.

Taxes.					
The Royal Aid in	1692,	£. 71	2	0
Poll-tax ——	1694, —	25	7	0
Land-tax —	1694, —	99	6	0
The ſame, at 3*s.*	1770, —	74	9	9

According to ſir Robert Atkyns, when his account of this pariſh was publiſh'd, there were 37 houſes, and about 180 inhabitants, whereof 6 were freeholders; yearly births 5, burials 4. But the following is a true ſtate of the regiſter. In a ſeries of ten years, from 1700 to 1709 incluſive, there were 38 baptiſms, and 31 burials. In a like ſeries of ten years, from 1760 to 1769, both incluſive, the births were 100, and the burials 43. The exact number of houſes is 56, of inhabitants 241; ſo that upon an average of ten years, the proportion of annual burials to the number of ſurviving inhabitants, is nearly as 1 to 56; an inconteſtible proof of the healthy ſituation of this place, where the inhabitants are increaſing very faſt.

RUDFORD

IS a ſmall pariſh, lying one part in the hundred of Botloe, the other in the united hundreds of Dudſton and King's Barton, five miles diſtant ſouth-eaſtward from Newent, nine north-eaſt from Mitchel Dean, and four north-weſtward from Glouceſter.

The pariſh is bounded on the north by the river Leden, and a ſmall brook which riſes at Tainton runs through it, in its courſe to that river. Rudford may be ſo called from the *Road at the Ford*, or from the *Redneſs of the ſoil there*; for *red* was called *Rud* by our Saxon anceſtors. But if neither of theſe conjectures ſhould be ſatisfactory to the reader, it does not occur to me upon what other occaſion the name was given it.

The ſoil is deep and good, but it is in a bad ſtate reſpecting cultivation. The greater part is paſture, with orcharding and arable. The manor and moſt of the lands are held by leaſe under the church of Glouceſter, whence it happens, that, except the manor houſe, there is ſcarcely a habitable dwelling in the village. I mean not to reflect on that reverend body, for it is in general the caſe with the eſtates held under all fluctuating proprietaries, whoſe intereſt in ſuch eſtates being only for a ſhort duration, they will not be at the expence of improvements from which they cannot expect to reap ſuitable advantages. This is an evil which can only be lamented, as perhaps it does not admit of a remedy.

Of the Manor and other Eſtates.

'Madoch holds Rudeford, in Botelau hundred, 'of the king. He held it in the time of king 'Edward. There are two hides. In demean are 'two plow-tillages, and three villeins, and four 'bordars, with three plow-tillages; and a mill 'paying as much corn [*annonam*] as can be earned 'by it. It is worth and was worth 40*s.*' *D.B.* p. 80.

King William the Second gave Rodesford to the abbey of St. Peter at Glouceſter, when Serlo was abbat. Winebald de Balun, a great baron, with the conſent of Roger his ſon, gave the manor of Rudford to the ſame church, in the year 1126. The abbat of Glouceſter was ſeized of the manors of Rudford, Leden, and Mude Leden, and his right to free warren was allowed in a *Quo warranto* 15 E. 1.

The abbey continued poſſeſſed of the manor 'till the diſſolution, when it was granted to the dean and chapter of Glouceſter 33 H. 8. Mr. Edward Holder is the preſent leſſee of the manor under the dean and chapter. His arms are, *Sable, a chevron between three anchors argent.*

HAMLET. *High Leden* is a hamlet in this pariſh, and in the hundred of Dudſton and King's Barton. Richard de Wigmore gave his lands in Hyneledene, with the groves, paſtures, meadows, and all appurtenances, which had belonged to Jeoffry de le Dene, to the abbey of Glouceſter, in the year 1239. And king Edward the Third, by his charter, dated 23 Dec. in the 28th year of his reign, granted to the abbey of Glouceſter, free warren in all their demean lands in Hyneledene.

The tithes of High Leden were granted to the dean and chapter of Glouceſter 33 H. 8.

Of the Church, &c.

The church is a rectory, in the Foreſt deanery, worth 80*l.* a year. The dean and chapter of Glouceſter are patrons, and Mr. George Biſhop is the preſent incumbent.

The church is a ſmall building, dedicated to St. Mary, with a tower at the weſt end.

Firſt fruits £.10	0	0	Proc. & Syn. £.0	8	8
Tenths — 1	0	0	Pentecoſtals - 0	1	6

Rudford.

Taxes.					
The Royal Aid in	1692,	£. 35	2	0
Poll-tax — —	1694, —	3	8	0
Land-tax ——	1694, —	36	0	0
The ſame, at 3*s.*	1770, —	27	0	0

High Leden.

Taxes.					
The Royal Aid in	1692,	£. 56	9	4
Poll-tax ——	1694, —	3	5	0
Land-tax ——	1694, —	63	12	0
The ſame, at 3*s.*	1770, —	47	14	0

At

At the beginning of this century, there were 22 houſes in the pariſh, and about 106 inhabitants, of whom 4 were freeholders; yearly births 3, burials 3. *Atkyns.* The people are now about the ſame number.

RUERDEAN

IS a ſmall pariſh, in the hundred of St. Briavel's, in the Foreſt diviſion, two miles ſouth-weſtward from Mitchel Dean, five ſouthward from Roſs in Herefordſhire, and about fourteen weſtward from Glouceſter.

It is bounded on the eaſt by Great and Little Dean, on the north by Herefordſhire, on the ſouth by the Foreſt, and on the weſt by the river Wye, which ſeparates it from Welch Bicknor, a detached pariſh in Monmouthſhire.

It is called *Ruerdean*, (ſuppoſed to be a corruption of *Riverdean*) becauſe it is ſituated upon the river Wye, and to diſtinguiſh it from the neighbouring places of Mitchel Dean and Little Dean. All theſe places abound with pit-coal and iron ore, of which more is delivered under the general account of the Foreſt.

Of the Manor and other Eſtates.

Domeſday-book takes no notice of this manor, as diſtinct from the other Deans, whence I conclude that they became ſeparate manors ſince that record was compiled.

William de Alba Mara died ſeized of an eſtate called Ruerdean 40 H. 3. Thomas Deverty held the ſame, and St. Briavel's caſtle, 21 E. 1.

The ſheriff returned that Alexander de Byknore and William Hatheway were lords of the vill of Rewardyne 9 E. 1. Alexander de Byknore held one meſſuage in Ruerdean and Ludbrook, with the bailiwicks of Ruerdean and St. Briavel's caſtle in the foreſt of Dean, 34 E. 1.

A manor in Ruerdean belonged to the abbey of Flaxley, at the diſſolution ,and was granted to ſir Anthony Kingſton 36 H. 8. It was ſoon after conveyed to the Baynhams. Thomas Baynham and Joſeph Baynham were lords of this manor in the year 1608, from whoſe family it paſſed to the Vaughans. John Vaughan, eſq; was lord of the manor about the beginning of this century, and the ſiſters and coheireſſes of Richard Clark, of the Hill, in Herefordſhire, eſq; are the preſent proprietors of the manor.

Hatheways was a diſtinct manor, antiently, and for many generations, enjoyed by a conſiderable family of the ſame name. Thus the ſheriff returned that William Hatheway was lord of Rewardyne, as before recited, 9 E. 1. The eſcheator's inquiſition found that William Hatheway died 10 E. 2. ſeized of ſeveral lands and tenements in Ruardyne, which he held of Alexander de Bykenore, paying 4*s.* 9*d.* yearly, and left William Hatheway his ſon and heir. Thomas Hatheway died ſeized thereof 5 R. 2. and William Walleyn was ſeized of a tenement called Hatheways, 11 E. 4. This eſtate came afterwards to the Baynhams, and the diſtinction of the manors was by that means loſt by unity of poſſeſſion.

Walter de Clare was ſeized of one meſſuage and one plow-tillage in Ruerdean, 18 E. 2. Alexander Carent was ſeized of a mill, and of a yearly rent in Ruerdean, 50 E. 3. and John Carent, his ſon, was ſeized of the ſame mill, and of a yearly rent of 26*s.* 8*d.* in Ruerdean 6 R. 2.

Of the Church, &c.

The church is a curacy, in the deanery of Roſs, worth 15*l.* a year, to which the vicar of Walford in Herefordſhire preſents. Mr. Jones is curate. The ſmall tithes belong to the miniſter, and the great tithes to the præcentor of Hereford.

The church, dedicated to St. John Baptiſt, is large, and has a handſome ſpire at the weſt end.

Proc. & Syn. £. 0 2 0 Pentecoſt. £. 0 1 4

Benefactions.

Nine parcels of land, worth about 6*l.* a year, are given to the uſe of the poor, and for the repair of the church.

Mr. Greenway has given 60*l.* the intereſt of which to be expended in educating poor children.

Taxes.					
The Royal Aid in	1692,	£.	126	16	0
Poll-tax —	1694, —		38	17	0
Land-tax —	1694, —		142	15	0
The ſame, at 3*s.*	1770, —		104	5	0

At the beginning of this century, according to ſir Robert Atkyns, there were 100 houſes in the pariſh, and about 500 inhabitants, 12 of whom were freeholders; yearly births 16, burials 13. The preſent number of inhabitants is about 758.

SAINTBURY.

THIS pariſh lies in the upper diviſion of the hundred of Kiftſgate, about two miles weſtward from Campden, five ſouth-eaſt from Eveſham in Worceſterſhire, and about twenty-ſix north-eaſtward from Glouceſter.

The preſent manner of writing the name is a deviation from the antient and true orthography, and proceeded originally from want of knowing the true ſignification of it. In *Domeſday* it is written *Suineberie*, (*i.e. Suine's*, or *Swain's Camp*,) and it was ſo called from the *Berg*, or *Camp*, not far above the church, where the intrenchments are ſtill viſible, which the inhabitants call *Caſtle-Bank*.

This camp, which has ſo fixed its name on the pariſh, ſeems to have been dependent on another very large one, higher up on the top of the hill, incloſing near ſixty acres of ground, raiſed probably by the ſame people, and ſtill remaining pretty perfect; but the latter lies in the adjoining pariſh

pariſh of Willerſey. *Suine*, or *Swain*, to whom theſe intrenchments are attributed, was undoubtedly one of thoſe Daniſh locuſts who for many years carried deſolation wherever they went, and raiſed moſt exorbitant contributions all over England, and occaſioned that grievous tax called Dane Geld, which was at length ſtatedly levied on the people, and continued for ſeveral ages before the nation could get rid of it.

The village of Saintbury is ſituated on the north-weſt ſide of the great hill country, facing the vale of Eveſham, with a ſteep aſcent from the houſes to the church. It conſiſts of a few farm houſes and cottages, but affords nothing worth the traveller's attention.

Of the Manor and other Eſtates.

'Haſcoit Muſard holds Suineberie in Witelai 'hundred of the king. Chenuicelle held it. There 'are ten hides. In demean are three plow-tillages, 'and eighteen villeins, and three bordars, with 'nine plow-tillages, and ten among the *ſervi* and '*ancillæ*, and a mill of 6*d*. It was worth 12*l*. 'now 10*l*.' *Domeſday-book*, p. 78.

Of the above Haſcoit Muſard, many particulars are ſet down under Miſerden. Richard Muſard was ſon and heir of Haſcoit, and Haſcoit the ſecond, was ſon and heir of Richard, and held fifteen knights fees 12 H. 2. He died 33 H. 2. and was ſucceeded by Ralph his ſon and heir, who had livery of this manor 2 R. 1. and paid 100*l*. for his relief. He married Iſabel, the widow of John de Nevill, without the king's licence, and paid 100 marks for his tranſgreſſion. He was a baron, and built the caſtle of Miſerden, and was high ſheriff of Glouceſterſhire from the 17 Joh. to 9 H. 3. and died in the 14th year of the laſt mentioned reign.

Walter de Abbytot was ſeized of this manor 1 Joh. but it is probable that it was only in truſt, for the manor continued in the Muſards for ſeveral generations after.

Robert Muſard, ſon of Ralph, entered upon his lands without ſueing forth livery, wherefore his caſtle of Miſerden, and all his eſtates, were ſeized into the king's hands, but were ſhortly after reſtored upon compoſition. He died without iſſue 24 H. 3. leaving Ralph Muſard, his brother and heir, a minor, whoſe wardſhip was granted by the crown to Jeffery Deſpencer, in conſideration of 500 marks. Ralph had livery of his lands 31 H. 3. and died in the 49th year of that reign, leaving Ralph his ſon and heir, who died ſeized of this manor and of Muſarden 1 E. 1. John Muſard, the next poſſeſſor, died 17 E. 1. Maſculine Muſard became ſeized of this manor 28 E. 1. and in the 31ſt year of that reign granted it to the abbey of Eveſham; but he continued in poſſeſſion 2 E. 2.

It appears by the records, that this eſtate was afterwards in lay hands, but they could only be tenants, or truſtees for the abbey. Thus we find that Thomas de Beauchamp, earl of Warwick, and others, were ſeized of Seinbury in truſt, 24 E. 3. and John Rouſe, and others, held the ſame 49 E. 3.

The abbey of Eveſham was ſeized of the manor of Seinſbury, and of the impropriation of the church, in the reign of king Richard the Second, and continued in poſſeſſion 'till the general diſſolution of religious houſes.

The manor, and two mills, lately belonging to the abbey of Eveſham, were granted to Richard Bartlet 35 H. 8. whoſe ſon, Richard Bartlet, had livery 20 Eliz. He married Alice, daughter of —— Ruding of Worceſterſhire, and left Henry, his eldeſt ſon and heir, who married the daughter of —— Dutton, of Dutton in Cheſhire, but died without iſſue. Sir Thomas Bartlet, brother of Henry, had livery of this manor 25 Eliz. He married Mary, daughter of ſir John Dauntiſer, and was ſucceeded by John Bartlet, who married Jane, daughter of Robert Kelway of Dorſetſhire.

From the Bartlets the manor paſſed to the Brawnes. Sir Hugh Brawne was lord of it in the year 1608, and the three coheireſſes of the family of Brawne were proprietors of it at the beginning of this century. Hugh Brawne, eſq; was lord of this manor at the time of his death, in the year 1726. It has ſince been purchaſed by Mr. Joſeph Roberts, who is the preſent proprietor.

An eſtate in this pariſh, ſometimes alſo called a manor, conſiſting of lands and tithes, belonged to the abbey of Glouceſter, and was granted to the chapter of Glouceſter 33 H. 8. Other tithes in Saintbury, *alias* Senebrig, belonged to the abbey of Winchcombe, and were granted to ſir Thomas Seimour 1 E. 6.

Of the Church, &c.

The church is a rectory, in the deanery of Campden, worth about 170*l*. a year. The rev. Mr. Hudſon Boyce, the preſent rector, has two turns in the preſentation, and the lord of the manor has the third.

The manor having belonged to the abbey of Eveſham, the demeans thereof are free from tithes.

A piece of ground is aſſigned to the miniſter, in ſatisfaction for incloſures.

The church is dedicated to St. Nicholas, and has a chapel on the north, and a ſteeple on the ſouth ſide, in which are ſix bells.

Firſt fruits £.	19	9	2	Synodals £.	0	1	0
Tenths —	1	18	11¼	Pentecoſt.	0	0	6
Procurations	0	6	8				

Monuments and Inſcriptions.

Upon a blue ſtone in the chancel, is a painting of a venerable divine, in his gown, which was formerly taken out of the parſonage houſe, and placed there. Under the picture is this inſcription:

Wilulimus Warburton Sacræ Theologiæ Baccalavreus Teneris Unguiculis Scholaris Collegij Etonenſis ivxta Windeſoram, Inde Cooptatvs In Albvm Sociorum Collegij Regalis Cantabrigiæ.
Expedita fuit iſta Delineatio Anno Xni MDCXLIIII
Annoque Ætatis LXIX.

——He was preſented to this rectory in 1617, and was buried Nov. 8, 1649. Arms, *Azure, a chevron argent between three choughs proper.*

On

On a braſs plate, in the north chapel,

Sub terra gravi tumulatur Alicia Bartlett
Cum Chriſto exultet Spiritus in requie.
Here under foote lyethe compaſte w[th] colde claye
The Corps of Alice Bartlett faſte cloſyd yn a Cheſte
For her Soule to God devo[u]tly lette us praye
In heavē thorwe Chriſte it maye have Ioyefull reſte.
Obijt XXVII° die Aprilis A° dni M. CCCCCLXXIIII°.

On a flat ſtone in the chancel,

Here lyeth the body of Dame Theodoſia Biſhop Daughter of Sir Richard Brawne of Alſcoat in the County of Glouceſter Knight and Wife of Sir William Biſhope of Bridgtown in the County of Warwick Knight, who Departed this life December 16th 88. Theodoſia viz. The Gift of God.
The LORD Gave and the LORD hath taken away. *Iob.* 1, 21.

Here lyeth the Body of Hugh Brawne Eſq; Lord of this Manor who Departed this life Auguſt 31st 1726 Aged 72.———Arms, *Three bars, in the dexter canton a wolf's head erazed,* for Brawne.

To the Memory of the Reverend M[r]. Iohn Brawne, who ſucceeded his Father in this Rectory of Saintbury in the year of our Lord 1680. He lived and left a rare Example of Piety towards God, of Paſtoral Care towards his Pariſh, and of Benevolence towards all mankind. He died Sept[r]. 21st 1736, in the 81st Year of his Age.———Arms, Brawne as before.

Here lyeth the Body of Anne Brawne Daughter of William Byrd of Eveſham in the County of Worceſter, Gentleman, and Wife of John Brawne Rector of Saintbury, who Departed this life October the 6, 1680.———Arms, 1. Brawne. 2. *On a chevron ingrailed between three lions rampant as many fleurs de lis,* for Byrd.

Here lyeth the Body of Elizabeth Brawne Daughter of S[r]. Richard Biſhope of Bridgtown in the County of Warwick Knight, and Wife of John Brawne Rector of this place, who Departed this life January the 9th 1705 Aged 74.

Here Lyeth the Body of Elizabeth the wife of John Brawne Rector of Saintbury who Departed this life March the 21st Anno 1720.———Arms, 1. Brawne. 2. *A chevron ingrailed between three lions rampant.*

Here Lyeth the Body of Suſannah Mariet, Daughter of Thomas Mariet Eſq[r]; and Lucy-Ann his Wife, who departed this life December the 8th Ann. Dom. 1720.———Arms, *Barry of ſix, Or and ſable,* for Marriot of Preſton.

Benefactions.

A tenement and ſeven ridges of land are aſſigned to the pariſh clerk, who pays 4*s.* 6*d.* a year out of them for the repair of the church. Mr. Veal's land is charged with 2*s.* a year to the ſame uſe. Lady Theodoſia Biſhop charged her eſtate here with the payment of 5*l.* a year to the poor.

Taxes.					
The Royal Aid in	1692,	£. 146	2	0
Poll-tax ——	1694,	— 21	4	0
Land-tax ——	1694,	— 114	18	0
The ſame, at 3*s.*	1770,	— 86	3	6

At the beginning of this century, there were 54 houſes, and about 240 inhabitants in this pariſh, whereof 10 were freeholders; yearly births 7, burials 6. *Atkyns.* The preſent number of houſes is 31, and the people are decreaſed to 135.

****

Salperton, *or* Cold Salperton,

IS a ſmall pariſh, in the hundred of Bradley, twelve miles north from Cirenceſter, ſix ſouth-eaſtward from Winchcombe, four north-weſtward from Northleach, and ſixteen eaſtward from Glouceſter.

It lies very high and bleak on the Coteſwold, for which reaſon it obtained the addition of *Cold.* Notwithſtanding this expoſed ſituation, agriculture is carried on with a ſpirit and ſucceſs that do honour to the occupiers, and ſhame the indolence of many of the vale country farmers, who, with every advantage of a richer ſoil, and milder air, trudge on in the old beaten track of their anceſtors, almoſt without an attempt at improvement. It is diſguſting to ſee ſome of the beſt land in the county lie in a miſerable, unimproved ſtate, while the Coteſwold-hills, naturally bleak and barren, have, within a few years paſt, been rendered fruitful by judicious management, and the occupiers are become a thriving and opulent people.

The downs and common fields in this pariſh have been lately incloſed, greatly to the intereſt of the landholder, and no leſs to the advantage of the labouring people, becauſe thoſe lands, now chiefly converted to tillage, afford more conſtant and abundant employment for the labouring poor than in their former condition.

A ſmall ſtream riſes here, and runs down to Sherborne, in its courſe to the Windruſh.

Of the Manor and other Eſtates.

'Hugo Laſne holds Salpretune, in Bradelege 'hundred. There are ten hides taxed. Uuluuard 'held it. In demean are three plow-tillages, and 'ten villeins, and a prieſt, with ſeven plow-tillages, 'and eleven among the *ſervi* and *ancillæ,* and five 'acres of meadow. It was worth 9*l.* now 7*l.*' *Domeſday-book,* p. 78.

Among the particulars of the eſtates of the church of Worceſter, it is ſaid, 'Of the land 'belonging to this manor [Clive] Ralph holds four 'hides in Sapletone of the church.' *Ibid.* p. 70.

The knights templers were ſeized of the manor, and had a grant of court leet, waifs, and felons goods from king Henry the Third, which they pleaded in a writ of *Quo warranto,* 15 E. 1. and thoſe privileges were then allowed. The ſame knights continued ſeized of the manor 2 E. 3. when it was held of William de Clinton, earl of Huntingdon.

The manor was afterwards granted to the Benedictine nunnery of Stodely in Oxfordſhire, founded by Bernard de St. Waleric in the reign of king Henry the Second, and valued, at the diſſolution, at 102*l.* 6*s.* 7*d.* After the diſſolution, the manor was granted to Wincheſter college, to which it ſtill belongs. Thomas Browne, eſq; is the preſent leſſee of the manor, and proprietor of all the freehold lands in the pariſh. He has a very good ſtone-built houſe near the church, where he reſides.

Of the Church, &c.

The church is a curacy, in the deanery of Stow, worth 8*l.* a year from the impropriator. Mr. Browne is patron and impropriator, and Mr. Lawrence is the preſent incumbent. The living has been twice augmented with the queen's bounty.

 Robert

Robert de Chandos, who came in with the Conqueror, gave the advowſon of the church of Salperton to the monks of Lyra in Normandy. The impropriation was afterwards appropriated to the uſe of the nunnery of Stodely; and upon the diſſolution of that houſe, it was granted to Richard Andrews and Nicholas Temple, in truſt, 35 H. 8. The fee of the impropriation was veſted in Mr. Bee, about the beginning of this century, and was ſold, by him, to Mr. Coſley of Briſtol; of whom it was purchaſed by the earl of Weſtmoreland, and ſold to Thomas Browne, eſq; the preſent proprietor, who pays 4*s.* a year out of it to the crown.

The church is ſmall, dedicated to All Saints, and has a handſome new built tower at the weſt end.

Proc. & Syn. £. 0 4 4 Pentecoſt. £. 0 0 7

Benefaction.

Mr. Aylworth left 800*l.* to purchaſe land for the augmentation of four poor livings, *viz.* Charlton Abbats, Cold Salperton, Sevenhampton, and Compton Abdale.

Taxes.			£.	s.	d.
The Royal Aid in	1692,		23	9	0
Poll-tax	1694,	—	4	2	0
Land-tax	1694,	—	20	9	0
The ſame, at 3*s.*	1770,	—	14	13	$0\frac{3}{4}$

About ſeventy years ago, when ſir Robert Atkyns collected the materials for his Hiſtory, there were in this pariſh 15 houſes, and about 60 inhabitants, whereof 4 were freeholders; yearly birth 2, burials 1. But ſince that period, the condition of this country has been greatly altered. The downs and commons, which were eaſily managed by two or three ſhepherds and herdſmen, have been incloſed, and converted to tillage; and new cottages have been erected, ſo that the preſent number of houſes is 23, of inhabitants 155.

SANDHURST, *or* SANTHURST.

THIS pariſh lies in the Vale, in the united hundreds of Dudſton and King's-barton, thirteen miles eaſt from Newent, ſeven ſouth from Tewkeſbury, and three north from Glouceſter. It is bounded on the north by Norton, on the eaſt by Twigworth, on the ſouth by Longford, and on the weſt by the river Severn.

The ſoil is ſandy next the river, and being antiently overgrown with wood, gave occaſion to the name of the pariſh, which is ſuppoſed to be compounded of *Sand*, and of the Saxon word hyrſt, *a wood.* The reſt of the pariſh is much inclined to clay, and conſiſts chiefly of meadow and paſturage, with about a hundred acres of arable in common field.

Walſworth is a very handſome ſeat in this pariſh, belonging to Samuel Hayward, eſq; who has a good eſtate here, and in ſeveral other parts of the county. The houſe is new, with proper offices, and the gardens are well laid out, and very pleaſant. He has favoured the public with an elegant engraving of it, to decorate this work.

Not far from this houſe, there is a ſpring of medicinal or purging water, like the Cheltenham ſpaw, but it is ſometimes dry in the ſummer. And there is alſo a ſalt-ſpring, upon the diſcovery of which, about twenty years ſince, a pit was opened to a conſiderable depth, with an intention of erecting a ſalt-work; but not proving ſo ſtrong as was expected, that project was then dropt, and the mouth of the pit ſtopt up with bricks to prevent accidents.

Part of Wainlode's-hill lies in Sandhurſt, the reſt in Norton. It does not riſe to any great height, but ſtretching along the ſouth-eaſt ſide of the Severn, affords an extenſive proſpect over this part of the vale country, which lies flat and low, and therefore, in wet ſeaſons, is ſubject to inundations from the river.

Two brooks, which riſe at Shurdington and Witcombe, after uniting their ſtreams, fall into the Severn near Ablode's Court. The turnpike-road from Glouceſter to Tewkeſbury, and ſo to Worceſter, paſſes through the pariſh.

Of the Manor and other Eſtates.

'Edmar, a thane, held three manors in Dudeſtan 'hundred, Herſefel, Athelai, and Sanher. The 'ſame man could give or ſell his land to whom 'he pleaſed. This eſtate claimed to be taxed but 'for two hides [*pro* ii *hidis ſe defendebat*]. In de'mean are eight plow-tillages, and four villeins, 'and four bordars, and thirty *ſervi*, with five 'plow-tillages. There is meadow ſufficient for 'the plowed land.'

'Earl Herald took away theſe five eſtates '[Herſefel, Athelai, Sanher, Herſecome, and 'Broſtrop] after the death of king Edward, and 'Robert de Lurei put them to farm for 46*l.* 13*s.* 4*d.*' *Domeſday-book*, p. 67.

This manor, ſoon after the Norman conqueſt, belonged to the family of de Willington, from whom the manor houſe obtained the name of Willington-Court. Ralph de Willington and Olimpias his wife gave ſix ridges of land behind Ablode Court in this pariſh to the abbey of Glouceſter 12 H. 1. The ſheriff returned that John de Willington and the abbat of St. Peter at Glouceſter were lords of Sandhurſt 9 E. 1. John de Willington had a charter of free warren in Sandhurſt 4 E. 2. and died ſeized of this manor, and thoſe of Ablington in Bibury, Poulton in Awre, Frampton Cotterel, and Yate, 12 E. 3. Sir Ralph de Willington, ſon of John, held the ſame manors, and Weſtonbirt, at the time of his death 22 E. 3. whereupon livery was granted the following year to Henry his ſon, who was living 26 E. 3. Sir John de Willington, ſon of Henry, was ſeized of Poulton, Ablington, Yate, Frampton Cotterel, Sandhurſt, and Moreſlade, adjoining to Sandhurſt,

2 R. 2.

2 R. 2. and his son, Ralph de Willington, was lord of the same manors, and of Culverden in this parish, at the time of his death 6 R. 2. Joan his wife survived him, and was endowed with the third part of the manor of Sandhurst. She was afterwards married to Thomas West, whom she likewise survived, and died seized of her third part, and of tenements in Moreslade, 6 H. 4. Ralph, son and heir of Ralph and Joan de Willington, died 19 R. 2. possessed of the other two thirds of the manor, and was succeeded by his brother John de Willington, who died without issue 20 R. 2. seized of the manors of Poulton, Ablington, Westonbirt, Frampton Cotterel, Sandhurst, and Culverden and Moreslade in Sandhurst, all in the county of Gloucester, which thereupon came to Joan, his sister and heiress, who was married to John Wrath. John Wrath, son of John, and of Joan de Willington, died without issue 13 H. 4. and sir John Wadham was seized of this manor the same year; but he could be only in trust, for the last mentioned John Wrath left his two sisters coheiresses to his great estate; Elizabeth, married to sir William Poulton, and Isabel, the widow of William Beaumont.

Sir William Poulton and Elizabeth his wife levied a fine of the sixth part of this and other manors, to the use of themselves in taille, the remainder to Isabel the widow of William Beaumont. They dying without issue, Isabel became possessed of the whole family estate, which after the death of her son John Beaumont, without issue, descended to Isabel her daughter, who died unmarried 2 H. 6. seized of the manors of Ablington, Poulton, Yate, Westonbirt, Frampton Cotterel, and Sandhurst, all which were the patrimony of her ancestors the Willingtons.

Sir Thomas Beaumont, kinsman and next heir to Isabel, succeeded her, and dying 29 H. 6. this manor descended to his son, sir William Beaumont, (in some records stiled William Beaumont, esq;) who died in the thirty second year of the same reign. Philip Beaumont, brother and heir of William, died 13 E. 4. seized of the manors of Poulton, Ablington, Yate, Westonbirt, Frampton Cotterel, and Sandhurst, of all which Hugh Beaumont and Elizabeth his wife, John Basset and Elizabeth his wife, John Beaumont, clerk, John Chichester and Margaret his wife, and John Croker and Anne his wife, levied several fines 16, 18, & 20 H. 7. to Richard bishop of Durham, and other bishops and great persons, (among whom was Giles lord d'Aubeny) probably for the use of the king.

This and the before recited manors were granted to Giles lord d'Aubeny, who died seized of them 6 H. 8. and livery was granted to his son Henry lord d'Aubeny the same year. They afterwards reverted to the crown, and were granted to Edward duke of Somerset, upon whose attainder they came again to the crown. James Basset obtained a grant of the manors of Yate, Ablington, Westonbirt, Frampton Cotterel, and Sandhurst, 4 Mariæ, and the grant was confirmed to Arthur Basset 7 Eliz.

The manor of Sandhurst came afterwards to the Winston's. Philip Winston, of Willington Court, died in the year 1672, and lies buried in the church. John Viney, esq; was lord of the manor of Sandhurst-Willington at the beginning of this century, and John Viney, esq; a descendant of the above John, is the present proprietor.

Ablode's Court, written *Abbelode* in the time of king Edward the First, is another reputed manor, situate on the south side of the parish, and was so called, because it belonged to the abbey of Gloucester, and lies at the place where a brook empties itself into the Severn; for to such a confluence the name of *Lade*, or *Lode*, was frequently given by our Saxon ancestors.

King Henry the First granted lands in Ablode, and the grove of Barton, called Paygrove, to the abbey of Gloucester, in exchange for the place where the tower of the cathedral now stands, which was then an orchard belonging to the monks. The same king, in the 9th year of his reign, further granted to the abbey six ridges of land behind Ablode's Court. Ralph de Willington and Olimpias his wife gave six other ridges of land behind Ablode's Court to the same abbey 12 H. 1.

The sheriff returned, that the abbat of St. Peter of Gloucester was lord of a moiety of Sandhurst 9 E. 1. and it is probable that the abbat's part was what is now called Ablode. The abbey of Gloucester was seized of the manor of Abbelode 17 E. 3. and had three carucates of land there, worth 14*s*. each; rents of assize worth two marks; profits of the stock 10*s*. composition for work and taxes 6*s*. total 4*l*. 4*s*. 8*d*. and the same house had free warren in all their demean lands there 28 E. 3.

The manor continued in the abbey 'till the general dissolution, after which it was granted, together with half a wood called Woolridge in Ablode, to the dean and chapter of Gloucester 33 H. 8.

By an ordinance of parliament, Apr. 3, 1648, the scite or farm of the manor of Ablode, which belonged to the dean and chapter of Gloucester, and the yearly rent thereof, being 22*l*. 7*s*. 4*d*. was settled upon the mayor and burgesses of that city, for the support of preaching ministers. But after the Restoration of king Charles the Second, this ordinance was annulled, and the dean and chapter were reinstated in the manor of Ablode, which is now in lease from them to George-Augustus Selwyn, esq; whose arms are given under Matson.

Bruerne, is another antient manor in this parish, supposed to have been so called from the French word *Bruyer*, a *heath*, which might have been perfectly descriptive of its condition at the time the name was given it. A fair for cattle was formerly held here.

‘ Ældred

'Ældred archbiſhop [of York] claims Brewere, 'one member of this manor [Bertune]. There 'are three yard-lands, and three men. Milo 'Criſpin holds it.' *Domeſday-book*, p. 67.

'Milo Criſpin holds three yard-lands in Bruurne 'in Dudeſtan hundred. Wigot held them. There 'is one plow-tillage in demean, and ſeven bordars, 'with two plow-tillages, and half a fiſhery. It 'was worth 40*s.* now 30*s.*' *Ib.* p. 78.

In the extracts out of the pipe rolls in the exchequer, formerly ſent to the ſheriffs of the city of Glouceſter for levying certain ſums, it is ſaid, *De Almerico de Parco de firma duarum virgatum terræ in Brawer* 12 *den.* This Almeric of the Park was lord of the manor of Brawer in the reign of king Henry the Third. John le Boteler was ſeized of the manor of Bruarne, and of the Barton near Glouceſter 15 E. 1. at which time his right to ſeveral privileges in this manor was allowed in a writ of *Quo warranto*. John le Boteler of Lanſart held the ſame 2 E. 3. Beatrix le Boteler was ſeized of Bruarne, which ſhe held of the manor of Berton 33 E. 3. John Boteler of the Park held the manors of the Park in Haresfield, Morecot in Minſterworth, Bruarne, and Kingſholme, 36 E. 3. Elianor le Boteler held Bruerne and Kingſholme 46 E. 3. John Kenn died ſeized of the manors of Hardwick, la Bruerne in Sandhurſt, the Park in Haresfield, and Morecot in Minſterworth 6 H. 4. The late Thomas Vernon, eſq; died about the year 1775, poſſeſſed of this eſtate, by purchaſe from the deſcendants of the late general Carpenter.

Culverden, is another antient manor in this pariſh, the lordſhip of which is very extenſive. It has already been ſhewn, in the deſcent of the manor of Sandhurſt, that Culverden was part of the poſſeſſions of the antient family of de Willington, and it ſeems very probable that it paſſed through the ſame hands with Sandhurſt, down to the reign of king Henry the Seventh.

Chriſtopher Throckmorton died ſeized of Culverden 5 H. 8. and William his ſon had livery thereof, and of twenty meſſuages in Sandhurſt, the ſame year. Livery of the manor of Culverden was granted to Thomas Throckmorton 9 Eliz.

It came afterwards to the family of Bell, and was purchaſed, after the death of Mr. William Bell of Glouceſter, by Samuel Hayward, eſq; the preſent lord of the manor, who has built a handſome ſeat at Wallſworth, as mentioned in the introductory part of this account. His arms are, *Argent, on a bend ſable, between two roſes gules, a roſe between as many fleurs de lis Or; on a chief of the ſecond a lion paſſant of the fourth.*

Of the other eſtates, the records ſhew, that Robert le Savage held lands in Sandhurſt 44 H. 3. Adam de Ardeen was ſeized of lands in Sandhurſt and Culverden 56 H. 3. Robert de Aſton held lands in Sandhurſt 23 E. 3. of which John de Aſton, his ſon, died ſeized 7 R. 2. John Gaby, *alias* Withely, was poſſeſſed of one meſſuage, forty-two acres of arable, and ſix acres of meadow in Sandhurſt, 15 R. 2. Edward Brug held lands in Sandhurſt 16 H. 4. and Edward Brug, eſq; died ſeized of lands and tenements in the ſame place 15 H. 6. Two yard-lands in Sandhurſt belonged to the Auguſtin nunnery of St. Mary and St. Margaret at Dartford in Kent, which was founded by king Edward the Third, in the year 1373, and valued, at the diſſolution, at 400*l.* 8*s.* a year. Theſe lands were granted to Thomas Babington 36 H. 8. at which time they were in the poſſeſſion of Richard Amenell. Other lands in Sandhurſt, then in the tenure of Richard Gibbs, were granted to William Wit and William Bryton 2 Mariæ. Richard Wight died ſeized of ſix acres of meadow in Sandhurſt 44 Eliz.

Of the Church, &c.

The church is a vicarage, in the deanery of Glouceſter, worth 63*l.* a year, including 30*l.* a year given by Mr. Giles Coxe, for a lecture ſermon every Sunday morning. The biſhop of Briſtol is patron and impropriator.

The rectory and advowſon of the vicarage of Santhurſt belonged to the monaſtery of St. Oſwald in Glouceſter, and were granted to the biſhoprick of Briſtol 34 H. 8. and valued, in a ſurvey taken about that time, at 10*l.* 19*s.* *Willis.*

The church is dedicated to St. Lawrence, and conſiſts of the nave and chancel, with a low tower, in which are ſix bells, at the weſt end. The pews are in the old taſte, but in exceeding good preſervation. The church is fitted up with three handſome galleries, and the chancel has lately been repaired and ornamented at a very conſiderable expence, by the munificence of Samuel Hayward, and Thomas Vernon, eſq^{rs}.

Synodals 2*s.* Pentecoſtals 7*d.*

Monuments and Inſcriptions.

On a flat marble ſtone in the chancel,

Philippus Winſton de Willington's Court, Gen. obijt 14° Augu. Anno Salutis 1672, Ætatis 70.

If of afflictions patience is the Crown,
And to endure is to excell :
There's few deſerve a conqueror's renown
More than th' entomb'd within this cell.
If charity is preacht ye goſpel Sum,
And to be Chriſtian is to love :
Scarce any ere the name did more become
Then the bleſt ſoul hence fled above.

Arms, *Sable, a lion rampant argent, holding in the dexter paw a roſe of the ſecond.*

Next the above,

Here lyeth ye Body of Gyles Winſton, Gent. who departed this Life the 6th Day of September A^{o} D^{ni} 1662, aged 85 Yeares.

On the next ſtone,

Here lyeth the body of ye faithfull and paynfull preacher of ye goſpell Gerard Prior, who in his life time {dif / re} coueréd ye Concealed uicarage of Sandhurſt, built ye houſe, procured ye lecture, & after 53 years labor in ye Miniſtery put of y^{s} tabernacle and was buryed Auguſt 25th in the year of {his {age 76. / incumbency in y^{s} place 32} / our Lord 1654.}

Againſt

Againſt the ſouth wall,

This is to preſerve the Memory of Ioane the wife of Iohn Gyſe of this Pariſh Eſq; who departed this life the 20th day of April 1680, and out of her piety and love to this pariſh, gave 10 pounds per annum to a miniſter that ſhould be reſident here, to continue for 60 years after her death.——Arms, *Baron and femme*, 1. Gyſe. 2. *Argent, a cluſter of grapes gules*, ſuppoſed for Viney.

On a flat ſtone,

Here lyeth the Body of William Bell of yͤ Pariſh Gent. who departed yͤ Life the 3d of May, 1653, Aged 65 years.

Here lyeth alſoe the Body of William Bell, ſonne of the above named William Bell, who departed yͤ Life the 29th of Iuly 1669, Aged 29 Years.

Here lyeth alſoe the Body of William Bell, ſonne of yͤ laſt named Wm Bell, who departed this Life the 27 day of Septemb. Ano Dni 1706, Aged 45 Years.

Poſthumus Bell, Gent. ob. xxo Die Augti Ano Dni 1730, Ætat. ſuæ 60.

Elizaa Bell Vidua & Relict. Willi Bell, Gen. ob. 8o Die Novembris Ano Dni 1727, Ano Ætat. Suæ 86, & Viduitatis Suæ 58o.

Benefactions.

Giles Cox, of Ablode's Court, gent. in the year 1626, by his will, gave 30*l. per ann.* for a lecture ſermon in this church. He likewiſe gave a portion of rent iſſuing out of an eſtate in Upton St. Leonard's, (being originally the ſum of 5*l.*) to be divided among the poor labourers of this pariſh that receive no alms.

William Hayward, of Willington's Court, gent. built a gallery in the church; and in the year 1646, gave 5*l.* towards building the vicarage houſe; the *Book of Martyrs*, in two volumes; and a large ſilver bowl for the communion ſervice. He likewiſe ſubjected his eſtate to a rent charge of 3*l.* a year to find bread and wine for a monthly ſacrament for ever.

Thomas Church, gent. gave a houſe in Glouceſter, of the yearly rent of 2*l.* 10*s.* which is to be received by the churchwardens and overſeers, and by them to be diſtributed (after deducting 2*s.* 6*d.* for chief rent and their trouble) to twenty-four poor perſons of this pariſh not receiving alms.

Richard Cox, gent. and —— —— gave ſix acres of land in the pariſhes of Norton and Down Hatherley, and one acre in this pariſh, for the repair of the church houſe; or if that ſhould not want repairing, then for ſome other charitable uſe.

Mr. Shewell gave the intereſt of 40*l.* to buy coal for the poor.

Taxes.					
The Royal Aid in	1692,	£. 208	5	4
Poll-tax ——	1694, —	19	15	0
Land-tax ——	1694, —	251	4	0
The ſame, at 3*s.*	1770, —	188	8	0

In the year 1562, there were 42 houſholders in the whole pariſh; about the beginning of the preſent century, according to ſir Robert Atkyns, there were 60 houſes, and about 300 inhabitants, whereof 10 were freeholders; yearly births 9, burials 8. The people are now reduced to about 260 ſouls.

SAPERTON.

THIS pariſh lies in the hundred of Biſley, five miles diſtant north-eaſtward from Minchin-Hampton, five weſt from Cirenceſter, and fourteen ſouth-eaſt from Glouceſter.

The little river Froome runs by, and ſeparates Biſley from Saperton, and gives name to Frampton, a hamlet in this pariſh, ſtretching along the ſide of that river.

This village enjoys a healthy air, but it has long ſince been deprived of its greateſt ornament, the large and handſome manor houſe, which ſtood near the church, and was formerly the reſidence of the Atkyns family.

In the month of February, 1759, there was a large quantity of Roman coins found near a place called Lark's Buſh, in the hamlet of Frampton, by a waggon caſually paſſing over and breaking the urns that contained them. They had ſuffered by ruſt as little as could be expected from lying ſo long under ground, for they are ſuppoſed to have been placed there by the Romans. They were ſoon diſperſed into many hands, but no perſon, I believe, collected a more compleat ſeries of them than Mr. James Dallaway, who has favoured me with the following particulars.

Silver Coins.

Severus Empr.	SEVERVS PIVS AVG. *Reverſe.* A prieſt going to offer at a low altar. *Legend.* VOTA SVSCEPTA XX. Vows made for the emperor's ſafety.
Julia, wife to *Severus.*	IVLIA PIA FELIX AVG. *Reverſe.* MAT. AVGG. M. SEN. M. PATR. [*Mater Auguſtorum, mater ſenatus, mater patriæ.*]
Albinus, commander in Britain under *Severus.*	D. CLOD. SEPT. ALBINVS. *Reverſe.* Minerva with her helmet, ſpear, ſhield, and olive branch. *Legend.* MINER. PACIFIC.
Caracalla Emp.	ANTONINVS PIVS AVG. GERM. *Reverſe.* P. M. TR. P. XVII. COS. IIII. P. P.
Plautilla, wife to *Caracalla.*	PLAVTILLAE AVGVSTAE. *Reverſe.* Two perſons joining hands. *Legend.* CONCORDIAE AETERNAE.
Geta Cæſar.	SEPT. GETA CAES. PONT. *Reverſe.* The figure of Security reſting on one hand, a mound, or ball, in the other. *Legend.* SECVRITAS IMPERII.
Julia Mæſa.	IVLIA MAESA AVG. *Reverſe.* PVDICITIA.
Julia Sœmias, mother of *Heliogabalus.*	IVLIA SOEMIAS AVG. *Reverſe.* VENVS CAELESTIS.
Heliogabalus Emperor.	IMP. CAES. ANTONINVS AVG. *Reverſe.* Mars bearing a trophy on his ſhoulder, and a ſpear in his hand. *Legend.* MARS VICTOR.
Julia Aquilia, wife to *Heliogabalus.*	IVLIA AQVILIA SEVERA AVGVSTA. *Reverſe.* A man and woman joining hands. *Legend.* CONCORDIA.
Julia Mamæa, mother of *Alexander Sev.*	IVLIA MAMAEA AVG. *Reverſe.* Juno with her peacock. *Legend.* IVNO CONSERVATRIX.
Alexander Severus Empr.	IMP. C. M. AVR. SEV. ALEXANDER. AVG. *Reverſe.* Mars. *Legend.* P. M. TR. P. COS. P. P.
Orbiana, wife of *Alexander.*	SALL. BARBIA ORBIANA AVG. *Reverſe.* CONCORDIA AVGG.
Maximinus Emperor.	MAXIMINVS PIVS. AVG. GERM. *Reverſe.* Peace with her olive branch. *Legend.* PAX AVGVSTI.
Gordian Empr.	IMP. CAES. M. ANT. GORDIANVS AVG. *Reverſe.* Jupiter with his thunderbolts. *Legend.* IOVI CONSERVATORI.
Philippus Emp.	IMP. IVL. PHILIPPVS CAES. *Reverſe.* A perſon on horſeback. *Legend.* ADVENTVS AVGG.

Otacilla

Otacilla, wife of *Philippus*.	OTACILLA SEVERA AVG. *Reverse*. CONCORDIA AVGG.
Philippus the Son.	M. IVL. PHILIPPVS CAES. *Reverse*. PRINCIPI IVVEN.
Decius Empr.	IMP. C. M. Q. TRAIANVS DECIUS AVG. *Reverse*. Two female figures representing the countries of the two Pannonias. *Legend*. PANNONIAE.
Etruscilla, wife of *Decius*.	HER. ETRVSCILLA AVG. *Reverse*. Fruitfulness with a cornucopia, and a child by her side. *Legend*. FECVNDITAS AVG.
Gallus Empr.	IMP. CAE. C. VIB. TREB. GALLVS AVG. *Reverse*. Liberty with her cap. *Legend*. LIBERTAS AVGG.
Volusian, son of *Gallus*.	IMP. CAE. C. VIB. VOLVSIANO AVG. *Reverse*. CONCORDIA AVGG.
Valerian Empr.	IMP. VALERIANVS AVG. *Reverse*. Hope with a flower in her right hand. *Legend*. SPES PVBLICA.
Mariniana, wife of *Valerian*.	DIVAE MARINIANAE. *Reverse*. CONSECRATIO.
Gallienus Emp.	GALLIENVS P. F. AVG. *Reverse*. Two captives bound at the foot of a trophy. *Legend*. GERMANICVS MAXIMVS.
Salonina, wife of *Gallienus*.	SALONINA AVG. *Reverse*. VENVS FELIX.
Valerianus, son to *Gallienus*.	VALERIANVS CAES. *Reverse*. An infant riding on a goat. *Legend*. IOVI CRESCENTI.
—— A consecration piece.	DIVO VALERIANO CAES. In Speed, p. 245. *Reverse*. CONSECRATIO.
Valerianus, brother to *Gallienus*.	VALERIANVS P. F. AVG. *Reverse*. Vulcan and his temple. *Legend*. DEO VOLCANO.

Brass Coins.

Mariniana, wife of *Valerian*.	. . . . . MARINIANAE. *Reverse*. CONSECRATIO.
Gallienus Emp.	IMP. GALLIENVS AVG. *Reverse*. A griffin. *Legend*. APOLLINI CONSERV.
Salonina, wife of *Gallienus*.	SALONINA AVG. *Reverse*. VENVS VICT.
Valerian Empr.	IMP. C. P. LIC. VALERIANVS P. F. AVG. *Reverse*. Apollo with the tripod and olive branch. *Legend*. APOLLINI CONSERV.
Postumus Emp. a tyrant in Gaul.	IMP. C. POSTVMVS P. F. AVG. *Reverse*. A galley. *Legend*. LAETITIA.
Postumus the Son.	IMP. POSTVMVS AVG. *Reverse*. CONCORDIA EQVITVM.
Victorinus Emp. a tyrant in Gaul.	IMP. C. PI. VICTORINVS AVG. *Reverse*. Justice with her ballance. *Legend*. AEQVITAS.
Victorinus the Son.	. . . . . VICTORINVS P. F. AVG. *Reverse*. The sun. *Legend*. INVICTVS.
Tetricus Emp. a tyrant in Gaul.	IMP. C. PES. TETRICVS P. F. AVG. *Reverse*. FIDES MILITVM.
Tetricus the Son.	C. PIV. TETRICVS CAES. *Reverse*. PIETAS AVG.
Marius Emp. a tyrant in Gaul.	IMP. C. M. MARIVS AVG. *Reverse*. VICTORIA AVG.
Claudius Empr.	IMP. CLAVDIVS AVG. *Reverse*. Lætitia, or Joy, with a cornucopia and garland. *Legend*. LAETITIA AVG.
Quintillus Emp.	IMP. C. M. AVR. CL. QVINTILLVS AVG. *Reverse*. VIRTVS AVG.
Aurelian Empr.	IMP. AVRELIANVS AVG. *Reverse*. Peace with her symbols. *Legend*. PAX AVGVSTI.

Not far distant from the place where the above coins were deposited, are the remains of a camp, where it is supposed those soldiers were posted to whom the money belonged. When this treasure was hid is uncertain, but some probable conjectures may be formed of the occasion of it.

It was a prudential maxim with the Romans to conceal their money before they were drawn out to battle, or went on distant expeditions, lest any part should fall into the hands of the enemy; and because the soldiery had relaxed in this necessary precaution, it is related by Sparcian, that Pescennius Niger published an edict, commanding them to carry no gold nor silver coin with them at any such time. This money, therefore, must have been concealed immediately before some engagement or expedition, from which the owners never returned; or else, perhaps, was hid at the time of the final departure of the Romans out of Britain, which happened in the year 476, when, by their troubles at home, they were unable to return any more.

Upon a high spot of ground, a little south-eastward of the camp, stood an antient beacon, wherefore the field is called the *Beacon-field*, and the turnpike-road from Cirencester to Minchin Hampton and Stroud leads through it, close by the beacon-hill.

Of the Manor and other Estates.

Under the title *Terra Roberti de Todeni* it is recorded after this manner:

'Robert de Todeni holds Sapeltorne and Frantone, in Biselege hundred. There are five hides 'in each. Ulf held them. There are seven 'plow-tillages in demean, and seventeen villeins, 'and nine bordars, with ten plow-tillages. There 'are thirteen *servi*, and two mills of 6*s*. and a 'wood half a mile long, and two furlongs broad. 'These two manors together were worth 14*l*. in 'the time of king Edward, and are now worth 16*l*.' *Domesday-book*, p. 76.

The above Ulf might possibly be the fourth son of king Harold, who had a son of the name of Ulf, or Wolfe, according to Speed. In sir Robert Atkyns's quotation from *Domesday*, it is said, *He was third Son of King Harold, and therefore in the Reign of King William the Conqueror, he was deprived of these manors, and confined, &c.* But the record says no such thing, and the whole passage printed in Italics was injudiciously inserted by the compiler of the *Ancient and Present State of Glocestershire*.

Robert de Todeni gave a plow-tillage in Saperton to the priory which he had founded at Belvoir in Lincolnshire, to pray for the soul of Adela his wife. He died seized of Great Risindon, Horedon, Saperton, and Frampton, in Gloucestershire, in the year 1088, and the manors of Saperton and Frampton descended from him to the several proprietors, as it is related of Great Risington, down to the time of king Richard the Second, when one moiety thereof was vested in William de Lisle, who died 8 R. 2. and Anchoret, widow of Henry Hussey, the elder, was endowed with the other moiety of Saperton, and died in the 13th year of the same reign.

Sir William Nottingham purchased both the moieties, and died without issue, seized of the intire manor, 2 R. 3. leaving it to Elizabeth his wife, for her life, the reversion in trustees.

Richard

Richard Poole, of Cotes, fon of John Poole, of the antient family of that name in Chefhire, married Elizabeth, the widow of fir William Nottingham, and purchafed the inheritance of the manor from the truftees, 7 H. 7. and was high fheriff of the county in the 13th year of the fame reign. Sir Leonard Poole, fon of Richard, fucceeded to this manor, and marrying Katherine, daughter of fir Giles Brydges, died 30 H. 8. Sir Giles Poole, fon of fir Leonard, married Elizabeth, one of the fix daughters and coheireffes of Thomas Whitington of Pauntly. He ferved the office of high fheriff of Gloucefterfhire, in the year 1565, and died in 1588. Sir Henry Poole fucceeded his father fir Giles in this manor, and was eminent for his great houfekeeping and hofpitality. He married Anne, daughter of fir William Wroughton, and having ferved the office of high fheriff 31 Eliz. died in 1616, and lies buried under a noble monument in Saperton church. Sir Henry Poole, fon of fir Henry, was high fheriff of Gloucefterfhire 8 C. 1. and married Beatrix, daughter of Grey lord Chandos. He was fequeftered for his attachment to the royal caufe in the great civil war, and paid 1494*l.* 6*s.* 6*d.* compofition for his eftates. Sir William Poole, fon of the laft fir Henry, married Marial, daughter of lord Tracy, and was fucceeded by his fon, fir Henry Poole, who was the laft male heir of his family, and fold the manor of Saperton, in the year 1660, to

Sir Robert Atkyns,[a] knight of the Bath, and chief baron of the court of exchequer, who died in the year 1709, and was fucceeded by his fon fir Robert Atkyns. He died in 1711, and the manor of Saperton paffed out of his family, by purchafe, to Allen firft earl of Bathurft, whofe fon, Henry earl of Bathurft, lord high chancellor of Great Britain, is the prefent lord of this manor. His lordfhip's pedigree and arms are given under *Cirencefter*.

Saperton was held of Cicely dutchefs of York, mother to king Edward the Fourth, as of the manor of Bifley.

HAMLETS. 1. *Frampton*, which lies weftward from the church, and belonging antiently to the Manfels, was called *Frampton Manfel*, to diftinguifh it from two other parifhes of the name of *Frampton*, in this county. Henry earl of Bathurft is lord of the manor.

2. *Hayly* is another fmall hamlet in this parifh, lying a mile fouth-weftward from the church. It is a manor within a manor, and belongs to Charles Coxe, of Kemble, in the county of Wilts, efq; whofe arms are given under *Rodmarton*.

Of the Church, &c.

The church is a rectory, in the deanery of Stonehoufe, improved of late to about 200*l.* a year, by inclofing the parifh, and allotting lands to the rectory in lieu of tithes. The earl of Bathurft is patron, and James Benfon, LL.D. and chancellor of this diocefe, is the incumbent.

The church is dedicated to St. Kenelm, and built in the form of a crofs, with a fmall fpire in the middle.

The parfonage houfe was built by Mr. Davis, a rector of this church, about feventy years ago; but it has been fince repaired, and greatly improved, by the honourable and reverend Allen Bathurft, the late incumbent, who died Aug. 21, 1768, and lies buried in the chancel.

Firft fruits £.	17	0	0	Synodals £.	0	2	0
Tenths —	1	14	0	Pentecoftals	0	1	3
Procurations	0	6	8				

Monuments and Infcriptions.

There is a noble monument in the north crofs aile, for fir Henry Poole and his lady, who are reprefented kneeling, with books before them, and richly habited in the drefs of their time. A marble table bears this infcription:

Here Refteth the Bodies of Sir Henry Poole Knight & of Anne his Wife, Daughter to Sir William Wroughton of Broadehinto in The Cōty of Wilts Knight By Whome hee had Iffu 3 Sonns & 4 Daughters, That is to fay, Deuereux, Gyles, & Henry, Elinor Francis Dorothey & Anne, Elinor married Sir Richard Fettiplace of Bezelfleigh in the County of Barck[s] Knight Francis

[a] The family of Atkyns formerly refided in Monmouthfhire. Thomas Atkyns lived in the reign of king Edward the Third, and dying in London, was buried in the church of St. Peter Cheap, in the year 1401, 2 H. 4. Richard Atkyns, fon of Thomas, followed the profeffion of the law, in Monmouthfhire, and Thomas Atkyns, his fon, was of the fame profeffion. Richard Atkyns, fon of Thomas, died 11 H. 7. and Thomas Atkyns, his fon, died 4 H. 8. He was fucceeded by David Atkyns, who married Alice, daughter of and was an eminent merchant in Chepftow, from whence he moved to Tuffley, near Gloucefter, and died in the year 1552. Thomas Atkyns, fon of David, married Margaret, daughter of John Cook of London, and was judge of the Sheriff's court there. He argued the firft cafe in *Plowden's Commentaries*, and dying before his father, in the year 1551, was buried in Aldermanbury church, in London.

Richard Atkyns, fon of Thomas, was under age at his father's death, and was granted in ward to Thomas Wendy, efq; phyfician to king Edward the Sixth. He was found by inquifition to be feized of the manors of Tuffley, Hempfted, Morecot in Minfterworth, and Brickhampton in Churchdown, held of the king in *capite*; and of lands in Sodbury, Betefley, and Tudenham, all in the county of Gloucefter. He married Elianor, daughter of Thomas Marfhe, of Warefley in Huntingdonfhire, efq; and was one of the judges of Wales, and one of the council of the Marches there, and dying in the year 1610, was buried at Hempfted, where there is a handfome monument erected to his memory. Sir Edward Atkyns, third fon of Richard, (whofe elder brothers and their iffue have fince been extinct) married Urfula, daughter of fir Thomas Dacres, of Chefhunt in Hertfordfhire, and died one of the barons of the court of exchequer, at the age of 82 years When king James the Second removed fome of the judges for denying his difpencing power, he replaced them with others of more pliant tempers, of whom this fir Edward was one. Sir Robert Atkyns, fon of fir Edward, was created knight of the Bath at the coronation of king Charles the Second, and was chief baron of the court of exchequer. He purchafed the manor of Saperton of fir Henry Pool, in the year 1660. He married, firft, Mary, daughter of fir George Clerk, of Watford in Northamptonfhire; fecondly, Anne, daughter of fir Thomas Dacres, fon of fir Thomas, and dying in 1709, aged 88, was fucceeded by his fon, fir Robert Atkyns. Sir Robert, the fon, married Lovife, daughter of fir George Carteret, of Hawnes in Bedfordfhire, and was the author of that well known book, the *Ancient and Prefent State of Glocefterfhire*, printed in the year 1712, but he did not live to fee it publifhed, for he died in 1711.

It is remarkable that there has been always one of this name and family prefiding in fome of the courts of judicature in this kingdom above three hundred years. *Atkyns.*

Married

Married Sir Neuell Poole of Oakſey in the County of Wilts Knight, Dorothey Married Sir Iohn Sauedg of Elmley in the County of Worceſter Knight, & Ann Married Sir Theobald Gorges of Aſhley in the County of Wilts Knight. Theiſe Both loued & liued Together Many Yeeres Much Giueuen to Hoſpitallity, He Was Alwayes Faithfull to his Prince, & louinge to his Cuntry, True to His Frinde, & Bountifull to his Seruants, Being 75 yeeres of age, Deceſſed ANNO Dõni 1616.

Arms, *Baron and femme*, 1. *Quarterly*, 1ſt *and* 4th, *Azure, ſemé of fleurs de lis Or, a lion rampant argent*, for Poole. 2d & 3d, *Argent, a chevron ſable between three ſtags heads caboſhed gules.* On the femme ſide, *Quarterly*, 1ſt & 4th, *Argent, a chevron gules between three boars heads ſable.* 2d & 3d, *Argent, three chevronels azure*; *in chief a creſcent gules.*

In the ſouth aile is a very handſome freeſtone monument for ſir Robert Atkyns, with his effigy in white marble, in a recumbent poſture, leaning on his left elbow. Behind him, on a marble table, is this inſcription:

In memory of S^r^. ROBERT ATKYNS of Pinbury Park in Glocefter Shire Knight, Son of S^r^. ROBERT ATKYNS, one of ye Iuſtices of ye Court of Common Pleas in ye Reign of K. C. II. afterwards Lord Chief Baron of ye Exchequer and Speaker of ye houſe of Lords and Grand Son to S^r^. EDWARD ATKYNS who was one of ye Barons of y^e^ ſaid Court.

While He lived He was beloved and honoured, and when He died ye loſs of him was lamented by all who knew his private and his publick Vertues.

He was always Loyal to his Prince, Loving to his Wife, Faithful to his Friends, Charitable to ye Poor, Kind & Courteous to his Neighbours, Iuſt to All, Sober and Serious in his Converſation, and a Peace-Maker to his utmoſt Power.

His obligeing Vertues endear'd him to his Country, who choſe him for their Repreſentative in Parliament as often as He would accept of their Choice. He lived with great indifference for life, and without ye fear of Death: and dyed of a Dyſentery at his Houſe at Weſtminſter, on ye XXIX day of November, in ye year of our Lord MDCCXI, and of his Age LXV. He left behind him LOVISE Lady ATKYNS, Daughter of S^r^. GEORGE CARTERET of Hawns in Bedford-Shire, his moſt dear and ſorrowful Widow, who erected this monument to his memory, though He left behind him one more durable, The Ancient and Preſent State of Glofter-Shire.

This Lady who was altogether worthy of ſo Good and Great a Man, Was Her-Self Interred in the ſame Vault with him. She died the 2^d^ of Dec. 1716, Aged 63.

Arms, at top, *Per pale, baron and femme*, 1. *Argent, a croſs cotized with demy fleurs de lis between four mullets ſable, pierced of the field*, for Atkyns. 2. *Gules, four fuſils in feſs Or*, for Carteret.

Under a niche in the eaſt wall of the north aile, is the effigy in freeſtone of a man in armour, girt with a ſword, and over him are the arms of Poole. There is no inſcription, except the date, 1574.

Benefactions.

Leonard Poole, eſq; gave the church-houſe, two acres of arable in each field, and one beaſt paſture, for the uſe of the church. Nathaniel Butler, who was preſented to this rectory in the year 1603, gave 10*s*. a year, of which 6*s*. 8*d*. for a ſermon on the 5th of November, the remainder for the poor. By a decree in chancery, an eſtate worth 23*l*. a year has been purchaſed with money left by lord chief baron Atkyns, and lady Atkyns; 5*l*. of which is allotted for a charity ſchool, the remainder to be given in bread to the poor.

Taxes.			£.		
	The Royal Aid in	1692,	65	12	0
	Poll-tax ——	1694, —	15	4	0
	Land-tax —	1694, —	43	6	0
	The ſame, at 3*s*.	1770, —	33	0	0

At the beginning of this century, there were 60 houſes in the pariſh, and about 320 inhabitants, of whom 12 were freeholders; yearly births 7, burials 6. *Atkyns*. The people are ſince decreaſed to about 300.

S A U L

IS a very ſmall pariſh, in the hundred of Whitſton, about four miles ſouth-eaſtward from Newnham, ſix northward from Durſley, and nine ſouthward from Glouceſter.

It is bounded on the eaſt by the Froome, which ſeparates it from Moreton Valence and Whitminſter; on the weſt by Frethorn; on the north by the great river Severn, and on the ſouth by the pariſh of Eaſtington.

A conſiderable proportion of the pariſh is arable, the reſt is rich paſturage and meadow ground.

The air is rendered impure and unwholeſome by the copious vapours and exhalations riſing from the Severn, and from the low lands that are conſtantly drowned by floods and ſpring tides, which particularly affect Saul, Moreton, and Frethorn. Yet here I was told, that this village was perfectly healthy, tho' it appeared to be far otherwiſe, from the pallid countenances of thoſe I converſed with, who allowed, however, that the two other above-mentioned neighbouring villages were greatly afflicted with agues and aſthmatic diſorders. On the contrary, the good people of Moreton aſſured me, that they were themſelves free from thoſe diſorders, but that Saul and Frethorn were very ſubject to them. Thus wiſely has providence reconciled mankind to their various ſituations, which Mr. Pope has elegantly expreſſed in the following lines:

Aſk where's the North? at York 'tis on the Tweed:
In Scotland, at the Orcades; and there
At Greenland, Zembla, and the Lord knows where.
No Creature owns it in the firſt Degree,
But thinks his Neighbour further gone than he.
Ethic Epiſt. B. 2.

Of the Manor and other Eſtates.

The ſheriff returned, that the abbat of St. Peter's at Glouceſter, and Galfrid de Frethorne, were lords of the vill of Salley, in the hundred of Wyſton, 9 E. 1. Galfrid de Fretherne died 14 E. 2. at which time he was ſeized in fee of one meſſuage and one plow-tillage in Fretherne. *Eſch.*

The manor came afterwards to the Staffords of Thornbury, and continued for many generations in that family. Sir Hugh Stafford was ſeized of the manor of Salle 1 H. 6. It came afterwards to the Lloyds of Wheatenhurſt. George Lloyd, eſq; was lord of the manor at the beginning of this century, and Mr. Richard-Owen Cambridge is the preſent proprietor.

Lands and tithes in Saul, which belonged to the abbey of Glouceſter, were granted to Edward duke of Somerſet 1 E. 6.

Of the Church, &c.

The church is a perpetual curacy, in the deanery of Glouceſter, to which the vicar of Standiſh preſents. Mr. Davis is the preſent incumbent. The curate has ſmall tithes, and ſome glebe, worth about 7*l*. a year. The living has been augmented with

with the queen's bounty, and by a benefaction from Mr. Hodges, with which money an eftate has been purchafed at King's Stanley, worth 30*l.* a year.

The tithes of Saul belonged to the abbey of Gloucefter, and were granted to the bifhoprick 33 H. 8. and confirmed 6 E. 6. The impropriation, worth 60*l.* a year, is in leafe to Mr. King.

The church is a fmall building, with a low embattled tower at the weft end, in which is one bell. It is dedicated to St. James, on whofe feaft day an annual fair was formerly held here.

There is a memorial on a tomb in the churchyard, for Thomas Swanley, who died in 1653, and for others of that family. The arms on the tomb are, *A fefs undy between three unicorns heads erazed.*

Land-tax at 3*s.* 1770, £. 34 19 6

At the beginning of the prefent century, according to fir Robert Atkyns, there were 30 houfes in the parifh, and about 130 inhabitants, whereof 7 were freeholders. There are now 29 families, and 151 inhabitants.

****

SEISINCOT

IS a fmall parifh, in the upper divifion of Kiftfgate hundred, four miles northward from Stow, fix fouthward from Campden, and about twenty-feven north-eaftward from Gloucefter.

The name of this place was antiently written *Chiefnecote*, and *Chefnecote*; and fince *Chefne*, according to fir Robert Atkyns, fignifies *an Oak*, and *Coed* is Britifh for a *Wood*, there is reafon to fuppofe that the name fignifies the *Oak Wood*, and expreffes the antient ftate of the place; yet there is nothing in the prefent condition of it to confirm this etymology.

The parifh was totally depopulated in the great civil war, and is intirely deftitute of antiquities and curiofities. The village confifts at prefent of fix or feven houfes, which fir William Juxton built for the ufe of the farmers, when he was lord of the manor.

Of the Manor and other Eftates.

This parifh was divided into feveral manors at the time of the general furvey; one of them lay in the old hundred of Celfledetorne, the others in Witelai, but both thofe hundreds are now comprized in that of Kiftfgate.

'Durand of Glowec' holds Chiefnecote in 'Celfledetorne hundred, and Walter holds it of 'him. There are two hides and a half. Leuuin 'and Leuui held it for two manors. In demean 'are two plow-tillages, and four bordars. It was 'worth 40*s.* and is now worth 60*s.*' *D. B.* p. 76.

'Walter the Deacon holds Chefnecote in Witelai 'hundred of the king. There are four hides and 'a half. Goduin held it, and could go where he 'pleafed, [*i.e.* was perfectly a free man.] There 'are two plow-tillages in demean, and eight 'villeins, with fix plow-tillages, and ten *fervi.* 'It is worth and was worth 3*l.*' *Ibid.* p. 77.

'Urfo de Abetot of Wireceftre holds one hide 'in Cheifnecote, in Witelai hundred. Eluuin 'held it for a manor, and paid tax. There is one 'plow-tillage in demean, and four *fervi.* It was 'worth 40*s.* now 10*s.*' *Ibid.* p. 78.

'Hafcoit Mufard holds one hide in Cheifnecote 'in Witelai hundred, and pays tax. Uluuin held 'it for a manor. There is one plow-tillage, and 'one bordar. It is worth and was worth 10*s.*' *Ibid.* p. 78.

'Hunfridus de Medehalle holds one hide in 'Cheifnecot, in Witelai hundred. Aluui held it 'for a manor, and paid tax. In demean were two 'plow-tillages, and fix *fervi*, and one bordar, and 'it was worth 50*s.* but it is now worth only 12*d.* 'on account of the meadows.' *Ibid.* p. 79.

Urfo de Abetot, hereditary fheriff of Worcefterfhire, left Emeline, an only daughter and heirefs, who was married to Walter de Beauchamp, whereby this manor came to the Beauchamps, and continued in that family for many generations. William de Beauchamp, earl of Warwick, fon of William de Beauchamp, and of Ifabel, the fifter and heirefs of William Manduit de Hanflape, earl of Warwick, died 52 H. 3. feized of the hamlet of Cheifnecot. William de Beauchamp, fon of the laft William, died 26 E. 1. and Guy de Beauchamp, earl of Warwick, his fon and heir, had livery the fame year, and died 9 E. 2. leaving Thomas, his infant fon, only two years old. He died 43 E. 3. and was fucceeded by Thomas de Beauchamp, earl of Warwick, his furviving fon and heir, who died feized of Seifincote 2 H. 4. whereupon the manor defcended to his fon Richard de Beauchamp, earl of Warwick, and lord Bergavenny, who died 17 H. 6.

The manor of Seifincot was foon afterwards vefted in the Grevils. Sir John Grevil died feized of it, and of the hundred of Kiftfgate, 20 E. 4. Ludowick Grevil was lord of the manor, and refided here in the reign of queen Elizabeth. The memory of this man feems to be preferved only to be execrated for his rapacious avarice, and inhuman barbarity. He invited to his houfe one Web, who had been his fervant, but was now grown rich, and there treacheroufly caufed him to be affaffinated in bed, by two domefticks, and afterwards, by means of a forged will, got poffeffion of the whole eftate of his murdered gueft. But one of the affaffins, afterwards in liquor, dropping fome hints that he could hang his mafter, fo alarmed Grevil, that he procured the other to difpatch him alfo. Divine providence, however, would not permit thefe complicated acts of wickednefs to remain long unpunifhed. Grevil was arraigned and executed for his crimes, who ftood mute to preferve his eftates in the family; but his family never flourifhed afterwards, and foon

 fell

fell to decay; as if heaven would ſhew that the horrible crimes of murder and forgery draw after them a curſe on poſterity for ſeveral generations.

Sir Edward Grevil was lord of the manor in the year 1608. Sir William Juxton, nephew of Dr. William Juxton, archbiſhop of Canterbury, was poſſeſſed of it in the reign of king Charles the Second, and ſold it to lord Guilford. The earl of Guilford is the preſent lord of the manor, and proprietor of a good eſtate in the pariſh.

A conſiderable eſtate here belonged to a family of the ſame name with the pariſh, for Thomas Cheſnecot died ſeized of one meſſuage, and two plow-tillages in Cheſnecot 33 E. 1. Alice his widow was married to Henry de Duffeld, and they joined in a fine, acknowledging the eſtate to be the right of Maud, daughter and heireſs of Thomas de Seiſincote. She was afterwards married to Peter de Wallingford.

John de Minera, and Alice his wife, granted lands in Cheſneton to William Camera, and Alice his wife, 20 H. 3. Nicholas de Sherborne was ſeized of one plow-tillage in Seiſincote 15 E. 1.

Of the Church, &c.

The church is in the deanery of Stow, and in the gift of the earl of Guilford, who pays about 8*l.* a year to the incumbent, and lets his eſtates tithe free. The living was augmented by lot in the year 1737. The pariſh was depopulated, and the church demoliſhed, during the civil wars, in the reign of king Charles the Firſt.

The glebe lands and tithes belonged antiently to the abbey of Bruern in Oxfordſhire, and were granted to Anthony Stringer, and John Williams, 34 H. 8. Other tithes in Seiſincot belonged to the abbey of Winchcombe, and were granted to ſir Thomas Seimour 1 E. 6.

	£	s.	d.		£	s.	d.
Firſt fruits	9	12	9½	Synodals	0	2	0
Tenths —	0	19	3½	Pentecoſt.	0	0	6
Procurations	0	6	8				

Taxes.		£	s.	d.
The Royal Aid in	1692,	99	8	0
Poll-tax ——	1694, —	6	16	0
Land-tax ——	1694, —	99	12	0
The ſame, at 3*s.*	1770, —	74	14	0

When ſir Robert Atkyns wrote his account of this pariſh, there were 7 houſes, and about 30 inhabitants, whereof 2 were freeholders. There are now 6 farm houſes only, with 43 inhabitants.

****

SEVENHAMPTON.

THIS large pariſh lies in the hundred of Bradley, in a lofty part of the Coteſwold country, about five miles eaſtward from Cheltenham, four ſouth from Winchcombe, and thirteen north-eaſtward from Glouceſter.

The village, like moſt others on the Coteſwolds, is ſeated in a bottom, ſheltered by bold riſing grounds, and the lands are principally in tillage. The river Coln riſes in two heads, here and at Whittington, and after paſſing by, and giving name to ſeveral villages, as Coln Dennis, Coln Rogers, Coln Aldwins, falls into the Thames below Fairford.

Of the Manor and other Eſtates.

The *Domeſday* account of this pariſh is given under Preſbury, on which it was once dependent, and was therefore ſometimes called *Preſbury on the Hill.*

The manor of Sevenhantone belonged to the biſhop of Hereford at the time of the general ſurvey, and Peter biſhop of that ſee had free warren in Preſbury and Sevenhampton 25 H. 3. and obtained a confirmation of that privilege 14 R. 2. In a taxation of the temporalties of the ſee of Hereford, in a MS. in the Cottonian Library, *Tiberius*, C. x. F. 76. is the following entry. *Item apud Pulcomb & Sevenhampton, de reditu 7l. 5s. 1d. ob. & 3 caruc. terre & valet caruc. 20s. Et unum molendinum aquaticum, quod valet 1 marc. et de placitis & perquiſitis 20s.*

Sir Robert Atkyns ſays, that Elizabeth Courtney, counteſs of Devonſhire, died 11 H. 8. ſeized of this manor, which thereupon deſcended to Elizabeth, her grandaughter and heir, married to ſir Arthur Plantagenet, who had livery granted them the ſame year. But that ſeems moſt likely to be the manor of Brockhampton in this pariſh, or perhaps ſome lands only, and not the manor, for the latter continued in the biſhoprick of Hereford 'till long afterwards, as appears by a grant of ſeveral particulars made to Scory biſhop of that ſee, by queen Elizabeth, March 23, 1562, in the fourth year of her reign, in conſideration of ſeveral manors therein mentioned, of which Sevenhampton was one.

Lands in Sevenhampton, which formerly belonged to the biſhoprick of Hereford, were granted to Chriſtopher Hatton 18 Eliz. Mr. Robert Lawrence died ſeized of the manors of Sevenhampton and Brockhampton in the year 1700. Mr. Anthony Lawrence was proprietor of the manor of Sevenhampton when ſir Robert Atkyns compiled his Hiſtory. It belonged afterwards to Walter Lawrence, eſq; and is now veſted in Mr. Walter Lawrence, who has a good eſtate in the pariſh, and reſides there. His arms are, *Argent, a croſs raguly gules.*

HAMLET. Brockhampton is a conſiderable hamlet in this pariſh, formerly belonging to the antient family of de Croupes. Edward Croupes, ſon of Richard de Croupes, died ſeized of the manors of Upper Dowdeſwell, Whittington, and Brockhampton, 35 E. 3. The manor was afterwards veſted in the Lawrences, of whom it was purchaſed by ſir William Dodwell, whoſe only daughter and heir, Mrs. Tracy, relict of Thomas Tracy, of Sandiwell in this county, eſq; is the preſent lady of the manor.

Puckham is the name of a place in this pariſh, antiently written *Pulcumb*, which belonged to the biſhop of Hereford. Puckham-farm is now the property of Mr. Reddall.

The prior of Lanthony had free warren in this pariſh 21 E. 1.

Of the Church, &c.

The church is an impropriation, in the deanery of Winchcombe. The incumbent receives 10*l.* a year out of the impropriation, which formerly belonged to the priory of Lanthony, and is now veſted in Mr. Lawrence and Mr. Hinckſman, who pay a ſmall quit-rent for it to the biſhop of Hereford. The living was augmented with Mr. Aylworth's benefaction, and by the queen's bounty, about the year 1733. There is no houſe for the curate.

The church is built in the form of a croſs, with a low embattled tower in the middle. It is dedicated to St. Andrew, and was built by John Camber, for whom there was the following inſcription upon a ſtone in the wall of the chancel,

Hic iacet Iohēs Camber, qui obiit xxvi Feb. 1448.

Procurations £. 0 6 8 Pentecoſtals £. 0 0 6½
Synodals — 0 2 0

Monuments and Inſcriptions.

On a flat ſtone in the chancel, engraved on braſs,

THE SACRED REMAINS OF
ROBERT LAWRENCE GENT.
Aged LXXII.
(Late)
Lord of the Manour of Sevenhampton
and Brockhampton
Repoſited here
June 19th
M. DCC.
His life on Earth was pious, prudent, juſt,
His Soul with God: his Body's here in Truſt.

Arms, at top, *Argent, a croſs raguly gules.* Motto. LOYAL AU MORT.

Againſt the ſouth wall of the chancel,

Subtus dormit quod extingui potuit Gulielmi Candelarij de Senhampton, pie demortui XXVI Ianuarij, Anno MDCLI, Ætat. LVII M. S.

Lumine mors corpus ſpoliauit, terra recondit
Splendet adhuc nomen, mens pia ſplendet: Idem
Luxerit hoc olim corpus, lumenq; Videbit
Non obcæcandum lumine [Chriſte] tuo.

Elianor Gulielmi uxor, labore indefeſſa, Senio autem laſſa, placide in deo obdormiuit xx Iunij Anno MDCLII Ætat. LXXII.
Repetunt primordia mentes.

Within the communion rails, is the following inſcription on a table of wood, in gold letters:

HEIC ALTUM DORMIT INTER AGNATOS CINERES ANNA PERDICIA, STIRPE ANTIQUA ET MEMORANDA, VXOR IOANNIS AVRIGARIJ DE CHARELTONIA EX ABBATE GEN. SVPRA MOREM FIDA PRVDENS PIA.
DEMORTVA FEBR. XXI ANNO { S. MDCLII / ÆTAT. LVI.
M. S.

Quæ fuit æternâ in terris digniſſima famâ
Terra [qua potuit parte iacere] iacet:
Mens cælo demiſſa, ſolo detenta caducas
Ruperat exuvias, læta reditq; domum.
Abijt non obiit.

Arms, at top, *Checky argent and ſable, over all on a bend gules, three eſcallops Or,* for Partridge.

On a flat blue ſtone, under the communion table,

In Memory of Iohn Carter Eſq[r] of Charlton Abbots, who died the 17th of December, 1722.

Alſo here lieth Alice the wife of Iohn Carter Eſq[r] of Charlton Abbots, and daughter of David Williams, Gent. of Cornden, who departed this Life the 20th of October, Anno Dom. 1726, in the 22d Year of her Age.——Arms, *Baron and femme,* 1. *Azure, two lions rampant combatant Or,* for Carter. 2. *A chevron between three fighting cocks, in chief three javelins erect.*

On a marble monument againſt the wall of the north croſs aile,

Here Lyeth the Body
of S[r] WILLIAM DODWELL K[t].
(Son to PAUL DODWELL of *Sevenhampton*
In the County of *Glouceſter* Eſq[r]
By Dame ELIZABETH only Daughter to
WILLIAM ROGERS Eſq[r]
and Relict of S[r] WALTER RALEGH K[t]. both
of *Sandiwell* in this County)
He married to his firſt Wife
ANNE eldeſt Daughter to S[r] JOHN LETHIEULIER
of *Lewiſham* in the County of Kent K[t].
and Relict of JOHN DELEAU of *Waddon* in
the County of *Surrey* Eſq[r]
by whom he had no Iſſue.
To his ſecond Wife he Married MARY, Daughter
to FRANCIS FULLER Gent.
and Relict of THOMAS MILLER Eſq[r]
by whom he left one only Daughter.
Dame ANNE firſt Wife died A° 1719
and lies Buried at *Croydon* in *Surry.*
Dame MARY ſecond Wife, died A°. 1724.
S[r] WILLIAM DODWELL died 1727.

Under the table are three coats, palewiſe, in one ſcutcheon. 1. *Argent, a chevron gules between three paroquets heads proper.* 2. *Vert, a feſs between three roſes argent,* for Dodwell. 3. *Gules, three bars argent, a canton of the ſecond.*

Againſt the north wall of the church,

Near this place lieth the Body of Mr. Thomas Longford, who departed this Life March y[e] 9th 1770 Aged 76 Years.
Memento Mori.
He gave in his life time Twenty Shillings per Ann. for ever to the poor of this pariſh in bread, five of which Quarterly, to be given out of the ground called or known by Dunnywell.

Taxes.					
The Royal Aid in	1692,	£. 75	0	0
Poll-tax ——	1694, —	18	13	6
Land-tax ——	1694, —	70	4	0
The ſame, at 3*s.*	1770, —	48	15	3¾

At the beginning of this century, there were 47 houſes in the pariſh, and about 180 inhabitants, of whom 8 were freeholders; yearly births 5, burials 4. *Atkyns.* There are now 63 families, and about 288 inhabitants.

SHENINGTON.

THIS pariſh lies in the upper diviſion of the hundred of Tewkeſbury, about five miles weſtward from Banbury in Oxfordſhire, ſix eaſtward from Shipſton upon Stour in Warwickſhire, and about thirty-nine north-eaſtward from Glouceſter.

The ſouth and eaſt ſides of this pariſh are bounded by Oxfordſhire, and the north and weſt by Warwickſhire; being intirely disjoined, and many miles diſtant from the county to which it belongs.

Part of Edgehill lies in this pariſh, and is rendered famous by the engagement fought on the 23d of October, 1642, between the forces of king Charles the Firſt and his parliament. Mr. Jago wrote a poem in blank verſe, intituled *Edgehill,* which was publiſhed about the year 1764. It

It is both deſcriptive and hiſtorical, comprehending the villas and towns which lie round about the hill he profeſſes to celebrate.

From the top of Shunlow-hill in this pariſh, there is a very pleaſant and extenſive proſpect into the counties of Oxford, Warwick, Glouceſter, Northampton, Bucks, Worceſter, Salop, and Stafford.

Two ſmall ſtreams run from hence, and fall, at laſt, one into the Severn, the other into the Thames.

Of the Manor and other Eſtates.

Domeſday-book, under the title *Terra Regis*, recounts the particulars of the extenſive manor and lordſhip of Tewkeſbury, and ſays,

'Ten hides in Senendone belong to the ſame 'manor [Teodecheſberie]. There are four plow-'tillages, and eight villeins, and four bordars, 'and five radchenifters, with eight plow-tillages. 'There are twelve *ſervi*, and a mill of 3 *s*. This 'eſtate is taxed for ſeven hides. In the time of 'king Edward it was worth 20 *l*. now 8 *l*. It is 'in the king's hands, and Robert de Olgi farms it.' *Domeſday-book*, p. 68.

The records relating to this pariſh, which was divided into two manors, are very confuſed and deficient, therefore as it would be difficult, if not impoſſible, to apply them with preciſion, they are ſet down in order of time.

The manor of Sheningdon was held of Richard de Clare, earl of Glouceſter and Hertford, 47 H. 3. John de Suor held this manor, with free warren, 15 E. 1. and John le More was ſeized of a manor in this pariſh, with free warren, the ſame year.

The family of the Peches held Shenington for ſeveral generations. John Peche died ſeized thereof 47 E. 3. and left two daughters his coheireſſes; Joan dying without iſſue, Margaret, the ſurviving daughter, married to ſir John Montfort, of Coleſhill in Warwickſhire, became ſole heir. Catherine the widow of ſir John Peche, William Montford [probably ſir John Montfort] of Coleſhull, and Margaret his wife, levied a fine of the manor of Shenington to the uſe of Catherine for life, the remainder to William and Margaret in taille, 12 H. 4.

John Saliſbury was ſeized of Shenington 11 R. 2. Joan the widow of —— Ruſtin of Norfolk, was ſeized of the manor of Shenington 7 H. 5.

Gerald earl of Kildare, and Elizabeth his wife, had a grant of the manor of Shenington, and of the advowſon, to them and their heirs males, 18 H. 7. which was confirmed 2 H. 8. Henry Fitz-Gerald, ſon of Gerald, granted the manor to his brother ſir Thomas Gerald, who died ſeized thereof 23 H. 8. and livery was granted to James Fitz-Gerald, ſon of ſir Thomas, 24 H. 8.

The manor of Shenington, and the advowſon of the rectory, were granted to John Coke, and John Baſſet, 4 E. 6. and it is recited in the grant, that the manor was lately John Fitz-Gerald's.

John Wigate, upon the death of his father, had livery of the manor of Shenington granted to him 20 Eliz.

Richard Pigot died ſeized of the manor 12 Eliz. and Robert Pigot, ſon and heir of Richard, dying unmarried, it came to Agnes, his ſiſter and heireſs.

Mr. Richard Gooding was lord of one manor in the pariſh at the beginning of this century, and it now belongs to Mr. Sheldon. Oriel college, Oxford, has another manor.

Henry le Fend and Iſabel his wife levied a fine of lands in Shenindon to William Giffard, archbiſhop of York, 7 E. 1. By another fine levied 20 E. 1. a third part of lands in Shenendon is acknowledged to be the right of Henry le Fend and of Iſabel his wife. John de Shokereſwell and Alice his wife levied a fine of lands in Shokereſwell and Shenendon, to John de Doweneved, 27 E. 1. John le Strange, of Knokyn, held one meſſuage, three yard-lands, and five acres of meadow in this pariſh 3 E. 2. John le Strange, of Walton, and Mabel his wife, levied a fine of lands in Shenington to Roger le Strange, and others, to the uſe of Philip le Strange, 15 E. 2. Henry Vyell and Alice his wife levied a fine of a rent in Shenington, to the uſe of Joan Scovile for life, the remainder to Henry Vyell and Alice, 3 H. 4. James Veel and Joan his wife levied a fine of a moiety of the manor of Shennington to ſir Reginald Bray, and others, 17 H. 7.

Of the Church, &c.

The church is a rectory, in the deanery of Campden, worth 160 *l*. a year, of which the earl of Litchfield is patron.

The advowſon of the rectory belonged to the abbey of Tewkeſbury, and was granted by the crown to Richard Andrews and Thomas Hyſley 36 H. 8. and was afterwards veſted in Mr. Sheldon.

The church is dedicated to the Holy Trinity, and has a tower at the weſt end, in which are five bells.

	£.	s.	d.		£.	s.	d.
Firſt fruits	15	3	4	Synodals	0	2	0
Tenths —	1	10	4	Pentecoſtals	0	0	8
Procurations	0	6	8				

Taxes.			£.	s.	d.
	The Royal Aid in	1692,	67	8	0
	Poll-tax ——	1694, —	33	2	0
	Land-tax ——	1694, —	82	1	0
	The ſame, at 3 *s*.	1770, —	61	10	9

At the beginning of this century, there were 60 houſes in the pariſh, and about 280 inhabitants, 24 of whom were freeholders; yearly births 10, burials 8. *Atkyns*. There are now about 300 inhabitants.

SHERBOURN.

THIS pariſh lies in the hundred of Slaughter, three miles diſtant eaſt from Northleach, five weſt from Burford in Oxfordſhire, and twenty-three eaſt from Glouceſter.

It

The village is ſituated on a brook, or *Bourn*, which riſes at Farmington, and being augmented in its courſe by ſome fine, clear ſprings, at the top of this pariſh, empties itſelf, a little below, into the Winruſh, near Barrington. It was undoubtedly this *Bourn* that gave name to the place, which was called *Sherbourn*, not becauſe it lies *on the border of the Shire*, as ſome have imagined, (for that is not the fact) but from the clearneſs of the water, for the Saxon word Scirebur̄n, in old writings, is tranſlated by *Fons Clarus*. Shakeſpeare, Milton, and other good writers, uſed the word *Sheer*, for *pure*, *clear*, *neat*, *unmixed*; and tho' it is now grown almoſt obſolete, yet we ſtill apply it to *wit*, in the like ſenſe or ſignification.

There is an eaſy deſcent on each ſide to this little river, and the ſlopes are covered with a beautiful verdure. Not two hundred yards diſtant, on the ſouth ſide, ſtands *Sherbourn-Houſe*, the ſeat of James Dutton, eſq; where the antient family of that name has reſided upwards of two hundred years. It conſiſts of two quadrangles. That on the eaſt, where the offices are, is the moſt antient building, ſuppoſed to have been one of the ſeats formerly belonging to the abbats of Winchcombe, who held the manor of Sherbourn 'till the diſſolution. The weſt quadrangle conſiſts of the principal apartments, and the grand entrance into the court, or area, is by a large gateway. The ſouth ſide, and part of the eaſt ſide of this ſquare, were built by Inigo Jones, but the reſt is about the age, and very much in the ſtile, of the public ſchools at Oxford.

Over the gateway, on the weſt ſide, are the Duttons arms, in freeſtone, with quarterings of the arms of other antient families, which by marriage they have a right to uſe.

There are two parks belonging to this ſeat, one adjoining to the houſe, the other lies at a little diſtance from it, with a beautiful lodge-houſe, and a paddock-courſe near it.

Of this ſeat, ſir Robert Atkyns has given a plate in his *Ancient and Preſent State of Glouceſterſhire*, but it is not a true repreſentation. One ſide of the weſt quadrangle does not appear in the engraving, tho' the houſe was exactly as it now ſtands, when that book was publiſhed. And beſides, the palliſadoes, gardens, and other decorations in the plate, are all imaginary, and never had exiſtence.

This ſeat will very ſhortly undergo conſiderable alterations. The late Mr. Dutton new built the coach-houſes and ſtables, which form a noble ſquare, but he was prevented by death from doing any thing further. The preſent proprietor has obliged the editor and the public with a beautiful plate of this ſeat, as it will appear when the deſign is compleated.

James Bradley, D. D. and Regius Profeſſor of Aſtronomy, who died in the year 1762, was a native of Sherbourn, but was buried at Minchin Hampton, in this county, where is an inſcription to his memory, on a braſs plate fixt to a tomb in the church-yard.

There is nothing further remarkable in this place, only it may not be amiſs to obſerve, that a bill is now depending in parliament for incloſing the common fields here, which, properly executed, will greatly improve and beautify the country.

Of the Manor and other Eſtates.

'The church of St. Mary of Wincelcumbe 'holds Scireburne in Salemones hundred. There 'are thirty hides, of which ten are free, as be-'longing to the court. There are five plow-'tillages in demean, and forty villeins, and ſeven 'bordars, with twenty-two plow-tillages. There 'are twelve *ſervi*, and four mills of 40*s*. and 'thirty acres of meadow. It was worth 20*l*. in 'the time of king Edward, and is now worth 14*l*.' *Domeſday*, p. 71.

This manor was diſcharged from the hundred court 8 H. 3.

The abbey of Winchcombe purchaſed a charter of free warren in Shirburn 35 H. 3. and aſſigned the manor to the abbey of St. Ebrulph in Normandy, 12 E. 2. Yet the firſt-mentioned abbey retained an eſtate here, for Richard Buſhel was ſeized of one meſſuage, two tofts, and of paſture for eight cows, in Winchcombe and Shirbourn, in truſt for the abbey, 18 R. 2.

After the diſſolution of religious foundations, this manor, and the rectory and advowſon of Sherbourn, were granted to ſir Chriſtopher Alleyn, who joins with Ethelreda his wife, and levies a fine of them to Thomas Dutton,[b] eſq; 6 E. 6. whoſe deſcendants have enjoy'd them ever ſince.

A mea-

[b] This family is of great antiquity. It appears by the antient roll of the barons of Halton in Cheſhire, that at the time of the conqueſt, Hugh Lupus, earl of Cheſter, brought with him out of Normandy one Nigell, a nobleman, and his five brothers, *viz*. Hudard, Edard, Wolmere, Horſwyne, and Wolfaith. And the ſame Nigell gave to Hudard, or Odard, the townſhip of Great Aſton, and a moiety of Weſton, in Cheſhire, *pro uno feodo militis*. This Odard was ſeated at a place called Duntune, in the ſame county, which was given him by Hugh Lupus, from whence his deſcendants took the ſurname of De Duntune, or Dutton, as appears by ſeveral deeds of great antiquity among the evidences of the Dutton family; and Hudard's ſword has paſſed over from heir to heir, as an *heir-loom*, and is ſtill very carefully preſerved.

Hugh, ſon of Odard, had thoſe lands, which he held, as it were *in capite*, of the earl of Cheſter, confirmed to him by Randle the Second, earl of Cheſter, about the latter end of the reign of Henry the Firſt.

Hugh de Dutton, ſon of Hugh, had thoſe lands which his father held of the baron of Halton confirmed to him by William ſon of Nigell, conſtable of Cheſter, and by William ſon of William, when they viſited Hugh de Dutton the elder, on his death-bed at Kekwick, about the end of the reign of king Henry the Firſt: and thereupon Hugh de Dutton, the father, gave to William the elder, his coat of mail, and his charging-horſe; and Hugh, the ſon, gave to William the younger, a palfry and ſparrow-hawk. This Hugh had iſſue Hugh, eldeſt ſon; Adam de Dutton, from whom the Warburtons are deſcended, who took their name from Warburton in Cheſhire, the place of their reſidence in the reign of Edward the Second; Geffrey de Dutton, another ſon, anceſtor of the Chedhills of Chedhill, and Aſhleys of Aſhley, who aſſumed thoſe names from the places of their reſidence, according to the cuſtom of antient times.

Hugh de Dutton, the third of that name, and great grandſon of Odard, married ——— daughter of Hamon Maſſy, of Dunham Maſſy, in the reign of king Henry the Second, and had iſſue

Hugh

A meadow in Sherbourn belonged to the priory of St. John the Evangelist in Burford, (which priory was valued at 13*l.* 6*s.* 6*d.*) and was granted to Edmund Herman 35 H. 8.

Of

Hugh Dutton, who married Muriel, daughter of Thomas le Dispencer, by whom he had Hugh, who died without issue, Thomas, John, and Adam; and a daughter Alice, married to William Boydell, of Dodleston. Randle, surnamed Blundevill, the sixth earl of Chester from Hugh Lupus, had been succesful in many conflicts against Llhewellin prince of North Wales, but was at last surprized, and forced, for his present security, to take refuge in the castle of Rothlent in Flintshire, to which the Welch laid siege. In this distress, Randle dispatched a messenger to his constable, Roger de Lacy, surnamed Hell, for his fierce spirit, to come to his relief with what forces he could collect. The news of the earl's distress reached Chester on Midsummer-day, which being the time of the principal fair, Roger de Lacy collected a rude multitude out of the city of Chester, composed of coblers, players, fidlers, and debauched persons of both sexes, and marched with them to the earl's relief. The Welch supposing a great army to be coming, raised their siege, and fled precipitately to their own country. In commemoration of this signal piece of service, the earl granted to Roger de Lacy authority over all the shoemakers, fidlers, &c. within the county, and the city of Chester. Some time afterwards, John, constable of Chester, son of Roger de Lacy, who had rescued the earl, reserving to himself and his heirs authority over the shoemakers, granted the patronage of the rest to his steward, Hugh de Dutton, of Dutton, and his heirs, (not Ralph de Dutton, as sir Robert Atkyns has it) as will more clearly appear by the grant, which follows:

Sciant presentes & futuri, quod ego Iohannes Constabularius Cestriæ dedi & concessi, & hac presenti charta mea confirmavi Hugoni de Dutton, & heredibus suis, Magistratum omnium Leccatorum & Meretricum totius Cestershiriæ, sicut liberius illum Magistratum teneo de Comite; salvo jure meo mihi & heredibus meis. Hiis testibus, Hugone de Boidele, Alano fratre ejus, Petro de Goenet, Liulfo de Twamlow, Adam de Dutton, Gilberto de Aston, Radulfo de Kingsley, Hamone de Bordington, Alano de Waleie, Alano de Mulinton, Willielmo filio Ricardi, Martino Angevin, Willielmo de Savill, Galfrido & Roberto filiis meis, Blethero, Herdberd de Waleton, Galfrido de Dutton.

This grant was made about the end of the reign of king John, from which time this family have exercised their jurisdiction with many ludicrous ceremonies; for on every Midsummer-day the heir of Dutton, or his steward, rides through the city of Chester, attended by all the fidlers in the county in procession, playing on their several musical instruments, to St. John's church; and after divine service, the cavalcade proceeds to the court house, where laws and ordinances are made for their better government; and here all the fidlers take out licences, none being permitted to follow their profession in that county without them.

A writ of *Quo warranto* was brought against Lawrence Dutton, of Dutton, esq; 14 H. 7. to shew cause why he claimed that all the minstrels of Cheshire, and the city of Chester, should meet before him at Chester, on the feast of St. John Baptist yearly, and give unto him *Quatuor Lagenas Vini et unam Lanceam, i. e.* four flaggons, or bottles, of wine, and one lance; and that every minstrel should pay unto him, at the said feast, four-pence halfpenny. And why he claimed from every whore in Cheshire and the city of Chester, *Officium suum exercente, i.e.* following her profession, four-pence yearly, to be paid at the feast aforesaid, &c. Whereunto the said Lawrence Dutton pleaded prescription.—— And here it must be observed, that in the statutes for punishing rogues and vagabonds, 39 Eliz. *cap.* 4. and 1 Jac. 1. *cap.* 25. the licenced fidlers of Cheshire are excepted; and care is taken, by an especial proviso, that no clause in those acts shall prejudice the right of John Dutton, of Dutton, esq; which he or his ancestors have lawfully enjoyed in the county and city of Chester.

Sir Thomas Dutton, second son of Hugh and Muriel, married Philippa, daughter and heir of Vivian de Sandon, or Standon, by whom he had Hugh, Thomas, and Robert; and two daughters, Margaret, married to William Venables, son and heir of Roger Venables of Kinderton, in the year 1253; and Katherine, married to John, son of Vrian de Sancto Petro. Sir Thomas was sheriff of Cheshire 1268, and died in the beginning of the reign of king Edward the First.

Sir Hugh Dutton, of Dutton, knight, son and heir of sir Thomas, married Joan, daughter of sir Vrian de Sancto Petro, *vulgo* Sampier, and by her had issue Hugh, William, and Robert; and a daughter Margaret. Sir Hugh, the father, died in the year 1294, and was succeeded by

Sir Hugh Dutton, his son and heir, born at Dutton, Dec. 8, 1276, 5 E. 1. He married Joan, daughter of sir Robert Holland, of Holland in Lancashire, by whom he had Thomas, William, Geffery, and Robert; and died in the year 1327, 1 E. 3.

Sir Thomas Dutton, of Dutton, knight, son and heir of sir Hugh, was fifteen years old on Whit-sunday, 1329. He purchased those lands in Dutton which had belonged to Halton fee; and likewise those lands in the same place which formerly belonged to Boydell of Dodleston, and so became possessed of the whole township of Dutton. He was made seneschal, governor, and receiver of the castle and honour of Halton in Cheshire, by William Clinton, earl of Huntingdon; and of his lands and manors in Cheshire and Lancashire, all which the earl farmed to him for 440 marks yearly, by his deed, dated at Maxstock, 19 E. 3. He was sheriff of Cheshire 30 & 33 E. 3. and married to his first wife, Ellen, eldest daughter and one of the coheirs of sir Peter Thornton, of Thornton, by whom he had sir Peter, who died without issue 35 E. 3. Thomas; Lawrence, his successor, who likewise died without issue; Edmund, the continuer of the family; Henry; and William. His second wife was Philippa, widow of sir Peter Thornton, but not the mother of his first wife. Sir Thomas died in the year 1381, 4 R. 2. aged 66.

Edmund Dutton, fourth son of sir Thomas, married Joan, daughter and heir of Henry Minshull, of Church Minshull, and by her had issue sir Peter, who was heir to his uncle sir Lawrence, and continued the elder branch of the family seated at Dutton; Hugh, second son, from whom the Duttons of Sherbourn are descended; Lawrence, and Thomas; and two daughters, Agnes, married to William Leycester, of Nether Tabley; and another daughter, Ellen.

Hugh Dutton, second son of Edmund, married Petronilla, daughter and heir of Ralph Vernon of Hatton, by whom he had four sons, John, Lawrence, Randle, and Hugh; and a daughter Elizabeth, married to Richard Manley of Manley.

John Dutton of Hatton, eldest son of Hugh, was mayor of Chester 30 H. 6. and married Margaret, daughter to William Atherton, of Atherton in Lancashire, by whom he had issue, Peter, Richard, and Geffrey; and two daughters, Cicely, and Ellen.

Peter Dutton of Hatton, son and heir of John, in the year 1464, married Elizabeth, eldest daughter and one of the coheirs of Robert Grosvenor of Holme, by whom he had Peter, eldest son, who married Elenor, daughter of Robert Foulishurst, of Crew in Cheshire, (and whose son, sir Piers Dutton, became heir to the lands of Dutton, on the death of Lawrence Dutton, of Dutton, esq; without lawful issue, in the year 1526,) and Ralph Richard, and Randle.

Richard Dutton, third son of Peter Dutton of Hatton, the elder, married Mary, daughter of ——— Mainwaring of Croxton, by whom he was father of

Ralph Dutton, who had two sons, William, his heir, and Richard, who settled at Cloughton in Pickering in Yorkshire, and was ancestor of the Duttons of Cloughton.

William Dutton of Chester, eldest son and heir of Ralph, married Agnes, daughter of John Conway of Flintshire, and had issue

Thomas Dutton, who purchased the manor of Sherbourn of sir Christopher Alleyn, 6 E. 6. He married three wives; by the first, Mary, daughter of Robert Taylour, of Gloucestershire, he had one daughter Anne, married to John Warneford, of Gloucestershire: By his second wife, Anne, daughter of Stephen Kyrton, alderman of London, and relict of sir Thomas Wyther, knight, he had issue William, his heir, Thomas, and Elenor. Thomas Dutton, of Sherbourn, died in the year 1581, aged 74, and was succeeded by his eldest son,

William Dutton, of Sherbourn, esq; who had livery of the manor and advowson of Sherbourn the same year his father died. He was high sheriff of Gloucestershire in 1590, and 1601, and having married Anne, daughter of sir Ambrose Nicholas, knight, lord mayor of London, deceased in the year 1618, leaving issue by his lady three sons, John, Ralph, and Giles.

John Dutton, of Sherbourn, eldest son of William, married first, Elizabeth, daughter of sir Henry Baintun, of Brumham in Wiltshire, by whom he had one son, over whose education he appointed Oliver Cromwell to be guardian, and the protector nominated a tutor to discharge his important trust; but the son died young. He had also three daughters, two of whom survived him, *viz.* Elizabeth, married to George Colt, esq; and Lucy, married to Thomas Pope earl of Down. To his second wife, he married Anne, fourth daughter of John King, bishop of London, who out-lived him, and was afterwards wedded to sir Richard How. John Dutton died Jan. 14, 1656, in the 63d year of his age, and was buried at Sherbourn.

Sir Ralph Dutton, knight, died before his elder brother John. He was gentleman of the privy chamber in extraordinary to king Charles the First, and high sheriff of this county in 1630. His estate, according to sir Robert Atkyns, was sequestered in the great rebellion, and he was forced to fly beyond seas, but being driven back by contrary winds, in his passage from Leith to France, he was cast on Burnt Island, and there died in 1646. He married Mary, daughter of sir William Duncombe, of London, by whom he had issue William, and Ralph.

William

Of the Church, &c.

The church is a vicarage, in the deanery of Stow, as it is said in bishop Benson's visitation book, but in the deanery of Fairford, according to sir Robert Atkyns, and is worth about 40*l.* a year. James Dutton, esq; is patron, and Mr. Twining is the present incumbent.

The vicarages of Sherbourn and Winrush were consolidated into one presentment in the year 1776, and a bill is now depending in parliament, whereby the lands belonging to the vicarage of Sherbourn are to be given up, and others of equal value to be allotted to the glebe at Winrush in lieu of them. The vicarage house at the former parish is to be taken down, and another built for the incumbent at the latter, and the lands laid contigious to it. The business was not compleated when this account was printed, but will be further advanced before that of Winrush goes to the press, where a more perfect account may be expected.

The church is newly built, at the sole expence of the late James-Lenox Dutton, esq; and consists of the nave only, with a portico on the north side, supported by two freestone pillars, of the Doric order, and has a handsome spire at the west end.

First fruits £.	14	6	4½	Synodals £.	0	2	0
Tenths —	1	10	8	Pentecost.	0	1	6
Procurations	0	6	8				

Monuments and Inscriptions.

Against the north wall of the church, is this inscription in capital letters:

In the vault vnder this monvment lies ye body of Thomas Dvtton Esqr. who died in ye yeare of our lord 1581.

And the body of William Dutton his sonne who died in the yeare 1618.

And Anne his wife the davght^r^ of Sir Thomas Nicholas of London.

And the body of Thomas Dvtton the sonne of William Dvtton who died in the year 1610.

Within the communion rails are two noble marble monuments. That on the left hand is the more antient. In a niche, between two Corinthian pillars supporting a pediment, is the figure, in white marble, of John Dutton, esq; standing erect, and covered with a winding sheet, the folds of which are very gracefully disposed, and the whole figure exceedingly well executed. On a table at his feet, it is thus engraven in capital letters:

IOHN DVTTON
Of Sherborne in Glovcester Shiere Esq; Son of William Dutton
& Anne ye Davghter of Ambrose Nicholas of London, K^t^;
A Person of a sharp Vnderstanding & cleer Ivdgment every Way
capable of those eminent Services for his Covntry which he
Vnderwent as Knight of ye Shiere in several Parliaments
and as depvty Lieftenant
One who was Master of a large Fortvne
and Owner of a Mind Æqvall to it.
Noted for his great Hospitality farr and neer;
and his charitable Relief of ye Poor.
Which makes his Memory honovred by ye best,
and his Loss lamented by ye last.
He deceased in the Year of his Age 63 & of ye Lord 1656.
IAN. 14.

On a small table, on the dexter side of the figure, it is written,

His first wife was
Elizabeth Daughter of Sr Henry Bainton
of Brumham in Wiltshire
by whom he had 1 son who dyed young
and three Daughters
whereof two only suruiued
Elizabeth married to George Colt esq;
& Lucy married to Thomas Pope Earle
of Downe. She deceased in ye 42 Yeare
of her Age A^o^ Dni 1648 apr. 28.

And over this inscription, in a scutcheon, *Sable, a bend lozengy gules.*

On the sinister side of the figure is this inscription:

ANN
His second Wife Fourth Daughter
of Iohn King Bishop of London
Descended from the Antient
Saxon Kings
of Deuonshiere
was married 8 yeares
unto whose care the erecting
of this Monument was by
will entrusted.

And over the table, in a lozenge, *Quarterly* 1st *and* 4th, *Sable, a lion rampant between three crosses croslets Or.* 2d *and* 3d, *Gules, within a bordure ingrailed Or, three lioncels passant in pale argent.*

Over the figure above the niche, *Quarterly* 1st *and* 4th, *Argent*; 2d *and* 3d, *Gules, a fret Or,* for Dutton: But the colours are not exprest in either coat.

The other is a very large monument of white marble, representing sir John Dutton in the

William Dutton, son of sir Ralph, succeeded his uncle John Dutton in the manor of Sherbourn, and other great estates. He married Mary, daughter of lord Scudamore, and widow of Thomas Russel, of Worcestershire, esq; and having served the office of high sheriff of Gloucestershire, in the year 1667, died without issue, and was succeeded by his brother,

Sir Ralph Dutton, baronet, son of sir Ralph, who married Grisle, daughter of sir Edward Pool, of Kemble in Wiltshire, by whom he had an only daughter, who died without issue. By his second wife, Mary, daughter of Dr. John Barwick, he had issue two sons, John and Ralph, and many daughters. He served in several parliaments as knight of the shire, and was lord of the manor of Sherbourn at the beginning of the present century.

Sir John Dutton, baronet, son of sir Ralph by his second wife, married first, Mary, only child of sir Rushout Cullen, of Upton in Warwickshire, baronet, by whom he had no issue; secondly, Mary, daughter of Francis Keck, of Great Tew, in the county of Oxford, esq; and by her had an only daughter, who died an infant. Sir John himself deceasing without issue, in the year 1742-3, bequeathed his estates to

James-Lenox Naper, esq; of the kingdom of Ireland, his sister's son, who assumed the name and arms of Dutton. He married two wives; by the first he had one son John, who died unmarried before his father. By his second wife, Jane, daughter of Edmund Bond, of Newland, in this county, esq; he left issue three sons, James, William, and Ralph; and four daughters, Anne, married to Samuel Blackwell, of Williamstrip, in this county, esq; Mary, married to Thomas Master, of Cirencester, esq; Frances, married to Charles Lambart, of Beaupark in the kingdom of Ireland, esq; and Jane, married to Thomas-William Coke, of Longford in Derbyshire, and Holkham in Norfolk, esq; one of the knights of the shire for the county of Norfolk. James-Lenox Dutton died in the year 1776, and was succeeded by his eldest surviving son,

James Dutton, esq; who married Elizabeth, the youngest sister of the before-mentioned Thomas-William Coke. He is the twenty-third in lineal descent from Hudard, or Odard, the Norman, who came into England with king William the First, and is the present lord of the manor of Sherbourn, where he resides. His arms are, *Quarterly*, 1st *and* 4th, *Argent*; 2d *and* 3d, *Gules, a fret Or.*

N. B. This is extracted from the elaborate and well authenticated pedigree of Dutton of Dutton, compiled about the year 1669, from original records and other evidences, by sir Peter Leycester, bart. of Nether Tabley in Cheshire, and continued down to the end of the year 1694, by George Ven, vicar of Sherbourn. All since that time falls within the reach of memory.

Roman drefs, ftanding on a pedeftal, and leaning his right arm on an urn. Upon the pedeftal it is thus written:

Sir JOHN DUTTON *Baronet*, [BARWICK,
Son of Sir RALPH DUTTON, by MARY the Daughter of JOHN
Doctor of Phyfic, departed this Life February the firft 174¾,
in the fixty firft Year of his Age.
He was twice Married
Firft, to MARY only Child of Sir RUSHOUT CULLEN of UPTON
in WARWICKSHIRE *Baronet*. by Her having no Iffue
His fecond Wife was MARY, Daughter of FRANCIS KECK
of Great TEW, in the County of OXFORD *Efquire*,
By whom He had One Daughter, who died an Infant.
He reprefented this County in Parliament
With great Integrity,
Was an excellent Juftice of Peace,
Hofpitable, Affable, and benevolent.

On the upper part of the monument are two fcutcheons, reprefenting the two marriages. The firft is *Baron and femme*, 1. Dutton as before. 2. *Or, an eagle difplay'd fable*, for Cullen. —The fecond fcutcheon bears, 1. Dutton, impaling, 2. *Sable, a bend ermine cotized with femi fleurs de lis*, for Keck.

Benefaction.

A ground called Cruckmore, worth 40*s*. a year, is given towards the maintenance of a fchool-mafter. *Atkyns*. Alexander Ready permitted the iffues and profits of this ground to be applied to the ufe of a fchool, fo long as there was a mafter; but I don't find that it was a permanent eftablifhment.

Taxes.					
The Royal Aid in	1692, £.	198	18	0
Poll-tax — —	1694, —	56	1	0
Land-tax ——	1694, -	106	13	4
The fame, at 3*s*.	1770, —	83	5	3

At the beginning of this century, there were 60 houfes, and about 300 inhabitants in the parifh, 5 of whom were freeholders; yearly births 10, burials 9. *Atkyns*. The prefent number of houfes is nearly the fame, but the people are increafed to about 360.

SHIPTON MOIGN *and* DOVEL

IS a pleafant, healthy village, in the hundred of Longtree, three miles fouth from Tetbury, three north-weftward from Malmefbury in Wiltfhire, and about twenty-one fouthward from Gloucefter.

The parifh is bounded on the eaft by Wiltfhire, and a fmall ftream, which rifes at Weftonbirt, runs through it, and falls into the Avon at Malmefbury.

Shipton, antiently written *Sciptune*, is of doubtful original. Sir Robert Atkyns conjectured that *it was fo called from the fheep kept here*. But *Scip* may be the name of the proprietor whofe town it was. *Moign* and *Dovel* are additional names, of later date, taken from the families of *Le Moygn*, and *De Dowe*, who were owners of the refpective manors fo called, and were given to diftinguifh them from two other places of the name of *Shipton*, in this county.

The village is ornamented with two gentlemen's feats, of which one belongs to the reverend Mr. Nowel, who, in right of his wife, is lord of the manor. It is of freeftone, built about half a century ago, with baluftrades over the Attic ftory, and the family arms of Hodges in a large fhield (*Azure, a fefs between three crefcents argent*) are placed in the centre of the principal front, facing the north.

The other is the antient feat of the Eftcourts. It is a large old houfe, with a great gate-way in front, and has a venerable and refpectable appearance. This is at prefent the feat and refidence of Thomas Eftcourt, efq; who is preparing to build a new houfe on his eftate at Long Newton, near Tetbury.

This parifh is diftinguifhed for having been the birth-place of John Oldham, an ingenious perfon of the laft age, who was the author of a well known, and much admired book of poems, and died in the prime of life, in the year 1683, aged 30.

Of the Manors and other Eftates.

Domefday-book takes notice of three manors in this parifh, but the accounts of the two moft confiderable were overlooked by fir Robert Atkyns. They are fet down under the title *Terra Mathiu de Moretanie*, and are thus defcribed in the record:

'Maci de Mauritania holds Scipetone in 'Langetrewes hundred, of the king. Strang, the 'Dane, held it. There are ten hides taxed. In 'demean are two plow-tillages, and four villeins, 'and two bordars, with four plow-tillages. There 'are four *fervi*, and a mill of 10*s*. and pafture 'worth 2*s*. It was worth 15*l*. now 8*l*.'

'The fame Maci holds Scipetone in Lange'trewes hundred, and Rumbald holds it of him. 'There are ten hides taxed. John held it in the 'time of king Edward. In demean are three 'plow-tillages, and four villeins, and eight bor'dars, with four plow-tillages. There are four '*fervi*, and a mill of 12*s*. and pafture worth 2*s*. 'It was worth 15*l*. now 8*l*.'

'The fame Maci holds one hide there, and 'Rumbald holds it of him. Aluuin held it, and 'could go where he pleafed, and Rainbert Flan'drenfis likewife enjoyed it. There is one plow'tillage in demean, and one villein, and one bor'dar, with half a plow-tillage. It was worth '20*fol*. now 14*fol*.' *Domefday*, p. 79.

There was another manor, thus defcribed in the antient furvey:

'The fame William [de Ow] holds Sciptone in 'Langetreu hundred, in the fame manner as 'Ralph de Limefi held it. Wlui held it in the 'time of king Edward. There are two hides. 'In demean are two plow-tillages, and two bor'dars, and eight *fervi*. It is worth and was worth '40*fol*. Wluui could go where he pleafed. Hugh 'holds it of William.' *Ibid*. p. 73.

William le Moygne was feized of a manor in this parifh 5 H. 3. which he held of the crown by the fervice of keeping the king's larder; and he pur-

purchased a charter of free warren in all his lands in Gloucestershire in the 37th year of the same reign. Walter de Stukeley, sheriff of Gloucestershire, in obedience to the king's writ, returned into the exchequer the names of all the vills in the county, with their respective proprietors; and in his list it is said, that Johanna le Moyn, Margaret Gifford, William Skay, and William de Dowe, were lords of the vill of Shipton Moynt, in Langtree hundred 9 E. 1. This return seems to have been preparitory to the writs of *Quo warranto* that were brought against almost every considerable landholder in the kingdom, by king Edward the First, in the fifteenth year of his reign, in order to oblige them to shew by what title they held their estates, or enjoyed certain privileges therein. However necessary such a method of preceeding might have been in certain cases, it was made use of by that king, who was chief lord of many manors, and other estates, as an expedient to fill his own coffers, by extorting exorbitant fines from the subject for fresh grants, where the title-deeds and evidences respecting estates were lost or destroyed, as was frequently the case, during the civil commotions that distracted the kingdom in his father's reign. And as the fines for renewal were arbitrary, and generally excessive, this measure was regarded by the subject in a light little better than confiscation by lawless violence.

A writ of *Quo warranto* was brought against William le Moygne, son of William, to oblige him to shew by what right he enjoyed divers privileges in Schipton, and his claim was allowed 15 E. 1. and he died seized thereof in the 23d year of the same reign. Henry le Moygne, son of the last William, was seized of the manor and advowson of Shiptone Moygne 1 E. 2. and dying 8 E. 2. the escheator's inquisition found that John le Moygne was his son and heir; but Joan, the widow of Henry, was endowed with the manor; upon whose death, 14 E. 3. livery was granted to Robert le Moygne, son of Henry, the same year. Sir Henry Moigne, son of Robert, succeeded his father, and died seized of Shipton Moigne and Hullecot [Hull-court] 49 E. 3. Sir John Moigne, son and heir of sir Henry, died seized of the manor of Shipton Moign, and left Elizabeth, his only daughter and heiress, who carried this estate by her marriage with William de Stourton, into that name and family. Upon occasion of this alliance, the Stourtons took for their crest, *A demy monk, with a penitential whip in his hand*, alluding to the name of *Moign*, which signifies a *monk*.

William de Stourton, descended from an antient family residing at Stourton in Wiltshire, was seized of Shipton 21 R. 2. in right of Elizabeth his wife, daughter of sir John Moigne, and died 1 H. 5. John de Stourton, son of William, was under age at his father's death, and had not livery of this manor until 9 H. 5. He was high sheriff of Gloucestershire 18 H. 6. and having been created a baron in the 28th year of that reign, died seized of Shipton Moign, Hull-court, and Hamvelle, *alias* Vetham, or Veelham near Berkeley, and was succeeded by William lord Stourton, who had livery of this manor the same year. He married Margaret, one of the daughters and coheiresses of sir John Chidiock, and died 17 E. 4. likewise seized of Shipton, and of Veelham near Berkeley. John lord Stourton, son and heir of William, had livery of the manor upon the decease of his father, and dying 2 R. 3. William lord Stourton, his son, had livery the same year, and having married the sister of John Dudley, duke of Northumberland, died 14 H. 8. William lord Stourton succeeded his father, but dying soon after, Edward lord Stourton, his brother, had livery 16 H. 8. and died seized of Shipton Moign in the 27th year of the same reign. William lord Stourton, son of Edward, had livery of this manor 33 H. 8. and dying 2 E. 6. left Charles lord Stourton, his son, who was hanged at Salisbury for murder, 3 Mariæ.

The manor came very soon after to the family of Hodges, or as they are sometimes called Hedges. John Hodges, or Hedges, esq; upon the death of his father, had livery of the manor of Shipton Moyne 20 Eliz. and died seized of Shipton Moyne and Shipton Dovell, and of the advowson of the church, in the 40th year of the same reign. He was likewise seized of the neighbouring manor of Eston Grey, in Wiltshire, and of the advowson of that church, at the same time. The escheator's inquisition found that Shipton Moyne and Shipton Dovell, and the advowson of the church, were held of the queen in *capite*, by the 40th part of a knight's fee, and were worth 21 *l.* 2 *s.* 0 *d.* *ob.* clear of all reprises. Thomas Hodges, son and heir of John, was twenty-one years old and upwards at the taking of the inquisition, and was lord of this manor in the year 1608, and high sheriff of Gloucestershire in 1622. Another Thomas Hodges, esq; was lord of the manor, and died in the year 1696. He married Edith, youngest daughter of Thomas Estcourt, of this parish, esq; who surviving him, died in the year 1717. Thomas Hodges, esq; son of the last-mentioned Thomas and Edith his wife, dying under age, in the year 1708, this manor and estate came to his younger brother, Estcourt Hodges, esq. The reverend Walter Hodges was lord of this manor, and the last male heir of his family. He was provost of Oriel college, Oxford, and vice-chancellor of that university, and died in the year 1757, aged 62. The reverend Mr. Nowel, in right of his wife, one of the coheiresses of the Hodges family, is the present lord of the manor, and resides here.

There is another very considerable estate in this parish, belonging to the antient family of the Estcourts, who have resided in this place upwards of 300 years, and seem to have taken their name from a manor they enjoyed here, called *Le Estcourt*, because it lay eastward of the before-mentioned manor.

John Eſtcourt died ſeized of a manor in Shipton Moigne 14 E. 4. And it appears by the eſcheator's inquiſition, taken 42 Eliz. that Thomas Eſtcourt, of Shipton Moigne, eſq; died Oct. 25, 41 Eliz. ſeized of a manor, and lands in Shipton Moigne called Le Eſtcourt, worth 8 *l. per ann.* which he held of Thomas Hedges, gent. as of his manor of Shipton Moigne. And of another manor and lands in Shipton Moigne, worth together 40 *s.* which he held of the queen in common ſoccage, as of her manor of Eaſt Greenwich in Kent; and of the manor of Wynſton, in the county of Glouceſter, worth 5 *l.* which he held of Anthony Hungerford, as of his manor of Wynſton. And that in the 39th year of the ſame reign he had enfeoffed. Ralph Sheldon, and others, with his manor or farm and lands at Combſend; and with lands in Old Sadbury, Little Sadbury, Dodington, Tormarton, and Yate, in this county, in truſt, by way of jointure for Mary, daughter of William Savage, and wife of Thomas Eſtcourt, his ſon and heir apparent. Thomas Eſtcourt, the father, died ſeized alſo of other very conſiderable eſtates in Long Newton, Weſtport, Malmeſbury, Burton Hill, Sherſton, Sherſton Magna, Pynckeney, Willeſley, Chippenham, Rowden, Waddeſwycke, Box, and Haſelbery, all in the county of Wilts, and left Thomas his ſon thirty years old at the time of his death. Walter Eſtcourt, eſq; ſon of Thomas, died in the year 1726, and left this manor and eſtate to Thomas Eſtcourt, eſq; upon whoſe death, in 1746, the manor came to Edmond Eſtcourt, eſq; his only brother and heir. He married Anna-Maria, third daughter and coheireſs of Charles Yate, late of Colthrope in this county, by whom he had one daughter, Anna-Maria, who was married to the late Thomas Earl, of Malmeſbury, eſq; deceaſed; but he bequeathed the bulk of his ample fortune to Thomas Eſtcourt, eſq; ſon of Matthew Eſtcourt, of Cam in this county, who is the preſent lord of this manor, and proprietor of many great eſtates in this pariſh and elſewhere. His arms are, *Ermine, on a chief indented gules three eſtoiles Or.*

Jeffry Pulham granted two yard-lands in this place to the abbey of Cirenceſter, 32 E. 1. Lands in Shipton Moign, belonging to the abbey of Cirenceſter, were granted to John Dudley and John Aſcough 17 Eliz.

Of the Church, &c.

The church is a rectory, in the deanery of Stonehouſe, worth 160 *l.* a year. Mrs. Nowel is patroneſs, and Mr. Huntely is the preſent incumbent.

The church, dedicated to St. John the Baptiſt, conſiſts of the nave and two ailes, with a tower, in which are five bells.

Firſt fruits £.	18	1	9	Synodals £.	0	2	0
Tenths —	1	16	2	Pentecoſtals	0	0	5
Procurations	0	6	8				

Monuments and Inſcriptions.

In the north aile, on a marble table, is this inſcription:

S. Æ. M.

THOMÆ HODGES, Armigeri, hujus Manerij Domini, Viri genuinâ Probitate, Prudentis, & ad ſtabilitæ Religionis Anglicanæ normam Pii, Eccleſiaſticorum munerum (quorum unum hæc Eccleſiâ) Patronus fuit digniſſimus, utpote qui neminem unquam ſimoniace promoverit. Maritus amantiſſimus, indulgens Pater, fidelis Amicus, Vicinus hoſpitalis, liberalis ingentibus, nemini injurioſus, oblatâ facultate omnibus beneficus, et omnibus (nec immerito) dilectus. Ex Uxore, quæ illi fuit unica, ſuſcepit tres filios atque unam filiam (ELIZABETHam) quos omnes in vivis reliquit, extra filium primogenitum (eodem quo Pater prænomine) in cunabulis morte præreptum.

Nec non

S. M. et V.

Ejus Conjugis EDITHæ HODGES, THOMÆ ESTCOURT de hâc Paræchiâ Armigeri Filiæ natu minimæ, Uxoris, Matris, Vicinæ, optimæ, Matronæ Virtute ſingulari. Pietate eximiâ, aliiſq; præclaris, quæ liberaliter educatam exornant fœminam, tum animi tum corporis dotibus, haud vulgariter inſignis: Viro fuit
ſuperſtes, ſed conjugii ſecundi neſcia.

Et etiam

P. M. S.

Eorum Filii præter unum natu maximi, THOMÆ HODGES, Armigeri; cujus vita, ſi computes annos, brevis, ſi ad bonum ingenium et probos mores reſpicias, longa fuit (eheu fuit) Indole adeo miti, adeo ſuavi, adeo placida, ut illorum quibuſcum verſatus eſt, nemini non charus vixerit, obierit
nemini non deſideratus.

Locum hunc circiter mortales Exuviæ conquieſcunt,
e quibus (non e vita) deceſſere,

Ille arthritica Paſſione Aprilis 14	A.D.	1696	Ætatis	37
Hic Phthiſi Julii 16		1708		20
Illa ſenili Atrophiâ Martis 18		1716-7		70.

ESTCOURT HODGES, Armiger, etq; Heres, cum pro Pietate in Parentes, et Charitate in Fratrem, tum honoris ergo

M. H. P.

Arms, *Baron and femme,* 1. *Azure, a feſs between three creſcents argent,* for Hodges. 2. *Quarterly* 1ſt *and* 4th, Eſtcourt, 2d *and* 3d, *Sable, a feſs between three falcons heads erazed Or.*

Within the communion rails, on a plain table of white marble,

Near this Place are interr'd the Remains
Of Will: Hodges, M.A. Rector of this Pariſh. [Eſq;
Of Bridget his Wife, Daughter of John Palmer, in ye C. of Worc.
And of Anne Hodges their Daughter.
The Praiſes of their late Spiritual Guide
Are deeply engraven in the Hearts
Of his ſurviving Pariſhioners:
To whom he ſhew'd the Way to that happy State
Which He Himſelf is now gone before them to Enjoy.
All who knew or heard Him
Want no Enumeration of His Virtues:
But the impartial Acknowledgment of the Public
Expreſs'd in the Printed N. Papers upon his Deceaſe,
May, in Juſtice to his Memory, without Offence,
Be tranſmitted down
For the Information of Poſterity
In the Pariſh of Shipton Moyne,
Of which he was Rector upwards of 40 Years:
He was an able Divine, a faithful reſident Paſtor,
And a true Engliſhman.
The Reader's Imagination will ſupply
The Omiſſion of more Particulars,
When He knows
That He was Chaplain to, & highly Eſteemed by
Sr William Trumbull,
One of the Principal Secretaries of State.

William	Died	April the 29th	1740	Aged	74	Years.
Bridget		October the 20th	1733		65	
Anne		April the 4th	1733		28	

H. M.

M. F. P.

Without the church, on the ſouth ſide, there is a marble monument, conſiſting of a baſe and pyramid, incloſed with iron paliſadoes; and on one ſide of the baſe is the following inſcription:

Underneath

Underneath are interr'd the mortal Remains of
The Revd WALTER HODGES D.D.
and ELIZABETH his Wife:
SHE was the Daughter of the Revd Robt RATCLIFF
B.D. Rector of Stone House near Gloucester,
HE the last Male Heir of the Family of HODGES
Lords of the Manor of Shipton Moyne and Dovel.
He presided as Provost of Oriel College in
Oxford from the Year 1728 to 1757, and had the
Honour for three Years of being appointed
Vice Chancellour of that University:
His Learning and Zeal in the Prosecution
of Scripture Knowledge appear in the
Books he hath written.
She died October 19th 1754 Aged 48
He died Jany 14th 1757 Aged 62.

Arms, *Baron and femme*, 1. Hodges. 2. *A bend engrailed.*

In a chancel, at the east end of the south aile, is a superb marble monument, which bears this inscripton:

Sacred to the never fading Memories
of
WALTER and THOMAS ESTCOURT Esquires
The former descended from an honourable and antient Family
Seated here for some Ages past;
Bequeathed his Estate to the latter,
That the Fame so long conserved of his Ancestors,
Might again revive and flourish,
Through the participation of his distinguished Merit.
An Intention so great, so glorious, in the bountiful Testator
was most happily accomplished
in
THOMAS ESTCOURT.
He was a Man Language wants Strength to paint.
Worthy of better Times, a kind of Prodigy in these.
Steady from Conviction of Mind,
To the true and unalterable Interests of his Country,
With a Zeal uninstigated by Profit; [Welfare,
He considered private Happiness as dependant on the publick
to which
His Thoughts, his Words, his Actions
were devoted.
In the wide Sphere of his Extensive Fortune,
Just, Generous, and Beneficent;
As Reason, Piety and Prudence demanded,
Tenants, Neighbours, Strangers,
Felt it;
And from an unsought, but not neglected Gratitude,
For he took pleasure in seeing others pleased,
He was universally
Esteemed, Respected, and Beloved.
In the more restrained Circle of Family Endearments,
Gentle, kind, and good;
Servants, Relations, Friends,
Received daily Instances of that Benignity of Soul
No Words can express.
Through all the Offices of Life,
A Clear Head, an open Heart,
Were always conspicuous
In whatever he said or did;
Until from this World, where Virtues are often misunderstood,
And can be only Applauded, [are known,
He was called to that where Even the most secret Acts of Goodness
And by the Author of all Goodness
Fully rewarded.

WALTER ESTCOURT Esq;	THOMAS ESTCOURT Esq;
Died October 23, 1726	Died October 6, 1746
Aged 82.	Aged 49.

On this monument are the arms of Estcourt, as before.

In the same chancel there is a very stately tomb, without any inscription, said to be intended for Judge Estcourt and his lady, who are represented lying along in full proportion, with hands lifted up in the posture of prayer. Round the tomb are seven sons, and one daughter, kneeling; all in the dress of the age of queen Elizabeth. Over the figures is a large canopy, supported by three handsome pillars on each side; and in front are two scutcheons, one of which bears the arms of Estcourt; the other, *Quarterly*, 1st & 4th, Estcourt; 2d & 3d, *Sable, a fess between three falcons heads erazed Or.* And at the top of the canopy, *Baron and femme*, 1. The two last-mentioned coats quarterly, impaling, *A fess ingrailed between three mules, or horses, passant.*

On a tomb in the church-yard,

Hic obdormit Domino placide ANNA OLDHAM, Virgo, Uxor, Mater maxime Pia, Quæ obiit A. D. 1699, Junii 21° Anno Ætat. 66.

Necnon Johannes Oldham V. D. M. Ejus Maritus, et Pater illius Johannis Oldham, Poetæ Celeberrimi, Nulli Pietate Secundus. Qui obiit A. Dom. 1716, Decemb. 5° Anno Ætatis 87.

There is also a latin inscription for Thomas Oldham, physician and surgeon, who died in 1688; and many others, of the same name and family, lie buried in the church-yard.

Benefactions.

Mr. Stourton, formerly lord of this manor, gave the church house for the repair of the church, but subject to a reserved rent of 4*d.* a year to the lord of the manor. Two shillings a year are paid out of Great Mead for the same use. Five pounds a year are left for five sermons.

Taxes.			£.	s.	d.
	The Royal Aid in	1692,	147	12	8
	Poll-tax ——	1694, —	32	6	0
	Land-tax ——	1694, —	5	9	4
	The same, at 3*s.*	1770, —	97	12	6¾

About the year 1710, according to sir Robert Atkyns, there were 60 houses, and about 250 inhabitants in the parish, 6 of whom were freeholders; yearly births 6, burials 5. The present number of souls is about 234.

SHIPTON OLIFFE

IS a small parish, in the hundred of Bradley, five miles distant east from Cheltenham, six north-westward from Northleach, and fourteen north-eastward from Gloucester.

It lies on the Coteswold hills, and has nothing curious of any sort to distinguish it. The etymology of *Shipton* is uncertain; but *Oliffe*, or *Olive*, is an addition taken from a family of that name, who were owners of the manor, and resided in the parish for several generations.

Of the Manor and other Estates.

This manor belonged to the archbishop of York, at the time of the general survey, wherein it is thus recorded, under the title *Terra Thome Archiepi, viz.*

'Gundulf held, and [still] holds, Scipetune, in 'Wacrescumbe hundred, [as] one manor of one 'hide, and pays tax. There is one plow-tillage 'in demean, and it is worth 8 *sol.* He holds it 'of archbishop Thomas.' *Domesday-book*, p. 69.

This manor is not always distinguished in the records from the neighbouring parish of Shipton Solers, which necessarily occasions confusion.

John de Turbervil died seized of this manor 17 Joh. In the sheriff's return of all the vills in this

this county, 9 E. 1. there is mention of one Shipton only, in the hundred of Bradley.

It came afterwards to the Olliffs, who continued in possession 'till the end of the seventeenth century, when Ralph Olliff, gent. sold it to William Peachy, esq; whose two daughters, Margaret Peachy, and Susanna Peachy, are the present ladies of the manor.

Lands in Shipton belonged to the priory of St. Oswald in Gloucester, and were granted to Cicely Pickerel 17 Eliz.

HAMLET. *Hampen* is a hamlet in this parish, in which there were two estates mentioned in *Domesday*. 'Pin held one manor, of one hide, 'in Hagepine, in Wacrescumbe hundred, and it 'paid tax. Ansger holds it of archbishop Thomas, 'and has one plow-tillage in demean. It was 'worth 20*s*. and is now worth 10*s*.' p. 70.

'William the son of Baderon holds Hagenepene 'in Wacrescumbe hundred, and Goisfrid holds it 'of him. Eduui held it, and there were five 'hides. There are two plow-tillages in demean, 'and six villeins, with three plow-tillages, and 'there are four *servi*. This land pays tax. It 'was worth 100*s*. now only 60*s*.' p. 74.

These estates were afterwards distinguished by Upper and Lower Hampen. King Henry the Third granted court leet, waifs, and felons goods in Shipton, (by which I understand Hampen in Shipton) to the knights templers, whose right to those privileges was allowed in the proceedings on a *Quo warranto* 15 E. 1. They were seized of Shipton near Withington (*i. e.* Hampen in Shipton) 2 E. 3. and the manor was held of William de Clinton, earl of Huntingdon, 28 E. 3. The order of knights templers was suppressed in England, and their estates given to the knights hospitallers of St. John of Jerusalem; and at the general dissolution of the knights hospitallers, this estate was granted to Edward Fiennes, lord Clinton and Say, and to Robert Tyrwit, 35 H. 8.

But there was another estate at Hampen, dignified with the title of a manor, held of the archbishop of York, by Thomas Lane, who died seized of the same 37 H. 8. and left Thomas his son eighteen years old. Hampen was afterwards the property of Lionel Rich, of Upper Dowdeswell, esq; out of whose family it passed lately, by purchase, to Mr. Van Notten, of London.

William Docket, and Elizabeth his wife, levied a fine of lands in Over Hampen, and Nether Hampen, to Edward Tame, 19 H. 7. Lands in Hannypen belonged to the priory of St. Oswald in Gloucester, and were granted to William Sharington 34 H. 8.

Of the Church, &c.

The church is a rectory, in the deanery of Stow, according to the bishop's visitation book; but was formerly accounted to lie in that of Winchcombe. It is worth 85*l*. a year. The ladies of the manor are patrons, and Mr. Chapone is the present incumbent.

Tithes in Shipton Oliffe, formerly belonging to Gloucester abbey, were granted to sir Edward Warner 4 Eliz. and are now the property of Thomas Browne, esq.

The church is small, with a cross aile on the south side, and a low spire at the west end.

There are memorials in the chancel, for Gyles Olliff, gent. who died in 1699, aged 72; Ralph Olliff, gent. who died in 1702, aged 39; Gyles and Robert Olliff, sons of Ralph Olliff, gent. who died in 1696 and 1697 respectively; and for several other persons of that family, whose inscriptions are now obliterated.

First fruits £	9	0	0	Synodals £.	0	2	0
Tenths —	0	18	0	Pentecost.	0	0	5½
Procurations	0	6	8				

Taxes.					
The Royal Aid in	1692,	£.	69	7	2
Poll-tax ——	1694,	—	13	15	0
Land-tax ——	1694,	—	57	18	4
The same, at 3*s*.	1770,	—	46	10	6

At the beginning of this century, there were 20 houses, and about 80 inhabitants in this parish, whereof 4 were freeholders; yearly births 2, burials 2. *Atkyns*. The present number of houses is 29, of inhabitants about 130.

****

SHIPTON SOLERS

IS a small parish, in the hundred of Bradley, about five miles eastward from Cheltenham, six westward from Northleach, and fourteen north-eastward from Gloucester.

It is severed in the middle, by the intervention of Shipton Oliffe, and the lands of both parishes are very much intermixed. The turnpike-road from Gloucester, to Oxford and London, leads through the parish, where there is a good inn, called *Frogmill*, on the east bank of the river Coln, which separates it from Withington.

Solers is the name of an antient family of eminence, who owned the manor, and had other considerable property in Gloucestershire, about the time of king Edward the Second.

Of the Manor and other Estates.

There were several estates in Shipton, at the time of the general survey.

'William Leuric holds three hides, less one 'yard-land, in Scipetune in Wacrescumbe hun'dred, and pays tax. Goisfrid holds them of him. 'Osgot held them. There is one plow-tillage in 'demean, and a priest, and one villein, and four '*servi*, without any plow-tillage. It was worth '40*s*. now 20*s*.' *Domesday*, p. 74.

'Durand of Glowec' holds Sciptune in Wacres'cumbe hundred, and Radulf holds it of him. 'Eduui held it. There are three hides and a half 'taxed,

'taxed. In demean are two plow-tillages, and 'three villeins, with two plow-tillages, and four '*fervi*, and ten acres of meadow. It was worth '4*l.* now 40*s.*' *Ibid.* p. 77.

'Hugh Lafne holds Sciptune in Wacrefcumbe 'hundred. There are five hides taxed. Uuluard 'held it. In demean are two plow-tillages, and 'four villeins, and one bordar, with two plow-'tillages. There are five *fervi*, and a mill of 10*s.* 'It was worth 4*l.* now 3*l.*' *Ibid.* p. 78.

'Ansfrid de Cormelies holds three yard-lands in 'Sciptune, in Wacrefcumbe hundred. Bil held them 'for a manor, and paid tax. There is one plow-'tillage in demean. It is worth and was worth '10*s.* This Bil could go where he pleafed. *Ib.* p. 78.

Sir Robert Atkyns fays, Walter de Lacy 'gave 'fixteen manors in Glofterfhire to Ansfrid de 'Cormeiles, who had married his niece. This 'Shipton was one of thofe manors, of which Ans-'frid de Cormeile was feized at the time of the 'general furvey, by virtue of the gift from Walter 'de Lacy.' But fir Robert was not aware that his affertion is a flat contradiction to the authority of *Domefday*, where, under the title *Terra Ansfridi de Cormeliis*, it is faid, *Thefe lands* [*i.e.* Pantelie, Chilecot, Chitiford, and Hege,] *and Winefian, and Tantefborne, above-written, Ansfrid received of Walter de Laci, when he married his niece. But he holds the other eftates of the king*; among which Shipton was one.

Richard de Cormeile was fon and heir of Anf-frid, and dying 23 H. 2. his wife, Beatrix, fur-viving him, enjoyed this manor in dower; but after her death, it defcended to Walter de Cor-meile, fon of Richard, who left three daughters coheireffes. Margaret, the eldeft daughter, was married to Hugh Poher, and died 20 H. 3. leaving iffue two daughters coheireffes, the elder married to Robert Archer, and the younger wedded to Simon Solers, who held this manor in right of his wife, and from him it obtained the name of Shipton Solers.

Thomas Solers was fon and heir of Simon, and John Solers, fon of Thomas, died feized of Ship-ton 4 E. 2. from which time I find no mention of this family at Shipton.

John Tyrrel held the manor of Shipton Solers 34 E. 3. which paffed afterwards into the family of the Twiniho's, who were proprietors of this manor for feveral generations. Edward Twiniho, the laft heir male, died 22 H. 8. and left two daughters coheireffes, who had livery of it the fame year. Anne, the elder daughter, was married to Henry Heydon; and Catherine, the younger, wedded to John Daunfey.

This manor was affigned to the Heydons. Edward Heydon, efq; was lord of it in the year 1608; and the heirefs of that family carried it by her marriage to William Peachy, efq; who was owner of it when fir Robert Atkyns compiled his account of it; and was fucceeded by his fon William, whofe fon, William Peachy, efq; is the present lord of this manor, but refides at Petworth in Effex. His arms are, *Quarterly*, 1ft *and* 4th, *Argent, within a bordure ingrailed azure.* 2d *and* 3d, *Azure, a bordure ingrailed argent.*

A meffuage in this parifh, which belonged to the abbey of Bruern in Oxfordfhire, was granted by the crown to Richard Andrews and Nicholas Temple 35 H. 8.

What fir Robert Atkyns fays of the knights templers being feized of Shipton, fhould not, as I apprehend, be applied to this manor; but to Hampen in Shipton Oliffe, where they had an eftate, which was granted away by the crown, at the general fuppreffion of knights hofpitallers, as mentioned in the proper place.

Of the Church, &c.

The church is a rectory, in the deanery of Stow, worth 65*l.* a year, of which Mr. Peachy is patron, and Mr. Chapone is the prefent incumbent.

Two yard-lands belong to the glebe.

A portion of tithes in Shipton Solers, which belonged to the abbey of Gloucefter, was granted to the bifhoprick 33 H. 8. and confirmed 6 E. 6.

The church is fmall, with a low turret at the weft end.

Firft fruits	£.7	3	4	Synodals	£.0	1	0
Tenths —	0	14	4	Pentecoftals	0	0	7½
Procurations							

Taxes.	The Royal Aid in	1692, £.	69	7	2
	Poll-tax —	1694, —	13	15	0
	Land-tax —	1694, —	57	8	4
	The fame, at 3*s.*	1770, —	46	10	6

There were 20 houfes, and about 120 inhabi-tants, whereof 5 were freeholders, at the beginning of this century; yearly births 3, burials 3. *Atkyns.* The number of fouls is now exactly 113.

SHURDINGTON

IS a fmall parifh, in the hundred of Dudfton and King's-barton, about five miles fouthward from Cheltenham, fix northward from Painfwick, and about fix eaft from Gloucefter.

It is pleafantly fituated under the weft fide of that ridge of hills which feparates the Vale from the hill country, and fhelters it from thofe chil-ling eafterly winds that generally prevail in the fpring. A fmall brook runs from hence into the Severn at Sandhurft.

There is a large *tumulus*, or barrow, in this parifh, which was opened by fome workmen, not many years ago, to dig for ftone, and having funk to the depth of about fixteen feet, they difcovered a ftone fepulchre, feven feet long, and four broad, and in it a perfect fkeleton. The bones were frefh and firm, and the teeth white as ivory. Over the head hung a helmet, which was fo in-tirely corroded by ruft, that it fell to pieces on the

the ſlighteſt touch. I am informed that there was nothing beſide the helmet, with the remains of the corps in the tomb, that could lead to any diſcovery, except ſome characters, which thoſe who ſaw them read for *One thouſand*; as if deſigned to point out the year when the corps was interred, anſwering to the 21ſt year of the reign of king Ethelred, commonly called the *Unready*. This was probably the corps of ſome great man, ſlain in the war between our own countrymen and the piratical Danes, who in the nineteenth year of that king's reign, ſailed up the mouth of the Severn, and made inroads up the country, perhaps to theſe parts.

Of the Manor and other Eſtates.

It was found by inquiſition, taken 8 E. 2. that the manor of Scherneton, with view of frank pledge, was held of Gilbert de Clare, the laſt earl of Glouceſter and Hertford of that name, at the time of his death. Peter de la Mere held this manor, with free warren, 12 E. 2. and John Maltravers was ſeized thereof the ſame year. John Maltravers, the elder, died ſeized of this manor 31 E. 3. whereupon ſir John Maltravers, his ſon, had livery the ſame year, and died 38 E. 3. Agnes, the widow of John Maltravers, died ſeized of the third part of this manor, which ſhe held in dower, 49 E. 3. John lord Maltravers, ſon of the laſt John, died 5 R. 2. and Henry Maltravers, his only ſon, deceaſing without iſſue, the manors of Shurdington, King's Stanley, Woodcheſter, and Stonehouſe, came to Elianor, ſiſter and heireſs of Henry Maltravers, who being married to John Arundel, ſometimes called John Fitz-Alan, ſecond ſon of Richard earl of Arundel, carried thoſe manors into that name and family. Eleanor Maltravers, after the death of John Arundel, was married to Reginald lord Cobham, who was ſeized of Shurdington, in her right, 4 H. 4. and ſhe continued to hold the manor 'till her death, 6 H. 4.

John Fitz-Alan, ſon of John, and grandſon of John Fitz-Alan and Elianor, the heireſs of the Maltravers's, became earl of Arundel, by the death of Thomas earl of Arundel without male iſſue. He was ſlain near Beauvois in France, and by an inquiſition taken 13 H. 6. was found to have died ſeized of the manors of Shurdington, Stonehouſe, Stoke Archer, King's Stanley, and Woodcheſter, in Glouceſterſhire, beſide great eſtates in other counties. Humphry earl of Arundel, ſon and heir of John, was ſix years old at his father's death, and dying ſoon afterwards, William earl of Arundel, his uncle, was next heir, and had livery of this manor 18 H. 6. But Elianor, the widow of John earl of Arundel, held the manor in dower. She was afterwards married to ſir Richard Poinings, and ſir Walter Hungerford, ſucceſſively, and died 33 H. 6. The before-mentioned William earl of Arundel married Joan, daughter of Richard Nevil, earl of Saliſbury; and dying 3 H. 7. was ſucceeded by his ſon, Thomas earl of Arundel, who married Margaret, daughter of Richard Widevile, earl of Rivers, and died ſeized of the manors of Shurdington, Archerds, King's Stanley, Stonehouſe, and Woodcheſter, 16 H. 8. William earl of Arundel, ſon of Thomas, had livery of theſe manors the ſame year, and having married Anne, ſiſter to Henry earl of Northumberland, died ſeized of all the above-mentioned manors, 35 H. 8.

The archbiſhop of York was ſeized of the manor of Shurdington 14 E. 3. and it ſeems that the great perſons before-mentioned held it of the archbiſhops; for in the grant of the manor to ſir Thomas Chamberlayne, 6 E. 6. it is mentioned to have belonged to the archbiſhop of York.

Edmond Chamberlayne, of Maugerſbury, eſq; great grandſon of ſir Thomas, was lord of it about the year 1691, and dying in 1755, was ſucceeded by his only ſon Edmond, upon whoſe death, in the year 1774, the manor deſcended to the reverend John Chamberlayne, his eldeſt ſon and heir, who is the preſent lord of the manor. His pedigree and arms are given under Maugerſbury, in the pariſh of Stow.

Henry de Pet held one plow-tillage in Great Shurdington, of John Giffard of Brimpsfield, and was ſeized of it 1 E. 3.

HAMLET. *Uphatherly* has been conſidered by ſome as a diſtinct pariſh, but it is now eſteemed a hamlet in Shurdington. It has its own conſtable, and overſeer of the poor. John de Chanſy held the hamlet of Atherley, of the honour of Wallingford, by the ſervice of half a knight's fee, 6 E. 2. and held a court, the perquiſites of which were valued at 12*d*. *Eſch.* Robert Preſbury was ſeized of lands in Uphatherly 18 E. 2. John Moor, the younger, levied a fine of lands in Uphatherly, to the uſe of Thomas Lane, 15 H. 7.

Of the Church, &c.

The church is an impropriation, within the deanery of Winchcombe, and is annexed to Badgworth. Jeſus college, Oxford, and Chriſt college, Cambridge, have the impropriation.

The tithes of Shurdington belonged antiently to the Benedictine nunnery of Uſke, in Monmouthſhire, and were granted, together with the chapel of Uphatherly and South Hatherly, to James Gunter and Walter Lewis, 37 H. 8.

Tithes in Shurdington and Uphatherly, lately belonging to the nunnery of Uſke, were granted to John Fernham 22 Eliz.

The chapel is dedicated to St. Paul, and has a handſome ſteeple at the weſt end, and an aile on the north ſide, called Hatherly aile, which is kept in repair by the inhabitants of the hamlet of Uphatherly.

Benefactions.

Nicholas Blount gave 40*s*. a year for ſix ſermons. William Mills, yeoman, gave 5*s*. a year to the poor, charged on lands in Little Shurdington.

Shur-

Shurdington, with Uphatherly.

Taxes.					
The Royal Aid in	1692,	£. 68	10	8
Poll-tax ——	1694,—	4	15	0
Land-tax ——	1694,—	86	16	4
The fame, at 3 *s.*	1770,—	66	6	0

At the beginning of the prefent century, there were 15 houfes in the parifh, and about 70 inhabitants, 6 of whom were freeholders; yearly births 2, burials 2. *Atkyns.* The people are now exactly 80 in number.

SIDDINGTON St. MARY

IS a fmall parifh, in the hundred of Crowthorne and Minety, one mile fouth from Cirencefter, fix north-weftward from Cricklade in Wiltfhire, and eighteen fouth-eaftward from Gloucefter. It is bounded by Cirencefter on the north and weft, by Lower Siddington and South Cerney on the eaft, and by part of Wiltfhire on the fouth.

The greater part of the parifh is in tillage, the reft is good meadow and pafture ground.

The antient and fignificant name is *Sudintone*, or *Suditone*, that is, the *South-town*, in refpect of Cirencefter; but it is moft ufually called *Upper Siddington.* Both the Siddingtons formerly made but one vill, tho' the manors were held independently of each other, and often by different owners; for which reafon the fheriff, in his return of all the vills of this county, 9 E. 1. mentions one Siddington only, under which both manors were included, for he fays, *Sodington, et funt Dni eiufd. vill. Hugo de Spencer, et Johannes de Langley, et Gualter de Langley*; that is, Sodington, and Hugh de Spencer, and John de Langley, and Walter de Langley are lords of the fame vill.

Doctor George Bull, was rector of this place, and afterwards bifhop of St. David's. He told Doctor Parfons, chancellor of this diocefe, a remarkable anecdote of the longevity of his parifhioners here, ten of whom he had buried, whofe ages together made about a thoufand years, and two of them were one hundred and twenty-three years old each.

Cotemporary with doctor Bull, was one John Roberts, *alias* Hayward, who lived here upon a little eftate of his own, which is ftill the property of a defcendant from him, of the fame name, now a merchant in London. That man was of a religious turn, and feems to have been the chief in thefe parts, of the people called Quakers. In the reign of king Charles the Second, when perfecution for religion ran high, he drank a potion of that bitter cup, as appears by the memoirs of his life, written by his fon, and publifhed in 1725. Bifhop Nicholfon, however, before whom he was many times cited, is reprefented in that narrative to have been a perfon of greater moderation than moft of his brethren, and was far from being difpleafed with the moral principles, plain dealing, and fenfible anfwers of that man, tho' he could not confiftently approve fome of his religious notions.

Of the Manor and other Eftates.

'The fame Humphry [the chamberlain] holds 'two hides in Sudintone, in Cireceftre hundred, 'and Anfchitil holds them of him. Aluuard held 'them for a manor. There is one plow-tillage 'in demean, and two bordars, with half a plow-'tillage, and a mill of 5 *s.* [rent]. It is worth and 'was worth 40 *s.* He that held it could go where 'he pleafed.' *Domefday*, p. 79.

'The fame William [the fon of Baderon] holds 'one hide in Suditone in Cireceftre hundred. 'Ofuuid held it in the time of king Edward, and 'could go where he pleafed. There is one plow-'tillage in demean, and four *fervi.* It is worth 'and was worth 24 *s.*' *Ibid.* p. 73.

The fheriff returned that Hugh de Spencer was lord of this manor 9 E. 1. as already obferved, and it is very probable that his family continued poffeffed of it 'till the latter part of the next reign, for the manor of Over Soddington was granted to Edmond earl of Kent, 1 E. 3. fubject to a referved rent of 23 *l.* and it is recited in the grant to have lately belonged to Hugh le Difpencer the younger. Edmond earl of Kent being attainted of treafon, and executed at Winchefter by the villainous contrivance of Roger Mortimer, earl of March, in the year 1330, this manor, together with great part of that nobleman's eftate, was granted to Jeffery Mortimer, third fon of the earl of March, 4 E. 3. who enjoyed his ill-got poffeffions but for a few months, when Roger Mortimer being himfelf attainted, and executed at a place called the Elms, about a mile from London, the fentence of Edmond earl of Kent was reverfed, his widow admitted to the enjoyment of her jointure, and his fon, John earl of Kent, was reftored in blood, and became poffeffed of this manor, of which he died feized 26 E. 3. without iffue; and Elizabeth his widow held it in dower, and died 12 H. 4.

Sir Edward le Difpencer, and Elizabeth his wife, daughter and heir of Bartholomew Burghurft, were feized of the manor of Soddington, 49 E. 3. probably in truft for the widow of John earl of Kent.

Edmond Mortimer, earl of March, defcended from the heirefs of the earls of Kent, died feized of this manor without iffue, 3 H. 6. and Joan his fifter, then the widow of fir John Grey, had livery thereof 4 H. 6.

The manor came foon afterwards to Walter Langley, lord of Lower Siddington, whofe widow, Ifabel, died feized of both thofe manors 14 E. 4.

Henry Kettleby was feized of Over Soddington, and Nether Soddington, in right of Ifabel his wife, (perhaps the heirefs of the Langleys) who died 31 H. 8. and John Kettleby, their fon, had livery granted to him 32 H. 8. Andrew Kettleby died

died 1 Jac. without iſſue, ſeized of the manors of Over Suddington, and Nether Suddington, then worth 19*l.* 10*s.* a year clear, which he held of the king *in capite*, and by will gave all his lands in Glouceſterſhire, and Wiltſhire, to his wife Jane, and her heirs. *Eſch.*

From the heir of Kettleby, the above-mentioned manors paſſed, by purchaſe, to the Danvers family, 5 Jac. Henry Danvers, earl of Danby, was lord of both manors in the year 1608, and ſold them to ſir Henry Poole, in the 13th year of the ſame reign. Sir William Poole ſettled the manor and hundred of Cirenceſter, and the manors of Upper and Lower Siddington, on Anne his daughter, who was married to James earl of Newburgh. Charles earl of Newburgh, their ſon and heir, left the above manors to Frances his widow, in fee; and ſhe ſold them, about the year 1695, to ſir Benjamin Bathurſt. Allen, firſt earl of Bathurſt, ſon and heir of ſir Benjamin, dying in the year 1775, theſe manors deſcended to his ſon, Henry earl of Bathurſt, the preſent proprietor. For his lordſhip's pedigree and arms, ſee *Cirenceſter*.

John de Langley, at the time of his death, 18 E. 2. was ſeized of one meſſuage, one plow-tillage, and fourteen acres and a half of meadow in Over Soddington, in truſt for a chantry in the church of Lower Soddington. Richard Urdle levied a fine of lands in Siddington Over, to John Young and William Lypiat, 18 R. 2.

Of the Church, &c.

The church is a rectory, in the deanery of Cirenceſter. This and the vicarage of Siddington St. Peter, are worth together 210*l.* a year. The lord chancellor is patron of both livings, and John Waſhbourne, M. A. is the preſent incumbent.

The church is a ſmall building, dedicated to St. Mary, and has a ſmall chapel on the north ſide, which was likewiſe dedicated to the ſame ſaint, as may be gathered from two verſes againſt the ſouth wall, which were legible a few years ago, but now obliterated, *viz.*

Cælos aſſumpt. cū nato virgo Maria
Crimina tu cuncta dilue virgo pia.

At the eaſt end is a niche, where the ſtatue of the ſaint ſtood; and the whole chapel was ornamented with a profuſion of painting, carving, and ſhort ſentences and verſes, which are decay'd, except the following lines in old characters, painted on the inſide of the door, which are very legible:

Annā ſolet dici tres concipiſſe Marias
Quas genuere viri Ioachim Cleophas Salomeq;
Has duxere viri Ioſeph Alpheus Zebedeus
Prima parit Chriſtum Iacobum ſecunda ſecundum
Et Ioſeph iuſtum peperit cum Symone Iudam
Tertia maiorem Iacobum volucremq; Iohannem.

Firſt fruits	£.8	11	$0\frac{3}{4}$	Synodals	£.0	2	0
Tenths	— 0	17	$2\frac{1}{2}$	Pentecoſtals	0	1	6
Procurations	0	6	8				

Monuments and Inſcriptions.

On a marble table, againſt the north wall of the chancel, is this memorial:

Hic juxta repoſitum Iacet quod mortale erat
Richardi Bridges Generoſi,
Iuvenis ingenio formaq; præcellentis
Qui ante quadriennium in Matrimonio exactum,
Amiſſa incomparabili Coniuge,
Filiâ unica Geo. Hanger de Driffeild, Arm.
(Qua mortua vix ipſi vita fuit mortalis)
Dein poſt menſes aliquot variolarum morbo correptus
(Amicis et quotquot ipſum norunt mœrentibus)
Hac vita ceſſit V Kal. Feb. MDCLXXVI.
Heu ſpes mundi fallaces.
Tu ſuperne quærito.

Within the communion rails, on a marble table againſt the wall,

I. S.
GULIELMUS DAY,
Iſtius Eccleſiæ Rector,
Vir
In omni Laudis Genere
Pleriſque Par.
Secundam Expectans
SALVATORIS EPIPHANIAM
In Primæ Feſto
Denatus eſt
A. D. 1743
A. N. 47.

On another table, within the ſame rails,

JOSEPHUS STEPHENS A. M. Archidiaconus & Prebendarius de Brecon, Cathedralis Eccleſiæ Meneveñſis Canonicus reſidentiarius, hujus Eccleſiæ Rector; Mortem obijt quinto Die Nov^ris^ Anno { Domini 1735to / Ætatis 80mo } Sub Spe Immortalitatis SS^to^ Dei Evangelio revelatæ——Cujus Pars terreſtris Terræ hic commiſſa eſt, Cum Anna Conjuge priore chariſſima. Spiritus ad Deum rediit, & ad Sanctorum Spiritus Fide ac Penitentia Conſummatorum, de Quo non pauca dici amplius oporteret, Diligentiam ejus in exequendis Muneris Sui Sacris propria Perſonâ, Mentis Tranquilitatem in adverſis, non obſtante Melancholia quadam Naturali indies Invaleſcente, Mores integros, Ingenium mitiſſimum Spectantia. Sed Manum de Tabulâ! Ne Laudes attribuantur poſt Mortem quas Ipſe vivens noluit audire, Hominum ab omni Oſtentatione alieniſſimus.

Hoc unicum illius Memoriæ tradi ſufficiat, quod doctiſſimo Præſuli GEO: BULLO, & Patrono ejus munificentiſſimo charus fuit, Negotiiſq; maximi Momenti conjunctiſſimus.———Arms, *Party per chevron azure and argent, in chief two falcons diſplay'd Or*, for Stephens.

Near the above,

M. S.

Annæ Chariſſimæ Uxoris Ioſephi Stephens A. M. Hujus Eccleſiæ Rectoris Filiæ Georgij Bulli S. T. P. Celeberrimi Natu Maximæ. Mulieris Patre ſuo dignæ, utpote eximia Pietate, gratiiſq; omnibus quæ ſexum ornant ornatiſſimæ, Quæ ad ſanctorum Cœtum tranſlata eſt Martii 3^tio^ A. D. 1703, Ætat. 41.

Amantiſſimo Conjugi, Cognatis, Amicis, Viciniſq; omnibus preſertim pauperioribus, quibus et Alimoniam et Medicinam liberaliter miniſtravit deſideratiſſima.———Arms, *Baron and femme*, 1. Stephens, as before. 2. *Or, three bulls heads caboſhed ſable, langued gules*, for Bull.

The pariſhes of Siddington St. Mary and Siddinton St. Peter are rated jointly to public taxes, except that they maintain their poor independently of each other.

Taxes.					
The Royal Aid in	1692,	£. 69	7	0
Poll-tax ——	1694, —	13	15	0
Land-tax —	1694, —	57	8	4
The ſame, at 3*s.*	1770, —	46	10	6

At the beginning of this century, there were 14 houſes, and about 60 inhabitants; yearly births 5, burials 4. *Atkyns.* The preſent number of houſholders is 17, of inhabitants exactly 74.

SID-

SIDDINGTON St. PETER

IS a ſmall pariſh, in the hundred of Crowthorne and Minety, one mile ſouth from Cirenceſter, ſix north-weſtward from Cricklade in Wiltſhire, and eighteen ſouth-eaſtward from Glouceſter.

It is ſeated on a flat, on the banks of the Churn, which runs through the pariſh; and it is commonly called *Lower Siddington*, in contradiſtinction to the adjoining village of *Upper Siddington*, which lies on a pleaſant elevation at the diſtance of about half a mile. The pariſh has likewiſe been diſtinguiſhed by the addition of *Langley*, which it received from the family of that name, who were lords of the manor for many generations, and had a large manſion houſe near the church; but it has been long ſince razed to the ground, and nothing remains to ſhow where it ſtood, but part of the moat with which it was ſurrounded.

During the winter, and the former part of the ſpring, the farmers here lead the water over the meadows, (which they call drowning) by means of ſluices from the river Churn, after the example of their neighbours at Driffield, under which pariſh I have given the method of doing it, with a view to promote the public good.

Of the Manor and other Eſtates.

'The ſame Haſcoit [Muſard] holds Sudintone, 'in Cireceſtre hundred. There are ten hides 'taxed beſides the demean. Erneſi held it. In 'demean are three plow-tillages, and eight villeins, 'and ten bordars, with a prieſt, having five 'plow-tillages and a half. There are ſeven *ſervi*, 'and twenty acres of meadow. It was worth 10*l.* 'now 8*l.*' *Domeſday*, p. 78.

From the above Haſcoit Muſard, who accompanied king William the Firſt in his invaſion of England, this manor deſcended, like Miſerden, down to 1 E. 1. when Ralph Muſard died ſeized of it. Jeffry de Langeley held Southington and Weſton the following year, and Walter de Langley, ſon of Jeffry, was lord of the manor of Sodington 8 & 9 E. 1.

It was held of Gilbert de Clare, earl of Glouceſter and Hertford, 15 E. 1. againſt whom a writ of *Quo warranto* was then brought, to ſet forth his right to the privilege of a court leet in Siddington; and he pleaded a grant to his anceſtor Richard de Clare, 47 H. 3. and his claim was allowed.

John de Langley, ſon of Walter, was high ſheriff of Glouceſterſhire 1 E. 2. and died ſeized of this manor in the 18th year of the ſame reign. William de Caroſwell, and Mary his wife, levied a fine of the manor of Nether Sodington to the uſe of themſelves for their lives, the remainder to Jeffry Langley, ſon of Jeffry, in taille, 4 E. 3. Joan, the widow of John Trillow, died ſeized of Nether Sodington 49 E. 3. It muſt be ſuppoſed that ſhe had been the wife of Jeffry Langley, and held the manor in dower. John Langley, grandſon of John, was ſeized of Soddington Langley, *alias* Nether Soddington, Rodmarton, and Torleton, 10 H. 4. Jeffry Langley held Sodington of Edmond earl of March, 3 H. 6. and John Langley, eſq; died ſeized of it, and of a manor in Turk Dean, in the 39th year of that reign. The manors of Upper and Nether Sodington, and Turk Dean, came next to Walter Langley, whoſe widow, Iſabel, died ſeized of them 14 E. 4. and from that time both the Siddingtons have been enjoy'd by the ſame proprietors. The earl of Bathurſt is the preſent lord of the manor.

Of the Church, &c.

The church is a vicarage, in the deanery of Cirenceſter, worth about 30*l.* a year, and has the ſame patron and incumbent as Siddington St. Mary, under which pariſh the outgoings are ſet down; except that the vicarage pays 7*s.* 8*d.* yearly to the crown, for tithes and glebe in Cheſterton.

Jordan de Clinton gave the manor of Sodington, conſiſting of lands and tithes, with their appurtenances, to the knights hoſpitallers of St. John of Jeruſalem. The impropriation was veſted in Mr. Coxwell of Turk Dean, at the beginning of this century, and paſſed afterwards to ſir John Nelthorp, of whom it was purchaſed, in the year 1776, together with the impropriation of Cheſterton, in Cirenceſter, by the earl of Bathurſt, the preſent proprietor.

The church is dedicated to St. Peter. It has a handſome chapel on the north ſide, and an unfiniſhed tower, with three bells, at the weſt end of the chapel.

The chapel was built by Edmund Langley, in honour of the ſalutation of the virgin Mary. It is a handſomer ſtructure than the church, from which it is ſeparated by pillars. There is a cut through the ſtone-work that divides the chancel from the body of the church, that the people in the chapel might ſee the elevation of the hoſt.

In the upper part of the eaſt window of the chapel, there are three large figures painted in the glaſs, of which only that of the virgin mother remains intire; and under their feet it is thus written:

Orate: p: aīabs: edmūdi: lāgley.—et: iohē: et elizabeth: ux: ei': qui:—hāc: capellā: ī honor: ſalutacionis: bē. marie: fecit:

Beneath are ſeveral of the Langleys, kneeling, with books before them, and the family arms on their ſurcoats, *viz. Gules, a ſaltire Or.* Their reſpective names are written over their heads, *viz. Benet Langley armig. Richard, William, William, William, Waltr, Edmude.* There are ſeveral ſcutcheons of arms cut in ſtone, and fixed in the walls, and over the pillars; but they are filled up with white-waſh, ſo that only the two following can now be diſtinguiſhed; 1. *(Argent) a feſs, in chief three pellets.* 2. *Quarterly, per feſs indented (Or and ſable.)* both which coats have likewiſe been born by perſons of the name of Langley.

 The

The east window of the chancel is likewise ornamented with paintings, representing several of the same family, and others, in compleat chain armour, kneeling, and the following names inscribed on the glass, *viz. Galfrus langel', Iohes, Galfrus, Iohanna, Iohes fil' Iohis fili Iohis langel'. Iohes Worth, miles,* and his arms, *A fess, in chief three pellets.*

There is a scutcheon in the south window of the chancel, bearing *Argent, two chevronels gules, in chief a label of five points azure,* with the name, *Nichole de Semour* . . . . .

In the north window is this coat, *Paly of six, Or and azure,* with the name, *Thom. Gurney* . . . .

Monuments and Inscriptions.

There is a large grey marble stone in the chancel, which had once the effigy of a man in armour upon it, said to have been intended for one of the Langleys, but the brass is now torn off.

Upon a white marble in the chancel, is this inscription:

Here lyeth the Body
of THOMAS DEACON, Esqr.
late of ELMSTREE
in the Parish of TETBURY
and County of GLOUCESTER
who Departed this life
the 24th Day of April
in the Year of our LORD
MDCCXXXVI
and in the 46th Year of his Age.

Arms, at top, [*Argent*] *a cross between four lions rampant* [*sable*], *on a chief* [*azure*] *three roses proper.*

A neat table of white marble, against the south wall, bears this inscription:

Here lye the Remains
of
The Honble BENJAMIN BATHURST,
Eldest Son of
ALLEN LORD BATHURST.
He was born the 12th: of August 1711,
And died the 23^{d}: of January 1767.
He married ELIZABETH BRUCE,
Second Daughter of
CHARLES EARL of *Ailesbury,*
on the 14th of December 1732.
He was a true Friend to the Poor.
This Monument is erected
by his affectionate Widow.

Arms, at bottom, *Sable, two bars ermine, in chief three crosses paty Or,* for Bathurst. On a scutcheon of pretence, *Quarterly,* 1st *and* 4th, *Or, a saltire and chief gules, in a canton argent a lion rampant azure,* for Bruce earl of Ailesbury. 2d *and* 3d,

Sir Robert Atkyns has not given the state of population as it stood at the beginning of the present century; but there are now 35 housholders, and 153 inhabitants.

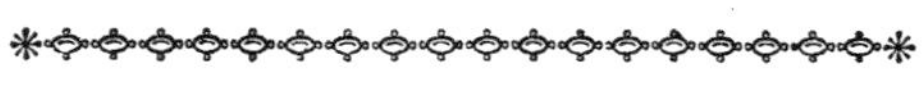

SIDE.

THIS small parish lies in the hundred of Rapsgate, about seven miles distant northwestward from Cirencester, four northward from Bisley, and ten south-eastward from Gloucester.

It was called *Side,* from its lying on the *sides* and slopes of hills; for the country hereabout is remarkably uneven and turgid, as at Edgworth and Miserden. The lands are chiefly arable, with some pasture ground, and woodlands, in which the herb Valerian is found in great plenty.

It is separated from Brimpsfield by a small rivulet, which is one of the heads of the river Froome, that runs to Stroud, and gives name to several places lying in its course towards the Severn.

Of the Manor and other Estates.

The manor is thus described in the antient survey:

'Ansfrid de Cormeile holds Side, in Respigete 'hundred, and Turstin holds it of him. Leuuin 'held it of king Edward. There are three hides 'which pay tax. In demean are two plow-tillages, 'and one villein, with a priest, and three bordars, 'with one plow-tillage, and six *servi,* and four 'acres of meadow. It was worth 4*l.* now 40*s.*' *Domesday,* p. 78.

This manor came to the Giffards of Brimpsfield, soon after the Norman conquest, and continued in that family 'till the reign of king Edward the Second, when John Giffard of Brimpsfield was seized of the manor of Side and Walliswood, and of the advowson of the church; but joining with the earl of Lancaster, and other barons, in endeavouring to expel the Spencers, he was taken prisoner at the battle of Burroughbridge, in Yorkshire, attainted, and executed at Gloucester as a traitor.

Upon Giffard's attainder, the manor was granted to Hugh le Dispencer the elder, with remainder to Hugh le Dispencer the younger, 15 E. 2. The Spencers, however, enjoyed it but for a short time, and then fell a sacrifice to the fury of an injured people, the father being executed at Bristol, and the son at Hereford, in the year 1326, 20 E. 2.

The manor of Side was soon after granted to John Maltravers the younger, as a reward for murdering king Edward the Second, and he procured a fine of it from John de Çallew, who was heir to the Giffards by a daughter, 4 E. 3. But Maltravers did not long enjoy the reward of his villainy, for he was soon convicted of high misdemeanors, and obliged to fly into Germany, where he lurked for many years; 'till having found means to perform some signal service for king Edward the Third, he threw himself at his feet, and obtained a pardon for the murder of the late king, and was restored to some of his estates. But this manor had been before granted to the Berkeleys, and Thomas lord Berkeley, the third of that name, was seized of it, and founded a chantry in his manor of Side, in the reign of king Edward the Third.

Sir John Berkeley was seized of Side, and of the advowson of the church, held of the manor of Brimpsfield, 6 H. 6. Sir Maurice Berkeley of Beverston was possessed of the manor in the 38th & 39th years of the same reign, and died seized of it 14 E. 4. as did sir William Berkeley 5 E. 6. and John Berkeley, son of sir William, had livery of it the following year.

Robert

Robert Partridge died seized of the manor of Side, *alias dict. Side et Leckehampton*, 42 Eliz. *Esch.* John Partridge, esq; was lord of it in the year 1608, and conveyed it to sir William Sandys, in trust. Mr. Nathaniel Ridler, of Edgworth, was lord of the manor at the beginning of this century. It passed afterwards to Nigel Kingscot, of Kingscot, esq; whose nephew, —— Kingscot, esq; is the present proprietor of it.

Of the Church, &c.

This is a rectory, in the deanery of Stonehouse, worth about 40*l.* a year, of which the lord of the manor is patron.

The church is a small building, dedicated to St. Mary, with a low tower at the west end. There was formerly a chantry in this church, which was founded by William de Side, who took his name from the parish.

	£						
First fruits	3	18	3	Synodals £.	0	2	0
Tenths —	0	7	10	Pentecost.	0	0	8
Procurations							

Benefaction.

Mr. Thomas Muggleton, who died in the year 1659, gave a portion of rent, about 15*s.* a year, issuing out of Bullbank-leaze, in Duntisbourn Abbats, to the use of the poor of this parish.

Taxes.			£.		
The Royal Aid in	1692,				
Poll-tax — —	1694, —		2	12	0
Land-tax ——	1694, -		17	12	0
The same, at 3*s.*	1770, —		14	6	10½

At the beginning of this century, according to sir Robert Atkyns, there were 17 houses, and about 70 inhabitants in the parish, 3 of whom were freeholders; yearly births 2, burials 1. The present number of houses is only 11, and the people are decreased to 47.

SISTON.

THIS parish lies in the hundred of Pucklechurch, seven miles distant north-eastward from Bristol, eight northward from Bath, and about thirty-six southward from Gloucester.

It is situate in the Vale, and consists principally of rich pasture ground. A rivulet rises here, and runs to Bitton, the next parish, where it falls into the Avon.

Siston House is the seat of Trotman, esq. It consists of an extensive front, and two large wings, and is ornamented with a great number of arms of families which the Dennys's have a right to quarter with their own; for the house was built by one of that family, about the time of king Charles the First, as appears by the style of the architecture, and has undergone no alterations. It is not seen at any great distance, tho' seated upon a little eminence, as it is approached to from the south and west; but the best front faces eastward.

Moon's Court, or *Mound's Court*, was an antient seat belonging to the Stranges, who resided there for several hundred years; and tho' now a farm house, it is rendered famous by queen Catherine Par keeping her court there, seven or eight weeks, after visiting Bath and Bristol.

This parish constitutes part of the forest of Kingswood, where coal is found in the greatest plenty; and I have it on the authority of Dr. Parsons's Manuscript *Collections*, which he finished about the end of the last century, that at a place called Berry, in this parish, there was then lately discovered a vein of tin-ore, intermixed with grains of silver. I made some enquiry concerning this matter, without being able to get any further information from the present inhabitants, who know nothing of it; and therefore I conclude, that the vein was very inconsiderable, and either exhausted in working, or would not bear the expence of it, and so became neglected and forgotten.

There is a large work, in the hamlet of Warmly, for converting copper into brass. They fetch the *Lapis Calaminaris* used in that process from Mendip-hill, in Somersetshire. There are also five or six furnaces for making of Speltre. This work now belongs to a company in Bristol; but it was carried on, 'till lately, in a more extensive manner, by gentlemen, who, about the year 1770, sold it to the present proprietors. Under the first masters, the machinery was put in motion by water, and there was a fire engine to return into the pond that water which had passed thro' the works. But the engine is now taken down, and part of the manufacture carried on at the adjacent works in the parish of Bitton.

Of the Manor and other Estates.

'The same Roger [de Berchelai] holds Sistone, 'in Pulcrecerce hundred. Anne held it. There 'are five hides taxed. In demean are two plow-'tillages, and eight villeins, and ten bordars, 'with four plow-tillages. There are four *servi*, 'and eight acres of meadow. It is and was 'worth 100 *sol.*' *Domesday*, p. 75.

—— Serlo died seized of this manor, and left his two sisters coheiresses, Agatha, the wife of Henry ——, and Juliana, the wife of William de Stratton; but Anne, the widow of Serlo, had the manors of Siston, Campden, and Whittington assigned to her in dower, 4 H. 3. at which time she was the wife of Hugh de Stratton.

Siston came soon after to the Walerans. Robert Waleran married Maud, the daughter of Ralph Russel, of Durham in this county, and purchased a charter of free warren in Siston 31 H. 3. He was governor of St. Briavel's castle, warden of the forest of Dean, and four times sheriff of Gloucestershire in that reign, and died without issue 1 E. 1. Robert Waleraund, uncle of John Waleraund, died seized of the manor of Siston 2 E. 2. which he held only for the life of his sister Cecilia. And the escheator's inquisition found that the manor

manor was holden of the heir of William de Berkeley, by the ſervice of one knight's fee; and that it ought to devolve to Alan Plokenet, ſon of Alan Plokenet, ſon of Alice, daughter of Iſabel, daughter of Thomas de Rochesford and Agatha his wife, who was the daughter of Roger de Berkeley, and had Siſton given to her in free marriage by her father. Alan Plokenet, whom ſir Robert Atkyns, by miſtake, calls Alan Blakeman, held Siſton 19 E. 2.

Sir Peter Corbet died ſeized of this manor 36 E. 3. He had married the daughter of Walter of Glouceſter, and with her had the manors of Alveſton and Urcot, which paſt, by the marriage of Margaret his daughter and coheireſſes, to ſir Gilbert Dennis, who was ſeized of the manors of Siſton, Alveſton, and Erdecot, 44 E. 3.

Richard Dennis levied a fine of the manor to ſir Maurice Dennis, 7 E. 6. Sir William Dennis was ſon of ſir Maurice; and Maurice Dennis, ſon of ſir William, died ſeized of the manor 5 Eliz. and left Walter Dennis his brother and heir, who was then ſixty years old, and had livery of this eſtate the ſame year.

Henry Billingſley, eſq; was lord of the manor in the year 1608. It was veſted in Samuel Trotman, eſq; at the beginning of this century, and deſcended to Thomas Trotman, whoſe ſon, Trotman, eſq; is the preſent lord of the manor, and reſides here. His arms are, *Argent, a croſs between four roſes gules.*

Henry Gildeney, and Joan his wife, levied a fine of lands in Siſton, to Henry Harſhfield, clerk, to the uſe of themſelves in taille, 7 H. 5. John Kemys died ſeized of lands here, 16 E. 4. and Roger Kemys, his ſon and heir, was found to be a lunatick, 21 E. 4. Sir John Bar was ſeized of an eſtate in Siſton 22 E. 4.

HAMLETS. 1. *Warmly.* 2. *Breach Yate,* which lies one part in Abſton and Wick, the other in this pariſh.

Of the Church, &c.

The church is a rectory, in the deanery of Hawkeſbury, worth 130*l.* a year. Mr. Trotman is patron, and Chriſtopher Haynes, M. A. is the preſent incumbent.

The preſent church is ſmall, and dedicated to St. Anne, the mother of the virgin Mary. There were formerly two others in the pariſh; one dedicated to St. Bartholomew, which was the mother church, the other to St. Cuthbert, biſhop of Lindisfern, now called Holy Iſland, on the coaſt of Northumberland, to whom many miracles were attributed in the dark ages of ignorance and popiſh ſuperſtition. The wakes, or feaſt days, of all three churches are obſerved by the inhabitants to this day.

	£.	s.	d.		£.	s.	d.
Firſt fruits	5	14	4½	Synodals	0	1	0
Tenths —	0	11	5¼	Pentecoſt.	0	0	5
Procurations							

Benefaction.

Dr. Harmer, of Marſhfield, in the year 1690, gave 4*l.* 10*s.* a year for the uſe of the poor.

Taxes.			£.	s.	d.
	The Royal Aid in	1692,	104	16	0
	Poll-tax —	1694, —	40	12	0
	Land-tax —	1694, —	115	6	0
	The ſame, at 3*s.*	1770, —	82	18	11¼

When ſir Robert Atkyns compiled his Hiſtory, there were 98 houſes in the pariſh, and about 450 inhabitants, 12 of whom were freeholders; yearly births 12, burials 11. I have not been able to obtain any ſatisfactory information concerning the preſent ſtate of population.

SLAUGHTER (LOWER)

IS a ſmall pariſh, in the hundred of its own name, three miles diſtant ſouth-weſtward from Stow, ſix northward from Northleach, and twenty-three north-eaſtward from Glouceſter.

The name was antiently written *Scloſtre,* that is, *Sclo's Place,* for I have ſhewn, in ſeveral inſtances, that *tre,* ſignifies a *Place.*

George Whitmore, eſq; has a ſeat here, with handſome coach-houſes, and ſtables, newly built. The houſe is ſituated in the midſt of the village, which conſiſts of one ſtreet, with a pretty trout river running through the middle of it; and a pin lying on the gravelly bed of the river, may be ſeen through the tranſparent ſtream, which makes it very pleaſant in the ſummer. This ſtream falls into the Winruſh, near Bourton on the Water, and is one of the heads of that river.

Of the Manor and other Eſtates.

In the antient ſurvey, are the following particulars:

'Roger de Laci and his mother hold Scloſtre, 'in Saleſmaneſberie hundred. There are three 'hides. Offa and Leuuin held it for two manors, 'and might go where they would. There are 'four plow-tillages in demean, and four bordars, 'and eight *ſervi,* and a mill of 12*s.* [rent]. It 'is worth and was worth 6*l.* One of theſe three 'hides paid 10*s.* tax every year for the king's uſe.' *Domeſday,* p. 75.

This manor, ſoon after the conqueſt, belonged to the alien priory of Mountberg in Normandy, the poſſeſſions of which houſe being taken away by act of parliament, 2 H. 5. this eſtate, together with the manor of Cheltenham, and the hundreds of Salemaneſberie and Cheltenham, paſſed to the nuns of Syon in Middleſex. Maud, abbeſs of Syon, levied a fine of this manor, and of the hundred of Salemaneſberie, to the biſhop of Exeter, to the uſe of the nunnery of Syon, 22 H. 6. and that houſe had a confirmation of the above particulars 1 E. 4.

Upon the diſſolution of religious foundations, this manor came to the crown, in which it continued,

tinued, 'till it was granted in fee, together with the hundred of Slaughter, to George Whitmore, eſq; by king James the Firſt, in the 8th year of his reign.

Richard Whitmore, ſon of George, married Katherine, daughter of John George, of Baunton, eſq; and dying in the year 1667, being then high ſheriff of Glouceſterſhire, was ſucceeded by his eldeſt ſon, Richard Whitmore, eſq; to whom the manor of Lower Slaughter belonged at the beginning of this century. The late lieutenant general William Whitmore, (next brother to ſir Thomas Whitmore, knight of the Bath) died in the year 1771, and was ſucceeded by his ſon, George Whitmore, eſq; the preſent lord of the hundred and manor of Slaughter, and proprietor of many good eſtates in the county. His arms are, *Vert, fretty Or.*

Thomas Everdon, and Alice his wife, levied a fine of lands in Lower Slaughter and Upper Slaughter, to William Wiggeſton, and others, 19 H. 7.

Of the Church, &c.

The church is a rectory, in the deanery of Stow, but annexed to Bourton on the Water. The patronage is veſted in All Souls college, Oxford, and Mr. Vernon is the preſent incumbent.

The advowſon of the chapel of Lower Slaughter was granted to ſir Chriſtopher Hatton, 21 Eliz. and paſſed, like Bourton on the Water, to the preſent patrons.

The church is ſmall, but neat, having been lately freſh pewed, and otherwiſe repaired. The inhabitants buried at Bourton on the Water 'till within theſe ſeven or eight years, but they have ſince obtained right of ſepulture, and now bury here.

Monument and Inſcription.

A flat ſtone in the north aile bears the following inaccurate inſcription :

Here lyeth Interred the Body of Richard Whitmore Eſq[r] who Departed this Life the 20th Day of Auguſt Anna Dom. 1667 Being then High Sherriff of the County of Glouceſter, who left Behinde him Katherine his Wife And four Children Elizabeth Richard Katherine and George.

Near this Place alſo Lyeth Interred the Body of the ſaid Katherine the Wife who Departed this Life the laſt Day of November Anna Dom. 1673.

Here alſo Lye Interred the Remains of Lieutenant General William Whitmore Eſq[r]. who Dyed 22[d] July 1771 Aged 57 Years.

Taxes.					
The Royal Aid in	1692,	£. 64	10	8
Poll-tax ——	1694, —	24	13	0
Land-tax —	1694, —	38	10	0
The ſame, at 3 *s.*	1770, —	30	12	9

At the beginning of the eighteenth century, when ſir Robert Atkyns drew up his account of this pariſh, there were 32 houſes, and about 150 inhabitants, 11 of whom were freeholders; yearly births 5, burials 4. There are now 39 families in the pariſh, and the people are increaſed to 194, by actual numeration.

Slaughter (Upper) and Eyford.

THIS pariſh lies in the hundred of its own name, three miles diſtant ſouth-weſt from Stow, ſeven miles north from Northleach, and twenty-three north-eaſtward from Glouceſter.

Several large ſprings riſe in the upper part of it, and run through the village to Lower Slaughter, and at length empty themſelves into the Winruſh.

The pariſh is divided into farms, and has no gentleman's ſeat within it ; for Eyford, which has ſometimes, tho' improperly, been conſidered as a hamlet belonging to it, is extraparochial ; yet I ſhall ſo far follow the example of other topographers, as to place the account of it after this pariſh.

There are no antiquities here, but nature has diſplay'd herſelf in a moſt extraordinary manner, in the growth and ſize of a child, the ſon of Mr. John Collet, a gentleman farmer of this village. He was not eight years old in February, 1777, when this account was taken ; but meaſured over the breaſt, fifty-two inches round, and round the thigh twenty-eight inches. His height I cannot exactly aſcertain, but when I ſaw him, it appeared to be about four feet nine or ten inches. He has a jolly, manly countenance, and florid complexion ; is healthy, active, ſprightly, and ſenſible, and is much diſpleaſed with the curioſity of ſtrangers coming to ſee him.

Of the Manor and other Eſtates.

This manor was part of the antient demeans of the crown, as appears by the following tranſlation from *Domeſday :*

'King Edward held Scloſtre in Salemaneſberie 'hundred. There were ſeven hides, and three 'plow-tillages in demean, and nine villeins, and 'eleven bordars, with eight plow-tillages. There 'are ſeven *ſervi*, and two mills of the rent of one 'mark of ſilver ; and meadow of [the rent of] 10*s.* 'and 10*s.* [rent iſſuing] out of one of theſe hides, 'and 5*s.* for the dogs. The ſheriff paid what 'he would for this manor, in the time of king 'Edward, ſo that they [the inquiſition] know 'not how to value it. Now the ſheriff hath added 'one plow-tillage there, and five bordars, with 'one plow-tillage; and he now pays for the 'manor itſelf, and for the hundred, 27*l.* by tale.' *Domeſday*, p. 67.

Edward de Bona Vera held Sclaughtre with its appurtenances 5 Joh. Thomas Baſſet held twenty librats of land in Sloutres, Wales, and Cotes, which were in the poſſeſſion of Edward de Bona Vera, 4 H. 3.

But it was afterwards veſted in the crown, for king Henry the Third, in the 36th year of his reign, granted the manors of Cheltham and Sclaugtre, and the hundreds of Cheltham and Salemaneſberie, with free warren, to the abbey of Fiſchamp in Normandy, in exchange for lands in

 Win-

Winchelsea and Rye in Suffex. Their claim to free warren and other great privileges in Cheltenham and Slouſter was allowed in the proceedings on a writ of *Quo warranto*, 15 E. 1. and they purchafed a licence from the crown, in the 18th year of the fame reign, to fell the above-mentioned manors and hundreds. The abbey, however, did not part with this manor, but continued poffeffed of it 5 E. 2. and it appears by the records that it was held of William de Clinton, earl of Huntingdon, 28 E. 3.

Upon the diffolution of alien priories, this eftate was difpofed of to feveral religious houfes. A meffuage in Slaughter belonged to the abbey of Bruern in Oxfordfhire, and was granted to Edward Powel 36 H. 8. A meadow, called the Hay-meadow, which belonged to the abbey of Evefham, was granted to fir Philip Hobby 37 H. 8. Lands in Slaughter, called No Man's Lands, belonged to the bifhop of Hereford, and were granted to Robert earl of Leicefter 16 Eliz.

The antient family of the Slaughters were lords of the manor for many generations, and took their name from the parifh, in which they refided upwards of three hundred years.

John Slaughter, efq; of Over Slaughter, died in the year 1583, and Paris Slaughter, his fon and heir, died in the year 1597. Chambers Slaughter, efq; was lord of this manor in the year 1608, Another Chambers Slaughter died in the year 1718, and William Slaughter, efq; fon of a third Chambers Slaughter, was lord of this manor, and died in the year 1740. From this family the manor and advowfon paffed, by purchafe, to Mary, daughter and fole heirefs of fir William Dodwell, of Sevenhampton, knight, afterwards married to the late Thomas Tracy, of Sandiwell in this county, efq; deceafed, and fhe is the prefent lady of the manor.

Of the Church, &c.

The church is a rectory, in the deanery of Stow, worth about 120*l.* a year. Mrs. Tracy is patronefs, and the reverend Mr. Ferdinando-Tracy Travel is the prefent incumbent. It was formerly appropriated to the abbey of Evefham.

Two yard-lands belong to the glebe.

The church, dedicated to St. Peter, confifts of two ailes, and has a handfome tower at the weft end.

Firft fruits £. 14	14	1½	Proc. & Syn. £. 0	5	4
Tenths — 1	9	5	Pentecoftals - 0	0	4½

Monuments and Infcriptions.

The chancel being repaired about the year 1775, three antient brafs plates, with infcriptions, were taken down from the wall, which I copied exactly thus :

Here lyeth bvryed the Body of Iohn Slavghter of Over Slavghter in the Covntye of Glovc. Efqvire who departed this Lyfe in the yeare of ovr Lord God one thowfand fyve Hundred fovrfcoore and three Memento Mori.

Here lyeth bvried the Body of Elianor Slavghter the Wife of Iohn Slavghter aforefaid and the eldeft Davghter vnto William Baghott of Prefbvry in the Covnty of Glovc. Efqvire which fayde Elianor departed this Lyfe the ninth of Ianvarie in the yeare of ovr Lord God one Thowfand five hvndred fovrfcore and feaventene Hodye mihi : Cras tibi.

Here lyeth bvried the body of Paris Slavghter fonne and heire vnto Iohn Slavghter Efqvire who died the XVIIIth of Febrvary in the yeare of ovr Lord 1597 and in the 55 yeare of his age.

Upon a ftone in the chancel is this memorial :

Edmond Slaughter of Upper Slaughter Gen^t^ ye 5 fon of Chambers Slaughter Efq; defired to bee buried Vnder this Stone, july the 29 day, aged 71 Years. Anno Dom. 1698.

Upon a table of white marble,

In Memoriam Viri optimi Plurimifq; Nominibus Defideratiffimi CHAMBERS SLAUGHTER de Braceleigh in Agro Vigornienfi Armigeri, Obijt Ian: 13° An° Ætatis fuæ 66to Dom^i^ 1718. Hoc Monumentum SUSANNA filia RICH^di^ HILL De Bachcombe in Agro Hereford: Armigeri, & Relicta ejufdem CHAMBERS SLAUGHTER amoris Ergo
P.

A plain white marble in the chancel bears this infcription :

Sacred to the Memories of SARAH, Daughter of OBEDIAH SEDGWICK, Merchant, and Wife to CHAMBERS SLAUGHTER, Efq; She was born Octo. 29, 1675, died Sept. 16, 1736.

Endow'd with all the virtues Mortals know
The knowledge of them, and the practice too;
Propitious Heaven indulged her Life to fee
Generall efteem attend her piety.
Then grown too perfect for this low abode,
Death gave the ftroke, and wing'd her to her God.

And

of WILLIAM SLAUGHTER Efq^r^ her only Son. He was born March 20, 1710, died March 23, 1740.

If Fame in what fhe fays fincere can be,
(When in the fame her hundred tongues agree)
More fond, more dutifull, or more fincere
No Friend, no Son, no Brother will appear :
In Manners fkill'd, in Books well read, of truth
A Lover, ftrict in Morals, tho' a Youth.
Adieu, dear Friend, and facred be the ftone
Which fpeaks the truths can be deny'd by none.

Arms, at the top of the monument, *Baron and femme*, 1. *Quarterly* 1ft *and* 4th, *Argent, a faltire azure*, for Slaughter. 2d *and* 3d, *Ermine, on a fefs fable a caftle of three towers argent.* On the femme fide, *Argent, on a crofs azure five bells of the field.*

On a tomb, under an arch in the north wall of the chancel, it is thus written :

THIS no Monument of Greif, but the Happy & Bleffed Memoriall of A Vertuous Woman, who hauing liu'd in A uery Eminent manner, Religious towards God : The Comfort of her Parents : The Delight of her Friends : & The greateft Bleffing to her Hufband, By A peacefull death fhee ended her Peacefull and Pious life, & was tranflated to Glory.

Her name FRANCES eldeft Daughter to Iohn Hutton of Marfke in ye County of York Efq: Wife to Andrew Wanley of Evford in this County & neighbourhood Gent: fhee left only one fonn named William, & dyed in ye 29 yeare of her Age March 8th Anno Dom. 1682.

HERE alfo in this defired Place of Reft doth lye interr'd the Body of ANDREW WANLEY of Eyford Gent. who dyed in the 46: yeare of his aGE Auguft 3^d^ Anno Dom. 1688.

For wee knew that our Redemer liueth, & though wormes deftroy theife Bodyes, yet in our Flefh fhall wee fee GOD.

There are the arms of Wanley impaling thofe of Hutton in a fcutcheon over the monument, *viz.* 1. *Argent, a crofs paty fitchy inverted, and on the point a crefcent gules*, for Wanley. 2. *On a fefs, between three cufhions placed lozengewife and taffelled at the corners, as many fleurs de lis*, for Hutton.

Near this monument, on three flat ftones, it is thus written :

F. W. 1682. Alfo under this Stone lyeth the Body of M^rs^ ANN Wanley the Wife of M^r^. William Wanley, the Son of Mr Andrew Wanley Aged 53 Years Died April the 26th 1744.

In Memory of WILLIAM WANLEY Efq; of EYFORD who dy'd JULY the 22^d^ 1747 in the 66th year of his Age.

Here lyeth the Body of WILLIAM WANLEY Efq; of EYFORD the Son of WILLIAM WANLEY Efq^r^. of EYFORD who Died May the 4th 1762. Aged 56 Years.

Benefactions.

Benefactions.

Mr. Charles Baghot, of Staple's Inn, London, 33 Eliz. gave a yard-land, containing 55 acres, now let at 30*l.* 10*s.* a year, for the repair of the church; but if that ſhould not want repairing, then for the uſe of the poor.

The intereſt of two ſums of 10*l.* each is given for the uſe of the poor.

Taxes.					
The Royal Aid in	1692,	£.65	12	8
Poll-tax — —	1694, —	21	10	0
Land-tax ——	1694, -	32	10	0
The ſame, at 3*s.*	1770, —	26	12	3

About ſeventy years ago, when ſir Robert Atkyns compiled his account of this pariſh, there were 70 houſes, and about 150 inhabitants, of whom 12 were freeholders; yearly births 4, burials 3. The preſent number of families is 84, and the people having been numbered, are found to be increaſed to 178.

E Y F O R D.

THIS little place lies in the hundred of Slaughter, three miles diſtant ſouth-weſtward from Stow, twelve north-weſtward from Burford in Oxfordſhire, and twenty-two north-eaſtward from Glouceſter.

It adjoins to the pariſh of Upper Slaughter, within which ſir Robert Atkyns underſtood it to be a hamlet; but he was miſtaken in that particular. The antient grants and evidences ſtile it the pariſh of Eyford, and declare it to be *Parochia de ſe*, and the conſtant uſage ſupports its claim to independency. It is extraparochial, having no church, and maintains its own poor.

Eye, ſays the above-mentioned learned hiſtorian, ſignifies *water*, and *Eyford* is the ſame with *Waterford*. The turnpike-road from Stow to Glouceſter leads through it, and the place unqueſtionably took its name from the road croſſing the rivulet, formed by the union of ſeveral fine ſprings of water, which riſe here, and run purling down to Slaughter.

On the weſt ſide of this ſtream, in a little ſequeſtered valley, ſtands a pleaſant villa, with large gardens, canals, and beautiful plantations and pleaſure-grounds, now the ſeat, and ſometimes the reſidence of John Dolphin, eſq; but formerly the retreat of the duke of Shrewſbury; where, in a ſummer-houſe, built over a caſcade, long ſince fallen into ruins, the inimitable Milton wrote part of his *Paradiſe Loſt*. The duke ſometimes retired hither, being delighted with the ſolitarineſs of the place, and the pleaſantneſs of the neighbouring country for recreations. King William the Third made the duke a viſit, and was wonderfully taken with his ſolitude and privacy, ſo different from a royal court, that he thought himſelf out of the world.

Before the Norman conqueſt, this place was a diſtinct manor, which is next to be conſidered.

Of the Manor and other Eſtates.

Eyford eſtate conſiſts of one thouſand two hundred and fifty acres of land, of which *Domeſday* gives the following particulars:

'Haſcoit Muſard holds Aiforde in Salemaneſ- 'berie hundred. There are five hides, which pay 'tax. Erneſi held it. There are two plow- 'tillages in demean, and twelve villeins, and one 'bordar, with five plow-tillages; and there are 'eight among the *ſervi* and *ancillæ*. It is worth 4*l.*' *Domeſday*, p. 78.

Richard de Clare, earl of Glouceſter and Hertford, held Heyford 47 H. 3. The ſheriff returned to the treaſurer and barons of the exchequer that Roger de la Mare was lord of Hayford, in the hundred of Salmoneſberie, 9 E. 1.

John le Rous, and others, held this manor, and the advowſon of the church, 49 E. 3. in which year John le Rous of Raggeleye, William Gille, clerk, William Alewy, chaplain, and Richard Patty, chaplain, obtained a licence of the king to grant to the abbat and convent of Eveſham, and their ſucceſſors for ever, the manor of Eyford, with the appurtenances, and the advowſon of the church of the ſame manor, and one meſſuage, three yard-lands and a half, and nine acres of land, and ſix acres of meadow, with their appurtenances, in Stow St. Edward's, Malgareſbury, Burghton, and Wykeryſyndon, worth together twelve marks and nine ſhillings *per annum*, as it was found to be by the eſcheator's inquiſition; and the abbat and convent had a licence at the ſame time to empower them to take this eſtate.

After the diſſolution of the abbey of Eveſham, Eyford, called the pariſh of Eyford, part of the poſſeſſions of that abbey, was granted by the crown to ſir Philip Hobby, knight, 11th May, 37 H. 8. Sir Thomas Hobby, knight, brother to ſir Philip Hobby, died ſeized of Eyford 9 Eliz. His widow was married to lord Ruſſel, whom ſhe ſurvived, and after his death ſhe demiſed Eyford to the earl of Huntingdon, and the lord treaſurer Burleigh, 18th Jan. 34 Eliz. all which particulars appear by authentic evidences in the poſſeſſion of the preſent owner.

The earl of Worceſter was lord of this manor in the year 1608. It was afterwards purchaſed by Mr. Andrew Wanley, and deſcended from him through ſeveral generations, 'till it came to the late William Wanley, eſq; who died ſeized of Eyford in the year 1762. After his death, it paſſed, by purchaſe, to John Dolphin, eſq; of Shenſtone in the county of Stafford, who has made a large addition to, and greatly improved the houſe, and frequently reſides here. He married Margaretta Eeles, daughter of Iſaac Eeles, of Amerſham in the county of Bucks, eſq; by whom he hath iſſue two ſons, and two daughters. His arms are, *Azure, three dolphins nayant Or.*

Taxes.					
The Royal Aid in	1692,	£. 52	18	0
Poll-tax ——	1694, —	2	12	0
Land-tax ——	1694, —	42	0	0
The ſame, at 3*s.*	1770, —	31	18	3

There were, moſt probably, about thirty inhabitants in this place at the time of the general ſurvey, in the Conqueror's reign, for the villeins and bordars were thirteen, who had five plow-tillages; and there were eight other plow-tillages, which the *ſervi* and *ancillæ* had between them, ſo that they may be eſtimated at fifteen or ſixteen more. But ſir Robert Atkyns ſays, 'this place 'was appropriated to the abbey of Eveſham, for 'a ſtipend to teach youth, in the year 1472, at 'which time it had no inhabitants.' So deſtructive had the civil wars between the Yorkiſts and Lancaſtrians been to this country, as to depopulate whole villages. Eyford now conſiſts of two houſes, two families, and twenty-five ſouls.

SLIMBRIDGE.

THIS pariſh lies in the hundred of Berkeley, ſix miles diſtant north from the town of that name, four north-weſt from Durſley, and eleven ſouth from Glouceſter.

The name is written *Hiſlinbruge* in *Domeſday*, the ſignification of which I don't underſtand.

It is bounded on the north-weſt and north-eaſt by the rivers Severn and Cam, and conſiſts chiefly of rich paſture and meadow land, with ſome arable, and produces good cheeſe and cyder.

Here is a large tract of land called the *Dumballs*, but more commonly the *New Grounds*, conſiſting of above a thouſand acres, which have been gained from the Severn many ages ago, and belong to the earl of Berkeley, becauſe his manors extend to the middle of that river. King Charles the Firſt, by his attorney general, commenced a ſuit in the exchequer againſt lord Berkeley, for thoſe lands; but after the jury was impannelled, and evidence begun, the attorney general dropt the ſuit.

I could never learn when this acquiſition was firſt made from the river, and perhaps it is not any where recorded. The like has happened at Lidney, on the other ſide, but lower down the river. And the ſame has been in much greater degree in other countries. One Hubert Thomas, who was ſecretary to the elector palatine of the Rhine, in his deſcription of the country of Liege, affirms, that the ſea once came up to the walls of Tongres, now ſaid to be about fourſcore miles diſtant from it; which he proves (among other reaſons) by the great iron rings then to be ſeen there, to which the ſhips were uſed to be faſtened. So Michael Hoſpitalis, giving an account of the preſent ſtate of a place, antiently the *Forum Julij*, on the coaſt of Narbonne in France,

Apparet moles antiqui diruta portûs
Atqui ubi portus erat, ſiccum nunc littus & horti.

The ruins of an antient port are ſeen,
And lands and garden grounds where ſhips have been.

Theſe great changes were moſt likely occaſioned by earthquakes or volcanos, which have happened in diſtant parts of the globe, and of which it is impoſſible for us to eſtimate the effects, or to aſcertain how far their influence extends.

But to return to Slimbridge. Againſt one ſide of the New Grounds, next the river, the earl of Berkeley (I believe the grandfather of the preſent earl) built a vaſt wall of large ſtones, firmly cramped together, to break the violence of the waves, and to preſerve the land from being waſhed away by floods and high tides. This work is called the Hock Crib.

Great numbers of cattle are depaſtured upon theſe grounds; and it is thought that the herbage has ſtronger nutritive powers, and makes cattle fat ſooner, than the graſs of common meadows. Here grows the true Samphire in great plenty, which is much eſteemed in pickling, and ſometimes uſed in medicine.

There is another very large piece of rich ground in this pariſh, called the *Wharfe*, or *Warthe*. It is in common all the year, and, as well as the Dumballs, ſubject to floods and ſpring-tides. If it could be incloſed, it would be worth 1500*l.* a year.

Of the Manor and other Eſtates.

This was a member of the manor of Berkeley, at the time of the general ſurvey, as it is expreſſly mentioned in *Domeſday*, where it is ſaid, that 'Roger [de Berkeley] holds two hides in Hiſlin-'bruge, belonging to the manor of Berkeley.'

Maurice lord Berkeley died ſeized of Slimbrugge in the year 1281, 9 E. 1. and his grandſon, Thomas lord Berkeley, held it 17 E. 3. and died ſeized of it in the 35th year of the ſame reign. Maurice lord Berkeley, ſon of Thomas, died ſeized of Slimbruge 42 E. 3. of the wounds he had received ten years before at the battle of Poictiers.

Ralph Walers was ſeized of this manor 49 E. 3.

Thomas lord Berkeley, ſon of Maurice, held the manor 6 R. 2. and Nicholas Barſtable was ſeized of Slimburg 13 H. 4. but it ſeems to have been only in truſt for Thomas lord Berkeley, who did not die 'till July 13, 1416, at which time he was poſſeſſed of the manor, and of a tenement called Sage's Place, in Slimbridge.

Richard Beauchamp, earl of Warwick, married Elizabeth, the only child of Thomas lord Berkeley, and by that means became poſſeſſed of this manor, and many others in Glouceſterſhire, notwithſtanding a ſpecial entail and fine in favour of James lord Berkeley. He had iſſue, by Elizabeth his wife, three daughters, Margaret, married to John Talbot, earl of Shrewſbury; Elianor, married to Edmund duke of Somerſet; and Elizabeth, married to George Nevil, lord Latimer; and died poſſeſſed of this manor 17 H. 6.

Sir Edward Ingoldſthorp was ſeized of Slimbridge 35 H. 6. probably in truſt, for

Margaret

Margaret countefs of Shrewfbury, eldeft daughter of Richard Beauchamp, earl of Warwick, and Elizabeth his wife, died feized of Slimbridge, Goffington, Hurft, Cambridge, Arlingham, &c. 7 E. 4.

William lord Berkeley, created earl of Nottingham, and earl marfhal, levied a fine of this manor, and of the manor and caftle of Berkeley, and other great eftates, to the ufe of king Henry the Seventh, and his heirs males; by virtue of which fine they came to the crown, and continued in it 'till the death of Edward the Sixth, when they reverted to Henry lord Berkeley, the fifth in lineal defcent from Maurice, brother of William lord Berkeley, who had livery granted to him 1 Mariæ; and from him the manor of Slimbridge defcended to Frederick-Auguftus, earl of Berkeley, the prefent lord of the manor.

HAMLETS, and places of diftinct names.

1. *Hurft*. Maurice lord Berkeley died feized of the manor of Hurft 9 E. 1. and was fucceeded by his fon, Thomas lord Berkeley, who was feized of it in the 17th, and died in the 35th year of the reign of king Edward the Third. Maurice lord Berkeley, fon of Thomas, died feized of it 42 E. 3. It paffed afterwards to the crown by fine, as already related under Slimbridge, Berkeley, &c.

2. *Sages*, probably fo called from a family of the name of Sage, one of whom gave lands in Brickhampton in Churchdown, to the abbey of Hayles, 6 E. 2. This manor likewife belonged to the Berkeleys, but was not conveyed to king Henry the Seventh. Thomas lord Berkeley died feized of it 24 H. 8. and Thomas lord Berkeley, his fon, had livery of it the fame year.

3. *Church-end*.

4. *Moor-end*.

5. *Goffington*. Lands in this place belonged to the abbey of Kingfwood, and were granted to fir Baptift Hickes, 7 Jac.

6. *Kingfton*.

7. *Slimbridge Street*. Slimbridge Wharfe was given, by one of the Berkeley family, to the abbey of St. Auguftin in Briftol; and after the diffolution of that houfe, it was granted to the bifhoprick of Briftol 34 H. 8. A tenement in Slimbridge belonged to the priory of St. Ofwald in Gloucefter, and was granted to fir Baptift Hickes, 7 Jac. Nicholas Hawling was feized of lands in Slimbridge 36 E. 3.

8. *Cambridge*, lies on the little river Cam, from which it takes its name. Huntingdon, Hoveden, and Florence of Worcefter, make mention of a great victory obtained here by king Edward the elder over the plundering Danes, whom he attacked as they returned from an excurfion, loaded with booty, and killed many thoufands of them on the fpot, together with Healfden, Cinvil, and Inguer, three of their princes. Here was formerly a chapel, in which Thomas lord Berkeley founded a chantry 17 E. 3. Lands in this place, which belonged to the chantry in the chapel of Cambridge, were granted to fir Oliver Cromwell, 5 Jac.

William lord Berkeley, by the name of earl marfhal, and earl of Nottingham, levied a fine of lands in Slimbridge, to Edward Willoughby and Robert Legg, 3 H. 7. in order to convey them to the king. Thomas Baker levied a fine of lands in Slimbridge to John Efterfield, John Walfh, John Heming, Richard Bolton, and Thomas Broom, 9 H. 7. Thomas Laney and Catherine his wife levied a fine of lands in Slimbridge and Goffington to Edmund Tame 16 H. 7. John Woodard levied a fine of lands in Slimbridge to John Bower; and William Bridgman and Anne his wife levied a fine of lands in Slimbridge and Goffington, to Francis Cotherington, 3 E. 6. John Pleydell levied a fine of feven meffuages in Slimbridge, Ham, Hinton, and Berkeley, to his fon, in fee taille, 31 Eliz. *Efch.*

Of the Church, &c.

The church is a rectory, in the deanery of Durfley, worth about 300*l.* a year. The patronage is vefted in Magdalen college, Oxford, and the reverend Mr. John Stone is the prefent incumbent.

The patronage of the church was antiently in the Berkeley family, and was granted to the priory of Stanley St. Leonard's, by Roger de Berkeley. But Thomas de Bredon, abbat of Gloucefter, afterwards releafed the advowfon of Slimbridge to Thomas lord Berkeley, in confideration of lands near Cam, called Lorlynge, or Lorrenge, as the reader may fee more at large under Stanley St. Leonard's.

The rector pays 10*l.* a year to Magdalen college, for choir-mufic on the top of the college tower on May-day.

Twelve acres of arable land, and about thirteen acres of fmall inclofures, belong to the glebe.

The church is dedicated to St. John the Evangelift. It is a very neat one, newly pewed, and confifts of the nave, and two fide ailes, with a gallery, and a handfome lofty fpire at the weft end.

The Berkeley arms are painted in the windows of the chancel and fouth aile. And in the fouth window of the chancel, *Quarterly, Per pale and per fefs indented, ermine and gules.*

There were two chantries in the parifh, dedicated to St. Catherine, and St. John Baptift. One of them was founded by Thomas lord Berkeley, in the chapel of Cambridge, in this parifh, 17 E. 3. The laft incumbents were John Browne, who had a penfion of 4*l.* and William Willington, who received a penfion of 5*l.* in the year 1553. *Willis.* Lands belonging to one of thefe chantries, were granted to Ralph Sherman, by king E. 6.

James Berkeley, third fon of Thomas lord Berkeley, was rector of Slimbridge, and afterwards confecrated bifhop of Exeter, in the year 1326. Henry Stokefley, prefented to this rectory in 1509, and confecrated bifhop of London in 1536, diftinguifhed himfelf as a violent perfecuter of the proteſtants, in the reign of king Henry the Eighth. Owen Oglethorpe, likewiſe rector of this church, was advanced to the biſhoprick of Carliſle in 1556, by queen Mary. He crowned queen Elizabeth Jan. 15, 1559, being the only biſhop that could be prevailed on to aſſiſt at the ceremony; but he was deprived the ſame year, with thirteen other popiſh biſhops, for refuſing to comply with the laws enacted in favour of the reformation.

Firſt fruits £. 28	2	4	Synodals £. 0	2	0
Tenths — 2	16	$3\frac{1}{2}$	Pentecoſt. 0	0	8
Procurations 0	6	8			

Monuments and Inſcriptions.

On a ſmall monument, againſt the wall of the chancel,

Hic Iacet Gulielmus Cradock, S. T. P. Nec non hujus Eccleſiæ Rector. Cætera quis Neſcit?

Obijt 26th Martij Anno Salutis 1727 Anno Ætat. 68.

Arms, *Baron and femme*, 1. *Argent, three boars heads ſable*, for Cradock. 2. *Gules, a feſs between two chevronels argent*, for Nourſe.

On a marble table in the church,

Near this place lieth the Body of William Davies of Moor-end in this Pariſh, Gent. who departed this Life the 17th of July in the Year of our Lord 1742, aged 68.

Near this Place lyeth the Body of Robert Davies of this Pariſh Gent. Ob. April 27th 1749 Æt. 37.

Alſo near this Place lyeth the Body of Grace the Wife of William Davies of Roll's Court in this P. Gent. Ob. 25th Maij 1750, Æt. 41.

Deborah Davies, Relict of William Davies of Moor-end Gent. died Janʸ. 14th 1759, Aged 86.

William Davies of Roll's Court Gent. died Aug. 1, 1762, aged 56.

Arms, at top, *Gules, a chevron between three mullets Or, pierced of the field.*

A ſtone table, over one of the pillars of the church, bears this inſcription:

In Memory of Robert Awood, Practitioner of Phyſick, of Frampton upon Severn, and Elizabeth his Daughter. She died Jan. 21, Æt. 7. He Jan. 27, Æt. 58, A. D. 1734.

Here lies a Father with his Offspring dear,
Joy of his Heart, and Solace of his Care;
She freſh in Years, & tender in her Frame,
Wither'd and fell by Febris' waſtful Flame.
The Parent anxious to allay the Fire,
Unguarded, ſtricken, did near her expire.
Oh gloomy State of Man! when void of Fence
Not Virtue ſtands, nor yet can Innocence!
But ſure the Good awaits a better Lot;
A Child of God's can never be forgot.

Taxes.					
The Royal Aid in	1692, £.	185	16	0
Poll-tax —	1694, —	44	1	0
Land-tax —	1694, —	215	8	0
The ſame, at 3*s.*	1770, —	161	17	0

At the beginning of this century, there were 120 houſes in the pariſh, and about 560 inhabitants, 40 of whom were freeholders; yearly births 16, burials 15. *Atkyns.* The preſent number of ſouls is eſtimated at about 800.

SNOWSHILL.

THIS pariſh lies in the lower diviſion of the hundred of Kiftſgate, ſeven miles north-eaſt from Winchcombe, five ſouth-weſt from Campden, and twenty-three north-eaſtward from Glouceſter.

A fine ſpring riſes in the village, and being joined with others a little below, they form a ſmall brook, which falls into the Avon near Eveſham.

The pariſh is ſituated on the high part of the Coteſwold country, and conſiſts chiefly of arable land; but the village and church ſtand in a little bottom, and are not to be ſeen, except from the brow of thoſe high lands which encompaſs them.

Near the north-eaſt border of it, in the fineſt open hunting country imaginable, the honourable John-Coventry Bulkeley has built an elegant houſe, called *Spring Hill*, ſtanding upon an eminence, with a large piece of paſture ground ſloping from the front, which he has improved to a good verdure, and adorned the face of this naked country with fine plantations of beech and fir, that before produced nothing but furze. Part of this gentleman's eſtate lying in Snowſhill, gave me an opportunity of taking notice of his ſeat, which, however, ſtands juſt without the boundaries of the county, in the pariſh of Broadway, in Worceſterſhire.

Snowſhill was incloſed by parliamentary authority, about the year 1761. Were the manor houſe in a better ſituation, it would be called handſome. It is occupied by the principal farmer; but not many years ago, it was the reſidence of a family of the name of Sambach, who have now left the county.

Of the Manor and other Eſtates.

This manor is ſaid to have been given to the abbey of Winchcombe, by Kenulph, or Kenwolf, the thirteenth king of Mercia, who died in the year 819, and was buried in that monaſtery, of which he was the founder. And it was part of the poſſeſſions of that abbey at the time of the antient ſurvey, as appears by the following extract from *Domeſday*:

'The church of St. Mary of Wincelcumbe holds 'Snaweſille, in Holefordes hundred. There are 'ſeven hides taxed. In demean are three plow-'tillages, and twelve villeins, and two bordars, 'with ſix plow-tillages. There are ſix *ſervi*. It 'is worth and was worth 100 *ſol.*' *Domeſday*, p. 71.

The abbey was ſeized of this manor 35 H. 3. and the ſame year purchaſed a charter of free warren, which privilege was allowed in the proceedings on a writ of *Quo warranto*, 15 E. 1. The abbat and convent of Winchcombe aſſigned the manor to the monaſtery of St. Ebrulf, at Utica in Normandy, 12 E. 2. but it returned to them again, moſt probably by another grant, at the time when alien monaſteries were diveſted of their lands in England, 2 H. 5. and it continued in the poſſeſſion of the abbey of Winchcombe, 'till that houſe was diſſolved.

King Henry the Eighth aſſigned the manor of Snowſhill to queen Catherine, in part of her dower. After her death it was granted, by king Edward the Sixth, to John earl of Warwick, afterwards created duke of Northumberland, and executed

executed for treaſon in the beginning of the reign of queen Mary. Henry Willoughby had livery of the manor granted to him 4 Eliz. And John Warren died ſeized of it 19 C. 1. William Sambach, eſq; was lord of the manor of Snowſhill when ſir Robert Atkyns wrote his Hiſtory; and from him it deſcended to his ſon, William Sambach, eſq; who died without iſſue, in the year 1743.

This manor and eſtate was purchaſed in 1759, by Samuel Blackwell, eſq; who ſold it, ſoon afterwards, to John Small, of Clapham in Surrey, eſq; the preſent lord of the manor, whoſe family arms are emblazoned p. 471.

William Fravileſworth held lands in Snowſhill 33 E. 3. as did John Daſton 6 E. 4.

Brockhampton is a ſmall hamlet in this pariſh, conſiſting of two farms.

Of the Church, &c.

The church is annexed to Stanton. It is a rectory, in the deanery of Campden, worth about 85*l.* a year. The reverend Mr. Reginald Wynniat is patron, incumbent, and impropriator.

The impropriation belonged to the abbey of Winchcombe; and a portion of tithes, lately belonging to that houſe, was granted to ſir Thomas Seymour 1 E. 6.

The manor of Stanton, and the free chapel of Snowſhill, were granted by the crown, 4 & 5 Phil. & Mar. to John Elliot, who obtained a licence to alienate them to Thomas Doleman the ſame year; and John Doleman, ſon of Thomas, had livery of the advowſon of this church 15 Eliz.

Two hundred and two acres of land were allotted to the rector, at the incloſing of the downs and common fields, in lieu of all tithes in Snowſhill, except of the two farms in Brockhampton; and thoſe lands are now let at 85*l.* a year.

The church is ſmall, and has a tower at the weſt end, ornamented with pinnacles and battlements.

Pentecoſtals - - - - 2½*d.*

Monument and Inſcription.

A ſmall marble monument in the church, bears this inſcription:

In the Chancell of this Church near the Communion Table is depoſited the Body of William Sambach, Eſq^r. (ſon of William Sambach, Eſq; who alſo is interred in the Chancell of this Church) He was a zealous Friend to the Church of England, and the true Intereſt of his Country. He married Ann third daughter of William Batſon, Eſq^r. of Bourton on the Hill in this County, and died the twenty ninth Day of July, 1743, aged 40, without Iſſue.

This Monument was erected to his Memory by his equally loving and beloved Widow Ann Sambach.

At top are theſe arms; *Baron and femme,* 1. *Azure, a feſs between three garbs Or,* for Sambach. 2. *Argent, three bats wings ſable, on a chief gules a lion paſſant of the firſt,* for Bateſon.

Taxes.					
The Royal Aid in	1692,	£. 74	1	0
Poll-tax ——	1694, —	13	14	0
Land-tax ——	1694, —	70	2	0
The ſame, at 3*s.*	1770, —	49	6	6

At the beginning of the preſent century, there were 38 houſes, and about 192 inhabitants, of whom 9 were freeholders; yearly births 6, burials 5. *Atkyns.* The preſent number of families is 48, and the people, by a late ſurvey, were found to be exactly 236.

SODBURY (CHIPPING.)

THIS is a ſmall pariſh, in the hundred of Grumbald's-aſh, twelve miles diſtant north-eaſtward from Briſtol, ſeven north-weſtward from Marſhfield, thirteen north from Bath, and thirty ſouth from Glouceſter.

It lies in the Vale, about a mile weſtward of the great Howby hill, (which is part of that chain that ſtretches lengthways through the county) and is watered by a little brook which runs from hence into the Froome, and ſo to Briſtol.

There are three places, all lying together, of the name of Sodbury, which they take from the camp on Little Sodbury hill; and in general, the termination *bury*, in the names of places, is taken from the Saxon beoɲȝ, a *camp*, or *fortification*, as I have frequently obſerved in the courſe of this work. If *Sopeberie*, as I find it in *Domeſday*, were the true reading, it would lead me to conjecture, that *Sope* was the name of ſome conſiderable perſon in theſe parts, to whom the manor belonged; and this opinion is in ſome meaſure ſtrengthened by the name of another place, a few miles diſtant, being *Sopworth*; which, in all likelihood, belonged to the ſame perſon. But if it ſhould be alledged, that the name is ill written in the antient record, and that *Sodbury* is the true orthography, then it may ſignify the *South Camp*, for *Sod* is often put for *South*. And in that caſe, I ſhould ſuppoſe it to have been ſo called on account of its ſituation from the *Caſtles*, another camp, lying about a mile northward, upon the edge of Horton-hill. The prenomen, *Chipping*, has been already explained under Campden, and it remains only to obſerve, that it was firſt added to the name of this place, after the market was eſtabliſhed here, in the reign of king Henry the Third, and ſerved to diſtinguiſh it from the other Sodburies.

This is a ſmall market town, conſiſting of two ſtreets, lying ſomething in the form of the letter L, upon the turnpike-road from Briſtol, through Oxford, or Abingdon, to London; and is lately much improved in its buildings. The market, which is held on Thurſday, is very little frequented, being nothing more than a few neighbouring people aſſembled in the public houſes. The town lies in a great dairy country, and formerly the market is ſaid to have been very conſiderable for cheeſe; but things are diverged from their proper point, and markets in general are reduced to almoſt nothing, owing to factors, jobbers, and foreſtallers buying up the great neceſſaries of life at the farm and dairy houſes. It is a pernicious, if not an illegal practice, fraught with

with many evils, and particularly injurious to market towns, which are taxed higher than villages, and made ſubject to many charges unknown to the latter; but are thus more and more deprived of the means of bearing them. Here are two fairs in the year, held on Holy Thurſday, and on the 24th of June, for cattle and pedlery.

There is a great deal of travelling through the town to Briſtol, and waggons are continually paſſing through it to the coal pits, which lie two or three miles further weſtward, whence many parts in Glouceſterſhire, Wiltſhire, and even ſome places in Berkſhire, are ſupply'd with coal. And the whole tract of country from Sodbury and Lanſdown hills weſtward, as far as the city of Briſtol, ſeems to be full of that neceſſary foſſil.

Here, alſo, is an excellent ſort of lime ſtone, called the White-lays, of a blue caſt, very compact and ponderous, and burns into a ſtrong lime, as white as ſnow. Conſiderable quantities of this lime are ſent into various parts of the country, not only on account of its goodneſs, but it is rendered cheap, alſo, from the low price of coal.

Here is no prevailing manufacture at preſent. One maſter clothier employs a few hands, but the women and children have ſufficient ſpinning-work brought them from other parts.

This town was made a corporation by charter, in the year 1681, whereby the government of it was veſted in a mayor, ſix aldermen, and twelve burgeſſes, with a high ſteward, recorder, and town-clerk; and a court of record was erected for trying all manner of perſonal ſuits, actions of debt, &c. ariſing within the borough, and not exceeding the value of five pounds. But this weight of honour was too great to be ſuſtained by ſo weak and feeble a body, and ſo the charter was annulled by proclamation, at the requeſt of the inhabitants themſelves, as I am informed, in the year 1688; and from that time the town recurred to its antient government by a bailiff, who is annually choſen by the lord of the manor, or his ſteward, out of three perſons returned to him by the jury at the leet.

By very antient grants from two perſons, who were lords of the manor in the reigns of king Henry the Second and king John, (as will be more particularly ſhewn under the account of the manor) the bailiff, and bailiff burgeſſes, (who are ſuch as have been bailiffs) have the diſpoſal of two eſtates, of which one is called the Stub Riding, conſiſting of about one hundred acres. And annually on the 14th of May, they grant the ſummer paſture of it, under ſuch regulations as they think proper, for ſixty-eight cow-beaſts, to perſons who have inhabited the town fourteen years; one paſture to each.

The other eſtate, called the Meadow Riding, is divided into eighty-one lots, or portions, beſides two others, called the Bailiff's Piece, and the Hayward's Piece. Each of thoſe eighty-one lots, being more than a ſtatute acre, they leaſe out to certain perſons for the lives of the leſſees, and for the lives of their widows.

The lord of the manor receives five pounds yearly out of the Ridings, and the vicar of Old Sodbury 1 *l.* 13 *s.* 4 *d.* in lieu of tithes. The bailiff, beſides his allotment, receives 50 *s.* and the cuſtom is, for him to provide an ox, and two barrels of ale, at an annual feaſt on St. Stephen's day, to entertain the inhabitants.

The moſt memorable tranſactions at this place have been of the melancholy kind. Here one John Piggot was burnt at the ſtake, to ſatisfy the ſanguinary ſpirit of the popiſh religion, in the ſecond year of the reign of queen Mary; and two other perſons, John Barnard, and John Walſh, were ordered to be apprehended and proſecuted, becauſe they often came to the town, and ſhowed Piggot's bones, with a deſign of animating the people to a perſeverance in the reformed religion. It is alſo related in *Fox's book of Martyrs*, that doctor Whittington, who was vicar-general for ſome part of this dioceſe, having condemned a woman to death for hereſy, about the ſame time, and attending himſelf at the execution, a bull that had broke out of the town, ran furiouſly to the place, and without doing the leaſt injury to any other perſon, killed the doctor on the ſpot, and carried his entrails away upon his horns.

Of the Manor and other Eſtates.

This belonged to the antient demeans of the crown, and was part of the manor of Old Sodbury at the time of the general ſurvey, wherefore there is no diſtinct account of it in *Domeſday*, which was finiſhed in the fourteenth year of the Conqueror's reign. Sometime afterwards, king William gave this manor to Odo earl of Champagne, his near kinſman, who attended him in the invaſion of England, and for his good ſervice was rewarded with the earldom of Holderneſs in Yorkſhire, and with that of Albermarle in Normandy.

Stephen, ſon of Odo, ſucceeded his father in theſe earldoms, and marrying Hawiſe, daughter of Ralph de Mortimer, died ſeized of this manor. William was ſon and heir of Stephen, and was ſurnamed Le Groſs from his great corpulency. He had made a vow to go a pilgrimage to Jeruſalem, but growing very fat, obtained a diſpenſation from the pope to releaſe him from the performance of it. He was a great benefactor to this place, and granted to the burghers of Sodbury the like liberties which the burghers of Briſtol enjoyed, with licence for every burgher to have common for one heifer in the place now called the Ridings, which they ſtill enjoy; and dying 25 H. 2. left Hawiſe his only daughter and heireſs. She carried her great poſſeſſions by marriage, firſt, to William de Mandeville, earl of Eſſex, who dying without iſſue, ſhe was married, ſecondly, to William de Fortibus, an admiral, and very gallant officer, by whom ſhe had a ſon, called alſo William de Fortibus.

tibus. She was married, a third time, to Baldwin de Betune, earl of the iſle of Wight, whom ſhe ſurvived, and died 16 Joh. She was ſucceeded by her ſon William de Fortibus, whoſe original confirmation of the aforeſaid privileges to the burgeſſes of Sodbury the editor has ſeen, and it is now in the poſſeſſion of the bailiff of the town; but time has impaired the parchment itſelf, ſo that the writing is deſtroyed in ſome parts. By that confirmation it appears that he aſſumed the name of *Craſſus*. It runs thus, ...

Will. Craſſus primogenitus filius Willi Craſſi junioris ſalutem. Noveras nos conceſſiſſe & hac preſenti carta n'ra confirmaſſe burgenſibus noſtris de Sobbur' et heredibus ſuis totum quod Willus Craſſus primogenitus avunculus noſter eiſdem fecit & per cartam ſuam confirmavit, videlicet, Quod habeant et teneant omnes libertates que ſpectant et pertinent ad leges de Britoill; &c. &c. &c.

About this time, William Green of Sodbury, by his deed without date, gave Gaunt's fields to the burgeſſes of Sodbury. And at the ſame time Jurdan Biſhop, who was lord of Little Sodbury, granted them common of paſture for cattle in Dymerſhed and [c] Norwood. Theſe grants are ſuppoſed to have been made in the reign of king Henry

[c] The original grant runs thus:

CEST endenture teſmoyne lacord entre Jurdan Biſſop de un p't et Thomas atte Hulla Johan Whitchened Thomas atte Mulle William Watersſhip & touz les aultres Borgeys de la Vylla de Chepyngſobb'i de aultre p't ceſt a ſavoyr q' le avauntdyt Jurdan ad graunte pur luy & pur ces heyres & pur ces aſſygnes a les avauntdyt Thomas Joh'n Thomas Willyam & a touz les aultres bergeys de la Vylla de Chepyngſobb'i q'ils ayount & tynent commune de paſture cheſkune de eaux ou un Vaſch a communer mon boys de Dewermeſſyde et Forchwode en petite Sobb'i com eauz & les tres tenaunz ount ew & uſa la dyte commune a lour Franctenements en la Vylle avauntdyt de temps dount memorye ne con're A avoyr & tener a les avauntdyt Thomas John Thomas & Willyam & a touz les aultres bergeys de la Vylla de Chepyngſobb'i la commune de paſture en mes boys avauntdyt a ceux & lour heyres & a lour aſſygnes ſans chalenge ou deſtourbaunce de moy auauntdyt Jurdan ou de mes heyres ou de mes aſſygnes. Et jeo le avauntdyt Jurdan & mes heyres & mes aſſygnes la auauntdyt commune de paſture en les boys avauntdyt a les avauntdyt Thomas John Thomas & Willyam & touz les aultres Bergeys de la Vylle de Chepyngſobb'i en countre touz gents garrauntera aquytera & defendera. En teſmonyaunce de ceſtes les p'tyes contrethaunchablement ount mys lour ſeals.

The townſmen's privileges were diſputed by the lord of the manor of Little Sodbury, in the reign of king Edward the Sixth, and both parties appealing to the council of the Marches, the following order was made to ſettle the right, *viz.*

Apud Chipping Sodbury decimo die Septembris anno Regni Regis Edwardi Sexti, ſexto.

WHEREAS great controverſie and debate before this time hath riſen and been depending between John Wirrett the younger, bailiff of Chipping Sodbury, Richard Norris, and Thomas Smith, and all other the burgeſſes and inhabitants of the town of Chipping Sodbury, within the ſaid county of Glouceſter, complainants, and Maurice Welch of Little Sodbury within the county of Glouceſter aforeſaid Eſq; and other his tenants and inhabitants of Old Sodbury, within the ſaid county of Glouceſter, of, for, and concerning certain common which the ſaid burgeſſes and inhabitants of Chipping Sodbury aforeſaid pretend and claim to have in certain parcels of ground now incloſed, called the Nokes and Hangers, and in a certain paſture called the Leyes, and in another parcel of ground called the Kinley, and of and in certain parcels of ground called the Meadows and Marſhes, which ſaid parcels of ground be the inheritance of the ſaid Maurice Welſh, and be parcels of the manor of Old Sodbury aforeſaid. Whereupon the ſaid bailiff and burgeſſes before this time have made their complaint to the lord reſident and others the king's majeſty's council in the marches of Wales: Whereupon the ſaid Maurice Welſh and other defendants made their anſwers, and ſo the ſaid parties deſcended to an iſſue concerning the premiſſes. By their books of record remaining before the ſaid council, it doth appear, for the trial whereof divers witneſſes have been produced by the ſaid parties before the ſaid council and there examined, whoſe ſayings and depoſitions in that behalf do likewiſe remain before the ſaid council of record; which matter being well weighed and conſidered by the ſame council, the ſaid lord preſident and council, by the mutual aſſent of the ſaid parties, directed the king's majeſties letters hereunto annexed, dated the 10th day of July, in the ſixth year of our ſovereign lord's reign king Edward the Sixth, to ſir Walter Dennis, knight, David Brook, the king's ſerjeant at law, ſending them the ſaid books, together with the ſaid letters, giving them authority by the ſame letters to call the ſaid parties before them, and thereupon to conſider the whole matter with the circumſtances thereof, and to make ſome final end between the ſaid parties concerning the premiſſes: By virtue whereof, we the ſaid ſir Walter Dennis, knight, and David Brook, calling before the ſaid parties, have, by good advice, peruſed the contents of the ſaid books, and deliberately heard the alligations of the ſaid parties, and thereupon conſidered the ſame, earneſtly travailing therein, Have and do, by their mutual aſſent, conſent and agreement of the ſaid Maurice Welſh, and the ſame bailiff and burgeſſes, and by virtue of the ſaid letters to us directed, and for the avoiding of further ſuit and trouble that otherwiſe might enſue, grow and ariſe between the ſaid parties concerning the ſaid premiſſes, do make this our preſent order, final and determinate end, in manner and form following, that is to ſay: We order and decree by the authority aforeſaid, and by the aſſent and full agreement of the ſaid Maurice Welſh, that the ſaid burgeſſes and inhabitants that now be, or hereafter ſhall be, of the town of Chipping Sodbury aforeſaid, ſhall from henceforth have, uſe and enjoy common for their cattle in the ſaid waſte ground called Horwood, in all places of the ſame waſte, ſit, lying and being without the hedge of the ground called Little Sodbury Park, and lately diſparked, and in the way or lane leading unto the Yate that divideth and incloſeth the ſaid waſte ground from the common meadow of Old Sodbury aforeſaid, in like manner and form as they have had and uſed the ſame in times paſt, and ſhall likewiſe uſe, and enjoy, have common for their cattle in the ſaid ground called Kinggroves wood, and likewiſe upon the conſideration hereafter expreſſed, it is further ordered by the aſſents aforeſaid, that the ſaid burgeſſes and inhabitants which now be, or hereafter ſhall be, of the town of Chipping Sodbury aforeſaid, ſhall have their common in one parcel of ground called the Gaunt's field, in Old Sodbury aforeſaid, as they have at this preſent time, or have uſed or had moſt uſually within the ſpace of xxth years next before the date hereof: Further it is ordered and decreed by the ſaid ſir Walter Dennis, knight, and David Brook, Eſq; that the ſaid burgeſſes that now be, or hereafter ſhall be, in the ſaid town of Chipping Sodbury, ſhall not at any time hereafter claim, have, or uſe any common for their beaſts or cattle in any lands ſeveral or waſte ground, commonly called the Hangers, the Nokes, the Kinly, the Leys, the Marſhes, the Meadows, or elſewhere, ſet, lying and being in the eaſt part or eaſtward from the ſaid waſte ground called Horwood, and from the eaſt part and eaſtward from the ſaid ground called Kinggrove wood, nor eaſtward from the Yate before reherſed. And foraſmuch as on the examination of the matter concerning the premiſſes, it appeared to us the ſaid ſir Walter Dennis and David Brook, that before this time there were certain grounds incloſed in the Meadows and Marſhes aforeſaid, by the aſſents of the copyholders aforeſaid, which ſeverally and particularly were limitted and appointed to the copyholders hereafter mentioned, which grounds do at this preſent remain ſtill incloſed, and are occupied in ſeveral by the ſame copyholders, whereof there was very little in quantity appointed and limitted to any cottager, cottageholder, or half yard-land within Old Sodbury aforeſaid, by reaſon whereof the ſame cottages were impaired by loſs of ſuch common as they pretended to have in the meadows and marſhes aforeſaid, and the ſaid copyholders thereby much bettered and amended; it is therefore ordered by the authority aforeſaid, and by the aſſent of the ſaid Maurice Welſh, and alſo his aſſent for his tenants as much as in him lieth, or may do, that the copyholders of the ſaid manor of Old Sodbury hereafter named, and all ſuch as hereafter ſhall have and hold ſuch copyhold lands as they now have, ſhall not at any time after the feaſt of St. Michael the Archangel, which ſhall be in the year of our lord God MDLiij uſe, have, or enjoy any common for any manner of cattle in the ſaid waſte ground called Horwood, and that the cottagers of the manor of Old Sodbury which now be, or hereafter ſhall be, dwelling in the cottages or half yard-lands where they now dwell, ſhall have reaſonable common after the rate of their cottages or half yard-land in the waſte ground called Horwood, any thing before expreſſed to the contrary notwithſtanding. And furthermore, for a furthur quietneſs to be had between the ſaid parties, it is ordered by their aſſents, and the aſſent of the aforeſaid Maurice Welſh, that the ſaid bailiffs and burgeſſes of Chipping Sodbury aforeſaid, for the time being, ſhall yearly chuſe a Hayward from time to time,

Henry the Third, becauſe John Biſhop, who was grandſon to Jurdan Biſhop, was ſeized of Little Sodbury as early as 9 E. 1.

The earl of Albemarle was ſeized of Sodbury, with fairs and markets, 10 H. 3.

William de Weyland was afterwards ſeized of this manor, with which Marcella, his wife, was endowed. She ſurviving him, was married to John de Bradeſton; and Thomas de Weyland, ſon of William, acknowledged their right by a fine levied 4 E. 1. But Thomas de Weyland had been poſſeſſed of this eſtate before that time, which he held jointly with Margery his wife, and had markets and fairs, court leet and gallows granted to him 55 H. 3. and was ſeized thereof 8 E. 1. and pleading his right in a writ of *Quo warranto*, his claim was allowed in the fifteenth year of the laſt-mentioned reign.

Sir Edward Burnell died ſeized of this manor, and Elianor his widow was endowed with it, and with the borough, of which ſhe died ſeized 37 E. 3. Edward Burnell, ſon and heir of ſir Edward, had livery of the town, and of two fairs, the ſame year.

Hugh le Diſpencer, and Elizabeth his wife, levied a fine of the manor of Sodbury, to the uſe of themſelves in fee, 38 E. 3. and Edward lord Diſpencer, and Elizabeth his wife, daughter and heir of Bartholomew Burghurſt, held it, and died ſeized thereof, and of the borough of Chipping Sodbury, 49 E. 3.

It paſſed ſoon afterwards into the family of the Stanſhaws. Elizabeth Stanſhaw was ſeized of the manor of Chipping Sodbury 13 H. 4. as was John Stanſhaw, at the time of his death, 37 H. 6. He was ſucceeded in this eſtate by his ſon, Robert Stanſhaw, who died ſeized of it 12 E. 4.

The manor paſſed to the Walſhes in the time of king Henry the Seventh, and was ſold out of that family, in the reign of king James the Firſt, to Thomas Stephens, eſq; attorney-general to prince Henry and prince Charles. Winchcombe-Henry Hartley, eſq; one of the knights of the ſhire for the county of Berks, is the preſent lord of the manor, of whoſe family and arms, ſome account may be ſeen under Little Sodbury.

John Cotherington, and Alice his wife, levied a fine of lands in Chipping Sodbury, to the uſe of themſelves for life, the remainder to Humphry, John, and Thomas, their ſons, ſucceſſively, in taille; the remainder to Margaret Baſiles, late wife of ſir Peter Baſiles, in taille; the remainder to the king, 49 H. 6. which was the year when that king, for a ſhort time, recovered the crown. Richard Forſter, and John Moor and his wife, levied a fine of lands in Chipping Sodbury, to the uſe of John Walſh, 1 & 6 H. 7. John Stanſhaw, and Humphry his brother, levied a fine of lands in Chipping Sodbury, to William Fream, and others, 12 H. 7.

A gild was founded in this borough, and dedicated to St. Mary, in the reign of king Henry the Sixth, of which John Glover was the laſt incumbent, and received a penſion of 4*l.* a year, in 1553. The lands belonging to this gild were granted to Miles Patrick 2 E. 6. who granted them, the ſame year, to Richard Pate, who alſo granted them, 5 Mar. to the burghers of Sodbury, part for a town-hall, and part for an almſhouſe. An information was brought in the court of exchequer 14 Eliz. for lands in Sodbury, called Town-lands, formerly belonging to the diſſolved gild, which information was diſmiſſed upon a full hearing.

time, which ſhall have full power and authority to take and impound all ſuch cattle which ſhall be taken in or upon Horwood and King grove aforeſaid, of all ſuch perſons which have not common there, and the ſame to impound in the lord's pound at Old Sodbury appointed for the ſame, and to have yearly half the profits of the pound to be taken for the ſame for his labour and travel in that behalf: And for a final concluſion and peace to be had and concluded concerning the premiſſes, at the requeſt and deſire of the ſaid parties, the ſaid ſir Walter Dennis, knight, and David Brook, the king's ſerjeant at law, humbly deſireth this honourable council, that they will by their honourable order, affirme and confirme all theſe former orders contained herein, that to the intent that the ſame may remain of record, and alſo the ſame and every part thereof wherein they ſhall diſlike to add, diminiſh, or more plainly declare according to the true meaning of the ſaid parties before rehearſed, adding thereto if it may ſtand their pleaſures that if any ambiguities, doubt, or doubts ſhall happen hereafter to ariſe in any order or branch concerning the premiſſes, or any part thereof, that then the ſame ambiguities, doubt, or queſtions ſhall by a commandment out of this honourable court be expounded, judged, and ordered by the ſaid ſir Walter Dennis and David Brook; and on lack thereof, the parties to be called into this honourable court, to abide ſuch further order therein as to juſtice ſhall appertain, and as to them ſhall ſeem good in that behalf. In witneſs whereof to this our preſent order filed unto this book, and ſent unto this honourable council, we the ſaid ſir Walter Dennis, knight, and David Brook, the king's ſerjeant at law, have ſeverally put to our ſeals, and ſubſcribed our names to this our order, made the xth day of September, in the ſaid ſixth year of the reign of our ſaid ſovereign lord Edward the Sixth, by the grace of God, of England France and Ireland king, defender of the faith, and in earth of this church of England, and alſo of Ireland the ſupream head.

The Names of the Copyholders of the Manor of Old Sodbury, for Term of their Lives, who have their Common in Horwood within the County of Glouceſter.

John Woodward holdeth a meſſuage, with a yard land, with his appurtenances.

John Saunders holdeth a meſſuage, a yard land, with his appurtenances.

John Alridge holdeth a meſſuage, a yard land, with his appurtenances.

Maurice Alridge holdeth a meſſuage, a yard land, with his appurtenances.

Thomas Hopkins holdeth a meſſuage, a yard land, with his appurtenances.

Richard Francombe holdeth a meſſuage, a yard land, with his appurtenances.

John Coxe holdeth a meſſuage, a yard land, with his appurtenances.

The Names of the Cottagers of the Manor of Old Sodbury, which are appointed to have Common upon King Grove and Horwood, according to the Rate of their Cottages.

John Biſhop holdeth two cottages.
Thomas Tilly one cottage.
Willm. Dark one cottage.
John Martin one cottage.
W^m^. Francombe one cottage.
Henry Saunders one cottage.
John Jervice one cottage.
Willm. Balle one cottage.
Willm. Colls one cottage.
John Hill one cottage.
Thomas Anſtee one cottage.
John Adams one cottage.
Francis Codrington one cottage
Will: Whiting one cottage.
Robert Barrow one cottage.
John Yeoman one cottage.
Nicholas Wickſon one cottage.
Robt. Hopkins one cottage.
John Adams one cottage.

Walter Dennis.
Per me David Brook.

hearing. The lands belonging to this gild were again granted to William Herick and Arthur Ingram, 5 Jac. and another information was brought in the exchequer 32 C. 2. ſuppoſing them to have belonged to the monaſtery of Bradenſtoke, but that was likewiſe diſmiſſed.

Of the Church, &c.

The church is a chapel of eaſe to Old Sodbury.

The church conſiſts of the nave and two ailes, of the ſame length with the body, and a large gallery. It is handſome, but not uniformly pewed. The tower, which ſtands at the weſt end, is ornamented with pinnacles and battlements, and has in it a clock and chimes, and ſix muſical bells. There was a chantry in this church, called Borler's chantry, of which William Williams was the laſt incumbent, and received a penſion of 6*l.* in the year 1553. *Willis.*

In a window in the north aile, is the figure of St. George vanquiſhing the dragon.

Firſt fruits £.	14	5	10	Synodals £.	0	2	0
Tenths —	1	8	7	Pentecoſt.	0	1	0
Procurations	0	6	8				

Monuments and Inſcriptions.

There is an antient tomb, without inſcription, at the end of the north aile. It belongs to the Walſhes, as appears by their arms thereon, *viz. Azure, five mullets in ſaltire Or.*

In the ſame part of the church, are ſeveral memorials on braſs plates, for the family of the Burcombes, of which the following is the moſt obſervable:

Here lyeth the Body of ANNE the Wife of SAMUEL BURCOMBE, who departed this life the 27th of Auguſt 1703 Aged 64 Years.

Farewell, vain World, What Good in thee is found,
Where Sickneſs, Sorrow, Sinne and Shame abound?
Where tedious Paines, and anxious Troubles dwell,
And Cares and Fears perplex: Vain World farewell.

Upon the table of a white marble monument, fixed to a pillar in the chancel, is this inſcription:

Juxta hoc Marmor Sepultum eſt
Quicquid Mori potuit
Petri Hardwicke M. D.
Oxonienſis;
Qui in Civitate Briſtolienſi, et Viciniâ,
Felici Medendi Uſu inclaruit:
Quem Eruditio conſummata, Ingenijq; Acumen,
Inter Vicinos abunde diſtinxere:
Pietas autem, Morum Comitas,
Vitæq; Integritas,
Iiſdem reddidere chariſſimum.
Quum aliorum Saluti non datum ſit
Amplius invigilare;
Fractum Laboribus indefeſſis,
Nervisq; Paralyſi ſolutis;
Spei Æternitatis in Chriſto plenum
Mors ad eam Evocavit,
Imo die Sept. Anno Dom. MDCCXLVII.
Ætat. ſuæ LXIV.
Juxta etiam depoſitæ ſunt Exuviæ
Mariæ Uxoris dilectiſſimæ,
Henrici Smith in Agro Derbienſi, Armigeri,
Filiæ natu minoris:
Quæ Febre Puerperali confecta
Ineluctabili fato ſuccubuit,
4to die Martij MDCCXV
Ætat. ſuæ XXII.
Defuncti Executorum impenſis Monumentum hoc fuit erectum.

At the top of the monument are theſe arms: *Argent, a ſaltire ingrailed azure. On a chief of the ſecond three roſes of the firſt*, for Hardwicke. On a ſcutcheon of pretence, *Per chevron azure and Or, three eſcallops counterchanged*, for Smith.

On a well executed monument in the chancel, it is thus inſcribed:

Sacred to the Memory of GEORGE HARDWICKE Son of GEORGE and ANN HARDWICKE of this Borough, A Youth of the gentleſt Manners and moſt untainted Morals. He died juſtly lamented by all who knew him, on March the 3d 1770, in the 19th Year of his Age, and is interr'd in a Vault near this Marble. His Life a Source of Happineſs to his Parents, his Death, they truſt, the Commencement of his own.

GEORGE, WILLIAM and ELIZABETH, who died Infants, Children of the above GEORGE and ANN HARDWICKE, are buried in this chancel.

Alſo GEORGE and AGNES HARDWICKE, formerly of this Borough, Grandfather and Grandmother to the above Children.

The ſcutcheon upon this monument is, *parted per pale, baron and femme*, 1. Hardwicke as before. 2. *Ermine, a bend gules.*

On a flat ſtone,

In Memory of Joſeph Hardwicke, Eſq; late of Tytherington in this County, who died the 12 day of Octr 1771 Aged 78 Years. And likewiſe of Sarah his Wife, aged 50 Years.

The following is written on a large marble table fixed to the north wall:

In Memory
of JAMES BUSH late of the City of BRISTOL, Apothecary,
ELIZABETH his Wife,
and four of their Children
ANNE, WILLIAM, ANNE, and ELIANOR.
Alſo
of GEORGE BUSH, late of the ſaid City, Apothecary;
the laſt ſurviving iſſue of the above named JAMES and ELIZABETH:
Who, formed by the dictates of a religious Education,
to the conſtant exerciſe of Piety and Virtue;
ſupported the frequent attacks of an oppreſſive Diſorder,
with entire acquieſcence in the ſupreme will;
and firm aſſurance of a better ſucceſſion.
At length exempted from ſufferings,
He arrived at the period of his labors,
on the 30th day of July
in the year of our Lord 1760:
And the fiftieth of his Age.

On a braſs plate in the ſouth aile:

To the Memory of Elizabeth, late Wife of George Oldfield, Gent. and Daughter of Robert Haviland of the Citie of Briſtol Mercht. who departed the 4th of Oct. Ano Domi. 1642, being aged 26.

Here is the wardrobe of my duſty clothes,
Which hands divine ſhall bruſh, & make ſoe gay
That my immortal ſoule ſhall put them on,
And weare the ſame vpon my weddinge day,
In which attire my Lord ſhall me convoy,
Then to the lodginge of eternal joy.

Benefactions.

There are certain lands lying in the pariſhes of Chipping Sodbury, Old Sodbury, and Wickwar, the rents of which amount, at preſent, to above 100*l. per ann.* which are ſettled by a decree in chancery 30 Car. 2. to the following uſes; *viz.* 20*l.* yearly to be paid to the maſter of the free ſchool; 20*l.* yearly to apprentice out poor children with 4*l.* each. 4*l.* yearly to be laid out on the roads of the pariſh; and 20*l.* to be given annually to ſuch perſons of this pariſh, of good name, as do not receive alms; and, according to ſir Robert Atkyns, 10*l.* to the repair of the church.

Beſide the above proviſion for the maintenance of the free gramar ſchool, Mr. Robert Davis of Little Sodbury, who died May 16, 1680, added 10*l.* yearly to the ſchool-maſter's ſalary, and there have lately been ſome donations from doctor Hardwicke,

wicke, and Mr. Samuel Hardwicke, late of the city of Briſtol, but natives of this place, towards providing a houſe for the maſter.

Mr. Oldfield of Briſtol gave 20*l.* to the uſe of the poor.

Mrs. Martha White, by her deed, dated July 19, 1731, gave 200*l.* for the uſe of the poor of Chipping Sodbury and Yate, to be applied diſcretionally by her truſtees.

Mr. Daniel Woodward of London, who was a native of this place, by his will, dated Mar. 30, 1771, gave 50*l.* to the uſe of the workhouſe. And lately, Mr. Richard Blake of Briſtol, but originally of this place, gave 50*l.* the intereſt of which to be diſtributed annually in bread to the poor.

Taxes.					
The Royal Aid in	1692,	£. 62	8	0
Poll-tax — —	1694, —	59	6	0
Land-tax ——	1694, —	130	6	0
The ſame, at 3*s.*	1770, —	62	15	10½

At the beginning of this century, there were 140 houſes, and about 650 inhabitants in this pariſh, whereof 30 were freeholders; yearly births 18, burials 16. *Atkyns.* The inhabitants are now about 800.

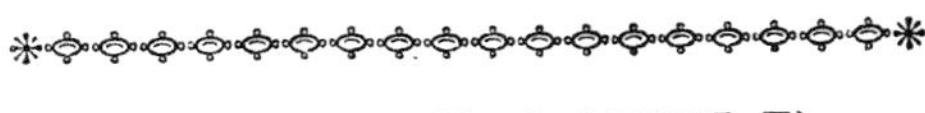

SODBURY (LITTLE)

IS a ſmall pariſh, in the hundred of Grumbald's Aſh, one mile diſtant eaſtward from Chipping Sodbury, ſix north-weſtward from Marſhfield, and about twenty-nine ſouth from Glouceſter.

A ſmall part of the pariſh lies in the hill country, on the borders of which, on the brow of the hill, is a very ſtrong camp, of an oblong form, ſtill remaining as perfect as when originally made. It has a double *agger*, thrown up very high, except on the weſt ſide, where it overlooks the vale, and there it is ſingle, becauſe the hill is ſo ſteep, that the camp was thought inacceſſible from that quarter. It is about three hundred and twenty yards long, as I found by pacing it, and two hundred broad. The interval, or ditch, between the *aggera*, is twenty-two yards wide, and the way into it is towards the eaſt. Some think it a Daniſh camp, others will have it to be Roman, forming their opinions merely from the conſtruction of it, as it is no where taken notice of in hiſtory, and no coins, or other things, have been found in or near it, to determine the point: But this we know, from Leland, that king Edward the Fourth's army occupied it a little before the battle of Tewkeſbury.

Juſt below this camp, on the ſide of the hill fronting weſtward, ſtands the manor houſe, an antient building, formerly the ſeat of the Stephens's, a very reſpectable family, that has been long reſident in this county. It is now the property of Winchcombe-Henry Hartley, eſq; who is deſcended, on his mother's ſide, from that family. From this houſe, there is an extenſive proſpect over the vale, as far as the Briſtol channel; and four clumps of large trees, growing above it, are objects particularly obſervable, and taken notice of, through a large extent of country on that ſide the hills.

A dreadful thunder ſtorm fell on this ſeat in the year 1556, when Maurice Walſh, eſq; was lord of the manor. The lightning entered at the parlour door, and forced its way out at the window on the oppoſite ſide of the room, when Mr. Walſh and his family were at dinner. One of the children was killed on the ſpot, and ſix others, with the unfortunate father, were ſo much hurt, that they all died of the ſhock in leſs than two months afterwards.

The learned William Tyndale lived in this houſe with ſir John Walſh, as tutor to his children, about the time of king Henry the Eighth, where he tranſlated the New Teſtament into the Engliſh language, and wrote ſeveral books to promote the reformation, which drew a ſtorm upon his head, not leſs dreadful than that before-mentioned, tho' of a different nature. He fled from his perſecutors into the low Countries, but was purſued by the intemperate zeal which diſtinguiſhed thoſe times, and impriſoned in Filford caſtle in Flanders, under whoſe walls he was burnt for hereſy, in the year 1556.

Of the Manor and other Eſtates.

The particulars of this manor, taken from the antient ſurvey, are miſplaced by ſir Robert Atkyns to the pariſh of Old Sodbury. The following is a literal tranſlation from the original language of the record, with which the reader may compare it, as it ſtands in the 73d page of this book:

'Hugo Maminot holds Sopeberie in Grimboldeſtou hundred, of the ſame biſhop [of Liſiaux in Normandy]. Aluuard held it in the time of king Edward. There are five hides taxed, and two plow-tillages in demean, and four villeins, and two bordars, with two plow-tillages. There are four *ſervi*, and twenty acres of meadow, and a little wood. It was worth 8*l.* and is now worth 4*l.*'

Jurdan Biſhop held the manor of Little Sodbury in the reign of king Henry the Third, and granted common of paſture to the burghers of Chipping Sodbury, as particularly mentioned in the account of that place. He was cotemporary with William Craſſus, and was a witneſs to his confirmation of privileges to the town of Chipping Sodbury. The ſheriff returned, that John Byſhoppe was lord of Sudbury 9 E. 1. and he continued poſſeſſed of it in the 15th year of the ſame reign, when he defended the privileges of his manor, in the proceedings on a writ of *Quo warranto.*

This manor paſſed afterwards to the Diſpencers, who held it in the reigns of king Edward the Second and king Edward the Third.

Richard de Alerdine, and Edith his wife, levied a fine of it 11 R. 2. After whom it came to the Stanſhaws,

Stanſhaws, who continued poſſeſſed of it down to the reign of king Edward the Fourth.

Richard Forſter was ſeized of this manor in the beginning of the reign of king Henry the Seventh, and joined with Thomas Moor and his wife in levying a fine of the manor of Little Sodbury, and of the advowſon of the church of St. Adeline there, to John Walſh of Olveſton, who had married Elizabeth his daughter and heir; by virtue of which fine this manor paſſed into the family of the Walſhes, 1 H. 7.

Sir John Walſh, ſon and heir of John Walſh, married Anne, daughter of ſir Robert Pointz, and having ſerved the office of high ſheriff of Glouceſterſhire 18 & 27 H. 8. died ſeized of Little Sodbury in the 38th year of the ſame reign, leaving Maurice his ſon thirty years old, who had livery of the manor the ſame year, and married Bridget, daughter of —— Vauſe. Nicholas Walſh, was ſon of Maurice, and ſucceeded him in the manor of Little Sodbury. He was high ſheriff of this county 4 Eliz. and having married Mary, daughter of ſir John Berkeley, died in the 20th year of that reign. Henry Walſh, ſon and heir of Nicholas, had livery of the manor of Little Sodbury on the death of his father, and was killed by Edward Winter, in the reign of queen Elizabeth. Walter Walſh, couſin of Henry Walſh, and ſon of another Henry, who was a younger brother of Nicholas before-mentioned, was lord of the manors of Little Sodbury and Old Sodbury, in the reign of queen Elizabeth, and continued poſſeſſed of them in the year 1608.

The manors of Little Sodbury and Old Sodbury paſſed by purchaſe, from the heir of the Walſhes, to Thomas Stephens, eſq; third ſon of Edward Stephens of Eaſtington, in the reign of king James the Firſt. This Thomas Stephens was eminent in the profeſſion of the law, being attorney general to the princes Henry and Charles. By his wife Elizabeth, daughter and coheireſs of John Stone of London, he had three ſons, Edward, the eldeſt, who ſucceeded him in the manors of Sodbury; John, the ſecond, anceſtor of the Stephens's of Lypiat; and Nathaniel. Thomas Stephens died in the year 1613, and was ſucceeded in the manors of Sodbury by his eldeſt ſon Edward, who married Anne, the daughter of —— Crew, and ſerved the office of high ſheriff of this county 10 C. 1. Sir Thomas Stephens, ſon and heir of Edward, married Katherine, the daughter of —— Combs, and was high ſheriff of Glouceſterſhire in the years 1644 & 1671. He was ſucceeded by his ſon Thomas Stephens, eſq; who married Anne, the daughter of —— Neale.

From him the manor and eſtate deſcended to Edward Stephens, after whoſe death, in the year 1728, they came to Robert Packer, eſq; as heir at law, whoſe mother was a daughter of Richard Stephens of Eaſtington.

Robert Packer married Mary, one of the daughters and at length ſole heireſs of ſir Henry Winchcombe, of Bucklebury in the county of Berks, baronet, ſon of ſir Henry Winchcombe, baronet, by Frances, one of the daughters and coheireſſes of Thomas earl of Berkſhire, and had iſſue four ſons, Winchcombe-Howard, John, Robert, and Henry, who all died without iſſue; and one daughter, Elizabeth, ſecond wife to David Hartley, M.D. a perſon of great abilities, extenſive learning, and diſtinguiſhed eminence in his profeſſion. He was ſon of the reverend John Hartley, and was lord of this manor in right of his ſaid wife Elizabeth, by whom he had iſſue one ſon, Winchcombe-Henry, and one daughter, Mary.

His ſon, Winchcombe-Henry Hartley, eſq; is the preſent lord of this manor, and one of the knights of the ſhire for the county of Berks, where he has ſeveral eſtates, particularly Donnington and Bucklebury, at the latter of which he reſides. His arms are, *Argent, on a croſs azure, voided in the center, four cinquefoils Or, and in the firſt and fourth quarters a martlet ſable.* Crest, *A martlet ſable holding in its mouth a croſs croſlet fitchy of the third.*

The records ſhew, that John Smith held lands in Little Sodbury. John Smith was his ſon and heir, and dying ſeized of them 9 C. 1. left John his ſon nine years old.

Of the Church, &c.

The church is a rectory, in the deanery of Hawkeſbury, worth 100*l.* a year. Winchcombe-Henry Hartley, eſq; is patron, and the reverend Mr. Coats is the preſent incumbent.

The church is dedicated to St. Adeline. It is a low building, with an aile on the north-eaſt, belonging to the lord of the manor. There is no chancel, and the inhabitants bury at Old Sodbury, for which 10*s.* *per ann.* is paid to the miniſter.

	£.				£.		
Firſt fruits	7	0	0	Synodals	0	2	0
Tenths —	0	13	1	Pentecoſtals	0	0	5
Procurations	0	0	0				

Taxes.			£.		
The Royal Aid in	1692,		60	16	0
Poll-tax ——	1694,	—	23	0	0
Land-tax —	1694,	—	75	12	0
The ſame, at 3*s.*	1770,	—	55	17	9

At the beginning of this century, there were 24 houſes, and about 90 inhabitants in this pariſh, whereof 5 were freeholders; yearly births 2, burials 2. *Atkyns.* The preſent number of ſouls is 115.

SODBURY (OLD)

IS a pariſh in the hundred of Grumbald's Aſh, about one mile diſtant north-eaſt from Chipping Sodbury, ſix north-weſt from Marſhfield, and twenty-nine ſouth from Glouceſter.

One part of it ſtretches over that ridge or chain of hills that divides the Coteſwold country from the vale, and the other lies in the vale. It affords nothing obſervable in natural hiſtory or antiquities, except part of the camp deſcribed under

under Little Sodbury, which lies within its boundaries. The turnpike-road from Gloucefter to Bath runs through the parifh, and a fmall brook from hence empties itfelf into the Froom.

The etymology of the name is given under Chipping Sodbury, which was originally a part of this parifh, and is now intirely encompaffed by it; wherefore this was called Old Sodbury, with refpect to the former.

Of the Manor and other Eftates.

The particulars which *Domefday* gives of this manor, are totally omitted in fir Robert Atkyns's Hiftory, and part of thofe belonging to Little Sodbury are placed, by miftake, in their room. The following is a tranflation of the record:

'Brictric the fon of Algar held Sopeberie in 'Edereftan hundred. In the time of king Edward 'there were ten hides, and four plow-tillages in 'demean, and twelve villeins, with five plow-'tillages; and four bordars, and eighteen *fervi*, 'and one park, and a mill of 5*s*. [rent]. The 'fteward hath lately added one mill of 40 *den*. 'There is a wood one mile long, and one broad. 'Hunfrid pays for this manor 16*l*. 10*s*. One 'yard-land in Wiche belongs to it, which paid 'twenty-five fextaries of falt. Urfus the fheriff 'has fo oppreffed the men, that now they cannot 'pay the falt.' *Domefday*, p. 68.

This manor antiently belonged to the earls of Gloucefter and Hertford, and continued by defcent in that family, 'till the reign of king Henry the Seventh. During this long fucceffion, it paffed by female heirs into the great families of Difpencer and Beauchamp, and at laft ended in Anne, the great heirefs and fifter of Henry Beauchamp, duke of Warwick. She was married to Richard Nevil, generally called the Stout earl of Warwick, who being flain in Barnet field, fighting for the houfe of Lancafter, this Anne, his widow, became obnoxious to the fucceeding reigns: But upon the turn of affairs, by the fuccefs of king Henry the Seventh, that fubtle prince prevailed on her to fettle the greateft part of her vaft inheritance on him and his heirs, and accordingly fhe levied a fine to that purpofe 3 H. 7.

King Henry the Eighth gave the manor of Old Sodbury to fir John Walfh, who had been his champion, and it continued in the family of the Walfhes 'till it was purchafed, in the reign of king James the Firft, by Thomas Stephens, attorney general to prince Henry. From him it defcended, like Little Sodbury, down to Winchcombe-Henry Hartley, efq; who is the prefent lord of the manor.

Several other perfons were feized of lands in this parifh, as appears by records of the following dates. John de la Wild held lands in Sodbury 10 E. 3. Elizabeth Stanfhaw died feized of lands in Old Sodbury 13 H. 4. John Stanfhaw held lands in Old Sodbury 37 H. 6. which were held by Robert Stanfhaw, together with an eftate called Kengrove, 12 E. 4. John Stanfhaw, and Humphry his brother, levied a fine of lands in Old Sodbury to William Freem 12 H. 7.

The capital meffuage of Old Sodbury belonged to the college of Weftbury, and was granted to fir Ralph Sadleyr 35 H. 8.

Hamfteed, an eftate in this parifh, formerly belonged to the monaftery of Bradenftoke in Wiltfhire. It was granted, by the name of the manor, grange, or farm of Hampfteed, to Anne, widow of fir Adrian Fortefcue, for her life, and after to her fon, John Fortefcue, in fee, 4 & 5 Phil. & Mar. It was fold by that family to Edward Stephens, efq; 9 C. 1. Sir Thomas Stephens fold it to William Clutterbuck, in 1675; after which it was purchafed by —— Okey, from whofe family it paffed, by purchafe, to the truftees of Henry Woolnough, efq; and it is now the property of John-Hugh Smyth, of Long Afton in the county of Somerfet, efq; in right of Elizabeth his wife, fole daughter and heirefs of the faid Henry Woolnough. His arms are, *Gules, on a chevron between three cinquefoils argent, as many leopards faces fable.*

Lygrove is a confiderable eftate in this parifh, where was a good houfe, now in decay, and a park. John Cotherington, and Alice his wife, levied a fine of lands in Lygrove, to the ufe of themfelves for life, the remainder to Humphry, John, and Thomas, fucceffively in taille, the remainder to Margaret Bafile, late wife of fir Peter Bafile, in taille, 49 H. 6. Lygrove eftate is now the property of Mr. Hartley.

Of the Church, &c.

The church is a vicarage, in the deanery of Hawkefbury, worth about 300*l*. a year. The dean and chapter of Worcefter are patrons, and the reverend Mr. Duvall is the prefent incumbent. The chapel of Chipping Sodbury is annexed to it.

In the year 1218, the bifhop of Worcefter gave the rectory of Old Sodbury to the monaftery of Benedictine monks at Worcefter, founded originally by king Ethelred, for fecular canons; but Ofwald placed the Benedictines in it in the year 991. The advowfon, which had belonged to the fame monaftery, was granted to the chapter of Worcefter 33 H. 8. confirmed 6 Jac. and ftill continues in the fame.

The church has two crofs ailes, and a low tower at the weft end. It is dedicated to St. John the Baptift. It is the mother church to Chipping Sodbury, but yields the fuperiority in fize, beauty, and convenience to her rival daughter.

Firft fruits £.	14	5	10	Synodals £.	0	2	0
Tenths —	1	8	7	Pentecoftals	0	1	0
Procurations	0	6	8				

Monuments and Infcriptions.

In the north aile, which is the burying place of the Stephens's, under two niches, lie the effigies in ftone of two perfons, with their legs acrofs, after the manner of the knights templers, and fcutcheons on their arms, but the bearings are not

not diſtinguiſhable, and there is no tradition concerning them.

Againſt the north wall of the ſame aile, upon the table of a marble monument, it is thus written:

Here lyeth the Remains of
EDWARD STEPHENS of Little SODBURY, Eſq[r].
Who had all the Vertues that adorn
A Gentleman, a Magiſtrate and a Chriſtian;
In his Sincere Piety to GOD,
In his impartial Juſtice and Benevolence to Mankind,
In his Fidelity and Zeal for his Friend,
In an Inſtructive Converſation,
And a particular Happineſs of Addreſs,
Which never failed to gain him the Good will
Of all that approached him;
IN SHORT,
In every Religious, in every ſocial Virtue,
He was a Pattern equalled by few, Excelled by none.
He dyed the 6th Day of April, MDCCXXVIII,
In humble Hope of a Glorious Reſurrection,
Through HIM who is the Reſurrection,
And the Life.

Upon this monument are the following arms, *Baron and femme*. On the baron ſide, *Quarterly* 1ſt *and* 4th, *Per chevron azure and argent, in chief two falcons with wings elevated Or*, for Stephens; 2d, *Azure, a chevron argent between three lions paſſant Or*; 3d, obliterated. On the femme ſide, *Quarterly* 1ſt *and* 4th, *Argent, four bars azure, on a chief ſable a lion paſſant Or*, for Burthogg; 2d *and* 3d, *Argent, a croſs ingrailed gules*, for Trevill.

Upon a flat ſtone is this memorial:

Here are depoſited the Remains of Sarah Stephens, Widow of Edward Stephens, late of Little Sodbury, Eſq; One of the Daughters & Coheireſſes of Richard Burthogge of Totnes in y[e] County of Devon Eſq[r] & Grandaughter and Sole Heireſs of Andrew Trevill of Ethe in y[e] County of Cornwall Eſq[r]. For her religious Regard of her Duty toward God and Man, her Charity to y[e] Poor, her friendly Correſpondence with her Neighbours, her exact Order and Oeconomy in her way of life, She was Eminent. She Died y[e] 19th Day of February 1737 Aged above 70 Years, Full of good Works, the Remembrance whereof will remaine a more laſting Monument of her Virtues.

N. B. There are the ſame arms on Mrs. Stephens's ſtone, as upon her huſband's monument; and in this, the 3d quarter on the baron ſide is, *three greyhounds courant in pale*, but the colours are not expreſſed in the ſculpture.

Under the eaſt window, in the chancel:

The body of Edward Potter, Vicar, Aged 77 years, here interred the 10th day of Avgvſt Anno Dom. 1676.
Peccata deplorans, miſericordiam implorans, morior.
In terris Peregrinvs Eram, dum Corpore Vixi
Nunc Patriam viſo, terra aliena Vale.
Hæ ante obitvm ſvvm Per Seipſum Compoſitæ.

On a tablet againſt the eaſt wall:

The Body of William Sheen Bachelour of Arts and Miniſter of ye Goſpell at Old Sodbury in the County of Glouceſter 17 years & at Kingſwood in the County of Wilts 14 years, here interred ye 27th of November Anno Dom. 1676 Ætatis ſuæ 59.
In Obitum repentinum eius.
Ducit ad æternam te mors brevis, ut via, vitam,
Ut mors interitus non ſit, at introitus.
Sed luctantem animam Clotho imperioſa Coegit
Ad Cœlum, invitos traxit in aſtra pedes.

In the ſouth aile is the following:

In Memory of HENRY BEDFORD, A.M.
Rector of LITTLE SODBURY,
who died July 10, 1717, Æt: 49;
And of ELIZABETH his Wife,
who died Septr 8th 1701 Æt: 26:
Likewiſe of EDWARD their Son,
who died Octo[r] 25th 1732, Æt. 32;
And alſo of SAMUEL COLBORNE
of STROUD WATER, Gent.
who died Feby 11th 1767, Æt: 69.

Upon the above monument are theſe arms, *viz. Quarterly* 1ſt *and* 4th, *Gules, a chevron between three quatrefoils Or*; 2d, *Argent, a bear ſeiant ſable, muzzled, collar'd, and chain'd Or*; 3d, *Argent, on a chevron between three hunting horns ſtringed ſable, as many mullets Or.*

Taxes.			£.	s.	d.
The Royal Aid in	1692,		182	0	0
Poll-tax ——	1694,	—	25	3	0
Land-tax ——	1694,	—	192	12	6
The ſame, at 3*s*.	1770,	—	145	14	7½

At the beginning of the preſent century, there were 48 houſes in this pariſh, and about 200 inhabitants, whereof 16 were freeholders; yearly births 7, burials 6. *Atkyns*. And there are now about the ſame number of ſouls.

SOUTH HAMLETS.

THESE hamlets lie in the hundred of Dudſton and King's-barton, on the ſouth ſide of the city of Glouceſter; and being either extraparochial, or within ſome of the city pariſhes, are therefore jointly called the South Hamlets.

1. *Lanthony*, the ſcite of an antient priory of that name. The reader will ſee a large account of this hamlet placed among the pariſhes in alphabetical order, under the proper title of *Lanthony*.

2. *Sudmead*, ſo called from its lying ſouth from Glouceſter. It is extraparochial, and formerly belonged to the priory of Lanthony, and after the diſſolution of that houſe, was granted to Richard Andrews and Nicholas Temple 35 H. 8. but it belongs at preſent to ſeveral proprietors.

Lanthony and Sudmead.

Taxes.			£.	s.	d.
The Royal Aid in	1692,		63	9	4
Poll-tax —	1694,	—	4	16	0
Land-tax —	1694,	—	121	12	0
The ſame, at 3*s*.	1770,	—	91	4	0

3. *Tuffley*. This place lies in the pariſh of St. Mary de Load, in the city of Glouceſter, but in the hundred of Dudſton and King's-barton. It is a place of conſiderable extent, about two miles ſouth-eaſt from the city, conſiſting of rich meadow and paſture, and very good arable land. In the time of king Edward the Confeſſor, Tuffelege was held by the church of St. Peter at Glouceſter, as a member of the great manor of Bertune, of which the particulars from *Domeſday* are ſet down p. 206. It had been alienated from the church of Glouceſter, but was again recovered to them by Oſborn biſhop of Exeter, when Serlo was abbat, and king Henry the Second confirmed it to them by his charter. It continued in the abbey of Glouceſter 'till that houſe was diſſolved, and was then granted to the dean and chapter of Glouceſter, 33 H. 8. But the tithes of Tuffley, and a paſture called Sudgrove, late belonging to the abbey of Glouceſter, were granted to Arthur Porter 32 H. 8.

The Atkyns's were antiently tenants of the manor, and of a large eſtate in this place, where they had a good houſe and park, which they held for ſeveral generations, by leaſe under the dean and chapter. Colonel Richard Atkyns, the laſt of that name who was poſſeſſed of this eſtate, ſuffered much for his loyalty to king Charles the Firſt. He raiſed a troop of horſe at his own charge, and was afterwards ſequeſtered, and paid 140*l*. compoſition. He was ſon of Richard Atkyns, of Tuffley,

Tuffley, esq; who married Mary, the daughter of sir Edwin Sandys, and not the daughter of lord Sandys of the Vine, as sir Robert Atkyns represents it, for she was sister to colonel Henry Sandys, the father of that lord Sandys, as appears by a well authenticated pedigree of the Sandys family, communicated to me by William Bayntun, of Gray's Inn, esq; who married Catherine, eldest daughter of Windsor Sandys, lord of the manors of Miserden and Winston in this county.

Taxes.			£.	s.	d.
	The Royal Aid in	1692,	48	6	8
	Poll-tax ——	1694, —	8	14	8
	Land-tax ——	1694, —	88	8	0
	The same, at 3*s.*	1770, —	38	14	0

There are about 140 inhabitants in this hamlet.

4. *Wolstrop*, antiently written *Wolrichesthorp* and *Wolverstrop*. This place is extraparochial, and lies in the hundred of Dudston and King's-barton, about two miles from Gloucester, adjoining to the parish of Quedgley, and is bounded on the north-west by the river Severn. Robert de Pont de Larch held Wolrichesthorp 30 H. 3. and granted the same, with Lanwarrine, to William de Valencia, earl of Pembroke; and king Henry confirmed the grant in the 36th year of his reign. William le Walsh died seized of Wolverstrop 3 E. 3. which was held by Giles Walsh, of Richard lord Talbot and Anchoret his wife, by the eighth part of a knight's fee 20 R. 2. and it was held of Gilbert Talbot 7 H. 6. Here Thomas Hayward, esq; has a pleasant seat, and a large estate in this and other places. His arms are, *Argent, on a bend sable, three fleurs de lis Or, on a chief of the second a lion passant of the third.*

Taxes.			£.	s.	d.
	The Royal Aid in	1692,	18	0	0
	Poll-tax ——	1694, —	8	5	0
	Land-tax ——	1694, —	32	8	0
	The same, at 3*s.*	1770, —	24	6	0

5. *Littleworth*, or *Lower South-gate-street*, so called because it joins to the south gate at Gloucester. It is extraparochial, and lies in the hundred of Dudston and King's-barton. It contains about 100 inhabitants.

The land-tax at 3*s.* 1770, £. 6 4 6

SOUTHROP.

THIS parish lies in the hundred of Britwell's Barrow, eight miles distant south-east from Northleach, five south from Burford in Oxfordshire, and twenty-six east from Gloucester.

It consists chiefly of arable land, and the river Lech runs through it to Leachlade, where it empties itself into the Thames.

There are four manors described in *Domesday* by the name of Lecce, all lying on the river of the same name. Three of them are now called Northleach, Eastleach-Martin, and Eastleach-Turville; and this is the fourth, which, for distinction, obtained the name of *Southrop*, from its being situated more *southward* than the others; for *Southrop* signifies the *South Village*.

The air of this village is wholesome, and the soil, tho' light, produces good corn.

Of the Manor and other Estates.

The following are the particulars of this manor from the antient survey:

'Walter the son of Ponz holds Lece in Bricstuoldes hundred of the king. There are ten hides taxed. Earl Tofti held it. There are four plow-tillages in demean, and sixteen villeins, and six bordars, and a priest, with eight plow-tillages. There are twelve *servi*, and a mill of 10*s.* [rent] and twenty acres of meadow. It was worth 12*l.* and is now worth 15*l.*' *Domesday*, p. 77.

Robert Creping and Nicholaa his wife held the manor and advowson 31 H. 3. and Benedict Blakenham, and Joan his wife, levied a fine of the manor to the use of themselves 1 E. 1. which said Benedict obtained a licence to alienate two plow-tillages in Southrop to Henry de St. Philebert 26 E. 1.

John de St. Philebert, son of Henry, was seized of Southrop, with free warren, 10 E. 2. and died 7 E. 3.

Henry de Grey died seized of a manor in Southorpe 8 E. 2. which he had of John the kinsman and heir of Robert de Grey, and held it by the service of one fourth part of a knight's fee; and sir Ralph Grey, son of Henry, levied a fine of those lands 22 E. 3.

John de St. Philebert, son of John, levied a fine of Southrop to the king 27 & 31 E. 3. and the king granted the same (lately belonging to John de St. Philebert, as the grant expressly mentions) to William Herney and Mary his wife, and to the heirs males of their bodies, 50 E. 3. The same year, also, the king granted one plow-tillage in Southrop, held by John Short for life, to William Herney and Mary his wife, and to their heirs males. Mary the wife of William Herney survived him, and died seized of Philebert's Court, and Grey's Court, in Southrop, 7 H. 4.

Robert Leversedge died seized of this manor 4 E. 4. and it was granted by the king to Robert Horsely, for life, in the twelfth year of the same reign. The crown granted it, as part of the dutchy of Lancaster, to Peter Bradshaw, 3 Jac. and it was again granted to Robert earl of Salisbury 5 Jac. Sir Thomas Row was lord of this manor in the year 1608, which passed soon afterwards to Wadham college, in Oxford, to which it now belongs.

Of the Church, &c.

The church is a vicarage, in the deanery of Fairford, worth 100*l.* a year. It is in the presentation of Wadham college, and Mr. Baldwin is the present incumbent.

Alice de Clermont gave the church of Southrop to the knights hoſpitallers of St. John of Jeruſalem, in Clerkenwell, London, which grant was confirmed by Richard de Clare, earl of Hertford.

The church is ſmall, without any thing to diſtinguiſh it, except a monument in the ſouth aile for ſir Thomas Conway and his lady, with his arms, *viz. Sable, on a bend cotized argent, a roſe proper between two annulets*; but there is no inſcription. Sir Thomas had been lord of this manor.

Firſt fruits £. 4	4	0	Synodals £. 0	2	0
Tenths — 0	11	0	Pentecoſt. 0	0	10
Procurations 0	6	8			

Benefaction.

Mr. Thomas Buſh, late butler of Chriſt-church college, Oxford, gave 100 *l.* to the uſe of the poor of this pariſh.

Taxes.					
The Royal Aid in	1692,	£. 65	12	2
Poll-tax ——	1694, —	24	9	0
Land-tax ——	1694, —	58	8	0
The ſame, at 3 *s.*	1770, —	43	16	0

At the beginning of this century, there were 38 houſes, and about 170 inhabitants in this pariſh, whereof 8 were freeholders; yearly births 5, burials 4. *Atkyns.* There are now, by an exact ſurvey, 47 families, and 216 ſouls.

STANDISH.

THIS pariſh lies in the hundred of Whitſton, four miles diſtant north-weſtward from Stroud, eight north from Durſley, and ſeven ſouth from Glouceſter.

It conſiſts of rich paſture ground, with ſome arable and woodlands, and produces excellent cheeſe and good cyder.

Here was antiently a pretty large houſe, with ſeveral offices, belonging to the abbey of Glouceſter. It was called the Almery of Standiſh. Part of it ſtill remains, and particularly the arches of the gateway. An old building, which belonged to that houſe, ſtands intire on one ſide of the church-yard, ſtrongly ſecured by buttreſſes; and the farm houſe, cloſe by the church, ſeems to be a part of the old Almery, of which the reader, turning to p. 141 of this book, may ſee many particulars.

There is a ſpring in Standiſh park, called the Red Well, which moſt probably runs thro' a bed of iron ore, as it tinges the ſtones with a red ochry colour; and it incruſts ſticks, and other ſubſtances lying in the courſe of its waters, with a ſtony ſubſtance. Theſe waters may be beneficial in diſorders for which preparations of iron are preſcribed.

Of the Manor and other Eſtates.

Beornulph king of Mercia, in the year 821, gave fifteen hides in Standiſh under Ezinbury to the church of St. Peter at Glouceſter, which was then occupied by ſecular canons. Eldred archbiſhop of York afterwards became poſſeſſed of the manors of Stanedis, Otintune, and Lece, (now called Northleach,) as a ſecurity for the money he had expended in the repair of the monaſtery of Glouceſter, a little before the Norman invaſion; and Thomas archbiſhop of York held Stanedis at the time of the general ſurvey, as appears from a paſſage in *Domeſday*, of which the following is a literal tranſlation:

'Archbiſhop Eldred held Stanedis, in Witeſtan 'hundred. It was [part] of the demean of St. 'Peter of Glouuceceſtre. There were fifteen hides 'in the time of king Edward. There are three 'plow-tillages in demean, and nine villeins, and 'fourteen bordars, with ſixteen plow-tillages; 'and ſeven radecheniſters, having ſeventeen plow-'tillages. There are eight *ſervi*, and half a fiſhery; 'a wood half a mile long, and one furlong broad.

'In the time of king Edward the whole manor 'was worth 16 *l.* now [only] 12 *l.* Archbiſhop 'Thomas holds it, and it pays tax in the ſame 'manner.

'The abbat of Glouuec' holds two hides of the 'land of this manor, and he ought of right to 'hold them.

'Earl Hugh holds one hide unjuſtly. Durand 'the ſheriff holds three hides which earl William 'gave to Roger his brother. Archbiſhop Thomas 'claims them.' *Domeſday*, p. 70.

The before-mentioned Thomas archbiſhop of York reſtored this manor to the abbey of Glouceſter, about the year 1094-5, and that houſe continued poſſeſſed of it 'till the diſſolution of the monaſtery. But it had been held by meſne lords, as in the 7th of H. 8. when John Huntley was tenant under the abbey.

Edward duke of Somerſet had a grant of the manor 1 E. 6. and after his attainder, it was granted to ſir Anthony Cook, in the 6th year of the ſame reign.

Sir Henry Winſtone was lord of it in 1608. Sir Ralph Dutton, baronet, was ſeized of it at the beginning of this century; and from him it deſcended to his great grandſon, James Dutton, eſq; who is the preſent lord of the manor. His pedigree and arms are given under Sherbourn, the place of his reſidence.

TITHINGS and HAMLETS.

1. *Colthrop*, or *Coldrup*, which is ſeparated from the reſt of the pariſh by the intervention of part of Haresfield. Thomas Crook held Coldthrop 10 E. 3. Charles Yate, eſq; was proprietor of it, and had a good ſeat here, about the beginning of this century. He was the youngeſt ſon of William Yate, eſq; and married, to his ſecond wife, Elizabeth, eldeſt daughter of Richard Yate of Arlingham, and dying in the year 1721, left iſſue, by his ſaid wife, ſix daughters coheireſſes. Elizabeth, the eldeſt, and Sophia, the fourth daughter,

 died

died unmarried:—Dorothy, the ſecond, was married to Powell Snell, of Guiting Grange in this county, eſq; by whom ſhe had three ſons, Powell, John, and Charles; and one daughter, Dorothy:—Anna-Maria, the third daughter, was married to Edmund Eſtcourt, of Shipton Moign, eſq; whoſe only child, Anna-Maria, was wedded to William Earle, late of Malmeſbury in the county of Wilts, whom ſhe ſurvived, and died in the year 1775:—Caroline, the fifth daughter, was married, firſt to Jacob Elton, ſon of ſir Abraham Elton, baronet; and ſecondly, to John Aſpinel, eſq; ſergeant at law, but died without iſſue by either:—Henrietta, the youngeſt, was the wife of Mr. Richard Warren, of Briſtol, by whom ſhe had one daughter. Charles Snell, third ſon of Powell Snell, eſq; and Dorothy his wife, ſold this eſtate to Mr. Samuel Niblet, of the city of Glouceſter, who is the preſent proprietor of it. Colthrop, and part of Hardwick make one tithing.

Livery of a cloſe in Coldrup was granted to John Bound 4 Eliz.

2. *Putloe.* Livery of this manor was granted to ſir John Lutterel 1 Eliz. It is now the property of James Dutton, eſq.

3. *Standiſh Morton.* 4. *Little Hareſfield.* 5. *Oxlinch*; all which belong to Mr. Dutton. Lands in Nether Oxlinch belonged to the abbey of Tewkeſbury, and were granted to Edward duke of Somerſet 1 E. 6.

6. Part of *Pitchcombe*, which is intirely ſeparated from the main body of the pariſh, by the interpoſition of Randwick. This eſtate belonged to John Bridgman, of Prinknaſh, at the beginning of the preſent century, and is now veſted, by purchaſe, in Mr. Page, of Painſwick in this county.

Of the Church, &c.

The church is a vicarage, in the deanery of Glouceſter, worth about 230*l.* a year, and in the patronage of the biſhop of Glouceſter.

The church, dedicated to St. Nicholas, is ſmall, but neatly pewed with Dutch oak, and has a handſome ſpire at the weſt end.

Firſt fruits £. 44	2	$8\frac{1}{2}$	Synodals £.	
Tenths — 4	8	$3\frac{1}{4}$	Pentecoſt.	
Procurations				

Monuments and Inſcriptions.

There is an old monument for ſir Henry Winſtone, but the inſcription and arms are covered with white waſh.

Upon a flat ſtone, within the rails incloſing the communion table, is this inſcription, exactly taken.

Robertus Frampton
Epiſcopus Glouceſtrienſis,
(Cætera quis neſcit?)
Ob. 8 Calend: Junij,
Ætatis ſuæ 86
Anno Conſecrationis 28
Æræ Chriſtianæ 1708.

On the upper part of the ſtone are the arms of his dioceſe, impaling *Gules, three bars argent, in chief three creſcents Or,* for Frampton.

Againſt the ſouth wall of the chancel, there is a marble monument, with this inſcription:

Near this place lies interred the Body of Charles Yate, late of Colthrope in this County, Eſq. He was the youngeſt Son of William Yate, Eſq; & died the Day of May, 1721, Aged 79 Years.

He married two Wives, y[e] firſt was Elizabeth, the only Daughter of Iohn Scote, Doctor in Divinity, by whom he had one Daughter Mary. And his ſecond was Elizabeth, eldeſt Daughter of Richard Yate, late of Arlingham in this County, Eſq; his now Widow & Relict, by whom he left ſix Daughters, viz. Elizabeth, Dorothy, Anna-Maria, Sophia, Carolina, & Henrietta.

Elizabeth Yate, Relict of the above Charles Yate, died July 17th 1759, Aged 76. Elizabeth their eldeſt Daughter died June 7th 1756, Aged 49.

Arms at top, *Baron and femme*, Yate impaling Yate.

Putloe.

Land-tax at 3*s.* 1770, £. 41 0 6

Oxlinch.

Land-tax at 3*s.* 1770, £. 142 1 $4\frac{1}{2}$

About the beginning of the preſent century, there were 123 houſes in the pariſh, and about 500 inhabitants, of whom 14 were freeholders; yearly births 16, burials 15. *Atkyns.* Here the ſmall farms have been joined together, and the cottages ſuffered to fall down, which has obliged the poorer ſort of people to remove to other places, and reduced the number of inhabitants to about 400.

STANLEY, *or* KING's STANLEY.

THIS pariſh lies in the hundred of Whitſton, three miles diſtant ſouth-weſtward from Stroud, ſeven north-eaſtward from Durſley, and ten ſouth from Glouceſter.

Sir Robert Atkyns was of opinion, that *Stanley* is derived from the Saxon Stan, *a ſtone*, and leag, *a paſture ground*, as though it were a ſtony ſoil; but the pariſh in general conſiſts of ſtrong, deep land, not at all conſiſtent with that explanation. It is probable, that in the time of the Saxons, the capital manſion-houſe being of ſtone, (a thing not then very common in the vale country) gave name to the pariſh; for Leag ſignifies *a place*, and Stanleag, the *Stone-place*, i.e. *the houſe*; as we ſometimes ſay the manor place for the manor houſe. And I am the rather of this opinion, ſince other villages and towns derive their names from the ſame thing. Thus Stanley, and Stonehouſe, the name of an adjoining village, tho' different in ſound, have a like ſignification; and both are ſimilar to *Bodmin*, Britiſh, the name of a town in Cornwall.

This is ſuppoſed to have been the reſidence of one of the Mercian kings, wherefore it was called *King's Stanley*, to diſtinguiſh it from the pariſh of Leonard Stanley, next adjoining.

Part of the village is called the *Borough*, for which two bailiffs are annually choſen, who execute the office of conſtable within its precincts. In it, ſtands a building which the inhabitants ſay was once a jail, and a piece of ground, now belonging

longing to the rectory, is called *Hanging Close*, where it is ſaid criminals were formerly executed. Theſe are as ſo many ſhadows of particular privileges, which I ſuppoſe the place antiently enjoy'd when it was a borough, and of greater conſequence than at preſent, for ſo it appears to have been by the names of Pig-ſtreet, High-ſtreet, &c. mentioned in old writings.

The poor people are chiefly employ'd in the clothing buſineſs, which is the general manufacture of this part of the county.

Here are two meadows, called Selſley-meadow, and Stanley-meadow, each containing about fifty acres, which after the hay is taken off, are common to all the inhabitants.

Of the Manor and other Eſtates.

The manor was given to Walter Deſpencer by king Henry the Second, to whom he was [d]uſher of the chamber. This Walter was [d]eldeſt ſon of Thurſtan le Deſpencer, the ſon of William le Deſpencer, who were both of them [d]ſtewards to king Henry the Firſt; and Robert Deſpencer, father of William, bore the ſame office under king William the Conqueror, with whom he came into England, and received the name of [e]Deſpencer, *i.e.* ſteward, from his employment. Walter died without iſſue, and was ſucceeded by his ſecond brother, Almerick le Deſpencer,[f] who was ſheriff of Rutlandſhire 34 H. 2. & 1 R. 1. and being ſteward to the latter, enjoyed, of his gift, the manor of King's Stanley. And in the 5th year of the reign of king John, he had a confirmation in fee of the lordſhips of Wurdie and Stanley in the vale of Glouceſter; which lordſhip of Wurdie king Henry the Second had formerly given to Walter, brother of Almerick, for his homage and ſervice, paying for the ſame a pair of gilt ſpurs, or 12*d.* yearly into the exchequer, on the feaſt of St. Michael the archangel, and to be held by the ſervice of half a knight's fee. He married Amabel, daughter of Walter de Cheſnei, or Chenei, by whom he had iſſue three ſons, Thurſtan, Almerick, and Philip.

Almerick le Deſpencer, the ſecond ſon, enjoyed the manor of Stanley, but joining with his brother Thurſtan, and other barons, in taking up arms againſt king John, his lands were ſeized, and granted by that king to Oſbert Giffard, his own natural ſon[g].

Sir Robert Atkyns ſays that this Almerick le Deſpencer was ſeized of King's Stanley, and had a grant of free warren, fairs, and markets 53 H. 3. which he pleaded in the proceedings on a writ of *Quo warranto* 15 E. 1. and died in the 34th year of the ſame reign; and that Almeric, ſon of the laſt Almerick, was ſeized of two yard-lands, and of eight acres in this place 4 E. 2. But it appears by a liſt of all the vills in the county, and their reſpective lords, which was returned into the exchequer by Walter de Stukely the ſheriff 9 E. 1. that John Gifford was then ſeized of the vill of Stanſley Regis, in the hundred of Wyſton. He married Maud, the widow of William Longeſpee, and died 27 E. 1.

John Giffard of Brimpsfield, ſon of John and Maud his wife, was ſeized of the manor of King's Stanley, of the advowſon of the church, and of Walliſwood 6 E. 2.

Stephen Mareſchall held the manor, and one meſſuage, and one yard-land therein, 7 E. 2.

John Giffard of Brimpsfield laſt mentioned, continued ſeized of King's Stanley 16 E. 2. but being taken in open rebellion againſt that king, at the battle of Burroughbridge in Yorkſhire, he was executed at Glouceſter as a traitor, and his lands confiſcated. John lord Maltravers obtained a grant of this manor, and procured a fine of it to be levied by John Calew, heir to John Giffard by a female. He was ſoon after convicted of ſundry miſdemeanors, whereupon his eſtates were ſeized, and this manor, with ſeveral others, was granted to Maurice, ſon of Maurice lord Berkeley, 11 E. 3. but Maltravers being again received into the king's favour, recovered this manor in the 27th, and died ſeized of it in the 31ſt year of the ſame reign. John lord Maltravers, ſon of John, ſucceeded his father, and died 38 E. 3. but Agnes, the widow of John lord Maltravers the elder, was endowed with this manor, and died 49 E. 3.

A third John lord Maltravers, ſon of the laſt John, died ſeized of the manor of King's Stanley 5 R. 2. and his ſon Henry deceaſing without iſſue, the manor came to Elianor, ſiſter of Henry, who by her marriage with John Fitz-Alan, or Arundel, ſecond ſon of Richard earl of Arundel, carried it into that name and family.

John Arundel, ſon of John and Elianor, had likewiſe a ſon John, who became earl of Arundel, on the deceaſe of Thomas earl of Arundel without iſſue male. He was ſlain near Beauvois in France, and by an inquiſition taken 13 H. 6. was found to have been ſeized of King Stanley, Stonehouſe, Shurdington, Archers [Stoke Archer,] and Woodcheſter in Glouceſterſhire, beſides great eſtates in other counties.

Elianor the widow of ſir Walter Hungerford, late wife of ſir Richard Poinings, and formerly the wife of ſir John Arundel, and mother of John earl of Arundel, held this manor in dower 'till her death 33 H. 6.

Humphry earl of Arundel was ſon and heir of John, but dying under age, the honour and manor of King Stanley came to his uncle, William earl of Arundel. He married Joan, daughter of Richard Nevil, earl of Saliſbury, and dying 3 H. 7. was ſucceeded by his ſon Thomas earl of Arundel, who married Margaret, daughter of Richard Widvile earl of Rivers, and died ſeized of King Stanley 16 H. 8.

William earl of Arundel, ſon of Thomas, had livery of the manors of King's Stanley, Stoke Archer, Shurdington, and Woodcheſter upon the deceaſe of his father; and having married Anne, ſiſter

ſiſter to Henry earl of Northumberland, died 35 H. 8. Henry earl of Arundel, ſon of William, had livery of King's Stanley the following year, and died 22 Eliz. He was a zealous friend to queen Mary, and greatly inſtrumental in her advancement to the throne; an action laudable perhaps in the intention, but direful in its conſequences, and productive of thoſe ſhocking barbarities which marked the ſhort but tragical reign of that female zealot; when fire and faggot were thought the fitteſt inſtruments to promote that religion whoſe diſtinguiſhing characteriſticks are patience, meekneſs, and univerſal philanthropy; when the biſhops Cranmer, Ridley, and Latimer were burnt at the ſtake; men that for learning, piety, and exemplary manners, were the moſt illuſtrious of their age, an honour to the nation wherein they lived, and whoſe names will be remembered with veneration by lateſt poſterity. But to return:

The manor was in the crown 6 Jac. and was granted the next year to George Walter, and John Williams, in truſt for William Garraway, and others. It came ſoon afterwards to the Ducie family, and lord Ducie is the preſent lord of the manor.

Of the other eſtates the records ſhew, that John de Clavile died ſeized of half a yard-land in King's Stanley 4 E. 2. and his ſon John de Clavile was likewiſe ſeized of the ſame lands 11 E. 3.

John Notelin was ſeized of lands in King's Stanley; and Joan, his widow, was endowed with them, and died 14 E. 3. John Notelin, ſon of John, died ſeized of the ſame lands 36 E. 3. and John Notelin, his ſon, likewiſe died ſeized of them 1 R. 2. Another John Notelin, a deſcendant from the laſt-mentioned John, died ſeized of an eſtate in King's Stanley 29 H. 6.

Hugh Twiſel held one meſſuage, twenty-four acres of arable, and two acres of meadow in King's Stanley 7 R. 2. John Twiſel died ſeized of lands here 32 H. 6. and John Twiſel, ſon of John, died poſſeſſed of the ſame lands 11 E. 4. John Barton, and Richard Ruſſel and Margaret his wife, levied a fine of lands in King's Stanley to William Cale 1 E. 6. Thomas Rogers of Wotton Baſſet, ſon and heir of Agnes, died ſeized of lands in this pariſh 15 Eliz. leaving Thomas, a poſthumous ſon, his heir. Lands in King's Stanley, which belonged to Henry earl of Arundel, were granted to Chriſtopher Hatton 18 Eliz.

TITHINGS and *HAMLETS.*

1. The *Borough* is a diſtinct tithing, of which Nathaniel Peach, eſq; is the preſent lord.

2. *Dudbridge*, where Mr. Richard Hawker has a very handſome new-built houſe.

3. *Stanley's End.* Thomas Pettat, eſq; has a good houſe and eſtate here, which belonged to John Jefferis, eſq; at the beginning of the preſent century.

4. The *Leighs.*

5. *Pig Street*, where Mr. Richard Clutterbuck has a good houſe and eſtate.

6. *High Street.*

Of the Church, &c.

The church is a rectory, in the deanery of Stonehouſe, worth 160*l.* a year. The patronage is in Jeſus college, Cambridge, and the reverend Kinard Baghott is the preſent incumbent. The church is dedicated to St George.

	£.	s.	d.		£.	s.	d.
Firſt fruits	18	15	$1\frac{1}{2}$	Synodals	0	2	0
Tenths —	1	17	$8\frac{1}{4}$	Pentecoſt.	0	0	7
Procurations	0	6	8				

Monuments and Inſcriptions.

Againſt the ſouth wall is this inſcription:

Near this Place lieth the body of Richard Clutterbuck of this Pariſh, Gent. who died y^{e} 10th of Auguſt 1714 in the 64th Year of his Age.

Alſo near this Place lieth the Body of Richard the Son of the ſaid Richard Clutterbuck of this Pariſh Gent. who died the 3^{d} of Ianuary 1718 in the 42d year of his age.

Arms, *Baron and femme,* 1. *Azure, a lion rampant argent, in chief three eſcallops of the ſecond,* for Clutterbuck. 2. *Azure, on a chevron between three fleurs de lis Or, as many mullets pierced ſable.*

At the eaſt end of the church, on the table of a handſome monument,

Ad Sacros cineres et piam Memoriam Guliel. Clutterbuck Gen. Dorcas Clutterbuck Relicta ſua (filia Joſephi Bayneham de Weſtbury in agr. Gloceſtrien: Ar.) pii & coniugalis amoris Sui monumentum affert.

Obiit An^{o} Dom 1655
ætat. ſuæ 74.

In terris hoſpes qui Chriſto vixit eodem
In cœlis fruitur ciuis eoq; ſatur.

Arms, *Baron and femme,* 1. Clutterbuck as before. 2. *Gules, a chevron between three bulls heads caboſhed argent,* for Baynham.

On another handſome monument,

Near this Place are interred the bodies of Jaſper Clutterbuck of this Pariſh Gent. who died the 18th Feb. 1752, in the 62^{d} year of his Age. Elizabeth his firſt wife died 11th Augst. 1723, in the 25th year of her Age. Anne his ſecond Wife who died 9th Novr. 1745, in the 60th Year of her Age. Jaſper his Grandſon who died 23^{d} March 1771 in the 22^{d} year of his Age.

Arms, Clutterbuck, as before.

Next to the above,

Near this Place lieth the Body of Anne ye Wife of Nathaniel Paul of this Pariſh who died the 29th of Octob. 1723 Alſo four Children, Holmun, Mary, Oneſiphorus, and Obadiah.

Alſo near this Place lieth ye Body of ye above mentioned Nathaniel Paul, who died the 19th of June 1737, in the 65th year of his Age. Alſo Anne his Daughter died Jany ye 29th 1739 aged 38 y^{rs}. Sarah Elliott Daughter of Nathaniel and Anne Paul died Feby. 22, 1740, aged 35.

Arms, *On a feſs three croſſes croſlets;* no colours.

Within the communion rails, there is a handſome marble monument, conſiſting of a vaſe and pyramid. Over the vaſe are two *genii* ſupporting a ſkeleton, repreſenting mortality; and on the vaſe it is thus written:

This Monument is erected to the Memory of OBADIAH PAUL of this Pariſh Gentleman, who died the 9th of *September* 1724, aged 46 years.

SUSANNAH PAUL his Widow who died the 29th of *May* 1737 aged 56 years.

JOHN PAUL, Son of the ſaid OBADIAH and SUSANNAH, who died the 13th of *July* 1752 aged 39 years.

SAMUEL PAUL of *Rodborough Eſq;* Son of OBADIAH and SUSANNAH PAUL died the 5th of *May* 1768, aged 59.

The arms are placed on the pyramid, *Baron and femme,* 1. *Argent, on a feſs azure three croſſes croſlets Or,* for Paul. 2. *Argent, a battle-ax gules between three roundlets ſable.*

Againſt the north wall, there is another handſome pyramidal marble monument, with two weeping

weeping *genii*, one holding an inverted torch, the other an olive branch, both ſitting on a vaſe. Beneath, on a table, it is thus written:

To the Memory of NATHANIEL PAUL Son of *Nathaniel* and *Anne Paul* of this Pariſh, who died April 6th 1742 aged 40 years.

ELIZABETH WATHEN Siſter of the ſaid *Nathaniel Paul* died March 14th 1749 aged 43 years.

ONESIPHORUS PAUL Brother of *Nathaniel Paul* died March 19th 1770 aged 57 years.

Benefactions.

Lady Hungerford, who was born in this pariſh, gave two ſilver bowls, and two ſilver patens, for the communion ſervice. Thirty ſhillings a year are given to teach poor children to read; and the income of an eſtate which lets for about 7 *l.* a year is left one half for the ſame purpoſe, the remainder for clothing widows and old people.

Taxes.					
The Royal Aid in	1692,	£. 108	16	0
Poll-tax ——	1694,	— 31	9	0
Land-tax ——	1694,	— 155	1	0
The ſame, at 3 *s.*	1770,	— 118	3	1½

At the beginning of this century, according to ſir Robert Atkyns's account, there were 250 houſes in the pariſh, and about 1100 inhabitants, of whom 60 were freeholders; yearly births 22, burials 19. The average of annual burials is now 32, and there are at preſent 1257 inhabitants; ſo that about one in 42 dies annually.

STANLEY St. LEONARD's.

THIS pariſh lies in the hundred of Whitſtone, four miles diſtant ſouth-weſt from Stroud, ſix north-eaſt from Durſley, and eleven ſouth from Glouceſter.

It is bounded by King's Stanley on the eaſt, Eaſington on the weſt, Stonehouſe to the north, and Woodcheſter on the ſouth; and is ſituated on the north ſide of a lofty wood, called *Bucholt*, which in the Saxon language ſignifies the *Beechwood*, and without doubt did antiently, as it does at preſent, conſiſt chiefly of the beech tree. The greater part of the pariſh is rich paſturage and orcharding, and produces good cheeſe, and ſtout cyder.

The etymology of *Stanley* is given in the preceding pariſh. This was called *Leonard Stanley*, (from a priory here, dedicated to St. Leonard) to diſtinguiſh it from the adjoining pariſh of King's Stanley.

King Edward the Second granted a charter of a weekly market, to be held on Saturday, at Stanley St. Leonard's; and of two annual fairs, one on the 6th day of November, which is St. Leonard's day; the other on the Saturday after the 15th of July, which is St. Swithin's day; theſe being the ſaints to whom the priory and the pariſh church were reſpectively dedicated; and that charter was renewed in the year 1620.

This was the only market-town in the hundred, and was formerly more populous than at preſent, having been much reduced by a dreadful fire, which happened in May, 1686, and almoſt conſumed it. There was a brief, ſoon after, for the benefit of the poor ſufferers; but the national revolution taking place about that time, and men's minds being employ'd on greater concerns, the cataſtrophe was too much neglected, and not one ſixth part of the money collected was remitted to the pariſh, nor was the remainder ever accounted for by the farmers and officers of briefs at that time. It continues, however, to rank as a market town in our books and maps, and has a right to hold markets and fairs, but wants intereſt and conveniencies to bring people together. In ſhort, the market has been long ſince diſuſed, and is totally loſt. The houſes ſtand in a diſcontinued, ſtragling form, and the only appearance of its having been a market town, is a little ſhed, which was the market houſe, ſtill remaining about the middle of the place.

There was a ſmall monaſtery founded here, dedicated to St. Leonard, of a prior and canons, as they are expreſſly called, in archbiſhop Theobald's confirmation of ſeveral gifts to them, a tranſlation of which I have inſerted in the Appendix, N°. 24. And here it is proper to obſerve, that only the former part of that confirmation, as far as the word *appurtenances*, (which ſtands in the twelfth line, as I have printed it) is given in ſir Robert Atkyns's Hiſtory; and that what follows in that book, is the latter part of king Henry the Second's charter to the priory of Newent, which, by ſome unaccountable miſtake, was joined to it, and makes an incongruous medley of two diſtinct writings.

It is not abſolutely certain who was the founder of this priory, but it has been commonly attributed to Roger de Berkeley, who gave it the advowſons of the ſeveral churches of Ozleworth, Cowley, Erlingham, Uley, and Slimbridge; and in the year 1146, gave the patronage of the priory, with all its rights, to the abbey of Glouceſter, with the conſent of Sabrith, or Sabrath, the prior of the monaſtery, and the reſt of the monks, and with the approbation of Simon, biſhop of Worceſter, whereby it became a cell of Benedictine monks to that abbey. And in the year 1156, the ſame Roger de Berkeley gave the church of Cam, with the appurtenances, to this priory, and a grove called Fyſacre; which were afterwards confirmed by king Henry the Third, and by John, biſhop of Worceſter. But this Roger de Berkeley could not be that Roger who came in with the Conqueror, to whom ſir Robert Atkyns (p. 25.) has attributed ſeveral of theſe donations. Robert de Berkeley, ſon of Maurice, gave alſo to this priory, a mill in Cowley[h], and a meſſuage with lands, belonging to the ſame mill, in the reign of king Henry the Second.

There was afterwards a law-ſuit commenced concerning the church of Slimbridge, between Thomas lord Berkeley, and Thomas de Bredon, abbat

[h] Dugdale's *Monaſticon*, Vol. 1. p. 119.

abbat of Gloucester, which was adjusted by composition. Maurice lord Berkeley, grandson of Harding, had founded an hospital at Lorwing, or Lorling, by the name of the *Master and brethren of Lorwing*, and endowed it with lands there; which hospital, lands and appurtenances, Thomas lord Berkeley gave to the priory of Stanley, in consideration whereof the church of Slimbridge was released to him 8 H. 3. And thus it happened, that Lorenge-farm became appurtenant to this parish, tho' seven or eight miles distant from the body of it; and the occupiers of the farm have paid the parochial taxes, and served the offices to this parish time immemorially; but the land-tax goes in aid of the parish of Cam, to which Lorenge is contiguous.

Sir Robert Atkyns, in his History of Gloucestershire, and Mr. Stevens, in his *Supplement to the Monasticon*, were both mistaken, in representing Geoffry Mandevil, earl of Essex, as a great benefactor to this priory; in which they have confounded it with that of Stonely in Huntingdonshire, of the order of St. Augustin, founded by William Mandeville, earl of Essex, who lived in the year 1180; whereas this priory of Stanley St. Leonard's was of the Benedictine order.

I have no where found a catalogue of the priors, nor can I make out a list of them from the papers which have fallen into my hands. Doctor John Crosse was prior here in 1189, and not in 1449, as sir Robert Atkyns has it. He lies interred in the south aile of the church, with an old monkish inscription on the stone, (as I have it in some manuscript papers concerning the priory) and tho' the date has been effaced for above a century past, yet it appears, from the most probable accounts of him, that he died in 1199. The inscription was as follows:

Qui jacet hoc tumulo Doctor John Crosse nominatur
Ille Prior Stanly Sancti fuerat Leonardi
Hunc sancto rotulo scribat Deus et tueatur.

This priory was dissolved with the abbey of Gloucester; but before that event took place, there being only two monks in the priory, king Henry the Eighth, by a letter, dated June 11, in the 30th year of his reign, desired that those monks might be recalled to the abbey, and that the abbat and convent would grant a lease of this cell, for ninety-nine years, to sir William Kingston, knight; which was done accordingly, July 18, at the yearly rent of 36*l.* 13*s.* 4*d.* with some few reservations, as appears by abbat Malvern's manuscript. The annual revenues of the priory, at the dissolution, amounted to 126*l.* 0*s.* 8*d.* according to Speed's account; and the clear value was 106*l.* 17*s.* according to a table of valuations in *Stevens's Supplement*.

The scite of the cell of Stanley, formerly belonging to the abbey of Gloucester, and all the lands in England belonging to that cell, were granted to sir Anthony Kingston, reserving a rent of 40*s.* *per ann.* 36 H. 8. Sir Anthony conveyed them, by licence of alienation, to Anthony Bourchier, esq; 2 E. 6. Mr. Bourchier conveyed them to John Sandford, on the 2d of Feb. 3 E. 6. and they were then properly enrolled in chancery, as appears by evidences and writings in the possession of Robert Sandford, esq; the present owner of the scite of the priory. He is descended from an antient family in Shropshire, who sprung from the same stock with the Sandfords in Westmoreland, mentioned by Leland, among the familes of note there in the reign of king Henry the Eighth, one of whose descendants, Thomas Sandford, esq; of Hougil-castle in that county, was created a baronet 17 C. 1. Anselm Sandford was son of the above-mentioned John Sandford, and upon his father's death, had livery of the priory of Stanley, and of the manor of Stonehouse, in this county, 13 Eliz. Robert Sandford, gent. was a direct descendant from Anselm. He died in the old priory of Stanley, which was the seat of his family, in 1719; and was succeeded by his only son Robert Sandford, esq; who resided at Stratton, and was an acting magistrate in the commission of the peace for the county of Gloucester, which office he discharged with judgment and integrity upwards of forty years; and dying in 1769, he was succeeded by his son Robert Sandford, esq; the present proprietor of the priory, and lord of the manor of Stanley. His arms are, *Per chevron, sable and ermine, in chief two boars heads couped Or.*

The old priory house was taken down about thirty years ago, and the outward walls of a good house were built on the very spot of ground whereon it stood; but the inside is not yet finished.

Of the Manor and other Estates.

The earliest account of this manor is thus recorded in the antient survey:

'Radulf de Berchelai holds Stanlege in Blacelew 'hundred. There are four hides and a half. 'Godric and Wisnod held it for two manors. 'There are two plow-tillages in demean, and six 'villeins, and fourteen bordars, with twelve plow-'tillages. There are five *servi*, and ten acres of 'meadow. It was worth and is worth 100*s.*' *Domesday*, p. 75.

Henry de Berkeley was seized of the manor of Stanley St. Leonard's, and of the advowson of the church; and his right to certain privileges formerly granted to him, was allowed in the proceedings on a *Quo warranto* 15 E. 1. John Berkeley of Dursley, and Hawise his wife, levied a fine of this manor, to the use of themselves in taille, 5 E. 3. and were seized of it 19 & 22 E. 3. Sir Nicholas Berkeley held lands in Stanley St. Leonard's 2 & 6 R. 2.

Maud de Cantelupe, descended from the Berkeleys, died seized of this manor 4 H. 4. Richard Cheddre married a daughter of Robert de Cantelupe by Maud his wife, and by her had a daughter

and

and heireſs, married to Thomas Wekys, who, in right of his wife, died ſeized of this manor 13 E. 4. Nicholas Wekys died alſo ſeized of it 5 Mar. and livery was granted to Robert Wekys, his grandſon and heir, the ſame year.

The manor paſſed afterwards to the Whitmores, a Staffordſhire family, who enjoyed it for a conſiderable time, 'till it was purchaſed not long ago of the late William Whitmore, of Slaughter in this county, by Robert Sandford, the father of Robert Sandford, eſq; the preſent lord of the manor, of whoſe family and arms, I have given a ſhort account under that of the priory.

Roger Barber was ſeized of four meſſuages, and three ſhops, in Glouceſter and Stanley St. Leonard's, for the uſe of the abbey of Glouceſter, 16 R. 2.

Of the Church, &c.

The church is in the deanery of Stonehouſe. It is a donative, and was for many years an impropriation, ſubject only to the annual payment of 6*l.* 13*s.* 4*d.* to the curate. There uſed to be a leaſe granted by the impropriator, of moſt of the tithes, except of the priory lands, to the curate; which ſeldom amounted to more than 36*l.* a year; but the church has received a double augmentation from queen Anne's bounty, with ſome further additions from the impropriator and others, about forty years ago; ſo that by the purchaſe of an eſtate, and the ſettlement of the greater part of the tithes of the pariſh, except of the priory lands, the benefice is now worth 60*l.* a year neat, and is ſubject to epiſcopal juriſdiction. Robert Sandford, eſq; is patron, and his brother, the reverend John Sandford, D.D. is the preſent incumbent.

The church is dedicated to St. Swithin. It is built in the form of a croſs, and the tower, which is very large, ſtands in the middle of it, containing four great bells, and a clock. There are private receſſes between the outer and inner walls of the tower, the uſe of which is not certainly known; and there was formerly a high ſpire on the top of it.

Procurations £. 0 6 8 Pentecoſtals £. 0 0 7
Synodals — 0 2 0

Monuments and Inſcriptions.

Upon flat ſtones in the chancel, are the four following memorials:

Here lyeth the Body of Ralph Sandford B. A.
of Trinity College in Oxford,
Third Son of Robert Sandford, Eſq;
of Stratton in this County.
A Youth of amiable Diſpoſitions
And of an Exemplary Conduct.
Earneſtly deſirous of Knowledge,
He purſued his Studies with a laudable Induſtry,
yet confined not his Search to Knowledge alone,
But joined with his Improvements in uſeful Learning
The more valuable Attainments of Piety & Virtue.
As he lived under the habitual Influence of Religion
So was he ſupported by it in Death:
He met the Approaches of it with Peace & Compoſure,
Declaring his Confidence in the Merits of Xſt's Blood,
And his intire Reſignation to the Will of God.
Reader, imitate thou the Example of his Life
That thy laſt End may be like his.
He died June 10th, 1749, Aged 23.

M. S.
ROBERTI SANDFORD de Stratton in Com. Gloceſtr. Armigeri
Manerii Hujuſce Domini
Vir fuit certe Graviſſimus
Humanioribus Literis excultus
Et Chriſtianæ Pietatis Exemplar.
Genus antiquum iis Virtutibus illuſtravit
Quæ virum Probum decent et Sanctum. [indefeſſus,
Irenarchæ munus L per annos prope ſuſtinuit alacer promptus ac
Iuris Municipalis peritus idem ac incorruptus Adminiſtrator.
Ad Lites vicinorum pacifice dirimendas egregiè compoſitus;
Virtutis quippe veræ cuſtos, ſibi ſemper conſtans
alios non Vi et Imperiis
Sed Benevolentiâ et Exemplo Rexit.
Honeſto Ruris Seceſſu Deliteſſere
Maluit quam rebus verſari Publicis
Viciniæ, amicorum et Familiæ ſuæ commodis invigilare.
Maritus, Parens, Paterfamilias, Amicus, Patronus optimus!
Caſtiſſimam morum ſeveritatem grata commendavit alloquii Comitate.
Officia Sacra tam publicè quam Privatim conſtanter obiit
Deo tamen inſervire tum maxime ſibi videbatur cum Hominibus Prodeſſet.
Annorum et Famæ Satur,
Ex hâc vita Deceſſit
Futuræ per Chriſtum tribuenda, Præmia votis Præſumens
Nov^bris^ 14, A. Ætatis 81, Dom. 1769.

Juxta Robertum
Janæ Willett Uxoris ſuæ Johannæ Sororis
Deponuntur Reliquiæ.
Fœmina Quidem vixit Innupta
Sed in Moribus Caſta,
Et in Officiis Pietatis ac Prudentiæ Peragendis
Nunquam non Laudabilitèr Conſtans.
Senio tandem confecta
Ob^t^ Dec^ris^ 16° A. D. 1771. Æt. 77°.
Adveniet Dies
Cum Tuba Canet ac Mortui Reſurgent.
1. Cor. c. xv. v. 52.

H. S. E.
Juxta Matrem
SARÆ SANDFORD Generoſæ
Quod fuit mortale.
Cœlebs Exemplo comprobavit
Quantum ad religionis Cultum valet
Mens ingenua, Caſta, Pia, ac Benefica.
Semper hujuſce Loci pauperibus benignè fuit Liberalis.
At Quinquaginta Gloceſtrenſi Noſocomio Libras
Perpetuum Miſeris Solamen
Legavit Moriens.
Cœlo diù Matura
Caducam æternæ Vitam
Feliciter Per Chriſtum tandem Permutavit
Julii 25° A. Æt. 81° Dom. 1771.

On a ſmall monument at the eaſt end of the church, is this inſcription:

HOC PAVLVLVM POSVIT
IOHES CLIFFORD GEN. AD MEMORIAM
FÆLICEM MARIÆ FILIÆ MAXIMÆ NATV
WILLI SHEPPARD ARMIG. VXORIS DICTI
IOHIS CVI QVATVOR PEPERIT FILIAS
MARIAM ANNAM ROSAMVNDAM ET ELIZABETHAM
QVARVM VNA (VIZT) ANNA GLORIÆ CORONAM
ÆTERNÆ ANTE MATREM ACCEPIT TRES AVTEM
CÆTERÆ PATRI MOESTO VT AMORIS SVI PIGNORA
VIVENTIA SVPERSVNT. { DOMINI MDCLI
OBIIT XII° DIE FEBR. AN° { ÆTATIS XXXI°
{ CONIVGII XII°

The arms upon the monument are, *Baron and femme*, 1. *Checky Or and azure, on a bend argent three lions of the firſt*, for Clifford. 2. Sheppard, as at Hampton.

There is an elegant latin inſcription for Henry Riſhton, A.M. who died in the year 1741, and for his wife Elianor, who were both buried here, and who gave 200*l.* for the uſe of the poor of this pariſh for ever, which has been laid out in the purchaſe of land here, and the profits of it are applied to that uſe by the patron and incumbent, who are perpetual truſtees.

There

There is alſo a monument in the church for Mr. Nathaniel Badger, clothier of this pariſh, who dying in 1707, ſettled 40*s*. a year for ever, to be paid out of lands in Slimbridge, for the eſtabliſhment of a charity ſchool in this pariſh, to teach children to read, &c. which, with ſome additions by ſubſcription, is at preſent kept up by the miniſter, who is truſtee for this purpoſe.

Taxes.			£.	s.	d.
The Royal Aid in	1692,	£.	80	2	8
Poll-tax ——	1694,	—	22	12	0
Land-tax ——	1694,	—	96	6	0
The ſame, at 3*s*.	1770,	—	77	15	6

There were, about ſeventy years ago, according to ſir Robert Atkyns, 90 houſes, and about 400 inhabitants in this pariſh, whereof 17 were freeholders; yearly births 12, burials 11. The number of ſouls at preſent is about 512.

STANTON, *or* STAUNTON.

THIS pariſh lies in the lower diviſion of the hundred of Kiftſgate, ſeven miles diſtant ſouth-weſt from Campden, ſeven north from Winchcombe, and twenty-two north-eaſt from Glouceſter.

One part of it lies in the Vale, the other on the ridge of hills that divides the vale from the Coteſwolds. Here are no curious natural productions, nor any antiquities, except a large camp on Shunborow-hill, fortified with double intrenchments, and overlooking the vale, but to what age or people it owes its exiſtence, is utterly unknown.

This place was probably called *Stanton* from the *ſtone-quarry* on the ſide of the hill.

The parſonage houſe is a very good one. It was built by the reverend Mr. Henry Izod, as appears by his arms on the chimney-piece in the hall.

A ſmall brook runs from hence into the river Iſbourn, which empties itſelf into the Avon below Eveſham.

Of the Manor and other Eſtates.

This manor is ſuppoſed to have been given to the abbey of Winchcombe, by its founder, Kenulph king of Mercia, who died in the year 819; and it continued in the poſſeſſion of that houſe at the time of the general ſurvey, as appears by a paſſage from *Domeſday*, of which the following is a tranſlation:

'The church of St. Mary of Wincelcumbe 'holds Stantone in Greteſtanes hundred. There 'are three hides. In demean are two plow-'tillages, and fourteen villeins, with ſeven plow-'tillages. There are three borders, and ſix *ſervi*, 'and ſix acres of meadow. A wood one mile 'long, and half a mile broad. It is worth and 'was worth 3*l*.' p. 71.

The abbey of Winchcombe purchaſed a charter of free warren in Stanton and Snowſhill 35 H. 3. and their right to that privilege was allowed in the proceedings on a writ of *Quo warranto* 15 E. 1. Peter de Stanton was tenant of the manor 16 E. 1. The abbey of Winchcombe aſſigned the manors of Stanton and Snowſhill to the abbey of St. Ebrulph at Utica in Normandy, 12 E. 2.

Upon the general diſſolution of abbies, this manor came to the crown, and was aſſigned as part of the jointure of queen Katherine, and holden, together with the advowſon of the church, as of her manor of Eaſt Greenwich.

The king and queen granted their houſe in Stanton, and the manor, with its rights and members, to John Elliot, to hold by the fourth part of a knight's fee, 4 & 5 Ph. & M. and Elliot, abtaining a licence of alienation, conveyed them to Thomas Doleman the ſame year. John Doleman, ſon of Thomas, had livery of the manor, and of the advowſon of the church of Snowſhill, 15 Eliz. Matthew Doleman, of London, haberdaſher, was ſeized of the manor, and of lands here, which he ſold to William Jackſon, *alias* Boothe, Thomas Warne, Nicholas Kirkham, Humphry Wrighte, Nicholas Izode, and others.

William Jackſon died in the year 1602, ſeized of part of the demean lands of the manor, of common of paſture in Dukemead and Berry Wormington, of the Sheephouſe, and of the tithes of Sheephay; which particulars, except the tithes, were part of the late manor of Stawnton; and William Jackſon, ſon and heir of the ſaid William, was upwards of forty years old at his father's death, as appears by the eſcheator's inquiſition 2 Jac.

Mr. Izod had a good eſtate here, which he gave by will to Reginald Wynniat, eſq; from whom it deſcended to his ſon, the reverend Reginald Wynniat, M.A. who has lately purchaſed ſeveral others in the ſame place, ſo that he is now poſſeſſed of the greater part of the pariſh; but all courts and royalties have been long ſince neglected. For his arms ſee Dimmock.

Of the Church, &c.

The church is a rectory, in the deanery of Campden, worth about 180*l*. a year. The rev[d]. Mr. Reginald Wynniat, M.A. is patron, incumbent, and impropriator.

The chapel of Snowſhill is annexed to this church, and the advowſon of them was lately given in exchange, by the reverend Lionel Kirkham, B.D. with the preſent patron, for the rectory of Salford in Oxfordſhire.

The rector has one fourth of the great tithes, and the impropriator has the other three parts. The demean lands are free from tithes.

One yard-land belongs to the glebe.

The church is dedicated to St. Michael, and built in the form of a croſs, with a ſteeple at the weſt end.

	£.	s.	d.		£.	s.	d.
Firſt fruits	17	11	4	Synodals	0	2	0
Tenths —	1	15	1½	Pentecoſt.	0	0	9½
Procurations	0	2	0				

Monu-

Monuments and Inſcriptions.

Maurice Tewkeſbury is ſuppoſed to have built the ſouth aile, from his name [Mauricivs tvexbury] appearing in carved letters round the figure of a dove in the roof.

Againſt the ſouth wall of the chancel is this inſcription :

H. S. E.
Reverend[s] Vir HENRICUS IZOD, Art. M[r].
Hujus Eccleſiæ Rector quam per Annos 27
Mirâ Pietate et Candore exornavit.
Non minus Exemplo quam Doctrina diu illuſtris
Eccleſiæ Anglicanæ, licet oppreſſæ,
Non Deſertor ſed acerrimus Vindex.
Ideoq; REGI ſuo etiam exulanti
perquam fidelis,
Amor et Deliciæ Vicinorum occubuit
Multo magis Parochianorum Deſiderium
Novem: 9: Anno { Ætatis 52 / Domini 1650.
ALICIA uxor, Filia Rich. Vernon Rectoris
de Hanbury, Com. Wigorn. Præivit Junij 8, 1642.
Maria Parſons Filia natu minima
Obſequij ergo Poſuit 1675.

Arms, at top, *Baron and femme*, 1. *Argent, ſix leopards heads vert*, 3, 2, 1, for Izod. 2. *Or, upon a feſs azure three garbs of the field*, for Vernon. At bottom, 1. *Gules, a leopard's head caboſhed between three croſſes paty fitchy argent*, for Parſons, impaling, 2. Izod as before.

On another monument in the chancel,

Subtus jacet vir venerabilis Henricus Kirkham, hujus Eccleſiæ Rector. Natus Octob. XXVIII MDCXXXII. Sepultus Mart. XXVIII MDCCV.

Necnon Sarah

Uxor ejus Reverendi Henrici Izod hujus Eccleſiæ quondam Rectoris filia quarta. Nata Feb. x[mo] MDCXXXV. Sepulta Dec. xxx[o] MDCCIIII.

Arms, at top, *Party per pale, baron and femme*, 1. *Ermine, three lions rampant gules within a bordure ingrailed ſable*, for Kirkham. 2. Izod, as before.

A handſome marble table, againſt the wall, bears this inſcription :

Near this Place
are interred the Bodies of
LIONEL & ROBERT Son and Grandſon of
HENRY KIRKHAM,
All ſucceſſively Rectors of this Pariſh.
As alſo of
HENRIETTA KIRKHAM, & PENELOPE
the Wife of THO[s] WOODS, CLERK,
Daughters of the above named HENRY :
THO: WOODS the ſon of PENELOPE :
SARAH the Wife of IOHN CHAPONE, CLERK,
and Daughter of LIONEL above mentioned,
MARY the Wife of ROBERT KIRKHAM,
and three of their Daughters
who died in their Infancy,
To whoſe Memory this Monument was erected
in the Year of our Lord MDCCLXVII.

There is likewiſe a memorial for John Warren, grandſon of Thomas Warren, of this pariſh, gent. who died in 1728, with his arms, *viz. Ermine, a feſs counter company, Or and azure, between three talbots paſſant ſable.*

Benefaction.

Mr. Lawrence Banks, rector, who died in 1651, gave a tenement in Eveſham, worth 1 *l.* 8 *s.* a year, out of which 6 *s.* 8 *d.* is to be applied to the repair of the church, the remainder to the poor.

Taxes.					
	The Royal Aid in	1692,	£. 95	10	0
	Poll-tax ——	1694, —	23	9	0
	Land-tax ——	1694, —	96	10	0
	The ſame, at 3 *s.*	1770, —	66	6	6

Sir Robert Atkyns reckons 60 houſes in the pariſh, and about 300 inhabitants, whereof 29 were freeholders; yearly births 8, burials 7. The preſent number of people is about 310.

STANTON *or* STAUNTON.

THIS pariſh lies in the hundred of St. Briavell's, in the Foreſt diviſion of the county, five miles eaſt from Monmouth, two weſt from Colford, and twenty-three ſouth-weſtward from Glouceſter.

It is full of iron ore, the getting of which is the chief employment of the labouring people, who make very good wages at it.

The name of the village is derived from the Saxon Stan, *a ſtone*, and *ton*, a common termination ; but whether it was ſo called from the ſtony ſoil, or from a ſtone of a prodigious ſize ſtanding here, I ſhall not determine. This ſtone is placed as it were on a point, ſo as to fill the beholder with apprehenſions of its being ready to fall. It is ſuppoſed to have been a *Rocking Stone*, placed here in the time of paganiſm, and if ſo, it is the only one of that kind in Glouceſterſhire; but it has now loſt its motion. There are various opinions concerning theſe ſtones. Some have ſuppoſed them to be rude, pagan deities, which the people worſhipped on particular occaſions; but I rather think the Rocking Stone was not the immediate object of worſhip. The more probable opinion ſeems to be, that it was an inſtrument in the hands of the prieſt to aſſiſt his authority in matters of moment and difficulty; who, the better to affect his purpoſe, taught the people, by example and precept, to approach it with great veneration and reſpect. Being ſo nicely adjuſted as to move with eaſe, it ſeemed calculated to decide any queſtion that might be put, by its motion one way or the other, agreeably to the will of the perſon officiating; and ſo of anſwering the purpoſe intended by the antient oracles among the Greeks and Romans.

This village ſtands at the bottom of a high hill, which overlooks the town of Monmouth, and part of the counties of Monmouth and Hereford.

Of the Manor and other Eſtates.

'Turſtin the ſon of Rolf holds Stantone in 'Blachelaue hundred. There are five hides. Tovi 'held it of king Edward. In demean are two 'plow-tillages, and eight villeins, and ſix bordars, 'with ten plow-tillages. There are four *ſervi*, 'and two mills of 35 *ſol.* and ten acres of meadow; 'a wood one mile long, and half a mile broad. 'It is worth and was worth 100 *ſol.* Tovi holds 'two hides of this land by the gift [*elemoſina*] of 'king William.' *Domeſday*, p. 78.

An inquiſition taken 15 E. 1. before William de Saham, Richard de Boyland, Roger Toveday, and John de Mettingham, itinerant juſtices for the county of Glouceſter, recites, That Thomas

Walding de Stanton ought to hold the vill of Stanton with the bailiwick, of the king, *in capite*, *viz.* one carucate of land, which paid 26*s.* 8*d.* a year; and that Richard de la More then held it, together with the bailiwick, but the jurors knew not how.

John Walding held this manor 13 E. 3. He is ſoon afterwards called John de Stanton, and held the manor and bailiwick of Stanton in the foreſt of Dean, with its fees and profits, in the 16th, and died ſeized thereof in the 22d year of the ſame reign. Thomas Walding de Stanton died ſeized of the manor, and of the advowſon of Stanton, 8 R. 2. and another Thomas Stanton died ſeized of Stanton 16 E. 4.

The manor came afterwards to the family of Baynham. John Baynham died ſeized of it 20 H. 8. William Baynham, ſon of John, had livery of it 26 H. 8. and levied a fine of it, and of Newland, 6 E. 6.

From the Baynhams it came to the Brains, a reſpectable family in this part of the county. Robert Brain, upon the death of his father, had livery of the manor 1 Eliz. George Winter, eſq; younger brother of ſir William Winter of Lidney, married Anne, one of the ſiſters and coheireſſes of Robert Brain, and in her right was ſeized of this manor, and died poſſeſſed of it, and of Dyrham and Hinton in this county, in the year 1581. John Winter, ſon of George, had livery of Stanton, Dyrham, and Hinton, the ſame year his father died. He commanded the Elizabeth, of eighty tons burthen, as vice admiral under ſir Francis Drake, in his famous voyage round the world in 1577, but he did not accompany him thro the expedition, for being ſeparated from the admiral in a violent ſtorm, on the 8th of October, 1578, he repaſſed the ſtraits of Magellan, and returned to England.

The Halls were afterwards lords of the manor. Benedict Hall, ſon of Henry-Benedict, and grandſon of Benedict Hall, of Highmeadow, eſq; was proprietor of it at the beginning of this century. His only daughter and heireſs, Beata-Maria-Thereſa, was married to ſir Thomas Gage, created viſcount Gage of Caſtle-Iſland in the county of Kerry, and baron Gage of Caſtlebar in the county of Mayo, Sep. 14, 1720. She deceaſing in the year 1749, was buried at Newland, and his lordſhip likewiſe dying in 1754, was buried at Firle in Suſſex, and was ſucceeded in title and eſtate by his eldeſt ſon, William-Hall viſcount Gage, the preſent lord of the manor of Stanton. His lordſhip married Elizabeth, daughter of Sampſon Gideon, eſq; and ſiſter of ſir Sampſon Gideon, of Spalding in Lincolnſhire, baronet, and has a fine ſeat at Highmeadow, one part (as it is ſaid) in this pariſh, the other in that of Newland, under which head it has already been taken notice of. His lordſhip's arms are, *Per ſaltire ſaphire and pearl, a ſaltire ruby.* Crest. *On a wreath, a ram proper, armed and ungued topaz.* Supporters. *Two greyhounds tenne, gorged with coronets of fleurs de lis topaz.* Motto. Courage sans Peur.

William Hall, who married Juliana Nurſe, died ſeized of lands in Staunton, Aſhrug, and Highmeadow 37 H. 8. and left Chriſtopher his ſon twenty-three years old. James Bell died ſeized of lands in Newland, and of a cloſe in Aſhrydge in this pariſh 43 Eliz. *Eſch.*

Of the Church, &c.

The church is a rectory, in the foreſt deanery, worth about 70*l.* a year, of which lord Gage has the patronage.

The advowſon of the rectory of Stanton was granted to William Rigg and Peter Gering 5 Mar. and it was again granted to Richard Robſon 6 Eliz. Miſtakes often ariſe from two places being of the ſame name; thus, what ſir Robert Atkyns ſays of queen Katherine being endowed with this rectory, and of the grant to John Elliot and Alexander Cheſnal 4 Mar. muſt be underſtood of Stanton in Kiftſgate hundred.

The church, dedicated to All Saints, is a double building, ſupported by pillars, and has a handſome tower in the middle, adorned with pinnacles.

Firſt fruits £. 6	11	0	Proc. & Syn. £. 0	7	0
Tenths —	14	0	Pentecoſtals - 0	1	4

Benefaction.

Henry Hall, ſecond ſon of William Hall of Highmeadow, who died in 1644, left 40*l.* a year to be equally diſtributed between the poor of this pariſh and Newland. The money is paid out of lands called Trepenkennet, in the pariſh of St. Wenard's in Herefordſhire. See *Inſcriptions* at Newland.

Taxes.			£.	s.	d.
	The Royal Aid in	1692,	85	12	0
	Poll-tax — —	1694, —	29	11	0
	Land-tax ——	1694, —	158	18	0
	The ſame, at 3*s.*	1770, —	72	0	3

About ſeventy years ago there were 54 houſes in the pariſh, and the people were computed to amount to 220, 14 of whom were freeholders; yearly birth 6, burials 5. The preſent inhabitants are eſtimated at about the ſame number.

STANWAY.

THIS pariſh lies in the upper part of Tewkeſbury hundred, ſeven miles diſtant ſouth-weſt from Campden, ſix north from Winchcombe, and twenty-one north-eaſt from Glouceſter.

The great road from Tewkeſbury to London leads up Stanway-hill, from which the place took its name, for *Stanway*, ſignifies the *ſtony road*.

The abbats of Tewkeſbury had a country ſeat here, ſituated a little eaſtward of the church. It was rebuilt and enlarged by abbat Richard Cheltenham,

tenham, in the time of king Henry the Seventh, and Leland calls it *a fayre Mannour Place*, in the ſucceeding reign. The preſent manor houſe is large and handſome, ſituated on the ſlope of the hill, with good gardens, and a caſcade of water, ſeen from the vale below at the diſtance of ſeveral miles. It was built by ſir Paul Tracy, in the reign of king James the Firſt, and was the ſeat and reſidence of Robert Tracy, eſq; 'till the time of his death, in the year 1767. The famous doctor Dover, who inſtituted the *Coteſwold Games*, died at this houſe in the year 1742, and was buried, at his own requeſt, in the vault belonging to the Tracy family. No gentleman reſides at Stanway-houſe at preſent.

A ſmall brook, called the Leame, runs from hence into the river Iſbourn, which empties itſelf into the upper Avon, near Eveſham; and another ſpring, riſing in the higher part of the pariſh, runs into the river Winruſh, and ſo into the Thames.

Of the Manor and other Eſtates.

It is ſaid that this manor was given to the abbey of Tewkeſbury by the two brothers Odo and Dodo, who founded that monaſtery in the year 715. It was part of the poſſeſſions of the ſame abbey at the time of the general ſurvey, as appears by the following extract from the record:

'Seven hides in Stanwege belong to the church '[of Tewkeſbury]. There are two plow-tillages 'in demean, and eight villeins, and two bordars, 'with eight plow-tillages. There is a monaſtery, 'and five [plow-tillages] among the *ſervi* and '*ancillæ*, and a ſalt pit at Wich, and eight acres 'of meadow. A wood three furlongs long, 'and one broad. In the time of king Edward it 'was worth 8*l.* now 7*l.*' *Domeſday*, p. 68.

From this time I find no further mention in the records of the monaſtery at Stanway.

King William the Second granted to the abbey of Tewkeſbury court leet, waifs, and felons goods in Stanway, which grant was pleaded and allowed in a *Quo warranto* 15 E. 1. Thomas de Cannings was tenant of the manor 9 E. 3.

This eſtate continued in the abbey of Tewkeſbury 'till the diſſolution of monaſteries, and was then granted by the crown to William Tracy, of Toddington, eſq; anceſtor of the preſent lord Tracy. He ſettled it on Richard Tracy, his ſecond ſon, who married Barbara, daughter of Thomas Lucy, of Charlecot in Warwickſhire, and was high ſheriff of this county 3 Eliz. Sir Paul Tracy, baronet, ſon and heir of Richard, married Anne, daughter of ſir Ralph Shakerly, and ſerved the office of high ſheriff of this county 11 Jac. 1. Sir Richard Tracy, ſon of ſir Paul, married Anne, daughter of ſir Thomas Coningſby, of Hampton in Herefordſhire, and was high ſheriff of Glouceſterſhire 4 C. 1. Sir Humphry Tracy, ſucceeded his father ſir Richard, and ſerved the office of high ſheriff 15 C. 1. His attachment to the royal cauſe in the great civil war, which diſtracted the kingdom in that reign, occaſioned the ſequeſtration of his eſtates by the victorious party, nor did he recover the poſſeſſion of them 'till he had paid 1600*l.* compoſition. Upon his death, without iſſue, in the year 1651, the manor of Stanway devolved to his next brother, ſir Richard Tracy, who alſo died without iſſue, and was ſucceeded by ſir John Tracy, his younger brother; but he likewiſe deceaſing without iſſue, in the year 1677, left the manor of Stanway to

Ferdinando Tracy, younger ſon of John third lord Tracy, who married —— daughter of ſir Anthony Keck, lord commiſſioner of the great ſeal, and left John Tracy, eſq; his only ſon and heir. He married Anne, daughter of ſir Robert Atkyns, lord chief baron of the exchequer, by Anne his ſecond wife, daughter of ſir Thomas Dacres of Hertfordſhire, and was lord of this manor at the beginning of the preſent century. By his ſaid wife Anne he had iſſue five ſons, Robert and John, twins; Ferdinando, Anthony, and Thomas; and five daughters, Anne, Catherine, Martha, Elizabeth, and Frances. Robert Tracy, eſq; ſucceeded his father John, and marrying Anna-Maria, daughter of ſir Roger Hudſon, knight, died at Stanway without iſſue, Aug. 26, 1767. And Edward Devereux, lord viſcount Hereford[1], in right of his lady, Henrietta-Charlotte, daughter of the late Anthony-Keck Tracy, eſq; is the preſent lord of the manor of Stanway.

HAM-

[1] This noble family derive their furname from Evereux, a town in Normandy. The firſt of them who ſettled in England was Robert, youngeſt ſon of Walter earl of Roſmar. This Robert, who in antient records is ſometimes ſtiled de Ebrois, and de Ebroicis, accompanied William duke of Normandy in his invaſion of England, and had an only ſon and heir, Reginald d'Evereux, whoſe ſon and heir, William d'Evereux, had to his wife Helewyſe, who ſurvived him, and gave to the monks of St. Peter's at Glouceſter, certain lands called the Hyde, in Herefordſhire, which were given her in marriage by Walter de Laci.

Euſtace d'Evereux, ſon of William, impleaded Herbert Waleran for one knight's fee in Kington, 5 Joh. Stephen, only ſon of Euſtace, having attended the king in his wars againſt the Welch, as appears by the Clauſe Rolls 7 H. 3. had ſcutage of his tenants in the counties of Glouceſter and Hereford. By Iſabel his wife, he had a ſon William d'Evereux, who was one of the barons marchers, and was ſlain fighting againſt the king in the battle of Eveſham, 49 H. 3. By Maud, ſiſter to Walter de Gifford, he had an only ſon William, who paid a compoſition of three years value to have livery of his father's lands. He was ſummoned to parliament in 1298, and, by Alice his wife, left a ſon ſir William d'Evereux, knight, whoſe ſon, ſir Walter d'Evereux, knight, by Margery his wife, had iſſue ſir John d'Evereux, his heir, and ſir William d'Evereux, ſeated at Bodenham and Whitechurch in Herefordſhire, of whom hereafter.

Sir John married Margaret, daughter of John Vere, earl of Oxford, and having ſerved under the Black Prince in France and Spain, and in various wars by ſea and land, was made a knight banneret, and inſtalled knight of the garter 9 R. 2. He filled many places of great truſt and honour, and was ſummoned to parliament among the barons, from the 8th to the 16 R. 2. He died in 1394, leaving iſſue one daughter Joan, and one ſon ſir John d'Evereux, who married Philippa, daughter of Guy de Bryan, and died without iſſue.

I now return to ſir William Devereux, of Bodenham and Whitechurch, before mentioned, who by Anne his wife, daughter of ſir John Barre, had iſſue ſir Walter Devereux, who married Agnes, daughter of Thomas Crophull, and left iſſue four ſons and two daughters, *viz.* Walter, John, Richard, Thomas, Elizabeth, and Margaret. Walter, the eldeſt, marrying Elizabeth, daughter of ſir Thomas Bromwich, knight, had iſſue ſir Walter, his ſon and heir, and a daughter Elizabeth; which ſir

Walter,

HAMLETS. 1. *Church Stanway.* 2. *Taddington*, lying two miles eaftward from the church. 3. *Wood Stanway.*

Of the Church, &c.

The church is a vicarage, in the deanery of Campden, worth about 50*l.* a year, of which the lord of the manor is patron and impropriator.

The vicar receives 2*l.* a year out of the hamlet of Taddington, in lieu of tithe of hay; and 8*l.* a year out of Church Stanway, as fatisfaction for all great tithes.

The church is dedicated to St. Peter. It is large and handfome, and has a tower at the weft end, adorned with pinnacles and battlements.

Firft fruits £	9	0	0	Synodals £.	0	2	0
Tenths —	0	18	0	Pentecoft.	0	1	1½
Procurations	0	6	8				

Benefactions.

Lady Billingfley gave 40*l.* for the ufe of the poor; and there is a ftock of 20*l.* the intereft of which is applied to the repair of the church.

Taxes.					
The Royal Aid in	1692, £.	212	4	0
Poll-tax — —	1694, —	24	8	0
Land-tax ——	1694, -	100	1	8
The fame, at 3*s.*	1770, —	81	1	3

About feventy years ago, here were 49 houfes, and about 240 inhabitants, of whom 7 were freeholders; yearly births 8, burials 7. *Atkyns.* The people at prefent are eftimated at about 260.

Walter, by Elizabeth his wife, daughter and heir of fir John Merbury, knight, had iffue fir Walter, his heir; fir John; and two daughters, Anne and Sibil.

The laft mentioned fir Walter married Anne, fole daughter and heir to William lord Ferrers of Chartley, and was fummoned to parliament by the title of lord Ferrers, 1 E. 4. and had a grant the fame year of feveral manors, &c. in recompence of his fervices in the wars againft king H. 6. He was flain, Aug. 22, 1485, in Bofworth-field, fighting for king Richard the Third, leaving iffue three fons, fir John, fir Richard, and fir Thomas; and one daughter Elizabeth.

John, the eldeft fon, was fummoned to parliament from the 3d to 12 H. 7. and wedding Cecilie, fifter and heir of Henry Bourchier, earl of Effex, had iffue by her Walter, his only fon, and one daughter Anne, married to Henry lord Clifford. Which Walter, for his gallant behaviour in the king's wars, was elected one of the knights companions of the garter, 15 H. 8. and afterwards, in further recompence of his great prudence, loyalty, and valour, was advanced to the dignity of vifcount Hereford, to him and his heirs males for ever, 4 E. 6. He had iffue by Mary, daughter of Thomas Grey, marquis of Dorfet, three fons, *viz.* Henry, who died unmarried; fir Richard Devereux, who died before his father; and fir William Devereux, who, by his firft wife Jane, daughter of John Scudamore, of Home Lacy in com. Hereford, efq; having no male iffue, after her deceafe married Margaret, daughter of Robert Garnifh, of Kenton in Suffolk, by whom he had iffue fir Edward Devereux, of Caftle Bromwich, in the county of Warwick, of whom hereafter as continuator of the male line.

Sir Richard Devereux, by Dorothy his wife, eldeft daughter of George the firft earl of Huntington, had iffue two fons, Walter and George; and two daughters, Elizabeth and Anne, and dying in his father's life-time, 1 E. 6. Walter, his fon, became 2d vifcount Hereford, and was created earl of Effex 14 Eliz. By Lettice his wife, daughter of fir Francis Knolles, knight of the Garter, he had iffue three fons, Robert, his fucceffor; Walter, flain at the fiege of Rouen, without iffue; Francis who died young; and two daughters, Penelope and Dorothy.

Robert, the eldeft fon, 3d vifcount Hereford and 2d earl of Effex, the famous favourite of queen Elizabeth, was beheaded in 1601, leaving iffue by Frances his wife, daughter and heir to fir Francis Walfingham, one fon and two daughters, *viz.* Robert, Frances, and Dorothy, who were reftored in blood 1 Jac. 1. whereby

Robert, the fon, fucceeded as 4th vifcount Hereford, and 3d earl of Effex, and was general of the parliament's forces in the reign of king Charles the Firft. His lordfhip dying without furviving iffue male, in 1646, the earldoms of Effex and Eu became extinct; but the title of vifcount Hereford devolved on fir Walter Devereux, eldeft furviving fon of fir Edward Devereux, of Caftle Bromwich, before mentioned, only fon of fir William Devereux, by his fecond wife, Margaret Garnifh: which fir Edward Devereux, by Catherine his wife, daughter of Edward Arden, of Park-hall in Warwickfhire, had fix fons and four daughters. Ambrofe, the eldeft, died unmarried; the others were fir Walter; William; fir George, the continuator of the male line; Edward, who died unmarried; and Henry: The daughters were Margaret, Anne, Howard, and Grace.

Sir Walter Devereux, the fecond fon, fucceeded to the title of vifcount Hereford, in 1646. He married Elizabeth, daughter of Thomas Knightley, of Borough-hall, in the county of Stafford, efq; and had iffue by her five fons, Effex, Leicefter, Walter, Edward, and John; of whom the firft, third, fourth, and fifth died without iffue.

Leicefter, the fecond fon, fucceeded as 6th vifcount Hereford. He had iffue, by Elizabeth his firft wife, daughter and heir to fir William Withipole, knight, one daughter Frances, married to William vifcount Tracy. And by Prifcilla, his fecond wife, daughter of John Catchpole, of the county of Suffolk, efq; left iffue two fons, Leicefter and Edward; and two daughters, *viz.* Elizabeth, who died unmarried; and Anne, mifreprefented in *Collins's Peerage* (V. 6, p. 213) as the wife of John-Symes Berkeley, efq; and mother of the prefent dutchefs dowager of Beaufort; whereas he married Elizabeth, relict of Edward the 8th vifcount Hereford, as appears by his memorial in the church of Stoke-Giffard, in this county.

Leicefter, the eldeft fon, fucceeded as 7th vifcount Hereford; but dying in 1682-3, being then about nine years of age,

Edward Devereux, his brother, became 8th vifcount Hereford. He married Elizabeth, daughter and coheir to Walter Norborne, of Calne in the county of Wilts, but died without iffue in 1700, and in him the male iffue of this branch became extinct.

I return therefore to fir George Devereux, fourth fon of fir Edward Devereux; which fir George, by Blanch his wife, daughter and heir of fir John Ridge, of Ridge in Shropfhire, left an only fon and heir, George, who by his wife Bridget, daughter and heir to Arthur Price, of Vaynor in Montgomeryfhire, efq; had two fons, Price, his heir apparent; and Vaughan Devereux, efq; feated at Nantaribba in the laft mentioned county, and the continuer of the male line. Price, the eldeft fon, died in his father's life-time, leaving, by Mary his wife, daughter of —— Stephens, of the city of Briftol, efq; an only fon,

Price, the 9th vifcount Hereford, who married Mary, fecond daughter of Samuel Sandys, of Omberfley-court, in the county of Worcefter, efq; by whom he had iffue one fon, Price Devereux, born in 1694; and one daughter, Mary; and dying in 1740, aged 77, was fucceeded by his faid only fon,

Price Devereux, 10th vifcount Hereford. His lordfhip was twice married, but died in 1748, without iffue; wherefore the honour defcended to the male heir of Vaughan Devereux, efq; who, as before recited, was feated at Nantaribba in the county of Montgomery, and by Mary his wife, daughter of —— Fox, efq; left a fon Arthur Devereux, who married two wives; firft, a daughter of Evan Glynn, of Glynn, efq; and by her had two fons, Arthur, buried at Forden in 1737, without iffue; and Vaughan, who died an infant in 1712. By his fecond wife Elizabeth, daughter of Richard Glynn, efq; he had iffue

Edward, 11th vifcount Hereford, who took his feat in the houfe of peers in 1750. His lordfhip married Catherine, daughter of Richard Mytton, of Gartle in the county of Montgomery, efq; by whom he had iffue three fons and two daughters, *viz.* Arthur Devereux, born in 1740, and died in 1743; Edward, the prefent vifcount Hereford; George, Bridget, and Catherine. And dying in 1760, his lordfhip was fucceeded by his faid eldeft furviving fon,

Edward, now 12th vifcount Hereford, who married Henrietta-Charlotte, daughter of Anthony-Keck Tracy, efq; and in her right is lord of the manor of Stanway. His lordfhip's arms are, *Argent, a fefs gules, in chief three torteauxes.* CREST. *In a ducal coronet Or, a talbot's head argent, eared gules.* SUPPORTERS. On the dexter fide, *A talbot argent, eared gules, with a ducal coronet of the fecond.* On the finifter, *A Rein-deer of the laft, attired, gorged with a ducal coronet, and chained Or.* MOTTO. BASIS VIRTVTVM CONSTANTIA. His lordfhip's chief feat is at Nantaribba, in the county of Montgomery.

This pedigree is extracted from *Collins's Peerage*, where the reader may fee the authorities.

STAPLETON.

STAPLETON.

THIS pariſh lies in the hundred of Barton Regis, three miles diſtant north-eaſt from the city of Briſtol, nine weſt from Marſhfield, and thirty-three ſouth-weſtward from Glouceſter.

It is a very pretty village, with ſeveral good houſes, of which the following are the chief:

Heath Houſe is ſituate on a great eminence, about half a mile on the north ſide of the turnpike-road to Briſtol. The terras commands an exceeding fine proſpect of Stoke Houſe, of the village of Stapleton, and of the above-mentioned city, with the pretty villas and populous country about it. The proſpect is cloſed by Lanſdown and Sodbury hills on one ſide, and by Dundery and the Somerſetſhire hills on the other; and in the intermediate ſpaces of this extenſive landſcape, are beautiful and well cultivated incloſures and plantations, thro' which the river Froome, with various meanders, takes its courſe to Briſtol, and forms the quay of that port. There is nothing, for healthineſs of air, can exceed this ſituation, in which reſpect it may emulate even Stoke itſelf. This houſe and eſtate belong to Mrs. Whitchurch, the ſole heireſs of the family of the Walters, who have reſided in this pariſh ever ſince the ſecond year of the reign of king Edward the Sixth.

Oldbury Houſe is the ſeat of Thomas-Hayward Winſtone, eſq; who reſides there. Near to it, upon the hill, is a ſmall camp, which gave name to the place.

At *Ridgway* Doctor Drummond has a good houſe, pleaſantly ſituated in the road leading to Chipping Sodbury, a little more than two miles diſtant from Briſtol.

Mr. Lockwood, Mr. Hart, and Mr. Harford have very handſome houſes, and pleaſant gardens, in the village of Stapleton, and others may poſſibly deſerve mention that have eſcaped particular notice.

Here is a well, whoſe waters guſh out from many places in a perpendicular direction, like a boiling caldron, and has been uſed as a cold bath, with great ſucceſs, in diſorders for which cold bathing is preſcribed; however, my inquiries concerning it will not authorize me to attribute to this water any greater virtues than cold ſprings poſſeſs in general. This is called the Boiling-well, and is ſo copious as to drive a mill at about a quarter of a mile from its ſource.

Of the Manor and other Eſtates.

There is no particular mention of Stapleton in *Domeſday*, wherefore it muſt be included in the account of ſome other manor. Sir Robert Atkyns, in the 26th page of his *Ancient and Preſent State of Gloſterſhire*, ſpeaking of Robert de Todeni, ſays, ‘He was poſleſt of eighty one Mannors, ‘whereof Riſendon, Horton, Stapleton, and ‘Frampton were in Gloſterſhire. He gave a ‘Plow's Tillage in Stapleton to the Priory which ‘he had founded at Belvoir, to pray for the Soul of ‘Adela his Wife.’ But this is all miſtake reſpecting Stapleton, of which it does not appear that Robert de Todeni was ever poſſeſſed; but Saperton and Frampton in the hundred of Biſley, were antiently the eſtates of Robert de Todeni.

This manor belonged to the Berkeleys of Stoke Giffard for a long courſe of time. Richard Berkeley, eſq; was lord of it in the year 1608. Sir Maurice Berkeley ſold out divers tenements to the citizens of Briſtol, and others, but reſerved the royalty, which is now veſted in her grace the dutcheſs dowager of Beaufort, ſiſter and heireſs of the late Norborne Berkeley, lord Botetourt, a more particular account of whoſe family is given under Stoke Giffard.

John de Alleber (Delabere) held one yard land in Stapleton, by the ſervice of carrying the king's writs one day's journey from the caſtle of Glouceſter at his own charges, and the reſt of the journey at the king's expence, 5 H. 3. Roger de Goſſenton was ſeized of lands in Stapleton for guarding the king's foreſt of Kingſwood 15 E. 1. Roger Kemys, a lunatick, held lands in Stapleton 21 E. 4. John White levied a fine of lands in this place to Roger Walroon 1 E. 6.

HAMLETS. 1. *Oldbury.* William Dodiſham levied a fine of the manor of Oldbury in Stapleton, to the uſe of William Dodiſham his ſon, and Joan his wife, in taille, 8 H. 6. Thomas Winſtone, eſq; died ſeized of it in 1757, and gave it to Mrs. Winſtone, his widow; in virtue of whoſe will it paſſed afterwards to Thomas Hayward, (ſecond ſon of her brother Thomas Hayward, of Quedgley, eſq;) who marrying a niece of the late Mr. Winſtone's, aſſumed his family name, and is the preſent proprietor of Oldbury, and high ſheriff of this county, 1777.

2. *Ruggeway*, or *Ridgway*, is a diſtinct manor, lying one part in this pariſh, the other in Mangotsfield, under which head ſome account of it has already been given. Sir Jarrit Smyth, baronet, is lord of the manor.

Of the Church, &c.

The church is a curacy, in the deanery of Briſtol, worth about 20*l.* a year, before it was augmented, in the year 1720, by a donation from Edward Colſton and Thomas Edwards, eſqrs and with the queen's bounty. Mrs. Whitchurch is patroneſs, and the reverend Mr. Shute is the preſent incumbent.

The impropriation belonged to St. James's monaſtery in Briſtol, and was granted to —— Brain 35 H. 8. It came afterwards to the Walters, and is now veſted in Mrs. Mary Whitchurch, widow of the late Joſeph Whitchurch, eſq; and ſole heireſs of the Walter family. The arms of the Walters are, *Azure, upon a nut bough iſſuing from the ſiniſter baſe proper, a ſquirrel ſejant Or.*

The church is ſmall, but neat, dedicated to the Holy Trinity, and has a low pinnacled tower at the weſt end, with ſix bells in it.

Monuments and Inſcriptions.

A braſs plate, fixt to a flat ſtone in the chancel, bears this inſcription :

Hic jacet Sepultum Corpus
Matthæi Walteri Generoſi hujus Parochiæ
Incolæ qui e uita deceſſit die Aprilis
uigeſimo octauo Anno Domini 1680
Ætatisq; Suæ Octogeſimo.

Quod me genuit idem occidit Ex
inquinato Semine ortus ejuſdem uenenô
mortuus ſum Ah ſæua genitrix ipſoq;
Struthio camelo crudelior quæ ſuam
ipſius auſa eſt necare prolem Alte . . . .
beatus Phœnix ille qui moriendo
e cineribus hiſce faciet uivus reſurgerem
ac in æternum viverem.

Againſt the north wall, near the communion table, there is a very handſome marble monument, with the following inſcription :

In the Family Vault near this Place
reſt in Hopes of a bleſſed Reſurrection,
THOMAS WALTER, *Eſq*[r] who dyed 28th December 1728.
He married MARY, Daughter of WILLIAM ROWLES, *Eſq*[r]
of *Newnham* in this County, who dyed 25th January 1744.
ROWLES WALTER their Son dyed 24th April 1733.
He married 3[d] January 1712, JANE Daughter of
NATHANIEL PYRKE of *Little Dean* in this County *Eſq*[r]:
by whom he left one Son THOMAS, & one Daughter MARY.
THO[s] Son of ROWLES & JANE, dyed 8th October 1738 aged 19.
JOSEPH WHITCHURCH, *Eſq*[r]: dyed 6th Auguſt 1772.
He married 19th Auguſt 1736 MARY Daughter of
ROWLES WALTER, *Eſq*[r]: by whom he left an only Daughter
JANE, married 11th Auguſt 1767, to THO[s] SMITH of
Long-Aſhton, in the County of *Somerſet*, *Eſq*[r].
This Monument was erected by MARY WHITCHURCH,
in reſpectful Memory of her much beloved Huſband & Friends.

Arms, *Gules, three talbots heads* 2 *and* 1 *erazed Or* ; *on a chief argent, gutty du ſang, a lion paſſant ſable,* for Whitchurch.

Upon a braſs plate in the chancel,

Under this Stone by his own appointment lie interred the Relicks of JOSEPH WHITCHURCH, Eſq; who dyed 6th Auguſt 1772. He was an affectionate Huſband, a kind Father, and a ſincere Friend, and rejoiced in every Opportunity of rendering Service to the Diſtreſſed.

Upon the vaſe of a neat marble monument againſt the ſouth wall, it is thus inſcribed :

SACRED TO THE MEMORY
of
THOMAS WINSTONE of this Pariſh Eſq[r]
A Gentleman of unblemiſhed Honour & Integrity ;
who died July 4th 1757 in the 60th Year of his Age.
IN TESTIMONY
of her Love and Gratitude,
this Monument was erected by his faithful Relict
ALBINA WINSTONE.

The arms upon this monument are, *Per pale gules and azure, over all a lion rampant argent, holding in his paws a tree proper.*

Againſt the north wall of the church,

M. S.

Hic juxta inhumatur Thomas Bubb hujuſce Parochiæ Generoſus, ex Natis Thomæ Bubb ibidem Armigeri Primogenitus et Hæres. Vir Ingenio Sagaci admodum ac faceto, Scientiâ literis et Artibus omnimodò excultus, aliiſq; Virtutibus ornatus; Quibus tamen illuſtrandis nimis obſtrarunt ſua Verecundia et Receſſûs Amor. Obijt decimo ſexto Calend. Maij Anno poſt Natum D. Chriſtum MDCCIX Ætatis ſuæ 64.

Lactea perſequitur Genius Veſtigia Cœlis
Dum tuus, atq; Choros micat inter (amice) beatos,
Hoc jaceant Cineres ſub ſacro limine dulces
Immortæ donec (terrâ flagrante) reſurgent,
Sollicitæ tandem geniales quærere ſedes,
Quas facile invenient, cœleſti Lampade ductæ,
Ac inibi æternum requie potientur amenâ.

At the top of the monument are theſe arms, *Per pale Or and ermine, over all on a bend gules three unicorns heads erazed ſable.*

There is likewiſe a memorial for John Wyatt, of this pariſh, gent. who died in 1713, aged 90 ; for Anne his wife, daughter of William Self, of Milſham, in the county of Wilts, who died in 1696, aged 70 ; and for two of their children, Mary, the wife of Thomas Webb, who died in 1729, aged 80 ; and Elizabeth, who died an infant ; with their arms, *viz. Baron and femme,* 1. *Or, on a feſs gules between three boars heads couped ſable, as many mullets of the firſt.* 2. *Ermine, three chevronels gules.*

Benefactions.

Mrs. Anne Whittington gave 5 *l. per ann.* together with the intereſt of 115 *l.* 16 *s.* to be diſtributed to the poor ; alſo, 1 *l.* 1 *s.* 6 *d.* to the miniſter, at Chriſtmas, for ever.

Thomas Webb, eſq; gave the intereſt of 50 *l.* to the poor ; and Mrs. Mary Webb gave 10 *s.* a year to the miniſter for a ſermon, 2 *s.* to the clerk, and 2 *s.* in bread to the poor on Good Friday, for ever.

Mrs. Sarah Packer, in 1754, and Mrs. Mary Packer, in 1757, gave the intereſt of 100 *l.* each to ſuch poor people as do not receive alms.

Mrs. Frances Berkeley gave 20 *s.* yearly for ever, for a ſermon on the 30th of January, and the like ſum to the poor in bread on that day.

Thomas Bubb, eſq; gave 10 *s.* a year for a ſermon on Trinity Sunday, for ever. And Mr. John Widlake gave 10 *s.* a year to the rector of St. Peter's church in Briſtol, for a ſermon here on St. John's day, for ever.

Here is a charity ſchool, founded and ſupported by the following contributions : Mrs. Mary Webb, in 1729, gave 450 *l.* A perſon unknown, in 1731, gave 100 *l.* Mr. Berkeley, in 1744, gave 85 *l.* 10 *s.* George Packer, eſq; in 1745, gave 50 *l.* And in 1754, Miſs Elizabeth Bayly gave 50 *l.* So that from the intereſt the ſchool-maſter's income is about 24 *l.* a year, beſides a houſe to live in.

Taxes.					
The Royal Aid in	1692,	£. 131	0	0
Poll-tax —	1694,	— 83	16	0
Land-tax —	1694,	— 195	4	0
The ſame, at 3 *s.*	1770,	— 141	13	6

At the beginning of this century, there were about 160 houſes, and 700 inhabitants in this pariſh, whereof 30 were freeholders ; yearly births 16, burials 13. *Atkyns.* Since that time population has very much increaſed, for the average of annual baptiſms from 1773 to 1776, both incluſive, have been 41, of burials 42. And deducting 10 from the burials, on account of perſons brought hither from other places, and then reckoning the number of living in the proportion of 40 to 1 of the annual burials, the preſent number of inhabitants will be about 1280.

STAVERTON

IS a ſmall pariſh, in the lower diviſion of the hundred of Derhurſt, five miles diſtant ſouth from Tewkeſbury, four weſt from Cheltenham, and five north from Glouceſter.

It lies in the Vale, yet the greater part is in tillage, and moſt of the arable lands in common fields.

fields. It has nothing curious in natural hiftory or antiquity.

The turnpike-road from Gloucefter to Cheltenham leads thro' the fouth part of the parifh, and all befides are very miry and founderous. The poor are chiefly employ'd in hufbandry.

Of the Manor and other Eftates.

The following is all that is recorded of this manor in *Domefday*:

'The church of St. Dyonifius at Paris holds 'three hides in Starventon.' p. 72.

John Browning held the manor of Staverton and Yenington 3 H. 5. Sir Richard Baker was lord of the manor of Staverton in the year 1608. The earl of Oxford was proprietor of it, and of Uckington in the parifh of Elmfton, at the beginning of this century. From his heirs it paffed, by purchafe, as a member of the manor of Uckington, to Mr. Rogers of Dowdefwell, and Mrs. Rogers, widow of the late John Rogers, efq; is the prefent lady of the manor of Uckington in Elmfton, where fhe holds a court leet, at which the inhabitants of Staverton attend.

Edward Brugge, efq; held lands in Staverton 15 H. 6.

Part of *Haydon* lies in Staverton, and pays to the parochial levies; the other part is in the parifh of Bodington.

Of the Church, &c.

The church is a vicarage, within the peculiar of Derhurft, worth about 120*l.* a year, to which Bodington is annexed. Mrs. Lock is patronefs, and Mr. Kipling is the prefent incumbent. The vicar has the great tithes of the manor of Staverton.

The advowfon of the church, as well as the manor, formerly belonged to the priory of Derhurft; but when that houfe was fuppreffed with other alien priories, the advowfon was granted to the abbey of Tewkefbury, in which it continued 'till the general diffolution of religious foundations, in the reign of king Henry the Eighth. It was afterwards granted to Thomas Gatwick and Anfelm Lamb, 5 Mariæ.

The church has a very low tower, with three bells, at the weft end, and is dedicated to St. Catherine, who is faid to have been a virgin, martyred in the year 307, by means of a wheel ftuck full of iron hooks, which from her is called a Catherine Wheel.

Firft fruits £.	12	0	0	Synodals £.			
Tenths —	1	4	0	Pentecoft.	0	0	4½
Procurations							

Benefactions.

Lands worth 6*l.* a year are given for the ufe of the poor, and there is befides, a fmall donation of 6*s.* a year left for fuch poor people as do not receive parifh collection. The lands given to the poor were formerly of much greater value, but a confiderable part has been long fince loft.

Uckington, tho' a hamlet in Elmfton, is joined in fome payments with this parifh.

Staverton and Uckington.

Taxes. The Royal Aid in	1692,	£. 69	0	0
Poll-tax ——	1694, —	11	0	0
Land-tax ——	1694, —	64	7	4
The fame, at 3*s.*	1770, —	49	14	0

About the beginning of the prefent century, according to fir Robert Atkyns, there were 40 houfes in the parifh, and about 200 inhabitants, 8 of whom were freeholders; yearly births 6, burials 6. But fir Robert's eftimate muft have been much too high; for I am informed by a perfon who has refided in the parifh upwards of feventy years, that there are now three houfes more than when he firft knew it, and the prefent number is only 24. His extract from the regifter is equally incorrect, for in ten years, from 1700 to 1709 inclufive, there are entered 34 baptifms, and 19 burials; and in the fame number of years, from 1760 to 1769 inclufive, there are regiftered 58 baptifms, and 29 burials. The people are fuppofed to have increafed fince the beginning of this century, and are now eftimated at about 120.

STINCHCOMBE

Is a parifh in the hundred of Berkeley, four miles diftant eaft from the town of that name, two weft from Durfley, and fifteen fouth from Gloucefter.

It adjoins to the parifh of Cam, of which it was formerly a part, and confifts chiefly of fine pafture land, with fome good arable, and produces excellent cheefe, and pretty good cyder.

This village is fheltered on the eaft by a lofty hill, on whofe top there is a large plain, which formerly the people of this part of the country very much frequented to play at the robuft game of ftoball. The weft fummit of this hill commands a bird's-eye view of Berkeley-caftle, and a moft extenfive profpect into Somerfetfhire, Monmouthfhire, Herefordfhire, Worcefterfhire, and feveral parts of South Wales. Some indeed pretend, that thirteen counties, and thirty parifh churches may be feen from it in a very fair day, but I mention this only from Dr. Parfons's manufcript Collections, and not from my own knowledge. The feveral profpects are no lefs rich than extenfive. North-weftward, the fine verdure and beautiful inclofures in the Vale, and the long courfe of the river Severn, with its windings, make the fore ground of the landfcape; beyond, are the venerable oaks of Dean foreft, towering one above the other, and waving in all the grandeur of fylvan majefty; and laftly, the Welch Mountains, at a great diftance behind, appear like a cloud faintly coloured, and clofe the profpect.

Great quantities of foffils, confifting of petrifications of the cockle, mufcle, fcallop, and other fifh fiſh of the bivalvular kind, are found incorporated in a reddiſh ſtone, of a coarſe grit, at a place called Newnham's quarry; and ſeveral of the *Cornua Ammonis* have alſo been found there. Theſe are all the curious natural productions which the pariſh affords, and it ſeems to be totally deſtitute of antiquities.

Of the Manor and other Eſtates.

William de Alba Mara held the manor of Stinchcombe and Thorp 40 H. 3.

Thomas de Braddeſton, a very eminent perſon in his time, was advanced to the dignity of a peer of the realm 16 E. 3. and died ſeized of the manors of Stinchcombe, Horton, and Bradeſtone (from the latter of which he took his name) in the 34th year of the ſame reign. Agnes, the widow of Thomas de Braddeſton, died ſeized of Stinchcombe, Arlingham, and Horton, in dower, 43 E. 3. Thomas lord Braddeſton, ſon of Robert, and grandſon of Thomas, was poſſeſſed of the manors of Stinchcombe, Arlingham, Horton, and Bradeſtone in Berkeley, at the time of his death, 48 E. 3. and Ela, his widow, died ſeized of Stinchcombe and Stancombe 11 H. 4.

Richard Seimour ſeems to have been a truſtee of the Bradſtones, for he was poſſeſſed of all the before-mentioned manors 2 H. 4.

Sir Walter de la Pool, in right of Elizabeth his wife, daughter and heireſs of the laſt Thomas de Braddeſton, was ſeized of Stinchcombe, Arlingham, Draycot's Place in Horton, and Bradſtone in Berkeley, 12 H. 6. And ſir Edward Ingoldſthorp was ſeized of this manor, and of others which had belonged to the Bradſtones, in the 35th year of the laſt-mentioned reign.

Stinchcombe came afterwards to lord Wentworth, who ſold it to divers perſons, in the reign of queen Elizabeth. John Holliſter was lord of it in the year 1608. It was veſted in Thomas Pinfold, eſq; when ſir Robert Atkyns compiled his account of it, and John Pinfold, eſq; is the preſent lord of the manor, and reſides at Peer's-Court in this pariſh. His arms are, *Azure, two couple cloſes Or, between three hickwalls, or French pies, argent, beak'd and member'd of the ſecond.*

The Tyndales, (from whom the reverend Mr. Richard Tyndale of Charfield is deſcended) were a very reſpectable family, long reſident in this pariſh, where they had a good eſtate. Thomas Tyndale died ſome time before 33 H. 8. as appears by a deed of that date, to which Edward Tyndale of Pull Court in Worceſterſhire, (anceſtor of the preſent Tyndales of Bathford) was a party. By Alicia his wife, daughter and ſole heir of Thomas Hunt, he had iſſue five ſons, Richard, William, Henry, Thomas, and John; and one daughter Elizabeth. Richard, the eldeſt ſon, had a ſon and heir Richard, who had iſſue eight ſons, and four daughters. Thomas Tyndale of Stinchcombe, clothier, was his eldeſt ſon and heir. He married Catherine, the daughter and heir of John Harris, gent. by whom he had iſſue Thomas Tyndale, and making his will, died in 1637, as appears by the Probat dated Oct. 12, the ſame year. Thomas Tyndale, his ſon, lived at Stinchcombe in the reign of king Charles the Firſt, and being inimical to the king's cauſe, fled from his houſe at the approach of a party of royaliſts, and hid himſelf for three days and nights in a large yew-tree, now growing at the top of Stinchcombe wood, whence he had the mortification to ſee Mr. Pinfold's houſe and his own burnt to the ground.

Richard Tyndale, uncle to the laſt Thomas, and fourth ſon of the laſt Richard, had iſſue Daniel Tyndale of Stinchcombe, who married Katherine, daughter and heir of John Wilkins, by whom he had two ſons, Richard, who died a batchelor, and John Tyndale, clerk; which ſaid John, about the year 1724, married Mary, daughter of Thomas Lodge, clerk, and had iſſue four ſons, and one daughter, Mary. William, the firſt ſon, married Mary, daughter and heir of Nicholas Lodge, of Briſtol, and had iſſue one ſon William, who died an infant; and one daughter Mary. He died rector of Charfield in 1764. John and Daniel, the ſecond and fourth ſons, died without iſſue; and Richard, the third ſon, is now rector of Charfield. See more of the Tyndales under the account of Eaſtwood, in the pariſh of Thornbury.

Langley-hill in Stinchcombe, with the chapel called St. Michael's chapel, and lands in Stancombe, were granted to Thomas lord Seimour, after whoſe attainder, they were granted to William marquis of Northampton, 5 E. 6.

HAMLETS. 1. *Clinger.* 'Roger [de 'Berchelai] holds one hide in Claenhangare, part 'of the land of this manor [Berchelai].' *D.B.* p.68.

2. *Stancombe* is another hamlet.

Of the Church, &c.

The church is a curacy, in the deanery of Durſley, worth about 45*l.* a year. The biſhop of Glouceſter is patron and impropriator, and the rev. Mr. John Webb is the preſent incumbent.

The living has been augmented by a donation from Mr. Pinfold, and the queen's bounty, with which lands in Bradſtone have been purchaſed, now let at 25*l. per ann.* 'Till then, the incumbent only received 20*l.* a year from the leſſee of the great tithes.

The church is dedicated to St. Cyril, and has a ſmall ſteeple with one bell in it. The whole building was repaired in the year 1763, and is now both handſome and convenient.

Monuments and Inſcriptions.

Againſt the ſouth wall of the chancel, is this inſcription:

M. S.
Ionathani Smith,
Viri in S. Scripturis docti,
Verbi divini præconis aſſidui,
Pietatis, humilitatis, hoſpitj, et Chriſtianæ
vrbanitatis exemplaris viri,
in vita dilecti, in morte defleti.

Natus

Natus fuit in Civitate Roffenfi Aprilis XVI Anno
MDCIX in Hibernia vero educatus, inde reverfus
Vxorem duxit
Abigail filiam unigenitam Richardi Miles Civis Cantuarienfis
defunctam poftquam peperiffet filium unicum Ionathanum
Poftea duxit Ianam fororem Iohannis Markey Armigeri
Superftitem.
In Ecclefia Roffiana in agro Herefordienfi per duodecim
annos Chrifti Evangelium publice docuit, et poft regis
ingreffum inde expulfus manfit tamen in vinea domini
quotidie ad finem ufque laborans
Ex hac vitâ migravit, Febri duplici quartanâ
decimo die decembris Anno
Domini M. DCLXX
ætatis vero fuæ
LXII.
Et jacet hic fepultus.
Quid opus unimodæ legis folvantur habenæ
(Gloria in Excelfis) lingua foluta canit.
From preaching Chrift to us, to Chrift he's gone
Praifes to fing before his glorious throne.

In the fame chancel, is the following infcription in gold letters:

H. S. E.
Elizabetha Compeer, Uxor Roberti Compeer, Gen:
Filia unica Iohanis King, A.M. hujus Eccle[ae]. Paftoris,
Ingenuæ Indolis, judicii fupra Sexum et ætatem fublimis.
Probitatum Modeftiæ, utramq; Pietati et Charitati
Eo modo Superaddidit, quo Solo melius Religioni,
Uti par eft, Ancillarentur.
Sic divinas Virtutes cum humanis in fe una conjuxit,
Conjunctas excoluit, excultas exemplo fuo infignivit.
Filiam obfequentem Parentes,
Amantiffimam Conjugem Maritus,
Amicam comem et benignam Neceffarij,
Singuli quia charam Univerfis
Defiderant.
Obijt gravida, Maij 20, A. D. 1713 Ætat. 23°
Quam juxta etiam jacet condita,
Elizabetha,
Filia unica, quæ cum annos duos vix numeraffet,
Et vel hac ætatula egregia ingenij edidit fpecimina,
Mortalitati valedixit Octob. die 4to
A. D. 1712
Monumentum hoc Iohanes King
Pater Mœrens pofuit.

And near it,

To the Memory of Robert Compeer Gent. who was buried the 22[d] Day of June 1720 Aged 28 Years.

A handfome monument of white marble, placed againft the north wall of the church, is thus infcribed:

In the Churchyard
Near this place lie interred the Remains of
JOHN PINFOLD Sen[r] of this Parifh,
and *ELIZABETH* his Wife [*MAN*)
(one of the Daughters of *JOHN* and *ELIZABETH TROT-*
He } died { Jan[y] 30th. 1705 } Aged { 94 } Years.
She } died { Mar. 14th. 1701 } Aged { 83 } Years.
Alfo of *JOHN* their eldeft Son and *CATHERINE* his Wife;
He } Died { Dec[r] 26th 1726 } Aged { 82 } Years.
She } Died { May 10th 1723 } Aged { 72 } Years.
Alfo of *THOMAS ANNA* and *MARY* Son and Daughters
of the aforefaid *JOHN* and *ELIZABETH PINFOLD.*
THOMAS } died { Jan[y] 14th 1738 } Aged { 83 } Years.
ANNA } died { Aug[st] 10th 1667 } Aged { 24 } Years.
MARY } died { Sept[r] 10th 1716 } Aged { 68 } Years. [*FOLD*
Alfo of *JOHN* Son of the faid *JOHN* and *CATHERINE PIN-*
and *MARY* his Wife:
He } Died { Jan[ry] 17th 1732 } Aged { 59 } Years.
She } Died { Oct[r] 11th 1739 } Aged { 66 } Years.
Alfo of *ELIZABETH* Daughter of the aforefaid *JOHN* and
CATHERINE PINFOLD, who died May 10th 1708 aged 24 years
Alfo of *MARTHA* Wife of *JOHN PINFOLD* Jun[r] who Died
May 9th 1756 Aged 51 Years.

The monument is ornamented at top with a fcutcheon of two coats, *Baron and femme*, 1. *Azure, a chevron voided Or between three hickwalls, or French pies, argent*, for Pinfold. 2. *Azure, on a chevron between three owls argent, as many mullets fable, within a bordure ingrailed ermine*, for Hill.

There is likewife a memorial for Samuel Tyndale, merchant, fon of William Tyndale of Stinchcombe, who died in 1673; but the whole of the infcription is not legible.

Benefactions.

Lands worth 7*l.* a year were vefted in feoffees for charitable ufes, by a perfon unknown, 1 Jac. 1. Matthew Tyndale of London, merchant, in 1676, gave two grounds, worth about 8*l. per ann.* the income of which to be thus difpofed of; one third to the minifter, one third for teaching children to read, and the remainder to the poor. And Mr. Henry Stubbs, a diffenting minifter, left 10*s.* a year to buy New Teftaments for poor children.

Taxes.			£.	s.	d.
	The Royal Aid in	1692,	92	2	0
	Poll-tax ——	1694, —	16	15	0
	Land-tax —	1694, —	74	12	0
	The fame, at 3*s.*	1770, —	74	14	3

At the beginning of this century, there were 120 houfes in the parifh, and about 500 inhabitants, 18 of whom were freeholders; yearly births 15, burials 14. *Atkyns.* The inhabitants are now eftimated to be about 450.

STOKE GIFFARD.

THIS parifh lies in the hundred of Henbury, four miles diftant northward from Briftol, nine fouth-weft from Chipping Sodbury, and twenty-two fouth-weftward from Gloucefter.

It is a large parifh, confifting of fome arable and woodlands, but the greater part is pafturage.

There are feveral Stokes in this county, as Stoke Archer, Stoke Bifhop, and this *Stoke*, which received the additional name of *Giffard*, by way of diftinction, from the family of that name, who enjoyed it for many generations immediately after the conqueft.

Stoke Houfe is the feat of the dutchefs dowager of Beaufort. It was built originally in the time of queen Elizabeth, by fir Richard Berkeley, and was greatly damaged in the civil wars in the reign of king Charles the Firft. The prefent houfe was partly rebuilt, and otherwife beautified and repaired, by the late lord Botetourt, about the year 1760; and the motto, (MIHI VOBISQVE) placed in the front by his lordfhip, is ftrongly expreffive of the amiable difpofition and generofity that fo eminently diftinguifhed its owner.

It is a noble pile, exquifitely fituated, like Windfor Caftle, to command a great extent of rich country to the eaft and fouth of it, with a large view of the city of Briftol, and its populous environs. The profpect clofes with the great chain of hills about Sodbury on one fide, and with the Somerfetfhire hills on the other.

The lofty terras in front gives it an air of grandeur and magnificence not to be defcribed. It ftands about three hundred yards diftant from one of the great roads leading to Briftol, and a

beautiful

beautiful lawn, interſperſed with trees, ſlopes down from it, in all the unaffected elegance of nature.

The muſe that ſung of Clifton, paid her devoirs to Stoke; but, like the writer of this account, ſhe was too deficient in deſcriptive powers to do it juſtice.

I cannot find, upon inquiry, that Stoke affords any curious natural productions, or antiquities.

Of the Manor and other Eſtates.

Oſbern Gifard aſſiſted king William the Firſt in the conqueſt of England, and was rewarded, for his ſervices, with twenty manors, of which four were in Glouceſterſhire, *viz.* Rochemtune, Brimesfelde, Aldeberie, and Stoche; which latter is the ſubject under immediate conſideration, and *Domeſday* gives the following particulars of it:

'Oſbern Gifard holds Stoche, in Letberg hun-'dred. There are five hides taxed. Dunne held 'it. In demean are four plow-tillages, and eight 'villeins, and three bordars, and a prieſt, with 'eight plow-tillages. There are four *ſervi*. It 'was worth 6*l.* and is now worth 8*l.*' p. 76.

The Giffards had a caſtle at Brimpsfield, which was the reſidence of the family, and continued in the name, 'till John Giffard was taken priſoner at the battle of Boroughbridge, in open rebellion againſt king Edward the Second, and afterwards attainted, and executed at Glouceſter as a traitor; 'till which time this manor of Stoke deſcended in ſucceſſion, like Brimpsfield, to the ſeveral branches of that family.

The manor of Stoke was held of the honour of Glouceſter, and was granted to ſir Maurice de Berkeley, after the death of Margaret Giffard, the third wife of John Giffard, 11 E. 3. This Maurice de Berkeley was the ſecond ſon of Maurice lord Berkeley, of Berkeley caſtle, by Eve his firſt wife, daughter of Eudo la Zouch, lord Zouch, as may be ſeen more at large, (p. 274) in the account of the anceſtors of the earl of Berkeley. He died at Calais, 21 E. 3. leaving iſſue by Margaret his wife,

Sir Thomas Berkeley, who married Catherine, daughter of ſir John de Bitton, knight, and dying in the year 1360, left iſſue one ſon,

Maurice, who married Catherine, youngeſt daughter and coheir of John lord Botetourt. He was ſeated at Stoke Giffard, and dying in 1361, left iſſue,

Sir Maurice Berkeley, who took to wife Joan, daughter of ſir John Dynham, knight, and dying in the year 1400, left her with child of

Maurice Berkeley, who held Stoke Giffard and Uley 10 H. 5. He married Ellen, daughter of ſir William Montford, knight, and died 4 E. 4. leaving by her an only ſon,

Sir William Berkeley, who was made a knight of the Bath at the coronation of Richard the Third, and was high ſheriff of Glouceſterſhire in the third year of that reign. He left the kingdom when king Richard was ſlain in Boſworth-field, and being attainted 1 H. 7. his eſtates were ſeized into the king's hands, and the manor of Stoke Giffard was granted the ſame year to Jaſper duke of Bedford, and his heirs males; but ſir William was afterwards received into favour, and Stoke Giffard was granted to him 4 H. 7. after the entail on the duke of Bedford, who died without iſſue 11 H. 7. when ſir William came into poſſeſſion again; but his eſtates were much impaired during the alienation. He died ſeized of Stoke Giffard in 1501, leaving iſſue, by his wife Anne, daughter of ſir Humphry Stafford, knight, one ſon,

Sir Richard Berkeley, who married Elizabeth, daughter of ſir Humphry Coningſby, knight, and by her had iſſue two ſons, and three daughters, *viz.* ſir John, ſir Maurice, afterwards of Bruton in Somerſetſhire, anceſtor of the lords Berkeley of Stratton; Mary, Frances, and Anne, married to Thomas Speke, eſq. He died in 1514, and was ſucceeded by his eldeſt ſon,

Sir John Berkeley, of Stoke Giffard, who died in 1546, having married Iſabel, daughter of ſir William Dennis, knight, by whom he had iſſue a ſon and heir,

Sir Richard Berkeley, who received the honour of knighthood Aug. 1, 1574. He married two wives, *viz.* Elizabeth, daughter of ſir William Read, of Glouceſter, knight, and Elianor, daughter of Robert Jermie, of Norfolk, eſq; and relict of ſir Robert Roe, knight, and alderman of London. By the former he had iſſue two ſons, Henry and William; and three daughters, Elizabeth, Mary, and Catherine; and dying in 1604, was ſucceeded by his eldeſt ſon,

Henry Berkeley, eſq; who dying Feb. 7, 1607, left iſſue by his wife Mariel, or Myrriel, daughter of Thomas Throckmorton, of Coughton in Warwickſhire, eſq; an only ſon,

Richard Berkeley, eſq; who had two wives, Mary, daughter of Robert Roe, eſq; by whom he had a ſon Maurice; and Jane, daughter of Thomas Mariet, of Berkſhire, by whom he had no iſſue. He deceaſed May 12, 1661, and was ſucceeded by his grandſon Richard, ſon of ſir Maurice Berkeley, who died in his father's life-time, in 1654. This ſir Maurice was twice married, firſt to Elizabeth, daughter of ſir Edward Coke, lord chief juſtice of the king's bench, by whom he had one daughter Frances, who died in 1660, without iſſue; ſecondly, to Mary, daughter of ſir George Tipping, of the county of Oxford, knight, by whom he had iſſue the ſaid

Richard Berkeley, who married Elizabeth, daughter of Henry Symes, of Frampton Cotterel in Glouceſterſhire, eſq; by whom, at his death in 1671, he had iſſue two ſons, George, and John-Symes.

George Berkeley, eſq; married Jane, daughter of Maurice Berkeley, viſcount Fitz-Harding, and died without iſſue in 1685, and was ſucceeded by his brother,

John-

John-Symes Berkeley, who married firſt, Suſan, daughter and ſole heireſs of ſir Thomas Fowles, knight, banker, and citizen of London, but by her, who died in 1696, had no iſſue. His ſecond wife was Elizabeth, daughter and coheir of Walter Norborne, of Caln in Wiltſhire, eſq; (by his wife Frances, daughter and coheir of ſir Edmund Bacon, of Redgrave in Suffolk, baronet,) and relict of Edward viſcount Hereford, by whom he had iſſue a ſon Norborne; and a daughter Elizabeth, married to Charles-Noel, duke of Beaufort, by whom ſhe is mother of the preſent duke of Beaufort.

Norborne Berkeley, eſq; claiming the barony of Botetourt, which had long been in abeyance, after a ſolemn hearing in the houſe of peers, had his claim allowed; and his majeſty was pleaſed to ſummon him to parliament, as baron Botetourt, by deſcent, 5 Geo. 3. While his lordſhip was a commoner, he ſerved in the 9th, 10th, 11th, and 12th parliaments of Great Britain, as knight of the ſhire for the county of Glouceſter; and upon his preſent majeſty's acceſſion to the throne, was appointed groom of the bed-chamber, which he reſigned when he took his ſeat in the houſe of peers. In 1768, the government of Virginia was committed to his care, and during his reſidence in that colony, he was ſeized with a fever, of which he died, unmarried, greatly lamented by all, in 1770, and in the 53d year of his age. He was ſucceeded in this eſtate by his ſiſter,

Elizabeth, dutcheſs dowager of Beaufort, who is the preſent lady of the manor of Stoke Giffard. The Beaufort arms are given under Badminton. Her grace's paternal coat is thus blazoned, *Gules, a chevron ermine, between ten croſſes pattee (ſix above, and four below) argent.*

HAMLETS. 1. *Great Stoke,* of which already.

2. *Little Stoke.*

3. *Harris Stoke.* Elias de Filton was ſeized of Stoke Herry 4 E. 3. Edward Blount and Margaret his wife were ſeized of the manor of Harriſtoke 4 R. 2. Sir Thomas Fitz-Nichols held the ſame manor 7 R. 2. and Thomas Fitz-Nichols, ſon of ſir Thomas, was ſeized thereof 6 H. 5. John Browning, ſon of John, was ſeized alſo of this manor 8 H. 5.

Of the Church, &c.

The church is in the deanery of Briſtol, but in the dioceſe of Glouceſter. It is a vicarage, valued at 6*l.* in 1534; and now of the clear value of 20*l.* 12*s.* 5*d.* It was antiently appropriated to the priory of Little Malvern in Worceſterſhire, for which John Giffard was ſeized of the advowſon, in truſt, 20 E. 1. The dutcheſs dowager of Beaufort is patroneſs, and the reverend Mr. Shute is the preſent incumbent.

The church is ſaid to be dedicated to St. Michael. It is neatly and uniformly pewed, and has a north aile ſeparated from the nave by two fluted pillars, and as many pillaſters, with capitals. The inhabitants of one part of the pariſh bury at Stapleton; and others bury at Almondſbury.

Firſt fruits £.			Synodals £. 0	1	0
Tenths —			Pentecoſt. 0	1	6
Procurations 0	6	8			

Monuments and Inſcriptions.

There is a monument againſt the ſouth wall of the chancel, with the following inſcriptions, on two plates of braſs:

TO RICHARD BERKELEY ESQ^r AND MARY HIS WIFE (DAUGHTER OF ROBERT ROE OF LONDON, ESQ^r) HIS DEARE FATHER AND MOTHER, A DUE TO THEIR LOVE, OF WHOM ROBERT BERKELEY THEIR YOUNGEST SON AND ONLY NOW LIVING HATH SET UP THIS REMEMBRANCE OF THEM.

SHEE WHEN SHEE HAD PASSED NEARE 36 YEARES IN THE EXERCISE OF RELIGIOVS AND MORALL DUTIES, AND THEY BOATH HAD LIVED TOGETHER ALMOST HALFE A YEARE UPWARDS OF 17 (WITHOVT KNOWEING THE OTHER 2: WHOSE COMFORTS THEY ENVYED) DIED THE 24th OF IVLY IN THE YEARE OF OVR LORD 1615.

HEE LIVED VPWARDS OF 46 YERES AFTER AND DYED IN THE 83^d YERE OF HIS AGE THE 12th DAY OF MAY 1661: THEIRE SOVLES ARE IN HEAVEN, THEIRE BODIES LYE HERE: HERE HEE LAYD HERS, AND HERE WHEN DEATH SHOVLD DIVIDE HIM HIS WILL WAS HIS BODIE SHOVLD BE LAID, TRUSTING IN GODS MERCY HIS SOULE SHOULD SOONE BE WITH HERS, AND THEIRE BODIES IN THE MEANE TIME LYINGE HERE TOGETHER, TOGETHER FROM THENCE AT OUR SAVIOURS CALL SHOULD ARISE: FOR EVER AFTER BODIES AND SOULES TO ENIOY THE ALL HAPPYING VISION.

HERE LYETH THE BODY OF *Henry Berkeley* ESQ^r SON AND HEIRE OF Sr *Richard Berkeley* KN^t: THIS BLESSED CHANGE HE MADE ABOUT THE 48 YEARE OF HIS AGE VPON THE 7th OF FEB: IN THE YERE OF OUR SAVIOUR 1607: HE HAD BY MYRRIELL HIS WIFE (DAVGHTER OF *Thomas Throgmorton* ESQ^r) DIVERS SONNES AND DAUGHTERS: THE OTHERS DYED YOUNG THERE ONELY SURVIVED VIZ^t. RICHARD, ELIZABETH AND MARGARET.

ELIZABETH DYED IN THE YEARE OF OUR LORD 1605 (IN THE 22^d YEARE OF HER AGE AND WAS HERE INTERRED.

There are, upon the monument, theſe arms, 1ſt *and* 4th Berkeley of Stoke. 2d *and* 3d, *Argent, a ſaltire engrailed ſable*; with this motto, DESPICIT QVAE VULGVS SVSPICIT.

Oppoſite to the above, is a ſuperb marble monument, with the Berkeleys arms only, and upon the table this memorial:

Near this Place
Lyeth the Body of JOHN SIMES BERKELEY *Eſq*;
(Second Son of RICHARD BERKELEY *Eſq.)*
Who ſucceeded his Anceſtors in the Lordſhip of this Mannor,
Which has been enjoyed by the Family
For ſome Hundred Years.
He was twice Knight of the Shire *for this County,*
AND
Married firſt SUSAN *daughter and ſole Heireſs of*
Sr THOMAS FOWLES Knight,
Banker *and* Citizen *of* London,
And Relict of JONATHAN COPE
Of Ranton Abbey *in* Staffordſhire *Eſq*:
His ſecond Wife was
ELIZABETH Viſcounteſs Hereford,
Relict of EDWARD Lord Viſcount Hereford
And Coheireſs of WALTER NORBORNE Eſq:
Of Caln *in the* County *of* Wilts,
By whom he had one Son Norborne,
And one Daughter Elizabeth,
Who are now living.
He died December *the* 13th 1736
In the 74th *Year of his Age.*

On a plain table of white marble, on the ſouth ſide of the chancel, it is thus written:

SACRED

SACRED
To the Memory of
NORBORNE BERKELEY
BARON De BOTETOURT,
who was only Son of JOHN BERKELEY Efq[r].
of Stoke Gifford,
and the LADY VISCOUNTESS HEREFORD,
Daughter of WALTER NORBORNE, Efq[r].
of Calne in the County of Wilts.
In four fucceffive *Parliaments*
He was unanimoufly elected
KNIGHT of the SHIRE for this County.
In 1760
He was appointed one of the Grooms
of his MAJESTY's Bedchamber.
In 1762
Lord Lieutenant and Cuftos Rotulorum
For the County of Gloucefter, &c.
The BARONY of BOTETOURT having been long in Abeyance,
In 1764
His MAJESTY was gracioufly pleafed to reftore to him
Thofe antient Honours,
And foon after appointed him
One of the Lords of his Bedchamber.
In 1768
The *Government* of *Virginia* was committed to his Care.
During his Refidence in that Colony,
He was feized with a Fever,
Which on the 15th of October, in 1770,
In the 53[d] Year of his Age,
Put a Period to his Life.
His Body was depofited
In the *College of William* and *Mary*
In the Town of WILLIAMSBOURG.
How much the Virginians ow'd
To his Paternal, and well-conducted Government,
They have gratefully teftified,
By unanimoufly voting
In their Council and Affembly,
A magnificent Statue to his Memory.
Thus were his public Virtues acknowledged.
But how fhall his Relations
And his more intimate Friends
Who alone could truly eftimate
The private Qualities of his Heart,
In Words expreffive of their Grief, lament
Their irreparable Lofs?
Extenfive Charity, unbounded Generofity,
Ardent Friendfhip, and Affection;
An unwearied Attention to every public Good,
A ftrict and zealous Loyalty,
The politeft, the moft engaging Manners
Gave him an indifputable Claim
To this moft enviable Title,
THE FRIEND OF MANKIND.
He directed
Long before his Death,
This plain Marble to be here affixed.
His Friends have only infcribed
His true Character.

On a flat ftone in the church,

Here lyeth the Body of John Silcocks of this Parifh Yeoman,
who died November the 14th 1741 Aged 58.
He was a Man of ftrict Honefty,
Integrity, and friendly Behaviour,
And tho' thefe good Qualities
Became extinct with him,
Yet his
Provifion for an early Knowledge of Religion,
And his great Benefaction to the Poor,
Are lively Inftances
And will remain lafting Examples
of his Piety, and Charity.

Benefaction.

In 1741, John Silcocks of this parifh, yeoman, left by will the intereft of 200*l.* to be given weekly in bread to twelve poor people, not receiving alms; and the intereft of 100*l.* in reverfion, to be applied to the fame ufe. He alfo gave the intereft of 50*l.* for teaching poor children to read; and the intereft of 50*l.* for preaching four fermons yearly, one on the firft Sunday after each quarter day for ever.

Taxes.					
The Royal Aid in 1692,	£. 167	4	0
Poll-tax — 1694, —	31	18	0
Land-tax — 1694, —	147	2	4
The fame, at 3*s.* 1770, —	110	5	0

At the beginning of this century, there were 42 houfes, and about 200 inhabitants in this parifh, whereof 8 were freeholders; yearly births 5, burials 4. *Atkyns.* There are now about 60 families, and 283 inhabitants.

STONE

IS a fmall parifh, in the hundred of Berkeley, two miles diftant fouth from the town of that name, five weft from Wotton-underedge, and nineteen fouth from Gloucefter.

It is generally accounted but a tithing to the parifh of Berkeley. The turnpike-road from Gloucefter to Briftol runs thro' it, croffing a large brook, collected from feveral heads rifing about Boxwell and Wotton-underedge, and forming the Berkeley Avon, which empties itfelf into the Severn, below that town.

Mr. Jenkins has a good houfe near the church.

Of the Manor and other Eftates.

This manor is not diftinctly mentioned in *Domefday*, but is undoubtedly included in the particulars of the barony of Berkeley. There are records, however, of the following dates, which mention others to have been poffeffors of the manor. Joan, the widow of Robert Grendour, or Grinder, was feized of it 24 H. 6. and fo was fir John Bar 22 E. 4. But it reverted to the Berkeley family, and the earl of Berkeley is the prefent lord of the manor.

John Sergeant was feized of lands in Stone 36 & 47 E. 3.

Of the Church, &c.

The church is in the deanery of Durfley. It is a curacy annexed to Berkeley. The vicar of Berkeley pays 8*l.* a year, and there is another donation of 40*s.* a year to the curate, who has a houfe, with an orchard and garden. About thirty years ago, Mr. Morfe left 300*l.* to purchafe land, and directed that 10*l.* of the profits of it fhould be paid to the curate, on condition of his refiding there; the reft to be diftributed to the poor. And by means of this donation, the queen's bounty has been obtained, fo that the curacy is now worth about 40*l.* a year.

The tithes of this place belonged to the priory of Bradenftoke in Wiltfhire, and were granted to the dean and chapter of Briftol 34 H. 8.

The church or chapel is dedicated to All Saints. It is a handfome building, adorned with battlements, and has a pretty fpire at the weft end.

There

There were two chantries in this chapel, one founded by John Sergeant 30 E. 3. Richard Lane, the laft incumbent, received a penfion of 6*l.* in the year 1553. The revenues of it were granted to Thomas Throckmorton 6 E. 6. The other chantry, dedicated to All Saints, Mr. Willis gives no account of. It was endowed with lands in Ham, Alkinton, Cam, and Berkeley, which were granted to fir John Thynn 6 E. 6.

The benefactions have been mentioned in the account of the curacy.

The public payments, and yearly baptifms and burials, are fet down under Berkeley.

Sir Robert Atkyns reckoned 44 houfes, and about 200 inhabitants in this parifh, and there are now about the fame number of houfes and people.

STONEHOUSE.

THIS parifh lies in the hundred of Whitfton, four miles diftant weft from Stroud, feven north from Durfley, and nine fouth from Gloucefter.

It is fituated in the Vale, and confifts chiefly of pafture, with fome good arable land. It was fo called from the chief or manor houfe being of *ftone*, which was not common in the vale. The fame thing gave denomination to other places, as obferved under Stanley.

The turnpike-road from the town of Stroud to the next paffages over the Severn, at Framilode and Arlingham, runs thro' this parifh; and a canal is now cutting thro' it, to open a navigation from that town to the above-mentioned river.

Mr. Ellis has a very handfome new houfe at Ebley, built by his uncle Mr. Jofeph Ellis, who acquired a large fortune in the clothing bufinefs, with the higheft reputation, and was in the commiffion of the peace for this county when he died, in the year 1771. Mr. Elliott, Mr. Reddall, and Mr. Andrews have alfo very good houfes and eftates in this parifh.

The clothing bufinefs has flourifhed here for many generations, to which the fine appearance and improved condition of this country is to be attributed; for nothing is more certain, than that trade and manufactures encourage agriculture.

Here are no antiquities, nor curious plants. The natural productions of the place confift at prefent of grain, cheefe, and cyder, all excellent in their kinds. But it appears on record, that there was a vineyard in this parifh above feven hundred years ago. The expreffion is, *Ibi duo arpenz vinee*, which fir Robert Atkyns tranflates two acres of orchard, for he had conceited that there could be no vineyards in England, becaufe our climate is not fo favourable to the ripening of the grape as fome others. But that way of reafoning might be extended to prove, with equal truth and certainty, that melons and cucumbers do not grow in our country, becaufe there are climates that fuit them better.

Here are two fairs in the year, one on the 1ft of May, the other on the 10th of October.

Of the Manor and other Eftates.

The following is a tranflation from *Domefday:*
'William de Ow holds Stanhus in Blachelew 'hundred. Tovi held it in the time of king 'Edward. There were feven hides. In demean 'are two plow-tillages, and twenty-one villeins, 'and nine bordars, with twenty plow-tillages. 'There are four *fervi*, and two mills of 17*fol.* and '6 *den.* There are two arpenz of vineyard. It is 'worth and was worth 8*l.* This manor pays tax.' *Domefday*, p. 73.

This manor was held of the bifhop of Worcefter. John Giffard of Brimpsfield had a grant of free warren in Stonehoufe 9 E. 1. Upon the attainder of another John Giffard, the laft male heir of that family, in the reign of king Edward the Second, Stonehoufe came to the crown, and was granted to John lord Maltravers by king Edward the Third, who procured a releafe and confirmation from John Calew, heir to the Giffards by one of their daughters, 4 E. 3. But John lord Maltravers incurring the king's difpleafure by committing certain mifdemeanours, his lands were feized by the crown, and Stonehoufe was granted to Maurice de Berkeley, after the death of Margaret Giffard 11 E. 3.

The lord Maltravers being foon afterwards reftored to the king's favour, and to his eftates, joins with Agnes his wife in levying a fine of this manor to the ufe of themfelves in fpecial taille, the remainder to the right heirs of the lord Maltravers, 30 E. 3. and he died in the 31ft year of that king. Another John lord Maltravers, with the before-mentioned Agnes, levied a fine of this manor to the ufe of themfelves in taille; the remainder to John, fon of Richard earl of Arundel, and to Eleanor the wife of John in taille, for John Fitz-Alan, fecond fon of Richard earl of Arundel, had married Eleanor, the daughter of John lord Maltravers, and fifter and heirefs of Henry lord Maltravers, whereby the manor of Stonehoufe came by defcent to the Fitz-Alans, earls of Arundel, defcended from Alan lord of Clun in Shropfhire, who came into England with king William the Conqueror; for John Fitz-Alan, grandfon[k] of John and of Eleanor, came to be earl of Arundel, by the death of Thomas earl of Arundel without iffue. The before-mentioned Eleanor Maltravers married to her fecond hufband Reginald Cobham the elder, of Sternbrugh, by whom fhe had no iffue; and furviving him, died feized

[k] Sir Robert Atkyns fays *fon of John* in this place; but he has made him to be the grandfon, who became lord Arundel after the death of Thomas earl of Arundel, in his account of thefe perfons under King's Stanley.

of Stonehouſe, Shurdington, and other eſtates in this county, 6 H. 4.

This eſtate continued for ſeveral generations in the earls of Arundel. Thomas earl of Arundel died ſeized of it 16 H. 8. and was ſucceeded by his ſon William earl of Arundel, upon whoſe death 35 H. 8. livery was granted to Henry earl of Arundel, ſon of William.

This manor came ſoon afterwards to the Sandford family. William Sandford was ſeized of it 9 Eliz. and in that year aſſigned it to William Fowler, who died ſeized of it 41 Eliz. as appears by the eſcheator's inquiſition taken that year. Daniel Fowler, his ſon and heir, was upwards of thirty years old at his father's death, and was lord of the manor in the year 1608. Daniel Fowler was his ſon and heir, whoſe daughter and heireſs, Mary, was married to Thomas Smyth, eſq; of the family of that name then reſiding at Nibley in this county, who, in her right, was lord of this manor, and was ſucceeded by Thomas Smyth, his ſon and heir, who died in 1684. He left a daughter and heireſs, married to Mr. Ball of London, whereby the manor paſſed into another name; and Mrs. Ball, widow of Robert Ball, eſq; is the preſent lady of the manor. The family arms of Ball, as I find them in the church, are, *A lion rampant, holding a ball or roundlet in his dexter paw.*

The hamlets of *Ebley* and *Weſtrip* lie partly in this pariſh. Richard, ſon of John Browning, was ſeized of Ebbelegh 2 H. 4.

William Elland and his wife levied a fine of lands in Stonehouſe and Ebley to Robert Kyll 7 H. 7. John Stanſhaw and Humphry his brother joined in levying a fine of lands in Stonehouſe 12 H. 7. The abbey of Glouceſter had a water mill here, and a fulling mill, called Coneham Mill, with ſome lands, 8 H. 8. A meſſuage and a mill in Stonehouſe belonged to the priory of Lanthony, and were granted to the city of Glouceſter 34 H. 8.

Of the Church, &c.

The church is a vicarage endowed, in the deanery of its own name, worth 180*l.* a year. It is in the immediate preſentation of the crown, and the rev. John Pettat, M.A. is the preſent incumbent.

The advowſon formerly belonged to the nunnery of Hellenſtow, to which houſe the vicar paid 6*l.* a year, and the ſame annual ſum is ſtill due to the crown.

Twenty-one acres of paſture, and ten of arable land, belong to the glebe.

The church is dedicated to St. Cyril, and has a low tower at the weſt end, in which are ſix bells. It was newly roofed, leaded, and otherwiſe beautified, and repaired, in 1713. And I find the following memorandum in the regiſter: *The congregation being much larger than the church would receive with convenience, and the church itſelf darkened and deformed by two galleries in the midſt of it; in the year 1746 I built a new iſle, with ſtone from Dovro wood, which was given by Robert Ball, eſq; and brought gratis to the church-yard by Mr. Richard Merret of Ebley; beſides this, I had great encouragement by fair promiſes, but no other aſſiſtance, ſo that the building coſt me above 150 l. which I ſhall think well laid out, if it ſerves, as I intended it ſhould, to the Glory of God, the convenience of the people, and for the benefit of my ſucceſſors. S. Harris.*

The miniſter receives an annual ſum for the pews in this aile.

	£.	s.	d.		£.	s.	d.
Firſt fruits	22	0	0	Synodals	0	2	0
Tenths —	2	4	0	Pentecoſt.	0	0	9
Procurations	0	6	8				

Monuments and Inſcriptions.

On a flat ſtone in the chancel,

Hic Jacet Thomas Smyth de Stonehouſe in Comitatu Glouc. Armiger, Obijt Sexto die Martij Anno Ætatis ſuæ Sexageſimo tertio, Annoq; Salutis 1684.

There is a ſcutcheon at top, containing three coats palewiſe. 1. *Quarterly* 1ſt *and* 4th, *A lure*; 2d *and* 3d, obliterated. 2. *On a chevron between ſeven* [by miſtake for ſix] *croſſes paty fitchy* 4 *and* 3, *three fleurs de lis*, for Smyth. 3. *A lion rampant holding in his dexter paw a roſe.*

Againſt the ſouth wall of the chancel,

In Memory of Mary ye Wife of Thomas Smyth of Stonehouſe Gent. who departed this Life the Firſt day of October in the Yeare of our Lord God 1675.

Reſurgam

Solus Chriſtus Mihi Sola Salus.

Near this place alſo lies ye Body of Mary ye Wife of John Ball of London Gent. & Daughter of ye s^d^ Thomas Smyth by the abovementioned Mary his Wife, who died ye 15th of June 1703.

The Smyths arms on this monument are, *Azure, on a chevron between ſix croſſes paty fitchy Or, three fleurs de lis of the field.*

Againſt the ſame wall,

In Memory of Anſelm Fowler of Moorehalls in this Pariſh Gent. who died Auguſt ye 4th in the Yeare 1700, in the 63^d^ Year of his Age.

Alſo in memory of Rebeccah his Wife, and Daughter of Henry Partridge Gent. who died March the 18th in the year 1707, being about the 75th Year of her Age.

Arms at top, *Baron and femme*, 1. *Quarterly azure and Or, in the firſt a lure of the ſecond.* This coat was granted to Daniel Fowler of this pariſh, ſon of William Fowler, by William Camden, Clarencieux King at Arms, Mar. 13, 1606. 2. *Checky argent and ſable, on a bend gules three eſcallops Or*, for Partridge.

Upon a flat ſtone,

Here lyeth the Body of John Ball, Eſq; Son of John Ball of London Gent. by Mary his Wife, Exempt & Captain of his Majeſties 1ſt Troop of Horſe Guards, who departed this life the 31^ſt^ of July 1729, in the 32 year of his Age.

Arms at top, *Quarterly* 1ſt *and* 4th, *A lion rampant holding a ball or roundlet in his dexter paw.* 2d *and* 3d, Smyth, as before.

On another flat ſtone,

Underneath are depoſited the Remains of Robert Ball, Eſq, Lord of this Manor. A Gentleman of refined Senſe and Politeneſs; a Magiſtrate of diſtinguiſhed Abilities, and an affectionate Huſband, Father, and Friend. He died Oct. 19, 1760, aged 51. Alſo Robert his Son, aged 5 Months.

Arms, *Baron and femme*, *Quarterly* 1ſt *and* 4th, Ball. 2d *and* 3d, Smyth. 2. *A chevron between three croſſes paty, in chief a quaterfoil.*

Upon a monument in the church-yard, incloſed within paliſadoes, is this inſcription:

This Monument is erected to perpetuate the Memory
*Of the late Rev^d^* Samſon Harris *M. A.*
(Thirty five Years Vicar of this Pariſh)
A Divine
Eminently diſtinguiſhed for his exemplary piety
Learning, and indefatigable Diligence
In the Work of the Miniſtry:
Deeply impreſſed with the ſacred Truths of the Goſpel,
He recommended them to others

with

with a moſt perſwaſive Energy, & truly Xtian Example,
Diſplaying
In his own Conduct the moſt lively Evidence
of Sincerity,
His whole Life being one continued Practice
Of every Chriſtian and Social Virtue.
*He died deſervedly lamented Nov*r. 10th 1763;
in the 66th *Year of his Age.*
Reader, Go, & imitate.

On the other ſide is this inſcription:

*Here alſo is inter'd the Body of Sophia Relict of the late Rev*d Samſon Harris, *who departed this Life April* 10th 1767, *in the* 80th *Year of her Age.*

Another tomb, likewiſe incloſed with paliſadoes, bears the following inſcription:

*This Monument is erected in ſincere regard to the Memory of M*rs *Sophia Pettat, late Wife of the Rev*d *John Pettat, the preſent Vicar of y*e *Pariſh And Niece to his worthy Predeceſſor y*e *Rev*d *Samſon Harris.*
The unaffected Piety and Affability
Which regulated her Conduct
Might reflect ample Evidence
to the Value of her Character
Did not reſpect to that Modeſty
Which ſhunn'd all public Teſtimony to her Merits
check the Enlargement of this Tribute
Even to her lifeleſs Remains.
The Submiſſion and Fortitude
With which ſhe ſuſtained the Torture
Of a long and painful Illneſs,
Until Patience had her perfect Work,
gave amazing Proofs of the
Amiableneſs of her Temper;
And ſtrongly illuſtrated the comforts
Of the Chriſtian Hope.
By the Merciful Call of divine Providence
She was admitted to that Place
Where the Weary be at reſt
April the 24th 1764:
Aged 24 *Years.*

Cloſe to the above, upon a tomb,

Underneath this Tomb are depoſited the Remains of Thomas Pettat Eſq; late of this Pariſh, who departed this Life the firſt Day of February 1767, *aged* 78 *Years. Alſo are depoſited the Remains of* Catherine *late Wife of the above Thomas Pettat, who departed this Life the Sixth Day of May* 1766, *aged* 66 *Years.*

On another tomb,

In Memory of
ROBERT RATCLIFF B.D.
Born in Devonſhire, Fellow of Exeter College, Oxford
Chaplain to the forces of King Charles & King James ye Second
In America, in which he lived ten Years
By Royal Licence of King Charles the Second
And Direction of the Biſhop of London
Conſtituted the Epiſcopal Miniſter at Boſton in New England
(where he founded a Church)
And in the Iſland of Saint Chriſtophers
Chaplain to their Majeſties houſhold
Vicar of Stonehouſe eighteen } Years
And Rector of Coln-Rogers ten }
who departed this life Ian: ye 7th
Anno { Salutis 1707; Ætatis Suæ 53.

On the top of the ſame tomb, engraven on braſs,

In Memory of *JOHN RATCLIFF* D.D.
Maſter of Pembroke College *Oxford*
and Prebendary of *Glouceſter*, the
laſt Survivor of the Deſcendants
of *ROBERT RATCLIFF*, B.D. and
MARY his Wife, He departed this Life
July 13th 1775 Aged 76 *Years* and lies
Interred in the Pariſh Church of
S*t*. *Mary de Crypt* in the City of
Glouceſter.

On the other ſide of the tomb,

Here alſo lieth Interred three Children of Robert Ratcliff and Mary his Wife
Viz. Richard, Mary, Anne } Buried { Nov. 10th, Dec. 9th, Nov. 13th } Anº Domi { 1701, 1704, 1707
Alſo by this Tomb lyeth the Body
of Robert Eldeſt Son of Mr. Robert Ratcliff
late Vicar of Stonehouſe
who departed this life the 26 day of July 1711
Aged 14 Years.

Arms, *Baron and femme*, 1. [*Argent*] *a bend ingrailed* [*ſable*] for Ratcliff. 2. *A feſs between three creſcents*, ſuppoſed for Hodges.

There was a handſome monument erected in the church-yard, in the year 1776, which is now taken down to be repaired. Upon one table was the following memorial:

This Monument
is erected to the Memory
of JOSEPH ELLIS, Eſqr.
of *Ebley* in this Pariſh,
who died greatly regretted
Sepr. 3d, 1771, Aged 53,
at *Spa* in *Germany*;
and his Remains lie interred
in the Chancel
of the Proteſtant Chapel of *Olne*,
in the adjacent *Dutch* Territory.

On the other table, this inſcription:

Beneath this Tomb
are interred the Remains of
CHRISTIAN ELLIS,
Widow and Relict of JOSEPH ELLIS, Eſqr.
of *Ebley* in this Pariſh,
to whoſe Memory
ſhe erected this Tomb.
She died March 28th 1776,
in the 57th Year of her Age.

On the north ſide of the church-yard, incloſed within iron rails, is a handſome marble tomb, in memory of Giles Naſh, eſq; who ſerved the office of high ſheriff of this county in the year 1764, and was for many years in the commiſſion of the peace. He departed this life the 12th of January, 1767, aged 63. This gentleman, for a long time, employed a very large fortune in the clothing buſineſs, with the greateſt honour and integrity, and was ſuppoſed to be the beſt ſcarlet dyer in the kingdom. There are alſo two old tombs adjoining, in memory of perſons of this reſpectable family.—Sir Nathaniel Naſh, knight, (the laſt of his name and family) younger brother of the late Giles Naſh, eſq; and for ſome years alderman of Caſtle-baynard ward, in the city of London, died Auguſt 28th, 1769, and his remains are depoſited in the ſame grave with his lady, in St. Paul's cathedral.

Benefactions.

In the year 1775, the principal inhabitants raiſed upwards of 600*l*. by ſubſcription, for the eſtabliſhment of two ſchools, one at each end of the pariſh, for teaching the poor children to read, and inſtructing them in the principles of the Chriſtian religion. Some part of the money has been ſince laid out in the purchaſe of a ſchool-houſe, with an orchard adjoining; and the remainder placed out on government ſecurity, and the intereſt duly applied to the maintenance of thoſe ſchools, wherein about forty children are taught by this charity.

Taxes.			£.	s.	d.
The Royal Aid in	1692,		155	12	8
Poll-tax —	1694,	—	42	9	0
Land-tax —	1694,	—	268	18	0
The ſame, at 3*s*.	1770,	—	196	1	0

About the beginning of this century, there were, according to ſir Robert Atkyns, 100 houſes in the pariſh, and about 500 inhabitants, of whom

30

30 were reputed to be freeholders; yearly births 18, burials 16. But by an accurate furvey, taken a few years ago, the people were found to be increafed to 759.

****

S T O W.

THIS parifh lies in the hundred of Slaughter, ten miles diftant fouth from Campden, nine north-weft from Burford in Oxfordfhire, and twenty-five north-eaftward from Gloucefter.

Stow, in the Saxon language, fignifies a *Dwelling*. It is fometimes called *Stow on the Wold*, becaufe it lies in the high Cotefwold country; but in antient deeds it is written *Edwardeftou*, and *Stow St. Edward's*, for king Athelred gave one hide of land in this place to the church of St. Edward.

It is a market town, fituated, in a very peculiar manner, on the fummit of a high hill, about three miles diameter in bafe, and expofed to every inclemency of the weather, without the leaft fhelter or protection. The bafe of the hill is encircled by a kind of narrow valley, and the great Roman Fofs Way runs a little northward of the town.

It is commonly faid, that *Stow wants three elements out of the four*. It wants water, from its high fituation, and having little or no land belonging to the town, and confequently no produce of fewel, it is deficient in earth and fire; but it has air enough, which in this mountainous and expofed fituation, muft neceffarily be very fharp and piercing, tho' pure, and perhaps, for ftrong conftitutions, healthy. The church is pretty lofty, and as there is nothing to obftruct the view, it is feen, like a land mark, from every place for many miles all round that part of the country.

The town is fmall, and very irregularly built, with two or three mean houfes in the midft of the principal ftreet. It has a weekly market on Thurfday, pretty well frequented; and two fairs in the year, held, fince the rectification of our Calendar, on the 12th of May, and the 24th of October, for all forts of cattle, hops, cheefe, Birmingham wares, linen of the manufacture of this part of the country, and other valuable commodities. The fairs were formerly very large, but are much declined; tho' it is faid, that the tolls of them, and of the markets, are at prefent worth 80*l*. a year.

Its charter for fairs and a market was granted in the fourth year of king Edward the Third, and has fince been confirmed by king James the Firft.

The turnpike-road from Coventry and Warwick leads thro' this town to Bath and Briftol, and the antient Roman Fofs is high, and very vifible in many places, for miles between this town and Cirencefter.

There is a free-fchool, hofpital, and almfhoufe in this place, of antient eftablifhments, of which further particulars are given under the account of Benefactions.

Of the Manor and other Eftates.

At the time of the general furvey, Stow does not feem to be a manor diftinct from Maugerfbury, and as both places are connected in the antient record, I have placed the account of them under this head, as follows:

'The church of St. Mary of Evefham holds 'Malgerefberie at Edwardeftou, in Salemones 'hundred. There were eight hides in the time 'of king Edward, and the ninth hide, which 'adjoins to the church of St. Edward, king Adelred gave quit from tax. There are three plow-'tillages in demean, and twelve villeins, and one 'free man, and a prieft, having amongft them 'feven plow-tillages. There are fix *fervi*, and a 'mill of 8 *folid*. and a little quantity of meadow. 'In the time of king Edward, it was worth 100 *fol*. 'and is now worth 7 *lib*.' *Domefday*, p. 72.

The abbey of Evefham purchafed a charter of free warren in Stow, Maugerefbury, &c. 35 H. 3. and had a grant of markets and fairs in Stow 4 E. 3. of which it was feized in the 45th year of that reign. It is mentioned, notwithftanding, in another record, that Thomas de Beauchamp, earl of Warwick, and others, were feized of Stow St. Edward, Donington, and Maugerfbury 24 E. 3. but it does not appear on what account, and the manor continued in the abbey of Evefham 'till its diffolution.

The manor of Stow, and of Nethercot near Stow, and a yearly rent of 20*s*. in Stow, lately belonging to the abbey of Evefham, were granted to fir Thomas Seymour 1 E. 6. and upon his attainder, were afterwards granted to John earl Warwick, 3 E. 6. It was again granted to —— Willoughby; for Henry Willoughby, upon the death of his father, had livery thereof granted to him 4 Eliz.

It paffed, foon afterwards, to the Chamberlains, and the reverend John Chamberlain is the prefent lord of the manor, and refides at Maugerfbury, a hamlet in this parifh, under which head there is fome account of his family.

HAMLETS. 1. *Donnington*, where lord Afton was totally defeated by colonel Morgan, on the 21ft of March, 1645; upon which all hopes of preferving the king's garrifon in Oxford were loft. Gilbert de Clare, earl of Gloucefter and Hertford, was feized of Donnington 7 E. 2. Livery of this manor was granted to the coheireffes of Thomas Hale 1 & 15 Eliz. In the year 1765, the common fields here were inclofed by act of parliament, and lands allotted to the rector in lieu of tithes.

2. *Maugerfbury*. The abbey of Evefham purchafed a charter of free warren in Malgerfbiry and Dinington 35 H. 3. After the diffolution of religious foundations, Maugerfbury was granted to fir Thomas Leigh. Rowland Leigh, fon of fir Thomas, had livery of Maugerfbury granted to him 15 Eliz. It foon afterwards came to the Cham-

Chamberlaynes. The reverend Mr. John Chamberlayne[1] is the present lord of the manor of Maugersbury, and has a handsome seat in this place, and a large estate in this and other parts of the county.

John Rouse and others were seized of lands in Stow St. Edward, and Malgersbury, 49 E. 3. Lands in Stow belonged to the abbey of Bruern in Oxfordshire. They were in the possession of Richard Jirvis, 36 H. 8. and were then granted to Edward Powell.

Of the Church, &c.

The church is in the deanery of Stow, to which it gives name. It is a rectory worth 400*l.* a year. The reverend Mr. Hippisley is patron and incumbent. The rector had only a third part of the great tithes in Donnington and Maugersbury, and the other two parts belonged to the impropriators of those places; but in the years 1765 and 1766, the common fields of both places were inclosed by act of parliament, and then the rector had lands allotted to him in lieu of tithes.

The rectory of Stow on the Wold, and a portion of tithes, formerly belonging to the abbey of Evesham, were granted to William Wright, esq; and William Breme, 8 Jac. The rectory pays 5*s.* yearly to the crown, and 20*s.* yearly to the patron.

The church is large, and the tower, which is 81 feet high, and adorned with battlements and pinnacles, stands on the south side of it. The original church was built in the 10th century, by Ethelmare, (sometimes called Ailmere) earl of Cornwall, and of Devonshire, on a ground then called St. Edward's Close, and dedicated to St. Edward, who is said to have been an hermit of great sanctity, and an eminent confessor.

There was a chantry founded in this church 4 H. 6. by William Chestre, and dedicated to the Holy Trinity. It was valued at 15*l.* 12*s.* 8*d.* a year 21 E. 4. and the officiating priest had a salary of 5*l.* There was another chantry, dedicated to All Saints, which was endowed with a messuage in Overswell.

	£.				£.		
First fruits	18	0	0	Synodals	0	2	0
Tenths —	1	16	0	Pentecostals	0	1	1½
Procurations	0	6	8				

Monuments and Inscriptions.

Near the vestry door in the chancel, is a marble monument, with this inscription:

Adesdum lector, qualis quantusq; cinis hic juxta conditus, paucis te monitu velim.

Dormit humatus Joannes Chamberlayn Armiger, Vir multis notus, nulli non mirabilis; clarus prosapia, sed virtute clarior; suis multa debens avis, at plura sibi; fidelis Principi (vel exulanti) Subditus, devotissimus Eccles: Anglicanæ (vel spoliatæ) filius;

[1] This antient family is descended from John count de Tankerville, of Tankerville-castle in Normandy, who came into England with king William the Conqueror, but returned again into Normandy. John de Tankerville was a younger son of the former earl, and was lord chamberlain to king Henry the First. Richard Chamberlayne, son of the last John, was lord chamberlain to king Stephen, and thereupon assumed the surname of Chamberlayne. He married the daughter of ——— Galfrey. William Chamberlayne, lord of North Rifton, was son of Richard. He also was lord chamberlain to king Henry the Second, and married the daughter of ——— Clifton. He had taken prisoner Robert de Bellemont, earl of Millain in Normandy, and earl of Leicester in England, commonly called Blanchmains, who had taken part with young king Henry against the king his father; and for that service the king granted him to quarter the arms of the earl of Leicester with those of Tankerville, in the year 1174. Robert Chamberlayne was son of William, and sir Richard Chamberlayne was son of Robert. He married Jane, daughter and heir of John Gatesden. Sir Robert Chamberlayne, son of sir Richard, married the daughter of ——— Griffeth of Northamptonshire; by whom he had issue sir John Chamberlayne, who married Jane, daughter and heir of John Mortein, descended from an antient family of that name, and whose mother was an heiress of the name of Ekney.

Sir Richard Chamberlayne, son of sir John, married Jane, daughter of sir John Reins, of Clifton Reins. Their eldest son, sir Richard Chamberlayne, settled at Sherborne in Oxfordshire, where his posterity continued 'till John Chamberlayne, the last of that branch, died in the reign of king James the First, and left two daughters coheiresses, the elder of whom was first married to sir Thomas Gage, and afterwards, to sir William Goring of Sussex; and the younger daughter was married to the lord Abergavenny.

John Chamberlayne, of Hopton in Derbyshire, was second son of sir Richard, the elder, and brother to sir Richard Chamberlayne, the younger. He married the daughter of ——— Bensted, and had issue Thomas Chamberlayne, who married Isabel, the daughter of ——— Knifton. John Chamberlayne, son of Thomas, married the daughter of ——— Elton, and had a son John, who married Agnes, the daughter of ——— Keynes. William Chamberlayne, son of the last John, married Elizabeth, daughter of ——— Fleming, of Dartmouth.

Sir Thomas Chamberlayne of Presbury, son of William, married Anne Vander Zenny, of the house of Nassaw in the Low Countries. His second wife was Elizabeth, daughter of sir John Luddington, and widow of ——— Machine, from whom are descended the Chamberlaynes of Maugersbury. His third wife was Anne, sister of sir ——— Monke of Devonshire, grandfather to the duke of Albemarle, from whom the Chamberlaynes of Oddington were descended. This sir Thomas was eminent for his many embassies in the reigns of king Henry the Eighth, king Edward the Sixth, and queen Elizabeth.

Edmond Chamberlayne, of Maugersbury, esq; was son of sir Thomas, and brother and heir to sir John Chamberlayne of Presbury. He married Anne, the widow of ——— Moulton, of Surry. His second wife was Grace, daughter of John Strangeways, of Melbury in Dorsetshire. He was high sheriff of Gloucestershire 39 Eliz. and died in 1634. John Chamberlayne, son of Edmond by his second wife, married Elizabeth, daughter of sir William Leigh of Longborough; and having been sequestered for his loyalty to king Charles the First, paid 1246*l.* for composition. He died in 1668, and was succeeded by his son John Chamberlayne, who married Mary, daughter of Walter Savage, of Broadway in Worcestershire, esq; and died in 1691. Edmund Chamberlayne, son of John, married Emma, the daughter of James lord Chandos, and served the office of high sheriff of Gloucestershire 4 Anne. He died in the year 1755, and was succeeded by his only son Edmund, who married one of the daughters and coheiresses of Robert Atkyns, of Nether Swell in this county, esq; by whom he had a numerous issue. He died in the year 1774, and was succeeded by his eldest son, John, rector of Little Ilford in the county of Essex, who married Martha, third daughter of Henry Doughty, of Broadwell, in this county, esq; by whom he has one son and one daughter. This family bears two coats, *Quarterly*, 1st *and* 4th, *Gules, an inescutcheon argent between eight stars in orle Or*, for Chamberlain; 2d *and* 3d, *Gules, a chevron between three escallops Or*, for Tankerville.

To the above pedigree, sir Robert Atkyns subjoins, that sir John Chamberlayne, of this family, was a great soldier, and eminent in the court of king Edward the Third. It appears by a record in the tower of London, that the king granted to him, by the name of count Chamberlayne, earl of Tankerville, viscount de Millaine, and high constable of Normandy, a warrant to receive 10,000 marks, which he had lent to the king's son in the wars with France. He married the daughter and heir of the lord Harling, governor of Paris, who was seized of the manor and castle of East Harling in Norfolk, and of many other considerable estates in that and other counties. She was reputed the greatest heiress in England, and refused many suitors of the chiefest nobility, and with leave of the king, married this sir John Chamberlayne. She afterwards married the lord Scrope, and had for her third husband ——— Benefield, of Norfolk; but she chose to be buried near her husband sir John Chamberlayne, in the church of East Harling; all which was inscribed in the window of the great chamber of East Harling castle.

ftrenuus patriæ patronus. Nefcio an legum peritior an pacis ftudiofior. Jufticiarius veriffime fic dictus curiæ fedifq; Judicialis ornamentum ac decus ingens. Ingenio fimul & facundia præpollens, Moribus ipfe ille quem finguli optarint, ut verbo dicam, omnium vivus defiderium et dolor mortuus. In hujus tam chari capitis memoriam Monumentum hoc Conjux Relicta L. M. Q. P. pium feris nepotibus amorem teftatura. Obiit in Menfe Februarij 1667.

There is a fcutcheon over the monument, *Parted per pale baron and femme*, 1. Chamberlayne. 2. *Gules, a crofs engrailed, and in the dexter quarter, a lozenge argent.*

There is a memorial on a flat ftone in the chancel, for colonel Edmund Chamberlayne, who died in 1676; and an infcription upon another flat ftone there, for Edmund Chamberlayne, gent. eldeft furviving fon of colonel Edmund Chamberlayne, who died in 1696, aged 52. And upon another flat ftone, it is thus written:

Quiefcit hic humatus inclytus atq; eruditus Vir Johannes Chamberfbury, nuper de Maugerfbury Armiger. Spiritum efflavit fexto Nonarum Martij 49 annos 3 menfes 12q; dies natus Annoq; Salutis humanæ M. DCLXXXI.

There is alfo a handfome mural monument in the chancel, and upon the table this infcription:

H. S. E.
Johannes Chamberlayne
Filius natu maximus Edmundi Chamberlayne
De Maugerfbury in Com. Gloceftrenfi Armig. et
Uxoris ejus Emmæ filiæ Prænobilis Jacobi Domini Chandos
Baronis de Sudely
Antiquiffimæ familiæ
Quamdiu vixerit Decus
Per duodecem fere Annos unica fpes
Et Proli ex ejufdem demum Parentibus Ortæ optimum Exemplum.
Oxonii in Collegio Wadhamenfi bonis Literis
Et virtutis præceptis inftitutus
In Templi interioris Hofpitio
Patriis legibus fideliter ftuduit.
Hifce dotibus ornatus a Burgenfibus
De Rye in Com. Suffex ad Parliamentum
Electus erat viceffimo primo Æt. anno.
Menfe Februarij 1713-14 ad peregrinas fedes invifendas proceffit
Ut nihil generofo Animo deeffet
Vel quod ipfi ornamento
Vel quo ipfe Alijs effet Præfidio.
Sed Eheu! Parifiis Sphafelo correptus
Defiderium fui reliquit omnibus bonis
Parentibus præcipue et fuis.
Quicquid matura ingenij vis et fumma potuit induftria
Optimus juvenis Patriæ Foro et Senatui promifit;
Quicquid fevera potuit Religionis Reverentia
Pientiffimus Filius Ecclefiæ reddidit Matri.
Hifce Artibus hâc Pietatis difciplinâ
Nobilitatem veram adeptus
Et vivere didicit et mori.
Nat. Mart. 30 1693 Obijt Julij 31 1714
Pridie illius Diei
(Mœftiffimæ Britannis Æræ)
Quâ interiit
Anna Principum Optima.

This monument is ornamented with a fcutcheon, bearing the family arms, quartered as already mentioned in the clofe of their pedigree.

There is alfo upon a flat ftone, a latin infcription for James-Montague Chamberlayne, eldeft fon of Edmund Chamberlayne, efq; who died in 1754, in the 25th year of his age. And another for Edmund Chamberlayne, efq; who died in 1755, aged 84; and for the honourable Emma Chamberlayne, his wife, who died in 1738.

On another flat ftone in the chancel,

Depofitum Roulandi Wilde, Clerici, in fpe certa refurrectionis.

H. S. E.
R. Hippifley A. M.
huj. Eccle. Rector
ob. Nov. XXVI
M DCC LXIV.

On a very large raifed tomb ftanding in the middle of the chancel, is engraven the burft of a foldier, and this memorial beneath it:

Sacræ Memoriæ

Inclytiffimi Ducis Haftings Keyt Filii Johannis Keyt de Ebrington Agro Glouceftrenfi Armigeri Wigorniæ Cohortium ex Parte Regis Præfecti, in Prælio juxta Stow 21mo die Martij 1645 occifi.

Over the buft, and round the tomb, are fcutcheons of the arms of Keyt, late of Ebrington.

Benefactions.

Ethelmere, founder of the church, erected an hofpital in this place, which was valued at 25*l.* 4*s.* 8*d.* yearly, and is charged, in the firft fruits office, with the annual fum of 13*s.* 4*d.*

Thomas Belleny, chief juftice of England, Henry Spelman, and others, were feized of lands called the Gleame, fituate in the parifh of St. Olave, Southwark, and conveyed them to William Cheftre, Richard Cheftre, &c. and their heirs. William Cheftre, by his will, dated in May 16 E. 4. gave thofe lands for divers ufes, *viz.* part for an almfhoufe in Stow for eight poor men and women, and a woman to wafh for them, each to have 8*d.* weekly, but a man and his wife 12*d.* Another part was for the maintenance of Trinity chantry. Thefe lands came to Richard Cheftre by furvivorfhip, having only one daughter, Joan, married to Thomas Bittlefden, againft whom William Martin recovered in Trinity term 3 H. 7. and he conveyed the fame lands, then worth 18*l. per ann.* to feven truftees in Stow, to be applied to the above ufes, and appointed 6*l.* a year to the chantry prieft, who was to keep a fchool, and inftruct the children of the town. At length the leffees of thofe lands built upon them, and greatly improved the rents, fo that they now amount to feveral hundred pounds a year; and the eftate is charged with 40*l.* a year for the ufe of the fchool and almfhoufe. In the front of the fchool-houfe is this infcription:

SCHOLA INSTITVTIONIS PVERORVM IMPENSIS RICHARDI STEPHAM CIVIS ET MERCATORIS LONDINENSIS EXTRVCTA ANNO DOMINI 1594.

Lands in Maugerfbury, worth upwards of 3*l.* a year, are given for the repair of the church; and 5*s.* yearly are paid out of the meadows there, which formerly belonged to fir James Rufhout, in lieu of rufhes, which by cuftom were cut in thofe meadows, to be fpread over the floor of the church.

Mr. Thomas Chadwell, Mr. Richard Hodges, and Mr. Anthony Hodges have given 20*s.* a year each to the poor.

George Townfend, efq; gave 4*l.* yearly to teach children to read, and 2*s.* weekly in bread for the poor.

In 1690, William Cope, of Icombe in this county, efq; gave 12*l.* a year for the ufe of the poor, and 5*l.* a year for ever for apprenticing out poor children. He alfo gave 100*l.* for ftock to fet the poor at work.

In 1702, lady Juliana Tracy gave 50*s.* a year for ever. In 1715, Mr. Thomas Compere, of London,

don, gave the intereſt of 150*l.* In 1716, Mr. John Grayhurſt, of Bledington, gave the intereſt of 50*l.* In 1720, Joſhua Aylworth, of Aylworth, eſq; gave the intereſt of 100*l.* all to be diſtributed yearly in bread to the poor.

In 1744, Richard Freeman, of Batsford, eſq; gave 20*l.* a year for ever to the uſe of the poor. And about the year 1767, Mr. Mince, by his will, gave the intereſt of 200*l.* to buy clothes, to be given, on New-years day, to the nine poor people in the almſhouſes.

The town of Stow, and the two hamlets of Maugerſbury and Donnington, are rated diſtinctly to the land-tax.

Stow.

			£.	s.	d.
Taxes.	The Royal Aid in	1692,	£. 46	14	0
	Poll-tax ——	1694,—	54	0	0
	Land-tax —	1694,—	47	2	8
	The ſame, at 3*s.*	1770,—	32	9	0

Maugerſbury.

			£.	s.	d.
Taxes.	The Royal Aid in	1692,	£. 114	10	8
	Poll-tax ——	1694,—	23	7	0
	Land-tax ——	1694,—	82	13	4
	The ſame, at 3*s.*	1770,—	63	16	3

Donnington.

			£.	s.	d.
Taxes.	The Royal Aid in	1692,	£. 84	4	0
	Poll-tax ——	1694,—	15	8	8
	Land-tax ——	1694,—	34	14	0
	The ſame, at 3*s.*	1770,—	27	1	3

At the beginning of this century, there were 329 houſes, and about 1300 inhabitants in this pariſh, whereof 60 were freeholders; yearly births 32, burials 31. *Atkyns.* I examined the pariſh regiſter, and found that the average of annual baptiſms in ten years, begining with 1700, was 39.1; and of burials in the ſame number of years, (beginning with 1708, the burials not being entered 'till that time) 29.2. Again, the medium of annual baptims for ten years, beginning at 1760, was 36.9; and of burials 23.6; whereby it appears that the pariſh declines in population. And reckoning the proportion of the living to the medium of annual burials as 50 to 1, the preſent number of ſouls will then be 1180, which is ſuppoſed to be very near the truth.

STOWELL.

THIS pariſh lies in the hundred of Bradley, two miles ſouth-weſtward from Northleach, nine northward from Cirenceſter, and eighteen eaſt from Glouceſter.

The great Roman Foſs leads along the eaſt ſide of it, and the river Coln waters it on the ſouth-weſt ſide, on whoſe banks there are ſome meadow grounds; but the greater part of the pariſh lies high, and is of a light ſtony ſoil, moſt ſuitable to, and chiefly employ'd in tillage.

The antient name of it was *Stanuuelle.* And ſince the little river *Lech*, in this neighbourhood, which in the Britiſh language ſignifies a *ſtone*, was ſo called on account of the petrifying quality of its water; it is not improbable that the name of *Stanuuelle*, i.e. *Stone-well*, was given to this place, from a ſpring within it, that incruſts with a ſtrong ſtony ſubſtance, ſticks, and other things lying in its courſe. The ſoil is naturally ſtony; and there is plenty of petrified ſhell-fiſh, of the ſmaller kinds, turned up in the fields almoſt every where about it.

Lord Chedworth has a ſeat here, where he reſides. The turnpike-road upon the Foſs runs above a mile along the ſide of the deer park, and his lordſhip's houſe is ſituated about half a mile northweſtward from it, but the plantations prevent its being ſeen from that quarter. It ſtands upon an eminence fronting to the weſtward, with the river Coln about a quarter of a mile below it, and very pleaſant woods on the oppoſite ſlope, on the other ſide of the bourn. The houſe was built about the reign of king James the Firſt, by one of the Atkinſons, as appears by the arms of that family, carved in freeſtone over the north door, *viz. Azure, a croſs flory argent, between four lions rampant Or.*

Of the Manor and other Eſtates.

This ſeems antiently to have been a member of the large manor of Northleach, for which reaſon I have given the extract from *Domeſday* concerning it under that head; but it may be proper to repeat it in this place, and thus ſays the record:

'Stanuuelle adjoins to this manor [Lecce.] 'There are two plow-tillages in demean, and five 'villeins, with five plow-tillages, and a mill of 40*d.* 'and four *ſervi*, and two *ancillæ*, and there is one 'hide in Culberlege belonging to this manor.' [*i.e.* to Lecce, and not to Stanuuelle]. p. 70.

Richard Martell died ſeized of the manor of Stowell 56 H. 3. and Adam Martell, a deſcendant from Richard, purchaſed a charter of free warren in it 19 E. 3. How long it continued in that name and family I cannot tell; but it paſſed afterwards to the Tames, the elder houſe of which family reſided at Stowell in the time of John Leland the antiquary. *Mr. Horne of Oxfordſhire*, ſays he, *dwelling by Langeley, hath maried this Tame doughter and heir, and ſhal have by her a* 80*li. land by the yere.* Itin. vol. 6, p. 16. Edmond Horn levied two fines of the manor and advowſon of Stowell, 1 & 4 E. 6. His only daughter and heireſs was married to Anthony Bourn, who had livery of the manor granted to him, in right of his wife, 2 Mar.

Stowell paſſed afterwards to the Atkinſons, and Henry Atkinſon, eſq; was lord of it in 1608. He was ſon of Robert Atkinſon, of the Inner Temple, and grandſon of Richard Atkinſon, of the city of Briſtol. Anne, his eldeſt ſiſter, was married to ſir William Wentworth, of Wentworth-Woodhouſe in Yorkſhire; and ſir Henry Atkinſon

Atkinſon, the laſt heir male of this family, dying without iſſue, gave this manor to William earl of Strafford, ſon of Thomas earl of Strafford, and grandſon of the before-mentioned William Wentworth.

John How, eſq; purchaſed the manor of the earl of Strafford, and it has deſcended from him in a direct line to Henry-Frederick How,[m] lord Chedworth, the preſent lord of the manor.

Of the Church, &c.

The church is in the deanery of Cirenceſter. It was annexed to Hampnet in the year 1660, by the conſent of the biſhop and patron. Agnes Harcourt, the widow of John Harcourt, preſented to it in 1503.

The church was built in the form of a croſs, but the north aile has been long ſince taken down. Divine ſervice is not performed in it.

Monuments and Inſcriptions.

Some of the Atkinſons have been buried in the church; as was John How, father of the firſt lord Chedworth, but there are no monuments for them. Upon a plain marble table, againſt the north wall of the chancel, is this memorial:

In Memory of the Truly Pious the Lady ANNABELLA HOWE, one of the Daughters of Emmanuel Lord Scrope, earl of Sunderland, the Widow of JOHN-GRUBHAM HOWE of Compton; and the moſt Indulgent Mother of JOHN-GRUBHAM HOWE of Stowell in the County of Glouceſter. She died the 20th of March, 1703-4.

Quem ſemper Acerbum
Semper Honoratum . . . . Habebo.

[m] This family has been long ſeated in Somerſetſhire and Wiltſhire, John How, of Stanligth, in the dioceſe of Bath and Wells, by his will, dated in 1529, (to which Henry How was one of the witneſſes) among other things, bequeathed 6*s.* 8*d.* each, to fifteen churches where he had lands, and to three others 3*s.* 4*d.* each.

Henry How was father of John How, gent. who dwelt in the pariſh of St. Helen's London. Which John, by his will 16 Eliz. among other things, bequeaths to his ſon John Howe, his beſt chain of gold, weighing 16 ounces; and to the poor of the pariſh of Uſculme, where he was born, 6*l.* 13*s.* 4*d.* His will was ſealed with his ſeal, *a feſs ingrailed, between three wolves heads*, as born by his deſcendants. He had lands in the counties of Somerſet, Devon, Eſſex, and in the city and ſuburbs of London; and bequeathed his manor and lordſhip of Hunſpel de la Heies, with many other eſtates in London and elſewhere, to John his ſon and heir.

Which John took to wife Jane, daughter of Nicholas Grubham, of Biſhop's Lidiard, com. Somerſet, who brought him a very large fortune. He had iſſue by her three ſons, John, George, and Lawrence; and one daughter Elizabeth, married to John Bainton, eſq. George the ſecond ſon, was created a baronet on the reſtoration of king Charles the Second; but the title became extinct with his ſon James, who died without iſſue.

John, the eldeſt ſon, had the manor of Compton in Glouceſterſhire, and Wiſhford, and other eſtates in Wiltſhire, by the gift of his uncle ſir Richard Grubham. He was created a baronet in 1660, and had iſſue by Bridget, daughter of Thomas Rich of North Cerney, maſter in chancery, three ſons, ſir Richard-Grubham How; John, anceſtor to the preſent lord Chedworth; and ſir Thomas How, who died without iſſue.

Sir Richard-Grubham How married Anne, daughter of John King, biſhop of London, and widow of John Dutton of Sherbourn, in the county of Glouceſter, eſq; and had by her one ſon Richard, his heir.

Which Richard married Mary, daughter of ſir Henry-Frederick Thynne, of Kempsford in the county of Glouceſter, baronet, and was one of the repreſentatives for the county of Wilts in nine parliaments. But dying without iſſue in 1730, the title became extinct.

John How, eſq; ſecond ſon of ſir John How, baronet, abovementioned, married Annabella, third daughter of Emanuel Scrope, earl of Sunderland, and had, in her right, the manor and ſeat of Langar in Nottinghamſhire, with other eſtates. She ſurvived him, and dying in 1703-4, was buried at Stowell, having had iſſue by her ſaid huſband, four ſons and five daughters, whereof Bridget was married to John Bennet, lord Oſulſton; Elizabeth to ſir John Guiſe, of Rendcombe in this county, baronet; and Diana to ſir Francis Molineux, of Tiverſall in Nottinghamſhire, baronet; but of the two others I find no account. The ſons were Scrope, John, Charles, and Emanuel.

Scrope How was born in 1648, and ſerved in ſeveral parliaments as knight of the ſhire for the county of Nottingham, in the reign of king Charles the Second, by whom he was knighted, and in ſeveral parliaments afterwards. He concerted with the earl of Devonſhire the means of bringing the prince of Orange into England, and on his landing, united with the earl of Nottingham in a declaration of their principles, on Nov. 22, 1688, *We own it rebellion to reſiſt a king that governs by law; but he was always accounted a tyrant that made his will the law; and to reſiſt ſuch a one, we juſtly eſteem no rebellion, but a neceſſary and juſt defence.* He was one of the grooms of the bed chamber to king William, and was created baron of Clenawly, in the county of Fermanagh, and lord viſcount How, of the kingdom of Ireland, by patent dated May 6, 1701. He died Jan 16, 1712-13, having been twice married. By his firſt wife, lady Anne, daughter of John, 8th earl of Rutland, he had iſſue one ſon, John-Scrope How, and two daughters. By his ſecond wife, Juliana, daughter of William lord Allington, he had Emanuel-Scrope lord viſcount How, and three daughters. Which Emanuel-Scrope lord viſcount How, was appointed governor of Barbadoes in 1732, and died there in 1735; leaving iſſue by his lady Mary-Sophia-Charlot, daughter of the baron Kilmanſegg, three ſons, George-Auguſtus, Richard, and William; beſides ſix daughters. George-Auguſtus, ſucceeded his father, but being killed on July 6, 1758, near Ticonderoga in North America, the honours and eſtate devolved upon his brother Richard, the preſent lord viſcount How, who is an admiral in the Britiſh navy. But I leave this elder branch, and return to

John How, ſecond ſon of the before-mentioned John How, and lady Annabella. He ſerved in ſeveral parliaments for the borough of Cirenceſter, and afterwards as knight of the ſhire for the county of Glouceſter, and diſtinguiſhed himſelf very remarkably by his ſpeeches in the houſe of commons, which ſhewed his extenſive knowledge in the laws, and averſion to unconſtitutional meaſures. It is ſaid, that when the partition treaty was under conſideration of that houſe, he expreſſed his ſentiments of it in ſuch terms, that king William declared, that if it were not for the diſparity of their rank, he would demand ſatisfaction with the ſword. In the reign of queen Anne, he was ſworn of the privy council, conſtituted vice-admiral of the county of Glouceſter, and pay-maſter general of her majeſty's guards and garriſons, which laſt place he enjoy'd 'till after the acceſſion of king George the Firſt. He married Mary, daughter and coheireſs of Humphry Baſkerville, of Pentryllos in Herefordſhire, eſq; and widow of ſir Edward Morgan, of Llanternam in Monmouthſhire, bart. and dying in 1721, left iſſue by her, his ſon and heir

John How, of Stowell, eſq; who, on the deceaſe of ſir Richard How, of Compton in Glouceſterſhire, and Wiſhford in Wiltſhire, bart. in 1730, without iſſue, ſucceeded to thoſe eſtates, and was ſeveral times elected one of the knights of the ſhire for the county of Wilts. In 1741, he was created lord Chedworth, baron of Chedworth in Glouceſterſhire. His lordſhip married Dorothy, eldeſt daughter of Henry-Frederick Thynne, eſq; and had iſſue by her ſix ſons and two daughters; John-Thynne How, his ſucceſſor; Henry-Frederick, now lord Chedworth; Thomas; Charles; James, who in 1755, married ——— daughter and heir of Humphry Howorth, of Maſelwych in Radnorſhire, knight; and William. The daughters were Mary, and Anne. His lordſhip departed this life in April 1742, and was ſucceeded in honour and eſtate by his eldeſt ſon,

John-Thynne How, ſecond lord Chedworth, who in 1758, was declared lord lieutenant and Cuſtos Rotulorum of the county of Glouceſter, and conſtable of the caſtle of St. Briavell's, upon the reſignation of Matthew lord Ducie. His lordſhip married, on Sept. 23, 1751, Martha, daughter and coheir of ſir Philip-Parker Long, of Arwarton in Suffolk, baronet, but died without iſſue May 10, 1762, and was ſucceeded in title and eſtate by his next brother,

Henry-Frederick, now lord Chedworth.

His Lordſhip's ARMS are, *Or, a feſs between three wolves heads couped ſable, a creſcent for difference.*

CREST. *On a wreath, a dexter arm in armour, erazed below the elbow, lying feſs-ways, and holding in the hand a ſcimetar erected, all proper, hilted and pomelled Or, pierced through a boars head couped ſable.*

SUPPORTERS. *On the dexter ſide a lion argent, pellected, armed and langued gules; and on the ſiniſter ſide an angel proper, the face profile, with browniſh hair, habited crimſon, the under garment azure, the wings argent, pinioned of the fourth, and ſupporting the ſhield with both hands.*

MOTTO. JUSTUS ET PROPOSITI TENAX.

Over

Over the table, in a lozenge, are, 1. the arms of How, impaling 2. *Azure, a bend Or,* for Scrope.

Oppoſite to the above, on a ſmall marble monument, is this inſcription:

In Memory of the truly excellent Mrs ANNE MORGAN Daughter and Coheireſs of Sr EDWARD MORGAN late of *Llanternam* in the County of *Monmouth*, Bart. who dyed the 24th of *Augst* 1712, in the 35th *Year* of Her Age.

Her Perſon was Beautifully Agreeable. She had Wit without Levity, Knowledge without Affectation, a penetrating Underſtanding, with a ſound Judgment. She was Pleaſant in Converſation, Modeſtly Reſerved, without Severity; Juſt, Beneficient, Charitable, and Generous. Endued with a Sweetneſs and Firmneſs of Temper above the power of common Accidents, civil & well-bred towards all; but where ſhe profeſſed Friendſhip, in every Part of that Duty without Equal. For ever to be Honoured, Lov'd, and Lamented.

The Lord giveth, and the Lord taketh away. Bleſſed be the Name of the Lord.

Over the monument, are her family arms, *viz. Or, a griphon rampant ſable.* The ſame arms are given by the Morgans of Fairford alſo, as well as thoſe emblazoned p. 444; for both families ſprung from one common ſtock; which is mentioned here, becauſe it was not taken notice of under Fairford.

Taxes.						
	The Royal Aid in	1692,	£.	31	7	0
	Poll-tax — —	1694,	—	8	4	0
	Land-tax ——	1694,	—	28	0	0
	The ſame, at 3*s*.	1770,	—	19	9	0

Sir Robert Atkyns obſerved, that in his time there was only the manor-houſe within the pariſh; and there is only that houſe at preſent.

STRATTON

IS a ſmall pariſh, in the hundred of Crowthorne and Minety, one mile north-weſtward from Cirenceſter, ſeven eaſtward from Biſley, and ſixteen ſouth-eaſtward from Glouceſter.

The village is ſeated in a little bottom, thro' which the Dunteſbourn water runs, and falls into the river Churn at Cirenceſter. The lands in the upper part of the pariſh are employ'd in tillage, and like moſt in the Coteſwold country, are light and ſtony; but ſince the common fields were incloſed, about the year 1771, few places have received greater improvement.

The *Irminſtreet*, one of the great Roman ways, paſſes through and undoubtedly gives name to this place, for Bede and other antient writers call the Roman ways *Stratæ*; and it is obſervable, that there are other villages of the ſame name, ſituated upon Roman ways; particularly *Stratton St. Margaret*, in the north part of Wiltſhire, which lies upon the ſame road.

Mr. Camden was of opinion, that the *Irminſtreet* was ſo called in honour of Mercury, who is repreſented, in heathen mythology, as preſiding over highways, and was worſhiped by the Germans under the name of *Irmunſul*. But I cannot help thinking that the explanation of the name is to be ſought nearer home, in the language of our anceſtors; and ſince Here is an *army*, and Hereman a *ſoldier*, it ſeems pretty clear that *Irminſtreet* ſignifies the *ſoldier's road*, and is nothing more than the term *Via Militaris*, tranſlated into the Saxon language.

Sir Robert Atkyns obſerves, that a buſh called Crowthorn, in Stratton field, gives name to Crowthorn hundred. But from what has been ſaid of this matter under Minety, it may ſeem wonderful that the learned author ſhould adopt a notion ſo vulgar and improbable.

Of the Manor and other Eſtates.

'Roger de Laci holds Stratone in Cireceſtre 'hundred. There are five hides taxed beſides the 'demean. Edmund held it in the time of king 'Edward. There are three plow-tillages in de-'mean, and ſixteen villeins, and ſeven bordars, 'with a prieſt, having nine plow-tillages. There 'are five *ſervi*, and two mills of 20*s*. It was 'worth 8*l*. now 6*l*.' *Domeſday-book*, p. 75.

The pariſhes of Stratton and Daglingworth ſeem to have been but one vill, when the above-mentioned record was compiled, and very probably were known by both names indifferently for many generations; for tho' we find Stratton in *Domeſday*, there is no mention of Daglingworth. On the contrary, Daglingworth ſtands in the liſt of vills, 9 E. 1. but Stratton is unnoticed.

Walter de Laci, ſon of Roger, ſucceeded his father in this manor, and gave one villein, one villeinage, and two thirds of the tithes of his demeans in Stratton to the priory of St. Peter in Hereford, which he had founded, and the grant was confirmed by king William the Firſt. Hugh de Laci, ſon of Walter, confirmed the before-mentioned donation, and in the year 1101, gave the ſaid priory with all its appurtenances, to the abbey of Glouceſter, to which it thence-forward became a cell.

Richard Martin levied a fine of the manor of Stratton, and of other lands belonging to the dutchy of Lancaſter, to king Edward the Fourth, to the uſe of himſelf for one month, remainder to Elizabeth the queen, to the archbiſhop of Canterbury, and to others, 15 E. 4.

William Caſſey, ſon of John Caſſey, eſq; died ſeized of this manor, and of Caſſey Compton in Withington, 1 H. 8. leaving three infant ſons, Leonard, William, and Robert, who ſucceeded each other, and the latter died ſeized of Stratton, Caſſey Compton, and Wightfield in Derhurſt, 1 E. 6. leaving Henry Caſſey his ſon and heir.

Thomas Watſon died 12 Eliz. ſeized of the manor of Stratton, and left Thomas his ſon and heir eleven years old. Thomas Nicholas, eſq; was lord of the manor in the year 1608, and died in 1638. It came afterwards to the Sheldons, from one of which family it was purchaſed by Jaſper Chapman, eſq; who died in the year 1713. Thomas Maſter, eſq; married Joanna, ſole daughter and heireſs of Jaſper Chapman, and with her had the manor of Stratton, which is now the property of his grandſon, Thomas Maſter, of the Abbey at Cirenceſter, eſq.

Adam de Rolby levied a fine of lands called Mead's Croft in Stratton, to Adam de Stratton, 6 E. 1. Eight acres of land in Stratton belonged to the hofpital of St. John the Baptift in Cirencefter 33 E. 1. and a confiderable eftate in the fame place now belongs to that hofpital. Walter Wrilock, and others, granted one plow-tillage in Stratton to the abbey of Cirencefter, 13 E. 2. William Boys, and others, held lands in Stratton, 32 E. 3. William Nottingham and Elizabeth his wife levied a fine of lands in this place to John Kendall, and the heirs of Elizabeth, who regranted them to William Nottingham and Elizabeth his wife in fpecial taille, 20 H. 6. Humphry Brydges of Cirencefter, died 40 Eliz. feized, among other things, of a capital meffuage in Caftle-ftreet in Cirencefter, and of two clofes of pafture thereto adjoining and appertaining, called Ayfhcroftes; of two meffuages, two cottages, two tofts, a dove houfe, three orchards, 200 acres of land, ten of meadow, fixteen of pafture, the Myll Hames, formerly parcel of the manor, and of a meadow called Mayms Meade, *alias* Our Lady's Meade, in Stratton, then in the occupation of Edward Chapman; all which particulars he gave by will to Anthony Brydges, his fecond fon. *Efch.*

Of the Church, &c.

The church is a rectory, in the deanery of Cirencefter, worth about 180*l.* a year. Thomas Mafter, efq; is patron, and the reverend Mr. Daubeny is the prefent incumbent.

Fifteen acres of pafture, and forty-eight acres of arable in each common field, belonged to the glebe, before the parifh was inclofed by act of parliament, about the year 1771, when lands were allotted to the rector in lieu of his former glebe and tithes.

The church, dedicated to St. Peter, is very fmall, and has a low flated tower in the middle, with two bells in it.

Firft fruits £. 12	7	9	Synodals £. 0	2	0
Tenths — 1	4	9	Pentecoft. 0	1	1½
Procurations 0	6	8			

Monuments and Infcriptions.

There is a marble monument againft the fouth wall of the chancel, with the bufts of a man and his two wives; and under them is the following infcription, in gold letters:

Here refteth the Body of Thomas Nicholas Efqvire late Lord of this Manovr, and Patron of this Chvrch, fometime high Sheriffe of this Covnty, and a lover of Hofpitalitie, who had to his firft wife, Iane Avdley, worthily defcended of the antient family of the Avdleys, and to his fecond wife Bridget Strange, davghter to Michael Strange of Somerford, Efq; who changed this Lyfe the 14 day of Avgvft 1638.

Memoriæ eivfdem Tho: Nicholas Armig.
facrvm.

Hic fitus eft Iri ac Crœfi communis amator,
Doctrinæ fautor, religionis honos;
Qui fatur annorum, famæq; euafit ad auras
Ethereas, novus & gratus vbi hofpes adeft.
Hofpes at interea folitus, folita oftia fruftra
Pulfat, & efuriens nunc mifer Irus abit.
Dum fpectas imitare, fidem fic exprime factis.
Diuide, da, cura, dilige, talis eris.
Ætat. 63.

Over the man's buft are thefe arms, *Argent, on a chevron fable between three blackbirds two lions rampant Or*, for Nicholas. Over his firft wife's buft, Nicholas, as before; impaling, *Gules, a fret Or*, for Audley. And over his fecond wife's buft, Nicholas, impaling, *Gules, two lions paffant argent debruifed by a bend ermine*, for Strange.

In the chancel is likewife this infcription, but now covered by the pews:

Conduntur hic ingentis viri Exuviæ
Radulphi Willett A.M. hujufq; Ecclefiæ non ita pridem
Rectoris digniffimi.
Qui præclaro ingenii acumine, eximiis animi Dotibus
Omnigenâ, qua prodeffe poffet, Literatura exornatus,
Vel Ruris obfcuritate Emicuit
Haud medocriter illuftris.
In concionibus
Doctrinæ Sanitate Bullum;
Concinna Styli Simplicitate, Tillotfonum;
Rationum Soliditate fe unum Referebat:
Concionator urbi Aulæve Petendus;
Medicinæ Jurifq;
Longe fupra Sortem peritum fatentur omnes
Quibus, Morbis Litibufve vexatis, fidiffimum erat
Subfidium et Tutamen.
Quum vero Diu Deo, Proximo, fibiq; Vixiffet
Vir optimus, abfq; omni fuco faftuve Pius,
Senio tandem confectus
Mortalitati placide ceffit Aug. 20° A.D. 1738,
Ætatis fuæ 84°.

Taxes.	The Royal Aid in 1692,	£. 40	12	0
	Poll-tax — 1694, —	19	14	0
	Land-tax — 1694, —	36	16	0
	The fame, at 3*s.* 1770, —	28	1	0

At the beginning of this century, there were 30 houfes, and about 150 inhabitants in this parifh, whereof 7 were freeholders; yearly births 3, burials 3. *Atkyns.* But the regifter fhews that in ten years, beginning with 1720, the baptifms were 42, the burials 45. And in the fame number of years, beginning with 1760, the baptifms were 43, and the burials 58. The excefs in the burials is owing to feveral families at Cirencefter having fepulture here. The prefent number of families is 35, of inhabitants exactly 173.

****

STROUD.

THIS parifh lies in the hundred of Bifley, betwixt three and four miles north-weft from Minchin Hampton, about the fame diftance weft from Bifley, and nearly ten fouth from Gloucefter.

The firft mention I have found of the name is in a compofition between the rectors of the church of Bifley and the inhabitants of *La Stroud*, dated 1304. Sir Robert Atkyns was of opinion that it was *fo called from* Strogd, *which in the Saxon language fignifies fcattered, from their houfes being difperfed at a diftance.* But fome perfons have taken *Stroud* and *Strand* for fynonimous expreffions; and it feems not improbable that this place obtained its name from thofe houfes which were firft built here, ftanding on the *ftrand* or banks of the river Froom, which runs through and feparates it from the parifhes of Hampton and Rodborough on the fouth.

Froom, or *Froome*, (perhaps from the Britifh *ffrom*, rapid) is an appellation given to many rivers

vers in this kingdom. This river has been erroneoufly called the Stroud. It rifes at Brimpsfield, and is known there by its proper name, which it communicates to feveral places lying in its courfe, as Frampton, Froomill, Froombridge, another Frampton, and laftly Framilode, where it fall into the Severn, about nine miles below Stroud.

Befide the Froom, Stroud is extremely well watered by feveral rivulets, fome of which conftitute the boundaries between it and neighbouring places. One rifes near Lypiat, and running thro' Todefmore-bottom, divides part of this parifh from Bifley eaftward; another runs through the Slade-bottom, and divides a part from Painfwick northward; a third comes from, and feparates Painfwick from Pakenhill on the eaft; and a fourth divides part of Stroud from Randwick.

The parifh is in fome places five miles long, and two broad, and confifts of high grounds, and declivities thence on all fides to the waters, where the meadow and pafture-lands are. Above them, the foil being moftly light and ftony, is employ'd in tillage; but the upper part of the declivities confifts of beech woods, which are continually fuffering a diminution by the incroachment of the hufbandman, and a defire of turning the land to a more immediate account.

The intermixture of gently rifing hills and dales, with woods and lawns, produces in this country a great variety of pleafing landfcapes and profpects, ftill heightened and improved by the beautiful tints of fine woollen clothes ftretched upon the tenters, and villages of good ftone-buildings, all whitened, every where interfperfed, and almoft contiguous; fo that ftrangers are greatly ftruck with the profpects, and think them fuperior to moft they have feen.

Within the parifh there is a market-town of the fame name, fituated on the ridge of a declivity, near the confluence of the river Froom and the Slade-water, in the midft of the principal clothing country of Gloucefterfhire, with which it maintains a good trade; but there is not much travelling through it, becaufe of the fteep hills that encompafs it almoft on every fide except to the weftward. It is not large, in proportion to the populoufnefs of the country; for the clothiers don't refide in the town, but generally near the rivulets where their refpective mills ftand; whence the *Bottoms*, as they are called, are an almoft continued range of houfes and villages, and from the hills exhibit a moft pleafing view of a populous country.

This town has a weekly market on Friday, and two fairs, one on the 12th of May, the other on St. Lawrence's day, but now held on the 21ft of Auguft, for cattle, &c. the profits of which belong to Mr. Hoard and Mr. Chamberlayne.

One turnpike-road leads from it through Painfwick to Gloucefter; another by Cain's-crofs, Stonehoufe, and Whitminfter to Frampton on the Severn, which is ten miles diftant; and a third to Rodborough and Hampton-common, where it divides, the right hand branch leading to Tetbury; the left to Cirencefter, and fo onwards to London.

The latitude of the town was accurately taken fome years fince by the ingenious Mr. Canton, who was a native of this place, and F.R.S. and it was found to be 51° : 44′ : 21″ north.

The trade of this part of the country, tho' frequently fluctuating, is in general confiderable. They make here a great variety of broad clothes, both for home confumption and foreign trade, from thofe of low value to the beft Spanifh. Thefe are fent away either white, or dyed in the cloth; and in particular great quantities are dyed fcarlet, for which branch of trade the place is noted. The beauty of their colours is very great, to the perfection of which the Froom water has been erroneoufly fuppofed to contribute, for it is moft affuredly owing to the fkill of the artift. Many hands are employ'd in the various branches of the manufacture, as in cleanfing the wool by picking and wafhing it; in fcribbling and fpinning it; fpooling and warping the yarn; weaving the cloth; burling, milling, and rowing it; then in fhearing and dreffing it; and, if to be fent off coloured, in dying it; and laftly, in preffing and packing it; and moft of thefe proceffes are carried on by diftinct workmen. As fpinning requires moft hands, fome of the clothiers fend their wool to the diftance of twenty miles or more, and the poor women and children, for that extent of country, work at this branch, which makes it difficult to afcertain the numbers employ'd in the manufacture. Moft of the other branches are carried on at the mills, or at the clothiers houfes; but the weavers work at home. There are in this parifh eighteen clothing mills, and about thirty mafter clothiers. The editor of the *Magna Britannia* eftimates the returns of the clothiers of thefe parts at 50,000*l. per ann.* "fome making" fays he, "1000 clothes a year for their own fhare." What he means by *thefe parts* is not very certain; but his calculation is much too low, and efpecially for the prefent time; for the cloth made annually within this parifh only, is fuppofed to amount to near 200,000*l.* and there is one perfon that makes above 3000 clothes a year. Very large fortunes have been acquired in this bufinefs, and it is an obfervation of Mr. Camden's, that feveral of the moft eminent families among the nobility in this nation have had their rife from it.

This large trade has brought together a very numerous poor, who are not, however, fo burthenfome in proportion to their number as in many other places. In common years, when trade has been good, and provifions reafonable, four levies of 82*l.* each, have been fufficient for the fupport of the poor of the whole parifh; but

ever

ever ſince the year 1766, ſix or ſeven ſuch levies have been expended upon them annually.

Lands let here at a high rate; paſture and meadow ground from 30*s.* to 3*l.* the acre, and arable from 10*s.* to 20*s.* And conſequently the produce ſells almoſt as dear as in any part of the kingdom, which makes ſome amends to the landed intereſt for the burthen of the poor.

The great trade and populouſneſs of the country occaſioned an application to parliament for a power to make the Froom navigable from this town to the Severn, and an act paſſed for that purpoſe in 1730, but from an apprehenſion afterwards of injuring the clothing mills upon the river, it was never carried into execution. In 1759, a ſcheme offered to obviate all objections reſpecting the mills, by which it was propoſed that all loading ſhould be laid in ſquare cheſts to be placed in boats, two of which to ply on the river between every two mills, and that at each mill a crane ſhould be erected to ſhift the cheſts of loading from one boat to another, through the whole navigation. This ſcheme was tried for a ſmall part of the way; but it did not ſucceed. In 1775, an act paſſed for making a navigable canal from Walbridge, near Stroud, to the Severn, near Framilode; in conſequence whereof a handſome canal, forty-two feet wide, is already cut part of the way, and when compleated, will be of great advantage to this country and the neighbouring parts, by the importation of all heavy goods, and eſpecially of coal, of which there is a great conſumption amongſt the clothiers and dyers. There is a remarkable circumſtance attending this navigation: From Walbridge to Framilode along the turnpike-road is ten miles and two furlongs, whereas it is only eight miles down the canal, which makes it two miles and a quarter farther by land than water.

The natural hiſtory of the pariſh of Stroud may be comprized in a ſmall compaſs. Above the town of Stroud, the hill gradually aſcends to the higher grounds. On the ſides of this acclivity, to the north and ſouth, are two plentiful ſprings, called *Gainey's* and *Hemlock's Wells*, that pour out a great quantity of water in a ſhort time. They both iſſue immediately from a great depth under ground; and by obſervations made with a thermometer, the water has been found of an equal temperature, within one degree, in winter and ſummer. The water of Gainey's Well has been lately conveyed to the town in leaden pipes, to the great convenience of the inhabitants.

In Manſel's mead, ſouth of the town, is a chalybeate, mineral ſpring, that tinges lightly with galls, and is uſed for ſore eyes; and above this ſpring, and in other parts of the neighbourhood, in the blue clay, and the earth near it, are found *pyrites*, in very ponderous, yellow, irregular balls, or nodules, ſome of which, I am informed, have been tried at Redbrook works, and yielded a ſmall proportion of copper.

The higher grounds are every where lined with ſtone, which lies near the ſurface, and conſiſts chiefly of free-ſtone, and what is called here weather-ſtone, The former appears like a congeries of the *ovula* of fiſh, and the minuter ſhells. The latter is full of ſhells of the larger ſort, moſtly of the bivalvular kind, as cockles, *anomiæ*, and oyſter-ſhells, tho' many other different ſpecies may be obſerved. In many places the ſubſtance of the ſhell may be ſeen ſufficiently diſtinct, but in general they are incruſted and filled with a hard ſtony concretion, ſo ſtrongly adhering that they are not ſeparable from it. *Nautuli* and *Cornua Ammonis* are found in plenty in the beds of blue clay and marle; *lac lunæ*, *ſtalactitæ*, and incruſtations are found in the cavities and quarries, and a variety of ſpars in the ſtones every where. But I am informed that there are no plants worth the curious botaniſt's notice growing in the pariſh.

The following anecdote, which ſir Robert Atkyns has told imperfectly, is found in Dr. Parſons's MS. Collections. It is ſaid that ſometime in the reign of queen Elizabeth, the earl of Tyrone's daughter, Florence, fled with her jewels and valuables from her father's houſe, with a ſervant, to London, and there lived privately married to him; but burying her huſband, ſhe came into this country, and married a cloth-worker, concealing her birth and parentage for many years. At laſt, falling deſperately ſick, ſhe diſcovers the whole, and left in money and jewels 1000*l.* a piece to her ſons, and 500*l.* each to her daughters, and was interred in Stroud church-yard.

Of the Manor and other Eſtates.

Domeſday takes no notice of this place, for when that record was compiled, this was part of the pariſh and manor of Biſley. Sir Robert Atkyns ſays, the Whitingtons were formerly lords of this manor. The Whitingtons were indeed lords of the manor of Rodborough, in the reigns of king Henry the Sixth, and king Henry the Eighth. They contributed to the building of the ſouth aile of the church of Stroud, as may be preſumed from their arms being carved in the ſtone-work of the porch, where they are ſtill to be ſeen; but what eſtate, if any, they had in Stroud, I have not been able to diſcover. The ſame learned author obſerves, that the manor was in his time divided amongſt many conſiderable freeholders; but I am informed that it belongs at preſent to John Stephens, eſq; who is alſo lord of the manor of Biſley.

William Nottingham, and Elizabeth his wife, levied a fine of lands in Stroud to John Kendal and the heirs of Elizabeth, who regranted the ſame to William Nottingham and to Elizabeth, in taille, 20 H. 6. Robert Hill and his wife levied a fine of lands in Stroud to the uſe of John Maſon 1 H. 7.

TITHINGS

TITHINGS and *HAMLETS.*

1. *Upper Lypiat*, or *Over Lypiat*. This manor was held of the honour of Hereford, and was antiently in the family of the Manſells. William Manſell died ſeized of Over Lupeyate, which he had by the grant of Alexander de Domeſbourne, as appears by an inquiſition after his death, 18 E. 2. and Philip Manſell died ſeized of the ſame 19 R. 2. It was for ſeveral ſucceeding generations in the family of the Wyes, who are mentioned by Leland (*Itin.* V. 6.) as reſiding at Lipiate. Thomas Wye died ſeized of this manor, and of ten meſſuages, two hundred acres of land, ſixty of meadow, one hundred of paſture, forty of wood, and other particulars in Overlypiat, Stroud, Biſley, and Winſton, as appears by the eſcheator's inquiſition taken at Cirenceſter 18 Sept. 26 Eliz. The manor, according to ſir Robert Atkyns, belonged afterwards to Throckmorton, who was concerned in the popiſh powder-plot. However that might be, they now ſhew a room in the manor-houſe where it is ſaid that plot was concerted; but I don't remember that hiſtory takes notice of any one of the name of Throckmorton concerned in it. There was a ſir Nicholas Throckmorton tried for high teraſon, and acquitted, in the firſt year of the reign of queen Mary, who may poſſibly be the perſon ſir Robert alludes to. This manor was afterwards purchaſed in the reign of king James the Firſt, by Thomas Stephens, eſq; who was attorney-general to prince Henry and prince Charles, and a younger brother of the Stephens's of Eaſington. He died in 1613, and left three ſons; the eldeſt was anceſtor to the Stephens's of Sodbury; the ſecond progenitor to the Stephens's at Lypiat; and the youngeſt anceſtor to the Stephens's of Cherington. John Stephens, eſq; ſecond ſon of Thomas, ſucceeded him in the manor of Lypiat. Thomas Stephens, ſon of John, married Anne, daughter of —— Child, of Northwick in Worceſterſhire, and ſerved the office of high ſheriff of this county in the year 1693, and was afterwards choſen one of the knights of the ſhire. Thomas Stephens, was ſon and heir of Thomas, whoſe ſon, John Stephens, is the preſent lord of the manor of Upper Lypiat, and has a very antient ſeat, with a chapel, and a great eſtate in this place, where he reſides.

In the time of the great civil wars, colonel Maſſy placed a garriſon of the parliament's forces in this houſe, which was afterwards taken by ſir Jacob Aſhly, in the abſence of the captain who commanded there.

Richard Arundell died ſeized of a capital meſſuage called Huckevale's Place, with lands thereto belonging, together with Prowle-grove in Lyppiate Superior, as appears by the eſcheator's inquiſition 42 Eliz.

2. *Lower Lypiat*. This manor was alſo held of the honour of Hereford. The Freames were an antient family, and had a ſeat here, called Lypiat Hall. Robert Freame died ſeized in fee-taille of Nether Lyppiate 41 Eliz. *Eſch.* Charles Coxe, eſq; married one of the heireſſes of that family, and with her had this manor. He was deſervedly appointed one of the judges of Wales, and ſerved in ſeveral parliaments for the borough of Cirenceſter. He was ſucceeded in this eſtate by his ſon, John Coxe, eſq; who was alſo elected a repreſentative in parliament for the borough of Cirenceſter, in the year 1748, and is the preſent proprietor of Lower Lypiat, where he has a handſome houſe, and a large eſtate. His arms are blazoned under Rodmarton.

There was alſo another Lypiat, which belonged to the knights hoſpitallers of St. John of Jeruſalem. It was granted to John Pope 36 H. 8. and is now the eſtate of Mr. Peter Leverſedge.

Brimſcomb is a little hamlet in the Lower Lypiat diviſion, ſituated in a pleaſant valley, on the banks of the Froom, ſurrounded with woods, and lies in the common road between Minchin Hampton and Stroud. There is in this place an antient houſe, formerly called Bigge's Place, with clothing-mills adjoining, which was the property of the late William Dallaway, eſq; who ſerved the office of high ſheriff of this county in the year 1776, and carried on a large trade in the clothing buſineſs 'till the time of his death, in the year 1775. The lands belonging to it are ſaid to have been part of the poſſeſſions of the priory of Stanley St. Leonard's, and ſome pieces retain the name of the Friers meadows to this time. The arms of this family are, *Or, on a bend gules between ſix martlets a javelin.*

New Houſe, in this hamlet, is a very handſome building, the reſidence of Joſeph Wathen, eſq; who is in the commiſſion of the peace, and one of the greateſt clothiers in the county.

3. *Pakenhill*, or *Pagan Hull*. This diviſion lies in the weſt part of the pariſh, intirely ſeparated from the reſt, by the intervening of part of Painſwick pariſh, which runs down to the Froom, or Stroud river. This manor, and Upper and Lower Lypiat, were held of Humphry de Bohun, earl of Hereford and Eſſex, and of Joan his wife, 46 E. 3. Henry de Dean died ſeized of the manor of Pagenhul 20 E. 1. John Baſſet was ſeized thereof, and had a confirmation of free warren, 28 E. 3. and William Laſborough had another ſuch confirmation in Paganhull 4 R. 2. Thomas Warner died ſeized of Pakenhill 17 C. 1. and was ſucceeded by his ſon William, who was twelve years old at his father's death. To him ſucceeded Thomas Warner, whoſe ſon, Thomas Warner, eſq; died in 1736, and his ſiſter's ſon, Henry Wyatt, eſq; is the preſent poſſeſſor of the Warners eſtate at Pakenhill.

The Fields were an antient family long reſident in this diviſion. Thomas Field, eſq; of Pakenhill, died in the year 1510, and was buried on the fouth fide in Stroud church, where his effigy was placed. His eftate defcended from father to fon, down to Thomas Field, efq; who enjoyed it in the prefent century, and it is now the property of the defcendants of his nephew, the late John de la Field Phelps, of Durfley, efq.

4. *Steanbridge.* In this divifion Mr. Thomas Baylis has a handfome and fpacious new-built houfe, called the *New Mills*, of which he has obliged the editor with the engraving annexed.

There are feveral other good houfes and eftates in this parifh; as at *Griffin's Mill*, which is the eftate and refidence of Thomas Griffin, efq; one of his majefty's acting juftices of the peace for this county; at the *Thrup*, the property of James Clutterbuck, efq; at *Gannicock's*, belonging to William Knight, efq; at *The Field*, near the town, the property of Fream Arundell, efq; and at *Stretford*, where Mrs. Gardiner has a good eftate.

Of the Church, &c.

The church is in the deanery of Stonehoufe. It is an impropriation, belonging to the earl of Coventry, out of which the curate receives 10*l.* a year. In 1722, and 1728, the curacy received a double augmentation from monies raifed by Mr. Bond, the minifter, and fome of the principal inhabitants, and from queen Anne's bounty, which were laid out on the purchafe of an eftate called the Radways, worth 32*l.* a year; fo that, with other revenues herein after mentioned, and the contributions of the inhabitants, the minifter's income is pretty confiderable. The inhabitants have nominated to the curacy, but the bifhop of Gloucefter prefented to it on the two laft vacancies, and the reverend Mr. James Webfter is the prefent incumbent.

This was antiently a chapel of eafe to Bifley, and in the year 1304, a certain compofition was made between the rectors of the firft and fecond portion of the church of Bifley, and the inhabitants of Stroud, in which, after reprefenting, 'That 'whereas between the faid chapel of Stroud, and 'the mother church of Bifley, there is fo great and 'dangerous a diftance, that men can't well pafs 'betwixt, by means of which great danger of fouls 'may very likely happen, in baptizing of infants 'and adminiftring other ecclefiaftical facraments: 'It is agreed, that at the charge of the inhabi'tants, baptifms fhall be ufed in the fame chapel 'of Stroud, and a chaplain chofen by the fore'faid perfons fhall continually remain. And that 'the faid inhabitants fhall take on themfelves the 'repairs of the chancel of the faid chapel, and 'that in confideration of thefe things, the faid 'rectors give up a certain vacant plot of ground 'called *Area feu Tenementum in La Stroud quam* '*vel quod Johes de Pridie pro Certa Reditu hactenus* '*tenuit de Rectoribus antedictis*, which plot of 'ground the faid inhabitants are competently 'to build upon, and to keep the buildings in re'pair at their proper cofts and charges, paying 'therefore yearly to the faid rectors eighteen 'pence as before accuftomed, and to the aforefaid 'chaplain fifteen fhillings yearly.' This compofition was fince confirmed in the ecclefiaftical court, in the years 1493 and 1598. On the aforefaid plot of ground, it is fuppofed the markethoufe and feveral adjacent houfes were fince built. Thefe, with three other houfes in the town, of antient donation, and two acres of ground, called Church Furlong, yielding now in the whole about 129*l. per ann.* fubject to taxes, are vefted in feoffees, and by an order of chancery in 1741, 20*l. per ann.* are to be paid to the curate of Stroud out of the rents and profits, in full fatisfaction for all his right in the fame, and the reft is left for the reparation of the church, and the fupport of the poor.

The prefent church is handfomely pewed with Dutch oak. It confifts of the nave, with two ailes, and two chancels, with a fpire fteeple and eight bells at the weft end, where are two galleries, and there is one alfo in each aile. The original chapel is now the inner chancel, with a fmall kind of fpire, in whofe bafe hung two little bells, juft above the roof of the chapel. That which is now the nave, with the fteeple, feems to be the firft addition to the chapel; but the people ftill inceafing, the fouth aile and chancel were next built, very probably by the affiftance of the Whitingtons, as their arms are placed on the left hand of the entrance, in the wall of the porch adjoining to that aile. So on the right were the arms (tho' now defaced) of another family, who, it is fuppofed, were large contributors to the building of the fame aile. The north aile was built in 1759, by the joint contributions of thofe perfons whofe names appear in the lift of Benefactions, and who have the property of the feats vefted in them; but the congregation is fo numerous that the church is ftill infufficient for the inhabitants.

There are, befide the parifh church, two meeting houfes in the town, one for independents, the other for the followers of Mr. Weftley.

Pentecoftals - - - 6*d.*

Monuments and Infcriptions.

There is a very handfome monument in the fouth chancel, with the figure, in full proportion, of a gentleman habited in a doctor of law's gown, and kneeling; and upon a fmall tablet it is thus written in letters of gold:

THOMAS STEPHENS Armiger legum municipalium Regni Angliæ peritiffimus, HENRICO et CAROLO principibus Walliæ Attornatus generalis, obiit 26 Aprilis An. Dom. 1613 Ætatis fuæ 55.

Lege perit Stephanus? væ nobis lege perimus
Omnes peccanti lex datur una mori:
Non periit Stephanus: Fertur lex altera Chrifti,
Quæ *Stephanon* Staphano dat prohibetq; mori.

In a fcutcheon at the top of the monument are thefe arms, Quarterly 1ft *and* 4th, *Per chevron azure and argent, in chief two falcons with wings elevated Or*, for Stephens; 2d *and* 3d, *Gules, upon a bend cotoifed argent a* *fable.*

Near the above, on a fmall tablet:

In Memory of Edward Field, late of Field Place in this Parifh Efq; many years one of his Majefties Juftices of the Peace for this

this County, who died the thirtyeth day of March, 1736, aged 67 years.

This Monument is erected by Anne his Widow and Relict who was his Second Wife and one of the daughters of Richard Plummer of this Pariſh Gentleman.

There is a ſcutcheon at bottom, bearing *Or, a feſs between an eagle diſplay'd in chief, and a buck's head caboſhed in baſe ſable.*

Upon a mural monument in the ſouth aile,

In Memory of Rich^{d}. Field of Field's Place Gent. and Elizth his Wife Daughter of Edwd Hill of Cam in ye County Eſq^{r}

He } dyed { Oct. 3, 1693 } Aged { 42.
She } { March 8, 1715 } { 78.

Joan^{a} Field Edvardi Field Armigeri, de Loco Fieldi, ſupra dicto, Uxor indulgentiſſima: Iohannis Delaberi, Armigeri, de Southam, in Parochia Epiſcop. Cliev. in Comit. Glocestr. Filia dilectiſſima, Ob. 15° Maij Anno Æt^{s} 63° currente, Redemptionis MDCCXXX^{mo}.

There is a ſcutcheon at the top of the monument, *Party per pale*, 1ſt, Field; 2d, *Azure, on a chevron Or within a bordure ingrailed and between three owls, as many mullets ſable.*

Upon a flat ſtone in the ſame aile,

Here lyeth the Body of Elizabeth eldeſt Daughter of Sr Edward Fuſt Baronet of Hill Court in this County, and Wife of Thomas Warner, Junior of this Pariſh Eſquire now living at Paynſwicke who departed this Life the 24th Day of April An^{o} Do. 1718.

Here lyes Interred the Body of Thomas Warner Eſq; who lived many Years in this Pariſh much eſteemed and well beloved of his Neighbours. He was an affectionate Huſband, a kind Father, a good Maſter, a generous and ſincere Friend, a charitable Benefactor to the Poor, and in all other Offices and Relations of Life, always behaved himſelf with Integrity and Honour. He departed this Life on the 11th of April 1736 much lamented and regretted by all about him.

The arms on this ſtone are, *Baron and femme*, 1ſt, *Or, a chevron between three boars heads couped ſable.* 2d, Fuſt, as at Hill.

On the table of a monument againſt the ſouth wall,

In Memory of Sarah, Wife of Richard Aldridge, who died Septr 10th 1761 aged 44. Thomas their ſon died Decr. 29th 1748; Benjamina their Daughter April 9, 1753; Sarah their Daughter Apr. 19th 1757.

The arms on this monument are, *Quarterly* 1ſt *and* 4th, *Argent, on a croſs ſable a leopard's head caboſhed Or*; 2d, *Or, a pile azure*; 3d, *Argent, a feſs between three martlets ſable.*——Note, there are other inſcriptions for perſons of this family name, with the ſame arms.

There is a mural monument in the north chancel, ornamented with ſeveral emblematical figures, and upon the table it is thus written:

Thomas Freame, Armiger, ex cohorte Centurio obiit 18 Aprilis an. dni. 1664 ætatis ſuæ 63.

Non cecidit Frœmus licet hîc cecidiſſe videtur
Ad ſuperas abijt, venerat vnde, domos:
Viua fides, charitas, ſpes, mens ſua firma manebant:
Cætera depoſuit, mors meliora dedit.
Hic etiam Anna Fream Thomæ quoundam Uxor
poſt xxx Viduitatis annos iterum Viro conjuncta fuit
Iun. 26° 1694.

And upon a ſmall tablet beneath,

In Memory of Thomas Clutterbuck the Son of Samuel Clutterbuck Great grandſon of Thomas Freame of Lower Lyppiat Eſq^{r} who died the 14th of March in the 9th year of his Age 1715.

At the top of the monument are theſe arms, *Baron and femme*, 1. *Argent, a feſs ingrailed gules, and a chevron in baſe ſable.* 2. *Gules, a dexter arm vambraced Or.*

Near to the laſt is this memorial,

M. S.

of Freame Clutterbuck (an Infant) the Son of Freame Clutterbuck Eſq; of this pariſh by his Wife Anne ye Daught^{r} of Francis Sims of Kempſcot in the County of Oxon Gent. who departed this life the 17th of July A. D. 1711 Aged one Year and ſeven Months.

When CHRIST commands away
'Tis Sin to wiſh to ſtay
Tho' ſoon thy Glaſs be run
For Heav'n thou'rt not too young
For all are like thee there
Go then and be Heav'n's Heir.

This monument is ornamented with the family arms, *viz. Argent, a lion rampant azure, in chief three eſcallops of the ſecond.*

In the ſame chancel is the following memorial,

Near this place was interr'd John Gryffin Gent. and Elizabeth his Wife in the year 1627. Alſo Elizabeth his Grandaughter wife of John Webb of the Throp Clothier was buried the 31st of July 1681. Alſo Elizabeth the Daughter of John Gryffin of this Pariſh Gent. Wife of Thomas Cliffold, Clothier, was buried the 18th day of October 1703.

John Gryffin of this Pariſh Gent. died the 28th of March 1719.

In the ſcutcheon over the monument are theſe arms, *viz. Baron and femme*, 1. *Sable, a griphon rampant argent.* 2. Webb, as at Painſwick.

Upon a table, againſt a pillar at the weſt end of the church, it is thus written:

H. S. E.
DANIEL CAPEL A.M.

Coll. Pemb. apud Oxon Socius et Ornamentum
Doctrina potius quam annis maturus,
Parentibus, Amicis, Eccleſ. Anglicanæ, ob pietatem ingenium et fidē carus.
Non modo nomine, ſed et virtutibus
Reverendum Avum Proavumq; expreſſit
Gravis et Urbanus, Prudens et facetus;
Politioribus quibus inclaruit artibus
Phæbæum Medicinæ Studium adjunxit,
In quâ tantum profecit Adoleſcens
Ut alterum Hippocratem Sponderet;
Donec Libitina imperij metuens
Hunc juvenem peremit
Ne de illâ provectior ſine modo triumpharet
Ob. Iul: 30 anō dōni 1709 Ætat. 24

DANIEL CAPEL Dicti Pater
Vir Pius, Probus, Gravis;
Medicus Peritiſſimus, qui Praxin
Non minus ſibi laborioſam,
Quam ægris ſuis commodam ſuſtinuit:
Sed Proh dolor! dum aliorum ſaluti
Attente nimis invigilavit,
Amiſit ſuam.
Obijt die Iunij 27 Anō Salutis Chriſtianæ 1714 Ætat. 55.

Over the tablet are the family arms, *viz. Checky Or and azure, on a feſs of the firſt, three lozenges of the ſecond.*

There is a neat monument, with this inſcription, at the eaſt end of the north aile:

To the Memory of JOHN HEART of this Pariſh Gentleman, who died the 19th of March 1763 aged 52 years. ELIZABETH Daughter of the ſaid JOHN HEART, by BETTY his Wife, died November 2^{d} 1767, aged 21.

There are two coats upon this monument, *viz. Baron and femme*, 1. *Gules, on a chief argent three hearts of the firſt.* 2. *Quarterly argent and ſable, over all, on a bend Or, three lions paſſant gules.*

On a ſmall marble tablet, at the weſt end of the ſame aile,

To the Memory of Thos. Arundel Gent. & Anne his Wife (daug^{r} of Thos. Gregory of Hordley in Oxfordſhire Eſq;) He died the 26th day of March 1742 aged 48 years. She the 29th of July in the ſame year, aged 50.

Fream Arundel their Son, died in the year 1721, aged one year and 6 months. Jno Gregory Arundel died July the 5th 1752 aged 6 months.

In a ſcutcheon placed at the bottom, are two coats, *viz. Baron and femme*, 1. *Sable, a chevron between three ſwallows argent.* 2. *Azure, on a feſs argent between three ſaltires croſſed Or, as many corniſh choughs ſable.*

Benefactions.

I have given the particulars of ſome antient donations in my account of the church, to which the reader is referred.

In 1636, Samuel Watts of London, merchant, gave 200*l.* afterwards laid out on lands in Colthrop, worth 10*l.* a year, one moiety of which by a decree in chancery in 1741, is directed to be applied to the maintenance of a Friday's lecture; the other to the uſe of the poor.

In 1642, Mr. Thomas Webb of the Hill, by his will, gave his houſe oppoſite the church for charitable uſes; and 10*l.* a year out of his lands at Huc-

Hucclecot, for the maintenance of a free-ſchool in Stroud, in which four poor children are to be taught to read, write, and caſt account; 20*l.* a year for their maintenance whilſt at ſchool; 6*l.* a year for their clothing, and keeping the houſe in repair; and 4*l.* a year out of the ſame lands, for two poor widows, to live in the ſaid houſe, and take care of the children. And in 1734, Henry Windowe, eſq; by his will, gave an eſtate in this pariſh, for ever, now worth 20*l.* a year, for the further advancement of Mr. Webb's ſchool; 5*l.* part of the rent, to the maſter for teaching two other boys; 4*l.* to the widows, and the remainder to be applied towards the maintenance, clothing, and placing out as apprentices the ſame two boys.

In 1676, William Hawker gave a rent-charge on his houſe and mills at Badbrook, of 2*l.* 10*s.* a year to the miniſter, and 3*l.* 10*s.* to the uſe of the poor, for ever.

Nathaniel Gardiner, by will, gave 20*s.* a year for ever, to be laid out in bread for the poor; and James Winchcombe, in the year 1731, gave 3*l.* a year out of lands in this pariſh to the ſame uſe.

In 1720, William Johns, clerk, by his will, gave the rents and profits of his houſe and orchard called the Knap, for ever, to the following uſes, *viz.* 20*s.* a year to the charity ſchool at Stroud; 10*s.* a year to keep the pump at the croſs in repair; 10*s.* a year for ringing the bell at eight o'clock at night, and four in the morning; 20*s.* to keep the church-clock and chimes in repair; and the reſidue to put out poor children apprentices.

There are four charity ſchools in this pariſh, for teaching the children of the poor to read, ſupported by a ſubſcription of the principal inhabitants, and a yearly collection at the church, on which occaſion there is a ſuitable ſermon, and the contributions of late have been liberal.

It appears by a table in the church, that the north aile, with the deſk and pulpit, were erected in the year 1759, at the ſole expence of the following perſons, *viz.* William Dallaway, Joſeph Wathen, Thomas Pegler, Fream Arundel, Samuel Arundel, Thomas Baylis, Samuel Baylis, Robert Ellis, Richard Aldridge, Peter Playne, William Knight, and Richard Capel.

Taxes.					
	The Royal Aid in	1692,	£.200	10	8
	Poll-tax —	1694,	— 100	11	0
	Land-tax —	1694,	— 314	4	0
	The ſame, at 3*s.*	1770,	— 243	10	6

At the beginning of this century, there were 750 houſes, and about 3000 inhabitants in this pariſh, whereof 100 were freeholders; yearly births 86, burials 84. *Atkyns.* By an exact account taken in the year 1756, there were 415 families, and 2024 inhabitants in the town of Stroud, and it is apprehended they have not varied much ſince. The proportion of adults, to thoſe under ſixteen, was obſerved to be as 21 to 11, or nearly as 2 to 1; and that of males to females, as 7 to 8. The number of inhabitants in the whole pariſh, including the town, is about 4000, of whom 120 are freeholders. The medium of births for twenty years, from 1747, has been 67 males, and 60 females, in the year; in all 127;—of burials for the ſame time, 38 males, and 41 females, in all 79; the births being to the burials as 16 to 10. And the medium of weddings from 1754 to 1766, incluſively, 36 in the year.

From this ſurvey, as well as from the ſtate of the buildings for many years, it appears that there has been no great increaſe or decreaſe of inhabitants; and that 48 may be ſpared yearly to ſupply the demands of the army, the navy, and our capital towns, without any diminution in the number of people in this pariſh.

S U D L E Y.

THIS pariſh lies in the lower diviſion of the hundred of Kiftſgate, near a mile diſtant ſouth from the town of Winchcombe, nine eaſtward from Tewkeſbury, and ſixteen north-eaſtward from Glouceſter.

It conſiſts of rich meadow and paſture ground, and is ſituated on the north ſide of that great chain of hills which runs through the county, and divides the deep vale from the high Coteſwolds of Glouceſterſhire. There was a large deer-park here, but it is now thrown open.

The name was antiently written *Sudlege*, which ſignifies the *South Place*, from the Saxon Suð, and leȝa, and has an obvious reference to Winchcombe, which lies a little northward of it. It is pronounced *Sewdley*, and ſometimes written *Sudely*, but without ſufficient authority.

Sudley was ſucceſſively the place of reſidence of great perſons from very early ages. It appears by *Domeſday* to have been the property of Ralph Medantine, or de Maunt, earl of Hereford, before the conqueſt, whoſe ſon Harold, was lord of Sudley, and his ſucceſſors took the name of *De Sudley*, after the manner of thoſe times.

There was an antient caſtle here, built, as ſuppoſed, about the time of king Stephen. Ralph Botiller, or Boteler, lord treaſurer of England, was created baron of Sudley by king Henry the Sixth, and had an annuity of two hundred marks given him out of the profits of Lincolnſhire, for the better and more honourable ſupport of his dignity, which Mr. Sheldon takes notice of in his *Titles of Honour*. This Ralph lord Sudley had ſerved as admiral of the Britiſh fleet, and with the ſpoils he had got in the wars with France, rebuilt the old caſtle, and made ſome additions to it; or rather, built a new one upon the old ſcite, for Leland expreſſly mentions that he made the caſtle *a fundamentis*. One part of it was called *Portmare's Tower*, after the name of the French admiral, who, if tradition may be credited, was taken

priſoner

prisoner by lord Sudley, to whom the king gave his randsom, which was supposed nearly sufficient to build the castle.

But so fluctuating was the state of public affairs in his time, that the subject was safe neither in person nor property; and the favourite of one reign was generally obnoxious to the succeeding. Ralph lord Sudley was suspected of a strong attachment to the Lancastrian family, and king Edward the Fourth attaining the crown, caused him to be apprehended at his castle, whence he was carried prisoner to London. Coming to the top of Sudley hill, he looked back, and said, *Sudley-castle, thou art the traitor, not I*; apprehending the king's design of seizing his castle, tho' he had committed no act that would legally subject his estate to confiscation. Accordingly, he found himself obliged to sell it to king Edward the Fourth; and constables were afterwards appointed by the crown.

Sir John Bruges, eldest son of sir Giles, was constituted constable of Sudley-castle 29 H. 8. and had a new grant of the constableship in the 34th year of the same reign, wherein Edmund, his son and heir, then one of the esquires of the king's body, was joined in that trust with him.

He afterwards obtained a grant in fee of the castle and manor, 1 Mar. and in 1554, her majesty was pleased to create him a peer of Great Britain, by the title of baron Chandos of Sudley; and the castle and manor belonging to it continued in his family for many generations.

At the breaking out of the civil war, in the reign of king Charles the First, this castle was garrisoned by about sixty men of the king's party, under the command of captain Bridges. In the evening of the first of January, 1642, colonel Massie, at the head of about 300 musketeers, with two sakers, from Gloucester, assisted by 80 horse, and four companies of dragoons, from Cirencester, drew up before it, and discharged several shot, with some execution. The next morning preparations were made for an assault, when a party of horse and dragoons possessing themselves of a garden close to the castle, set fire to some hay and straw, under the smoak of which the ordnance was brought up undiscovered. The garrison then beat a parley, and surrendered, on condition to return to their own houses, and never to serve against the parliament.

Soon afterwards, Cirencester was taken by prince Rupert, and the castle fell again into the king's hands, and for a long time greatly interrupted the intercourse between the parliament's garrisons at Gloucester and London, through Warwick, which was the only way of communication; so that even a scout could not pass without extreme hazard. But in the year 1644, when the king's army retreated from Oxford, before sir William Waller, the latter ordered Massie, governor of Gloucester, to meet him before Sudley-castle. Massie came up first, and fell in with a party of the garrison, who retreated within the walls, after a little skirmishing; and sir William Waller arriving within a few hours afterwards, summoned sir William Morton, the governor of the castle, who refused to surrender. But an accidental shot taking off the head of their cannoner, is thought to have daunted the common soldiery, and tho' the governor was an active man in the king's service, and had great reputation for his valour and general understanding, he gave up the castle and himself to the parliament, without providing for the indemnity of his person."[n] Nine captains, and twenty-two inferior officers were made prisoners of war, and a quantity of cloth was found in it, to the value of 4000*l*.

At that time it is supposed the castle was intire, but a great part has been since demolished. The remains shew it to have been a very beautiful building, and according to Leland, the windows of the hall had round beryls in them for glass. The beryl is a kind of precious stone, of a deeper and brighter red, and more transparent that the common cornelian, tho' something of the same kind. The fine ruins of this castle, in its present state, are well delineated in the annexed engraving, for which the editor and the public are indebted to the generosity of lord Rivers, the present owner.

Of the Manor and other Estates.

The records furnish the following particulars of this manor:

'Herald the son of earl Radulf holds Sudlege of 'the king, and Radulf his father held it. There 'are ten hides taxed, and four plow-tillages in 'demean, and eighteen villeins, and eight bordars, 'with thirteen plow-tillages. There are fourteen 'between the *servi* and *ancillæ*, and six mills of '52*s*. [rent] a wood three miles long, and two 'broad.' *Domesday*, p. 77.

This was a valuable manor, not so much from its great extent, as improved state; for as the richer soils were likely to turn to the best account, so were they earliest and best cultivated. The same Herald was lord of the manor of Todintun, and it appears by *Domesday*, that those two manors were worth 40*l*. in the time of king Edward the Confessor, as well as at the compiling that record.

The same family which held Sudley before the conquest, was continued in the possession of it afterwards; which is a rare instance for laymen; and Harold, who found such singular favour with the Conqueror, may thence be suspected of having been false to his country. He was descended from Goda, daughter of king Ethelred, and wife to Walter de Medantine. Radulf, or Ralph, son of the said Walter and Goda, and father of Harold, was official earl of Hereford, and so infamous for cowardice, that William the Conqueror removed him from his office.

John de Sudley was son and heir of Harold. Ralph de Sudley, son of John, married Emme, daughter of William de Beauchamp, and was succeeded

[n] Corbet's Military Government of Gloucester.

ceeded by Otnell his ſon; who dying without iſſue, his brother, Ralph de Sudley had livery of the manor granted to him 10 R. 1. Ralph de Sudley, ſon of Ralph, had alſo livery thereof 6 H. 3. and marrying Joan, ſiſter of William de Beauchamp, the firſt earl of Warwick, had iſſue Bartholomew de Sudley, his ſucceſſor, who purchaſed a charter of free warren in this manor 51 H. 3. and died 8 E. 1. John de Sudley, ſon and heir of Bartholomew, pleaded his charter of free warren in a writ of *Quo warranto* brought againſt him, and his claim was allowed 15 E. 1. He was afterwards lord chamberlain to king Edward the Second, and died without iſſue 10 E. 3.

John de Sudley, ſon of another Bartholomew, and next heir to the laſt John, married Eleanor, daughter of the lord Scales, who ſurviving her huſband, died ſeized of this manor, of which ſhe was endowed, 35 E. 3. whereupon their ſon John de Sudley had livery thereof; but he died without iſſue, 41 E. 3. and left Joan and Margery, his two ſiſters, coheireſſes.

Joan, the elder ſiſter of John de Sudley, was ſecond wife to William le Boteler, of Wem in Shropſhire, deſcended from Ralph le Boteler, who bore the office of butler to Robert earl of Mellent and Leiceſter, in the reign of king Henry the Firſt. The ſaid William and Joan had iſſue Thomas le Boteler, who upon partition of his father's eſtate, made 42 E. 3. had the manor of Sudley aſſigned to him, and died ſeized thereof 22 R. 2. leaving iſſue two ſons, John, and Ralph. John dying without iſſue, Ralph le Boteler was his heir. He was created baron of Sudley 20 H. 6. and built the caſtle, as already obſerved, and having ſold both that and the manor to king Edward the Fourth, died without iſſue 13 E. 4. leaving his ſiſters ſons, ſir John Norbury and William Belknap, his heirs.

The manor was granted many times afterwards by the crown to court favourites, and almoſt as often forfeited by the treaſon of its owners, 'till it came into the Chandos family. But to be more particular. King Henry the Seventh granted it to his uncle Jaſper duke of Bedford, and to his heirs male, 1 H. 7. It was again granted to Thomas lord Seymour 1 E. 6. who was created baron of Sudley; and the laſt abbat of Winchcombe being made the firſt dean of Weſtminſter, granted to the ſame lord Sudley, nineteen manors in Glouceſterſhire, for ninety-nine years. Upon the attainder of Thomas lord Seymour, the manor of Sudley was granted to William marquis of Northampton, 5 E. 6.

Upon the attainder of the marquis of Northampton, queen Mary, in the firſt year of her reign, granted both the caſtle and manor of Sudley to ſir John Bruges, who was created lord Chandos of Sudley, 4 Mar. and was anceſtor to the preſent duke of Chandos. His lordſhip married Elizabeth, daughter to Edmund lord Grey of Wilton, and died in the year 1557, ſeized of the caſtle and manor of Sudley, and was buried in the church there. Edmund lord Chandos, ſon and heir of John, married Dorothy, daughter and coheir of Edmund lord Bray, and dying 14 Eliz. was ſucceeded by his ſon, Giles lord Chandos, who had livery of Sudley the ſame year. He married Frances, the daughter of Edward earl of Lincoln, and dying without iſſue male, was buried at Sudley 36 Eliz. whereby his lordſhip's brother William ſucceeded to the honour, and by deed of entail, was intituled to the manor of Sudley. He married Mary, daughter of ſir Owen Hopton, and died 44 Eliz.

Grey lord Chandos was ſon of William. This lord was a noble houſekeeper, and by an engaging behaviour, gained ſo great an intereſt in Glouceſterſhire, and had ſo many attendants with him at court, that he was commonly called *The King of Coteſwold.* He married Anne, eldeſt daughter and coheir to Ferdinand earl of Derby, and dying 19 Jac. was ſucceeded by his eldeſt ſon, George ſixth lord Chandos, who was lord of the manor of Sudley. He diſtinguiſhed himſelf by his loyalty to king Charles the Firſt, and had three horſes killed under him, at the head of his regiment, in the battle of Newbury. In conſideration of his exemplary valour, the king would have made him earl of Newbury, which he modeſtly declined, 'till his majeſty ſhould be reſtored to the peaceable enjoyment of his crown. He died in 1654, and left the inheritance of the manor and caſtle of Sudley to Jane his ſecond wife, daughter of John earl of Rivers.

Jane, relict of George ſixth lord Chandos, was afterwards married to George Pitt, of Stratfield-Say in Hampſhire, eſq; whoſe deſcendant, George lord Rivers°, is the preſent lord of the manor of Sudley. *Of*

° His lordſhip's anceſtor, Nicholas Pitt, was living in the firſt year of king Henry the Sixth. He had a ſon, William Pitt, who lived in the time of king Henry the Eighth, and married Eleanor, daughter of ——— Naviland, by whom he had iſſue one ſon,

John Pitt, who was a clerk of the exchequer in the reign of queen Elizabeth. He married Joane, daughter of John Swayne, and by her had iſſue three ſons and two daughters, Agnes, married to Anthony Bennet; and Elizabeth, married to Jonadab Shirley. The ſons were 1. ſir William Pitt, knight, of whom hereafter; John Pitt, who ſettled in Ireland; and Thomas Pitt, of Blandford in the county of Dorſet, who took to wife Priſcilla, daughter of ——— Scarle, of Kayle in the county of Devon. This Thomas Pitt purchaſed the advowſon of St. Mary, at Blandford, and was anceſtor to the Pitts of Boconnock, the earls of Londonderry, &c.

Which ſaid ſir William Pitt, eldeſt ſon of John Pitt, was ſeated at Stepleton in the county of Dorſet, and at Stratfield-Say in Hants. He was employed as a commiſſioner in ſeveral weighty affairs tranſacted 1 Jac. 1. and is ſaid to have been comptroller of the houſhold, and a principal officer in the exchequer, in the reigns of Elizabeth, James the Firſt, and Charles the Firſt; or he was, as it is expreſſed upon his monument at Stratfield-Say, *Ærarii Miniſtrum Claſſis curandæ ac Aulæ Sumptibus corrigendis delectum.* He bore for his arms, *Sable, a feſs checky argent and azure, between three bezants,* which were granted to him by the name of William Pitt, of Ewern Stepleton, eſq; by William Camden, Clarencieux, in 1604, and it is ſuppoſed that the *feſs checky* was given in alluſion to his office in the exchequer. He was knighted at Newmarket in 1618, and died on the 29th of May, 1636, in the 77th year of his age, poſſeſſed of the manors of Ewern Stepleton, and Stratfield-Say, which he had purchaſed, and of the priory of Wareham, the manor and tithes of Little Preſton, the borough of Stowborough, and Redcliff-tenements there, with other very conſiderable eſtates in thoſe

Of the Church, &c.

The church is a rectory, in the deanery of Winchcombe, worth about 60*l.* a year in tithes, besides a small manor, lying within the manor of Sudley; and the lord of the manor of Sudley pays 20*l.* a year composition for tithes. Lord Rivers is patron. The rector holds a court baron.

There is nothing remaining of the church but the shell, or outer walls, (by which it appears to have been a neat building, adorned with battlements and pinnacles all round) except a small aile, called the chapel, where divine service is performed once a fortnight.

First fruits £	6	11	4	Synodals £.	0	2	0
Tenths —	0	13	1½	Pentecost.	0	0	6
Procurations	0	6	8				

Queen Catherine Parre, daughter of sir William Parre, knight, was first married to Edward Burghe; secondly to John Nevill, lord Latimer; thirdly to king Henry the Eighth, (being his sixth and last wife) and fourthly to Thomas lord Seymour, baron of Sudley, and high admiral of England. She died in child-bed, Sept. 5, 1548, and was buried, with much funeral pomp, in the chapel of Sudley-castle; of whose interment the following is a curious account, extracted from a MS. in the college of arms in London, intituled, *A Boke of Buryalls of trew noble P'sons.* N°. 1. 15. p. 98, 99.

A Brevyate of thentirement of the ladye Katheryn Parre Quene Dowager, late wiefe to Kinge Henrye theight, and aftre wiefe to S[r] Thomas lord Seymer of Sudeley & highe Admyrall of Englond.

Itm. on Wenysdaye the Vth of Septembre betwene ij & iij of the Clocke in the Morninge died the aforseid Ladye late Quene Dowager at the Castle of Sudley in Glocestre Shyre 1548 and lyethe buried in the Chappell of the seid Castle.

Itm. She was cearid & chestid in leade accordinglie, and so remaynid in her pryvie Chambre, untill things were in Aredynes.

Heraftre followethe the P'vision in the Chappell.

Itm. hit was hangid wth blacke clothe garnisshid wth Schoocheons of maryagys, vidz Kinge

those parts, as appears by the escheator's inquisition without date, and other evidences. He married Edith, daughter and coheir of Nicholas Cadbury, of Arne, by whom he had issue three sons, and four daughters, 1. Frances, married to Clement Walker, 2. Elizabeth, who had to her first husband Richard Wheeler, after whose decease, she was wedded to sir Francis Brandling, knight; 3. Mary, married first to sir Alexander Chocke, knight, and secondly, to John Rudhale; 4. Catherine, married to —— Venables. The sons were 1. Edward, of whom hereafter; 2. John; 3. William, who married Abigail, daughter of sir William Wake, baronet, and by her had issue three sons, Edward, Baldwin, and William, who all died *sine prole*; and one daughter Abigail, married to Ralph lord Stowell. I now return to Edward the eldest son of sir William Pitt.

The said Edward Pitt was seated at Stratfield-Say, and married Rachel, daughter of sir George Morton, of Milborn St. Andrew, in the county of Dorset, baronet, and by her had a very numerous issue, *viz.* ten sons, and four daughters. 1. Edith, the eldest daughter, was married to Charles Sydenham, son of sir Edward Sydenham, knight-marshal; 2. Rachel, wedded to John Kingsmill, of Sandelford in the county of Berks; 3. Catherine, wife of Francis Whitaker, of St. Martin's in the county of Middlesex; 4. Elizabeth, who died in her infancy. The sons were 1. William, 2. Edward, who both died without issue; 3. George, the continuator of the elder branch of this family; 4. John Pitt, who by his wife Catherine, daughter of Nicholas Venables of Andover, had a son George-Morton Pitt, seated at Twickenham, *com.* Middlesex, whose only daughter and heir Harriet, was married to Brownlow Bertie, brother to Peregrine duke of Ancaster; 5. Thomas Pitt, who took to wife Frances, daughter of Giles Cassey, of Compton in the county of Gloucester; 6. Nicholas; 7. Samuel; 8. Francis, who married Elizabeth, daughter of Jeffery Jeffereys, of Abercunick *in com.* Brecon; 9. Edward; 10. Christopher.

George Pitt, third son, by the death of his said two elder brothers, succeeded his father. He was an officer in the royal army during the civil wars in the reign of king Charles I. and compounded for his estate at 244*l.* 6*s.* He married Jane, relict of George lord Chandos, and the eldest of the four daughters of John earl Rivers, who were coheiresses of their nephew lord Morley and Montegle; and died 27 July, 1694. He had issue by her ladyship, 1. George, his son and heir; 2. William; 3. Edward; which two last died *sine prole*; 4. John, whose first wife was Mary, daughter of ——— Scrope. By his second wife Isabella, daughter of ——— Condon, he had two daughters, Lora, who died unmarried; and Isabella. The daughters of George Pitt, by lady Jane, were, 1. Mary, married to sir Charles Brown, baronet; 2. Elizabeth, wedded to Thomas viscount Fitz-Williams; 3. Jane, married to Christopher Hildyard; and 4. Anne, the wife of Frederick Tylney.

George Pitt, eldest son of George by the lady Jane Chandos, made great additions to the family estate, and was possessed of a noble fortune. He represented the borough of Wareham in parliament, and was afterwards one of the knights of the shire for the county of Hants. He married first, Lucy, daughter of Thomas Pile, of Buverstock in the county of Wilts, and relict of Lawrence Low of Shaftesbury, and by her had issue, 1. George Pitt, his eldest son and heir; 2. Thomas, who died without issue; and one daughter Lucy, who died unmarried. He had also a second wife, Lora, daughter and heiress of Auckley Grey, of Kingston in the county of Dorset, and had issue by this marriage, 1. Grey Pitt, who died an infant in 1700; 2. William Pitt, who married Elizabeth, daughter of —— Wyndham, but died *sine prole*; 3. John Pitt, of Encombe, who took to wife Marcia, daughter of Marcus Morgan, and by her had William-Morton Pitt; and George, Charles, and John, which three last died very young; and one daughter Marcia. 4. Thomas Pitt, who died without issue. The daughters of the second marriage were, 1. Elizabeth, married to William Burton; 2. Lora, wedded to Francis Gwyn of Ford Abbey; 3. Anne, unmarried; 4. & 5. both of the name of Mary, and died unmarried. The said George Pitt died February 28, 1734, and has a monument erected for him in the church of Stinsford, whereon his character is inscribed by his second wife Lora, who also died June 12, 1750.

George Pitt, eldest son of the said George, by his first wife Lucy, succeeded his father, and took to wife Louisa, daughter of —— Bernier, by whom he had issue four sons, *viz.* George Pitt, now lord Rivers; 2. James, 3. Thomas, both dead *sine prole*; 4. William-Augustus Pitt, of Heckfield in the county of Hants, a major-general, who married Mary, daughter of Scrope viscount Howe. He had also two daughters, *viz.* Lucy, married to James Kerr, of Scotland, esq; and Mary, buried Aug. 17, 1744. He died, and was buried Oct. 26, 1745.

George Pitt, eldest son of the last George, was appointed envoy extraordinary and minister plenipotentiary to the court of Turin, in November 1761; also in the year 1770, he was sent ambassador extraordinary and minister plenipotentiary to the court of Spain. And in consideration of his great abilities, and eminent services in those employments, his majesty was pleased to advance him to the dignity of a baron of Great Britain, by the title of baron Rivers, by letters patent, dated May 20, 1776. His lordship married Penelope, daughter of sir Henry Atkyns, and sister and heir of sir Richard Atkyns, and by her has issue one son, the honourable George Pitt; and three daughters, 1. Penelope, married to the present earl Ligonier; 2. Louisa, married to Peter Beckford, of Stepleton in the county of Dorset; and 3. Marcia.

His lordship's Arms are, *Sable, a fess checky argent and azure, between three bezants.*

Supporters. On the dexter side, *A falcon with wings elevated*; on the sinister side, *an unicorn argent.*

Motto. Æquam Servare Mentem.

His lordship resides at Stratfield-Say in Hampshire, the antient seat of his family.

Henrye

Henrye theight & her in pale undre the Crowne, her owne in lozenge undre the Crowne, Allſo tharmes of the lorde Admyrall & hers in pale w^th^out crowne.

Itm. Rayles cov'ed wth blacke clothe ffor the Mourners to ſytt in wth Stooles and Cuſsheons accordinglie w^th^owt eyther herſse ma^tie^ & vallence or tapres Savinge ij tapres wheron were ij Scoocheons wch ſtode uppon the Corps duringe the Servyce.

Thordre in proceadinge
to the Chappell.

Ffyrſt ij conductors in blacke wth blacke ſtaves.
Then Gentlemen and Eſquiers.
Then Knights.
Then Offycers of howſholde wth theyre whyte ſtaves.
Then the Gentlemen huiſshers.
Then Som'ſett heraulde in the Ks cote.
Then the Corps borne by vj Gentlemen in blacke gownes wth theire hodes on theyre heades.
Then xl ſtaffe Torchis borne on Eche ſide by Yeomen rounde abowte the Corps And at eche corner a Knight for Aſſyſtunce iiij wth theyre hodes on theyre heades.
Then the ladye Jane (Doughter to the lorde M'ques Dorſſett) chefe mourner, ledde by aeſtate, her trayne borne uppe by a yonge ladye.
Then vj other ladie mourners ij & ij.
Then all ladies & gentlewomen ij & ij.
Then Yeomen iij & iij in a Ranke.
Then all other ffollowinge.

The Mann' of the Seruice
in the Churche.

Itm. when the Corps was ſett w^th^in the Rayles and the mourners placid, the hole Quere began & ſonge certen Salmes in Engliſhe & reade iij leſſons; And aftre the iij^de^ leſſon the mourners accordinge to theyre degrees & as yt ys accuſtomyd offerid into the almes boxe And when they hadde don, all other as Gentlemen or Gentlewomen that wolde.

The Offeringe don Doctor Cov'dall the Quenes Almner began his Sermonde wch was verie good and godlie And in one place therof he toke A occaſion to declare unto the people howe that thei ſhulle none there thinke Seye nor ſpreade abrode that the offeringe wch was there don was don anye thinge to p'ffytt the deade but ffor the poore onlye And alſo the lights wch were caried & ſtode abowte the Corps were ffor the honnour of the parſson & for none other entente nor purpoſe, And ſo went thorowghe wth hys Sermonde, & made a Godlye prayer, And thole Churche aunſwerid and praied the ſame wth hym in thende.

The Sermonde don the Corps was buried duringe wch tyme the Quere ſonge Te Deum in Engliſse.

And this don aftre Dinn' the mourners and the reſt that wolde returnid homewarde agayne all wch aforſeid was don in a mornynge.

Doctor Parkhurſt compoſed the following Latin epitaph on this lady:

Incomparabilis fœminæ Catharinæ nuper Angliæ Franciæ et Hiberniæ reginæ dominæ meæ clementiſſimæ Epitaphium, 1548.

Hoc regina novo dormit Catharina ſupulchro
 Sexus fœminei flos, honor atque decus.
Hæc fuit HENRICO conjux fidiſſima regi
 Quem poſtquam e vivis Parca tuliſſet atrox,
Thomæ Seymero (cui tu Neptune tridentem
 Porrigis) eximio nupſerat illa viro
Huic peperit natam: a partu cum ſeptimus orbem
 Sol illuſtraſſet, mors truculenta necat.
Defunctam madidis famuli deflemus ocellis
 Humeſcat triſtis terra Britannica genas.
Nos infelices mœror conſumit acerbus
 Inter cœleſtes gaudet at illa choras.

Engliſhed thus:

The Epitaph of the incomparable lady Catharine, late queen of England, France, and Ireland, my moſt indulgent miſtreſs, 1548.

In this new tomb the royal Cath'rine lies,
Flow'r of her ſex, renowned, great, and wiſe!
A wife by ev'ry nuptial virtue known,
And faithful partner once of HENRY's throne.
To Seymour next her plighted hands ſhe yields,
(Seymour, who Neptune's trident juſtly wields)
From him a beauteous daughter bleſs'd her arms,
An infant copy of her parent's charms:
When now ſeven days this tender flow'r had bloom'd
Heaven in its wrath the mother's ſoul reſum'd.
Great Cath'rine's merit in our grief appears;
While fair Britannia dews her cheek with tears.
Our loyal breaſts with riſing ſighs are torn,
With ſaints ſhe triumphs,—we with mortals mourn.

Sudley.

Taxes.	The Royal Aid in	1692, £. 276	17	0
	Poll-tax ——	1694, — 15	18	0
	Land-tax ——	1694, — 248	11	4
	The ſame, at 3 *s.*	1770, — 175	15	2

Sudley Tenements.

Taxes.	The Royal Aid in	1692, £. 28	2	0
	Poll-tax ——	1694, — 12	14	0
	Land-tax ——	1694, — 122	16	8
	The ſame, at 3 *s.*	1770, — 84	3	0

There are only five families in this pariſh.

****

SUTTON under BRAYLES.

THIS pariſh lies in the upper diviſion of Weſtminſter hundred, ſeven miles diſtant eaſt from Campden, ten north-eaſt from Stow, and about thirty-five north-eaſt from Glouceſter.

It lies in a fine, rich country, on the bank of the Stour, and (tho' a part of Glouceſterſhire) is intirely ſurrounded by Warwickſhire, and many miles diſtant from any part of the county of which it is a member.

The antient name, *Sudtune, i.e.* the *ſouth town*, has a reference to Brayles, an adjoining pariſh in Warwickſhire.

Of the Manor and other Eſtates.

This manor belonged to the church of Weſtminſter before the Norman conqueſt, and is mentioned in *Domeſday-book* among the poſſeſſions of that houſe in Glouceſterſhire. The record, after enumerating the particulars of the large manor of Derheſt, recites that 'Sudtune was a 'berewic,

'berewic, or member, belonging to it'. See the whole account in the original language, p. 72.

The manor was held of the honour of Gloucester by the fifth part of a knight's fee, 10 R. 2. It continued to be part of the possessions of the abbey of Westminster 'till the general dissolution of monasteries, when it was given to the chapter of Westminster, 34 H. 8. But the manor of Sutton, a water-mill, and a tenement called Smith's Place, together with the manor of Todenham, were granted by the crown to sir William Petre and Anne his wife, in exchange for lands in Warwickshire, 36 H. 8. and Robert-Edward lord Petre[p] is the present proprietor of the manors of Sutton and Todenham. His lordship's arms are, *Gules, a bend Or between two escallop shells argent.* CREST. *On a wreath two lions heads erazed and addorsed, the first Or, the second azure, each gorged with a plain collar counterchanged.* SUPPORTERS. On the dexter side, *A lion regardant azure, collared Or*; on the sinister, *A lion regardant Or, collared azure.* MOTTO. SANS DIEU RIEN.

Of the Church, &c.

The church is a rectory, in the deanery of Stow, worth about 140*l.* a year. The bishop of London is patron, and the reverend Mr. George Upton is the present incumbent.

The advowson antiently belonged to the abbey of Westminster, after the dissolution of which

---

p By an inquisition taken 12 E. 4. after the death of Alice Storke (wife of John Storke, and formerly the wife of John Petre) it was found that William Petre was her grandson and heir, *viz.* son of John Petre, son of the said Alice, and at that time twenty-four years old.

This William Petre had a son John Petre, settled at Torre-Brian in Devonshire, who, by his wife Alice, daughter of John Collins, of Woodland in the same county, had issue five sons, and three daughters. The sons were, sir William, his heir; John, seated at Torre-Newton in Torre-Brian; ———, head customer of Exeter; Richard, chancellor of Exeter, and archdeacon of Buckingham; and Robert, an officer in the Exchequer.

Sir William Petre, eldest son and heir of John, was born at Exeter about the beginning of the reign of king Henry the Eighth, and having his education at Exeter college Oxford, made so great a proficiency in his studies there, that he was elected fellow of All Souls college, became principal of Peckwater's Inn, and in 24 H. 8. took the degree of doctor of laws. In 1535, 27 H. 8. he was commissioned, with some others, by Thomas Cromwell, the visitor general, to inquire into the behaviour of the monks and nuns throughout England, in order to collect sufficient matter for accusation against them, and to pave the way to the suppression of the monastic state; which great work being soon after fully accomplished, the king, in the 30th year of his reign, in consideration of the good service of this sir William therein, granted to him, and Gertrude his wife, in fee, the priory of Clattercote in Oxfordshire; and the next year he had a grant of the manor of Gyng-Abbats in Essex, (part of the possessions of the then dissolved monastery of Berkyng) with the advowson of the rectory of Ingarston, *alias* Gyng ad Petram. In 35 H. 8. he was sworn of the privy council, and appointed one of the principal secretaries of state; and in 36 H. 8. the king designing to invade France, for the prosecuting his claim to that crown, appoints this sir William one of the council to assist queen Catherine, his consort, in the administration of affairs during his absence. And in the last year of that reign, the king lying upon his death bed, nominated him one of the assistants to the council to king Edward the Sixth, his son and successor. He was very high in the esteem of Edward the Sixth, and queen Mary, in whose reign, foreseeing that the restoration of the Romish religion might endanger the enjoyment of those abbey lands he had acquired, he obtained a special dispensation from pope Paul IV. for the retaining them, by a bull, bearing date 4 cal. Dec. 1555. He was for some time principal secretary of state to queen Elizabeth, and one of her privy council 'till his death, Jan. 13, 1572, at which time he was possessed of seven manors in Devonshire, one in Dorsetshire, nine in Essex, three in Somersetshire, one in Kent, one in Suffolk, and of the manors of Sutton and Todenham in Gloucestershire. By Gertrude, his first wife, daughter of sir John Tirrell of Warley in Essex, knight, he had one child Dorothy, married to Nicholas Wadham, of Merrifield in Somersetshire, esq; the founder of Wadham college in Oxford. By Anne, his second wife, daughter of sir William Browne, knight, (lord mayor of London in 1514) and widow of sir Thomas Tirrell, of Heron Place in Essex, knight, he had issue John, his only son; and three daughters; Elizabeth, married to John Gostwick, of Willington in Bedfordshire, esq; Catherine, to John Talbot, of Grafton in Worcestershire, ancestor to the earls of Shrewsbury; and Thomasine, to Lodowick Grevil, of Milcot in Warwickshire.

John Petre, only son of sir William, was advanced to the dignity of a baron of England, by the title of lord Petre of Writtle in the county of Essex, (by letters patent, dated July 21, 1603, 1 Jac. 1.) and died Oct. 11, 11 Jac. 1. He married Mary, daughter of sir Edward Walgrave, of Berclay in Essex, knight, and by her had issue four sons, William, John, Thomas, and Robert; and four daughters, Mary, Elizabeth, Margaret, and Anne; but the daughters all died infants.

William, second lord Petre, (eldest son of John first lord Petre) taking to wife Catherine, second daughter of Edward Somerset, earl of Worcester, had issue seven sons, Robert, William, Edward, John, Thomas, Henry, and George; and also three daughters, Elizabeth, Mary, and Catherine. His lordship departing this life May 5, 1637, was succeeded by his eldest son,

Robert, third lord Petre, who in 1620, married Mary, daughter of Anthony viscount Montague, and by her had issue three sons, William, John, and Thomas, successively lords Petre; and two daughters, Mary, married to Edward, eldest son of William lord Stourton; and Dorothy, the wife of John Thimelby, of Irnham in Lincolnshire, esq. His lordship died Oct. 23, 1638, and by inquisition taken Dec. 14 following, it was found that he was seized of the following manors, besides lands &c. in other places; *viz.* The manor, rectory, and advowson of the vicarage of Great Bursteed, *alias* Bursteed-grange; the manors of Gurney's, *alias* Gurner's, White's, Challiveden, Writtle, East Horndon, West Horndon, Crondon, Blount's-walls, Waterman's, and Bacon's; the rectory of Buttersbury, and the manors of Cowbridge, Margaretting, Ingarston, Ging-Petre, Hanley, Mountneysing, Ingrave, *alias* Ging-Raffe, Tristinghall, Fieldhouse, and East, West, and South Hanningfield, all in the county of Essex; the manor and rectory of Osmington in Dorsetshire; the manors of Tatworth in Chatworth, and Chard in Somersetshire; the manors of South Brent, Churchstowe, Kingsbridge, Shute, South Leigh, Axminster, North Leigh, Wermingston, Laytwey, Uphay, Humfravile, Dowlshards, Haccomb-fee, Challonger, Comb-payne, and Downe-Humfravile, in the county of Devon; the manors of Tuddenham and Sutton in Gloucestershire; and the manor of Kennet in Kentford, in the county of Cambridge.

William, fourth lord Petre, was eleven years old at his father's death. He married first, Elizabeth, daughter of John earl Rivers, by whom having no issue, he married secondly, Bridget, daughter of John Pincheon, of Writtle in Essex, esq; and by her had an only child, Mary, born in 1679, and married to George Heneage, of Hainton in Lincolnshire, esq. In 1678, William lord Petre, William Herbert, earl of Powis, William Howard, viscount Stafford, Henry lord Arundel of Wardour, and John lord Bellasis were committed prisoners to the tower, and impeached, by the commons, of treason and other high crimes and misdemeanours. Lord Petre dying under his confinement, Jan. 5, 1683, the title devolved on his brother,

John, fifth lord Petre, who likewise became possessed of this estate by virtue of deeds of settlement. His lordship died unmarried in the year 1684, and was succeeded by his next brother,

Thomas, sixth lord Petre, who died June 4, 1707, leaving issue by Mary, daughter of sir Thomas Clifton, of Letham in Lancashire, bart. Robert, his only son, and a daughter Mary.

Robert, seventh lord Petre, married (Mar. 1, 1711-12) Catharine, daughter of Bartholomew, and sister and heir of Francis Walmesley, of Dunkehalgh in Lancashire, esq; and dying of the small-pox, Mar. 22, 1712-13, in the 23d year of his age, left her with child of

Robert, eighth lord Petre, born June 3, 1713. His lordship, on May 2, 1732, married Anne, daughter of James earl of Derwentwater, by whom he had issue one son, and three daughters, Catharine, Barbara, and Juliana; and dying in July 1742, was succeeded by his only son,

Robert-Edward, ninth lord Petre, who on April 19, 1762, married the honourable Miss Howard, niece to the duke of Norfolk, and is the present lord of the manors of Sutton under Brayles and Todenham, in this county.

house, it was granted to Thomas bishop of Westminster, 32 H. 8. It was afterwards given to the bishop of London, 4 E. 6. and the grant was confirmed by the crown, 1 Mariæ.

One yard-land belongs to the glebe.

The church consists of the nave only, with a tower on the south side, and is dedicated to Thomas Becket, who was canonized by the Roman pontiff for the great forwardness he shewed to extend the papal authority.

	£.	s.	d.		£.	s.	d.
First fruits	13	13	4	Synodals	0	2	0
Tenths —	1	7	4	Pentecost.	0	0	9½
Procurations	0	8	8				

Taxes.			£.	s.	d.
The Royal Aid in	1692,		94	4	0
Poll-tax —	1694,	—	30	17	8
Land-tax —	1694,	—	74	9	6
The same, at 3s.	1770,	—	55	17	1½

At the beginning of the present century, according to sir Robert Atkyns, there were 33 houses in the parish, and about 130 inhabitants, 4 of whom were freeholders; yearly births 3, burials 3. But I am informed that the people are since increased to at least 150.

SWELL (LOWER)

LIES in the hundred of Slaughter, in the Coteswold country, one mile south-westward from Stow, and about twenty-four north-eastward from Gloucester.

The village is pleasantly situated in a little valley, that like a moat surrounds the base of that hill on which the town of Stow is built; and a little rivulet called the Dickler, rises at Donnington, and runs through this place in its course to Bourton on the Water, where it falls into the river Winrush.

Thomas Hoard, esq; has a good house here, situated on the bourn, with a pleasant look-out over the meadows towards the south.

Of the Manor and other Estates.

'Radulf de Todeni holds Suelle, in Salemanesberie hundred, and Drogo holds it of him. 'Ernesi held it. There are seven hides taxed. 'In demean are four plow-tillages, and ten villeins, with six plow-tillages, and a mill of 7s. 6d. 'It was worth 8l. and is now worth 7l.' *Domesday-book*, p. 76.

'William de Ow holds Suelle, in Salemanesberie hundred. Ernesi held it in the time of 'king Edward. There are three hides taxed. 'It was worth 40s. now only 10s.' *Ibid.* p. 73.

The sheriff returned that the abbat of Hayles was lord of the manor of Netherswell in Salmonesburye hundred 9 E. 1. and the abbat pleaded his right to a court leet, waifs, strays, and felons goods, in the proceedings on a writ of *Quo warranto* brought against him in the 15th year of that reign, and his claim was allowed.

The abbey of Fischamp in Normandy sued the abbey of Hayles for hindering the tenants of Lower Swell from attending the court leet in the hundred of Salemanesberie, which had been granted to them by king Henry the Third, and obtained judgment 16 E. 1.

A wood and pasture in Nether Swell were held of the honour of Wallingford 20 E. 1.

The abbey of Hayles was seized of the manor, with lands, woods, and a pasture ground called the Park, containing 250 acres, 14 E. 2.

The manor was held of the honour of Gloucester, by the service of five knights fees, 16 R. 2. in which year the last-mentioned abbey had a grant of the hundred of Slaughter.

The manor came to the crown at the dissolution of religious foundations, and was not long afterwards vested in the Bartlets; of the heirs of which family it was purchased by Mr. Carter, and by him sold to sir William Courteen, after whose death it was purchased by sir Robert Atkyns, about the year 1659. He died in the year 1709, and was succeeded by his son sir Robert Atkyns of Saperton, who likewise died in the year 1711. Robert Atkyns, of Swell, esq; leaving two daughters coheiresses, the elder was married to Edmund Chamberlayne, of Maugersbury, esq; whose son, the reverend John Chamberlayne, and Thomas Hoard, esq; who married the other coheiress, are joint lords of this manor.

Edmond earl of Cornwall, (son of Richard earl of Cornwall, king of the Romans) held 140 acres of pasture in Lower Swell for the abbey of Hayles, and was buried in that monastery in the year 1300. The abbey of Hayles purchased two yard-lands, and nineteen acres of arable, and one acre and a half of meadow in Lower Swell of John Sage, 6 E. 2. By inquisition taken 8 E. 2. after the death of Gilbert de Clare, earl of Gloucester, it was found that Hugo le Poins held of him six knights fees in Tockinton and Swell, valued at 170l. *per ann.* Thomas Cole, and others, were seized of one messuage, one toft, and four yard-lands in Nether Swell, for the abbey of Hayles, 15 R. 2.

Of the Church, &c.

The church is a vicarage, in the deanery of Stow, worth about 50l. a year. Christ-church college, Oxford, has the patronage, and the reverend Mr. Henry Brown is the present incumbent.

The rectory, vicarage, and church of Nether Swell belonged to the priory of Osney in Oxfordshire, and were granted to the chapter of Oxford 34 H. 8. The impropriation belongs to Christ-church college, and is now in lease to Mrs. Mercy Ayshcombe, of the family of that name at Lyford, near Wantage, Berks, whose arms are, *Or, a lion rampant double queue gules, on a chief azure a crescent for difference.*

But there is a record which mentions that the manor of Lower Swell, with the procurations and tithes,

tithes, was granted to the bishop of London and his successors, in exchange for lands in Essex, 37 H. 8.

The abbey of Tewkesbury had tithes in Swell, as appears by two deeds without date, which I have here inserted from Stevens's *Supplement to the Monasticon*, Vol. 2, *Appendix*, N^os^. CLXI. 25, and 26.

De decima Dominii de Suella.

CARTA Simonis filii Poinz concedentis Ecclesiæ de Theok. tempore Simonis Wigorniensis Episcopi, in perpetuam Elemosynam Decimam totius Dominii sui de Suella, tam de Aldebiz quam de alio Dominico. Et ne aliqua in perpetuum oriretur controversia inter prædictam Ecclesiam de Theok. & Capellam de Suelle, dedit eidem Capellæ in perpetuum unam virgatam terræ, præter illas duas virgatas quas prius habebat.

Controversia inter Ecclesiam de Theok. *& Capellam de* Suelle *sic quievit super Decimas Dominii.*

COMPOSITIO facta inter Ecclesiam de Theok. & Mattheum Capellanum de Suelle super Decimis de Dominico auctoritate literarum Domini Papæ demandata Abbati de Buttlesden & R. de Northampton & ——— de Bukinham Archidiacono; scil. quod Monachi de Theok. percipient omnes Decimas de Dominico de Suelles, ita tamen quod si parochiani de Capella posuerint oves suas in ovili Domini de Suvella & in pastura de Dominico hiemaverint, rector Capellæ percipiet medietatem Decimarum illarum & Monaci reliquam medietatem. Monaci etiam percipient omnes decimas omnium servientium Domini quæ erunt in ovili Capellæ de Suvelle, 6*d*. pro loco Berthanæ quamdiu stabit in vilenagio. Erunt tamen quieti a præstatione eorum eo anno quo parochiani habuerint oves suas in Berthana Domini & in Dominico; & si remota fuerit Berthana; pœna etiam 100*s*. sub fidei præstatione interposita est, si aliter utraque partium a compositione resilient, parti eam observanti præstanda. Hanc compositionem prædicti Judices confirmaverunt.

One yard-land belongs to the glebe. The manor land, the church-piece, Tracy's ground, and four yard-lands of the impropriation are tithe free. The vicar has the third part of the corn tithes in all the tithable lands.

The church is a very small, mean building, without either aile or steeple.

First fruits £.	6	12	3	Synodals £.	0	2	0
Tenths —	0	13	2¼	Pentecostals	0	0	6½
Procurations	0	6	8				

Taxes.					
The Royal Aid in	1692, £.	99	4	8
Poll-tax ——	1694, —	25	7	0
Land-tax —	1694, —	98	8	4
The same, at 3*s*.	1770, —	64	18	7½

There were 37 houses, and about 160 inhabitants in this parish, 5 of whom were freeholders, when sir Robert Atkyns wrote his History of this county; yearly births 4, burials 4. The present number of houses is 44, and the people, by a late survey, were found to be exactly 213.

SWELL (UPPER)

IS a parish in the upper division of Kiftsgate hundred, one mile north-westward from Stow on the Wold, and about twenty-four north-eastward from Gloucester.

The village is called Upper Swell, because it lies higher upon the stream than the preceding parish. There is nothing in it worthy the traveller's notice.

Of the Manor and other Estates.

In the abstract from *Domesday* which sir Robert Atkyns has given concerning this manor, it is represented as belonging to the church of Winchcombe in the reign of king William the Conqueror; whereas it was then the property of the abbey of Evesham, as appears by the record, of which the following is an exact translation. This mistake arose from his using an incorrect copy of *Domesday*, as I have before had occasion to observe under Broadwell.

'The same church [St. Mary of Evesham] holds 'Svelle in Widelei hundred. There are three 'hides, and nine villeins, and two bordars, and 'a priest, with four plow-tillages amongst them 'all. There are six *servi*. It was worth 4*l*. now '5*l*. There are three plow-tillages in demean, 'and three mills of 20 *sol*.' *Domesday-book*, p. 72.

The abbey of Evesham pleaded their right of court leet in a writ of *Quo warranto*, 15 E. 1. and continued possessed of the manor 'till the general dissolution of religious foundations,

The manor of Over Swell, and the tithes of corn, wool, and lamb, lately belonging to the abbey of Evesham, and then in the tenure of William Fox, were granted to Richard Andrews, in trust, 33 H. 8.

The manor came afterwards to the Stratfords, and William Stratford died seized of it 9 Eliz. whereupon Anthony Stratford, his son, had livery the same year, and was lord of it in 1608. It was vested in sir James Rushout, of Northwick in Worcestershire, at the beginning of this century, and passed afterwards to sir Hildebrand Jacob, who sold it, about five years ago, to Mr. Fitz-Herbert, and others.

A messuage, and one acre of land in Over Swell, belonged to the chantry of All Saints in the church of Stow, and were granted to Francis Philips and Richard Moor 6 Jac.

Of the Church, &c.

The church is a rectory, in the deanery of Stow, worth 90*l*. a year. The advowson is vested, by purchase, in the reverend Mr. Henry Brown, and Mr. Lindsey is the present incumbent.

The advowson belonged to the abbey of Hayles, and after the dissolution of that monastery, was granted to Richard Andrews and Leonard Chamberlain 34 H. 8.

Formerly, four yard-lands, 240 sheep pastures, and thirteen beast pastures belonged to the glebe; but upon the inclosure of the parish, it was settled that the rector should receive 80*l*. a year, clear of all deductions, and he has besides a glebe worth 10*l*. *per ann*.

The church consists of the nave only, and is a small, mean building.

First fruits £.	7	0	0	Synodals £.	0	1	0
Tenths —	0	14	0	Pentecostals	0	1	3½
Procurations	0	6	8				

Monument

Monument and Inſcription.

A ſmall mural monument in the chancel bears the following inſcription :

M. S.
Hic juxta situs
JOHANNES CHAMBERLAYNE,
Medicinæ Baccalaureus,
Thomæ Chamberlayne, Armigeri,
Oddingtoniæ ſepulti,
Filius natu ſecundus.
Natus eſt MDCI,
Cœlebs denatus MDCLXVIII.
Hoc Monumentum
Amoris juxta et Mœroris
Teſtimonium
Poſuit Chariſſima Soror
MARIA OLDISWORTH.

The monument is ornamented at top with the arms of Chamberlayne and Tankerville, quarterly.

Taxes.					
	The Royal Aid in	1692, £.	34	18	0
	Poll-tax ——	1694, —	5	7	0
	Land-tax ——	1694, —	21	9	0
	The ſame, at 3*s.*	1770, —	16	16	9

About ſeventy years ago, according to ſir Robert Atkyns, there were 19 houſes in the pariſh, and about 82 inhabitants, 3 of whom were freeholders; yearly births 2, burials 1. There are now only 14 families, and the people are decreaſed to 69.

SWINDON

IS a ſmall pariſh, in the hundred of Cheltenham, one mile north-weſt from the town of that name, eight ſouth-eaſtward from Tewkeſbury, and nine north-eaſtward from Glouceſter.

It lies in the Vale, upon the banks of the little river Swilyate, which runs from hence to Tewkeſbury, where it empties itſelf into the Avon. The ſoil in ſome parts inclines to ſand, but in general is a ſtrong clay, and the lands are chiefly employed in paſture.

Of the Manor and other Eſtates.

The manor of Suindone belonged to the priory of St. Oſwald in Glouceſter before the compilation of *Domeſday-book*, but at that time it was held by Thomas archbiſhop of York, (as it had been by Stigand archbiſhop of Canterbury) to whoſe juriſdiction the priory of St. Oſwald was ſubject. The following is a tranſlation of the record :

'Stigand the archbiſhop held Suindone in 'Cilteham hundred. There were three hides, 'and two plow-tillages in demean, and ſeven 'villeins, and two bordars, having ſeven plow-'tillages [among them]. There are four *ſervi.* 'It was then worth 3*l.* now 4*l.* 10*s.* Thomas '[of Baieux] archbiſhop [of York] holds this 'manor, part of the eſtate of St. Oſuuald, and it 'pays tax.' *Domeſday*, p. 69.

The manor of Swindon was part of the poſſeſſions of St. Oſwald's priory, 'till that houſe was diſſolved, and then it paſſed into lay hands. James Clifford, eſq; of the antient family of that name, ſettled at Frampton upon Severn, was lord of this manor in the year 1608. It was afterwards purchaſed by Mr. Trotman, who ſold it to Mr. Aſhmead, from whom it paſſed in the ſame manner to Mr. Sturmy. Mr. John Sturmy was lord of the manor about the beginning of this century, and John Stratford, eſq; is the preſent proprietor.

John Hanborough, and Thomas Bruges and Maud his wife, levied a fine of lands in Swindone to William Whitington, and others, to the uſe of John Hanborough, and the heirs of John and Maud, 36 H. 6. John Garing and Elizabeth his wife levied a fine of lands in Swindon to the uſe of Thomas Bruges, and others, 2 E. 4. Lands in Swindon and Clopley belonged to the biſhoprick of Hereford, and were granted to Chriſtopher Hatton, 18 Eliz.

Of the Church, &c.

The church is a rectory, in the deanery of Winchcombe, worth about 60*l.* a year.

The church is dedicated to St. Lawrence. It has a low tower at the weſt end, without battlements, of an hexagonal form, but its ſides and angles are not equal.

Firſt fruits £.	13	0	1½	Synodals £.	0	2	0
Tenths —	1	6	1¼	Pentecoſt.	0	0	4½
Procurations	0	6	8				

Benefactions.

A ſmall parcel of land, which lets for about 10*s.* a year, is given for the repair of the church ; and Mr. John Walwyn has given a rent-charge of 50*s.* a year for the uſe of the poor.

Taxes.					
	The Royal Aid in	1692, £.	59	14	4
	Poll-tax ——	1694, —	10	13	0
	Land-tax ——	1694, —	47	17	0
	The ſame, at 3*s.*	1770, —	40	1	9

Sir Robert Atkyns ſets down the number of houſes in the pariſh at 24, and the inhabitants at about 90, of whom 6 were freeholders; the yearly births 2, and the burials 2. Examining the regiſter, I find that in ten years collectively, from 1760, there are entered 19 baptiſms, and 25 burials, which agrees pretty well with ſir Robert's eſtimate. But the people are now increaſed to exactly 105.

✻◇◇◇◇◇◇◇◇◇◇◇◇◇◇◇◇◇◇◇✻

TAINTON.

THIS pariſh lies in the hundred of Botloe, in the Vale country, about four miles diſtant ſouth-eaſtward from Newent, ſix north-eaſtward from Mitchel Dean, and ſeven weſtward from Glouceſter.

The roads at Rudford, Tibberton, and Tainton, are almoſt impaſſable in the winter. The ſoil is deep, and the lands are pretty equally divided between paſture and arable, but the occupiers ſeem not

not to be the moſt ſkilful nor the moſt induſtrious. Buſhes, brambles, and branches of trees lie in the courſe of the little brooks, whoſe waters ſo impeded, deluge the low lands on every conſiderable fall of rain, and overflow the public road, particularly at Tainton. Thoſe lands, from a wet ſtate, produce a coarſe herbage, intermixt with ruſhes, much inferior in quality and quantity to what they would bear if kept healthy, as might eaſily be done. Their corn-fields are no better managed, but from the natural ſtrength of ſoil, produce crops ſufficient to ſatisfy the farmer. Here, too, that execrable practice prevails with the tenant, of heading the young oaks, undoubtedly becauſe when once polled, they are intituled to the lop.

Some of our topographical books mention, that about the year 1700, there was an ore found at Tainton, from which the refiners extracted gold; and that they took a leaſe of the mine where the ore was found, but did not go on with the work, becauſe the quantity of metal was ſo ſmall as not always to anſwer the expence of ſeparation. I have made ſome inquiry into this matter, but without obtaining any ſatisfactory account. This however is certain, that an inexhauſtible treaſure will be found by a proper cultivation of the ſoil, which is deep and exceedingly fertile. This pariſh is famous for producing a very rich and pleaſant cyder, like that of Herefordſhire, in whoſe neighbourhood it lies, and for an excellent kind of perry, made of a fruit called the Tainton Squaſh-Pear.

Of the Manors and other Eſtates.

'William Goizenboded holds **Tetinton**, in 'Botelau hundred. Aluuin held it. There are 'ſix hides. In demean is one plow-tillage, and 'nine villeins, and ſeven bordars, with nine plow-'tillages. It was worth 6*l.* now 3*l.*' *Domeſday-book*, p. 74.

This manor was granted to Peter Burdune 2 Joh. John de Abernoon purchaſed a charter of free warren in Teynton 37 H. 3. It came ſoon after to the Muſgroſes. Robert de Muſgroſe died ſeized of the manor, and left Cecilia his widow, who held the bailiwick of Bicknor, in the foreſt of Dean, 10 E. 1. and pleaded, in the proceedings on a writ of *Quo warranto*, that ſhe and her anceſtors had held this manor, with court leet and waifs, time out of mind, and her claim was allowed 15 E. 1. She died in the 29th year of the ſame reign, at which time ſhe was ſeized of Tainton, and of a wood, 28 acres of aſſart land at Greenway, and of nine yard-lands and a half at Brat-Forton, all in the foreſt of Dean.

Robert de Muſgroſe, ſon of Robert, died 9 E. 1. leaving Hawiſe, an only daughter and heireſs, then the wife of ſir William Mortimer, younger ſon of Roger earl of March. She was likewiſe heireſs to Cecilia de Muſgroſe, her grandmother, who was ſeized of divers lands of inheritance, and being afterwards married to John de Ferrers, baron of Chartley, carried this manor into that name and family; for lord Ferrers had livery of it 30 E. 1. and died ſeized of it 18 E. 2. Robert lord Ferrers, ſon of John, was fifteen years old at his father's death, and diſtinguiſhed himſelf in the wars with France, in the reign of king Edward the Third, being with the king and prince of Wales at the memorable battle of Creſſy, fought Aug. 26, 1346, but died ſoon after. John lord Ferrers, ſon of Robert, married Elizabeth, daughter of Ralph de Stafford, and widow of Fulk le Strange, and with her had the manor of Engliſh Bicknor. He died 41 E. 3. Elizabeth, his widow, was afterwards married to Reginald Cobham, whom ſhe likewiſe ſurvived, and died ſeized of Tainton and Bicknor 49 E. 3. Robert lord Ferrers, ſon of John, married Margaret, daughter of Edward lord Spencer, and was poſſeſſed of the above manors, and of Bodington in this county, at the time of his death, 1 H. 5. whereupon they paſſed to his ſon Edmond lord Ferrers, who accompanied the gallant and victorious king Henry the Fifth in his wars in France, and died in the 14th year of the following reign, ſeized of all the before-mentioned eſtates, and of a woodwardſhip in the foreſt of Dean. William lord Ferrers, ſon of Edmond, being of full age, had livery of the manors of Teynton and Bicknor ſoon after his father's death; and deceaſing himſelf 28 H. 6. left Anne, his only child, eleven years and eight months old, who being married to Walter Devereux, eſq; carried the title of baron Ferrers to her huſband and his family; but the manor of Tainton was entailed on the male heirs, and ſo did not paſs to the Devereuxes, for Edmond Ferrers, brother to William, ſucceeded to this eſtate. And Elizabeth, the widow of William lord Ferrers, levied a fine of the manors of Tainton and Bicknor to the archbiſhop of Canterbury, and other great perſons, 32 H. 6. in which year Martin Ferrers was ſeized of a third part of this manor, and a perſon of the ſame name was ſeized of Great Teinton 1 R. 3.

This eſtate came ſoon afterwards to the Whitingtons. Thomas Whitington, of Pauntley, eſq; died poſſeſſed of it 38 H. 8. and left his eſtates to be divided among his ſix daughters and coheireſſes. Sir Chriſtopher Blount was ſeized of it, but he being attainted, it was granted to ſir Simon Weſton and John Wakeman, 1 Jac. 1.

Mr. Thomas Pury, jun. lord of the manors of Tainton and Minſterworth, died in 1693, in the 74th year of his age. He was one of thoſe principal citizens of Glouceſter who ſubſcribed the anſwer returned to the king's ſummons of ſurrender, Aug. 10, 1643, and took an active part in the management of public affairs during the ſiege of that city, of which he was afterwards mayor, in 1653. Piety, learning, great abilities, and extenſive charity, gained him the love and reſpect of his cotemporaries, and preſerved his memory from that obloquy which few eminent perſons of of his time had the good fortune to escape. Mr. Grove is owner of the Grove estate; and Mr. William Holder has another good estate in this parish.

HAMLET. *Little Tainton* is a hamlet and manor, to which, I apprehend, the following record should be applied:

'William the son of Norman holds Tatinton, 'in Botelau hundred. Ulgar held it of king 'Edward. This land is free [from tax]. There 'are six bordars, with one plow-tillage. It is 'worth and was worth 20*s*. There is one yard-'land in the same place which lies in the forest '[of Dean], and pays 12*d*.' *Domesday*, p. 74.

Hugh de Kilpec held the manor of Little Tainton of the king, by the service of guarding a hay, or wood, near Hereford, at his own charge. He died 32 H. 3. leaving two daughters coheiresses. Joan, the eldest, was married to Philip Marmion; and Isabel, the other daughter, was granted in ward to William de Cantelupe, the same year, and afterwards married to William Waleran. Maud Waleran died seized of Little Tainton 1 E. 1. Maud de Evors was likewise possessed of it, and of the manor of Kilcot in Hawkesbury, and pleaded her right to privileges in those manors 15 E. 1.

Bogo, or Bevis de Knoville, sheriff of Shropshire and Staffordshire, purchased this manor of William Waleran, and died seized of it, and of Kilcot in Newent, Knote Cleeve, and Yenington, 9 E. 1. Bogo de Knoville, son of Bogo, purchased a charter of free warren in Tainton 13 E. 1. and had a grant of the like privilege in Kilcot in Newent, the same year. A third Bogo de Knoville, son of the last Bogo, and Joan his wife, levied a fine of Tainton and Kilcot, to the use of themselves in special taille, 12 E. 2. and he died 12 E. 3. at which time he was likewise possessed of assart lands at Gravenhull and Zerkeley, near Lidney, in the forest of Dean.

Tainton passed to the Verdunes in the same reign. Sir John de Verdune levied a fine of it, and of Kilcot; and sir Thomas Moyne, knight, held this manor of the heirs of sir John de Verdune, at the time of his death, 1362, as appears by an inquisition taken 37 E. 3. and he left it to Edmund Moyne, his son and heir.

Little Tainton came afterwards to the Casseys of Cassey-Compton. William Cassey died seized of it 1 H. 8. leaving three infant sons, Leonard, William, and Robert, who succeeded each other, and the last died 1 E. 6. Henry Cassey, son of Robert, had livery 2 Mariæ, and died 38 Eliz. John Viney, esq; was lord of the manor at the beginning of this century, and Mr. Viney, of Gloucester, a descendant from him, is the present proprietor. His arms are, *Argent, a cluster of grapes, with its stalk truncated proper.*

Little Oakley in this parish, was parcel of the manor of Monmouth, and was granted to Edward Sallus and William Blake, scrivener, 3 Jac. 1.

William Nottingham, and Elizabeth his wife, levied a fine of lands in Teinton Great, to John Kendal, and the heirs of Elizabeth; and Kendal reconveys to William Nottingham and Elizabeth in taille, 20 H. 6.

Of the Church, &c.

The church is a rectory, in the forest deanery, worth about 100 *l.* a year. The dean and chapter of Gloucester are patrons, and the reverend Mr. Parker is the present incumbent.

Maud de Teynton gave the church of Teynton to St. Peter's abbey at Gloucester, to find lights; and Radulf Avenel confirmed it, and likewise gave a hermitage in this place, with a villein and his family, to the same house; which donations were confirmed by Gilbert Foliot, bishop of Hereford, when Hameline was abbat.

The old church, which stood at the north end of the parish, was burnt down, together with the parsonage, in the civil wars, probably about the time of the siege of Gloucester. The present church stands at a considerable distance from the scite of the old one, and was built during the protectorship of Oliver Cromwell, principally by the procurement and assistance of Thomas Pury, jun. who likewise founded, and was a great benefactor to the college library at Gloucester. It is dedicated to St. Lawrence, and has this remarkable circumstance attending it, that it is placed north and south, contrary to the prevailing custom, from which the truly pious builder chose perhaps to deviate, from a contempt of religious superstition in things of no moment.

	£	s	d		£	s	d
First fruits	9	6	8	Synodals	0	2	6
Tenths —	0	18	8	Pentecost.	0	1	6
Procurations	0	6	8				

Monuments and Inscriptions.

Four tombs in the church-yard bear the following inscriptions:

Post vitam occupatissimam & fere octoginta annorum fastidio gravatam; hic tandem requiescit THOMAS PURY, Qui indolem natura vegetam, ac ad summa comparatam, vel studijs humanioribus ita excoluit, vel rebus agendis adeò exercuit, ut sive artium peritia, sive negotiorum varietate, vix in pari fortuna quenquam sibi habuerit parem. Tot privatis occupationibus, tantisq; publicis aliquando motibus agitato, quidquam (temporum vitio magis quam suo) humanitùs accidisse non tam culpandum, quàm mirandum potius, cuiquam inter rebelles versanti pietatem & religionem, inter milites, artes & Scientias impensius placuisse: Ædificatum in proximo Templum extructaq; in celebriori Loco Bibliotheca hoc eousq; testantur: ut nec hisce literarum monumentis, nec sacrato lapide, nec posterorum memoria indignus esse videatur.

Ob. Aug. 26, A. D. 1693, Ætat. 74.

The arms upon the tomb are, *Baron and femme*, 1. *Quarterly* 1st *and* 4th, [*Argent*,] *on a fess between three martlets* [*sable*,] *as many mullets of the field* for Pury. 2d *and* 3d, *A chevron ingrailed between three fighting cocks.* On the femme side, [*Azure*,] *a chevron between three fleurs de lis* [*Or*,] for Kyrle.

Sub hujus Ædiculæ Moenibus
Quam Parentibus suis Thomæ Pury Pietas extruxit
Fas est
Ut Filiæ Saræ piæ Virginis cineres inviolati quiescant:
Quæ
Cum cætera omnia bonæ feminæ munia,
Vigili in Rebus domesticis sedulitate,
Voluntate erga Pauperes sublevandos propensa,
Benevoloque in vicinis excipiendis vultu,

Usque

Usque ad an. Ætat. LIV Salutisque MDCCIX
Cum laude peregisset
Coelo matura (Jun. I) terras reliquit.

Reducem Expectans Animam
H. S. I.
Pius atq; Eruditus ille Iohannes Guise Gen. ab Antiqua et Egregia stirpe D. Iohannis Guise de Elmore In Agro Glo. Baronetti Oriundus. Wilhelmi Guise De Civit. Glo: Armig. Filius natu Maximus:
Qui
In Meritis Christi totam fiduciam reponens et de
Misericordiâ Dei plene ac firmiter persuasus
4 Iulij A. D. 1703, Ætatis 21,
Ex hac Vita ad Cœlos Emigravit.
Filio optime Merenti
Mœrens Pater
H. M.

The arms of Guise are at the end of the tomb.

M. S.
Mortalitatis Exuvias hic deposuit Reverendus Vir Samuel Whittington, A. M. Ecclesiæ Anglicanæ Presbyter, Eruditione non Vulgari ornatus Scientiâ cum Graviori tum Politiori Egregia instructus Et Morum Candore Spectabilis Qui Animi Dotibus insignis At corporis Diuturna Confectus Invaletudine in Domino requievit 3° die Iulij
Anno { Salutis MDCCXXIV / Ætatis suæ XLII° }

Hoc Amoris Monumentum Mater Mœstissima Elizabetha Whittington (Thomæ Pury Ar. juxta sepulti Filia) Nato Optime Merenti P. C.

At the end of the tomb are these arms, *Quarterly* 1st *and* 4th, *Gules, a fess checky Or and azure,* for Whittington. 2d *and* 3d, Pury, as before.

There are likewise memorials for Barbara, wife of Thomas Pury, gent. and daughter of James Kyrle, of Walford in Herefordshire, esq; who died Dec. 6, 1688, aged 65: For Thomas, eldest son of Thomas Huggins, prebend of Limerick in Ireland, and of Barbara his wife, daughter of Thomas Pury, gent. who died March 12, 1694: And for Elizabeth Whittington, daughter of Thomas Pury, but the last is not legible.

Benefaction.

Some small pieces of land, worth about 40*s.* or 50*s.* a year, were given to the poor (according to tradition) by dame Cecilia Musgrose, antiently lady of the manor.

Taxes.					
The Royal Aid in	1692,	£. 121	12	0
Poll-tax ——	1694,	— 19	2	0
Land-tax ——	1694,	— 112	0	0
The same, at 3*s.*	1770,	— 84	0	0

Sir Robert Atkyns computed the number of houses in this parish at 45, and the inhabitants at about 200, 16 of whom were reputed to be freeholders; yearly birth 5, burials 4. And there are now about 250 inhabitants.

TETBURY.

THIS parish lies in the hundred of Longtree, five miles north from Malmesbury in Wiltshire, ten westward from Cirencester, twenty-six eastward from Bristol, and nineteen south from Gloucester.

It is about five miles long from east to west, and in some places more than two miles broad. The soil is mostly light and stony, but it has been greatly improved of late, and the lands now let at a high rate. It is situated upon high ground, on the south side of the county, bordering upon Wiltshire, from which it is separated by a rivulet, whose waters, in the winter, are here augmented by another little stream, and take their course to Malmesbury, Chippenham, Lacock, Bradford, and Bath, and are unquestionably the head, or highest source of the Bristol Avon; but in the summer those rivulets are frequently dry. Almost the whole parish is the property of its own inhabitants, but it is divided between so many owners, that no person has any great estate in it.

Within the parish, there is a market-town of the same name, with a bailiff for its chief officer, chosen annually for the better management of the public revenues. It is not large, but well frequented, and deservedly claims the third place in precedence among the towns in Gloucestershire. It is pleasantly situated upon the top of a knoll, which it almost covers, and surrounded with a deep and narrow dell, or bottom, greatly resembling the moat of a castle. The town is about a mile and a half in circumference, with four streets crossing in the center of it, consisting of about four hundred houses, chiefly built of stone, and which make a handsome appearance.

On the south-east side of the town, there was a very antient, strong camp, and there is a tradition, that before the camp was made, a castle stood upon the same spot of ground, called *Swinnerdown-Castle,* 'but it is now so intirely demolished,' says the *Magna Britannia,* 'that the ruins of it are scarce visible,' whence it might be inferred, that some faint traces of it were then to be seen. But I am clearly of opinion that the author never saw them, and in short, that no such thing as a castle ever existed there. Camden, who surveyed this country above a century before that book was compiled, and who was no cursory observer of antiquities, mentions the castles at Berkeley, Dursley, Beverstone, and that which had been long demolished at Cirencester; and if there had been any vestige of such a thing at Tetbury, or any account of it in the antient records, he would certainly have taken notice of it. But we will suppose for a moment that Camden overlooked it, yet it could hardly escape the many researches of the great antiquary Leland, and others both before and since his time, yet nobody pretends to have found any such account in them.

Speed relates, indeed, but I know not upon what authority, that one Donwallo Mulmutius, a king of the Britons, built this castle, about two thousand years ago, and that it was called *Caer Bladon.* But the very existence of that king is uncertain, and the whole story incredible; for who can believe that the Britons had any buildings like castles at that time, since Giraldus Cambrensis informs us what kind of fortifications were called castles in the reign of king Henry the First, and speaking

ſpeaking of the town of Pembroke, tells us, that Arnulf of Montgomery, brother to Robert earl of Shrewſbury, fortified that place with a caſtle of ſtakes and turves. Beſides, Cæſar, Tacitus, and all the writers on the Roman affairs in Britain, are totally ſilent on this head, and yet they deſcribe the method of fighting, and the warlike inſtruments of the Britons, and would not have omitted to mention their caſtles, if they had found any among them.

The Britons, we are told, called the place *Caer Bladon*, which was afterwards the Saxon Tette-beoꞃᵹ, or *Tetteberg*, and by gradual and ſucceſſive changes, came to be written *Teteberie*, or *Tetbury*, as it ſtands at the head of this account. As for *Tette*, I know not what it can mean, unleſs it be ſome great perſon's name who occupied the camp, or was proprietor of the manor. *Caer* originally ſignified a wall, and incloſure, and became at length to be uſed for a camp, caſtle, or any kind of fortreſs. The Saxon Beoꞃᵹ is nearly ſynonimous and equivalent to the Britiſh *Caer*, and doubtleſs the town took its name from this camp; and the extenſive ſignification of thoſe Britiſh and Saxon words, gave riſe to the notion of a caſtle, grounded, I think, chiefly on Speed's authority, who moſt probably took his account of Mulmutius from Geofry of Monmouth, and tranſlated the word *Caer* by *caſtle*; whereas the Britiſh writer meant nothing more by that word than ſome camp, or intrenchments. Thus I account for the miſtake concerning it, which is not peculiar to this place, for the ſame has happened reſpecting the camps, called Caſtles, on the heights at Saintbury, Titherington, Horton, and ſeveral other places in this county, where the inhabitants fancy that caſtles once ſtood, notwithſtanding it is very certain that there never was any ſuch thing at either of thoſe places.

There is, however, a gentleman of learning, and of laudable veneration for the antiquities of this town, who finding it difficult to remove the idea which tradition has early fixt in his mind, can hardly give up the point of a Britiſh caſtle. And if I have the leaſt doubt about the matter, it ariſes ſolely from that deference which I owe, in general, to his better judgment.

The camp here was levelled a few years ago by the owner of the field, when the workmen found ſeveral heads of arrows and javelins, with horſe-ſhoes of the antient form, and ſpurs without rowels, ſuch as were uſed by our firſt kings after the conqueſt, as they are repreſented on their ſeals in Speed's Hiſtory: And under the agger were found ſeveral antient Engliſh coins, particularly one of Edward the Confeſſor, one of king Stephen, and two of king Henry the Third. Roman coins have alſo been frequently found in and near the town, of the emperors Hadrian, Antoninus Pius, Conſtantine and his ſons, ſome of Poſthumus, Magnentius, and a very fine one of Carauſius in braſs, which are in the cabinet of the reverend Mr. Wight, the miniſter of the pariſh, who is well verſed in medallic hiſtory and antiquities. There were alſo ſeveral hewn ſtones found, which thoſe who had adopted the notion of the caſtle ſuppoſed to have belonged to that building; but it ſeems probable, from many circumſtances, that there was an antient houſe on this ſpot, belonging to the Braoſes, or Mowbrays, who were lords of the manor, and that theſe were ſome of its remains; and it is not unlikely, that ſome of the ſtones from that building were uſed in the walls of the tower, upon which the Mowbrays arms are now to be ſeen.

The field where the camp was is now improved into a kind of pleaſure-ground, with plantations of firs, and agreeable ſlopes and walks on the ſide next the rivulet; and there is a very pleaſant proſpect of the London, Bath, and Wiltſhire roads from the top of it.

There was formerly in this town a religious houſe, to which the monks removed, when they left the Grange at Haſleton, (as related under Rodmarton) for want of water. It ſtood at the eaſt end of the town, and was afterwards called Hacket's Court, belonging to the Denny's half a century back, upon part of the ſcite of which Mr. Matthew Sloper built a very handſome houſe, about the year 1765. But the monks being obliged to fetch wood for their uſe from Kingſwood, found Tetbury a very inconvenient ſituation for them, and ſo they removed a ſecond time to that place, whence they originally came. Beſide this, there were two other houſes, which ſome judicious perſons have ſuppoſed, from what is ſtill to be ſeen of them, to have been originally the habitations of perſons leading a monaſtic life; but tradition ſays little, and hiſtory ſtill leſs, or nothing at all about them. The one is in the Chipping, lately in the poſſeſſion of Mr. Thomas Pyke, and Mr. Gabriel Hadnot; and the other is the old vicarage houſe.

The *Chipping* is a ſpacious area in the north-eaſt quarter of the town, encompaſſed with houſes, where two fairs are held annually, on Aſhwedneſday, and the 22d of July, for horſes and other cattle; and it took its name from the Saxon Ceapan, to buy, becauſe it was the place where, at thoſe fairs, things were bought and ſold.

The market is held on Wedneſday, about the center of the town, where are two market-houſes, appropriated to diſtinct uſes; one for cheeſe and bacon, of which vaſt quantities were formerly brought from the great dairy countries in the Vale of Glouceſterſhire, and the north part of Wiltſhire; but very little of thoſe great neceſſaries of life come now to market, owing to the dealers buying them up in the countries that produce them. This practice manifeſtly tends to enhance the price of them, to the advantage of the land holder, but, as I conceive, to the injury of the community in general. The other market houſe is for wool and yarn, the tolls of which are reduced

reduced to about a fourth of what they were forty or fifty years ago; which, however, is not to be attributed to the decline of trade in thoſe commodities, but to the prevailing practice of ſelling them out of the market.

There was formerly ſome woollen cloth made here, but manufactures always decline under natural diſadvantages, and the clothing buſineſs could not long ſubſiſt at Tetbury, for want of conſtant water to drive the fulling mills, ſo neceſſary in that buſineſs. The chief manufactures now carried on here, are woolſtapling and woolcombing, in which latter about one hundred and fifty perſons find conſtant employment; and the combed wool is ſold at Coventry, Kidderminſter, Leiceſter, and other markets.

The inhabitants enjoy a fine, healthy air, and live to a great age, as appears from the following ſhort hiſtory of a family of five women lately dwelling in one houſe. Honour Powell, relict of the famous Mr. Powell mentioned in the Tatler, was one of thoſe perſons, who died at the age of ninety; a ſecond died in 1767, aged eighty-nine, and the other three were living when this account was taken, aged eighty-ſix, eighty-one, and fifty, the laſt being the daughter of one of the others; and all theſe, when living together, were able to wait on themſelves and each other, without aſſiſtance from abroad. But the moſt extraordinary inſtance of longevity to be produced in this county, is of one Henry Weſt, who reſided at Upton, a hamlet in this pariſh, in the time of king James the Firſt. He lived to be one hundred and fifty-two years of age, and it is written in a Bible, now in the poſſeſſion of one of his deſcendants, that he had five wives, but no child by the firſt four; that he had ten by the fifth, and lived to ſee a hundred grandchildren; and there is a traditional account that he gave to each of them a braſs pot, or kettle.

Tho' the elevated ſituation of the town gives it a pure air, yet it has been attended with a conſiderable inconvenience, the want of water, which the inhabitants uſed to purchaſe at 6*d.* and ſometimes at 10*d.* the hogſhead, 'till, in the year 1749, an antient well in the wool-market was ſunk lower, by ſubſcription, to the depth of 104 feet, and the preſent miniſter of the pariſh fixed a lead pump in it at his own expence; ſince that time many other wells have been ſunk for the uſe of private families, and the town is now pretty well ſupplied with water. But an accident that lately happened, in ſinking a quarry for the uſe of the turnpike-road, ſhews how it might be much better ſupplied, at no great expence; for the labourers ſtruck upon, and diſcovered an old aqueduct, which is ſuppoſed to have led from a ſpring called Whorwell, to ſome religious houſe in the town; and it ſeems unaccountable how a thing ſo neceſſary, where water was very ſcarce, could be neglected, and at length totally forgotten.

There is a petrifying ſpring, on the north ſide of the town, which incruſts pieces of wood, and other things, with a ſtrong ſtony ſubſtance, at a conſiderable diſtance from its riſe; and Mr. Wight, the miniſter, is poſſeſſed of a perfect ſtone, taken out of the courſe of that water, which ſeems formerly to have been a ſtick, with ſeveral rings, or concentrick circles at the end, indicating the years of its growth.

Two turnpike-roads run through the town, and croſs each other there. One leads eaſtward to Cirenceſter, and ſo to Oxford, or London; but weſtward from Tetbury, it leads to Bath and Briſtol. The other runs northward from this town to Minchin Hampton, Stroud, and Glouceſter; but ſouthward to Chippenham, Devizes, Saliſbury, and Southampton. At the weſt end of the town is a very deep hollow, part of the natural moat already taken notice of, over which the commiſſioners of the roads built a high bridge, of four large arches, in the year 1775, which makes the entrance into the town on that ſide exceedingly commodious, that before was up a ſteep acclivity, very difficult for carriages to aſcend.

The annual races are run upon a large common, about a mile eaſtward of the town, and are much frequented by the neighbouring gentry.

Of the Manor and other Eſtates.

In *Domeſday* it is recorded after this manner:

'Roger de Lurei holds Teteberie in Langetrewes hundred. There are twenty-three hides 'which pay tax. Siuuard held it in the time of 'king Edward. There are eight plow-tillages in 'demean, and thirty-two villeins, and two bordars, 'and two redcheniſters, with a prieſt, having 'amongſt them all fourteen plow-tillages. There 'are nineteen *ſervi*, and a mill of 15*d.* [rent] and 'paſture of 10*s.* and ten acres of meadow. The 'ſame Roger holds Uptone. There are two 'hides, and one yard-land taxed. Aluricus held 'it of king Edward. There are two plow-tillages 'in demean, and five villeins, and three bordars, 'with three plow-tillages. There are eight *ſervi.* 'Theſe two manors were worth 33*l.* in the time 'of king Edward, and they are now at farm for '50*l.*' *Domeſday*, p. 75.

Tetbury, ſoon after the Norman conqueſt, belonged to the family of St. Waleric, who took their name from the port of Saint Valeric in Normandy. Reginald de Saint Waleric founded a monaſtery of Ciſtercians at Haſleden, who, for want of water, removed from thence to Tetbury; and afterwards, for want of wood, removed from Tetbury to Kingſwood, where they continued 'till the diſſolution of that abbey.

Maud de St. Waleric, the heireſs of that family, was married to the great William de Braoſe, eldeſt ſon and heir of William de Braoſe, lord of Brecknock, and deſcended from William de Braoſe, who was one of thoſe who came into England to try their fortunes with the Conqueror; and by this marriage the manor of Tetbury paſſed into the family of de Braoſe. Maud was a lady of high ſpirit, and encouraged her huſband to oppoſe king John. Her huſband was greatly in debt for the province of Munſter in Ireland, which he farmed of the king, and his lands being ſeized for default of payment, he broke out in open rebellion, and was forced to fly into France, where he died in exile, whilſt Maud his wife, and their ſon William, were made priſoners, and both died in Corfe caſtle. But the hiſtory of the founders of Lanthony priory gives a different account of the king's diſpleaſure, and relates, that William fought with one Guenhunewyn, at Elwel, on the morrow after the feſtival of St. Lawrence, in the year 1198, and vanquiſhed him, with a ſlaughter of three thouſand of his followers, who were Welchmen; wherefore the king turned him out of all his eſtates, and baniſhed him the kingdom, without any legal proceedings, and ſo he died in exile.

William de Braoſe, deſcended from the laſt William, held the borough of Tetbury, with markets, fairs, courts-leet, waifs, and free warren, and his right was allowed in the proceedings on a writ of *Quo warranto*, 15 E. 1. This William left four daughters, coheireſſes, but the manor of Tetbury, notwithſtanding, continued in the ſame name; for Peter de Braoſe was ſeized of Rodmarton, Tetbury, Upton, and Charlton, with free warren, as part of the barony of Brembre, 29 E. 1. and died 5 E. 2. Thomas de Braoſe, ſon of Peter, had the grant of a fair in Tetbury 29 E. 3. and ſir John de Braoſe died ſeized of the manor in the 41ſt year of that reign. Richard de Braoſe was ſeized of the borough of Tetbury, with markets, fairs, and other liberties, 4 R. 2. which was at the time of his death; and he was ſucceeded, the ſame year, by William de Braoſe, whoſe right was allowed before the judges itinerant. Beatrix the widow of ſir Thomas de Braoſe was ſeized thereof 7 R. 2. And Margaret the widow of John Berkeley, and formerly the wife of another ſir Thomas de Braoſe, died ſeized of Tetbury 23 H. 6.

The manor of Tetbury deſcended to Maurice lord Berkeley, the fifth of that name, and brother to William marquis of Berkeley, as coheir to the laſt lord Braoſe, and it continued in that family 'till George lord Berkeley ſold it, with the borough, and tolls of the town, for the uſe of the inhabitants, in the year 1632, and they are now veſted in truſtees for the ſame uſe.

The *Warren* is a large common, ſtinted and regulated as the truſtees for the town think proper, and uſually brings in about 30*l.* a year for the winter paſture of ſheep.

The arms of the town are, *Two dolphins nayant.*

HAMLETS. 1. *Upton*, ſo called becauſe it lies high. It appears, by ſeveral foundations of houſes in the fields, that this village was much more populous than at preſent, and there have been coins found among the ruins, particularly one of king Henry the Second, and ſome of king Henry the Third. Perhaps it ſuffered in the civil wars. The *Domeſday* account of this manor is joined to that of Tetbury. Upton was held of Richard earl of Glouceſter and Hertford, 47 H. 3. Peter de Braoſa had free warren in Upton, Dufton, Elmundeſtree, and Charleton, 29 E. 1. and George Braoſa, eſq; was ſeized of Upton 6 H. 5. Sir Edmund Tame was lord of this manor, and leaving three ſiſters, coheireſſes, Alice was married to ſir Thomas Verney, who, in her right, was ſeized of the third part of ſir Edmund Tame's eſtates. Richard Verney, ſon and heir of Thomas, died July 26, 9 Eliz. ſeized in Glouceſterſhire, (as appears by the inquiſition taken at Glouceſter after his deceaſe) of the intire manor of Upton, and of two meſſuages and lands in Eaſtleech, twelve meſſuages with their appurtenances in Upton-Tedbury, Charleton, Doughton, and Tedbury; fifty-one meſſuages in Eaſtleech-Turville, Willingſtrup, and Colne Alwyns; and of the manor of Nymsfield; for it is expreſſly declared by the ſame inquiſition, that he, with his father, purchaſed the other two parts of theſe eſtates by indenture tripartite bearing date Feb. 26, 1 E. 6. George Verney, ſon of Richard, died ſeized of Upton 16 Eliz. leaving Richard Verney, his ſon, ten years of age at his father's death, who became a very eminent perſon, and was choſen one of the knights of the ſhire for the county of Warwick, 31, 35, 39, 43 Eliz. and 1 Jac. 1. Upton was afterwards part of the eſtate of ſir George Huntley, who entertained queen Elizabeth at Froceſter-court, in her way to Berkeley-caſtle. Thomas Cripps, eſq; is the preſent principal inhabitant, who has a good eſtate, and an elegant new-built houſe in this hamlet, where his family has reſided for many generations, and once enjoy'd a larger eſtate than it does at preſent.

The Grove eſtate at Upton, is the property of Samuel Saunders, of Tetbury, eſq; who is a branch of the Saunders's of Berkſhire. His arms are, *Per chevron, ſable and argent, three elephants heads erazed counterchanged.*

2. *Dufton*, or *Doughton*. This manor formerly belonged to the Stonors. Edward de Stonor was ſeized of Doughton 5 R. 2. as was Gilbert de Stonor, ſon of Robert, 3 H. 5. There is a large barrow in a field here, which was probably thrown up immediately after the battle fought at Sherſton, between the Engliſh and the Danes, about the year 1016, wherein the latter were routed, and have left their name to another field juſt by it, called *Danes End*. This hamlet belongs to ſeveral perſons, but Mr. Talboys, and Mr. Clark, have the principal eſtates. The former has a large old houſe here, built by Richard Talboys, eſq; who was high ſheriff of this county, and had an eſtate

eſtate of about 1500*l.* a year. This family is deſcended from one of the ſame name at Whiſton in Wiltſhire, whoſe arms are, *Argent, a ſaltire gules, on a chief of the ſecond three eſcallops of the firſt.*

3. *Elmſtree*, or *Elmudeſtre*, that is, *Elmude's place.* Reginald de St. Waleric gave the manor of Elmudeſtree to the monks of the Benedictine abbey of St. Ebrulph in Normandy. Alien monaſteries being deprived of their eſtates in England, by act of parliament, king Edward the Fourth, in the 4th year of his reign, granted to Henry Sampſon, dean of Weſtbury college, and to the chapter of the ſame, and to their ſucceſſors, the manor of Alminſtree, or Elminſtree, to hold in free and perpetual alms, with courts leet, frankpledge, &c. to pray for the ſouls of his father, mother, and brother, and for his own welfare. This eſtate continued in the college 'till the diſſolution, and was afterwards veſted in —— Tooke, who lies buried in Tetbury church; ſince whoſe time it paſſed to Thomas Deacon, eſq; formerly a ſilk-mercer in London, who married Mary, daughter of Thomas Haynes, a merchant in the city of Briſtol, and it continued in his family 'till the death of Mrs. Deacon, in the year 1769, who, by her will, deviſed this eſtate to Thomas Jenner, eſq; a member of the univerſity of Oxford, and a fellow of Merton college there, who is the preſent proprietor.

4. *Charlton.* William de Ballecot held ſix yard lands in Cherlington and Tetbury 33 E. 1. and another William Ballecot died ſeized thereof 20 E. 3. Edward de Mortimer, earl of March and Ulſter, was ſeized of a yearly rent of 41*s.* iſſuing out of Cherleton, a member of the manor of Tetbury, 5 R. 2. and died ſeized of the manor 3 H. 6. It was granted to Cicely dutcheſs of York, for her life, 38 H. 6. and confirmed to her 1 E. 4. It was afterwards made part of the dowry of Catherine, queen dowager of king Henry the Eighth, and was granted to Drew Drurey, and Edward Downing, 16 Eliz. An anceſtor to lord Ducie purchaſed it afterwards, and his lordſhip is the preſent lord of this manor.

5. The *Grange.* This is not properly a hamlet, but claims to be conſidered diſtinctly, as it formerly belonged to the abbey of Kingſwood, at the diſſolution of which it was granted to Richard Andrews, and Thomas Hyſley, 36 H. 8. It was afterwards the ſeat and eſtate of the Gaſtrells, who continued there ſeveral generations; but the houſe, with part of the eſtate, is now the property of Mr. William Fiſher. This eſtate is tithe free. Here was formerly a chapel, but it is now converted to common uſes. Mr. Fiſher's arms are, *a chevron vaire between three lioncels rampant.*

Of the Church, &c.

The church is in the deanery of Stonehouſe. It is a vicarage, endowed with all the tithes of Dufton, and with all but grain in every other part of the pariſh, except Upton, where the incumbent has only the ſmall tithes, and receives 5*s.* in lieu of tithe of hay; and except the Grange eſtate, which is exempt from tithes.

The rectory and advowſon were granted to the abbey of Eynſham, by Thomas de Waleric, and confirmed by the biſhop of Worceſter. *See the grant and confirmation in the Appendix to Stevens's Supplement to the Monaſticon*, pp. 99, 101. At the diſſolution of that abbey, they were granted to Chriſt Church college, Oxford, to which the impropriation ſtill belongs. The college, about the year 1563, granted the advowſon to Henry lord Berkeley, and his heirs, and George lord Berkeley ſold it to the inhabitants of Tetbury, who are patrons, and Mr. John Wight is the preſent incumbent. The glebe is very conſiderable, and the vicarage is worth upwards of 200*l.* a year.

The church was dedicated to the virgin Mary, and is ſaid to have been built originally by Reginald de Waleric, not long after the conqueſt. It appeared by the workmanſhip to have been ſince rebuilt at ſeveral times, and being very ruinous, is now taking down. The inhabitants have raiſed a large ſum of money themſelves, and received a few benefactions from others, particularly from the late doctor Johnſon, biſhop of Worceſter, the late lord Botetourt, Thomas Eſtcourt, eſq; captain Warren of Briſtol, Mr. Spencer of London, (a native of the town) Mr. William Earl of Malmeſbury, and Mr. Jackſon of Sneed Park; with which they are preparing to erect an elegant church, upon the ſcite of the old one, preſerving the preſent ſteeple, which is handſome, and in good condition; and the miniſter himſelf has given about 1500*l.* towards this neceſſary work. There is an exceeding fine ring of eight bells, with a clock, and a good ſet of chimes in the tower, on the weſt ſide of which, without, is a ſcutcheon, with *A lion rampant*, part of the arms of the Mowbrays.

A chantry was erected in this church 37 E. 3. by Walter de Tetbury, John de Weſton, Ralph Hale, and John de Colburn, dedicated to the virgin Mary, of which William Potte was the laſt incumbent, and had a penſion of 6*l.* 13*s.* 4*d.* in 1553. *Willis.* The lands belonging to it were granted to Edward Newport and John Crompton 5 Jac. There was another chantry erected by John de Grevil 19 E. 4. dedicated to the holy Trinity, and William Wotton, the laſt incumbent, had a penſion of 6*l.* in 1553. The lands belonging to this chantry were granted to Simon Wiſeman, and Richard Moor, 4 Jac. 1. There was alſo another, called Herne's chantry, of which Thomas Harman, the laſt incumbent, received a penſion of 4*l.* in the ſame year.

	£.				£.		
Firſt fruits	36	13	4	Synodals	0	2	0
Tenths —	3	13	4	Pentecoſtals	0	2	6
Procurations	0	10	0				

Monuments

Monuments and Inſcriptions.

On the ſouth ſide of the church was Braoſe's aile, where was a chapel belonging to that family, now deſtroy'd, and a vault beneath it full of bones. Near it ſtood an antient tomb, with the figure of a lord de Braoſe, lying in armour, with his legs acroſs, but it is wretchedly defaced, and broken to pieces.

There was a tomb in the north aile, with two very large figures of a man and woman lying along; the man in armour, with his feet reſting on a lion, to denote the courage and magnanimity that ſhould diſtinguiſh the ſoldier. At the woman's feet lies a dog, the proper emblem of fidelity and affection. There was no inſcription beſides the date, *Anno Domi* 1586; but it was deſigned for one of the Gaſtrells, as appears by the arms, *Quarterly* 1ſt *and* 4th, *Checky, argent and ſable, on a chief Or, three bucks heads couped of the ſecond,* for Gaſtrell. 2d *and* 3d, *Ten billets,* 4, 3, 2, 1, *a creſcent in chief.* On the femme ſide, 1ſt *and* 4th, either plain or obliterated. 2d *and* 3d, *An eagle diſplayed.* Doctor Gaſtrell, late biſhop of Cheſter, and one of the canons of Chriſt Church, was deſcended from a branch of this family, of whom many have been buried here without memorials.

On the tablet of a monument in the chancel was this inſcription:

Eſto fidelis vsque ad mortem, et dabo tibi Coronam Vitæ.
In Remembrance
of that Graue Gentleman,
RICHARD TALBOYS, ESQ.
Who after a Pilgrimage of 87 years
Departed this Life 3° Aug. A. D. 1663
KATHERINE HIS WIFE,
as a Pledge of ſurviving Loue hath erected. [this monument.]
Senibus mors eſt in Janua, Juvenibus
vero in inſidiis. Attende tibiipſi viator.

At the top, are the arms of Talboys, impaling, *Sable, a chevron between three croſs croſlets fitchy gules.*

There was a monument on the north ſide of the church for John Savage, who was repreſented kneeling before an altar, and this quaint inſcription upon the table in capital letters:

Our Bodyes all receiv'd of Earth, Earth muſt againe them keepe,
Untill the Lord ſhall raiſe them up, to Life from deadly Sleepe;
Our Soules aloft to Heaven ſhall mount, where Death them cannot preſſe
Death only is a Dore to us, the true Life to poſſeſſe;
Our Glory here ſtill vaniſhing, prone to decaye to fall:
Shall after Death be ſtabliſhed, be made Angelicall. (ſlayne
What then! what then! though Savage Death, our Savage thus hath
Regard it not, tis nothing, for, it was with Chriſt to raigne.
John Savage, Gent. deceas'd the 28 of Maye Anno Do 1608.

Many other perſons of the name of Savage, but of a different family, have been buried under flat ſtones in the ſouth aile, particularly Francis Savage, gent. who died in 1740, aged 63; Sarah, wife of William Savage, who died in 1767, aged 73; and ſome with only initial letters upon the ſtones; for the long expectation of a new church has prevented the erecting monuments in the old one. Upon two of thoſe ſtones were the Savages arms [q], *viz. Argent, ſix lioncels rampant ſable.*

Upon a flat ſtone in the ſouth aile,

Here reſteth ye body of MARY the Wife of NATHANIEL CRIPPS Gent. Daughter of SAMUEL BURCOME of Sodbury, Gent. who departed this Life the 13th day of July, 1710, Ætatis ſuæ 35.

Her body Earthly was, and to the Earth
Deſcended is, from whence it took its Birth.
Her Soul from a more High Original
Mounted aloft, became Angelical.
Clog not her Wings, then, with your dewy tears
On which She's rais'd above the Starry Spheres.
Ceaſe Huſband, Children, ceaſe, give God the Praiſe
Which She now warbles in immortal Layes.

Alſo Margaret the Daughter of ye ſaid Nathaniel and Margaret Departed ys Life ye 13th of July 1710.

Here alſo lyeth the Body of the abovefaid NATHANIEL CRIPPS, who departed this Life the 23d Day of March Anno Dom. 1739-40 Ætatis ſuæ 65.

On a ſmall marble tablet againſt the wall,

M. S.
Deboræ Uxoris Jacobi Roche de Merriott in Comitatu Somerſetenſi Generoſi, Quæ obijt quinto Die menſis Julij A. D. MDCCXX anno ſuæ ætat. XXIX. Nec non Patricij eorum filij infantuli, qui obijt ultimo die ejuſdem menſis et Anni.

At the top are theſe arms, *Gules, three roaches in pale proper.*

On flat ſtones in various parts of the church, were the following memorials, amongſt many others, with only dates and names.

Here lieth the Body of Mrs Mary Deacon Widow, eldeſt Daughter of M^r^. Thomas Haynes of the City of Briſtol, Merch^t^ who departed this life February the 22d Anno Dom. 1731-2 in the 73d year of her Age.

Here lyeth the Body of M^rs^. ESTHER DEACON, Daughter of THOMAS DEACON Gent. (late of ELMESTREE in this Pariſh) and of MARY his Wife, who lies buried near this Place. She died September ye 2nd in the Year of our Lord 1747, aged 56.

Upon both ſtones are theſe arms, *Argent, a croſs between four lions rampant ſable, on a chief azure three roſes proper.*

Benefactions.

There has been a free grammar-ſchool in the town for many years. It was founded in the reign of king James, by ſir William Rumney, alderman and ſheriff of London, who was a native of this town, to which he gave a leaſe for years, of the profits of the fairs and markets, and the produce was applied towards purchaſing the advowſon of the church, the tolls of the borough, the manor and commons, which were bought of George lord Berkeley. The truſtees continued the ſchool 'till the death of Mr. Henry Wightwick, a few years ago, ſince whoſe time no maſter has been appointed, as the tolls of the markets have not been ſufficient to raiſe a ſalary for one. Mr. Oldham, the poet, received part of his education at this ſchool, as did doctor Biſſe, biſhop of Hereford. Doctor Joſeph Trapp, born at Cherington in this neighbourhood, miniſter of Chriſt Church in London, and author of ſeveral valuable books, was here qualified for the uni-

[q] This family is deſcended from the Le Savages of Clifton and Rock Savage, in Cheſhire, and they from John le Savage of Sarcliffe in Derbyſhire, who was living 3 E. 2. John Savage married Margaret, the daughter and heir of ſir Thomas Daniel, of Bradley in Appleton, Cheſhire, knight; and Margaret ſurviving her huſband, granted to her ſon John Savage, and to his heirs, the right of bearing her coat of arms, *Argent, a pale fuſilly ſable,* by deed dated 3 H. 5. and the poſterity of Savage bore the arms of Daniel accordingly, with the creſt, *An unicorn's head couped argent,* 'till ſir John Savage of Clifton took the *ſix black lions,* in the reign of queen Elizabeth, as I find it in ſir Peter Leiceſter's *Hiſtorical Collections,* pp. 230, 231. There was a ſir John Savage, who married a daughter of ſir Henry Pool, of Saperton in this county, by which alliance this family came to be ſettled at Tetbury, where the reverend Mr. John Savage has now a good houſe, and a good eſtate.

verſity;

versity; and so was Mr. Gore, formerly of Sopworth in Wiltshire, a gentleman remarkable for his learning.

Out of the annual profits of the borough, &c. the trustees apply 10*l.* to buy garments for the poor; 5*l.* to bind out apprentices; and 10*l.* for a weekly lecture on Thursdays, by five neighbouring ministers. Doctor George Bull, afterwards bishop of St. David's, was one of the lecturers. The trustees also pay 5*l.* out of the tolls, to the poor, in lieu of money given to them by the wills of Mr. William Langstone, and Mr. John Malby.

Another school has been since founded here, by Mrs. Anne Hodges, of Shipton Moyne in this county, who, by her will, left 30*l.* a year to teach fifteen boys of this parish to read, write, and account; and 10*l.* a year to the second poor, charged on the Shipton estate.

Sir Thomas Estcourt, in the year 1624, gave 10*l.* yearly, arising from chief-rents in Tetbury, for the benefit of the poor, and 40*s.* yearly for sermons, which sums are charged on houses in Tetbury. John Veizey, in 1677, gave 30*s.* yearly, charged on lands, to the use of the poor, and for a sermon. Mr. John Savage gave 20*l.* to be let for four years, without interest, to four tradesmen. Mr. John Sheppard and his wife gave 30*l.* to the like use, which being lost by the insolvency of the borrowers, Charles Savage, esq; gave the like sum to the same use.

N. B. The benefactions from Mrs. Hodges and sir Thomas Estcourt were so long in arrear, that about the year 1765, they amounted to the sum of 420*l.* which was laid out on consolidated three *per cent.* annuities, vested in Mr. William Fisher, Mr. Robert Clark, Mr. Thomas Wight, and Mr. Edward Tugwell, trustees for the use of the poor.

Mr. Matthew Sloper, by his will, about the year 1770, gave 10*l.* to be laid out on the same security, and vested in the above-named trustees for the same use.

Mr. John Avery, late of the city of Bristol, has given eight sixpenny loaves, to be distributed every Sunday to the second poor for ever; and 10*s.* to the vicar, for a sermon on the anniversary of his death, with 3*s.* to the clerk, and 2*s.* to the sexton, for their attendance on that day. And a house in Bristol is charged with these benefactions.

Mr. Elton gave 20*s.* to the poor, and 10*s.* for an annual sermon, to the vicar.

Mrs. Mary Hone, (daughter of Mr. John Hone,) who was buried April 11, 1776, left 150*l.* (which legacy is enrolled in the court of chancery) the interest of which is to be equally divided between poor widows that are members of the established church, every year, on Christmas-day, by the vicar of the parish for the time being.

Mr. Giles Stedman gave 30*s.* to be disposed of in bread to the poor.

Mr. William Talboys gave 20*s.* yearly to buy books for the poor boys at the grammar-school; and both the two last charities are charged on a piece of ground in Tetbury, called Barley Croft.

Mr. Jonathan Shippen, clothier, gave 20*s.* in bread to the poor, and 10*s.* for a sermon. Mr. Hopeful Vokins and Mr. Joseph Lockey gave 50*s.* in bread to the poor. And Mr. Gilbert Gastrell gave 20*s.* to be disposed of in like manner, and 10*s.* for a sermon.

Thomas Talboys, of Hoxton in Middlesex, esq; who died in the year 1731, and was buried in Tetbury church, left 20*l.* a year for ever to the following uses, 4*l.* in bread, and 15*l.* in money, to the poor; and 20*s.* to the minister for a sermon on St. Thomas day. He also left 50*l.* to erect a monument for him in Tetbury church, which has not hitherto been done. There are several other sums of money left for monuments, which, it is presumed, will be erected in the new church.

Tetbury.

Taxes.	The Royal Aid in	1692, £.	107	5	4
	Poll-tax ——	1694, —	77	17	0
	Land-tax ——	1694, —	175	3	8
	The same, at 3*s.*	1770, —	133	0	0

Upton, Dufton, and Elmstree.

Taxes.	The Royal Aid in	1692, £.	93	11	4
	Poll-tax ——	1694, —	15	4	0
	Land-tax —	1694, —	95	8	4
	The same, at 3*s.*	1770, —	71	11	0¼
	Land-tax in Charlton	1770, —	36	10	2½

When sir Robert Atkyns compiled his account of this place, about seventy years ago, there were, according to him, 300 houses, and about 1200 inhabitants in the parish, whereof 80 were freeholders; yearly births 57, burials 55. About the year 1729, the people were numbered, and there were then 3115 souls, since which time they are increased to the number of about 3500.

T E W K E S B U R Y.

THIS parish lies in the hundred of Tewkesbury, about ten miles north-west from Cheltenham, nine westward from Winchcombe, and ten north-eastward from Gloucester.

It is situated in a fine rich vale, near the confines of Worcestershire, and watered by four rivers, like the garden of Eden. It has a corporation and borough-town within it, which gives name to the hundred; and is peninsulated by three of those rivers, the Avon, the Swilyate, and the Carrant. The first, after receiving the Swilyate, falls into the Severn at the *Lower Lode*, a little westward, or below the town; and the Carrant empties itself into the Avon a little above it. This is called the *Upper Avon*, to distinguish it from the river of the same name that runs from Bath to Bristol. It is navigable as high as Stratford in Warwickshire, and visits Evesham and Pershore in its course to Tewkesbury; whence,

 by

by means of the Severn, (in which it is ſaid the tide ſometimes flows to this place) the navigation is continued to Glouceſter, Briſtol, Worceſter, and to all places lying upon that river, or that have a communication with it.

It is the prevailing opinion that this place derives its name from one *Theocus*, who, as ſome ſay, was an eminent hermit, that dwelt here about the year 700, and had a chapel on the banks of the Severn. Leland, by a kind of unwarrantable licence, or at leaſt by miſtake, calls the town *Theoci Curia*, for *Theoci Buria*. But William of Malmeſbury, as if he had never heard of ſuch hermit, derives the name from the Greek word *Theotocos*, the mother of God, becauſe the firſt monaſtery that was built here was dedicated to the virgin mother. As to the firſt explanation, I am not without ſuſpicion that the ſtory of the hermit is fabulous; nor is the monk of Malmeſbury's derivation ſatisfactory, for who can ſuppoſe that Britons or Saxons would give names to places from a language they were almoſt totally ignorant of? Having firſt given the opinions of others, I ſhall take the liberty of ſubjoining my own. The earlieſt account we have of this place, is in the reign of Cenred, king of Mercia, when, we are told, two brothers, *Odo* and *Dodo*, great noblemen of that kingdom, were lords of this manor. And from this *Dodo*, or *Thodo*, (for in Saxon names the *D* and *Th* are often ſubſtituted for each other) comes *Thodocus*, the ſame name, only written after the Latin manner; and hence, probably *Teodecheſberie*, as it is in *Domeſday*. The Saxon writers, by contraction, call the town Ðeocſbuрẏ, and we their ſucceſſors, *Teuxbury*, or *Tewkeſbury*, as at the head of this account. The termination indicates that here was a camp or place of defence, now perhaps levelled and deſtroy'd, but there is no doubt of its once exiſting; and it was moſt probably in Oldbury field, for *Oldbury* ſignifies the *old camp*; and upon this ſuppoſition, *Teodecheſberie* ſignifies the *camp of Theocus*.

In the year 715, one of the above noblemen, or both, (for it is variouſly related) built a monaſtery here, as will be ſhewn more at large in the account of church affairs; and from the reſort to that monaſtery, the town very probably took its riſe, and ſeems to have increaſed gradually as the abbey flouriſhed. Upwards of three hundred years after that period, *Domeſday* was compiled, which takes notice of the particulars belonging to the manor, and that there were thirteen burgeſſes in the town, who paid twenty ſhillings a year; and that the queen eſtabliſhed a market, which paid eleven ſhillings and eight pence. A few ages afterwards, the town and the abbey were both improved and enlarged, by the patronage and munificence of the great earls of Glouceſter, who reſided here part of their time, and were lords of the large manor of Tewkeſbury.

King John, before he came to the crown, held this manor, and the honour of Glouceſter. He built the long bridge at Tewkeſbury, leading towards Worceſter, and gave the profits of the fairs and markets to keep it in repair. This bridge was very beneficial to the town, the approaches to which were ſubject to floods, from the frequent overflowing of the rivers that almoſt encompaſs it; and from that time Tewkeſbury was more frequented, becauſe more acceſſible.

After John acceded to the crown, the Clares were earls of Glouceſter, and lords of the borough and great manor of Tewkeſbury. They reſided part of their time at Holmes Caſtle, built upon an eminence near the town, and were great benefactors both to that and to the abbey. By the inquiſition taken after the death of Gilbert de Clare, which happened 7 E. 2. it appears, that there were then belonging to him, One hundred and fourteen burgages and a half, and a quarter part of a burgage, which paid 6*l.* 7*s.* 10*d.* and the toll of the borough was worth 100*s.* which was at that time a very conſiderable ſum, perhaps more than equal in value to the tolls of the borough at preſent. There were two views of frank pledge, one at Michaelmas, the other at Eaſter; the certain fines amounted to 7*l.* 12*s.* and the pleas and perquiſites of the court of the borough were worth 100*s.* beſide what aroſe from the other parts of the manor. Theſe particulars, compared with the foregoing, ſhew that the town was then greatly improved, and it became ſtill more and more populous 'till the time of the reformation.

In the reign of queen Elizabeth, when the nation was arming againſt the expected Spaniſh invaſion, the city of Glouceſter was appointed to provide one hundred men, and the borough of Tewkeſbury forty-ſix men for its quota. And in the year 1647, the county of Glouceſter was rated at 1212*l.* 3*s.* 4*d per* month for the maintenance of forces within the kingdom, and for carrying on the war in Ireland; at which time this borough was aſſeſſed 10*l.* 10*s.*

But to come nearer to our own times: When the new militia law was carried into execution in this county, in the years 1758, 1759, and 1760, one man out of every twenty-nine upon the liſts was taken by ballot, throughout the county, and there were fourteen men raiſed in Tewkeſbury, eighteen in Cirenceſter, and twenty-ſix in the city of Glouceſter; which ſhews the comparative ſtate of population in thoſe places, as far as the liſts can be relied on.

The town is an antient borough, but the ſheriff of Glouceſterſhire did not return it as ſuch 9 E. 1. and therefore it could not then be ſo reputed. It was firſt incorporated by charter 14 Eliz. by the name of the bailiffs, burgeſſes, and commonalty of the borough of Tewkeſbury; and king James the Firſt granted them another charter, much like the former, in the 3d year of his reign.

This

This laſt was ſurrendered, by writing under the common ſeal of the corporation, to king James the Second; and that king reincorporated them in the ſecond year of his reign, by the name of the mayor, aldermen, and common council, &c. However there was no mayor choſen by virtue of that new charter, and the government of the town, as a corporation, totally ceaſed 'till the thirteenth year of king William the Third, when that king granted the town their preſent charter, a tranſlation of which will be found in the *Appendix*, N°. XXVI.

The corporation conſiſts of twenty-four burgeſſes, out of whom two bailiffs are annually elected, who, with two aldermen, are the magiſtrates for the borough and corporation; and the juſtices of the peace for the county, by expreſs exemption in the charter, have no authority to act within the borough.

This town firſt elected two burgeſſes to parliament in the year 1609, as I find it in the black book belonging to the corporation; but Willis's liſt, in his *Notitia Parliamentaria*, commences in the year 1614.

The right of election is in the freeholders and freemen of the corporation, who together amount to above 500.

The town has had the honour of giving title to ſeveral noble perſons. There was a William earl of Tewkeſbury in the reign of king Henry the Firſt. Sir Henry Capel, brother to the earl of Eſſex, was created baron of Tewkeſbury, by king William the Third. And the electoral prince of Hanover, afterwards king George the Firſt, in the year 1706, was created baron of Tewkeſbury in the county of Glouceſter, viſcount Northallerton in the county of York, earl of Milford-Haven in the county of Pembroke, marquis and duke of Cambridge, &c.

But the place is moſt diſtinguiſhed in hiſtory for its celebrated abbey, and for the battle fought near it, between the houſes of York and Lancaſter, wherein the latter were ſo totally defeated, that they were never afterwards able to make head againſt king Edward the Fourth. The chief of thoſe that were killed in the field, and of thoſe who were made priſoners, and afterwards beheaded, or otherwiſe ſlain, were buried in the abbey church, wherefore Leland writes thus of the town:

Ampla foro, et partis ſpoliis præclara Theoci
Curia, Sabrinæ qua ſe committit Avona
Fulget; nobilium ſacriſq; recondit in antris
Multorum cineres, quondam inclyta corpora bello.

Which is thus tranſlated by the editor of Camden:

Where Avon's friendly ſtreams with Severn join,
Great Tewkeſbury's walls, renown'd for trophies, ſhine;
And keep the ſad remains with pious care,
Of noble ſouls, the honour of the war.

Of that deciſive battle our hiſtorians give the following particulars: Margaret, queen to king Henry the Sixth, landed on Eaſter-day, 1471, at Weymouth in Dorſetſhire, accompanied by her ſon, Edward prince of Wales, and Edmund Beaufort, duke of Somerſet, with a ſmall body of French forces; and ſoon taking the field, marched through Devonſhire, and Somerſetſhire, to the city of Briſtol. Her followers being increaſed to a very conſiderable army, ſhe advanced to Glouceſter, whence ſhe propoſed marching towards Wales to join the earl of Pembroke, but having been refuſed admittance into that city, ſhe proceeded to Tewkeſbury with the ſame deſign; but her ſcheme was defeated by the vigilance of king Edward, who proſcribed her and all her adherents by proclamation, and followed with his army ſo cloſe at her heels, that ſhe could not paſs the Severn without expoſing her rear to certain deſtruction. It was therefore reſolved, in a council of war, that the army ſhould be intrenched in the park adjoining to the town, and remain in that ſituation 'till the arrival of the earl of Pembroke, who had already ſent her ſome ſupplies, and was himſelf on his march to join her with a conſiderable body of forces raiſed in Wales. This plan was immediately put in execution, and Edward coming up, reſolved to attack them in their intrenchments, before they ſhould be more ſtrongly fortified or reinforced. He drew up his army in two lines, and gave the command of the firſt to his younger brother Richard duke of Glouceſter, and commanded the ſecond line himſelf, aſſiſted by his brother George duke of Clarence.

The duke of Somerſet diſpoſed the queen's army in three lines within the intrenchments, and he himſelf commanded the van, that he might ſuſtain the firſt ſhock of the enemy. The ſecond line was commanded by the lord Wenlock, under the prince of Wales, who was conſidered as general in chief; and the rear was conducted by John Courtnay, earl of Devonſhire.

King Edward obſerving that the duke of Somerſet had left ſome openings in the front, thro' which he might ſally; and being well acquainted with the impetuous diſpoſition of that nobleman, directed his brother Glouceſter, who began the attack, to decoy Somerſet from his intrenchments, by giving ground, and retreating with precipitation, until he ſhould ſee Somerſet and his line in the open plain, and then to turn and renew the charge, in which caſe he ſhould be properly ſuſtained.

Glouceſter having received his inſtructions, attacked the intrenchments with great vigour, and meeting with a very warm reception, retired with ſuch hurry and ſeeming confuſion, that Somerſet believing they fled, ſallied out of his intrenchments to purſue them, and at the ſame time ſent orders to lord Wenlock to follow and ſupport him in caſe of emergency. Glouceſter having by this ſtratagem drawn his antagoniſt into the open plain, immediately halted his troops, who inſtantly formed, and he led them back to the charge, which was made with ſo much fury, that the Lancaſtrians, who had begun the purſuit in diſorder, gave way, and retreated with the greateſt precipitation into their intrenchments; upon which the duke of Somerſet, perceiving that lord Wenlock had not made any advance from his ſtation to ſupport the firſt line, was ſo incenſed, that he rode up to him, and cleft his ſkull with a battle ax; and the duke of Glouceſter entering the intrenchments with the fugitives, made a terrible carnage. The young prince of Wales, being then but eighteen years of age, ſeeing all his army in confuſion, did not know on which ſide to turn; and the duke of Somerſet was ſo choaked with indignation, that he could hardly ſpeak, much leſs take the neceſſary ſteps for reducing his troops to order. King Edward following his brother with the ſecond line, compleated the overthrow of the queen's army, which was routed with great ſlaughter, the ſecond and third lines having run away without ſtriking a blow.

The earl of Devonſhire, ſir John Beaufort, brother to the duke of Somerſet, ſir John Delves, and other great men, were found among the dead, which amounted to 3000 men. The duke of Somerſet, John Langſtrother, great prior of St. John, ſir Humphry Handley, ſir Edmund Havarde, ſir William Wickingham, ſir John Leukenor, ſir William Vaule, ſir Gervaſe Clifton, ſir William Carr, ſir Henry Roſs, ſir Thomas Treſham, ſir William Lirmouthe, ſir John Urman, ſir Thomas Seinar, ſir William Rowys, ſir William Newborow, knights; John, ſon of ſir John Delves, Henry Wateley, eſq; Henry Barow, eſq; and —— Fielding, eſq; retired to the abbey church, thinking they ſhould be ſafe in that ſanctuary, from which, however, they were forcibly dragged and executed. The prince of Wales falling into the hands of his enemies, was brought into the preſence of king Edward, who with an air of inſolence demanded how he durſt preſume to enter his kingdom in arms? To this queſtion the prince replied with great fortitude and dignity, That he came to recover his father's crown and his own inheritance, which Edward had unjuſtly uſurped. He had no ſooner pronounced theſe words, than king Edward ſtruck him on the face with his gauntlet and retired, and immediately the dukes of Clarence and Glouceſter, the lord Haſtings and ſir Thomas Grey fell upon him like ſo many wild beaſts, and ſtabbed him in ſeveral places with their daggers. His mother, queen Margaret, being found on the field of battle in a waggon, where ſhe lay almoſt lifeleſs, was ſent priſoner to the tower of London, and kept there about four years, 'till the king of France redeemed her for 50,000 crowns.

The prince of Wales is ſuppoſed to have been murdered in the houſe belonging to, and in the poſſeſſion of Mr. Webb, an ironmonger; and the open plain where the battle was fought, is now called Glaſton meadow.

This town had ſome ſhare alſo in the military tranſactions in the reign of king Charles the Firſt, of which Corbet gives the following account: 'Sir William Vavaſour, ſir Walter Pye, and 'colonel Wroughton poſſeſſed themſelves of the 'town of Tewkeſbury on behalf of the king, and 'fortified it after the ſiege of Glouceſter. But 'before that ſiege, the king's forces under ſir 'Matthew Carew were poſſeſſed of Tewkeſbury, 'which they quitted on the firſt news of the 'Welch army being made priſoners near Glou'ceſter, and in leſs than twelve hours the town 'of Tewkeſbury was repoſſeſſed by the parlia'ment's forces, who immediately received an 'alarm, that the former forces were returned with 'a greater power: 'Twas a gallant brigade of 'horſe, commanded by lord Grandiſon, which 'came from Cheltenham. Captain Fiennes, with 'his party, had certainly been ſurprized by them, 'but for a ridiculous accident. Lord Grandiſon 'meeting with a man going from the town about 'a mile off, queſtioned him whether any forces 'were there, of what ſtrength, and by whom 'commanded. The man ſuppoſing them part 'of the parliament's forces, and willing to curry 'favour, talked of vaſt numbers, great ſtrength, 'and defied the cavaliers with much affected 'indignation. Upon this, they held a council of 'war, and were once about to turn back. This 'delay gave an hour's reſpite to thoſe within to 'prepare for flight, who had no ſooner recovered 'the end of the town, than the horſe entered it 'at the other, amazed to ſee themſelves ſo miſer'ably deluded.

'This town was afterwards fortified by the 'king's party, and became a bad neighbour to 'Glouceſter, the parliament's head garriſon; 'wherefore governor Maſſie, on the 5th of June, 'in the year 1644, with one hundred and twenty 'horſe, about thirty dragoons, and three hun'dred foot, reſolved to attempt the taking of it. 'The horſe and dragoons, commanded by major 'Hammond, advanced ſome few hours before 'the foot and atillery, and were to alarm the 'enemy 'till the foot came up. They made 'a halt about a mile from the town, and drew 'out a pretty ſtrong forlorn hope, conceiving 'they might poſſibly ſurprize them, if they had 'not as yet taken the alarm. And firſt, three 'men were ſent before to eſpy if the draw-bridge 'were down, and ſix more behind went undiſ'covered; next unto theſe marched the forlorn 'hope, and the main body in the rear. In this 'poſture they advanced up to the town, where 'they found the bridge down, the guards ſlender, 'the enemy without intelligence, and ſupinely 'negligent. On went the firſt party, killed the 'centinels, a pikeman, and a muſketier without 'match, and made good the bridge. The forlorn 'hope ruſhed in, and after them a full body of 'horſe and dragoons fell upon the guards, came 'up to the main guard before the alarm was 'taken, overturned their ordnance, and charged 'through the ſtreets as far as the bridge, Wor-

'ceſter-

'cester-way, where they took major Myn, governor of the town. The enemy threw down their arms, many escaped by flight, and many were taken prisoners. Of the king's party, colonel Godfrey, the quarter-master-general, and a lieutenant, with a few private soldiers, were slain in the first charge. But the parliament's forces dismounting, and neglecting to make good the bridge at which they entered, and to disarm the main guard, the latter at length took courage, charged some of them, and beat them out of the town. However, colonel Massie coming up with a few horse in the van of the foot, ordered the dragoons to fire on those that defended the works at the bridge next Gloucester, whilst he drew the foot round the town, it being now dark night; but before he could reach the further end, where he entered about midnight, the garrison were fled towards Worcester. There were found in the town two brass drakes, eighteen barrels of powder, and a few other military stores. The town itself was of great consequence to the parliament, as a frontier town, securing that side of the county, and commanding a great part of Worcestershire.'

In these actions several very extraordinary defects in generalship are observable in both parties, for which the time it relates to was remarkable. Both officers and men were mostly unexperienced countrymen, whom the confusion of action had bereft of memory and understanding; and whilst they were busied in every thing, could hardly effect any thing.

Having done with military affairs, it will not be improper to take notice of some other remarkable incidents that have happened here, as I find them recorded in the *Black Book* belonging to the corporation.

In 1586, there was a dearth in this country that bordered upon famine, and the justices of the peace joined with the bailiffs of the town to abridge the liberty of buying grain; and malting was intirely prohibited. And again in 1595, grain was so high before the harvest, that proclamations were published to restrain the prices to the rates they were at two months before. In 1597, wheat was at 12*s.* 6*d.* the bushel; barley at 8*s.* malt at 8*s.* and beans at 8*s.* which were excessive prices, considering the scarcity of money. During those times, the citizens of Gloucester stretched a chain across the Severn, that no vessel with provisions might pass beyond them; but the town of Tewkesbury petitioning the lords of the privy council, they caused the chain to be taken down. Pestilence commonly succeeds to famine, and accordingly the plague made its appearance the following year, tho' it carried off about forty persons only at that time; but four years afterwards it raged very furiously, when no less than 560 persons died of it within the year. And breaking out again in 1603, all those that died of it, says the book, 'to avoid the perill, were buried in coffins of bourde'; which shews that wood coffins were not then commonly in use.

It stands upon the credit of the same manuscript, that in 1604, there was so great a drought, that the river Avon was dry from Whitsuntide to Bartholomew-tide following; and in Wantner's papers in the Bodleyan library, is this very extraordinary story: On July 24, 1571, being fair-day, such a quantity of bats came floating down the Avon at this town, that they covered the surface of the water for above a land's length, in heaps above a foot thick; which so dammed up the mills for three days, that they could not go 'till the bats were dug out with shovels.

The county assizes were held in this town on the 4th of July, 1580, the plague, I suppose, being then at Gloucester. And the bailiffs, in their account with the chamberlain, charged 11*s.* for wine, and 13*s.* 4*d.* for tent, with which they had treated the court and their friends, and these sums were allowed them; which I mention as an example of the frugality of those times. What would two of his majesty's justices think of such a treat now-a-days?

The assizes were held here again, 14 C. 1. before sir Humphry Davenport, chief baron of the exchequer, and sir William Jones, knight; when the court made the following order:

Glouc. ss. WHEREAS a certain bridge called the Long Bridge, lying at the north end of the towne of Tewkesbury, and leading towards the cittie of Worcester, conteining above seven hundred yards in length is growne into great decay, and so hath beene for many yeeres last past, by reason whereof divers of his Majesties subjects travelling that way have beene unfortunately drowned: And for that it doth not appeare who in the memory of man have repayred the said bridge, nor who by law ought to do itt: Therefore to the end so necessary a worke should bee effected, IT IS ORDERED by assent, that the county of Gloucester shall forthwith rayse by way of contribution a competent some of money towards the repayre of the said bridge, which being once effected, the corporation of Tewkesbury doth offer to keepe and mainteyne the same: PROVIDED that the contribution of the whole county with the parish of Tewkesbury be no prejudice to the county, nor drawne into example for the future.

Per Curiam.

The town was divided into five wards in the year 1596, over which two high constables presided. They were 1. *Bridge-ward.* 2. *Church-ward.* 3. *Barton-ward.* These three had each a petty constable. 4. *St. Mary's-ward,* with two petty constables. 5. The *Middle-ward,* which the high

high constables themselves took charge of. There are now only four constables for the borough.

It consists of three principal streets, beside lanes. The High-street is of great length, sufficiently spacious and handsome, and well paved on each side for the convenience of walking. It leads from the town hall northwards towards Worcester. The modern houses are built of brick, and the more antient ones of timber, as there is very little stone for building in this part of the country. Not long since, the roads about the town were so founderous, that a carriage could not possibly pass; but for the last twenty years, the representatives of the borough have given large sums towards putting them in repair, and the turnpikes now support them.

This town had formerly some share in the clothing business, but that has been long since lost. Its chief trade, at present, is malting, stocking-frame knitting, especially of cotton, and a little nailing. But the making of mustard-balls, as taken notice of in every book that treats of this place, has been so long discontinued, as not to be within the remembrance of any person living.

Here are five yearly fairs, *viz.* on St. Matthew's day, on the 3d of May, the 11th of June, the 24th of August, and the 29th of September; and two weekly markets, on Wednesday and Saturday, which are plentifully supply'd from the rich country round about; so that provisions are generally cheaper here than in any other part of the county.

Of the Manor and other Estates.

Domesday gives the following ample account of this large manor:

'In Teodechesberie were fourscore and fifteen 'hides in the time of king Edward. Of these 'forty-five were in demean, and free from all 'royal service and tax, except the service due to 'the lord of the manor. The manor was in *capite*. 'There were in demean twelve plow-tillages, and 'fifty between the *servi* and *ancillæ*, and six-'teen bordars in waiting about the hall, and two 'mills of 20 *sol.* and one fishery, and a salt-pit at 'Wich belonging to the manor.

'There were three hides at Sudwich, six in 'Trotintune, six in Fitentone, eight in Pamintonie, 'three and a half in Natone, three in Waltone, 'and six in Estone. There were twenty-one 'villeins, and nine radchenisters, having twenty-'six plow-tillages, and five *coliberti*, and one bor-'dar, with five plow-tillages. These radchenisters 'plowed and harrowed for the sustenance of the 'lord's court.

'There were eight burgesses in Glouuecestre, 'paying 5 *sol.* and 4 *den.* and doing service at the 'court.

'In all Teodechesberie there are 120 acres of 'meadow, and a wood one mile and a half long, 'and as much broad.

'There are now thirteen burgesses at Teodekes-'berie, paying 20 *sol.* a year; a market established 'by the queen, pays 11 *sol.* and 8 *den.* And there 'is one plow-tillage more, and twenty-two be-'tween the *servi* and *ancillæ*; a fishery, and a 'salt-pit at Wich.

'Three radchenisters belonged [to the estate] 'there in the time of king Edward. One of them 'held six hides in Estone, which Girard now 'holds. Another held three hides in Waltone, 'which Radulf now holds. The third held two 'hides in Fitentone, which Bernard holds. In 'these eleven hides, ten plow-tillages are in de-'mean, and there are four villeins, and one bor-'dar, and nine *servi*, with one plow-tillage. There 'are eighteen acres of meadow. The whole was 'worth 10 *lib.* in the time of king Edward, and 'it is worth as much now.

'There was a country-seat, and five hides at 'Oxendone, belonging to Teodekesberie, in the 'time of king Edward. There are five plow-'tillages in demean, and five villeins, and two 'radchenisters, having seven plow-tillages, and 'twelve between the *servi* and *ancillæ*. There 'are twenty-four acres of meadow. At Wince-'combe are three burgesses paying 40 *den.* All 'this manor is worth and was worth 8 *lib.*'

'There are four hides in Hanlege, belonging 'to the same manor of Teodekesberie, without 'demean, but there were two plow-tillages in 'demean in the time of king Edward, and forty 'among the villeins and bordars, and eight among 'the *servi* and *ancillæ*, and a mill of 16 *d.* a wood 'in which there is an inclosure. This was earl 'William's estate, but it now belongs to the king's 'farm in Hereford. It was worth 15 *lib.* in the 'time of king Edward, now only 10 *lib.*

'Nine hides in Fortemeltone belonged to this 'manor. There are two plow-tillages in demean, 'and twenty among the villeins and bordars, 'and six among the *servi* and *ancillæ*; and a 'wood. It was worth 10 *lib.* in the time of king 'Edward, and is now worth 8 *lib.* Earl William 'held these two estates, and paid tax on account 'of Tedekesberie.

'Ten hides in Senendone belong to the same 'manor. There are four plow-tillages, and eight 'villeins, and four bordars, and five radchenisters, 'with eight plow-tillages. There are twelve '*servi*, and a mill of 3 *sol.* This estate pays tax 'for seven hides. It was worth 20 *lib.* in the time 'of king Edward, now only 8 *lib.* It is now in 'the king's hands, and Robert de Olgi farms it.

'Seven hides in Clifort belong to the same 'manor. There are three plow-tillages in de-'mean, and fourteen villeins, with five plow-'tillages, and a mill of 12 *sol.* and two acres of 'meadow. There were thirteen among the *servi* 'and *ancillæ*; and a church, and a priest with 'one plow-tillage. It was worth 8 *lib.* now only '6 *lib.* The queen gave this estate to Roger de 'Busli, and it paid tax for four hides in Tedeches-'berie.

'The

'The fifty hides above-mentioned, made up 'the fourfcore and fifteen hides which belonged 'to Tedechefberie, quit and free from all tax 'and royal fervice.

'This manor of Tedekefberie, when intire in 'the time of king Edward, was worth 100 *lib.* 'whereas Radulf received 12 *lib.* becaufe it was 'fpoiled and difordered. Radulf is now rated '40 *l.* neverthelefs he pays 50 *lib.*

'Brictric the fon of Algar held this manor in 'the time of king Edward, and at that time had 'the underwritten eftates of other thanes under 'his jurifdiction.

'One thane held a manor of four hides in 'Effetone. Girard holds it now, and has there 'one plow-tillage, and two villeins, with one 'plow-tillage. It is worth and was worth 40 *fol.*

'Let held a manor of eight hides in Chenemer-'tone. Girard holds it now, and has there three 'plow-tillages, and fourteen villeins, with four 'plow-tillages. There are eight *fervi*, and three 'mills of 15 *fol.* It was worth 8 *lib.* now only 6 *lib.*

'Three hides in Botintone belong to this 'manor. The fame Girard holds them, and has 'there two plow-tillages, and four villeins, with 'three plow-tillages. And there are three *fervi*, 'and a mill of 8 *fol.* and eight acres of meadow. 'It is worth and was worth 40 *fol.*

'A thane held three hides in Wenecote. The 'queen gave this eftate to Rainald the chaplain. 'There are three villeins, with half a plow-tillage. 'It was worth 40 *fol.*

'Dunning held fix hides and a half in Aldri-'tone, and four hides and a half in Dridedone. 'And a thane held one hide in Hundeuuic.

'Hunfrid holds thefe eftates of the king, and 'has there four plow-tillages in demean, and five 'villeins, and eight bordars, with three plow-'tillages, and one radchenifter, with one plow-'tillage, and one burgefs in Wicecombe, and it 'is computed that there are twelve acres of 'meadow. The whole was worth 11 *lib.* in the 'time of king Edward, now only 6 *lib.*

'Four villeins held two hides, and a thane held 'half a hide in Tuninge. There are four plow-'tillages, and three acres of meadow. The queen 'gave this eftate to John the chamberlain. It is 'worth and was worth 35 *fol.*

'Hermer and Aluuin held three hides, lefs one 'yard-land, in Stoches. Bernard holds them now 'of the king, and has there one plow-tillage in 'demean, and four acres of meadow. It was 'worth 60 *fol.* now only 40 *fol.*

'They who held thefe eftates in the time of 'king Edward, were, together with their lands, 'under the jurifdiction of Brictric.' *Dom.* p. 68.

This Brictric was a principal man in his country, and had the honour of Gloucefter, which was a noble feigneury, and many other great eftates, by inheritance from his grandfather, Hailward Snow. Having incurred the difpleafure of Maud, queen to William the Conqueror, and daughter to Baldwin earl of Flanders, by refufing to marry her, when he was ambaffador at her father's court, fhe revenged the infult by procuring his imprifonment, and the confifcation of all his poffeffions.

The large manors of Tewkefbury and Thornbury, and the honour of Gloucefter, were granted to queen Maud, and after her death, continued to be the demeans of the crown, 'till king William the Second granted them to Robert Fitz-Haiman, or Hayman, lord of Corboil and Thorigny in Normandy, kinfman and affiftant to the Conqueror. He married Sybelle, daughter of Roger Montgomery, and fifter of Robert de Belaime, earl of Shrewfbury, and by her had four daughters, Mabelle, Cicily, Hawife, and Amice.

Mabel was married to Robert Melhent, or Fitz-Roy, fometimes called Robert Rufus, conful and earl of Gloucefter. He was natural fon of king Henry the Firft, and had with her not only the manor of Tewkefbury, and all her other paternal eftates, but alfo all the land of Hamo Dapifer her uncle. He died in the year 1147, and left iffue by his faid wife, four fons, William, his fucceffor; Roger, bifhop of Worcefter; Haman, and Philip; and one daughter, named Maud.

William earl of Gloucefter, fon of Robert, fucceeded to the manor of Tewkefbury. He married Hawife, daughter of Robert earl of Leicefter, by whom he had a fon Robert, who died before him; and three daughters, Mabel, Amice, and Ifabel, or rather Avifa.

Ifabel, or Avifa, the youngeft daughter of William earl of Gloucefter, was married to John, commonly called *Sans-Terre*, or Lack-land, fourth fon to king Henry the Second, who had with her this manor, and the whole honour of Gloucefter. He was afterwards king of England, and having no child by his wife was divorced from her in the firft year of his reign. It is faid the king fold her afterwards, with all her lands and fees, except the caftle of Briftol, and the chaces belonging to it, to Geofry de Mandeville, earl of Effex, for 20,000 marks; after whofe death, fhe was married to Hugh de Burgh, juftice of England; but fhe had no iffue by either of her hufbands, whereby

Almeric, fon to the earl of Eureux in Normandy, by Maud, another daughter of William earl of Gloucefter, fucceeded to this manor, and the earldom of Gloucefter. He married the daughter of Hugh de Gournai, but dying without iffue, the manor of Tewkefbury devolved on Amice, the fecond and only furviving daughter of William earl of Gloucefter.

Richard de Clare, earl of Hertford, had married the faid Amice, in whofe right he became earl of Gloucefter, and lord of the manor of Tewkefbury. He was defcended from Giflebert, furnamed Crifpin, earl of Brien in Normandy, fon of Jeffery, who was natural fon to Richard the Firft, duke of Normandy. Richard, the eldeft fon of Giflebert earl of Brien, diftinguifhed himfelf in favour of the

Conqueror in the great battle of Haſtings, and was rewarded with great eſtates in England, and ſeized of thirty-eight manors in Surrey, thirty-five in Eſſex, three in Cambridgeſhire, two in Kent, one in Middleſex, one in Wiltſhire, one in Devonſhire, and ninety-five in Suffolk, of which Clare was the principal, and therefore he was ſometimes ſtiled Richard de Clare; but having purchaſed the caſtle of Tunbridge of the archbiſhop of Canterbury, he was more generally ſtiled Richard de Tonebrugge. He married Roheſe, daughter of Walter Giffard, earl of Buckingham, and was ſlain by the Welch near Abergavenny, about the year 1100. Gilbert, ſon and heir of Richard, married Adeliza, daughter of the earl of Clermont, by whom he had four ſons. Richard de Tonebrugge, or de Clare, was his ſon and heir, and had the title of earl of Hertford. Gilbert, his brother, ſurnamed Strongbow, from his ſtrength in drawing a ſtrong bow, obtained great victories and large territories in Wales. His ſon Richard Strongbow, obtained great victories in Ireland, and was earl of Pembroke and Strigule, now Chepſtow.

But to return to the Clares: Gilbert de Clare was the eldeſt ſon and heir of Richard, and ſucceeded him in the earldom of Hertford, and was alſo ſtiled earl of Clare. He died without iſſue in 1151, and was ſucceeded by Roger his brother, who married Maud, the daughter of James de St. Hillary, and died in 1173.

Richard de Clare, earl of Hertford, was ſon of Roger. He it was that married Amice, the laſt ſurviving daughter of the earl of Glouceſter, as before repreſented, and dying in 1206, was ſucceeded by his ſon and heir

Gilbert de Clare, who was earl of Glouceſter and Hertford, and lord of the manor of Tewkeſbury. He married Iſabel, one of the daughters, and afterwards coheir to the earl of Pembroke, and dying 14 H. 3. was buried in the choir of Tewkeſbury church.

Richard de Clare, earl of Glouceſter and Hertford, was ſon and heir of Gilbert. He married Maud, the eldeſt daughter of John de Lacy, earl of Lincoln, and dying in 1262, was buried in the choir at Tewkeſbury.

Gilbert de Clare, ſirnamed the Red, from his red hair, was ſon and ſucceſſor to the above Richard. He married the daughter of Guy earl of Angouleſme, from whom he was divorced; and then married Joan d'Acres, daughter of king Edward the Firſt, and dying in 1295, left iſſue by her his ſon and heir,

Gilbert de Clare, earl of Glouceſter and Hertford, who being ſlain at the battle of Bannockſburn in Scotland, 7 E. 2. without iſſue, his three ſiſters became his heirs. The inquiſition after his death, found, among other things, that he died ſeized of a park here, containing eighty acres, whoſe underwood and herbage were worth 30*s.* a year; of four hundred and ſixty acres of arable land, at 4*d.* the acre; of eighty-five acres and a half of meadow, at 2*s.* and of fifty acres of paſture, at 1*s.* the acre; of the rent of free tenants, 12*l.* 12*s.* 3*d.* of a mill worth 20*s.* of De la Home farm, *in manu cuſtomaria*, which paid 11*s.* 8*d.* of a meſſuage which the chaplain of Ayſhchurch held, worth 5*s.* of a meſſuage which Walter —— held, worth 4*s.* and of the More farm, worth 16*s.* a year: That there were one hundred and fourteen burgages and a half, and a quarter part of a burgage, which paid 6*l.* 7*s.* 10*d.* and that the burgeſſes rented lands within the hundred of the ſaid town, containing ſeventy acres and a half, and a third part of an acre, at 35*s.* 5*d.* and paid 20*s.* *per ann.* for a cuſtom called *Fulſtall*, and 12*s.* *per ann.* for ſtallage. That there were forty-ſeven cuſtomary lands and a half, every one of which was a virgate, and held in villeinage. That the total value of the whole manor, with the burg, was 131*l.* 5*s.* 6*d.* that there were two views of frankpledge, at Michaelmas and Eaſter, and the certain fines were 7*l.* 12*s.* The pleas and perquiſites of the court were worth 100*s.* the toll of the burg 100*s.* and the pleas and perquiſites of the ſaid burg, by itſelf, 100*s.* *per ann.* *Eſch.*

Hugh le Deſpencer the younger married Elianor, the eldeſt ſiſter of the laſt mentioned Gilbert, 7 E. 2. and in right of his wife, had livery of the manor of Tewkeſbury. But he dying an untimely death, as already related, left iſſue four ſons, Hugh, Edward, Gilbert, and Philip; and one daughter, the wife of Richard Fitz- Alan, earl of Arundel. Eleanor wife of the ſaid Hugh le Deſpencer ſurvived him, and was afterwards married to William la Zouch of Mortimer, and died ſeized of Tewkeſbury, Fairford, Sodbury, and Archer Stoke, June 30, 1337.

The reader may ſee a larger detail of the foregoing lords of this manor p. 93, under the account of the earls of Glouceſter.

Hugh le Deſpencer, ſon of the laſt mentioned Hugh, by Elianor his wife, married Elizabeth, widow of Giles de Badleſmere, and daughter of William de Montacute, earl of Saliſbury. He was ſummoned as a peer to parliament, but died without iſſue, ſeized of Tewkeſbury, Fairford, &c. Elizabeth his wife ſurvived him, and was endowed with the manor of Tewkeſbury, and was afterwards married to Guy de Brien, and died Feb. 8, 1349, 23 E. 3. *Collins's Peerage.*

Edward le Deſpencer was brother of the laſt Hugh, and ſecond ſon of Hugh le Deſpencer the younger, by Elianor his wife. He died in 1342, leaving by Anne his wife, daughter of Henry lord Ferrers of Groby, three ſons, Edward, heir to his uncle; Thomas le Deſpencer; and Henry, the warlike biſhop of Norwich.

Sir Edward, the eldeſt ſon, was made knight of the garter, and ſummoned to parliament among the barons 31 E. 3. He wedded Elizabeth, daughter and heir of ſir Bartholomew de Berghurſt, and dying at Caerdiff Nov. 11, 1375, was buried on the ſouth ſide of Tewkeſbury church, before the door of the veftry, leaving two fons, Thomas, his heir; and Hugh le Defpencer; and five daughters. His lady built the chapel of the Holy Trinity, in memory of him, and died in July 1409, endowed with a very great eftate in Wales, and with the manors of Tewkefbury and Fairford.

Thomas le Defpencer, fon of Edward, was created earl of Gloucefter. He married Conftance, daughter of Edmund de Langley, duke of York, fifth fon of king Edward the Third, and confpiring with the earls of Kent, Salifbury, and Huntingdon, to dethrone king Henry the Fourth, was taken and beheaded at Briftol, as more particularly related in the account of Cirencefter. He had by his faid lady, one fon Richard, who being under age at his father's death, was granted in ward to Edward duke of York, who married him to Elizabeth, daughter of Ralph Nevil, earl of Weftmoreland; but he died before he was fourteen years old, without iffue. Earl Thomas had alfo two daughters; Elizabeth, who died an infant; and Ifabel, born after her father's death, who was married to Richard Beauchamp, lord Bergavenny, and earl of Worcefter; who, in right of his wife, had livery of the manor of Tewkefbury 2 H. 5. but dying foon after, Ifabel his widow was married, by difpenfation from the pope, to Richard de Beauchamp, earl of Warwick.

This Richard de Beauchamp, earl of Warwick, had a large paternal eftate, befides great poffeffions which came by his mother, who was fifter and coheirefs of Thomas earl of Arundel; and now marrying Ifabel, who was the fole heirefs of the family of the Defpencers, he was feized of a vaft eftate. This earl was eminent not only for his wealth, but acknowledged by the emperor of Germany, and other foreign princes, to exceed all his cotemporaries in wifdom, valour, and courtefy. He was governor of Calais, and gained great honour to the Englifh nation by his generous and fplendid way of living. His firft wife was Elizabeth, heirefs to Thomas lord Berkeley, by whom he had three daughters, all married into noble families. He died 17 H. 6. and was buried at the collegiate church at Warwick, leaving iffue by his fecond wife Ifabel, one fon Henry, and one daughter Anne.

Which Henry de Beauchamp, earl of Warwick, was fourteen years old at his father's death, and was crowned king of the ifle of Wight by the king's own hand, and at the age of nineteen, was created duke of Warwick. He married Cecily, daughter of Richard Nevil, earl of Salifbury, and had by her an only child Anne, who died an infant; and the duke himfelf was taken away by death, in the twenty-fecond year of his age, 23 H. 6. leaving Anne, his fifter, fole heirefs to all his great inheritance.

Which Anne was married to Richard Nevil, earl of Salifbury, defcended from Gilbert de Nevil, who came into England with king William, commonly called the Conqueror, and was progenitor to the earls of Weftmoreland. But Richard Nevil, father of this Richard, marrying Alice, daughter and heir of Thomas de Montacute, earl of Salifbury, Richard the fon was created earl of Salifbury, and was afterwards, in right of his wife, earl of Warwick. He is celebrated in the Englifh annals for his power and martial atchievements, and commonly called the *Stout Earl of Warwick*, and the *King Maker*; for king Henry the Sixth and king Edward the Fourth held the crown by turns, as this earl favoured the fide; but he was at laft killed at the battle of Barnet, April 14, 1471, wherein, and in the battle fought a few days after at this place, king Edward fecured the crown to himfelf. This great earl was buried at the monaftery of Bifham in Berkfhire, leaving iffue by his countefs Anne, the great heirefs, two daughters, Ifabel, (by fome called Alice) and Anne.

Ifabel, the eldeft daughter, was married to George duke of Clarence, brother to king Edward the Fourth, who was afterwards attainted by act of parliament, and drowned in a butt of Malmefey wine, (his brother, Richard duke of Gloucefter, affifting at the execution) and was buried at Tewkefbury. His children were Edward Plantagenet, earl of Warwick, and Margaret countefs of Salifbury. Edward was beheaded, unmarried, 15 H. 7. in the 24th year of his age, for a pretended confpiracy with Perkin Warbeck; for the king viewed him with a jealous eye, as being the only heir male of the houfe of York. Margaret his fifter was wedded to fir Richard Pole, and was beheaded 33 H. 8. upon an act of attainder paffed againft her for correfponding with her fon cardinal Reginald Pole.

Anne, the younger daughter of Richard earl of Salifbury and Warwick, was married, firft, to king Henry the Sixth's only fon, Edward prince of Wales, who being made prifoner at the battle of Tewkefbury, May 4, 1471, was bafely affaffinated by Richard duke of Gloucefter. She was afterwards married to the murderer, and by him had Edward prince of Wales, who died in 1484, in the eleventh year of his age, not long before his mother; who is faid to have been poifoned by Richard to facilitate his intended marriage with his niece the princefs Elizabeth, afterwards queen to king Henry the Seventh. The acts of cruelty and inhumanity which are related of this duke are not to be parallelled in the Englifh annals. He procured the murder of his two nephews, the fons of king Edward the Fourth, to make way for himfelf to the crown; and having thus glorioufly attained it, fell himfelf a victim to juftice in a decifive battle at Bofworth-field in Leicefterfhire, about two years afterwards, when king Henry the Seventh was victorious, and obtainted the crown.

King Edward the Fourth had procured an act of parliament to diveft Anne, the great heirefs, of her large inheritance, after the death of her hufband huſband the earl of Warwick, and had ſettled it on her daughters and their iſſue; but king Henry the Seventh obtaining the crown, alledged the injuſtice of it, and procured another act, in the beginning of his reign, to reinſtate the mother. The king pretended juſtice, but was actuated by intereſt, and prevailed with the counteſs dowager to levy a fine of her eſtate, and ſettle it on himſelf, which ſhe did 3 H. 7. and died two years afterwards; whereby that large eſtate came to the crown, and amongſt many other manors, the following were in Glouceſterſhire: Tewkeſbury, Stoke-Archer, Whittington, Fairford, Sodbury, Tredington, Pamington, Fidington, Northway, the Mythe, King's Barton near Briſtol, Barton hundred, Kemmerton, Chedworth, and Lidney.

The manor of Tewkeſbury was granted from the crown to ſir Thomas Seymour 1 E. 6. and upon his attainder reverted back again; and was again granted, with the borough, and with many free tenements, Severnham, and other lands, to the corporation of Tewkeſbury 7 Jac. who are the preſent lords of the manor.

TITHINGS and *HAMLETS.*

1. The *Mythe*, and part of *Mythe-Hook*, ſituated a little northward of the town. Mr. Richard Jackſon, and Mr. William Buckle, have both very good houſes in this hamlet, and are proprietors of the greateſt part of the lands within it. Their houſes ſtand on high ground, on the weſt ſide of the Avon, and command a fine proſpect over the rivers, and the neighbouring vale.

Mythe-wood, now intirely aſſarted, formerly belonged to the abbey of Tewkeſbury, to which it was given by Gilbert de Clare, earl of Glouceſter and Hertford, in the year 1230; and the abbey obtained a licence to incloſe the wood 47 E. 3. The manor of Mythe belonged ſucceſſively to the lords of the manor of Tewkeſbury, and ſir Thomas Seymour had a grant of it, wherein it was called Warwick's lands, 1 E. 6. After lord Seymour's attainder, it reverted to the crown, and was granted, together with Mythe-Hook, and a meadow called King's Mead, a fiſhery in the Severn, and another in the Avon, to Daniel Pert, and Alexander Pert, in truſt, 7 E. 6. And it is now divided amongſt ſeveral freeholders.

2. *Southwick.* This hamlet is briefly mentioned in the large extract from *Domeſday*, ſtanding at the beginning of the account of the manor of Tewkeſbury.

Robert le Pearl was ſeized of lands in Supiſhull and Southwick 37 E. 3. Sir John Tracy was alſo ſeized of the manor of Southwick 37 E. 3. It afterwards belonged to the abbey of Tewkeſbury, and together with lands called Goſebuts, was granted to Thomas Stroud, Walter Earl, and James Paget, 36 H. 8. A cloſe in Southwick, called Panter's, was granted to Walter Compton; and lands in Southwick, in the tenure of John Jones, were granted to John Pope, 36 H. 8. Lands called Culverhouſe, in Southwick, were granted to Edward Cooper and Valentine Fairweather, 7 E. 6. Lands called Dearhurſt Place, in Southwick, were granted to William Read, and John Read, 7 E. 6. Other lands called Walton's Field, in Southwick, were granted to William Fitz-Williams, and Arthur Hilton, 7 E. 6.

Of the Abbey of Tewkeſbury.

It is not to be expected that in the hiſtory of this abbey, which according to all accounts was founded above a thouſand years ago, there ſhould be every particular recorded to make it complete. There is indeed a large account of it in the *Monaſticon*, chiefly collected from the Chronicle of Tewkeſbury, in the Cotton Library, and from the writings of William of Malmeſbury, and of Ordericus Vitalis, whence the following is chiefly extracted.

Odo and Dodo were two noble dukes of Mercia, who flouriſhed in the reigns of Ethelred, Kenred, and Ethelbald, kings of Mercia, and were poſſeſſed of large eſtates in various parts. About the year 715, theſe noblemen founded a monaſtery, to the honour of the virgin Mary, upon their own eſtate near the Severn, where, ſays the Chronicle, a certain hermit, called *Theocus*, had made his abode, from whom the place was called *Tewxbury*: And they granted the manor of Stanway, with its members, and other ſmaller poſſeſſions, for the maintenance of the monks, who were few in number, not exceeding four or five, placed under the government of a prior, to live after the rule of St. Benedict. Theſe noble perſons dying, were buried in the church of Perſhore, to which they had been great benefactors, as they alſo had been to ſeveral other monaſteries, built by themſelves or their anceſtors.

From this time, for almoſt a century, we have no certain account who had the patronage of this little monaſtery, which it is ſaid ſuffered, with others, by the civil wars that diſtracted Britain during the heptarchy, and from the incurſions of the Danes. The monks were often driven away, the monaſtery plundered, and twice conſumed by fire.

In the year 800, Hugh, a great nobleman of Mercia, was patron of this priory, and Brictric, king of the Weſt Saxons, dying the preceding year, was buried, by his procurement, in the chapel of St. Faith there; and the ſame Hugh dying in the year 812, was himſelf buried in this priory.

Here again is a large vacancy in our account, for I find nothing material mentioned of this monaſtery 'till about the year 930, when there flouriſhed a noble knight called Haylward, or Ailward, ſurnamed *Snew*, or *Snow*, from his fair complexion. He was royally deſcended from king Edward the Elder, and was patron of this priory. He founded a ſmall monaſtery on his demean lands at Cranbourn in the county of Dorſet,

Dorfet, and fubjected the priory of Tewkefbury to that abbey, where at length he was buried. His wife's name was Algive, by whom he had a fon Algar, father of that Brictric fo often mentioned in *Domefday*, as proprietor of many large eftates in Gloucefterfhire; and he was alfo lord of the vaft feigneury of Gloucefter. This Brictric finifhed and much enlarged the church of Cranbourn, which was founded by his anceftors.

At the conqueft of Britain by William duke of Normandy, Brictric's perfon was feized and imprifoned, and all his eftates confifcated by that monarch, as already more largely related in the defcent of the manor of Tewkefbury, and other parts of this work. By which means the patronage of the before-mentioned monafteries was vefted in the crown, and fo continued during that reign; but in the next, William Rufus gave the honour of Gloucefter, and all Brictric's eftates, with the patronage of thefe monafteries, to Robert Fitz-Haimon; and from that time the latter was vefted in the great lords of the manor of Tewkefbury. And as they have been already fet down in the account of the manor, the reader is referred to that account, as it would be equally tedious and unneceffary to go over them again. I fhall therefore take notice, in this place, of fuch of them only who have been

Particular Benefactors to the Abbey.

In the year 1102, the above Robert Fitz-Hamon, or Haimon, at the inftance of his wife Sybil, and of Girald the abbat of Cranbourn, rebuilt and enlarged the church of Tewkefbury, with all the offices, and endowed it with many lands, rents, and large poffeffions. And becaufe it was thought to exceed Cranbourn in fruitfulnefs of foil, and pleafantnefs of fituation near a navigable river, he removed abbat Girald and his monks from Cranbourn to Tewkefbury, leaving only a prior and two monks at the former, to keep up the memory of the founders of that church, which was now reduced to a priory, and made fubject in future to that of Tewkefbury, thus advanced to the high honour of an abbey. At the fame time the following charter of ordination was made, and entered in the Regifter-book of the abbey. *Stevens*, V. 2. *Appendix*, 206.

Carta Ordinationis Ecclefiæ Theokefburienfis, tempore Giraldi Abbatis, & Roberti filii Haimonis.

IN nomine Patris & Filii & Spiritus Sancti, Amen. Ordinata eft Ecclefia Sanctæ Mariæ Theokefburienfis Cœnobii. Divifa funt viz. ejufdem Ecclefiæ quæque Minifteria; & nominatim funt diftributa quæque quibufque & fingulis minifteriis pertinentia in eifdem minifteriis perpetualiter, quamdiu fcilicet feculum duraverit Deo opitulante firma affertione permanfura & convenienter & divife funt conftituta ad fingulas utilitates Domus Dei regendas & promovenda quæque neceffaria, ficut fubfequenti capitulatione infcribitur. Sunt autem hæc ad Monachorum menfam pertinentia. In ipfa Theodekefburia Molendina duo, pifcaria una, terra de Phytentona, Decima Domini & hominum ejufdem villæ, Decimæ quorundam vicinorum, tertia pars omnium Elemofynarum quæ fiunt in Ecclefia, vel in Capitulo quocunque modo fiunt in eadem Domo Dei, præter Confuetudines Parochiæ, Ecclefia Sancti Petri de Briftol, Obedentia de Wallis præter terram quæ fuit Walchelini Belingehopa, juxta Hereford, Waffeburna, Stanleya, Staneweya, Tatintona, Leomintona, Amenel, Altentuna, Werftona, Tarenta. Hoc autem Manerium Tarenta dedit Abbas ejufdem Ecclefiæ nomine Gyraldus, prece Roberti filii Haymonis ad emendationem victus Monachorum die hujus ordinationis. Unde tunc definita fuit fore cotidiana melioratio victus eorum 12*d.*

Erant vero tunc in Ecclefia Monachi numero 57.

Ad veftes Monachorum pertinet Ecclefia de Wairford, terra de Middelonda, omnes Ecclefiæ quæ fuerunt Roberti Capellani, Kingeftona, poftquam Cœnobium edificatum fuerit. De manu Abbatis centum folidi, donec conftituantur in terra.

Ad fecretariam pertinent omnes confuetudines Parochiæ, præter Decimas. De Elemofyna Dominici 40*s.* tertia pars omnium extrinfecarum Elemofynarum quæ fiunt in eadem Ecclefia.

Ad emendum Parcamentum, pertinet quædam terra in Wallis quæ fuit Walchelini, Decima Roberti de Bafkereville.

Ad Elemofynam pertinet Ceotel in Dorfete, terra de Pequemintona, una Haya ad Wyncelcumbam, Decima totius victus Coenobii, Decima Cenfus de Briftol.

Cæteri redditus & terræ quas privilegium Ecclefiæ nominando diftinguit, ad emendum terras, ornamenta, ad fupplenda omnia deficientia prædictorum, ad agenda quælibet opera, ad explendas omnes res Abbatis ordinantur.

Facta eft hæc Ordinatio a prædicto Abbate monitu & confilio Roberti filii Haymonis ejufdem Ecclefiæ Fundatoris & Domini, ipfo præfente & Sibilia uxore fua, atque filia fua Mabilia, Gylbertoque de Deulframvilla, Ricardo de Croyle, multifque aliis, prefente etiam toto Conventu ipfius Ecclefiæ, 5° Kal. Octobris, anno fcilicet ab Incarnatione Domini 1105: quo eodem Henricus Rex Anglorum deftruxit Baiocas incendio. Hujus Ordinationis Violatorem, fi forte ullo tempore furrexerit, excommunicavit eodem die Abbas prædictus ut a confortio cœlefti feparatus in pœnis gehennalibus permaneat fine fine cruciandus, nifi fatiffaciens recipuerit, toto Conventu Ecclefiæ & omnibus qui aderant refpondentibus AMEN.

It cannot be eafily conceived, fays William of Malmefbury, how much Robert Fitz-Haimon adorned and beautified this monaftery, where the ftatelinefs of the buildings ravifhed the eyes, and the pious charity of the monks the affections of all perfons that came thither.

Robert Fitz-Roy, earl of Gloucefter, who married Mabile, the eldeft daughter of Robert Fitz-Haimon, built a priory, dedicated to St. James, on his own demeans at Briftol, endowed it with lands, ornaments, and poffeffions, and made it fubject to the abbey of Tewkefbury. He died in 1147, and William, his fon, confirmed all the charters, confirmations, liberties and donations which his father and all his anceftors had granted to the abbey. Not long afterwards the abbey was burnt down, a common accident in thofe days, but it was foon rebuilt, and the abbat entertained king John, and many of his royal retinue; and Matthew Paris mentions that the fame king afterwards kept his Chriftmas there.

In the year 1230, Gilbert de Clare gave the Mythe wood to the abbey; and about a century afterwards Hugh le Defpencer, the third of that name, amongft other good gifts, appropriated the church of Lantriffa to the abbat and convent in fucceffion, from which they received fifty marks annually.

Guido de Brien, who lived in the reign of king Edward the Third, alfo appropriated certain rents in Briftol, and annexed the profits to the office of Sacrift in Tewkefbury, and to the prieft who fhould fay the firft mafs for the faid Guido every day at the altar of St. Margaret, in the church there, with thefe prayers, *God of his mercy, &c.* for his furviving kindred; and *Incline, O Lord, &c.* for the dead kindred; the mafs of the *Trinity* on Sunday; the mafs of the *Holy Ghoft* on Monday; the mafs of St. *Thomas* on Tuefday; the mafs of the *Holy Rest* on Wednesday; the mass of the *Ascension* on Thursday; the mass of the *Holy Cross* on Friday; the mass of St. *Mary* on Saturday; and whatever priest should so officiate for a week, should receive 21 *d.* and whosoever should celebrate mass on his anniversary day, or on the anniversary of his wife Elizabeth, if the abbat, he should receive 5 *s.* if the prior 3 *s.* 4 *d.* who reads the Gospel on those days should have 8 *d.* who reads the Epistle should have 8 *d.* who holds the paten 8 *d.* the præcentor and his two assistants 8 *d.* a piece; the prior 12 *d.* and every monk should have 4 *d.*

Edward le Despencer, great grandson of Hugh earl of Winchester, gave a gold cup to the monastery, and a precious jewel, says the Chronicle, neatly contrived, to hold the sacrament on solemn days. And the lady Elizabeth, his wife, gave a suit of scarlet vestments, embroidered with lions of gold; *viz.* one coat with three royal robes and white vestments, and fifteen mantles or copes.

Isabel countess of Warwick gave three hundred marks a year to this abbey, that six monks more might be added to pray for her soul, and for the souls of her ancestors and successors. She also gave all the ornaments which she wore when alive, valued at three hundred marks, and procured the church of Tarrande in the diocese of Salisbury, and the church of Penmarshe in the diocese of Landaffe, to be appropriated to the abbey.

Robert de Chandos, in the year 1113, founded the church of Goldclive, for a prior and twelve brethren, to follow the rule of St. Benedict, and made it subject to the abbey of Bec in Normandy; but after his death, the patronage of Goldclive priory was seized by the crown, and held by the kings of England 'till the reign of king Henry the Sixth. This king granted the patronage to Henry duke of Warwick, and the priory itself to the abbat and monks of Tewkesbury, in the year 1442; and king Henry confirmed all former donations to the church of Tewkesbury at the same time. The duke also gave the church of Sherston to this abbey, and all the ornaments which he wore, to make vestments for the monks.

Richard Nevil, earl of Salisbury and Warwick, confirmed the appropriation of the church of Sherston, and all former charters which the duke of Warwick had granted, particularly that of fishing in the Severn, the Avon, and in the Taff at Caerdiff.

The royal charters and confirmations to this church are printed in the Appendix to this book, N°. 25. And various other charters of donations, confirmations, compositions, and instruments of less consequence, copied out of the Register-book of the abbey, are published in Mr. Stevens's *Supplement to the Monasticon*, V. 2. Appendix N°. CLXI. from 1 to 86.

Abbats, from Mr. Willis's Catalogue.

1. Giraldus, formerly a monk of Winchester. He was brought hither from Cranbourn in the year 1104, and made the first abbat by Robert Fitz-Haimon the founder. Not caring to gratifiy the covetous disposition of king Henry the First, he was forced to leave his abbey, and return to Winchester, as appears by the annals of that monastery, published in the *Anglia Sacra*; whereupon, the year following

2. Robert was made abbat. He died in 1124, and was succeeded by

3. Benedict, who dying *anno* 1137, was also succeeded the same year by

4. Roger, sometimes called Robert, who dying in 1161,

5. Fromond was made abbat, in whose time the church of Tewkesbury was burnt *anno* 1178; and he died the same year, whereupon there seems to be a vacancy, for

6. Robert, who was the next abbat after him, did not receive the benediction 'till September 29, 1182. After him

7. Alan, prior of Canterbury, was made abbat, and received the benediction 17 Cal. Julij, 1187. He was a man of great learning, and on his death, which happened in the year 1202,

8. Walter became abbat. He dying in 1213, was succeeded by

9. Hugh, who had been prior of this place. He received the benediction from Giles, bishop of Hereford, by the permission of the bishop of Worcester, the year after which he died, and was succeeded by

10. Bernard, one of the monks of this place; but his election not being approved of,

11. Peter, a monk of Worcester, was appointed abbat, and received the benediction April 3, 1216, from the bishop of Worcester. He died in 1232, and was succeeded by

12. Robert, prior of this place, whose surname, as I take it, was Fortington. He died in 1253, and had for his successor

13. Thomas de Stokes, who died in 1275, and was succeeded by

14. Richard de Norton, confirmed abbat in 1276. He died in 1282, and was succeeded the same year by

15. Thomas Kemsey; after whose decease, in the year 1328,

16. John Cotes was made abbat, who dying in 1347,

17. Tho: de Legh was elected abbat Aug. 20, 1347. He died Oct. 17, 1361, and was succeeded the same year by

18. Thomas Chesterton, elected Nov. 24, 1361, who presided thirty-seven years, and dying in 1398, was succeded by

19. Thomas Parker, *alias* Pakare, who was a great benefactor to this monastery; and in the year 1397, caused a very handsome chapel of carved stone work to be erected over the grave of Robert Fitz Haimon, who had been the principal benefactor to the abbey, and was considered as its founder; for whom, and for his wife, this abbat also appointed a mass for the dead to be daily celebrated in perpetual memory of them. Abbat Parker died in 1421, and was succeeded by

20. William Bristow, of whom I know nothing further than that he was in great favour with his patrons, and dying about the year 1442, was succeeded by

21. John Abingdon, who in the year 1443, stood godfather to Anne, daughter of Henry duke of Warwick, but Mr. Willis, by mistake, says it was the daughter of Richard Nevill, earl of Salisbury. When this abbat died I cannot find, neither the institution or death of

22. John de Salis, the next abbat, who occurs in 1468, and was succeeded by

23. John Strensham, in whose time, or his successor's, as I judge, this was made a parliamentary abbey. He died in 1481, and was succeeded by

24. Richard Cheltenham, elected the same year. He re-edified and augmented Stanway manor-place in the time of king Henry the Seventh, and died 1 H. 8.

25. Henery Beoly succeeded in the year 1509. He occurs in 1519, and 1529. It does not appear when he died, but his successor was

26. John Walker, who deceasing in 1531, 23 H. 8. was buried in this abbey church under a marble stone, whereon was his coat of arms affixed. On his death

27. John Wich, *alias* Wakeman, (whom A. Wood calls Robert) succeeded; who continuing 'till the Dissolution, on Jan. 9, 1539, then surrendered up his monastery, with thirty-five of his monks, and obtained a pension of 266 *l.* 13 *s.* 4 *d.* *per ann.* which he gave up on being consecrated, in September 1541, to the see of Gloucester; and there is some further account of him in the catalogue of the bishops of that see, p. 155.

This abbey was the last of the religious foundations in Gloucestershire that surrendered to the king. The introduction to the surrender was the same as most of the rest, and in this form:

'*To all Christian people to whom these presents shall 'come, We the abbat, &c. and brothers of the said 'monastery, send greeting. Know ye that we, upon 'full consideration, certain knowledge, and mere 'motion, and for divers causes just and reasonable, 'moving*

'*moving our ſouls and conſciences, have freely and* '*voluntarily given and granted to our lord the king,* '*&c. &c.*

About half the number of the monks were living and unpreferred in the year 1553, and received the penſions ſet down againſt their names, *viz.* Robert Cireceſter 13*l.* 6*s.* 8*d.* Phill. Cardiff 8*l.* Tho: Newport 7*l.* John Welneforde 6*l.* 13*s.* 4*d.* Richard Winbole 6*l.* Tho. Twining 6*l.* William Stremiſh 6*l.* 13*s.* 4*d.* Robert Aſton 6*l.* 13*s.* 4*d.* John Gates 6*l.* 13*s.* 4*d.* Tho. Briſtow 6*l.* 13*s.* 4*d.* John Hertland 6*l.* 13*s.* 4*d.* Tho. Thornborough 6*l.* 13*s.* 4*d.* Hen. Worceſter 6*l.* 13*s.* 4*d.* Richard Cheltenham 6*l.* 13*s.* 4*d.* Thomas Stanwey 6*l.* 13*s.* 4*d.* John Aſton 6*l.* 13*s.* 4*d.*

In biſhop Burnet's Hiſtory of the Reformation, Vol. 1, p. 151, in the Appendix, is the following inventory of the goods and revenues of this monaſtery, together with an eſtimate of the lands and buildings belonging to it, which is here inſerted as a ſpecimen of the proceedings in ſuppreſſing monaſteries. Dr. Burnet took it from a book in the augmentation office, which begins thus:

'The Certificate of Robert Southwell, Eſq; &c. Will. Petre, 'Edward Kairne, and John London, Doctors of Law; John 'Aprice, John Kingſman, Richard Paulet, and Will. Bernars, 'Eſqs; Commiſſioners aſſigned by the King's Majeſty, to take 'the Surrenders of divers Monaſteries, by force of his Grace's 'Commiſſion to them, ſix, five, four, or three of them, in that 'behalf directed, bearing Date at his Highneſs's Palace of Weſt-'minſter, the 7th Day of November, in the 31st Year of the 'Reign of our moſt dread Sovereign Lord Henry the VIIIth, by 'the Grace of God, King of England and France, Defender of the Faith, Lord of Ireland, and in Earth immediately under 'Chriſt ſupreme Head of the Church of England; of all and 'ſingular their Proceedings, as well in and of theſe Monaſteries 'by his Majeſty appointed to be altered, as of others to be 'diſſolved, according to the Tenours, Purport and Effect of his 'Grace's ſaid Commiſſion; with Inſtructions to them likewiſe 'delivered, as hereafter enſueth.

Co. GLOCESTER.

Teuxbury late monaſtery ſurrendered to the uſe of the king's majeſty, and of his heirs and ſucceſſors for ever, made bearing date under the convent ſeal of the ſame late monaſtery, the 9th day of January, in the 31st year of the reign of our moſt dread victorious ſovereign lord king Henry the 8th; and the ſaid day and year clearly diſſolved and ſuppreſſed.

The clear yearly value of all the poſſeſſions belonging to the ſaid monaſtery, as well ſpiritual as temporal, over and beſides 136*l.* 8*s.* 1*d.* in fees, annuities, and corrodies, granted to divers perſons by letters patents under the convent ſeal of the ſaid late monaſtery, for term of their lives, 1595*l.* 15*s.* 6*d.*

Penſions aſſigned to the late religious diſpatched, That is to ſay, To John Wich, late abbat there, 266*l.* 13*s.* 4*d.* John Beley, late prior there, 16*l.* J. Bromeſgrove, late prior of Dele-hurſt, [*i. e.* Deerhurſt, co. Glouceſter] 13*l.* 6*s.* 8*d.* Robert Circeſter, prior of St. James, [Briſtol] 13*l.* 6*s.* 8*d.* Will. Didcote, prior of Cranbourn, [co. Dorſet] 10*l.* Robert Cheltenham, B.D. 10*l.* two monks 8*l.* a piece, 16*l.* one monk 7*l.* twenty-ſeven monks 6*l.* 13*s* 4*d.* each, 180*l.* in all 551*l* 6*s.* 8*d.* and ſo remains clear 1044*l.* 8*s.* 10*d.*

Records and evidences belonging to the late monaſtery, remain in the treaſury there, under the coſtody of John Whittington, K[t]. the keys thereof being delivered to Richard Paulet receiver.

Houſes and buildings aſſigned to remain undefaced, *viz.* the lodgings called the Newark, leading from the gate to the late abbat's lodging, with Buttery, Pantery, Cellar, Kitchin, Larder, and Paſtry thereto adjoyning; the late abbat's lodging; the Hoſtery; the great gate entering into the court, with the lodging over the ſame; the abbat's Stable, Bakehouſe, Brewhouſe, and Slaughterhouſe; the Almry, Barn, Daryhouſe; the great Barn next Aven; the Maltinghouſe, with the garnes in the ſame, the Oxhouſe in the Barton gate, and the lodging over the ſame, committed to the coſtody of John Whittington K[t].

Deemed to be ſuperfluous, *viz.* the Church, with Chapels, Cloiſter, Chapter-houſe, Miſericord; the two Dormitaries, Infirmary, with chapels and lodgings within the ſame; the Workhouſe, with another houſe adjoyning to the ſame; the convent Kitching; the Library; the old Hoſtery; the chambers, lodgings; the new Hall; the old Parlor, adjoyning to the abbat's lodging, the cellarer's lodging; the Poulter-houſe; the Gardner; the Almary, and all other houſes and lodgings not above reſerved, committed as abovesaid.

Leads remaining upon the choir, iſles, and chapels annext; the cloyſter, chapter-houſe, frater, St. Michael's chapel, Hall's fermory, and gate-houſe, eſteemed to 180 foder.

Bells remaining in the ſteeple there, are 8 poize, by eſtimation 14600 weight.

Jewels reſerved to the uſe of the king's majeſty, *viz.* two mitres garniſhed with gilt rugged pearls, and counterfeit ſtones.

Plate of ſilver reſerved to the ſaid uſe, *viz.* ſilver gilt 329 *oz.* ſilver, parcel gilt 605 *oz.* ſilver white 497 *oz.* Total 1431 *oz.*

Ornaments reſerved to the ſaid uſe, *viz.* one cope of ſilver tiſſue, with one cheſible, and one tunicle of the ſame, one cope of gold tiſſue, with one cles, and two tunicles of the ſame.

Sum of all the ornaments, goods and chattels belonging to the ſaid late monaſtery, ſold by the ſaid commiſſioners, as in a particular book of ſales thereof, made ready to be ſhewed, as more at large may appear, 194*l.* 8*s.*

Payments by the late religious ſervants diſpatched, *viz.* to 38 late religious perſons of the ſaid late monaſtery, of the king's majeſty's reward, 80*l.* 13*s.* 4*d.*

To an 144 late ſervants of the ſaid late monaſtery, for their wages and liveries, 75*l.* 10*s.*

Payments for debts owing to the ſaid late monaſtery, *viz.* To divers perſons for victuals and neceſſaries of them had to the uſe of the ſaid monaſtery, with 10*l.* paid to the late abbat there; for and in full payment of 124*l.* 5*s.* 4*d.* by him to be paid to certain creditors of the ſaid late monaſtery, by covenants made with the aforeſaid commiſſioners, 18*l.* 12*s.* And ſo remains clear, 19*l.* 12*s.* 8*d.*

[Then follows a liſt of ſome ſmall debts owing to and by the ſaid monaſtery, of no conſequence at preſent; and a general account of the livings in their gift, *viz.*]

Co. Glouceſt. 4 parſonages, and 10 vicarages. Co. Wigorn. 2 parſonages, and 2 vicarages. Co. Warwic. 2 parſonages. Co. villæ Briſtoll. 5 parſonages, and 1 vicarage. Co. Wilts 2 vicarages. Co. Oxon. 1 parſonage, and 2 vicarages. Co. Dorſ. 4 parſonages, and 2 vicarages. Co. Somerſ. 3 parſonages. Co. Devon. 1 vicarage. Co. Cornub. 2 vicarages. Co. Glamorg. and Morgan. 5 vicarages. In all 21 parſonages, and 27 vicarages.

It appears by an antient deed tranſcribed into an old council-book, that before, and at the time of the diſſolution, the body of the abbey church was uſed as the pariſh church, and that the pariſh purchaſed of the king the chancel, ſteeple, and bells, with the clock and chimes, for 483*l.*

The cloiſters, chapter-houſe, &c. of this monaſtery, are reported to have been burnt down at the diſſolution by the king's viſitors, on account, as 'tis ſaid, of the monks reſiſting them at their firſt coming.

The arms of the abbey were, *Gules, a croſs Or.*

Of the Church, &c.

The church is a curacy, worth about 130*l.* a year. The patronage is in the crown, and the reverend Mr. James Tatterſall is the preſent incumbent. The curate has no houſe nor glebe. The impropriation is divided, but the greater part belongs to lord Craven.

In the year 1609, king James the Firſt, by letters patent, charged the rectory of Tewkeſbury with the payment of 10*l.* yearly to the vicar. And in 1616, granted 5*l.* 15*s.* 8*d.* yearly to be paid by his auditor to the aſſiſtant, or curate of the church.

The donations for the augmentation of the curacy are particularly ſet down with other public benefactions.

There is a plate of this church in the *Monaſticon*, and in Stevens's *Supplement* to it is another plate of the ichnography of it. It is a magnificent building, in the form of a croſs, vaulted at top with ſtone work, and ſupported by two rows of large round pillars, ſeven in each row. It has an aile on each ſide, and the whole is covered with lead, but not kept in very good repair. The chancel is divided from the choir by an organ, erected at the expence of the pariſhoners in the year 1736. The Lady-chapel, long ſince deſtroy'd, and the ſcite of it turned into a garden ground, ſtood at the eaſt end, and is ſaid to have been a 100 feet long. The preſent building from eaſt to weſt is 300 feet; the length of the great croſs aile 120 feet; the breadth of the body and ſide ailes 70 feet; and of the weſt front 100 feet. The tower, in which are eight muſical bells and a ſet of chimes, ſtands in the middle, upon four arches. It is very large, 132 feet high, and had formerly a lofty wooden ſpire on the top of it, which fell down in the time of divine ſervice on Eaſter-day, 1559.

The choir and chancel are likewiſe ſupported by ſix pillars, and enlightened by ſeven large windows, placed at a great height, and ornamented with painted glaſs. The two firſt windows, at the entrance, *viz.* one on each hand, are divided into four compartments each, in which are painted the figures in armour of eight earls of Glouceſter, diſtinguiſhed by their arms. In the next window on the right, is the prophet Daniel; and on the left, Jeremiah; in the middle window king Solomon; next to him on the right, the prophet Joel; on the left a ſcutcheon parted per pale, 1ſt, *Argent, a lion rampant ſable.* 2d, *Quarterly argent and gules, in the 2d and 3d a fret Or, over all on a bend ſable three eſcallops of the firſt*, for le Deſpencer.

There are beſides in theſe windows, 1. The arms of the Clares, *Or, three chevrons gules.* 2. Thoſe of the abbey, *Gules, a croſs Or.* 3. *Argent, five bars azure.* 4. *Barry undy Argent and Gules, a baton in bend azure*, for Damory. 5. *A lion ſable crown'd Or.* 6. *Azure, a lion rampant gardant Or*, for Fitz-Haimon. 7. *Gules, ten bezants*, for Le Zouch.

In the weſt front of the church are ſeveral coats, *viz.* 1. *Gules, a lion rampant regardant Or.* 2. *Or, a feſs vaire between ſix labels of three points ſable.* 3. *Gules, a croſs raguly Or.* 4. *Gules, a ſaltire argent.* 5. *Per bend Or and ſable, a lion rampant counterchanged.*

Under the weſt window within the church, 1. *Or, between two bends ruby an eſcallop in the chief point ſable*, for Tracy of Stanway; impaling, *Gules, a bend Or.* 2. *Azure, a lion rampant argent*, for Pool of Saperton. 3. *Baron and femme* 1. *Gules, a dexter hand couped argent, on a chief of the ſecond three fighting cocks of the firſt*; impaling, 2. *Or, a feſs wavy between ſix labels of three points ſable. viz.* Hancock of Twining impaling Baugh of the ſame place.. Theſe families were probably benefactors to the church, amongſt many others, whoſe arms are diſplay'd in various parts of it, and are ſo numerous, that to emblazon them would fill ſeveral pages.

Monuments and Inſcriptions.

Robert Fitz-Haimon was buried in the chapter-houſe in the year 1107, but removed into the preſbytery in 1241, and thence in 1397, to the north ſide of the choir, where his bones, wrapt in fine diaper, were laid in a tomb of grey marble, which had braſſes at top, with his figure and ornaments, long ſince torn off. Abbat Parker incloſed the tomb in a chapel, now ſtanding, and round the top was written, *In iſta capella jacet Dnus Robertus Filius Hammonis, hujus loci Fundator.*

Near the above, is another chapel, with a very curious arched roof, originally ſupported by ſix ſmall marble pillars, of which only two are intire. It was ornamented with the pictures of our ſaviour and his apoſtles, and with many coats of arms; and round the upper part of it is written,

Mementote d'ne Iſabelle ledeſpenſer Cometiſſe de Warrewick que hanc capellam fundauit in honorē vir' Marie Magdalene Et obiit Londiniis apud Mīnores A° dnī M° CCCC° XXXIX die ſcī Jhīs eūnglie Et ſepulta ē ī chora ī dextrā patris ſui cuj' aīe ppiciet' deus Amen.

On the ſame ſide, under a canopy of very curious arched work of four ſtories, gradually diminiſhing, and finiſhing at top in one arch, highly ornamented in the Gothic taſte, are the figures, in white marble, of George duke of Clarence and Iſabel his dutcheſs, lying at full length. She was buried in 1479, in a vault behind the high altar, over-againſt the door of the chapel of St. Edmund the martyr, known by the ſymbols of him on the top of the chapel. He was ſhot with arrows, and beheaded, and a wolf is ſaid to have defended his head from other beaſts.

The ceremonial of the funeral of the dutcheſs of Clarence, taken from the *Chronicle of Tewkeſbury*, may ſerve as an example of the cuſtom among the great in thoſe days. Her body was brought from Warwick to Tewkeſbury on the 4th of January, 1476. John Strenſham, abbat of Tewkeſbury, with divers other abbats, in their prieſtly habits, and the whole convent, receiving it in the middle of the choir; and the funeral office was preſently after performed by the ſuffragans of the biſhop of Worceſter, and the biſhop of Landaff, and by the dean and chaplains of the lord duke; and the vigils were obſerved by the duke's own family all night to the next day, which was the vigil of the Epiphany. The ſuffragan of the biſhop of Landaff celebrated the firſt maſs of St. Mary, in the chapel of St. Mary; the ſecond maſs of the Trinity was celebrated by the lord abbat, at the high altar. The ſuffragan of the biſhop of Worceſter celebrated the third maſs, of eternal Reſt, at which Peter Weld, doctor of divinity, and of the order of the Minors at Worceſter, preached a ſermon in the choir, before the prelates and the reſt there preſent. Maſs being ended, the body of the dutcheſs was left under the herſe, in the middle of the choir for thirty-five days, and on every one of thoſe days ſolemn

exequies

exequies were performed in the convent, for the good of her foul. Afterwards, a week before the feaft of the purification of the bleffed Mary, the fame day after mafs ended, her body was committed to be buried in a vault behind the high altar, and before the door of the chapel of the bleffed virgin, in the abbey church, over againft the door of the chapel of St. Edmund the martyr.

The chapel on the fouth fide of the choir was erected by Cicely dutchefs of Warwick, in memory of the duke her hufband, and over it is the effigy of Richard Nevil, the earl of Warwick, in armour, kneeling, with his hands in a fupplicating pofture.

Oppofite to the duke and dutchefs of Clarence, under another arch of hollow work, lies the figure of lord O'Brien, with fcutcheons of his arms round the tomb, *Or, three piles meeting near the bafe azure*; impaling his wife's family arms, *viz. Argent, three fufils in fefs gules,* for Montacute, earl of Salifbury. They were both buried in the aile near the high altar.

At the upper end of the fouth aile, near the choir, is an altar monument under an arch, for Edmund Beaufort, duke of Somerfet.

Directly oppofite to it in the north aile, is fuch another, in a niche, with the effigy of lord Wenlock lying thereon, and upon a fhield over the left arm this coat, *Gules, a chevron Or between three lions argent.*

In the middle fpace under the tower, is a large grey marble, which had brafs plates affixed to it, and is faid to have been for the unfortunate prince Edward, only fon to king Henry the Sixth.

On the fouth fide of the choir, under two arches, are two grey marble altar-monuments for two abbats; and beyond them is the effigy of another abbat lying in full proportion, with thefe arms, *A chevron between three efcallops, over all a palmer's ftaff in pale*, fuppofed to be for Robert Fortington, or Forthampton, abbat of this place, who died in 1253.

On the fouth fide of the choir is another antient altar-monument, with a crofs on the top, and round the verge IOÞANNES ABBAS ÞVIVS LOCI. and above this is a monument for another abbat.

There were alfo buried in this church, for whom there are now no monuments:

1. Gilbert de Clare, earl of Gloucefter, buried in 1290, near the communion-table, under a plain ftone, with an infcription round the edge, now defaced.

2. John, fon of the third Gilbert de Clare, buried in the virgin Mary chapel.

3. Edward le Defpencer, who died in 1375, and was buried before the door of the veftry near the prefbytery, or chancel, where his wife, daughter of Bartholomew de Burghurft, built a chapel, dedicated to the Holy Trinity; and in 1401 fhe died, and was buried under a marble ftone in the choir, on the left hand of her hufband.

In the body of the church, round a flat ftone, it is thus written: + LEGER : DE : PARR : GYT : YCY · DYEVX : DE : SA : ALME : EN : EYT : MERCI.

There are very few modern infcriptions in the church worth tranfcribing. I fhall however infert two or three of them, and take notice of the family arms on the monuments. In the north crofs aile is the following:

Edwardus Wakeman Armiger qui obijt 3° die Decembris An° Dni 1634. Refurget et Vivet per illum qui dixit Ego fum Refurrectio et Vita.——Arms, *Vert, a faltire wavy ermine.*

On a flat ftone,

Here lies the Hon[ble] Elianor Stanford, Daughter of Edward Stanford, Efq; of Sawford in the County of Warwick, by his Wife Katherine Cocks of Northey in the County of Gloucefter. She was Wife of the Hon[ble] Francis Stafford, Son of William Lord Vifcount Stafford, and Lady Mary Counteffe of Stafford, his Wife, defcended from the antient Princes, the Staffords Dukes of Buckingham, and Earls of Stafford, &c. She had Iffue by him one Son named Henry, who puts this Stone upon her, in Memory of a pious Wife and tender Mother. She departed this Life the 26th Day of October, *Anno Dni* 1707.——The arms on this ftone are, within a lozenge, *Party per pale*, 1. Stafford, *viz. Or, a chevron gules, a mullet for difference.* 2. *Quarterly*, 1ft *and* 4th, *three bars*, for Stanford; 2d *and* 3d, Cocks, as at Dumbleton.

On a monument againft the wall,

This Monument is erected by Thomas Hale, Gent. in Memory of his Pious and Virtuous Confort Letitia the Daughter of the Honourable S[r] Thomas Penniſton, late of Cornwell in the County of Oxon Baronet, deceafed, & Dame Elizabeth his Wife, fole Daughter and Heirefs of S[r] Cornelius Fairmeadow deceafed. She died the 3d of November, 1700, aged 32 Years.

The monument is ornamented with thefe arms, *viz. Baron and femme*, 1. *Argent, a fefs fable, and in chief three cinquefoils vert.* 2. *Argent, three Cornifh choughs proper*, for Pennifton.

There are various other infcriptions in feveral parts of the church, *viz.* for John Roberts of Fiddington, gent. who died in 1631; with his arms, *Per pale, argent and gules, over all a lion rampant fable.* For Mary Oldifworth, (daughter of Thomas Chamberlayne) who died in 1684; with a fcutcheon, Oldifworth impaling Chamberlayne. For feveral of the Bridges's of Wilton caftle, with the arms of Bridges. For Richard, Samuel, and Marmaduke Rofe, who died refpectively in the years 1726, 1757, and 1770; with *three rofes on a bend.* For Edward Popham of Tewkefbury Lodge, who died in 1753; and Dorothy his wife, and Letitia their daughter; with the arms of Popham, impaling, *Vert, a chevron between three greyhounds courant argent.* For Thomas Kemble, gent. who died in 1707, with his arms, *Azure, on a bend Or three bulls heads couped fable, gutty du fang.*

Benefactions to the Poor.

The abbey, by its foundation, was obliged to maintain thirteen almfmen with 10*d.* a week each for diet, 6*s.* 8*d.* a year for gowns; and 3*l.* 6*s.* 8*d.* for the rent of all their houfes. This charity was continued by king Henry the Eighth after the reformation, and queen Mary, on the 3d of April, 1553, granted thofe fums to be paid by the auditors for this county for ever.

Mr.

Mr. Gyles Geeft by his will, in 1558, gave the rent of twenty-two houfes, and as many gardens, near the Church-ftreet. Mrs. Margaret Hicks, by will in 1562, gave the rent of a meffuage in Barton-ftreet. Alfo the rent of half an acre in Avonham was given by a perfon unknown, and has been received ever fince 1564. Mrs. Juliana Beft, gave a rent charge of 3*s.* 4*d.* out of a houfe in High-ftreet. The rent of two acres in Severnham is received and annually diftributed by Mr. Geeft's truftees. Mrs. Anne Slaughter, by her deed in 1618, gave the great Saffron garden near Swilyate. William Ferrers, of London, efq; in 1625, gave 5*l.* a year out of Shellingthorp manor in Lincolnfhire. Mr. William Alye, of London, gent. by his will in 1625, gave 100*l.* which purchafed the Seek-rents. The Right Hon. Baptift vifcount Camden, by will in 1629, fettled the rectory and church of St. Ifmaels, in Rofe in Pembrokefhire, half to the poor, and half to the minifter. Mr. John Roberts of Fiddington, by will in 1631, gave the intereft of 20*l.* for ever, to buy coals. John Wright, by deed in 1636, gave a rent charge of 20*s.* a year on a meffuage in Kemmerton, and lands in Breedon meadow. Lord Coventry, in 1652, gave a rent charge of lands in Breedon of 15*l.* a year, and 200*l.* for a ftock to fet the poor to work. And Mr. Edward Richardfon, by his will in 1651, gave 60*l.* for a ftock, with which were purchafed feven houfes and fix gardens in Gander-lane. Sir Francis Ruffel, baronet, by his deed in 1674, confirmed his mother's gift of ten houfes and a garden near the church-yard, with fome land in Smith's lane. Mr. William Curtis, by deed in 1681, gave the Moors in Twining. William Wakeman, gent. by will in 1681, charged lands called Red Pools and Middle grounds with 20*s.* a year to the poor, and 10*s.* for a fermon. Mr. John Read, by his will in 1683, gave 50*l.* fince laid out on lands called the Abbat's-lays in Gretton. Mr. John Porter, by will in 1698, gave two thirds of two acres in Severn-ham. The reverend Mr. Robert Wriggan, by will in 1701, gave 5*l.* William Wilfon, gent. by will in 1720, gave 100*l.* capital ftock in the South Sea company. Mr. William Hayward, by will in 1727, gave the intereft of 50*l.* to the poor, and of 20*l.* to the minifter for two fermons. Mrs. Elizabeth Hopton of Briftol, by will in 1732, gave 100*l.* fince laid out in land in the parifh of Upton. Daniel Kemble, efq; by will in 1732, gave his lands in Severn-ham, adjoining to thofe given by Mr. Porter, alfo the profits of 100*l.* now laid out in land in Upton parifh. Sir William Strachan, baronet, by deed, vefted an eftate at Caftle Morton in Worcefterfhire, worth 8*l.* a year, in truftees for the ufe of the poor.

To repair the Church, and augment the Living.

Mr. Cook, by will, about 1558, gave a meffuage in High-ftreet for repairing the church; and Mrs. Ellyne Eckynfale, in 1568, by her will, gave 12*d.* a year for the fame purpofe.

Mr. Thomas Poulton, in 1607, gave 20*s.* yearly towards maintaining a preaching minifter. Alfo 40*l.* to be lent without intereft, which are now loft.

In 1629, lord vifcount Camden fettled half the rectory and church of St. Ifmaels in Rofe, in Pembrokefhire, on the minifter for ever.

In 1681, William Wakeman, gent, gave 10*s.* a year for a fermon on Good Friday.

In 1683, Edwin Skrimfhire of Aquilat in Staffordfhire, by his deed, gave the tithes of Tredington and Fiddington, out of which to pay the minifter of Tredington and Afhchurch 12*l.* yearly each, the reft to the minifter of this place.

In 1685, Thomas Geers, by his deed, fettled the privy or fmall tithes of this town and borough on the reader, or affiftant to the minifter of this church for ever.

In 1685, Mrs. Elizabeth Townfend, by will, gave 200*l.* fince laid out on land in Gretton, for the minifter.

In 1716, Charles Wynde, efq; by his will, charged his eftate in Stoke Prior, *com. Wigorn.* with 20*s.* a year for a fermon, and 5*s.* for prayers on the anniverfary of his death, and 40*s.* for reading prayers on Sunday evenings, between Lady-day and Michaelmas.

In 1722, Mrs. Elizabeth Dowdefwell, by will, gave 100*l.* for the better maintenance of the minifter, and 50*l.* to repair the church, both which fums are laid out in the purchafe of the Abbat's Lays in Gretton. Alfo 20*l.* to buy a filver flaggon for the church.

Mrs. Catherine Hancock gave a large filver cup and cover to the church, fince exchanged for two filver plates. Alfo 50*l.* laid out on land towards repairing the church windows.

In 1727, Mr. William Hayward gave the intereft of 20*l.* for two annual fermons.

In 1732, Mrs. Elizabeth Hopton gave Williams's Meadow, and one butt and two lands in Oldbury field to the minifter, to preach fix fermons preparatory to the facrament on the laft Friday in every month, between Lady-day and Michaelmas for ever.

To the Schools.

In 1609, fir Dudley Diggs gave 160*l.* with which land called the Holms, one acre in the Oldbury, and lands in Downbell's meadow were purchafed and fettled to the ufe of the free fchool.

In 1625, William Ferrers gave 20*l.* a year out of Shillingthorp in Lincolnfhire.

In 1625, William Alye gave 70*l.* with which chief-rents were purchafed, for the education of fix poor children in the grammar fchool.

In 1722, Mrs. Elizabeth Dowdefwell gave 40*l.*

In 1724, Mr. Thomas Merret charged his lands with the payment of 50*s.* yearly to the charity fchool.

In 1721, lady Capel gave her eftate called Perry Court, in the county of Kent, to fupport twelve charity fchools, one twelfth part of which to the charity fchool here.

To the Roads and Bridge.

In 1562, Mrs. Margaret Hicks gave the rent of an acre of land in Oldbury to repair the roads.

In 1567, Mrs. Beſt gave 3*s.* 4*d.* yearly to repair the long bridge.

In 1665, Mr. Richard Mince gave 40*s.* a year out of the latter-math of Avon-ham to repair the long bridge.

Borough of Tewkeſbury.

Taxes.	The Royal Aid in	1692, £. 347	4	6
	Poll-tax ——	1694, — 207	7	0
	Land-tax ——	1694, — 350	12	8
	The ſame, at 3*s.*	1770, — 267	1	3

Mythe, and Mythe Wood.

Taxes.	The Royal Aid in	1692, £. 94	0	0
	Poll-tax ——	1694, — 6	16	0
	Land-tax ——	1694, — 70	13	4
	The ſame, at 3*s.*	1770, — 54	7	3

Southwick and Park.

Taxes.	The Royal Aid in	1692, £. 255	15	0
	Poll-tax ——	1694, — 10	3	4
	Land-tax ——	1694, — 225	15	0
	The ſame, at 3*s.*	1770, — 47	15	$3\frac{3}{4}$

When ſir Robert Atkyns compiled the account of this place, he eſtimated the houſes in the pariſh to be 470, and the inhabitants 2500; but the latter are now ſaid to be upwards of 3000; however, no calculation can be made from the pariſh regiſter, as the diſſenters (including the quakers) have ſepulture in their reſpective burying yards.

THORNBURY.

THIS large pariſh lies in the lower part of the Vale of Glouceſterſhire, within the hundred of its own name. It is bounded for ſeveral miles on the north-weſt by the river Severn, from whence to the oppoſite extremity, it is upwards of ſix miles in length, and croſſing that direction, it is above five miles in breadth.

Thro' all this extent of rich country, there is at preſent but very little tillage-land, and it is obſervable, that for the laſt forty or fifty years paſt, the corn fields here, as well as in general throughout the vale, have been gradually converted to paſture, whilſt the very contrary practice takes place on the hills.

Large quantities of Wormwood and Marſhmallows grow in the meadows, alſo Aſparagus and ſeed Purſlain, which the inhabitants gather for their tables. And there are many other plants growing ſpontaneouſly, that the curious botaniſt would not paſs over unnoticed; among which are the *Acanthus*, or Bear's Breech, the black Maidenhair, Agrimony, the wholeſome Wolfeſbane, common Maidenhair, yellow Centaury, Wild Germander, great Celadine, Pilewort, Hounds Tongue, Eyebright, Fumitory, Wild Clary, St. John's Wort, Betony, Wild Marjoram, Polypody of the wall, Comfry, common Vervain, Heartſeaſe, Miſſeltoe, and ſome others.

A great part of the pariſh next the Severn is very ſubject to inundations from that river. Near two thouſand acres of land are rated to the repair of the ſea walls in the upper level, but a much greater tract is liable to floods, whoſe waters ſtagnate on the marſhes and low lands. Hence the inhabitants of that part of the pariſh are very unhealthy from the putrid air they breathe; and if any go from the hill-country to reſide there, ſuch perſons are uſually attacked with a violent ague on their firſt ſettling, which emaciates them, and proves fatal in a little time. Doctor Franklin's ſentiments on moiſt ſituations, in a letter to his friend Dr. Percival, are new and ſingular, and merit conſideration. 'The gentry of England,' ſays he, 'are remarkably afraid of moiſture and 'of air. But ſeamen, who live perpetually in 'moiſt air, are always healthy if they have good 'proviſions. The inhabitants of Bermudas, St. 'Helen, and other iſlands far from continents, 'ſurrounded with rocks, againſt which the waves 'continually daſhing, fill the air with ſpray and 'vapour, and where no wind can ariſe that does 'not paſs over much ſea, and of courſe bring 'much moiſture, are remarkably healthy. And 'I have long thought mere moiſt air has no ill 'effect on the conſtitution; though air impreg'nated with vapours from putrid marſhes is 'found pernicious, not from the moiſture, but 'from the putridity. It ſeems ſtrange that a man, 'whoſe body is compoſed in great part of moiſt 'fluids, whoſe blood and juices are ſo watery, who 'can ſwallow quantities of water and ſmall beer 'daily without inconvenience, ſhould fancy that 'a little more or leſs moiſture in the air ſhould 'be of ſuch importance. But we abound in ab'ſurdity and inconſiſtency. Thus, though it is 'generally agreed that *taking the air* is a good 'thing, yet what caution againſt air! what ſtop'ping of crevices! what wrapping up in warm 'cloaths! what ſhutting of doors and windows! 'even in the midſt of ſummer. Many London 'families go out once a day to take the air, three 'or four perſons in a coach, one perhaps ſick; 'theſe go three or four miles, or as many turns 'in Hyde Park, with both the glaſſes up, all 'breathing over and over again the ſame air they 'brought out of town with them in the coach, 'with the leaſt change poſſible, and rendered 'worſe and worſe every moment; and this they 'call *taking the air*. From many years obſer'vations on myſelf and others, I am perſuaded 'we are on a wrong ſcent in ſuppoſing moiſt or 'cold air, the cauſe of that diſorder we call a cold: 'ſome unknown quality in the air may ſometimes 'produce colds, as in the *influenza*; but generally 'I apprehend they are the effects of too full 'living, in proportion to our exerciſe.'

The town of Thornbury ſtands in the midſt of the pariſh, a little above the marſhes, but the air there is in ſome degree contaminated by the ſtagnated waters on the low lands. It is ſeven miles diſtant ſouth from Berkeley, ſix weſtward from Wickwar, eleven north from Briſtol, and twenty-four ſouth-weſtward from Glouceſter. It is a borough by preſcription, and is governed by a mayor and twelve aldermen, but ſends no repreſentatives to parliament. The mayor is annually choſen out of the aldermen, and the latter, upon a vacancy, out of the freeholders reſiding in the borough. The mayor attends the borough court, collects the lord's chief-rents, and examines weights and meaſures; but it is difficult to aſcertain the duties of his office with any degree of preciſion, as I find them no where deſcribed. And it may be preſumed that much of that power which was antiently delegated to him, is loſt for want of uſing it, ſo that his office is now become little more than nominal.

We know very little of the antient ſtate of this borough. About the Norman conqueſt it had a market, whoſe profits were then worth twenty ſhillings, according to *Domeſday*. Leland made a viſit to it in the reign of king Henry the Eighth, and deſcribes it in his *Itinerary* as 'ſet almoſte 'upon an equalle grounde, [*i.e.* nearly level] 'beinge large to the proportion of the letter Y, 'havinge firſt one longe ſtrete, and two hornes 'goyne owt of it. There hathe bene, (ſays he) 'good clothing in Thornebyry, but now Idelnes 'muche reynithe there.' To which I ſhall ſubjoin, that the clothing buſineſs is now intirely loſt, and no manufacture ſupplies its room, except that the women and children are furniſhed with ſpinning work by maſter clothiers from other places.

The town ſtretches from north-eaſt to ſouth-weſt, parallel to the courſe of the Severn, at the diſtance of about two miles and a half from that river. It conſiſts, as in Leland's time, of one ſtreet of a good breadth, and about three quarters of a mile long, with two other ſtreets, or rather lanes, of very little account.

The great turnpike-road from the north of England, through Glouceſter to Briſtol, runs upon a conſiderable eminence by the town, but there are only the church and a few houſes to be ſeen from the road, becauſe many lofty trees intercept the view on that ſide. The beſt proſpect of the town is from the heights at Lidney and Woollaſton, in the foreſt of Dean, about five or ſix miles diſtant on the oppoſite ſide of the Severn, whence it ſeems to be larger than it really is. Some of the houſes are built of brick, a few of ſtone, but the greater part ſeem to be wood buildings; and from the preſent condition of them, the town appears to be declining. It has loſt its market from its vicinity to Briſtol, and carrying the road by the ſide of it, has deprived it of the benefit of travelling buſineſs, whereas, before the turnpike was erected, the great road led through it. Theſe loſſes, and the defect of its manufacture, muſt neceſſarily impoveriſh and depopulate the place.

The market, of which there is very little appearance, is held on Saturday, and there are three yearly fairs for the ſale of horned cattle and hogs, *viz.* on Eaſter-monday, on the 15th of Auguſt, and on the Monday before St. Thomas-day.

The public buildings are the Boothall, the corn market-houſe, and the Shambles. There are four diſtinct courts held in the Boothall, *viz.*

1. The court of the Honour of Glouceſter. Of this Honour I have already given ſome account, p. 91. It remains only to obſerve, that in it pleas are held for the recovery of debts from 40*s.* to any amount, within its juriſdiction, which extends over the following places in the county of Glouceſter, *viz.* Thornbury, Kington, Oldbury upon Severn, Cowhill, Morton, Mars, *alias* Mares and Falfield, Philpots, Saltmarſh, [*i.e.* the Marſhes in Olveſton and Almondeſbury] Rowles, Buckover, Hope, Rangeworthy, Titherington, Iron Acton, Charfield, Dodington, Marſhfield, Mangotsfield, Bitton, Upton Cheney, Beech, Barr's Court, Oldland, Hanham, Doynton, Gaunt's Erdicot, Over, Tockington, Coate, Tewkeſbury, Oxendon, Alderton, Boddington, Walton Cardiff, Kemmerton, Frampton Cotel, Hampton Meſey, and Holyrood Amney. The action commences by affidavit of the debt before the ſteward or his deputy, who iſſues an attachment againſt the defendant's goods, to be condemned and forfeited at the next court, unleſs two ſufficient perſons reſiding within the juriſdiction become pledges, in the nature of bail, for the debt and coſts, if the defendant ſhould be condemned in the action. Pledges being given, the goods are releaſed, and the plantiff proceeds by declaration, as in the courſe of common law. Matthew Hale, eſq; is the preſent ſteward of this court.

2. The hundred court, held on Thurſday every three weeks, before the ſteward, and two free ſuitors, for the recovery of debts under 40*s.* ariſing within the hundred.

3. The borough court, held alſo on Thurſday every three weeks, before the ſteward of the manor, in the preſence of the mayor, attended by the ſerjeant at mace, where are tried actions of debt under 40*s.* ariſing within the borough.

4. The manor court, or court baron, held occaſionally before the ſteward of the manor and tenants, where, beſides ordinary buſineſs, tenants are admitted to their copyholds. And the cuſtom of the manor is, that ſuch eſtates deſcend to the next heir like freeholds, with this exception, that the tenants children being all daughters, the eldeſt inherits, and ſo of nieces.

Of Thornbury Caſtle.

There was very antiently a caſtle at this place, but by whom it was originally built is at this time altogether uncertain. Hugh de Audley, earl of Glou-

Gloucefter, refufing to obey the fummons of king Edward the Second, to come to the king at Gloucefter on the 3d of April, in the 14th year of that reign, the earl's caftle at Thornbury, and his other eftates, were feized into the king's hands; but they were reftored in the firft year of the next reign. Doctor Holland obferves that Ralph lord Stafford built a houfe at Thornbury, in the reign of king Edward the Third. Perhaps this was done upon the fcite of the old caftle. And in the fecond year of the reign of king Henry the Eighth, Edward duke of Buckingham took down part of the houfe built by Ralph lord Stafford, and began a caftle near the church, at the north end of the town; but he was prevented from finifhing it by his attainder and death in the thirteenth year of the fame reign. John Leland faw it foon after the duke was beheaded, and gives the following account of it in the feventh volume of his *Itinerary:*

'There was of auncient Tyme a Maner Place, 'but of no great eftimation, hard by the Northe 'Syde of the Paroche Churche. Edward late 'Duke of Bukkyngeham likynge the Soyle aboute, 'and the Site of the Howfe, and fette up magni-'ficently in good fquared Stone, the Southe Syde 'of it, and accomplifhyd the Weft Parte alfo 'withe a right comely Gatehoufe to the firft Soyle; 'and fo it ftondithe yet withe a Rofe forced for 'a tyme. This Infcription on the fronte of the 'Gatehowfe: This Gate was begun in the yere 'of Our Lorde Gode M CCCCC XI The ii yere 'Of The Reyne Of Kynge Henri the VIII By me 'EDW duc of Bukkinghā Erlle of Harforde 'Stafforde ande Northamtō. The Dukes Worde: 'DORENTE SAVANT, [upon a label]. The 'Foundation of a very fpacious Bafe Courte was 'there begon, and certeyne Gates and Towres in 'it Caftelle lyke. It is of a iiii or v Yardes highe, 'and fo remaynithe a Token of a noble Peace of 'Worke purpofid. There was a Gallery of 'Tymbre in the Bake Syde of the Houfe joyning 'to the Northe Syde of the Paroche Churche.— 'Edward Duke of Bukkyngham made a fayre 'Parke hard by the Caftle, and tooke muche faire 'Ground in it very frutefull of Corne, now fayr 'Launds for Courfynge. The Inhabytaunts 'curfyd the Duke for the Lands fo inclofyd.

'There cummithe an Armlet of Severne eb-'bynge and flowyng into this Parke. Duke 'Edward had Thowght to have trenchyd there 'and to have browght it up to the Caftle.—There 'was a Parke by the Maner of Thornebyry afore, 'and yet is caullyd Morlewodde.—There was 'alfo afore Duke Edward's Tyme a Parke at 'Eftewood, a Myle or more of: But Duke Edward 'at 2 Tymes enlarged it to the Compace of 6 'Myles, not without many Curfes of the Poore 'Tenaunts. The Severne Se lyethe a Myle and 'more from Thornebyrie, the Marches lyenge 'betwene.'

Thus far Leland. But I have been favoured with a more particular defcription of this caftle, written, as I conjecture, about the time of king James the Firft, which, as it may be acceptable to many readers, is here inferted in the language of the writer.

'The houfe or caftle of Thornbury ftandeth 'within two miles of the river Seaverne, which 'runneth on the north fide thereof. It is ad-'joining unto the church-yard of the parifh 'church of Thornbury on the fouth part; the 'parke there, called New Parke, on the north 'and eaft parts, and a piece of ground called the 'Pitties on the weft part. At the firft entry is a 'faire back court containing two acres and a 'halfe, compaffed about with buildings of ftone 'for fervants lodgings, to the hight of 14 or 15 'foote, left unfinifhed without timber or covering, 'fet forth with windows of freeftone, fome having 'bars of iron in them, fome none.

'At the entry into the caftle on the weft fide 'are two gates, a greater and a leffer, with a 'wicket in the fame. At the left hand thereof is 'a porter's lodge, conteyning three roomes, with a 'dungeon or place of imprifonment underneath. 'Next adjoining is a faire roome called the Duke's 'Wardrobbe, and within the fame a faire roome 'or lodging chamber with a cellar or vaught 'underneath; over all which are fower lodging 'chambers with chimneys. On the right hand 'of the gates are two faire roomes called the 'Duches Wardrobbe, and over the fame are two 'faire chambers called the Steward's Chambers.

'Within all which is a court paved with ftone, 'conteyning halfe an acre, encompaffed with the 'caftle buildings and leading from the gates afore-'said to the great hall, at the entry whereof is a 'porch, and on the right hand a fmall room 'called the Ewery.

'On the left or north fide of the court is a 'faire wett larder, a dry larder, a privy bakehoufe, 'and a boyling houfe, with an entry leading from 'all the faid houfes of offices to the great kitchin, 'over all which are five chambers for privet 'lodgings, & over all the fame againe is one long 'roome called the Cockloft. The great kitchin 'having two great large flewes or chimneys, & 'one leffer chimney, & within the fame kitchin 'is a privy kitchin with two flewes or chimneys 'in it, over the which laft recited kitchin is a 'lodging chamber for cookes.

'On the backfide of all which recited buildings 'are certaine decayed buildings fometimes ufed 'for a bakehoufe, & an armory wth certaine de-'cayed lodgings over the fame. From the great 'kitchin leading to the great hall is an entry, on 'the one fide is a decayed roome called the fkul-'lery, with a large flew or chimney therein, & a 'pantry adjoyning. On the other fide of the 'entry are two old decayed roomes heretofore 'ufed for cellars, on the backfide whereof is a 'little court adjoyning to the great kitchin, & in 'the

'the ſame is a faire well or pump for water, 'partley decayed; betweene the decayed cellars 'and the lower end of the great hall is a buttery; 'over all which laſt recited roomes are fower 'chambers called the Earle of Stafford's Lodgings, 'partly decayed, with one roome thereunto ad- 'joyning called the Clerkes Treaſury.

'From the lower end of the great hall is an 'entry leading unto the chappell, at the corner of 'which entry is a ſellar. The utter part of the 'chappell is a faire roome for people to ſtand in 'at ſervice time, & over the ſame are two roomes 'or partitions with each of them a chimney, 'where the duke & the duches uſed to ſitt & 'heare ſervice. The body of the chappell it ſelfe 'fairely built, having twenty & two ſettles of 'wainefcott about the ſame, for prieſts, clerkes, '& quieriſters.

'The great hall, faire and large, with a hearth 'to make fire on in the mideſt thereof. Adjoyning 'to the upp end of the ſame is one faire roome 'called the Old Hall, with a chimney in the ſame. 'Next adjoyning to the ſame is a faire cloyſter 'walke paved with bricke, leading from the 'Duke's Lodging to the privy garden, which 'garden is fower ſquare, conteyning about one 'third part of an acre, three ſquares whereof are 'compaſſed about with a faire Cloyſter or walke 'paved with bricke, & the fowerth ſquare is 'bounded with the principal parts of the Caſtle 'called the New Buildings; over all which laſt 'recited Cloyſter is a faire large gallery, & out of 'the ſame gallery goeth another gallery leading 'to the pariſh church of Thornbury, at the end 'whereof is a faire roome with a Chimney, and a 'Window into the ſaid Church, where the Duke 'uſed ſometime to heare ſervice. Neere adjoyn- 'ing unto the ſaid large gallery are certain roomes 'or lodgings called the Earle of Bedford's 'lodgings, conteyning 13 roomes, whereof ſix 'are below, three of them having chimneys in 'them, & ſeaven above, whereof fower have 'chimneys likewiſe. All which houſes, buildings '& roomes aforementioned are for the moſt part 'built with freeſtone, & covered with ſlatt or tyle.

'The lower part of the principall buildings of 'the caſtle is called the New Buildings, at the weſt 'end whereof is a faire tower, in which lower 'buildings is conteyned one great chamber, with 'a chimney in the ſame, the ſealing & timber 'worke whereof is decayed. Within the ſame is 'another faire chamber with a chimney therein. 'And within the ſame againe is another faire 'lodging chamber, with a chimney therein, called 'the Duke's Lodging, with one little Roome or 'Cloſſett betweene the two laſt recited chambers. 'Within all which is one roome, being the foun- 'dation or lowermoſt part of the tower called the 'Duke's Cloſſett, with a Chimney therein. From 'the which ſaid Duke's lodging leadeth a faire 'gallery paved with bricke, & a ſtayer at the end 'thereof aſcending to the Duke's Lodging, being 'over the ſame, uſed for a privy way.

'From the upp end of the great hall a ſtayer 'aſcendeth up towards the great chamber, at the 'top whereof are two lodging roomes. Leading 'from the ſtayers head to the great chamber is a 'faire roome paved with bricke, & a chimney 'therein, at the end whereof doth meete a faire 'gallery leading from the great Chamber to the 'Earle of Bedford's Lodging on the one ſide, & 'the Chappell on the other ſide.

'The great Chamber very faire with a chimney 'therein. Within the ſame is one other faire 'Chamber, called the Dineing Chamber, with a 'chimney therein likewiſe. And within that 'againe, is one other faire chamber alſoe, called 'the Privy Chamber, with a chimney in that 'likewiſe. And within the ſame againe is one 'other chamber or cloſſett called the Duke's 'Jewell Chamber. Next unto the Privy Cham- 'ber on the inner part thereof, is a faire round 'chamber, being the ſecond ſtory of the Tower, 'called the Duke's Bedchamber, with a chimney 'in the ſame. From the Privy Chamber a Stayer 'leadeth up into another faire round chamber 'over the Duke's Bedchamber, like unto the 'former, being the third ſtory over the Tower, '& ſoe upwards into another like chamber over 'the ſame, called the Treaſury, where the Evi- 'dences do lye. All which laſt recited buildings, 'called the New Buildings, are built faire with 'freeſtone, covered with lead, & embattelled.

'On the eaſt ſide of the Caſtle is one other 'garden, conteyning three quarters of an acre, 'adjoining upon the Earle of Bedford's Lodgings, 'at the weſt corner whereof is a little void court 'of waſt ground. On the north ſide of the Caſtle, 'adjoyning upon the Chappell, is a little Orchard 'conteyning half an acre, well ſett with trees of 'diverſe kinds of fruites. All which Caſtle 'buildings, with Orchards & Gardens aforeſaid, 'are walled about with a Wall of Stone, part 'embattelled, ruined and decayed in diverſe places 'thereof, conteyning in circuit and quantity, by 'eſtimation, twelve Acres of Ground, or there- 'abouts. On the eaſt Side of the ſaid Caſtle, 'adjoining unto the outer Side of the Walls 'thereof, is one faire Orchard quadrente, con- 'teyning by Eſtimation fower Acres, palled about 'well, & thick ſett with trees of diverſe Kinds of 'fruites.'

I ſhall cloſe this account of the caſtle by ob- ſerving, that the gatehouſe, and much of the caſtle walls, and the outer wall that incloſed the whole, with loop holes at convenient diſtances to ſhoot thro' with bows and croſs bows, are now ſtanding; and ſome of the rooms of the caſtle are occupied as a farm houſe. The foregoing inſcription on the gatehouſe is as I found it myſelf, and not exactly as in the *Itinerary*, for Leland had not copied it accurately. Beſides the inſcription, there

there are ſeveral ornamental devices upon it, with the Staffords Knot; and the preſent remains of the caſtle ſhew the deſign to have been noble and magnificent, tho imperfectly executed.

In the year 1539, king Henry the Eighth and Anne of Bulloigne were entertained at this place for ten days.

The town of Thornbury was fortified for the king in the great rebellion, by ſir William St. Leger, to reſtrain the garriſon at Glouceſter.

Of the Manor and other Eſtates.

The following abſtract from *Domeſday* ſtands under the title *Terra Regis:*

'Brictric the ſon of Algar held Turneberie in 'Langelei hundred. In the time of king Edward 'there were eleven hides, and four plow-tillages 'in demean, and forty-two villeins, and eighteen 'radchenifters, with twenty-one plow-tillages; 'and twenty-four bordars, and fifteen *ſervi*, and 'four *coliberti*. There were two mills of 6*s*. 4*d*. 'a wood a mile long, and a mile broad. There 'was a market of 20*s*. The ſteward hath now 'added a mill there of 8*d*.

'This manor was queen Maud's. Hunfrid 'paid 50*l*. for it by tale. In this manor is a 'meadow of 40*s*. and at Wiche, forty ſextaries 'of ſalt, or 20*d*. and the fiſhery of Glouceſter of '58*d*.' *Domeſday*, p. 68.

The manor of Thornbury deſcended like that of Tewkeſbury, and the honour of Glouceſter, 'till it came into the poſſeſſion of Ralph lord Stafford, in right of his wife Margaret, ſole daughter and heireſs to Hugh de Audley, earl of Glouceſter.

The above Ralph lord Stafford was deſcended from Roger de Toeni, who was ſtandard-bearer of Normandy, and deſcended from Malahulctus, uncle to Rollo duke of Normandy. Robert, a younger ſon of Roger, was founder of the abbey of Conches. Nicholas Toeni was ſon of Robert, and another Robert, ſon of Nicholas, came into England with king William the Firſt, who rewarded him with one hundred and thirty-one manors, whereof eighty-one were in Staffordſhire. He was alſo made governor of a caſtle in Stafford, and thence he aſſumed the name of Stafford. He married Avice de Clare, and lies buried at Stone in Staffordſhire, where he had founded a priory for canons regular, of the order of St. Auguſtin.

Nicholas de Stafford, ſon and heir of Robert, was high ſheriff of Staffordſhire in the reign of king Henry the Firſt, and was buried with Maud his wife in the monaſtery of Stone. Robert de Stafford, ſon and heir of Nicholas, was alſo high ſheriff of Staffordſhire from the 2d to the 6th year of king Henry the Second. He likewiſe was buried at Stone, and left a ſon named Robert, who died without iſſue, whereby Miliſent, ſiſter to this laſt Robert, became his heir.

Which Miliſent was married to Hervey Bagot, of an antient family in the ſame county, who, in her right, ſucceeded to the barony of Stafford. Hervey Bagot, ſon and heir of Hervey and of Miliſent, aſſumed the name of his mother, which was the cuſtom of thoſe times, when the mother was a conſiderable heireſs He married Petronilla, ſiſter to William de Ferrers, earl of Derby, and died 21 H. 3. A third Hervey de Stafford, ſon of the laſt, ſucceeded to the barony and eſtate, but dying without iſſue, his brother, Robert lord Stafford, became his heir, and had livery granted to him of all his brother's lands 25 H. 3. He married Alice, one of the coheirs of Thomas Corbet, of Caus in Shropſhire, and dying 10 E. 1. was buried with his anceſtors at Stone.

Edmond lord Stafford, ſon of Robert, married Margaret, daughter of Ralph lord Baſſet, of Draiton, whereby the eſtate of the Baſſet family, for want of heirs male, deſcended afterwards to the Staffords. He died 2 E. 2. and was buried in the monaſtery of the Friers Minors in Stafford.

Ralph lord Stafford, ſon of Edmond, was nine years old at his father's death. He had livery of his paternal eſtate 17 E. 2. and became eminent in military employments. He married Margaret, the daughter and heir of Hugh de Audley, earl of Glouceſter, and was created earl of Stafford. He died ſeized of the manors of Thornbury and Rendcombe, in right of his wife, 46 E. 3. and was buried at Tunbridge in Kent. Ralph his eldeſt ſon had married Maud, daughter of Henry de Lancaſter, earl of Derby, but died without iſſue before his father.

Hugh earl of Stafford, ſurviving ſon and heir of Ralph, and of Margaret de Audley, was twenty-eight years old at the death of his father, whom he ſucceeded in title and eſtate. He followed the wars in France and Scotland, and married Philippa, daughter of Thomas Beauchamp, earl of Warwick. Dying at Rhodes, in his return from a pilgrimage to Jeruſalem, 9 R. 2. his body was brought into England, and buried at Stone. He died ſeized of Thornbury, with its members, Oldbury, Kington, Morton, Falfield and Mares, and of the manors of Rendcombe and Eſtington; and was ſucceeded by his ſon

Thomas earl of Stafford, who married Anne, the daughter of Thomas of Woodſtock, duke of Glouceſter, by his wife Eleanor, eldeſt daughter and coheireſs of Humphry de Bohun, earl of Hereford. But this Thomas died before he could conſummate the marriage, and was buried at Stone 16 R. 2. whereby his brother William, who was his next heir, ſucceeded to the title and eſtates; but he died unmarried 18 R. 2.

Edmond earl of Stafford was brother and heir to William, and by ſpecial licence from the king, he married Anne, his brother Thomas's widow, with whom he had the manor of Wheatenhurſt. He was ſlain at the battle of Shrewſbury, fighting for king Henry the Fourth againſt Hotſpur, ſon of Henry earl of Northumberland, 4 H. 4. and was buried in the Auguſtine friery at Stafford. He died ſeized of Thornbury, with its members aforeſaid, and of the manors of Rendcombe and Wheaten-

Wheatenhurſt, and of the caſtle of Caldecot in Glouceſterſhire. The counteſs Anne, his relict, died 17 H. 6. and was then buried at the priory of Lanthony, near Glouceſter.

Humphry earl of Stafford, ſon and heir of Edmond, was very young at his father's death, and married Anne, daughter of Ralph Nevil earl of Weſtmoreland. He was governor of Calais, and was created duke of Buckingham 23 H. 6. A diſpute ariſing concerning precedency between him and Henry Beauchamp, duke of Warwick, it was decided by act of parliament, and ordered, that theſe two dukes ſhould take precedency by turns, one one year, the other the next; and that precedency ſhould be given to ſuch of the poſterity of each as ſhould firſt have livery of their lands. He was ſlain at the battle of Northampton 38 H. 6. wherein king Henry the Sixth was taken priſoner.

Humphry earl of Stafford was the eldeſt ſon of Humphry duke of Buckingham. He married Margaret, daughter and coheir of Edmond duke of Somerſet, and was ſlain at the battle of St. Albans, in his father's life-time.

Henry duke of Buckingham, ſon of Humphry earl of Stafford, and grandſon of Humphry duke of Buckingham, ſucceeded his grandfather in honour, and in the manor of Thornbury. Being under age at his grandfather's death, he was in ward to the king, and the care of his education was aſſigned to Anne, dutcheſs of Exeter, the king's ſiſter. He married Catherine, daughter of Richard Wodeville, earl of Rivers. He was highly inſtrumental in king Richard the Third's unjuſtly obtaining the crown, and afterwards, thro' remorſe of conſcience, took up arms againſt him, and being taken, he was beheaded at Saliſbury 1 R. 3. without any judicial proceedings. A proclamation had been iſſued, offering a thouſand pounds reward to whomever ſhould apprehend the duke, which tempted Humphry Banniſter, his ſervant, to betray him; but he went without the reward, for king Richard ſaid, *That he who would betray ſo good a maſter would be falſe to all others*. This, however, was no juſtification for the king's breaking his faith. Richard's morals and politics were equally bad, and as by this inſtance of his conduct he appeared to be one that could not be relied on, ſo very few would have entered into his ſervice on future occaſions.

Edward duke of Buckingham was ſon of the laſt Humphry. He had livery of his lands 14 H. 7. and obtained a licence to impark a thouſand acres of land in Thornbury 2 H. 8. He married Alianora, daughter of Henry Percy, earl of Northumberland. The king conceived a jealouſy of him for ſome very hot and indiſcreet expreſſions, for which he was tried by his peers upon an accuſation of high treaſon, and found guilty; and diſdaining to aſk his life, was beheaded 13 H. 8. The principal witneſs againſt him was Charles Knevet, whom he had diſcharged of his ſervice at the clamour of his tenants His haughty ſpirit, and contemptuous carriage towards cardinal Wolſey, contributed to his ruin. The duke was preſenting the baſon on his knees for the king to waſh his hands after dinner, and when the king had done, and was turned away, the cardinal ſportingly dipt his hand in the baſon whilſt the duke was on his knees. The duke reſented it as an affront, and riſing up, poured the water into the cardinal's ſhoes. The eccleſiaſtic was nettled in his turn, and threatened the duke to ſit upon his ſkirts. The duke, therefore, came the next day to court, without ſkirts to his doublet, and being aſked the reaſon of it, told the king that it was to avoid the cardinal's anger, for he had threatened to ſit upon his ſkirts. The duke had his jeſt, but the cardinal had his head afterwards. All the monuments of this great family, upon the diſſolution of the priory of Stone, were removed, 30 H. 8. to the friers Auguſtins at Stafford, in hopes that the Mendicant friers might be ſpared; but thoſe coſtly tombs were deſtroy'd, and buried in the ruins of that monaſtery.

Henry Stafford, eldeſt ſon of Edward duke of Buckingham, was by act of parliament reſtored in blood, but not to his father's honours and eſtate, 14 H. 8. However, the king ſoon afterwards granted ſeveral of the lands of the late duke of Buckingham to this Henry Stafford, and to Urſula his wife, and their heirs. She was the daughter of ſir Richard Pole, by Margaret his wife, who was the daughter of George duke of Clarence, brother to king Edward the Fourth. The manor, caſtle, town, and park, &c. of Thornbury, and the manor of Bedellanam in Thornbury, were granted to Henry lord Stafford, and to Urſula his wife, 2 Mar. He was a perſon of great learning and virtue, and having tranſlated ſeveral pieces of divinity, died in the year 1558.

Edward lord Stafford, ſon and heir of Henry, married Mary, daughter of Edward earl of Derby, and left Edward lord Stafford his ſon and heir, who had livery of the manor of Thornbury, and of the reſt of his father's lands, in 1592. He married Iſabel, daughter of Thomas Foſter, of Tonge in Shropſhire, and died in 1625.

Edward lord Stafford, ſon of the laſt Edward, married Anne, daughter of James Wilfords, of Newnham-hall in Eſſex, and died before his father, leaving a ſon Henry, and a daughter Mary. Henry died young in 1637.

Mary Stafford, daughter of the laſt-mentioned Edward, and heireſs of the family, was married to William Howard, a younger ſon of Thomas earl of Arundel and Surry, who, in her right, was ſeized of the manor of Thornbury. He was created viſcount Stafford by king Charles the Firſt, and was beheaded in the reign of king Charles the Second, upon the teſtimony of the famous doctor Oates, as being guilty of the popiſh plot. In the reign of king James the Second, an attempt was made to reverſe the attainder of this lord by a bill in parliament, againſt which ſome of the lords proteſted, and the commons threw it out.

Henry

Henry-Stafford Howard, fon of William vifcount Stafford, was created earl of Stafford by king James the Second, and was lord of the manor of Thornbury at the beginning of the prefent century. The duke of Norfolk is the prefent lord of the manor.

William Heron, of London, haberdafher, and Joan his wife, levied a fine of lands in Thornbury to the ufe of themfelves 33 H. 6. John Stanfhaw, and Humphry his brother, levied a fine of lands in Thornbury 12 H. 7. Richard Forfter levied a fine of the moiety of lands in Thornbury, Oldbury, and Falfield, 12 H. 7.

TITHINGS and *HAMLETS*.

By an act paffed in the reign of king Charles the Second, the tithings of Oldbury, Kington, Morton, and Falfield, all in the parifh of Thornbury, were confolidated into one manor, called the manor of Thornbury. Of which tithings in their order.

1. *Oldbury*, fometimes written *Aldbury*, and *Ealdbury*, from the Saxon Ealð-beꞃᵹ. We now call it *Oldbury upon Severn*, to diftinguifh it from Oldbury upon the Hill, in the hundred of Grumbald's Afh. It ftretches along the fhore of the Severn, and is fuppofed to be the Roman ftation called the *Trajectus*, or ferry, mentioned in Antoninus's fourteenth *Iter*, from *Ifca*, now Caerleon in Monmouthfhire, to *Calleva*, now Wallingford in Berkfhire. It received its prefent name from the Saxons, on account of the antient camps which they found there, and of which fome traces ftill remain. The fmaller one, or *Campus Minor*, was on the eaft fide of the hill near the church, where every thing paffing upon the Severn hereabout might be feen, and many Roman coins have been found upon the fpot. A little eaftward of that, about a quarter of a mile on the plain, was the *Campus Major*; and part of the intrenchments, with high banks, forming two fides of a fquare, ftill remain pretty perfect, tho' the other parts are levelled. Juft by thefe, in a piece of ground which ftill fhews many tumps and unevenneffes, a great many old foundations have been dug up in the memory of perfons living in the place. Thefe circumftances very much corroborate the opinion that here was the Roman *Trajectus*, and not at Auft, as fome have fancied. The diftance between the *Abone*, another Roman ftation, and the *Trajectus*, is fet down to be nine miles by Antoninus, which not agreeing with the real diftance between the places where thofe ftations are fuppofed to have been, has occafioned much difficulty in fixing the fituation of the *Abone*; but as this fubject has been fully difcuffed under Lidney, the reader is referred to that head for further fatisfaction.

This part of the parifh is very unhealthy, from ftagnated water lying on fome of the lands; and it is made more fo from the great number of Elm trees ftanding fo thick about the houfes, that the air has not a free current.

Sir Robert Atkyns has mifapplied the account of Edward the Elder paffing over the Severn at this place, to meet Leoline prince of Wales; for according to Mapes, and others, it happened at Auft, and not here.

The Defpencers are faid to have been fometime feized of this manor, in the reign of king Edward the Second. Eubulo le Strange, and Aleria his wife, levied a fine of Oldbury to the ufe of Hugh le Defpencer 18 E. 2.

The knights templars were feized of Oldbury 2 E. 3. and upon the diffolution of that order, the manor was granted to the Veals. John Veal died feized of the manor of Oldbury 36 H. 6. as did Robert Veal, fon of John, 13 E. 4.

The Kemyfes fucceeded the Veals. Roger Kemys, who was found by inquifition to be a lunatick, died feized of Oldbury 21 E. 4. Hugh Kemys and John Kemys levied a fine of the manor of Oldbury to William George, and William Overton, 4 E. 6. Sir James Harrington was lord of this manor in the year 1608, but it is now confolidated with Thornbury.

John Newton and Joan his wife levied a fine of lands in Oldbury to the ufe of themfelves in taille, 8 H. 5. Lands in Oldbury and Holeham belonged to the abbey of Tewkefbury, and were granted to Daniel Pert and Alexander Pert, in truft, 7 E. 6. A portion of tithes in Oldbury, and a meadow called Holeham, which belonged to the abbey of Tewkefbury, were granted to the lord Fenton 5 Jac.

There is a chapel in Oldbury, and the chapelry is annexed to Thornbury. It is called the Rectory of Oldbury in the prefentation, and is worth 50*l.* a year. The chapel ftands on the top of a hill. The inhabitants fay, that their anceftors attempted to build it on Shaw's Green, near the middle of the village; but what they effected in the day was deftroy'd by night, which made them defift. They were then advifed to yoke two heifers that never had been milked, and wherefoever they fhould firft ftop, there to build the chapel. The poor beafts ftraggling along, at laft halted on the top of the hill, and fo the chapel was built there.

Cowhill, or *Cowell*, is a hamlet in this tithing. Henry Campneys was feized of Cowhull 15 E. 4. Anthony Campneys died feized thereof 27 H. 8. and livery was granted to Henry Campneys, brother and heir to Anthony, the next year. Livery of Cowell was alfo granted to John Campneys 13 Eliz. Cowell was lately purchafed out of the family of fir Thomas Campnefs, by Peter Holford, of Wefton Birt in this county, efq.

Mr. Thomas Adams has a good eftate at Cowhill.

2. *Kington*. The church of Thornbury ftands in this tithing. The lands antiently belonged to the

the family of the Staffords, and were granted to Dorothy Stafford, and to her sons, in taille, 26 Eliz. Aryld, a virgin, is said to have been murdered here by one Muncius, a tyrant, who cut off her head. She was afterwards canonized, and buried in St. Peter's abbey at Gloucester.

Marlewood is within this tithing, where was an antient seat and a park belonging to the Staffords, which Edward Stafford sold, about the beginning of this century, and Mr. Knight, whose ancestor purchased it, is the present owner of it.

3. *Morton.* Eastwood is a very large estate in this tithing, where was formerly a park. It is situated on a fine eminence, on the east side of the town, and has a large mansion house belonging to it, now converted to a farm house. This estate came to the crown by the attainder of Edward duke of Buckingham, and was granted to Thomas Tyndale[r] 7 Eliz. Sir Richard Rogers, son of Robert Rogers of Bristol, died seized of Eastwood in 1635. It afterwards passed to sir Richard

---

[r] This family came antiently from Tyndale in the north of England, so called from the north Tyne, which rises in the mountains on the borders of England, and waters that dale. Robert de Tyndale had three sons, Adam, Robert, and John. Adam de Tyndale was living in 1199, and had issue by Helewisa his wife, one daughter Philippa, married to Nicholas, baron of Bolteby, in the time of king Henry the Third. Robert, the second son, seated himself at Transover in Northamptonshire, *temp.* E. I. and had issue two sons, sir William Tyndale, knight, who died without issue; and Robert Tyndale, living in 1293. Which Robert had issue two sons, Richard, and William. Richard died *sine prole*; but sir William Tyndale of Transover, the second son, married Elizabeth, the niece and heir of sir Henry Deane, of Deane in Northamptonshire.

John Tyndale, son of sir William, was living in the year 1391, and by his wife Catharine Zouch, had issue two sons, Richard, who died 3 H. 5. *sine prole*; and sir William Tyndale, who by his wife Alana, (daughter and heir of sir Simon Bigod, *alias* Felbrigge, of Felbrigge in Norfolk, knight of the garter, by his wife Margaret, daughter to the duke of Theise, and niece to the king of Bohemia) had issue sir Thomas Tyndale, of Deane, knight. Which sir Thomas Tyndale married Margaret, daughter of sir William Yelverton, and by her had sir William Tyndale, of Hockwold in Norfolk, made knight of the Bath in 1496; and three daughters, Anne, married to Henry St. Germain; Jane, wedded to John Blanerhasset; and Elizabeth.

The said sir William Tyndale of Hockwold, by Mary his wife, daughter and heir of Osbert Montford, of Norfolk, had issue four sons, *viz.* 1. sir John; 2. William, the ancestor of the Tyndales of Bathford, of whom hereafter; 3. Robert; and 4. Edward, settled at Pull-court in Worcestershire. Sir John Tyndale, eldest son of sir William Tyndale of Hockwold, married Amphillis, daughter of —— Coningsby, and by her was father of two sons, sir Thomas, and Humphry; and four daughters, Anne, Mary, Beatrix, and Dorothy. Sir Thomas Tyndale, the eldest son, married first, Anne, daughter of sir William Paston, by whom he had issue a son William, who died in 1591, having married a daughter of sir Ambrose Germain, by whom he was father of one son, Felix Tyndale, who died without issue. Sir Thomas Tyndale's second wife was Anne, daughter of sir Henry Fermer, by whom he had issue six sons, sir John; ———; Francis, who died a batchelor, and his will was proved in 1631; Henry; Humphry, D. D. dean of Ely, president of Queen's college, Cambridge, and chancellor of Litchfield, who died and was buried at Ely in 1614; and Arthur: The daughters were Susan, Ursula, Elizabeth, Anne, and Amye.

Sir John, eldest son of sir Thomas Tyndale, by Anne his second wife, settled at Great Maplestead in Essex, where he built a house called New Chelmeshoo House. He was a master in chancery, and was murdered by John Bertram, as he was going to his chambers in Lincoln's Inn, Nov. 12, 1616. He married Anne, daughter of Thomas Egerton, esq; and widow of sir William Deane, of Great Maplestead, and by her had issue three sons and three daughters, *viz.* Deane, Arthur, Roger; Sarah, Margaret, and Hester. Deane Tyndale, eldest son of sir John, married Amye, daughter and heir of Robert Weston, of Prested Hall in Essex, and died in 1678, aged 92. He had issue by his said wife four sons, *viz.* Deane, buried March 23, 1633; Francis, who died young; John, of whom presently; Drue, a Hamborough merchant; and two daughters, Anne, and Elizabeth. John, the third but only surviving son of Deane Tyndale of Maplestead, married Elizabeth, daughter of Anthony Deane, of Dynes Hall, esq; by whom he had issue an only daughter Elizabeth, wedded to Jasper Blitheman. At the death of the said John Tyndale, the male heirs of this branch became extinct: I return therefore to the other sons of sir William Tyndale, of Hockwold in Norfolk, who, as before recited, were William, of whom hereafter; Robert; and Edward.

Edward Tyndale, fourth son of sir William, settled at the Pull, otherwise called Pull court, in Worcestershire, and married two wives. By the first he had issue two sons, Thomas, and William; and five daughters: By Joan his second wife, daughter of William Lawrence, he had three sons, John, Edward, and Henry; and three daughters. He died in the year 1546, as appears by the *probat.* of his will.

Thomas Tyndale, eldest son of Edward, settled at Eastwood in the parish of Thornbury, in the county of Gloucester, of which he had a grant 7 Eliz. 1565, and by Avice his wife, daughter of John Bodie, had an only son Edward, and one only daughter Elizabeth, who both died before their father. Thomas survived 'till the year 1571, and by his will gave the estate at Eastwood to his cousin Thomas Tyndale, a minor, whose descent I shall now proceed to trace from sir William Tyndale, of Hockwold in Norfolk.

William Tyndale, second son of sir William Tyndale of Hockwold, and brother of Edward of Pull-court, died about the year 1558, leaving issue one son Thomas; and two daughters, Joan, and Faith.

Thomas Tyndale, son of William, married a daughter of ——— Lloyd, of Grismond-castle in Monmouthshire, and of Whitminster in Gloucestershire, and had issue

Thomas, to whom Thomas Tyndale of Eastwood left that estate, in the year 1571. Thomas, the son, died in 1619, having married Oriana le Bon, daughter of John le Bon, counsellor in the parliament of Roan in Normandy, and one of the sisters and heirs of Claudius le Bon, of Farnaux in that province. By her he had issue four sons, Thomas, Francis, Edmund, and George, of whom the three last had no children; and three daughters, who all died unmarried.

Thomas Tyndale, the eldest son, sold the estate at Eastwood in this parish, to sir Richard Rogers, a grocer in Bristol, about the year 1628, and went to reside at the priory at Kington St. Michael, near Calne in Wiltshire, where he died Feb. 22, 1671. The following curious letter from this gentleman to his cousin, Mr. ——— Tyndale, of Stinchcombe in this county, may be acceptable to some of my readers:

' *Cousin,*

' *I have received your late letter, and am very glad to hear so well*
' *of you; and shall much rejoyce to understand of any good which*
' *may arrive to the familie of Stinchcombe, so as I can not but hope that*
' *the thing you write of to me looks that way, tho' you mention it not.*
' *The name of Tyndale is well known in the Harold's office to bee of*
' *great antiquity and reputation, but branched out into many and divers*
' *families, as all ancient names have been from age to age, without*
' *observing or keeping any knowledge of the times, or any certain*
' *genealogie of their descents, albeit they are of the same extraction and*
' *originall with the rest. The first familie of Tyndale in credit and*
' *reputation was of Dale castle in South Tyndale in Northumberland,*
' *and called, by writ, to the upper house of parliament in the time of*
' *Edward the 1st, and were barons of Langley in South Tyndale.*
' *That house extinguished by an heir general married to Boultebey,*
' *whose heir general was after married unto Percie. The second brother*
' *of that Tyndale seated himself in Northamptonshire, at a place called*
' *Transover, and after they married the heir of sir Henry Deane, of*
' *Deane by Transover, and then the heir of sir Symond Bygod, of*
' *Felbrigge, one of the knights of the garter, and it was a great match,*
' *and with one of the heirs of the lord Scales of Nacelles, dividing that*
' *inheritance with the earl of Oxford; afterwards they married the*
' *heir of Montfort in Norfolke, whether Tyndale removed his seat to*
' *Hockwold. This familie was in great reputation 'till the beginning*
' *of queen Elizabethe, at what time sir Thomas Tyndale made an end*
' *of all which his father sir John Tyndale had not spent before. Sir*
' *John Tyndale, second son to sir Thomas Tyndale, did leave his son*
' *Deane Tyndale, who (if living) is just my age, and dwelleth in Essex,*
' *near Heningham-castle, and hath some eight hundred Pound per*
' *annum left, and is the best Tyndale now remaining. From that*
' *familie my great grandfather came. There is also another familie of*
' *Tyndale of Brotherton in Yorkshire, of good estate and reputation, but*
' *giving some what a different coat, as you may perceive by what I*
' *have set down here underneath; but I cannot at this time see certain*
' *to blazon Brotherton's coat aright. I have heretofore heard that the*
' *first of your familie came out of the North in the times of the wars*
' *between the houses of York and Lancaster, at what time many of good*
' *sort (their side going down) did fly for refuge and succor where they*
' *could*

Richard Aſhfield, in right of Mary his wife, eldeſt daughter, and one of the coheireſſes of ſir Richard Rogers; and is at preſent the eſtate of ſir Banks Jenkinſon, of Oxfordſhire, baronet, whoſe arms are given under Hawkeſbury.

Hope is the name of a place in the pariſh of Thornbury. Sir William Compton died ſeized of ten meſſuages, five hundred acres of arable, and two hundred acres of paſture, and of other lands in Hope, near Thornbury, 20 H. 8. Mr. Thomas Morris has a good eſtate at Hope.

Buckover is the name of another place. Lands in Buckover in Thornbury, lately belonging to Edward duke of Buckingham, were granted to Elizabeth Harwell 15 H. 8. Lands called the Barrys, late the duke of Buckingham's, were granted to Thomas Henege, and Catherine his wife, for their lives, 23 H. 8.

4. *Falfield*, ſo called from the Saxon Falð, *an incloſure*. It was reputed a manor, and belonged to ſir John Berkeley, of Beverſtone, 6 H. 6. and to ſir Maurice Berkeley 14 E. 4. William Berkeley was ſeized of it, and being outlawed for treaſon, it was granted to Thomas Brug, and his heirs male, 1 H. 7. But William Berkeley was afterwards reſtored to his eſtates. Sir William Berkeley died ſeized of Falfield 5 E. 6. and John Berkeley, ſon of ſir William, had livery of it granted to him 6 E. 6. Livery of the manor of Falfield was alſo granted to Edward lord Stafford 9 Eliz. This manor, as before obſerved, is conſolidated with that of Thornbury. Mr. Thomas Skey has a good eſtate here, which has been in his family for many generations.

Of the Church, &c.

The church is a vicarage, in the deanery of Durſley, worth about 200*l.* a year. Chriſt Church college, Oxford, are patrons, and the reverend Mr. Holwell is the preſent incumbent. It was formerly given to the abbey of Tewkeſbury, by Gilbert de Clare earl of Glouceſter; and the abbey recovered it from the biſhop of Worceſter 26 E. 1. It was appropriated[a] to the uſe of the monaſtery

'*could find it. That it was your predeceſſor his fortune to come into*
'*Gloceſterſhire, changing his name to that of Huchins, and that after-*
'*wards he married there, and ſo having children, he did before his*
'*death declare his right name, and from whence and upon what ſubject*
'*he came thither; and ſo taking his own name, did leave it unto his*
'*children, who have ſince continued it, as it was fit they ſhould. This*
'*I have heard from your good father himſelf. Two of my ſons do know*
'*them of Brotherton and my ſon Thomas (now married in London)*
'*hath been there. I have made you now (as you ſee) an ample relation*
'*of all that I can at preſent call to mind that may be proper to acquaint*
'*you withal, and ſhall think well thereof if it may any way ſatisfie your*
'*deſires. My ſon William is now with me, and deſires to be very*
'*kindly remembered unto you, as having (by his ſaying) been known*
'*and received courteſies from you in the Low Countreys. If you*
'*pleaſe to write any more unto me, you ſhall not need to put my name*
'*Thomas, nor the priory to the ſuperſcription; I am much known*
'*without thoſe additions. My wife is alſo yet living, though in a ſad*
'*condition this long time, but ſhe hath not forgotten you, praying me*
'*to remember her love unto you. It is now time to give over and make*
'*an end, ſo concluding with my affectionate reſpects and good wiſhes*
'*to yourſelf and to your nephew, tho' unknown, I reſt*

'*Your loving kinſman, and*
'*aſſured friend,*
'*Thomas Tyndale.*'

'*Kington St. Michael,*
'*Febr.* 3*d* 1663.

This Thomas Tyndale took to wife Dorothy, daughter of William Stafford, of Northamptonſhire, by whom he had five ſons and four daughters, *viz.* Stafford, who died childleſs; William, Thomas, George, and John; and four daughters, Frances, married to John Poree, of Roan in Normandy; Anne, wedded to captain Doughty; Dorothy, and Orian.

William Tyndale, of Kington St. Michael, ſecond ſon of Thomas, died Nov. 3, 1675. He took to wife Margaret, daughter of Anderſon Atcherley, of Shropſhire, and by her had five ſons, Thomas, George, John, Athelſtan, and Henry.

Thomas Tyndale, the eldeſt ſon, born June 2, 1667, removed to Bathford near Bath, where he died in the year 1747. He married firſt, a daughter of ——— Winchcombe, of Witney in Oxfordſhire, and by her had a ſon Thomas, who died young, and one daughter, Dorothy. By Elizabeth his ſecond wife, daughter of George Booth, of Woodford in Cheſhire, eſq; he had iſſue two ſons, John, who died unmarried in 1728; and George; and four daughters, Martha-Maria, Elizabeth, Mary, and Arabella.

George Tyndale, ſecond ſon of Thomas, married to his firſt wife, Vere, daughter of the honourable and reverend Robert Booth, D.D. and dean of Briſtol, fifth ſon of George lord Delamere, by whom he hath iſſue one ſon, George-Booth Tyndale, born Sep. 8, 1743; who being bred to the law in the Inner Temple, was called to the bar in 1768; and one daughter, Elizabeth-Vere, who died young. His ſecond wife was Margaretta, daughter of John Bamfylde, of Heſtercombe in Somerſetſhire, eſq; by whom he has iſſue two ſons, John, and Thomas-Bamfylde; and three daughters, Margaretta, Elizabeth, and Charlotta-Maria. Which George Tyndale, eſq; reſides at Bathford in Somerſetſhire, where he has a good houſe and eſtate. His arms are, *Argent, a feſs gules between three garbs ſable.*

[a] In the twelfth and thirteenth centuries, the laity began to think they had done enough for monaſteries; therefore the monks ſought out other means to increaſe their revenues, by deſpoiling the ſecular clergy, who were the true labourers in the church, and thereupon appropriation of tithes to regular monks became more frequent. The following is a tranſlation of the appropriation, as given by ſir Robert Atkyns:

TO all ſons of holy mother the church, to whom theſe preſents ſhall come, Walter, by God's permiſſion, biſhop of Worceſter, ſendeth grace, health, and eternal benediction. Tho' we are obliged out of the duty of common charity, to extend ſome favour to all perſons in miſery, towards the relief of their neceſſities; we are however bound more principally to exert ourſelves in the aſſiſtance of the religious under our care, who whilſt they are buſied in the fruits of good works, we ſee reduced and fallen into great want, and not by any fault of their own. Therefore we having a due regard to the monaſtery of Tewkeſbury, and to the religious men the abbat and monks of the ſaid monaſtery, within our dioceſe, which was heretofore founded by the progenitors of famous memory of the lord Gilbert de Clare, late earl of Glouceſter and Hertford, and endowed with ſpiritualties and temporalties ſituated in remote parts, and particularly in Wales, which was ſubject to the frequent incurſions of enemies, by which means it is but meanly endowed, and not able to ſubſiſt the convent, and maintain the poor, and other neceſſary charges and burthens of the ſame monaſtery, as ought to be; and it alſo lies oppreſt under divers calamities of fire, and inundation of waters on their lands and poſſeſſions, and by other adverſities and malice of this preſent world, will be daily brought into great and notorious decay, which unleſs timely relieved, can ſcarce in probability be ever recovered. And we taking notice that the pariſh church of Thornbury within our dioceſe, is under the patronage of the ſaid monaſtery, and that it was heretofore duly and canonically appropriated to the ſaid abbat and monks for the time being, and to their ſucceſſors, for the better ſupport of the burthens and charges aforeſaid; and that they for a long time had actually and peaceably enjoyed the poſſeſſion thereof, and that a great part of the revenue of the ſaid monaſtery, at the time of the appropriation did conſiſt herein, and that ſince they have been deprived of the ſame by ſome ſecular men, upheld with the power of ſome great nobles, who have divers times wrongfully preſented to the ſaid church, by their own damnable unjuſtice, and not thro' any fault of the ſaid monaſtery, who, notwithſtanding, have continued to maintain the functions of their monaſtery, in like manner as if they had enjoyed the profits of that impropriation, in as full manner as at their firſt foundation and appropriation, and their expences by theſe means have exceeded their yearly revenue, whereby they have unavoidably incurred on themſelves and their monaſtery, a heavy and inſupportable debt. And further, they are at this day

monaftery by Walter bifhop of Worcefter, in the year 1314. The impropriation is now vefted in Chrift Church college, by grant from the crown 38 H. 8. But the rectory of Thornbury was granted to William Fitz-Williams, and Arthur Hilton, 7 E. 6.

The tithes of lady Symonds's lands, and all the fmall tithes, belong to the vicarage. There are three chapels annexed to this church, Oldbury, Rangeworthy, and Falfield.

The church is dedicated to the virgin Mary. It is large and handfome, with a fpacious aile on each fide the nave, and two crofs ailes, and a beautiful high tower at the weft end. The great chancel belongs to Chrift Church college. It is faid that the body of the church and the tower were built by Fitz-Harding, who dwelt at Roll's Place; and that the fouth aile was built by Hugh lord Stafford.

There were four chantries in this church, one

---

day fubject to a great and unufual charge, by reafon of the great travelling which is thro' that place both by land and water, it being fituated between two great rivers, the Severn and the Avon, which bring a great concourfe of people, who expect to be entertained by the faid monaftery, and has brought a charge upon the monaftery, beyond what it is able to bear, and has neceffarily reduced the monaftery, and abbat, and monks, to great poverty, which can no way be relieved and redreffed without the augmentation of their poffeffions and revenues. And we being fully advifed of the truth of all and fingular of thefe circumftances, we therefore beholding with grief and an eye of compaffion, the oppreffion and mifery of thefe faid religious men and the monaftery, and defirous to affift them to the beft of our power, as becomes our holy office, and that thefe religious men fhould not be incumbred with the anxious neceffities of this life, who have devoted themfelves to the fervice of God alone, during their whole lives, under the obfervance of pious rules; and we further confidering how we may deliver them out of this impendent ruin into which they have fallen, and reftore them to a more eafy and plentiful augmentation of their profit, whereby they may keep better hofpitality for the future, and may perform greater acts of charity, and may uphold the chapel founded by the aforefaid earl, to the honour of the bleffed Mary mother of God, and glorious virgin, which chapel hath lately been built anew, at the burthen and charge of the faid abbat and monks of the faid monaftery, and that the mafs of the bleffed virgin may be daily faid therein, to the praife of God and of his mother, and of All Saints, to the increafe of divine worfhip, for the profperity of the living, and the reft of the fouls of the dead; and that the officers and minifters who affift in the celebration of the fame, and the other charges thereunto belonging, may be fuftained, we, by the influence of divine piety and pontifical authority, do give, grant, affign and appropriate the parifh church of Thornbury within our diocefe aforefaid, in which the faid religious men have a juft right of patronage, to the faid monaftery of Tewkefbury, and to the abbat and monks of that place, and to their own proper ufe for ever, having a due regard to the right and intereft of the faid mafter Roger Marfhall the prefent rector of Thornbury, and all others who can have any intereft or claim, being firft fummoned, and their confent on this behalf being firft obtained.

We further will and grant, that after the ceffion or death of the faid mafter Roger, the prefent rector of the church, the actual poffeffions of the fame church, with all its chapels thereon depending, and all its rights, members, and appurtenances whatfoever, without any interpofition of us or any of our fucceffors, fhall be converted to the proper ufe of the faid monaftery, for the better fupport of their charges, referving neverthelefs a moderate portion to the vicarage of the faid church of Thornbury, which we do fix to be the fum of 25 marks fterling, yearly to be received out of the profits of the faid church, by the vicar, to be prefented by the faid religious men, for the performing the duty of the faid church and chapels thereunto belonging, faving all rights which belong to our cathedral church at Worcefter.

In witnefs whereof we have hereunto fixt our feal, dated at London in the year of our Lord 1314, and in the fecond year of our confecration.

The fame bifhop Walter eftablifhed an endowment for the vicar, which is thus tranflated by fir Robert Atkyns:

TO all fons of holy mother the church, to whom thefe prefents fhall come, Walter, by divine permiffion, bifhop of Worcefter, fendeth eternal health in our Lord. Know ye, that whereas for certain good caufes we have lately appropriated the church of Thornbury in the deanery of Durfley, within our diocefe, to the religious men the abbat and convent of Tewkefbury, and to their fucceffors, and to the monaftery of that place, referving to ourfelves the power of ordering and taxing unto the value of 25 marks, for the ufe of the vicar of the church, all which does in our faid appropriation more fully appear. Therefore, by a legal inquifition of divers worthy rectors and vicars of the faid deanery, and others, laymen, in form of law being fummoned, who being rightly informed of the true value of all the oblations, obventions, and other the leffer tithes, rights, and appurtenances of the faid parochial church of Thornbury, and therein certified by them, that the oblations, obventions, and the other leffer tithes due to the altar, to wit, of milk, wool, lambs, cows, calves, fwine, poultry, pidgeon-houfes, eggs, bees, herbs, flax, fifhings, and gardens, and likewife the tithes of the hay in the whole parifh, whether a fum of money be paid for it, or elfe gathered in kind: Befides and except the tithes of hay of the demean lands of the manor of Thornbury, lying within the bounds, limits, and tithing places of the faid church, belonging to the lady Symonds, are eftimated at 18 marks and 10*s.* and being willing to tax and make up the reft of the intended revenue of the vicarage to the full, (as in juftice ought to be) out of money arifing by the wax, which thro' devotion and reverence to the holy virgin Mary, whofe image is placed in the chancel of the faid church, or the ready money, or gold or filver, which may be there offered, and alfo with a fufficient houfe in the town of Thornbury, ftanding on the ground belonging to the church, lately held by one Relibron for his life, together with a garden adjoining to the faid houfe, and belonging to the rectory before the appropriation was made.

Wherefore we the bifhop, having fummoned the above mentioned perfons, and all things being obferved in form as ought to be, and confidering that the aforefaid taxation and affignation to be juft and equal in all refpects, and that the faid oblations, obventions, and leffer tithes, together with the houfe and garden, and other contingent profits, will one with another arife to make five marks, and will be fufficient to maintain the vicarage and vicar, with his and all the charges of the vicarage, do appoint, decree, and confirm, that the further fupply to the vicarage ought to confift in thofe faid portions, and that the faid vicar at prefent, and all the vicars his fucceffors, ought to be contented with the faid offerings, obventions, fmall tithes, and other portions, as is above enumerated, without any further profit to be demanded from the faid religious men.

We do moreover order, appoint, and decree, that the faid vicar in the church of Thornbury, now canonically inftituted, and all the vicars his fucceffors in the fame, fhall be firmly obliged and bound to difcharge all procurations to the archbifhop, and fhall furnifh lights in the cathedral fynods, and fhall find and keep in repair all books and veftments, and other ornaments neceffary to the faid church, as heretofore has been accuftomed by the rectors of the faid church, and by right they ought to have done; and to fuftain all thefe afore-mentioned things, and all other ufual and ordinary burthens whatfoever and howfoever, at their own proper cofts and charges, excepting the reparation, amendment, and building of the chancel of the church of Thornbury aforefaid; for which end all other extraordinary charges which are impofed on the church of Thornbury, or fhall any way hereafter be impofed, the faid vicar and his fucceffors, fhall be rated for their fhare at the proportion of 15 marks, except in the payment of four marks, which by the confent and affent of the faid abbat and convent, we have ordered and referved, and by them truly fubmitted unto on their part (which fubmiffion has been made appear unto us) to be yearly paid unto us and our fucceffors, when the fee of Worfter fhall be full, and unto the chapter of the place when the fee fhall be vacant, which burthen we have laid upon the church of Thornbury for our proper ufe, by authority of an ordinary, with their confent as aforefaid, and do impofe the fame on the faid church, under the name of an annuity. In witnefs therefore of this our free and perpetual decree, we have caufed it to be drawn in three parts, whereof we will one, figned with our feal, and with the feal of the vicar of Thornbury, fhall remain with the faid abbat and convent; another part figned with our feal, and the feal of the abbat and convent, fhall remain with the faid vicar and his fucceffors; and a third part figned with the feal of the abbat and convent, in token of their fubmiffion and confent to all the premiffes, fhall remain to us and our fucceffors.

We the abbat and convent aforefaid, in fign and confirmation of our fubmiffion, and confent to all the premiffes, have hereunto affixed our feal.

Dated at our chapter in Tewkefbury, the eleventh day of Auguft, in the year of our Lord 1315.

dedicated

dedicated to the virgin Mary, and erected in the year 1499; another called Barne's chantry, of which Thomas Smyth was the last incumbent, and received a pension of 5*l.* in 1553; the others were Bruis chantry, and Slimbridge chantry, whereof the abbat of St. Augustin's in Bristol was patron. The lands belonging to the two latter were granted to sir Arthur Darcie 7 E. 6.

Monuments and Inscriptions.

At the foot of the altar, there formerly stood a large raised tomb of black marble, inlaid with brass. But when the chancel was afterwards repaired, the tomb was taken down, and the upper slab fixed in the floor, with the following inscription on a plate of brass:

Thomas Tyndale dyed the 28 of April, buried 31st May, 1571.

Ye se how death doth Spare no age no Kynd
How I am lapt in Claye and dead you fynde
My Wife and Childeren lye here with me
No Gould, no friend, no Strength could randsome bee
The End of Vayne delighte and Ill Intente,
The end of Care and Matter to repent,
The End of faere for frynd and Worldly Wo,
By Death we have; and of lyke Thousande mo.
And death of Tymes in us hath made an End,
So that nothing can ower Estate amend.
Who would not be Content such Change to make
For Worldly thinges Eternal Life to Take.

A free-stone monument, against the north wall of the chancel, is thus oddly inscribed:

Here *Lieth the* Body of Sr. Iohn Stafford Knight. A Gentleman Pensioner *During the Space* of 47 YEARES to QVEENE ELIZABETH AND King IAMES HEE had as A REWARD of his VALOUR & fidELITY conferRED VPON him BY HER MAtie, THE ConstabLESHIP of BRIStOLL CAStLE WHEREIN HEE continued A long time. HEE LIUED (as himselfe on his DEATH bed confessed) in THE fraiLE AND SLIPPERY course of A SOULDIER AND A COURTIER FROM THE time of his MANhood NEERE VNTO THE time of his DEATH: Notwith*standing* sensible of *his end and that accompt hee* was to *give* at *the last Day*, HEE DID FVLLY *and freely* forgiue *all men Sealing the same* by *calling* for *and* Receiuing *the* bLEssed *Sacrament*, *as a pledge* of his *forgiving other men*, *and* of *the* forgivenesse of his owne sinnes, for whatsoeueR *the* frailty of his LIFE OR bitternes *of the* DISEASE where*of* HEE DIED might be, his hope of *a* better LIFE through *the mercies* and sufferings of HIS REDEEMER *made* him a conquerOVR over *and* beyond *those* humane fRAILTIES, *hee* dying IN THE SOVND *faith of a* penitent sinner, *a Loyall* SERVANT to his *prince*, *a* LOVER of his *Country*, *wherein* HEE did BEARE *the* chiefest offices of *trust* and creditt, *and a* founder of *an* ALmeshouse in *the* PariSH *where hee* LIUED endowing *the* same with 10 pounds p' *Annũ to* be payd for euer. Obiit 28° DIE Septemb: A° Dñi 1624.

In cuius MEMORIÃ, et VERitatis huius testimonium Nepos eius sciens vidensque, hoc Monumentũ posuit, hac fretus spe, votoque inquiens, Non aLITER cineres *mando* IACERE MEOS.

Within a scutcheon, upon the stone, are these *insignia*, *Gules*, *in fess*, *on the dexter side*, *the Stafford's knot*, *on the sinister side*, *A wolfe's head erazed Or.*

Opposite to the above, against the south wall,

Heere lyeth the Body of Richard, Son & Heire to Sr Richard Ashfield Bart. of Neither-Hall in Suffolke, by Mary his Wife eldest Davghter, & one of the Coheires of Sr. Richard Rogers Kt. who deceased May ye 17th ANO DNI 1656, Ætat. svÆ 5.

Vnhappy Losse! Nay happy Gaine bee't se'd
When by Earth's Losse Heauen's Kingdom's PVRCHASED
Christ's bloud the PRICE, God's word ye EVIDENCE
Heauen settle's Crounes on Childrens Innocence.
This Branch soe soone cropt' off, earth cast thereon
Add's TVRFE to TWIG, and giues POSSESSION.
Thy TITLE's good, thy TENURE'S CAPITE;
Death past the FINE, Christ the RECOVERIE.

Against the south wall of the church,

In Memory of Iane the wife of John Baker Gent. and Daughter of Richard Newman Gent. whoe had Issue by the said Iohn Baker 15 childrẽ 11 of which survived her. She was buried 20° die Octob: 1646: As for her Life and Conversation shee imitated her Parents in vertue: was constant in her Love to her husband: tender to her children, provident in her family, charitable to all, and zealous in God's service, which crowneth the Rest. The said Iohn Baker hath as his last Farewell erected (at the Place where hee first brought and last left her) this Monument.

Hoc tumulo inclusa virtus pietasq; perennant
Mors licet eripuit, Fama Superstes erit.

Arms, *Quarterly* 1st *and* 4th, *Sable*, *three mullets argent.*

Near it is an inscription on a monument for John Baker, of this parish, gent. with these arms, *Barry of ten pieces*, *argent and azure*, *on six scutcheons sable as many lions rampant of the first.*

Upon a table of a large handsome marble monument, against the same wall, it is thus written:

In the middle Isle under a marble Stone lies with his Ancestors, the Body of John Atwells, Gent. who died Feb. ye 18th 1729-30, Having by his last Will dated May 16, 1729 (Which was proved in the Prerogative Court of Chancery) bequeathed to this and other Parishes, for charitable Uses, the Sum of 1200*l.* He was the only Son and Heir of Richard Atwells lately of this Town Gent. by Jane his Wife, one of the Daughters of John Ridley Gent. formerly of Shrivenham in the county of Berks, who are all extinct.

The arms on this monument are, *Argent*, *a pile sable*, *over all a chevron counterchanged.*

On a white marble monument, against the wall of the north aile, is this inscription:

In Memory of William Raymond late of this Parish, Esq; who died the 28th of July, 1729, aged 56.

Also in Memory of Hester, Daughter of John Tayer of this Parish Gent. and Relict of William Raymond Esq; who departed this Life the 4th of April 1764, Aged 76.

DOMINE
Notum fac Mihi Salutis viam;
Tuum enim Vultum semper commitatur Summa Felicitas
Ps. xvi. 12.

Arms, *Sable*, *a chevron argent between three eagles display'd Or*, *on a chief of the third three martlets gules.*

Near it, on another marble monument,

In the Church Yard
Behind this Monument
are deposited the Remains of
WILLIAM RAYMOND
of SIBLAND, in this Parish Esq;
Who died the 14th April 1756, aged 57.
He married MARY Daughter of
JACOB VANDERESCH of HAGUE
In the Province of HOLLAND, Esq;
By whom he had ELIZABETH, Wife to
Mr. RALPH GROVE
Of the Borough of THOROBURY.
By MARY his next Wife,

Third Daughter and Coheir of *Philip Hampton*, of WESTBURY, in the Forest of DEAN, and ANNE his Wife, Daughter and Coheir of THOMAS SYMONDS of Cleer-Well, in this County Esq; he had Issue five Sons and six Daughters: of whom six lie buried with their Mother at WESTBURY, Two, PHILIP and ANNE, with their Father. The Survivors, MARY, Wife to RICHARD BIGLAND, of FROCESTER in this County, FLORENCE RAYMOND, and THOMAS RAYMOND, from Duty and Affection, have erected this Monument to the Memory of the Deceased, A. D. 1770.

At bottom, on the dexter side, Raymond, impaling *Azure*, *an estoile Or*; *on a chief of the second two carpenters squares in saltire of the first.* On the sinister side, Raymond, and on an escutcheon of pretence, *Argent*, *a chevron gules between three cinquefoils azure.*

In the same aile, is a small monument for the Tysons of Hope-farm, in this parish, with their arms, *Vert*, *three lions rampant regardant argent*, *ducally crowned Or.*

Benefactions.

Mr. William Edwards of Alveston built a free-school in the town, which Mr. White afterwards endowed with 14*l.* a year.

Sir

Sir John Stafford built an almſhouſe for ſix poor people, and endowed it with 10*l.* a year, charged on his eſtate at Buckover.

Thomas Slimbridge built an almſhouſe for four poor people, and endowed it with lands worth 11*l.* 9*s.* 4*d.* a year. And by his will dated Sept. 27, 1605, gave all his houſes, gardens, and lands within the borough and lordſhip of Thornbury, to the uſe of the poor of the ſaid borough, at the diſpoſal of the mayor and eldeſt burgeſſes for ever.

John Hilp of Thornbury, gent. by deed dated the 1ſt of June, 2 Jac. 1. gave 52*s.* a year charged on his houſes and lands there, to be diſtributed weekly to the poor. Alſo a meſſuage, with a garden in the ſaid borough, called the lower almſhouſe, for four poor people for ever.

John White of Thornbury, by his will in 1590, gave 17*s.* 4*d.* charged on a tavern in that borough, to the uſe of the poor.

Katherine Rippe of Thornbury, by her will, proved in 1594, gave a houſe there for an almſhouſe, and charged her tan-houſe there with 3*s.* 4*d.* a year for the reparation of the ſame almſhouſe.

Cecily Harwood, of the city of Glouceſter, widow, by her will in 1668, gave the intereſt of 20*l.* for placing out poor children of this pariſh apprentices.

Chriſtian Morſe gave the intereſt of 20*l.* to the ſame uſe.

Mr. Thomas Haynes of Wick, gave 20*l.* to the poor, which was diſtributed accordingly.

John Atwells of Thornbury, gent. by his will, proved in 1730, gave 500*l.* for eſtabliſhing a free ſchool in Thornbury, for teaching to read, write, knit, and ſew. Alſo a further ſum of 200*l.* to be laid out on lands, the rents to be applied to apprentice out poor boys of Thornbury to trades.

William Stephens, of Littleton upon Severn, gave 20*l.* a year to ſuch poor of Thornbury as have not relief of the pariſh.

Here is alſo a free grammar ſchool, but I could not obtain the exact particulars of its eſtabliſhment.

Thornbury and Coat.

			£.	s.	d.
Taxes.	The Royal Aid in	1692,	£. 45	16	0
	Poll-tax — —	1694, —	40	3	0
	Land-tax ——	1694, —	82	6	0
	The ſame, at 3*s.*	1770, —	40	10	0

Oldbury upon Severn.

			£.	s.	d.
Taxes.	The Royal Aid in	1692,	£. 250	8	0
	Poll-tax ——	1694, —	27	13	0
	Land-tax ——	1694, —	174	14	5
	The ſame, at 3*s.*	1770, —	161	18	3

Morton.

			£.	s.	d.
Taxes.	The Royal Aid in	1692,	£. 186	4	0
	Poll-tax —	1694, —	33	12	0
	Land-tax —	1694, —	207	16	0
	The ſame, at 3*s.*	1770, —	154	19	0

Kington.

		£.	s.	d.
Land-tax at 3*s.*	1770, —	167	2	9

According to ſir Robert Atkyns, when he compiled his account of this pariſh, there were 270 houſes, and about 1100 inhabitants, whereof 100 were freeholders; yearly births 33, burials 31. The inhabitants are now about 1971.

TIBERTON

IS a ſmall pariſh in the Foreſt diviſion, and in the hundred of the Dutchy of Lancaſter, about four miles diſtant ſouth-eaſtward from Newent, ſeven north-eaſtward from Mitchel-Dean, and ſix north-weſtward from Glouceſter.

The name is ſometimes written Tibberton, but the antient orthography is *Tebriſton*, as in *Domeſday*; and it ſeems to indicate that the place belonged to one Tebri, or in other words, that it was *Tebri's Town*, perhaps early in the Saxon times.

The pariſh was comprized in the hundred of Botloe, 'till, by act of parliament, in the fiftieth year of the reign of king Edward the Third, Lancaſhire was erected into a county palatine, and John of Gaunt, ſon of that king, was honoured with the title of duke of Lancaſter. Then all thoſe eſtates in Glouceſterſhire which came to him in right of Blanch his wife, daughter of the preceding duke of Lancaſter, of which Tiberton was one, were ſevered from the hundreds to which they antiently belonged, and erected into a new one, then firſt, and ever ſince, called the hundred of the dutchy of Lancaſter.

Tiberton enjoys an unlimitted right of common in the foreſt of Dean, and in Huntley common. It lies in the vale, and the ſoil is naturally rich and fertile; but, like the adjoining pariſhes of Tainton and Rudford, is not in the higheſt ſtate of cultivation. Here, and in moſt other parts of the foreſt diviſion, is plenty of iron ore, and ſome orcharding, from which they make an excellent ſort of cyder, much eſteemed for its rich and pleaſant flavour. They alſo make good cheeſe, and the corn fields produce fine wheat and other grain. But the place affords no other curious productions of art or nature.

A brook divides this pariſh from Tainton and Newent, and taking its courſe to Rudford, runs through two arches under the river Leden. This under paſſage was enlarged when thoſe arches were made, about ſix years ago, and by that means the meadows, which before were almoſt continually in a wet and rotten ſtate, have been drained and very much improved.

Of the Manor and other Eſtates.

'William the ſon of Baderon holds Tebriſton, 'in Botelau hundred. There are five hides. 'Ulfelin held it of king Edward, and could go 'where he pleaſed. There are three plow-tillages 'in demean, and ten villeins, and eight bordars, 'with eight plow-tillages. There are four *ſervi*, 'and a wood three miles long, and one broad. 'It was worth 6*l.* 10*s.* now 100*s.*' *Domeſday*, p. 73.

Henry

Henry earl of Lancaſter, deſcended from Edmond earl of Lancaſter, ſon of king Henry the Third, was lord of this manor 2 E. 3. at which time the lands were held under him by ſeveral tenants, *viz.* William Lunge held Tiberton by the ſervice of one knight's fee; Jeffry de Feerre held other lands here by the fifth part; as did Ralph Marmion by the eighth part; William Franklyn by the twentieth part; and John ſon of Stephen by the fortieth part of a knight's fee. The above Henry became duke of Lancaſter, and dying of the plague 35 E. 3. left two daughters, Maud, and Blanch. Maud was married to the duke of Bavaria, and had the manor of Tiberton aſſigned to her, but dying without iſſue, her eſtates came to Blanch, the younger ſiſter, married, in 1359, to John of Gaunt, (fourth ſon of king Edward the Third) who, in her right, ſucceeded to the eſtates of the former duke of Lancaſter; and he and Blanch his wife levied a fine of Tiberton, Rodley in Weſtbury, and Minſterworth, to the uſe of themſelves in taille, 39 E. 3. He died in 1399, and his ſon Henry became king of England the ſame year, by the reſignation of Richard the Second, whereupon this manor came to the crown.

But, leſt the houſe of York ſhould recover the crown, king Henry the Fourth procured an act of parliament to be paſſed, in the firſt year of his reign, whereby the dutchy of Lancaſter was ſevered from the crown, and entailed on his heirs. And king Henry the Fifth, in the year 1414, probably with the ſame view, procured another act of parliament, by which all thoſe great eſtates that deſcended to him from Mary his mother, daughter and coheireſs of Humphry de Bohun, earl of Hereford, were likewiſe annexed to the dutchy of Lancaſter.

Notwithſtanding theſe precautions, the houſe of York became poſſeſſed of Tiberton, together with the crown, in the perſon of king Edward the Fourth, who levied a fine of it to the uſe of Elizabeth his queen, in the 15th year of his reign. The manor was in the crown in the year 1608, and was granted to Edward Ramſey, and Robert Ramſey his brother, by king James the Firſt. Mr. Payne, and Mr. Twitty, both of Worceſter, were joint proprietors of it about the beginning of this century, but Mr. Edward Elton, of the city of Glouceſter, is the preſent lord of the manor. He is deſcended from an antient family, ſeated near Ledbury in Herefordſhire, and gives for his arms, *Paly of ſix, Or and gules, on a bend ſable three mullets pierced of the firſt.*

The abbey of Glouceſter held Hawker's Place in Tiberton, and granted a leaſe of it 2 H. 8. It is now the property of the dean and chapter of Glouceſter, and is in the poſſeſſion of Mr. Daniel Ellis, as leſſee under the college. Almoſt all the other lands are copyholds of inheritance.

Of the Church, &c.

The church is a rectory, in the Foreſt deanery, worth 100*l.* a year. There has been a diſpute about the advowſon. Mr. Elton claims the whole, and the heirs of Mr. Somerſet Jones claim two preſentations out of three. The reverend Mr. Joſeph Parry is the preſent incumbent.

John de Langley held the advowſon of the church, of Henry earl of Lancaſter, 2 E. 3.

The church is a ſmall building, in good repair, dedicated to the Trinity, with a low tower at the weſt end, covered with tiles.

There is a parſonage houſe and garden, with a new barn, and about ſeven or eight acres of glebe land.

Firſt fruits £.	7	16	0	Proc. & Syn. £.	0	10	0
Tenths —		15	7¼	Pentecoſtals -	0	1	6

Benefaction.

Four acres of land, worth about 40*s.* a year, are given for the repair of the church.

Taxes.					
The Royal Aid in	1692,	£. 97	12	0
Poll-tax ——	1694,	— 10	19	0
Land-tax —	1694,	— 92	12	0
The ſame, at 3*s.*	1770,	— 65	9	6

At the beginning of this century, according to ſir Robert Atkyns, there were 33 houſes in the pariſh, and about 150 inhabitants, 8 of whom were reputed to be freeholders; yearly births 5, burials 5. There are now about 230 inhabitants.

TIDENHAM.

THIS pariſh formerly conſtituted the intire hundred of Tedeneham, but it now lies in the hundred of Weſtbury, in the Foreſt diviſion. It is ſituated eaſtward from the town and pariſh of Chepſtow, from which it is ſeparated by the river Wye. It is ſeven miles diſtant ſouth from Colford, and twenty-five ſouth-weſt from Glouceſter; and there is a turnpike-road leading through it to that city from the ſouth of Monmouthſhire. The lands are chiefly paſture, with ſome good arable; and there is plenty of coal here, and in moſt other parts of the foreſt. Some petrifications of ſhell fiſh are found in the cliffs and banks of the Wye and the Severn; but Tidenham produces no plants that are curious and uncommon.

The ſouth-weſt part of the pariſh is hemmed in by the Severn on one ſide, and the Wye on the other, and forming a narrow promontory, runs into the broad channel of the Severn where the waters of the two rivers join; and ſir Robert Atkyns was of opinion that Tidenham took its name from the high tides which aſſault both ſides of it. About two miles above the mouth of the Wye, there is a bridge over that river, commonly called Chepſtow Bridge, becauſe one end ſtands in the pariſh

pariſh of Chepſtow, and leads to the town of that name. The other end is in Tidenham, and by a ſtatute, 28 Eliz. it was enacted, that one half of the bridge ſhould be repaired by Monmouthſhire, the other by Glouceſterſhire. It is built of timber, at a prodigious height above low water, for the tide here flows ſixty feet high at particular times, and it is thought that it does not riſe higher in any part of the world.

The famous intrenchment, called by the Britons *Claudh Offa*, i.e. *Offa's Dyke*, which was thrown up by the Mercian king of that name, about the year 760, to divide and protect his dominions from the Welch, began in this pariſh; and there are at this time large remains of it, extending almoſt from the Severn to the Wye, in length near half a mile, croſſing the turnpike-road that leads from Chepſtow to Beachley, at a place called Buttington's Tump. It was a prodigious work, and was carried from this place northward, to the mouth of the river Dee, in Flintſhire, croſſing Radnorſhire near Knighton, to which town the Welch, upon that account, gave the name of *Tref-y-claudh*, that is, the place of the ditch. And John of Saliſbury writes, that king Harold made a law, that if any Welchman ſhould be found with a weapon on this ſide the dyke, he ſhould loſe his right hand.

The dyke now ſeparates Beachley from Sudbury, two hamlets in this pariſh, the latter of which was ſo called in reference to the bulwarks, or camp, about two miles northward of it. Beſides theſe, there are traces of other old fortifications upon Beachley-green, which at this time alſo go by the name of the Bulwarks.

When or by whom theſe works were made is altogether uncertain, but moſt likely at different times; for as Beachley is a ſtrip of land running out between the before-mentioned great rivers, it was eaſily fortified, and the poſſeſſion of it was thought of importance in the many civil wars which this kingdom has ſo frequently and fatally experienced.

In the reign of king Charles the Firſt, as Corbet relates it, prince Rupert ſent five hundred horſe and foot into the foreſt, who began to fortify Beachley for a laſting guard, and which was then the only commodious ferry, or paſſage, from Wales to Briſtol, and the weſtern parts. 'The governor,' (ſays my author) meaning colonel Maſſie, 'advanced upon them four days after they 'began the fortifications, and had drawn the 'trench half way from the banks of one river to 'the other, when the other part was well guarded 'with an high quick-ſet hedge, which they lined 'with muſquetteers, and a ditch within, with a 'meadow beyond, wherein they had made a re-'intrenchment. At high water the place was 'inacceſſible, by reaſon of their ſhips which 'guarded each river with ordnance, lying level 'with the banks, and clearing the face of the 'approach from Wye to Severn. Wherefore the 'governor taking the advantage of low water, 'ten muſquetteers were ſelected out of the for-'lorn hope, to creep along the hedges. Theſe 'gave the firſt alarm, and cauſed the enemy to 'ſpend their firſt ſhot in vain. Upon the gover-'nor's ſignal, the forlorn hope ruſhed on, being 'followed by the reſerve, and fell upon the hack, 'when the whole and each part of the action was 'carried on without interruption. Of the king's 'troops ſome were killed, the reſt taken priſoners, 'beſides ſome few that recovered the boats, and 'many of them that took the water were drowned.

'The king's friends attempted a ſecond time 'to fortify this place, but before the works were 'compleat, colonel Maſſie attacked and defeated 'them, but had like to have fallen in the attempt, 'for the foremoſt of his party forcing two or 'three palliſadoes, found themſelves between the 'line of palliſadoes and a quick-ſet hedge lined 'with muſquetteers. The governor, in this 'critical ſituation, who was now the leader of 'the forlorn hope, with not a little difficulty 'forced his horſe over the hedge, fell in among 'the king's men, by whom he was furiouſly re-'charged, his head-piece knocked off with the 'but-end of a muſket, and was in the utmoſt 'danger, when ſome of his men came to his 'aſſiſtance, and bore down the enemy before 'them, ſlew thirty, and took priſoners a lieu-'tenant-colonel, a major, two captains, three lieu-'tenants, three enſigns, with other officers and 'ſoldiers to the amount of two hundred and 'twenty. They forced ſir John Winter down 'the cliff into the river, where a little boat lay to 'receive him. Many took the water and were 'drowned, others by recovering the boats ſaved 'themſelves.'

Theſe particulars are extracted from Corbet's *Military Government of the City of Glouceſter*, and have a connexion with the hiſtory of the village. The place where ſir John Winter eſcaped is called *Winter's Leap*, and there is a tradition that he leaped his horſe, at once, from the high rock on the ſide of the Wye, into the water. But that could not be the fact, for both horſe and rider muſt have been daſhed to pieces againſt the declivity of the rock in the attempt.

It is ſaid that antiently, near the confluence of the Severn and the Wye, there ſtood a chapel, dedicated, according to Leland, to St. Terendake, but others ſay to St. Tecla, who was martyred in the year 47. What they call the ruins of it may be ſeen among the rocks, at low water, but at high water they are overflowed, and at leaſt a hundred yards diſtant from the ſhore. Hence it may be inferred, with ſome degree of probability, that if it really was a chapel, either the tides did not flow ſo high as they now do, when it was firſt built; or elſe, that it muſt ever have been an uſeleſs building.

At Beachley in this pariſh is a ferry or paſſage over the Severn, between Briſtol and Wales. It is is called Beachley, or the Old Paſſage, and 'till lately was the loweſt upon the river. The oppoſite paſſage-houſe is at Auſt, in the pariſh of Henbury. The times for paſſing are already ſet down in the 47th page of this book, to which the reader is referred. I come now to treat

Of the Manors and other Eſtates.

When *Domeſday* was compiled, there were ſeveral great proprietors of eſtates in this pariſh, as appears by the following tranſlation of the paſſages in the record concerning it.

'The abbey of Bath had one manor, Tedeneham by name, in Tedeneham hundred. They had thirty hides there, of which ten were in demean. There were thirty-eight villeins, having thirty-eight plow-tillages, and ten bordars, eleven fiſheries in the Severn in demean, and forty-two fiſheries of the villeins; one fiſhery in the Wye, and two fiſheries and a half of the villeins.

'Earl Roger added two fiſheries in the Wye. There is a wood two miles long, and half a mile broad, and twelve other bordars.

'Earl William gave one yard-land of this eſtate, with one villein, to O. the biſhop, his brother. And he gave two fiſheries in the Severn, and half a fiſhery in the Wye, with one villein, to Walter de Laci. And he gave two fiſheries in the Wye, with one villein, to Ralph de Limeſi. And he gave half a hide of land, and the church, with the tithes of the manor, to the abbey of Lyra.

'This manor paid no tax in the time of king Edward, except proviſions for the monks. Archbiſhop Stigand held it when earl William took to it. Now it pays 25 *lib.* twenty of it in *Ora* and white money. There is now a mill of 40 *den.*' *Domeſday*, p. 69.

'William de Ow holds one yard-land and a half in Tideham, and they were taxed. Stigand the archbiſhop held them. There is one villein, with one plow-tillage, and two fiſheries. It is worth and was worth 10 *ſol.*' *Ib.* p. 73.

'Roger de Laci holds half a hide in Tedeham. Archbiſhop Stigand held it. There is one villein, with one plow-tillage, and four fiſheries and a half. It is worth and was worth 20 *s.*' *Ib.* p. 75.

Some time after the compilation of *Domeſday*, the Welch poſſeſſed themſelves of Tidenham and Woolaſton, from whom they were taken by Walter and Roger, younger brothers of Gilbert earl of Clare, which happened in the year 1160, in the reign of king Henry the Second. Gilbert de Clare, ſurnamed Strongbow, left Richard Strongbow his ſon and heir, who became earl of Pembroke and Strigule, now called Chepſtow. His only daughter Iſabel was married to William Mareſchal, who, in right of his wife, was earl of Pembroke, whereby this manor came into that family. They were deſcended from Gilbert Mareſchal, who bore the office of Mareſchal to king Henry the Firſt; which office deſcended hereditarily in that family to the famous William earl of Pembroke, who died 3 H. 3. and left five ſons and four daughters.

William earl of Pembroke, ſon of William, gave a conſiderable eſtate in the manor of Tudeham to the abbey of St. Mary of Tintern in Monmouthſhire, founded by Walter de Clare in 1131, with common of paſture, and of wood, and other benefits in his chaſe of Tudeham, 8 H. 3. All the five brothers were ſucceſſively earls of Pembroke, and all died without iſſue, whereby the ſiſters became coheireſſes. Maud, the eldeſt, was married to Hugh Bigot, earl of Norfolk, who, in her right, and for her ſhare, was ſeized of the manor of Tidenham.

This Hugh Bigot was deſcended from Roger Bigot, who came into England with king William the Conqueror, and died 7 H. 1. William Bigot, ſon of Roger, was ſteward of the houſhold to king Henry the Firſt, and was drowned coming from Normandy with the king's childred 20 H. 1. Hugh Bigot was brother and heir to William, and alſo ſteward to the king. He is eminent in hiſtory for making oath that king Henry the Firſt, on his death bed, gave the crown of England to king Stephen, in diſinheriſon of his own daughter Maud, the empreſs. He died in pilgrimage to the Holy Land 23 H. 2.

Roger Bigot ſucceeded Hugh his father in the earldom of Norfolk, and ſtewardſhip of the king's houſhold, and died 5 H. 3. Hugh earl of Norfolk, ſon of Roger, married Maud, coheireſs of William Mareſchal earl of Pembroke, as abovesaid, by whom he had a ſon Roger, earl of Norfolk, who died ſeized of Tidenham, and of 10 *s.* rent in the village of Beteſlegh, and of the hamlet of Lancaut, 25 E. 1. This earl Roger had levied a fine of his honour, and of his lands, to the king, taking back an eſtate taille to himſelf and Alice his wife, and dying without iſſue, the manor of Tidenham came to the crown.

King Edward the Second granted the title of earl of Norfolk, and all the eſtate of the former earl of Norfolk, 6 E. 2. to his brother Thomas, the fifth ſon of king Edward the Firſt, generally called Thomas of Brotherton, a place in Yorkſhire, where he was born. He died ſeized of the manor of Tidenham 12 E. 3. leaving two daughters coheireſſes, Margaret, and Alice.

Margaret was firſt married to John de Segrave, and afterwards to ſir Walter de Manny, who, in her right, was ſeized of the manor of Tidenham 46 E. 3. She was afterwards created dutcheſs of Norfolk for life, 21 R. 2. Elizabeth, ſole daughter and heireſs of Margaret, by her firſt huſband John de Segrave, was married to John de Mowbray, who was therefore created earl of Norfolk, and earl Mareſchal.

The family of the Mowbrays deſcended from Nigel de Albini, who was of noble extraction, and

and together with his brother William de Albini, came into England with king William the Conqueror. Nigel, by his mother's ſide, was a Mowbray, and had done eminent ſervice in the wars for king William, and alſo for king William the Second, and king Henry the Firſt, and was therefore rewarded with all the eſtates of Robert Mowbray, earl of Northumberland, who had been guilty of treaſonable conſpiracies. He married Maud, the wife of that earl, whilſt her huſband was living, by a ſpecial diſpenſation from the pope; but having no children by her, was the cauſe of their divorce. He then married Gundred, daughter of Girald de Gournay.

Roger de Mowbray was ſon and heir of Nigel de Albini, and of Gundred; and by command of king Henry the Firſt, took the name of Mowbray. He married Alice de Gaunt, and was buried near Gundred his mother, in the abbey of Biland in Yorkſhire, which he had founded for Ciſtercian monks, in 1138. Nigel de Mowbray, ſon and heir of Roger, married Mabel, daughter of the earl of Clare, and died in pilgrimage to the Holy Land.

William de Mowbray, ſon of Nigel, married Agnes, daughter of the earl of Arundel, and fiercely eſpouſed the cauſe of the barons againſt king John. Nigel Mowbray was ſon of William, and married the daughter and heir of Roger de Camvil, but died without iſſue 13 H. 3. Roger de Mowbray, brother and heir of Nigel, married Maud, the daughter of William Beauchamp, of Bedford, and came of age 25 H. 3. He had a ſon Roger, who had livery of his lands 6 E. 1. and was ſummoned as a baron to parliament. He married Roſe, ſiſter to Gilbert earl of Clare, and died 26 E. 1. John de Mowbray, ſon of the laſt Roger, married Aliva, daughter, and afterwards coheir, of William de Brewes of Gowher. He was governor of York, and ſheriff of Yorkſhire, and being taken in rebellion againſt king Edward the Second, was hanged at York. John de Mowbray, ſon of John, was in favour of king Edward the Third. He married Joan, one of the daughters of Henry earl of Lancaſter, and died of the plague at York 35 E. 3. John de Mowbray, ſon and heir of the laſt John, married Elizabeth, daughter and heir of John lord Segrave, by Margaret, daughter and heir of Thomas of Brotherton, as before related, and was, in her right, created earl of Norfolk, and earl Mareſchal, and was lord of the manor of Tidenham. He was ſlain by the Turks, near Conſtantinople, 42 E. 3.

John de Mowbray, ſon of the laſt John, was four years old at his father's death. He was created earl of Nottingham 1 R. 2. and died 6 R. 2. whereupon his brother Thomas de Mowbray was created earl of Nottingham. He married, firſt, Elizabeth, daughter and heir of John le Strange, of Blackmore, and was created earl Mareſchal for life. His ſecond wife was Elizabeth, the daughter of Richard earl of Arundel, and had the grant to him and his heirs to be earls Mareſchal, and to bear a golden truncheon. He joined with the debauched favourites of king Richard the Second, and to gratify them promoted the death of his father-in-law the earl of Arundel, and guarded him to execution. He was a principal contriver of the death of Thomas of Woodſtock, duke of Glouceſter, uncle to the king, who was murdered at Calais, which obtained him ſuch favour from the king, that he was created duke of Norfolk; but that day twelve-month, on which the duke of Glouceſter was murdered, this duke of Norfolk was baniſhed the realm, and died of the plague at Venice, in his return from Jeruſalem, 1 H. 4. and that year the manor of Tidenham was ſeized by the crown. He left two ſons, Thomas, and John; and two daughters, Iſabel, married to James lord Berkeley, and Margaret, married to ſir Robert Howard.

Thomas Mowbray, eldeſt ſon of Thomas duke of Norfolk, had no other title than Earl Mareſchal. He married Conſtance, daughter of John Holland, earl of Huntingdon, which drew him into rebellion againſt king Henry the Fourth, and he was beheaded at York 6 H. 4. John, his brother, and next heir, married Catherine, daughter to Ralph Nevil earl of Weſtmoreland, and was reſtored to the dukedom of Norfolk. He died 11 H. 6. and Catherine his widow was endowed with many great eſtates, and with the manor of Tidenham. He was ſucceeded by his ſon John, duke of Norfolk, who married Elizabeth, daughter of John the firſt earl of Shrewſbury, and died 15 E. 4. leaving an only daughter, Anne, who was married to Richard duke of York, ſecond ſon of king Edward the Fourth, but died without iſſue, whereby a vaſt eſtate came to the families of Berkeley and Howard, whoſe anceſtors had married Iſabel and Margaret, daughters of Thomas Mowbray, the firſt duke of Norfolk; and a partition of that great eſtate was made between their heirs 14 H. 7.

The manor of Tidenham came ſoon afterwards to the earls of Worceſter. Henry earl of Worceſter died ſeized of it 3 E. 6. from whom it has regularly deſcended down to Henry duke of Beaufort, the preſent lord of the manor of Tidenham.

John ap Adam held one mill in Tudenham, and one hundred and ſixty acres of land lying within the liberties of Chepſtow, 6 E. 2. And by the eſcheator's inquiſition taken 9 E. 4. n. 21. it appears, that William Herbert earl of Pembroke, who was taken priſoner in the battle near Banbury, between the Yorkiſts and Lancaſtrians, and beheaded the next day, died ſeized of the caſtle, manor and lordſhip of Chepſtow, of the manor of Tudenham, and of other very great eſtates. But this muſt not be underſtood of the principal manor of Tidenham. Thomas Atkyns was ſeized of fifty acres of arable land, twenty of meadow,

meadow, thirty of paſture, and twenty of wood in Tudenham, by the grant of Henry earl of Worceſter, 4 H. 8.

HAMLETS, and places of diſtinct names.

1. *Church-End*, in which are twenty families. Mr. Charles Williams has a good houſe near the church, late the property of Mr. William Jones.

2. *Biſhton*, formerly written Biſten, containing nineteen families.

3. *Sudbury*, in which are nineteen families. William Webley, of Chancery Lane, London, eſq; has a handſome houſe called the Mead, and a good eſtate in this hamlet.

4. *Beachley*, antiently *Betteſley*, containing eleven families. There is a houſe of good accommodation, and a paſſage over the Severn, at this place, very much frequented in the route between Wales and the city of Briſtol. The river is upwards of two miles over, and the oppoſite paſſage-houſe is at Auſt, in the pariſh of Henbury. It is called the Old Paſſage, in reference to another lately ſet up a few miles below, at St. Pierre in Monmouthſhire. It is high water at new and full moon, a little after ſeven o'clock, in general, but the wind may occaſion a ſmall variation. Proper directions for paſſing are given at p. 47. Henry Lewis, eſq; was ſeized of the manor of Betteſley, from whom it deſcended to George Lewis, his ſon, who died ſeized thereof 10 Car. 1. and left William his ſon and heir ſeven years old. Morgan Lewis, eſq; is the preſent lord of this manor; but the ferry belongs to four proprietaries, *viz.* the ſame Morgan Lewis, eſq; William-Bromley Cheſter, eſq; Mr. Samuel Hill, and Mr. Charles Williams. There was formerly a chapel dedicated to St. Ewin, near the paſſage-houſe, now totally demoliſhed.

5. *Wibden*, or *Widden*, formerly belonging to John Madocke, eſq; who had a good eſtate and a handſome ſeat here, now fallen into ruins, and the eſtate is gone out of the name. The ſame John Madocke was deſcended from Owen Gwineth, a prince of South Wales. Some of his anceſtors reſided for ſeveral generations at Alvington, and removed thence to Wibden. John Madocke died ſeized of Wibden in 1587, and the eſtate continued in the ſame name and family 'till within our memory; but it now belongs to William Sheldon, of Weſton in Warwickſhire, eſq. Morgan Lewis, eſq; has the manor of Walden in this hamlet. There are twenty-ſix families in Wibden.

6. *Stroat*, or *Strote*, where the James's have for many ages enjoy'd a good eſtate, which is now the property of Mr. Selwyn James. There are fourteen families here.

7. *Lancaut*, containing three families. There is a chapel in this hamlet dedicated to St. James, where divine ſervice is performed once a month. It was formerly a diſtinct rectory, to which Henry earl of Worceſter preſented in 1548; but it has lately been annexed to Wollaſton.

Of the Church, &c.

The church is a vicarage, in the Foreſt deanery, worth about 100*l.* a year. James Davis, eſq; is patron, and the reverend Mr. William Seys the preſent incumbent.

The impropriation formerly belonged to the priory of Sheen in Surrey, who gave thirteen buſhels of wheat, and 13*d.* in money yearly to the poor, on the Thurſday before Eaſter; and it was granted to Thomas James, 5 Jac. reſerving that yearly payment, which has been continued to the poor ever ſince. Mr. William Webley, and Mr. Charles Williams are the preſent impropriators.

The church is dedicated to St. Mary. It is a double building, ſupported by pillars in the middle, and has a low tower, with ſix bells, at the weſt end. It ſtands on high ground, and is ſeen from many parts at a conſiderable diſtance on the other ſide of the Severn.

Firſt fruits £.	9	0	0	Proc. & Syn. £.	0	9	2
Tenths —	0	18	0	Pentecoſtals	0	1	6

Monuments and Inſcriptions.

There is a raiſed tomb in the church-yard, incloſed with iron palliſadoes, with ſhort inſcriptions for the following perſons, who died in the years ſet after their names, *viz.* John Madocke of Wibden, gent. in 1587; Edmund his ſon, 1626; Anſelm ſon of Edmund, 1615; John ſon of Anſelm, 1643; Edmund ſon of John, 1693; John ſon of Edmund, 1732-3. At one end of the tomb are the family arms, *viz. Argent, a chevron between three foxes heads erazed ſable.*

On another raiſed tomb are inſcriptions for the following perſons, with the dates of their deceaſe, *viz.* William Webley, 1712; Walter Webley, his ſon, 1763, &c. &c. And their family arms, *viz. Or, a bend between three mullets pierced ſable.*

Benefactions.

Thirteen buſhels of wheat, and 13*d.* in money are given annually out of the impropriation to the poor.

Mrs. Bridget Madocke of Wibden, by her will, proved in chancery in 1736, gave 5*l.* a year in land, 50*s.* part thereof, for teaching poor children to read; 40*s.* to the miniſter for catechiſm in the church, from the firſt ſunday in April to the firſt ſunday in June; and 10*s.* a year for keeping the tomb of her anceſtors in the church-yard in repair.

William Stevens gave 5*s.* a year to the poor; and John Stevens of Briſtol gave 10*s.* a year to the ſame uſe.

Taxes.	The Royal Aid in 1692,	£. 229	0	0
	Poll-tax — — 1694,	— 55	6	0
	Land-tax —— 1694,	- 250	8	0
	The ſame, at 3*s.* 1770,	— 187	16	0

There were 140 houſes in this pariſh at the beginning of this century, and about 600 inhabitants, whereof 32 were freeholders; yearly

 births

births 16, burials 15. *Atkyns.* In ten years, from 1708, to 1717, both inclufive, there were entered in the parifh regifter 165 baptifms, and 138 burials; and in the fame period of time, from 1767 to 1776, the baptifms were 163, and the burials 150. The prefent number of families is 112, and of inhabitants about 500.

TITHERINGTON.

THIS parifh lies in two hundreds. The hamlet of Itchington is in the hundred of Henbury. The part called Titherington is in that of Thornbury, diftant three miles fouth-eaftward from the town of that name, three and a half weftward from Wickwar, and twenty-four fouthward from Gloucefter. It is bounded on the eaft by Cromhal, on the weft by Alvefton, on the north by Thornbury, and on the fouth and fouth-eaft by Iron Acton and Wickwar.

The village is feated on the fouth fide and at the foot of a high rock, called Tower Hill, whofe top is pretty level, and adjoins to Milbury Heath, which lies part in Thornbury, and part in this parifh. To the fouth of the village the lands form a flat vale of very rich pafture ground.

About a quarter of a mile weftward from the church, there is a ftrong intrenchment on an eminence called *Caftle Hill.* It is an oblong fquare, inclofing about four or five acres of ground, and overlooks the vale to the eaft and fouth-eaft. It is generally fuppofed, from its conftruction and other circumftances, to be the work of the Romans, who had certainly a lodgment here, as may be concluded from a teffellated pavement dug up at Stidcot in this parifh, towards the clofe of the laft century. This was one of thofe forts fuppofed to have been thrown up by that people to protect their road between the *Trajectus* and *Aqua Solis.* There is a prevailing notion in the neighbourhood, that a caftle formerly ftood upon this ground, but that is a miftake arifing from the name of the place, which was called Caftle Hill from the camp there, in like manner as feveral other intrenchments in this county have obtained the name of caftles.

About the year 1772, fome perfons employed to dig materials in this parifh for repairing the roads, found a large ftone like a ftep, not far below the furface of the ground, and then another fuch ftone, and fearching further, difcovered two perfect fkeletons, inclofed in ftone coffins, lying in a direction to the north and fouth; whence fome perfons have concluded, but I think upon very flender foundation, that the corps were placed there before the general eftablifhment of Chriftianity in this country. One of the fkeletons was fix feet and a half long, as a gentleman who meafured it affured me, but they both fell to pieces on being flightly touched; and no coin, armour, nor other thing that I can hear of, was found in the fepulchre to give any light as to the time of interment, or the people to whom thefe reliques belonged.

A fmall brook, called the Laden, runs from hence, and empties itfelf into the Lower Froom, which falls into the Briftol Avon.

Of the Manor and other Eftates.

'Ofbern bifhop of Execeftre holds Tidrentune 'in Bacheftanes hundred. Aluui held it in the 'time of king Edward. There are five hides, 'and two plow-tillages in demean, and one villein, 'and five bordars, and two *fervi*, and twenty 'acres of meadow. A wood half a mile in length 'and breadth. It was worth 100*s.* now 40*s.*' *Domefday*, p. 70.

This manor was held of the honour of Gloucefter, and is now within the jurifdiction of the honour court.

Walter de Stukeley, fheriff of Gloucefterfhire, being commanded by the king's writ, to return into the exchequer the names of all the vills in his county, with their refpective proprietors, certified that William Corbet was lord of Tederinton 9 E. 1. and Roger Corbet was feized of it in the 15th and 18th years of the fame reign. William Corbet, fon of Roger, purchafed a charter of free warren in Titherington 33 E. 1. By an inquifition taken 8 E. 2. after the death of Gilbert de Clare, earl of Gloucefter, it was found that Roger de Corbet held Tetherington of the faid Gilbert, by the fervice of one knight's fee, value 34*l.* William Corbet of Chadfey held the fame 17 E. 2.

Thomas de Bradefton, a very eminent perfon, was fummoned to parliament among the barons 16 E. 3. and died feized of Titherington, Ichenton, Stinchcombe, Horton, Winterbourne, and Bradeftone in Berkeley, 34 E. 3. Agnes the widow of Thomas lord Bradefton held the four firft of thefe manors, together with Arlingham, in dower, and died 43 E. 3. Thomas lord Bradefton, fon of Robert, fucceeded his grandfather Thomas in all the before-mentioned eftates, of which he died feized 48 E. 3. leaving Elizabeth his only daughter and heirefs, afterwards married to Walter de la Pool, who had livery of her lands 13 R. 2. the fame year in which fhe came of age.

Robert, fecond lord Willoughby of Broke, was feized of this manor at the time of his death, 1521, 13 H. 8. He was fon of Robert lord Willoughby of Broke, and grandfon of John, and great grandfon of Thomas Willoughby, the third fon of Robert lord Willoughby (and of Alice his wife, the daughter of fir William Skipwith, of Ormefby in Lincolnfhire, knight, who died chief baron of the exchequer, 1366, 40 E. 3.) lineally defcended from fir John de Willoughby, a Norman knight, who had the lordfhip of Willoughby in Lincolnfhire, by the gift of king William the Firft, with whom he came into England.

England. The before-mentioned Robert, ſecond lord Willoughby of Broke, married, to his firſt wife, Elizabeth, eldeſt of the three daughters and coheireſſes of Richard lord Beauchamp, by whom he had an only ſon Edward, who died before his father, but left iſſue, by Elizabeth his wife, daughter of Richard Nevil lord Latimer, three daughters, coheireſſes, Elizabeth, Anne, and Blanch.

Elizabeth, eldeſt daughter of Edward Willoughby, was granted in ward to ſir Edward Greville, of Milcot in Warwickſhire, and after the death of her two ſiſters, without iſſue, became one of the richeſt heireſſes in England. Her guardian deſigned to have matched her with John his eldeſt ſon, but ſhe choſe, and took for her huſband, ſir Fulke Grevil, the ſecond ſon, who died ſeized of this manor 1 Eliz. leaving by his ſaid wife three ſons, and four daughters.

Sir Fulke Grevil, the eldeſt ſon, was knighted 7 Eliz. and having married Anne, daughter of Ralph Nevil, earl of Weſtmoreland, died in 1606, 4 Jac. 1. leaving an only ſon Fulke, and a daughter Margaret, married to ſir Richard Verney.

Fulke Grevil, ſon of ſir Fulke, was alſo knighted, and made a conſpicuous figure both as ſtateſman and ſoldier, in the reigns of queen Elizabeth, king James, and king Charles the Firſt. He obtained a grant of the ruined caſtle of Warwick, 2 Jac. 1. and converted it into a magnificent ſeat, at the expence of 20,000*l.* In the 18th year of the ſame reign, he was advanced to the dignity of baron Brooke, by letters patent, Jan. 9, 1620-21, with remainder (in default of male heirs of his own body) to Robert ſon of Fulke, and grandſon of Robert the ſecond ſon of Fulke Grevil and Elizabeth Willoughby before-mentioned. Neglecting to reward one Hayward, or Haywood, an old ſervant, he was ſtabed by him at Brooke-houſe in London, and dying unmarried Sep. 30, 1628, in the 75th year of his age, was buried at Warwick, under a monument he had erected for himſelf, with this remarkable inſcription:

Fulke Grevile,
Servant to Queen *Elizabeth,*
Councellor to King *James,*
and Friend to Sir *Philip Sidney.*
Trophæum Peccati.

Upon the death of Fulke lord Brooke without iſſue, the title devolved on his kinſman Robert, but the manor of Titherington deſcended to ſir Richard Verney, knight, who had married Margaret Grevile, as before recited, and by her had iſſue four ſons, Grevile, John, Richard, and George; and four daughters.

Sir Grevile Verney, knight, ſucceeded his father in this eſtate, and died May 12, 1642, having married Catherine, daughter of ſir Robert Southwell, of Woodriſing in Norfolk, by whom he had four ſons, and one daughter; Grevile, John, Richard, George, and Elizabeth.

Sir Richard Verney, of Belton in Rutlandſhire, third ſon, on the death of William, great grandſon of Grevile his elder brother, without iſſue, in the year 1683, ſucceeded to this eſtate; and laying claim to the antient barony of Willoughby, it was allowed him in parliament, and he had ſummons accordingly, as baron Willoughby of Brooke by deſcent, Mar. 25, 1695, and died July 18, 1711, in the 91ſt year of his age. By Mary his firſt wife, daughter of ſir John Prettiman, of Lodington in Leiceſterſhire, bart. he had three ſons, John, George, and Thomas.

George lord Willoughby, D.D. the ſecond ſon, ſucceeded his father in honour, and was proprietor of Titherington when ſir Robert Atkyns compiled his account of it. He died Dec. 26, 1728.

The manor of Titherington paſſed afterwards to James Hardwicke, eſq. Joſeph Hardwicke, eſq; was afterwards proprietor of it, and dying in the year 1771, was ſucceeded by his ſon John Hardwicke, eſq; who is the preſent lord of the manor of Titherington. His arms are, *Argent, a ſaltire ingrailed azure*; *on a chief of the ſecond three roſes of the firſt.*

Sir Walter de la Pool and Elizabeth his wife, daughter of Thomas lord Bradeſton, were ſeized of eighteen acres of meadow in Titherington 12 H. 6.

HAMLETS. 1. *Itchington,* which lies in the hundred of Henbury. 2. *Stidcot,* where the remains of a Roman teſſellated pavement were diſcovered, about the cloſe of the laſt century.

Of the Church, &c.

The church is a vicarage, in the deanery of Hawkeſbury, worth 95*l.* a year. John Hardwick, eſq; is patron, and the reverend Mr. Shellard is the preſent incumbent, and holds the impropriation for life; after which it devolves to the lord of the manor. It was formerly appropriated to the priory of Lanthony.

The parſonage houſe was built in the year 1662, by William Eldridge, vicar, who died Nov. 20, 1677, and lies buried in the chancel.

The church conſiſts of the nave, with an aile on each ſide, and a tower at the weſt end, in which are three bells. It is ſeventy-one feet long, and fifty broad, including the chancel and ſide ailes, and is kept in good repair.

From the top of the ſcar, or hill, above the church, there is an extenſive proſpect over the Severn; and I am told that ſeventeen or eighteen pariſh churches may be ſeen from it in a fair day.

	£.	s.	d.		£.	s.	d.
Firſt fruits	10	0	0	Synodals	0	2	0
Tenths —	1	0	0	Pentecoſt.	0	1	0
Procurations	0	6	8				

Monuments and Inſcriptions.

Againſt the north wall of the chancel, is this inſcription,

S. M.

Reuerendiſſimi viri Dni Richardi Bridges, filij Roberti Bridges de Wood-cheſter gen: natu 3tii Art. Mag. & Eccles: paroch: de Cromhall (dū inter viuos fuerat) Rect: qui duxit in Vxorē Eleanoram,

Eleanoram, filiam Guil: Lawrence de Shurdington gen. ex quâ 5 fuſcepit Liberos; quorū 2 reliquit ſuperſtites Richardū & Elizabetham, & febre tandem correptus, quicquid habuit mortale depoſuit 4to iduū maij A° Dni 1657 Anoq; Ætat. 45.

Hoc Eleanora relicta L. M. Q. P.

Siſte o viator Quisquis huc venis gradū;
Fletuſq; ſolve debitos loco tuos.
Pauper ades? olim pede quē calcas cinis,
Clarum Patroni nobiLis corpus erat:
Seu Dives? infra conditur quem vel tibi
Fortuna fecit ampla Mens atq; parem.
Divina pandis Myſtes Oracla? fratris
Curare Mortem Literas fata negant.
Iactas Amici nomen? en fidum caput,
Integritatis veteris exemplar novum!
Commune quam ſit vir bonus Loci Bonu,
Et quam caducum docuit, ac moræ brevis.
Abi, et fac SimiLe.

Stay Paſſenger, whoer Thou art,
And dropp a teare ere Thou depart:
Griefe claymes that tribute as a due
From aLL Who this Inſcription view.
If Poore, here Lye's Thy Patron, he
Who whiL'ſt he Liv'd breath'd charity:
If Rich, Thy FeLLow, who by none
In Courteſyes Would be out-gone.
Art of the Learn'd fraternity?
The book Saves no man; cLerks muſt dye.
A friend? Lament en-tomb'd to ſee
True friend-ſhipp's None-ſuch, this was He.
His Life made Vertue's Value knowne,
His Death hath beſt men's fraiLty ſhowne.
Goe hence, & Imitate.

On the monument are the arms of Bridges, as already blazoned in ſeveral places of this work.

On a marble monument againſt a pillar, is this inſcription,

Near this Place lies Interred ALICE HOBBS (Spinſter) one of the Daughters of Edward and Sarah Hobbs of this Pariſh Clothier; who died Aug^st. 28th. 1750, Aged 28, To whoſe Memory this Monument was erected.

In Memory of MARTHA HOBBS (Spinſter) Siſter to the above; who departed this Life Octo^r. 24th 1765, Aged 42.

A real example of Patience Meekneſs and Fortitude;
Her Submiſſion to the decrees of Providence;
Her effectionate Behaviour to all her Relations;
were ever uniform and exemplary; A tender & ſincere Friend
A ſhining pattern of Chriſtian Piety.

Arms, *Argent, a bend wavy between two hawks, or hobbys, proper.*

Taxes.			£.	s.	d.
	The Royal Aid in	1692,	103	18	0
	Poll-tax —	1694, —	33	5	0
	Land-tax —	1694, —	115	17	0
	The ſame, at 3*s.*	1770, —	86	18	4½

Sir Robert Atkyns ſet down the number of houſes in this pariſh at 85, and eſtimated the people at 320, of whom 15 were freeholders; yearly births 6, burials 5. It appears by the pariſh regiſter, that in ten years, from 1760, the baptiſms were 96, burials 81; and the people now amount to about 310, of whom 132 were upwards of fourteen years of age at the time this account was taken.

TODENHAM.

THIS pariſh lies in the upper diviſion of Weſtminſter hundred, about eight miles diſtant northward from Stow on the Wold, ſix eaſtward from Campden, and about thirty-four north-eaſt from Glouceſter.

Sir Robert Atkyns aſſerts, that the name is derived from *Toedoen*, a noble family which came in with king William the Conqueror; but I apprehend he was miſtaken, for before, as well at the time of the conqueſt, and afterwards, the manor belonged to the abbey of Weſtminſter, and not to any of that family. In *Domeſday* it is written *Teodeham*, and it ſeems probable that the place took its name from *Thodo*, or *Dodo*, one of the dukes of Mercia, who lived about the beginning of the eighth century. He had a palace at Derhuſt in this county, which he converted into a monaſtery, and was lord of that large manor, of which this place was a member; and ſo it might from him be called *Thodham*, or *Teodeham*, with great propriety.

There is nothing very curious or remarkable in this pariſh. It lies at the north-eaſt extremity of the county, where Worceſterſhire, Warwickſhire, and Glouceſterſhire are very much intermixt. It is bounded on the eaſt, north, and ſouth by Warwickſhire, from which it is ſeparated by two brooks that empty themſelves into the Stour; on the weſt by a detached part of Worceſterſhire; and on the ſouth-weſt by Lemington in Glouceſterſhire.

Of the Manor and other Eſtates.

This manor belonged to the abbey of Weſtminſter at the time of the general ſurvey, and is ſet down, in *Domeſday-book*, as one of thoſe *berewics*, or hamlets, dependant on the extenſive manor of Derhurſt. See the whole account in the original language of the record, p. 72.

Robert Fitz-Hamon took Todenham from the abbey of Weſtminſter, in the reign of king William the Second; but Lawrence, the twenty-fifth abbat, recovered it by a ſuit at law, in the reign of king Henry the Second.

Ralph de Papilion, the twenty-eighth abbat of Weſtminſter, was deprived for dilapidations, by Nicholas biſhop of Tuſcany, by the ceremony of breaking his ſeals; and the abbat of Waltham (to whom the making proviſion for his maintenance had been referred) aſſigned him the manor of Todenham for life, in the poſſeſſion of which he was confirmed by William de Hume, the ſucceeding abbat of Weſtminſter.

After the diſſolution of the abbey, and erection of the ſee of Weſtminſter, this manor was granted to that ſhort-lived biſhoprick, 34 H. 8. from which it was afterwards taken, and granted to ſir William Petre and Anne his wife, in exchange for lands in Warwickſhire, in the 36th year of the ſame reign. From this time the manors of Todenham and Sutton under Brayles have been enjoyed by the ſame owners, and lord Petre is the preſent proprietor of both. His lordſhip's pedigree and arms are given p. 721.

A rent in Todenham, formerly belonging to the biſhop of Weſtminſter, and afterwards to the biſhop of London, was granted to ſir William Petre 7 E. 6.

HAMLET. Upper Lemington is a hamlet in this pariſh, and is ſet down in *Domeſday* among thoſe

thoſe members of the great manor of Derhurſt that were held by radchenifters in the reign of king Edward the Confeſſor, and belonged to the abbey of Weſtminſter at the time of the general ſurvey. See p. 72.

Richard Grevill levied a fine of the manor of Lemington Over to Thomas Grevill, and others, 8 H. 7. William Palmer, and Anne his wife, levied a fine of the manor of Lemington Over, and of lands in Todenham, to John Newdegate, 2 Mariæ. It belonged to ſir William Juxton at the beginning of this century, and is now the property of lady Fane.

Of the Church, &c.

The church is a rectory, in the deanery of Campden, worth 150*l.* a year. The biſhop of London is patron, and the reverend Mr. George Upton is the preſent incumbent.

One yard-land belongs to the glebe.

The advowſon formerly belonged to the abbey of Weſtminſter, and was granted to Thomas biſhop of Weſtminſter, by king Henry the Eighth; but the ſee of Weſtminſter being ſoon ſuppreſſed, the advowſon was granted to Nicholas biſhop of London, 4 E. 6. and confirmed 1 Mariæ.

Tithes in Todenham, which had belonged to the abbey of Tewkeſbury, were granted to Daniel Perte and Alexander Perte, in truſt, 7 E. 6.

Sir Robert Atkyns ſays, ‘ the abbat of Weſt-‘ minſter reſerved the tithes of his own farm, ‘ which now belong to lord Petre, and are in leaſe ‘ to Mr. Kite.’ But I am informed by the rector, that no tithes appear to have been reſerved. The leaſe granted to Mr. Keyte was of lands worth 200*l.* a year, which, by the death of Mrs. Agnes Keyte, are now fallen into lord Petre's hands, and that eſtate pays tithes.

Dr. Parſons, in his MS. Collections, which he made about the cloſe of the laſt century, obſerves, that the pariſh clerk's name was John Green, and that the names of all the pariſh clerks for near two hundred years paſt had been the ſame, which is remarkable.

Robert Wickens, rector of this church, and maſter of the free-ſchool at Campden, publiſhed a Concordance to the Engliſh Bible, and wrote ſeveral grammatical treatiſes. He died in 1682.

The church has an aile on the north ſide, called Upper Lemington chapel, another on the ſouth ſide, and a handſome ſpire at the weſt end, in which are ſix bells. It is dedicated to Thomas Becket, archbiſhop of Canterbury.

	£.	s.	d.		£.	s.	d.
Firſt fruits	18	19	9½	Synodals	0	2	0
Tenths —	1	17	11	Pentecoſtals	0	1	1½
Procurations	0	6	8				

Benefactions.

A tenement is given to the poor; and archbiſhop Juxton gave 50*l.* to the ſame uſe. Mrs. Mary Rawlinſon gave 20*l.* to teach poor children to read.

Taxes.			£.	s.	d.
The Royal Aid in		1692,	175	2	0
Poll-tax	——	1694, —	30	8	0
Land-tax	——	1694, —	125	0	0
The ſame, at 3*s.*		1770, —	88	10	0

About the beginning of this century, according to ſir Robert Atkyns, there were 38 houſes in the pariſh, and about 160 inhabitants, 7 of whom were reputed to be freeholders; yearly births 5, burials 5. But the people have increaſed very much ſince ſir Robert's time, and are now eſtimated at upwards of 450.

TODINGTON.

THIS pariſh lies in the lower diviſion of Kiftſgate hundred, nine miles eaſtward from Tewkeſbury, eleven north-weſtward from Stow on the Wold, and ſixteen north-eaſt from Glouceſter.

The river Iſbourne runs through it from Winchcombe, in its courſe to the upper Avon, which it joins a little below the town of Eveſham in Worceſterſhire.

This village lies in the vale, and is diſtinguiſhed for the richneſs of its ſoil, but more particularly for its being the reſidence of the lord viſcount Tracy. His lordſhip's houſe is large and handſome, and was built about the cloſe of the laſt century, ſince which it has undergone but little alteration. There is a large oak chimney-piece in the great hall, brought from Hayles Abbey, where it was ſet up by the Hobbys, as appears by a large ſcutcheon in the centre of it, divided into ſix quarterings, the firſt being the Hobbys arms, *viz. A feſs between three hobbies or hawks,* but the colours are not expreſſed in the carving. The hall windows are ornamented with painted glaſs, brought from the ſame place, and among other things, have in them the arms of France and England quarterly, and thoſe of Richard duke of Cornwall in a large ſcutcheon, *viz. Or, an eagle diſplay'd with two heads ſable,* and round, *Ricard. Plantagenet Semper auguſtus fundator Noſter.*

Of the Manor and other Eſtates.

Todington exhibits a very extraordinary inſtance of an eſtate deſcending for upwards of ſeven hundred years in the male line of the ſame family, in uninterrupted ſucceſſion. The preſent noble proprietor is deſcended from the blood of the antient Saxon kings of England.

Ethelred the Second, ſon of Edgar, was crowned at Kingſton upon Thames, April 14, 979. During his reign, the Danes frequently invaded the kingdom, but were ſometimes prevented from committing depredations, by the payment of a large ſum of money; which however, being only a preſent relief, the king planned a general maſſacre of them, which was accordingly executed, Nov. 13, 1002.

1002. He died at London in 1016, after an unhappy reign of thirty-feven years.

Goda, the youngeft of king Ethelred's daughters, was the wife of Walter de Medantine, or de Maigne, a noble Norman, and by him was mother of

Radulf earl of Hereford, lord of the manors of Sudley and Todington, in the reign of king Edward the Confeffor. He was fucceeded in both eftates by his fon

Herald, who was poffeffed of them in the reign of king William the Firft, as appears by the record, of which the following is a tranflation:

'The fame Herald holds Todintun. His father [earl Radulph] held it. There are ten hides taxed. In demean are three plow-tillages, and feventeen villeins, and feven bordars, and two free men, having among them all eight plow-tillages. There are ten [plow-tillages] among the *fervi* and *ancillæ*, and two mills of 20*s*. A falt pit pays fifty meafures [*mittas*] of falt. Thefe two manors [Sudlege and Todinton] are worth and were worth 40*l*.' *Domefday*, p. 77.

John de Sudley, fon and heir of Herald, fucceeded his father, and married Grace, the daughter of Henry de Traci, lord of the honour of Barnftaple in Devonfhire, which he had by the gift of king Stephen, as a reward for his valour and faithful fervices in the Weft. This family of the Tracies took their name from the town of Traci in Normandy, and accompanied king William in his invafion of England, in 1066. By this lady, John had two fons, Radulph, or Ralph, who fucceeded to the barony of Sudley, and

William, who affumed his mother's family name, and lived in the time of king Henry the Second. He held lands (probably the Todington eftate) of his brother Ralph de Sudley, by the fervice of one knight's fee, in the laft-mentioned reign, and is fuppofed to be one of thofe four knights who killed Thomas Becket,[t] archbifhop of Canterbury, Dec. 29, 1171.

Oliver de Tracy, fon of William, occurs among the knights in Gloucefterfhire who paid fcutage 2 Joh. and was father of

William de Tracy, who prefented to the church of Todington 53 H. 3. In 1289, 17 E. 1. he is recorded among the knights of the county of Gloucefter, and, with Ralph de Sudley, his kinfman, commanded under that king in his victorious expedition into Scotland. He left a minor fon,

Sir William Tracy of Todington, who in a return of the gentry in Gloucefterfhire, made 25 E. 1. 1298, being then in ward to Lawrence Trefham, is certified among thofe who had 40*l*. a year in lands, and were qualified to receive the honour of knighthood. He was fheriff of Gloucefterfhire 12 & 17 E. 2. and left iffue a fon Henry, and a daughter Margery, wedded to John, fon of John Archer, of Umberflade in Warwickfhire, and anceftor to the prefent lord Archer.

Henry Tracy, fon of fir William, had likewife a fon

Henry, whofe fon and heir,

Thomas Tracy, was high fheriff of this county in 1359, and fo continued for four years fucceffively.

John Tracy, fon of Thomas, was knighted by king Edward the Third, and, together with Thomas Moygne, John Clifford, and John Sloghter, commiffioned to view and take order for the repair of the banks and drains for the prefervation of the low lands upon the Severn between Briftol and Gloucefter, 36 & 38 E. 3. He gave the advowfon of the church, and an acre of land in Todington, to the abbey of Hayles, 37 E. 3. and was high fheriff of Gloucefterfhire in 1366, and ferved as knight of the fhire in the parliaments convened in the 32d, 37th, 40th, and 43d years of that reign.

Henry Tracy, fon of John, was father of

John Tracy, high fheriff of Gloucefterfhire in 1379, 2 R. 2. whofe fon

William Tracy likewife ferved that office in the 18th year of the fame reign, 1395.

William Tracy, fon of William, was high fheriff in 1416, and married Alice, one of the daughters and coheireffes of Guido de la Spine, lord of Coughton, (whofe great grandfather, William de la Spine, had to wife Joan, daughter and heirefs of fir Simon de Cocton) and by her had iffue William, his heir; John, living 27 H. 6. and Alice, wife of Hugh Culme, or Cullum, anceftor to the prefent baronet, fir John Cullum, of Haftide in Suffolk.

---

[t] The other three were fir Richard Brito, fir Hugh de Morville, and fir Reginald Fitz-Urfe.—The ficklenefs of the human mind is perhaps in no cafe more obfervable, than in this event; for thofe who detefted the pride and arrogance of this ecclefiaftic when alive, began to worfhip him after his death, and thus they fang of him:

Tu per Thomæ fanguinem, quem pro te impendit,
Fac nos, Chrifte, fcandere quo Thomas afcendit.

Imitated thus:

By Thomas's blood, which for thee was expended,
O Chrift, may we rife whither Thomas afcended.

Such a prodigious number of miracles were reported to have been performed at his tomb, as neither Chrift nor his apoftles wrought in fupport of the Chriftian difpenfation. Indeed the great variety of them exhibited on every trivial occafion, would, in an age lefs fuperftitious, and more enlightened, have utterly deftroyed their credibility; for the monks paid no attention to Horace's maxim,

Nec Deus interfit, nifi dignus vindice nodus
Inciderit.

Becket's biographers pretend, that all thofe perfons who had been concerned in his death, died miferably in three or four years afterwards, as it fhould feem, by fome particular interpofition of providence in his behalf. But little or no credit is to be given to monkifh writers, in matters that affect the reputation of their favourite faints, and the champions of papal authority; for it appears upon record, that this fir William de Tracy was in arms, with other barons, againft king John, 17 *regni*, for which offence his lands were feized by the crown, but were reftored to him again 2 H. 3. and that in the 6th year of the laft mentioned reign, 1222, he ferved in an expedition againft the Welch; fo that he furvived the commiffion of that murder upwards of fifty years: It is equally certain, that Hugh de Morville was living in the reign of king John, and held the manors of Kirk Ofwald and Lefingby in Cumberland, which he enjoyed in right of his wife Heloife de Eftouteville.

William Tracy, eldeſt ſon of the laſt William, was high ſheriff in the years 1442, and 1443, and left a ſon

William Tracy, who was high ſheriff of this county in 1449. By Margery his wife, daughter of ſir John Pauncefoot, he had two ſons, Henry, and Richard.

Henry Tracy, eldeſt ſon of William, married Alice, daughter and heireſs of Thomas Baldington, of Adderbury in Oxfordſhire, eſq; and by her was father of three ſons, William his heir; Richard; and Ralph, a monk; and two daughters.

Sir William Tracy, eldeſt ſon of Henry, was knighted, and ſerved the office of high ſheriff of Glouceſterſhire in 1512. He was one of the firſt that embraced the reformed religion in England,[u] and, by Margaret his wife, ſecond daughter of ſir Thomas Throckmorton, of Corſe-court in this county, had iſſue three ſons, William, his heir; Richard, who, as well as his father, was a zealous reformer, and wrote ſeveral treatiſes on religious ſubjects, (ſome of which king Henry the Eighth by proclamation forbad to be read) and was living in 1556; and Robert, who left no iſſue.

William Tracy of Todington, ſon of ſir William, married a daughter of ſir Simon Digby, of Coleſhill in Warwickſhire, and by her was father of Henry, his heir; and of Richard, who had the manor of Stanway ſettled upon him, and became the anceſtor of the baronets of that place, the male line of which family ended in the perſon of ſir John Tracy, in the year 1677.

Henry Tracy, eldeſt ſon of William, took to wife Elizabeth, ſecond daughter of John firſt lord Chandos of Sudley, anceſtor to the duke of Chandos, and dying in 1551, left iſſue John, Giles, Edward, Francis, and Nicholas; and a daughter Eleanor, wife to William Kingſton, of Quenington in this county, eſq.

Sir John Tracy, the eldeſt ſon, was knighted by queen Elizabeth, in her progreſs to Briſtol, 1574, and in the 20th year of that reign, 1578, was high ſheriff of the county of Glouceſter, and died in 1591. By Anne his wife, daughter of ſir Thomas Throckmorton, of Corſe-court, knight, he left iſſue five ſons, *viz.* John, his heir; Thomas, William, Anthony, and Henry; and two daughters, Dorothy, married firſt, to Edmond Bray, of Barrington in this county, and ſecondly, to ſir Edward Conway, of Arrow in Warwickſhire, created lord Conway; and Mary, wedded firſt to Mr. William Hobby, and ſecondly, to that renowned general, ſir Horatio Vere, baron of Tilbury.

Sir John Tracy, eldeſt ſon of ſir John, was knighted by king James the Firſt, and ſerved the office of high ſheriff in 1609. He was advanced to the dignity of viſcount Tracy of Rathcoole, in the county of Dublin, in the kingdom of Ireland, by king Charles the Firſt, Jan. 12, 1642; and having married Anne, daughter of ſir Thomas Shirley, of Isfield in Suſſex, knight, left iſſue by that lady,

Robert, ſecond viſcount Tracy, who took to wife Bridget, third daughter of John Lyttelton, of Frankley-court in Worceſterſhire, eſq; by whom he had one ſon John, and a daughter Anne, wedded to William Somerville, of Edſton in Warwickſhire, eſq. His lordſhip married ſecondly, Dorothy, daughter of Thomas Cocks, of Caſtle-ditch in Herefordſhire, and by that lady was father of Robert Tracy, one of the juſtices of the king's bench to king William, and one of the judges of the court of common pleas to queen Anne, and commiſſioner of the great ſeal in 1710: He was again in the commiſſion of the great ſeal, with ſir John Pratt and ſir James Montague, in 1718, but retired from his employments, on

[u] Before the Reformation in religion was fully eſtabliſhed, numbers of thoſe who favoured it were cruelly perſecuted and burnt at the ſtake. Sir William Tracy eſcaped the flames in his life-time, yet ſome paſſages in his laſt will, deviating from the ſtandard of church orthodoxy, as then eſtabliſhed, excited ſo violent a reſentment in the popiſh party, that he was condemned as an heretick after his death, and an order was ſent to Parker, chancellor of Worceſter, to raiſe his corps. The officious chancellor, however, deſirous to ingratiate himſelf with his ſuperiors, exceeded the bounds of his commiſſion, and burnt the body, in which proceeding he could not be juſtified, even by the laws of the church of Rome, as ſir William was not a relapſe. So two years after, the chancellor being ſued by Tracy's heirs, was turned out of his office, and fined 400*l.*

The obnoxious paſſages in the will are ſubjoined for the ſatiſfaction of the reader, who will eaſily perceive, that ſir William's contempt of purgatory, and of prayers for the dead, gave occaſion of offence.

The WILL.

'IN the name of God, Amen. I William Tracy, of Todington in the county of Glouceſter, eſq; make my Teſtament and laſt Will as hereafter followeth:

'Firſt, and before all other things, I commit myſelf to God, and to his mercy, believing, without any doubt or miſtruſt, that by his grace and the merits of Jeſus Chriſt, and by virtue of his paſſion and reſurrection, I have, and ſhall have remiſſion of all my ſins, and reſurrection of body and ſoul, according as it is written, *I believe that my Redeemer liveth, and that at the laſt day I ſhall riſe out of the earth, and in my fleſh ſhall ſee my Saviour*: This my hope is laid up in my boſom.

'And touching the wealth of my ſoul, the faith that I have taken and rehearſed is ſufficient (as I ſuppoſe) without any other man's works or merits. My ground and belief is, that there is but one God, and one meditator between God and man, which is Jeſus Chriſt; ſo that I accept none in heaven or in earth to be mediator between me and God, but only Jeſus Chriſt; and all other to be but as petitioners in receiving of grace, but none able to give influence of grace; and therefore will I beſtow no part of my goods for that intent, that any man ſhould ſay or do to help my ſoul, for therein I truſt only to the promiſes of Chriſt. *He that believeth and is baptized ſhall be ſaved, and he that believeth not ſhall be damned.*

'As touching the burying of my body, it availeth me not whatſoever be done thereto; for St. Auguſtine ſaith, *De cura agenda pro mortuis*, that the funeral pomps are rather the ſolace of them that live, than the wealth and comfort of them that are dead, and therefore I remit it only to the diſcretion of my executors.

'And touching the diſtribution of my temporal goods, my purpoſe is, by the grace of God, to beſtow them to be accepted as the fruits of faith. So that I do not ſuppoſe that my merit ſhall be by the good beſtowing of them, but my merit is the faith of Jeſus Chriſt only, by whom ſuch works are good, according to the words of our Lord, *I was hungry, and thou gaveſt me meat, &c.* and it followeth, *That ye have done to the leaſt of my brethren, ye have done it to me, &c.* And ever we ſhould conſider that true ſaying, *That a good work maketh not a good man, but a good man maketh a good work: For faith maketh a man both good and righteous, for a righteous man liveth by faith, and whatſoever ſpringeth not of faith is ſin.*

'For my temporal goods, &c.' Dated 22 H. 8.

account

account of his ill health, in 1726, and died Sep. 11, 1735, having filled his feveral pofts, equally to the honour and advantage of himfelf and his country.

John, third vifcount Tracy, eldeft fon of Robert, married Elizabeth, eldeft furviving daughter of Thomas lord Leigh, of Stoneleigh in Warwickfhire, and by her ladyfhip had iffue William, his heir; Charles; and Ferdiando, to whom fir John Tracy, the laft baronet of Stanway, bequeathed that manor, which continued in the Tracies, his defcendants, 'till it paffed, very lately, to the prefent vifcount Hereford, by the marriage of an heirefs. He had alfo one daughter Mary.

William, fourth vifcount Tracy, married firft, Frances, daughter of Leicefter Devereux, vifcount Hereford, by whom he was father of Elizabeth, wife to Robert, fon and heir apparent to fir Robert Burdet, of Bramefh in Warwickfhire, and mother of fir Robert Burdet, of Foremark in Derbyfhire, bart. His lordfhip married, fecondly, Jane, third daughter of fir Thomas Leigh, and fifter of lord Leigh, of Stoneleigh, and by her ladyfhip had one fon Thomas-Charles, and one daughter Anne, married to fir William Keyte, of Ebberton in this county, bart.

Thomas-Charles, fifth vifcount Tracy, on Dec. 27, 1712, efpoufed Elizabeth, eldeft daughter of William Keyte, efq; fon of fir William Keyte, of Ebberton, bart. and had iffue William, who died in 1752; Thomas-Charles, his fucceffor; and one daughter Jane, wedded to Capel Hanbury, of Pont-y-pool in Monmouthfhire, efq. His lordfhip took to wife, fecondly, Frances, daughter of fir John Packington, of Weftwood in Worcefterfhire, baronet, by whom he had three fons, John, D.D. warden of All Souls college, Oxford; Packington, who died young; and Henry; likewife three daughters, Frances, woman of the bedchamber to the queen; Anne, the wife of John Smith, of Comb-hay in Somerfetfhire, efq; and Elizabeth, who died unmarried in 1764. His lordfhip furvived his fecond lady, and departing this life, June 4, 1756, was fucceeded in title and eftate by his fecond but eldeft furviving fon,

Thomas-Charles, the prefent vifcount Tracy, and lord of the manor of Todington. His lordfhip, on February 6, 1755, married Harriot, one of the daughters of Peter Bathurft, of Clarendon-Park, in the county of Wilts, efq; by Selina his fecond lady, daughter of Robert Shirly, earl Rivers; but his lordfhip has no child now living.

His lordfhip's paternal arms are, *Or, an efcallop in the dexter chief fable, between two bends gules.*

CREST. *On a cap of maintenance gules, turned up ermine, an efcallop fable between two wings erected Or.*

SUPPORTERS. *Two falcons proper, beak'd and bell'd Or.*

MOTTO. MEMORIA PII ÆTERNA.

HAMLET. *Stanley Pontlarch* is a hamlet in this parifh, which has its own officers, and a chapel within it, where divine fervice is performed once a month, but the people bury at Todington.

'Four hides and a half in Stanlege belong to 'the church of Teodekefberie. There is one 'plow-tillage, and four villeins, with two plow-'tillages, and three bordars, and five *fervi*. This 'eftate was free from tax. It was worth 4*l.* 'now 40*s.*' *Domefday*, p. 68.

Robert de Pontlarch, or Pont de L'arch, held this eftate under the church of Tewkefbury; and it is probable that it received the addition of Pontlarch, from him, by way of diftinguifhing it from two parifhes in this county of the name of Stanley.

John de Sudley was feized of Stanley Pontlarch 41 E. 3. and Hugh Croft, and Agnes and Leon Croft, levied a fine of the fame manor to fir William St. Maur 18 H. 7.

Walter Havanage recovered lands in Stanley, and in Thorp, Greet, and Greeton in Winchcombe, againft Adam Havanage and Alice his wife, 28 E. 1. Lands in Stanley Pontlarch belonged to the vifcount Lifle, and were granted to Thomas earl of Effex, upon whofe attainder they were again granted to fir William Kingfton 32 H. 8.

This hamlet contains feven houfes.

Of the Church, &c.

The church is a vicarage, in the deanery of Campden, value 32*l.* in the king's books. There are twenty-eight acres of arable land, and eleven of meadow and pafture, belonging to the glebe, which have been let at 23*l.* a year; and there is a compofition of 6*l.* 13*s.* 4*d.* The chapel of Stanley Pontlarch is annexed to it, on which account the impropriator pays the vicar a further fum of 4*l.* a year, as I find it in bifhop Benfon's vifitation book.

The advowfon formerly belonged to the Tracies, and was given by fir John Tracy to the abbey of Hayles, 37 E. 3. And in the year 1403, the bifhop of Worcefter fettled a compofition with the abbat of Hayles for the maintenance of the curate of Todington. After the diffolution of Hayles abbey, the advowfon returned into the fame family, and Thomas lord vifcount Tracy is patron and impropriator.

The church is fmall, but neat, and was rebuilt in the year 1723, by Thomas-Charles lord vifcount Tracy.

Firft fruits £	8	13	4	Synodals £.	0	2	6
Tenths —	0	17	4	Pentecoft.	0	0	8½
Procurations	0	6	8				

Monuments and Infcriptions.

There are four monuments in the chancel, with the following infcriptions: Againft the fouth wall,

Hic jacet Dominus Iohannes Tracy Miles, quondam Dominus de Todington, &c. (Filius et Hæres Henrici Tracy Armigeri, et Elizabethæ Filiæ Iohannis Domini Chandos Baronis de Sudely) qui obijt Septembris 25° Anno Dni 1591.

On the fame fide,

The Body of this Church was rebuilt in the Year of our Lord One Thoufand feven Hundred and twenty-three, by the Right Honourable

Honourable Thomas-Charles Lord Viſcount Tracy, who died on the 4th of June, 1756, in the 66th Year of his Age.

His lordſhip's buſt ſtands over the tablet, and beneath it a ſcutcheon, *Quarterly* 1ſt *and* 4th, Tracy; 2d *and* 3d, *Argent, a chevron between three mullets ſable.*

Againſt the north wall,

Here lyeth the Body of Margaret one of the Daughters and Coheires of Thomas Whittington of Pavntley, Eſquior, and Wife of Sir Thomas Throckmorton of Torthworth, Knight, who deceaſed Feb. 1° Anno Dni 1577.

As alſo the Bodies of Anthony Throckmorton and Margaret, her Sonne and Daughter.

On this monument are the arms of Whittington and Throckmorton.

Againſt the eaſt wall,

M. S.

Nobiliſſ[i] juvenis Caroli Tracy, filij tertij Honoratiſſ[i] Dni Ioh: Vice-comitis Tracy. Juvenis non natalibus ſolùm ſed et egregiâ indole, et ſummis ingenij Dotibus illuſtriſſ[i]: Qui poſt pueriles annos fæliciter ſtudijs liberalibus impenſos, migravit Oxonium, ubi ſeſquianno vix dum elapſo, non ſine ſuſpirijs omnium quibus innotuit, immature (proh dolor!) obijt 3° die Maij 1676.

Sed Heus! Lector, oculis cave, ſi enim vivum nôſſes cujus jam mortui Epitaphium legis, verendum eſſet ne inſtar Niobes, indulgens lachrymis rigeres in ſtatuam.

Taxes.	The Royal Aid in	1692,	£. 211	7	0
	Poll-tax — —	1694, —	22	15	0
	Land-tax ——	1694, -	188	4	0
	The ſame, at 3*s.*	1770, —	104	16	10½
	Stanley Pontlarch.				
	Land-tax at 3*s.*	1770, —	28	5	9½

At the beginning of this century, there were 48 houſes, and about 200 inhabitants in this pariſh, whereof 6 were freeholders; yearly births 6, and burials 6. *Atkyns.* But examining the regiſter, I found, that in ten years, beginning with 1700, there had been 58 baptiſms, and 53 burials; and in a like period, beginning with 1760, the baptiſms were 53, the burials 49; and the inhabitants are now about 186.

TORMARTON

IS a pariſh in the hundred of Grumbald's Aſh, about four miles northward from Marſhfield, four ſouth-eaſtward from Chipping Sodbury, and thirty-two ſouth from Glouceſter.

The village is ſeated upon high ground, in a fine, healthy, champaign country, through which three turnpike-roads are carried; one from Glouceſter and Cirenceſter to Bath, a ſecond from Chippenham to Sodbury and Briſtol, and the third from Chriſtian Malford in Wiltſhire, to Pucklechurch, Mangotsfield, and Briſtol. The pariſh is bounded on the eaſt by Weſt Kyneton in Wiltſhire, on the weſt by Dodington, on the north by Old Sodbury, and has Weſt Littleton on the ſouth, which latter was formerly taken out of it.

The name is of doubtful original, yet ſir Robert Atkyns ſuppoſed it to be taken *from the tower of the church, and from* Meark, *which in the Saxon language ſignifies a boundary*; *and this town,* ſays he, *ſtands in the borders between the Mercian and Weſt Saxon kingdoms.* But he formed his judgment from the modern name, for Tormentone, as it is written in *Domeſday*, does not favour his conjecture.

The ſame learned author takes notice of a ſort of ſtones found in the north fields in this pariſh, about the bigneſs of piſtol bullets, which being broke, look ruſty like iron ore. Upon inquiry, I find that thoſe ſtones, as he calls them, are not uncommon at this time, and are really no other than iron bullets, diſcharged, I apprehend, in the battle and ſkirmiſhing that happened in theſe parts in the reign of king Charles the Firſt, between the king's troops, and thoſe under the command of ſir William Waller.

Of the Manor and other Eſtates.

'Richard the legate holds Tormentone, in 'Hedredeſtan hundred, of the king. There are 'eight hides. Alric held it of king Edward. 'There are ſix plow-tillages in demean, and 'twenty villeins, and four bordars, and a prieſt, 'and one radchenitter, having among them all 'twelve plow-tillages. There are twelve *ſervi.* 'It was worth 12*l.* and is now worth 15*l.*' *Domeſday-book*, p. 76.

The records ſhew, that Henry de Willington, ſon of Ralph de Willington, held Tormarton 23 E. 3. in which year he had livery of the manors of Poulton, Ablington, Yate, Weſtonbirt, Frampton Cotterel, and Sandhurſt, all in the county of Glouceſter. John de Willington, of Willington-court in Sandhurſt, great grandſon of Henry, was ſeized of Tormarton, Littleton, and all the before mentioned manors, at the time of his death, 20 R. 2. and left Joan his ſiſter and heir, who was married to John Wrath.

This manor was held of the Willingtons, as chief lords, by ſome of the perſons following:

Richard de la Rivere, or de Ripariis, had a grant of fairs in Tormarton, and of free warren in all his lands in England, 38 H. 3.

The ſheriff, in his liſt of all the vills in the county, and their reſpective proprietors, 9 E. 1. omits Tormarton and Littleton, but ſays, John, the ſon of John de la Rivere, is lord of Acton Turville, in Grymbaldeaſhe hundred, and in ward to the earl of Arundel; and I conclude that he was then likewiſe proprietor of this manor, for it appears by the eſcheator's inquiſition 8 E. 2. that he died ſeized of Tormarton, and of the hamlet of Littleton, both together worth 30*l.* a year, which he held of John de Wylintone by the ſervice of two knights fees; and alſo of half a knight's fee in Actone Turvyle, worth 6*l.* *per ann.* which he held of the earl of Arundel, and left John, his ſon and heir, two years old.

Richard de la Rivere forfeited all his lands for rebellion againſt king Edward the Second, and Edward earl of Arundel had a grant of them, and was ſeized of Tormarton in the 20th year of that reign; but Richard de la Rivere recovered poſfeffion 1 E. 3. The manor was held of Edward earl of Kent, by knight's fervice, 4 E. 3.

John de la Rivere held Tormarton and the hamlet of Littleton, with markets and fairs, 6 E. 3. and John de la Rivere, his fon, was feized thereof in the 13th year of the fame reign. Henry de la Rivere had a confirmation of markets and fairs in Tormarton 22 R. 2.

Sir John Drayton held this manor, and Acton Turville, 5 H. 5.

Ifabel. the widow of fir Thomas de la Rivere, and daughter of fir Maurice Ruffel, died feized of Tormarton, Littleton, and Skirewell, 15 H. 6. Maurice de la Rivere, fon of fir Thomas and Ifabel, had a fon Robert, whofe daughter and heirefs, Ifabel, was married to fir John St. Loe, and carried the inheritance of the manors of Tormarton, Littleton, and Acton Turville, into that name and family. She was afterwards wedded fucceffively to fir John Drayton, fir Geoffry Scrope, and Stephen Hatfield, efq; but had no child by the three laft. Sir John St. Loe, fon of fir John, and of Ifabel the heirefs of the de la Riveres, married a daughter of fir John Guyfe, by whom he had fir William, his heir; Nicholas, Edward, and Clement. Sir William St. Loe, eldeft fon of fir John, married Elizabeth,[w] daughter, and at length heirefs of John Hardwicke, of Hardwicke in Derbyfhire, and widow of fir William Cavendifh, of Chatfworth in the fame county, and fettled upon her the inheritance of this eftate, which paffed, on her fourth marriage, to George earl of Shrewfbury, whofe fon, Gilbert earl of Shrewfbury, was poffeffed of it in 1608. The manor afterwards became the property of William marquis of Newcaftle, who conveyed it to fir Francis Top, from whom it defcended to fir John Top, baronet, who refided here. He left two daughters, one of whom was married to —— Hungerford, whofe only fon John Hungerford, of Dingley-hall in Northamptonfhire, efq; is the prefent lord of the manors of Tormarton and Acton Turville. His arms are, *Sable, two bars argent, in chief three plates.*

John Cotherington and Alice his wife levied a fine of lands in Tormarton, to the ufe of themfelves for life, remainder to their fons, Humphry, Thomas, and John, fucceffively in taille, remainder to Margaret Bafiles, late wife to fir Peter Bafiles, 49 H. 6. 1470, in which year Henry, that pageant king, recovered and enjoyed his crown for a few months, 'till he was again dethroned in 1471.

Lands in Tormarton belonged to the priory of Black Canons at Bradenftoke in Wiltfhire, and were granted to John Pope 37 H. 8.

The fimilarity in names of places frequently produces confufion, and to this caufe it muft be attributed that fir Robert Atkyns has applied fome records to Tormarton which evidently belong to Farmington, as already obferved under the account of that parifh.

Of the Church, &c.

The church is a rectory, in the deanery of Hawkefbury, worth upwards of 400*l.* a year. Nathaniel Caftleton is patron, and the reverend Mr. Newdigate Pointz is the prefent incumbent. He is defcended from the antient family of that name, formerly lords of the manor of Iron Acton.

The bifhop of Winchefter appropriated this church to the abbey of Malmefbury, 35 E. 3.

Ninety-five ftatute acres belong to the glebe.

The whole parifh was inclofed about the year 1760, when the glebe was laid together, but the other lands were not exonerated from tithe.

The church is dedicated to St. Mary, and has an aile on the fouth fide, and a low embattled tower at the weft end. It was built by fir John de la Rivere, who is alfo faid to have founded a chantry in this church, dedicated to St. Mary.

Firft fruits £. 27	0	0	Synodals £. 0	2	0
Tenths — 2	14	0	Pentecoft. 0	0	10
Procurations 0	6	8			

Monuments and Infcriptions.

Leland fays, *There lyeth buried in the Body of the Paroche Churche of Thormerton one Petrine de la Ryvers, with a Frenche Epitaphie. He was owner of the Lordfhype of Tormerton.* And fir Robert Atkyns obferves, that in his time, the effigies of fir John de la Rivere, with the model of the church in his hand, remained in the chancel; but the braffes of both thefe monuments are now torn off and loft.

Upon a brafs plate, fixed to a black marble ftone, in the body of the church, is the effigy of a man, with a purfe hanging before him, and

[w] This beautiful and accomplifhed lady had been married, at fourteen years of age, to Robert Barley, of Barley in Derbyfhire, who was likewife very young, and died foon after, Feb. 2, 1532-3; but fhe enjoyed the whole of his large fortune, by fettlement on her and her heirs. After living a widow fome years, fhe was married, fecondly, to fir William Cavendifh, by whom fhe was fo intirely beloved, that at her requeft, he fold his poffeffions in the fouthern counties, to purchafe eftates in Derbyfhire, where her relations chiefly refided; and by her perfuafion, he began building a noble feat at Chatfworth, which, however, he did not live to finifh, dying 4 & 5 Phil. & Mar. She accepted for her third hufband, fir William St. Loe, captain of the guard to the queen Elizabeth, and proprietor of Tormarton, and other confiderable eftates in Gloucefterfhire, all which, in failure of iffue by him, were fettled on her and her own heirs. She furvived him, but not her charms of wit and beauty, by which fhe captivated George Talbot, fixth earl of Shrewfbury, then the greateft fubject in the realm, whom fhe took for her fourth hufband; and had the honour of being keeper to Mary queen of Scots, during feventeen years of her imprifonment in England. She was a fourth time left a widow, in 1590, and fo continued 'till her death, Feb. 13, 1607, in the 87th year of her age. Happy in her feveral marriages, fhe rofe by each hufband to greater wealth and higher honours; but had iffue only by the fecond, *viz.* 1. Henry, who died childlefs in 1616; 2. William, created baron Cavendifh of Hardwicke, May 4, 1605, and earl of Devonfhire, Aug. 8, 1618; 3. Charles, father of William, earl, marquis, and duke of Newcaftle; and three daughters. It is not unworthy obfervation, that fhe built three of the moft elegant feats that were ever raifed by one perfon in any county in England, *viz.* Chatfworth, Hardwicke, and Oldcotes, all tranfmitted intire to the firft duke of Devonfhire.

his

his hands in a ſupplicating poſture. Round the verge, in old character, is this inſcription :

✠ Orate pro Anima Iohannis Ceyſyll quondam famulus Reverendi Dni Iohīs Sendlow militis qui quidem Iohannes Ceyſyll ſuum clauſit extremum in vigilia Sancti Bartholomei Apoſtoli Anno Dni Millimo ccccIxxxxiii° Et anno regni Regis Henrici Septimi nono. Cuius anime propitietur D' Altiſſimus Amen.

On a white ſtone in the chancel,

Here lyeth the Body of John Baber, Doctor of Divinity, in his life time parſon of this Church of Tormarton, and Chaplain in ordinary to K. James of bleſſed memory; who by his care preſerved that which remaineth to his ſucceſſors. He departed this life ye 9 May, 1628, being aged threeſcore and five years, having for many years undergone with great credit ſeveral places of eminency in the commonwealth, and enjoy'd this parſonage of Tormarton 37 years.

Againſt a pillar in the church,

Near by lyeth interred the Body of Edward Topp, Son of Lingen Topp of Witton in the county of Salop, Eſq; late High Sheriffe of that county, and Son of Alexander Topp of Witton Eſq; Son of John Topp of Stockton in the county of Wilts Eſq; who departed this life the 15th Day of May in the 50th yeare of his age, and in the yeare of our Lord 1699.

Arms, *Argent, in a canton gules a dexter hand clinched and erected azure.* Creſt. *On a wreath, a dexter hand holding a ſiniſter arm couped below the elbow gules.* Motto. FORTIOR EST QUI SE.

Taxes.			£.		
The Royal Aid in	1692,				
Poll-tax — —	1694, —		20	12	0
Land-tax ——	1694, —		95	7	0
The ſame, at 3*s.*	1770, —		75	3	11$\frac{3}{4}$

When ſir Robert Atkyns compiled his Hiſtory, there were 30 houſes in this pariſh, and about 130 inhabitants, 4 of whom were freeholders; yearly births 4, burials 3. The people are ſince increaſed to 207.

TORTWORTH.

THIS pariſh lies in the hundred of Grumbald's Aſh, four miles diſtant ſouth from Berkeley, four weſt from Wotton-underedge, and twenty ſouth-weſtward from Glouceſter.

It conſiſts of ſome woodland, with a ſmall proportion of arable, but much the greater part is rich paſture ground, and dairy farms, that yield as good cheeſe as any in Glouceſterſhire.

Tortworth, or Torteword, is a name of the ſame claſs with Badgworth, Brockworth, Pebworth, &c. already explained under thoſe heads.

The pariſh is diſtinguiſhed by an antient ſeat near the church, where the anceſtors of the preſent lord Ducie ſometime reſided, and the park ſtill remains incloſed with a high ſtone wall. The houſe is large and irregular, and was built by one of his lordſhip's family. There is a cheſnut-tree in the garden of great antiquity and ſize, having been there, it is ſaid, ever ſince the year 1216. The greater part of it is dead, but ſome of the branches bear fruit every year, and the writer of this account meaſured it two or three years ago, and found it eighteen yards in circumference. Some have ſuppoſed it to be ſeveral trees incorporated together, but the notion is abſurd, and the appearance of the tree is ſufficient to refute it.

Of the Manor and other Eſtates.

Tortworth is thus deſcribed in the ſurvey, made in the reign of king William the Firſt:

'Turſtin the ſon of Rolf holds Torteword in 'Bacheſtan hundred. There is one hide. Aluuold 'held it. In demean are two plow-tillages, and 'ſix villeins, and ſeven bordars, with ſeven plow-'tillages. There are ſix *ſervi*, and two mills of '15*s.* [rent] and ten acres of meadow. A wood 'one mile long, and half a mile broad, pays 5*s.* 'The manor was worth 7*l.* now 100*s.*' *Domeſday-book*, p. 78.

The ſheriff returned that Nicholas de Kyneſton was lord of Totworth 9 E. 1. and it is extremely probable, that his mother was one of the daughters and coheireſſes of a former proprietor; and that Margaret, the other coheireſs, was married to ſir William Manſel, of Lypiat; for ſir William Manſel, and Margaret his wife, releaſed all their right in the manor and advowſon of Tortworth to ſir Nicholas, who at the ſame time releaſed his right in other lands to them, in the 27th year of that reign. He purchaſed the privilege of fairs, markets, and free warren in this manor 32 E. 3. and died ſeized thereof 9 E. 2. Hawiſe, his only daughter and heireſs, had been married to, but was then the widow of Robert de Veel, or le Veel, as appears by ſir Nicholas's charter to the abbey of Kingſwood, 9 E. 2. wherein he releaſes all his right in a piece of meadow called Joneſham in Charfield, which had been given to that houſe by Hawiſe his daughter.

Sir Peter le Veel held Tortworth 14 E. 2. Nicholas le Veel, ſon and heir of ſir Peter, died ſeized of Tortworth, which he left in dower to Margaret his widow, who died 23 E. 3. John Veel was poſſeſſed of Tortworth, at the time of his death, 36 H. 6. and was ſucceeded by Robert his ſon, who married Elizabeth, daughter of John Pointz, eſq; and by her had an only daughter and heireſs Alice, married to ſir David Matthews, of Glamorganſhire, who was lord of this manor, in right of his wife, in the reign of king Henry the Seventh.

William Throckmorton, deſcended from the antient family of that name, ſeated at Fladbury in Worceſterſhire, married Margaret, the eldeſt of the five daughters of ſir David Matthews. He was high ſheriff of Glouceſterſhire 21 H. 8. and was ſucceeded by his ſon ſir Thomas Throckmorton, who married Margaret, one of the ſix daughters and coheireſſes of Thomas Whittington, of Pauntley, eſq. He ſerved the office of high ſheriff of this county 6 Phil. & Mar. and was ſucceeded by his ſon

Sir Thomas Throckmorton, who had livery of the manor 9 Eliz. and was high ſheriff of Glouceſterſhire in the 30th and 43d years of the ſame reign. He married, firſt, Elizabeth, daughter of ſir Richard Berkeley of Stoke Giffard, and ſecondly, —— daughter of ſir Edward Rogers, and dying in in the year 1607, was succeeded by his son sir William Throckmorton, who married Cicely, daughter and coheiress of Thomas Baynham, of Clowerwall. He was lord of the manors of Charfield and Tortworth in the year 1608, but he sold the latter to —— Webb.

Sir Robert Ducie, baronet, alderman of London, descended from the Ducies in Staffordshire, purchased the manor of Tortworth of —— Webb. Sir Richard Ducie, baronet, son of sir Robert, was high sheriff of Gloucestershire 12 C. 1. He was taken prisoner in the civil wars by sir William Waller, and dying unmarried, was succeeded by his next brother, sir William Ducie, baronet, who served the office of high sheriff in the year 1660, and was made knight of the Bath at the coronation of king Charles the Second, by whom he was also created viscount Down in the kingdom of Ireland. He died without issue, whereupon the manor descended to Elizabeth, only child of Robert Ducie, esq; his younger brother. She was married to Edward Morton, of Morton in Staffordshire, esq; and had issue Matthew-Ducie Morton, created lord Ducie, June 13, 1720. From him the manor of Tortworth descended to Matthew lord Ducie, and after his death, to Thomas the present lord Ducie, whose pedigree and arms are given under Woodchester.

But there was another manor in this parish, which was held of the king, as of the hundred of Grumbald's Ash.

Henry Wogan was seized of it, in right of Katherine his wife, and dying 9 H. 8. left an only daughter Joan, then eleven years old, heiress to her mother. Thomas Hicks, in right of his wife Joan Dorney, was seized of lands in Tortworth, and of a fulling mill, which passed to John Hicks, his son, who died possessed of them 38 H. 8. leaving John his son, three years old.

There are places in this parish of the following names, which are too inconsiderable to be considered as hamlets, *viz.* 1. *Tafarn-Bàch*, corruptly called *Tavern-bath*, of which already, under Charfield. 2. *Avening*. 3. *Avon's-green*. 4. *Damery*. and 5. *Crockley*.

Of the Church, &c.

The church is a rectory, in the deanery of Hawkesbury, worth about 250*l*. a year. The advowson passed with the manor for many ages, but is now vested in Oriel college, Oxford, and the reverend Dr. Bosworth is the present incumbent.

Sixty acres belong to the glebe.

The church is dedicated to St. Leonard, and has an aile on the south side, and an embattled tower at the west end.

First fruits £.	16	3	4	Synodals £.	0	2	0
Tenths —	1	12	4½	Pentecost.	0	1	0
Procurations	0	6	8				

Monuments and Inscriptions.

Near the chancel, there is a handsome monument for sir Thomas Throckmorton, with his effigy lying upon it in full proportion.

A monument on the south side of the church bears the following inscription:

Near this place lies the body of the Right Honourable Matthew the first Lord Ducie, Baron of Moreton in the county of Stafford, who departed this life May the 22[d] 1735, in the 72d year of his age.

Here also is interred the Right Honourable Arabella Lady Ducie, relict of the first Lord Ducie, one of the coheiresses of Sir Thomas Prestwich of Lancashire, baronet. She died Mar. 14, 1749, aged 90.

Over the monument hang a helmet and gauntlet; and beneath it are the Ducies arms, *viz. Argent, a chevron gules between three square buckles sable.* Motto. PERSEVERANDO.

Benefactions.

A house and land worth about 12*l*. a year are given for the use of the church. And the reverend Mr. Brooke, rector of this church, who died Aug. 1, 1757, left a library of books for the use of his successors.

Taxes.	The Royal Aid in	1692,	£. 142	0	0
	Poll-tax —	1694, —	30	17	0
	Land-tax —	1694, —	150	17	0
	The same, at 3*s*.	1770, —	117	9	0

About the beginning of this century, there were 45 houses in the parish, and about 240 inhabitants, 8 of whom were freeholders; yearly births 8, burials 8. *Atkyns.* The people having been accurately numbered a few years ago, were found to be 241, so that population has remained nearly in the same state for the last sixty years.

TREDINGTON

IS a parish in the lower division of Tewkesbury hundred, two miles and a half south-eastward from the town of that name, five north-westward from Cheltenham, and nine north from Gloucester.

It lies in a healthy part of the Vale, free from those floods and inundations to which lower situations are frequently exposed; and the face of the parish is diversified by an agreeable variety of gentle slopes and swells, without any eminence of consequence; but the traveller is disgusted with the badness of the roads, which have never been attended to 'till within these few years, and are still in a miry condition, tho' considerably improved.

The little river Swilyate runs through this parish, and is here augmented by two small streams, one from Aston, the other from Stoke Archer, and empties itself into the Upper Avon, a little below the town of Tewkesbury.

Of the Manor and other Estates.

Tredington was appendant to, and dependant on, the great lordship of Tewkesbury, at the time of of the general ſurvey taken in the reign of king William the Firſt, as the reader may ſee in the copy of that record at p. 68 of this book. And the manor deſcended to the ſeveral ſucceſſive proprietors of Tewkeſbury, 'till it came to Anne, widow of Richard Nevil, the great earl of Warwick, who levied a fine of this and many of her other eſtates to the king, 3 H. 7. by which means it came to the crown.

Queen Mary, in the 5th year of her reign, granted the manor, by the name of late Warwick's lands, to Anne Forteſcue, widow of ſir Adrian Forteſcue, and to the heirs males of ſir Adrian. The manor belonged to ſir Francis Forteſcue in the year 1608, and lord Craven is the preſent proprietor of it.

Ralph Seimour and Iſabel his wife levied a fine of lands in Tredington, to ſir Richard Croft, 16 E. 4.

Lands, called Penny-land, belonged to the counteſs of Warwick, and were granted to William Fitz-Williams and Arthur Ingram 7 E. 6.

Tithes in Tredington belonged to the abbey of Tewkeſbury, and were granted to Thomas Stroud, Walter Earl, and James Paget, 36 H. 8. Several lands here, likewiſe belonging to the ſame abbey, were reputed a manor, and granted to Daniel Pert and Alexander Pert, 7 E. 6.

John Surman, eſq; has a houſe and a large eſtate in the pariſh, deſcended to him from his anceſtors. William Surman, eſq; was owner of them at the beginning of this century, and dying in 1742, was ſucceeded by his ſon William-Packer Surman, whoſe ſon William-Packer dying without iſſue, the houſe and eſtate came to John Surman, eſq; his younger brother. The arms of Surman, as I find them on a hatchment in the chancel, are, *Or, a lion rampant ſable, armed and langued gules, between three holly leaves ſlipped proper.*

Of the Church, &c.

The church is a curacy, in the deanery of Winchcombe, worth about 20*l.* a year, to which the biſhop of Glouceſter preſents by ſequeſtration. It was formerly reputed a vicarage, and belonged to the priory of Lanthony.

The church is a ſmall building, dedicated to St. John Baptiſt, with a low wooden tower at the weſt end, in which are five bells.

There was formerly a lofty ſtone croſs in the church-yard, of which nothing remains, at preſent, but the ſteps and column that ſupported it.

Monuments and Inſcriptions.

There is a tomb in the church-yard, formerly ſurrounded with paliſadoes, for John Surman, eſq; who died in 1687, and others of the ſame family.

Near the communion table, in the chancel, are the two following inſcriptions upon a flat blue ſtone:

In Memory of William Surman, of Tredington in the County of Glouceſter, Eſq[r]. who died the 14th Day of July, Ann[o] Dom. one Thouſand ſeven Hundred and forty two, Ætat. Suæ 75.

Anne the Wife of William Surman, of this Pariſh Eſq[r]. and Sole Daughter and Heir of William Packer, late of Cricklade in the County of Wilts, Gent. who died the 26th of May, Anno Dom. 1728, Ætat. Suæ 56.

At the top of the ſtone are theſe arms, *Baron and femme*, 1. *Or, a lion rampant ſable, armed and langued gules, between three holly leaves ſlipped proper*, for Surman. 2. *Gules, a croſs lozengy Or between four roſes argent*, for Packer.——*Note*. The colours are not expreſſed on the ſtone, but are taken from an hatchment over the communion table.

Upon another flat ſtone, cloſe to the laſt,

Here lyeth the Body of W[m] Packer Surman, Eſq; who departed this Life y[e] 7th day of January, 1764, Aged 60.

And alſo the Bodys of W[m] and Ann Son and Daughter of the above W[m] Packer Surman, Eſq[r]. Ann died Jan. the 17th 1747, Aged one year and 10 Months. W[m] died March the 9th 1747, Aged 11 Months.

Here lyeth the Body of Elizabeth Daughter of William Surman, Eſq; who died the Nineteenth day of January, 1761, Aged 60.

There are likewiſe inſcriptions for ſeveral of the Cartwrights, once a conſiderable family in this pariſh, with their arms, *A feſs embattled between three cart wheels.*

Benefactions.

Several parcels of land are given for the repair of the church. Edwin Scrimſhire, of Aquilat in Staffordſhire, eſq; gave the tithes of Tredington and Fidington to the miniſter of Tewkeſbury, but ſubject to the annual payment of 12*l.* each to the miniſters of Tredington and Aſhchurch.

Taxes.					
The Royal Aid in	1692,	£. 78	12	0
Poll-tax ——	1694, —	21	11	0
Land-tax —	1694, —	56	0	0
The ſame, at 3*s.*	1770, —	42	12	0

About ſeventy years ago, according to ſir Robert Atkyns, there were 23 houſes in the pariſh, and about 100 inhabitants, 8 of whom were freeholders; yearly births 3, burials 3. But population is very much increaſed, for it appears by an exact liſt taken this year, (1777) that the preſent number of families is 30, of inhabitants 169.

TURKDEAN.

THIS pariſh lies in the hundred of Bradley, three miles diſtant north from Northleach, eight ſouth-weſtward from Stow, and nineteen eaſt from Glouceſter.

It conſiſts chiefly of open fields, and lies in the high Coteſwold country, but affords no antiquities, nor any thing curious in natural hiſtory.

Of the Manor and other Eſtates.

The lands in this pariſh were divided between two proprietors at the time of the general ſurvey, as appears by the following extract:

'William Leuric holds Turghedene in Bradeleg 'hundred, and Goisfrid holds it of him. Oſgot 'held it. There are five hides, and one yard land 'and a half, but nothing in demean. There are 'two villeins, and three bordars, with one plow-'tillage. This eſtate pays tax. It was worth 4*l.* 'and is now worth 10*l.*' *Domeſday*, p. 74.

 'Robert

'Robert de Olgi holds Turchedene. There 'are five hides, and two yard lands and a half 'which pay tax. Siuuard held them. There 'are four plow-tillages in demean, and twelve 'villeins, with ſix plow-tillages, and there are 'eight among the *ſervi* and *ancillæ*. It was worth '6*l.* now only 100*s.*' *Ib.* p. 76.

It is difficult to diſtinguiſh theſe manors in their deſcent to their ſeveral proprietors. Two religious houſes were ſeized of the greater part of the pariſh, and the remainder was veſted in lay proprietors, *viz.*

Upper-Turkdean belonged to Weſtbury college, near Briſtol, and after the diſſolution of that houſe, was granted to ſir Rafe Sadleir 35 H. 8. William Banniſter died ſeized of Turkedeane 2 Jac. 1. leaving Thomas his ſon and heir, as appears by the eſcheator's inquiſition, taken the ſame year. Thomas Banniſter was ſeized of it in 1608, from whom it deſcended to Mr. ſerjeant Banniſter, who enjoy'd it when ſir Robert Atkyns compiled his account of this pariſh: Since which time it paſſed out of that name, and Edmund Waller, eſq; is the preſent proprietor of it.

Lower Turkdean belonged to the priory of Lanthony, near Glouceſter. Richard Poncy gave certain lands in Turchdene to the canons regular of Lanthony, which were afterwards confirmed to them by the king's charter 1 Joh. and a writ of *Quo warranto* was brought againſt the prior to ſet forth his right to a court leet and waifs in Turkdean, and his claim was allowed 15 E. 1. After the diſſolution of that priory, this eſtate was granted to Richard Andrews and Nicholas Temple, in truſt, 35 H. 8. John Walter, upon the death of his father, had livery of this manor granted to him 1 Eliz. It came afterwards to Oliver lord St. John, who died ſeized thereof 24 Eliz. and John lord St. John, his ſon, had livery of it the ſame year. It paſſed afterwards to Mr. Coxwell, who enjoyed it about half a century ſince; but it is now the property of ſir John Nelthrop, baronet. His arms are, *Argent, on a pile ſable, a broad ſword of the field, with a martlet in chief ſiniſter for difference.*

Beſide the above-mentioned manors, or reputed manors, there was another which continued in lay hands. Robert de Tormin held Turkdean by one knight's fee 3 Joh. John Langley died ſeized of the manor of Turkdean 2 E. 1. as did another John Langley, eſq: 39 H. 6. Walter Langley was ſurvived by Iſabel his wife, who died ſeized of this manor, and of Upper and Lower Siddington, in dower, 14 E. 4. Sir Ralph Dutton was ſeized of it at the beginning of this century, and was ſucceeded by his ſon ſir John Dutton, baronet; from him it paſſed thro' two deſcents, like Sherbourne, to James Dutton, eſq; who is the preſent lord of the manor.

Of the other eſtates the records ſhew, that Philip Burnell died ſeized of lands in Turkdean 22 E. 1. Thomas Ralegh held one meſſuage and two plow-tillages in Turkdean, of the honour of Wallingford, 21 R. 2. and Thomas his ſon died ſeized of the ſame 6 H. 4. Walter Ralegh, ſon and heir of the laſt Thomas, died ſeized of the manor of Turkdean 8 H. 5.

Of the Church, &c.

The church is a vicarage, in the deanery of Stow, worth about 60*l.* a year. It has been augmented by the queen's bounty. Chriſt Church college in Oxford, are patrons, and the reverend Mr. Thomas Bowen is the preſent incumbent. It formerly belonged to the priory of Black Canons of Oſney. The rectory and advowſon of the vicarage were granted to Chriſt Church college 34 H. 8. and confirmed 38 H. 8. and the impropriation is now in leaſe to Mr. Miller.

The vicar has all privy tithes, half the hay tithes, and the corn tithes of three yard lands.

The church is ſmall, with an aile on the ſouth ſide, and an embattled tower at the weſt end.

Firſt fruits £.	10	0	0	Synodals £.	0	2	0
Tenths —	1	0	0	Pentecoſtals	0	1	0
Procurations	0	6	8				

Taxes.					
The Royal Aid in	1692,	£. 53	18	10
Poll-tax ——	1694, —	19	1	6
Land-tax ——	1694, —	56	4	0
The ſame, at 3*s.*	1770, —	34	3	9

There were 32 houſes in this pariſh at the beginning of this century, and about 120 inhabitants, whereof 7 were freeholders; yearly births 3, and burials 3. *Atkyns.* Thers are now 25 families, and exactly 113 inhabitants.

TURLEY *and* HAW.

TURLEY is only a part of the pariſh, lying in the lower diviſion of Weſtminſter hundred. The Haw, another part, lies in the lower diviſion of the hundred of Derhurſt. The pariſh is four miles diſtant ſouth-weſt from Tewkeſbury, eight eaſt from Newent, and eight north from Glouceſter. It is ſituated upon the weſt bank of the Severn, and very ſubject to floods from that river.

The etymology of Turley, or Tirley, as it is ſometimes written, is uncertain; but Haw ſignifies a green plot in a valley, and is deſcriptive of the ſituation of the place.

It is a rich, loamy ſoil, with ſome clay, and produces excellent herbage. The houſes in general are mean cottages, built of brick and wattling, notwithſtanding there is a quarry near, if not in the pariſh, of fine blue ſtone, with a very ſtrait ſmoth ſurface, proper for building.

It is a common practice at this place, particularly after floods, to fiſh, as they call it, in the Severn for coals, and the buſineſs is performed in in the following manner: They ſink a net, with its mouth extended by an iron hoop of a ſemi-circular form, and a perſon ſtirs the bottom of the river with a long pole juſt before the net, by which means, and by the aſſiſtance of the current, the coals roll into it. Five or ſix boats are ſometimes employ'd in this buſineſs at a time.

They ſtill retain the antient cuſtom at this place, which formerly prevailed at many others, of ſtrewing the floor of the church over with graſs on Whitſunday and Trinity ſunday, and there is an acre of ground given to maintain it.

Of the Manor and other Eſtates.

This was part of the manor of Derhurſt at the time of the general ſurvey.

'Edric held two yard-lands and a half at 'Trinleie, in the time of king Edward, but 'William the ſon of Baderon holds them now.' *Domeſday*, p. 72.

Turley belonged to the abbey of Weſtminſter 'till that houſe was diſſolved. It was then granted to the chapter of Weſtminſter 34 H. 8. But queen Mary coming to the crown, the monaſtery was reſtored, and this manor was regranted to the abbey and convent of Weſtminſter in the fourth year of her reign. After the death of that princeſs, the monaſtery was again diſſolved, and the manor of Turley regranted to the chapter of Weſtminſter 2 Eliz.

Thomas Throckmorton had livery of the manor of Turley 9 Eliz. and ſir William Throckmorton, or Throgmorton, was lord of it in 1608. Thomas earl of Coventry was lord of the manor when ſir Robert Atkyns drew up his account of it, and the preſent earl of Coventry is now lord of the manor. For his lordſhip's arms, ſee Derhurſt.

Lands in this pariſh, given to maintain lamps in the church of Turley, were granted to ſir William Rider 7 Jac. A meadow in Turley, which belonged to the abbey of Tewkeſbury, was granted to Lawrence Baſkerville, and William Blake, ſcrivener, 3 Jac. Chriſtopher Raſtall died ſeized of Woodend and Baul's Meadow in Turley, and left Thomas his ſon thirty years old. Mr. Griffin has a good eſtate in this place, which formerly belonged to Mr. George Hurdman.

The Haw is the other diviſion of the pariſh, where there is a paſſage over the Severn. The prior of Derhurſt was ſeized of Haws 56 H. 3. After the ſuppreſſion of alien priories, the manor of Haws was granted to the abbey of Tewkeſbury 7 E. 4. And after the ſuppreſſion of that abbey, it was granted to Giles Throckmorton 35 H. 8.

Of the Church, &c.

The church is a vicarage, within the peculiar of Derhurſt, worth 40*l.* a year. The lord chancellor is patron, and the reverend Mr. Charles Parker is the preſent incumbent. There is no glebe, and the impropriation belongs to the earl of Coventry.

The church is dedicated to St. Michael. It is ſmall, with a low embattled tower at the weſt end.

Firſt fruits £. 9 6 8 Tenths £. 0 18 8

Monuments and Inſcriptions.

The following inſcription is upon the table of a monument in the chancel:

Beneath lyes William the ſon of George Hurdman, of Sandpitts Gent. Grandſon of Edward Hurdman ye firſt Maior of the City of Worceſter. He dy'd Auguſt ye 5th 1684, aged about 55 Y^rs^.

The monument is decorated with the family arms, *viz. Argent, upon a feſs between three creſcents gules, as many fleurs de lis Or.* —There are alſo inſcriptions for ſeveral others of the ſame name.

Upon a monument, againſt the ſouth wall of the chancel, it is thus written:

To the Pious Memory of Mrs Mary Browne, third Daughter of Iohn Browne Senr of Cumberwood in y^s^ Pariſh Gent. who exchanged this Life for a better Ian^ry^ 18th 1717. She was a Perſon eminent for her Piety, Liberality and Charity, and like Tabitha, was allways employ'd in doing Good and in Diſpenſing her Bounty to all about her: But in a more particular Manner to her Relations.

Upon the monument are theſe arms in a lozenge, *Or, on a feſs gules three cheſs rooks of the firſt; in chief as many martlets ſable.*

There are inſcriptions for John Brown of Tirley, gent. who died in 1656; for John Brown of Cumberwood, gent. buried in 1681; and for Jane his wife, daughter of Giles Driver, of Rendcombe, gent. who died in 1683; for Henry Browne, ſon of John and Jane, buried in 1688; and for Charles and Anne Browne, ſon and daughter of John and Jane, who were buried in the year 1722.

Benefactions.

A houſe and land called Turley's Elm are charged with 10*l.* a year for the uſe of the poor. Mr. Joſeph Millard, who was buried in 1727, by his will, gave 5*l.* a year for ever out of his eſtate at the Rye, to buy five coats, ſhoes, and ſtockings, for as many poor men. The reverend Mr. Bateman, vicar of this pariſh, gave 20*l.* with which an acre of land in Kingſend was purchaſed, for the uſe of the poor. And Mrs. Suſanna Gwyn gave three acres of land in Harley, and one in Churchfield to the ſame uſe. Mrs. Jane Atwood, and Mrs. Mary Atwood of Tewkeſbury, gave about an acre of paſture ground and orcharding, called Netherſtone Leaſow, in Turley, to the uſe of the miniſter, for a ſermon in the church on Holy Thurſday, and on Aſcention-day, for ever. In default, the profits to go to the poor.

Turley.

Taxes.	The Royal Aid in 1692, £.		50	6	0
	Poll-tax ——	1694, —	12	0	0
	Land-tax ——	1694, —	89	4	0
	The ſame, at 3*s.*	1770, —	67	8	0

The Haw.

Taxes.	The Royal Aid in 1692,	£.	34	0	0
	Poll-tax —	1694, —	18	17	0
	Land-tax —	1694, —	80	0	0
	The ſame, at 3*s.*	1770, —	61	5	10½

At the beginning of this century, there were 76 houſes in this pariſh, and about 300 inhabitants, whereof 20 were freeholders; yearly births 8, and

and burials 7. *Atkyns.* Examining the pariſh regiſter, I found that in ten years, beginning with 1700, the baptiſms were 111, and the burials 78; and in the ſame number of years, beginning with 1760, the baptiſms were 76, and the burials 87. There are now 65 houſes in the pariſh, and about 280 inhabitants.

TWINING.

THIS pariſh lies in the lower diviſion of Kiftſgate hundred, three miles diſtant north from Tewkeſbury, twelve ſouth-ward from Worceſter, and thirteen north from Glouceſter.

It is pleaſantly ſituated in a point of land between the rivers Severn and Avon, and very probably took its name from Tpi, which in the Saxon language ſignifies *two*, and inge, a *meadow*, becauſe it has meadows on the banks of thoſe two rivers.

It is the only pariſh in the county that lies wholly on the north-weſt ſide of the Avon, over which it has a ferry at a place called Twining's Fleet; and the turnpike-road from Glouceſter and Tewkeſbury to Worceſter runs through the midſt of the village.

It conſiſts chiefly of meadow and paſture, with a conſiderable quantity of very good arable land; and is within the juriſdiction of the leet of Winchcombe, where the court is held for Kiftſgate hundred.

The middle part of it lies high, and on the weſt ſide there is a little head of land ſhooting out from the continent, with which it is level, but it ſtands on a great eminence above the meadows next the Severn. The top of it conſiſts of ſeveral acres of ground, and is fortified all round with double intrenchments. This camp is not above a mile diſtant from the river, which it ſurveys for a conſiderable length, and commands a great extent of country on that ſide. It is called Towbery Hill, but Leland miſtakes it for Tetbyri Caſtelle, and ſays, 'It is a 2 miles from Theokeſ-'byri, above it, *in ripa leva Sabrinæ*. It is now,' continues he, 'overgrowne with Trees and Buſhes 'of Juniper. It longgid to Winchelcumbe Ab-'bay. Peradventure it was King Offa or King 'Kenulphus Houſe.' *Itin.* V. 6. p. 71.

I don't know why Leland fixed on this for the ſcite of the royal palace; but leaving that matter in uncertainty, as it is ever likely to remain, I ſhall only obſerve, that it was moſt probably a Roman camp; yet upon the ſtricteſt enquiry, I cannot diſcover that any Roman coins have been found thereabout, as might be expected.

The pariſh is well ſupplied with ſprings of water, and in a piece of ground called the Park, where it is ſuppoſed the antient manor houſe formerly ſtood, is a ſpring, whoſe water is ſaid to be a prevalent remedy for cutaneous diſorders, and even the leproſy itſelf. It turns the vegetables that ſtand in its courſe of a reddiſh yellow colour, which ſhews it to have paſſed thro' a bed of ochre.

The order of the different *ſtrata* near the ſurface of the ground is uncertain and irregular. In ſome places, firſt, a competent depth of loam, then gravel, next marle, then clay; but marle is to be found in almoſt every part of the pariſh, at ſome depth or other, tho' the inhabitants never uſe it for manure.

The principal houſe and eſtate in the village, belong to Mrs. Hancock, relict of the late Peter Hancock, eſq. But there are ſeveral other good houſes, which are taken notice of in the account of the hamlets to which they belong.

Stubhill-gardens, in this pariſh, is a very pleaſant rural place, belonging to Mr. Warren, conſiſting of two or three acres of ground, laid out in walks, with beautiful ſhrubs and flowers, in a very pretty taſte. There is a ſummer-houſe, and pleaſant ſeats agreeably diſpoſed, and kept in the neateſt order; and many perſons of good faſhion reſort thither in the ſummer ſeaſon to a public breakfaſting.

Of the Manor and other Eſtates.

There were two great proprietaries of lands in this pariſh when *Domeſday* was compiled, from which the following is extracted:

'The church of St. Mary of Wincelcumbe 'holds Tueninge in Greteſtanes hundred. There 'are three hides taxed, and two plow-tillages in 'demean, and twenty-four villeins, and eight 'bordars, with twenty-ſeven plow-tillages. There 'are eight *ſervi*, and two *ancillæ*, and forty acres 'of meadow; a wood two furlongs long, and 'one broad. It was worth 8 *l.* now 7 *l.*' *Domeſday*, p. 71.

At the time of the conqueſt, the other eſtate was held under the great but unfortunate Brictric, lord of Tewkeſbury, who was diveſted of it, and the record ſhews how it was diſpoſed of.

'Four villeins held two hides in Tuninge, and 'a thane held half a hide. There are four plow-'tillages, and three acres of meadow. The queen 'gave this eſtate to John the chamberlain. It is 'worth and was worth 35 *ſol.*' *Ibid.* p. 68.

The firſt mentioned eſtate continued in the abbey of Winchcombe 'till its diſſolution. The abbat purchaſed a charter of free warren in Twining 35 H. 3. and was impleaded for it in a writ of *Quo warranto* 15 E. 1. John Cole and others granted one yard land in Twining near Tewkeſbury, to the abbey of Winchcombe 34 E. 1. That abbey aſſigned the manor of Twining to the abbey of St. Ebrulph at Utica in Normandy 2 E. 2. but it reverted again to the monks of Winchcombe.

After the diſſolution of Winchcombe abbey, the manor of Twining, and a meadow ground on the ſide of the Avon, called Upham, were granted to ſir Rafe Sadleir 1 E. 6. and Ralph Sadler, eſq; was

was lord of this manor in the year 1608. It paſſed afterwards to Richard Baugh, eſq; who died ſeized of Twining in 1682, and left three daughters coheireſſes, of whom the eldeſt was married to Charles Hancock, eſq; who died ſeized of the manor of Twining in the year 1717. It paſſed afterwards to Peter Hancock, eſq; who dying on the 5th of May, 1776, his widow, Mrs. Anne Hancock, became poſſeſſed of it as part of her jointure. By her he left iſſue two daughters, Anne, married to George Maxwell, of Twining, eſq; and Charlotte, wedded to John Embury, of the ſame place, eſq; to whom, as coheireſſes, the manor will deſcend on the death of their mother. Mr. Maxwell's arms are, *Argent, within a bordure gules a ſaltire between two creſcents, one in chief the other in baſe, ſable.*

John Conqueſt died ſeized of the manor of Gobe's Hull, within the manor of Tewkeſbury 26 E. 1. The place is now called Gubber Hill. It is an antient ſeat, moated round, formerly belonging to the Reads, but is now the property of

HAMLETS. 1. Part of *Mythe-Hook*, which lies in the hundred of Tewkeſbury.

2. *Wood-end*, where Thomas Kemble, eſq; has a good eſtate. His arms are given under Tewkeſbury.

3. *Church-end*, in which is the ſeat of the late Peter Hancock, eſq.

4. *Shuthanger*, which lies upon the great turnpike-road. Mr. George Turberville died ſeized of a good houſe and eſtate in this hamlet about the year 1775, which are now his widow's. The Turbervilles are an antient family, and bear *Checky vert and gules, a feſs ermine.*

The Neaſts were a reſpectable family, formerly reſiding here, who enjoyed a good eſtate, now gone out of that name by the marriage of the heir general with the late Mr. Havard, whoſe ſon, Mr. Neaſt Havard of Tewkeſbury is the preſent owner of it. Mr. Havard gives for his arms, *Argent, a bull's head caboſhed between three mullets.*

The Miſs Woolleys have alſo a good houſe and eſtate here, formerly belonging to the Aycriggs.

5. *Hill-end*, where John Martyn, of Overbury, eſq; has a good eſtate. Mr. Martyn of Pebworth, who ſerved the office of high ſheriff of Glouceſterſhire in the year 1732, gave for his arms, *Sable, on a feſs Or three maſcles azure, between as many ſwans heads erazed argent gorged of the ſecond.* But I am not abſolutely certain that the Martyns of Overbury bear the ſame arms.

6. *Green-end*, where Mr. Baldwin's houſe and eſtate lay, now the property of the reverend Mr. Vernon.

Puckrup is not properly a hamlet, but an eſtate formerly Mr. Baldwin's, but now Mr. Phelps's. And *Phelps* is another good eſtate, belonging to Mr. Warren.

Of the Church, &c.

The church is an impropriation, in the deanery of Winchcombe, worth about 43*l.* a year to the curate. The dean and chapter of Chriſt Church college in Oxford are patrons, and the reverend Mr. Francis Mines is the preſent incumbent. The impropriation and advowſon of the vicarage formerly belonged to the abbey of Winchcombe, and were granted to the chapter of Oxford 38 H. 8. The impropriation pays 30*l.* a year to the curate. The vicarage has no glebe belonging to it.

There was a diſpute in the time of Malger biſhop of Worceſter, and of William abbat of Tewkeſbury, between the church of Tewkeſbury, and that of Twining, concerning certain tithes in this pariſh; which diſpute was amicably adjuſted in the manner expreſſed in the regiſter-book of Tewkeſbury abbey, whence the writing is copied and printed in Mr. Stephens's *Supplement to the Monaſticon*, p. 201.

Lying near the deanery of Perſhore in Worceſterſhire, this church, by agreement, is viſited by the archdeacon of Worceſterſhire, in exchange for Broadway in the dioceſe of Worceſter, which is viſited by the archdeacon of the dioceſe of Glouceſter.

The church is dedicated to Mary Magdalen, and has a low embattled tower, with ſix muſical bells, at the weſt end.

Firſt fruits £.	7	9	7	Synodals £.	0	2	0
Tenths —	0	14	11½	Pentecoſt.	0	1	0
Procurations	0	6	8				

Monuments and Inſcriptions.

There is a marble monument on the ſouth ſide of the chancel, with the following inſcription:

Qui multa ſolus meruit, unius jacet Monumenti particeps,
Nempe Edwinus Baldwyn,
Patre ſuo Thoma ante annos circiter viginti ſepulto,
Hîc una reconditur.

Generoſus a virtutibus ſuis ſine ære aut marmore celebris futurus, Egregiæ quidem indolis, et qualem paucis contigiſſe ſatis conſtat, Quam autem eâ excoluit induſtriâ, ut hâc ſola minor videretur. Legibus, quibus inſtitutus erat, pari ſucceſſu incubuit, ac integritate Exercuit, utrinq; hominum gratiam et amorem abunde promeruit. Febre tandem hujus unius fato nimium peſtilenti correptus, Virtute, quam annis gravior, et univerſum ſui deſiderium relinquens, occubuit 10mo die Mart. Anno ætatis ſuæ 55° Æræ Chriſtianæ 1669.

The monument is adorned with theſe arms, *Argent, a ſaltire ſable.*

Upon another monument, with an exceedingly well finiſhed alabaſter figure of a lady, in the dreſs of her time, and an infant in her arms, it is thus written:

Heare lyeth buried the bodyes of Sybill Clare wyffe to Fraunces Clare Eſquier and Anne their daughter, wch Sybill was only daughter & heire apparant unto Gabriel Blycke Eſquier & Margaret his wyffe whoe in ye 18 yeare of her age gave her in marriage to ye ſayed Fraunces, a Gentilman bothe worſhipfull in parentage & commendable in good qualites between whom ſuch was the affection & good lykinge as was ſeldom ſeen in their age, ſoe as if they had not ben prevented by deathe they had continewed a rare example, but when they moſte rejoyced their matche they weare ſoneſte devided: for the ſayed Sybill being conceavid with child and after a dewe tyme delivered of a daughter, within one forthnight fell ſycke, & after ſhe had languiſhed certen dayes, ſhe willinglye yealded her innocente ſoule into ye handes of God the xiii daye of Februarie in the

 yeare

yeare of our Lord 1575, to the unspeakable losse & sorowe of her deare Parentes, Frendes, and of all that knewe her but moste especiallye of her lovinge husband beinge departed from so deare a wyffe, well endewed wyth sondrye rare gyftes bothe of bodye & minde, in whos Remembraunce as an eternal pledge of good will, the sayed Fraunces caused this Monumente to be erected at his proper Costes and Charges the 12 of Auguste in the yeare of our Lord 1577. To whos Soule God graunte a joyfull Resurrection. Amen.

At the top of the monument are the following arms, *Quarterly*, 1st *and* 4th, *Argent, three chevrons ermine.* 2d and 3d quarters are, *Quarterly* 1st *and* 4th, *Sable, on a chevron argent three pellets, on a chief of the second three black birds.* 2d *and* 3d, *Two lions passant.*

There is a very large monument against the east wall of the chancel, with inscriptions,

For William Hancock, of Norton in the parish of Bredon, in the county of Worcester, esq; who died in 1676, aged 82.

For William Hancock, his eldest son, by his first wife, who died in 1674, aged 49.

For Charles Hancock, of this parish, esq; who died in 1717, aged 73.

Under the figure of the first William Hancock are his arms, *viz. Gules, a dexter hand couped argent, on a chief of the second three fighting cocks of the first.*

The last-mentioned monument is ornamented with paintings of ships, as if the family had been much concerned in naval affairs.

On the table of another monument in the chancel, it is thus written:

Juxta sepultæ sunt mortales Reliquiæ Thomæ Neast, Generosi, Et quod corruptabile est, Spe resurgendi Anima evolavit superiores ad auras, sanctasq; sedes Aprilis duodecimo, Annoq; salutis Milesimo sexcentesimo octagesimo octavo, Redamatus ab omnibus, multisq; desideratus. Iam pergas, Lector, et si possis imitare. Anna Neast mœrens posuit.

Over the monument are these arms, *Per pale, baron and femme,* 1. *Argent, two lions paws erazed in saltire gules,* for Neast. 2. *Argent, on a cross sable a leopards face caboshed Or,* for Bridges.

There are several inscriptions for the Baughs, particularly for Edward Baugh, gent. late one of the coroners for this county, who died in 1773. Their arms are, *Gules, a fess vaire between three mullets Or.*

Benefactions.

Richard Edgock gave a farm in Twining, worth about 25*l.* a year, half to the minister, and half to the poor for ever. And Richard Portman, clerk, gave 40*s.* a year for ever, one half to the minister, and the other to the poor. As did John Reeks 6*s.* 8*d.* to the minister, and 13*s.* 4*d.* to the poor for a term.

John Best gave 50*s.* a year to the poor, and John Turberville gave twelve pecks of wheat to be distributed to the poor on St. Thomas day, yearly, for ever.

Charles Hancock, esq; gave two silver flaggons for the communion, and 3*s.* 4*d.* a year is charged on a house at Tewkesbury towards the repair of the church.

Twining.

Taxes.			£.		
	The Royal Aid in	1692,	75	14	0
	Poll-tax —	1694, —	71	8	0
	Land-tax —	1694, —	190	0	0
	The same, at 3*s.*	1770, —	133	15	6

Mythe.

Taxes.			£.		
	The Royal Aid in	1692,	94	0	0
	Poll-tax —	1694, —	6	16	0
	Land-tax —	1694, —	70	13	4
	The same, at 3*s.*	1770, —	54	7	3

There were 140 houses, and about 600 inhabitants in the parish, at the beginning of this century, whereof 37 were freeholders; yearly births 15, burials 13. *Atkyns.* The number of souls is now about 567.

****

U L E Y.

THIS parish lies in the hundred of Berkeley, above four miles north-eastward from Wotton-underedge, two east from Dursley, and fourteen south from Gloucester.

The name of it has been variously written, as *Euuelege, Iweley,* and *Uley,* and was given it on account of the many springs that rise here, for, like that of Dursley, it signifies the *Watry Place.*

The middle, and perhaps the greater part of the parish is pasture ground, interspersed with orcharding, but there is some arable, and a great deal of woodland. The herbs Centaury, Lady's Mantle, Maidenhair, Agrimony, Vervain, and several other medicinal plants, are found in various parts of it.

It is bounded on the east by part of the little village of Olepen, and, together with it, forms a deep comb, or valley, about a mile over, beautifully adorned with borderings of beech-wood, and plantations of fir, on the sides of the lofty hills that everywhere encompass it, except to the west. Defended by those hills from the chilling blasts to which open situations are exposed, vegetation is forward in the spring, and the winter not so severe as in most of the neighbouring places. It has an opening westward to the Vale, and a small bourn, formed of the springs which rise here, takes its course that way, and together with the Dursley water, runs into the Severn at Slimbridge.

Part of the hill on the north side of the village shoots out in a rocky head, and is united by a narrow neck of land to the open plain adjoining to the parish of Nimpsfield. This spot of ground is called the *Berry,* from the oblong camp on the top of it, for *Berry,* or *Bury,* is but another name for a camp. Thus we have Berrybank in Staffordshire, Berryhill in Hampshire, Egbury, Dunbury, Okebury, and many other Berries in various parts of the kingdom besides Gloucestershire. That which I am now describing is very strong by situation, with double intrenchments round the edge of the hill, inclosing the whole space of ground on the top, consisting of thirty or forty acres; and the declivity without is so great as to secure it from any powerful attack, except at the entrance. This was certainly a Roman camp, as I prove by the coins which have been found about

about it, (the greater part being of the emperors Antoninus and Conſtantine) of which Mr. Small, late owner of the eſtate, has made a collection.

Our anceſtors delighted in ſheltered ſituations, and Uley, from early ages, ſeems to have been the reſidence of many good families; but leaving the antient ſtate of the village, to be reſumed under the account of the manor, the following places engage our preſent attention.

Stout's-Hill is a handſome new houſe, with octagonal projections, turreted, and ornamented in the Gothic taſte. It ſtands in a lawn of excellent verdure, upon an eminence that commands a view of the village in front, with a curtain of fine beech wood, hanging, as it were, from the ſlope of the hill, at a very agreeable diſtance to the ſouth. It is the property and reſidence of Timothy Gyde, eſq; who has a good eſtate in the pariſh, and gives for his arms, *Azure, on a chevron between three fleurs de lis Or, as many mullets of the field.* This is alſo the place of the writer's nativity, where he collected his firſt ideas, and for which he ſtill indulges a natural partiality.

Ille terrarum mihi præter omnes
Angulus ridet. . . . .
Ver ubi longum, tepidaſque præbet
Jupiter brumas. . . . . Hor. O. vii.

There are two other good houſes at the Green, near the church. One of them is the property of John Holbrow, eſq; where he reſides, and has alſo a very good eſtate in the pariſh. He is the ſon of the late William Holbrow, eſq; who was high ſheriff of Glouceſterſhire in the year 1741. The preſent Mr. Holbrow is in the commiſſion of the peace for the county, and gives for his arms, *Azure, a bend between ſix mullets argent.*

The other was built in the time of king James the Firſt, by one of the Dorneys, (a family of antient ſtanding in this pariſh) as appears by their name in the front, and who then poſſeſſed the eſtate belonging to it. It was afterwards ſold to the Smalls, and is now the property of Mrs. Small, relict of the late Mr. John Small, who died in January, 1778.

Bencombe is a good houſe, where the Dorneys have long reſided, and now belongs to Mr. Edward Dorney, who has a good eſtate there. His arms are, *Gules, a chevron vaire between three creſcents Or.*

This village, tho' not large, is very populous, from a manufacture of fine broad cloth long eſtabliſhed here. It is ſtill carried on by ſeveral perſons in a very extenſive manner, and furniſhes employment for the lower claſs of people. But idleneſs and debauchery are ſo deeply rooted in them, by means of thoſe ſeminaries of vice called Alehouſes, that the poor are very burthenſome. Theſe houſes are ſcattered all over the country, and are daily increaſing, which we owe either to the magiſtrates inattention, or indulgence; or, perhaps, to a miſtaken notion of ſerving the community by increaſing the public revenue from licences; but they may be aſſured that nothing can compenſate for depravity of morals, and the loſs of induſtry.

Of the Manor and other Eſtates.

This place was a member of the great lordſhip of Berkeley at the time of the general ſurvey, as appears by a paſſage in *Domeſday*, p. 68, and by the tranſlation of it under Berkeley, p. 271, where there is nothing further recorded than that 'In 'Euuelege are two hides.'

It has been fully related under the account of the laſt-mentioned town, that the lordſhip of Berkeley, with its members, was given by king Henry the Second to Robert Fitz-Harding, anceſtor to the preſent earl of Berkeley; and this eſtate continued in the elder branch of his lordſhip's family, 'till it was ſettled on Maurice Berkeley, ſecond ſon of Maurice lord Berkeley, ſome time in the reign of king Edward the Third. That Maurice Berkeley was anceſtor to the Berkeleys of Stoke Giffard, whoſe deſcendants held Uley in an uninterrupted ſucceſſion to the end of the reign of king Richard the Third, when ſir William Berkeley took part with that king, and was in the battle of Boſworth. Victory declaring for the earl of Richmond, afterwards king Henry the Seventh, ſir William fled into Britainy, and was attainted 1 H. 7. and his eſtates were ſeized by the crown.

Jaſper duke of Bedford, the king's uncle, had a grant of Uley to himſelf, and the heirs male of his body, 1 H. 7. But afterwards ſir William Berkeley made his peace with the king, and took a grant of the reverſion after the duke's eſtate taille, 4 H. 7. whereby this eſtate returned to his family. The earl of Berkeley is the preſent lord of the manor of Uley.

There were two dependant manors in the pariſh. Baſſet's court was a reputed manor, wherein the Baſſets had an antient ſeat. Sir Anſelm Baſſet married Margaret, daughter of Thomas lord Berkeley, and of Joan, the daughter of Ralph Somery, lord of Campden, and with her had this eſtate. William Baſſet was lord of Baſſet's court in the year 1608. Richard Baſſet was ſequeſtered in the great rebellion, and paid a compoſition of 653*l.* William Baſſet, a deſcendant from the laſt William, left two daughters, Elizabeth and Margaret, coheireſſes, of whom Elizabeth, the ſurvivor, was married to William Weſcombe, who ſold this eſtate to ſeveral perſons upwards of twenty years ſince, and there is now only a ſmall part of the antient manſion houſe remaining. The Baſſets gave for their arms, *Ermine, on a canton gules a mullet Or.*

The White Court was another reputed manor, which is ſaid to have had two parks formerly belonging to it. The manor houſe has been totally

totally demoliſhed time immemorially, but there is a kind of hamlet that ſtill retains the name of the White Court.

Bencombe lies on the ſouth ſide of the pariſh, upon an eminence at the head of the combe, or valley, which gave occaſion to its name, and is mentioned in records.

It belonged to the Berkeley family when they firſt had Uley. Peter de Iweley died ſeized of it 1 R. 1. John de Benecomb died alſo ſeized of it, and left Agnes, his only daughter and heireſs, married to John de Couel (de Coaley) in the reign of king Edward the Third.

It has been obſerved that Mr. Edward Dorney has a good houſe and eſtate there.

The records mention, that Elianor the widow of John de Veel, ſon of ſir Peter le Veel, held lands in Uley for her life. Sir William Rumſey levied a fine of the reverſion of thoſe lands to ſir John Popham and Elizabeth his wife 3 H. 4.

Beſides the above, there are places in Uley of the following names, *viz.* Toney, Crawley's Shard, Shoreditch, Shadwell, Ellcombe, Rowdon, Bawcot, which in the Britiſh ſignifies a little wood; Angerſton, perhaps more truly Hengaerſton, the town at the antient camp; Reſdon, the Hurn, and ſome others; which names are ſuppoſed to be all ſignificant, and expreſſive of ſome ſtriking circumſtances peculiar to the reſpective places.

Of the Church, &c.

The church is a rectory, in the deanery of Durſley, worth about 140*l.* a year. Roger lord Berkeley gave the advowſon of it to the priory of Stanley St. Leonard's; and thirty acres in the pariſh now pay tithes to Stanley. The lord chancellor is patron, and the reverend Mr. John Gregory is the preſent incumbent. There are ſixteen acres for the glebe. The rectory pays 13*s.* 4*d.* a year to the crown.

Sir Herbert Croftes, baronet, afterwards biſhop of Hereford, was rector of this church in 1667.

The church is dedicated to St. Giles. It has no aile, but there are two handſome galleries at the weſt end, and a low embattled tower on the north ſide.

Firſt fruits £. 12	3	4	Synodals £. 0	2	0
Tenths — 1	4	4	Pentecoſt. 0	0	6
Procurations 0	6	8			

Benefactions.

Mr. William Pegler, who died in 1695, gave a parcel of land, and 10*l.* in money, to the uſe of the poor; and an eſtate belonging to Mr. John Holbrow is charged with 10*s.* a year in lieu of the latter.

The reverend Mr. Henry Stubs gave 50*l.* to the pariſh, to eſtabliſh a ſchool for teaching poor children to write. And he alſo gave 10*s.* a year in books for the poor.

Mr. Tether gave 30*s.* a year to be diſtributed to the poor on St. Thomas day, and 10*s.* for a ſermon. And Thomas Parſlow gave 10*s.* a year to the poor.

Taxes.			£.		
	The Royal Aid in	1692,	103	4	0
	Poll-tax — —	1694,	37	8	0
	Land-tax ——	1694,	114	1	1
	The ſame, at 3*s.*	1770,	84	17	6

It is ſaid there were 200 houſes in this pariſh, and about 900 inhabitants, of whom 80 were freeholders, at the beginning of this century; yearly births 21, and burials 19. *Atkyns.* In the year 1748, the number of ſouls was 1162, and ſince that time they are increaſed to about 1310.

UPLEADEN

IS a ſmall pariſh, in the hundred of Botloe, three miles eaſtward from Newent, and about ſix north-weſtward from Glouceſter.

It lies in the Vale, on the weſt bank of the river Leden, by which it is bounded, and from which it takes its name. The lands, like the circumjacent fine country, are abundantly rich in corn and paſture, but the pariſh has nothing particular to recommend it to the notice of the antiquary or naturaliſt.

Of the Manor and other Eſtates.

This manor belonged very antiently to the abbey of Glouceſter, as appears by a paſſage in *Domeſday-book*, of which the following is a tranſlation:

'The ſame church [St. Peter at Glouceſter] 'holds Ledene in Botelawes hundred. There are 'four hides. In demean are two plow-tillages, 'and eight villeins, and one bordar, with eight 'plow-tillages. There are four *ſervi*, and a mill 'of 4*s.* and ten acres of meadow. A wood two 'miles long, and two furlongs broad. It is worth 'ſcarcely 30 *ſol.*' *Domeſday*, p. 71.

The abbat of Glouceſter had a writ of *Quo warranto* brought againſt him, to oblige him to ſet forth his right to free warren here, and his claim to that privilege was allowed 15 E. 1.

The manor continued in the abbey 'till the general diſſolution, when it paſſed to the crown, by which it was afterwards granted to John Arnold, who died ſeized of it 37 H. 8. and livery was granted to ſir Nicholas Arnold, his ſon and heir, the ſame year. Rowland Arnold, ſon of ſir Nicholas, left an only daughter Dorothy, married to ſir Thomas Lucy, of Charlecot in Warwickſhire, who was lord of the manor in the year 1608. It paſſed afterwards to Thomas Brown, eſq; alderman of Glouceſter, who was owner of it at the beginning of this century, and Mrs. Broxoline is the preſent proprietor.

Of

Of the Church, &c.

The church is a curacy, in the Foreft deanery, worth 20*l.* a year, to which the dean and chapter of Gloucefter prefent.

The impropriation, formerly belonging to the abbey of Gloucefter, was granted to the chapter of that fee, 33 H. 8. It is now in leafe to Mrs. Broxoline, and pays 14*l.* 10*s.* a year to the curate.

Taxes.					
The Royal Aid in	1692,	£.78	14	0
Poll-tax — —	1694, —	7	16	0
Land-tax ——	1694, —	69	14	0
The fame, at 3*s.*	1770, —	52	5	6

Sir Robert Atkyns reckoned 25 houfes in this parifh, and eftimated the people at about 100, 7 of whom were freeholders; yearly births 2, burials 2. The prefent number of houfes is only 19, and the inhabitants are fuppofed to be proportionably decreafed.

UPTON St. LEONARD's.

THIS parifh lies in the united hundreds of Dudfton and King's-barton, about three miles north from Painfwick, and three fouth-eaftward from Gloucefter.

With refpect to *Upton*, or *Optune*, as it was antiently written, it will be fufficient juft to obferve, that the village is feated on a gentle elevation, in the vale, which certainly fuggefted the firft idea of the name.

Creed's Place is a very handfome new brick houfe, the property and refidence of Robert Campbell, efq; who built it upon an eftate which he purchafed of John Guife, efq; about the year 1770.

Whitley Court is alfo a handfome feat, belonging to Peter Snell, efq; who refides there.

I don't find that there are any antiquities or curious natural productions here, but the hills adjoining to the fouthward yield iron ore, or ochre, as appears from a fpring of water that runs down the road, tinging the ftones in its courfe of a redifh yellow colour.

Of the Manors and other Eftates.

Upton was a member of the great manor of Bertune, before, and at the time of the general furvey, and is entered in the record among the demeans of the crown, under the title *Terra Regis*.

'Aluui, the fheriff, claims Optune, another 'member [of the manor of Bertune]. There is 'one hide of land, and there are four [free] men. 'Hunfridus holds it.' *Domefday*, p. 67.

But fir Robert Atkyns has placed another abftract from *Domefday* to the account of this parifh, which has nothing to do with it, but belongs to Utone, or Wotton, near Gloucefter.

There were formerly two manors in this parifh of the common name of Upton. Want of diftinction occafions great difficulty in applying the records with precifion, but I fhall endeavour to point out the defcent of each manor in regular fucceffion.

Walkelyn de Fabrica held Uptone of king Edward the Firft, by the fervice of paying two hundred arrow heads. He pleaded his right in the proceedings on a writ of *Quo warranto* brought againft him 15 E. 1. and his claim was then allowed.

Edmond Fitz-Alan, earl of Arundel, was feized of the manor of Upton; but being beheaded at Hereford, in the unfettled reign of king Edward the Second, all his lands here came to the crown, and were granted to Richard de Munemuth 4 E. 3. Richard earl of Arundel, fon of Edmond, was feized of one tenement, and one mill in Upton St. Leonard, and of the hundred of King's Barton, 21 R. 2. Elizabeth, widow of Thomas duke of Norfolk, and daughter of Richard earl of Arundel, was feized of Upton 3 H. 6. John duke of Norfolk was feized of the manor of Upton St. Leonard's 11 H. 6. John duke of Norfolk, and Elizabeth his wife, levied a fine of it 8 E. 4. Joan, the widow of William de Beauchamp, lord de Bergavenny, one of the fifters and heirs of Thomas earl of Arundel, died feized of the manor of Upton St. Leonard's 14 H. 6. as did Beatrix, the widow of Thomas earl of Arundel, 18 H. 6. Eleanor, the widow of fir Walter Hungerford, late wife of fir Richard Poinings, and formerly the wife of John earl of Arundel, died feized of Upton 33 H. 6.

Another manor of the name of Upton belonged to the Berkeley family for feveral ages fucceffively.

Thomas lord Berkeley died feized of Upton St. Leonard's 35 E. 3. as did Maurice lord Berkeley, his fon, in the 42d year of the fame reign. Thomas lord Berkeley, fon of Maurice, had livery the next year, and dying 5 H. 5. left Elizabeth, his only daughter and heir, married to Richard Beauchamp, earl of Warwick. Edward Nevil, lord Bergavenny, married Elizabeth, the daughter of Richard Beauchamp, earl of Warwick, in whofe right he was feized of the manor of Upton, and died 16 E. 4. Thomas lord Berkeley died poffeffed of this manor 24 H. 8. whereupon Thomas lord Berkeley, his fon, had livery granted him the fame year, and died in the 26th year of that reign. Henry lord Berkeley, fon of the laft Thomas, had livery 3 Mariæ.

The manor of Upton was granted to Walter Pye and William Beal 2 Jac. It is now divided among feveral freeholders, but the late Mr. Singleton, lord of Dudfton and King's Barton hundred, was lord paramount.

Bullins is a reputed manor in this parifh, belonging to Mr. Selwyn.

Grove Court is another reputed manor, formerly the property of a family who feem to have taken their name from this eftate. Jeoffery de la Grave held one yard-land in Upton by the fervice of attending

attending the king, in his wars againſt Wales, with bow and arrows forty days at his own charge, and afterwards at the king's coſt, 5 H. 3. and Sibilla de la Grave held lands in Upton St. Leonard's of the king in *capite*, by the ſame ſervice, 10 E. 2. *Eſch*. This eſtate paſſed afterwards to the Berkeleys, and was the property of Richard Walter, eſq; at the beginning of the preſent century. It now belongs to Mrs. Bliſſet, of Chancery Lane, London.

John the ſon of Nicholas le Broke granted divers lands in Upton St. Leonard, Glouceſter, Barton Abbats, Kynemerſbury, and Sneedham, to the abbey of Glouceſter 3 E. 2. and that abbey held two plow-tillages in Upton, each worth 30*s*. *per ann*. 17 E. 3. William Nottingham, eſq; the king's attorney-general, gave the manor of Sneedham, &c. to the abbey of Glouceſter, for the purpoſe of erecting a chantry in the abbey, 10 E. 4.

Part of Snedeham in the pariſh of Upton St. Leonard, late belonging to the abbey of Glouceſter, and containing twenty-ſix acres and a half, was ſold by the crown, Sep. 11, 34 H. 8. to the mayor and burgeſſes of Glouceſter, who conveyed it to Thomas Lane, eſq; the following year. Theſe lands, with ſome others, were to be held by the 20th part of a knight's fee, and by the payment of 3*s*. 6*d*. *ob*. to the court of augmentation.

Lands and tithes in Upton belonged to the abbey of Perſhore, and were granted to John Butler 37 H. 8.

Of the Church, &c.

The church is a curacy, in the deanery of Glouceſter, worth 20*l*. a year from the impropriation. The rectory and advowſon of the vicarage of Upton St. Leonard belonged to the abbey of Glouceſter, and were granted to the biſhoprick 33 H. 8. and confirmed 6 E. 6. The biſhop of Glouceſter is patron and impropriator, and the reverend Mr. Charles Biſhop is the preſent incumbent.

The church, dedicated to St. Leonard, has an aile on the north ſide, and an embattled tower at the weſt end, in which are five bells.

An eſtate worth about 15*l*. a year is given for the repair of the church.

Synodals 1*s*. Pentecoſtals 1*s*. 2*d*.

			£.		
Taxes.	The Royal Aid in	1692,	151	6	8
	Poll-tax ——	1694, —	17	1	0
	Land-tax ——	1694, —	238	8	0
	The ſame, at 3*s*.	1770, —	179	2	0

There were 110 houſes in the pariſh, and about 450 inhabitants at the beginning of this century, 40 of whom were reputed to be freeholders; yearly births 12, burials 10. But the people are now decreaſed to about 300.

WALTON CARDIFFE

IS an inconſiderable pariſh, in the lower diviſion of Tewkeſbury hundred, about one mile ſouth-eaſtward from the town of that name, and nine northward from Glouceſter.

The pariſh conſiſts chiefly of rich meadow and paſture, and is watered by the little river Tirle, or Turle, which comes from Aſhchurch, and after joining the Swilyate at this place, runs down to Tewkeſbury.

What is the ſignification of Walton, I ſhall leave to the determination of others, but the cognomen of *Cardiffe* was certainly taken from the family of *de Kaerdyff*, to whom the manor belonged, and diſtinguiſhes this place from *Walton* in the neighbouring pariſh of Derhurſt.

Of the Manor and other Eſtates.

Walton was dependant on the great manor of Tewkeſbury in the reign of king Edward the Confeſſor, as appears by the tranſlation from *Domeſday-book*, inſerted under Tewkeſbury.

It continued to be a member of the ſame lordſhip, and was held of Richard de Clare, earl of Glouceſter and Hertford, 47 H. 3.

In the ſheriff's liſt of all the vills of the county, with their reſpective lords, returned into the exchequer 9 E. 1. it is ſaid, that William de Kerdiffe was lord of Walton Kerdiffe in Tewkeſbury hundred, but that it was then in the hands of Margaret counteſs of Glouceſter and Hertford.

It appears by the eſcheator's inquiſition, taken 8 E. 2. after the death of Gilbert de Clare, earl of Glouceſter, that Paulinus de Kerdyff then held Walton of the ſaid earl; and by another inquiſition, it likewiſe appears, that the ſame Paul de Kaerdyff died 9 E. 2. ſeized of the hamlet of Walton, which he held of the counteſs of Glouceſter, as of the honour of Tewkeſbury, by the fourth part of a knight's fee, and left William de Kaerdyff his ſon and heir, ſixteen years old. Joan the widow of —— Kaerdiff, and afterwards the widow of John de Wynecote, was endowed of Walton Kaerdiff, and died 23 E. 3. Robert Underhill and Evet his wife levied a fine of Walton Kaerdiffe, to Edward de Kaerdiff and Joan his wife, to —— Imprinham of Tewkeſbury, to Thomas Geſtock, and to John Bandrip and Elizabeth his wife, 37 E. 3. And Edward de Kaerdiffe and Joan his wife were ſeized thereof in the 43d year of the ſame reign.

William de Cheſterton, and others, were ſeized of the manor of Walton Kaerdiff 7 R. 2. as was Edward earl of Stafford 4 H. 4.

John Baſſet, of Bentbury in Glamorganſhire, in right of Elizabeth his wife, was ſeized of Walton at the time of his death, 4 H. 8. William Baſſet, ſon of John, dying before his father, William Baſſet, ſon of William, became heir to his grandfather, and had livery of the manor granted to him 22 H. 8.

William

William lord Willoughby, and Thomas Hurmage and Catherine his wife, levied a fine of the moiety of the manor of Walton Caerdif to the king, 3 E. 6. James Gunter and Anne his wife, levied a fine of Walton Cardiff, and Walton Basset, to Thomas Barew and Margaret his wife, 1 Mar.

The manor came afterwards to the Reads, who enjoyed it for many years. Giles Read, esq; was lord of it in 1608, and Foulk Read, esq; was proprietor of it in 1658. The manor is now vested in the corporation of Tewkesbury.

Three closes in Walton, which had belonged to the abbey of Tewkesbury, were granted to Thomas Sheldon and Lawrence Poyner, 36 H. 8. The tithes of Walton Caerdiffe, and divers lands, reputed to be a manor, part of the possessions of Tewkesbury abbey, were granted, together with a moiety of lands in Derhurst Place, to William Read and John Read, 7 E. 6. Another portion of tithes, formerly the property of that house, was granted to Daniel Perte and Alexander Perte, the same year. Another portion of tithes in Nether Gaston in Walton Cardiff, and tithes of hay in Walton Cardiff, which had belonged to the same monastery, were granted to Francis Maurice and Francis Phillips, in trust for sir William Ryder, 7 Jac.

Of the Church, &c.

The church is an impropriation, in the deanery of Winchcombe, worth 17*l.* 10*s.* to the curate, who is nominated by All Souls college, Oxford. Foulk Read, esq; in 1658, gave the small tithes to the curate, and the same year built the chapel, which is dedicated to St. James. The parishioners bury at Tewkesbury and Ashchurch.

Taxes.					
The Royal Aid in	1692,	£. 79	17	0
Poll-tax ——	1694, —	7	10	0
Land-tax ——	1694, —	116	0	0
The same, at 3*s.*	1770, —	88	5	1½

At the beginning of this century, there were 14 houses in the parish, and about 56 inhabitants, 4 of whom were freeholders; yearly births 1, burials 1. *Atkyns.* There are now 6 families in the parish.

WAPLEY *and* CODRINGTON.

THIS parish lies in the hundred of Grumbald's Ash, about six miles distant northwest from Marshfield, three south-westward from Chipping Sodbury, and about thirty-two southward from Gloucester.

The soil is fruitful, and the greater part of the parish is in pasturage. The river Boyd rises in the hamlet of Codrington, and runs thro' Bitton, where it empties itself into the Avon. The face of the country is exceedingly diversified with slopes, swells, and agreeable declivities, but the parish yields nothing curious for the entertainment of the naturalist or antiquary.

The large manor house, called Codrington Court, is now occupied as a farm house.

Of the Manors and other Estates.

A part of Wapley was considered as a member of the great manor of Betune, in Suinheve, now Langley and Swineshead hundred, and is entered under the title *Terra Regis* in *Domesday-book.* There were likewise two other estates here, which are thus described in the record:

'The bishop of St. Laud at Constance holds 'Wapelie in Polcrecerce hundred, and Aldred 'holds it of him. The same person held it in 'the time of king Edward. There is one hide, 'and one plow-tillage in demean, and two *servi.* 'It is worth and was worth 20 *sol.*' *Domesday*, p. 71.

'Radulf the brother of Roger [de Berchelai] 'holds Wapelie, in Pulchecerce hundred, of the 'king. There is one hide. Godric held it. 'There is one plow-tillage in demean, and four '*servi.* It is worth and was worth 20 *sol.*' *Ibid.* p. 75.

The manors of Wapley and Codrington were granted by king Henry the Second to Radulph son of Stephen, who immediately gave them to the abbey of Stanley, in the diocese of Salisbury, to pray for the soul of the king, and for the souls of himself and his family.

The sheriff returned that the abbat of Stanley was lord of the manor of Codrinton, in Grymbaldeashe hundred, 9 E. 1. and a writ of *Quo warranto* was brought against the abbat, in the 15th year of the same reign, to oblige him to set forth his right to court leet and felons goods within the manor of Codrington, and his claim to those privileges was then allowed.

The abbat of Stanley obtained a licence for alienating the manor of Wapley, reserving a rent of 11*l.* a year, for the repair of his abbey. Accordingly it was sold to John de Codrington, and to the heirs of his body, 33 H. 6. and John de Codrington obtained from pope Martin the Fifth, in the 12th year of his pontificate, a licence for having a portable consecrated altar for the celebration of mass in what places he pleased.

Simon Codrington, esq; was lord of the manor in the year 1608, as was his descendant, Robert Codrington, of Didmarton, esq; at the beginning of the present century. The manor continued in the Codrington family, 'till it passed out of that name to sir Richard Bamfylde, by his marriage with Jane, daughter and sole heir of colonel John Codrington, of Wraxall in Somersetshire. Sir Richard Bamfylde, baronet, died in the year 1776, and his relict, lady Bamfylde, is the present owner of the manors of Wapley and Codrington. The arms of Bamfylde are, *Or, upon a bend gules three mullets argent.*

HAMLET. *Codrington* is a considerable hamlet, once the residence of the Codringtons, who

who took their name from it, agreeable to the custom of antient times. The abbey of Stanley in Wiltshire was seized of Cudelington, *alias* Cotherington, 33 H. 6. John Sloper, lord of this manor, died in the year 1550, and left an only daughter and heiress, married to sir Walter Dennys, who likewise left an only daughter and heiress, married to Simon Codrington. From this time the manors of Wapley and Codrington have been enjoyed by the same persons, and lady Bamfylde is the present proprietor.

Mouswell is a place in this parish, where sir Thomas Roe had an estate, which he charged with the payment of 25*l*. a year to the town of Cirencester for apprenticing out poor boys, &c. These lands now belong to Mrs. Dorrington of Chipping Sodbury.

Robert Stanshaw, esq; died seized of lands in Wapley 12 E. 4. John Stanshaw and Humphry his brother levied a fine of lands in Wapley and Codrington 12 H. 7. Lands in Wapeley belonged to St. Augustin's abbey in Bristol, and were granted to the dean and chapter of that city 34 H. 8.

John Cotherington and Alice his wife levied a fine of lands in Cotherington to the use of themselves for life, remainder to Humphry, John, and Thomas, their sons, successively in taille; remainder to Margaret Besiles, late wife of sir Peter Besiles, in taille, 49 H. 6.

Lands in Cotherington belonged to the Benedictine nunnery of Pynely in Warwickshire, and were granted to Thomas Reeve and Richard Bullet 5 Mariæ. Lands called Magdalen's Croft, in Codrington, belonged to the Magdalen hospital in Bristol, and were granted to Henry Brain and John Marsh 37 H. 8.

Of the Church, &c.

The church is a vicarage, in the deanery of Hawkesbury, worth 35*l*. a year, and in the patronage of the lady of the manor, who holds the rectory and advowson of the vicarage by lease from the dean and chapter of Bristol. The reverend Mr. Gold is the present incumbent. The advowson belonged to St. Augustin's abbey in Bristol, and was granted, together with the impropriation, to the dean and chapter of that see, 34 H. 8.

The abbat of Stanley would have erected a chapel in Codrington, but the measure was opposed by the abbey of St. Augustin, as being prejudicial to the church of Wapley, of which they were patrons. This controversy was settled in the year 1280, when the abbat of Stanley had permission to build a chapel for the sole use of the capital messuage at Codrington; but no other persons were to resort to it without leave from the minister of Wapley.

The church, dedicated to St. Peter, is small, and has an aile on the south side, which was the burying place of the Codrington family.

First fruits £.	7	18	0	Synodals £.	0	2	0
Tenths —	0	15	9½	Pentecost.	0	1	6
Procurations	0	6	8				

Monument and Inscription.

Several of the Codringtons lie buried in the south aile, particularly John Codrington, esq; for whom there is an altar monument, and upon a small freestone tablet against the wall, this inscription:

Hic jacet Iohēs Codrynton Armiger qui obijt nono die Mensis Octobris Anno Dni M°CCCC°LXXV° Cujus Ætas erat die quo obijt CXI annor. V mensium XIII dierum. Cujus aie p'piciet' de' Amen.

Taxes.					
The Royal Aid in 1692,	£.	170	2	8
Poll-tax —	1694, —	18	2	0
Land-tax —	1694, —	191	12	0
The same, at 3*s*.	1770, —	150	7	3

There were 45 houses in this parish at the beginning of the present century, and about 180 inhabitants, 5 of whom were freeholders; yearly births 5, burials 4. *Atkyns*. The people are increased within the last sixty years, and are now about 200 in number.

WASHBOURN (GREAT)

IS a small parish, in the upper division of Tewkesbury hundred, seven miles eastward from the town of that name, five north from Winchcombe, and about fifteen north-eastward from Gloucester.

It lies in the Vale, and has a small brook which runs into the river Carrant. It is one of those places of which there is but little mention, except in rent-rolls and books of account, where, I suppose, it makes a handsome figure; for the soil is rich and fertile, and the greater part of the land is pasture. However, Anthony a Wood takes notice, that the great traveller John Cartwright was of this parish, and published his travels into Judea, Persia, and other eastern parts, in the year 1611.

Of the Manor and other Estates.

Waseborne belonged to the church of Tewkesbury when *Domesday*, was compiled, for the record takes notice that the abbey held three hides in Waseborne, and that there were two plow-tillages, and six villeins, with three plow-tillages; and one bordar, and nine *servi*, with one *ancilla*. p. 68.

After the dissolution of the abbey of Tewkesbury, this manor was granted to Anne Fortescue, widow of sir Adrian Fortescue, and to the heirs males of sir Adrian, 5 Mariæ. Sir Francis Fortescue was lord of it in the year 1608. It passed afterwards to Mr. Starkey, and is now vested in lord Craven, who holds a court leet.

Of

Of the Church, &c.

The church is a curacy, in the deanery of Campden, worth 5*l.* 10*s.* a year. Mr. Dark is patron and impropriator, and Mr. Roberts is the preſent incumbent.

The rectory formerly belonged to the abbey of Tewkeſbury, and was granted to Drew Drurey and Edward Downing 16 Eliz. The curate has no houſe nor glebe.

The church is a ſmall building, with a wooden turret in the middle. It is dedicated to St. Mary, and has divine ſervice performed in it only once a fortnight.

Pentecoſtals - - 4½*d.*

Taxes.					
The Royal Aid in	1692,	£. 88	18	0
Poll-tax ——	1694, —	3	10	0
Land-tax —	1694, —	29	14	0
The ſame, at 3*s.*	1770, —	29	14	0

There were 14 houſes in the pariſh, and about 60 inhabitants, 3 of whom were reputed to be freeholders, at the beginning of the preſent century. And the people are about the ſame number at this time.

WELFORD.

THIS pariſh lies in the upper diviſion of Derhurſt hundred, nine miles diſtant north from Campden, four ſouth from Stratford upon Avon in Warwickſhire, and thirty-ſix north-eaſtward from Glouceſter.

It is bounded by Weſton upon Avon on the eaſt, by Dorſington on the ſouth, and on the north and north-weſt by the river Avon, which ſeparates it from Warwickſhire.

It is a rich ſoil, abundantly fertile in corn and paſture; but the public roads in all this part of the county are very incommodious, and almoſt impaſſible in the winter ſeaſon. They are either carried through miry lanes, or along head lands in the common fields, ſo that the traveller is obliged to ſhape his courſe in a zig-zag direction, as the ground will permit.

Of the Manor and other Eſtates.

Domeſday takes notice of Welford among the vills in Derhurſt hundred, which were held by the church of St. Dennis at Paris, and obſerves, that there were fifteen hides. But as the record will not bear abridgment, the reader is referred to p. 72. where he will find the whole account in the original language.

The priory of Derhurſt, which was a cell to the abbey of St. Dennis, held the manor of the earls of Glouceſter, and the ſame houſe continued poſſeſſed of it 'till the diſſolution of alien priories, when this manor was granted to the abbey of Tewkeſbury.

After the general diſſolution of religious houſes, this manor was granted by the crown to William Willington, of Barcheſton in Warwickſhire, in taille, the remainder to Edward Grevil of Milcote, and Margaret his wife, daughter of William Willington, and to her heirs, 7 E. 6.

Lodowick, or Lewis Grevil, only ſon of Edward and Margaret, had livery of this manor granted to him 1 Eliz. Sir Edward Grevil of Milcot, only ſon of Lodowick, was lord of this manor in the year 1608; but being much involved in debt, he ſold his whole eſtate to Lionel Cranfield earl of Middleſex, whoſe daughter Frances carried this manor, by her marriage, to Richard Sackville, fifth earl of Dorſet. Charles Sackville, ſixth earl of Dorſet, died Jan. 29, 1705-6, and was ſucceeded by his only ſon Lionel-Cranfield, ſeventh earl and firſt duke of Dorſet, who was lord of the manor of Welford at the beginning of this century, and the duke of Dorſet is the preſent lord of the manor. His grace's arms are, *Quarterly Or and gules, over all a bend vaire.* CREST. *Out of a ducal coronet Or, an eſtoile of eight points argent.* SUPPORTERS. *Two leopards argent, ſpotted ſable.* MOTTO. AUT NUNQUAM TENTES AUT PERFICE.

The records mention other perſons as proprietors of the manor. Thus it is ſaid, ſir Thomas Weſt and Alice his wife were ſeized of the manor of Welford 10 R. 2. and John Grevil, eſq; died ſeized of it 23 H. 6. But they could only be tenants under the priory of Derhurſt.

William Hoeſe and Margaret his wife purchaſed lands in Welford of Ralph de Welford, which lands had been formerly purchaſed by the ſaid Margaret, and by William Comyn her former huſband, 5 H. 3. A tenement in Welford belonged to the Ciſtercian abbey of Bordeſley in Worceſterſhire, and was granted to Robert earl of Leiceſter 16 Eliz.

HAMLETS. 1. *Bickmarſh*, containing one family. In the antient ſurvey, made in the reign of king William the Firſt, Bichemerſe is ſaid to be in Ceolflede hundred, which is now comprized in that of Kiftſgate. But how derogatory ſoever it may ſeem to that record, the hamlets belonging to this pariſh now lie in Warwickſhire, and pay land-tax in aid of that county, but contribute to the parochial levies of Welford. Hence it may be inferred, that ſome alterations have taken place in the diviſion of counties, as well as of hundreds, within the laſt ſeven hundred years. The record runs thus:

'Eddiet holds Bichemerſe in Ceolflede hundred, 'of the king. She held it in the time of king 'Edward. There is one hide, and in demean 'two plow-tillages, and one villein, and one 'bordar, and four *ſervi*. It is worth and was 'worth 20 *ſol.*' *Domeſday*, p. 79.

2. *Little Dorſington*, where are three families.

3. *Bedlam*, which does not ſeem at preſent intituled to the diſtinction of a hamlet, as the only houſe within it was originally a barn.

Of the Church, &c.

The church is a rectory, in the deanery of Campden, worth 180*l.* a year. The duke of Dorfet is patron, and the reverend Mr. Green is the prefent incumbent.

Two yard-lands in Welford, and two in Bickmarfh belonged to the glebe, but are now intirely loft from the living.

There was antiently a chapel at Bickmarfh in this parifh, and a compofition was made in the reign of king John, between Walter abbat of Tewkefbury, and Robert Foliot, parfon and patron of the chapel of Bikemareys, concerning tithes, of which the reader may fee fome account in Stevens's *Supplement to the Monafticon, Appendix*, p. 201.

In the year 1497, the bifhop of Worcefter, at the requeft of the inhabitants, made a fpecial vifitation in the parifh, for which he received four marks.

The advowfon paffed from the priory of Derhurft to the abbey of Tewkefbury, and after the general diffolution of monafteries, was granted to fir Ralph Sadler, 1 E. 6.

The church is dedicated to the Trinity, and has a high tower at the weft end.

Firft fruits £.	29	15	10	Synodals £.	0	2	0
Tenths —	2	9	7	Pentecoft.	0	1	0½
Procurations	0	6	8				

Monuments and Infcriptions.

On a flat ftone in the body of the church, is this infcription:

☧ Hic jacet dns Waltherus Williams quondam Rector ifti' Ecclie qui obiit die . . . . Menfis Augufti Anno dni MCCCCLXXXIIIJ° Cuj' Aie ppiciet' deus Amen.

Againft the outfide of the fouth wall of the chancel,

Underneath is the Grave of Richard Rawlings of Wolford, who by Will bearing Date the 22^d Day of October 1727 did give 3 Pounds per Annum charged upon his Half yard land in Welford (one moiety whereof to be paid half year) for the Maintenance of a Schoolmafter there for ever to teach eight poor boys of the parifh to read and write Englifh, to inftruct them in the Church Catechifm, in the ufe of figures, & to make them ready Accountants.

This little Charity the Founder Gave
to excite the rich who larger Sabftance have
to increafe its Fund & fo refpect his Grave.

Benefactions.

John Frecketon gave 13*s.* 4*d.* and a further fum of 6*s.* 8*d.* a year, payable out of the Millhams, to the poor for ever. Thomas Mills gave 3*l.* yearly to the poor, and 3*s.* 4*d.* *per ann.* for the repair of the highways of this parifh, both which fums are charged on a meadow called Synderham. A full account of Richard Rawling's charity is given in the infcription for him.

Taxes.			£.	s.	d.
	The Royal Aid in	1692,	200	16	0
	Poll-tax — —	1694, —	39	17	0
	Land-tax	1694, -	202	4	0
	The fame, at 3*s.*	1770, —	140	3	0

At the beginning of this century, there were 98 houfes in the parifh, and about 450 inhabitants, 18 of whom were freeholders; yearly births 13, burials 11. *Atkyns.* But at prefent the people fall fomething fhort of that number.

WESTBURY.

THIS parifh lies in the Foreft divifion, and in three different hundreds. It is two miles diftant north-eaft from Newnham, four fouth-eaft from Mitchel Dean, and ten fouthweftward from Gloucefter.

It is bounded for feveral miles on the fouth by the river Severn, and forms a very extenfive tract of rich ground, of which the greater part is meadow and pafture, interfperfed with orcharding and fome arable land.

The name of the place fignifies the *Weft Camp*, yet I cannot difcover any traces of antient intrenchments now exifting.

Weftbury-Court is an elegant houfe, in modern tafte, with beautiful canals and extenfive pleafure gardens, ftanding about half a mile from the Severn, on the fide of the road leading from Monmouthfhire to Gloucefter. It is the feat of Maynard Colchefter, efq; who refides there. In the pediment over the Attic ftory are the family arms, impaling three crefcents; and the following infcription ftands over the door in the front:

D.
O. M.
N. M. M. H. E. P. N. C.

This houfe was built by Maynard Colchefter, efq; father of the prefent owner, whofe piety and gratitude are well expreffed in the firft three letters of the infcription, which I read *Deo Optimo Maximo*. The fubfequent line contains the initials of this hexameter:

Nunc mea, mox hujus, et poftea nefcio cujus.

alluding to the fucceffive defcent of property from one generation to another.

In this large parifh the foils are various, and the natural productions numerous. The Foreft divifion is allowed by competent judges to yield the beft cider in the kingdom, and there is more truth than poetic fiction in the following verfes:

— *To the utmoft bounds of this*
Wide univerfe, Silurian cider born,
Shall pleafe all taftes, and triumph o'er the vine.

So Phillips fang: And Weftbury may juftly claim her fhare of the general commendation. Iron ore is found not only here, but in almoft every part of the foreft; and I have no doubt but that there is plenty of coal in Weftbury, tho' no particular inducement to fearch for it, the inhabitants being fo well accommodated with that moft ufeful foffil from the next parifh.

There is alfo a thin kind of ftone found in the cliffs next the Severn, of a fine glittering colour on the furface like gold, which was lately tried in the

the furnace. Much of its ſubſtance evaporates in ſmoak, but it contains no metal of any kind.

I believe this to be the only place in Glouceſterſhire where the *Carduus Fullonum*, or Teaſle, is cultivated for the uſe of the clothing manufacture. Several common medicinal plants grow in different parts of the pariſh, and I obſerve the herb Celery flouriſhes vigorouſly on the banks by the ſides of the high roads, which indicates a great ſtrength of ſoil.

There is a ferry over the Severn at this place, to Framilode on the other ſide, where is an inn for the accommodation of travellers; but no ſuch conveniency on the Weſtbury ſide.

My inquiries for antiquities in this place have not been very ſucceſsful. I viſited the pariſh church in 1776, and ſaw a piece of a bone lying in the chancel window, which was ſaid to be a part of the thigh bone of ſome prodigious giant. It was about two feet long, appearing very porous at the broken end. I could make no eſtimate of the length of it when intire, but it was twenty-two inches in circumference. The inhabitants knew not how it came there, nor indeed any thing about it.

Doctor Hakewill, in his learned *Apology of the Power and Providence of God in the Government of the World*, relates, that about the year 1634, there were ſeveral bones of a prodigious ſize found not far diſtant from Glouceſter, but does not ſay where; and that king Charles the Firſt appointed lord Herbert of Cherbury to examine them, who collected a huckle bone, a piece of a ſhoulder blade, ſome part of a tooth, and the bone of the noſe, all of aſtoniſhing ſize. Doctor Hervey, a great anatomiſt of that age, and Doctor Clayton, the king's profeſſor of phyſic in Oxford, with ſeveral other judicious perſons, examined them, and concurred in opinion that they were not human, but the bones of an elephant, brought hither, as may be ſuppoſed, by the Romans; for according to Dion, Claudius brought elephants into Britain. The bone of the noſe in particular was not like a man's, which confirmed them the rather in opinion that none of the others were human. They were all found together, mixt with the bones and horns of ſheep and oxen, and the tuſk of a boar, and a great ſquare ſtone, like the top ſtone of an altar, lay by them, whence it is imagined that they were the relicks of ſome great ſacrifice made near the place where they lay. And it is not improbable that the piece of the bone which I ſaw in Weſtbury church was found at the ſame time with the above.

I am next to ſhew what ſhare this pariſh has had in military affairs. In the time of the great civil wars, the governor of Glouceſter placed a garriſon at Weſtbury, to keep the market of that city open, but Corbet relates that the garriſon was loſt 'by the treachery of captain Thomas 'Davis, who ſold them at a rate to ſir John Win-'ter. This Davis,' ſays he, 'commanded the 'guard at Huntley, where himſelf by night, ſome 'diſtance from the houſe, attended the enemy's 'coming, went in before them, as friends from 'Glouceſter, gave them poſſeſſion, and having 'accompliſhed that piece of treaſon, immediately 'marched to Weſtbury, where he was received 'for a friend, and led in his train of cavaleers, ſo 'that both places were ſurprized in two hours, 'and about eighty men and arms loſt in that 'great exigency.' The ſame author relates that afterwards, '150 muſkettiers, and the whole 'ſtrength of horſe were drawn out [from 'Glouceſter] towards the foreſt ſide, and came 'upon Weſtbury. Here the enemy held the 'church, and a ſtrong houſe adjoining. The 'governor [Maſſie] obſerving a place not flanked, 'fell up that way with the forlorn-hope, and 'ſecured them from the danger of ſhot. The 'men got ſtools and ladders to the windows, 'where they ſtood ſafe, caſt in granadoes, and 'fired them out of the church. Having gained 'the church, he quickly beat them out of their 'works, and poſſeſſed himſelf of the houſe, where 'he took about thirty priſoners without the loſs 'of a man.'

Before the reformation, there lived at this place one Mr. James Baynham,[x] who was burnt at the ſtake for religion in the reign of king Henry the Eighth.

Of

[x] The following detail of his ſufferings will excite an abhorrence of the perſecuting principles of the times he lived in, and tend to make the preſent age happy in the religious liberty they enjoy.—Mr. James Baynham was ſon of ſir Alexander Baynham, the elder, who had conſiderable poſſeſſions in this pariſh, in St. Briavel's, and other parts of the foreſt of Dean. The ſon was bred up at the inns of court, and was of a virtuous and religious turn. He married the widow of Simon Fiſh, the author of a famous book intituled the *Supplication of the Beggers*, which contributed greatly to the reformation of religion. King Henry the Eighth had read and approved the book, and gave his protection to the author to ſkreen him from perſecution. Mr. Baynham was ſuſpected to be of reforming principles, and not long after his marriage, was accuſed to ſir Thomas Moor, then chancellor of England, and taken by a ſerjeant at arms out of the Temple to ſir Thomas's houſe at Chelſea, where he remained a kind of priſoner at large for ſome time. But ſir Thomas not being able to prevail with him to renounce his principles, uſed him with greater ſeverity, caſt him into a priſon in the ſame houſe, whipped him at a tree in his garden, called afterwards the *Tree of Truth*, and at length ſent him to the tower of London to force him by the rack to accuſe ſuch gentlemen of the Temple as were of his judgment, and to confeſs where his books were, attending in perſon to ſee this cruelty executed on him. And becauſe his wife could not be prevailed with to diſcover his books, ſhe was ſent to the Fleet, and their goods were confiſcated.

When ſir Thomas found all his attempts to reduce him to the church were vain, he ſent him to the biſhop of London, who put him in Lollard's Tower, examined him ſeveral times upon articles and interrogatories, and at laſt, by fair words and threats, brought him to recant; and ſo doing penance at St. Paul's croſs, he was ſoon diſmiſſed and ſent home. But he was ſo troubled in conſcience, that within a month afterwards he aſked forgiveneſs of God, and the proteſtant congregation in Bow-lane; and openly declared in St. Auſtin's church, that he had denied God, and prayed all the people to forgive him. Upon this, he was ſoon apprehended, condemned, and delivered to the ſheriff to be executed. When he came to the ſtake in Smithfield, where he ſuffered April 30, 1531, he ſpoke thus to the people: 'Good 'people, I am come hither to die as an heretic, and theſe be the 'articles I ſuffer for: I ſay that it is lawful for every man and 'woman to have God's book in the mother tongue: That 'the pope is antichriſt: That there are no other keys of 'heaven gate but preaching of the word: That there is no other

'purgatory

Of the Manor and other Eſtates.

This and Hueſberie, which we now call Weſtbury upon Trim, were two large manors, and as the accounts ſtand in *Domeſday*, there appears to be ſome difficulty, at firſt ſight, eſpecially, to diſcriminate between them.

For as Chire, that is Shirehampton, and Cliftone immediately follow the account of Weſtbury in the record, it is natural enough to imagine that the account relates to Weſtbury upon Trim, in whoſe neighbourhood thoſe places lie. But that could not be the caſe, becauſe the record declares Weſberie to be the demeans of the crown, and it appears by the ſame authority, that Hueſberie, now Weſtbury upon Trim, belonged at that time to the church of Worceſter.

This difficulty ſeems to have been the reaſon why ſir Robert Atkyns gave no abſtract from *Domeſday* concerning this manor. The record runs thus:

'There are thirty hides in Weſberie. King 'Edward had five plow-tillages there in demean, 'and thirty-two villeins, and fifteen bordars, 'with twenty-eight plow-tillages. There is 'one *ſervus*. This manor paid a farm of one 'night in the time of king Edward, and ſo it did 'likewiſe for four years in the time of king 'William. But ſix hides were afterwards taken 'from the manor. There are ten hides in Chire 'and Cliftone, eight in Noent and Chingeſtune, 'and one in Ladenent.

'The abbey of Cormeile, and Oſbern, and 'William the ſon of Richard, hold theſe lands 'now, but nevertheleſs the ſheriff pays the whole 'farm for the remainder.

'The men of the county ſay, that Sapina be'longed to the farm of king Edward in Weſtberie.' p. 67.

Beſides the principal manor, there were two ſmall eſtates in Weſtberie hundred, held of the king's farm, and a third that was independent of it, as appears by *Domeſday-book*.

'William ſon of Baderon holds two yard lands 'and a half, and has there one villein, and one 'bordar. Wihanoc his anceſtor held it, but the 'county affirms that this eſtate is held of the 'king's demean farm in Weſtberie, and is worth '3 *ſol.*' p. 74.

'William Goizenboded holds half a hide of 'land, and half a fiſhery in Weſtberie hundred. 'Aluuin the ſheriff held it, and gave it to his 'wife. This eſtate belonged to the king's farm 'in Weſtberie.' p. 74.

'Durand the ſheriff holds one manor of three 'hides in Weſtberie hundred. Aluuold held it 'and paid tax. There is one plow-tillage in 'demean, and four villeins, and three bordars, 'with four plow-tillages. There are two *ſervi*, 'and it was worth 60 *ſol.* now only 40 *ſol.*' p. 76.

It is obſervable that the book does not mention what pariſh theſe eſtates lay in, but only the hundred; yet there is reaſon to ſuppoſe they were a part of Weſtbury, and that the records of the following dates relate chiefly to theſe, and not to the principal manor.

Henry de Myners reſided in this pariſh, and purchaſed a licence to incloſe a park near his houſe 2 Joh.

The manor of Weſtbury was granted to Ralph de Beauchamp 18 Joh. and paſſed afterwards to the Burghulls, or Bornhulls, for Baſilia de Burghull died endowed thereof 55 H. 3. Roger de Burghull, ſon of Roger, died ſeized of the ſame manor, and of the hundred of Weſtbury, 31 E. 1. Roger Burghull, ſon of the laſt Roger, died ſeized of Weſtbury 1 E. 3. and Robert de Sapy held it 10 E. 3.

Jeffery de Mareſchal was ſeized of Weſtbury 32 E. 3. It was held of Humphry de Bohun, earl of Hereford and Eſſex, and of Joan his wife, 46 E. 3.

Sir John de Aylesford, *alias* Eynesford, died ſeized of the manors of Weſtbury and Bolley 19 R. 2. Iſabel the wife of ſir John de Aylesford ſurvived him, and was endowed with the manor of Weſtbury, and afterwards married Richard de la More, whom ſhe likewiſe ſurvived, and died ſeized of Weſtbury 9 H. 5.

John Milborn and Elizabeth his wife were ſeized of the manor of Weſtbury 1 & 15 H. 6. John earl of Shrewſbury was ſeized thereof in the 32d year of the ſame reign; as was Alice the widow of William Codder 34 H. 6.

This manor paſſed afterwards to the Baynhams, for John Baynham died ſeized thereof, and of twenty meſſuages, and three hundred acres of paſture, &c. in Weſtbury, 20 H. 8. William Baynham, ſon of John, had livery of it 26 H. 8. Robert Baynham had alſo livery granted to him 9 Eliz. as had Joſeph Baynham in the 14th year of the ſame reign.

The hundred of Weſtbury is now in the crown, and the court leet is kept by the ſheriff. But Maynard Colcheſter, eſq; is lord of the manor. His arms are, *Or, a chevron between three eſtoiles gules.*

Of the other eſtates the records ſhew, that Nicholas de Bath was ſeized of one meſſuage, 260 acres of arable, &c. in the pariſh of Weſtbury next Newnham, 20 E. 2. John Knight and others were ſeized of ſix acres in Weſtbury, and of the advowſon of the church, and of twenty libratas of land in Whitington and Weſtbury,

'purgatory but Chriſt's blood; and that the ſouls of the faithful 'go immediately to heaven: That Thomas Becket was no 'ſaint, but a traitor: That there is no tranſubſtantiation in 'the ſacrament, but that 'tis idolatry to worſhip the bread, &c.' ——One Pavy gave him the lie in thus ſpeaking, and haſtened to burn him. While he was in the midſt of the flames, and his arms and legs were half conſumed, he cried out, 'O ye papiſts, ye look 'for miracles, behold here ye may ſee one, for in this fire I feel 'no more pain than if I were in a bed of down, but it is to me 'as a bed of roſes:' And then expired ſoon after.

for

for the use of the church of St. Athelbert in Hereford, 4 R. 2. which church was founded by Milefrid king of the Mercians in the year 825. William Aston was seized of a tenement called Aston's Court in the parish of Westbury 3 H. 4. Richard Beke levied a fine of lands in Westbury to Edward Veel 1 Mar. The manor of Cellers in Westbury belonged to the priory of Lanthony, and was granted to Thomas Reeve, William Ryvet, and William Hechins, 6 Eliz.

HAMLETS. There are several large hamlets in this parish, of which in their order.

1. *Rodley*, which lies in the hundred of the dutchy of Lancaster, and is situated about two miles eastward from the church. *Domesday* gives the following particulars of the manor. 'Walter 'Balistarius holds Rodele. There is one hide 'taxed. Tovi held it. There is one plow-tillage 'in demean, and two villeins, and four bordars, 'with two plow-tillages. It was worth 40 *sol.* 'but now only 10 *sol.*' p. 77.

Sir Robert Atkyns, in his account of this manor, has confounded it with Ruddle in the parish of Newnham, which was given to the abbey of Gloucester; but the manor of Rodele in Westbury was never any part of the possessions of that monastery, as sir Robert asserts.

The records shew, that Henry de Bohun released all his right in Rodley to king John, in the first year of that king's reign; and Simon Montfort, the great earl of Leicester, died seized of Rodleigh 43 H. 3.

Gilbert Talbot, son of Richard and of Aliva, daughter of Alan Basset, justiciar of England, married Guenthlian, or Guendoline, daughter of Rhese ap Griffith, prince of Wales, and died seized of Rodleigh and Longhope 2 E. 1. In an inquisition taken 4 E. 1. it is said, Rodeley was of the antient demeans of kings, and was then in the hands of Richard Talebott, but the jury did not know by what means; and that it used to yield to the king a revenue of 42 *l.* a year.

Edmond earl of Lancaster, second son of king Henry the Third, was seized of Rodleghe, and had his right of court leet allowed in a writ of *Quo warranto* 15 E. 1. Henry earl of Lancaster, second son of earl Edmond, and brother and heir to Thomas earl of Lancaster, was seized of Rodeley, and of twelve acres of pasture in the forest of Dean belonging to the manor of Rodeley, 10 E. 2. Henry earl of Lancaster, son of earl Henry, and afterwards duke of Lancaster, was seized of Rodleye, and of estovers in the forest of Dean, 10 E. 3. He died of the plague at Leicester-castle 35 E. 3. and left two daughters coheiresses. Maud, the elder, was married to the duke of Bavaria, and had the manors of Rodelegh, Tiberton, and Minsterworth assigned to her, but dying without issue, her sister Blanch, married in 1359, to John of Gaunt, duke of Lancaster, became her heir, from whom are descended the kings of England of the line of Lancaster. John duke of Lancaster and Blanch his wife levied a fine of the manors of Rodleyh, Tiberton, and Minsterworth, to the use of themselves in taille 39 E. 3. Joan the widow of Robert Grinder died endowed with Rodley 24 H. 6. This manor is part of the dutchy of Lancaster, and king Edward the Fourth levied a fine of it to Richard Martin to hold for one month, the remainder to Elizabeth the queen, and to the archbishop and other great persons, 15 E. 4. Sir William Guise, baronet, is the present lord of this manor.

The records also shew, that William de Dean died seized of Rodeley, which he held of Thomas le Blount by the service of 12 *s.* he was also seized of one yard-land worth 6 *s.* a year, and of six borachs in the Severn worth 6 *s.* a year, and of two acres of meadow worth 5 *s.* a year. *Esch.* Richard de Blensedon was seized of two messuages, sixty acres of arable land, and of a fishery in the Severn at Rodeley 20 E. 2. Philip Hook of Little Dean died seized of the manor of Stantways in Rodeley, 16 H. 6. and it was granted the same year to Richard Barton and Morgan Merideth, to hold for their lives.

The tenants of this manor antiently paid, and still continue to pay, to the lord, a rent called Pridgavel, for liberty of fishing in the Severn, of which see more under Minsterworth.

2. *Walmer* is a distinct manor within this parish, consisting of very large commons by the side of the Severn. Ralph de Abbenhall was seized of ten acres of meadow in Walmer 29 E. 1. Richard de Poulton held Walmore and Northwoode *in capite*, paying to the king three bearded arrows as often as he should hunt *in propria persona* in the forest of Dean; and he died seized of the same, and of one messuage, fifty acres of arable, and three acres of meadow, 12 E. 2. *Esch.* John Ate-Yate was seized of Walmore and Littlemore within the manor of Rodley, as parcel of the manor of Stanteway 41 E. 3. Sir Brian Tuke died seized of Walmer 37 H. 8. and Charles Tuke, son of sir Brian, had livery the same year. Richard Andrews and Ursula his wife levied a fine of the manor of Walmer to Edward Wilmot and others 2 Mar. of which manor, and of a large house called the Grange, Anthony Kemp, esq; of Slyndon in Essex, was seized at the beginning of the present century. The manor of Walmer, and the Grange, are now, by marriage, vested in the earl of Newburgh.

3. *Chaxhill*, which lies eastward from the church.

4. *Bolloe*, which also lies eastward from the church. The two hamlets of Bolloe and Chaxhill have one tithingman.

5. *Upperleigh*, which lies about two miles north-east from the church. This place belonged to the chantry of St. Mary in Westbury, and was granted to sir Anthony Cope 10 Jac.

 6. *Northwood*,

6. *Northwood,* which lies north from the church. Northwood and Upperleigh have one tithingman.

7. *Netherleigh,* which lies about two miles north-eaſt from the church. Nicholas Gamage died ſeized of this manor 24 E. 3. It belonged afterwards to ſir John Scudamore, who being attainted, it was granted to ſir Richard Herbert, and his heirs males, 4 E. 4. George Rawleigh, eſq; died ſeized of the manor of Netherlaugh 37 H. 8. and left Simon his ſon twenty-two years old, and Leonard a brother, who had a ſon Thomas. The manor then paſſed to the Baynhams. Sir George Baynham died ſeized thereof 38 H. 8. and livery was granted to his ſon ſir Chriſtopher Baynham 3 E. 6. and Richard Baynham, brother of Chriſtopher, had livery of it 5 Mar. This place has its own tithingman.

8. *Boſeley,* which lies north-weſtward from the church. John Sabyn and others held one meſſuage, one toft, and one plow-tillage in Boſely, Leye, and Rodlegh, 10 R. 2. This place hath a tithingman.

9. *Cleeve,* which lies ſouth-eaſtward from the church. 10. *Adſet,* lying north-eaſtward from the church. 11. *Stanteway.* Theſe three have one tithingman.

12. *Elton,* which lies weſtward from the church, is a large hamlet, and has its proper tithingman.

Of the Church, &c.

The church is a vicarage, in the Foreſt deanery, worth about 140*l.* a year. The Vicars Choral of the cathedral of Hereford are patrons, and the reverend Mr. Kidley is the preſent incumbent. The impropriation, which belongs to the ſame Vicars of the church of Hereford, is worth 300*l.* a year, and is in leaſe to Doctor John Cam, a phyſician at Hereford, whoſe arms are, *Paly of ſix argent and azure.*

There are two churches in the church-yard. The old church has a handſome wooden ſpire at the weſt end. The new one, in which divine ſervice is performed, was built in the year 1530, and ſtands at a conſiderable diſtance from the other. It conſiſts of the nave, with an aile on each ſide, ſupported by pillars, and is dedicated to the virgin Mary.

There were two chantries in Weſtbury church, whereof one was dedicated to St. Nicholas, and the lands belonging to it were granted to ſir Nicholas Arnold 5 Eliz. The other chantry was dedicated to the virgin Mary, and John Shawe was the laſt incumbent, who enjoyed a penſion of 3*l.* 6*s.* 8*d.* in 1553. The lands, and a meſſuage in Adſet, which belonged to this chantry, were granted to Anthony Cope and others 10 Jac.

A licence was granted to the vicar of Weſtbury to purchaſe land to enlarge his houſe 26 E. 3. Doctor John Hooper, biſhop of Glouceſter, at the deſire of the inhabitants, made a ſpecial viſitation in this pariſh, for which was paid 2*l.* 13*s.* 4*d.* for procuration.

Firſt fruits £. 20	2	10	Proc. & Syn. £. 0	9	2
Tenths — 2	0	3$\frac{1}{4}$	Pentecoſtals - 0	1	4

Monuments and Inſcriptions.

Upon a tablet in the chancel,

MEMORIÆ NICHOLAI ROBERTS AR. QVONDAM HVIVS
MANERIJ DOM. QVI MORTALITATEM EXUIT 19 IAN. 1636.
HOC QVALECVNQ; CHARISSIMI AVUNCVLI
MERITIS QVAM LONGE IMPAR
SACRATVM VOLUIT
E SORORE NEPOS RICHVS COLCHESTER AR.
MODERNVS EIVSDEM MANERIJ DNS.

This monument is ornamented with two coats, the one *Party per pale ermine and gules, a lion rampant ſable,* for Roberts. The other Colcheſter, as already given.

There are alſo four very handſome marble monuments in the chancel, with the following inſcriptions:

Deo Opt. Max. Sacrum
Ut laudetur in
Pia Memoria
DUNCUMBI COLCHESTER, Eq. Aurati,
Qui obiit Maij 25to A^{o} D^{ni} 1694° Æt. 65.
Hic (ut olim SOLOMON) in viis Cordis ſui
Pede heu! libero nimis AMBULANS,
Non infructuoſo tandem EXPERIMENTO didicit,
VANA OMNIA PRÆTER NUMINIS CULTUM.
Eximiis NATURÆ dotibus pollens,
MUNERA PUBLICA non unius generis obivit;
Nec ſine LAUDE Sæculi:
Sola defuit MATURA SANCTITAS,
Sed MORBO tandem, velut NUNCIO Cœlitus miſſo, admonitus,
Quicquid Supererat VITÆ
Id totum PIETATIS ſtudijs impendit.
Nec ſufficere ſibi ratus PRIVATAM POENITENTIAM,
OMNIBUS, quotquot EXEMPLO ſuo nocuiſſe videri poterat,
POENITENTIAM, etiam ſuam NOTAM eſſe voluit.
Non metuens de FAMA, nec moratus
Dicacem IMPROBORUM hominum ſtultitiam.
REM etiam in TEMPLIS PUBLICARI curavit ipſe,
NOVO et SINGULARI Exemplo
SE VIVUM præſtans OMNIBUS,
Maxime DIERUM VANITATIS ſuæ ſociis, (TUM.
ILLUSTRISSIMUM GENEROSÆ POENITENTIÆ MONUMEN-
Etiam MORTUUS loquitur, LECTOREM ſerio MONENS
Vt DEVM ſibi quam citiſſime AMICUM conciliet,
Quem ASYLUM omnes optabunt.

MAINARDUS COLCHESTER, F. natu maximus,
Hoc Marmor PATRI
P.
Necnon DOROTHEÆ SORORI Chariſſimæ, quæ diu LANGUENS
Pia CURA ÆGROTANTIS Patris,
MORTUI DESIDERIO,
TERRENORUM omnium TOEDIO,
Ad COELESTEM Patrem MIGRAVIT
Maij 10mo. A^{o}. D^{ni}. 1696, Æt. . . .

This monument is decorated with two coats, *Baron and femme,* 1. Colcheſter. 2. *Argent, three ſiniſter hands couped at the wriſt gules,* for Maynard.

To the left of the above,

Dominæ Elizabethæ Colcheſter,
Uxoris Duncumb Colcheſter Militis,
Filiæ Iohan. Maynard Equitis Aurati,
Servien. ad Leg: et Regis Conciliarij in Lege peritiſſimi,
Cineribus Sacrum.
Vitæ Sanctimoniâ,
Morum Suavitate et Candore,
In rebus Oeconomicis Peritiâ,
Charitate erga Pauperes,
Medicamentis arga Infirmos,
Præceptis erga Errantes,
Clementiâ erga Ignorantes,
In ſe Omnium benevolentiam Conciliantis:
Sed Eheu! per multos annos,
Varijs morbis et cruciantibus conflictata,
Tandem Animam immaculatam
Deo reddidit Septemb: 19, 1681.
Filios duos, tres Filias Superſtites reliquit moriens.
Optimæ Conjugi Amantiſſimus Maritus
Hoc poſuit Monumentum.

There are the ſame arms on this monument as on the foregoing.

On

On the right hand of the communion table,

Near this place are depoſited y[e] precious Remains
of *Maynard Colcheſter*, Eſq[r]; dec[d]. honourably deſcended
being y[e] eldeſt Son of S[r] *Duncomb Colcheſter*
late of this Pariſh by Eliz. daughter of S[r] *Io. Maynard*,
dec[d]. one of the Lords Commiſſioners of the Great Seal of
ENGLAND;
But much more honourable & worthy to be had in everlaſting
Remembrance for thoſe truly noble qualities w[ch] by the Grace of
God he was early poſſeſſed of, & perſevered in to the laſt &
whereby he was enabled to diſcharge wth great judgment
inflexible Integrity, & undaunted Courage the ſeveral
Offices & Truſts w[ch] without ſeeking he was called to by his
Prince & Country, & to deviſe & do many great & liberal things
for y[e] Honour of God & y[e] Good of mankind, having been
A principal Founder & Supporter of the Societies for
Reformation of Manners & promoting Chriſtian Knowledge
by Charity Schools of w[ch] he ſet up & maintained ſeveral at his own
charges. And likewiſe one of y[e] firſt Members of y[e] Society for
propagating y[e] Goſpel in foreign Parts, and A generous
Encourager of that & many other good Deſigns.
This excellent Perſon was ſtrictly pious himſelf & zealous to
promote true Piety in others within his reach, eſpecially in
his own Family, & was thought to have been ſo ſingularly
happy herein, as to have even overpaid y[e] debt of filial
Duty & Gratitude, by being an inſtrument of
Spiritual Life to him, from whom he had only
Received that which was Natural.
He was an effectionate Huſband,
a tender & careful Parent, A kind and faithfull Friend,
A true lover of all good Men (tho' differing from him)
And ready to every good worke;
particularly to thoſe of Charity to y[e] Poor & diſtreſſed,
For whom he yearly ſet apart
A large proportion of his Income, w[ch]
was ſtrictly, tho' ſecretly applyed
to y[e] moſt uſefull Charities.
This Chriſtian Hero was exerciſed for many
Years with almoſt conſtant ſickneſs and the
moſt accute pains, which he bore with exemplary
patience, and an intire Submiſſion to y[e] Divine
Will & Pleaſure, & at length joyfully reſigned
up his pious Soul into y[e] hands of his faithful
Creator & merciful Redeemer y[e] 25th of June
1715 in y[e] 51st year of his Age; leaving 3 Daughters
Anne, *Jane*, & *Eliz.* by *Jane* y[e] only
Daughter of S[r]. Edward Clarke, K[t].
dec. late L[d] Mayor of London
his loving & dutifull
wife & now mournfull
widdow.

At top of the monument are the arms of Colcheſter, impaling thoſe of Clarke, *viz. Argent, on a bend ſable a croſs croſlet fitchy Or.*

Near the laſt,

In Hopes of an happy Reſurrection,
Near this Place lies the Body
of MAYNARD COLCHESTER, Eſq[r]. Nephew and
Heir of COL[l]. MAYNARD COLCHESTER,
to whoſe Memory a Monument is here erected.
He was Grandſon of S[r]. DUNCOMB COLCHESTER,
and great Grandſon of that eminent Lawyer and Friend
to the Conſtitution and Liberties of England,
SERJEANT MAYNARD.
He retained thro' Life with his own Choice and Judgment
an hereditary Affection for the Laws, the Religion,
and civil Rights of Engliſhmen, as eſtabliſhed by the
Revolution. From this Principle he ever manifeſted a firm
Attachment to the illuſtrious Houſe of Hanover, and
the proteſtant Succeſſion, particularly during the Rebellion
in 1746: and approved himſelf by his Conduct at all Times
a vigilant, active, and prudent Magiſtrate, and a Friend
to Society.
In private Life he was a good Chriſtian, a kind Father, and
indulgent Maſter, was cautious and diſcerning in his
Choice of Friends, and ſteady and unchangable towards them
when choſen.
His whole Character did himſelf and Family Honour, and
needs not Praiſes, but deſerves Imitation.
Died May 25th 1756. Aged 53 Years.

At the top of this monument are the Colcheſters arms only.

Benefactions, from a Table in the Church.

John Young of Ley, gave by will 7*l.* a year, one moiety for a pariſh ſchool-maſter, the other for ſermons, for ever.

The church lands, let for 4*l.* 16*s.* yearly, are given by a perſon unknown, and are applied towards the repairs of the church.

Several tenements adjoining to the church-yard, and the church houſe, are given by perſons unknown, for the uſe of the poor of this pariſh.

The houſe, garden, and orchard, adjoining to the king's common pound, uſually let at 40*s.* a year, were given by a perſon unknown for the uſe of the pariſh for ever.

A tenement near the above, granted on leaſe formerly to Thomas Cook, and now occupied by Tobias Cowles, was left by a perſon unknown to this pariſh.

Cornelius Draper gave one piece of incloſed land in Huntley, now let to James Drinkwater at 40*s.* a year, to be given in bread to the poor.

Joſeph Bayſe gave the intereſt of 10*l.* (the principal now lying in the pariſh ſtock) to be given in bread to the poor of Elton tithing.

Joſeph Holſtead of Ley, gent. gave the intereſt of 20*l.* for the education of two boys at the ſchool.

John Mayn, of Staintway, gent. by will, gave ſeveral parcels of free-land in Walmore's hill, and one rudge and forehead of leaſe-land during the reſidue of his term, of the yearly value of 1*l.* 2*s.* 6*d.* to buy coal for the poor, in November yearly.

A chief-rent of 3*s.* 8*d.* on a tenement now belonging to John Sier, was given to the poor of this pariſh by a perſon unknown.

Mrs. Elizabeth Evans gave 20*l.* the intereſt to be given yearly for ever to the poor of this pariſh.

Taxes.			£.	s.	d.
	The Royal Aid in	1692,	436	12	0
	Poll-tax ——	1694,	106	11	6
	Land-tax ——	1694,	565	18	8
	The ſame, at 3*s.*	1770,	414	18	6

There were 290 houſes in this pariſh, and about 1200 inhabitants, at the beginning of the preſent century, whereof 100 were reputed freeholders; yearly births 34, and burials 32. *Atkyns.* But examining the pariſh regiſter, I find that in ten years, beginning with 1700, there were 451 baptiſms, and 308 burials; and in the ſame number of years, beginning with 1760, the baptiſms were 424, and the burials 340; and the inhabitants being numbered in the year 1765, were found to be 1275, and are ſince increaſed to above 1300.

WESTBURY *upon* TRIM.

THIS pariſh lies in the hundred of Henbury, two miles and a half diſtant northward from the city of Briſtol, thirteen ſouth-weſtward from Chipping Sodbury, and thirty-five ſouth-weſtward from Glouceſter.

The river Avon bounds it on the ſouth-weſt, and the great road from Wales, by the New and Old Paſſages, leads through it to the city of Briſtol. It

It has its name, ſays ſir Robert Atkyns, *from lying on the river Trim, and weſtward from the city of Briſtol.* But with due deference to that gentleman, the ſituation of the village, which is directly north from that city, will not juſtify his etymology. Indeed *Hueſberie*, ſeems to be the true name of the village, as it is found in *Domeſday:* And if it ſhould be contended that this was the way which the writer of that record expreſſed the ſound of W, the contrary will appear in an inſtance directly in point, where *Weſtberie* (thus written) ſtands for the name of a village in the foreſt of Dean. The former is compounded of *berie*, a camp, and *Hueſ*, (as I conjecture) from *Hue*, the name of ſome perſon who either occupied the fortifications, or poſſeſſed the lands about them. And that there was ſuch a camp I have not the leaſt doubt, tho' at preſent no traces of it ſhould remain.

In Mr. Wantner's papers, written about the year 1714, and now depoſited in the Bodleian library, it is ſaid, that at Pollbury in this pariſh, where the brook Trim falls into the Avon, 'much 'Roman coin hath been found'; and I am informed that great numbers of them, with pieces of Roman pottery, have been taken up at the ſame place ſince thoſe papers were written: And there are certain veſtiges of a Roman road leading from thence, acroſs Durdham down. Theſe circumſtances ſhew that the Romans had an encampment, or ſmall ſtation, there; but I don't pretend to ſay that it was from that camp, in particular, that the pariſh took its name.

Durdham down lies one part in this pariſh, the other in Clifton. It is a large tract of high and healthy ground, with a good turf for riding, and affords the fineſt opportunity for air and exerciſe to the citizens of Briſtol, and the inhabitants of this part of the country. Weſtbury lying in the vicinity of that opulent city, is ornamented with many gentlemen's houſes, of which the following are the principal:

Stoke Houſe is an exceeding good one, and inferior to few in the county for real comfort and utility. It was built by ſir Robert Cann, about the year 1669, as appears by an inſcription over the porch. It underwent a thorough repair by the late Mr. Jefferis; and Mr. Lippincott, the preſent owner, has ſince added conſiderably to the offices and gardens. It ſtands on a delightful eminence, with a charming view of the Severn and Avon, and of the ſhips as they turn Portſhead Point, and paſs up and down the river. The high road which ran very near the houſe, was turned to an eaſy diſtance, and a much pleaſanter and more open one made, Jan. 6, 1778, under the direction of the commiſſioners of turnpike, but at Mr. Lippincott's expence, by which he has the advantage of a fine lawn before his houſe, and the public are alſo greatly benefited by the alteration.

Sneed Park is another handſome ſeat in the tithing of Stoke Biſhop, under which head ſome deſcription is given of it, with a ſhort account of the family to which it belongs.

Redland Court is one of the moſt elegant houſes in this part of the country. The front is ornamented with Ionic pillaſters, and there is a flight of ſteps to the entrance. The gardens are kept in excellent order, and the green-houſe is ſtored with a well choſen variety of curious exotics. This ſeat ſtands on an eaſy elevation near the great road leading from the village of Weſtbury to Briſtol. It was built by the late Mr. Coffins, and is now the reſidence of John Innys, eſq. Not far from the houſe is a beautiful chapel, of which a further account will be given in the ſequel.

Weſtbury College claims the precedence of all in point of antiquity. Indeed there is but a ſmall part of the antient College remaining at preſent, which ſtood intire in the former part of the reign of king Charles the Firſt. It was turreted round, and had a large embattled tower on the ſouth ſide, but prince Rupert cauſed it to be ſet on fire in the time of the civil wars, and it was then in a great meaſure deſtroy'd, to prevent its being garriſoned by the parliament's forces, to annoy the city of Briſtol. That part which remains is incorporated with buildings erected ſince that time, and together conſtitute the ſeat of John Hobhouſe, eſq; who has, near adjoining to it, a new farm houſe and farm, remarkable for its neatneſs and elegance of culture. He gives for his arms, *Azure, three eſtoiles iſſuing out of as many creſcents Or.*

Pen Park is a delightful little villa, about a mile north of the church, with extenſive gardens and pleaſure-grounds, laid out in elegant taſte, from whence there is a proſpect of the country on the ſouth-eaſt ſide of the Severn, and of Kingroad, the mouth of that river. This little ſeat belongs to John Harmer, eſq; who gives for his arms, *Argent, on a chevron between three annulets gules, another of the field.*

Cote is a good houſe and eſtate on the north ſide of the road from the village of Weſtbury to Briſtol. It is turreted and embattled, and within the courſe of the laſt twenty years has been ſucceſſively the property of William Phelps, John Thomas, and John Webb, eſquires. By Mr. Phelps's demiſe it went to his widow, and paſſed afterwards by will to Mr. Thomas, who ſold it lately to captain Webb, the preſent owner, whoſe family arms are emblazoned p. 470.

John Fowler, eſq; a conſiderable merchant of Briſtol, has likewiſe a good houſe and eſtate at Cote, which he purchaſed of the creditors of the late Mr. Daniel Saunders, and has fitted up and ornamented the houſe in a genteel and modern taſte.

Mrs. Hort has alſo a good houſe, with a ſuitable eſtate, pleaſantly ſituated near Cote-houſe, upon the edge of Durdham-downs.

Cotham-houſe ſtands about a quarter of a mile from Redland Court. It is a genteel building, with

Fig. 1. An East and West Section of *PEN-PARK HOLE*.

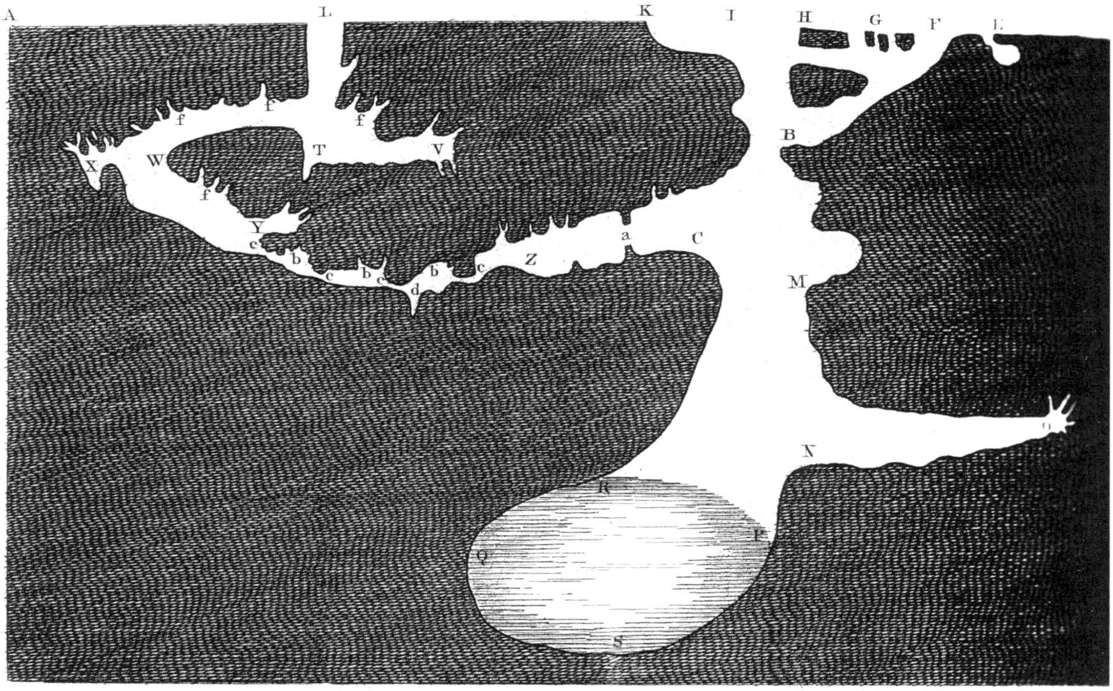

Fig. 2. A North and South Section of the Hole.

W. White delin.

with very handſome ſtables, &c. and there is a good eſtate belonging to it, of which Mr. Charles Partridge is owner. The Partridges family arms occur in the account of Miſerden.

Mr. Samuel Lloyd has a good houſe, very agreeably ſituated in the hamlet of Stoke Biſhop, with a garden laid out with great taſte and elegancy, and a conſiderable eſtate belonging to it, which has been for many years in the family.

The *Lodge* on Durdham down is a very pleaſant houſe, belonging to Thomas Jones, eſq; of the Park, Briſtol, who always makes it his ſummer reſidence.

Of the natural productions of this place the Cotham Stone (ſo called from the place where it is found) is the moſt curious and remarkable. It lies in a detached manner, within the ſurface of the ground. The upper ſide of it is full of nodules and bunches, and the prominences on ſome of theſe ſtones reſemble the interlacings of ivy, growing over each other, as it is ſometimes ſeen againſt old walls. The largeſt of them are about two feet and a half long, and ſeven or eight inches thick. They are uſed rough in the ruſtic work of gateways and other buildings, in which they have a good effect. Cut longitudinally through the thickneſs, and poliſhed, they exhibit a beautiful landſcape, like a drawing in Indian ink, and are often uſed in chimney-pieces. That part which in its native bed lies undermoſt, has the exact appearance of a river; beyond that there is a margin of trees and ſhrubs; next, another river; and a fertile fancy may very well imagine a high bank on the further ſide, covered with ſhrubs and hanging woods. The Cotham ſtones that I have ſeen have in them all the appearance of one or more rivers; but the other objects admit of variety in form and order in different ſtones. To give the reader a more perfect idea of this curious ſtone, there is a good engraving of it, by way of decoration to the map of the county, at the beginning of this work.

Lead ore and the Calamine ſtone are found in many parts of the pariſh, particularly in Pen-Park eſtate, but there is no mine of either worked at preſent.

There is a prodigious cavern in that eſtate, called Pen-Park Hole, about a mile and a half north-eaſt from the village of Weſtbury, and ſix miles eaſtward from the mouth of the Severn, with a vaſt depth of water in it at particular ſeaſons. Some account of this cavern has been publiſhed in the Philoſophical Tranſactions, but the moſt accurate ſurvey of it was taken in 1775, by Mr. White, an eminent land-ſurveyor of Briſtol, who deſcended into it ſeveral times, took the meaſure of its particular parts, and made drawings of two ſections of it, from which the annexed plate is engraven.

Fig. I. is the eaſt and weſt ſection.

A, L, K, I, H, G, F, E, D, repreſent the ſurface of the earth.

A, the eaſt end.

D, the weſt end.

E, a ſmall cave.

F, B, the weſtern paſſage, 13 yards long.

G, ſmall holes leading down to the ſame.

H, I, K, the great mouth of the cavern.

I, B, M, N, P, the paſſage down.

M, a ſhort cave to the weſt of the main funnel.

N, O, the lower weſtern cavity, 78 feet long.

P, Q, R, S, the ſurface of the water.

P, Q, the length of the water, 80 feet, but ſubject to vary.

R, S, the breadth of the water, 52 feet, alſo ſubject to variation.

L, T, the deſcent into the eaſtern funnel.

T, V, the firſt branch weſtward.

T, W, X, the extent eaſtward.

X, Y, Z, C, the lower branch weſtward.

a, a kind of door-way.

b, b, b, ſmall caves.

c, c, c, c, very ſtrait paſſages leading from one cave to another.

d, ſmall impaſſible chaſms running down in the rocks.

e, a pillar of ſtone.

f, f, f, f, ſmall funnels running upwards in the rocks.

N.B. There is another paſſage near X, that dips and runs a conſiderable way to the eaſtward, the mouth of which, not now diſcoverable, was ſtopt up a few years ago; and a perſon who was in it to ſearch for lead ore, before it was ſtopt up, ſays he was about half an hour going to the end and returning, making ſome obſervations as he went.

Fig. II. is the north and ſouth ſection.

A, I, the ſurface of the earth.

I, the great mouth of the hole.

a, a prop of ſtone.

C, the mouth of the eaſt branch.

R, the roof over the baſon.

T, V, the higheſt ſtate of the water, as appears from the mud left on the ſides, nearly 75 feet deep.

N, O, the height of the water, March 17, 1775, 66 feet.

P, Q, its height, 45 feet, the 25th of April following.

W, X, its loweſt ſtate, as found late in October 1777.

S, the bottom of the hole, 100 feet perpendicular from the roof.

I, b, the firſt deſcent, — —	40 feet.
b, c, the firſt perpendicular deſcent,	8
c, d, the ſecond deſcent, — --	12
d, e, the ſecond perpen. deſcent,	8
e, f, the third deſcent to the bay	50
f, h, irregular deſcent to the bottom,	97
I, a, b, c, d, e, f, h, the whole depth of the hole. — —	215 feet.

O, the mouth of the lower eaſt branch, near the ſame length and form of the weſt lower branch in Fig. I.

g, a maſſy rock, which appears to have fallen from the roof.

 This

This ſurvey had probably never been taken, but for the following melancholy accident: On Friday the 17th of March, 1775, the reverend Thomas Newman, one of the minor canons of Briſtol cathedral, in company with another gentleman, and two ladies (one his ſiſter, the other his intended wife) went to this place to examine the depth with a line; and approaching the mouth of the pit, laid hold, for the greater ſafety, of a twig that ſprung from the root of an aſh-tree, growing over the mouth of the cavern. But moſt unfortunately his foot ſlipt, the twig broke, and he fell to the bottom in ſight of his friends. Many perſons went down daily for a conſiderable time in ſearch of the body, and it was found thirty-nine days after the accident, floating in the water, with a large contuſion in the back part of the head, the eyes wide open, the face red as ſcarlet, and the body ſwelled nearly to double its natural ſize.

Mr. George Catcott, a gentleman of Briſtol, was one of the many whom curioſity prompted to view this remarkable cavern, and has written a very circumſtantial account of it, which was ſent me in manuſcript, by a gentleman, with his approbation. 'The roof,' ſays he, 'appears to 'be nearly of equal height in every part, and very 'much reſembles the cieling of a Gothic cathedral. 'The ſides are almoſt ſtreight, at leaſt as much 'as was then above water; and, *conſidering the 'whole to be intirely the work of nature, are remark-'ably regular.* The place is rendered ſtill more 'awful by the great reverberation that attends the 'voice when you ſpeak loud, and if thoroughly 'illuminated muſt have a very beautiful appear-'ance. When you view the place from hence, '[*i.e.* the bottom] objects of the moſt diſmal 'kind preſent themſelves from every quarter. 'The deep water almoſt directly under your feet, 'rendered ſtill more dreadful by the faint glim-'mering rays of light paſſing through the open-'ings of the chaſms above, and reflected from its 'ſurface; together with the black rugged rocks, 'horrid precipices, and deep caverns over head, 'brought to my remembrance the following lines 'of Milton:

'The diſmal ſituation, waſte and wild,
'A dungeon horrible on all ſides,
'No light, but rather darkneſs viſible,
'Serv'd only to diſcover ſights of woe,
'Regions of horror, doleful ſhades.'

The ſame ingenious gentleman gives the dimenſions of the ſeveral parts of the cavern; but the annexed plate, with the explanation, precludes the uſe of thoſe particulars, as a more perfect idea may be obtained from a drawing, than verbal deſcription is capable of giving. However, I acknowledge my obligations to Mr. Catcott for his papers, tho' I differ in opinion from him as to the origin of Pen-Park Hole.

By the paſſage diſtinguiſhed in Italicks, he declares it to be the work of nature; and ſpeaking of the eaſtern branch of the cavern, (Fig. I.) gives the following and only reaſon in ſupport of his opinion, *viz.* 'In the roofs of 'theſe caverns, and upper part of the ſides, are a 'great number of cavities in the ſolid rock, in 'form of inverted funnels, (ſee f, f, f, f, in 'the plate, Fig. I.) which as they widen in pro-'portion to their depth, prove they could not 'have been made by art, as ſome have abſurdly 'aſſerted; but by the retreat of the waters which 'flowed through them into the great abyſs be-'neath, at the time of the univerſal deluge, of 'which great and awful event they ſtill remain as 'ſo many undeniable proofs.'

I would by no means attempt to invalidate an argument in ſupport of Sacred Hiſtory; but it would be unfortunate if the truth of it reſpecting the deluge were to reſt on deductions to be made from Pen-Park Hole. If Mr. Catcott had obſerved that many places round about, in the ſame and the adjoining fields, appear to have been opened from the ſurface; and that along the field to the northward, the ground is much higher than in other parts, running into tumps like heaps of rubbiſh brought up out of a mine: If he had been informed of a tradition handed down in the family, that the great grandfather of the preſent owner received fifteen or ſixteen hundred pounds for his ſhare of ore raiſed there; and had known, from the information of the late Mrs. Anne Jefferis, that many places thereabout were worked by the company of Royal miners, he then would moſt likely have been of the general opinion of all competent judges of this matter, that it is no other than a large lead mine. Of that number is captain Hamilton, who has viſited all the principal mines in Europe, and deſcended into this no leſs than ſix times, where he generally continued for four or five hours together. As to the cavities which Mr. Catcott thinks could not have been made by art,—Are they not of the very ſhape commonly made by miners working over head? But that gentleman will have them formed by the retreat of the waters through them into the great abyſs; he ſhould, however, have ſhewn, that they now have, or at leaſt formerly had, a communication upwards through the rock to the ſurface; whereas no ſuch thing appears upon examination.

Upon the ſuppoſition of this being a Swallet hole, how can it be accounted for, that broken pipes of an old make, with very ſmall bowls, pieces of glaſs bottles, and fragments of old leather ſhoes, were found intermixt with ſome gravel and ſpar, brought up out of the eaſtern branch of it, about the year 1770, as I have been informed by Mr. Harmer, a gentleman of the ſtricteſt veracity? The workmen then offered to get out a thouſand tons of ſuch gravelly ſtuff, which had moſt probably been beat off from the ore, and was uniformly

formly thrown up on the ſides of the paſſages, ſo as to leave a clear carriage way. I would now aſk, Does not this look like mining? and can there remain a doubt that Pen-Park Hole is any thing but an old mine? Indeed Mr. Catcott himſelf ſeems to have been of the general opinion, when he wrote the beginning of his account, where deſcribing the part a, (Fig. II.) he ſays, *It is a prop or pillar of ſtone, which appears to be left with a deſign to keep the north part from falling down.* And it was undoubtedly left by the miners with that very deſign. I conjecture, however, from the antient make of the tobacco pipes found in the rubbiſh, that the hole was worked out in the early times of ſmoaking tobacco, and long before the Pen-Park lands were divided amongſt different proprietors, as they now are, which was done in the year 1650.

The only manufacture carried on in this pariſh is a pottery of coarſe, red ware; and it ſeems to be chiefly employ'd in making pans for the ſugar bakers in Briſtol.

Of the College of Weſtbury.

There was an antient monaſtery in this place, but of whoſe foundation is uncertain; and long before the conqueſt, the eſtates with which it had been endowed were appropriated to the church of Worceſter; for in thoſe days the biſhops had the cuſtody of all monaſteries in their dioceſes, and could appropriate their revenues to the colleges of their own cathedrals.

Oſwald was advanced to the ſee of Worceſter about the year 960. He reformed the monaſteries within his dioceſe, expelling the ſecular clergy, and placing monks in their ſtead, and the little monaſtery here partook of the general reform. The biſhop, with the aſſiſtance of king Edgar, was a good benefactor to the college, of which the monks were a new order of inhabitants, and therefore Oſwald was looked upon by ſome to be the founder. But as all human inſtitutions are ſubject to change, ſo this college experienced another alteration in the following century.

Sampſon, a Norman, was made biſhop of Worceſter in 1096. He annulled Oſwald's conſtitution, expelled the monks out of this college, and filled their places with ſecular canons; which gave no ſmall offence to the whole monaſtic order. He died at Weſtbury on the 5th of May, 1112; and the ſeculars kept poſſeſſion of the college during the time of Theulf his ſucceſſor.

In the year 1125, Simon ſucceeded to the ſee of Worceſter, in whoſe time the ſecular clerks ſaw a reverſe of fortune, for he diſplaced them from Weſtbury, and put monks in the poſſeſſion of the college, who maintained their ground there 'till the general diſſolution of monaſteries. Many of theſe particulars are related in the Survey of Worceſter Cathedral.

King Edward the Third gave the hoſpital of St. Lawrence, near Briſtol, towards the maintenance of the monks of this college. And Richard duke of York, and his third ſon Edmond earl of Rutland, were ſo great benefactors, that ſir Robert Atkyns affirms the college was founded by them, at which time it conſiſted of a dean and five canons; but in the particular of its foundation ſir Robert was certainly miſtaken.

King Edward the Fourth gave the manor of Aylminſter, (now Elmſtree) in the pariſh of Tetbury, to the monks of this college, when Henry Sampſon was dean, and a tranſlation of the royal grant is printed in the Appendix to this work, N°. 25.

William Canning, a rich merchant of Briſtol, after he had been five times mayor of that city, retired from buſineſs, and went into prieſt's orders, and ſeven years afterwards was made dean of this college, which, with the aſſiſtance of Dr. Carpenter, he new built, and was a great benefactor to it. He was a man of great generoſity and public ſpirit, and built an almſhouſe in Weſtbury, for poor men and poor women, and directed that the mayor of Briſtol ſhould have the placing in of one of the poor men, and the mayoreſs the appointment of one of the poor women. He alſo ſettled lands for the payment of 44 *l.* a year to the ſheriffs, in lieu of toll demanded by them at the gates of the city, for proviſion brought thither. He built the large and beautiful church of Redcliff in Somerſetſhire, adjoining to the city, where he lies buried in the ſouth aile, in his prieſt's robes, cut in white marble. He died in 1474.

Two thirds of the tithes of Biſley and Stroud were appropriated towards the maintenance of two prebendaries in this college; and a licence was obtained to erect the prebend of Auſt 49 E. 3. The college alſo obtained a licence to purchaſe lands of the yearly value of 10 *l.* for the maintenance of Richard Fulcher's chantry in their church, 35 H. 6.

At the general diſſolution of monaſteries, the yearly revenues of this houſe were valued at 232 *l.* 14 *s.*

The dimenſions of the college, in the reign of king Henry the Sixth, are given by William of Worceſter, as follows: *Collegium de Weſtberye continet in longitudine* 47 *virgas, latitudo ejus continet* 5 [25] *virgas. Eccleſia Collegij Dioconatus de Weſtbery continet in longitudine* 42 *virgas, vel* 60 *graſſus. Latitudo ejus continet* 24 *virgas, vel* 25. In Engliſh: The college of Weſtbury is 47 yards long, and 5 [ſuppoſed 25] broad. The college church 42 yards or 60 ſteps long, and 24 or 25 yards broad.

I have already given the ſtate of the building in the reign of king Charles the Firſt, from ſir Robert Atkyns, and its preſent ſtate from my own knowledge.

Of the Manor and other Eſtates.

It has been already obſerved, that in early ages the biſhops could appropriate the revenues of religious houſes to the colleges of their own cathedrals, and, with reſpect to Weſtbury college, that was actually done by the biſhop of Worceſter. Before the Norman conqueſt, the biſhop's reeve, or bailiff, received the profits of all ſuch eſtates, allowing to the monaſtery for ſuſtenance and clothing what the biſhop thought neceſſary. So that in fact there was little or no diſtinction between the proper lands of the biſhoprick, and thoſe antiently given to the uſe of ſuch impropriated monaſteries. This accounts for the manor of Hueſberie ſtanding in *Domeſday* under the title *Terra Eccle' de Wireceſtre*, as in the following extract from that record:

'The land of the church of Wireceſtre in 'Bernintreu hundred.

'Saint Mary of Wireceſtre held and ſtill holds 'Hueſberie. There were and are fifty hides. In 'demean are two plow-tillages, and eight villeins, 'and ſix bordars, with eight plow-tillages. There 'are four *ſervi*, and one *ancilla*. Theſe members, Henberie, Redeuuiche, Stoche, Giete, be'long to this manor. In theſe are nine plow'tillages in demean, and twenty-ſeven villeins, 'and twenty-two bordars, with twenty-ſix plow'tillages. There are twenty *ſervi*, and two '*ancillæ*, and twenty *coliberti*, with ten plow'tillages, and a mill of 20 *den*.

'Six radcheniſters belong to this manor, 'having eight hides, and eight plow-tillages, and 'they could not be ſeparated from the manor. 'And there are two houſes in Briſtou paying '16 *den*.

'Of the lands of this manor Turſtin the ſon of 'Rolph holds five hides in Auſtreclive, and 'Giſlebert the ſon of Turold three hides and a 'half in Contone, and Conſtantine five hides in 'Icetune. In theſe lands are five plow-tillages 'in demean, and ſixteen villeins, and twelve 'bordars, with twelve plow-tillages, and there 'are eleven *ſervi*.

'Oſbern Giffard holds five hides of the ſame 'land of this manor, and does no ſervice.

'All the manor, with its members, was worth '24 *lib*. in the time of king Edward, and now the 'demeans of St. Mary are worth 29 *lib*. 14 *ſol*. 6 *den*. 'That which the men hold is worth 9 *lib*.' *Domeſday*, p. 70.

This large manor continued a part of the poſſeſſions of the college of Weſtbury, under the church of Worceſter, 'till the general diſſolution of monaſteries. Weſtbury college was ſurrendered to king Henry the Eighth by John Barlow, dean thereof, on the 18th of February, in the 35th year of that king's reign. The king, by his letters patent, granted the ſame, with all manors, &c. thereunto belonging, to ſir Rafe Sadleir and his heirs for ever, 35 H. 8.

Sir Thomas Sadleir, or Sadler, knight, was ſon of ſir Rafe, and proprietor of the hundred of Henbury, and manors of Henbury, Weſtbury, and Stoke Biſhop, 32 Eliz. Sir Thomas left a ſon, Rafe Sadler, eſq; and a daughter Gertrude. Rafe Sadler leaving no iſſue, Gertrude, his ſiſter, who was wife to ſir Walter Aſton, of Tixal in Staffordſhire, became his heir. Walter lord Aſton, (ſon and heir of the ſame ſir Walter and Gertrude his wife) with lady Mary, wife to Walter lord Aſton, and Walter Aſton, eſq; their ſon and heir apparent, ſold the manor of Weſtbury Bryan, *alias* Weſtbury upon Trym, lately belonging to the college of Weſtbury, in the county of Glouceſter, to Thomas Yate and Gregory Gearing, eſquires, May 20, 1675.

Sir Samuel Aſtry, of Henbury, knight, purchaſed the ſame, July 2, 1680, of Thomas Yate, of Gray's Inn in the county of Middleſex, and Gregory Gearing, of Denchurch in the county of Berks, eſquires. Sir Samuel Aſtry left three daughters coheireſſes; Elizabeth, married to ſir John Smyth, baronet; Diana, the wife of Richard Orlebar, eſq; and Arabella, the lady of Charles-William earl of Suffolk, whom ſhe ſurvived; and dying without iſſue, ſhe left her third part to ſir John Smyth, baronet; whoſe ſon, ſir John Smyth, ſold a moiety of that third to the heirs of Edward Colſton, eſq; who had purchaſed the third part late Mr. Orlebar's. A moiety of the manor was then in ſir John Smyth, whoſe three ſiſters and coheireſſes ſold it to ſir Jarrit Smith, baronet, who married Florence, one of the ſaid coheireſſes. The other moiety deſcended to the two daughters and coheirs of Thomas Edwards, eſq; one of whom was married to Francis lord Middleton; the other wedded to Alexander Ready, eſq; who afterwards took the name of Colſton, and died in the year 1775. So that ſir Jarrit Smith, baronet, is the preſent owner of one moiety of this manor, and the honourable Thomas Willoughby, ſecond ſon of the late lord Middleton, and Alexander Colſton, eſq; at the time of his death, were proprietors of the other moiety.

This account is abſtracted from the original deeds, in the poſſeſſion of ſir Jarrit Smith.

The ſcite of the college belonged to Mr. Vigaur when ſir Robert Atkyns compiled his account of it, but it is now the property of John Hobhouſe, eſq; as already taken notice of in the account of the gentlemen's ſeats in this pariſh.

John Newton, ſon and heir of John, late merchant in Briſtol, levied a fine of lands in Weſtbury to the uſe of William More, 28 H. 6.

TITHINGS and *HAMLETS*.

1. *Stoke Biſhop* is a very conſiderable tithing. It was called Stoke Biſhop, or Biſhop's Stoke, becauſe it belonged to the biſhop of Conſtance in Normandy; and to diſtinguiſh it from Stoke Giffard in this neighbourhood. The particulars of the manor are thus recorded in *Domeſday*:

'The biſhop of St. Laud holds Eſtoch in 'Bacheſtanes hundred, and Tetbald holds it of 'him. Eldred held it of earl Herald, and could 'go where he pleaſed. There are two hides, one 'taxed,

'taxed, the other not. In demean is one plow-'tillage, and two villeins, and one bordar, with 'one plow-tillage. There are six *servi*, and five 'acres of meadow. It was worth 40*sol.* now '20*sol.*' *Domesday*, p. 70.

The manor of Stoke Bishop was afterwards vested in the bishops of Worcester, and held by them in succession, 'till it was alienated to the crown, by doctor Heath, 1 E. 6. and that king granted it the same year, among other particulars, late parcel of the possessions of the bishop of Worcester, to sir Rafe Sadler, and his heirs. Sir Thomas Sadler, knight, was lord of the manor of Stoke Bishop 32 Eliz. from whom it descended, like Henbury and Westbury, down to the present time, and with them is now vested in the same proprietors.

There is a handsome seat, and a large estate in this tithing, formerly belonging to the Canns. William Cann, of Compton, alderman of Bristol, married Margaret, sister to sir Robert Yeomans. Robert Cann, son and heir of William and Margaret, married to his first wife, Cicely, daughter of Humphry Hooke, alderman of Bristol. By her he had William, his son and heir, who married Elizabeth, daughter of sir Thomas Langton, of Bristol, knight. Their son and heir, William, married Elizabeth, daughter of Thomas Chester, of Knole, and by her had one daughter and heiress, Elizabeth, wedded to Thomas Master, of the Abbey at Cirencester, esq; which Elizabeth is mother to the present Thomas Master, of the same place, who married Mary, daughter of James-Lenox-Napier Dutton, esq; and by her has issue several children.

The before-mentioned Robert Cann was knighted by king Charles the Second, Apr. 22, 1662, and created a baronet on the thirteenth of September following. He married, to his second wife, Anne, daughter of sir Derrick Popley, by whom he had a son, Thomas, knighted by king James the Second, Apr. 18, 1686; in favour of whom he made a will, to the disinherison of his son William, which caused very long and expensive law-suits between the two branches of the family; when, after several hearings in chancery, and a bill of Revivor brought by the last sir William Cann, bar^t. the will was fully established. Sir Robert Cann served the office of high sheriff in the year 1676.

Sir Thomas Cann, knight, son of sir Robert, left issue two sons, Robert and William, of whom the latter was town-clerk of Bristol; and three daughters, Anne, married to Nicholas Jackson, of Sneed Park; Catherine, married to John Fog, alderman of Bristol; and Mary, who died unmarried. He served the office of high sheriff in the year 1686, and dying, was succeeded in estate by his eldest son

Robert Cann, who also, on the death of his cousin sir William Cann, Apr. 27, 1726, succeeded to the title of baronet. He served the office of high sheriff in 1726, and died a batchelor in 1748.

William Cann, town-clerk of Bristol, was brother to the last sir Robert Cann, whom he succeeded in honour and estate, and died in the year 1753.

Sir Robert Cann, son and heir of the last sir William, succeeded his father, and died without issue, July 20, 1765. His only sister, Catherine, had been married to Mr. Charles Jeffries, of Bristol, by whom she had issue one son, Robert-Cann Jeffries; and one daughter, Catherine.

Robert-Cann Jeffries was heir to his uncle sir Robert Cann, but dying a batchelor, May 16, 1773, the whole of his fortune descended on his sister Catherine, who, Feb. 10, 1774, was married to Henry Lippincott, esq; the present owner, in right of his wife, of the Canns seat and estate at Stoke Bishop, and lord of the manors of Compton, Olveston, and Elberton; and, by a late purchase, of Littleton upon Severn. He has likewise several good estates in other counties, and in the city of Bristol. They have issue one son, Henry-Cann Lippincott, born June 5, 1776. Mr. Lippincott is of an antient family in the county of Devon, and has twice served the office of sheriff for the city of Bristol, *viz.* in 1768, and 1771; and once for the county of Gloucester, in 1776, when there was an election of a knight of the shire, which was strenuously contested between the honourable George-Cranfield Berkeley, brother to the earl of Berkeley, and William-Bromley Chester, esq. The poll lasted thirteen days; but the business was afterwards carried, by petition, into the House of Commons, when Mr. Lippincott's conduct appeared so unexceptionable to the committee, that they unanimously came to the following resolution, *viz.* 'The committee, in justice to 'the high sheriff of the county of Gloucester, 'declare, that they have seen no reason, by any 'evidence adduced to them, to impeach his con-'duct with partiality, in the discharge of his duty 'in taking the poll.' Mr. Lippincott gives for his arms, *Quarterly*, 1st *and* 4th, *Per fess crenelle gules and sable, three mountain cats argent*, for Lippincott; 2d *and* 3d, *Sable, a chevron argent between three mermaids proper*, for Wyvely. Marrying an heiress, he bears a scutcheon of pretence, *Quarterly* 1st *and* 4th, *Azure, a fret Or, on a chief argent a lion passant gules*, for Jeffries; 2d *and* 3d, *Azure, fretty argent, on a fess gules three leopards faces Or*, for Cann.

Sneed Park lies in the tithing of Stoke Bishop, and was formerly a park belonging to the church of Worcester, but has been long since turned into farms, and is remarkable as well for the natural inequality and beautiful variety of the ground, as for the striking views it affords; particularly of the pendent rocks and woods on each side the Avon, which bounds it on the south and south-east. After the dissolution of monasteries, it became part of the very large estate of sir Rafe Sadler, of whose son it was purchased by Joseph Jackson,

Jackſon, an anceſtor to the preſent owner. He was fifth ſon of Nicholas Jackſon, by —— daughter of ſir Edward Stradling, knight. He married Mary, daughter of —— Hele, of Devonſhire, eſq; and built Sneed Park houſe, as appears by his arms on the maſonry over the entrance, impaling thoſe of Hele, *viz. A bend lozengy ermine.*

Joſeph Jackſon, only ſon and heir of the laſt Joſeph, married Catherine, daughter of Thomas Skinner, of Dewliſh in the county of Dorſet, eſq.

Nicholas Jackſon, eldeſt ſon and heir of the ſaid Joſeph and Catherine, married Anne, eldeſt daughter of ſir Thomas Cann, of Stoke Biſhop, by whom he had iſſue two ſons, Robert, and Nicholas; and two daughters, Catherine-Anne, and Mary; all living, except Catherine-Anne, who died in 1752.

Robert Jackſon, eſq; ſon and heir of Nicholas, is the preſent owner of Sneed Park, where he has a good eſtate, beſides others in the neighbourhood, and in the city of Briſtol. He bears *Or, on a chevron ſable, between three eagles heads erazed azure, as many cinquefoils of the firſt.* This family is originally from the county of York, and has been ſeated at Sneed Park about one hundred and thirty years. There is another branch of it, long ſince ſettled at Pentroilas in Herefordſhire, and is now in two heireſſes, the one married to Henry Shiffner, of the ſame place, eſq; and the other to Jonathan-Morton Pleydell, of the county of Dorſet, eſq.

Sneed Park houſe, tho' ſeated on an agreeable eminence, is ſheltered by hills on every ſide. It had ſuffered much by age, but was ſaſhed, and thoroughly repaired a few years ago, and is now a chearful and comfortable habitation. The terrace commands the river Avon, and the whole navigation of the city of Briſtol, at leſs than a quarter of a mile below it; and in full view, at the diſtance of two or three miles, on the oppoſite ſide of the river, ſtands the fine old houſe of Mrs. Gordon, one of thoſe places where king Charles the Second lay concealed, after the battle of Worceſter, as fully related by lord Clarendon; but it was then the property of Mr. Norton, and formerly a country houſe belonging to St. Auguſtin's priory in Briſtol. The ground, on every other ſide of Sneed Park houſe, falls, with an eaſy deſcent, to a little rill which feeds ſome fiſh-ponds, beyond which it riſes gradually again, and terminates the view not far from the edge of Durdham down; where, upon a delicious ſituation within the park walls, and near the point of Saint Vincent's rocks, ſtands an octagon tower, which forms a pretty object to the houſe, and to all the country thereabout. It commands a birds-eye view of the rocks, and of both ſides of the river Avon, as well as of the Severn, ſhut in by the mountains of Wales; and conſiſts of three good rooms, with an obſervatory at top. It was built two or three hundred years ago, as ſuppoſed, by one Cook, from whom it vulgarly obtained the name of *Cook's Folly.* The rooms are fitted up, and the tower is made uſe of as a Belvidere to Sneed Park houſe.

Say-Mills is an eſtate in this tithing, where, at the confluence of the Trim with the Avon, large docks for the preſervation of ſhipping were made ſeventy or eighty years ago. Rowles Scudamore, eſq; ſteward of the ſheriff's court in the city of Briſtol, is leſſee, under lord Clifford, of a good eſtate at Say-Mills, where he has a pretty villa. He is likewiſe the largeſt proprietor of the docks there. Theſe premiſſes are held by leaſe of a thouſand years, unimpeachable of waſte, from Edward Southwell, eſq; great grandfather to the preſent lord Clifford, at the rent of 81 *l. per ann.* The docks were planned and executed by Mr. Joſhua Franklyn, a wealthy citizen of Briſtol, who divided the ſame into thirty-two ſhares, moſt of which were purchaſed by his friends, and ſtood them in upwards of 300 *l.* a piece. Mr. Franklyn ſunk the greateſt part of his fortune in this undertaking, and the ſhares at preſent bear only an ideal value, ſome of them having been ſold at 10 *l.* a piece, and the docks have been utterly abandoned for ſeveral years.

Redland is a hamlet in the tithing of Stoke Biſhop. Redland formerly belonged to the abbey of Tewkeſbury, and the privilege of a court leet, waifs, and felons goods therein, was allowed to that abbey in a writ of *Quo warranto* brought againſt them 15 E. 1. Thomas Janitor, by his deed, reſtored to the church of Tewkeſbury, and to St. James of Briſtol, the land which Maud his wife gave to God and the church of St. James. He likewiſe gave to the ſame church of St. James, beſide other particulars, land worth 12 *s.* in Redland [*rubea terra*] to be held as freely as Robert earl of Glouceſter, his lord, gave it to him, and earl William, ſon of Robert, confirmed it. After the diſſolution of that abbey, it came to the Wilſons. Egion Wilſon and Dorothy his wife, and Miles Wilſon, joined in levying a fine of the manor of Rydland, *alias* Th' Ridland, to John Foxton 6 E. 6. John Innys, eſq; has an elegant houſe in this hamlet, built by the late Mr. Coſſins.

Thomas-Edwards Freeman, of Batsford in this county, eſq; has a good eſtate here.

This hamlet lying at a conſiderable diſtance from the church, the before-mentioned Mr. Coſſins, in the year 1740, built a chapel for the convenience of the inhabitants, upon an eminence not far diſtant from his houſe; and endowed it with lands, &c. which *communibus annis*, are worth about 130 *l.* a year. He alſo ſoon afterwards built a houſe for the miniſter, at the expence of 1000 *l.*

The chapel is of freeſtone. The entrance is at the weſt end, over which there is a pediment of the whole extent, ſupported by four Ionic pillaſters. It has one bell, which hangs under a handſome rotundo.

The

The floor and the ſteps to the altar are of black and white marble. The altar-piece is half an octagon, wainſcotted in compartments, and highly finiſhed with carvings of trophies and feſtoons, and ornamented with an excellent painting of the Embalming of Chriſt. The marble communion table is ſupported by a gilt eagle, and a little before it, upon pedeſtals, ſtand two other eagles, highly gilt, for placing books upon. The cieling is finiſhed in the beſt taſte, and it may be truly ſaid, that this chapel is one of the moſt elegant buildings of its kind.

In a ſmall veſtry room on the right of the entrance, there is a handſome monument, with the following memorials and family arms :

In the Vault under the Communion Table are depoſited the Remains of

Mrs. ANNE INNYS,	NICHOLAS MARISSAL	Mrs. MARY MARISSAL	IOHN COSSINS	Mrs. MARTHA COSSINS
Siſter to Mrs. COSSINS, who died 5th Decemb. 1747, Aged 69.	of Edmonton Eſq; who died 29th Auguſt, 1739, (brought from Chriſt Church in Middleſex in Decemb. 1747) Aged 52.	his Wife, Siſter to Mr. COSSINS, who died Septemb. 9, 1757, Aged 66.	of REDLAND COURT, Eſq; Founder of this Chapel, who died 19th April, 1759, Aged 77.	his Wife, Daughter of ANDREW INNYS of BRISTOL, Gent.
Beneath in a lozenge, *Quarterly* 1ſt *and* 4th, *Argent three eſtoiles azure*, for Innys. 2d, *Gules, three boars heads couped Or*, for Abercherder. 3d, *Or, three bars undy gules*, for Lovel.	Baron and femme, 1ſt, *Azure, a chevron between three cups Or*, for Mariſſal. 2d, *Quarterly* 1ſt *and* 4th, *Azure, a lion rampant Or, gutty du ſang*, for Coſſins. 2d *and* 3d, *Argent, on a bend ſable three owls of the field*, for Saville.	In a lozenge, the ſame coats, and alike diſpoſed as in the preceding column.	Baron and femme, 1ſt, Coſſins and Saville quarterly, impaling 2d, *Quarterly* 1ſt *and* 4th, Innys. 2d, Abercherder. 3d, Lovel, as in the firſt column.	In a lozenge, the ſame arms, and alike diſpoſed, as in the preceding column.

On one ſide the entrance, within, is the buſt of Mr. Coſſins, the founder, well executed in marble by Ryſbrack ; and on the other ſide, that of Mrs. Coſſins, his wife.

2. *Shirehampton*, is another large tithing, ſouthweſtward of the church, in the precincts of which are Kingroad, and Hungroad, two eminent ſtations for ſhips. This tithing is intirely detached from the reſt of the pariſh. It occurs by the name of Chire in *Domeſday*, and was a member of the large manor of Weſtbury, in the foreſt of Dean, as appears by the extract from that record.

Thomas Mallet, eſq; had livery of the manor of Shirehampton granted to him 9 Eliz. He died in the 22d year of the ſame reign, and left John his ſon and heir twelve years old. Henry Lewis, eſq; was ſeized of it, from whom it deſcended to George Lewis, ſon of Henry, who died poſſeſſed of it 10 Car. and left William his ſon ſeven years old.

There is a chapel in this tithing, where divine ſervice is celebrated once a fortnight.

South Mead is a manor within the pariſh of Weſtbury, formerly belonging to the nunnery of St. Mary Magdalen in Briſtol. The prioreſs granted a long leaſe of this manor to Thomas Haines, eſq; who obtained a reverſion in fee from king Henry the Eighth. The manor of Southmead in Weſtbury, lately belonging to the Magdalen nunnery in Briſtol, was granted to Richard Andrews and Thomas Hyſley, in truſt, 36 H. 8. Richard Haines died ſeized of Southmead 20 Eliz. and livery was granted to Thomas Haines, ſon of Richard. The heir of this family ſold it to Mr. Barker, anceſtor to the late Mr. Barker of Fairford, of whom it was purchaſed by Mr. Knight, and having ſince paſſed thro' ſeveral hands, has been lately ſold to Mr. Joſhua James, a diſtiller of Briſtol, who is the preſent lord of the manor of Southmead, and has made very conſiderable improvements on the manſion houſe and eſtate.

Of the Church, &c.

The church is in the deanery of Briſtol. It is an impropriation worth 10*l*. a year to the curate, before it was augmented, in the year 1719, by the queen's bounty, and the joint donations of Edward Colſton and Thomas Edwards, eſquires. The honourable Mr. Henry Fane is the impropriator and patron ; and the reverend Mr. Ray is the preſent incumbent.

The church is large and handſome, and dedicated to the Holy Trinity. It conſiſts of the nave, and two ailes, with a large chancel, and has a very handſome pinnacled tower at the weſt end. In the north window of the chancel are painted in the glaſs the figures of St. Auguſtine, St. Gregory, and St. Ambroſe, with their names ; and in the windows of the north aile are the arms of ſome of thoſe perſons who contributed to the building of it.

Monuments and Inſcriptions.

At the ſouth-weſt corner of the chancel, upon an altar tomb, lies the figure of a naked man, ill executed in ſtone, without arms or inſcription ; but it is ſaid to be intended for doctor Carpenter, biſhop of Worceſter.

Under an arch in the north aile is the figure of a man in armour, and this memorial :

HERE VNDER LIETH INTERRED THE BODIE OF S[r] RICHARD HILL, OF REDLAND COVRTE IN THIS PARISH, KNIGHT, WHO DECEASED THE 29th DAY OF MAY IN Y[e] YEARE OF OVR LORD GOD 1627, AGED 70 YEARES.

Over the monument are theſe arms : *Quarterly*, 1ſt, *Gules, a ſaltire vaire between four mullets argent.* 2d, *Gules, a lion rampant Or debruiſed of a bend ermine.* 3d, *Sable, a bend Or between ſix roundlets azure.* 4th as the 1ſt.

In the chancel, upon a handſome marble monument, it is thus written :

Near this Place lyeth the Body of Giles Hungerford, Son and Heir of Giles Hungerford, late of Willow in the County of Somerſet, Eſq[r]; deſcended from the Hon[ble] Houſe of the Hungerfords of Farley Caſtle in the ſaid County. He married Martha, eldeſt Daughter of Iohn Iacob of Norton in the County of Wilts, Eſq; by whom he had Iſſue only this Son, who died the twenty-third Day of Auguſt, in the One and twentieth Year of his Age, *Anno Domini* 1689.

Under the inſcription are theſe arms, *Sable, two bars argent, in chief three plates.*

On

On the table of another handfome monument:

Juxta tumulatur Corpus Jacob Knight de Southmead Armigeri, filij Johannis Knight Militis, Vico de Temple Civitate Briftol, olim habitantis.

Uxorem duxit Annam Dowdefwell filiam Caroli Dowdefwell, Armigeri, de Forthampton Court Gouc. Filios reliquit quatuor Johannem, Thomam, Jacob, & Carolum.

In Piam Memoriam Patris-Patriæ digniffimi, erga Parentes piiffimi, Mariti amantiffimi, Filiifq: indulgentiffimi, Hoc erigi juffit Monumentum Vidua Superftes. Obijt pridie Idus Julij, MDCCXX. Ætat. XXXVI.

Jacob tertius filius fupradict. Jacob Knight obiit 28 Nov. 1726, Ætat. 9.

Upon the monument are thefe arms: Baron and femme, 1ft, *Argent, three roundlets gules, on a chief of the fecond a buckle Or.* 2d, Dowdefwell, as under Forthampton.

There is alfo a memorial for Anne Knight, wife of the above Jacob, who died in 1736, aged 47.

On the table of a pyramidal monument:

Near this Place lies the Body of JOHN HENLEY, late of the Red Lodge in the City of Briftol, Efq; defcended from an antient Family in the County of Somerfet. He married Mary the eldeft Daughter of HENRY FANE, Son of Sir FRANCIS FANE, Knight of the Bath. He was an effectionate Friend, a charitable Benefactor to the Poor, and was greatly efteemed and regarded by all his Acquaintance. He departed this Life the 31ft Day of December, 1702, in the 59th Year of his Age.

The arms on this monument are, Baron and femme, 1ft, *Azure, a lion rampant argent, within a bordure of the fecond femee of roundlets gules*, for Henley. 2d, *Azure, three gauntlets Or*, for Fane.

Upon a flat ftone,

Here lie the Remains of Samuel Crefwick D. D. late Dean of the Cathedral Church of Wells, who departed this Life Jan. 14th 1766, aged 72 Years.

Upon another flat ftone,

Hic
repofitum quicquid mortale,
reverendi admodum viri,
GULIELMI STONE,
nuper hujus Ecclefiæ, necnon Comptoniæ,
Paftoris digniffimi.
Vir,
integerrimæ vitæ.
Eruditionis, in omni genere, fingularis.
Pietate fecundum Deum, maxime confpicuus.
diffufa in homines Benevolentia et Charitate,
non minus infignis.
Gravitate, mira quadam Comitate condita,
fpectabilis.
cæteris ad facram *Functionem* cunctis
Virtutibus ornatus.
Qui,
Poftquam Evangelium fumma, tum Conftantia,
tum Diligentia, quadraginta et fex circiter annos,
fideliffime predicâffet,
Mortem obijt,
4to Febii Anno { Salutis noftræ } MDCCXXIII
{ Ætatis fuæ } LXXIII.

On the table of a handfome pyramidal monument in the fouth aile,

Near this Place lyes interred
The Body of WILLIAM JEFFERIS, of Pen-Park in this Parifh, (Efqr.
whofe Induftry and Integrity in Mercantile Affairs
procured him an ample Reward.
Having gone through the Offices of *Magiftracy*
in the City of BRISTOL with great Reputation,
he died the 17th Day of April, 1752, in the 61st Year of his Age.
Alfo
ANN, fole Daughter and Heirefs of the above WILLIAM JEFFERIS,
born the 21st of Auguft, 1723, married the 30th of March 1752,
to JOHN HARMER then of the City of Briftol, *Merchant*,
and died the 9th of July, 1765.
The Sincerity of her Heart in all the Actions of her Life,
illuminated by the Practice of every commendable Virtue,
defervedly procured her
the Affection and Efteem of Relations, Friends, and Acquaintance;
and the folid Hope
of a more glorious Reward in a Life of Immortality.

Over the table are thefe arms: *Sable, a lion rampant between three fcaling ladders argent*, for Jefferis. Beneath, *Argent, on a chevron between three annulets gules another of the field.* On a fcutcheon of pretence, Jefferis, as before.

Upon a neat marble monument in the fame aile, it is thus written:

Near this Monument lies interred the Body of James Pipon of London, Merchant, who departed this Life at the Hot Wells, Briftol, the 12th of June, 1759, aged 48 Years. He was the 5th Son of Jofhua Pipon, Efq; Lieutenant Bailly, chief Magiftrate of the Ifland of Jerfey.

In a fcutcheon upon the pyramid are thefe arms, *viz. Party per chevron, azure and Or, in chief between two eftoiles of fix points a crefcent argent.*

There is alfo an elegant monument in the fame aile, with the following memorial on the vafe:

Near this Place are interred the Bodies of WILLIAM PHELPS, Efq; and MARY his Widow and Relict, both late of *Cote*, in this Parifh: He died the tenth Day of Auguft 1763, aged 43 Years. She died the firft Day of January, 1764, aged 53 Years.

This Monument is erected to their Memories in Purfuance of the Directions of the faid MARY, in a Codicil to her Will.

The monument is ornamented with a fcutcheon of two coats, Baron and femme, 1ft. *Argent, a lion rampant fable between fix crofs croflets fitchy gules*, for Phelps. 2d, *Or, a fefs between three griphons heads erazed fable.*

Befide thefe mentioned in the infcriptions, there are feveral other eminent perfons buried in the chancel, for whom there is no memorial, *viz.* Thomas earl of Weftmoreland, who died about feven years ago; and Henry Fane, of Wormefley in Oxfordfhire, efq; his brother: John earl of Weftmoreland, (fon to the above Thomas) and lady Burghurft, his wife: Mrs. Mary Crefwick, relict of doctor Samuel Crefwick, dean of Wells, and fifter to Thomas earl of Weftmoreland: And lady Anne Fane, eldeft daughter to the faid earl.

Benefactions.

Ralph Sadler, efq; formerly lord of the manor, gave two large houfes by the church-yard to the ufe of the poor. Mr. Robert Ardern gave two houfes without Laford's gate, worth 12*l.* a year, to the ufe of the poor. Mrs. Katherine Rutland gave 50*l.* the intereft whereof to be paid to the minifter for fix annual fermons. *Atkyns.*

The following particulars are hung up in a written table in the veftry room, *viz.* Robert Ardern gave the ground on which Robotham's houfe now ftands. William Afhley, the intereft of 10*l.* and Honor Bodman, the intereft of 50*l.* both to Shirehampton. Humphry Brown, 10*s.* for a fermon, and 40*s.* for bread, to Weftbury and Stoke only. William Burgis, fix fcore facks of coal to fix houfekeepers of Weftbury tithing only. Lady Cann, the intereft of 20*l.* Doctor William Cooke, fixty twopenny loaves on New-years day. Edward Colfton, efq; 100*l.* towards augmenting the living. Thomas Elbridge, the intereft of 100*l.* *viz.* 20*s.* for a fermon on the 30th of January, the reft in bread. Edward Haines, the intereft of 20*l.* Elizabeth Hellen, the intereft of 5*l.* Sir Richard Hill, of Redland Court, the intereft of 20*l.* Anthony Hill, the intereft of 20*l.* Mrs. Betty Hallifter, the intereft of 100*l.* Thomas Hart, efq; the intereft of 50*l.* John Jelf, the intereft of 30*l.* Robert Kitchin, 6*s.* 8*d.* for a fermon, and 6*s.* 8*d.* for bread, to the tithings of Weftbury and Stoke only. John Knight, the intereft of 10*l.* Thomas Moor, the intereft of

50*l.*

50*l.* John Morgan, the intereſt of 5*l.* Samuel Roach, for a ſermon at Shirehampton, 10*s.* and 10*s.* for coals to the poor there. Edmund Rutland, ſenior, and Edmund Rutland, junior, the intereſt of 5*l.* each. Mrs. Katherine Rutland, the intereſt of 10*l.* Chriſtopher Smith, 20*s.* for a ſermon at Shirehampton, and 20*s.* to the poor there. Joan Stainer, the intereſt of 75*l.* to Weſtbury and Shirehampton. Thomas Tilladam, the intereſt of 20*l.* Edward Wade, 15*s. per ann.* John Waſborow, the intereſt of 4*l.* George Webb, eſq; the intereſt of 200*l.* Mrs. Mary Webb, 10*s.* a year for a ſermon. William White, the intereſt of 10*l.* Mrs. Mary White, the intereſt of 20*l.* Robert Wood, the intereſt of 10*l.* Mr. Robert Yeomans, the intereſt of 20*l.* Mrs. Mary Innys, gave the intereſt of 200*l.* to the poor. The ſmall ſums are now put together to intereſt, and the produce diſtributed annually on the 6th of December.

Weſtbury.

Taxes.	The Royal Aid in	1692, £.	135	16	0
	Poll-tax — —	1694, —	37	14	0
	Land-tax ——	1694, -	144	0	0
	The ſame, at 3*s.*	1770, —	106	16	0

Shirehampton.

Taxes.	The Royal Aid in	1692, £.	135	8	0
	Poll-tax —	1694, —	23	5	0
	Land-tax —	1694, —	115	4	0
	The ſame, at 3*s.*	1770, —	86	17	0

Stoke Biſhop.

Taxes.	The Royal Aid in	1692, £.	139	8	0
	Poll-tax ——	1694, —	37	14	0
	Land-tax ——	1694, —	232	0	0
	The ſame, at 3*s.*	1770, —	176	14	0

When ſir Robert Atkyns compiled his account of this pariſh, there were, according to him, 140 houſes, and about 650 inhabitants, whereof 30 were freeholders; yearly births 23, burials 22. Since that time population is increaſed, and the inhabitants are now eſtimated at upwards of 900.

WESTCOT

IS a pariſh in the hundred of Slaughter, four miles ſouth-eaſtward from Stow, five northward from Burford, and twenty-ſix north-eaſtward from Glouceſter. It lies in a Vale, with Bledington to the eaſt, Little Riſington to the weſt, Icombe to the north, and Idbury in Oxfordſhire to the ſouth of it; and conſiſts chiefly of good meadow and paſture ground.

It is called *Icumbe* in *Domeſday*, from *Y-cwm*, which in the Britiſh language ſignifies *a valley*; but about the reign of king Stephen, the firſt letter was omitted, and then it was written *Combe*, and afterwards *Combe Baſkerville*, from a family who were lords of the manor, and whoſe name was added to diſtinguiſh this place from the adjoining hamlet of Icombe. In proceſs of time, the name of Combe was very little uſed, and the place was then called *Weſtcot*, as at preſent, perhaps for ſtill greater diſtinction. But there are ſome traces of the antient name ſtill remaining, in that of a wood in this pariſh, called *Gocombe*, i.e. Combe wood.

The river Evenlode bounds Weſtcot to the eaſt.

Of the Manor and other Eſtates.

At the time of the general ſurvey, there were two proprietors of eſtates in this place, as appears from two paſſages in *Domeſday*, of which the following is a tranſlation:

'Radulf de Todeni holds Icumbe, in Salemaneſberie hundred, and Roger holds it of him. 'There are ten hides which pay tax. In demean 'are three plow-tillages, and twelve villeins, and 'two bordars, with ſeven plow-tillages. There 'are eight *ſervi*. It is worth and was worth 7 *lib.*' *Domeſday*, p. 76.

'Roger de Laci holds Iccumbe in Salemaneſberie hundred, and Radulf holds it of him. 'Haldene held it. There are two hides. In 'demean are two plow-tillages, and two villeins, 'and two bordars, with one plow-tillage. There 'are four *ſervi*, and three *ancillæ*. It is worth 'and was worth 40 *ſol.* This eſtate pays tax.' *Ibid.* p. 75.

The Baſkervilles had property here ſoon after the conqueſt, for Hugard de Baſcheville gave one hide of land in Combe to the abbey of Glouceſter, and king Stephen confirmed the donation.

The ſheriff of Glouceſterſhire, in obedience to the king's writ, returned into the exchequer the names of all the vills in his county, with their proprietors, and he then certified that Combe was a vill in the hundred of Salmoneſburye, and that Sibilla Baſkerville was lady thereof, 9 E. 1.

It afterwards belonged to ſir Richard Baſkervill, and paſſed to the family of the Sheldons by the marriage of one of the daughters and coheireſſes of ſir John Blacket.

James Baſkervill levied a fine of Weſtcot Over and Nether Weſtcot, of the advowſon of the church, and of a fiſhery, to the uſe of William Sheldon, eſq; 1 E. 6. Ralph Sheldon had livery of theſe manors granted to him 13 Eliz. and a Ralph Sheldon was lord of Weſtcot in the year 1608. The late Mr. Owen, canon reſidentiary of St. David's, was lord of the manor at the beginning of this century, and had a good houſe near the church, which is now the property of the reverend Dr. Thomas Brookes; but the manor is divided among the freeholders.

Henry Huſee gave one hide and a half of land in Weſtcote, to the knights templers. *Dugd. Monaſt.* V. 2.

A tenement in Weſtcot, that had belonged to the Ciſtercian abbey of Bruern in Oxfordſhire, was granted to Edward Jewell 36 H. 8.

9 T Benjamin

Benjamin Baron, efq; enjoyed a good eftate here, at the time of his death, in 1693. His daughter and heirefs carried it, by her marriage, to fir Thomas Littleton, treafurer of the navy, and fpeaker of the houfe of commons, who was owner of it at the beginning of this century. It paffed afterwards, by purchafe, to Mr. Snell, and Powell Snell, of Guiting Grange, efq; is the prefent proprietor of it. This eftate was made tithe free, by appropriating a ground, called the Breach, to the rectory, as it was proved and fettled, by an iffue at law concerning the fame, about the beginning of the prefent century.

Of the Church, &c.

The church is a rectory, in the deanery of Stow, worth about 140*l.* a year, of which the reverend Thomas Brookes, D.D. is patron and incumbent. Two yard-lands belong to the glebe.

Firft fruits £.	9	7	3	Synodals £. 0	2	0
Tenths —	0	18	3¾	Pentecoft. 0	0	7½
Procurations	0	6	8			

Taxes.				
The Royal Aid in 1692,	£. 135	17	4
Poll-tax —— 1694,	— 20	8	0
Land-tax — 1694,	— 79	8	0
The fame, at 3*s.* 1770,	— 68	7	3

About the beginning of this century, there were 45 houfes in the parifh, and about 160 inhabitants, of whom 6 were freeholders; yearly births 3, burials 3. *Atkyns.* The people are now computed at 120.

WESTERLEIGH.

THIS parifh lies in the weft part of the hundred of Pucklechurch, whence its name; three miles diftant fouth-weft from Chipping Sodbury, feven north-weft from Marfhfield, and nine north-eaftward from the city of Briftol.

It confifts chiefly of pafturage, with large tracts of wafte land, or common, and abounds in coal; fo that a great part of the laborious inhabitants are employ'd in mining. There is alfo a manufacture of felt hats carried on in the village, which feems to be improving.

Doctor Edward Fowler, bifhop of Gloucefter, was a native of this place, and died at Chelfea, Aug. 26, 1714.

The *Ofmunda Regalis*, a very curious plant, grows fpontaneoufly in Wefterleigh common.

Of the Manor and other Eftates.

Wefterleigh was antiently a member of the extenfive manor of Pucklechurch, which was given to the monks of Glaftonbury, to pray for the foul of king Edmund the Firft, who was ftabbed in his palace at Pucklechurch, in the year 946. And being part of that manor at the time of the general furvey, it is not particularly mentioned in *Domefday*.

The monks of Glaftonbury quitted claim to the manors of Pucklechurch, Abfton, and Wefterleigh, to Joceline bifhop of Bath and Wells, 7 Joh. on condition that he would reftore to them the election of their own abbat; and Wefterleigh continued as part of the poffeffions of that fee 'till after the reformation. King Edward the Sixth took it from the bifhoprick of Bath and Wells in the fecond year of his reign, and it was granted to fir Nicholas Pointz 6 E. 6. Sir Nicholas Pointz, heir of fir Anthony Pointz, died feized of it 4 Mar. leaving Nicholas, his fon and heir, twenty-one years old.

John Roberts, alderman of Briftol, purchafed the manor of Nicholas Pointz, and was lord of it in the year 1608, as was Thomas Roberts, efq; at the time of his death, in the year 1673. Sir Samuel Aftry, knight, died poffeffed of it Sep. 22, 1704, and left it to Elizabeth his widow, afterwards the wife of Simon Harcourt, efq; whom fhe outlived, and dying Dec. 27, 1708, the manor paffed to her three furviving daughters and coheirs by fir Samuel Aftry, *viz.* Elizabeth, wife of fir John Smyth, of Long Afton, com. Somerfet, baronet; Diana, wife to Richard Orlebar, efq; and Arabella, afterwards lady of Charles-William, earl of Suffolk. From them the manor defcended like Henbury, to its prefent owners, who are fir Jarrit Smith, baronet, the honourable Thomas Willoughby, and Mrs. Colfton, relict of the late Alexander Colfton, efq.

Livery of the chapel of Wefterleigh, and of a meffuage called Sherwick, was granted to John Dennis 14 Eliz.

HAMLETS, and places of diftinct names in this parifh, are as follow: 1. *Nibley*; 2. *May's Hill*; 3. *Henvild*; 4. *Wotton's End*; 5. *Coal-pit Heath*; and 6. *Kendalfhire*; but none of them afford any thing worthy particular notice.

Of the Church, &c.

The church is in the deanery of Hawkefbury, and is annexed to Pucklechurch. A mortuary of 10*s.* is due to the vicar of the laft-mentioned church from the executors of all fuch houfholders of this parifh as die worth 40*l.*

The church is a neat building, fupported by eight octagonal pillars, and two pillafters; and has a handfome gallery at the weft end, erected at the expence of the parifh, in the year 1771. In the tower are fix mufical bells.

Monuments and Infcriptions.

On a flat ftone in the chancel, is this infcription:

P. M.

Richardi Hollifter eximii Ecclefiæ Alumni et columinis, qui obijt Maij 20° 1659, Æt. 47.

Epitaphium.

Vir virtute virens, Chrifti pugil, alter Elias,
Prudens, fidus homo, jam requiefcit humo.
Mater humus domus eft, tenebrofa nocte fed orto
Sole, datur fanctis luce tenenda Domus.

On

On a monument againft the fouth wall of the chancel :

In Memoriam Thomæ Roberts, Armigeri, hujus Manerij dudum Domini, Qui obijt

Julij 26° Anno Domini 1673 Ætatis fuæ 49.

The arms upon this monument are, Baron and femme, 1. *Party per pale argent and gules, over all a lion rampant fable*, for Roberts. 2. *Sable, a bend argent, on a canton a leopard's head cabofhed.*

On a brafs plate,

To the Memory of his dear Mother M[rs]. Mary Jones, Wife of William Jones, Efq; Lord of this Manor. She deceafed Oct. 22, A. D. 1661, Ætat. 38.

Tho. Jones filius pofuit.

Arms. Baron and femme, 1. *Ermine, a faltire gules*, for Jones. 2. Roberts, as before.

On an oval table, againft the eaft wall of the chancel,

Exuvias Mortalitatis fuæ infra depofuit Richardus Prigg, Gen. nuper de Ciuitate Briftol Pharmacopœus. Vir apto preditus Ingenio, Fortuna eminens, Arte fua præftans, Amicorum Solatium dum vixit Mortuus fufpirium. Natus fuit in hac Parochia, Denatus vero in Civitate prædicta

Anno Ætatis fuæ 65, Salutis noftræ 1723.

Over the monument, in a fcutcheon, are thefe arms: *Argent, a lion rampant regardant azure, between three trefoils proper.*

Benefactions.

John Roberts, lord of this manor, gave the church houfe, and a cottage called But Hays, to feoffees, for the benefit of the poor, 29 Eliz.

Mr. Edward Hill, who died in 1619, gave 100*l.* which fum has fince been laid out on lands that now produce about 14*l.* a year. The income is thus applied: 3*l.* for ten fermons; 3*l.* 10*s.* to be diftributed to the poor on Candlemas-day; and the remainder for apprenticing out poor children of this parifh.

The reverend Thomas Prigg, in 1986, gave a large filver flaggon, and other plate, for the communion fervice.

Mr. Robert Nailer, by will, in 1702, charged a tenement and lands at Acton with the payment of 5*l.* a year, for apprenticing a boy of this parifh.

Sir John Smyth, in the year 1715, by defire of his lady, fettled 20*l.* a year for ever, for teaching poor children of this parifh to read and write.

Taxes.				
The Royal Aid in	1692, £. 225	4	0
Poll-tax — —	1694, — 58	17	0
Land-tax ——	1694, — 274	14	8
The fame, at 3*s.*	1770, — 217	8	3

Sir Robert Atkyns reckoned the houfes in the parifh at 120, and the people at about 400, 14 of whom were reputed to be freeholders; yearly births 15, burials 13. Examining the parifh regifter, I find, that from 1700 to 1709, both inclufive, the baptifms were 218, and the burials 125; and in the fame number of years, beginning with 1760, the baptifms were 353, and the burials 247. The prefent number of inhabitants is about 930, and therefore they are in proportion to the annual burials nearly as 1 to 38.

WESTON *upon* AVON

IS a parifh in the upper part of Kiftfgate hundred, at the northern extremity of the county, four miles weft from Stratford upon Avon in Warwickfhire, nine north from Campden, and thirty-fix north-eaft from Gloucefter.

It lies in that vaft tract of rich country, fometimes called the *Vale of Evefham*, on the fouth bank of the Avon, over which there is a bridge at this place; and the lands confift almoft wholly of meadow and pafture. It has nothing to recommend it to the traveller's notice, but the common productions of nature, which indeed are very abundant.

At the time of the general furvey, there were many places in Gloucefterfhire of the common name of Weftune, or Weftone, which the experience of after ages found neceffary to diftinguifh by additions, and this parifh was then called Wefton upon Avon. The addition was given it for a reafon too obvious to need explanation; and indeed the word Wefton is almoft as obvious, being nothing more than the *Weft Town*, and commonly denotes the fituation of the place from fome other of greater confequence, near which it lies, or from the reft of the places in the fame hundred. So Eftone, or Afton, Norton, Sutton, are all names of like relative fignification.

Of the Manor and other Eftates.

'The church of St. Mary of Evefham holds 'Weftune in Widelei hundred. There are three 'hides, and one free [from tax]. In demean are 'two plow-tillages, and five villeins, and a prieft, 'with two plow-tillages. It was worth 20*s.* 'now 40*s.*' *Domefday*, p. 72.

How the manor paffed from the abbey of Evefham does not appear, but it belonged antiently to the Manduits, or Mauduits, earls of Warwick, which great family was defcended from William Manduit, chamberlain to king William the Conqueror. He married Maud, the daughter and heirefs of Michael de Hanflape, with whom he had a great eftate; and this parifh was frequently called Wefton Mauduit from his pofterity, to whom it belonged.

William Mauduit, baron of Hanflape in Buckinghamfhire, and hereditary chamberlain to the king in his exchequer, married Alice, daughter and at length heirefs of Waleran earl of Warwick, and dying 41 H. 3. left iffue William Mauduit, earl of Warwick, and baron of Hanflape, who died childlefs 52 H. 3. and Ifabel Mauduit, the wife of William de Beauchamp, baron of Elmley in Worcefterfhire. William de Beauchamp, eldeft fon of William and Ifabel, was baron of Elmley, hereditary fheriff of Worcefterfhire, and hereditary conftable of the caftle of Worcefter, in right of his father; and earl of Warwick, baron of Hanflape, and hereditary chamberlain

chamberlain to the king, in right of his mother. He died 26 E. 1. and was fucceeded by his fon Guy de Beauchamp, who held the manor of Wefton Mauduit, *alias* Wefton upon Avon, at the time of his death, 9 E. 2. Thomas de Beauchamp, fon of Guy, married Catherine, daughter of Roger lord Mortimer, and dying feized of Wefton Nov. 13, 1370, was fucceeded by his fon Thomas earl of Warwick, who likewife died feized of this manor 2 H. 4.

Wefton foon afterwards changed its owners, for John Grevil, efq; died feized of it 23 H. 6. as did his fon fir John Grevil, Aug. 6, 20 E. 4. and, by will, defired to be buried in St. Anne's chapel in the parifh church of Wefton upon Avon. Lewis Grevil had livery of it, and of Welford in this county, 1 Eliz. Sir Edward Grevil of Milcot was owner of thofe manors in the year 1608, and fold them to Lionel Cranfield, earl of Middlefex. Since that time, this manor has defcended like Welford, and the duke of Dorfet is the prefent proprietor of it.

The abbey of Evefham had court leet in Wefton 15 E. 1. Jeffery de Langeley was feized of Siddington and Wefton 2 E. 1. and John de Langeley, and Ela his wife, levied a fine of Wefton Mauduit to the ufe of themfelves for life, remainder to Jeffery their fon, and Mary his wife, in taille, 18 E. 2. John Rous, and others, held lands in Wefton upon Avon 49 E. 3. Sir Thomas Weft, and Alice his wife, held the manor of Wefton 10 R. 2.

Of the Church, &c.

The church is a vicarage, in the deanery of Campden, worth 32*l.* a year, and in the gift of the duke of Dorfet.

In the reign of king Henry the Fourth, a patent paffed the feal for appropriating the church of Wefton fuper Avon to the nunnery of Whitftane, or Wiftan, in the fuburbs of Worcefter, the revenue of which nunnery was valued at the diffolution at 53*l.* 3*s.* 7*d.* *per ann.* The impropriation is now vefted in the duke of Dorfet.

Twenty-five acres, in feveral inclofures, belong to the glebe.

The church is a fmall building, dedicated to All Saints.

Firft fruits £.	7	14	5	Synodals £.	0	1	0
Tenths —	0	15	5	Pentecoftals	0	0	8
Procurations	0	6	6				

Monuments and Infcriptions.

Two ftones in the chancel, inlaid with brafs, bore the following infcriptions :

Hic fitus eft Johannes Grevillus, Eques auratus, Milcoti olim Dominus, qui fatum implevit Anno Reparationis humanæ fupra milefimum quingentefimum quadragefim° fexto, Edvardi vero Sexti Anglorum Regis fecundo, Calendis Decemb.

Hic fitus eft Edvardus Grevillus, Eques Auratus, Milcoti olim Dominus, qui fato conceffit pridie natalis Chrifti Anno falutis humanæ quinquagefimo nono fupra milefimum et quingentefimum, imperante tum Anglis fereniffima Regina Elizabetha.

There were feveral other infcriptions for the family of the Grevils, many of whom were buried in St. Anne's chapel in this church; among whom was Edward Greville, who had been at the battle of the Spurs in France, and died 20 H. 8. But thofe infcriptions have been defaced time immemorially.

Taxes.					
The Royal Aid in	1692, £.	115	16	0
Poll-tax ——	1694, —	12	10	0
Land-tax ——	1694, —	133	16	0
The fame, at 3*s.*	1770, —	100	7	0

At the beginning of the prefent century, there were 14 houfes in the parifh, and about 60 inhabitants, 3 of whom were freeholders; yearly births 1, burials 1. *Atkyns.* The people are fince increafed to between 70 and 80 in number.

WESTONBIRT.

THIS parifh lies in the hundred of Longtree, three miles diftant fouth-weftward from Tetbury, eleven north-eaftward from Chipping Sodbury, and about twenty-four fouthward from Gloucefter.

It was antiently called Weftone, as being fituated in the weft point of the hundred to which it belongs; but the reafon why *birt* was afterwards added to it, is not fo apparent.

The turnpike-road from Tetbury to Bath and Briftol runs along the north fide of the parifh, and the fouth fide is bounded by Wiltfhire. The lands are chiefly arable, but there are neither antiquities, curious natural productions, nor any thing obfervable in the village, except the manor houfe, which belongs to Peter Holford, efq; one of the mafters in ordinary in the high court of chancery, who ufually refides here in the fummer feafon.

Of the Manor and other Eftates.

'William the fon of Baderon holds Weftone, 'in Langetreu hundred. Bricfi held it in the 'time of king Edward. There are three hides. 'In demean are two plow-tillages, and two vil-'leins, and three bordars, with two plow-tillages. 'There are four *fervi*, and fix acres of meadow. 'It was worth 6*l.* now 3*l.*' *Domefday*, p. 73.

'Earl Hugh holds Weftone in Langetreu hun-'dred. Elnod held it in the time of king Edward. 'There are three hides taxed. Leuuin held one 'hide in the fame hundred.' *Ibid.*

Sir Robert Atkyns was moft probably miftaken in reprefenting Maurice de Gaunt as lord of this manor in the reign of king John. Beverftone, King's Wefton, and many other eftates in Gloucefterfhire, belonged to Maurice de Gaunt 17 John, as I have related under Beverftone. He was a branch of the Berkeley family, and his poffeffions defcended to them. And as this manor and King's

King's Weston frequently occur in the records by the name of Weston, without any distinction, so there is good reason to suspect that some of the records which relate to the latter, have been misapplied by the before-mentioned learned historian to Westonbirt. Thus he says,

'This manor, and the manor of Beverstone did 'belong to Maurice de Gaunt earl of Lincoln '17 Joh. Margaret the widow of John Giffard 'held the same 6 E. 3. Thomas lord Berkeley 'held Westonbirt 35 E. 3. Sir John Berkeley 'held the same 6 H. 6. Sir William Berkeley 'died seized of this manor 5 E. 6. and livery thereof was granted to John Berkeley, son of sir 'William 6 E. 6.'—All these particulars are supposed to relate to King's Weston.

When there are two or more places in a county of the same name, it frequently creates confusion. The following records are supposed to concern Westonbirt:

Hugh le Dispencer the younger was seized of the manor of Westonbirt 5 E. 2.

Sir Ralph de Willington, son of John de Willington, died 22 E. 3. seized of the manors of Westonbirt, Ablington in Bibury, Poulton in Awre, Frampton Cotterel, Yate, and Sandhurst, of all which his son Henry had livery the following year, and was living 26 E. 3. Sir John Paulet and Margaret his wife were seized of Westonbirt and Poulton 15 R. 2. but it seems to have been only in trust, for John de Willington died without issue 20 R 2. seized of the manors of Poulton, Ablington, Westonbirt, Frampton Cotterel, Sandhurst, Culverden, and Moreslade, all in the county of Gloucester, and left Joan his sister and heir, who was married to John Wrath.

John Wrath, son of John and Joan de Willington, died without issue 13 H. 4. leaving his two sisters coheiresses to his great estate, of whom Elizabeth was married to sir William Poulton, and Isabel was the widow of William Beaumont.

Sir William Poulton and Elizabeth his wife dying without issue, Isabel Beaumont became possest of her father's estate, which after the death of her son John Beaumont, without issue, descended to her daughter Isabel, who died unmarried 2 H. 6. seized of the manors of Ablington, Poulton, Yate, Westonbirt, Frampton Cotterel, and Sandhurst, all which were the patrimony of her ancestors the Willingtons.

Sir Thomas Beaumont succeeded her, and died 29 H. 6. leaving a son William Beaumont, esq, afterwards knighted, who died in the 32d year of the same reign. Philip Beaumont, brother and heir of William, died 13 E. 4. seized of the manors of Poulton, Ablington, Yate, Westonbirt, Frampton Cotterel, and Sandhurst, of all which Hugh Beaumont and Elizabeth his wife, John Basset and Elizabeth his wife, John Beaumont, clerk, John Chichester and Margaret his wife, and John Croker and Anne his wife, levied several fines 16, 18, & 20 H. 7. to Richard bishop of Durham, and other bishops, to sir Giles D'Aubeny, or Giles lord d'Aubeny, and many other great persons. Giles lord d'Aubeny died seized of the said manors 6 H. 8. and livery was granted to his son Henry lord d'Aubeny, the same year. They afterwards were in the crown, and were granted to Edward duke of Somerset, upon whose attainder they came again to the crown, and this and several of the before-mentioned manors were granted to James Basset 4 Mar. and the grant was confirmed to Arthur Basset 7 Eliz.

Nicholas Dymery was lord of this manor in the year 1608. The Crews were afterwards proprietors of it, and it passed out of that name and family, by the marriage of an heiress, to sir Richard Holford, knight, who was appointed one of the masters in ordinary in the high court of chancery, in June, 1693. From him the manor descended to Robert Holford, esq; who was appointed a master in ordinary of the same court, in October, 1712; and from him it descended to Peter Holford,[y] esq; who now possesses it, and was also appointed a master in chancery, in the room of his father, by the earl of Hardwicke, in August, 1750. He is possessed of other good estates in this county, and elsewhere, and gives for his arms, *Argent, a greyhound passant sable.*

Of

[y] The family of Holford is of great antiquity in Cheshire, being descended from Hugh de Runchamp, who was lord of Loftock about the reign of king Stephen. He had a son Richard de Runchamp, whose son Gralan, or Gralam de Runchamp, sold Houlme juxta Nether Pever, in Cheshire, to Richard son of Randle Grosvenor, in the year 1234; and the town of Loftock was called Loftock Gralam, after his name. The Loftocks bore for their arms, *Argent, a greyhound passant sable.*

Gralam de Loftock, son of the last Gralam, had issue by Letitia his wife, three sons, Richard, Robert, and Galfrid. Richard, the eldest, married Emme de Merton, by whom he had issue two sons, Richard and Thomas, who both died *sine prole*; and one daughter Joan, married, in 1277, to William Toft, younger son of Roger de Toft, lord of Toft; whom she survived, and was married, secondly, to Thomas Vernon, about the year 1316, from whom the Vernons of Haslington in Cheshire descended. She was married, after the death of her second husband, to William de Hallum, in the year 1337. Which said William Toft gave for his arms, *Argent, a chevron between three text tees sable*, and by Joan his wife, had issue three sons, Roger, Henry, and Walter.

Roger de Holford, the eldest son, was living in the year 1316, and after the manner of those ages, assumed the name of Holford from the place of his residence. He married Margery, daughter of Richard le Dispencer, but died without issue 5 E. 3. whereby Henry, his next brother, became his heir, and assumed the name of Holford. Which Henry de Holford, by Margery his wife, had issue two sons, William and Roger, to which latter he gave lands in Plumley, 1344.

William de Holford, the eldest son, died in his father's life-time, having married Isabel, daughter of   by whom he had one son John.

John de Holford, son and heir of William, recovered the manor of Holford against Richard Vernon, of Loftock Gralam, 42 E. 3. and sealed usually with *a chevron between three text tees*; the chevron making the distinction between these and the arms of Toft of Toft, who bears the Tees without a chevron. He had issue by Joan his wife, daughter of Roger Bruyn, of Stapleford, one son Thomas, and died 9 H. 4.

Thomas Holford, son and heir of John, died before his father, 12 R. 2. having married Alice, daughter of William Buckley, of Oateworth.

William Holford, of Holford, was son and heir of Thomas. He married Margaret, daughter of sir Richard Venables, of Kinderton, and by her had issue three sons, Thomas, his heir; John, and Hugh; and two daughters, Jonet, wife of Randle

Of the Church, &c.

The church is a rectory, in the deanery of Hawkeſbury, worth about 80*l.* a year. Peter Holford, eſq; is patron. The living was augmented about the year 1725, by the donations of Robert Holford, eſq; and Doctor Godolphin, who gave 100*l.* each, and by queen Anne's bounty.

About forty acres belong to the glebe.

The church is ſmall, with a low tower at the weſt end.

Firſt fruits £. 6	2	0	Synodals £. 0	2	0
Tenths — 0	12	2¼	Pentecoſt. 0	1	0
Procurations 0	6	8			

Benefactions.

A houſe and garden, and an acre in the common field, are given for the benefit of the poor.

Mrs. Hodges left 3*l.* a year for teaching the poor children to read.

Land-tax at 3*s.* 1770, £ 47 5 0

The ſtate of population in this pariſh, about the beginning of the preſent century, as given by ſir Robert Atkyns, was 18 houſes, and about 80 inhabitants, whereof 5 were freeholders. There are now 22 families, and 106 inhabitants.

WESTON SUBEDGE

LIES in the upper diviſion of Kiftſgate hundred, about one mile weſt from Campden, ſix ſouth-eaſt from Eveſham in Worceſterſhire, and about twenty-eight north-eaſtward from Glouceſter.

The village is ſeated under the ſide of a hill, whence it received the addition of *Subedge*, but in all probability it was called *Weſton* from its ſituation from the town of Campden, or elſe from its weſtern aſpect on the ſide of the hill.

It is ſaid that the hundred court was formerly kept on the top of the hill, above the village; and ſir Robert Atkyns was of opinion, that the hundred received the name of Kiftſgate, from a gate near the place where the court was held.

Here is no great manufacture, but the women and girls are commonly employ'd in ſpinning flax.

Of the Manor and other Eſtates.

The lands in this pariſh were divided between two great proprietaries, when *Domeſday* was compiled, as appears by the record, of which the following is a tranſlation:

'Hugo de Grentemaiſnil holds Weſtone in 'Ceolflede hundred, and Roger holds it of him. 'There are four hides. Balduin held it. In de'mean are two plow-tillages, and ſix villeins, with 'three plow-tillages. There are four *ſervi*, and 'five *ancillæ*, and a mill of 10*s.* It was worth 7*l.* 'now 6*l.*' *Domeſday*, p. 77.

'Anſfrid de Cormeliis holds Weſtone in Celfle'ſtorn hundred. Two thanes (one a free man 'of earl Herald's, the other Leuric's) held ten 'hides there, for two manors, and could go where 'they pleaſed. In demean are four plow-tillages,

Randle Brereton of Malpas; and Margery. He died 38 H. 6. and was ſucceeded by

Thomas Holford, of Holford, eſq; his ſon and heir. Which Thomas, by his wife Joan, daughter of Richard Legh de Weſt-Hall, in High Leigh, had an only ſon Thomas Holford, and died in 1464.

Thomas Holford, of Holford, the younger, eſq; ſon of the laſt mentioned Thomas, married Maud, daughter of William Buckley, deputy judge of Cheſter, 1444, and by her had iſſue George, his ſon and heir; Randle, who had iſſue Humphry and Richard; Robert Holford, who had iſſue John, Philip, Bartholomew, Owen, Matthew, and Bryan. This Thomas died about 13 E. 4.

Sir George Holford, of Holford, knight, ſon and heir of Thomas, married Iſabel, daughter of Robert Legh, of Adlington, eſq; and widow of Lawrence Warren, and by her had two ſons, John, and George; and one daughter Conſtance, married to William, ſon of Edward Bradſhaw. Sir George was ſheriff of Cheſhire 16 H. 8. and bore Loftock's arms on his ſeal, *viz. Argent, a greyhound paſſant ſable.* He had alſo four baſtard ſons, 1. Thomas, 2. Arthur, from whom the Holfords of Davenham; 3. Raufe, 4. Robert. Alſo Ellen, a baſe daughter, all living 22 H. 7.

Sir John Holford, of Holford, knight, ſon of ſir George, was ſheriff of Cheſhire 33 H. 8. He married Margery, ſole daughter and heir of Raufe Brereton, of Iſcoit in Flintſhire, 22 H. 7. and had iſſue two ſons, Thomas, his heir; and Chriſtopher, who married Margaret, daughter of Thomas Danyell, of Over-Tabley, eſq; 1555; from whom the Holfords of London and Eſſex are deſcended. Alſo one daughter Alice, married to Piers Leyceſter, of Nether-Tabley, eſq. Sir John died in 1545.

Thomas Holford, of Holford, eſq; ſon and heir of ſir John, married, firſt, Margaret, daughter of ſir Thomas Butler, of Bewſy in Lancaſhire, by whom he had one ſon Chriſtopher. After the death of his ſaid wife, he married, ſecondly, Jane, the widow of Hugh Dutton, and daughter of ſir William Booth, of Dunham-Maſſey, by whom he had iſſue George Holford, of Newborough in Dutton, gentleman, the continuator of this family, of whom hereafter; Thomas, the ſecond ſon; and John. Alſo Ellen, married to John Carrington, of Carrington in Cheſhire, eſq; Dorothy, married to John Bruyn, of Stapleford in Cheſhire, eſq; and Elizabeth, married to Charles Manwaring, of Croxton in Cheſhire, eſq; 1560. This Thomas Holford died in 1569.

Chriſtopher Holford, of Holford, eſq; ſon of Thomas by the firſt venter, had alſo two wives; firſt, Anne, daughter of Hugh Dutton and Jane aforeſaid, by whom he had iſſue Thomas Holford; and another ſon John, and a daughter Anne, who both died infants. His ſecond wife was Elizabeth, the widow of Peter Shakerley, and daughter and coheir of ſir Randle Manwaring, of Over-Pever, by whom he had iſſue one daughter Mary.

Thomas Holford, ſon and heir of Chriſtopher, having married Dorothy, daughter of Peter Shakerley, of Hulme, eſq; and Elizabeth, aforeſaid, died without iſſue, and was buried at Nether Pever, in 1561; whereby the ſaid Mary Holford became ſole heir to Chriſtopher her father, and was married to ſir Hugh Cholmondley, of Cholmondley in Cheſhire, and had a numerous iſſue.

I return now to George Holford, brother to Chriſtopher, and next heir male of the Holfords. Between whom and the ſaid Mary Cholmondley were law ſuits concerning the Holford eſtates for upwards of forty years, which at laſt were ſettled by mediation of friends, and the eſtates were parted between them. The ſaid George Holford married Jane, daughter and heir of Charles Awbrey, of Camriff in Brecknockſhire, and widow of Henry Maſterſon, and by her had iſſue ſeven ſons, Thomas and John, twins; Edward, Peter, (continuator of the male line) George, Charles, and William; and one daughter Mary, married to William Harcourt, of Winſham, gentleman. He died in 1635; and Thomas Holford of Iſcoit, his ſon and heir, died without iſſue male, wherefore the inheritance deſcended to James Holford, of Newborough, ſon and heir of Peter, fourth ſon of George; for all the brothers of Peter died without iſſue male. Which James Holford married Margaret, daughter of Matthew Carleton, of Lincoln's-inn, London, and dying in 1666, left iſſue one ſon Thomas, and one daughter Mary.

Sir Richard Holford, knight, lord of the manor of Weſtonbirt, by family tradition, was a branch of this houſe; but no care having been taken to continue the Holfords pedigree, neither in the heralds office, nor in family papers, it is uncertain where he ought to be joined to the antient ſtock.

Robert Holford, eſq; was ſon of ſir Richard, and dying in the year 1750, was ſucceeded by his ſon Peter Holford, eſq; the preſent lord of the manor of Weſtonbirt.——This pedigree is chiefly extracted from ſir Peter Leiceſter's *Hiſtorical Antiquities*, and the particulars are authenticated by antient deeds from which he extracted them.

'and

'and eighteen villeins, and one bordar, with nine 'plow-tillages, and twelve *fervi*. It was worth '100*s*. now 7*l*.' *Ibid*. p. 78.

Thefe manors are defcribed in the records by the fame common name; which making it difficult to apply the accounts of them with certainty, they are therefore fet down in chronological order.

Jeffry Giffard, archbifhop of York, was feized of the manor of Wefton Subedge 7 E. 1. and Henry de Penbrugge held it the fame year. The fheriff returned that John Giffard was lord of Wefton 9 E. 1.

Godfrey Giffard, was lord chancellor of England, and bifhop of Worcefter. A court leet and free warren in Wefton and Norton were allowed him in the proceedings on a writ of *Quo warranto* 15 E. 1. and he died feized of thofe manors in the 30th year of that reign. The Giffards of Wefton, afterwards, the better to announce their defcent from this prelate, gave for their arms, *Argent, ten torteauxes*, which are thofe of the bifhoprick of Worcefter.

John de Feckenham was feized of the manors of Wefton and Norton 34 E. 1. John Giffard of Wefton, or of Doyton, died 13 E. 2. poffeffed of the manors of Wefton Underegge, and Norton Underegge, and of the advowfon of the church of Wefton; and the efcheator's inquifition found, that John Giffard, his fon, held the fame of the king for life. A John Giffard, probably the fame perfon noticed in the inquifition, held the before-mentioned eftates 1 & 38 E. 3.

Thomas de Evefham held Wefton Underegge 17 E. 3. as did William de Acton 47 E. 3. John Solers was feized of two yard-lands, and of feven acres of meadow, in Wefton Underegge, 20 R. 2. and William Solers was poffeffed of an eftate dignified in the records by the name of Wefton Underegge 5 H. 4. Thomas Wefton, the chaplain, was likewife feized of an eftate of the fame name, 6 H. 4.

Roger Giffard, efq; was feized of the manors of Wefton Underegge, and Norton Underegge, 25 H. 6. Margaret, the widow of Thomas Herward, was feized of the manor of Wefton Subege 12 E. 4. Joan the widow of fir John Merney, late wife of Robert Giffard, and formerly the wife of —— Barendine, was poffeffed of the manors of Wefton Underegge, and Norton, 18 E. 4. Livery of the manor, park, and advowfon of Wefton Underegge, and of Norton, was granted to George Giffard 15 Eliz.

Sir Edward Grevil was lord of this manor in the year 1608. Francis Throgmorton was alfo feized of it, but being attainted of treafon, it was granted by the crown to Henry Spiller, efq; and others, in truft for George Giffard, 7 Jac. 1. It was again granted to the fame perfons, 9 Jac. and they fold it to Henry Fleetwood, efq; and others.

Richard Graves, efq; purchafed the manors of Wefton Subedge, Afton Subedge, and Mickleton, with the royalty of the hundred of Kiftfgate, about the middle of the laft century. He fold Wefton Subedge to William Morgan, efq; who had married one of his daughters. Richard Morgan, grandfon of William, by his will, dated May 29, 1740, gave this manor to Morgan Graves, efq; great grandfon of Richard Graves, before-mentioned; and his fon, Walwyn Graves, efq; is the prefent lord of the manors of Wefton Subedge, Afton Subedge, and Mickleton, all in this county.

Nicholas le Chamberlain held two yard-lands in Wefton Subedge 29 E. 1. Agnes de la Chambre held lands here 2 E. 3. and Alice at Chambre was likewife feized of lands in this place 37 E. 3. Thomas Bifhop was feized of one meffuage, and of one yard-land in Wefton, 18 E. 2.

A large wood, called Wefton Park, on the fide of the hill, together with fome other lands, were fold from the manor, by Henry Fleetwood and the other owners, to fir Baptift Hicks, in the year 1610. This eftate, by defcent, is now vefted in the earl of Gainfborough.

HAMLETS. There are three hamlets in this parifh of the name of Norton.

'Ansfrid de Cormeliis holds five hides in 'Nortune, in Celfleftorn hundred. Two thanes 'held them for two manors, and could go where 'they pleafed. In demean are four plow-tillages, 'and nine villeins, and two bordars, with four 'plow-tillages, and ten *fervi*. They were worth '4*l*. now 6*l*.' *Domefday*, p. 78.

It has already been fhewn, that the Giffards enjoyed this eftate (called Norton Giffard from them, but generally Norton Underedge) for many fucceffive generations; but it afterwards became divided into three diftinct hamlets, and fo it continues.

1. *Upper Norton*. Richard Fiennes, lord Say and Seal, fon of Richard lord Say, died 11 Jac. feized of the manors of Wefton and Norton, and left William lord Say, his fon and heir, twenty-eight years old. This eftate paffed afterwards to fir William Keyt, baronet, who being burnt in his own houfe, in the year 1741, his fon fold it to fir Dudley Ryder, lord chief juftice of England, whofe fon, Nathaniel Ryder, efq; is the prefent proprietor of Upper Norton.

2. *Middle Norton*, which belonged to Mr. Sprig at the beginning of this century, is now, by purchafe, the property of Mr. Ryder.

3. *Lower Norton*, where was formerly a chapel of eafe. Lady Langley, of New-Houfe in Herefordfhire, and Laurence Fiennes, efq; were proprietors of Lower Norton at the beginning of this century. The Fiennes family fold it to Mr. Maunder, of whom it was purchafed by Thomas Eden, efq; the prefent owner.

Of the Church, &c.

The church is a rectory, in the deanery of Campden, worth 500*l*. a year. The reverend Mr. Peeley is patron a d incumbent.

Tithes

Tithes in Weſton Subedge belonged to Winchcombe abbey, and were granted to ſir Thomas Seymour 1 E. 6.

The church land, worth 40*s.* a year, is aſſigned to the uſe of the pariſh clerk. Three yard lands belong to the glebe.

The parſonage houſe is of good hewn ſtone, and, together with the gardens, is ſurrounded with a ſtrong wall of conſiderable antiquity. In one of the rooms the letters W. L. are many times expreſſed on the painted glaſs, and are ſuppoſed to be the initials of the perſon's name who built it.

The church is a ſtrong building, dedicated to St. John Baptiſt, with a tower at the weſt end. The walls have been decorated with paintings, as of the Aſcenſion, the four Evangeliſts, &c. but time has much impaired the colours.

John Bell, rector of this church, was archdeacon of Glouceſter, prebendary of Lincoln and Litchfield, warden of the collegiate church of Stratford upon Avon, vicar-general of the dioceſe of Worceſter, and afterwards biſhop of that ſee in 1539. But he reſigned his biſhoprick in 1543, and retired to a private life at Clerkenwell, where he died in 1556.

Firſt fruits £.	31	0	0	Synodals £.	0	2	0
Tenths —	3	2	0	Pentecoſt.	0	1	0½
Procurations	0	6	8				

Monuments and Inſcriptions.

On a braſs plate, fixed to a blue marble ſtone, is the figure of a man, and underneath this inſcription:

Here lyeth the bodye of William Hodges, who Maried ye Daughter of Sir George Throgmorton of Kawghton, knyght, and was the wyddowe of John Gifford, of Weſton Underedge, Eſquire, who Departed this lyfe the XXIII of Auguſte An°. 1590.

H. S. E.

Iohannes Ballard, M. B. Vir perquam doctus, artiſq; præſertim Apollineæ, quam ſumma cum laude ſucceſſuq; admodum felici exercebat, Peritiſſimus. Anatomiam, Chymiam, herbas, adeo calluit, ut nemo magis dignus qui vel Gallenum ætate ſuperaret; nondum annos ſeptuaginta natus, Oxonii (inter Muſas & literatos ſibi gratiſſimos) animam efflavit, Maij 2, Anno Dom. 1678, Ætatis ſuæ 66.

On the table of a marble monument, againſt the north wall of the chancel, is this inſcription:

H. S. E.
Pharamus Fiennes LL. D.
Gulielmi Vicecomitis Say et Seal
Nepos;
Collegij Winton Socius;
Hujus Parochiæ Rector.
In quâ Domum Dei et Rectoris,
Illam Vaſis deauratis;
Hanc Ædificijs hortiſq; Cultiſſimis,
(Hoſpitalitate vero magis
et Liberalitate)
Utramq; ſuâ ſuorumq; pietate
et moribus ſanctiſſimis
Ornavit.
Populum ſibi concreditum
Fideliter docuit,
Prudenter rexit,
Unice amavit.
Obijt Dec. Anno { Dni MDCCVIII / Ætatis LXII.

Over the monument are theſe arms, *Baron and femme*, 1. *Azure, three lions rampant Or.* 2. *Argent, upon a chevron between three cinquefoils gules a leopard's face inter two roundlets Or.*

Benefaction.

Twenty pounds a year, payable out of an eſtate at Lower Norton, are given to four poor widows of this pariſh.

Taxes.					
The Royal Aid in	1692, £.	319	14	0
Poll-tax ——	1694, —	32	19	4
Land-tax ——	1694, —	252	18	6
The ſame, at 3*s.*	1770, —			

There were 58 houſes in the pariſh when ſir Robert Atkyns compiled his account of it, and he eſtimated the inhabitants to be about 300, of whom 26 were reputed to be freeholders. He alſo ſets down the annual births at 8, and burials at 6. But ſir Robert's eſtimate was too high, for according to the regiſter, in ten years, from 1700 to 1709 incluſive, there were only 60 baptiſms, and 42 burials; and in the ſame number of years, from 1760 to 1769, there were 105 baptiſms, and 47 burials. Thus it appears that population has advanced ſince ſir Robert's time, and the preſent number of inhabitants being 197, exceed that of the annual burials in the proportion of 42 to 1.

****

W H A D D O N

IS a ſmall pariſh, in the united hundreds of Dudſton and King's Barton, about ſix miles north from Stroud, and four ſouth from Glouceſter.

It lies in the Vale, and conſiſts chiefly of rich paſture land, but has nothing very curious, in the works of art or nature, to diſtinguiſh it.

Of the Manor and other Eſtates.

'Durand the ſheriff holds Wadune, in Duneſtane hundred. There are five hides. Five brothers held them for five manors, and could go where they pleaſed, and were equals [*i.e.* had equal ſhares]. In demean are five plow-tillages, and one villein, and ſeven bordars, with five plow-tillages. In the time of king Edward it was worth 8*l.* and is now worth 100*ſol.*' *Domeſday*, p. 76.

The manor belonged to Robert de Pont de Larch, or Pont de l'Arch, 30 H. 3. Robert Waleran, ſheriff of Glouceſterſhire, was ſeized of it 31 H. 3. in which year he obtained a grant of an annual fair in Whaddon, to be held on the eve, the day, and the morrow after the feaſt of St. Margaret the virgin.

William de Valence, earl of Pembroke, uterine brother to king Henry the Third, was ſeized of Whaddon and Moreton Valence, by the gift of Robert de Pont de Larch. He had a confirmation of the grant of thoſe manors from the king, 36 H. 3. and the privileges of court leet and free warren were allowed him 15 E. 1. He was ſlain by the French at Bayonne, 23 E. 1. and died ſeized of Moreton and Whaddon, the latter of which was held in dower by Joan his wife, daughter

daughter and at length heireſs of Gwarine de Montchenſy.

Audomar de Valence, earl of Pembroke, ſurviving ſon of William, was killed in France, on account of the part he had taken in the death of the earl of Lancaſter, 17 E. 2. He left no iſſue, and the eſcheator's inquiſition found that he died ſeized of Payneſwyke, Morton, and Whaddon; that there were in Whaddon *quidem gurges in Sabrina*, worth 20*s.* *per ann.* 125 acres of arable land, worth 4*d.* *per* acre; and 100 acres worth 2*d.* *per* acre; 30 acres of ſteril land, worth only 1*d.* an acre; 40 acres of meadow, at 1*s.* 6*d.* an acre; 15 acres of paſture at 1*s.* and a park without deer; and that John de Haſtinges, Johanna the wife of David de Strabolgi earl of Arthelos, and Elizabeth Comyn were his heirs.

From this Audomar the manor of Whaddon paſſed, like thoſe of Moreton Valence and Painſwick, 'till it came into the poſſeſſion of ſir William Kingſton, who levied a fine of Painſwick and Whaddon to ſir Nicholas Pointz, 5 E. 6.

The manor paſſed from the Kingſtons to the Jerninghams of Coſſey in Norfolk; and Henry Jerningham had livery of it 15 Eliz. Sir William Dorrington was lord of the manor in the year 1608, and ſir Samuel Eckley died poſſeſſed of it in the reign of queen Anne. It paſſed afterwards to Mr. John Small, and is now veſted in Samuel Peach, eſq; a ſilk-merchant in London. His arms are, *Gules, three martlets between two chevronels argent.*

Of the Church, &c.

The church is a curacy, in the deanery of Glouceſter, worth 25*l.* a year. The leſſee of the prebendary of Hereford is patron and impropriator, and Mr. John Jones is the preſent incumbent.

The impropriation is now worth 52*l.* a year, and pays 15*l.* a year to the curate.

The church is a ſtrong building, dedicated to St. Margaret, and has an embattled tower at the weſt end.

Firſt fruits £.	7	15	0	Synodals £.	0	1	0
Tenths —	1	5	6	Pentecoſt.	0	0	5½
Procurations	0	3	0				

Benefaction.

Mrs. Harris, of Abergavenny, left 1000*l.* now laid out on the purchaſe of an eſtate at Upton St. Leonard's, for the following purpoſes, *viz.* 20*s.* for an anniverſary ſermon on the 27th of June, the day of her death; 5*s.* for a ſacrament; and 2*s.* 6*d.* to the clerk; with the ſame donations to the pariſh of Hempſted. Four widows are to be clothed on that day; and the remainder of the income, if any, is to be employed in apprenticing poor boys of this pariſh and Hempſted, or in clothing poor men. See Hempſted.

Taxes.					
The Royal Aid in	1692,	£. 56	14	8
Poll-tax —	1694, —	11	2	0
Land-tax —	1694, —	65	12	0
The ſame, at 3*s.*	1770, —	49	4	0

At the beginning of this century, there were 27 houſes in the pariſh, and about 110 inhabitants, 4 of whom were freeholders; yearly births 2, burials 2. *Atkyns.* The inhabitants are now about 123.

Wheatenhurſt, *or* Whitminſter,

IS a pariſh in the hundred of Whitſton, in the Vale part of the county, about five miles diſtant weſt from Painſwick, ſeven north from Durſley, and eight ſouthward from Glouceſter.

It conſiſts chiefly of rich paſture and meadow ground, proper for dairy and grazing, and produces very good cheeſe and cider.

Witenherſt, as the name is written in *Domeſday*, ſignifies the *ſtrong wood*, and denotes the antient condition of the place when the name was given it. The pariſh was afterwards vulgarly called *Whitminſter*, (contracted from *Whitenherſt*, and *Minſter*, a *Monaſtery*) in honour of the abbey of Glouceſter, becauſe the monks had acquired a manor here; and the latter is the name moſt commonly uſed at preſent, but *Wheatenhurſt* occurs in all deeds, and formal writings.

The river Froom, or the Stroud river, which is a boundary between Saul and this pariſh, falls into the Severn at the diſtance of ſomething more than a mile from the church, and a navigable canal from the Severn at Framilode, croſſes this pariſh, and will ſhortly be extended to the town of Stroud, under which head the reader will find an hiſtorical account of the proceedings on that buſineſs.

Two turnpike-roads paſs through Whitminſter, one leading from the eaſt part of the county, by Minchin Hampton and Stroud, and ſo weſtward towards the paſſages over the Severn at Framilode and Newnham; the other, is the great road from Glouceſter to Bath and Briſtol. And ſurely there cannot be a more infamous turnpike-road, for ſeveral miles of it, than the latter; for, incredible as it may ſeem, the writer of this account, in the winter of 1776, ſaw a chaiſe mired in it, about half a mile from the Swan inn in this pariſh, and was there told, that a horſe had like to have been ſmothered in the ſame place two days before, but was luckily ſaved by ſome perſons coming accidentally to the poor animal's aſſiſtance. Several cauſes operate to this evil; the ſcarcity of ſtone, the remiſſneſs of the commiſſioners; and the total ignorance of the ſurveyor. There may be, however, one lucky circumſtance attending this road. If it could once be put in repair, the canal will eaſe it of a great part of the coal, and other heavy carriage, and it may then, with no great exertion, be prevented from relapſing into its preſent founderous condition.

Richard-Owen Cambridge, eſq; has a good old houſe and gardens near the church, where Frederick prince of Wales, the father of his preſent majeſty, did him the great honour of a viſit, when he made an excurſion into Glouceſterſhire, a little before his death. But this ſeat has been for ſome years intirely unoccupied.

Of the Manors and other Eſtates.

Domeſday gives the following account of this manor:

'Hardinc holds Witenherſt in mortgage of 'Brictric. The ſame Brictric held it in the time 'of king Edward. There are five hides taxed. 'In demean is one plow-tillage, and a prieſt, and 'two villeins, and ſix bordars, with five plow-'tillages. There are three *ſervi*, and a mill of '10 *ſol.* and ten acres of meadow. It was worth '100 *ſol.* now 30 *ſol.*' *Domeſday*, p. 80.

This was not the great, unfortunate Brictric, who was poſſeſſed of the lordſhip of Glouceſter, but one of the king's thanes of the ſame name. Who was the next poſſeſſor to Hardinc does not appear; but Jeffery Fitz-Peirce, earl of Eſſex, was afterwards ſeized of this manor. He had one daughter Maud, married to Henry Bohun, earl of Hereford, to whom he gave the manor of Wheatenhurſt in frank marriage, and died 14 Joh. He had alſo three ſons, who died without iſſue, whereby the Bohuns, deſcendants of the aforeſaid Maud, became earls of Eſſex. Henry de Bohun died ſeized of Wheatenhurſt 4 H. 3. and was ſucceeded by his ſon Humphry de Bohun, who was taken in rebellion in the battle of Eveſham, and his lands were ſeized by the king; but the manors of Wheatenhurſt and Southam were reſtored to him 50 H. 3. and he died 3 E. 1. Henry de Bohun, earl of Hereford, obtained a licence to fortify his manor houſe of Wheatenhurſt, 21 E. 3 and died in the 34th year of the ſame reign. Another Humphry de Bohun, the laſt earl of Hereford, died 46 E. 3. having married Joan, daughter of Richard earl of Arundel, by whom he left two daughters coheireſſes, Eleanor, the wife of Thomas of Woodſtock, youngeſt ſon of king Edward the Third; and Mary, married to Henry earl of Derby, who was afterwards king Henry the Fourth.

Thomas of Woodſtock, duke of Glouceſter, held the manor of Wheatenhurſt in right of his wife. He was ſmothered under a feather bed at Calais, 21 R. 2. and left Humphry, his ſon, who dying without iſſue, Anne Plantagenet, his only ſiſter, was his heir. She was married firſt to Thomas earl of Stafford, who dying before conſummation, ſhe was afterwards married, by ſpecial licence from the king, to Edmond earl of Stafford, younger brother of Thomas, who died ſeized of Wheatenhurſt 4 H. 4. In which name and family this manor continued for a long time, and of whom there is a further account under Thornbury.

King James the Firſt granted the manor of Wheatenhurſt to Peter Vanlore, merchant, and William Blake, ſcrivener, in the third year of his reign, and recites in the grant, that it came to the crown by the attainder of ſir Walter Rawleigh, and that it formerly belonged to the abbey of Glouceſter.

William Bayly, eſq; was lord of this manor in the year 1608, in whoſe family it continued 'till another William Bayly, eſq; conveyed it to ſir Samuel Eckley, whoſe brother and heir Mr. Eckley was lord of it at the beginning of this century. It paſſed afterwards to lord Middleton and Alexander Colſton, eſq; in right of their wives, and has lately been purchaſed by Nathaniel Peach, eſq; who is the preſent lord of the manor. His arms are, *Gules, three martlets between two chevronels argent.*

There is another manor in the pariſh, which formerly belonged to Richard Bird, who died in 1612. Thomas Lloyd, eſq; deſcended from the family of that name in Monmouthſhire, married Sybil, daughter and heireſs of Richard Bird of Whitminſter, and with her had this eſtate. Thomas Lloyd, ſon of Thomas, ſucceeded his father, and married Rebecca, daughter of Thomas Hinſon, of Taviſtock in Devonſhire. Thomas Lloyd, ſon and heir of the laſt Thomas, married Elizabeth, daughter of ſir Theobald Gorges, of Aſhley in Wiltſhire; but dying without iſſue, in 1658, George Lloyd, his brother and heir, became ſeized of this eſtate, and marrying Anne, daughter of Giles Pain, of Rodborough, died in the year 1703. George Lloyd, eſq; ſon of George, married Elizabeth, eldeſt daughter of William Bayly of Frethorn, and was proprietor of this manor, and of a good houſe near the church, at the beginning of the preſent century. The houſe and eſtate now belong to Richard-Owen Cambridge, eſq; whoſe arms are, *Argent, on a pile gules a croſs croſlet of the field, between ſix croſſes croſlets fitchy ſable.*

Of the Church, &c.

The church is an impropriation, in the deanery of Glouceſter, worth in the whole about 50 *l.* a year to the curate. Mr. Jaſper Selwyn is patron and impropriator, and Mr. Jaſper Selwyn, his ſon, is the preſent incumbent. The impropriation, now worth 80 *l.* a year, antiently belonged to the priory of Bruton in Somerſetſhire. The abbey of Troars in Normandy had the advowſon of the church of Wheatenhurſt 56 H. 3.

The living was formerly valued at only 8 *l.* a year, but it has been augmented by the queen's bounty, and by the donation of Mrs. Dorothy Bayly,

Bayly, who left the reverfion of an eftate called Jackfons's farm, in this parifh, now let at 84*l.* a year, to augment the livings of Frethorn and Wheatenhurft; and the curate now receives half the profits. There is neither houfe nor glebe for the minifter.

The church is dedicated to St. Andrew, and has a handfome embattled tower at the weft end, with four bells in it.

Proc. 6*s.* 8*d.* Syn. 2*s.* Pentecoft. 9*d.*

Monuments and Infcriptions.

A handfome black marble monument, on the north fide of the chancel, bears the following infcription:

Near Underneath reft the Bodies of Thomas Lloyde the Elder, Efq; who departed this Life October 15, 1658, aged 70. whofe firft wife was Rebecca, daughter of Tho. Hynfon, Efq; Alfo Margery his 2[d] Wife, daughter of Leonard Iefferys, Efq; who departed this Life April the 24 An° 1643. Alfo Tho. Lloyde the Younger Efq; with Elizabeth his wife daughter of S[r] Theobald Gorges K[t]. She departed this life April the 16, 1666, aged 43, & he departed this life Octob. the 14th An° 1668 Aged 49.

Alfo Anne the Wife of George Lloyde, Efq; daughter of Gyles Payne, Gent. who departed this life September the 10th An° 1670, Aged 44.

Alfo Philippa a 2[d] Wife (Daughter of Walter Parker of Lyffell in y[e] County of Wilts, Efq;) Died y[e] 20th of Aug[st]. 1696.

Alfo George Lloyde, Sen[r]. Efq[r]. who died March the 15th 1703, Ætat. Suæ 80.

Edmond the fon of George and Anne Lloyde died 1670.

Elizabeth the D[r]. 1680.

Elizabeth a 2[d] D[r].

Radegund 3[d] D[r]. died 1669.

Difcimus Exemplis quam totus Homuncio nil eft,
Vive igitur, Lector, (dum licet effe) Deo.

Againft the fame wall, there is a fmall neat marble monument, with the effigy of a woman kneeling, and this infcription:

Here lyeth Rebecca Wife of Thomas Lloyde, Efq; daughter of Thomas Hinfon Efquire, by Ann daughter of the Lady Springe, daughter of Margaret Countefs of Bath. She deceafed the 16 day of Februā 1625.

Virgo modefta fuit; pia Mater; optima Conjux:
Sed Parcas pietas flectere tanta nequit.
Victa tamen vivit; Gentifq; infignia, Soles *
Occiduos, mutat Splendidiori Solo.

* The family arms of Hinfon, which are placed on the finifter fide of the fcutcheon upon this monument, *viz. Azure, on a chevron between three funs in their fplendor Or, a crefcent gules.* On the dexter fide is this coat, *Azure, a crofs fable between four bucks Or,* fuppofed for Lloyd, whofe arms are thus blazoned in the laft herald's vifitation, *viz.* 1 *and* 4. *Quarterly Or and azure, four bucks trippant counterchanged.* 2 *and* 3. *Argent, a quiver gules, banded and replenifhed with arrows Or, between three pheons fable.*

Againft the fouth wall of the church,

Near this place lies the Body of George Bigland, of Bigland in the County Palatine of LANCASTER, Efq[r]. who died in this PARISH, upon his Return from BRISTOL, (where he had been for the Recovery of his Health) on the 19th Day of September, 1752, aged 49 Years. He married MARY, the only Daughter of JOHN FOX, of WHITEHAVEN, in the County of CUMBERLAND, Gent. by whom he left iffue two fons, viz. GEORGE and THOMAS.

At the top of the monument are thefe arms, *Baron and femme,* 1. *Azure, two ripe ears of wheat erect proper.* 2. *Or, on a chevron between three foxes heads erazed gules, as many fleurs de lis argent.*

Taxes.					
The Royal Aid in	1692, £.	80	10	8
Poll-tax ——	1694, —	10	1	0
Land-tax ——	1694, —	126	12	0
The fame, at 3*s.*	1770, —	103	3	9

About the beginning of this century, there were 46 houfes in the parifh, and about 200 inhabitants, 12 of whom were freeholders; yearly births 5, burials 4. *Atkyns.* Examining the parifh regifter, I find that in ten years, beginning with 1765, the burials were 87, and the prefent number of people is exactly 231, fo that about one in 27 dies every year.

WHITTINGTON.

THIS parifh lies in the hundred of Bradley, near five miles fouth-eaftward from Cheltenham, five fouth from Winchcombe, thirteen north from Cirencefter, and thirteen eaft from Gloucefter.

It is a fmall parifh, in the Cotefwold country, confifting of more arable than pafture ground. The village is fheltered on the north by fome very lofty fields, whofe tops are adorned with plantations of firs. The Coln, a very pretty trout river, rifes in a fmall head at this place, and growing more confiderable, gives name to feveral villages thro' which it paffes in its courfe to Fairford, where it empties itfelf into the Thames.

Of the Manor and other Eftates.

In *Domefday* it is thus recorded:

'William Leuric holds Witetune, in Wacref-'cumbe hundred. Ofgot held it. There are 'three hides, and they are taxed. In demean are 'two plow-tillages, and fix villeins, and one rad-'chenifter, and four bordars, with four plow-'tillages. There is a mill of 10 *fol.* [rent] and a 'wood one mile long, and half a mile broad. It 'was worth 100 *fol.* now 60 *fol.*' *Domefday*, p. 74.

A few ages afterwards, one Serlo was proprietor of this manor, of Broad Campden, and of Bradley in Wotton. He died without iffue, and left Agatha and Juliana his fifters and coheireffes. Anne his wife furviving him, was married to Hugh de Stratton, and had the manor of Whittington affigned to her for dower by the fifters and coheirs of her former hufband 4 H. 3.

Richard de Crupes poffeffed this manor in the fame reign, and had a grant of markets, fairs, and free warren in Whittington 41 H. 3. which grant was pleaded and allowed in the proceedings on a writ of *Quo warranto* 15 E. 1. Another Richard de Crupes, defcended from the former Richard, died feized of this manor 10 E. 3. as did Edward Crupes his fon, in the 35th year of the fame reign.

Edward, fon of Edmond de Langley, duke of York, fifth fon of king Edward the Third, was flain at the battle of Agincourt, feized of Whittington, 3 H. 5.

Richard le Difpencer, earl of Gloucefter, died feized of this manor, whereby Ifabel his fifter became his heir. She was firft married to Richard Beauchamp earl of Worcefter, and afterwards by a fpecial a ſpecial diſpenſation from the pope, ſhe was married to Richard Beauchamp earl of Warwick, who, in her right, died ſeized of the manor of Whittington 15 H. 6. Iſabel died 18 H. 6. and ſome ſhort time before her death, levied a fine of this manor to the uſe of her laſt will. She left iſſue Henry and Anne; Henry was afterwards created duke of Warwick, and his iſſue dying without iſſue, Anne his ſiſter was heir to his vaſt eſtate. She was married to Richard Nevill, the great earl of Warwick, and ſurviving him, was prevailed with by king Henry the Seventh, to convey this manor, amongſt many others, to himſelf, 3 H. 7. A more particular account of this family may be ſeen under Tewkeſbury.

King Henry the Seventh granted this manor to the Cottons, and Richard Cotton, eſq; died ſeized of it, and of the advowſon of Whittington, 3 Mar. John Cotton had livery of the ſame, and died 42 Eliz. William Cotton, the laſt male heir of that family, was lord of the manor in the year 1608. The heir female was married to ſir John Denham, author of that excellent poem, called Cooper's Hill. He was ſurveyor general of the works and buildings to king Charles the Second, and left two daughters coheireſſes; one married to ſir Thomas Price, who died without iſſue, whereby her inheritance devolved to her ſiſter, who was married to ſir William Morley, of Halnaker in the county of Suſſex, nephew to the reverend prelate of that name, biſhop of Wincheſter.

Sir William Morley likewiſe left two daughters coheireſſes, of whom one died unmarried, whereby Mary, the ſurviving ſiſter, was intituled to the whole eſtate. She was married to James earl of Derby, who, in her right, was lord of the manor of Whittington.

The manor paſſed afterwards to lord Conway, of whom it was purchaſed by the late Thomas Tracy, eſq; whoſe widow, Mrs. Tracy, is the preſent lady of the manor, and proprietor of ſeveral other good eſtates in this county.

William Bradehurſt and Alice his wife held lands in Whittington 2 R. 2. John Tayler was alſo ſeized of lands in Whittington 9 R. 2. Lands in Whittington, a water mill, and the advowſon of the rectory, which formerly belonged to the Deſpencers, and to the earls of Warwick, were granted to Thomas Stroud, Walter Earl, and James Paget, 36 H. 8. Other lands called Hill, Colemore, Plots, and Colewell, and a wood, called Hall-wood, belonged formerly to the abbey of Winchcombe, and were granted to William Berners 36 H. 8.

HAMLET. *Syreford* is a hamlet in this pariſh, containing about ſix or ſeven houſes. Lands called Wally in this hamlet, formerly belonged to a religious foundation, and pay only 4*s.* a year in lieu of tithes.

Of the Church, &c.

The church is a rectory, in the deanery of Winchcombe, worth about 100*l.* a year, to which Mrs. Tracy has the preſentation.

Twenty-two acres incloſed, and about ſeventy in the common fields, belong to the glebe.

The church is ſmall, with an aile on the ſouth ſide, built by the Cottons, and a low wooden turret in the middle.

	£.				£.		
Firſt fruits	13	6	8	Synodals	0	1	0
Tenths —	1	6	8	Pentecoſtals	0	0	7½
Procurations	0	6	8				

Monuments and Inſcriptions.

Under an arch, between the chancels, are the figures in ſtone, larger than life, of two knights in armour, lying with their legs acroſs. One is diſtinguiſhed with a large ſhield upon the left arm, bearing *ſix lozenges Or*, 3, 2, 1. And there is another figure of a female, lying along in the ſouth aile, diſtinguiſhed by the ſame arms.

Upon a plate of braſs, fixed to a flat ſtone, under the figures of a man and woman, with two children between them, it is thus engraven:

HERE LYETH THE BODDYES OF RICHARD COTON ESQVIER AND MARGARET COTON HIS WIFE. HE DECESSED THE NINE AND TWENTYTH DAYE OF MAYE IN THE THYRD AND FOWRTH YEARE OF THE REYGNE OF KINGE PHILLYPP AND QVEENE MARYE ANNO DOMINI 1556 AND THE SAYD MARGARET DECESSED THE DAYE OF MAY IN THE FYRST YEARE OF THE REYGNE OF OVR SOVERAINE LADYE QVEENE ELIZABETH ANNO DOMINI 1560.

Note, The arms are torn off this ſtone.

Upon a table againſt the wall in the chancel,

In Memoriam
Viri admodum literati
Morum et Religionis integerrimi
Iacobi Ingram
Qui S. S. Theologiæ merito Doctor
Hujuſce Paræciæ Paſtor fidiſſimus
Eccleſiam decoravit
Vitam cum Morte mutavit
Anno { Ætatis ſuæ 70,
Domini 1670.
Iuxta quem
ſepultus jacet
Filius ejuſdem natu maximus
Iacobus Ingram
Cujus morum probitas ſimplicitas ſuavitas
Effecit
ut omnibus lugubre deſiderium reliquit
Ian. 20
Anno Ætatis ſuæ 36
Domini 1678.

And beneath,

Haud procul poſitum eſt
Q^d reliquum Margaretæ
D^ris Ingram Filiæ
Antonii Barns 1mo deinde Rob^ti Speat,
Conjugis
Lumina condidit Id. Maiis
An: Ætatis ſuæ 52,
Æræ X^nae 1692.

In chariſſimam Memoriam Margaretæ Barns Antonij et Margaretæ Prolis unicæ, Quæ præpropera Patris morte orba antequam nata, relicta Matri triſtiſſimæ ſolamen nimis breve præbuit; Variolis nempe Correpta immatura morte Quinto Novemb. Expiravit,

Anno Ætatis ſuæ 7
Domini 1677.

In a ſcutcheon upon this monument are two coats, *Baron and femme.* 1. *Ermine, on a feſs gules three eſcallops Or.* 2. *Barry of ten pieces argent and azure, over all a lion rampant gules.*

There

There is an elegant marble monument, confisting of a vafe fupporting an urn, with proper decorations, in the fouth chancel, and upon the front is the following memorial:

To the beloved Memory
Of Thomas Tracy, Efq[r] of Sandywell in Glocefterfhire,
Youngeft Son of Iohn Tracy, Efq[r] of Stanway
in the faid County,
who deceas'd Iune 24th, 1770, Aged 53.
This excellent Man was diftinguifhed in
Private Life
By an uncommon Sweetnefs of Temper
and Benevolence of Heart,
and poffeffed in an eminent degree thofe focial
and amiable Virtues
Which not only procured him the Love of his
Relations and intimate Friends,
But the univerfal Efteem of all
His Acquaintance.
He was unanimoufly Chofen by his Country,
in two fucceeding Parliaments, to reprefent the
County of Glocefter;
Which important truft he difcharged
with the ftricteft Integrity
and
Difinterefted Zeal.
He married Mary only Daughter and Heirefs of
Sir William Dodwell, Kn[t].
And had by her one only Son, Dodwell Tracy,
A Youth (from his amiable Difpofition and
diftinguifhed Parts) of the moft
promifing Hopes.
But thefe, alas! were blafted when in the
flower of his Age he was fnatched
From the Arms of his Afflicted Parents and Friends,
Ian: 11, 1768, at Paris, on his return
from his Travels,
in the 21st Year of his Age.
Mary their lamenting Wife and Mother
placed this Mournful Teftimony of
Her tendereft Affection
to her Dear Hufband
and her beloved Son.

Their Remains are depofited in the Tracy Vault at Stanway.

Upon a fhield placed at top of the monument, are thefe arms, *Quarterly*, 1ft *and* 4th *Or, on a bend voided gules an efcallop fable.* 2. *Azure, a crofs croflet fitchy Or.* 3. *Sable, a bend ermine cotized flory Or.*——Over all a fcutcheon of pretence, *Quarterly*, 1ft *and* 4th *Vert, a fefs between three rofes argent,* for Dodwell. 2d *and* 3d *Argent, three bars gules, a canton of the fecond.*

Taxes.					
	The Royal Aid in	1692, £.	58	11	2
	Poll-tax ——	1694, —	6	10	0
	Land-tax —	1694, —	62	16	0
	The fame, at 3*s.*	1770, —	36	19	3

At the beginning of this century, there were 32 houfes, and about 126 inhabitants in this parifh, whereof 4 were freeholders; yearly births 3, burials 3. *Atkyns.*

Wickham, *or* Child's Wickham.

THIS is a fmall parifh, in the hundred of Kiftfgate, four miles diftant fouth-eaftward from Evefham in Worcefterfhire, near fix weftward from Campden, and twenty-two north-eaftward from Gloucefter.

It is fituated on the great road leading from Worcefter to London, and was antiently called *Wicuene*, and afterwards *Child's Wickham*, from the Childs of Northwick, who, it feems, were once lords of this manor.

It lies in the Vale, yet the greater part is arable; and the common fields were inclofed by authority of parliament, about the year 1765. A fmall brook, rifing in two heads, one in Broadway, the other in Buckland, runs from hence into the Avon above Evefham; but the parifh is chiefly diftinguifhed in natural hiftory by a falt fpring, which not being work'd, is of no immediate advantage.

Here is a cuftom from time immemorial, for the lord of the manor to give a certain quantity of malt to brew ale to be given away at Whitfuntide and a certain quantity of flour to make cakes; every one who keeps a cow fends curd, others plumbs, fugar, and flour; and the payers to church and poor contribute 6*d.* each towards furnifhing out an entertainment, to which every poor perfon of the parifh who comes, has, with a quart of ale, a cake, a piece of cheefe, and a cheefecake.

Of the Manor and other Eftates.

'Rotbert Difpenfator holds Wicuene, in Gretestane hundred. There are ten hides taxed. 'Balduin held it. There are three plow-tillages 'in demean, and thirty-two villeins, and ten bor-'dars, with twelve plow-tillages. There is one '*fervus*, and two mills of 10*s.* and ten acres of 'meadow. In Wincelcumbe is one burgefs pay-'ing 16*d.* It was worth 12*l.* and is now worth '16*l.*' *Domefday*, p. 76.

'The church of Wincelcumbe holds one hide 'in Wicquenn.' *Ibid.* p. 71.

The above Robert Difpenfator, or Defpencer, came into England with William the conqueror, to whom he was fteward, and had by his gift the manor of Wicuene in Gloucefterfhire, befides four in Warwickfhire, fifteen in Lincolnfhire, and feventeen in Leicefterfhire, of all which he was poffeffed at the time of the general furvey, as appears by the record juft quoted.

Sir Robert Atkyns fays, 'It is very probable 'that the Peches were afterwards owners of this 'manor; for king Edward the Second confirmed 'a grant of fir Gilbert Peche, of lands in Wick-'ham, to the abbey of Leyftone in Suffolk, 6 E. 2. 'The confirmation doth not indeed mention in 'what county Wickham lay, but fince other lands 'in Glofterfhire are named with it, and that the 'Peches were owners of very confiderable pof-'feffions in this county, it is the more probable.'

Upon this paffage I obferve, that there is good reafon to believe that the Peches were not owners of the Wickham of which I am now treating, for the fheriff returned that the earl of Warwick [William de Beauchamp] was lord of Wickwane in Holford and Grefton hundred 9 E. 1. The efcheator's inquifition found, that his fon Guido de Bello Campo, earl of Warwick, died 9 E. 2. feized of the manor of Wikewayne, which he held of the king *in capite*, but by what fervice the jurors were ignorant; of 360 acres of arable land there, at 4*d.* an acre; of fixteen

 acres

acres of meadow, at 3*s.* an acre; and of three acres of paſture, at 2*s.* the acre; of 6*l.* 3*s.* 1*d.* of the rent of free tenants, and 119*s.* rent of the natives, and not more, becauſe 20*l.* rent is aſſigned to the chantry of the caſtle of Aumley [Elmley] by the king's charter, with the conſent of the lord Guy de Beauchamp. He left Thomas de Beauchamp, his ſon and heir, almoſt two years old.

The manor belonged to ſir William Cornwallis in the year 1608. It came afterwards to the Sheldons, of whom it was purchaſed by the Fermors. James Fermor, eſq; was proprietor of it about the beginning of this century, and his grandſon, William Fermor, of Stockeld Park, near Tadcaſter in Yorkſhire, eſq; is the preſent lord of the manor of Child's Wickham, and gives for his arms, *Argent, a feſs ſable between three lions heads erazed gules.*

HAMLET. *Murcot* is a hamlet in this pariſh, lying north-weſtward from the church, and had formerly a chapel belonging to it, of which William Belſon was the laſt incumbent, and had a penſion of 2*l.* 10*s.* paid him in the year 1553. *Willis.* There is a piece of ground now called the Chapel cloſe.

Of the Church, &c.

The church is a vicarage, in the deanery of Campden, of which Mr. Fermor is patron, and Mr. Robert Burgis is the preſent incumbent. The advowſon of it formerly belonged to the abbey of Bordeſley in Worceſterſhire.

Mr. Fermor has the impropriation both of Wickham and Murcot.

In the year 1763 an act paſſed for incloſing the common fields in this pariſh, when lands, now let for 51*l.* a year, were allotted to the vicar in lieu of tithes, which together with the vicarage houſe and orchard, eaſter offerings, &c. make the living worth about 60*l.* a year. For every perſon dying worth 30*l.* there is a mortuary of 10*s.* paid to the vicar.

This is a peculiar, and is viſited by the biſhop and arch-deacon in the manor houſe. And the lord of the manor, by cuſtom, entertains the viſitor with a cake, a loaf, a pound of butter, a quarter of a ſage cheeſe, and a quarter of a plain cheeſe, a dozen of ale, and ſix bottles of ſtrong beer. The vicar has the probat of wills within the peculiar.

The church is built in the form of a croſs, and has a handſome ſpire at the weſt end, with five bells. There is, painted on the glaſs in the chancel window, *Sable, a feſs between ſix croſs croſlets Or.* And upon ſome bricks in the church, *Three chevrons Or.*

Benefactions.

In the year 1683, Mr. Samuel Wharton, ſometime ſheriff of Briſtol, gave 27*l.* to purchaſe land for the uſe of the poor, which was laid out accordingly; and the ground ſo purchaſed, and another piece called the church head-land, were exchanged, upon incloſing, for land now let for two guineas a year.

Four ſmall tenements are given towards the repair of the church.

Taxes.					
The Royal Aid in	1692,	£. 115	18	0
Poll-tax —	1694, —	17	8	0
Land-tax —	1694, —	117	8	0
The ſame, at 3*s.*	1770, —	82	10	6

At the beginning of this century, there were 75 houſes, and about 340 inhabitants, whereof 12 were freeholders; yearly births 8, and burials 8. *Atkyns.* But ſir Robert's account of the baptiſms is very erroneous, for in ten years, beginning with 1700, the baptiſms were 116, the burials 78. In the ſame number of years, beginning with 1760, the baptiſms were 102, and the burials 88. But in 1761, and 1764, the burials were double the average number. The inhabitants are now about 306, ſo that population ſeems to be ſomething declining.

WICKWAR.

THIS pariſh lies in the hundred of Grumbald's Aſh, five miles ſouth-weſt from Wotton-under-edge, four north from Chipping Sodbury, and about twenty-ſix ſouth from Glouceſter.

It is ſituated in the Vale, and conſiſts chiefly of paſturage, with ſome arable, and a conſiderable proportion of waſte land, pretty much inclined to clay.

The antient name was *Wichen*, from *wic*, which has various ſignifications, as a village, or hamlet, a caſtle, a dairy farm, &c. It was afterwards called *Wickwar*, from the family of *La Warr*, who for many generations were lords of the manor.

In this, and the neighbouring pariſhes of Chipping Sodbury, Yate, and Cromhall, are rocks of a very compact and ponderous ſtone, which, from its colour, is called the White Lays. It is a ſpecies of marble, and makes a moſt excellent lime. Broken ſmall, it wears as ſmooth as a gravel walk on the public roads, and is very durable. The calamine ſtone, and ſome lead ore, have alſo been found in theſe places.

This part of the country is bleſt with plenty of pit coal, which is of great advantage to the inhabitants, and ſeems not to be counterballanced by any natural inconveniencies, except that grain is uſually ſomething dearer than upon the hills, becauſe the lands here are chiefly uſed in grazing and dairy, many of which were formerly corn fields, as appears by the ridges ſtill remaining.

Within the pariſh ſtands a ſmall market town, of one ſtreet, whoſe privileges of a weekly market, and yearly fair, were firſt granted in the reign of king Edward the Firſt. King Henry the Eighth

alſo

alſo granted to Thomas Weſt, lord La Warr, the like privileges of a weekly market, and of two annual fairs, in the twenty-fourth year of his reign; and I have ſeen an *Inſpeximus* and confirmation of the laſt-mentioned grant, dated July 4, in the fourth year of the reign of king Charles the Firſt. It was ſhewn me by the mayor, as a charter of incorporation, for the town is a borough by preſcription, like Wotton and Berkeley, with a mayor and twelve aldermen, who have the mace carried before them on particular days: The profits of the market and fairs belong to the mayor, and ſuch as have ſerved that office are deemed aldermen.

The market day is on Monday, and there are two fairs, one on Lady-day, the other on the ſecond of July. But the market is unfrequented, and the town declining. There are two courts, one held for the borough, the other for the tithing, or foreign, which have ſeparate conſtables.

The clothing buſineſs was probably ſettled here very early, for Leland, in the time of king Henry the Eighth, calls it a *pratye clothinge tounlet*, and the manufacture has continued here ever ſince, with various ſucceſs; but is at preſent in a very languiſhing condition, there being only one maſter, who does but little in it. However, the women and children have uſually full employment in ſpinning for the clothiers about Stroud and Chalford.

Of the Manor and other Eſtates.

'Humphry the chamberlain holds Wichen, in 'Bacheſtanes hundred. There are four hides. 'Three free men of Brictric the ſon of Algar 'held it for three manors in the time of king 'Edward, and they could go where they would. 'There were three plow-tillages in demean, and 'nine villeins, and fourteen bordars, with nine 'plow-tillages. There are five *ſervi*, and twenty 'acres of meadow, and ſix furlongs of wood. It 'is worth and was worth 12 *lib.* Theſe two vills, 'Actune and Wichen, the queen gave to Hum'phry.' *Domeſday* p. 79.

John earl of Glouceſter, brother to king Richard the Firſt, gave this manor to John la Warre, and afterwards confirmed it to him when he was king, 8 Joh. to hold of that king by the ſervice of half a knight. Jordan la Warre was ſon and heir to John. He often joined in rebellion againſt king John and king Henry the Third; but prudently took care to make his peace. John la Warre ſucceded Jordan in this manor, and was himſelf ſucceeded by Roger la Warre, who held it 9 E. 1. and purchaſed a weekly market in Warre-Wike, on Tueſday; a yearly fair on Whit-monday, and the two following days; and free warren within the manor, in the 13th year of the ſame reign; and all theſe privileges were allowed him in the proceedings on a writ of *Quo warranto*, 15 E. 1. He married Clarice, eldeſt daughter and coheireſs of John lord de Tregoz, of Herefordſhire, an eminent baron, after whoſe death, this Roger la Warre had ſummons as a baron to parliament, 22 E. 1. He died 14 E. 2. ſeized of the manors of Wykewarre and Briſtlington, and the eſcheator's inquiſition found, that Wykewarre was then held of Thomas ap Adam, ſon of John ap Adam, as of the manor of Caſtleharpetre, by the ſervice of half a knight's fee. John lord la Warre, ſon of Roger, died 21 E. 3. and (John his eldeſt ſon dying before him) was ſucceeded by his grandſon Roger lord la Warre, who was eminent in the reign of king Edward the Third, whom he attended in his wars in France; and being preſent at the battle of Poictiers, Sept. 19, 1356, when the French king and his ſon, the earl of Tankerville, ſir Jaques of Bourbon, the earls of Ponthieu and Eue, with many other noblemen, were taken, he was one of thoſe knights who challenged the French king as their priſoner, and this ſir Roger had the crampet, or chape, of that monarch's ſword aſſigned him for his ſhare in that exploit, and he and his family afterwards bore it, as an honourable augmentation, in their armorial bearings. He and Elizabeth his wife levied a fine of the manor and advowſon of Wickwar to the uſe of themſelves in taille, the remainder to John his ſon, 28 E. 3. and he died in the 44th year of the ſame reign. John lord De la Warre, ſon of Roger, died without iſſue 22 R. 2. and was ſucceeded by his brother Thomas lord de la Warre, rector of Mancheſter, who levied a fine of this manor to the uſe of himſelf in taille, the remainder to Thomas Weſt in taille, the remainder to Reginald Weſt, ſon of Thomas Weſt, 12 H. 4. and died without iſſue, 4 H. 6.

Reginald Weſt, ſon of ſir Thomas Weſt by Joan the daughter and heireſs of the laſt Roger lord de la Warre, ſucceeded to this manor in virtue of the before-mentioned entail, (notwithſtanding John Griffin was next heir male at law) and had livery of the lands of his mother's inheritance. Petitioning the ſame year to have place and precedency among the barons as lord de la Warre, he had ſummons to parliament accordingly from 5 to 28 H. 6. and died in the 29th year of that reign, ſeized of Wyke-Warr, leaving Richard lord de la Warr, his eldeſt ſon and heir, who died 16 E. 4. Thomas lord de la Warr, eldeſt ſon of Richard, bore ſeveral important truſts under king Henry the Seventh, with whom he was in great favour. He made his will Oct. 8, 1524, and died ſoon after, as appears by the probat, which bears date Feb. 12, 1525. Thomas lord de la Warr, eldeſt ſon of Thomas by his firſt wife, had a grant of the abbey of Whorwell in Hampſhire, which afterwards became the ſeat of his family. He died without iſſue, ſeized of the manor of Wickwarre, and of the advowſon of the church, Sep. 25, 1554.

William Weſt, ſon of ſir George Weſt, who was brother by the father to the laſt-mentioned Thomas

Thomas lord de la Warr, was bred up in his uncle's houſe as his preſumptive heir, and impatient of delay, attempted to diſpatch him by poiſon; which being complained of in parliament, 2 E. 6. he was diſabled to ſucceed him in honour and eſtate, and had only an allowance of 350*l.* a year. But behaving with diſtinguiſhed valour in the Engliſh army at the ſiege of St. Quintin, in 1557, and carrying himſelf well for ſeveral years afterwards, he received the honour of knighthood at Hampton-court, Feb. 5, 1568; and obtained a new creation to the title of lord de la Warr, and by act of parliament, which paſſed on the 12th of March following, had full reſtitution in blood, and became poſſeſſed of this manor. He died 38 Eliz. and was ſucceeded by his ſon Thomas lord de la Warr, who, by petition to the queen in parliament, was reſtored to the precedency of his anceſtors, 39 Eliz. and dying in the 44th year of that reign, left Thomas lord de la Warr, his ſon and heir. This lord was conſtituted captain-general of the colonies planting in Virginia, whither he went with three ſhips, in 1609, and was very active in forming ſettlements and making diſcoveries; whereby his health was greatly impaired, and he died at ſea, in his return home, June 7, 1618.

Wickwar was afterwards purchaſed by ſir Robert Ducie, from whom it deſcended, like Tortworth, and lord Ducie is the preſent lord of the manor.

HAMLET. *Bagſtone* is a hamlet in this pariſh, which is ſuppoſed to have given name to the hundred called Bacheſtane hundred in *Domeſday-book*, and now comprized in the hundreds of Thornbury and Grumbald's-aſh. The abbey of Kingſwood was ſeized of the manor of Bageſton 12 H. 4. and Matthew Hale, eſq; was lord of it at the beginning of this century.

Andrew Sudenham granted an eſtate in Wikewarre to John and Thomas Howes, at the annual rent of two pounds of wax, to be paid at the altar of St. Mary, in the north part of the church of Wickwar, on the feaſt of the bleſſed virgin; and one pound of wax, to be paid at the altar of St. Lawrence, in the ſame church, on the feaſt of that ſaint, 12 E. 3. and the original grant is now in the hands of Mr. Rudge of this place.

John Newton, citizen of Briſtol, and Joan his wife, levied a fine of lands in Wickwar to the uſe of themſelves in taille, 8 H. 5. and John Newton, ſon of John, levied a fine of lands in the ſame place, to the uſe of William More, 28 H. 6.

Of the Church, &c.

The church is a rectory, in the deanery of Hawkeſbury, worth 300*l.* a year. The reverend Mr. Cheſter is patron and incumbent.

The church is a handſome ſtructure, dedicated to St. Mary, with an aile on the north ſide, and a well built tower at the weſt end. It ſtands on an eminence, at ſome diſtance from the town, and is ſaid to have been erected by one Woolſworth, an eminent clothier of this place, who likewiſe built a houſe at the pool in the bottom near the church. Againſt the eaſt end of this houſe, which now belongs to Mr. Jobbins, is the figure of St. John the Baptiſt, in an erect poſture, pointing with his left hand towards the church, and over him this inſcription in antient characters:

Ste Iohẽs Baptiſta ora . . . .

Beneath the figure,

In ye zere of our Lord God M° CCCC° IIIj
ſcore & xvi trinete monday XXII day of May.

Firſt fruits £.	18	0	0	Synodals £.	0	2	0
Tenths —	1	16	0	Pentecoſt.	0	0	6
Procurations	0	6	8				

Monuments and Inſcriptions.

Upon a plain ſtone in the north aile it is thus written:

VNDER THIS STONE LYETH THE BODY OF
ROBERT SPERT OF WICKWARE IN THE
COVNTY OF GLOVC: ESQV WHO DEPARTED
THIS LIFE THE 27th DAY OF OCTOBER A. D. 1638.
VT DAVID IONATHÆ MORTEM DEFLEVIT AMANTIS:
SIC FLEO DECESSVM CHARE MARITE TVVM,
SPES TAMEN VNA MANET CÆLO NOS ESSE SODALES
PERPETVISQVE BONIS ABSQVE DOLORE FRVI.

On the ſide of a freeſtone altar tomb in the ſame aile, are the following inſcriptions, in three compartments:

M. S.
GVLIELMI FILIJ
NATV MAXIMJ JOHANNIS HICKS
HVJVS PAROChiæ GENEROSI
QVI OBIJT
JAN. 14° ANNO { DOMINI 1674
ÆTATIS SVÆ 21.
Hoc ô Viator Marmore Conditæ
Charæ RecvMbunt Exuviæ brevem
Viventis OPTANTiſq; VITAM
PRæcoce Cœlum Anima Petentis:
Muſarum Alumnus Jam fuit Artibus
Præfectus Sacris, quas Studio Pio
Atq; Aure quam fida receptas,
Oxonij Coluit Parentis.
Sed SPrevit Artes Vah nimium breves
Vitamq; longam Credidit heu Brevem
Triſtiſq; Plenum Errore multo
Ipſum Helicona Scatere vidit.

M. S.
Iohanĩs Hickes hujus parochiæ Generoſi,
qui arthritico morbo confectus
mortem libenter oppetit
In explorata fide beatæ reſurrectionis
menſis Julij decimo quarto die
Ano ſalutis milleſimo
ſexcenteſimo nonageſimo quarto
Ætatis ſuæ ſeptuageſimo.
H. I. S.
Juxta Mariti Exuvias
Elizabetha Hickes
Filia Gul. Oldiſworth
de Coln Rogers in Com. Gloc.
Armigeri
Ob. Sepris 6to A. D. 1727
Æt. 81°.

Dum cœlum habet animam
Sub hoc tumulo hypogœum
caros conſervat cineres
Mariæ Filiæ
Iohanis et Elizabethæ Hickes
maxime piæ Virginis
Quæ immedicabilibus Variolis laborans
placide in Chriſto obdormivit
octobris die Viceſimo ſexto
æra chriſti
Milleſima ſeptingenteſima undecima
paulo poſt anos quadraginta impleverat.

A hand-

A handſome marble monument, in the ſame aile, bears this inſcription :

SACRED
To the Memories
of Mr. John Purnell,
Late of the Pool-Houſe, in this Pariſh,
Gentleman,
And of Jane his Wife,
Who was the youngeſt Daughter
of John Hickes, of Weſt End
In this Pariſh,
Gentleman,
By Elizabeth Daughter of
William Oldiſworth, of Coln Rogers, in this County
Eſquire.
Mr. Purnell dyed Aug. 16th 1726 Ætatis 46.
His Wife dyed Ap[l]. 5th 1743 Ætat. 60.
Iohannes Purnell S. T. P. et Novi Collegij In Oxon
Cuſtos,
Eccleſiæ item Appropriatæ de Cwmdu Com. Brecon
et Dioc. Menevenſis Rector,
Optimis Parentibus
P. C.

Arms, *Baron and femme*, 1. *Argent, on a feſs between three maſcles azure, as many cinquefoils of the field*, for Purnell. 2. *Gules, a feſs undy between three fleurs de lis Or*, for Hickes.

There is likewiſe the following memorial on a flat ſtone :

Here Lyeth
A Rare Example of much goodneſs
Mr. JOHN PURNELL,
Late of ye Pool-houſe in this Pariſh
who died Auguſt the 16th
Anno Salutis 1726
Ætatis 46.
He was
A Zealous Member of ye Church of England,
a loving Huſband, a Tender Father,
A king Relation, a Generous Friend,
Always acceptable to the Rich,
and Liberal to the Poor.
Injurys between others He eaſily reconciled,
His own as readily forgave.
A Bleſſed Peace-maker.
He was through the whole Cours of his Life
A Sincere Chriſtian without Oſtentation,
And a Lover of all Mankind without Deſire of Praiſe.
Reader !
Go Thou and do likewiſe
That Thou mayeſt Reſt in Peace
and Riſe in Glory.
Alſo THOMAS his Youngeſt Son died Aug[t]. the
6th, 1728, aged 4 Years 9 Mo.

On a marble table in the ſame aile,

Near this Monument, in the Burying Place of her Anceſtors, lies interred the Body of ELIANOR late the Wife of THOMAS STOKES of y[e] Par[sh] Gent. and Second Daughter of IOHN HICKES the Elder, Formerly of Weſt End in this Pariſh Gentleman deceaſed, by ELIZABETH his laſt Wife Alſo deceaſed, Who was a Daughter of WILLIAM OLDISWORTH of Coln Rogers in y[e] County Eſquire, long ſince deceaſed. She departed this Life the 24th Day of July 1754, Aged 75 Years.

Arms, *Baron and femme*, 1. *Sable, a lion rampant argent*, for Stokes. 2. Hickes, as before.

On a marble table, againſt a pillar, in the ſame aile,

Near this Monument is interr'd the Body of ELIZABETH the Wife of EDWARD YATE of Malmeſbury in the County of Wilts Clothier, and Daughter of IOHN HICKES of this Pariſh Gent: by SYLVESTER his Wife who departed this Life the 16th Day of *October* Anno Dom. 1721, Ætatis ſuæ 67.

Arms, *Baron and femme*, 1. *Argent, three gates gules, 2 and 1*, for Yate. 2. Hickes, as before.

On a table of copper, againſt the ſouth wall,

In a Vault beneath the oppoſite Alley lie interred the Remains of Alexander Dorney, the younger, of this Pariſh Gent. He died Sept. the 21st Anno Dom. 1668, in the 38th Year of his Age, leaving behind him Sarah his Wife, and by her two Daughters, viz. Eliz. & Jane.

The above mentioned Sarah afterwards y[e] Wife of Thomas Stokes, youngeſt Son of Samuel Stokes formerly of Stanſhaw's Place in the Pariſh of Yate in y[e] County Gent. by Iſabella his Wife third Daughter of Samuel Codrington heretofore of Dodington in y[e] County Eſq; both long ſince deced lyeth alſo interr'd in the above-mentioned Vault. She Dy'd March y[e] Tenth 1721 in y[e] 94th Year of her Age, leaving behind her y[e] before-named Eliz: & Jane, as alſo Thomas her Huſband, & by him one Son only viz. Thomas.

Thomas y[e] Father lyeth alſo Inter'd in y[e] afores[d] Vault as do likewiſe y[e] ſaid Eliz. & Jane, who reſpectively departed y[e] Life in y[e] following Order of Time, viz.

Thomas Auguſt the 12, 1732 Aged 87 }
Iane April the 2, 1738 Aged 75 } Years.
Elizabeth Octo[r] y[e] 7, 1745 aged 86 }

Sacred to whoſe Memories y[e] Monument was here placed by y[e] aforementioned Thomas y[e] Son Nov. 7, 1753.

At the top are theſe arms, *Azure, a chevron between three dolphins nayant Or*. At bottom, *Sable, a lion rampant argent*, for Stokes.

On a marble altar tomb, in the church-yard, are the following memorials :

Here lies Sarah the Wife of Daniel Woodward
of the City of Briſtol Merchant, and Daughter of
Thomas Springett Eſq; of Groſmond in the County
of Monmouth, by Sarah his Wife,
Who
(Dear to her Relations
Valuable to her Acquaintance,
Charitable to the Poor
Pious towards God)
Died the 13th of June 1749 Aged 31,
and has left a Name behind her
more laſting than this marble can perpetuate.

On another compartment,

Alſo her two Daughters Elizabeth and Sarah, Elizabeth being interr'd with her, Aged 11 Days, and Sarah the 8th Day of January following, Aged 7 Months.

Alſo two of her Brothers James and Giles, James was buried Nov. 22[d] 1746, Aged 11 Months, Giles Jan. 25, 1733, Aged 12 Years.

At the end,

Here likewiſe lies interred William Giles of this Pariſh, Eſq; who died the 29th Day of Sept. 1750 Aged 80.

Here alſo lies Sarah the Daughter of the ſaid William Giles, Widow of Thomas Springett Eſq; and Mother of Sarah Woodward ſeverally aforementioned. She died the 19th of Aug. 1759, Ætatis ſuæ 65.

N. B. Upon a monument in the chancel, for the above William Giles, are theſe arms, *viz. Azure, a chevron Or between three caſtles argent.*

On the other ſide,

Here alſo lyeth interred the Body of William Woodward Son of Daniel Woodward Eſq; and the ſaid Sarah his Wife. He died the 31st Day of May 1754 Aged 6 Years.

The arms at one end of the tomb are, *Baron and femme*, 1. *Three oak leaves proper*. 2. *A feſs undy between three creſcents.*

On a marble monument, in the chancel,

In Memory of George Hobbs, ſon of William Hobbs, Clothier, by Sarah his Wife. He died Sept[r] 5th 1740, Aged 21 Years.

Alſo of the ſaid William Hobbs, who died Feb. 23[d] 1747-8 Aged 55 Years.

And Sarah his Wife who died May 6th 1754 Aged 72 Years.

Alſo of John the Son of the aforeſaid William and Sarah Hobbs who died June 3[d] 1759 Aged 35.

Arms, *Baron and femme*, 1. *Argent, a bend wavy azure between two hawks, or hobbys, proper*, for Hobbs. 2. *Sable, an unicorn Or, on a chief argent three pinks gules.*

Benefactions.

In 1655, John Wolford gave 4*l.* a year to the uſe of the poor, charged on a ground called the Moors, in the pariſh of Charfield. Mrs. Elizabeth Spurt gave 40*s.* yearly, one part for a ſermon, the other for the poor. Mr. Henry Cann gave 3*l.* a year to the poor ; and John Cox gave a houſe in the borough, and 10*l.* to the ſame uſe. —— Prout gave a field called Cook's Leaze, worth 4*l.* a year; and Mr. William Hobbs, clothier, gave a rent charge of 30*s.* a year out of the Bell at Wickwar, both to buy clothing for the

the poor. —— Yeates gave 60*l.* that the intereſt of it may be applied to the apprenticing out poor boys to London. And Mrs. Elizabeth Hicks gave 12*l.* to buy a branch for the church, and the intereſt of 20*l.* to be given to the poor.

But the principal benefactor was Mr. Alexander Hoſea, who, by his will, in 1684, eſtabliſhed a free grammar-ſchool in this borough, and endowed it with a very good houſe in Gray's inn lane, in Holbourn, London. He alſo gave 600*l.* to build a ſchool houſe for the maſter to live in. The maſter receives 28*l.* a year. There is another free-ſchool in this place, for teaching poor children to read and write, endowed with 10*l.* a year, and a houſe for the maſter. The corporation are truſtees to both ſchools, and appoint the maſters. —Mr. Hoſea had been a poor boy apprenticed to a weaver in the town, and upon a particular day in the year, when it was the cuſtom with the inhabitants to make a diſh, called *Whitepot*, his miſtreſs ſent him with a panfull to the bakehouſe. Poor Hoſea had the misfortune to break the pan, which ſo terrified him that he durſt not return to his maſter, but ſet out immediately for London, where he was proſperous, and acquired a large fortune.

Taxes.					
The Royal Aid in	1692, £.	145	17	4
Poll-tax ——	1694, —	37	3	0
Land-tax ——	1694, —	180	16	6
The ſame, at 3*s.*	1770, —	133	14	6¾

At the beginning of this century, there were 220 houſes, and about 1000 inhabitants, whereof 36 were freeholders; yearly births 27, and burials 24. *Atkyns.* Since that time the town has loſt its trade, and the preſent inhabitants are computed to be about 850.

WIDFORD.

THIS is a ſmall pariſh, in the hundred of Slaughter, two miles diſtant eaſt from Burford in Oxfordſhire, ten ſouth-eaſt from Stow, and thirty eaſt from Glouceſter.

It is one of thoſe inſtances of the inconvenient and unnatural allotment of pariſhes to hundreds and counties, which I have had frequent occaſion to mention, and ſerves to mark the capricious humour even of the greateſt and wiſeſt of men. For what can be more abſurd than to appropriate this pariſh to Glouceſterſhire, when it lies ſome miles diſtant from any part of it, and is totally ſurrounded by Oxfordſhire?

The river Winruſh is of conſiderable breadth here, and is famous for fine trout and cray fiſh. It has a ford through it, which gave name to the place, for what is *Widford*, but the *Wide ford*?

The pariſh conſiſts chiefly of arable lands and wood lands. A houſe, called Cap's Lodge, tho' lying within the boundaries of the foreſt of Whichwood, belongs to Widford, where, by antient cuſtom, the inhabitants of the town of Burford aſſemble, on Whitſunday yearly, and chuſe a lord and lady. They likewiſe claim the privilege of cutting wood, and of hunting with dogs, and killing deer in the foreſt; but the latter is compounded for, by delivering to them two bucks annually, on a certain day, with which the principal inhabitants of that town make an entertainment.

Of the Manor and other Eſtates.

'Saint Oſwald of Glouuceceſter held Widiforde, 'in Berniton hundred. In the time of king 'Edward there were two hides, and two plow-'tillages in demean, and four villeins, and three 'bordars, with two plow-tillages. There are 'four *ſervi*, and eight acres of meadow, and a 'mill of 10*s.* In the time of king Edward it was 'worth 40*s.* and is now worth 60*s.* Rannulf 'holds it of Saint Oſwald. It has the ſame 'owner now as it had in king Edward's time.' *Domeſday*, p. 70.

How, or at what time, the manor paſſed from the priory of St. Oſwald, does not appear; but it was in lay hands 9 E. 1. when the ſheriff returned into the exchequer the names of all the vills in his county, with their reſpective proprietors, certifying that Wideforde was a vill in the hundred of Salmoneſburye, and that Robert de . . . . was lord of it.

It was ſome time afterwards veſted in the Lovels, who reſided at a place, called Minſter-Lovel, under Whichwood, where conſiderable remains of their manſion houſe are ſtill to be ſeen. John lord Lovel died ſeized of Widford and Little Riſington, 4 E. 4. and Joan his wife, the ſiſter of William viſcount Beaumont, was endowed with this manor, and died in the 6th year of the ſame reign. Francis lord Lovel, ſon of John, was in great favour with king Richard the Third, and a partaker with him in his wicked practices, and was therefore advanced to be lord chamberlain. His ill behaviour and undeſerved preferment drew on him the odium of the people, ſo that he was attainted 1 H. 7. for divers miſdemeanors; and entering the kingdom in arms, was ſlain near Newark, 3 H. 7. leaving no iſſue.

Widford was granted to Jaſper duke of Bedford, uncle to the king, 1 H. 7. but he died without iſſue, in the 11th year of the ſame reign. It was afterwards mortgaged by the crown, together with other conſiderable eſtates, to Paul Withepool, and other citizens of London, 36 H. 8.

The manor came afterwards to the Johnſons, for Herman Johnſon, eſq; was lord of it in the year 1608. Out of that name and family it paſſed to the Fettiplaces, about the cloſe of the laſt century. Sir Charles Fettyplace, baronet, was owner of Widford when ſir Robert Atkyns wrote his Hiſtory; and Robert Fettyplace, eſq; is the preſent lord of the manor, and has a ſeat, with a large

large deer-park, and a good eſtate in the pariſh. His arms are, *Argent, two chevrons gules.*

Henry de Berkeley and Annabel his wife levied a fine of lands in Widford, to the uſe of Walter de Eſchale and Alice his wife, 51 H. 3. but this muſt be underſtood of Widford in Berkeley, and not of this place. John Martyn and Margaret his wife levied a fine of lands in Widford, to the uſe of William Conbrook, 22 R. 2. and William Conbrook levied a fine of the ſame lands, to the uſe of John Faellore de Filking, 6 H. 4.

Of the Church, &c.

The church is a rectory, in the deanery of Stow, worth about 30*l.* a year, and in the gift of Mr. Fettyplace. The earl of Warwick formerly preſented to this church.

There is no houſe nor glebe for the miniſter.

The advowſon of the rectory of Widford, and a toft of land which lately belonged to the priory of St. John the Evangeliſt in Burford, were granted to Edmond Herman 37 H. 8.

The church is ſmall, without any ſteeple.

Taxes.					
The Royal Aid in	1692,	£. 25	16	0
Poll-tax —	1694, —	2	12	0
Land-tax —	1694, —	26	13	4
The ſame, at 3*s.*	1770, —	20	17	3

There were 7 houſes in the pariſh, and about 36 inhabitants, 2 of whom were freeholders; yearly births 1, burials 1. *Atkyns.* I think there are now only 3 houſes, and about 20 inhabitants.

WILLERSEY.

THIS is a ſmall pariſh, in the upper diviſion of Kiftſgate hundred, about three miles weſt from Chipping Campden, five ſouth-eaſtward from Eveſham, and twenty-ſix north-eaſtward from Glouceſter.

The village is ſeated in the Vale, and lies under the weſt ſide of thoſe hills which every where mark the limits of the Coteſwold country with a bold and well defined outline. On the ſummit of the hill above the village, but within the pariſh, there is a large camp, incloſing about ſixty acres of ground, ſuppoſed to have been formed in the time of the Daniſh ravages, and it ſtill continues pretty perfect.

From this camp there is a fine bird's-eye view of the vale below, interſected with beautiful hedge-rows, and ſcattered with villages and farm houſes. The river Avon meanders through the middle of the vale, and the town of Eveſham at an agreeable diſtance, preſents itſelf as the principal object, with the Breedon and Malvern hills in the back ground to cloſe the view. This camp and proſpect principally diſtinguiſh Willerſey; but in proſecuting my inquiry after curioſities, I was informed by the rector, as a matter worthy notice, that there is an eſtate here, ſubject to a rent-charge, proportioned by the rate of the land-tax, payable to a certain family as a recompence (tho' an inadequate one) for preſerving the life of king Charles the Second, by hiding him in the oak. When the land-tax is at three ſhillings in the pound, the annuity, or payment, is four guineas.

Of the Manor and other Eſtates.

At the time of the Norman conqueſt, Willerſey belonged to the abbey of Eveſham, according to *Domeſday*; but ſir Robert Atkyns has repreſented it as being then the property of the church of Winchcombe, which error I apprehend he was led into by uſing an imperfect copy of *Domeſday*, as already obſerved under Broadwell. The following is a literal traſlation of the record:

'The ſame church [St. Mary of Eveſham] 'holds Willerſei, in Widelei hundred. There 'are eight hides, and one at Wiquenna [Child's 'Wickham]. There are three plow-tillages in 'demean, and ſixteen villeins, and four bordars, 'and a prieſt, with ſix plow-tillages. There are 'two *ſervi*, and a little meadow. It was worth '4*l.* and is now worth 100*s.*' *Domeſday*, p. 72.

The abbey of Eveſham purchaſed a charter of free warren in this and many other manors, 35 H. 3. The ſame houſe was ſeized of the manor 9 E. 1. and their right to court leet and free warren was allowed, in the proceedings on a writ of *Quo warranto*, in the 15th year of that reign. Sir Thomas Weſt and Alice his wife held Willerſey 10 R. 2. as tenants to the abbey of Eveſham, in which year ſir Thomas died; and the ſame monaſtery continued ſeized of this manor 'till the general diſſolution of religious houſes.

The manor of Willerſey, and the demean lands thereof, lately belonging to the abbey of Eveſham, were granted to John Cock and John Wrath, 36 H. 8. and the manor and the advowſon of the rectory were granted to ſir John Bourn, ſecretary of ſtate to king Philip and queen Mary, and to Dorothy his wife, 5 Mar. and the grant to them recites that the lands formerly belonged to the abbey of Eveſham.

The manor was veſted in Charles Kettleby, eſq; in the year 1608. Edward Winnington, eſq; ſon of ſir Francis Winnington, of Worceſterſhire, attorney-general to king Charles the Second, was owner of it at the beginning of this century; and ſir Edward Winnington is the preſent lord of the manor of Willerſey.

John Dereham died ſeized of a meſſuage and a yard land called Parſon's, and of an eſtate called Spragges's, and of ſeveral other lands, cloſes, and common of paſture in Willerſey, 43 Eliz. leaving William Dereham, his ſon and heir, twenty-eight years old. *Eſcheat. Inquiſ.* 2 Jac.

Of the Church, &c.

The church is a rectory, in the deanery of Campden, worth about 150*l.* a year. The reverend

reverend Mr. William Scott is patron and incumbent. The patronage formerly belonged to the abbey of Evefham.

The whole lordfhip contained about thirty-fix yard lands. The impropriator had the great tithes of twenty-eight of them, paying the rector eight bufhels of wheat, eight of barley, and eight of beans; and the rector had the tithes of the remaining eight yard lands. But in the year 1767, the common fields and wafte lands were inclofed by act of parliament, when Anne George, the impropriatrix, had 145 acres allotted her in lieu of her tithes, and the rector 83 acres in lieu of his glebe and tithes.

The church, dedicated to St. Peter, is built in the form of a crofs, with a tower in the middle; and the founder of it is fuppofed to lie buried in a niche in the chancel.

Firft fruits £.	13	2	6	Synodals £.	0	1	0
Tenths —	1	6	3	Pentecoftals	0	0	8½
Procurations	0	3	0				

Taxes.			£.	s.	d.
The Royal Aid in	1692, £.		97	6	0
Poll-tax ——	1694, —		18	5	0
Land-tax ——	1694, —		60	11	0
The fame, at 3s.	1770, —		46	18	5

About the beginning of this century, there were 56 houfes in the parifh, and about 250 inhabitants, 35 of whom were freeholders; the yearly births were 5, and the burials 5. *Atkyns.* I am not particularly informed of the ftate of population at prefent.

****

WINCHCOMBE.

THIS parifh lies in the hundred of Kiftfgate, ten miles diftant fouth-weft from Campden, nine eaftward from Tewkefbury, and fixteen north-eaftward from Gloucefter.

The river Ifborne, which rifes in Charlton Abbats, receives the Poftlip ftream, and feveral fprings out of Sudley manor, and taking its courfe northward through this parifh, empties itfelf into the Avon a little below Evefham in Worcefterfhire. It produces fome trout and fmall fifh, particularly eels and gudgeons.

It is remarkable that tobacco was firft planted in England in this parifh, and yielded a confiderable profit to the inhabitants, until they were reftrained by act of parliament.

The parifh confifts chiefly of rich meadow and pafture, and is pretty extenfive. It has a market town feated on the weft fide of it, which was antiently called *Wincelcumbe*, from the Saxon pincel, a *corner*, and *comb*, a *valley*, becaufe it lay in a nook, or corner of the vale, encompaffed with hills, except to the north-eaftward.

The town was formerly of much greater account than at prefent. It derived its confequence from an abbey founded in the eighth century, by Kenulfe king of Mercia, who had a palace here; for the founding of religious houfes, in the early times of Chriftianity, occafioned a great refort of people, and had pretty much the fame effect on population in fome places as the increafe of trade had afterwards in others.

There was a fmall territory adjoining to the town, and dependent upon it, which is faid to have been a fheriffdom, or county, in the Anglo-Saxon time, and fo to have continued 'till the reign of king Canute, whofe vice-roy Edric, furnamed Streona, divefted it of its independence, and adjoined it to Gloucefterfhire. But after the conqueft the town was a diftinct hundred, as it is expreffly mentioned in *Domefday*; and it is remarkable, that the account of it ftands in that record between the particulars of fome manors and eftates in Wales, and thofe in Gloucefterfhire, as though the borough was not, even at that time, laid to the county at large. It is alfo obfervable, that it is called a borough in *Domefday*, when no other towns in the county, except Gloucefter and Briftol, were fo dignified. The following is a tranflation from that record:

'In the time of king Edward, the borough of 'Wincelcumbe paid a farm of 6 *lib.* of which 'earl Herald had the third penny, that is, 40 *fol.* 'It paid 20 *lib.* afterwards with the whole hun'dred of its vill. Durand the fheriff added 100 *fol.* 'and Roger de Ivrei 60 *fol.* Now the three hun'dreds being joined pay 28 *lib.* of which 20 are 'in *Ora*.' *Domefday*, p. 67.

I fuppofe the 100*s.* and the 60*s.* fo added as above, were paid on account of the two additional hundreds, but the record does not mention what they were, nor can I form any probable conjecture about them.

There were three burgages in the town, of 40 *den.* appendant to the manor of Oxendone; one appendant to Aldritone; one, paying 3 *fol.* held by the church of Wireceftre; one paying 18 *den.* held by the church of Hereford; two paying 10 *den.* belonging to the church of St. Dennis at Paris; William Goizenboded held one burgage; Roger de Laci held three of 32 *den.* Roger de Lueri held ten, paying 65 *den.* Robert Difpenfator held one of 16 *den.* and Henry de Ferrers held two paying 16 *den.* Thefe make together twenty-five burgages, fet down in *Domefday* among the poffeffions of the feveral before-mentioned proprietors.

In its moft flourifhing ftate, the town was large, and had a wall built round it, as appears by the Legend, or Life of St. Kenelm, and as Leland teftifies,[a] who faw the appearance of the town wall when he vifited this place in the time of

[a] His words are thefe: 'The towne of certaine, as it ap'peareth in divers places, and efpecially by fouth, towardes 'Sudeley-Caftle, was walled; and the Legend, or Life of St. 'Kenelme doth teftifie the fame.' *Itin.* 2d Edit. Hearne, V. 4.

of king Henry the Eighth. He collected some particulars of it from one Avery, the parson of Dene, who informed him, that Winchcombe was *oppidum muro cinctum,* and that a great part of the town stood on the side of the river next to Sudley-castle, where there were no houses in Leland's time; and that it extended on the other side above the church, 'where the Farme of Corwedene is.' From this account it is evident that the river Isborne, which waters the foot of the present town, ran through the middle of the old one, *so that of old tyme*, says my author,[b] *it was a mighty large Towne*. It was defended by a fortress, or castle, which stood near the south side of the present parish church, where are now some cottages and gardens; and was called the *Ivy Castle*, as appeared from writings in Winchcombe abbey, perhaps because the walls of it were covered with ivy, which grows very commonly in the decay'd walls of old buildings. But the castle was not standing in Leland's time, nor had the last prior of Winchcombe ever seen it, having only heard[c] that there was such a fort which stood about the east-north-east part of the borough.

This is all we know of the antient state of the town, and perhaps all that can now be collected about it. Richard Kidderminster, the last abbat except one, wrote a history of the foundation of his abbey, &c. but his book was unfortunately burnt by the fire of London, in the year 1666, which accident has most likely prevented many historical matters concerning it from coming to our knowledge; so that we can neither fix the æra of its greatest prosperity, nor the time of its first decline. We find that in Leland's time it had fallen much to decay; and as it rose to its eminence by means of the monastery, so after the suppression of that house, it ran still more rapidly to ruin, as I conclude from the preamble to queen Elizabeth's grant of a fair and market, which recites, that *by the relation of Dorothy the lady Chandos, and the humble petition of the inhabitants of the borough or town of Winchcombe, the said borough* appeared to be *fallen into so great ruin and decay, that its inhabitants* were *not able to support and repair* it *for the great poverty that* reigned *amongst them.*

It now consists of two streets, crossing each other. One leads northwards towards Tewkesbury and Evesham; the other, which is by much the most considerable, leads on the east side to Campden; on the west towards Cheltenham and Gloucester. There is no great road through it, and consequently it is but little frequented, except by those who have immediate concerns with the inhabitants. It is a borough by prescription, governed by two bailiffs, and their assistants, not exceeding ten in number, and out of those twelve the bailiffs are taken by rotation, and annually at the court-leet are sworn into their office.

Queen Elizabeth, by letters patent, granted a fair to be holden within the borough, upon the eve, upon the feast, and upon the morrow after the feast of St. Mark; and a market upon Tuesday in every week. But there are now two annual fairs, held on the 6th of May, and the 28th of July, and the market is on Saturday. As the town is seated in a rich vale, the fairs are usually well supply'd with cattle and draught horses; but the market is very inconsiderable. The corporation have the tolls, which usually let at about 10*l.* a year.

Of the ABBEY.

In the year 787, king Offa built a nunnery here, and in 798, Kenulph king of Mercia laid the foundation of a stately abbey in the place of the nunnery, wherein three hundred monks of the order of St. Benedict were maintained on its first foundation. But it is supposed that not more than forty or fifty of them were in holy orders, the rest working to supply the priests and themselves in all necessaries that might be wanting.

This monastery was dedicated with great pomp to St. Mary, and consecrated by Wulfrid archbishop of Canterbury, and by twelve other bishops, in the presence of king Kenulph, and of Cuthred king of Kent, and of Sired king of the West Saxons, and of ten dukes, and other noblemen; king Kenulph, in honour of the solemnity, releasing at the high altar Eadbert king of Kent, whom he had then lately taken prisoner. At that time, besides the rich presents which he gave to the noblemen, the king gave a pound weight of silver to all such who had no lands, and a mark in gold to all priests, and a shilling to every monk, and distributed many other valuables to the people.

King Kenulph died about the year 820, in the 24th of his reign, and was buried in the eastern part of this abbey church, leaving two daughters, Quendrid and Burgmill, and an infant son Kenelme, but seven years old, whom he committed to the care of his daughter Quendrid. But she conspired with Askebert, the young king's tutor and governor, to murder him, that she might succeed to the kingdom. The wicked Askebert accordingly taking him into a wood called Clenth, cut off his head in an obscure place between two hills, where a white cow frequented, and was therefore called the *White Cow's Valley*.

What follows in our antient historians[d] concerning the discovery of this murder and treason, savours too much of the marvellous to gain credit with many of the present age. I shall, however, give the substance of it for the reader's entertainment. They relate, that the murder was for a short time unknown, 'till it was miraculously discovered at Rome, where a dove flying over the altar of St. Peter, let a parchment drop, on which it was thus written:

In Clent in Cowberche hed bewevyd lyth Kenelme.

Which being in the English langugage, was not understood by any except an Englishman that was very luckily present, and interpreted the writing to the pope, who by his apostolical letters discovered the murder to the English princes. Multitudes of people are said to have been present at the taking up of the body of the infant king, and a contention arising between the inhabitants of Gloucestershire and Worcestershire which should have his relicks, it was at last determined that he should be buried at Winchcombe: And whilst the corps was bringing into the town, accompanied by the clergy and laity, singing holy hymns, the wicked Quendred stood looking out at her window, and with a loud voice sung the 109th psalm, to disturb the celebration of her brother's funeral: But when she came to the 19th verse, where are these words, *Let it thus happen from the Lord unto my enemies, and unto those who speak evil against my soul*, her eye balls instantly droped out of her head, and besmeared the place with blood, which, it is said, was to be seen many ages afterwards.

This is the story of king Kenelm, who was canonized for a saint upon the account of these miracles, and his relicks brought infinite riches to the monastery. What reader will not abhor the cruel murder, and at the same time detest the lying tale of the miraculous discovery, invented by the monks, to raise a superstitious veneration for Kenelm, and so to excite many to visit their abbey, and make offerings at his tomb!

In process of time,[e] this monastery became a college of Seculars. It suffered severely by the Danish ravages, and was in a very ruinous condition in the reign of king Edgar, when archbishop Oswald rebuilt it, and restored it to great splendor. It was then consecrated anew to the virgin Mary and St. Kenelm, whose story the bishop cultivated to the great enriching of the monastery.

In the fourth year of king William the Second, a vehement lightening shook the abbey, and the roof and steeple of the church, and threw down the crucifix and image of the virgin Mary.

This was a mitred and peeral abbey, and the first summons of the abbat of Winchcombe to parliament, which is now to be found on record, was in the year 1265, 49 H. 3. *Dugd. Summons.*

Catalogue of Abbats, taken from Mr. Willis's *History of Mitred Parliamentary Abbeys.*

1. Germanus, prior of Ramsey, was made abbat by king Edgar upon the rebuilding of this abbey, *anno* 985. After he had governed several years, he retired to Ramsey, and was there buried. The next that I meet with is

2. Godwinus, whom I take to be the same that is called Eadwinus in the *Decem Scriptores*. He lived in the time of king Canutus, *anno* 1026, and dying *anno* 1054, as Florence of Worcester has it, was succeeded by

3. Godricus, called Eadricus, for I take them to be the same in the *Decem Scriptores*, who *anno* 1066, opposing the Norman invasion, the conqueror deprived him of his abbatship, and made him close prisoner in Gloucester castle, committing the charge of the monastery to the abbat of Evesham, 'till such time as he constituted

4. Galandus abbat in his stead. Whose successor

5. Radulphus, dying *anno* 1095, this abbey was, after two years vacancy, conferred upon

6. Girmundus. He died *anno* 1122, 4 *Id. Junii*, and was succeeded by

7. Godefridus, prior of this church. He died *anno* 1137, and was succeeded by

8. Robert, in whose time this church was burnt. He governed 20 years, and dying *anno* 1157, was succeeded by

9. Gervase, who died *anno* 1172, and was succeeded by

10. Henry, prior of Gloucester. He died *anno* 1184, (or as others *anno* 1181) and was succeeded by

11. Crispin, prior of this place, who died the same year, and was succeeded *anno* 1185, by

12. Ralph; to whom succeeded *anno* 1193,

13. Robert. He ordained that on the morrow after All Souls, *viz.* on Nov. 3, an hundred people should be relieved here with bread, meat, and drink. He redeemed the manors of Yanworth, Hasleton, Halling, &c. which were mortgaged for above 558*l.* to William, advocate of Bitton. He also laid out 570 marks and 12*s.* sterling in disafforesting the manor of Twining. He also, at a great charge, made an aqueduct to bring spring water in lead pipes from Hanwell to his monastery. He died *anno* 1220, and was succeeded by

14. Thomas, prior of this place. He died 5 *Non.* Octob. 1232, and was succeeded the same year by

15. Henry de Tudinton, installed abbat the 29th of the same month. He died *anno* 1248, and was succeeded the same year by

16. John de Yarmouth, or Ganeworth, as Wharton calls him; or as in the Monasticon Yanworth. He obtained the manor of Dry Marston, worth about 1130 marks, and many other good estates in tithes and farms were added to the church in his time. He died *anno* 1284, having resigned two years before his death, on account of his age, to

17. Walter de Wickwane; who thereupon commenced abbat *anno* 1282, and held this dignity 'till the time of his death, which happened *anno* 1314. After his decease

18. Tho. de Scirburn became abbat 4 *Id. Junii*, 1314; who dying the same year

19. Richard de Ydeburi, sacrist, succeeded. He bought the fee of the manor of Rowel for 550*l.* and purchased the farm of Cotes for ever, and the assart lands in Ennefton for 100 marks. He resigned *anno* 1339, and had for his successor, *anno* 1340,

20. Will. de Shirborn; whose successor

21. Robert de Ippewell, confirmed abbat 24 Sept. 1352; resigning *anno* 1359,

22. Walter de Winfortune, burser or cellarer of Worcester, was substituted in his stead. This abbat obtained the hundreds of Kiftsgate, Holford, and Gretestan, for the abbey. He died June 22, *anno* 1395, and was succeeded the same year, *viz.* July 6 following, by

23. Will. Bradely. He died Dec. 28, *anno* 1422, and was succeeded January 15 following by

24. John Cheltenham; who dying *anno* 1452, was succeeded by

25. Will. Winchecombe, elected abbat Dec. 21, 1452. He was a considerable benefactor by removing the parish church out of the abbey. He died *anno* 1474, and was succeeded by

26. John Twinning; who received the benediction Aug. 22, the same year. He was a great promoter of learning, and dying *anno* 1488,

27. Richard Kederminster was confirmed abbat July 10, 1488. He had been educated in Gloucester college, afterwards called Gloucester hall, and now Worcester college in Oxford, where there was an appartment belonging to this abbey, called Winchcombe Lodging. He was a learned man, and by his wise government, and his encouragement of virtue and good letters, made the monastery flourish so much, that 'twas equal to a little university. *Anno* 1500, he travelled to Rome, and became afterwards a celebrated preacher. In the year 1515, the privileges of the clergy being attack'd, he preached a remarkable sermon on that account, shewing that 'twas against the law of God, who, by his prophet David says, *Touch not my anointed, and do my prophets no harm.* He wrote a very valuable history of the foundation of this monastery, and another of the lives of the abbats, beginning with Germanus, *anno* 7 of King Edgar, *anno* 988, and reaching down to his own time; which desirable book was unhappily lost in the fire of London, *anno* 1666. He died *anno* 1531, and was buried in the abbey church, in beautifying which, &c. he had expended a great deal, and in inclosing it with a stone wall *ex quadrato Saxo* towards the town. He was on his death succeeded by

28. Richard Ancelme, *alias* Mounslow, the last abbat; who, with 24 others of his convent, subscribed to the king's supremacy *anno* 1534. After which, with the rest of his monks, surrendering his abbey into the hands of the king's visitors, on Dec. 3, 1539, he obtained a pension of 160*l. per ann.* which I find him possessed of *anno* 1553, tho' with an abatement of 40*l.* on account, as I persume, of his having some preferment given him to quit his pension in part. *Anno* 1554, I meet with the presentation of one Richard Mounslow to the rectory of Radwinter, near Colchester, co. Essex, which about 4 years afterwards became vacant by his resignation, or rather death, as I conclude: Whether he were

[e] Tanner's Notitia Monastica.

were the ſame with our abbat I cannot be certain; and all I have elſe to add is, that *anno* 1553, there was 14*l*. 6*s*. 8*d*. remaining in charge in fees, and 46*l*. in annuities, out of the revenues of this late monaſtery, beſides the following penſions:

Richarde Mounſlowe, late abbott, 140*l*. and 40 lodes of firewod owt of Depewode yerelie, by th' aſſignement of the receiver for the tyme being, John Hancock, prior, ſexten and maſter of the chappell, 8*l*. Will. Craker, ſen. and chaunter, Will. Bloſſom, ſen. almener and pitenſſer, Will. Bradley, hoſteler, Richard Freeman, B.D. John Whalley, ſupprior and fermorer, Walter Cowper, ſub-chanter, Hugh Cowper, A.B. Richard Bidon, kechinner and ſubcellerer, George Foo, ſub ſexten, 6*l*. 13*s*. 4*d*. each: Richard Parker, Will. Trentham, Will. Howard, terce prior, Richard Williams, Walter Turbot, chaplen, Richard Baniſter, keeper of the liberary, Chriſtopher Chawnfut, 6*l*. each. Sum 250*l*.

Kenulph, king of Mercia, and his ſon and ſucceſſor, Kenelm, were buried in the abbey church; as were Henry Boteler, who covered the body of that church with lead, and ſeveral other perſons of the family of the Botelers of Sudley. *Leland.*

There is no deſcription of this abbey church extant, and it is thought that the whole was demoliſhed, very ſoon after the ſurrender, by lord Seymour, the firſt proprietor. Since which time the very ſcite of the buildings being levelled, and turned into plowed fields, it is only conjectured that they ſtood on the eaſt ſide of the preſent pariſh church.

See the charters relating to this abbey in the *Appendix*, N°s. 34, 35, 36.

Of the Manor and other Eſtates.

The manor of Winchcombe was veſted in the abbey 'till the latter was diſſolved, and it was then granted, with the ſcite of the monaſtery, to ſir Thomas Seymour, 1 E. 6. upon whoſe attainder, it was granted to William Parr, marquis of Northampton, June 24, 5 E. 6. to be held in free ſoccage, as of the manor of Eaſt Greenwich, without quit-rent. The marquis was attainted 1 Mar. for taking up arms on behalf of the lady Jane Grey, whereby the manor reverted to the crown, which was in the poſſeſſion of it in the year 1608. It came afterwards into the poſſeſſion of the Chandos family, who ſold it to the Whitmores; and doctor Lloyd, chancellor of the dioceſe of Worceſter, was lord of it at the beginning of this century. He had two daughters coheireſſes, one married to John Soley, of Bewdley in the county of Worceſter; the other to John Cox, of Clent in the county of Stafford; who were ſeized of it in right of their wives. From them it paſſed, by purchaſe, to George Pitt, eſq; and lord Rivers is the preſent lord of the manor.

Gilbert de Laci, nephew to Hugh de Laci, *temp. Steph. reg.* granted to the knights templers three burgages in Winchelcumbe. *Dugd. Bar.* Roger de Wateville was ſeized of houſes in Winchcombe, and granted them to the maſter of the knights templers 15 E. 1. who were ſeized of them 2 E. 3. John Alderwine was ſeized of one meſſuage, and 2*s*. rent in Winchcombe 9 R. 2. Richard Buſhel was ſeized of five meſſuages, three yard-lands, two acres of arable, ſix acres and a half of meadow, and four acres of paſture, lying in Winchcombe, Coat, and Dry Marſton, for the uſe of the abbey, 15 R. 2. Richard Buſhel, for the abbey of Winchcombe, was ſeized of one meſſuage, two tofts, three acres of meadow, and of a paſture for eight cows in Winchcombe and Sherbourn, 18 & 20 R. 2. and of lands in Winchcombe 2 H. 4. Richard Chamberlain was alſo ſeized of divers tenements, and of a mill in Winchcombe, 3 H. 4. Thomas Bruges and Maud his wife levied a fine of lands in Winchcombe, Gret, and Greton, to the uſe of John Hanborough, and to the heirs of John and Maud, 36 H. 6. John Garine and Elizabeth his wife levied a fine of lands in Winchcombe, Gret, and Greton, to Thomas Bruges, and others, 2 E. 4.

A toft and lands in Winchcombe, lately belonging to the abbey, were granted to Richard Andrews and Nicholas Temple, in truſt, 35 H. 8. Other lands in Winchcombe, which belonged to the abbey, were granted to Richard Andrews and Thomas Hyſley, 36 H. 8.

The ſcite of the monaſtery of Winchcombe was granted to John lord Chandos 1 Mar. and he dying the ſame year, Edmond lord Chandos had livery, and died ſeized thereof Sept. 11, 14 Eliz. *Eſch.*

Dancer's meadow in this pariſh, formerly belonging to Hayles abbey, was granted to Henry Ruſſel and Charles Brockton, 2 Mar.

Two woods, called Depwood and Hemlyehoo, in this pariſh, which belonged to the abbey, were granted to Edmond lord Chandos 1 Eliz. and other lands in the pariſh, which likewiſe belonged to the ſame houſe, were granted to Robert earl of Leiceſter, and to John Morley, 24 Eliz.

Tithes in Winchcombe, late the abbey's, were granted to ſir Chriſtopher Hatton, 24 Eliz. and other tithes there, which belonged to the abbey, were granted to ſir John Forteſcue, and Richard Tomlins, 4 Jac. 1.

Two mills in this pariſh, which had been granted to William marquis of Northampton, were, upon his attainder, granted to Edward Ferrers and Francis Philips, 7 Jac. 1.

TITHINGS and *HAMLETS*.

1. *Sudley Tenements.* This eſtate belongs to George lord Rivers. It has, for many centuries, had the ſame proprietors with the manor of Sudley, under which there is a particular account of them.

2. *Cotes.* This hamlet joins to the borough. The abbey of Winchcombe purchaſed a charter of free warren in Cotes 35 H. 3. John Cole, and others, granted one meſſuage, and one yard-land in Cotes near Winchcombe, to the abbey there, 34 E. 1. Richard de Ydebury, who ſucceeded to the abbacy about the 7 E. 2. purchaſed for the abbey the farm of Cotes for ever, and the aſſart lands in Enneſton, for one hundred marks. Walwyn Graves, eſq; is the preſent lord of the manor, and holds a court leet, called Greteſtan-court, to which ſeveral adjoining pariſhes owe ſuit.

3. *Poſtlip.*

3. *Poſtlip.* This hamlet is taken notice of in *Domeſday*, where it is thus recorded:

'Ansfrid de Cormeliis holds Poteſlepe in Grete-'ſtan hundred. Godric held it. There are three 'hides taxed. There are two plow-tillages in 'demean, and three villeins, and five bordars, 'with two plow-tillages. There are eleven *ſervi*, 'and two mills of 15*ſol.* A wood one mile long, 'and one broad. It was worth 100*ſol.* now 4*lib.*' *Domeſday*, p. 78.

William de Poſtelip was ſeized of one yard land in Poſtlip, and was convicted of felony 27 E. 1. William de Cheſterton, and others, were ſeized of the manor of Poſtelip, in truſt for the abbey of Tewkeſbury 7 R. 2. Tithes in Poſtelip, which belonged to the abbey of Winchcombe, were granted to ſir Thomas Seymour 1 E. 6. and by his attainder reverted to the crown, and were granted to ſir Chriſtopher Hatton 24 Eliz. Poſtlip is now the eſtate of the earl of Coventry, and has been in his family for many years. His lordſhip has a large houſe here, ſituated on the ſide of an eminence, with a chapel, now converted to prophane uſes. The houſe is occupied by Mr. William Durham, who is one of the moſt conſiderable paper-makers in the kingdom.

4. *Cockbury.* The name of this place is probably from *Coch*, which ſignifies *red* in the Britiſh language. John earl of Shrewſbury was ſeized of a tenement called Cockburns near Winchcombe 38 & 39 H. 6. One part of this hamlet belongs to the earl of Coventry, the other to William Rogers, of Dowdeſwell, eſq.

5. *Langley.* This hamlet lies upwards of two miles from the church, and is only one farm houſe. Maurice Sheppard died ſeized of this manor 20 Eliz. and left an only daughter married to Richard Houghton, who, in right of his wife, had livery granted to him the ſame year. It belonged to Richard Freeman, eſq; at the beginning of this century, and Thomas-Edwards Freeman, of Batsford in this county, eſq; is the preſent lord of the manor.

6. *Greet.* This hamlet lies about a mile from the church. It contains about ſixty houſes, and had formerly a chapel, now converted into a dwelling-houſe. The maſter of the knights templers had a grant of a court leet, with waifs and felons goods, in Greet and Greton from king Henry the Third, which grant was allowed in the proceedings on a writ of *Quo warranto* 15 E. 1. John de Sudley held two meſſuages, two yard lands and a half, and two acres of meadow, in Greet and Greeton, in truſt for William de Wotton, 17 E. 2. John de Sudley was ſeized of Greet 27 & 41 E. 3. William de Wotton was ſeized of Greet and Greeton 48 E. 3. Lands in theſe places were granted to Thomas lord Seimour, and upon his attainder they were again granted to William marquis of Northampton 5 E. 6. Other lands in Greet, which belonged to the chantry of St. Mary in Winchcombe, were granted to Anthony Cope 10 Jac. Mrs. Freeman, and Mr. William Carnal, are proprietors of good eſtates here.

7. *Gretton.* There is a chapel of eaſe in this hamlet, with divine ſervice once a month. John de Beſmamicele and Alice his wife granted three meſſuages, and ſeventy-ſix acres of land in Greeton and Aldrington to the abbey of Tewkeſbury 35 E. 1. The knights templers held lands in Greeton 2 E. 3. and the hamlets of Greet and Greeton were held of William de Clinton, earl of Huntingdon, 28 E. 3. John Wotton was ſeized of eighteen acres of land, called Swinſbrook land, lying in Greeton, 2 R 2. It appears by the regiſter book of the abbey of Tewkeſbury, that in the time of Simon biſhop of Worceſter, there aroſe a diſpute between the abbies of Tewkeſbury and Winchcombe concerning the tithes of a hide of land which Roger de Dicleſdon held in Gretton of the fee of the earl of Glouceſter, which was thus ſettled; that the chapel of the vill of Gretton, and half the tithes of the aforeſaid hide, ſhould remain to the church of Winchcombe, and that the other half of the tithes ſhould be enjoy'd by the abbey of Tewkeſbury. Tithes in Gretton, which belonged to the laſt-mentioned abbey, were granted to Edward earl of Lincoln, and to Chriſtopher Gouſe, 22 Eliz. Other tithes in Gretton, which belonged to Winchcombe abbey, were granted to ſir Chriſtopher Hatton 22 Eliz. Lord viſcount Tracy is lord of this manor.

8 *Frantone.*

9. *Naunton.* Sir Robert Atkyns, by miſtake, has miſapplied the particulars of this manor to the pariſh of Naunton upon the hills. The following is tranſlated from *Domeſday*:

'The church of Wincelcumbe holds Niwetone 'in Greteſtanes hundred, and two knights hold 'it of the abbat. There are three hides and a 'half. In demean are three plow-tillages, and 'three *ſervi*, and two villeins, with one plow-'tillage, and there may yet be ſix more. It is 'worth and was worth 40*ſol.*' *Domeſday*, p. 71.

This manor continued in the abbey of Winchcombe 'till that houſe was diſſolved. It was then granted to Thomas Culpeper 33 H. 8. and Alexander Culpeper had livery of it 1 Eliz. A leaſe of lands in Naunton, lately belonging to Winchcombe abbey, was granted to Henry Tracy 36 H. 8. Henry Tracy and Elizabeth his wife had a grant of lands here 7 E. 6. The tithes in Naunton, formerly belonging to the abbey of Winchcombe, were granted to ſir Thomas Seymour 1 E. 6. This manor is in the Tracy family.

10. *Corndean.* This is the eſtate of Mr. Blizard.

Of the Church, &c.

The church is in the deanery of Winchcombe, to which it gives name. It is worth from the impro-

impropriation about 16 *l.* a year. Lord viſcount Tracy is patron, and the reverend Mr. Roberts is the preſent incumbent of this curacy, and of the chapel of Gretton. Daniel Tanturier, eſq; barriſter at law, gave 200 *l.* towards augmenting the living, and Dr. Benſon, late biſhop of Glouceſter, procured the further augmentation from the governors of queen Anne's bounty, with a moiety of 500 *l.* left by Mr. Becker, and veſted in ſouth ſea annuities.

The impropriation is divided amongſt many proprietors, and is worth about 400 *l.* a year, and pays 12 *l.* 9 *s.* 7½ *d.* to the crown. The impropriation and advowſon formerly belonged to the abbey. Lord Tracy has the vicarage and ſmall tithes. The chantry lands which belonged to the ſame monaſtery are tithe free.

There was a church very antiently in the eaſt part of the town, dedicated to St. Nicholas, which falling to decay, the pariſhioners aſſembled to hear divine ſervice in the body of the abbey church, 'till the reign of king Henry the Sixth; when the then abbat, William Winchcombe, by the conſent of the town, began a pariſh church at the weſt end of the abbey, where a little chapel of St. Pancras ſtood. The abbat finiſhed the eaſt part, and the pariſhioners began the body, towards which they had collected 200 *l.* but that not being ſufficient, Ralph Boteler, lord Sudley, finiſhed the work, after which it was dedicated to St. Peter; and that is the preſent pariſh church. It is a large handſome building, with an aile on each ſide, and a tower at the weſt end; and both church and tower are embattled and adorned with pinnacles. There were figures in the ſouth aile of the choir, deſigned for Thomas Boteler, lord Sudley, and his four ſons, John, William, Thomas, and Ralph; and for Elizabeth, wife of Ralph lord Sudley; but they have been long ſince deſtroy'd.

By a decree in chancery 10 C. 1. the impropriators are obliged to pay towards the repair of the chancel.

There were ſeveral chantries and chapels in this church. The chapel of St. Nicholas belonged to the Botelers of Sudley, and was their burying place. There was another dedicated to the virgin Mary, and was curiouſly ornamented. The bailiff and pariſhioners preſented to a rich chantry in this church, in the year 1503.

Firſt fruits £. 3	4	0	Synodals £. 0	2	0
Tenths —	6	4¾	Pentecoſt. 0	0	5
Procurations 0	6	4¼			

Monuments and Inſcriptions.

There is a ſtone mural monument on the north ſide of the chancel, with the figure of a man in armour, kneeling, with a book before him; and upon a ſmall tablet beneath is this memorial:

This is the Effigies of Thomas Williams, Eſq; of Cornden, the ſecond Son of Sr Dauid Williams, Baronet, of Gwernewett in Brecknockſhire, one of his Majeſties Iudges in Weſtminſter, who was buried here the 28th day of May in the year 1636.

The monument is decorated with theſe arms, *viz.* Baron and femme, 1. *Argent, a chevron between three fighting cocks gules, on a chief ſable three pheons heads argent.* 2. *Per pale and per chevron argent and ſable, three mullets counterchanged.*

Near the above,

D. S.

Thomas Williams Filius hæres Dauidis Williams Arm. de Cornden, proſapiam à nobilibus et principibus viris longa ſerie deductam et illuſtrem legum et pietatis ſtudijs vlterius illuſtrauit; obijt Septem. viijo Ano 1669.

On a blue ſtone in the chancel,

H. S. E.

Vir inſigniſſimus David Williams Armr. de Cornden; Tam ſuis quam Atavorum virtutibus vere Nobilis Et à ſeris Nepotibus piè celebrandis, Numeroſæ prolis pater chariſſimus, Famulorum clemens juſtuſq; Dominus, Nec Laboris plus quam par exigens, Neq; minus præmij rependens. Non ſibi ſuiſq; ſolum Quin et Alijs, Regi, Reip. Eccleſiæ, Deo natus; Utriuſq; Juris qua Eccleſiaſtici qua Civilis cū peſſimis periculis ad Exitiū fere colluctantis propugnator et Vindex. Sic diù vixit vir bonus commune bonum, Honoribus æque ac Annis plenus. At! at! Extremæ tandem ſenectutis, Graviſſimo ſanè morbo depreſſus, Summaq; ſpe fretus Reſurrectionis beatæ, Lubens ac Lœtus occubuit, Importunum relinquens ſui Deſiderium, Grande pietatis & virtutum omnium Exemplar. Jan. xviijo Ano Dni 1698. Ætat. ſuæ 85. Hinc diſce vivere Viator, Hinc diſce Mori.

Near the above, are memorials for Carew Williams (ſon of David Williams, eſq; of Cornden) and Mary his relict, the former died in 1722, the latter in 1730; — for Heſter the wife of Thomas Williams, who died in 1674; —and for Elizabeth Williams, gent. who was buried in 1713.

Upon a marble table againſt the eaſt wall of the ſouth aile,

Intra Sacros Hoſce parietes juxta reconduntur exuviæ THOMÆ HAWES viri deſideratiſſimi: Filij Natu ſecundi Revdi SAMUELIS HAWES, A.M. & Eccleſiæ Budbrook juxta Warwicū Vicarij: Qui vocatus in Familiam THOMÆ COMITIS Coventriæ Prænobili Domino a Cenſibus, Ejuſq; poſt mortem, Comitiſſæ Dotariæ indefeſſâ Diligentiâ, illibatâ juſtitiâ & eodem in Cæteris vitæ tenore pariter Inſervijt.

Hoc inſuper Diſce Lector ac imitare. Inter varias & vitæ et officij curas Deum jugi & eximia pietate coluit et omnes Morum Elegantiâ demeruit. Obijt Jan. 9, 1700 Ætat. 29.

The arms upon this monument are, *Azure, a feſs undy between three lions paſſant Or.*

Upon a flat ſtone,

Hic jacet Elizabetha Uxor Iohannis Thorne ſenr quæ decimo octavo die Aprilis obijt 1679.

Hic quoque jacet Edmundus Thorne A.M. Socius Coll. Oriel Oxon. ſepultus decimo Octavo die Decemb. 1711.

Sub eodem lapide conditur Em. Rainsford Relict Edmundi Rainsford A.M. Obijt viceſimo die Maij Anno Xti 1741.

Upon another ſtone,

Hic jacet Edmundus Rainsford Paſtor huius Ovilis in expectatione ſupremi illius diei et qualis ille fuit iſte dies indicabit. Obijt XXVIIII die Menſis Maij MDCCXXVI.

Upon another,

Hic jacet Henricus Thorne, hujus Eccleſiæ Miniſter fuit 44s Ans Obijt 29o die Aprilis Anno Dom. MDCCXVIII.

D. S.

IACET, HEV IACET THOMAS MARKLEIVS, VIR VERE BONVS, ERVDITE PIVS, ECCLESIÆ ANGLICANÆ LVCERNA RESPLENDENS, ALLIS LVMEN ET VITAM LARGIENDO PROPRIAM ABSVMSIT: Denatus Maij XVI, Ano Chriſti Nati MDCLXXI.

Alſo here lyeth the body of Cicely Markley Gen. Relict of Thomas Markley Gen. ſomtime Miniſter of this place. She departed this Life the 29 of July 1706, Aged 75.

Upon another flat ſtone,

Hic jacet Gulielmus Harvey Rector de Burlington, qui mortem oppetijt triceſimo die Martij Anno Domini 1686.

And near it, engraven on braſs,

Hic jacet Elizabetha vxor amiciſſima Gulielmi Haruey cleri, triduo labore defeſſa obſtetricantis manus vix et ne vix quidem auxilio tertiam enixa ſobolem Modeſtiæ ceterarumq; virtutum encomijs alicubi ſatis elaudatam æq; piam ac quietam (anno Ætatis plus minus triceſſimo ſexto) intermiſit animam Maij quart. Anno Chriſtianæ Redemtionis MDCLXXXV

 Bene-

Benefactions.

There are three free ſchools in Winchcombe; the firſt is a grammar ſchool, founded by queen Elizabeth, and endowed with 10*l.* a year, for teaching eight or ten boys. The ſecond is another grammar ſchool, founded 13 Jac. by lady Frances Chandos, with a ſchool-houſe in St. Nicholas ſtreet for the maſter; and ſhe endowed her ſchool with certain lands formerly belonging to the ſexton's office in the monaſtery, for the maintenance of a maſter, and the education of fourteen boys, born in Winchcombe. The maſter receives 20*l.* a year out of the profits, and the remainder is applied towards repairing the houſe. The other ſchool was founded by George Townſend, of Lincoln's-inn in the county of Middleſex, eſq; who, by his will, in 1683, gave lands in Wormington in the county of Glouceſter, in truſt for ſecuring the payment of 4*l.* yearly to each of the towns of Winchcombe, Northleach, Campden, and Cheltenham, for teaching poor children to read. Alſo 3*s.* to be diſpoſed of weekly in the church of Winchcombe to ſuch poor as ſhall be uſual frequenters of the church; and 12*d.* weekly in bread to the poor of each of the towns of Northleach, Campden, and Nether Guiting; and 5*l.* yearly to each of the towns of Winchcombe, Northleach, Campden, Cheltenham, and Nether Guiting, for apprenticing one boy yearly out of each of the ſaid places.

In 1685, George Harvey gave two acres of land, the profits to be given to the poor of this pariſh for ever.

In 1692, lady Juliana Tracy gave ſixteen ridges of land, the profits of which, amounting to upwards of 4*l.* a year, to be laid out in garments for the poor at Chriſtmas.

William Thorndale gave 22*l.* to the uſe of the poor. *Atkyns.*

In 1715, Mr. Thomas Compere, of London, gave the intereſt of 150*l.* to be diſtributed to the poor.

In 1743, John Harvey gave the intereſt of 10*l.* to the uſe of poor widows.

In 1752, Anne Blaby gave 50*l.* to be laid out in land, and the rent to be given annually to poor families not receiving alms.

The lady Dorothy Chandos, wife of Edmund lord Chandos, and daughter and coheir of Edmund lord Bray, built an almſhouſe in this place for twelve poor women, but it has no endowment.

Winchcombe.

Taxes.	The Royal Aid in	1692,	£. 24	15	8
	Poll-tax ——	1694, —	26	19	0
	Land-tax ——	1694, —	55	8	0
	The ſame, at 3*s.*	1770, —	32	11	0

Gretton.

Taxes.	The Royal Aid in	1692,	£. 86	4	0
	Poll-tax — —	1694, —	6	13	0
	Land-tax ——	1694, -	74	8	0
	The ſame, at 3*s.*	1770, —	52	9	0

Greet.

Taxes.	The Royal Aid in	1692,	£. 60	2	0
	Poll-tax — —	1694, —	7	3	0
	Land-tax ——	1694, —	60	13	0
	The ſame, at 3*s.*	1770, —	41	17	0

Poſtlip.

Taxes.	The Royal Aid in	1692,	£. 71	11	0
	Poll-tax —	1694, —	3	18	0
	Land-tax —	1694, —	52	16	0
	The ſame, at 3*s.*	1770, —	37	2	3½

Coat.

Taxes.	The Royal Aid in	1692,	£. 18	0	4
	Poll-tax ——	1694, —	2	11	0
	Land-tax —	1694, —	32	16	0
	The ſame, at 3*s.*	1770, —	21	19	6

At the beginning of this century, there were 564 houſes, and 2715 inhabitants in this pariſh, of whom 56 were freeholders; yearly births 53, burials 48. *Atkyns.* But examining the regiſter, it appears that in ten years, beginning with 1700, there were 526 baptiſms, and 435 burials; and in the ſame number of years, beginning with 1760, the baptiſms were 562, and the burials 401. And there are now about 1960 ſouls in the whole pariſh, by which it ſhould ſeem that there is a conſiderable miſtake in the number of inhabitants given by ſir Robert Atkyns.

****

WINRUSH

LIES in the hundred of Slaughter, about nine miles diſtant ſouthward from Stow-on-the-Wold; four weſtward from Burford in Oxfordſhire, and twenty-four eaſt from Glouceſter.

It enjoys a healthy air, and conſiſts chiefly of corn fields. The lands decline on the north ſide to the banks of a pretty river of the ſame name, which bounds the pariſh, and produces trout and cray fiſh; and after viſiting Burford and Witney in Oxfordſhire, empties itſelf into the Thames at a place called the New-bridge.

The name is written *Wenric* in *Domeſday*, of which the etymology is uncertain. Perhaps the place was ſo called from *Wen*, ſome antient proprietor of it, and *ric*, which in the Anglo-Saxon language denotes *a dominion*, *province*, or *diſtrict*, in which ſenſe it is underſtood in the word *biſhoprick* at this time. Sir Robert Atkyns's notion of its being *derived from a battle heretofore won amongſt the ruſhes of this place*, was formed from the modern orthography, and is too forced to be adopted. There are, however, antient intrenchments, and ſeveral *tumuli*, or barrows here, which ſhew it to have been a ſcene of military actions.

There is a curious ſpecies of foſſil, called the *Siliquaſtra*, or foſſil pods, found in the quarries here, and in the neighbouring pariſh of Sherbourn. They are ſuppoſed to be the bony palates of different

different fifhes, and refemble half the pod of the Lupine, or other leguminous plant, filled with ftony matter. Some of them are extreamly minute, others near two inches long, and varioufly coloured, as brown, black, and bluifh. There are alfo petrifications of the bivalvular kind, in thefe parifhes, as of the *Cardium*, or cockle; and other fhell fifh; and the indefatigable doctor Woodward found the *Afteria Columnaris*, particularly at Sherbourn. It is of a cylindrical but pentangular form, generally about an inch long; and of the thicknefs of a goofe-quill. Thefe are all the particulars in natural hiftory which I have been able to collect worthy the reader's notice. I come now to fhew the defcent

Of the Manor and other Eftates.

There were feveral proprietors of eftates in this place at the time of the general furvey, for it is thus recorded in *Domefday:*

'Roger de Laci holds Wenric in Bernintone 'hundred, and Radulf holds it of him. There 'are two hides. Wluric held it in the time of 'king Edward. In demean is one plow-tillage, 'and three villeins, and two bordars, with one 'plow-tillage. There are five *fervi*, and a mill 'of 5 *fol.* and ten acres of meadow. It was worth '100 *s.* now 4 *lib.*

'The fame Roger holds one hide and one yard-'land there, and Hugo holds it of him. Godric 'held it, and was one of king Edward's thanes. 'There is one plow-tillage in demean, and two 'bordars, and one *fervus*, and a mill of 3 *fol.* and 'eight acres of meadow. It is worth and was 'worth 24 *fol.*' *Domefday*, p. 75.

'Elfi de Ferendone holds three hides and a half 'in Wenric of the abbey of Wincelcombe. Bolle 'held it and gave it to the abbey. He could dif-'pofe of himfelf and his land as he pleafed. 'There are five plow-tillages in demean, and nine 'villeins, and feven bordars, with one plow-'tillage, and ten *fervi*, and a mill and a half of '12 *folid.* and 6 *den.* It is worth 8 *lib.* in the 'whole. Uluric held two hides of this land for 'a manor, and Tovi five yard-lands for a manor, 'and Lewin one yard-land for a manor.

'This manor, which Elfi holds unjuftly of the 'abbey, lay in Salemonefberie hundred after Bolle 'was dead. Now it lies in that of Bernitone, 'according to the verdict of the men of the fame 'hundred.' *Ibid.* p. 71.

'Elfi de Ferendone holds three hides and a half 'in Wenric in Bernintone hundred, of the king. 'Wluric and Tovi and Lewin held them for three 'manors, and could go where they would. There 'are five plow-tillages in demean, and one villein, 'and feven bordars, with one plow-tillage. There 'are ten *fervi*, and a mill and a half of 12 *folid.* 'and 6 *den.* This eftate was worth 3 *lib.* now '8 *lib.*' *Ibid.* p. 79.

'Chetel holds one hide and one yard-land in 'Wenric, in Gerfdones hundred, and he held it 'in the time of king Edward. There is one 'plow-tillage, and four *fervi*. It is worth and 'was worth 20 *folid.*' *Ibid.*

Pope Alexander the Third confirmed to the abbey of Winchcombe all their land in Wenric, 21 H. 2.

John Delamere was feized of Wenrech 8 E. 1. The fheriff returned into the king's exchequer that Wenrich was held by the abbey of Wynchelcombe, William Pynchpole, and Robert de Marys, 9 E. 1. the two latter having taken their names from the hamlets of Pinchpole and Maris in this parifh. Benjamin Bereford held Wyke and Wenrich, by one knight's fee, of Robert de Mortimer, earl of March, 22 E. 2. and the manors continued for a long time in the fame family, for another Benjamin de Bereford and Philippa his wife were feized of the manor of Winrifh and Wike 3 H. 6.

This manor was in the crown in the year 1608. It was afterwards the property of fir Ralph Dutton towards the end of that century, and continuing in the fame family, it defcended like Sherbourn, to James Dutton, efq; who is the prefent lord of the manor of Winrufh.

Of the other eftates the records fhew, that Henry de Norton levied a fine of lands in Wenric to Richard Wale 54 H. 3. And Chriftopher Allen and Ethelreda his wife levied a fine of lands in the fame place to Thomas Dutton 6 E. 6.

HAMLETS. 1. *Maris.* 2. *Pinchpool.* 3. *Lan Maris.*

Of the Church, &c.

The church is a vicarage, in the deanery of Stow, worth about 40 *l.* a year. James Dutton, efq; is patron, and Mr. Twining is the prefent incumbent.

The vicarages of Sherbourn and Winrufh were confolidated into one prefentment in the year 1776.

Seventy-four acres of land belonged to the glebe; but as the parifh is inclofing, the vicarage will be improved, and it is propofed to lay other lands to the glebe in lieu of thofe which belonged to the vicarage of Sherbourn, and to build a new houfe for the vicar in this parifh.

The prior of Lanthony was feized of the impropriation 13 H. 4. The rectory, church, and tithes of Winrufh, formerly belonging to the priory of Lanthony, were granted to Francis Philips and Richard Moor, 6 Jac. 1. The impropriation belongs to the lord of the manor, and pays 4 *l.* 13 *s.* 4 *d.* yearly to the crown.

The church is dedicated to St. Peter. It has a fmall aile and a chapel on the fouth fide, and a tower at the weft end. The chapel is dedicated to St. Mary. It is called Hungerford's chapel, becaufe it was repaired by the family of that name, feveral of whom lie buried in it.

It is mentioned in *Stow's Chronicle*, that fir John, the vicar of this place, was ordered penance for keeping

keeping a concubine, to walk three times round the croſs at Burford, with a faggot at his back.

Firſt fruits £.	4	18	5	Synodals £.	0	1	0
Tenths —	0	10	0	Pentecoſt.	0	0	10
Procurations	0	6	8				

Benefactions.

An eſtate worth 3*l.* 10*s.* a year is given towards the repair of the church; and half a yardland, and three tenements, are likewiſe given to the ſame uſe.

Taxes.	The Royal Aid in 1692, £.	63	19	4
	Poll-tax —— 1694, —	18	6	0
	Land-tax —— 1694, —	37	5	10
	The ſame, at 3*s.* 1770, —	23	18	3

There were 36 houſes, and about 140 inhabitants, whereof 8 were freeholders, at the beginning of this century; yearly births 4, and burials 3. *Atkyns.* Since which time population hath increaſed here, and the inhabitants are now about 190.

WINSTON

IS a ſmall pariſh, in the hundred of Biſley, ſix miles diſtant north-weſtward from Cirenceſter, nine ſouth from Cheltenham, and about twelve ſouth-eaſtward from Glouceſter.

It is bounded on the north-eaſt by that great Roman road, the *Irminſtreet,* ſo often mentioned in the courſe of this work. The greater part of it is arable land. It lies high, and much expoſed to the bleak north and eaſterly winds, which exceedingly retard vegetation in the ſpring, ſo that in general theſe fields produce but thin crops at harveſt.

It is written *Wineſtane* in *Domeſday,* which ſeems to be no other than *Wine's Town,* denoting whoſe property it was when it began to be cultivated, and had firſt a name given it. But as the ſignification of names is not always to be inveſtigated with certainty, ſo in the preſent caſe I may be miſtaken, eſpecially if ſir Robert Atkyns conjectures right, who derives its name *from a battle having been fought and won in this place, and the barrows where each ſide buried,* ſays he, *are yet to be ſeen.* There are, indeed, ſeveral tumps, which ſome have ſuppoſed to be *tumuli,* or burying-places, and the fields, from them, are called *Jackbarrows.* But there is no appearance of an encampment near them, nor have we the leaſt account in hiſtory of any engagement happening hereabout: But however that be, I am far from adopting the common notion, that *Win,* in the names of places, always denotes them to have been the ſcene of ſome military engagement, upon which ſir Robert ſeems to have framed his etymology.

Of the Manor and other Eſtates.

There is, in the pariſh of Bibury, a tithing of the name of Winſon, which lies in the hundred of Bradley, and ſir Robert Atkyns has miſapplied to this pariſh the *Domeſday* account belonging to that tithing. The following is a literal tranſlation from the record, relative to this manor:

'Ansfrid de Cormeliis holds Wineſtane in Biſelege hundred. There are five hides. Uluuard held it. In demean are three plow-tillages, and ten villeins, and four bordars, and one *francigena,* with eight plow-tillages. There are eight *ſervi,* and a mill of 20 *den.* It is worth and was worth 7 *lib.*' *Domeſday,* p. 78.

John le Brun was ſeized of this manor 50 H. 3. and John le Brun, ſon of John, was ſeized thereof 31 E. 1.

Hugh le Deſpencer, the elder, the great favourite of king Edward the Second, was by that king created earl of Wincheſter, and purchaſed a charter of free warren in Winſton and Miſerden 5 E. 2. Being afterwards attainted and executed at Hereford, in the 20th year of the ſame reign, the manor of Winſton was granted to Roger de Mortimer, earl of March, 2 E. 3. He alſo was attainted in parliament, and ſuffered at the common gallows, then called the Elms, near Smithfield; but his poſterity was reſtored in blood and honour, and the manor of Winſton continued long in the family of the Mortimers earls of March; but between the attainder of Roger earl of March, and the reſtoring his poſterity, ſeveral grants and aſſignments were made of this manor. Richard Bellers held it 3 E. 3. The manor and advowſon were granted to John de Aſpath in the 14th year, and Thomas de Burton held the manor in the 16th year of the ſame reign.

Edmund Mortimer, the laſt earl of March, died ſeized of Winſton 3 H. 6. whereby Anne his ſiſter became his heir. She was married to Richard of Coningſburgh, ſecond ſon, and afterwards heir to Edmund of Langley, duke of York, fifth ſon of king Edward the Third, and progenitor to the kings of England of the houſe of York, and ſo the manor of Winſton came to the crown.

Richard duke of York, ſon of Richard of Coningſburgh, by Anne his wife, levied a fine of this manor 14 H. 6. And he and Cicely his wife, the youngeſt daughter of Ralph earl of Weſtmoreland, joined in levying another fine of Winſton, in the 27th year of the ſame reign. The manor was granted to Cicely dutcheſs of York, for her life, 38 H. 6. and the grant was confirmed 1 E. 4. She outlived her huſband thirty-five years, and died 10 H. 7.

Winſton was intended to have been part of the dower of queen Catherine, had ſhe ſurvived king Henry the Eighth, but was afterwards granted to the Tames. Sir Edmund Tame died ſeized of it 26 H. 8. and Edmund Tame, his ſon, had livery the ſame year, and died 36 H. 8. leaving his three ſiſters coheireſſes. Margaret, one of the ſiſters, was

was married to Humphry Stafford, and they had livery of Winſton 37 H. 8.

King Edward the Sixth, by letters patents, dated Feb. 12, in the Seventh year of his reign, granted the manor of Winſton to Anthony Kingſton; but it did not continue long in his family, for Anthony Hungerford, gent. was lord of it 41 Eliz. as was ſir Thomas Hungerford in the year 1608, whoſe arms, (as emblazoned under Down Amney) remain very perfect over the door of the old manor houſe. It was afterwards purchaſed by the Sandys family, and Samuel Sandys, eſq; is the preſent lord of the manor. His pedigree and arms are given under Miſerden.

But there was another manor, dependant on the greater; for the eſcheator's inquiſition found that Thomas Eſtcourt, gent. died 41 Eliz. ſeized of a manor called Le Eſtcourt, in Shipton Moigne, which he held of Thomas Hedges, gent. and of the manor of Wynſton, and of three meſſuages, three cottages, four gardens, 200 acres of land, ſeven of meadow, forty of paſture, of 12*d.* rent, and of 100 ſheep paſtures, and eleven beaſt paſtures in Wynſton, worth 5*l. per ann.* all which particulars he held of Anthony Hungerford, gent. as of his manor of Wynſton, by fealty, and by the rent of 7*s.* 7*d. per ann.* He left Thomas Eſtcourt, his ſon and heir, thirty years old.

Nicholas, ſon of Nicholas le Arch, was ſeized of ſixty acres of land, and of a rent of 40*s.* in Wineſton, 31 E. 1. Thomas Neole held fourteen meſſuages, and ſixteen yard-lands in Wineſtone, 2 E. 2. John de Acton and Sybill his wife were ſeized of ſixty acres of land, and 40*s.* rent in Wineſtone, 6 E. 2. and George Acton held one meſſuage, one hundred acres of land, and ten marks rent in the ſame place, in the 8th year of that reign. Sir John de Acton was ſeized of the ſame lands 17 E. 3. Richard Forſter levied a fine of a moiety of lands in Winſton to John Walſh, and others, 12 H. 7. Andrew Kettleby died 1 Jac. 1. without iſſue, ſeized of the manors of Over and Nether Siddington; of one meſſuage and two yard-lands in Daglingworth, worth 40*s. per ann.* which he held of Henry Pool, knight, in free ſoccage, as of his manor of Daglingworth; and of one meſſuage, and half a yard-land in Wynſton, worth 6*s.* 8*d. per ann.* which he held in free ſoccage, of Anthony Hungerford, eſq; as of his manor of Wynſton; and left all his lands in Glouceſterſhire and Wiltſhire to his wife Jane. *Eſcheat.*

Sir Robert Atkyns takes notice that lands in Winſton belonged to the Auguſtine priory of Oſney in Oxfordſhire, and were granted to the chapter of Oxford 34 H. 8. And that other lands which had been granted to the biſhoprick of Oxford, were likewiſe granted to the chapter of that ſee, in the 38th year of the ſame reign; but this muſt be underſtood of Winſon in the pariſh of Bibury, and not of this pariſh, where the priory of Oſney had never any poſſeſſions.

HAMLET. *Waſhbrook* is a ſmall hamlet in this pariſh, of one houſe only.

Of the Church, &c.

The church is a rectory, in the deanery of Stonehouſe, worth about 90*l.* a year. Samuel Sandys, eſq; is patron, and the reverend Mr. Longdon is the preſent incumbent.

About forty-ſeven acres in the Park-field, and forty-four acres in the Foſs-field, beſide ſome ſmall incloſures, belong to the glebe.

The church is a ſmall building, dedicated to St. Bartholomew.

Firſt fruits £	7	10	0	Synodals £.	0	2	0
Tenths —	0	15	0	Pentecoſt.	0	0	7
Procurations	0	6	8				

Monuments and Inſcriptions.

There is a white marble table in the ſouth wall of the chancel, with this inſcription:

VPON THE INGENIOVS AND IVDICIOVS ARTIST, Mr. IOHN HAVILAND SONNE TO THAT REVEREND PROFESSOR AND DISPENCER OF GODS WORD Mr. IOHN HAVILAND, SOMETIMES INCVMBENT HERE AT WINSTON.

Anag. { IOHN HAVYLANDE / HOLD AY IN HEAV'N } { OBIIT NOVEMB. 19 / A° DNI. 1638.

NONE PRINTED MORE, AND ERRED LESSE IN PRINT,
NONE LED A LIFE THAT HAD LESSE ERRORS IN'T;
NONE HAD A STATE THAT DID MORE GOOD WITH IT,
NONE LESSE APPEARING, AND MORE FVLL OF WIT;
NONE LESSE AFFECTED TO FANTASTICK FASHION,
NONE MORE ADRES'T TO CHRISTIAN COMPASSION;
NONE BETTER KNOWNE TO TH' MYST'RY OF HIS ART,
NONE OF A STRONGER BRAINE OR CLEARER HEART.
WELL HAS HE FINISH'D THEN HIS PILGRIM RACE,
WHO EVER LIV'D IN FORM, AND DIDE IN CASE.
THIS CONSTANT IMPREZE THEN SHALL SEALE HIS GRAVE,
EACH YEAR MY WORKS MVST NEW IMPRESSIONS HAVE.

EPITAPH.

A MATRICE GAVE ME LIFE, A MATRICE GAIN,
AND EARTH'S THE MATRICE THAT DOES ME CONTAIN.

Mrs. Joan Webb, wife of Francis Webb, rector of this church, died in 1645, and was buried in the chancel, with this epitaph:

Epitaphium merito ſuum.
Virgo nupta prius, poſtquam Matrona pudica
Uni juncta viro, dum tibi vita manet:
Tam caſtè vivens, Tu ſancta Exempla dediſti,
Fæmineum caſtum; ſic foret omne genus.
Poſt mortem, triplici, ſolaris, prole, maritum
Ut ſint virtutis Stemmata viva tuæ.

Upon a flat ſtone in the chancel is the following,

IN OBITUM FRANCISCI WEBB,
IN ARTIBUS MAGISTRI
RECTORIS DE WYNSTON
EPITAPHIUM.
Obiit Junii 7° 1648.

VV ltum quis ſtantem? certum quis poſcit amicum?
E x animo ſanctum Paſtorem, et ad omnia doctum?
B iblia ſacra ſuis et vitâ et voce tenentem?
B elle novos contra Doctores bella gerentem?
V icinis gratum poſcis? vis denique charum
S anctis? FRANCISCUS ſanctus fuit omnia WEBBUS.

Benefaction.

Thomas Muggleton, of Miſerden, gave 15*s.* a year to the poor of this pariſh, which donation is now paid by the overſeers of the poor of Duntiſbourn Abbats.

 Taxes.

Taxes.					
The Royal Aid in 1692,		£. 34	10	0
Poll-tax —	1694, —	3	3	0
Land-tax —	1694, —	21	13	2
The ſame, at 3*s.*	1770, —	18	2	4½

When ſir Robert Atkyns compiled his account of this pariſh, there were 26 houſes, and about 100 inhabitants, whereof 5 were freeholders; yearly births 3, burials 2. The preſent number of families is 30, and of inhabitants exactly 160.

WINTERBOURN.

THIS pariſh lies in the hundred of Langley and Swineſhead, ſix miles weſtward from Chipping Sodbury, thirty ſouthward from Glouceſter, and ſix northward from the city of Briſtol.

It is bounded on the ſouth by the river Froom, which divides it from Weſterleigh and Mangotſfield; and is ſaid to have received its name from a *bourn*, or ſmall river, running through it in the *winter* ſeaſon, as if there were no current of water in the ſummer. However ſpecious this may ſeem, it is inconſiſtent with the fact at preſent, for there is a conſtant ſtream in ſummer as well as winter, and the little bourn, which riſes at Stoke, produces good jack and eel.

The ſoil is a reddiſh loam, intermixt with ſand, and the pariſh is moſtly divided into pleaſant paſture grounds. A great road leads through it to Briſtol, which has occaſioned many of the houſes to be built on the ſides of it like a market town, for the convenience of buſineſs, and for the amuſement which the mind receives from the ſight of different objects paſſing to and fro; but the church ſtands half a mile diſtant from the ſtreet.

Edmund Probyn, of Newland in this county, eſq; has a good houſe here.

Nearer towards Briſtol, lies the hamlet of Frenchay, in this pariſh; a very pretty village, where many families of good faſhion have genteel houſes, with elegant gardens and plantations. The moſt diſtinguiſhed of them belong to Mr. Joſeph Beck, Mr. Perry, Mr. Mark Harford, Mr. Barnet, Mr. Read, Mr. Dean, Mr. Gordon, Mr. Ames, Mr. Lewis, Mr. Gwin, and perhaps other gentlemen, whoſe names I have not been favoured with.

Winterbourn furniſhes no antiquities, nor any thing curious in natural hiſtory. I muſt not, however, omit to mention a manufacture of felt hats carried on here, and in ſome of the neighbouring places, which furniſhes employment for many of the labouring people. And there are two annual fairs for pedlery goods, one held on the 29th of June, the other on the 18th of October.

Of the Manor and other Eſtates.

We learn from *Domeſday*, that Wapelie and Wintreborne, for ſo they are written in that record, were members of the manor of Betune, in Suinheve hundred, and together with the whole manor, were the antient demeans of the crown, and held by king William at the time of the general ſurvey.

Philip de Albeniaco died ſeized of this manor 17 Joh. as did Richard de Wales 9 H. 3. Ralph de Wallis alſo died ſeized of Winterbourn 30 H. 3. and left two daughters coheireſſes, who were married to Jeffery de Wrokſhall, and Ralph de Hadele, againſt whom a writ of *Quo warranto* was brought to ſhew by what right they held court leet, free warren, and other privileges in the manor of Winterbourn, and their claim was allowed 15 E. 1. Robert de Hadele, ſon of Ralph, died ſeized of one meſſuage, and one plow's-tillage in Winterbourn 17 E. 2.

Thomas lord Bradeſton, of Bradeſton in the pariſh of Berkeley, died ſeized of the manor of Winterbourn 34 E. 3. He had been ſummoned to parliament among the barons, having been active in depoſing of king Edward the Second. He founded a chantry at the altar of St. Michael in the church of Winterbourn, and gave ſix meſſuages, four acres of arable, twelve acres of meadow, twelve acres of wood, and a rent of 100*s.* out of Winterbourn, for the maintenance of the ſame. Robert Bradeſton, ſon of Thomas lord Bradeſton, died before his father, whereby Thomas lord Bradeſton, ſon of Robert, became heir to his grandfather, and died ſeized of this manor 48 E. 3. He left Elizabeth his only daughter and heir, married to Walter de la Pool, and ſhe had livery of Winterbourn, when ſhe came of age, 13 R. 2. Blanch Bradeſton, widow of Robert Bradeſton, died ſeized of Winterbourn, with fairs, markets, and free warren, 15 R. 2.

Notwithſtanding the deſcent to an heir female, the manor continued for a long time afterwards in the name of the Bradeſtons. Ela, the widow of the laſt Thomas lord Bradeſton, was endowed with this manor, and died ſeized thereof 11 H. 4. Thomas Bradeſton and Edith his wife were ſeized of this manor 16 H. 6. She ſurviving her huſband, had it in dower, and died ſeized of it in the 23d year of the ſame reign.

The Bradeſtones of Winterbourn bore for their arms, *Argent, on a canton gules a roſe Or, barbed proper.* This antient family went to decay about the time of queen Elizabeth, when James Buck, eſq; purchaſed this manor, and John Buck, eſq; was lord of it in the year 1608. It continued only four deſcents in that family, and then paſſed to the Browns. Hugh Brown, eſq; died ſeized of Winterbourn in the year 1691. John Jones, eſq; was lord of it when ſir Robert Atkyns compiled his account of it; and Mr. Whalley is the preſent lord of the manor of Winterbourn.

Thomas de Marlborough and Joan de Haddon levied a fine of lands in Winterbourn, and of the advowſon of the church, to the uſe of Henry de Haddon

Haddon for his life; the remainder to William Fitzwarren and Amice his wife, in taille, 11 E. 3. Richard Forster levied a fine of a moiety of lands in Winterborn and Hambrook, to John Walsh, and others, 12 H. 7.

HAMLETS. 1. *Hambrook* is a large hamlet in this parish, in which there is a chapel of ease. The following is extracted from *Domesday*:

'The bishop of St. Laud of Constance holds 'Hanbroc in Sineshovedes hundred, and Osulf 'holds it of him. Algar held it of king Edward, 'and could go where he pleased. The land is 'five plow-tillages. There are two hides. In 'demean are two plow-tillages, and two villeins, 'with two plow-tillages, and two *servi*, and six 'acres of meadow. It was worth 100*sol.* now '60*solid.*' *Domesday*, p. 70.

John Folliot of Bristol and Lucy his wife levied a fine of lands in Hambrook, and acknowledged the right of Richard le Cook of Winterbourn and Juliana his wife, 43 E. 3. Sir Robert Ashton was seized of one messuage, one plow-tillage, and of a yearly rent of 40*s.* in Hambrook, within the manor of Winterbourn, 7 R. 2. Thomas Moreton, esq; died seized of the manor of Hambrook, and was succeeded by his son and heir sir Robert Moreton, who also died seized thereof 6 H. 8. and left William his son, five years old, who died 14 H. 8.

2. *Frenchay*, but more rightly *Froomshaw*, is a genteel hamlet, of which mention has been already made in the introductory part of this account. Richard Cook and Juliana his wife levied a fine of lands in Froomshaw in this parish 20 R. 2.

3. *Stourden* was an antient manor in Winterbourn. William Hoese and Margaret his wife purchased lands in Stourdon of Ralph de Wellford, which had before been sold to the said Margaret, and to William Comyn, her former husband, 5 H. 3. William Towkeram, or Tukeram, was seized of Stourdon 41 H. 3. and of lands in Hendon, and left two daughters coheiresses. Cicely, (one of them) and Robert Mermion, her husband, levied a fine of these estates to the use of Adam de Machine, and Amabell his wife, who was the other daughter, 51 H. 3. John de la Rivere died seized of the hamlet of Stourdon near Bristol, 35 E. 3. and Richard de la Rivere held it in the 36th year of the same reign. Emme, the widow of John Merston, and formerly the wife of Richard de la Rivere, was endowed of this manor, and died 41 E. 3. as did Thomas de la Rivere 48 E. 3. The abbey of Westminster held lands in Stourdon 49 E. 3. Nicholas Stanshaw died seized of Stourdon, and left it in dower to Margaret his wife, who died 14 H. 6. Sir Jarrit Smith, baronet, purchased this manor of the coheirs of the late sir John Smyth, of Long Ashton in the county of Somerset, and is the present proprietor of it.

The family of de Stern, or Hicinstern, one of whom, according to tradition, was a great robber in this country, were long possessors of a manor in this parish, and had a large house called Stern-court, which is ruined, but still preserves its name, and belongs to sir Jarrit Smith.

The mayor and corporation of Bristol were seized of another manor in this parish, for the use of Gaunt's hospital in Bristol.

There is a distinct constable for Winterbourn, and one tithingman for Hambrook, Frenchay, and Stourdon.

Of the Church, &c.

The church is a rectory, in the deanery of Bristol, worth about 400*l.* a year, of which St. John's college in Oxford are patrons.

Robert Gernoun gave the advowson of the church of Winterbourn to the abbey of Gloucester, in the year 1112, and Helias Boy Giffard confirmed the same in 1160. But that was probably another Winterbourn, for in the grant it is called the chapel of St. Andrew in Winterbourn, whereas this church is dedicated to St. Michael. John Giffard of Brimpsfield was seized of the advowson of Winterbourn 1 E. 3. and John Calew, heir of the Giffards, levied a fine of it, and acknowledged the right of John lord Maltravers 4 E. 3. The advowson was granted to Thomas de Bradeston 11 E. 3. who founded a chantry in the church, of which John Rastale was the last incumbent, and in the year 1553, received a pension of 3*l.* 13*s.* 4*d.* *Willis.* The lands which belonged to the chantry were granted to John Baynham by king Edward the Sixth.

The church consists of the body, and an aile on the north side, handsomely and uniformly pewed, with a gallery at the west end. It has a tower, with a steeple, and a handsome vestry room on the south side, and there is an oratory against the north wall of the church. In the west window are the Berkeleys arms, impaling, *Azure, three couple closes braced Or, a chief of the second.* There is another scutcheon, with these arms, *viz. Azure, two bars within a bordure argent.*

First fruits £.	27	7	0	Synodals £.	0	1	0
Tenths —	2	14	8	Pentecostals	0	1	1½
Procurations	0	6	8				

Monuments and Inscriptions.

There is the figure of a man in compleat armour, lying along, upon a tomb in the chancel, with his hands in a supplicating posture. His head rests upon a bear's head, couped and ducally gorged, and his feet upon a lion couchant. And close by, upon another tomb, is the effigy of a lady lying along in a loose robe, and her feet resting on a dog, the emblem of fidelity. These are supposed to represent some of the Bradstone family; but the arms upon the man's shield are not discernable.

There is another figure lying along in armour, under an arch in the north wall of the church, the

the head refting upon a ram, the feet on a lion; fuppofed to be for Tukeram, the proprietor of Stourdon. And a figure of a woman lies in the belfry.

On the tablet of a monument againft the wall, in gold letters:

M. S.
VIRI OPTIMI ET ORNATISSIMI
PATRIS SVI COLENDISSIMI
IACOBI BVCK, ARMIGERI,
QVI IN DOMINO
PLACIDE OBDORMIVIT
AN: DO: CIↃIↃCXII°
MARTII XIII°
ÆTATIS LXVI°
QVOD BRVTI STATVÆ SUBSCRIPSIT ROMA SEPULCHRO
INSCRIBAM PATRIO; VIVERAT, OPTO, PATER.
SED PATRIS PIETAS, PROCVL ISTO DISSITA MUNDO,
HVNC RAPVIT PATREM, RESTITVITQVE DEO.
PIET. ERGO LVGENS
POSVIT
MATTHEVS BUCK, FILIUS ET HÆRES.

And on flat ftones are thefe infcriptions:

HERE LYETH THE BODY OF MATHEW BVCK ESQ[r] WHO DECEASED THE 17th OF SEPT. A° DMI 1631.

Although the fubject of thefe fatall Rymes
(This Mathew) liu'd in th' Cuftome of the times
Reader, thou muft (like him) beefore thou dieft
Leave the worlds Cuftome for to follow Chrift.
And then his Cenfure fhall fhutt vp thy Storie,
Hee that did rise to Grace fhall rife to Glorie.

Here lyeth the body of THOMAS BVCK ESQ[r] LORD of this Mannor, who deceafed the 14th day of Apr: Ano Dmi 1658. Ætat. 47.

Upon thefe ftones are the family arms, *viz. Per fefs nebule, argent and fable, three bucks attires fixed to the fcalps counterchanged.*

On the table of a large monument,

In Memory of Amy the Wife of Thomas Symes Efq[r] of this parifh, Daughter of Edward Bridges of Kaynfham in the County of Somerfet Efq[r] defcended from the noble family of the Lord Chandois baron of Sudely Caftle in the County of Gloucefter, who though her Extraction was Honourable, yet by her Exemplary life and maners became an honor to her family, and after 17 years fpent in her minority, and 20 years in wedlock, in which intervall fhe was mother of twelue fons and fower daughters, changed this mortal ftate for an immortall the 30th of Aprill 1662.

Hear alfo lyes the body of Thomas Symes of this parifh Efq[r] fon of John Symes of Pounsford in the County of Somerfet Efq[r] who ddced the 22 day of January 1669 aged 48 years.

Hear alfo lyes the Body of Benjamin fon of Thomas Symes Efq[r] and Amy his wife who ddced Auguft the 12th 1662, aged 6 months.

Hear alfo lyes the body of Elizabeth daughter of Thomas Symes Efq[r] and Amy his wife, who ddced the 18th of January aged 19 Years.

On a fmall monument it is thus written:

M. S.

HVGONIS BROWNE Nuper de WINTERBOVRN Court Armigeri, qui obiit primo die Septembris Anno Domini Millefimo Sexcentefimo Nonagefimo primo, Ætatis fuæ Quadragefimo Septimo.

Hoc Amoris fui Pignus Chariffima Conjux Pofuit Monumentum.

Here alfo lyeth ye Body of Ann Browne Wife of ye above named Hugh Browne Efq[r] who Died ye 19th of March 1725.

The arms upon this monument are, *Baron and femme,* 1. *Argent, on a bend Or three eagles difplay'd fable.* 2. *Paly of fix argent and fable, over all three eagles difplay'd counterchanged.*

Upon a flat ftone,

Here lyeth y[e] Body of M[rs] Sophia Williams, Daughter of M[rs] Ann Browne by her firft Hufband Charles Williams Efq, Sometime Sheriffe of y[e] City of Briftol, who died y[e] 11 of April 1730 aged 50 Years.

Benefactions.

In 1691, Hugh Brown, efq; gave 5*s.* to be diftributed weekly in bread to the poor for ever. And in 1720, William Bayly, efq; a native of this place, and once fheriff of Briftol, gave the intereft of 50*l.* to be given in bread to the poor annually on the 25th of March for ever. And in 1760, Mr. Gregory Bufh, of Briftol, apothecary, gave the intereft of 50*l.* for ever, to four poor houfekeepers of this parifh.

Winterbourn.

			£	s.	d.
Taxes.	The Royal Aid in	1692,	121	1	4
	Poll-tax ——	1694,	48	2	0
	Land-tax ——	1694,	125	4	0
	The fame, at 3*s.*	1770,	93	18	0

Hambrook.

			£	s.	d.
Taxes.	The Royal Aid in	1692,	110	3	4
	Poll-tax ——	1694,	22	0	0
	Land-tax ——	1694,	123	6	0
	The fame, at 3*s.*	1770,	89	3	6

At the beginning of this century, there were 120 houfes, and about 500 inhabitants in this parifh, whereof 26 were freeholders; yearly births 10, burials 10. *Atkyns.* The number of fouls is now about 567.

WITCOMBE

IS a fmall parifh, in the hundred of Dudfton and King's Barton. It lies about eight miles diftant north from Stroud, feven fouth from Cheltenham, and fix fouth-eaftward from Gloucefter.

The greater part of the parifh confifts of a wide combe, or valley, with an opening northwards to the great vale country, but environed on the eaft, fouth, and fouth-weft quarters by that chain of hills which runs length-ways through the county. Hence arifes a variety of foils and of produce. The lower parts and acclivities are chiefly pafture, and the higher hills moftly woodlands.

It is fometimes called Great Witcombe, to diftinguifh it from the tithing of Witcombe, in the parifh of Badgworth. The reafon and propriety of the name is obvious. Witcombe is a fmall deviation from *Widcombe*, or *Wide Combe*, made fo very naturally, and almoft inevitably, by quick pronunciation, that it is wonderful it fhould efcape fir Robert Atkyns's difcernment: But it is ftill more unaccountable that a gentleman of his experience and learning fhould fall into the following inconfiftence and abfurdity: Speaking of Rendcombe, *It is fo called,* fays he, *from being encompaffed with valleys, for Ring is Saxon for a Circle, and Comb for a Valley.* Unmindful of this explanation, in the account of Winchcombe, he very gravely informs the reader, that *Comb fignifies a hill*; and a little further on, gives the following etymology of Witcombe: *It is called Witcomb Magna. The name,* continues he, *fignifies a White Hill,*

Hill, and it lies under Birdlip Hill, where the roads make it look white. This ferves to confirm the truth of that obfervation, that men of genius fometimes commit the greateft miftakes.

Part of this parifh ftretches over the hill to the fouthward, and joins to Brimpsfield.

Howe Hicks, efq; has a good houfe, which ftands in the center of the valley, with a park, and a large eftate here. The park lies upon a confiderable acclivity on the fouth fide of the houfe, and at the foot of a fteep hill covered with beech wood. From a vifta upon the hill, not a mile from the houfe, is a fine bird's eye view of the fubjacent vale, and the river Severn. Part of the foreft of Dean, and the conic mountain near Abergavenny in Monmouthfhire, are feen to the left: The blue hills of Malvern in Worcefterfhire, (with the Welch mountains at a great diftance behind) prefent themfelves in front: And to the right is a view of the town of Tewkefbury, and of the city of Worcefter, near thirty miles diftant.

Of the Manor and other Eftates.

It does not appear whofe property this manor was, about the time of the Norman conqueft, as there is no mention of it in *Domefday*; but Edmond earl of Cornwall was feized of it 4 E. 1. probably for the ufe of the priory of St. Ofwald in Gloucefter. And the archbifhop of York was feized of this manor for the ufe of the fame priory, in confequence of an agreement between the archbifhop and that houfe, as more particularly related in the account of St. Ofwald's priory, p. 189.

Upon the diffolution of monafteries, this manor was granted to fir Thomas Chamberlain 6 E. 6. and fir John Chamberlain was lord of it in the year 1608.

From the Chamberlains it was purchafed by the widow of fir Michael Hicks, in which name and family it has continued ever fince, and Howe Hicks, efq;[f] is the prefent lord of the manor. His arms are, *Gules, a fefs undy between three fleurs de lis Or.*

Of the Church, &c.

The church is a rectory, in the deanery of Gloucefter, worth about 50*l.* a year. Howe Hicks, efq; is patron, and Mr. Nafh is the prefent incumbent. The advowfon of the rectory belonged formerly to St. Auftin's abbey in Briftol, and it now pays 13*s.* 4*d.* a year to the dean and chapter of Briftol cathedral.

Tithes in Witcombe, which formerly belonged to the priory of St. Ofwald in Gloucefter, were granted to John Hercey and John Edwards 20 Eliz.

The church is a fmall building, dedicated to St. Mary, and has an aile on the north fide.

Firft fruits £.	4	6	8	Synodals £.	0	2	0
Tenths —	0	8	8	Pentecoft.	0	0	6
Procurations	0	3	4				

Monuments and Infcriptions.

There is the following infcription on a marble monument in the chancel:

---

[f] This family has been very antiently feated in Gloucefterfhire. Sir Ellis Hicks was made a knight banneret in the reign of king Edward the Third, and had the three fleurs de lis given him for his arms on account of his bravery, and taking a pair of colours, when in the fervice of the Black Prince.

John Hicks, of Tortworth in Gloucefterfhire, was defcended from fir Ellis Hicks, and died 2 H. 7.

Robert Hicks, fon and heir of the faid John, was a citizen of London, and raifed a very confiderable eftate by his bufinefs. He married Julian, daughter to Arthur Chapham, of the county of Somerfet, efq; and had iffue three fons, Michael, Francis, and Baptift. Francis, the fecond fon, died young. Baptift taking to bufinefs, and by the intereft of his elder brother, having great dealings with the court, for rich filks and other commodities imported from abroad, acquired a large fortune, and came afterwards to great honours. He was knighted by king James the Firft, and was created a peer 4 Car. by the title of baron Hicks, of Ilmington in the county of Warwick, and vifcount Campden, of Campden in the county of Gloucefter; which honours are now enjoy'd by the prefent earl of Gainfborough, his lordfhip's anceftor Edward lord Noel, who married Julian, eldeft daughter and coheir of the faid Baptift lord Campden, having obtained a grant of them to himfelf and his heirs male, on failure of iffue male of the faid Baptift lord vifcount Campden.

Michael Hicks, eldeft fon and heir of the faid Robert Hicks, was bred to learning at Trinity college in Cambridge, whence he removed to Lincoln's inn to ftudy the law, and was afterwards fecretary to lord treafurer Burleigh. He was a wife and religious perfon, and his excellent parts endeared him exceedingly to fir Robert Cecil, fon to the lord treafurer. He was knighted, and in the year 1604, purchafed the caftle and manor of Beverftone, in the county of Gloucefter. He married Elizabeth, daughter of Mr. Colfton, of Lowlayton in Effex, merchant, with whom he had Ruckholts; and dying in 1612, his widow purchafed the manor and eftate of Witcombe, in this county. He left by her two fons, William and Michael, of whom the latter died unmarried.

William, the eldeft fon, was created a baronet in 1619, and diftinguifhed himfelf for his loyalty in the great civil wars. He married Margaret, daughter of William lord Paget, and died Oct. 22, 1680, in the 84th year of his age, leaving iffue two fons, William and Michael, both knighted in their infancy by king Charles the Second, at Ruckholt.

Sir William Hicks, the eldeft fon, was created a baronet, and ferved the office of high fheriff of the county of Effex. He married Marthagnes, daughter of fir Henry Coningfby, knight, and dying in 1703, left iffue by her two fons, Henry and Charles, of whom the latter married the daughter of ——— Coningfby, efq; and died in 1760, leaving one fon, John-Baptift, who, upon the failure of the elder branch, is the prefent baronet.

Sir Henry Hicks, elder fon and heir of fir William Hicks, fucceeded his father, and married, to his firft wife, Margaret, daughter to fir John Holmes, knight, by whom he had one fon Henry, who died unmarried. He married to his fecond wife Barbara, daughter of Mr. Johnfon, of the county of Effex, and dying in 1754, left iffue by her two fons, Robert and Michael. The latter died unmarried in 1764.

Sir Robert Hicks fucceeded his father in title and eftate, but died without iffue in 1768, whereby the title of baronet devolved on fir John-Baptift Hicks, beforementioned.

I now return to fir Michael Hicks, fecond fon of fir William Hicks, baronet. He was lord of the manor of Witcombe, and married Sufanna, daughter of fir Richard Howe, and dying in 1710, left one fon,

Howe Hicks, efq; who married Mary, daughter of Jeffry Watts, efq; of the county of Effex, and died in 1728. He had iffue one fon,

Howe Hicks, efq; the prefent lord of the manor of Great Witcombe. He married Martha, daughter of the reverend Mr. Browne, and by her has two fons, William and Michael, and one daughter, married to the reverend Mr. Pettat, rector of Stonehoufe in this county.

 Near

Near this Place
lies interr'd the Body of
S^r^. MICHAEL HICKES K^t^.
Younger Son of
S^r^. WILLIAM HICKES Baronet,
of Beverstone Castle in this County,
who departed this life May 4th
in the Year of our LORD 1710
and the 65th of his Age.
Near whom is reposited the body of
MICHAEL HICKES his 3^d^ Son
who dyed an Infant.

See Ag'd experience submits to Death
And Infant Innocence resigns its breath,
Happy ye Soul whose first Essay of Praise
Is Joyn'd in Consort with the Heavenly Layes,
Much Happyer those whose virtuous acts engage
A Weight of Glory for a Load of Age.

Near this Place lyeth Dame Susanna Relict
of sir Michael Hicks K^t^. and Daughter of
Sir Richard Howe of the County of
Surry K^t^. she died Novem^r^ 1724.
Here also lyeth Michael ye Son of
Howe Hicks Esqr & Mary his Wife
he died 6 March 1721
aged 9 months.

At top of the monument is a scutcheon, with two coats, *viz.* Hicks, impaling Howe.

On the table of another monument,

Near this place resteth what was Mortal of Howe Hicks Esqr Son of Sir Michael Hicks. He died Feby 12th 1727-8 Aged 38.

Here also lies the remains of Mary Relict of Howe Hicks Esqr. & Daughter of Jeffry Watts, Esqr. of the County of Essex. She died Aug^st^ 6 1728 Aged 36.

Here also lieth Howe Hicks, Son of Howe Hicks Esqr. He died Jan^ry^ 7th 1744 in the 5th Year of his Age.

In Memory of Susanna Elizabeth Hicks, Daughter of Howe Hicks Esqr & Martha his Wife. She died June 17th 1747 Aged one Year & 23 Days.

Here also lieth Mary Hicks Daughter of Howe Hicks Esqr & Martha his Wife. She died July 30th 1758 in the 15th Year of her Age.

The arms on this monument are 1. Hicks, impaling, 2. *Argent, two bars azure, in chief three pellets*, for Watts.

On a flat stone in the chancel,

Here rests the Body of Mary Hicks who departed this Life the 30th Day of July 1758 in the 15th year of her Age.

Tho' few her Years, She not untimely died,
Who richly was with heav'nly Gifts supplied.
Thus GOD decrees - When ripe for Heav'n - the soul
Quits her terrestrial House without controul.
Of Youth, Physician's Care, or Parents Love,
T' enjoy her blest Abode prepar'd Above.

Here lyes the Body of Michael Son of Sr Michael Hicks K^t^. and Susanna His Lady, Who in the Innocence of Childhood Departed this Life Jul. III. MDCLXXXIX.

On another flat stone,

Here lieth Mary Williams Daughter of Howe Hicks Esqr & Mary his Wife. She Died Feb^ry^ 14th 1755 Aged 35.

Taxes.		£.	s.	d.
The Royal Aid in 1692,		50	8	0
Poll-tax ——	1694,—	5	11	0
Land-tax ——	1694,—	61	18	0
The same, at 3*s.*	1770,—	46	8	3

There were 24 houses, and about 90 inhabitants in this parish, whereof 4 were freeholders, about the beginning of this century; yearly births 2, and burials 2. *Atkyns.* The number of houses at present is 24, and of inhabitants exactly 96.

WITHINGTON.

THIS parish lies in the hundred of Bradley, six miles distant south-eastward from Cheltenham, six west from Northleach, and fourteen east from Gloucester.

The river Coln runs through, and waters the lower part of it, where are some meadow and pasture lands; but generally the soil is stony, and best adapted to tillage. The sides of the hills and acclivities on the southward are covered with one continued wood for a considerable extent, and since the antient name of the place was *Wudiandun*, as it is written in in the old charters belonging to the see of Worcester; and that the names of several of the hamlets, as Hilcot, Foscot, Upcot, are compounded of *Coed*, the British word for *wood*; it is very probable that the parish was formerly almost over-run with it; but in the progress of population, agriculture was improved, and many of these lands were gradually cleared, and appropriated, as we now see them, to the produce of corn and pasture.

There was a nunnery at this place in the Saxon times, and it was most probably endowed with the manor. In those ages the bishops had the custody of all monasteries in their respective dioceses, and Wilfrith[g] bishop of Worcester, in the eighth century, obtained a synodal decree that this monastery should be annexed to his see, after the death of the abbess who then presided over it. However, Mildred, the succeeding bishop of Worcester, in whose time it lapsed, made a fresh grant of it in the year 774, to the lady Æthelburga, who was abbess of a religious house at Worcester, on condition that both this and her own monastery at Worcester should devolve to that see upon her death. This accounts for the bishop of Worcester's property here, and brings me next to treat

Of the Manor and other Estates.

The following is translated from *Domesday:*

'The church of Wirecestre holds Widindune in 'Wacrescumbe hundred. There are thirty hides, 'of which three never paid tax. There are two 'plow-tillages in demean, and sixteen villeins, 'and eight bordars, with seven plow-tillages. 'There are six *servi*, and ten acres of meadow; a 'wood one mile long, and half a mile broad. And 'in Contone is one plow-tillage, and two villeins, 'and two bordars, with one plow-tillage, and 'two *servi*, and a mill of 5 *solid.*' *Domesday*, p. 70.

'There are in the same manor four radchenis-'ters having two hides, and three yard lands, and 'they have two plow-tillages; and a priest having 'half a hide, and one plow-tillage. In Glouuec. 'four burgesses pay seven-pence half-penny.

'Morinus holds of the bishop three hides in 'Fuscote, of the land of this manor; Anschitil 'two hides in Colesburne and Willecote; Robert 'four hides and a half in Dodesuuelle and Pecle-'furde; Scheline five hides in Nategrave; Drogo 'ten hides in Estone. In these lands there are 'sixteen plow-tillages in demean, and fifty-one 'villeins, and seven bordars, with twenty-eight 'plow-tillages. There are forty-one *servi*, and 'three mills of 13*s.* 4*d.* In Wicelcumbe one 'burgess

[g] Heming. Chart. p. 464, 465, 467.

'burgess pays 3 *sol.* There is some meadow and 'wood in certain places, but not much. The 'whole manor was worth 38 *lib.* in the time of 'king Edward, now 33 *lib.* in all. Bishop Ulstan 'holds this manor.' *Domesday*, p. 70.

John Musgrose was tenant under the bishop of Worcester 3 E. 1. A writ of *Quo warranto* was brought against the bishop to set forth his right to court leet and free warren in Withington, and his claim was allowed 15 E. 1.

This manor continued in the bishoprick of Worcester 'till doctor Hooper surrendered that see to the king, in order that he might be collated to the two bishopricks of Worcester and Gloucester, as they were intended to be united. But according to doctor Heylin, bishop Hooper was never afterwards suffered to enjoy the temporalties, but only received some small allowance for them; and Mr. Willis observes, that in the patent and grant of king Edward the Sixth, to John Hooper bishop of Gloucester and Worcester, dated Dec. 10, 1552, the manors of Hartlebury, Fladbury, Ripple, Bredon, and Withington, are omitted, and thence infers, that they were reserved by the crown, but afterwards restored by queen Mary.

The bishop of Worcester is the present lord of the manor, and holds a court leet, and has a good house near the church, now in lease to John Guise, of Highnam in this county, esq.

HAMLETS. 1. *Compton*, or *Conton*, as it is written in *Domesday*. It lies on the little river Coln, and is now generally called *Cassey Compton*, from the family of the Casseys, who were owners of it for many generations, and have been of antient standing here, and in other parts of the county. John Cassey, esq; died seized of Compton in the reign of king Henry the Seventh, and was succeeded by William Cassey his son, who died seized thereof 1 H. 8. Leonard Cassey, son of William, was five years old at his father's death, but dying without issue, William Cassey, his brother, obtained livery of this manor 21 H. 8. and Robert Cassey, esq; another brother of Leonard, died seized of Compton 1 E. 6. Henry Cassey, son of Robert, had livery 2 Mar. and died 38 Eliz. leaving Thomas his son then thirty-seven years old, who had livery of the manor the same year. This manor now belongs to lord Chedworth. The tithes of Cassey Compton belonged to the priory of Bonhommes at Eddington in Wiltshire, and were granted to the bishop of Bristol 34 H. 8.

2. *Fuscote*, which is also mentioned in the preceding abstract from *Domesday*, and is now called Foscote, and commonly written Foxcot. Hugh le Despencer was seized of Foxcote 4 & 5 E. 3. It was afterwards granted to Westbury college, near Bristol, and upon the dissolution of religious foundations, was again granted to Ralph Sadleir 35 H. 8. William Jonets and Isabel his wife levied a fine of lands in Foxcot and Withington to William Vauce 7 E. 4. William Dalby and his wife also levied a fine of lands in Foxcote to William Derset and Edmond Burshell 11 H. 7. Mr. Edward Ansell has a good estate in this hamlet, which he enjoys in right of his wife, whose family name was Jordan.

3. *Broadwell End.*

4. *Little Colesbourn.* It is not easy to distinguish the particulars in *Domesday* concerning this hamlet from those relating to the parish of Colesbourn, adjoining. It appears from the foregoing extract from *Domesday*, that Anschitil held two hides in Colesbourn and Willecote; and it is said in another place, that 'Eluuin held one hide and 'a half in Colesbourne, for a manor.' p. 78. Lands in this place formerly belonged to the Cistercian abbey of Bruern in Oxfordshire, and at the dissolution were granted to Edward Hermon 35 H. 8. Mr. Roberts has a good estate in this hamlet.

5. *Owdeswell.* There was formerly a chapel here, but it is now disused. This manor belonged to the priory of Black canons at Studley in Warwickshire, and was granted to Richard Andrews, and Nicholas Temple, in trust, 35 H. 8. and livery of it was granted to Francis Heydon 1 Eliz. It now belongs to Robert Lawrence, of Shurdington, esq.

6. *Hilcot* is a reputed manor, and formerly belonged to the Casseys. It is now the property of lord Chedworth.

7. *Rosley*, or *Rosely*. This place is separated from the parish to which it belongs by that of Dowdeswell. The extract from *Domesday* which sir Robert Atkyns applied to it belongs to Cowley, in Rapsgate hundred. Lands called Roseley in Withington belonged to the abbey of Winchcombe, and were granted to John Dudley earl of Warwick, afterwards duke of Northumberland, 1 E. 6. This manor was held of Temple Guiting, and William Rogers died seized thereof 17 C. 1. leaving Daniel his son seven years old. William Rogers, of Dowdeswell, esq; one of the masters in chancery, was proprietor of it at the beginning of this century; from whom it descended like Dowdeswell, to William Rogers, esq; who is the present lord of the manor.

Of the Church, &c.

The church is in the deanery of Winchcombe. It is a rectory and peculiar, worth about 500*l.* a year, having a great quantity of glebe land belonging to it. The bishop of Worcester is patron, and the reverend Mr. John Hayward is the present incumbent. This parish and that of Dowdeswell are included in the peculiar. The churches are subject to the visitation of the bishop of Gloucester, but exempted from that of the archdeacon, the rector of Withington exercising archidiaconal power, proving wills, and granting administration in both parishes.

The

The church is dedicated to St. Michael. It has a handſome tower in the middle, adorned with pinnacles and battlements, and furniſhed with ſix muſical bells. There is a ſmall croſs aile on the ſouth ſide, belonging to Compton eſtate, and is the burying place of lord Chedworth's family.

Firſt fruits £. 30	0	0	Synodals £. 0	2	0
Tenths — 3	0	0	Pentecoſt. 0	1	6
Procurations 0	6	8			

Monuments and Inſcriptions.

There is a handſome marble monument in the aile, with the following inſcription, in ſmall capitals:

Bridgett one of the Davghters of Tho: Rich of North Cerney in this Covnty of Glovc. Eſq; one of the Ma^{rs}. of the highe Covrte of Chavncery & Anne his wife one of the Davgh^{rs} & Coheires of Thomas Bovrchier of Barneſly in the ſaid County Eſq; the 23th of Ivly 1620 was married to Iohn Howe of Little Compton in this pariſh Eſq; nephewe & Heire of Sr Richard Grobham of Greate Wiſhford in ye Covnty of Wiltes, K^{t}. deceaſed; with whome ſhee lived a vertvovs and lovinge wife 21 yeares & a XI Moneths & had Iſſue 9 Children (Viz) firſt Richard Grobham Howe, borne ye 28th of Avgvſt 1621, who Married Lvcie one of the Davghters of S^{r}. Iohn S^{t}. Iohn of Lyddiard Tregoze in the ſaid Covnty of Wiltes K^{t}. & Barr^{t}. 2^{ly} Iohn Grobham Howe borne ye 25th of Ianvary 1624, who Married Annabella one of ye Davghters & Coheires of Emanvell late Earle of Svnderland; 3dly December ye 4th, 1626, Svſanna was borne, who married Iohn Ernle of Berry Towne in the ſaid Covnty of Wiltes Eſq^{r}.

4^{ly} the third day of March 1629, Thomas Grobham Howe was borne.

5^{ly} the 13th day of Ivne 1630, William Howe was borne, *ſlayne at Limbrick in the Kingdom of Ireland.*

6^{ly} the 4th of March 1632, Anna Howe was borne, who died very yovnge and lyeth heere buryed.

7^{ly} the 21th day of December 1633, Elizabeth Howe was borne, *nowe the wife of Thomas Cheſter of Aunſbury in this County Eſq^{r}.*

8^{ly} the 22th of October 1635, George Howe was borne, who died yovnge & lyeth bvried at Wiſhford in ye Vavlt.

9^{ly} the 27th of November 1637 Charles Howe was borne.

And on the 15th day of Ivne 1642, Annoqvæ Ætatis Svæ 46; left them to the protection of the Almighty and her owne Mortality to this Earth, Expectinge a Ioyfvll Reſvrrection.

At top are the figures of a man and woman, and between them a ſcutcheon of their arms, Party per pale, 1. *Or, a feſs between three wolves heads couped ſable*, for Howe. 2. *Per pale ſable and gules, a croſs botonny fitchy between three fleurs de lis Or*, for Rich.

On a ſmall table in the chancel,

Si Hões tacverint, lapis hic clamabit vitam mortemq; Perinde imitandā Viri clariſſimi

Gvlielmi Oſbern
Qui; Antiquâ Proſapia ortus; Literis
Humaniorib' imbutus, in Academiam Oxonienſem
aſcitus, in Socium Om: An: creatus: S: Theologiæ
Doctoratu inſignitus; in Canonicum Reſidentiar'
Eccleſiæ Sariſburienſis aſcriptus; in Rectorem
huius Eccleſiæ electus; Cuius Curâ fideliter
Obeundâ, Senio tandem confectus; annos plus
minus Octoaginta natus; denatus eſt j^{o} Aprilis
ANNO DNI: 1646.

Arms at top, *Quarterly azure and ermine, over all a croſs ingrailed Or.*

On the table of a handſome monument it is thus written:

MEMORIÆ SACRVM
Viri reuerendi Gilberti Oſberne S.S.T.B.
Præbendarij Eccleſiæ Cathædralis Glouceſt'
Necnon Rectoris de Withington.
Qui cum in temporibus plus-quam difficillimis
Egregium Charitatis Exemplar, grandeq;
Fidei ſpecimen edidiſſet, et in omnibus
Vitam *aſpilon kai anepilepton* egiſſet,
In Beatorum conſortiam lubens ſeceſſit.

Anna (D^{ni}: Richardi Oſberne Baronetti de
Knockmon Hiberniæ filia, mœſtiſſima Relicta,
Amoris in defunctum Coniugem, et Mœſtitiæ pignus,
Hoc lachrymis humidum erexit Marmor.
Obijt Feb. 16 Ætat. ſuæ 56. Salut. 1656.
Eis eme oroon euſebees eſto.

On a ſmaller table below,

Diſce ab Hoc vno eſſe Mori beatum,
Vita cuius Mors erat, et ſupultus
Prædicat, viuens moriens vocetur
Jure ſacerdos.
Norma viuebat Pietatis, hoc ſtet
Marmor, vt poſſint homines futuri
Scire, verum hic peſſima ſæcla ferre
Eccleſiaſten.

The ſcutcheon upon this monument is parted per pale, 1. Oſberne as before, impaling Oſberne.

N. B. This inſcription is exactly taken from the ſtone, and varies a little from that in p. 167, which was ſent me by a friend.

On a braſs plate againſt the wall,

VITA CHRIST. MORI LVCRVM.
VBI SISTIS IACET SYBILLA VXO^{r} ROB: KNOLLIS GEN. ART.Q. MAG. STIRPE PAT: EX GENEROS: OWENO^{rum} MONÆ INSULÆ MAT: EX ANTIQ: NOBILISS^{aq}. BARKLEYOR^{um}: FAM: ORTA CVIVS PIETA^{em}. PRVD^{am}: CAS: FIDEMQ: CONIVGAL^{em}: HOC ÆS POSTER: COMMENDAT IMITANDAS. 1614. SEPT: 25, MORT^{em}: CV^{m}. VITA COMMVTAVIT.
LECT: PIO.
ES Q^{d}. ERĀ Q^{d} SV^{m} FVERIS TV SCRIPTA LEGENDO
SIS MEMOR IPSE MEI, SIS MEMOR IPSE TVI.

On a flat ſtone in the chancel,

M. S.
ROBERTI FIELDING,
M. D. ET. COL. MED. LOND. SOC.
OB.
MAII XXII A. D. MDCCIX. ÆTAT: LXXXVII.
ARMA PORTABAT PATRIÆ SALUTI,
HUNC SALUS TRIVIT PATRIÆ TOGATUM,
ET PIIS ARMIS INIMICA FATA
ARTE PREMEBAT.
RES TAMEN FLUXÆ HAUD TENUERE TOTUM
NAM SUÆ MORBIS ANIMÆ VACAVIT,
VITA CUM CEDAT MEDICUSQUE QUOD DAT
EUTHANASIAN.

There are two coats placed palewiſe upon this ſtone, *viz.* 1. *Argent, on a feſs ſable three lozenges Or*, for Fielding. 2. —— *a croſs raguly* ——.

Benefactions, taken from a Table in the Church.

William Oſbern, D.D. rector of this pariſh, and John Rich, eſq; gave 100*l.* each for apprenticing out poor children; and both ſums have been ſecured by the purchaſe of land in the pariſh of Charlton King's.

John Gilman, formerly rector here, and Robert Fielding, M.D. and Charles Fielding, gent. of the Inner Temple, (who died Dec. 15, 1737) gave 20*l.* a piece to this pariſh for charitable uſes. And lady Howe, relict of ſir Richard Howe, gave a ſervice of gilt plate for the communion.

Taxes.	The Royal Aid in	1692, £. 188	6	8
	Poll-tax ——	1694, — 32	18	8
	Land-tax ——	1694, — 209	13	0
	The ſame, at 3*s.*	1770, — 116	12	$3\frac{3}{4}$

When ſir Robert Atkyns compiled his account of this pariſh, there were 73 houſes, and about 320 inhabitants, whereof 18 were freeholders; yearly births 10, burials 9. Since that time population hath greatly increaſed, and there are now upwards of 500 inhabitants.

WOLSTONE.

WOLSTONE.

THIS is a fmall parifh, in the lower part of the hundred of Derhurft, about four miles eaft from Tewkefbury, five weft from Winchcombe, fix north from Cheltenham, and eleven north-eaft from Gloucefter.

The church and village are feated on the fide of a hill, with a north-weft profpect over the vale. The fituation is pleafant and healthy, and the parifh confifts of good pafture and arable land.

Of the Manor and other Eftates.

This manor was part of the poffeffions of the church of St. Dyonifius at Paris, at the time of the general furvey, and afterwards belonged to the priory of Derhurft. Upon the diffolution of that priory, it was granted to the abbey of Tewkefbury 7 E. 4. and after the final diffolution of monafteries, it was granted to the Throckmortons.

Thomas Throckmorton had livery of the manor and advowfon of Wolfton 9 Eliz. and fir William Throckmorton was lord of the manor in the year 1608. He fold it to the lord keeper Coventry in the year 1630, and the earl of Coventry is the prefent lord of the manor of Wolftone, for which he pays 36*s*. yearly to the crown.

Of the Church, &c.

The church is a rectory, in the deanery of Winchcombe, worth about 90*l*. a year, of which the earl of Coventry is patron. There is no glebe belonging to it. The priory of Derhurft was feized of the advowfon of this church 56 H. 3. and the provoft of Eaton college near Windfor has prefented to it.

The church is dedicated to St. Martin. It was new built in 1499, with an aile on the north fide, and an embattled tower at the weft end.

Firft fruits £.	13	6	3	Synodals £.	0	2	0
Tenths —	1	6	7½	Pentecoft.	0	0	4
Procurations	0	6	8				

Taxes.					
The Royal Aid in 1692,	£.	95	1	0
Poll-tax — 1694,	—	6	3	0
Land-tax — 1694,	—	55	0	0
The fame, at 3*s*. 1770,	—	41	5	0

At the beginning of this century, there were 23 houfes, and about 90 inhabitants in this parifh, whereof 12 were freeholders; yearly births 3, burials 2. *Atkyns*. The inhabitants are now upwards of 100.

****

WOODCHESTER.

THIS is a fmall parifh, in the hundred of Longtree, three miles diftant weft from Minchin-Hampton, three fouth from Stroud, and thirteen fouth from Gloucefter.

The principal part of the village lies on the fide of a bold rifing ground, facing eaftward, and feen from the great road on Rodborough-hill forms a pretty landfcape, with a little river in the fore-ground, gently gliding along through the valley. Higher in the view, are many good houfes and gardens, thickly fcattered and diftributed for about a mile in length; and above them, the profpect clofes with natural woods and plantations, nodding from the acclivities behind.

Lord Ducie has a feat in this parifh, with an extenfive park, and very fine fifhponds. It is his lordfhip's ufual country refidence; but it cannot be feen at the fame time with the village, as it ftands two miles diftant weftward from it, in a very narrow valley, amongft large and lofty beech-woods, and may be juftly admired as a place of rural retirement.

Woodchefter moft probably obtained its name from thofe woods, and from its having been a fmall poft or ftation of the Romans, for where-ever the Saxons found a Roman camp, it was ufual with them to terminate the name of fuch place with ceaꞅꞇꞃe; and as it is written *Udeceftre*, in *Domefday*, the place is fuppofed to have been one of the Roman *Caftra*, or at leaft an antient camp of one fort or other. But there is good reafon to attribute it to the Romans in particular, from a curious teffellated pavement having been difcovered here in the laft century, about four or five feet below the furface of the ground, on the fouth-weft fide within the church-yard. This could be no other than a Roman work. Part of it remains in pretty good prefervation, and lying at a proper depth, many coffins are placed upon it; but it has been frequently broken through at the requeft of fome families, who defired to have their friends interred at a greater depth. It is of very large extent, decorated with birds and other figures, but not having been wholly uncovered, its dimenfions cannot be exactly afcertained.

There was alfo another very interefting difcovery made in this parifh in the year 1687. It was of a confiderable quantity of the gold coin of king Edward the Fourth, which had been hid, as it is fuppofed, in the time of fome public convulfion, or civil war.

Woodchefter is famous for its fine broad cloth manufacture, carried on in a very extenfive manner by feveral mafter clothiers. And it is remarkable that the firft Napping-mill in thefe parts was erected here by the late fir Onefiphorus Paul. It is a machine for raifing the nap upon cloth in little knots, at regular but very fmall diftances, that give it a fingularly pleafing appearance. Near the fame time, another was fet up by one Mr. Freame, and fome years afterwards a third, by Mr. Richard Hawker, both of this neighbourhood, which latter is ftill employ'd, and yields great profit to the proprietors. I thought proper to make public mention of thefe machines,

machines, in honour of the inventors and improvers of an art, tending to extend the great and leading manufacture of the kingdom.

The wealth acquired in the clothing bufinefs has occafioned improvements in agriculture, and almoft every fpot of ground in this part of the country has the appearance of high cultivation.

Of the Manor and other Eftates.

There were two manors in this parifh. The antient record relating to the principal of them, exhibits a ftriking inftance of a mind abhorrent of the cruelty and injuftice of earl Godwin, who by a wicked contrivance, ftripped the nuns of Berkeley of their poffeffions, as already related under that head. The paffage may be thus tranflated:

'Gueda the mother of earl Herald held Udeceftre in Langetreu hundred. Goduin bought 'it of Azor, and gave it to his wife for her 'maintenance whilft fhe fhould refide at Berche-'lai; for fhe would not eat any thing of the pro-'duce of that manor, on account of the deftruc-'tion of the abbey. Eduuard holds this eftate in 'his farm of Wiltefcire, but unjuftly, as the 'county fays, becaufe it does not belong to any 'farm. Of which manor none gave any account 'to the king's commiffioners, nor was there any 'of them [*i.e.* of the county] prefent at the taking 'this writing. This eftate pays 7 *lib.*' *D. B.* p. 69.

The other manor lay in the hundred of Blacheleu, which is now comprized in that of Whitfton, according to the following extract:

'Brictric holds of the king Wideceftre in 'Blacheleu hundred. He held it in the time of 'king Edward. There is one hide taxed. There 'are fixteen villeins, and twelve bordars, with 'fixteen plow-tillages, but nothing in demean. 'In Glouueceftre one burgefs pays twenty bars of 'iron. There is a mill of 10 *folid.* It is worth 'and was worth 100 *folid.*' *Ibid.* p. 80.

John Maltravers held Wodecheftre of William earl Marefchal, and died feized thereof 24 E. 1. and John Maltravers, his fon, had livery of it in the 25th year of that reign. King's Stanley and Stonehoufe came afterwards into the poffeffion of the family of Maltravers, and this manor continued in that name and family, by defcent, 'till the reign of king Richard the Second, when Elianor, fifter and heirefs of Henry Maltravers, being married to John Arundel, fecond fon of Richard earl of Arundel, carried this manor and other eftates into the name and family of the earls of Arundel, as related under King's Stanley, in which family they continued for many generations. Sir Robert Atkyns is not quite confiftent in his accounts of the defcent of thefe manors to the Arundels, as may be feen by comparing them together.

The manor of Woodchefter was granted to George Huntley and John Huntley 6 Eliz. and it is mentioned in the grant to have been lately the earl of Arundel's. It was afterwards purchafed of the Huntleys by fir Robert Ducie. Sir Robert had feveral fons, who all died without iffue, whereby Elizabeth, his daughter, became his heir, from whom this manor defcended, like Tortworth, down to Thomas lord Ducie,[h] who is the prefent lord of it.

There

[h] This noble lord is paternally defcended from the Mortons of Morton in Staffordfhire, denominated of that place in the reign of king Edward the Firft, the faid lordfhip and other manors having been granted by that king to his anceftor for his good fervices in Scotland; and are devolved on the prefent lord Ducie.

The Ducies were defcended from a family in Normandy, one of which having raifed a regiment there, brought it over to England to the affiftance of queen Ifabel, (confort to king Edward the Second) againft the Spencers; and for his fervices had a grant of lands in Staffordfhire, which his defcendants enjoyed for many ages, 'till about the latter end of the reign of king Henry the Eighth, when the greateft part was fold by James Ducie, efq; who had to wife, firft, Eleanor, fifter to Edmund lord Sheffield; and fecondly, Alice, fifter to fir Richard Pipe, of Belfton in Derbyfhire, knight. By the laft he had iffue Richard, his fon and heir; and Henry, fecond fon, who married Mary, daughter and at length heir of Robert Hardy, by whom he had, amongft other children, fir Robert Ducie, knight and baronet, who married Elizabeth, daughter of Richard Pyot, alderman of London.

Which fir Robert Ducie was free of the company of merchants in London (commonly called merchant-taylors) and in 1620, 18 Jac. 1. was one of the fheriffs of that city, whereupon he was knighted; and, being one of the aldermen of the city of London, was, in the fifth year of king Charles the Firft, advanced to the dignity of a baronet, by letters patent, bearing date Nov. 28, 1629. He was lord mayor of the city of London in 1631, 7 Car. 1. and, being immenfely rich, was made banker to king Charles; and on the breaking out of the civil war, loft 80,000*l.* owing to him by his majefty. Neverthelefs, he is faid to leave at the time of his death, to the value of 400,000*l.* in land, money, &c. to his four fons, who were fir Richard Ducie, baronet, fir William Ducie, Henry, and Robert Ducie, efqrs, to which laft he gave Little Afton in Staffordfhire.

Sir Richard Ducie, the eldeft fon, was a great fufferer in the wars between king Charles the Firft, and his parliament, and being taken prifoner by fir William Waller, remained for fome time under confinement. He died unmarried, and was fucceeded in his dignity and eftate by his brother, fir William Ducie, bart.

Which fir William Ducie, bart. was made one of the knights of the Bath, at the coronation of king Charles the Second. He had his principal refidence at Tortworth in the county of Gloucefter, where he lies buried; but died at Charlton in Kent, in the 65th year of his age, on September 9, 1697; having been created vifcount Down of the kingdom of Ireland by king Charles the Second. He married Frances, daughter of Francis lord Seymour of Troubridge, grandfather of Charles the fixth duke of Somerfet; but leaving no iffue, his eftate defcended to Elizabeth, daughter and fole heir of Robert Ducie, efq; his brother.

Which Elizabeth was married to Edward Morton, of Morton and Engleton in the county of Stafford, efq; and left iffue Matthew-Ducie Morton, her fon and heir, created lord Ducie.

He ferved under king William during the war in Flanders, 'till the conclufion of the peace of Ryfwick, A. D. 1697. In the reign of queen Anne, he was twice chofen one of the knights of the fhire for the county of Gloucefter; and was alfo returned for the fame to the firft parliament called by George the Firft, who, in 1717, conftituted him vice-treafurer and pay-mafter of Ireland, whereupon he was rechofen for the faid county. Alfo, on June 13, 1720, he was advanced to the dignity of a peer of this realm, by the ftile and title of lord Ducie, baron of Morton in Staffordfhire.

His lordfhip married Arabella, daughter and coheir of fir Thomas Preftwich, of Holm, in the county palatine of Lancafter, bart. by whom he had iffue three fons and four daughters; 1. Matthew-Ducie Morton, his fucceffor; 2. Rowland-Lewis-Ducie Morton, who was colonel of a company in the foot-guards, and, in November 1739, was appointed colonel of a regiment of marines; 3. Charles-Ducie Morton, efq; who married Anne, daughter to ——— Wyat, of Windfor in Berkfhire, efq; and had iffue by her a fon named Benjamin, deceafed. Elizabeth, eldeft daughter, was married firft to Richard Symms,

of

There is a very good houfe near the church, which formerly belonged to Mr. Robert Bridges. This houfe, and the eftate belonging to it, paffed by the marriage of Mr. Bridges's fifter, to Mr. Browning, whofe daughter and heir was married to Mr. Dowell, of Over in this county, whofe eftates came by will to the late Mr. Degge; and this part was purchafed by the late Mr. Samuel Paul, and given by him to Nathaniel Peach, efq; the prefent owner.

Pudhill is a good houfe and eftate in this parifh, formerly belonging to the Smalls, but now the property of Thomas Wade, efq; where he refides.

Of the Church, &c.

The church is a rectory, in the deanery of Stonehoufe, worth about 100*l.* a year. Lord Ducie is patron, and the reverend Mr. Peter Hawker is the prefent incumbent.

The church is dedicated to St. Mary. It has an aile on the fouth fide, and a low embattled tower, with fix bells, at the weft end.

Firft fruits £.	10	0	0	Synodals £.	0	2	0
Tenths —	1	0	0	Pentecoftals	0	0	7
Procurations	0	6	8				

Monuments and Infcriptions.

There is a handfome raifed tomb in the chancel for fir George Huntley and his lady, who are reprefented lying along under a canopy fupported by pillars, with their ten children round the tomb. There are the Huntleys arms with quarterings upon the canopy, but no infcription.

On a marble monument on the fouth fide of the chancel, it is thus written:

Near to this place is Depofited all that is Mortal of
ROBERT BRIDGES Efq.
Who departed this life the 6th Day of March 1722 Aged 72.
In Memory of whom this Monument was Erected and of
His BROTHER in law Mr. RICHARD HICKS and IANE his wife fifter
of the faid Mr. BRIDGES who lies in the Chancel
of this Church.
Alfo near to this Place lies the Body of Mrs. ELIZABETH BROWNING,
Sifter to the Said Robert Bridges Efq; who departed this Life
December the 4th 1733.

At the top of the monument are the arms of Bridges.

On a fmall monument againft the chancel,

M. S.
IOHANNIS KING, A. M.
Hujufce Ecclefiæ Rector.
Ob. 4° Iulii Anno Domni 1723°
Ætat. Suæ 70mo
Et ELEANORÆ KING
Viduæ Ejus
Ob. 31mo Janrii Anno Domni 1728°
Ætat. fuæ 72do
Omnia Mors æquat.

Againft the fame wall is a marble monument, of which the defign is two *genii* holding up a fkeleton. Upon the front of the vafe it is thus written:

This Monument is erected
In Memory of
NATHANIEL PEACH of this Parifh Clothier
who died Auguft the 19th 1719 Aged 43.
MARGARET his Widow who died October the 18th 1741. Aged 58.
Alfo DEBORAH Wife of Nathaniel Peach Son of the faid
Nathaniel and *Margaret Peach*, and Sifter of *Samuel Paul* of
Rodborough Efq: She died May the 16th 1765 Aged 58.

At top is a fcutcheon, *Baron and femme*, 1. *Gules, three martlets between two chevronels argent*, for Peach. 2. *Azure, a bend embattled between two unicorns heads erazed Or*, for Pearfe. At bottom, *Baron and femme*, Peach, as before; impaling, 2. *Argent, on a fefs azure three croffes croflets Or.*

Between the two laft, ftands a marble pyramidal monument, with this infcription:

This MONUMENT is erected
in Memory of
EDWARD PEACH late of EBLEY in this County Clothier
eldeft Son of NATHANIEL and MARGARET PEACH
he died July 5, 1770 Aged 60 Years.
And alfo of
JOHN PEACH late of the City of BRISTOL MERCHANT
Second Son of the faid NATHANIEL & MARGARET PEACH,
he died at BATH September 20 1774 Aged 63.

Arms, Peach, as before.

In the church-yard, on a tomb,

Sr Onefiphorus Paul, Bart. died Sept. 21st 1774, Aged 68.

On the oppofite fide,

To the Memory of Catherine Lady Paul, fecond Wife of
Sr Onefiphorus Paul, Bart.
Eldeft Daughter of Francis Freeman of Norton Malereward in
the County of Somerfet Efqr. She
departed this Life ye 20th day of
Octr. 1766 in ye 56 year of
her Age.

Benefactions.

In 1699, Mr. Nathaniel Cambridge of Hamburgh, merchant, gave 1000*l.* to endow a fchool

of Blackheath, in the county of Kent, efq; and fecondly, on February 5, 1729-30, to Francis Reynolds, only fon and heir of Thomas Reynolds, efq; formerly a South-fea director, by whom fhe had two fons, Thomas Reynolds, and Francis Reynolds, efqrs. The other daughters, Mary, Arabella, and Penelope, died unmarried.

The faid Matthew lord Ducie departing this life at his houfe in Jermyn-ftreet, on May 22, 1735, was fucceeded by Matthew, his eldeft fon and heir.

Which Matthew lord Ducie, in the life-time of his father, was elected for the borough of Calne and Cricklade in Wiltfhire, in the laft parliament of George the Firft, and was a member for Tregony in Cornwall, in the firft parliament of George the Second. On February 14, 1754, he was appointed lord lieutenant of and in the counties of Gloucefter and of Briftol; and of the city of Gloucefter, and county of the fame; and cuftos rotulorum of Gloucefterfhire. He had alfo a grant of the offices of conftable of St. Briavel's, and keeper of the deer and woods in Dean foreft; and was likewife appointed vice-admiral of Gloucefterfhire. His lordfhip enjoyed all the faid places and offices until Nov. 1758, when, upon his refignation, they were conferred on John-Thynne How, fecond lord Chedworth.

His lordfhip, forefeing that upon the failure of iffue male of his own body, and the deceafe of his brothers without fuch iffue, the title of lord Ducie would become extinct, obtained a new patent, on April 23, 1763, granting to himfelf and his heirs male, and in default of fuch iffue, then to Thomas Reynolds, efq; his lordfhip's nephew, and to his heirs male, and in default of fuch iffue, then to Francis Reynolds, efq; brother to the faid Thomas Reynolds, and alfo nephew to his lordfhip, and his heirs male, the dignity of baron of the kingdom of Great Britain, by the title of lord Ducie, baron Ducie of Tortworth in the county of Gloucefter; and deceafing Dec. 27, 1770, the title, with his lordfhip's eftates, devolved upon the faid Thomas Reynolds, who, in virtue of the laft-mentioned grant, is now lord Ducie, baron of Morton in Staffordfhire, and lord Ducie of Tortworth in Gloucefterfhire. His lordfhip's arms are, *Argent, a chevron gules, between three fquare buckles fable.*

CREST. *Out of a wreath a moor-cock rifing proper, combe and wattles gules.*

SUPPORTERS. *Two unicorns argent, arm'd, maned, tufted, and hoofed Or, each gorged with a ducal coronet, party per pale Or and gules.*

MOTTO. PERSEVERANDO.

for

for the education of poor boys of this pariſh, which money was laid out in the purchaſe of Saintloe farm, in the pariſh of Minchin-Hampton, and a ſchool was there erected, and is ſtill continued in purſuance of the donor's intention: And in 1729, Mr. Richard Cambridge of London, gave 100*l.* to augment the ſame ſchool.

In 1705, Mrs. Elizabeth Seys gave 400*l.* to purchaſe an eſtate, the profit to be divided between three or more poor women, for teaching poor girls to read and work; which money, with 215*l.* intereſt, is laid out on two eſtates, one lying at Hamfallow in the pariſh of Berkeley, the other is called Hipp's-hill in this county.

In 1722, Robert Bridges, eſq; gave 500*l.* with which an eſtate has been purchaſed in the pariſh of Wheatenhurſt, and the profits are applied to teach three boys to read and write, and to clothe and apprentice out one or more of them every year, agreeably to the donor's directions.

In 1729, Mr. Richard Cambridge, of London, gave 20*l.* the intereſt of which to be diſpoſed of at the diſcretion of the overſeers, for ever.

Taxes.					
The Royal Aid in	1692,	£. 80	5	4
Poll-tax — —	1694, —	19	11	0
Land-tax ——	1694, —	89	0	0
The ſame, at 3*s.*	1770, —	66	18	0

At the beginning of this century, there were 120 houſes in this pariſh, and about 460 inhabitants, whereof 24 were freeholders; yearly births 11, and burials 10. *Atkyns.* In the year 1756, the people were numbered, and found to be 792, and they are ſomething increaſed ſince that time.

WOOLLASTON.

THIS pariſh lies in the hundred of Weſtbury, in the Foreſt diviſion of the county, about four miles diſtant north-eaſtward from the town of Chepſtow in Monmouthſhire, ſeven ſouth from Colford, and twenty-two ſouth-weſtward from Glouceſter.

It ſtretches along the north-weſt ſide of the Severn, and riſing gradually from that river to a conſiderable height, affords a beautiful proſpect of it, and of the towns of Berkeley and Thornbury, with Hill, Oldbury, Knole, and other villages in the vale on the oppoſite ſide of the river, and the hills and woods at a diſtance behind them.

The name of it is conſiderably altered from its original. It was taken from that of its owner, and written *Odelaveſton* in *Domeſday*, about ſeven hundred years ago; and we of the preſent age, to expreſs the ſame idea, ſhould write it *Odelave's Town.* The pariſh conſiſts of good paſture and arable land, and a ſmall brook running through it empties itſelf into the Severn. The turnpike-road from Glouceſter to Glamorganſhire is carried over an eminence through the pariſh, and is extreamly pleaſant upon account of the extenſive proſpect abovementioned.

Of the Manor and other Eſtates.

Sir Robert Atkyns omits the *Domeſday* account of this manor, which runs thus:

'William de Ow holds Odelaveſton in Twiferde hundred. Brictric the ſon of Algar held it. There are two hides. There is nothing in demean except five villeins, with five plowtillages. There is one fiſhery in the Severn of 5 *ſol.* and a mill of 40*d.* It is worth and was worth 20 *ſol.* This eſtate pays tax.' *Dom.* p. 73.

The hundred of Twiferde was a very ſmall diſtrict, including only this pariſh, a ſmall part of Tiddenham, and a place called Modiete, in this neighbourhood; but there is no ſuch diſtrict at preſent.

The Welch poſſeſſed themſelves of Tiddenham and Woollaſton, but both places were retaken from them by Walter and Roger, brothers of Gilbert de Clare, in the year 1160. And it is probable that Woollaſton was afterwards granted to the abbey of Tintern in Monmouthſhire, founded in the year 1131, by William earl of Pembroke, for monks of the Ciſtercian order; and that the manor continued in that houſe 'till the diſſolution.

Henry earl of Worceſter died ſeized of the manor and Grange of Wolveſton, *alias* Woollaſton, 3 E. 6. as appears by an inquiſition taken at Wotton-underedge, Feb. 21, 4 E. 6. Edward earl Worceſter was lord of this manor in the year 1608, and the duke of Beaufort is the preſent lord of the manor of Woollaſton, and proprietor of the Grange eſtate; but the latter is in leaſe to Mr. Barrow. The Grange houſe is an antient building, with a chapel, now converted to a malthouſe.

Elizabeth Harriſon, widow, formerly the wife of Thomas Stanſhaw, and daughter and heir of Alice daughter of James lord Berkeley, levied a fine of lands in Woollaſton to John Walſh and others 13 H. 7.

HAMLETS. There are places in this pariſh of the following names: 1. *Keynſham*; 2. *Everend*; 3. *Gumſtod*; 4. *Pluſterwyne*; and 5. *Brookend.* But the extract from *Domeſday*, which ſir Robert Atkyns places under *High Woolaſton*, belongs to Hewelsfield, and not to this place.

Of the Church, &c.

The church is a rectory, in the Foreſt deanery, worth about 130*l.* a year, of which the duke of Beaufort is patron, and the reverend Robert Penny, D.D. is the preſent incumbent, and of the chapel of Lancaut in Tiddenham, which has lately been annexed to this church.

The tithes were given to the abbey of Tintern by William earl of Pembroke, and earl marſhal of England, in 1131; and after the diſſolution, were

were held by the lords of the manor, and paid 2*l.* 13*s.* 4*d.* yearly to the crown; and the living was formerly held as a vicarage, 'till the tithes were recovered, not long ſince, by Mr. Griffith, a late incumbent.

Firſt fruits £. 13	11	3	Proc.& Syn. £. 0	1	8
Tenths —	1	7	$1\frac{1}{2}$	Pentecoſtals - 0	1	4

Benefactions.

Henry Newland, abbat of Tintern, gave the church-houſe and green in 1501.

One acre in Thornhill is given towards the reparation of the church.

Mr. Richard Clayton of Chepſtow gave 22*s.* a year to the poor, 37 Eliz. And Mrs. Margaret Clayton, his widow, gave 40*s.* a year for teaching four poor children to read.

Mr. Thomas James, alderman of Briſtol, in 1618, gave 100*l.* to be lent without intereſt, on giving ſecurity, to ten poor widows, to enable them to employ themſelves in ſpinning.

In 1685, Mrs. Mary Smart gave 20*s.* a year to be diſtributed to the poor in bread, and the payment thereof is charged on an eſtate in this pariſh, late belonging to Mr. Charles Gough, who married Elizabeth, ſiſter to Mrs. Smart.

Taxes.					
	The Royal Aid in	1692, £.	118	4	0
	Poll-tax ——	1694, —	33	6	0
	Land-tax ——	1694, —	170	13	0
	The ſame, at 3*s.*	1770, —	127	19	0

At the beginning of this century, there were 96 houſes, and about 400 inhabitants in this pariſh, whereof 17 were freeholders; yearly births 9, and burials 8. *Atkyns.* The inhabitants are now about 459.

WORMINGTON

IS a ſmall pariſh, in the lower diviſion of Kiftſgate hundred, five miles diſtant ſouth from Eveſham in Worceſterſhire, five north from Winchcombe, and nineteen north-eaſtward from Glouceſter.

It is ſituate in the Vale, and a brook runs through it into the Avon at Hampton, near Eveſham. The greater part of the land is arable, but the village has nothing particular to diſtinguiſh it in natural hiſtory, or antiquities.

Of the Manor and other Eſtates.

The following is tranſlated from *Domeſday* :

'Roger de Laci holds Wermetun in Greteſtan 'hundred. Walter the ſon of Ercold holds it 'under him. There are five hides taxed. Eduui 'held it. In demean are two plow-tillages, and 'ſix villeins, with two plow-tillages. There are 'two *ſervi*, and a mill of 8 *ſolid.* and ten acres of 'meadow. It was worth 100 *ſol.* now only 4 *lib.*' *Domeſday*, p. 75.

King Henry the Third granted court leet, waifs, and felons goods in Wormington to the maſters of the knights templers, and his grant was allowed in a writ of *Quo warranto* 15 E. 1. The manor was afterwards given to Weſtbury college, near Briſtol, and upon the diſſolution of religious foundations, this eſtate, and others belonging to that college, were granted to ſir Rafe Sadleir, 35 H. 8.

Sir Robert Atkyns makes mention that Henry Acton died ſeized of Wormington 20 Eliz. and that livery thereof was granted to his ſon Valentine Acton, the ſame year; but that muſt be underſtood of Wormington Grange in Didbrook, and not of this place.

John Newton, eſq; was lord of this manor in the year 1608, out of which name it paſſed by the marriage of a daughter of the Newtons to Mr. Gwinneth, who ſold it to Mr. Dobbins, and it was by him conveyed to Mr. Townſend. Mr. Kenrick laid claim to the manor of Wormington at the beginning of the preſent century, and that claim was continued by Mr. John Partridge, who died about the year 1776; but a great part of the demeans of the manor was given to charitable uſes by George Townſend, eſq; about eighty years ago.

The Daſtons were antiently ſeized of a manor, or reputed manor, in this pariſh, which from them was called Wormington Daſton. John Daſton was ſeized thereof 15 E. 4. Anthony Daſton alſo died ſeized of lands in Wormington 12 C. 1. and left Richard his ſon and heir, twelve years old.

Lord Aylmer has a good eſtate in this pariſh, but his lordſhip's uſual reſidence is at Greenwich in the county of Kent. His lordſhip's arms are, *Pearl, a croſs diamond between four Corniſh choughs proper.* CREST, *In a ducal coronet a chough with wings diſplay'd proper.* SUPPORTERS, *Two mariners habited, the dexter holding in his hand a foreſtaff, and the ſiniſter a lead-line, all proper.* MOTTO, STEADY.

Of the Church, &c.

The church is a rectory, in the deanery of Campden, worth about 70*l.* a year, of which is patron, and is the preſent incumbent. Two yard-lands belong to the glebe, but eleven yard-lands, being the demeans of the manor, are tithe free.

The church is ſmall, dedicated to the Holy Trinity, or, as ſome ſay, to St. Catherine, whoſe figure, with her wheel, appears in one of the painted windows.

Firſt fruits £. 7	15	0	Synodals £. 0	1	0
Tenths —	0	15	$6\frac{1}{2}$	Pentecoſt. 0	0	$8\frac{1}{2}$
Procurations	0	3	0			

Taxes.					
	The Royal Aid in	1692, £.	43	10	0
	Poll-tax ——	1694, —	9	12	0
	Land-tax —	1694, —	20	16	10
	The same, at 3s.	1770, —	14	16	4½

When sir Robert Atkyns compiled his account of this parish, there were 19 houses, and about 80 inhabitants, whereof 4 were freeholders; yearly births 2, and burials 2. The inhabitants are now about 85.

WOTTON-UNDEREDGE.

THIS parish lies in the hundred of Berkeley, four miles distant south from Dursley, five north-east from Wickwar, and nineteen south from Gloucester; but these distances are to be taken from the market town, which lies within the parish.

The town of Wotton-underedge is situated upon a pleasant eminence, overlooking a comb, or little valley, to the north-eastward. It lies near the foot of a ridge of hills to the north, which being partly covered with woods, have a very pleasing appearance. Hence the town certainly obtained its name, which is easily resolved into *Wood-town-under-ridge*. It is quite open to the other quarters, with an ample vale richly beset with villages and farm houses before it, and commanding an extensive and beautiful prospect, including the populous parish of Kingswood, formerly famous for its monastery, the towns of Wickwar and Sodbury, with Lansdown hill near Bath on one hand, and Berkeley castle, the Severn, Dean forest, and the Welch mountains on the other.

It is called a borough, but sends no members to parliament. In the 37th year of king Henry the Third, Maurice lord Berkeley caused a leet, consisting of the resiants within the borough, to be taken out of the great hundred of Berkeley, agreeable to the custom of great lords in those days; and he, and lady Jane his mother, who held the manor of Wotton in jointure, by their deed of that date, granted to the inhabitants of the borough the same liberties, usages, and customs, as the borough of Tetbury then enjoy'd, having, the preceding year, obtained from the king a grant of a market each Friday at Wotton, and of a fair every year, to be held upon the eve, upon the day, and the morrow of the Exaltation of the cross. These privileges were afterwards confirmed by Thomas lord Berkeley, in the tenth year of the reign of king Edward the First.

In the first year of the following reign, the jury, at the leet holden at Michaelmas, had leave to choose one person out of the burgesses to be the supreme governor amongst them, 'till that time twelve-month, and to call him the Mayor, which they have continued to do from time to time ever since. The origin of the custom, and the ceremony of choosing the mayor, are particularly set down in a manuscript written by Mr. John Smyth, a very learned and judicious person, who was steward to lord Berkeley in the reign of king Charles the First, and took great pains to extract from the records many curious particulars relating to the places within the hundred of Berkeley. The jury present, in writing, the names of three persons (the old mayor, and two others) to the steward, out of whom he makes choice of one for the new mayor, and administers to him the oath of office. The old mayor then rising from his seat, and leaving the silver-gilt mace upon the table where he sate with the steward, the new one sits down in his place, and elects one of the other two that were returned with him for his serjeant, who, in the language of the court-rolls, is called *Serviens ad Clavem*. The court being ended, the serjeant, with his mace, walks before the mayor to his house, whom the other burgesses also attend. The serjeant, by the custom, is obliged to collect the lord's rents and profits within the borough, and to pay them to the auditor; and if he fail, the mayor is answerable for them.

Refusing to serve the office of mayor in this borough is punishable by fine. In the year 1639, Richard Pool being chosen, refused to serve, and was fined 10*l*. John Leigh was then chosen by the steward, and refusing in like manner, paid a fine of 6*l*. 13*s*. 4*d*. The legality of the steward's imposing such fine has been determined in the case of Thomas Daws, who was fined 10*l*. in the year 1693, which he would not pay, whereupon he was arrested in virtue of a *Capias* sued out of the court of king's bench in Michaelmas term 1695, and a verdict was obtained against him at the Lent assizes, and judgment entered in the same court the Easter term following.

This town gave name to an usurped jurisdiction, called the Hundred of Wotton, set up by the descendants of Richard de Beauchamp, earl of Warwick, who had possessed themselves of the manors of Wotton and Nibley, and of other considerable estates within the hundred of Berkeley; and during the long law-suits between them and the heirs male of the Berkeley family, affected to call their possessions in these parts *the Hundred of Wotton*. An estate was actually granted by that name to John duke of Northumberland, upon whose attainder, in the first year of the reign of queen Mary, it reverted to the crown, and was again granted by the same name to Ambrose earl of Warwick, and to Robert earl of Leicester, in the fifteenth year of queen Elizabeth. Accordingly there is a certain district so distinguished in some of our old maps, tho' no such independent jurisdiction was ever legally and rightfully established.

Thomas Talbot, viscount Lisle, grandson of that Richard de Beauchamp, by Elizabeth the heiress of William lord Berkeley, resided in this borough,

borough, and there are ſome remains of his lordſhip's houſe, conſiſting of the arches of doorways, &c. ſtill diſtinguiſhable in the buildings belonging to Mr. Veel, ſituate in the lower part of the town.

Wotton was burnt down in the reign of king John. It then ſtood a little northward of the preſent ſcite, as may be gathered from the name of a place called the *Brands*, from the fire which then happened there.

It has not been diſtinguiſhed by any very intereſting tranſactions, only in the great civil war, the king had a temporary garriſon here, conſiſting of a regiment of horſe, which, according to Corbet, were driven out of the town by the parliament's party, under the command of colonel Maſſie, and having ſuffered the loſs of ſix killed, and twelve made priſoners, the reſt eſcaped to Briſtol. It was again garriſoned for the king by eight hundred men, and attacked by captain Backhouſe with two hundred horſe and dragoons, who fell ſuddenly on, ſays the before-mentioned hiſtorian, marched up to the main guard, and for ſome time were maſters of four pieces of ordnance; but being over matched, were forced to retreat, which they did without the loſs of a man.

There was a conduit erected in the town, in the year 1630, at the expence of ſir Richard Venn, and his ſon-in-law, Hugh Perry, both aldermen of London, and natives of this place, by which water was brought from a ſpring in Edbrook field to the market croſs; but the conduit is now intirely deſtroy'd.

Leland, in his *Itinerary*, written in the reign of king Henry the Eighth, calls it *A praty Market Towne, welle occupyed withe Clothiars, havyinge one faire longe Strete, and welle buyldyd in it, and it ſtondithe clyvinge toward the rotes of an hill.* But tho' Leland takes notice of but one ſtreet, it is probable that there were others in his time, and that he ſpeaks of the high ſtreet only, becauſe the reſt comparatively were of little account. The following names appear in the writings of the next century, *viz.* High-ſtreet, Sow-lane, the Chipping, or Market-place, Chipping-lane, Bradley-ſtreet, Hawe-ſtreet, Church-lane, and Symlane; the whole borough then comprizing an extent of about ſixty acres of ground.

It is pretty well built, and the clothing buſineſs, chiefly in the fine way, is of very antient ſtanding. There are now ſeven or eight maſter clothiers, and the trade is ſtill in a flouriſhing ſtate, tho' not equal to what it has ſometimes been.

The market is held on Friday, and there is a fair on the 25th of September, formerly noted for cheeſe and cattle; but now of much leſs account for either.

The hills on one ſide of the town rendering it difficult for carriages to paſs and repaſs, is a circumſtance unfavourable to its market, which like that of moſt other little towns, is dwindled to nothing. There is, however, a turnpike-road branching from it northward to Glouceſter, and eaſtward to Tetbury, and another extending ſouth-weſtward towards Wickwar, Sodbury, and Briſtol; but theſe are not the great roads leading from Glouceſter to Bath and Briſtol; ſo that there is but little travelling through the town, except by people of the neighbourhood, and by ſuch as are connected in trade with the inhabitants.

The pariſh of Wotton is very extenſive. Upon the brow of a hill called Weſtridge, looking towards Tortworth, there is a ſquare camp, with double intrenchments, incloſing an area of about four acres of ground. It is now over-grown with beech wood, and is called *Becket's Bury*, but for what reaſon I cannot conjecture.

Of the Manor and other Eſtates.

This manor was a member of the great lordſhip of Berkeley at the time of the general ſurvey; but there are no further particulars of it recorded in *Domeſday*, than that there are 'In Uutune 'fifteen hides and half a yard-land.' Roger de Berkeley was ſeized of it in the reign of king William the Conqueror, and it deſcended in that family, with the manor of Berkeley, 'till the death of Thomas lord Berkeley, the fourth of that name. This Thomas lord Berkeley married Margaret, daughter of Gerard Warren, lord Liſle, by his wife Alice, the daughter and heir of Henry lord Tyes, with whom he had a very great eſtate. He died 5 H. 5. and left an only daughter, Elizabeth, married to Richard Beauchamp, earl of Warwick.

This Elizabeth counteſs of Warwick was heir general to the whole eſtate of the Berkeley family; but James lord Berkeley, ſon of James, younger brother to Thomas lord Berkeley, father of the ſaid Elizabeth, was heir male, and derived his title by an eſtate taille limited to the heirs males; for Thomas lord Berkeley, grandfather to the before-mentioned Thomas, levied a fine of Berkeley, Wotton, and divers other manors, 23 E. 3. whereby he ſettled thoſe manors on his heirs males, and James lord Berkeley being heir male, had right to the eſtate by virtue of that ſettlement. However, the ſame Richard Beauchamp being in Berkeley caſtle at the death of Thomas lord Berkeley, his wife's father, ſeized upon all the deeds and writings that concerned the eſtate, which made it difficult for James lord Berkeley to prove his title.

Richard Beauchamp, earl of Warwick, died leaving three daughters coheireſſes. Margaret, the eldeſt, was ſecond wife to John the great earl of Shrewſbury, who had iſſue by her John, afterwards created viſcount Liſle. He with his deſcendants proſecuted their pretenſions againſt the lords Berkeley with great violence and illegality; and Thomas viſcount Liſle, ſon of John, loſt his life at Nibley-green in this quarrel, as related under that pariſh. But after many years conteſt, the quiet poſſeſſion was yielded to the Berkeley family,

family, and the earl of Berkeley is the prefent lord of the manor of Wotton.

Joan Skey, widow, levied a fine of lands in Wotton-underedge to John Walworth and Eleanor his wife, 8 H. 7. John Stanfhaw and Humphry his brother levied a fine of lands in Wotton borough, and Wotton forreigne, to William Freame, and others, 12 H. 7. A meadow called the Vineyard in Wotton, formerly belonging to the abbey of Kingfwood, was granted to George Huntley, and others, 2 Jac. 1. Two tenements in Wotton, called Spencer's Heye, and Nayler's Heye, with the tithes of the fame, belonged to the priory of St. Ofwald, in Gloucefter, and were granted to Peter Grey and Edward his fon 19 Eliz.

TITHINGS and *HAMLETS*.

There are four tithings in this large parifh.

1. *Sinwell* and *Bradley* make one tithing. Sinwell adjoins to the borough, and the parifh church ftands within it. Mr. Web had a good houfe and eftate at Sinwell, at the beginning of this century, which are now the property of Mr. Veel, of Simondfhall.

Bradley gave name to an eminent family to whom it belonged, and Hugh de Bradley was living in the reign of king Richard the Firft. One Serlo died feized of Bradley, and left Agatha and Juliana his two fifters coheireffes; the former married to Henry ——, the latter to William de Straton. Anne the widow of Serlo was married to Hugh de Straton, and had the manor of Bradley affigned to her for dower 4 H. 3. Robert de Pleffy was feized thereof 29 E. 1. as were Thomas de Luda and Elizabeth his wife in the 33d year of the fame reign. Sir Maurice Berkely held this manor 2 H. 4. and fir Maurice Berkeley of Uley died feized of Bradleigh 4 E. 4. John Berkeley died feized of the manor of Bradley 5 Mar. and left Brice Berkeley his brother and heir. Arnold Oldfworth died feized of this place, and left Edward Oldfworth his fon, who alfo died feized of it 4 C. 1. when Robert his fon was fourteen years old. This was an antient family defcended from the Oldfworths of Yorkfhire, and fir Lancelot Halifax, of Halifax, was their anceftor, who died 15 E. 1. Many lands in this place were given by Thomas lord Berkeley to the abbey of St. Auftin's in Briftol, for which reafon the chief meffuage is called *Canons Court*, and after the diffolution of religious foundations, they were granted to the dean and chapter of Briftol. Bradley came afterwards to Thomas Daws, efq; whofe great niece, Mrs. Smart, is the proprietor of Bradley-houfe, and of a good eftate there, and holds Canons Court under the dean and chapter of Briftol.

2. *Simondfhall* and *Combe* conftitute another tithing. Simondfhall is the higheft ground in all this country. It is for the moft part a large plain, with an antient manfion houfe, which has been the refidence of the Veels for many generations. And it is faid, that in a clear day, eighteen counties may be feen from fome parts of the down near the houfe. Between this and Bagpath, ftands a large barrow, which never having been opened, nothing can be faid of the contents of it with certainty, only it is fuppofed to have been the burying place of fome perfons who fell in battle hereabout. In the evidences belonging to Bartholomew hofpital in Gloucefter, of the year 1280, there is an account of a fardel of land lying between the land of Adam de Tedepen on the north, and the land belonging to the church of Symondefhale on the fouth; which I quote only to fhew that there was at that time a church or chapel belonging to this place, but it has been long fince difufed. In *Domefday* it is recorded, that 'Half a hide in Symondefhale belonged to 'the lordfhip of Berchelai.' The inheritance of this manor has ever fince been vefted in the proprietors of that lordfhip, and is now the property of the earl of Berkeley; but the eftate is in leafe to William Veel,[i] efq; who is defcended from a very antient family, which came into England with William the Conqueror.

Combe

[i] Jeffrey le Veel married Maud, daughter and heir of Harding, fon of Elias Harding of Hunterford, *alias* Huntingford, which Elias was younger brother of Robert Fitz Harding, anceftor of the Berkeley family. He was in great efteem with king John.

Henry le Veel, fon of Jeffrey, was living 37 H. 3.

Robert le Veel of Charfield lived in the time of E. 1. and E. 2. and married Hawife, daughter of —— le Gore, with whom he had the manor of St. Faggon 25 E. 1.

Sir Peter le Veel, fon of Robert, married Hawife, daughter and heir of —— Kingfton of Tortworth 5 E. 3. and with her had the manor of Tortworth.

Sir Peter le Veel, fon of fir Peter, married Cecilia, daughter and heir of —— Maffey of Charfield, with whom it is faid he had the manor of Charfield. He was high fheriff of Gloucefterfhire 49 E. 3. and died 20 R. 2.

Sir Peter le Veel, knight, fon of fir Peter, married Catherine, daughter and heir of fir John Clevedon. Her fecond hufband was Thomas lord Berkeley.

Thomas Veel, fon of fir Peter, (or Pierce) married Hawife ——. Her furname feems to have been Torrington, as the arms afcribed to her belong to the Torringtons, *viz. Gules, an annulet between two bars Or, in chief a lion paffant of the fecond.*

John Veel, fon of Thomas, married Margaret ——, and died 9 H. 6.

Sir John Veel, fon of John, married Alice, daughter of —— Brookfby. Her arms were *Barry undy argent and fable, on a canton gules a mullet Or.* He was high fheriff of Gloucefterfhire 31 H. 6. and died in the 36th year of that reign, leaving two fons, Robert and William.

Robert Veel, the eldeft fon, married Alice, daughter of John Pointz, efq; and by her had an only daughter and heir Alice, married to fir David Matthews, of Rayder in Glamorganfhire, by whom fhe had four daughters, of whom Margaret, the third daughter, was married to fir William Throckmorton, and carried the manor of Tortworth into that family. I now return to

William Veel, fecond fon of fir John Veel, and brother to Robert. He married Sufanna, daughter and coheirefs of —— Vyell, whofe arms were *Argent, a fefs raguly gules between three annulets fable.*

William Veel of Over in Almondfbury, fon of William, married Margaret, daughter of William Fettiplace, of Maiden-Cott in the county of Oxford, whofe arms were *Gules two chevrons argent.*

Edward Veel, eldeft fon of the laft William, married Catherine, daughter of John Holloway.

Edward Veel, fon of Edward, married Jane, daughter of George Burley, of Whifte in Wiltfhire. But we leave this branch and return to William Veel of Over, who had a third fon, of the name of William.

Which

Combe lies eaſtward of the church. This eſtate was given by the empreſs Maud to Nigel de Kingſcote, anceſtor to the Kingſcotes of Kingſcote, for his ſervices to her in the wars; but that family was probably diſpoſſeſſed of it on the change of affairs. Thomas Davis, of Minchin Hampton, eſq; died ſeized of Wotton-Combe 37 H. 8. and left Giles his ſon eighteen years old; whoſe ſon, Francis Davis, died ſeized of the manor of Wotton-Combe 5 Mar. leaving two daughters coheireſſes, of whom Mary, the eldeſt, was married to William Weſtden, and Elizabeth, the youngeſt, was married to John Poll; and they had livery of this manor granted to them the ſame year. Mr. Hicks had a good eſtate at Combe, which is deſcended to the reverend Mr. Somerville, of Bibury, whoſe mother was daughter of that Mr. Hicks. What ſir Robert Atkyns obſerves of Combe belonging formerly to the abbey of Bordeſley in Worceſterſhire, and of its being granted to Thomas Smith 7 E. 6. is all miſtake, and ſhould have been applied to Combe in the pariſh of Campden.

The *Rudge* is an eſtate ſometimes in antient writings dignified with the title of a manor. It belonged formerly to the abbey of Kingſwood, and was granted to ſir Nicholas Pointz 36 H. 8. But Rudge farm belonged to the Pointz's before the above grant, for ſir Robert Pointz died ſeized thereof 12 H. 8. and was ſucceeded by ſir Anthony Pointz, whoſe ſon and heir, ſir Nicholas Pointz, died ſeized thereof 4 Mar. and left Nicholas his ſon twenty-one years old. The manor of Rudge, with a good eſtate here, is now the property of the reverend Mr. Brereton of Glouceſter, in right of his wife.

Nynd is a place in this pariſh.

3. *Wortley* is a diſtinct and populous tithing, where was formerly a chapel of eaſe, founded by Thomas lord Berkeley, and dedicated to St. John; and William lord Berkeley, earl mareſchal and of Nottingham, levied a fine of the advowſon of the chapel 3 H. 7. There was alſo a chantry in this chapel, of which John Collins was the laſt incumbent, and received a penſion of 2*l.* 16*s.* in the year 1553. *Willis.* John Engayne was ſeized of Wortley 30 E. 1. It was part of the manor of Wotton, and ſold by George lord Berkeley and his mother, by their deed inrolled in chancery, dated 28 Nov. 7 Car. for 1500*l.* to Richard Pool, gent. and his heirs, by the name of a manor. It is now the eſtate of Matthew Hale, eſq; in whoſe family it has been for ſeveral generations.

4. *Huntingford* is another tithing in this pariſh. Elias Harding, younger brother of Robert Harding, anceſtor to the Berkeley family, died ſeized of this manor in the reign of king John. John Veale was ſeized of Huntingford 36 H. 6. Catherine ——, an heireſs to this manor, was married to Henry Wogan, who died ſeized of Huntingford 9 H. 8. and left Joan his daughter and heir eleven years old. The manor was then held of the king, as of the hundred of Grumbald's Aſh. Mr. Adey has a good eſtate here, with manerial rights; but lord Berkeley is lord paramount.

Of the Church, &c.

The church is a vicarage, in the deanery of Durſley, worth 43*l.* 6*s.* 8*d.* from the impropriation; but it has no ſort of tithes belonging to it. It has been augmented by a donation from the late Edward Colſton, eſq; by another from the feoffees of the market, and by queen Anne's bounty; ſo that the income is now upwards of 100*l.* a year. Chriſt Church college in Oxford are patrons, and the reverend William Tatterſall, M. A. is the preſent incumbent. The impropriation belongs to the ſame college.

The advowſon belonged to the nunnery of Berkeley before the Norman conqueſt, and was

Which William the third ſon, and brother of the firſt mentioned Edward Veel, lived at Acton, and married Elianor, daughter of John Gover of Wotton-underedge. Her arms were *Argent, on a bend azure a fret Or.*

Nicholas Veel of Alveſton, ſon and heir of William, married the daughter of Richard Brydges of Combe, and had iſſue ſeven ſons, Peter (of whom there was iſſue remaining about Axbridge in Somerſetſhire *anno* 1685) William, Richard, Thomas, Edward, Nicholas, and Philip; and two daughters, Margaret and Maria.

Thomas Veel of Alveſton, ſon of Nicholas, married to his firſt wife Dorothy, daughter of John Wynneate, of Hampton, com. Middleſex, whoſe arms were, *Sable, a bend argent cotized Or, between ſix martlets of the ſecond.* By his firſt wife he had one ſon William, and three daughters, Suſanna, Eleanor, and Dorothy, which Dorothy was married to William Holland of Briſtol; and Eleanor, the ſecond daughter, was married to Edward Hill of Cam, in this county. He had iſſue by his ſecond wife, two ſons, Nicholas and Thomas; Nicholas Veel was of Olveſton in this county, in the commiſſion of the peace, who married Alice, daughter of —— Blanchard, of Wroxall in the county of Wilts, and by her had iſſue an only child Nicholas, who died unmarried. Thomas Veel, ſecond ſon by the ſecond marriage, married Mary, daughter of Henry Butler, eſq. She was buried at Wotton-underedge, and there is now an inſcription for her in Wotton church. Thomas Veel, the father, was ſequeſtered in the civil wars, and paid 704*l.* 13*s.* 4*d.* and died about the year 1663.

William Veel of Simondſhall, ſon and heir of Thomas, married Elizabeth, daughter of Robert Culliford, of the iſland of Purbeck in Dorſetſhire. Her arms were, *Argent, a feſs between three bulls ſable.* They had iſſue two ſons, Robert, who died unmarried; and Thomas Veel of Simondſhall, ; alſo one daughter Margaret, married to Robert Culliford of Southampton.

Thomas Veel, ſon of William, married Elizabeth, daughter of John Smyth, of Nibley in the county of Glouceſter, eſq; and by her had iſſue two ſons, Thomas, who died unmarried, and William; Alſo two daughters, Elizabeth, married to the reverend Mr. Thomas Snell, of Bampton in the Buſh, com. Oxon; and Anne, married to the reverend Timothy Millechamp, of Newton in Wilts.

William Veel, ſon of Thomas, was ſeven years old in 1682. He married Heſter, daughter and heir of Robert Web, of Sinwell in Wotton-under-edge, whoſe arms were, *Sable, three eſcallops in bend argent.* They had iſſue three ſons, Thomas, who died unmarried in 1752; Robert, who died unmarried in 1742; and William; alſo one daughter Elizabeth, married to William Davis, of Slimbridge in this county.

William Veel, third ſon of the laſt William, married Anne, eldeſt daughter and one of the coheireſſes of Stephen Compeer of Wotton-underedge, whoſe arms are *Or, on a feſs azure between three martlets ſable as many croſs croſlets fitchy of the field.* By her he has iſſue three ſons, William, Robert, and Thomas, now living; and three daughters, Anne, Elizabeth, and Mary. He reſides at Simondſhall, and is poſſeſſed of ſeveral good eſtates in this county. He gives for his arms, *Argent, on a bend ſable three calves Or.* The Creſt, *A garb Or, enſeigned with a ducal coronet gules.* Motto, FACE AUT TACE.

treacherouſly obtained from them by earl Godwin, from whom it came to the crown, and was granted by king Henry the Second to Robert the ſon of Harding, progenitor to the Berkeley family, and by him given to the monaſtery of St. Auguſtine in Briſtol. It was appropriated 35 E. 1. and the abbey of St. Auguſtine was ſeized of the advowſon 3 E. 2. It was again reſtored to the Berkeley family, and Maurice lord Berkeley granted it to the abbey of Tewkeſbury in the reign of king Henry the Seventh. The tithes were again appropriated, and after the diſſolution of monaſteries, were at different times granted to Chriſt Church college in Oxford; *viz.* a portion of tithes in Wotton which belonged to the abbey of Glouceſter, and another portion which belonged to the priory of St. Oſwald there, were granted to the chapter of Chriſt Church 33 H. 8. And the rectory of Wotton Subedge, and the advowſon of the vicarage, were granted to that college 38 H. 8. which before were in the poſſeſſion of the abbey of Tewkeſbury. Henry lord Berkeley laid claim to this advowſon, and by a decree in chancery 3 Eliz. the advowſon of Tetbury was given to his lordſhip, and this of Wotton to Chriſt Church college.

The tithes of Spencer's Heye and Nayler's Heye in Wotton, which belonged to the beforementioned priory of St. Oſwald, were granted, as already obſerved, to Peter Grey and Edward his ſon 19 Eliz. Other tithes and lands in Wotton, which belonged to the ſame priory, were granted to John Hercey and John Edwards 20 Eliz. And other tithes in Wotton, which belonged to the abbey of Kingſwood, were granted to George Huntley and others 2 Jac. 1.

The church is dedicated to the virgin Mary. It ſtands in the tithing of Sinwell and Bradley. It is large and handſome, conſiſting of the nave, and two ſide ailes, with a lofty pinnacled tower at the weſt end. The earl of Berkeley's arms are in ſeveral windows of the church.

There were ſeveral chantries in this church; one dedicated to St. Mary, and after the diſſolution, the lands belonging to it were granted to Edward Seimour, duke of Somerſet, 1 E. 6. and afterwards to William Heirick and Arthur Ingram, 5 Jac. 1. Other chantries were dedicated to the Holy Croſs, to St. Nicholas, to St. Catherine, and to All Saints. And there was a houſe founded in Wotton for friers of the Holy Croſs, who obtained licence to purchaſe a ſcite and lands to the amount of 10*l.* a year, 23 E. 3.

Firſt fruits £.	13	10	0	Synodals £.	0	2	0
Tenths —	1	7	0	Pentecoſt.	0	1	6
Procurations	0	6	8				

Monuments and Inſcriptions.

There is a large handſome tomb of grey marble in the north aile, with two figures engraven on braſs plates, in memory of Thomas lord Berkeley, the fourth of that name, and of the lady Margaret his wife, ſole heireſs of Gerrard Warren, lord Liſle. There is no inſcription upon the tomb, but he died in 1417, and his lady in 1392.

Upon a large monument of white marble, are the following inſcriptions:

D. O. M. S.
Infra deponitur quod reliquum eſt
RICARDI DAWES, Arm.
Ex honeſtâ et antiquâ noſtros inter Dobunos
proſapia oriundi.
COLL: WADH. apud Oxon olim alumni
Ubi Academiâ Auguſtiſ. ANNÆ triumphos
Solemni ritu celebrante,
ad res ſublimes depingendas deſignatus
quàm optime munus implevit.
Hinc in ſocietatem TEMPLI INT: adſcitus
juri municipali operam dedit,
atq; inter Cauſidicos repagulares adſcriptus eſt.
OPTIMUS ADOLESCENS
ingenij acumine et gravitate ſpectabilis,
morum integritate et elegantiâ magis conſpicuus,
animi candore et magnitudine ornatiſſimus,
pietate deniq; in Deum et in parentes obſervantiâ
nunquam ſatis laudatus.
Si vivum ſciveris viator,
habes cùr impenſius mortuum plores.
Ille 9no Cal. Jun. An. { Sal. 1712. / Æt. 26.

Necnon
ROBERTI DAWES
RICARDI jam memorati fratris natu min.
Qui etiam optimarum artium Studijs
in eadem inclytâ muſarum ſede
per triennium non infeliciter incubuit;
fraternæ virtutis æmulus.
Sed proh dolor! utrumq; tantæ ſpei juvenem,
delicias omnium, decus et ornamentum familiæ,
(cujus nominis perpetuandi in ijs ſpes ſola manſit)
eadem dira variolarum peſtis corripuit
ac quicquid mortale fuit
oblivioni et tenebris mandavit,
non niſi tubâ ultimâ revocandum.
Animæ interim ad Coelum avolarunt,
eaſq; occupavêre ſedes,
quas DEUS SALVATOR juſtis preparavit.
Hæc nobis indubitata fides:
Uterq; enim dignus ævo in terris extento,
niſi ad vitam iſtam meliorem feſtinaſſent.
Hic 3[tio] Id. Jun. An. Sal. 1711. / Æt. 22.

Hoc ſepulchrale marmor (haud procùl a quo et ſuas reliquias condi volunt { Filijs / Nepotibus } deſideratiſſimis { Pater / Patruus } mœſtiſſimi poſuere.

Likewiſe was interred near this place, the body of Thomas Dawes of Bradley, Eſq[r]. who died the 4th day of Iuly A. D. 1713 in the 62[d] year of his age, Lamented by All that knew him, becauſe when living he was doing good to all. He was devout and conſtant in religious exerciſes, hoſpitable and generous in his houſe, kind and charitable to the poor, meek in his temper, affable and pleaſant in converſation, courteous and benevolent to all men. He was a loving Huſband, a good Maſter, and a faithful Friend. But why ſhould we praiſe him by our Words whoſe Works both praiſe and follow him and are an example for our Imitation.

Laſtly, Here lie repoſed the only mortal Remains of
Lydia Dawes

Relict of y[e] Said Th. Dawes, Eſq[r] who Died 15 Feb. 1739 Ag. 88. Who moſt amiably conjugal in every Virtue of His, as well as in her Love towards Him, not only bore a part in thoſe excellent Graces that adorn'd Him living, but after his Death, ingrafting, as, it were, upon Her Self the whole, Shone forth a moſt illuſtrious Pattern of every humane and Chriſtian Virtue. Sincerely pious, unaffectedly Devout, Munificent, Hoſpitable, Charitable, Affable, & Courteous.

Stranger (if ſuch Thou Sh[st] be to her Vertues) drop a Tear. Lament the Degeneracy of thy Times, and teach thy Self from this faint & too Faithleſs Record of her Merit, to imitate whom Thou muſt ſo Shortly Follow.

The monument is ornamented with the arms of Dawes, *viz. Azure, three mullets argent, 2 and 1.*

On a large marble pyramidal monument are the two following inſcriptions, written by the ſide of each other:

To

To the Memory of DANIEL ADEY, *Esqr.* of *Combe*, who having thro' Life approv'd Himſelf a Character of Piety, Virtue, and general Uſefulneſs to Mankind, left this World for the Rewards of a better on ye 4th of Feb. 1752, aged 86.

To the Memory alſo of ELIZABETH his Wife, who died March 5th 1717, aged 52.

DANIEL, & FREDERICK, two Sons of THO^s CURTIS of the City of BRISTOL, Eſq; His Grandſons, were buried here.

To the Memory alſo of DANIEL ADEY, Eſq^r. of Sinwell, who died on the 11th of Novr. 1763, aged 67 Years.

Mrs. BRIDGED ADEY, the Wife of DANIEL ADEY, Eſq; of SINWELL, was Here buried on the 11th of October 1740, in ye 41st year of her ege.

Interred Here alſo lye ſix of their Sons and two Daughters, with two Children unbaptiſed. One other Son lies buried at WICKWAR.

Over the firſt inſcription are theſe arms, *Baron and femme*, 1. *Argent, on a bend azure three leopards faces caboſhed Or*, for Adey. impaling 2. *Azure, three cinquefoils argent, on a chief indented Or, three annulets gules.*

Over the ſecond inſcription, Adey, as before, impaling *Azure, a lion rampant argent*, for Crew.

Near the Dawes's monument,

H. S. E.

Elizabetha filia Mauritij Trotman uxor Gul. Nelmes de Cam; cui peperit Johannem Nelmes de Bradſtone Cap: Mariam Roberto Hoſkins de Wotton connubio junctam; Janam Gulielmo Gardiner de Stroude; Lydiam Thomæ Dawes de Bradley; Saram Gulielmo Stokes de Horton; Inſigne pietatis erga Deum et charitatis erga egenos præcipue verbi divini miniſtros exemplar. cum vixiſſet Lxxv annos ſupremum diem in Domino obiit Feb. xxvi A. D. MDCLXXXXII°. Hic etiam reponuntur reliquiæ Saræ Uxoris Gulielmi Stokes de Horton Gen. et Gul. Nelmes de Cam Gen. filiæ Obiit et Quievit Maij 24° Anno Æræ Chriſtianæ 1691. Elizabetha eorum filia e cunabulis ad cœlum evaſit Auguſt 28° 1691 Ætatis ſuæ primo.

Near the laſt,

In Memory of ELIZABETH Wife of IOHN NELMES, of this Town MAYOR, who being ſeized (in time of Child-birth) with the Small-pox, departed this life Oct. 21, 1713, Ætat. ſuæ 26.

Her virtues could not be buried, who having exactly copied Solomon's excellent woman, was Summoned to receive the fruit of her hands and to leave her works to praiſe her in the gates.

Filia, Uxor, Mater,
Fœminarum Decus Eximium
LYDIA alſo D. of IOHN NELMES Aged 16 days
Alſo Iohn Nelmes, Eſq;

A very eſtimable Pattern of Temperance, Prudence, Integrity, and Juſtice, Uſeful in Council, careful in Truſt, and ſteady in Principle. He diſcharged with a becoming Credit the uarious Duties of Life in wch he was concerned. He was an uncommon Example of Patience, & even Chearfulneſs (that Temper ſo peculiarly Chriſtian) in as uncommon a ſeries of Pain & Torture, from which God was graciouſly pleaſed to releaſe him on 15 Novr. 1742, Aged 61.

Inſcribed on an elegant marble monument, ornamented with the arms of Adey:

This Monument
is erected to preſerve the Memory of
WILLIAM ADEY
of COMB in this Pariſh *Eſq^r*;
who having for ſeveral years
laboured under an infirm ſtate of Body,
at length calmly reſigned up his Soul
into the Hands of his Creator
on the 31st of July 1765:
Aged 67 Years.

In the chancel are the following: Round the verge of a grey marble flat ſtone, which had a braſs plate fixed on it, with the figure of a man, now torn off, are theſe lines in Saxon characters:

Natus in hâc villa cognomine dictus ab illâ
Qui Rector fuit hic, aptum nomenq; ſibi ſic
R. de Wottonâ jacet hic, cui cælica dona,
Impetret ipſa pia pulcherrima virgo Maria. Amen.

In the middle of the ſtone,

Es mihi virgo pia, Dux et Lux, ſancta Maria.

On a white marble tablet,

Juxta Hoc Marmor Mortales deponuntur Exuviæ Thomæ Rouſe Arm. cui Hoc Oppidum natalem Locum dedit. Iuris-Prudentia primos Iuventutis Labores exercuit, in Quâ curruete Ætate notabiliter ſagacem eximiumq; ſe præſtitit. Hactenus aptiſſime inſtructus ad Iuſtitiarii Munus—evectus fuit, in Quo pari et fæliciſſima Iuſtitiæ et Miſericordiæ Temperantia Se gerens, modo Manſuetudine, modo Authoritate valens,——— Provinciam hanc cum Dignitate perfunctus eſt. Neque privatæ vitæ Officiis indecoram egit Partem, Seu Maritum, Parentem, Amicum, aut Vicinum reſpicimus, Seu denique Comitem imprimè alacrem, urbanum et facillimum. Obiit 28° Feb. 1737, Æt. 63.

Nec non Ianæ dilectiſſimæ ejus Uxoris quæ Marito non diu ſuperſtes Obiit 8° Oct. 1740, Æt. 69.

Near the above,

Near this place lyes interred Iane eldeſt daughter of Mr. Thomas Rous of this Town, and Wife of Mr. Thomas Coſter of Redbrooke in this County, who left this life for a better the 7th Day of June 1721, Aged 23 years.

She was an obedient daughter, a true Friend, and an excellent Wife. She lived in the exact practice of Piety and Virtue, and dyed with a perfect Reſignation of herſelf to the Will of her Maker.

Upon the monument are theſe arms, Baron and femme, 1. *Ermine, a chevron per pale Or and ſable*, for Coſter; impaling, 2. *Or, an eagle diſplay'd azure*, for Rouſe.

On a tablet of white marble,

In Memory of MARY BLAGDEN, Widow, Daughter of Daniel Adey, Eſq; of Comb in this Pariſh. She reſigned her ſoul to God who gave it on the ninth Day of September, in the Year 1761, Aged 75.

Arms, Baron and femme, 1. *Sable, three trefoils ſlipt argent, on a chief indented Or three annulets gules*, for Blagden; impaling, 2. Adey, as before.

In the ſouth aile: A raiſed marble tomb, with this inſcription:

Ego Domina ELIZABETHA LONG filia natu maxima GEORGII MASTER de Cirenceſtria in Com. Glouceſt. Armigeri primo connubio juncta EDVARDO OLDISWORTH de Bradley in hac parochia Armig. deinde GVALTERO LONG de Draicott-Cerne in agro Wilt. Equiti aurato, ex hac uita diſceſſi Nou. 14° A° S^tis MDCLVIII Ætatis 58 et hîc requieſco, at Reſurgam.

The tomb is decorated with two ſcutcheons at the head, one bearing the arms of Maſter, impaling, *Gules, three creſcents argent, a chief ermine*; the other, Maſter, impaling, *Argent, on a feſs ſable three plates fretty of the ſecond.* There are alſo two ſcutcheons at the foot, on one Oldiſworth, impaling Maſter; on the other, 1. *Azure, a lion rampant, and ſemi of croſs croſlets argent*, for Long, impaling, 2. Maſter.

Upon the table of a well executed monument,

Reſurrectionem in Chriſto hic expectat reveren. Dn. Robertus Web, pietate comitate et Charitate vix ulli ſecundus, ut dives ſic largus opum qui vivus pauperes paterno amore fovit, et moriens teſtamento cavit, ut in æternum e fundis ſuis viginti et ſex libræ quotannis in egenos erogarentur ita ut quatuor ſolidi unoquoque die dominico in templo finitis precibus matutinis viginti quatuor indigentibus Wottoniæ ubi vixit, totidemque Regiſſylve* ubi natus diſtribuerentur. Hiſce moribus qualis eſſet teſtatum reliquit, monumentumq; ſibi in animis hominum diutius manſurum ſtruxit, quâm hoc quod memoriæ eius, amoris & coniugalis fidei ergo ſuis ſumptibus poſuit Anna chariſſima uxor filia Ricardi Draper Mercatoris Londinenſis quæ illi Annam unicam filiam peperit, Nicholao Web de Aſhwick in Com. Glouc. Gen. connubio iunctam. Obijt totius vicinæ lachrymis defletus 14° Jan. A. S. 1662 Ætat. 74.

ROBERTUS WEB
O TU REBUS UBER

Te Deus UBERtim ditavit REBUS opimis:
Pauper inopſque tuis REBUS et UBER erat.
UBER TU ſemper nam quæ donantur egenis
Has tecum ſolas ſemper habebis opes
Fama perennis erit præclari nominis; et ſi
In cineres abeas author, at extat opus
Caviſti prudens, jejunos qui tot alebas
Vivus, ne pereant te moriente ſimul
Iam vivant inopes, dum vivunt, tu quoque vives,
REBUS ut UBER eras, REBUS et UBER eris.

In a ſcutcheon at top of the monument, Party per pale, 1. R. W. the initials of Robert Web, impaling 2. *Sable, a croſs moline Or*, for Draper.

3. Near

* *Kingſwood* in *Wiltſhire*.

Near the foregoing,

THOMAS GRAIL MEDICINÆ PROFESSOR IN QVA NON MEDIOCRITER VERSATUS, GALENI METHODO ET VESTIGIJS MAXIME INSISTENS NON SINE OPTATO SUCCESSU ET APPLAUSU MUNUS OBIVIT, QUI ESTI NON TOTO ORBI TAMEN VICINIÆ SALUTIFER FUIT ET JUVAMEN ALIJS QUOD SIBI PRÆSTARE NON POTUIT, PRÆSTITIT; APOPLEXIÂ LABORANS VITAM JUN: V° A. S. MDCLXIX° ÆTATIS LXI° FINIVIT. IN CUJUS MEMORIAM UXOR EJUS SARAH FILIA LAURENTIJ POTS MERCATORIBUS ANGL: METELLIBURGI SACELLANI HOC MONUMENTUM EXTRUI CURAVIT.

Here Underneath Interr'd doth lie
One that bids Thee prepare to die.
I lov'd in upright Paths to go,
Phyfick my Practice was, but loe
Death is too Stronge for Any Man,
For Phyfick and Phyfitian.

Infcribed on a handfome marble monument,

Near this Place are depofited the Remains of WILLIAM ADEY of *Uley* in this County *Efq*r Whofe Military Abilities exerted in the Service of his Country acquired him the Rank of *Lieut. Col*l. in the 68th Regiment. In his private Character he difcharged the focial Duties of Life with Tendernefs & Humanity. He died the 7th Novr. 1763, Aged 39. His Widow's Affectionate Regard to his Memory caufed this Monument to be erected.

At top are thefe arms, Baron and femme, 1. Adey, impaling, 2. *Azure, on a chevron between three fleurs de lis Or, as many mullets of the field*, for Gyde, having married Anne, fifter to Timothy Gyde, of Uley, efq; which Anne is fince deceafed.

Near the foregoing,

M. S.
Richardi Ofborne de Wortley Arm:
Quem mira Animi alacritas,
Nuda Veritas, Morefq; puri,
Charum reddiderunt ac bonis flebilem,
Humanitas Egenis defideratiffimum,
Graviffimos Arthritidis cruciatus
Per Annos quamplurimos fuftinuit
Tali conftantia ac fortitudine
Qualem fola miniftrat Virtus,
Ac vere Chriftiana Fides.
Labefacto tandem ac devicto corpore,
Animam pie et placide efflavit,
Die Aprilis 28 A. D. 1749 Æt. 60.
Juxta requiefcit
Quicquid terreftre fuit Saræ Ofborne,
Prædicti Conjugis dilectiffimæ.
Ob. Jan. 25, 1742, Æt. 51.
Nec non eorum feq; Liberorum
Johannis Infantis
Richardi, Ob. Dec. 12, 1723, Æt. 6.
Thomæ, Ob. Julij 25, 1736, Æt. 17.
Gulielmi Infantis.

The arms on this monument are, Baron and femme, 1. *Argent, a bend between two lioncels rampant fable*; impaling, 2. Blagden, as before.

Placed over Mr. Veel's family feat,

Maria Uxor Thomæ Veel filij Thomæ Veel de Alvefton in Com. Gloc. Armig. filia vero Henrici Butler de Hanly in Agro Dorceftrienfe Armig. immaturos ex itineris moleftijs gemellos enixa, non fine maximo conjugis dolore expiravit Dec. 16 A. D. 1658° Æt. 24°.

Huc ufq; peregrina, nunc domi.
My Journey's at an end my travaile's done,
I'm brought to bed, and now I am at home.
Maria Veel
irâ me leva
Me Deus oppreffit; quis ab illius at *levet ira?*
Me Chriftus velet, liberet, atque *levet*.
3d Gen. 16.
1 Tim. 2-15.

Againft the wall, in the nave of the church,

M. S. GVLIELMI WILLET FILIJ NATU MAXIMI RADVLPHI WILLET GENEROSI, QVI PHTHISI LABORANS PIE ET PLACIDE MORTALE CORPUS DEPOSVIT SEPT. 11 A. D. 1657, ÆTATIS SVÆ 22 ANIMA VERO FIDVCIA SALVTIS ETSI JNPRIMIS LANGVIDA TANDEM VIVIDA ET CERTA ERECTA CÆLVM ADIBAT: QVO ET SVSANNÆ SORORIS, PETRI ET MATTHÆI WILLET FRATRVM ANIMULÆ, NON MVLTO ANTE TRANSLATÆ, EXPECTANT VNA FELICITATIS CONSUMMATIONEM.

ONE HOVSE, NAY WOMBE THESE FOVRE ONCE HAD, ONE GRAVE
THEYR BODIES NOW, THEIR SOVLES ONE HEAVEN HAVE.
DEATH DOTH NOT THEM DIVORCE BVT AS THEY WERE
JN LIFE VNITED NOW IN DEATH THEY ARE.
JN THEM THERE WAS WHAT E'RE DESERVED PRAISE
THEY WANTED NOVGHT COVLD BE DESIR'D BUT DAYES.
JN SPRING THEYR AVTUMNE WAS, TOO RIPE THEY WERE
TOO HOPEFVLL, PIOVS, PRETTY TO BE HERE
PRESERVERS WEAK ARE STONES, THEIRE NAMES SHALL LAST
WHEN BRASSE AND MARBLE VNTO DUST SHALL WASTE.

Gulielmus Willet
Luget jllum Levius.

HIC VIVUS TOTIES PROPTER PECCATA DOLEBAT
VT MADIDÆ LACHRYMIS NOCTE DIEQVE GENÆ.
CONSTITERAT QVOCVNQVE LOCO PECCATA VIDEBAT
ANTE OCCVLOS HABVIT CRIMINA CVNCTA SVOS.
NON CITHARÆ CANTVS, NON VESTES, PRÆDIA LARGA
NON CORDI MVNDI REGIA QVICQVID HABET.
PANIS ERANT LACHRYMÆ, POTVM, VICTVMQVE PEROSVS
CONFECTVS MACIE, FVNERIS JNSTAR ERAT.
LONGA REFERRE MORA EST, PER QUOT DISCRIMINA, PLANCTVS
PECCATO, SATANA, MORTE, TROPHEA TVLIT.
PER CHRISTVM TANDEM VICTOR, CARET ATQVE PERICLI
LUGET EVM LEVIVS QVISQVIS AMICVS ERAT.

Near the foregoing,

Near this Place lie the Remains of EDWARD GREGORY,
Son of ABRAHAM GREGORY S. T. P.
Born at GLOUCESTER,
Educated at EATON SCHOOL,
Afterwards STUDENT of CHRIST CHURCH in OXFORD
And at the Taking of VIGO under ADMIRAL ROOKE,
CHAPLAIN to the TORBAY Man of War:
Sometime *Lecturer* of *All Hallows Staining* in *London*
And laftly VICAR of this Parifh,
Where he continued above Thirty Years,
Indefatigable in the Duties of his Function,
Loving and beloved by his Parifhioners.
At length worn out with a lingering Illnefs
He quitted this Life in Hopes of a Better
October 31, 1738, Aged 62.
EDWARD, ABRAHAM, THOMAS, & FRANCIS,
Out of a true Love & filial Piety,
Erected this Monument
To the Memory of their Father.

Arms, *Or, two bars azure, in chief a lion paffant of the fecond.*

Benefactions.

Lady Catherine Berkeley, widow of Thomas lord Berkeley, founded a free grammar fchool in this place 8 R. 2. and endowed it with forty marks a year. A licence to purchafe land in Nubbely, Stancombe, and Woodmancot, for its maintenance, was obtained at the fame time; and Walter Burnel, and others, were made feoffees of two acres, feven meffuages, and a garden in Wotton-underedge, for the ufe of the fame fchool. The mafter is appointed by the Smyths of Nibley, and the bifhop of the diocefe is vifitor. The mafter has 40*l.* a year, and a houfe. Ten boys have 4*l.* a year each from ten to eighteen years of age, who wear caps and gowns. There is befides an overplus of income of about 20*l.* a year, applied to the maintaining one or more of the boys at the univerfity, or putting them out apprentices.

Robert Dudley, earl of Leicefter, defcended from the Berkeley family, founded an hofpital at Warwick 13 Eliz. for twelve poor men, wounded in the wars; but if there fhould be none fuch, then two poor men out of Wotton-underedge are to be placed in the hofpital.

Lady Anne, countefs of Warwick, gave the new Tolfey to the ufe of the town, and the reft of the tenements belonging to it to the poor. She likewife built an almfhoufe at Cheney in Buckinghamfhire, 38 Eliz. and appointed that two of the almsfolks fhould be from this place, with an allowance of 5*l.* a year each. Henry lord Berkeley, upon agreement with her for the manor of Wotton, confirmed this donation 7 Jac. 1.

Sir Richard Venn, knight, alderman of London, and a native of this parifh, gave 10*l.* a year to the poor,

poor, charged on his lands in Wotton and Nibley. He alſo gave two large ſilver flaggons for the ſervice of the communion table, beſides other gifts to the town and poor.

Hugh Venn, of this pariſh, clothier, gave 20*s.* a year out of lands in North Nibley, and a tenement in Durſley, worth 30*s.* a year, to the poor.

Margaret Mallows, of London, widow, gave money, with which Cauſeway-mead and Mill-mead were purchaſed, for the uſe of the poor, by deed dated Dec. 1, 1619, 17 Jac.

Hugh Perry, eſq; alderman of London, and a native of this place, built an almſhouſe for ſix men and ſix women, with a chapel, and appointed a weekly lecture to be preached in the pariſh church, and prayers to be read twice a week to the almſpeople, for which the miniſter receives 5*l.* a year. The lectureſhip, afterwards increaſed with 6*l.* a year by Richard Meads, is now 18*l.* a year, and is given to ſix clergymen. He gave lands worth 50*l.* a year, and upwards, for the maintenance of his charity; and in 1630, joined with his father-in-law, ſir Richard Venn, in erecting an aqueduct to convey water from a ſpring in Edbrook-field to the market-croſs.

Sir Jonathan Dawes, ſheriff of London, and ſon of Robert Dawes of this pariſh, clothier, left 1000*l.* with which his widow purchaſed lands in Hill, for the uſe of the poor, and the application of the rents has ſince been ſettled by decree in chancery.

William and Robert Hyett, nephews of ſir Jonathan Dawes, gave 600*l.* to the poor of this their native place; which ſum was laid out in the purchaſe of lands at Wotton and Berkeley, in or about 1693.

Thomas Dawes, of Bradley, eſq; gave an eſtate at Bournſtream, worth near 30*l.* a year, to the poor; and likewiſe gave a fire-engine to the town.

Joan Gower, or Cooper, widow, gave a tenement and cloſe in Bradley-ſtreet in Wotton, worth 4*l.* a year, to the poor.

Robert Webb, of Sinwell, clothier, gave 4*s.* weekly to be diſtributed every Sunday to the poor, and 40*s.* yearly to forty poor houſholders, at 1*s.* each, on St. Thomas day, for ever; the money to be paid out of an eſtate called the Grange in Kingſwood.

Robert Hale, of Alderley, eſq; father of lord chief juſtice Hale, gave the reverſion of an eſtate in Rangeworthy, worth 26*l.* a year, to the poor. And Margaret Hale, widow, gave tne reverſion of lands in Rockhampton, worth 7*l.* a year, to the ſame uſe.

The old almſhouſe, and eighteen tenements beſide, are given for the benefit of the poor, but the donor is not known.

The church houſe, with the tenements in Simlane, a tenement near the Horſe-pool, and William Wallington's houſe, are given for the repair of the church.

Richard Meades, alderman of this town, gave 6*l.* a year to ſix miniſters for preaching a lecture, as already mentioned, and a like ſum to be diſtributed annually on the 2d of February, to the poor; no perſon to have more than 5*s.* nor leſs than 2*s.* 6*d.* each.

The feoffees of the market, with the approbation of the mayor and aldermen, gave 50*l.* towards recovering the grammar ſchool, and ſettling it in truſtees; 100*l.* towards improving the vicarage; and 80*l.* towards the maintenance of the curate.

John Okes, M.A. a native of this place, by his will, gave 600*l.* and upwards for the uſe of the church of Wotton, and 20*l.* to the poor; and bequeathed his library to the pariſh.

George lord Berkeley built the old gallery in the year 1626.

Mrs. Sarah Winſton, in 1686, gave a large ſilver paten for the communion table.

The honourable colonel Morton gave the timber for the charity working ſchool, in the year 1714.

Mr. William Bailey, of this pariſh, clothier, in 1721, gave 20*l.* to the poor, and 20*l.* in truſt for the uſe of the charity ſchool, for ever.

Richard Oſborne, of Wortley, eſq; in 1722, gave 3*l.* *per ann. viz.* 10*s.* for a charity ſermon, and 50*s.* to the charity ſchool.

Mrs. Mary Blagden, of Nind, in the year 1723, gave 20*l.* in truſt, to be diſtributed every Good Friday in bread to the poor of the hoſpital; and 10*l.* for the benefit of the charity ſchool.

In 1734, Mr. Thomas Blagden gave a crimſon velvet pulpit cloth.

In 1748, Richard Oſborne, eſq; gave a crimſon velvet cloth for the communion table, and two ſilver plates for the offertory.

William Moore, eſq; gave the rich chandelier, in 1763.

The ſame year, Mr. Robert Purnell bequeathed 550*l.* for bread for ſuch poor inhabitants as have not received alms; and 100*l.* to the charity ſchool.

And in 1769, Mr. Edward Bearpacker gave 100*l.* to the charity ſchool.

Wotton.

			£.	s.	d.
Taxes.	The Royal Aid in	1692,	42	16	0
	Poll-tax —	1694, —	64	8	0
	Land-tax —	1694, —	107	15	4
	The ſame, at 3*s.*	1770, —	74	8	3

Sinwell and Bradley.

			£.	s.	d.
Taxes.	The Royal Aid in	1692,	82	12	0
	Poll-tax ——	1694, —	23	4	0
	Land-tax ——	1694, —	143	16	0
	The ſame, at 3*s.*	1770, —	111	0	0

Simondſhall and Combe.

			£.	s.	d.
Taxes.	The Royal Aid in	1692,	72	4	0
	Poll-tax ——	1694, —	18	2	0
	Land-tax ——	1694, —	72	0	0
	The ſame, at 3*s.*	1770, —	54	3	0

Wortley.

Taxes.	The Royal Aid in	1692,	£. 73	8	0
	Poll-tax — —	1694, —	9	11	0
	Land-tax ——	1694, -	39	3	0
	The ſame, at 3 *s.*	1770, —	29	5	0

Huntingford.

Taxes.	The Royal Aid in	1692,	£. 26	6	0
	Poll-tax ——	1694, —	2	8	0
	Land-tax ——	1694, —	20	2	0
	The ſame, at 3 *s.*	1770, —	14	17	6

At the beginning of this century, there were 840 houſes, and about 3500 inhabitants in this pariſh, whereof 70 were freeholders; yearly births 81, burials 78. *Atkyns.* There are now near 4000 inhabitants.

Y A T E.

THIS pariſh lies in the hundred of Henbury, one mile diſtant weſt from Chipping Sodbury, ten north-eaſt from the city of Briſtol, and thirty-one ſouthward from Glouceſter.

It is written *Giete* in *Domeſday*, of which the ſignification is uncertain. It is ſituated in a flat part of the vale, with a large tract of common belonging to it, lying open to the commons of Weſterleigh and Rangeworthy.

Of the natural productions of this place, the moſt remarkable are, a little lead ore, ſome calamine ſtone, and great plenty of pit-coal. There is alſo a remarkable rock of ſtone, called the White Lays, which runs through Yate, Cromhall, Thornbury, Almondſbury, Clifton, and acroſs the Avon to the Leigh and Mendip in Somerſetſhire; and taking a large ſweep from thence eaſtward, returns a little ſhort of Lanſdown, to Wick, Sodbury, and ſo to Yate, forming a circle of fourteen or fifteen miles in diameter; and it is ſaid that coal may be dug every where within the circumference of that circle. I will not vouch for the abſolute truth of this opinion, but it is certain, that there now are or have been coal mines in moſt of the places within theſe limits. The white lay ſtone is a kind of marble, and burns into a ſtrong lime of an exquiſite whiteneſs.

The ſoil in general is rich and fertile, and the lands are employ'd in dairy and grazing. Great improvements might be made by incloſing the waſtes and commons, yet it may not be expedient to incloſe them, as it would incapacitate many poor families from purſuing their preſent buſineſs, who now employ themſelves in carrying coal from the pits to ſell round about the country, and depaſture their horſes on theſe commons.

One of the lord Berkeleys built a handſome ſeat here, which was called Yate Court. It was moated round, and Maurice lord Berkeley, the fifth of that name, reſided there ſome time. It was garriſoned by the parliament's forces in the great civil war, who burnt it, and it was never rebuilt afterwards.

Thomas Neal, the learned Hebrew Profeſſor in the univerſity of Oxford, was born in this pariſh. He died and was buried at Caſſington in Oxfordſhire, in the year 1590.

Of the Manor and other Eſtates.

At the time of the general ſurvey, this place was a member of the great manor of Hueſberie, in the hundred of Bernintreu, as appears by the extract from *Domeſday* relating to Weſtbury, p. 800. At that time the manor of Weſtbury belonged to the church of Worceſter, but Yate paſſed ſoon afterwards into lay hands.

Ralph de Willington and Olympia his wife purchaſed the manor of Yate of Robert d' Evercide 9 Joh. and Richard de Willington died ſeized of it, and of markets within it, 2 H. 3. Ralph de Willington had a licence to erect a caſtle in this place 21 E. 1. and John de Willington held the manor of Yate, with free warren, 3 E. 2. and died in the 12th year of king Edward the Third. Sir Ralph de Willington was ſummoned as a peer to parliament, and died ſeized of Yate 22 E. 3. Reginald de Willington was his uncle and heir, and ſir John de Willington was ſeized of the manor of Yate 2. R. 2. Sir John Paulet, in right of Margaret his wife, was ſeized of Yate 15 R. 2. and Ralph de Willington, grandſon and heir of ſir John de Willington, died ſeized of this manor 19 R. 2. and John de Willington, uncle and heir of Ralph, had livery of Yate, and of the advowſon of the church, 20 R. 2.

Iſabel the daughter of William Beaumont was ſeized of Yate 2 H. 6. as was Iſabel the widow of ſir Thomas de la Rivere in the 15th year of the ſame reign. Philip Beaumont, eſq; was alſo ſeized of this manor 13 E. 4. Hugh Beaumont and Elizabeth his wife, John Baſſet and Elizabeth his wife, John Beaumont, clerk, John Chicheſter and Margaret his wife, John Croker and Anne his wife, levied ſeveral fines of the manor of Yate to Richard biſhop of Durham and other biſhops, to John earl of Oxford, ſir Giles D'Aubeny, and to ſeveral other great perſons 16 H. 7. Giles lord D'Aubeny had a grant of this manor from the crown, and died ſeized of it 6 H. 8. and livery was granted to his ſon Henry lord D'Aubeny the ſame year.

The manor of Yate was granted to Edward duke of Somerſet, and after its reverting to the crown upon that duke's attainder, it was granted to James Baſſet 4 Mar. and was again granted to Arthur Baſſet 7 Eliz.

Mr. Oxwick was lord of the manor at the beginning of this century; but ſir Francis Knollis is the preſent lord of the manor.

Stanſhaw is an antient manor in this pariſh. Elizabeth Stanſhaw was ſeized of the manors of Stanſhaw and Yate 13 H. 4. Robert Stanſhaw, eſq; was alſo ſeized of the manors of Stanſhaw and

and Yate 12 E. 4. Mr. Stokes is the present owner of Stanshaw, where he has a good house and estate. His arms are, *Sable, a lion rampant, his tail double, ermine*; and the family arms upon the monument at Wickwar should have been the same.

Brimsham is another manor in this parish, which continued for many generations in the name and family of the Burnells, from the reign of king Edward the Third. Thomas Burnell, the last heir male of that family, married Elizabeth, daughter of Thomas Chester, of Knole, esq; and dying without issue, gave this manor to Thomas Chester, brother to his wife.

One part of the parish is distinguished by the name of *Church End*, the other by *Hall End*. In the latter division the late Richard Hill, esq; had a good estate, which is now the property of Mr. Veel, of Simondshall.

Of the Church, &c.

The church is a rectory, in the deanery of Hawkesbury, worth about 190*l.* a year, to which the reverend Mr. Thomas Tournay, (now D. D.) was presented in 1765, by William Tournay, esq; patron for that turn only. The glebe is worth about 80*l.* a year.

The church is dedicated to St. Mary. It is built with a cross aile on each side. The chancel has also an aile on each side; and there is a large handsome tower at the west end. The south aile belongs to the manor of Stanshaw, and the north aile to that of Yate.

The lands which belonged to a chapel in this church were granted to Francis Maurice and Richard Moor 6 Jac.

First fruits £.	27	16	4	Synodals £.	0	2	0
Tenths —	2	14	10½	Pentecostals	0	1	4
Procurations	0	6	8				

Monuments and Inscriptions.

There is a large brass plate fixt upon a flat stone, upon which are engraven the figures of a man between his two wives, Avis, and Elizabeth, with eleven children, and under them this inscription:

Corpus Alexandri Staples lapis iste tuetur:
Spiritus ætherea sede beatus erit.
Rursus supremum tuba cum taratantara clanget
Spiritui junget mortua membra Deus.
Tercentum lustris octodenoq; fluente,
Bernardi, a Christo, concidit ipse die
Saxum hoc mœsta suo ponebat Eliza marito
Conjugij signum quod pietatis erit.
22° Augusti. 1590.

On a plate of brass fixt to a flat stone in the chancel,

Hic iacet corpus Hodges Godwin, jun. armigeri, Legum Angliæ periti, qui obijt 2° die Novemb. Anno Dni 1677, Spe Beatæ Resurrectionis, Ætatis suæ 40.

Upon a freestone monument in the chancel,

Juxta hunc tumulum reconditur urna continens cineres Henrici Wogan armig: qui natus apud Wiston in Comitat. Pembroke e familia antiqua, obijt apud Yate in Comitat. Glofter. 1° die Febr. Anno Ætat. 22° Annoq; Dni 1661.
Vivit post funera Virtus.

The arms are obliterated.

There is a monument for William Mason, rector of this parish, who died in 1740, and for his wife, and several of their family, with their arms, *viz.* Baron and femme, 1. *Party per pale Or and azure, a chevron counterchanged between three billets sable*, for Mason. 2. *Argent, on a chevron gules three roses of the field.*—There are also memorials for Richard Hill, of this parish, esq; who died in 1755.—For Mary Rouse, daughter of Thomas Rouse of Wotton-underedge, esq; who died in 1759.—For Richard Wallington, rector of this parish, who died in 1764.—And for Thomas Blagden; but there is nothing in them that can be the least instructive or entertaining.

Taxes.					
The Royal Aid in	1692, £.	119	4	0
Poll-tax — —	1694, —	55	17	0
Land-tax ——	1694, —	375	11	0
The same, at 3*s.*	1770, —	280	9	3

At the beginning of this century, there were 80 houses, and about 320 inhabitants in this parish, whereof 26 were freeholders; yearly births 8, and burials 7. *Atkyns*. But it appears by the register, that the average of baptisms in ten years, beginning with 1700, was 10.4, and of burials 7.7. And in the same number of years, beginning with 1760, the average of baptisms was 13.6, and of burials 12.1; by which it appears that the parish increases in population, and there are now about 412 inhabitants.

F I N I S.

APPENDIX.

Containing GRANTS, CHARTERS, CONFIRMATIONS, *and other* PAPERS *of considerable Length, referred to in the Body of the Work.*

NUMBER I.

The Bounds of the Forest of Dean, as set forth at a Justice Seat held at Gloucester, 10 Edw. I.

THE bounds of the forest of Dean begin at Glocester bridge, and so extend themselves by the thread of the water of Severn, going down the same unto a place where the river of Wye falls into the Severn, and so going by Wye unto the bridge of Strogoyle *, and still ascending by Wye to the passage of the castle of Goodrich, and so unto Dunnescross, and so, by a certain path called Pevesley, unto Alecune, and so by the brook of Alecune unto the public road coming from Rosse unto an ash beyond Weston, and so by the highway beyond the bridge unto a certain tree called Halletree†, and so by the highway unto the millpond of Birctune, which is Richard Talebot's, and so by the highway unto a certain cross called Lucecross, and so by the highway of Gorsteley unto Gorsteley's foorde, and so descending by the brook unto the bridge of Oxenhalle, and so by the king's highway unto the bridge of the prior of Newent, and by the same highway unto the bridge of Gloucester.

* *Now Chepstow.*

† *Now Bollatree.*

NUMBER II.

The Names of the Vills, &c. which had been afforested after the Coronation of Hen. II. *and which, by the Commissioners in the Reign of King* Edw. I. *ought to be disafforested.*

THE vill of Biriton which Richard Talebot holds, the vill of Ekeleswell with the wood, a moiety of the vill of the Lee, the vill of Weston, the vill of Cokton which the said Richard Talebot holds, the vill of Penyard with the wood which John Abadam holds, the vill of Welleford which John of Welleford holds, the vill of Hull, the wood of the bishop of Hereford which is called Wydyhay, which the said bishop holds, the vill of Huwaldefelde with the wood and Herthull which the abbot of Tynterne holds, Alvynton, with the wood and appurtenances, which the prior of Lanthony of Gloucester holds, a moiety of the vill of Aylbriton which the said prior holds, a moiety of the vill of Lydenaye which the Earl of Warwick holds, the vill of Nass which Walter of the same holds, Pyritone which John Abadam holds, Blakeneye (except the lands of Thomas Blakeney which he holds of our lord the king *in capite*) the vill of Ettelawe which Maud de Chaward holds, Blideslowe which the tenants of Alan Plokenet holds, Aure which Joan de Valence and Maud de Mortimer hold, Boxe which Sybil Pancener holds, Rodele which the abbot of Gloucester holds, the vill of Sandforde under the way towards Severn (except the tenants of our lord the king of Blakeneye unto the vill of Newenham) the vill of Staure, Elnetone, Clive, Adscote, Rodelye, Chakeshull, Stanetwey, Bolley, Menstreworth, Dunye, Hamptone, Morecote which Pury of Lancastre holds, Westbury, Overlye, Netherlye, Besseley, with the woods which Nicholas de Ba, Roger de Borowhulle, and Nicholas de Gamage hold in purparty, a moiety of the vill of Bleckedone which Ralph de Abbenhale and Elias de Blakeneye hold, Sebyche with the wood of Birdwode and other appurtenances, Moretone, Lylletone, Hynnham with the wood which is called Pyraresgrave which the abbot of Gloucester holds, Overe which the said abbot holds, Balley which Philip de Lude holds, Thybertone which William Long holds, a certain part of Redeford which the abbot of Gloucester holds, Tayntone, with the groves which extend from Hymteley by the middle of Northfield unto the mill which is called Abbelandes-Mulne, a certain part of Ocheley, Shawe, Southorte, Malewyke, which the prior of Newent holds, Little Teyntone, which Bogo de Onevile holds, Newent (except Loxelond and a moiety of Nywestrete.

NUMBER III.

Perambulation of the Forest of Dean towards the end of the Reign of King Charles II.

THE metes and bounds of the forest begin at Hope's Well in the Purlieu green, and thence on the left hand between the counties of Gloucester and Hereford unto Bereley's Green, and thence descending between the said counties unto a certain stream called Bishop's Brook, following the antient course thereof into the river of Wye, and so descending through the midst of Wye unto a certain place called Juttline, and thence leaving Wye and ascending a certain path or way called Slow Path, into a place where formerly a yew tree grew (below Symon's Yatt) keeping the bounds between the counties aforesaid, and thence descending down overthwart those craggy rocks or hill unto Wye, and so descending through the midst thereof unto a little stream running down by Lady-park wall, and so up that stream unto the corner of Lady-park grove, and thence ascending up by that grove unto an old oak called Bellman's Oak, and thence turning short on the left hand up a certain meadow or pasture called the Ridings unto a certain ash, and from that ash athwart that meadow or pasture ground unto a great beech on the south side of the Ridding's Barn, and from that beech ascending up a meer or ditch by a coppice wood or grove unto the upper end thereof, and thence to the Scarrs (being an edge of rocks) unto a certain well called St. John Baptist Well, and from thence to Staunton's Gate, and thence descending down the highway unto a great stone called Broadstone, and thence to a well of water called Drybrook, and thence following the antient course thereof into the river of Wye, and so descending through the midst of Wye unto a certain water called Brockweare's Brook, and so ascending that brook or stream which is the bound between the parishes of Hewelsfield and St. Briavell's, until it cometh to Meerwall adjoining Meresmore Well, and thence turning short on the right hand by the upper end of a little moorish green unto the corner of a hedge adjoining to the common there called Harthill, and so leaving Harthill on the right hand, and the parish of St. Briavell's on the left hand, following the bound between the parishes of Hewelsfield and St.

St. Briavell's unto Aylesmore Brook, and so descending that brook until it cometh unto Conebrook, following the stream thereof unto Alvington's Woods, and thence by the bounds of Rodmore Grove unto the lower corner thereof, and thence crossing the stream there called Woodward's Brook unto a certain old meer or mound, and so up that meer or mound to a place called Stedfast Pound (being an heap of stones which formerly was a pound) and thence following that meer or mound through Sir John Wintour's park unto Chelfredge Well, and from that well up the aforesaid meer unto the highway leading from Breem to Lidney called Marleway, and then leaving the wood called Warwick's Tuff on the right hand unto a little stream called Meerbrook, and so descending that stream into Newarn's Brook, and down that brook by the antient course thereof unto the lower corner of the Sneed, and thence ascending up a little stream called Lipmeer unto Yorkley Mead, and so directly up that mead or pasture unto the place in the wall where antiently an hazle grew called Tachment's hazel, and thence crossing the highway unto Soilwell, and so following the stream thereof unto Tachment's stream (being the next stream on the left hand) and thence up that stream unto the upper corner of the Hey's grounds, and thence following the Hey's grove on the left hand unto the Hey's well, and so descending the stream thereof which is called Lansbrook into the river of Severn (near Pirton's village) and so ascending up through the midst of Severn unto a certain place called Fullmeadow Pill, and so ascending that stream unto Chicknell's Well, and thence to the highway leading from Awre to Awreleford, keeping the said way until it cometh to Awreleford, and thence ascending that brook unto a certain path called Shipway, and following that way unto a way called Rudgeway, and thence descending, leaving the manor or lordship of Ruddle on the right hand unto a certain water course rising in a grove of Richard Hillgeat's, following the said water course unto the river of Severn, and through the midst thereof unto Newnham's Pill, and thence ascending that stream unto a certain pasture formerly a grove called Piper's, (alias Palmer's grove) and thence up that stream unto the highway leading from Newnham to Dean, ascending that highway unto Dean's hill, and thence leaving the bounds of the manor of Rodley on the right hand, and the hundred of St. Briavell's on the left hand unto the pool of Flaxley's Forge, and thence to Blesdon, alias Blaisdon's hedge, and thence to Poulton's Hill, and thence leaving the hundred of Westbury on the right hand unto Brimstone's Yatt, and thence including the lands of the of Walmore to the highway leading towards Framulard, and thence to the leaving the said hand round about it, and so to a place called White a certain way leading under the Park of the Ley, and from that way unto a grove called Birchingrove, and from that grove unto Rareham, and from thence to the place where antiently was a mill called Seymore's Mill, and from that place to the brook of Blesdon (alias Blaisdon) ascending that brook unto Gavell's Gate, (alias Gawlett's Yatt) and so ascending that brook unto a little stream called Tinbridge Sych, and so stretching up by the said stream between the woods late of the abbot of Flaxley, and the woods called Hope's Woods unto Hope's shard, and thence to a path called Justy Path, and crossing that path keeping strait forwards unto the water that leadeth from Mitchel Dean to Hope, and so crossing over that water up under the edge of a coppice wood called Langrove, leaving it on the left hand unto the bounds of the parishes of Longhope and Mitchel Dean, and thence directly to Bradley Grove, leaving the grove on the right hand unto the little lane that leadeth from the highway into the said grove, and so down that lane unto the highway, and thence unto Bradley House, and thence athwart the meadow there unto Owley Grove, leaving the grove on the left hand unto a lane near the middle of the said grove, and thence turning up the said lane on the right hand, and crossing the highway leading from Mitchel Dean to the Lea-line directly to Hannkin's Well, and thence athwart to the highway leading from Gloucester towards Hereford by the Lealine tree, following the said way to the said line tree, and thence leaving a certain freedom of William Phillips on the left hand (being a cottage garden and about an acre of orchard close adjoining to the said line tree) and thence to a lane called Lane, and so up that lane unto a ditch and foot path in Owley Grove aforesaid, (being at or near a place in the said grove where we came out a little before) leading down through the grove unto a piece of pasture ground called the Nockolds, (being the round under the grove) and thence leaving the hedge on the left hand directly to the mill called Clacerford Mill, leaving the said mill on the left hand, and then turning up a lane or highway leading towards Cawnadge until it cometh to the lane turning on the right hand towards the Lea Baily unto the hither side of a piece of ground called Cudley Broom, and then entering into the said ground and leaving the hedge on the right hand unto the ground called the Noake, leaving it on the right hand, and thence crossing Noakham Lane unto a well called Gingerly Well, and so descending from that well unto an oak called Walton's Oak, and thence turning upon the left hand by a certain little water course unto the upper end of a certain parcel of arable or pasture land called Udnells directly to the upper end of Pouce Lane, and from that lane unto the yew tree in a certain parcel of pasture ground called Hartshill, leaving a certain coppice grove on the right hand, and turning down under the Lea-Baily hedge unto a stream called Megtrance's Stream (being the first stream running out of the Lea-Baily) and so down that stream unto Hope's brook, and thence ascending by a certain meer or old hedge to the lower end of a piece of pasture or arable land formerly a grove called Hooper's Grove, and thence along by the lower side of that said pasture (formerly a grove) unto a certain yew tree in Blast's grounds near the brook running down from Hazeley, and so up that brook unto Hillam Lane, and so by the Baily-Hedge unto the Lea-Way, and thence turning on the left hand under the edge of the Lea-Baily unto the upper corner of the Lea-Baily, and thence athwart, leaving the forest on the left hand, and the purlieu of the bishop of Gloucester on the right hand, unto a certain place where antiently an oak did grow called Silver Oak, which was a meer and mark between the counties of Gloucester and Hereford, in place whereof is a meer stone pitched, and thence to the bank near Blackewell Mead, following the same to the stream, and so down that stream unto Hope's Well.

The NAMES *of the* REGARDERS *of the* FOREST OF DEAN.

JOHN WITT	JOHN BIRKYN
WILLIAM AILBERTON	JEREMIAH HIET
THOMAS PYRKE	EDWARD MORSE
WILLIAM GOUGH	GEORGE BOND, *of Colford*
GEORGE BOND	EDWARD MACHEN
GEORGE BERROW	RICHARD NASH
CHRISTOPHER WOODWARD	THOMAS WALTER
EDWARD WHITE	EDWARD SKIN
THOMAS WORGAN	WILLIAM BROWN
WILLIAM CARPENDER	

☞ The above perambulation was rode by the above regarders in the latter end of the reign of Charles the IId. from one of whom I had it, but whether any record thereof be to be found I know not.

MAY 29, 1767. WILLIAM GOUGH.

NUMBER IV.

The Order of the Court of Exchequer concerning the Miners digging Mine, Ore, and Cinders, in the Forest of Dean.

Glouc' Hillary, 10 Jac.

WHereas the 25th day of May, in Easter Term last, the court was informed by his majesty's attorney general, that the king's majesty by his letters patent under the great seal of England, had granted to the Right Hon. the Earl of Pembroke (*inter alia*) the mine, ore, and cinders, to be found out and gotten within the forest of Dean in the county of Gloucester for 21 years, for the yearly rent of 2433l. 6s. 8d. and that to the prejudice of his majesty's farmer, one Thomas Monjoye, the elder, Thomas Monjoye, the younger, John Hill, and others, mine diggers, and carriers of mine and cinders within the said forest, do daily dig and carry away out of the said forest the mine and ore there gotten; whereupon it was then ordered, that his majesty's writ of injunction under the seal of this court should be awarded to the said parties, commanding them and every of them, upon pain of 500l. not to carry nor transport any of the mine and cinders to be digged or gotten in the said forest, except they should shew good cause to this court by or before the first Saturday of Trinity term then ensuing, and thereupon the court would then take other order, as by the said recited order it plainly appears; whereupon the said Monjoye and other the said parties before mentioned came, and by Mr. Escourte of their counsel named, informing this court that they were poor labouring men, and were wholly sustained, with their wives and families, by digging and carrying of such mine, ore, and cinder; acknowledging, as well by their answer to the said information as by the council at the bar, the soil to be his majesty's, and that they had no interest therein, humbly praying they might be permitted to continue their digging and carrying the said mine, ore, and cinder, as they had been accustomed, having no other means to relieve their poor estates; whereof the court taking due consideration, and upon the humble submission of the said parties for their offences formerly past, and considering also that his majesty's farmer of the

the ſaid iron works, paying a great rent, ſhould not be furniſhed of matter to keep his forges in work if the ſaid ore and cinder ſhould be carried away; it pleaſed the court to move that the ſaid parties before named, and ſuch others as have been accuſtomed to dig and get mine, ore, and cinder, in the ſaid foreſt, of charity and grace, and not of right, might be permitted, for the maintenance of their wives and children, who muſt by means of their labour live, to continue to dig for the ſaid mine, ore, and cinders, to be carried to his majeſty's forge and iron works within the ſaid foreſt, and not to any other place; and being paid for the ſame according to ſuch rates as they have been accuſtomed to ſell to other men before his majeſty leaſed the ſame; to which motion his ſaid majeſty's ſaid attorney general, in conſideration of the ſaid poor men's eſtates, did aſſent; it being as good for his majeſty's farmer to employ thoſe that are always exerciſed in the ſaid works as others; and thereupon it was then ordered by ſuch conſent as aforeſaid, that the ſaid parties above named, and ſuch others as have been accuſtomed to dig and get mine, ore, and cinders, in the ſaid foreſt, ſhould, of charity and grace, and not of right, be permitted to continue the digging and getting of the ſaid ore and cinders, ſo as they carry, or cauſe the ſame to be carried to his majeſty's iron works and forges, receiving for the ſame ſuch rateable price as they had been uſually accuſtomed to ſell to other men before his majeſty leaſed the ſame, until ſuch time as by the cauſe now depending by Engliſh bill, brought in the names of divers of the inhabitants by way of petition, their claims in the ſaid foreſt ſhall be heard and decreed, and thereupon this court will take other order: And for the better performance of the ſaid order, it was then alſo further ordered by the court, that his majeſty's writ of injunction ſhould be awarded to the ſaid parties aforenamed, to Thomas Maddock, John Gwillym, John Fryer, and to all other the inhabitants, diggers, miners, and workmen in the ſaid foreſt, for the due obſerving and performing of the ſaid order, upon pain of 100l. to be levied upon him that ſhould break the ſame. Now, upon the motion of Mr. attorney general this day in court, ſhewing, that notwithſtanding the ſaid former order and injunction, divers perſons inhabiting within the ſaid foreſt, have, ſince the ſaid order, carried out of the ſaid foreſt great quantities of cinder and mine ore unto other places, and not unto the king's works within the ſaid foreſt, as by the affidavit of William Whitefoot, of the pariſh of Chapel Hill, in the county of Monmouth, wiredrawer, made the 28th day of October, in Michaelmas term laſt paſt, and this day read in court, appeareth; and that thereupon proceſs of attachment being awarded againſt ſome of the ſaid perſons for the ſaid contempts, ſome of them have appeared this day in perſon, the court again entered into conſideration of ſome courſe to be taken for the moderate carrying away of the ſaid mine, ore, and cinder, from the king's works in the ſaid foreſt, to other places out of the ſaid foreſt, and yet having regard to the poverty of the ſaid inhabitants, who receive moſt part of their maintenance and relief thereby, for the better eſtabliſhing the ſaid matter hereafter, have thought fit, and it is this day ſo ordered, that the inhabitants of the ſaid foreſt who have heretofore uſed to dig and carry mine, ore, and cinder, ſhall be permitted, of favour and grace, and not of right, to continue the ſame until the hearing of the ſaid cauſe now depending by Engliſh bill as aforeſaid, ſo as they carry the ſame, or offer it, to the king's works; and if the ſame ſhall be refuſed by the farmers, or other officers of his majeſty's works, then the ſaid diggers and carriers of mine and cinders may ſell the ſame to any other works within and near about the ſaid foreſt, for the ſervice of ſuch works; and further, that no new diggers or carriers of mine and cinder, whereof the court is informed there are very many, ſhall hereafter be allowed, but only ſuch poor men as are inhabitants of the ſaid foreſt: And it is further ordered, that a commiſſion ſhall be drawn, with articles thereunto annexed, by ſuch as follow for the king, and the ſame to be ſhewed to the defendant's council; upon which, if they cannot agree, then the barons will conſider thereof, as alſo of the commiſſioners to be therein nominated, which commiſſioners ſhall have power to appoint what number of new diggers and carriers ſhall be allowed, and to conſider of their eſtate, quality, and condition, and at what rate they and all other the diggers and carriers of mine, ore, and cinder, ſhall ſell the ſame to the king's works, conſideration being had of the diſtance of places where the cinder and ore are digged, and the king's works to which they ſhall be carried, and to ſet down ſuch prices for the ſaid mine, ore, and cinders, as ſhall be thought fitting in reſpect of their labour therein; and alſo when and in what manner they ſhall be paid for the ſame. And, as touching the two defendants, Randal Marks and William Sibborns, now appearing upon the aforeſaid attachments, it is ordered that they may, in the mean time till the commiſſion be executed, carry their ore and cinder to the king's works, at ſuch rates and prices as have been heretofore moſt uſually paid to them for the like, to be paid to them every two months, when the ſame ſhall be meaſured, and the reſt of the ſaid inhabitants who have uſed to dig and carry mine, ore, and cinders, as aforeſaid, are in the like manner permitted to do; and if the farmer of the king's works refuſe to give the ſaid rates as is above mentioned, and ſuch other further rates as ſhall be appointed by the aforeſaid commiſſioners, then they are left at liberty to carry the ſame elſewhere, at their pleaſures, to other works within and near about the ſaid foreſt, for the ſervice of ſuch other works: And touching the contempts of them, and all the other ſaid perſons, the court is pleaſed to ſuſpend them till the hearing of the ſaid cauſe.

NUMBER V.

A Paper delivered by the Inhabitants of the Foreſt, &c. to the Right Hon. Henry *Lord* Herbert, *Lord Lieutenant of the County of* Glouceſter, *and Conſtable of the Caſtle of St.* Briavell's, *and the reſt of his Majeſty's Commiſſioners for the Foreſt of* Dean.

WE who have hereunto ſubſcribed, being freeholders and inhabitants of the ſeveral pariſhes, towns, villages, and places, within the hundred of St. Briavell's, and the perambulation of the foreſt of Dean, within the county of Glouceſter, and adjacent pariſhes thereunto, that is to ſay, St. Briavell's, Newland, Hualdsfield, Staunton, Bicknor, Ruardean, the Lea, Mitchel Dean, Little Dean, Flaxley, Bleeldon, Abenhall, Newnham, Awre, Lidney, Alvington, Manor of Rodley, and Long Hope, taking into conſideration the exceeding great trouble your honours muſt of neceſſity be at, if every lawful commoner ſhould bring in his claim, or ſeverally make out his juſt right to common of paſtures, pannage, and eſtovers, that is to ſay, of houſe-boot, fire-boot, hay-boot, and other privileges, which he hath within the waſte ſoil of the ſaid foreſt of Dean, and the 18,000 acres formerly part thereof, but lately diſafforeſted by his majeſty's letters patent to Sir John Wintour, knt. have thought fit, as well on behalf of all the freeholders and inhabitants within the pariſhes, towns, villages, and places as aforeſaid, as of ourſelves alone, to preſent unto your honours, as in our claim (which we acknowldge to be unlawful, were it to be ſo done at a juſtice ſeat) the antient, lawful, and juſt rights and privileges, which we, they, and thoſe whoſe eſtate we and they do hold, have had, taken, and enjoyed for divers hundreds of years laſt paſt, until the uſurped power of the late Oliver Cromwell, as by the claim hereafter following more fully doth and may appear.

The aboveſaid freeholders and inhabitants within the ſeveral pariſhes, towns, villages, and places, of the hundred of St. Briavell's, do ſay, and each of them jointly, and ſeverally, and reſpectively, for themſelves, and every of them, ſaith: That by reaſon of their attendance and ſuit of court at the caſtle and manor of St. Briavell's aforeſaid, and by reaſon that the ſaid pariſhes, villages, and hundred, are within the perambulation of the foreſt of Dean; they have uſed and enjoyed in the ſaid foreſt, and in the woods and waſtes of the ſame, as belonging to their antient meſſuages, lands, and tenements, common of paſture, herbage, and pawnage, for all their commonable cattle, all times of the yearly freely, without attachment; and alſo common of eſtovers to be taken in the woods of the ſaid foreſt; that is to ſay, houſe-boot, for the reparation and amendment of their antient meſſuages, houſes and edifices of huſbandry thereunto belonging, and hey-boot for making incloſures about the ſame, and alſo convenient and neceſſary fire-boot to be ſpent in their ſaid antient meſſuages, and alſo liberty to dig and get lime-ſtone, tile ſtone, and other ſtones, neceſſary to be employed in and upon the ſaid antient meſſuages, lands, and tenements, and alſo to get and to make mill-ſtones and grindſtones, under and according to the government of the court of ſwanimote, and attachments, within the ſaid foreſt; paying therefore into his majeſty's exchequer the yearly rent of one penny, called ſwine ſilver or herbage money, and one penny called ſmoke penny, or mark money, for every houſe in the ſaid hundred, as by antient records it doth and may appear. And the miners and colliers within the ſaid hundred do ſay, that they and every of them have had, and do claim, liberty to dig and get mine and coal in all places within the ſaid foreſt at their pleaſure and liberty; alſo to have and take ſufficient timber within the ſaid woods for their neceſſary ſupport, and building of the ſaid mines and coal works, according to their antient uſage and cuſtomed rents and duties to his majeſty for the ſame. And the freeholders and inhabitants of the hundred of Bledſloe do claim the ſame, and the like common paſture, herbage, pawnage, eſtovers, houſeboot, and other the profits and commodities as unto their ſaid antient meſſuages, lands, and tenements, belonging or appertaining, and under the ſame, or the like rents the hundred of St. Briavell's do pay. The tenants and owners of lands and tenements

ments in the lordſhips of the dutchy, and Longhope, claim common of paſture and pawnage, and dead and dry wood only, to be had and taken within the waſte and woods of the ſaid foreſt. The town and pariſh of St. Briavell's ſay, that they uſually have had and taken within the waſte of his majeſty called Huddenalls, liberty to take and cut wood there, at all times, at their pleaſure, without view or attachment of any officer whatſoever of the ſaid foreſt; and for their and every of their ſeveral and reſpective titles to this their claim, they ſay, and all thoſe whoſe eſtates they have in the ſaid ſeveral meſſuages, lands, tenements, and buildings aforeſaid, have uſually had, and uſed and enjoyed the ſaid liberties, privileges, and franchiſes, from the time whereof the memory of man is not to the contrary, according to the form, force, and effect, of their ſaid claim. And we whoſe names are underwritten, apprehending the gracious inclination of his ſacred majeſty and his parliament towards the preſervation of wood and timber in the ſaid foreſt of Dean, and in the ſenſe of public advantage to his majeſty and the kingdom, do humbly offer and propoſe, on behalf of ourſelves, and all other the freeholders in the ſaid foreſt, to bind ourſelves by any lawful act, to forbear our claims and rights to wood and timber in the ſaid foreſt, for ſo long time as his majeſty ſhall be graciouſly pleaſed to ſuſpend the employing of his iron works, and cutting the woods of the ſaid foreſt, provided that our rights and claims before mentioned be ſecured unto us after the ſaid time of forbearance as aforeſaid; and that we, and all the inhabitants of the ſaid foreſt, may be freed from the power and exerciſe of the foreſt laws, upon any of our and their particular lands and inheritance; and that we humbly deſire, that the 18,000 acres may be reafforeſted, and that the letters patent for the ſale thereof to Sir John Wintour, knt. may be made void, and that the foreſt law may be put in execution on the waſte ſoil of the ſaid foreſt, whereby the woods and timber may be the better preſerved.

NUMBER VI.

The preſent CHARTER *of the City of* GLOUCESTER.

CHARLES the Second, by the grace of God king of England, Scotland, France, and Ireland, Defender of the Faith, &c. To all to whom theſe preſents ſhall come, greeting. Whereas our city of Glouceſter, and county or vill of the city of Glouceſter, hath of long time been a burrough and vill very ancient and populous, and by its ſituation borders upon the bank of the famous navigable river of Severn; where alſo into the ſpacious haven of the ſame city, called the Key, ſhips and boats laden with goods, as well to be exported as imported, by the daily ebbing and flowing of the ſea, continually do arrive: And whereas the citizens and burgeſſes of the ſaid burrough, vill, or city, as well by land as by water, have, uſe, and enjoy, divers franchiſes and privileges, by virtue of ſeveral charters and letters patents, by our late moſt dear father, king Charles, of bleſſed memory, and divers other of our progenitors and predeceſſors, late kings and queens of England; and alſo by us to them and their predeceſſors heretofore granted; and alſo by preſcription and cuſtoms in the aforeſaid city or haven obſerved and kept: And whereas our beloved ſubjects the mayor and burgeſſes of our city of Glouceſter aforeſaid, have under their common ſeal ſurrendered up our charter bearing date on the 16th day of November in the 16th year of our reign to them before granted; which ſurrender we have accepted, and by theſe preſents do accept: And whereas the aforeſaid mayor and burgeſſes of the city of Glouceſter have humbly beſought us to grant anew to them the mayor and burgeſſes of the city of Glouceſter aforeſaid, and their ſucceſſors, all and all manner of liberties, franchiſes, privileges, freedoms, inheritances, and rights whatſoever, in the ſaid former charters and grants of our anceſtors contained; and that we would be pleaſed to confirm them for the future for ever: And that we, for the better government of the city aforeſaid, would join the citizens and burgeſſes of the city of Glouceſter, by whatſoever name or names of incorporation they were heretofore incorporated, or whether they were before incorporated or not, in one body politic, by the name of the mayor and burgeſſes of the city of Glouceſter in the county of the ſame city; and that we would by our letters patents ratify and confirm it, or by what other means ſhall ſeem to us expedient:

We therefore willing that in the city of Glouceſter aforeſaid, there may be one certain and undoubted manner of form and rule for the keeping of the peace and government of the people there; and that the ſaid city may henceforward be and remain a city of peace and quietneſs, and as we hope, for the terror of evil doers, and the reward of thoſe that do well; and that our peace and other acts of juſtice may be well and truly there kept; and hoping, that if the ſaid burgeſſes and inhabitants of the city aforeſaid, do by this our grant enjoy their liberties and privileges, that then they will hold themſelves eſpecially bound to exhibit and employ their utmoſt powers and endeavours in the ſervice of us, our heirs, and ſucceſſors: *Know ye*, That we, in conſideration of your faithful ſervice to us heretofore done, and hereafter to be done, of our eſpecial grace and favour, of our own accord and mere motion, have willed, ordained, conſtituted, declared, and granted, and by this preſent charter do will, ordain, conſtitute, declare, and grant, that our city and vill of Glouceſter for the future for ever be named and called by the name of the city of Glouceſter in the county of the city of Glouceſter; and that the ſaid city of Glouceſter in the county or vill of the city of Glouceſter, henceforth for ever may, and ſhall be one free city and county of itſelf; and that the citizens, burgeſſes, and inhabitants of the city aforeſaid, who at the time of the aforeſaid ſurrender, were burgeſſes or freemen of the city aforeſaid, and their ſucceſſors may, and ſhall hereafter be, by virtue of theſe preſents, one body corporate and political, by the name of the mayor and burgeſſes of the city of Glouceſter in the county of the city of Glouceſter.

And we do for us, our heirs, and ſucceſſors, by theſe preſents grant, erect, make, appoint, confirm, and declare them, a body corporate and political really and fully, by the name of the mayor and burgeſſes of the city of Glouceſter, and of the county of the city of Glouceſter, and by the ſame name may have a perpetual ſucceſſion; and that they, by the name of the mayor and burgeſſes of the city of Glouceſter, and of the county of the ſame city, may, and ſhall hereafter for ever be fit perſons, and in law capable of having, getting, receiving, and poſſeſſing manors, lands and tenements, liberties, privileges, juriſdictions, franchiſes, and inheritances, of what nature and kind ſoever they be, to them and their ſucceſſors in fee, or for ever, or for term of a year or years, or any otherwiſe howſoever: As alſo goods or chattles, or any other things, of what kind, name, nature, or quality ſoever. As likewiſe, to have and retain all manors, lands, and tenements, liberties, privileges, juriſdictions, franchiſes, and inheritances whatſoever: As alſo, all goods and chattles of which they were any way ſeized or poſſeſſed before the aforeſaid ſurrender: And alſo, to give, grant, let, ſet, aſſign, or diſpoſe of manors, lands, tenements, and inheritances, and to do and execute all things by that name; and by the ſame name, the mayor and burgeſſes of the city of Glouceſter in the county of the city of Glouceſter, may plead and be impleaded, anſwer and be anſwered, defend and be defended, in all courts and places, and before all judges, juſtices, and other perſons and officers of us, our heirs and ſucceſſors whatſoever; and all others in all and ſingular actions, ſuits, plaints, cauſes, matters, and demands, of what kind or nature ſoever, in the ſame manner and form as all other our liege ſubjects of this kingdom of England, being any other body politic or incorporate within our kingdom of England, and fit men and capable in law, may have, get, receive, poſſeſs, enjoy, retain, give, grant, let, ſet, aſſign, or diſpoſe of, plead and be impleaded, anſwer and be anſwered, defend and be defended, do, promiſe, and execute.

And that the aforeſaid mayor and burgeſſes of the city of Glouceſter aforeſaid, and their ſucceſſors, have for ever a common ſeal, to be uſed in whatſoever buſineſs may happen to them, or their ſucceſſors: And be it lawful for the ſame the mayor and burgeſſes of the city aforeſaid, from time to time at their pleaſure, to break, change, alter, and make anew the ſaid ſeal, as to them ſhall ſeem good.

And whereas, ever ſince the memory of man, there was a cuſtom within the ſaid village, burrough, or city of Glouceſter aforeſaid, that certain *capital burgeſſes* of the ſame burrough, city, or village, in number ſometimes more, ſometimes leſs, who by the reſt of the burgeſſes were thought moſt diſcreet, were choſen into the common council of the ſaid burrough, vill, or city; and that upon the death of any one or more of them, that ſome one or more of the ſaid burrough, village, or city, was choſen freely, and without any conſtraint or compulſion, into the common council of the ſaid burrough, vill, or city aforeſaid: We therefore, at the humble petition of the mayor and burgeſſes of the city of Glouceſter, intending and deſigning to reduce the number of the ſaid capital burgeſſes to a greater certainty, do will, and for us, our heirs, and ſucceſſors, by theſe preſents grant to the aforeſaid mayor and burgeſſes of the city aforeſaid, and their ſucceſſors, that for the future for ever there are, and ſhall be within the city aforeſaid, thirty capital burgeſſes at the leaſt, and not more than forty, to be choſen out of all the burgeſſes, who ſhall be named the common council of the city of Glouceſter: And that there be, and ſhall be, twelve of the burgeſſes aforeſaid, being of the common council of the city aforeſaid, (in the form in theſe preſents following, choſen and appointed) who ſhall be named aldermen of the city

city aforesaid, and that there be, and shall be, one of the aldermen aforesaid (as in the form in these presents following chosen and appointed) who shall be named mayor of the city of Gloucester aforesaid; and that the other eleven aldermen of the city, for the time being, be from time to time respectively assistant in council to the mayor of the said city for the time being, in all matters, causes, and businesses, any ways touching or concerning the government of the city aforesaid; and that the rest of the common council of the same city shall all and every of them attend and assist the mayor and aldermen of the city aforesaid for the time being, in all matters, causes, and businesses, concerning the said city, whensoever they, or either of them, shall be summoned or called by the command of the mayor and aldermen, or the major part of them.

Also our will and pleasure is, and we by these presents do grant for us, our heirs and successors, to the said mayor and burgesses of the city aforesaid, and their successors, that their successors for ever have one honourable man, and learned in the laws of this our kingdom of England (as in the form in these presents following) who shall be named Recorder of the city of Gloucester aforesaid, from time to time to execute all things belonging to his office, for the public good of the same city.

And our farther will and pleasure is, and we, for us our heirs and successors, by these presents grant to the mayor and burgesses of the city aforesaid, and their successors, that the mayor, aldermen, and the rest of the common council of the city of Gloucester, for the time being, or major part of them, who upon public summons have gathered together, and if upon any such occasion their votes happen to be equal, that then that part of whom the mayor of the city aforesaid for the time being is one, may, and shall have from time to time, full power and authority of making, ordaining, and constituting such laws, statutes, and decrees, in writing, as shall seem safe, honest, and necessary, according to the discretion of them, or the major part of them, or in equal votes to that part of them whereof the mayor for the time being is one, for the good rule and government of the city aforesaid, and of all and singular officers, ministers, artificers, inhabitants, or residents, within the city aforesaid, or the liberties or suburbs of the same; and for a model in what method or order they the said mayor and burgesses of the city aforesaid, and all and singular officers, ministers, burgesses, tradesmen, or residents, within the said city or liberties, or suburbs of the same, may behave themselves, and use, exercise, and perform their several and respective offices, functions, and trades, for the public good and profit of the said city, and for the well managing of all things whatsoever, touching and concerning the government and good provision for the said city.

And that they the said mayor, burgesses, and common council of the city aforesaid, or the major part of them, or in case of equal votes, that party whereof the mayor of the city for the time being is one, having ordained, made, and established, any institutions and decrees of this kind, may punish the offenders against the laws and institutions of this nature, by imprisonment of body, by fines, and amerciaments, or by either of them, as for the better observation of the said laws and institutions shall seem necessary, fit, and requisite, to the said mayor, aldermen, or common council men, or the major part of them, or in equal vote to that part whereof the mayor of the city aforesaid for the time being is one, to appoint, limit, and provide; and that the sheriffs, and other ministers and officers of the city aforesaid, may have power to levy the said fines or amerciaments by distress or otherwise, at their pleasure, for the use of the said mayor and burgesses of the city, and their successors, without any hindrance from us, our heirs or successors, or from any officer or officers, or minister of us, our heirs or successors, or without any account thereof to be given to us, our heirs or successors. All which respective laws or institutions made or to be made, we will to be observed under the penalties in them contained; provided that such laws, institutions, imprisonments, fines, and amerciaments be reasonable, and not repugnant, nor contrary to the laws, statutes, customs, or rights, of our kingdom of England.

And for the better execution of our will and grant in this part mentioned, we have assigned, named, appointed, and made, and by these presents do, for us, our heirs and successors, assign, name, appoint, and make our well beloved Henry Fowler, esq; the present mayor of the city aforesaid; farther willing, that the said Henry Fowler continue in the office of mayor of the city aforesaid, from the date of these presents, until the Monday next ensuing the feast of St. Michael the archangel next; and that then one other of the aldermen of the city aforesaid be duly chosen and sworn to the office of mayor, according to the ordinances and provisions in these presents following expressed and declared, if the said Henry Fowler shall so long live, unless in the mean while he be duly removed from his office, according to the ordinances and provisions hereafter in these presents expressed:

And we have also assigned, named, created, appointed, and made, and do, by these presents, for us, our heirs and successors, assign, name, create, appoint, and make our well beloved Sir William Morton, knt. one of our justices of our court of common pleas, before us, wheresoever we may be, to be holden, to be the present recorder of the city aforesaid; farther willing, that the said Sir William Morton shall continue in the office of recorder of the city aforesaid during his natural life, from the date of these presents, unless he shall be duly removed from that office by surrender, or according to the ordinances and provisions in these presents hereafter expressed.

Also we have assigned, named, created, appointed, and made, and do by these presents assign, name, create, appoint, and make, Henry Norwood, William Cooke, Duncombe Colchester, esquires, Henry Bret, William Selwyn, esquires, William Russel, Thomas Price, John Wagstaffe, the aforesaid Henry Fowler, John Guithens, Thomas Aram, and John Rogers, to be the present aldermen of the city aforesaid; and in that office respectively to be continued from the date of these presents, during the natural life of them, and either of them, unless in the mean time, for their ill government and behaviour in their office, or for any offence or offences, default or defaults, by them committed and done, they or any of them, according to the orders and provisions in that case made and provided, be duly and lawfully from that office removed.

We have likewise assigned, nominated, created, appointed and made, and do, for us, our heirs and successors, by these presents nominate, create, appoint, and make, William Lambe and Samuel Rose, to be the present bailiffs of the city of Gloucester, and sheriffs of the said city and county of the same, to be continued in that office respectively, from the date of these presents until the Monday next following the feast of St. Michael the archangel; and that then two more of the burgesses of the city aforesaid, being of the common council, shall be duly chosen and sworn, according to the orders and provisions in these presents hereafter following expressed and declared, if the said William Lamb and Samuel Rose, or either of them, shall so long live, unless in the mean time they, or either of them, be (according to the orders and provisions in these presents hereafter expressed) duly removed.

We have also assigned, nominated, created, appointed, and made, and do, by these presents, for us, our heirs and successors, assign, nominate, create, appoint, and make, John Powell, esq; Robert Halford, John Marston, Francis Singleton, Arnold Aram, William Lambe, Samuel Rose, William Jordan, John Price, Thomas Luge, Matthias Bower, Richard Stephens, Nicholas Phelps, Giles Weblye, John Cromwell, John Campion, Joseph Ludlow, Walter Vecie, Joseph Phelps, Thomas Gosslinge, Daniel Comeline, John Perkes, John Webb, William Corseley, Cornelius Plott, Daniel Collins, Nicholas Lane, and John Bishop, to be of the common council of the said city, and to be continued in the office of common council men from the date of these presents, during the natural life or lives of them, and every of them, unless in the mean time for their ill government and behaviour in that office, or for any fault or offence by them, or any of them, committed and done, or to be committed and done, they, or either of them, shall, according to the laws, provisions and orders hereafter expressed, be from that office duly removed.

And our farther will and pleasure is, and we have ordered, that if any of the aldermen, sheriffs, or bailiffs afore named, or either of them, or any other burgess of the common council afore-named, shall, upon notice given, refuse to take upon him the burthen of any office of this kind, as of alderman, bailiff, sheriff, or common council man, that then in that case it shall be lawful for the mayor and burgesses of the city aforesaid, to chuse another aldermen, bailiff, sheriff, or common council man, instead of him so refusing; and, in such an election, to proceed as if the said alderman, bailiff, sheriff, or common council man were dead, or lawfully removed from his office.

And we further will, and by these presents ordain, that, if any one of the aldermen or burgesses of the common council afore named were not a freeman of the city aforesaid, at the time of the surrender aforesaid, that then, and in that case, such alderman and burgess, having within one month next after the date of these presents taken the sacrament respectively required by due form of law, he shall be admitted and made a freeman of the city aforesaid; and notwithstanding his defect at admission, yet the sacrament respectively required being first taken, he shall, by vertue of these letters patents, be for ever reputed a freeman of the city aforesaid, to all intents and purposes whatsoever; and shall continue alderman, or common council man, in the same manner and form as he could, or ought, if he had been a freeman at the time of the surrender aforesaid, any defect of admission to the contrary notwithstanding.

And we farther will, and do, for us, our heirs and successors, by these presents, grant to the mayor and burgesses of the city of Gloucester aforesaid, that the mayor, aldermen, and common

mon council men of the city aforefaid, for the time being, or the major part of them, or in equal votes, that part or equal number of them, whereof the mayor of the city aforefaid for the time being is one, may have full power and authority to chufe fuch, and fo many of the moft honeft and difcreet burgeffes to make up the number of thirty in the common council in the whole at the leaft; or to increafe that number, fo that they exceed not the number of forty at the moft, as fhall feem expedient to them, the mayor, aldermen, and common council men oforefaid, or the major part of them, to be the reft of the burgeffes of the common council of the city aforefaid, being thirty at the leaft, and not above forty at the moft; and that the faid burgeffes fo chofen into the common council, fhall remain and continue in the faid office, during the natural lives of them, or either of them, unlefs they, or either of them, fhall for any faults by them, or either of them, committed and done, or to be committed and done, by the mayor, aldermen, and common council, or the major part of them; or in cafe of equal votes, by that part whereof the mayor of the city aforefaid for the time being is one, be from that office lawfully and duly removed.

And whereas Richard the IIId, late king of England, by his letters patents, willed and ordained, that there fhould be an yearly election made, as well of the mayor of the city aforefaid, as of other officers of the fame city, by four and twenty electors, viz. by the twelve aldermen of the city aforefaid, and twelve other of the moft legal and difcreet burgeffes of the faid city; which words being fubject to an uncertain and doubtful conftruction, have caufed divers elections to be made at uncertain times: We therefore, of our fpecial grace and favour, defiring to reduce the election of the mayor and other officers of the city aforefaid, to a certainty, for the honour and common good of the faid city, and avoiding of popular tumults, do will, and for us, our heirs, and fucceffors, by thefe prefents, grant to the aforefaid mayor and burgeffes of the city aforefaid, and their fucceffors, that every year henceforward, on the Monday next following the feaft of St. Michael the archangel, the mayor and aldermen, and reft of the burgeffes of the common council of the city aforefaid, in great folemnity, fhall meet together in the guildhall, or fome other convenient place within the city aforefaid, or fuch and fo many as fhall then remain and continue; and then and there, the mayor, aldermen, and the fenior fheriff, or fuch of them as are then and there prefent; and fo many other of the burgeffes of the common council of the city aforefaid, by order of election firft in that office, and feniors to the reft of the common council, being there prefent, as fhall make up the number of twenty in the whole, be, and fhall be for that time, electors of the mayor, bailiffs, and chamberlain of the city aforefaid, and coroner and fheriffs of the county of the fame city for the year enfuing; which twenty electors being called together by themfelves in the council chamber of the faid guildhall, or any other convenient place within the city aforefaid, may proceed to the election of the mayor, and other officers afore named, for the year enfuing; and in that election the faid twenty electors, or the major part of them, fhall feverally nominate and elect the mayor and other officers of the city aforefaid; and if thofe electors votes fhall in the election of either of thofe officers be equal, fo that ten of them fhall defend, and the other ten deny the election, that then, and in every fuch cafe, the election of the mayor of the city aforefaid, and other officers of the fame, fhall be made and concluded by thofe ten electors, of whom the mayor, or in his abfence, the fenior alderman fhall be one; and that thofe twenty electors, from time to time henceforward for ever, may, and fhall, have power and authority in manner and form aforefaid, to nominate and elect yearly for ever, on the Monday next following the feaft of St. Michael the archangel, one of the aldermen of the city aforefaid, for the time being, to be mayor for the whole year then next following; as alfo, another of the aldermen of the city aforefaid, for the time being, to be the coroner of the county of the fame city, for one whole year then next enfuing; and likewife, two of the burgeffes of the common council of the faid city, for the time being, to be bailiffs of the city, and fheriffs of the county of the city aforefaid, for one whole year then next following; and one other honeft and difcreet man to be chamberlain of the faid city, to be continued in that office for one whole year, unlefs he be for fome reafonable caufe, according to the orders and provifions in thefe prefents expreffed, from that office duly removed: And that that alderman who, as before, fhall be nominated and elected mayor of the city aforefaid, before he be admitted to the execution of his office, fhall take a corporal oath in the prefence of the laft and next precedent mayor of the city aforefaid, if he fhall be there prefent, and the reft of the aldermen aforefaid, or fix or more of them; and in the prefence of fo many of the common council, and the reft of the burgeffes of the city aforefaid, as fhall be then and there prefent, well, truly, and faithfully to execute the office of mayor of the city aforefaid, in all things belonging thereunto: To which precedent mayor and aldermen of the city aforefaid, or fix or more of them, we, for us, our heirs, and fucceffors, do, by thefe prefents, give and grant full power and authority to adminifter this oath to the mayor elect; and that this alderman aforefaid being chofen and fworn mayor, after this oath taken, may, and fhall execute the office of mayor of the city aforefaid, for one whole year then next enfuing, until another be duly chofen and fworn to that office, according to the orders and provifions in thefe prefents expreffed and declared, unlefs for fome fault or faults, offence or offences, by him the mayor of the faid city, for the time being, committed and done, he fhall by the aldermen and common council of the city, folemnly called together, fo that there be four and twenty at the leaft there prefent, or the major part, or any other lawful way, be from his office removed: Which mayor of the city aforefaid failing, as in the form aforefaid, we, for our heirs and fucceffors, do, by thefe prefents, will and declare to be liable to be removed and divefted of his office.

And if it fhould happen that the mayor of the city aforefaid fo chofen, or hereafter to be chofen, fhould die, or be removed, after his election or fwearing, and before the Monday next following the feaft of St. Michael the archangel then next following, that then, as often as this cafe fhall happen, the aldermen of the city aforefaid, the Sheriffs, or fuch of them as fhall be then and there prefent, and as many of the fenior burgeffes of the common council of the city aforefaid being there prefent, as fhall make up the number of four and twenty, being gathered together in the guildhall, or fome other convenient place within the city of Gloucefter aforefaid, or the major part of them; and in cafe of equal votes, that part whereof the fenior aldermen there prefent is one, immediately after the death or removal of the mayor of the city aforefaid, may, and fhall have power, and fhall choofe one other of the aldermen of the city aforefaid for the time being, to be mayor of the faid city; and after the oath in that part required, in manner and form aforefaid, by him taken, be continued until another be chofen and fworn to that office.

And farther, our will and pleafure is, that one other of the aldermen of the city aforefaid, who, as before, fhall be nominated and elected coroner of the city aforefaid, before he be admitted to the execution of that office, fhall take a corporal oath before the mayor of the city aforefaid, newly chofen and fworn, or, in his abfence, before the aldermen of the faid city, or fix or more of them, that he will well and truly perform the office of coroner of the county of the city aforefaid, and faithfully execute all things to that office belonging; to which mayor fo newly elected and fworn, and to the aldermen of the city aforefaid, or to any fix or more of them, we, for us, our heirs, and fucceffors, do, by thefe prefents, give and grant full power and authority, from time to time, to adminifter the oath of a coroner to him chofen; and that the aforefaid alderman being fo chofen and fworn to the office of a coroner, after he hath taken the aforefaid oath, fhall execute the office of a coroner for one whole year then next following, and then until another be, according to the orders and provifions in thefe prefents expreffed and declared, in due manner and form, to that office elected and fworn; unlefs, in the mean time, for any fault or defaults, offence, or offences, by him the faid coroner of the city aforefaid, committed and done, or to be committed and done, he fhall, by the mayor, aldermen, and common council men of the city aforefaid, on this part folemnly called together, fo that there be four and twenty at the leaft then and there prefent, or by the major part or number of them, be from that office duly and lawfully removed.

And that they, the two burgeffes of the common council of the city aforefaid, who fhall be chofen and nominated to be bailiffs of the city aforefaid, and fheriffs of the county of the fame city, before they be admitted to the execution of that office, fhall take a corporal oath, before the mayor of the city aforefaid, then duly elected and fworn, or, in his abfence, in the prefence of the aldermen of the faid city, or any fix or more of them, that they, or either of them, will well and truly, and faithfully, perform the office of bailiffs of the city aforefaid, and fheriffs of the county of the fame city, and faithfully execute all things to that office belonging; to which mayor newly elected and fworn, and the aldermen of the city aforefaid, or any fix or more of them, in manner aforefaid, we, for us, our heirs, and fucceffors, do, by thefe prefents, give and grant full power and authority to adminifter the faid oath to the bailiffs of the city aforefaid, and the county fheriffs of the fame city; and that the faid burgeffes being chofen bailiffs and fheriffs, fhall execute the office of bailiffs and fheriffs for one whole year then next following; and thence till two more be duly elected and fworn to that office, according to the orders and provifions above declared and expreffed, unlefs in the mean while, for any fault or faults, offence or offences, by the bailiffs and fheriffs for the time being committed and done, or to be committed and done, they, or either of them, fhall, by the mayor, aldermen, and common council of the city aforefaid, folemnly called together, fo that there be four

and

and twenty at the leaſt then and there preſent, or by the major part of them, be from that office lawfully and duly removed.

And that the chamberlain of the city aforeſaid, ſo nominated and elected as aforeſaid, before he be admitted to that office, ſhall take a corporal oath before the mayor of the city aforeſaid, then newly choſen and ſworn, or, in his abſence, before the aldermen of the ſame city, or any ſix or more of them, and ſhall find and give ſuch good and ſufficient ſecurity, for the true and faithful execution of the office of a chamberlain, and all things thereunto belonging, as the mayor for the time being, and the burgeſſes of the ſaid city, being then and there preſent, ſhall approve of; to which mayor ſo newly choſen and ſworn, and to the aldermen of the city aforeſaid, or any ſix or more of them, we do, for us, our heirs, and ſucceſſors, by theſe preſents, give and grant full power and authority to adminiſter the oath of chamberlain of the city aforeſaid, and to take and approve of the ſecurity tendered by the chamberlain aforeſaid; and that the ſaid burgeſs then choſen and ſworn chamberlain, ſhall continue in the office of chamberlain until, for any fault or faults, offence or offences, by him committed and done, or to be committed and done, he ſhall be by the mayor, aldermen, and common council of the city aforeſaid, in that caſe ſolemnly called together, ſo that there be four and twenty at the leaſt then and there preſent, or the major part or number of them; or in caſe of equal votes, that part whereof the mayor of the city for the time being is one, or, in his abſence, the ſenior of the aldermen then and there preſent, be from that office lawfully and duly removed; which ſaid coroner, ſheriffs, and bailiffs, or chamberlain, in manner aforeſaid failing, we, for us, our heirs, and ſucceſſors, by theſe preſents, declare liable to be removed.

And if it ſhould happen that any of the ſaid officers, as ſheriff, coroner, or chamberlain, ſhould die, or be removed from his office after his election, and before the ſaid Monday next following the feaſt of St. Michael the archangel, that then and in ſuch caſe, as often as it ſhall happen, the mayor, aldermen, and ſenior ſheriff of the city aforeſaid, or ſuch of them as ſhall be then and there preſent; and as many other of the ſenior burgeſſes of the common council of the city aforeſaid being there preſent as ſhall make up the number of twenty in the whole, being gathered together in the guildhall aforeſaid, or any other convenient place within the city aforeſaid, or the major part of them; or in caſe of equal votes, the part whereof the mayor for the time, or, in his abſence, the ſenior of the aldermen there preſent is one, ſhall immediately after the death or removal of any the ſaid officer or officers, nominate and elect another to that office, to be continued after the oaths taken, until another be to that office duly elected and ſworn.

And our farther will and pleaſure is, and we do, for us, our heirs, and ſucceſſors, by theſe preſents, grant, that as often as the office of recorder of the city aforeſaid ſhall, by the death, ſurrender, or removal of any one, happen to be void, that then it ſhall be lawful, and be it lawful, for the mayor, aldermen, and common council aforeſaid, or the major part of them that ſhall be preſent at the election, to nominate one honourable and famous man, learned in the law of this our kingdom of England, to be recorder of the city aforeſaid, to be continued in that office, and to exerciſe and execute all things thereunto belonging, until by death, ſurrender, or any other reaſonable cauſe, or according to the orders and proviſions in theſe preſents expreſſed, he ſhall be from that office duly removed; and that he the ſaid recorder, being nominated and elected, ſhall, before he be admitted to the execution of his office, before the mayor of the city aforeſaid for the time being, or, in his abſence, before the aldermen of the city aforeſaid, or any ſix or more of them, take a corporal oath for the performance of his office in all things, for the greateſt profit and advantage and public good of the ſaid city: To which mayor and aldermen we, for us, our heirs, and ſucceſſors, do, by theſe preſents, give and grant full power and authority to adminiſter the aforeſaid oath to the perſon choſen to be recorder aforeſaid.

And our farther will and pleaſure is, and we do, for us, our heirs, and ſucceſſors, by theſe preſents, give and grant to the mayor and burgeſſes of the city of Glouceſter, and their ſucceſſors, that the mayor, aldermen, and common council of the city aforeſaid, being ſolemnly for that purpoſe called together, ſo that there be four and twenty there preſent at the leaſt, or the major part of them, may, and ſhall have full power and authority to remove and expel any one or more of the aldermen of the city aforeſaid, from the office, place, and authority of an alderman of the city aforeſaid; and as often as it ſhall happen that any one or more of the aldermen of the city aforeſaid ſhall die, or be removed from his or their office or offices in manner aforeſaid, it ſhall be lawful, and be it lawful, for the mayor and aldermen of the city aforeſaid then remaining, or the major part of them, to nominate and elect ſome one or more of the ſix ſenior burgeſſes of the common council of the ſaid city for the time being, under the degree of an alderman, as they ſhall think moſt fit, into the place or places of the ſaid alderman, or aldermen, removed or deceaſed, to be an alderman, or aldermen, of the city aforeſaid, to be continued in that office, and to exerciſe and execute all things thereunto belonging, during their natural lives, unleſs for ſome defect or defects, fault or faults, offence or offences, by him or them committed and done, they, or either of them, ſhall be from that office lawfully and duly removed.

We alſo farther will, and do, for us, our heirs, and ſucceſſors, by theſe preſents, grant to the mayor and burgeſſes of the city of Glouceſter, and to their ſucceſſors, that from time to time henceforth it may be lawful for the mayor, aldermen, and common council of the city aforeſaid, or the major part of them, by act or order of common council, to place and diſpoſe any member or members, in any place or order in theſe preſents mentioned, higher than the ſaid member, or members before were, any thing herein contained notwithſtanding.

And our farther will is, and we do, for us, our heirs, and ſucceſſors, by theſe preſents, grant to the mayor and burgeſſes of the city aforeſaid, and their ſucceſſors, that they and their ſucceſſors for ever may, and ſhall have, within the liberties, limits, and precincts of the ſaid city, one honeſt and diſcreet man to be town clerk of the city aforeſaid, to execute all things belonging to and concerning that office, within the liberties and precincts of the county of the city aforeſaid, from time to time to be choſen by the mayor, aldermen, and common council of the city aforeſaid, or the major part of them, being preſent at the election: And we have aſſigned and nominated, and do, for us, our heirs, and ſucceſſors, by theſe preſents, conſtitue and make our well beloved John Dorney, eſq; to be the preſent town clerk, willing that the ſaid John Dorney ſhall continue in the ſaid office during his life, unleſs by ſurrender, or for ſome other reaſonable cauſe in theſe preſents hereafter expreſſed, he ſhall be from that office duly removed.

And we have farther granted, and do, for us, our heirs, and ſucceſſors, by theſe preſents, grant to the aforeſaid mayor and burgeſſes of the city aforeſaid, that they may, and ſhall have one other honeſt and diſcreet man, to be ſword bearer, within the city and ſuburbs, limits, and liberties of the ſame, to perform all things touching and concerning that office within the ſaid city, limits, liberties, and precincts of the ſame, to be choſen by the mayor, aldermen, and common council of the ſame city, or the major part of them, as many as are willing to be preſent at the election; and that the ſword bearer of the city aforeſaid ſhall from time to time wait and attend upon the mayor, aldermen, and ſheriffs of the city aforeſaid, for the time being, in all things touching and belonging to his office: And he ſhall bear before the mayor of the city aforeſaid for the time being, within the ſaid city and limits, liberties and precincts of the ſame, one ſword, with a ſheath of any colour, having the arms of us, our heirs, and ſucceſſors, and the arms of the city aforeſaid, in gold and ſilver engraven upon it: And that the abovesaid town clerk and ſword bearer, before they, or either of them, be admitted to the performances of their reſpective offices, ſhall take a corporal oath, that they will well and faithfully execute their offices, before the mayor of the city aforeſaid for the time being, or, in his abſence, in the preſence of the aldermen of the ſaid city, or any ſix or more of them: To which mayor and aldermen of the city aforeſaid, we, for us, our heirs, and ſucceſſors, do, by theſe preſents, grant full power and authority to adminiſter the oath of a town clerk or ſword bearer in form aforeſaid: And that the ſaid town clerk and ſword bearer being elected and ſworn, ſhall execute and perform the reſpective offices of town clerk and ſword bearer during their natural lives, unleſs for ſome fault or faults, offence or offences, by them, or either of them, committed and done, or to be committed and done, they, or either of them, ſhall, by the mayor, aldermen, and common council, in that caſe ſolemnly called together, ſo that there be four and twenty at the leaſt then and there preſent, or the major part of them; or in caſe of equal votes, that part whereof the mayor, if he be preſent, or, in his abſence, the ſenior of the aldermen there preſent, is one, be from their reſpective offices duly removed; which town clerk and ſword bearer, or either of them, ſo failing, we, for us, our heirs, and ſucceſſors, will and declare liable to be removed.

And our farther pleaſure is, and we do, for us, our heirs, and ſucceſſors, by theſe preſents, grant to the mayor and burgeſſes of the city aforeſaid, and their ſucceſſors, that they and their ſucceſſors, may and ſhall henceforth for ever, have within the city aforeſaid, limits, liberties, and precincts of the ſame, four ſerjeants at mace, to execute and perform all things belonging to that office within the city aforeſaid, limits, liberties, and precincts of the ſame, to be choſen in the ſame manner and form, and the ſame perſons as they were wont heretofore; and each of them ſhall carry before the mayor, aldermen, and ſheriffs of the city aforeſaid, for the time being, according to the cuſtom long ſince there obſerved, a ſilver mace, with the arms of us, our heirs, and ſucceſſors, and the arms of the city aforeſaid,

ſaid, wrought and engraven upon it: And alſo, that the mayor and burgeſſes of the city aforeſaid, may, and ſhall have, within the city aforeſaid, ſuch and ſo many officers to execute and perform all things touching and belonging to thoſe reſpective offices, in ſuch manner and form, from time to time to be choſen, continued, and removed, within the city aforeſaid, and limits and liberties of the ſame, as they were wont to be choſen, conſtituted, continued, and removed: And that the ſaid ſerjeants at mace, and other officers of the city aforeſaid, from time to time to be nominated and elected, ſhall, before they, or either of them, be admitted to the execution of their offices, take a corporal oath, well and faithfully to perform all things relating to their office, before the mayor of the city aforeſaid, or ſuch other perſon or perſons as are wont to be preſent at the ſwearing of thoſe officers: To which mayor and other perſons aforeſaid, we, for us, our heirs, and ſucceſſors, do, by theſe preſents, grant full power and authority to adminiſter the oath to the ſerjeants at mace, and other officers aforeſaid, according to the cuſtom in that city long ſince obſerved and kept.

And we do farther will, and do, for us, our heirs, and ſucceſſors, by theſe preſents, grant, to the mayor and burgeſſes of the city aforeſaid, and their ſucceſſors, that if any one or more of the aldermen of the city aforeſaid, or burgeſſes of the common council of the ſame city, whether he be inhabiting or reſident within the city aforeſaid, and limits, liberties, and precincts of the ſame, or without, ſhall be elected and nominated to the office of mayor, alderman, bailiff, chamberlain, burgeſs of the common council of the ſaid city, or coroner or ſheriff of the county of the ſame city, or conſtable, or any other inferior officer, except the office of recorder, town clerk, ſword bearer, or ſerjeant at mace; and having notice and cognizance given them of the election of them, or either of them, ſhall refuſe to take the oath, or comply with the ſubſcriptions in that caſe by ſtatute eſpecially provided, to make them capable of, and fit to execute the offices on them impoſed, that then it ſhall be lawful for the mayor, aldermen, and common council of the city aforeſaid, for the time being, or the major part of them, to commit him or them ſo refuſing to execute the office or offices, to which he or they were elected, to the goal of the city aforeſaid, there to remain until he or they ſhall be willing to undertake the ſaid office or offices; and to impoſe ſuch a fine or amerciament on him or them ſo refuſing, as to the mayor, aldermen, and common council, or to the major part of them, ſhall reaſonably ſeem expedient; and that they may lawfully keep him or them ſo refuſing in the ſaid gaol, until they ſhall pay, or cauſe to be paid, thoſe fines and amerciaments as aforeſaid, for the public uſe of the city aforeſaid; and, if it ſhall ſeem fit to the mayor, aldermen, and common council men of the city aforeſaid, or the major part of them, to expel, remove, or deprive him or them of the liberties and franchiſes of the city aforeſaid.

And we have farther granted, and do, for us, our heirs and ſucceſſors, by theſe preſents, grant to the mayor and burgeſſes of the city aforeſaid, and their ſucceſſors for ever, that if any cuſtom herein contained be deficient, or not compleat, or any new cuſtoms have ariſen that want altering and mending, they, the mayor, aldermen, and common council of the city aforeſaid, for the time being, or the major part of them, may find a remedy, agreeable to honeſty and reaſon, for the public good of the citizens and burgeſſes of the ſaid city, and of other our faithful ſubjects thereto reſorting, as often as to them ſhall ſeem expedient; provided that the alterations of this kind be profitable to us and our people, and agreeable to honeſty and reaſon as aforeſaid; and that they be not repugnant to the royal prerogative of us, our heirs, and ſucceſſors, and contrary to the laws and ſtatutes of this kingdom of England then in force.

And we farther will, and do, for us, our heirs and ſucceſſors, by theſe preſents, to the mayor and burgeſſes of the city aforeſaid, grant, that the mayor, biſhop of the dioceſe of Glouceſter, for the time being, the recorder of the ſame city, the dean of the cathedral church of the holy and indiviſible trinity in Glouceſter, the aldermen of the ſame city, and two ſuch of the prebends of the ſame church, for the time being, as we, our heirs, and ſucceſſors, ſhall from time to time appoint and name, ſhall for the future for ever, they, and every of them, be juſtices, to be kept, and keep the peace, of us, our heirs and ſucceſſors, within the city of Glouceſter and county of the ſame, and limits, liberties, and precincts of the ſaid city and county thereof; and for the putting in execution of the ſtatutes and laws concerning tradeſmen and labourers, and enquiring into weights, meaſures, and all other things belonging to the office of a juſtice of the peace; which ſaid biſhop, dean, and two prebendaries of the cathedral church aforeſaid, ſhall from time to time for ever, by us, our heirs and ſucceſſors, by commiſſion under the great ſeal of England, and at the pleaſure of us, our heirs and ſucceſſors, from time to time to be renewed, we will that they, and either of them, be authorized and appointed to the office of juſtice of the peace, of us, our heirs and ſucceſſors; and that the ſaid mayor, biſhop, recorder, dean, two prebendaries, and aldermen of the city aforeſaid, made, and to be made, conſtituted, and to be conſtituted juſtices of the peace, by virtue of theſe preſents, or any three or more of them, of whom the mayor, biſhop, recorder, dean, two prebendaries, or any of the ſix ſenior aldermen being two, may appoint, keep, and hold, ſeſſions of the peace, in the ſame manner and form as any other juſtices of the peace being aſſigned to enquire into treſpaſſes and crimes, and to hear and determine controverſies, may or can; and that they have full power and authority to enquire into any offences, neglects, or defaults whatſoever, committed within the city aforeſaid, or the limits, liberties, and precincts of the ſame, or that may any time hereafter be committed and done; and there to do and execute all things which any other juſtices of the peace within any county, city, vill, or borough, incorporate within the kingdom of England, may or can inquire into, do and execute: Alſo, we will and do, for us, our heirs, and ſucceſſors, by theſe preſents, grant to the ſaid mayor and burgeſſes of the city aforeſaid, and their ſucceſſors, that the mayor, the biſhop of Glouceſter, for the time being, the dean of the cathedral church aforeſaid, the recorder, the two prebendaries, and the aldermen of the city aforeſaid for the time being, and every one or more of them, of whom the mayor, biſhop, dean, recorder, one of the ſaid two prebendaries, or any of the ſix ſenior aldermen of the city aforeſaid, for the time being, being two, ſhall be of the quorum, ſhall from time to time be juſtices of the peace, of us, our heirs and ſucceſſors, to make a gaol delivery in the city aforeſaid, and county of the ſame city, of all priſoners therein kept, according to the laws, cuſtoms, and ſtatutes of our kingdom of England: And that the ſheriffs and coroner of the county of the city aforeſaid, ſhall make return of all juries, pannels, attachments, and indentures, by them taken, or henceforward to be taken, before the mayor, biſhop, dean, recorder, two prebendaries, and aldermen of the city aforeſaid, of whom the mayor, biſhop, dean, recorder, one of the ſaid two prebendaries, and any of the ſaid ſix ſenior aldermen of the city aforeſaid, ſhall be of the quorum, and ſhall be attendant whenever it ſhall pleaſe to make a gaol delivery in all things thereunto belonging; and from time to time execute and obey the precepts of the mayor, biſhop, dean, recorder, two prebendaries, and aldermen of the city aforeſaid, for the time being, or any of them, in the ſame manner and form as other ſheriffs and coroners within our kingdom of England before any juſtices in the ſaid kingdom, of us, our heirs, and ſucceſſors, have been wont and ought to do, return, and execute, as touching any goal delivery; and that they the ſaid mayor, biſhop, dean, recorder, two prebendaries, and aldermen of the city aforeſaid, for the time being, or any of them, may by them and their ſervants and deputies take and arreſt all murderers, manſlayers, robbers, felons, and other malefactors, within the ſaid city, county, limits, liberties, and precincts of the ſame to be found; and bring, or cauſe to be brought, to the gaol within the city aforeſaid, there to be kept, until by due proceedings at law they ſhall be delivered, any other order, decree, or cuſtom to the contrary notwithſtanding: And alſo, that they, or any of them, may not proceed to determination of any treaſon, or miſpriſion of treaſon, without the ſpecial command of us, our heirs, or ſucceſſors, within the city aforeſaid, and the limits, liberties, and precincts of the ſame.

Alſo we will, and do, for us, our heirs and ſucceſſors, by theſe preſents, grant to the mayor and burgeſſes of the city aforeſaid, and their ſucceſſors, that the mayor of the city, for the time being, and his ſucceſſors, may, from time to time for ever, have, uſe, and execute the office of clerk of the market, of us, our heirs, and ſucceſſors, together with all things belonging to the ſaid office, in all and ſingular matters and cauſes concerning that office within the city aforeſaid, limits, liberties, and precincts of the ſame, and within the county of the ſame city, as well in the preſence of us, our heirs, and ſucceſſors, as in our abſence, and they ſhall enjoy this office ſucceſſively; and, at their goings out, levy all fines and amerciaments to and for the uſe of the mayor and his ſucceſſors, without any account to be made to us, our heirs, and ſucceſſors: And, for the time to come, that no clerk of the market of us, our heirs, and ſucceſſors, except the mayor of the city aforeſaid, ſhall enter upon any thing belonging to the execution of the ſaid office, or, under colour of his office, any ways poſſeſs himſelf of any thing in the ſaid city, or within the limits, liberties, and precincts of the ſame, or within the county of the ſaid city, or any part or parcel of it.

Alſo we will, and do, for us, our heirs, and ſucceſſors, by theſe preſents, grant to the ſaid mayor and burgeſſes of the city aforeſaid, and their ſucceſſors, that the mayor of the city aforeſaid, and his ſucceſſors, may do, exerciſe, and execute all and ſingular things belonging to the office of ſteward and marſhal of us, our heirs, and ſucceſſors, within the limits, liberties, and precincts of the city aforeſaid, and county of the ſame city;

and

and may do, execute, and exercise those things, as well in the presence of us, our heirs and successors, as in our absence, without the contradiction of us, our heirs and successors, as quietly, freely, and entirely, as if they, or either of them, had before exercised and executed the office of marshal and steward, and all things thereunto belonging, or before might have exercised and executed the same: And that the said mayor and burgesses, or any inhabitant or resident within the city aforesaid, or within the limits, liberties, and precincts of the county of the same city, being called to execute any precepts or commands of the steward or marshal of the houshold, of us, our heirs and successors, or any officers of the court of the steward or marshal of the said houshold, of us, our heirs or successors, or any deputy, or deputies, being called to appear before them, or either of them, are not holden and bound to obey: And that no steward or marshal of the house of us, our heirs and successors, or any officers of the court of the steward or marshal of the said houshold, besides the mayor and his successors, and their officers, may enter the city aforesaid, the limits, liberties, and precincts of the same, or the county of the city aforesaid, either in the presence or absence of us, our heirs or successors, to hold any sessions, make any enquiry, or execute any commands, of us, our heirs and successors, or of the steward or marshal of the houshold aforesaid, to make any gaol delivery, or to perform any of the respective offices of them, for any emergent occasion whatsoever.

And we also will, and do, for us, our heirs and successors, by these presents, grant to the mayor and burgesses of the city aforesaid, and their successors, that the mayor, aldermen, and common council of the city aforesaid, for the time being, or the major part of them, of whom the mayor of the city aforesaid for the time being is one, may and shall have full power and authority, from time to time, as often as to them shall seem necessary, to tax and assess all burgesses, citizens, inhabitants, and residents within the city aforesaid, and liberties and precincts of the same, some certain pence to be paid and answered by them, for the maintaining and repairing of the bridges within the city aforesaid, and towards the necessary and requisite expences of the said city and county of the same, and for other causes and matters touching and concerning the city aforesaid, and county of the same; and upon refusal of payment of such pence by them from time to time to be taxed and assessed, to levy them upon all citizens, burgesses, inhabitants, and residents within the city aforesaid, and county of the same city, to and for the use aforesaid, by distress, imprisonment of their bodies, or any other lawful way whatsoever, according to the laws and customs of our kingdom of England, and as in any other city, burrough, or vill incorporate, within this kingdom of England, it is used and accustomed: And these our letters patents, or an inrolled copy of the same, shall from time to time, be to the said mayor and burgesses of the city aforesaid, and their successors, a sufficient warrant and security.

And we farther will, and do, for us, our heirs and successors, by these presents, grant to the mayor and burgesses of the city aforesaid, and their successors, that no guild or fraternity within the city aforesaid, may have the power, authority and jurisdiction of making, appointing and constituting any statutes or constitutions whatsoever, to oblige or bind any of the burgesses of the city aforesaid, or any one or more of any fraternity within the said city, unless they may and shall have power, authority, and licence to make such statutes, orders, and constitutions, from the mayor, aldermen, and common council of the city aforesaid, under the common seal of the said city, witnessing such licence, power, and authority: And that all and singular laws, orders, statutes, constitutions, and decrees whatsoever, made, or to be made, by any fraternity or guild within the city aforesaid, without such power, authority, and licence, under the common seal of the city aforesaid, shall be void in law, and had and reputed of none effect; any statute, act, order, or provision, or any matter or cause to the contrary notwithstanding.

And whereas, by the letters patents of our predecessor Richard the IId. made in the 21st year of his reign, it was granted, that the burgesses of the vill of Gloucester, and their successors, should for ever have cognizance of all pleas of lands or tenements within the said vill, suburbs, limits, liberties, and precincts of the same, as well of assize of novel disseisin, as of mort d'auncestre, and certificates of persons arraigned, as of the debts, trespasses, and any other pleas, real or personal, within the said vill, suburbs and precincts of the same, before the said bailiffs in the said guildhall to be holden; from which time, by other several letters patents, or by some other our letters patents, and of our predecessors of this kingdom of England, the said vill of Gloucester was erected and brought into a city, enlarged also by the hundreds aforesaid annexed to it; and the bailiffs of the vill aforesaid were translated and altered into the mayor and sheriffs of the city aforesaid, and county of the same city: We therefore, willing to extend and establish the aforesaid privileges and jurisdictions of the aforesaid bailiffs within the vill aforesaid and precincts of the same, and through the whole city aforesaid, and county of the same city; and limits, liberties, and precincts of the same, into a mayor, bailiffs, and chamberlain of the city aforesaid, and sheriffs of the county of the same city, we will, and do, for us, our heirs and successors, grant to the mayor and burgesses of the city aforesaid, and their successors, that they the said mayor and burgesses, and their successors, may from time to time have a court within the city aforesaid, before the mayor or his deputy, the sheriffs and bailiffs of the said city for the time being, or any two or more of them, (so that the mayor or his deputy be one) on every Monday to be holden: And that the said mayor or his deputy, the aforesaid sheriffs or bailiffs for the time being, or any two or more of them, (so that the mayor or his deputy be one) may from time to time for ever hold in that county all the aforesaid pleas, suits, and plaints, as well of assize of novel disseisin, as of mort d'auncestre, and certificates of the same, as all other the said pleas, real and personal, of all lands or tenements, as well within the city aforesaid as the county of the same city, the precincts, liberties, and franchises of the same; and of all other matters and causes issuing, and to be issued, out of the city aforesaid, and county of the city, to be holden before the mayor or his deputy, and the sheriffs and bailiffs for the time being, or before any two or more of them, (so that the mayor or his deputy be one) on every Monday from time to time within the city aforesaid; and that they have cognizance of all the said pleas of assize and certificates, and all other pleas, and of all other things issuing within the said city and county of the same city; and that the mayor or his deputy, the sheriffs and bailiffs aforesaid, and any two or more of them, (so that the mayor or his deputy be one) may proceed in all and singular pleas, actions, suits, and plaints aforesaid, in that court moved or to be moved, prosecuted or to be prosecuted by such like brief, summons, and distresses, and other proceedings, judgments, and executions, according to the law and custom of the court in the guildhall of the city aforesaid hitherto observed, in as ample manner and form as in former times, any bailiffs of the vill of Gloucester, or any mayors, sheriffs, and stewards, of the city or vill of Gloucester, or any mayors, sheriffs, and bailiffs, and chamberlain of the city aforesaid, were wont lawfully to proceed in the said guildhall of the city aforesaid.

We will also, and do, for us, our heirs and successors, grant, by these presents, to the aforesaid mayor and burgesses of the city aforesaid, and their successors, that the bailiffs of the said city, and sheriffs of the county of the same city for the time being, and their successors, may have and hold all and singular the pleas aforesaid, for any matters and causes issuing within the said city and county thereof, and within the limits, liberties, and precincts of the same, in the tolsey court in the city aforesaid, from hour to hour, and day to day, to be holden before the said sheriffs and bailiffs in the same manner and form as it was formerly wont to be holden before the bailiffs of the said vill of Gloucester, or before the sheriffs and bailiffs of the city of Gloucester and county of the same; and that the said sheriffs and bailiffs for the time being, and their successors, in all actions and suits of debts, accounts, trespasses, detaining of chattels, actions on the case, and all other actions, plaints, pleas, and suits personal whatsoever, issuing or happening within the said city of Gloucester, the suburbs, and precincts of the same, or within the county of the same city, which have been moved or begun, or hereafter shall be moved and begin before the said sheriffs and bailiffs for the time being, or their successors, in the aforesaid tolsey court, may and shall have full power and authority by themselves, or by any of their bailiffs, in that part specially assigned by the precept and command of the said sheriffs, under the seal of their office, to the said bailiffs or sheriffs directed, or to be directed, may proceed against all and singular persons being defendants, against whom such plaints, pleas, or actions shall happen to be moved or laid in the aforesaid court, for defect of chattels or lands of the defendants within the city aforesaid, and county of the same city, and the limits, liberties, and precincts of the same, where they may be summoned, attached, or distrained, or their bodies taken; so that the sheriffs aforesaid proceed to hear and determine all and singular such actions, plaints, and pleas severally; and likewise to determine and deduce proceedings of judgment, and executions of judgments, as other sheriffs, bailiff or bailiffs, have in that place been heretofore lawfully accustomed.

Moreover, we will, and do, for us, our heirs and successors, grant, by these presents, to the aforesaid mayor and burgesses of the city aforesaid, and their successors, that the sheriffs aforesaid may and shall for ever hold a county court for the county of the said city, from month to month, to be holden on a Tuesday, and a law day twice in a year; once within a month after Easter, and again in a month after Michaelmas, as it was aforetime lawfully used to be holden; and that all things may there be done that are used to be done in the county court of any sheriff of the same county; and in the same manner and form, and by the same proceedings as have been hitherto used in other

county

county courts: And that the coroner of the city aforefaid, and others refpectively attending in thefe courts, fhall do, execute, and perform all and fingular offices belonging to their refpective places; and that the fheriffs of the county of the city aforefaid may have, ufe, and exercife all fuch power, jurifdiction, authority, and liberty, and all other things whatfoever belonging to the office of fheriff within the faid city and county, and the limits, liberties, and precincts of the fame, as any other fheriffs and bailiffs, of us and our heirs, within our kingdom of England, within their refpective bailiwicks, may have, or ought to ufe: And that we, our heirs and fucceffors, fhall for the future for ever direct, and caufe to be directed, all and fingular briefs, bills, precepts, and commands, of us, our heirs and fucceffors, which fhall in any matter, or for any caufe, or in and for any matters and caufes iffuing and happening within the city of Gloucefter aforefaid, or the county of the fame city, the limits, liberties, and precincts of the fame, to the county fheriffs of the city of Gloucefter, and to no other fheriffs: And that no other fheriff in the kingdom of England, or bailiff, or ferjeant of any fheriff in the faid kingdom (only excepted the aforefaid fheriffs of us and our heirs) for the county of the faid city, to be chofen and conftituted in manner and form aforefaid, and their bailiffs fhall enter the city aforefaid, in any wife to exercife and execute any thing whatfoever belonging to the office of a fheriff, (only excepted the fheriffs of the county of the city of Gloucefter, who are to keep a county court for the county of the city of Gloucefter, to be holden in the ufual place in the charter of king Richard the IIId fpecified): And that all the fheriffs of the county of the city of Gloucefter, and bailiffs of the fame, who ought at the going out of their office to give an account into the exchequer, belonging to us, our heirs aud fucceffors, ought every year to do it before the barons and treafurer of the exchequer of us, our heirs and fucceffors, or before the barons of the faid exchequer by their fufficient attorney or attornies, to be appointed by their letters patents under the feal of their office, to be directed to the barons aforefaid: And that no fheriff of the county of the city of Gloucefter fhall any way be compelled to come out of the limits of the faid county, to give an account of any thing belonging to their office, fo that his attorney or attornies would do it in manner and form aforefaid.

And whereas our aforefaid predeceffor Richard the IId, late king of England, by his letters patents made in the one and twentieth year of his reign, hath willed and ordained, that the bailiffs of the vill of Gloucefter for the time being, fhould have full power and authority to take all recognizances whatfoever between merchant and merchants, and execution thereon to be made according to the ftatute of merchants, and the ftatute of Acton Burnell lately fet forth: Whereas alfo, Richard the Third, in the firft year of his reign, by his letters patents hath willed and granted, that the aforefaid vill of Gloucefter, together with all villages and hamlets within the hundreds of Dudftone and King's Barton near Gloucefter, fhould be and remain one entire county by itfelf incorporate for ever in deed and in name diftinct; and that the bailiffs of the city aforefaid fhould for ever be fheriffs of the county of the faid vill of Gloucefter, doing and executing all things, belonging as well to the office of bailiffs as fheriffs within the faid vill and county of the fame; from which time the faid fheriffs have received, and were wont to receive recognizances of debts according to the form of the ftatute aforefaid: But by thofe letters patents there is no certain provifion in whofe hands the greater or leffer feal of the recognizances fhould be kept; we therefore, willing to reduce all things neceffary to be taken into thefe recognizances to a certainty, do will, and do, for us, our heirs and fucceffors, by thefe prefents, grant to the aforefaid mayor and burgeffes, and their fucceffors, that the fheriffs of the county of the city aforefaid for the time being, and the clerk affigned to take recognizances of debts, according to the form of the ftatute of merchants, and the ftatute made at Acton Burnell, may for ever have full power and authority to take and receive any recognizances whatfoever, and executions on the fame to be made according to the ftatute of merchants, and the ftatute at Acton Burnell, lately fet forth; and alfo do and execute all things within the city of Gloucefter and county of the fame city, which by virtue of the ftatutes, or either of them, may belong to any mayor, bailiff, officer, and to any clerk in any city or borough incorporate within this our kingdom of England, being appointed to take recognizances of debts, according to the form of the ftatutes aforefaid, or either of them; and that the faid fheriffs and clerk for the time being may, and fhall have, and by vertue of thefe prefents fhall make, affume, and apply one feal of two parts, one part of which fhall be called the greater, and the other the leffer part, henceforward to feal recognizances coming before them, according to the form of the ftatutes of merchants, and the ftatute of Acton Burnell lately fet forth; which feal fhall for ever hereafter be the king's feal, to feal the aforefaid recognizances to be taken within the city aforefaid, the greater part of which fhall always remain in the cuftody of the fheriffs of the county of the faid city for the time being, and the other part in the hands of the clerk appointed and deputed to write and enroll the recognizances aforefaid, according to the intention of thefe our letters patents: And that the town clerk of the city aforefaid for the time being, as long as he fhall continue in that office, may and fhall be the clerk, of us, our heirs and fucceffors, to take recognizances of debts according to the ftatutes aforefaid, or either of them, within the city aforefaid, and county, limits, liberties, and precincts of the fame; and to write and enroll them, and to keep all rolls and records, and to keep the leffer part of the feal aforefaid, and to do and execute all things which may be done and executed by any clerk appointed and deputed to take recognizances of debts according to the form of the ftatutes aforefaid, or either of them: And we do, for us, our heirs and fucceffors, appoint and ordain, without any brief in that cafe to be obtained, or any other election, the faid town clerk of the city aforefaid, clerk of us, our heirs and fucceffors, to write and enrol recognizances of debts within the city aforefaid, according to the form of the ftatute aforefaid, or either of them, and to keep the leffer part of the feal aforefaid, and to do all other things belonging to the office of any clerk appointed and deputed to take recognizances of debts, according to the form of the aforefaid ftatutes.

And farthermore, we, of our great and fpecial favour, and of our certain knowledge and meer motion, have granted and confirmed, and do, for us, our heirs and fucceffors, by thefe prefents, grant and confirm to the aforefaid mayor and burgeffes of the city aforefaid, and their fucceffors, that the mayor and burgeffes of the city aforefaid for the time being, may from time to time for ever, have and enjoy all and fingular chattles of outlaws, for whatfoever caufe, being brought before any juftices of the peace whatfoever, and the chattles of felons and fugitives, deodands, and all manner of fines and amerciaments of all burgeffes, and their heirs and fucceffors, of and in the faid city, limits, and precincts of the fame, although the faid burgefs or burgeffes be a fervant or officer of us and our heirs, as alfo of all refidents in the city aforefaid, and precincts of the fame, and their heirs and fucceffors, to be determined before us and our heirs, and the juftices of labourers and tradefmen, the treafurer and barons of the exchequer of us and our heirs, and before the clerk of the market of us and our heirs, and the juftices appointed to hear and determine, and before other juftices, officers, and minifters, of us and our heirs whatfoever; all forfeits made, and to be made, for or through any caufe whatfoever, to be levied and taken by the fheriffs and bailiffs aforefaid for the time being, without any lett, impediment, or fcandal, from us or our heirs, or from the chancellor, treafurer and barons of the exchequer, juftices, fheriffs, or any other of our officers and minifters whatfoever: And that the aforefaid mayor and burgeffes, and their fucceffors, may have all goods and chattles whatfoever, taken or to be taken, with any perfon whatfoever, and found with the faid perfon, being before a juftice of the peace within the faid city, fuburbs, limits, and precincts of the fame.

And whereas the mayor and burgeffes of the city aforefaid are day by day at great cofts and charges for the maintenance and reparations of the gates and pavements of the faid city, and the two wharfs called the Old and New Key, for the lading and unlading of fhips and boats by the river of Severn, thither arriving; as alfo, of feveral bridges called the Weft Bridge and the Foreign Bridge, of one of which great part is fealed and parjetted, being fixteen foot high, or thereabouts, built with divers arches and vaults, and half a mile in length, or thereabouts: And whereas, in confideration that the burgeffes of the city aforefaid have been oppreffed with very many burthens and payments, and divers grants by feveral letters patents under the great feal of England, have been made by our predeceffors and progenitors, for divers terms now ended, to the bailiffs and burgeffes of the city of Gloucefter aforefaid, that they fhould take of all things coming to be fold at the faid vill divers and feveral cuftoms, viz. (among others) for every horfe or mare, ox or cow, coming thither to be fold, one penny, and feveral other cuftoms for other things paffing to be fold through the gates of the faid city; as alfo, other cuftoms and tolls, moorage, pontage, and tonage; which cuftoms and tolls, as well by land as by water, and fome other duties, the burgeffes of the city aforefaid have received, and been wont to receive: And whereas, by a ftatute made in parliament of Henry the VIIth late king of England, at Weftminfter, on the 25th day of February, in the 19th year of the reign of the faid king, it was enacted, that whatfoever perfon or perfons, of what degree, eftate, or condition foever they be, or fhall be, who henceforth fhall take of any of his majefty's fubjects any impofitions for any troughs or boats, or any other veffels, for the carriage of any goods or merchandize in or upon the river of Severn, fhall incur the penalties and forfeitures limited in the faid ftatute: In which ftatute it is farther provided, that if any perfon or perfons, fpiritual or temporal, or body incorporate, before the moft honourable

nourable the lords of the king's moſt honourable privy council, in the ſtar chamber at Weſtminſter, at any time before the feaſt of the aſcenſion of our Lord, which ſhall then be in the year of our Lord one thouſand four hundred fifty and five, ſhall appear, and by ſufficient proof ſhall exhibit his or their title or claim to any due or impoſt to be levied and received for any goods or merchandize carried in or upon the ſaid river of Severn, that then, after the title and claim produced before the lords of the council aforeſaid for the time being, and by the decree of the ſaid lords in the ſtar chamber approved, it ſhall be lawful for any ſuch perſons whatſoever, having ſuch lawful and approved title, to receive all ſuch dues and impoſitions of any of the king's liege ſubjects, for any ſuch boat or veſſel paſſing on the river of Severn, as ſhall be admitted and allocated by the decree of the lords of the council aforeſaid, as by the aforeſaid ſtatute fully appears: And whereas, after and before the aforeſaid feaſt of the aſcenſion of our Lord, according to the proviſion of the ſtatute aforementioned, the mayor and burgeſſes of the vill of Glouceſter then being, exhibited their petition to the moſt reverend father in God, William, then archbiſhop of Canterbury, and lord chancellor of England, and the reſt of the lords of the council of king Henry the VIIth in the ſtar chamber; by which petition, they the ſaid mayor and burgeſſes, in conſideration of the annual coſts and payments with which they, for the repair of the great bridge of the aforeſaid vill, built with arches and ſtone vaults on the aforeſaid river of Severn, and of the havens of the ſaid city on the bank of the ſaid river, and for divers other good cauſes and conſiderations mentioned in the petition aforeſaid, have laid claim and title to divers tolls, ſums of pence, impoſitions, and cuſtoms, time out of mind, due to them and their predeceſſors, and by them levied and taken, of and for boats and other veſſels paſſing in or upon the river Severn under the bridges aforeſaid, and for the goods and merchandize in them carried, and for the goods and merchandize unladen at the havens aforeſaid, towards the payment of the annual expences aforeſaid; upon which, at the time of Eaſter, being the 29th day of April, in the twentieth year of the reign of king Henry the VIIth, in the ſtar chamber at Weſtminſter aforeſaid, before the aforeſaid lord chancellor of England, and other lords of the council of the ſaid king being then and there preſent, (the aforeſaid petition of the ſaid mayor and burgeſſes of the vill of Glouceſter being often read, and very well underſtood) as alſo the depoſitions and examinations, and other proofs and evidences, as well of the part of the aforeſaid mayor and burgeſſes of the vill of Glouceſter, as of the mayor and citizens of the city of Coventry, and the burgeſſes and inhabitants of the vill of Bewdly and Tewkſbury, and other villages and places, being produced and read publickly, heard and fully underſtood, upon mature and diligent deliberation, by the aforeſaid lord chancellor, and the reſt of the council of the ſaid late king then and there preſent, by vertue of the ſaid ſtatute in that parliament ſet forth, and by vertue and authority of the ſtatute given and granted to that council, it was ordained, decreed, and adjudged, concerning the matters ſpecified in the petition aforeſaid, by the aſſent and conſent, as well of the mayor and burgeſſes of the vill of Glouceſter, as of the mayor and citizens of the city of Coventry, and of the burgeſſes and inhabitants of the vills of Bewdly and Tewkſbury, in manner and form following, viz. that the mayor and burgeſſes of the ſaid vill of Glouceſter, and their ſucceſſors, ſhould have and take of all citizens of the ſaid city of Coventry, and their ſucceſſors, towards the payment of the fee farm of the ſaid vill, and other expences in the decree aforementioned, for every hogſhead of wine, and ton of other merchandizes, paſſing in any boat, trough, or veſſel, from or through the ſaid vill of Glouceſter towards the city of Worceſter, three-pence; and for every hogſhead of wine and ton of other merchandize unladen in the ſaid vill of Glouceſter, at or upon the wharf, key, or land, three-pence, without any thing to be paid for the carriage of the ſaid goods, by carts, drays, or horſes, for the uſe of the mayor and burgeſſes, or without any ſum of pence to be aſked or received, by the name of any cuſtom whatſoever, for the ſaid wines, or the veſſels wherein they were laden, in or upon the river aforeſaid, paſſing at, by, or under, or about the bridge aforeſaid; or for any of them bound with ropes and hooks near the adjacent bridge, or by any art or ingenuity, to be drawn and conducted under the bridge, into any place within the ſaid vill of Glouceſter, and the privileges and franchiſes of the ſame: And it was farther adjudged, decreed, and ordained, by the lord chancellor and lords of the council aforeſaid, that the mayor and burgeſſes of the ſaid vill of Glouceſter, and their ſucceſſors, ſhould for ever have and take for cuſtom the like number of pence of all other perſons, for every hogſhead of wine and ton of other merchandize, to be unladen in the ſaid vill, the vill of Tewkſbury, together with the burgeſſes and inhabitants within the franchiſes of the ſame; and other cities, vills, burroughs, or perſons, being excepted, who have made compoſition with the mayor and burgeſſes aforeſaid, with ſome other proviſions for the leſſening and eaſing of thoſe goods for which the cuſtom was formerly paid, although things might be by water exported, not at all altering the property, as is ſpecified in the decree aforeſaid; and that the mayor and burgeſſes aforeſaid ſhould have, of every boat or veſſel paſſing from one ſide or other under the ſaid bridge, laden with timber, board, or lath, four-pence, for every time it ſhall paſs by or under the ſaid bridge, and for every boat or veſſel laden with firewood or fewel, two-pence, without any cuſtom or toll to be paid for the ſame; always provided that that decree extend not to the detriment of the vill of Tewkſbury, nor the burgeſſes, nor any perſons within the ſaid vill priviledged and excepted; provided alſo, that the aforeſaid mayor and burgeſſes of Glouceſter ſhould take no cuſtom for any houſhold neceſſaries, nor any thing bought or provided for the private uſe of a family, being not to be merchandized: And moreover, the mayor and burgeſſes ſhall have, for every ton of wheat paſſing from either ſide under the aforeſaid bridge, being to be made merchandize of, three-pence, and for all other grain, two-pence; and this to be paid, until ſome perſons can ſufficiently prove before the chancellor aforeſaid in the ſaid council, that leſs than three-pence ſhould be levied and taken for the ſame, ſo that this proof be made within ſeven years: And then there was a further ordinance made for the toll of corn in the place aforeſaid by the council aforeſaid, as by the aforeſaid decree of the lord chancellor aforeſaid, and the lords of the king's council then and there preſent in the ſtar chamber aforeſaid, made the day and year aforeſaid, which we have looked into, as plainly and fully appears: We therefore willing to confirm, approve, and ratify, all the kinds of dues, tolls, cuſtoms, and ſums of pence, by the mayor and burgeſſes of the city of Glouceſter heretofore, by vertue of the decree aforeſaid, or any other ways lawfully received and levied, to them the aforeſaid mayor and burgeſſes, will, and do, for us, our heirs and ſucceſſors, by theſe preſents, grant to the aforeſaid mayor and burgeſſes, and their ſucceſſors, that it may be lawful for the ſaid mayor and burgeſſes, and their ſucceſſors, for the time being, from time to time for ever, to have, receive, take, and levy, for oats, bread-corn, and all ſorts of grain and other merchandizes, and things to be ſold, brought and carried to the city aforeſaid; and for all boats paſſing there, or lying in the river of Severn, and for the goods wherewith they are laden or unladen at, or upon the haven aforeſaid, ſuch and ſo many cuſtoms, tolls, and reaſonable ſums of pence, as by the burgeſſes or bailiffs in their reſpective turns have, by vertue of thoſe grants, or any other lawful way, been heretofore received and levied.

And whereas, from the time of the making theſe letters patents, in the firſt year of the reign of the ſaid Richard the IIId, although by theſe letters patents the aforeſaid vill of Glouceſter was made a city, two burgeſſes only were ſummoned at all parliaments elected by the major part of the burgeſſes to ſerve and ſit in parliament, never any other were choſen knights for the county of the ſame city; and yet it was a cuſtom in other cities that two were choſen burgeſſes for ſuch a city, and two more knights for the county of the ſame city: We therefore for the future, to avoid and aboliſh all ſcruple and doubt in that caſe, do will and ordain, and for us, our heirs and ſucceſſors, by theſe preſents, grant to the mayor and burgeſſes of the city aforeſaid, and their ſucceſſors, that upon ſummons of any parliament of us, our heirs or ſucceſſors, it may and ſhall be lawful for the mayor and burgeſſes of the city aforeſaid, and their ſucceſſors, and the major part of them, at a full country court next after the ſummons to be holden in that caſe, lately made and provided, to elect, nominate, and return two only diſcreet men of the ſaid city to be burgeſſes for that city and county of the ſame city; and that thoſe two burgeſſes ſo choſen, ſhall ſerve and ſit in parliament as burgeſſes of the city aforeſaid, and knights of the county of the ſame: And that the mayor and burgeſſes of the city aforeſaid ſhall in no wiſe be forced or compelled to elect, nominate and return for burgeſſes of the city aforeſaid, and knights of the county of the ſame; but they two only ſhall ſerve and ſit in parliament, who ſhall from time to time be lawfully elected and returned by the mayor and burgeſſes of the city aforeſaid, or the major part of them, according to the form of the ſtatute in that caſe made and provided, as before the time of the reign of king Richard the IIId, the like burgeſſes of parliament for the burrough or vill of Glouceſter, were wont to be nominated, elected and returned, and no otherwiſe.

And whereas the bailiffs and burgeſſes of the vill of Glouceſter of old held the ſaid burrough, with the appurtenances of the kings of England in fee farm, by the yearly payment of ſixty and five pounds of lawful money of England, we do, for us, our heirs and ſucceſſors, by theſe preſents, grant, and of our ſpecial grace and favour, give and confirm to the mayor and burgeſſes of the city aforeſaid, and their ſucceſſors, the ſaid whole city of Glouceſter, with all and ſingular its privileges, rights and appurtenances, having been hitherto uſed to have been paid to us, our predeceſſors, and progenitors, and remain to be paid to us, our heirs and ſucceſſors, in as ample manner and form as they were heretofore granted to the mayor and burgeſſes

gesses of the city aforesaid, and their predecessors, by whatsoever name or names of incorporation, or by any former charters or letters patents of any of our anceſtors and progenitors, and as the said mayor and burgesses, and their predecessors, by vertue or pretext of any charter or letters patents, have heretofore lawfully holden and possessed it.

And we do further, of our special grace and favour, for us, our heirs and successors, by these presents, grant, approve, ratify and confirm to the aforesaid mayor and burgesses of the city aforesaid, and their successors, all and singular such like manors, messuages, lands and tenements, court leets, assize of frank pledge, sheriffs courts, and all other courts whatsoever, markets, fairs, customs, liberties, franchises, freedoms, fines, and amerciaments, exemptions, jurisdictions, and inheritances whatsoever, as the said mayor and burgesses now lawfully enjoy and use, or that they, or either of them, or their predecessors, by any names of incorporation, or by vertue and pretext of any charters or letters patents by any of our predecessors and progenitors, late kings and queens of England, made and granted, were wont to have, use, and enjoy, before the said surrender was made; or by pretext of any law, prescription, or custom, or any other lawful way, right, or title, had and accustomed, although they or some of them have been ill used or abused, or any way lost and forfeited, yet to be kept and enjoyed by the aforesaid mayor and burgesses of the city aforesaid, and their successors for ever, only paying to us, our heirs and successors, such fee farm and sums of pence as have been hitherto due and used to be paid: Wherefore we will, and do, for us, our heirs and successors, by these presents, by strict injunction, command, that the aforesaid mayor and burgesses, and their successors, may for ever have, hold, use, exercise, and enjoy, all and singular the aforesaid courts, and all other authorities, jurisdictions, franchises, and immunities, together with all manors, lands, tenements, and inheritances aforesaid, according to the tenor and effect of these our letters patents, without any lett or impediment from us, our heirs or successors, or any justices of the peace, sheriffs, or other officers or ministers of us, our heirs or successors whatsoever, any surrender of former charters to the contrary notwithstanding.

Being also unwilling that the said mayor and burgesses of the city aforesaid, or any of them, or their successors, should by occasion of the premisses, by us, our heirs or successors, justices, sheriffs, or any other officers or ministers of us, our heirs or successors whatsoever, be molested, vexed, aggrieved, or any way disturbed, we will, and by these presents, for us, our heirs and successors, strictly command the treasurer, chancellor, and barons of the exchequer at Westminster, and other officers and justices of us, our heirs and successors, our attornies general, and attornies in any courts whatsoever for the time being, and all officers and ministers of us, our heirs and successors, that they and every of them do not prosecute or continue, or cause to be prosecuted and continued, any brief or summons de quo warranto, or any other brief, briefs, or processes, against the said mayor and burgesses of the city aforesaid, for any causes, things, or matters, offences, claims, or usurpations, or either of them, duly claimed, attempted, had, or usurped, before the day of the date of the making of these our letters patents.

We willing also that they the said mayor and burgesses of the city aforesaid should not, by any justices, officers, or ministers aforesaid, in and for the due use, claim, or abuse of any liberties, franchises, or jurisdictions, within the city aforesaid, or the precincts of the same, be molested, aggrieved, or hindered, or compelled to answer any of them before the day of the date of these our letters patents, we will, and we do, by these presents, for us, our heirs and successors, grant to the mayor and burgesses of the city aforesaid, and their successors, that this present charter so generally made, may and shall be of the same vertue and effect as if all the premisses above specified were specially and particularly in this our charter expressed; and that it be understood and adjudged in the best and most favourable sense on the part of the mayor and burgesses of the city aforesaid, and their successors, though it might be toward us, our heirs and successors, better understood, any omission, defect, repugnancy, or contradiction in the same to the contrary notwithstanding.

Nevertheless, we will that the justices of assize of nisi prius and general goal delivery in the county of Gloucester, as also the justices of the peace of the said county being assigned, or to be assigned, to keep their sessions, and also the sheriffs of the county of Gloucester, they and either of them may freely enter the said city to keep their sessions concerning any matter or business happening or issuing without the county of the city, and within the county of Gloucester, as they were wont before these times, and before the letters patents of the said late king Richard the IIId, made in the first year of his reign, this present grant in any wise notwithstanding.

Moreover we will, and by these presents declare, that all and singular justices assigned to keep the peace in the county of Gloucester for the future for ever, may take and receive within the said city, informations, recognizances, and all other acts, matters, and things, as being justices of the peace they may any where do; and that all commissioners of sewers, and commissioners for charitable uses, may execute their respective commissions within the said city of Gloucester, for all matters and things whatsoever issuing without the county of the city, and within the county of Gloucester, this present grant of ours in any wise notwithstanding.

Always provided, and we will, and do, for us, our heirs and successors, by these presents, firmly enjoin, order, and command, all and singular the mayor, recorder, town clerk, aldermen, capital burgesses, and all other our officers and ministers of our city aforesaid, and all others their deputies; as also, all justices of the peace of us, our heirs and successors, within that city, by vertue and according to the tenor of these our letters patents, or charters heretofore made, for the future to be nominated and elected, shall, before they or either of them be admitted to enter upon the execution of their respective offices, take as well the corporal oath, commonly called the oath of obedience, as the corporal oath, commonly called the oath of supremacy, upon the holy gospel, before such person or persons as shall be assigned and appointed to administer such oaths.

And we farther will and declare our royal pleasure and intention, that no recorder or town clerk of our city aforesaid shall be admitted to the execution of his or their respective offices, before they or either of them be or shall be approved of by us, our heirs or successors, any thing in these presents contained to the contrary notwithstanding.

Always provided, that those letters patents, or any thing in them contained, shall not extend to be expounded or interpreted to grant the hundreds of Dudstone and King's Barton near the city of Gloucester aforesaid, or the villages, parishes, hamlets, or any other places within the said hundreds, to be a parcel of the county of the city aforesaid, as in former times have been, or to give, grant, and confirm to the aforesaid mayor and burgesses of that city, and their successors, any liberties, privileges, franchises, immunities, jurisdictions, powers, profits, or advantages whatsoever, to be had, taken, and enjoyed within the said hundreds, or any of them, or within any parishes, villages, or hamlets within the said hundreds, or either of them; but we will and declare our royal intention, that those hundreds, and all inhabitants of the same, or either of them, and all villages, places, and hamlets whatsoever, within the said hundreds and hamlets, and every part and parcel of them, or either of them, shall henceforth for ever remain parcels of our said county of Gloucester to all intents and purposes; and that all things, jurisdictions, liberties, privileges, powers, and authorities, by any of our progenitors and predecessors, kings or queens of England, heretofore granted to the vill or city of Gloucester aforesaid, or corporation of the same, by any name or names within the said hundreds, to be had, taken and enjoyed, to be void and of none effect, as for and concerning the said hundreds and either of them, and all inhabitants of the same, according to the form of the statute in that case made and provided, any thing in these presents contained to the contrary in any wise notwithstanding.

Always provided that those letters patents and this said charter and grant of liberties and privileges, or any thing in them contained, be not any way prejudicial to the dean and chapter of the cathedral church of the city aforesaid, or their successors; but we will, and by these presents declare our royal intention, that the said dean and chapter, and their successors, may from time to time for the future for ever hold and enjoy all such rights, privileges, franchises, jurisdictions, and immunities whatsoever, as the said dean and chapter do now lawfully enjoy, and are rightfully due and belonging to the said church, any thing in these presents contained to the contrary notwithstanding.

Always provided, that if at any time or times it shall seem expedient to us, our heirs or successors, to remove the mayor or any of the aldermen or burgesses of the common council, or any officer or officers within the said city or county of the same, (except the chamberlain, sword bearer, and serjeants at mace) and ease him or them of his or their respective office or offices, and we, our heirs or successors, shall signify such will or pleasure of us, our heirs or successors, by order to be made in the privy council, of us, our heirs or successors, that then immediately from and after notice of such order given to the mayor and burgesses of the city aforesaid for the time being, they the said mayor and burgesses, if it be not a mayor to be removed, and if it be, the aldermen and common council of the city aforesaid, or the major part of them that shall be there present, shall proceed to the election of a new mayor, alderman, burgess of the common council, or other officer or officers as abovesaid, removed, or to be removed, as if he or they had died in the said office or offices, any thing in these presents contained to the contrary notwithstanding.

In witness whereof we have caused these our letters to be made patents. Witness ourself at Westminster this 18th day of April, in the four and twentieth year of our reign.

By Writ of Privy Seal.——PIGGOTT.

NUMB.

NUMBER VII.

The CHARTER *of Foundation of the Bishoprick of* GLOUCESTER.

HENRY the VIIIth, by the grace of God, king of England and France, defender of the faith, lord of Ireland, and supreme head on earth of the church of England, to all to whom these presents shall come, greeting: Whereas the great convent or monastery, which, whilst in being, was called the monastery of St. Peter of Gloucester, and all and singular its mannors, lordships, messuages, lands, tenements, hereditaments, endowments, and possessions, for certain special and urgent causes, were, by Gabriel Moreton, prior of the said abbey or monastery and the convent thereof, lately given and granted to us and our heirs for ever, as by the deed of the said prior and convent, under their common conventual seal inrolled in our court of chancery, fully appears; by vertue whereof we are rightfully seized in our demesne, as of fee, of and in the scite, bounds and precinct of the said convent or monastery; and of all and singular manors, lordships, messuages, lands, tenements, hereditaments, endowments, and possessions of the said late prior and convent; and we being so seized, and being influenced by divine goodness, and desiring above all things, that true religion, and the true worship of God may not only not be abolished, but intirely restored to the primitive and genuine rule of simplicity; and that all those enormities may be corrected into which the lives and profession of the monks for a long time had deplorably lapsed, have, as far as human frailty will permit, endeavoured to the utmost that, for the future, the pure word of God may be taught in that place, good discipline observed, youth freely instructed in learning, the infirmities of old age relieved with necessaries, alms given to poor christians, highways and bridges repaired; and that all offices of piety in every kind may there abound, and thence spread to the neighbourhood far and near, to the glory of God, and the common good and benefit of our subjects.

Wherefore, considering that the scite of the said late monastery of St. Peter of Gloucester, in which many famous monuments of our renowned ancestors, kings of England, are erected, is a very fit and proper place for erecting, instituting and establishing an episcopal see, and an episcopal church, of one bishop, one dean a presbyter, and six prebendaries presbyters, for the service of Almighty God for ever, we have decreed, and by these presents we do decree, the scite of the said monastery of St. Peter in Gloucester, and the place and church thereof, to be an episcopal see, and to be created, erected and established a cathedral church; and the said cathedral church we do, by these presents, fully and indeed create, erect, found, ordain, make, appoint and establish, of one bishop, one dean a presbyter, six prebendaries presbyters, which we will and command, by these presents, from henceforth unalterably, to continue and endure, and to be established for ever.

And we also will and ordain, by these presents, that the said cathedral church shall be from henceforth for ever a cathedral church and see episcopal; and that our whole town of Gloucester be from henceforth and for ever a city; and we will and decree that the same be from henceforth for ever nominated and called the city of Gloucester: And whereas our said late town or vill of Gloucester, together with all and singular the vills and hamlets of Dudston and King's Barton near Gloucester, have for a long time past been an entire county by itself, rightfully incorporated in deed and name; and whereas one Thomas Payne, now mayor of our vill aforesaid, and the burgesses of our said late vill of Gloucester, now have, hold, and do enjoy several liberties, franchises and privileges within the said late vill of Gloucester, and within the county of the same vill; and the predecessors of them, the said now mayor and burgesses, within our said late vill of Gloucester, and within the county of the same our late vill of Gloucester, by letters patents of our progenitors, by use, prescription, or otherwise, in what manner soever had, held and enjoyed, the same as by right, and by the laws of our kingdom they lawfully might use, hold and enjoy the same; we will, and by these presents, do grant, that now our city of Gloucester, together with all and singular the vills and hamlets of Dudston and King's Barton, be, and for ever hereafter shall be, the county of our city of Gloucester, by the same meets and bounds by which our said late vill of Gloucester, together with all and singular the vills and hamlets of Dudston and King's Barton aforesaid, is limited and known; and we do, by these presents, ordain, make, erect and establish our said city of Gloucester, together with the vills and hamlets of Dudston and King's Barton aforesaid, one entire county in deed and name, distinct and absolutely separated from our county of Gloucester for ever.

And out of our farther grace, we will, and by these presents do grant, that the aforesaid Thomas of the said city, and the now mayor, the burgesses of the said city, and their successors, for ever have, hold and enjoy, and have full power and authority to have, hold and enjoy within our county aforesaid, and within the county of our city aforesaid, so many, such, as great and like liberties, courts leet, views of frank pledge, and all things belonging to view of frank pledge, return of writs, rights, jurisdictions, franchises, and privileges whatsoever, as many, as great, and in like cases, and in the same manner and form as the now mayor and burgesses of our city of Gloucester, or any one, or any of their predecessors within our said late vill of Gloucester, had, held or enjoyed, or ought for any reason, or in any manner whatsoever, to have, hold or enjoy.

And the said city of Gloucester, and all the county of the said city, and all our county of Gloucester, as the same is by meets and bounds limited and known, from all jurisdiction, authority and diocese, as well of the bishop of Worcester as of the bishop of York and bishop of Hereford for the time being, and their successors, we do separate, divide, exempt, exonerate, and, by these presents, do free and discharge; and we do adjoin and unite all episcopal jurisdiction, as well as all profits, emoluments and hereditaments whatsoever, right or jurisdiction episcopal, belonging, appertaining, or arising within our said city of Gloucester, or county of the said city, and within the whole county of Gloucester, to the bishop of Gloucester, to be by us named and elected by these our letters patents, and to his successors for ever, bishops of Gloucester, and to the bishoprick of Gloucester: And we do by these presents, make and ordain the said city and county to be the diocese of Gloucester; and we will and ordain that it be for ever hereafter nominated and called the diocese of Gloucester; and all that diocese of Gloucester, and every part thereof, we will and ordain to be of the province of Canterbury, and so for ever hereafter to be nominated, reputed and taken, to all intents and purposes, and in the same manner as the diocese of Worcester was, and was taken and reputed to be.

And because our vill of Bristol which is situate and being within the bounds and limits of our county of Gloucester, is a county of itself, and is part within the diocese of Bath and Wells, and part within the diocese of Worcester, therefore, to prevent and take away all ambiguity and doubt hereafter, we will, ordain and appoint, and by these presents do grant, that all that part of our vill and county of Bristol which heretofore was in the diocese of Worcester, be from this time forward, and for ever, in the diocese of Gloucester, to all intents and purposes, in the same manner as it was wont to be within the episcopal jurisdiction of Worcester.

And to the end that this our intention may obtain due and ample effect, we very much confiding in the knowledge, good manners, probity and virtue of our well-beloved chaplain, John Wakeman, clerk, do nominate and elect, and by these presents we do elect, nominate and create him the said John bishop of Gloucester: And we will, and by these presents do grant and ordain, that the said bishop be a body corporate in deed and in name: And we do by these presents declare, accept, ordain, make and constitute him a body corporate for ever, and that he have a perpetual succession, and that he and his successors, by the name of bishop of Gloucester, shall be called and nominated; and that he and his successors by and under that name, may prosecute, claim and plead, and be impleaded, defend and be defended, answer and be answered, in all the courts and places of law, of us, our heirs and successors whatsoever, and elsewhere; and in all and singular causes, actions, suits, writs and plaints, real, personal, or mixed, as well temporal as spiritual, and in all other things, causes and matters whatsoever; and by that name to take, receive, enjoy and acquire any manors, lordships, lands, tenements, rectories, pensions, portions, and other hereditaments whatsoever; possessions, profits and emoluments, as well spiritual and ecclesiastical as temporal, and all other things whatsoever, by our letters patents to the aforesaid bishop and his successors, by us, our heirs, in due manner to be made, or which shall be given or granted by any other person or persons, according to our laws, or the laws of any of our heirs or successors; and that he and they may, and can have full power and authority to give, alien, or demise, and generally all other things to receive and do, in the like and in the same manner and form as any other bishop or bishops of our kingdom of England may, or can receive, or do, but not otherwise, nor in any other manner.

And because we will that our said bishop of Gloucester and his successors be honourably endowed, we give, and by these presents do grant to the said bishop, all that our hall covered with lead, commonly called the leaden hall, one room or pantry, one buttery, with one kitchen, two little houses for putting meat, one square pool or stew for keeping of fish, to which fresh water runs, situate at the east end of a certain hall, a large bed chamber where the servants of the late abbot did use to eat, situate at the west end of the said hall; and also, one pantry, one buttery, one office under ground, with the way leading thereto, situate on the south part of the aforesaid great bed chamber; and also a certain square or void place containing in length by estimation two perches, and in breadth one perch and

 three

three foot, adjoining to the ſaid great bed chamber; and alſo, one other bed chamber commonly called the ſquare bed chamber, ſituate on the north part of the great bed chamber, with three other bed chambers built over the ſaid ſquare bed chamber, and one other great bed chamber where the abbot of the ſaid monaſtery did uſe to eat, with one pantry, one buttery, and one office under ground, ſituate and being at the end of the ſaid great bed chamber; and alſo, one gallery ſituate at the ſouth-eaſt end of the ſaid bed chamber; and alſo, one bed chamber ſituate on the ſouth part of the ſaid bed chamber, and one bed chamber ſituate on the ſouth part of the ſaid gallery, with three bed chambers built all together, and ſituate on the north part of the ſaid gallery; and alſo, all thoſe three inner bed chambers with one middle room, one chapel, and another gallery joining to the ſaid three chambers, being the ſaid late abbot's own apartment, on the north end of the ſaid great bed chamber where the late abbot did uſe to eat, and on the ſouth ſide of the ſaid bed chamber; as alſo, one other hall, one pantry, one buttery, one kitchen, and two bed chambers, ſituate at the eaſt end of the ſaid gallery; and all and ſingular chambers, houſes, edifices, buildings, offices under ground, and other offices whatſoever, ſituate or built under or over the ſaid halls, bed chambers, galleries, and all and ſingular other buildings under or over the premiſſes, or any part thereof; and all that flower garden, containing in length by eſtimation ſix perch and ten foot, and in breadth ſeven perch thirteen foot and a half; which garden reaches and extends itſelf to the three inner chambers and other buildings which was the abbot's own apartment, and all and ſingular meſſuages, dwellings, houſes, buildings, ſtructures, with the ground and ſoil thereto belonging, gardens, orchards, void places, walls, and all and ſingular other hereditaments that are known by the name or names of the abbot's lodgings, or ſituate and being within all that precinct, circuit and encloſure known or called the abbot's lodgings; which ſaid circuit or encloſure in the ſouth part contains by eſtimation nine perches and ten foot, and in the north part nine perch and ſix foot, and on the weſt end eight perch nine foot and eight inches, and at the eaſt end eight perch and ſixteen foot, each perch containing eighten foot and a half and three inches; which ſaid hall, houſes, buildings, galleries, walks, and all and ſingular other the premiſſes; and alſo, all the lands and ſoil whereon the ſame ſtand, are ſituate, lying and being within the precinct of the ſaid late abbey or monaſtery: And we do alſo give, and by theſe preſents grant to the ſaid biſhop, all that ſtable, commonly called the abbot's ſtable, containing in length four perch eight foot and a half, and in breadth one perch and four foot; and alſo, one garden being at the eaſt end of the church-yard, containing in length ſix perch ſeventeen foot and a half, and in breadth ſix perch and ſixteen foot; and alſo, that houſe commonly called the wood barton, containing in length one hundred and eight foot, and in breadth thirty-four foot; and alſo, two other ſtables, two ſlaughter houſes, and one dog kennel, containing in length eighty-four foot, and in breadth thirty foot; which ſaid ſtables, ſlaughter houſes, and all and ſingular the premiſſes are ſituated and lie in the pariſh of St. Mary de Lode in our ſaid city of Glouceſter without the precinct of the ſaid monaſtery; and alſo, free ingreſs, egreſs and regreſs, and all manner of other liberties and benefits, of going, returning, carrying and recarrying to and from all and ſingular the places aforeſaid, and all other the premiſſes, and of doing all other things at all times of the year, at the will and pleaſure of the ſaid biſhop and his ſucceſſors; to have and to hold all and ſingular the aforeſaid halls, chambers, galleries, walks, offices, ſtables, houſes, edifices, and all and ſingular other the premiſſes to the ſaid biſhop and his ſucceſſors; to be held of us and our ſucceſſors as of free alms: And we will that the ſaid meſſuages, dwellings, halls, chambers, and all and ſingular other the premiſſes be for ever hereafter taken to be nominated and called the palace of the biſhop of Glouceſter and his ſucceſſors.

And moreover, and by theſe preſents we do ordain, that the ſaid cathedral church from henceforth forward for ever ſhall be the cathedral church and ſee epiſcopal of the ſaid John biſhop of Glouceſter, and of his ſucceſſors biſhops of Glouceſter; and the ſaid cathedral church we do by theſe preſents adorn with the honours, dignities and enſigns of an epiſcopal ſee; and the ſaid epiſcopal ſee we do by theſe preſents give and grant to the ſaid John and his ſucceſſors, to have and to hold to the ſaid John and his ſucceſſors for ever.

And farthermore, of our farther grace, we will and ordain, and by theſe preſents do grant, that the biſhop of Glouceſter that now is, and every one of his ſucceſſors, amongſt other things already mentioned, may, and can from time to time nominate, depute and appoint, one vicar general or vicars general, commiſſary or commiſſaries, regiſter or regiſters, in and through the whole dioceſe of Glouceſter, as the ſame by meets and bounds is known and limited, in the ſame manner as the biſhop of Worceſter might, ought, and was wont to nominate and appoint them; and that ſuch vicar general, commiſſary and commiſſaries, regiſter and regiſters, ſo by the biſhop hereafter to be nominated and deputed, and every one of them, all and ſingular profits and emoluments to their reſpective offices now belonging, may and have full power and authority to collect, receive and have, in and through the ſaid city, in manner as the vicar, commiſſary and regiſter of the biſhop of Worceſter for the time being heretofore might, was wont, or accuſtomed to collect, receive, or have, any grants or commiſſions by the ſaid now biſhop of Worceſter, or any of his predeceſſors or ſucceſſors already made, granted, or done, or to be made, granted or done, notwithſtanding.

And moreover we will, and by theſe preſents do ordain, that the aforeſaid John, and his ſucceſſors, biſhops of Glouceſter aforeſaid, may, can and ought to exerciſe, perform and uſe all and all manner of juriſdiction, power and authority, as well ordinary as extraordinary within the cathedral church of Glouceſter and dioceſe aforeſaid, from this time forth and for ever, in as ample manner and form as the biſhop of Worceſter by our laws might, could, or ought to exerciſe, perform and uſe.

And we farther will that the ſaid John biſhop of Glouceſter, and his ſucceſſors biſhops of Glouceſter, from henceforth and for ever have one or more authentic ſeal or ſeals, for the doing of all matters and buſineſſes, which is to ſerve and be of the ſame effect in law, in the ſame manner and form as the biſhop of Weſtminſter now has, or may have.

And we will that the cathedral church aforeſaid be filled and adorned with fit perſons in all places and degrees; and we by theſe preſents do make and ordain our well beloved chaplain, William Jennyns, batchelor in divinity, to be the firſt original and modern dean of the ſaid cathedral church, and that he the ſaid dean, and every of his ſucceſſors to be by us named, have and poſſeſs the firſt place of dignity in the ſaid cathedral church next to the ſaid biſhop; and that our well beloved chaplain, Nicholas Wotton, archdeacon of Glouceſter, and every one of his ſucceſſors, by the biſhop of Glouceſter to that archdeaconry henceforth to be nominated and choſen, have and poſſeſs the ſecond place of dignity in the ſaid catheral church; and our beloved chaplain, Richard Brown, clerk, batchelor in civil and common laws, to be the firſt and preſent preſbyter prebendary, and Henry Willis, clerk, batchelor in divinity, to be ſecond preſbyter prebendary, and John Rodley, clerk, batchelor in divinity, to be the third preſbyter prebendary, and James Vaughan, clerk, maſter of arts, to be the fourth preſbyter prebendary, and Edward Bennet, clerk, to be the fifth preſbyter prebendary, and John Huntley, clerk, late prior of Dandri in our county of Surrey, to be the ſixth preſbyter prebendary.

We will alſo and ordain, and we do by theſe preſents grant to the ſaid dean and prebendaries, that the aforeſaid dean and ſix prebendaries from henceforth be of themſelves in deed and in name a body corporate, and that they have a perpetual ſucceſſion, and that they ſhall demean, appear and employ themſelves according to certain ordinances, rules and ſtatutes by us, in a certain indenture to them hereafter to be made, ſpecified and declared; and that the ſaid dean and prebendaries, and their ſucceſſors, ſhall for ever hereafter be called the dean and chapter of the holy and individed trinity of Glouceſter; and that the aforeſaid dean and prebendaries of the cathedral church aforeſaid, and their ſucceſſors, be, and for ever after ſhall be, the chapter of the biſhoprick of Glouceſter; and that the ſaid chapter be for ever hereafter annexed, incorporated and united to the beforementioned John and his ſucceſſors, biſhops of Glouceſter, in the ſame manner and form in which the dean and chapter of the cathedral church of St. Peter in our city of Weſtminſter, to the biſhop of Weſtminſter, or epiſcopal ſee of Weſtminſter, is annexed, incorporated, or united; and we make them, the ſaid dean and prebendaries, one body corporate in deed and name; aud them for one body we do make, declare, ordain and accept, and that they have a perpetual ſucceſſion.

And that the ſaid dean and chapter, and their ſucceſſors, by the name of the dean and chapter of the holy and individed trinity of Glouceſter, may proſecute, claim, plead and be impleaded, defend and be defended, anſwer and be anſwered, in all our courts and places of law and elſewhere, in and upon all and ſingular cauſes, actions, ſuits, demands, writs and plaints, real, ſpiritual, perſonal and mixt, and in all other things, cauſes and matters, in the ſame manner as the dean and chapter of St. Peter of Weſtminſter may or can make or do, and by the ſame name, manors, lordſhips, lands, tenements, and other hereditaments whatſoever, poſſeſſions, profits and emoluments, as well ſpiritual or eccleſiaſtical as temporal, and all other things whatſoever, to take by letters patents of us, our heirs or ſucceſſors, or of any other perſon or perſons whatſoever, to them or their ſucceſſors, or otherwiſe according to the laws of us, our heirs or ſucceſſors, to be given or granted, may and can take, receive and acquire, give, alien and demiſe; and generally all and ſingular other things, take, receive, acquire, give, alien and demiſe, and do and execute in like, and in the ſame manner and form in which the dean and chapter of the aforeſaid cathedral church of St. Peter in our city of Weſtminſter can take,

take, receive, acquire, give, alien, demife, and do or execute, but not otherwife, nor in any other manner.

And that the dean and chapter of the cathedral church of the holy and individed trinity of Gloucefter, and their fucceffors for ever, may ufe one common feal to feal all charters, evidences and writings, by them made or to be made, or any ways touching or concerning the faid cathedral church aforefaid.

And moreover we will, and by thefe prefents do grant and ordain, that the aforefaid bifhop of Gloucefter, and every of his fucceffors for the time being, and the aforefaid dean and chapter of the cathedral church of the holy and individed trinity of Gloucefter, and every one of their fucceffors, have full power and faculty of making, receiving, giving, aliening, demifing, executing, and doing all and fingular things which the bifhop of Weftminfter jointly and feverally can make, receive, give, alien, demife, execute, or do.

And becaufe we will that the faid cathedral church of the holy and individed trinity of Gloucefter be honourably endowed, we of our farther grace have given and granted, and by thefe prefents do give and grant to the aforefaid dean and chapter of the holy and individed trinity of Gloucefter all the aforefaid fept, circuit, enclofure and precinct of the abovenamed late abbey or monaftery of St. Peter of Gloucefter, with all ancient privileges, liberties and free cuftoms of the faid late abbey or monaftery, and all the church there, together with all chapels, leads, bells, and all things belonging to bells, cloyfters, church-yards, meffuages, houfes, edifices, certain curtillages, flower gardens, gardens, orchards, fifh ponds, and all other places, lands, territories and places within the fame fcite, fept, circuit, enclofure, and precinct of the faid late abbey or monaftery, and all that was reputed or efteemed part or parcel thereof, and which lately were the faid priors and convents, in right of their monaftery aforefaid, together with all and all manner of veffels, ornaments, goods, chattles and implements of the faid late abbey or monaftery, with their appurtenances whatfoever, except and always referved to the aforefaid bifhop and his fucceffors, all and fingular halls, chambers, galleries, walks, offices, ftables, houfes, buildings, and other hereditaments and liberties whatfoever to the faid bifhops and his fucceffors herein in thefe prefents before granted; to have, hold and enjoy the aforefaid fcite, fept, circuit, enclofure and precinct of the faid late abbey or monaftery beforementioned, together with all ancient privileges, liberties and free cuftoms abovementioned; together with the church, chapels, bells, and all things belonging to bells, cloyfters, church-yards, meffuages, houfes, curtilages, flower gardens, gardens, orchards, fifh ponds, lands, territories, and places within the fcite, fept, circuit, enclofure and precinct of the faid late abbey or monaftery; together with the veffels, jewels, ornaments, goods, chattles and implements of the faid late abbey or monaftery, with all and fingular their appurtenances whatfoever; and with all and fingular other the premiffes above fpecified, with their appurtenances, (except before excepted) to the aforefaid dean and chapter of the faid cathedral church of the holy and individed trinity of Gloucefter, and their fucceffors for ever, of us, our heirs and fucceffors, in pure and perpetual alms.

We will alfo, and by thefe prefents do grant to the dean and chapter of the faid cathedral church of the holy and infeparable trinity of Gloucefter, that the dean of the faid church for the time being, all and fingular inferior officers and minifters of the faid cathedral church, and all other perfons of the faid cathedral church, as the cafe or cafes do require, fhall make, conftitute, appoint and accept from time to time for ever; and that he may and have authority fuch perfons, and every of them fo admitted or to be admitted, for lawful caufe to correct, and alfo to depofe, remove and expel from the faid cathedral church, faving to us, our heirs and fucceffors, the right, title and authority of nominating, affigning and preferring, and by our letters patents to ordain, prefer and prefent all deans, prebendaries, and all the poor living there on our liberality from time to time, howfoever and as often as the faid cathedral church of a dean, prebendaries, or poor people, either by the death of any of them or otherwife, fhall happen to be vacant, any thing in thefe prefents before mentioned contained in the contrary, notwithftanding.

And we will alfo and ordain, and by thefe prefents do decree, that the archdeacon of Gloucefter that now is, and his fucceffors, be from henceforth for ever feparated, difcharged, and altogether freed from the jurifdiction, power, right and authority of the bifhop of Worcefter; and the faid archdeacon, and his fucceffors, we do, by thefe prefents, feparate, exonerate, and for ever free from the fame; and him the faid archdeacon, and his fucceffors, we do decree, enact, ordain and eftablifh from henceforth and for ever, to be in the aforefaid church of Gloucefter in the fame manner, form and plight, in which he or any of his predeceffors were in the cathedral church of the bleffed virgin Mary of Worcefter.

We alfo enact and ordain, and by thefe prefents we will and grant, that the aforefaid John, bifhop of Gloucefter, and his fucceffors bifhops of Gloucefter, have, hold and poffefs in all things, and through all things, authority, power, right, plight and jurifdiction of, in and on the archdeaconry of Gloucefter, and the archdeacon that now is, and his fucceffors, as fully and abfolutely to all and intents and purpofes as the bifhop of Worcefter that now is, or any of his predeceffors now hath, or had, or ought to have, or did ufe or exercife.

We will alfo, and by thefe prefents do grant, as well to the aforefaid bifhop as to the dean and chapter, that he and they have, and fhall have, thefe our letters patents under our great feal of England, made and fealed in due form, without fine or fee great or fmall, in our hamper or elfewhere, in any manner to be rendered, paid, or made; notwithftanding there is no exprefs mention at this time in thefe prefents made of the true yearly value or certainty of the premiffes, or any of them, or of any other gifts or grants by us made to the faid bifhop or dean and chapter, or their fucceffors; and notwithftanding any ftatute, act, ordinance, provifion, or reftriction to the contrary thereof made, publifhed, ordained, or provided, or any other thing, caufe, or matter whatfoever, in any wife notwithftanding.

In teftimony of which, thefe our letters we have made patents. Witnefs our felf at Weftminfter, the 3d day of September, in the 33d year of our reign.——S.

CUPPER.

By Writ of Privy Seal of the fame Date, and alfo by Authority of Parliament.——S.

NUMBER VIII.

The ENDOWMENT *of the Bifhoprick of* GLOUCESTER.

HENRY the VIIIth, by the grace of God, king of England and France, defender of the faith, lord of Ireland, and fupreme head upon earth of the church of England, to all to whom thefe prefent letters fhall come, greeting: Know ye, that we of our fpecial grace, certain knowledge, and mere motion, have given aud granted, and by thefe prefents do give and grant to the reverend father in Chrift, John Wakeman, bifhop of Gloucefter, all thofe our manors of Maifmore, Brokethorpp and Hafecomb, Prefton, Longford and Droifcorte, in the county of our city of Gloucefter, with all their rights, members and appurtenances; and our manor of Rudge and Tufleigh in our county of Gloucefter, with all their rights, members and appurtenances; and alfo all thofe our manors of Hope-Melefhal, Dewchurch and Kilpeck in our county of Hereford, with all their rights, members and appurtenances; which manors, and other the premiffes, with all their appurtenances, did fometime belong and appertain to the late monaftery of St. Peter in Gloucefter, or were part of the poffeffions of the faid late monaftery; and alfo all and fingular meffuages, mills, houfes, buildings, lands, tenements, meadows, feedings, paftures, woods, underwoods, rents, reverfions, fervices, rents-charge, rents-feck, and rents-referved, upon all demifes and grants whatfoever, annuities, yearly rents, farms, fee farms, waters, fifheries and fifhings, and rents of all our tenants and farmers whatfoever; and alfo waifs, villains with their confequences, knights fees, wards, marriages, efcheats, reliefs, herriots, fairs, markets, tolls, cuftoms, holy days, warrens, commons, firze heaths, moors, wafts, penfions, portions, tythes, oblations, quarries, marfhes, pools, fifh ponds, courts leets, view of frank pledge, and all things which do or hereafter may or ought to belong to view of frank pledge, and affize and affay of bread, wine and ale, eftrays, goods, and chattles wayfed; and all other our rights, profits, emoluments, commodities and hereditaments whatfoever, with all and fingular their appurtenances, fituate, lying and being in the villages, fields, parifhes of Brokethorpp, Harefcomb, Prefton and Brokworth, in the county of our city of Gloucefter, and in the parifh of St. Mary de Lode within our faid city of Gloucefter, and in the parifhes of St. Ofwald and St. Mary de Lode within our faid city of Gloucefter, and in Standifh in our faid county of Gloucefter, and in Dewchurch in our faid county of Hereford, or elfewhere, in the fame counties of our city of Gloucefter, Gloucefter and Hereford, and elfewhere, within our kingdom of England, to the faid manors, or either of them, in any wife belonging or appertaining, or have been heretofore known, taken or reputed, as being members or parcels of the fame manors, or either of them, or have before this time been let, fet, or occupied with the fame manors, or either of them, or any parcel of either of them.

We give alfo, and by thefe prefents do grant, to the fame reverend father in Chrift, John Wakeman, bifhop of Gloucefter, cester, all that scite of a certain mansion house called the vineyard, and also a certain close of pasture adjoining to the said scite of the vineyard aforesaid, called the Park, containing about 15 acres and three rods, and now or late in the tenure or occupation of John Arnold, esq; or his assignees, situate, lying, and being in the parish of St. Mary de Lode, in our said county of the city of Gloucester, and did sometime belong and appertain to, and were part of the possessions of the said late monastery of St. Peter in Gloucester.

And also, all that our meadow commonly called Importams, otherwise Porthame, containing by estimation 67 acres of meadow, lying and being in the said parish of St. Mary de Lode, in our said county of the city of Gloucester, and the first shoot of the same meadow, being part of the demesnes of Barton Abbots, and did some time belong and appertain to the said late monastery of St. Peter in Gloucester.

And also, all that our part of the manor of Lassington in our said county of the city of Gloucester, with all its rights, members and appurtenances, and some time belonging and appertaining to the said late monastery of St. Peter's in Gloucester, and being parcel of the possessions of the said late monastery; and also all and singular messuages, lands, tenements, rents, reversions, meadows, feedings, pastures, woods, underwoods, commons, courts, leets, view of frank pledge, and all things which belong to view of frank pledge, chattles, waifs, estrays, services, and all other our profits, commodities, emoluments and hereditaments whatsoever, in any wise to the said part of our manor belonging or appertaining, or that have been heretofore known, taken, used, or reputed members or parcels of the same part. or any parcel thereof, situate or being in the parishes of St. Oswald and St. Mary de Lode, or elsewhere, in the county of our said city of Gloucester: And also, all that moiety or half part of a certain wood of ours called Woolridge, containing by estimation fifty acres; and also, all that moiety or half part of another wood of ours there called the Perch, containing by estimation sixteen acres, together with the land and soil of the said moiety of the same woods, lying and being in the said parish of St. Mary de Lode within the said county of our city of Gloucester, and some time belonging and appertaining to the said late monastery of St. Peter in Gloucester, and being parcel of the possessions of the said late monastery.

We also give, and by these presents do grant, for ourselves, our heirs and successors, to the aforesaid reverend father in Christ, all those our rectories and churches of Hartpury, Maisemore and Upton St. Leonard, in our said county of our city of Gloucester; and also, all those our rectories and churches of Cam, Northleach, Kempsford, Whelford, South Cerney, and Standish, in our said county of Gloucester; and likewise, all those our rectories and churches of Dewchurch, Kilpeck, Glasbury, Devennocke, Cowern, and Ewias Harold, in our said county of Hereford; and also, all that our rectory and church of Stewport in our said county of Wenlock in Wales; and likewise, all that our chapel of Cam in our said county of Gloucester; and all that our chapel of Piperton in our said county of Hereford; and all that our chapel of Maisemore in our said county of the city of Gloucester; which rectories, churches and chapels, did some time belong and appertain to the said late monastery of St. Peter in Gloucester, and were part of the possessions of the said late monastery; and also, all and all sorts of manors, messuages, glebes, meadows, feedings, pastures, rents, reversions, services, tithes, oblations, obventions, pensions, portions, and all and singular other our hereditaments and emoluments whatsoever to the said rectories, churches and chapels, or any of them, belonging or appertaining, or that have been heretofore had or known to be part or parcel of the same rectories, churches or chapels, or any of them, or have been let or demised with the said rectories, churches or chapels, or any of them; and also, all and singular our tithes, glebes, pensions, portions, oblations and obventions whatsoever, issuing from, or being in the villages, fields, parishes, or hamlets of Standish, Caldrup, Hardwick, Over-Oxlinch, Little Runwike, Harsefield, Nether Oxlinch, Sall, Putley, Farley, and Holyrood Ampney, in our said county of Gloucester; and in Devennock, Wentworth and Talgarthe, in our said county of Hereford, sometime belonging and appertaining to the said late monastery of St. Peter in Gloucester, or being part or parcel of the possessions and revenues of the same late monastery.

Moreover we give, and by these presents do, for ourselves, our heirs and successors, grant to the aforesaid reverend father in Christ, the bishop of Gloucester, a certain pension of fifty-three shillings and four-pence, issuing out of the rectory or church of Kempsford in our said county of Gloucester, and yearly paid by the vicar of the same church for the time being; and likewise, a certain pension or yearly rent of twenty-six shillings and eight-pence, issuing out of the rectory or church of Teynton in our said county of Gloucester; and also, a certain pension or yearly rent of nine shillings, issuing out of the rectory or church of Rendcomb in our said county of Gloucester; and also, a certain pension or yearly rent of twenty-six shillings and eight-pence, issuing out of the rectory or church of Nympsfield in our said county of Gloucester; and also, a certain pension or yearly rent of twenty-six shillings and eight-pence, issuing out of the rectory or church of Newport in our said county of Wenlock in Wales, and yearly paid by the vicar of the same church for the time being, which pensions were yearly paid by the several rectors and vicars of the same churches for the time being, and did sometime belong and appertain to the said late monastery of St. Peter in Gloucester, and were parcel of the possessions of the said late monastery.

We give also, and by these presents, for ourselves, our heirs and successors, do grant to the aforesaid bishop all those portions of tithes whatsoever arising, growing or renewing in Aldesworth, Linton, and Shipton Solers, in our said county of Gloucester, and now or lately in the several tenures or occupations of George Daston, and the farmer of the rectory of Aldesworth aforesaid; and also, all those portions of tithes whatsoever arising, growing or renewing in Ash-Leomyster, Ferm, Barn, Bunches, Strood and Lake in our said county of Hereford, which portions did sometime belong and appertain to the said late monastery of St. Peter in Gloucester, and were parcel of the possessions of the said late monastery.

We give also, and by these presents, for our selves, our heirs and successors, do grant to the same bishop all and singular the advowsons, donations, presentations, free dispositions, and rights of patronages, of all and singular the rectories and churches to the said manors, or any of them, belonging or appertaining; and likewise, all and singular advowsons, donations, presentations, free dispositions, and right of patronage, of all and singular the vicarages of Hartpury, Maisemore, Upton St. Leonard, in our said county of the city of Gloucester; and of Cam, Northleach, Kempsford, Whelford, South Cerney and Standish, in our said county of Gloucester; and of Dewchurch, Kilpeck, Glasbury, Devennock, Cowern and Ewias Harold, in our said county of Hereford; and of Newport in our county of Wenlock in Wales, sometime belonging and appertaining to the said late monastery of St. Peter in Gloucester, and being parcel of the possessions of the same monastery; and likewise, the donations, presentations, and free dispositions, of all those chaplains, chanteries, or of the stipends of all those chapels of Maisemore, Cam, Stinchcomb, Piperton, in our said county of Gloucester, and in the county of our city of Gloucester, and in our said county of Hereford, which did sometime belong and appertain to the said late monastery of St. Peter in Gloucester, as fully and wholly, and in as ample manner and form as the last abbot and late convent of the said late monastery of St. Peter in Gloucester, or any of their predecessors, in right of that late monastery any time before the dissolution of the same late monastery, or before that late monastery came into our hands, had, held and enjoyed the said manors, lands, tenements, and other the premisses, or any parcel thereof, or ought to have had, held and enjoyed; and as fully and wholly, and in as ample manner and form as all and singular of them came or ought to have come into our hands, and now are, or ought to be in our hands, by reason or pretence of any deed of gift, grant or confirmation made unto us by the late prior of the said late monastery under the seal of his convent, or any other way whatsoever, to have, hold and enjoy all and singular the aforesaid manors, messuages, lands, tenements, rents, reversions, services, courts, leets, view of frank pledge, meadows, feedings, pastures, woods, underwoods, pensions, tithes, and portions of tithes, oblations, obventions, advowsons, donations, presentations, free dispositions, and rights of patronages, and all and singular other the premisses abovementioned and specified, with all and singular their and every of their appurtenances, to the aforesaid reverend father, the bishop of Gloucester, and his successors for ever, to be held of us, our heirs and successors, in pure and perpetual alms; and also yielding to us, our heirs and successors, at our court of augmentations of the revenues of our crown, yearly from thenceforth for ever, thirty-three pounds, sixteen shillings, and four-pence, of good and lawful money of England, to be paid on the feast of St. Michael the archangel every year for ever.

Furthermore, out of our more abundant grace, certain knowlege and mere motion, we have given and granted, and by these presents do give and grant to the aforesaid bishop, all and all manner of issues, rents, revenues and profits, of all and singular the aforesaid manors, messuages, lands, tenements, hereditaments, and other the premisses, and each parcel of them, from the feast of St. Michael the archangel last past, before the date of these presents until this time, to be had and received by the same bishop as of our gift, as well by his own proper hands, as by the hands of those that are or shall be the farmers, bailiffs or occupiers, receivers or other our officers and ministers whatsoever, of all and singular the premisses, and every parcel of them, without account, or without yielding, paying, or doing any thing for the same, to us, our heirs or successors.

And whereas, by a certain act in our parliament begun at London, the 3d day of November, in the one and twentieth year of our reign, and from thence adjourned to Westminster, and by divers prorogations then and there continued and held until

until the 3d day of November, which was in the twenty-fixth year of our reign, amongft other things it was declared, provided, enacted and ordained, that we, our heirs and fucceffors, kings of this realm, fhould have and enjoy from time to time for ever to come, of all fuch perfon and perfons, who at any time after the firft day of January then next following fhould be nominated, chofen, profeffed, prefented, or any other way appointed to any archbifhoprick, bifhoprick, abbey, monaftery, priory, college, hofpital, archdeaconry, deaconry, deanery, prebendary, rectory, vicarage, chauntry, free-chapel, or any dignity, benefice, office, or fpiritual promotion, within this kingdom or elfewhere, within any of our dominions, of what name or quality foever they fhall be, or to whatfoever foundation, patronage or donation they fhall belong, the firft fruits of the revenues and profits for one year of every fuch archbifhoprick, bifhoprick, abbey, monaftery, priory, college, hofpital, archdeaconry, deanery, prebendary, rectory, vicarage, chauntry, free-chapel, or any other dignity, benefice, office, or fpiritual promotion, or to what fuch perfon or perfons nominated, after the aforefaid firft day of January, fhould be nominated, elected, preferred, prefented, collated, or any other way appointed, as in the fame act of parliament, amongft other things, it does more plainly appear: Know ye, that we being willing to difcharge and acquit the faid bifhop of Gloucefter, and his executors, as well of the faid firft fruits, revenues and profits of the premiffes, and every of the premiffes, as of every fum of money to be paid to us on account of the faid act of parliament for firft fruits, of our fpecial grace, certain knowledge, and mere motion, for ourfelves, our heirs and fucceffors, do grant to the fame bifhop and his executors, that we, our heirs and fucceffors, will not have, require, claim, nor challenge any firft fruit or fruits of or for the faid bifhoprick of Gloucefter, nor of or for the aforefaid manors, lands, tenements, and other the premiffes, nor of or for any parcel thereof, nor any iffues, revenues or profits, nor any fums of money in the name of the firft fruits, of or for the premiffes, or any part of them, nor for the firft fruits of the fame, or any parcel of them, for this time only, but that the fame bifhop and his executors are and fhall be difcharged and acquitted, as to us, our heirs and fucceffors, of and for the firft fruits of all and fingular the premiffes, and every parcel of them; and of and from all and all forts of iffues, profits, revenues of the premiffes, and every part of them; and of and for all and all manner of fums of money whatfoever, to be paid to us, our heirs and fucceffors, for and in the name of the firft fruits for the premiffes, and every parcel of them, for this time only; and alfo, we have pardoned, remitted and releafed, and by thefe prefents do pardon, remit and releafe, to the beforementioned bifhop, the aforefaid firft fruits, revenues and profits of the premiffes, and every parcel of them; and all and all manner of fums of money, for and in the name of firft fruits of the faid bifhoprick, and the aforefaid manors, lands, tenements, and all and fingular other the premiffes, and every parcel of them, due or to be paid unto us by ourfelves, by thefe our letters patents granted to the fame bifhop for this time only; and alfo, by thefe prefents we give unto the fame bifhop all and every fum and fums of money whatfoever, for the firft fruits, revenues and profits of the premiffes, or any parcel of them, or for or in the name of the firft fruits of the premiffes, to be yielded, paid or done by the faid bifhop of Gloucefter unto us, by reafon of the aforefaid act, or any other act, law, ufage, prefcription, cuftom, or otherwife, or any other manner whatfoever, to be had by the fame bifhop, of our gift, without any account, and without yielding, paying or doing any other thing therefore to us, our heirs and fucceffors, faving unto us, our heirs and fucceffors, the firft fruits for the premiffes, to be yielded hereafter by his fucceffors, bifhops of Gloucefter, according to the form of the ftatute aforefaid.

And furthermore, out of more abundant grace, certain knowledge and mere motion, we give and grant unto the fame bifhop and his fucceffors, that the fame bifhop and his fucceffors fhall have, hold and enjoy, and fhall be impowered and enabled to have, hold and enjoy, within the faid manors, and all and fingular other the premiffes, and within each parcel of them, as many, as great, and fuch and the fame fort, and the like courts leets, view of frank pledge, and alfo all things that belong to view of frank pledge, affize and affizes of bread, wine and ale, and other drink whatfoever, chattles waifed, eftrays, free warrens, and all things that belong to free warren, quarries, lands, fairs, markets, tolls, liberties, franchifes, privileges and jurifdictions whatfoever, as and which the aforefaid late abbot and convent of the faid late monaftery of St. Peter in Gloucefter, or any of his or their predeceffors have had, held and enjoyed, or ought to have had, held and enjoyed in the aforefaid manors, lands, tenements, and other the premiffes, or in any parcel of them, by vertue of any other letters patents by us, or one or other of our progenitors, to the faid abbot or any of his predeceffors made or granted, or by reafon of any prefcription, ufage, cuftom, corodies, or any other manner whatfoever, in as ample manner and form as the faid late abbot, or any of his predeceffors have had, exercifed and enjoyed, or ought to have had, exercifed and enjoyed.

And furthermore, we out of our more ample grace, and by thefe prefents, do grant for us, our heirs and fucceffors, that the fame bifhop and his fucceffors, from henceforth for ever, fhall have, hold and enjoy, and to their own proper ufe fhall convert, have and enjoy, and be empowered to convert to their own proper ufe all and fingular the aforefaid rectories which were any ways appropriated; and all and every the lands, tenements, tithes, commodities, profits and emoluments whatfoever, to the fame rectories, or any of them, in any wife belonging or appertaining, with all their appurtenances, to the beforementioned bifhop and his fucceffors before granted; and that the faid rectories, with their appurtenances, from henceforth for ever, be appointed to the faid bifhop and his fucceffors, in as ample manner and form as the faid late abbot and convent of the faid late monaftery of St. Peter in Gloucefter, or either, or any of his or their predeceffors, in right of the late monaftery or the faid rectories, or any, or either of them, with their appurtenances, had, held or enjoyed, or ought to have had, held or enjoyed, on any account or manner whatfoever, any act, ftatute, ordinance, law, cuftom, prohibition or reftriction heretofore made, had, publifhed, ufed or provided, or any other matter or caufe whatfoever to the contrary in any wife notwithftanding or impeding; and this without any prefentation, admiffion, or induction of any incumbent or incumbents to the faid rectories, or any of them, to the faid bifhop and his fucceffors.

And we will alfo, and do by thefe prefents, for ourfelves, our heirs and fucceffors, grant to the beforementioned bifhop and his fucceffors, that we, our heirs and fucceffors, for ever, and from time to time, fhall acquit, difcharge and fave harmlefs, as well the fame bifhop, his fucceffors and affignees, as the aforefaid manors, lands, tenements, and all and fingular other the premiffes, with their appurtenances, againft every perfon and perfons, their heirs and fucceffors whatfoever, of and for all and every penfions, portions, rents, fees, commodities, annuities, charges, and fums of money whatfoever, any ways iffuing, or to be paid out of, or for the faid manors and premiffes, or any parcel of them, or that are or fhall be charged upon the premiffes, or any of them, except the rent above by thefe prefents to us referved, and except a fee of forty fhillings yearly, paid to the bailiff of the manor of Maifemore aforefaid for the time being, and of eleven fhillings yearly paid to the woodward of Woolridge aforefaid, and of fix fhillings and eightpence yearly paid to the woodward of the Perch aforefaid, and of twenty-fix fhillings and eight pence yearly paid to the bailiff of Brokethorp and Hafecomb aforefaid, and of eleven fhillings and eight-pence yearly paid to the bailiff of Prefton aforefaid, and of fix fhillings and eight-pence yearly paid to the bailiff of Longford aforefaid, and of eight fhillings and four-pence yearly paid to the bailiff of Rudge and Farleigh aforefaid, and of thirteen pounds fix fhillings and eight-pence yearly paid to the vicar of the church of Cam aforefaid, and to the chaplain celebrating divine fervice in the chapel of Stinchcomb in the parifh of Cam to the fame church annexed, in augmentation of their falaries and ftipends; and of fifteen pounds five fhillings yearly paid to the vicar of Standifh aforefaid, and a fee of thirteen fhillings and four-pence yearly paid to the collector of the penfions of Kempfford, Teynton, Rendcomb, and Nympsfield aforefaid, and a fee of fourteen fhillings and one penny yearly paid to the bailiff of Hope-Melefhall aforefaid, and a fee of one pound fix fhillings and eight-pence yearly paid to the bailiff of Dewchurch and Kilpeck aforefaid, and of five fhillings yearly paid to the chancellor of Hereford for procurations and annual iffues out of the rectories of Dewchurch and Kilpeck aforefaid, and of two fhillings and two-pence yearly paid to the archdeacon of Brecknock, in the diocefe of St. David, for procurations and fynodals, and of ten pence yearly paid to the church of Glafbury aforefaid, and of five-pence yearly paid to the church of Devennock aforefaid, and the fee of thirteen fhillings and four-pence yearly paid to the farmer of the rectory of Glafbury and Devennock aforefaid for his livery, and of two fhillings yearly paid to the vicar of York for a certain portion of tithes iffuing out of the rectory of Cowern aforefaid, and a fee of three fhillings and four-pence yearly paid to the collector of portions in Afh-Leomyfter, Ferm, Farne, Briches, Strode and Lake aforefaid, and the fee of fix fhillings and eight-pence yearly paid to the bailiff of Droifcort aforefaid for the time being.

Moreover, we will, and for ourfelves, our heirs and fucceffors, do ftrictly charge and command, as well our chancellor of the court of firft fruits and tenths, and chancellor and convent of the court of augmentations of the revenues of our crown for the time being, as all other our receivers, auditors, and other officers and minifters whatfoever, that they, and every of them, upon the only producing of thefe our letters patents, or inrolment of the fame, without any other writ or warrant from us, our heirs and fucceffors, in any wife to be obtained or profecuted, fhall make, or caufe to be made, full entries and due allowance, defalcation, deduction and plain difcharge to the beforementioned

mentioned bishop, his successors and assigns, of all and every such pensions, portions, rents, fees, commodities, annuities, charges, and sums of money (except before excepted) charged or to be charged on the said manors, or on the premisses, or any part of them; and these our letters patents shall yearly, and from time to time, be as well to the said chancellor of the court of tenths and first fruits, as the chancellor and counsel of our court of the augmentations of the revenues of our crown for the time being, as to every of our receivers, auditors, and other our officers and ministers, a sufficient warrant and discharge on his part.

And moreover, out of our more ample grace, we will, and by these presents, for ourselves, our heirs and successors, do grant, that these our letters patents, and every word, sentence and clause in the same contained or specified, shall be interpreted, expounded, taken, understood, adjudged and determined, as well before us, our heirs and successors, in every of our courts, and the courts of our heirs and successors, both temporal and spiritual, and in all other places, and before whatsoever judges, justices, or other person or persons whatsoever, to the greatest advantage and profit of the aforesaid bishop and his successors, and most strictly against ourself, our heirs and successors, altho' the name or surname of the aforesaid bishop, or the certain true value of the aforesaid bishoprick of Gloucester be not specially and certainly in these our letters patents expressed, declared and specified; or for any omission, defect, negligence, repugnancy, contrariety in these presents, or any of them, or for express mention not being made in these presents of the true yearly value and certainty of the premisses, or other gifts and grants made to the aforesaid bishop before this time, any statute, act, ordinance, or restriction to the contrary of the premisses, or any of them, before this time published, made or ordained, or any other cause or matter whatsoever, in any thing notwithstanding.

We will also, and by these presents do grant, to the beforementioned bishop, that he may and shall have these our letters patents made, sealed and to be sealed in due manner under our great seal of England, without yielding, paying or doing therefore in any manner to us, any fine or fee, great or small, in our hamper or elsewhere, to our use, although express mention be not made in these presents of the true yearly value or certainty of the premisses, or any of them, or any other gifts or grants by us to the aforementioned bishop of Gloucester heretofore made, or any statute, act, ordinance, provision or restriction to the contrary thereof made, published, ordained or provided, or any other thing, cause or matter whatsoever, in any case notwithstanding.

In witness whereof we have caused these our letters to be made patents. Witness ourself at Westminster, the 4th day of September, in the three and thirtieth year of our reign.

NUMBER IX.

The ENDOWMENT *of the Dean and Chapter of* GLOUCESTER.

HENRY the VIIIth, by the grace of God, king of England and France, defender of the faith, lord of Ireland, and supreme head of the church of England upon earth, to all to whom these present letters shall come, greeting.

Know ye, that we of our special grace, certain knowledge, and mere motion, have given and granted, and by these presents do give and grant to the dean and chapter of the cathedral church of the holy and undivided trinity of Gloucester, by us now newly erected and founded, all those our manors of Tuffley, Ablode and Sainthurste, Barnewood and Croneham, Mattisdon and Wotton, in our county of the city of Gloucester, with all and singular their rights, members and appurtenances.

As also all those our manors of Churcham, Rudford, Culne-Rogers, with Ablington, Colne-Alwyn, Estletch-Martyn, otherwise called Burethroppe, with Cotes, Tyberton, Tayneton and Bulley in our county of Gloucester, with all and singular their rights, members and appurtenances.

And our manors of Willingiswike and Monk-Hide, otherwise called Hide of the Monks, in our county of Hereford, with all their rights, members and appurtenances.

And our manors of Tregosse and Pennon, in our county of Morgan and Glamorgan in Wales, with all their rights, members and appurtenances.

And also our manors of Linkynholte, Littleton and Walloppe, in our county of Southampton, with all their rights, members and appurtenances; which said manors, and all other the premisses with their appurtenances, did belong and appertain to the late monastery of St. Peter of Gloucester, now lately dissolved, or were parcel of the possessions of the said late monastery.

We do also give, and by these presents grant, to the aforesaid dean and chapter, all and singular messuages, houses, edifices, barns, dove-houses, lands, tenements, meadows, feedings, pastures, woods, underwoods, rents, reversions, services, rents charges, rents seck, and rents reserved, upon any demises or grants, annuities, annual rents, farms, fee-farm rents, and the farms of all our tenants and farmers, mills, waters, piscaries, fishing, moors, marshes, fish-ponds, knights fees, wards, marriages, escheats, reliefs, herriots, villaines, with their consequences, markets, fairs, tolls, passages, parks, warrens, commons, furze, wasts, heath, mines of coal, pensions, portions, tithes, oblations, obventions, courts leet, views of frank pledge, and all that to view of frank pledge belongs, and all that hereafter may, can, or ought thereto to belong; assize and assay of bread, wine and beer, waifs, estrays, liberties, and all and singular other hereditaments, commodities, emoluments, and our profits whatsoever, with all and singular their appurtenances, situate, lying, or being within the vills, fields, parishes or hamlets of Tuffley, Ablode and Sainthurste, Barnewood and Croneham, Mattisdon and Wotton, in our county of the city of Gloucester; and Churcheham, Rudforde, Culne-Rogers, with Ablyngton, Colne-Alwyn, Estletch-Martyn, otherwise called Burethroppe, with Cotes, Tyberton, Tayneton and Bulley, in our said county of Gloucester; and in Willyngyswike and Monk Hide, otherwise Hide of the Monks, in our said county of Hereford; and also in Tregosse and Pennon, in our said county of Morgan and Glamorgan; as also in Lynkinholte, Littleton and Walloppe, in our said county of Southampton, and elsewhere, wheresoever in the said counties of Gloucester, city of Gloucester, Hereford, Morgan and Glamorgan, and Southampton, or in either of them, or elsewhere, wheresoever in our kingdom of England, to the said manors, or any one of them, in any manner whatsoever belonging or appertaining, or as members or parcel of the said manors, or of any one of them heretofore being had, known or reputed, or with the said manors, or with any of them, or as parcel of any of them being leased, occupied or demised.

We also give, and by these presents do grant, to the said dean and chapter, all that our tenement or inn called the White Hart in Holborn, near our city of London, in our county of Middlesex, with all its buildings, gardens and appurtenances, together with a certain annual rent of eight shillings, which was wont to be paid for the said tenement to the late monastery of Carthusians near our said city of London now dissolved, and all that our meadow called Meneham in our said county of the city of Gloucester, containing by estimation 39 acres of meadow; and all that our meadow called Archdeacon's Mead in the same county, containing by estimation 18 acres of meadow, and also the first herbage of the said meadows. We also give, and by these presents do grant, to the said dean and chapter, all that moiety or half part of all that our wood called Woobridge, lying in the parish of St. Mary de Lode, in our said county of the city of Gloucester, which said wood contains in the whole by estimation 500 acres of wood; and all that moiety or half part of our whole wood called le Perche, lying and being in the said parish of St. Mary de Lode, in our said county of the city of Gloucester, which said wood contains in the whole by estimation 16 acres of wood. We also give, and by these presents grant, to the said dean and chapter, all that our wood called Barnewood Grove, in our said county of the city of Gloucester, containing by estimation 10 acres of wood; and all that our wood called Buckholte in the same county, containing by estimation 200 acres of wood; and also all that our wood called Byrdewood, lying and being in the parish of Churcheham, in our said county of Gloucester, containing by estimation 100 acres of wood; and all that our wood called Westwoodes, lying and being in Lynkynholte, in our said county of Southampton, containing by estimation 60 acres of wood; and all that our wood and underwood called Littleton-Coppice, lying in Littleton in our said county of Southampton, containing in the whole by estimation 48 acres of wood; and also all that annual or fee-farm rent of four pounds, issuing, and yearly to be received out of our manor of Wallop, in our said county of Southampton; which said tenement, meadows, woods and yearly rents aforesaid, with their appurtenances, did lately belong and appertain to the late monastery of St. Peter of Gloucester, or were parcel of the possessions of the said monastery.

We give also, and by these presents do grant, to the said dean and chapter, all and all manner of aqueducts and water-courses whatsoever which did belong and appertain to the said late monastery of St. Peter of Gloucester, or were parcel of the possessions of the said late monastery, in as ample manner and form as the last late abbot and convent of the said late monastery, or any one, or any of their predecessors, in the right of their late monastery, at any time before the dissolution of the said late monastery, had, held or enjoyed, or might or ought for any reason, or in any manner whatsoever, to have, hold or enjoy the same.

We give also, and by these presents do grant, to the said dean and chapter, all those messuages, houses, edifices, shops, cellars, sollars,

ſollars, gardens, lands, tenements, rents, reverſions, ſervices, tofts, cottages, penſions, portions, tithes, oblations, courts leets, view of frank pledge, and all things to view of frank pledge belonging; markets, fairs, toll, and all and ſingular our profits, commodities and hereditaments whatſoever, ſituate, lying or being within our city of Glouceſter, or within the ſuburbs of the ſaid city, which did of late belong and appertain to the ſaid late monaſtery of St. Peter of Glouceſter, or were parcel of the poſſeſſions of the ſaid late monaſtery.

We alſo give, and by theſe preſents do grant, to the ſaid dean and chapter, all that rectory church and chapel of Barnewood, in our ſaid county of the city of Glouceſter; and all that our rectory and church of Brokethroppe in the ſaid county; and all that our rectory and parochial church of the bleſſed virgin Mary near the gate of the ſaid late monaſtery of St. Peter in the ſaid county; and alſo, all that our rectory and church or chapel of Grace-lane in the ſame county; and alſo thoſe our rectories and churches of Churcheham and Colne-Alwyn in our ſaid county of Glouceſter; and all that our rectory and church of Lancarnan in our ſaid county of Morgan and Glamorgan; and all that our rectory and church of Chipping-Norton in our county of Oxon; which ſaid rectories, and churches or chapels, did lately belong and appertain to the ſaid late monaſtery of St. Peter of Glouceſter, or were parcel of the poſſeſſions of the ſaid late monaſtery.

And we alſo give, and by theſe preſents do grant, to the aforeſaid dean and chapter, our rectories and churches of Fayreford and Eſtletch in our ſaid county of Glouceſter; and alſo our rectory and church of Sherſton and Aldrington in our county of Wilts; and our rectory and church of Great Marlow in our county of Bucks; and alſo our rectories and churches of Lantwit, Lamblethian, Lantriſſan, Senmarke and Cardiffe, with the chapel of St. Donats, and to the other ſaid rectories annexed in our ſaid county of Morgan and Glamorgan; which ſaid rectories and churches, with the chapels aforeſaid, did lately belong and appertain to the late monaſtery of Tewkſbury in our county of Glouceſter now diſſolved, or were parcel of the poſſeſſions of the ſaid late monaſtery.

We give alſo, and by theſe preſents do grant, to the aforeſaid dean and chapter, all and ſingular the manors, lordſhips, meſſuages, barns, edifices, gardens, lands, tenements, rents, reverſions, ſervices, glebes, granges, meadows, feedings, paſtures, woods, underwoods, knights fees, eſcheats, reliefs, wards, marriages, herriots, commons, furze, waſtes, heath, tithes, oblations, obventions, penſions, portions, and all and ſingular other our profits, poſſeſſions, and hereditaments whatſoever, ſituate, lying or being in the vills, fields, pariſhes or hamlets of Barnewood, Brokethroppe, of the bleſſed Mary near the gate of the ſaid late monaſtery of St. Peter in Glouceſter, Grace-lane, Churcheham, Colne-Alwyn, Lancarnan, Chipping-Norton, Fayreford, Eſtletch, Sherſton, Aldrington, Great Marlowe, Lantwit, Lamblethyan, Lantriſſan, Senmarke and Cardiffe aforeſaid, or in either of them, or elſewhere whereſoever in our kingdom of England, to the ſaid rectories, granges, churches or chapels, or to any one of them in any manner belonging or appertaining, or which being at any time heretofore had, known or reputed to be, as part or parcel of the ſaid rectories, granges, churches or chapels, or of any one of them.

We alſo give, and by theſe preſents do grant, to the ſaid dean and chapter, all that portion of tithes in Barton-Abbots, within the pariſh of St. Mary de Lode, in our ſaid county of the city of Glouceſter; and all that portion of tithes iſſuing and yearly to be taken out of the manor of Senebrug in the ſame county; and all that portion of tithes of Upleaden and Hyneleaden in the ſame county; and all that portion of tithes of Ablode and Sainthurſte in the ſame county; and all that portion of tithes of Wotton in the ſame county; and all that portion of tithes of Ewrendyefield and Kings-Furlonge in the ſame county; and alſo, all that portion of tithes iſſuing and yearly to be taken out of the rectory of Hilmerton in our county of Wilts; and all that portion of tithes of Innyſworthe in our ſaid county of the city of Glouceſter; and alſo, all that portion of tithes iſſuing and yearly to be taken out of the rectory of Okeborne in our county of Bucks; which ſaid portions of tithes with their appurtenances to the ſaid late monaſtery of St. Peter of Glouceſter, did of late belong and appertain, or were parcel of the poſſeſſions of the ſaid late monaſtery.

We alſo give, and by theſe preſents do grant, to the ſaid dean and chapter, all that portion of tithes within the rectory of Fayreford in our ſaid county of Glouceſter, late belonging and appertaining to the ſaid late monaſtery of Tewkſbury, or being parcel of the poſſeſſions of the ſaid late monaſtery; we give alſo, and by theſe preſents do grant, to the ſaid dean and chapter, all that penſion or annual rent of twenty ſhillings iſſuing and yearly to be taken out of the rectory or church of St. John baptiſt in our ſaid city of Glouceſter; and all that penſion or yearly rent of ten ſhillings iſſuing and yearly to be taken out of the rectory or church of Mattiſden in our ſaid county of the city of Glouceſter; and all that penſion or yearly rent of thirteen ſhillings and four-pence iſſuing and yearly to be taken out of the rectory or church of St. Nicholas within our ſaid city of Glouceſter; and alſo, all that penſion or annual rent of ten ſhillings to be paid yearly by the guardians of the royal college of Brazen-noſe in Oxon; and all that penſion or annual rent of fifty-three ſhillings and four-pence iſſuing and yearly to be taken out of the rectory or church of Alcannynge in our county of Wilts; and all that penſion or annual rent of twenty ſhillings iſſuing and yearly to be taken out of the rectory or church of Lydyard Tregoz in the ſame county; and all that penſion or yearly rent of four pounds iſſuing and yearly to be taken out of the rectory or church of St. Peter de Mancroft within our city of Norwich in our county of Norfolk; and all that penſion or yearly rent of forty ſhillings iſſuing and yearly to be taken out of the rectory or church of St. Martin in Vintry in our ſaid city of London; which ſaid penſions or yearly rents aforeſaid, with their appurtenances, did belong and appertain, or were parcel of the poſſeſſions of the ſaid late monaſtery of St. Peter of Glouceſter.

We alſo give, and by theſe preſents do grant, to the ſaid dean and chapter, all and all manner of advowſons, nominations, donations, collations, preſentations, free diſpoſitions and rights of patronage, to our rectory and church of Mattiſdon in our ſaid county of the city of Glouceſter; and of our rectories and churches of Rudford, Culne-Rogers, with Ablington and Tayneton, in our ſaid county of Glouceſter; and alſo, of our rectory and church of Lynkynholte in our ſaid county of Southampton, to the ſaid late monaſtery of St. Peter of Glouceſter belonging and appertaining, or being parcel of the poſſeſſions of the ſaid late monaſtery.

We give alſo, and by theſe preſents do grant, to the ſaid dean and chapter, all and all manner of advowſons, nominations, donations, preſentations, collations, free diſpoſitions and rights of patronage, to the vicarage church of Brokethroppe in our ſaid county of the city of Glouceſter; and to the vicarage church of the Holy Trinity within our ſaid city of Glouceſter; and alſo to the vicarage churches of Churcheham, with the chapels of Lyncham and Colne-Alwyn in our ſaid county of Glouceſter, to the ſaid late monaſtery of St. Peter of Glouceſter, lately belonging and appertaining, or being parcel of the poſſeſſions of the ſaid late monaſtery; and alſo to the vicarage church of Fayreford in our ſaid county of Glouceſter; and to the vicarage church of Sherſton and Aldrington in our ſaid county of Wilts; and to the vicarage church of Great Marlow in our county of Bucks; and of all and ſingular the vicarage churches of Lantwit, Lamblethian, Lantriſſan, Penmarke and Cardiffe, with the chapel of St. Donats in our county of Morgan and Glamorgan, to the ſaid late monaſtery of Tewkſbury, late belonging and appertaining, or being parcel of the poſſeſſions of the ſaid late monaſtery; and alſo the advowſons, nominations, donations and rights of patronage, of every of the vicarages aforeſaid; and alſo all and all manner of advowſons, nominations, donations, preſentations, collations, free diſpoſitions and rights of patronage, of all and ſingular rectories or vicarages of the churches, chapels or chanteries, to the ſaid manors, or to any one of them in any manner belonging or appertaining, or in our ſaid city of Glouceſter, or in the ſuburbs of the ſaid city being, which did of late belong or appertain to the ſaid late monaſtery of St. Peter of Glouceſter, or were parcel of the poſſeſſions of the ſaid late monaſtery, as fully and wholly, and in as ample manner and form as the laſt late abbot and convent of the ſaid late monaſtery of St. Peter of Glouceſter, or any one of them, or any one or any of their predeceſſors, or the laſt late abbot and convent of the ſaid late monaſtery of Tewkſbury, or any one of them, or any one or any of their predeceſſors, in the right of thoſe monaſteries, or of either of them, before the diſſolution of them the late ſeveral monaſteries, or of either of them, or before the ſame late monaſteries came, or either of them, did come to our hands; or that they, or any one of them, the ſaid manors, lands, tenements, rectories, penſions, and all and ſingular other the premiſſes or any parcel of them, had, held and enjoyed the ſame, or might or ought to have, hold and enjoy the ſame, and as fully and wholly, and in as ample manner and form, as all and ſingular thoſe things, by reaſon or pretence of the diſſolution of the ſaid ſeveral monaſteries, or of any one of them; or by reaſon or pretence of any charter, gift, grant or confirmation, by the aforeſaid late abbots of the ſaid late monaſteries, or of any one of them, under their conventual ſeal to us thereof made, or in any other manner they came or ought to come, or now are or ought to be, in our hands; to have, hold and enjoy all and ſingular the aforeſaid manors, lordſhips, meſſuages, houſes, buildings, gardens, lands, tenements, rents, reverſions, ſervices, courts leet, liberties, rectories, chapels, advowſons, churches, rights of patronage, tithes, penſions, portions, and all and ſingular other the premiſſes above expreſſed and ſpecified, with all and ſingular their rights, members and appurtenances whatſoever, to the ſaid dean and chapter of the cathedral church of the holy and undivided trinity of Glouceſter aforeſaid, and to their ſucceſſors for ever, to be held of us, our heirs and ſucceſſors, in pure and perpetual alms; and alſo yielding to us, our heirs and ſucceſſors, at at our court of augmentations for the revenues of our crown yearly, from this time for ever, ninety pounds, fourteen ſhillings, and one halfpenny, of lawful money of England, at the feaſt of St. Michael the archangel, in full recompence and ſatisfaction of all ſervices, ſum and ſums of money whatſoever, annual rents or tenths, to us, our heirs or ſucceſſors, by reaſon of the premiſſes, by the ſaid dean and chapter, and their ſucceſſors, or by any or any one of them, or by any or by any one of their ſucceſſors, or by any perſon or perſons whatſoever, which to the ſaid deanery of the cathedral church aforeſaid, or to any prebendary in the ſaid church, or to any benefice, office, dignity, or other promotion whatſoever, in the cathedral church aforeſaid, now nominated, aſſigned or appointed, or hereafter to be nominated, aſſigned or appointed, by vertue, or reaſon, or force of a certain act of parliament in the 26th year of our reign, made for firſt fruits, revenues and profits, or in the name of firſt fruits, revenues and profits, of the aforeſaid manors, lands, tenements, and other the premiſſes of one year, or for one year, or for firſt fruits of the revenues or profits of the deanery, prebendaries, or of any other benefice, office, dignity, or other promotion of the ſaid cathedral church, or of any yearly value, or of any yearly rent, penſion or annuity, or of any other ſum of money whatſoever, of or for the ſaid manors, lands, tenements, rectories, and other the premiſſes, or out of any parcel thereof iſſuing, and to us, our heirs or ſucceſſors, to be made, paid or rendered, or being parcel of the profits of the manors, and other the premiſſes aforeſaid, or of any parcel thereof being, or aſſigned, or limited, or to be aſſigned or limited to the ſaid dean and prebends, or to any one of them, or to any other perſon or perſons, and to their ſucceſſors, or to the ſucceſſors of any one of them now promoted or aſſigned, or hereafter to be promoted or aſſigned to any benefice, office or dignity in the ſaid church, for annual rent or penſion, or in the name of annual rent or tenth parts, or of perpetual penſions, extending to the tenth part of the yearly value of the ſaid manors, lands, tenements, and other the premiſſes, or of the deanery of the ſaid cathedral church aforeſaid, or of the prebendaries, or of any benefices or offices whatſoever in the ſaid church, or of any prebendary, benefice, office, dignity or promotion in the ſaid church, or of any one of them; or to the annual rendering of a penſion, or to the tenth part of the yearly value of the aforeſaid manors, lands, tenements, rectories, and other the premiſſes, or out of any parcel thereof iſſuing or to be paid, or parcel of the profits of the ſaid manors, and other the premiſſes, or being any parcel thereof, being and aſſigned or limited, or to be aſſigned or limited, to the ſaid dean and prebends, or to any one of them, or to any other perſon or perſons whatſoever, and their ſucceſſors, or to the ſucceſſor of any one of them, to any benefice, office or dignity in the ſaid church, now promoted or aſſigned, or hereafter to be promoted or aſſigned by any perſon or perſons whatſoever, now, or at any time hereafter, in any manner to be paid, made or rendered.

Know ye, moreover, that we out of our ſpecial grace, for us, our heirs and ſucceſſors, do by theſe preſents pardon, remit and releaſe, to the aforeſaid dean and chapter, and their ſucceſſors for ever, and to all and ſingular perſon and perſons whatſoever, and to every one of them who now are, or is, or hereafter ſhall be dean of the cathedral church aforeſaid, or prebend in the ſaid church, or promoted to any benefice, office or dignity in the ſaid church, all and ſingular ſum and ſums of money whatſoever, to us, our heirs or ſucceſſors, by the ſaid dean and chapter or their ſucceſſors, or by any dean of the cathedral church aforeſaid, or by any prebend in the ſaid church, or by any perſon or perſons whatſoever, that now are or is, or hereafter ſhall be promoted to any benefice, office or dignity in the church aforeſaid, as well for firſt fruits, revenues and profits, or in the name of firſt fruits, revenues and profits of the ſaid manors, lands, tenements, and other the premiſſes, or of any of them, or of any parcel of them, or any of them, or of one year's value of the deanery of the church aforeſaid, or of the prebendaries, or of any other benefice, office or dignity whatſoever, in the cathedral church aforeſaid, to whom, to which, or to what he is promoted, aſſigned or appointed, or at any time hereafter, to whom, to which, or to what he or they ſhall be promoted, aſſigned, appointed or collated, for any annual rendering of the tenth part, or of any penſion, or of any yearly value, or of any yearly rent, penſion or annuity, or of any other ſum of money whatſoever, out of the aforeſaid manors, lands, tenements, rectories, and other the premiſſes, or out of any parcel of them iſſuing or to be paid, or parcel of the profits of the aforeſaid manors, lands, tenements, and other the premiſſes, or of any parcel of them being and aſſigned, or limited, or to be aſſigned or limited to the ſaid dean and prebends, and to any one of them, or to any other perſon or perſons, and the ſucceſſor and ſucceſſors of them, and every of them, to any benefice, office or dignity in the ſaid church, now promoted or aſſigned, or hereafter to be promoted or aſſigned; or in the name of any annual rent, tenth part, or penſion extending to the yearly value of a tenth part, or to the tenth part of all and ſingular the aforeſaid manors, lands, tenements, and other the premiſſes, or any of them, or of any parcel of them; or of the deanery of the cathedral church aforeſaid, or of any prebendary, benefice, office, dignity, or of any other promotion whatſoever in the ſaid church, or to the tenth part of any yearly value, rent, penſion or annuity, or of any other ſum whatſoever before ſpecified, or of any value of them, or by vertue or reaſon of the act of parliament made in the aforeſaid twenty-ſixth year of our reign, to us, our heirs and ſucceſſors, to be paid, rendered or made, the aforeſaid ſum of ninety pounds, fourteen ſhillings, and one halfpenny, by us (before mentioned) reſerved only excepted, and to us, our heirs and ſucceſſors, yearly reſerved.

And beſides, out of our farther grace, we, for us, our heirs and ſucceſſors, do pardon, remit and releaſe, to our well beloved chaplain, William Jenyns, clerk, batchelor in divinity, now dean of the cathedral church aforeſaid; to our well beloved chaplain, Richard Brown, clerk, batchelor in the civil and canon laws, the firſt and preſent preſbyter prebend; to Henry Willis, clerk, batchelor in divinity, ſecond preſbyter prebend; to John Rodley, clerk, batchelor in divinity, the third preſbyter prebend; to James Vaughan, clerk, maſter of arts, the fourth preſbyter prebend; to Edward Bennette, clerk, the fifth preſbyter prebend; and to John Huntley, clerk, late prior of the abbey of Tandriche, in our county of Surry, the ſixth preſbyter prebend, now prebends in the cathedral church aforeſaid; and to every one of them, all and ſingular ſums of money by the aforeſaid William, Richard, Henry, John, James, Edward and John, or by any one of them to us, for firſt fruits, revenues and profits, or in the name of firſt fruits and profits, or in the name of firſt fruits of the deanery aforeſaid, or prebendaries in the ſaid church, or any one of them, or of any annual rent, penſion or portion, or of any other ſum of money whatſoever to them, for their ſeveral portions in the cathedral church aforeſaid, limited or aſſigned, or to be limited or aſſigned, or for annual rendering of the tenth part, or in the name of a penſion extending to the tenth part of the value of the deanery aforeſaid, or prebendaries aforeſaid, or of any of them, or of any rent, penſion or portion, or of any of them, to them or to any one of them, for his part or portion, limited or aſſigned, or to be limited or aſſigned in the ſame church, to be paid, rendered or made.

And we, of our more abundant grace, do, for us, our heirs and ſucceſſors, kings of this kingdom of England, by theſe preſents, give and grant to the aforeſaid dean and chapter and their ſucceſſors for ever, all and ſingular ſums and ſum of money by the aforeſaid dean and chapter, or their ſucceſſors, or any, or any one of their ſucceſſors whoſoever, which may any way whatever, either by the dean of the ſaid cathedral church, or the prebends, or any other perſons in the ſaid church, or by any of them, or by any other perſon or perſons whatſoever, who at any time hereafter ſhall be, or ſhall be nominated, aſſigned or appointed to the deanery aforeſaid, or to any prebendary in the ſaid church, or to any benefice, office, dignity or promotion in the ſaid church, or ſub-dean of the ſaid church, or prebend in the ſame church, or promoted to any benefice, office or dignity, in the cathedral church aforeſaid, to us, our heirs or ſucceſſors, kings of this kingdom of England, by virtue or reaſon of any act of parliament made in the aforeſaid ſix and twentieth year of our reign, for the uſes of any of the premiſſes, to be paid, rendered or made, the aforeſaid ſum of ninety pounds, fourteen ſhillings, and one halfpenny, by us as aforeſaid reſerved only excepted; to have and enjoy all and ſingular the ſaid ſums, and every ſum of money aforeſaid, except only as before excepted, to the ſaid dean and chapter, and their ſucceſſors for ever, of our ſpecial gift, without any account, or any other thing therefore, to us, our heirs or ſucceſſors, to be rendered, paid or done.

And we farther will, and by theſe preſents do, for us, our heirs and ſucceſſors, grant to the ſaid dean and chapter, and their ſucceſſors, and to every perſon and perſons that now is, or are, or hereafter ſhall be, dean of the church aforeſaid, or prebend in the ſaid church, or nominated, appointed or promoted to any benefice, office or dignity in the ſaid church, that we, our heirs and ſucceſſors, will not have, aſk, claim, challenge any firſt fruits, revenues or profits, or any ſum of money whatſoever for firſt fruits, revenues or profits of the aforeſaid manors, and other the premiſſes, or any of them, or any parcel of them, or for firſt fruits of any annual rents, penſions or annuities, or of any other ſum before ſpecified, or in the name of firſt fruits of them, or any one of them, or of any parcel of any one of them, or any penſion or annual rent extending to the tenth part of the yearly value of the ſaid manors, and other the premiſſes, or any of them, or of any parcel thereof, or to the tenth part of any annual rent, penſion or annuity, or of any other ſum whatſoever before ſpecified, or any ſum whatſoever, or any other thing whatſoever, by virtue or reaſon of the aforeſaid act of parliament, made in the aforeſaid twenty-ſixth year of our reign, by the ſaid dean and chapter, or their ſucceſſors, or any perſon whatſoever that now is, or at any time hereafter ſhall be, dean of the cathedral church aforeſaid, or prebend in the ſame church, or promoted

to

to any benefice, office or dignity in the faid church, therefore to be rendered, paid or made, befides the faid fum of ninety pounds, fourteen fhillings, and one halfpenny, as is above premifed, by us above yearly referved.

But that as well the faid dean, prebends and chapter, and their fucceffors, as all and every fingular perfon and perfons who now are or is, or hereafter fhall be dean of the church aforefaid, or prebend in the faid church, or promoted to any benefice, office or dignity in the fame church, he and they fhall be exempted and acquitted by thefe prefents, againft us, our heirs and fucceffors, from all and fingular, and every fum and fums of money, to us, our heirs or fucceffors, by vertue or reafon of the faid act of parliament, made in the aforefaid twenty-fixth year of our reign, for the deanery of the faid church, or for any prebendary, or any benefice, office, dignity or promotion in the faid church, and every thing concerning the faid deanery, prebendaries, benefices, offices, dignities and promotions, or any of them, to be rendered or paid, any claufe, matter, fentence, thing, article, ordinance, provifo, gift, grant, or any caufe whatfoever in the faid ftatute contained or fpecified to the contrary notwithftanding.

And we will, and for us, our heirs and fucceffors, by thefe prefents, do grant to the faid dean and chapter, and their fucceffors, to enter into all the aforefaid manors, lands, tenements, rents, fervices, and all other the premiffes, and into every parcel thereof, and thofe to enjoy, to have and to hold, to them and their fucceffors for ever, by the tenor, force, form and effect of thefe our letters patents; and that it fhall be lawful for all and every perfon and perfons whofoever, who now is, or are, or hereafter fhall be dean of the church aforefaid, or prebend in the faid church, or promoted to any benefice, office or dignity in the faid church, and for all and every one of them, to enter, take and have actual and real poffeffion of that to which he hath been nominated, appointed and promoted in the cathedral church aforefaid; and to have, take and receive the iffues, revenues and profits thereof to his own proper ufe, without any other fatisfaction or payment, to the ufe of us, our heirs or fucceffors, for any firft fruits, revenues or profits, of that to which he is, or fhall be nominated, appointed or promoted, in the cathedral church aforefaid, and without any licence, concord, fuit, compofition, or profecution of any livery to be made from us, our heirs or fucceffors, or our officers, in any of our courts for that caufe, befides the aforefaid annual fum of ninety pounds, fourteen fhillings, and one halfpenny, to us, our heirs and fucceffors, for tenths and firft fruits of all and fingular the manors, lands and tenements before granted, referved as aforefaid.

And befides we will, and for us, our heirs and fucceffors, kings of this kingdom of England, by thefe prefents, do grant to the aforefaid dean and chapter, and their fucceffors, and to all and every perfon and perfons that now are, or is, or hereafter fhall be dean of the cathedral church aforefaid, or prebend in the fame church, or promoted, nominated or affigned to any benefice, office or dignity in the faid church, that it fhall and may be lawful that they, and every one of them, may enter, take, and have actual and real poffeffion of fuch aforefaid deanery, prebendary, benefice, office or dignity, to which he hath been nominated, appointed or promoted, in the faid cathedral church; and alfo that he and they may have, take and receive, the iffues, revenues and profits, rents and emoluments of fuch deanery, prebendary, benefice, office, dignity or promotion, or any one of them, in the faid cathedral church, without any fatisfaction or payment, to the ufe of us, our heirs or fucceffors, for any firft fruits, revenues and profits, of the premiffes, or any of them, or for any firft fruits of the deanery, prebendary, or other benefice, office or dignity in the faid cathedral church, to which they, or any one of them, now are, or is, or at any time hereafter fhall or may be nominated, appointed or promoted, and without any compofition or agreement therefore to be made; fo that we, our heirs or fucceffors, or any other, for us, our heirs or fucceffors, or in our name, or in the name of our heirs or fucceffors, fhall not for that caufe difquiet, impeach, difturb nor moleft, or vex the aforefaid dean and chapter, or their fucceffors, or any perfon or perfons whatfoever, to the deanery in the faid cathedral church, or to any prebendary in the faid church, or any benefice, office, dignity or promotion in the faid church, nominated, affigned or appointed, or to be nominated, affigned or appointed, of, for, or concerning any intrufion, or other offence or forfeiture whatfoever, in any of the premiffes; but that as well the faid dean and chapter, and their fucceffors, and all and fingular perfons whatfoever, who to the deanery of the faid cathedral church, or to any prebendary in the fame church, or to any benefice, office, dignity or other promotion whatfoever in the faid church, now nominated, affigned or appointed, or at any time hereafter fhall be nominated, affigned or appointed, and every of them, fhall be altogether exonerated, acquitted, pardoned and releafed, againft us, our heirs and fucceffors, and every one of us, from any fine, for all and fingular fuch entries, intrufions, offences, penalties and forfeitures, and other things whatfoever, limited or fpecified in any ftatute or act of parliament made in the aforefaid twenty-fixth year of our reign, concerning the payment of firft fruits, and the payment of annual rents and penfions extending to the yearly value of any benefice, office, dignity or promotion, or any of them, any ftatute, ordinance, provifo or act made in the faid 26th year of our reign, to the contrary notwithftanding.

Moreover willing, and by thefe prefents firmly enjoining and commanding, all and fingular archbifhops and bifhops within this our kingdom of England, and the chancellor of our court of our tenths and firft fruits, as alfo all and fingular the officers and minifters of us, our heirs and fucceffors, and every one of them, that they, or any one of them, in any manner whatfoever, fhall not impeach, difturb, vex, difquiet or moleft the dean and chapter aforefaid, and their fucceffors, or the fucceffor of any one of them, or any perfon whatfoever that now is, or at any time hereafter fhall be dean of the cathedral church aforefaid, or prebend in the fame church, or nominated, appointed or promoted to any benefice, office or dignity in the faid church, of, for or concerning the payment of any fum or thing whatfoever, for firft fruits, revenues or profits, or in the name of firft fruits of the premiffes, or of any of them, or of the deanery of the cathedral church aforefaid, or of any prebendary, benefice, office or dignity, in the faid cathedral church, or of, for or concerning the payment of any fum or thing whatfoever, for or in the name of an annual rent or penfion, extending to the tenth part of the value, or yearly value of the premiffes, or any of them, or of the deanery of the cathedral church aforefaid, or of any prebendary, benefice, office, or dignity in the faid church, or by reafon or pretence of any ftatute made in the aforefaid 26th year of our reign; but that all and fingular the aforefaid archbifhops, bifhops, chancellors, officers and minifters, of us, our heirs and fucceffors, upon the only fhewing of thefe our letters patents, fhall permit and caufe the faid dean and chapter, and their fucceffors, and every other perfon aforefaid, to be quiet and in peace, of, for and concerning the premiffes.

And farther, we, out of our more abundant grace, do give and grant to the faid dean and chapter, and their fucceffors, that they the faid dean and chapter, and their fucceffors, fhall have, hold and enjoy, and that they may and have full power to have, hold and enjoy, within the manors and lordfhips aforefaid, and all and fingular other the premiffes, and within every part and parcel of them, as many fuch, as great, the fame, and like courts leet, view of frank pledge, and all that to view of frank pledge belongs; affize and affay of bread, wine, beer, wayfes, eftrays, free warrens, and all that to free warren belongs; fairs, markets, liberties, franchifes and jurifdictions whatfoever, as, and which the aforefaid late abbot and the late convent of the faid late monaftery of St. Peter of Gloucefter, or any one of them, or any of their predeceffors, or the aforefaid late abbot, or late convent of the faid late monaftery of Tewkfbury, or any one of them, or any, or any one of their predeceffors had, held or enjoyed, or might, or ought to have had, held and enjoyed, in the manors, lands, tenements, rectories, and other the premiffes, or in any parcel thereof; and that fo fully and wholly, and in as ample manner and form as all and fingular thofe premiffes, by reafon or pretence of the diffolution, furrender or grant of the faid feveral monafteries, or any or either of them, or otherwife howfoever, came or ought to come to our hands, or at this time are or ought to be in our hands.

And farther, out of our more ample grace, we will, and by thefe prefents do grant, for us, our heirs and fucceffors, that the faid dean and chapter, and their fucceffors, fhall from henceforth for ever have, hold and enjoy, and to their own proper ufe convert, and alfo, that they may, and have full power and authority to have, hold and enjoy, and to their own proper ufes, to convert all and fingular the aforefaid rectories and chapels that lately were in any manner appropriate; and all, and all manner of lands, tenements and tithes, commodities, profits and emoluments whatfoever, to the faid rectories and chapels, or to any one of them, in any manner belonging or appertaining to the faid dean and chapter, and to their fucceffors before granted, with all and fingular their appurtenances; and that the faid rectories and chapels, with their appurtenances, fhall for ever hereafter be appropriate to the faid dean and chapter, and their fucceffors, in as ample manner and form as the faid late feveral abbots, or either of them, or any, or any one of their predeceffors, in the right of their late feveral monafteries, or in their own right, or in the right of either of them, had, held and enjoyed, or might or ought to have had, held or enjoyed, all or any, or any one of the faid rectories or chapels, with their appurtenances, in any kind or manner whatfoever, any act, ftatute, ordinance, law, cuftom, prohibition or reftriction, before this time had, made, enacted, ufed or provided, or any other matter, thing or caufe whatfoever to the contrary in any wife notwithftanding or hindering, and this without any prefentation, admiffion or induction of any incumbent or incumbents to the faid rectories and chapels, or any of them granted as aforefaid to the faid dean and chapter, and their fucceffors, by thefe prefents.

And alfo we will, and by thefe prefents, for us, our heirs and fucceffors, do grant to the aforefaid dean and chapter, and their fucceffors, successors, that we, our heirs and successors, shall and will, from time to time, and for ever discharge, acquit and keep indemnified, as well the said dean and chapter and their successors, as the manors, lands, tenements, and all and singular other the premisses, with their appurtenances, against all and every person and persons whomsoever, and their heirs and assignees, of and from all, and all manner of pensions, portions, rents, fees, corrodies, annuities, charges and sums of money whatsoever, of or for the manors and other the premisses, or of or for any parcel thereof already charged, or to be charged, besides the aforesaid sum of ninety pounds, eighteen shillings, and one halfpenny, to us, our heirs and successors, above by these presents reserved; and besides a certain rent of ten shillings yearly to be paid to Anthony Kingston, knt. in right of the late monastery of Flaxley; and of eighteen-pence yearly to be paid to the rector of the church of St. Mary de Cript, in our said county of the city of Gloucester; and of two shillings and eleven-pence yearly to be paid to the steward of our said city of Gloucester for the time being; and of fifteen shillings yearly to be paid to the master and brethren of the hospital of St. Margaret of Duddeston, in our said county of the city of Gloucester; and of fifty-seven shillings and one penny yearly to be paid to the sheriff of the said county of our city of Gloucester, for longable rent; and of ten pounds yearly to be paid to the bailiff and collector of the rents and farms within our said city of Gloucester for the time being for his fee; and of twenty shillings yearly to be paid to the bailiff of Tuffley aforesaid for the time being for his fee; and of forty shillings yearly to be paid to the bailiff of Ablode and Sainthurste, with Direhurste and Walton aforesaid for the time being for his fee; and of six shillings and eight-pence to be paid yearly to the farmer there for his livery; and of forty shillings yearly to be paid to the bailiff of Barnewood and Cronham aforesaid for the time being for his fee; and of six shillings and eight-pence yearly to be paid to the woodward or keeper of the woods there for the time being for his fee; and of five shillings yearly to be paid to the bailiff of Mattisden aforesaid for the time being for his fee; and of twenty shillings yearly to be paid to the bailiff of Wotton aforesaid for the time being for his fee; and of two shillings yearly to be paid to the archdeacon of Gloucester for procurations and synodals, and yearly issuing out of the chapel of Barnewood aforesaid; and of a certain annual pension of ten pounds, thirteen shillings and four-pence yearly to be paid to the vicar of the parochial church of the blessed virgin Mary near the gate of the late monastery of St. Peter of Gloucester; and of thirteen shillings yearly to be paid to the bishop and archdeacon of Gloucester, for procurations and synodals there; and of ten shillings yearly to be paid to the collector of divers pensions and portions yearly issuing out of some of the rectories, vicarages, hospitals and churches, in our said county of the city of Gloucester for the time being; and of twenty-six shillings and eight pence yearly to be paid to the bailiff of Churcheham aforesaid for the time being for his fee; and of twenty shillings yearly to be paid to the woodward or keeper of the woods there for the time being for his fee; and of ten shillings yearly to be paid to the bailiff of Culne-Rogers, with Ablington aforesaid, for the time being, for his fee; and of twenty-six shillings and eight-pence yearly to be paid to the bailiff of Colne-Alwyns aforesaid for the time being for his fee; and of six shillings and eight-pence yearly to be paid to the farmer there by covenant indented; and of twenty shillings to be paid yearly to the bailiff of Estletch-Martyn aforesaid, otherwise called Burethroppe with Cotes, for the time being, for his fee; and of five shillings yearly to be paid to the collector of the rents of Tyberton, Tayneton and Bulley aforesaid, for the time being, for his fee; and of thirteen shillings and four-pence yearly to be paid to the dean of the church of Churcheham aforesaid, for the time being, for his salary or stipend; and of six shillings and eight-pence yearly to be paid to the farmer of the scite of the rectory of Colne-Alwyn aforesaid, for his regard by covenant indented; and of ten shillings yearly to be paid to the bailiff of Willingswike aforesaid, for the time being, for his fee; and of thirteen shillings and four-pence yearly to be paid to the bailiff of Monk-Hide, Asperton and Tonston aforesaid, with the hamlets of Stoke Edythe, Yarkhill and Taddington aforesaid, for the time being, for his fee; and of six shillings and eight-pence yearly to be paid to the steward there for the time being, for his fee; and of ten shillings yearly to be paid to the bailiff of Lynkingholt aforesaid, for the time being, for his fee; and of ten shillings yearly to be paid to the bailiff of Littleton aforesaid, for the time being, for his fee; and of four shillings yearly to be paid to the collector of the pensions and portions issuing out of the rectories of Alcannyngs, Lydiard-Tregoz, and Hilmerton, in our said county of Wilts, for the time being, for his fee; and of six shillings and eight-pence yearly to be paid to the collector of a certain pension issuing out of the aforesaid church or rectory of St. Peter de Mancrofte, within our said city of Norwich, for the time being, for his fee; and of seventeen shillings and nine-pence farthing yearly to be paid to the bishop of Gloucester for his visitation, issuing yearly out of the rectory of Fayreford; besides also twenty shillings yearly to be paid to the farmers of the rectories of Lantwit, Lamblethian, Lantrissen, Penmarke, and Cardiffe aforesaid, with the chapel of St. Donats, for the time being, for carriage of the money and rent aforesaid.

And out of our more ample grace, we farther give and grant to the aforesaid dean and chapter, all issues, revenues and profits of all and singular the aforesaid manors, lands, tenements, rectories, pensions, portions, tithes, and of all and singular the premisses above expressed and specified, arising or growing from the feast of St. Michael the archangel last past, until this time.

We will moreover, and by these presents firmly enjoining, do command, as well our chancellor and council of our court of augmentations of the revenue of our crown, for the time being, as all receivers, auditors, and other our ministers whatsoever, that they, and every one of them, upon only shewing of these our letters patents, without any writ or warrant from us, or our successors, in any manner to be sought, obtained or prosecuted, do accept, make, and cause to be made, a full, whole and due discharge, allowance, defalcation, and manifest deduction, to the said dean and chapter, and their successors, of all and all manner of annuities, rents and sums of money whatsoever, out of the premisses as aforesaid, issuing or to be paid, or thereon charged or chargeable, besides those rents, fees and sums of money which are above nominated, and expresly excepted: And these our letters patents shall be to our said chancellor and council of our court of augmentations of the revenue of our crown for the time being, as well as to the aforesaid auditors, receivers, and other our officers and ministers whatsoever, a sufficient warrant and discharge in this thing: And besides, out of our more ample grace, we will and grant, for us, our heirs and successors, by these presents, that these our letters patents, and every word, sentence and clause in them contained and specified, shall be interpreted, expounded, taken, understood, adjudged and determined, as well before us, our heirs and successors, as in all and every of our courts whatsoever, and in the courts of our heirs and successors, as well spiritual as temporal; and in all other places, and before whatsoever judges, justices, and other person and persons whatsoever, to the greatest commodity and profit of the said dean and chapter, and their successors, and of every person that now is, or at any time hereafter shall be, dean of the said cathedral church, or prebend in the same church, or nominated, assigned, appointed or promoted, to any benefice, office or dignity in the said church, and most strictly against us, our heirs and successors; and this, although the names and sirnames, or name and sirname of them, or any one of them, who hereafter shall be dean of the church aforesaid, or prebend or prebends in the said church, or named, assigned, appointed or promoted, to any benefice, office or dignity in the said church, or certainty of the value of the deanery of the said church, or of the prebendaries in the said church, or of the other benefices, offices, dignities or promotions in the said church, or any one of them, are not in these our letters patents specially and certainly expressed, declared or specified; or any omission, defect, negligence, repugnancy or contrariety in these presents, or any of them, or for that express mention of the true yearly value, or of the certainty of the premisses, or no mention is made in these presents of any other gifts or grants by us before this time made to the said dean and chapter, any statute or act of parliament enacted or made in the aforesaid twenty-sixth year of our reign, or any statute, act, ordinance or restriction to the contrary of the premisses, or any of them before this time enacted, made or ordained, or any other thing, cause or matter whatsoever in any kind notwithstanding.

We will also, and by these presents do grant to the aforesaid dean and chapter, that they have these our letters patents, under our great seal of England, in due manner to be made and sealed, without fine or fee, great or small, to us in our hanaper, or elsewhere, to our use, in any manner to be rendered, paid or made, notwithstanding in these presents there is no express mention made of the true yearly value, or of any value, or of the certainty of the premisses, or of any of them, or of other gifts or grants by us, or by any of our progenitors or predecessors, to the said dean and chapter before this time made, or any statute, act, ordinance, proviso or restriction to the contrary thereof made, enacted, ordained or provided, or any other thing, cause or matter whatsoever to the contrary in any wise notwithstanding.

In testimony of which we have caused these our letters to be made patents. Witness myself at Westminster, the 4th day of September, in the 33d year of our reign.

By Writ of Privy Seal, and Authority of Parliament of the same Date.

SOUTHAMPTON.
SOUTHWELL.

Inrolled before William Barnes, auditor.

NUM-

NUMBER X.

To the supreme AUTHORITY, *the* PARLIAMENT *of the* COMMONWEALTH *of* ENGLAND,

The humble Petition of the MAYOR, BURGESSES, *and divers Hundreds of Inhabitants of the City of* GLOUCESTER,

SHEWETH,

THAT the city of Gloucester being a garison for the parliament's service, in 1643, and of vast importance to the commonwealth, upon the approach of the late king's army, to besiege the said city, it was resolved by the governor and council of war there, that the said city and garrison could not be preserved against the enemy, unless the whole suburbs of the said city (which was a full third part thereof) were pulled down and demolished.

That in pursuance of the said resolve, two hundred forty and one houses, besides barns, stables, out-houses, gardens, orchards and goods, of the suburbs of the said city, wherein so many families lived, were burned, pulled down, and utterly destroyed, the night before the leaguer was laid to the said city by the late king's forces, whereby most of your petitioners were reduced to most miserable poverty, and the estates of most of them much impaired, and the said city in general very much impoverished.

That it was proved upon oath to the grand inquest, at an assizes held for the county of the said city, that your petitioners losses, by the burning and destroying their said houses, amouted to the sum of twenty-six thousand pounds, and upwards, as by the certificate of the grand inquest to the lord chief baron, a copy whereof is hereunto annexed, may appear.

That your petitioners willingly suffered the loss of their houses and goods for their affections to the parliament service, and it was a great means, under God, to preserve the said city and garrison, and by consequence the whole country, from the power of the enemy: And your petitioners have ever since continued constantly faithful to the commonwealth, and the present government thereof, in the times of greatest danger and trial unto this day, and have always hoped, that according to the parliament's declarations, their losses and ruins for the commonwealth's service, should be repaired out of the estates of the commonwealth's enemies who occasioned the same.

Your petitioners therefore humbly pray, that their losses and ruins may be repaired, and their distressed families relieved, out of the estates of such delinquents as shall be appointed to be sold, or in such other way as shall seem best to your wisdom, justice and charity.

And they shall be bound to pray, &c.

NUMBER XI.

The CHARTER *of* STEPHEN, *King of* ENGLAND, *reciting and confirming the several* DONATIONS *to the church of St.* PETER *of* GLOUCESTER.

IN the year 1138, from the incarnation of our Lord Jesu Christ, I, Stephen, king of England, in the third year of my reign, at the request of Walter de Laci, abbot of Gloucester, and of several of my nobles, do grant and confirm unto the church of St. Peter of Gloucester, all those lands, churches and tithes, and other donations which the barons of England have heretofore given to the said church, and which my predecessors, kings of England, have confirmed by their charters; that is to say, Berton, Standish, Lech, Oddington, and the manor of Maisemore, with the wood and the adjoining lands given by king Henry the First; and Brokrup given by Atheline of Hibreio; and Colne St. Andrew, and two commons, and one church, with one hide of land, and a water-mill given by Roger of Gloucester; and the church of St. Peter of Hereford, with the prebendaries, lands, tithes, and all other things belonging to the same, which were the gift of Hugh de Laci; and the land changed for the monks orchard on which the tower was built, which was executed by the sheriff; and the church of St. Cadoc of Lancarvan, with the land called Treigos, given to them by Robert Fitzhamon; and the land in Hampshire called Littleton, given by Hugh of the port; and Lincheholt, of the gift of Ernulph de Hesding; and Ledene, restored to them by Walter de Laci; and Plumtreu in Devonshire, given by Odo the son of Gamiline, which abbot Serlo did change with Nicholas de Pool for land called Alnodeston and Clehangre, the gift of Roger of Berkeley; and one hide at Afpreton in Herefordshire, given by William de Ebroicis; and the land in Erchenefelt called Vestewde, given by Walter of Gloucester; and a small parcel of land at Guitings, given by Luric de Loges; and a water mill at Framalode, which Winebald of Baderon restored to the church; and Clifford, the gift of Roger de Buslei; and Rudfort, the gift of king Henry the First; and Rudle, the gift of Radolph Bloet; and the church of Hatherop, with the tithes of the vill, and the priests land, and a water-mill in the same place, with the land belonging to it; and the church of Kempsford, with the tithes and the priests lands; and the church of Norton, with five yard lands and the tithes, and whatever is adjoining to it, which were given by Ernulph de Hesding and Emeline his wife; and the tithes of Chesterton, given by Nigel Doily; and a part of a wood, with three cottages, given by Elias Giffart; and one yard land in Kempsford, given by Patrick de Chauworth, free from all charges except those due to the king; and one house in the moor of Black Ditch, free as the former; and the houses of Edric, the king's lieutenant, in the same moor, and the land belonging to them, and the tithes of meadows in the same village, and one water mill with the land belonging to it, and the tithes of two other water-mills in the same place; and one hide of land in Ammeny, of the fee and grant of Patrick; and one half hide in the same vill, which Tovi held in alms of king Henry the First; and Glasebery at Brecchenne, with the lands and woods, and all other things belonging to the same; and all the tithes of all his demesnes in Brecchenne, of corn, cattle, cheese, venison, honey; moreover, the church of Cover, with all the tithes of that parish, and the land belonging to that church; and one hide called Berche, given by Bernard of Newmarket; and the church of Gunlui, with the land and tithes belonging to the same, given by king William the First; and the mill given by Roger Giffart; and the church of Cerney, with the tithes of the same; and the church of St. Helene, with one yard land given by Walter the sheriff; and two new plowed grounds with the small meadows adjoining to them; and a small wood lying in the king's fee of Celeswood, and were given by king William the First; and the land in Rugge which Thomas de St. John restored to the church; and Duntesburne, the gift of Emmeline, the wife of Walter de Laci; and one water-mill, with a small yard land adjoining to it, free and quit as given by William de Owe; and the land at Soteshore, which was restored by Roger de Berchelai; and the water-mill which runs by the abbey, given to them by the kings my ancestors; and the church of St. Peter which stands in the market place at Norwich, and was the gift of king William the First; and all the plowed lands of Bully at Homme, and the tithes of William of Bully, which were given by the said William; and all the tithes of all my venison which shall be taken in the county of Gloucester, and was granted to them by king Henry the First; and wheresoever they shall buy or sell any thing for the benefit of the monastery, they shall be exempted from toll and payments of passage, and may go through any place without any molestation, as it was granted to them by king Henry the First; and wheresoever they shall take any sturgeon in any of their fisheries, they may retain it entirely to their own use; this was granted to them by king William the First; and all their lands shall be free from carriage, summonage and conduct, as they were granted to them by king Henry the First; and the church of St. Martin, standing near the Thames at London, and all the land which the priest of that church did hold, free and discharged from all customs and imposts, which was the gift of Ranulph Peverell; and the church of St. Guthlac in Hereford, with all its appurtenances, given to them by our venerable brother, Robert, bishop of Hereford; and the church of Westbury; and the church of Laverstoke, of the gift of Robert Gernan, with the consent of Alexander bishop of Lincoln; and the church of St. Leonard Stanley, with whatsoever belongs to it; and the chapel of St. John the Baptist, in the wood called Basing, with all its appurtenances; the church of Norton, with all its appurtenances; the church of St. John Baptist of Gloucester, with all its appurtenances; and the church of St. Patrine, with the chapels and lands thereunto belonging, which were given by Richard, the son of Gislebert; and the church of Teynton, with the chapel of the wood, and a yard land; and the chancel of Chilpect, and the lands and tithes, and whatsoever belongs to the same; and the church of St. Michael of Ewias, with all belonging to it; and moreover, the tithes of all the manors of Robert Ewias, and the church of St. Michael of Uggemore, and St. Bridget the virgin, with all their appurtenances; and all the lands within the manor of Estletch, which they had in exchange for the manor of Glasbury with Walter de Cliffort; and also the church of Quenington, with a yard land, and the tithes of the vill, and all other things belonging to it; and the parish of the castle of Gloucester, without being a member of any other church; and all places, as well within the walls of the city as without, as they held the same in the time of Wolston bishop of Worcester, or in the time of Sampson his successor; and one hide of land in Combe, which was the gift of Hugard de Bascheville.

Simon,

Simon, the biſhop of the church of Worceſter, ſends all obedience and duty to his father and Lord Theobald, by the grace of God archbiſhop of Canterbury, and primate of all England. Foraſmuch as all donations have their full power and efficacy, when confirmed by apoſtolical authority, therefore, at the requeſt of our beloved brother, the abbot of Glouceſter, and his brethren, we have inſpected the charters of the church of St. Peter of Glouceſter, and do hereby teſtify the truth of them, and certify the ſame to your grace, that you may be pleaſed to confirm them by your authority, and that you may without difficulty order them to be atteſted in your apoſtolical preſence: May it therefore be known to your grace, that all theſe things contained in the charter of king Stephen were actually granted to the church of St. Peter of Glouceſter by donation from himſelf, or of the kings his predeceſſors, or of ſome great noblemen, and were confirmed by their ſeveral charters and ſeals. Farewell.

NUMBER XII.

The CHARTER *of King* HENRY IV. *for the better Endowment of St.* BARTHOLOMEW'S HOSPITAL *in* GLOUCESTER.

HENRY, by the grace of God king of England and France, and lord of Ireland, to all to whom theſe preſents ſhall come, greeting. Know ye, that whereas the hoſpital of St. Bartholomew, between the bridges in Glouceſter, founded by our progenitors formerly kings of England, and now belonging to our patronage, is but meanly endowed, and the lands, tenements, rents and poſſeſſions are not ſufficient for the ſuſtentation of the ſaid hoſpital, and of the prior or guardian, and of the brothers or chaplains, and of the poor men and women now reſiding in the ſame hoſpital, who are obliged to aſſiſt by faſtings and continual interceſſions, and other devout and divine ſervices by night and by day, to pray for their benefactors, and for the ſouls of ſuch others as they are thereunto required; nor for the reparation and amendment of their church, houſes, buildings and edifices of the ſaid hoſpital, and for the ſupport and ſuſtaining other burthens daily neceſſary for the good of the hoſpital, without the aſſiſtance of us and our heirs, and the charitable benevolence of good chriſtians and well diſpoſed perſons; and their charters, writings, muniments and evidences concerning their lands, tenements, rents and poſſeſſions, by the careleſneſs and negligence of the former priors or guardians, and of the brothers and chaplains of the ſaid hoſpital, being burnt, ſubtracted, purloined or loſt, by which means the preſent prior or guardian, and the brothers or chaplains, and the alms people, have not only ſuffered great damages and prejudice, but the ſaid hoſpital muſt apparently come to utter ruin, which God forbid, unleſs we on our part ſhall ſuccour and relieve them.

We therefore, out of a charitable compaſſion, and taking the premiſſes into a due conſideration, and being willing of our ſpecial grace to provide in a convenient manner that the ſaid prior or guardian, and the brothers or chaplains, and alms people, ſhould in all quiet and ſafety, with a chearful heart, pray unto the Moſt High, particularly for the good eſtate of us whilſt we are living, and for our ſoul when we are departed out of this life, and for the ſouls of our moſt dear father John, late duke of Lancaſter, and of Mary, our conſort, lately deceaſed, and alſo for the ſouls of our progenitors, and of all others dead in the true faith.

And for the preſervation of the rights of the ſaid hoſpital, eſpecially being founded by our ſaid progenitors, and the patronage thereof, now belonging to us as aforeſaid; and leaſt by the like folly and negligence it ſhould be utterly ruined, we for ourſelves and ſucceſſors, as much as in us lies, do accept, approve, ratify and confirm the ſtate and poſſeſſions which the ſaid preſent prior or guardian, and brothers or chaplains, and alms people have in the ſaid hoſpital, and in the ſeveral churches thereunto annexed and appropriated, and in their lands, tenements, rents and poſſeſſions, with their appurtenances.

And we do hereby farther give and grant, (if need be) the ſaid churches, lands, tenements, rents and poſſeſſions aforeſaid, to them and their ſucceſſors for ever: Moreover, we will that the ſaid hoſpital be always held and reputed to be of the foundation of our progenitors, and the patronage thereof to belong to us and our heirs; and that the ſaid prior or guardian, and brothers or chaplains, and alms people, ſhall have and hold to them and their ſucceſſors for ever, the churches, lands, tenements, rents and poſſeſſions aforeſaid, as freely, quietly, and in as full manner as if the ſaid charters, writings, muniments and evidences were now entirely in being, and remaining within the ſaid hoſpital in the cuſtody of the ſaid prior or guardian, and brothers or chaplains: And we do by theſe preſents take, diſpoſe and receive under our eſpecial protection, guardianſhip and defence, the ſaid preſent prior or guardian, and brothers or chaplains, or the alms people, and all their ſucceſſors, and their proctors and agents, wherever they ſhall go or come, who ſhall be employed in aſking, demanding and gathering any elemoſynary gifts, or other charitable ſubſiſtencies for the uſe and benefit of the preſent prior or guardian, and brothers or chaplains, or alms people, and the ſucceſſors of them, and we ſhall protect the ſaid hoſpital, its lands, tenements, rents and poſſeſſions whatſoever.

Alſo we will not, that any clerks, purveyors or buyers of proviſion for the uſe of our houſhold, or for the uſe of our heirs, or any of them, or for the uſe of any of our carriages, or any other officers, bailiffs or miniſters of us, or of our heirs, or of any other perſon whatſoever, ſhall at any time take the corn, hay, horſes, carts, carriages, oxen, cows, hogs or other cattle, victuals or other goods or chattles, or things belonging to the ſaid prior or guardian, and brothers or chaplains, and alms people, or their ſucceſſors, in any of their houſes or places whatſoever, or in the cuſtody of the ſaid prior or guardian, and brothers or chaplains, and alms people, or of their ſucceſſors, or of their bailiffs, miniſters, or their tenants whatſoever, againſt their good wills.

And that the ſaid preſent prior or guardian, and brothers or chaplains, and alms people may partake of our eſpecial favour, and the languiſhing condition of the ſaid hoſpital may be relieved, we do farther will and grant, for us and our ſucceſſors, as much as in us lies, to the ſaid preſent prior or guardian, and brothers or chaplains, and their ſucceſſors, that as often as the ſaid hoſpital, by the death, ceſſion, depoſing, deprivation or reſignation of any prior or guardian of the ſame for the time being, or by any other means whatſoever, ſhall happen to be void, that then the brothers or chaplains of the ſaid hoſpital for the time being, and their ſucceſſors, ſhall with free aſſent and conſent, elect from time to time one able and ſufficient perſon from amongſt themſelves; or in caſe none ſhall be thought proper, then they ſhall elect ſome other ſufficient perſon to be the prior or guardian of the place, without our royal licence being firſt aſked and obtained, and without the licence of any of our ſucceſſors; and when ſuch election ſhall ſo be made, that then the biſhop of the place may proceed to confirm ſuch elected perſon, without our royal aſſent, or the aſſent of our ſucceſſors, being firſt aſked and obtained; and the ſaid perſon ſo elected, ſhall be admitted by the ſaid biſhop to be prior or guardian of the ſaid place, and paſtor thereof, and ſhall receive all the temporalties of the ſaid hoſpital as from God himſelf, and ſhall diſpoſe of them for the benefit of the ſaid hoſpital, without any procuring any livery of the ſaid temporalties out of our hands, or the hands of any of our ſucceſſors, as the cuſtom heretofore has been; and ſuch elections, and the confirmations of them, and the admittances of the ſaid prior or guardian of the ſaid place, without the licence and aſſent of the king, ſhall in no wiſe be prejudicial to the ſaid hoſpital, or turn to their loſs or prejudice; for in all vacancies of the ſaid hoſpital, the brothers or chaplains of the ſaid hoſpital for the time being ſhall, during ſuch vacancies, have the cuſtody of their temporalties, without rendering any account to us, or to any of our ſucceſſors, or paying any thing for the ſame; and no ſheriff or eſcheator of us or our ſucceſſors, in the county of Glouceſter or elſewhere for the time being, or any other officer of us or our heirs, by reaſon of ſuch vacancy, ſhall any ways intermeddle with the ſaid hoſpital, or any of their temporalties, provided notwithſtanding, that the eſcheator of the ſaid county for the time being ſhall, on every vacancy, make ſeiſin at the gate of the ſaid hoſpital in the king's name, and ſo having done ſhall forthwith depart; and that the ſaid eſcheator ſhall not, by reaſon of ſuch ſeiſin, be obliged or compelled to give any account or eſtimate to us, or to our heirs.

We do alſo farther will and grant, out of the abundance of our grace and favour, to the ſaid prior or guardian, and to the brothers or chaplains, and to their ſaid ſucceſſors, that they and their ſucceſſors ſhall ever be diſcharged and freed from all penſions and ſallaries required by our command, or the requeſt of us or our ſucceſſors, notwithſtanding the ſtatute againſt giving lands and tenements into mortmain, or any other ſtatute or ordinance to the contrary whatſoever; and notwithſtanding the ſaid prior or guardian, the brothers or chaplains, and their predeceſſors, were heretofore, by reaſon of their foundation, obliged to aſk licence and conſent, before they made any ſuch election and admittance of their prior or guardian of the ſaid place, and after admittance were obliged to ſue forth livery of their temporalties out of the hands of the king in the court of chancery, and notwithſtanding any other cauſe whatſoever: In witneſs whereof we have cauſed theſe our letters to be made patents.

Witneſs ourſelf at Glouceſter, the 19th day of November, in the 9th year of our reign.

NUMBER XIII.

The CHARTER *of King* EDWARD *the* IIId, *reciting the Foundation of the Priory of* CIRENCESTER *in the County of* GLOUCESTER, *and confirming the same.*

THE king to archbishops, &c. We have inspected the charter of Henry the First, of famous memory, heretofore king of England, our progenitor, in these words: Henry, king of England, to archbishops, bishops, abbats, priors, earls, barons, justices, sheriffs, and all the sons of holy church established throughout England, greeting: Know all men, that I, by the consent and authority of Pope Innocent, of pious memory, and by the advice and common approbation of the archbishops and bishops, princes and barons of my kingdom, have given to God and the church of the blessed Mary of Cirencester, of which I was the unworthy founder, for the good of the souls of my parents and ancestors, and for the remission of my sins, and for the welfare and safety of my kingdom, and to Serlo the first abbat, and to all his successors, and to the regular canons serving God in that place, in pure alms, all the estate of Reimbald the priest, in lands and churches, and other things, as followeth; to wit, two hides of land in the town of Cirencester, and the third part of the tolls of the market, which is held on Sunday in the several streets; and two parts of the tithes of the demesnes of Cirencester, and the whole tithe of all the rest of the parish; in Gloucestershire, eight hides of land in Preston, and the church thereof; one hide of land in Norcott, seven hides in Drifeild, four hides and one yard land in Amney, and the church thereof; two hides in Walle, which did belong to Balchi Daci, one hide in Elmundestan, one yard land and a wood in Wik, the church of Chiltenham, with the land thereof, and the mill, and the chapels, and all other appurtenances to the said church belonging; in Wiltshire, nine hides in Latton and Eisy, and the churches of both those places with their land, and the chapel of Eaton which belongs to the church of Eisy; three houses in the town of Cricklade, and the church of Pevesy, with the lands, tithes and customs appertaining unto the said church; the church in Avebiry, with the lands, chapels, tithes and customs appertaining to the said church; in Somersetshire, the church of Melborn, with the lands, chapels, tithes and other things belonging to the said church; the church of Frome, with the lands, chapels, tithes and all other things, whether woods or plains, appertaining to the said church; the church of Walon, with the lands, chapels, tithes and all customs, whether woods or plains, appertaining to the said church; in Dorsetshire, ten hides of land in woods and meadow in Puley; in Berkshire, the church of Scriveham, with the lands, chapels, tithes, and all other customs appertaining to the said church; the church of Cocheham, with the lands, chapels, tithes, and all other things appertaining to the said church; the church of Bray, with the lands, chapels, tithes and all things appertaining to the said church; ten hides in Eston; eleven hides and three yard lands in Hatcheburne, and the church of the same, with the chapels and tithes of the other Hatcheburn; in Oxfordshire, one hide of land in wood and plains, and one mill in Boicot; the church of Passeham in Buckinghamshire, with the lands, tithes and all things appertaining to the said church; in Northamptonshire, the church of Rowel, with the lands, chapels, tithes, and all customs belonging to the said church; the church of Bristoke, with the lands, chapels, tithes, and all customs, whether in woods or plains, appertaining to the said church; three houses in Winton: And I have farther granted to the said church of Cirencester, of my own demesnes, for ever, one hide of land in Cirencester, called Scereve-Hide, to make orchards, copses, and a place for a water-mill; and the abbat, Serlo, with my licence, has exchanged two messuages of that hide with the burgesses of Cirencester, for the conveniency of the priests: I have also granted a water-course, and the wood called Acley, with the forest, and all its lands; and I retain to myself nothing out of the wood besides my hunting, and the abbat may not plow up any part of it.

We moreover ordain, concerning the estates belonging to Reimbald, that whatsoever part of it the bishop of Salisbury hath, shall remain to him during his life, but after his death it shall return to the proper use and demesne of the canons regular: We ordain the like concerning the lands held by William Fitz Warin the sheriff; and the like of the lands held by Nicholas, nephew of the bishop of Winton; and the like concerning the lands which the secular canons held by their prebends: We do also grant to the said church, throughout all their possessions, soc and sac, toll, theam, infang-theof, and all other liberties, immunities, customs and privileges, in as free manner as the said church held the same in the reign of king Edward the confessor, or in the reign of my father or brother, or in my time; and as free as any other eleemosynary lands in the kingdom are held; therefore I approve, and by my royal authority do corroborate this my grant and concession, and by the power given to me by God, I decree, that the said church shall for ever enjoy the same; and I declare that I reserve those lands so given in alms, in my own hand, and under my protection, as if those alms-lands had been my own proper gift.

Witnesses, William, archbishop of Canterbury; Turstan, archbishop of York; Roger, bishop of Salisbury; Henry, bishop of Winchester; Alexander, bishop of Lincoln; Jeoffry, bishop of Durham; Nigell, bishop of Ely; Robert, bishop of Hereford; John, bishop of Rochester; Robert, keeper of the seal; Robert de Vere, Miles Gloec. Robert Doiley, Hugh Bigott, Robert de Curcy, and Pagan, the son of John; and Eustace and William his brothers; and William de Albia Britone.

Done at Burne, as I was crossing the seas, in the year of our Lord 1133, and in the 33d year of our reign.

We therefore the said grants, &c. do confirm, &c.

Given under the hand of the king at Berwick upon Tweed, on the first day of July.

NUMBER XIV.

The CONFIRMATION *of the Grants to the Abbey of* CIRENCSTER *by King* JOHN.

JOHN, by the grace of God, king of England, &c. to archbishops, &c. greeting: It is becoming our dignity, and is necessary for our salvation, that we should defend, keep and preserve those holy and religious places which were founded by our great grandfather, king Henry the First, and were confirmed by king Henry the Second, our father; therefore we give and grant, and by this present charter confirm to God, and to the holy church of St. Mary of Cirencester, and to the canons regular serving God in that place, in free and perpetual alms, for the good of the soul of the aforesaid king Henry, who was founder thereof, and for the soul of our father aforementioned, and for the souls of king Richard our brother, and queen Anne our mother, and of our brethren and all others departed this life in the true faith, all our manor of Cirencester, with all its appurtenances; with the town of Minchey, which is a member of the said manor, with the seven hundreds belonging to the said manor and farm, with all their appurtenances; to hold of us and our successors, yielding and paying 30l. yearly for all services, at our exchequer, at the feast of St. Michael: And know ye, that for the good of our soul, and all others abovementioned, we have given, released, and quit claimed, in perpetual alms, to the honour of St. Mary, and to our said canons of Cirencester serving God, forty shillings yearly rent which the said manor was accustomed to pay, so that for the future they shall pay only a rent of 30l. as aforesaid; and this we have done, that the canons of our demesnes, who are so named herein, may the more freely, quietly and safely serve God, in praying for us, for our father, and the rest abovementioned; wherefore we will, &c. We will also and command, that they enjoy that manor as fully and quietly, with all its liberties and free customs, as king Richard, our brother, enjoyed the same, when it was in his hands, except pleas of the crown, and our forest of Minchey, which we reserve to ourselves, as the charter of king Richard, our brother, can testify.

Witnesses, Robert, earl of Leicester; William, earl of Pembroke; William de Albeniaco, Garine de Glapum, Peter Estokes, and many others.

NUMBER XV.

The CHARTER *of* HENRY *Duke of the* NORMANS, *reciting the Grants of the Benefactors of the Abbey of* FLAXLEY *in the County of* GLOUCESTER, *and confirming the same.*

HENRY duke of Normandy, and earl of Anjou, to archbishops, &c. greeting: Know ye, that I have granted and confirmed to God and St. Mary, and to the monks of the cistertian order, for the good of the souls of my ancestors, and of my own soul, in perpetual alms, all those donations which Roger earl of Hereford gave to those monks in alms, according to the tenor of those charters, to wit, a certain place in the valley of Castiard, called Flaxley, to build an abbey there; and all that land called Wastadene, which did belong to Walfric, and an iron work at Edland; and all the land under the old castle of Dene which remains to be asserted, and that which is already assarted; and

and a certain fiſhery at Redley called Newerre, and a meadow in Pulmeade; and all eaſements in the foreſt of Dean, and all the demeſnes in Dymmock, and the lands belonging to Walfric; but ſo, that if Uthred the clerk continues in the abbey with the lands he exchanged, to wit, two yard lands, that then he ſhall give no account of it to any body but the abbot; half the wood at Dymmock, and all the tithes of cheſnuts in Dean every year; and all the land of Jeoffry, ſon of the aforeſaid Walfric, which the earl of Hereford did releaſe; and all the land of Leffric de Stanra, which the earl of Hereford did likewiſe releaſe: Wherefore I will, &c.

We do not only confirm to them theſe aforeſaid grants, but we alſo confirm all others which the ſame Roger, earl of Hereford, does intend to give unto them in alms.

Witneſſes, Roger, earl of Hereford; William de Crevecour; Richard de Humett, conſtable; Philip de Columbariis, Robert de Virgum, William de Angervil, William Cumin, at Eveſham.

NUMBER XVI.

The CHARTER *of king* HENRY *the* IId. *to the Abbey of* FLAXLEY.

HENRY, by the grace of God, king of England, and duke of Normandy and Aquitain, and earl of Anjou, to archbiſhops, &c. and to all faithful, as well Engliſh as Normans, both preſent and to come, greeting: Know ye, that I have given and confirmed to God and the bleſſed Mary, and to the monks of Dean, which I have received into my protection, for the good of my ſoul, and of my anceſtors, in perpetual alms, a certain place within the foreſt of Dean, to wit, all the valley of Caſtiard, and the place called Flaxley, where an abbey is founded of the ciſtertian order, in honour of the bleſſed virgin Mary, for the love of God, and the benefit of the ſoul of my grandfather king Henry, and of the ſoul of my father the earl of Anjou, and of Maud the Empreſs, my mother, and of the ſouls of all my parents and anceſtors, and for the good of my own ſoul, and of my heirs, and for the proſperity and peace of the kingdom of England; I have alſo granted to them, and have confirmed all the donations which Roger earl of Hereford gave to them in alms, in the ſame manner as thoſe charters do expreſs; moreover I have granted and confirmed to them all eaſments within my foreſt of Dean, to wit, common of paſture for their young cattle and hogs, and for all other beaſts, and wood and timber to repair their houſes and buildings, and for other neceſſaries, without committing waſte in the foreſt; and I have given them tithes of cheſnuts out of the ſame foreſt, and the farm called Waſtdean, and one iron forge free and quit, and with as free liberty to work as any of my forges in demeſne; and all the land under the old caſtle of Dean, with liberty to plow it up, to wit, one hundred acres, and a fiſhery at Redley called Nowere, and a meadow of Reidley called Pulmead, containing four acres; and all the land which Leuveric de Stanra gave to them in alms, and the farm which I gave them at Wallemere, out of my new plowed grounds, containing two hundred acres, with the meadows and paſtures, and all other eaſments; and four acres of Northwood, and all my demeſnes at Dymmock; and five yard lands and an half, beſides the demeſnes, and half my wood at Dymmock, and half my nets which I have in my hands, for the conveniencies of my men, becauſe I would have my monks enjoy that part of the wood peaceably and quietly, without any interfering with any other perſons, and I ſtraightly command, that no perſon offer to diſturb them upon this account; I further give to them my new plowed grounds under Caſtiard, called Vincent's Land: All thoſe I give unto God and to the bleſſed Mary, and to my monks devoutly ſerving God, to have and to hold for ever, quit and diſcharged from all regards and other ſecular exactions, whereof I will, &c.

Witneſs, Richard de Humett, William de Crevecour, Philip de Columbariis, William de Angervil, at Eveſham.

NUMBER XVII.

The CHARTER *of the* FOUNDATION *of the Abbey of* HAYLES.

TO all ſons of holy mother the church, to whom this preſent writing ſhall come, Richard earl of Cornwall ſendeth greeting in the Lord: Know all of ye, that we, in honour of Almighty God, and of the glorious virgin Mary, and of all ſaints, for the good of our ſoul, and the ſouls of our anceſtors, have founded a certain abbey of the order of the ciſtercians, in the manor of Hayles, which was given to us by Henry king of England, our brother; and the ſaid manor we have given and granted, with all its appurtenances, and by this preſent charter have confirmed unto the abbot and monks ſerving God, and the bleſſed Mary, in that place, and to their ſucceſſors, in free, pure and perpetual alms, with the advowſon of the church of that manor, with all its appurtenances, liberties, homages, and the ſervices of the free men, and all eſcheats in villains and villainages, in rents and woods, in meadows, plains and paſtures; in waters, mills, ponds and fiſh-ponds; in ways and paths, and in all things appertaining to the ſaid manor, freely, quietly, peaceably, and intirely free and diſcharged from all ſecular ſervices, from any exaction and demand; to have and to hold for ever, freely, quietly, and as fully as any other alms can poſſibly be granted; and we and our heirs will warrant the ſaid manor, with all its appurtenances aforeſaid, to the ſaid abbot and monks, and their ſucceſſors, againſt all men and women, and as free and quit, and perpetual alms, will we acquit and defend the ſame for evermore: And that this our grant and conceſſion may be of utmoſt and laſting force, we have hereunto ſet our ſeals.

Witneſs, Simon de Montfort, earl of Leiceſter; Peter of Savoy; the lord William of York; lord preſident of Beverlai; Robert Paſſilewe, archdeacon of Lewis; Simon de Everdon, archdeacon of Cheſter; Hugh de Vivone, Peter de Geneve, Robert de Muſgrove, Pauline Pejure, William de Ireby, Gyles Chancell, William Blundell, Philip de Eye, clerks, and many others.

NUMBER XVIII.

The CHARTER *of* MILO, *Conſtable of* GLOUCESTER, *to the Priory of* LANTHONY.

MILO, conſtable of Glouceſter, to Simon, by the grace of God, biſhop of Worceſter, and to Robert, biſhop of Hereford, and to all the barons of Worceſterſhire and Herefordſhire, and all the faithful of holy church, greeting: We will it to be known to all people preſent and to come, that I, for the good of my ſoul, and of the ſouls of my anceſtors, have, by the hand of Robert biſhop of Hereford, given to God and St. Mary, and to the canons of the church of Lanthony, in perpetual alms, the church of Burchelle, with all benefits thereunto belonging, one hide in Glouceſter free from all ſervices, a meadow called Caſtlemead, the tithes of hay of the meadow of Preſtenham, the tithes of all fiſh in the water and mill of Quedreſſe, and in the moat round the caſtle, the church of St. Owen with all its appurtenances. Theſe particulars following are appurtenant to the ſaid church, and were given by my anceſtors Roger of Glouceſter, and Walter the conſtable, to wit, a chapel within the caſtle, a ſmall piece of land upon the bank of the Severn to find a light to the ſaid chapel; all offerings which ſhall be made by the keepers of the tower, and of the caſtle, and of the barons reſiding there; a moiety of all offerings given by myſelf or my family, if my chaplain be preſent, but the whole of my offerings if my chaplain ſhall be abſent; alſo the chapel of St. Kyneburg, and all the pariſh in the hand of the conſtable within the ſouth gate, and all the pariſh without the ſaid gate, and all the land which Roger de Tocheam and Richard the chaplain held within the ſaid gate or without; the tithes of all the fiſh taken in the fiſhery under the caſtle; the chapel of Heccamſtude, with the tithes of all the villains in all things; the chapel of Quedreſſe, with the tithes of the demeſnes in all things, and the tithes of all the villains in all things, and a ſmall piece of land to collect the tithes; two parts of the tithes of Caldecot in all things; all the tithes of Wadon; all the tithes of the manor of Brocrup in all things; and of all the villains, with a ſmall parcel of land to collect the tithes; all the tithes of the manor of Longford, and the tithes of the orchard of Coveſley; all the tithes in the manor of Sutham in all things, and a ſmall parcel of land to collect them; all the tithes of Hide in Glouceſter in all things, two parts of the tithes of the manor of Berninton in all things, two parts of the tithes in Coleſburn Sampſon, two parts of the tithes of Elias Loholt of Coleſburn, the chapel of Elmor, with all the tithes of the demeſnes in all things, with all the tithes of the villains, with a ſmall parcel of land to collect the tithes; two parts of the tithes of Cerney, all the tithes of Cuckerton, the church of Tocheham with its appurtenances; all the tithes of the manor of Tocheham, with its appurtenances; half the tithes of the manor of Lotheridge, and of the manor of Cireton, and all the tithes of Sutgrove Reſtald: And I made the grant of all the ſaid tithes to the canons of Lanthony of the church of St. Mary at Glouceſter, upon the ſame day

day and hour as the church was dedicated, in the year of our Lord, 1137.

Witneſſes, Simon, biſhop of Worceſter; Robert, biſhop of Hereford; Robert, abbat of Tewkſbury; Serlo, abbat of Cirenceſter; William de Mara, William de Bercale, Alan, ſon of Main; Roger, ſon of Richard; Richard Wicet, Roger Wicet, Roger de Tocheam.

Afterwards I gave unto them the church of Berton near Wincheſter, with half an hide of land belonging to it, both which were part of my fee, deſcended to me from my anceſtors, and now in my poſſeſſion; and in the year 1141, being at Briſtol, and being made conſul thereof, I gave them the manor of Hethamſtede, with the meadows, and all its appurtenances, by land or by water, free and diſcharged from all ſervice and cuſtom, in as full and free manner as my father or ſelf did at any time hold the ſame. This donation I and my wife Sybille, and my ſons Roger, Walter and Henry, did make in the church of the canons of Glouceſter: Roger, who is now married, took an oath upon the altar of St. Mary, and upon the four evangeliſts, that he would never hereafter give them any diſturbance concerning that manor, and would never do them any damage or diminution in any thing, either by himſelf or any other; and my ſon Walter took the ſame oath. This was ſome days after my return from Briſtol, in the preſence, and atteſted by my ſaid ſons, by Drogo the ſteward, Robert Corbet, William de Bercale, Alan, ſon of Main, Hugh de Heſeley, Turſtin, ſon of Simon, William Britton, Roger the Little, Radulph Avenel, Walter de Broſeley, Robert, ſon of Hugh.

The witneſſes to the firſt donation at Briſtol were, the empreſs; Robert, earl of Glouceſter; Brien, ſon of the earl; and Robert, ſon of Martin.

I likewiſe gave them half the fiſhery at Haſpool which belongs to the ſaid manor, with the fiſhing places on one ſide or the other belonging to it; and not long after I gave unto them the other moiety of that fiſhery, by delivering a golden ring upon the altar in the ſame church, which I did in gratitude for the recovery of my ſon Roger. Two years afterwards, when my ſon Walter lay ſick with them, I then gave them a meadow in Elmore, which Roger of Tocheam had granted out of a grove; and in this gift I particularly aſſigned a rent to find a light before the body of our Lord on the altar, as I had promiſed them before, and had made alſo a vow unto God.

NUMBER XIX.

The CHARTER *of King* JOHN, *reciting the Grants of the benefactors to the Priory of* LANTHONY, *and confirming the ſame.*

JOHN, by the grace of God, king of England, &c. Know all men, that we out of love to God, &c. have confirmed in perpetual alms to God, and to the church of the bleſſed Mary and St. John Baptiſt, and the canons regular of Lanthony, theſe underwritten donations which have been juſtly given unto them: The chapel within the caſtle of Glouceſter, given by king Henry, my father, and a ſchool houſe in the ſame town, and half the fiſhery of Herſepool which is in our demeſne, and four libratas of land in the manor of Bernington, in perpetual alms, and four other libratas of land in the ſame manor, in fee farm, for four pounds to be yearly paid; and alſo all the lands given by Hugh de Lacy, and Pagan, ſon of John Ominour, in Bethreſhant, in Redwerren, and in Oldville and Little Freme, and half an hide at Aclam, and certain lands in Herchenfield, and a fiſhery in the Ham, with four acres of land, and a tenement which Ord and his anceſtors held, with the fiſhery of Tudenham, and the wears of Hodenai, and all the fiſhery belonging to it, as Pagan did ever hold the ſame in the moſt free and honourable tenure; and alſo all the lands given by Walter de Lacy, which lie between the mountains of Iriſebroke quite to Anſmere, and the land which Richard Poncy gave to them in Turchdean; and alſo two plow lands in the vill of St. Michael, given to them by Brien the ſon of the earl; and whatſoever was given by Nigelle the ſon of Hordfaſt, and granted by Henry de Albeny, and by his ſon Robert; whatſoever the ſaid Nigelle held in ſocage at Hanelowe in Aylricheſey, with the church of Hannelanne; whatſoever was given by Roger de Chandos and Robert his ſon, in Boneſhul in Chenceſtre, and Felilie; whatſoever Aldred held, with a yard land in Hope; the church of Brokewordin, given by Robert de Chandos, with half an hide of land, and an houſe on the weſt ſide of the church yard, and the land called Norbroc in Brockwordyn, unto the old way near the park of the earl; and two new plowed grounds which Richard de Brockwordyn gave unto them, and half a yard land which was Alred's, and the land which was Folley, which was Hugh de Donnoc's, with his ſervices and common of paſture for cattle, with the cattle of the Lord, and two mills in Mardeford, with thirty acres of land, and ſo much of a wood as will ſuffice to repair the mills, and twenty-four acres more of land which were added to the former, and another thirty acres, and one acre of meadow; the church of Begerdone with its appurtenances, and whatſoever was given by Roger de Chandos the younger in Brockwordyn; one yard land conſiſting of twenty-four acres, and all the new plowed ground which was Goremond's, and ten acres adjoining to the new plowed ground, and five acres which John the preſbyter held, and one yard land which was Richard's, and all the algarde on the eaſt ſide near the monaſtery, and the lands called Kitetoſhull, and Heglane, Frudung and Pilemode, and one yard land which was Lonewic's, of the ſtreet, and common of paſture for the cattle of the canons to go with the cattle of the lords, and the lands in Brockwordyn which the canons had in exchange for Kyneceſtre; the donation of Radulph de Baſkervil, of all the tithes of all lands belonging to his right of inheritance, and the church of Herdeſley, with twelve acres of land and an orchard, with part of the wall under the church-yard; the church of Janeſore, and the chapel of Streton; the church of Chiveſhope, the chapel of Pulule, the church of Herſope, the new plowed ground of Herderſley, with part of the wood as it is bounded out; all Hardeſhope, with Brechul and Foxley, with all their appurtenances, and the land called Canondinan; whatſoever was given by earl Milo; the church of Burchull, with all its appurtenances; the church of Bertone, with half an hide of land lying under the caſtle of Glouceſter, and the meadow called Caſtle-Mead, and the tithes of the hay of the meadow of Preſtenham and the manor of Hechamſted with its appurtenances, with a moiety of the fiſhery of Hereſpole, and the meadow at Elmore which Roger de Cokehams grubbed up; the church of St. Owen with two prebends, and all things belonging to them, and four acres in Knight's Meadow, and two acres in the meadow of William de Mara, and two acres of meadow of Robert ſon of Jordan, with both their conſents, and the land which was Guncelin's, and the land which was Redmer Bracinton's, and the tithes of the cyder of Brocwerne; whatſoever was given by Walter the conſtable and confirmed by earl Milo; the moiety of Bernington, with the church and all its appurtenances; whatſoever was given by earl Roger, the other moiety of Bernington, for the proviſion of thirteen lepers; whatſoever was given by Hugh de Laci and confirmed by earl Roger; the church of Wyhe with its appurtenances; whatſoever was given by Walter de Hereford; the village called Alvyntone with its appurtenances; whatſoever was given by Gerard de Limeſy; the land which was Roger de St. Juan's in Ramurthewyke; whatſoever was the gift of Robert biſhop of Exeter; the church of St. Mary in Glouceſter, with the chapel of All-Saints; whatſoever was given by Radland Malherle; four acres in Hanelane; whatſoever was given by Henry of Hereford; the church of Herſefield, the church of Caldicote and Gortune under the caſtle of Glouceſter, and a moiety of the meadow called Preſter; and whatſoever was given by Mahel of Hereford, the other moiety of the meadow, and the orchard under the caſtle of Glouceſter; and whatſoever was given by Margaret de Bohun, two parts of Quedgeley which remained to her after ſhe had made a partition with her ſiſter Lucy; and whatſoever was given by the ſaid Margaret de Bohun, and was confirmed by Humphry de Bohun her ſon; the church of Cheritone, with one hide of land; alſo ſome land in Cerney, in ſatisfaction of fifteen quarter-acres of land which the brothers of the ſaid Margaret had given and confirmed to the ſaid canons; alſo the twenty quarter-acres in Cudeſley, given by the ſaid Margaret de Bohun in perpetual alms; what was given by Walter of Hereford, ſome new plowed grounds in Cheltenham; alſo what was given by Radulph Picard, all the land which he had in Glouceſter; what was given by Richard Murdoc, one hide of land in Dunteſburn; alſo ſome land in Sutham, which Margaret de Bohun gave to the canons in exchange of land in Blekemere, which Roger de Harsforth had given to them; alſo all the alms lands which the freemen of the ſaid Margaret, with her conſent and confirmation, had given to the ſaid canons; alſo what was given by Walter de Laci, the church of St. Mary de Drogheda in Ireland. All theſe things aforeſaid, and whatever elſe has been legally given to the ſaid canons, or ſhall hereafter be given, either in England or Ireland, we do grant unto them: Wherefore we will, &c.

Given by the hand of Henry, archbiſhop of Canterbury, our chancellor, at Rupem Aurival, on the 13th day of July, in the firſt year of our reign.

NUMB-

NUMBER XX.

The CHARTER *of* WALTER DE LACY, *reciting and confirming divers Charters and Lands in* IRELAND, *given by his Father* HUGH *to the Prior of* LANTHONY.

TO all the faithful in Chrift, to whom this prefent writing fhall come, Walter de Lacy, fon of Hugh de Lacy, lord of Midia, fendeth eternal health in the Lord: Know ye, that no holy intentions of doing good ought to be hindered or obftructed by the unadvifed rafhnefs of men, but we are all obliged with the beft means which God has given us, to protect and uphold religious men, and all their goods which our anceftors had given them out of a pious mind for the good of their own fouls, and the good of our fouls; I therefore, in imitation of the devout intention of my father, the lord Hugh de Lacy, for the good of my own foul, and the fouls of my mother and wife, and for the good of the fouls of my anceftors and fucceffors, have given, and by this prefent writing have confirmed to God and to the church of St. John Baptift at the firft Lanthony, and to the canons ferving God in that place, all the tithes and profits and goods which the faid Hugh de Lacy, my father, of bleffed memory, had affigned to the faid canons for the good of his foul, with the affent of the archbifhops and bifhops in Ireland, and with the confent of their chapters, before he had infeoffed his freemen in Ireland, which lands he had obtained in Ireland, to wit, the church of Calp, with the tithes of Commgerie and Duvenelavy; the church of the town of Marmeri, with the tithes of the fifhery; the church of Anye, the church of Valle Clonelewy, the church of the town of Oggary in Midia, the church of Stathmolin, and the advowfon of the vicarage of Lillen; the church of Kilmeffan, the church of Kilculy, the church of Delvene, the church of Killimethe, the church of the town which did belong to Reginald de Turbervile, the church of Kilcarwarn, the church of Dunboin, the church of Rathbegan, the church of Kilbray, and the church of Dumrath; and the land of Balibin, and the land which Gilbert the Cornifhman held in the honour of Rafhouthe: All which I have confirmed to be enjoyed by them for ever, with all the chapels of all the feveral churches and their appurtenances, and with all the lands and ecclefiaftical benefices belonging to me in my land of Midia, or which fhall hereafter belong; and I and my heirs will warrant the rights of thofe patronages, with their chapels and appurtenances, unto the faid prior and canons, againft all men and women whatfoever, &c.

Witneffes, Robert de Turbervile, Walter, fon of Alured; Philip de Colevillc, Simon de Tylefhop, &c. and many others.

NUMBER XXI.

The CHARTER *of King* EDWARD *the Second, reciting and confirming the* GRANTS *and* CONCESSIONS *of* WALTER DE LACY *and others.*

EDWARD, by the grace of God, king of England, lord of Ireland, and duke of Aquitain, to all archbifhops, &c. We have infpected a deed which Walter de Lacy, late lord of Midia, made to the canons of the firft Lanthony in thefe words: To all faithful people who fhall fee or hear this prefent writing, Walter de Lacy, lord of Midia, fendeth greeting in our Lord: Know ye, that I, by the influence of divine piety, have granted to the canons of the firft Lanthony, that, according to ancient cuftom, without my leave, or my heirs and fucceffors, it may be lawful to the faid canons, when their church fhall happen to be void, to elect an orderly fit perfon out of their own body, or elfewhere, to prefer to be their paftor, to be prefented to the bifhop of the diocefe to receive confirmation from him; and I, nor any of my fucceffors, will intermeddle or difturb any of their goods, lands or poffeffions, during the vacation, until fuch time as their paftor fhall be elected; and that this liberty of election may remain unto them inviolable for ever, I have therefore to this writing fet my feal.

We have alfo infpected a deed which Walter de Lacy, fon of Hugh de Lacy, made to the faid canons in thefe words: Know all men, prefent and future, that I Walter de Lacy, fon of Hugh de Lacy, have given, granted, and by this prefent charter have confirmed, in pure and perpetual alms, to God and the bleffed Mary, and to the church of St. John Baptift, of the firft Lanthony, and to the canons ferving God in that place, for the good of my own foul, and the foul of the Lady Margery, my wife, and the fouls of my anceftors and fucceffors, all the valley, with all its appurtenances in which the faid church is fituated; to wit, on one fide, by Kenen Taffet and Afharefway, and by Ruggewey unto Antefin, and on the fide of Hateroll from the land of Seifel, the fon of Gilebert, by Ruggewey to the bounds of Talgargh, free and quit from all fervices, cuftoms and demands; and I grant that they may have all hunting and free warren within the bounds of their lands, and I do prohibit all perfons to enter into the faid bounds, to hunt, feed, or cut wood, without the leave and confent of the faid canons; and if they fhall chance to apprehend any one hunting, feeding, or cutting of wood, it fhall be lawful to the faid canons and their men, to feize them and bring them before their own court, to be adjudged what fatisfaction they fhall make; and I will, that no fteward, conftable, bailiff, keeper or forefter, fervant, huntfman, or any other perfon's bailiff, paffing through their lands, fhall be entertained at the charge of the faid canons, or of their men, nor fhall expect any provifions of meat or drink from the faid canons or their men, but what fhall be freely given unto them. I have granted to the faid canons and their men, that they fhall have full common of pafture in Wrynen, and Haybot and Houfebot therein, and all other conveniencies which they or theirs can receive in the faid place, without the interruption, demand, or difturbance of any; and I will, that no bailiff of mine, or of my heirs, under pretence of any forfeiture, fhall make an entry into their lands; and I will, that the faid canons and their officers fhall have common in my wood of Mafcoit for their fwine, free and quiet from pannage and toll; and I will, that the faid canons and their men, fhall be quit from all toll and demands throughout all my lands; and I will, that the faid canons and their men be quit from plowing, mowing, reaping, and all other cuftoms and exactions in all places, and in all things; and I grant to the faid canons, that they fhall enjoy all privileges, power, immunities, and liberties, in the land of Ewias, in as full manner as I do enjoy, or may enjoy, or any of my heirs may enjoy the fame.

I will, and ftraitly command, that the canons of the firft Lanthony, fhall hold all their tenements in the land of Ewias, whether lay-lands or church-lands, whether in their prefent poffeffion, or they fhall obtain them hereafter by purchafe, gift, or by any other title, peaceably, freely and quietly in all places and in all things; free from all pleas and plaints; from aids, horfe carriages, carts and carriages; from repairs of bridges or caftles, from guarding our treafure, and from all work; from tunnage and ftallage, and from all fummons, affizes and fuper affizes, and from all fines and amerciaments, upon what occafion foever, and from penalties for new plowing up wood grounds; and no forefter fhall intermeddle in any of the woods of the prior and canons of the firft Lanthony, but they fhall have as full power in their own woods, as I or my heirs have, or can have; and the faid prior and canons, and their men, and their goods, fhall be free from all toll, exactions and demands, in all fairs, courts and markets, and in all places and things, throughout all the whole land of Ewias.

The faid prior and canons fhall have jurifdiction of affaults, murthers and fhedding of blood, and breach of peace, and treafure found, and whatever belongs to our prerogative; no falaries or rewards upon any occafion whatfoever fhall be demanded of the faid canons, their lands or fervants; and if demanded, they fhall not be obliged to pay the fame, but all things to them fhall be free and quiet, and accountable only to the canons themfelves.

I grant that the faid prior and canons fhall have all pleas of theft, manflaughter, rapes and burnings, within their prefent poffeffions, or fuch poffeffions they fhall hereafter have within the land of Ewias, over all their own men, and over all ftrangers which fhall negotiate there, or fhall be taken there, and the fact fhall be found upon them, and all other pleas which can be tried in the court of Ewias; with trials of all thefts committed in their lands, or by perfons fled thither; and all amerciaments which fhall arife on fuch pleas, held before the faid canons or their bailiffs, fhall be due to the faid canons; and I grant that they fhall have a gallows to belong to their court of juftice, and to do juftice in what part of their lands they fhall think fit.

I grant that the faid prior and canons fhall enjoy all the aforefaid liberties and free cuftoms, as freely, quietly, peaceably and fully, as ever I or my anceftors did moft fully and freely enjoy the fame; and I grant that they fhall have as great privileges in the land of Ewias, as ever I or my fucceffors have, or can have, by grant of any king of England, or by any other; and I and my heirs will for ever warrant this grant and conceffion to the faid canons, againft all men and women whatfoever; and that this grant and conceffion may for ever continue firm and inviolable, I have ftrengthened and corroborated the fame by fetting my hand, and affixing my feal thereunto.

Witneffes, the lord Simon de Clifford, the lord Walter de Bafkervyll, the lord Richard de Hampton, the lord Walter, Walter Condecot.

We therefore, all the gifts, grants and confirmations aforefaid, and alfo the grant, &c. which John, the fon of Reginald, by his deed

deed made to the ſaid canons, of their peaceable depaſturing the horſes of the ſaid canons, through all the lands of the ſaid John in Wales, as well in foreſts and free chaſes, as in all other places, except in his park already incloſed, without any let or hinderance; with free egreſs and regreſs, to go and lead out their horſes, or to bring them back at their pleaſure; and alſo leave to go and take fiſhes in the meer, and to perform any other affairs as often, and when they ſhall think fit; and the releaſe and quitclaim which the ſaid John made by his deed to the ſaid canons, of the payment of certain money, or poultry, or any other thing which the ſaid canons were accuſtomed to pay unto the ſaid John, or to any of his predeceſſors, we, for us and our heirs, as much as in us lyes, do ratify and ſtrengthen the ſame, and do grant and confirm every part thereof unto our beloved in Chriſt the prior and canons of the place aforeſaid, in as full manner as their writings do reaſonably teſtify.

And moreover, although it be found by inquiſition, taken at our command by our beloved and faithful John de Breek, and John de Botiller of Lanlutwyt, and returned into our court of chancery, that the ſaid prior and canons, and their predeceſſors, have not made uſe of the ſaid liberties and quittances for ſome time paſt, we will however, in conſideration of a fine paid to us by the ſaid prior and canons, and out of our ſpecial favour to them, grant, for us and our heirs, as much as in us lyes, unto the ſaid prior and canons, that they and their ſucceſſors, ſhall for the time to come, uſe and enjoy all thoſe ſeveral liberties and quittances in the ſaid deeds contained, when, and as often as it ſhall ſeem expedient to them, without any let or hinderance from us or our ſucceſſors, &c.

Given under our hand at Langeley, on the 26th day of January, in the 18th year of our reign.

NUMBER XXII.

The BULL *of Pope* ALEXANDER *the* IIId, *confirming divers Donations in* NORMANDY *and* ENGLAND *to the Priory of* NEWENT.

TO all ſons of the holy mother the church: We, William by divine permiſſion, biſhop of Lexonienſis, and we, abbats of Becce, Pratelle, Greſton and Cormeille, greeting in our Saviour: Know ye, that we have diligently inſpected the charter of privileges granted by Pope Alexander, of happy memory, correct and uncancelled, and no way prejudiced, in this form following.

Alexander, biſhop T , ſervant of the ſervants of God, to our beloved ſons, Robert, abbat of the monaſtery of Cormeille, and to the brethren of the ſame, as well preſent as future, who profeſs always a regular life, chuſing a religious life. It behoves you to have the apoſtolical aſſiſtance, that no perſon by a raſh attempt may endeavour to withdraw you from your good reſolution, or ſhall pervert you in the true religion, which God forbid; therefore, my beloved ſons in the Lord, we readily comply with your juſt requeſts, and we take the ſaid monaſtery in which you have vowed obediance to God under the protection of St. Peter, and our own protection, and do ſecure the ſame by the privileges granted by this preſent writing: Firſt, we ordain, that the monaſtical order in your monaſtery, inſtituted by God according to the rule of St. Benedict, be for ever ſtrictly obſerved: Moreover, whatever poſſeſſions, whatever goods the ſaid monaſtery do juſtly and canonically enjoy at preſent, or ſhall hereafter, by the grants of biſhops, the bounty of kings and princes, the free-will offering of the faithful, and by any other juſt means obtained, through the bleſſing of God, ſhall remain firm and undiminiſhed to you and to your ſucceſſors; and we think fit to expreſs the ſame in more particular words; as followeth: the church of St. Peter, the church of Holy Croſs, the church of St. Silveſter with all its appurtenances, the town of Cormeille, &c. In England, the manor of Noent, with all its appurtenances; to wit, five hides of land and the church, with all tithes, oblations, meadows, mills, and the woods of Iarcleſdune and of Tedeſwude, Cumpton, Linde, Eclam, and Meleſwit, with the mills and woods; Ligeſley, with all the new plowed grounds which belong to Nuentz; Stantling, and Boleſdon, with the chapel; the church of Tedinton, the chapel of Panteley, the church of Dimmock, with all its appurtenances and tithes, and the tithes of all the demeſnes, and one yard land in the ſame town; the church of Bekeford, with the chapels and tithes, and other appurtenances; the tithes of all the demeſnes in the improved and in the new plowed grounds, and half an hide of land; the church of Aſton, with the chapels and all its appurtenances, and one yard land, and the tithes of the demeſnes; in Toniton, all the tithes of the demeſnes in all things, and one yard land in the ſame town; in Compton, all the tithes of the demeſnes, and one yard land; ſeventy-five ſhillings rent in Glouceſter, and forty ſhillings in Dimmock.

Dated at Benevent the 26th day of April, in the year 1168, and in the 10th year of the pontificate of pope Alexander the IIId.

We therefore, at the inſtance of thoſe religious perſons, the abbat and convent of Cormeille, have hereunto cauſed our ſeals to be fixed.

Given in the year 1242, on the ſecond day of the month November.

NUMBER XXIII.

The CHARTER *of King* HENRY *the* IId, *confirming the Grant of the Manor of* NEWENT, *and divers other Lands and Churches in the Counties of* GLOUCESTER, HEREFORD, WORCESTER, MONMOUTH, SOUTHAMPTON, *&c. within this Kingdom of* ENGLAND.

HENRY, king of England, and duke of Normandy and Aquitaine, and earl of Anjou, to our juſtices and ſheriffs, and barons, and all our officers throughout England, greeting: Know ye, that we have given and granted to God and St. Mary of Cormeille, and to the abbat and monks ſerving God in that place, the churches, lands, alms, tithes, and all other their tenements, to hold them as beneficially and peaceably, as juſtlly, honourably and quietly, as they ever held them in the reign of king Henry my grandfather; and particularly all the manor of Newent, with all its appurtenances; to wit, five hides of land, and the church, with all the tithes, oblations, meadows, mills, and the woodsof Iarcleſdune, and of Tedeſwude, Compton, Lind, Eacle, and Melſwiche, with the mill and meadows; and Onghelie, with all the new plowed grounds belonging to Newent and Stanling; and Buledune, with its chapel; and the church of Tedington, with the chapel of Pantley; the church of Dimmock, with all its appurtenances, and the tithes, and the tithes of the demeſnes, and one yard land in the ſame town; the church of Beckford, with all its appurtenanes, with its tithes and chapels; and all the tithes of the demeſnes in the improved grounds, and in the new plowed grounds, and half an hide of land; the church of Aſton, with all its tithes and chapels and appurtenances, and one yard land, and all the tithes of the demeſnes; all the tithes of the demeſnes of Tockington, with all other things, and one yard land in the ſame town; all the tithes of the demeſnes of Compton, and one yard land; and all the tithes of the demeſnes of Cadybroke, and all the tithes of the demeſnes of Eure; all the tithes of the demeſnes of Alkſton, and all the town of Kingſton, with all its appurtenances; to wit, with two hides of land and a chapel in the ſame town; the tithes of the demeſnes of Weſtkingſton, and one yard land; the church of Mawrdy, with all the tithes and appurtenances, and all the tithes of the demeſnes, and one yard land; and the church of Kingſton, with all its tithes and appurtenances, and chapels and oblations, and all the tithes of the demeſnes, and one yard land; all the tithes of the demeſnes at Pioney, and one yard land; and the church of Suckley, with all the chapels, tithes and appurtenances, and all the tithes of the demeſnes, and one yard land; the church of Merley, with all the chapels and tithes, and appurtenances, and three yard lands, and all the tithes of the demeſnes; our right in the ſalt pits at Wich; all the tithes of the demeſnes at Hollway, and one yard land; all the tithes of the demeſnes at Sidham, and half an hide of land; all the tithes of the demeſnes at Reinham, and one yard land; all the tithes of the demeſnes at Turkiſton, and half an hide of land and a meadow; the church of Lidiar, with all the tithes and appurtenances, and half the tithe of the demeſnes and a meadow; the church of Kandel, with all the tithes and appurtenances, and all the tithes of the demeſnes, and two yard lands; the tithe of the rents in the town of Monmouth, and of Troy, and of Cumcarvan; and half the tithes of the demeſnes of Newvill, and half the tithes of the demeſnes of Richard, ſon of earl Gilbert, lying between Uſk and Wye, in woods and in plains; of fiſheries and of honey; of pannage, that is, the benefit of maſts in the wood; and pleas, that is, of profits of courts; the fourth part of the tithes of Strigule, and one bleſſaga at the ſaid manor of Newent, and coal in the wood of Eædulveſhelle, to plow it up, if it be not within our foreſt; the church of Strigule, with the chapels, and all tithes and rents, and appurtenances, and 12 l. which are paid into our exchequer out of the town of Hereford, and 9l. 10s. paid at Southampton; in which town the monks and the men of their demeſnes, and of their houſe, are free from paying any cuſtoms; ſeventy-five ſhillings paid out of the tithes of Suckley and Merley, and forty ſhillings paid at Glouceſter and Dimmock.

Witneſs, R. earl of Cornwall, at Weſtminſter.

NUMBER XXIV.

The Confirmation of the Gifts to the Priory of STANLEY, *in the County of* GLOUCESTER, *by* THEOBALD, *Archbishop of* CANTERBURY.

THEOBALD, by the grace of God, archbishop of Canterbury, primate of England, and legate of the apostolical see, to his venerable brother and friend, Simon, bishop of Worcester, and to our beloved in the Lord, all the sons of holy mother the church, health and blessing: We, out of a due regard to the peace and welfare of the church, do, out of a pious good will, grant and confirm by our authority, all those things which the churches have acquired by the bounty of good princes, or by any other justifiable means; and understanding therefore that the church of Eston, and the church of Erlingeham, and the church of Comberley, and the church of Oslewords, and the church of Cam, with all their appurtenances, and one prebend which belonged to Bernard the chaplain in Berkeley, and all the eleemosynary dues which the said Bernard held of the church of St. Leonard, in Berchelai Hernesse, and which were some time ago rightly given to Sabriethus the prior and canons of Stanley; and having a fuller knowledge of this matter by an attestation from royal charters, and from the writing deeds of our beloved son, Roger de Berkeley, patron of the said church, we do grant the full sanction of our authority for the church of Stanley St. Leonard, to have possession of these same churches; and we do hereby, by means of this present writing, confirm the aforesaid churches to the church of Stanley for ever. Farewell.

NUMBER XXV.

An INSPEXIMUS, *reciting and confirming the Charters of several Kings of England to the abbey of* TEWKSBURY.

THE king to all archbishops, &c. health: We have inspected the charter which William of famous memory, heretofore king of England, our progenitor, had granted to the church of St. Mary of Tewksbury, in these words: I William, king of the Englishmen, do grant for ever unto the monastery of St. Mary of Tewksbury, these particulars following, which Robert Fitz-Hamon and his tenants did give; to wit, his fishing, with the royalty of the river, the mills, and a meadow with the tithe, and a meadow near the pasture grounds by the fishery, and the meadow of Edmondshall, and the meadow of Selden, and the land of Roger of the Vineyard, and the churches of Walis, with the lands, tithes, rents, and all other things; and one beid, with a fishery, as the island divides the beid, and a meadow adjoining to the beid; and the tithes of colts, and of the skins of venison, and all manor courts, with full privileges throughout all the lands of St. Mary, and the common of Tewksbury, for all cattle which shall be kept in the demesnes.

Witnesses. William, the chancellor; Robert Fitz-Hamon, Roger Fitz Gerard, and Walter Giffard.

We have also inspected the charter of Henry, of pious memory, heretofore king of the Englishmen, our progenitor, granted to the blessed Mary of Tewksbury, in these words: In the name of the Holy Trinity, be it known to all good people present and to come, that I Hairic, by the grace of God king of the Englishmen, at Marlborough, in the year of our Lord 1100, do grant, and for ever confirm, these underwritten things and lands to the church of the blessed Mary of Tewksbury, which Robert Fitz-Hamon and other my great men have given to the said church; to wit, Gingeston and Stanley, and one hide at Mildelland, and two hides at Bermerton, one at Berchelai, a fishery at Tewksbury, and the meadow adjoining to it; and the mills, and the church of Walis, and the tithes and church of Fairford, and the church of Cetesly, and the tithes of Denely, and the tithes of Chenucey, and half an hide at Alureton, and the tithes of Ceotol which Robert de la Haye gave to the said church, and all the churches of his demesnes, and a fishery in Walis and Amney, which Winebald de Balaon gave to that church, with the king's leave, and the land of Robert the son of Werton, which he gave to the said church.

Signed Henry, king, with a cross before his name, and with crosses for the names of all the witnesses.

Hugh Earle, Robert de Belaime, William de Moriam, Roger de Poictivin, Heanric de Warwick, William the chancellor, Edward, William de Wrievvast, Eodorunus the steward, Robert Fiz-Hamon, and Hamon his brother, William de Albegni, Miles Crispin, Hugh de Belchamp, Roger de Nuvant, Nigell de Moneville, Roger le Bigod, Robert Malet, Hugh Maminot.

We have also inspected another charter which the said king Henry granted to the said church, in these words: In the name of the holy and undivided trinity, to all the sons and lovers of the catholick church, king Henry sendeth health: Be it known unto you all, that I Henry, by the grace of God king of the Englishmen, for ever have granted and freely confirmed to the church of Mary, the holy mother of God, and always virgin, in the year 1106, at Winchester, all things hereunder written, which Robert Fitz-Hamon and many others have given, or which the abbat hath purchased; and this I do for the good of my soul, and of the souls of my father and mother, and of my ancestors; to wit, the land of Byrnete one hide, and land in Bulling-Hope, and in Rerevalls, and one hide at Amney, which did belong to Humphry the cook; two hides at Purbike, and one hide with two tithings of Alfrede de Nicholas, and one hide in Pamington, and one yard land in Aston, and the church of St. Peter of Brigston, and the tithes of the rents of Brigston, and the churches which did belong to Robert the chaplain, with the lands and tithes thereof; those churches are thus severally named, as followeth; one church in London called Semanneskirk, the church of Merlane, the church of Hamelden, the church of Ascenten, the church of Marshfield, the church of Sodbury, the church of Thornbury, the church of Pentric, the church of Essemere, the church of Frome, the church of Lapaford, the church of Wincheley, the church of Edusley, the church of Sut-Molton, the church of Chitelmenton, the church of Bideford, the church of Liteham, the church of Chilthenton: And I, king Henry, did give unto the church one vill, which held of the honour belonging to Robert Fitz-Hamon; I gave it after his death for the good of his soul; the vill is called Ferthelmenton; one fishery, in Tewksbury, with the royalty of the water of the fishery, as far as the land of the town doth go, and one water mill; a meadow, with the tithe of the meadows; one meadow out of the common, the meadow of Eadmundeselle, the meadow of Selden, and common of pasture in all places within Tewksbury for the cattle feeding on the demesnes; the land of Roger of the Vineyard, and the new plowed ground of North Haye, soc and sac, toll and tein, in all the lands of the church; the court house, with the houses near the church, which Robert Fitz-Hamon gave to the church in the town of Tewksbury; one haye given by Godwin, two hayes given by Eglaf, and a small parcel of land given by Godwin the baker, lying near Suthmeade; and in Malverne wood whatsoever is necessary for the use of the church, and quiet pasturage for swine in the same wood: also Kingston, Stanley, Mildeland, Bermerton, Berthele, Wodechesande; half an hide in Hamme; one yard land in Alangeford; the church of Fairford; the church of Ceteslev; the tithes of Heytrodobery, the tithe of Chenuke, the tithe of Tarente; the church of Umberley, the church of Bikenton, Amney, Wertone, Chetel; with an hide in Aiulsi; with the land of Walter; two houses in Bureford, of the gift of Radulph the priest; one yard land in Bisley, of the gift of Sybill; one hide of land in Oxendon, bought of Godric, Dydicot, in exchange made by Alexander; thirty-two solidatas of land by the year, lying in a village called Aise in Somersetshire, which Gilbert de Umphrevil gave for the good of his wife's soul; two hides and a yard land in Ascenton, given by Robert the son of Nigell; in Wales the parish church of St. Mary of the town of Cardiffe, with one plow's tillage; the chapel in the castle of Cardiffe, with one plow's tillage; and the tithes of all the rents of the demesnes of the town of Cardiffe; the tithes of all the demesnes which Robert the son of Fitz-Hamon held in Wales; the tithes of all the barons holding of Robert Fitz-Hamon throughout all Wales; all that branch of water of Taff which is near the church, from the issuing out of Taff till it goes into Taff again, to make fish-ponds therewith, or any other conveniencies for the church; and the meadow on the other side of the water near the church; the village called Landoho; the land given by Walter de Landbethien; the tithes of the land which the abbat of Gloucester hath in Landcarven; the church of Landhiltunit; the land which Wakelyn gave; the water mill at Raz, and the fisheries which Robert de Hay gave; the land which Robert the son of Nigel gave; the church of Newcastle; all these have been confirmed by me, and my barons with me; signed with a cross by the several persons following:

King Henry; Walter, the chancellor; Gerard, the archbishop; Robert, bishop of Nicholo; Sampson, bishop of Worcester; Hugh, the abbat; Humphry de Bohun; Haymon, the steward; Robert, earl of Mellent; the abbat of Glastenbury; Robert, son of Nigell; the abbat Germund; the abbat Pharis; Roger, bishop of Salisbury; Thomas, the chaplain; William, bishop of Exeter; and the abbat Nigell.

We have also inspected the charter which the same king Henry made to St. Mary, and to the monks of Tewksbury, in these words: Henry, by the grace of God king of England and duke of Normandy, to all archbishops, bishops, earls, barons, justices, sheriffs, and all our officers, health: Know ye, that I, in honour of God, and of the holy Mary, mother of God, and for the good of my soul, and the souls of king William my father, and of king

king William my brother, and of queen Maud my mother, and of queen Maud my wife, and of the fouls of all my anceftors, and for the good of the foul of Robert Fitz-Hamon, have granted and confirmed to St. Mary, and to the abbat and monks of Tewkfbury, all their poffeffions in churches and tithes, in lands and waters, in mills and fifheries, in paftures and woods, and in all other things, to hold to them in perpetual almonage, as free and difcharged as Robert Fitz Hamon held the fame, who founded the fame church, and as they were when in the demefne of king William my father, or queen Maud my mother, from all payments to the fhires or hundreds, from all taxes or dane money, and from all cuftoms and other pretenfions.

Witneffes. Roger, bifhop of Salifbury; Robert, bifhop of Lincoln; Robert, earl of Mellent; Robert, earl of Gloucefter; Brience, fon of earl Hamo, fteward of the houfhold; Walter of Gloucefter, at Winchefter.

We have alfo infpected the charter which the fame king Henry granted to St. Mary of Tewkfbury in thefe words: Henry, king of the Englifhmen, to all archbifhops, bifhops, juftices, earls, barons, fheriffs, and all other officers of the refpective places wherein the abbat of Tewkfbury has any lands, fends greeting: Know ye, that I have granted and confirmed to St. Mary of Tewkfbury thefe following particulars in perpetual almonage, freely and quietly, for the good of my foul, and the fouls of my father and mother, and of all my anceftors, the church of Chedefley, the church of Lethe, the tithes of Chaldewel and Fifhide, the tithes of Sutton, the tithes of Bacheberge, the tithes of Wefton, given by Robert de Bafkerville, the tithes of Harefelde, the tithes of Muchelefberge; the land called Lancadel, which Walchelin gave to the church; the land in Didicot, which the church had by exchange from Alexander de Cormeille; the land in Polton, which Adaliza de Lifle gave to the fame church, for the good of the foul of Reginald de Dunftanville her hufband; two hides in Porbec, of the fee of Robert de Claville; and I farther will and command, that all poffeffions of St. Mary of Tewkfbury be free and difcharged from all pleas and taxes, and all other charges, as when they were the demefnes of Robert Fitz-Hamon, and as they are now the demefnes of Robert my fon.

Witneffes. Ranulph, the chancellor; and Hamon, the fteward, at Burnam.

We have alfo infpected the charter which Henry of pious memory, king of England, our great grandfather, granted unto the faid monks, in thefe words: Henry king of England, and duke of Normandy and Aquitaine, earl of Anjou, to our juftices, fheriffs, barons, and other officers, and all his good people throughout England and Wales, fend greeting: Know ye, that I have granted to the monks of Tewkfbury, that they may freely and quietly buy and fell all manner of things neceffary for themfelves throughout all England and Wales; and I forbid all perfons from giving any difturbance to them under the penalty of 10l.

Witnefs. Humphry de Bohun, at Gloucefter.

We therefore intending to ftrengthen and make good the feveral gifts, grants and confirmations abovefaid, to our well beloved in Chrift, the abbat and convent of the place abovefaid, and to their fucceffors, do, for us and our heirs, as much as in us lies, grant and confirm all things in the feveral charters fpecified.

Witneffes. The venerable fathers, A. bifhop of Durham; John, bifhop of Carlifle; William bifhop of Coventry and Litchfield; John de Warren, earl of Surrey; Thomas, earl of Lancafter; Henry de Lacy, earl of Lincoln; John de Haftinges; John de Segrave; Hugh le Difpencer, and others.

Given under our hand at Carlifle, the firft day of July, by a fine levied in the exchequer.

NUMBER XXVI.

The CHARTER *of the Town and Borough of* TEWKSBURY.

WILLAM the IIId, by the grace of God of England, Scotland, France and Ireland, king, defender of the faith, &c. to all to whom thefe letters patents fhall come, greeting: Whereas our great grandfather, James the Firft, late king of England, &c. by his letters patents under his great feal of England, bearing date the 23d day of March, in the year of his reign of England, France and Ireland, the feventh, reciting: That whereas our fovereign lady Elizabeth, late queen of England, by her letters patents fealed with her great feal of England, bearing date at Gorhambury, the 4th day of April, in the 17th year of her reign, amongft other things had willed, ordained, conftituted, granted and declared, that the town of Tewkfbury, in her county of Gloucefter, and the whole fee called the abbey fee in Tewkfbury aforefaid, and alfo the whole manor and liberty of the late abbey, or late diffolved monaftery of Tewksbury, called the abbey fee, parcel of the poffeffions of the late monaftery fhould be and are a free borough, incorporated in deed, fact and name, for ever, of two bailiffs, and of burgeffes and commonalty of the faid town or borough of Tewksbury, by the name of the bailiffs, burgeffes and commonalty of the borough of Tewksbury, in the county of Gloucefter; and that the bailiffs, burgeffes and commonalty of the fame borough for the time being, and their fucceffors, be and fhould be one body corporate and politick, and one perpetual community in deed and name, and fhould have perpetual fucceffion; and them the faid bailiffs and burgeffes, one body corporate and politick, really and to the full had created, erected, ordained, declared and incorporated by the fame letters patents, as by the fame letters patents, amongft other things, may more fully appear.

And alfo reciting, that whereas the faid James the Firft, late king of England, &c. by his letters patents, fealed with his great feal of England, bearing date at Weftminfter, the 18th day of October, in the year of his reign of England, France and Ireland, the 3d, and of Scotland the 39th, (amongft other things) had willed, granted, ordained, conftituted and declared, that the borough of Tewksbury aforefaid, fhould be, and remain for ever hereafter, a free borough of itfelf; and that the bailiffs, burgeffes, and commonalty of the borough of Tewksbury thereafter for ever, be, and fhould be one body corporate and politick, in deed, fact and name, by the name of the bailiffs, burgeffes, and commonalty of the borough of Tewksbury, in the county of Gloucefter; and them, by the name of the bailiffs, burgeffes, and commonalty of the borough of Tewksbury, in the county of Gloucefter, one body corporate and politick, really and to the full, for himfelf, his heirs and fucceffors, had erected, made, ordained and created, by his faid letters patents; and that, by the fame name, they fhould have perpetual fucceffion, as by his faid letters patents (amongft other things) in like manner more fully may appear.

And alfo reciting, that whereas his beloved and faithful fubjects, the bailiffs, burgeffes, and commonalty of the borough of Tewkfbury afforefaid, in the faid county of Gloucefter, had purchafed of him the faid king, for a great fum of money, his whole manor and borough of Tewkfbury in the county of Gloucefter, and his divers meffuages, lands, tenements and hereditaments in Tewkfbury, in the faid county of Gloucefter, late parcel of the poffeffions of the late monaftery of Tewkfbury, and the manor of Tewkfbury in the faid county of Gloucefter, and his hundred of Tewkfbury in the faid counties of Gloucefter and Worcefter, or in one of them; and divers meffuages, lands, tenements and hereditaments there, late parcel of the lands of Thomas late lord Seymour of Sudely, attainted; and alfo the manor and borough of Tewkfbury, in the faid county of Gloucefter, and divers meffuages, lands, tenements and hereditaments there, late parcel of the lands called Warwick's and Spencer's lands; as well for and in confideration of the purchafe aforefaid, as for divers other good caufes and confiderations, him to the fame prefents efpecially moving, for the better rule, government and improvement of the borough of Tewkfbury aforefaid, of his fpecial grace, and of his certain knowledge and mere motion, had willed, granted, conftituted ordained and declared, for himfelf, his heirs and fucceffors, that the faid manor and borough of Tewksbury in the county of Gloucefter, and the other hereditaments aforefaid, late parcel of the lands of the late monaftery of Tewkfbury, and the aforefaid manor of Tewkfbury in the faid county of Gloucefter, and the aforefaid hundred and liberty of Tewkfbury, in the faid counties of Gloucefter and Worcefter, or in one of them, and the other hereditaments aforefaid, late parcel of Thomas late lord Seymour of Sudely, attaint, and alfo the aforefaid manor and borough of Tewkfbury in the faid county of Gloucefter, and other the hereditaments aforefaid, late parcel of the lands called Warwick's and Spencer's lands, be and fhould be, and reputed to be, part and parcel of the incorporation of the town and borough of Tewkfbury aforementioned; and the aforefaid town of Tewkfbury in the county of Gloucefter, and all that fee called the abbey fee in Tewksbury aforefaid; and alfo all that manor and liberty of the late abbey, or late diffolved monaftery of Tewkfbury, called the abbey fee, parcel of the poffeffions of the late monaftery; and all that manor and borough of Tewkfbury, parcel of the poffeffions of the late monaftery: and all that manor of Tewkfbury in the faid county of Gloucefter; and all that hundred and liberty of Tewksbury, in the counties of Gloucefter and Worcefter, or in one of them, parcel of lands of Thomas late lord Seymour of Sudely, attaint; alfo all that manor and borough of Tewksbury, parcel of the lands called Warwick's and Spencer's lands; and all other meffuages, lands, tenements and hereditaments as aforefaid, of him purchafed, to be one intire free borough corporate, in deed, fact and name, from thence for ever had, ordained, created and incorporated by his faid letters patents; and alfo had given and granted to them the faid bailiffs, burgeffes, and commonalty of the borough aforefaid, and their fucceffors, divers liberties, powers, privileges, authorities,

rities, and other things, as by the faid letters patents, bearing date the twenty third day of March, in the feventh year of the reign of the faid late king James the firft, more fully may appear:

And whereas the bailiffs, burgeffes and commonalty of our borough of Tewksbury aforefaid, have furrendered the charter or letters patents, bearing date the faid twenty third day of March, in the feventh year of the reign of the faid late king James the firft, to them or their anceftors formerly granted; and all the liberties, privileges, emoluments and advantages, by the fame charter, or by any former or other charters or letters patents to them granted, to James the fecond, late king of England, by their writing, fealed with their common feal, bearing date the twenty fourth day of March, in the firft year of the reign of the faid late king James the fecond, and duly inrolled in our court of chancery:

And whereas the aforefaid James the fecond, late king of England, by his letters patents under his great feal of England made, bearing date the twelfth day of March, in the fecond year of his reign, did will, conftitute and declare, that the faid town of Tewksbury, in the faid county of Gloucefter, and the other meffuages, lands, tenements and hereditaments in the fame letters patents mentioned, be, and fhould be a free borough of itfelf; and the burgeffes and inhabitants of the fame borough be, and fhould be one body corporate and politick, in deed, fact and name, by the name of the mayor, aldermen, and common council of the borough of Tewksbury, in the county of Gloucefter; and granted to them divers liberties, franchifes, powers, and other things.

And whereas no election of mayor, aldermen, or perfons of the common council of the borough aforefaid, or of any officer in or for the borough aforefaid, nor any government in the fame borough, according to the form and effect of the fame letters patents of James the fecond, or of any other charter of incorporation of the borough aforefaid, for divers years laft paft have been had or executed, or is now executed, as we are informed, by reafon of which, all acts of government and adminiftration of juftice in the fame borough (as a body corporate) have totally ceafed, and as yet do ceafe, to the great prejudice of our fubjects inhabiting there:

And whereas the burgeffes of the fame borough have humbly befought us, and our late moft dear confort Mary, late queen of England, &c. to grant to them our royal charter, and to reftore and confirm to them fuch liberties and privileges as they had and enjoyed at the time of the furrender aforefaid: We therefore, being willing that from henceforth for ever there be had in the borough aforefaid, a certain and undoubted manner of, and for the keeping of the peace, and for the good rule and government of our people there, and others coming thither; and that our peace in future times may be kept inviolated there, and that other acts of juftice and good rule within the borough aforefaid, may be rightly adminiftered and executed, to the terror of the wicked, and the reward of the good.

And we being alfo willing that the burgeffes and inhabitants of the borough aforefaid, for ever hereafter, may have and ufe the ancient liberties, franchifes, privileges and preheminences, from the burgeffes and inhabitants of the borough aforefaid, before this ufed and enjoyed, together with our fuller grants for the better confervation of the peace in the borough aforefaid, and government and rule of our people there: Know ye, that we of our fpecial grace, certain knowledge and mere motion, have willed, granted, conftituted, ordained and declared, and by thefe prefents for us, our heirs and fucceffors, do will, grant, conftitute, ordain and declare, that the faid manor and borough of Tewkfbury, in the county of Gloucefter, and the other hereditaments aforefaid, late parcel of lands of the late monaftery of Tewkfbury; and the aforefaid manor of Tewkfbury, in the faid county of Gloucefter; and the aforefaid hundred and liberty of Tewkfbury, in the counties of Gloucefter and Worcefter, and in either of them; and the other hereditaments aforefaid late parcel of lands of Thomas late lord Seymour of Sudely, attaint; and alfo the aforefaid manor and borough of Tewksbury, in the faid county of Gloucefter, and other the hereditaments aforefaid, late parcel of lands called Warwick's and Spencer's lands; be, and fhall be, and reputed to be part and parcel of the incorporation of the town and borough of Tewksbury beforementioned; and the aforefaid town of Tewksbury, in the county of Gloucefter; and the whole fee called the abbey fee, in Tewksbury aforefaid; and alfo the whole manor and liberty of the late abbey or monaftery of Tewksbury lately diffolved, called the abbey fee; parcel of the poffeffion of the faid late monaftery, and whole manor and borough of Tewksbury, part of the poffeffions of the faid late monaftery; and whole manor of Tewksbury, in the faid county of Gloucefter; and the whole hundred and liberty of Tewksbury, in the counties of Gloucefter and Worcefter, and in either of them, parcel of lands of Thomas late lord Seymour of Sudely, attaint; and alfo all that manor and borough of Tewksbury, parcel of lands called Warwick's and Spencer's lands; and all other meffuages, lands, tenements and hereditaments, as aforefaid purchafed; we do ordain, create and incorporate by thefe prefents, one entire free borough corporate, in fact, deed and name, henceforth for ever.

And that the burgeffes and inhabitants of the fame borough of Tewksbury, for the future and for ever, are, and fhall be one body corporate and politick in fact, deed and name, by the name of bailiffs, burgeffes and community of the borough of Tewkfbury, in the county of Gloucefter; and them by the name of bailiffs, burgeffes and community of the borough of Tewksbury, in the county of Gloucefter, one body corporate and politick, really and fully, for us, our heirs and fucceffors, we erect, make, ordain and create by thefe perfents; and that by the fame name they may have a perpetual fucceffion. And that they and their fucceffors, by the name of bailiffs, burgeffes and community of the borough of Tewksbury, in the county of Gloucefter, may and fhall be perpetually for the future, perfons fit and capable in the law, to have, demand, receive and poffefs lands, tenements, liberties, franchifes, jurifdictions and hereditaments, to them and their fucceffors, in fee and perpetuity, or for term of life or lives, year or years, or otherwife howfoever; and alfo goods and chattles, and all other things of whatfoever fort, nature, kind or quality they fhall be; and to give, grant, demife and affign the fame lands, tenements and hereditaments, goods and chattles, and other deeds and things whatfoever, or any parcel thereof; and all other things do and perform by the name aforefaid: and that by the fame name of bailiffs, burgeffes and community of Tewksbury, in the county of Gloucefter, they may and can plead and be impleaded, anfwer and be anfwered, defend and be defended, in all courts and places whatfoever, and before us, our heirs and fucceffors; and all judges and juftices, and other perfons and officers whatfoever, of us, our heirs and fucceffors, in all and fingular actions, pleas, fuits, complaints, caufes, matters and demands whatfoever, of whatfoever fort, nature or kind, in the fame manner and form as any other of our fubjects of our kingdom of England, perfons fit and capable in the law, or any other body corporate and politick, whithin this our kingdom of England, may, and can have, receive, purchafe, poffefs, give, grant, demife, affign or difpofe, and plead and be impleaded, anfwer and be anfwered, defend and be defended, do or perform.

And we further will, and by thefe prefents for us, our heirs and fucceffors, do give, grant, reftore and confirm to the faid bailiffs, burgeffes and community of the borough of Tewksbury aforefaid, and their fucceffors, full power and authority to execute, enjoy and exercife fo many, fo much, fuch, the fame, of the fame kind, all, all manner, and the like cuftoms, liberties, privileges, franchifes, immunities, acquittances, fines, amercements, exemption of goals, merchandizing, tolls, cuftom, and all other rights and jurifdictions whatfoever, within the faid town of Tewksbury in the county of Gloucefter; and within the whole fee, called the abbey fee, in Tewksbury aforefaid; and within the whole manor and liberties of the late abbey or monaftery of Tewksbury, lately diffolved, called the abbey fee, parcel of the poffeffion of the faid late monaftery; and within the whole manor and borough of Tewksbury, parcel of the poffeffion of the faid late monaftery; and within the whole manor of Tewksbury, in the faid county of Gloucefter; and the whole hundred and liberty of Tewksbury, in the faid counties of Gloucefter and Worcefter, and in either of them, parcel of lands of Thomas late lord Seymour of Sudely, attaint; and alfo within the whole manor and borough of Tewksbury, parcel of lands called Warwick's and Spencer's lands; and alfo within all and fingular meffuages, lands, tenements and hereditaments, as aforefaid, before purchafed; and within every and either of them, and part and parcel of each of them, as many, as much, fuch, and which the aforefaid bailiffs, burgeffes and community of the borough aforefaid, or their predeceffors, or any of them, by whatfoever names, or by whatfoever name, or by whatfoever incorporation, or pretence of any incorporation (at or before the time of the furrender aforefaid) lawfully had, poffeffed or enjoyed, or ought to have, poffefs, ufe or enjoy, within the borough, town, hundred, manor, tenements, liberties and places aforefaid.

And we farther will, and by thefe prefents for us, our heirs and fucceffors, do give and grant to the aforefaid bailiffs, burgeffes and community of the borough aforefaid, and to their fucceffors, free liberty, power and authority, and that it well may and fhall be lawful for the aforefaid bailiffs, burgeffes and community of the borough aforefaid, and their fucceffors, to perambulate and make perambulation or perembulations thereof, and to erect and put bounds and limits there, or in the outward parts thereof, or any part of it, for to have true and better knowledge thereof, as often as it fhall pleafe them, or fhall feem neceffary to them; and this without any writ, or other warrant therefore from us, our heirs or fucceffors, in this part howfoever to be requefted or profecuted.

We will alfo, and by thefe prefents for us, our heirs and fucceffors, do grant and ordain, that from henceforth for the future, there are and fhall be in the borough aforefaid, two of the burgeffes of the borough aforefaid, in manner below in thefe prefents named,

named, to be chosen and named, who ſhall be, and ſhall be nominated bailiffs of the ſame borough; and for the better execution of our grant in this part, we have aſſigned, nominated, appointed and made, and by theſe preſents, for us our heirs and ſucceſſors, do aſſign, nominate, appoint and make our beloved Joſeph Jones and Henry Dobbins, gent. to be the firſt and modern bailiffs of the borough aforeſaid; willing that they the ſame Joſeph Jones and Henry Dobbins ſhall be and continue in the offices of bailiffs of the ſame borough, from the date of theſe preſents, until and in the ſecond Thurſday in the month of October next to come, and from the ſame day until two other of the burgeſſes of the borough aforeſaid ſhall be elected, appointed, and ſworn to the office of bailiffs aforeſaid, at the time, in the manner and form in theſe preſents here under mentioned, if the ſame Joſeph Jones and Henry Dobbins, or either of them ſhall ſo long live. And we will alſo, and by theſe preſents, for us our heirs and ſucceſſors, do grant and ordain, that from henceforth for ever, there may and ſhall be in the borough aforeſaid, four and twenty men, of the better, honeſter, and more diſcreet burgeſſes of the ſame borough, who ſhall be, and perpetually called principal burgeſſes of the borough aforeſaid; which principal burgeſſes, together with the bailiffs of the borough aforeſaid, may, and ſhall be, and for ever hereafter ſhall be called the common council of the borough aforeſaid, for all things, matters, cauſes and buſineſſes of the borough aforeſaid, and the good rule, ſtate and government of the ſame borough, touching or concerning; and they may, and ſhall be from time to time aſſiſtant and helping to the ſaid bailiffs, for that time being, in all things, matters, cauſes and buſineſſes relating to the ſame borough.

And we farther have aſſigned, nominated appointed and made, and by theſe preſents, for us our heirs and ſucceſſors, do aſſign, nominate appoint and make our beloved Robert Tracy, eſq; Richard Dowdeſwell, eſq; Henry Collet, jun. eſq; Charles Wynde, the aforeſaid Joſeph Jones, Nicholas Streight, Theophilus Holland, William Streight, Henry Peyton, Nicholas Wrenford, William Wilſon, John Mann, Abraham Farren, Samuel Hawling, Robert Porter, the aforeſaid Henry Dobbins, William Jones, Francis Leight, John Jeynes, Thomas Warkeman, William Merrett, Thomas Hale, merchant, Thomas Bartholomew, and Daniel Kemble, gent. to be the chief and modern four and twenty principal burgeſſes of the borough aforeſaid, to be continued in the ſame offices and places as long as they ſhall behave themſelves well; which indeed principal burgeſſes, and every of them before named, and principal burgeſſes, of the borough aforeſaid, for the time being, for himſelf or themſelves ill behaving, we will to be moveable at the good pleaſure of the bailiffs and principal burgeſſes, being common council of the borough aforeſaid, or the greater part of them, either of which bailiffs of the borough aforeſaid, for the time being, we will to be one.

And we farther will, and by theſe preſents, for us our heirs and ſucceſſors, do grant to the bailiffs, burgeſſes, and community of the borough aforeſaid, and to their ſucceſſors, that whenſoever it ſhall happen that either or any of the four and twenty principal burgeſſes of the borough aforeſaid, for the time being, do die, or be removed from their office as aforeſaid, that then and ſo often, it may and ſhall be well and lawful for the aforeſaid bailiffs, and principal burgeſſes, being a common council of the borough aforeſaid, or for the greater part of them, (of whom either of the bailiffs of the borough aforeſaid, for that time being, we will to be one) one other, or more of the burgeſſes of the borough aforeſaid, into the place or places of a principal burgeſs, or thoſe principal burgeſſes ſo dead, or removed from his or their office or offices, to elect, nominate and appoint, to ſupply the aforeſaid number of four and twenty principal burgeſſes of the borough aforeſaid; and that he or they ſo elected and appointed as aforeſaid, may have and exerciſe that office or offices as long as he or they ſhall behave himſelf or themſelves well in the ſame office or offices, a corporal oath before the bailiffs and principal burgeſſes, being common council of the borough aforeſaid, for the time being or the greater part of them (of whom either of the bailiffs of the borough aforeſaid we will to be one) of that office, in all things touching that office, rightly, well and faithfully to execute(being performed.

And farther, of our more abundant ſpecial grace, certain knowledge, and mere motion, have willed, ordained and granted, and by theſe preſents, for us our heirs and ſucceſſors, do will, ordain, and grant to the aforeſaid bailiffs, burgeſſes, and community of the borough aforeſaid, and their ſucceſſors, that from henceforth for ever there be, and ſhall be within the borough aforeſaid, four and twenty other men, honeſt and diſcreet, of the ſame borough, who ſhall be, and be named aſſiſtants of the ſame borough which indeed four and twenty aſſiſtants may, and ſhall be from time to time aſſiſting and helping to the bailiffs of the borough aforeſaid, for the time being, and to the aforeſaid four and twenty principal burgeſſes, for the good rule, ſtate, and government of the borough aforeſaid, in all things, cauſes, matters and buſineſſes touching the ſame borough.

And we have aſſigned, nominated, created, appointed and made, and by theſe preſents, for us our heirs and ſucceſſors, do aſſign, nominate, create, appoint, and make our beloved Joſeph Sheene, Stephen Millington, Iſaac Merret, Robert Wilkins, John Reeks, Robert Morris, George Moore, William Heyward, Edward Leight, John Farren, Ralph Jeynes of the Barton ſtreet, Matthew Maid, Thomas Nutt, Edward Phelps; Samuel Dobbins, Ralph Jeynes of the high ſtreet, Philip Bruſh, George Waters, alias Hawkins, Richard Pitt, Joſeph Smith, John Clifton, John Chaundler, Edward Peirce, and Samuel Penell, to be four and twenty chief and modern aſſiſtants of the borough aforeſaid, to be continued in the ſame offices as long as they ſhall behave themſelves well; which very aſſiſtants before named, and either or any of them, and the aſſiſtants of the borough aforeſaid; for the time being, and either or any of them, not behaving himſelf or themſelves well in their offices, we will to be moveable at the good pleaſure of the bailiffs and principal burgeſſes, being common council of the borough aforeſaid, or the greater part of them, of whom either of the bailiffs of the borough aforeſaid for the time being, we will to be one.

And we farther will, and for us, our heirs and ſucceſſors, do give and grant to the ſaid bailiffs, burgeſſes and community of the borough aforeſaid, and to their ſucceſſors, that whenſoever it ſhall happen, that either or any of the aforeſaid four and twenty aſſiſtants of the borough aforeſaid, do die, or are removed from his or their office, as aforeſaid, that then and ſo often, it may and ſhall be well and lawful for the ſaid bailiffs, and the reſt of the common council of the borough aforeſaid, for the time being, or the greater part of them (of whom either of the bailiffs of the borough aforeſaid, for the time being, we will to be one) one other or more of the burgeſſes of the borough aforeſaid, into the place or places of the ſame aſſiſtant or aſſiſtants, ſo happening to die or be removed, to elect, nominate and appoint, to ſupply the aforeſaid number of four and twenty aſſiſtants of the borough aforeſaid; and that he or they ſo as aforeſaid elected and appointed to the office or offices of an aſſiſtant or aſſiſtants of the borough aforeſaid, having performed before the bailiffs and the reſt of the common council of the borough aforeſaid, for the time being, or the greater part of them (of whom either of the bailiffs of the borough aforeſaid, for the time being, we will to be one) a corporal oath, well and faithfully to execute that office, he and they ſhall be of the number of the aforeſaid four and twenty aſſiſtants of the borough aforeſaid; and this from time to time as often as it ſhall ſo happen.

And we farther will, and by theſe preſents, for us our heirs and ſucceſſors, do grant to the ſaid bailiffs, burgeſſes, and community of the borough aforeſaid and their ſucceſſors, that from heneforth for the future, the bailiffs, burgeſſes aforeſaid, ſhall be elected, nominated, and ſworn yearly, and every year, in and upon the ſecond Thurſday in the month of October, and not upon the Thurſday next after the feaſt of St. Simon and Jude apoſtles, by and before ſuch perſon and perſons, and in the ſame manner and form as was wont to be in the ſame borough, at and before the time of the ſurrender aforeſaid; and that they who ſhall be elected, nominated and ſworn, as aforeſaid, to the office of bailiffs of the borough aforeſaid, may have and exerciſe that office for one whole year then next following, and thenceforth until two other burgeſſes of the borough aforeſaid to the offices of bailiffs of the borough aforeſaid ſhall be elected, appointed, and ſworn in due manner.

And moreover we will, and for us, our heirs and ſucceſſors, do grant to the bailiffs, burgeſſes, and community of the borough aforeſaid, and their ſucceſſors, that if it ſhall happen that the bailiffs of the borough aforeſaid, or either of them for the time being, within one year after they ſhall be elected, appointed, and ſworn to the offices of bailiffs of the borough aforeſaid, ſo as aforeſaid, do die, or be removed from his or their office or offices, that then and ſo often, one other fit perſon, or two other fit perſons, ſhall be elected, appointed and ſworn into the bailiwick or bailiwicks of the borough of Tewkſbury aforeſaid, by and before ſuch perſon and perſons, and in ſuch manner and form as was wont in the ſame borough at and before the time of the ſurrender aforeſaid; and that he or they ſo elected and ſworn, may have and execute that office or offices during the reſidue of the ſame year, and ſo often as it ſhall ſo happen.

And we farther will, and by theſe preſents, for us our heirs and ſucceſſors, do grant to the aforeſaid bailiffs, burgeſſes and community of the borough aforeſaid, and their ſucceſſors, that they and their ſucceſſors may and ſhall have in the borough aforeſaid, one honeſt and diſcreet man to be choſen and nominated, in form beneath in theſe preſents expreſſed, who ſhall be, and be named high ſteward of the borough aforeſaid; and we have aſſigned, nominated, appointed and made, and by theſe preſents, for us our heirs and ſucceſſors, do aſſign, nominate, appoint and make our well beloved and faithful kinſman Algernoon, earl of Eſſex, to be the firſt and modern high ſteward of the borough aforeſaid, to be continued in the ſame office ſo long as he ſhall behave himſelf well.

We alſo will, and by theſe preſents, for us our heirs and ſucceſſors, do grant to the bailiffs, burgeſſes and community of the borough aforeſaid, and their ſucceſſors, that from and after the death of the ſaid Algernoon, earl of Eſſex, or any other determination

mination of his office, the bailiffs and principal burgeſſes of the borough aforeſaid, for the time being, or the greater part of them, (of whom either of the bailiffs of the borough aforeſaid we will to be one) may, and can elect, nominate and appoint one other honeſt and diſcreet man, from time to time, to the office of high ſteward of the borough aforeſaid; and that he who ſhall be elected, appointed and nominated, ſo as aforeſaid, after the death of the ſaid Algernoon, earl of Eſſex, or any other determination of the ſaid office of high ſteward, ſhall and may execute and enjoy that office of high ſteward of the borough aforeſaid, during the good pleaſure of the aforeſaid bailiffs and principal burgeſſes of the borough aforeſaid, or the greater part of them, (of whom either of the bailiffs of the borough aforeſaid we will to be one) and ſo as oft as it ſhall ſo happen.

We will alſo, and for us our heirs and ſucceſſors, do grant to the ſaid bailiffs, burgeſſes and community of the borough aforeſaid, and their ſucceſſors, that they, from henceforth for ever, may have in the borough aforeſaid, one honeſt, fit and diſcreet man, ſkilful and learned in the laws of this kingdom of England, who ſhall be, and be named recorder of that borough, to be continued in that office, and to execute the ſame by himſelf or his deputy, as long as he ſhall behave himſelf well: And we have aſſigned, nominated, appointed and made, and by theſe preſents, for us our heirs and ſucceſſors, do aſſign, nominate, appoint and make the aforeſaid Robert Tracy to be chief and modern recorder of the borough aforeſaid, to be continued in the ſame office, and the ſame office to execute by himſelf or his ſufficient deputy, as long as he ſhall behave himſelf well.

And we farther will, and by theſe preſents, for us our heirs and ſucceſſors, do grant to the bailiffs, burgeſſes, and community of the borough aforeſaid, and their ſucceſſors, that after the death or removal of the ſaid Robert Tracy, from the office aforeſaid, and ſo oft as the office of recorder of the borough aforeſaid ſhall happen to be vacant, it may, and ſhall be lawful for the bailiffs and principal burgeſſes of the borough aforeſaid, for the time being or the greater part of them (of whom either of the bailiffs of the borough aforeſaid we will to be one) to elect, name and prefer one other honeſt and diſcreet man, learned in the laws of this kingdom of England, into the office of recorder of the borough aforeſaid, to be continued in the ſame office ſo long as he ſhall behave himſelf well; which ſaid Robert Tracy, and all other perſons who for the future ſhall be elected, nominated and appointed, ſo as aforeſaid, into the office of recorder of the borough aforeſaid, before he ſhall be permitted to execute that office, ſhall take a corporal oath before the bailiffs of the borough aforeſaid, for the time being, or either of them, to rightly, well and faithfully execute that office, in all buſineſſes touching or concerning it.

And we farther, of our more abundant ſpecial grace, certain knowledge, and mere motion, have willed and granted, and by theſe preſents, for us our heirs and ſucceſſors, do will and grant to the aforeſaid bailiffs, burgeſſes and community of the borough aforeſaid, and their ſucceſſors, that the bailiffs and recorder of the borough aforeſaid, for the time being, during the time in which they ſhall happen to be in their offices, and four other of the honeſter and more diſcreet burgeſſes of the borough aforeſaid, to be choſen and nominated by the bailiffs and principal burgeſſes of the borough aforeſaid, or by the greater part of them, (of whom either of the bailiffs of the borough aforeſaid we will to be one) may and ſhall be, and every of them may and ſhall be our juſtices, and our heirs and ſucceſſors, to keep the peace, and to keep and cauſe to be kept the orders and ſtatutes ſet forth for the good of the peace of us, our heirs and ſucceſſors, and for the keeping of the ſame, and for the good and quiet rule and government of our people, our heirs and ſucceſſors, and in all their articles in the borough and liberty, and precincts by theſe preſents, to the aforeſaid bailiffs, burgeſſes and community of the borough aforeſaid before granted, according to the ſtatute, form, and effect of the ſame; and to chaſtize and puniſh all offending againſt the force, form and effect of the ſame orders and ſtatutes, or either of them, as ſhall be to be done according to the form of the ſame orders and ſtatutes; and to cauſe to come before them, or either of them, all thoſe who have threatened either or any of our people, concerning their bodies, or burning of their houſes, to find ſufficient ſecurity of the peace, or their good behaviour towards us and our people; and if they ſhall refuſe to find ſuch ſecurity, then them to cauſe to be kept ſafe in our priſon in the borough aforeſaid, until they ſhall find ſuch ſecurity; and to hear and determine all and all manner of fellonies, and other miſdeeds in the ſaid borough, and liberty and precinct of the ſame, before mentioned, committed and to be committed, and to keep and correct, and cauſe to be kept and corrected, the ſtatutes concerning artificers, labourers, weights and meaſures, within the borough aforeſaid, and liberty and precinct of the ſame.

And that the ſaid bailiffs and principal burgeſſes, or the greater part of them, within one month after the date of theſe preſents, ſhall chuſe four ſuch burgeſſes as aforeſaid, to be juſtices of the peace, which ſaid four burgeſſes ſhall continue in the offices of juſtices of the peace within the borough aforeſaid, until and upon the ſecond Thurſday in the month of October next to come; and that in and upon the aforeſaid ſecond Thurſday of October next to come, and upon every ſecond Thurſday in the month of October for ever, four ſuch burgeſſes of the borough aforeſaid, ſhall be yearly choſen as aforeſaid, to be juſtices of the peace as aforeſaid, within the borough aforeſaid; and that the bailiffs and recorders of the ſame borough, for the time being, and four other burgeſſes to be elected and nominated ſo as aforeſaid, in the offices of juſtices of the peace, or any three of them (of whom either of the bailiffs or recorders of the borough aforeſaid we will to be one) may have full power and abſolute authority, to enquire from time to time by the oath of honeſt and lawful man of the borough aforeſaid, liberty and precinct of the ſame, concerning all and all manner of petty treaſons, murders, voluntary manſlaughter, manſlaughters, felonies, witchcrafts, incantations, ſorceries, magick art, foreſtallings, ingroſſings, regratings and extortions whatſoever; and concerning all and ſingular other witchcrafts, tranſgreſſions, faults and offences whatſoever, of which the juſtices appointed to keep the peace in any county of our kingdom of England, may, or ought lawfully to enquire. And that they may or ſhall hear and determine all and ſingular felonies, offences, tranſgreſſions, crimes and articles whatſoever, that belong to the office of a juſtice of the peace within the borough aforeſaid, liberty and precinct of the ſame, to be done, heard, performed and determined ſo fully and wholly, and in ſo ample manner and form as any other juſtices appointed to keep the peace in any county of our kingdom of England, by the laws and ſtatutes of the ſame kingdom of England, or otherwiſe. And that they, or any three of them, may and can from time to time keep ſeſſions in the ſame manner and form as any other juiſtices appointed to keep the peace in any county of our kingdom of England, may and can: ſo nevertheleſs that at the determination of any treaſon, murder, manſlaughter, felony, or other offence whatſoever, touching the loſs of life or a member within the borough aforeſaid, liberty and precinct of the ſame, without our ſpecial mandate of us our heirs or ſucceſſors, howſoever, for the future, they may not proceed.

We will alſo, and for us our heirs and ſucceſſors, do command and forbid by theſe preſents, that no juſtice of the peace within the county of Glouceſter, do any ways introduce, to do or execute any thing within the town or pariſh of Tewkſbury, and precinct of the ſame, that belongs to the office of a juſtice of the peace there to be done.

And we farther will, and by theſe preſents for us our heirs and ſucceſſors, do grant to the aforeſaid bailiffs, burgeſſes and community of the borough aforeſaid, and their ſucceſſors, that they and their ſucceſſors henceforth for ever, may have and hold within the borough aforeſaid, a certain court of record before the bailiffs of the ſame borough, for the time being, in a certain houſe called the Tolſey (or other convenient place in the ſame borough) upon Friday in every week yearly to be kept; in which court they ſhall keep the pleas of all and all manner of debts, treſpaſſes, and perſonal actions, proceeding from within the liberty of the borough aforeſaid, ſo that they do not exceed the ſum of 50 l. of lawful money of England, nor touching a free tenement within the liberties of the borough aforeſaid, by complaints thereof before the bailiffs aforeſaid, to be levied, made and entered; and that the ſame bailiffs, burgeſſes and community, and their ſucceſlors, upon the like ſort of complaints, pleas, quarrels and actions, may have power, authority and faculty to implead defendants againſt whom the like complaints, pleas or actions in the ſaid court ſhall happen to be levied or removed, by an attachment of their bodies, to be directed to the ſergeants at mace of the borough aforeſaid, or other officer or officers, or any of them, to be appointed or aſſigned by the bailiffs aforeſaid, or either of them, for the time being.

And that the like pleas, complaints, ſuits and actions, may be there heard and determined before the bailiffs of the ſaid borough, for the time being or either of them, together with the recorder of the borough aforeſaid, or his ſufficient deputy for the time being by ſuch and the like proceſſes and means, according to the laws and cuſtom of this our kingdom of England, by their peers, and as is agreeable to our laws, and in as ample manner and form as is or ought to be uſed and accuſtomed in any court of record in any city, borough or town incorporate, within our kingdom of England: provided always, and it is our good pleaſure, and for us our heirs and ſucceſſors, do will and forbid, that no attachment or other proceſs be directed to the ſergeants at mace of the borough aforeſaid, or ſhall be executed or ſerved by the ſame in any place, unleſs within the town and pariſh of Tewkſbury aforeſaid, and precinct of the ſame town.

And we farther will, and for us our heirs and ſucceſſors, do grant to the bailiffs, burgeſſes and community of the borough aforeſaid, and their ſucceſſors, that there may and ſhall be perpetually in the borough aforeſaid, one honeſt and diſcreet man, to be choſen in form in theſe preſents mentioned, who ſhall be, and be nominated common clerk of the borough aforeſaid, and clerk of our peace within the borough aforeſaid, to be continued in the ſame office ſo long as he ſhall behave himſelf well. And we have

have farther appointed, nominated and conſtituted, and by theſe preſents, for us our heirs and ſucceſſors, do appoint, nominate and conſtitute the aforeſaid Henry Collet, junior, to be the firſt and modern common clerk of the borough aforeſaid, and clerk of our peace within the borough aforeſaid, ſo long as he ſhall behave himſelf well, and to do and execute all things which reſpectively belong to the office of common clerk, and clerk of the peace within the borough aforeſaid.

And we alſo will, and by theſe preſents, for us our heirs and ſucceſſors, do grant to the aforeſaid bailiffs, burgeſſes and community of the borough aforeſaid, and their ſucceſſors, that from henceforth for the future, there be and ſhall be within the borough, liberty and precinct of the ſame, one honeſt and diſcreet man, to be choſen in form in theſe preſents, who ſhall be and be called coroner of the borough aforeſaid, who ſhall have full power and authority to do and execute all and ſingular thoſe acts and things whatſoever within the borough aforeſaid, and precinct of the ſame, which tend and belong to the office of a coroner within the borough aforeſaid to be done and executed. And we have appointed, nominated and conſtituted, and by theſe preſents do appoint nominate and conſtitute the aforeſaid Henry Collet to be firſt and modern coroner of the borough aforeſaid, to be continued in the ſaid office during the good pleaſure of the bailiffs and principal burgeſſes of the borough aforeſaid, or the greater part of them (of whom either of the bailiffs we will to be one.) And we farther will that after the death or removal of the aforeſaid Henry Collet from the office of coroner aforeſaid, then and thenceforth, it may and ſhall be well and lawful for the bailiffs and principal burgeſſes of the borough aforeſaid, for the time being, or the greater part of them who ſhall be then preſent (of whom either of the bailiffs of the borough aforeſaid we will to be one) at their pleaſure from time to time to elect, nominate and appoint one other honeſt and diſcreet man of the burgeſſes of the borough aforeſaid, into the office of coroner of the borough aforeſaid, to be continued in the ſame office during the good pleaſure of the aforeſaid bailiffs and principal burgeſſes of the borough aforeſaid, or the greater part of them (of whom either of the bailiffs we will to be one) a corporal oath being firſt taken before the bailiffs of the borough aforeſaid, or either of them, to rightly, well and faithfully perform that office in all things touching or concerning that office.

We farther will, and by theſe preſents, for us our heirs and ſucceſſors, do grant to the ſaid bailiffs, burgeſſes, and community of the borough aforeſaid, and their ſucceſſors, that the bailiffs and principal burgeſſes of the borough aforeſaid, for the time being, or the greater part of them (of whom either of the bailiffs of the borough aforeſaid, for the time being, we will to be one) may and ſhall from time to time elect, conſtitute and create one of the burgeſſes of the borough aforeſaid, to have, exerciſe and execute the office of chamberlain of the borough aforeſaid, ſo long as it ſhall ſeem fit to the aforeſaid bailiffs and principal burgeſſes of the borough aforeſaid, or the greater part of them (of whom either of the bailiffs of the borough aforeſaid for the time being, we will to be one) or until the aforeſaid chamberlain ſhall leave the office of his own own accord, or dye; and that every burgeſs of that borough elected, choſen and created chamberlain of the borough aforeſaid, or to be elected, choſen or created, ſhall take a corporal oath in due manner, to do and faithfully execute all thoſe things which belong to the office of chamberlain of the borough aforeſaid. And that the chamberlain of the borough aforeſaid for the time being, ſhall, and may receive all manner of rents, fines, amercements, revenues, profits, commodities emoluments whatſoever, to the aforeſaid bailiffs, burgeſſes and community of the borough aforeſaid, and their ſucceſſors, by right of any corporation, or howſoever belonging, appertaining, incured, due or payable, and keep the ſame in his power to and for the uſe of the bailiffs, burgeſſes and community of the borough aforeſaid, and expend and diſburſe the ſame from time to time, at their command and requeſt. And the aforeſaid chamberlain of the borough aforeſaid, for the time being, ſhall keep all and ſingular writings, deeds, evidences and muniments whatſoever to the ſaid bailiffs, burgeſſes and community of the borough aforeſaid for the time being, belonging, or in any wiſe appertaining; and ſhall keep the ſeal as well of the aforeſaid bailiffs burgeſſes and community of the borough aforeſaid, as of the maſter of the ſchool beneath written, in the chamber of the borough aforeſaid, and ſhall cauſe to come the writtings and muniments, and ſeal, before the aforeſaid bailiffs and principal burgeſſes, or either of them, as often and whenſoever by them they ſhall be commanded, that they may look into them, and duely determine and diſpoſe or uſe them, and let him perpetually give a true and juſt yearly account at every feaſt of James the apoſtle, or within fifteen days next following the ſame feaſt, to the ſaid bailiffs and principal burgeſſes of the borough aforeſaid, for the time being, or the greater part of them, of all things by him ſo received or levied, kept or had. And let him execute and do all thoſe things as in times paſt were uſed and accuſtomed by the chamberlain aforeſaid; and alſo that every chamberlain of the borough aforeſaid, for the time being, who ſhall happen to be removed from his office, or ſhall leave his office aforeſaid of his own accord, and the heirs, executors and adminiſtrators of ſuch who ſhall dye, having the office of chamberlain aforeſaid, within one month next after the death or removal, or voluntary leaving of his office beforeſaid, may give a true and faithful account of all things in his office, by virtue of his ſaid office, by him accepted, had or done, to the bailiffs and principal burgeſſes of that borough, or ſo many of them as will be there, when it ſhall be required of him. And for the better execution of our will and grant in this part, we have appointed, created, nominated, conſtituted and made, and by theſe preſents, for us our heirs and ſucceſſors, do appoint, create, nominate, conſtitute and make the aforeſaid William Wilſon to be the firſt and modern chamberlain of that borough, to be continued in the office aforeſaid as long as he ſhall behave himſelf well. And that from time to time, and at all times after the death, ſurrender, or other determination of the office aforeſaid, at the good pleaſure and will of the bailiffs and principal burgeſſes of the borough aforeſaid, for the time being, or the greater part of them (of whom either of the bailiffs of the borough aforeſaid, for the time being, we will to be one) the aforeſaid bailiffs and principal burgeſſes of the borough aforeſaid for the time being, or the greater part of them as aforeſaid, may elect, nominate, and appoint one other diſcreet man of the burgeſſes of the borough for the time being, from time to time, to be chamberlain of the borough aforeſaid; and that he who ſhall be elected, appointed, and nominated to be chamberlain of the borough aforeſaid, ſo as aforeſaid, after the death, ſurrender, or other determination of the aforeſaid office, may have, enjoy, and exerciſe that office of chamberlain of the borough aforeſaid, during the good pleaſure of the bailiffs and principal burgeſſes of the borough aforeſaid, for the time being, or the greater part of them (of whom either of the bailiffs of the borough aforeſaid, for the time being, we will to be one) a corporal oath being firſt taken before the bailiffs and principal burgeſſes of the borough aforeſaid, or ſo many of them as will be there, (of whom either of the bailiffs for the time being we will to be one) to execute that office of chamberlain of the borough aforeſaid, rightly, well and faithfully, in and by all things touching that office; and ſo often as it ſhall ſo happen.

And farther, of our more abundant ſpecial grace, certain knowledge, and mere motion, by theſe preſents, for us our heirs and ſucceſſors, we do will and grant to the aforeſaid bailiffs, burgeſſes and community of the borough aforeſaid, and their ſucceſſors, that the bailiffs of the borough aforeſaid, for the time being, together with our clerk, our heirs and ſucceſſors of the ſame borough, aſſigned to receive recognizance of debts, may for ever have full power and authority to receive recognizances, by virtue of the ſtatute of *Acton Burnell*, between merchant and merchant, merchants and merchants, and between every and all other perſon and perſons whatſoever, or either of them, concerning any debt, and any ſum, and the execution thereof to be made, acording to the form and effect of the ſaid ſtatutute of *Acton Burnell*, ſtatute of *Merchants*, or either of them, or other ſtatute in that part ſet forth and provided; and alſo to do and execute all other things in the premiſſes, or the premiſſes any ways touching or concerning, which by the vigor of the ſaid ſtatute of *Acton Burnell*, and the ſtatute of *Merchants*, and other ſtatutes in that part ſet forth and provided, or either or any of them belong to be done and executed; that for ever hereafter there be and ſhall be a clerk, of us our heirs and ſucceſſors, of the ſaid borough of Tewkſbury, to receive ſuch like recognizances of debts, according to the form of the ſtatutes aforeſaid; and that he may and ſhall perpetually have power and authority to do and perform all and ſingular matters, which in any wiſe belong to the office of clerk of the recognizances, according to the form of the ſtatutes aforeſaid, or either of them, to be taken in the vigour of thoſe ſtatutes, or either of them to be done and executed; and we do ordain, nominate, conſtitute, create, erect and appoint, by theſe preſents, for us our heirs and ſucceſſors, the aforeſaid Henry Collet to be our clerk our heirs and ſucceſſors, of the recognizances aforeſaid, within the borough aforeſaid, and the aforeſaid liberty and precinct of the ſame according to the form of the ſtatute aforeſaid, as long as he ſhall behave himſelf well in the ſame office; and that the aforeſaid bailiffs, and the aforeſaid clerk of the like recognizances for the time being, may for ever have a ſeal for ſealing the recognizances aforeſaid, according to the form of the ſtatute aforeſaid; and that the ſame bailiffs and clerk of ſuch like recognizances, for the time being, may have for ever henceforth the keeping of the ſaid ſeal; and that the ſaid bailiffs and clerk of the like recognizances for the time being, may have from henceforth for ever ſo much, and ſo great and entire, and abſolute authority, faculty and power from henceforth for the future, to take, ſeal and record, and certifie ſuch like recognizances, and to perform, do and execute all other, according to the exigence of the ſaid ſtatute, by and in all things, with the ſureties, fees, and regards thereunto belonging and appertaining, as any other mayor, mayors, bailiff, bailiffs, and ſuch clerk or clerks in any city, borough, or town whatſoever, within this our kingdom of England hath, or have, or ought to have; and we do make, create, conſtitute, appoint and ordain by theſe preſents, the

the ſaid bailiffs and clerk of the recognizances of the ſaid borough for the time being, to do and perform all the premiſſes.

And we farther will, and by theſe preſents, for us our heirs and ſucceſſors, do grant to the bailiffs, burgeſſes, and community of the borough aforeſaid, and their ſucceſſors, that after the death or removal of the aforeſaid Henry Collet from the aforeſaid offices of common clerk, clerk of the peace, and clerk of the recognizances, within the borough aforeſaid, or from either of them, and from and after any other determination of the offices aforeſaid of common clerk, clerk of the peace, and clerk of the recognizances, within the borough aforeſaid, or either of them, and as often as ſuch offices, or either or any of them ſhall be void, then and ſo often it may and ſhall be well and lawful for the bailiffs and principal burgeſſes of the borough aforeſaid, for the time being, or for the greater part of them, (of whom either of the bailiffs of the borough aforeſaid for the time being, we will to be one) to elect, nominate, and appoint one other fit perſon, or more fit perſons to be common clerk, clerk of the peace, and clerk of the recognizances, within the borough aforeſaid, to be continued in the like office or offices to which he or they ſhall be elected and appointed, ſo long as he or they ſhall behave himſelf or themſelves well. Provided always, and we will that every perſon and perſons, ſo as aforeſaid, hereafter to be elected to the aforeſaid offices of common clerk, clerk of the peace, and clerk of the recognizances, within the borough aforeſaid, or to either or any of thoſe offices, before he or they be admitted to the execution of thoſe offices, or either, or any of them, ſhall take a corporal oath for the due execution of the offices of common clerk, clerk of the peace, and clerk of the recognizances within the borough aforeſaid, or for the due execution of ſuch office or offices to which he or they ſhall be ſo elected, before the bailiffs and principal burgeſſes of the borough aforeſaid, for the time being, or the greater part of them.

And moreover we will, and by theſe preſents, for us our heirs and ſucceſſors, do command, that the bailiffs, recorders, common clerk, principal burgeſſes, juſtices of the peace, aſſiſtants, chamberlain, coroner, clerk of the peace and recognizances, and other officers, by theſe preſents nominated and conſtituted, before that they or either of them be reſpectively admitted to the execution of their ſeparate truſts and offices, in theſe preſents mentioned, they and every of them ſhall take and perform their ſeparate corporal oaths, upon the bible, for the due execution of their truſts, and reſpective offices, in manner and form following: viz. The bailiffs and recorder, by theſe preſents nominated and appointed, ſhall take their oaths before the aforeſaid Richard Dowdeſwell, Stephen Baldwyn, eſq; Henry Collet, ſenior, and James Bengough, gent. or any two or more of them, to which, or any two or more of them, we give and grant by theſe preſents full power and authority to give and adminiſter the like oath. And we have alſo granted, and by theſe preſents, for us, our heirs and ſucceſſors, do grant that the aforeſaid bailiffs and recorder in theſe preſents nominated, or two of them, (of whom either of the bailiffs we will to be one) may have full power and authority of giving and adminiſtring a corporal oath to the reſt of the principal burgeſſes, juſtices of the peace, chamberlain, common clerk, clerk of the peace and recognizances, coroner, aſſiſtants, and other officers aforeſaid, in theſe preſents before mentioned, and alſo the aforeſaid four juſtices of the peace, by virtue of theſe preſents as aforeſaid to be elected, within one month after the date of theſe preſents.

And we farther will, and by theſe preſents, for us our heirs and ſucceſſors, do grant to the aforeſaid bailiffs, burgeſſes, and community of the borough aforeſaid, and their ſucceſſors, that the aforeſaid bailiffs, burgeſſes, and community of the borough aforeſaid, and their ſucceſſors, may and ſhall for ever have within the borough aforeſaid, liberty, and precinct of the ſame, one priſon or jail, for the preſervation and keeping of all and ſingular perſons attach't and to be attach't, or to be any ways adjudged to the priſon or jail of the borough aforeſaid, within the liberty of the borough aforeſaid, or precinct of the ſame, for any cauſe which could be inquired, proſecuted, puniſhed or determined in that borough, to abide there ſo long, and until they ſhall be freed in a lawful manner; and that the bailiffs of the borough aforeſaid, for the time being, be and ſhall be keepers of the ſame jail.

We will alſo, and by theſe preſents, for us our heirs and ſucceſſors, of our more abundant ſpecial grace, certain knowledge, and mere motion, do grant to the aforeſaid bailiffs, burgeſſes, and community of the borough aforeſaid and their ſucceſſors, that they and their ſucceſſors may have all fines, redemptions, recognizances and amerciaments whatſoever, for tranſgreſſions and other miſdeeds whatſoever, or other cauſes and matters within the borough aforeſaid, liberty and precinct of the ſame, committed and to be committed, and alſo all and all manner of penalties and forfeitures, forfeited or to be forfeited, of all burgeſſes and inhabitants of the borough and liberty of the ſame aforeſaid, there reſiding, and henceforth happening to reſide, and their ſucceſſors, for the peace of us, our heirs and ſucceſſors, and otherwiſe howſoever, and alſo of all other reſiding in the borough aforeſaid, and liberty of the ſame, forfeited or to be forfeited, to us, our heirs and ſucceſſors, within the ſame borough, liberty, and precinct of the ſame, and all and all manner of iſſues, fines, redemptions and amerciaments of the aforeſaid burgeſſes and reſidents, their heirs and ſucceſſors, before the bailiffs of the borough aforeſaid, as before the juſtices of us, our heirs and ſucceſſors, appointed to take the aſſizes or jail delivery, keepers of the peace, and juſtices itinerant, and the inſtitutes of us, our heirs and ſucceſſors, to hear and determine, and other commiſſionary juſtices of us, our heirs and ſucceſſors, whatſoever forfeited or to be forfeited, done or to be done, impoſed or to be impoſed, from or by any cauſe, by the chamberlain of the borough aforeſaid, who ſhall be for that time, to the uſe of the ſaid bailiffs, burgeſſes and commonalty of the borough aforeſaid, and their ſucceſſors, to be aſked, levyed and demanded, without the occaſion or hindrance of us, our heirs and ſucceſſors, ſheriffs, juſtices, and other commiſſionary officers and miniſters whatſoever, of us, our heirs and ſucceſſors.

We have alſo granted, and by theſe preſents, for us our heirs and ſucceſſors, do grant to the aforeſaid bailiffs, burgeſſes, and community of the borough aforeſaid, and their ſucceſſors, that they and their ſucceſſors, henceforth for ever, may and ſhall have, to the proper uſe of them the bailiffs, burgeſſes, and community of the borough aforeſaid, and their ſucceſſors, all and all manner of goods and chattels of all felons and fugitives, outlawed and waved, to be outlawed and to be waved, adjudged, condemned, and to be adjudged, attaint, and happening to be attaint, convicted and to be convicted, fled and to be ſought after, for felony, murther, or petty treaſon, tranſgreſſion, or other matter or cauſe whatſoever; and other forfeitures and offences beforeſaid, touching or concerning all and ſingular burgeſſes and inhabitants, reſiding and not reſiding within the borough aforeſaid, and liberty and precinct of the ſame, and all other things whatſoever within the borough aforeſaid, liberty and precinct of the ſame, found out, and happening for the future to be found out; and that if any perſon that ought to loſe his life or limbs for his offence, ſhall either fly, and will not ſtand to judgment, or ſhall commit any other crime, for which he ought to loſe or forfeit his goods and chattels, whereſoever juſtice ought to be done him, whether it be in our court, our heirs and ſucceſſors, or in any other court whatever, his goods and chattles being, or henceforth for the future happening to be, within the borough aforeſaid, liberty and precinct of the ſame, ſhall be to the bailiffs, burgeſſes, and community of the borough aforeſaid, and their heirs for ever; and that it may and ſhall be well and lawful for the ſame bailiffs, burgeſſes, and community of the borough aforeſaid, and their ſucceſſors, by the chamberlain of the borough aforeſaid, who for that time ſhall be, or by any other or others in their name, without the hinderance of us, our heirs or ſucceſſors, or any officers of our heirs and ſucceſſors whatſoever, to put himſelf or themſelves in ſeiſure of the goods and chattels aforeſaid, and them receive and keep for the uſe of the bailiffs, burgeſſes, and community of the borough aforeſaid, and their ſucceſſors, although the ſame goods and chattels ſhall be firſt ſeized by us, or our heirs or ſucceſſors, or by our or their ſervants.

And we farther will, and by theſe preſents, for us our heirs and ſucceſſors, do grant to the aforeſaid bailiffs, burgeſſes and community of the borough aforeſaid, and their ſucceſſors, that the bailiffs of the borough aforeſaid, for the time being, and their ſucceſſors, may and ſhall have full authority and power to preſs for the ſervice of us, our heirs and ſucceſſors, at any of our wars, and muſterings, and trainings of our ſubjects within the town and pariſh of Tewkſbury aforeſaid, the limits and precincts of the ſame, as often and when they ſee fit, from time to time to be done, taken and overlooked, and to cauſe to be chaſtiſed and puniſhed thoſe that refuſe the premiſſes, or any of them, at the lawful command of the ſaid bailiffs of the borough aforeſaid, for the time being, by impriſonment of their bodies, according to their diſcretion; and that no man poſſeſſing a place, or a commiſſioner of us, our heirs or ſucceſſors, appointed or to be appointed to preſs, or train in the aforeſaid county of Glouceſter, may introduce himſelf in any preſſing or training of men, abiding or inhabiting within the town and pariſh of Tewkſbury aforeſaid, limits and precinct of the ſame, nor enter into the town or pariſh aforeſaid, limits or precinct of the ſame, to do or execute any thing that doth in any wiſe belong to his office of preſſing or training, unleſs with the aſſent and conſent of the bailiffs of the borough aforeſaid for the time being.

And farther, of our more ample ſpecial grace, certain knowledge, and mere motion, we will, and by theſe preſents, for us our heirs and ſucceſſors, do grant to the aforeſaid bailiffs, burgeſſes, and community of the borough aforeſaid, and their ſucceſſors, that neither they the bailiffs and principal burgeſſes, and their aſſiſtants, the high ſteward, chamberlain, and their ſucceſſors, and other their officers within the borough aforeſaid, ſhall ſerve, nor any of them may be compelled or bound, nor either of them be compelled or bound any ways to come before us, our heirs and ſucceſſors, the juſtices of the bench of us and our heirs, the

the juſtices of us and our heirs, appointed keepers of the peace, to take the aſſizes and jail delivery, and the juſtices of us and our heirs, appointed to hear and determine divers felonies, tranſgreſſions and miſdeeds, or the juſtices of us and our heirs of the *Niſi Prius*, or the juſtices of us and our heirs aſſigned to ſurvey the ſea walls, ditches, gouts, ſewers, paths, bridges and rinds, or other commiſſioners of us or our heirs, the high ſheriff, eſcheator, coroner, high ſteward, mareſchal, or clerk of the market, of our houſhold, or other officers and ſervants of us, our heirs and ſucceſſors, nor may any or either of them in any aſſizes be put or impannelled on a jury, or other inquiſition, without the borough aforeſaid; nor may they or either of them forthwith forfeit to us, or our heirs, in any iſſue or amerciament, on any occaſion whatſoever, but thereof let them be quiet for ever unleſs they have, or either of them hath, lands and tenements without the borough aforeſaid, liberty and precinct of the ſame, for which he or they ought to be charged.

And we have farther given and granted, and by theſe preſents for us, our heirs and ſucceſſors, do give and grant to the aforeſaid bailiffs and burgeſſes of the borough aforeſaid, and their ſucceſſors, that the bailiffs of the borough aforeſaid, for the time being, may and ſhall have the return of all writs, precepts, bills and warrants of us, our heirs and ſucceſſors, and alſo ſummons, eſtreats and precepts of our exchequer, our heirs and ſucceſſors, and the eſtreats and precepts of our juſtices itinerant, as well at the foreſt pleas, as at the common pleas, or other offices whatſoever; and alſo attachments, as well of the pleas of the crown as others, coming from and happening in the ſaid borough, liberty and precinct, or any part of them, and the execution of them, to be made by the bailiffs of the borough aforeſaid, for the time being, ſo that no high-ſheriff, under-ſheriff, bailiff, or any ſervant of us, our heirs, and ſucceſſors, may enter into our borough aforeſaid, the ſuburbs or precinct of the ſame, for any thing or things belonging to his office to be done in this part, to be done, (*ſic*) unleſs in defect of thoſe bailiffs, or their ſucceſſors, or their ſervants for the time being.

And we will alſo, and by theſe preſents for us, our heirs and ſucceſſors, do grant and ordain, that henceforth for ever there be, and ſhall be in the ſaid borough of Tewkſbury, two burgeſſes of the parliament of us, our heirs and ſucceſſors. And that the bailiffs, burgeſſes, and community of the borough aforeſaid, and their ſucceſſors, upon a writ of us, our heirs and ſucceſſors, concerning the election of burgeſſes of parliament, to them directed, may and ſhall have power, authority and faculty of electing and nominating two diſcreet and honeſt men, to be burgeſſes of the parliament of us our heirs and ſucceſſors, for the ſame borough, and to ſend the ſame burgeſſes ſo elected, at the charges and coſts of the ſaid bailiffs, burgeſſes and community of the borough aforeſaid, and their ſucceſſors for the time being, into the parliament of us, our heirs and ſucceſſors, where it ſhall be then held, in the ſame manner and form as is uſed and accuſtomed in any boroughs of our kingdom of England; which burgeſſes ſo elected and nominated, we will to be preſent, and to abide at the parliament of us, our heirs and ſucceſſors, at the charges and coſts of the ſaid bailiffs, burgeſſes and community of the borough aforeſaid, for the time being, during the time in which the parliament ſhall happen to be held, and they to have places and votes in the like manner and form as other burgeſſes of parliament for any other boroughs or borough whatſoever, within our kingdom of England do and have, or have been wont to do or have; and theſe burgeſſes in the parliaments of us, our heirs and ſucceſſors, ſhall have their votes as well affirmative as negative, and ſhall there do and execute all and ſingular other matters, as any other burgeſſes or burgeſs of our parliament, for all other boroughs or borough whatſoever, may or can have, do and execute, by reaſon or manner whatſoever.

And we farther will, and by theſe preſents for us, our heirs and ſucceſſors, do grant to the aforeſaid bailiffs, burgeſſes and community of the borough aforeſaid, and their ſucceſſors for ever, that they and their ſucceſſors may and can have, hold, and keep in the borough aforeſaid, yearly for ever, all and ſingular ſuch wakes, fairs and markets in the ſame borough, as by the aforeſaid charter made in the ſeventh year aforeſaid of the late king James the firſt, or by any charters of our anteceſſors and predeceſſors to the ſame bailiffs, burgeſſes and community of the borough aforeſaid, or to their predeceſſors granted, before that time were granted, and which at or before the time of the ſurrender aforeſaid, were lawfully held or uſed by the aforeſaid bailiffs, burgeſſes and community of the borough aforeſaid, within the borough aforeſaid, together with the Pye-Powder-Court, there held in the time of thoſe wakes and fairs, and with all liberty and free cuſtom of roll, [*ſic in copia*] ſtallage, piccage, fines, amercements, and all other profits, commodities and emoluments whatſoever belonging, happening, proceeding or touching the ſame wake or fair, and Pye-Powder-Court, and with all other free cuſtoms and liberty whatſoever, to the ſame wake, fair and Pye-Powder-Court appertaining or belonging.

And we farther will and grant to the bailiffs, burgeſſes and community of the borough aforeſaid, and their ſucceſſors, that the bailiffs of the borough aforeſaid, for the time being, henceforth for ever, be and ſhall be clerks of the market within the borough aforeſaid, liberty and precinct of the ſame.

And we farther will, and by theſe preſents, for us our heirs and ſucceſſors, do grant to the aforeſaid bailiffs, burgeſſes and community of the borough aforeſaid, and their ſucceſſors, that the bailiffs and principal burgeſſes of the borough aforeſaid, for the time being, or the greater part of them (of whom either of the bailiffs of the borough aforeſaid, for the time being, we will to be one) may and ſhall have power and authority, from time to time, to elect, nominate, appoint and conſtitute ſo many and ſuch, as well without the borough aforeſaid as within that borough, limits or precincts of the ſame, inhabiting and abiding, to be burgeſſes of the ſaid borough, as to the ſaid bailiffs and principal burgeſſes of the borough aforeſaid, or to the greater part of them, as aforeſaid, for the publick profit of the ſaid borough, ſhall ſeem more profitable, in the ſame manner and form, and with the ſame corporal oath, to be taken by every of the ſaid burgeſſes ſo choſen and appointed, as the burgeſſes of that borough were heretofore wont to take within the ſaid borough of Tewkſbury; and that theſe burgeſſes of the borough aforeſaid, and every of them, henceforth for ever, may and can perpetually, fully and peaceably poſſeſs and enjoy all liberties, privileges, franchiſes and immunities by either or any of our progenitors or predeceſſors, kings or queens of England, to the bailiffs, burgeſſes and community of the borough of Tewkſbury, or incorporated by any other name or names, before given and granted, at and before the time of the ſurrender aforeſaid.

And farther, of our more plentiful and ſpecial grace, certain knowledge, and mere motion, we have given and granted, and for us our heirs and ſucceſſors, by theſe preſents do give and grant to the aforeſaid bailiffs, burgeſſes, and community of the borough aforeſaid, and their ſucceſſors, full power, authority and juriſdiction, that the aforeſaid bailiffs of the borough aforeſaid, for the time being, may and can have and exerciſe within the borough aforeſaid, and liberty and precinct of the ſame, henceforth for ever, the puniſhing and correcting of all and ſingular drunkards, and all and ſingular harlots, whores, bawds, concubines, and all others whatſoever living laſciviouſly and incontinently; and alſo all and ſingular diſhoneſtly or maliciouſly communicating, upon any occaſion, whether they are ſcolds, abiding or inhabiting within the borough aforeſaid, and liberty of the ſame, or are delinquents, as well by the verdict and preſentment of twelve honeſt and lawful men of the borough aforeſaid, for that time being, as by other lawful ways and means, to which ſaid bailiffs for the time being, it ſhall ſeem to be moſt expedient.

And farther, of our more abundant ſpecial grace, certain knowledge and mere motion, we have granted, and by theſe preſents for us, our heirs and ſucceſſors, do grant, and give ſpecial and free liberty and faculty, power and authority, to the aforeſaid bailiffs, burgeſſes and community of the borough aforeſaid, and their ſucceſſors, to have, receive, and purchaſe to them and their ſucceſſors for ever, the manors, meſſuages, lands, tenements, meadows, paſtures, woods, rectories, tithes, rents, reverſions, and other hereditaments whatſoever, within our kingdom of England, or any where within our dominions, purchaſed of us, our heirs and ſucceſſors, as of any other perſon or perſons whatſoever, ſo that the ſame manors, meſſuages, lands, tenements, meadows, paſtures, woods, underwoods, rectories, tithes, rents, reverſions, and other hereditaments, ſo by them to be had, received, and purchaſed, above the aforeſaid manor, borough and hundred of Tewkſbury, and other the premiſſes in theſe preſents before mentioned, and other manors, lands, tenements and hereditaments purchaſed before the making of the aforeſaid letters patents, in the ſeventh year of king James the firſt, by the ſame bailiffs, burgeſſes and community of the borough aforeſaid, or their predeceſſors, by any name or names incorporated or purchaſed, by virtue of any incorporation, do not exceed in the whole, the clear yearly value of 200 l. *per ann.* beſides all charges. And we do give alſo, and by theſe preſents, for us, our heirs and ſucceſſors, to every of our ſubjects, our heirs and ſucceſſors, ſpecial and free liberty, power and authority, that they, or either, or any of them, may give, grant or ſell meſſuages, lands, tenements, meadows, paſtures, woods, underwoods, rectories, tithes, rents, reverſions, ſervices and other hereditaments whatſoever, to the aforeſaid bailiffs, burgeſſes and community of the borough aforeſaid, and their ſucceſſors; ſo that all the aforeſaid manors, meſſuages, lands, tenements, meadows, paſtures, woods, underwoods, rectories, tithes, rents, reverſions, ſervices and other hereditaments, to the ſame bailiffs, burgeſſes and community of the borough aforeſaid, and their ſucceſſors, by virtue of theſe preſents ſo to be given, granted, leaſed and aliened, as aforeſaid, do not exceed in the whole the clear yearly value of 200 l. *per ann.* beſides all charges and repriſes.

And we farther will, and by theſe preſents for us, our heirs and ſucceſſors, do give, grant, confirm, ratify, reſtore and approve to the aforeſaid bailiffs, burgeſſes and community of the borough aforeſaid, and their ſucceſſors, all and all manner of liberties, franchiſes, immunities, exceptions, privileges, acquittances,

tances, jurisdictions, lands, tenements, wastes, funds, commons and hereditaments whatsoever, which the bailiffs, burgesses and community of the borough aforesaid, or any of their successors, by any names or name, or by any incorporation, or under pretence of any incorporation, in time of making the aforesaid charter, made in the seventh year of the aforesaid king James the first, had, possess'd, used or enjoyed, or ought to have, possess, use or enjoy, from an hereditary state, by reason or under pretence of any charters or letters patent, by any of our progenitors or predecessors, kings or queens of England, however before then made, confirmed or granted, or by any other lawful means, right, title, custom, use or prescription before then lawfully used, had or accustomed, although the same, or any of them have not heretofore been used, or have been abused, or ill used, or discontinued; and although the same, or either, or any of them are, and have been forfeited, or lost, or surrendered, to be had, possessed, exercised, used and enjoyed by the aforesaid bailiffs, burgesses and community of the borough aforesaid, and their successors for ever, and to restore, and pay therefore to us, our heirs and successors, yearly, so much, so many, such, the same, and the like rents, services, sums of money and demands whatsoever, as for the same were heretofore wont to be paid, or they ought to pay to us or our predecessors. Wherefore we will, and by these presents, for us, our heirs and successors, that the aforesaid bailiffs, burgesses and community of the borough aforesaid, and their successors, may fully and entirely have, possess, use and enjoy all liberties, free customs, privileges, authority, jurisdictions and acquittances aforesaid, according to the tenor and effect of these our letters patent, without the occasion or hindrance of us, or any of our heirs or successors, nilling that the same bailiffs, burgesses, and community of the borough aforesaid, and their fnccessors, or any, or either of them, by reason of the premisses, or either of them, by us, our heirs, our justices, sheriffs, escheators, or other bailiffs or servants of us, our heirs and successors whatsoever, be occasioned, molested, vexed, grieved, or disturbed in any thing; willing, and by these presents, for us our heirs and successors commanding, as well the commissioners for our treasury, the treasurer, chancellor and barons of the exchequer, of us, our heirs and successors, as our attorney and solicitor general for the time being, and every of them, and all other officers and servants whatsoever of us, our heirs and successors, that neither they, nor either, nor any of them, may prosecute or continue, or shall cause to be prosecuted or continued, any writ or summons of any warrant, or any other our writ, writs or process whatsoever, against the bailiffs, burgesses and community of the borough aforesaid, or either or any of them, for any causes, things or matters, offences, claims or usurpations, whether of any of them, by them or any of them due, claimed, attempted, used, had or usurped before the day of the making of these presents. Willing also, that the bailiffs, burgesses and community of the borough aforesaid, or either of them, be no ways molested or hindered by either, or any justices, officers and servants aforesaid, in or for due use, claim, usurpation or abuse of any liberties, franchises or jurisdiction, before the day of the making of these our letters patent, or be compelled to answer to any, or either of these things.

And farther, for the better education and instruction of boys and youth within the same borough, liberty and precinct thereof, in good arts, learning, virtue and education, perpetually to be educated and informed, of our more abundant special grace, certain knowledge and mere motion, we have willed, granted and ordained, and by these presents for us, our heirs and successors, do will, grant and ordain, that from henceforth for ever there be, and shall be within the borough aforesaid, liberty and precinct of the same, one grammar school, which shall be called the free grammar school of William Ferrers, citizen and mercer of London, in Tewksbury in the county of Gloucester, and that school, by the name of the free grammar school of the aforesaid William Ferrers, of Tewksbury in the county of Gloucester, we do erect, ordain, create, found, and firmly establish by these presents. And that the free grammar school aforesaid be, and do consist of one master and one usher, and scholars, in the same school, to be taught and instructed according to the ordination and constitution in these presents below specified and declared. And that our foresaid intention may better take effect, and that the manors, messuages, lands, tenements, rents, reversions, hereditaments, annuities, goods and chattels, and other profits and hereditaments, to be granted, assigned and appointed, to the sustenance of the free grammar school aforesaid, may be better governed, for continuation of the same school, we will, grant and ordain, that the aforesaid bailiffs, justices of the peace, chamberlain of the borough aforesaid, and town clerk in Tewksbury aforesaid, and their successors, henceforth for ever, shall be, and be called, governors of the goods, possessions and revenues of the aforesaid free grammar school of William Ferrers, in Tewksbury in the county of Gloucester.

And farther, of our more abundant special grace, certain knowledge and mere motion, we do will, ordain and establish by these presents, for us, our heirs and successors, that the aforesaid bailiffs, justices, chamberlain and town-clerk of the aforesaid borough of Tewksbury for the time being, and their successors, for ever henceforth be, and shall be, one body corporate and politick of itself, in deed, fact and name, by the name of governors of the goods, possessions and revenues of the free grammar school of Willam Ferrers, in Tewksbury in the county of Gloucester; and them, and their successors, into one body corporate and politick, really and to the full, for us, our heirs and successors, we do incorporate, erect, create, ordain, make and establish by these presents; and that by the same name of governors of the goods, possessions, and revenues of the free grammar-school of William Ferrers, in Tewksbury, in the county of Gloucester, in all future times they shall be known, called and nominated, and shall have a perpetual succession.

And we farther will and ordain, and by these presents for us, our heirs and successors, do grant to the aforesaid governors, and their successors, that they and their successors, from henceforth for ever, may have a common seal to serve for their business touching the free-grammar-school aforesaid, according to the tenor and true intent of these our letters patent; and that it may and shall be well and lawful for them and their successors, to break, change, and make new that seal, from time to time, at their pleasure, as it shall seem fit to them to be done; and that they and their successors, by the name of governors of the goods, possessions, and revenues of the free grammar-school of William Ferrers, in Tewksbury, in the county of Gloucester, be and shall be perpetually persons fit and capable in the law, to have, purchase, receive and possess, to them and their successors, the goods and chattels, and also manors, messuages, lands, tenements, meadows, pastures, feedings, rents, reversions, services, rectories, tithes, and other possessions and hereditaments whatsoever, to the sustenance and maintenance of the said grammar-school, as well from us, our heirs and successors, as from any other person or persons whatsoever, in manner and form in these presents below specified; and that the aforesaid governors and their successors, by the name of governors of the goods, possessions, and revenues of the free grammar-school of William Ferrers, in Tewksbury, in the county of Gloucester, may and can plead and be impleaded, defend and be defended, answer and be answered, in all and singular causes, complaints, actions, suits and demands whatsoever, of whatsoever sort, nature or kind they be, in whatsoever places and courts of us, our heirs and successors, and before whatsoever judges and justices of us, our heirs and successors, or any of them, within our kingdom of England, and to do and execute all other facts and deeds, by the name aforesaid, as other our subjects of our kingdom of England, persons fit and capable in the law, within our kingdom of England, do or may do, in the places and courts aforesaid, and before the justices abovesaid.

And we farther will, and by these presents, for us, our heirs and successors, do give and grant liberty, power and authority to the aforesaid governors and their successors, to elect, nominate and appoint, and that they may and can elect and appoint one honest man, learned, and fearing God, to be master of the free grammar-school aforesaid, and one other man, discreet and fit, to be usher of the same school; which master and usher, so as aforesaid elected, nominated and appointed, shall be and continue, and either of them shall be and continue in their offices aforesaid, during the good pleasure of those the governors and their successors, for the time being; and that as often as it shall happen that any master or usher of the free grammar-school aforesaid does die, or be removed from the office and place aforesaid, that then and so often, it shall and may be well and lawful for the aforesaid governors, and their successors, to elect, nominate, and appoint one other honest man, learned and fearing God, in the place of the master, so dead or removed from his office; and also one other honest and fit man in the like place of the usher, so happening to die or be removed; and that every master, so as aforesaid nominated and appointed, shall be and continue in the office or place of master or usher of the same free-grammar-school, during the good pleasure of those governors of the goods, possessions, and revenues of the free grammar-school aforesaid, and their successors; and that the same governors of the goods, possessions, and revenues of the said free grammar-school of William Ferrers, of Tewksbury, in the county of Gloucester, for the time being, and their successors, shall and may make fit and wholesome statutes, ordinances and writings, touching and concerning the nomination, election, ordination, government, punishment, expulsion, removal and direction of the said free grammar-school, the master and usher of the same school, and the scholars in the same school being: and concerning and touching the ordination, government, dismission, location, disposition, recovery, defence, and preservation of the manors, messuages, lands, tenements, possessions hereditaments, goods and chattels, to be given, granted, or assigned to the maintenance of the aforesaid grammar-school. Which Statutes and ordinances so to be made, we will and ordain, and for us, our heirs and successors, do command, from time to time, inviolably to be observed for ever. So nevertheless that the aforesaid statutes and ordinances,

nances, ſo as aforeſaid to be made, or any of them are not repugnant or contrary to the laws, ſtatutes, rights or cuſtoms of this our kingdom of England.

And farther, of our more abundant ſpecial grace, certain knowledge and mere motion, we have given and granted, and by theſe preſents, for us, our heirs and ſucceſſors, do give and grant to the aforeſaid governors of the goods, poſſeſſions and revenues of the aforeſaid free grammar-ſchool of the aforeſaid William Ferrers, in Tewkſbury, in the county of Glouceſter, and their ſucceſſors, liberty, ſpecial free-will, power, faculty and authority to have, purchaſe, receive and poſſeſs, to them and their ſucceſſors for ever, for the perpetual ſuſtenance and maintenance of the free grammar ſchool aforeſaid, manors, meſſuages, lands, tenements, meadows, paſtures, woods, under-woods, rectories, rents, reverſions and ſervices, and other hereditaments whatſoever, within our kingdom of England, or any where within our dominions, as well from our heirs and ſucceſſors, as from any other perſon or perſons whatſoever, ſo that the ſame manors, meſſuages, lands, tenements, meadows, paſtures, woods, underwoods, rectories, tithes, rents, reverſions, ſervices, and other hereditaments, do not exceed in the whole the clear yearly value of 30 l. per An. beſides all charges and repriſes.

And we do alſo give and grant, for us, our heirs and ſucceſſors, by theſe preſents, to every of our ſubjects, our heirs and ſucceſſors whatſoever, ſpecial and free liberty and power, faculty and authority, that they and every of them may give, grant, ſell, leaſe, or alien manors, meſſuages, lands, tenements, meadows, paſtures, feedings, woods, underwoods, rectories, tithes, rents, reverſions, ſervices, and other hereditaments whatſoever, to the aforeſaid governors of the goods, poſſeſſions, and revenues of the aforeſaid free grammar-ſchool of William Ferrers, in Tewkſbury, in the county of Glouceſter, and their ſucceſſors, ſo neverthleſs that all the aforeſaid mannors meſſuages, lands, tenements, meadows, paſtures, feedings, woods, underwoods, rectories, tithes, rents, reverſions and ſervices, and other hereditaments, ſo as aforeſaid to be given, granted, leaſed or aliened to the ſame governors and their ſucceſſors, by virtue of theſe preſents, do not exceed in the whole the clear yearly value of 30 l. beſides burthens and repriſes.

We will alſo, and by theſe preſents, for us, our heirs and ſucceſſors, do grant to the aforeſaid bailiffs, burgeſſes, and community of the borough aforeſaid, and their ſucceſſors, that theſe our letters patent, and all and ſingular things in them contained, ſhall ſtand and be good, firm, valid, ſufficient and effectual in the law, and that all and ſingular things in theſe preſents expreſſed and ſpecified, may be expounded, declared, conſtrued, interpreted and adjudged, as well to the ſenſe and intention, as to the words, moſt kindly, favourably, graciouſly, and for the profit and benefit of thoſe bailiffs, burgeſſes, and community of the borough aforeſaid, and their ſucceſſors, towards us, our heirs and ſucceſſors.

In witneſs whereof we have cauſed theſe our letters to be made patents.

Witneſs our ſelf at Weſtminſter, the thirteenth day of July, in the thirteenth year of our reign.

NUMBER XXVII.

The CHARTER *of the Borough of* CHIPPING CAMPDEN.

JAMES, by the grace of God, king of England, Scotland, France and Ireland, defender of the faith, &c. To all to whom theſe preſents ſhall come, greeting. Whereas our borough of Chipping Campden, in our county of Glouceſter, is a very ancient and populous borough, and the burgeſſes and inhabitants of that borough have from time out of mind, had, uſed, and enjoyed divers liberties, franchiſes, immunities, and preheminences, as well by virtue of divers letters patents, and charters of divers of our progenitors and anceſtors, late kings of England, made and granted heretofore to them and their predeceſſors, by the name of bailiffs and burgeſſes of Chipping Campden, in the county of Glouceſter, or by what other name or names of incorporation ſo ever heretofore made and granted, which charters and letters patents, by negligence or misfortune, are loſt, as alſo by reaſon and colour of divers preſcriptions, uſages and cuſtoms uſed and practiſed in that borough. And whereas our beloved ſubjects, the burgeſſes and inhabitants of that borough have humbly beſought us, that we would, on this occaſion, exhibit and extend our royal grace and magnificence to the burgeſſes and inhabitants of that borough: And that for the better regulation, government and improvement of that borough, as to us ſhall ſeem expedient, we would vouchſafe, by our letters patents, to make, reduce and create the ſaid burgeſſes and inhabitants of that borough of Chipping Campden (by whatſoever name or names of incorporation they have been heretofore incorporated, or whether heretofore incorporated or not) into one body corporate and politick, by the name of bailiffs and burgeſſes of the borough of Chipping Campden, in the county of Glouceſter. We therefore being willing that for ever hereafter one certain and undoubted manner of and for keeping the peace, and regulating and governing our people there, ſhall be conſtantly obſerved in that borough; and that the ſaid borough may for ever hereafter be a borough of peace and quietneſs, to the fear and terror of evil men, and the encouragement of the good: And that our peace and the due courſe of juſtice may and ſhall be there the better conſerved: And hoping that the ſaid burgeſſes and inhabitants of the ſaid borough and their ſucceſſors will, in conſideration of their enjoying, by our grant, more ample liberties and privileges, think themſelves more eſpecially and ſtrongly obliged to pay and perform all the ſervices, as lies in their power, to us, our heirs and ſucceſſors, have, of our ſpecial grace, certain knowledge, and mere motion, willed, ordained conſtituted, declared and granted, and by theſe preſents do, for us our heirs and ſucceſſors, will, ordain, conſtitute, declare and grant, that our ſaid borough of Chipping Campden, in the county of Gloceſter, may and ſhall be for ever hereafter a free borough of itſelf, and that the burgeſſes and inhabitants of the ſaid borough, and their ſucceſſors, may, and ſhall be for ever hereafter, by virtue of theſe preſents, one body corporate and polick, in deed, fact and name, by the name of bailiffs and burgeſſes of the borough of Chipping Campden, in the county of Gloſter. And do by theſe preſents, really and fully, for ourſelves, our heirs and ſucceſſors, erect, create, make, ordain, conſtitute, confirm and declare them one body corporate and politick, in deed, fact, and name, by the name of bailiffs and burgeſſes of the borough of Chipping Campden, in the county of Gloceſter. And that they ſhall, by the ſame name, have a perpetual ſucceſſion.

And that, by the name of bailiffs and burgeſſes of the borough of Chipping Campden, in the county of Glouceſter, they may and ſhall, at all times, for ever hereafter, be perſons qualified and capable in law to have, purchaſe, receive and poſſeſs manors, meſſuages, lands, tenements, liberties, privileges, juriſdictions and other hereditaments, of what nature, kind, or ſort ſoever, to themſelves and their ſucceſſors, in fee and for ever, or for the term of a year or years, or in any other manner; and alſo goods, chattels, and all other things of what kind, names, nature, quality and ſort ſoever they ſhall be. And alſo to give, grant, demiſe, alienate, aſſign and diſpoſe lands, tenements, and hereditaments, and to do and execute all other and ſingular acts and deeds, by the name aforeſaid.

And that, by the ſame name of bailiffs and burgeſſes of the borough of Chipping Campden, in the county of Glouceſter, they may and be impowered to plead and be impleaded, anſwer and be anſwered, defend, and be defended, in any courts, ſtreets and places, and by the judges, juſtices and other perſons and officers whomſoever, of us, our heirs and ſucceſſors, in all and ſingular actions, pleas, ſuits, complaints, cauſes, matters and demands, of whatſoever kind, name, nature, quality and ſort they may or ſhall be, in the ſame manner and form as our other liege people of our kingdom of England, being perſons qualified and capable in law, or any other body corporate and politick within our kingdom of England, can and may have, purchaſe, receive, enjoy, retain, give, grant, demiſe, alienate, aſſign and impoſe, plead and be impleaded, defend and be defended, anſwer and be anſwered, do, permit or execute.

And that the bailiffs and burgeſſes of the ſaid borough, and their ſucceſſors, ſhall for ever have a common ſeal for the execution of all manner of cauſes, and matter, of them and their ſucceſſors. And that it may and ſhall be lawful for the ſaid bailiffs and burgeſſes, and their ſucceſſors, from time to time, to break, change and make anew that Seal, as to them ſhall ſeem beſt to be done.

And farther we will, and by theſe preſents, for us, our heirs and ſucceſſors, do grant to the ſaid bailiffs and burgeſſes of the borough aforeſaid, and their ſucceſſors, that there may and ſhall be choſen fourteen of the burgeſſes of the ſaid borough, in form hereafter mentioned in theſe preſents, who ſhall be and be nominated capital burgeſſes of the ſaid borough, of which fourteen capital burgeſſes two from time to time ſhall be elected and nominated, in form hereafter mentioned in theſe preſents, to be bailiffs of the borough aforeſaid. And that in like manner there may and ſhall be choſen within the ſaid borough, twelve of the burgeſſes of the ſaid borough, in form hereafter mentioned in theſe preſents, who ſhall be and be nominated inferior burgeſſes of the ſaid borough, of common council of the ſame; which fourteen capital burgeſſes, and twelve inferior burgeſſes, for the time being, ſhall be of the common council of the ſame borough. And that the reſt of the aforeſaid fourteen capital burgeſſes of the ſaid borough, for the time being, not being in the offices of bailiffs of the ſaid borough, and the aforeſaid twelve inferior burgeſſes of the ſaid

ſaid borough, for the time being, ſhall from time to time be aiding and aſſiſting to the bailiffs of the ſaid borough for the time being, in all cauſes, things, affairs, and matters touching or any way concerning the aforeſaid borough.

And farther, of our abundant grace, we will, and by theſe preſents for us, our heirs and ſucceſſors, do grant to the aforeſaid bailiffs and burgeſſes of the ſaid borough, and their ſucceſſors, that the bailiffs and capital burgeſſes of the borough aforeſaid, for the time being, or the major part of them (whereof we will that the bailiffs of the ſaid borough for the time being be two) ſhall have, and by theſe preſents have, full authority, power and faculty of compiling, conſtituting, ordaining, making and eſtabliſhing, from time to time, ſuch and ſuch manner of laws, ſtatutes, ordinances and conſtitutions, as in ſound diſcretion ſhall ſeem to them, or the major part of them (whereof we will that the bailiffs of the ſaid borough for the time being be two) to be good, profitable wholſome and neceſſary, for the good government and regulation of the bailiffs and burgeſſes of the ſaid borough, and all other and ſingular the other burgeſſes, officers, miniſters, artificers, inhabitants and reſidents whomſoever, within the ſaid borough for the time being. And for declaration in what manner and order the bailiffs and burgeſſes of the borough aforeſaid, and their ſucceſſors, and all other and ſingular the officers, miniſters, artificers, inhabitants and reſients within the ſaid borough, ſhall, for the time being, behave, demean, and uſe themſelves in their offices, miniſtries, trades and buſineſſes, within the ſaid borough and liberties of the ſame, for the farther publick good, common advantage, and good government of the borough aforeſaid, and victualling of the ſame. And alſo for the better preſervation, ordering, diſpoſing, letting and demiſing the lands, poſſeſſions, revenues and hereditaments given, granted or aſſigned, and for the future to be given, granted and aſſigned to the aforeſaid bailiffs and burgeſſes of the ſaid borough, or their ſucceſſors, and other things and cauſes whatſoever, touching, or any way concerning the ſaid borough, or the ſtate, rights and intereſts of the ſame.

And that the bailiffs and capital burgeſſes of the borough aforeſaid, for the time being, or the major part of them, (of whom we will that the bailiffs of the ſaid borough for the time being be two) as oft as they ſhall compile, make, ordain or eſtabliſh ſuch laws, ſtatutes, ordinances and conſtitutions, in form aforeſaid, may and ſhall be impowered to make, ordain, limit and provide ſuch pains, puniſhments and penalties, by corporal impriſonment, or by fines and amerciaments, or both of them, againſt and upon all delinquents, againſt ſuch ſtatutes, laws, ordinances, conſtitutions, or any of them, or any other puniſhments, as to them, the bailiffs and burgeſſes of the borough aforeſaid, for the time being, or the major part of them (of whom we will that the bailiffs of the ſaid borough for the time being, be two) ſhall ſeem moſt neceſſary, reaſonable and requiſite to be made, for the obſervation of the ſaid laws, ordinances and conſtitutions; and levy and receive the ſaid fines and amerciaments to the benefit and uſe of the ſaid bailiffs and burgeſſes of the borough aforeſaid, and their ſucceſſors, whithout impeachment of us, our heirs or ſucceſſors, or any of the officers or miniſters of us, our heirs or ſucceſſors, and without any account to be rendered thereof to us, our heirs and ſucceſſors, which all and ſingular laws, ordinances, ſtatutes and conſtitutions, ſo as aforeſaid to be made, we will to be obſerved under the penalties therein to be contained. Nevertheleſs, ſo that ſuch laws, ordinances, ſtatutes and conſtitutions, fines and amerciaments ſhall be reaſonable, and not repugnant or contrary to the laws, ſtatutes, cuſtoms or rights of our kingdom of England.

And for the better execution of our will and grant in this behalf, we have aſſigned, nominated, created, conſtituted and made, and by theſe preſents for us, our heirs and ſucceſſors, do aſſign, nominate, create, conſtitute and make our beloved John Price, gent. and William Dampart, yeoman, burgeſſes of the ſaid borough, to be the two firſt modern bailiffs of the ſaid borough, to be continued in the ſaid offices of bailiffs of the ſaid borough, from the date of theſe preſents to Wedneſday immediately before the feaſt of St. Michael the archangel then next enſuing, and from thenceforth until two other of the capital burgeſſes of the ſaid borough ſhall be duly elected, deputed and ſworn to the ſaid offices, according to the ordinances and proviſions in theſe preſents hereafter expreſſed and declared, if the ſaid John Price and William Dampart ſhall ſo long live. Alſo we have aſſigned, nominated and conſtituted, and by theſe preſents for us, our heirs and ſucceſſors, do aſſign, nominate and conſtitute the above-named John Price, William Dampart, and our beloved Thomas Baſſonals, butcher, Anthony Garret, John Jenk, William Jenk, Thomas Eddon, Thomas Clerkſon, Henry Overbury, Roger Harriſon, Thomas Read, John Freeman, Thomas Clerk and Richard Coleman, to be the firſt and preſent fourteen capital burgeſſes of the ſaid borough, to be continued in the ſaid offices of capital burgeſſes of the ſaid borough during their natural lives, unleſs, in the mean times, they or any of them ſhall be removed from their offices for male-adminiſtration or miſdemeanor in the ſame, or ſome other reaſonable cauſe.

Alſo we have aſſigned, nominated, created and conſtituted, and by theſe preſents for us, our heirs and ſucceſſors, do aſſign, conſtitute, name and make our beloved Robert Bompas, John Higgins, Thomas Joyce, Laurence Croſs, Triſtram Warne, Richard Garret, William White, John Tiſſoe, John Turner, John Trevis, John Wilſon and George Freeman, burgeſſes of the ſaid borough, to be the firſt and preſent twelve inferior burgeſſes of the common council of the ſaid borough, to be continued in the ſaid offices during their natural lives, unleſs, in the mean time, they or any of them ſhall be removed for male-adminiſtration, or miſdemeanor in their ſaid offices, or for any reaſonable cauſe.

And farther we will, and by theſe preſents do, for us, our heirs and ſucceſſors, give and grant to the above-named bailiffs and burgeſſes of the ſaid borough, and their ſucceſſors, that the ſaid fourteen capital burgeſſes of the borough aforeſaid, for the time being, or the greater part of them, may and ſhall from time to time, for ever hereafter, have power and authority yearly, and every year, upon the Wedneſday which ſhall firſt and immediately happen to be before the feaſt of St. Michael the archangel, to chuſe and nominate, and that they may and ſhall chuſe and nominate two of themſelves, the aforeſaid capital burgeſſes of the borough aforeſaid, for the time being, who ſhall be bailiffs of the ſaid borough for one whole year thereafter next enſuing; and that they who in form aforeſaid ſhall be elected and nominated into the offices of bailiffs of the ſaid borough, before they are admitted to execute their offices, ſhall take their corporal oaths before the laſt bailiffs their predeceſſors, the ſteward, and the reſt of the capital burgeſſes of the ſaid borough, or as many of them as ſhall be then preſent, well, and truly and faithfully to execute the ſaid offices in all things thereunto belonging. And that after taking ſuch oaths, they may and ſhall from thenceforth execute the offices of bailiffs of the borough aforeſaid, for one whole year next enſuing.

And moreover we will, and by theſe preſents, for us, our heirs and ſucceſſors, do grant to the aforeſaid bailiffs, and burgeſſes, of the borough aforeſaid, and their ſucceſſors, that if it ſhall happen that the bailiffs of the borough aforeſaid, or either of them, at any time within one year after they ſhall be elected and ſworn, ſo as aforeſaid, to the offices of bailiffs of the ſaid borough, ſhall die, or be removed from their offices, that then and as often it ſhall and may be lawful for the capital burgeſſes of the borough aforeſaid, for the time being, (or the major part of them) to chooſe and depute one or two others of the aforeſaid capital burgeſſes of the borough into the offices of bailiff or bailiffs of the ſaid borough, according to the ordinances and proviſions in theſe preſents declared. And that he or they ſo elected or deputed into the office or offices of bailiff or bailiffs of the borough aforeſaid, ſhall have and exerciſe the ſaid offices during the reſidue of the year, having firſt taken the corporal oaths in form aforeſaid, and ſo as often as the caſe ſhall ſo happen.

And farther we will, and by theſe preſents, for us our heirs and ſucceſſors, do grant to the aforeſaid bailiffs and burgeſſes of the ſaid borough, and their ſucceſſors, that whenſoever it ſhall happen that any one or more of the aforeſaid capital or inferior burgeſſes of common council of the borough aforeſaid ſhall die, or for ſome reaſonable cauſe be removed from their offices of capital or inferior burgeſſes of common council of the borough aforeſaid; which ſaid burgeſſes or any of them, our will is, ſhall for miſdemeanor be removed from their offices at the diſcretion of the bailiffs and capital burgeſſes of the ſaid borough, for the time being, or the major part of them, that then, and as often, it ſhall and may be lawful for the ſurviving and remaining capital burgeſſes of the borough aforeſaid, or the major part of them, to elect, nominate and depute one other, or more, of the burgeſſes of the borough aforeſaid, in the room of him or them of the capital or inferior burgeſſes of the common council of the borough aforeſaid, ſo happening to die or be removed, for ſupplying the aforeſaid number of fourteen capital burgeſſes, or twelve inferior burgeſſes, of common council of the borough aforeſaid, and that he or they ſo elected and deputed, as aforeſaid, to the offices of capital or inferior burgeſſes of the common council of the ſaid borough, having taken their corporal oaths before the bailiffs and ſteward of the ſaid borough for the time being, well and truly and faithfully to execute the ſaid offices, ſhall be of the number of the aforeſaid fourteen capital burgeſſes, or twelve inferior burgeſſes of the common council of the borough aforeſaid, and ſo from time to time as the caſe ſhall ſo happen.

And farther we will, and by theſe preſents, for us, our heirs and ſucceſſors, do grant to the aforeſaid bailiffs and burgeſſes of the ſaid borough and their ſucceſſors, that they and their ſucceſſors, for ever hereafter, may and ſhall have in the borough aforeſaid one perſon, diſcreet and learned in the laws of England, choſen and nominated in form following in theſe preſents, who ſhall be, and be nominated ſteward of the borough aforeſaid; and we have aſſigned, nominated, ordained, conſtituted and made,

and

and by these presents for us, our heirs and successors, do assign, nominate, constitute and make our beloved subject Nicholas Overbury, esq; to be the first and present steward of the said borough, during the pleasure of the bailiffs and capital burgesses of the borough aforesaid, or the major part of them, (of whom we will that the bailiffs of the said borough for the time being be two) or until any other shall be duly elected, deputed and sworn to the office of steward of the aforesaid borough, by the bailiffs and capital burgesses of the same for the time being, or the major part of them, (of whom we will that the bailiffs of the said borough for the time being be two) and we will, and by these presents for us, our heirs and successors, do grant to the said bailiffs and burgesses of the borough aforesaid, and their successors, that whensoever it shall happen that the office of steward of the said borough shall be vacant, by death, surrender, removal, or any other manner whatsoever, that then, and as often, it may and shall be lawful for the aforesaid bailiffs and capital burgesses of the said borough, for the time being, or the major part of them, (of whom we will that the bailiffs of the said borough for the time being be two) to elect and depute one other person, discreet and learned in the laws of England, to be steward of the said borough; and that he being so elected and deputed, in form aforesaid, and having taken his corporal oath well and faithfully to execute the office of steward of the said borough, in all things touching or any ways concerning that office, before the bailiffs, and as many of the capital burgesses as will then be present, may and shall execute and exercise the office of steward of that borough, during the pleasure of the bailiffs and capital burgesses of the said borough, or the major part of them, (of whom we will that the bailiffs of the said borough be two) and this so often as the case so happens.

And furthermore we will, and by these presents for us, our heirs and successors, do grant unto the aforesaid bailiffs and burgesses of the borough aforesaid, and their successors, that they and their successors from henceforth for ever, have and hold, and may and have power to have and to hold, within the borough aforesaid, one court of record, on Friday every fourth week yearly, before the bailiffs and steward of the borough aforesaid for the time being, or a sufficient deputy of the same steward for the time being; and that in the court they be enabled, and may hold by plaint in the same court, to levy all and all manner of pleas, causes, suits and demands personal, concerning whatsoever trespasses, by force of arms, and other personal actions whatsoever, within the borough aforesaid, the liberties and precincts of the same, moved, arising or committed, or for the future may be moved, arise, had, or committed, and of all and all manner of debts, pleas on the case, frauds, compositions, covenants, deteinors of writings, muniments and chattles, taking and detaining of beasts and cattle, and other contracts whatsoever, within the borough aforesaid, the liberties and precincts thereof arising, or that for the future may happen to arise, although the same trespasses, debts, compositions, covenants, frauds, deteinors or other contracts, do amount to, or not amount to, or exceed the sum or value of forty shillings, so that they do not exceed the sum of six pounds, thirteen shillings and four-pence; and that such pleas, plaints, suits and actions, shall be there heard and determined before the said bailiffs and steward of the borough aforesaid, for the time being, or the sufficient deputy of the steward for the time being, by such and such like process, means and manners, according to the law and custom of our kingdom of England, and what have been consonant unto our law, and that in as ample manner and form, as has been used and accustomed in any other court of record, in any city, borough or town corporate, within this our kingdom of England.

And that the bailiffs and capital burgesses of the borough aforesaid for the time being, or the major part of them, (of whom we will that the bailiffs for the time being shall be two) from time to time have, and shall have power and authority in full court aforesaid to choose, nominate, appoint, admit and swear, so many discreet, experienced and fit men to be attorneys, and to attend the court of record aforesaid, as often as their presence, ministery and service shall be required, as to the aforesaid bailiffs and capital burgesses of the borough aforesaid, for the time being, or the major part of them, (of whom we will the bailiffs of the borough aforesaid for the time being shall be two) shall seem necessary to be chosen and nominated, as is used in any other courts of record within this our kingdom of England.

And moreover we will, and by these presents for us, our heirs and successors, do grant to the foresaid bailiffs and burgesses of the borough aforesaid, and their successors, that from henceforth for ever, there may and shall be two officers, which shall be called serjeants at mace, in the borough aforesaid, for proclamation, arrest and execution of process, mandates, and other business belonging to the office of serjeants at mace, in the borough aforesaid, its limits, bounds and precincts, and from time to time to be performed and executed; which serjeants at mace shall be appointed, nominated and chosen by the aforesaid bailiffs of the borough aforesaid, for the time being, and shall be to attend from time to time upon the bailiffs of the borough aforesaid for the time being; and that the aforesaid serjeants at mace, so to be chosen and nominated, shall in due manner be sworn to exercise their offices aforesaid before the bailiffs and steward of the borough aforesaid, or the deputy of the same steward; and after such oath so taken, they may and shall have power to exercise and enjoy those offices, during the pleasure of the bailiffs of the said borough. And that the aforesaid serjeants at mace, in the borough aforesaid, to be deputed, shall bear and carry gilt or silver maces, engraved and adorned with the ensign of our arms, before the bailiffs of the borough aforesaid, for the time being, every where within the said borough, suburbs, liberties and precincts of the same.

And farthermore we will, and by these presents for us, our heirs and successors, do grant to the aforesaid bailiffs and burgesses of the borough aforesaid, and their successors, that they and their successors from henceforth for ever, have, hold and keep, and may have power to have, hold and keep yearly for ever, in the borough aforesaid, two fairs, to be held every year in the said borough; the first of the said fairs to begin on the feast of St. Andrew the apostle, and to continue all that feast, and the other fair of the two fairs to begin in and upon Ash-Wednesday, and to continue all that day, together with a pye-powder court, to be there held in the time of the said fairs, with all liberties and free customs, tolls, stallage, picages, fines, amerciaments, and all other profits, commodities and emoluments whatsoever, belonging or happening to, arising from or touching such fairs, or pye-powder courts, with all other free customs and liberties whatsoever, to such kind of fairs and pye-powder courts belonging or appertaining, but so that the said fairs be not to the damage of any near ajacent neighbouring fairs.

And farthermore, out of our more abundant special grace, certain knowledge, and mere motion, we have given and granted, and by these presents for us, our heirs and successors, do give and grant to the aforesaid bailiffs and burgesses of the borough aforesaid, and their successors, special licence, free and lawful power, faculty and authority, of having, purchasing, receiving and possessing, to them and their successors for ever, to the use and benefit of a free grammar-school within the borough aforesaid, and the poor inhabitants of the said borough, or any other business necessary to be done in and about the borough aforesaid, messuages, lands, tenements, meadows, pastures, feedings, woods, underwoods, rectories, tithes, rents, reversions, and other hereditaments whatsoever, within our kingdom of England, or elsewhere within our dominions, as well of us, our heirs and successors, as of any other person or persons, which are not immediately held *in capite*, nor by knights service from us, our heirs and successors, so that the same messuages, lands, tenements, meadows, pastures, feedings, woods, underwoods, rectories, tithes, rents, reversions and other hereditaments, do not in the whole exceed the yearly value of forty pounds, above all charges and reprisals, the statute of *mortmain*, or any other statute, act, ordinance or provision heretofore had, made, ordained or provided, or any other thing, cause or matter whatsoever to the contrary hereof in any wise notwithstanding.

We give also and grant for us, our heirs and successors, by these presents, to every subject or subjects of ours, our heirs and successors, licence, free and lawful power, faculty and authority, that they or any of them may have power to give, set, devise or alienate, to the aforesaid bailiffs and burgesses of the borough aforesaid, and their successors, messuages, lands, tenements, meadows, pastures, feedings, woods, underwoods, rectories, tithes, rents, reversions and hereditaments whatsoever, which are not held of us, our heirs and successors *in capite*, or by knights service, so that the same messuages, lands, tenements, meadows, pastures, feedings, woods, underwoods, rectories, tithes, rents, reversions and other hereditaments, so to the same bailiffs and burgesses of the borough aforesaid, and their successors, by virtue of these presents to be given, granted, devised or alienated, do not exceed, in the whole, the clear yearly value of forty pounds by the year, above all charges and reprisals; the statute of *mortmain*, or any other thing, cause or matter whatsoever heretofore had, made, set forth, ordained or provided to the contrary hereof notwithstanding.

And farthermore out of our more abundant special grace, certain knowledge and mere motion, we have granted and confirmed, and by these presents for us, our heirs and successors, do grant and confirm to the aforesaid bailiffs and burgesses of the borough aforesaid, and their successors, all and all manner of liberties, franchises, exemptions, discharges, jurisdictions, customs, privileges, lands, tenements and hereditaments, which the bailiffs and burgesses of the borough aforesaid now have, hold, enjoy and use, or ought to have, hold, use and enjoy, or that some or any of them or their predecessors, by whatsoever name or names, or by whatsoever incorporation, or by pretence of whatsoever incorporation, have, had, used or enjoyed, or ought to have, had, held, used, enjoyed, or hath, had, used and enjoyed by reason or pretence of any charter or letters patents heretofore confirmed or granted, any manner of way, by any of our progenitors or ancestors, or by any other lawful means, right, use or presumption heretofore had and used, to have and hold and enjoy to the foresaid bailiffs and burgesses of the borough aforesaid, and their successors for ever; yielding and paying to us, our heirs and successors, such manner of and such like rents, services and sums of money, which of right have been accustomed heretofore to be due and payable therefore to us, our progenitors or predecessors.

We will also and grant to the foresaid bailiffs and burgesses of the borough aforesaid, and their successors, that they have, hold, use and enjoy, and may have power fully to have, hold, use and enjoy for ever, all the liberties, free customs, privileges, jurisdictions and discharges aforesaid, according to the tenor and effect of these our letters patents, without any let or hindrance of us, our heirs or successors whomsoever, not being willing that the same bailiffs and burgesses of the borough aforesaid shall, by reason of the premisses or any of them, be let, molested, vexed or aggrieved, or in any wise disturbed by us, our heirs or successors, or by the justices, sheriffs, eschetors, and other bailiffs or ministers of us, our heirs and successors whatsoever. Willing, and by these presents strictly charging and commanding, as well the treasurer, chancellor, and barons of our exchequer, and of our heirs and successors, and all and singular others our justices, and of our heirs and successors, as our attorney and solicitor general, for the time being, and every of them, and all other our officers and ministers whatsoever, that neither they nor any nor either of them shall prosecute or continue, or any of them cause to be prosecuted or continued, any writ or summons of *quo warranto*, or any other writ or process of ours whatsoever, against the aforesaid bailiffs and burgesses of the borough aforesaid, or either or any of them, for any causes, things or matters, offences, claims or usurpations, or any of them, by them or any of them due, claimed, attempted, used, had or usurped before the day of the making of these.

Willing also that the bailiffs and burgesses of that borough, or any of them, shall not by any of our justices, officers or ministers aforesaid, in or for any debt, usage, claim, or abuse, liberties, franchises or jurisdictions, within the borough aforesaid, the suburbs and precincts of the same, before the making of these our letters patents, be molested or disturbed, or be compelled to answer to them or any of them.

Saving nevertheless always to Anthony Smith, esq; his heirs and assigns, all and all manner of such, the same, and such like liberties, franchises, privileges, immunities, preheminences and jurisdictions whatsoever, which the same Anthony Smith, at the time of the making of these presents, lawfully had, used and enjoyed, or ought lawfully to have, use or enjoy, within the foresaid borough of Chipping Campden, in as ample manner and form as if these letters patents had never been made, any thing in these presents to the contrary thereof notwithstanding.

We will also, and by these presents do grant to the aforesaid bailiffs and burgesses of the borough aforesaid, that they have and shall have these our letters patents, made and sealed in due manner, under our great seal of England, without yielding or paying great or small fine or fee to us in the hanaper of our chancery, or elsewhere, to our use in any manner, notwithstanding express mention of the true yearly value, or any other value, or certainty of the premisses or any of them, or any other gifts or grants by us, or any of our ancestors or progenitors, to the foresaid bailiffs and burgesses of the borough aforesaid, before these times, in these presents does not appear, or any other statute, act, ordinance, provision, proclamation or restriction to the contrary hereof heretofore had, made, set forth, ordained or provided, or any other thing, cause or matter whatsoever in any wise notwithstanding.

In witness whereof we have caused these our letters to be made patents. Witness ourself at Westminster the thirteenth day of June, in the third year of our reign over England, France, and Ireland, and Scotland, 38.

By Writ of the Privy Seal, &c.

T. RAVENSCROFT.

NUMBER XXVIII.

STATUTES *and* ORDERS, *for the better Rule and Government of the* CATHEDRAL CHURCH *of* GLOUCESTER, *appointed and prescribed by the Command of King* HENRY *the Eighth, in the Thirty-sixth Year of his Reign.*

HENRY the Eighth, by the grace of God, king of England, France and Ireland, defender of the faith, and supreme head upon earth of the church of England and Ireland: To all Sons of Holy Mother the church, to whom this present writing shall come greeting:

Whereas it has seemed good unto us, and to our nobles, and to our whole senate, stiled the Parliament, being influenced, as we trust, by God himself, to suppress and abolish the monasteries dispersed throughout the kingdom for their many and great enormities, and for divers other good causes and reasons, to transfer them to better uses. We therefore, judging it more conformable to the divine will, and more christian-like, that the pure worship of God and the holy gospel of Christ should be diligently and sincerely preached in those places, where ignorance and superstition had before prevailed; and that the youth of our kingdoms should be instructed in good literature, for the greater increase of the christian faith and piety; and that the poor be charitably relieved, have erected and constituted in the place of those monasteries divers churches, whereof some we will to be called Cathedral Churches, and others Collegiate Churches. For the better rule and government whereof, we have caused the following laws and statutes to be prescribed, which the deans and canons of both orders, and other officers, children, and the poor who are of, and belong to the said churches, ought to submit unto and obey, and be ruled and governed by the same, as if decreed and ordained by ourselves. Which if they shall observe, will produce, as we trust in God, a great increase of true piety in this kingdom; and then we shall not be deceived or disappointed in our expectation and good wishes, who have erected those churches for the honour of Almighty God, and the increase of the christian faith, and have adorned the same with divers orders and degrees of officers.

CHAP. I.

The whole Number of those who are to be maintained in the Cathedral Church *of* Gloucester.

In the first place, we decree and ordain, that there be for ever in the said church one dean, six canons, six minor-canons, whereof one shall be a sacrist, another shall be deacon, another sub-deacon; six lay-clerks, one master of the choristers, eight choristers, two masters to instruct children in the grammar, whereof one shall be the head master, the other the under master; four poor people to be maintained at the charges of the said church; two under sacrists, two door-keepers, who shall also be virgers; one butler, one cook, one under cook.

All who, according to this fixed number, shall in their several ranks and orders serve in this church, and punctually obey our statutes and orders.

CHAP. II.

Of the Qualification of the Dean.

We decree and ordain, That the dean shall be in priests orders, of a good life and reputation, and not only learned and skilful in sciences, but have also been honoured with a degree of learning, that is, he shall be either a doctor in divinity, or batchelor in divinity, or doctor of law. But whensoever the office of dean shall hereafter become void by death, resignation, deprivation or cession, or by any other means, we will that such person shall be dean, and be so accepted, and shall enjoy the office of dean in all respects, whom we or our successors shall nominate, elect and prefer under our letters patents, to be sealed under the great seal of us or our successors, and shall think fit to present to the bishop of Gloucester. Which said dean so nominated, elected and presented, and having been instituted by the bishop, the canons for the time being shall accept and admit for dean of the cathedral church of Gloucester.

And the dean, upon such his admission, before he shall take upon him any government in the church, or concern himself in any affairs thereunto belonging, shall take an oath in this form:

The DEAN'S OATH.

I. N. *who am elected and instituted dean of this cathedral church, do call God to witness, and do swear upon the holy evangelists, that I will, to the best of my power, well and truly rule and govern this church, according to the statutes and ordinances of the same, so far as they agree with God's word, and the laws of this realm. And that I will well and justly preserve and keep, and cause to be preserved and kept by others, all the goods, lands and tenements, the rents and possessions, rights and liberties and privileges, and all other things moveable and immoveable, saving the bare use of them; and all other profits belonging to the said church. These, and all other the ordinances of king Henry the Eighth, our founder, as far as they concern myself, I will diligently procure to be observed. So help me God, and the holy evangelists.*

We moreover will, That the dean and canons, and other officers of our church, before admission, do take the oath of succession and supremacy, according to the statutes of the realm in this case provided.

CHAP. III.

Of the Office of Dean.

Whereas it behoves a dean to be vigilant, (like the eye in the body, which takes care of the reft of its members) we will and ordain that the dean, for the time being, fhall with all diligence govern, and at all times, and upon all occafions admonifh, reprehend, reprove and perfuade the canons, and all other minifters of the church, as one that watcheth for the good of his flock committed to his charge. Let him particularly take care that divine fervices be performed with all decency, that fermons be preached upon days appointed, that the children be profitably inftructed, that alms to the poor be diftributed, and that all perfons do faithfully difcharge thofe duties wherein they are intrufted.

Moreover it is requifite, That the dean, as often as he is refident, do keep a fober and competent family, and relieve the poor with alms; and herein we charge him upon his confcience, that he honeftly and frugally demeans himfelf. If the dean proves a fcandalous covetous man, the bifhop fhall correct him, and the dean fhall reprehend the canons if they fhall prove fo. He fhall alfo correct and punifh all others, who fhall be wicked and defective in their duties, according to the ftatutes.

Moreover the dean fhall diligently and faithfully diftribute, difpofe, keep and preferve the treafure, jewels, and ornaments of the church, the golden and filver veffels, the veftments, utenfils, the charters, muniments, court-rolls, writings, and all other goods and fubftances whatfoever, belonging to the church aforefaid, without any diminution or damage done to them, and without any farther ufe of them than our ftatutes and ordinances do reafonably allow and direct.

And he fhall take care that the faid goods be diftributed, difpofed, kept and preferved by others to whofe care they belong, that he may leave all things entire to his fucceffor.

Finally, we will and ordain, That in all caufes of a more than ordinary concern (as in granting of leafes, and fetting of lands, and fuch like) the dean's confent be obtained, if he be refident, but if abfent, his confent fhall be however firft afked, if he be within the limits of our kingdom of England.

CHAP. IV.

Of the Vifitation of the Lands.

Farther we will, That the dean or his receiver, or one of them, which receiver fhall be elected and deputed by the dean, or the fub-dean and chapter, [*By the chapter every where in thefe ftatutes, underftand the one half part, at leaft, of the whole number of the canons.*] fhall once every year (beginning after Eafter) vifit, and thoroughly infpect all and fingular the manors, lands, tenements, houfes, edifices, groves, woods and under-woods belonging to our faid church.

To which the dean, or his receiver, fhall be joined, throughout all the vifitation, a fteward or clerk of the lands, who fhall faithfully ferve him, keep his courts, and give him good counfel. In which vifitation, whatfoever is to be new built or repaired fhall be accordingly built and repaired, that there may not be found in any of them any ruins, devaftations, deftructions, abatement of rents, or other diminution of the farms, thro' want of a due care and infpection.

We alfo will, That the true ftate of the manors and edifices be carefully regiftred, and what reparations are wanting. Befide, let all be regiftred which the dean or canon did agree unto, what he did bargain, direct, or order to be done. The dean or canon fhall, within the fpace of eight days after his return to his cathedral, lay all thefe things before the other canons then prefent, and give up his account in writing. We have thought good to allow 4s. only for each day to the dean thus vifiting, and employed about the needful affairs of the college, and only 2s. a day to the receiver who fhall be fo employed.

CHAP. V.

The letting of Lands and Tenements to Farm.

Farthermore, We decree, that neither the dean, nor any one of the canons fhall fell to any perfon any groves or trees, or fet to any one any lands or tenements for a fet term of years, or let them to farm without the counfel and confent of the chapter. It is alfo our will that no land be let to farm above one and twenty years; and not from time to time, as from three years to three years, or from feven years to feven years, or upon the obligation of renewing any term of time when it fhall be expired.

However we confent that houfes or edifices in cities and villages may be fet for the fpace of fifty, or at moft of fixty years. We alfo will, That in the indentures of farms, the farmers be obliged to pay the fums of their rents in the cathedral, to our receiver, or to his deputy. But we utterly forbid the alienation or mortgaging of any manor, land, revenue, tenements, or other immoveable thing: For our defire is, that our church fhould be enriched, not impoverifhed.

Let not the dean, nor any one of the canons commence, profecute, let fall or put an end, to any caufe or fuit in law, for the defence, recovery or prefervation of any of the rights of our faid church, without the confent of the chapter.

Let the dean, or in his abfence the fub-dean, difpofe of the benefices, rectories, vicarages, and other ecclefiaftical preferments belonging to the prefentation of our church, with the confent of the chapter.

CHAP. VI.

Concerning the furrendering of Goods to the Dean.

That the goods of the church aforefaid may be the more fafely and fecurely preferved, we do ordain and appoint, That as foon as the dean hath taken his oath, all they to whom the keeping of any things were committed, either in the time of the preceding dean, or in the vacancy, that is, all they who now have, or before had, any goods in their care and keeping, by indentures or otherwife, fhall before the chapter fingly give up a true and perfect account of all things by them done or committed, to their care and cuftody, and fhall furrender, or caufe to be furrendered to the dean, all goods, jewels, all ornaments and other goods whatfoever, to the aforefaid church belonging; and whatfoever things they before held by their indentures they fhall, by new indentures, to be made between the dean and them, again receive them from the dean's hands. Of all which things the dean himfelf fhall forthwith make a new and general inventory, and fubfcribe to it; which inventory, after it fhall by the chapter be read, approved and fubfcribed, let the treafure, the jewels, ornaments, and other things before-named, which are not neceffary for daily ufe, and which ought not to lie in the keeping of the officers, by their indentures, be laid up in places appointed for this purpofe, according to our ftatutes.

CHAP. VII.

Concerning the Refidence of the Dean.

Since nothing is more beneficial than the watchful eye of the governor, that all things may be rightly managed, we will and ordain that the dean fhall always refide in his own church, except fome lawful impediment does prevent him. We declare a lawful impediment to be the domeftick fervice of the king or queen, which they call ordinary; the fervice of them who fupply the places of dean, chaplain, almoner, or a tutor of the prince in the king's court. To thefe add, the king's extraordinary fervice enjoyned and required, infirmity of body, care of the bufinefs of the church, violent detention, or laftly, the going to the parliament, or the convocation upon the account of the church, and the continuance there.

If thro' any of thefe impediments it fhall chance that he be abfent from our church, we will however that, in refpect of his receiving the fruits and profits of the church, he fhall be efteemed as prefent; provided that upon his return he prove before the chapter the caufe of his abfence.

But, if he fhall happen to be abfent for other caufes, we will that he be look'd upon as abfent, according to the time; and let him not expect the profits which they who are duly refident ought to receive. Moreover we grant leave to the dean to be abfent from his church 100 days at one, or feveral times in a year, to mind his parochial concerns, and other benefices, if he hath any, and to difpatch his own other private bufineffes; for which times of his abfence, he fhall receive his emoluments the fame as if he had been conftantly refident.

CHAP. VIII.

Of Obedience to be yielded to the Dean.

Since St. Paul teacheth us that obedience is to be payed to fuch as bear rule over us, we will and command, that the canons as well as the petty canons and all other minifters of the church, and each of them do own the dean to be their head and governor: That they reverence him, and in all lawful and honeft things and commandments which concern our ftatutes, or do appertain to good government and the ftate of our church: That they obey, fubmit to, aid and affift the dean himfelf or his deputy, or in their abfence, the fenior canon according to admiffion.

CHAP. IX.

Concerning the Qualities, Election and Admiffion of the Canons.

We ordain, and it is our will, that as often as it fhall happen that any canon of our church aforefaid fhall depart, leave, or be expelled from our church, either by death, refignation, deprivation,

tion, ceffion, or any other way, that then he fhall be owned and accepted as a canon, whom we or our fucceffors fhall think fit to nominate and chufe, and by our letters patents under our great feal, and the feal of our fucceffors, to prefent to our bifhop of Gloucefter. We will notwithftanding, that no one be admitted to be a canon who is not in priefts orders, of good name, not only learned and fkilful in the fcriptures, but dignified with fome title of learning, either a profeffor of divinity, or a batchelor of divinity, a doctor of law, or a mafter of arts, or at leaft a batchelor of law.

And we farther will, that no one be admitted a dean or canon of this church, who is a dean or canon of any other cathedral church, or college of our late foundation, or of our college of Windfor, or of St. Stephen at Weftminfter. Neverthelefs, we grant leave to our own, and to our queen's domeftick chaplains, whom they call ordinary; as alfo, to the dean of our chapel, our almoner, and to the tutor of the prince our fon, that although they already have a dean or prebend's place in one of the aforefaid churches or colleges, they may however be admitted to another in this church, provided that in our aforefaid churches they may not have more than two canons places. Moreover we will that the dean, or his fub-dean, fhall in the prefence of the canons receive and admit a canon thus nominated and prefented after the bifhop hath given him inftitution.

CHAP. X.

Of a Canon's Oath.

Whoever fhall be thus admitted as a canon, fhall fwear in the prefence of the dean or his deputy, together with the other canons, in this form.

I N. who am nominated, elected and inftituted a canon of this church of the holy and undivided Trinity in Gloucefter, laying my hand upon the facred gofpel, do fwear, that to my ability I will keep and caufe to be kept all the lands, tenements, revenues, poffeffions, rights, liberties, privileges and all other things belonging to this church; and will myfelf myt faithfully keep, and as much as in me lies, will caufe to be kept by others, all and fingular the ftatutes and ordinances of king Henry the Eighth our founder, fo far forth as they are agreeable to the word of God, and the laws of this realm: Nor will I wittingly obftruct any thing that may be done for the benefit and reputation of this church, but will procure and augment its profit: And if I fhall be called, chofen and defigned to bear any office in this church aforefaid, I will not refufe to undertake it, and diligently to act thirein, according to my ability. All and each of thefe things I will perform. So God help me and this holy gofpel.

CHAP. XI.

Of the Refidence of the Canons.

Forafmuch as it is not expedient that the members fhould be very remote from the head, it is our will that, as the dean, fo the canons alfo fhall keep themfelves at home, and be always refident in our church, except fome lawful impediment does prevent.

We declare the domeftick fervice of the king or queen (which they call ordinary) the fervice of thofe who in the king's court ferve as deans, chaplains, almoners or inftructors of the prince in grammar; any employment enjoyn'd by the king; ficknefs, the care of the concerns of our church; any violent detention; and laftly, going and attending in the parliament or convocation; all thefe we call lawful impediments.

If therefore he is abfent from our church for any of thofe impediments, it is our will that he be accounted as refident, in refpect of his receiving any fruits and benefits from the faid church; fo that when he is returned, he makes good the alledged caufe of his abfence before the dean or the fub-dean, the canons alfo being then prefent.

Befides, we give leave to every one of the canons to be abfent from our church in every year eighty days at one, or at feveral times, to vifit their cures or other benefices, if they have any, and to mind their own private concerns. For the time of which abfence they fhall receive the fame falary as a refident doth.

Farthermore, we ordain, and it is our will, that as often as any dean or canon travels within fifteen miles of our church to preach, if he be abfent one whole day, he fhall however receive the profits of that day, the fame as if he had been at home: And if he goes to preach more than fifteen miles, and lefs than twenty-four miles from our church, he fhall receive the fame emoluments which they have who remain at home, though he be abfent two full days.

And withal we decree, and it is our will, that the third part at leaft of the whole number of canons be always refident in our church: and except the third part do continue at home, we command that all they who fhall be abfent without a lawful impediment, fhall lofe their dividends, and alfo the money due to the corps of any prebend, fo long as the third part of the canons, as has been faid, fhall nor be refident.

CHAP. XII.

Of Sermons to be preached in our Church.

Becaufe the word of God is a lanthorn unto our feet, we ordain and will that the dean and our canons, and withal we befeech them by the mercies of God, be diligent in feafon and out of feafon, in fowing the word of God, as in other, fo more efpecially in our cathedral church.

And we will that every canon fhall every year make four fermons at leaft to the people in the church aforefaid, in Englifh, either by himfelf or by others, and that upon the Lord's days; once between the nativity of Chrift and the feaft of the annunciation of the bleffed Virgin Mary; once between the feaft of the bleffed Virgin Mary and the nativity of John; once between the nativity of St. John and the feaft of Michael; and once between the feaft of Michael and the nativity of Chrift; fo that almoft no one Lord's day in the whole year fhall be without a fermon. But we will that the dean, either by himfelf or by his proxy, fhall preach every year in our Englifh tongue at Eafter, upon *Corpus Chrifti* day, and at Chriftmas.

CHAP. XIII.

Of the Canons Table.

We ordain and will that all the refident canons fhall live apart with their feveral families, and fhall fo difpofe of the revenues which they fhall receive by our liberality to good purpofes, that they may not feem to have fought fhifts and excufes for their covetoufnefs, or to have been guilty of too much prodigality. But if any one be notorioufly guilty of one of thefe vices, let him be rebuked by the dean, or in his abfence, by the fub-dean; or if occafion be, let him be punifhed by a fine as fhall be thought reafonable.

Moreover, if there be any canon who hath not 40l. of a conftant yearly rent, befide the falary of our church, all his payments being deducted, we will not that he be conftrained to maintain his family apart, but ordain that he go to the table of the dean, or fome canon or minor-canon within the circuit of our church.

But if there be more canons in this circumftance, they may maintain a common table of their own. All who thus living together at a common table, fhall be efteemed but as one refident, and fhall receive out of the common dividends, but fo much as one of them who maintain their families apart. But we utterly forbid all others who have no common table amongft themfelves, but go to another's table, to be partakers of the dividends, arifing from the abfence of the dean and other canons.

CHAP. XIV.

Of the Salary of the Dean and Canons.

We know that hofpitality is very acceptable to God, which that the dean and canons may obferve, we ordain and appoint that the dean fhall every year receive for the corps of his deanery, by the hands of the treafurer, 27*l.* of lawful money of England. And that every canon fhall yearly receive for the corps of his prebend, by the hands of the treafurer, 7*l.* 17*s.* and 8*d.* of lawful money of England.

We farther decree and will, That the dean for every day in which he fhall be either in all the mattins, or at mafs, or in the even-fervices, apparell'd with his proper attirements, and alfo for thofe days he fhall be abfent by the toleration of our ftatutes, he fhall receive from our church 4*s.* of lawful money of England. And in like manner we ordain, that every canon, for every day in which he fhall wear his proper ornaments, either in all the mattins, or at mafs, or in the vefpers, or in which he is abfent by the permiffion of our ftatutes, fhall receive from our church 8*d.* of lawful money of England.

We alfo will and ordain, That all the four moft ufual quarters of the year, that is, at the feaft of Michael, the nativity of Chrift, the annunciation of the bleffed Virgin Mary, and the feaft of John Baptift, all and every falary be paid, as well to the dean and canons, as to all other officers and minifters; and alfo all thofe moneys which ought to be paid for their common table each month; and alfo all that money which every year doth arife out of the abfence of the dean and canons, and which is to be divided amongft the refidents.

Which money is thus to be collected: The precentor, for the time being, fhall faithfully note thofe days in which the dean and canons are abfent. From the dean fhall be detained, for every day of his abfence, 4*s.* and from each canon, for every day of his abfence, fhall be taken 8*d.* and let the treafurer detain it.

Let this fum, thus arifing out of the abfence of the dean and canons, be divided at the end of the year, in the feaft of St. Michael, by a proportionable diftribution between the refident dean and the refident canons. Now thofe we call refidents, who

for

for one and twenty days together are at divine ſervice, according to the orders of our ſtatutes, and do maintain their families apart. And it is our pleaſure that the dean receive twice as much as a canon; that is, if a reſident canon receives for his portion 8 d. out of the dividends, the dean ſhall receive 16 d.

Chap. XV.

Of the Election of Officers.

The dean and prebendaries ought to remember that they are united together as one body. And we will and command that they being mindful of it, ſhall in common conſult together in love and charity; yet ſo that the power of reprehending be left wholly to the dean, or in his abſence, to the ſub-dean, who may gently and mildly admoniſh even the reſident canons, and may check and prudently reprove every one in their ſeveral places.

Therefore let the dean, or in his abſence, the ſub-dean, every year (the canons being convened upon the laſt day of November) chuſe and eſtabliſh the following officers, with the common conſent of the chapter, out of the canons, that is, the ſub-dean, the receiver and treaſurer. And we will that ſuch as ſhall refuſe the office aſſigned them, without ſuch an excuſe as ſhall be approved of by the electors, ſhall be for ever expelled from our church.

And we will that all the canons, except ſuch as are excuſed by our forenamed lawful impediments, do meet and be preſent in our foreſaid church at this election of officers; otherwiſe, as many as ſhall be then abſent, ſhall be utterly deprived of that whole ſum of money which they ſhould have received that year for the corps of their prebends.

Chap. XVI.

Of the Office of the Sub-Dean.

We do decree, and will, that the ſub-dean for the time being, whilſt the dean is abſent, or the deanery vacant, ſhall preſide and have charge over the canons, and all the miniſters and officers of our church, and keep them in order; that whatſoever things ought to be done by the dean being reſident, belonging to the affairs or government of the church, whilſt he is abſent, or his office vacant, the ſub-dean ſhall well and truly perform and execute: And whilſt the dean is preſent, he ſhall be next to him, and reſpected above the reſt, as well in the choir as elſewhere; and therefore in all affairs of our church, he ought to be more diligent and circumſpect, that he may ſeem to be one and the ſame head with the dean. Moreover, we will that the dean's place being void, the ſub-dean ſhall have the full and entire power of ruling and governing in our church in all things, and in like manner as is given and granted in our ſtatutes to the dean himſelf, until a new dean ſhall be elected and ſubſtituted; and he in preſence of thoſe who elected him to this office, laying his hand upon the bible, ſhall ſwear that he will faithfully perform all theſe things.

Chap. XVII.

Of the Office of a Receiver.

We ordain that whoſoever is admitted into the office of a receiver, ſhall collect and receive all moneys and rents of lands and tenements, and all debts belonging to our church; and as ſoon as conveniently he can, he ſhall deliver them to the treaſurer for the time being.

It ſhall be the charge of the receiver alſo to take care of all the goods of the ſaid church, eſpecially thoſe abroad, and timely to look to the ruins and neceſſary reparations of the diſtant.

To him alſo it ſhall belong to undertake and perform all ſuch things as are before preſcribed to him under the title of the office of dean, that is, the viſitation of lands and tenements; and then laying his hand upon the holy evangeliſts in the preſence of his electors, he ſhall bind himſelf by an oath, that he will faithfully and diligently perform all theſe things.

Chap. XVIII.

Of the Treaſurer's Office.

We appoint and ordain, That the treaſurer for the time being ſhall duly pay, as well thoſe ſalaries which every month are to be paid to the miniſters and others belonging to the choir, for their diet and commons, as thoſe which are to be paid quarterly, and thoſe alſo which are to be paid at the end of the year for dividends. To him alſo it belongs, to take care that the buildings of the church be kept in good reparation; and with the advice of the dean, or in his abſence, of the ſub-dean, to mend and repair the houſes of all the miniſters of our church, except thoſe of the dean and canons, as often as need ſhall require; and to provide whatſoever doth neceſſarily belong to the repairing and adorning of the church and choir. He ſhall alſo provide materials and timber for building. He ſhall alſo look to the buildings of the dean and canons; which if they do not repair after notice given, the treaſurer, out of their ſalaries, ſhall ſee that they be repaired.

Moreover, that the houſes of the canons may be the better and more diligently kept in repair, we ordain, that a canon newly choſen may ſucceed in the houſe of one that's dead, or that hath reſigned, or upon any account hath withdrawn; and that he have and enjoy it, with the gardens, ſtable, and other conveniences thereunto belonging. In fine, let him take care of the veſtry, and let him diligently do his utmoſt to preſerve the ſacred veſtments, the holy veſſels and garments, and all muniments.

All which he ſhall ſwear that he will obſerve, laying his hands upon the holy evangeliſts, in the preſence of them who did elect him.

Chap. XIX.

Of the Quality, Election, and Admiſſion of the Minor-Canons.

Becauſe we have decreed that God ſhall be praiſed in this our church in hymns and pſalms, and prayers for ever, we have ordained, and do appoint that thoſe ſix prieſts whom we call minor-canons, as alſo the ſix laick-clerks, and alſo the deacon and ſub-deacon (who ſhall read the goſpel and the epiſtle) all whom we have conſtituted daily to celebrate the praiſe of God in our church, be, as much as may be, learned, of a good name, and honeſt converſation; and laſtly, that they be men of judgment in ſinging, which ſhall be approved of by the judgment of thoſe who do well underſtand the art of muſick, in the ſame church. And they ſhall be choſen, when their places are vacant, by the dean, or in his abſence, by the ſub-dean and chapter, and at their admiſſion they ſhall take the following oath.

Chap. XX.

The Oath of the Miniſters.

I N. *being choſen a minor-canon in the church of the holy and undivided Trinity in Glouceſter, do ſwear, that ſo long as I ſhall continue in this church I will inviolably obſerve, to the utmoſt of my ability, as much as in me lyeth, all the orders and ſtatutes made by the moſt potent king Henry the Eighth, founder of this church. And will pay due obedience and reverence to the dean and canons. And laſtly, that I will carefully promote the good and honour of this church. So help me God, and the Holy Goſpels.*

Which oath we will that all miniſters ſhall take at their admiſſion.

Chap. XXI.

Of the Reſidence of the Miniſters.

We will and ordain that the reſidence of the minor-canons, and all other clerks doing ſervice in our church, be perpetual; for it ſhall be lawful to no one to be abſent from our church a whole day, or a whole night, without leave being firſt obtained, either from the dean, or in his abſence, from the ſub-dean. And whoſoever ſhall do otherwiſe, he ſhall be puniſhed by the dean, or in his abſence, by the ſub-dean, at their diſcretion.

And if any of the miniſters of the choir ſhall undecently ſtay away from our church for three months, the dean, or the ſub-dean, being not fore-acquainted with it, we will that he be deprived of his ſalary for three months. And whoſoever of the minor-canons ſhall be abſent from the greater maſs, or from mattins, ſhall loſe a penny; and whoſoever ſhall be abſent from the veſpers, or the complin, ſhall forfeit a halfpenny; and whoſoever ſhall be abſent after the firſt or third, or ſixth or ninth hour, ſhall be ſconced a farthing; whoſoever is not in the choir before the firſt pſalm is finiſhed, or before Kyrie eleeſon, in the maſs, ſhall forfeit a farthing; whoſoever ſhall refuſe to do as the precentor requires him, ſhall forfeit two-pence.

But the puniſhment of the clerks ſhall be determined by the pleaſure of the dean, or of the major part of the canons who are preſent, to whoſe ſentence the clerks ſhall ſubmit.

Let the money that is forfeited by thoſe who are abſent be equally divided amongſt thoſe who were not abſent, at the end of every quarter. And according to the number of the days in which any one was preſent, he ſhall receive more of the dividends; he that was preſent fewer days ſhall receive the leſs.

However, that the minor-canons, and preſbyters of our church, may be encouraged the more diligently to attend their charge, we do permit that they do enjoy one eccleſiaſtical benefice jointly with their office in the church; provided that the ſaid benefice be not above twenty-four miles diſtant from the city of Glouceſter. And whilſt they continue in the ſervice of our cathedral, we give them licence, and do diſpence with their abſence from ſuch benefice; any act or ſtatute of this realm to the contrary notwithſtanding.

Chap. XXII.

Of the Precentor and his Office.

We decree and ordain, that by the dean, or he being abſent, by the ſub-dean and the chapter, out of the minor canons, one elder than the reſt, and more eminent, both for his behaviour and for his learning, ſhall be choſen precentor; whoſe office it ſhall be handſomely to direct the ſinging men in the church, and, as a guide, to lead them by his previous ſinging, that they make no diſcords whilſt they ſing; whom the reſt ſhall obey.

As to the buſineſs of the choir, all the minor-canons and clerks, and others who ſhall ſing in the church, ought readily to obey whatever he hath ordered them to read.

Beſide, he ſhall faithfully obſerve the abſence from divine ſervice, as well of the dean and canons, as of all who ſerve in the choir; of which abſence he ſhall give a true account every fortnight in the chapter-houſe, before the canons there preſent.

And if any of the minor-canons gives a reaſon of his abſence, it ſhall prevail, if the dean, or in his abſence, the ſub-dean, allow of it.

He ſhall alſo ſee that the books for the ſervice of the choir be carefully laid up. And, in fine, as oft as he ſhall be abſent from our church, he ſhall ſubſtitute a deputy, who ſhall faithfully perform what he ought to have done.

All which, by a ſolemn oath, he ſhall promiſe that he will faithfully perform.

Chap. XXIII.

Of the Sacriſts and Sub-Sacriſts.

We ordain and will, that one of the minor-canons, being a careful and honeſt man, ſhall be choſen by the dean, or in his abſence, by the ſub-dean and chapter, who ſhall be called the ſacriſt, to whom ſhall be committed the care of the church, the altar, the chapels, the veſtments, the books, the calices, the muniments, and other ornaments, which he ſhall receive from the treaſurer, in the preſence of the dean or ſub-dean, and the canons then preſent; and he ſhall be bound by indentures, or ſome ſuch way, to deliver them up. With the advice of the treaſurer he ſhall alſo take care that there be no want of wine, water, or wax-candles, for the celebration of divine ſervices in the church aforeſaid, at times proper for their celebration.

The ſame ſacriſt ſhall alſo viſit the ſick in our church, and (as often as there is occaſion, or time ſhall require it) he ſhall diligently and reverently adminiſter the ſacraments, as well to the ſick as to thoſe that are in health.

The offerings alſo in the church, if there be any, he ſhall take, and keep to be delivered up for the uſe of the church.

We will alſo that he have under him two honeſt and induſtrious men (to be nominated by the dean, or, in his abſence, by the ſub-dean and chapter) who ſhall be obedient to the commands of this ſacriſt, who ſhall lay up the veſtments, light the candles, keep the altars, take care that the church be ſwept and kept clean, toll the bells, or ſee that they be tolled at times appointed by the dean or ſub-dean.

Laſtly, we will, that as well the ſacriſts as their ſub-ſacriſts, when it ſhall happen that they are abſent from our church, ſhall ſubſtitute others in their places, who, in their abſence, ſhall faithfully execute their office.

Which ſacriſt, and his ſub-ſacriſts, ſhall oblige themſelves by oath to be faithful in their places.

Chap. XXIV.

Of the Choriſters and their Maſter.

We decree and ordain, that in our church aforeſaid, by the election and deſignation of the dean, or in his abſence, of the vice-dean and chapter, there be eight choriſters, youths who have good voices and are inclined to ſinging, who may ſerve, miniſter and ſing in our choir.

For the inſtruction of theſe youths, and training them up, as well in modeſt behaviour, as in ſkilfulneſs of ſinging, we will that by the dean, or in his abſence by the ſub-dean and chapter, beſide the eight choriſters before named, there ſhall be one choſen who is of a good life and reputation, ſkilful both in ſinging and in playing upon the organs, who ſhall diligently ſpend his time in inſtructing the boys in playing upon the organs, and at proper times in ſinging divine ſervice. But if he be negligent, and careleſs in teaching them, let him be depoſed from his office, after the third admonition. He ſhall alſo be bound by an oath faithfully to diſcharge his duty.

Chap. XXV.

Of the School-Maſters.

That piety and good learning may alway ſpring, grow, flouriſh, and in due time prove fruitful in our church, to the glory of God, and the good and honour of the commonwealth, we will and ordain, that by the dean, or in his abſence, by the ſub-dean and chapter, one be choſen who is ſkilful in Greek and Latin, of good fame, and a godly life, well qualified for teaching, who may train up in piety and good learning, thoſe children who ſhall reſort to our ſchool to learn grammar. And let him have the firſt charge, and be the chief ſchool-maſter. We alſo will that by the dean, or in his abſence, by the ſub-dean, there be one other choſen, of good repute, and of a virtuous life, well ſkilled in the Latin tongue, and who hath a good faculty in teaching, who ſhall inſtruct the youths under the head maſter, in the firſt rudiments of grammar, and ſhall therefore be called the under-maſter, or uſher. And we will that thoſe inſtructors of youth do carefully and faithfully obſerve thoſe rules and orders which the dean, or in his abſence, the ſub-dean and chapter, ſhall think fit to preſcribe unto them.

But if they prove idle, negligent, or not fit to teach, let them be expelled, and deprived of their places, after a third admonition from the dean, or in his abſence, from the ſub-dean and chapter.

Theſe ſhall be obliged by oath that they will faithfully perform all duties belonging to their places.

Chap. XXVI.

Of the Poor and their Duty.

We ordain and will, that by the deſignation and election of us, or of our ſucceſſors, by the letters of us or them, ſigned with our or their hands, there be in our church aforeſaid, maintained out of the profits of our church, four poor men, oppreſſed with want and poverty, maimed in the wars, weakened with age, or any other ways diſabled, and reduced to want and miſery; whoſe office it ſhall be, as far as their infirmity will permit them, to be daily preſent in the church in the time of divine ſervice, to give themſelves to prayer; to ſerve, aſſiſt, and help the preſbyters in their preparing themſelves for prayers; to keep the body of the church and choir clean from all filth and naſtineſs; to aſſiſt, as much as they are able, the ſub-ſacriſts in lighting the candles, and in tolling the bells; and laſtly, to obey the dean and ſub-dean in ſuch things as belong to the decency of the church. But if they be found negligent in thoſe offices, they ſhall be corrected according to the pleaſure of the dean, or in his abſence, of the ſub-dean. And if any of them be abſent, and reſide not in our church, or at leaſt in the houſes thereunto adjoining, we will that according to the time of their abſence they loſe their ſalary. Yet we grant leave to tbe dean, or in his abſence, to the ſub-dean, to give them leave to be abſent twenty days in a year, for ſome cauſe to be approved of by the dean, or in his abſence, by the ſub-dean. And they ſhall give aſſurance that they will do their duties, by the like oath that other officers of our church do take.

Chap. XXVII.

Of the inferior Officers of the Church.

Since no one can worthily ſerve in the offices of the church, and at the ſame time be intangled with worldly concerns, and that they who miniſter in our choir may not be obſtructed in their duty, we ordain, that inferior officers ſhall be ſubſtituted.

We will therefore that the dean, or in his abſence, the ſub-dean, according to his diſcretion and prudence, do make choice of, and admit as a butler or manciple, an induſtrious man, one of a good repute and converſation, who, at ſeaſonable hours, ſhall ſupply with bread and drink thoſe who eat at the common table, and carefully ſee the buttery ſupplied; and (together with the cook, by the aſſiſtance of the ſteward) ſhall diligently take care to buy proviſions for the table of the minor-canons and officers.

Moreover we will, that the dean, or in his abſence the ſub-dean, chooſe two door-keepers, who ſhall alſo do the office of virgerers, careful men, of a good life and reputation, who ſhall alſo faithfully keep the keys of the gates; and ſhall alſo keep the gates, and outward doors of the bounds of our church, and ſhall ſhut, keep, and open them at the command of the dean, or in his abſence, of the ſub-dean. But in the night time they ſhall not ſuffer them to lye open for any one, unleſs with the expreſs command of the dean, or in his abſence, of the ſub-dean.

Laſtly, the dean, or in his abſence the ſub-dean, ſhall chuſe a cook and an under-cook, men that are induſtrious, of good repute, and of an honeſt life, who ſhall diligently provide the meat and drink for the table of thoſe who eat together.

And all theſe ſhall take the like oath as they take who ſerve in the choir.

Chap. XXVIII.

Of the common Table of the Officers.

That they who live together, and praiſe God together in the choir, may alſo eat together, and praiſe God together at table, we ordain and will, that as well the minor-canons and officers in the

the choir, as the teachers of the grammar-ſcholars, and all other inferior officers of our church, and the children who learn to ſing, ſhall feed together in the common hall, if it may be conveniently done. In which hall the precentor, or in his abſence the ſenior petty-canon, ſhall ſit uppermoſt at the upper table; then the head ſchool-maſter, and the minor-canons, and the maſter of the choriſters. In the ſecond rank let the deacon, the ſix lay-clerks, the ſub-deacon, and the under ſchool-maſter ſit.

In the third rank let the ſinging boys of the choir ſit.

Theſe having dined, let the ſub-ſacriſts, the manciple, the door-keeper, the cook and the cenſor ſit down.

In the hall ſhall be the precentor, or if he be abſent, the ſenior petty-canon, who ſhall rebuke ſuch men as be of an ill behaviour. But in the firſt place they ſhall reprove the boys, and alſo their maſters. And, that all things may be done quietly, in order, and with decency in the hall, upon the five and twentieth day of November, one ſhall yearly be choſen out of the prieſts of the church, by the conſent of the major part of them who eat together in the firſt and ſecond rank, who ſhall do the office of an yearly ſteward, who ſhall be ſteward for one whole year; who ſhall alſo provide wood, coal, ſalt, and other ſuch like things as ſhall be thought neceſſary for a ſtore, (as they call it) againſt the following year, to ſerve the common table.

He ſhall examine the accounts of the monthly ſteward (who ſhall be ſteward only for one month) every week; and in the end of every month, ſhall give an account to the major part of the commoners of the firſt and ſecond rank, at the end of the year, of all their charges. Moreover, one out of the petty-canons and the commoners of the ſecond rank (either by himſelf, or by ſome one elſe) ſhall every year in like manner, each month do the office of a monthly ſteward, whoſe advice the butler and the cook ſhall obſerve in buying the victuals, with whom he alſo ſhall go into the market, if it ſeem good, and with them he ſhall buy and provide meat. Nevertheleſs, we will and grant that it ſhall be lawful for the dean, or for the ſub-dean in the dean's abſence, to aſſign and cauſe to be paid to the clerks of our church who are married, and to any that are ſick, a portion of money in lieu of their commons. And to the other preſbyters and clerks, and alſo to the boys who learn muſick, having their victuals freely given them from the church, we give leave, that a portion of money ſhould be aſſigned and paid for their commons, provided that conſtantly every month they allow a competent ſum of money to the common table of their companions, according to the order of the dean and chapter.

We ordain alſo, and appoint that the treaſurer of our church, at the begining of every month, do deliver and pay to the monthly ſteward for the table and commons of all of them who eat together, after this manner following: That is, for them who eat in the firſt rank, for each minor-canon, for the head maſter of the grammar-ſcholars, and for the maſter of the choriſters, ſix ſhillings monthly. And ſhall pay for the commons of them who eat in the ſecond rank, for each of the clerks, the deacon, the ſub-deacon, and the lower maſter of the grammar-ſchool, monthly, five ſhillings and eight-pence. Laſtly, for the table of the choriſters, monthly, three ſhillings and four-pence. Again, for the table and the commons of all thoſe who ſit down after the others are riſen, for the ſub-ſacriſts, the manciple, the door-keepers, and the cook, monthly, four ſhillings. Which monthly ſums, by the monthly ſteward, with the advice of the yearly ſteward, ſhall be honeſtly and frugally diſpoſed of; and at the end of each month, he ſhall give an account of the ſum diſpoſed of to the yearly ſteward, or ſome other prudent man of the firſt or ſecond rank.

And that they may the more faithfully execute their offices, both the ſtewards ſhall be bound by an oath given to the college. Laſtly, all the miniſters of our church eating together, ought to obſerve and yield obedience to thoſe orders, forms and ſtatutes which by the dean and chapter ſhall hereafter be made therein.

CHAP. XXIX.

Of the Veſtments of the Officers, called Liveries.

We decree and will, that the minor-canons, clerks and other officers of our church, and the choriſters alſo, and four poor men, have their outward garments as near as may be, of the ſame colour, or the like; and they already named, ſhall receive yearly for the making of their outward garments, after the manner we here ſit down: All the minor-canons and the upper ſchool-maſter, four yards of cloth for their gowns, at 5*s.* *per* yard; and the maſter of the choir ſhall have for his gown, three yards of cloth, price 5*s.* *per* yard.

The deacon, ſub-deacon, all the clerks, the uſher of the grammar ſchool, ſhall receive for their cloaths three yards of cloth, at the rate of 4*s.* 6*d.* And the other officers, that is, the ſub-ſacriſts, baker, door-keepers, and the cook, every one ſhall receive for himſelf three yards of cloth for his garments, at the price of 3*s.* 4*d.* Each of the choriſters, and the ſub-cook, for their garments, two yards and a half, price 3*s.* 4*d.* Which cloth being delivered to them, whoſoever ſhall not take care that it be decently made up fit for him, and ſhall not wear it greateſt part of the year, he ſhall be deemed unworthy of our gift; and therefore let him be conſtrained to refund to our church ſo much of his ſtipend as the cloth ſhall be valued. The dean, or in his abſence, the ſub-dean, ought every year to provide the cloth and livery garments, together with the receiver for the time being; and they ſhall deliver to every one their portions of cloth, before Chriſtmas, that they may celebrate the birth-day of our Saviour Jeſus Chriſt, with new cloaths and new ſouls: But the poor men ſhall always wear on the left ſhoulder of their gowns, a roſe made of red ſilk; and when they walk either in the church or elſewhere abroad, they ſhall every where walk in the ſaid gowns.

CHAP. XXX.

Of the Salaries of the Officers of the Church

We ordain and will, that out of the common ſtock of our church, beſide their commons and liveries before aſſigned, certain ſtipends be paid quarterly to all the officers of our church, by the treaſurer, by equal portions, in manner following: That is, to each minor-canon for his ſhare, 5*l.* 2*s.* To the head ſchool-maſter, 8*l.* 8*s.* 8*d.* To the maſter of the choriſters, 5*l.* 7*s.* To the uſher, 59*s.* and 2*d.* To the ſub-deacon, 59*s.* and 2*d.* To every clerk, 59*s.* and 2*d.* To the ſacriſt, 26*s.* and 8*d.* To the manciple, 58*s.* To the cook, 58*s.* To the door-keepers, 58*s.* To the choriſters, 15*s.* To each of the four poor men, 6*l.* 3*s.* and 4*d.* To the ſub-dean, 26*s.* and 8*d.* To the precentor, 26*s.* 8*d.* To the receiver, 5 marks. To the treaſurer, 26*s.* 8*d.* To the ſteward, or clerk of the lands, 53*s.* and 4*d.* To the ſub-cook, 26*s.* 8*d.* To the ſub-ſacriſts, 33*s.* and 4*d.*

CHAP. XXXI.

Of the Celebration of Divine Service.

That prayers and ſupplication may decently and in good order be every day performed in our church, and that every day the praiſe of God may be made with joy and rejoicing: We decree and ordain, that the minor-canons and clerks, together with the deacon and ſub-deacon, and the maſter of the choriſters, do daily perform divine ſervice in the choir of our church, according to the right and cuſtom of other cathedral churches; but we will not oblige them to ſing their ſervices by night. Moreover, we will, that in all principal feaſts, the dean, but in the greater double feaſts, the ſub-dean, and in other double feaſts, the other canons, every one in his place ſhall officiate in celebrating the divine ſervice. We ordain alſo, that no one of the canons, or of others miniſtering in the choir, ſhall come thither in time of divine ſervice, except he be cloathed with ſuch ornaments as are proper for that place.

We will alſo, that the maſters of the grammar ſchool, upon feſtival days be in the choir, wearing habits fit for that place; whereof one ſhall have his place above the minor-canons, the other ſhall ſit next below them. We will alſo, that as ſoon as I am departed out of this life, obſequies be made for my ſoul in my church at Glouceſter, all the canons of our church, and other officers and poor men being called together and aſſiſting: And that the day of our death be written in the ſtatute-books, upon which ſame day anniverſary obſequies and maſſes ſhall for ever be celebrated for us.

CHAP. XXXII.

Of the common Treaſury, and keeping of the ſeal and Muniments.

We ordain and will, that one inward and more private room be ſet apart, and an outward one large enough, and adjoining to the inward one; which rooms ſhall be called the treaſury.

In the outward room ſhall be placed a cheſt, and a coffer to keep the writings in; in which the books of the accounts of all the officers, ſervants, and of all others who are obliged to give up any accounts, ought to be kept and laid up. In thoſe cheſts and coffers ſhall be laid up the court rolls, both by themſelves and apart. All obligatory writings apart, and by themſelves. The books concerning revenues, called the rentals: Inventories of the goods and lands apart, and by themſelves. In this room let there be placed an iron cheſt, to keep the moneys put into the treaſury, which may be needful for daily expences. In this room alſo let there be a counter-houſe, where the accounts of all farmers, bailiffs, officers, and of others, are to be examined and proved.

In the inward room we would have one ſtrong iron cheſt placed, wherein let there be laid up the ſum of 40*l.* which we would have to be taken out of what remains as overplus, in the end of every year, that that ſum may always remain and be ready to ſerve the neceſſities of our church, if there ſhall any happen. And in this room let there be kept one ſmall cheſt, in which let there be put and carefully kept the common ſeal of our church; by which common ſeal we command, that nothing be at any time ſealed but what was firſt at large and plainly written in a certain regiſter,

regiſter, and be publickly compared, and at large read over with the ſame regiſter. And as often as the ſeal is put upon any writing, there ſhall never be required of any one above 13*s.* and 4*d.* for the ſigning of that writing. We will alſo, that in this room there ſhall be kept another cheſt, in which let theſe our ſtatutes, ordinances and letters patents of the foundation and endowment of our church, and other writings and muniments of the manors, lands, tenements, revenues, poſſeſſions and rights and liberties which our church by any right hath, be depoſited. But every cheſt, even the little one, ſhall have three locks, with ſo many keys of a different faſhion: and of each of theſe cheſts, and of the little one, the dean ſhall keep one key, the ſub-dean another, and the treaſurer the third; and none of the cheſts, no not the little one, ſhall be open but when all the keepers of them, or their deputies are conſenting and preſent. Finally, we forbid any one man to keep two keys with him at the ſame time; and as often as any one of the key-keepers goes forth from our ſaid church, let him leave his key with ſome one canon that ſtays at home, and hath neither of the other keys.

CHAP. XXXIII.

Of the Accounts given up every Year.

We will, that within two months after the feaſt of Michael, all bailiffs, farmers, officers and ſervants, both foreign and domeſtick, do give in, and make a full and true account of all thoſe things that do belong to their offices. And we farther ordain and decree, that at the ſame time alſo, both the receiver and the treaſurer, do give a full and true account of all things belonging to their offices before the dean and the canons then preſent, and the auditor, whether he be preſent, or whether he ſubſtitutes another in his place, of what they have received, and of what they have laid out; what the church oweth, and what is due unto the church. And finally, let all the indentures of the goods of the church, which are in uſe, be ſhewed and renewed, that in all things the dean and canons may be ſatisfied in the ſtate and condition of the church.

CHAP. XXXIV.

Of correcting Exceſſes.

That a good behaviour may be obſerved in our church, we ordain and will, that if any one of the petty-canons or other officers ſhall be guilty of any leſſer fault, he ſhall be puniſhed according to the diſcretion of the dean, or in his abſence, of the ſub-dean; but if he hath offended by any great fault, if it ſhall be thought fit, he ſhall be expelled by thoſe by whom he was admitted. And if any one of the canons be in any fault or crime, whereby any notorious ſcandal may ariſe to our church, let him that is found guilty be admoniſhed by the dean, or in his abſence, by the ſub-dean; but if he mend not his behaviour, being the third time admoniſhed, let him be called before the biſhop his viſitor, and at his pleaſure let him be puniſhed: But we reſerve the puniſhment of the poor men, as oft as they offend, to the diſcretion of the dean, or in his abſence, of the ſub-dean; and if they continue incorrigible, let them be expelled from the church by the dean, with the conſent of the chapter, and let them loſe all benefit from the church.

CHAP. XXXV.

Concerning Alms.

Beſide our alms beſtowed upon thoſe four poor men, we have given alſo an annual ſum of 40*l.* to our church, both for the relief of the poor and needy, and alſo toward the repairing of the high ways. We will that one half of that ſum be diſtributed by the dean, or his receiver, when in his circuit he viſits the lands, manors, and impropriate churches; in which churches let it be diſtributed to the poor, according to their need; leſt they ſeem from hence to reap all and ſow none. But let the dean or treaſurer diſpoſe of the aforeſaid ſum, partly to the poor and needy nigh our church. The account of which diſtribution let it be ſhewn in the general account. The biſhop, in his viſitation, ſhall take notice of this money, after it be faithfully diſpoſed of. Another ſum of 20*l.* we have aſſigned for the repairing of bridges and the mending of highways, according to the diſcretion of the dean, or in his abſence, of the ſub-dean and chapter. But ſince the grammar-ſchool, and almoſt all the buildings, in which we would that the minor canons and other officers of our church ſhould lodge, are run to ruin, waſte, out of repair, and unhandſome, we give leave that that ſum of 20*l.* which we aſſign for the repairing of bridges, may be made uſe of to repair thoſe buildings, making them more habitable, and to make them fit for thoſe uſes they ſhall be deſigned, for the ſpace of three years. But when thoſe three years are expired, after the date of theſe preſents, we do ordain that the ſame ſum ſhall be made uſe of to repair bridges and highways. The biſhop alſo, in his viſitation, ſhall take care that this be faithfully executed.

CHAP. XXXVI.

Of keeping Chapters.

We decree and will, that the dean, or in his abſence, the ſub-dean, with the reſident canons, once at leaſt in every fortnight, or oftener, as it ſhall ſeem expedient, ſhall keep a chapter in the chapter-houſe, and there piouſly and prudently confer about the affairs of our church. We alſo will, that in every year there ſhall be kept two chapters, one upon the laſt day of November, and the other upon the veſpers of St. John Baptiſt; in which chapters we will, that whatſoever ſhall be ordained and appointed by the dean, and the canons preſent, ſhall be obſerved by all perſons of our church, ſo far as they concern them, provided they do not contradict theſe our ſtatutes.

CHAP. XXXVII.

Of the Viſitation of the Church.

There's no work ſo piouſly begun, ſo proſperouſly continued, or ſo happily conſummated, which is not ſoon deſtroyed, and utterly ſubverted by careleſſneſs and negligence. There are no ſtatutes ſo ſacred, and firmly made, but in length of time they are expoſed to oblivion and contempt, if there be not a conſtant care and zeal for religion. Which that it may never happen, or come to our church, we, truſting in the faith and diligence of the biſhop of Glouceſter for the time being, have conſtituted him to be the viſitor of our cathedral of Glouceſter, willing and commanding, that according to his chriſtian faith, and earneſt zeal for religion, he watch, and diligently take care that thoſe ſtatutes and ordinances which we have made for our church be inviolably obſerved; that the poſſeſſions, and the ſpiritual as well as temporal affairs may flouriſh in a proſperous ſtate; that the rights, liberties, and privileges be preſerved and defended.

And that theſe things may be ſo, we ordain and will, that the biſhop himſelf, as often as he ſhall by the dean, or by two canons, be aſked; and if not aſked, yet once in every three years ſhall come in perſon to our church, except ſome very urgent neceſſity ſhall obſtruct him, or elſe that he come by the proxy of his chancellor, that he there, in a convenient place, call together the dean, canons, minor-canons, clerks, and all other officers of our church. To which biſhop, by virtue of this preſent ſtatute, we grant a full power and authority to examine the dean, canons, minor-canons, and the other officers, concerning all the articles contained in our ſtatutes, and concerning all other articles relating to the ſtate, welfare and reputation of our college: And that he urge every one of them, by the oath they gave unto the church, to ſpeak the truth concerning all faults and crimes whatſoever: And that the biſhop puniſh them who ſhall be found and proved guilty, according to the nature of the fault and crime; and that he reform them. And that he do all things that may ſeem proper for the ſubduing of vice, and which are known to belong to the duty of a viſitor. And we will and command all, as well the dean as the canons, and other officers of our church, that they obey the biſhop in reſpect of the premiſſes.

And we ordain, by virtue of the oath given to the church, that no one ſay or inform any thing againſt the dean or the canons, or any one of the officers of our church, but what he believes to be true, and is publickly reported ſo to be.

Moreover we will that the dean, at the common charges of the church, prepare and ſet before the biſhop viſiting, and attended with eight perſons, two entertainments at moſt within the lodgings of our church. Farthermore, becauſe we wiſh that theſe our ſtatutes may laſt for ever, we will, that if any ambiguity, contention, or diſſention ſhall hereafter ariſe between the dean and canons, or between the canons themſelves, about the true and genuine meaning of our ſtatutes, (all which we would have underſtood according to the plain grammatical ſenſe) we will and ordain, that that ſtatute, or any clauſe of the ſtatute, concerning which the contention is riſen, ſhall be referred to the archbiſhop of Canterbury; to whoſe interpretation we command all to ſubmit without any delay or contradiction, provided it be not repugnant to our ſtatutes. But we utterly forbid the viſitor, and the interpreter of our ſtatutes, and all other men, of what dignity or authority they ſhall be, to make any new ſtatutes, or to diſpence with any of the old.

And we do forbid the dean and canons of our church to receive any ſuch ſtatutes, under the penalty of perjury, and perpetual expulſion from our church.

Notwithſtanding we reſerve to ourſelf, and to our ſucceſſors, a full power and authority to change and alter theſe ſtatutes, and if it ſhall ſeem good, even to make new ones.

In witneſs of all and ſingular the premiſſes, &c.

Of the Prayers in the Church.

We decree and ordain, that during my natural life theſe following prayers be every day uſed for us, for our royal conſort, and for the prince our ſon, in the high maſs, *viz. Deus, in cujus*

manu

manu sunt corda Regum, &c. Suscipe, quæsumus Domine, &c. Præsta quæsumus, &c. Pro animabus autem Invictissimi Patris nostri Regis Henrici *Septimi, & nobilissimæ matris nostræ* Elizabethæ *reginæ & charissimæ nuper conjugis nostræ* Janæ *hæ Orationes dicantur, Deus, cui proprium, &c. Intuere, quæsumus, &c. Prosit, quæsumus Domine. &c.*

Prayers to be said by all in our Church in the Morning, as they are rising.

Libera nos, Salve nos, &c. with this prayer, *Omnipotens, Sempiterne Deus, &c.* with this psalm, *De profundis*, and with the following suffrages.

Prayers in the Evening.

As they are going to bed, let them say the hymn *Salvator Mundi Deus*, with the psalm *De profundis*, and with the suffrages following.

Prayers to be used in the School in the Morning.

As soon as the usher and all the scholars are come into the school, at six of the clock in the Morning, let them alternately repeat the psalm *Domine in virtute tua lætabitur Rex, &c.* 1. *Kyrie Christe, Kyrie.* 2. *Pater noster, & ne nos, &c.* 3. *Ostende nobis Domine, &c.* 4. *Domine, salvum fac Regem, &c.* 5. *Esto ei Turris fortitudinis, &c.* 6. *Nihil perficiat Inimicus, &c.* 7. *Domine exaudi.* 8. *Quis Omnipotens Deus, &c.* 9. *Actiones nostras quæsumus Domine.*

Prayers in the School, to be said in the Evening.

At five of the clock, the scholars being ready to go out of the school, shall alternately repeat the psalm *Ecce nunc benedicite Dominum, &c. Kyrie, Christe, Kyrie, Pater noster, &c. Exurge Domine adjuva nos, &c. Domine Deus virtutum, &c.* with this prayer, *Tenebras nostras illumina, quesumus Domine.*

The Prayers of the Poor.

Let the poor men, who are maintained at the charges of our church, daily say in the morning, at the evening, and at noonday, the Lord's Prayer, the Angel's Salutation, the Apostles Creed, the Ten Commandments of God, all of them in English, with the prayer translated into English, *Quæsumus Omnipotens Deus.*

We Nicholas Wigorn', George Cicestren', and Richard Cox archdeacon, do now present unto you the dean, canons, and all other officers of the said church of the sacred and undivided Trinity at Gloucester, by the command and authority of our dread sovereign the king, these his statutes to be diligently observed by you, in the thirty-sixth year of the reign of the same our Lord the king, and upon the fifth day of the month July.

NICHOLAUS WIGORN'.
GEORGIUS CICESTR'.
RIC. COX.

NUMBER XXIX.

Difficult Words which occur in the Charters of Liberties explained; taken from a Manuscript containing Charters, &c. relating to the Monastery of the Holy Trinity, near Algate, London.

SOC, That is, the suing of men in their own court, according to the custom of the kingdom.

SAC is the power of impleading and punishing transgressors in their court, because *sake* in *English* signifies *encheson* in *French*, *(which is occasion, cause, or reason)* and it is said *for siche sake (that is for such sake or reason)* being the same as *quele encheson*, and *sake* is said for *forfeit*.

TOL imports, that you, and all your men, throughout all your homage lands, be exempt in all markets from toll, for things bought or sold.

THEAM. This is, that you have all the generation of your villains, with their services and chattels, wheresoever they shall be found in England: excepting any one born in servitude, shall continue for a year and a day undisturb'd in any privileged town, so that he be received into their company, or gild, and as one of them, by the same he shall be exempted from villainage.

INFANGETHEF is, that thieves or robbers, taken in your lordship, or fee, and convicted of their theft, be adjudg'd in your court.

OUTFANGETHEF is, that thieves or robbers, which belong to your land, or fee, if taken with a robbery out of your land or fee, be brought back to your court, and there try'd.

HAMSOKENE. That is, that you be exempt from amerciaments for entering houses violently and without leave, against the peace of our lord the king, and that you hold pleas of this sort of transgression committed on your land, in your court.

GRYTHEBRICHE. That is, the breach of the king's peace, for *gryth* in *English*, is *pax* in *Latin*, and *pees* in the *Roman*; *briche* in *English*, is *freynt* in the *Roman*.

BLODWYTE. That is, that you be exempt from amerciament for blood spilt, and that you hold pleas thereupon in your court, and that you have the amerciament arising from thence; because *wyte* in *English*, is the same as *injuria* in *Latin*.

PHILTWYTE is, that you be exempt from amerciaments for frays, and that you hold pleas of the same, in your court, and have the amerciaments thence arising; for *philt* in *English* is *medle* in the *Roman*.

PHLYTHWYTE. That you be exempt from contention and assemblies, and that you hold pleas thereof in your court, and have the amerciaments proceeding from the same; for *phlyth* in *English* is *contentio* in *Latin*.

PORDWYCHE is, that you be exempt from amerciaments when any fugitive outlaw comes to the peace of our lord the king, either of his own accord, or upon licence.

PLEMENESFRITH is, that you have the chattels or amerciaments of a fugitive.

LECHERWITE is, that you take a fine of him that lies with a bond-woman born, without your leave.

CHILDWYTE. That you take a fine from a bond-woman born, that is with child, who has lost her virginity without your leave.

PORSTALL is, that you be exempt from amerciaments for chattles seized, either within or without your lands, and that you have and hold pleas concerning such cases so arrested within your lands, in your court, and the amerciaments arising from the same.

SCHOT is, that you be exempt from a certain custum, as of the common toll imposed by the sheriff or his bailiffs.

GELDE is, that you be exempt from servile customs, which once us'd to be paid, as of *horngilde*, and the like.

HITAGE, or CARRUAGE is, that you shall be exempt, if our lord the king should tax all the land by *carucates*.

DANEGELDE. That is, exemption from a custom us'd in another place, which the Danes once exacted in England.

HORNGELDE. That you be exempt from a certain custom exacted at fairs and markets.

WAPENTAKE is, that you be exempt from suit of the hundred, which is called *wapentake*.

LESTAGE. That is, exemption from a duty exacted at fairs and markets.

STALLAGE is exemption from a duty exacted for standings taken or assign'd in fairs and markets.

STHENG, or HEDWYNG is exemption from attachment in any court, and before any persons whatsoever, for trespasses presented and not avow'd.

MISHERYNG. That is, exemption from amerciaments for any trespasses whatsoever brought into court, without exemplification.

BURGBRICHE is a discharge from any passing thro' cities or boroughs, against the peace.

AVERPAYE is exemption from paying a penny for average to our lord the king.

HUNDREDAT is exemption from paying the penny, or contributing to the hundred.

BORDALPANY. That is, exemption from the exaction us'd in markets, where they paid a halfpenny for taking away their stalls.

BURGBOTE is exemption from contributing to the relief of the city, or borough, or for building of walls fallen.

BRUGEBOTE is exemption from contributing to build bridges.

THECLEPENY is exemption from tallage of the tenth for the council.

MUNDEBRYCHE is exemption from amerciaments for transgressions committed against our lord the king.

NUMBER XXX.

A Grant from Henry de Hamtonel, Abbat of Cirencester, to John de Latton.

TO all christian people who shall either see or hear this present deed, Henry, by divine permission, abbat of Cirencester, and the convent of that place, send health in our Lord. Know ye that we have granted to John de Latton and Isabel his wife, in form and under condition following, these several things hereafter specified, to receive every week, so long as they shall jointly live; Fourteen white loaves and nine gallons of beer, whereof five gallons of the beer shall be such as the convent useth, and the other four gallons shall be of the chaplain's beer, and they shall receive one mess every day out of our kitchen, in like manner as our day officers do receive it from our house. Provided that if the said Isabel shall survive, that then and immediately from the death of the said John, one moiety of all above granted shall altogether cease. And in consideration of the aforesaid grant, the aforesaid John hath wholly released to us and to our church, and hath quit claimed for himself and his heirs

heirs for ever, all right and claim which he had or any way can have, with the reverſion thereof, in all the lands and tenements, with all their appurtenances, which Walter father of the ſaid John did hold by leaſe from us in Latton. And the ſaid John and his heirs ſhall fully and intirely warrant the ſaid lands and tenements to us and to our church, without any diminution whatſoever. And if it ſhould happen, which we hope will never be, that the ſaid John and Iſabel ſhall any way be deficient in the ſaid warranty, or ſhould lay claim, or pretend any right to the ſaid tenements, that from thenceforth the ſaid abbat and convent ſhall be for ever diſcharged from the performance of every part of this grant, without any pretence whatſoever. In witneſs whereof the parties aboveſaid have interchangeably ſet their ſeals to this indenture.

Given at Cirenceſter, at the feaſt of the purification of the bleſſed Virgin, in the thirty-third year of the reign of king Edward, ſon of king Henry.

NUMBER XXXI.

King Henry the Fourth's Grant to the Men, &c. of Cirenceſter.

THE king, to all unto whom theſe preſents ſhall come, greeting. Know ye that of our ſpecial grace, and for the good and laudable and acceptable ſervices which the men of the town of Ciceter have performed, in reſiſting the malicious attempts of Thomas late earl of Kent, and John late earl of Saliſbury, and other traitors and rebels, who had traiterouſly taken up arms againſt us and our crown, contrary to their allegiance; we do give and grant to the men aforeſaid, all the goods and chattels, in whoſe hands ſoever they may be found, which did belong to the ſaid late earls, and the other traitors, and were found in the ſaid town when the ſaid earls and other traitors were there arreſted by the men aforeſaid; excepting all gold and ſilver, and money, and veſſels of gold or ſilver, or guilded, and except all jewels of all kinds; to hold unto the ſaid men of our gift. In witneſs whereof, &c.

Given at Weſtminſter the twenty-eighth day of February, 1 H. 4.

The ſame Year, the King rewards them with another Conceſſion.

THE king, to all unto whom theſe preſents ſhall come, greeting. Know ye that of our eſpecial grace, and for the good ſervice which our beloved liege-people and commons of the town of Cirenceſter, as well men as women, have performed unto us, in the taking of the earls of Kent and Saliſbury, and of others their followers, in the late rebellion, do grant unto the men four does in ſeaſon, to be delivered unto them by our chief foreſter, for the time being, or his deputy, out of our foreſt of Bradon; and alſo one hogſhead of wine, to be received every year out of the port of our town of Briſtol, by the hand of our officer therein for the time being. We alſo grant unto the women aforeſaid ſix bucks, to be delivered them in right ſeaſon, by our chief foreſter aforeſaid, or his deputy, out of the foreſt aforeſaid; and alſo one hogſhead of wine, to be delivered to them out of the port of our ſaid town of Briſtol, by the hands of our officer therein for the time being. This grant to continue during our pleaſure. In witneſs whereof, &c.

NUMBER XXXII.

An Ordination made by William King of England, concerning Derhurſt.

WILLIAM king of the Engliſhmen, earl of Normandy, and *Cænomanenſium* to the faithful believers in Chriſt of whatſoever nation. Our bleſſed ſaviour and merciful God, patient and full of pity, amongſt other his precepts concerning mercy, faith, *That all the things of this world are as nought, in communion with eternal happineſs*, and therefore cammands us that we ſhould out of what we now poſſeſs, lay up everlaſting treaſure in theſe words, *Lay up to yourſelves treaſure in heaven, where neither ruſt nor moth can corrupt.* We therefore being excited by that good precept, and by our wife Maud, with the prudent council of our nobles, and for the good of own ſoul, and the ſouls of all our children, do aſſign and confer the church of Deorherſt, ſituated within the juriſdiction and county of the city of Gloſter, with all its appurtenances, unto St. Dennys, who was the happy apoſtle of France, in as full manner as our
did grant the ſame to our faithful ſubject Baldwin, then a monk of that ſaint, now the abbat of St. Edmondſbury; and in like manner as we our ſelf did grant the ſame to him after we poſſeſt the kingdom. Let this monaſtery, and all belonging to it, be free from all earthly ſervices. We alſo grant the ſame privilege to Tainton and its appurtenances, which the aforeſaid king had given to the ſame ſaint, thereby to gain an eternal reward, decreeing that it be likewiſe free as this which we now give; that we and our children, by the prayers of that ſaint, and of his companions Ruſtious and Eleutherius, may be proſperous in this world, and obtain an eternal happy manſion hereafter. If any one ſhall detract from this our gift, let him be of what degree ſoever, let him by the vengance of almighty God have the ſame fate with Dathan and Abiram, unleſs he repent and make ſatiſfaction and amends to that ſaint, and to the brethren intituled to that monaſtery. This privilege was confirmed in the monaſtery of St. Swithin, in the city of Wincheſter, in the year of our Lord 1069, in the reign of king William the Firſt, on the
of Eaſter, after the celebration of maſs: Theſe witneſſes agreeing thereunto.

I king William do corroborate this our grant and confirmation with the ſign of the holy croſs.
I Maud, queen of the ſaid king, do acknowledge my content therein.
I Richard, ſon of the king, do approve the grant of my father and mother.
I Stigand, archbiſhop of Canterbury, do confirm it.
I Aldred, archbiſhop of York, do confirm it.
I William, biſhop of London, do confirm it.
I Aileric, biſhop.
I Herman, biſhop.
I Liuric, biſhop.
I Odo, biſhop, brother to the king.
I Goſfrid, firſt biſhop of Landaff.
I Baldwin, biſhop Ebreiencis.
I Ernald, biſhop Cenemænenſis.
I Robert, earl, and brother of the king, do agree to it with a good will.
I William, earl, ſon of Oſborn.
I Robert, earl of Caſtle.
I Radulfe, earl of Brien.
I Radulfe de Alneo.
I Henry Ferrars.
I Hugh de Montfort.
I Richard, ſon of earl Giſlebert.
I Roger de Ivri.
I Haimon, the king's ——
I Robert, brother of Haimon.

NUMBER XXXIII.

The King's Patent, making Derhurſt which is an alien Priory to be denizen.

THE king to all, &c. greeting. Know ye, that whereas the priory of Derhurſt in the county of Glouceſter, is an alien priory of the order of St. Benedict, in which priory (ſaid to be a monaſtery in the year 1006) St. Alphege at that time was a monk profeſt, who afterwards in the reign of king Ethelred our progenitor, heretofore king of England, was conſtituted archbiſhop of Canterbury, as in the legend of St. Alphege it does more fully appear. And whereas St. Edward, of pious and famous memory, heretofore king of England, our anceſtor, out of his ſincere and hearty devotion which he did bear to St. Dennis, did give and grant the ſaid priory to the abbey of St. Dennis in France; from the time of which grant the priory has continued a perpetual and conventual priory and cell of that abbey, and ſo continues at preſent. And whereas the ſaid prior, and convent of the ſaid priory, and their preceding priors and convents have ever had, time out of mind, cloyſters, dormitories, refectories, and a common ſeal, and other neceſſary and fitting conveniencies for a priory and convent, ſuitable to their revenues and decency of religion; and whereas the ſaid prior and convent do to this day enjoy the ſame, as we are credibly informed: By virtue of which grant and donation, the abbat and convent of the abbey of St. Dennis, whenever the place of prior in the ſaid priory did become void, did always preſent ſome religious perſon of the abbey of St. Dennis unto the ſaid priory, who by virtue of that preſentation was the right and lawful prior thereof; until of late, by reaſon of war begun between us and France, the ſaid priory can have but ſlow and difficult acceſs to the ſaid abbey to procure a new preſentation, wherefore

wherefore at the humble requeſt of our beloved in Chriſt Hugh the preſent prior of the ſaid priory, and of the convent thereof, we are beſought to take into our conſideration, and to find a remedy whereby this evident danger in procuring a preſentation from abroad may be hereafter beſt avoided. We therefore being inclined to favour their humble petition, do of our eſpecial grace, after having fully and maturely conſidered the premiſſes, grant unto the ſaid Hugh the preſent prior of the ſaid priory, and to the convent of the place, that they and their ſucceſſors ſhall be denizens in the ſame manner and form, and as fully and intirely to all intents and purpoſes as any other Engliſh priors are held, deemed, and reputed; and that the ſaid prior and convent ſhall hereafter have and hold the ſaid priory as an Engliſh priory, together with all their manors, lands, tenements, and poſſeſſions of the ſaid priory, with all their appurtenances; and ſhall have all and all ſorts of liberties, immunities, and privileges, and ſhall uſe and enjoy the ſame as freely as any other religious men of the ſame order *Ance Oriundi* did uſe or enjoy the ſame yielding and paying tithes, ſubſidies, and dues, as other denizens of that order do throughout the kingdom of England. And moreover of our farther grace, we grant for us and our heirs, as much as in us lies, to the ſaid prior and convent, and their ſucceſſors, that when and how often the place of prior ſhall become void, whether by death, reſignation, or acceptance of other perferment by the prior of the ſaid priory, that then the ſaid convent and monks of that place, in every ſuch vacancy of the ſaid priory, ſhall and may freely elect one of themſelves to be prior, firſt obtaining a licence for the ſame from us and our ſucceſſors. In witneſs whereof, &c.

Witneſs the king at Cheſwick, the twenty-fourth day of February.

By writ under the privy ſeal of the ſame date, and by authority of parliament, and for 20l. paid into the Hanaper.

NUMBER XXXIV.

The Charter of the moſt glorious King Kenulph, concerning the firſt Foundation of the Monaſtery at Winchcombe.

IN the 811th year of the incarnation of our bleſſed Lord Jeſus Chriſt the ſaviour of the world, who reigned in the heavens from all eternity, in the fourth year of the indiction, and in the ſixteenth year of our reign by the grace of God, and on the ninth day of November. I Kenulph king of the Mercians, by God's favour and aſſiſtance, did begin an imperfect work at a place called antiently by the inhabitants Wincelcombe, in the province of the Wixes: It is now a noble church, and not inglorious in its firſt deſign. It was dedicated by Wulfred archbiſhop of Canterbury to the honour of our Lord Jeſus Chriſt, and the bleſſed Mary his mother, who held him in her boſom, whom heaven and earth could not contain, where I intend to lay my body to reſt in the Lord. It ſeemed good to me to invite all the great men of the kingdom of Mercia, all biſhops, princes, earls, deputies, and my own kindred, as alſo Cuthred king of Kent, Sired king of the Weſt Saxons, with all thoſe who were members of our ſynod, to be preſent and witneſſes at the dedication of the ſaid church; which church I have built to the honour and glory of our Lord Jeſus Chriſt, for the love of heaven, and for the expiation of my ſins, and for procuring a bleſſing on my endowment, and to ſecure thoſe privileges which the Roman biſhops by authority of St. Peter the prince of apoſtles have indulged to me.

I Kenulph, by the favour of God, king of the Mercians, out of gratitude for their good will, who by the authority of the apoſtles have ſtrengthened and confirmed the grants and decrees of my ſynods to the ſecurity of my endowment, by me granted to the monaſtery of Wincelcomb, and particularly for the confirmation of my endowment, made by the authority of pope Leo, and afterwards by pope Paſchal, by the authority of his power, and farther confirmed in three ſynods of the men of Mercia, with their unanimous conſent, whereby the grant of the endowments by me made for the good of myſelf and my heirs is corroborated; and alſo all my gifts, which with a free heart I gave to the great men of the kingdom of Mercia, and of other kingdoms, in gold, ſilver, and other utenſils; and alſo in choice horſes given to them, according to their ranks and qualities, and a pound of pure ſilver to thoſe who had no lands, and a mark of gold to every prieſt, and one ſhilling to every one of the ſervants of God; and all theſe gifts were becoming our royal dignity, and were in number ſo many, and in value ſo great, that they are ineſtimable. All which I beſtowed to procure that the endowment by me granted to the ſaid monaſtery might be firm and irrecoverable, and might be ſettled for ever for the good of me and my heirs.

I Kenulph, king of the Mercians, have alſo obtained the banner of the holy croſs on which Jeſus Chriſt our Lord did ſuffer, that it might be a ſafeguard and protection of my ſoul, and of all my temporal affairs, and of all my heirs, againſt the deſigns of the wicked one. And if any perſon whatſoever, be he great or ſmall, ſhall attempt by violence to do wrong to this holy banner, let him be excommunicated and accurſed, and by God's juſt judgment let him be ſever'd from any benefit thereof, unleſs he ſhall make amends to the ſaid church by full ſatisfaction. And know ye, that all this is corroborated by the favour of the bleſſed trinity, and by the protection of angels, archangels, patriarchs, prophets, apoſtles, martyrs, confeſſors, virgins, and all ſaints. And I Kenulph, and all the great men who were preſent, and witneſſes hereof, in our great ſynodical councils, do ordain and decree, that if any perſon who has forfeited his life, or is guilty of any other crime, open or ſecret, and ſhall eſcape to the bounds of my inheritance by me granted, and ſhall enter the church, and demand the holy banner of the croſs, ſuch perſon ſhall find entire ſafety and protection; and that no perſon preſume to be ſo bold, or to entertain any wicked thoughts to embezle any thing for fear, or to ſell, give, or mortgage any of the lands of my endowment, unleſs for a certain time, and for the life only of one perſon. But let all things continue inviolable, and remain for ever as we firmly decreed the ſame in three general ſynods.

Witneſſes of the truth hereof, and confirmed by them under the ſign of the croſs, as followeth:

I Kenulph, king of the Mercians, do eſtabliſh this decree with the ſign of the croſs.

I Cuthred, king of Kent, do agree hereunto, and do affix the ſign of the holy croſs.

I Sired, king of the Weſt Saxons, do confirm the ſame, and ſign it with the holy croſs.

I Wulfred, archbiſhop of Canterbury, do agree and ſubſcribe.
I Aldulf, biſhop of Litchfield, do agree and ſubſcribe.
I Denebert, biſhop of Worceſter, do agree and ſubſcribe.
I Wulfhard, biſhop of Hecanæ (now Hereford) do agree and ſubſcribe.
I Woerenbrith, biſhop do agree and ſubſcribe.
I Tilferd, biſhop do agree and ſubſcribe.
I Ethelwolph, biſhop of the Eaſt Angles, do agree and ſubſcribe.
I Alchbart, biſhop of the South Saxons, do agree and ſubſcribe.
I Ethelnot, biſhop of London, do agree and ſubſcribe.
I Wilbarte, biſhop of do agree and ſubſcribe.
I Beornard, biſhop Roveceſtrenſis, do agree and ſubſcribe.
I Wignot, biſhop of Exeter, do agree and ſubſcribe.
I Ecombenet duke.
I Heardbeorth duke.
I Beornoth duke.
I Cymkelone duke.
I Ceolbert duke.
I Aldred duke.
I Wulfred duke.
I Heafreth duke.
I Colfarth duke.
I Heatfarth duke.
I Pleſe, duke, do agree and ſubſcribe.

NUMBER XXXV.

The Bull of Alexander the Third, Pope of Rome, confirming all the Churches, Towns, and Rents belonging to the Monaſtery of Winchelcombe, in the year 1175.

ALexander, biſhop, ſervant of the ſervants of God, to our beloved ſons Henry, abbat of the monaſtery of the bleſſed Mary, and St. Kenelme of Winchelcumbe, and to the brethren there, both preſent and future, who have profeſt a regular life. Foraſmuch as it behoveth the apoſtolical benediction to be a defence unto all ſuch who have choſen a religious life, leſt the inconſiderate raſhneſs of any ſhould divert them from their good reſolutions, or ſhould violate the band of holy religion, which God forbid.

We therefore do readily comply with the juſt deſires of our well beloved ſons in the Lord, and do take the ſaid monaſtery in which you live in all godly obedience, into St. Peter's and our own protection, and by the authority of this preſent writing, we defend the ſame, ordaining that whatſoever poſſeſſions or goods the ſaid monaſtery juſtly and canonically have or ſhall hereafter thro' the bleſſing of God, by juſt means obtain, by the grants of biſhops, kings, or princes, or by the oblation of other good people, ſhall ever remain firm and inviolable to them and their ſucceſſors; and we think fit herein to ſpecify them in expreſs

expreſs terms. Firſt, the ſcite of the place whereon the ſaid monaſtery is built, with all its appurtenances; the church of Twining, with its appurtenances; the church of Sherburne, with its appurtenances; the church of Enneſtone, with the chapel of Chawford, with all its appurtenances; the church of Alney, with all its appurtenances; the church of Bladington, with all its appurtenances; the church of Staunton, with all its appurtenances; the church of Snowſhill, with all its appurtenances; the church of St. Kenelme, with the chapel of St. Peter, with the chapel of Hailes, the chapel of Southley, the chapel of Aldrinton, the chapel of Dicleſdon, the chapel of Preſtecot, the chapel of Charlington, with all their appurtenances.

The town of Twining, with all the lands, orchards, meadows, paſtures, waters, mills, and all their appurtenances; the town of Shirburne, with the men, lands, meadows, paſtures, waters, mills, and all their appurtenances; the town of Enneſton, with the men, lands, woods, meadows, paſtures, mills, waters, and all their appurtenances; the town of Alney, with the men, lands, meadows, paſtures, woods, and all appurtenances; the town of Bladington, with the men, lands, meadows, paſtures, mills, and all its appurtenances; the town of Snowſhill, with the men, lands, paſtures, and all its appurtenances; the town of Ethelmington, with the mills, men, lands, meadows, paſtures, and all its appurtenances; the town of Newton, with all its appurtenances; the land in Wenric, with all its appurtenances; and the lordſhip which you have in Wincelcomb, and all the lands which you have in that town, either by gift or purchaſe, and the two mills in the ſame town; the lordſhip which you have in Cote, half an hide of land which Harold de Sudely gave in alms to the church; the commons of paſture between Winchelcomb and Sudely; one yard-land and three acres which you bought of Robert Ruſſel, with its appurtenances; one yard-land which Radulph de Sudely gave in alms to your church, with its appurtenances; a hide of land which you have in Greton, two hides which you have in Aldrinton, the land which you have in Freolinton, two hides which you have in Hudicote, three houſes in London, your ſalt-pits in Wiche, one houſe in Oxford.

Moreover we forbid you my ſon the abbat, and all your ſucceſſors, to alienate any of the churches or poſſeſſions, or treaſure of your monaſtery, without the conſent of the major part or more diſcreet part of your chapter; but it ſhall be lawful for you and your ſucceſſors to chuſe prieſts, and preſent them to the biſhop, for your pariſh churches, which if the biſhop approves them, he may commit the cure of ſouls to them, who ſhall account to you for their temporal profits, and to the biſhop concerning the ſouls of the people: And as to the corn of ſuch lands which you ſhall keep in your own hands, let no man preſume to demand any tithes thereof. We alſo decree, that the right of ſepulture in thoſe churches ſhall be free, and that no man oppoſe the burial of any perſon who ſhall deſire to be buried there, except ſuch perſon be either excommunicated or interdicted, reſerving the dues of burial to ſuch churches from whence the corps ſhall be brought; and tho' the whole nation ſhould incur an interdict, yet it ſhall be lawful to you to celebrate divine ſervice within your monaſtery, provided it be in a low voice, your doors ſhut, and no bells rung, and that you admit no excommunicated or interdicted perſon amongſt you. And we do farther by theſe preſents decree and ſtraitly command, that no fee ſhall be exacted of your abbat for this our benediction hereby indulged.

It is moreover lawful for you to retain in your monaſtery, in order to their converſion, both clerks or lay-brethren, who are free and unmarried, without diſturbance from any perſon whatſoever. And we farther forbid any of thoſe brethren, after they have profeſt themſelves monks, upon light occaſions to quit the cloyſter, without leave from the abbat; and whoever ſhall ſo depart without a certificate from the ſociety, let none preſume to receive him, unleſs it be in order for a ſtricter rule of life. But you ſhall receive from the biſhop of your dioceſe, the criſm, the holy oyl, conſecration of your altars or churches, and the admiſſion or promotion into holy orders of any of your clerks or monks, provided that the biſhop be a true catholick, and in communion with the apoſtolical ſee, and ſhall confer the orders without any fee and reward, or any other ill meaning, otherwiſe it ſhall be lawful upon ſuch occaſion to go to any other biſhop, who ſhall be firſt well certified by you, to receive from him what ſhall in any of thoſe caſes be deſired.

After your deceaſe, and ſo after the deceaſe of any of your ſucceſſors, no perſon ſhall be impoſed as abbat, by any device or force, but who ſhall be elected by common conſent of the brethren, or the major part of them, or the major part of the moſt diſcreet in the fear of God, and according to the rule of St. Benedict.

We further decree that no perſon whatſoever preſume raſhly to diſturb the ſaid monaſtery, or to deprive them of their poſſeſſions, or to retain any of them, or to diminiſh the ſame, or any ways to vex or moleſt them, but let all things be preſerved whole and intire, and aſſigned to the ſeveral uſes of them for whoſe convenience and maintenance they were at firſt intended, provided that it no ways doth infringe the authority of the apoſtolical ſee, nor the canonical juriſdiction of the biſhop of the dioceſe; whoever therefore, be he a perſon eccleſiaſtical or lay, knowing this our conſtitution and order, ſhall raſhly endeavour to oppoſe the ſame, let him be admoniſhed a ſecond or third time, and if he makes not plenary ſatisfaction for his fault, let him be deprived of all power and honour, and let him expect that divine vengance will attend him for the wickedneſs which he hath committed, and let him be debarred from the body and blood of our Lord and God, and redeemer Jeſus Chriſt, and let him be liable to the ſevere account at the day of judgment; but on the other ſide, let all thoſe who ſhall obſerve the rules and rights of this monaſtery, partake of the peace of our Lord Jeſus Chriſt, that they may receive the bleſſing of their good works in this life, and eternal rewards of peace before the ſevere judge at the laſt day. Amen.

NUMBER XXXVI.

The Charter of Richard Biſhop of Worceſter, confirming the Appropriations of the ſeveral Churches already made to the Monaſtery of Winchcombe.

KNow all men by theſe preſents, that we Richard by the divine permiſſion, biſhop of Worceſter, in our perſonal viſitation of our dioceſe, according to our accuſtomed right, have ſummoned our beloved ſons in Chriſt, thoſe religious perſons the abbat and convent of the monaſtery at Winchcombe, to appear before us at a certain time and place, to ſhew by what right and title they hold and have the ſeveral churches, indowments, and penſions hereafter mentioned, to wit, the parochial churches of Wincelcomb, Rowell, Shirburne, Twining, Bladington, which are appropriated and united to them and their monaſtery; and alſo their portions of tithes and annual penſions, to wit, 20*s.* from the church of Bladington, 10*s.* from the church of Muckleton, within the pariſh of Quenington, the tithes of their demeans in Bladington, the tithes of their demeans in Adelmington, the tithes of their demean lands in Marſton Sicca, the tithes of their demean lands in Staunton and Snowſhill; and alſo two parts in three of the greater tithes throughout the pariſh of Staunton aforeſaid; and alſo the tithes of their demean lands in Alney in the pariſh of Kynemarton; and alſo the tithes of their demean lands in Charleton, Halling, Haſleton, and Yanworth, all within our dioceſe. And whereas the ſaid religious perſons did judicially appear before us at the appointed time and place, and did offer to ſhew their writings, titles, and claims, and prove that the above mentioned churches, their portions of tithes and penſions, did of right belong to them, and that they have held, poſſeſſed, and enjoyed the ſame from the time of their grants quietly and peaceably, and have often earneſtly deſired of us to admit them to prove in form before us their juſt right, and to pronounce judgment for their canonical poſſeſſion of them, and that we would confirm the ſame, and diſmiſs them from our court, and from any farther examination. And we being willing to do full juſtice herein to the ſaid religious perſons, have therefore inſpected, peruſed, and diligently examined their apoſtolical letters and bulls, and their other evidences and proofs, which had been judicially exhibited before us concerning the premiſſes, by which they did ſufficiently make good their allegations; we therefore rightly proceeding, do by a definitive ſentence in theſe words declare, That the ſaid religious perſons have a good right, title, and poſſeſſion to the ſeveral churches, portions of tithes, penſions, and tithes aboveſaid, and the ſaid churches, portions of tithes, and penſions, and the ſeveral tithes and every one of them do of right belong to the ſaid religious perſons and to their monaſtery, in like manner and form as they claim the ſame, and ſo ought to continue to them for ever; and all the ſaid churches, tithes, portions of tithes, and penſions, and every and ſingular of them ſo claimed by the ſaid religious perſons, we of our certain knowledge and legal authority do confirm unto them and their monaſtery, and do decree that thoſe religious perſons and monks were and are the rightful poſſeſſors of the ſaid churches, tithes, portions of tithes, and penſions; and we will that they enjoy the ſame firm and ratify'd for ever, and we by our decree, diſmiſs the ſaid religious perſons as to all and ſingular the premiſſes, from farther attendance at our court, and from any farther examination. In teſtimony of all which, we have hereunto cauſed our ſeal to be affixed.

Given at our manor of Blockly, the ſixteenth day of the month of November, in the year 1404, and in the fourth year of our tranſlation to this ſee.

INDEX

I N D E X.

N. B. The Names of Parifhes are not inferted in this Index, becaufe the Accounts of fuch Places are arranged in alphabetical Order, in the Body of the Work.

ARMS

ARMS

Bleythe's

Fabrica.

Grevil

Long,

Netheruge

Pithoufe

F I N I S.